ENCYCLOPEDIA OF PSYCHOLOGY

ENCYCLOPEDIA OF PSYCHOLOGY

Editors

H.J. Eysenck, London
W. Arnold, Würzburg
and
R. Meili, Berne

CONTINUUM · NEW YORK

1982

The Continuum Publishing Company
575 Lexington Avenue
New York, New York 10022

Encyclopedia of Psychology was originally published in 1972 in three volumes. This one-volume edition is a complete and unabridged edition of the original.

Printed in the United States of America

Library of Congress Cataloging in Publication Data
Main entry under title:

Encyclopedia of psychology.

1. Psychology—Dictionaries. I. Eysenck, H. J. (Hans Jurgen), 1916– . II. Arnold, Wilhelm, 1911– . III. Meili, Richard. [DNLM: 1. Psychology—Encyclopedias. BF 31 E563]
BF31.E52 1982 150'.3'21 82–8001
ISBN 0–8264–0097–3 AACR2

FOREWORD

This *Encyclopedia of Psychology* is an international venture, both in the sense that the authors for the definitions and articles have been drawn from many different countries and also because it is being published in English, German, French, Spanish, Portuguese and Italian. Entries in this Encyclopedia are of two kinds. First there are the ordinary definitions, occupying a line or two, which can be found in most dictionaries; second, there are articles covering important terms and concepts, specially written by well-known authorities, ranging in length up to 4,000 words, and containing suitable bibliographies for further study. This combination seemed particularly suitable for a readership which would include professional psychologists as well as students, and also psychiatrists, sociologists, educators, social workers, anthropologists and quite generally anyone interested in modern psychology, its achievements, its theories and its problems.

Such an ambitious venture must stand or fall by the quality of the people writing the articles and definitions. We have been exceptionally lucky in obtaining the co-operation of well-known experts in all the fields covered; a brief mention of just a few of these will give the reader some idea of the quality of authorship.

From the United States, Anne Anastasi has written on Differential Psychology and A. Bandura on Socialization; L. Berkowitz on Aggression; I. Bilodeau on Motor Skills and Practice; J. E. Birren on Aging and Gerontology; H. R. Blackwell on Decision Processes; J. Brozek on Soviet Psychology; R. B. Cattell on Factor Analysis; E. R. Hilgard on Behaviorism; A. L. Irion on Reminiscence; H. A. Murray on Need; J. Zubin and F. Schumer on Projective Tests. From Britain, H. J. Butcher has written on Questionnaires; C. Cherry on Communication; Alan and Anne Clarke on Mental Defect; D. Furneaux on Hypnosis; H. G. Jones on Habit; R. Lynn on Arousal; Irene Martin on Emotion and Stress; P. McKellar on Imagination and Fantasy; Ian Oswald on Sleep and Dreams; S. Rachman on Behavior Therapy and Aversion Therapy; H. Tajfel on Prejudice; P. E. Vernon on Personality; and A. Yates on Conflict and Frustration. From the Soviet Union, A. R. Luria has written on Aphasia and Localization of Psychological Functions, the Frontal Lobes, and Soviet Psychology; E. N. Sokolov on the Orienting Reflex and A. N. Sokolov on Thinking and Inner Speech. In addition there are many German, French and Japanese authors who may not be so well known to English-speaking readers, but who are regarded as international experts in their fields. The list given above is only a random sample of well-known contributors; many others could have been named in addition or instead of those actually mentioned.

It is our hope that this Encyclopedia will be found useful by those for whom it is intended; we also hope that it will play a part in making our science more truly international than it has been hitherto, by helping to standardize terms and information, drawing attention to work done in other countries, and generally making people more aware of the international character of modern psychology.

H. J. Eysenck

PREFATORY NOTE

This Encyclopedia for the most part presents psychology as increasingly understood and accepted in the English-speaking world; nevertheless, some entries represent views that now occur predominantly in the literature of other linguistic and cultural areas. An international work with contributors from twenty-two countries which takes into account the standard divisions and nomenclature of the university departments and institutes of the countries to which it is addressed, offers a unique opportunity to compare and obtain information on the diverse views and methods of the theoreticians and practitioners of a still young science; it necessarily includes some concepts which diverge significantly from their English analogues.

The bibliographies appended to each major article, and to many shorter entries, in most cases list the sources of the author's references to the essential Anglo-American literature, but in areas where theory and research have been written up largely in other languages, the appropriate books and articles are recorded. Unless the author has referred specifically to the original or current foreign-language edition, or the English version differs in some pertinent respect from the edition cited, only English translations are given. In the case of untranslated Russian works, French or German translations are cited whenever possible. Editions later than the first are indicated by a number before the date (e.g. ^{2}1971). It is hoped that the sometimes extensive (though always selective) bibliographies will prove one of the most valuable features of the Encyclopedia.

A list of the main articles and contributors is provided at the beginning of this volume, together with a key to the initials of the authors of the shorter entries. Short, unsigned definitions are the work of a group of psychologists and lexicographers in the Herder Lexicographical Institute.

Wherever it seems appropriate, headwords are followed by the main synonymous (or approximately equivalent) terms. In the case of pharmaceutical preparations, however, complete lists of the corresponding trade names for even the English-speaking countries would be beyond the scope of this Encyclopedia; nevertheless, examples of such products on the market during the preparation of this work are usually cited. Less common synonyms are sometimes given at the end of an entry. The main abbreviations to be found in the Encyclopedia are listed in these preliminary pages; other abbreviations, too numerous to be listed initially, appear in context.

J.C.

MAIN ARTICLES

Catecholamines (Janke, W., Giessen, W. Germany)
Character (Arnold, W., Würzburg, W. Germany)
Child Psychology (Yule, W., London, England)
Clinical Psychology (Schraml, W., Freiburg, W. Germany)
Cognitive Orientation (Kreitler, H. & Kreitler, S., Tel Aviv, Israel)
Color Blindness (Plattig, K. H., Erlangen, W. Germany)
Color Perception (Kanizsa, G., Trieste, Italy)
Color Vision (Plattig, K. H., Erlangen, W. Germany)
Communication (Cherry, C., London, England)
Comparative Psychology (Holland, H. C., Beckenham, England)
Conditioning, Classical & Operant (Holland, H. C., Beckenham, England)
Conflict (Yates, A., Nedlands, Australia)
Conscience (Trasler, G., Southampton, England)
Consciousness (Pongratz, L.; Arnold, W., Würzburg, W. Germany)
Consciousness, Disorders of (Ehrhardt, H., Marburg, W. Germany)
Construct Validity (Horn, J. L., Denver, USA)
Correlational Techniques (Maxwell, A. E., London, England)
Creativity (Kaulfush, G., Hamburg, W. Germany)
Credibility (Topič, O., Karlovy Vary, Czechoslovakia)
Criminality (Trasler, G., Southampton, England)
Crowd Behavior (Jodelet, F., Nancy, France)
Cybernetic Education (Frank, H., West Berlin, Germany)
Cybernetics and Psychology (Klix, F., Berlin, German Democratic Republic)
Decision Processes (Blackwell, H. R., Columbus, USA)
Defiance (Meister, H., Saarbrücken, W. Germany)
Depression (Sattes, H., Würzburg, W. Germany)
Depth Psychology (Miles, T. R., Bangor, Wales)
Development (Oerter, R., Augsburg, W. Germany)
Differential Psychology (Anastasi, A., New York, USA)
Dream (Oswald, I., Edinburgh, Scotland)
Drive (Bolles, R. C., Seattle, USA)
Drug Dependence (Teasdale, J. D., London, England)
Ear (Monje, M., Kiel, W. Germany)
Educational Guidance (Illyés, F. & Lányes, A. E., Budapest, Hungary)
Educational Psychology (Mialaret, G. C., Caen, France; Pelzer, K. E., Würzburg, W. Germany)
Educational Science (Husén, T., Stockholm, Sweden)
Ego (Meili, R., Berne, Switzerland; Pawlik, K., Hamburg, W. Germany; Toman, W., Erlangen, W. Germany)
Emotion (Martin, I., London, England)
Encephalopathy (Engels, H. J., Bonn, W. Germany)
Energy, Psychic (Toman, W., Erlangen, W. Germany)
Existence Analysis (Boss, M. & Hicklin, M., Zürich, Switzerland)
Experiment (Merz, F., Marburg, W. Germany)
Experimental Esthetics (Berlyne, D. E., Toronto, Canada)
Exploration (Nahoum, C., Vanves, France)
Expression (Kirchhoff, R., West Berlin, Germany)
Eye (Monjé, M., Kiel; Rix, R., Erlangen, W. Germany)
Factor Analysis (Cattell, R. B., Champaign, USA)
Family (Toman, W., Erlangen, W. Germany)
Fantasy (McKellar, P., Dunedin, New Zealand)
Fatigue (Gubser, A., W. Germany)

Feedback System (Rohracher, H., Vienna, Austria)
Folk Psychology (Schmidbauer, W., Feldafing, W. Germany)
Forensic Psychology (Müller-Luckmann, E., Brunswick, W. Germany)
Frequency Distributions (Mittenecker, E., Graz, Austria)
Frontal Lobes (Luria, A. R., Moscow, USSR)
Frustration (Yates, A. J., Nedlands, Australia)
Ganzheit, *Gestalt*, Structure (Metzger, W., Münster, W. Germany)
Geisteswissenschaftliche Psychologie (Novak, F., Würzburg, W. Germany)
General Psychology (McKellar, P., Dunedin, New Zealand; Müller, P., Neuchâtel, Switzerland)
Genital Stage (Toman, W., Erlangen, W. Germany)
Geometrical-optical Illusions (Rausch, E., Frankfurt, W. Germany)
Gerontology (Birren, J. E., Los Angeles, USA)
Gonadotropic Hormones (Maisch, H., Hamburg, Germany)
Grammar (Abraham, W., W. Germany)
Graphology (Pokorny, R., Tel Aviv, Israel; Novak, F., Würzburg, W. Germany)
Group Dynamics (Braun, P., Würzburg, W. Germany)
Group Formation (Schmidt-Mummendey, A., Mainz, W. Germany)
Guilt (Ehrhardt, H., Marburg, W. Germany)
Habit (Jones, H. G., Leeds, England)
Hermaphroditism (Maisch, H., Hamburg, W. Germany)
History of Psychology (Wesley, F., Portland, USA; Wehner, E., Würzburg, W. Germany)
Homeostasis (Vormfelde, D., West Berlin, Germany)
Homosexuality (Maisch, H., Hamburg, W. Germany)
Hormones (Janke, W., Giessen, W. Germany)
Humanistic Psychology (Cohen, J., Manchester, England; Bühler, C., Los Angeles, USA)
Humor (Victoroff, D., Paris, France)
Hypnosis (Furneaux, D., Uxbridge, England)
Id (Lischke, G., Freiburg, W. Germany)
Identical Retinal Points (Rix, R., Erlangen, W. Germany)
Identification (Toman, W., Erlangen, W. Germany)
Imagery, Mental (Süllwold, F., Frankfurt)
Impression (Kiener, F., West Berlin, Germany)
Imprinting (Tschanz, B., Diemerswil, Switzerland)
Incest (Maisch, H., Hamburg, W. Germany)
Incubation (Ramsay, R. W., Amsterdam, The Netherlands)
Industrial Psychology (Wilson, G. D., London, England)
Infancy (Malrieu, P., Toulouse, France)
Information (Weltner, K., Wiesbaden, W. Germany)
Information, Psychology of (Frank, H., West Berlin, Germany)
Information Theory (Weltner, K., Wiesbaden, W. Germany)
Inhibition (Blöschl, L., Düsseldorf; Spreng, M., Erlangen; Schönpflug, W., Bochum, W. Germany)
Inner Speech (Sokolov, A. N., Moscow, USSR)
Instinct (Broadhurst, P. L. & Wilcock, J., Birmingham, England)
Instructional Technology (Glaser, R., Pittsburgh, USA)
Intelligence (Meili, R., Berne, Switzerland)
Intelligence Tests (Steck, P., Würzburg, W. Germany)
Interview (Bellebaum, A., Freiburg, W. Germany)
Language (Kaminski, G., Tübingen, W. Germany)
Latency (Toman, W., Erlangen, W. Germany)
Laterality (Ullmann, J. F., Bonn, Germany)
Leadership (Marschner, G. R. W., Bardenberg, W. Germany)
Learning (Metz, F., Marburg, W. Germany)

Learning Curves (Bärtl, M., Augsburg, W. Germany)

Learning Theory (Foppa, K., Berne, Switzerland)

Libido (Toman, W., Erlangen, W. Germany)

Life History (Bühler, C., Los Angeles, USA)

Literature, Psychology of (Cumming, J., London, England)

Localization of Psychological Functions (Luria, A. R., Moscow, USSR)

Logical Reasoning (Wason, P. C., London, England)

Longitudinal Studies (Meili, R., Berne, Switzerland)

Mania (Sattes, H., Würzburg, W. Germany)

Manipulation (Autrum, H.-J., Munich; Haas, H., Mannheim, W. Germany)

Marriage Guidance (Dominian, J., London, England)

Mathematical Psychology (Faverge, J.-M. F., Brussels, Belgium)

Maturation; Maturity (Engels, H. J., Bonn, W. Germany)

Meditation (Lotz, J. B., Rome, Italy; Dumoulin, H., Tokyo, Japan)

Memory (Underwood, B. J., Evanston, USA; Schubert, F. C., Würzburg, W. Germany)

Mental Defect (Clarke, A., Hull, England)

Mental Hygiene (Friedemann, A., Bienne, Switzerland)

Methods of Psychology (Traxel, W., Kiel, W. Germany)

Military Psychology (Mitze, G., Bonn, W. Germany)

Mind–Body Problem (Pongratz, L., Würzburg, W. Germany; Rohracher, H., Vienna, Austria)

Models (Tack, W., Hamburg, W. Germany)

Motivation (Nuttin, J. R., Louvain, Belgium)

Motor Skills (Bilodeau, I., New Orleans, USA)

Music, Psychology of (Lundin, R. A., Sewanee, USA)

Music Therapy (H.-N. Genius, Würzburg, W. Germany)

Need (Murray, H. A., Cambridge, Mass. USA)

Neuroanatomy (Bosque, P. G., Valladolid, Spain)

Neuropsychology (Guttmann, G., Vienna, Austria)

Neurosis (Wolpe, J., Philadelphia, USA)

Nervous System (Guttmann, G., Vienna, Austria)

Non-parametric Tests (Lienert, G. & Sarris, V., Düsseldorf, W. Germany)

Objective Tests (Wilson, G. D., London, England)

Occupational Psychology (Leplat, J., Paris, France)

Oedipus Complex (Toman, W., Erlangen, W. Germany)

Operational Definition (Buggle, F., Hamburg, W. Germany)

Opinion Polls (Noelle-Neumann, E., Allensbach, Germany)

Orienting Reflex (Sokolov, E. N., Moscow, USSR)

Pain (Sternbach, R. A., San Diego, USA)

Parapsychology (Beloff, J., Edinburgh, Scotland)

Perception (Droz, R., Lausanne, Switzerland)

Perseveration (Mittenecker, E., Graz, Austria)

Person (Arnold, W., Würzburg, W. Germany)

Personality (Vernon, P. E., Calgary, Canada; Takuma, T., Tokyo, Japan)

Personnel Selection (Marschner, G. R. W., Bardenburg, W. Germany)

Perversions (Broadhurst, A., Birmingham, England)

Phenomenology (Rudert, J., Heidelberg, W. Germany)

Philosophy and Psychology (Braun, P., Würzburg, W. Germany)

Physiology (Plattig, K. H., Erlangen, W. Germany)

Physiological Psychology (Plattig, K. H., Erlangen, W. Germany)

Physiology of Behavior (Grossmann, K., Freiburg, W. Germany)

Political Psychology (Baeyer-Katte, W., Heidelberg, W. Germany)

Practice (Bilodeau, I., New Orleans, USA)

Prejudice (Tajfel, H., Bristol, England)

Probability Theory (Maxwell, A. E., London, England)
Prognosis (Schneider, H.-J., Hamburg, W. Germany)
Programmed Instruction (Frank, H., West Berlin, Germany)
Projection (Toman, W., Erlangen, W. Germany)
Projective Techniques (Zubin, J. & Schumer, F., New York, USA)
Psychagogy (Schmidbauer, W., Feldafing, W. Germany)
Psychoanalysis (Ancona, L., Rome, Italy)
Psychodiagnostics (Meili, R., Berne, Switzerland)
Psycholinguistics (Kaminski, G., Tübingen, W. Germany)
Psychopathy (Hare, R. D., Vancouver, Canada)
Psychopathy: a Psychoanalytic View (Toman, W., Erlangen, W. Germany)
Psychopharmacology (Janke, W., Giessen, W. Germany)
Psychophysics (Stevens, S. S., Cambridge, USA)
Psychoses (Lorr, M., Washington, USA)
Psychosomatics (Hamilton, M., Leeds, England)
Psychotechnics (Thomas, A., Münster, W. Germany)
Psychotherapy (Bergin, A. E., New York, USA)
Punishment (Church, R. M., Providence, USA)
Questionnaires (Butcher, H. J., Sussex, England)
Reaction Timers (Thomas, A., Münster, W. Germany)
Regression (Toman, W., Erlangen, W. Germany; Mikula, G., Graz, Austria)
Reinforcement (Bolles, R. C., Seattle, USA)
Religion, Psychology of (Keilbach, W., Munich, W. Germany; Spinks, G. S., Bury, England; Vergote, A., Louvain, Belgium)
Reminiscence (Irion, A. L., St Louis, USA)
Restitution of Mental Processes (Luria, A. R., Moscow, USSR)
Repression (Toman, W., Erlangen, W. Germany)
Retention Curve (Hofer, M., Marburg, W. Germany)
Retina (Rix, R., Erlangen, W. Germany)
Risk Taking (Kogan, N., Princeton, USA)
Rôle (Rocheblave-Spenlé, A., Paris, France)
Satiation (Karsten, A., Frankfurt, W. Germany)
Scaling (Eyferth, K., Darmstadt, W. Germany)
Schizophrenia (Cooper, J. E., London, England)
School Readiness (Mandl, H., Augsburg, W. Germany)
Semantics (Bar-Hillel, J., Jerusalem, Israel)
Sensation (Plattig, K. H., Erlangen, W. Germany)
Sense Organs (Monjé, M., Kiel, W. Germany)
Sexuality (Broadhurst, A., Birmingham, England)
Sexuality in Childhood (Thomas, K., West Berlin, Germany)
Sign and Symbol (Kreitler, S. & Kreitler, H., Tel Aviv, Israel)
Simulation (Drösler, J., Brunswick, W. Germany)
Skin Diseases (Vaitl, D., Münster, W. Germany)
Sleep (Oswald, I., Edinburgh, Scotland)
Socialization (Bandura, A., Stanford, USA)
Social Perception (Pagès, R. C., Paris, France)
Social Psychology (Hartley, E. L., Green Bay, USA; Victoroff, D., Paris, France)
Social Scale (Schmidt-Mummendey, A., Mainz, W. Germany)
Sociogram (Schmidt-Mummendey, A., Mainz, W. Germany)
Soundness of Mind (Topič, O., Karlovy Vary, Czechoslovakia)
Soviet Psychology (Brožek, J., Bethlehem, USA; Luria, A. R., Moscow, USSR)
Space Perception (Pick, H., Minneapolis, USA)
Sport, Psychology of (Schilling, G., Magglingen, Switzerland)
Statistics (Faverge, J.-M., Brussels, Belgium)

AUTHORS OF SHORTER ARTICLES

KEY TO INITIALS

A.A.	A. Anastasi
A.B.	A. Broadhurst
A.Ba.	A. Bandura
A.Be.	A. Bellebaum
A.B.K.	A. B. Kristofferson
A.D.B.C.	A. D. B. Clarke
A.E.B.	A. E. Bergin
A.E.L.	A. E. Lányi
A.E.M.	A. E. Maxwell
A.F.	A. Friedemann
A.G.	A. Gubser
A.H.	A. Hajos
A.Hi.	A. Hicklin
A.J.Y.	A. J. Yates
A.K.	A. Karsten
A.L.	A. Lang
A.N.S.	A. N. Sokolov
A.R.	A. Rausche
A.R.L.	A. R. Luria
A.R.-S.	A. Rocheblave-Spenlé
A.S.-M.	A. Schmidt-Mummendey
A.T.	A. Tanda
A.Th.	A. Thomas
A.V.	A. Vergote
A.W.	A. Wellek
A.W.-F.	A. Weill-Fassima
A.Y.	A. Yates
B.B.	B. Brooker
B.H.	B. Heinze
B.J.U.	B. J. Underwood
B.L.	B. Louis
B.R.	B. Rollett
B.S.	B. Schmidt
B.Sp.	B. Spiegel
B.T.	B. Tschanz
B.W.	B. Wittlich
C.B.	C. Brinkmann
C.Bü.	C. Bühler
C.C.	C. Cherry
C.D.F.	C. D. Frith
C.G.	C. Guttmann
C.G.H.	C. G. Hoyos
C.M.	C. Münkel
C.N.	C. Nahoum
C.S.	C. Scharfetter
D.B.	D. Bartussek
D.E.	D. Eaves
D.E.B.	D. E. Berlyne
D.F.	D. Furneaux
D.G.	D. Görlitz
D.P.	D. Pfau
D.V.	D. Vaitl
D.Vo.	D. Vormfelde
E.D.	E. David
E.F.K.	E. Furch-Krafft
E.G.W.	E. G. Wehner
E.H.	E. Heineken
E.J.	E. Jorswieck
E.L.	E. Lehmann
E.L.H.	E. L. Hartley
E.M.	E. Mittenecker
E.M.-L.	E. Müller-Luckmann
E.N.M.	E. Noelle-Neumann
E.N.S.	E. N. Sokolov
E.R.	E. Rausch
E.R.H.	E. R. Hilgard
E.U.	E. Ullrich
E.W.	E. Wehner
F.B.	F. Bomio
F.Bu.	F. Buggle
F.-C.S.	F.-C. Schubert
F.H.	F. Haeberlin
F.J.	F. Jodelet
F.K.	F. Keller

F.Ki.	F. Kiener
F.Kl.	F. Klix
F.K.I.	F. K. Illyés
F.M.	F. Merz
F.Ma.	F. Mattejat
F.N.	F. Novak
F.S.	F. Süllwold
F.Sch.	F. Schumer
F.W.	F. Wesley
G.A.	G. Arnold
G.B.	G. Bachmair
G.B.T.	G. B. Trasler
G.C.M.	G. C. Mialaret
G.D.	G. Debus
G.D.W.	G. D. Wilson
G.E.	G. Erdmann
G.G.	G. Guttmann
G.H.	G. Huber
G.J.	G. Jones
G.K.	G. Kaulfush
G.Ka.	G. Kanizsa
G.Ki.	G. Kaminski
G.K.S.	G. K. Stürup
G.L.	G. Lischke
G.Li.	G. Lienert
G.M.	G. Mikula
G.Mi.	G. Mitze
G.P.	G. Prystav
G.R.W.M.	G. R. W. Marschner
G.S.	G. Stocker
G.Sch.	G. Schilling
G.S.S.	G. S. Spinks
G.T.	G. Trasler
H.A.M.	H. A. Murray
H.C.H.	H. C. Holland
H.D.	H. Dumoulin
H.D.S.	H. D. Schmidt
H.E.	H. Ehrhardt
H.F.	H. Frank
H.G.	H. Giessen
H.H.	H. Haase
H.He.	H. Hediger
H.H.J.K.	H. H. J. Keil
H.I.	H. Illner
H.-J.A.	H.-J. Aebi
H.-J.Au.	H.-J. Autrum
H.J.B.	H. J. Butcher
H.J.En.	H. J. Engels
H.-J.E.	H.-J. Eysenck
H.-J.K.	H.-J. Kornadt
H.-J.S.	H.-J. Steingrüber
H.-J.Sch.	H.-J. Schneider
H.K.	H. Knauer
H.Kr.	H. Kreitler
H.L.	H. Lippert
H.M.	H. Maisch
H.Ma.	H. Mandl
H.Me.	H. Meister
H.N.G.	H. N. Genius
H.P.	H. Pick
H.R.	H. Riedel
H.Ro.	H. Roth
H.Rr.	H. Rohracher
H.R.B.	H. R. Blackwell
H.S.	H. Schmalfuss
H.Sa.	H. Sattes
H.Schr.	H. Schröder
H.T.	H. Tajfel
H.W.	H. Wagenknecht
H.Z.	H. Zemanek
H.Zu.	H. Zumkley
I.B.	I. Bilodeau
I.L.	I. Lindner
I.M.	I. Martin
I.M.D.	I. M. Deusinger
I.O.	I. Oswald
J.B.	J. Beloff
J.Bi.	J. Birren
J.Br.	J. Brožek
J.B.G.	J. B. Grize
J.B.-H.	J. Bar-Hillel
J.B.L.	J. B. Lotz
J.C.	J. Cumming
J.Co.	J. Cohen
J.D.	J. Drösler
J.D.H.	J. D. Hundleby
J.D.T.	J. D. Teasdale
J.Fa.	J. Fahrenberg
J.F.	J. Friedrichs
J.F.U.	J. F. Ullmann

J.G.	J. Griffiths
J.L.	J. Leplat
J.L.H.	J. L. Horn
J.L.I.	J. Lopez Ibor
J.M.	J. Mields
J.Ma.	J. Maxwell
J.Me,	J. Maisonneuve
J.-M.F.	J.-M. Faverge
J.N.	J. Nitsch
J.O.	J. Osterland
J.P.	J. Price
J.R.	J. Rudert
J.R.N.	J. R. Nuttin
J.S.	J. Schenk
J.W.	J. Wittkowski
J.Wi.	J. Wilcock
J.Wo.	J. Wolpe
J.Z.	J. Zoltobrocki
J.Zu.	J. Zubin
K.D.G.	K. D. Graf
K.D.N.	K. D. Nissen
K.-D.S.	K.-D. Stoll
K.E.	K. Eyferth
K.E.G.	K. E. Grossmann
K.E.P.	K. E. Pelzer
K.F.	K. Fiedler
K.Fo.	K. Foppa
K.G.	K. Grossmann
K.H.P.	K. H. Plattig
K.M.	K. Mizushima
K.Mi.	K. Mierke
K.P.	K. Pawlik
K.T.	K. Thomas
K.W.	K. Weltner
L.A.	L. Ancona
L.B.	L. Blöschl
L.J.I.	L. J. Issing
L.J.P.	L. J. Pongratz
L.S.	L. Shaw
M.A.	M. Amelang
M.Ad.	M. Adler
M.B.	M. Brambring
M.Ba.	M. Bartl
M.Bo.	M. Boss
M.H.	M. Haider
M.Ha.	M. Hamilton
M.He.	M. Henke
M.Ho.	M. Hofer
M.-J.B.	M.-J. Borel
M.L.	M. Lorr
M.Mo.	M. Monjé
M.R.	M. Reinhardt
M.S.	M. Spreng
M.Sa.	M. Sachs
M.Y.	M. Yela
N.K.	N. Kogan
N.S.-R.	N. Schmidt-Relenberg
O.S.	O. Schrappe
O.T.	O. Topič
O.W.	O. White
P.B.	P. Braun
P.-B.H.	P.-B. Heinrich
P.C.W.	P. C. Wason
P.D.	P. Dietsch
P.G.	P. Graw
P.G.B.	P. Gomez Bosque
P.J.	P. Jankowski
P.L.	P. Leyhausen
P.Le.	P. Ley
P.L.B.	P. L. Broadhurst
P.M.	P. Müller
P.Ma.	P. Malrieu
P.McK.	P. McKellar
P.S.	P. Steck
P.Sch.	P. Schmidt
P.T.	P. Tholey
P.V.	P. Vernon
P.W.B.	P. W. Bradshaw
P.Z.	P. Zimmermann
R.A.S.	R. A. Stamm
R.A.St.	R. A. Sternbach
R.B.C.	R. B. Cattell
R.C.	R. Chocholle
R.C.B.	R. C. Bolles
R.C.P.	R. C. Pagès
R.D.	R. Droz
R.D.H.	R. D. Hare
R.G.	R. Glaser
R.H.	R. Hetherington
R.Hä.	R. Hänni

R.K.	R. Kirchhoff	*V.Sa.*	V. Sarris
R.L.	R. Lynn	*W.A.*	W. Arnold
R.M.	R. Meili	*W.Ab.*	A. Abraham
R.M.C.	R. M. Church	*W.B.*	W. Boucsein
R.O.	R. Oerter	*W.Ba.*	W. Bauer
R.P.	R. Pokorny	*W.B.-K.*	W. Baeyer-Katte
R.P.S.	R. P. Swinson	*W.D.F.*	W. D. Fröhlich
R.R.	R. Rix	*W.F.N.*	W. F. Neubauer
R.S.	R. Simon	*W.H.B.*	W. H. Butollo
R.W.L.	R. W. Lundin	*W.J.*	W. Janke
R.W.R.	R. W. Ramsay	*W.J.S.*	W. J. Schraml
R.Z.	R. Zazzo	*W.K.*	W. Kretschmer
S.K.	S. Kanizsa	*W.Ke.*	W. Keilbach
S.Kr.	S. Kreutzer	*W.L.*	W. Lauterbach
S.R.	S. Rachman	*W.M.*	W. Metzger
S.S.	S. Sapon	*W.N.*	W. Neubauer
S.S.S.	S. S. Stevens	*W.P.*	W. Pieper
T.H.	T. Husén	*W.S.*	W. Sperber
T.O.	T. Oyama	*W.Sc.*	W. Schmidbauer
T.R.M.	T. R. Miles	*W.Sch.*	W. Schönpflug
T.T.	T. Takuma	*W.Se.*	W. Seitz
U.H.S.	U. H. Schindler	*W.T.*	W. Toman
V.K.J.	V. K. Jain	*W.Ta.*	W. Tack
V.M.	V. Martinu	*W.Tr.*	W. Traxel
V.P.	V. Preuss	*W.W.*	W. Wittling
V.S.	V. Sigusch	*W.Y.*	W. Yule

MAIN ABBREVIATIONS USED IN THIS WORK

AA = Achievement age
abb. = abbreviation
ACh = Acetylcholine
ACTH = Adrenocorticotrophic hormone
AL = Adaptation level
Am. = American
ANS = Autonomic nervous system
ant. = antonym
anthropol. = anthropological
A.P.A. = American Psychological Association
AQ = Achievement quotient
b. = born
biol. = biological
CA = Chronological age
c. = *circa* = about
cc = cubic centimeter (centimetre)
cf. = *confer* = compare
ch., chs = chapter(s)
CFF = Critical flicker frequency
chem. = chemical
CNS = Central nervous system
cps = cycles per second
CR = Conditioned response
CS = conditioned stimulus
d. = died
db = decibel
d.f. = degrees of freedom
DNA = Desoxyribonucleic acid
E., Es = Experimenter(s)
EA = Educational age
Ed., Eds = Editor(s)
ed. cit. = edition cited
EEG = Electroencephalogram
e.g. = *exempli gratia* = for example
EKG = Electrocardiogram
Eng. = English
EQ = Educational quotient
ERG = Electroretinogram
esp. = especially
ESP = Extrasensory perception
et al. = *et alii* = and others
etc. = *et cetera* = and so forth
et seq. = *et sequens, sequentia* = and the following
ex., exs = example(s)
f., ff. = and the following
FFF = Flicker-fusion frequency
fig., figs = figure(s)
fn. = footnote
Fre. = French
GABA = Gamma-amino-butyric acid
GAS = General adaptation syndrome
Ger. = German
Gr. = Greek
GSR = Galvanic skin response
Hz. = Hertzian wave
Ib. = *ibidem* = in the same place
Id. = *idem* = the same person(s)
i.e. = *id est* = that is
introd. = introduction by
IQ = Intelligence quotient
IRM = Innate releasing mechanism
It. = Italian
IU = Interval of uncertainty
j.n.d. = Just-noticeable difference
Lat. = Latin
loc. cit. = *loco citato* = in the place (passage) cited
m. = meter (metre)
MA = Mental age
math. = mathematical
med. = medical
min. = minute
mm. = millimeter (millimetre)
n.d. = no date
No., Nos = number(s)
n.p. = no place of publication
n.s. = new series
NS = Nervous system
O = Observer
op. cit. = *opere citato* = in the work cited
o.s. = old series
OT = Occupational therapy
p = probability
p., pp. = page(s)

PE	= Probable error	S., Ss	= Subject(s)
philol.	= philological	SD	= Standard deviation
philos.	= philosophical	SE	= Standard error
phys.	= physical	sec.	= second(s)
physiol.	= physiological	sect.	= section
PR	= Percentile rank	ser.	= series
pref.	= preface	S-R	= Stimulus-response
q.v.	= *quod vide* = which see	stat.	= statistical
R	= Response	syn.	= synonym
REM	= Rapid eye movement	TAT	= Thematic Apperception Test
resp.	= respectively	TE	= Trial-and-error learning
rev.	= revised by	trans.	= translation
RI	= Retroactive inhibition	UR	= Unconditioned response
RNA	= Ribonucleic acid	US	= Unconditioned stimulus
rpm	= revolutions per minute	V	= volt
RS	= Reinforcing stimulus	vol.	= volume
RT	= Reaction time	VTE	= Vicarious trial and error
S	= Stimulus	WHO	= World Health Organization

ACKNOWLEDGEMENTS

It is possible to mention only a few of those who have contributed to the making of this Encyclopedia. Special thanks are due to Professor O. Köhler of Verlag Herder and Freiburg University, and to Herr F. Novak of Würzburg University. In production Mr D. Cahill's proofreading and the advice and help of Frau G. Pallat, Herr A. Zimmermann and Mr J. Gibbons were invaluable. The translations into English were made by J. Cumming, D. Geoghegan, V. Green, J. Griffiths, J. F. Hargreaves, W. Hargreaves, D. Livingstone, J. Maxwell and H. Repton. *J.C.*

Abasement. A general term for behavior indicative of submission to, e.g., aggression or punishment. See *Appeasement gestures.*

Abasia. The inability to walk, in the absence of nerve lesions or disorders of the muscular apparatus, i.e. of apparent organic causation. Abasia is recognized in a condition of mental conflict which would seem to inhibit further vocal and other protest in the individual affected. Occurs mainly in neurotic disorders, especially as a symptom of hysteria. *Astasia* is the inability to stand, similarly without recognizable organic cause; *astasia-abasia*, the combination of both afflictions. *A.H.*

Aberration. 1. See *Chromatic aberration.* **2.** *Spherical aberration:* Marginal rays bend more than those refracted by the inner surface of the lens; i.e. focal points on the optical axis are not identical. *R.R.*

Abience. Tendency to avoid or withdraw from a stimulus. Hence *abient behavior* or *response*, behavior withdrawing the organism from the stimulus, or negating or even cancelling the stimulus in some way. *J.G.*

Abilities: a psychometric account. Many modern psychologists, particularly in America, have given up the use of the term "intelligence" in the technical sense, and prefer to use terms like "human abilities"; "intelligence", if it is retained at all, is used to denote a particular area of inquiry. At the same time, doubt is being thrown on the usefulness of the IQ, and preference is often given to "ability profiles". The British school (Burt, Vernon, Eysenck) considers the concepts of "general intelligence" and "special abilities" as complementary, and continues to use the concept of IQ as well as that of ability profiles. The arguments employed by protagonists reach back into the past, and a brief account of the development of these divergent notions is essential, if only because the facts have often been misrepresented. The concept of "intelligence", very much as used later by more experimentally-oriented writers, owes its inception to Spencer and Galton; Binet constructed his tests very much along the lines of their expressed views. The crucial step toward quantitative testing of theories, as opposed to simple quantification of measurement, was taken by Spearman, who used the techniques of correlational analysis and factor analysis (q.v.), both of which had been developed by Pearson, in relation to the scores obtained by groups of children on various intelligence tests. He was concerned to test the theory that these correlations were due entirely to a general intellective factor, "g"; in addition to this he recognized specific factors, "s" factors, which were specific to particular tests. Essentially his point was that under these conditions matrices of intercorrelations between tests should be of rank one; he did not use matrix algebra himself, but his formulas are the equivalent of more modern versions.

Thurstone generalized Spearman's methods and formulas, translated them into matrix algebra, and carried out large-scale studies, using as many as fifty-seven tests on one group of subjects; on the basis of these studies he concluded that Spearman was wrong in postulating a single "g" factor, and that an alternative description in terms of several "primary abilities" fitted the data much better. The main factors he discovered were S (spatial ability), P (perceptual speed), N (numerical ability), V (verbal meaning), M (memory), W (verbal fluency), and R (inductive reasoning). There are several reasons why this apparent conflict between the two systems is much less real than appears at first. Spearman had laid down two main conditions under which he said his "g" would be found. The first related to populations sampled; he worked with random samples of the population (usually children), and while very low IQs would probably be missing in these groups (being confined to mental defective colonies or special schools for the educationally subnormal), nevertheless the range of IQs would be approximating to 100 points. Thurstone contravened this first rule by working only with students, and with specially selected students at that; all his subjects had IQs around the 95th percentile! By thus reducing the range of "g" to less than 10 per cent, he naturally reduced his chances of discovering traces of it in his experiment. The second difference between Spearman and Thurstone relates to choice of tests. Spearman had stated explicitly that tests should not be too similar to each other; if they were, then the "s" factors would overlap and cause additional correlations which would emerge as separate factors and disturb the unit rank of the matrix. Thurstone used groups of tests which were very similar, often almost identical, and consequently his study could certainly not be considered as a test of Spearman's hypothesis.

Thurstone later on recognized the force of these objections, particularly as a consequence of his work with children. Having originally elaborated a system of rotation of axes based on the principle of "simple structure", he found that with random samples of the population he could no longer keep his factors orthogonal (independent) and yet retain simple structure; accordingly he gave up orthogonality and allowed his factors to be correlated. These correlated factors correspond quite well to the types of tests Spearman had called for, and indeed Thurstone found that when the matrix of intercorrelations between his factors was analyzed, a single "g" factor was indeed found. This suggests a hierarchical structure of intellect, with "g" at the top, and the "primary abilities" (whose intercorrelations necessitated the postulation of "g") at a lower level; the actual tests used, whose intercorrelations gave rise to the "primary abilities", would of course be at a lower level still. The agreement between Spearman and Thurstone is almost perfect, and it should also be noted that in his work Spearman had also found evidence of group or "primary" factors, such as verbal ability and fluency, which could not be explained entirely in terms of similar "s" factors.

More recently, Guilford has suggested a model of human intellect which takes Thurstone's set of factors even further, and which admits no "g" at all. Guilford postulates four types of mental contents (figural, symbolic, semantic, and behavioral), upon which five types of operations can be performed: cognition, memory, evaluation, divergent production and convergent production. This leads to one or more of six products: units, classes, relations, systems, transformations, or implications. Thus we have 120 possible combinations of these three classes of variables, and Guilford points out that examples of most of these are already in existence in the mental testing literature; he himself and his students have added many of the missing ones. Psychometrically, Guilford's work is subject to several criticisms. He has concentrated most of his studies on populations with a restricted range of intelligence, thus reducing the scope of "g"; and he has used orthogonal methods of rotation, thus ignoring the correlations between "simple structure" factors which would have emerged only if he had used an oblique method of rotation. Certainly the scores on his tests, when administered to random samples of the population, are highly correlated, even though they come from different parts of his three-dimensional "box"; an appropriate analysis of the intercorrelations would almost certainly give rise to some form of hierarchical system. In spite of these criticisms, Guilford's long-continued work has certainly been useful in producing a whole range of novel tests, and in linking mental testing much more firmly than was previously the case with experimental and theoretical psychology. Of more practical importance is the criticism that Guilford's factors are so narrow and specialized that they have little value in prediction, as in educational and vocational guidance. This is almost certainly true; knowledge of a child's "g" and a few of the broader "primary abilities" is probably as predictive as any amount of further testing and probing.

While there are still many points of detail on which experts disagree, on the whole most would probably now agree on some form of hierarchical model, although they might not be at one in assessing the practical importance of "g" as opposed to "primary abilities". Fortunately such decisions are seldom needed; in most practical situations tests would provide information on both types of factors. Furthermore, the problem is an empirical one, and in due course enough information should be available to make a decision possible.

The division of "intellect" into these various factors is not the only kind that is possible; Cattell, for instance, has suggested that we should distinguish "fluid" from "crystallized" ability, i.e. potentiality for intellectual achievement from acquired knowledge. Jensen has suggested a division between level 1 (associative ability) and level 2 (reasoning ability), measured by tests of rote learning and of the education of relations respectively. A thorough discussion of these and other schemes is given by Butcher; like all descriptive systems there is no one "true" scheme which must prevail, but different schemes may serve different purposes. Objections to any form of analysis, on the grounds that the mind "acts as a whole", are not very useful; scientific understanding is predicated upon analysis, and analysis has proved extremely useful already. Other criticisms of such concepts as "intelligence" and "primary abilities" suggest that they imply "reification"; intelligence is not a thing, but an abstraction. Exactly; scientific concepts like gravitation, electricity and intelligence are abstract in that they relate to certain properties of the data. No psychologist has ever publicly talked about "intelligence" as a reified unity; it is a hypothetical concept having certain mathematical properties the presence or absence of which can be tested in relation to data from given samples of tests and subjects. This is precisely the purpose of most of the experimental work done in this field.

Other criticisms have been made of these factorial studies of mental abilities, and these are more difficult to answer. What is normally correlated is the score on one test with the score on another; these scores may be derived in quite different ways from different subjects, yet be identical for all of them. Consider subject A who gets twenty answers right, working straight through from the easiest to the twentieth, and then fails to get the twenty-first or any more difficult ones right; compare him with subject B who gets only twelve right out of the first twenty (perhaps because he hurries and does not bother to check his wrong answers), but goes on to get another eight right out of the more difficult problems succeeding number 20. Both get the same score, namely 20, but they have behaved in a very dissimilar fashion, and have solved quite different problems in many cases. Or consider subject C, who gives up easily, but does not make any errors; he too may solve twenty problems, but those solved by him may only overlap very partly with those solved by A or B. In what sense can we say that these three subjects, although having the same score, are equivalent for the purpose of statistical analysis? Eysenck has suggested that the unit of analysis should be the individual problem; this can be attempted and solved correctly; attempted and solved erroneously; attempted and given up before any solution becomes apparent; or not attempted at all. Furneaux has taken up this suggestion and provided an analysis of intellect in terms of such concepts as mental speed, error-checking mechanism, and continuance (or persistence); he has shown that these are relatively independent of each other. Only the first of these may be regarded as a proper "ability"; the other two are probably related to personality (e.g., extraverts are known to be quicker and more prone to error than introverts). Analysis along these lines is as yet relatively novel, but in due course it should throw much light on the problem of mental abilities. Certainly the customary failure of psychometrists to take into account personality differences in analyzing intelligence tests is a source of weakness; the fact that there are few overall correlations between total scores on tests and personality traits does not prove that there is not considerable interaction, and it even seems that the very nature of the factors found in a given sample may be affected by the personality make-up of the subjects involved.

Little use has hitherto been made of electrophysiological recording in work on mental abilities. Ertl has demonstrated repeatedly that when evoked potentials on the EEG are compared for bright and dull subjects, marked differences can be observed; the records of the bright subjects (as measured by IQ tests) are characterized by EEG patterns which suggest the speedy transmission of information. This finding may link up with Furneaux's isolation of menta speed as the main (perhaps the only) truly cognitive factor in intelligence test performance. This type of work has not yet touched on the different "primary abilities", but has been concerned entirely with "g"; its extension to other problems will be awaited with interest. In particular it seems that the inclusion of such electrophysiological tests in a factorial study should facilitate the identification and interpretation of "g". It also seems likely that such tests would throw much light on the hereditary nature of "g"; no tests of this kind have as yet been carried out on uniovular and binovular twins.

Racial differences in human abilities have been frequently studied, and the evidence has been reviewed by Eysenck; most of the work has been done on American Negroes. Results seem to show that when Negroes are compared with whites, the Negroes have IQs some 15 points lower than the whites; this is true whether testing is carried out by white or black testers. Contrary to the belief that these differences are due to poorer environment, it is found that when working-class whites are compared with middle-class Negroes, differences in favor of the whites still persist; it is also found that differences are largest in respect to "fluid" intelligence, as measured by relatively "culture free" tests, and least with respect to "crystallized" ability, as measured by tests involving culture-transmitted knowledge. Orientals in California, although inferior to whites in socio-economic status, are somewhat superior on tests of "fluid" ability, suggesting innate racial differences. American Indians, although as much below Negroes with respect to socio-economic status as Negroes are below whites, yet equal to Negroes on IQ tests. Maoris, though inferior to whites in IQ, are superior to them on verbal fluency. There are many detailed findings which suggest that there are important racial differences between different populations, but much work remains to be done until any worthwhile generalizations become possible.

Bibliography: Burt, C.: The evidence for the concept of intelligence. Brit. J. Educ. Psychol., 1955, *25*, 158–77. **Butcher, H. J.:** Human intelligence. London, 1968. **Cattell, R. B.:** Theory of fluid and crystallized intelligence: a critical experiment. J. Educ. Psychol., 1963, *54*, 1–22. **Ertl, J. P. & Schafer, E. V. F.:** Brain response correlates and psychometric intelligence. Nature, 1969, Vol. 223, 421–2. **Eysenck, H. J.:** Intelligence assessment: a theoretical and experimental approach. Brit. J. Educ. Psychol., 1967, *37*, 81–98. **Id.:** Race, intelligence and education. London, 1971. **Furneaux, W. P.:** Intellectual abilities and problem-solving behavior. In: **Eysenck, H. J.** (Ed.): Handbook of abnormal psychology. London, 1960. **Guilford, J. P.:** The nature of human intelligence. New York, 1967. **Jensen, A. R.:** Environment, heredity, and intelligence. Harvard, Reprint Ser. No. 2, 1969. **Id.:** Hierarchical theories of mental ability. In: **Dockrell, W. B.** (Ed.): On intelligence. London, 1970. **Spearman, C.:** The abilities of man. London, 1927. **Thurstone, L. L. & Thurstone, T. G.:** Factorial studies of intelligence. Psychometric Monogr., 1941, No. 2. **Vernon, P. E.:** The measurement of abilities. London, 1956.

H. J. Eysenck

Abilities: a conceptual account. Some other notions ("*Begabung*", q.v., "talent" and "capacity"—the latter no longer being in common use) are virtually synonymous with "ability"; there is no clear distinction between these concepts. Linguistic overlap occurs in a number of languages, and contradictions may be found in a single dictionary. A given word may have different meanings in different languages: while the word "aptitude" as used in the English literature (*Eignung* in German) signifies the "ability" to exercise a profession or acquire certain forms of knowledge or skill, the French word "*aptitude*" corresponds to the English term "ability", designating ability in the narrower sense as it is used in empirical research—although unfortunately not in general practice. Here ability means *all the psychological conditions needed to perform an activity*. Ability is therefore operationally defined by the activity with which it is associated; in this sense, e.g., even the ability "intelligence" (q.v.) is frequently defined today as that which is measured by an intelligence test. It follows from this definition of the term ability that there are as many different abilities as there are activities, and that the question as to the number and nature of abilities is meaningless. The word is therefore primarily an abbreviation for "all the psychological conditions needed to perform an activity". It should, however, be noted that ability includes only the necessary conditions; some influences which might facilitate the activity, such as interest, degree of activation, practice and certain experiences are therefore excluded. This does not, however, mean that ability is reduced to innate conditions, as was frequently the case in the past and as applies to the word *Begabung*. Some of the conditions may well be explained by experience and general learning processes. It has been generally recognized that it is empirically impossible to make a reliable distinction between acquired and innate conditions of psychological phenomena.

Activities and the abilities normally associated with them may be quite specific: e.g. knitting, adding, writing advertising slogans, and so on; or complex, such as manual crafts, trades, mechanical engineering, and so on. It is necessary to distinguish between complex abilities and those which are more general and cover a group of relatively similar activities. (See *Attention; Memory*.)

Empirical findings and conclusions. The decisive change brought about by empirical research into the notion of ability is that abilities are no longer considered—as were "capacities"—as innate, uniform and clearly distinct "powers", but (in a much less precise manner) as a *set of conditions*. This attitude has been motivated primarily by research into the relations between abilities, using correlational techniques (q.v.). Correlations may be determined between performances in a variety of cognitive problems (i.e. highly specialized ability) or between performances in different school subjects (e.g. mathematics and languages), or between intelligence and motor abilities (skills) (e.g. drawing). These studies have shown that there are very many relations within the range of intellectual abilities, and that, e.g., mathematical aptitude is not so very different from linguistic aptitude as is often assumed; indeed, it has even been shown that there is a definite correlation between manual skill and intelligence. It follows that many abilities (not only those which are specialized or relatively complex) overlap partially; this means that the basic conditions for different abilities are sometimes the same.

The age-old debate between those who assumed a central capacity in man and those who believed in several, or a wide range of, capacities has therefore finally been settled by empirical research. We now know that the conditions on which performance is based are complex, even in the case of specialized activities; in other words there are several conditions for performance, none of which can be attributed to any individual achievement.

Factor analysis (q.v.) provides a method of determining and defining basic conditions (factors) common to different activities. It therefore becomes possible to determine the inner structure of an ability defined with reference to an activity. Through this research we have come to realize above all that the conventional classification of ability into intelligence, memory, attention, motor skills and sensorimotor activities is extremely superficial and has little basis in the light of psychological principles. The correlations are sometimes very slight between different feats of intelligence, and almost wholly absent between memory and motor skills, etc.

Nevertheless the notion of ability is still used today in connection with such activities or ranges of activity. Since ability is no longer viewed as a uniform, clearly defined capacity, we come up against the question of the meaning of general or complex ability. Two answers are given: (*a*) the conditions which are common to a group of partial abilities; (*b*) the totality of the conditions effective in all of them. If we define intelligence by the general factor "g", as Spearman has suggested, we will opt for the first concept; but if we measure intelligence by a complex test such as the Binet–Simon intelligence scale, intelligence is then defined by the total set of conditions for the different tasks.

The concept of ability is primarily important in applied psychology, in the case of all types of aptitude test. At first, unsuccessful attempts were made to subdivide the ability proper to a certain profession into partial abilities such as intelligence, motor skills, perception, etc. Later, the emphasis was placed on testing specific activities approximating most closely to those of the vocation in question. Recently, attempts have been made to use aptitude tests to determine the basic factors of vocational achievement; but it has been found that many factors other than ability play a part in vocational success and in school achievement.

Bibliography: Cox, J. W.: Mechanical aptitude. London, 1928. **Id.:** Manual skill: its organization and development. Cambridge, 1934. **Meili, R.:** Lehrbuch der psychologischen Diagnostik. Berne, [5]1965. **Piéron, H.** *et al.*: L'utilisation des aptitudes. Paris, 1954. **Révész, G.:** Talent und Genie. Berne, 1952. **Vernon, P.:** The structure of human abilities. London, 1950.

R. Meili

Ability grouping. In many countries series of tests have been devised to select those suitable for secondary (or even tertiary) education, and to divide them into relatively homogeneous groups according to their presumed general, or specialized, scholastic ability. Syn. *Homogeneous grouping*. Only the intellectual aspect of suitability can be covered since effort and so on vary greatly and depend on external circumstances. See *Abilities*.

R.M.

Ability research. Branch of psychological research dealing with questions of ability.

It clarifies, e.g., what the prerequisites for some particular activity are, and whether and to what degree anyone possesses them and hence can participate in this activity. Still currently engaging most attention is the elucidation of the intellectual prerequisites. See *Abilities*. *H.-J.A.*

Ability to dissociate. See *Spaltbarkeit.*

Abklingen (Ger.). Fading out. The slow cessation of a tone, emotional process or sensation.

Ablation. 1. The surgical removal of an organ or bodily part (*Amputation*). **2.** The separation of one organ from another. **3.** The removal, interruption or weakening of a psychic relationship or dependency (e.g. of children and parents) during or for psychic maturation, especially in the case of the displacement of affect, i.e. *transference*, in psychoanalysis (q.v.).

Ablation experiments: term for animal experiments in which—after acquisition of a certain behavior—cerebral tissues are excised, and the relation between the extent of excision (*Extirpation*, q.v.) and location (neural centers and pathways) on the one hand and the functional loss on the other is observed. Lashley's (q.v.) experiments (c. 1929) were important in this field: rats which had learnt to negotiate a maze retained their orientation there even after extirpation of specific motor centers and cutting of pathways.

Bibliography: Lashley, K. S.: Nervous mechanisms in learning. In: **Murchison, C.** (Ed.): The foundation of experimental psychology. Worcester, Mass., 1929. **Id.:** Brain mechanisms and intelligence. Chicago, 1929.

F.S.

Ablösung (Ger.). The dissolution of a psychic bond between two individuals, or of the dependence of one on the other. Used in Freudian psychoanalysis for the termination of a psychotherapeutic reliance (transference, q.v.) of the analysand (q.v.) on the analyst, and deemed requisite before treatment can be said to have come to an end. *H.N.G.*

Abnormal psychology is the study of "abnormal behavior" or "abnormal personality", i.e. "abnormalities" of sensory perception, of psychomotor function, of cognitive, motivational and other psychological functions; abnormalities of personality including psychoses, neuroses, psychosomatic disorders, character disorders, mental deficiencies, etc.; abnormalities of social behavior such as crime or delinquency, drug addiction and other sociopathic behavior.

1. *Concept of abnormality.* The word "abnormal" is used in several different senses and also in various combinations of them. The major dimensions of differentiation are: (*a*) whether it is defined as deviation from the ideal norm or as the statistical unusuality; (*b*) whether the definition of abnormality is to be universal or to differ according to the culture; (*c*) whether it is based on objective characteristics of behavior, or on the fact that a person is objectionable to himself or to others, or calls forth sanctions from others.

Satisfactory definition of the discipline also depends on and is made problematic by studies of the development and health of personality, of cultural norms, of the reaction of individuals and society to deviant behavior, and so on.

2. *Mental illness* (general and classificatory approach). Scientific approaches to mental illness have been developed since the end of the eighteenth century by Pinel, Mesmer, Esquirol, Bernheim, Charcot and several others. Janet (1895–1947) saw the neurotic process as the reduction of the energy level, and distinguished two principal types: psychasthenia and hysteria. Kraepelin (1856–1926) regarded certain symptoms of mental illness which tended to appear in clusters as manifestations of specific types of mental illness. His contribution to the

description of "*dementia praecox*" (later elaborated as schizophrenia by Bleuler) and manic-depressive illness introduced an epoch in psychiatry. The description of abnormal character developed by K. Schneider and others has stimulated biopsychological studies of criminals and other sociopaths.

Recently, statistical methods have been used in classification. For example, Jenkins and his colleagues found three major syndromes of children's behavior problems: over-inhibited, unsocialized-aggressive, and socialized-delinquent. Eysenck, using factor analysis, found three independent variables: introversion–extraversion, neuroticism and psychoticism.

Classification and description depend also on the researcher's view of the origin and treatment of abnormalities. There are biological, behavioristic, psychodynamic, sociodynamic and other theories. From an eclectic viewpoint, Meyer evaluated the influence of the inherited structures and tendencies, of life experiences and of environmental stress. The present classification of the American Psychiatric Association distinguishes two classes: "disorders caused by or associated with impairment of brain tissue function", and "disorders of psychogenic origin or without clearly defined physical cause of structural change in the brain". The latter category includes psychotic, psychophysiological, autonomic and visceral, psychoneurotic, personality, and transient situational personality disorders. See also *Psychiatry, Clinical psychology, Psychoses, Psychoneurosis, Mental defect, Psychopathology, Delinquency, Drug dependence.*

3. *Biological approaches.* The inheritance of abnormal tendencies has been studied by family investigation and other more sophisticated methods. Observations of monozygotic twins, especially in comparison with dizygotic twins, have been reported with psychotics, neurotics and sociopaths (Lange, Rosanoff, Kallmann, Salter, Yoshimasu, Inoue). The genetics of some psychological factors, e.g. intelligence, motor skills, neurotic tendencies, has also been studied. (See *Heredity.*) In a constitutional approach to the problem, Kretschmer described physical types which he correlated with psychotic disorders and their pre-morbid personality patterns. More recently, Sheldon's system of somatotypes, Lindegard's method, factor analysis method and other new techniques have been employed in constitutional approaches (see *Traits*).

4. *Experimental approaches.* Jackson's hierarchical model of the dissolution of function stimulated the early experimental studies. Pavlov's experiments in conditioning and induced neurosis have been highly influential. Conflict between neural excitation and inhibition was regarded by Pavlov as the precipitating factor of neurosis. Many studies of aggression, fixation and other maladaptive habits of animals have been reported (Lashley, Liddel, Maier, Masserman). (See *Aggression, Animal psychology.*) Effects of early experiences have been studied in animals (Denenberg, Levine, Thompson, Harlow). Some studies have dealt with abnormalities of human behavior in such experimentally induced situations as sensory deprivation. Laboratory techniques with psychiatric patients have been developed (Luria, Malmo, Eysenck). These techniques are used also as objective tests in clinical practice. From experimental evidence and behavioral theory, Eysenck, Wolpe and others developed behavior therapy (q.v.).

The effects of drugs have been studied experimentally and clinically. (See *Psychopharmacology, Hormone.*) Neurophysiological studies on brain damage have been developed by direct observation or by means of neurological techniques such as EEG. (See *Neuropsychology, Brain pathology.*) Biochemical studies have tried to determine the chemical causes of mental disorders or to clarify a chemical process under abnormal mental conditions. (See *Psychopharmacology, Neuropsychology.*)

5. *Psychodynamic approaches.* Since Freud, a number of psychoanalytic and other

psychodynamic studies have been reported, based on orthodox Freudian theory, Jungian, Adlerian, neo-Freudian theories, or other eclectic theories (see *Psychoanalysis*). In the field of child psychiatry (q.v.) or clinical-educational psychology, since Healy and others, the psychodynamic approach has become especially dominant in diagnostic and therapeutic practice. Related to this field are many observations of children under certain environmental conditions, and especially under abnormal home conditions (Bowlby, Goldfarb, Spitz). Experimental and clinical observations of the dynamics of personality have also been attempted. They include the recording of dreams, imagery and other characteristic phenomena. Behavioral theories and other theories based on the experimental approaches have been synthesized using psychodynamic concepts (Mowrer and Kluckhorn, Dollard and Miller, Maier). Although psychodynamics has been faulted for its lack of objective clarity (Eysenck), the psychodynamic approach is dominant in projective diagnosis and psychotherapy (q.v.) in the clinical field.

6. *Socio-cultural approaches*. Much anthropological research related to socio-psychological approaches in psychoanalysis has been carried on into the "abnormal psychology" of primitive societies (Fortune, Benedict, Mead, Malinowski). (See *Anthropology*.) Comparative studies have been made of personality and behavior disorders in different modern countries, and among different ethnic or social groups. There have been many ecological (or epidemiological) studies of mental disorders (Hollingshead, Redlich, *et al.*), of crime and delinquency (Shaw, McKay, *et al.*) and other behavior disorders. (See *Criminality*.) Deviant acculturation or group reference is emphasized even in individual clinical practice, especially in the case of crime and delinquency (Jenkins, Mizushima). Group dynamics (q.v.) and other socio-psychological theories have been evaluated and adopted in social therapy (q.v.). Socio-cultural approaches have also influenced the recent development of community psychiatry, community psychology, social work and other related practices. But there are as yet few systematic studies of the historical sociodynamics of abnormal behavior and societal reaction to it.

7. *Ontological approaches*. In the European tradition of psychiatry, Jaspers' "*Verstehende Methode*" has had a great influence. More recently, Binswanger, Von Gebsattel, Minkowski, Boss and others have developed "existential analysis" (q.v.), based on the existential philosophies. The "existential analyst" rejects the objective orientation of psychodynamics and tries to understand the patient in the context of his subjective world and its meaning. Related to this are such new approaches as Frankel's "*Logotherapie*" or clinical applications of Eastern thought (Yoga and Zen). Rogers' self theory, Gestalt theories, and some organismic theories, with their emphasis on the phenomenal world, and the totality and uniqueness of a person, occasionally approximate to the "existential" tendency.

8. *Summary*. As an objective science, abnormal psychology uses biological, physiological, behavioral, psychodynamic, socio-cultural, and other experimental and observational approaches to statistically unusual or deviant behavior. It is related to diagnostic and therapeutic psychiatry, clinical psychology and other scientific approaches to mental health, in which subjective and artistic methods are included or integrated.

Bibliography: Arieti, S. (Ed.): American handbook of psychiatry. New York, 1959. **Binswanger, L.**: Schizophrenie. Pfüllingen, 1957. **Eysenck, H. J.** (Ed.): Behaviour therapy and the neuroses. London, 1960. **Id.** (Ed.): Handbook of abnormal psychology. New York, 1961. **Fenichel, O.**: The psychoanalytic theory of neurosis. New York, 1945. **Hunt, J. McV.** (Ed.): Personality and the behavior disorders. New York, 1944. **Jaspers, K.**: Allgemeine Psychopathologie. Berne, 1913. **Kraepelin, E.**: Lehrbuch der Psychiatrie. Leipzig, 1883–1927. **Kanner, L.**: Child psychiatry. Springfield, Ill., 1935. **Lemert, E. M.**: Social pathology. New York, 1951. **Pavlov, I. P.**: Selected works. Moscow, 1955. **Ullman, L. P. & Krasner, L.**: A psychological approach to abnormal behavior. Englewood Cliffs, N.J., 1969. *K. Mizushima*

Abortion. In the strict medical usage, synonymous with *miscarriage*, i.e. the interruption of pregnancy either through natural processes or artificial induction. Non-technically, however, "abortion" is often used to refer only to the intentional termination of pregnancy as a method of *birth control* (q.v.) (still illegal in many parts of the world), while "miscarriage" is reserved for naturally occurring rejections of the fetus. *G.D.W.*

Spontaneous abortion is the natural expulsion of an abnormally developing fetus; *therapeutic abortion* is the term used to describe a (usually surgically) induced termination which satisfies the medico-legal conditions of the particular country or state: these usually require that continuation of pregnancy would endanger the mother's life, or her physical or psychic health, but vary considerably.

Criminal abortion describes a termination which does not satisfy such conditions. Abortion can be followed by more or less severe feelings of deprivation in the mother. Most vaginal terminations for psychiatric reasons are therefore carried out in the first three months.

Abortifacient: an agent which produces abortion (syn. *Abortient*).

Bibliography: Baker, A. A.: Psychiatric disorders in obstetrics. Oxford, 1967. **Clark, M.** *et al.*: Sequels of unwanted pregnancy. Lancet, 1968, No. 2, 501ff. **Tredgold, R. F.:** Psychiatric indications for termination of pregnancy. Lancet, 1964, No. 2, 1251ff.

Abreaction. A term used in psychiatry, and especially in psychoanalysis, to describe the more or less rapid discharge of long pent-up affects (tension). The process is unconscious—unlike, say, the working off of "actualized", or relived, repressed contents of experiences (though the word is used, less precisely, in this sense). Popular abuse of the term has tended to rob it of any consistent value outside the early literature. See *Cathartic method.* *R.Hä.*

Absence. 1. A form of *petit mal* (q.v.); term for the attack characteristic of children. The consciousness is clouded for 5–15 sec., and the sufferer is wholly or largely immobile (e.g. exhibits only eye movements). This form of attack gives a typical 3/sec. spikes and waves EEG pattern. Absence can be so transient that the child is unconscious of it, and it is subsumed into the total process of movement or speech. Such "absences" are to be distinguished from attacks of psychomotor epilepsy (temporal lobe epilepsy), which are sometimes called "pseudo-absences". **2.** "Absence" is also encountered in the (Freudian) psychoanalytic literature as descriptive of a fleeting loss of consciousness in hysteria, or even sexual orgasm. *C.S.*

Absolute error. The observed value plus or minus the true value; the true value being most probably the mean of the measurements.

Absolute pitch. 1. The generally recognized definition of the standard pitch of A as 440 vibrations a second, internationally adopted in 1960, and therefore the new "concert pitch". **2.** A special sense for actual pitch (as opposed to relative pitch). This special ability is very rare and occurs mostly among musicians (placed by Wellek at 8·8% and by G. Revesz at 3·4%).

Absolute pitch in this sense is not necessarily an accompaniment of musical ability. Wellek distinguishes three types of absolute pitch recognition according to criteria of retroactive experience (relation of new sounds to retained experience of a sound), and the tendency to confusion (in the "polar" type within the 4th and 5th, in the less common "linear" type within the chromatic note-row—Am. tone-row).

Bibliography: Neu, D. M.: A critical review of the literature on "absolute pitch". Psychol. Bull., 1947. **Wellek, A.:** Das absolute Gehör und seine Typen. Leipzig, 1938. *B.S.*

Absolute threshold. See *Threshold.*

Absolute value. A numerical value (−X) whose negative sign becomes positive: i.e. a number without regard to its sign. See *Scale.* *W.H.B.*

Absorption. When light (radiation) quanta pass through a medium, as a rule they divide into three parts. One part is *reflected,* one is *absorbed* (transduced, or transformed into heat), and one is *transmitted.* Taking light as a whole as 1, the relationship is: reflection + absorption + transmission = 1. The graphic representation of absorption as a function of the wavelength of light is an *absorption curve* (absorption coefficient); and, analogously, we have a reflection curve and a transmission curve. *Absorptivity* is the ratio of the amount of radiation absorbed to the amount incident, and, as *a,* stands in the following relationship to *e* (the emissivity, or constant to which the rate of emission of radiation is proportional): $e = a$ (Kirchoff's relation, or law). The absorption curve decides the color of the surface in question (see *Color mixture*). For a *black body* the absorption for all wavelengths is uniformly 1 (i.e. $a = 1$, since a black body absorbs all radiation incident on it); for a *grey body* the absorption for all wavelengths is uniform, i.e. less than 1.

Bibliography: Eisberg, R. M.: Fundamentals of modern physics. New York, 1961. **Weale, R. A.:** Photochemistry and vision. In: Photophysiology, Vol. 4. New York, 1968. *A.H.*

Abstinence. Voluntary self-deprivation of a substance, or the act of refraining from some action. Used in psychoanalysis to refer to sexual restraint (occasionally in something like the sense of "chastity"): i.e. refraining from, e.g., masturbation (q.v.), petting (q.v.), coitus (q.v.). Abstinence in this sense is often bound up with the proscriptions of a sexual ethics in which reproduction is seen as the overriding aim of sexuality, and which permits and even legalizes sexual relations only within marriage (e.g. Christianity, Islam). Abstinence is also used to describe the action of the voluntary drug-abstainer, whose restraint may, of course, be ritual (a temporary return to "drug virginity") or a planned tolerance-reductive measure. *J.F.*

Abstraction. 1. The process of developing a concept. A distinction is made between abstraction as *generalization, isolation,* and *idealization.* In generalization, the apparently essential characteristics of things, classes and their relations are ideally separated from the apparently inessential by considering them under one particular aspect. In isolation, the characteristics, relations and so on are considered independently: i.e. individuals are classed according to a common feature. In idealization, ideal models are constructed. The ability to abstract is possessed only by man, characterizes a stage of mental development (Piaget), and is thought of as a mark of adult "normality". *V.M.*

2. A general term for introspection (q.v.), emphasizing inattention to or obliviousness of the external world. **3.** A pejorative term for an intellectual construct that has suppressed properties deemed essential to any discussion of the individuals thus classed.

Bibliography: Piaget, J.: The psychology of intelligence. London, 1950.

Absurdity test. A task in which discovery of the contradiction or incongruity of a picture or story is the objective. Syn. *Absurdities test.*

Abulia. Abnormality of volition characterized by extreme apathy and indecisiveness.

Often subjectively described as a total absence of will-power or drive and accompanied by feelings of automatism in which the person experiences himself only as "reacting to" rather than "operating on" the environment and is completely unable to direct his own thoughts or behavior. *P.W.B.*

Acalculia. Inability to calculate mathematically as the result of the loss of the capacity for numerical ideation (damage to the left parietal area in right-handed people) or as one of the presenting symptoms of an *aphasia* (q.v.). *C.S.*

Acceleration. An increase in the speed of the development process. Bodily growth and maturation are out of step. Acceleration shows itself primarily in an increase in body size and weight; early growth of the milk teeth and the permanent teeth, and an earlier start to puberty (particularly significant in girls) are also symptomatic. Acceleration has been observed in all civilized nations since the first half of the last century. The phenomenon has increased in frequency in the last few decades. Attempts have been made to explain acceleration as consequent on environmental changes leading to a rise in pituitary hormone production (changes in nutrition, excessive stimulus, added stress in urban life, general changes in the conditions of life and work). Investigations which show the number of accelerates in the above sense to be much higher in urban than in agricultural areas would seem to confirm the relation between environmental influences and acceleration. See *Retardation; Maturation; Development.*

Bibliography: Carmichael, L. (Ed.): Manual of child psychology. New York, [2]1954. **Günther, H.:** Säkulare umweltbedingte Variationen der Körpergestalt des Menschen. Endokr., 1951, *28*. **Id.:** Die säkulare Progression der Körpergrösse des Menschen. Münchner Med. Wschr., 1954, *96*. **Hathaway, M. L.:** Heights and weights of children and youth in the United States. U.S. Dept. Agr. Home Econ. Res. Rpt. (Washington), No. 2, 1957. **Id. & Ford, E. D.:** Heights and weights of adults in the United States. U.S. Dept. Agr. Home Econ. Res. Rpt. (Washintgon), No. 10, 1960. **Martin, W. E. & Stendler, C. B.:** Child development: the process of growing up in society. New York, [2]1959. **Stott, L. H.:** Child development. New York & London, 1957. **Tanner, J.:** Education and physical growth. London, 1961. **Tanner, J. M.:** Growth at adolescence. Oxford, [2]1962. **Thomae, H.:** Längsschnittuntersuchungen zum Problem der Beziehungen zwischen körperlicher und seelischer Entwicklung. Z. exp. angew. Psychologie, 1957, *4*. *G.S.*

Acceptance. See *Rejection.*

Accident proneness. The theory of accident proneness implies a personal predisposition which makes some people more liable to accidents than others. As accidents present a serious social problem, this concept is an important field of psychological research. Unfortunately it has also become so fertile a field for psychological controversy that, even after fifty years, the validity of the concept is still questioned. Some of this disbelief is caused by the difficulty of substantiating the concept by statistical means; or to the rigid way in which it is so often defined. But some of it can also be traced to the natural reluctance of certain behaviorists to accept a concept implying the existence of deep-seated personality traits. In view of this controversial thinking, it is very advisable for any student or would-be researcher to study the literature; although it would be surprising if a truly objective assessment of this did not convince him that there is ample research support for the concept, if viewed in a realistic manner.

Accident proneness is by no means a simple phenomenon. It can be caused by any number of human failings or maladjustments and will therefore show itself in different ways in different people, and to different degrees. A person could be more prone to one type of accident than to another; he could have the skill to cope with one task but not another; or he could be motivated to behave carefully in one sphere and recklessly in another. And not only do people change both physically and psychologically as they develop, but their behavior can be modified by factors like experience or discipline, or the pressures of social opinion. It is therefore essential to view accident proneness as a multi-dimensional problem of complex human beings functioning in a complex environment; failure to appreciate this has been one of the main reasons for the rather poor quality of much of the research in this field, and the confusion over the validity of the concept.

For the better-planned experimental studies have demonstrated that people display markedly different accident rates and that these differences are associated with recognizable personal characteristics. A recent major study on road accidents has shown that it is possible to lower the accident rate substantially in a transport company by using psychological tests (which have been subjected to repeated cross validation) to screen out the bad accident risks on the basis of their intelligence, psychomotor functions, personality, social attitudes and interpersonal relations. Findings like these emphasize the important practical implications of differential liability to accidents.

Bibliography: Arbous, A. G. & Kerrich, J. E.: Accident statistics and the concept of accident proneness, 1951, Biometrics, 7, 340–432. **Shaw, L. & Sichel, H. S.:** Accident proneness. London & New York, 1970. **Walbeehm, T. B.:** The accident-prone driver. London, 1960.

Lynette Shaw

Accident research. Accidents are the greatest killer of our modern age and therefore provide an extremely important field of psychological research. But it is by no means a homogeneous one where the same causes are operative or the same preventative measures applicable. Accidents occur among people of very different ages, and in the course of activities which make very different demands on their capabilities or serve very different psychological needs. Accidents in different spheres of life are therefore best regarded as fields of specialized research.

1. *Methods and results.* There are various research approaches: studying the causes of individual accidents or the characteristics of accident offenders; exploring the value of psychological tests as accident predictors; studying the efficacy of preventative measures such as training, therapy, discipline, or safety propaganda, or the influence of such factors as morale or social opinion. As in many other branches of behavioral research, greater attention has been paid to the causative than to the preventative factors, since it is easier to determine the causes of human behavior than to find ways of modifying it. But accident research has suffered from another common bugbear of psychologic complaint, namely the conflict between the rival doctrines of dynamic psychology and behaviorism (q.v.) (especially the American behavioristic doctrine of "specificity", where conduct is believed to consist of specific and almost unrelated S-R bonds or habits). This clash has resulted in two widely divergent schools of thought: (*a*) that accidents are virtually unpredictable as they are predominantly situation-dictated events, and (*b*) that accidents can be predicted as they are often the outcome of a relatively consistent pattern of behavior dictated by dynamic personality traits. This controversy, which has at times been a very heated one (as over the question of accident proneness), is most unfortunate; for research has shown that although there is something to be said for both points of view, there is nothing to be gained by too rigid an adherence to either; accidents have many causes, some environmental and some person-centered, and the only realistic way to study the problem is in this context.

But this very complexity presents great methodological difficulties, and is really the main reason for rather slow progress, especially in the field of experimental research, where it is virtually impossible to control all the independent variables. Failure to appreciate this complexity has also led to many of the misleading statements found in the research literature, where the low correlations between accidents and single characteristics have been repeatedly cited as evidence that such factors as intelligence and personality have little or nothing to do with accidents—findings which have been refuted by the better studies, where adequate controls and a more realistic multivariate approach have yielded very positive results. But these controlled experimental studies are possible only with such subjects as professional drivers or factory workers engaged on a particular task. With the general public, or with children, often the best one can do is to compare groups with high/low accident rates to see whether they display different characteristics. However, this somewhat crude method has proved very productive, for findings of these studies have displayed remarkably consistent trends. Most of these comparative studies have been done on traffic accidents, and on factors related to personality; and very different research methods have been used: personality inventories, projective techniques, attitude scales, clinical interviews, and studies of home background and personal history. In the psychological studies, the high-accident groups have displayed marked anti-social attitudes and a number of distinctive personality characteristics, such as immaturity, irresponsibility, impulsiveness, aggressiveness, emotional instability, or neurotic anxiety. Of course the characteristics differ from person to person, but in each case they are indicative of personality imbalance. In the sociological studies, these groups have contained a preponderance of people with histories of crime, drunkenness, traffic offenses, debt, and other manifestations of social maladjustment. Findings like these are very compatible with three controlled experimental studies: in one it was possible to predict future accident rates on the basis of a comprehensive personality rating derived from projective tests; in the second, a factor analysis (q.v.) of personality traits revealed two higher-order factors of extraversion and neuroticism which correlated significantly with a graded accident criterion; and in the third, the accident offenders displayed a number of psychomotor malfunctions such as hasty and impulsive movements, or shock reactions, all indicative of personality disturbances.

But it is also very interesting to note that similar findings have emerged from studies of industrial and childhood accidents, showing that accidents in any sphere are one manifestation of personal and social maladjustment. But different circumstances will undoubtedly impose different controls on accident-producing behavior. The rather similar personality traits (especially those of extraversion) found in accident-prone children and adult traffic offenders, indicates that this sort of acting-out behavior must fulfill rather similar psychological needs. But in the industrial working context there is stronger evidence of the neurotic traits, and the extravert ones seem to be under better control—possibly because of stricter supervision, or because the consequences of extraverted behavior are more readily appreciated. It seems possible that the people who are liable to industrial accidents are, on the whole, more deeply maladjusted, and that their accidents are often associated with personality functions not under conscious control.

Whereas the relationship between personality and accidents is largely a linear one (i.e. the more pronounced the defects the higher the accident potential) the effects of other psychological factors cannot be measured in this way. Group studies on experience show a pronounced learning curve, starting with a high accident rate which soon levels off. The effects of intelligence and skill seem to follow the same curvilinear trend, though the curve is less steep in a complex operation like driving, where lack of intelligence often accentuates the personality defect. (For example, it is dangerous enough for a person's driving behavior to be motivated by exhibitionism or aggression; it is doubly so when he is too stupid to appreciate the consequences of his action, or to think quickly in a crisis.) The age factor, on the other hand, shows a U-shaped curve, with the young and the old as the worst offenders. But these are only general trends, as liability to accidents has proved to be a very individual matter—so much so that the only reliable way of predicting it is to assess each person individually, on his own merits.

2. *Preventative measures.* Controlled studies of the efficacy of preventative measures are still rare, but several studies of traffic accidents have shown that accident rates can be reduced by: (*a*) thorough training to improve driving skills, (*b*) eliminating the people with bad accident records; (*c*) using comprehensive psychological tests to screen out potential offenders, (*d*) enforcing discipline, and (*e*) as in one unusual study, by combining discipline with propaganda aimed at changing the image of reckless driving from "clever" to "psychologically sick" behavior. But there are formidable difficulties in applying some of these methods on a large scale and to the general public. The whole question of translating research findings into prevention policies, which are both practicable and socially acceptable, offers a tremendous challenge to psychological research.

Bibliography: Brody, L.: Human factors research in occupational accident prevention (Am. Soc. Safety Engineers). Chicago, 1962. **Haddon, W., Suchman, E. A. & Klein, D.:** Accident research. New York, 1964. **Hakkinen, S.:** Traffic accidents and driver characteristics (Finland's Inst. of Technology). Helsinki, 1958. **Shaw, L. & Sichel, H. S.:** Accident proneness. London & New York, 1970. **U.S. Pub. Health Serv.:** A review of mental health in industry. Washington, D.C., 1958. **Viteles, M. S.:** Industrial psychology. New York, 1932.

Lynette Shaw

Accommodation. Adaptation: changes take place in the curvature of the lens of the eye in order to accommodate variations of distance. The curvature of the anterior surface of the lens is adjusted more than that of the posterior surface by the action of the ciliary muscle. The lens is kept flat for distant objects, and is made to bulge—become spherical—for near ones. The *near point* (nearest point at which something can be seen distinctly) and *far point* (the most distant point at which something can be seen distinctly when accommodation is relaxed) are limit points for the accommodative power of the eye. Accommodative failure occurs in old age with increasing loss of elasticity of the lens. Accommodation of 14 diopters (q.v.) when young is reduced to 2 diopters in old age. *Absolute accommodation:* accommodation of one eye; *binocular accommodation:* of both eyes at once.

Bibliography: Campbell, F. W. & Gubisch, R. W.: Optical quality of the human eye. J. Physiol., 1966, *186*, 558–78. **Weale, R. A.:** From sight to light. London, 1968.

R.R.

Accommodation of information. The adjustment of the subjective expectation of the probability of events or signals to their actual probability of occurrence. The subjective information (q.v.) of the *receiver* is reduced to accord with the objective information of the *sender*; the necessary apperception and reaction times are minimalized. Accommodation of information (i.e. of surprisal value) occurs unconsciously, but can be influenced by conscious processes. The average speed of the process increases up to app. twenty years of age and then gradually decreases. The process is speeded up by an increase in motivation.

Bibliography: Riedel, H.: Psychostruktur. Quickborn, 1967.

H.R.

Acculturation. A term originating in American ethnology (q.v.) for processes of cultural change arising through intensive and continuous contact or influence between two or more culturally distinctive groups. The specific cultural features of the other group or groups are assimilated to, and in a more or less altered form adopted by, or rejected eventually but for a few characteristics by, the other group or groups. In the case of a mutual exchange of features between groups, the result of acculturation can be a novel, widely influential form of culture or even civilization which then becomes the dominant form for all groups participating in the process. The original use of this now somewhat too inclusive and non-specific term referred only to unilateral influences: e.g. the influence on "primitives" and their traditions of the customs of the "civilized majority", leading to the adoption of these customs. See *Assimilation*. *W.D.F.*

Acetoxycycloheximide. See *Antibiotics*.

Acetylcholine (abb. ACh). A nerve hormone traditionally thought to be the chemical transmitter substance in the parasympathetic system, which it activates. It is now known that ACh is a transmitter substance (*a*) in all postganglionic fibers of the parasympathetic division of the autonomic nervous system, and in a few postganglionic fibers of the sympathetic division (e.g. sweat glands), (*b*) in the preganglionic fibers of the parasympathetic *and* sympathetic divisions, (*c*) in the motor nerves of the skeletal muscles. Recently the function of ACh in the central nervous system has been recognized, which has given rise to many hypotheses in regard to the connection between ACh and behavior, and especially learning and sleep (see *Psychopharmacology*). High concentrations of ACh are found in particular in the cortex, nucleus caudatus, hypothalamus, thalamus, midbrain, and corpus callosum. ACh is difficult to identify since it occurs only in minute quantities, and is very speedily inactivated by cholinesterase (ChE) (q.v.). However, inhibition of ChE (see *Cholinesterase inhibitors*) allows of indirect opportunities for studying relations between ACh and behavior.

Bibliography: Carlton, P. L.: Cholinergic mechanisms in the control of behavior. In: **Efron, D.** (Ed.): Psychopharmacology 1957–1967, Washington, 1968. **Koelle, G. B.** (Ed.): Cholinesterases and anticholinesterases. Hdb. d. exp. Pharmakol. Vol. 15. Berlin, 1963. **Reeves, C.:** Cholinergic synaptic transmission and its relationship to behavior. Psychol. Bull., 1966, *65*, 321–35. **Rosenzweig, M. R., Krech, D. & Bennett, E. L.:** A search for relations between brain chemistry and behavior. Psychol. Bull., 1960, *57*, 476–492. **Id.:** Brain chemistry and adaptive behavior. In: **Harlow, H. F. & Woolsey, C. N.** (Eds): Biological and biochemical bases of behavior. Madison, 1965. **Russell, R. W.:** Neurophysiological and biochemical correlates of effects of drugs on behavior: The acetylcholine system. In: **Steinberg, H.** (Ed.): Animal behavior and drug action. London, 1964. *W.J.*

Achievement. 1. General term for the successful attainment of some goal requiring a certain effort. **2.** The degree of success attained in a task, e.g. solving a test. **3.** The result of a certain intellectual or physical activity defined according to individual and/or objective (organizational) prerequisites: i.e. proficiency. *G.R.W.M.*

Achievement age. The chronological age at which a specific level of achievement is usually attained.

Achievement, assessment of. There are various methods designed to measure (an) individual achievement against a specific achievement norm (standard): e.g. achievement batteries (groups of tests covering several areas of academic performance), achievement quotient (q.v.), Thematic Apperception Test (q.v.), and so on. See *Abilities*. *G.R.W.M.*

Achievement curve. A graphic representation of the process of achievement over a period of time (performance in a specific area, test values, etc.). *G.R.W.M.*

Achievement motive; achievement motivation. A hypothetical construct designed to explain inter- and intra-individual differences in the orientation, intensity and consistency of achievement behavior. In terms of content, achievement motivation may be characterized as the tendency to maintain and increase individual proficiency in all areas in which a standard of quality is taken as binding (Heckhausen, 1963). Research into achievement motivation was established on the basis of a recently-developed theory of motivation (McClelland & associates, 1953, 1969). According to McClelland, the basic principle for *definition* of a motive is the connection (dependent on experience) of an expected change in affect with specific key conditions; and, for *delimitation* of different motives, the particular class of content of expectations. In the case of achievement motivation, these expectations of positive or negative affective changes refer to the attainment or non-attainment of the individual standard of quality. According to whether *hope of success* or *fear of failure* is provoked by a situation, adient or abient behavior will result; a conflict can arise when expectations are equally intense. On this theoretical base, McClelland (1953) developed a special thematic apperception test (q.v.) to measure achievement motivation. On the basis of new results, J. W. Atkinson and (in Germany) Heckhausen have further developed the theory and methods of measurement.

A large number of experimental and cultural investigations have been carried out for construct validation (see *Construct validity*) of achievement motivation, which has been demonstrated as relatively constant as an individual characteristic in the course of diverse achievement situations and of time. Childhood experiences especially, i.e. the nature of early independence training, are positively related to achievement-orientation in adult life. According to Heckhausen, the average correlation between scholastic achievement and achievement motivation is $r = 0{\cdot}40$; if scholastic knowledge, anxiety and so on are taken into account, it can be $r = 0{\cdot}60$. On the whole, success-motivated individuals show an average, and the failure-motivated an unrealistically high or very low degree of risk-taking behavior and aspiration level. The significance of achievement motivation for national economic development was shown by McClelland and associates in a number of studies and a program for alteration of motive in this regard.

Bibliography: Atkinson, J. W. (Ed.): Motives in fantasy, action, and society. Princeton, N.J., 1958. **Heckhausen, H.:** Hoffnung und Furcht in der Leistungsmotivation. Meisenheim, 1963. **McClelland, D. C., Atkinson, J. W., Clark, R. A. & Lowell, E. L.:** The achievement motive. New York, 1953. **McClelland, D. C. & Winter, D. G.:** Motivating economic achievement. New York, 1969. *H.-J.K. & C.M.*

Achievement quotient (abb. AQ). The ratio between the expected and the actual measured level of performance in school. Chronological age (CA) or mental age (MA) may be used to estimate the theoretical performance, and achievement or educational age to measure the actuality. *J.M.*

Achievement society (*Achieving society*). A model of advanced industrial societies in which the individual achievement in the work process determines status in the work organization and also the predominant range of possible life-satisfactions as defined by that society. As a societal model, it is opposed to privilege as a principle governing the distribution of income, prestige, and so on, and therefore derives from egalitarian theory; yet, as a normative principle, it supports the legitimization of inequality.

Bibliography: McClelland, D. C.: The achieving society. Princeton, N.J., 1961. *C.B.*

Achievement tests. In general, measures of the effect of a special training. School performance tests form the most popular category. There are also vocational achievement tests, e.g. for skills such as those involved in stenography and so on, which are used both to check success in learning and (to some extent in conjunction with aptitude tests) for selection purposes. *R.M.*

Achromatic lens. Lens corrected for reduction of chromatic *aberration* (q.v.), which cannot be wholly compensated. Lenses of different materials with different focal powers are combined one behind the other in order partly to correct an eye's inability simultaneously to bring to a single focus light of all relevant wavelengths. *R.R.*

Achromatop(s)ia. Complete color blindness: no colors but only degrees of luminosity—shades of grey—can be distinguished. Partial color blindness is *color anomaly*: e.g. *anomalous dichromatism*—only two colors are seen; *anomalous trichromatism*—abnormal ratios of primary color mixtures (usually red-green). *R.R.*

Ach-Vygotsky method. A method used by Ach (1921) to study concept formation. Nonsense words were attached to stereometric objects of varying size and weight for which there was no ready concept and word. For example, *gatsun* indicated "large and heavy". After a short time with these blocks, the initially meaningless word came to mean something for S. (*gatsun* gradually came to *mean* "large and heavy"). S. formed the concept *gatsun*, and subsequently used it as a general term for large, heavy objects. Rimat varied the method to study concept formation in adolescents; it was modified by Vygotsky, who describes (1962) its implications, one of which is that concept formation is a creative process, and not a passive one based on mechanical associative connections.

Bibliography: Ach, N.: Über die Begriffsbildung. Bamberg, 1921. **Rimat, F.:** Intelligenzuntersuchungen anschliessend an die Ach'sche Suchmethode. Göttingen, 1925. **Vygotsky, L. S.:** Thought and language. Cambridge, Mass., 1962 (Orig. Russ., Moscow-Leningrad, 1934). *H.J.A.*

Acoustics. A division of psychology concerned with the nature and investigation of sound. It includes the physics of sound or noise, the physiology of the ear and the psychology of hearing. See *Auditory perception*.

Bibliography: Békésey, G. von: Experiments in hearing. New York, 1960. **Hirsh, I. J.:** The measurement of hearing. New York, 1952. **Kryter, K. D.:** The effects of noise on man. J. Speech Hear. Disorders. 1960, Monogr. Supp., No. 1. **Rodda, M.:** Noise and society. London, 1967. **Wever, E. G.:** Theory of hearing. New York, 1949. *V.M.*

Acoustic type. A type who perceives and remembers above all acoustically. Belongs among the *sense types* (q.v.).

Acquiescence (syn. *Acquiescence tendency*). Originally the term for a *response set* (q.v.) or bias in answering personality inventories: the subject tends, regardless of the content of the test-item, to answer "Yes", "Correct", "Right" rather than "No", "Incorrect", "Wrong", and so on (*acquiescent response set*—L. J. Cronsbach). In the course of the debate on the traits of the "authoritarian personality" (q.v.) classifiable as "acquiescence", the concept was "socio-psychologized": in this sense, the *acquiescence tendency* is a characteristic of authoritarian, conformist behavior or an aspect of a more general personality syndrome (Couch & Keniston, 1960). Although a conceptual distinction is usually made between formal and social acquiescence, high positive correlations have been obtained (e.g. Couch & Keniston, Overall Agreement Score; B. M. Bass, Social Acquiescence Scale).

Bibliography: Bass, B. M. & Berg, I. A.: Objective approaches to personality assessment. Princeton, 1959. **Berg, I. A.** (Ed.): Response set in personality assessment. Chicago, 1967. **Couch, A., & Keniston, K.:** Yeasayers and naysayers: agreeing response set as a personality variable. J. abnorm. soc. Psychol., 1960, *60*, 151–74. **Messick, S., & Jackson, D. N.:** Acquiescence and the factorial interpretation of the MMPI. Physchol. Bull., 1961, *58*, 299–304. *H.D.S.*

Acquired responses. Behavior primarily learned through experience; as opposed to *innate responses*, behavior primarily ascribed to inheritance. The distinction does not imply an absolute separation between environmentally learned and inherited behaviors, whereas popular usage tends to such absolutism and therefore to devalue the terms.

Acromegaly (*Acromegalia*). Unusual growth of the "acral" (or extreme peripheral) parts of the face, such as nose, ears and malar bones, and of fingers and toes. This enlargement is caused by hypersecretion of the growth hormone somatotrop(h)in in the anterior lobe of the pituitary body, and is usually a sign of pituitary adenoma, which is frequently accompanied by disturbances of other glands (q.v.), e.g. the thyroid gland (q.v.) and sexual glands. Mechanical pressure of this adenoma on nearby nerves and parts of the brain can lead to disorders of vision and psychic changes. Acromegaly in children can lead to gigantism, or overgrowth of the long skeletal bones. *E.D.*

Acrophobia. An exaggerated or abnormal dread of being in (very) high places.

Act. See *Act psychology*.

ACTH (abb. for *Adrenocorticotrophic hormone*) (corticotrophin; corticotropin). A glandotropic hormone produced from the anterior pituitary, which stimulates the output of corticosteroids (q.v.) in the adrenal gland. The production of ACTH is regulated (*a*) by the level of corticosteroid circulating in the blood (negative feedback), (*b*) by the corticotrophin-releasing factor (CRF) via the pituitary, and (*c*) by the level of adrenalin(e) (q.v.) (epinephrine) circulating in the blood. The relative value of the three control factors has not yet been determined. ACTH is available in a number of forms for therapeutic application. An overdose of ACTH can have quasi-psychotic effects. Little is known about the psychic effects of physiological doses of ACTH. Euphoric effects are most often noticed in patients, but it is not clear whether these are anything other than mere accompaniments of successful therapeutic effects. The small number of investigations carried out on healthy testees show no evidence of any stronger psychic effects. ACTH plays a special role in response to stress. According to H. Selye, all stressors (psychically and physically effective) induce increased production of ACTH via the sympathetic nervous system, hypothalamus and anterior pituitary.

Bibliography: Hodges, J. R.: The control of pituitary corticotrophic function. J. Psychosom. Res., 1965, *9*, 63–6. **Malitz, S., Hamburg, D. A. & Modell, S.:** Effects of ACTH on mental function. J. nerv. ment. dis., 1953, *118*, 315–31. *W.J.*

Acting out. The attempt of the patient in psychotherapy or psychoanalysis, who is afraid of his unconscious conflicts, not to allow them to become conscious. Instead he tries to transfer, displace, or "act them out" by finding immediate, illusive, "real" solutions. For instance, a girl who is afraid of men because of some traumatic family experience, but who refuses to face up to the extent of the trauma during psychotherapy because of increasing fear of it, will begin suddenly to flirt with a number of men. In this way she "proves" to herself and the therapist that she is not afraid of men and therefore does not really need to discover any cause of her fear. The opposite to acting out is *reality-testing*, which is the attempt to find genuine explanations for the consciously realized conflicts. Reality-testing usually takes place toward the end of, and after, psychotherapy, whereas acting out comes usually in mid-course.

Bibliography: Toman, W.: An introduction to the psychoanalytic theory of motivation. London & New York, 1960. *W.T.*

Actinomycin. See *Antibiotics.*

Action. 1. Intentional behavior. **2.** A unified series of behaviors. **3.** A change brought about by force or a natural agency. **4.** A deliberative act of will with some external sign or result, particularly change. **5.** The process of change. **6.** A physiological or mechanical process. **7.** The movement or function of the body or one of its parts. **8.** Performance. See *Activity.* *J.M.*

Action potential (syn. *Action current*). In general, this is the term for any change in electrical potential during intense physiological activity of functional units (nerves and muscles) in organisms.

Stimulation causes, e.g., nerve cells to be influenced so that the functional membrane surrounding the cell is locally depolarized, and the resting potential due to the differential permeability of the cell membrane to sodium and potassium ions is reduced. There is a local reversal of potential in response to above threshold stimulus: i.e. if the stimulus exceeds a certain minimum intensity, spontaneous activation of the entire cell occurs with complete depolarization of the membrane, and a much greater action potential is established. Once the membrane is depolarized, resting potential, or polarization, is reestablished. *M.S.*

Activation. Nowadays the term is used mostly when referring to the functions of the ascending reticular activating system (ARAS) (q.v.). This system regulates the level of general attention in relation to environmental stimuli on the one hand, and cerebral processes on the other. In consequence, the organism is continually in varying states of activation, or in an "activation continuum". The organism reaches its highest activation level at an average stimulus intensity, whereas the level of activation via the ARAS remains low at very intense and very weak stimulation. Sleep, of course, is not simply consequent upon cessation of activation, but is an active process in this sense. Activation level can be determined in terms of brain cell potential, breathing and pulse rate, and galvanic skin response (q.v.). See *Arousal.*

Bibliography: Lindsley, D. B.: Psychophysiology and motivation. Nebraska Symposium on Motivation, 1957, 44–104. **Id.:** Attention, consciousness, sleep and wakefulness. In: **Field, J.,** *et al.* (Eds): Handbook of physiology. Sect. 1, Vol. 3. Washington, D.C., 1960, 1553–94. *R.Hä.*

Activation pattern. The activation pattern of the EEG (q.v.) indicates desynchronization, or suppression of alpha waves (q.v.), in favor of low-voltage fast activity when the individual suddenly engages in visual activity (e.g. opens his eyes to look at a presented object). *Diffuse* (affecting all areas of both cerebral hemispheres) and *localized* (affecting only certain cortical areas) forms have been distinguished; together with a *tonic* (long-term wakefulness), and a *phasic* (short-term shifts of attention to presented modulations of stimuli) form. Syn. *Alpha blocking; Arousal reaction.*

Bibliography: Morrell, L. K.: Some characteristics of stimulus-provoked alpha activity. Electroencephalog. Clin. Neurophysiol., 1966, *21*, 552–61. *J.C.*

Active hypnosis, gradual. A psychotherapeutic technique forming part of the "dual standard approach" (E. Kretschmer). After a "basic practice" consisting of the "weight" and "heat" stages of autogenic training (q.v.), an autohypnotic state is induced and deepened. In clinical practice, gradual active hypnosis is always coupled with a parallel analysis. The method attempts a combination of two psychotherapeutic approaches: analysis and a form of "conditioning".

Bibliography: Kretschmer, E.: Über gestufte Aktivübungen und den Umbau der Hypnosetechnik. Dtsch. med. Wschr., 1946, *71*, 281–83. *H.N.G*

Active therapy. Therapy in which the therapist makes some kind of active intervention rather than passively recording and interpreting information from the patient. In active therapy an attempt is usually made to break up a neurotic habit by forcing the patient to act against his symptoms, e.g. making the drug addict go through withdrawal, or forcing the phobic patient to confront the situation which he fears in the hope that he will become accustomed to it and overcome it. In psychoanalysis, active therapy is usually employed in order to break down a *resistance*. *G.D.W.*

Activity. In psychology, activity is either a behavior (movement) of an organism or of a human individual which is directly released by inner conditions, or the readiness or capacity to behave, when the term "arousal" (q.v.) or "activation" is usual. The term is applied to psychological and physiological phenomena. It does not imply that the process in question has no external initial stimulus, but only that it can be traced to an energy peculiar to the individual in question. In this sense, a response to an environmental stimulus is also conceivable as an active process, insofar as the stimulus releases energy resulting in a determinate, specific answer on the part of the organism.

The concept of activity has a long history in psychological thought, and might be said to be conterminous with that of the conception of the "psyche", or "soul", as possessing not only cognitive ability but the capacity for aspiration and effort. Only the rigorous variety of association psychology (q.v.) wholly neglected the aspect of activity. Other schools paid more or less attention to this moment of the psychological process (in the nineteenth century, for example, the theories of Herbart, Fechner, Brentano and Wundt), and it was a basic principle of all divisions of dynamic psychology (q.v.).

More recently, conceptions of activity have tended to the *arousal* (q.v.) or *activation* (q.v.) model. Especially since the findings of Woodworth & Schlosberg (1954), activity is conceived as a psychophysical variable which on the one hand is expressed in specific physical symptoms as a level of readiness of the organism or of individual functional systems to behave, or expend energy, and on the other can appear in individual experience as tension release or excitation. Accordingly, the living organism always manifests a specific *activation level* which is very low in deep sleep (q.v.), but significantly higher in the relaxed waking state. A high activation level corresponds to an emotional state (released, e.g., by an organic need or an external situation), whereas an even higher one is characteristic of a strong affective state (such as rage). Activation level therefore can also be seen as comprising a dimension of emotional or motivational behavior.

The relation between activation (arousal) and achievement has often been investigated. It is assumed that there is a curvilinear relation between these two variables. This implies that a medium activation level is most favorable for performance, whereas both a very low and very high activation level reduces performance.

Bibliography: Duffy, E.: Activation and behavior. New York & London, 1962. **Fahrenberg, J.:** Psychophysiologische Persönlichkeitsforschung. Göttingen, 1967. **Heckhausen, H.:** Activierung und Leistung. 25th Cong. of German Psychological Society, 1966. Göttingen, 1967. **Lindsley, D. B.:** Emotion. In: **Stevens, S. S.** (Ed.): Handbook of experimental psychology. New York & London, 1951. **Schönpflug. W.** (Ed.): Methoden der Aktivierungsforschung, Berne, 1969. **Traxel, W.:** On the scaling of activation. 16th International Psychology Congress, 1960. Amsterdam, 1962. **Id.:** Gefühl und Gefühlsausdruck. In: **Meili, R. & Rohracher, H.** (Eds): Lehrbuch der experimentellen Psychologie. Berne, [2]1968. **Woodworth, R. S. & Schlosberg, H.:** Experimental psychology. New York & London, [2]1954. *W. Traxel*

Activity bed. Specially devised bed used to register, e.g., nocturnal restlessness in psychiatric patients, and thus, e.g., to study the effects of drug therapy.

Activity cage. A device used by Campbell & Sheffield to measure general activity level in rats: the revolving drum records the distance run by the rat. There are many similar devices, including the spring-suspended cage. Activity (restless activity) is closely related to motivation (q.v.); measurements of activity can therefore be used as indirect evidence for determining motivation.

Bibliography: Campbell, B. A. & Sheffield, F. D.: Relation of random activity to food deprivation. J. comp. physiol. Psychol., 1953, *46*, 320–22. **Foppa, K.:** Lernen, Gedächtnis, Verhalten. Cologne, 1968. *V.M.*

Activity quotient (syn. *Action quotient*). Busemann's formal index of the linguistic style typical of a certain age-group. The ratio of the number of verbs (activity words) to adjectives (qualitative words, or qualifiers) is the activity quotient, which varies according to age. Throughout an individual's life, Busemann found there was a rhythmic alternation of "actional" (high a.q.) and "qualitative" phases (low a.q.). A high activity quotient indicated emotional lability and a relatively low achievement level for the specific age-level.

Bibliography: Busemann, A.: Die Sprache der Jugend als Ausdruck der Entwicklungsrhythmik: Sprachstatistische Untersuchungen. Jena, 1925. *S.Kr.*

Activity-specific potential (syn. *Action-specific potential;* abb. ASP). The potential that must be reached for a specific activity. ASP is essentially distinct from all those factors which, however necessary for a certain activity, take effect non-specifically. *R.Hä.*

Actone. 1. H. A. Murray's term for an act or pattern of action examined as specific to the individual, or in regard to the specificity of the act and therefore without regard to its effects, e.g. on others. **2.** A simple reflexlike response considered in isolation. *J.G.*

Act psychology. A view of psychology represented by Franz Brentano (q.v.) (1838–1917), and later mainly by his pupil Carl Stumpf (1848–1936), emphasizing "psychical phenomena" as "intentionally containing an object in themselves". This fundamental "intentionalism" derives from a long tradition (Aristotle, Philo of Alexandria, Anselm, Thomas Aquinas, Sir William Hamilton, etc.), with the emphasis on Aristotelian–Scholastic philosophy. The viewpoint of act psychology is opposed to that of empiricism (q.v.) and sensationalism, and in regard to the development of the particular complex of problems it represents, belongs to the pre-history of Husserl's phenomenological psychology and Dilthey's cultural science psychology.

Brentano classifies the subject-matter of psychology as distinct from that of the natural sciences. It is exclusively concerned with "inner perception", as a category of phenomena whose specific nature is elicited by analytic description as "intending" some object.

The essence of psychical phenomena is their "intentionality". They are "acts" whose mode of existence is "being for an *other*", i.e. an object which they themselves, as acts, are not. Neo-scholastic philosophy calls this the "intentional (or mental) *inexistence* of an object". In the visual modality, for example, one "intends" the actual object seen, which then "inexists" (immanently) in the act of seeing.

In Brentano's view, ideas are the "fundamental principle of other psychical phenomena", and to that extent act psychology is a psychology of consciousness. Two further classes of psychical phenomena are distinguished, and, together with ideas, comprise all possible psychological events. They are characterized by the specific way in which they realize the intentional inexistence of objects: namely, ideating and judging; i.e. rejecting or recognizing and feeling; i.e. *loving* or *hating*. The three kinds of acts and classes of mental phenomena are: *ideas judgments* and *feelings* (movements of the heart, or *Gemüt*).

In this view, the concept of experience means the apprehension ("directly" and "evidently" experienced by "inner perception" in analytic description) of acts of consciousness (q.v.). For act psychology, the individual—in accordance with his general nature as a vehicle of consciousness—is the subject of and ground for the possibility of intentional acts. It sees psychology as concerned with the analysis and description of the general nature of conscious processes in order to establish a fundamental discipline for the human sciences (*Geisteswissenschaften*). See *Philosophy and psychology*.

Bibliography: Brentano, F.: Psychologie vom empirischen Standpunkt (Vol. 1), Ed. O. Kraus. Hamburg, [6]1955. **Id.:** Von der Klassifikation der psychischen Phänomene (Vol. 2), Ed. O. Kraus. Leipzig, [2]1925. **Id.:** Vom sinnlichen und noetischen Bewusstsein (Vol. 3), Ed. O. Kraus. Leipzig, 1928. *P. Braun*

Actual anxiety. According to Freud, the anxiety which occurs as a result of frustrations or interruptions of, or inadequate, sexual excitement or satisfaction.

Actual neuroses are, in Freud's terminology, neuroses (q.v.) whose symptoms, contrary to those of transference neuroses, derive from inadequate satisfactions, particularly in sexual activity.

Bibliography: Freud, S.: Introductory lectures on psycho-analysis. London, [2]1929. *W.T.*

Actual genesis. A term from gestalt psychology (F. Sander). An initially diffuse, undifferentiated pre-gestalt can, under favorable conditions, develop into a gestalt. The subject can actively forward these conditions by bringing the object under observation closer, scrutinizing it more carefully, and so on. "Actual genesis" also refers to typical processes of productive thought (q.v.) in which a "gestalt" evolves from an imprecise idea. See *Ganzheit*. *V.M.*

Actuality of emotions. A term used by Külpe (q.v.) for the phenomenon that emotions cannot be remembered or conceived without the simultaneous recurrence of all associated phenomena. Hence it is impossible to have an "image" of an emotion; instead it recurs, or becomes actual, in itself.

Bibliography: Külpe, O.: Outlines of psychology: based upon the results of experimental investigation. New York, 1895. *R.Hä.*

Actualization. The process by which memory contents become conscious and actual. A distinction is made between active searching for memory contents and their sudden coming to mind (without the active participation of the individual). This actualization occurs variously according to the conscious or unconscious association with it of certain occasions or fragmentary memories.

Bibliography: Selz, O.: Zur Psychologie des produktiven Denkens und des Irrtums. Bonn, 1922. *H.-J.A.*

Actual neurosis. See *Actual anxiety*.

Acuity, visual. Sensitivity of sight, particularly the ability to resolve minute spatial detail in the visual field. Tested either by the familiar letter chart or by more sophisticated laboratory displays, and commonly stated as a ratio between the distance at which the subject can make a given discrimination and the normal distance for that discrimination. The best-known index uses a constant numerator of 20, so that 20/15 is better than average vision, and 20/40 is rather worse than average. Acuity is affected adversely by many factors, including *myopia*, *diplopia*, and *astigmatism*. *G.D.W.*

Adaptation. The adaptation of the activation of a sense cell to a prolonged stimulus. In general, sensory adaptation (see *Sense organs*) implies that absolute threshold is raised and the responsiveness of sensory function is decreased. *J.G.*

Adaptation level (abb. AL). **1.** H. Helson found (1947) that after responding to a number of stimuli, Ss could say which stimulus was "in the middle", i.e. from what point of magnitude they could describe the stimulus as "big" or "small". Such reference points (i.e. neutral points) occur on every dimension of perception, either in the course of experience (hence we characterize a play as good or bad) or in regard to a situation (an object remains bright in the evening). Our perceptual apparatus adapts to the situation, and this simultaneously ensures constant and sensitive perception. *V.M.*

2. According to Helson (e.g., 1959), AL is the frame of reference by which the colors seen are determined according to different light stimuli. Under strongly colored lighting, objects with an albedo (q.v.) higher than the AL are inclined to appear under the hue of the lighting, those with a lower albedo to assume the hue complementary to that of the lighting, and those with an albedo approximating that of the AL to appear gray. *G.K.*

3. A general term for emotional equilibrium or neutrality.

Bibliography: Helson, H.: Adaptation level as frame of reference for prediction of psychophysical data. Amer. J. Psychol., 1947, *60,* 1–29. **Id.:** Adaptation level theory. In: **S. Koch** (Ed.): Psychology. A study of a science. Vol. 1. New York, 1959.

Adaptation, social. See *Adjustment, social.*

Adaptation syndrome. See *Stress.*

Adaptive system. The quantity of possible behaviors of an adaptive system changes in accordance with the influences of the system's environment, in such a way that it maintains its distinctive function. In the simplest case this is due to a control system (q.v.) depending on a fixed, programmed connection between system inputs and outputs. In complex instances adaptation occurs by alteration of the system itself. Examples are: changes in the retina during adaptation to darkness; changes in human behavior as the result of learning. *K.-D.G.*

Addition theorem. 1. The addition theorem of *probability* (q.v.): if $A_1, A_2, \ldots, A_n$ are exclusive events (q.v.) in a random experiment, then in this experiment $P(A_1 + A_2 \ldots A_n) = P(A_1) + P(A_2) + \ldots P(A_n)$. $P(A_1 + A_2 + \ldots A_n)$ represents the probability that either A_1 or A_2 or $\ldots A_n$ will occur. If A and B are random events, i.e. under certain conditions compatible with the probability $P(A)$ or $P(B)$, then in a random experiment the event $A + B$ has the probability $P(A + B) = P(A) + P(B) - P(AB)$. **2.** The addition theorem for *means*: the arithmetic mean of a quantity of random variables whose means exist, is equal to the sum of these means, $E(X_1 + X_2 + \ldots + X_n) = E(X_1) + \ldots E(X_n)$. Here $E(X_1)$ represents the expected value of the random variables X_1. **3.** The addition theorem for *distributions* (see *Frequency distributions*): the sum of a determined distribution of a series of values corresponds to this distribution. See *Deviation.* *W.H.B.*

Adiadochokinesis. A symptom of acute diseases of the cerebellum, presenting as the inability to carry out alternating movements, e.g. alternate extension and bending of the fingers. Together with other coordination disturbances such as intention tremor and nystagmus, adiadochokinesis is a complex of cerebellar asynergies, and is often coupled with myasthenia. It does not appear in chronic cerebellar prolapse when parts of the cerebrum take over cerebellar function. It can be improved by optical control and practice. *E.D.*

Adience. Tendency to approach or increase exposure to a stimulus. Hence *adient behavior* or *response*, behavior leading the organism to, or prolonging, the stimulus in some way.

Adjustment. **1.** A state in which the needs of the individual on the one hand and the claims of the environment on the other are fully satisfied. Harmony between the individual and the objective or social environment. **2.** The process by which this harmonious relationship can be attained. The state is of course expressible only in theoretical terms, since in practice no more than a relative adjustment is reached in the sense of optimal satisfaction of individual needs and untroubled relation to the environment. Adjustment takes the form of variation of the environment and variation in the organism through the acquisition of responses appropriate to the situation; the variation in the organism may be biological (see *Phylogenesis*). *R.Hä.*

Adjustment, social. A process, or state resulting from that process, of physical, socio-systemic or organizational changes in group-specific behavior or relations, or a specific culture. In a functionalist perspective, the meaning and purpose of such a process depend on an improvement in individual or group survival prospects, or in the mode of attaining to significant goals. The biological connotations of the concept show its close relation to the theory of evolution (q.v.). The adaptive character of behavior modifiable through learning is also part of the total problematics of social adjustment, and owes its introduction into the debate above all to H. Spencer. The term is also used to indicate the process by which an individual or a group reaches a state of social equilibrium in the sense of experiencing no *conflict* (q.v.) with the milieu (ant. *Social maladjustment*). *W.D.F.*

Adler, Alfred. B. 7/2/1870 in Vienna; d. 28/5/1937 in Aberdeen. Graduated in medicine, Vienna, 1895. Began work as an opthalmologist in Vienna in 1897, later practiced as an internist. First meeting with Freud 1899–1900. Adler defended Freud's ideas at the Viennese School of Medicine, in local medical circles and in the press. From 1902 he took part in the small discussion circle at Freud's home. Wrote *The Doctor as Educator* (1904). His first decision to break with the circle was withdrawn at Freud's request. In 1970 he published his monograph on organ inferiority (Eng. trans.: *Study of Organ Inferiority and its Psychical Compensation.* Washington, 1917). Lecture in Vienna, 1908: "The Instinct of Aggression". In 1910 he became the president of the Viennese branch of the Psychoanalytic Association. Co-editor with Freud and Stekel of the *Zentralblatt für Psychoanalyse.* In January and February 1911, he gave four lectures forming "A Critique of Freud's Sexual Theory of Mental Life". After the fourth lecture the majority of Freud's supporters present decided (despite Stekel's objection) to make the "justification for remaining a member of our Society dependent on acceptance of Freud's sexual theory". Adler and seven other doctors left the meeting. In August 1911, in Vol. I, No. 10/11 of the *Zentralblatt für Psychoanalyse*, Adler announced his resignation from the Editorial Board. *The Neurotic Constitution* was published in 1912 (Eng. trans.: New York, 1917); Adler saw this work as establishing "Individual Psychology" (i.e. the theory of the unity of the individual: indivisible, free, goal-directed, responsible for his actions, whole in himself) as the basis of a new form of psychotherapy (q.v.). Other works: *The Practice and Theory of Individual Psychology*, 1920 (Eng. trans.: New York & London, 1927); *Understanding Human Nature*, 1928–30 (Eng. trans.: New York & London, 1928); *The Education of Children*, 1929 (Eng. trans: New York & London, 1930); *Superiority and Social Interest.* London, 1965. After World War I, he organized child-guidance clinics in Vienna. In 1926–7

Adler made a lecture tour in the U.S.; and another in 1928. In 1927 he was appointed Visiting Professor at Columbia University. From 1932 to 1937 he was Visiting Professor of Psychiatry at Long Island College of Medicine (New York).

Through a widespread misunderstanding, Adler's theory of neurosis has been taken to be the Adlerian psychology of normality. In fact, he describes neurosis as the sum of *social maladjustments* whose common characteristic is an *egocentricity* of experience and behavior. The contrasting, normal state is centered on the *group* in its "community feeling", "social interest" and social goals, and is directed to a striving for perfection in the accomplishment of social ideals. Normality is the experiential knowledge that personal happiness ("fulfillment") can never be won at the expense of others and of the task benefiting all, but only together with others, and is most accessible for the individual who does not pursue it too avidly and who does not make egocentric claims. The purpose of Individual Psychology is to convince the neurotic of the desirability of this normal state and to help him to see clearly the modalities of his self-centeredness and possible will-to-power, and, if necessary, to help to unify the unique psyche by means of social tasks and interpersonal relationships.

Bibliography: Ansbacher, H. L. & R. R.: The individual psychology of Alfred Adler. London, 1955. **Bottome, P.:** Alfred Adler: a biography. New York, 1939 (Alfred Adler: Apostle of freedom. London, 1947). **Orgler, H.:** Alfred Adler: the man and his work. New York, [2]1948. **Rom, P.:** Alfred Adler und die wissenschaftliche Menschenkenntnis. Frankfurt a.M., 1966. **Sperber, M.:** Alfred Adler, oder das Elend der Psychologie. Vienna, 1970. **Way, L.:** Alfred Adler: an introduction to his psychology. Harmondsworth, 1956.

W.M.

Adolescence. The post-puberal period in which individual self-responsibility is established. The characteristics of physical maturity are already present. The psychic phenomena of puberty (q.v.) are gradually discarded. A search for freedom, and increasing self-confidence and self-consciousness, are characteristic of this phase of development (q.v.). In the literature, the beginning of adolescence is sometimes equated with that of puberty. The age-ranges conventionally associated with adolescence are 12–21 years for girls, and 13–22 for boys.

Bibliography: Bühler, C.: Das Seelenleben des Jugendlichen. Jena, 1929. **Id.:** From birth to maturity. London, 1935. **Carmichael, L.:** Manual of child psychology. New York, [2]1954. **Erikson, E. E.:** The challenge of youth. Garden City, N.Y., 1965. **Henry, N. B.** (Ed.): Adolescence. Yearbook Nat. Soc. Stud. Educ., 43(I), 1944. **Hoffman, M. L., & Hoffman, L. W.** (Eds.): Review of child development research. Vols. 1 & 2. New York, 1964; 1966. **Jersild, A. T.:** The psychology of adolescence. New York, 1957. **Kay, W.:** Moral development. London, 1968. **Stolz, H. R., & Stolz, L. M.:** Somatic development of adolescent boys. New York, 1951. **Strang, R.:** The adolescent views himself. New York, 1957. **Tanner, J. M.:** Growth at adolescence. Oxford, 1962. **Wattenberg, W. W.:** The adolescent years. New York, 1955.

K.E.P.

Adrenal glands. The *glandulae suprarenalis*, suprarenal glands, or adrenal glands, are two endocrine glands weighing app. 11–18 g. and situated above the kidneys. Each consists of a firmer, yellowish-brown cortex outside, and a softer, reddish-brown medulla inside. The *adrenal cortex*, consisting of three histologically distinctive layers, produces *steroids* (*cortisone*, q.v.; hydrocortisone). According to effect, the "corticosteroids" can be divided into three groups: (*a*) the *mineralocorticoids* and aldosterone, as regulators of the mineral metabolism; (*b*) the *glucocorticoids* and cortisol (q.v.), which influence the carbohydrate and sugar supply to produce an increase in blood sugar, and inhibit non-specific reactions of the body (e.g. in allergies); and (*c*) the *andrococorticoids*, which co-determine post-puberal body-growth and the development of female secondary sexual characteristics. The *adrenal medulla*, deriving historico-developmentally from the sympathetic nervous system, produces the hormones *adrenalin*(*e*) (q.v.) (epinephrine) and *noradrenalin*(*e*) (q.v.) (norepinephrine). *E.D*

Adrenalin(e) (*Epinephrine; Suprarenine*). A natural hormone of the adrenal medulla and a derivative of pyrocatechin (catechol). It was prepared in 1901 by T. B. Aldrich, H. Fürth and J. Takamine as 1-(3·4 dihydroxy-phenyl-)-2-methylamino-ethanol. Its effects mimic those of stimulation of the sympathetic nervous system (it is a sympathetic transmitter substance). Like *noradrenalin(e)* (norepinephrine), it raises blood pressure by constriction of peripheral blood vessels and increasing heart activity, but inhibits, e.g., intestinal peristalsis, bronchial muscular contraction, and sweat secretion. In particular, by catabolism of liver and muscle glycogen, unlike insulin (q.v.), it increases the blood sugar level, and thereby promotes metabolic activity, physical and mental capacity, and performance readiness. Since additional natural adrenaline is released under stress, anxiety and fright, and psychic behavior is altered in consequence, it is counted among the psychogenic hormones (see *Catecholamines; Hormones*). *E.D.*

Adrenergic. 1. A term used to characterize the effects of chemical substances which mimic the effects of adrenalin (q.v.). **2.** Descriptive of nerve fibers or nervous systems in which noradrenalin or adrenalin functions as a transmitter substance (q.v.). Adrenergic activity patterns are peripheral-vegetative expressions of sympathetic activation. The once conventional equation of sympathicomimetic and adrenergic is inaccurate, as "adrenergic" is also used to refer to the central nervous system (q.v.) insofar as adrenalin, noradrenalin or related substances act as transmitter substances (see *Catecholamines; Biogenic amines*). *W.J.*

Adrenergics (*Adrenergic substances*). Substances which have the same effects as, or similar effects to, adrenalin (q.v.) or noradrenalin (q.v.) in the nervous system. *W.J.*

Adrenocorticotrop(h)ic hormone. See *ACTH*.

Adultomorphism. The attempt to interpret children's behavior in terms proper to adults. (Syn. *Enelicomorphism*; ant. *Pedomorphism*). *K.E.P.*

Adult psychology. A dimension of developmental psychology. The psychology of adults has only recently come to be considered as a separate area of research. It is necessary to divide development into several, largely independent dimensions. Adult psychology must be distinguished from juvenile psychology and gerontology (see *Aging*). Biological factors and various socio-cultural considerations must be taken into account in determining the dimension of adulthood, therefore a clear and uniform distinction is difficult to arrive at; in general the time span lasting from the third decade of life to the commencement of old age (about the sixth decade of life) is taken into consideration. In the opinion of various authors, this time span contains the peak of abilities (e.g. C. Bühler) (see, on the other hand, *Abilities; Intelligence; Intelligence tests*). The relation of age to productivity, performance, creativity, and so on; problems of development in marital life; problems of retirement and leisure activities: these are among the various research areas which might be considered parts of adult psychology.

Bibliography: Breckinridge, E. L.: Effective use of older workers. Chicago, 1953. **Bühler, C.:** Der menschliche Lebenslauf als psychologisches Problem. Göttingen, [2]1957. **Id., & Masserick, F.:** Lebenslauf und Lebensziele. Stuttgart, 1969. **Dennis, W.:** Variations in productivity among creative workers. Sci. Mon., 1955, *80*, 277–8. **Id.:** The age decrement in outstanding scientific contributions: Fact or artifact? Amer. Psychologist., 1958, *13*, 457–60. **Harris, D. B.** (Ed.): The concept of development. Minneapolis, 1957. **Kleemeier, R. W.** (Ed.): Aging and leisure: A research perspective into the meaningful use of time. New York, 1961. **Lehman, H. C.:** Age and achievement. Princeton, 1953. **Id.:** The age decrement in outstanding scientific creativity. Amer. Psychologist., 1960, *15*, 128–34. **Pressey, S. L., & Kuhlen, R. G.:** Psychological development through the life span. New York, 1957. *F.C.S.*

Advantage by illness. Psychologically, the subjective benefit or degree of relative satisfaction which the sick person gains from his sickness. Freud made a distinction between primary (*paranosis*) and secondary (*epinosis*) advantage by illness. The primary variety is the reduction of anxiety or anxiety-aggression that has arisen through the withdrawal of possible satisfaction or by reason of inadequate defense (q.v.) mechanisms. The secondary variety is an environmental gain enjoyed because of the sickness.
Bibliography: Freud, S.: Collected papers, Vol. 1. London, 1924–25. *W.T.*

Advertising psychology. See *Marketing psychology.*

Aesthesiometer. See *Esthesiometer.*

Aesthetics. See *Esthetics.*

Aetiology. See *Etiology.*

Affect. A term that is not defined uniformly. In general, it is used to characterize a feeling-state of particular intensity. Sometimes an "affect" is characterized as a state brought about by actions almost wholly devoid of intentional control in accordance with moral and objective viewpoints. The term is also found in the literature as practically synonymous with "emotion" in certain senses. See *Emotion; Depth psychology.* *R.M.*

Affect, displacement of. The change of the object of an affect in the course of the duration or recurrence of that affect. E.g. a boy might express his acute anger at his father in ill-treatment of his dog; a girl might displace the affective element of her fear of her father onto a teacher, and therefore express it as fear of the teacher. (Syn. *Transposition of affect.*) *W.T.*

Affect, flattening of. Acute inability to give an emotional response. Usually the result of two contradictory "affects" (anger, joy), motives or behavioral tendencies. Stupor is a variant of flattening of affect. See *Ambivalence.* *W.T.*

Affect, projection of. The perception of one's own affective states in other individuals or groups who (in the judgment of neutral observers) show no signs of any such states. One's own affective state is suppressed or occurs in isolation, either being experienced unconsciously or as not appertaining to oneself. See *Projection.* *W.T.*

Affection. 1. A general term for emotion (q.v.) or feeling. **2.** A general term for tenderness or love. **3.** Influence or alteration of a psychic state or constitution by the environment; the state of being affected by something external. **4.** An obsolete synonym for disposition, inclination, trait. *R.Hä.*

Affective logic; affective reasoning. Propositions or sequences of propositions which appear to have a logically exact, unambiguous, and regular structure but, when analyzed, are seen to proceed by emotional transitions peculiar to an individual, and therefore to have no intersubjective validity. See *Logical reasoning.* *J.M.*

Affective psychoses. Psychoses in which the primary disturbance is an alteration of mood and the ensuing alterations in thought and behavior are secondary processes. They include involutional melancholia and illnesses of the manic-depressive continuum. The illness is regarded as functional although biochemical and genetic factors play a part. Affective disorders in which etiological factors are predominantly environmental are usually milder and do not amount to an illness of psychotic intensity. *D.E.*

Affectivity. 1. All, the whole range of, or generalized emotional experience. **2.** Tendency to react with emotion. **3.** The quality of a stimulus which produces an emotional reaction. A behavior is sometimes termed "affective" when evoked by strong emotions. *R.Hä.*

Afference. A collective term for afferent nerves (q.v.) and axon (q.v.) transmission. Often used only to refer to the transmission of information as nerve impulses from the peripheral to the central nervous system.

Bibliography: Locke, S.: Modern neurology. Boston, 1969. *G.A.*

Afferent conduction; afferent transmission. The conduction of neural impulses toward the central nervous system.

Afferent nerves. Neurites, or long nerve-cell processes which convey information in the form of nervous impulses from the periphery (e.g. the sense cells of the eye, ear, vestibule, nose, tongue and skin, or other receptors) to the central nervous system (q.v.) (brain, brainstem and spinal cord). This definition applies both to animal neural fibers with conscious transmission, and to vegetative fibers with unconscious transmission. *E.D.*

Affiliation. The formation of social contacts. Mainly at Schachter's instigation, the need for self-evaluation by means of social comparison was experimentally investigated as an important affiliation motive: uncertainty about the appropriateness of emotional reactions, about the correctness of opinions or one's own abilities lead to affiliation with individuals who are experienced as similar to oneself. Factorial analysis in personality (q.v.) research has revealed factors (q.v.) characterizing differences in affiliation readiness ("gregariousness" or "sociability").

Bibliography: Radloff, R.: Affiliation and social comparison. In: **Borgatta, E. F. & Lambert, W. W.:** Handbook of personality theory and research. Chicago, 1960. **Schachter, S.:** Psychology of affiliation. Stanford, Calif., 1959. *D.B.*

Afterimages. Visual perceptions experienced *after removal* of visual stimuli. They belong to the class of phenomena known as *aftersensations* (q.v.). Secondary stimuli (e.g. change from light to dark) can influence afterimages. *Negative afterimages* can be of the color complementary to that of the original stimulus, or less bright than the original stimulus. *Positive afterimages* correspond in brightness to the original image (whatever is bright/dark in the original image, appears bright/dark in the afterimage), or are of the same color as the original image.

An accepted explanation of the phenomenon is that activation in the visual system persists after removal of the stimulus. Jung (1961) offered a psychophysiological explanation of the afterimage process (afterimage phases) based on neurophysiological research. He was able to show that in the case of some types of neuronal activity in the visual system, there is correlation between afterimage phases, Charpentier's bands, Hering afterimages, Purkinje-Sanson images, Hess afterimages, successive contrast, and the corresponding dark intervals.

Bibliography: Jung, R.: Neuronal integration in the visual cortex and its significance for visual information. In: **Rosenblith, W. A.** (Ed.): Sensory communication. New York & London, 1961. *A.H.*

Aftersensation. The continuation of a sensory experience after withdrawal of the stimulus. Most readily observable in the visual modality (where they are more commonly called *afterimages*) but applicable to some extent in most modalities. In vision the aftersensations are usually *negative*, i.e. complementary in hue and brightness, but they may be *positive* following exposure to intense stimulation. Also called *aftereffects* (a slightly more general term). *G.D.W.*

Aged, sexuality in the. Changes in hormone secretion during and after the menopause bring about physiological alterations in the sexual organs and in the sexual reaction cycle of the aging woman. However, hormone-conditioned anatomical and physiological changes alone do not suffice to explain a diminution of sexual capacity in the older woman; cultural schemata are also influential. A drop in the frequency of coitus with increasing age, though induced by the abovementioned factors, is thought to be dependent on irregular practice.

The aging process also affects the male reaction cycle: the various phases are considerably extended, whereas the ejaculation and erection phases are less clearly distinct, erection taking longer and ejaculation diminishing in force and duration. The refractory period of the male resolution phase is usually extended, and secondary refractory periods after loss of erection without ejaculation have been observed. Erections can often be maintained for some time without reaching orgasm. Impotence in the older man would seem usually to be secondary in nature, and very frequently reversible. Frequency of coitus is probably dependent on sexual behavior in the individual's past life. There would not seem to be any physiological age limit for full sexual activity. See *Sexuality*. *U.H.S.*

Agent. The transmitter or sender in a telepathy (q.v.) experiment.

Age ratio. Chronological age (CA) at one testing divided by the chronological age at a later testing. The age ratio provides a rough indication of an aptitude (ability) test's predictive power. Predictive power is usually better the shorter the interval between tests, and the older the age. Some would claim that social class has more predictive power than *pre-school* tests. *J.G.*

Agglutination. 1. The clumping together or flocculation of heterogeneous cells in the blood serum of previously sensitized or immunized individuals. It is a sign of an antigen-antibody reaction. *Agglutination tests* are used in medicine for bloodgrouping, and the identification of micro-organisms. *E.D.*

2. A group of dissimilar individuals. **3.** In linguistics: a compound word, or the formation of such a word by combining individual words each of which has a single specific meaning.

Aggregate, social. A term derived from the sociology of V. Pareto and adopted by T. Parsons for any kind of more or less enduring social mass, and distinguished from the *group* in social psychology, where it indicates a collection of individuals formed by external conditions (e.g. geographical proximity) or isolated in the course of an investigation using definite categories or classes (e.g. socio-economic status). Relations between individuals in such a plurality are, if detectable at all, intermittent and accidental: no relatively persistent forms of interaction and/or goals of action are observable. (Syn. *Aggregation.*) *W.D.F.*

Aggression. Controversy reigns in the study of human aggression (here defined as behavior intended to be injurious). Conflicting stances have been taken as to the fundamental nature of man, the role of learning and experience in the development of aggressive tendencies, how aggression is best controlled, the relation between the instigation to aggression and other types of motivation, and even what standards of evidence are required for theoretical propositions. This article will briefly review and evaluate some of the best-known positions that have been taken on these matters.

1. *The roots of aggression.* Although the

non-specialist is apt to view much of the controversy as a dispute between those whose biological orientation stresses the role of innate determinants (here he probably will think of orthodox psychoanalysis and European ethology), and those who emphasize the role of learning and experience (such as, most notably, American psychologists and social scientists), the major arguments really center upon endogenous versus exogenous causation. Writers such as Freud (1948), Storr (1968), and Lorenz (1963), trace the mainsprings of aggression primarily to internal sources, and assume that man has a spontaneously engendered drive impelling him to attack and even destroy other persons; they maintain that this energy must be discharged (whether by direct aggression, the observation of violence, the destruction of inanimate objects, participation in competitive sports, or achieving positions of dominance and mastery), if uncontrolled explosions of violence and perhaps even suicide are not to occur. However, some critics of this reasoning have also expressed a strong biological emphasis while still disputing the idea of an internally generated aggressive drive. The zoologist, J. P. Scott (1958), for example, holds that fighting behavior develops under the influence of a variety of genetic and environmental factors, but says the hereditary determinants affect the organism's predisposition to aggression rather than create a spontaneously produced instigation. Scott points out that an animal or human being can live satisfactorily for a long period of time without engaging in fights, unless external conditions stimulate aggressive reactions. Proponents of the endogenous causation thesis have accused their opponents of "naive optimism" about human nature, but still lack adequate evidence for their own position.

Also highly questionable is the Freudian–Lorenzian conception of a unitary aggressive drive that supposedly powers a wide variety of non-aggressive as well as aggressive actions. In agreement with many other students of animal behavior, Scott insists that there is no single instigation to aggression. Fighting serves a number of different functions and has a multiplicity of causes. Moyer (1968) has presented a list of different kinds of aggression (predatory, inter-male, fear-induced, irritable, territorial defense, maternal, and instrumental), and suggests that each type has a somewhat different basis in physiological mechanisms and eliciting stimuli. At the human level, Berkowitz (1962, 1970c) maintains that instrumental aggression, which is governed by anticipated rewards, must be differentiated from impulsive aggression which is evoked by situational cues in a manner akin to conditioned responses. The unitary aggressive-drive conception is highly dubious, and, by leading investigators to neglect or deny the operation of many different casual factors, may even be an impediment to more adequate formulations, as R. A. Hinde (1959) has argued in his discussion of unitary drive theories.

In addition to using gross analogies, extremely speculative leaps of inductive reasoning, and highly selective documentation (see Montagu, 1968; Berkowitz, 1969a), endogenous-causation theorists often refer to indications of appetitive aggression. As has been demonstrated in a number of experiments (e.g., Azrin *et al.*, 1965; Lagerspetz, 1964; Ulrich, 1966), animals at times exhibit a clear preference for aggressive activity. Instead of regarding this preference as an expression of a spontaneously generated drive, however, the opportunity for aggression is better viewed as a reinforcer, with the reinforcing quality of aggression being limited to certain conditions and functioning much like other reinforcers.

Nor is the apparent generality of aggressive behavior adequate support for the unitary-aggressive-drive theory. A hostile person may display certain other traits, but the correlation between hostility and these other characteristics is no proof that one trait had caused the others. Furthermore, the unitary-drive idea of energy flowing from one type of behavior to another must be differentiated from the more precisely defined response-generalization concept developed by experimental psychologists. Research has shown that reinforcements provided for a certain reaction can strengthen other, similar responses. Rewarding one class of aggressive responses, such as hostile remarks, can increase the likelihood of other kinds of aggressive behavior. The reinforcement influence generalizes from one act to the others because they have something in common; perhaps the aggressor regards all of these as hurting someone. Whatever the exact meaning of the various aggressive actions, it is theoretically unparsimonious to interpret response generalization as an energy transfer from one response channel to another.

As discussed by some of its proponents, the frustration-aggression hypothesis (frequently seen as the major alternative to the Freudian–Lorenzian conception) also seems to posit a "built-in" influence on aggression. Dollard, Doob, Miller, Mowrer & Sears (1939) had said that they took no position on this issue, but many readers believed that their classic presentation of the frustration-aggression doctrine implied an innate connection between an antecedent stimulus event, the frustration, and the subsequent aggression. The Yale group had maintained that a frustration, defined as "an interference with the occurrence of an instigated goal response at its proper time in the behavior sequence", will universally arouse an instigation to aggression. Some American psychologists (e.g., Bandura & Walters, 1963) have questioned this thesis by citing demonstrations of learned modifications of frustration reactions as evidence of the inadequacy of the frustration-aggression hypothesis. However, the presence of learning does not necessarily exclude the possibility of innate behavioral determinants; built-in behavior patterns may be modifiable by learning but can still play a crucial role in motivating action. The frustration-aggression relationship may be learnable without being entirely learned. Experiments with animals (see Ulrich, 1966) have shown that thwartings can produce aggression even without prior learning, and what holds for other species may also be true for man.

Some other criticisms of this traditional social science doctrine can also be answered readily (see Berkowitz, 1962, 1969b). It is especially important to distinguish between frustrations and mere deprivations. As the Dollard, Doob *et al.* formulation clearly indicates, if the individual is to be regarded as frustrated, he must be performing anticipatory goal responses (i.e. must be anticipating the satisfaction to be gained from reaching his goal), and then be prevented from achieving adequate consummation. This blocking can have a number of consequences, as Dollard and his colleagues had recognized, and some of these may be stronger than the instigation to aggression, but as the frustration (in the present limited sense of the term) continues, the likelihood of aggression presumably increases. All in all, Berkowitz (1962, 1969b) has proposed two alterations of the frustration-aggression hypothesis while still accepting its basic validity: (*a*) contrary to the 1939 discussion, every aggressive action does not necessarily rest on a prior frustration: aggressive behavior can be learned much as other modes of conduct are learned; (*b*) the linkage between frustration and aggression may be weaker than was assumed by the Yale group, and may not be revealed in overt behavior unless there are appropriate situational conditions, such as external stimuli associated with aggression, which facilitate the occurrence of aggression.

Along with other writers (see Ulrich, 1966), Berkowitz (1969b) has also suggested that the frustration-aggression relation may be a special case of the connection between aversive stimuli and aggression. Thwartings are noxious events in important respects, and pain is a reliable stimulus to fighting (see

Ulrich, 1966). In this regard, Scott believes social fighting has evolved from defensive reactions to pain. We should note, however, that the aversive stimulus also produces a heightened arousal state which can increase responsivity to the dominant aggressive cues in the environment.

2. *The control of aggression.* Followers of the Freudian–Lorenzian conception generally advocate "discharging" one's supposedly pent-up aggressive drive in various aggressive or even non-aggressive activities. Simple though this prescription seems to be, the findings uncovered by experimental research are far more complex than this reasoning would have us expect and are better explained by standard experimental-psychological analyses (Berkowitz, 1970a, b).

Engaging in, or even seeing, aggressive behavior frequently increases the probability of further aggression. In many cases, according to recent research, angry people do feel better and may even experience a temporarily reduced inclination to attack their tormentors upon learning that these persons have been hurt. Their aggressive goal has been reached and they are gratified. The long-term consequences may be very different, however. The information about the injury inflicted on the intended target is also a reinforcement, and as such, can heighten the likelihood that aggression will occur again in the future (Patterson, Littman & Bricker, 1967). Moreover, those people who believe they did not have adequate justification for their aggression are later apt to invent reasons to show their behavior was indeed appropriate and proper (Brock & Pallak, 1969). These rationalizations can also increase the chances of further aggression. Then, too, the injured party may retaliate, thereby provoking yet another attack. For many reasons, aggression is all too likely to lead to still more aggression.

This does not mean that all violent actions should be excused or that every effort should be made to avoid all frustrations. Extreme permissiveness can also heighten the chances of aggressive behavior, and people should learn to react constructively and non-aggressively to the thwartings they inevitably will encounter in life. Punishment conceivably could be employed as a means of controlling aggression (see Berkowitz, 1970b). Evidence suggests that punishment can be effective if it is employed early in the disapproved-behavior sequence, is carried out consistently, is combined with reasoning, and if the punished individual has readily discriminated the attractive alternative responses available to him. Nevertheless, punishment is also painful and may give rise to aggressive responses, especially if other people with aggressive stimulus properties are nearby.

Effective control of aggression requires that we avoid reinforcing this behavior without re-instigating it. Extreme permissiveness may also be hazardous since the aggressor may believe other people tacitly approve of his action when they fail to condemn it. With children, at least, it may be better to remove them quickly and temporarily from the provoking situation when they become violent rather than ignore their aggression, and then permit them to return only when they have quieted down. This "time out" procedure can be combined with explanations to show why the disapproved behavior is wrong. Aggression can also be lessened by minimizing the number of aggression-evoking stimuli in the environment, and by teaching people to act in ways that are incompatible with aggression when they do encounter stimulation to violence. They should not be encouraged to attack someone or some object, or to express their anger in the hope that they will drain some hypothetical energy reservoir. This notion of hostility catharsis is, in its traditional form, an outmoded theoretical conception lacking adequate empirical support; it also has potentially dangerous social implications. Aggression ultimately produces more aggression.

Bibliography: Azrin, N. H., Hutchinson, R. R. & McLaughlin, R.: The opportunity for aggression as an operant reinforcer during aversive stimulation.

Journal of Experimental Analysis of Behavior, 1965, *8*, 171–80. **Bandura, A. & Walters, R. H.**: Social learning and personality development. New York, 1963. **Berkowitz, L.**: Aggression: a social psychological analysis. New York, 1962. **Id.**: Simple views of aggression. American Scientist, 1969a, *57*, 372–83. **Id.**: The frustration-aggression hypothesis revisited. In: **Berkowitz, L.** (Ed.): Roots of aggression: a re-examination of the frustration-aggression hypothesis. New York, 1969b. **Id.**: Experimental investigations of hostility catharsis. Journal of Consulting and Clinical Psychology, 1970a. **Id.**: The control of aggression. In: **Caldwell, Bettye & Ricciuti, H.** (Eds): Review of Child Development Research, Vol. 3. New York, 1970b. **Id.**: The contagion of violence. In: **Page, M.** (Ed.): Nebraska symposium on motivation, 1970. Lincoln, Nebr. 1970c. **Brock, T. C. & Pallak, M. S.**: The consequences of choosing to be aggressive. In: **Zimbardo, P. G.** (Ed.): The cognitive control of motivation. Glenview, Ill., 1969, 185–202. **Dollard, J., Doob, L., Miller, N., Mowrer, O. Sears, R.**: Frustration and aggression. New Haven, 1939. **Freud, S.**: Beyond the pleasure principle. London, 1948. **Hinde, R. A.**: Unitary drives. Animal Behavior, 1959, *7*, 130–41. **Lagerspetz, K.**: Studies on the aggressive behaviour of mice. Helsinki, 1964. **Lorenz, K.**: Das Sogenannte Böse. Vienna, 1963. Eng. trans.: On aggression. New York & London, 1966. **Montagu, M. F. A.** (Ed.): Man and aggression. New York, 1968. **Moyer, K. E.**: Kinds of aggression and their physiological basis. Communications in Behavioral Biology, 1968, *2*, 65–87. **Patterson, G. R., Littman, R. A. & Bricker, W.**: Assertive behavior in children: a step toward a theory of aggression. Monographs of Society for Research in Child Development, 1967, *32*, 5, 1–43. **Scott, J. P.**: Aggression. Chicago, 1958. **Storr, A.**: Human aggression. New York, 1968. **Ulrich, R.**: Pain as a cause of aggression. American Zoologist, 1966, *6*, 643–62.

L. Berkowitz

Aggressiveness; aggressivity. 1. The tendency to display aggression (q.v.). **2.** The quality of a will to dominance, or even achievement.

Aging, psychology of. The psychology of aging is concerned with the explanation of changes in behavior over the adult phase of the life span—app. three-fourths of the average length of life. The subject-matter includes the changes that occur in capacities such as perception, memory, learning, intelligence, thinking and problem solving. It also embraces age changes in skills and patterns of behavior such as those involved in emotions, and interpersonal relationships. Since many of the behavior changes with age are not easily subjected to experiment, much of the basic information available in the psychology of aging has been descriptive, although experimental studies are coming to be more frequent.

The psychology of aging has a biological and a social orientation, since genetic and other biological factors determine the limits set upon behavior by the capacities of the nervous system, as well as other organ systems, and our habits and social roles are determined by the nature of the group or society in which we have grown up and grown old. For example, chronological age is an important factor in determining how members of society relate to one another. The characteristics of age status systems of a society are not as yet fully known, but social psychologists are increasingly concerned with the social status and roles of different age levels.

Specialists emphasize different aspects of the psychology of aging; different weight is given to the importance of the biological limitations of aging, or to the importance of the social environment, much as in child psychology. Similarly, the psychology of aging tends to be concerned with whether man ages because of "nature" or "nurture". At present, few formal theories of the psychology of aging have been proposed. Those offered in the past have mostly been borrowings from or derivatives of theories developed in some other area of psychology such as brain damage, learning, personality, or psycho-pathology.

The psychological theory of aging is directed toward systematic explanation of age differences in the behavior and capacities of adults. Because each of the many aspects contain such dissimilar observed facts it is not likely that there will be any single theory of aging that will prove universally serviceable for all psychologists.

1. *History*. One of the first scientists to be concerned with the empirical aspects of aging was a Belgian, Quetlet (1835). His concept of the "average man" took into account a central tendency around which extremes, both positive and negative, were distributed. He evidently believed that there are marked individual differences in man's longevity and in his behavior with age, and that the characteristics of aging are partly a function of the environment in which the individual lives. The English psychologist Francis Galton was also concerned with the aging of various behavioral capacities. His work in the second half of the nineteenth century, while pioneering in many respects, was not directly followed up by other scientists, and the field lay relatively dormant. The first psychologist systematically to review the literature and facts of the psychology of aging was G. S. Hall (1922). His book *Senescence* reflected a developmental psychological point of view of the whole life span, reminiscent of his earlier work on adolescence. On retirement, he addressed himself directly to the processes of aging. Hall saw the superficiality of regarding aging merely as a regression toward an earlier stage of life, and emphasized the high degree of variability among older persons, as well as the point that aging is not an inverse process of earlier development. The question of individual differences increasing with age is often discussed, but as yet insufficient data prevent postulation of a law in this regard.

Following World War II, a number of laboratory investigators began an accelerated phase of investigation into the psychological processes of aging. The work of Kallmann & Jarvik and their colleagues (1959) suggests that aging is indeed multivariate. Studies of one-egg twins over the age of sixty-five suggests that monozygotic twins show more similar patterns of aging in appearance, intelligence and cause of death than do fraternal twins and siblings. There is thus a continuing genetic influence on late-life similarities, as seen earlier in one-egg children. Therefore the patterns of aging are to some extent genetically determined.

2. *Life span differentiation*. The adult, like the child, appears to evolve toward greater differentiation. Differentiation in both child and adult is brought about by social as well as biological processes. At each age level or phase of life, individuals are presented with characteristic tasks that require resolution. In this sense there is as much dynamic quality in the life of the seventy-year-old as there is in the fifty-year-old or in the adolescent. In part, the tasks facing individuals at characteristic ages give life a pattern. Some, such as Bühler (1951), have inferred there is a basic tempo or rhythm to adult life. Analysis of biographical information has led Bühler to opine that there are demarcated phases of construction, combination and reduction. In terms of social behavior, individuals as they grow older are thought to change from a pattern of achievement orientation and striving to a withdrawal from life and reduction of activity. This pattern, while not universally accepted as normal or typical, has been described as a process of "disengagement" (Cumming & Henry, 1961). The concept behind the term is that individuals as they grow older undergo a reduction in energy and become willing accomplices in the gradual loss of an active role in society.

The extent to which an individual shows high motivation in later life must depend to some degree on the state of his nervous system. Insufficient information is available about the anatomical and biochemical changes in the nervous system with age, to predict detailed behavioral consequences. But there is little doubt that the nervous system is in a key position to influence aging in the rest of the body. Not only is the nervous system critical in integrating behavior but it also mediates the vegetative processes of the body, and can presumably distribute the influences of its aging capacities. Nerve cells have a particular significance since they are fixed post-mitotic cells; that is, they do not divide after their origins in embryonic life. The cells of the nervous system are of great importance not only in the organization of behavior, but as a limiting factor in the ability to survive and function. It is not surprising that, unlike studies of childhood, studies of aging have more frequently involved measured aspects of the biological capacities of the organism along with observed behavior characteristics.

3. *Theories of behavior and aging.* Behavior of the older adult, whether perceptual, associative, or motor, tends to be slower than might be expected in a young adult. The basis for this has been given considerable attention, since evidence suggests that all behavior mediated by the central nervous system tends to be slow in the aging organism. Whereas young adults are quick or slow to respond in their behavior in accordance with their estimation of the demands of the environment, older adults may show a generalized slowness of behavior. One likely explanation is the known gradual loss of nerve cells that occurs diffusely in the nervous system with advancing age. Other explanations have involved reduced neural excitability, physical-chemical changes at the synapse that limit transmission speed, and a lowering of subliminal excitation of the nervous system. In addition, two functional hypotheses have been advanced to explain the slowness, the *neural noise hypothesis* and the *excitability hypothesis.*

The neural noise hypothesis postulates that with advancing age there is increased random neural activity, or neural noise, against which background any signal must be distinguished; the signal-to-noise ratio is assumed to be reduced with advancing age because of an increase in the noise level. Among factors contributing to such an increase might be spontaneous firing of hyper-irritable neurons, or perhaps local conditions of irritation produced by dying cells. Crossman & Szafran (1956), interpreting their data on visual and somaesthetic discrimination, have suggested that the nerve impulses conveying signals along the sensory pathways occur against a background of ambient neural activity that increases with age. It should follow that differential thresholds are likely to be relatively less affected by aging than are absolute thresholds. Some evidence in favor of this contention is to be found in a study of tachistoscopic recognition thresholds, in which a comparison of information-transfer functions, with and without distorted input, revealed no consistent decline with age among professional pilots (Szafran, 1966). Similarly, the older pilots did not show the traditionally expected more severe change of the effective threshold in the presence of white masking noise input to the contralateral ear. A preference of the older adult for guidance in his skilled activities by the largest possible picture of the immediate environment could also be ascribed to a decrease in the signal-to-noise ratio. Seeking additional sensory cues may indicate a need for stronger input, required perhaps to effect the intermediate processes between perception and action (Szafran, 1951; 1955).

Statistical decision theory, as applied to perception, should make it feasible to determine experimentally whether the observed decrement in performance with age is due entirely to a decrement in sensitivity or at least in part to a change in response criterion (Green & Swets, 1966). As yet there have been very few experiments of this nature, although F. I. M. Craik (1969) has reported no evidence of any substantial age differences in the estimates of the relative signal strength, and some tendency for the older subjects to adopt a more cautious criterion under one of the experimental conditions employed. From the theory, one would also predict that the human observer of faint or very brief signals can vary in confidence about his judgments, and that shifts in the criterion which he must use to arrive at a decision may be promoted by training and further enhanced by experience. A study of the effectiveness of increased sensory thresholds under unfavorable circumstances, using pilots as subjects, suggests that an important change of "strategy" in detecting distorted signals may occur as a result of prolonged experience, and that this strategy change can be relatively immune to the adverse effects of aging (Szafran, 1968).

Although many older adults may be able to minimize the very subtle relative functional losses in perceptual input by using efficiently stored hypotheses or information, there is evidence that perceptual identification may be impaired to some extent in later life (Birren, 1955; Wallace, 1956; Welford, 1958; Birren & Riegel, 1962). Older subjects have been reported to be less able than the younger to detect simple designs embedded in more complex ones (Axelrod & Cohen, 1961). Since an explanation merely in terms of known changes in the sensory input is obviously unsatisfactory in these cases, the observations provide some support for the view that with advancing age the ability to shift from one perceptual hypothesis to another may be reduced (Welford, 1958; Birren, 1964).

The other hypothesis of a functional character assumes that the excitability or arousal of the older nervous system is low. In this view, readiness to rapid response is low because neurons are not in a high state of subliminal excitation such as might result from a relative sensory deprivation of the older person, and perhaps an inherent lessening of activity of the reticular activating system. The finding of increased response time in relation to increasing task difficulty does not preclude an alternative interpretation along the lines of delayed synaptic transmission. Hence, if the single synapse takes longer for transmission with advancing age, the greater the number of synapses involved in any complex behavior the greater will be the time of response in the older adult. The lengthening of the time need not be a linear function of the time delay at any single unit, but may grow as a power function of the number of synapses, as the excitation spreads over a network.

It was pointed out earlier that slowness of behavior is not only associated with advancing age, but is seen in subjects with brain damage, mental retardation and certain forms of psychosis. Whether the same mechanism underlies the slowness shown in all four groups, is to be questioned. This assumes, for purposes of discussion, that behavioral slowing is a general factor: slowness of all behavior mediated by the central nervous system (Birren, 1965). It is possible that there is a basis in the nervous system for a generalized slowing consisting of the extra-pyramidal centers, midbrain and reticular formation with rostral and caudal connections. The structure likely to influence the elements of the speed of complex behavior is the reticular activating system of the brain stem. In turn, the extra-pyramidal system functions in cooperation with the reticular formation. Hassler (1965) emphasized the control of the extra-pyramidal system on slowness of behavior. The loss of cells in the extra-pyramidal structures of the nervous system could contribute substantially to the slowness of behavior seen with advancing age. Such an anatomic point of view is of course related to an activation hypothesis which in effect says that the tonic influences on the older nervous system diminish and result in a lower preparedness to respond or to organize responses.

4. *Information theory and "intelligence theory"*. Evidence has been collected by Szafran (1966) and others that with advancing age the nervous system can process fewer units of information per unit time. Information theory lends itself to an explanation of such age changes. One unresolved issue is the constancy of the *bit* of information, particularly when dealing with complex stimuli. Rabbitt (1965), for example, showed that when irrelevant information is introduced into the stimulus, older persons will take a longer time to respond. The amount of information in a stimulus would appear to depend upon the subject's purpose in responding to it. There is always more

information in the environment than we are responding to. How then, with age, does the subject ignore or handle the massive amount of information from which he is withholding response? One implication of research by Rabbitt is that older subjects find increasing amounts of irrevelant information a distraction. This may reflect what some researchers regard as a weak set, or others as weak inhibitory processes, attention or vigilance.

Increased conceptual organization of information may permit the older subject to process fewer bits, but larger chunks of information per unit time. This would increase the total effectiveness of his behavior by allowing him to deal with larger chunks of information through the formation of concepts, although at the same time a decrease in processing time per unit may be observed.

Results of standardized intelligence tests (Guilford, 1969) suggest that certain functions rise in scores with advancing age. Results of vocabulary measurement show, for example, that the healthy adult will generally know more words after an increase in age: that is, with advancing age the individual accumulates more experience. If each element of experience remained as an isolated bit, the individual would be searching an increasingly large store of information and his performance would probably slow down. Concomitant with rises in stored information with age shown on intelligence test scores, other measures—such as speed on decoding tests—show a decrease. Thus the aging nervous system contains an increasing mass of stored information to process, yet seems to have a slower processing mechanism. How does the middle-aged and older adult maintain effectiveness? Tentatively, it would seem that an explanation might lie in the fact that, with increasing experience, verbal and other information is reorganized conceptually and need neither exist nor be retrieved as isolated bits.

A study of successful middle-aged individuals carried out at the University of Chicago (Birren, 1969) suggests that successful middle-aged professionals tend to concentrate on crucial aspects of a situation, whereas the young professional person must deal with more information since he doesn't know what crucial information to look for. With additional experience, the individual forms concepts and can classify categories of crises, clients, or interpersonal relations according to their assumed nature. Though this increases his effectiveness, in a limited sense he may be processing fewer bits of information than he did as a young professional; nevertheless, as an older person, he can use his larger mass of experience and retrieve it in larger chunks or concepts.

Consequently the effectiveness of the older man in adapting to a technological environment is not necessarily indicated directly by the number of bits of information he can process per unit time. Possibly, his experience or information may be organized so that he can deal with larger chunks of information or experience acquired with age. Effectiveness, in response to a complex environment, is a joint function of the conceptual organization of the individual's experience and his processing time. At some age this joint function may result in declining effectiveness, but it would appear to occur later in life than our curves of choice-reaction time with age would imply. One cannot extrapolate directly to effectiveness of behavior from either a simple curve of information processing of bits of information per second, or from total information stored as in a vocabulary test. As suggested, the "bit" itself may not be a constant quantity. Studies of isolated elements of experience do not tell us how they are grouped under concepts and hence available to the retrieval mechanisms of the nervous system. In this view, aged individuals are more or less efficient in terms of the organization of their retrieval mechanisms and concepts as well as their processing time.

5. *Major problems.* There has been a tendency in the social psychology of aging to regard older persons as constituting a

minority group. In general, social surveys indicate that older persons tend to be disadvantaged with regard to income, services and prestige in society. But there is little substantial evidence that older persons identify with others of the same age as constituting their reference group. This would be necessary were older persons really to constitute a minority group within societies. However, access to study populations has often been limited; therefore the literature on aging appears to be concerned with institutionalized adults available and amenable to investigation. The literature is biased in suggesting high levels of dependency and incapacity, for such characteristics reflect the nature of the populations institutionalized rather than the characteristics of older individuals leading an independent life in society. Because of the lack of easy access to older members of the population for study of these and other topics, little detailed information is usually available about the factors influencing the life satisfaction and functioning of older adults independently living in society. Therefore psychologists have tended to revert to points of view about the development of children. As research explores the details of aging with the same enthusiasm and effort that has been given to child psychology, much more should be revealed about the conditions that lead to optimum life satisfaction and functioning throughout the life span, including old age.

Bibliography: Axelrod, S. & Cohen, L. D.: Senescence and embedded-figure performance in vision and touch. Percept. Motor Skills, 1961, *12*, 283–8. **Birren, J. E.:** Age changes in speed of simple responses and perception and their significance for complex behavior. In: Old age in the modern world. London, 1955, 235–47. **Id.:** The psychology of aging. Englewood Cliffs, New Jersey, 1964. **Id.:** Age changes in speed of behavior; its central nature and physiological correlates. In: **Welford, A. T. & Birren, J. E.** (Eds): Behavior, aging, and the nervous system. Springfield, Ill., 1965, 191–216. **Id.:** Age and decision strategies. In: **Welford, A. T. & Birren, J. E.** (Eds): Decision making and age. Basle and New York, 1969, 23–6. **Birren, J. E. & Riegel, K.:** Lights, numbers, letters, colors, syllables, words and word relationships. In: **Tibbitts, C. & Donahue, W.** (Eds): Social and psychological aspects of aging. New York, 1962, 751–8. **Bühler, Charlotte:** Maturation and motivation. Personality, 1951, *1*, 184–211. **Craik, F. I. M.:** Applications of signal detection to studies of aging. In: **Welford, A. T. & Birren, J. E.** (Eds): Decision making and age. Basle, 1969. **Crossman, E. R. F. W. & Szafran, J.:** Changes with age in the speed of information intake and discrimination. Experientia, Suppl., 1956, *4*, 128–35. **Cumming, M. Elaine & Henry, W. E.:** Growing old; the process of disengagement. New York, 1961. **Green, D. M. & Swets, J. A.:** Signal detection theory and psychophysics. New York, 1966. **Guilford, J. P.:** Intellectual aspects of decision making. In: **Welford, A. T. & Birren, J. E.** (Eds): Decision making and age. Basle, 1969. **Hall, G. S.:** Senescence. New York, 1922. **Hassler, R.:** Extrapyramidal control or the speed of behavior and its change by primary age processes. In: **Welford, A. T. & Birren, J. E.** (Eds): Behavior, aging, and the nervous system. Springfield, Ill., 1965, 284–306. **Quetlet, A.:** Sur l'homme et le développement de ses facultés, 2 vols. Paris, 1835. **Rabbitt, P. M. A.:** Age and discrimination between complex stimuli. In: **Welford, A. T. & Birren, J. E.** (Eds): Behavior, aging, and the nervous system. Springfield, Ill., 1965, 35–53. **Szafran, J.:** Changes with age and with exclusion of vision in performance at an aiming task. Quart. J. Exp. Psychol., 1951, *3*, 111–18. **Id.:** Experiments on the greater use of vision by older adults. In: Old age in the modern world. London, 1955, 213–35. **Id.:** Age differences in the rate of gain of information, signal detection strategy and cardiovascular status among pilots. Gerontologia, 1966, *12*, 6–17. **Id.:** Psychophysiological studies of aging in pilots. In: **Talland, G. A.** (Ed.): Human aging and behavior. New York, 1968, 37–74. **Wallace, J. G.:** Some studies of perception in relation to age. Brit. J. Psychol., 1956, *47*, 283–97. **Welford, A. T.:** Ageing and human skill. London, 1958.

J. E. Birren

Agnosia. A disorder of recognition despite intact functioning of the sense organs, intelligence, and consciousness. A perceived object is not recognized, i.e. is not identified by reference to memory content. (*a*) *Optical* or *visual agnosia* can affect optical-spatial orientation and recognition, and identification of the outward appearance of individual objects (lesion of the upper parieto-occipital region); recognition of characteristic features of objects or persons (injury to the visual cortex of the occipital lobe); or knowledge of the (acquired) significance of colors (parieto-occipital lesion). (*b*) *Acoustic* or *auditory agnosia* might be described as a sensory *aphasia* (q.v.) extended to the entire acoustic field, and consists of a disorder of the recognition of noises, melodies (sensory amusia), etc. Localization of the lesion: temporal lobes of the dominant hemisphere. (*c*) *Tactile agnosia* (*stereoagnosis, astereognosis*): inability to recognize an object by touch despite the retention of sensitivity. Tactile agnosia was at one time thought to be caused by a parietal lesion, whereas the occurrence of an isolated tactile agnosia is now thought doubtful. *C.S.*

Agonistic behavior. A collective term for behavior in social confrontations; it includes attacks (offensive and defensive), threats, fighting, evasion, subjection, appeasement gestures (q.v.), flight. This group of behaviors forms a unity for theorists who attempt to explain aggressive behavior as arising out of the conflict between tendencies to attack and to flight. Neurophysiological findings would seem to support this hypothesis. Electrical stimulation of the midbrain reveals transitions between attack, threat behavior and flight.

Bibliography: Holst, E. von & St Paul, U.: Vom Wirkungsgefüge der Triebe. Naturwiss., 1960, *47*, 464–76. **Hunsperger, R. W.:** Affektreaktion auf elektrische Reizung im Hirnstamm der Katze. Helvet. physiol. acta., 1956, *14*, 70–92. *R.S.A.*

Agoraphobia. An exaggerated or abnormal dread of traversing or being in open spaces.

Agrammatism. Ungrammatical speech. Each word is correctly formed and pronounced but the order is wrong, or there is an incorrect conjugation of verbs, declension of nouns, and comparison of adjectives and adverbs. Parts of speech (say, a verb or preposition) may be omitted. If the message is present to a minor degree, it may be possible to decipher it. More severe cases speak nonsense. Often accompanied by perseveration or stereotypy (q.v.). Syn.: (in organic states) *jargon* or *syntactical aphasia*; (in functional states) *incoherence, drivelling*. *B.B.*

Agraphia. An inability to write consequent upon injury to a specific cerebral area. With a lesion in the area of the (in the right-handed, left) parietal lobe, as "apractic" (or apraxic) or ideokinetic agraphia, it forms part of an *apraxia* (q.v.). It is to be distinguised by the site of the lesion in Broca's area (q.v.) from the "aphasic" agraphia that accompanies *aphasia* (q.v.). *C.S.*

Agreement coefficient. A measure of the degree of agreement among rankings.

$$CA = 100\left[1 - \frac{\frac{\Sigma T - \Sigma B}{N}}{2(H - L)}\right]$$

where CA = coefficient of agreement, T = the top 50% of rankings, B = the bottom 50% of rankings, $H - L$ = the highest less the lowest possible ranking, and N = the number of cases. *J.M.*

Aha experience (*Ah-ah experience*). The experience of direct understanding or insight that announces or accompanies the sudden occurrence of a solution (often only illusive) in the thought process. *H.-J.A.*

Alalia. Not in common use now, the term means without the ability to talk. This meaning is now carried by *aphasia*, which is divided into many sub-categories; these in turn have no completely accepted system of classification. If it is ever to be of use, the term must be restricted to those mute (aphonic) patients who have no peripheral disturbance of articulation (anarthria), and yet appear to be able to formulate ideas and can communicate them in some other way, such as writing. However, this disorder is at present commonly called *motor aphasia*, or when present in a lesser degree, *verbal aphasia* (see *Aphasia*). *B.B.*

Alarm function. Function ascribed to the ascending reticular activating system (q.v.). It effects the transition from the relaxed waking condition to a state of general attention (q.v.). *R.Hä.*

Alarm reaction(s). 1. (syn. *Alarm calls*). Varying calls elicited in certain species by the presence of a predator, and serving to communicate danger: e.g. "mobbing" calls in birds. **2.** An emergency reaction in the initial phase of general adaptation. *J.G.*

Albedo. The albedo of a surface is the reflective power of that surface: i.e. the ratio of reflected to incident light. *Albedometer:* a device for measuring albedo.

Bibliography: Berlyne, D. E.: The influence of the albedo and complexity of stimuli on visual fixation in the human infant. Brit. J. Psychol., 1958, *49*, 315–18. *G.K.*

Alcoholism. No one discipline has yet found any conclusive evidence to indicate the etiology of alcoholism. Physiological study, psychiatric appraisal, psychoanalytic interpretation, and socio-cultural formulation all yield divergent opinions (Yates, 1970, pp. 305ff.). Several additional factors contribute to the equivocation: the variety of disciplines each viewing the topic primarily from its own vantage point; the failure to discover any underlying common premorbid personality structure; the lack of agreement with respect to therapeutic goals and criteria for their evaluation; controversy over whether alcoholism is a disease *per se*, symptom of malaise or product of socio-psychological aberration; and diverse estimates of incidence, depending upon the criteria adopted.

Many non-behavioral scientists (not to mention members of Alcoholics Anonymous) hold that there is some physiologically based deficiency or predisposition to become an alcoholic. This implies that alcoholism is some form of disease entity which a person carries with him until he is cured, a paradigm so far unsubstantiated. Other scientists retain a functional definition of sickness but reject the necessity for a physiological basis. Alcoholism as a disease is then viewed in socio-psychological terms. Certain learning theorists (e.g. Ullmann & Krasner, 1969, pp. 498ff.) totally reject the disease concept and view alcoholism entirely in terms of learning theory. For the psychoanalytically oriented, alcoholism is often a symptom of some underlying infantile fixation to be treated by psychodynamic means. Sometimes it is argued that alcoholism is a symptom which has also become a disease. Others attempt to combine these diverse views into a multi-variate omnibus approach. But, to date, no general factors have emerged that would encompass the hypothesized psychological, behavioral, social, genetic and physiological components of the alcoholism syndrome. It may well be that the concept of alcoholism is little more than a convenient—if misleading—reification.

It is within the above context that the following definition of alcoholism is offered: "Alcoholism is a chronic behavioral disorder manifested by repeated drinking of alcoholic beverages in excess of the dietary and social uses of the community and to an extent that interferes with the drinker's health or his social or economic functioning" (Keller, 1958). But such a definition is by no means universally accepted. Many would object to the emphasis on description and symptomatology at the expense of etiology (for instance, Zwerling & Rosenbaum).

Regardless of orientation, it is necessary to know more about the physiological and socio-psychological effects of alcohol. Naïveté rather than scientific rigor has marked most of the earlier studies in this area (se reviews by Carpenter, 1962; Lester, 1966). More recent investigations (see Franks, 1970) challenge hitherto generally accepted conclusions, such as that of Jellinek & MacFarland (1940) to the effect that the use of alcohol consistently brings about a deterioration in mental performance and that the effect of alcohol is a simple linear function of the amount ingested. Too many studies suffer from being predicated upon single dosages rather than sustained alcohol intake. Although individuals do not differ widely in their brain tissue tolerance to alcohol, there are wide differences among them in their subjective and manifest reactions to alcohol: these cannot yet be satisfactorily accounted for in theoretical terms despite several attempts to do so (Eysenck, 1957; Franks, 1967).

Despite a wide variety of approaches there is hardly more reason now to be optimistic about therapy than there was in the 'forties. The present trend seems to be toward greater sophistication in the conceptualization and execution of treatment models, and recognition of the need to develop multiple interdisciplinary programs, each geared toward different patient populations (see Pattison, 1966; Blum & Blum, 1967). But adequate scientific standards and criteria for program evaluation and comparison are still lacking.

The behavioral approach to alcoholism, with its assumption that deviant drinking behavior is, in part, a conditioned response subject to the same learning principles that determine any other form of behavior, has its clinical origins in the naïve and now outmoded aversive conditioning procedures of the 'forties. Later, experimental psychologists came to the forefront, advocating a scientifically rigorous but clinically not very successful S-R regimen which focused largely upon the drinking *per se*. Gradually, a more integrative approach developed which extended itself to pertinent aspects of the patient's total life style, including behavioral, biogenetic, developmental and socio-environmental influences (Lazarus, 1965).

If alcohol-drinking behavior is reinforced by its tension-reducing effect, then it becomes necessary to develop other and more acceptable devices for reducing tension, including direct environmental manipulation. Much needed research into the drinking patterns of alcoholics and the rewarding effects of alcohol in a variety of settings is under way (e.g. Mello *et al.*, 1968; Nathan *et al.*, 1970; Vogel-Sprott, 1970).

Behavior is malleable; therefore it is sometimes argued that it should be possible to teach selected ex-alcoholics to engage in limited social drinking with no adverse consequences. This unlikely contention, contrary to generally accepted practice and opinion, has yet to be validated. Perhaps prophylaxis is of greater importance. Prevention can occur at various levels: direct treatment of the alcoholic; early detection of the potential alcoholic with a view to changing the processes in his life that seem likely to lead to alcoholism; and a more general reduction of the personal and societal tensions that, in a complex society, lead to a variety of aberrations, of which alcoholism is but one.

Little is known with confidence about the kind of alcoholic most likely to respond to a particular type of therapeutic regimen. Techniques for sustaining motivation in the recovered alcoholic, and the establishment of alcoholism-training programs for therapist specialists and the technicians who can be trained for much of the work, require attention in the future. Computerized longitudinal studies of potential alcoholic populations through health and sickness, and into the post-sickness stages when appropriate, are desirable.

Investigation of any aspect of alcoholism is now facilitated by the existence of a continually updated documentation program duplicated throughout the world (Keller, 1964).

Bibliography: Blum, E. M. & Blum, R. H.: Alcoholism: modern psychological approaches to treatment. San Francisco, 1967. **Carpenter, J. A.:** Effects of alcohol on some psychological processes: a critical review with special reference to automobile driving skill. Quart. J. Stud. Alc., 1962, *23*, 274–314. **Eysenck, H. J.**: Drugs and personality. 1: Theory and methodology. J. Ment. Sci., 1957, *103*, 119–31. **Franks, C. M.**: The use of alcohol in the investigation of drug-personality postulates. In: **Fox, Ruth** (Ed.): Alcoholism—behavioral research, therapeutic approaches, 55–79. New York, 1967. **Franks, C. M.**: 1970 Alcoholism. In: **Costello, C. G.** (Ed.): Symptoms of psychopathology: a handbook. New York, 1970, 448–80. **Jellinek, E. M. & MacFarland, R. A.**: Analysis of psychological experiments on the effects of alcohol. Quart. J. Stud. Alc., 1940, *1*, 272–371. **Keller, M.**: Alcoholism: nature and extent of the problem. Ann. Amer. Acad. Polit. Soc. Sci., 1958, *315*, 1–11. **Id.**: Documentation of the alcohol literature. Quart. J. Stud. Alc., 1964, *25*, 725–41. **Lazarus, A. A.**: Towards the understanding and effective treatment of alcoholism. S. Afr. Med. J., 1965, *39*, 736–41. **Lester, D.**: Self-selection of alcohol by animals, human variation, and the etiology of alcoholism: a critical review. Quart. J. Stud. Alc., 1966, *27*, 394–438. **Mello, Nancy K., McNamee, H. B. & Mendelson, J. H.**: Drinking patterns of chronic alcoholics: gambling and motivation for alcohol. Psychiatric Research Report No. 24, American Psychiatric Association, March 1968, 83–118. **Nathan, P. E., Title, N. A., Lowenstein, L. D., Solomon, P. & Rossi, M.**: Behavioral analysis of chronic alcoholism: interaction of alcohol and human contact. Arch. Gen. Psychiat., 1970. **Pattison, E. M.**: A critique of alcoholism treatment concepts with special reference to abstinence. Quart. J. Stud. Alc., 1966, *27*, 49–71. **Ullmann, L. P. & Krasner, L.**: A psychological approach to abnormal behavior. Englewood Cliffs, N.J., 1969. **Vogel-Sprott, Muriel**: Alcoholism and learning. In: Biology and Alcoholism (Chapter 10), 1970, *11*. **Yates, A. J.**: Behavior therapy. New York, 1970. **Zwerling, I. & Rosenbaum, M.**: Alcohol addiction and personality (non-psychotic conditions). In: **Arietti, S.** (Ed.): American Handbook of Psychiatry, Vol. 1, New York, 1959, 623–44.

C. M. Franks

Aldosterone. An adrenal hormone (see *Corticosteroids*) which is one of the so-called mineralocorticoids and is by far the most potent natural hormone in view of its effect on electrolyte concentration. Detailed knowledge of the effective mechanism of aldosterone is not yet available. The amount of aldosterone in urine probably varies according to emotional stress. Little is known of the psychic effects of this hormone in healthy individuals.

Bibliography: Baulien, E. E. & Potel, R.: Aldosterone. Oxford, 1964. **Laragh, J. H. & Kelly, W. G.**: Aldosterone: its biochemistry and physiology. In: **Levine, R. & Luft, R.** (Eds): Advances in metabolic disorders. New York, 1964. **Mason, J. W., Jones, J. A., Ricketts, P. T., Brady, J. V. & Tolliver, G. A.**: Urinary aldosterone and urine volume responses to 72-hr avoidance sessions in the monkey. Psychosom. Med., 1968, *30*, 733–45. **Nowakowski, H.**: Aldosterone. Berlin, 1963.

W.J.

Alexia. Caused by a lesion in a specific cortical area (angular gyrus of the left temporal lobe in the right-handed), alexia is an inability to read because the affected individual has lost any understanding of written or printed characters. Word blindness = sensory alexia. "Aphasic alexia", on the other hand, refers to a loss of expressive speech. See *Aphasia*. *C.S.*

Algedonic. Concerning the pleasure-pain dimension. The algedonic is one of the three dimensions of the emotions in the typology of W. Wundt (q.v.). *R.Hä.*

Algesia (syn. *Algesis*). Sense of, or sensitivity to, pain. Subject to considerable variations (subjective attitude, earlier experiences, etc.). Certain diseases and the surgical reduction of nerve fibers can lead to a higher or lower pain threshold (see *Hypalgesia; Hyperalgesia; Pain*). *M.S.*

Algesimeter (syn. *Algesiometer*). An instrument for measuring sensitivity to pain by means of defined mechanical (calibrated pressure needle, etc.), thermal (heat radiation), or electrical pain stimuli. *M.S.*

Algolagnia. Sexual arousal by administering or suffering pain. *Active algolagnia:* sadism (q.v.); *passive algolagnia:* masochism (q.v.). *G.L.*

Algometer. An instrument for recording pain sensitivity in certain individuals. Defined pain stimulation is applied, e.g. by electrical current, and the pain response is determined subjectively by question and answer, or objectively by measuring reflexes or EEG variations. A very problematical method because of the considerable differences in pain evaluation. See *Pain*. *E.D.*

Algopareunia. See *Dyspareunia*.

Algorithm. An unambiguous, fixed, step-by-step system of operations for solving a class of problems. The sequence of operations is specified in the simplest case. The next operation is usually made to depend on the result of the previous one. *H.R.*

Alienation. 1. A term in social psychology and clinical psychoanalysis for states causing conflict (self-alienation, loss of a sense of identity, a feeling of depersonalization), the cause of which is traced back to some environmental pressure (e.g. the excessive demands of social or performance standards). As *Entfremdung*, the concept originated with Hegel, who used it to denote the distance between mind and reality. *W.D.F.*

2. In the Marxian sense, the objectification of labor is the loss of the object of labor, and bondage to it; it is alienation inasmuch as "the more powerful labor becomes, the more powerless becomes the laborer" (Marx, 1964). An ambitious theoretical attempt to reconcile this view with the Freudian theory of the negation of the pleasure principle is to be found in Marcuse (1955), who also offers an analysis of a more progressive stage of alienation under technological rationality, in which alienation masquerades as fulfillment (1964). Skinner's fictional *Walden Two* envisions a proficiently socialized "non-alienated" society of the kind that Marcuse would classify as "pure alienation".

Bibliography: Bensmen, J. & Rosenberg, B.: The meaning of work in bureaucratic society. In: **Stein, M. R.** (Ed.): Identity and anxiety. New York, 1960. **Marcuse, H.:** Eros and civilization. Boston, 1955. **Id.:** One-dimensional man. Boston, 1964. **Marx, K.:** The economic and philosophic manuscripts of 1844. New York, 1964. **Schacht, R.:** Alienation. New York & London, 1971. **Shepard, J. M.:** Automation and alienation. Cambridge, Mass., 1971. **Skinner, B. F.:** Walden two. New York, 1948. *J.C.*

Allele (syn. *Allelomorph*). Either of two genes located at one chromosome locus and controlling alternative (Mendelian) characters. In diploid (q.v.) organisms, both alleles can be in the same cell. In characteristics one allele can dominate (dominant-recessive inheritance, e.g. brown or blue eyes dominate in man), or else the characteristic is expressed in an intermediate form (pink pea-flowers in the case of alleles for white and red).

Multiple allele: any of more than two different genes for the same characteristic (e.g. human blood groups). *H.S.*

Allergy. An abnormal tendency to react to specific stimulus objects and situations which is conditioned by physical (and possibly psychic) hypersensitivity. Among the allergies are hay-fever, asthma, and certain skin irritations. See *Psychosomatics*. *K.E.P.*

Allochthonous dynamics. According to Gutjahr (1959), in an actualization process, a distinction must be made between motivational (allochthonous, according to R. Bergius) and autochthonous (individual-specific) dynamics. Allochthonous dynamics represents powers which occur as a result of active searching by the individual. Bergius (*Handbuch der Psychologie*, Vol. 1/2, 209) sees autochthonous dynamics as consisting "of the forces occurring through the functional interaction of the limbs". According to Gutjahr, autochthonous dynamics can occur "only in a behavioral process released by a specific motivation". Autochthonous dynamics is subject to the individual behavioral process. For example, all memories that "come suddenly to mind" without any conscious searching are actualized autochthonously.

Bibliography: Gutjahr, W.: Zur Psychologie des sprachlichen Gedächtnisses. II. Über Aktualisierungsdynamik. Z. Psychol., 1959, *163*, 1–108.

H.-J.A.

Allolalia. Meaning a different, unusual or abnormal state of speech. More specific words for particular varieties of speech disorder are favored now. *B.B.*

Allopreening. One adult bird preens another in answer to preening invitation postures. This social preening among certain families of birds may be compared with similar behaviors in mammals in which one adult cleans another as if attending to its young. Allopreening has the effect of checking aggression, or acting as a form of greeting or courtship, especially in pairing. Tongue-play and so on in humans can be interpreted as derived from analogous mutual preening actions. *V.P.*

All-or-none law (syn. *All-or-nothing principle*). A functional unit subject to the all-or-none law within the organism reacts to every above-threshold stimulation with a potential ungraded in relation to the stimulus size or intensity. Stimulation produces a maximal response or none at all. The validity of the law in the case of excitable functional units (neurons) in the organism depends on the electrical processes of excitation. The functional membrane surrounding every excitable cell is at first locally depolarized by every stimulus not occurring within the refractory period. This local depolarization, or reduction of resting potential, is reversed by metabolic processes (the sodium-potassium "ion pump") during below-threshold stimulation, but during above-threshold stimulation brings about a considerable ungraded (in relation to stimulus intensity) increase in membrane permeability, and thus a further locally unrestricted depolarization which very quickly leads to a complete (reversible) reversal of membrane potential (see *Action potential*). Examples where the law applies are cardiac muscle contraction and the frequency coding of stimulus-intensity information conveyed to sensory nerves with a uniform amplitude.

Bibliography: Grossman, S. P.: A textbook of physiological psychology, New York, 1967. *M.S.*

Allport, Gordon Willard. B. 11/11/1897, in Montezuma (Indiana), d. 7/10/1967 in Cambridge (Mass.). An American psychologist specializing in the study of personality who studied at Harvard, Berlin, Hamburg and Cambridge (Eng.) Universities, and returned to teach at Harvard in the Psychology Department, and in the School of Social Relations (from 1924 to 1930, social ethics; and from 1930 to 1966, psychology). For twelve years he edited the *Journal of Abnormal and Social Psychology*. In addition to personality theory and research, Allport concerned himself with diagnostic psychology and prejudice (*The Nature of Prejudice*, 1954). In his main works *Personality: A Psychological Interpretation* (1937), and *Becoming* (1955), he emphasized the individuality, individual world and uniqueness of personality, and represented an image of man dominated neither by the pleasure-pain principle nor by the stimulus-response schema. At the same time Allport recognized the importance of biology and the study of traits. His theory of "functional autonomy" stresses the present moment and the relative unimportance of antecedent (e.g. genetic) explications of behavior. The uniqueness of motives in the adult is emphasized at the expense of the instincts, etc., from which they derive. Allport distinguishes between individual and interindividual, or common, traits (which are, however, only *more like* those of other individuals). Of ultimate importance is the forward striving of the individual self—the "*proprium*" ("propriate striving", "propriate functions")—to ideal self-realization, and the categories of maturity, organization, the new, development, and self-dynamic activity.

Main works: Personality: a psychological interpretation. New York, 1937. ABCs of scapegoating, 1944. The use of personal documents in psychological science. New York, 1947. The nature of prejudice. Reading, Mass., 1954. Becoming: basic considerations for a psychology of personality. New Haven, Conn., 1955. Personality and social encounter, Boston, 1960. A study of values: a scale for measuring the dominant interests in personality (with P. E. Vernon & G. Lindzey). Boston, [3]1960. Pattern and growth in personality. New York, 1961.

Bibliography: Allport, Gordon W.: In: Boring, E. G. & Lindzey, G. (Eds): A history of psychology in autobiography, Vol. 5, New York, 1967, 3–25. **Hall, C. S. & Lindzey, G.:** Theories of personality. New York, 1957. *G.S.*

Alpha-methyldopa (syn. *Aldomet; Methyldopa; Hydromet*—with hydrochlorothiazide). A substance which leads to the formation of false transmitter substances in adrenergic nervous systems. Alpha-methyldopa inhibits decarboxylase in the conversion of dopa (q.v.) into the noradrenaline precursor dopamine (q.v.), and probably brings about substitution of the natural neurotransmitter noradrenaline by the false transmitter (alpha-) methylnoradrenaline. As a result of this substitution, the CNS and ANS tissues are deprived of noradrenaline. Alpha-methyldopa causes a fall in blood pressure and is used therapeutically against hypertension. The psychic effects of alpha-methyldopa are not clearly established, although depression has sometimes been reported.

Bibliography: Acheson, G. H. (Ed.): Second symposium on catecholamines. Pharmacol. Rev., 1966, *18*, 1–804. **Thoenen, H.:** Bildung und funktionelle Bedeutung adrenerger Ersatz-transmitter. New York, 1969. *W.J.*

Alpha movement (syn. *Alpha motion*). M. Wertheimer's term for an illusion of movement: the perception of a change in size when objects otherwise alike are rapidly presented and one object appears to grow or diminish. See *Motion, apparent*. *V.M.*

Alpha waves (syn. *Alpha rhythm; Berger rhythm*). Slow wave-form variations in potential (0·1–40 Hz) which can be recorded at the cerebral cortex or scalp (electroencephalogram: EEG) by means of electrodes, and which represent the temporal-spatial integral of slow postsynaptic impulses of the cortical cells. EEG waves in the 8–12 Hz (8–12 c/s) frequency range are characterized as alpha waves. When the adult subject is inactive these waves occur predominantly at occipital locations. Alpha waves are inhibited by sensory stimuli and intellectual activity and are replaced by *beta waves* (q.v.) of a lower amplitude. Their frequency drops with a diminution of the level of cerebral excitation (sleep). *M.S.*

Alternate forms. Two collections of test items so similar that they are taken to be not different tests but versions of the same one.

Alternating method. A term sometimes applied to the use of programmed instruction (q.v.) together with conventional methods. *H.I.*

Alternative (syn. *Alternative hypothesis*). In statistical hypothesis testing: an hypothesis which represents an alternative to the hypothesis (H_0) which is to be tested. See *Statistics*. *W.H.B.*

Alternative reinforcement. Reinforcement (q.v.) by fixed temporal intervals between, or a fixed ratio of, responses, according to a *reinforcement schedule*.

Altruism. Unselfish behavior. A collective term for all modes of behavior directed to the advantage of others and not to one's own profit. The conditions for the occurrence and acquisition of altruism have been investigated in recent years. Positive correlations between various tests for unselfishness would seem to indicate the existence of a general personality trait that would accord with the above definition.

Bibliography: Krebs, D. L.: Altruism: an examination of the concept and a review of the literature. Psychol. Bull., 1970, *73*, 258–302. **Hartshorne, H.,** *et al.*: Studies in the nature of character. II: Studies in service and self-control. New York, 1929. *D.B.*

Amaurotic idiocy. Also known as cerebromacular degeneration or Tay-Sach's disease, this is a rare condition at one time thought to occur only in Jewish families. A degenerative disease of the central nervous system due to a recessive gene. The child is normal at birth and develops normally until the onset of the disease. Symptoms are arrested mental development, muscular weakness and rapidly developing blindness (amaurosis). Death occurs within two years of onset. *V.K.J.*

Ambidexterity. Equal dexterity, or skill, with both hands. How skilled hands are depends, among other factors, on heredity, education and imitation. Usually the right hand is the guiding hand and the left the helping. By practice one can train both hands equally. In work processes requiring a different performance from each hand, ambidexterity proves to be of little use, since rhythmic action is disturbed and there is the danger of accidents. Adj. *Ambidextrous.* See also *Handedness.* *W.S.*

Ambivalence. The existence of two (possibly contradictory) values, goals or directions. The term was introduced into psychology by E. Bleuler to indicate the simultaneous occurrence of two antagonistic emotions (q.v.) (e.g. inclination and disinclination, hate-love). Affective ambivalence is a general characteristic of schizophrenia (q.v.). *R.Hä.*

Ambivalent behavior. Often the same behavioral situation releases different responses alternating in conflict (q.v.). For instance, if a female wrasse (*Labridae*) appears at a male's nest, this means "strange fish in my preserve" and at first releases attack behavior, until there is an increasing alternation between attack and courtship, and finally the female's readiness for spawning inhibits the male's hostility. The stickle-back's zig-zag dance also arises from ritualized movements indicating both attack and leading-to-the-nest.

Bibliography: Bastock, M., Morris, D. & Moynihan, M.: Some comments on conflict and thwarting in animals. Behav., 1953, *6*, 66–84. *K.F.*

Amblyopia. Functional dimness of vision in the absence of organic defect. It occurs, e.g., in squinting (strabismus). To avoid double images, the image from one eye is suppressed. This can affect vision in the suppressed eye; if the condition is allowed to persist, it can prove irreversible. *R.R.*

Toxic amblyopia: a reduction in vision associated with excessive consumption of tobacco, alcohol and certain drugs.

Amenorrh(o)ea. The condition in which a woman's menstrual periods are missed. A distinction is made between *primary* and *secondary* amenorrhea. In the first case, menstruation has never occurred since the beginning of sexual maturation, e.g. because of hypofunction of the primary sex glands (ovaries) or thyroid gland. In the second case, menstruation *has* occurred before cessation, which is normal during pregnancy as a result of placental hormone production and uterine changes, but also occurs as a result of a specific method of birth control using slowly absorbed and long-term effective sexual hormones. Amenorrhea also occurs after cessation of ovarian function during the menopause. In all three cases, secondary amenorrhea is physiological and not indicative of any disease. Secondary amenorrhea may be termed pathological if it is caused by lesions of the pituitary gland, the thyroid gland, or the ovaries. A disturbance of gonadotrophin production (essential for menstruation) by the anterior pituitary can also be psychically conditioned. Amenorrhea is often observed in cases of depression (q.v.), schizophrenia (q.v.), extreme psychological stress (q.v.), and as a result of sexual neuroses and abstinence from sexual intercourse.

Bibliography: Hamburg, D. A. *et al.*: Studies of distress in the menstrual cycle and the post-partum period. In: **Michael, R. P.** (Ed.): Endocrinology and human behaviour. London, 1968. **Sturgis, S. H.** *et al.*: The gynaecological patient: a psycho-endocrine study. London, 1962.

G.L.

Amentia. Synonymous with "oligophrenia", "mental defect", "mental deficiency", "mental subnormality". Tredgold defined amentia as a condition in which the mind has failed to reach complete or normal development. The term is no longer used and since the introduction of the British Mental Health Act (1959) has been replaced by the terms "subnormality" and "severe subnormality". In German the term is sometimes used to designate subacute delirious states. *V.K.J.*

Ametropia. Defective vision resulting from a pathological change in the refractive mechanism of the eye or a non-physiological distance between retina and lens. (See *Myopia; Hyperopia; Astigmatism.*) Not to be confused with *Presbyopia.* *R.R.*

Amnesia. Strictly speaking, the term refers to a complete loss of memory for past events. In practice it is used to refer to a general impairment of memories previously acquired, due to some temporary or permanent pathological process which may be organic or functional. It is not used to refer to an inability to recall past events, the memory for which has faded with time.

R.H.

Amnesic syndrome. This embodies impairment of memory for recent past events and a marked impairment of the ability to learn new material. Intellectual ability is not otherwise affected, nor are perception and clarity of consciousness. Confabulation (q.v.) also occurs in some cases. Possible causes are alcoholic Korsakoff psychosis, bitemporal lesions, encephalitis and severe head injury, and there may be damage to deep cortical and sub-cortical structures, particularly the mesial aspects of the temporal lobes, hippocampus and mammillary bodies. *R.H.*

Amodal. In contradistinction to *modal completion* (i.e. amplification, gestalt completion, or dynamic gestalt activity), A. E. Michotte defines amodal completion as that with no underlying sensory equivalence between the gestalt to be completed and the completing part. Hence, e.g., the perceived half of a ball is completed to become a total form as the "whole ball". Without amodal completion our limited capacity for perception would not allow us to adjust adequately to our environment. See *Ganzheit.*

Bibliography: Metzger, W. (Ed.): Handbuch der Psychologie, Vol. 1/1. Göttingen, 1966. *V.M.*

Amok. A rare psychiatric disturbance which occurs specifically in Malays, although it has counterparts in other cultures. Patients run wild and become homicidal, the hyperactive state persisting until exhaustion occurs. It may be of epileptic origin or arise from chronic intoxication with cannabis. *D.E.*

Amorphous type. An unemotional, inactive, unobtrusive character.

Amphetamines. Stimulant drugs (psychomotor stimulants) used therapeutically to combat listlessness, and formerly in clinical use as anti-depressants: e.g. as amphetamine sulfate (Benzedrine), methamphetamine (Methedrine), and dextroamphetamine (dexamphetamine; Dexedrine) (very often used in psychopharmacological investigations). The amphetamines have peripheral sympathicomimetic (e.g. in raising pulse rate and blood pressure) and central effects in the sense of increased arousal of the reticular formation. *Psychic effects:* a feeling of subjective alertness (usually before objective changes in performance), in most cases a positive influence on mood, increase of vigilance (q.v.), often a reduction in reaction times, higher results in clerical tests, and certain simple and complex motor skills tests (e.g. pursuit rotor, q.v.). Effects on motor endurance in certain respects have been demonstrated in soldiers and athletes ("doping"). The effect is dependent on initial condition. The most favorable effects were reported after sleep deprivation and extended psychic stress. Side effects observed are tremor, irritability, loss of appetite, and sleep disorders. Chronic recourse to large doses can produce habituation, dependence and addiction, and even psychotic states (*Amphetamine psychoses*).

Bibliography: Cole, S.: Experimental effects of amphetamine. Psychol. Bull., 1967, *68*, 81–90.

K.-D.S.

Amphetamine-barbiturate mixtures. Compounds which, through the addition of barbiturates, can add physical addiction to psychic drug dependence. Drinamyl ("purple hearts") is one such mixture widely used or abused, especially among the social groups of housewives and teenagers, being (in the United Kingdom) generally legally prescribed for the former, and illegally obtained by the latter.

Bibliography: Legge, D. & Steinberg, H.: Actions of a mixture of amphetamine and barbiturate in man. Brit. J. Pharmacol., 1962, *18*, 490–500.

Ampliation. A. E. Michotte has carried out experiments toward an explanation of the perception of causality. When a self-propelled object A begins to move, a previously immobile object B is set in motion in such a way that both movements are perceived as identical. Ss then assert that B's movement is caused by A, even though there is actually no causal relation. Michotte calls this illusion *ampliation*, and postulates an *ampliation structure* underlying the perception of causality.

Bibliography: Metzger, W. (Ed.): Handbuch der Psychologie., Vol. 1/1. Göttingen, 1966.

V.M.

Amplification. A psychotherapeutic method (C. G. Jung, q.v.) which—in contradistinction to the Freudian method of *reductio in primam figuram* by free association—attempts to extend and enrich dream-contents in analysis and interpretation by directed associations and by comparison of individual dream motifs with analogous material in the form of images, symbols, legends, myths, and so on. In this way dream-contents are supposed to be revealed in all possible nuances of meaning and in their various aspects. *H.N.G.*

Amusia. Loss of the ability of musical expression (*expressive amusia*), or also of the ability to apprehend, remember, and recognize melodies (*receptive amusia*), as a result of a lesion in the cerebral centers (usually the left parietal lobe in right-handed people) responsible for this function. *C.S.*

Amylobarbitone (*Amytal; Sodium Amytal*). A barbiturate synthesized in 1923. A hypnosedative or minor tranquilizer which in animals reduces certain aggressive behaviors and is highly anticonvulsant. Used clinically to treat certain disorders featuring fear and conflict.

Bibliography: Miller, N. E.: The analysis of motivational effects illustrated by experiments on amylobarbitone sodium. In: **Steinberg, H.,** *et al.* (Eds):

Animal behavior and drug action. London, 1964, 1–18.

Amytal. See *Amylobarbitone.*

Anaglyphs. Pictures composed of two similar views partly superimposed as to stimulate the *retinal disparity* relationships in normal binocular vision. When viewed through spectacles which allow only one image to be presented to each eye, a *stereoscopic* effect is obtained. *G.D.W.*

Anagogic. In psychoanalytic psychiatry, the term pertains to moral ideals, or to the spiritual or profound significance of dreams, thoughts, and other behavior. More specifically, C. G. Jung employed the term to denote those tendencies of the unconscious which are morally uplifting (opposite to the Freudian concept of *id*). *G.D.W.*

Analeptics. Substances which excite or stimulate the control centers of the ANS, or the CNS. If psychic effects are in question, the term *psychoanaleptics*, or *stimulants*, is sometimes used. Among other applications, analeptics are used therapeutically in the case of intoxication from hypnotics (q.v.), or of overdoses of narcotics (q.v.). Some important analeptics are caffeine (q.v.), pentamethylene tetrazol (Cardiazol, Metrazol, Pentetrazol), nikethamide (Coramine), strychnine (q.v.), camphor.

Bibliography: Hahn, F.: Analeptics. Pharmacol. Rev., 1960, *12*, 447–530. *W.J.*

Anal eroticism (syn. *Anal erotism*). Sensuous preoccupation with defecation and particularly with feces and the gaining of pleasure from the manipulation of feces. See *Anal stage.* *T.W.*

Analgesia. Insensitivity to pain while in possession of the other senses. Analgesia is always present as well in cases of anesthesia (q.v.). Localized analgesia occurs with mechanical or pharmacological treatment of corresponding pain nerves, or generalized analgesia after the administration of pain-killing drugs (see *Analgesics*). To some extent analgesia can be induced by distraction by means of, or the superimposition of, powerful sensory stimuli such as light or sound, or by the temporary elimination of certain brain centers. Analgesia is often the aim of non-specific pain therapy. However, analgesia is symptomatic of illness when caused by organically perceptible nervous, or psychic, changes. *E.D.*

Analgesics (syn. *Analgetics*). Psychotropic substances used therapeutically to relieve or remove pain. Narcotics (q.v.) and local anesthetics are not counted among the analgesics. Functional distinctions between the actions of analgesics, say between those affecting central (hypothalamus and thalamus) and peripheral (origin and conduction of pain afference) areas are possible only to a very limited extent, since the etiology of pain (q.v.) and of the interactions of peripheral and central structures are as yet unclear. Among the centrally effective analgesics are the so-called *narcotic analgesics*, which can produce drug addiction or dependence (q.v.): opium alkaloids such as morphine (q.v.) and its natural derivatives methyl morphine (see *Codeine*), dihydrocodeine, diamorphine (see *Heroin*), thebacodone, hydromorphone, etc., and the synthetic opiates (q.v.) pethidine, methadone, propoxyphene, levorphanol, etc. The morphine antagonists nalorphine and pentazocine are analgesics, but are not addictive. The so-called *peripheral analgesics* include the non-addictive and also antipyretic and antirheumatic pyrazol derivates (amidopyrine, phenylbutazone), the salicylates (salicylic acid, acetylsalicylic acid) and the aniline derivative phenacetin. In addition to increased stimulation of receptors, psychic factors (as expectations, affects, cognitions) are also involved in the experience of pain. The action of many analgesics consists in the alteration of sensory and psychic elements of pain. When tranquilizers (q.v.) and neuroleptics (q.v.) are used as analgesics, psychic elements are probably affected for the most part. The testing of analgesics in animals centers upon threshold determinations and measurements of the latency and duration of reactions: spinal reflexes, vocalization during (medullar) and after stimulation (thalamic reflexes) serve as pain indicators. Electrical and thermic stimuli are mainly used. In analgesics testing in animals, in addition to post-operative, mainly experimentally induced, states of pain are used: e.g. mechanical stimuli, heat radiation, electrical stimulation of epidermis of tooth pulp, and chemical stimulation (e.g. bradykinin injection). Control substances used for comparison are usually morphine (q.v.) or acetylsalicylic acid. In addition to recording pain waves, physiological (e.g. breathing and heart rates) and psychological variables (e.g. symptom and characteristic word lists, reaction time) are used to test efficacy. Most analgesics can induce a slight drowsiness.

Bibliography: **Desstevens, G.** (Ed.): Analgetics. New York, 1965. **Grimlund, K.:** Phenacetin and renal damage at a Swedish factory. Acta med. Scand. (Supp.), 1963, *405*, 1–26. **Mellett, L. B. & Woods, L. A.:** Analgesia and addiction. In: **Jucker, E.** (Ed.): Fortschritte der Arzneimittelforschung. Vol. 5. Basle, 1963. **Soulairae, A., Cahn, J. & Charpentier, J.** (Eds): Pain. New York, 1968. See also under *Morphine*.

W. Boucsein

Analgesimeter. A device for measuring the intensity of pain. Marked frontal areas are subjected to short-term heat radiation resulting in pain. Wolf developed a pain scale on the basis of his measurements of such pain waves, with the *dol* (Lat. *dolor*, pain) as the unit (a dol is one tenth of the scale covering the pain sensation induced by the least perceptible stimulus to that at which a further increase in stimulation induces no further increase in pain). These measurements are used to confirm the effects of analgesics. See *Pain*. *V.M.*

Anal intercourse. Anal stimulation can have a strongly erotic effect and occasionally induce orgasm. The physiological and psychological mechanisms concerned approximate those of other erotic responses. Novel recording methods have permitted the confirmation of previously unrecognized rhythmic contractions of the external anal sphincter during sexual stimulation (Masters & Johnson, 1966). Individual differences in anal response are due to intensity of varying nerve supply and psychological impressionability. Anal techniques are used in heterosexual intercourse, in sexual play among children, in male homosexual intercourse, as a form of masturbation, or as additional stimulation during normal vaginal intercourse.

Bibliography: Masters, W. H. & Johnson, V. E.: Human sexual response. Boston, 1966.

G.L.

Analogy. 1. Analogous behavior is functionally like but genetically different. Morphological and behavioral structures are probably analogous if they occur in species of the same form of life. Very similar patterns of behavior in closely related types are termed *homologous* (see *Homology*). *Analogue:* an organ or structure having an analogous or corresponding function in different species. *K.F.*

2. Mathematical proportion, or the equality of ratios. *Analogy of Pythagoras:* the proportion between the lengths of strings affording the distinct though concordant notes of the musical scale. **3.** The inferring of further similarities between two things similar in one respect from that one similarity. See *Problem-solving*.

Analogy test (syn. *Analogies test*). A form of test used mainly in intelligence testing. E.g.: *Bird* is to *air*, as *fish* is to ? . . . The testee must find the missing word or select it from a list in order to establish the analogy between the two sets of terms. Such tasks can also use pictures, geometrical figures or numbers. *R.M.*

Anal-sadistic stage. Equivalent to anal stage (q.v.). The term "sadistic" refers to the destructive possibilities increasingly available to a child with the refinement of motor skills and understanding of conditions of power in the environment, but normally less and less invoked by him. *W.T.*

Anal stage. According to Freud, the phase of child development in which the expulsion of feces and the manipulation of the child's own body are of primary interest. On average, the anal stage includes the second and third years of age. In the early part of the stage, the interests of the oral stage (q.v.) are increased by interest in locomotion, and in bodily and manual activity. Among the physical activities is defecation, a function that a child at first performs relatively without control, and on impulse. In social relations, the power aspects of his parents and his own power begin to be perceived and exercised in an all-or-nothing form. In the later anal stage, locomotion and body and hand movements are refined. Defecation comes under the control of the child himself and of his parents. A distinction is made between the exercise of power toward the child's parents, and the perception of their power. In this stage, the child learns to work, to cooperate, to emulate, and to resist. According to Freud, K. Abraham, and Fenichel, regression to the early anal stage can lead to paranoia, masochistic perversions and pregenital conversion neuroses, and fixation; and later regression to the late anal stage can lead to compulsive neuroses, sadistic perversions, and milder forms of pregenital conversion neuroses. Instead of specific neurotic symptoms, a certain deformation of personality—the "anal character"—can result. Freud includes pedantry, stinginess and frugality among the characteristics of this disordered personality.

Bibliography: Abraham, K.: Selected papers on psychoanalysis. London, 1927. **Freud, S.:** Three essays on the theory of sexuality. London, [2]1962. **Id.:** Introductory lectures on psycho-analysis. London, [2]1929. **Id.:** Collected papers, Vol. 2. London, 1924–5. **Fenichel, O.:** The psychoanalytic theory of neuroses. New York, 1945. **Toman, W.:** An introduction to psychoanalytic theory of motivation. London & New York, 1960. *W.T.*

Analysand. An individual undergoing psychological analysis or psychoanalytic therapy.

Analysis of Reading Ability. Graded tests by M. D. Neale consisting of oral reading passages and three diagnostic tests. Word recognition, comprehension, auditory discrimination, sound production, syllable recognition as well as reading. For 6 to 13 years.

Bibliography: Neale, M. D.: Analysis of reading ability. London, [2]1966. *J.M.*

Analysis of variance. See *Variance, analysis of.*

Analytical Intelligence Test (abb. AIT). A group of six primarily non-verbal tests. One of the first group tests (q.v.) designed to determine the intelligence profile for vocational and school counseling. Two forms for use from 12 and 15 years.

Bibliography: Meili, R.: Der analytische Intelligenztest. Berne, 1967. *R.M.*

Analytical psychology. Generally, an approach to the subject-matter of psychology which emphasizes reduction to its elements. Specifically (and more usually), the school of psychoanalytic psychiatry associated with Jung (q.v.), as opposed to that of Freud. Jung's theory of personality is less deterministic than that of Freud, more mystical and sometimes even religious, and he lays much less stress on the role of sex and aggression. In addition to the *personal unconscious*, Jung postulated a *collective unconscious* which contains the latent memories inherited from man's evolutionary past, and is manifested in universal symbols and myths called *archetypes*. Thus the aim of Jungian analysis and dream interpretation is not just to bring memories of personal experiences into consciousness, but to release the creative potential of the collective unconscious. The term is sometimes used to refer to any psychological method which might be termed "analytic". *G.D.W.*

Analytic(al) situation. The socio-dynamic process between the analyst (therapist) and analysand (patient), which is largely dependent on psychoanalytic techniques. It is based on the following factors: (*a*) The fundamental rule of analysis (the "analytic contract") requires the patient to declare everything that occurs to him during analysis (free association, q.v.), even though he may find it irrelevant, meaningless, painful or impolite; the analyst guarantees absolute discretion and expert assistance. This should produce an asymmetry of verbal communication. (*b*) The analyst tries to eliminate from the therapy all elements regarding his own private sphere, thus enabling the patient to transfer to the analyst his earlier emotional relations and expectations from specific individuals. Of course, in this process the analyst can provide only an approximation to neutrality in the shape of freedom from any "individual valuation". (*c*) The so-called rule of abstinence requires that the patient's wishes—either real (e.g. drugs) or arising out of transference (i.e. those directed onto the analyst and emanating from early childhood)—are not actually satisfied by the analyst. The analyst cannot and should not exert any influence on the actual situation (e.g. in marriage or vocation). This abstinence, or non-fulfillment of wishes by the analyst, raises affective pressure and hence therapeutic potential during analysis. (*d*) The patient's position on the couch enables the analyst to register every deviation from the agreed posture, and also from verbal communication, as special behavior, or acting-out (q.v.). The prone position also helps induce the regression (q.v.), or return to childhood, which is requisite for analysis. This phase traditionally follows the cathartic phase, during which hypnosis is used. Modern methods of analysis, which are adapted to the type of analysand, or the particular social situation of the analysis, involve technical modifications (parameters) deviating from the classical analytic situation (analyses of children, adolescents, delinquents or psychotics; analytic group therapy, minor analysis). See *Psychoanalysis*.

Bibliography: Becker, A. M.: Die Behandlungstechnik der Psychoanalyse. In: **Schraml, W. J.** (Ed.): Klinische Psychologie. Berne, 1970. **Freud, S.:** Standard edition of the complete psychological works. Vols. 1, 5, 16, 17. **Id.:** Group psychology and the analysis of the ego. London, [2]1959. **Id.:** Introductory lectures on psycho-analysis. London, [2]1929. **Id.:** New introductory lectures on psycho-analysis. London, 1933. **Id.:** An outline of psychoanalysis, [2]1959. **Greenson, R.:** The technique and practice of psychoanalysis. New York, 1967. **Glover, E.:** The technique of psychoanalysis. London, 1955. *W.J.S.*

Anamnesis. 1. All the information regarding an individual's life collected by questioning him or by some other means. The anamnesis is often neglected by psychologists. Developmental psychology, however, would seem unmistakably to show that test results can only be correctly interpreted in conjunction with an anamnesis. *R.M.*

2. Recollection. In Platonic philosophy, the soul's gradual rediscovery of all that it experienced in a previous existence. Learning as the eliciting of innate knowledge, or its implications.

Anancasm. A compulsive, repetitious behavior pattern.

Anancastia. The anancastic reactive type (or compulsive or obsessive character) is the counterpart of the hysteric reactive type. Anancastia represents a possible initial stage of compulsion neurosis, and is characterized by scrupulosity, minutely ordered, pedantic control over self and others, obsessive cleanliness, fear of loss, hypochondria, obsessive anxieties at inappropriate moments. A rigid form of reaction.

Bibliography: Kretschmer, E.: Der sensitive Beziehungswahn. Berlin, [4]1966. **Id. & Kretschmer, W.:** Medizinische Psychologie. Stuttgart, [13]1970. *W.K.*

Androgen(e)s. Male sexual hormones (steroid hormones) mostly produced in the testes (see *Gonads; Hormones*), and to a lesser extent (where the biological significance is not wholly clear) in the adrenal cortex (see *Corticosteroids*). The most important of the androgens produced by the testes are (in order of significance): testosterone, Δ^4-androstenedione, dehydroepiandrosterone (DHEA: androsterone). Primarily the two last-mentioned hormones are produced by the adrenal cortex, in larger quantities than by the testes. Androgens break down in a complex series of stages to form primarily the biologically inactive 17-ketosteroids (q.v.). Unmodified testosterone (q.v.) is excreted in the urine only in very small amounts.

Bibliography: Dorfman, R. L. & Shipley, K A.: Androgenes. New York, 1956. **Rose, R. M.:** Androgen excretion in stress. In: **Bourne, P. G.** (Ed.): The psychology and physiology of stress. New York, 1969. **Tonutti, E., Weller, O., Schuchardt, E. & Heinke, E.:** Die männliche Keimdrüse, Stuttgart, 1960. *W.J.*

Androgyny. A term for a certain historically and ideologically conditioned conception of a mixture of male and female characteristics: Physically and psychically men and women exhibit characteristics thought proper to the other sex. Androgyny is to be distinguished from *hermaphroditism* (q.v.), which is a somatic dual sexuality, and from *pseudo-hermaphroditism*, which is characterized by abnormal development of the external sex organs. In androgyny the generative glands are those of a specific sex. More usually a distinction is made between androgyny and *gynandry* (q.v.), in which the former refers to the condition of a male exhibiting female characteristics, and the latter to a female exhibiting male characteristics. Adj. *androgynous*; n. *androgyne*. *D.V.*

Andromania (syn. *Nymphomania*). Pathologically excessive sexual desire (for men) in women with occasional limitation of consciousness (M. Bleuler). *D.V.*

Andropause. Cessation of male sexual activity at some time after sixty years of age. Since the investigations of Kinsey *et al.*, however, it is known that such a definite postulate is untenable. Male sexuality gradually wanes (a process beginning after the culmination point at approximately age sixteen), while its manifestations alter and become more dependent on stimuli. In addition there is a considerable increase in the interindividual variability of frequency of sexual behavior. The problem of the "andropause" is part of the psychology of *aging* (q.v.). See *Aged, sexuality in the.*

Bibliography: Kinsey, A. C., Pomeroy, W. B. & Martin, C. E.: Sexual behavior in the human male. Philadelphia & London, 1948. *G.L.*

Anencephalia. In this condition the cranial vault is deficient and practically the entire brain is missing, with the exception of some nervous tissue at the base of the posterior cranial fossa. Among the possible explanations of this condition are irradiation of the fetus or maternal malnutrition. This condition is incompatible with life. *V.K.J.*

Anesthesia. Insensitivity to all sensory stimuli. Includes loss of pain and skin sensitivity.

Occurs in a generalized form during narcosis (q.v.) and is usually accompanied by loss of consciousness. A result of medical treatment of specific skin areas with novocaine, etc. (*local anesthesia*), or agents to block nerve pathways. *Anesthesiology* is the special branch of medicine concerned with anesthesia and *anesthetics* (or agents producing anesthesia), which first made modern surgery possible; it is practised by qualified specialists. *E.D.*

Anesthetic type (syn. *Anesthetic*). Insensitive pole of the schizoid marginal temperament according to E. Kretschmer: "Indifferent, frigidly nervous", some "eccentrics", "coldly despotic", "irascible", "fanatic", coldly calculating, egocentric. "Indolent, apathetic, dull loafers"; "loss of immediacy between emotional stimulus and motor response". In individual cases it is arguable whether sympathy is permanently absent or is only masked and responsive to specific motivation.

Bibliography: Kretschmer, E.: Physique and character. London, 1925. *W.K.*

Angiotensin. A tissue hormone (see *Hormones*) with powerful vasoconstrictive action, which raises blood pressure more than any other known substance. Angiotensin leads to increased production of catecholamines (q.v.) from the adrenal medulla and of aldosterone (q.v.) from the adrenal cortex. It is assumed that angiotensin plays a part in the causation of essential hypertonia. A distinction is made between angiotensin I and angiotensin II, the latter being produced biosynthetically from the former.

Bibliography: Page, I. H. & Bumpus, F. M.: Angiotensin. Physiol. Rev., 1961, *41*, 331–90. **Peart, W. S.:** The rentin-angiotensin system. Pharmacol. Rev., 1965, *17*, 143–182. *W.J.*

Angle illusion. A more general name for those geometric illusions which induce the perceptual distortion of angles, e.g. *Poggendorf illusion, Lipps illusion* (q.v.). *C.D.F.*

Anhedonia. An absence of pleasure or pleasantness, usually together with lifelessness—when it is known as the "anhedonic-apathetic" syndrome. Anhedonia in situations which are usually pleasurable can appear as a symptom of depressions (q.v.) of various causation. *C.S.*

Anima. In Jung's analytical psychology, the *anima* and *animus* represent the opposed personified characteristics and tendencies of the two sexes, which everyone has but to a considerable extent represses from the self-image, and masks with (male or female) sex stereotypes. The anima is one of the archetypes (q.v.) and is the supraindividual soul-image of the woman in the unconscious of the man; according to Jung it is inherited from primordial orgins, appears in fantasies or in dreams (see *Dream*), or in a fantasy- or emotionally-conditioned reality, and becomes clear for the individual in the process of individuation (q.v.). Unconscious projection of the anima (or animus) on the female (or male) partner can disarrange the relationship between man and woman by preventing confrontation with the true personality of the other person. *H.N.G.*

Animal psychology. Nowadays animal psychology is, in some quarters, unjustly considered to be an antiquated study. Ethology, or comparative psychology (q.v.), is the favored objective approach. Various animal psychologists have in recent years more or less suddenly become ethologists. In fact, ethology is not so novel a science as some would think; the term appeared even in 1920 in the zoological dictionary edited by Knottnerus-Mejer, where it was defined as "the theory of animal life and behavior" (Hediger, 1963). Heinroth, the founder of modern ethology, published his fundamental work "Contributions to biology: the ethology and psychology of the Anatidae" in 1910. It is significant that in 1969, i.e. in its twenty-sixth year of publication, the *Zeitschrift für Tierpsychologie* (Journal of Animal Psychology), began to appear with the English sub-title, "Journal of Comparative Ethology". The last major comprehensive work on animal psychology was that of Hempelmann (1926), or, in the Anglo-American world, Maier & Schneirla (1935)—which came out in a new, enlarged edition in 1964. Of course, their *Principles of Animal Psychology* is concerned more with behaviorism (q.v.), the dominant approach in Britain and the U.S.A. for many years, which considers animal or man as a more or less complex stimulus-response mechanism.

Animal psychology has not undergone a harmonious, unilinear development: its two extreme approaches were largely determined by, on the one hand, Cartesianism (the mechanical conception of the animal put forward by Descartes, 1596–1650), and, on the other hand, an excessive anthropomorphization of animals. Even the so to speak "anecdotal" phase of animal psychology which survived until the first half of the twentieth century was characterized by a strong anthropomorphic tendency. This largely subjective trend was then replaced by an experimental, objective method, interested only in measurable behavior.

A dominant tendency at present is to consider man merely as an animal (Hill, 1957; Morris, 1967), and thus to make him part-object of a general ethological approach which discards all interest in subjective, mental phenomena (Eibl–Eibesfeldt, 1967), and ultimately sees him purely in neurophysiological and mechanistic terms (Tinbergen, 1951). The separation of animal and human psychology which was once conventional has disappeared in favor of a comparative psychology. The many achievements of anatomical research and physiology, of the study of problems such as aggression, learning, stress, frustration, etc., have in no small way resulted from comparative studies. The pioneers in the field were Scheitlin (1840) and C. G. Carus (1866). "It is only a step from comparative anatomy to comparative psychology"; Carus took this step. This method investigates the analogies and homologies, but also the essential differences, between the individual groups.

The history of animal psychology may be seen largely as the history of the struggle against anthropomorphization. Humanization led to such extremes as the ascription to the spider of a high degree of (human) intelligence on account of its web, and to the police dog of something like a sense of duty in the pursuit of criminals, and so on. The anthropomorphic tendency is a persistent source of erroneous judgments, and has its equivalent in animals in zoomorphism. This assimilative tendency results in the consideration, and consequently the treatment, of different species as the same. Hence the circus lion zoomorphizes the tamer, and the dog its master, who in turn anthropomorphizes his dog, gives it a human name, and even talks to it as if it were human, and so on. Anthropomorphism often leads to over-evaluation (and just as often to under-evaluation) of animal behavior. In order to avoid such errors, at the height of the anecdotal and anthropormorphic stage of animal psychology, Lloyd Morgan's canon was established, which held that an animal act such as the construction behavior of the bee was not to be interpreted in terms of higher mental abilities (intelligence) if it was possible to interpret it in a less complex fashion (e.g. as instinctive- or drive-activity). Bierens de Haan (1935) found it necessary to emphasize, however, that it was not so much a matter of explaining animal behavior as economically as possible, as of searching for the *correct* explanation. Economy of interpretation is advisable not only in the explication of animal behavior, but in situations where it might be said that animals are too often placed in complex experimental devices before their normal behavior has been adequately assessed. Ethology requires a behavioral catalog (or "ethogram": Eibl–Eibesfeldt, 1967) for each species, but no really adequate example has been forthcoming. The two headwords "instinct" and "intelligence" characterize a trend in animal psychology which—especially in Europe—has specified the major points of debate for half a century. The anecdotes used to defend the concept of animal intelligence were justly rejected, but on the other hand modes of behavior were declared to be mythical which were later shown to be actual, as, e.g., in the case of parent beavers carrying their young in their arms (Hediger, 1970). There was an increasing tendency for untrue conceptions (such as the idea that the ostrich sticks its head in the sand) to lead to overcompensation in the form of a complete rejection of any study of animal behavior that might in any way be classed as "anecdotal". The classic example of this process is that of the so-called "thinking" horses and dogs which caused a worldwide sensation before, during and after World War I (Krall, 1914). These seemed to be animals which were able to express human thoughts and complex calculations by tapping. Of course, all these apparent achievements could be attributed to signals from the experimenter. Instead of this highly interesting finding becoming the object of intensive research, the negative conclusion was drawn that human influence should be as far as possible excluded from all experiments which were to be recognized as scientifically responsible. Significantly, it was Koehler (1937) who required that all contact between researcher and animal during the experiment was to be strictly excluded, and that the animal was "to make its own free decisions". In some experiments, Koehler would even read intensively in order to avoid any suspicion of "thought transference". But of course this did not exclude the specifically human element from the experimental situation. Indeed, it is doubtful whether this could be achieved at all, since experimental animal and experimenter are to be conceived of not only as two partners in the action–reaction sense, but as two systems which influence one another in a multitude of ways. Communications (q.v.) research and semiotics (q.v.) (Osgood & Sebeok, 1965) require us to re-examine the relations between animal and experimenter with all the instrumental and conceptual means now at our disposal. In this regard, the important experiments of Rosenthal (1966) require attention: very often the experimenter finds exactly what he (perhaps unconsciously) expected of the experiment. This applies to some extent to the maze experiments which have been so popular for some decades, and which have been used mainly for the study of intelligence, or learning behavior and orientation. The Dutch animal psychologist Bierens de Haan (d. 1958) declared in 1936: "Since Small's experiments (c. 1900) thousands and thousands of creatures—from children to toads and cockroaches—have negotiated . . . innumerable mazes. In the process, animals have been made to starve and go thirsty, their nerves have been severed and their sense organs extirpated, they have been poisoned and deprived of vitamins, and their memory and ability to transfer what has been learnt to other mazes have been studied. In the U.S.A., especially, in the course of the years the labyrinth has become almost a standard apparatus for all research into animal psychology . . .". Fischel (1932) has opined that "the results obtained in this way have not been worth the immense time and trouble expended". The multitudinous variations on the maze experiment owe their existence to the desire objectively to measure and compare the psychic performance and capabilities of the most varied individuals and species. The Skinner box (q.v.) (Ferster & Skinner, 1957) is in principle devoted to the same end. Both devices are used essentially to obtain directly comparable, quantitative results. The directly measurable, that which can be represented in terms of scores and curves, is also to the fore in ethology and even approaches the condition of the only valid object of study, even though—as at times in psychiatry—considerable interest is attached to the individual, special case, or exception. Ethology is concerned more with the average, species-specific behavior, and not with the behavior of isolated individuals, which, on the other hand, the animal psychologist makes it his concern (and the zoologist his duty) to understand as far as possible. Ethology is concerned with an understanding of the causes of mechanisms, and applies itself not to individual "personalities" but to innate, average behavior. Tinbergen (1951) understands by "behavior" all the movements of the healthy, undamaged animal. The animal psychologist, however, is also concerned with sick, injured animals and those subjected to extraordinary situations. He believes he is able in a certain sense to achieve a certain "empathy" with the situation of an individual animal, with, of course, the aid of ethological data and precise information about the specific environment—the key to which was provided by von Uexküll (1928). In this sense, the animal psychologist's approach can be quite free from any anthropomorphism, and is wholly subject to critical control. On the basis of his biologically grounded "empathy", he has to be able to offer behavioral prognoses for every animal in every situation. The justness of these predictions is open to precise verification. If in the past the comparative assessment of intelligence, of acquired behavior or learning ability, was in the foreground, in the last few decades the emphasis has been on innate, instinctive, behavior (see *Instinct*). Some special forms of learning occurring as imprinting (q.v.) within quite short periods of time, and which are possibly decisive for the entire later life of the individual concerned, have remained the objects of comprehensive investigations (Thorpe, 1956; Lorenz, 1967; Sluckin, 1964).

The problem of the abovementioned "dichotomous" oppositions of innate and acquired behaviors, i.e. of instinct and intelligence, has been stressed particularly by Lehrman (1953). Instinctive activities were thought of as rigid; learning as plastic. Instinctive behaviors are therefore allowed taxonomic significance in something like the same sense as morphological characteristics. This idea has to some extent been overstressed. Ultimately, even bones and other organs are not absolutely "rigid", but just as subject to evolution (Hediger, 1963).

For some time, (especially European) behavior researchers (among whom one may number ethologists and animal psychologists) have been divided to some extent into two camps. Bierens de Haan (1940) defended the thesis that instinct and instinctive activities are in a certain sense plastic, whereas the ethologists kept to the idea of absolute rigidity. A kind of compromise was reached by ethologists—especially Lorenz and Tinbergen—in the division of the individual instinctive actions into appetitive behavior and "end" behavior. According to this idea, e.g., the bird's selection of a nesting place and material depends on a plastic appetitive behavior which takes account of specific conditions. The special kind of nest construction, the end activity, on the other hand, is wholly fixed; it occurs in accordance with fixed, innate patterns. Schneirla (Maier & Schneirla, 1964, 643) believes that it is possible to see this decisive dichotomy of rigid innate and plastic acquired behavior as analogous with computer performance: in the inherited ability to carry out a specific behavior, and in the actual behavior in a particular situation, he finds an analogy to what the computer has stored and the task that it has to perform at a particular moment. Contrary conceptions are also proposed currently in view of the human position—for man is to be taken into account in comparative psychology or ethology. The characteristics shared by men and animals were (under Darwin's influence) overemphasized for a long time, whereas whatever separates them was overlooked or belittled.

For centuries, spiritual (intellectual) characteristics were ascribed to animals (even bees). If one is to see the "spirit" as comprising language, history, religion, art, and so on, clearly there are significant and fundamental differences between animal and man. For example, it has never been possible to teach the creatures closest to man, the anthropoid apes, more than three words; they are without the decisive speech center in the brain. Accordingly attempts have been made recently to circumvent this difficulty by using ASL (American Sign Language)—a "deaf-and-dumb" language (Gardner, 1969). However, apart from the area of the human spirit, there are other profound differences between animal and man: e.g. the use of fire. Here there are no transitional stages: either one makes and uses fire, or one has no control over it. A halfway house is inconceivable. The exclusive use of fire has been of fundamental importance in human development.

Lorenz (1967) has recently reaffirmed the spiritual aspect as a human monopoly, and rejected the idea of chance as dominant in the phylogenesis of animals and man. Previously, random mutations and selection were held to be solely responsible for all evolution. Now Lorenz too has stated, in opposition to the assumption of a supreme randomness in biological events: "It is a misconception to believe that 'pure chance' rules over the development of organisms."

Bibliography: Bierens de Haan, J. A.: Die tierpsychologische Forschung, ihre Wege und Ziele. Leipzig, 1935. **Id.:** Labyrinth und Umweg. Leyden, 1937. **Id.:** Die tierischen Instinkte und ihr Umbau durch Erfahrung. Leyden, 1940. **Carus, C. G.:** Vergleichende Tierpsychologie. Vienna, 1866. **Eibl-Eibesfeldt, I.:** Grundriss der vergleichenden Verhaltensforschung. Munich, 1967. **Ferster, C. B. & Skinner, B. F.:** Schedules of reinforcement. New York, 1957. **Fischel, W.:** Methoden zur psychologischen Untersuchung der Wirbeltiere. Handbuch biol. Arbeitsmethoden. Sect. 6. Part D. Leipzig, 1932. **Gardner, R. A. & Gardner, B. T.:** Teaching sign language to a chimpanzee. Science, 1969, *165*, 664–72. **Hediger, H.:** Wild animals in captivity: an outline of the biology of zoological gardens. London, 1950. **Id.:** Studies of the psychology and behavior of captive animals in zoos and circuses. London, 1955. **Id.:** Tierpsychologie im Zoo und im Zirkus. Basle, 1961. **Id.:** Tierpsychologie und Ethologie. Schweiz. Arch. Neurol. Neurochir. u. Psychiatrie. (Festschrift for M. Bleuler), 1963, *91*, 281–90. **Id.:** Verstehens- und Verständigungsmöglichkeiten zwischen Mensch und Tier. Schweiz. Z. Psychol., 1967, *26*, 234–55. **Id.:** Zum Fortpflanzungsverhalten des Kanadischen Bibers. Forma et Functio, 1970, *2*, 336–51. **Heinroth, O.:** Beiträge zur Biologie, namentlich Ethologie und Psychologie der Anatiden. Vortr. 5. Intern. Ornithol. Congr. Berlin, 1910. **Hempelmann, F.:** Tierpsychologie vom Standpunkte des Biologen. Leipzig, 1926. **Hill, O. W. C.:** Man as an animal. London, 1957. **Knotterus-Mejer, T.:** Zoologisches Wörterbuch. Leipzig & Berlin, 1920. **Koehler, O.:** Die "zählenden" Tauben und die "zahlsprechenden" Hunde. Der Biologe 1. Munich, 1937. **Krall, K.:** Denkende Tiere. Leipzig, 1914. **Lehrman, D.:** A critique of Konrad Lorenz's theory of instinctive behavior. The Quarterly Rev. Biol., 1953, *28*, 337–63. **Lorenz. K.:** On aggression. London, 1966. **Id.:** Die instinctiven Grundlagen menschlicher Kultur. Die Naturwiss., 1967, *54*, 377–88. **Id.:** Studies in animal and human behavior, Vol. 1. London, 1970. **Maier, N. R. F. & Schneirla, T. C.:** Principles of animal psychology. New York, [2]1964. **Morris, D.:** The naked ape. London, 1967. **Osgood, C. E. & Sebeok, T. A.:** Psycholinguistics. Indiana, 1965. **Rosenthal, R.:** Experimental effects in behavioral research. New York, 1966. **Scheitlin, P.:** Versuch einer vollständigen Thierseelenkunde. Stuttgart & Tübingen, 1840. **Sluckin, W.:** Imprinting and early learning. London, 1964. **Thorpe, W. H.:** Learning and instinct in animals. London, 1956. **Tinbergen, N.:** The study of instinct. Oxford, 1951. **Id.:** Social behavior in animals. London, 1953. **Id.:** On aims and methods of ethology. Z. Tierpsychol., 1963, *20*, 404–33. **Uexküll, J. von:** Theoretische Biologie. Berlin, 1928. **Id. & Kriszat, G.:** Streifzüge durch die Umwelten von Tieren und Menschen. Frankfurt, 1971.

H. Hediger

Animism. The view that ascribes anthropomorphic behavior (see *Anthropomorphism*) to objects and natural phenomena: i.e. the attribution to inanimate objects of such conditions of human activity as life, thought, free decision, by projecting them outward from the human state. Piaget has described an animistic phase in the development of human intelligence. In E. B. Taylor's anthropological studies of religion, animism in so-called primitive societies is seen as a form of "understanding of the supernatural".

A.T.

Animosity. Strong enmity, hatred or hostility which may be covert or manifest. *G.D.W.*

Animus. 1. An intention or objective, or the effort directed toward that end. **2.** A characteristic approach or "animating" principle. **3.** Inspiration. **4.** Hostility—usually deep-set—or animosity. **5.** Jung's term for the archetypal masculinity component of the soul-image: "a very feminine woman has a masculine soul" (see *Anima*). On the whole, "animus" is an imprecise term, and one to be avoided in exact discourse. *J.M.*

Anisometropia. Unequal sight: the result of inequality of refractive power. *R.R.*

Anisotropy. Unequal evaluation. We perceive space in a different way from so-called Euclidean space. E.g.: a vertical is often taken as being longer than a horizontal which is objectively of the same length. *V.M.*

Anklingen (Ger.). The slow entry or occurrence of an emotional process or sensation. *R.Hä.*

Anlage (Ger.). *Anlage:* fundamental disposition or arrangement. *Anlagen* are the first recognizable bases of a morphological or functional differentiation toward a specific organ, or a specific characteristic of a self-developing organism. One may speak of the *anlage* of the optic vesicle, etc., but also, in the sense of *disposition*, of an "*anlage* to", say, confirmed rational or emotional behavior. The term is now more usually met with in the German literature in the sense of the first recognizable accumulation of cells basic to a specific developmental process.

In all self-developing individuals of a species (apart from special cases of defective development) the same *anlagen* always appear in the same spatial and temporal sequence. This organizational plan and the spatio-temporal arrangement of further *anlagen* differentiation or development into organs, systems of organs, functions and functional systems, together with the point in time, kind and extent of the interaction of self-developing systems, and the point in time, kind and extent of the influence of external factors on development and its outcome, are passed on from generation to generation by means of elementary, material information units.

The bearers of the specific items of information are known as *genes* (q.v.), though, of course, a gene is an abstraction and the *actual* carriers are *chromosomes* (q.v.); the totality of characteristics transmitted by an individual form of life is known as a *genotype* (q.v.). The totality of structures and functions produced by the interaction of genotype, cytoplasm ("cellsap") and environment is known as the *phenotype* (q.v.). The branch of science concerned with the investigation of the process of reaction chains from the gene to the ultimate, perceptible characteristic is known as *phenogenetics* (q.v.). *Cytogenetics* (itself a combination of experimental cytology and genetics) is concerned with the structures within the living cell which are bearers and transmitters of inherited information, and with their possible variations. Phenogenetics and cytogenetics now compose the additional study of *molecular genetics.* Genes "mutate" within a population of individuals of the same species at a rate (alteration or loss of function of a gene = gene mutation) which stays the same so long as conditions of life do not change essentially. Therefore every population contains a specific number of *mutations*, or mutant genes (see *Allele*): a result of natural selection. With a change in the environment, therefore, new selection pressures favorable to the preserved mutant forms find already present and "waiting" in the population the allelomorphic material necessary for corresponding, harmonious total alteration of the particular organism.

The question of *innate* and *acquired* characteristics (also in behavior and experience) does not directly concern the nature of the *anlage*(*n*), but the phenotypes developing from its (their) interaction with the environment. The dominant phylogenetic selection pressures determine whether a component observable feature of a phenotype will behave in an ontogenetically environment-stable or environment-labile manner. Since selection (q.v.) can directly affect only the phenotype and not the genotype, the degree of environmental stability of a phenotype component is independent of the complexity or relative simplicity of its genetic basis.

Bibliography: Gerking, S. D.: Biological systems. London, 1969. **Loewy, A. G. & Siekevitz, P.:** Cell structure and function. New York, 1969. **Oparin, A. I.:** Genesis and evolutionary development of life. New York, 1968. **Sinnott, E. W., Dunn, L. C. & Dobzhansky, T.:** Principles of genetics. New York & London, [5]1958.

P. Leyhausen

Anomaloscope. A device (W. Nagel, 1907) for presenting color mixtures in order to measure color sense and deficiency. The instrument consists essentially of a drum and a scale of 73 gradations. The test color is sodium yellow (light), which may be varied in intensity and is compared with the color mixtures in two approximate fields. If 40 gradations of lithium red are mixed with 33 gradations of mercury green (Rayleigh equation) in one field, and this mixture is set against 14 gradations of sodium yellow in the other field, a subject with normal vision will experience no difference in color and intensity. *R.R.*

Anonymization. The process of reification (objectification) and reduction of the intensity of socio-emotional interpersonal contacts which is characteristic of modern highly-organized, bureaucratized industrial societies under the division of labor. Anonymization is characterized by a loss of individual distinctiveness and by a feeling of personal alienation in view of the increasing urbanization that accompanies intensified horizontal and vertical mobility of the population. *W.N.*

Anop(s)ia. Blindness even though the retina is intact: caused by damage to the optic pathway. A lesion of the *fasciculus opticus* (between the retina and the optic chiasm) leads to unilateral anopia; a lesion of the optic tract (between the optic chiasm and the optic cortex) leads to hemiopia (q.v.), or blindness in half of the visual field. *R.R.*

Anorexia nervosa. A term (proposed by Sir William Gull, 1874) for a syndrome the main feature of which is a considerable reduction or a loss of appetite and hunger. A neurotic or psychosomatic symptom, especially in adolescent girls though it also occurs as a reaction in poor eaters among children. No primary organic findings, but frequently secondary disturbances of inner secretory organs. *F.-C.S.*

Anorgasmy (syn. *Anorgasmia*). Absence of the orgasmic phase in the sexual reaction cycle. Primary anorgasmy can occur in any form of physical sexual stimulation capable of leading to orgasm, including masturbation (q.v.) and anal intercourse (q.v.), both in heterosexual and homosexual activity. Primary anorgasmy seldom occurs in men but quite frequently in women. Apart from anatomical and neurophysiological defects, incompatible sexual attitudes in the partners and/or faulty imprinting (q.v.) and/or socio-cultural conditioning may be responsible.

Physiological pain accompanying anorgasmy, sometimes after coitus interruptus (q.v.), or in the woman after premature ejaculation in the man, has been reported. *G.L.*

Anosmia, Absence of the sense of smell after traumatic brain damage, in tumors of the frontal lobes, the olfactory sulcus and the sellar region, also after diseases of the peripheral olfactory apparatus. *R.R.*

Anosognosia. Non-recognition of a state of sickness or disease in one's own body (e.g. a patient does not recognize that he is paralyzed on one side). Anosognosia occurs in a combination of any cerebral locus with a diffuse brain lesion and is diagnostically non-specific. It is often psycho-dynamically interpreted as a defense mechanism (q.v.), in the sense of a refusal to recognize actuality. *C.S.*

Anoxemia, cerebral. A reduced supply of oxygen to the brain caused by anoxemia = an oxygen deficiency in the arterial blood. The brain (q.v.) is the most sensitive organ in terms of reaction to oxygen deprivation, so that even slight general oxygen deficiency in the blood can lead to deprivation symptoms such as lassitude, loss of discriminative ability, euphoria and loss of restraint. High-degree anoxemia leads to loss of consciousness, and after approximately 3 to 5 minutes to irreversible brain damage.

Anoxia: deficient supply of blood to the tissues. See *Brain pathology*. *E.D.*

Antagonists (syn. *Antagonistic muscles*). Every physical movement represents a play of agonists and antagonists, an interaction controlled by the pyramidal system. The antagonist of an extensor would be a flexor, and vice versa. *E.D.*

Anterior cerebrum. See *Forebrain*.

Anthropocentrism. A doctrine or theory which elevates man as the center of the world and sees the well-being of humanity as the ultimate purpose of things. This idea is related to the geocentric view of the universe, as represented by, say, Ptolemy, the Fathers of the Church, and Scholasticism. Since the Renaissance, however, thinking has concentrated more upon man himself than upon his relation to the supernatural. The anthropocentrism of the Italian philosopher Vico (1668–1744) and that of the French materialists of the eighteenth century were the forerunners of anthropology (q.v.). With Ludwig Feuerbach and Karl Marx, man became the only object and goal of philosophy. Scheler, Jaspers, Heidegger and Sartre are essentially concerned with man, the midpoint of their philosophies. Man is the absolute, even though imperfect and difficult to conceive adequately; hence the interplay between the investigation of his essence (nature) and the elucidation of his existence (freedom). *M.R.*

Anthropology. Anthropology studies man as a living, social being with certain habits, who exists in a context of human interrelations, makes tools, institutions and laws, forms values and beliefs, strives for cultural identity, and is subject to forces beyond his control. In order to attain to the status of a scientific discipline (i.e. in order to apprehend its object systematically, and to describe and explain it by means of appropriate concepts), anthropology must clearly determine the area of application of its methods, and its possible systems of reference. It includes a variety of fields of research, which (except for morphological anthropology) have as their common concern the observation of man in an optimally inclusive and direct fashion in all the complexity of his actual existence, while concentrating on differences and variations rather than on human identity as such.

Although anthropology is as old as philosophy, it has used scientific methods only since the nineteenth century; its present individual areas of research have been distinct fields only since the turn of the century. These areas are related by the common pursuit of objectivity and a more exact understanding of human existence as a whole whose every part functions in conjunction with all other parts, and not as a mere sum of component elements.

The dominant theory in nineteenth-century anthropology was that of evolution, which tended to ascribe to every human society a unified form of development on the Western model. This doubtful simplification nevertheless led to a concern for scientifically respectable explication (Herbert Spencer; E. B. Taylor). Similarly, the various diffusionist theories compensated for their excessive atomism with highly proficient observations (H. Graebner; W. Schmidt). At quite an early stage in modern anthropology, a primary distinction was made between natural-scientific, or morphological, and social or cultural anthropology (q.v.), which arose from the difference in perspectives (man as a biological "life-form" as distinct from man as a "social being") and in the methods used (comparative/differential; extensive/intensive).

Natural-scientific anthropology studies man's origin and the causation and mechanisms of his biological development—his "specificity"; and tries—using morphological, genetic and environmental criteria—proficiently to define the notion of "race" (q.v.), geographically conditioned variations, and so on.

Social and *cultural anthropology* (and also ethnology), as developed in the twentieth century, is a theoretical discipline which assimilates the evidence of ethnography (monographic and empirical representation of the specific nature of individual and, particularly, archaic social forms), palaeontology, archaeology and history, and attempts the extremely difficult task of a comparative study of these discrete materials. In a search for greater clarity, modern ethnology examines the structure and function of social systems and constructs models for this purpose. Two main tendencies are apparent: (*a*) that orientated to *sociology* (social anthropology), which examines human interrelations in the context of social structures (functionalist and structuralist tendencies: E. Evans-Pritchard; A. R. Radcliffe-Brown; B. Malinowski; E. Durkheim; M. Mauss; C. Lévi-Strauss); (*b*) that orientated to *psychology* (cultural anthropology), which studies the different manifestations of culture in regard to the relation between the individual and cultural schemata (R. Benedict; M. Mead; A. Kardiner). It distinguishes between "culture" as a number of collective and unified schemata of behavior and belief) and "society" (as a special form of cultural schematization) when studying its object in its dynamic course of development (cultural variations, acculturations: R. Linton; M. Herskovits; E. Lebach; G. Balandier).

Bibliography: Balandier, G.: Phénomènes sociaux totaux et dynamique sociale. Cahiers d'histoire mondiale, 1961, *6*, No. 3. **Benedict, R.:** Patterns of culture. Boston, 1934. **Comas, J.:** Manual of physical anthropology. Springfield, 1960. **Durkheim, E. & Mauss, M.:** Primitive classification. London, 1963. **Evans-Pritchard, E. E.:** Nuer religion. Oxford, 1956. **Herskovits, M. J.:** The economic life of primitive people. New York, 1940. **Kardiner, A.:** The individual and his society. New York, 1939. **Leach, E. R.:** Rethinking anthropology. London, 1961. **Lévi-Strauss, C.:** Structural anthropology. New York, 1963. **Lowrie, R. H.:** An introduction to cultural anthropology. New York, 1940. **Mauss, M.:** Manuel d'ethnologie. Paris, 1947. **Radcliffe-Brown, A. R.:** Structure and function in primitive society. London & Glencoe, Ill., 1952.

M.-J. Borel

Anthropology, psychological. Anthropology attempts a summary approach to the various aspects of human reality: *synchronically*, at a given moment; and *diachronically*, in their process of development. The pertinent problems can be considered from a *positive* viewpoint which takes into account man's physical, biological, psychological, social and cultural characteristics. But a *philosophical* viewpoint is also possible which, according to Scheler, takes up a position midway between the natural sciences and metaphysics, and studies the nature and meaning of man and culture.

Anthropology in its physical, social, cultural and philosophical aspects was enriched in the nineteenth century by the addition of psychological anthropology, which emerged from the development and mutual influence and interpenetration of general psychology, social psychology, sociology, cultural anthropology, and social anthropology. Its field is the *relations between personality and culture*, which are the object of multifarious investigations. These are concerned with the interdependences between (*a*) differences in the areas of perception, emotion, motivation, intellect, and above all the various aspects of psycholinguistics and nurture and education, in the development of attitudes, essential traits and structures of temperament, character and personality, and (*b*) different cultures, societies and institutions, especially in regard to language, myths, stereotypes, beliefs, sexual life, and social and familial structure, and the nature and modes of child care and treatment. Numerous examples may be found in Hsu (1961), who was the first to use the term "anthropological psychology", and other authors (see bibliography).

Social and cultural anthropology (q.v.) have always shown interest in psychological themes—as is apparent, e.g., in the studies that came from the Torres Strait expedition of 1898 and later investigations (B. Malinowski, F. Boas, M. Mead, E. Sapir, etc.). The attempts (above all those of a psychoanalytical bent) to ground a theory of man in the psychological processes of ego formation and in the unconscious elements of personality, or at least to give a psychological basis to the origin of various beliefs, rites, customs and institutions, are well known. A related effort is that of R. Benedict, who sees the particular aspects of a national culture as determined by the personality characteristics of a nation.

The reverse attitude is more frequently met with: i.e. that which stresses the formative influence of a national culture on the personality of its component individuals. The thesis of R. Linton and A. Kardiner is important in this regard: Each culture determines a *basic* or *modal* personality, which then becomes the field of operation of further individual differences. The decisive influence of cultural patterns in the various stages of development in the course of which personality is constituted, is the central theme of modern psychological anthropology, especially in its psychoanalytical and structuralist emphases.

The strongest tendency in psychological anthropology is a concern to use empirical, and as far as possible experimental, methods to examine the interdependences between psychological and anthropological variables. It takes two main directions: (*a*) the intercultural verification of psychological hypotheses; (*b*) the development of theories of human behavior, which in an *empirically verifiable* way integrate the psychological, sociological and historical aspects of human social behavior within a community.

The anthropological perspective of psychology proper should also be mentioned. Even in the first treatise on psychology, the *De Anima* of Aristotle, the psychic is defined as the psychosomatic behavior of the *whole man* (403 a). One of the first texts in which the word "psychology" occurs is entitled "Anthropological Psychology" (*Anthropologische Psychologie*, by O. Casmann. Hanau, 1594). This trend is emphasized nowadays. Even after the split between the physical and the psychic (Descartes), retained in the theoretical parallelism and methodological introspectionism of the first stage of experimental psychology, the interest in anthropology was still apparent (e.g. the folk psychology (q.v.) of W. Wundt). Contemporary psychology has once again made human *behavior* its object.

Bibliography: Benedict, R.: Patterns of culture. Boston, 1934. **Hsu, L. K.**- Psychological anthropology. Homewood, Ill., 1961. **Hunt, R.:** Personalities and cultures: Readings in psychological anthropology. New York, 1967. **Kardiner, A.,** *et al.*: The psychological frontiers of society. New York, 1945. **Kluckhohn, C., Murray, H. A. & Schneider, D.:** Personality in nature, society and culture. New York, 1953. **Kroeber, A. L.:** Anthropology today. New York, 1965. **Lindzey, G. (Ed.):** Handbook of social psychology. Cambridge, Mass., 1954; [2]1968. **Tyler, S. A.:** Cognitive anthropology. New York, 1969. *M. Yela*

Anthropometry. The scientific method of comparative measurement of the skull, externally and internally (craniometry), of individual bones (osteometry), and other structures of the human body. Used to some extent in anthropology. *M.S.*

Anthropomorphism. The tendency to interpret the manifestations of the animate and inanimate environment analogously to human behavior and experience. Anthropomorphism is not only a feature of mythic thinking (see *Myth*), but in the history of science played a part in animal psychology, and was only overcome by the proficient methodology of comparative psychology (q.v.) and behaviorism (q.v.). *W.Sc.*

Antibiotics. Substances derived as natural products of various micro-organisms (bacteria, molds), and which more or less selectively inhibit or block the growth of other micro-organisms. They are used in the treatment of infectious diseases. The best-known antibiotics are penicillin and streptomycin. Antibiotics have become of especial interest to psychologists since the discovery of the significance of ribonucleic acid (RNA) (q.v.) for learning and retention, and of the way in which antibiotics affect the synthesis of RNA and protein. Animal experiments (rats, goldfish) would seem to show that, e.g., actinomycin D, puromycin and acetoxycycloheximide block long-term memory, whereas learning and short-term memory remain unaffected. The way in which antibiotics act in influencing retention is not yet clear. In particular it is still questionable whether it is a question of specific disturbances of retention or of reproduction. Investigations in which disturbances of retention caused by puromycin were removed by other substances would seem to support the disturbed reproduction theory.

Bibliography: Agranoff, B. W., Davis, R. E., Lim, R. & Casola, L.: Biological effects of antimetabolics used in behavioral studies. In: **Efron, D.** (Ed.): Psychopharmacology 1957–1967. Washington, 1968. **Deutsch, J. A.:** The physiological basis of memory. Ann. Rev. Psychol. 1969, *20*, 85–104. *W.J.*

Anticholinergics. Substances which block the action of acetylcholine (q.v.) and hence (peripherally and autonomically) parasympathetic activity (parasympathicolytic). The most important substances with an anticholinergic effect are atropine (q.v.) and scopalamine (q.v.). Many psychopharmaceutical drugs which are used for therapeutic purposes, for instance against depressions (see *Antidepressives*) or spasms (see *Spasmolytics*), have unpleasant side-effects (e.g. dryness of the mouth). Anticholergic drugs are frequently used as experimental stimuli in investigations of learning in animals, in which they retard habituation to new stimuli.

Bibliography: Bignami, G.: Anticholinergic agents as tools in the investigation of behavioral phenomena. In: **Brill, H.** (Ed.): Neuro-psycho-pharmacology. Amsterdam, 1967. **Carlton, P. L.:** Cholinergic mechanisms in the control of behavior. In: **Efron, P.** (Ed.): Psychopharmacology 1957–1967. Washington, 1968. *W.J.*

Anticholinesterase agents. See *Cholinesterase inhibitors.*

Anticipation. 1. Mental adjustment to a coming event, etc. **2.** A schematic presemblance of the solution in problem solving (Selz). *H.-J.A.*

Anticipation error (syn. *Anticipatory error*). A term of C. L. Hull's. In serial learning experiments, Ss have learned a series of nonsense syllables. The fact that they repeat some syllables prematurely, i.e. before the right syllables according to the series, is ascribed by Hull to anticipation of the later syllables. In general, if a response in serial learning occurs earlier than it should, it is an anticipation error which confirms the existence of an *anticipation response*.

Bibliography: Hull, C. L.: Essentials of behavior. New Haven, Conn., 1951. *V.M.*

Anticipation neurosis. In Kraepelin's theory, excessive anxiety about the outcome of a future experience is said to disturb the normal mental attitude to that experience, or in the case of certain basic activities such as speech, writing, and so on—to produce a partial response, or even to block the intended response. The latter is usually known as an *anticipation* (or *anticipatory*) *response*. *J.M.*

Anticonvulsives. Agents which reduce or prevent convulsions. In high doses hypnotics and tranquilizers can act as anticonvulsant drugs in tetanus and status epilepticus.

Bibliography: Irwin, S.: Anti-neurotics: practical pharmacology of the sedative-hypnotics and minor tranquilizers. In: **Efron, D. H.** (Ed.): Psychopharmacology 1957–1967. Washington, 1968. *E.L.*

Antidepressives (syn. *Antidepressants*). The antidepressive drugs are used to treat depressions (q.v.) of varying etiology. Chemically, antidepressives are divided primarily into the tricyclic iminodibenzyl derivatives (e.g. imipramine [G22355, Tofranil], q.v.; desipramine [Pertofran]; trimipramine [Surmontil]), the dibenzocycloheptene derivatives (e.g. amitriptyline [Tryptizol, Laroxyl, Elavil]; nortryptaline [Aventyl, Allegron]), and the dibenzodiazepine derivatives (e.g. dibenzazepine), which may be classed together as thymoleptics in the narrower sense in contrast to the thymeretics—represented mainly by the monoamine oxidase inhibitors (q.v.) (MAO inhibitors: e.g. iproniazid [Marsalid]; nialamide [Niamid]; isocarboxazid [Marplan]). Lithium is also used for prophylaxis of phasic endogenous depressions. The therapeutic effects of antidepressives are broadly classed as alleviation of mood, increase of drive and removal of anxiety or reduction of agitation. Anxiety-reductive and stimulant effects are largely excluded in the case of only one agent (Pöldinger), whereas improvement of mood can be brought about in combination with the other two aims (thymoleptic or thymeretic effect). The mechanism by which these effects are obtained is as yet inadequately explained. Animal experiments with the tricyclic antidepressives, which are particularly relevant clinically, showed symptoms of central inhibition as well as central excitation (Sigg). Biochemically, anticholinergic and noradrenaline-potentiating effects are to be observed simultaneously in this group. MAO inhibitors effect a rise in the concentration of intraneuronal *biogenic amines* (q.v.). Substances which have only anticholinergic or noradrenaline-potentiating effects are shown to be unsuitable for reduction of depressive moods (Davis *et al.*). Lithium also affects noradrenaline concentration, though on another level: mania can be alleviated at the same time as phasic depressions are prevented (Schou). The differentiation of biochemical action and indication of different types of preparations permit conclusions to be drawn on the biochemical basis and the etiological differentiation of depressions (Davis *et al.*). Tests of the specifically antidepressive action of antidepressant agents on healthy individuals are difficult to carry out, since the requisite initial emotional conditions are not so obviously present, or cannot be induced. Nevertheless, it would seem possible to demonstrate differences in effect dependent on habitual tendencies to depression (recorded by means of questionnaires). Information on effects in healthy individuals obtained by controlled experiments are available only for imipramine (q.v.). Overdosage with the tricyclic antidepressives can produce a form of delirium (q.v.).

Bibliography: Davis, J. M., Klerman, G. L. & Schildkraut, J. J.: Drugs used in the treatment of depression. In: **Efron, D. H.** (Ed.): Psychopharmacology 1957–1967. Washington, 1968. **Pöldinger, W.:** Vergleichende Untersuchungen antidepressiv wirkender Psychopharmaka an gesunden Vpn. In: **Bente, D. & Bradley, P. B.** (Eds): Neuro-Psychopharmacology. Amsterdam, 1965. **Schou, M.:** Lithium in psychiatry—a review. In: **Efron, D. H.** (Ed.): Psychopharmacology 1957–1967. Washington, 1968. **Sigg, E. B.:** Tricyclic thymoleptic agents and some newer antidepressants. In: **Efron D. H.** (Ed.): Psychopharmacology 1957–1967. Washington, 1968. *P.D.*

Antiemetics. Drugs used to treat the tendency to vomit (hyperemesis), and motion and sea sickness (nausea). The various antiemetics have little in common apart from the intended therapeutic effect. Many of them are anticholinergics (q.v.) (e.g. scopalamine, q.v.), antihistamines (q.v.), or phenothiazines (q.v.). The psychic effects of antiemetics vary according to their chemical structure; however, most of them have a sedative effect and can influence performance.

Bibliography: Brand, J. J. & Perry, W. L. M.: Drugs used in motion sickness. Pharmacol. Rev., 1966, *18*, 895–924. *W.J.*

Antihistamines. Substances which block or reduce the effects of *histamine* (q.v.). The antihistamines are not entirely histamine-antagonizing (especially questionable in the CNS); they are for the most part substances which reduce or inhibit allergic and anaphylactic reactions and the fall in blood pressure after the application of histamine. This occurs with most antihistamines by means of a blocking of the histamine receptors; with others by means of an inhibition of biosynthesis or a biological inactivation of histamine (e.g. potentiation of the enzymes which inactivate histamine). Chemically and pharmacologically, the antihistamines belong to different groups: ethanolamine (e.g. diphenhydramine [Benadryl]), ethyldiamine (e.g. tripelenamine [Pyribenzamine]) and propylamine (e.g. pheniramine). Antihistamines with other primary therapeutic applications are, e.g.: anticholinergics (q.v.) (scopalamine, q.v.), spasmolytics (q.v.), phenothiazine (q.v.) (e.g. piomethazine), and drugs used to control Parkinsonism. Most antihistamines have central effects. Sedative effects occur even with therapeutic doses. Influences on performance are difficult to demonstrate (reaction time, concentration tests).

Bibliography: Handbuch der experimentellen Pharmakologie. Vol. 18. Part 1: Histamine. Its chemistry, metabolism and physiological and pharmacological actions. Berlin, 1966. **Wagner, H. J.:** Uberprüfung des Leistungsverhaltens unter dem Einfluss verschiedener Antihistaminica. Arzneimittel-Forsch. (Drug Res.), 1962, *12*, 1065–1070. **Turk, J. L.:** Immunology in clinical medicine. London, 1969. *W.B.*

Antihypertensives. Antihypertensive drugs are substances which reduce blood pressure (hypertension). There are several agents which can be called antihypertensive; they bring about a fall in blood pressure (q.v.) by means of very different physiological mechanisms (e.g. peripheral, central). In addition to their required specific action, most antihypertensive drugs have numerous other effects, e.g. on the CNS, with the corresponding psychic changes (subjective sedation and influence on performance). Many antihypertensives belong to the sympathicolytics (q.v.), the ganglionic blocking agents (q.v.), or the reserpine (q.v.) group; some are also parasympathicomimetics (q.v.).

Bibliography: Green, A. F.: Antihypertensive drugs. Advances in pharmacology, 1962, *1*, 161–225. **Schlittler, E.:** Antihypertensive agents. New York, 1967. *W.J.*

Anti-Semitism. A social disease measured by (among other rating techniques) the Anti-Semitism Scale reported on by Adorno and others (See *Authoritarian personality*). Underlying trends of the anti-Semitic ideology would seem to be: stereotypy; rigid adherence to middle-class values; high moral estimation of one's own group; desire for the power and dominance of one's own group; fear of sensuality and immorality, of overthrow and victimization; a desire to strengthen group-divisive phenomena. The connection between (anti-Semitic) prejudice and emotional instability has been confirmed. See *Authoritarianism; Prejudice; Stereotype.*

J.G.

Anxiety. *Origins of the concept.* Like its Latin original *anxietas*, *anxiety* commonly connotes an experience of varying blends of uncertainty, agitation and dread. The

Latin usage included a suggestion of strangulation which is sometimes implied in the present-day connotation. The term was introduced into psychology when Freud (1894) described the anxiety neurosis as a syndrome distinct from neurasthenia. But its acceptance in the discipline did not become general until more than forty years later. May (1950) has noted that, outside the publications of psychoanalytic writers, anxiety was not even listed in the indexes of psychological books written before the late 1930s.

In his earliest formulations, Freud considered anxiety to be the outcome of repressed somatic sexual tensions (*libido*, q.v.). He believed that libidinal images that were perceived as dangerous were repressed; and that the libidinal energy was cut off from normal expression and transformed into anxiety. He later replaced this notion with the much broader conception of anxiety as a signal for danger; distinguishing now between objective anxiety (fear) and neurotic anxiety, depending on whether the danger came from the outside world or from internal impulses (Freud, 1936). Freud's followers in the course of the years proposed many modifications of his views. For example, May (1950) characterized anxiety as "the apprehension cued off by a threat to some value the individual holds essential to his existence as a personality", and Sullivan (1953) referred to it as the state of tension arising from the experience of disapproval in interpersonal relations.

2. *An operational definition.* All the foregoing formulations, and many others like them, seem to be attempts to capture the essence of an assumed "entity" called anxiety. But no yardstick is available to indicate which, if any, of them is "right". In any event, none of them is precise enough to be of use in scientific investigation. Only by an operational definition can such objections be circumvented. According to one fairly widely used definition, anxiety is the autonomic response pattern characteristic of a particular individual organism after the administration of a noxious stimulus (Wolpe, 1952). The pattern varies from one individual to the next. A *noxious stimulus* is an extrinsic agent (such as an electric current) that produces local tissue disturbance which the subject may report as pain, and which, if strong enough, can produce tissue damage. The unconditioned response to noxious stimulation generally has both motor and autonomic components. Unconditioned autonomic responses similar to those produced by noxious stimulation can also be evoked by other agents; for example, by very intense auditory stimuli and by ambivalent stimulus situations—which are situations in which strong and incompatible action-tendencies are simultaneously aroused. Fonberg (1956) has impressively demonstrated the essential similarity between the effects of ambivalent stimulation and those of noxious stimulation.

When unconditioned anxiety responses are evoked they can be conditioned to "neutral" stimuli that impinge on the organism at about the same time. The conditioned generally resembles the unconditioned anxiety response, though exceptions have been noted (Hein, 1969). The anxiety that conditioned stimuli evoke is in turn conditionable to other stimuli. Because of serial conditionings, most organisms, and certainly most human beings with "normal" histories, come to have anxiety evocable by a great many conditioned stimuli before reaching adulthood. However, the extent of such conditioning is controlled by various innate factors (Eysenck, 1957). The operational definition demands in every case a specification of the antecedents of the emotional response. If this is done, there is clearly little point in the distinction proposed by Freud between fear and anxiety—especially since the determination whether the controlling stimuli come from within or without must often be left to the subject. In any case, to vary the name of the response according to its antecedents can only lead to confusion. Another distinction between fear and anxiety that is commonly promulgated is that the former is episodic and the latter chronic. For this to be operationally usable, a temporal dividing line would have to be established; but the inevitable arbitrariness of this would severely limit its usefulness.

3. *The topography of anxiety responses.* The autonomic events that make up an anxiety response are predominantly functions of the sympathetic division of the autonomic nervous system. Common manifestations of the sympathetic response are: increased heart rate, raised blood pressure, increased respiratory rate, sweating of the palms, dilatation of the pupils, and dryness of the mouth. Some parasympathetic responses may also participate in the anxiety pattern; common ones are diarrhea, nausea, vomiting, and frequency of urination. Studies by Hess (1947) suggest the additional occurrence of diffuse autonomic effects manifested by increased general irritability. This is possibly related to the general rise in muscle tension that is ordinarily so constant an accompaniment of anxiety (Jacobson, 1938). Whereas the combination of autonomic events constituting the anxiety response varies greatly from one individual to the next, it is quite consistent within individuals. Nevertheless, it may change for the individual if he is subjected to new conditioning events that add new components to the constellation, or through selective operant conditioning (Miller Banuazizi, 1968) that may change the balance of response elements already present. At least some autonomic responses are subject to operant conditioning; that is, they can be strengthened by arranging for them to be followed by rewards, and weakened by withdrawing the rewards. In one set of experiments (DiCara & Miller, 1968), cardiac acceleration was conditioned in one group of animals, and cardiac deceleration in another, by relating the given response to the "reward" of escape or avoidance of shock.

The autonomic responses characteristic of anxiety have been the subject of steadily increasing research efforts in recent years. This has been inspired by the intrinsic interest of the subject as well as by the central role of anxiety in most neuroses. It has been shown in both animal and human subjects that anxiety responses can be specifically conditioned to selected stimuli, and deconditioned. Deconditioning is usually accomplished by counter-conditioning, which depends on inhibiting the anxiety by a response incompatible with it. (See *Neuroses.*)

4. *Unadaptive ("pathological") anxiety responses.* Anxiety responses conditioned to stimulus situations objectively associated with danger are judged *adaptive.* Anxiety responses to stimuli without relation to danger are *unadaptive.* Persistent unadaptive conditioned habits are called *neurotic.* Under certain circumstances a low degree of anxiety may enhance such functions as performing on stage (the Yerkes–Dodson Law); but if the level is considerable it interferes with the effective performance of many classes of behavior. The generalized rise in muscle tension impairs coordination of movement. Mental concentration, the ready flow of associations, and the registration of impressions may all be diminished. There may be reduced efficiency at work, impaired social functioning, or inadequate sexual behavior—manifested as impotence in males and frigidity in females.

Unadaptive anxiety can also result from physiological pathology. Generalized anxiety is a feature of severe cases of Vitamin B1 deficiency (beri-beri), and apparently results from a widespread lowering of the thresholds of sympathetic synapses. Anxiety without determinable stimulus antecedents, and presumably of organic origin, is frequently observed in cases of schizophrenia. Other organic sources of anxiety are the hypoglycemic syndrome, thyrotoxicosis, tumors of the adrenal medulla (pheochromocytoma), and limbic lobe seizures.

Bibliography: DiCara, L. V. & Miller, N. E.: Long-term retention of instrumentally learned heart-rate changes in the curarized rat. Comm. behav. biol., 1968, *2,* 19–23. **Eysenck, H. J.:** The dynamics of anxiety and hysteria. London, 1957. **Fonberg, E.:** On the manifestation of conditioned defensive reactions in stress. Bull. Soc. sci. lettr. lodz. class III. Sci. math. natur., 1956, *7*, 1–10. **Freud, S.:** 1894. Quoted in **Jones, E.**, The life and work of Sigmund Freud. New York, 1961. **Id.:** The problem of anxiety. New York, 1936. **Hein, P. L.:** Heart rate conditioning in the cat and its relationship to other physiological responses. Psychophysiol., 1969, *5*, 455–64. **Hess, W. R.:** Vegetative Funktionen und Zwischenhirn. Basle, 1947. **Jacobson, E.:** Progressive relaxation. Chicago, 1938. **May, R.:** The meaning of anxiety. New York, 1950. **Miller, N. E. & Banuazizi, A.:** Instrumental learning by curarized rats of a specific visceral response, intestinal or cardiac. J. comp. physiol. psychol., 1968, *65*, 1–7. **Sullivan, H. S.:** The interpersonal theory of psychiatry. New York, 1953. **Wolpe, J.:** Experimental neuroses as learned behavior. Brit. J. psychol., 1952, *43*, 243–68. **Yerkes, R. M. & Dodson, J. D.:** The relation of strength of stimulus to rapidity of habit formation. J. comp. neurol. psychol., 1908, *18*, 459–82.

J. Wolpe

Anxiety scales. Inventories for measurement of the specific reaction or set of *anxiety* (q.v.): e.g. J. A. Taylor's Manifest Anxiety Scale, MAS, 1953; children's version, CMAS; IPAT Anxiety Scale Questionnaire, 1957–63; Sarason's Test Anxiety Scale for children and students.

F.K.

Apathetic type. An unemotional, inactive, listless and indirect character.

Apathy: an absence of feeling. *Disorganization apathy:* mass despair or loss of morale.

Aperture color. A vague, soft, texture-free expanse of color seen through an opening in a neutral screen.

Aphasia. A speech disorder which occurs as a result of localized brain lesions, especially in the so-called *speech areas* of the dominant cerebral hemisphere (in right-handed people the left hemisphere).

Aphasic speech disorders are distinguished from other, more elementary, speech disorders in that they disturb speech in the sense of a complex form of symbolic activity, whereas in the more elementary forms only the motor components of speech (dysarthria), the phonation processes (dysphonia), or the fluid innervation of the act of speaking (stuttering, q.v.) are disturbed.

Aphasia can take various forms depending on the localization of the lesion of the cerebral cortex. As early as 1861, P. Broca reported that damage to the caudad section of the third (inferior) frontal lobe convolution of the left cerebral hemisphere (*Broca's area*, q.v.), while causing no functional disorders of lip or tongue movement, could impair "motor speech", and therefore lead to an inability to speak actively and expressively (*motor aphasia*), even though the spoken matter might remain relatively comprehensible. In 1873, C. Wernicke confirmed that injury to the posterior part of the superior temporal convolution of the left hemisphere could lead to the reverse: a disorder of "sensory speech", causing impaired comprehension of spoken matter, even though acoustic perception of non-articulated sounds might be retained. This form of speech disorder, known as *sensory aphasia*, is not accompanied by any impairment of articulated speech, although the patient's active speech can be incorrect and agrammatical. In addition to these two basic forms of aphasia, an amnesic aphasia was distinguished in which both comprehension of spoken matter as well as the ability to articulate are retained, but the names of objects or people are forgotten (*nominal aphasia*). The localization of the brain damage causing nominal aphasia has not yet been established, although many authors have postulated its connection with injury to the inferior parietal area of the left hemisphere, which has been seen as the cortical area responsible for concept formation.

Attempts to trace the different aphasias to lesions of specific areas of the cerebral cortex did not, however, offer a scientific explanation of disorders of speech in the sense of complex forms of symbolic activity. Consequently, a number of authors maintained that brain injuries led to a disturbance of complex "abstract" or "categorized" behavior, and that every lesion of highly complex areas of the cerebral cortex must lead to a disorder of highly complex "symbolic" forms of activity depending on holistic operations of the entire brain (K. Goldstein *et al.*). However, the mechanisms of extremely complex forms of symbolic behavior were still unexplained; consequently, asphasia began to be viewed as a disorder of the highest mental processes whose anatomical and physiological basis was taken as largely unknown. A conflict arose between mechanistic attempts to derive speech disorders from precisely localized brain lesions, and holistic views of speech as a holistic symbolic activity which could be examined without reference to its cerebral substrate.

Progress in modern neuroanatomy, neurophysiology (q.v.) and neuropsychology (q.v.) permitted much more accurate analyses of speech disorders, and a more satisfactory explanation of aphasic symptoms.

It was demonstrated that damage to each of the abovementioned areas of the cerebral cortex eliminated one of the factors essential to speech activity, and led to partial forms of aphasic speech disorder.

Damage to the posterior sections of the upper temporal area of the left hemisphere (the secondary sections of the auditory area) leads to impairment of complex forms of sound analysis, makes it impossible to differentiate similar phonemes, and leads to acoustic (sensory) aphasia, which is shown in an inability to comprehend phrases (which are perceived with insufficient acuity), to difficulty in repeating words accurately (with inappropriate sounds within words = *literal paraphasia*; or inappropriate syllables within words = *verbal paraphasia*), and to an inability to give accurate spoken descriptions of objects, together with inaccurate analysis of word-sounds, necessary for writing.

Damage to the secondary cortex of the sensorimotor area of the dominant hemisphere (especially of the inferior sections of the post-central and pre-motor area) does not directly impair the auditory analysis of spoken sounds, but can lead to a significant disturbance of expressive (articulated) speech.

Damage to the secondary sections of the inferior part of the post-central area (central fissure) leads to a disturbance of the kinesthetic afference of speech movements, causing diminished accuracy of articulated speech and confusion of similar articulemes: e.g. the lip consonants *b–m*, and the point consonants *d–l–n* (tongue and gums). In the worst cases, this makes clearly articulated speech impossible and leads to ("afferent" or "kinesthetic") motor aphasia, evidenced both in speech and in a characteristic disorder of written language.

Damage to the inferior sections of the *pre-motor region* of the left hemisphere produces a marked impediment in denervation of resultant articulations, and impairment of "kinetic melodies", and leads to an "efferent" (or kinetic) aphasia, which becomes evident in a major disturbance of speech flow and in a pathological persistence of specific verbal stereotypies in speaking and in writing.

The abovementioned forms of speech disorder are partial disturbances of speech activity which occur because the lesion eliminates major factors essential to the act of speech.

Damage to individual sections of the cerebral cortex is not in itself a sufficient explanation of disturbances of complex verbal behavior; an important part of the total explanation is provided by analysis of the *pathophysiological changes* which occur in the activity of the damaged regions of the cerebral cortex.

An injury of the posterior parts of the cortex of the left (dominant) hemisphere inevitably leads to a pathological condition in these cortical areas, evident especially in a disturbance of normal concentration of neural processes and in characteristic "phasic" inhibitions of the cortex, in the course of which stimuli producing the traces of various systems are assimilated to one another in intensity, thus lose their selectivity (q.v.), and are easily confused with one another. The result is that attempts to find the appropriate word produce an uncontrolled mass of equally probable associations, and that the normal process of selecting the required (descriptive) verbal terms is disturbed. A pathophysiological mechanism of this kind produces the typical symptoms of "amnesic" (nominal) aphasia, or paraphasias (q.v.) (confusions of words).

On the other hand, injuries to specific regions of the cerebral cortex of the left (dominant) hemisphere can lead to a significant impairment of the plasticity of neural processes, causing neural stereotypies that have occurred once to become pathologically stable. This can easily disturb the formation of new and mobile reference systems and affect the process of constant switching from one set of verbal references to others (i.e. the basic prerequisite for all verbal behavior), and result in an inability to produce active, detailed speech. This kind of pathological condition of the cerebral cortex (and especially of the cortex of the anterior sections of the "speech area") is often the prime cause of those forms of speech disorder which manifest themselves in disturbances of spontaneous speech.

Bibliography: Brain, R.: Speech disorders. London, 1961; [2]1965. **Conrad, K.:** New problems of aphasia. Brain, 1954, *77*, 491–509. **De Reuck, A. V. S. & O'Connor, M. (Eds):** Disorders of language. London, 1964. **Goldstein, K.:** Language and language disorders. New York, 1948. **Head, H.:** Aphasia and kindred disorders of speech, Vols 1, 2. Cambridge, 1926. **Landsell, H.:** Laterality of verbal intelligence in the brain. Science, 1962, *135*, 922–3. **Luria, A. R.:** Higher cortical functions in man. New York & London, 1966. **Id.:** Traumatic aphasia. The Hague, 1970. **Ombredane, A.:** L'aphasie et l'élaboration de la pensée explicite. Paris, 1951. **Piercy, M. F.:** The effects of cerebral lesions on intellectual function: a review of current research trends. Brit. J. Psychiat., 1964, *110*, 310–52.

A. R. Luria

Aphemia. Loss of the ability to enunciate; generally used in the sense of a loss only of the ability to proceed from thought to verbal enunciation. See *Aphasia.*

Aphrasia. Inability to utter (expressive aphrasia), or understand (sensory aphrasia), phrases. Single words are understood or can be used correctly. It is one of the group of aphasias, none of which is sharply delineated from another. The comprehension by a patient of a word sequence will depend upon his emotional state and its emotional significance as well as the length of the phrase, its construction or subtlety of meaning. In this wider sense it is common in both organic and functional states. It is rare if restricted to patients limited to the use or comprehension of single words. *B.B.*

Aphrodisiacs. Pharmaceutical compounds to increase sexual reactivity, sexual hormones, and various folk medicines, all of disputed efficacy. Some serve to prolong orgasm (e.g. yohimbine) by inhibition of the sympathetic nerve. There are sometimes unpleasant aftereffects. See *Anorgasmy.* *G.L.*

Aplasia. The failure of organs and tissues to develop.

Apollonian type. In accordance with the mythological conception of the Greek god Apollo, the Apollonian type represents striving for order, measure, harmony and form. The opposite is the Dionysian type; in accordance with the Greek god Dionysus, this is the dynamic, creative and passionate type. Schelling postulated the combination of the two as ideal: "To be simultaneously inebriated and sober is the secret of true poetry". Nietzsche adopted and developed the conceptual opposition in his *The Birth of Tragedy.*

Bibliography: Klein, O.: Das Apollinische und Dionysische bei Nietzsche und Schelling. Stuttgart, 1935.

W.K.

Apparent motion; apparent movement. See *Motion, apparent.*

Apparition. Hallucinated figure. Often associated with spontaneous ESP (q.v.), e.g. in connection with a telepathic communication from a person in distress (= "crisis apparition"), or in connection with a haunt (q.v.) (= ghost). A phantom or phantasm. *J.B.*

Appeasement gestures. Certain species exhibit effective aggression-inhibitory, ritualized behavior. For instance, they make themselves appear as small as possible, flatten hair or feathers, or retract limbs, and withdraw combat-releaser weapons such as teeth or bill from the superior adversary (gulls elicit inhibition by looking away and down). Immobility often accompanies these wholly submissive attitudes. The victor is inhibited. In the mating season (q.v.), appeasement gestures play an important role and bring male combat to an end.

Bibliography: **Carthy, J. D. Ebling, F. J.** (Eds): The natural history of aggression. London, 1964. **Lorenz, K.:** On aggression (Eng. trans.). London, 1966. **Tinbergen, N.:** Einige Gedanken über Beschwichtigungsgebärden. Z. Tierpsychol., 1959, *42*, 651–65. *K.F.*

Apperception. According to Wundt, a process by which a mental (psychic) content is recognized, or *clearly* perceived. Apperceptive perception is characterized in that physical stimuli are not perceived in isolation but in an "apperceptive mass" from which we select the contents that are meaningful for us.

Bibliography: **Wundt. W.:** An introduction to psychology. London, 1912. *V.M.*

Apperception categories. W. Stern distinguishes the following phases of apperception (q.v.) through which a child normally passes in the course of mental development: (*a*) substance stage (0–8 years); (*b*) action stage (9–10 years); (*c*) relation stage (11–13 years); (*d*) quality stage (from 14 years).

Bibliography: **Stern, W.:** Allgemeine Psychologie auf personalistischer Grundlage. The Hague, [2]1950.

K.P.

Appetitive behaviors. Modes of behavior with for the most part an inherited base, which continue instinctively (and without their normal specific releaser) in order to maintain psycho-physiological equilibrium. Appetitive behaviors may therefore be seen as instincts (q.v.), or "appetitive drives", produced endogenously and without a releasing stimulus. But see *Aggression*; *Drive; Instinct; Emotion; Sexuality.*

Bibliography: **Craig, W.:** Appetites and aversions as constituents of instincts. Biol. Bull., 1918, *34*, 91–107.

H.S.

Applied psychology. The application of psychological knowledge and research to tasks arising out of the needs of life. The fundamentals of applied psychology are *general psychology* (q.v.) and *characterology* (q.v.) or *personality* (q.v.) assessment as a special aspect of the theory of human behavior. Applied psychology is, therefore, the useful, practical application of scientific knowledge. When specific empirical principles are used in order to assist men to direct their lives in various ways, one speaks of *practical psychology*. Scientific psychology adopts a proficient methodological approach, and is concerned to establish adequate modes of classification and verifiable results, whereas "pre-scientific" psychology approaches its objects in ways that might be classed as exclusively intuitive (see *Intuition*).

1. *Psychology as a profession.* A man or woman who intends to become a practising psychologist must combine a basic scientific attitude, a desire to gain and add to knowledge, with a measure of social dedication and a basic desire to help others out of common humanity. It is not only a question of applying scientific knowledge already verified and established, but of the possibility of

discovering new methods. Essential prerequisites for the practice of psychology—as for that of every other profession requiring a rigorous academic training—are an above average intellectual ability, and mature judgment in the sense of being able clearly to distinguish contradictory opinions and estimate the value of different viewpoints. It is also essential that a practical psychologist should not be of a wavering or unstable disposition.

2. *Basic principles of applied psychology.* More, almost, than in any other profession, the ethical aspects of applied psychology require constant and careful consideration. Professional dangers specific to the psychologist would seem to be above all of a psychic nature: disturbances of mental equilibrium, and concerns affecting acuity of thought, moral sensitivity, and dedication to and joy in life and work, which tend to affect human relations.

Profit ought not to be a basic consideration in the practice of psychology; power-seeking and competitiveness are also essentially foreign to its aims. Excessive egotism, self-assertion and envy, and any form of aggressive tendency can obviously affect adversely any relationship between psychologist and client.

Just as the medical practitioner is bound by the Hippocratic oath, the psychologist is bound to help any who come to him for advice and assistance. Principles for an international code of ethics for psychologist have been proposed by F. Baumgarten (*Revue internationale d'éthique professionelle*, 1953, and *Psychologie und Praxis*, 1961). The German Psychological Association has also made proposals in this regard (G. Kaminsky, 1965). The definitive work on questions of professional ethics is, however, the American Psychological Association's *Casebook on Ethical Standards of Psychologists* (1968). Developments in research methods have given rise to the question of experiments on human beings, both in diagnosis and therapy. Experiments on supposedly less valuable human beings, the mentally deficient, or prisoners, are of course inhuman and unjustifiable. The boundaries of applied psychology are defined by injury to one's fellow men.

Problematical areas in this regard are certain psychologists' and psychiatrists' recommendations for treatment of mental disorders with drug therapy (see *Psychopharmacology*), narcoanalysis (q.v.) and the use of "lie detectors" (q.v.). Similar possibilities of interfering with the liberty of one's fellow men exist in the field of advertising psychology ("subliminal perception" and stimuli producing unconscious reactions). Tape-recordings, film records, television observation and one-way-screen observations essentially presuppose the agreement of the person recorded or observed. All diagnoses, consultations and treatments are concerned with individual human beings whose *dignity* must be respected. In addition the psychologist must allow the matter in hand, and not extraneous factors such as inappropriate sympathy and antipathy, to direct his degree of concern.

Whenever psychologists have reason to expect that situations of conflicting responsibility might arise (e.g. in educational or vocational guidance), they must remember that they are bound by *professional secrecy* in regard to the testee or client in question. The possibility of withdrawal from a client relationship must also be ensured, especially if there is any possibility of complex transference. Client relations within one's own family, or one's own circle of friends and acquaintances, should be avoided. The professional duty of discretion of course also includes proficient discrimination: the obligation of secrecy on the psychologist is lifted where the client would otherwise be endangered.

The psychologist is also bound to maintain standards in his professional activity that are qualitatively as high as possible. Therefore he is bound to abandon activities which cannot be humanly justified. For instance, the independent psychologist employed by an organization or business concern is bound to carry out his duties as required by the employer; but where this involves him in a conflict of interests, he is also bound by the general rule that the interests of the *individual* in question must take precedence over those of, say, an industrial concern or government agency.

3. *Methods of applied psychology.* Proficient judgments require the determination of symptoms (test results, modes of behavior) and their logical classification according to psychological categories (syndromes, etc.), and the careful confirmation and presentation of findings. Where the observation or judgment of a man as a whole (in terms of achievement and character traits) is concerned, test methods, questionnaires (q.v.), and interviews (q.v.) are not the only methods to be applied. The psychologist must also practice adequately the arts of personal encounter and expression, and be proficient in exploration (q.v.), behavioral observation, and analysis of expression, according to the specific case. Special attention must also be given to *social conditions* (for example, parents or teachers often see children only in one aspect of their lives).

Psychologists required to give evidence regarding an individual must remember the possibility of this being taken as applying to that individual in all life situations, and should therefore take into account the temporal limits to the relevance of their findings.

Since psychology implies service to the individual, a psychological diagnosis made in connection with a report is never permissible in the total absence of the patient or subject. Even though some diagnostic methods that do not require the subject's presence can be of help, they should never be used alone. In the actual individual case, *typological systems* can only afford valuable assistance to the diagnostician. *Typology* (q.v.) has to be supplemented by an individual diagnosis in the sense of differential psychology (q.v.), which is concerned to observe and describe a person in terms of his individual characteristics with regard to inter-individual and intra-individual differences. Frequently the psychologist has to call on other experts for assistance. Team work (see *Team*) and the rating system are invaluable, for the checking of ratings by several diagnosticians can help to overcome the possibility of subjective assessments. The psychologist also has to take into account the internal and external conditions of his work situation as they may affect the client, his partner in the work, and the assessment. This includes not only his degree of obvious motivation and concern, but conditions such as a quiet atmosphere in suitable premises and the avoidance of such disturbances as a window opening on to a noisy street—both positive and negative factors of influence must always be considered. Finally, as regards methodology, it must be stressed that as full a range as possible of proven techniques must be invoked in the description and assessment of human personalities.

Characterological analysis is a construct analysis: i.e. the interpretation of a specific character trait, e.g. aggressivity, depends on the nomothetic nexus of relations governing the concept in question. At the beginning of every character analysis, the intuitive approach forms a hypothesis which must be confronted with the results of scientific procedure, i.e. the phenomenologically intuitive process requires verification by operational and statistical criteria. The particular trait must be determined in relation to other traits (q.v.).

4. *Reports.* A report, where there is no prescribed model, can take the form of a rating, a personality profile, advice as the result of counseling, or a predictive summary. A report commissioned by, say, a prospective employer might consist of a statement of the terms of reference, followed by a short description of the rating method and process used. Reports can include a description of aptitude, performance, intelligence, special

abilities, essential traits, motivation, emotivity, sociability, development, professional achievement, social conditions, and even the attitude to and estimate of self of the person concerned—all according to situation and purpose. Various models are possible: (*a*) a description of fixed traits (static personality model); (*b*) an analysis based on behavior determinants; (*c*) a causal analysis tracing the grounds, causes and motives of behavior (dynamic model); (*d*) the behavior of a personality in regard to development; (*e*) the possible meaning and purpose of a specific behavior or behavior pattern.

5. *Tasks and fields of application.* The tasks proper to applied psychology focus in general on the determination of character traits. A frequent task is to ascertain the ability and aptitude of an individual in order to advise him accordingly (school and educational counseling, vocational guidance, therapeutic counseling—e.g. advice on learning problems; psychologists cooperating in rehabilitation and resocialization). The psychologist is required to present his findings in various—usually documentary—forms, which differ from country to country, and from institution to institution.

One of the most pressing fields of application is the area of *work and vocation.* Industrial psychology can be psycho-technically oriented, and concern itself principally with human behavior during work and the discovery of optimal working conditions (workplace conditions; light, color, temperature, noise, human factors research, and so on); but work can also occupy psychologists with problems of vocational aptitude and inclination, occupational mobility, labor market prospects, and socio-political motivation. Questions of working atmosphere and morale, industrial relations, and modes of rationalization intended to make labor more humane, belong to the wide range of tasks that require the expertise and research potential of industrial psychologists.

Educational counselors are concerned with the varied field of mental defects and various problems met with by young people, such as legasthenia, stuttering, lack of concentration, sexual problems, neglect. They are required to diagnose, counsel, apply therapy, and on occasion have recourse to the specialized methods of clinical psychology (q.v.). Educational psychologists also play an important part in teacher training, and research into new educational methods (e.g. in programmed instruction, q.v.). A distinction is sometimes made between educational psychologists and *school* psychologists, whereby the latter are those particularly concerned with testing, rating, remedial measures, and conflict situations among schoolchildren.

Forensic, or legal, *psychology* (q.v.) is sometimes thought of as ancillary to the administration of justice. Testimonies and evidence, the credibility of witnesses and defendants, and the fitness of individuals to stand trial, can come within the competence of the forensic psychologist, who can, in some countries, be called on to act as a graphologist and attest to the genuineness of or identify a sample of handwriting. He can also be asked to confirm psychological disturbances in cases of suspected diminished responsibility or guilt. Psychologists also play an important part in the links between courts, schools and probation officers, and in reform institutions and the prison service.

Psychopharmacology (q.v.) is concerned with the effects of chemical substances (e.g. narcotics, stimulants, sedatives) on human drives, emotions, perception, ideation, behavior, expression, character, development and culture, and so on, and such phenomena as the effects of hallucinogens and addiction to medically prescribed drugs. The use of psychopharmaceutical compounds is properly reserved to psychotherapists with a medical training or to psychiatrists. Questions proper to the psychologist are reactions and dangers dependent on personality, e.g. in traffic psychology (behavior of drives under the influence of alcohol) or in sport (doping), and any unjustifiable use of drugs to manipulate human beings.

Traffic psychology includes anthropological and objective tasks. Behavior in traffic, driving capability and accident proneness are related to personality. Technical possibilities in traffic psychology (e.g. simulators) still require psychological elucidation.

Management psychology and related fields present major problems for the psychologist: group relations and leadership, risks and security, administration problems and management training, and teamwork planning are among them.

Advertising, publicity, market research and opinion polls are related areas requiring psychologists to estimate, e.g., appropriate ways of sampling or influencing large numbers of people. (See Marketing.)

Military psychology dates back to the experiences of American psychologists in World War I. Officer selection and pilot selection and training are only two of the many sub-fields in this regard.

Among the fields of application under development at present is *political psychology* (q.v.), which embraces, e.g., the psychological suasions of government and social justice, peace research, the causes of authoritarianism and prejudice (q.v.), the treatment of refugees, and problems of developing nations.

The psychology of *religion* (q.v.) examines the principles of religious experience. The psychology of *sport* (q.v.) offers assistance in training, learning processes, and the selection of appropriate techniques. The conditions for adequate performance, attitude to success and failure, personal experiences leading to depression or euphoria, are psychological questions as important for, e.g., the athlete, as is technical proficiency in the particular pursuit.

In view of unrest in universities, the contribution of psychologists to university life is essential, particularly in guidance on study problems. Here the psychologist has to deal not only with performance problems but with particular neuroses and even suicidal tendencies.

There are many other areas of applied psychology that come under the above heads, ranging from statistics to counseling, not the least important of which are of course, marriage guidance and individual vocational advice.

Bibliography: Anastasi, A.: Fields of applied psychology. New York, 1964. **Argyle, M.:** Psychology and social problems. London, 1964. **Arnold, W.:** Person und Schuldfähigkeit. Würzburg, 1965. **Id.:** Angewandte Psychologie. Stuttgart, 1970. **Dorsch, F.:** Geschichte und Probleme der angewandten Psychologie. Berne, 1963. **Dudycha, G. J.:** Applied psychology. New York, 1963. **Eysenck, H. J.** (Ed.): Handbook of abnormal psychology. London, 1961. **Fraser, J. M.:** Industrial psychology. New York, 1962. **Fryer, D. H. & Henry, D. R.** (Eds): Handbook of applied psychology. New York, 1950. **Gray, J. S.:** Psychology applied to human affairs. New York, [2]1954. **Guilford, J. P.:** Fields of psychology. New York, [2]1950. **Joyce, C. R. B.** (Ed.): Psychopharmacology: Dimensions and perspectives. London, 1968. **Koch, S.** (Ed.): Psychology, a study of a science, Vols. 1–6. New York, 1959–66. **Webb, W. B.:** The profession of psychology. New York, 1962.

W. Arnold

Apport. Object supposed to have been paranormally transported into a closed room during a *séance* (q.v.) or during a *poltergeist* (q.v.) disturbance. *J.B.*

Apprehension. 1. The act of becoming aware. Apperception (q.v.). Conscious central processing of newly received perceptions and ideas on the basis of the existing experiential matrix. In developmental psychology, the transition from holistic to analytic apprehension is important in the 7–8 years range. **2.** Anxiety (q.v.).

Apprehension span: Measured by the number of objects that can be correctly apprehended at one exposure. See *Attention.*

Bibliography: Miller, G. A.: The magical number seven plus or minus zero. Psychol. Rev., 1956, *63*, 81–97. *K.E.P.*

Approach-approach conflict. A term used by K. Lewin (q.v.) for a conflict situation in which the individual has to choose between two equally attractive alternatives: e.g. the fable of the ass who starved because it could not choose between two bundles of hay.

Approach-avoidance conflict: A goal is as attractive as it is unattractive, hence the situation that arises is often called an *ambivalence conflict*. Some visits to the dentist might be classed here.

Double approach-avoidance conflict: Two or more aspects of the goal are simultaneously as attractive as they are unattractive.

Avoidance-avoidance conflict: An individual is asked to choose between two equally unattractive alternatives. *Leaving-the-field* (q.v.) may be the result. See *Conflict*.

Bibliography: Lewin, K.: Principles of topological psychology. New York, 1936. **Id.:** Field theory and learning. Yearb. nat. Soc. Stud. Educ., 1942, *41*, 215–42. **Miller, N. E.:** Experimental studies in conflict. In: **Hunt, J. McV.:** Personality and the behavior disorders (ch. 14). New York, 1944. *R.Hä*

Approach gradient. See *Gradient*.

Approximative consciousness. According to C. J. Jung (q.v.), when ego-activity is diminished a quasi- or near-conscious state can exist intermediate to the conscious and unconscious. The contents of this allegedly highly-complex state are said to manifest themselves occasionally in dreams as *scintillae*, or sparks of light. *J.G.*

Apraxia (syn. *Dyspraxia*). Impairment of learned purposeful movements which is not attributable to paralysis, disorders of coordination, sensibility, language comprehension or apprehension (intelligence, consciousness).

1. *Ideational apraxia:* disturbance of the conception of a movement. The volitional impulse is incorrect (e.g. the patient puts the match and the cigarette in his mouth). Occurs with diffuse brain lesions which are the cause of simultaneous dementia.

2. *Motor apraxia:* Awkwardness in executing certain movements as a result of damage to the corresponding limb center, which does not lead to paralysis but to disturbance of kinesthetic memory images.

3. *Ideomotor* (*ideokinetic*) *apraxia:* Confused execution of an act as a result of interruption of the connection between the ideational and limb centers (e.g. the patient nods when asked to make a threatening gesture with his fist). The very simplest minor movements can be performed successfully, since they are controlled from the limb centers alone. *C.S.*

Aptitude might be thought of as potential ability. Traits (q.v.) are determined and assessed with regard to certain future ends (e.g. work) without considering underlying talent and its development. An attempt is made simultaneously to predict *future ability* to hold down a job, and to examine, e.g., capability, achievement motivation, reliability, and responsibility. See *Abilities; Objective tests.* *W.S.*

Aptitude tests. Tests of aptitude for some activity or occupation. H. Münsterberg (1863–1916) was one of the first to suggest such tests, which were used during World War I for pilots and lorry drivers and then in industry. Today combinations of several tests (test batteries) are usually administered; one part is not designed to measure any specific activity but aims at assessing more general and above all intellectual performance. Special aptitude tests have been constructed, e.g., for algebra, engineers, dentists, musicians, office staff. The success of these methods depends very much on careful psychological analysis of the relevant activities. *R.M.*

ARAS. Abb. for *Ascending reticular activating system* (q.v.).

Archetypes. Primeval images and ideas which are said to be genetically inherited and to be common to all men (C. G. Jung, q.v.). They are contained in the racial unconscious or "collective unconscious" (whereas the personal or individual unconscious contains the feeling tones, or affective components). These primordial symbols are said to have been meaningful at all times and for all races, and are found in many forms, especially in fairy tales, myths, religion and art. In the language of the unconscious, which is pictorial discourse, these archaic images reappear in a personified or symbolic form. The notion of the archetype is, of course, a hypothetical construct. See also *Mandala*.

Bibliography: Jung, C. G.: Introduction to the science of mythology. London, 1951. *H.N.G.*

Area sampling. A survey method making for more accurate sampling than quota sampling (q.v.), and ensuring random sampling (q.v.). The given area to be sampled is divided into districts, and the districts into dwelling units. Specific dwelling units are selected and specific respondents within them. Repeated calls are necessary to ensure the interviewing of all respondents in the total area. An expensive method used by official bodies.

Bibliography: Cantril, H.: Gauging public opinion. Princeton, 1947.

Arecolin(e). Alkaloid obtained from betel (q.v.) or areca nut. It has a cholinergic action. Peripheral-autonomic effects are weaker than with the pharmacological substances muscarine (q.v.) and pilocarpine (q.v.). Arecoline excites the reticular formation; in low to medium doses it can produce subjective stimulation and euphoria.

Bibliography: Herz, A.: Wirkungen des Arecolins auf das Zentralnervensystem, Naunyn-Schmiedebergs Arch. exp. Path. Pharmacol., 1962, *242*, 414–19. *W.J.*

Areflexia. Absence of reflexes in state of profound unconsciousness; a sign of absence of spinal function.

Argyll-Robertson pupil. The pupil does not respond to light (or negligibly), whereas accommodation (q.v.) is retained. Occurs in neuro-syphilitic disorders (CNS). *A.Hi.*

Arithmetic mean. The statistical measure of the central tendency of a distribution:

$$\bar{X} = \frac{\Sigma X_i}{N}$$

The mean value is defined by $\Sigma(X_i - \bar{X}) = 0$. *W.H.B.*

Armchair psychology. E. W. Scripture's term (usually pejorative) for psychological theories conceived and propagated wholly without experimental verification. *H.-J.A.*

Army Alpha Test. Developed by a number of leading American psychologists for group testing of intelligence on the entry of the U.S.A. into World War I. The test consists of various series of tasks, such as sequences of instructions, counting, arranging words in sentences, analogies. The Army Alpha provided an impetus for the use of tests in American schools. *R.M.*

Army Beta Test. A test developed at the same time as the Army Alpha, but designed for illiterates and those unable to understand English. The constituent tests are non-verbal and the instructions have to be given without any use of language. *R.M.*

Army General Classification Test (abb. AGCT). A test designed for U.S. army use in World War II and given to more than ten million individuals; made available for civilian use after the war. The test contains an equal number of word-recognition, numerical reasoning, and block counting tests (perceptual relations). The crude score is converted into an IQ. This test series was later replaced by the Army Qualification Test (AFQT). *R.M.*

Arousal. In its most limited meaning, arousal refers to the increase in frequency and decrease in amplitude of EEG rhythms (desynchronization) which occur as a result of stimulation. The animal is then said to show an increase in arousal. The term *activation* is also used more or less synonymously.

The stimulation may take a number of forms. Any novel or intense external stimulus will produce an increase in arousal, but with repetition the stimulus has less and less effect, and finally none at all. Certain internal stimuli can also increase arousal. In a classical experiment, Moruzzi & Magoun (1949) showed that arousal increases as a result of electrical stimulation of the brain stem reticular formation by means of implanted electrodes. Under this stimulation neural impulses are transmitted from the brain stem to the cerebral cortex, thus producing the EEG desynchronization. It is now generally accepted that the brain stem reticular formation plays a vital role in the maintenance of arousal levels.

The other area of the brain principally involved in the maintenance of arousal is the thalamic reticular formation. The brain stem and thalamic divisions of the reticular formation operate in different ways. Stimulation of the brain stem reticular formation produces a relatively long-lasting increase in arousal, possibly lasting for several hours in the case of a subject awoken from sleep. This is known as the generalized arousal reaction. It produces activation over the whole of the cerebral cortex and takes a relatively large number of trials to habituate. In contrast, stimulation of the thalamic reticular formation produces the "localized reaction", which lasts for a shorter period, is confined to the particular area of the cortex served by the thalamic nucleus concerned, and is relatively quickly habituated in something of the order of ten trials.

EEG desynchronization is not the only physiological manifestation of an increase in arousal. Other effects are the activation of the sympathetic nervous system, leading to the acceleration of heart rate and respiration rate, the psychogalvanic reaction, and pupil dilation. There is also an increase in the sensitivity of the sense organs and a speeding up of reaction times. Parlor called this group of reactions the *orientation reaction*, which is used synonymously with the *arousal reaction.*

The concept of arousal has interested psychologists for five principal reasons. Firstly, it appears to provide the physiological basis for the concept of a general activation drive, which many have postulated without understanding the physiological mechanisms involved. Such a concept has been assumed in various guises, including "excitation" (Duffy), "general emotional state" (Cannon) and "drive" (q.v.) (Hull). With the discovery of the physiology of arousal the postulation of these drive states seems to have been vindicated.

Secondly, arousal seems to provide the physiological basis for certain personality differences. There are several similarities between arousal and the personality characteristic of anxiety, since both involve an abnormally high level of sympathetic reactivity. Eysenck (1967) has suggested that his two personality dimensions of neuroticism (q.v.) and introversion—extraversion (q.v.) are, respectively, functions of the strength of the two divisions of the arousal system, the thalamic and the brain stem. Hence introverts behave in many respects as if they were chronically highly aroused. For instance, they have greater reactions to pain, habituate slowly and have faster EEG rhythms.

Thirdly, some of the baffling problems of mental illness may be explicable in terms of malfunctions of the arousal system. There is much evidence that neurotics are characterized by overreactive arousal systems. The evidence relating psychosis to disturbance of the arousal system is less strong, but there is support from various sources for the view that the majority of chronic hospitalized psychotics are under-aroused. There is probably also a smaller group of acute psychotics who are hyper-aroused (Gellhorn, 1957; Lynn, 1966).

Fourthly, it has been suggested by Berlyne (1960) that many human activities can be understood as a search for increases in arousal. For these he has coined the term "arousal jags". Such popular human activities as gambling, sports competitions, adventure enjoyed either in reality or vicariously through fiction or television, drug taking and esthetic experiences frequently involve increases in arousal. This theory, however, has yet to make the impact on psychologists which it seems to deserve.

Fifthly, arousal has proved a useful concept to those working on the psychological effects of drugs. These may be classified broadly into those which increase arousal and those which decrease it. The stimulants, amphetamines and hallucinogens appear to increase arousal, whereas the depressants, sedatives and tranquilizers decrease it. This formulation gives the investigator a framework in which to consider the details of the site and mode of action of a particular drug.

Arousal is now generally regarded as a scale. At the lowest level is the state of coma, then deep and light sleep, and drowsiness. From the middle of the scale upwards are the states of relaxation, alertness, excitement, anxiety and finally terror. Many stimulus situations shift the individual from one of these states to another according to the intensity with which the stimulus is applied. For instance, being driven in a car slowly can induce drowsiness, but as the speed increases one may be taken through all the stages on the scale, right up to terror. This scale of states of consciousness seems to reflect an underlying physiological scale of the extent of neural activity in the reticular formation. Hence a considerable degree of synthesis between psychological and physiological states has been achieved in this field.

Bibliography: Berlyne, D. E.: Conflict, arousal and curiosity. London, 1960. **Eysenck, H. J.:** The biological basis of personality. Illinois, 1967. **Gellhorn, E.:** Autonomic imbalance and the hypothalamus. Minneapolis, 1957. **Lynn, R.:** Attention, arousal and the orientation reaction. Oxford, 1966. **Moruzzi, G. & Magoun, H. W.:** Brain stem reticular formation and activation of the EEG. EEG Clin. Neurophysiol. 1949, *1*, 455–73.

R. Lynn

Arrangement. A term used by A. Adler to refer to an unconscious organization of attitudes, symptoms, behavior, etc., which mediates between the *striving for superiority*, and the limitations of reality discovered through experience, in determining the *life plan* of the patient. Also used more generally to describe a pattern of ideas which is developed by the patient in order to account for, or justify, his neurotic behavior. Cf. the defense (q.v.) mechanism of *rationalization*.
G.D.W.

Arthur Scale. A performance test for children of 5 to 15 years. A test battery formed from the best performance tests (1930), using concrete materials (e.g. S. C. Kohs' mosaic test). A slightly different form has been in use since 1947. *R.M.*

Articular sensations. See *Organic sensations*.

Articulation. 1. The movements effectively producing or modifying speech sounds. The production of such sounds. **2.** The production of consonantal sounds. **3.** Clarity of speech. **4.** A joint between bones or cartilages. **5.** Interrelation or clarification: e.g. of items or ideas. *D.G.*

Artifact (artefact), statistical. An error (q.v.) resulting from incorrect assessment of parameters (q.v.), or the use of inadequate or inaccurate experimental methods, or the improper use of methods. *W.H.B.*

Art, primitive. The very term is symptomatic of the problems confronting the anthropological psychologist studying contacts between cultures. The esthetic question of "primitive" art was first raised when its various forms were measured against European conceptions of art, and attempts were made to accommodate more magical-religious artifacts (see *Ethnology; Folk psychology*). The psychology of art studies the occurrence in archaic art-forms of typical structures that are clearly partly determined by the holistic (gestalt) nature of human perception.

Bibliography: Smith, M. W. (Ed.): The artist in tribal society. London, 1961. *W.S.*

Art, psychology of. In a wider perspective, the psychology of art forms an important part of the general theory and science of art, and, according to its founder M. Dessoir, is to be distinguished as an objective science from esthetics (see *Experimental esthetics*, however), which is an evaluative science. More precisely, the psychology of art is the psychology of the *visual arts*, and in this narrower sense forms, together with the psychology of *literature* (q.v.) and the psychology of *music* (q.v.), an essential component of an inclusive psychology of culture (see *Cultural anthropology*). Instead of the psychology of sound or auditory phenomena and psychophonetics, the psychology of visual perception is essentially important in regard to the visual arts, together with the study of the sense of touch and form for sculpture. Spatial sensitivity is, of course, a major theme here. The questions of comprehensibility of content and empathy are also posed somewhat differently, say in the matter of allegorical painting and sculpture, where the problems of form and content, etc., are materially different to those arising in music and literature. Because of their basic geometric and architectonic contents, the visual arts became the essential, paradigmatic object of gestalt psychology (see Sander, 1932, 1967; Arnheim, 1954).

More general psychological and sociological contributions to the study of "modern" abstract or non-objective art are to be found in Malraux (1949), and particularly in the works of the psychiatrist Winkler (1949) and the sociologist and philosopher Gehlen (1960, [2]1965). Gehlen examines (among other questions) such special areas of psychological interest as the *eidetic* and *kinesthetic* ability of the painter Kandinsky. Wellek (1966) provides a summary discussion of this theme. The interpretation of such phenomena and the connections between artistic intention and objective reception offer many problems for discussion, and not only in the field of so-called modern art. Siddig and Thieme (1969) carried out an investigation in which art experts and laymen were used experimentally to analyze the lack of correlation between painters' declared intentions and the actual judgments of observers. What R. Francès calls "L'age esthétique d'un sujet", i.e. the maturity of esthetic judgment in the individual, can be measured by the yardstick of the *consensus* of opinion obtained among those of supposedly mature judgment, the experts. There is a considerable amount of statistical information on musical taste in this regard. Burt (1924, 1933) followed up C. Spearman in attempting a factorial analysis of questions of taste; the work was extended by R. W. Pickford and H. J. Eysenck. These investigators postulate a "general factor of esthetic ability" in Spearman's sense, which (according to Pickford) aims at a balance between "emotional expressiveness" and "harmony of form", and therefore *implicitly* justifies an "esthetics of *form and expression*" (cf. Wellek). In addition to this general factor, all the types of painting, music and literature investigated exhibit a *bipolar* factor, showing an opposition of the more colorful, emotionally expressive, emotionally impressionistic or expressively distorted types of art to those which are less colorful, and so on. The first group is usually preferred by extraverted and the second group by introverted types (see *Type; Traits*); often the contrast is between the more and less modern, or between romantic and classical (Pickford, 1967, esp. p. 926). In principle, these findings recall Wölfflin's contrasts in his *Principles of Art History* (Eng. trans., London, 1932), and Wellek's *Typologie der Musikbegabung*

(1939). Psychology (especially since H. Prinzhorn) has shown more interest in the art-products of the psychologically disturbed than in their verse and music (up to Jakáb, 1956; Pickford, 1967; Plokker, 1969); recently drawing and painting under hypnosis have awakened interest. In addition, the viewpoint of comparative developmental psychology as represented by Krueger (1915) and Werner ([2]1948) is particularly fruitful in this area, not least of all with regard to the theory of art itself. There is a vast amount of literature devoted to children's art (cf. summary in Mühle, 1967); Westrich (1968) has produced a developmental psychology of drawing during the puberal phase. As early as 1934, Münz (a teacher of the blind) and the psychologist V. Löwenfeld made an interesting survey of sculpture by the blind and produced a comparative-psychological analysis (cf., for a more general view, Révész, 1950).

A survey of the British and American views and literature can be found in the collection of readings edited by Hogg (1969) and the summary account in Schrickel ([2]1968). (See also: *Literature; Music; Ganzheit*).

Bibliography: Arnheim, R.: Art and visual perception. New York, 1954. **Burt, C.**: The psychology of art. In: **Burt, C.** (Ed.): How the mind works. London, 1933. **Gehlen, A.**: Zeit-Bilder. Frankfurt & Bonn, [2]1965. **Hogg, J.** (Ed.): Psychology and the visual arts. Harmondsworth, 1969. **Jakáb, I.**: Zeichnungen und Gemälde der Geisteskranken. Budapest & Berlin, 1956. **Krueger, F.**: Über Entwicklungspsychologie. Leipzig, 1915. **Malraux, A.**: Psychology of art. New York, 1949–50. **Morgan, D. N.**: Psychology and art today. In: Aesth. Art Critic., 1950, *9*. **Mühle, G.**: Entwicklungspsychol. des zeichnerischen Gestaltens. Munich, [2]1967. **Munro, T. M.**: Methods in the psychology of art. In: Aesth. Art Critic., 1948, *6*. **Münz, L. & Löwenfeld, V.**: Plastiche Arbeiten Blinder. Brünn, 1934. **Odgen, R. M.**: The psychology of art. New York, 1938. **Perrer, S. C.**: Principles of art appreciation. New York, 1949. **Pickford, R. W.**: Studies in psychiatric art. Springfield, Ill., 1967. **Plokker, J. H. & Wiesenhütter, E.**: Zerrbilder. Schizophrene Gestalten. Stuttgart, 1969. **Prinzhorn, H.**: Bildnerei der Giesteskranken. Darmstadt, [2]1970. **Reitman, F.**: Psychotic art. London, 1950. **Révész, G.**: Psychology and art of the blind. London, 1950. **Sander, F.**: Elementarästhetische Wirkungen zusammengesetzter geometrischer Figuren. Wundts Psychol. Stud., 1913, *9*. **Id.**: Gestaltpsychol. und Kunsttheorie. Neue Psychol. Stud., 1932, *4*. **Id.**: Gestaltpsychologisches zur modernen Kunst. In: **Mühlher R. & Fischl, J.** (Eds): Gestalt und Wirklichkeit. Festschrift für Weinhand. Berlin, 1967. **Schrickel, H. G.**: Psychology of art. In: **Roback, A. A.** (Ed.): Present-day psychology. New York, [2]1968. **Siddig, A. & Thieme, T.**: Die verlorenen Botschaften. Über die Urteilsstruktur bei Künstlern . . . Z. f. expt. u. angew. Psychol., 1969, *6*. **Vándor, T.**: Visuelle Erlebnisse in Hypnose. Meisenheim, 1969. **Wellek, A.**: Das Farbenhören und seine Bedeutung für die Bildende Kunst. Palette (Basel), 1966, *23*; Exakte Ästhetik (Frankfurt a. M.), 1966, *3–4*. **Werner, H.**: Comparative psychology of mental development. Chicago, [2]1948. **Westrich, E.**: Die Entwicklung des Zeichnens während der Pubertät. Frankfurt a. M., 1968. **Winkler, W.**: Psychol. der modernen Kunst. Tübingen, 1949. *A. Wellek*

Ascendance-submission. A bipolar continuum from complete dominance to complete submission in interpersonal relations.

Allport Ascendance-Submission Reaction Study (A–S Reaction Study): an inventory to measure the individual's location on this continuum; one of the first self-evaluation scales in which the individual must choose the behavior appropriate to him in a certain situation. *R.M.*

Ascending reticular activating system (ARAS). A non-specific sensory system located in the reticular formation (q.v.). The ARAS is fed by primary afferent and cortico-reticular fibers. Activation (i.e. arousal) of the ARAS effects a general activation of the organism. It would seem to be responsible for the transition from a state of wakefulness to one of general attention. See *Alarm function.* *R.H.*

Asceticism. A voluntary renunciation of "all" sensuous gratification, sometimes in an attempt to train the will to endure enforced deprivation of pleasure. Usually associated with the fulfillment of the ideal way of life postulated by certain religious and even political systems. *J.G.*

Asexual. 1. A term descriptive of an individual wholly without secondary sexual characteristics, and who possesses only rudimentary sex organs. **2.** Term for a process of reproduction (e.g. spore formation) without the union of individuals or cells of different sexes: asexual generation; asexual reproduction. *G.L.*

As if (Ger. *als ob*). A term deriving its currency from Hans Vaihinger's *Die Philosophie des Als Ob* (1911; Eng. trans.: *The Philosophy of "As If"*. New York & London, 1925) and referring to reality-enhancing, non-verifiable hypotheses or "guiding fictions". Whereas Vaihinger conceived of man's knowledge (classes, categorizations, concepts, and so on) as largely a network of such "as if" strategies, the term is also applied less inclusively to suppositions deliberately assumed in order to judge the consequences of such a situation. Adler (q.v.) applied Vaihinger's relativist conception to, e.g., the incorporation of novel experience and ideas into one's "scheme of apperception": the new is treated "as if" it were (or were not) the individually known, and thus assimilated by relation. The unified individual acts "as if" he knew his goal; and so on. *J.C.*

Asphyxia. Arrested breathing. The CO_2 content of the blood responsible for breathing control rises above a partial pressure of 56 mm Hg and poisons the breathing center; consequently artificial respiration is necessary. Asphyxia occurs in the newborn during birth either as a blue, non-dangerous, or a white, dangerous form. It results from blocking of the respiratory passages or lesions of the brain resulting from birth trauma. *E.D.*

Aspiration level. The level of aspiration is the possible goal (score) an individual sets himself in his performance. Hoppe (1930) traced personal achievement to the experience of success and failure: a specific action only becomes success or failure because of its relation to a momentary goal or norm which can serve as a yardstick for the action considered in the sense of achievement. In experiments with different tasks Hoppe observed an increase in aspiration level after repeated success in the same achievement, and a decrease after repeated failure, which he described as typical shifts in aspiration level. An atypical shift would be an increase after failure and a decrease after success. Hoppe used the term *ego level* for the attempt to keep one's self-image as high as possible by a high standard of achievement. In experiments with children (10 to 15 years) and adults, Jucknat used two series of tasks: a success series (ten cards with solvable maze tests and a scale of increasing difficulty) and a failure series (ten similiar though insoluble tasks). Measurement of the choice time for the task in a decision conflict (i.e. the time from the start of the problem-solving process to decision taking) revealed the following: a final decision for a specific, easy or difficult, task is made only after a more or less protracted period of consideration and trying of several tasks. After successful solution of a task, on average the time taken to select the new task constantly decreases. After success, encouragement is shown not only in the increase of aspiration level but in the speed of selection and in immediate application to more difficult tasks. After failure, the average selection time either remains approximately the same, or even increases. The drop in self-estimation is expressed not only in the decrease in aspiration level but in considerable fluctuation or a slow, lingering process of selection.

1. *Aspiration level and achievement motivation.* Confrontation with a standard of excellence is a central theme of achievement motivation (q.v.) (D. D. McClelland, J. W. Atkinson, H. Heckhausen, etc.). The personality-specific expression of achievement motivation decisively influences the aspiration level preferred by the individual. Not only its intensity but above all its orientation

plays a part in achievement motivation, whether hope of success or fear of failure is predominant (Heckhausen, 1963). Jucknat and others trace the formation of an aspiration level to the interaction of momentary achievement, longstanding achievement confidence, momentary achievement impulse, seriousness of the situation and type of subject. Heckhausen indicates that social situations, e.g. the presence, prestige and behavior of onlookers, also influence aspiration level. The goal discrepancy of subjects, i.e. the difference between the level of aspiration and the level of achievement attained previously, would seem to be an indicator of individual achievement motivation. It is constantly evident that those confident of success prefer an aspiration level somewhat above the actual achievement, whereas those concerned with the possibility of failure prefer an aspiration level far above or far below their actual capacity. Sears found that the average positive discrepancy in children after failure is greater than after success. This would indicate that estimation of ability is more realistic after success than after failure. Confident, realistically adjusted children behave reasonably in regard to aspiration level. Socially maladaptive children showing disturbed performance are mainly characterized by their affective wishes in regard to aspiration level. After protracted success-and-failure experiments with school and college students, Nuttin recorded effects on perception, learning and memory. In comparisons of normal and manic-depressive subjects, cumulative occurrences of success and failure often result in destructive deformations and traumatic operations of judgment. Both successes and failures are experienced as stress situations by children with speech defects.

2. *Aspiration level and group achievement.* When a group of individuals are faced with the task of deciding between goals of varying degrees of difficulty, one problem is how a common group goal is established from the individual goals set. It has been shown that group members with a high desire for group achievement chose tasks of average difficulty, whereas members with a low desire for group achievement chose either very difficult or very easy tasks (Zander, Medow *et al.*). Differences in the estimation of subjects' own individual performance were found among members with a central or peripheral position in the group (Zander & Medow). Members with a central position evaluated their own performance after failure at a level lower than that at which members with a peripheral position judged theirs; but after success there was hardly any difference in self-evaluations. With failure, group members evaluated the group result at a lower level than their personal performance ($X = 3{\cdot}21$ or $4{\cdot}67$). With success, on the other hand, they evaluated their personal and the group performance at approximately the same high level ($X = 5{\cdot}09$). With success and failure, the group performance is usually judged more favorably by those with a central position in the group than by those with a peripheral position. E. Mayo has indicated positive effects of success on the climate of work (see *Industrial psychology*). Harmonious understanding, a feeling of responsibility and recognition of individual importance are features of a harmonious work group. Although failure can stimulate enthusiasm for work, it will often be a dogged or bitter rather than happy enthusiasm.

Research into the relations between performance (achievement) and aspiration level, and into the dynamic processes of success and failure, has become increasingly significant since Hoppe's classical investigation, and is carried out in widely varying fields: in psychology, education, sociology, economics and politics.

Bibliography: Atkinson, J. W.: Motivational determinants of risk-taking behavior. Psychol. Rev., 1957, *64*, 359–372. **Id. & N. T. Feather:** A theory of achievement motivation. New York, 1966. **Festinger, L.:** Wish, expectation, and group standards as affecting level of aspiration. J. abnorm. soc. Psychol., 1942, *37*, 184–200. **Heckhausen, H.:** Hoffnung und Furcht in der Leistungsmotivation. Meisenheim/Glan,

1963. **Id.**: Allgemeine Psychologie in Experimenten. Göttingen, 1969. **Hilgard, E. R., Sait, E. M. & Margaret, G. A.**: Level of aspiration as affected by relative standing in an experimental social group. J. exp. Psychol., 1940, *27*, 411–21. **Hoppe, F.**: Erfolg und Misserfolg. Psychol. Forsch., 1930, *14*, 1–62. **Jucknat, M.**: Leistung, A. und Selbstbewusstsein. Psychol. Forsch., 1937, *22*, 89–179. **Lewin, K.**: Feldtheorie in den Sozialwissenschaften. Berne, 1963. **Lewin, K., Dembo, T., Festinger, L. & Sears, P.**: Level of aspiration. In: **J. McV. Hunt** (Ed.): Personality and the behavior disorders, Vol. 1. New York, 1944, 333–378. **Mayo, E.**: The human problems of an industrial civilization. Cambridge, Mass., 1933. **Id.**: The social problems of an industrial civilization. Cambridge, Mass., 1945. **Medow, H. & Zander, A.**: Aspirations for the group chosen by central and peripheral members. J. Pers. soc. Psychol., 1965, *1*, 224–28. **Nuttin, J.**: Tâche, réussite et échec. Théorie de la conduite humaine. Louvain, 1953. **Zander, A. & Medow, H.**: Individual and group levels of aspiration. Human Relations, 1963, *16*, 89–105.

A. Karsten

Assignment therapy. Psychotherapeutic treatment by assigning to an appropriate play, work or discussion group. See *Group therapy*.

Assimilation. 1. Generally, the process of incorporation of some aspect of the surrounding environment into the self or whole. Among the variety of uses in psychology is that of the distortion of new facts and stimuli to accord with expectations based on previous experience. Thus the details of a rumor are modified in accordance with one's prejudices before being transmitted to others. In perceptual psychology, assimilation phenomena (the accentuation of stimulus similarities) are opposed to *contrast* phenomena (the accentuation of stimulus differences). *Cultural assimilation*, also called *acculturation* (q.v.), is the process of becoming like the social environment in some respects, e.g. adopting the prevailing attitudes of that society.

G.D.W.

2. In the *biological* sense, assimilation is the conversion by living organisms (with the aid of sunlight and chlorophyll) of simple, low-energy chemicals into more complex, energy-rich compounds. *H.Sch.*

3. *Physiologically*, assimilation is the formation of substances proper to the body from basic chemical substances, ultimately absorbed from food and directly from the intermediary metabolism. In E. Hering's color theory, assimilation refers to the building-up of the three color-sensitive substances in the retina (q.v.) (corresponding to the antagonistic colors green-red, blue-yellow and black-white) under light stimulation. Assimilation and dissimilation (q.v.) take place to varying degrees at the same time; the resulting color sensation depends on the dominance of one or the other process. *R.R.*

Assimilation-contrast theory. A theory of information processing (Yale group). Information which falls within the tolerance of one's own opinion is accepted and "processed" by reciprocal approximation of divergent viewpoints. Information diverging from one's own viewpoint is rejected. In extreme cases, the receiver of the information puts forward his own opinion even more radically in opposition to the viewpoint received by him ("boomerang effect").

H.-J.A.

Associate chain theories. See *Associative chain theory*.

Association. Thunder has always been connected with lightning and such associations probably go back to the beginning of human thought. Various types and degrees of associations have been postulated whenever man began to reflect more systematically about the nature and the origin of his knowledge, thoughts, images and ideas. The *Psychological Abstracts* indicate "learning" as a cross-reference for "association" and list studies in conditioning, verbal learning, sensation, memory, recall, and so on, under this combined category.

1. *History of associationism.* The concept of associationism appears first in Plato's

Phaedo where it is pointed out that the mere sight of a lover's lyre or gown will bring thoughts and feelings similar to those caused by the lover himself. Aristotle, in *On Memory and Reminiscence*, established several principles of association which influenced much later psychology. He thought that we recall an object because it is either similar or dissimilar to the one in our present thought, or because the two objects were originally perceived by us closely in time and space. These Aristotelian principles of association became known as the laws of similarity, contrast, and contiguity. Aristotle thought that repetition, emotion, attention, and certain forms and shapes of objects also influence the formation of associations.

For Aristotle, association implied that thoughts are environmentally determined and not "god-given". This was not acceptable to the Scholastic philosophers, and speculations about association lay dormant for about 2000 years, until they were revived as "associationism" or the "doctrine of associationism" by the British empirical philosophers Hobbes, Locke, Hume, Hartley, Bain and others. As summarized by Esper (1964), these writers closely followed Aristotle's laws of association in postulating that all mental life stems from sensory stimulation, and that similar experiences may later occur as ideas or as mental elements in the absence of the original stimulation. Hartley extended the laws of association to include muscular movements and suggested certain neurophysiological rules as the basis for associationism. Bain proposed the additional principles of pleasure and pain, and pointed out that those associations which lead to pleasure will be repeated, and those which lead to pain will not.

The experimental basis of associationism was established mainly by Sechenov. In *Reflexes of the Brain* (1863), he explained certain mental and purposive acts in terms of neurological mechanisms which had been demonstrated in laboratories.

Sechenov's work paved the way for Pavlov who spent many years investigating the circumstances under which animals and humans learn or form associations between new and previously known stimuli and responses. Pavlov (1934) maintained that there was no difference between the psychologist's term "association" and the psychologist's terms "conditioning" (q.v.) or "temporary nervous connections". Pavlov's work has influenced much of present psychology, in theory as well as in practice.

2. *Modern associationist theories.* Modern psychology encompasses many areas, and associationistic principles play an important part in several of them. Developmental psychology (q.v.) has been strongly influenced by Watson's behaviorism (1919). Watson demonstrated that Pavlov's findings apply equally well to human infants, as many of their fears and desires can be conditioned by direct or indirect associations with physical pain or pleasure. Watson's classical conditioning procedures have been augmented by Skinner's (1953) operant conditioning methods. These methods use the naturally occurring behavior fluctuations, and reward those which approach "wanted" behavior, and neglect those which are not wanted. Many of the principles of conditioning and their experimental studies pertaining to sucking, feeding, toilet training, and other child-rearing problems, are currently reported in the *Journal of Experimental Child Psychology*.

The psychology of learning (q.v.) leans most heavily on associationistic principles. Robinson (1932) listed the following laws of association as important to learning theorists: contiguity, assimilation, frequency, intensity, duration, context, acquaintance, and so on. Various theorists, however, have investigated and emphasized different aspects necessary for the establishment of associations. As pointed out by Hilgard Bower (1956), Guthrie stressed mere time or contiguity, Hull the reduction of physiological needs, and Tolman the formation of mental patterns. Congruent with current trends of specialization, research in learning has examined more discrete problems of association. As frequently reported in the *Journal of Verbal Learning and Verbal Behavior*, investigators seek to understand the mechanisms of learning by examining specialized problems such as whole vs. part learning, massed vs. distributed practice, interference of retention, perceptual generalization, unlearning, inhibitions, and so on.

The social implications of modern associationistic theories are perhaps most evident in the areas of education, counseling, and clinical psychology, where they have found many practical applications. Eysenck (1968) has pioneered the investigation and description of procedures which uncondition or desensitize socially undesirable behavior. A homosexual, for instance, may be given an electric shock while looking at pictures of men; an alcoholic may be given a drug which will cause nausea at his next intake of alcohol; and so on. Behavior modification techniques based on Skinnerian operant conditioning are also expanding rapidly into fields of education, juvenile delinquency, psychopathology, and into other areas where retraining is an issue.

Pongratz (1967; pp. 58, 173) has pointed out that associationism has been criticized by gestalt psychology and other phenomenological approaches. Psychoanalytic views have also been opposed to knowledge gained through the investigation of association, because they hold that human thought and conduct cannot be dissected into elements and laws of association. Despite these various counter-currents, associationism has occupied much of psychology's theory and practice and is likely to make many further contributions to the understanding of human behavior. See *Conditioning*.

Bibliography: Esper, E. A.: A history of psychology. Philadelphia & London, 1964. **Eysenck, H. J.:** Fact and fiction in psychology. London, 1965. **Hilgard, E. R. & Bower, G. H.:** Theories of learning. New York, [3]1956. **Jowett, B.:** The Republic of Plato (trans.) Oxford, [3]1908. **Pavlov, I. P.:** Selected works. Moscow, 1955. (Original publication, 1934). **Pongratz, L. J.:** Problemgeschichte der Psychologie. Berne & Munich, 1967. **Robinson, E. S.:** Association theory to-day. N.Y., 1932. **Ross, W. D.** (Ed.): The works of Aristotle. Oxford, 1908–1931. **Sechenov, I.:** Reflexes of the brain. Cambridge, Mass., 1965 (originally publ. in: Meditsinsky Vestnik, Nos. 47 & 48, 1863). **Skinner, B. F.:** Science of human behavior. New York, 1953. **Watson, J. B.:** Psychology from the standpoint of a behaviorist. Philadelphia, 1919.

F. Wesley

Association coefficient. A term for forms of measurement of the degree of relationship between two alternative characteristics within a fourfold table. *H.-J.S.*

Association, free. The non-purposefully linked course, trend or flow of thoughts, ideas and memories that arises in dreams (q.v.), daydreaming, and free fantasy, in psychotherapy (q.v.) and psychoanalysis. The subject or the observer (the psychotherapist) is said to be able to discern in free associations the motives and wishes which control these associations without his agency or volition.

Bibliography: Freud, S.: The interpretation of dreams. London, 1955. **Jung, C. G.:** Studies in word association. London, 1969.

W.T.

Association, induced. Related thoughts, ideas or memories induced or directed by stimulus or orienting ideas, goals or motives. In everyday life, associations may occur in the context of searching for a name, or a technique to solve a specific task; in psychology as divergent thought (under an overall theme); and in psychotherapy as the working out of a theme, a relationship with a certain person, or a traumatic event—when the orienting ideas are examined to uncover motives and wishes. *W.T.*

Association, laws of. Since Aristotle, the following psychological laws governing association have been postulated with minor variations: *similarity* (two similar memory-contents are linked); *contrast* (two contrasted elements are linked with one another);

contiguity in space and time (two simultaneous or immediately successive elements are linked together). See *Association. H.-J.A.*

Association pathways. The neural association pathways in the cerebral cortex (intracortical pathways) are distinguished from those which pass largely beneath the cerebral cortex (subcortical pathways). The former represent mainly tangential connections of neighboring nerve cells (ganglionic cells, q.v.); the latter, in the form of nerve fibers (axons, q.v.) transmitting resting and action potential (q.v.), link cortical areas to their hemisphere. The *fibrae arcuatae cerebri* (bow-shaped nerve fibers) connect the convolutions on the surface of the cortex (see *Gyrus*). The *fasciculus longitudinalis superior* extends between the frontal and occipital lobes of the cerebrum. The *fasciculi intersegmentales* connect nerve cells of the same side with different spinal segments.

Association areas: The term sometimes used for the largest cortical areas, the frontal association area (in the frontal lobe) and parietal-temporal-occipital association area (PTO), which overlaps the parietal, the temporal, and the occipital lobes.

Bibliography: Braus, H. & Elze, E.: Anatomie des Menschen. Berlin, 1960. **Grossman, S. P.:** Physiological psychology. New York, 1967. **Teitelbaum, P.:** Physiological psychology. Englewood Cliffs, N.J., 1967.

G.A.

Association psychology. A school or trend in psychology seeking to explain all mental states and processes in terms of associations (see *Association*). The founders and principal proponents of this theory of mental organization might be said to be Hobbes, Hume, Hartley, James Mill, J. S. Mill, and A. Bain. The term is often used to refer only to psychology before the second half of the nineteenth century. Association psychology still plays a not insignificant role in learning (q.v.) theory. *H.-J.A.*

Association-sensation ratio. Ratio of mass of total association cortex to total sensory cortex. Sometimes used to indicate learning ability.

Association test. The subject is required to respond with association to stimuli, usually words. The method is used in psychoanalysis to uncover repressed complexes, and sometimes in forensic psychology (in certain countries) to confirm evidence. It is, of course, applied in marketing psychology to determine reactions to a brand name and so on. Occasionally, an attempt is made to decide the degree of "originality" of the subject by comparing his associations with those typical in the population. *V.M.*

Associative chain theory. The postulate that one act in a series is caused by (causes) another.

Associative fluency. In divergent thinking: a factor assessed by tests in which, e.g., as many synonyms as possible have to be given for a predetermined word, or sentences must be completed with adjectives, or words must be made out of one initial word. *M.A.*

Associative inhibition. See *Memory*.

Astasia; astasia-abasia. See *Abasia*.

Asthenic type. According to E. Kretschmer's typology, a long, lean and dysplastic version of the leptosome (q.v.) constitution (physique), with a similar tendency to psychic disturbances. According to K. Conrad, the hypoplastic pole of the "secondary variant" body-build types. E. Kretschmer assesses the asthenic character as simply submissive under stress, and featuring no particular defense reactions: "weak-willed, thin-skinned natures which suffer the stresses of life without being able to defend themselves from them, neither hating nor showing anger".

Bibliography: Kretschmer, E.: Der sensitive Beziehungswahn. Berlin, [4]1966. **Id.:** Physique and character. London, 1925. **Conrad, K.:** Der Konstitutionstyp. Berlin, [2]1963. *W.K.*

Astigmatism. The refractive surfaces of the eye, cornea and lens can feature irregularities, or variable degrees of refraction in varying visual fields. Usually the variations of refraction extend to 0·5 diopters, but more extensive irregularities are experienced as disturbances of vision and classed as astigmatism. Astigmatic lenses are used to correct the deviation. Corneal astigmatism is usually predominant. *R.R.*

Astigmometer (syn. *Astigmatometer*). A device for measuring the degree of astigmatism of the eye's refractive system in different visual fields. First described by Hemlholtz (1855); various modifications since—e.g. by E. Javal and H. Schiötz. *R.R.*

Asymmetry. Asymmetry (the opposite of symmetry) refers to the *skewness* (q.v.) of distributions. An asymmetrical frequency distribution is one without a mean value $\bar{X}$ to which $f(X - \bar{X})$ is applicable. In mathematics and logic, asymmetry means that a relation R, which is applicable for xRy, is not applicable for yRx. *W.H.B.*

Ataractic drugs. See *Tranquilizer.*

Atavistic regression (*Atasvim*). A throw-back or *reversion* to a more primitive ancestral form. In genetics, the reappearance in an organism of a character or trait which has not manifested itself for several generations. Also used more loosely to refer to primitive modes of behavior in general. *G.D.W.*

Ataxia (syn. *Ataxy*). Incoordination of the groups of muscles responsible for movement, with the result that both oriented movements (e.g. reaching out for an object), sequential movements (e.g. walking or talking), and the equilibrium of trunk and limbs in a certain position, are disturbed. Ataxic movements tend to overshoot the goal.

The causes of ataxia are not located in the corresponding muscle group but in the spinal and cerebral centers responsible for control of movement.

Spinal ataxia: In disorders of the conductors responsible for depth sensitivity (e.g. in polyneuritis), or the nerve roots or ganglia of the spinal cord, e.g. in *tabes dorsalis*, or locomotor *ataxia* (ataxy), usually a sequel of syphilis. The tabetic patient generally sways or even falls if asked to stand upright with eyes closed (Romberg's sign, q.v.).

Cerebellar ataxia: Occurs during nonfunctioning of certain areas of the cerebellum as the result of tumors, atrophy, and so on; here, too, the patient sways when asked to stand with eyes closed (astasia) or to walk (abasia, q.v.).

Cerebral ataxia: Occurs with lesions of frontal, temporal and parietal lobes, of the thalamus and mesencephalon. Loss of coordination is not so pronounced as with cerebellar ataxia. *D.V.*

Ataxiameter. A device which records and measures all an individual's involuntary movements, when he is trying to stand upright and motionless, with eyes closed. The ataxiameter is often used in experimental investigations of suggestibility (q.v.). *F.-C.S.*

Athletic type. Robust physique, massive or slim. The locomotor apparatus (bones, muscles, etc.) is well developed, and there is occipital protuberance. Solid, high-set head with abundant hair and thick skin. Affinity to the barykinetic (q.v.) temperament, schizophrenia, epilepsy.

Bibliography: Kretschmer, E.: Physique and character. London, 1925. **Id. & Kretschmer, W.:** Medinische Psychologie. Stuttgart, [13]1970. *W.K.*

Atmosphere effect. Woodworth & Sells observed (1935) that in a syllogism affirmative premisses tended to induce a positive formulation of the conclusion, even when the conclusion was logically false. Negative premisses tended to induce negative conclusions. This suggestive effect exerted by the "atmosphere" or context of the premisses, they termed an "atmosphere effect". E.g.: All these candies are chocolate-creams.

All these candies are delicious.

Chocolate-creams are delicious.

Bibliography: Woodworth, R. S. & Sells, S. B.: An atmosphere effect in formal syllogistic reasoning. J. exp. Psychol., 1935, *18*, 451–60. *H.-J.A.*

Atomism. 1. *Atomistic psychology* tries to obtain insight into psychological processes or mental states by reducing them to their elements or discrete components, and is therefore opposed to gestalt psychology (see *Ganzheit*, etc.). Gestaltist theoreticians sometimes use the term pejoratively to characterize association psychology (q.v.), sensualism (q.v.) and extreme forms of neobehaviorism (q.v.). **2.** *Logical atomism* is the philosophical view that certain entities are ultimately unanalyzable, related only contingently, or wholly independent: e.g. there are unanalyzable atomic propositions from which other propositions are generalized. *H.-J.A.*

Atonia (syn. *Atony*). The absence of all normal muscular tension. In the smooth tissue musculature this can lead to circulatory collapse; in the gastro-intestinal tract, to ileus (cessation of bowel peristalsis); and in the pregnant uterus to a dangerous arrestation of the birth process. *E.D.*

Atrophy. Decrease in volume and loss of function in organs or parts of organs, usually as the result of inactivity or a lack of oxygen or nourishment. *E.D.*

Atropine (*Hyoscyamine*). A parasympathetic-inhibiting substance found together with the other belladonna drug hyoscine (scopalamine, q.v.) in deadly nightshade and similar plants. Main physiological effects in small doses (0·5–5 mg): dilatation of pupils, paralyzed accommodation, inhibition of aqueous humor flow, reduction of sweat and saliva (increase in skin resistance, dryness of the mouth), antispasmodic effect (especially in gastro-intestinal area), peristalsis inhibition, rapid pulse (but slows down heart rate with very low doses, up to 0·5 mg). In the CNS there is slow electrocortical activity (5–8 Hz), and reduction of the arousal reaction of the reticular formation under stimulation (e.g. light). The main psychic effects (several hours) with low doses (0·5–5 mg administered orally): subjective deactivation; performance non-uniform but largely affected. At higher doses (10 mg): activation. Hallucinations occasionally with very high doses. In numerous animal investigations (some in animals reacting differently from men) symptoms of sedation at lower dosage seem less pronounced than in men. The EEG behavior dissociation described by A. Wikler (EEG retardation unaccompanied by deactivation) is theoretically significant. No satisfactory explanation is as yet forthcoming for the coexistence of activating and deactivating symptoms, both in animals and in man. It is extremely probable that many psychic effects are not "centrally" but "peripherally" conditioned by the considerable autonomic effects (unusual vegetative sensations). There are numerous substances related to or derived from atropine (e.g. naltropine, homatropine, scopalamine). Their effects are to some effect quite different to those of atropine, especially in the relations between central and autonomic action. Several of these drugs have relatively slight peripheral-physiological effects, but more powerful central effects (e.g. naltropine).

Bibliography: Longo, V. G.: Behavioral and electroencephalographic effects of atropine and related compounds. Pharmacol. Rev., 1966, *18*, 965–96. **Soyka, L. F. & Unna, K. R.:** A comparison in man of the autonomic and behavioral effects of N-Allylnoratropine with atropine. Psychopharmacologia. 1964, *6*, 453–61. *W.J.*

Attention. There are several concepts of attention. Knowledge concerning attention is developing rapidly, especially in cognitive-perceptual psychology, physiological psychology, psychophysics, and behavior theory. But these developments proceed independently to a great extent; different meanings of the term are found in the different fields as well as within each field. It is possible to discern some continuity with historical meanings of attention in most cases.

In the older literature, attention was defined in terms of conscious awareness and played crucial roles in the great theories of consciousness. Structural psychology and functional psychology each made use of the term and two quite different conceptions emerged.

Structural psychology associated attention with the clearness of items in consciousness. Wundt described consciousness as consisting of a clear core or focus and a less-clear periphery, and considered attention to be the process by which items in peripheral consciousness are brought into the focus of consciousness. Attention transforms perception into apperception and imparts clarity (Boring, 1929). Titchener went further, implying a continuum of clearness produced by attention and giving clearness the status of a dimension of sensation which he called "attensity". Attensity, along with intensity, extensity, duration and others, became a fundamental dimension of the structure of consciousness (Boring, 1929).

Rather than placing attention "within" consciousness, as the structuralists appeared to do, William James (1890), representing the functionalists, located it prior to consciousness and described attention as a process of selection among items not yet in consciousness: a selection of some items to enter consciousness while other items remain excluded. James argued that attention is a necessary condition for conscious clearness but he specifically denied that it is sufficient; additional cognitive operations are also required. Hence James emphasized the importance of attention in the relationship between an organism and its environment. Through the selective action of attention a psychological environment is created out of the physical environment and thereby attention gains adaptive significance. But James did not confine attention only to selection among stimuli. He recognized intellectual as well as sensorial attention, and volitional as well as passive attention.

Few references to attention are to be found in the literature of gestalt psychology, behaviorism and psychoanalysis, and for many years the concept was ignored. Its revival was heralded by an influential book by Donald Hebb (Hebb, 1949). Citing new evidence for spontaneous central neural activity, Hebb posited attention as an autonomous central process acting as a reinforcement of sensory processes and strongly influenced by learning. Attention determines perceptual organization and the selection of a response, given a particular sensory input. Response selection rather than stimulus selection is emphasized, and a similarity between attention and set is apparent.

A book by Broadbent (1958) proposed a new theory of attention, couched in the terminology of information theory and based on stimulus selection. This event marks the beginning of modern attention theory in cognitive-perceptual psychology. Broadbent's theory was based on the results of extensive experiments of two kinds: "listen-and-answer" and "split memory span". In the former, subjects listen to several speech messages simultaneously and then are interrogated about the messages. Broadbent showed how limited one is in performing such a task, and worked out some of the factors involved.

In the split-span experiment, immediate memory for digits is tested with successive pairs of digits presented dichotically, i.e., one member of each pair to the right ear, the other to the left ear. The main finding was that subjects organize their responses according to ear rather than according to order of presentation when the number of pairs is small and they are presented rapidly.

Broadbent's theory is most like the position taken by William James. The function of attention is to prevent overloading of the individual's information-processing capacity. The cognitive structure (P-system, in Broadbent's terms) has an information-processing capacity which is much less than the total entering the organism by the sensory pathways; attention serves as a gate to admit some and exclude the remainder: it is a "filter" interposed between sensory input and P-system. The filter is all-or-none, admitting the contents of one input channel at a time and completely blocking the remainder, but it can switch rapidly between channels, and the boundaries of channels are flexible, being in part a function of the amount of information in the sensory pathways.

This filter theory of selective attention stimulated many experiments which have led to several modifications of the theory. These have recently been reviewed (Swets & Kristofferson, 1970; Moray, 1969). A dominant experimental method in this work is the shadowing technique, in which two different messages of continuous speech are presented simultaneously, one to each ear, and the subject follows one of the messages by repeating it as he hears it. The message which is not being repeated conveys little information to the subject although under certain conditions it does convey some. If, for example, it contains the subject's own name, there is some chance that it will be heard. Such findings have been taken to mean that there must be some interpretation of sensory input prior to attention, and several more recent theories differing from Broadbent in various ways on this point have been proposed (Moray, 1969).

The idea of selective attention as a sensory filter has been studied in psychophysics (q.v.) for some years, and several methods have been developed for the quantitative investigation of some aspects of attention. For example, the probability of detecting a weak stimulus is higher if the subject knows in advance the identity of the sensory channel in which the signal will occur. This literature, particularly that which relates attention to signal detection theory, has been reviewed recently (Swets & Kristofferson, 1970).

Initial presentation of a novel stimulus is likely to produce a complex response pattern which has behavioral, central-neural and autonomic components. This "orienting reflex" (q.v.) habituates rapidly and may reappear if the stimulus is changed slightly. It is interpreted as a state of heightened attentiveness and has been studied extensively (Sokolov, 1963): both physiologically (Lindsley, 1960), where it is related to activation or arousal (q.v.), and behaviorally (see Jerison, 1968, for a brief summary). As behavior, it is related to observing responses, such as eye-movements, which are often used to indicate attending, and to instrumental and classical conditioning.

The importance of observing responses in learning has been recognized by behavior theorists for many years, especially by those who study discrimination learning. The sufficiency of observing responses as attentional mechanisms is now being questioned and learning theorists are turning to hypothetical constructs of selective attention in the analysis of discrimination learning (Trabasso & Bower, 1968).

The arousal systems of the brain are being mapped out. Their response to external stimuli is observed as a desynchronization of the electroencephalogram (q.v.) and the relationships among attentiveness, arousal and levels of consciousness are being determined. There is some evidence that the arousal systems are involved in selective attention through inhibition and facilitation of sensory inputs (Lindsley, 1960).

Attention enters into certain areas of applied psychology. In engineering psychology, for example, attention sets limits on the design of those information-processing systems which include human operators. Of particular importance are limits on the ability to receive information simultaneously from multiple sources and to sustain attention for long periods of time. Much research has been done on the latter under the heading of "vigilance" (q.v.) (Swets & Kristofferson, 1970). Another example is the considerable recent literature on attentional deficits associated with various pathological conditions, particularly schizophrenia.

Bibliography: Boring, E. G.: A history of experimental psychology. New York & London, 1929. **Broadbent, D. E.:** Perception and communication. Oxford, 1958. **Hebb, D. O.:** The organization of behavior. New York & London, 1949. **James, W.:** The principles of psychology. New York, 1950 (1890). **Jerison, H. J.:** Attention. Int. Encycl. Soc. Sci., 1968, 444–9. **Lindsley, D. B.:** Attention, consciousness, sleep and wakefulness. Vol. 3, 1553–1593, in Am. Physiol. Soc., Handbook of Physiology. Section 1: Neurophysiology. Ed. **Magoun, H. W.** *et al.*, Baltimore, 1960. **Moray, N.:** Attention. Selective processes in vision and hearing. London, 1969. **Sokolov, E. N.:** Perception and the conditioned reflex. New York, 1963. **Swets, J. A. & Kristofferson, A. B.:** Attention. Ann. Rev. of Psychol., 1970, *21*, 339–66. **Trabasso, T. & Bower, G. H.:** Attention in learning: Theory and research. New York-London-Sydney, 1968.

A. B. Kristofferson

Attention, distributive. Attention distributed over several processes or objects. See *Attention.*

Attention, fluctuation of. Attention (q.v.) cannot be given with the same intensity to a single process or object after a certain period of time, but is subject to fluctuations or periodic changes evidenced in fluctuating performance. H. Rohracher postulates a cause in regeneration of the ganglionic cells.

H.-J.A.

Attention span. The number of objects (e.g. random digits) which can be grasped in one short presentation.

Attention theories. 1. *Physiological:* G. E. Müller believed that certain processes increased the stimulability of certain areas of the brain, thus leading to improved receptivity. H. Ebbinghaus and E. Dürr derived attention from effects occurring in the nerve pathways of the brain, and assumed that impulses passing through certain frequently-used pathways must lead to more precise perception ("*Bahnungstheorie*").

More modern theories treat attention for the most part physiologically, and refer to increased activation by the ARAS (see *Ascending reticular activating system; Alarm function*).

2. *Psychophysiological*: H. Henning's "sensibilization" theory sees attention as the result of a sensitization of the sense organs and neural pathways brought about by external and internal stimuli. Similarly, H. Rohracher sees attention as an activation of individual mental functions, provoked by powerful external stimuli or by drives, interests and volition. These theories are based on stimulation; P. K. Hofstätter explains attention in terms of the "suppressor-fields" which lead to a "reduction in the effective stimulation of the environing field".

3. *Psychological:* B. Erdmann sees attention as psychic energy pure and simple which cannot be derived more accurately. Mach and Wundt (like Kant) view attention as a consequence of volitional activity.

4. *Mechanical model:* D. E. Broadbent (1957): see *Attention.*

Theories of attention are largely determined by the fundamental conception of attention itself.

Bibliography: Broadbent, D. E.: A mechanical model for human attention and immediate memory. Psychol. Rev., 1957, *64*, 205–15.

H.-J.A.

Attention types. Experimental investigations (especially those of O. Vollmer), both with visual and acoustic stimuli, showed the existence of two attention types which can be categorized according to Kretschmer's constitutional typology. Schizothymes (q.v.)

showed a narrow attention span: their attention was detailed and their perception more objective. Cyclothymes (q.v.) featured a broad attention span; their attention tended to fluctuate, and perceived the whole in a more subjective manner.

Bibliography: Vollmer, O.: Die sogenannte Aufmerksamkeitstypen und die Persönlichkeit. Suppl. Vol. 14. Leipzig, 1929. *W.K.*

Attitude. An *attitude* is normally defined as a perceptual orientation and response readiness in relation to a particular object or class of objects. Some qualifications must be added however:

(*a*) Attitudes are reasonably *enduring*, thus distinguishing them from *sets* and *expectations* which normally refer to more temporary states of readiness. This does not mean that attitudes can never change (for attitude change is a very important field in social psychology), just that they are extremely resistant to alteration.

(*b*) Attitudes must show *variation* between individuals and between cultures, i.e. they relate to issues upon which people disagree. In this way they are distinguished from various other concepts referring to response predispositions and characteristic behavior, such as *instinct* (q.v.) and *habit* (q.v.). As Sherif *et al.* (1965, 19) point out, "the fact that we customarily walk downstairs instead of tumbling down does not require explanation in terms of an attitude, nor does the characteristic response of eating when a hungry person is offered food". This fact of variance within and between cultures is often taken to mean that attitudes are *learned* through experience. Although this appears to be true in the main, it seems likely that certain genetic predispositions, e.g. aggressiveness, (which also show variance in the population) may be partial determinants of certain attitudes (McGuire, 1969).

(*c*) Possibly the most important distinguishing feature of attitudes is that they are necessarily *evaluative* or *affective*. *Beliefs* may be constituents of attitudes ("Negroes are dirty"), or they may be largely unrelated to attitudes ("Negroes are tall").

(*d*) The attitude concept in psychology has the scientific status of a *hypothetical construct*. It cannot be directly observed, but must be inferred from observable behavior such as verbal statements of *opinion*, physiological changes due to exposure to the attitude object, or overt acts in relation to the object. None of these observables may be equated with attitudes; they can only be used as indicators, measures, or "operational definitions".

1. *Measurement.* Attitudes are most commonly measured through analysis of patterns of response to questionnaires and other *self-report* techniques. These fall into two major groups: (*a*) *Scales which present directional statements of opinion* (e.g. "Homosexuals ought to be publicly whipped"), to which S responds with some amount of agreement or disagreement. Among the best-known scales of this kind are the *F-Scale* (Adorno, Frenkel-Brunswik, Levinson & Sanford, 1950), the *Dogmatism Scale* (Rokeach, 1960), and the *Social Attitudes Inventory* (Eysenck, 1954). (*b*) *Scales which present non-directional concepts* (e.g., "Father", "death penalty") and require the respondent to evaluate them. The *Semantic Differential* (Osgood, Suci & Tannenbaum, 1957), and the *Conservatism Scale* (Wilson & Patterson, 1968) are scales of this kind. When applicable, the latter item format would seem to be preferable on a number of counts. It is economical, less susceptible to acquiescence response bias, eliminates certain sources of ambiguity (e.g. differences in the perceived point of emphasis in the opinion statement), and avoids algebraic addition problems for the subject (e.g. having to disagree with a negatively worded statement).

Of the various techniques for selecting scale items, most of the traditional methods (e.g. those of Thurstone and Guttman) were concerned with the construction of *unidimensional* scales (Scott, 1969). With the advent of the computer, the mathematical models upon which they are based have been largely superseded by the technique of *factor analysis*, which permits the development of *multidimensional* attitude scales.

In addition to the self-report technique, various *disguised* measures of attitudes have also been investigated, on the argument that they are less contaminated by various inhibitory factors (such as "social desirability") which might lead to faking. Actually, this problem is not very insistent in the area of attitude measurement because of the evaluative nature of attitudes themselves. Whereas with variables such as intelligence and neuroticism there is considerable agreement as to which end of the scale is desirable, an individual's own position in relation to an attitude object is by definition perceived as good.

Nevertheless, attitudes can be measured without the subject's awareness in terms of their effects upon memory and perceptual processes (e.g. recall thresholds, binocular resolution), or performance on certain tasks involving materials relevant to the attitude object (e.g. classifying opinion statements as favorable or unfavorable toward an issue instead of indicating one's own agreement). Several physiological measures of attitudes have also been used, especially autonomic measures such as the GSR (Cook & Selltiz, 1964). Apart from the fact that they are very cumbersome by comparison with questionnaires, the major disadvantage of most physiological measures is that they indicate only the *intensity* of an attitude response, not its *direction*. The recent hope that pupil size might constitute a measure of direction as well as intensity (Hess, 1965) now appears to be subsiding (McGuire, 1969).

2. *Structure*. There is widespread agreement amongst researchers that attitudes relating to various areas of social controversy (religion, politics, art, sexual behavior, race, and so on) tend to be intercorrelated, forming a *general factor* in social attitudes. This major dimension has been variously called fascism, authoritarianism, dogmatism, and rigidity, but is probably best described as *conservatism*, a tendency to resist change (Wilson, 1970). The extreme or "ideal" conservative is characterized by the following attitude clusters: religious dogmatism, right-wing political orientation, intolerance of minority groups, insistence on strict rules and punishments, anti-hedonistic outlook (the tendency to regard pleasure as bad), preference for conventional art, clothing, and institutions, and opposition to scientific progress. The individual opposite in each of these groups of attitudes would be described as *liberal*. See *Authoritarian personality*.

Eysenck (1954) has shown that, particularly in the field of political attitudes, it is also useful to study variation along a second, independent dimension which he called *toughmindedness-tendermindedness*. The toughminded individual is characterized by attitudes that are realistic, worldly, and aggressive (and tends to be an extraverted personality type), while the tenderminded individual has attitudes which are idealistic, moral, and submissive (and tends to be introverted). See *Traits; Type*.

3. *Functions*. McGuire (1969) discusses four types of adaptive functions which might be served by holding certain attitudes. These are not regarded as either mutually exclusive or exhaustive.

(*a*) *Utilitarian functions*—Attitudes may dispose us toward objects and paths that are instrumental in achieving valued goals, e.g. adopting the attitude of a group in order to gain acceptance within that group.

(*b*) *Economy functions*—Like all categories and generalizations, attitudes provide a simplification of the complex world and give guidance as to appropriate behavior in a new situation, e.g. holding a "stereotyped" image of a natural group enables one to treat all members of that group alike.

(*c*) *Expressive functions*—Attitudes may have self-assertive and cathartic functions, and may be adopted to bolster or justify one's behavior. The theory of *cognitive dissonance* (Festinger, 1957) draws attention to the fact that a change in attitude often follows rather than precedes a change in behavior, apparently serving a supportive function.

(*d*) *Ego-defense functions*—Some attitudes may be held not because of any characteristics of the object in question, but because they help to resolve certain inner conflicts, cf. the notion that anti-Semitism originates as a defense mechanism to facilitate the repression of oedipal hostility toward an authoritarian father (Adorno *et al.*, 1950).

McGuire notes that attitudes may be extremely resistant to change because they serve several or all of these functions at once. For example, a racial prejudice originating for ego-defensive reasons would soon be bolstered by a network of supportive attitudes and become a preferred way for the individual to assert himself and give meaning to his world. It would be a basis of selecting friends and would thus have utility as a means of remaining acceptable to the group. The difficulty in changing such an attitude is apparent.

4. *Attitude change*. In discussing the history of the attitude concept, McGuire (1969) notes that in the early part of this century it was so central to social psychology that it was often equated with it. After passing through an era in the 1950s when it was overshadowed by studies of group dynamics, the attitude concept has regained its dominant status within social psychology, and this has been largely through the work of Hovland, Festinger, Sherif, and others, on the variables and processes involved in attitude change. While it would be impossible to summarize the findings in this vast field here, it may be worthwhile to list some examples of fairly well-established findings.

(*a*) The extent to which a communication is effective in changing attitudes depends upon the perceived *credibility* of the source (e.g. the prestige of the communicator).

(*b*) Certain *personality* characteristics, e.g. low self-esteem and general passivity, dispose an individual toward high persuasibility.

(*c*) There are advantages in having both the first say (*primacy*) and the last say (*recency*) in persuading an audience. These variables have relevance to the fair conduct of political debates and trial by jury.

(*d*) Attitudes which are close to those already held by the audience are likely to be *assimilated*, while those which are very far removed are likely to result in a reaction away from the communicator (*contrast effect*).

(*e*) Communications which present *both sides* of an argument while favoring one, are more effective than one-sided communications.

(*f*) Presenting and dismissing the opposite side of an argument ("*inoculation*") results in a greater resistance against later counter-communications.

(*g*) Establishing conditions favorable to *cooperation toward common goals* is an effective means of reducing intergroup hostility (the "common enemy" approach).

Bibliography: Adorno, T. W., Frenkel-Brunswik, E., Levinson, D. J. & Sanford, R. N.: The authoritarian personality. New York, 1950. **Cook, S. W. & Selltiz, C.:** A multiple-indicator approach to attitude measurement. Psychol. Bull., 1964, *62*, 36–55. **Eysenck, H. J.:** The psychology of politics. London, 1954. **Festinger, L.:** A theory of cognitive dissonance. Stanford, 1957. **Hess, E. H.:** Attitude and pupil size. Sci. Amer. 1965, *212*, 46–54. **McGuire, W. J.:** The nature of attitudes and attitude research. In: **Lindzey, G. & Aronson, E.** (Eds): Handbook of social psychology 2nd ed. Vol. 3. London, 1969. **Osgood, C. E., Suci, G. J. & Tannenbaum, P. H.:** The measurement of meaning. Urbana, Illinois, 1957. **Rokeach, M.:** The open and closed mind. New York, 1960. **Scott, W. A.:** Attitude measurement. In: **Lindzey, G. & Aronson, E.** (Eds.): Handbook of social psychology, 2nd ed., Vol. 2, London, 1969. **Sherif, C. W., Sherif, M. & Nebergall, R. E.:** Attitude and attitude change. Philadelphia, 1965. **Wilson, G. D.:** Is there a general factor in social attitudes? Evidence from a factor-analysis of the Conservatism Scale. Brit. J. Soc. Clin. Psychol., 1970. **Wilson, G. D. & Patterson, J. R.:** A new measure of conservatism. Brit. J. Soc. Clin. Psychol., 1968, *7*, 264–9.

G. D. Wilson

Attitude change. A process in which an attitude (or an opinion, a judgment, etc.) is changed (see *Attitude*).

From a socio-psychological viewpoint, an attitude is a dependent variable of a process of social influence. The independent variables conditioning it are elements of a communication process: source variables, message variables, channel variables, receiver variables and destination variables. The more adequately these variables, and in particular their general mode of operation as well as their significance for a specific situation, are known, the easier it is to predict the direction and degree of a change of attitude.

Attitude change as a dependent quantity is regarded as a stochastic process in which the individual (the recipient) has to pass in turn through the stages of attention, comprehension, yielding, retention, and action, if the communication process is to effect a change in attitude.

In order to forecast and explain changes of attitude (and also changes of opinion and judgment), a series of models (attitude change theories) has been produced. Among these, consistency models regard such changes as subserving the restoration of a state of equilibrium (the principle of homeostasis) (see *Dissonance, cognitive*). There are also models with a greater psychophysical orientation, and "functional" models which stress the role of needs. See *Communication*.

Bibliography: Insko, C. A.: Theories of attitude change. New York, 1967. **Rosenberg, M. J. & Hovland, C. J.:** Attitude organization and change. New Haven, Conn., 1960. *H.D.S.*

Attitude types. According to Jung's classification these are *introverts* and *extraverts*, and determine *function types* (q.v.). Introversion (q.v.) and extraversion (q.v.) indicate the nature of the probable reaction, of "expectation", and "direction" or "orientation". See *Type*.

Bibliography: Jung, C. G.: Psychologische Typen. Zürich, [9]1960. (Eng. tran.: Psychological types. In: Contributions to analytical psychology. London, 1928. But see: Collected works, Vol. 6, in preparation). *W.K.*

Attributes. 1. Any quality, property, character (usually elementary) of a subject or his behavior, or of a spiritual or material substance, that is deemed indispensable to the nature and therefore to any conception of the phenomenon in question. **2.** That which is predicated of the subject of a proposition. **3.** An invariant (discriminatory) response. **4.** Sometimes used loosely for *traits* (q.v.). In general, a term more appropriate to metaphysics than to exact psychology. *J.G.*

Atypical. A marked deviation from the typical, e.g. in an individual differing from the social or group norm, or in a test-score.

Aubert-Förster phenomenon. At the same visual angle, objects that are nearer (e.g. letters) are recognized more easily than those that are more distant. The objects that are nearer take up a larger area of the retina. *V.M.*

Aubert phenomenon. When an illuminated vertical line has been fixated in a dark room for some time, if the head is tilted to one side one has the impression that the line is displaced in the direction opposite to the tilting. The center of equilibrium alone is insufficient for full spatial orientation. *V.M.*

Audile (syn. *Auditive type; Auditory type*). A type whose ideas are affected by auditory stimulation, by the passing of time, and by movements. T. Kiefer in particular distinguishes between the visual and audile imagery types.

Bibliography: Kiefer, T.: Der visuelle Mensch. Munich & Basle, 1956. *W.K.*

Audiogram. The result of an audiometric investigation (see *Audiometry*), it represents the loss of auditory sensitivity as the function of amplitude of a just perceptible sound. The unit of measurement is given in dB. *M.B.*

Audiology. The theory of testing and investigating auditory acuity in order to diagnose and treat hearing disorders. The most important area of examination is *audiometry* (q.v.). In testing hearing the patient's own impressions of his auditory acuity (problem of *simulation*, q.v., child audiometry) are usually necessary; therefore an audiological examination or experiment can suffer from the usual sources of error that beset all psychological experimentation (fatigue, monotony, background noises, and so on). Problems also arise in regard to the subject's tonal adaptation and sensitization. *M.B.*

Audiometer. A device for determining auditory acuity. The acumeter (Politizer's version) is an instrument producing a noise of constant intensity. The distance at which the noise can just be heard is taken as the auditory threshold. The basic audiometer is a device generating sounds of different frequencies (discrete or continuous); the tones can also be varied in intensity (discretely in 5 dB stages, or continuously). The amplifier is graduated in dB, and is fitted with earphones and usually has a loudspeaker too. There are various other forms of noise generator (e.g. for above-threshold audiometry). *M.B.*

Audiometry. The measurement of auditory acuity by means of electro-acoustic noise generators (see *Audiometer*). The result of an audiometric investigation is usually recorded as an audiogram (q.v.). In addition to basic audiometry (diagnosis of disorders of the outer and inner ears, and combined disturbances), audiometry is also concerned with above-threshold audiometry (the differential diagnosis of the impairment of auditory acuity of the inner ear); speech audiometry (suitability of hearing aids; counting and word-recognition tests, etc.). There are various other divisions, ranging from child audiometry to objective audiometry (psycho-galvanic skin reaction, etc.). *M.B.*

Audio-visual aids. Means of presenting information during instruction, which is directed to the eye and ear. This definition would cover wall-charts and maps as well as the more modern media, such as slides, loops, films, gramophone records, tapes, radio, and television. Audio-visual aids are intended to make the material of the lesson more "actual", and clearly apprehensible, and to stimulate the pupil's attention and motivation. In programmed instruction (see *Instructional technology*), and particularly in machine learning (q.v.), audio-visual techniques are no longer mere aids but integral components of the instructional process.

Bibliography: Lumsdaine, A. A. & Glaser, R.: Teaching machines and programmed learning. Vol. I. Washington, 1962. The following journals, among others, provide information on a fast-moving field: Programmed Learning and Educational Technology (U.K.); Audio-Visual Communication Review (U.S.A.). *H.I.*

Audition colorée. See *Colored hearing.*

Auditory acuity. See *Auditory perception.*

Auditory ossicles (syn. *Ossicular chain*). The three bones (hammer, anvil and stirrup) of the middle ear. Part of the mechanical transmission system between the external auditory canal and the cochlea of the inner ear, the ossicles increase the force but reduce the amplitude of the transmitted vibration (adaptation of 26 dB). The hammer (manubrium and malleus), which is connected to the drum, transmits the mechanical vibrations by way of the anvil (incus) and the stirrup (stapes) to the oval window of the cochlea. *M.S.*

Auditory perception. The decoding by the central nervous system of certain stimuli processed physiologically by the sense of hearing. As in all the sensory modalities, a distinction must be made between *perception* and *sensation.* Auditory perception is far more complex than auditory sensation, since it leads to the identification (recognition) of composite sound stimuli (sound patterns) or elements. Auditory sensation is brought about by the stimulation of specific elements in the ear, and is the elementary form of nervous response to sound stimuli. *Sound* is the adequate stimulus. The objective, physical parameters for sound are *frequency* (audible range from about 16 to 22,000 c/s) and *amplitude*. In the case of frequencies under 16 c/s, one speaks of *infrasonic* waves (which produce vibratory or "fluttering" sensations); in the case of frequencies over 30,000 c/s, of *ultrasonic* waves. *Pitch* is closely related to frequency but may vary with intensity. *Intensity* (known as *loudness* in subjective terms) depends on the amplitude of the oscillations, which are measured in phons or decibels (dB). Auditory sensitivity varies with frequency. It is greatest (lowest absolute auditory threshold; threshold of audibility) in the middle frequency range (1000 to 3000 c/s). The sensitivity of hearing is good in regard to variations in intensity and frequency (see *Sense organs*). The measurement of auditory thresholds and the determination of hearing defects are the functions of *audiometry* (q.v.).

See *Sense organs: the ear* for detailed information on sound; the reception of stimuli (external ear to ear drum); mechanical amplification by the middle ear; transformation into nervous impulses in the cochlea; sensitivity to frequencies; measurement of loudness, and adaptation; auditory range and localization; and estimation of the distance of a sound source.

1. *Auditory perception* is very complex and depends on many factors; it allows the following possibilities: specific judgments of sound sensations; determination of the spatial location of sound sources; separation of several different simultaneous sound stimuli (a specific type of sound can be recognized accurately in the presence of other sounds); and comprehension of language and all the precise distinctions of intonation (we recognize an individual by his speech). Finally, auditory perception has many important functions in speech. Auditory perception relies on a series of operations in the higher centers of the central nervous system (q.v.), starting from information received (sensations); it is essentially based on the availability of all previous experience (mnemic traces stored in the memory); on conditioning, on associations, and on (for the most part) unconscious cognitive and affective operations (music).

2. *The subjective characteristics of sound* (auditory phenomena). Depending on its individual nature, sound may be perceived as pleasant, neutral or unpleasant. The "auditory area" consists of more than 300,000 distinguishable qualities; this allows perception of the most finely-nuanced language and music. The subjective qualities of auditory perception are either directly dependent on frequency, e.g. "light" (high frequencies) and "dark" sounds (low frequencies), or they are produced by physically defined sound qualities. A distinction may be made between:

(*a*) *Tone*, consisting of sound made up of harmonic partial vibrations (oscillations).

(*b*) *Noise*, stimulated by mixed vibrations (partial vibrations associated in an irregular frequency ratio).

(*c*) *Surface noise*, a persistent, monotonous sound free from fluctuations in intensity.

(*d*) *Excessive noise*, defined by the subjective characteristic of excessive loudness.

(*e*) *Timbre*, the characteristic quality which enables us to distinguish between different (musical) tones which have the same fundamental frequency (or pure tone) but a different "spectral" composition (overtones). It is dependent on the relative intensity of the overtones contained in its "spectrum", or group of frequencies. The tone impression can be analyzed by frequency analyzers (spectrum analyzers), spectrometers or resonators.

3. *Space orientation*. Auditory perception plays a major part in spatial orientation,

which is based on the synergic operation, or coordination, of several senses. Hearing provides information on distant, intangible, inaccessible and invisible objects. Estimation of the distance of a sound source and directional hearing are important here (see *Sense organs: the ear*). Acoustic estimation of distance is highly accurate up to a distance of about one meter. The assumption that the distance of the sound source could be determined by the pressure difference between the two ears was refuted by von Békésy. In reality several factors are involved: one factor is loudness (the louder sound is heard as the nearer one); a second, the frequency spectrum. It is possible to estimate the distance of noise and speech more accurately than that of pure tones.

The absolute auditory directional threshold is estimated at about 3°, but is in reality 8–12°; the direction of relatively complex sound sources can be determined quite adequately. The very old (and initially very vague) assumption that the direction of a sound source could be determined from the difference in *acoustic pressure* (since the head acts as an obstacle to sound) has been precisely investigated in recent years (Trendelenburg, 1950) and is taken into account in telecommunications engineering and stereophony. Von Hornbostel's and Wertheimer's temporal theory of acoustic localization is based on the measurable retardation of sound impinging on the ear facing away from the sound source (localization to right and left of the median plane) (see *Differential running time*). Recent experimental research based on "trade" tests and ablation experiments has proved that both theories are justified; temporal difference comparison is primarily effective up to a sound level of 60 dB, while the comparison of intensity gives optimal results in the high frequency and intensity range. The phase difference between the two ears allows directional hearing at low and middle frequencies (up to about 1000 c/s), whereas intensity difference comes into play at higher frequencies. The difference in arrival time at the two ears is also important (e.g. in the case of loud reports).

Bibliography: Békésy, G. von: Experiments in hearing. New York, 1960. **Chocholle, R.:** Das Qualitätssystem des Gehörs. In: **Metzger, W.** (Ed.): Handbuch der Psychologie, Vol. 1. Göttingen, 1966. **Davis, H.** Psychophysiology of hearing and deafness. In: **Stevens, S. S.** (Ed.): Handbook of experimental psychology. New York, 1951. **Hirsh, I. J.:** The measurement of hearing. New York, 1952. **Ranke, O. F. & Lullies, H.:** Gehör, Stimme, Sprache. Lehrbuch der Physiologie in zusammenhängenden Einzeldarstellungen. Berlin, 1953. **Stevens, S. S., & Davis, H.:** Hearing; its psychology and physiology. New York, 1938. **Stevens, S. S.:** Handbook of experimental psychology. New York, 1951. **Trendelenburg, F.:** Akustik. Berlin, [2]1950. **Wever, E. G.:** The theory of hearing. New York, 1949. **Zwicker, E. & Feldkeller, R.:** Das Ohr als Nachrichtenempfänger, Stuttgart, [2]1967.

R. Chocholle

Auditory type. See *Audile.*

Aura. Kind of halo believed by spiritualists (see *Spiritualism*) to envelop the human body and to be visible to a suitably trained sensitive (q.v.) who may infer from its coloration facts about the mental state of the person. Sometimes used of normal field-forces of an electromagnetic nature surrounding the body. *J.B.*

Aura, epileptic. A direct premonition of the convulsive attack occurring in approximately half of all epileptics. It is variously constituted, and can be emotional (anxiety, happiness); proportional (e.g. altered color sense, illusions of sense); occur in thinking (e.g. rapidity, retardation, compulsive thinking, confusion); or as sweating, cold, warmth, flushing, and so on. An aura is seldom experienced without a subsequent attack.

C.S.

Ausdruck. See *Expression.*

Austrian school. A school of psychology founded by F. Brentano (q.v.) at the end of the nineteenth century. In contrast to W. Wundt (q.v.), Brentano conceived of psychology as concerned not with psychic *contents*, but with psychic *acts* (see *Act psychology*). The representatives of the Graz School are considered to belong to this group of psychologists. The most important are C. von Ehrenfels (q.v.), the precursor of gestalt psychology (see *Ganzheit*), A. Meinong (q.v.) and his pupils S. Witasek (1870–1915) and V. Benussi (1878–1927). In a broader sense, the Austrian school also includes C. Stumpf (q.v.), T. Lipps (q.v.), H. Cornelius (1893–1947), and E. Mach (q.v.), O. Külpe (q.v.), and A. Messer (1867–1937).

Bibliography: Boring, E. G.: A history of experimental psychology. New York, [2]1957. **Pongratz, L.:** Problemgeschichte der Psychologie. Berne, 1967. *F.M.*

Authoritarianism (syn. *Authoritarian attitude*). A collective term for various antidemocratic and potentially fascist social attitudes, which are seen as constituting one of the main components of the authoritarian personality (q.v.).

Authoritarian attitudes are commonly characterized by: (*a*) *conventionalism* (q.v.): ossified or rigid attachment to traditional middle-class norms and values; (*b*) *authoritarian submission:* a submissive and uncritical attitude to the idealistically viewed moral authorities of one's own reference group; (*c*) *authoritarian aggression:* the tendency to look out for, despise, condemn, penalize and punish those who offend against traditional and conventional values; (*d*) rejection of more individual and personal inventive or creative attitudes, and of "soft-hearted" and "subjective, psychological, human approaches to personal and social problems" (*anti-intraception*); (*e*) *superstitious and stereotyped behavior:* belief in mystical powers determining individual human destiny, and the disposition to think in rigid categories; (*f*) a preference for positions of *power*, and "toughness": a preoccupation with dimensions such as dominance-submission, strong-weak, leader-followers; identification with those in positions of power, excessive emphasis on one's own power, strength and toughness; (*g*) *destructiveness and cynicism:* a generalized hostility and readiness to vilify other men and the human; (*h*) *projectivity;* the projection of unconscious emotional impulses on the environment; (*i*) an exaggerated concern with *sexual* "goings-on" in society. (See *Attitude.*)

Adorno *et al.* developed the F scale, or fascism scale, which consists basically of the above variables, and is still used (in the modified form resulting from various methodological critiques—e.g. Christie & Jahoda, 1954) to measure fascistic tendencies.

Bibliography: Adorno, T. W., *et al.*: The authoritarian personality. New York, 1950. **Christie, R. & Jahoda, M.** (Eds): Studies in the scope and method of "The authoritarian personality". New York, 1954.

A.S.-M.

Authoritarian personality (syn. *Antidemocratic personality*). Numerous characteristics form a syndrome or major pattern in certain individuals whose personalities might be defined as "potentially fascist" according to the research carried out by Adorno *et al.* (1950) using attitude scales, interviews and projective techniques. The authors also distinguish typical variations within the pattern (critique by Pettigrew, 1958).

The most important characteristics of the authoritarian mentality are: (*a*) *anti-Semitism* as a stereotype composed of negative attitudes to Jews, who are viewed as personally offensive, socially threatening, too assimilative, too seclusive, too intrusive, and generally "other than" non-Jews; (*b*) *ethnocentrism* (q.v.), in the sense of a stereotyped, relatively consistent attitude of rejection of alien groups (non-Jewish foreigners or strangers, those of different skin pigmentation, culturally unlike societies) to whom the individual in question may in fact be positively disposed rather than hostile; (*c*) *fascism* (q.v.) (or authoritarianism); (*d*) politically economic *conservatism*, i.e. right-wing conservative ideas regarding the value of property and possessions (both one's own and in general), money and work; a positive attitude toward social inequality arising from economic competition—a supposed relation between efficiency/worthiness and riches.

In addition to the distinction between social attitudes characteristic of the authoritarian and non-authoritarian types, the authors describe differing cognitive styles. Authoritarians are classed as cognitively more rigid and intolerant in regard to equivocal situations (intolerance of ambiguity) than are non-authoritarians.

A relation is also postulated between characteristics of the authoritarian personality and specific experiences in early childhood and the parental home situation, and an attempt is made to explain this by recourse to the psychoanalytic model.

Bibliography: Adorno, T. W., Frenkel-Brunswik, E., Levinson, D. J. & Sanford, R. N.: The authoritarian personality. New York, 1950. **Christie, R. & Jahoda, M.** (Eds.): Studies in the scope and method of "The authoritarian personality". New York, 1954. **Pettigrew, T. F.:** Personality and sociocultural factors in intergroup attitudes: A cross-national comparison. T. confl. Resol., 1958, *2*, 29–42. *A.S.-M.*

Authority. A person's status in a relationship between two or more individuals, which allows him to influence and to dominate the opinions, judgments, valuations and decisions of the other or others in this relationship or group. (See *Group dynamics*.)

Individuals are granted authority formally or informally by reason of their group role (e.g. a teacher in the classroom, a father in a family, an officer, and so on), or because of their expertise in some group-relevant field (e.g. specialist knowledge, superior general education, or special physical aptitudes). Such persons are granted, or tacitly acknowledged as having, authority, inasmuch as they signify the possibility of satisfying, or manifest the ability to satisfy, the needs of the other group members. Authority is usually bound up with the social power of the individual.

Adams & Romney (1959) have attempted a model analysis of the relationship and behavior apparent between those who are invested with authority and those who acknowledge it in them.

Bibliography: Adams, J. S. & Romney, A. K.: A functional analysis of authority. Psychol. Rev., 1959, *66*, 234–51. **Homans, G. C.:** Social behavior: Its elementary forms. New York, 1961. *A.S.-M.*

Autism. 1. *History*. Much confusion and misunderstanding surround the word "autism". In lay language autism (from the Greek *autos*, self) implies preoccupation with one's thoughts and daydreams. The superficial relationship between this usage and autism as used in such expressions as "infantile autism", and "the autistic child", is highly misleading. The term "autism" was applied by Leo Kanner in 1944 to a very rare and unique type of childhood psychosis, first described by him in a classic paper published a year earlier. A striking characteristic of the children with "Kanner's syndrome" was their pensive, totally absorbed facial expression, which resembled that of a normal person who was daydreaming or "lost in thought". For this reason, and because it was difficult to attract the attention of, or communicate with, these children, Kanner entitled his second paper "Early Infantile Autism". As a result of uncritical thinking, Kanner's loose analogy with adult autism has been misconstrued; therefore it is unfortunately widely believed that infantile autism involves a more or less voluntary rejection of the real world in favor of fantasy. Needless to say, such an interpretation is unwarranted. Kanner has insisted that infantile autism is "inborn", and has repudiated the idea that it is caused by faulty child rearing. Others, notably Bettelheim, insist that autism is psychologically caused.

2. *Specificity*. Further confusion results from the widespread use of the term "autistic" to refer to almost any young child with a profound behavior disorder who shows some of the symptoms of Kanner's syndrome. Kanner has stated that only ten per cent of

children diagnosed by others as autistic proved to be true cases when seen by him. The writer's experience confirms this: of the nearly 1,800 cases of severely disordered children for whom I have collected detailed diagnostic information, only about 150 show the striking configuration of symptoms described by Kanner. My data also confirm Kanner's complaint that the diagnosis of autism has been applied indiscriminately to children who resemble the true autistic only superficially. Of 346 psychotic children in my files whose case histories contain at least two diagnoses, 169 had autistic listed as the first diagnosis, and 107 had autistic as the second diagnosis. Of these children, only 43 were diagnosed as autistic on both occasions, the remaining "autistic" children being reclassified as schizophrenic, retarded, emotionally disturbed, brain damaged, and so on.

3. *Incidence.* Studies by Lotter in England and by Treffert in the USA have established an incidence of about four psychotic children per 10,000 births. Since true autism seems to represent about ten per cent of children loosely called autistic, about one child in 25,000 would be a realistic estimated incidence of classical autism.

4. *Description.* The onset of classical autism is usually at birth (or before), although a few cases appear normal till the thirtieth month. In no case is the onset later than thirty-six months.

The child with infantile autism is usually attractive and well-proportioned, and is often described as having the appearance of high intelligence. Unless the mother is experienced she will not realize her infant is abnormally unresponsive and fails to adapt himself to her body when held. Most parents report early concern that the child may be deaf, but the child's intense interest in music, and often his extraordinary ability to reproduce it by singing or humming, belies deafness. Sudden onset of walking, with little prior crawling, is common. About half of autistic children never develop speech—these are the children who tended to be quiet and passive infants. Those autistics who later develop speech tend to be very alert and sensitive, though not socially responsive, as infants. When speech occurs it is of an unusual sort and is not used for communication. The child merely repeats what he has heard. The voice is puppet-like, and has a hollow, monotonic quality. The words "Yes" and "I" are not used until the child is seven or eight years old. "Yes" is expressed by repeating the question, and "I" is expressed by saying "You". Kanner has termed these speech characteristics "affirmation by repetition" and "pronominal reversal". He has also identified and named several other unique speech patterns.

Two of the most significant symptoms are "autistic aloneness"—the child is socially inaccessible or (apparently) self-isolated; and what Kanner has termed "obsessive insistence on the preservation of sameness". The latter refers to the child's extreme agitation when his physical environment is changed—the arrangement of furniture or playthings, position of window blinds, route taken to grandmother's house, utensils or containers used in feeding, and so on. Strong eccentricities in feeding are common, such as drinking only milk, or no milk, or refusing foods that require chewing. Excellent finger dexterity is common, and is often manifested by spinning small objects. Autistic children are very agile and graceful, and are skilful climbers. They rarely fall or hurt themselves accidentally, although insensitivity to pain is common. They are fascinated by mechanical objects or appliances, in contrast to their antipathy toward humans or pets. Idiot savant abilities in arithmetic, memory, music, calendar skills, and sometimes art, are common among true cases of autism.

5. *Prognosis* has been closely tied to speaking ability. Those who have some meaningful speech by age 5½ have a fifty per cent likelihood of at least partial recovery. Prognosis has been very poor for the mute children, but recent biochemical discoveries may change this picture. Among the few

cases who have recovered spontaneously are several gifted composers and mathematicians.

6. *Causation*. Cause is unknown. Kanner's original report that parents of true autistic children showed unusual drive and intelligence were at first discounted, but later reports by Rimland, Lotter, and Treffert, in which Kanner's diagnostic criteria were heeded, have confirmed his finding. Rimland regards autism as a crippling genetic deviation from high intelligence. Recent blood serotonin studies of accurately diagnosed cases of autism have revealed a serious metabolic defect. Further research promises to remove much of the mystery surrounding classical autism.

Bibliography: Bettelheim, B.: The empty fortress. New York, 1967. **Boullin, D. J., Coleman, Mary & O'Brien, R. A.:** Abnormalities in platelet 5-hydroxytryptamine efflux in patients with infantile autism. Nature, 1970, *226*, 371–2. **Eisenberg, L.:** The autistic child in adolescence. Amer. J. Psychiat., 1956, *112*, 606–12. **Kanner, L.:** Autistic disturbances of affective contact. Nerv. Child, 1943, *2*, 217–50. **Id.:** Early infantile autism. J. Pediat., 1944, *25*, 211–17. **Id.:** The specificity of early infantile autism. Ztschr. f. Kinderpsychiat., 1958, *25*, 108–13. **Kanner, L. & Lesser, L. I.:** Early infantile autism. Pediat. Clinics N. Amer., 1958, *5*, 711–30. **Lotter, V.:** Epidemiology of autistic conditions in young children. II: Some characteristics of the parents and children. Soc. Psychiat., 1967, *1*, 163–73. **Rimland, B.:** Infantile autism: The syndrome and its implications for a neural theory of behavior. New York, 1964. **Id.:** On the objective diagnosis of infantile autism. Acta Paedopsychiat., 1968, *35*, 146–61. **Treffert, D. A.:** The epidemiology of infantile autism. Arch. of Gen. Psychiat., 1970, *25*, 431–8.

J. Rimland

Autobiography. A special version of the biographical method (q.v.) in personality research. The autobiographer is both observer and the subject-matter of the observation.

G.K.

Autochthonous action. The precursor of displacement activity or, more generally, an action originating within the individual, as opposed to allochthonous actions, or instinctive movements activated by an external source.

Bibliography: Kortlandt, A.: Wechselwirkung zwischen Instinkten. Arch. Neerl. Zool., 1940, 10, Suppl. 2, 64–78.

K.F.

Autochthonous dynamics. See *Allochthonous dynamics*.

Autochthonous ideas. A term which refers to ideas which occur independently of the prevailing stream of thought. They are experienced by the subject as being foreign to his normal mode of thinking. This is an obscure term which may include such diverse phenomena as obsessional thinking, the experience of thought insertion and primary delusions. It is of little descriptive value.

R.H.

Autoeroticism. Sexual activity directed to one's own self or one's own body. Sometimes used as synonym for masturbation (q.v.). See also *Narcissism*.

Autogenic training. A technique developed by the Berlin nerve specialist J. H. Schultz on the basis of experience with hypnosis; it is applicable in individual and group therapy. It is essentially a form of self-hypnosis. Exercises induce a hypnotic state and a form of relaxation. The basic stage consists of six individual exercises: experience of weight (muscular decontraction); experience of warmth (decontraction of tissues); heart exercise; breathing exercise; control of abdominal area; adjustment of head (feeling of frontal coolness). Some meditative and contemplative processes are connected with the technique, which should be acquired only under medical supervision. In addition to therapeutic possibilities in the case of functional irregularities of organs, etc., the technique can prove extremely invigorating, intellectually and physically, in healthy subjects.

Bibliography: Schultz, J. H.: Das autogene Training. Stuttgart, [13]1970.

H.N.G.

Autohypnosis. A hypnosis (q.v.) induced by autosuggesion, in contradistinction to hetero-hyponosis, which is induced by another person. Although autohypnosis is induced by the subject himself, it depends on certain conditions such as repeated, simple optical, acoustic, or sensory stimuli.

Self-hypnotic practices are age-old (yoga techniques). One of the best-known auto-hypnotic techniques used today in medical therapy (in certain countries) is autogenic training (q.v.). *H.N.G.*

Autokinetic effect (syn. *Autokinetic illusion; Autokinetic phenomenon*). If one watches a fixed point of light in a dark room, the point eventually appears to move. After some time the eye musculature becomes tired and causes a slight eye movement. Although the movement is compensated, because of the darkness, the perception-processing system has no points by which it can judge to what extent the movement on the retina (q.v.) is caused by the movement of the eye. The experiment has been used in social psychology to determine suggestibility. *V.M.*

Automata theory. The theory of automata is concerned with the classes and principles of possible abstract automata. Applications are the mathematical construction of cybernetic systems and, e.g., teaching and learning systems. *K.-D.G.*

Automatic writing. A psychological phenomenon in which a person's hand writes spontaneously and produces meaningful sentences, but without that person being consciously aware of what is being written. Usually associated with mediumship (q.v.). *J.B.*

Automation in education. The use of modern technology to solve the various problems of mass instruction of students of varying ability, the planning of curricula and timetables, and even the use of mass media (especially radio and television) in the classroom. See *Instructional technology; Learning; Machine learning*.

Automatism. Locomotor movements are not the result of chain reflexes but of rhythmic, automatic activation. The fins of a fish manifest distinctive rhythms; if one dominates, the result is superposition. The most stable is absolute coordination 1:1. In relative coordination the phasic relations vary. *K.F.*

Automatisms. In psychology and psychiatry, "automatisms" are actions performed without conscious control. Most catatonic symptoms (see *Catatonia*) may be described as automatisms. Compulsive acts also usually take this form. *R.Hä.*

Automatist. Person, usually a medium (q.v.), who produces automatic writing (q.v.). *J.B.*

Automatization. Process of developing an activity or behavior until it is performed wholly or virtually without conscious control. An automatized activity usually takes place uniformly. *H.-J.A.*

Automatograph. An instrument for measurement of involuntary (e.g. arm) movements, which records the process graphically.

Automaton, abstract. Mathematical models of learning, and, more generally, the relation between the organism and the environment, can be represented in terms of automata theory. The environment and organism may be viewed as abstract automata which exist in interaction. As a mathematical system, an abstract automaton requires no concrete form. *K.O.G.*

Autonomic balance. The postulated balance between the antagonistic functions of the sympathetic (adrenergic) and parasympathetic (cholinergic) nervous systems. M. A. Wenger (1941, 1942, 1948, 1957) extracted a factor which he termed "autonomic imbalance", and which could be phasic or chronic, or obtain for either system: "Autonomic imbalance, when measured in an unselected population, will be distributed continuously about a central tendency . . . autonomic balance." Other authors have disagreed, reporting reliable patterns of autonomic activation. Lacey (1958) termed this autonomic response specificity, "autonomic response-stereotypy": "For a given set of autonomic functions, Ss tend to respond with an idiosyncratic pattern of autonomous activation in which maximal activation is shown, whatever the stress."

Bibliography: Eysenck, H. J.: The biological basis of personality. London & Springfield, 1967. **Lacey, J. I. & Lacey, B. C.:** Verification and extension of the principle of autonomic response-stereotypy. Amer. J. Psychol., 1958, *71*, 50–73. **Wenger, M. A.:** Pattern analysis of autonomic variables during rest. Psychosom. Med., 1957, *19*, 240–244. *D.B.*

Autonomic nervous system (Abb. ANS). Also known as the *vegetative*, or *visceral*, *nervous system*, the ANS consists of all nerve fibers of the central nervous system (CNS) and peripheral nervous system (PNS) mediating involuntary functions. Its activation is mainly unconscious. Its preganglionic (sympathetic and parasympathetic) fibers are myelinated, whereas its postganglionic fibers (extending from sympathetic ganglia) are not myelinated. These fibers convey impulses slowly at speeds of 5 to app. 20 m/sec. The ANS controls and coordinates the functions of all internal organs, such as the heart, lungs, blood vessels, stomach, intestine, gallbladder, urogenital system, and glands. Through innervation of all smooth muscle fibers and the internal sense organs known as enteroceptors, the ANS plays an important role in the transmission of information for the regulation of blood pressure (q.v.), heart activity, breathing, water balance, blood sugar, and so on. It is divided into the *sympathetic* (thoraciolumbar division) with an ergotrophic function in stimulating physical activity, and a *parasympathetic* (cranial-sacral division) with a tropotrophic activity for refreshment, alimentation, and elimination of waste. The vagus (or tenth cranial nerve) belongs to the parasympathetic. *E.D.*

Autonomy, functional. According to Allport's principle of functional autonomy, means originally used to attain to a specific end continue to be used even when the original goal has long since been reached: i.e. motives can become independent of their origins: e.g. capital is acquired for its own sake rather than for the life-enhancing things it once provided.

Bibliography: Allport, G. W.: Personality. New York, 1937. *R.Hä.*

Autosuggestion. Self-suggestion through the largely unconscious, but also conscious, influence of one's own ideas and judgments (*Heterosuggestion* is suggestion by others). A frequent phenomenon in that emotional expectations, wishes and fears can condition certain views, convictions and attitudes. When used as a conscious method, autosuggestion can, within certain limits, help to control affectivity. E. Coué demonstrated an autosuggestive method of strengthening the unconscious will in order to lead the patient to health and a sense of well-being (see *Couéism*). See also *Autogenic training*. *H.N.G.*

Auxiliary ego. In psychodrama (q.v.), a participant who assists or substitutes for the "ego", i.e. the patient, whose conflicts are portrayed in dramatic form. In this way the sick person learns possible rational ways of mastering his conflicts, that he can put into practice later. Either the psychotherapist himself or a specially trained assistant enacts the part. *W.Sc.*

Average. A general term for the measure of the central tendency of a distribution (see *Frequency distribution*). But average usually refers to the arithmetic mean. *W.H.B.*

Average deviation. See *Deviation.*

Average error. An old measure of the variability (q.v.) of test data caused by error, and $= \pm 0{\cdot}6745$ of standard error. Sometimes called *probable error* (PE). See *Deviation.*

W.H.B.

Aversion therapy is one of the methods of behavior therapy (q.v.). The purpose of aversion therapy is to produce an association between an undesirable behavior pattern and unpleasant stimulation *or* to make the unpleasant stimulation a consequence of the undesirable behavior. In either case, it is hoped that an acquired connection between the behavior and the unpleasantness will develop. There is a further hope that the development of such a connection will be followed by a reduction of the target behavior. Ideally, the therapeutic program includes attempts to foster alternative, acceptable behavior. Aversion therapy is used predominantly for the treatment of those behavior disorders (e.g. alcoholism and sexual deviations) in which the patient's conduct is undesirable but nevertheless self-reinforcing. The appetitive characteristics of these disorders frequently involve the therapist in problems concerning the introduction of other, suitable forms of satisfying behavior. Sometimes it is not sufficient only to eliminate the unsuitable behavior: the therapist should attempt to foster alternate forms of behavior which are incompatible with the unacceptable behavior. A variety of unpleasant (aversive) stimuli have been employed in this form of treatment, but the most widely used are electrical or chemical forms of aversion.

In the electrical form of treatment, the therapist administers a mildly painful shock to the patient whenever the undesirable behavior, or its imaginal equivalent, is elicited. In the chemical method, the patient is given a nausea-producing drug (emetine or apomorphine), and is then exposed to the deviant stimulus, or required to carry out the deviant act when the drug produces its maximal effect. The chemical method has found its widest application in the treatment of alcoholism, and the electrical method is used predominantly in the treatment of sexual disorders. The advantages and disadvantages of these two techniques are discussed by Rachman (1965), who recommended the preferential use of electrical aversion on several grounds, including the fact that this method allows for increased control over the treatment situation, closer definition of the treatment process and increased theoretical clarity.

Aversion therapy is based on a conditioning paradigm, the basis of which is to be found in Pavlov's work (1927). The earliest clinical application of aversion therapy appears to have taken place in Russia some forty years ago. One of the earliest Western accounts of aversion therapy was provided in 1935 by Max, who described the treatment of a patient with a homosexual fixation by the administration of electrical shocks. During the late 'thirties and 'forties, however, chemical aversion therapy was widely employed—predominantly in treating alcoholics. The resurgence of interest in this form of therapy occurred as a result of the increasing interest in behavior therapy from 1950 onwards. During the past decade it has been adopted fairly widely in Britain, and to a lesser extent on the Continent and in the United States. In current practice the electrical form of treatment is more widely employed and the disorders which are most frequently chosen for this type of treatment are alcoholism and sexual disorders. Although there is now sufficient evidence to conclude that the treatment is an effective procedure (Rachman & Teasdale, 1969), it is also recognized that the technique requires refinement, and the underlying theory is only partially satisfactory.

The explanation of aversion therapy which is based on a classical conditioning model can still be used to encompass many of the phenomena encountered with this form of treatment. It has become increasingly clear, however, that the classical conditioning theory is limited, and that greater importance must be attached to the cognitive factors which are part of this or any other form of treatment. This theoretical development is paralleled by the exploration of a new form of aversion therapy based largely on cognitive manipulations. Covert sensitization, like aversion therapy proper, attempts to build up an association between an undesirable activity and an unpleasant effect. However, this treatment is carried out entirely at the imaginal level—the patient is required to imagine the deviant activity or stimulus and *then* to imagine some extremely undesirable consequence, such as nausea, shame, pain and so forth. Although research on this form of cognitive treatment is still at the rudimentary stage (Rachman & Teasdale, 1969) it coincides with, and indeed is part of, the shifting emphasis from a purely conditioning approach to a more sophisticated view of aversion therapy. It seems probable that aversion therapy, both practically and theoretically, will combine conditioning theory and cognitive variables.

Bibliography: Blake, B.: The application of behavior therapy to the treatment of alcoholism. Behav. Res. Ther., 1967, *5*, 78–85. **Cautela, J.:** Covert sensitization. Psychol. Reports, 1967, *20*, 459–68. **Eysenck, H. J. & Rachman, S.:** The causes and cures of neurosis. London, 1965. **Feldman, M. P.:** Aversion therapy for sexual disorders. Psychol. Bulletin, 1966, *65*, 65–79. **Lemere, G. & Voegtlin, W.:** An evaluation of the aversion treatment of alcoholism. Quart. J. Stud. Alcohol., 1950, *11*, 199–204. **Rachman, S. & Teasdale, J.:** Aversion therapy and the behavior disorders. London, 1969.

S. Rachman

Aviation psychology (syn. *Aeronautical psychology*). A branch of applied psychology (q.v.). Aviation psychologists investigate the special conditions to which human behavior is subjected in aviation; among their practical concerns are aspects of the selection and training of pilots, stewardesses, maintenance personnel, and so on, the avoidance of possible accidents, and the construction of adequate instruments and displays, etc. See also *Motor skills; Accident research; Stress.*

Bibliography: Aitken, R. C. B.: Prevalence of worry in normal aircrew. Brit. J. Med. Psychol., 1969, *42*, 283–6. **Cartellieri, D.:** Einführung in die Luftfahrtpsychologie. Schriftenreihe der HTS der deutschen Luftwaffe, 1965. **Gourney, A. B.:** Psychological measures in aircrew. Aerospace Med., 1970, *41*, 18–91. **Miller, R. B.** *et al.*; Survey of human engineering needs in maintenance of ground electronics equipment. Pittsburgh, 1954. **Sells, S. B. & Berry, C. A.** (Eds): Human factors in jet and space travel: a medical-psychological analysis. New York, 1961. **Whiteside, T. C. D.:** Problems of vision in flight at high altitude. London, 1957.

F.M.

Avitaminosis. A deficiency or complete absence of one or more vitamins, marked by specific symptoms. Beri-beri, for example, presents as inflammations of the motor nerves together with disturbed gait and movement, and cardiovascular disease; it is caused by a lack of vitamin B_1. Beri-beri is unknown among peoples with a mixed diet but is found in those with an exclusive diet of, e.g., polished rice. Scurvy is a vitamin C deficiency disease, and in the past occurred on sailing ships which were without fresh citrus fruit and green vegetables: a characteristic symptom was degeneration of the teeth and gums. Rickets is a disease of small children who lack adequate sunlight and therefore cannot convert the first stage of vitamin D into its active form, and who because of calcium deficiency develop irregular bone formation and softening. These and all other genuine avitaminoses can be prevented or cured by correcting dietary deficiencies or, in certain cases, by injecting special vitamin preparations. See *Vitimans.* *E.D.*

Avoidance-avoidance conflict. See *Approach-approach conflict; Conflict.*

Avoidance behavior (syn. *Aversive behavior*). Abient behavior, or withdrawal, liable to increase distance between the subject and a goal (a physical object, a social partner or a situation). Barriers on the way to the goal play a part in avoidance. The intensity of the avoidance behavior is a function of the distance to the goal (*avoidance gradient*). Avoidance can be a learned reaction to specific situations. It is also to a certain extent explicable as instinctive activity derivable from the "innate releasing mechanism". It is displayed in the motor phenomena of flight (escape) and defense, but is also interpreted as an inner ego-protective process (Freud), as an inner process for removal of possibly threatening cognitive patterns (Lazarus), of specially tabooed words, etc. (*perceptual defense*, subliminal perception), and for protection against painful and persistent stimulation (J. M. Sokolov). Avoidance in thinking and perception is usually known as *defense* or *defensive behavior*. The disposition to avoidance or defensive behavior differs from individual to individual and is mainly diagnosed by the use of *projective techniques* (q.v.). See *Gradient*.

Bibliography: Campbell, B. A. & Church, R. M. (Eds.): Punishment and aversive behavior. New York, 1969. **Lazarus, R. S.:** Psychological stress and the coping process. New York, 1966. *W.Sch.*

Avoidance gradient. See *Gradient*.

Avoidance reaction. See *Conditioning, classical and operant*.

Awareness (*Bewusstheit*). A concept used by N. Ach (Würzburg school). In his experiments Ach instructed the testees to perform some activity, e.g. adding, upon an agreed signal. Ss performed the action after the signal without consciously realizing the instruction. In this way, Ach showed that Ss were in a psychic state which he called "task-awareness", or "readiness". He defined several kinds of awareness in this sense, which was connected with the Würzburg school's theory of *Bewusstseinslagen*, or "conscious" attitudes, which could not be separated into sensory or imaginal contents.

Bibliography: Humphrey, G.: Thinking. London, 1951. *V.M.*

Axial gradient. A gradient (q.v.) or change in metabolic activity along, e.g., the primary axis of the body.

Axiom. An axiom, or axiomatic system, in contrast to a theorem, is an *unproved* proposition. The older philosophic systems (as even today non-technical thinking) conceived an axiom as a proposition whose truth-content is self-evident. The development of mathematics after the mid-nineteenth century led to an abandonment of the idea of self-evident truth, since when an axiomatic system for a specific theory has been understood as a collection of *elementary* unproved postulates known as axioms, which are *taken as* given, and from which all other propositions, or theorems, of the theoretical system are then deduced. The only restriction on the choice of axioms is that they are non-contradictory, when the system is known as consistent. *J.B.G.*

Axis cylinder (syn. *Axis cylinder process; Axite; Neuraxis; Neurite*). The central core of an *axon* (q.v.); also used synonymously with "axon". The basic components of the core itself are axolemma, neuronemes and axoplasma.

Bibliography: Chévremont, M.: Notions de cytologie et d'histologie. Liège, 1960. *G.A.*

Axon(e). Nerve cells (*neuron(e)s*) consist of a cell body, a number of dendrites (or fibers) branching off from the cell body, and an elongated part leading from the cell body to the specific organ or to other neurons: the conducting core, or axis cylinder, of this longer section is known as an *axon*, which divides into several *end feet*, or synaptic knobs (see *Synapses*). In lower animals these nerve fibers have practically no medullary sheath (or fatty layer or *myelin*) insulating them from surrounding tissue, but only a thin covering (*endoneurium*) and a cellular layer (sheath of Schwann); they show continuous conductivity (i.e. the impulse proceeds continuously along the fiber) and therefore conduct slowly (app. 1 m/sec). Most vertebrate axons have an insulating myelin sheath which is interrupted at app. 1 mm intervals by the nodes of Ranvier, points at which the cell membrane is laid bare. The primary nerve impulse (depolarization) proceeds only from node to node along the nerve fiber and therefore travels faster (5 to 100 m/sec), since between the nodes (*internodium*) conductivity does not depend directly on chemical processes and relatively slow stimulation by and displacement of sodium ions, but on a spreading *electrochemical* disturbance. An axon can extend to a length of 1 m; the diameter of non-medullar nerve fibers in vertebrates is between 1–2 μ and of those with myelin sheaths between 3–20 μ. *M.S.*

B

Babinski reflex. This reflex was recorded by the Paris neurologist J. F. Babinski in 1901 as a pathological reflex in organic nervous diseases in the region of the spinal cord and the pyramidal tract (upper motor neurons). It is produced by stroking the sole of the foot and manifests itself in dorsiflexion (upward extension) of the big toe instead of a normal plantar flexion (contraction). Its occurrence in infancy is physiological, and normal, as long as the pyramidal tract has not yet fully matured. Syn. *Babinski sign.* *E.D.*

Bahnung (Ger.). See *Attention theories.*

Balance, loss of. An objective or subjective disorder of control over equilibrium while standing and/or walking (swaying, staggering, tendency to fall) resulting from the loss of labyrinthine sense in the inner ear of one or both sides of the head (often accompanied by vertigo and nausea); or from a disorder of the central vestibule (e.g. in diseases of the CNS, q.v.), or of the *archicerebellum* (with typical cerebellar *ataxia*, q.v.; spontaneous nystagmus). See *Equilibrium.* *F.C.S.*

Balanced experiment. If a measurement is repeated in such a way that the first observation sometimes takes place under the one experimental condition and the second under the other (e.g. control), a systematic error (q.v.) must be expected (dependence of measurements, q.v.). To prevent this, one half of the whole sample is always observed under the one experimental condition and then under the other or vice versa (experimental planning, q.v.). This arrangement is known as a balanced experiment. *Balancing* refers to this technique and, more generally, to all measures to ensure that the variation of the extraneous variable in each repetition is the same for all conditions of the independent variable. *W.H.B.*

Ball-and-field test. A Stanford–Binet test (q.v.) item: the testee is asked to show by drawing how he would look for, e.g., a ball in a large field.

Ballard (-Williams) phenomenon. "Reminiscence": described by Ballard (1913), confirmed by O. Williams (1926). Phenomenon that what has been learnt is remembered (reproduced) better after several days than after the termination of the learning period. However, this increment is only observed when between this period and the test certain activities are practiced which have some connection with what has been learnt. These activities (in the case of Ballard, e.g., a retention test) themselves offer another opportunity for learning. Therefore the phenomenon is—as C. J. Hovland has demonstrated—an artifact.

Bibliography: **Ballard, P. B.:** Obliviscence and reminiscence. Brit. J. Psychol. Monogr. Suppl. 1, 1913, *2*. *H.-J.A.*

Bandwag(g)on effect. To withhold one's opinion, then vote in accordance with the majority view once that view is known, is in popular usage to "hop (or get, climb, etc.) on the bandwagon". The *bandwagon effect* is a noticeable result of public opinion polls, and is observable, e.g.. during voting for political parties or at revival meetings, and refers to the increasing tendency to associate with or even switch to the dominant view. A bandwagon was a railroad (railway) pay car in the USA. *J.C.*

Barany test. A test, especially in the selection of pilots, to record nystagmus (q.v.) after rotation of the subject about the three axes of the vestibule, i.e. the semicircular canals of the inner ear. A special chair is used. *A.L.*

Barbiturates. Salts of barbituric acid or malonylurea. Psychotropic group of substances discovered in 1862, and homologous with the hypnotics (q.v.). In chemical terms, barbiturates are cycloureids. Since the first clinical use of barbitone (barbital) (1903), more than 2500 barbiturates have been synthesized, and are used as sedatives (q.v.), anticonvulsants (q.v.), narcotics (q.v.) for the purpose of narcoanalysis (q.v.), but chiefly as hypnotics. Depending on the varying speed of precipitation the barbiturates are divided into those slow to take effect and those of long duration (barbitone, phenobarbitone); those of intermediate duration of action (amylobarbitone, cyclobarbitone, pentobarbitone, secobarbitone); and those of ultra-short duration of action (hexobarbitone, thipentone). Their effects are very similar qualitatively. They produce a general and central sedation with increased dosage. This is shown, e.g., in a lowered flicker-fusion frequency (q.v.), shorter duration of afterimage, underestimation of time, poorer performance in vigilance tests, increased bodily unsteadiness, reduced conditionability, decreased intellectual performance and some loss of motor skill. There is also a reduction of anxiety and an increase in extravert behavior. Sleep induced by barbiturates is distinguished in various ways from that not due to medication: electrophysiologically (e.g. inhibited peripheral and central electrocortical arousal response—blocked EEG arousal); and in behavior (diminished proportion of paradoxical sleep-phases and reduced bodily movement). Chronic use of barbiturates leads to tolerance and physical and psychic dependence, and also to withdrawal symptoms ("withdrawal sickness") when weaning from drug dependence (q.v.).

Bibliography: Adams, B. G., *et al.*: Patients receiving barbiturates in an urban general practice. J. Coll. gen. Practitioners, 1966, *57*, 24–31. **Black, P.** (Ed.): Drugs and the brain. Baltimore, 1969. **Maynert, E. W.** Sedatives and hypnotics II. In: **Di Palma, J. R.** (Ed.): Drills pharmacology in medicine. New York, 1965, 188–209. *E. Lehmann*

Bar diagram (syn. *Bar chart*). **1.** A graphic representation of magnitudes by means of narrow rectangles of a uniform width but varying lengths, the lengths corresponding to the magnitudes. **2.** A graphic representation of a whole so divided as to display the relation between its parts. *J.M.*

Barrier (*Barrière*). Concept from K. Lewin's vector or topological psychology (q.v.). "Barrier" is used by Lewin to denote factors inhibiting behavior in the "life space": i.e. everything that hinders or prevents a course of action corresponding to the forces at work in the field. The "barrier" itself also exerts forces counteracting those in existence. In daily life every obstacle that has to be circumvented or overcome represents a barrier. *H.-J.A.*

Bartlett, Sir Frederick Charles. B. 20/10/1866 at Stow-on-the-Wold (*England*). Studied at St. John's College, Cambridge, and London University. Professor of Experimental

Psychology and Director of the Psychological Laboratory, Cambridge. Worked in the field of experimental psychology, investigated thinking, perception, memory. He related the function and nature of memory to social psychology, and also worked in the area of military psychology. Barlett's researches led to a rejection of the "storage" conception of memory, and emphasized remembering as a "construction" (i.e. "schemata" used to absorb new information), and therefore an active process of reinterpretation. Editor and co-editor of the British Journal of Psychology; Mind; Psychological Abstracts; Journal of General Psychology.

Works include: An experimental study of some problems of perceiving and imaging, *Brit. J. Psychol.*, 1916; Feeling, imaging and thinking, *Brit. J. Psychol.*, 1925; with **Myers, C. S.**: Text book of experimental psychology, Part 2, 1925. Remembering: A study in experimental and social psychology, 1932. Thinking: An experimental and social study, 1958.

Bibliography: Boring, E. G.: A history of experimental psychology. New York, 1950. **Murchison, C.:** A history of psychology in autobiography, Vol. 3. Worcester, 1936. **Id.:** The psychological register. Worcester, 1929.

W. S.

Bartlett test. A simultaneous test (named after S. Bartlett, 1932) of the statistical significance (q.v.) of more than two variant samples. It is sometimes used to check the homogeneity of variance (q.v.) in an analysis of variance (q.v.). See *Mathematical psychology; Statistics.* *W.H.B.*

Barykinetic type. Temperament related to the athletic in which the entonic proportion (q.v.) of fluidity (q.v.) is prominent: the reactions are characterized by "heaviness", no matter whether they seem to be rather clumsy or rather supple (simultaneous, antagonistic application of tension). Moderate adaptability. Dull expression of emotions. Apparent imperturbability, often however concealing sensitiveness and lability of mood. Intense emotional reactions are at first held back and then compressed into one moment with a consequent abrupt or explosive effect. Genially sociable or dysphorically mistrustful, constant and reliable. Introverted and extraverted characteristics seem to be counterbalanced.

Bibliography: Kretschmer, E.: Physique and character. New York, 1931. **Kretschmer, E. & W.:** Medizinische Psychol. Stuttgart, [13]1970. **Kretschmer, E. & Enke, W.:** Die Persönlichkeit der Athletiker. Stuttgart, 1936.

W.K.

Basal ganglia. The term *ganglia* (q.v.) is here used exceptionally for masses of nerve cells in the subcortex with an identical or similar function within the central nervous system (q.v.). The following are among the basal ganglia: *corpus striatum* (striate body), *globus pallidus, corpus amygdaloideum*, and *claustrum.* *G.A.*

Basal text. An extremely brief formulation of the subject-matter of a lesson which is to be given directly or in a teaching program. In cybernetic education the target of a program is usually defined with the aid of a basal text. *H.F.*

Basedow's disease. Described in 1840 by K. A. von Basedow; due to enlargement and overactivity of the thyroid gland. It is characterized by exophthalmic (protuberant) eyes, struma (soft, frequently pulsating enlargement of the thyroid gland), tachycardia (heart rate increased up to 160 per minute), raised basal metabolic rate, ready sweating, tremors, motor disturbance, subfebrile temperatures, diarrhea, emaciation, reduced virility, and menstrual disorders, but especially by nervousness and psychic hyperexcitability. Its etiology is largely unexplained. In addition to hereditary predisposition, various factors may act as "triggers" and provoke its onset. Treatment is not uniform and extends to radiation and surgical excision of parts of the thyroid gland. Syn. *Exophthalmic goiter; Graves' disease; Hyperthyroidism, Parry's disease; Thyreotoxicosis.* *E.D.*

Basilar membrane. The coiled, fluid-(perilymph-)filled, inner auditory canal (cochlea) is divided into two halves by the basilar membrane, which carries the organ of Corti (q.v.) with its four rows of hair cells. Longitudinally, the basilar membrane features continuously changing mechanical properties; it is set in motion when mechanical sound impulses are transmitted via the auditory ossicles and the oval window; and, together with the organ of Corti, enables the cochlea to function as a transducer which translates these mechanical into electrical impulses. It is assumed that the sound frequency is transmitted by maximum deformation of different parts of the membrane, leading to maximum stimulation of groups of hair cells in different places (dispersion): i.e. there is a distribution of low to high frequencies along the membrane. *M.S.*

Batterie de tests d'aptitude scolaire (abb. BASC). Intelligence tests (q.v.) of scholastic ability; four parallel series, each with different tests, agree in their factorial structure.

Bibliography: Cardinet, J. & Rousson, M.: Etudes factorielles de tests d'aptitudes scolaires. Schweiz. Z. Psychol. Anwend., 1967, *26*, 256–70; *27*, 362–80.

R.M.

Bayes' theorem. An inferential statistical model representing an alternative to the classical testing of hypotheses. Instead of single decisions in favor of H_0 or H_1 on the basis of the results of individual samplings, it permits a successive revision of the probabilities of the hypotheses which are to be compared. Syn. *Bayes' principle.*

Bibliography: Lindley, D. V.: Introduction to probability and statistics. Cambridge, 1965. *W.H.B.*

Beat. The periodical reinforcement of two simultaneously sounded, and therefore simultaneously heard, notes (tones) which are near to one another in vibration frequency.

Bed wetting. See *Enuresis.*

Begabung. 1. *A general view. Begabung* may be defined as the whole range of innate abilities to achieve qualified performances in various cultural fields. In this view, "ability" is an *endogenous fact* which, however, is realized in the achievements and creations of actual life. Therefore the specific experiential context of achievement is very important: it can crucially motivate, innervate, promote, repress, hinder or even arrest individual fulfillment. *Begabung* is revealed in achievement characteristics; modes of behavior and even attitudes are involved, since every achievement can result only from a behavior, and this only from a certain attitude. (See *Abilities.*)

This definition of ability has a substantial basis in the psychophysical constitution of the human *person* (q.v.). It is multidimensional, for it includes cultural factors (general ability, e.g.: vitality, emotional capacity and the will, motor skills and so on; and special abilities such as linguistic or numerical thinking). It also includes personal constitutional causative factors, and ability types and capacities (theoretical and practical; nature, talent, genius; normal and subnormal ability) that are graduated (and therefore measurable) in terms of cultural dimensions differentiated according to number and especially quality. Dynamic plasticity (q.v.) is one of the features of ability defined as a multidimensional, graduated, substantial datum. Ability in this sense can be both developed and unfold. The nucleus of ability can grow; it can be differentiated in greater or smaller, stronger or weaker branches.

Begabung is more comprehensive than *intelligence* (q.v.) which is essentially the capacity to produce and understand meanings, relationships and significant contexts.

Begabung is genetically conditioned; its unfolding depends on environment.

Ability as defined here and *aptitude* (q.v.) can be established diagnostically by analyses of achievement and performance; the following at least are factors in all achievement: intelligence, personal temperament, adaptability, and capability of practice. Mental and moral considerations, positive and negative, cannot be disregarded in research into ability. *Begabung* is conceived more inclusively from the standpoint of *characterology* (q.v.), which sees each individual's achievement, despite its situtational determination, as dependent just as much on essential *traits* (q.v.)—displayed in sentiments and attitudes—as on *anlagen* (q.v.).

Begabung, therefore, is also the special capability of exerting a personal influence on the environment in action and reaction (objectively, and in personal, spiritual modes). This definition makes it possible to speak also of ability in regard to emotion, thinking, imagination, memory, fantasy, and mind ("spirit").

Intelligence has been identified with ability. Ziehen used the special term "*Beanlagung*" to define ability as the "general nature of the more important psychical processes of the individual in so far as it does not depend on practice but on the innate or very early acquired organization of the brain". By *Beanlagung*, he understands ability in the narrower sense, i.e. in regard to active achievement and the special and individual value of its various manifestations. Such a division of the concept is no longer tenable.

Klages includes the qualities of ability in the sense of *Begabung* in his *Stoff des Charakters*, or "character material". By this he understands quantitative traits, as distinguished from directive characteristics (type and motivation of the character). He sees differences in abilities or capacities from one person to another; a greater or lesser degree of "ability" qualifies the "character" (q.v.). A. Wenzel, in his *Theorie der Begabung* (1934), adhered to the view of ability as intelligence.

A recent denaturizing tendency has interpreted ability as a process of learning (Roth, 1970). The question must arise whether such a process can be effected insubstantially, without any need for a human agent. A person, i.e. a unity of body, soul and mind, is always individually furnished with natural gifts. Every person can be supplied by his milieu with further gifts, but the natural gifts (dispositions) are prerequisites for the exogenous process of unfolding and education. It is disastrous if strained and artificial constructions cause ability to be interpreted as a "gift from without", and if a theoretical construct eliminates the real, factual disposition which has always been present in each individual, and will be in future. The concept would be too narrow and unilateral if it were restricted solely to the capacity for learning. "Ability" also means independent *creativity* (q.v.). In current linguistic usage *gift* is used not only in the sense of "gift received", but in the sense of "innate attributes, or talent".

Whereas *Begabung* is actualized as the basis of achievements in a definite sociocultural area, *talent* (q.v.) extends beyond normal, average qualities and surpasses them in its achievements. *Genius* (q.v.) is supreme ability which the mind inspires and impregnates.

2. *Methodology of research.* It seems inadmissible to try to define the phenomenon of ability solely from the operational standpoint (E. L. Thorndike), just as it is one-sided to try to elucidate the problem in a purely "humanistic" (*geisteswissenschaftlich*) way (e.g. Seeberger, 1966). The operational technique of factor analysis has produced a general intelligence factor (G factor). The following individual ability factors were determined: memory, linguistic ability, logical thinking, technical thinking, spatial thinking, arithmetical abilities (L. L. Thurstone; W. Arnold found corresponding factors in 1960). Ability research is chiefly directed to distinguishing between operating numerically and scientifically, and thinking logically with words. In our time there has also been a noticeable shift of emphasis in regard to ability and aptitude, in the socio-political and educational-political spheres, to the creation and development of specialist colleges and even universities to encourage special abilities in predominantly economic and technical subjects.

Bibliography: Arnold, W.: Begabung und Bildungswilligkeit. Munich & Basle, 1968. **Klages, L.:** The science of character. London, 1928. **Mierke, K.:** Bildung, Bildsamkeit. Stuttgart, 1963. **Roth, H.** (Ed.): Begabung und Lernen. Stuttgart, 1970. **Seeberger, W.:** Begabung als Problem. Stuttgart, 1966. **Thurstone, L. L.:** Primary mental abilities. Chicago, 1938. **Wenzl, A.:** Theorie der Begabung. Heidelberg, [2]1957.

W. Arnold

Begriff. See *Concept.*

Behavior. 1. The activity of an organism. **2.** The observable activity of a specific organism. **3.** The measurable activity of a specific organism. **4.** The responses of an individual, species or group to stimuli. **5.** A specific response of a specific organism. **6.** A part-response of a response pattern. **7.** Movement or a movement. **8.** The total activity, subjective and objective, non-observable and observable, of an individual or group.

The above definitions represent only a small number of the existing views of the object of psychology. For more detailed expositions of differing viewpoints see, e.g.: *Act psychology; Behaviorism; Comparative psychology; General psychology; History of psychology.* For specific aspects, see, e.g.: *Aggression; Drive; Habit; Learning.*

Behavioral. Methods, theories and phenomena which are determined by behavior are termed behavioral, and are thus distinguished from those which are physiological or determined by experience. Also used in a general sense to characterize an objective as opposed to a subjective approach. Must not be confused with *behaviorist* and *behavioristic* (q.v.). *R.H.*

Behavior, animal. See *Animal psychology; Comparative psychology; Drive; Instinct.*

Behaviorism is a radical form of objective psychology in which all references to introspection and consciousness are rejected in favor of a discussion of psychologically relevant events primarily in terms of stimulus and response. This radical form was first proposed in America by John B. Watson (1878–1958) in a paper entitled "Psychology as the behaviorist views it" (1913). His position, although repeatedly under attack, gained favor in America. Less popular in other parts of the world than in the United States, related views are prominent in the U.S.S.R. and Eastern Europe (though there more commonly thought of as physiology), and a belated recognition has come to behaviorism in England (e.g., Broadbent, 1961).

1. *Precursors of behaviorism.* The definition of psychology as the study of consciousness, with introspection as the preferred method, was widely accepted in the late nineteenth century and early twentieth century. Cattell (1904), McDougall (1908), and others sought to extend the domain of psychology to cover behavior, while retaining consciousness and introspection. This was not radical enough for Watson.

More radical objectivisms had also emerged, such as that of Sechenov in Russia, followed by the observations of Pavlov and Bekhterev. Germany produced Loeb with his doctrine of tropisms (he emigrated to America and taught at Chicago while Watson was a student there); objective views like his were promulgated in Germany by Beer, Bethe, and von Uexküll. Throughout the world students of animal activities carried out objective studies of behavior.

Philosophers, too, had begun to raise doubts about consciousness and introspection as ways to get at the fundamental nature of mind. E. A. Singer (1911) influenced E. R. Guthrie (1886–1959), an American psychologist important in promoting behaviorism. In France there had been the mechanistic conception of La Mettrie and, later, Comte's positivism.

It is not surprising to find that others created a fertile soil for Watson's doctrines, but this does not detract from his originality, boldness, and personal influence.

2. *Watsonian behaviorism.* The central tenet of behaviorism is, of course, the objectivity of the data to be accepted by science. The facts of observation are to be limited to those of any other science: observable events that can be recorded by an experimenter, often with the aid of precision instruments. The events to be included are, first of all, the antecedent stimuli, and then the consequent responses of muscles and glands. Muscles and glands are the only effectors; there is no additional "mental activity". The behaviorist was also interested in the *products* of behavior, which can also be objectively measured. Verbal responses, although produced by muscular movements, are really products of movement, quite as much as words typed on a page or check-marks on a psychological test. This interest in the products of behavior saved behaviorism from becoming a "muscle-twitch" psychology —an unfavorable description mentioned by Watson in the preface to his *Psychology from the Standpoint of a Behaviorist* (1919), and often attributed to Tolman (1932, p. 5), who was merely repeating something that Watson had said he had been charged with (and denied) much earlier. The acceptance of verbal responses as behavior also freed behaviorism from restrictions that would otherwise have been imposed: for instance, it permits the study of dreams, without calling this introspection.

Watson did not wish only to eliminate imprecision and subjectivity. There were at least three more aspects of this theory as it developed: associationistic atomism, peripheralism, and extreme environmentalism.

The search for an analytic unit led first to the central concept of habit; it became the core systematic concept until the *conditioned reflex* (q.v.) doctrine took its place. In theoretical terms, the conditioned reflex was an analytical unit, serving his system in much the same way as the sensation in the introspective psychology that he was opposing. The attacks by the gestalt psychologists on behaviorism and sensationism focussed on this "molecular" or "atomistic" feature. Despite Watson's great interest in the brain (his 1919 chapter on the neurophysiological basis of action contains no less than 26 diagrams of the brain and cord and neurones, apart from numerous diagrams of sense organs and effectors in other chapters) he gradually came to espouse what is called a *peripheralism*—by contrast with a centralism. The centralist believes that thinking takes place in the brain; Watson had it take place in the vocal cords, as the thinker talks to himself. The emotions, too, might be thought of as having central representation, but Watson was more interested in what happened in the body, and defined the emotions accordingly. This is an aspect of Watsonian behaviorism from which modern students have diverged, particularly as newer methods for studying brain activity have developed. For example, the notion that hunger depends upon stomach contractions (a peripheralist view) is generally modified now to the belief that it depends on something happening in the hypothalamus (a centralist view).

The third additional Watsonian dogma was that of *extreme environmentalism*, to which he came gradually. It is something of a surprise to find a chapter on instincts in his 1919 book, after his behaviorism was well established; although he then believed the role of innate tendencies was chiefly to provide a background for habit formation, he did not deny innateness. Later he became bolder, and rejected hereditary potentials in man in favor of a learning basis for individual differences (Watson, 1925).

The essence of behaviorism lay in its

emphasis upon making psychology an objective science; the associationistic atomism, peripheralism, and environmentalism were not essential to the position, but at the height of Watson's influence they had an important impact upon psychology (and other social sciences) in America.

3. *Tolman's purposive behaviorism.* Early in his career, Edward C. Tolman (1886–1959) became fascinated by Watson's behaviorism, but critical of it, and he soon began to develop his independent position, first in a paper entitled "A new formula for behaviorism" (1922), and later in his major book, *Purposive Behavior in Animals and Men* (1932). His system is most simply characterized by three statements:

(*a*) It is a *behaviorism* in that it rejects introspection as a method. Although a subjective vocabulary is sometimes used (e.g. "inventive ideation"), such conceptual formulations are always considered to be *inferences* from observed behavior. The data are behavioral.

(*b*) It is characterized as a *molar* behaviorism by contrast with Watson's *molecular* behaviorism. An act of behavior has distinctive properties of its own, to be identified and described irrespective of the underlying muscular, glandular, or neural processes.

(*c*) It is a non-teleological *purposivism.* This means only that behavior is organized and regulated in accordance with objectively determinable goals, often a matter of expectations (probabilistic outcomes) based on prior experience.

An important concept of Tolman's, accepted later by Hull, but rejected by Skinner, is that of an *intervening variable.* A stimulus response psychology, modeled after the simple reflex arc, was not acceptable to Tolman; very much takes place between stimulus and response to modify the stimulus-response correlation: any careful account of behavior must respect the prior history of the organism, its present drive state, etc., in addition to the present stimulating conditions.

4. *Hull's behavior system.* Clark L. Hull (1884–1952), greatly impressed by Pavlov's *Conditioned Reflexes* (1927), began a series of theoretically guided experimental studies that seemed to him to fulfill the work left undone by Watson. Although he continued later to contribute to theory and experiment, the system reached its height of confidence in *Principles of Behavior* (1943). Instead of assuming that a chain of conditioned reflexes provided a simple explanation of habit, Hull developed an elaborate model in which the triggering stimulus was the first term of a complicated set of events which resulted in the response as the end term. Between stimulus and response there were many intervening variables (as made familiar by Tolman, but not with Tolman's content). These included tendencies to respond acquired in the past, stimulus generalization, drives based on physiological deprivation or noxious stimulation, and other features, both associative and non-associative, affecting the actual evoked response. One important intervening variable which served to integrate many forms of behavior was the fractional anticipatory (or antedating) goal response (^{r}—G), which became in his system a surrogate for ideational processes. The presence of these complex intermediaries distinguished his system from Watson's. Otherwise, in spirit, it was equally behavioristic, and essentially peripheralist. Despite the prominence of Hull's system for some twenty years, the emergence of other kinds of mathematical models, more sophisticated than his empirical curve-fitting, led to its rapid decline in influence in the 1960s, despite the strong discipleship of Kenneth W. Spence (1907–67) and others.

5. *Skinner's experimental analysis of behavior.* B. F. Skinner (b. 1904) kept a strict behaviorism alive in the midst of a climate of opinion rather antithetical to it, and if there was any "school" of psychology in the United States in the early 1970s it was that associated with his approach to behavior. His followers developed a society of their

own, a central journal (*Journal of the Experimental Analysis of Behavior*), and some satellite journals; and those close to Skinner's position spoke a common language of operant conditioning, schedules of reinforcement, and shaping of behavior, and shared common taboos of the kind associated with earlier radical behaviorism, as against any inner processes not describable in behavioral terms. By contrast with Tolman and Hull, intervening variables or other inferential terms were felt to be unnecessary excesses.

Skinner views his standpoint as essentially a powerful technology, rather than a scientific system; it is indeed a very radical behaviorism (Skinner, 1938; 1952; 1959). The basic terms and relationships can be learned quickly. There is, to begin with, an *operant level*, according to which any organism behaves in a given environment. This is the "entering behavior", and one need not ask if it is innate or acquired, species-specific or culturally derived. It is this behavior which presents itself for modification and control. It is controlled by manipulating the discriminatory stimuli and the stimuli serving as reinforcements (rewards). The teaching or training process is one of *shaping* the behavior by *reinforcing* (rewarding) any shifts in the desired direction and *extinguishing* (by non-reinforcement or non-reward) any shifts in the undesired direction. The method can be used to produce *discriminations* between stimuli, and *differentiation* of response patterns. This is all the information that is needed to apply Skinner's technology to various individual and social problems. There are of course more complex aspects having to do with intermittent reinforcements of various kinds, with secondary reinforcements, with chaining of responses—but these are accessory details. The important result is that behavior is brought under the control of the stimulus, and hence can be managed.

The successes of the method are readily documented: in animal training (as in the various "marine-lands" in America in which dolphins and killer whales perform remarkable tricks to the delight of the audience, after being "shaped" by Skinner's methods); in programmed instruction, which Skinner invented as a form of teaching that made use of his principles; and in various forms of psychotherapy. Therefore Skinner has come nearer than anyone to achieving what Watson set out to do: to predict and control behavior, without reference to subjective processes or states.

6. *The permanent contributions of behaviorism to general psychology*. The success of Skinner's technology has led to its acceptance by his disciples as an ultimate psychology, but many other psychologists, who have no hesitation about accepting its successes, and even making use of its methods, do not believe it to be the final answer to psychology's understanding of man. It glosses over the problems of the biological bases of behavior (heredity, hormonal control, and so on), the subjective states represented by dreams and hallucinations (as well as imagining and planning), and dismisses the possibilities of systematic science (e.g. hierarchical organization; mathematical models with interchangeable constants). Some of these reservations have to do with Skinner's personal preferences, rather than with the possibility of a behaviorism, but some alternative methods of dealing with subjective processes still seem plausible to many, if not most, contemporary psychologists. In expressing these doubts, some essentially behaviorally oriented writers have described their position as a "subjective behaviorism" (Miller, Galanter & Pribram, 1960, 211–14).

The major contribution of behaviorism may have been to give confidence to students of human and animal nature that they were dealing with a subject-matter sufficiently like that of other sciences to place them in the tradition of Darwin, Mendel, Newton and Einstein. Having gained the new perspective that behaviorism provided, and the new scientific status that it enhanced, they have found that the positives of behaviorism can now be incorporated into modern psychology without its negatives.

Bibliography: **Bergmann, G.**: The contributions of John B. Watson. Psychol. Rev., 1956, *63*, 265–76. **Broadbent, D. E.**: Behaviour. London, 1961. **Broadhurst, P. L.**: John B. Watson, Int. Ency. Soc. Sciences, 1968, *16*, 484–7. **Cattell, J. McK.**: The conceptions and methods of psychology. Pop. Sci. Mo., 1904, *46*, 176–86. **Hull, C. L.**: Principles of behavior. New York, 1943. **McDougall, W.**: Introduction to social psychology. London, 1908. **Miller, G. A., Galanter, E. & Pribram, K. H.**: Plans and the structure of behavior. New York, 1960. **Pavlov, I. P.**: Conditioned reflexes. London, 1927. **Singer, E. A.**: Mind as an observable object. J. Phil. Psychol. sci. Meth., 1911, *8*, 180–86. **Skinner, B. F.**: The behavior of organisms. New York, 1938. **Id.**: Science and human behavior. New York, 1953. **Id.**: Cumulative record. (Rev. ed.) New York, 1961. **Id.**: Behaviorism at fifty. Science, 1963, *140*, 951–9. **Tolman, E. C.**: A new formula for behaviorism. Psychol. Rev., 1922, *29*, 44–53. **Id.**: Purposive behavior in animals and men. New York, 1932. **Watson, J. B.**: Psychology as the behaviorist views it. Psychol. Rev., 1913, *20*, 158–77. **Id.**: Psychology from the standpoint of a behaviorist. Philadelphia & London, 1919. **Id.**: Behaviorism. New York, 1925. **Woodworth, R. S. & Sheehan, M. R.**: Contemporary schools of psychology. New York, [3]1964.

E. R. Hilgard

Behaviorism, descriptive. 1. B. F. Skinner's learning theory (q.v.), which explains behavior largely in terms of linguistically formulated observations and their relations to one another and thus dispenses with mathematical constructs, intervening (theoretically necessary) variables and formal representations. **2.** Descriptive behaviorism is also used as a collective term for the techniques of operant conditioning by which operants, or emitted responses, are examined without necessary reference to originating rather than reinforcing stimuli. *R.Hä. & J.C.*

Behaviorism, molar. Term used for the learning theory of E. C. Tolman (q.v.) who does not start from the smallest possible elements of behavior but instead considers the holistic, purposive units or aspects. *Molar behavior:* one of these units. Syn. *Purposive behavior (ism); Molarism.* *R.Hä.*

Behaviorism, molecular. Behaviorism is called molecular when it seeks to explain all behavior as built from the smallest possible units (e.g. the concept of J. B. Watson, q.v.). C. L. Hull (q.v.) does not consider his theory molecular because he reserves the notion for physiological behavior theories. See *Behaviorism.* (Syn. *Molecularism.*) *R.Hä.*

Behaviorist; behavioristic. Appertaining to behaviorism (q.v.). The concept is used both to denote the method, and in a pejorative sense by, e.g., authors who reject operational definitions and deny the relevance of animal experiments—often carried out by behaviorists—for human psychology. *Behaviorist* (n.) indicates a practitioner or adherent of behaviorism. *R.Hä.*

Behavior, physiology of. See *Physiology of behavior.*

Behavior rating. 1. Observing, scoring and measuring a specific behavior or class of behaviors. **2.** (also *Behavior-rating schedule*). An alternative-choice questionnaire on behavior in a range of situations.

Behavior sampling. A record of an individual's behavior (possibly a specific behavior) during a certain period of time.

Behavior therapy is a term used to describe a number of therapeutic methods developed in recent years. Although the actual procedures vary from desensitization to aversion treatment they share certain theoretical conceptions. The rationale adapted by practitioners of behavior therapy is that neurotic behavior and other types of disorder are predominantly acquired. If neurotic behavior is acquired, then it should be subject to the established laws of learning. Knowledge about the learning process concerns not only the acquisition of new behavior patterns, but the reduction or elimination of existing behavior patterns. Behavior therapy derives its impetus from experimental psychology and is essentially an attempt to apply the findings and methods of this discipline to the disorders of human behavior. The aspect of experimental psychology with the most immediate and obvious value for therapy is the study of learning; the literature on this subject provides a valuable starting-point for the development of scientific methods of treatment.

Although some of the ideas used in the theory and practice of behavior therapy have a long history, the subject was firmly established less than twenty years ago. The most important stages in development can be attributed to the work of Wolpe, Eysenck and Skinner. Historically, major influences on the course of development of behavior therapy are found in the works of Pavlov and of Watson. Their approach to abnormalities of behavior, in conjunction with the rapid growth of learning theory, provided a suitable climate for the development of behavior therapy. This form of therapy grew partly as a consequence of growing dissatisfaction with depth psychotherapy. Wolpe's research made a timely appearance in the early 1950s and was supported and developed by the work of Eysenck and his colleagues. Skinner's contribution to the subject can be traced to 1953 with his interest in the shaping of behavior of chronic psychotic patients. This work was continued and developed by Lindsley and by Ayllon, who made the first systematic attempt to apply the techniques of operant conditioning in a psychiatric ward. This research has mushroomed and the establishment of psychiatric and other special facilities for the psychological management of abnormal behavior has undergone rapid expansion during the past five years. Most of these research and treatment programs are described as "token economy" projects. Desirable and constructive behavior is shaped and reinforced by therapists and nurses. Rewards are often given in the form of tokens to be exchanged for special privileges or items. Currently, behavior therapy is being developed and investigated extensively in Britain, the U.S., and various European countries. At present the most widely used therapeutic methods are desensitization for anxiety conditions, aversion therapy for deviant behavior, and operant conditioning for deficit behavior.

Broadly speaking, problems of behavior can arise in two ways. If the person fails to acquire a necessary, adaptive form of behavior this deficit can constitute a problem (e.g. enuresis, q.v.). Most neurotic disorders in adults are, however, essentially surplus reactions: the patient has acquired a persisting unadaptive form of behavior (e.g. anxiety, phobic states, etc.). The learning and un-learning techniques which have been used for therapeutic purposes include the following: (*a*) Desensitization (Wolpe, 1958; Eysenck & Rachman, 1965; Marks, 1969); (*b*) Aversion therapy (q.v.) (Rachman & Teasdale, 1969; Feldman, 1966); (*c*) Operant conditioning (q.v.) (Ayllon & Azrin, 1968; Ullman & Krasner, 1968; Sloane & Macaulay, 1968); (*d*) Negative practice (q.v.) (Yates, 1970); (*e*) Special techniques—bell and pad conditioning treatment for enuresis, feedback procedures for stuttering (Turner, Young & Rachman, 1970; Yates, 1970).

Behavior therapy has been successfully used in the treatment of a variety of neurotic conditions including, most notably, the phobias, and sexual, obsessional, children's speech and other disorders. It has also been of considerable value in the rehabilitation of severely ill patients with deficit disorders or inadequate behavior. The most significant advances to date have been made in the treatment of phobic disorders (Marks, 1969). Encouraging successes have also been obtained in the treatment of sexual disorders and alcoholism (Rachman & Teasdale, 1969). The use of conditioning procedures in the rehabilitation of chronic schizophrenics is described by Ayllon & Azrin (1968). Other applications of operant conditioning procedures are described by Sloane & Macaulay (1968) and by Ullman & Krasner (1968). General accounts of the clinical effectiveness of these methods are provided by Meyer & Chesser (1970) and by Yates (1970).

The methods of behavior therapy have also been the subject of a large number of experimental investigations. In particular, desensitization treatment has been studied extensively (Rachman, 1967). Much of this experimental work has been carried out on non-psychiatric volunteers who have an excessive, irrational fear of some object or situation. The experimental findings are virtually unanimous in showing that the treatment is capable of producing significant and lasting reductions in fear. It has also been shown that the two major components of the treatment, relaxation and graded imaginal presentations of the fearful stimulus, contribute to therapeutic effectiveness. They appear to act in combination. After the patient has been trained to obtain deep relaxation, he is asked to imagine scenes of increasing fearfulness. Successive repetitions of these imaginal presentations are given until the patient reports decreasing anxiety. Eventually he is able to tolerate the imaginal fearful situations with tranquility, and this change generally transfers to the real-life situation without difficulty. Wolpe's (1958) original theory, on which this and other forms of treatment are based, has received a fair degree of support but is not entirely unchallenged. Wolpe's theory proposed that the main basis for the therapeutic effect was the development of condition inhibition and that this could best be achieved by eliciting the anxiety reaction and then superimposing upon it an antagonistic and incompatible response (e.g. relaxation).

Both the clinical and experimental evidence show that significant and lasting reductions in anxiety can be achieved by desensitization; furthermore, it appears to be unnecessary for the therapist or patient to undertake extensive exploration into the possible origins, since deeper significant reductions in fear obtained with this form of treatment are not followed by the appearance of new or substitute symptoms.

Aversion therapy is based on a conditioning paradigm and involves the repeated association of stimuli which provoke some form of undesirable behavior and aversive stimuli (chemical or electrical). This form of treatment has been used predominantly in the treatment of sexual disorders and alcoholism (q.v.).

The operant conditioning techniques derive largely from the work of Skinner and rest on the central concept of reinforcement (q.v.). Behavior which produces satisfying consequences is strengthened, but behavior which produces unsatisfactory consequences is weakened. In order to generate and maintain behavior, the reinforcing or satisfying consequences must be made contingent on the responses in question. In speech training, e.g., the correct enunciations are followed by reinforcing consequences (e.g. praise, rewards). Similar principles are used in the management and rehabilitation of chronic psychotic patients in whom encouraging advances have been recorded (Ayllon & Azrin, 1968). The overall clinical effectiveness of the operant procedures is still under investigation.

A number of special treatment techniques have also been developed: the two most prominent are used for the management of enuresis and of stuttering. The enuresis treatment was developed by Mowrers in 1938 and was based on a classical conditioning model. The aim was to produce a conditioned connection between the interoceptive stimuli preceding urination and an alarm bell which would awaken the child and prevent or interrupt urination. Lovibond (1964) proposed an alternative theory based on avoidance conditioning. However, the theory and its deductions have recently been queried

(Turner *et al.*, 1970). Clinically, this technique is highly effective in arresting bed-wetting, but relapses remain a problem.

Some important theoretical advances have already been attained. Significant improvements in neurotic and other types of abnormal behavior can be achieved with behavioral methods even in the absence of deep exploratory psychotherapy. The reduction or elimination of abnormal behavior is rarely followed by the development of substitute symptoms. These, and related findings, are of significance not only for behavior therapy but have wider implications for our understanding and explanations of behavioral abnormalities in general.

Progress has been rapid and encouraging but there is still a great need for large-scale field trials and intensive experimental investigations of the theory and methods of behavior therapy.

Bibliography: Ayllon, T. & Azrin, N.: The token economy. New York, 1968. **Eysenck, H. J. & Rachman, S.:** The causes and cures of neurosis. London, 1965. **Feldman, M. P.:** Aversion therapy for sexual deviations. Psychological Bulletin, 1966, *65*, 65–79. **Lovibond, S.:** Conditioning and enuresis. Oxford, 1964. **Meyer, V. & Chesser, E.:** Behaviour therapy in clinical psychiatry. London, 1970. **Marks, I.:** Fears and phobias, London, 1969. **Rachman, S.:** Systematic desensitization, Psychological Bulletin, 1967, *67*, 93–103. **Rachman, S. & Teasdale, J.:** Aversion therapy and the behaviour disorders. London, 1969. **Sloane, H. & Macaulay, B.:** Operant procedures in remedial speech and language training. Boston, 1968. **Turner, R. K., Young, G. & Rachman, S.:** Treatment of nocturnal enuresis by conditioning. Behav. Res. Therapy, *8*, 1970. **Ullman, L. & Krasner, L.:** A psychological approach to abnormal behavior. New York, 1968. **Wolpe, J.:** Psychotherapy by reciprocal inhibition. Stanford, 1958. **Yates, A.:** Behavior therapy. New York, 1970.

S. Rachman

Bekhterev, Vladimir M. B. 22/1/1857 in Vjatka, d. 24/12/1927 in Leningrad; Professor of psychiatry at Kazanz; later Professor of psychology and neurology in St. Petersburg (at the Army Medical School). Ranks with Pavlov (q.v.) as the founder of *objective psychology* (q.v.) (later known as *reflexology*, q.v.; conditioned reflexes, q.v.). Worked on problems of the central nervous system, of the spine (Bekhterev's disease) and on "associative reflexes". Bekhterev's emphasis on the physiological approach (which extended also to thought processes) and his pioneer work on "motor responses" make him one of the precursors of behaviorism.

Works: Die Bedeutung der Suggestion im sozialen Leben, 1905. Objektive Psychologie. Leipzig, 1907. (La psychologie objective. Paris, 1913.) Die Funktionen der Nervenzentra. Jena, 1908–11. General Principles of human reflexology, New York, 1932.

Bibliography: Boring, E. G.: A history of experimental psychology, New York, [2]1950. **Schniermann, A. L.:** Bekhterev's reflexological school. In: **Murchison, C.:** Psychologies of 1930. Worcester, 1930, 221–42.

W.S.

Belief-value matrix. In E. C. Tolman's *Purposive Behaviorism*, the system of *expectancies* (including classifications and categorizations) and *valences* (value judgments) which the individual brings to any new situations and which partly determine his response to the environment. *G.D.W.*

Bell Adjustment Inventory. A personality questionnaire measuring emotionality, social, domestic and other adjustments, and yielding higher emotionality scores for females than for males in high school, college and delinquent groups.

Bibliography: Bell, H. M.: The theory and practice of personal counseling. Stanford, 1939. *J.G.*

Belladonna alkaloids. Psychotropic substances occurring in numerous plants, especially in the genus *solanum* (deadly nightshade, thorn apple). Belladonna alkaloids have been known for centuries. The most important are *atropin*(*e*) (q.v.) and *scopolamin*(*e*) (q.v.). There is a wide range of natural, semi- and wholly synthetic related preparations. They have strong anticholinergic and CNS effects.

In stronger doses they have psychosomimetic effects. See *Psychosomimetics*. *W.J.*

Bell–Magendie law (syn. *Bell's law*). The principle laid down by the Scottish physiologist C. Bell (1811) that the anterior (ventral) roots of the nerves of the spinal cord are motor, the posterior (dorsal) roots sensory. *F.-C.S.*

Bell's palsy. A phenomenon named after the Scottish anatomist C. Bell (1774–1842): owing to a peripheral paralysis of the facial nerve, the eyeball moves upward under the upper lid of the paralyzed half of the face. *D.V.*

Bender Gestalt Test. A widely used procedure for testing gestalt comprehension and reproduction. The person tested must copy nine geometrical figures. The test has been used to determine the level of intelligence in the range of 5 to 10 years, and as an aid in evaluation for the projective method of personality diagnosis; the spatial errors made have also been invoked in the diagnosis of brain damage. The validity (q.v.) of several evaluation formulas is guaranteed by a large number of investigations on a rough selection basis.

Bibliography: Tolor, A. & Schulberg, H. C.: An evaluation of the Bender Gestalt Test. Springfield, Ill., 1963. *A.L.*

Bennett tests. 1. *College Qualification Test* (1955–61): six-category intelligence group test: verbal, numerical, science information, social studies information, total information, total. **2.** *Differential Aptitude Test:* for school grades 8 to 12: verbal, numerical, abstract, and mechanical reasoning; spatial relations; clerical speed and accuracy; language usage (spelling and sentences). **3.** *Hand-tool Dexterity Test* (1946): manual dexterity test using screw and screwdriver. **4.** *Short Employment Tests* (1951–56): clerical, numerical, verbal tests for management and professional grades. **5.** *Tests of Mechanical Comprehension* (1940–55): high-school and adult mechanical aptitude tests with several difficulty levels. Mathematical and technical drawings requiring right-wrong-better judgment. *J.G.*

Benton Test. A procedure similar to the Bender–Gestalt test but using different models and instructions designed to test gestalt comprehension and reproduction from recent memory. *A.L.*

Berdache. A sexual role among the Sioux Indians of North America. The Sioux consider a berdache to be both male and female. The role is formally assigned by the medicine man after the youth has told him certain dreams. A berdache dresses like a woman, takes no part in military expeditions and is often a kind of jester (or even teacher). He is said to take no interest in sexual activities with women. Yet he is not necessarily homosexual. Now that the Indians have to a large extent adopted the sex roles of Western civilization, that of the berdache is no longer assigned.

Bibliography: Erikson, E. H.: Observations on Sioux education. J. Psychol., 1939, 7, 101–56. *G.L.*

Berger rhythm. See *Alpha rhythm.*

Bernoulli distribution. See *Binomial distribution.*

Beschreibung. See *Introspection; Description method.*

Bestiality. Sexual contact between humans and animals. Most societies condemn or ridicule this behavior, but it is not infrequent in some, e.g. Copper Eskimos, Hopi Indians, Masai. Kinsey estimates the frequency of bestiality as 8% for males and 3·6% for females in his sample. Syn. *Erotic zoophilia, Zoophilia.* *P.Le.*

Beta movement. According to M. Wertheimer, apparent movement during which an impression is created that an object is moving from one place to another. If, e.g., in a dark room a small lamp is allowed to flash at a place A and a second small lamp at a place B, alternately, Ss perceive the "movement" of a small lamp from A to B and back. See *Motion, apparent.* *V.M.*

Beta rhythm; beta waves. EEG waves in the frequency range 13 to 30 c/s which appear predominantly when there is a high level of cerebral activation (sensory stimulation, mental activity). See *Alpha rhythm.* *M.S.*

Betel. The betel nut, or kernel of the betel palm: chewed as a stimulant when ground and mixed with (or wrapped in) betel leaves together with burnt coral paste: i.e. a *masticatory stimulant*, especially in India and the Far East. See *Arecolin; Intoxicants.* *J.G.*

Betz cells. Large pyramid(al) cells in the motor cortex.

Bewusstheit. See *Awareness.*

Bezold-Brücke phenomenon. The greater visibility of red and green under reduced light intensity, and the predominance of yellow and blue when the intensity is heavily increased. A similar effect occurs with changes in the spatial dimensions of the stimuli: when the angle of vision is reduced, it becomes more difficult to distinguish between yellow and blue than between red and green. See *Tritanopia; Purkinje effect.* *G.Ka.*

Bias. A term used in statistics to denote a systematic error (q.v.). Random samples with bias can no longer be regarded as representative of all the cases in question. The reasons for this are not due to the intended experimental variation. *W.H.B.*

Bibliotherapy. Making use of reading for therapeutic gain. Books may be prescribed by the therapist for many different reasons: to help the patient understand the terminology of therapy, to remedy deficiencies in knowledge, to give vicarious satisfactions not available in reality, to facilitate vocational rehabilitation, and so on. *G.D.W.*

Bifactor method. The extraction first of a factor general to all the tests, and then the extraction of more limited group factors among test clusters. See *Factor analysis.*

Bilingualism. 1. The ability to speak fluently and as "mother tongues" two languages learned at approximately the same time. Known as *coordinate* bilingualism when the learning situations are distinct (e.g. one language from one parent, one from the other), and the sets of meaning responses in each language are independent. **2.** The ability to speak fluently two languages one of which is learned later than the first. Known as *compound* bilingualism, when the set of meaning responses is common to both languages. Successful second-language learning has been thought to approximate more to the coordinate model, and various educational strategies are used to provoke original responses in the new language. Chomskyian models, however, have been influential recently. No *conclusive* evidence of general adverse effects on mental development has been shown in bilingual children. (But see, e.g., Arsenian, 1945; Darcy, 1946; Leopold, 1948; Macnamara, 1966; Smith, 1949; Thompson, 1952.) IQ, socio-economic situation, and parents' attitude are important factors.

Polyglottism, the ability and will to acquire fluency in several languages, has been variously assessed, the Adlerian school judging it favorable as an outgoing tendency (e.g. Brachfeld, 1932), some psychoanalytic commentators finding it neurotic, and the polyglot a "linguistic Don Juan" (see Vereecken, 1966).

The problem of bilingualism (and polyglottism) is best considered in the context of abilities (q.v.) and the family, as well as in terms of the language-and-mind debate, i.e. especially between the idea of universal grammar as an innate schematism (Chomsky) and the Skinnerian concept of language acquisition in terms of reinforcement—a debate which can hardly be said to have been concluded). See *Differential psychology; Grammar; Language.*

Bibliography: Arsenian, S.: Bilingualism in the post-war world. Psychol. Bull., 1945, *42*, 65–86. **Brachfeld, O.:** Zur Individualpsychologie des Sprachenerlernens. Int. Z. Ind. Psychol., 1932, *10*, 201–7. **Chomsky, N.:** Language and mind. New York, 1968. **Darcy, N. T.:** The effect of bilingualism upon the measurement of the intelligence of children of preschool age. J. Educ. Psychol., 1946, *37*, 21–44. **Elwert, Th.:** Das zweisprachige Individuum. Akad. Wiss. Lit., 1959, 267–344. **Fisher, J. A.:** Readings in the sociology of language. The Hague, 1968. **Leopold, W. F.:** The study of child language and infant bilingualism. Word, 1948, *4*, 1–17. **Macnamara, J.:** Bilingualism and primary education. Edinburgh, 1966. **Skinner, B. F.:** Verbal behavior. New York, 1957. **Smith, M. E.:** Measurement of vocabulary of young bilingual children in both of the languages used. J. Genet. Psychol., 1949, *74*, 305–10. **Thompson, G. G.:** Child psychology. Boston, 1952. **Vereecken, J. L. T. M.:** Quelques considérations sur le polyglottisme. Psychother. Psychosom., 1966, *14*, 66–77. *J.C.*

Bimodal. A term used for a distribution with two peaks (maxima, or modes). See *Frequency distributions.*

Binary digit (*Bit*). A measure introduced by C. E. Shannon for the information unit *H*. It is defined as the number of information units necessary in order to be able to make a decision between two equally probable or two unequally probable alternative outcomes. The magnitude *H* depends on the number of alternatives (*N*), which are available for selection, and on the probability (p_i) of the single alternatives. With two equally probable possibilities one needs an information unit ($H = 1$ bit) in order to make a decision. With four such possibilities two information units are needed; and so on. In general terms, the following formula holds good: $2^H = N$, or more simply: $H = \log 2\,N$, where logarithms to the base 2 are used. It has been calculated on the basis of answers given that the information units at the expert's disposal are in the order of magnitude 10^6.

If unequal probabilities are the two alternatives (*A,B*) for selection, E. B. Newman's law is used: condition $p_A = p_B$

$$H \underset{L}{=} -p_A \log 2p_A - p_B \log 2p_B$$
$$\doteq \log 2\,2 = 1.$$

The value lies between 1 and 0 and follows the curve calculated by Newman. If there are more than two possibilities, the law can be generalized:

$$H = -\frac{\Sigma}{N} p_i \log 2p_i$$

See *Information theory.* *W.S.*

Binary system. In mathematics, the use of only two symbols, a zero and a digit, to construct a system of numbers. By using 0 and 1 we get for the numbers 0 to 9 of the decimal system: 0, 1, 10, 11, 100, 101, 110, 1000, 1001. The importance of the binary system is its application in fields such as computer calculation (Boolean algebra), data processing, and information theory (q.v.).

K.E.P.

Binet, A. B. 11/7/1857 in Nice; d. 18/10/1911 in Paris. An important representative of classical experimental psychology in France. After studying law, medicine and biology, together with Henri Beaunis he founded in 1889 the first psychology laboratory in France, at the Sorbonne, and in 1894 became its director.

He published much of his research in the first French psychological journal *L'année psychologique*, which appeared in 1895, and which he founded and edited. Binet's main field was research into "higher mental processes" in children and adults. In answer to a request from the French Ministry of Education, he devised his first standardized test to discover defective primary-school children in collaboration with Th. Simon. The test was developed from intelligence scales for the investigation of normally gifted and subnormal children, which were extended to become an intelligence test for the age range 3 to 15. First published in 1905, it was revised in 1908 and 1911. The 1911 version offered more accurate assessments of general ability and was the model for countless imitations. Each of the tests in a series of increasing difficulty accords with a specific developmental level. There is a revised American version by L. Terman (Stanford Revision).

Works: La psychologie du raisonnement. Paris, 1886. Les altérations de la personalité. Paris, 1891, L'étude expérimentale de l'intelligence. Paris, 1903. Le développement de l'intelligence chez les enfants. L'année psychologique, 1908 (Eng .trans.: Binet, A. & Simon, T.: The development of intelligence in children. London, 1916). Les idées modernes sur les enfants. Paris, 1909.

Bibliography: **Claparède, E.:** A. Binet. Archives Psychologiques, 1911, *11*, 376–88. **Simon, T.:** A. Binet. L'année psychologique, 1912, *18*, 1–14. *G.S.*

Binet-Simon Scale. Historically the most influential procedure for examining intellectual ability, the first intelligence test was developed in 1905 on behalf of the French Ministry of Education by A. Binet and Th. Simon to select children of defective intelligence for transfer to special schools. To begin with, it consisted of thirty verbal, perceptive and manipulative tasks in a series of increasing difficulty. In the decisive revision of 1908 the mental age principle was introduced: those tests which were almost always done correctly by $\frac{2}{3}$ to $\frac{3}{4}$ of a representative sample of children of a certain age, but only seldom by younger children and almost always by older ones, were grouped into test levels typical for respective ages. The Binet–Simon test contains levels at which normal children can pass for each year between 2 and 13; later procedures employ partly differentiated age scales and widen the age range downwards (see *Development tests*), and upwards to include adults. The sum of all the tasks which a testee can do indicates the level of his development on an intelligence age scale (abb. MA; see *Mental age; Intelligence quotient:* IQ).

Typical of all tests conforming to the Binet–Simon principle is the grouping of tasks of a heterogeneous nature (as regards task standard, material, assumptions about knowledge, solution processes, etc.) into a global measure of intelligence. The MA scale and the IQ concept quickly spread everywhere. They signified a decisive breakthrough in the measurement of abilities (q.v.); on the other hand they were the reason—at least in practice—why a differentiated consideration of the forms and structure of intellectual achievements was delayed and made difficult.

Adaptations, revisions and modifications of IQ tests on the mental age-level principle were published at an early date in many countries. Some influential examples were those of E. Claparède and A. Descoeudres in French-speaking Switzerland, O. Decroly in Belgium, C. Burt in Britain, G. H. Jaederholm in Sweden and W. Stern, O. Bobertag, P. Chotzen and E. Hylla in Germany. One of Burt's major contributions was the substitution (1911) of paper-and-pencil Yes–No and cross-out or underlining responses to printed tests for Binet's *verbal* tests and responses. It was Wundt (1912) who introduced the IQ index. In the U.S.A., after the first adaptations of H. H. Goddard, F. Kuhlmann and others, the new and carefully developed Stanford–Binet test (q.v.), by L. M. Terman & M. A. Merrill, 1937 and 1960, became one of the most widely used intelligence tests. In German-speaking countries importance was attached especially to the "*Binetarium*" of I. Norden as well as to the comprehensive Viennese development test series by Ch. Bühler, H. Hetzer and others; those in use today also include the test series for Swiss children by H. Biäsch, the J. Kramer's intelligence test, and an adaptation of the Stanford–Binet by H.-R. Lückert. In French-speaking countries, the Stanford–Binet test has been revised as the Terman–Binet test, and is widely used. *A.L.*

Binocular fusion; binocular integration. The fusion of the two separate retinal images as the two eyes function in unison.

Binocular rivalry. Radically different colors or figures presented simultaneously to corresponding areas of the two eyes are not usually combined. If, for example, a red and a green square are presented the observer sees each of these squares alternately rather than a single brown square. The rate of alternation of the two percepts and the prevalence of one or the other are determined by factors such as light intensity and the content of the stimuli. *C.D.F.*

Binomial distribution. If an alternative event A in any experiment has a probability B, the probability is that this event will occur x times in N experiments:

$$_{N}p_{x} = \binom{N}{x} \cdot [P^{x} \cdot (1 - P)^{N-x}]M,$$

This is the binomial distribution, or Bernoulli distribution. The expression for $_{N}p_{x}$ consists of the probability of a certain sequence of alternative events the aggregate result of which $f(A) = x$ in N experiments has a probability of $p^{x} \cdot (1 - P)^{n-x}$, as well as of the number of all possible sequences of the length N all of which lead to the result $f(A) = x$, $\binom{N}{x}$.

Bibliography: Maxwell, A. E.: Basic statistics in behavioural research. Harmondsworth, 1970, 62–72.

W.H.B.

Biocenosis. The living community in which an animal or a plant species exists, i.e. all the organisms of a biotope (see *Ecology*), among which there is often a range of direct or indirect relationships. For example, in a beech wood the principal organic factor is the copper-beech; this tree is responsible for the conditions of light and humidity that determine which other plants will occur there (e.g. wild anemones). Certain kinds of worm, beetle and slug in turn live on beech leaves; certain spiders on the slugs; and certain birds on the beetles; and so on. *H.S.*

Bioclimatics. **1.** The branch of biology dealing with the influence of climate (weather, air temperature, air humidity, etc.) on living creatures. **2.** The way in which an organism interrelates with climate. Syn. *Bioclimatology.* *K.E.P.*

Biodynamics. **1.** The physiology of the active relations between organisms and their environment. **2.** The name given to a theory associated with J. H. Masterman, in which an ambitious attempt is made to combine the basic principles of psychoanalysis, behaviorism, and so-called "psychobiology".

Biogenetic law. A principle postulated by E. Haeckel: ontogeny recapitulates phylogeny: i.e. the individual development of any kind of organism is a brief recapitulation of its phylogeny, or stages of species-specific evolutionary development. This is not an actual law, as the repetition does not necessarily take place, but can be demonstrated in very many cases. In the human embryo, the pharyngeal arches, homologous to the gill bars of lower vertebrates (fish), and the primary hair of the fetus may serve as examples. Such instances of the law offer clear evidence for the accuracy of Darwin's theory of evolution. *H.S.*

Biogenic amines. A group of biologically active substances which are main, intermediate or end products in cellular metabolism and have a number of physiological functions, especially in the nervous system. In part, biogenic amines act as *transmitter substances* (q.v.). The term "biogenic amine" refers in its most restricted sense to substances which are obtained from aromatic amino-acids as decarboxylation products (separation of CO_2 from the carboxyl group [COOH]).

Substance	Conversion into next substance under influence of enzyme	Enzyme activity disturbed by	Effects
(biosynthesis) Phenylalanine ↓	Hydroxylase	Inborn error of metabolism	Phenylketonuria
Tyrosine ↓	Tyrosine hydroxylase	α-methyl-tyrosine	Reduction of endogenous noradrenaline concentration
Dopa ↓	Dopa decarboxylase	α-methyldopa	Replacement of noradrenaline by α-methylnoradrenaline (false transmitter)
Dopamine ↓	Dopamine-β-hydroxylase	Adrenalone, Arterenone, Disulfiram	Decrease in noradrenaline concentration
(decomposition) Noradrenaline ↓ (a)	(a) Catechol-o-methyl transferase (COMT)	COMT-inhibitors	
	(b) Monoamine oxidase (MAO)	MAO-inhibitors (e.g. Iproniazid)	Increase in noradrenaline concentration in brain
Normetanephrine ↓ (b)			
3,4-Dehydroxymandelic acid			

Biosynthesis and decomposition of natural noradrenaline, and some possible pharmacological effects.

The most important of these substances are the neurohormones *histamine* (q.v.) (from histidine), *tryptamine* (q.v.) (from tryptophane), *serotonin* (q.v.) (from 5-hydroxytryptophane) and *tyramine* (q.v.) (from tyrosine). From other (basic and aliphatic) amino-acids the following are derived by decarboxylation: *cadaverine*, *putrescine*, *agmatine* (all three constituents of ribosomes), *propanolamine*, *cysteamine*, *β-alaline* and *γ-aminobutyrate* (GABA, q.v.), which plays a part in brain metabolism.

In the wider sense, biogenic amines also include substances which are not obtained by decarboxylation, especially the *catecholamines* (q.v.) (e.g. *noradrenaline*, q.v., and *dopamine*, q.v.].

Biogenic amines have been at the center of pharmacological, biochemical and clinical-therapeutic research since 1950. It is often assumed that the biosynthesis and decomposition of the biogenic amines are disturbed in psychiatric illnesses (depression, schizophrenia). In particular, numerous studies discuss the pathogenetic significance of the metabolism of noradrenaline and serotonin (the catecholamine and serotonin hypothesis of mental illnesses). The main starting-points for these discussions are the possibilities of pharmacological intervention, and morbid (inborn) errors of the biosynthesis and decomposition of the biogenic amines. Some possible pharmacological effects are indicated, using noradrenaline as an example (see tabular summary).

Bibliography: Brune, G. G.: Biogenic amines in mental illness. International Review of Neurobiology, 1965, *8*, 197–220. **Euler, U. S. von, Rosell, S. & Uvnäs, B.** (Eds): Mechanisms of release of biogenic amines. Oxford, 1966. **Franzen, F. & Eysell, K.:** Biologically active amines found in man: their biochemistry, pharmacology and pathophysiological importance. Oxford, 1969. **Guggenheim, M.:** Die biogenen Amine. Basle, 1961. **Himwich, H. E.** (Ed.): Amines and schizophrenia. Oxford, 1967. *W.J.*

Biographical methods in personality research. These consist mostly of a life-history analysis in order to obtain as full and well-rounded a picture as possible of the structure and dynamics of some personality (q.v.). Since the conclusions drawn often owe much to inexpert observations and documents, errors are usually rife. *G.K.*

Bio information. Corresponds largely to the term ESP (q.v.). Used often in Warsaw Pact countries. *H.H.J.K.*

Biology and psychology. As the "science of life", psychology might be considered part of biology. As a discipline in its own right, psychology studies specifically human problems transcending anatomy, physiology, (phylo)genetics and molecular biology. When it relinquishes the objective methods of an experiential science in studying forms of existence and change, it approximates to philosophy (see *Philosophy and Psychology*). The principal founders of empirical psychology were biologists and natural scientists: H. L. F. von Helmholtz, E. H. Weber, G. T. Fechner, W. Wundt, E. Hering, G. E. Müller, and so on. Since then, scientific psychology has been closely allied with biological research in numerous areas: e.g. the physiology of the senses, nerves, brain, metabolism, and development; electrophysiology; endocrinology (q.v.), ecology, molecular biology, etc. Comparative psychology, the psychology of learning, and motivational psychology overlap research into evolution, behavioral physiology, ethology and biocybernetics. Psychological statistics is closely related to biometry. The application of purely biological methods to the study of human behavior and experience is called "biologism", and the over-stressing of psychological principles "psychologism".

Psychology is most obviously distinct from biology in the areas where social and cultural influences on the basis of individual differences and experiences (learning in the broadest sense) produce behavioral differences, restrictions and combinations: e.g. socialization, group behavior, the development of "internal modes of behavior control" (often called "character", "personality", or—in their partial aspects—"motives", "traits", etc.). The increasing influence of biological anthropology and comparative psychology (q.v.) can be noticed here. A psychology of learning oriented solely toward environmental influences is being replaced by research into learning processes which are broader in scope and based on biology: the RNA-DNA system now enters into ontogenetic considerations; and the biological analysis of behavioral potentials—in, say, human and population genetics—is helping to extend our knowledge of the causes of behavior.

Bibliography: Hess, W. R.: Psychologie in biologischer Sicht. Stuttgart, 1968. **Lorenz, K.:** Evolution and modification of behavior. Chicago & London, 1965. **Tembrock, G.:** Grundriss der Verhaltenswissenschaften. Jena, 1968.

K. E. Grossman

Biometry. The application of quantitative methods to research into biological phenomena.

Biorhythm. Life rhythm. The rhythmic course of the life processes of organisms, e.g. corresponding to the day or season, or according to the rhythms inherent in the organism (endogenous rhythm). The biorhythmic phenomena which manifest themselves psychically in man have scarcely been explored but they appear in the female periodic cycle as well as in the phases of juvenile growth. Some ingeniously precise suppositions (such as that of W. Flies that the life of a man moves in rhythmic phases of 23 days, that of a woman in phases of 28, and that the life span can be subdivided into seven year phases) are confirmed neither biographically nor statistically.

F.-C.S.

Biotic experiment (K. Gottschaldt). An experiment in a real-life situation, but without the awareness of the subject; hence disturbing field forces that might come from the test situation are excluded. It is distinguished from pure behavioral observation because the facts to be observed have been deliberately contrived by the experimenter.

The quasi-biotic experiment also takes place without S's awareness, but the situation is not quite true to life. Disturbing field forces are nevertheless excluded since S., while aware that he is taking part in an experiment, knows neither his own role nor the object of the test. This situation is achieved by inserting the critical phase, i.e. the actual test, in an extended framework from which it differs considerably in theme, thereby assuming a "biotic" character (e.g. S., according to instructions, experiences the critical phase only as a preparatory action for a subsequent task which he thinks will be the real test).

Bibliography: Spiegel, B.: Uber die Notwendigkeit biotischer Versuchsansätze in der Verhaltensforschung. Bericht über den 24. Kongress der Deutschen Gesellschaft für Psychologie, Göttingen. 1965, 409–13.

B.Sp.

Biotonus. M. Verworn's (1863–1921) (initially wholly physiological) term for the potential life energy of an individual in regard to the physiological processes of an organism. Biotonus depends on the quality and rate of the metabolism and determines the functional rate and intensity of all organs. It is in equilibrium when the synthesizing and decomposing forces are balanced; high when the synthesizing forces are stronger, low when the decomposing forces are stronger. G. Ewald (b. 1883) extended the term to a man's total state of tension, which is bound up with his temperament, and made biotonus the basic concept of a typology (q.v.): biotonus is said to condition the intensity of mental events, mental alertness and the tonality of the vital emotions (temperament, q.v., vitality, q.v.). Biotonus varies from the melancholic (with a "limp" biotonus) to the circumspect type (in whom it is "average") and to the hypomanic (with a "taut" biotonus).

Bibliography: Ewald, G.: Temperament und Charakter. Berlin, 1924.

F.-C.S.

Bipolarity of traits. Personality traits whose extreme degrees of expression represent opposites (e.g. dominance-submission; extraversion-introversion, q.v.). The zero point of the scale indicating the lowest degree of expression does not coincide with the end of the scale (unipolar trait), but is at the (qualitatively neutral) mid-point between the two opposites. See *Traits*. *K.P.*

Birth order. Adler was the first psychologist to describe the psychological features of specific birth order. Toman has systematized his observations: A family of two children may consist of two brothers, two sisters, or one brother and one sister (sibs, or siblings); in the last case either the boy or the girl is older. Families of three children give eight possibilities, and of n children 2^n possibilities, if only the sex and age sequence vary. The birth order of a given person is one of $n2^{n-1}$ possibilities. If there are only two children, one boy may be the elder or younger brother of a brother or sister. The same applies to a girl in a family of two children. There are therefore eight types of birth orders or sibling relationships. These eight types form the basis of all more complex family constellations. An only child does not have a birth order or sibling relationship.

Studies of children in permanent social contacts outside the family with persons of similar age have shown a preference (based on experience in their original families) for leadership and responsibility roles by the oldest brother or sister of a family and for dependence and opposition roles among the youngest members. Persons with siblings of the opposite sex were more successful in exercising this role toward non-family members of the opposite than of the same sex. Persons with siblings of the same sex only, tended to exercise these roles toward persons of the same rather than of the opposite sex.

Mixed birth orders (e.g. the elder brother of a sister and brother; a sister who has an older and younger brother as well as an even younger sister) are built up from the principal types of birth orders and sibling relationships. Their tendencies in social behavior are therefore correspondingly mixed. Twins generally acquire seniority and juniority characteristics from their environment, while both assume characteristics of their birth position in relation to their brothers and sisters. An only child is distinguished from other only children according to the sib position of the parent of the same sex. Only children always show a need for personal relations in which the partner assumes the role of a father or mother. See *Family*.

Bibliography: Ansbacher, H. L. & Ansbacher, R. R.: The individual psychology of Alfred Adler. New York, 1956. **Dechêne, H. Ch.:** Geschwisterkonstellation und psychische Fehlentwicklung. Munich, 1967. **Toman, W.:** Family constellation. New York, [2]1969. *W.T.*

Birth trauma. Considered by Rank to be the original ontogenetic form of anxiety determining future anxiety reactions in the individual. Birth transfers the individual from an intra-uterine state of uninterrupted satisfaction of his requirements (warmth, soft contact, food and oxygen supply through the mother's bloodstream) to a state of global deprivation (coldness, physical pressure, breathing problems, unfamiliar effects of light and sound, hunger).

However, Rank made no serious attempt to study the effects of the act of birth on birth anxiety and subsequent anxiety reactions as well as individual susceptibility to anxiety. It is probable, too, that the particular characteristics of a birth (easy or difficult) also depend on the social and mental circumstances of the mother's life (e.g. happy marriage, illegitimate birth, first or *n*-th birth), and that the continuation of these circumstances after birth and the mother's attitude to them have a more significant influence on the development of the child and its susceptibility to anxiety than does the more physical act of birth.

Bibliography: Rank, O.: The trauma of birth. New York, 1929. **Toman, W.:** Motivation, Persönlichkeit Umwelt. Göttingen, 1968. *W.T.*

Biserial correlation. A correlation measurement for the degree of frequency of the common occurrence of the classes of a quantitatively and an alternatively measured (dichotomous) continuous variable. The *point-biserial correlation* is applied when, instead of the dichotomous, there is a genuine alternative variable. See *Correlational techniques*. *W.H.B.*

Bisexual. A term applied to women and men who show both homo- and heterosexual behavior. According to psychoanalytic theory, everyone is bisexual. Precise evidence is not yet available, but it can be concluded at least indirectly from material presented by Kinsey and others that bisexual desires are very often met with. *G.L.*

Bit. Abbreviation for binary digit (i.e. number in the binary system). In information theory, the amount of information which will reduce known alternative possibilities by one half. See *Mathematical psychology*.

Bivariate distribution. In contrast to a one-dimensional (univariate) variable, a two-dimensional variable (X_1, X_2) constitutes a bivariate distribution which (for a continuous case) can be expressed as

$$dF = (x_1, x_2)\ dx_1 dx_2$$

In the case of discrete data or such as are comprised in classes, there is a bivariate *frequency distribution* (q.v.) or a *correlation table* (q.v.). The *correlation coefficient* (q.v.) is a measurement for the degree of statistical dependence of the variables of this distribution. *W.H.B.*

Blacky pictures. A projective method developed by G. S. Blum (1946) for diagnosing psychosexual development according to psychoanalytical concepts, using twelve scenes in the life of a family of dogs—the leading character is the little black dog Blacky. The child invents stories about the cartoons and answers questions. The reliability (q.v.) and validity (q.v.) of the method (which suggests, e.g., family conflict situations such as the Oedipus conflict) have been questioned; there is less argument about its clinical utility. *A.L.*

Bleuler's syndrome. The "psycho-organic syndrome" described in 1916 by E. Bleuler

(1857–1939), the Swiss psychiatrist whose main work *Dementia Praecox or the Group of Schizophrenias* appeared in 1911 (Eng. trans.: New York, 1950); later this was called the "organic psychosyndrome", equated with the amnes(t)ic syndrome and finally, as "diffuse cerebral", contrasted with a "cerebrally local" or "endocrine" psychosyndrome (M. Bleuler). It always refers to those psychic combinations of symptoms which can be recorded descriptively and phenomenologically (in the sense of Jaspers' psychopathology) and which are to be found in chronic and diffuse cerebral disorders of a primary and secondary nature, in which disturbances of perception and memory, emotionally hyperesthetic debility, and other impairments of efficiency due to organic brain lesions can be demonstrated. See *Psychoses*.

Bibliography: Bleuler, E.: Lehrbuch der Psychiatrie. (Ed. M. Bleuler) Berlin, [11]1969. (Textbook of psychiatry. New York, 1924.)

O.S.

Blind analysis. The evaluation of data without any contact with the subject. Hence it is not influenced by any subjective impression, yet cannot draw on any information that might be derived from direct observation. On the whole, the tendency is to make the diagnosis solely from the objective data. Comparative investigations have shown that, given good tests, on average blind analysis produces no worse results. *R.M.*

Blind, education of the. In the education of the blind, attempts are made to compensate by systematic training for difficulties in personality development caused by the total or partial loss of sight (such as dependence on strangers' help, restricted possibilities of cognition, inability to conceive esthetic values in the visual modality); and to enable the blind or partially-sighted child, as he grows up, to share in our cultural or intellectual heritage as a full member of the community. The greater dependence of such children has to be considered in the structure and conditions of their education; and the cause of the absence or defect of vision (blindness at birth, early in life or later) influences the choice of teaching methods, which (with such aids as braille, tape libraries, and defect-specific devices) try to make full use of even the least degree of sight.

H.S.

Blind experiment (syn. *Blind test*). A control procedure designed to exclude undesired variables from the experiment. Testees are diagnosed without the experimenter being able to speak to them, etc.; i.e. the diagnosis is made solely by tests.

Double blind test. In this form of the blind test the experiment is conducted without the person in charge or the testee having any knowledge of the variables. E.g. drugs are administered to one group of testees, whereas another group receive placebos. The research director then determines the effect without knowing to which group the testees belonged.

V.M.

Blind, psychology of the. A branch of psychology concerned with the effects of the absence of sight on the sensory, motor, intellectual and personality traits of the blind person, and with research into measures for rehabilitation of the blind in general.

Differences between the sighted and the blind in regard to the discrimination of tactile and auditory signals derive from the additional practice blind people have had. The sense of touch is especially important for reading and the differentiated apprehension of environmental phenomena. Hearing is important for communication and for moving about.

Disablement due to blindness is especially noticeable in motor skills (q.v.), peculiarities in blind children, and difficulties in moving about in the street (recognition of objects: obstacles, traffic signs; see *Orientation*).

There is no difference in intellectual performance between the sighted and the blind. There are more cases of extreme variants among the blind in the lower distribution range (multiple damage: blindness and deafness, blindness and brain damage, etc.).

In regard to specific personality traits, how the blind person comes to terms with his affliction is of major interest. Resignation and adaptation by compensation (q.v.) are assumed. Psychologically important distinctions among the blind are the degree of blindness and when it happened, and the age and sex of the blind person.

The partially sighted seem to have more difficulties in performance and achievement than the totally blind. Investigations to see whether people who have lost their sight profit from their visual experience have yielded no uniform results. Studies dealing with the question (important in cognition theory) of the spatial awareness of those born blind arrive at different conclusions: no primary spatial notions (von Senden, 1932) versus the different nature of tactile-kinesthetic space (Juurmaa, 1966).

Rehabilitation measures are directed primarily to adapting technological advances for the blind (the development of automatic reading appliances, electronic appliances for guiding the blind, light prostheses, etc.).

Bibliography: Research Bulletin: Publication of the American Foundation for the Blind. New York (quarterly). **Juurmaa, J.**: An analysis of the ability for orientation and operations with spatial relationships. Work—Environment—Health, 1966, *2*, 45–52. **Révész, G.**: Psychology and art of the blind. London, 1950. **Senden, M. von**: Raum- und Gestaltauffassung bei operierten Blinden vor und nach der Operation. Leipzig, 1932. **Zahl, P. A.** (Ed.): Blindness: modern approaches to the unseen environment. Princeton, 1950.

M. Brambring

Blind spot. The point where the optic nerve leaves the eyeball. It corresponds to the *papilla nervi optici* and is situated 12 to 18 degrees on the nasal side of the *fovea centralis*. There are no light receptors here. *R.R.*

Blocks (*Blocking*). The terms *block* and *blocking* are often used synonymously in psychology and physiology for an inhibition, barrier, obstacle or an interrupted action. In hierarchical function models (as, e.g., in reflex and instinct theory, Tinbergen, 1951), blocking is adduced to explain prepotent reflexes (q.v.).

The usual applications of the terms: (*a*) in physiology: *synaptic blocking*, *anodic blocking*, *depolarization* and *hyperpolarization blocking*, *heart blocking*, all of which are terms to denote obstructions of the transmission of electrical impulses in nerve fibers and cells. *Ganglionic blocks:* chemical substances in vegetative ganglia; their effect is to inhibit excitation. *Alpha-wave blocking:* the suppression of the alpha-wave activity in the electroencephalogram. (*b*) In psychology and psychopathology: *mental block:* see below. *Memory block:* a name or concept normally easy to recall cannot at the moment be brought to mind. *Affective block:* psychopathological obstruction of the emotional capacity for experience and response; to be distinguished from "*emotional block*": an inhibition of perceiving, thinking or acting as a result of emotional arousal, e.g., caused by examination anxiety or stage fright. (*c*) In the experimental sense, a block can also be: an external obstacle which obstructs the realization of some reaction (e.g. a barrier in a maze). In the planning of experiments (block design): the smallest responsive group of contiguous experimental lots (or subjects), to which the different experimental conditions are allotted at random or systematically. Since Bills (1931), "*psychic*" or "*mental*" blockings have come to mean brief interruptions of thought processes or continuous stimulus-response activities where no specific external stimulus or subjectively perceptible motive (q.v.) can be made responsible.

Subjective accompaniments of blocks are: a "mental vacuum", "sensory dissociation" in the perception of stimuli or in the train of thought, as well as momentary motor inability to give the response which until a very short time before had been given correctly. There are significant colloquial expressions for the phenomenon, such as: "short circuit", "losing the thread", "breaking off one's train of thought", "on the tip of my tongue", etc.

From the standpoint of behavioral psychology, blocks are best observed during continuous behaviors with relatively homogeneous stimulus- and activity-structures (e.g. during the continuous naming of colors, or the continuous addition of digits). They appear then as relatively long interruptions of the activity (duration of a block is between app. 0·5 and 10 sec., and in rare cases even as much as 1 min. or more). In continuous activities, e.g. the numbers 2 + 3 suddenly cannot be added ("the answer won't come"), or the figures appear as unintelligible characters ("like hieroglyphs"), or the testees recognize, e.g., the color green, but are momentarily unable to pronounce the associated word "green". A few seconds later the specific response is given quite normally once more. Blocks can appear in series, and can be announced by responses which become longer and longer but which also frequently appear with extreme suddenness in the midst of the response activity. Blocks can also disappear with the same suddenness. Blocks cannot voluntarily be prevented from appearing. Fatigue and anxiety states especially can give rise to intensified blocking.

There is as yet no satisfactory theoretical explanation for blocking. Bills regarded it as a defensive inhibition of fatigue (*refractory period theory*).

Mental blocking is related to severa psychological phenomena of attention, thought, activity and motivation, as well as certain psychopathological effects (e.g. the interruption of a thought process in schizophrenic thought disorders, etc.).

Bibliography: Bäumler, G.: Statistische, experimentelle und theoretische Beiträge zur Frage der Blockierung bei fortlaufenden Reaktionstätigkeiten (Dissertation). Würzburg, 1967. **Bills, A. G.:** Blocking: a new principle of mental fatigue. American Journal of Psychology, 1931, *43*, 230–45. **Tinbergen, N.:** The study of instinct. Oxford, 1951.

G. Bäumler

Blood-brain barrier (BBB). A term coined by Stern & Gautier (1921) to denote the fact that most chemical substances pass with relatively greater difficulty from the blood into the tissues of the central nervous system than into other bodily tissues. The barrier is conceived as a system regulating the passage of substances present in the blood into the CNS. It cannot be clearly delineated either anatomically or physiologically and biochemically, but has the character of an intervening variable in the sense of a collection of numerous factors. The extent to, and speed with which different substances pass the barrier depend on their chemical and physical properties (e.g. molecular size, fat solubility). Gases pass with especial ease (e.g. O_2; inhalant narcotics); many hormones pass with difficulty, or not at all, e.g. adrenalin(e).

Bibliography: Dobbing, J.: The blood-brain barrier. Physiological Review, 1961, *41*, 130–88. **Lorenzo, A. V.:** Mechanism of drug penetration in the brain. In: **P. Black** (Ed.): Drugs and the brain. Baltimore, 1969.

W.J.

Blood pressure. The prevailing pressure in the blood vessels, which can be measured physically. It can be measured directly with a manometer introduced into the vessel, or indirectly (according to S. Riva-Rocci) with an inflated sphygmomanometer strapped round the arm. There are two components, one hydrostatic and the other hemodynamic. The latter is the consequence of the heart's activity, serves to overcome resistance to flow and decreases continuously in the circulatory system in the direction of the blood flow (from 120 mmHg via the aorta, via 35 mmHg in the capillary circulation to 0 in the veins near the heart). In the arteries it fluctuates with the rhythm of the heart beat between a systolic (120 mmHg) and a diastolic (80 mmHg) value.

These fluctuations of pressure appear as the pulse and can be recorded as a sphygmogram. The mean blood pressure is regulated by the vasomotor center in the brain stem by way of pressure points in the blood vessels and heart activity, as well as vascular contractile power. (For morbid changes of the blood pressure see under *Hypertonia* and *Hypotonia*). *E.D.*

Blumenfeld illusion (syn. *Blumenfeld alley*). If Ss are given the task of making two parallel rows with small gas lamps in a dark room, they will arrange the lamps other than when they are asked to take the corresponding lamps in pairs to the same distance in depth. This optical illusion (see *Geometric-optical illusions*) is an argument against the "parallel axiom" (or "parallel postulate" of Euclid's geometry) in space perception. See *Visual perception*. *V.M.*

Body build index (syn. *Body type index*). According to H. J. Eysenck, the body may be considered as a rectangle in terms of two independent dimensions: height and width. Height is measured by length of arms, of leg, total height, etc.; width by chest width, and chest or hip circumference. General, total body size is calculated by height multiplied by width (i.e. transverse chest width). Body build, or shape (whether the body is relatively long or relatively squat), is calculated by dividing the height by the width (or one hundred times the height divided by six times the transverse chest width = IB). Macrosomatics, mesosomatics and microsomatics are descriptive terms for body size 1 SD above, within ±SD of, and 1 SD below the mean of the population respectively (SD = % standard deviation). Eurymorphs, mesomorphs and leptomorphs are descriptive terms for body build, similarly determined.

Bibliography: **Rees, L. & Eysenck, H. J.:** A factorial study of some morphological and psychological aspects of human constitution. J. ment. Sci., 1945, *91*, 8–21. *J.C.*

Body concept. See *Body image*.

Body ego. An aspect of the "ego" (q.v.) concept: all ego-experiences in regard to one's own body. Equivalent to L. Kleist's "somatopsyche". *H.-J.A.*

Body image (syn. *Body schema*). In general, a spatial idea of one's own body which changes according to information received from one's body and the environment; in this image the parts of the body have a different appearance. Schilder (1935) and Head (1926) described the distortion of the body image from a neurological and psychiatric angle, and extended their findings to the field of normality. (*a*) The change of the body image through each new position and movement of the body; (*b*) the development of the body image depends on social contact. The body image mainly operates unconsciously, and is used as a standard by which all positions, movements and perceptions of the body are compared before there is any response.

Bibliography: **Fisher, S. & Cleveland, S. E.:** Body image and personality. New York & London, 1958. **Head, H.:** Aphasia and kindred disorders of speech. London, 1926. **Schilder, P.:** The image and appearance of the human body. London, 1935. *J.O.*

Body size. See *Body build index*.

Body Sway Test of Suggestibility. A test for primary (motor) suggestibility from Eysenck's battery. Basically, the Hull Body Sway Test is used: the subject listens to a record while standing upright; the degree of movement on being told that he is falling forward is measured.

Body temperature. Organisms which are poikilothermic, i.e. with a variable body temperature, adapt it to the environment and may reach even higher levels than man (e.g. the lizard when the sun is very hot). Homoiothermic (warm-blooded) creatures such as man maintain a uniform *interior body* temperature in the cranial, pulmonary and abdominal cavities. The rectal temperature varies between approximately 36·2 and 37·5°C, being at its lowest at about 6 a.m., and at its highest at about 6 p.m. In the outer body, which in man may also be described as poikilothermic, the temperature as the skin is approached drops more or less to that of the environment. Body temperature is subject to a complicated biocybernetic process controlled by centers—a "cooling center" in the rostral hypothalamus and a "heating center" at the back of the hypothalamus. The control value is the temperature of the arterial blood, any rise in which after transmission through corresponding hypothalamic or even spinal points produces vasodilation, sweating, and a feeling of heat; any drop in arterial blood temperature leads to vasoconstriction, and an increase in the metabolic rate, shivering and numbness. Fever may be regarded as a change in the normal values of the hypothalamic control centers. *K.H.P.*

Bone conduction. The conduction of sound through the skull bones to the cochlea. (Air) sound waves above 800 Hz create cranial vibrations and their oscillation nodes, or nodal points, pass through the petrosal bone and compress the cochlea according to the sound rhythm. Because of the unequal elasticity of the two (oval and round) windows (Békésy's compression theory) each bulges to a different degree and there is thus displacement of fluid in the two scalae (lymphatic canals in the cochlea). Since the fluid mass of the semicircular canals is also joined to one of the two scalae (von Ranke's mass coupling theory), the asymmetry of the scalae (and hence the displacement of fluid) is further intensified. The associated vibration of the basilar membrane separating the two scalae leads to the excitation of auditory cilia, and thus the sound is perceived. *E.D.*

Bonhoeffer's syndrome. Karl Bonhoeffer (1868–1948) described in 1912, in an article on psychoses and infections and other diseases (in: Aschaffenburg, G.: *Handbuch der Psychiatrie.* Leipzig & Vienna, 1912) the "acute exogenous reaction-type". Under this term he grouped all the acute psychic concomitant symptoms of physical (i.e. not just primarily cerebral) illnesses. M. Bleuler and K. Conrad have done much to develop the concept. See *Psychoses; Psychosomatics.*

Bibliography: Bleuler, M., Willi, J. & Buehler, H. R. *et al.*: Akute psychische Begleiterscheinungen körperlicher Krankheiten. Stuttgart, 1966. **Conrad, K.:** Die symptomatischen Psychosen. In: **Gruhle, H. W., Jung, R., Mayer-Gross, W. & Müller, M.** (Eds): Psychiatrie der Gegenwart, Vol. 2, 369–436. *O.S.*

Boredom. A psychological condition associated with environmental monotony and characterized by negative affect, loss of interest, wandering attention, low arousal and impaired working efficiency. In its extreme form boredom may give rise to symptoms ranging from depression to agitation and hallucinations, and is being held increasingly responsible for many social problems including delinquency, suicide and martial unhappiness. *G.D.W.*

Bovarism (syn. *Bovaryism*). Holding an unreal, glamorized conception of oneself to the extent that one fails to distinguish between romance and reality. Also: such a conception. From Emma Bovary in Flaubert's novel *Madame Bovary.*

Bowel training (syn. *Cleanliness training; Toilet training*). According to Freudian theory, exceptionally severe or too early anal training in regularity of stool, etc., can result in later abnormal orderliness, obstinacy and stinginess. Attempts have been made to test the hypothesis of the existence of an anal trait and some evidence has been obtained, but the relation to coercive or speedily-completed bowel training has not been demonstrated.

Bibliography: Barnes, C. A.: A statistical study of the Freudian theory of levels of psychosexual development. Genet. Psychol. Monogr., 1952, *45*, 105–24. **Beloff, H.:** The structure and origin of the anal character. Genet. Psychol. Monogr., 1957, *55*, 141–72.
J.G.

Brace Scale of Motor Ability. A test to estimate ability to learn motor skills. Useful for determining gross motor coordination difficulties. The scale can be applied throughout the age-range of 5 to 18 years and contains thirty-nine tasks testing motor abilities (e.g. agility). Revisions by McClory & Young (1954) and Vickers *et al.* (1942) are available: Iowa–Brace Scale.

Bibliography: Brace, D. K.: Measuring motor ability. A scale of motor ability tests. New York, 1927. **McCloy, C. H. & Young, N.:** Tests and measurements in physical education. New York, [3]1954. **Vickers, V. *et al.*:** The Brace used with young children. Res. Quart., 1942, *13*, 299–302.
J.M.

Bradykinesia (*Bradykinesis; Hypokinesis*). A motor disorder. Slowness of movement as a result of central organic disturbance.

Bradykinin. A polypeptide contained in the tissues the significance of which is as yet unexplained. Pain of limited duration can be produced by the injection of bradykinin into arteries leading to the extremities or to the intestines, or by use on skin blisters. Hence bradykinin is used for the experimental induction of pain and for testing, *inter alia*, analgesics (q.v.). In therapy bradykinin is used as a peripheral vasodilator, when it brings about a considerable fall in blood pressure.

Bibliography: Erdös, E. G.: Structure and function of biologically active peptides: bradykinin, kallidin, and congeners. Annals of the New York Academy of Science, 1963, *104*, 1–464. **Lim, R. K. S. & Gurman, F.:** Manifestations of pain in analgesic evaluation in animals and man. In: **Soulairac, A., Cahn, J. & Charpentier, J.** (Eds): Pain. New York, 1968.
W.B.

Bradyphrasia (syn. *Bradyarthria; Bradylalia; Bradyphasia; Bradyglossia*). An organically conditioned speech disorder. Retardation of speech by drawing out the syllables, and by pauses of varying length as a result of central organic disturbance: in lesions of the cerebellum and associated structures, especially in multiple sclerosis; often combined with other motor disorders. *F.-C.S.*

Bradyphrenia (syn. *Hypophrenia*). Retardation of the mental functions through a lack of inner drive consequent upon central organic disturbance, e.g. encephalitis (q.v.). *F.-C.S.*

Brain. Conscious processes cannot occur without a properly functioning brain: every experiential content depends on the activation of specific nerve cells. If these cells are activated by specific stimuli (see *Neuropsychology*), the related psychological processes occur; if the nerve cells are destroyed, the mental processes dependent on them are irrevocably lost: the totality of neuronal activity in our brain represents our individual world.

Even in simply organized forms of life, the nerve cells are associated in larger groups which receive stimuli from the sense cells or transmit corresponding information to the effectors. This tendency to centralization is particularly marked in all the vertebrates. These have a central nervous system (brain and spinal cord) in which the mass of brain substance dominates that of the spinal cord with an increasing level of differentiation.

The cell bodies of the neuron(e)s (grey matter) are either combined in nuclei embedded deep in the brain in the fibrous masses of other nerve cells (white matter), or form a superficial cell layer with many transverse connections, i.e. the (cerebral) cortex. In the primates there is a very substantial multiplication of cells in the anterior section of the brain (the endbrain, or telencephalon, q.v.), and in particular in the main cerebral cortex (covering the hemispheres of the endbrain) in which the terminals of all specific, sensory stimuli are located and the pathways for control of the voluntary motor system originate. The caudal brain sections adjoining the endbrain, i.e. the interbrain (diencephalon, q.v.) and midbrain (mesencephalon, q.v.), which still play a dominant part in controlling the behavior of the lower vertebrates, are much less important in all the higher vertebrates (especially in man), and are almost completely covered by the hemispheres of the endbrain. This structural principle led to the assumption that the "higher" parts of the brain which developed later took over the functions of their phylogenetic precursors in a differentiated form (hierarchical function model). In this assumption, the cerebral cortex, as the most recent differentiation in brain development, is thought to be the highest central nervous unit on whose activity the control of all more complex behavioral processes and the occurrence of psychic (mental) processes depend. This view has been revised more recently with the discovery of a cell system which extends as a functional unit in the longitudinal axis of the brain, through all the hierarchical levels, and on the activity of which the activation level of the living being is dependent at any given time. This *non-specific activation system* includes a group of multiform nerve cells in the midbrain and in the hindmost section of the brain, the hindbrain (rhombencephalon, q.v.), with many transverse links, by reason of which it is known as the reticular formation or substance (*formatio reticularis*). It continues, without any clear demarcation, into the interbrain (thalamus: non-specific thalamic projection system), and—functionally at least—into the endbrain (*limbic system*). Stimulation of the non-specific activation system controls the activity of the cerebral cortex and hence all experience and behavior. If this stimulation is blocked (by pathological processes or interventions in animal experiments) the organism falls into a state of permanent coma even though the cortex remains intact; the activity of the cerebral cortex determines the specific content of a conscious process, whereas the non-specific activation system determines the kind of awareness and the experiential (emotional or motivational) background for this process.

The changes in electrical potential which accompany stimulation of the cortical neurons (see *Nervous system*) can be amplified and recorded from the scalp without surgical intervention (see *Electroencephalogram*). Specific intervention has recently allowed stimulation components fundamental to a specific conscious content to be isolated from all other simultaneous stimulation, and to be observed separately, even though their current amounts to only a few millionths of a volt (see *Neuropsychology*). This advance into the region of just measurable cerebral phenomena has given initial access to an objectively observable correlate for heterogeneous psychic phenomena.

Bibliography: Crosby, E. C., Humphrey, T. & Lauer, E. W.: Correlative anatomy of the nervous system. New York, 1962. **Ferner, H.:** Anatomie des Nervensystems und der Sinnesorgane des Menschen. Munich & Basle, 1970.

G. Guttmann

Brain pathology. The branch of medicine concerned with the analysis of changes (especially in mental processes) which occur in the event of brain damage.

Brain damage may be of two kinds: *organic* and *dynamic*. Organic damage to cerebral activity is associated with irreversible destruction of the nerve cells (ganglionic cells) or pathways (nerve fibers). This damage may be caused by hemorrhage or circulatory disorders in the brain, lesions resulting from injury, brain tumors or inflammatory processes. It may be local or affect the whole brain; the involvement of the entire brain occurs quite often in the event of vascular weakness or atrophic processes resulting from defective development, or aging. The second type of brain damage consists of dynamic lesions which are either perifocal (on the limits of the pathological focus) or at points which are linked functionally with the focus. This damage is based on a temporary inhibition of functions which occurs primarily in connection with a disturbance of the synaptic conductivity of stimuli due to disturbance of the chemical equilibrium between acetylcholine (a chemical substance—transmitter-substance—carrying nerve impulses) and cholinesterase (an enzyme which inactivates acetylcholine). Dynamic damage to brain activity is sometimes referred to as "diaschitis" (K. von Monakow). The main problem in brain pathology is to determine the basic mechanisms of functional disorders (above all disturbance of mental functions) in the event of focal damage to the brain.

The traditional approach to this problem was based on the assumption that each brain section (or each group of brain cells) had a specific function, simple in one case and complex (mental) in another. The proponents of this classical theory (of "narrow localization") believed that in addition to the sections of the cerebral cortex with sensation or motor functions there were also cortical areas specifically concerned with the highest mental functions (ideation, conceptualization, speech, writing, calculating, etc.); injury to these cortical areas would therefore result in the failure of the associated functions. This was the theory of Gall, who established the "science" of phrenology (q.v.) early last century: this located the most complex "abilities" in certain limited brain "centers"; this opinion was shared by Broca who believed the inferior frontal gyrus of the left cerebral hemisphere to be the "motor verbal imagery center"; the same theory was held by O. and C. Vogt and in particular by K. Kleist who introduced the term "brain pathology" and believed that functions such as the understanding of words or sentences, calculation, or even the "personal, social or religious ego" were located in specific parts of the brain. He therefore believed that destruction of the corresponding brain sections would lead to the isolated cessation of these specific functions.

Clinical practice has not confirmed these theories; it has shown that a given function (e.g. writing) can be disturbed by brain injury in various, different areas, whereas the destruction of a single, limited section of the brain may give rise to a whole range of disturbances of mental functions (e.g. cortical injury to the left temporal lobe—in a right-handed person—can affect the understanding of words, naming of objects, writing, and so on).

These facts have led a number of scientists to the opposite assumption: namely, that the human brain always works as a whole, and that the complex mental processes are not localized in specific areas of the brain, but are a function of the whole cortex. This theory of "anti-localization" was propounded by F. L. Goltz, and has been supported more recently by K. S. Lashley, K. von Monakow, and, to some extent, by K. Goldstein. These researchers consider that a disturbance of the complex forms of rational (or categorial) activity depends on the extent of the injury rather than on the particular area of the brain which it affects.

Neither of the two theories outlined above has stood the test of time. While the "localizationists" worked from the incorrect assumption that the highest mental functions were innate abilities which could not be broken down into component parts and could be traced to the functions of individual nerve cells, the "anti-localizationists" considered (wrongly as it turned out) that the highest mental processes were categories of intellectual life which could not be subjected to detailed analysis and were in some undefined manner dependent on the brain as a whole.

Recent scientific developments have led to a thorough revision of the notion of "function", and to a radical reappraisal of the nature of disturbances of mental functions in the event of brain damage.

Scientists now assume that there are two completely different interpretations of the term "function": it may be understood on the one hand as the activity of a tissue (e.g. the photosensitive functions of the retina, or the secretory functions of the glands); and on the other hand as a complex adaptive activity designed to carry out a specific task (e.g. the function of digestion, of breathing, or of locomotion). In the latter case, the "function" is complex and consists of a complicated functional system which works toward a permanent (invariable) goal with varying means. Breathing, which primarily involves the muscles of the diaphragm, may be taken over by the intercostal muscles if the diaphragm muscles are damaged; if the former are damaged, it can be performed by swallowing air; and so on. Most biological "functions" consist of such complex functional systems involving the joint activity of a wide range of nerve mechanisms located to some extent on different planes. All the higher psychological "functions" enjoy the same complex nature. Unlike the biological "functions", these are even more complex functional systems whose origins are socio-historical, while their structure is heterogeneous (dependent on a range of aids), and their method of functioning voluntary (i.e. they are subject to self-control).

It is therefore clear that these "functions" cannot be carried out by isolated cell groups, but are dependent on the common activity of all the different brain areas, each of which makes a specific contribution to the performance of these "functional systems". The process of writing, for example, can only take place if the cerebral cortex is in a certain state (which is guaranteed by subcortical structures); and a further condition is precise phonematic analysis of the sound content of the words to be written (this is ensured by the mechanisms of the temporal-auditory cortex); a simultaneous kinesthetic (articulatory) analysis of the sounds (by the apparatus of the post-central, kinesthetic cortex) is essential, and can only take place if the spatially organized visual patterns of the letters to be written (governed by the visual parietal areas of the cortex) are unimpaired. The following are also requisite for writing: a continuous sequence of movement impulses and the implementation of fluid "kinetic" functions (functions of the pre-motor areas of the cortex), and maintenance of initial intentions with a continuous check on performance of the corresponding actions (which would be impossible without participation of the frontal lobes).

The complex "function" may therefore be disturbed by damage to almost any brain area, but the disturbances will always differ, depending on the contribution of the particular zone to the structure of the functional system as a whole.

This idea has completely changed the orientation of brain pathology. The function of the research worker is no longer to determine which function is disturbed in the event of a limited (local) brain lesion, but rather to isolate the main factor whose failure led to the disturbance of the whole functional system; and to show how the given "function" is disturbed in the event of local brain injury.

This trend—the search for the primary damage which occurs in the event of a local brain lesion, and analysis of the secondary (system-dependent) damage which occurs as a consequence of the primary damage—is the main orientation of modern brain pathology or neuropsychology. The aim is first to describe meticulously the disorder of mental activity which occurs in the event of local brain injury and then to "qualify" the symptom, i.e. to detect its cause and isolate the factor whose failure has led to the disturbance, after which the secondary "system disturbances" can be determined; only when all this has been done is it possible to carry out a local ("topical") analysis of the injury. Brain pathology, or neuropsychology, is of fundamental importance to psychology as a whole. It allows an analysis to be made of the factors which constitute complex psychological processes, and permits more accurate research into the psychophysiological structure and brain mechanisms of these factors. It therefore provides criteria for differentiation between "functions" which appear externally similar but are in reality fundamentally different, and vice versa: it establishes an inner system of links between "functions" which may at first sight appear completely disparate. The auditory perception of music and that of language (phonematic perception) may seem to be related processes, but the fact that a lesion of the left temporal lobe leads to impairment of phonematic hearing, whereas musical hearing remains unaffected, proves that they are in fact very different. On the other hand, processes such as spatial orientation, calculation, and the comprehension of complex logico-grammatical structures are completely different forms of activity; however, the fact that injuries to the lower parietal areas of the cortex leads to disturbance of *all* these processes suggests that they are all dependent on a single region. Research into brain damage (neuropsychological analysis) can therefore be of great significance for psychology, because it investigates the detailed inner structure of psychological processes and their mechanisms in the brain.

Bibliography: Ajusioguerra, J. & Hécean, H.: La cortex cérébrale. Paris, 1966. **Ivanov-Smolenski, A. G.:** Grundzüge der Pathophysiologie der höheren Nerventätigkeit. Berlin, 1954. **Kleist, K.:** Gehirnpathologie. Leipzig, 1934. **Luria, A. R.:** Higher cortical functions in man, New York, 1966. **Id.:** Traumatic aphasia. The Hague, 1970. **Monakow, K. von:** Die Lokalisation im Grosshirn und der Abbau der Funktionen durch lokale Herde. Wiesbaden, 1964.

A. R. Luria

II

Brain stem. The part of the brain (q.v.) left after the exclusion of the cerebrum and cerebellum.

Brainwashing. The subjection of an individual to conditions of physical and even psychic duress in order to persuade him to disclose secrets, bear false witness, or alter his political viewpoint or moral convictions, or otherwise to "convert" him to a desired viewpoint or action. Measures used (usually in exceptional situations, e.g. imprisonment), which eventually bring about intellectual and emotional disorganization, are, e.g.: deprivation of food and sleep, excessive physical stress, refusal of medical attention, isolation. Syn. *Menticide; Coercive persuasion.*

Bibliography: Biderman, A. D. & Zimmer, H.: The manipulation of human behavior. New York, 1961. **Eysenck, H. J.:** Crime and personality. London, 1964. **Lifton, R. J.:** Thought reform and the psychology of totalism. New York, 1961. **Schein, E. H., Schneier, I. & Barker, C. H.:** Coercive persuasion. New York, 1961.

M.A.

Branching. A technique in the construction of teaching programs: one or several subprograms are linked to a main program. These alternative learning paths either offer complements to and elucidations of the main program, or afford an opportunity for repetition. On the basis of his replies to a criterion unit the learner is guided into one of these pre-programmed learning paths according to his individual knowledge or ability; he may be taken to a remedial frame: when he has finished it, he will be taken back into the main program or sequence of frames: e.g. each step ends with a multiple-choice question; the answer chosen decides the next step taken. This is the multiple path or branching program technique originated by Norman Crowder. See *Instructional technology; Machine learning; Programmed learning.*

L.J.I.

Bravais–Pearson correlation coefficient. This coefficient gives the correlation (q.v.) of two continuous *normal distributions* (q.v.). It is not identical with the product-moment correlation (q.v.), but can be satisfactorily estimated from it. *W.H.B.*

Breeding and parental care. Certain creatures take or plan measures in advance which serve directly to protect their offspring, such as placing the nests in protected spots, making protective covers and supplying their progeny with food (e.g. the breeding pellets, or spherical dung-balls in which eggs are laid, of the *Scarabaeus sacer* and Spanish Copris beetles and other members of the Scarab family). Parental care serves indirectly to look after the nests and the young who are watched over and supplied with oxygen or food. *External parental care:* some pipe-fish (e.g. *Nerophis ophidion*), the midwife toad (*Alytes obstetricans*), leeches, crabs, spiders and bugs carry the eggs around with them. *Internal parental care:* those which incubate in body cavities are certain cichlids (in the mouth), needle-fish and sea-horses (in pockets); the frog *Rhinoderma darwinii* even carries its offspring in the sound vesicles. Viviparous creatures: in ovoviparous species the young are still in the egg case at birth. Apart from the egg-laying Greenland Shark, sharks develop a yolk-sack placenta. Cloacal mammals, while laying eggs, have neither placenta nor nipples but lacteal areas. Marsupials give birth to living young but usually have no placenta, and premature young grow together with the nipples. The eutheria have a placenta which enables gas and food to pass between the embryo and the mother. Insessores have a short (rabbits 28 days), autophagi a long gestation (porpoises 63 days). There is prolongation of pregnancy with embryonic development arrested temporarily. E.g. roe-deer and badgers have a prolonged gestation period with temporarily arrested embryonic development.

Bibliography: **Hesse, R.** & **Doflein, F.:** Tierbau und Tierleben, Vol. 2. Jena, 1943. *K.F.*

Brentano, Franz. B. 16/1/1838 in Marienberg near Boppard on the Rhine; d. 17/3/1917 in Zürich. 1864 ordained priest, 1866–73 *Privatdozent* (lecturer), and later Professor of philosophy at Würzburg, 1874–80 Professor at Vienna University, and until 1895 a lecturer in Vienna. His philosophy was neo-Aristotelian in origin, and his psychology was descriptive. Brentano opposed the analysis of consciousness into contents. His theory of the intentionality of psychic phenomena, and his "empirical", rationally argumentative account of mind and experience as a mode of acting, make him the founder of act psychology (q.v.). His recognition of the importance of the intentional orientation of all psychic phenomena to some inner "given" entitles him to rank as a forerunner of phenomenology (q.v.) (see *Husserl*). His understanding of inner perception as prerequisite for all psychology, and his distinction between psychic acts and non-psychic contents influenced (among others) A. Meinong (q.v.) and C. von Ehrenfels (q.v.).

Works: Die Psychologie des Aristoteles, insbesondere seine Lehre vom *nus poetikòs*. Mainz, 1867 (reprinted: Darmstadt, 1967). Psychologie vom empirischen Standpunkt, Ed. O. Kraus. Leipzig, 1924–28. Vom Ursprung sittlicher Erkenntnis. Leipzig, 1907. Von der Klassifikation der psychischen Phänomene. Leipzig, 1911.

Bibliography: **Barclay, J. R.:** Franz Brentano and Sigmund Freud, J. Existentialism, 1964, *5*, 1–36. **Brett, G. S.:** Associationism and "act" psychology. In: **Murchison, C.** (Ed.): Psychologies of 1930. Worcester, Mass., 1930, 39–55. **Kraus, O.:** Franz Brentano. Zur Kenntnis seines Lebens und seiner Lehre. Munich, 1919. **Utitz, E.:** Franz Brentano. Kantsstudien, Vol. 22. Cologne, 1918. *K.E.P*

Brentano's illusion. If in the first of two adjacent pictures we have a circle, and in the second a circle of equal size but surrounded by a larger, concentric circle, the circle in the second picture appears larger than the circle in the first picture which, objectively, is of the same size. See *Delboeuf's illusion; Geometrical-optical illusions.* *V.M.*

Breton's law. A new formulation of Weber's law (q.v.): the relation between the stimulus and the smallest just-noticeable stimulus difference is parabolic. *V.M.*

Brightness. The luminous intensity experienced in visual perception is defined as brightness. A distinction is made between photometric brightness (=luminous intensity) and the specific brightness characteristic of colors (yellow and green being brighter than violet and red). G. T. Fechner assumed that brightness is proportional to the logarithm of light intensity (luminous intensity, retinal illumination). Depending on the duration of exposure to light, Aiba & Stevens (1964) found power functions with different exponents.

Bibliography: Aiba, T. S. & Stevens, S. S.: Relation of brightness to duration and luminance under light and dark adaptation, Vis. Res., 1964, *4*, 391–401).

A.H.

Broca's area. The inferior frontal gyrus of the left cerebral hemisphere (in the right-handed). It is particularly important as the location of the motor language center (but see *Aphasia; Brain pathology*) in the dominant hemisphere. *C.S.*

Bundle hypothesis. Gestalt theorists' term (pejorative) for the view that a whole is only the sum of its parts.

Bühler–Hetzer test. A test for pre-school children (1932); see *Development tests.*

Bibliography: Bühler, C. & Hetzer, H.: Testing children's development from birth to school age. London, 1935.

Bühler, Karl. B. 27/5/1879 at Meckesheim (Baden); d. 24/10/1963 in Pasadena (Calif.); M.D. 1903, Ph.D. 1904; 1907–09 one of the most important researchers of the Würzburg school (q.v.); worked in Bonn from 1909, in Munich from 1913, in Dresden from 1918, and finally in Vienna from 1922 to 1938 (the high point of his academic activity). He was arrested by the Nazis, and sought refuge in Oslo in the autumn of 1938. He went to St Paul (Minn., U.S.A.) in 1940, and lived from 1945 in Los Angeles. His contributions to the psychology of thought belong to his Würzburg period: he defended his method of observation under experimental conditions against W. Wundt (q.v.), G. E. Müller (q.v.), etc. The results of his research work into types of thought are recorded in his articles "Über Gedanken" (1907), "Über Gedankenzusammenhänge" (1908), "Über Gedankenerinnerungen" (1908), and in "Tatsachen und Probleme zu einer Psychologie der Denkvorgänge" (Archiv der Gestaltpsychologie, 1907, *9* and 1908, *12*). These articles also contributed to the defeat of the elementarism (q.v.) and sensualism (q.v.) of classical psychology, and to the recognition of the *Ganzheit* (q.v.) principle. The holistic view of psychic processes was the explicit theme of his *Die Gestaltwahrnehmungen* (Stuttgart, 1913) and, once again, of his last work: *Das Gestaltprinzip im Leben des Menschen und der Tiere* (Berne & Stuttgart, 1960). Bühler gained lasting merit with his book *Die Krise der Psychologie* (Jena, ²1927), in which he endeavors by his theory of aspects to rescue the unity of psychology from the controversies of the schools. His books *Ausdruckstheorie* (Jena, 1933) and *Sprachtheorie* (Jena, 1934) have considerable significance for social psychology. In 1962 his theory of language, and particularly the functions and phenomena of spoken language, formed the central topic of a semantics (q.v.) congress in Indiana; the newly-developing psycholinguistic research (see *Psycholinguistics*) cannot disregard it. Finally, with his *Die geistige Entwicklung des Kindes*

(Jena, 1918; Eng. trans.: *The Mental Development of the Child.* New York & London, 1930), Bühler gave a decisive impetus to developmental psychology. His fundamental, far-reaching and spirited works make Bühler one of the basic personalities of modern psychology.

Bibliography: Festschrift für K. Bühler. In: Zeitschrift für experimentelle und angewandte Psychologie, 1959, *6*, 1–118. **Wellek, K.:** K.B. 1879–1963. Archiv der Gestaltpsychologie, 1964, *116*, 3–8. *L.J.P.*

Burt, Sir Cyril Lodowic. B. 3/3/1883; d. 10/10/1971 in London; studied at Christ's Hospital, London, and at Oxford and Würzburg. Read natural science and psychology, and was a disciple of W. McDougall (q.v.) and O. Külpe (q.v.).

1907–12: taught experimental psychology and physiology at Liverpool University, where he carried out research into the measurement of intelligence; 1913–32 official educational psychologist to the London County Council; 1924–31 Professor of Education in the University of London; 1931–51 Professor of Psychology at University College, London; 1951: Professor Emeritus, University of Oxford. Investigations into and publications on problems of general intelligence, methods of testing intelligence and mental differences between individuals; some of the best standard intelligence tests. Burt also investigated backwardness in children, and delinquency. In the nineteen thirties, he introduced factor analysis into England, and developed the view of factors as classifications of consistent correlations between different test results (the multi-level view of ability—see *Abilities*).

Works: Joint editor of the *British Journal of Psychology, Pedagogical Seminary and Journal of Genetic Psychology, Genetic Psychology Monographs;* Ed. *British Journal of Statistical Psychology.* His publications include: Experimental tests of general intelligence, *Brit. J. Psychol.*, 1909. The distribution and relations of educational abilities, 1917. Mental and scholastic tests, 1921; [4]1949. Handbook of tests for use in schools, 1923. The mental differences between individuals, Brit. Ass. Presidential address, 1923. The young delinquent, 1925. The backward child, 1937. The factors of the mind, 1940. Intelligence and fertility, 1946. The structure of the mind—a review of the results of factor analysis, *Brit. J. Educ. Psychol.*, 1949, *19*, 110–11, 176–99. The evidence for the concept of intelligence, *Brit. J. Educ. Psychol.*, 1955, *25*, 158–77. Intelligence and heredity, *Irish J. Educ.*, 1969, *3*.

Bibliography: Boring, E. G.: A history of experimental psychology. New York, [2]1950. **Burt, C.:** Cyril Burt. In: **Boring, E. G.** (Ed.): History of psychology in autobiography. Vol. 4. Worcester, Mass., 1952, 53–73. **Murchison, C.:** The psychological register. Worcester, Mass., 1929. *W.S.*

Butyrophenones. Chemical subgroup of the neuroleptics (q.v.). Clinically important derivatives are haloperidol, meperone, fluanisone, trifluperidol, fluoropipamide, droperidol, benperidol and pimozide. The butyrophenones are related pharmacologically and clinically to the phenothiazines (q.v.). There have been hardly any psychological investigations. Some results indicate situationally dependent effects. See *Haloperidol.*

Bibliography: Goldstein, B. J., Clyde, D. J. & Caldwell, J. M.: Clinical efficacy of the butyrophenones as antipsychotic drugs. In: **Efron, D. H.** (Ed.): Psychopharmacology 1957–1967. Washington, 1968. **Janke, W. & Debus, G.:** Double-blind psychometric evaluation of pimozide and haloperidol versus placebo in emotionally labile volunteers under two different work load conditions. Psychopharmacologia, 1970, *18*, 162–83. **Lehmann, H. E. & Ban, T. A.:** The butyrophenones in psychiatry. First North American Symposium on the butyrophenones. Quebec, 1964. *G.D.*

C

CA. See *Chronological age.*

Cadre formation. 1. The training and further training of executive staff in all areas of an organization. **2.** The training or indoctrination of theoretically aware and wholly trustworthy key members of a (revolutionary) political party. See *Leadership; Management.* *G.R.W.M.*

Caffeine. A psychopharmacological drug (which is chemically identical with *theine*) to be found in coffee, tea, cola, maté, etc. It ranks as a stimulant (q.v.). Since the end of the last century, caffeine has been frequently studied in psychopharmacological experiments (in doses up to approximately 500 mg). It is less stimulating than the amphetamines and has relatively strong side-effects (e.g. tremor). As a rule (after about 30 min.) caffeine induces a feeling of increased wakefulness although no positive changes in performance can be detected.

Bibliography: Weiss, B. & Laties, V.: Enhancement of human performance by caffeine and the amphetamines. Pharmacol. Rev., 1962, *14*, 1–36. *K.D.S.*

Calibration. Calibration of a random sample of raw values is standardization (q.v.), i.e. determining distribution standards and checking how far they are representative. The term calibration is used especially in connection with the standardization of a newly constructed test (test calibration). The raw value distribution of the previous test is checked by using the calibration sample to see if it agrees with the distribution (see *Frequency distribution*) of the test values in the population (q.v.). If that is not the case, the necessary correction is made. Subsequently the raw values are transformed into standard values in conformity with a standard criterion. *W.H.B.*

California Test of Personality. Personality questionnaires dealing with personal and social adjustment. Five different scales from the nursery-school to the adult level with percentile grading norms for sixteen personality variables such as self-confidence, self-esteem, nervous symptoms, social and total adjustment, antisocial tendencies, etc.

Bibliography: Thorpe, L. P., Clark, W. W. & Tiegs, E. W.: California Test Bureau, 1942–1953. Monterey, Calif. *R.M.*

Call. In parapsychology: subject's response at a given trial in a card-guessing test. *J.B.*

Calorie (*Calory*). **1.** In physics: the amount of heat at 1 atm required to raise the temperature of one gram of water from 14·5 to 15·5°C (1000 cal = 1 kcal.). **2.** In physiology: a value for measuring energy or heat production. *G.R.W.M.*

Canalization 1. A general term for a process in human development involving the *consolidation* of certain kinds of behavior from a range of many developmental possibilities.

2. In a narrower sense, according to G. Murphy, the consolidation and thus the preference of definite means of drive satisfaction from among several initially possible choices. The canalization process is discussed mainly in connection with socialization (q.v.). *W.D.F.*

Cancellation tests. B. Bourdon was the first to have a set of letters cancelled as a test of attentiveness. To exclude habituation to letters, E. Toulouse and H. Piéron have used symbols, and some other tests of this kind have been suggested. Since memory can play a part in the use of symbols, Meili has constructed a "non-model" cancellation test.

Bibliography: **Meili, R.:** Lehrbuch der psychol. Diagnostik. Berne, [5]1965. **Id.:** Durchstreichtest ohne Modell. Berne, 1956. *R.M.*

Cannabis. A variety of hemp, *cannabis indica v. sativa.* Parts of the female hemp plant, after various modes of preparation, are eaten, drunk or smoked for their narcotic effects. A number of hemp products are met with; their pharmacological efficacy depends in large measure on their composition and the conditions under which they have been grown. The best known are hashish (q.v.), or Indian hemp, which comes from India, and marihuana (q.v.), from South America. The active elements in cannabis have been identified as tetra(hydro)cannabinols which are contained especially in the resin of the female plant. See *Narcotics; Psychotomimetics.*

Bibliography: **Bewley, T. H.:** Heroin and cocaine addiction. Lancet, 1965, No. 1, 808–10. **Isbell, H.** *et al.*: Effects of 1-Δ^9-*trans*-tetrahydrocannabinol in man. Psychopharmacol., 1967, *11*, 184–8. **Wholstenhome, G. E. W. & Knight, J.** (Eds): Hashish: its chemistry and pharmacology. Boston & London, 1965. *G.E.*

Cannon emergency function. An adaptation process in the organism as a reaction to sudden serious mental or physical stress, especially to meet some danger, i.e. in an emergency; the process was described by W. B. Cannon after extensive experiments. By temporarily shifting the autonomic balance toward sympathicotonia the organism prepares for a quick release of energy for the purpose of fight or flight, thereby reducing the restitutive processes. Onset and control are set in train by the hypophyseal-midbrain system; and this leads to an increased release of adaptive hormones from the hypophysis and adrenal medulla (especially adrenalin). This induces a fairly stereotyped series of reactions in three stages: the alarm-reaction stage (with hypotonia, increased blood flow, increased permeability, hypothermia and other symptoms of shock, which partly revert in the "counter shock" phase, i.e. when the adaptation begins); the resistance stage (defense phase; release of energy, and adaptation); the exhaustion stage. See *Emotion.* *F.-C.S.*

Bibliography: **Cannon, W. B.:** Bodily changes in pain, hunger, fear and rage. New York, [2]1929.

Capacity. 1. A general term for the retentiveness, or storage capacity, of *memory* (q.v.). Information theory (q.v.) attempts to provide a measurement of capacity in terms of the amount of information retained (bit, q.v.). *Flow capacity* is the amount of information which can be absorbed in a unit of time (bit/sec.).

2. A general term for ability (see *Abilities*). *E.H.*

Capillary. One of the capillaries, or smallest blood vessels. The capillary wall is a single layer of endothelial cells allowing the passage of liquid nutrients and metabolic waste. *H.L.*

Cardiac neurosis. Imprecise designation for the varied complex of symptoms in an organ neurosis involving cardiac disorders: e.g. heart pains, irregular or rapid heart beat, a sensation of pressure or constriction in the area of the heart, and feelings of anxiety. No objective demonstrable symptoms of an organic heart condition are present. These functional heart disorders are generally the result of repressed mental conflict situations. See *Conversion neurosis*. *A.-N.G.*

Cardiazol shock. A general convulsive reaction produced by cardiazol, a central analeptic (q.v.).

Cardinal point; cardinal value. The point or value, according to Fechner, in a quantitative series of sensations at which *difference threshold* (q.v.) begins to increase in proportion to stimulus.

Case history method. The use of case histories (histories of psychotherapeutic and psychiatric cases, reports on education and the home, forensic documents, biographies and autobiographies) in the "anthropological" disciplines (psychoanalysis, psychiatry, psychology, pedagogy, sociology, ethnology, and criminology). This biographical method was developed and refined predominantly by the proponents of psychoanalysis (q.v.) as an instrument of research; to the analysis of the life they added the investigation of experience. Case histories can be interpreted either qualitatively or quantitatively. The qualitative interpretation corresponds to the research approach of the psychology of "understanding" (*Verstehende Psychologie*), and thus psychoanalysis or depth psychology (q.v.) too; the quantitative calculation of solid data (birth, family details, school, occupation, etc.) corresponds to the ideal of an exact natural or social science. Numerous concepts and hypotheses are based on case histories: psychoanalysis owes much to Freud's and Breuer's Anna case, and four cases of hysteria: "little Hans", the wolf man, the rat man, and the famous Dora; child psychology employs parents' (Darwin, W. & C. Stern, E. & G. Scupin) and adolescent diaries (C. Bühler, W. Küppers); cultural-anthropological field research uses studies of "primitive" cultures (M. Mead, P. Parin). Individual emphases and a variety of information on the one hand, and quantitative evaluation on the other will always to some extent remain the bases of conflicting approaches.

Bibliography: Allport, G. W.: The use of personal documents. Psychological science. Social Science Research Council Bulletin, New York, 1942, 49. **Dollard, J.:** Criteria for the life history. New Haven, 1935. **Schraml, W. J.:** Die Psychoanalyse und der menschliche Lebenslauf. Psyche, 1965, *19*, 250–68. **Thomae, H.:** Die biographische Methode in den anthropologischen Wissenschaften. Studien Gen. 1952, *5*, 163–77. *W.J.S.*

Case study. A method of personality psychology which aims to define the "qualitatively unique" individual character of a human being (G. W. Allport). The case study requires a highly detailed study (often continued over a lengthy period) of the individual in the course of which all available data on this person are collected and processed (results of psycho-diagnostic tests, anamnestic-biographical details, creative performance, etc.). The case study is used in ideographic personality research and above all in clinical psychology for practical and diagnostic purposes.

Bibliography: Allport, G. W.: Pattern and growth in personality. New York, 1961. **Anastasi, A.:** Psychological testing. New York, 1961. **Gathercole, C. E.:** Assessment in clinical psychology. Harmondsworth, 1968. **Hetherington, R. R.** *et al.*: Introduction to psychology for medical students. London, 1964. *K.P.*

Caspar Hauser complex (also *Kasper–Hauser*). Alexander Mitscherlich used the name Caspar Hauser (a compulsive impostor who died in 1833 from self-inflicted injuries, and allegedly a foundling who had grown up in complete solitude) to designate a "complex" (q.v.) characteristic of the inner loneliness and emotional atrophy of city dwellers (inability to make contacts). *W.Sc.*

Caspar Hauser experiments. A method in comparative psychology (q.v.): animals are reared under optimum experience deprivation (care has to be taken that no organic injury is inflicted on the animal). The aim is to separate genetically conditioned from acquired behavioral components. *W.Sc.*

Castration. Removal of the sexual glands (in males the testicles, in females the ovaries), thus changing the organism's hormonal function and sterilizing the person. Male castration has occurred as a cultic or religious practice, or as a punishment, for thousands of years. Castration can also be accidental or therapeutic. Female castration is only used therapeutically in cases of physical disease in or around the ovaries. Castration before physical development is complete (i.e. about twenty years of age) results in inhibition of the development of the sexual organs, prolongation of bone growth, "babyface"-change, as well as changes in the body's metabolic processes. In adults (when growth is complete) therapeutic castration is used to diminish libido. Psychic changes and general fatness seldom occur. A change in fat-distribution to more fat on the breasts and hips is common. Therapeutic castration has been used since 1892 in Switzerland, and is now also employed in several other countries. The first law permitting therapeutic castration was passed in 1929 (Denmark). When used in cases whose sexual drive involves them in considerable psychic sufferings or social devaluation, and when supplemented with psychiatric help, the results are excellent. 3,186 cases have been reported: 2% have relapsed into criminal sexual activity.

Bibliography: Langelüddeke, A.: Die Entmannung von Sittlichkeitsverbrechern. Berlin, 1963. **Stürup, Georg K.:** Treatment of sexual offenders in Herstedvester, Denmark. Copenhagen, 1968. *G.K.S.*

Castration complex. According to Freud, a boy's anxiety that he may lose his sexual organs; or the alleged fear experienced by a girl who, after recognizing that she does not have a (male) sexual organ, is afraid that she may lose other parts of her body as well. This castration complex is said to appear in the early genital phase (q.v.) in connection with the prevention of, and threats against, masturbation or heterosexual genital interest in members of the same family. Castration anxiety is the mildest of infantile fears. In the anal phase (q.v.) the child develops the fear that he might be seriously mutilated or even crushed to pieces and killed; in the oral phase (q.v.) there is the fear of being eaten up, swallowed or dissolved.

In association with developmental disorders in the early genital phase the castration complex is said to persist into adulthood, and is claimed to be the cause of a neurotic inability to make love, involving in particular fear of the opposite sex, symptoms of impotence in a man and frigidity (q.v.) in a woman, and even resulting in perversions (q.v.). *W.T.*

Catalepsy. Preservation of posture for an inordinately long period of time. This posture itself may or may not be abnormal and may be spontaneous or induced by an observer. Some writers include in this group only those whose postures have been imposed by an observer or by fortuitous events, reserving the term catalepsy for them only. In this restricted group the postures are preserved without reason but are not again assumed spontaneously by the patient. This restricted form is often associated with *flexibilitas cerea* (waxy flexibility), and may be due to heightened suggestibility. However, this restriction of the group is not logically or practically defensible. As well as in schizophrenia, catalepsy is found in organic brain disease, epilepsy, disturbed personalities and hysterical and subnormal people. *B.B.*

Catamnesis. 1. That part of a case history reporting on the effect of therapy (or counseling) and the rehabilitation of the patient (or client). The report is based on external observation of, or on self-observation by, the patient, and deals with this condition and behavior (usually some considerable time) after the termination of the therapy or counseling.

2. A case history from onset of a problem or sickness to, or even including, admission to a clinic or hospital. *F.-C.S.*

Cataplexy. Transient attacks of powerlessness triggered off by emotional experience, most commonly by laughter but also by anxiety, annoyance or anger. This may be partial or complete both in distribution or degree. The condition may coexist with *narcolepsy* (q.v.), both conditions resulting from the same cause. *J.P.*

Catathymia. A psychic change brought about by the influence of some affect. It occurs in prelogical and magical thought, in primitive everyday thinking and also in mental illness: e.g. thunder is heard and shortly afterwards somebody falls down dead. The two events are linked by the affect (fright) accompanying them. Catathymia is significant in the study of the falsification of memory. *A.Hi.*

Catathymic amnesia: Transient amnesia.

Catatonia. See *Schizophrenia*, in which catatonic symptoms are prominent. These embrace a number of predominantly motor deviations: catalepsy (*flexibilitas cerea:* waxy flexibility), stupor, hyperkinesis, etc. Acute and chronic forms are observed. Symptoms of intense arousal, tension and anxiety are found in *pernicious* catatonia which, if not treated, soon proves fatal. *A.Hi.*

Catecholamines. A group of hormones (q.v.) at the center of interdisciplinary psychophysiological research. The most important are adrenalin(e) (q.v.) and noradrenalin(e). Most of the catecholamines are formed in the adrenal medulla (q.v.), adrenaline and noradrenaline being approximately in the ratio 3:1 but varying according to the nature of the "stimuli". They can be measured in blood plasma or urine and used as dependent variables in psychological experiments. Catecholamines are also produced in the central and autonomic nervous systems (sympathetic NS), where noradrenaline is predominant. The significance of adrenaline in the central nervous system is not yet clear. Direct evidence of catecholamines in the central or autonomic nervous system cannot readily be established in humans *in vivo*. Psychophysiological catecholamine research concentrates on three groups of problems: (*a*) catecholamines as CNS transmitter substances; (*b*) catecholamines as objective indicators of emotional and motivational arousal; (*c*) their administration in order to induce non-specific or specific excitation.

(*a*) Catecholamines certainly act as transmitter substances in the central nervous system. The presence of noradrenaline in the brain (particularly concentrated in the hypothalamus, q.v.), and that of dopamine (a natural precursor of noradrenaline) have been demonstrated. The biosynthesis and decomposition of noradrenaline are of great importance in elucidating the processes by which psychoactive drugs (q.v.), and especially antidepressives, take effect. It is assumed that the biosynthesis of noradrenaline is disturbed in cases of depression (Schildkraut, 1965). Concentrated noradrenaline is biologically inactivated either inside the cell by monoamine oxidase (see *Monoamine oxidase inhibitors*), or outside it at the receptors by means of catechol-*o*-methyl transferase. Noradrenaline is synthesized in four stages (several enzymes are involved; see *Biogenic amines*). This synthesis can be blocked specifically by certain substances (e.g. by alpha-methyl tyrosine, or biogenic amines). Adrenaline is synthesized from noradrenaline by splitting off the methyl group CH_3.

(*b*) Numerous experiments in recent years have demonstrated the relations between the secretion of catecholamines (urine or plasma) and emotions. In particular, research teams led by U. S. von Euler, Elmadjan, L. Levi and M. Frankenhäuser demonstrated that stressors (such as flying, parachute jumps, examinations, exciting films, stress interviews, threats of electric shocks, sensory deprivation), as well as pleasant affects, caused catecholamines to *be released in larger quantities*. There is an unvarying relation between the mean values of scaled emotions or stimulus intensities and the release of catecholamines. Adrenaline release is usually the more sensitive indicator. It is not yet clear to what extent there are interactions between the ratio of noradrenaline to adrenaline and emotional qualities. Hypotheses according to which anxiety corresponds to the release of adrenaline, and annoyance (anger) to that of noradrenaline (Ax, 1953; Funkenstein *et al.*, 1957), do not as yet have adequate experimental support. However, it has been proved that there is a relatively greater release of noradrenaline in the case of physical, and of adrenaline in that of mental, stress. Intraindividually, the release of catecholamines is only moderately constant, and catecholamine detection is not reliable enough for individual determinations; especially when measuring the concentration in urine, several factors, e.g. meals, must be kept constant. There are as yet no proven correlations between the release of catecholamines and constant personality traits.

(*c*) Adrenaline and noradrenaline exist in synthetic forms, and can be administered intravenously. As neither drug will penetrate the blood-brain barrier, any direct action in the central nervous system is ruled out. Physiological doses of both substances in healthy subjects induce symptoms of sympathetic excitation with varying patterns of effect. With increased dosage, adrenaline leads to subjective excitation, and a feeling of general arousal. This emotional and motor excitation is usually experienced as slightly unpleasant. According to the situation (S. Schachter) the "non-specific" excitation resulting from small doses of adrenaline can be "transformed" into specific emotions (unpleasant, e.g. anxiety, annoyance; and possibly even pleasant, e.g. joy). There is little effect on performance. Speed tests (q.v.) sometimes show quantitative improvements; low doses also have a negative effect on motor constancy. Small amounts of noradrenaline have only an insignificant, if any, psychic effect. Animal experiments show that both substances directly activate the reticular formation (q.v.). It is not yet known how infused catecholamines, or those detectable in the blood or urine, relate to central catecholamine variations.

Bibliography: Anden, N.-E., Carlsson, A. & Häggendal, J.: Adrenergic mechanisms. Ann. Rev. Pharmacol., 1969, *9*, 119–34. **Ax, A. F.:** The physiological differentiation between fear and anger in humans. Psychosom. Med., 1953, *15*, 433–42. **Breggin, P.:** The psychophysiology of anxiety: With a review of the literature concerning adrenaline. J. nerv. ment. dis., 1964, *139*, 558–68. **Chessick, R. D., Bassan, M. & Shattan, S.:** A comparison of the effect of infused catecholamines and certain affect states. Amer. J. Psychiatr., 1966, *123*, 156–65. **Euler, U. S. von.:** Noradrenaline. Illinois, 1956. **Frankenhäuser, M.:** Biochemische Indikatioren der Aktiviertheit: Die Ausscheidung von K.n. In: **W. Schönpflug** (Ed.): Methoden der Aktivierungsforschung. Berne, 1969. **Funkenstein, D. H., King, S. H. & Drolette, M. E.:** Mastery of stress. Harvard, 1957. **Kroneberg, G. & Schümann, A. J.** (Eds): New aspects of storage and release mechanisms of catecholamines. Berlin, 1970. **Landis, C. & Hunt, W. A.:** Adrenaline and emotion. Psychol. Rev 1932, *39*, 467–85. **Levi, L.:** Biochemische Reaktionen bei verschiedenen experimentell hervorgerufenen Gefühlszuständen. In: **P. Kielholz** (Ed.): Angst. Berne, 1967. **Marley, E.:** Behavioral and electrophysiological effects of catecholamines. Pharmacol. Rev., 1966, *18*, 753–68. **Mason, J. W.:** A review of psychoendocrine research in the sympathetic adrenal medullary system. Psychosom. Med., 1968, *30*, 631–53. **Schachter, S. & Singer, J.:** Cognitive, social and physiol. determinants of emotional states. Psychol. Rev., 1962, *69*, 379–99. **Schildkraut, J. J.:** The catecholamine hypothesis of affective disorders: a review of supporting evidence. Amer. J. Psychiatr., 1965, *122*, 509–22. **Wurtman, R. J.:** Catecholamines. Boston, 1966.

W. Janke

Category. In general usage, categories are classes, kinds or types offering the necessary subdivisions of conceptual systems for ordering objects in the environment. The concept of category is essential to a theory of judgment; for example, Aristotle distinguished ten categories of predicates (substance, quantity, quality, relation, place, time, position, state, action, passion) which may be asserted of any object, while Kant proposed a number of classes of "transcendental concept", or conditions necessary for judging experience.

In his theory of types, Bertrand Russell tried to provide a non-paradoxical concept of class and predicate. Ryle's category theory, based on his analysis of the use of concepts in natural language, is intended to determine the conditions for sound predication. *M.J.B.*

Cathartic method. A psychotherapeutic technique used by Breuer and Freud to treat neurotic symptoms, and intended to produce a "catharsis" (purging, or release). Hypnosis is used to arouse (by hypermnesia, q.v.) memories of repressed affective experiences thought to be originally responsible for the neurotic disorder. The therapeutic efficacy of this process is thought to reside in the abreaction of the affects repressed until then (see *Repression*), a process which takes place during hypnosis or in the course of the accompanying dialogue. *H.-N.G.*

Cathexis (syn. *Cathection*). In psychoanalytical terminology cathexis signifies a concentration or investment of mental energy or libido (q.v.) in a certain direction: e.g. toward some object or person. *J.L.I.*

Cattell, James McKeen. B. 25/5/1860 in Easton (Pa.), d. 20/1/1944 in Garrison (N.J.). Studied under H. Lotze and W. Wundt (q.v.) and at the universities of Göttingen Leipzig, Paris and Geneva. 1887: lecturer at the University of Pennsylvania; 1888: lectured at Cambridge, England; 1888–91: Professor of psychology at Pennsylvania; 1891–1917: Professor at Columbia University; 1929: President of the International Congress of Psychologists held for the first time in America. Cattell introduced exact experimental psychology into America. He encouraged research into reaction times and associations (q.v.). He gave much time to the rank-order method for pair comparison (see *Psychophysics*). His main interest was the diversity of human nature and human abilities (differential psychology). He developed mental tests and was the first to use the term.

In 1921, Cattell founded the Psychological Corporation, whose object was primarily to bring psychological discoveries to the notice of the public and the administration, and to promote applied psychology.

Works: 1894–1940: Editor and manager of numerous journals, such as the *Psychological Review*, and the *American Naturalist*. Publications include: The inertia of the eye and brain, *Brain*, 1885, *8*, 295–312. Mental tests and measurements, *Mind*, 1890, *15*, 373–81. With C. S. Dolley: On reaction-times and the velocity of the nervous impulse, *Psy. Rev.* 1896. The conceptions and methods of psychology, *Pop. Sci. Mo.*, 1904, *46*, 176–86. The interpretation of intelligence tests, *Scient. Mo.*, 1924. Some psychological experiments, I, II, *Science*, 1928. Psychology in America, *Scient. Mo.*, *30*, 1930, 114–26.

Bibliography: Boring, E. G.: A history of experimental psychology. New York, [2]1950. **Garrett, H. E.:** Great experiments in psychology. New York, 1930. **Murchison, C.:** The psychological register. Worcester, 1929. **Poffenberger, A. T.** (Ed.): James McKeen Cattell: Man of science. Vol. 1: Psychological research; Vol. 2: Addresses and formal papers. Lancaster, 1947. **Woodworth, R. S.:** James McKeen Cattell, 1860–1944, Psychol. Rev., 1944, *51*, 201–9.

W.S.

Cattell's factorial theory of personality. See *Personality*.

Caudal. In animals with a recognizable head region the end of the body opposite this head region is known as *caudal* (Latin, *cauda:* tail region). Ant.: frontal (Latin, *frons:* forehead; cephalic). *H.S.*

Caudate nucleus. Mass of grey matter in the subcortical area of the cerebral hemispheres; part of the *corpus striatum* (q.v.).

Causality. An asymmetrical relationship between two terms, the antecedent being known as the *cause*, and the consequent as the *effect*. The terms can be events, phenomena, or objects. The relation itself is such that the effect necessarily follows on the occurrence of the cause, and the cause always precedes the effect. The *cause* of a phenomenon is often distinguished from its *condition* (or "necessary cause"), the cause ("sufficient cause") being *sufficient* for its production, whereas the condition is *necessary*.

Principle of causality: the postulate that every phenomenon has a cause. "Nothing ever happens without a cause or at least a determining reason; that is, without some thing affording an *a priori* reason why something exists rather than does not exist, and why it exists in this and not in any other way" (Leibniz, *Theodicy*). *J.B.G.*

Ceiling effect. If a task or a test is too easy, and many testees who obtain the highest score ought to obtain one still higher according to the factual criteria, then one speaks of a ceiling or "plafond" effect, which influences standard deviation (q.v.) and correlation (q.v.). *W.H.B.*

Censorship. According to Freud (*The Ego and the Id*, first German edition, 1923), censorship is a functional sphere which checks forbidden impulses (motives), or those which can no longer be satisfied; or modifies them before their gratification or partial gratification in such a way that they are no longer directly recognizable as those forbidden or no longer gratifiable motives. In his later structural theory of the psyche, Freud ascribed this function of censorship (objective counter-cathexis, inner defense or repression, q.v.) on the one hand to the ego (q.v.). But the ego was said to be concerned with the organization of gratifications of permissible or at least not forbidden impulses. On the other hand, the super-ego (q.v.) also includes certain aspects of censorship among its functions.

Bibliography: Freud, S.: Introductory lectures on psycho-analysis. London, [2]1929. **Id.:** The ego and the id. London, [2]1962.

Centile (*Percentile*). A standard measure frequently used in psychology, especially in the calibration (q.v.) of diagnostic instruments. The whole area of frequency distribution (q.v.) of raw values is divided into 100 sections. Hence exactly 1% of all cases occurs in a centile area. *Centile rank:* the relative rank of a score in a distribution. *W.H.B.*

Central convolution (syn. *Central gyrus*). The anterior central convolution (*Gyrus precentralis*) is the rearmost convolution of the frontal lobe, and is separated by the central fissure or sulcus (*Sulcus centralis*) from the posterior central convolution (*Gyrus postcentralis*). The anterior central convolution contains the representational fields for the motor behavior of the striate musculature. *G.A.*

Central nervous system (abb. CNS). All the nervous elements, cells and conducting pathways within the brain (q.v.) and spinal cord (q.v.). This system is responsible for the entire nervous control of the activity of the living organism. All afferent sensory nerve paths receiving information from the sense organs (q.v.) regarding the state of the environment end in the CNS, where, in terms of reflexes, reactions, behavior patterns and volitions, this information is processed and conveyed once more by means of efferent motor nerve fibers to the motor effectors, and hence to the environment. The CNS has a hierarchical construction. See *Nervous system; Neuroanatomy.* *E.D.*

Centrifugal nerves (syn. *Centrifugal neuron(e)s*). Nerve fibers of the peripheral system which conduct information from the periphery of the body to the brain and spinal cord. Since they for the most part conduct sensory information from the eye, ear, vestibule, the organs of smell and taste, the cutaneous sense points, and the entero-ceptors, they are also known as sensory nerve fibers. See *Sense organs.* *E.D.*

Centroid method (*Center of gravity method*). A factor-analytical method developed by C. L. Burt (1917) and L. L. Thurstone (1931) to extract factors (q.v.) from intercorrelation matrices. The variables (e.g. tests) can be represented as vectors in a certain space. A common factor of these tests can be represented as a vector (q.v.) passing through the "centroid" of the end points of the variable vectors. *W.H.B.*

Cephalic. Forming part of, or appertaining to, the head (ant. *Caudal*, q.v.).

Cephalization. The formation of a head at the frontal end of higher animals, especially with regard to the nervous system, which localizes a relay and control center in the head (see *Brain*), thus making possible a biologically meaningful coordination of all the vital processes in an individual. *H.S.*

Cerebellum. The smaller main part of the brain; it is noticeably wrinkled, and is situated in the lower part of the occiput close to the cranial bone. It consists of three parts, the *archi-*, *paleo-*, and *neocerebellum.* The first has developed from the vestibulary nuclei, helps to maintain the balance and is responsible for seasickness. The other two parts help to maintain muscular tonus and to coordinate all muscular movement in response to the information coming from the sense organs. Therefore the cerebellum has fibrous links with all the sensory channels, with the cerebrum (q.v.), and with the extra-pyramidal motor system. Acute disturbance seriously affects balance, and movement and coordination; in cases of slow deterioration or congenital defect the cerebrum partly takes over the function of the cerebellum.

Bibliography: **Eccles, J. C.:** The physiology of synapses. Berlin, 1964. *E.D.*

Cerebral arteriosclerosis (*Diffuse sclerosis;* group of leucodystrophies). Generic name for a group of rare sclerotic processes affecting the cerebrum. The condition (which leads very quickly to death) is classed as a hereditary disorder of the metabolism with tissue degeneration (hereditary-degenerative diseases). Three principal symptoms are common to all forms of this disease: spasticity on both sides, blindness on both sides (caused by atrophy of the optical nerve), and dementia. *G.A.*

Cerebral cortex (*Cortex cerebri*). The grey layer of nerve cells which is only a few mm thick and is situated directly below the surface of the cerebrum. According to location on the cerebral cortex, individual areas are distinguished by the architectural structure of the nerve-cell layers. While the anatomical division into frontal, parietal, temporal and occipital lobes does not indicate any functional units, the cortical projection areas are functionally uniform. Broca's area in the temporal lobe would seem to be connected with the active formation of speech (see *Brain pathology*), the precentral gyrus (as the origin of the pyramidal tract) with voluntary motor activity, and the primary optical cortical projection field in the occipital lobe with image recognition (if it is destroyed, there is visual amnesia). While those of some other areas are known, the functions of most parts of the cortex are unexplained, but it is supposed that they can selectively assume different tasks. *E.D.*

Cerebral nerves. The brain (q.v.; see *Encephalon*) consists of the forebrain, midbrain and hindbrain. The twelve pairs of cerebral nerves originate in the encephalon and run through the base of the skull to the head, while others branch off into other parts of the body. The *corpus pineale* is a continuation of the midbrain. The *cortex cerebri* (cerebral cortex) consists of grey matter and mainly contains nerve cell bodies. The brain stem is the midbrain, hindbrain and *pons.* *G.A.*

Cerebral palsy. A traumatic condition resulting from intrauterine brain lesions of extremely varied genesis, i.e. birth injuries or injuries suffered during early infancy, such as cerebral malformations, congenital syphilis, toxoplasmosis, encephalitis, etc. It usually presents as a spastic (q.v.) paralysis (spasticity) of one or both sides of the body; the latter form is known as Little's disease (q.v.). Frequent accompaniments are defective intelligence, tremor, and choreatic movements of the affected limbs. Cure is usually impossible; treatment is restricted to alleviation of the symptoms. *E.D.*

Cerebral stimulation. The electrical release of behavior patterns in animals allowed to move freely; this is done by implanting micro-electrodes in the brain. The method of auto-stimulation in which the experimental animal actuates a contact of its own accord gives valuable results. Indifferent stimulus centers were stimulated about 25 times per hour and positive centers with a reward effect between 200 to 7000 times per hour; habituation symptoms were noted. The position of the electrode tip is marked by micro-electrolysis, electro-coagulation or Berlin blue reaction, histologically fixed, and entered on brain charts.

Bibliography: Olds, J. & Olds, M. E.: The mechanisms of voluntary behavior. In: **Heath, R. G.** (Ed.): The role of pleasure in behavior. New York, 1964, 23–53. *K.F.*

Cerebration. See *Encephalization.*

Cerebrospinal system. The human nervous system is divided into the central and autonomous nervous systems. In the CNS the central nervous system proper, consisting of the cerebrum and spinal cord, is distinguished from the peripheral nervous system. The latter includes the two major groups of the brain and spinal nerves. The ANS comprises the (largely antagonistic) sympathetic and parasympathetic systems. *G.A.*

Cerebrotonia. According to Sheldon's constitutional theory of personality, cerebrotonia is a temperamental quality correlated with ectomorphic (q.v.) bodily components: characteristic traits are postural restraint, sensitivity, expressive inhibition, and difficulty of adaptation.

Bibliography: Sheldon, W. H.: The varieties of temperament. New York, 1942. *W.K.*

Cerebrum (*Telencephalon* and *Diencephalon*). It represents the main mass of the brain (q.v.) and consists of the *pallium*, the brainstem ganglia, the olfactory brain, the *corpus callosum*, the *fornix* and the *septum pellucidum.* It is divided almost completely into two parts by a longitudinal fissure. Its histological structure is characterized by a grey substance containing cells and a white substance containing fibers. The *cortex cerebri* or cerebral cortex (q.v.), and the basal ganglia form part of the grey substance, while the mass of fibrous links between the nerve cells belongs to the white substance. The function of the cerebrum is very complex and has scarcely been investigated in detail; in addition to the mental functions which can be recognized even in animals, it especially includes those which distinguish man from animals, such as recognizing (q.v.), abstracting, learning (q.v.), thinking (q.v.), criticizing, speaking (q.v.), and artistic creation, but also *drive* (q.v.) and the processes of the consciousness (q.v.).

Bibliography: Pribram, K. H.: Brain and behavior (4 vols). Harmondsworth, 1969. *E.D.*

CFF. Abb. for *Critical flicker frequency* (q.v.).

Chain behavior. See *Chain reflex.*

Chaining. See *Conversational chaining.*

Chain reflex (syn. *Chain behavior; Chain reaction*). A number of individual responses linked to one another so that the same sequence is always maintained. Presumably the effects of preceding links act as cues for the release of the next. Chain reflexes in any existing form are always learnt. *H.Ro.*

Chain theory (Ger. *Kettentheorie*). Metzger's term (1954) for the perception theories of association psychology. Chain theory is opposed to the explanations of gestalt psychology.

Bibliography: Metzger, W.: Psychologie. Darmstadt, [2]1954. *R.Hä.*

Channel. The channel is that part of a communications system (communications unit) which transmits signals (q.v.) from an input (sender) to an output (receiver). According to the kind of signals, a distinction is made between discrete and continuous channels. The transmission system interferes with (distorts) the signals to a greater or lesser extent.

Channel capacity: the maximum amount of information which can be transmitted through a channel per unit of time (measured in bit/sec.). *B.R.*

Character. The word comes from the Greek *kharakter* (meaning: an engraved or stamped mark). In current usage, it has two different basic meanings: the first denotes the purely factual characteristics of a thing or a person as distinguished from other things or persons. The second refers to the purely psychic distinctiveness of a living creature. In this second sense, *being a person is the foundation for developing a character*. In regard to man, the concept of character also has an ethical content. If the concept of *person* (=self) refers to the individual being of man, character denotes the *specific thus-ness* of man.

Since antiquity, character has been a subject for research. Theophrastus wrote character studies which have come down to us. Aristotle investigated the polarity and the affinity of character traits, and postulated a basic structure of character. Kant introduced the concept of the "empirical" character to mean man now, at this moment, and in his special "thus-ness". Empirical character is dependent on age, educational and environmental influences, climate, nutrition, whereas the fundamental character is hardly affected by these influences.

In the natural-scientific mode of the nineteenth century, J. Bahnsen saw a man's character as derived from the general characteristics of all those things which have to be brought into action for their distinctive features to be recognized. This attitude made him a precursor of systematic research. According to A. Pfänder, character has its foundations in a primal drive (the instinct of self-development). The empirical character is the creation (self-expression) of the fundamental character. For A. Gehlen, character is a product of education: it is the total expression of stable habits and views by virtue of which a person prefers certain things to others. Accordingly, character would be a form of behavior with an invariant value-tendency: a product of cultivation by the society in which man lives and of its particular division of interests.

G. Kerschensteiner speaks of an "instinctive character"—a predisposition restricted to life in terms of the emotions, instincts and impulses. Out of this instinctive and emotional life there develop intellectual life and a capacity for experience. In this view, the concept of character would also comprise mind. Hence the concept of character would lie between that of natural dispositions and that of ethical values. For Le Senne, character is elementally tripartite: the "innate", the "firm", and the "lasting" are the three structural aspects of the inner life. (See *Drive; Instinct.*)

Characterology in the wider sense deals with the ways in which man develops, specializes, compensates and responds to his natural dispositions. Layer models allow characterologists some theoretical foundation (P. Lersch, A. Wellek).

Characterology in the narrower sense was originally developed mainly in German-speaking countries. Its concerns are in many ways identical with those of personality research in Britain and America.

The notion of character cannot be divided into elements conceivable in isolation; it has to be grasped as a whole. It is an objective unity.

As every character behaves in a peculiarly distinctive way, there are many modes of individual expression for observation and diagnosis. This is the theoretical point of departure for the psychology of *expression* (q.v.).

For character diagnosis, *typologies* (q.v.) are used (e.g. those of E. Kretschmer, H. W. Sheldon, G. Ewald, E. R. Jaensch, C. G. Jung, E. Spranger), together with the methods of general *personality diagnosis* and psychometric *factor analysis* (q.v.) (R. B. Cattell). In research into the vital part played by character inheritance, use was made of longitudinal *genealogy* (F. Galton) and twin studies (K. Gottschaldt). The central theme of this work is *abilities* (q.v.). Character is further molded in the development of fundamentals (i.e. basic experiences): *emotions* (q.v.), *thinking* (q.v.), *intelligence* (q.v.), *memory* (q.v.), *attention* (q.v.), and *will* (q.v.).

Summary: Character is the indivisible, individual distinctiveness of a person (more precisely, of a *self*), which is exhibited in certain modes of individual experience and experiencing; these modes are organized as wholes and are subject to change, but they persist in essence. Character is the *form* of a person, and a stage in the forming, or development, of his personality. See *Personality; Traits; Type.*

Bibliography: Allport, G. W.: Pattern and growth in personality. New York, 1961. **Arnold, W.:** Person, Charakter, Persönlichkeit. Göttingen, [3]1970. **Hebb, D. O.:** A textbook of psychology. Philadelphia, Pa., 1958. **Klages, L.:** Grundlagen der Charakterkunde. Bonn, [13]1966. **Lersch, Ph.:** Aufbau der Person. Munich, [10]1966. **Rohracher, H.:** Kleine Charakterkunde. Munich, [12]1969. **Rostand, J.:** L'Hérédité humaine. Paris, 1966. **Wellek, A.:** Polarität im Aufbau des Charakters. Munich, [3]1966.

W. Arnold

Characteropathy. An irreversible, *abnormal* change (absence, deficiency, excess or faulty structure of the emotional-volitional possibilities of action and reaction) as the result of a disease that can be clearly shown to have been somatic, or of a condition that followed the illness.

Such a genesis must be sharply divided from marked inherited inadequacies or defects of feeling and volition (see *Psychopathy*), from character disturbances due to harmful social or environmental influences, and from endogenously and episodically conditioned behavioral disorders.

Characteropathy occurring after damage to the brain (see *Encephalopathy*) is usually an ensuing abnormal change in the quantity and structure of the basic mental disposition or of the persistency in experiencing and acting which are determinative of and significant for the individual's attitude. *H.-J.E.*

Charpentier-Koseleff illusion. Also known as the *size-weight illusion.* Of two objects which are of the same weight but of different sizes, the smaller will be considered the heavier. Analogously, a mistake is made in regard to volume when two objects of identical dimensions but of different weights are presented. The heavy object appears smaller.

Bibliography: Koseleff, P.: Eine Modifikation des Charpentier-Effektes. Psychol. Forschung, 1936, *21*, 142–5. **Usnadze, D.:** Über die Gewichtstäuschung und ihre Analoga. Psychol. Forschung, 1931, *14*, 366–79.
P.S.

Charpentier's bands. A series of alternate light (white) and dark (black) stripes perceived as the afterimage (q.v.) of an illuminated (white) sector rotated on a black background. Named after A. Charpentier (1852–1916).

Charpentier's illusion. The apparent movement of a small point of light in a darkened room. See *Autokinetic effect.* *K.E.P.*

Charpentier's law. A. Charpentier (1852–1916): the product of the object's light intensity and of the stimulus or image area (size of the retina, dependent on the angle of vision) is a constant for the magnitude of the threshold value of light sensitivity (optical threshold stimulus).

Bibliography: Graham, C. H. (Ed.): Vision and visual perception. New York & London, 1965.
F.-C.S.

Chemoreceptors. The sense organs (q.v.) which are affected by a change in the chemical environment (e.g. taste, smell).

Chemotaxis. See *Chemotropism 2.*

Chemotropism. 1. A spatially orientated growth movement of plants in response to a chemical stimulus source. **2.** More generally, orientation of a cell or organism at any stage of development in relation to a chemical stimulus. *H.H.*

Chiasm, optic. The point where the optic nerves cross behind the anterior cranial fossa in front of the hypophysis (q.v.). Here the fibers of the nasal retina halves cross over to the contralateral *tractus opticus* (q.v.), whereas the fibers of the temporal retina halves

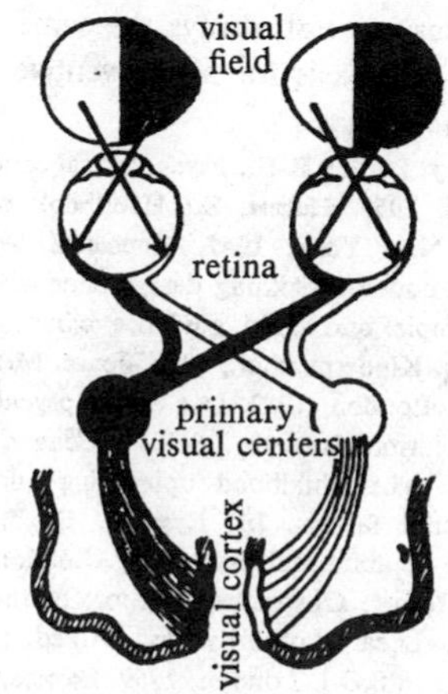

From: Pauli & Arnold, *Psychologisches Praktikum* (Stuttgart, [6]1957).

continue on the same side. The fibers of the *macula lutea* (yellow spot, q.v.) cross in part, so that the point where visibility is sharpest is represented in both parts of the brain. Because of this crossing over, there is synchronization of both eyes. Pathological processes in the area where the crossing over takes place cause hemiano(p)sia (q.v.). *R.R.*

Child guidance. A method originating in the U.S.A. and England which embraces the diagnosis and treatment of behavioral, performance (learning), and psychosomatic disturbances in children, and parent-counseling.

The *child-guidance clinic* is the basic institutional unit. The approach depends on the team-work of psychiatrist, psychologist and social worker (or psychiatric social worker). The psychiatrist examines and treats the child; psychological diagnosis and test administration are the responsibilities of the psychologist; and the social worker interviews the parents to obtain the life history and offer advice. The training which combines all three subjects (dynamic psychiatry, psychology and sociology) and underlies the child-guidance method has become a model for child psychiatric and psychotherapeutic institutions, although in many places all three professions are represented in the team, and the emphasis is not always the same. Child guidance is a basis for all preventive work. See *Psychohygiene*.

Bibliography: Bordin, E. S.: Psychological counseling. New York, 1955. **Harms, E.:** Handbook of child guidance. New York, 1947. **Hopmann, W.:** Zur Bedeutung und Entwicklung der psychoanalytischen Psychotherapie und child guidance clinics in den USA. Prax. Kinderpsychol., 1952. **Jones, M.:** Social psychiatry. London, 1952. **Id.:** Social psychiatry in practice. Harmondsworth, 1968. **O'Connor, N. & Franks, C. M.:** Childhood upbringing and other environmental factors. In: **Eysenck, H. J.** (Ed.): Handbook of abnormal psychology. London, 1960. **Seebohm Report:** Government Report of the Committee on Local Authority and Allied Personal Services (H.M.S.O.). London, 1969. **Savage, R. D.:** Psychometric assessment of the individual child. Harmondsworth, 1968.

W.H.S.

Childhood. Childhood proper might be said to begin with the first "defiance" period at the age of 3 to 4. Its first phase (approximately from 4 to 7) is characterized by a form of realism colored by fantasy and magic. Then comes a phase of naïve realism (from 7 to 10) in which analytical thought and the first signs of abstract thought develop. Childhood ends with a short phase of somewhat "critical" realism (from the age of 9 to 10 until the beginning of puberty) when a second period of defiance leads into youth. But the term is often used for the whole period from birth to puberty. See *Child psychology; Concept formation; Piaget.*

M.Sa.

Childhood experiences. Psychoanalysis (q.v.) has called attention to the (traumatic) effects which early childhood experience can have on the entire development of an individual and his character. Such experiences may be episodic, and isolated events. But "chronic" forms (e.g. bowel training) are also said to occur.

M.Sa.

Child, only. Growing up in a family situation where there are no brothers or sisters must have definite consequences for a child's development, but empirical investigations of the subject seem to offer, contradictory evidence on intelligence and school work, and certain personality traits. A fairly consistent finding would seem to be that only children seek the supportive company of others (and particularly others in a similar situation) when unhappy or under anxiety stress (Lewis; Schachter).

Bibliography: Lewis, H.: Deprived children. London, 1954. **Schachter, S.:** Psychology of affiliation. Stanford, Cal., 1959.

K.E.P.

Child psychiatry. Psychiatry (q.v.) as applied to mental disorders in children.

Child psychology is concerned with the development of psychological processes in the child from birth and before, through infancy and childhood to adolescence and maturity. All the processes of interest to psychologists in general are studied, but in developing as opposed to mature organisms.

1. *History and methods.* Interest in child development is as old as recorded history. The study of children is only now breaking away from the realm of sentimental mythology and entering the domain of objective science. Early theories of child development range from William James's empiricist view of the infant as being aware of only a "big,

booming, buzzing confusion", to the nativist view of Gestaltist psychologists that the infant can make sense of his world at birth. Freud regarded the infant as a bundle of instincts whereas Watson eschewed such speculation and studied only what was directly observable. He overemphasized the environmental influences of children's development, at the expense of ignoring genetically determined individual differences.

Naturalistic observations play an important part in the methodology of child psychology. Early studies of children relied on observations of varying quality. The baby diaries written by people such as Charles Darwin were not so productive as those of Jean Piaget, but such records can only serve as starting-points for more controlled study of representative samples.

Direct, controlled observations of children's behavior in both natural and laboratory settings have been fruitful when the usual requirements of the reliability of observation have been met. Tests and questionnaires have dominated child psychology, particularly in the area of intellectual development and educational attainment. In the field of personality testing, very few tests measure up to the minimum psychometric requirements, and projective techniques have proven to be of as little value as with adults.

In recent years, the experimental method has been applied to child psychology with renewed vigor. Conditioning techniques, in particular, have allowed more systematic study of the pre-linguistic child's repertoire of behavior.

The cross-sectional studies pioneered by such workers as Gesell served to establish broad norms of development. However, they tended to overemphasize the importance of chronological age and to underplay the importance of social and environmental influences. They also championed the concept of discrete stages of development, while underemphasizing individual differences in the rate of development. Currently, the methodology of cross-sectional studies has been influenced by the epidemiological model, and greater sophistication is evident in sampling and measuring techniques.

Longitudinal studies are the most appropriate for answering the many questions about the later effect of particular events in childhood and, conversely, about the antecedents of later deviant development. The best-known such study is probably the Berkeley Growth Study associated with the name of Nancy Bayler. Kagan (1964) described ten American longitudinal studies, and in Britain the National Survey and the National Child Development Study have extended the methodology by studying large-scale national samples, in the case of Douglas, for over twenty-one years.

2. *Neonatal period and early experience.* The newborn child is not a *tabula rasa* on which can be written the desires of his parents. Both Watsonian "behaviorism" and psychoanalysis conspired to ignore the genetic and biological predispositions of infants and concentrated instead on the effects on the child of its environment, and particularly on the effects of parental child-rearing practices. However, recognition of biologically determined individual differences forces the child psychologist to adopt an interactionist rather than a solely genetic or environmental position in seeking explanations for the development of behavior (Berger, 1971).

In fact, studies of the effects of child-rearing practices on children's later development have been singularly unproductive. Yarrow attempted to replicate some of the major studies, including the oft-quoted Sears, Maccoby & Levin, *Patterns of Child Rearing*, which had related dependency and aggression in children to specific patterns of maternal practices. Yarrow was forced to conclude from her own study that the "compelling legend of maternal influences on child behavior that has evolved does not have its roots in solid data".

Studies of delinquents have implicated "inconsistent" parental discipline, showing a correlation between that and antisocial behavior. However, most such studies can only be regarded as suggestive since they are retrospective and not based on direct, concurrent observation. Experimental studies of behavior modification techniques have demonstrated a causal relationship between adult management practices and children's behavior, so that a methodology is now available to examine this in the context of the parent-child interaction.

3. *Personality*. Starting from a multiplicity of theoretical positions, studies of personality in children are in broad agreement in isolating two major dimensions: extraversion and neuroticism (Rachman, 1969). The evidence is in favor of there being a continuity in the growth of personality. However, much of the evidence is based on self-rating inventories such as the Junior Eysenck Personality Inventory, or Cattell's HSPQ. Since the child must have a reading age of about eight years to be able to complete these satisfactorily, this effectively limits their use. Observational studies of children as young as four years have yielded factors closely similar to the *E* and *N* dimensions. What is needed is to relate self-ratings with objective behavioral measures, as has been done profitably in adults.

Extraverted children are scholastically superior to introverted children. The relationship between attainment and neuroticism is less clear-cut, since there are interactions between neuroticism, extraversion and sex. There is some suggestion that introverts tend to develop more slowly than extraverts, but this needs confirming in longitudinal studies.

It has now been established that in the neonatal period there are stable patterns of behavior, both in the type of behavior shown and in its manner or formal characteristics. Hence, whatever the behavior, some infants will display it at greater intensities than others. Some will be more regular than others in its emission. Such characteristics have been labeled "temperamental factors"; in the New York Longitudinal Study, Thomas has reliably identified nine temperamental characteristics. Bridger views temperamental factors in terms of excitatory and inhibitory processes in the central nervous system. This ties in well with the Eysenckian two-dimensional model of personality (q.v.) structure.

The New York Longitudinal Study has shown that temperamental characteristics tend to cluster together, and they have identified three types of children: *difficult* ones who are characterized as being irregular in function and who react at high levels of intensity; *easy* children who are regular and react at low levels of intensity; and children who are *slow to warm up* to new situations. In this follow-up study, they found that proportionately many "difficult" children later presented with behavioral and adjustment difficulties. Although this work needs to be replicated, it has helped to shift the focus of interest in the area of children's behavior disturbances from mere consideration of parental mishandling to an appraisal of the significance of biologically based individual differences between children, and the interaction between the child management and the child's characteristics.

4. *Cognitive development*. One of the strongest influences on research into cognitive development has been the Swiss psychologist, Jean Piaget. Stemming from his interest in "genetic epistemology" (the origin and growth of knowledge), he has stimulated much research into children's thinking. His own early work suggested that there were fixed sequences of "stages" in the growth of thought. He also believed that thinking at one stage is qualitatively different from thinking at another.

Piaget has described the three main stages of intellectual development as: (*a*) Sensory motor intelligence (from birth to 18 months); (*b*) concrete operations: (i) the pre-operational stage (from 18 months to 7 years); (ii) concrete operations (7 years to 12 years); (*c*) formal operations (from 12 years onwards).

Perhaps his most influential work has been that concerned with the attainment of object permanence and the conservation of liquids and solids. Methodologically, Piaget's own early work was very weak, but his major findings have been broadly confirmed in large-scale replication projects. Most importantly for his theories, it has been shown that infants rarely acquire the responses said to be characteristic of a later stage of intellectual development, without having attained those of earlier stages. Bruner's work has demonstrated that it is possible to accelerate the child's progress through the Piagetian stages provided appropriate teaching methods are used. Currently, research is needed to find the limits of such procedures.

5. *Perception.* Fantz has demonstrated that form perception exists in young infants. They show preference for pattern over uniform surfaces from birth, and there is some evidence for the preference of the human face over other objects.

Using operant conditioning procedures, Bower has demonstrated that as early as two months, infants have a limited visual memory. He has also shown that size constancy is present at a very early age. It is not until about six months however that most infants are capable of discriminating novel stimuli from familiar ones, and it is at this age that attachments to familiar people become most apparent.

6. *Language.* The 1960s saw the growth of psycholinguistics (q.v.), and its influence is now felt in developmental psychology. The sterile description of vocabulary growth so common in the 1920s has been replaced by studies of children's grammar. Chomsky, Lenneberg and Roger Brown have made their mark, but as yet no normative studies of language development analyzed in their terms have appeared. (See *Grammar.*)

The psycholinguists emphasize the structure of a child's grammar rather than its content. Somewhere in the second year of life, most children acquire a grammar utilizing simple two-word combinations of "pivot words" such as "see" or "all-gone", which can be combined with other single words to form novel, telegraphic sentences. There are large social-class differences in the way in which parents expand these simple sentences, with middle-class parents extending not only the grammatical complexity but also the range of ideas expressed by the child. It is probable that this is one of the reasons for the middle-class child's advantage in the area of language development.

7. *Intelligence.* Intelligence tests are used for both descriptive and predictive purposes. The older tests yielding global estimates of intelligence are being replaced by tests describing different cognitive processes in greater detail. However, the global IQ score is still useful in making predictions within certain limits.

Concern has been expressed about the stability of the IQ measures. There are difficulties over basing predictions on Developmental Scale scores obtained on infants largely because of the different content of the test and the different functions measured. But psychometric assessments are more useful than clinical judgments in predicting children who will develop atypically.

Much work has revolved around the question of the relative hereditary and environmental contributions to intelligence. This has been ably reviewed by Jensen, who concluded that 80% of the variance measured in IQ scores is attributable to genetic rather than environmental influences. Clearly, any individual's actual functioning depends on the interaction between his inheritance and the environment in which he finds himself.

8. *Social—emotional.* Following the Spitz, Goldfard & Bowlby work on the effects of institutionalization and separation from the mother, the attachment behavior of young children has been subjected to much intensive study. The main methodological and theoretical shifts have been away from psychodynamic formulations toward the study of psychological processes such as perception underlying the attachment. Separation is

no longer viewed as a unitary phenomenon having all-or-none effects on emotional development. The effects of the breaking of an existing attachment are now differentiated from the consequences of institutional placement. It is also recognized that short, intense separations may have immediate effects without any long-term consequences. Nowhere in child psychology has the influence of ethology been so much in evidence, as can be seen in Bowlby's most recent work.

The family, peer groups and the school as socializing influences continue to be studied. The most important development in this area has been the increase in direct observational studies, coupled to the increase in experimentation. Bandura's work on the learning of social behavior by imitation commands an important place.

9. *Educational.* Much of the laboratory work on learning remains divorced from actual teaching practices in the classroom. This was clearly shown in the failure of programmed learning (q.v.) to be implemented more generally. One reason for its failure was that the assumption that success was self-rewarding appears not to hold for all children. They have to learn that success is a positive experience.

There have been relatively few studies of pupil-teacher interaction in the classroom situation. Most have been done by those interested in behavior modification techniques for modifying disruptive, aggressive behavior.

Concern over the educational failure of the underprivileged led to mass social intervention in the form of compensatory educational programs. Many attempted to raise the level of attainment by first boosting general intelligence, and these largely failed in their aims. Those which tackled the problems directly and used specific structured techniques met with more success.

Reading failure has been the subject of many studies. Depending on the definitions employed, anything from 5% to 25% of ten-year-old children are identified as having reading problems. There is now a large consensus that few of these cases are "dyslexic" in the sense of having one particular neurological syndrome. Quality of teaching, motivational factors and the influence of the home are equally important factors in the etiology of reading difficulties.

10. *Abnormal behavior.* Research into children's disorders has tended to concentrate on neurotic behavior, despite the evidence that such disorders largely remit without treatment and carry no risk of later disturbance in adulthood. Knowledge of the genesis and treatment of antisocial disorders, apart from the work on delinquency, is much more limited. Yet antisocial disorders are notoriously difficult to treat and often lead to gross problems in adulthood, as the thirty-year follow-up study of Robins showed.

Epidemiological studies have established the prevalence of disturbance in the middle years of childhood as being at least 6%. Many more boys than girls are affected. Examining possible etiological processes, it has been shown that boys react more adversely than girls to stresses within the family. Research now needs to be structured so that intra-familial processes can be directly observed.

The problems of treatment of disturbances in childhood differ from those in adulthood, in that the aim is more frequently to build up patterns of behavior which have not developed, rather than to break abnormal patterns. Developmental disorders such as language delays are peculiar to this period. Traditional treatment methods based on psychoanalytic techniques have not proved useful. In contrast, behavior modification techniques, including operant conditioning and modeling techniques, are being successfully applied in an ever-increasing variety of problem behaviors. Careful evaluation studies of these powerful techniques are required to establish their limits.

The field of child psychology is vast, and this review has touched only on some of the more important growth points. Premature theorizing is being replaced by empirical observation and experimentation. The next decade should see the appearance of empirically based theories of child development.

Bibliography: **Bandura, A.:** Principles of behavior modification. New York, 1969. **Becker, W. C., Madsen, C. H., Arnold, R. & Thomas, D. R.:** The contingent use of teacher attention and praise in reducing classroom behavior problems. J. spec. Educ., 1967, *1*, 287–307. **Berger, M.:** Early experience and other environmental factors: An overview. In: **Eysenck, H. J.** (Ed.): Handbook of abnormal psychology. London, 1971. **Bowlby, J.:** Attachment and loss, in: Attachment, Vol. 1. London, 1969. **Bruner, J. S., Olver, R. R. & Greenfield, P. M.:** Studies in cognitive growth. New York, 1966. **Clarke, A. M. & Clarke, A. D. B.** (Eds): Mental deficiency: the changing outlook. London, 1965. **Douglas, J. W. B., Ross, J. M. & Simpson, H. R.:** All our future. London, 1968. **Elkind, D. & Flavell, J. H.** (Eds): Studies in cognitive development: Essays in honor of Jean Piaget. London, 1969. **Eysenck, H. J. & Eysenck, S. B. G.:** Personality structure and measurement. London, 1969. **Fantz, R. L. & Nevis, S.:** Pattern preferences and perceptual-cognitive development in early infancy. Merrill-Palmer Quarterly, 1967, *13*, 77–108. **Flavell, J. H. & Hill, J. P.:** Developmental psychology. Ann. Rev. Psychol., 1969, 1–56. **Foss, B. M.** (Ed.): Determinants of infant behavior, Vols 1–4, 1963–69. **Hess, R. D. & Shipman, V. C.:** Cognitive elements in material behavior. In: **Hill, J. P.** (Ed.): Minnesota Symposia on Child Psychology, Vol. 1. Minneapolis, 1967. **Hoffman, M. L. & Hoffman, L. W.** (Eds): Review of child development research, Vols 1 & 2. New York, 1964 & 1966. **Jensen, A. R.:** How much can we boost I.Q. and scholastic achievement? Harvard Educ. Rev., 1969, *39*. **Kagan, J.:** American longitudinal research on psychological development. Child Devel., 1964, *35*, 1–32. **McNeill, D.:** Developmental psycholinguistics. In: **Smith, F. & Miller, G. A.** (Eds): The genesis of language. Cambridge, Mass., 1966. **Mussen, P. H.** (Ed.): Handbook of research methods in child development. New York, 1960. **Newton, R. & Levine, S.** (Eds): Early experience and behavior. Springfield, Ill., 1968. **Pringle, M. L. K., Butler, N. & Davie, R.:** 11,000 seven-year-olds. London, 1966. **Rachman, S.:** Extraversion and neuroticism in childhood. In: **Eysenck & Eysenck,** *op. cit.*, 1969. **Robins, L. N.:** Deviant children grown up. Baltimore, 1966. **Rutter, M., Tizard, J. & Whitmore, K.** (Eds): Education, health and behaviour, London, 1970. **Thomas, A., Chess, S., Birch, H. G., Hertzig, M. E. & Korn, S.:** Behavioral individuality in early childhood. London, 1964. **Thomas, A., Chess, S. & Birch, H. G.:** Temperament and behavior disorders in children. London, 1968. **Thomas, H.:** Some problems of studies concerned with evaluating the predictive validity of infant tests. J. child Psychol. Psychiat., 1967, *8*, 197–205. **Tizard, J.:** New trends in developmental psychology. Brit. J. educ. Psychol., 1970, *40*, 107. **Yarrow, M. R., Campbell, J. D. & Burton, R. V.:** Child rearing. San Francisco, 1968. *W. Yule*

Children as witnesses. From antiquity until the last century, children's statements remained suspect as evidence. Only when experimental research into testimonies began in the early years of this century were those of children thought to merit psychological examination. The first findings of forensic psychology in this regard were reported by Stern (1903). For some time after that the testimony of pre-adolescent girls was considered unreliable, partly because of medical prejudice (Möbius, 1908; *et al.*). Since World War II, more attention has been given to children's evidence because of new approaches in psychological testing. Although legal conditions vary in different countries and states, the evidence of minors in cases of sexual assault and so on is often considered.

Bibliography: See *Forensic psychology*. *M.M.*

Chirognomics. A pseudoscientific theory about the expressiveness of the shape and nature of the hand. Certain sections (e.g. the fingers) and parts (e.g. joints) are made to refer symbolically to character traits, although there is no proof of such a connection. The degree of definition in the shape of the hand and its parts is taken to be the expression of symbolically analogous character traits (e.g. the thumb as a symbol of power; a strong thumb as a sign of violence). The hand may be thought of as expressive in the sense mainly of "constitutional" psychology: E. Kretschmer, W. H. Sheldon. Medical diagnostics also attaches importance to the state of the hand.

Bibliography: **Bürger, M.:** Die Hand des Kranken. Munich, 1956. **Kretschmer, E.:** Physique and character. London, 1925. **Sheldon, W. H.:** The varieties of human physique. New York & London, 1963. *P.K.*

Chirology. The art of reading the hand, originating in ancient chiromancy; the art of prophesying from the shape and the lines of the hand, which were thought to relate to the stars (in imitation of astrology) or to organs of the body. Chirology has renounced its mantic purpose and now concerns itself with the interpretation of character (q.v.) from the shape, state and lines of the hand, but its findings have no validity: in the main they are based on unjustified and empirically unfounded analogies or metaphorical generalizations. In addition to chirology, there is scientific research into the lines of the hand and the patterns of callosities.

Bibliography: Kiener, F.: Hand, Gebärde und Charakter. Munich, 1962. *F.K.*

Chi-square distribution (*χ^2-distribution*). A random distribution of magnitudes which represent functions of observation values (e.g. frequencies). It is used to test statistical hypotheses and is therefore sometimes called a test distribution. The function

$$C = \left[\left(\frac{r-2}{2}\right)! \cdot 2^{\frac{r-2}{2}}\right]^{-1}$$

gives the functional value of χ for a specific r (number of independent, normally distributed random variables). This allows calculation of the probability $d\Phi(\chi^2)$ that an observed χ^2 lies between the values χ^2 and $d(\chi_1^2)$. *W.H.B.*

Chi-square test (χ^2 test). An inferential-statistical test based on the chi-square distribution (q.v.). Probably the most frequent application is the random testing of deviations (q.v.) of observed values (e.g. frequencies) from the values of a random spot-check expected on the basis of the χ^2 distribution (test for the validity of the adaptation). In addition, the χ^2 test is used to test the randomness of deviations between observed and hypothetical variances (q.v.) as well as in the combination of significance tests (see *Significance*). *W.H.B.*

Chlordiazepoxide (syn. *Librium*). A tranquilizer (q.v.) with which, after meprobamate (q.v.), a new class of chemical substances, the benzodiazepines (*inter alia:* diazepam [Valium], oxazepam [Serax]), were introduced into pharmacotherapy; they have anti-neurotic, but minor sedative, effects over a wide dosage range. In therapeutic doses, chlordiazepoxide has a central effect, predominantly in the limbic system. Large doses induce sleep but are not narcotic. Autonomic effects are largely non-existent. The effects on healthy persons have been tested in numerous experimental investigations. The effects in daily life depend on habitual personality characteristics and situational conditions (see *Differential psychopharmacology*). Emotional relaxation can occur with doses of up to 60 mg., and will be greater with the emotionally unstable and those under emotional stress. Under certain conditions (e.g. mental stress) paradoxical arousal is possible. At up to 30 mg., scarcely any influence on performance can be shown. Impairments of performance are most noticeable in speed tests of perception and cognition. When the dose is increased to more than 30 mg., there is more likelihood of subjective sedation and impairment of performance.

Bibliography: Janke, W. & Debus, G.: Experimental studies on anti-anxiety agents with normal subjects: methodological consideration and review of the main effects. In: **Efron, D. H.** (Ed.): Psychopharmacology 1957–1967. Washington, 1968. See also *Tranquilizers*. *G.D.*

Chloroform. A narcotic (q.v.) in use since 1847, very potent in a limited area of narcosis, with undesirable toxic effects on the myocardium and liver parenchyma. Now little used for humans. *E.L.*

Chlorpromazine (syn. *Amargil, Largactil, Megaphen, Thorazine*). Clinically the best-known neuroleptic (q.v.) of the phenothiazine (q.v.) derivatives, it has been widely used since J. Delay & P. Deniker (1952) described its beneficial effects in psychiatric therapy. Among the phenothiazines, chlorpromazine affords a comparatively medium neuroleptic effect with moderate extrapyramidal but stronger autonomic side-effects (circulation) in large doses. In healthy persons, chlorpromazine (up to 200 mg.) has an effect on performance independently of the nature of the tests; it is not emotionally relaxing, but in isolated cases increases tension and as a rule is sedative. A reduction of experimentally induced anxiety could not be demonstrated positively. Paradoxal sleep is prolonged by small doses, and shortened by large ones. See *Dream*.

Bibliography: Brodie, C. M.: Chlorpromazine as anxiety-reducer: effects on complex learning and reaction time. J. exp. Res. Pers., 1967, *2*, 160–67. **Hartlage, L. C.:** Effects of chlorpromazine on learning. Psychol. Bull., 1965, *64*, 235–45. **Janke, W. & Debus, G.:** Experimental studies in anti-anxiety agents with normal subjects: methodological considerations and review of the main effects. In: **Efron, D. H.** (Ed.): Psychopharmacology 1957–1967, Washington, 1968. **Lewis, S. A. & Evans, J. I.:** Dose effects of chlorpromazine on human sleep. Psychopharmacologia, 1969, *14*, 342–8. *G.D.*

Choice reaction (syn. *Choice experiment*). Choice reactions are all those reactions in which Ss have to respond variously to several, different stimuli. E.g. they must press a button with the left hand in response to a red light, with the right hand in response to a blue light, and with both feet in response to a white light. In such experiments, Ss are primarily required to apply sensory discrimination and appropriate motor coordination. In choice experiments, reaction times are significantly longer than in other reaction situations. *A.T.*

Choleric type. According to medieval tradition an irascible, vehement temperament; an emotionally active, direct personality. *W.K.*

Cholinergic. 1. Characteristic of the effect of chemical substances comparable to that of acetylcholine (q.v.). **2.** Nerve fibers or nervous systems in which acetylcholine or acetylcholine-related substances function as transmitters (q.v.). To equate cholinergic with parasympathetic is incorrect, since "cholinergic" is used in connection with the central nervous system when acetycholine functions as a transmitter. According to many authors, cholinergic nervous systems are of fundamental importance for learning. See *Psychopharmacology*. *W.J.*

Cholinergics. Substances with a cholinergic effect.

Cholinesterase (abb. ChE) (syn. *Acetylcholinesterase*, abb. AChE). An enzyme under the influence of which the acetylcholine (q.v.) released in the organism is inactivated within a very short time (in the region of milliseconds). *W.J.*

Cholinesterase inhibitors. Substances which block or delay the rapid enzyme decomposition of acetylcholine (q.v.). In consequence the effect of acetylcholine at the receptor is strengthened and/or prolonged. Important cholinesterases are neostigmine (prostigmin) (q.v.), physostigmine (q.v.), pyridostigmine, edrophonium (Tensilon). Certain substances (organic phosphates, e.g. diisopropylfluorophosphate [isofluorophate; Fluoropryl], DFP) inhibit cholinesterase irreversibly, and cause death by convulsions and impairment of the breathing and circulation. Some of these substances are used as insecticides (e.g. nitrostigmine). Some substances related to DFP have been considered for use in chemical warfare as "nerve poisons" (e.g. sarine, somane, tabune). Small doses of cholinesterase inhibitors impair the performance of healthy persons; large doses create symptoms resembling psychosis. Cholinesterases are used extensively to investigate the relations between acetylcholine and behavior. See *Psychopharmacology*.

Bibliography: Koelle, G. B.: Cholinesterases and anticholinesterase agents. In: Hdb. d. exp. Pharmakol. Vol. 15. Berlin, 1963. See also *Acetylcholine; Anticholinergics.* *W.J.*

Chorea. An extrapyramidal (see *Pyramidal tract*) motor disorder in the form of constantly repeated spasms of particular muscles or groups of muscles. The intention to move, together with emotional excitement, increases the disturbance of movement. The following are distinguished: (*a*) *Chorea minor* (Sydenham's chorea; St Vitus' dance) as the result of a rheumatic cerebral inflammation, a childhood disease; (*b*) *Huntington's chorea:* a dominant inherited, degenerative complaint in which there is cellular atrophy in the *caudatum* and *putamen*, i.e. the *corpus striatum*. In addition to the motor disturbance (and often preceding this), there is psychic damage in the sense of increasing "coarsening of the personality", loss of restraint, and dementia (q.v.). (N.B.: This chorea, with its cerebral pathological causation, must not be confused with *chorea major*, a term once used for serious hysterical attacks.) *C.S.*

Choriongonadotrophine (syn. *Chorionic gonadotrophin*). An extrahypophyseal gonadotrop(h)ic hormone (protein hormone), which is formed during pregnancy in the trophoblast and later in the fetal section of the placenta. Biological significance and effect: prevents cyclic modification of the *corpus luteum* (yellow body) in the follicle, which it stimulates to further growth during the first months of pregnancy, thus maintaining its function. Choriongonadotrophine therefore mainly has a luteinizing action similar to that of gonadotrophic hormone. The placenta begins to produce choriongonadotrophine some four to five weeks after fertilization, and reaches the maximum value in about the sixth week of pregnancy: this facilitates early diagnosis of pregnancy, since large quantities of choriongonadotrophine are detectable in the urine and blood plasma. *H.M.*

Chromatic. In general, "chromatic" means colored. (*a*) Visual perception: *monochromatic* and *polychromatic light stimuli; monochromatic* refers to radiation with one wavelength. *Polychromatic light stimuli* are radiation composed of several wavelengths. The color of mono- and polychromatic light can be the same. Afterimages are *homochromous* (*homochromatic*) when they show the same color as the primary stimulus, and *heterochromous* (*heterochromatic*) when they show a different color. (*b*) In music, the twelve-part scale is called chromatic in contrast to the seven-part scale, which is diatonic. (*c*) *Chromatisms:* see *Synesthesia. Chromatopsia:* morbid varicolored vision due to many different reasons such as a cataract operation, poisoning, etc. *A.H.*

Chromatic aberration. In optics: a chromatic image-forming defect. In a convex lens the rear focal point for short-wave light rays (blue) is in front of the rear focal point for long-wave light rays (red). If one examines the image of a point source in the focal plane (retina), it is seen to feature colored (chromatic) rings, or chromatic *dispersion circles.* Since in the human eye, too (with the exception of the retinal layer in the narrow foveal area), all optic media have a convex effect, these produce a chromatic aberration (color deviation). Although, as a rule, nothing of this considerable degree of chromatic aberration is noticed in perception, we do see colored dispersion circles immediately the chromatic aberration of the eye is artificially increased or diminished. It is not yet known how chromatic aberration in the human eye is corrected or suppressed for the purpose of perception. *A.H.*

Chromatic adaptation. Reduction of the hue and saturation of a color when fixated.

Chromatoptometer. Light rays which are perceived as different colors are distinguished physically by their wavelengths. Since the angle of refraction as the ray passes from one optic medium to another depends on the wavelength, rays of different wavelengths unite in the eye at different points on the optic axis. The point of union (focal point) of light-blue rays is nearer to the cornea than the focal point of red rays (see *Chromatic aberration*). The chromatoptometer makes use of this chromatic aberration: when the emmetrope (see *Emmetropia*) looks at an electric lamp (bulb) through an interposed cobalt glass (which transmits red and blue light only), he sees violet; the myope (see *Myopia*) sees red with a blue edge; the hyperope (see *Hyperopia*) sees blue with a red edge. *R.R.*

Chromomeres. When cells begin to divide, small nodules known as chromomers, become recognizable on the strands from which chromosomes are formed. They are considered to be the beginning of a spiralization. *H.S.*

Chromesthesia. See *Color hearing; Synthesia.*

Chromosomal aberration. A chromosomal anomaly, discovered in 1959 (Lejeune, Gautier, Turpin), which consists of either a missing or an additional gene; there are somatic and psychic consequences. Trisomia 21 (chromosome 21 according to the Denver nomenclature) is the cause of Down's disease (see *Mongolism*). The XO aberration (instead of XX) brings about the Turner syndrome (q.v.) (gonadal dysgenesia), the XXY aberration (instead of XY) causes the Klinefelter syndrome (q.v.) (men with a marked feminine aspect); men with the XYY aberration are usually tall with disturbed social behavior. There are other forms of chromosomal aberration which all cause brain disturbances.

Bibliography: **Züblin, W.:** Chromosomale Aberrationen und Psyche. Basle & New York, 1969. *F.Ki.*

Chromosomes. Minute, thin strands with a fibrous, rod-like structure in the cell nucleus whose number remains constant with the species (forty-six in humans); as a rule they are only recognizable by refined spectroscopic techniques when a cell divides, and they each split into two. Each chromosome is a DNA (desoxyribonucleic acid) molecule (for structure of DNA helix, see Watson, 1968); the chromosome theory of heredity holds that the genes strung along the molecule are fundamentally responsible for the transmission of inherited characteristics. Some inheritance processes and changes can be traced to the molecule responsible.

Bibliography: **Watson, J. D.:** The double helix. London, 1968. **Id.:** Molecular biology of the gene. London, 1969. *H.S.*

Chronaxie. A characteristic dimension in testing nerve function: an index of tissue excitability calculated in terms of the reaction time for stimulation with a current double the threshold intensity.

Chronograph. Usually an electronic appliance with the help of which (e.g. in continuous reaction experiments) the smallest periods of time can be measured and recorded. See *Chronoscope.* *K.E.P.*

Chronological age (abb. CA). The subject's age from his birth to a specific point.

Chronoscope. Term used for an accurate stop-watch (capable of measuring 1/1000 sec.). Inventors: C. Wheatstone & M. Hipp.

Cinema. See *Film.*

Circuit processes. Processes which, as they take place, retroact on their initial conditions, e.g. the changes in a river bed caused by water pouring over it. The functional principle underlying circuit processes is known as *feedback* (q.v.). *K.-D.G*

Circular psychosis. French psychiatrists in the 1850s (Falret & Bailarger) described *folie circulaire* as an episodic illness with normal intervening periods, each episode being characterized either by extreme cheerfulness or depression. Because of variations in associated disorders of movement and thought, classifications multiplied until Kraepelin subsumed all such illnesses under *manic depressive psychosis* (q.v.). Since then, other attempts have been made to separate discrete types of circular illness according to their patterns of mood, behavior, thought and perceptual symptoms; these are labeled variously periodic psychosis, cycloid psychosis, recoverable schizophrenia, schizophreniform psychosis and schizoaffective psychosis. The field is variously charted and overlaps with that of the recoverable psychoses, i.e. those mentioned above, together with degeneration psychosis, reactive psychosis, psychogenic psychosis and acute psychosis. See *Psychoses*. *B.B.*

Circulation response. A response by the organism to a change in internal or external conditions. Cardiac and circulation responses are observed during physical exertion, e.g. muscular work, passive rotation or tilting of the body, in experiences with a strong emotional content, or in cases of physical trauma (shock), but also as a phenomenon accompanying changes in arousal, e.g. emotions and stress, and also as a consequence of simple sensory stimuli (orienting reflex). These reactions are not only demonstrable in cardiac activity (pulse, beat, EKG), but in the arterial system (systolic and diastolic blood pressure, pulse wave velocity, peripheral resistance and volume) and in venous pressure, vein condition and capillary circulation. The cardio-circulatory system is able to adjust in many, interdependent regulating circuits to changing requirements; a general distinction must be made between an ergotropic (sympathetic) and trophotropic, vagotonic functional condition (autonomic system). See *Arousal*.

Because of the close, neurovegetative connections, mental stress and emotive excitation primarily influence the cardio-circulatory system: blushing, loss of color, pulse acceleration, blood pressure reaction, etc. The pulse frequency and systolic blood pressure are used most commonly as activation indicators because they can still be measured relatively simply, and generally vary in direct relation to the degree of physical effort and mental stress. It has not yet been possible to demonstrate specific patterns of circulation response during individual emotions (see *Emotion*). See *Psychophysiological methods*.

Bibliography: Donat, K.: Herz und Kreislauf. In: **Bartelheimer, H. & Jores, A.** (Eds): Klinische Funktionsdiagnostik, Stuttgart, *3*, 1967. **Legewie, H.:** Indikatoren von Kreislauf, Atmung u. Energieumsatz. In: **Schönpflug, W.** (Ed.): Methoden der Aktivierungsforschung. Berne, 1969. *J.Fa.*

Circumcision. The partial or total medico-surgical or ritual removal of the prepuce. In depth psychology, circumcision is often described as a ritualized approximation to, or threat of, castration (castration complex, q.v.); in some cultures it forms part of an initiation ritual (see *Initiation*). Even today circumcision is sometimes used as a "therapy" and (or) punishment for infant masturbation (q.v.), but is usually a form of treatment for phimosis (chronic contraction of the prepuce). Circumcision is often indicated or rationalized —according to the point of view—as a measure to intensify sexual hygiene. A comparison of large social groups in which circumcised men form a minority or a majority, shows that at any moment the minority is regarded as sexually more effective, both in respect to the auto- and the stereotype. This heightened effectiveness is supposed to result from a more than average ability to control ejaculation (q.v.), based in the circumcised on a diminished sensitiveness of the glans penis, in the non-circumcised on decreased stimulation by the vagina during intercourse, since the glans penis is extensively protected by the prepuce. Both views seem to be refuted by neurological and sexological investigations.

There are three main kinds of circumcision: (*a*) *Incision:* only the *frenulum* is incised. (*b*) *Circumcision:* the entire foreskin is removed (e.g. among Jews and Arabs). The above statements refer to this form. (*c*) *Subincision:* the urethrá is cut open to the root of the penis (New Guinea and Melanesia). *G.L.*

Clairvoyance. A form of ESP (q.v.) where the information acquired by the subject is assumed to derive directly from an external physical source, not from the mind or brain of another person as in telepathy (q.v.). *J.B.*

Clairvoyant. Person with special ability for clairvoyance (q.v.). Must not be confused with its colloquial usage where it refers to a fortune-teller. *J.B.*

Clang. A term for the acoustic phenomenon produced by the superimposition of harmonic partials. The latter, which comprise the fundamental tone and its overtones, represent the simplest periodic sound vibrations, the frequencies of which rise in the ratio of whole numbers. The number, choice and intensity of the individual partials basically determine the *timbre*, while the pitch is fixed by the fundamental tone even if it is not heard. Other features of clang are its loudness and duration.

In clang analysis, both partials and clang are distinguished qualitatively and quantitatively with respect to pitch and intensity. This can be done by the human ear alone or by means of resonators, interference valves, electric filters, Fourier analysis. See *Music, psychology of.*

Bibliography: Wellek, A.: Musikpsychologie und Musikästhetik. Frankfurt, 1963. *B.S.*

Claparède, Edouard. B. 24/3/1873, d. 29/9/1940, in Geneva. Doctor and psychologist; professor at Geneva where in 1912 he founded the "Institut J.-J. Rousseau". Devoted himself to comparative psychology, especially to child psychology, and is considered to be the co-founder of applied psychology; advanced the development of industrial psychology, and put forward proposals for the use of psychology in medicine. Claparède considered psychological processes from the standpoint of their biological utility. See *Functionalism.*

Works. Psychologie de l'enfant et pédagogie expérimentale, 1905. Psychologie judiciaire (in: *Année psychol.*), 1906. L'éducation fonctionelle, 1931. Le développement mental, ^{2}1946. 1901: founded the "Archives de Psychologie" (with Flournay).

Bibliography: Claparède, E.: Edouard Claparède. In: **Murchison, C.** (Ed.): A history of psychology in autobiography, Vol. 1. Worcester, Mass., 1930, 63–97.
F.-C.S.

Classification. The operation of dividing into classes the elements of a group of objects with the aid of some *common characteristic* (relation of equivalence or similarity). Each object thus classified belongs to one class only. The term also denotes the result of the process. In traditional logic, classification was dichotomous and culminated in a "tree" structure (Tree of Porphyry, c. 232 to 301 A.D.). It progressed in each case in accordance with the next, higher generic concept (*genus proximum*) and the difference constituting the species (*differentia specifica*). The concept of "grouping" (Piaget) shows that the concrete thinking of the child also progresses according to a "tree-structure" classification. See *Concept.* *M.-J.B.*

Classification methods are used to group events in categories or classes. According to the nature of the characteristics classified, qualitative may be distinguished from quantitative classification.

Classification tests are either those in which a testee is asked to classify objects, or those used to classify a group of people according to some predetermined set of categories (e.g. "streaming" by IQ, etc., in schools). *G.M.*

Class, social. A term used in sociology and social psychology (q.v.) in regard to social stratification; it is applied to individuals or small groups (families) in a given society or community who show relative similarities in regard to certain possibilities: choice of vocation, and/or income, and/or living conditions and standards, and/or social prestige (vocational group); there are many other modes of division, or "classes"—e.g. linguistic usage. Empirical research is constantly concerned to establish the characteristics of new social strata in the process of formation. In general, the *Marxist* concept of class (but see Lukàcs, 1971) differs in postulating that ownership or non-ownership of the means of production and of the products (property or no property) is sufficient to develop *class consciousness*, expressed as a form of solidarity among members of a class. In the first case, class is defined in terms of the complex of characteristics relevant at a given time, place, and so on; in the second case, in terms of economic circumstances and the resulting emotions.

Bibliography: Barber, B. & E. G.: European social class: stability and change. New York, 1965. **Bendix, R. & Lipset, S. M.** (Eds): Class, status and power. New York, [2]1966. **Bergel, E. E.:** Social stratification. New York, 1962. **Brandis, W. & Henderson, D.** (Eds): Primary socialisation, language and education, Vol. 1: Social class, language and communication. London, 1969. **Bronfenbrenner, V.:** Socialization and social class through time and space. In: **Maccoby, E. E.,** *et al.* (Eds): Readings in social psychology. New York, 1958. **Centers, R.:** The psychology of social classes. New York, 1949. **Lukàcs, G.:** History and class-consciousness. London, 1971. *W.D.F.*

Classical conditioning. See *Conditioning, classical and operant.*

Claustrophilia. A desire to be confined or to withdraw to a small, enclosing space. *Claustrophobia:* a fear of such confinement or withdrawal.

Cleanliness. See *Bowel training.*

Client-centered therapy. A form of psychotherapy or counseling developed by C. Rogers. The approach is *non-directive*, involving no attempts to diagnose, interpret or persuade, the aim being to provide a climate of *warmth*, *empathy*, and *acceptance* in which the *client* will be free to gain insight into his unique *self* enabling him to mobilize his potentialities in the solution of his own problems. The job of the therapist is to communicate his sincere feeling that the client is a person of *unconditional self-worth*, of value regardless of his attitudes, ideas, and behavior, and to reflect what the client is saying in such a way as to clarify his thoughts and make it clear that his feelings are fully understood. The method has gained widespread popularity, particularly in the U.S.A., and is the basis of the group technique called *sensitivity training* or *T-groups.* *G.D.W.*

Climate of work. This comprises factors in the social structure of a factory which lie outside the worker but influence him. Among them are good factory organization, communication facilities between worker and employer and between the workers themselves, some voice in affairs, direct and indirect recognition, group relationships, etc.

An unfavorable atmosphere decreases productivity and individual activity, and quantities produced, and finds expression, e.g. in discontent, work-shyness and increased absenteeism. See *Industrial psychology; Occupational psychology.*

Bibliography: Friedmann, G.: The anatomy of work. Glencoe, Ill., 1961. **Davison, J. P.** *et al.*: Productivity and economic incentives. London, 1958. **Gouldner, A. W.:** Wildcat strike. London, 1955. **Sayles, L. R.:** Behavior of industrial work groups. New York, 1958. **Winn, A.:** The laboratory approach to organization development: a tentative model of planned change. J. manag. Stud., 1969, *6*, 155–66. **Zalezinik, A.,** *et al.*: The motivation, productivity and satisfaction of workers: a predictive study. Harvard, 1958. *W.S.*

Climax (*Orgasm*). The peak of excitement during sexual intercourse or masturbation.

Normally corresponding with ejaculation in the male, and ideally, vaginal contractions immediately following ejaculation for the female. (See also *Clitoral orgasm.*) In medicine, the height of a fever or disease process.
G.D.W.

Clinical psychology. 1. *Definition.* There is no single generally accepted definition of clinical psychology. We can therefore do no more than outline the main trends of thought on the subject: (*a*) Clinical psychology is the activity of the psychologist in a clinic or hospital, confined normally to diagnosis and, within certain limits, to advice (Meyerhoff, 1959). (*b*) Clinical psychology is a *special method* (exploration and observation) which was first introduced into child psychology by Jean Piaget. (*c*) Clinical psychology is the application of the results and methods of all the basic psychological disciplines (general, developmental, differential, social, and dynamic psychology or psychoanalysis), and related disciplines such as comparative psychology (q.v.), sociology and methodology in the "clinical sector" (Schraml, 1970; Wolman, 1965). Clinical psychology is also understood as the application in the clinical sphere of psychology stemming from a unified conception (e.g. learning theories or C. R. Rogers' conception); depending on the interpretation concept which is adopted, emphasis is placed on individual sectors (e.g. social aspects or learning disorders) (e.g. Sundberg & Taylor, 1963). Definition (*c*) is stressed here because clinical psychology is an applied, i.e. a pragmatic, discipline.

2. *Historical background.* Three phases can be distinguished in the development of clinical psychology. (*a*) During and after World War I, methods of psychological examination developed in the laboratory were used to evaluate brain damage caused by injury or accident (W. Poppelreuther, O. Lippmann). A psychological laboratory already existed at the time in the clinic run by the famous psychiatrist E. Kraepelin. Clinical psychology combined experimental laboratory psychology, hospital psychology and industrial psychology, and was a precursor of rehabilitation methods. (*b*) A new trend developed with the introduction of psychoanalysis in psychology and psychiatry, primarily in the English-speaking countries. Whether psychoanalysis is used in the strict sense of the word, or of an eclectic use of procedures borrowed from many different psychological systems, or of the results of learning theories combined with those of dynamic psychology or psychoanalysis (O. H. Mowrer), the clinical psychologist is not merely a diagnostician but an adviser and therapist. This situation developed with some speed in the U.S.A. after World War II, when the hospitals of the Veterans' Administration were set up. (*c*) In a final phase of development, clinical psychologists have begun to work in psychiatric, psychosomatic, psychotherapeutic, pediatric, neurological and orthopedic establishments as diagnosticians, therapists (especially in group therapy, q.v.) and consultant social workers, or counseling psychologists. The function of the psychologist as a methodological expert in clinical research is almost entirely novel. Since the average doctor has no training in quantitative methods, a new sphere of clinical psychology has developed.

3. *Applications.* According to internationally accepted terminology, the clinical sector not only covers fixed establishments for the care of patients (hospitals, clinics) but also out-patient departments and the whole range of guidance centers (educational or child guidance, vocational guidance, marriage, family, geriatric, and alcohol and drug addict guidance as well as guidance for suicide risks), and remand establishments, old people's homes and psychiatric establishments and hospitals. In addition, clinical psychologists act in an advisory capacity in the education and health planning institutes of advanced countries and international organizations.

4. *Clinical social psychology.* Clinical social psychology has developed considerably in

the last decade; the boundaries between social psychiatry, psycho-hygiene, social education and clinical social psychology are fluid, but in this sector, too, the activities of social psychiatrists, social workers, sociologists, social education experts and psychologists are often identical. The work is therefore determined by function and method rather than by professional disciplines. (*a*) *Prevention:* (i) Information through mass media (press, radio, television) on mental disorders and how to treat and prevent them (e.g. sex education, child nurture and training). Advice in planning new housing developments, kindergartens, schools and old people's homes, etc. (ii) Participation in the training of all types of educators, social workers and hospital staff by imparting psychological knowledge and by sensitivity training, etc., in dynamic group therapy. (iii) Institutional preventive therapy in all establishments for preventive care. (*b*) *Study and improvement of the social structure of clinical establishments:* (i) Group relations in hospitals (doctors, nurses, administrative staff, specialists and patients). (ii) Group relations in educational establishments and remand homes: educators, psychologists, teachers and pupils. (iii) Social structure in clinics, old people's homes and psychiatric establishments. (*c*) *Rehabilitation and resocialization:* (i) Help in integrating children born with physical or mental defects into society (together with special educational methods). (ii) Reintegration of persons physically handicapped as a result of accidents or disease (examination, retraining and mental rehabilitation). (iii) Reintegration and mental care of the chronically sick. (iv) Reintegration of psychiatric patients and persons who have been in hospital for long periods. (v) Resocialization of delinquents (overlap with the education and rehabilitation of criminals, and with criminal psychology, q.v.).

5. *Clinical diagnosis.* (*a*) As in medicine, a *case history* is compiled to study the previous development of patients or third parties (biological, sociological or biographical data). (*b*) *Exploration:* As in psychiatry, the intellectual and psychic state of the patient is determined by observing his verbal and para-verbal responses to stimuli. (*c*) The clinical *interview* used primarily in the early stages of psychotherapy (q.v.), psychosomatics (q.v.), and similar areas, allows the patient to speak freely and therefore enables the basis of a conflict and possibilities of interaction to be clarified by association.

6. *Clinical test diagnosis.* A distinction must be made between integrated psychodiagnosis, which is an inseparable part of the clinical process, and purely cooperative psychodiagnosis, which makes results available for clinical practice. The methods (tests) can usefully be divided up according to intention, method and sphere of application. (*a*) *Intention:* intelligence, aptitude and interest studies; *methods:* psychometric; *application:* child psychiatry and educational guidance; neurology and rehabilitation. (*b*) *Intention:* determination of normal or pathological personality structure by projective methods (q.v.); *method:* interpretative, with some measurements; *application:* psychiatry, child psychiatry and educational guidance; psychotherapy and guidance. (*c*) *Intention:* individual conflict, biographical genesis and social relations by thematic methods (e.g. TAT, CAT for children, Four-Picture test); *application:* early stages of psychotherapy and psychosomatics; child psychiatry and educational guidance; guidance centers. (*d*) *Intention:* classification of patients by personality inventories (e.g. MPPI, MPI); *methods:* metric, quantitative; *application:* in hospitals and out-patient departments to classify patients for therapeutic methods. (*e*) *Intention:* analysis of the relation of personalities to individual psycho-physical or physiological data; *method:* experimental, quantitative; *application:* in clinical research.

7. *Psychological guidance, treatment and care.* In most instances, an eclectic, pragmatic method of clinical psychology adapted to the specific situation is used. However, the clinical psychologist must be acquainted

with the principles of all the methods listed below; if he does not have the necessary training himself he must at least be able to refer patients for the appropriate special treatment. (*a*) *Guidance and counseling:* (i) informational guidance, i.e. explanation of research results and general knowledge (e.g. from group and development psychology); (ii) guidance based on knowledge of the case history but with a strong directive emphasis (e.g. referral to different guidance centers); guidance of patients who are not accessible to introspective treatment aimed at clarifying the conflict (e.g. certain psychiatric patients). (*b*) *Symptom-oriented methods:* (i) physiotropic or organismic methods: including hypnosis (q.v.), narcosis-hypnosis, suggestion and relaxation methods (autogenic training, q.v., progressive relaxation according to E. Jacobsen, etc.); in these methods the therapists use verbal stimuli to contact the organism directly, either to cure the symptom or to change the responses; (ii) behavior or aversive therapy: the aim is either to eliminate negative stimulus-response associations (e.g. systematic desensitization, aversion therapy, q.v.), or to build up necessary stimulus-response associations which have not yet been acquired (see *Conditioning*). (*c*) *Psychodynamic and conflict-oriented methods:* (i) psychoanalysis (q.v.): attempts are made to cure symptoms by changing the psychodynamic personality structure, gaining insight into the unconscious conflict process, and studying social relationships; derivatives of psychoanalysis (parameters) in child therapy, psychoses and delinquency and all forms of short-term therapy; (ii) deviations from psychoanalysis (changes in the theoretical concept: K. Horney, E. Fromm, H. Schultz-Hencke & H. Sullivan; the early depth-psychology schools of A. Adler & C. G. Jung); and existential analysis (less important from the standpoint of clinical psychology); (iii) non-directive psychotherapy, or client-centered (discussion) therapy (q.v.) according to C. R. Rogers, in which *non*-specific conflict is assumed (suitable for relatively minor conflicts). (*d*) *Group psychotherapy:* (i) all forms of non-analytical group psychotherapy: e.g. play and constructive groups with children and adolescents, directive discussion groups, psycho-drama (J. L. Moreno) rehabilitation groups for former psychiatric patients and alcoholics; (ii) analytical group psychotherapy; important here are multilateral transference and specific forms of catharsis (q.v.). (*e*) *Clinical* (psychological) *exploitation of other methods* such as rhythm, work and occupational therapy. See *Group therapy*.

8. *Research in clinical psychology.* Primarily progress control and study of the success rate of psychotherapeutic methods, psychopharmacology (q.v.), and psychophysiology (q.v.).

Bibliography: Bulletin de Psychologie. Numéro Spécial: Psychologie Clinique, 1968, *21*, 15–19. **Benton, A. L.** (Ed.): Contributions to clinical neuropsychology. Chicago, 1970. **Gathercole, C. E.:** Assessment in clinical psychology. Harmondsworth, 1968. **Lubin, B. & Levitt, E.** (Eds): The clinical psychologist. Chicago, 1967. **Meyerhoff, H.:** Leitfaden der Klinischen Psychologie. Munich & Basle, 1959. **Schraml, W. J.** (Ed.): Hdb. der Klinischen Psychologie. Berne & Stuttgart, 1970. **Stern, E.** (Ed.): Hdb. der Klinischen Psychologie, Vols 1 & 2. Zürich, 1954/58. **Sundberg, N. D. & Tyler, L. E.:** Clinical psychology. London, 1963. **Wolman, B. B.** (Ed.): Handbook of clinical psychology. New York, 1965. **Wolpe, J.:** The practice of behavior therapy. New York, 1969.

W. J. Schraml

Clisis. According to Monakow, the investment of some object of a drive or instinct with *positive emotional qualities*. Investment with *negative* emotional qualities is *ecclisis*.

W.T.

Clitoral orgasm. 1. A pattern of changes in the *clitoris* (the penis analogue in the female) involving tumescence and retraction, which are believed to be associated with sexual climax in the female during intercourse or masturbation. **2.** Sexual climax in the female achieved through physical stimulation of the clitoris rather than the inside of the vagina.

G.D.W.

Closure. A principle proposed by gestalt psychologists to explain how stable percepts can be achieved by the subjective closing of gaps and the completion of incomplete figures to form wholes. *C.D.F.*

Closure Faces Test. C. M. Mooney's test of visual perception, used, e.g., to examine the long-term effects of temporal lobectomy.

Bibliography: Mooney, C. M.: Closure with negative afterimages under flickering light. Canad. J. Physiol., 1956, *10*, 191–9. **Id.:** Closure as affected by configural clarity and contextual consistency. Canad. J. Physiol., 1957, *11*, 80–8.

Closure, law of. Mental and physical processes tend to formal completeness, e.g. asymmetrical figures will be seen as symmetrical. See *Ganzheit*.

Cluster. An accumulation of elements (points, observations) relative to the environment; e.g. an accumulation of points in part of the coordinate system. R. C. Tryon's cluster analysis is a method related to factor analysis (q.v.), and used for the grouping of variables on the basis of intercorrelations (e.g. in a correlation table). *W.H.B.*

Cocaine. An alkaloid synthesized from ecgonine and obtained from leaves of South American coca shrubs (*Erythroxylon coca*), chewed by the Andean Indians on account of their stimulating, invigorating and intoxicating effects. The effect of cocaine on the central nervous system is at first exciting and then inhibiting. It inhibits monamine oxidase (q.v.) and thus increases the effect of the catecholamines (q.v.) present in the body. By blocking conduction in the peripheral nerves it has a strong local anesthetic effect. Acute cocaine intoxication passes through several phases: a euphoric phase, in which there is a feeling of enhanced physical and mental power, is replaced by an intoxicated phase in which the mood is anxious and irritable and there are acoustic and micro-optic hallucinations (q.v.); the final phase is depressive. Cocaine use can be addictive. It has little significance nowadays in medical use.

Bibliography: See *Drug dependence; Narcotics.* *G.E.*

Co-consciousness. A term coined by Rohracher for those items of knowledge and information that people are not consciously aware of, but which can be retrieved instantly without effort of memory or verbalization, e.g. one's name, address, etc. *C.D.F.*

Code. A system of symbols, or a specification for the unambiguous arrangement ("coding") of the symbols of a (relatively large) array and those of another (relatively small) array.

A large number of special codes have been developed for the different areas of information processing (q.v.), which are studied in information theory (q.v.). Existing codes can be classified according to different criteria, e.g. the degree of redundancy (q.v.).

Computer code (syn. *Machine code*): a system of symbols for the operations built into a computer. *P.-B.H.*

Codeine (*Methyl morphine*). A psychotropic (q.v.) substance, contained in opium (q.v.), related chemically and pharmacologically to morphine (q.v.), but a weaker analgesic than the latter. Only small amounts of morphine occur as a decomposition product, therefore withdrawal symptoms cease in cases of morphine addiction; codeine itself scarcely causes addiction. It inhibits the "cough center"; large doses impair breathing. It acts centrally, as does morphine. Codeine has a mild sedative effect.

Bibliography: Kay, D. C., Gorodetsky, C. W. & Martin, W. R.: Comparative effects of codeine and morphine in man. J. Pharmacol. exp. Therap. 1967, *156*, 101–6. *W.B.*

Coding. See *Code*.

Coeducation. The joint education or training of boys and girls. Full segregation of the sexes during primary, and even secondary, education is tending to disappear in Western culture, and in certain countries is more often associated with religious or socially privileged educational systems.

Coefficient. **1.** In mathematics: a constant value by which another value is multiplied. **2.** In statistics: a value expressing the degree to which an information characteristic occurs under certain conditions. Some coefficients, e.g. the correlation coefficients (q.v.), are so defined that they assume values between 0 and 1. *G.M.*

Cognition. **1.** An expression for every *process* by which a living creature obtains knowledge of some object or becomes aware of its environment. Cognition processes are: perception, discovery, recognition, imagining, judging, memorizing, learning, thinking, and often speech. **2.** Knowing as distinct from volitional or emotional processes. **3.** The product of cognizing, or knowing; the knowledge acquired. *H.W.*

4. Like the word "knowledge", "cognition" refers to a human activity which is intellectual and communicable. The many varied meanings of the word can be reduced to two principal ones: (*a*) the representation or grasping in conceptual terms of a (concrete or abstract) object by perception, imagination or conceptualization; (*b*) understanding or explanation: the understanding of an object as specific because it fits into a system of relationships which justifies it by its very nature. In both meanings, the cognitive action determines the object as such, and differentiates between that which is known and the person who has cognizance of it. Cognition therefore contrasts with the pure subjectivity of the states of consciousness, feeling and belief, because it merely aims at revealing the truth. Problems in regard to cognition concern its origin (reason, experience), nature (intuitive, discursive), and range (phenomenal, absolute). See *Epistemology; Empiricism.* *M.-J.B.*

Cognition theory (*Theory of knowledge;* Ger., *Erkenntnistheorie*). A collective term for philosophical theories which seek to explain the nature, mechanisms and value of cognition by studying the general relationship between subject and object, thought and world. The term *Erkenntnistheorie* was first used by K. L. Reinhold (*Attempt at a New Theory of Human Ideation*, Jena, 1789) but the problem is as old as philosophy itself. Historically speaking, the first explanations were *dogmatic:* (*a*) there is an object outside thought which is conceived by the latter (*realism, idealism, rationalism,* q.v., *empiricism,* q.v.); (*b*) there is no object outside thought (*phenomenalism*); (*c*) if there is an object, it cannot be known (*skepticism,* q.v.). Later explanations were *critical:* the question of the existence of objects outside thought was replaced by an inquiry into the conditions for cognition, which were looked for at its source, i.e. in the structure of the "cognizing" or "knowing" subject. Finally *dialectical* explanations developed: it is not the type of elements which determines the relationship between cognition and subject; on the contrary, subject and object form a unity in which elements are determined reciprocally. See *Epistemology*. *M.-J.B.*

Cognitive map (syn. *Cognitive schema*). The picture built up by an organism on the basis of experiences, e.g. the image of a maze constructed by an animal, or an individual's image of an organization.

Cognitive orientation. According to the CO theory, cognitive processes, such as recognition, combination and elaboration of meaning, are necessary conditions for the elicitation of orienting reflexes and the acquisition of conditioned reflexes (q.v.), and determine the direction and course of human molar behavior. It suggests a model of cognitive processes intervening between stimulation and behavior: Interaction between the stimulus representation and CO components (beliefs about goals, norms, self and world) creates a CO cluster which produces a goal-directed behavioral intention, actualized in behavior when implemented by inherited, learned or *ad hoc* adapted plans. Conflicts appear when simultaneously several CO clusters and hence several behavioral intentions arise, or when several plans are activated for implementation of one behavioral intention. Experiments show that CO clusters, measured by questionnaires, correlate highly with behavior (e.g. level and course of achievement after success and failure, acted-out defense mechanisms, and so on) when plans are held constant. Studies reveal that schizophrenics (q.v.) have abnormal CO clusters, whose change by clinical means is followed by a decrease in symptoms. Concerning the genesis of CO it was found that children of four to six years already have differentiated CO clusters referring to various aspects of behavior.

Bibliography: **Kreitler, H. & S.:** Die weltanschauliche Orientierung der Schizophrenen. Munich & Basle, 1965. **Id.:** Die kognitive Orientierung des Kindes. Munich & Basle, 1967. **Id.:** Cognitive orientation: a model of human behavior. ETS, Princeton, N.J., RM 23, 1969. **Id.:** The cognitive antecedents of the orienting reflex. Schweiz. Z. Psychol. Anwend., 1970, *29*, 37–44. **Id.:** Cognitive orientation and behavior. New York, 1971.

H. & S. Kreitler

Coherence, coherence factors. Müller proposed coherence factors to explain the formation of "*Gestalten*". These factors included: spatial vicinity, identity, similarity, symmetry and contour (i.e. differentiation of figure from ground). Such factors produce coherence between different parts of the stimulus array, that is, the parts hang together and form a unit. *C.D.F.*

Cohesion (syn. *Cohesiveness*). A term for the forces which induce the individual to remain a member of a group. In general, cohesion is equated with the *attractiveness* of a group, which depends especially on: (*a*) The degree to which the interaction within a group possesses positive qualities for the individual members (the cohesion is greater when interaction produces a greater reward for group members); (*b*) the extent to which group activities are rewarding for each individual (e.g. the recreative effect of leisure activities available in the group); (*c*) the degree to which membership of a group can be used as a means for attaining individual objectives.

The cohesion and attractiveness of a particular group depend also on the value of possible alternatives outside the particular group (the group affords a comparison level for alternatives). The cohesion of a group and the conformity (q.v.) of its members are directly related; the greater the cohesion, the stronger the possible negative sanctions against the non-conforming behavior of an individual without the latter leaving the group. See *Group dynamics*.

Bibliography: **Cartwright, D. & Zander, A.:** Group dynamics: research and theory. New York, ²1960.

A.S.-M.

Coital foreplay (syn. *Pre-coital techniques; Foreplay*) consists of techniques used by one or both partners for stimulation before heterosexual intercourse proper (coitus, q.v.) and to induce readiness for penetration. Methods vary within Western culture according to individual and socio-moral factors: kissing, tongue-play, manual or oral stimulation of the woman's breasts, manual stimulation of the male or female genitals, oral-genital stimulation (see *Cunnilingus; Fellatio*), mutual manual-genital stimulation, genital apposition without introduction of the penis into the vagina, intercrural intercourse. If foreplay does not culminate in coitus, it is usually known as "petting". Some of these techniques (especially fellatio and cunnilingus) are still erroneously held to be "abnormal" or even "perverted" in our culture, even though since Kinsey's findings (1948–53) there has been widespread public awareness of the "normal", widespread use of such methods. The reasons for the persistence of such disapproval would seem to be largely moral and religious.

Recent research in Western Germany (Schmidt & Sigusch, 1970) has confirmed the social-class correlation of foreplay as recorded by Kinsey & Masters in the U.S.A. It is practiced in the form of manual-genital contacts, cunnilingus and fellatio more frequently by upper and middle-class than by lower social groups, where sexual activity more often consists of simple coitus. It is worthy of note that foreplay is more frequently prolonged (eleven minutes to one hour) and used (73% compared with 53%) more before than after marriage. Kinsey & Masters (1953) draw attention to the fact that the findings certainly do not support a widely-held assumption that premarital coitus is necessarily quicker and consequently less satisfying than coitus when married.

Whatever form it takes, coital foreplay fulfills the important task of increasing sexual excitement before, and readiness for, coition.

Bibliography: **Ford, C. S. & Beach, F. A.:** Patterns of sexual behavior. London, 1952. (See *Coitus* for additional literature.)

H.M.

Coitus. Heterosexual intercourse, the most common form of sexual behavior among the majority of adults in all known societies, but very rarely indeed the *sole* form of sexual activity. Preference for certain *positions in coitus* depends on a particular culture; the "active male" and "passive female" roles in coitus are not dependent on "nature" and have nothing to do with a biological pattern of "male" and "female". The duration of coitus depends on the speed with which the man reaches orgasm. When such activity begins depends very much (in Western societies) on social class (Kinsey, 1948; 1953); this applies just as much to males as to females: workers of both sexes first engage in coitus about four years before students of both sexes (Schmidt & Sigusch, 1970); this seems to result not from greater sexual freedom but from earlier material independence, and the earlier age at which workers marry. Greater *mobility of partners* (i.e. number of partners in coitus) for men is frequently written about (Kinsey, 1964; Schofield, 1968, and others), but this also seems to depend to a large extent on class (a greater tendency to change partners is found among workers and not among students, Schmidt & Sigusch, 1970). The average *frequency of coitus* depends on experience and decreases gradually both with men and women as they grow older; this is not a result of any decrease in a woman's capacity to respond sexually as she ages but of physiological processes taking place in the man; yet healthy males have "a capacity for sexual performance that frequently may extend beyond the eighty-year age level" (Masters & Johnson).

Bibliography: **Brecher, R. & E.:** An analysis of "Human sexual response." New York & London, 1967. **Kinsey, A. C.** ***et al.*****:** Sexual behavior in the human male. Philadelphia & London, 1948. **Id.:** Sexual behavior in the human female. Philadelphia & London, 1953. **Masters, C. & W. H.:** Human sexual response. Boston, 1966. **Schmidt, G. & Sigusch, V.:** Sexuelle Verhaltensmuster bei jungen Arbeiter und Studenten. In: **Schmidt, G.** *et al.* (Eds:): Tendenzen des Sexualforschung. Stuttgart, 1970. **Schofield, M.:** The sexual behaviour of young people. Harmondsworth, 1968.

H.M.

Coitus interruptus. A coital technique: after insertion into the vagina, the penis is removed shortly before ejaculation of the semen. Together with condoms and oral contraceptives, it is the most used technique of contraception. Freud's supposition that frequent coitus interruptus could bring on anxiety neuroses is disputed. *J.F.*

Coitus reservatus. A confusing term since it is used to refer to coitus interruptus (q.v.), to the intentional inhibition of the male orgasm until orgasm has commenced in the female, and to full, intentional inhibition of the male orgasm in coitus. The third denotation is preferred.

Cold, paradoxical. See *Paradoxical cold and warmth.*

Collective idea (syn. *Collective image*). G. E. Müller was foremost in trying to explain the genesis of idea or image complexes as the effect of a collective idea. In the collective idea, successive elements of a learning sequence (e.g. nonsense syllables) are all grasped simultaneously, detached from the mass of available impressions, and associated to form a group, whether the elements are presented uniformly one after the other, or simultaneously. The elements of such a complex are bound together by extremely strong associations (q.v.) and when they become conscious tend to reproduce the entire complex from the beginning (initial reproduction tendency). Two forms may be distinguished: collective ideas of simultaneous, and those of successive, impressions. According to G. E. Müller (1924) mental images of common words and known musical signals depend on the collective idea.

Bibliography: Müller, G. E.: Abriss der Psychologie. Göttingen, 1924.

F.-C.S.

Collective unconscious. A form of the unconscious postulated by C. G. Jung (q.v.) and considered by him to be distinct from the "personal" unconscious. The collective part of the unconscious does not include the contents which are specific to our individual ego (q.v.) or which arise from personal experience, but is said to be the powerful spiritual inheritance of human development, reborn in each individual brain-structure. The contents of the collective unconscious are the so-called archetypes (q.v.), which are universally human and enjoy a supra-personal validity. They are supra-individual forms into which the personal element of the individual enters as content, and they are said to be passed on like instincts. *H.-N.G.*

Color antagonists. Color pairs with maximum dissimilarity of hue. When they are mixed together, color antagonists (red-green, yellow-blue) produce dull colors (white or grey). Illogically, the term *complementary wavelength* has become usual in colorimetry instead of *compensatory wavelength*. This term denotes the wavelengths (or bands) which are perceived as color antagonists. See *Complementary colors; Ideal colors. A.H.*

Color blindness. Defective physiological color vision with intact perception of form. May be total (= achromatop(s)ia, achromatism) or partial as in "anomalous trichromatism" (all three receptor pigments present in the retina, q.v., but all or some with unphysiologically lower efficacy); and "dichromatism", in which two of the pigments are effective but the third is absent. Depending on whether the first pigment (yellow), the second (green) or the third (blue-violet) of the trichromatic theories of color vision (q.v.) is affected, use is made of the prefixes "proto", "deutero" or "trito". Protanomaly, deuteranomaly and tritanopia or tritanopsia indicate lack of perception of the colors in question. Dichromatism and anomalous trichromatism are congenital conditions and, save for the extremely rare cases of autosomal tritanopia (q.v.), sex-linked, usually recessively. They therefore affect both the eyes and all retinal parts in the same degree.

Color blindness is diagnosed with the aid of pseudoisochromatic charts (q.v.), e.g. those designed by J. Stilling–E. Hertel (see *Stilling color charts*) or by S. Ishihara (see *Ishihara test*) on which numbers and letters are made up of points differing in color but of the same brightness; or, better still, with a color mixer that produces spectral colors (see *Anomaloscope*). In addition to this

Table. Characteristics of color-vision defects and their distribution among the inhabitants of Europe and North America (Kalmus, p. 147, Klein & Franceschetti, pp. 121ff. and Pschyrembel, p. 355).

Protoforms		Men	Women
Anomaly:	Restricted sensitivity to red. Dark red confused with black, green with white or grey, violet with blue.	0.7%	0.03%
Anopia:	No sensitivity to red (red blindness). Red, yellow, green and brown confused with each other; also violet with blue, dark red with black.	1.1%	0.01%
Deuteroforms			
Anomaly:	Restricted sensitivity to green. Green confused with yellow, brown and grey.	4–5%	0.35%
Anopia:	No sensitivity to green (green blindness). Confusion of colors practically the same as in protanopia, although dark red can be better distinguished from black.	1.8%	0.35%
Tritoforms (very rare)			
Anomaly:	Restricted sensitivity to blue. Green confused with blue, delicate pink with pale yellow, light blue with grey.	0.01%	0.01%
Anopia:	No sensitivity to blue (blue blindness). Red confused with orange, blue with green, greenish yellow with grey and violet, light yellow with white.	0.01%	0.01%

genetically determined *innate* color blindness, there is *acquired* color blindness caused by traumatic or toxic damage to the optic sensory path (detached retina, scotoma, q.v., atrophy of the optic tract or of the sclerotic coat), often in the form of *circumscribed* color-blindness (affecting only parts of the visual field). Occasionally such disorders of the optic tract lead to total color-blindness (see *Achromatop(s)ia*). *K.H.Plattig.*

Color blindness tests. Used to determine the various kinds and degrees of color blindness (q.v.). In the widely used pseudoisochromatic charts developed by J. Stilling, S. Ishihara and others, dots of various hues (q.v.) are so arranged that different shapes (letters, numbers) are distinguished by Ss, depending on whether they have good color vision or suffer from varying degrees of color blindness. The Holmgren test (q.v.) involves the matching for hue of differently colored skeins of wool. Deuteranopia and protanopia can be clearly distinguished with E. H. Nagel's anomaloscope (q.v.) which makes it possible to determine the exact components of monochromatic red and green light, which, in additive mixture, are perceived as standard yellow. By plotting a chromaticity diagram, color vision defects can be accurately diagnosed. See *Color vision.* *A.L.*

Color circle. See *Color square.*

Color constancy. See *Color vision.*

Color contrast, simultaneous. See *Simultaneous contrast.*

Color contrast, successive. When a large number of white, black or colored strips, disks, etc., are laid on a grey or colored background, normal simultaneous contrast (q.v.) gives way to equalization of brightness and hue. The white strips lighten the background, the black ones darken it, the yellow ones add a yellow component to it, and so on. This phenomenon was first noted by W. von Bezold and thoroughly investigated by C. Musatti.

Bibliography: Musatti, C.: Luce e colore nei fenomeni del contrasto, della costanza e dell'eguagliamento. Archivio di Psicologia, Neurologia e Psicologia, 1953, *5*.
G.Ka.

Colored smelling. See *Synesthesia.*

Color hearing. Tones are often associated with specific colors. Slow music, e.g., conjures up a blue hue; a rapid tempo is connected with red; high-pitched tones evoke light colors, low-pitched tones dark colors. Beyond these associations, rare cases occur of actual synesthesia (q.v.), i.e. individuals who hear tones and simultaneously "see" colors. This phenomenon, probably based on inherited tendencies, has not yet been satisfactorily explained. *G.Ka.*

Color mixer. A disk with colored angular sectors the width of which can be varied as desired. When the disk is rotated fast enough (over 60 rev/sec) the colors fuse. The result is an additive mixture in which each color component is present in proportion to the width of the corresponding sector. Rotating the disk at a speed below that necessary for the colors to fuse (flicker fusion frequency) produces the phenomenon of *flicker*, i.e. the rotating disk is animated by an irregular pulsation of colored lights. *G.Ka.*

Color mixture. The coincidence of rays emitted or reflected by two or more objects, either in space or in time. In the first case, rays issuing from several sources simultaneously excite the same area of the retina. In the second, the various light stimuli strike the same point of the retina in rapid succession, with the result that what is perceived is not the individual colors but a product of fusion (see *Color mixer*). The two processes result in an additive color mixture. A subtractive color mixture is obtained by superposing two or more transparent colored plates. In this case the absorption coefficients coincide in such a way as to produce a new color different from that of any of the individual plates on its own. See *Pigment color mixture.* *G.K.*

Color perception. Colors can be defined from the viewpoints of physics, physiology and psychology.

1. For physics, colors are specific instances of radiant energy, i.e. nothing but different wavelengths of the electromagnetic spectrum ranging from c. 380 to 750 mμ. In addition to wavelength (or frequency), there are two further properties of radiated light of importance to color vision, namely, the amplitude (or intensity) of the wave and the composition of the spectrum (or purity) of the radiation.

2. As an experienced phenomenon, however, color is not the direct registering of a property of physical radiation but the end-product of physiological processes inside the organism. Although the physiological level is crucial for rounding off these processes and for understanding color sensations, it must be admitted that our physiological knowledge is still far from advanced, so closely are the various processes interwoven and so enormous is the difficulty presented by experimental research in this field. We are faced more with a

---

COLOR PLATE, KEY TO. A Additive color mixture. **B** Subtractive color mixture. **C** The four primary colors of the color square. **D** of the 24-scale hue circle. **E** Physiological spectrum of almost normally sighted person (green vision slightly impaired). **F** Physiological spectrum of sufferer from red-green blindness. **G** Examples of color harmony. **H** Mixed colors produced by means of superposed screens (four-color printing). **I** Longitudinal section through color solid (a triangle of identical hue for each of the 2 complementary colors 11 and 23 with grey scale as a common base). **K** Grey scale. **L-N** Spectra: **L** Incandescent neon gas, **M** Sun with Fraunhofer absorption lines. **N** Incandescent strontium vapor. **O** Colors of solids heated to 1,300–500°C. (Plate prepared by Müster-Schmitt, K.G., Göttingen.)

profusion of theories (e.g. Goethe's theory of color) than with firmly established and generally accepted facts. The theories still thought highly of today are the *three-color theory* of T. Young and H. Helmholtz, and the *four-color theory* of E. Hering and J. Müller, recently improved upon by L. M. Hurvich and D. Jameson. The three-color theory postulates that all that is necessary to make any color appear is to mix the wavelengths corresponding to red, green and blue (primary colors), carefully adjusting their intensity. Similarly, the theory assumes the existence on the *retina* (q.v.) of three types of receptor, each specifically sensitive to one of the main wavelengths. Even though each of the three visual pigments reacts in a specific way to the rays of all wavelengths, its reaction is at a maximum for one of the three main rays, and each of the possible combinations of the specific reactions of the spectrum sets in train a physiological process to which corresponds one of the 200–250 hues distinguished by the human eye. According also to the four-color theory or the theory of "antagonistic color pairs", all color-vision phenomena are explained once the existence of three visual substances is admitted. The course of events according to this model, however, greatly differs from that of Young and Helmholtz. It postulates a light-sensitive red-green substance, a yellow-blue substance and a white-black substance. With the dissimilation processes set in motion by specific wavelengths (see *Dissimilation*), it is claimed that such substances are associated with visual perception of red, yellow and white, whereas green, blue and black are seen as a result of the assimilation processes (see *Assimilation*) of the same substances on exposure to other wavelengths. In addition to the above theories, there are many others which are for the most part modifications of the two theories mentioned, or attempts to embody them into a single system capable of accounting for all normal and pathological color phenomena. None of these attempts has so far yielded a satisfactory result. Consequently, interest in physiological theories has today greatly diminished.

3. For psychology, the problems presented by colors arise in connection with: (*a*) suitably classifying our color impressions; (*b*) ascertaining regular correlations between color phenomena and the variable quantity of the stimuli; (*c*) the meanings and aspects of color sensations. In ordering colors, account is taken of three basic properties, i.e. *hue* (q.v.), *brightness* (q.v.) and *saturation* (q.v.), which show a fairly regular correlation with wavelength and amplitude and spectral composition of the radiated light. Of the countless combinations that can be obtained by mixing these three physical variables in different proportions, the human eye can distinguish only about 350,000 color qualities, each of which exhibits a unique mixture of hue, brightness and saturation. All these qualities are classified in diagrams or stereometric models of "color geometry", which illustrate how the various colors are related to each other on the phenomenal plane. These classifications are rounded off by taking into account the "modes of appearance" of colors. With these in mind, colors can be arranged by *surface colors* (q.v.), *film colors* (q.v.), *color volume* and *transparent colors*. In addition, the modes of appearance are distinguished by gloss, glitter, sparkle and direct light sources. One of the key problems of color vision arises from the relative "*constancy*" (q.v.) of the color and the brightness of the objects. "Constancy" is in turn ensured by an outstanding performance on the part of the visual system, i.e. by the phenomenal separation of a single color event into the color of the object and its illumination. *Two* physical variables (intensity and spectral composition on the one hand, and degree of reflection and absorption of the object on the other) are represented by a *single* physical stimulus (intensity and spectral composition of the reflected light) which sparks off a *single* sensory process. To this, in the sphere of sensation, correspond *two* perceptual factors (color of object and light to which it is exposed) which reflect the duality of the physical situation fairly closely. This problem has been tackled by some of the best-known investigators of perception, and has given rise to a literature rich in experimental observations, discussions and theories. (See Gelb, 1929, Katz, 1911 for the history of the problems.) It widely held that "constancy" is the effect of "transformation" exercised by central processes on peripheral processes to make them correspond to external reality. The biological function of color constancy, like other cases of constancy of perception, is to enable us to move about with certitude in a world of familiar objects whose appearance is not constantly changing. Some well-known experiments by Gelb, Kardos and Wallach have shown, however, that the phenomenal separation of light reflected from a surface can take place in such a way that constancy phenomena may be accompanied by cases of inconstancy that are just as conclusive. This suggests that "constancy" is a special effect and not necessarily bound up with phenomenal separation which, on the other hand, appears to obey precise general laws of perception (q.v.). The known facts do not yet permit us to define these laws with certainty. There appears, however, to be a widespread conviction that the phenomena of "constancy" are the result of field factors: the colored appearance of a zone of the visual field is believed to depend on the *relationship* that exists between an area of stimulation and the adjoining areas.

Bibliography: Boring, E. G.: Sensation and perception in the history of experimental psychology. New York, 1942. **Committee on Colorimetry, O.S.A.:** The science of color. New York, 1953. **Evans, R. M.:** An introduction to color. New York, 1948. **Gelb, A.:** Die Farbenkonstanz der Sehdinge. Handbuch der normalen und pathologischen Physiologie, Vol. 12/1. Berlin, 1929. **Helmholtz, H.:** Handbuch der physiologischen Optik. Hamburg, 1909–11; Eng. trans.: Handbook of physiological optics. London, 1924–5. **Hering, E.:** Grundzüge der Lehre vom Lichtsinn. Berlin, 1920. **Hurvich, L. M. & Jameson, D.:** Theorie der Farbwahrnehmung. Handbuch der Psychologie, Vol. 1. Göttingen, 1966. **Kanizsa, G.:** Die Erscheinungsweise der Farben. Handbuch der Psychologie, Vol. 1. Göttingen, 1966. **Kardos, L.:** Ding und Schatten. Zeitschrift Psychol. Erg., 1934, *23*. **Katz, D.:** Die Erscheinungsweisen der Farben. Zeitschrift Psychol. Erg., 1911, *7*. **Le Grand, Y.:** Light, color and vision. New York, 1957. **Segal, J.:** La mécanisme de la vision des couleurs. Paris, 1953. **Wallach, H.:** Brightness constancy and the nature of achromatic colors. Journal of Experimental Psychology. 1948, *38*.

G. Kanizsa

Color perception types. R. Scholl & O. Kroh distinguish between color perception and shape perception types. The two types were found by Scholl (in children) and by Kroh (in adults) to have distinct personalities. *Color perception types:* (*a*) children are lively and wide-awake; (*b*) adults are responsive, vivacious, communicative, rarely self-critical and not always thoroughgoing. *Shape perception types:* (*a*) children are bashful, nervous, anxious, cautious and taciturn; (*b*) adults reserved, self-controlled, critical, ambitious, composed, inadaptable.

Bibliography: Spieth, R.: Der Mensch als Typus. Stuttgart, 1949.

W.K.

Color pyramid. The best-known three-dimensional system of "color geometry". On the central axis, which joins up the two vertices of the double pyramid, are arranged all hueless colors ranging from white to black (brightness). The common base of the two pyramids forms the color square (q.v.) whose angles represent the full colors red, yellow, green and blue. On the lateral area all full colors are arranged in accordance with a given gradation of brightness. As saturation (q.v.) diminishes with an increase or decrease of brightness (q.v.) the distance from the central grey axis is also reduced in the upward and downward directions, so that a model in the form of a double pyramid is obtained. See *Color square*.

Bibliography: Ebbinghaus, H.: Grundzüge der Psychologie. Leipzig, 1902.

G.K.

Color pyramid test. A process for assessing personality developed by M. Pfister (1942),

R. Heiss & H. Hiltman (1951). The subject chooses from among a batch of small plates in twenty-four (more recently fourteen) different hues, and is required to build a number of pyramids each comprising fifteen fields. In the main it is the color-choice frequency that is evaluated, together with the structure of the pyramids and the color-selection procedure. Some doubt exists as to the validity of the findings concerning the subject's affectivity (response, regulation, disposition, introversion–extraversion, maladjustment).

Bibliography: **Schaie, K. W. & Heiss, R.:** Color and personality. Berne, 1964. *A.L.*

Color sense. See *Color vision.*

Color square. The various hues can be arranged along the sides of an ideal square whose angles form the four basic colors (red, yellow, green and blue). On each side are arranged the hues which are experienced as lying between two adjacent basic colors. The colors can be visualized as being arranged on a circle instead of a square (color circle). *G.K.*

Color stimulus test. A psychophysical method of measuring the color stimulus in order to establish a system for grading colors, on the basis of which laws expressing relations between certain properties of stimuli and the responses of an "average receiver" can be determined under strictly uniform conditions. This technique is based on the circumstance that in any visual situation each color stimulus can be equated with a single combination of three different suitably chosen colors.

Bibliography: **Committee on Colorimetry:** The Science of Color. New York, 1953. *G.K.*

Color symbolism. From time immemorial, colors have possessed symbolic significance, especially in ceremonial rites (e.g. color of clothing or special symbolic objects) and in paintings with a religious or mythical content. No uniform significance, however, is attached to color by various cultures, epochs and liturgies.

The following classification is often made: *red* = activity, excitement, passion, courage, will to win; *yellow* = love of change, mobility, salvation and release, intuition, speech, faith; *green* = acceptance of emotion and experience, sense of reality, joy; *blue* = coldness, intellectuality, truth, security, loyalty; *white* = purity, loneliness, barrenness; *black* = mourning, mysterious power. See *Color vision.*

Bibliography: **Berkusky, H.:** Zur Symbolik der Farben. Zeitschrift des Vereins für Volkskunde, 1913, *23.* **Bopst, H.:** Color and personality. New York. 1962. **Gutter, A.:** Märchen und Märe. Solothurn, 1968. *F.-C.S.*

Color tests. Used to evaluate favorable and adverse judgments on colors in assessing personality, e.g. color-choice test (M. Lüscher, 1949), color pyramid test (q.v., M. Pfister & R. Heiss). The color symbolism and characterological significance of the colors on which both these tests are based are without empirical verification, and are ambiguous. The re-test reliability of the color choices is also limited. *A.L.*

Color theory. See *Color vision.*

Color triangle. The different saturation rates of a hue can be so arranged as to cover a triangle whose base is determined by the range of degrees of brightness. A triangle is used because, while the highest saturation rate for each color is reached at a medium degree of brightness, saturation goes on falling steadily, regardless of whether brightness increases or decreases, until the color component completely disappears and the brightness corresponds with that of white or black. *G.K.*

Color variator. A color mixer (q.v.) the width of whose sectors can be varied while it is rotating.

Color vision. The optic tract (eye with connected neural conducting and processing elements) is a system highly sensitive to color and light. It can, in suitably coded form, display hue, i.e. the wavelength of the light stimulus (between 400 and 800 nm.) and call up a corresponding sensation. *Color coding theories:* (*a*) Trichromatic theory of color vision (three-receptor hypothesis, three-color theory, three-component theory) put forward by Th. Young (1802) and H. von Helmholtz (1852) is based on the possibility of color mixing, on the laws of color blindness (q.v.), and on the successful isolation of various receptor substances (rhodopsin, iodopsin, cyanopsin, porphyropsin) by G. Wald and co-workers (Nobel Prize 1967) among others. (*b*) Dominator-modulator theory represented by R. Granit (1943, Nobel Prize 1967). (*c*) Complementary color theory (four-color theory) of E. Hering (1874).

(*a*) Young & Helmholtz postulated for the retina three types of light receptors, each excited to the maximum by a particular wavelength. With the incidence of monochromatic or mixed-chromatic light, in every case all three types of receptor are excited, though in varying degrees (see Fig. *a*); and a clear excitation correlative is obtained, by mixing the individual spectral components, for each of the approximately 160 hues distinguishable by man. This three-receptor theory is in close agreement with the findings obtained with color vision defects. Although these led to the view that the three primary colors of the human eye must be the same as those which enable all the hues to be composed in color printing and television—i.e. red, yellow and blue—visual pigments with the following sensitivity maxima were isolated from the cones (q.v.) of primates: (i) 577 nm. (yellow), (ii) 540 nm. (green) and (iii) 447 nm. (blue-violet) (E. F. MacNichol, jr., 1964). With these pigments all hues can also be represented, as shown in Fig. *b*.

(*b*) Granit's dominator-modulator theory is likewise trichromatic and amplifies the Young–Helmholtz three-color theory. It assumes the dominator system to be made up of broad-band ON-elements in the retina, i.e. receptors that are briefly excited by a broad

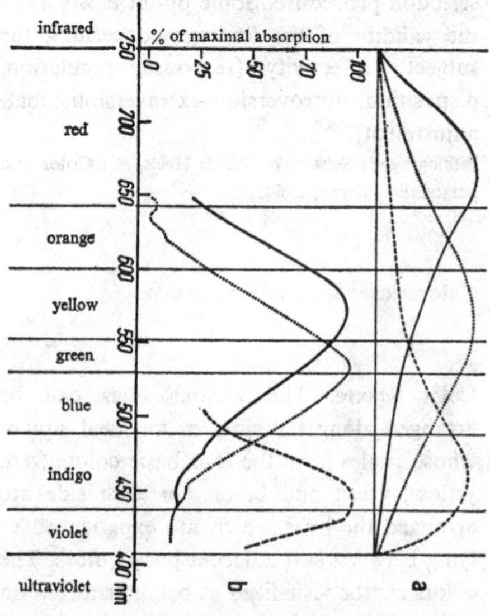

The spectral sensitivity or absorptivity of the three retinal color receptors postulated by T. Young and H. L. F. von Helmholtz (a) and of the retinal pigments recently isolated from the cones of monkeys' eyes (b). The common abscissa gives the light wavelength in nm; the hues perceived are given below. The lower ordinate refers to percentage of maximal absorption of the particular pigment; the upper ordinate uses arbitrary absorption units. The actual spectral sensitivity and absorption maxima (though not measured in humans) show a shift toward the short wavelengths in comparison with those originally put forward by Young and Helmholtz.

frequency band (without distinct maxima) at the start of stimulation, and the modulators to consist of narrow band elements for particular frequencies or wavelengths that correspond to the receptor pigments described under (*a*).

(*c*) Hering, in the light of psychological investigations, also postulates three visual substances with four colors forming two complementary pairs, i.e. red-green, yellow-blue and, in addition, black-white. Assimilation (q.v.) and dissimilation (q.v.) processes lead to displacements of the balance of excitation and therefore to color coding. This complementary color theory clearly does not hold for retinal receptor substances but does apply to "code conversion" in the nervous controls of the retina (q.v.).

Bibliography: **MacNichol, E. F., jr.:** Three-pigment color vision. Scientific American, 1964, *211*, 48–56.

K. H. Platlig

Color weakness. See *Color blindness.*

Color-word test. Used in differential psychology for investigating "cognitive style"; suggested in 1935 by Stroop under the influence of E. R. Jaensch. Performance in naming colored words ("red", "blue", etc.) printed in colors other than those to which they refer, is poorer than in naming colored dots because the tendency to read the words interferes (see *Interference*).

Bibliography: **Hörmann, H.:** Konflikt und Entscheidung. Experimentelle Untersuchungen über das Interferenzphänomen. Göttingen, 1960.

A.L.

Colored hearing. See *Color hearing.*

Colored shadows. An effect of simultaneous contrast (q.v.) brought about by illumination. When a wall is illuminated by two suitably spaced light sources (one white, one red) and a small opaque screen is interposed, two shadows will appear on it. The shadow caused by interception of the white light will appear red because it is illuminated by the red lamp (the background is pink because it receives white and red light simultaneously). It might be expected that the shadow resulting from interception of the red light would be white, since only white light reaches it. In fact, it appears *green* as a result of antagonistic induction caused by the pink background.

G.K.

Coma. 1. An optical aberration of spherical lenses which occurs when light strikes the lens at a specific angle. **2.** A state of *unconsciousness* from which the individual cannot be wakened. It appears when there are serious changes in the electrolytic balance, and in various kinds of poisoning and disease. A coma may always prove fatal, and its treatment demands complex clinical diagnosis. Depending on their genesis, comas are accompanied by varying physiological reactions, by increased or diminished reflex activity, delirium, and by brain lesions (coma in hypoglycemia).

U.H.S.

Combination. Study of the possible arrangements of a number of different elements. A distinction is made between permutations, combinations and variations. The theory of combinations provides the basis in probability theory for many non-parametric (q.v.) operations.

G.M.

Combination tones. Additional tones which are heard when two or more tones are sounded together. The *difference tone* is heard at the frequency equal to the difference in frequency between the tones sounded. The *summation tone* is heard at a frequency equal to the sum of the two frequencies sounded.

C.D.F.

Commissures. Nerve fiber tracts connecting the hemispheres of the brain or the two sides of the spinal cord and containing the commissural fibers or neurons. These conduction tracts coordinate bilaterally analogous areas of the central nervous system (q.v.). The *corpus callosum* represents the largest commissural tract; in it, impulses conduct information from the cortex on one side to that on the other and vice versa.

Bibliography: **Lockhart, R. D., Hamilton, G. F. & Fyfe, F. W.:** Anatomy of the human body. London, 1965.

G.A.

Communality. That part of the total variance of a variable which coincides with other variables in a given set. The communality of a variable is equal to the sum of squares of its factor loadings. Communality may also be understood as the *squared multiple correlation* of the factors with the variable. See *Factor analysis*. *G.M.*

Communication is a subject which has received increased attention within many fields since World War II; for example, in technology, psychology, sociology, international relations, epistemology, and in art, advertising and labor relations. This is perhaps one sign of an increasing awareness of national interdependences, in trade, defense, science, travel, culture, broadcasting and our many institutions. A major force in this movement has been technology, especially that of global communication and air-travel, and of computers.

Communication is therefore still not a unified subject, to any degree, but is studied within many academic disciplines, in various ways. There seems no likelihood of any unifying scientific theory with direct relevance to all fields emerging within the foreseeable future.

1. *Philosophy of communication.* In order to discuss this wide subject rationally, and as a guide to setting up experiments in, say, psychology, some consistent guide to thinking—some philosophy—is advisable. The subject is on the one hand practical (telecommunication, computers, automation, and so on, which have developed the subject most scientifically, as yet), and on the other hand concerns people, their thoughts and knowledge, and their individual and social behavior. To unite these aspects in discussion, the writer has found most useful the philosophy of Charles Sanders Peirce (1839–1914, the one-time teacher of William James), which he called *pragmatism* (see Peirce, 1931–35; Gallie, 1952; Cherry, 1957; Mead, 1934). Peirce set up, in particular, a theory of knowledge which was perhaps fifty years ahead of its time. This theory was essentially based upon practical outcomes (observables, behavior, and so on), but enabled him to define such value terms as *know, think, true*. Pragmatism relates the traditionally separate worlds "outside" us and "inside" us, by starting with the concept of *signs* (language, diagrams, icons, tokens, gestures, and so on). The worlds of "mind" and "matter" no longer remain a dualism, because knowledge exists only by virtue of signs, signification, significance: what "exists" is that which has any practical outcome which can then be signified.

2. *Pragmatism and human communication.* Communication proceeds by signs. It is always social, whether between people or when talking to oneself (or "thinking"). Hence it always involves relationships. There are two broad classes of sign: (*a*) linguistic signs (e.g. English, German, Italian, and so on), which are culturally dominant; and (*b*) sign-systems, invented, or needing definitions and rules (e.g. road signs, coinage, mathematics, and so on). Both raise the question: what *is* a sign? Do all perceptions, all *Gestalten*, constitute signs?

In order to distinguish one percept, or concept, from any other, it must be signified. Otherwise there is no logical distinction. A new concept requires a new sign; they cannot be separated. In its most primitive form, the sign may be an icon or "picture" of some new perception (e.g. we can distinguish between a table and a chair either by using these names, or by visualizing the objects). Perception, knowledge and communication all rest upon sign-usage, a usage within some systems, based upon cultural habits (e.g. language) or upon defined rules of a specific system (road-signs, mathematics, and so on).

3. *Observation and communication.* For such logical reasons, our question can be answered: all perceptions do indeed constitute signs, but we should be careful to distinguish between two, quite different, situations of their usage. These are in (*a*) observation (e.g. looking at a tree *as* "a tree"), and in (*b*) communication. Situation (*a*) is non-social, or an I/it situation; situation (*b*) is social, or an I/thou situation. And it is the

latter, communication, which is dominant upon us, and the main source of all our knowledge of the world as it seems today, and of the whole of history. We each build up our own, individual, models of the world *not* so much through our direct observation but very largely by being taught: by parents, schools, books, newspapers, radio and TV, and hosts of other social institutions which form our culture. Knowledge is socially derived, for even our most personal and "original" thoughts we have been led to through our language, our sign-systems, and all our social institutions (Mead, 1934).

4. *Communication: the self and society.* The great sociologist Emile Durkheim (1858–1917) was the first to show clearly the dualism between a person and society (Bierstedt, 1966). In brief, when one was born one formed part of one's mother, who taught one self-awareness, and one's earliest concepts. Admittedly this broad statement can raise questions about "instincts" and various innate or chromosomic constraints. Nevertheless one's knowledge (knowing *what, who, that*, and so on) derives from acquisition of verbal and other signs. Therefore, argued Durkhcim, nobody can know anything, even that he exists, without society. Conversely, society cannot exist without persons. The person and his society form an inseparable dualism (see Mead, Bierstedt).

It is essential to bear this in mind in all discussion about "international communication" or "understanding". One is largely as one has been taught, through the many institutions of a society; and one can understand other countries' peoples only through the eyes of one's own institutions. Understanding emerges most clearly only when institutions are shared in common (Mangore, 1954; Europa Year Book, 1967) (e.g. of science, of language, of sports, of trade, and so on). Communication is only possible with common habits—not only of language and word usage, but essentially other institutional customs as well. The global spread of telecommunication, news services, cheap travel and tourism, etc., since the end of World War II has therefore raised acutely certain problems in the minds of millions of people (in both the industrial and in the developing countries) who were previously protected. That old cliché "Knowledge is power" has become inverted to read: "Knowledge is an increasing sense of helplessness".

Therefore it is not surprising that studies of "communication" have entered into the academic fields of political philosophy and sociology (Pye, 1963), nor that we are witnessing many challenges today for reappraisal of the purposes, values and methods of education. The technology of communication, globally spread within one generation, has presented us with a great dilemma: how can we adjust ourselves to this overwhelming body of news-items, rumours of changing national images, and partial truths, when we still have emotional capacities more suited to communities of village size? Some writers have predicted a future in which we all carry our personal radio-telephones in our pockets, and are "instantly able to communicate with anyone else in the world". This cannot possibly be the case; one person can have acquaintance, or dealings, at a personal level, with only a relatively small number of people. He can only generalize about the other thousands of millions, and speak of them as "*the* Chinese", "*the* Africans", "*the* Arabs", and so on. In this writer's opinion, what is more likely to happen will be a great improvement in standards of journalism, play-writing, films, and in many other forms of *intermediaries*, or *interpreters* or *mediators* at a first-class professional level —an improvement that will be demanded by coming generations of better-educated people.

International law is another mediator which has greatly improved since World War II, not because we are better people but because it can now be far better *defined* (Mangore, 1954). The existence of global communication (telephones, telegraphy, airways), of computers and many other *information technologies*, is rendering this increasingly and practically possible. The explosive growth of the international organizations since World War II is one source of evidence (see Mangore, 1954; Europa Year Book, 1967).

5. *Pragmatic theory of meaning* (see Peirce, 1931–35; Gallie, 1952; Cherry, 1966; Mead, 1934). Peirce argued that a sign, standing alone, cannot be said to have any meaning. Its meaning results from somebody's response to it. "Meaning" is not a property of the sign itself, in linguistic sign-usage, but the relation between the sign and the person hearing or seeing (responding to it). Furthermore, the nature of that meaning does not emerge (to any observer) until the responder makes *his* sign, in reply. In simplest terms, if someone says "Good morning", one may respond in several ways, thereby showing that this remark was perceived *as* a sign and that it had a certain meaning *to oneself*. Thus one might reply: "Good morning, George!" (meaning a greeting), or "Go to hell!" (meaning aggravation), or one could totally ignore it (meaning what? Conceit, deafness, rudeness, embarrassment . . . or? Nobody can say). In this pragmatic, or psychological sense, "meaning" involves triadic relations between *sign*, *sign-user* and *concept* signified (see Peirce, Gallie; Morris, 1946).

Peirce then observed that *conversation* involved a continual series of stimulus signs and response signs, each successive one interpreting the preceding one; and, therefore, that it was in the nature of conversation that it need never end. It is always possible to add a further, relevant, remark. Fortunately, conversations are ended by some kind of ritualistic sign (for instance, "Goodbye!").

This pragmatic view of meaning is as relevant to psychology as the semantic view is to linguistics. Linguists are concerned with the customary usages of language by whole populations, rather than with momentary use by individuals. They speak of "meaningful sentences", and even of "meaningless sentences" (e.g. Noam Chomsky's example: "Colorless green ideas sleep furiously") (Smith, 1966). The two views of meaning are not to be confused.

6. *Communication: syntactics, semantics and pragmatics*. The theory of knowledge, as it has descended from the early empiricists in particular, has evolved into the science today called "*semiotics*", largely under the guidance of Charles Sanders Peirce (Morris, 1946). It is convenient to divide this field into three related branches.

(*a*) *Syntactics*. Signs, themselves, their classifications and their orderings, without reference to meaning.

(*b*) *Semantics* (q.v.). The formal relations between signs and their designata (signified concepts as in mathematics, logic, linguistic theory, and so on).

(*c*) *Pragmatism*. Signs and their varied usage, by specific persons, in specific situations. This latter branch (*c*) concerns psychology especially. Semantics is more the interest of logicians, linguists and others less concerned with specific persons and events. Syntactics is the branch which has received the most elaborate scientific and mathematical attention, which is to be outlined next.

7. *Information theory*. The global strategy of World War II, with its fluid fronts, was greatly dependent upon communication. It forced attention upon two fields of technology, later taken up by industrial needs of post-war conditions: (*a*) systems of communication capable of handling great quantities of information, at high speeds; and (*b*) the possibility of machines which could adapt their actions to changing conditions, using "information", and so to carry out seemingly human-like tasks (cybernetics) (Wiener, 1961) which evolved eventually into the practical realizations of the computer control of processes. Both offered challenges to mathematicians to define "information" (Shannon, 1949).

As it has evolved, information theory is a part of syntactics (Cherry, 1966; Shannon, 1949). It concerns only signs, their encoding, their frequencies, and errors in transmission. It is most strictly relevant to well-defined technical systems of telecommunication such as teleprinters. How do such systems "send information"? First, there is an identical keyboard at both ends, having a number of keys N. When in use, some human being presses these keys, one at a time, in sequence, each time sending a coded signal which causes the right key to be selected at the receiving-end machine. The first question answered by the theory is (Shannon, 1949): what are the *conceivably possible* simplest and fewest signals needed to convey the message correctly? It is adequate here to illustrate by using a very reduced keyboard of only $N = 8$ letters, shown below.

	A	B	C	D	E	F	G	H
1st Selection	1	1	1	1	0	0	0	0
2nd Selection	1	1	0	0	1	1	0	0
3rd Selection	1	0	1	0	1	0	1	0

The letters here are in an agreed order. When any letter is selected, the coded signal must first indicate whether it lies to the left or right of the dividing line, by using one of two signs (binary digits; one or nought or, in computer tape, hole or no-hole, and so on). A second selection is then needed, thereby quartering the alphabet A . . . H; then a third selection. Each code-group of three digits here uniquely identifies any one of the keys. (E.g. the code 101 selects C, etc.).

From simple mathematics, the fact that three binary selections are needed arises from the equation $3 = \log_2 8$. If now there are N keys, or letters, the number of 1, 0s (binary digits) needed for each code group would be n, where $n = \log_2 N$.

In practice, however, the various keys or letters are not used with equal frequency. In English, for example, the letter A is used most often, followed by T, E . . . Z. A letter used very frequently is said to convey less information content than a rare one (because it could be *guessed* correctly, more often). The idea of probability (q.v.) is therefore brought in. Suppose these letter probabilities are assembled, and denoted by $p(\text{A})$, $p(\text{B})$ . . . $p(x)$ . . . $p(\text{Z})$, and so on. Then it may be shown that *on an average* (i.e. statistically) the least number of binary signals is H, where

$$H = \text{average of } \log_2 \frac{I}{p(x)} = -\Sigma p(x) \log p(x)$$

binary digits per letter.

Again, in practice, all channels of communication are affected by disturbances known as *noise*, and often the statistical properties of this can be assessed too. In this case, the disturbed signals at the receiving end become distorted and do not specify uniquely the letter selected by the sender; they give only *evidence*. The mathematical theory of inference may then be used, in order to compute the *true* rates of information.

One great contribution made by information theory is guidance to those who are concerned with *coding*, for it is possible to compare and measure the efficiencies of various codes. More advanced treatment of the theory does not concern us here.

8. *Information theory. Relevance to psychology*. The first publications, in the early 1950s, regarding information theory aroused great interest in many fields of social science, including psychology and linguistics, and a burst of applications followed (Jackson, 1953; Cherry, 1966). In particular, it seemed directly relevant to choice-reaction time experiments, and to others where *rates of information* within the human subject were of interest. To a great extent, however, this early promise was not maintained, and indeed it misled a number of workers. For the theory is applicable *numerically* only where the set of signs N and their probabilities are defined and known, and this is true in few fields outside technology. There has been very little development of information theory since the early 1950s, apart from applications to coding theory.

Nevertheless, it would be false to say that the theory is irrelevant to psychology, for it does have some relevance to experimental method, by clarifying certain concepts. Without the greatest care, it may not be very useful as a measuring tool (Broadbent, 1958). For example, the probabilities of signs (letters, words, keys, etc.) *to* a person are subjective probabilities—perhaps rank-ordered but not known numerically. Perhaps the most valuable contributions to psychology have been the stimulus the theory gave to new ideas and experiments and, above all, the means it offered for bringing together, in some better understanding, scientists in several disciplines whose traditional boundaries it has overstepped (Cherry, 1966). See *Cybernetics and psychology: Information theory.*

Bibliography: Bierstedt, R.: Emile Durkheim (includes selected bibliography). London, 1966. **Broadbent, D. E.:** Perception and communication. London, 1958. **Cherry, E. C.:** On human communication. Cambridge, Mass. & London, 1957 (2nd ed. 1966). **Europa Year Book** 1967. London, 1967, etc. **Gallie, W. B.:** Peirce and pragmatism. Harmondsworth, Middx., 1952. **Jackson, W.:** Proc. symp. on information theory (London). New York, 1953. See also: Proceedings of three later London symp. (Ed. Colin Cherry). London, 1952, 1955 and 1961. **Mangore, G. J.:** A short history of international organizations. New York, 1954. **Mead, G. H.:** Mind, self and society. Chicago, 1934. **Morris, C.:** Signs, language and behavior. New York, 1946. **Peirce, C. S.:** The collected papers of Charles Sanders Peirce. Vols. 1 to 6, ed. C. Hartshorne & P. Weiss, Harvard, 1931–35. **Pye, L. W.** (Ed.): Communications and political development. Princeton, N.J., 1963. **Shannon, C. E.:** The mathematical theory of information. Illinois, 1949. **Smith, A. G.** (Ed.): Communication and culture. New York, 1966. **Wiener, N.:** Cybernetics. New York, 1961[2].

C. Cherry

Communications, animal. These can be acoustic, olfactory, optical or tactile. They can take place between species or be confined to one. When understood, communication signals can change the behavior of the animal or animal group. Animal communications are used in sexual activity, mating and group formation as well as in the establishment of territory ownership. The courtship songs and dances of birds and insects, the particular odor of social insects (q.v.), the re-establishment of territory by song, e.g. in birds, or by the depositing of excrement or urine by dogs are well known. See *Comparative psychology.*

V.P.

Communication(s) systems. "Communications" is generally taken to mean the interaction of systems by the exchange of signs (q.v.) and signals (q.v.). Communications theory and research study the exchange and processing of information in living creatures, especially man. Information theory (q.v.) as science deals with the quantitative aspect, as engineering with the technical aspect. Communication often involves the interposing of technical systems (telephone, radio). Schematically, it is represented as a chain consisting of input (sender; transmitter), (transmission) channel, interference source and output (receiver). See *Communication.*

K.W.

Communicator. In spiritualism (q.v.): the deceased person who is said to be communicating with the sitter (q.v.) at a séance (q.v.) through the medium (q.v.). *J.B.*

Community. A term applied by F. Tönnies to social systems and their genesis. The word community denotes social groups which, through firm bonds between their members (cohesion, cohesiveness, q.v.) seek spontaneously to achieve common objectives, which frequently have emotional overtones (e.g. family, religious groups). Society is a more complex form which develops from communities. *W.D.F.*

Community feeling (syn. *Communal spirit*). In Adler's individual psychology the force counteracting the egotistic desire for power; community feeling maintains the individual's ties with the community (F. Tönnies): recent research in developmental psychology (R. A. Spitz, J. Bowlby) points to its origins in the mother-child relationship (basic trust).

Bibliography: Bowlby, J.: The nature of the child's role to his mother. Int. J. Psychoanal., 1958, *39*, 350–73. **Spitz, R. A.:** The smiling response: a contribution to the ontogenesis of social relations. Genet. Psychol. Monogr., 1946, *34*, 57–125.

W.Sc.

Comparative judgment. See *Judgment, comparative.*

Comparative psychology. Students of human behavior in increasing numbers are making use of the greater tractability of non-human species in order to make credible comparisons with problems of human organization and conduct. They do so, whether their essential motivation is practical, therapeutic, or frankly academic, in order to further knowledge and to increase the comfort of men. From reports appearing in the literature, it can be seen that there is a continual re-working of old ground and a ceaseless confirmation of past work, in addition to the daily advance of comparative methods into new fields of research.

The use of animal subjects to further understanding about human beings, though historically old, is at best a compromise; like all compromise solutions it has both advantages and disadvantages. Its advantages lie directly in the basic genetic and environmental controls that can be exercised, the animals providing the investigator with subjects of known heredity and nurture, and possessing homogeneity of those elements, features and functions under examination. They are exemplars of types suitable for analysis which would be unlikely to be found by accident; it is possible to produce in them characteristics which it would be ethically improper (on any criterion of moral action) to produce in humans. The price paid, however, is high, for no matter how expert he may become, the comparative practitioner cannot communicate directly with the subject of his study. Imperfect though it may be, language is the pre-eminent form of human communication, and no equivalent facility is found among the forms of communication (zoosemiotics) available to infra-human species (see, however, Drewe *et al.*, 1970; Goodall, 1965; Thorpe, 1967). To a limited extent, the inability to communicate is compensated for by elaborate investigatory methodologies (common to all studies of behavior) which give credence to conclusions derived from assumptions about the motivation, purpose and intention of observable and measurable action.

Space does not permit anything but the briefest outline of the use made of animals in all branches of biology and in those areas of research whose development would be greatly impaired without their unique contribution (Fox, 1968; Lane-Petter, 1963). Likewise, lack of space does not allow descriptions of the history or origins of comparative psychology found in ethology (Lorenz, 1970), ecology (Scott, 1958), comparative anatomy (e.g. neuro-anatomy) (Zeman & Innes, 1963), and so on. Subjects such as animal husbandry (Lane-Petter, 1963), experimental methodology (Gay, 1968), biometrics and instrumentation must be thought of as subjects in their own right. It is hoped that the few topics it is possible to indicate will serve to illustrate the breadth of the subject and the difficulties of including a discussion of its participation in areas like dentistry and organ transplants which at first sight appear to be particularly and almost exclusively "human". For example: knowledge of *maternal behavior* in humans has benefited considerably from observation of both the epimeletic (care-giving) and et-epimeletic (care-seeking) behavior of animals (Fox, 1968; Grota & Ader, 1969). It is within the orbit of this initial relationship, and largely out of the interactions of mother and offspring, that the vital determining characteristics of the individual's adult social and physical behavior are established (Fox, 1968; Levine, 1966). Although social behavior is clearly discriminable from maternal behavior, there is at least a temporary overlap between the two when the nuclear family (with or without the fathering male) has a structure which arises from the interactions of its members, and can be said to constitute a social group with a greater cohesion within it than there is outside it (Dimond, 1970). The family ties determining the group grow progressively less strong as the offspring mature, or are rejected by the mother, and the interactions between individuals widen to include not only the immediate peer group but members of other families. At this point intra- as well as inter-group play (Jewell & Loizos, 1966) appear to cause the animal to become aware of its physical capacities as well as the behavioral characteristics of its play objects.

Perhaps the greatest use of animal subjects is in the study of the effects of drugs (Kumar *et al.*, 1970; Steinberg, 1965; Steinberg *et al.*, 1964; Thompson & Schuster, 1968), particularly in the study of those chemicals which affect such biological processes as (preferred) food and water intake, fear reactions (Wilson & Dinsmoor, 1970) and other functions which arise within a behavioral repertoire instead of in a straightforward physiological context. In recent years these studies have been exemplified and epitomized by comparative investigations outlining the effects of the so-called psycho-active and psycho-tropic drugs. The study of sedation, memory and learning at all levels, whether by a progressive or consensus approach (Miller, 1964), requires the use of (and in many cases the sacrifice of) many individuals and species. Despite the anthropomorphic implications and ultimate application of the research, the infra-human species plays an indisputably primary role in this context. Animals, too, figure largely in studies of *nutrition*. Although it is not true to say (and never has been) that "an animal is what an animal eats" (Lat, 1969), there is no doubt that the physical, neurological and behavioral characteristics of an organism can be altered by dietary manipulation (Brozek, 1962; Lat, 1969; Worden, 1968). The existing and encroaching imbalances of human ecology add an urgent necessity to the systematic appraisal of this kind of work. In the field of *genetic* research, though it is not confined to animals, it is in the interaction of the genotype with its environment that many exciting applications are to be found. The credibility of the basic laws of inheritance is increased by the study of organisms whose genetic expression is modifiable and whose behavior repertoire contains an element of volition or choice. Genetics is acquiring a profound influence in all branches of biology where the homogeneity of material, referred to in the opening paragraph, is proving to be vital. The efficient way of obtaining such "pure" stocks is by the techniques of special breeding and selection and these methods cannot be used with, or on, humans.

It is necessary, also, to consider the vast contribution made by infra-human species to the semi-permanent modifications of conduct called *learning*. The largest single application of comparative psychology (if one is to judge from reports) is in behavioral modifications of all kinds, from simple habituation to the habit complexities of primate intelligence. The classical conditioning experiments of Pavlov and his colleagues, the recent successful and developing operant procedures of the Skinnerians and the hybrid paradigms of the behavior therapists (Davison, 1968; Eysenck & Rachman, 1965; Stampfl, 1966; Wolpe, 1958) have all established the fundamental principles of their systems by direct experiments on animals, and it is likely that crucial differences between them will be resolved in a like manner.

Animals are used in numerous forms of research for many reasons, some of which are good because they enhance the knowledge of humans about themselves and lead to an understanding of problems and malfunctions which it would be impossible to clarify without their analogous contribution. Apart from those subjects already referred to, there are many others in comparative psychology which have a particular human relevance. For instance, there are the studies of isolation stress, immobilization stress (Mikhail & Broadhurst, 1965), and punishment (Bandura, 1970) which have an immediate application in penology, in the study of institutionalization and in all forms of aversive treatment. Associated with penology, discipline and social control is the study of the behavioral factors involved in addictive processes (Nicholls, 1963) and in deviancy of all kinds, either of which may involve immediate or postponed gratification (Eysenck, 1963). There is also the area of frustration and drive energization (Amsel, 1962), the abnormal concomitant of which may be self-directed or externalized aggression (Fox, 1968; Lorenz, 1970). Another form of investigation lies in those studies whose psychological/behavioral component is not so clear. In some of these, non-physiological factors appear to combine with structural elements to produce pathologies of anatomy which are, in turn, associated with deteriorations in the functional efficiency of behavior. This type of study is most clearly illustrated within the hybrid discipline of psychosomatics, e.g. ulcer studies, anorexia studies (Russell, 1969) and even tumour studies (Matthes, 1963), where researchers employ animal subjects chosen or pre-treated on a basis which emphasizes and permits evaluation of the contribution made by their functional rather than by their physical capabilities.

The foregoing emphasizes, and the few examples illustrate, that research in comparative psychology assumes a relationship between man and animals. Such an assumption, which requires only that man be located on a phylum appropriate to him and to his progenitors, has dangers, not the least of which lies in the reciprocal errors of under- and over-generalization. These include the easy assumption of complete behavioral similarity between human and non-human species, and also the misleading anecdotes which evaluate animal behavior within a man-orientated anthropomorphic, mentalistic and self-relevant system. All must be avoided if investigations employing non-human subjects are to make an effective contribution to what is advanced as "the proper study of mankind".

Finally, a caution: an informed and ceaseless vigilance is necessary to ensure that a balance is maintained between the needs of science, the health of mankind and the inalienable dignity of the infra-human species. If the first and second can be achieved only at the cost of the third plus a loss in the humanity of those using them, comparative psychology and its practitioners may well share in scientific advance and benefit to the world of men, but may, in the process, lose something more precious than they gain.

Bibliography: Amsel, A.: Frustrative nonreward in partial reinforcement and discrimination learning: Some recent history and a theoretical extension. Psychol. Rev., 1962, *69*, 306–28. **Bandura, A.:** Principles of behavior modification. London, 1970. **Brozek, J.:** Soviet studies on nutrition and higher nervous activity. Anns. N.Y. Acad. Sci., 1962, *93*, Art. 15, 665–714. **Davison, G. C.:** Systematic desensitization as a counterconditioning process. J. Abnormal Psychol., 1968, *73*, 91–9. **Dimond, S. J.:** The social behaviour of animals. London, 1970. **Drewe, E. A., Ettlinger, G., Milner, A. D. & Passingham, R. E.:** A comparative review of the results of neuropsychological research on man and monkey. Cortex, 1970, *VI*, 129–63. **Eysenck, H. J.:** Emotion as a determinant of integrative learning: an experimental study. Behav. Res. Therap., 1963, *1*, 197–211. **Id. & Rachman, S. J.:** The causes and cures of neurosis. San Diego, Calif., 1965. **Fox, M. W.:** Abnormal behavior in animals. Philadelphia, 1968. **Gay, W. L.:** Methods of animal experimentation, Vols. 1, 2 & 3. New York, 1968. **Goodall, J.:** Chimpanzees of the Gombe Stream Reserve. In: **De Vore, I.** (Ed.): Primate behavior, New York, 1965. **Grota, L. J. & Ader, R.:** Continuous recording of maternal behaviour in *Rattus Norvegicus*. Anim. Behav., 1969, *17*, 722–9. **Jewell, P. A. & Loizos, C.** (Eds): Play, exploration and territory in mammals. London, 1966. **Kumar, R., Stolerman, I. P. & Steinberg, H.:** Psychopharmacology. Ann. Rev. Psychol. 1970, *21*. **Lane-Petter, W.** (Ed.): Animals for research. London, 1963. **Lat, J.:** Nutrition, learning and adaptive capacity. In: **Kare, M. R. & Maller, O.** (Eds): The chemical senses and nutrition. Baltimore, 1967. **Id.:** Some mechanisms of the permanent effect of short-term, partial and total overnutrition in early life upon the behaviour in rats. Proc. VIII, International Congress of Nutrition, Prague, 1969, Symposium on Nutrition and Behaviour. **Levine, S.:** Infantile stimulation and adaptation to stress. In: Endocrines and the Central Nervous System. Association for Research in Nervous and Mental Disease. Baltimore, 1966. **Lorenz, K.:** Studies in animal and human behaviour, Vol. 1. London, 1970. **Matthes, T.:** Experimental contribution to the question of emotional reactions on the growth of tumours in animals. Proc. Eighth Anti-Cancer Congress, 1963, *3*, 1617. **Mikhail, A. A. &**

Broadhurst, P. L.: Stomach ulceration and emotionality in selected strains of rats. J. Psychom. Res., 1965, *8*, 477. **Miller, N. E.**: The analysis of motivational effects illustrated by experiments on amylobarbitone sodium. In: **Steinberg, H., de Reuck, A. V. S. & Knight, J.** (Eds): Animal behaviour and drug action, London, 1964, 1–18. **Nicholls, J. R.**: A Procedure which produces sustained opiate-directed behavior (morphine addiction) in the rat. Psychol. Rep., 1963, *13*, 895–904. **Russell, G. F. M.**: Metabolic, endocrine and psychiatric aspects of anorexia nervosa. Scientific Basis of Medicine, Annual Reviews, London, 1969, 236–55. **Scott, J. P.**: Animal behavior. Chicago, 1958. **Stampfl, T. G.**: Implosive therapy: The theory, the subhuman analogue, the strategy and the technique. In: **Armitage, S. G.** (Ed.): Behavior modification techniques in the treatment of emotional disorders. V. A. Publication, Battle Creek, Michigan, 1966. **Steinberg, H.**: Methods of assessment of psychological effects of drugs in animals. In: **Marks, J. & Pare, C. M. B.** (Eds): The scientific basis of drug therapy in psychiatry. Oxford, 1965. **Id., de Reuck, A. V. S. & Knight, J.** (Eds): Animal behaviour and drug action. London, 1964. **Thompson, T. & Schuster, C. R.**: Behavioral pharmacology. Englewood Cliffs, New Jersey, 1968. **Thorpe, W. H.**: Animal vocalization and communication. In: **Millikan, J. & Darley, F.** (Eds): Brain mechanisms underlying speech and language. New York, 1967. **Wilson, E. H. & Dinsmoor, J. A.**: Effect of feeding on "fear" as measured by passive avoidance in rats. J. comp. physiol. Psychol., 1970, *70*, 431–6. **Wolpe, J.**: Psychotherapy by reciprocal inhibition. Stanford, 1958. **Worden, A. N.**: Nutritional factors and abnormal behavior. In: **Fox, M. W.** (Ed.): Abnormal behavior in animals. Philadelphia, 1968. **Zeman, W. & Innes, J. R. M.**: Craigie's neuroanatomy of the rat. New York, 1963.

H. C. Holland

Compensation. Covering up, or making up for conscious or unconscious inferiority or insecurity in regard to social, family and individual ideals. First described by A. Adler (q.v.) as a dynamic process resulting from innate "organ inferiority", and later extended by C. G. Jung to cover the relation of the unconscious (q.v.) to the conscious (q.v.), and of dreams to waking life in general. In personality psychology, Lersch distinguishes *direct compensation* ("of the first order")—which corresponds to Adler's concept—from the compensation of the *next chance* ("of the second order"), which G. W. Allport terms "substitution". Unsuccessful compensation or "as-if compensation" ("of the third order") occurs when the adjustment is made possible by a secondary advantage by illness (q.v.) with neurotic symptoms. Recent research classifies compensation among the general biological control processes.

Bibliography: Lersch, P.: Aufbau der Person. Munich, [8]1962. **Orgler, H.**: Alfred Adler: the man and his work. London, 1947. **Menninger, K.**: Regulatory devices of the ego under major stress. Int. J. Psychoanal., 1954, *35*, 1–14.

W.Sc.

Complementary colors. The hues which do not produce any intermediate colors when they are mixed but only different degrees of saturation of one of the members of the pair and—in corresponding proportions—an achromatic or grey color. In general those colors are complementary which lie at the extremities of any diameter in the Hering or Ostwald color circles, in particular the color pairs red and green, and yellow and blue.

G.K.

Complementary phenomena. A collective concept for the phenomenon that incomplete visual groups of stimuli are restructured into totalities. In contrast to the purely physiological stimuli images on the retina, there are complementary phenomena such as the "filling up", enlarging and completing of the perceptual field: e.g. the completion of the blind spot (q.v.), of the visual field in hemianopsia (q.v.), in modal phenomena, and in the overlapping of opaque images. The phenomenon of perceptual reliability is explained by gestalt laws such as pregnance, compactness, similarity, proximity, etc. (see *Ganzheit*). Familiarity of experience also plays a part.

Bibliography: Metzger, W.: Figural-Wahrnehmung. In: Hdb. der Psychol., Vol. 1/1, Göttingen, 1966, 693–744. **Michotte, A., Thinès, G. & Crabbe, G.**: Die amodalen Ergänzungen von Wahrnehmungsstrukturen. In: Hdb. der Psychol., Vol. 1/1. Göttingen, 1966, 978–1002.

P.S. & R.S.

Completion test. A variety of task in which a unit has to be completed: e.g. a gap in a sentence, word or picture; the missing part of a sentence or a story; missing numbers, figures or pictures, in a series, etc. The factorial significance of such tests varies according to whether completion occurs as a result of logical reflection, of imagination or of learned mechanisms. *R.M.*

Complex. 1. In the older psychology of thought, a complex is a group of memory contents which are especially strongly associated, and originate during learning, e.g. when individual components of a series are apprehended as a group. *R.Hä.*

2. Something (e.g. a theory) possessing distinguishable parts structurally related so as to allow the whole a certain unity.

3. A concept introduced by C. G. Jung (q.v.) into psychoanalytical terminology, and later extended to other fields. It is used to indicate the presence of ideas and thoughts which are repressed and have a strong emotional charge. It is because of this emotional charge that complexes which remain in the unconscious influence a person's behavior. Other writers speak of complexes when they merely wish to indicate overemphasized ideas, without necessarily referring to the supposition that a complex only has some effect when it has been repressed into the unconscious. *J.L.I.*

Complex psychology. C. G. Jung called his own psychoanalytical approach a "psychology of complexes". The most important differences between this and the psychoanalysis (q.v.) of Freud are: the assumption of a collective unconscious, the process of individuation (q.v.) in a person's development, the assumption of general psychic energy instead of psychosexual energy (see *Libido*) as in the case of Freud, and also the use of compensatory and complementary relations to explain the development of the ego (q.v.). *J.L.I.*

Complex qualities. A term used by Krueger (Leipzig school, q.v.) with reference to wholes which do not possess a readily partitioned structure. The term is particularly applied to emotions. *C.D.F.*

Complication experiment. A classical experiment designed to illustrate the so-called *law of prior entry*, which states that of two simultaneous stimuli the one which is being attended to will be perceived as having occurred first. In the complication experiment the task was to read the position of a rotating clock hand (or pendulum) at the moment a bell was sounded. The reading apparently differs measurably according to whether attention is directed to the visual or auditory stimulus. *G.D.W.*

Comprehension test. 1. A test which requires the testee to answer a number of questions set on a (usually short) text in order to show quality, speed and extent of understanding of the subject-matter, or to test various other factors which the text is designed to correspond with. **2.** A test in which the testee is asked to describe his response to a given situation.

Compulsive neurotic. A person who is prone to *obsessions* (q.v.) which compel him to perform certain thought rituals or overt actions such as hand-washing, in an attempt to reduce the anxiety level engendered by the unpleasant obessional thoughts. Such people usually score highly on both introversion and neuroticism scales. The term *anancast* is sometimes used synonymously. *R.H.*

Computational linguistics (syn. *Mechanolinguistics*). The use of automata theory and/or computers themselves to aid research into the structure of language, or to study specific tasks such as the possibilities of machine translation between a pair of natural languages.

Bibliography: Gross, M.: On the equivalence of models of language used in the fields of mechanical translation and information retrieval, Infor. Storage and Retrieval, 1964, *2*, 43–57. **Lamb, S. M.:** The digital computer as an aid to linguistics. Language, 1961, *37*, 382–412. **Turner, G. J. & Mohan, B. A.:** A linguistic description and computer program for children's speech. London, 1970. *J.C.*

Computer, electronic. A program-controlled, information-storing and processing device. A primarily electrical and electronic system which permits the input and output of data from peripheral appliances (e.g. magnetic tape units) and their processing in a central processor. The latter comprises the computing and control mechanism and storage facilities for data and programs. Computer programs are coded instructions which have to be written in program language (a computer or machine code). Computers are outstanding for their high speed in processing, immense storage capacity, extensive operational range and variable planning possibilities. They are used whenever large amounts of information have to be processed rapidly and frequently, e.g. in evaluating experiments, commercial accounts and process controls. See *Communication; Cybernetics and psychology.*

Bibliography: Cluley, J. C.: Electronic computers. London, 1967. *K.D.G.*

Computer language. See *Machine language.*

Conation. 1. A term (A. Ward, W. McDougall) for purposive mental drive or striving toward action. Conative forces can appear as "blind impulse" or as purposeful effort. **2.** Voluntary activity. *I.L.*

Concentration. 1. A special form of attention (q.v.); according to Mierke (1966) disciplined organization and fixation of subjective attention on the grasping and shaping of matter containing meaning and value. The following outward aspects may be observed: vital force, and energy impulses in the person concerned, maturity and practice in paying attention (Mierke); volitional control (N. Ach); conscious restriction of the field of attention (W. Wundt, N. Ach); focusing motive forces by determination and structuring (*Gestaltung*) (A. Wellek); aiming for an excellent, well-planned performance, and finding functional links to develop the idea or thoughts (Mierke). Concentration is dependent on physiological factors such as fatigue (E. Kraepelin), state of satiation (D. Katz), hormone balance (G. Venzmer), and sound functioning of the central nervous system (E. Kleist), as well as on mental and other factors such as interest, general outlook and tradition (E. Spranger), or situation (Mierke). The concept of concentration is taken from educational psychology, where it represents the requisite condition for optimal cognitive achievement. Concentration is prominent in techniques in which the field of consciousness is closely restricted: e.g. in hypnosis (q.v.) and autogenic training (q.v.), which I. H. Schultz calls "concentrative relaxation". In yoga (q.v.), concentration is the first stage leading to meditation (q.v.) and profound contemplation. See *Concentration tests.*

Bibliography: Mierke, K.: K. fähigkeit und K. schwäche. Berne-Stuttgart, 1966. *E.U.*

2. In Pavlovian theory, "concentration" (i.e. of excitation, indifferent stimulations, inhibition, etc.) refers to the limitation of certain neural processes to a certain area of the cortex. Pavlov speaks in this connection of a "law of concentration of excitation": "the irradiated excitation gathers along certain lines and toward certain foci".

Bibliography: Pavlov, I. P.: Lectures on conditioned reflexes. Vol. 1. New York & London, 1928.

Concentration tests. Methods generally classified as performance tests, and designed to measure concentration, as a rule demand continuous and sustained attention in dealing with optical or acoustical material, and are characterized—at least in theory—by their independence from intelligence (q.v.). The study of the dependence of concentration on the kind of stimulus field on the one hand and on intrapsychic factors on the other is the object of perception experiments. Three kinds of concentration tests can be distinguished: 1. *Exercises in addition* (KLT, KBT, Pauli test); 2. *Cross-out tests* of letters (d2, Bourdon test), figures, or meaningless symbols (Meili); 3. *Selection* and *sorting* exercises (KVT).

Apart from the Pauli test, the *concentration performance test* (KLT) developed by Düker and standardized by Lienert (1959) represents the best-known method. In it 250 simple additions and subtractions have to be completed in thirty minutes. The evaluation based on the number done, quality, the percentage of errors and their quotient is economical and objective. Standard values (age, sex, employment and school) are available for reference. Reliability criteria and validity (q.v.) were checked several times and proved satisfactory. In contrast with KLT, the *concentration-stress* test developed by Kirsch (1959) and used for assessing the ability of future pilots consists of arithmetical exercises with *coded* figures. In the *concentration-time test* (KVT) devised by Abels (1954), sixty cards have to be sorted into four groups. Scoring the test involves the evaluation of time and errors taken together, distinguishing between different kinds of errors and recording the point at which they were made. Reliability and validity checks made so far show that the method can be recommended (Bartenwerfer, 1966). Among the *cross-out tests*, the "d2" by Brickenkamp (1962) is the most important. Letters with certain reference marks have to be crossed out. Evaluation criteria are total number of exercises worked, number and percentage of errors, their distribution, and the range of variation shown. Standards are available for four age groups from 15 to 59. The coefficients of stability, equivalence and inner consistency have proved very satisfactory; the validity of the method was established in several studies made by the writer.

Bibliography: Abels, D.: Konzentrations-Verlaufstest (KVT). Handweisung. Göttingen, [2]1961. **Bartenwerfer, H.:** Allgemeine Leistungstests. In: **R. Heiss** (Ed.): Hdb. der Psychol., Vol. 6. Göttingen, [2]1966, 385–410. **Brickenkamp, R.:** Aufmerksamkeitsbelastungstest (d2). Handanweisung. Göttingen, 1962. **Düker, H. & Lienert, G. A.:** Konzentrations-Leistungstest (KLT). Handanweisung. Göttingen, 1965. *G.P.*

Concept (Ger., *Begriff*). The "categorization of objects and events on the basis of features and relationships which are either common to the objects perceived or are judged to be so by the individual" (K. Foppa). Features essential to the concept are termed "relevant", those which are unimportant, "irrelevant". Usually a concept is given a symbol (q.v.), a name. The word, therefore, is not the concept itself but only a symbol.

Concept formation as a process of development from childhood to adolescence takes place by way of "qualitative new acquisitions" (Vygotsky). Various phases can be distinguished. Vygotsky (1962) describes three (each of which is divided into stages): (*a*) The child unites diverse concrete objects in groups under a common "family name" and on the basis of external relationship. (*b*) He forms "potential concepts" by establishing objective relationships and connections, "uniting and generalizing single objects", "singling out certain common attributes". This is objective and connective thinking. (*c*) He considers the elements "outside the actually existing bond" between objects, "detaches", "abstracts" and "isolates the individual elements". He then attains to the formation of genuine concepts. Words are integral to the first two developing processes and maintain their guiding function in the third. Similar phases are found in Piaget's schema of concept development. The term is also applied to the process of abstraction and generalization of qualities or properties in any individual conceptualization. See *Child psychology; Piaget*.

Concept centers: areas of the cerebral cortex in which the concepts are said by some to be "localized". (*Conceptual nervous system*, however, refers to a hypothetical model or construct used to study the neural system.)

Bibliography: Bruner, J. S., Goodnow, J. J. & Austin, G. A.: A study of thinking. New York, 1956. Vygotsky, L. S.: Thought and language. Cambridge, Mass., 1962.

H.-J.A.

Concept progress (abb. *v*). The (median) number of added concepts per teaching *step* (q.v.) occurring in the basal text (q.v.) (basal concepts) along a teaching path in a teaching program (q.v.). If *z* is the median number of basal concepts which appear in a teaching step, then v/z is called the concept concision, $1\text{-}v/z$ the concept redundancy. The magnitudes *v* and *z* can be illustrated by the Anschütz-diagram.

Bibliography: Anschütz, H.: Über die Verteilung der semantischen Information in Lehrprogrammtexten. GrKG 1965, *6*, 1–10.

H.F.

Conceptual model. See *Model thought.*

Concert pitch. An international standard of pitch used by musicians based on the "normal-a" of 440 Hz. *C.D.F.*

Condensation. In psychoanalysis, the term refers to the fusion of two or more ideas in the unconscious giving rise to a single idea in the conscious mind. This process is supposed to occur particularly in dreams, where several elements in the *latent content* are represented by a single detail in the *manifest content*, e.g. a character appearing in the conscious part of a dream may be derived from the fused memories of several different people, real and fictional. Thus the dream itself is thought to be meager by comparison to the vast complex of unconscious ideas which are presumed to underlie it, and the analysis of a dream lasting only a few minutes may take many hours. Certain *neologisms* and distorted words such as "alcoholidays" are also described in terms of condensation.

G.D.W.

Conditioned inhibition (syn. *Inhibitory potential*). According to the hypothesis put forward by C. L. Hull in his "mathematico-deductive" theory of learning, stimuli and stimuli traces which are associated with the reduction of reactive inhibition (q.v.), i.e. with the termination of some activity (the cessation of a response), themselves acquire the tendency to produce some inhibition. The inhibition learnt in this way is said to be conditioned (*SIR*). The reactive and conditioned inhibition together form the inhibition potential (*IR*).

Bibliography: Hull, C. L.: Principles of behavior. New York, 1943.

L.B.

Conditioned reflex. See *Conditioning, classical and operant.*

Conditioned response. See *Conditioning, classical and operant.*

Conditioning, classical and operant. At all phylogenetic levels, behavioral acts occur without a specific genetic or physiological background; they have biological utility and rely entirely on a particular sensory event. These acts, or segments of performance, are called *reflexes;* and the systematic way these are brought under alternative stimulus control forms the subject-matter of learning (q.v.)—perhaps the cardinal problem of psychology.

One method of accomplishing control, and of describing the data of such modification of behavior on conceptual and physical levels, is conditioning. Conditioning was and, although theoretically sophisticated, still is an experimental procedure for bringing natural reflexes within experimental manipulation. It can be shown that, by pairing a reflex with a neutral intra-organismic event or exteroceptive stimulus, it is possible to establish the capacity of the latter with the capabilities of the former. When evoked by the "normal" stimulus, the reflex is called an "unconditioned reflex"; when elicited by a provided (i.e. not "normal") stimulus it is called a "conditioned reflex": more generally, the term "reflex" having fallen from fashion, the outcome is known as a "conditioned response". Both the procedure and the terminology stem from the work of Pavlov (q.v.), whose experimental methods are standard and definitive (classical) and whose conceptualizations remained unquestioned for several decades.

Responses within the repertoire of many species may be conditioned by the classical method (Hilgard, 1940), but it has limitations apart from the response capacity of the organism. Once established, not only is the CR an imperfect replication of the UCR but it is subject to interference by a number of factors. Its evocation, e.g., is dependent upon the temporal contiguity of the CS and the UCS, the bond which is hypothesized to exist between them being reinforced (strengthened) by some aspect of their association. On the other hand, the reaction is progressively weakened by inhibition of stimulus and response, by stimulus equivalences and the unfavorable biochemical or physiological status of the organism, until extinction (cessation) ensues: although the phenomenon of "spontaneous recovery" suggests that the established bond may persist beyond its elicitability. Classical conditioning appears to be largely confined to reactions which originate in the autonomic nervous system (ANS), and is difficult to demonstrate in "spinal reflexes" and those cases which require a high degree of mediation. There are also inter-individual differences in several of the parameters of the response which make "differential conditionability" a meaningful concept. A feature of the conditioned response is *generalization.* A response made to a particular CS will be partially elicited by stimuli dimensionally similar to it. Such stimulus generalization is both a boon and a curse; without it perception of the world would be limited (stimuli and events are rarely, if ever, identical) but, alternatively, omnipresent fear would be absent. Indeed, a number of treatments (Wolpe & Lazarus, 1966) of people (victims of severely traumatic occurrences, coupled with the endowment of a labile nervous system) possess rationales based upon generalization. The gradients of responses which emerge from generalization can be understood by an appeal to the principles involved, and their employment in the removal (i.e. extinction) of pathological symptoms is a corollary. The way in which uncontrolled generalization is limited is due to *discrimination.* Initially emerging from the classical situations of Pavlov (within the context of a method of contrasts), with whom it is therefore historically linked, the nature and use of discrimination and its effects on the shape of generalization, have recently received attention within the context of operant conditioning (see Gilbert & Sutherland, 1969).

1. *Instrumental conditioning.* The shortcomings and constraints of the classical procedure with its dependence upon experimenter-controlled programs of reinforcement, led to the first deviation from the paradigm of Pavlov. Called *instrumental conditioning,* and historically associated predominantly with Bekhterev, it differed from the classical form only insofar as the reinforcement, upon which the conditioned bond rested, occurred after the response had been made. Because of this order, the response was said to be "instrumental" in obtaining the reinforcement. The instrumental response could be strengthened in one or admixtures of four different ways: by positive reward, by escape, by avoidance, or by higher order training; the first two represent primary reinforcements, and the second two, secondary.

2. *Operant conditioning.* This form of learning which, as a theory or principle of learning,

has existed for a bare thirty years (see, however: Bitterman, 1969; Skinner, 1938, 1948a, 1950, 1966), differs from classical conditioning in a number of important ways (Hoffman, 1966). It does not differ, except methodologically, as distinctly from instrumental conditioning (Honig, 1966); although a true Skinnerian (Skinner being the principal exponent of the method), while allowing that operant conditioning deals with instrumental behavior in the overall sense, would deny any useful similarity between them. Operant conditioning examines the consequences of largely voluntary and unprompted actions; consequences which are evaluated by the vigor of the action after it has been associated with reinforcement. Vigor of action (strength of learning) is characterized by the rate of elicitation of the behavior being studied, and the reinforcement which leads to its increase. Likewise, a contingent event is said to be non-reinforcing or punishing (Azrin, 1966) if it leads to a decrease in response rate. The terminology of operant conditioning lies in the language of behavioral response (the operant[s]) rather than of the reflex, and it is primarily concerned with those acts which are mediated by the central nervous system. The data of the technique are the rates of responding, and the changes which occur in them, produced by the organism within a response frame of reference set by itself and its physiological limitations. Responding can be varied by arranging that reinforcement conform to schedules dependent upon fixed or changeable intervals of time, or permanent or temporary ratios of action (Ferster & Skinner, 1957). By these "fixed" or "variable" intervals and ratios, their combination into sequential or concurrent assemblies ("multiple schedules"), the experimenter can produce and maintain behavior of specific dimensionality, and permit analysis of it to a fine degree.

One of the costs of the freedom of operant conditioning is the phenomenon of superstition. "Superstition" is the term given to the behavior, usually transient, which occurs under conditions of its consistent correlation with reinforcement. It is usually the terminal behavior of adventitious or arbitrary reinforcement contingencies; whether they be primary or secondary, positive or negative. It is likely to be thought a stereotyped act when no explanation or purpose is apparent. The reader is referred to Herrnstein (1966) for the way in which human superstitions are formed and transmitted, and the way in which animal superstitions differ (speech in the former case circumventing the ordinary process of conditioning) (Honig, 1966).

A number of supporters of the principles of operant conditioning and the views of Skinner (1950) have been attracted by the way in which "statistics" and "the planned experiment" are questioned, and the "wasteful" process of formal hypothesizing is abjured, as principles of planning. In operant conditioning, flexibility is emphasized, and the manipulation of variables in a developing situation is encouraged. Skinner's views on methodology are at once a credo of scientific method, a sensitive means of studying the individual, and an answer to his critics who complained that (by emptying it) he has degraded the organism to the level of the machine. The limitations of the single response datum (rate) are discussed by Honig (1966).

3. *Similarity with a difference*. The essential similarity between classical and operant conditioning has led students to pose questions about the parsimony or necessity of more than one principle to account for this type of learning. It has been suggested that instrumental conditioning can account for most of the facts of operant conditioning. The Skinnerian denial of this viewpoint remains unconvincing: Skinner argues that behavior "operates" on the environment to *produce* reinforcement and, therefore, that the term "operant" conditioning is appropriate.

But, despite the similarities outlined, differences are considerable. Many forms of "operant" conditioning are only effective after the response in question has first been established by classical methods. An example of this type is seen in the escape/avoidance paradigm, in which avoidance takes place only after the administration of the aversive stimulus and its association with the conditioned stimulus. See Sidman (1966) and Herrnstein (1969) for a discussion of the two-factor theory advanced by Mowrer (1946) to account for aversive learning. Whereas there is no difficulty in establishing most autonomic responses by a simple process of temporal contiguity with an ineffective CS, it is virtually impossible (without deliberate or accidental chaining [Kelleher, 1966]) to do this with ordinary reinforcement in an operant situation.

The differences between operant and classical conditioning appear to give the basis of an answer to the question "What is the difference between conditioning and learning?" It would seem possible to work backwards from classical conditioning to the simpler forms of behavior modification, including habituation and adaptation, and forwards from operant conditioning to mediated responsiveness at all levels of sophistication. (Honig, 1966 *et al.*; Skinner, 1948b). The view taken of the degree to which the procedures overlap, the different predictions which stem from their acceptance, and the manner in which one may be more heuristic in generating explanations of a comprehensive theory of behavior may depend more on the affiliations and philosophies of the assessor than on true differences in outcome.

Bibliography: Azrin, N. H. & Holz, W. C.: Punishment. In: **Honig, W. K.** (Ed.): Operant behavior, Ch 9. New York, 1966. **Bekhterev, V. M.:** Objective Psychologie. Leipzig & Berlin, 1913. **Bitterman, M. E.:** Thorndike and the problem of animal intelligence. Amer. Psychologist, 1969, *24*, 444–53. **Evans, R. I.:** B. F. Skinner, the man and his ideas. New York, 1968. **Ferster, G. B. & Skinner, B. F.:** Schedules of reinforcement. New York, 1957. **Gilbert, R. M. & Sutherland, N. S.:** Animal discrimination learning. London, 1969. **Herrnstein, R. J.:** Superstition: a corollary of the principles of operant conditioning. In: **Honig, W. K.** (Ed.): Operant behavior, Ch. 2. New York, 1966. **Id.:** Method and theory in the study of avoidance. Psychol. Rev. 1969, *76*, 49–69. **Hilgard, E. R. & Marquis, D. G.:** Conditioning and learning. New York, 1940. **Hoffman, H. S.:** The analysis of discriminated avoidance. In: **Honig, W. K.** (Ed.): Operant behavior, Ch. 11. New York, 1966. **Honig, W. K.:** Operant behavior—areas of research and application. New York, 1966. **Kelleher, R. T.:** Chaining and conditioned reinforcement. In: **Honig, W. K.** (Ed.): Operant behavior, Ch. 5. New York, 1966. **Mednick, S. A.:** Learning. Englewood Cliffs, N.J., 1964. **Mowrer, O. H. & Lamoreaux, R. R.:** Fear as an intervening variable in avoidance conditioning. J. Comp. Psychol. 1946, *39*, 29–50. **Pavlov, I. P.:** The reply of a physiologist to psychologists. Psychol. Rev., 1923, *39*, 91–127. **Id.:** Conditioned reflexes. London, 1927. **Sidman, M.:** Avoidance behavior. In: **Honig, W. K.** (Ed.): Operant behavior, Ch. 10. New York, 1966. **Skinner, B. F.:** The behavior of organisms. New York, 1938. **Id.:** "Superstition" in the pigeon. J. exp. Psychol., 1948a, *38*, 168–72. **Id.:** Walden Two. New York, 1948b. **Id.:** Are theories of learning necessary? Psychol. Rev., 1950, *57*, 193–216. **Id.:** Operant behavior. In: **Honig, W. K.** (Ed.): Operant behavior, Ch. 1. New York, 1966. **Watson, J. B.:** The place of the conditioned-reflex in psychology. Psychol. Rev. 1916, *23*, 89–116. **Wolpe, J. & Lazarus, A. A.:** Behavior therapy techniques. Oxford, 1966. *H. C. Holland*

Conduction. 1. The transmission of nervous impulses through neuron(e)s (see *Axon*). **2.** The transmission of (sound) waves. **3.** The transmission of energy.

Conduction unit. Thorndike's term for the supposed neural mechanism or action system responsible for a specific adaptive behavior.

Conductivity. The capacity for conduction.

Cones. Receptors within the retina which transform light energy into nervous impulses. See *Eye; Visual perception.*

Confact. Behavior acquired as the result of some learning process for a certain situation is transferred to another situation (see *Generalization; Transfer*). According to

Symonds, however, this only happens when both situations contain identical elements.

Bibliography: Symonds, P. M.: The dynamics of human adjustment. New York, 1946. *K.E.P.*

Confidence limits (syn. *Fiducial limits*). A term used to define that area round a statistical value of a sample distribution, in which there is a certain probability that the corresponding parameter (q.v.) of the population (q.v.) is to be found. The size of this area, or distance between its limits, is known as a *confidence interval* (q.v.), and is determined by the standard error. *G.M*

Conflict. 1. *Definition of conflict.* Conflict has often been defined as present in an organism when two drives (q.v.) (e.g. hunger and thirst) are simultaneously present. As Haner & Brown (1955) have pointed out, this is illogical, since drive states will conflict only when alternative possibilities of action exist (for instance, water and food are both present, but only one may be chosen). Conflict may more logically be defined as "any pattern of stimulation presented to an organism which has the power to elicit two or more incompatible responses, the strengths of which are functionally equal" (Maher, 1966, p. 138).

2. *The work of Luria.* The first serious experimental study of conflict was carried out by Luria (1932) who devised many conflict situations, both experimental and real-life. For example, he made use of Jung's word-association technique by requiring the subject to give a part response to a generic stimulus (e.g. house-room) and then suddenly introducing an "impossible" stimulus (e.g. moon—?). The existence of conflict was indexed by an increase in reaction time. More generally, he devised the "Luria technique" of the "combined motor method" in which both voluntary and involuntary motor responses, as well as verbal reaction-time, were measured. He distinguished three major types of conflict, arising respectively from the prevention of excitation from issuing into action ("conflicts of the setting"); from lack of preparedness for reacting ("conflicts of defection"); and from the diversion of suppressed activity into central processes.

3. *The work of Lewin.* The contribution of Luria was overshadowed by the simultaneous work of Lewin (1935) who defined conflict as "a situation in which oppositely directed, simultaneously acting forces of approximately equal strength work upon the individual" (Lewin, 1935, p. 122). He described three basic types of conflict situation (Type I: approach-approach; Type II: approach-avoidance; and Type III: avoidance-avoidance). His major contribution was to apply these notions to the interpretation of the effects of rewards and punishments on behavior. Hence, he distinguished situations involving command with threat of punishment (Type III conflict); command with prospect of reward (Type II); prohibition with threat of punishment (Type II); and prohibition with prospect of reward (Type I).

Lewin's work was extended by Hovland & Sears, who made use of a board with one or two lights of different colors placed in each corner of the board diagonally opposite a start point placed in the middle of the near edge. The subject's task was to move a pointer toward a positive light or away from a negative light. With this apparatus, Hovland & Sears were able to demonstrate Lewin's three types of conflict situation and their effect on motor behavior, as well as the effect of a fourth type of conflict situation (double-approach avoidance, in which positive and negative lights appeared simultaneously in each corner) (Hovland & Sears, 1938; Sears & Hovland, 1941). They demonstrated four kinds of conflict resolution (single, double, or compromise reactions; and blocking of response). Interest in this technique has recently been revived by studies by Epstein and associates.

4. *The work of Miller.* The most complete account of Miller's work on conflict may be

found in Miller (1959). He based his analysis of conflict mainly on the work of Brown (1948) with rats. Brown demonstrated empirically gradients of approach and avoidance in rats running in straight alleys; showed that the heights of the approach and avoidance gradients are modified by the strength of appetitive and noxious drives respectively (as well as other factors); and claimed that the slope of the avoidance gradient is steeper than that of the approach gradient. Thus, conflict between approach and avoidance tendencies will be maximized at the point of intersection of the gradients. From this model, Miller deduced that an approach response would be displaced from the original goal object to an alternative one. Murray & Berkun (1955) extended the analysis of conflict by using a three-dimensional model of conflict to predict displacement (Figure 1). The model involves strength of behavioral tendency, degree of similarity between original and displaced goal, and nearness to original and displaced goal. By means of a three-alley straight maze, they were able to demonstrate displacement as a result of conflict.

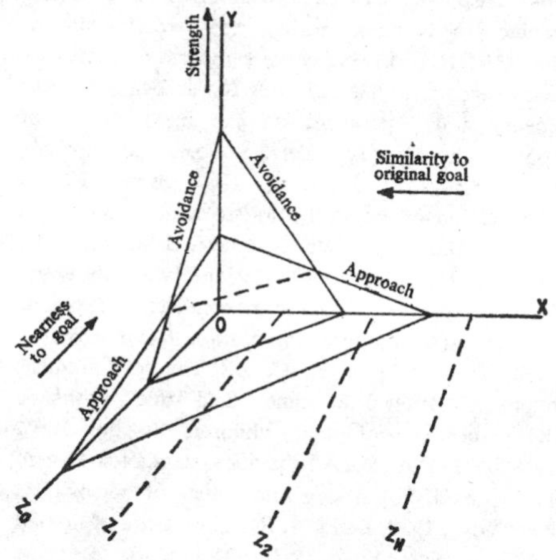

Fig. 1. A three-dimensional model of conflict and displacement. (Source: Murray, E. J., and Berkun, M. M., Displacement as a function of conflict. *J. abnorm. soc. Psychol.*, 1955, **51**, 47–56.)

5. *Extensions of conflict theory.* Hull (1938) reinterpreted Lewin's model of conflict to account for the behavior of children, and later (1952) extended Miller's model to account for conflict behavior in free space, regarding detour behavior as a special case of approach-avoidance behavior. Many of the novel predictions made by Hull (1938, 1952) have never been tested.

Williams (1959) and, more recently, Delhees (1968) have made use of Cattell's dynamic calculus model in which conflict is defined as a situation in which opposite attitudes are evoked to statements which have positive loadings on one factor and negative loadings on another, both factors being represented in a particular statement. Attitude (q.v.) strength in such a situation may be measured by various indices (reaction time, number of times each attitude is chosen, and so on).

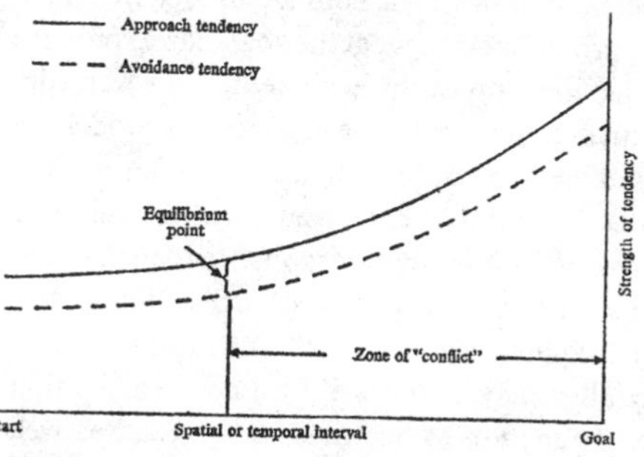

Fig. 2. Parallel gradients of approach and avoidance. (Source: Maher, B.A., The application of the approach-avoidance conflict model to social behavior. *J. Conflict Res.*, 1964, **8**, 287–91.)

Maher (1964) has distinguished between spatial and temporal gradients of approach and avoidance and has experimentally demonstrated temporal gradients (Maher *et al.*, 1964). He has also stressed the importance of distinguished strength of response from probability of response as a dependent variable. Most importantly, he has suggested an alternative model involving parallel rather than intersecting gradients of approach and avoidance, and defined a "zone of conflict", as shown in Figure 2, from which many novel predictions may be made.

Worrell (1963) has related degree of

conflict to intra-individual variability. The person in a state of conflict will possess nearly equally strong response tendencies to a given stimulus situation, and his actual response will therefore vary from one occasion to another even though the stimulus situation is identical. Worrell has stressed the effects of prior experience of conflict in producing conflicting response dispositions which will manifest themselves in a wide range of situations, including objectively non-conflict situations, such as simple reaction time.

Epstein (1962) has produced a modified version of Miller's conflict model in which approach is stronger at the goal than avoidance (the *net* approach increment, however, declines as the goal is neared). In his model the gradients of approach and avoidance to a simultaneously feared and desired goal refer to drives rather than response tendencies, and the summation of these drive tendencies determines the level of activation. Hence conflict may be indexed by a rise in activation as a function of nearness to the goal, as well as by a decrease in adequacy of performance and a relative increase in strength of approach responses to stimuli of low relevance. Epstein has investigated the validity of his model in real-life conflict situations, such as parachute-jump training and in studies making use of projective techniques (q.v.).

6. *Conflict and psychopathology*. The proposition that experimental neurosis may be produced by demanding more and more difficult discriminations derives, of course, from the original work of Pavlov with dogs; the results of this work have been generalized to explain neurotic behavior in human subjects. A good summary of much of this work will be found in Maher (1966). The so-called "neurotic paradox" (in which behavior persists even though repeatedly punished) has also been explained in terms of conflict theory, involving differential delay of reinforcement and punishment.

7. *Conflict and frustration*. The relationship between conflict and frustration is unclear. Thus, behavior in a frustrating situation has sometimes been explained as resulting from conflict arising in the frustrating situation; whereas it has also been argued that frustration arises as a result of conflict. The differing viewpoints of the relationship have been discussed by Yates (1962, pp. 178–81), who has also proposed a solution to the problem. See *Drive; Frustration; Instinct*.

Bibliography: Brown, J. S.: Gradients of approach and avoidance responses and their relation to motivation. J. comp. physiol. Psychol., 1948, *41*, 450–65. **Delhees, K. H.:** Conflict measurement by the dynamic calculus model and its applicability in clinical practice. Multivar. behav. Res., 1968 (special issue), 73–96. **Epstein, S.:** The measurement of drive and conflict in humans: theory and experiment. In: **Jones, M. R.** (Ed.): Nebraska symposium on motivation. Lincoln, 1962, 127–206. **Id. & Fenz, W. D.:** Theory and experiment on the measurement of approach-avoidance conflict. J. abnorm. soc. Psychol., 1962, *64*, 97–112. **Haner, C. F. & Brown, P. A.:** Clarification of the instigation to action concept in the frustration-aggression hypothesis. J. abnorm. soc. Psychol., 1955, *51*, 204–6. **Hovland, C. I. & Sears, R. R.:** Experiments on motor conflict: I. Types of conflict and their modes of resolution. J. exp. Psychol., 1938, *23*, 477–93. **Hull, C. L.:** The goal-gradient hypothesis applied to some "field-force" problems in the behavior of young children. Psychol. Rev., 1938, *45*, 271–99. **Id.:** A behavior system. New Haven, 1952. **Lewin, K.:** A dynamic theory of personality. New York, 1935. **Luria, A. R.:** The nature of human conflicts. New York, 1932. **Maher, B. A.:** The application of the approach-avoidance conflict model to social behavior. J. conflict Resol., 1964, *8*, 287–91. **Id.:** Principles of psychopathology. New York, 1966. **Id., Weisstein, N. & Sylva, K.:** The determinants of oscillation points in a temporal decision conflict. Psychon. Sci., 1964, *1*, 13–14. **Miller, N. E.:** Liberalization of basic S–R concepts: extensions to conflict behavior, motivation, and social learning. In: **Koch, S.** (Ed.): Psychology: a study of a science. New York, 1959. **Murray, E. J. & Berkun, M. M.:** Displacement as a function of conflict. J. abnorm. soc. Psychol., 1955, *51*, 47–56. **Sears, R. R. & Hovland, C. I.:** Experiments on motor conflict: II. Determination of mode of resolution by comparative strengths of conflicting responses. J. exp. Psychol., 1941, *28*, 280–86. **Williams, J. R.:** A test of the validity of P-technique in the measurement of internal conflict. J. Person., 1959, *27*, 418–37. **Worrell, L.:** Intraindividual instability and conflict. J. abnorm. soc. Psychol., 1963, *66*, 480–88. **Yates, A. J.:** Frustration and conflict. New York, 1962.

A. J. Yates

Conflicting behavior. If a stimulus produces two types of behavior simultaneously and if a conflict arises between the two, they can either extinguish one another, alternate (ambivalent behavior), repress or encourage one another, or completely reorientate behavior. If fighting cocks are made simultaneously to want to fight and to run away, they begin to pretend to peck at the ground. See *Instinct; Conflict.* *V.P.*

Conformity; conformist behavior (conformism versus non-conformism). Behavior or behavioral tendency or attitude which takes its norms, standards, etc., from a reference group. For example, it can be shown even in perception experiments that there is considerably less variance in perceptual judgments among a number of test subjects when interaction is possible.

However, not every approximation of individual behavior to that of a group is conformity. Such adaptation of behavior can, for example, also be explained as *contagion* (imitation of behavior without any pressure from the group), or social facilitation (patterns of behavior, already habitual, are easier to act upon after the observation of models). See *Socialization.*

Conformity also needs to be distinguished from *compliance*, in which an individual yields to behavioral precepts more from obedience. Since different individuals react in varying degrees to the behavior of a reference group, conformity represents a personality variable (see *Group dynamics*). In the case of authoritarian individuals (see *Authoritarian personality*), there is usually more conformity in power-holding groups (see *Group*). Members of minority groups can display conformism in regard to behavioral patterns which, from a general perspective, are non-conformist.

Bibliography: Berg, I. A. & Bass, B. M. (Eds): Conformity and deviation. New York, 1961. **Collins, B. E. & Raven, B. H.:** Group structure: Attraction, coalitions, communications, and power. In: **Lindzey, G. & Aronson, E.** (Eds): Handbook of social psychology. Vol. 4, Reading, Mass., 1969. *H.D.S.*

Congenital. A characteristic originating during the fetal stage or during birth.

Congruence, cognitive. This central term in the interpersonal congruence theory of Secord & Backman (1961) refers to a perceptive-cognitive state which some person desires to reach and maintain and which demands congruence between the following three components: (*a*) a particular point of view relative to the conception which that person has of himself; (*b*) the interpretation of this person's behavior which is relevant to this point of view; (*c*) the opinion of this person about how a second person will behave with regard to the first two components when considering this point of view. It is assumed that the three components are congruent when the behavior of the two persons manifests definitions of the first person's self which imply congruence between the relevant aspects of that conception of the self. The model of cognitive congruence enables predictions to be made about interpersonal attraction. An individual will seek to establish contact with those others who will help him to maintain congruence between the abovementioned components.

Bibliography: Secord, P. F. & Backman, C. W.: Personality theory and the problem of stability and change in individual behavior. An interpersonal approach. Psychol. Rev., 1961, *68*, 21–32. *A.S.M.*

Connector. A neuron(e) located between other neuron(e)s.

Connotations. Linguistic symbols carry meanings. "Meaning" signifies not only the transmission of neutral subject-matter but the abstract qualities connected with it, e.g. emotional and affective aspects. Hayakawa (1949) used the terms "extensional" and "denotative" for reference to a given subject-matter; he used the terms "intensional" and "*connotative*" for cases where there was conceptual-verbal or emotional resonance ("informative" or "affective" connotations). *Informative* connotations are now usually known as *denotations*, and those which are *affective* are known as *connotations* (Osgood, Suci & Tannenbaum, 1957). By "denotative meaning", Osgood understands that correspondence between non-linguistic and linguistic events which has been established by agreement; and by "connotation" he understands mediating processes as a result of which the meaning of a word loses its firmly defined character and becomes a dynamic process (See *Communication; Semantics.*)

Bibliography: Hayakawa, S. I.: Language in thought and action. New York, 1949; London, 1952. **Osgood, C. E.** *et al.*: The measurement of meaning. Urbana, Ill., 1957.

H.W.

Conscience. A term used in several distinct (but related) senses concerning the individual's response to the moral principles and behavioral norms of the social groups of which he is a member, and in particular to refer to "the cognitive and affective processes which constitute an internalized moral governor over an individual's conduct" (Aronfreed, 1968). It may therefore denote *cognitive* processes—awareness of the nature and origin of rules of conduct, and ability to evaluate one's own actions and intentions; avoidance of proscribed behavior, and the tendency to act in ways regarded as meritorious, in the absence of punishment or external reinforcement (the *behavioral* aspect); and *affective* components of morality; that is, feelings of obligation, guilt and remorse. Aronfreed suggests that the term should be restricted to "those areas of conduct where substantial changes of affective (emotional) states have become attached to either actions or their cognitive representations"; in contemporary Western cultures these relate to aggressive and sexual behavior, honesty cleanliness, truthfulness and respect for authority.

1. *The development of moral values.* Research into the cognitive aspects of conscience has been greatly influenced by Piaget's (1932) studies of the development of morality in children, in which he explored children's attitudes toward the rules of a game (marbles), and also required them to make moral judgments upon social situations presented in the form of stories. Piaget identified two stages of moral development: until he is seven or eight years of age a child regards rules "not only as obligatory, but as inviolable", independent of individuals, and externally imposed by authority. In this phase ("heteronomy"), penalties are seen as the inexorable consequence of infractions of literal rules; the intentions of the offender are not important. This view of morality gradually gives place to a recognition that the justification for rules is the mutual advantage of members of the group and their consent to them ("autonomy"); punishment comes to be regarded as a means of restitution; and the notion of "equity" emerges: i.e. the child tends increasingly to evaluate cases on their merits, taking into account the circumstances and the intentions of the offender; morality is to some extent internalized. Piaget and those who have developed his work (especially Kohlberg, 1969) emphasize maturational processes in moral development linked with (and dependent upon) intellectual development; however, there is evidence of class differences in the attainment of internalization (Harrower, 1934; Lerner, 1937; Aronfreed, 1969), and of substantial individual differences within social-class groups (Morris, 1958).

The psychoanalytic theory of moral development, based mainly on retrospective clinical studies, is in some ways complementary to Piaget's scheme (Peters, 1960), but offers an account of the mechanism of internalization of moral values which emphasizes the role of parent-child interaction; it also attempts to explain why some children develop consciences which are more severe and punitive than those of their parents (Sears *et al.*, 1957).

2. *Behavioral aspects of conscience.* The similarity between the suppression of socially-proscribed behavior (internalization) and passive avoidance conditioning forms the basis of theoretical models intended to explain the mechanism of this form of social learning and the origin of individual differences in the effectiveness of behavioral suppression. It is suggested that avoidance behavior is mediated by conditioned anxiety responses, previously established through the temporal association of forbidden behavior with punishment (Mowrer, 1960). Hence failure to inhibit proscribed behavior may result from resistance to conditioning (Eysenck, 1960), or a more specific inability to form anticipatory responses; alternatively it may result from inadequate socialization. See *Psychopathy; Criminality*.

The schemes proposed by Piaget and Kohlberg, and the psychoanalytic theory of the super-ego, imply the general development, in the individual, of moral values and socially-conforming behavior (Bandura & Walters, 1963). But attempts to demonstrate this have not been very successful. Hartshorne & May (1928) used a battery of tests designed to reflect various forms of dishonesty (particularly lying and cheating) among children of varying ages. The resulting correlations were low, and they concluded that there was no evidence of a general trait of honesty. Although a more sophisticated analysis of their data reveals some degree of generality, a substantial part of the variance of their tests was specific to certain situations (Burton, 1963). Burton offers an explanation in terms of the interaction of two generalization gradients—one relating to stimulus elements, the other to verbal mediation. The extent to which parents promote both forms of generalization by appropriate methods of child training and verbal explanation of moral rules appears to be partly a function of their socio-economic status and education (Bernstein, 1961; Sears *et al.*, 1957; Trasler, 1970), which may explain the class-related differences in moral development noted above.

Suppression of socially-proscribed behavior cannot always be attributed to previous punishment; evidence relating to mechanisms of imitation, "modeling" and vicarious experience is reviewed in Aronfreed (1969), Berkowicz (1964) and Bandura & Walters (1963).

3. *Affective components of morality.* The emotional states associated with conscience are usually denoted by the terms: fear (or anxiety), guilt and shame. Mowrer's (1960) theory assigns a central role to conditioned fear responses; socially-conforming or moral behavior is the means by which the individual reduces this fear. Mowrer reserves the term *guilt* for the heightened state of fear which follows the completion of an act which (on previous occasions) has attracted punishment; this fear, being no longer reducible by learned avoidance responses, tends to persist. The notion that the need to reduce post-transgressional fear (guilt) may cause the individual to solicit punishment by committing other delinquencies is prominent in psychoanalytic theory (see *Criminality*); severe self-criticism, self-abasement and confession may also be regarded as strategies for reducing guilt.

The term *shame* is commonly employed to denote the unpleasant emotion which attends public revelation of one's wrong-doing or shortcomings. It has been suggested that techniques of socialization which rely upon shame rather than guilt as the major sanction are less effective in securing internalization of moral values; the evidence is equivocal, and in practice the distinction between shame and guilt is difficult to draw (Aronfreed, 1968).

The connection between the affective components of conscience and moral behavior is apparently complex. Kohlberg (1964) was unable to demonstrate any relation between the tenacity with which a child will conform to a behavioral rule and the intensity of the guilt which he exhibits if he is induced to break the same rule.

Bibliography: Aronfreed, J.: Conduct and conscience. New York & London, 1968. **Id.:** The concept of internalization. In: **Goslin, D. A.** (Ed.): Handbook of socialization theory and research. Chicago, 1969. **Bandura, A. & Walters, R. H.:** Social learning and personality development. New York, 1963. **Berkowicz, L.:** The development of motives and values in the child. New York, 1964. **Bernstein, B. B.:** Social structure, language and learning. Educ. Research, 1961, *3*, 163–76. **Burton, R. V.:** Generality of honesty reconsidered. Psychol. Rev., 1963, *70*, 481–99. **Eysenck, H. J.:** The development of moral values in children—the contribution of learning theory. Brit. J. Educ. Psychol., 1960, *30*, 11–21. **Harrower, M. H.:** Social status and moral development. Brit. J. Educ. Psychol., 1934, *4*, 75–95. **Hartshorne, H. & May, M. A.:** Studies in deceit. New York, 1928. **Kohlberg, L.:** Development of moral character and moral ideology. In: **Hoffman, M. & Hoffman, L. W.** (Eds): Review of child development research, Vol. I. New York, 1964. **Id.:** Stage and sequence: the cognitive-developmental approach to socialization. In: **Goslin, D. A.** (Ed.): Handbook of socialization theory and research. Chicago, 1969. **Lerner, E.:** Perspectives in moral reasoning. Amer. J. Sociol., 1937, *63*, 249–69. **Morris, J. F.:** The development of moral values in children—the development of adolescent value-judgments. Brit. J. Educ. Psychol., 1958, *28*, 1–14. **Mowrer, O. H.:** Learning theory and the symbolic processes. New York, 1960. **Peters, R. S.:** Freud's theory of moral development in relation to that of Piaget. Brit. J. Educ. Psychol., 1960, *30*, 250–8. **Piaget, J.:** The moral judgment of the child. London, 1932. **Sears, R. R., Maccoby, E. E. & Levin, H.:** Patterns of child rearing. Evanston, 1957. **Trasler, G. B.:** Criminal behavior. In: **Eysenck, H. J.:** Handbook of abnormal psychology. London, [2]1970.

G. B. Trasler

Consciousness. 1. It was under the banner of "consciousness" that psychology won its independence round about the middle of the last century. Consciousness was the undisputed subject-matter of "classical" psychology, which investigated mainly the sensory manifestations of consciousness, considering sense-data to be the foundations of all mental life and holding that they were more suitable for the experimental approach than the "higher" contents of consciousness. In later years, the Würzburg school (q.v.) broke with this use of experimentation (which was restricted to "simple" psychic processes), and showed that thought processes and volitions can also be observed under experimental conditions: the complex of methodological problems posed by research into consciousness can be seen to enter in here. Scruples about method also led "objective psychology" to abandon consciousness as the object of psychology in favor of research into behavior "*more physico*". But, as early as the nineteen-thirties, the objectivist taboo on consciousness was removed, and consciousness (according to Tolman, the most real reality which we possess and can desire) was again recognized as an object of psychology. The attempt to bring the data of consciousness to the level of manifest behavior made new definitions imperative. Hence, e.g., differentiation was called a criterion of consciousness. It became possible to record "consciousness" even in animal experiments. On the human plane, the criterion of verbalization accords with the demand for objective data of consciousness. Accordingly, everything is conscious which is communicated or, at least, is communicable. Consciousness in this sense is possessed, e.g., by a baby before it is aware of objects or of itself. Even electrophysiological processes can be shown to be correlates of conscious phenomena; hence the (physiological) body is also an indicator of consciousness. Along with intentionality, the physical nature of consciousness is also stressed by contemporary phenomenologists (see *Phenomenology*). On the basis of an historical survey, L. J. Pongratz (1967) describes consciousness as the cognitive presence of something: i.e. consciousness always implies a more or less clear knowledge of something here and now. See *Depth psychology*.

Bibliography: Abramson, H. S.: Problems of consciousness. New York, 1951–55. **Boring, E. G.:** Physical dimensions of consciousness. New York, 1933. **Ey, H.:** La conscience. Paris, 1963. **Graumann, C. F.:** Bewusstsein und Bewusstheit. In: Handbuch der Psychologie, Vol. 1/1. Göttingen, 1964. **Gurwitsch, A.:** Théorie du champ de la conscience. Paris, 1957.

Hofstätter, P. R.: Die Psychologie und das Leben. Vienna, 1951. **Miller, J. G.:** Unconsciousness. New York, 1942. **Pongratz, L. J.:** Problemgeschichte der Psychologie. Berne & Munich, 1967. **Schaefer, H.:** Bemerkungen zu einer Theorie des Bewusstseins. Psychologische Beiträge, 1960, *4*. **Thomae, H.:** Bewusstsein und Leben. Archiv ges. Psychologie, 1940, *105*. **Id.:** Das Bewusstseinsproblem in der modernen Psychologie. Der Nervenarzt, 1962, *33*. **Tolman, E. C.:** Purposive behavior in animals and men. New York, 1932. **Zutt, J.:** Was lernen wir aus den Bewusstseinsstörungen über das Bewusstsein? Der Nervenarzt, 1962, *33*, 483. *L. J. Pongratz*

2. With the introduction of the natural sciences into the field of psychology, the problem of consciousness came to the fore. Knowledge can only be formed by rational, logical, hence conscious endeavors. To that extent, science must have recourse to consciousness. Whereas, in the early stages of traditional psychology, sensation and perception played the chief role in psychophysics (q.v.), the scientific possibilities of psychology later multiplied, especially in the field of the semi- (sub-)conscious and of the wholly unconscious. By conscious effort, introduced by (purposive) intention and (volitional) concentration, and controlled by the application of attention (from the unconscious via the subconscious to the clearly conscious; to be conceived in the form of three concentric circles), its province is steadily becoming more clearly and sharply defined. In more recent times, especially as a result of Soviet psychology (q.v.), consciousness and the possibilities it offers for methodical observation and criticism, as well as its significance in the activation of behavior, have become steadily more important, while in the West, in depth psychology (q.v.) and psychotherapy (q.v.), attempts are still made to apply the concept of consciousness scientifically (e.g. logotherapy, q.v.).

To this extent, psychology might be said to be developing into a science dealing with the different degrees of clarity of consciousness which are expressed (or are at least noticeable) in physically observable behavior (expression, q.v.; gesture, etc.), as well as in emotional experience. If, finally, one considers that conscious doing, thinking and acting in man are subject to control, it might be deduced that in the future research into consciousness will become increasingly important, not least in connection with information theory (q.v.) and computer techniques.

Bibliography: Hiebsch, H.: Ergebnisse der sowjetischen Psychologie. Berlin, 1967. **Manis, M.:** Cognitive processes. Belmont, Calif., 1966. **Neisser, U.:** Cognitive psychology. New York, 1967. **Rubinstein, S. L.:** Grundlagen der allgemeinen Psychologie. Berlin 1958. **Id.:** Das Denken und die Wege seiner Erforschung. Berlin, 1967.

W. Arnold

Consciousness, degrees of. If consciousness is taken to mean wakefulness, its level can be approximately recorded by means of a verbal scale ranging from the state of unconsciousness through dullened states of consciousness (stupefaction, confusion, twilight state) to a condition of optimal clarity of consciousness. See *Arousal*. *V.M.*

Consciousness, disorders of. From clinical observation we know the kind and degree of very different disorders of consciousness. Yet every attempt to grasp these disorders systematically more or less falls short of the reality, because disturbances of consciousness vary considerably and overlap and interact with other psychic changes. The "highest" degree of disturbed consciousness is unconsciousness (q.v.), the full arrestation of conscious mental processes, which (in certain organic diseases, e.g. diabetes) is a warning symptom of coma. Stupefaction, somnolence, twilight condition (q.v.) characterize restrictions of consciousness, especially of awareness of objects. These are usually disoriented twilight conditions which are often and more advantageously studied in the range of illnesses marked by a rapid onset. Typologically, but with certain limitations, one can distinguish mere restriction of consciousness, stupor (stupefaction), dimming of consciousness and dreamlike or delirious consciousness. Mild twilight states and delirium usually present as a dimming of consciousness. Delirium always contains elements of stupor. In addition, comprehension and all purposive processes are impeded, concepts tend to disintegrate, behavior becomes purely instinctive, ideation incoherent, and the individual undergoes hallucinatory, pseudo-hallucinatory and illusory experiences, together with motor arousal of varying intensity. In pathological disorders of consciousness diminished awareness is rarely absent. Hypnosis (q.v.) (as an experimental disturbance of consciousness) can avoid the stupefaction and dullness. In hypnotic states there is a characteristic splitting of the contents of consciousness or elimination of certain part-contents by the hypnotist. Recently there has also been talk of an "extension of consciousness" by the use of certain hallucinogens. It is doubtful that this could be genuine extension, but there is no doubt that every case is a result of intoxication. "Normal" disorders of consciousness can be caused by intense emotional disturbance. Fear, anger, ecstasy are experienced as intensive and sudden emotional arousals of relatively short duration and considerable though varying intensity. A common symptom is a restriction or darkening of the noëtic horizon, i.e. of the horizon of "clearly ordered perceptions, notions and ideas, by which man organizes his image of the world, comprehends it, and behaves consciously and purposively" (Lersch). Other post-traumatic or "post-hysterical" psychogenic or functional disorders of consciousness arise from affective needs: an actual or supposed advantage is sought more or less consciously. From a differential-diagnostic angle, functional disorders of consciousness can occasionally present considerable difficulties, especially as mixed and superimposed images are not infrequent. The forensic evaluation of non-pathological disorders of consciousness is a special problem; individual cases always require some reference to morbid disorders of consciousness. See *Psychoses; Schizophrenia*.

Bibliography: Bleuler, E.: Textbook of psychiatry. New York, 1924. **Brach, J.:** Conscience et connaissance. Paris, 1957. **Ehrhardt, H.:** Die Schuldfähigkeit in psychiatrisch-psychologischer Sicht. In: **Frey, E. R.:** Schuld-Verantwortung-Strafe. Zürich, 1964. **Ey, H.:** La conscience. Paris, 1967. **Eysenck, H. J.** (Ed.): Handbook of abnormal psychology. London, 1969. **Lersch, P.:** Aufbau der Person. Munich, [8]1962. **Staub, H. & Thölen, H.** (Eds): Bewusstseinsstörungen. Stuttgart, 1961. **Störring, G. E.:** Besinnung und Bewusstsein. Stuttgart, 1953. **Zutt, J.:** Was lernen wir aus den Bewusstseinsstörungen über das Bewusstsein? Nervenarzt, 1962, *33*, 483. *H. Ehrhardt*

Consciousness, restricted. Only a limited number of contents can enter our consciousness at any given moment, and we can turn our attention in only one direction at any given moment. *V.M.*

Consciousness, threshold of. Concept related to restricted consciousness (q.v.).

Conservatism. The tendency to keep to tradition, the opposite of liberalism or radicalism. Different independent factor analyses (q.v.) of attitude measurements each yielded a factor which was interpreted in this sense. In R. B. Cattell's personality system, the inventory factor "radicalism versus conservatism" which correlates with J. P. Guilford's T factor ("thinking introversion", a tendency toward reflection) describes the degree of independence in the formation of opinion. See *Attitude*.

Bibliography: Eysenck, H. J.: Psychology of politics. London, 1954. *D.B.*

Consistency. 1. *Internal consistency* is the homogeneity of the individual elements of a method of measurement (e.g. of test items), and may be determined by discovering the average intercorrelation between the elements, and the correlation of each with the total score. The *internal consistency coefficient* (which may be calculated by Kuder-Richardson formula 20) is a measure of the reliability (homogeneity) of the score obtained from individual test components.

2. A *statistical* test is called consistent when, as the size of the sample increases, the test covers differences with increasing certainty. *G.M.*

3. A synonym for (behavioral) *reliability* (q.v.).

4. Individual *constancy*, i.e. the degree to which a testee displays identical behavior in different situations, at different times, and when performing different tasks. Consistency also determines the extent to which individual behavior can be predicted. It has not yet been established whether different forms of consistent behavior can be traced back to a common personality factor. *K.P.*

Consonance; dissonance. Terms used of the combination of two or more tones. Because of the structural complexity, consonance and dissonance (q.v.) cannot be defined universally, but only from different points of view: mathematically (frequency, H. von Helmholtz), acoustically (coincidence of overtones, or harmonics, C. Husmann), psychologically (degree of fusion, C. Stumpf), and in regard to sequential form (harmony or melodic line). The notion of consonance and dissonance has constantly changed over the centuries. Wellek (1963) attempted a comprehensive definition in his multiplicity theory. See *Music, psychology of.*

Bibliography: Wellek, A.: Musikpsychologie und Musikästhetik. Frankfurt, 1963. *B.S.*

Constancy. Perceptual compensation by which objects retain constant perceptual properties in spite of objective changes, e.g. objects appear the same size even when seen at different distances and the same color even when seen in different illuminations. *C.D.F.*

Constant stimulus method. A psychophysical procedure for estimating an absolute or differential sensory threshold. One stimulus is held invariant (the standard) while a series of similar stimuli are presented in random order for comparison on the variable in question (e.g. brightness, loudness, thickness). The threshold is computed from the proportion of correct responses given for each comparison stimulus. Syn. *Method of right and wrong cases.* *G.D.W.*

Constants. See *Method of constants.*

Constellation theory. G. E. Müller's attempt to explain why in a specific thought process only concepts appropriate to that process impinge upon the conscious mind. The task acts as an orienting idea encouraging the associative tendencies of certain concepts and inhibiting those of others. This system of advancement and blocking is known as *constellation*, and the complex of unified, associated ideas as *a constellation.*

Bibliography: Müller, G. E.: Zur Analyse der Gedächtnistätigkeit und des Vorstellungsverlaufs. Part 3. Leipzig, 1913. *R.Hä*

Constitution. See *Constitutional theory.*

Constitutional theory. "Constitution" may be understood as human reactive potential and reaction style (form and performance). It is grounded in heredity and *anlagen* (q.v.), or fundamental dispositions and those acquired in early childhood, or more rarely at a later date, and can be determined as a type (q.v.) or an individual constitution. Constitutional theory studies mental and physical principles of the healthy and ailing organism as a whole. It can be thought of as a biological science based on description, measurement and correlational statistics. It uses analytical methods to discover typical elements of character or temperament, organic functional systems, and physical proportions. It throws light on basic mental and physical abilities, tendencies to social deviation, and proneness to disease. See *Criminality; Traits.*

Bibliography: Kretschmer, E.: Physique and character. London, 1925. *W.K.*

Constitutional types. Theoretical groupings of psychophysical (occasionally exclusively physical: the "biotype") characteristics which are assembled either by a statistical frequency method or by arbitrary selection. Kretschmer's *physique types:* pyknic (q.v.), leptosomic (q.v.), athletic (q.v.) are derived correlatively from manic depressive and schizophrenic *psychoses* (q.v.), and in turn form the starting-point for statistical elucidation of the cyclothymic (q.v.), schizothymic (q.v.), and barykinetic (q.v.) types. Statistically, Sheldon (1942) found three physical growth variables: endomorphy (q.v.), ectomorphy (q.v.), and mesomorphy (q.v.). These provide a basis for describing the viscerotonic (q.v.), cerebrotonic (q.v.), and somatotonic (q.v.) temperaments (Sheldon's constitutional theory of personality). Conrad (1963), using rough measurements, groups the proportions of the body in series of variations ranging between the extremes *compact-elongated* (pyknomorphic-leptomorphic) and *robust-thin* (athletic-hyperplastic-asthenic-hypoplastic). Types based on age and sex are also recognized as psychophysical constitutional types. See *Body build index; Type.*

Bibliography: Eysenck, H. J.: The structure of human personality. London & New York, [2]1960. **Kretschmer, E.:** Physique and character. London, 1925. **Sheldon, W.:** The varieties of temperament. New York, 1942. **Conrad, K.:** Der Konstitutionstyp. Berlin, [2]1963. *W.K.*

Construct validity. 1. *Origin of the phrase.* The phrase *construct validity* came into widespread use in the behavioral sciences in the nineteen fifties. In an article entitled "Construct validity in psychological tests" that did much to establish this usage, Cronbach & Meehl (1955) trace the origin of the term to the work performed by an APA Committee on Psychological Tests. According to these authors, "The chief innovation of the Committee's report was the term *construct validity.* This was first formulated by a subcommittee (Meehl and R. C. Challman) . . . and later modified and clarified by the entire Committee (Bordin, Challman, Conrad, Humphreys, Super and the present writers)". As concerns the reasons for introducing the term, Cronbach & Meehl state that although "construct validity calls for no new scientific approach", the concept is needed to more clearly . . . "specify types of research required in developing tests for which conventional views on validation are inappropriate".

2. *Controversy relating to use of the phrase.* Several behavioral scientists, perhaps most notably H. P. Bechtoldt and R. B. Cattell, have expressed serious objections to use of the term construct validity. They have argued cogently that at best it is merely an old wine in a new bottle, and that in some of its formulations it is confusing, misleading and could even support a . . . "non-empirical, non-scientific approach to the study of behavior" (Bechtoldt, 1959). Cattell (1964) has recommended use of the term *concept validity* in place of construct validity, on the grounds that it has the desirable connotations and few of the undesirable connotations of the latter, and because . . . "an empirical construct, in logic and epistemology, is only a particular form of a concept . . . [and] the psychologist is often interested in validity for other kinds of concepts, such as are logically deducible from general postulates" (Cattell & Butcher, 1968). Bechtoldt also argues to the effect that the scientifically accurate connotations of construct validity are well represented by the idea of explication of a concept, as indicated by logical positivism and operational metholdology, and that construct validity should . . . "be eliminated from further consideration as a way of speaking about psychological concepts, laws and theories".

But, however compelling these arguments may be, they appear to have had little influence on use: construct validity continues to be a widely-used phrase and a number of writers (e.g. Campbell, 1960) have argued compellingly for its continued use. The fact that space has been made available for it in this reference work probably bespeaks of a reality: use of the phrase has become too well-established to expect that it will be supplemented by another term, or cease to be used, in the near future.

3. *A basis for definition.* Available attempts at definition of construct validity are extended essays considerably longer than this entry. Most have been similar to essays designed to explain theory construction generally, or such aspects of this as model specification, hypothesis testing, operationalism, concept explication, functional unity and intervening variables. This is not to say that the concepts represented by these various labels are indistinguishable from those of construct validity, but merely to alert the reader to similarities, and to the fact that the thrust in each case is toward specifying the necessary and sufficient conditions for establishing credence in science for a concept or set of concepts.

In most attempts to describe construct validation, one central idea is that to validate a construct is to identify the observables which denote it, and to show that these observables vary and co-vary in ways that indicate that all represent the same thing—i.e. form a functional unity (Cattell, 1950). It is generally, if implicitly, agreed that the extreme form of operationalism which requires a different construct—and a different construct name—for every distinguishable operation (however trivial the difference) is not desirable in science or for construct validity. Hence, it is implied that to validate a construct is to designate operationally distinct manifestations of the construct and to show that these are unitary.

But this raises some very knotty problems. On the one hand, it invites confusion of construct validity with internal consistency reliability (see *Test theory*); and on the other hand it can confuse the validation of a particular set of measurement operations (a test) with the elaborate process of building support for an entire theory. Indeed, these would appear to be extremes along a continuum near the middle of which are the conditions specified for construct validity, the continuum representing convergence of different observations of the same phenomenon or correlation (in a broad sense of this term) among different variables. To break the *tertium quid* implied here, theorists have suggested that reliability be defined as convergence among highly similar kinds of observations, and that theory verification be thought of in terms of interrelationships among different constructs, whence the convergence required for construct validity can be defined as that among operationally quite distinct measures of the same construct. But, clearly, behind this verbal solution lurk some very difficult problems of specifying what it is that makes measurement operations "highly similar", and "quite distinct". Toward a solution to this kind of problem, R. B. Cattell has proposed that the basic observations upon which psychological measurements are built can be classified into mutually exclusive and exhaustive categories of media of observations: Data either derive from observations made by the subject himself, from observations made by others, or from the effects of the subject's behavior on the impersonal environment. Measurements based upon observations made through different media may then be regarded as operationally "quite distinct", and yet indicate the same construct. Reliability is then to be understood in terms of convergence within a particular mode of observation; construct validity can be defined (in part, see below) by convergence in measurements of the same attribute based upon observations through different media; and theory construction can be understood in terms of the broader concerns of interrelationships among different constructs, verification of interacting stimulus-response hypotheses, and so on. There remains in each case a practical problem of specifying the degree of relationship required to support an hypothesis of convergence, but this can be treated as a technical issue. In this regard, too, several theorists have emphasized the need to demonstrate a lack of convergence—i.e. the distinctiveness—among supposedly different constructs (see Campbell & Fiske, 1959; Horn & Cattell, 1965).

To provide truly compelling evidence for construct validity in the sense of what R. B. Cattell has defined as a functional unity, it is necessary to go beyond demonstration of convergence and distinctiveness for the observables which represent the concept, and to show that those observables appear together, disappear together, change together or, in general, interact in one of the many ways in which things can interact when they represent a unitary phenomenon. This means, e.g. that in controlled-manipulative experiments independent variable conditions should produce cohesive effects on all of a set of operationally separable measures of the same construct; that in studies of development it should be found that the construct observables "grow" together in a unitary way; and that in studies of process, an occurrence in one manifestation of a construct should be accompanied by a corresponding occurrence in other manifestations. Construct validity in this sense thus becomes very similar to theory verification. There is a difference in emphasis, however, for in construct validation the focus is on establishing credence for a particular measurement operation, and only incidentally are tests of an entire theory at issue, whereas in theory verification the adequacy of measures of constructs is implicitly assumed and the emphasis is upon showing that several constructs "behave" as specified in the theory.

Clearly, construct validation continues to be one of the more controversial topics in the behavioral sciences.

Bibliography: Bechtoldt, H. P.: Construct validity: a critique. American Psychologist, 1959, *14*, 619–29. **Campbell, D. T.:** Recommendations for APA Test Standards regarding construct, trait, or discriminant validity. American Psychologist, 1960, *15*, 546–53. **Id. & Fiske, D. W.:** Convergent and discriminant validation by the multitrait-multimethod matrix. Psychological Bulletin, 1959, *56*, 81–105. **Cattell, R. B.:** Personality. New York, 1950. **Id.:** Beyond validity and reliability: some further concepts and coefficients for evaluating tests. Journal of Educational Measurement, 1964, *33*, 133–43. **Id. & Butcher, J. H.:** The prediction of achievement and creativity. New York, 1968. **Cronbach, L. J.:** Essentials of psychological testing. New York, [3]1970. **Id. & Meehl, P. E.:** Construct validity in psychological tests. Psychological Bulletin, 1955, *52*, 281–302. **Horn, J. L. & Cattell, R. B.:** Vehicles, ipsatization and the multiple method measurement of motivation. Canadian Journal of Psychology, 1965, *19*, 265–79.

J. L. Horn

Consumer research. See *Marketing*.

Contact. By the ability to make contact(s) one understands the speed and facility with which a person can establish a positive social relationship with his fellows. An inability to make contacts can indicate neurotic incapacity or be a sign of self-sufficiency (a preference for one's own company rather than the group). See *Sociability*. *G.K.*

Contact behavior. This can be mainly observed in the care of the young. A grey goose chick remains in acoustical and optical contact with its mother. If this fails, it "cries". Young perch often seek to establish contact with the parent by touch. Contact behavior can easily be produced by dummy sign stimuli (q.v.). *V.P.*

Contagion, psychic. A supposed process by which certain behavior (e.g. rhythmic movement) is rapidly passed from individual to individual to affect a whole group. Also associated with the "ideo-real law" (q.v.) postulated by Hellpach, and, like that hypothesis, ultimately dependent upon very precise confirmation of the modes of mutual interdependence of mental and physical phenomena. *J.M.*

Contamination. 1. Psychopathologically: mixing or fusing words or parts of words with a usually meaningless resultant. Occurs in normal people in a state of great fatigue or in dreams, but especially in schizophrenia (q.v.) as the result of pathological disorders of speech and thought. 2. Diagnostically: in shape-interpretation methods, the condensation of two heterogeneous contents to produce a false interpretation (e.g. in the Rohrschach test: a combination of specific schizoid or schizophrenic behaviors.) 3. A subjective interference with any interpretation of scores or analyses. *G.P.*

Content analysis. According to B. Berelson, a research technique which seeks to describe objectively, systematically and quantitatively the manifest content of communication; according to H. D. Lasswell: "quantitative semantics". The method is used especially in the study of publicity, in social psychology and political science, but also in the study of literature and the psychology of development. Verbally communicated material in particular (newspaper articles, texts of speeches, films, diaries, etc.) can be analyzed quantitatively by determining frequencies or their ratios in defined classifications (categories). More recently, content analysis has come to be used as a means for deciding research hypotheses, and sophisticated applications now demand the use of computers. See *Computational linguistics.*

Bibliography: Holsti, O. R.: Content Analysis. In: Lindzey, G. & Aronson, E. (Eds): Handbook of social psychology, Vol. 2. Reading, Mass., 1968, 596–692.

H.D.S.

Contiguity. The coexistence or proximity, in time or space, of different experiences.

Law of contiguity: When events occur simultaneously or in close proximity, they are then associated, which is a precondition for learning. In the strict sense, the law is often synonymous with contiguity theory: when stimulus and response occur together once, a final and (some claim) non-reinforceable connection is established between them. Principles for explaining phenomena such as association (q.v.) and conditioning (q.v.) are based on this law.

E. R. Guthrie's contiguity theory (Guthrie's contiguous conditioning theory): if a stimulus affects an organism while this is in motion, the stimulus will subsequently release this movement. The formation of associations on the basis of *simultaneity* of stimulus and movement is a necessary and sufficient condition for learning.

Bibliography: Guthrie, E. R.: The psychology of learning. New York, 1935.

H.W.

Contingency. 1. The degree to which one variable depends on another variable or other variables. 2. A term descriptive of the phenomenon that within a whole group of individuals featuring certain characteristics, certain combinations of these are especially frequent. The sets of psychological characteristics that are related are "typical"; and the individuals featuring these sets are "types". *W.Se.*

3. *Logical contingency:* a state of affairs which, in regard to the laws of logic, may and also may not be. 4. *Physical contingency:* a state of affairs which, in regard to the laws of physics, may and also may not be. More loosely, x is contingent on y if the occurrence of x is dependent on the occurrence of y, and y may or may not occur in accordance with the laws of nature.

Contingency coefficient. The coefficient of a non-parametric correlation method the object of which is to determine the degree of interrelationship between two variables of more than one class. *G.M.*

Continuity, correction of. Its use is required when with small samples a characteristic which is actually continuous is taken to be discrete, and the theoretical distribution of the statistic is also continuous. *W.H.B.*

Continuous scales. 1. Scales in which all values situated between two limits can occur, at least in theory. In psychology such scales are rare although it is often assumed that variables measured by means of discrete scales are also actually continuous (e.g. memory performance in a test). In general, measurable variables are said to be continuous, those obtained merely from measures representing whole numbers are *discontinuous*, or *discrete*. **2.** Scales of infinitesimal increments of gain. *G.M.*

Contour. See *Figure-ground.*

Contraception. The prevention of conception. Various contraceptive measures in current use are: coitus interruptus (q.v.), the "safe" period, mechanical devices such as condoms (sheaths), or intrauterine coils (although the use of such devices, together with abortion, q.v., is properly classed as birth-prevention *after* conception), and various anti-spermicidal creams, etc. The regular self-administration of hormonal contraceptives is a popular and economic method (the "pill"), although various, even fatal, side-effects with certain types in certain individuals have been recorded. Male and female sterilization is sometimes classed as a contraceptive measure, but the term is usually reserved for methods other than the (usually) irreversible. *U.H.S.*

Contraction. The drawing together of a muscle. In the case of the transversal skeletal muscle a distinction is made between individual contractions lasting 0·1 sec, and *tetanic* contractions the duration of which depends on how long the series of stimuli lasts; between *isometric* (those where there is no change of length but only some development of energy), *isotonic* (where only length and not tension changes), and *auxotonic* contractions (a mixture of isometric and isotonic). The contraction of the heart muscle lasts 0·3 to 0·5 sec., and consists of isometric, auxotonic, isometric, and then isotonic phases. *E.D.*

Contrast. Two juxtaposed surfaces of differing brightness and color influence one another in the sense that each surface tends to produce a complementary color in its neighbor (*simultaneous contrast*). The results are as follows: (*a*) if the two surfaces differ in brightness, the difference is more strongly accentuated (*brightness contrast*); (*b*) if the two surfaces have complementary (q.v.) colors, the saturation increases (a maximum saturation of green occurs when it is placed on a red ground); (*c*) if the two colors are not complementary they change according to the rules of summative color mixing. The following also apply: (*a*) the intensity of the contrast effected is proportional to the area affected (*induction area*, or *surface*); (*b*) the smaller the brightness contrast, the greater the simultaneous color contrast; (*c*) the intensity and direction of the contrast are also influenced by structural (gestalt) factors (Benary, 1924); (*d*) simultaneous color contrast is very strongly accentuated if the reciprocally impinging surfaces are covered with a sheet of flimsy white paper (fluorescent contrast).

Bibliography: Benary, W.: Beobachtungen zu einem Exp. über Helligkeitskontrast. Psychol. Forsch. 1924, 5. *G. Ka.*

Contrectation drive. A term introduced by Moll to denote the contact drive as one of the components of the sex drive. When contact or touch is established, this drive loses its force and the so-called *detumescence* drive is substituted. *G.L.I.*

Control group. A group of Ss in an experiment who are not subjected to any experimental treatment, but are equal to the Ss in the experimental group (q.v.). In general, the control-group results must be compared with those for the experimental group before any pronouncement can be made about the degree and direction of the effect of the experiment. *G.M.*

Controlled variable. See *Variable.*

Convention. A term for rules of social behavior, or customs which have been formed in the course of time and are not explicitly formulated inside the group but are known to all the members. They are considered not so much as generally binding precepts or norms but rather as matters which are self-evident in social interaction. A particularly rigid and stereotyped adherence to social rules and precepts or conventions which actually do not demand such a degree of submission is known as *conventionalism;* it is considered to be a characteristic of the "authoritarian personality" (q.v.). See *Conformity.* *A.S.-M.*

Convergence. 1. A position, or a change in position, of the two eyes produced by their force of fusion (fusion reflex, making both retinal images coincide), and by the eye muscles, with the result that the visual axes cross at the fixation point. The angle of convergence is the angle between the lines of regard in the visual plane. *Angle of fusion:* the angle between the line of regard and the parallel position. The opposite of convergence is *divergence.* The general term for both is *vergence.* A distinction is sometimes made between accommodative, fusional and proximal convergence, depending on what induces the convergence movement: state of accommodation, disparate retinal points (q.v.), and apparent decrease in the distance of a seen object. Accommodation (q.v.), convergence and pupillary reaction are interconnected.

2. The term "convergence" is also used for development processes, etc., when there is a tendency or law for variables to agree with or tend toward one another. (W. Stern's convergence theory: convergence between genotype, q.v. and environment, q.v.) *A.H.*

Convergent thinking. According to J. P. Guilford, one of the two kinds of productive-thinking operations (see *Divergent thinking*). Convergent thinkers look for the one (predetermined) right, or best, or conventional answer to a problem. Convergent thinking can, in certain respects, be examined by tests with one correct solution.

Bibliography: Guilford, J. P.: Three faces of intellect. Amer. Psychologist, 1959, *14*, 469–79. *J.G.*

Conversational chaining. A type of non-branching program introduced by J. A. Barlow (see *Branching*) in which the desired answer that will fill the blank space in statement 1 occurs at some point in statement 2, where it is emphasized (e.g. in bold type) in the text. The question in each frame, or step (q.v.), is therefore an incomplete statement. This variation of the linear method has the advantage of appearing more discursive.

Bibliography: Barlow, J. A.: Conversational chaining in teaching machine programs. Psychol. Rep. 1960, 7, 187–93. *H.F.*

Conversion. The transformation of a mental conflict into a physical symptom which represents a disguised drive gratification or wish fulfillment, or (more frequently) an inhibition of such a drive gratification or wish fulfillment, or both. Conversions appear in hysteria (q.v.) as anesthesias and paresthesias, as motor paralysis, convulsive attacks, and (in more serious regressive conditions) as pregenital conversion neuroses. In contrast to psychosomatic illnesses (see *Organic neuroses*) which subjectively have no "meaning" for the patient, conversions are "meaningful".

According to Freud, conversion neuroses

are *conversion hysteria* and *pregenital* conversion neuroses (especially tics and stuttering). According to Freud and Fenichel, fixations on the later or early anal stages (q.v.) (depending on the gravity of the symptoms) lie at the root of these illnesses. See *Psychopathology; Psychosomatics.*

Bibliography: Fenichel, O.: The psychoanalytic theory of neurosis. New York, 1945. **Freud, S.:** Three essays on the theory of sexuality. London, [2]1962. **Toman, W.:** An introduction to psychoanalytic theory of motivation. London & New York, 1960. *W.T.*

Convulsion. A general, involuntary muscular contraction.

Convulsive therapy. This was first introduced by Ladislas von Meduna (1896–1964) into the treatment of schizophrenia (q.v.) and other psychoses. By intravenously injecting cardiazol, metrazol and other analogous substances, Meduna succeeded in artificially inducing an epileptic state. The idea was based fundamentally on his observation that schizophrenia and epilepsy (q.v.) almost never occur together. He therefore supposed that they were mutually antagonistic. Later, Cerletti and Bini obtained convulsive crises by means of electricity and introduced treatment by electric shock into hospitals. The appearance of psychopharmacological drugs for use in medicine has decreased the frequency with which electric shock treatment is used, especially in cases of depression. Present practice is to use it with intravenous anesthesia, and to combine it with drugs which reduce the violence of the convulsions.

Bibliography: Meduna, L. J.: The convulsive treatment. In: **Sackler, A. M.** (Ed.): The great physiodynamic therapies in psychiatry. New York, 1956, 76–90. *J.L.I.*

Cooperation. 1. The manner in, and degree to which an individual's activity is linked with that of others or depends on it, e.g. in shared work places, group therapy, teamwork, and so on, through the influence of the overall organization of group dynamics (q.v.) and of appropriate leadership (q.v.),

2. Readiness to participate, share a workload, etc., respond to counseling, and so on. *G.R.W.M.*

Cooperative School and College Ability Tests (abb. SCAT). Tests which attempt to assess the abilities (q.v.) developed by the school. The calculations comprise a total level and values for verbal and "quantitative" abilities. There are four series for different high-school grades; two series for colleges.

Bibliography: Educational testing service. Princeton, 1955–63. *R.M.*

Coordination. A function of the central nervous system: bringing the perceptual organs into operation so that certain stimuli can impinge which are required for further responses (e.g. visual-motor coordination); to control the function of antagonistic muscles so that they support one another in regard to the intended behavioral goal instead of impeding or preventing it. The process of coordination can be either innate or acquired, and can operate both consciously and unconsciously. See *Brain.* *A.Ro.*

Coprophagy. The eating of excrement, which can occur in serious cases of imbecility, and occasionally among the insane. *C.S.*

Copulation. The process of sexual intercourse. With higher-order animals, copulation is only one aspect of pairing (mating), which also involves care of the brood. The frequent isolation of sexuality in experimental research led for a long time to an underestimation of the general social aspects of mating. For instance, aggression aroused by sexual approach has to be restrained, not only for copulation but for the restitution of friendly contact. This is helped by courtship (q.v.), and presumably by coital after-play—which as yet has scarcely been investigated but can be found among parrots, seagulls and ducks. Syn. *Coition; Coitus* (q.v.). *R.A.S.*

Cornea. Circumscribes the eye almost spherically at the front, is 1 mm thick, and consists of five layers. Its structure allows rays of visible light to pass; they are refracted on the cornea. *R.R.*

Corona effect. See *Halo effect*.

Corpus luteum (syn. *Yellow body*). The endocrine organ which forms in the female ovary from the spent follicle, the remains of the ovum which has burst during ovulation. It is here that the *corpus luteum* hormones estrogen and progesterone are formed. The latter transforms the uterine lining (which has grown under the influence of the estrogen) so that the fertilized ovum can establish itself. From the third month of pregnancy the *corpus luteum* degenerates, and the placenta takes over the formation of *corpus luteum* hormones, and with it the maintenance of the uterine lining; it also has a beneficial effect on the uterine musculature. If the burst egg is not fertilized and is passed, the hormone production ceases after about fourteen days and the uterine mucus membrane is evacuated during menstruation (q.v.). See *Hormones*. *E.D.*

Corpus quadrigemina. Part of the mesencephalon, and consisting of two masses of tissue believed to contain visual and auditory reflex centers.

Corpus striatum (syn. *Striate body*). Part of the base of each cerebral hemisphere in the prosencephalon, consisting of the internal capsule and the caudate and lenticular nuclei.

Correlational techniques. 1. *History.* The idea that characteristics of individuals are often related (height and weight, intelligence and achievement, and so on) has long been accepted in civilized societies. Yet no effort was made to express the extent of such relationships in quantitative terms before the end of the nineteenth century. The first person to tackle the question seriously was Francis Galton. One of the problems he considered (Galton, 1886) was the relationship between the heights of fathers and sons. As a result of his investigations he succeeded in deriving linear equations (or regression lines) for predicting a son's height from that of his father, and, conversely, a father's height from that of his adult son. He also showed that when the variabilities of the two sets of measurements were equated the slopes of the two lines, relative to the horizontal and vertical axis respectively, were equal. This slope, which was now a unit-free measure, became known as the correlation coefficient between the two sets of measurements.

Galton's work was soon extended by other writers, notably Karl Pearson and G. U. Yule. Pearson (1896) developed a formula for the direct calculation of a correlation coefficient—the Pearson product-moment correlation coefficient. He also provided techniques for correlating data when one or both of the variables could be measured only in a qualitative way. Yule (1907) contributed notably to the extension of the theory of correlation and regression to include any number of variables. Early in the present century, too, the value of correlational techniques for psychological experimentation was realized. A leading pioneer in this field was Charles Spearman (1904).

By the end of the first decade of the present century most of the basic work on the derivation of correlation and regression coefficients had been done and attention was being directed to questions concerning the sampling errors of these statistics. At first these proved very intractable. One main difficulty was the fact that the distribution of a correlation coefficient is skew, in particular when its numerical value approaches the limits of plus and minus unity. This major difficulty was largely overcome when Fisher (1921) introduced the *z-transformation* of the correlation coefficient, which has a distribution approaching closely to a normal distribution. The development, also by Fisher, of the methods of analysis of variance and co-variance (Fisher, 1925) contributed greatly to the solution of problems concerned with the general theory of linear and multiple regression, and to the interpretation not only of these techniques but of the correlation coefficient itself. The effect of Fisher's and later work on correlational theory is discussed in detail by Hotelling (1953).

2. *The bivariate normal distribution.* This distribution is basic to correlational theory. It arises when, for a sample of N subjects, we have scores or other measurements on two variables X and Y each of which can be measured on a continuous scale and is normally distributed in the population. This is one of the necessary conditions of a bivariate normal distribution. The other condition is that when the N pairs of scores are plotted in a diagram using orthogonal axes (say the X-axis horizontal and the Y-axis vertical), the scatter of points thus obtained shows an elliptical or circular distribution which decreases consistently in density outwards from the point representing the mean scores of the two variables. The diagram is called a *scatter diagram* or *scattergram.*

The density function for a bivariate normal distribution (see Kendall & Stuart, 1961) requires five constants, or population parameters, to define it. These are the means and standard deviations of the two variables and the correlation coefficient between them. The latter, where the whole population of subjects is concerned, is denoted by the Greek letter ρ. An estimate r of ρ, obtained from the scores of a sample of subjects drawn randomly from this population, is found by the formula

$$r = \frac{\Sigma xy}{\sqrt{(\Sigma_{x^2} \,.\, \Sigma_{y^2})}}, \tag{1}$$

in which Σ_{x^2} is the sum of the squares of the deviations of the N-scores on variable X from their mean. Σ_{y^2} is defined similarly for the Y-scores, while Σ_{xy} is the sum of the products of the N pairs of deviational scores. Formula (1) is Pearson's product-moment formula for the correlation coefficient. It can be expressed in several equivalent forms.

3. *Regression lines.* In the case of a distribution which is approximately bivariate normal there are two regression lines. If the X-axis is divided into intervals, then for values of X within a given interval the mean of the corresponding Y-scores can be obtained. When this is done for all intervals, the Y-means derived will be found to lie roughly on a straight line. This line can be expressed in the form

$$\hat{Y} = a + bX, \tag{2}$$

in which b is the slope of the line relative to the X-axis, what is called the *regression coefficient* of Y on X; a is the intercept of the line on the Y-axis and $\hat{Y}$ is the estimated value of Y for a given value of X. The regression line is also called a "least square" line, as the constants a and b are found such that the sum of the squares of the distances of all points in the scattergram (taken parallel to the Y-axis) from the line is a minimum.

A process similar to that just described can also be carried out by dividing the Y-axis into intervals and then calculating the X-means corresponding to each interval of Y. This process will lead to a linear equation of estimating X for given values of Y, namely

$$\hat{X} = a' + b'Y. \tag{3}$$

When the standard deviations of the X and Y scores are equal it is found that b is equal to b' and each is equal to r.

In cases in which scores on one variable, say the Y variable, are measured on a continuous scale but these scores are ascertained only for certain predetermined values of the X-variable it is customary to consider only the "regression" line of Y on X. If bivariate normality cannot be assumed it may be necessary to test for *linearity of regression* (see McNemar, 1962). If the test indicates a non-linear relationship then a more complicated equation than that given by expression (2) is required. When this is the case, the relationship between the two variables cannot be adequately expressed by a product-moment correlation coefficient but a coefficient called the *eta coefficient*, which is a measure of curvilinearity, may be used.

4. *Other correlational methods.* In psychological investigations it is not always possible to collect data in the form required by expression (1), and other procedures for estimating correlation coefficients then become necessary. The most commonly occurring situations and the coefficients appropriate to each are summarized below. Basic reference books are those by McNemar (1962), Lord & Novick (1968), and Kendall & Stuart (1961, 1966).

(*a*) *Tetrachoric coefficient.* This correlation coefficient may be used in the case of data which basically are distributed in a bivariate normal manner but for which scores on the two continuous variables are not available. Instead it is known for each member of a sample of subjects only whether he lies above or below some given point on each of the variables. Tetrachoric correlations are difficult to calculate without a computer and are generally estimated from nomograms.

(*b*) *Biserial coefficient.* This coefficient gives an estimate of the product moment correlation between two variables which have a bivariate normal distribution, but for one of which scores are available only in dichotomous form (e.g. "alcoholic" and "non-alcoholic").

(*c*) *Point biserial coefficient.* This coefficient gives an estimate of the product-moment correlation between two variables one of which is continuous but the other is truly dichotomous (e.g. "male" versus "female"). Bivariate normality is not assumed.

(*d*) *The fourfold point or phi coefficient.* When both variables are dichotomous in form, the scatter diagram is reduced to a fourfold table. The product-moment correlation for such a table is known as the *phi coefficient.* The coefficient is primarily used for correlating test items but unfortunately it is not independent of item difficulty.

(*e*) *The kappa coefficient.* Fourfold tables also arise when two judges separately interview a sample of subjects and note the presence or absence of some characteristic. A *phi* coefficient might again be used as a measure of agreement between the judges, but a preferable measure is the *kappa coefficient*, which takes possible bias between the judges into account (see Spitzer *et al.*, 1967; Everitt, 1968).

(*f*) *Rank correlation.* When a sample of subjects is arranged in order according to some characteristic which they possess to a varying degree, they are said to be ranked. When rankings exist for the subjects on two separate characteristics, the relationship between the rankings can be determined by the use of rank correlation techniques. The two most commonly used coefficients are Spearman's *rho* and Kendall's *tau.*

(*g*) *Intraclass correlation.* The simplest example of this correlation arises in the comparison of identical twins. If we have a sample of N pairs of twins with scores for each on a single variable, then in arranging the scores it is immaterial which score in a pair is placed first. When correlating the data each pair of scores is entered twice in reverse order so that there are then $2N$ pairs of scores in all.

(*h*) *Partial correlation.* The observed correlation between two variables may be influenced by the fact that one or both are linearly related to other concomitant variables. A partial correlation is the correlation between the two variables after the effect of these extraneous influences has been removed.

(*i*) *Serial correlation or autocorrelation.* Given a series of measurements

$$x_1, x_2, x_3, \ldots, x_i, \ldots, x_t,$$

taken at equal intervals of time, correlations may be obtained between the $(t-1)$ pairs of measurements $(x_1, x_2), (x_2, x_3), \ldots$, or between the $(t-2)$ pairs of measurements $(x_1, x_3), (x_2, x_4), \ldots$, and so on. The first is known as a serial correlation of *lag one*, the second as a serial correlation of *lag two*, and so on. Examination of the values of the successive correlations may reveal trends in the series. A plot of the correlations for lags of increasing size is known as a *correlogram*.

(*j*) *Multiple linear regression and multiple correlation*. Multiple regression arises when we examine the relationship between one variable, generally referred to as the dependent or criterion variable, and the combined effects, assumed to be linear, of several other variables, generally referred to as the independent or predictor variables. In this case the regression equation takes the form

$$\hat{Y} = a + b_1X_1 + b_2X_2 + \ldots + b_pX_p, \quad (4)$$

where $\hat{Y}$ is the estimated value of the dependent variable Y for given values of the p independent variables X_1 to X_p. As with simple regression a is the intercept on the Y-axis, but now b_i is the rate of change in Y as X_i varies and the other dependent variables are held constant at their mean values; the b's are known as *partial regression coefficients*, and they are determined so that the sum of the squares of the discrepancies $(\hat{Y}_i - Y_i)$ for $i = 1, 2, \ldots, N$, is a minimum. The correlation between the N pairs of values $(\hat{Y}_i, Y_i)$ is known as the *multiple correlation*.

(*k*) *Canonical correlations*. Canonical correlational analysis is an extension of multiple regression analysis. It arises when a set of p variables X_1 to X_p can be divided meaningfully into two subsets p_1 and p_2, where $p = p_1 + p_2$. The problem here is to find that weighted sum of the first set which correlates maximally with a weighted sum of the second set. The correlation thus obtained is known as the first *canonical correlation* between the two sets. In general p^* independent sets of weights can be found, where p^* equals p_1 or p_2 whichever is the smaller, so that p^* canonical correlations of successively decreasing magnitude are obtained (Hope, 1968).

Bibliography: Everitt, B. S.: Moments of the statistics kappa and weighted kappa. Brit. J. Math. & Stat. Psychol. 1968, *21*, 97–103. **Fisher, R. A.:** "On the probable error" of a coefficient of correlation deduced from a small sample, Metron, 1921, *1*, 1–32. **Id.:** Statistical methods for research workers. Edinburgh, 1925. **Galton, F.:** Regression towards mediocrity in hereditary stature. Jour. Anthrop. Inst., 1886, *15*, 246–70. **Hope, K.:** Methods of multivariate analysis. London, 1968. **Hotelling, H.:** New light on the correlation coefficient and its transforms. J. Roy. Stat. Soc., 1953, *15*, 193–224. **Kendall, M. G. & Stuart, A.:** The advanced theory of statistics, Vols 2 and 3. London, 1961 and 1966. **Lord, F. M. & Novick, M. R.:** Statistical theories of mental test scores. Reading, Mass., 1968. **McNemar, Q.:** Psychological statistics. New York & London, 1962. **Pearson, K.:** Regression, heredity and panmixia, Phil. Trans. Roy. Soc., 1896, Series A, *187*, 253–67. **Spearman, C.:** The proof and measurement of association between two things, Amer. J. Psychol., 1904, *15*, 88–103. **Spitzer, R. L. *et al.*:** Quantification of agreement in psychiatric diagnosis. Arch. Gen. Psychiatry, 1967, *17*, 83–7. **Yule, G. U.:** On the theory of correlation for any number of variables treated by a new system of notation, Proc. Roy. Soc., 1907, Series A, *79*, 182–93.

A. E. Maxwell

Correlation coefficient. A statistical value which indicates the degree of relationship between two or more variables. Correlation coefficients (except for contingency coefficients, q.v.) vary between −1.00 and +1.00; 0.00 indicates the complete absence of any correlation, while the coefficients −1.00 and +1.00 indicate a wholly negative or positive correlation.

G.M.

Correlation indices. Known also as z' transformations, these are transformed correlation coefficients. As such coefficients cannot normally be distributed, they are frequently transformed into more or less normally distributed correlation indices. The formula for transformation of the product-moment correlation r is:

$$z' = \frac{1}{2}[\log_e(1 + r) - \log_e(1 + r)].$$

Tables of transformed values are available, and are used to carry out significance tests on correlation coefficients. They are distributed more or less normally round zero independently of the sample size. See *Correlational techniques*.

G.M.

Correlation ratio. A statistical index for the degree of correlation between two variables when the relation is curvilinear. See *Correlational techniques.* *G.M.*

Correlation table. The frequency table for a bivariate distribution (q.v.) which is used as the basis for calculating a correlation coefficient (q.v.). In a correlation table the values of the two variables are arranged in order of magnitude, horizontally and vertically, so that their quantitative relationship is clear. *G.M.*

Correspondence, law of. The theory that whatever is true of "molecular" behavior is also true of "molar" behavior, and that a unifying principle can be found. This theory is taken over from physics. *C.D.F.*

Corresponding (retinal) points. The points in the retina which correspond to one another in both eyes, so that when images are formed on both retinas double vision (q.v.) does not occur, but a single visual image is perceived. If these points are determined geometrically by retinal coordinates, they are called coincident points or *identical (retinal) points* (q.v.). *A.H.*

Cortex cerebri. See *Cerebral cortex.*

Cortical. Pertaining to the *cortex cerebri.* In physiological terminology it denotes brain processes which occur rationally and consciously, such as thinking (q.v.), recognizing, abstracting, calculating, etc., in contrast to subcortical brain processes which occur unconsciously. *E.D.*

Cortical blindness. See *Agnosia.*

Cortical deafness. This term is not much employed nowadays and once referred to a form of receptive aphasia in which sounds were heard but words could not be identified or understood. *B.B.*

Cortical type. A term introduced by Kraus (1919) for a type of person in whom the intellect is most prominent and whose actions are controlled by the cortex.

Bibliography: **Kraus, F.:** Allgemeine und spezielle Pathologie der Person (2 vols). Leipzig, 1919–26.

W.K.

Corticosteroids. A group of steroid hormones, more than thirty in number, which—with the exception of aldosterone—are stimulated by the secretion of ACTH, and are formed in the adrenal cortex; in contrast to the hormones produced in the adrenal medulla they are essential to life because of their action on the carbohydrate, fat and mineral metabolic functions. The following are distinguished: (*a*) mineral corticoids (e.g. aldosterone, q.v.; 11-desoxycortisone; 11-desoxycorticosterone), which act on renal tubules and cause water and Na retention; (*b*) glucocorticoids, with an extensive effect on carbohydrate and sugar metabolism (e.g. cortisone, q.v., hydrocortisone, q.v., 11-dehydrocorticosterone [corticosterone]); (*c*) hormones concerned with protein metabolism or androgenic cortical hormones (e.g. androsterone, androstenedione) which in addition to promoting protein formation influence sexual behavior. Over- (or under-) activity of the adrenal cortex leads to serious physical and mental disorders (e.g. Addison's disease with under-activity; Cushing's disease and the adreno-genital syndrome, with over-activity). The secretion of corticosteroids varies distinctly according to the time of day (maximum in the early morning, minimum around midnight). In man, about 15–30 mg. are produced each day. Since 1950, numerous synthetic corticosteroids have been available, the most important being prednisone (Deltra, Deltasone), prednisolone (Delta Cortef, Meticortelone) and dexamethasone (Decadron, Deronil). Corticosteroids play an important part in psychology in demonstrating the emotional effect of stress stimuli; hydrocortisone (q.v.) in particular is a sensitive indicator of emotional tension. It has not yet been proved whether, as Selye maintains, there is a greater non-specific secretion of corticosteroids under all kinds of stress (physical or mental).

Bibliography: Currie, A. R., Symington, T. & Grant, J. K. (Eds): The human adrenal cortex. Baltimore, 1962. **Dorfman, R. I. & Ungar, F.**: Metabolism of steroid hormones. New York, 1965. **Eisenstein, A. B.** (Ed.): The adrenal cortex. London, 1967. **Hübner, H. J. & Staib, W. H.**: Biochemie der Nebennierenrindenhormone. Stuttgart, 1965. **Mason, J. W.**: A review of psychoendocrine research on the pituitary-adrenal cortical system. Psychosom. Med., 1968, *30*, 576–607. **Murphy, B. E. P.**: The determination of plasma levels of corticoids and their diagnostic significance. In: **Bajusz, E.** (Ed.): An introduction to clinical neuroendocrinology. Basle, 1967. **Rubin, R. T.**: Adrenal cortical activity in pathological emotional states: A review. Amer. J. Psychiat., 1966, *123*, 387–400. See also *Cortisone*.

W.J.

Corticosterone. A hormone secreted by the adrenal cortex (see *Corticosteroids*), serving (as glucocorticoid) to regulate the carbohydrate metabolism. *W.J.*

Corticotrop(h)ine. See *ACTH*.

Corticotrop(h)ic hormone. See *ACTH*.

Cortisol. See *Hydrocortisone*.

Cortisone. A natural hormone (q.v.) of the adrenal cortex and prototype of the glucocorticoids (see *Corticosteroids*). Used (now less often) in the treatment of a number of diseases (e.g. Addison's disease, arthritis, allergies, inflammations). ACTH, or adrenocorticotrophic hormone (q.v.), stimulates the production of cortisone. Exogenous administration of cortisone blocks its natural production in the body. Psychological effects correspond closely to those of ACTH. It has been the object of only a few psychological investigations. There are no certain effects on performance and subjective condition when taken in physiological doses. Nor is there any statistical confirmation of euphoric reactions reported in patients.

Bibliography: Delay, J. *et al.*: Etude expérimentale des modifications psychologiques produites par les traitments à l'ACTH et la cortisone. Encéphale, 1952, *41*, 393–406. **Kaiser, H.**: Cortisonderivate in Klinik und Praxis. Stuttgart, 1968. **Lidz, T.,** *et al.*: Effects of ACTH and cortisone on mood and mentation. Psychosom. Med., 1953, *14*, 363–77. *W.J.*

Couéism. A method of psychotherapy by *autosuggestion* employed by E. Coué. The patient is first taught the effects of autosuggestion by physical exercises such as telling himself he is falling backwards, or that he is unable to release his clasped fingers. He is then instructed to repeat to himself frequently every day a suggestion relating to his symptoms or affect, e.g. that he is beginning to feel much better. *G.D.W.*

Counseling. An interpersonal relationship in which one person (the counselor) attempts to help another (the counselee) to understand and cope with his problems in the areas of education, vocation, family relationships, and so on. The term covers a wide range of procedures, including the giving of advice and encouragement, providing information concerning available opportunities, and the interpretation of test results. Counseling differs from psychotherapy in that it is usually applied to help "normals" rather than patients, although the two processes merge imperceptibly on many occasions, as in C. Rogers' *Client-centered therapy* (q.v.). In *non-directive counseling* the counselor merely "lends a friendly ear" to the counselee, perhaps reflecting his thoughts and feelings, and detailing the alternative forms of behavior. A *directive* counselor, on the other hand, is likely to lead the conversation and to try to persuade the counselee (or client) to behave in certain prescribed ways. *G.D.W.*

Coupling (in genes, q.v.). Some hereditary factors are in most cases coupled when they are transmitted from the parents to their offspring. This is explained by the chromosome theory of heredity: coupled genes are to be found in the same chromosome (q.v.) which is generally transmitted as a whole so that only those maternal and paternal genes can combine freely which are located in different chromosomes. Coupling can be interrupted by crossing-over (q.v.). *H.S.*

Courtship behavior. Modes of expression during pairing and the prelude to mating behavior and copulation (q.v.). Courtship includes ritual behaviors such as mating dances and mating song. At this time strikingly showy features are displayed. It cannot always be clearly distinguished from aggressive *displays* (q.v.), etc. Courtship may have numerous functions. It is: (*a*) an indication of presence, serves (i) to attract the sexual partner, (ii) to ward off rivals; it aids recognition of: (*b*) the identity of species (courtship rituals of closely related species in the same location are often different), and (*c*) readiness to pair; it inhibits (*d*) non-sexual activities (especially aggression); it reinforces (*e*) intimacy between mates; and serves especially to (*f*) stimulate the individual, the partner, and synchronization for the act of copulation. That mating fits into a social framework can be seen in subsidiary functions of courtship such as feeding the mate, indicating the nest, and so on.

Bibliography: Bastock, M.: Courtship. London, 1967.

R.A.S.

Counterprobability is a term used in statistical hypothesis testing. It denotes the probability α of erroneous rejection of the null hypothesis in the case of a (significant) deviation of a sample result from the random expectation. *W.H.B.*

Couvade. A custom according to which the father of a child assumes the mother's role by taking to his bed immediately after the birth, while the mother quickly returns to her usual work. This custom has survived longest in southern France (Béarn) and among the Basques (in Europe at least). The couvade often developed from the ceremony which lent a magic emphasis to fatherhood at the transition from a matrilinear (see *Matriarchate*) to a patrilinear society. In general it reflects the structural principles of exchange and social symmetry demonstrated by Lévi-Strauss (1965) in the rules of exogamy. The man and woman "perform" and suffer the birth in equal measure.

Bibliography: **Lévi-Strauss, C.:** The elementary structures of kinship. New York, 1965. **Id.:** The savage mind. London & New York, 1966. *W.Sc.*

Covariance. The measurement of the tendency of two series to vary concomitantly. Given two normalized series, $x_1, x_2, \ldots x_n$ and $y_1, y_2, \ldots y_n$, their covariance $= \sum_{i=1}^{n} (x_i y_i)/n$. *C.D.F.*

Covariance analysis. An extension of the method of analysis of variance: (*a*) in order to reduce experimental error, (*b*) in order to analyze the effect of independent variables on the covariance of two dependent variables. E.g., the use of covariance analysis is necessary when the effect of two teaching methods on retention performance has to be studied in two groups of differing intelligence, since it can be assumed that intelligence and retention performance are not independent of one another. See *Variance, analysis of*. *G.M.*

Covariant phenomenon. An illusion of depth perception first described by Jaensch. Three threads are hung in front of the observer in a frontal parallel plane. If one outer thread is moved backward and forward the middle appears to move in the opposite direction forward and backward. *C.D.F.*

Covariation. The concomitant variation between two or more characteristics (variables). The prerequisite for determining statistical dependence or relation. See *Covariance*. *G.M.*

Covert response. Behavior which cannot be directly established by an observer but must be concluded from measurement values, from the observation of the further behavior of the subject, or from the verbal report obtained by the introspection (q.v.) of the subject. The distinction between *covert* and *overt* (q.v.) responses was at first strongly stressed by behaviorism in deposing the traditional psychology of consciousness, but was finally attenuated by the admission of verbal answers as equally objective data. In programmed instruction (q.v.) the purely mental response procedure offers the advantage of a generally shorter learning period over overt response procedure. *L.J.I.*

Craniology. See *Phrenology*.

Creative synthesis. Apperception (q.v.): the combination of elements into a significant whole in, e.g., conceptualization.

Creativity. The ability to see new relationships, to produce unusual ideas and to deviate from traditional patterns of thinking. One of the prime objects of psychological research is the analysis of creative personality, the creative process, and the products of the creative process, together with the problem of how to encourage creativity. See *Abilities; Personality*.

Bibliography: Gruber, H. E. *et al.*: Contemporary approaches to creative thinking. New York, 1962. **Mooney, R. L. & Razik, T. A.** (Eds): Explorations in creativity. Chicago, 1967. **Taylor, C. W. & Barron, F.:** Scientific creativity: its recognition and development. New York, 1963. **Taylor, C. W.** (Ed.): Creativity: progress and potential. New York, 1964. **Vernon, P. E.** (Ed.): Creativity: selected readings. Harmondsworth, 1970. *G.K.*

Creativity tests. Experiments to measure creativity accurately have been conducted since 1930 (C. Spearman); significant studies however have only been made in recent years (C. W. Taylor, J. P. Guilford). In particular it was Guilford's concept of divergent (q.v.) thinking which led to the construction of serviceable tests. What is required in these tests is essentially the production of as large a number of answers as possible (e.g. as many suitable titles as possible have to be found for some story).

Bibliography: Goldman, R. J.: The Minnesota tests of creative thinking. Educ. Res. 1964, *7*, 3–14. **Guilford, J. P.:** The nature of human intelligence. New York, 1967. **Wilson, R. C., Guilford, J. P. *et al.*:** A factor-analytical study of creative thinking abilities. Psychometrika, 1954, *19*, 297–311. *G.L.*

Credibility (syn. *Trustworthiness*). In the legal sense, a deposition (testimony) is evidence that helps a court (or other body) to establish the facts of a case. The court is obliged to take all depositions into account in arriving at its judgment, and to check each of them for credibility, or probable compatibility with the true facts.

A psychologist can appraise the deposition for prosecution purposes in the light of the following criteria: (*a*) the probability of accurate *perception* of the facts (this depends on corrections of customary errors of perception and estimation, e.g. of time, speed, and number), and the probability of *distortion*, under the influence of strong emotion, of the events perceived; (*b*) the probability of accurate *retention* of remembered incidents, i.e. the distinction between original and subsequent events, between personal experience and the influence of suggestion; (*c*) the *ability to reproduce* the facts accurately. The ability to give testimony depends upon the whole personality of the person concerned. This calls for careful appraisal, and special account has to be taken of any evidence of character traits that have a special bearing on the deposition made. Accuracy of perception is influenced by a person's intellectual capacity, his state of mind at the time of the act, and motivation control (selectivity of perception). Similar factors also influence suggestibility. Investigation of the possible motivation that might lead to a deposition lacking in credibility helps psychologists to judge whether a statement is credible.

The methods used in assessing credibility are extremely problematic. Agreement has not yet been reached as to the utility of general criteria for its assessment. Most psychologists are trying to establish such criteria and apply them. Some, however, consider that each case is too specific to admit of such general criteria. If, in judicial proceedings, only credibility with respect to a specific case is taken as significant, general credibility, i.e. credibility established in the light of general criteria, would seem to be of doubtful immediate utility.

Bibliography: Abercrombie, M. L. Johnson: The anatomy of judgment. London, 1967. **Britt, S. H.:** The rules of evidence: an empirical study in psychology and law. Cornell Law Quart., 1940, *25*, 556–80.

O. Topič

Crespi effect. Some increment in learning which appears suddenly and intensely and which is disproportionate to the increased reinforcement (q.v.).

Bibliography: Crespi, L. P.: Quantitative variation of incentive and performance in the white rat. Amer. J. Psychol., 1942, *55*, 467–517.

K.E.P.

Cretinism (*Congenital myxedema*). A congenital condition in which there is a complete absence or defective functioning of the thyroid gland (see *Hypofunction*) of unknown causation. An iodine deficiency, endogenous influences or a goitrous mother have been suggested as responsible for fetal damage in these cases. Cretinism frequently occurs in districts where goiter is endemic. The characteristic features of the cretin are stunted physical growth, disturbances in the development of the central nervous system, the skeleton and the skin, and severe subnormality of varying intensity, and a retardation of metabolism. The cretin presents a bloated appearance with a lack of expression; the nose is flat, the hair thick and bristly, the tongue large, and the fingers short; he is hard of hearing and may even be deaf; speech is retarded; there may be constipation and occasionally goiter. The disease can be prevented by prophylactic iodine therapy of expectant mothers and young babies in districts where goiter is prevalent. *E.D.*

Criminality. The tendency to exhibit behavior which is contrary to the criminal law; more usually, repeated or persistent commission of criminal offences. The utility of this term as a description of individuals has been questioned on the ground that it defines too heterogeneous a class of people (Wootton, 1959) and that—because the scope and limits of the criminal law vary from time to time and from place to place—it entails an arbitrary and psychologically-irrelevant distinction between criminal acts and other forms of deviant social behavior (Mannheim, 1962). Many actions which fall within the scope of the criminal law escape notice, or cannot be traced to their authors; it follows that the group of persons identified as criminals by reason of conviction in the courts inevitably reflects the biases inherent in police practice (Walker, 1965). These limitations upon the empirical definition of criminality constitute a major obstacle to attempts to develop systematic explanations for these forms of deviant social behavior.

The majority of recorded crimes are offenses against property—mainly thefts of various kinds, but also frauds, embezzlement and robbery (i.e. theft involving personal violence or threat). Assaults, murders, crimes of wounding, and sexual offenses are much less frequent, at least in contemporary Western countries. With the two exceptions of shoplifting and offenses related to prostitution, crime is overwhelmingly a male matter; the ratio of the sexes in respect of criminal convictions in Britain being about six to one, a figure typical of Western states. Crime is also predominantly an activity of the young; the peak incidence of convictions tends to occur a little before the age of leaving school, although there is some evidence that future recidivists start earlier than those offenders whose criminal histories are comparatively brief (Walker, 1965). On the whole (and taking into account the immense differences in the frequency of offenses of different kinds), recidivists are seldom specialists, except for those who commit frauds and crimes of breaking-and-entering; most of those with several convictions have committed crimes of more than one kind (Hammond & Chayen, 1963).

1. *Classical theories of criminality.* The early development of criminological theory was dominated by three schools of thought which have exerted considerable influence upon contemporary research. The positivist and crimino-biological schools (Mannheim, 1965) stressed the belief that persistent criminals were atavistic deviants in the process of man's evolution; this view prompted a search for physical signs of primitivism, and an interest in constitutional correlates of criminality which has its modern counterpart in the study of physique and chromosomal endowment in persistent offenders. A second stream of research has concentrated upon the intellectual characteristics of offenders: the imprudent, unprofitable nature of much crime gave rise to the belief that most criminals were too stupid to understand the consequences of their actions. It now appears that early estimates of the incidence of subnormality in criminal populations were much too high (Woodward, 1955), but the investigation of cognitive characteristics of offenders continues to be an important field of research. The third major source of criminological ideas has been psychoanalysis, whose influence is apparent in two respects. First, it has drawn attention to the irrational nature of much criminal behavior. Freud (1915) described the phenomenon of "criminality from a sense of guilt"—that is, offenses committed in order to provoke punishment which will alleviate guilt originating in the Oedipus complex. The notion that intra-psychic conflicts may be responsible for antisocial actions was further developed by Alexander & Staub (1929) and Friedlander (1947). Contemporary psychoanalytic theory assigns great importance to early parent-child relationships in the development of moral behavior; this has stimulated interest in the childhood experiences of criminals and delinquents (Bowlby, 1946; Glueck & Glueck, 1956).

2. *Contemporary developments.* Central to current thinking in relation to criminality is a learning-theory model, "passive avoidance conditioning". Early attempts to explain criminality in terms of learning emphasized the acquisition of criminal techniques or habits: e.g. Sutherland's principle of differential association (Sutherland & Cressey, 1955). But this is now the central problem; few crimes demand skills beyond the repertoire of most people. What is necessary is to show how normal individuals learn to inhibit socially-proscribed acts which they are able and motivated to perform, and to explain why this learning process is sometimes ineffective. Mowrer (1960a) suggested that the appropriate paradigm was that of passive avoidance conditioning; forbidden actions occurring spontaneously in childhood are punished, and (after several repetitions) these categories of behavior become associated with the aversive state induced by punishment. The contemplation of the forbidden action is thereafter sufficient to elicit resurgence of this aversive emotional state, blocking the consummatory phases of the behavioral sequence.

Mowrer's model has obvious implications for the problem of criminality. Lykken (1957) demonstrated a specific defect in the capacity to acquire conditioned avoidance responses in a group of persistent offenders ("primary sociopaths", selected according to Cleckley's criteria: see *Psychopathy*), a finding replicated by Schachter & Latané (1964). Eysenck (1964) argued that persistent criminality is usually (though not always) the consequence of an inherent unresponsiveness to conditioning procedures of all kinds which—according to his general theory of personality—is largely a function of extraversion. Thus highly-extraverted individuals will tend to become criminals unless they are subjected to particularly intense and efficient training. Whether conditionability is a general trait is still a matter of dispute; however, there is considerable experimental evidence to support Eysenck's theoretical arguments in so far as they relate to criminals.

3. *Constitutional bases of criminality.* Eysenck's theory is one of several recent contributions to criminology discourse which have revived interest in constitutional and genetic factors in the causation of criminal behavior. Several investigators of physical type (body build) have found a marked preponderance of mesomorphic physique among criminals, a discovery which compares interestingly with the known relationship between mesomorphy and extraversion (Eysenck, 1964). There have been many demonstrations of differences in autonomic functioning between those who commit crimes and those who do not (Hare, 1970), indicating the possibility of alternative explanations of the relations between physical type and criminality.

Johannes Lange (1929) furnished striking evidence for the existence of a genetic element in the causation of criminality, based upon a study of thirty pairs of twins, thirteen of which appeared to be uniovular. A number of twin studies (q.v.) conducted during the following three decades also yielded patterns which appeared to indicate the operation of a genetic mechanism, although (because identical twins tend to experience similar childhood environments) such observations present major problems of interpretation (Slater, 1953). More recently attention has been focussed upon the discovery that chromosomal anomalies occur more frequently in certain groups of criminals than in the population at large. Early studies (using the Barr method of staining for sex-chromatin) showed an excess of individuals with supernumerary *X*-chromosomes among criminal subnormal men detained in state institutions; subsequent studies, using more sophisticated methods of karotyping, seem to indicate that there is a more direct connection between extra-complementary *Y*-chromosomes and criminal tendencies, a relation which sometimes occurs as the *XXYY* pattern, so concealing the real nature of the anomaly (Casey *et al.*, 1966). These observations are peculiarly difficult to interpret; although some writers (such as Slater) offer an explanation in terms of the relation between male sexuality and disposition to commit crimes, others argue that subclinical cortical damage may be a crucial link in the connection (see Trasler, 1970, for references).

4. *Techniques of socialization.* The Mowrer model (like classical psychoanalysis) has directed interest to the interaction of parents and children in the process of socialization (that is, the acquisition of appropriate avoidance responses). There is undoubtedly some connection between family breakdown (the interruption of parent-child interaction) and delinquency, but whether this is to be attributed to "maternal deprivation" (as Bowlby would suggest), to the absence of the father at a critical period of the child's development (Grygier *et al.*, 1969), or merely to suspension of the socialization process, is not clear.

The avoidance-conditioning model has extensive implications concerning the sources of inefficiency in parental techniques for the training of children. The characteristics of conditioning procedures developed in the laboratory—the systematic pairing of conditional and unconditional stimuli, the phenomena of generalization, transfer and discrimination learning—have direct counterparts in the parameters of child-training methods, and constitute promising links between this psychological paradigm and the substantial body of sociological observations of patterns of parental behavior. The conjunction of these apparently disparate areas of criminological science has suggested a number of hypotheses which may help to explain consistent differences between socio-economic classes in the incidence of criminality; they may also have implications for long-term trends in the pattern and frequency of criminal behavior (Trasler, 1971).

In recent years increasing attention has been devoted to the role of language in mediating avoidance conditioning. It is clear that the efficiency of this process (in the Mowrer-Eysenck formulation) depends upon generalization from a few examples of punished wrongdoing, occurring spontaneously in childhood, to an extensive range of adult behaviors which have few features in common with the child analogue (Mowrer, 1960b). It is also apparent that the high resistance to extinction exhibited by social avoidance responses relies upon very effective discrimination cues. Bernstein argues that it is possible to distinguish at least two styles of language employed between parents and child, one of which ("elaborated code") is much better adapted to the task of securing efficient avoidance training than the other (termed "restricted code", q.v.). Ability to make use of the more sophisticated style of verbal interaction is a function of education, and is consequently correlated with the socio-economic status of the parents, an observation which may be relevant to the high incidence of delinquency among children of lower-class families (Lawton, 1968).

Although it is now established that the distribution of intelligence (using non-verbal tests) among criminals is not significantly different from that in the population as a whole, the incidence of serious school failure is very high in delinquent groups, apparently because of a specific handicap in the use of verbal and other symbols (Prentice & Kelly, 1963; Graham & Kamano, 1958). This is consistent with the contention that grasp of language is a condition of effective social avoidance training, and points to the importance of further investigation of the cognitive characteristics of persistent offenders (Trasler, 1971; Hare, 1970).

Contemporary developments in the theory of criminality thus reflect the integration of several major lines of inquiry, each of which (as it happens) has its roots in classical criminology.

Bibliography: **Alexander, F. & Staub, H.:** Der Verbrecher und seine Richter. Vienna, 1929. **Bowlby, J.:** Forty-four juvenile thieves. London, 1946. **Casey, M. D., Blank, C. E., Street, D. R. K., Segall, L. J., McDougall, J. H., McGrath, P. J. & Skinner, J. L.:** YY chromosomes and antisocial behaviour. Lancet, 1966, 859–60. **Eysenck, H. J.:** Crime and personality. London, 1964. **Freud, S.:** Some character-types met with in psycho-analytic work. Imago, Vol. 4, 1915. **Friedlander, K.:** The psycho-analytical approach to juvenile delinquency. London, 1947. **Glueck, S. & Glueck, E.** Physique and delinquency. New York, 1956. **Graham, E. E. & Kamano, D.:** Reading failure as a factor in the WAIS subtest patterns of youthful offenders. J. clin. Psychol. 1958, *14*, 302–5. **Grygier, T., Chesley, J. & Tuters, E. W.:** Parental deprivation: a study of delinquent children. Brit. J. Criminol., 1969, *9*, 209–53. **Hammond, W. H. & Chayen, E.:** Persistent criminals. London, 1963. **Hare, R. D.:** Psychopathy—theory and research. New York, 1970. **Lange, J.:** Verbrechen als Schicksal. Leipzig, 1929. **Lawton, D.:** Social class, language and education. London, 1968. **Lykken, D. T.:** A study of anxiety in the sociopathic personality. J. abnorm. soc. Psychol., 1957, *55*, 6–10. **Mannheim, H.:** The study of crime. In: **Welford, A. T.** (Ed.): Society. London, 1962. **Id.:** Comparative criminology. London, 1965. **Mowrer, O. H.:** Learning theory and behavior. New York, 1960a. **Id.:** Learning theory and the symbolic processes. New York, 1960b. **Prentice, N. M. & Kelly, F. J.:** Intelligence and delinquency—a reconsideration. J. soc. Psychol., 1963, *60*, 327–37. **Schachter, S. & Latané, B.:** Crime, cognition and the autonomic nervous system. In: **Jones, M. R.** (Ed.): Nebraska symposium on motivation. Lincoln, 1964. **Slater, E.:** Psychotic and neurotic illness in twins London, 1953. **Sutherland, E. H. & Cressey, D. R.:** Principles of criminology. Chicago, 1955. **Trasler,**

G. B.: The explanation of criminality. London, 1962. **Id.**: Criminal behaviour. In: **Eysenck, H. J.** (Ed.): Handbook of abnormal psychology. London, ²1971. **Walker, N. D.**: Crime and punishment in Britain. Edinburgh, 1965. **Woodward, W. M.**: Low intelligence and delinquency. London, 1955. **Wootton, B.**: Social science and social pathology. London, 1959.

G. B. Trasler

Criminal psychology. Criminal psychology is concerned with the causes of criminality (q.v.), and tries to discover the factors which make an individual a criminal. Criminal psychology is to be distinguished from forensic psychology (q.v.), which is a branch of applied psychology, and comprises two directions of research, one orientated to constitutional psychology, and the other to social psychology.

Bibliography: Conger, J. J. & Miller, W. C.: Personality, social class and delinquency. New York, London & Sydney, 1966. **Glueck, S. & Glueck, E.**: Five hundred criminal careers. New York, 1930. **Lombroso, C.**: Crime, its causes and remedies. Boston, 1911. **Rosebuck, J. B.**: Criminal typology. Springfield, Ill., 1967.

F.M.

Criminology. There is only general agreement that criminology is criminal etiology, i.e. that it deals with the causes or factors producing crime. The most important areas of criminology are: (*a*) the observation, description, analysis and classification of crimes and criminals (criminal sociology); (*b*) research into factors producing crime which can be traced back to the organism, or to personality factors (criminal biology and psychology); (*c*) research into the significance of hereditary factors for criminality (criminological research into heredity); (*d*) the prognostication of criminality and recidivism (prognostic research); (*e*) victimology; (*f*) the sociological and sociopsychological study of prison communities. All these tasks are shared by different branches of empirical science: sociology, psychology, psychiatry, and the medical sciences adjacent to criminology; legal sociology, psychology and psychiatry. In addition to the above, further aspects of criminology studied in the U.S.A. are *prophylaxis* and *penology*.

H.M.

Crisis. The term came into psychology from medicine; Hippocrates used it for the sudden cessation of a state which was gravely endangering life (in contrast to the slow *lysis*). Analogously, a crisis is thought of as being a dramatic decision, or coming to terms with mental conflicts.

W.Sc.

Criterion. 1. A *decisive* characteristic with which other characteristics are compared. A criterion (e.g. in a validity test) is an indisputable or undisputed measurement of what a test is required to measure. 2. *Critical values* are said to be criteria when, after they have been reached or exceeded, an alternative decision changes into its opposite (e.g. passing an examination—not passing it).

Criterion group: a reference group with known characteristics used to test validity.

G.M.

Critical flicker frequency; critical flicker fusion. The rate at which the flicker, or rapid change in perception resulting from change in the stimulus, is replaced by a smooth fusion. See *Flicker photometry*.

Critical ratio. The ratio of a difference between two statistics, or of a statistic, to the *standard error* (q.v.) of that difference, or of that statistic.

Critical theory (Ger. *Kritische Theorie*). The name applied to the body of theory emanating from the Frankfurt school of sociology (the Institut für Sozialforschung), and mainly associated with T. W. Adorno, Max Horkheimer, Herbert Marcuse and, in recent years, Jürgen Habermas. Critical theory combines insights of Marxist and Freudian thought in its examinations of the various ways in which "interest" affects knowing, and has produced valuable studies of prejudice in areas ranging from family and education to epistemology, the best known of which in the English-speaking world is *The Authoritarian Personality*. Recently, critical theorists have concerned themselves with the attempts of (positivistic) scientists to establish an intersubjectively binding language of factual statement in the social sciences.

Bibliography: Adorno, T. W. *et al.*: The authoritarian personality. New York, 1950. **Habermas, J.:** Erkenntnis und Interesse. Frankfurt, 1968. **Horkheimer, M. & Adorno, T. W.:** Dialectic of enlightenment. New York, 1972. **Wellmer, A.:** Critical theory of society. New York, 1971.

J.C.

Criticism, compulsive. An irresistible yet subjectively unconscious urge to find fault with (almost) everything. It is often an expression of inner discontent; there is an absence of self-criticism in the affected subject.

H.J.A.

Cross-cultural studies. The comparison and combination of certain cultures to see if similar behavior in different environments occurs under certain common conditions; or to see if certain results are produced by certain emphases (e.g. in learning or the use of folk remedies) that do not occur but might be valuable in the base culture; and so on. The field of research is vast and ranges from pioneering general studies (e.g. Mead, 1937) to cross-cultural studies of alcohol use (e.g. Child, Bacon & Barry, 1965). See *Anthropology; Social psychology.*

Bibliography: Child, I. L., Bacon, M. K. & Barry, H A cross-cultural study of drinking. Quart. J. Stud. Alc., 1965, Supp. 3. **Mead, M.** (Ed.): Cooperation and competition among primitive peoples. New York, 1937.

J.G.

Crossing-over. An "exchange of factors", or exchange of segments of two of the four homologous chromatids during meiosis, i.e. the reductive division of a diploid cell, part of which process is the splitting of each chromosome (q.v.) into two chromatids.

Bibliography: Loewy, A. G. & Siekeritz, P.: Cell structure and function. New York, 1969. **Sinnott, E. W.** *et al.*: Principles of genetics. New York & London, [5]1958.

I.M.D.

Cross-section(al) method (syn. *Cross-section(al) investigation*). In contrast to the longitudinal method (q.v.), a means of investigating a large number of variables as they are found at a given period of time.

Crowd behavior. Crowd psychology (mass psychology) was one of the first areas of debate and investigation in social psychology, especially in France (Le Bon, 1895; Tarde, 1890). The development of interest in group dynamics, however, eventually took precedence. Recently, various types of event (demonstrations and conventions among the young, "violent" strikes, disasters—whether technical or military, and so on) have reawakened interest in crowd studies. If we define a "*small group*" as a collection of individuals who are "face to face", we may think of a *crowd* as a collectivity whose members are "side by side": i.e. unorganized, temporary, irregular assemblies featuring a certain activity (which serves to distinguish them from *aggregations*, or collections of people without a common purpose, and "passive" public assemblies or totalities, e.g. *audiences*). The activity in question is categorized according to purpose and outcome: aggression (riots, lynchings), appropriation (occupation of buildings or localities, looting), avoidance or flight (reactions to disasters), and "expression" and play (festivals). Recent research (e.g. Cantril, R. Brown) is still more or less indebted for initial inspiration to Le Bon's descriptive schema (homogeneity of behavior and attitudes in crowds; the emotivity and irrationality which inspire them), and retains his hypothesis of unconscious tendencies freed from a certain form of social control in the anonymous context of the crowd (a point developed later by Freud), though of course it rejects

Le Bon's theory of a "spirit of the race" giving rise to the "crowd soul", or "collective mind". Nowadays research is directed toward explaining how the absence of any regulative interaction between individuals in such an assembly produces in them an illusion of power and of "universality": a kind of contagion allowing a transition to action and a collective "leveling" of manifest behaviors on the basis of a relative similarity of latent predispositions and, ultimately, of processes of emotional fusion and leader-identification. Analyses are also made of the various degrees of "implication" of the individual in the crowd, which can differ considerably according to personality and the occasion. See *Le Bon, G.*

Bibliography: Brown, R.: Social psychology. New York, 1965. **Cantril, H.:** The psychology of social movements. New York, 1941. **Id.:** The pattern of human concerns. New Brunswick, N.J., 1965. **Le Bon, G.:** La psychologie des foules. Paris, 1895. **Sprott, W. J. H.:** Human groups. Harmondsworth, 1958. **Tarde, G.:** Les lois de l'imitation. Paris, 1890. **Id.:** L'Opinion de la foule. Paris, 1901. *F. Jodelet*

Crude score (syn. *Raw score*). In contrast to a *derived score*, an original, statistically unanalyzed or transformed score, or observational value.

Cryptesthesia. An assumed hyperacuity of the senses sometimes invoked as an explanation of alleged ESP (q.v.). *J.B.*

Cryptomnesia. Recall without recognition. A buried memory for some fact; sometimes invoked to explain an apparent paranormal awareness. *J.B.*

Cryptorchism. The failure or retardation of descent of one or both testes into the scrotum; instead, they remain in the body cavity or in the inguinal canal. For sperm to be produced normally and to make procreation possible, the testes must descend into the scrotum before puberty, or there is a danger of malignant degeneration. If descent has not occurred at puberty, hormone therapy is usually necessary, though surgery may be recommended. Mental disturbance must be avoided, e.g. by careful explanation of the condition and treatment. *K.-D.N.G.*

Cue appreciation, recognition. See *Sign learning.*

Culpability. See *Conscience; Guilt.*

Cult. In modern cultural anthropology (q.v.), a cult or rite is regarded as an activity—as distinct from a myth, which summarizes and interprets the spiritual or intellectual content of cults. Myth and cult are inseparably linked. After some years of religious-phenomenological analysis of "primitive" cults (Jensen, 1960), attention is now being devoted to their (group) psychotherapeutic function.

Bibliography: Durkheim, E.: The elementary forms of the religious life. London, 1915. **Eliade, M.:** Patterns in comparative religion. London & New York, 1958. **Jensen, A. E.:** Mythos und K. bei Naturvölkern. Wiesbaden, 1960. **Schmidbauer, W.:** Psychohygienische und (gruppen)psychotherapeutische Aspekte "primitiver" Riten. Jb. Psychol. Psychother, med. Anthropol. 1970, *18*, 238–57.

W.Sc.

Cultural anthropology. 1. Whereas *ethnology* (q.v.) is chiefly concerned with the analysis of so-called "primitive" societies, cultural anthropology uses comparative methods to study intercultural possibilities in order to establish typical conceivable patterns of human behavior, both individual and social. It works in close alignment with ethnology (see *Ethnopsychology*) and social psychology on the one hand, and with comparative psychology (q.v.) (research into animal, and especially primate behavior), on the other hand. From the methodological point of view, this comparative approach provides answers to questions which cannot be studied experimentally; it was on such grounds that W. Wundt based his somewhat too extensive separation of experimental from ethnological psychology (see *Folk psychology*). *W.Sc.*

2. In the sense of *cultural sociology*, cultural anthropology is concerned with the analysis of expectations, norms and symbols, the ways in which they are passed from generation to generation (see *Socialization*), and their effects on the structuring of individual existence and the shaping of (individual) life styles. The last is the particular study of cultural anthropology and the psychology of culture in a narrower sense. See *Social anthropology; Culture, psychology of.*

Bibliography: Kroeber, A. L.: The nature of culture. Chicago, Ill., 1952. **Malinowski, B.:** A scientific theory of culture. Chapel Hill, N.C., 1944. **Mühlmann, W. E. & Müller, E. W.** (Eds): Kulturanthropologie. Cologne & Berlin, 1966. **Znaniecki, F.:** Cultural sciences. Urbana, Ill., 1952. *W.D.F.*

Cultural determinants. Factors, mostly norms and ideals, with a unifying influence which determine events and actions for groups of people (such as ways of perceiving, thinking and acting) but also control diversity and differentiation (e.g. the distribution of roles, and their mutual adjustment and complementation as the case may be). Language (q.v.) is one of the most important cultural determinants.

Bibliography: Child, I. L.: Personality in culture. In: **Borgatta, E. F. & Lambert, W. W.** (Eds): Handbook of personality theory and research. Chicago, 1968, 82–145. *M.A.*

Cultural lag. A term introduced in connection with cultural change and with the analysis of disturbances of an existing cultural system (e.g. by industrialization); it indicates a falling-behind, or a period of time between the point when some technological goal is reached and the point when the attainment of that goal has been absorbed by society. In general, the reason is a discrepancy between set norms and the state of society at the time when the norms are accepted. It is assumed that social planning will help to avoid such discrepancies, or reduce the intervals of time. *W.D.F.*

Cultural neurosis. Although neuroses (q.v.) are ubiquitous, in their genesis they are often structurally related to the cultural medium in which they make their appearance. At present, one hears much about "neuroses" developing in contemporary society and it is implied that the same dynamics are active as in neuroses proper. This phenomenon might lead to the conclusion that the anxiety-ridden constitution of man is more manifest now than at other times. The secularization of modern life, the transformation of sex into merchandise, and the toleration of aggressiveness are some of the underlying problems. See *Aggression; Alienation.*

Bibliography: Horkheimer, M. & Adorno, T. W.: The dialectic of enlightenment. New York, 1972. **Marcuse, H.:** One dimensional man. Boston, 1964.

J.-L.I.

Cultural puberty. A distinction is made between *primitive* puberty and *cultural* puberty according to the significance of the sexual drive. Whereas the former refers to the uninhibited, the latter corresponds to the inhibited form. Spiritual, inward values are prominent and their acquisition is preferred to sexual interests. Young people look for a purpose in life. Intellectual affinity and common interests determine friendships with the opposite sex.

Bibliography: Busemann, A.: Pädagogische Jugendkunde. Frankfurt, 1953. *M.Sa.*

Cultural science psychology. See *Geisteswissenschaftliche Psychologie.*

Culture-free intelligence tests. Constructed at the Institute of Personality and Ability Testing under the direction of R. B. Cattell. They have to be as independent *as possible* of any cultural influences, and therefore contain only exercises with figures (series, classification, matrices and overlapping figures).

Bibliography: Cattell, R. B. & Cattell, A. K. S.: IPAT Culture Free Intelligence Test. Inst. Pers. Abil. Test. Champain, Ill., 1950–59. *R.M.*

Culture, psychology of. Founded by W. Dilthey; a mode of interpreting individual areas of culture in the past or present by *understanding* them. The tasks of the psychology of culture have now to a large extent been taken over by cultural anthropology (q.v.), as a comparative approach allows of much more sensitive analyses of cultural elements and biological determinants. *W.Sc.*

Cumulation. A term in statistics for a method of calculation in which every value of a distribution is added to the sum of the lower values. It occurs in the representation of frequency distributions (q.v.). *G.M.*

Cumulative frequency. A term for the sums of frequencies of a distribution which are calculated by the successive addition of score or class frequencies in order of magnitude. The total number of cases is determined up to a certain point of a distribution. A graphic representation of the arrangement is known as a *cumulative frequency curve.* *G.M.*

Cunnilingus. Oral contact with female genitals (*cunnus*), largely taboo in Jewish-Christian cultural areas. Historical tradition shows that cunnilingus was accepted in many older cultures. Ethology (q.v.) shows that oral-genital contacts are widespread among mammals. The use of cunnilingus correlates quite positively with the level of education. As a masturbation (q.v.) technique, cunnilingus in female homosexual relationships (see *Homosexuality*) is not so widespread as fellatio (q.v.) in those between males. In heterosexual relationships, cunnilingus is more often requested by the male than permitted by the female partner, by reason of the taboo.

Bibliography: Kinsey, A. *et al.*: Sexual behavior in the human female. New York, 1953. *G.L.*

Curare. A collective name for arrow-poisons (of a strychnine-like kind) obtained from plants by South- and Central-American Indians. Curare contains several alkaloids with a similar pharmacological effect. The most important substances isolated are *d*-tubocurarine and toxiferine. Numerous substances have curare-like effects and are produced semi- or wholly synthetically (e.g. gallamine) and included with curare in the group of curare-like ganglion blocking agents. Curare blocks the transmission of acetylcholine (q.v.) to the muscles (neuro-muscular junction), so that the result is muscular paralysis, and in larger doses death from cessation of breathing. Some substances related to curare are used as spasmolytics (q.v.). There are very few central and autonomic effects from curare-like substances; as they do not pass the blood-brain barrier (q.v.), the central and autonomic effects which have occasionally been observed are apparently conditioned by a reduction in the adrenalin released in the adrenal medulla and by the release of histamine (q.v.). *D*-tubocurarine is used in experimental research on the emotions to explore the relationship between proprioceptive feedback and emotion, especially anxiety. Doses of *d*-tubocurarine reduce anxiety under aversive stimuli.

Bibliography: Davison, G. C.: Anxiety under total curarization: Implications for the role of muscular relaxation in the desensitization of neurotic fears. J. nerv. ment. dis., 1966, *143*, 443–8. **De Ruek, A. v. S.:** Curare and curare-like agents. London, 1962. **Solomon, R. L. & Turner, L. J.:** Discriminative classical conditioning in dogs paralyzed by curare can later control discriminative avoidance responses in the normal state. Psychol. Rev., 1962, *69*, 202–19. **Thomas, K. B.:** Curare: its history and usage. London, 1964. *W.J.*

Curriculum. The meaning has been widened to include nowadays the unity of the subjects taught, teaching methods and aims. Proficient research endeavors to formulate curricula which fit teaching methods to the particular exigencies of individual subjects or inter-subject aims (e.g. moral education). Nowadays curriculum planning is of increasing importance in regard to the organizational restructuring of schools and educational institutions in order to cater for varying abilities (q.v.), but at the same time to foster a spirit of democratic equality. Strategies have to be developed locally or nationally in accordance with legal requirements, dominant socio-cultural norms, national economic requirements, the distribution of intelligence in a population or area, and availability of trained teachers and counselors. See *Educational science*. *G.B.*

Curvature illusion. A class of illusions involving the misperception of curvature. An example is provided by *Hering's illusion* (q.v.), in which straight lines appear curved and by the illusion below in which the two central lines are of equal curvature, but appear to be different by contrast with their surroundings. *C.D.F.*

Curve fitting. The use of, e.g., the least-square method (q.v.) to discover the curve most appropriate to the data.

Cutaneous resistance. See *Skin resistance*.

Cutaneous sense. Cutaneous sensitivity is aroused by the stimulation of different nerve ends, or skin receptors. It allows of three modalities of cutaneous feeling: *mechanical* (pressure, vibration), *thermic*, and *pain-induced*. Sensitivity varies according to the part of the body. The hands, soles of the feet, lips and sexual organs are most sensitive; the back and buttocks least sensitive. *V.M.*

Cybernetic education covers all definitions, problems, suggested solutions and results which come under both cybernetics *and* education. It replaces holistic-intuitive methods by methods of calculation which have proved successful in the modern natural sciences; in cybernetic education, mathematical methods are used not only (as in non-cybernetic education) for statistical analyses, but for the development of workable and verifiable models. The aim of cybernetic education is to objectify teaching by the use of technical systems such as teaching machines (*cybernation*).

Cybernetic education is divided into three stages of increasing complexity. At the *first stage* the six components ("dimensions") of instruction are analyzed separately and interpreted in mathematical terms; at the *second stage* their interdependence, and at the *third stage* their dependence on the socio-cultural environment and feedback to it comprise the object of cybernetic research.

The six cybernetico-educational disciplines at the first stage (basic educational sciences) are as follows: (*a*) theory of subject-matter (information); (*b*) theory of media (in particular teaching machines and computer-assisted instruction); (*c*) psychostructural theory (see *Information, psychology of*); (*d*) sociostructural theory (programs); (*e*) theory of teaching aims; (*f*) theory of instructional algorithms. Information theory (q.v.) enables quantitative statements to be made on subject-matter and connected with learning ability. Abstract machine (automata) theory forms the cybernetic basis of the theory of media and instructional algorithms.

The second-stage disciplines are "didactic". In all, there are sixty-two possible combinations of these disciplines. They consider specific instances ("conditional fields") in the context of the six dimensions referred to above, and determine which didactic decisions are compatible with these instances in the remaining dimensions ("decision fields"). For example, the didactic method of programmed instruction (q.v.) tries to establish instructional algorithms (decision field) which will enable given information to be imparted by a given medium to a psychologically defined group of learners under the influence of certain statistically predictable sociocultural conditions, in accordance with a given target-criterion (five condition fields).

The third-stage cybernetico-educational disciplines include, e.g., educational economics, instructional organization, the history and geography of education (to be expressed in mathematical terms), and educational and futurology research based on all these concepts.

Cybernetico-educational theory has developed specific methods of programmed instruction, based on information psychology, and using computers to produce instructional algorithms. See *Instructional technology.*

Bibliography: Atkinson, R. C. & Wilson, H. A.: Computer-assisted instruction: A book of readings. New York, 1969. **Coulson, J. E.** (Ed.): Programmed learning and computer-based instruction. New York, 1962. **Frank, H.:** Kybernetische Grundlagen der Pädagogik. Baden-Baden, [2]1969. **Hickey, A. E. & Newton, J. N.:** Computer-assisted instruction: A survey of the literature. Newburyport, Mass., 1966. **Holtzman, W.** (Ed.): Computer-assisted instruction, testing and guidance. New York, 1970. **Mager, R. F.:** Preparing instructional objectives. Palo Alto, Cal., 1962. **Pask, G.:** An approach to cybernetics. London, 1961. **Smallwood, R. D.:** A decision structure for teaching machines. Cambridge, Mass., 1962. **Unwin, D. & Leedham, J.:** Aspects of educational technology. London, 1967.

H. Frank

Cybernetic organism. An information-processing system which can fulfill at least the following functions: perception, motivated operational thinking and outward-directed activity. In this sense, every adult human is a cybernetic organism. Cybernetics endeavors to construct technical simulation models of such organisms.

Bibliography: Stachowiak, H.: Denken und Erkennen im kybernetischen Modell. Heidelberg, 1965.

K.-D.G.

Cybernetics and psychology. 1. *The terms of reference of cybernetics and the interrelation of cybernetics and psychology.* Cybernetics is a *cross-sectional science* in which general laws (regularities) are developed from different individual sciences, examined, and formulated on a suitable level of abstraction. Formal means of representation have been developed for this purpose within the framework of the mathematical sciences. These enable relationships and interactions between complex systems or part-systems to be expressed. A universal characteristic of complex, highly organized systems is the ability to record, process and transmit information. In the present state of scientific development, *research into the structure and functions of data (information) processing systems* has emerged as the specific sphere of study of cybernetics. The research methods of cybernetics are directed toward the presentation and analysis of, and its research objective is, the synthesis and optimization of data-processing systems. Systems of this kind, which are treated in abstract terms in the context of cybernetics, are found in different branches of science: e.g. in physiology (receptor systems, sensorimotor coordination processes, nerve cells functioning as information storage-systems, and nerve networks); in genetics (specification of inherited information, coding and transmission of this information from one generation to another); in operational research (organization of the exchange of information within and between groups); in technological control (development of self-optimizing, technical systems which are capable of "learning"); and in communications and information (optimization of data transmission, self-adapting receiver and sign-recognition systems). One area of experimental psychology which is closely related with this subject is concerned with the analysis of cognitive structures and functions (in particular those of perception, learning, concept formation, thought and speech). These processes are specifically dependent on emotional and affective influences or on differing inner activation levels, while at the same time influencing these conditions. Precise analysis of these processes is therefore concerned with more than a mere description of their own structural laws. It relates them to problems of personality research and clinical psychology.

All the *cognitive* processes in man are very closely related to the exchange of information between the organism and its environment: the laws of perception are based on the modes of data processing by the receptor and analyzer systems; the strategies of concept formation are based on procedures of information generation and utilization (formation and testing of hypotheses). Learning processes are expressed in behavioral changes to the extent that they occur as a consequence of individual data processing; thought processes such as those involved in problem-solving are based on specific interactions between classification and transformation processes, which form a basic algorithmic structure. This applies right up to the level of heuristic processes as the potentially most effective and at the same time most dangerous strategies for the human acquisition of information. Linguistic competence (as an internal, cognitive linguistic structure) and language use (as the ability to form comprehensible sentences) are the bases of linguistic communication as the most advanced form of information exchange between living beings. To the extent that psychophysical processes are essentially processes of information acquisition and processing, they are the object of research by both experimental psychologists and cyberneticians. Research into the structure and function of such complex system-characteristics can help to enrich the theory and construction of cybernetic models; at the same time, cybernetic methods and means of representation can assist psychological research.

2. *The development of cybernetics.* The current means of representation and research in cybernetics are characterized by four independent discoveries, although cybernetics existed even before these advances: (*a*) The discovery that stable system-behavior in the presence of unpredictable causal disturbances (noise interference) can be achieved by feedback of the instantaneous error if the error value (or its dynamic pattern) is used as a correction parameter (Wiener, 1948). In technology this principle has led to the development of control theory; analogies can be drawn with biological control processes: the self-stabilization of homeostatic functions (Ashby, 1956), eye movement, the regulation of muscular tension and sensorimotor coordination are all subject to the same principle (Küpfmüller, 1959). (*b*) The discovery that the information conveyed by a signal (q.v.) can be expressed, and that information content can be measured in physical terms (Shannon & Weaver, 1949). The coding principle of information theory, the capacity of an information-conveying system (channel capacity, q.v.), and the influence of disturbances ("noise") on the reliability of recognition, are all fundamental in the characterization of the capacity of organismic receptor systems ("perceptrons") (Rosenblatt, 1958; Arkadjew & Brawermann, 1966). (*c*) The discovery that transmission structures of the type represented by nerve networks are able to maintain the reliability of recognition of *transformed* input signals or signs (McCulloch & Pitts, 1943; von Neumann, 1958). (*d*) The discovery that information-processing systems can be represented in a theoretically self-contained form with unified means (Gluschkow, 1963). This has contributed in large measure to the development of the theory of abstract automata (Starke, 1969), of higher programming and algorithmic languages, and of the simulation of problem-solving behavior (Feigenbaum & Feldmann, 1963) on computers. *Control theory, information theory, algorithm and automata theory* now constitute the fundamental disciplines of cybernetics,

and in turn lead to specific developments such as learning systems, semantic information theory, formal language theory, and artificial intelligence. All three basic disciplines have resulted in greater knowledge in experimental psychology.

3. *Application and results of cybernetic research methods in experimental psychology.* (*a*) The methods and means of presentation of control theory have been used in the analysis of highly practiced and learning-dependent, sensorimotor coordination processes (e.g. tracking; motor skills, q.v.). The basic approach may be represented thus

$$\xrightarrow[x(s)]{x(t)} \boxed{\begin{matrix} h(t) \\ H(S) \end{matrix}} \xrightarrow[y(s)]{y(t)}.$$

We assume a continuous input function $x(t)$ (on which stochastic disturbances may be superimposed), and the consequential movement $y(t)$ as the output function. We then look for the internal system-structure $h(t)$ which simulates the transmission behavior characteristic of the system under investigation:

$$h(t) = \frac{x(t)}{y(t)}.$$

It has been shown (E. S. Krendel, D. T. McRuer, etc.) that the communicative behavior characteristic of man under specific, limited input conditions can be described by the following equation:

$$A(S) = \frac{e^{-T_o(S)}(\alpha T_1 s + 1)}{(T_2 s + 1)(T_3 s + 1)} K(\sigma),$$

in which T_o is the reaction time, dependent on the input signal. T_1 are time constants, and s shows that the input and output functions are transmitted in the range of Laplace transforms. The second component of the numerator is a differential component. It describes the anticipatory content of the transfer system, or the ability of the human being to anticipate processes from specific input functions. The denominator contains two linear first-order time-elements. They describe the adaptability of the system behavior to changes in the state of the input functions. (The factor K includes non-linearities.) The same approximation is also possible if the input and output signals are stochastically disturbed. The adaptation is then formed through the performance spectra of the input and output functions. (The performance spectrum of a signal is the Fourier transform of the auto- or cross-correlational function.) This approach has been generalized and extended (Schweizer, 1968). The aim of this process is to optimize certain work or control actions. In particular it is necessary to design optimal man-machine systems (q.v.) of the kind studied in human engineering. It has been shown that if sensorimotor demands are inadequately adapted to human transfer behavior, highly-skilled individuals (e.g. pilots in supersonic aircraft simulators) show worse performance than unskilled test subjects in optimized systems. To analyze the optimal design of a man-machine system, the phase characteristic is determined and the range with good compatibility proposed to the designers for preparation of the machine system. Similar methods have also been developed for the analysis of sensorimotor learning behavior.

4. *Methods, and means of representation, of information theory* have been used primarily in the analysis of signal recognition processes, in choice reaction experiments, in processes of complex pattern identification (organismic sign recognition), and in connection with problems of language generation and linguistic communication in psychology. We may take as an example findings made in connection with recognition performance in choice reaction experiments. One basis is Shannon's (1949) measure of information. According to this assumption, the information content $I(x_i)$ of an event is inversely proportional to the logarithm (to base 2) of the probability of its occurrence:

$$I(x_i) = 1d \frac{1}{p(x_i)} = -\log_2 p(x_i).$$

The mean information content of a source X

with the elementary events (x_i) is determined by the entropy $H(X)$:

$$H(X) = -\sum_{X} p(x_i) \log_2 p(x_i).$$

It was found that the recognition time (measured in reaction times R_i) is proportional to the mean information content of a source event:

$$R_t = K \cdot H(X) + C,$$

if $H(X)$ exhausts the maximum information content of the elementary events. H_{max} (X). . . $\log_2(n)$ for all x_i values with $i = 1 \ldots n$. $O \ldots H(X) \ldots \log_2(n)$. The values between O and $\log_2(n)$ determine the redundancy R of an information source:

$$\left(R = 1 - \frac{H(X)}{\log_2(n)}\right).$$

If the information source is redundant, the recognition time is in non-linear dependence on $H(X)$. Learning processes enable the mean probability of the source events to be assimilated. Changes in the recognition times depend on expectations or attitudes formed on the basis of conditional probabilities between the symbols (or signs). They determine the reciprocal information content between the elementary events. Perception structures are formed by utilizing the redundancy between elementary events. Specific source structures (Markoff sources; syntactic information sources in which the sequence of symbols is determined by fixed rules) lead to special (inner or cognitive) recognition algorithms. They are not only found in language recognition; recognition performance related to specific concepts has a similar basic structure: an object is recognized as an element in a class if it is the vehicle of a special (learnt) association of features. The resulting association with fixed memory content seems to be the basic principle of recognition processes. The formation of perception structures, and in particular higher-level recognition processes, exhibit an extraordinary reduction in the stimuli transmitted by the senses. The filtering out of behavior-relevant environmental data is the cognitive principle for testing behavioral decisions. The statistical definition of information-content is not sufficient for its analysis. *Semantic* characteristics (i.e. the dependence of an item of information on a context and the effect of that context on behavioral attitude) and *pragmatic* characteristics (i.e. the evaluation of an item of information according to its instantaneous significance for a behavioral decision) must be drawn on to extend classical information theory, in order to make proficient predictions in regard to emotionally codetermined or achievement-motivated behaviors. Relevant research is in progress in many institutes today.

5. *The application of automata theory and algorithms* is mainly focussed on the simulation of perception-, thought- and (especially) problem-solving processes in man, and on computer simulation of these processes (see *Simulation of mental processes*). "Simulation" in the cybernetic sense means genuine experimentation with psychological data on computers. The aim is to use the results of computer programs to decide the reliability of research into laws (regularities) and performance characteristics of cognitive (mental) processes. Special importance attaches to sign-recognition algorithms, classification algorithms and problem-solving algorithms. In the simulation of sign-recognition processes we are concerned with the structural simulation of the recognition of (stochastically disturbed, or even geometrically distorted) samples. These objects must be identified as class elements on the basis of characteristic features. The basis for such identification is provided by the functional properties of organismic recognition processes. In the structure of classification algorithms we are concerned with the computer simulation of concept formation processes. Objects are assigned to specific categories on the basis of characteristic features and their association. Learning algorithms for class formation and inductive recognition algorithms have

been developed (Klix, 1971). The development of algorithms for problem-solving is becoming particularly important. These are means of recognition for analysis of the components of complex strategies for human information processing, including heuristic techniques—which are man's most sophisticated forms of data processing. Their increasing practical significance resides in the synthesis of mental performance, e.g. for the automation of production-planning processes, or for programmed instruction specifications in learning psychology.

Cybernetic disciplines (including cybernetico-psychological research) have now reached a high degree of theoretical development through progress in algebra (structural theory, category theory: Klix & Krause, 1969). They comprise means and methods of representation in control, information, and automation theory. See *Communication; Instructional technology.*

Bibliography: Arkadjew, A. G. & Brawermann, E. M.: Zeichenerkennung und maschinelles Lernen. Munich, 1966. **Ashby, W. R.:** An introduction to cybernetics. New York, 1956. **Feigenbaum, E. A. & Feldman, J.** (Eds): Computers and thought. New York, 1963. **Gluschkow, W. M.:** Theorie der abstrakten Automaten. Berlin, 1963. **Klix, F.:** Information und Verhalten. Einführung in die naturwiss. Grundlagen der Allgemeinen Psychologie. Berlin, 1971. **Id. & Krause, B.:** Zur Definition des Begriffs "Struktur", seine Eigenschaften und Darstellungsmöglichkeiten in der Experimentalpsychologie. Berlin, 1969. **Neumann, J. von:** The computer and the brain. New Haven, Conn., 1958. **Rosenblatt, F.:** The perceptron. Psychol. Rev. 1958, *65.* **Id.:** Principles of neurodynamics. New York, 1961. **Shannon, C. & Weaver, W.:** The mathematical theory of communication. Urbana, 1949. **Schweizer, G.:** Probleme und Methoden zur Untersuchung des Regelverhaltens des Menschen. Friedrichshafen, 1967. **Wiener, N.:** Cybernetics, or control and communication in the animal and the machine. New York, 1948. **Id.:** Cybernetics. New York, 1961. **Id.:** God and golem, inc. New York, 1964.

D.Klix

Cycloid. A cycloid personality is one featuring relatively marked alternations of mood within the range defined as normal.

Cyclopropane. A highly effective narcotic (q.v.), both acting and subsiding rapidly, and with parasympathicomimetic side-effects.

E.L.

Cyclothymia. Irregular alternations of elation or excitement and sadness or depression. Abnormal alternations of mood. See *Psychoses; Source traits; Traits.*

Cytoarchitecture. A term for the cytoarchitectural organization of the cerebral cortex, or the fiber lamination, cellular structure and spatial characteristics of cortical areas.

Cytoplasm. What remains of the cell (i.e. a clear solution) after removal by centrifugation of the nuclei, mitochondria and microsomes. The cytoplasm contains enzymes, sodium, potassium and phosphate ions and certain other constituents.

D

Daedaleum. A term for the simplest form of stroboscope invented by J. F. Horner. See *Stroboscope.*

Daltonism. Red-green blindness. John Dalton, the English physicist, described (1798) this defect from which he himself suffered.

Dancing language. On the basis of von Frisch's and Lindauer's theories and experiments (e.g. with a glass hive and paint-marked bees) it has been established that bees convey information regarding, e.g., distance, direction, kind of food, energy required for the flight, to one another by means of elaborately described figures or "dances", which sometimes continue in darkness within the hive. Various researchers have postulated innate and/or acquired characteristics as responsible for this communications system. It has been noted that tempo differs from race to race; one researcher (Steche) has succeeded in artificially instructing bees. Lindauer showed that bees decide where to go to found a new nest by a process of "debate" in terms of repeated inspection of various sites, and danced reports, until unanimity is reached. Haldane characterized the bees' dance as a highly ritualized intention movement, and (in Russell and Whitehead's terminology) as "a propositional function with four variables: 'There is a source of food with smell *A* at a distance *B* in direction *C* requiring *D* workers.'"

Bibliography: Chauvin, R.: Animal societies. London, 1968. **Frisch, K. von:** Der Farbensinn und Formensinn der Biene. Zool. Jahrb. Allg. Zool. Physiol., 1914, *35,* 1–188. **Id.:** Aus dem Leben der Bienen. Heidelberg, [5]1953. **Haldane, J. B. S.:** Communication in biology. In: Studies in communication. London, 1955, 29–43. **Ribbands, C. R.:** The behaviour and social life of the honey bee. London, 1950. *J.C.*

Danger-from-without situation. General term introduced by R. A. Stamm (*Behavior*, 1962, *19*, 22) for situations where a social community or its possessions are threatened. The threat may come from members of the same species, ecological competitors, predators, the sudden appearance of unfamiliar objects, loud noises, etc. The reaction to all such situations is similar. The partners close their ranks to counter the danger. They are found to move closer together, make more contact movements, and synchronize and coordinate their subsequent behavior. *R.A.S.*

Dark adaptation (syn. *Scotopic adaptation*). Adaptation of the visual system to dark surroundings; more accurately: an increase of sensitivity to light intensity when the general illumination drops from a higher to a lower level. The opposite process, when there is an increase of general illumination, is *light adaptation* (q.v.) (decrease of sensitivity to light intensity). Dark and light adaptation designate both the process of adaptation and the state of the visual system (the eyes adapted to darkness or light). When there is a sudden change from light to dark, or vice versa, all visual performance is noticeably reduced (functional blindness, glare). As dark or light adaptation increases, visual performance increases, but with the dark-adapted eye, it does not reach the same level as with the light-adapted eye (static characteristics of visual sensitivity as against dynamic characteristics). With a dark-adapted eye the ability to distinguish between colors is absent (see *Duplicity theory*). In the process of adaptation, immediate adaptation (adaptation of the cones, duration three to ten minutes) is distinguished from prolonged adaptation (adaptation of the rods which has not terminated after some hours).

Adaptation range: the range of light intensity between just-perceptible light intensities and the light density which, despite the light-adaptation time, produces glare (according to some writers, from 10^{-9} to 10 lamberts, or units of luminance). See *Glare*.

Bibliography: Bridges, C. D. B.: Bio-Chemistry of visual processes. Compreh. Biochem., 1967, *27*, 31–78. **Davson, H.** (Ed.): The eye, Vol. 2. New York & London, 1962. **Graham, C. H.** (Ed.): Vision and visual perception. New York & London, 1965, 185ff **Hamburger, F. A.:** Das Sehen in der Dämmerung. Vienna, 1949.

A.H.

Darwinism. Charles Darwin's theory of the origin of species by (means of) natural selection (1859). In the struggle for existence only those species and individuals can hold their ground whose organisms are able to adapt themselves to environmental conditions. Essential factors are considered to be the structure of the genes (conditioned also by mutation) and the ability to respond to the pressure of selection with suitable behavior. In addition, the phylogenetic aspect (see *Phylogenesis*) of Darwinism stressed the relationship between man and animal and so gave new life to many departments of psychology. There now seemed, for example, to be more justification for comparing the behavior, development, expression, etc., of men and animals, and taking the results of animal psychology into account in human psychology. Recently, because of additional factors (e.g. culture and tradition), the findings of animal psychology (q.v.) are applied to human psychology only when the connection is equivalent. See *Comparative psychology*.

Bibliography: Barnett, S. A.: A century of Darwin. London, 1958. **Darlington, C. D.:** Darwin's place in history. London, 1959. **Darwin, C.:** On the origin of species. London, 1859. **Id.:** The descent of man and selection in relation to sex. London & New York, 1871. **Id.:** The expression of the emotions in man and animals. London, 1872. **Id.:** A biographical sketch of an infant. Mind, 1877, *2*, *2*, 285–94. **Smith, S.:** The origin of "The Origin", Advancement of Sci., 1960, *64*, 391–401.

P.S. & R.S.

Daseinsanalyse. See *Existential analysis*.

Dating. Making an appointment or engagement with a person of the opposite sex. This, especially in the U.S.A., is a complex behavioral pattern of unmarried young persons in search of a marriage partner; the relationship to the person "dated" or "dating" is not binding. The number of dates (in the sense either of escorts or occasions) is often regarded as the mark of a girl's prestige.

Bibliography: Coleman, J. S.: The adolescent society. New York, 1961.

J.F.

Day blindness. See *Nyctalopia*.

Daydream (syn. *Waking dream; Waking vision*). In daydreams, the individual surrenders to more or less hypertrophied fantasies which he finds pleasurable in some way. They occur frequently in adolescents and children, and can continue to appear throughout some individuals' lives. Daydreams usually serve to fulfill specific wishes. *J.L.I.*

Day residues. According to Freud, day residues—together with an individual's early and unconscious wishes—operate to produce a dream. They are memories of events of the past day, in which wishes similar to the early unconscious wishes were activated and as a rule could not be gratified. The daytime situation, from which the day residue derives, has already been apprehended by the dreamer (while awake) analogously to early temptation and denial situations. The more recent, though often insignificant, daytime frustration (q.v.) activates, during the dream, more primitive forms of such wishes and frustrations, which are then metamorphosed by the secondary dreamwork into the manifest dream-content (see *Dream*).

Bibliography: **Freud, S.:** The interpretation of dreams. London, 1955.

W.T.

Dazzle. See *Glare*.

Deafferentation. Separation of the spinal cord from the sensory components by severing the dorsal roots. Used to demonstrate the spontaneity of locomotor movements (see *Automatism*). Complete deafferentation prevents coordinated swimming in sharks and *teleostei* but not in toads. In the tench, *Tinca tinca*, two, and in the pricked dogfish, *Squalus acanthus*, three pairs of intact sensory spinal-cord roots suffice for organized swimming after contact stimuli. Toads make coordinated movements even with one intact sensory root.

Bibliography: **Holst, E. V.:** Erregungsbildung und Erregungsleitung im Fischrückenmark. Pflüger's Arch., *235*, 345–59. **Gray, J.:** Animal locomotion. London, 1968.

K.F.

Deaf-mute blindness. Blindness and deafness together with dumbness or high-degree speech loss. Multiple defects usually arise from disease (cerebral infection), but in rare cases are wholly congenital. Dumbness is often a consequence of deafness (see *Deaf-mutism*). There is a high mortality rate as a result of extensive brain damage, and increased accident proneness as a result of multiple loss of sense of distance. *F.-C.S.*

Deaf-mutes, education of. Deaf children become dumb after the babbling stage. The absence of linguistic communication impairs the general mental, and especially intellectual, development. Special remedial education, undertaken as early as possible, attempts to develop a non-acoustic or substitute sign-language. Pictures, writing, finger language and lip reading are taught to compensate for the absence of spoken language. In addition, it is technically possible to convert spoken language into vibrations applied to the skin, or into visual signs. In this way speech can be apprehended by means of non-acoustic sensory channels.

G.B.

Deaf-mute speech. A deaf person cannot acquire linguistic competence in the usual way if hearing is lost before language acquisition begins. Even after appropriate training, the speech of deaf-mutes is still imprecise by normal standards, despite the increased emphasis on articulation. Proficient vowel formation is hardly possible when hearing is absent; pitch is frequently too high; and volume varies inappropriately. Deaf-mute speech is generally unmelodious. *H.B.*

Deaf-mutism. Dumbness, or high-degree loss of speech capacity, as a result of congenital deafness, or deafness occurring before or during language (speech) acquisition. Deafness does not bring about any defect of the speech mechanism, and is to be distinguished from mutism accompanied by normal hearing, the various forms of aphasia (q.v.), and spasmodic speech disorders. The absence of speech may be viewed as the specific cause of the many psychological and social inadequacies and disorders of deaf-mutes. *F.-C.S.*

Deafness. Considerable or complete absence or loss of the ability to hear as a result of (recessive) inheritance, perinatal injury, disease or injury, and sometimes also hysterical conditioning. Defects in the sound-conduction mechanism, and/or in the neutral area (nerve fibers, ganglionic cells in the organ of Corti and/or the cortical hearing center) are met with (see *Sense organs: the ear*). Deafness can also lead to certain alterations of expressed personality (paranoid traits have been reported). *F.-C.S.*

Death instinct (syn. *Death drive; Death impulse; Thanatos instinct*). According to Freud, the "counterpart" of the life instinct or love instinct (or libido, q.v.). Freud postulates that the organism has an innate tendency to revert to its initial state. This instinct, which would lead to self-destruction, has to be diverted outward by the developing organism. The death instinct contradicts the pleasure principle, and is controlled by the compulsion to repetition. The death instinct may be characterized as more neutral than the aggressive instinct (e.g. Hartmann, Rapaport), and hence represents one of the two major classes of drives and motives, which—for psychoanalysts—comprise all motivational processes. Toman has characterized aggression (q.v.) as representing more primitive forms of motive gratification, which hinder the gratification of other's motives to a greater extent than is requisite for the average gratification of an individual. The distinctions between "libidinous" and aggressive gratifications are fluid, and the assumption of two classes of drive is only a rough division. See *Drive; Instinct.*

Bibliography: Freud, S.: Beyond the pleasure principle. London, [2]1959. **Hartmann, H., Kris, E. & Loewenstein, R. M.:** Notes on the theory of aggression. Psychoanalytic Study of the Child, 1949, *3–4*, 9–36. **Rapaport, D.:** The structure of psychoanalytic theory: a systematizing attempt. In: **Koch, S.** (Ed.): Psychology: a study of a science, Vol. 3. New York, 1959, 55–183. *W.T.*

Decerebration. The removal of (an animal's) cerebrum; the subject is then known as a *decerebrate*.

Decision processes have been studied most extensively in connection with human sensory discriminations, where the stimulus is best known and controlled. A distinction first suggested by Fechner, as reported by Boring (1942), is appropriate to a description of the present status of this concept. Fechner differentiated between outer and inner psychophysics to describe the interfaces between physical stimuli and physiological correlates on the one hand, and physiological and psychological correlates on the other. In the present context, this distinction implies separate consideration of the transfer function relating physiological correlate to physical stimulus, and the decision process used to derive a sensory discrimination. Use of two-stage models for sensory discrimination is merely an explanatory convenience, and need not imply that such stages actually exist and occur in sequence.

Four models of sensory decision processes will be described in terms of two-stage analysis. Stimulus conditions will be standardized as follows: There is considered to be an extended field of uniform luminance, L. Three decision processes will be used to describe the detection of a luminance increment, ΔL, added briefly to a portion of the field. The fourth will describe judgments of relative magnitude of luminances L' substituted briefly for L over a portion of the field.

1. *Temporal variability of sensory effects.* According to Boring (1929), Fechner first reported variability among successive measures of sensory discrimination, believing them to be due to measurement error. Separately, Urbantschitsch (1875) reported temporal fluctuations in the sensory magnitude resulting from a steady stimulus. Marbe (1895) suggested that these two phenomena were dual evidence of a fundamental variability in sensory effects, a concept supported by the work of Guilford (1927) and many others. All decision processes to be considered here ascribe a key role to such time-varying sensory effects.

2. *The neural quantum model.* Boring (1926) first suggested that sensory magnitudes should reflect the discreteness of peripheral receptive elements by exhibiting small steps

or sensory quanta. Evidence for sensory quanta in discriminatory data obtained from the auditory modality was presented by von Bekesy (1930, 1936). A general model of sensory decision processes known as the neural quantum model has been developed in these terms. Descriptions of the model and experimental data in support of it have been

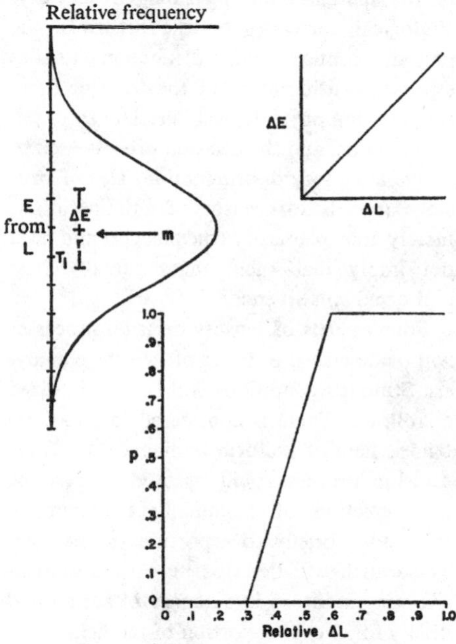

Fig. 1. Representation of the Neural Quantum Model. Upper left: distribution of effect E from steady luminance L, with quantum steps shown by tick-marks. At a moment, m, level of E exceeds quantum step T_1 by residual r. For detection of ΔL, E must increase by two quantum steps and $\Delta E + r = 2Q$, where Q is the difference in E between quantum steps. Upper right: linear transfer function of ΔL to ΔE. Lower right: predicted variation in probability p of detecting ΔL as a function of ΔL.

reported by Stevens & Davis (1938); Stevens & Volkman (1940); Stevens, Morgan & Volkman (1941); Flynn (1943); and Miller & Garner (1944).

According to this model, the effect E due to a steady prevailing luminance L will be represented by the normal frequency distribution shown in the upper left portion of Figure 1. The magnitude of E, due to L, is time-varying, and different values are obtained with different frequencies during any sampling period. Momentary changes in E are continuous, E varying from one level to another by passing through all values between the two. Values of E are, however, quantized into the relatively few discrete levels or steps shown by the tick-marks, each quantum step being of essentially the same size. Since E varies continuously, only a one-quantum jump can occur from L alone. The residual r is defined as the difference between m, a momentary value of E, and T_1, the level of the quantum step it just exceeds. The addition of a luminance increment ΔL produces an increment effect ΔE which is added to the momentary value of r. Detection of ΔL requires that $(\Delta E + r)$ reach a criterion value. One such criterion is that $(\Delta E + r)$ must be sufficient to produce a two-quantum jump in E, a sensory change unachievable from momentary changes in E due to L alone. Thus, $(\Delta E + r) = 2Q$, where Q is the size of a quantum step in E.

The value of ΔE required to produce the two-quantum jump will vary from trial to trial, depending upon the value of r existing when ΔL is added; and the distribution of ΔE will depend upon the distribution of r. All values of r from 0 to Q will occur with equal frequency, provided the total range of variability in E covers a fairly large number of quantum steps. If r varies from 0 to Q in this manner, ΔE will vary from Q to $2Q$ in accordance with a rectilinear frequency distribution.

Assume that ΔE is linearly related to ΔL as shown in the upper right portion of the figure. Then, values of p, the probability of detecting ΔL, will be related to the magnitude of ΔL as shown in the lower right portion of the figure. The value of p is zero until $\Delta L = 0{\cdot}3$, assumed to be the value at which $\Delta E = Q$. Then, p increases linearly until it reaches unity when $\Delta L = 0{\cdot}6$, at which value $\Delta E = 2Q$. Experimental data have been reported which apparently verify these predictions.

3. *The fixed criterion model.* According to the model proposed by Blackwell (1952, 1963), the effect produced by a steady luminance L is time-varying in accordance with the normal frequency distribution shown in the upper-left portion of Figure 2. This distribution of E is time-sampled and a criterion level E_c is selected which occurs from L only a few per cent of the time at most. Addition of a luminance increment ΔL gives rise to a distribution of E due to $(L + \Delta L)$, with mean value greater by ΔE than the distribution of E due to L alone. The magnitude of ΔE is linearly related to ΔL, as shown in the upper right portion of the figure. Distributions of E due to L or $(L + \Delta L)$ have essentially equal values of σ.

Detection of the presence of ΔL occurs whenever the value of E produced by $(L + \Delta L)$ reaches or exceeds the criterion level of E_c. Then, the relation between p, the probability of detection, and ΔL will be described by the normal ogive shown in the bottom right portion of the figure labeled $S = 0$.

When detection probability is inferred from Yes-No responses, spurious Yes responses may occur, as revealed by blank trials. Assuming independence, the total probability of a Yes response is:

$$p' = p + (1 - p)S,$$

where S is the proportion of Yes responses when $\Delta L = 0$.

The curves in the lower right portion of the figure labeled $S = 0{\cdot}25$ and $S = 0{\cdot}50$ represent predictions from two levels of spurious Yes responses. Experimental data have been reported which apparently verify these predictions.

4. *The variable criterion model.* The model reported by Tanner & Swets (1954), and by Green & Swets (1966), also assumes that the effect E produced by L is time-varying in accordance with a normal frequency distribution, and that distributions of E produced by the addition of different values of ΔL to L are normal also with approximately equal σ, as shown in the upper left portion of Figure 3. However, it is assumed that ΔE, the difference between means of the distributions of E produced by L and $(L + \Delta L)$, is related to ΔL by the non-linear transfer

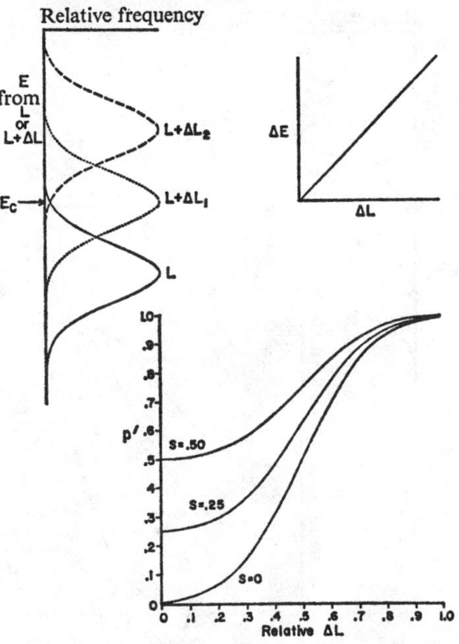

Fig. 2. Representation of the Fixed Criterion Model. Upper left: distributions of effect E from steady luminance L and from L plus each of two values of ΔL. The distribution of E from L is time-sampled and a criterion value E_c selected to have low probability of occurrence from L alone. Detection occurs whenever E from $(L + \Delta L)$ equals or exceeds E_c. Upper right: linear transfer function of ΔL to ΔE. Lower right: predicted variation in probability p' of responding Yes as a function of ΔL for different levels of spurious Yes responses, S.

function $\Delta E = 5{\cdot}9\Delta L^{2{\cdot}7}$ shown in the upper right portion of the figure.

Different criterion levels of E, $E_{c1} \ldots E_{c_n}'$ may be selected corresponding to different ratios of two classes of response error, false alarms when Yes responses are given to L alone, and detection failures when No responses are made to $(L + \Delta L)$. Selection of one or another value of E_c depends upon the values assigned to the two-error classes, and reflects an approach to response optimization.

The relation between p, the probability of a Yes response, and ΔL will depend upon the value of $E_{c'}$ as shown in the bottom-right portion of the figure. Experimental

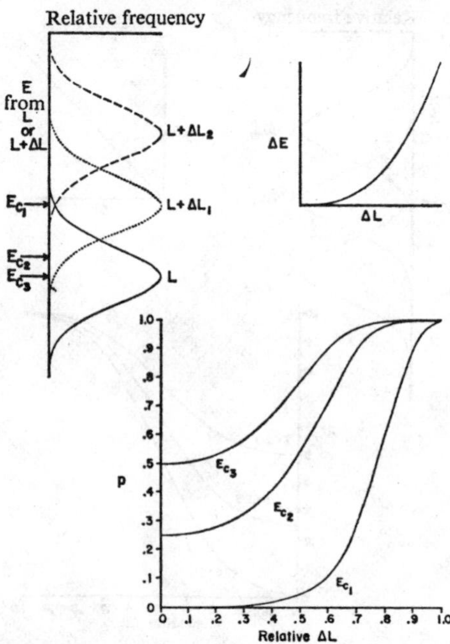

Fig. 3. Representation of the Variable Criterion Model. Upper left: distributions of effect E from steady luminance L and from L plus each of two values of ΔL. Criterion values of E, E_{c_1} .... E_{c_n}, may be set corresponding to different ratio of false alarms and correct detections of ΔL. Upper right: non-linear transfer function in which $\Delta E = 5{\cdot}9\ \Delta L^{2{\cdot}7}$. Lower right: predicted variation in probability p of responding Yes as a function of ΔL for different criterion values of E.

data have been reported which apparently verify these predictions.

5. *The phi-gamma model.* Müller (1904) and Urban (1909) described a generalized model of sensory discrimination based upon the assumption that temporal variability in human sensory systems is normally distributed. Boring (1917), and Brown & Thomson (1925), postulated normal distributions of factors considered favorable or unfavorable to discrimination, and assumed that smaller stimulus magnitudes require more of the factors to be favorable than do larger magnitudes. Thurstone (1927) employed the model to describe experimental situations involving judgments of the relative magnitude of two stimuli, each of which was assumed to produce time-varying effects. We shall consider this form of the phi-gamma model, drawing upon the description given by Guilford (1936).

For a stimulus magnitude comparison experiment, the stimulus situation must be altered slightly as follows: The steady prevailing luminance L is momentarily replaced by a field of non-uniform luminance having a small central area of luminance L' either greater or less than L, with the remainder of the field having luminance L. The value of L' is varied from trial to trial. Judgments are made of the relative magnitude of L' with respect to L on each trial, with only the responses Greater and Less being permitted.

As shown in the upper-left portion of Figure 4, L and each value of L' produce separate time-varying normal distributions of effect E. These normal distributions have approximately equal values of σ. Mean values of the distributions of E produced by L and L' are separated by ΔE. This quantity is linearly related to ΔL, the difference between L' and L taken without regard to sign, as shown in the upper-right portion of the figure. Temporal variability of the effects due to L and L' is uncorrelated from trial to trial, and values of E do not change during the duration of a stimulus exposure.

Discrimination is infallible, each judgment correctly reflecting whether or not the sample drawn from the distribution of E produced by L' had greater or less magnitude than the sample drawn from the distribution of E produced by L. Then, the probabilities of response, p_0 for Greater and p_1 for Less, will be related to the magnitude of L' as shown in the lower-right portion of the figure. Experimental data have been reported which apparently verify these predictions.

6. *Additional models.* Alternative decision-process models have been described by Atkinson (1963), Luce (1963), Broadbent (1966), Krantz (1969), and many others, with experimental data supporting each. Clearly, there can be no single model describing decision processes in human sensory systems.

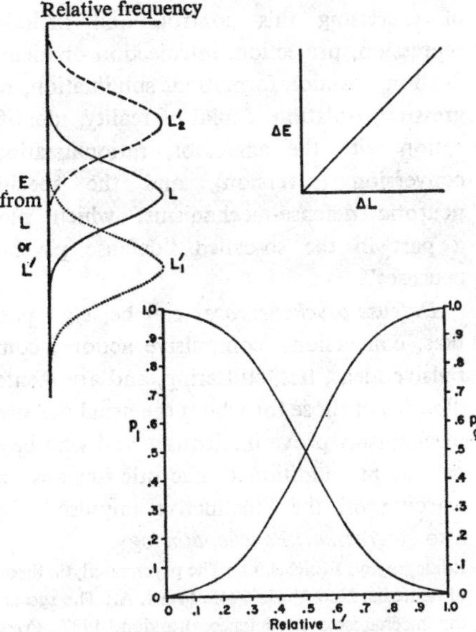

Fig. 4. Representation of the Phi-Gamma Model. Upper left: distributions of effect E from standard luminance L and from two values of comparison luminance L'. Evaluation of the relative magnitude of L' with respect to L involves drawing pairs of samples from uncorrelated distributions of effect due to L and L', with infallible judgment of relative magnitude. Upper right: linear transfer function of ΔL to ΔE. Lower right: predicted variation in judgments p_l (lesser) and p_g (greater) as a function of L'

Rather, the stimulus and response conditions of an experiment will determine the decision process used in making the discrimination.

Bibliography: Atkinson, R. C.: A variable sensitivity theory of signal detection. Psychol. Rev., 1963, *70*, 91–106. **von Bekesy, G.:** Über das Fechnersche Gesetz und seine Bedeutung für die Theorie der akustischen Beobachtungsfehler und die Theorie des Hörens. Ann. d. Phys., 1930, *7*, 329–59. **Id.:** Über die Hörschwelle und Fühlgrenze langsamer sinusförmiger Luftdruckschwankungen. Ann. d. Phys., 1936, *26*, 554–66. **Blackwell, H. R.:** Theory and measurement of psychophysical thresholds. Ann Arbor, 1952. **Id.:** Neural theories of simple visual discriminations. J. Opt. Soc. Amer., 1963, *53*, 129–60. **Boring, E. G.:** A chart of the psychometric function. Amer. J. Psychol., 1917, *28*, 465–70. **Id.:** Auditory theory with special reference to intensity, volume, and localization. Amer. J. Psychol., 1926, *37*, 157–88. **Id.:** A history of experimental psychology. New York 1929. **Id.:** Sensation and perception in the history of experimental psychology. New York, 1942. **Broadbent, D. E.:** Two-state threshold model and rating scale experiments. J. Acous. Soc. Amer., 1966, *40*, 244–5. **Brown, Wm. & Thomson, G. H.:** The essentials of mental measurement. London, 1925. **Flynn, B. M.:** Pitch discrimination: The form of the psychometric function and simple reaction time to liminal differences. Arch. Psychol. N.Y., 1943, *280*, 1–41. **Green, D. M. & Swets, J. A.:** Signal detection theory and psychophysics. New York, 1966. **Guilford, J. P.:** Fluctuations of attention with weak visual stimuli. Amer. J. Psychol., 1927, *38*, 534–83. **Id.:** Psychometric methods. New York, 1936. **Krantz, D. H.:** Threshold theories of signal detection. Psychol. Rev. 1969, *76*, 308–24. **Luce, D. R.:** A threshold theory for simple detection experiments. Psychol. Rev. 1963, *70*, 61–97. **Marbe, K.:** Schwankungen der Gesichts, empfindungen. Phil. Stud., 1895, *10*, 620–41. **Miller, G. A. & Garner, W. R.:** The effect of random presentation on the psychometric function; implications for a quantal theory of discrimination. Amer. J. Psychol., 1944, *57*, 451–67. **Müller, G. E.:** Die Gesichtspunkte und die Tatsachen der psychophysischen Methodik. Wiesbaden, 1904. **Stevens, S. S., & Davis, H.:** Hearing: its psychology and physiology. New York, 1938. **Stevens, S. S., Morgan, C. T. & Volkman, J.:** Theory of the neural quantum in the discrimination of loudness and pitch. Amer. J. Psychol., 1941, *54*, 315–35. **Stevens, S. S. & Volkman, J.:** The quantum of sensory discrimination. Science, 1940, *92*, 583–5. **Tanner, W. P. Jr. & Swets, J. A.:** A decision-making theory of visual detection. Psychol. Rev., 1954, *61*, 401–9. **Thurstone, L. L.:** Psychophysical analysis. Amer. J. Psychol., 1927, *38*, 368–89. **Urban, F. M.:** Die psychophysischen Massmethoden als Grundlagen empirischer Messungen. Arch. ges. Psychol., 1909, *15*, 261–355. **Urbantschitsch, U.:** Über eine Eigentümlichkeit der Schallempfindungen geringster Intensität. Centralbl. f. d. med. Wiss., 1875, *23*, 625–8.

H. R. Blackwell

Decortication. The removal of (an animal's) cerebral cortex; the subject is then known as a *decorticate*.

Deculturation. A term from American ethnology, which concentrates on cultural changes within the frame of a dynamic anthropology (q.v.). In general it represents the negative aspect of *acculturation* (q.v.). Both terms denote mechanisms of acceptance, rejection or reorganization of cultural characteristics, institutions or behavioral patterns within one society in contact (or conflict) with another. These phenomena have appeared in, e.g., the integration of the American minorities into American society (Herskovits, Linton). Recently similar phenomena have appeared in the states of Asia and Africa which as a result of decolonialization have to struggle for their own identity (Balandier, Leach).

Bibliography: Herskovits, M. J. (Ed.): Acculturation. New York, 1938. **Linton, R.**: Acculturation in seven. American Indian tribes. New York, 1940. See also *Cultural anthropology*. *A.T.*

Deduction. The analytical transition from one or several propositions (premisses) to one proposition (conclusion). Deduction as a process of transition from the general to the particular is often contrasted with induction, where the opposite occurs. By *transcendental deduction*, Kant understands the application of *a priori* principles to experience. *J.B.G.*

Defect, mental. See *Mental defect*.

Defemination. This appears in a woman, e.g., as the result of a tumor in the *zona reticularis* of the adrenal cortex. The term *virilism* (q.v.) is also used. The secondary sexual characteristics change and become more like those of the male. The voice becomes deeper, a beard begins to grow, and the most reliable diagnostic sign is that the upper limit of the pubic hair changes toward the male form. There is partial atrophy (q.v.) of the external and internal sexual organs. The changes disappear after the removal of the tumor, or estrogen therapy. Contrary to a widely held view, psychological changes do not always follow on defemination. *G.L.*

Defense; defence. In depth psychology, the inner, automatic inhibition of the satisfaction of an impulse that was once possible for the individual, but from a certain point in development was prevented by others or checked by the threat of "punishment". Defense aims at avoidance or control.

Defense-mechanisms are distinctive means of exercising this control, and include: repression, projection, introjection or identification, reaction formation, sublimation, regression, isolation, denial of reality, identification with the aggressor, rationalization, conversion (reversion), and the specific neurotic defense-mechanisms, which play a part in the so-called "defense psychoneuroses".

Defense-psychoneuroses can be, e.g., phobias, conversions, compulsive actions, compulsive ideas, tics, stuttering, and are mental illnesses of those for whom the usual defense-mechanisms prove inadequate and who have to adopt additional neurotic means of warding off the "instinctive impulse". See also *Regression; Psychopathology*.

Bibliography: Fenichel, O.: The psychoanalytic theory of neurosis. New York, 1945. **Freud, A.**: The ego and the mechanisms of defence. London, 1937. **Freud, S.**: New introductory lectures on psycho-analysis. London, 1933. **Id.**: The ego and the id. London, [2]1962. **Id.**: Inhibitions, symptoms and anxiety. London, [2]1936. **O'Connor, N. & Franks, C. M.**: Childhood, upbringing and other environmental factors. In: **Eysenck, H. J.** (Ed.): Handbook of abnormal psychology. London, 1960. *W.T.*

Defensive reflex (syn. *Defense reflex; Protective response*). An automatic (reflexive) response in answer to a dangerous or painful stimulus.

Defiance, age of (syn. *Obstinacy*). In the older (German) developmental psychology, the period from three to five years of age was defined as the "first phase of defiance", and that from twelve to fifteen as the "second phase of defiance". In these periods one can observe an increase in behaviors characterized by strongly affective and motor resistance reactions to individuals and things (stamping, crying, refusal to obey, fits of anger, sulking, silences, passivity, "negative attitudes"). Such behaviors are interpreted in the literature as "intrinsic volition"; the first emergence of the ego from the non-ego; an experimental breaking of the physiognomic barrier; first emotional crises; lability of mood as a result of adjustment processes in the internal secretory organs; compensation of inferiority feelings in regard to female characteristics, parental authority, or the restriction of gratification by society; and so on. Systematic investigations of defiance in early infancy carried out by Kemmler (1957) would seem to indicate that it is not primarily a general, endogenously conditioned phenomenon; not every child manifestly experiences a phase of defiance, and there are considerable interindividual variations in extent. The frustration of needs (e.g. for independence and self-sufficiency), and the experience of a discrepancy between what was previously allowed and one's own desire to experiment, together with an inability adequately to master the situation, can primarily condition defiance (as a kind of panic reaction). "Defiance" can be reinforced by parental reactions (see *Reinforcement*), and thus become an acquired form of domination. The child's experiences in such situations are relevant for the entire development of the personality.

Bibliography: Kemmler, L.: Untersuchungen über den frühkindlichen Trotz. Psychol. Forsch., 1957, *25*, 279–338.

H.M.

Deficiency, mental (syn. *Mental defect; Amentia; Feeblemindedness; Oligophremia*). Mental deficiency (now used only in clinical practice) is the older term for mental subnormality or mental retardation. This and the term feeblemindedness are sometimes used for the least degree of what, according to the (British) Mental Health Act of 1959, is now generally known as subnormality (i.e. not amounting to *severe subnormality*). It might be thought of as a condition in which there is a minus variation, or some slight form of retardation conditioned by heredity, or a mental disability resulting from brain damage, such as a pre- or postnatal cerebral inflammation, or after injury from cerebral hemorrhage, or some traumatic experience. Sometimes the condition is equated with an IQ of 50–70, but the correspondence is unsatisfactory in the case of adults. An inherited or acquired deficiency in ability is expressed as retarded intellectual maturity, difficulty in acquiring knowledge and dealing with unusual situations. The range of interests is restricted, apprehension is limited, thinking is basically concrete and skill in abstracting is only developed to a slight degree.

It is precisely in regard to this mental subnormality that the aspect of character which is independent of intelligence is decisively significant; with children suffering from mental deficiency it is vitally important to prevent any harmful development of character: an attempt may be made in this direction by employing suitable therapy, avoiding isolation in the family and the environment, and appropriately developing and training existing abilities. Mental deficiency can, but need not, imply a marked absence of personality. It must not be equated with infantilism or primitivism. In general, the treatment is therapeutic (counseling).

N.B. The WHO classification recommends that a distinction be made between the *mentally defective* (organically damaged) and the *mentally retarded* individual (suffering from a learning disability). In general, the term "mental deficiency", though not so evidently negative as some older designations, is best avoided outside a clinical situation in which it is the specifically defined usage of a certain practitioner. See *Mental defect; Autism*.

Bibliography: Benda, C. E.: Die Oligophrenie (Entwicklungsstörungen und Schwachsinnszustände). In: Psychol. der Gegenwart, Vol. 2. Berlin, 1960. **Clarke, A. M. & Clarke, A. D. B.:** Mental deficiency: the changing outlook. London, [2]1965. **Masland, R. L., Sarason, S. B. & Gladwyn, T.:** Mental subnormality.

New York, 1958. Tredgold, R. F. & Soddy, K.: Mental retardation. London, 1969. *H.Sa.*

Deficiency motivation (syn. *Deficit motivation*). If motivation is understood as a phenomenon resulting from certain conditions of the organism, deficiency motivation is the result of some disturbance in the sense of the homeostatic principle. Such disturbing stimuli which may be conditioned by a lack of food, liquid, etc., cause the individual to seek ways and means of removing the deficit and restoring equilibrium. In his system, Maslow contrasts "deficiency motives" with "growth motives" (abundancy motivation).

Bibliography: Maslow, A. W.: Deficiency motivation and growth motivation. Lincoln, Neb., 1955.

P.S. & R.S.

Definition. A statement which either makes clear what one is talking about (real definition) or the way in which one is talking about something (nominal definition). A real definition puts the concept requiring definition into the framework of a classification system. In the simplest cases, the next higher genus (*genus proximum*) and the specific difference (*differentia specifica*) are shown: e.g. "A rhombus is an equilateral parallelogram". "Parallelogram" is the next higher genus, "equilateral" the specific difference. A nominal definition shows which word denotes a concept assumed to be known. Thus it is conventional and serves mostly to abbreviate discourse: e.g. "UNO = df. United Nations Organization". The sign = "df." means "equal *per definitionem*"; the new notation on the left is the *definiendum*; the known term for which it will stand, on the right, is the *definiens*. In formal systems frequent use is made of inductive definitions. These consist of three propositions: (*a*) initial proposition, (*b*) inductive proposition, (*c*) final proposition; e.g.: "(*a*) nought is a number, (*b*) if *n* is a number, *n'* is a number, (*c*) nothing is a number unless it agrees with (*a*) and (*b*)". These definitions make it possible to elicit gradually all the elements (and only those) of a class. See *Deduction*.

J.B.G.

Deflation. A state of negative affect (e.g. disappointment) marking a relatively sudden return to the *status quo* (or lower) following some cause for and feeling of elation. For example, one is likely to feel deflated when the winning horse one has backed is later disqualified. *G.D.W.*

Defloration. The piercing of the vaginal hymen during the first coitus. An intact hymen (*virgo intacta*) is even today a highly-valued attribute in a bride. It is sometimes asserted that a woman feels specially dependent on the man who has deflowered her. In various civilized cultures defloration was a privilege (*jus primae noctis*) of certain persons of standing. *U.H.S.*

Degeneration in the CNS. If an axon (q.v.) is severed and thus separated from the proximodistal flow from the perikaryon (cell body) of the nerve cell (neuron), the proximal portion undergoes retrograde degeneration, and the distal continuation secondary, or Waller's, degeneration. In myelin fibers, the myelin sheath first of all undergoes fatty degeneration and can be stained black with osmium tetroxide (Marchi's method); later the axons fragment. Retrograde degeneration leads to chromatolysis of the Nissl bodies in the perikaryon (soma). Transneuronal degeneration sets in when a neuron is cut off from a considerable part of its afferent connections, since the synapses converging on it are affected by terminal degeneration.

Bibliography: Singer, M. & Schade, J. P. (Eds): Degeneration patterns in the nervous system. Progress in Brain Res., *14*, Amsterdam, 1965. *K.F.*

Degrees of freedom. In a set of *k* observations, $k - 1$ values can be freely chosen within a system, the last value being fully determined.

The number of degrees of freedom (*df*) is therefore $k - 1$. For example, the statistic $\Sigma(X_i - X)^2$, the sum of the squared deviations of a sample (q.v.) of N elements, has $N - 1$ degrees of freedom, since, given the definition of the mean ($\Sigma x = 0$), the last value can no longer be freely chosen. The number of degrees of freedom is of prime importance in determining the critical values of test distributions. *W.H.B.*

Déjà vu experience. Sometimes called *fausse reconnaissance:* an illusion of memory which occasionally occurs in healthy people in a state of exhaustion, but more frequently in neurotics and psychotics. A new situation is experienced for a moment as already known. This an illusion not of the senses but of a paradoxical emotional experience. The following explanations of the phenomenon have been suggested: (*a*) continuance of an emotional state from the preceding situation: the feelings undergo no immediate new orientation because of fatigue or some psychological defect; (*b*) associations of the perceived stimuli with repressed memories; (*c*) partial similarity of certain features, or cues, of the situation to those of a former one, which is then completed on the "part-for-the-whole" principle. *P.S.*

Delayed conditioning. If a pause occurs between a conditioned and an unconditioned stimulus (see *Conditioning*), this is known as delayed conditioning.

Delayed reaction (syn. *Delayed response*). A reaction to certain stimuli after some delay.

Delayed reaction test. To test memory, Hunter carried out a delayed-response experiment which consisted of leaving the subject (an animal) without access to the incentive for some time after presentation. A concealing shield was withdrawn after the delay, and the accuracy of the animal's choice of the object's location served to indicate acuity of memory. It is doubtful whether this is an adequate way of assessing biologically significant memory. According to Baerends, the sand wasp *Ammophilia* is capable of a "delayed reaction" of up to fifteen hours. In the morning, on its first visit of inspection to all the nests, it decides what activities it will carry out on each one throughout the day.

Bibliography: Baerends, G. P.: Fortpflanzungsverhalten und Orientierung der Grabwespe Ammophilia campestris. Jur. Tijdschr. Entomol., 1941, *84*, 68–275. **Hunter, W. S.:** The delayed reaction in animals and children. Behav. Monogr., 1913, *2*, 21–30.

K.F.

Delboeuf's illusion. Large circles which objectively are equally large seem to be different in size when other concentric circles are added to them, whether inside or outside. See *Brentano's illusion.* *K.E.P.*

Delinquency and personality. In numerous investigations—chiefly of juvenile behavior—only moderate correlations were observed between personality traits and delinquent or criminal behavior (see *Criminality*). Delinquency would seem to correlate most reliably with aggressiveness (see *Aggression*), hostility, impulsiveness, neuroticism (q.v.), and (in agreement with Eysenck's theory) extraversion (q.v.). There are problems of method, principally in regard to the unreliability of criteria for delinquency, and the separation of pre-delinquent expressions of traits from those which are relatively conditioned (e.g. by imprisonment).

Bibliography: Eysenck, H.-J.: Crime and personality. London, 1964. **Quay, H. C.:** Personality and delinquency. In: **Quay, H. C.,** (Ed.): Juvenile delinquency. Princeton, 1965, 139–66.

M.A.

Delirium. An exceptional mental state with partial or complete disorientation (q.v.), hallucinations (q.v.), delusions and usually general restlessness. It occurs in the acute exogenous reaction-type during serious somatic illnesses and intoxications affecting the CNS. *Delirium tremens* is probably the best-known variety; it is related to chronic *alcoholism* (q.v.). *A.Hi.*

Delta movement. This is an apparent movement (q.v.): the position of an object seems to change when the lighting is changed.

Delusion. See *Paranoia; Schizophrenia.*

Delusions of reference. These are said to occur when a person unjustifiably believes that others are talking about him, slandering him and spying on him. He may believe that passages in the newspapers or programs on television are referring to him. Such experiences occur in schizophrenia and in severe depression. In the latter case the person believes that such persecution is justified by his wickedness. *R.H.*

Dementia. An acquired defect of intelligence, usually accompanying the final stage of an endogenous or exogenous psychotic change; often the result of cerebral traumata and infectious diseases of the brain. Congenital mental subnormality, or that acquired at a very early age, is sometimes referred to as *oligophrenia* (q.v.). See *Psychoses; Psychopathology.* *U.H.S.*

Dementia, arteriosclerotic. Arteriosclerosis is one of the two common causes of dementia in the elderly. Fairly distinct from senile dementia, the underlying cause is a thickening of the medium-sized arteries of the brain, resulting in diminished blood flow. Deterioration takes place in a step-wise fashion, usually following a series of strokes. Personality is preserved to a late stage, memory loss often being the first sign. Life expectancy is considerably reduced. *D.E.*

Dementia praecox. A term of only historical interest. A synonym for schizophrenia. Morel in 1860 coined the term *démènce precoce*, or premature dementia, to describe severe intellectual deterioration in an adolescent. In 1873 Kraepelin grouped together the syndromes *dementia praecox*, hebephrenia, catatonic and *dementia paranoides* and called the group the *psychological degeneration processes.* In 1899 he changed the name of this group to *dementia praecox* because the illnesses led to intellectual deterioration and usually occurred with young people. Hence the term no longer referred to a specific clinical state. Confusion arose over the implication of youth and permanent dementia until, in 1911, E. Bleuler coined the term *schizophrenia* (q.v.) for this group. *B.B.*

Dementia, presenile. Pick described in 1892 a dementing state associated with aphasia, now known to be a distinct pathological entity inherited as a Mendelian dominant. Occurring before the age of 60, the progressive dementia is accompanied by brain atrophy which is particularly marked in the frontal and temporal lobes. Special features are early emotional changes, but memory is retained until a late stage. Deterioration is usually rapid. *D.E.*

Democracy (syn. *Democratic atmosphere*). A decision-making or discussion atmosphere characterized by freedom of expression, tolerance of individual and minority viewpoints, respect for the worth of each group member, and equal opportunity to contribute to the group decision or activity.

Democratic leadership: A democratic group leader not only informs the group of aims in advance and allows them to be discussed, but is open to the discussion changing those aims.

Bibliography: Berkowitz, L.: Sharing leadership in small, decision-making groups. J. Abnorm. soc. Psychol., 1953, *48*, 231–8. **Fetscher, I.:** Die Demokratie. Stuttgart & Berlin, 1970. **Haythorn, W.:** The effects of varying combinations of authoritarian and equalitarian leaders and followers. J. Abnorm. soc. Psychol., 1956, *55*, 210–19. **Maier, H. R. F. & Solem, A. R.:** The contribution of a discussion leader to the quality of group thinking: the effective use of minority opinions. Hum. Relat., 1952, *5*, 277–88.

J.C.

Demography. In the narrower sense, demography means the statistical assessment and description of a population by means of such variable characteristics as sex, age, income, size of family, etc.: the so-called demographic variables. In a wider sense, the term refers to the study of the natural and social structures of a population, and the causes and consequences of its changes. *A.Hä.*

Demoor's illusion. A defective estimation of weights, especially among the mentally subnormal: the normal overestimating of larger weights and underestimating of smaller weights occurs with gross miscalculation of the proportion of size to weight, or vice versa. *F.-C.S.*

Demoscopy. The terms "demoscopy", "survey" and (public) "opinion poll" denote a method of investigation based on the statistical analysis of (random) samples, and on inquiries, which enables large numbers of people to be observed and analyzed in regard to some specific attitude, etc. The word "demoscopy" arose from a suggestion (1946) made by the American sociologist S. C. Dodd, and at first it was only adopted in Germany (the Allenbach Institute for Demoscopy was founded in 1947), but recently its use has spread increasingly to other countries. In Britain surveys or opinion polls are used.

The term "demoscopy" was introduced because the use of the word "opinion" gives the misleading impression that inquiries were used only or chiefly to ascertain opinions. In fact, the subjects investigated cover a much wider field; the sampling method is used also to investigate facts (e.g. demographic characteristics or housing conditions), knowledge, behavior, attitudes, effects and the connections between these factors. Even the word "demoscopy" is too narrow in one respect: demoscopy investigates not only "people", but groups of every kind (e.g. doctors or teachers), and not only individuals but also bodies (aggregates), such as neighborhoods, school classes, military units, and government agencies. For the method of demoscopy see *Opinion polls.* *E.N.-N.*

Demythologization. 1. The liberation of a myth (q.v.) from its magical character and supernatural features. An attempt is made to divest the myth of its sacred character and ritual function by reducing it to purely human phenomena of a historical, rational, scientific, linguistic (Max Müller) and sociological (see *Cultural anthropology*) nature. A process that occurred in numerous primitive societies during cultural changeovers.

2. In existential and religious-anthropological usage: the elucidation of the essence of a myth in a form that will make its relevance immediately clear to modern man.

M.R.

Dendrites. Nerve cells (neurons) consist of a cell body, several dendrites branching from it, and the axon (q.v.), the extended nerve fiber leading to the effector, or to other nerve cells. Numerous nerve fibrils coming from other nerve cells end at synapses (q.v.), or junctions between them and the relatively short dendrites, thus enlarging the extent of impulse conduction into the nerve cell.

Bibliography: Eccles, L. C.: The physiology of nerve cells. Baltimore, 1957.

M.S.

Denial. See *Reality, denial of.*

Density mean. A measurement for the central tendency of a distribution (see *Frequency* *distribution*). It is the value on the score continuum of a single-peak distribution which shows the greatest frequency ($f'(x) = 0; f''(x) < 0$). In the case of a distribution with several peaks there are several density means; it is a measure of the central tendency in this special case only for the section of the distribution between the two adjacent minima. The density mean has weaknesses, especially in regard to samples (q.v.).

W.H.B.

Dependence. In the measurement of probability, dependence of events (q.v.) means that the probability (q.v.) of the occurrence of these events is influenced by the occurrence or non-occurrence of other events:

$$P(A) = P(A|B) \quad \text{and} \quad P(B) = P(B|A).$$

The probability of the common occurrence of events A and B in the case of stochastic dependence is $P(AB) = P(A)P(B)$. See *Mathematical psychology; Statistics.* *W.H.B.*

Dependence, social; dependency. The state of an individual when economically, emotionally or otherwise dependent on other individuals. Also used to refer to the relation of the immature child to those who care for or guide it.

In socialization (q.v.), dependence of the child on a person to whom it can relate (mother or parents, and so on) is the necessary premiss for the social imitation (q.v.) of different behavior patterns and for the internalization of social norms and values.

A condition for the development of the child's dependence on, or trust in, its parents is the presence of an appropriate person to whom it can refer and with whom it can identify. If such a person is not available, partly irreversible damage can result in all areas of child development (e.g. hospitalism, q.v.) (see Spitz, 1945).

A possible explanation for the origin of dependent behavior in the child is the principle of *secondary reinforcement* (Mowrer, 1950). The behavior of the persons to whom it refers takes on reinforcing (reward) qualities for the child, through repeated association with the satisfaction of primary or bodily needs by these persons. The reinforcement value is transferred to all aspects of those persons' behavior: the child learns to place a positive value on their presence and attention. Dependence is also intensified by an upbringing and education oriented to warmth and love (see Sears *et al.*, 1957).

See, e.g., Bronfenbrenner (1961) for the relation of dependence to the child-rearing conventions of different social classes, to children's sex, or to family structure.

Bibliography: Bronfenbrenner, U.: The changing American child: A speculative analysis. J. soc. Issues, 1961, *17*, 6–10. **Mowrer, O. H.:** Learning theory and personality dynamics. New York, 1950. **Sears, R. R., Maccoby, E. E. & Levin, H.:** Patterns of child rearing. New York, 1957. **Sears, R. R., Rau, L. & Alpert, R.:** Identification and child rearing. London, 1966. **Spitz, R.:** Hospitalism: An inquiry into genesis of psychiatric conditions in early childhood. The Psychoanalytic Study of the Child, 1945, *1*, 53–74.

A.S.-M.

Dependent distribution. When the relative frequency of the simultaneous occurrence of events X and Y is unequal to that calculated according to $F(x) \cdot F(y)$, the distribution of these dependent random variables is a "dependent distribution". The degree of dependence (q.v.) can be expressed, e.g., in the form of a correlation coefficient (q.v.). See *Mathematical psychology; Statistics.* *W.H.B.*

Dependent samples. In contradistinction to independent samples, dependent (correlational) samples are obtained either by parallelization (q.v.) according to control characteristics, or by the repetition of measurements on the same objects. In the case of parallel samples, the sampling error (q.v.) will decrease with the increase in covariance (q.v.) between the pretest variables and the dependent variables to be tested. In the case of repeated measurements, the sampling error will be smaller than with random samples, and will correspond to the extent of the correlation between the measurements. *W.H.B.*

Dependent variables. In connection with analyses of dependence (regression analyses, q.v.), dependent variables represent the variable to be measured. Dependent variables are examined to see whether, how and to what extent they are covariant with the systematically changing independent variables. In general terms, X and Y are dependent random variables in a two-dimensional distribution

$$f(x, y) = f_1(x) . F^2(y)$$

where F_1 and F^2 are the marginal distributions of X and Y. *W.H.B.*

Depersonalization. The feeling of a patient that he has lost his identity. The clear awareness that everything one feels, says or does comes from oneself is partially or entirely missing. This occurs especially in cases of *schizophrenia* (q.v.) or serious *depression* (q.v.). *A.Hi.*

Depression. The term "depression" is used for a complex of symptoms: a "depressed", despondent condition, unresponsiveness and loss of drive, motor and mental inhibition, typically depressive ideas and definite somatic disorders. One most significant variety is endogenous depression, which is constitutionally grounded, dependent on heredity, and tends to manic-depressive illness. E. Kraepelin distinguished it from *schizophrenia* (q.v.). The characteristic symptoms of *endogenous depression* are a groundless, deeply-felt sadness (melancholia), anxiety (q.v.), or excitement, and typical, sometimes imaginary, ideas of impoverishment; self-accusation, a conviction of sinfulness, as well as depersonalization (q.v.), with a tormenting loss of emotional life. In addition there is an inadequacy which is experienced mentally and physically as hypochondria, as well as pathognomonic somatic disorders in the form of insomnia, periodical fluctuations of emotional condition with a morning "low", loss of appetite and weight, and vegetative disorders.

Forms of depression. According to the symptoms, there are *inhibited depressions* in which the inhibition can be intensified and become stupor (q.v.); agitated, i.e. anxiously *excited, depressions; hypochondriac depressions*, which are felt entirely somatically and occur within the area of physical feeling and the related anxieties. *Paranoiac depressions* are characterized by imaginary feelings of guilt and ideas of injury; *anancastic* depressions are determined by compulsive notions. In *vegetative depressions*, as in other forms, actual melancholia may be quite absent. In manic-depressive psychoses (q.v.), approximately half of all cases experience the various phases in the form of depressions; in a quarter of the cases there are both depressive and manic phases; and in another quarter there are only manic phases. There is an essential danger of suicide (q.v.) in endogenous depressions. It is rare for the thought of suicide not to occur, and in 10–15 per cent of the cases the patient actually attempts to take his own life. The condition runs in phases, with an average duration of six months. The single phase does not lead to any change in personality, in contrast to the schizophrenic shift.

Unlike the endogenous depression, in a *reactive depression* the depressive resentment remains more or less explicable on normal psychological grounds, as a quantitative increase of normal sadness; it thus appears as an adequate reaction to stressful events of an acute or chronic nature, whose contribution to the causation of the depression can be recognized by the patient too. *Exhaustion depressions* are also largely to be understood in a normal psychological sense, as cases of depressive reactions to chronic somatic and mental over-strain. *Neurotic depressions* are said to arise from unresolved conflicts (q.v.)

in the unconscious; they are more or less repressed and mostly of a chronic nature, and frequently derive from childhood. They often feature aggressive, hysterical and demonstrative characteristics which are not found as a rule in endogenous depressions. A causative factor in *symptomatic depressions* is temporary exogenous or endogenous somatic damage linked to some cerebral injury (infectious diseases, chronic circulatory disturbances, cerebral poisoning from drugs and medicines, disorders of internal secretions, etc.). *Organic depressions* (P. Kielholz) are also due to cerebral damage, e.g. to organic processes in the brain and to cerebral sclerosis. Hence these depressions also feature organic disturbances of reasoning processes which are not found in depressions without any somatic cause, or in endogenous depression. In contrast to these endogenous and symptomatic depressive moods, which can be limited in time, in depressive psychopaths (see *Psychopathy*) there is a very deeply-rooted and lasting depressive mood without enjoyment of life or confidence, and a tendency to treat everything with pessimism. In this group of psychopathic personalities, the constitutionally melancholy take everything to heart and yet often have very strong emotions, and have to be distinguished from others in whom the basic depressive mood is bound up with bitter resignation and contempt for any enjoyment of life. The pathophysiology of endogenous depressions is still unexplained, although it is undoubtedly somatic in origin.

Psychiatry in the English-speaking world (see Kendall, 1968) does not distinguish as rigorously as traditional psychiatry between the individual depressions. The treatment of depressions is oriented by etiology, and is therefore either psychopharmacological or psychotherapeutic. See *Antidepressives; Psychoses, functional; Schizophrenia.*

Bibliography: Coppen, A. & Walk, A.: Recent developments in affective disorders. Brit. J. Psychiat., Special publ., No. 2, 1968. **Hill, D.:** Depression: disease, reaction, or posture. Am. J. Psychiat., 1968, *25*, 37ff. **Hippius, H. & Selbach, H.:** Das depressive Syndrom. Munich, 1969. **Kendall, R. E.:** The classification of depressive illnesses. London, 1968. **Lange, J.:** Die endogenen und reaktiven Gemütserkrankungen und die manisch-depressive Konstitution. Hdb. der Geisteskrankheiten, Vol. 6, Berlin, 1928. **Murphy, H. B. M.** *et al.*: Cross-cultural factors in depression. Transcultural Psychiat. Res., 1964, *1*, 5–21. **Schulte, W. & Mende, W.:** Melancholie in Forschung, Klinik und Behandlung. Stuttgart, 1969. **Tellenbach, H.:** Melancholie. Berlin, 1961. **Weitbrecht, H. J.:** Depressive und manisch-endogene Psychosen. In: Psychiatrie der Gegenwart, Berlin, 1960. **Wolpe, J.:** The practice of behavior therapy. New York, 1969.

H. Sattes

Deprivation experiments. Experiments in which animals or humans are placed in situations in which desired objects are absent or needs are not gratified. Experiments of this kind are carried out, e.g., in motivation research, when food, sleep, etc., are withheld.

Bibliography: Brozek, J., Guetskow, H. & Baldwin, M. V.: A quantitative study of perception and association in experimental semistarvation. J. Pers., 1951, *19*, 245–64. **Epstein, S.:** The measurement of drive and conflict in humans. In: **Jones, R. J.** (Ed.): Nebraska Symposium on Motivation. Lincoln, Neb., 1962.

K.E.P.

Deprivation, social. Social isolation affecting individual well-being and capacity, personality, development and the socialization process (see *Socialization*). The effect of social deprivation on work has been shown by investigation to depend on personality traits. Developmental psychology draws on animal experiments, case studies of feral children, and studies of institutionalized or hospitalized children, for data concerning social deprivation. Social deprivation leads to disturbances of development and behavior. See *Child psychology; Depth psychology.*

Bibliography: Anastasi, A.: Fields of applied psychology. New York, 1964. **Id.:** Differential psychology. New York, [3]1958.

D.B.

Deprivation symptoms. See *Withdrawal symptoms.*

Depth perception. The localization of perceived objects in phenomenal (perceived) space in regard to the distance between the objects of perception and the individual (egocentric depth localization, or absolute depth localization), or in regard to the distance between objects of perception (relative). Depth perception can occur in various modalities, though most precisely in the visual modality (the term often means only one's awareness of the distance between one and the visually perceived object); it also occurs in hearing (loudness, frequency spectrum) and by means of the tactile-haptic system (see *Sense organs*). In contrast to some animals, in man the sense of smell plays hardly any part in depth localization. Although different senses can be implicated, a unified impression of phenomenal distance is obtained (unified phenomenal or perceived space, and also active space). See *Space perception.* *W.P.*

Depth psychology. 1. *Introductory.* "Depth psychology" (Ger. *Tiefenpsychologie*) is a term which has been used extensively on the continent of Europe in the last sixty years but less frequently in American and British writings. Some authors simply equate it with "psychoanalysis" (q.v.) (see, e.g., Rycroft, 1968); others, however, give it a wider meaning: thus English & English (1958, p. 145) characterize it as "any psychology that postulates dynamic psychic activities that are unconscious", while Wyss (1966), under the title *Depth Psychology*, surveys not only the work of Freud but that of Adler, Rank, Fromm, Binswanger, and many others. On this showing the term appears to be roughly coextensive with "psychodynamics"—a word which is currently used to refer to the study of unconscious wishes and conflicts without implying any particular theory, Freudian or otherwise, about their nature or origin. Here, consideration will be given to a variety of ways in which these "deeper" aspects of human personality have been studied.

Perhaps the key point in the notion of "depth" is that of surface appearance in contrast with what lies "within" or "beneath". Just as we may be misled by the surface appearance of, e.g., a box or a pond, so a person may seem friendly or aloof at a "superficial" level, but may manifest quite different behavior if intimate details of his life are under discussion, his deeper feelings sometimes "erupting" in conditions of stress. Sometimes the contrast is between "inside" and "outside", as in the phrase "innermost feelings", while often there is the suggestion that it is the *real* personality which lies below or within, with the implication that one can be misled if one considers only what is at the surface. The spatial analogy should not, of course, be pressed too far. The notion of "distance away" from the findings of common-sense observation is not without value, but clearly any reference to actual units of measurement would be quite out of place, and one needs to be aware both of the limitations and of the value of this kind of language. A helpful critique of the notion of "depth" in clinical psychology is given by Levy (1963).

2. *Methods of investigation.* (*a*) One of the main methods of investigation has been the *therapeutic interview*. Under this heading may be included not only full-scale psychoanalysis as practiced by Freud (1856–1939) and his close followers, but also the methods of treatment adopted by those who deviated to a greater or lesser extent from the original Freudian tradition, e.g. C. G. Jung (1875–1961), A. Adler (1870–1937), Karen Horney (1885–1952), and Melanie Klein (1882–1960). (For samples of their work see Freud, 1922; Jung, 1954; Adler, 1925; Horney, 1946; Klein, 1932.) "Depth" interpretations are sometimes made even when there is no full-scale psychotherapy, as has been shown by Malan (1963) and by some psychiatric social workers, e.g. Irvine (1956). In all these cases, particular pieces of behavior on the part of the patient (e.g. verbal remarks about present and past difficulties of adjustment) are commented upon by the therapist,

who attempts to indicate what seems to him to be their deeper emotional significance. Criteria for the correctness of interpretations have been discussed by many writers, e.g. Isaacs (1933) and Farrell (1962). There are largely the same procedures in group therapy (see, e.g., Foulkes & Anthony, 1957), except that up to about nine patients are present with the therapist simultaneously. Other types of depth-orientated work with groups have been described by Balint (1957), Bion (1961), and Rice (1965).

(*b*) A second method of investigating these "deeper" aspects of personality is by means of *projective tests* (q.v.). The earliest and best known is the Rorschach inkblot test (see Klopfer & Davidson, 1962). Here the subject or patient (the setting is usually a clinical one) is presented with a series of cards containing patterns resembling ink-blots, and is required to say "what he sees" there. From a consideration of how he uses the various features of the blots in his successive responses, testers try to reconstruct the unconscious feelings and attitudes which appear to be influencing his life-style. The procedure is basically similar in the case of Murray's Thematic Apperception Test and Bellak's Children's Apperception Test (for a discussion of both see Bellak, 1954), except that in these two tests the cards do not contain meaningless shapes, but pictures of humans and animals in lifelike situations. Phillipson's Object Relations Test (Phillipson, 1955) has been specially constructed on the assumption that the subject's past and present experiences of human relationships will play an important part in determining his responses.

(*c*) Thirdly, attempts have been made to study "below-surface" tensions in the industrial situation. The pioneer worker here has been Jaques (see, especially, Jaques, 1961). He describes his role as that of "social analyst", and his basic method has been to sit in on industrial committee meetings and discussions and to examine with those present the deeper significance of their remarks and emotional displays. For example, when there were wrangles over payment, this often appeared to reflect underlying discontent or insecurity over status. In addition Jaques suggests that, with suitable safeguards, the formula "length of time over which responsibility is carried" (or "time-span") can be used as a basis for paying people a salary or wage which they themselves will inwardly feel to be equitable.

(*d*) Fourthly, use has been made of the method of systematic record-keeping, particularly in respect of the behavior of children. From many possible examples, two will be given by way of illustration. (i) Isaacs (1948) has recorded samples of the social behavior of children at a nursery school, most of them aged between three and six; and she claims that these records provide evidence of "the deeper sources of love and hate", such as children's fantasies of oral and anal aggression and their feelings of guilt at their own "bad" impulses (see, especially, *op. cit.*, pp. 280 *seq.*). (ii) Bowlby (1966) has collated a large amount of evidence purporting to show the effects on young children of maternal deprivation; and on the basis of this evidence he asserts that "the prolonged deprivation of the child of maternal care may have grave and far-reaching effects on his character and so on the whole of his future life" (*op. cit.*, p. 46).

(*e*) Finally, mention should be made of a group of more speculative pronouncements involving in various ways the notion of "depth". Examples include the application by Money-Kyrle (1951) of depth principles to the study of political behavior, the use of the "depth interview" for advertising purposes, as described by Packard (1957), and attempts to understand the "deeper" sources of artistic creation, as in Freud's study of Leonardo da Vinci (Freud, 1963). The basic principle in all these cases is that of applying ideas derived from clinical procedures to situations of everyday life.

3. *A scientific critique.* Accurate evidence in this whole area is not easy to come by. It

is arguable, however, that the "deeper" aspects of personality are of such fundamental importance and interest that even poorly controlled experiments are of more value than rigorous experiments on more trivial matters. On the other hand, there are special dangers if far-reaching claims are made by those inadequately trained in evaluating evidence; in particular, ingenious though doubtful speculations, if passed from one person to another, may come to acquire the cachet of established fact when they are nothing of the kind.

(*a*) A detailed account of psychoanalysis is given elsewhere in this encyclopedia, and the present discussion will be limited to some general remarks about the evaluation of evidence derived from all forms of psychotherapy. For scientific purposes it is necessary to isolate those factors in the stimulus-situation which, in conjunction with earlier stimuli, are influencing a particular response. Thus if an interpretation in terms of aggressive wishes is put forward, it could be that the interesting behavioral changes which result are due not to the patient's recognition of these aggressive wishes for what they are, but to the fact that the therapist is showing that he can tolerate them and that they are not fatally destructive. In general it is arguable that a re-description of the therapy situations in the language of "operant conditioning" (q.v.) would be very advantageous: firstly, it would force investigators to take seriously the problem of analyzing the stimulus-situation into its components; secondly, interesting parallels would immediately be suggested with laboratory findings, and fuller theoretical understanding would be possible as to why particular interpretations given in a particular context have a particular effect. Since laboratory studies have conclusively shown that verbal comments such as "good" and "mphm" can sometimes act as reinforcers (see, e.g., Greenspoon, 1962), therapists would be forced to make sure that they themselves were not *unwittingly* reinforcing certain types of behavior (e.g. responses relating to sexual matters in a Freudian analysis); also they would be in a position to exert more rational control over the number and timing of particular kinds of interpretation in the light of what is known about reinforcement in other contexts. What is required, in this view, is not replacement of psychotherapy by therapies based on conditioning principles, but a synthesis as a result of which experts in these different fields can learn from each other (compare Skinner, 1956, and Miles, 1966).

(*b*) The scientific status of projective tests remains a matter of dispute. It seems safe to say that test results can sometimes contribute in a distinctive way to the making of appropriate practical decisions; but the theoretical justification for the term "projection" is more questionable, and the claim that these tests enable us to investigate the "depths" of personality is by no means universally accepted.

(*c*) The industrial work of Jaques (1961) could well turn out to be important, and there is no dearth of testable hypotheses (see, e.g., pp. 142 *seq.* and pp. 216 *seq.*). Validation on a large scale, however, has not so far been attempted.

(*d*) Isaacs' work (1948) exemplifies the value of natural history methods when properly used. The quality of the evidence adduced in studies of maternal deprivation has been called in question (see, e.g., Wootton, 1959, Chapter IV, Andry in Bowlby, *op. cit.*, pp. 223–35, and Munro, 1966), but it is hard to avoid the conclusion that maternally deprived children are at risk.

(*e*) The main difficulty in the more speculative ideas described under (*e*) above is the lack of any clear procedure for evaluation. It is not that evaluation is intrinsically impossible, as has been shown by Farrell in his interesting commentary on Freud's Leonardo da Vinci (Freud, 1963, pp. 11–18); but what counts for or against particular claims is sometimes a matter for dispute, and the evidence in these areas is insufficient to permit any assured verdict.

In general, the function of the term "depth psychology" may be said to be that of orienting and steering; it commends certain areas in the study of personality as being worth special investigation and emphasizes the danger of "superficiality" if these areas are ignored. Even if in the future the loose metaphor of "depth" becomes supplanted by more precise and literal formulations, this warning will remain pertinent.

Bibliography: Adler, A.: Individual psychology, tr. P. Radin. London, 1925. **Andry, R. G.:** see Bowlby, *op. cit.* **Anthony, E. J.:** see Foulkes & Anthony, *op. cit.* **Balint, M.:** The doctor, his patient, and the illness. London, 1957. **Bellak, L.:** The TAT and CAT in clinical use. New York, 1954. **Bion, W. R.:** Experience in groups and other papers. London, 1961. **Bowlby, J.** *et al.*: Maternal care. New York, 1966. **Davidson, H. H.:** see Klopfer & Davidson, *op. cit.* **English, H. B. & English, A. C.:** A comprehensive dictionary of psychological and psychoanalytic terms. New York & London, 1958. **Farrell, B. A.:** The criteria for a psychoanalytic explanation. Aristotelian Society, 1962, Suppl. Vol. 36, 77–100. **Id.:** see Freud, *op. cit.* (1963). **Foulkes, S. H. & Anthony, E. J.:** Group psychotherapy. Harmondsworth, 1957. **Freud, S.:** Introductory lectures on psychoanalysis, tr. Joan Rivière. London, 1922. **Id.:** Leonardo da Vinci and a memory of his childhood, tr. Alan Tyson. Harmondsworth, 1963. **Greenspoon, J.:** Verbal conditioning and clinical psychology. In: **Bachrach, A. J.** (Ed.): Experimental foundations of clinical psychology. New York, 1962, 510–53. **Horney, K.:** Our inner conflicts. A constructive theory of neurosis. London, 1946. **Irvine, E. E.:** Transference and reality in the casework relationship. Brit. J. Psychiat. Soc. Work, 1956, *III*, 1–10. **Isaacs, S.:** Social development in young children. London, 1933. **Id.:** Childhood and after. London, 1948. **Jaques, E.:** Equitable payment. London, 1961. **Jung, C. G.:** The practice of psychotherapy, tr. R. F. C. Hull. Collected works, Vol. 16. London, 1954. **Klein, M.:** The psychoanalysis of children, tr. Alix Strachey. London, 1932. **Klopfer, B. & Davidson, H. H.:** The Rorschach technique: an introductory manual. New York, 1962. **Levy, L. H.:** Psychological interpretation. New York, 1963. **Malan, D. H.:** A study of brief psychotherapy. London, 1963. **Miles, T. R.:** Eliminating the unconscious. Headington, 1966. **Money-Kyrle, R. E.:** Psychoanalysis and politics: A contribution to the psychology of politics and morals. London, 1951. **Munro, A.:** Parental deprivation in depressive patients. Brit. J. Psychiat., *112*, 1966, 443–57. **Packard, V.:** The hidden persuaders. London, 1957. **Phillipson, H.:** The object relations technique. London, 1955. **Rice, A. K.:** Learning for leadership: interpersonal and intergroup relations. London, 1965. **Rycroft, C.:** A critical dictionary of psychoanalysis. London, 1968. **Skinner, B. F.:** Critique of psychoanalytic concepts and theories. In: The foundations of science and the concepts of psychology and psychoanalysis. Minnesota, 1956, 77–87. **Wootton, B.:** Social science and social pathology. London, 1959. **Wyss, D.:** Depth psychology. A critical history, tr. Gerald Onn. London, 1966.

T. R. Miles

Derma (syn. *Dermis; Corium; Cutis*). The inner, sensitive mesodermic layer of the skin beneath the epidermis, containing sensory receptors.

Dermal sense. The sensitivity of the sensory receptors in the derma.

Dermatographia. Signs written on the skin with a blunt object become visible after a few seconds as a reddening and possibly as a swelling (welts). This physiological reaction is caused by expansion of the dermal capillaries after mechanical irritation; when excessive (hyperirritability), it is thought to be a sign of morbid vegetative hyperexcitability (*Urticaria factitia*). *E.D.*

Description (method). The subject describes his own experiences without interpreting them. See *Introspection.*

Descriptive psychology. The academic psychology which came into being in Germany at the beginning of this century. In contrast to experimental psychology, it is concerned with the description and understanding (see *Intuitive understanding psychology*) of psychic phenomena, and does not try to explain them causally and mechanically. Its founders were F. von Brentano (q.v.) and W. Dilthey. Other prominent representatives are K. Jaspers, E. Spranger.

Bibliography: Brentano, F. von: Psychologie. 2 vols, Leipzig, 1924. **Dilthey, W.:** Gesammelte Schriften, Vol. 1. Leipzig & Berlin, 1922. *P.S.*

Desexualize. 1. To sublimate (see *Sublimation*) by diverting attention or energy from sexual to other goals. **2.** To deprive an object or communication medium of sexual associations, reference, or symbolism. **3.** To castrate (see *Castration*).

Desmolysis. H. Schultz-Hencke's term for the psychotherapeutic dissolution of unconscious inhibitions, inappropriate to the age-group of the subject, which are thought to prevent the development of personality.

De(s)oxyribonucleic acid (abb. DNA). The hereditary substance. Together with protein (which consists of amino acids), the nucleic acids are the principal chemical constituents of chromosomes (q.v.) (fibrous strands in the cell nucleus which can be seen by electron microscope during cell division, and of which there is a characteristic number for each species of animal and plant). DNA consists of very large molecules (macromolecular chains), each molecule having a weight in the order of tens of millions, and consisting of nucleotides combined from a sugar (de(s)oxyribose), a phosphate group, and the four bases adenine, guanine, cytosine and thymine. The DNA helix according to Watson and Crick consists of two DNA chains latched together through these bases: an adenine on chain 1 opposite a thymine on chain 2; and the same for guanine and cytosine. The nucleic acids are the carriers of heredity characteristics, whose information code is distinguished by the different arrangement of the nucleotides in the molecular structure. DNA would appear to be the prime carrier of heredity.

Bibliography: Watson, J. D.: The double helix. London, 1968.

E.D.

Destruction (syn. *Destructive instinct; Destrudo*). Destruction is best defined psychologically (i.e. psychoanalytically) as the human frustration of the satisfaction (gratification) of human needs (motivation). Destruction sought for or attained is the more serious according to the degree of individual frustration, its duration, and its extension to others. The complete frustration of human motivation is synonymous with death. The complete frustration of one's own motivation is self-destruction.

Freud considered the destructive instinct as the second energy source of human motives and human behavior after libido (q.v.). Others (Hartmann, Lorenz) conceive it as a large class of motives (see *Death instinct; Aggression*). Destructive behavioral tendencies can also appear in response to frustration (q.v.).

Bibliography: Freud, S.: Beyond the pleasure principle. London, [2]1959. **Hartmann, H., Kris, E. & Loewenstein, R. M.:** Notes on the theory of aggression. Psychoanalyt. Study of the child, 1949, *3/4*, 9–36. **Lorenz, K.:** On aggression. London, 1966. **Toman, W.:** Introduction to psychoanalytic theory of motivation. London & New York, 1960.

W.T.

Desublimation. The removal of libidinal objectifications, which—according to H. Marcuse—result from the failure of repressive social institutions. Desublimation is achieved by the self-sublimation of all sexual part-instincts in the eros under a non-repressive reality principle free from authoritarianism, and is the basis of a utopian, free society.

Bibliography: See *Alienation*.

U.H.S.

Detail response. In the Rorschach test: the observation of and response to larger (*D*) or smaller (*d*) partial areas of the whole inkblot.

K.E.P.

Deterioration. Progressive impairment of physical or mental function. See also *Aging; Gerontology*.

Determinants. 1. In a biological sense: heredity factors (*anlagen*, q.v.). **2.** In psychology: (*a*) in general: factors determining some process or development; (*b*) in depth psychology: "boundaries of individual possibilities"

(Schottlaender); (*c*) in psychoanalysis: the decisive aspects of a dream; (*d*) in the Rorschach test: inkblot qualities which settle the testee's answer (i.e. image perceived: e.g., color, shape); (*e*) in general: limiting factors or terms, e.g. in activity, postulation, diagnosis. See *Traits*. *K.E.P.*

3. Causative or limiting factors. The entire science of psychology is based upon the assumption that thoughts, feelings, and behavior are predictable on the basis of previous conditions, i.e. that they are not random, but *determined*. For example, Freud argued that many apparently meaningless phenomena such as dreams and slips of the tongue are largely determined by unconscious motivational processes. *G.D.W.*

Determination, coefficient of (syn. *Index of determination*). The square of the product-moment correlation (q.v.) of two variables, r^2_{xy}. The term indicates that the coefficient (q.v.) expresses the proportion of variance of the dependent variable *Y*, which is "determined" by the independent *X*, i.e. which it has "in common" with *X*. See *Correlation; Statistics*. *W.H.B.*

Determining tendency (syn. *Set*). A term introduced by N. Ach for the idea that the course our consciousness takes is partly determined by and dependent on our consciously or unconsciously operative conceptions of a goal or aim. The course of a thought process is definitely directed by a predisposing set formed by the expected result.

Bibliography: **Ach, N.:** Über die Begriffsbildung. Bamberg, 1921. **Watt, H. J.:** Experimentelle Beiträge zu einer Theorie des Denkens. Arch. ges. Psychol., 1905, *4*, 289–436. *K.E.P.*

Determinism. **1.** All the conditions (determinants) which are necessary for the appearance of a phenomenon. The same phenomena can, however, be caused by different "determinisms": biological, social, geographical, etc. **2.** In a philosophical sense: the doctrine that the phenomena (facts) of the universe depend so closely on those preceding them that they represent their sole effect. **3.** In the Aristotelian theory of causality determinism denotes the concept of "*efficient cause*", i.e. that producing an effect, as distinct from *material cause* (from which something arises), *formal cause* (which decides that a thing should come to be), and *final cause* (purpose). It is, however, sometimes used of formal cause. **4.** Any doctrine which (analogously to the physical world) interprets psychic life as dependent solely on (largely physiological) preconditions (*material*, or *mechanistic*, determinism). **5.** Loosely, any theory which denies freewill when postulating that all phenomena are directed by law. *M.-J.B. & J.M.*

Detour action. A detour action or behavior is the attainment of a goal not directly but by indirect routes: by means of behaviors which are not essentially connected with the goal. W. Köhler showed in chimpanzees, and K. Bühler in children, that when instinctive equipment, previous knowledge and situation give no direct indications regarding goal-getting, a detour is frequently sought and found which leads to the goal in question. According to K. Lewin, it is not connected to the direct appeal (valence) of the situation, but is controlled by the ego (q.v.); it presupposes control of drive, or leads as a substitute activity to an equivalent substitute goal; it is comparable to judicious behavior in an adult. Detour actions in the broadest sense comprise a large part of all adult actions. *H.W.*

Deuteranop(s)ia. Green blindness. The medium range of the color spectrum is not perceived. See *Color blindness; Color vision*. *R.R.*

Development. 1. *The concept*. The term "development" refers to a sequence of changes in organisms (animal or human), groups of organisms (e.g. nations), cultural fields (e.g. art), and dead matter (e.g. geological development). The concept was used by psychology in its early stages to denote the development of embryonic possibilities. In general, development extends from the origin (the beginning of mental or biological life) to the end of individual existence (death or extinction). Animal and human development comprises the whole course of life, although special attention is paid to child development. There is a dual relationship between development and learning: learning is a general term for development if the latter is considered as a special form of the former (long-term, irreversible, differential and structural), and the laws of learning are regarded as the general principles of human behavior. From another angle, development can be taken as the broader concept, not only for a comprehensive definition (such as the one above), but also in view of the processes of maturation and growth which take place in the organism and are independent of learning.

2. *Special interpretations.* Different theoretical conceptions led to two main areas of definition. On the one hand, development is regarded as growth and described as a quantitative increase (L. Carmichael, U. Undeutsch); on the other, it is understood as a qualitative change taking place in phases or stages (O. Kroh, O. Tumlirz, C. Bühler), leading (spirally) to higher developmental forms (A. Gesell), or comprising the superimposition of higher on lower layers (H. Rothacker, Ph. Lersch). A third approach to a definition considers the decisive factors of development such as the "principle of convergence" of *anlage* (q.v.) (natural endowment) and environment (W. Stern), development as *anlage* unfolding according to some plan (K. Bühler), or the combined effects of endowment, environment and personal activity (self-formation and self-realization) of the individual (G. W. Allport, q.v.). Today the question of a conceptual clarification of development is of secondary importance.

3. *History.* The roots of the psychology (or the concept) of development are to be found in Greek philosophy. Heraclitus taught that there was an eternal becoming; Empedocles explained that life originated in abiogenesis. For Aristotle, growth was development from potentiality to action. His principle of being as the realization of essence (entelechy, q.v.) has influenced German developmental psychology up to the present day. The same is true of the influence of Leibniz, who ascribed development and change to the spontaneous activity of "windowless" monads (i.e. elementary units containing the principle of their own changes). Development as learning can be traced back to Locke's empiricism. Darwin established the theory of heredity (q.v.), which explains the origin and development of animal species as arising from selection and mutation. This theory derives from phylogenetic sources not only the physical development of man but his experience and behavior. On the other hand, the concept of development was given a more humanistic interpretation in the nineteenth century. Its use in the philosophy of history was often directly transferred to individual development (ascending spirally toward some final end). The study of history led W. Dilthey to an intuitive characterization of human life as a mental process. W. Preyer's book of 1882 was an important landmark in the evolution of developmental psychology as a branch of objective science. In Germany the work of William and Clara Stern, and Karl and Charlotte Bühler soon took the theory of development to one of its peaks. Other important authors were Hildegard Hetzer, O. Kroh, O. Tumlirz, A. Busemann, especially H. Werner, but also F. Krueger (genetic psychology of totality), Freud (development of sexuality, importance of childhood for the genesis of personality traits) and C. G. Jung (development as active self-formation from the viewpoint of depth psychology). In the U.S.A. research into the psychology of development began at an early date with Stanley Hall and

J. M. Baldwin; in France with A. Binet, O. Decroly and E. Claparède. The most important influence even now is J. Piaget (q.v.), whose work is only just coming to be more widely known outside Europe.

4. *Methods.* There are the following *methods of compiling and interpreting data:* (*a*) systematic observation without prompting: studies of families and observation in the domestic situation, collection of data from a random sample of situations (e.g. play, meals, in school, etc.), and times during the day; in the optimum case the ethological method (see *Ethology*); (*b*) systematic observation with prompting: recourse to physical data (e.g. measurement of strength and speed, of reaction time, compilation of physiological data), psychometric techniques, experimentation (q.v.) (in the narrower sense). Specific possibilities in research into development are the evaluation of diary entries and the use of play to gain insight into children's behavior.

Research into the course of development: (*a*) Comparison of different age levels: longitudinal studies (observation of the same sample over prolonged periods of time), cross-sectional methods (comparison of representatives of different age groups at a given time); when considering the generation effect and test-retest effect, sequential models are used which couple longitudinal and cross-sectional studies; (*b*) simulation of development: control of conditions which seem to be important in "natural" development by using them as an independent variable and studying their short-term effects (over days or months).

5. *Present state of research.* (*a*) *Cognitive development.* The study of the development of intelligence was dominated for a long time by the conception of a rapid growth until the end of the second decade, followed by a slow decline in achievement. Often this growth curve obtained by cross-sectional studies could not be confirmed by longitudinal studies, which tended to show a progressively slow rise until old age (Bayle & Oden). As age increases, so does the number of intelligence factors (differentiation hypothesis of intelligence: H. E. Garrett, C. Burt). H. A. Witkin classifies mental development in terms of field-dependence and field-independence and differentiation: as age increases, there is greater ability to perceive embedded figures (q.v.), i.e. to detach elements (units) from the surrounding field. The development of "field articulation" is subject to fluctuations which may have physiological and social causes. Problem-solving strategies likewise change with age. H. H. Kendler concludes from his results that for young children the simple reinforcement model is still applicable, but with older children the explanation of performance in novel learning situations requires representative variables (concepts) (see *Apperception categories*). The development of thought strategies passes from primitive stereotyped practices (M. W. Weir) to methods which employ only positive examples of a concept, and from there to strategies which can make use of positive and negative information (S. Nadiraschwili). Piaget's approach to the description of cognitive development is being taken further and revised in very different circles. Assimilation and accommodation as component processes of adaptation in the first two years of life develop into sensorimotor intelligence, which coordinates perception and movement sequences. With the elaboration of basic schemata, thinking begins to develop, and moves from the pre-operational stage (beginning with the symbolic function) to concrete operational thought, and finally to formal operational thought, when the adolescent is able to think reflectively about the logical operations themselves and use them systematically (e.g. in mathematics). Characteristic progress to higher levels of thought which is associated with age depends on the nature of the exercises set. For the whole of cognitive development *curiosity and exploration* seem to be decisive. This behavior has its roots in the orienting reflex (q.v.) and in the affective excitation released by conflict situations (D. E.

Berlyne). See *Language; Conflict; Child psychology*.

(*b*) When considering *human development as a process of socialization* (see *Socialization*), the assumption of adult and sex roles is most important. Learning cultural standards can be described as the development of value judgments. The basic values of our culture are taken over at an early age but undergo revision in the second decade of life when the child or adolescent is strongly influenced by peer group culture. Norms are assimilated largely by imitative learning, said to include the establishment of the super-ego (q.v.) by the introjection of libidinal objects (parents) and their punitive energy. Classical conditioning (see *Conditioning; Conscience; Criminality*) can be adduced to explain the appearance and operation of the "bad conscience" (H. J. Eysenck).

(*c*) *Development of personality*. Here an increase of cognitive control seems to be generally characteristic of the development of personality traits. The complex interaction of the many components in each person's life leads to a result which is in every case unique. See *Personality; Character*.

(*d*) *Physical development*. This can be characterized by growth curves. On an average, there is a negative acceleration rate for entire body size and weight as well as for many individual organs. In physical development there is rapid growth of the brain, which possesses its full complement of cells even before birth and has already reached 80 per cent of its final weight at the age of four. J. Tanner speaks of a "skeletal age", a "dental maturity age" and a "morphological age". The speed at which maturity is reached is largely genetically programmed but there are environmental influences (acceleration, q.v., of total growth since the previous century), influences of nutritional standards, and dependence on social conditions (children from large families and underprivileged classes tend to be smaller and weigh less). During puberty there is a general advance in growth, and many physiological changes can be noticed (blood pressure, pulse and basal metabolism). See *Aging*.

6. *Explanatory principles*. Inherent in the concept of development is a sense of "unfolding from within"; this led to a descriptive model of development as *growth and maturation*. This view is very important in explaining the development of animal organisms, but is also applied to human psychological development when discussing physical and mental correlations (U. Undeutsch, F. Steinwachs, W. Arnold, C. Burt). Sequences of changes in experience and behavior are interpreted here as processes of maturation (q.v.). But the modern emphasis in human development is on learning processes. To describe the development of habits (see *Habit*), affective states, and the conditions underlying motivation, the model of classical and instrumental conditioning is useful (though not completely satisfactory). The process of socialization as incorporation of an asocial, uncultured being into the cultural community requires imitative learning as an additional explanatory principle. Neither of the two principles is adequate for the characterization of cognitive development, which requires a description and interpretation of learning as a process of organization and structuralization.

Independently of the dichotomy of learning and maturation, the two concepts differentiation and centralization are still used (H. Werner). With the progressive change of the organism, parts appear which were not visible in the undifferentiated whole. This process of differentiation may be observed in physiological as well as in phylogenetic development (development of the brain, q.v., in the animal world). The individual areas become independent insofar as they fulfill specific tasks; but they do not function independently because, as differentiation increases, central control sources increasingly take care of the coordination, inhibition and activation of the individual areas. As a whole, the principle of centralization enables distant aims to be set and approached; in specific instances, it allows control of motor impulses, selection and structuring in perception, and control of emotional excitation.

7. *Development as a science*. Like other branches of psychology, developmental psychology is changing from a purely descriptive into an "exact" science which endeavors to explain its statements with the aid of theories or at least of *models* (q.v.). Hence the scientific aim of developmental psychology is not primarily educational (to help and protect man), but to elucidate psychological phenomena by examining their genesis. It therefore serves general psychology. The use of the findings of developmental psychology for educational, political and religious ends is a value-oriented application of what is properly a scientific discipline.

Bibliography: Arnold, W.: Begabung und Bildungswilligkeit. Munich, 1968. **Baldwin, J. M.**: Mental development in the child and in the race: Methods and processes. New York, 1895, [3]1906. **Baltes, P.**: Sequenzmodelle zum Studium von Altersprozessen: Querschnitts- und Längsschnittssequenzen. In: Report of 25th German Psychology Association Congress. Göttingen, 1966, 423–30. **Bayley, N. & Oden, M. H.**: The maintenance of intellectual ability in gifted adults. J. Ger., 1955, *10*, 91–107. **Binet, A.**: Les idées modernes sur les enfants. Paris, 1932. **Bruner, J. S., Oliver, R. R., Greenfield, P. M.** *et al.*: Studies in cognitive growth. New York, 1966. **Bühler, C.**: From birth to maturity. London, 1935. **Bühler, K.**: Abriss der geistigen Entwicklung des Kindes. Leipzig, [7]1949. **Burt, C.**: The differentiation of mental ability. Brit. J. educ. Psychol., 1954, *24*, 76–90. **Id.**: Intelligence and heredity. In: The Irish Journal of Educat., 1969, *3*, No. 2. **Carmichael, L.**: Manual of child psychology. New York & London, [2]1954. **Claparède, E.**: Psychologie de l'enfant et pédagogie expérimentale. Geneva, 1926. **Eysenck, H. J.**: The development of moral values in children. VII—The contribution of learning theory. Brit. J. educ. Psychol., 1960, *30*, 11–21. **Garrett, H. E.**: A developmental theory of intelligence. Amer. Psychologist, 1946, *1*, 372–8. **Gesell, A.**: The ontogenesis of infant behavior. In: **Carmichael, L.** (Ed.): Manual of child psychology. New York & London, [2]1954. **Id.**: The first five years of life. New York, 1941. **Id.**: The mental growth of the pre-school child. New York, 1925. **Id.**: Biographies of child development. New York, 1935. **Id. & Ilg, F. L.**: Child development: an introduction to the study of human growth. New York, 1949. **Hetzer, H.**: Kind und Schaffen. Jena, 1931. **Kagan, J. & Moss, H. A.**: Birth to maturity. New York, 1962. **Kendler, H. H. & Kendler, T. S.**: Vertical and horizontal processes in problem solving. Psychol. Rev., 1962, *59*, 1–16. **Kroh, O.**: Entwicklungspsychologie des Grundschulkindes. Langensalza, 1944. **Krueger, F.**: Entwicklungspsychol. der Ganzheit. Rev. der Psychol., 1939/40, *2*. **Lersch, Ph.**: Aufbau der Person. Munich, [9]1964. **Merz, F. & Kalveran, K. T.**: Kritik der Differenzierungshypothese der Intelligenz. Arch. ges. Psychol. 1965, *117*, 287–95. **Nadiraschwili, S.**: Über die Modellierung von Verallgemeinerungsprozessen. Z. Psychol., 1965, *171*, 196–203. **Oerter, R.**: Moderne Entwicklungspsychologie. Donauwörth, [5]1969. **Piaget, J.**: The psychology of intelligence. London, 1950. **Preyer, W.**: Die Seele des Kindes. Leipzig, 1882. **Rothacker, E.**: Die Schichten der Persönlichkeit. Bonn, [4]1952. **Stern, W.**: Psychol. der frühen Kindheit bis zum sechsten Lebensjahre. [6]1928. **Tanner, J.**: Education and physical growth. London, 1962. **Thomae, H.** (Ed.): Entwicklungspsychologie. Handbuch der Psychologie, Vol. 3. Göttingen, 1959. **Tumlirz, O.**: Einführung in die Jugendkunde. Leipzig, 1927. **Undeutsch, U.**: Das Verhältnis von körperlicher und seelischer Entwicklung. Handbuch der Psychologie, Vol. 3. Göttingen, 1959, 329–57. **Weir, M. W.**: Development changes in problem solving strategies. Psychol. Rev., 1964, *71*, 473–90. **Werner, H.**: Einführung in die Entwicklungspsychologie. Leipzig, [2]1933. **Witkin, H. A., Dyk, R. B., Faterson, H. F., Goodenough, D. R. & Karp, S. A.**: Psychological differentiation. New York, 1962.

R. Oerter

Developmental age. The sum of all the items (multiplied by certain time values) which have been solved by the testee at any age from (theoretically) the first month of life. In the "normal" child this sum is equal to the age. The term and concept were first used in 1926 by Furfey and (quite independently) Penning.

Bibliography: Furfey, P. H.: Some preliminary results on the nature of developmental age. Sch. Soc. 1926, *23*, 183–4. **Penning, K.**: Das Problem der Schulreife in historischer und sachlicher Darstellung. Leipzig, 1926.

S.Kr.

Development tests (syn. *Development scales*). A collective name for methods used to assess developmental age and progress in comparison with average development (development quotient), especially for infants and pre-school children. Various aspects of achievement (performance: perception, psychomotor, language, socialization) are usually recorded separately by observation in standardized play situations and by questioning persons in charge. The results are presented as a development profile, and a developmental age and development quotient are established. Despite the easy transition to intelligence tests proper (e.g. the Binet-Simon Test, q.v.), longitudinal studies show only very slight correlations between the DQ in the first year of life and the IQ later. The practical value of these methods is to be found in the diagnosis of developmental disturbances. The best-known tests of this kind come from A. Gesell, Ch. Bühler and H. Hetzer, N. Bayley, P. S. Cattell, O. Brunet and I. Lézine.

Bibliography: **Stott, L. H. & Ball, R. S.:** Infant and pre-school tests: review and evaluation. Monographs of the Society for Research in Child Development. 1965, *30*, 1–151. *A.L.*

Deviation. 1. *Average deviation* (abb. AD), also known as *average variation*, or simply *deviation*, is the average value of the absolute deviations or departures of measures from their arithmetic means,

$$AD = \frac{\Sigma|X - \bar{X}|}{N}.$$

But this is seldom used, since the application of absolutes is disadvantageous in many cases. The *median deviation*, $\frac{x_i}{N}$, is a measurement for the central tendency of deviations $x_i = X_i - B$, where B can be any desired value. If a systematic error k is made in each individual observation, the median deviation will be k. If B is identical with the arithmetic mean, the median deviation will be zero. *W.H.B.*

2. Any departure from a norm.

Deviation, sexual. A deviation from the cultural norm in the selection and/or the arrangement of the stimulus situation helping the attainment of orgasm. Also some disagreement with this norm in relation to the frequency of sexual activity and avoidance of orgasm. See *Perversion*. *U.H.S.*

Dewey, John. B. 20/10/1859 in Burlington (Vermont); d. 2/6/1952 in New York. Social philosopher and educator. Educated at Vermont and Johns Hopkins universities. He first taught psychology at Michigan, and was later Professor in Chicago and Columbia, New York. Taking Hegel as his starting-point, Dewey helped to develop an empirical biological philosophy, functionalism, which emphasized consciousness and thinking as at the service of action and thus of habit formation, and the study of function as fundamental to psychology. Although Dewey made a significant contribution to the branch of American pragmatism known as "instrumentalism" and helped the advance of scientific psychology, his most lasting monument (apart from the multifarious influences of his democratic and ethical theories) has been the extension of child-centered techniques in Anglo-American education and the inspiration of countless teachers and educators to a new respect for cooperative approaches and classroom techniques.

Some Works: Psychology. New York, 1886. The reflex arc concept in psychology. Psychol. Rev., 1896, *3*, 357–70. How we think, N.Y.,1910. Democracy and education. N.Y., 1916. Essays in experimental logic. N.Y., 1916. Human nature and conduct. N.Y., 1922. Experience and nature, N.Y., 1925. Characters and events, 2 vols, N.Y., 1929. Problems of men. N.Y., 1946.

Bibliography: **Boring, E. G.:** John Dewey: 1859–1952. Amer. J. Psychol., 1953, *66*, 145–7. **Roback, A. A.:** A history of American psychology. New York & London, 1964. **Schilipp, P. A.** (Ed.): The philosophy of John Dewey. Evanston, 1940. *F.-C.S.*

Dexterity test. An individual test or a battery component which assesses manual speed and accuracy. See *Motor skills; Manual dexterity*.

Dextrality. See *Laterality.*

Diagnostics. See *Psychodiagnostics.*

Diagram. A schematic representation of essential (e.g. spatial) relations between parts or variables.

Diastole. A phase of inactivity during a cardiac cycle in which the heart muscle relaxes, and the ventricle dilates. It alternates rhythmically with the *systole* (contraction of the heart muscle) and lasts, according to the heart rate, 0·3 to 0·8 seconds. During this time the pressure of both ventricles sinks to its minimal value of about 0 mm Hg so that blood can flow from the auricles and adjacent veins into the ventricles. *E.D.*

Diathesis. Constitutional disposition or predisposition to some disease of the whole organism or of certain systems of the organism. A number of diatheses are distinguished according to the nature of the disease: e.g. *angiospastic diathesis* with vasolability, rapid fluctuations of blood pressure, loss of color and blushing, fainting fits and migraine; *exudative diathesis* with a congenital tendency in children's organisms to various diseases of the skin and the mucous membrane; *hemorrhagic diathesis,* with a tendency to persistent bleeding. *E.D.*

Diathetic proportion. Prominent scales of temperament with the cyclothymic and cycloid constitutions. An individual can pass through the stages, or experience one as a permanent temperamental emphasis.

Cyclothymic: elevated (cheerful, impulsively irascible), syntonic (easy-going, genial), subdued (quiet, melancholic).

Cycloid: hypomanic (excessively jolly, angry, mobile), sub-depressive (dejected, lacking in drive). *W.K.*

Diatonic. In music: the diatonic scale is the seven-tone major scale consisting of seven whole tones, and two semitones between the third and the fourth and the seventh and eighth intervals. *P.S. & R.S.*

Dichotomy. 1. The division into two of a population or a sample (distribution) according to an external criterion. **2.** The doctrine or theory that man consists of two parts: soma and psyche, body and soul.

Dichromatopsia (syn. *Dichromatism; Dichromatic vision*). Partial color blindness in which the person affected can only distinguish yellow from blue (red-green blindness) or only green from red (yellow-blue blindness). In the first case green and red are mistaken for one another and for grey; in the second case the person affected cannot distinguish a blue tone from a yellow but sees them both as two different tones of grey. See *Color blindness.* *G.Ka.*

Diction. Style of verbal presentation, particularly the clarity and precision of words and phrases spoken or sung. *G.D.W.*

Didactics. In educational theory the branch dealing with the formulation of aims in teaching, the choice of subjects to be taught, and the appropriate teaching method(s); however, the term is usually applied to instructional methodology.

Didactic analysis: an instructional psychoanalysis undergone by a prospective analyst. *G.B.*

Diencephalon (syn. *Betweenbrain; Interbrain*). Situated between the telencephalon (q.v.) and mesencephalon (q.v.), and consisting of the hypothalamus (q.v.), the thalamus (q.v.), and metathalamus and epithalamus. The metathalamus contains the geniculate bodies (*corpus geniculatum laterale* and *corpus geniculatum mediale*) which act as synaptic centers in the visual and auditory pathways. The pineal body is part of the epithalamus. (See *Pineal gland.*)

Bibliography: **Gardner, E., Gray, D. J. & Orahilly, R.:** Anatomy. Philadelphia, 1969. *G.A.*

Dietetics. The science of regulating food intake for reasons of health. *G.D.W.*

Difference tone. If two pure tones (primary tones) differing in pitch are sounded simultaneously, a third tone is heard in addition, the frequency of which is equal to the difference in frequency between the two primary tones. *P.S. & R.S.*

Differential Aptitude Test (abb. DAT). A test devised for educational and vocational guidance (q.v.); the subtests produce eight part-results (verbal reasoning, number ability, abstract reasoning, spatial relations, mechanical reasoning, clerical speed and accuracy in office work, language use: orthography and syntax), which are not differentiated factorially. Widely used in the U.S.A. (especially for grades 8 to 12).

Bibliography: **Bennet, G. K., Seashore, H. G. & Wesman, A. G.:** Differential Aptitude Tests. Psychol. Corp. N.Y., 1947–59. *R.M.*

Differential diagnosis. A diagnosis made in order to decide between different groups, e.g. clinical profiles, or occupations. *R.M.*

Differential inhibition. See *Inhibition, internal.*

Differential psychology is concerned with the nature and origins of individual differences in psychological traits. Such differences are not limited to man, but occur throughout the animal scale. Psychological studies of animals, from one-celled organisms to anthropoid apes, reveal wide individual differences in learning, emotionality, motivation, and other behavioral characteristics. So large are these differences within each species, that the ranges of performance overlap even when widely separated species are compared. When examined with the same learning task, the brightest rat in a group may excel the dullest monkey.

Although in popular descriptions persons are often put into distinct categories, such as dull or bright, and excitable or calm, actual measurement of any psychological trait shows that individuals vary in degree along a continuous scale. In most traits, the distribution approximates the bell-shaped normal probability curve, with the greatest clustering of cases near the center of the range and a gradual decrease in numbers as the extremes are approached. First derived by mathematicians in their study of probability, the normal curve is obtained whenever the variable measured results from a very large number of independent and equally weighted factors. Because of the extremely large number of hereditary and environmental factors that contribute to the development of most psychological traits, it is reasonable to expect that such traits should be distributed in accordance with the normal curve.

1. *Heredity and environment.* (*a*) *Concepts.* The origins of individual differences are found in the innumerable and complex interactions between each individual's heredity and his environment. Heredity comprises the genes transmitted by each parent at conception. If there is a chemical deficiency or imbalance in the genes, a seriously defective organism may result, with physical anomalies as well as severely retarded intelligence. Except for such pathological extremes, however, heredity sets very broad limits to behavior development. Within these limits, what the individual actually becomes depends upon his environment.

Environment includes the sum total of stimuli to which the individual responds from conception to death. It comprises a vast multiplicity of variables, ranging from air and food to educational facilities and the attitudes of one's associates. Environmental influences begin to operate before birth. Nutritional deficiencies, toxins, and other chemical or physical conditions of the prenatal environment may exert a deep and permanent effect upon both physical and mental development. Hence conditions present at birth, often loosely designated as innate or congenital, are not necessarily hereditary. Similarly, organic conditions need not be hereditary. Mental retardation resulting from brain injury in infancy, for example, has an organic but not a hereditary origin.

The relationship between heredity and environment can best be described in terms of interaction. Such interaction implies that a given environmental factor will exert a *different influence* depending upon the specific hereditary material upon which it operates. For example, the number and quality of symphonic recordings available in the home will exert a significant influence upon the musical development of a hearing child but none upon that of a deaf child. Conversely, any given hereditary factor will operate differently under different environment conditions. Two identical twins will differ markedly in body weight if one is systematically over-fed for six months and the other kept on a semi-starvation diet.

(*b*) *Methodology*. The methods used to investigate the operation of hereditary and environmental factors in behavior development may be subsumed under three major approaches: selective breeding, experiential variation, and statistical studies of family resemblances. Selective breeding for behavioral characteristics has been successfully applied to several species. From a single initial group of rats, for example, it proved possible to breed two strains representing "bright" and "dull" maze-learners, respectively. Another investigation on such selectively bred strains provided a good example of the interaction of heredity and environment. When reared in restricted environments, both strains performed almost as poorly as did the genetically "dull" rats reared in a natural environment. On the other hand, an enriched environment, providing a variety of stimulation and opportunities for motor activity, improved the performance of the "dull" strain; both groups now performed at about the level of the "brights" in a natural environment.

A second approach to the study of heredity and environment is concerned with the behavioral effects of systematic variations in experience. Experimental investigations of this question either provide special training or prevent the normal exercise of a particular function. Through such experiments, many activities formerly regarded as completely unlearned or "instinctive", such as nest-building and the care of the young by rats, have been found to depend upon prior experiences. A series of experiments with monkeys demonstrated the effects of training upon learning ability itself. Through the formation of learning sets, the animals were able to learn the solution of complex problems because of their prior experience in solving simpler problems of a similar nature. Some studies of young children have used the method of co-twin control, in which one identical twin is given intensive training in, e.g., stair climbing, while the other serves as the control. Others have compared the development of children reared in culturally deprived or restricted environments, such as orphanages, with that of children reared in more nearly average environments. Considerable retardation has been found in deprived environments, the retardation becoming more severe with increasing age. There is some evidence, however, that appropriate educational programs, particularly when introduced in early childhood, may counteract the detrimental effects of such environments on intellectual development.

The third approach uses statistical analyses of family resemblances and differences. In general, the closer the hereditary relation, the more similar will test scores be. On most intelligence tests, for example, identical twin correlations are close to 0·90; fraternal twin correlations cluster around 0·70; and siblings yield correlations around 0·50, as do parents and children. It should be noted, however, that a family is a cultural as well as a biological unit. The more closely two persons are related by heredity, in general, the greater will be the similarity of their environments and the extent of their influence upon each other. Investigations of foster children and of identical twins reared apart permit some isolation of hereditary and environmental factors, but several uncontrolled conditions in these studies preclude definitive conclusions.

3. *Nature of intelligence.* (*a*) *Composition.* Intelligence has been identified with the intelligence quotient (IQ) obtained in an intelligence test. Such tests do reflect at least partly the concept of intelligence prevalent in the culture in which they were developed. Most current intelligence tests measure chiefly scholastic aptitude, or that combination of abilities required for school achievement. Modern intelligence testing originated with Alfred Binet's development of a test to assess intellectual retardation among school children. Intelligence tests have frequently been validated against such academic criteria as school grades, teachers' ratings of intelligence, promotion and graduation data, and amount of schooling completed. In content, most intelligence tests are predominantly verbal, with some inclusion of arithmetic skills, quantitative reasoning, and memory. (See *Abilities.*)

With the increasing participation of psychologists in vocational counseling and personnel selection came the realization that supplementary tests were needed to measure aptitudes not covered by traditional intelligence tests. As a result, so-called special aptitude tests were developed for mechanical, clerical, and other functions. At the same time, basic research on the nature of intelligence was being conducted by the techniques of factor analysis. Essentially these techniques involve statistical analysis of the inter-correlations among test scores in order to discover the smallest number of independent factors that can account for their interrelations. Among the aptitudes or "factors" thus identified are verbal comprehension, word fluency, arithmetic skills, quantitative reasoning, perceptual speed, spatial visualization, and mechanical comprehension. Through factor analysis, the functions measured by intelligence tests were themselves identified as relatively independent verbal and numerical aptitudes, and these aptitudes, in combination with some of those underlying special aptitude tests, now provide a more comprehensive picture of human abilities.

(*b*) *Intellectual deviates.* The mentally retarded and the gifted represent the lower and upper extremes of the distribution of intelligence. Because the distribution is continuous, there is no sharp separation between these groups and the normal. In terms of intelligence-test performance, mental retardation is customarily identified with IQs below 70, covering about two to three per cent of the general population. Decisions regarding the disposition and treatment of individual cases are based not only upon the IQ, but also upon a comprehensive study of the individual's intellectual development, educational history, social competence, physical condition and familial situation. Although a few rare forms of mental retardation result from defective genes, many varieties can be traced to environmental factors operating before or after birth and including both physical and psychological conditions. (See *Mental defect*).

At the other end of the scale, children with IQs above 140, falling in the upper one per cent of the general population, have been found to be typically healthy, emotionally well adjusted, successful in school, and characterized by a wide range of interests. As they grow into maturity, these gifted children as a whole maintain their superiority in adult achievements. Other research on the intellectually gifted includes case studies of living scientists and an analysis of records of eminent men of the past. Since the 1950s, research on the nature and sources of creativity has expanded rapidly. The concept of intelligence has thereby been broadened to include a number of creative aptitudes, which have also been identified through factor-analytic studies.

(*c*) *Growth and decline.* Longitudinal studies of age changes in performance on traditional intelligence tests reveal a slow rise in infancy, followed by more rapid progress and eventual slowing down as maturity is approached. It should be noted, however, that intelligence tests measure a combination of several traits and that the nature of this composite differs with age. In infancy the IQ is based largely upon sensorimotor development, while in childhood it depends increasingly on verbal and other abstract functions.

Intelligence-test performance continues to improve at least into the twenties. Among intellectually superior persons, especially university graduates and those engaged in relatively intellectual occupations, such improvement may continue throughout life. In more nearly average samples, tested abilities tend to decline beyond the thirties, the drop being greatest in tasks involving speed, visual perception, and abstract spatial relations. Older persons can learn nearly as well as younger, but are more seriously handicapped when the task conflicts with well-established habits. Cross-sectional studies, utilizing different samples at different age levels, may give misleading results because of lack of comparability of groups in education, cultural milieu, and other conditions.

3. *Group differences.* (*a*) *Sex differences.* Psychological test surveys show that men as a group excel in speed and coordination of gross bodily movements, spatial orientation, mechanical comprehension, and arithmetic reasoning, while women excel in manual dexterity, perceptual speed and accuracy, memory, numerical computation, verbal fluency, and other tasks involving the mechanics of language. Among the major personality differences are the greater aggressiveness, achievement drive, and emotional stability of the male, and the stronger social orientation of the female. Sex differences in aptitudes and personality traits depend upon both biological and cultural factors. The influence of biological conditions may be quite direct, as in the effect of male sex hormone upon aggressive behavior. Or it may be indirect, as in the social and educational effects of the more rapid development of girls as compared to boys. The contribution of culture is illustrated by the wide differences in sex roles found in contemporary cultures and in different historical periods.

(*b*) *Racial and cultural differences.* If individuals are classified with regard to such categories as social class, occupational level, urban-versus-rural residence, or nationality, significant group differences are often found in child-rearing practices, sexual behavior, emotional responses, interests, and attitudes, as well as in performance on many aptitude tests. In all such comparisons, the direction and amount of group difference depends upon the particular trait investigated. Because each culture or subculture fosters the development of its own characteristic pattern of aptitudes and personality traits, comparisons in terms of such global measures as IQ or general emotional adjustment can have little meaning.

Races are populations that differ in the relative frequency of certain genes. They are formed whenever a group becomes relatively isolated, for either geographic or social reasons, so that marriage among its members is more frequent than marriage with outsiders. Since isolation fosters cultural as well as racial differentiation, the contributions of biological and cultural factors to race differences are difficult to separate. Although available data are inconclusive, studies using special experimental designs point more strongly to cultural than to biological causes of existing racial differences in psychological traits.

In racial comparisons as in all group comparisons, average differences between groups are far smaller than the range of individual differences within each group. Consequently the distributions of the groups overlap to a marked degree. Even when the averages of two groups differ by a large amount, individuals can be found in the low-scoring group who surpass individuals in the high-scoring group. Hence an individual's group membership is a poor guide to his standing in any psychological trait.

Bibliography: Anastasi, A.: Differential psychology. New York, [3]1958. **Id.:** Psychological testing. New York, [3]1968. **Id.** (Ed.): Individual differences. New York, 1965. **Cooper, R. & Zubek, J.:** Effects of enriched and restricted early environments on the learning ability of bright and dull rats. Canad. J. Psychol., 1958, *12*, 159–64. **Dreger, R. M. & Miller, K. S.:** Comparative psychological studies of negroes and whites in the United States: 1959–1965. Psychol. Bull. Monogr. Suppl., 1968, *70* (3, pt. 2), 1–58. **Fuller, J. L. & Thompson, W. R.:** Behavior genetics. New York, 1960. **Garai, J. E. & Scheinfeld, A.:** Sex differences in mental and behavioral traits. Genet. Psychol. Monogr., 1968, *77*, 169–299. **Guilford, J. P.:** The nature of human intelligence. New York, 1967. **Hebb, D. O.:** Heredity and environment in mammalian behavior. Brit. J. anim. Behav., 1953, *1*, 43–7. **Hirsch, J.:** Behavior-genetic analysis. New York, 1967. **Hunt, J. McV.:** Intelligence and experience. New York, 1961. **Maccoby, E.** (Ed.): The development of sex differences. Stanford, Calif., 1966. **Oden, M. H.:** The fulfillment of promise: 40-year follow-up of the Terman gifted group. Genet. Psychol. Monogr., 1968, *77*, 3–93. **Scheinfeld, A.:** Your heredity and environment. Philadelphia, 1964. **Sears, R. R., Maccoby, E. & Levin, H.:** Patterns of child-rearing. Evanston, Ill., 1957. **Tyler, L. E.:** The psychology of human differences. New York, [3]1965. **Vandenberg, S. G.:** Contributions of twin research to psychology. Psychol. Bull., 1966, *66*, 327–52.

A. Anastasi

Differential psychopharmacology. A branch of psychopharmacology (q.v.) concerned with the description and elucidation of inter- and intra-individual differences in psychological effects of psychopharmaceutical agents. Central areas of research in differential psychopharmacology are: (*a*) dependence of the effects of pharmaceutical agents on relatively constant, psychological personality and other characteristics of the testees. Such factors have been found to include: sex, age, race, neuroticism, psychoticism, extraversion, achievement motivation, type of constitution, innate metabolic dysfunction; (*b*) dependence of the effects of pharmaceutical drugs on actual personality characteristics. It has been shown that there are differential effects, *inter alia*, dependent on emotional arousal and attitudes to the experiment and the experimenter; (*c*) dependence of drug effects on situational factors such as the nature of the tests, behavior of the experimenter, whether group or individual test. As yet there is no comprehensive theory of the effective mechanism of factors (*a*) to (*c*) listed above. In particular, it is still an open question to what extent the covariation of the effects of pharmaceutical agents and relatively constant personality traits can be explained in the sense of individual differences in neurophysiological (e.g. Eysenck, 1963) and biochemical reactions, or with the aid of varying modes of assimilation (e.g., DiMascio, 1968; Janke, 1964) with different personality structures. The marked intraindividual inconstancy of psychopharmaceutical effects proves that there is always a significant participation of situation-adaptive processing mechanisms.

Bibliography: DiMascio, A. & Shader, R. I.: Behavioral toxity. In: **Efron, D.** (Ed.): Psychopharmacology 1957–1967. Washington, 1968. **Eysenck, H. J.** (Ed.): Experiments with drugs. Oxford, 1963. **Janke, W.:** Über die Abhängigkeit der Wirkung psychotroper Substanzen von Persönlichkeitsmerkmalen. Frankfurt, 1964. **Janke, W. & Debus, G.:** Experimental studies on antianxiety agents with normal subjects. Methodological considerations and review of the main effects. In: **Efron, D.** (Ed.): Psychopharmacology 1957–67. Washington, 1968. **Legewie, H.:** Persönlichkeitstheorie und Psychopharmaka. Meisenheim, 1968. **Rickels, K.** (Ed.): Non-specific factors in drug therapy. Springfield, Ill., 1968.

W.J.

Differential running time. The left-right localization of sound depends upon the time difference with which the sound strikes the two ears (Hornbostel). Localization occurs toward the ear struck first, the angle of the apparent source depending on the amount of precession. The ability to localize sounds indicates that people can discriminate time intervals in this way down to 0·015 seconds. *C.D.F.*

Differential sensibility. Ability to distinguish one sensory quality or intensity from another, as indexed by the *differential threshold*, or *just noticeable difference* (j.n.d.). *G.D.W.*

Differential threshold. See *Threshold.*

Differentiation. In psychology the concept of differentiation is used to refer both to differentiation as a basic process in organic and psychological development, and differentiation as a cognitive process.

In developmental psychology differentiation denotes the course taken by the organism from relatively simple to highly structured forms of behavior. Differentiation is necessarily accompanied by integration (q.v.) which incorporates each newly acquired behavioral unit into the totality of the organism in order to avoid any disorganization of behavior. The purpose of differentiation as developmental psychology sees it is to be found especially in an increase of adaptive capability. In conjunction with that, differentiation helps individuality to evolve.

Differentiation in the cognitive sense should be understood as enabling an individual to distinguish two or several environmental stimuli or to react differently to them. In learning theory, differentiation is thus the opposite of generalization (q.v.).

Bibliography: See *Child psychology; Development.*

P.S.

Differentiation inhibition. See *Inner inhibition.*

Differentiation theory of intelligence. The supposition that the development of the intelligence from childhood to adulthood is subject not only to the well-known quantitative but especially to qualitative changes in the sense of a differentiation of initially global capacities into aspects of intellectual performance which become increasingly independent.

Bibliography: Pawlik, K.: Dimensionen des Verhaltens. Berne & Stuttgart, 1968, 350–54. *M.A.*

Difficulty level. The level of an (intelligence) test item assigned to it in relation to the proportion of a sample successfully solving it. See *Abilities; Decision processes; Problem solving.*

Dilatation. The morbid enlargement of hollow organs such as heart, stomach or bladder. In the case of the heart one speaks of myogenous or tonogenous dilatation, depending on whether the muscular mass is hypertrophied (enlarged) from overstrain or overexpanded because of the increased residual volume. In both cases the total mass of the heart is larger and can be seen in an X-ray photograph of the thorax as the *cor bovinum* ("ox heart"). *E.D.*

Dimension. The concept denotes in general a definite quantity which can be measured in every direction in which it extends, and it has also been admitted into psychological terminology with this general meaning. Every psychological measurement embraces one or several dimensions of experience or behavior. W. Stern's theory of personality emphasized the concept of dimension. Recently "dimension" has been used with increasing frequency by some personality researchers in place of the traditional terms *characteristic* and *trait.* Behind this change in terminology is an attempt to determine personality quantitatively by establishing its positions numerically on prescribed bipolar continua, that is dimensionally. Hence the term "dimension" now refers to a construct of personality theory. See *Personality; Traits; Type.*

Bibliography: Arnold, W.: Person, Charakter, Persönlichkeit. Göttingen, [3]1970. **Eysenck, H. J.:** Dimensions of personality. London, 1947. **Graumann, C. F.:** Eigenschaften als Problem der Persönlichkeitsforschung. In: Handbuch der Psychologie, Vol. 4. Göttingen, 1960, 87–149. **Stern, W.:** Allgemeine Psychologie, Vol. 1, The Hague, 1935. *P.S.*

Dimension, psychological-personalistic theory of. An element in W. Stern's theory of personality. According to this conception, personal dimensions are directions and time processes within which a person realizes himself. The concept of dimension is thus understood not formally but dynamically. The basic dimension of any person is the polarity *within/without*. On this basis two groups of personal dimensions can be distinguished: *individual* and *world dimensions*.

Bibliography: Stern, W.: Allgemeine Psychologie. Vol. 1. The Hague, 1935. *P.S.*

Diminishing returns, law of. Improvement gradually decreases with each successive increment of application.

Dionysian type. See *Apollonian type*.

Diopter. A unit of measurement for the refractive power of an optical system, measured in m^{-1}. The refractive power is the reciprocal value of the focal distance.

Diplacusis. Diplacusis or unilateral displacement to one side of pitch sensitivity can be caused by changes in the perilymph (protein content, viscosity) or by metabolic disorders (e.g. by deafness) in the hair cells. See *Basilar membrane; Organ of Corti.* *M.S.*

Diploid. Possessing two pairs of chromosome sets. The genetic substance thus exists in duplicate. One chromosome (q.v.) always comes from the father, and one from the mother.

Diplopia. Seeing double. Diplopia in one eye is caused by a refractive defect. Diplopia in both eyes occurs when their visual axes are not focussed during fixation so that the image falls on identical retinal points (q.v.). *R.R.*

Dipsomania. A form of alcoholism (q.v.) considered to be rare. Described initially by von Bruhl-Cramer as "*die periodische Trunksucht*" which he said was distinct from "*die intermittende Trunksucht*". In the latter, intermittent, form the periods of abstinence were as little as three days, whereas in periodic alcoholism or dipsomania the sufferer remained abstinent for weeks or months. A prodromal phase of irritability and depression followed by a small intake of alcohol and a short period of sobriety is said to precede the phase of heavy pathological drinking, which is short-lived. The term may cover a number of etiological and symptomatological states. Syn. *Periodic alcoholism; Epsilon alcoholism.* *R.P.S.*

Directive therapy. Psychotherapy in which the therapist assumes a large amount of responsibility in controlling the course of the treatment and in deciding what is best for the patient. See also *Active therapy.* *G.D.W.*

Directivity (syn. *Directiveness; Directive method; Strictness*). One of the two principal dimensions (directivity vs. permissiveness and warmth and acceptance vs. coldness and rejection) with which the behavior of teachers and parents can be characterized in active teaching and upbringing. The distinguishing features of directivity are frequent orders, instructions, rebukes and questions as well as the irreversibility of judgments. It usually results in little cooperation, interruption of teaching, receptive and unoriginal behavior. See *Child psychology; Punishment.*

Bibliography: O'Connor, N. & Franks, C. M.: Childhood upbringing and other environmental factors. In: **Eysenck, H. J.** (Ed.): Handbook of abnormal psychology. London, 1960. **Riesman, D.** *et al.*: The lonely crowd. Yale, 1950. **Sears, R. R., Maccoby, E. E. & Levin, H.:** Patterns of child rearing. New York, 1957. *G.K.*

Direct vision (syn. *Foveal vision*). Optic perception by way of the *fovea centralis;* fixation on an object.

Disappointment. An emotional phenomenon accompanying *frustration* (q.v.), which occurs when expectation is not fulfilled or when a need is not gratified. *P.S.*

Discrete measure. A discrete measure makes it possible to carry out a discontinuous measurement of a possibly continuous quantitative variable. Such a variable is called a *discrete variable.* *W.H.B.*

Discriminated operant. B. F. Skinner's term for what, in his system, corresponds to a generalized response. See *Conditioning, classical and operant.*

Discrimination tests. A common method for studying learning, particularly with non-human species, is systematically to reward the subject's choice of one stimulus against another. For example, although rats are relatively non-visual in orientation, under suitable conditions they are able to learn to discriminate horizontal stripes from vertical stripes (i.e. react differently to them). Discrimination problems may of course be used to study perceptual as well as learning phenomena. *G.D.W.*

Discriminative learning. See *Learning, discriminative*

Discriminatory analysis. A statistical method for classifying individual values in one of several populations (q.v.) or for separating different populations. It is essential that the classification or separation should take place on the basis not of one but of several criteria. If, for example, an individual has to be classified on the basis of a score for one of x populations, this is done by discriminatory analysis so that the error (q.v.) on average is minimal. There must be (*a*) several scores for the individual to be classified and (*b*) the corresponding scores for other individuals whose classification with respect to the populations is known or has also to be ascertained. Knowledge of the scores for the members of the basic groups enables discriminant function to be obtained. *W.H.B.*

Disease. See *Sickness.*

Disengagement, theory of. This concerns the social and mental processes at work in a diminution of engagement in the social environment. Henry stresses the close connection between aging and disengagement, but other factors, such as variables (cultural values, attitudes, mode of life, economic and social conditions) play a part.

Bibliography: Henry, W. E.: The theory of intrinsic disengagement. Proc. Internat. Gerontology. Copenhagen, 1963. *P.S. & R.S.*

Disillusion. To disenchant; dispel illusions; bring an individual or group face to face with reality, no matter how discomforting this may be to them.

Disinhibition. 1. This denotes the removal of those factors which prevent a reaction.

2. In a narrower sense, the cessation of the regulative functions of the cerebral cortex (q.v.) under the influence of alcohol or drugs.
K.E.P.

Disintegrated type. See *Integrated type.*

Disintegration. See *Integration.*

Disjection. A splitting of the feeling of personality in dreams; one plays a double role, being simultaneously actor and spectator.
F.-C.S.

Disorientation. People are normally aware of who they are, where they are in time and space, and have a clear perception of their body image—especially in terms of the right-left orientation. When this awareness breaks down the person is said to be disorientated. Occurs in organic conditions which produce clouding of consciousness and/or amnesia; in mental disorders which produce delusions and/or hallucinations; and in neurotic disorders such as hysterical fugues which produce memory loss.
R.H.

Dispersion. The scatter (q.v.), or degree of difference, of individual scores in a population (q.v.) (see *Sample*). The usual statistics are either standard deviations (q.v.) from a central value, such as the mean variation mV (the sum of the absolute deviations divided by N) and the variance (q.v.) (mean value of the squared deviations), or positional parameters as, for example, the quartile deviation.
W.H.B.

Displacement in ESP is an unconscious phase shift by the subject between the sequence of calls (q.v.) and targets (q.v.). If this shift is of a fairly definite order, e.g. mainly by one trial over a large number of trials, evidence for ESP can be obtained through the analysis of displacement.

Forward displacement: The intended targets run ahead of the calls by a certain number of trials, i.e. the subject aims his, say, tenth call at the eleventh target, e.g. if the displacement is by one trial.

Backward displacement: The intended targets limp behind the calls by a certain number of trials, i.e. the subject aims his, say, tenth call at the seventh target, e.g. if the displacement is by three trials.
H.H.J.K.

Displacement activity (syn. *Irrelevant activity; Sparking over*). If the normal course of an instinctive activity (see *Instinct*) is disturbed by the absence of the releasing situation, or the occurrence of a conflict (q.v.) between irreconcilable drives, the drive energy can be "abreacted", or discharged, by means of a behavior which is "irrelevant" or inappropriate to the situation, but appropriate to another instinct. E.g.: for the stickleback, when a rival appears at the border of its territory, a conflict arises between fight and flight motives, which releases the displacement activity of sand-digging (part of nest-digging behavior). By ritualization, displacement activities can acquire specific significance as releasing actions, e.g. the sand-digging, originally an outlet, becomes a threat movement.
I.L.

Display-control relations. In ergonomics, the relationship between control or regulative processes (and particularly directed motion) and, e.g., moving-scale instruments. See *Motor skills.*

Displays. Coordinated movements and postures in the functional sphere of agonistic (fight and flight) and sexual behavior, which appear frequently, serve as signals for attraction or intimidation, and are often in themselves sufficient to decide the outcome of incipient conflicts. See *Appeasement gestures; Courtship; Threat behavior.*

Bibliography: Marler, P. R. & Hamilton, W. J.: Mechanisms of animal behavior. Chichester, 1966. **Tinbergen, N.:** Social behaviour in animals. London, [2]1965. *K.F.*

Disposition. A theoretical concept to explain the probabilities (which vary between individuals but are relatively constant) that certain forms of behavior, symptoms and other individual traits will appear. A distinction is made between innate and acquired dispositions. In Allport's personality theory the term "personal disposition" is synonymous with "trait" (q.v.).

Bibliography: Allport, G. W.: Pattern and growth in personality. New York, 1961. *D.B.*

Dissimilation. The breaking up of energy-rich compounds which are obtained by assimilation (q.v.). Dissimilation provides the energy which is necessary to maintain the processes of life and build up the organism. *H.S.*

Dissociation. A process by which some thoughts, attitudes, or other psychological activities lose their normal relationship to others, or to the rest of the personality, and split off to function more or less independently. In this way logically incompatible thoughts, feelings and attitudes may be held concurrently and yet conflict between them averted. A chronic state of dissociation is usually regarded as pathological. Some behaviors and phenomena which have been described in terms of dissociation include multiple or "split" personality, somnambulism (sleep-walking), automatic writing, certain delusional symptoms, hypnotism, and hysterical amnesia. *G.D.W.*

Dissociation of sensation. A specific collection of symptoms indicating a lack of response when half the spinal cord has been destroyed. In addition to other symptoms (loss of muscular response in the corresponding half of the body and, on both sides, a diminution of sensitivity to pressure), there is a dissociated paralysis of sensation: a feeling of pain, cold and warmth can be produced on the paralyzed side but no longer on the sound side. *P.S. & R.S.*

Dissonance. 1. Music: the simultaneous production of two sounds at a distance of a second and a seventh, which is found unpleasant in our cultural sphere. **2.** Psychology: the disturbance caused by two irreconcilable cognitions (see *Dissonance, theory of*).

Bibliography: Neisser, U.: Cognitive psychology. New York, 1967. *P.S. & R.S.*

Dissonance, cognitive. The central concept in L. Festinger's theory of cognitive dissonance, which endeavors to explain or predict changes in attitude (q.v.), and especially the connection between attitudes and behavior. Cognitive dissonance exists when there is a dissonant relation between two or more cognitive elements (i.e. knowledge, an opinion or an attitude concerning any objects, oneself or one's own behavior). Such a case arises when—if the elements are considered separately—one of them could be deduced from the opposite of the other. In addition, the relation between the elements must be relevant for there to be dissonance (q.v.) or consonance (q.v.).

According to Festinger, cognitive dissonance is experienced as unpleasant by the individual and creates pressure directed toward the reduction of the dissonance or toward consonance. The strength of this pressure to reduce dissonance depends on the strength of the existing dissonance, which in turn is a function of the relation between the importance and number of the dissonant elements on the one hand and the consonant elements on the other.

Fundamentally, three possibilities of dissonance reduction are described: (*a*) the changing of one's own behavior as a cognitive element; (*b*) the changing of the environment as a cognitive element; (*c*) the addition of a new cognitive element to lessen the weight of the dissonant as compared with that of the consonant models. See *Homeostasis*.

Bibliography: Festinger, L.: A theory of cognitive dissonance. New York, 1957. **Chapanis, N. P. & Chapanis, A.:** Cognitive dissonance: Five years later. Psychol. Bull., 1964, *61*, 1–22.
A.S.-M.

Dissonance, theory of. A theory of motivation propounded by L. Festinger according to which the motive for human action results from the dissonance (q.v.) of two cognitive elements. There is a case of dissonance when the two elements mutually exclude one another. From this disagreement comes pressure to restore the harmony which has been disturbed. *P.S.*

Distal. Considered away from the body's axis; outward; turned toward the environment. Ant.: *proximal*. For example, the upper arm is in the proximal position, the lower arm in the distal position relative to the elbow. *H.Sch.*

Distance hearing. See *Differential running time; Hearing, localized.*

Distance, social. A variable deduced from the attempt to describe group structures, social positions and interactive behavior among members of a group, or of groups among one another, in categories which are spatially analogous. By social distance, one means the relative accessibility of a person or group or the degree of desired contact with a second person or group. It depends on the spatial distance between two individuals, but also on the similarity of their social attitudes, their interests and preferences, occupations, aims, etc. The greater social distance is, the more the likelihood of contact between individuals or groups diminishes, and the more probable it is that negative or hostile attitudes will interpose themselves between them, and vice versa. The possibility of diminishing social distance by creating common interests, spatial proximity, etc., is seen as a way of reducing negative attitudes, prejudices and hostile actions between individuals or groups. Methods for measuring social distance are offered by the different forms of sociogram (q.v.) (Moreno, 1953; Lindzey & Borgatta, 1954), or the social distance scale according to Bogardus (1928).

Bibliography: Bogardus, E. S.: Immigration and race attitudes. Boston, 1928. **Lindzey, G. & Borgatta, E. T.:** Sociometric measurement. In: **Lindzey, G.** (Ed.): Handbook of social psychology, Vol. 1. Reading (Mass.), 1954. **Moreno, J. L.:** Who shall survive? New York, [2]1953.
A.S.-M.

Distance vision. Seeing, or discrimination of relative distance of, an object more than twenty feet away from the subject.

Distinctiveness. A variable of cues or learned signals, related not only to their appearance but to situational variables, influencing visual discrimination and choice: clarity of outline.

Distorted room. A location suitably designed for the purpose of demonstrating spatial and optical illusions: objects within the room are distorted.

Distributed practice. See *Distribution of practice*.

Distribution. A graphic representation or table of the functional values (scores) of a variable. See *Frequency distribution.*

Distribution of practice (syn. *Distributed practice*). The spacing out of periods of practice (learning) as widely as the total time allows.

Disulfiram (syn. *Tetraethylthiuram disulphide; Antabuse; Aversan; Abstinyl; Refusal*). A substance which is used as an adjunct in the treatment of chronic alcoholism. If administered before alcohol is taken, disulfiram causes pronounced vegetative disturbances (vertigo, vomiting, headache, etc.). *W.J.*

Divergent lines illusion. One of the geometric illusions whose effect is achieved in the same way as *Hering's illusion* (q.v.). The parallel lines appear to diverge where they cross the radiating lines. *C.D.F.*

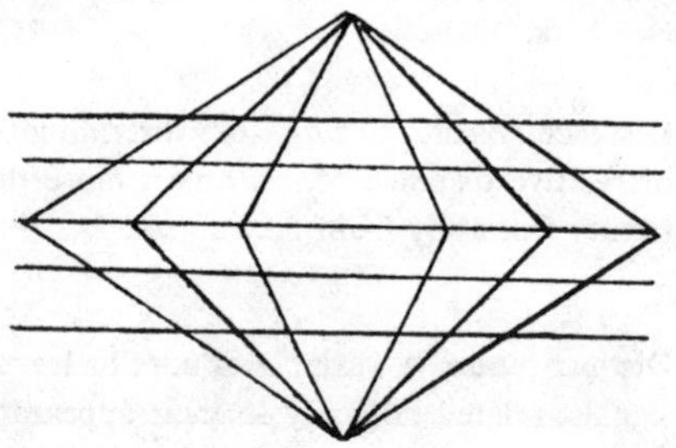

Divergent thinking. According to Guilford's intelligence-structure model, a part of intelligence. With divergent thinking the object is not, as with the traditional tests of general ability, to find a single correct solution but to record the variety and originality of the answers as well as the abundance of ideas and restructuring. It is assessed in terms of the factors of verbal and expressive fluency, and the factors of flexibility of thinking. Its definition coincides largely with that of creativity (q.v.).

Bibliography: Guilford, J. P.: The structure of intellect. Psychol. Bull., 1956, *53*, 267–93. **Id.:** Personality. New York, 1959. **Haddon, F. A. & Lytton, H.:** Teaching approach and the development of divergent thinking abilities in primary schools. Brit. J. educ. Psychol., 1968, *38*, 171–80. *G.K.*

Diversification quotient. See *Type-token ratio.*

Divining rod. See *Dowsing.*

Dizygotic twins. Twins from two separate eggs, as opposed to monozygotic twins. See *Twin studies.*

DNA. See *Desoxyribonucleic acid.*

Dogmatism. The term for a general tendency to rely strongly on "closed" in contrast to more "open" cognitions or frames of thought ("closed-mindedness" versus "open-mindedness", according to M. Rokeach). The more "closed" a system of opinions, attitudes, convictions is, the less an individual can perceive a multiplicity of different, relevant aspects in a situation. Flexibility of opinions and attitudes is rendered difficult; changes of opinion and attitude are only possible when the whole frame of thought is changed. This can encourage social attitudes like race-centeredness, authoritarianism (q.v.), intolerance, etc. "Dogmatism" is also used as a collective term for the cognitive aspect of such attitudes. See *Attitude.*

With his "dogmatism" scale M. Rokeach (1956) endeavored to formalize more distinctly the concept of authoritarianism and to free it from alleged one-sidedness. This, according to critics of the Adorno group (see *Authoritarian personality*), consists in the fact that scales to record "authoritarian", "anti-democratic", attitudes chiefly measure corresponding tendencies of those who lean to the right in politics. Connections between scales for "authoritarianism" and "dogmatism" mostly prove to be slightly positive. That members of the political left show just as high values with respect to "dogmatism" as do the "authoritarians on the right" has not been refuted. See *Conservatism.*

Rokeach (1960) deals with the problem of ideology from the sociopsychological angle when he defines dogmatism as "resistance to change" appearing in the shape of cognitive totalities of ideas and notions which are organized into relatively closed systems. Dogmatism is thus opposed to rigidity (q.v.) in the sense that a certain adaptation is not ruled out if the system itself can be maintained.

Bibliography: Livson, N. & Nichols, T. F.: Assessment of the general stability of the E, F and PEC scales. Psychol. Rep., 1957, *3*, 413–20. **Rokeach, M.:** Political and religious dogmatism: an alternative to the authoritarian personality. Psychol. Monogr., 1956, *70*, No. 18. **Id. & Fruchter, B.:** A factorial study of dogmatism and related concepts. J. abnorm. soc. Psychol., 1956, *53*, 356–60. **Rokeach, M.:** The open and closed mind. New York, 1960.

H.D.S. & M.-H.B.

Dolichocephalus. A technical term for long-headedness. The skull index (ratio of length to width of skull) is increased. It is used both as a characteristic of individuals and to distinguish supposed racial characteristics. *E.D.*

Dominance. A personality factor approximating to extraversion (q.v.): a striving for self-assertion and independence. See *Authoritarian personality.*

Dominance ranking (syn. *Dominance hierarchy*). **1.** The interindividual relations of dominance and submission in a group of animals or humans. **2.** A ranked series of behaviors.

Dominance, will to (syn. *Dominance; Will to dominate*). The disposition (q.v.) to rule in interpersonal relations. The striving for dominance has also appeared in personality research as an independent dimension (q.v.) which can to some extent be checked by factor analysis. The following may be regarded as indicatious of an aspiration to dominate: positive, self-convinced, stern, imperious, masterful and power-seeking modes of behavior. A. Adler in his monothematic drive theory gives this striving central importance as the *will to power.*

P.S. & R.S.

Dominant. In heredity theory, "dominant" denotes the heredity factor essential for the phenotype (q.v.). Ant. *Recessive.* *K.E.P.*

DOPA. An abbreviation for dihydroxyphenylanaline, an intermediate substance formed in the body during the biosynthesis of catecholamine (see *Biogenic amines*). DOPA is formed in the adrenal gland, in the sympathetic network and in the brain. In contrast to noradrenaline, dihydroxyphenylanaline passes the blood-brain barrier (q.v.). It can therefore be injected extra-cerebrally (e.g. intravenously). When small doses are given, after only a few minutes a striking increase in activity, an intensification of alertness and possibly euphoria appear. Little is known about the duration of effect of a single dose. The early hope that it could be used successfully in depression therapy has not been realized. However, it removes depressive states after large doses of reserpine (q.v.). Probably, when it is administered, the effective substance is not dihydroxyphenylanaline itself, but the natural final stage, noradrenaline. This is suggested by investigations in which the transformation of DOPA into the next stage (see *Dopamine*) is inhibited by decarboxylase inhibitors (see *Alphamethyldopa*).

Bibliography: Acheson, G. H.: Second symposium on catecholamines. Pharmacol. Rev., 1966, *18*, 1–804.

W.J.

Dopamine. A direct precursor in the biosynthesis of noradrenaline (see *Catecholamines*). Dopamine can be traced in the brain. It is only partially converted into noradrenaline, and partially reduced to other end-products. The conversion of dopamine into noradrenaline can be inhibited by a number of substances (e.g. by disulfiram = Antabuse). It can be detected unchanged in human urine. Therefore dopamine excretion can be used as a dependent variable in experiments. The few existing psychological investigations show that the excretion of dopamine decreases steadily from wakefulness through activated to non-activated sleep.

Bibliography: Baekeland, F., Schenker, V. S., Schenker, A. C. & Lasky, R.: Urinary excretion of epinephrine, dopamine and tryptamine during sleep and wakefulness. Psychopharmacologia, 1969, *14*, 359–70.
Hornykiewicz, O.: Dopamine (3-hydroxy tyramine) in brain function. Pharmacol. Rev., 1966, *18*, 925–64.

W.J.

Doppler effect (syn. *Doppler's principle*). A change in the frequency of sound or light waves in relation to an observer; the pitch of the sound or the hue of the light source appears to shift as it recedes from or approaches the observer.

Dorsal. The half containing the back is called dorsal in animals with only one symmetrical plane and a side with abdomen and back which is defined by the position of the nervous system in relation to the intestinal tract. Ant. *Ventral.* In vertebrates the nervous system is dorsal with respect to the intestines, in arthropods it is ventral. *H.Sch.*

Double-effect theory. See *Mind-body.*

Double images. Double images of an object appearing in binocular vision. They are either longitudinal or transverse, depending on whether the disparate condition is longitudinal (q.v.) or transverse (q.v.). Whereas longitudinal double images in practice appear only pathologically or optically (prisms), transverse double images appear in normal binocular vision also if sufficient attention is paid. If the point of fixation is in front of the object of the double image, there are homonymous or uncrossed double images (the double image in the right eye is to the right of the object of fixation, in the left eye to the left). If the object of fixation is behind the object of the double vision, there are non-homonymous or crossed double images. In cases of squinting there are pathological uncrossed double images if the squinting is inward and crossed if the squinting is outward. Double images are suppressed when binocular vision is corrected, occasionally they result from binocular rivalry, but are usually ignored. In spite of double images and image inhibition, an impression of depth is given by the object which is seen double. *A.H.*

Double organs. This refers to the symmetric organs existing in pairs, especially the eyes and ears. *K.E.P.*

Double vision. Also called *diplopia* (q.v.), it exists when one object can be seen twice. Diplopia can be either *functional* (see *Double images*) or *pathological.* Pathological *binocular* diplopia appears when there are positional anomalies of the eyes, due to squinting after paralysis, etc. *Monocular* diplopia may appear as a result of pathological changes of the eye media (see *Lens; Cornea*). There are also cases of polyopia. Binocular diplopia may also appear because of fatigue of the eye muscles or the effects of drugs (alcohol). *A.H.*

Down's disease (syn. *Down's syndrome; Langdon-Down syndrome; Imbecility; Mongolism,* q.v.; *Trisomia-21*). A frequent form of imbecility which is combined with distinctive physical characteristics. The basic cause is a chromosomal anomaly as a result of which there are three chromosomes instead of the chromosome pair 21.

Symptoms: usually serious imbecility together with a lively, sociable nature; retarded development; stature below normal; mongoloid slanting of the eyes with epicanthic folds of the eyelids; changes in connective membrane and iris, cataract frequently developing; brachycephalic skull; snub nose; tongue large and fissured; mouth usually open; fingers and hands misshapen, and malformations of the internal organs (heart and skeleton). Etiopathogenetically, three forms are distinguished nowadays: (*a*) the classical trisomia-21; (*b*) translocation-mongolism, in which the supernumerary chromosome is attached to another autosomal chromosome; (*c*) mosaic mongolism: different sets of chromosomes side by side in the same individual. With form (*a*) the mother is frequently no longer young and the risk of a repetition is slight. On the other hand, with form (*b*) there is the danger of a repetition of mongolism in the family. *C.S.*

Dowsing. The practice of attempting to locate underground water or other minerals, or some hidden object, by using a pendulum or "divining rod" (such as a forked twig) or similar instrument. The "dowser" traverses the target area until his instrument reveals by its movement the correct position. Possibly a form of clairvoyance (q.v.) that exploits a motor-automatism. Also known as "water-divining". *J.B.*

Draw-a-Man Test. Sometimes abbreviated to DAM, this test published by Goodenough in 1926 uses drawing to assess intelligence. Goodenough gave norms for children aged 3 to 13, W. E. Hinrichs (1935) and C. A. Oakley (1940) extended the scale up to the age of 18. The best drawing of a human produced by the testee is evaluated according to a standardized list (fifty-one items), and an IQ is calculated. Reliability $r = 0{\cdot}80$ to $0{\cdot}90$; validity: correlations with the Stanford-Binet test resulted in determination coefficients (q.v.) lying between $r^2 = 0{\cdot}17$ and $r^2 = 0{\cdot}58$; correlation with the teacher's assessment: $r = 0{\cdot}44$ (Goodenough).

In the drawing test by Goodenough & Harris (1963), three drawings, a man, a woman and a self-portrait, have to be completed, from them a mean IQ is calculated which the authors consider to be more reliable than the result of evaluating only one drawing.

Bibliography: **Goodenough, F. L.:** Measurement of intelligence by drawings. New York, 1926. **Id. & Harris, D. B.:** Drawing test. New York, 1963.

I.M.D.

Draw-a-Person Test (syn. *Machover Test;* Abb. DAP). A projective test in which the testee (from two years) is asked to draw a person and then tell a story about the sketch. The postulated projection of the child's body image (q.v.) to some extent determines analysis. *J.M.*

Dream. A dream is an experience during sleep and forms part of a fantasy life. It is generally distinguished from a hypnagogic hallucination on the grounds that the latter is a brief sensory experience during drowsiness in which the subject feels he is a non-participating observer. All sense modalities, unspoken communications, moods and feelings contribute to a dream. Those who have never experienced one sense modality (e.g. the congenitally blind) have dreams that are normal except for the missing modality. Whether a fantasy is called a dream depends upon the individual. Some subjects will call only bizarre experiences "dreams", and prefer to use the term "thinking" for sleep experiences which, though far removed in space and time from their beds, are internally consistent.

1. *History and methods.* For thousands of years before Sigmund Freud (1856–1939), dreams were interpreted in order to foretell the future. In dream symbolism, Freud saw a means of understanding the individual's motives. Unconscious impulses from the id (q.v.), together with memories which were unconscious owing to repression (q.v.), gave rise to the *latent dream,* which was itself wish-fulfilling. The efforts of the ego, exerted through the *dream-work,* resulted in the *manifest dream.* The *dream-distortion* meant that the dream was rendered less reprehensible and less anxiety-provoking, so that sleep

was not disrupted. In this way, dreams served as the *guardians of sleep*, which role they also served by disguising external stimuli as dream components. The forces of repression were considered to be somewhat relaxed during the dream, enabling it to contain features (for instance, of an incestuous nature) which were only thinly disguised or even openly expressed. The psychoanalyst, interpreting the dream as a whole, sought for its latent content.

Freud also believed that dreams contained material which was part of the *archaic heritage* deriving from the experiences of the patient's ancestors. The latter notion was analogous to the belief of C. G. Jung (1875–1961) that in dreams certain specific symbols or *archetypes* (e.g. of re-birth), which were representatives of the *collective unconscious*, frequently revealed themselves, as they also would in world-wide art forms, in myths and in the waking thoughts of the schizophrenic. The study of dreams proved a source of inspiration for both Freud and Jung, and their writings have had a profound influence on modern literature and art.

The clinical interpretation of dreams has been mainly based on day-time recall, but a number of psychologists about the end of the nineteenth century were awakening themselves by alarm clocks during the night in order to catch the freshly-experienced dream; in the 1950s a new technique enabled nocturnal awakenings to become a reliable proposition. Aserinsky and Kleitman observed recurrent periods of sleep with low voltage EEG, facial movements, and rapid conjugate eye movements, and suggested that during these periods dreaming was taking place. Dement and Kleitman later found 80 per cent dream recall from these rapid eye movement periods (paradoxical sleep) and only 7 per cent dream recall from non-rapid eye movement sleep (orthodox sleep). See *Sleep*.

2. *The present state of research*. It became clear that dreaming, like paradoxical sleep, must occupy at least a quarter of the sleep time. Old ideas were swept away: for example, that extended dreams occur in a flash of time, that brain injuries abolished dreams, that color is not usually experienced in dreams, that some people did not dream. Everyone, if awakened at the right times, will describe dreams.

Mental life of a less "dream-like" and more "thought-like" nature is described after awakenings from orthodox sleep, though in orthodox sleep, at the onset of sleep typical dream adventures are often experienced. Nightmares can be experienced in either kind of sleep. The profusion or number of rapid eye movements in a given time during paradoxical sleep is related to the dream content. The greater the profusion, the more active the events of the dream adventure. Barbiturate drugs reduce the eye movement profusion *and* the vividness of the dreams.

Dement conducted "dream deprivation" experiments in which he woke subjects for several nights whenever they began a period of paradoxical sleep. On a subsequent, undisturbed night of sleep, the subjects spent more than a normal proportion of time in paradoxical sleep, yet this did not happen if the awakenings had been made during orthodox sleep. The selective deprivation of paradoxical sleep is followed by dreams of enhanced vividness, accompanied by a greater profusion of rapid eye movements. The original claim that psychological abnormalities resulted from the selective awakenings has not been substantiated. It is now generally agreed that there is a need for paradoxical sleep, and that compensation will follow its loss, but no experiments have yet demonstrated a purely psychological need for dreams.

The environment influences dream content. When anxiety-provoking films are seen before sleep there is a greater profusion of eye movements during the paradoxical sleep periods, and the dreams contain more anxiety and incorporate elements from the films. Dreams elicited in the laboratory tend to be restrained in their content compared with home dreams. Times of general life anxiety, or depression, are associated with dreams containing themes of anxiety or depression. Anxiety in waking life is accompanied by adrenaline secretion, and in anxious dreams the level of free fatty acids, liberated into the blood by the action of adrenaline, is raised. The penile erections that normally accompany each period of male paradoxical sleep are diminished where dream anxiety is high. Penile tumescence increases sharply prior to seminal emission during sexual dreams. The time of menstruation is characterized by a greater degree of sexual and aggressive dream themes. Sensory stimuli presented without causing awakening during paradoxical sleep tend to become woven into the dream content on the basis of assonance, e.g. in the controlled experiments of Berger, the English girl's name "Sheila" led to a dream report about a "book by Schiller".

The extent of the dream narrative is greater when recall is made near the end of a period of paradoxical sleep, and is much reduced if awakening is delayed until orthodox sleep has just begun again. Dreams described immediately after night awakenings are only poorly recalled the next day, especially if sleep was quickly resumed or if rapid eye movement profusion was low. The successive dreams of a single night show some degree of continuity in their content.

The increased interest in dreams has led to many refinements in the scoring of such themes as anxiety, aggression or sexuality in the dream content. Particular mention should be made of the dream content analysis techniques of Hall and Van de Castle.

In delirium following withdrawal of alcohol or barbiturates from addicts, there is great intensification of paradoxical sleep, which often interrupts wakefulness. There is reason to believe that the experiences of delirium are, in essence, dreams. Despite the similarities in mental life between the dream and schizophrenic mental life, modern evidence has failed to reveal links between schizophrenia and any abnormality of paradoxical sleep. Paradoxical sleep, intoxication by such drugs as cannabis, mescaline or amphetamine, or even simple waking reverie, are states of altered consciousness during which there is thinking divorced from reality, to which such terms as dream-like, autistic, fantasy, or dream, may properly be applied without attempt at rigid distinction.

Bibliography: Abt, L. E. & Riess, B. F. (Eds): Progress in clinical psychology, Vol. 8; Dreams and dreaming. New York & London, 1968. **Baekeland, F. & Lasky, R.:** The morning recall of rapid eye movement period reports given earlier in the night. J. nerv. ment. Dis. 1968, *147*, 570–79. **Berger, R. J.:** Experimental modification of dream content by meaningful verbal stimuli. Brit. J. Psychol., 1963, *109*, 722–40. **Id. & Oswald, I.:** Eye movements during active and passive dreams. Science, 1962, *137*, 601. **Bonime, W.:** The clinical use of dreams. New York, 1962. **Carroll, D., Lewis, S. A. & Oswald, I.:** Barbiturates and dream content. Nature (Lond.), 1969, *223*, 865–6. **Dement, W. C.:** The effect of dream deprivation. Science, 1960, *131*, 1705–7. **Id. & Kleitman, N.:** The relation of eye movements during sleep to dream activity, an objective method for the study of dreaming. J. exp. Psychol. 1957, *53*, 339–46. **Dement, W. C. & Wolpert, E. A.:** The relation of eye movements, body motility and external stimuli to dream content. J. exp. Psychol. 1958, *55*, 543–53. **Fisher, C.:** Psychoanalytic implications of recent research on sleep and dreaming. J. Amer. psychoanal. Ass., 1965, *13*, 197–303. **Id.:** Dreaming and sexuality. In: **Schur, M., Solnit, A., Lowenstein, R. M. & Newman, L.** (Eds): Psychoanalysis—a general psychology. New York, 1966, 537–69. **Foulkes, D.:** The psychology of sleep. New York, 1966. **Hall, C. & Van de Castle, R.:** The content analysis of dreams. New York, 1966. **Karacan, I., Goodenough, D. R., Shapiro, A. & Starker, S.:** Erection cycle during sleep in relation to dream anxiety. Arch. gen. Psychiat., 1966, *15*, 183–9. **Kramer, M.** (Ed.): Dream psychology and the new biology of dreaming. Springfield, Ill., 1969. **Oswald, I.:** Sleeping and waking: physiology and psychology. Amsterdam, 1962. **Id.:** Sleep. Harmondsworth, Middlesex, 1970. **Pivik, T. & Foulkes, D.:** "Dream deprivation": effects on dream content. Science, 1966, *153*, 1282–4. **Swanson, E. M. & Foulkes, D.:** Dream content and the menstrual cycle. J. nerv. ment. Dis., 1968, *145*, 358–63.

I. Oswald

Dream analysis (syn. *Dream interpretation*). The interpretation of dreams is a part of psychotherapeutic measures designed to help elucidate unconscious motives in the patient (see *Psychoanalysis*). When unconscious motives activated in sleep cannot be warded off or repressed by the impaired inner control or censorship mechanism of the sleeper, they are converted into manifest dream-content, their partial gratification is attempted in dreams (q.v.), and (according to Freud) the state of sleep is thereby generally maintained. The account the dreamer gives of his dream is taken to be the manifest dream-content. By means of the patient's conceptions of the individual manifest dream-contents, the therapist and patient try to discover the unconscious motives (the latent dream-content) and, if possible, their ontogenetic origin, thus helping the patient to acquire better control over them.

Bibliography: Freud, S.: The interpretation of dreams. London, 1955. **Toman, W.:** Motivation, Persönlichkeit, Umwelt. Göttingen, 1968. *W.T.*

Dream censor(ship). See *Censorship.*

Drill. The acquisition of skills and knowledge by the repetition of some activity. As a result, mental and physical performance is increased as there is extensive automatization (q.v.) (subordinate part processes are excluded from the conscious operation of the will). Drill is dependent on fatigue (q.v.), general alertness and condition. See *Practice.* *W.Sp.*

Drill theory (syn. *Practice theory;* Ger. *Einübungstheorie*). K. Groos's theory of children's play: play primarily subserves the development of existing natural talent and is also an exercise preparatory to that vital activity which will later be required of the adult. See *Play theory.*

Bibliography: Groos, K.: Die Spiele des Menschen. Jena, 1899. *P.S.*

Drive. Certain physiological states, such as food deprivation, tend to increase animals' behavioral output. A number of early animal experiments showed that, in comparison with satiated rats, hungry rats would run more in activity wheels, and would explore more in a novel situation. These effects were commonly assumed to be unlearned and to be general with respect to the source of physiological disturbance, the kind of behavior affected, and the situation in which the effects occurred. The animal was believed to be inert unless motivated by some disturbance or threat to its well-being. Motivation was supplied by a hypothetical force or energy designated "drive".

The word "drive" was first used to describe this hypothetical force or energy by Woodworth in 1918, but the German equivalent *Trieb* had been used in essentially the same way by Freud in 1915. Within a few years, virtually everyone came to believe in some form of the drive concept. The concept was extended to include non-physiological sources of motivation, to give learned drives, social drives, higher drives, and so on. There were no convincing explanations of how learned drives were learned, but there was little doubt about the validity or usefulness of this kind of approach. The drive concept was applied as readily to human social behavior as to instinctive behavior in the lower animals.

These ideas were eventually combined, systematized and made explicit by Hull (1943) and Brown (1961). Hull emphasized the generality of drive. While there were many potential sources of drive, he said, they contributed alike to the total pool of energization. The resulting drive (*D*) gave energy to behavior, but did not direct it; direction came from the habits operating in a given situation, and *D* merely multiplied the strongest habit. *D* contrasts with another motivational concept, incentive, which Hull had introduced earlier. Drive was unlearned, general, and had a presumed physiological basis. By contrast, incentive depended upon prior learning, was specific to particular reinforcers and occurred in particular situations, and lacked any discernible physiological basis.

The fundamental question was: how much of the total motivation in a given situation could be attributed to drive and how much to incentive? One recent review of the relevant experimentation (Bolles, 1967) indicates that, in comparison with incentive, drive is relatively unimportant. Many of the unlearned and general motivational effects predicted by Hull's theory have turned out to be neither unlearned nor general. For example, the early discovery that hungry rats run more in activity wheels can now be discounted because of recent findings that this effect is relatively specific to the rat, to hunger and to the activity wheel. Other animals, in other situations, and under other kinds of deprivation conditions, may show increased activity, decreased activity, or no change (Campbell, *et al.*, 1966).

Many other hypotheses which drive theorists had proposed to bolster the drive concept have not been confirmed experimentally. Different sources of drive, such as food and water deprivation, are not intersubstitutable, and do not summate to give increased performance. The idea that the energy from one source of motivation can spill over to activate an irrelevant kind of behavior (i.e. displacement) has not been supported in laboratory experiments. The mechanistic philosophy which underlay the original drive concept is now outmoded. The idea that an animal is inert and has to be driven into activity is no longer popular. The drive concept does not fit the facts, even in the cases it was designed to handle—e.g. that of the hungry rat.

Most psychologists have abandoned the hope of explaining social motives in terms of acquired drives. A serious attempt was made to interpret learned fears as acquired drives, but the evidence favoring this interpretation was not very compelling, and there were always alternative explanations. Some psychologists prefer to explain behavior in terms of its intended aims, or its prior reinforcement history, rather than its motives. Others emphasize the importance of associative factors in what is called motivated behavior. The concept of motivation itself seems much less important than it once did. Therefore, we appear to be entering an era in which virtually no one believes in the concept of drive.

The word "drive" continues to be used, however; it will probably continue in use for some time, as it was originally; i.e. to describe the existence or operation of some motivation system with a physiological basis. This is poor usage, mainly because it lacks descriptiveness. Nothing is really conveyed by referring to a rat's "hunger drive" that is not implied by saying the rat is hungry.

Bibliography: Bolles, R. C.: Theory of motivation. New York, 1967. **Brown, J. S.:** The motivation of behavior. New York, 1961. **Campbell, B. A., Smith, N. F., Misanin, J. R. & Jaynes, J.:** Species differences in activity during hunger and thirst. J. Comp. Physiol. Psychol., 1966, *61*, 123–7. **Freud, S.:** Instincts and their vicissitudes. In: Collected Papers, IV. New York, 1959. **Hull, C. L.:** Principles of behavior. New York, 1943. **Woodworth, R. S.:** Dynamic psychology. New York, 1918.

R. C. Bolles

Drive theory. In general, the postulating of fundamental or elementary drives or "instincts" in human or animal behavior, and the establishment of criteria for differentiation or development. Freud (q.v.) was the first theorist to postulate that the sexual drive was the sole source of motivation; he later added the self-preservation or ego instincts and finally, in place of them, the two classes of libido (the life or love drive) on the one hand, and the death instinct, on the other. Jung (q.v.) assumed that libido was the basic drive, but emphasized progressive desexualization of libido in the course of individual development. Adler (q.v.) suggested that the power instinct or the search for security was the basic drive. See *Drive; Instinct.*

W.T.

Dropout. An individual who gives up before reaching his goal, particularly a student who does not complete a course, but also any individual who, either from sickness, lack of specific abilities, or for ethical reasons, attempts to opt out of a particular society or group within a society.

Drug. A product of natural (plant) origin in contrast to a synthetic substance. As a result of the widespread use of the word for medicines in English-speaking countries it has also become increasingly a synonym for natural and synthetic substances. *G.D.*

Drug addiction. See *Drug dependence.*

Drug dependence is "a state, psychic and sometimes also physical, resulting from the interaction between a living organism and a drug, characterized by behavioral and other responses that always include a compulsion to take the drug on a continuous or periodic basis in order to experience its psychic effects, and sometimes to avoid the discomfort of its absence. Tolerance may or may not be present. A person may be dependent on more than one drug" (World Health Organisation Expert Committee, 1969, p. 6).

1. *Physical dependence* is a state where the organism requires the presence of the drug for maintenance of bodily homeostasis; a definite, characteristic and self-limited abstinence syndrome occurs when the drug is withdrawn. The WHO definition implicates psychic (psychological) factors in all forms of drug dependence. However, some workers restrict the terms psychic, psychological, and psychogenic to states of dependence where the organism takes drugs for reasons other than the relief of the abstinence syndrome of physical dependence.

2. *Tolerance* describes a progressive decrease in the effects obtained from a given dose of drugs, and, conversely, the need to use larger doses to obtain the same effect with continued use of some drugs.

The drugs of dependence now mainly causing concern are grouped in six types, according to their similarity to morphine, barbiturates, alcohol, amphetamines, cocaine and cannabis; some would add LSD and other hallucinogens. Only the first three produce marked physical dependence, but a physiological withdrawal syndrome can be demonstrated in other classes using sensitive measures: for instance, the electroencephalogram in amphetamine withdrawal (Oswald, Evans & Lewis, 1969). The term "drug dependence" supersedes the previous terms *drug addiction* and *drug habituation*, which attempted—unsuccessfully—to distinguish between, respectively, more and less intense degrees of drug dependence. Research has investigated drug dependence in animals and man.

3. *Animal studies.* These have been reviewed by Schuster & Thompson (1969) and Teasdale (1971). It has been shown that most drugs abused by humans can serve as reinforcers for the establishment of operant habits in monkeys and rats. Such habits may be very persistent, and it can be said that the animals exhibit drug dependence. "Relapse" back to morphine-reinforced habits can occur long after animals have been withdrawn from the drug, and is more likely to occur in situations previously associated with drug consumption. Younger rats show more dependence-proneness than older ones. There is evidence to suggest genetically based individual variation in dependence-proneness. The drug reinforcement appears to consist either of relief of an unpleasant withdrawal state in physically dependent animals, or of a direct primary reinforcement effect of the drug. Secondary reinforcement can be established by pairing neutral stimuli with drug reinforcement, and the symptoms of the withdrawal state can be classically conditioned to neutral stimuli. The effect of variations in reinforcement schedule and size of reinforcement on drug-reinforced behavior has been investigated. These studies have demonstrated the existence of powerful behavior factors maintaining drug consumption. Such factors presumably operate in the same way in human addicts, in addition to whatever problems of personality, and so on, they may have. Wikler (1968) discusses the relevance of the animal studies to humans.

4. *Human studies.* Before becoming dependent on a drug, the individual must have experience of the drug; their availability among his friends seems an important determinant of exposure to drugs (Chein *et al.*, 1964; de Alarcon, 1969). The effects of drugs on the individual are not simply a function of the drug but depend on the quantity he takes, how often he takes it, and the route of administration; on his personality, his previous experience and present state; and on the social setting in which he uses the drug. The effects of drugs on man have been reviewed by Trouton & Eysenck (1960).

Haertzen (1965) has studied the subjective effects of addictive drugs and shown considerable overlap in the effects of pharmacologically distinct drugs. Oswald, Evans & Lewis (1969) have shown that addictive drugs cause a suppression of paradoxical (rapid-eye-movement) sleep (see *Sleep*), and a rebound increase on withdrawal. Weil, Zinberg & Nelsen (1968) have compared experimentally the effects of cannabis on naïve subjects and experienced users, and suggest the importance of prior experience in determining the drug reaction.

5. *Personality.* There seems to be no unique "addictive personality" common to all drug users, and distinct from other diagnostic groups. Tests such as the Minnesota Multiphasic Personality Inventory have been used to demonstrate the existence of a number of types (e.g. sociopathic, neurotic) within the addict population, some similar to types seen in criminals, delinquents and alcoholics (Hill, Haertzen & Davis, 1962). Von Felsinger *et al.* (1955) demonstrated the importance of personality differences in determining the nature of response to addictive drugs, comparing addicts with non-addicts, and groups within the normal subjects. There is evidence that drug use may be a form of self-medication in some drug users. Chein *et al.* (1964) offer psychodynamic descriptions of the personalities of the addicts they studied, and relate these to their family background.

Most workers have implicated personality defect in the etiology of drug dependence, but Dole & Nyswander (1967) have argued this is an effect rather than cause of drug use, which they attribute to metabolic abnormality. However, Vaillant (1969) presents evidence of maladjustment in addicts prior to drug use.

6. *Treatment.* Most forms of treatment have been aimed at reducing the addict's personality problems and re-integrating him in the community, and have generally included milieu therapy, psychotherapy, and other rehabilitative procedures. Results have generally been poor (e.g. Vaillant, 1969), with the exception of therapeutic communities run by ex-addicts (e.g. Rosenthal, 1969), for which considerable success is claimed, though good evidence is lacking. Other treatment programs (e.g. Dole & Nyswander, 1967) have included measures aimed more directly at the drug-taking itself and appear quite successful. Parole supervision in the community is associated with favorable outcome (Vaillant, 1969). Cessation of drug use with increasing age appears to occur in a proportion of addicts (Vaillant, 1969).

Bibliography: Chein, I., Gerard, D. L., Lee, R. S. & Rosenfeld, E.: Narcotics, delinquency and social policy: The road to H. London, 1964. **de Alarcon, R.:** The spread of heroin abuse in a community. Bulletin of Narcotics, 1969, *21*, 17–22. **Dole, V. P. & Nyswander, M. E.:** Heroin addiction—a metabolic disease. Arch. Internal. Med., 1967, *120*, 19–24. **Haertzen, C. A.:** Subjective drug effects: a factorial representation of subjective drug effects on the Addiction Research Center Inventory. J. nervous and mental Disease, 1965, *140*, 280–89. **Hill, H. E., Haertzen, C. A. & Davis, H.:** An MMPI factor analytic study of alcoholics, narcotic addicts, and criminals. Quart, J. Stud. Alcohol, 1962, *23*, 411–31. **Oswald, I., Evans, J. I. & Lewis, S. A.:** Addictive drugs cause suppression of paradoxical sleep and withdrawal rebound. In: **Steinberg, H.** (Ed.): Scientific basis of drug dependence. London, 1969. **Rosenthal, M. S.:** The Phoenix House therapeutic community: an overview. In: **Steinberg, H.** (Ed.): Scientific basis of drug dependence. London, 1969. **Schuster, C. R. & Thompson, T.:** Self-administration of and behavioural dependence on drugs. Annual Rev. Pharmacology, 1969, *9*, 483–502. **Steinberg, H.** (Ed.): Scientific basis of drug dependence. London, 1969. **Teasdale, J. D.:** Drug dependence. In: **Eysenck, H. J.** (Ed.): Handbook of abnormal psychology London, [2]1971

Trouton, D. & Eysenck, H. J.: The effects of drugs on behaviour. In: **Eysenck, H. J.** (Ed.): Handbook of abnormal psychology. London, 1960. **Vaillant, G. E.:** The natural history of urban drug addiction—some determinants. In: **Steinberg, H.** (Ed.): Scientific basis of drug dependence. London, 1969. **Felsinger, J. M. von, Lasagna, L. & Beecher, H. K.:** Drug-induced mood changes in man: 2. Personality and reaction to drugs. J. American Medical Association, 1955, *157*, 1113–9. **Weil, A. T., Zinberg, N. E. & Nelsen, J. M.:** Clinical and psychological effects of marihuana in man. Science, 1968, *162*, 1234–42. **Wikler, A.** (Ed.): The addictive states. Association for Research in Nervous and Mental Disease, Volume XLVI. Baltimore, 1968. **Wilner, D. M. & Kassebaum, G. G.** (Eds): Narcotics. New York, 1965. **World Health Organisation Expert Committee on Drug Dependence:** Sixteenth Report. WHO Technical Report Series, No. 407, 1969.

J. D. Teasdale

Drug dependence, theories of. Various psychological theories are adduced to explain the genesis of drug dependence. After psychoanalysis, learning theory has recently put forward explanations according to which the consequences of drug taking are regarded as reinforcers of a conditioning process (q.v.). (In animal experiments the method of drug self-administration is used to demonstrate the reinforcer effect.) However, most theories can only cover partial aspects of drug dependence, and a comprehensive explanation would have to take into account the complex interaction of physiological, psychological and sociocultural factors in the genesis of drug dependence.

Bibliography: AMA.: Committee on alcoholism and addiction and council on mental health. Dependence on barbiturates and other sedative drugs. Jama, 1965, *193*, 673. **Ausubel, D. P.:** Drug addiction: physiological, psychological, and sociological aspects. New York, 1966. **Collier, H. O. J.:** A general theory of the generics of drug dependence by induction of receptors. Nature, 1965, *9*, 181. **Eddy, N. B., Halbach, H., Isbell, H. & Seevers, M. H.:** Drug dependence: its significance and characteristics. Psychopharm. Bull., 1966, *3*, 1–12. **Essig, C. F.:** Addiction to non-barbiturate sedative and tranquilizing drugs. Clin. Pharmacol. Therap., 1964, *5*, 334. **Isbell, H. & Fraser, H. F.:** Addiction to analgetics and barbiturates. Pharmacol. Rev., 1950, *2*, 355–97. **Murray, J. B.:** Drugs and drug dependency. The American Ecclesiastical Review, 1967, *157*, 12–28. **WHO:** Scientific Group on the Evaluation of Dependence-Producing Drugs: WHO Technical Report Series No. 287, 1964.

H.K.

Drug habituation. See *Drug dependence.*

Drug postulate, Eysenck's. The hypothesis that CNS depressant drugs (e.g. alcohol and sodium amytal) increase inhibitory potential yet decrease excitatory potential, tending to extraverted behavior; and that CNS stimulant drugs (e.g. caffeine and dexedrine) decrease inhibitory potential yet increase excitatory potential, tending to introverted behavior. The postulate has been supported by experiments, and has proved extremely valuable in personality factor research.

Drug self-administration. A method in behavioral pharmacology (see *Psychopharmacology*) by which animals can administer drugs to themselves. Techniques for oral, intraperitoneal, intravenous, intracerebral administration and inhalation are available. The most common technique is oral administration, when a choice has usually to be made between an active and a dummy substance. Administration frequently takes place under conditions of stress (e.g. electric shocks). In certain situations the animals take increased quantities of alcohol, opiates, barbiturates, tranquilizers (such as chlordiazepoxide), and stimulants. Certain products are rejected after investigation (chlorpromazine, pemoline). The test animals are usually rats and monkeys. Localized intracerebral administration is especially important. It corresponds to the technique of electrical self-stimulation devised by J. Olds. Drug experiments offer findings which are expecially relevant to the problem of drug dependence (q.v.).

Bibliography: Schuster, C. R. & Thompson, T.: Self-administration of and behavioral dependence on drugs. Ann. Rev. Pharmacol., 1969, *9*, 483–502.

W.J.

Drunken driving. See *Traffic psychology.*

Drunkenness. See *Alcoholism.*

Dual effect theory. See *Mind-body problem.*

Dualism. A religious, cosmogonic, philosophical or metaphysical doctrine which takes as its starting-point the existence of two independent basic principles. In psychology, dualism postulates the twofold nature of physical and mental phenomena (psychophysical *parallelism,* q.v.); in philosophy, dualism postulates that both "mind" and "matter" are present in being (e.g. Descartes: extended substance [*extensio*] and thinking substance [*cogitatio*]); hence dualism is contrasted with monism and pluralism. *F.B.*

Dual morality (syn. *Double morality; Double moral standards*). The existence of double standards, chiefly in sexual morality, allowing one of the sexes greater freedom than the other. Especially in Europe and in the U.S.A., the sexual morality in question depends on supposed biological differences, and/or those sanctioned by religion, which allow men to indulge in pre-marital and extra-marital sexual contacts but expect abstinence from women. In his classification of sexual standards Reiss has characterized the attitude which allows men to have sexual contacts, especially extra-marital intercourse, but considers them reprehensible in women, as an "orthodox double standard". In the course of the last century, partly because of the emancipation of women, a "transitional double standard" has developed, which considers extra-marital sexual contacts permissible for women if they are in love or engaged to be married.

Bibliography: Reiss, I. L.: Premarital sexual standards in America. Glencoe, Ill., 1960. *J.F.*

Dual sensation. See *Synesthesia.*

Dual vision theory. See *Duplicity theory.*

Dummy sign stimuli. Used by K. Lorenz and N. Tinbergen to determine the key sign stimulus for the chick's pecking of regurgitated food from the bill of the herring gull. The bill of the adult bird is yellow and has a red spot on the lower mandible. Before they were fed, the chicks were systematically presented with dummy bills and heads varied in all dimensions. In this way it was possible to determine that the red color of the spot (at which the chick pecks) was the stimulus actually releasing the pecking and that, e.g., the color of the head and bill played no part. The technique is used above all in comparative psychology, but sometimes in human psychology. It is essential that S. should be presented not with natural environmental phenomena, but models of them that can be easily modified in order to discover the stimulus or combination of stimuli-releasing specific behavior patterns.

Bibliography: Harlow, H. F.: Love in infant monkeys. Frontiers of psychological research. San Francisco & London, 1959. **Lorenz, K.:** Der Kumpan in der Umwelt des Vogels. J. Ornithol. 1935, *83*, 137–215, 289–413. **Tinbergen, N.:** De functie van de rode vlek op de snavel van de zilverneeuw. Bijdragen tot de Dierkunde, 1949, *28*, 452–65. **Id. & Perseck, A. C.:** On the stimulus situation releasing the begging response in the newly hatched herring gull chick. Behaviour, 1950, *3*, 1–38. *R.Hä.*

Duncan Test. A special form of Student's Test. With the help of this procedure it is possible to compare pairs of median values when the results of more than two independent samples are available (e.g. in connection with an analysis of variance to identify the experimental condition[s] "responsible" for a possibly significant result). For this purpose the median values of the samples are ranked according to numerical magnitude. The adjacent median values can be tested for significance with the t test (q.v.), and all the others with the Duncan test. See *Statistics*.

W.H.B.

Duplicity theory (syn. *Duplicity principle*). This theory assigns different functional roles to the cones (q.v.) and the rods (q.v.), the photoreceptors, which are morphologically more or less distinct. The cones are said to be responsible for daylight vision and hence for color perception (q.v.). The rods are for seeing in faint or half-light. Cones and rods are also referred to as brightness and darkness receptors. The duplicity theory is supported by numerous morphological and functional facts. For example: nocturnal animals have a retina consisting of rods, those active by day a retina of cones or a mixed retina (cones and rods). Different visual functions (spectral sensitivity function, visual acuity, flicker fusion frequency, etc.; cf. Studnitz, 1952) have different corresponding parts for day or night vision, or differ for day or night vision (see, e.g., *Purkinje phenomenon*). In addition to rod substance (*rhodopsin*, q.v.), Studnitz (1952) identified *iodopsin* (the cone substance). Electron microscope investigations have revealed morphological differences between the cones (fibrous structure) and the rods (locular structure).

Bibliography: Graham, C. H. (Ed.): Vision and visual perception. New York & London, 1965. **Studnitz, G. V.:** Physiologie des Sehens. Leipzig, 1952.

A.H.

Dynamic-effect law. Attention and responses become habitualized to the degree to which they help an individual to reach a goal. A postulate of R. B. Cattell's.

Dynamic personality factors. In personality research based on factor analysis, dynamic personality factors refer to differences in the field of motivation, interests, attitude and adaptation to conflict. Whether an independent personality area exists, as is usually presupposed, is not yet clear. Five occupational interest factors seem to be established (science or scholarship, economics, social life, art, office work). Among extra-occupational interests, adventurousness versus desire for security, diversion and change were confirmed. No connections with aptitude factors have yet been demonstrated.

Bibliography: Guilford, J. F.: Personality. New York, 1959.

B.H.

Dynamic psychology. An approach which stresses the importance of energetics, or fundamental energy, in psychic life, as contrasted with the older, purely static conception (see *Association psychology*). The phenomena of psychic life are no longer understood as static conditions but as dynamic events, and research is conducted in this sense. Following suggestions from various schools of psychology (especially the effects of the ideas of Freudian psychoanalysis, q.v., as well as depth psychology as a whole, and the influence of Dilthey's ideas), the idea of dynamics found its way into scientific psychology in a twofold aspect: in the sense of change, and alteration, of the fluidity of mental life, and in the stress laid on the forces, drives and needs, i.e. the motivations, conditioning this constant change. It was especially in the hormic psychology (q.v.) of McDougall and the field theory (q.v.) of K. Lewin that the aspect of dynamic psychology was fundamentally emphasized. But great significance is also attached to dynamic thinking in the personality theories of G. W. Allport, S. L. Rubinstein, R. Heiss and H. Thomae. See *Depth psychology; Drive; Instinct.*

Bibliography: Allport, G. W.: Pattern and growth in personality. New York, 1961. **McDougall, W.:** The energies of men. London, 1932. **Heiss, R.:** Die Lehre vom Charakter. Berlin, [2]1949. **Lewin, K.:** A dynamic theory of personality. New York, 1935. **Rubinstein, S. L.:** Grundlagen der allgemeinen Psychologie. Berlin, 1958. **Thomae, H.:** Persönlichkeit: Eine dynamische Interpretation. Bonn, [2]1955. **Woodworth, R. S.:** Dynamic psychology. New York, 1918.

K.E.P.

Dynamics. **1.** In physics: a division of mechanics, which deduces tne processes of motion from effective forces. **2.** In general psychology: a construct which explains the observable variability of psychic phenomena by means of dynamic factors such as drive, need, aspiration, instinct, etc. This approach was evident in the psychology of perception (gestalt laws, actual- or dynamo-genesis); in motivational psychology in the drive theories of A. Adler, W. McDougall, W. Stern and others; and in the psychology of thought (see *Würzburg School*). See *Dynamic psychology*. *P.S. & R.S.*

Dynamic stereotype. Pavlov's term for a specific response pattern according to learned experience. One of a set of stimuli in different modalities may reproduce the characteristic responses of the other stimuli.

Dynamometer. An appliance with which the intensity of a physical response, e.g. manual pressure, can be determined.

Dysarthria. *Dysphasia* (q.v.) caused by brain lesions, especially CNS disease.

Dyscolia. See *Posodynics.*

Dysesthesia. The term designates diminished, increased or poorly-adapted sensitivity to pain, and abnormal sensations. See *Pain.*

Dysfunction. A disturbance of the normal functioning of organs, parts of an organ or of the body.

Dyshormia. Disturbed, unharmonious drive and motor behavior (e.g. shyness). Extremely pathological in catatonia.

Dyslalia. A disturbance in, but not absence of, the ability to talk. (See *Alalia.*) It is in use but its meaning and use vary, and its distinction from dysarthria (q.v.) is sometimes not made. Commonly used as a lesser degree of the condition defined under *alalia* in the sense of a motor aphasia. Syn. *Verbal aphasia; Verbal apraxia.* *B.B.*

Dyslexia. Disturbed ability to read, i.e. a disturbed comprehension of what is read, ranging from minor or fluctuating disability to a complete and permanent inability to read which is at odds with the individual's apparent intelligence and socio-economic background. The disability may include words and not letters, figures and not letters, and so on. Comprehension after finger tracing has been described. Causes are acquired brain damage or congenital disability. Special reading instruction can benefit some children with congenital or developmental dyslexia, thus demonstrating its protean nature. *B.B.*

Dysmelia. A defect in the embryonic development of the limbs. It is often the result of harmful exogenous factors such as oxygen, medicines or radiation during the period of limb formation in the fourth to sixth week of pregnancy, and appears as an absence or atrophy of the medullated bones with shortening and faulty positioning of the legs and arms. *E.D.*

Dysmenorrhea. A menstrual dysfunction. See *Amenorrhea; Hypermenorrhea; Hypomenorrhea; Oligomenorrhea.*

Bibliography: **Moon, A. A.:** Dysmenorrhoea and the climacteric: psychosomatic assessment and treatment. Med. J. Austral., 1950, *1*, 174. **Wittkower, E. D. & Wilson, A.:** Dysmenorrhoea and sterility: personality studies. Brit. Med. J., 1940, No. 2, 586.

Dyspareunia. A lack of harmony between couples; used especially when one of two sexual partners is frequently or habitually dissatisfied. In addition to psychosocial reasons (e.g. impotence, frigidity or vaginism), anatomical factors are often implicated which may cause pain during intercourse (e.g. phimosis, or inadequate vaginal lubrication). When some method of contraception other than oral contraceptives is used, there may be varying physiological intolerance of the method employed, which may result in chronic dyspareunia. The word originally denoted insufficient participation by the woman during coitus. *U.H.S.*

Dysphasia. Strictly means difficulty in speaking. It would seem more logical to use this term for the group of speech disorders now grouped under aphasia (q.v.), because few of them are actually without speech of any kind, as the term aphasia implies. It is now used loosely to describe a patient whose abnormal speech is awaiting a more specific label. *B.B.*

Dysphoria. See *Euphoria.*

Dysplastic type. A form of growth which is unharmonious or abnormal, and deviates from genuine biotypes (in proportions and superficial structure). The following are distinguished: malformations, intersexual dysplasia, retarded or accelerated dysplasia. The dysplastic type is not a uniform natural type, but a complex collective term embracing negative characteristics of structure or organization. Conceptually, it is quite different from the basic physical types, despite some schematic points of resemblance.

Bibliography: Kretschmer, E.: Physique and character. London, 1925. *W.K.*

Dysthymia. Originally meant an unpleasant mood state, with *autonomous dysthymia* being synonymous with endogenous depression. Currently used by Eysenck and most British psychologists to denote "the neurotic syndrome characterized by anxiety, reactive depression and/or obsession-compulsion features". The nearest term to this in former use was *psychasthenia.* People with dysthymia are usually introverted neurotics.

Bibliography: Eysenck, H. J.: The dynamics of anxiety and hysteria. London, 1957. *R.H.*

Dysthymic type. An imprecisely defined personality variant: introverted, slow to adapt to stress and tending therefore to protracted dysphoria. For ant.: see *Hysterical type.*

Bibliography: Franks, C. M.: Conditioning and personality. J. abn. and soc. Psychol., 1956, *52*, 143. *W.K.*

Dystonia. A disturbance of the normal condition of muscular tonus, especially of the vascular muscles. *Autonomic,* or *vegetative, dystonia* refers to an abnormal reaction of the parasympathetic and sympathetic nervous system. The results are circulatory weakness, disorders in blood distribution, cardiac activity, breathing, and the functioning of internal organs, with palpitation, restlessness, insomnia, irregularity of temperature, sweating, vertigo, stomach pains and headache. *E.D.*

Dystrophy. Malnutrition; an inability to assimilate food; used chiefly of infants. It may be a congenital dysfunction or due to an intestinal infection or incorrect feeding. The term dystrophy is also applied to individual organs and, when accompanied by dehydration and loss of weight, often indicates a possible transition to atrophy (q.v.). *E.D.*

E

Ear. See *Organs of sense.*

Ebbinghaus, Hermann. B. 24/1/1850 in Barmen, d. 26/2/1909 in Halle. Professor at Breslau and Halle. One of the pioneers and founders of experimental psychology. The first to carry out experimental investigations into the processes of learning and memorizing, beginning with numerous experiments on himself in which he had to learn neutral elements (nonsense syllables). For the speed at which things are forgotten he obtained the Ebbinghaus curve of retention (q.v.): what has been learnt is forgotten, at first quickly but progressively more slowly; and, for the ratio between quantity of matter to be learnt and time taken to learn it, he established the Ebbinghaus Law: if the quantity of matter to be learnt is increased slightly, the time taken to learn it increases considerably. He engaged in controversy with W. Dilthey concerning the methodical bases of psychology, and defended experimental psychology against the psychology of understanding (*Verstehende Psychologie*).

Works: Uber das Gedächtnis, 1885 (Eng. trans.: Memory: a contribution to experimental psychology. New York, [2]1964). Grundzüge der Psychologie, 2 vols, [4]1919. Abriss der Psychologie, [8]1922.

Bibliography: Boring, E. G.: A history of experimental psychology. New York & London, [2]1957. **Misiak, H. & Sexton, V. S.:** History of psychology. New York & London, 1966. **Shakow, D.:** Hermann Ebbinghaus. Amer. J. Psychol., 1930, *42*, 505–18. **Woodworth, R. S.:** Hermann Ebbinghaus, J. Phil., 1909, *6*, 253–56.

F.-C.S.

Ebbinghaus Law. This law states that an increase in the quantity of matter to be learnt necessitates a disproportionate increase in the time required to learn it. According to Ebbinghaus six or seven meaningless syllables will be reproduced without a mistake after having been presented once, twelve syllables after 16·6 sec., fifteen syllables after 30 sec., and so on. *H.H.*

Ecclesiogenic neuroses. These, according to E. Schaetzing (1955), are disorders in coping with experience due to a strict, precise, pseudo-Christian upbringing such as is common in ecclesiastical communities, especially in those with Nonconformist or pietistic leanings. The exclusion of certain subjects from discussion, prohibitions, and threats of punishment, lead to the body being despised and cause inhibitions (especially sexual), psychic castration and marital disasters.

40% of the neurotics I have treated for depression (elsewhere 10% to 20%) suffer from ecclesiogenic neuroses. In my experience, when a person finds a natural relationship with a member of the opposite sex blocked as being allegedly sinful, he often becomes a pervert (50% become homosexuals) or impotent (which includes frigidity). 90% of the 1,000 patients I have so far treated with these symptoms or scruples about masturbation were suffering from these neuroses.

Whereas genuine piety prevents neuroses, can cure marginal neuroses and acts as a protection against suicide, ecclesiogenic neuroses make it more likely that the sick will be driven to commit suicide in order to escape from the contradiction between the id (q.v.) and the super-ego (q.v.). *K.T.*

Echolalia. Repetition of the speech of another, especially when this occurs in the setting of an illness producing mental symptoms, e.g. schizophrenia, or brain disease. The same phenomenon can occur as a personality mannerism or in anxious individuals. Syn. *Echophrasia; Echospeech.* *B.B.*

Echopraxia. Repetition of the movements of another, i.e. imitation of actions (echokinesis) and gestures (echomimia). The term is reserved for describing patients with brain disease or functional psychosis who repeatedly imitate others. *B.B.*

Ecological representativeness (K. Lewin, E. Brunswik). A term for the presence of organisms appropriate to the conditions of the environment.

Ecology. The study of the relationship between organisms and their environment (living or inanimate). A distinction can be made between autoecology and synecology. Autoecology denotes the relationships between a type of organism and its environment (e.g. dependence on temperature, humidity, soil characteristics, food organisms, enemies, food competitors, etc.). Synecology covers the mutual relationships which prevail within a specific area (e.g. meadow, tree, pool, sea coast), each such area having in turn a relationship with other areas. *H.S.*

Economic principle. The principle formulated in the psychoanalytically-oriented psychosomatic research conducted by Alexander (1959): the non-sexual mental energy follows the principle of inertia or energy, while sexual energy follows the surplus principle according to which non-qualified surplus sexual stimulation can be directed by the sexual apparatus into outlet channels, while this is not the case with non-sexual energy.

Bibliography: **Alexander, F.:** Psychosomatische Medizin, Grundlagen und Anwendungsgebiete. Berlin, 1959. *D.V.*

Economic type. One of E. Spranger's ideal types which he includes in his "forms of life": a man who views the world from the standpoint of expediency; in extreme cases the means to an end may become an end in itself, e.g. money. This type is a creator rather than an enjoyer. He has little contact with esthetics or religion and much more with power. Sub-types: entrepreneur, speculator, saver, miser. *W.K.*

Economizing method. Method introduced by H. Ebbinghaus for quantitative determination of memory capacity. Material to be learnt is repeatedly presented to the subject; memory capacity is measured by the number of elements in this material which are retained without repetition, i.e. can be "economized". *P.S.*

Ecphoric inhibition. See *Inhibitions of memory*.

Ecphory. A term used by R. Semon to designate the activation of a memory trace or *engram*, resulting in a partial repetition of the original psychological event or experience (*ecphoria*). *G.D.W.*

Ecstasy. 1. A state of rapture characterized by a decrease of self-control, an exuberance of feeling (q.v.) and often excessive movement. Primary forms can be seen in fits of rage and in the orgasm (q.v.); secondary and derived forms appear in mass-psychological phenomena (see *Crowd behavior* and in certain forms of delirium the origin of which may be spontaneous and religious (*unio mystica*) or spontaneous and pathological; it could also be due to the use of narcotics (q.v.). **2.** In the form "ec-stasy", J. P. Sartre (*Being and Nothingness*) uses the term to denote the following: "The distance to the self which constitutes the for-self, which at the same time is not what it is" (it is not its past), "is what it is not" (it has to be its future), "in the oneness of a constant reference backwards is what it is not and is not what it is" (the present). *P.M.*

Ectoderm. A term for the outer cell-layer created during gastrulation (see *Gastrula*) and all tissues and organs which are formed subsequently by the further differentiation of this cell-layer (in vertebrates, e.g. the nervous system). *H.S.*

Ectomorph(ic type). A growth dimension (somatotype). The main characteristics are "linearity and leanness". The bones and musculature are deficient in strength. Sheldon elaborated this type for statistical emphasis, correlating it with the cerebrotonic (q.v.) character and approximating it to the leptosomic (q.v.) type.

Bibliography: Sheldon, W. H.: Varieties of human physique. New York, 1940. *W.K.*

Ectoplasm. Substance exuded from the mouth, nose or other orifices of a materializing medium assumed to be of a paranormal nature. See *Materialization; Medium.* *J.B.*

Educability. 1. A person's educational potentiality, or disposition to benefit from education as the combined result of innate and environmental factors. A unilateral attribution of significance to "talent" or environment leads to pedagogic pessimism (nativism, q.v.) or optimism (empiricism, q.v.). The irreconcilable antithesis of ineducability and hyper-educability is confuted by the convergence principle (W. Stern): a person is educable when "talent" and environmental factors converge. Of course, not only ability and environment are involved but the adequacy of both and the personal decisions of the individual. The cooperation of the person concerned is required to realize educability, for which both the emotional and linguistic aspects of inter-human communication are important. Educability is also related to the inner (spontaneous) cooperation of the pupil with the external educational aim. Educability always involves problems of spontaneity, one's own activity and receptivity to the environment. *H.Schr.*

2. To define educability as the ability to be educated is not very useful; it is more proficient to determine the form and level of ineducability, in order to establish a precise definition and define possible therapeutic measures and teaching methods.

Forms. There are several possible classifications. In a psychological perspective, they are (apart from severe subnormality of intelligence): (*a*) subnormality not amounting to severe subnormality, and susceptible to medical treatment and special training; (*b*) general but temporary incapacities; educators would include in this category asocial types who can improve, given certain pedagogic presuppositions; (*c*) partial or localized inabilities, e.g. those related to sense defects. *Level:* educability is directly related to IQ. An IQ below 0·40 makes it impossible to acquire even fundamental school knowledge (e.g. reading). For an exact diagnosis, other factors would have to be considered: family background, which is or is not favorable to primary-school education; character and motor skills, linguistic competence, timeliness of remedial measures already take, etc. See *Abilities; Autism; Learning.* *G.C.M.*

Education. See *Educational science.*

Educational guidance is dependent on education itself and therefore differs according to age, nationality, culture, economic conditions, philosophy, ethical considerations, human ideals of society and even family and personal factors—just as the objectives of education themselves differ. In the non-professional sense educational guidance has always existed. Intentional, planned, objective and scientifically based guidance with an expert orientation did not develop until the twentieth century. To some extent the two world wars drew attention to the problem of education; at the same time the difficulties of education were only fully recognized when the results of research in child psychology (q.v.) became available. Education based on parental and pedagogic authority changed and the emphasis shifted to the personality of the child. The conditions of life and work are becoming increasingly complex and requirements are growing: the problems and difficulties of education have therefore become one of the major concerns of society.

1. In the broad, comprehensive, sense, educational guidance designates generally valid indications and assistance for persons active in the educational process in order to achieve optimal control over and influence on the physical, intellectual and moral development of the normal child. The fundamental principles of education are those of love, patience, respect for the personality of the developing child, acceptance of otherness, a progression of demands, regularity, rewards and punishment, etc. Education is also of vital importance as a means of promoting independence and self-discipline. Education with these aims in mind can only be achieved if the environment of the child is calm, harmonious, honest and regular and provides an example which is worthy of imitation. There are periods in the life of a normal child and youth (phases of defiance, puberty, youth) when parents must frequently turn to the expert for guidance. The main task of educational guidance in the future will be to prevent educational conflicts.

2. In the narrower sense, educational guidance signifies carefully planned remedial measures for individual educational difficulties that are not normal problems. This is particularly important in the case of children who are handicapped or whose personality development is disturbed. (*a*) *Educational problems of handicapped children* (blind or suffering from defective vision, mute, deaf, mentally defective, physically handicapped, suffering from speech defects) are dependent on the specific defect. The perception processes, emotionality, and reactions to the outside world may be disturbed, mental development may deviate from the average, and the personality may have undergone a specific change. These children are characterized by failures, inhibitions, fear, distrust, isolation, a lack of self-confidence, anxiety, inability to work and social maladjustment. Parents adopt two extreme attitudes: such children are either spoilt and pampered or neglected and rejected. Parents therefore require expert advice at an early stage in order to prevent or reduce secondary personality problems. This will also facilitate compensation, correction and rehabilitation and influence those around the handicapped child to accept him as he is and view him objectively. (*b*) In the case of a number of other *defects in the development of the personality*, educational guidance again has an important part to play. A uniform taxonomy of these disturbances is not yet available. Reasons, symptoms or the degree of severity may be emphasized from case to case. Behavior problems, learning difficulties, character faults, social maladjustment, defective affective relations, impaired development, damage caused by the environment, etc., are characteristics of the exceptional problem child. The symptoms are varied and range from difficulties in learning to theft, from dyslexia (q.v.) to enuresis (q.v.) and from agressivity to inhibition in widely varying

however, is familiarity with the nature of the objects of educational activity, namely the pupils. No two pupils are alike in respect of their innate abilities. They develop in accordance with individual patterns. They do not behave in groups in the way they do as individuals. For subject-matter to be communicated, it will not suffice to know the individual pupils. One must also know the principles and conditions under which learning takes place. These principles, together with knowledge of individual differences, maturity and development, are taught by *educational psychology* (q.v.), a field which borders on general and experimental psychology and scientifically relates to it in fruitful interaction.

The theory of how learning opportunities ought to be organized forms the core of what has traditionally been called "didactics".

(*c*) The third and last stage of the educative process was designated above by the appraisal of the didactic measures, the attempt to assess how far the objectives formulated have been achieved. These measures are usually described in educational terminology by the word *evaluation*. This term is concerned in part with examining, testing and grading. However, evaluation does not pertain solely to the more tangible and cognitive results of education, but also to affective results, such as values, attitudes and esthetic taste. The aim of educational research is to measure the results of the educational process. For this reason, the theory of testing and measurement is an important branch of educational psychology. Of basic relevance in this connection is the construction of achievement tests, which are used to measure comprehensively the acquisition of knowledge and skill. Attempts are also made to construct instruments in order to assess more subtle qualities in the moral and esthetic sphere, that is valuative, attitudinal and similar qualities of education.

Remedial education (q.v.), a sector not accounted for in the above itemization of education as a discipline, is also closely related to educational psychology. It is concerned with negative deviations: with pupils who, because of intellectual retardation, find it hard to keep up with their classmates: with pupils beset by reading and writing disabilities; with emotionally disturbed pupils, and so on. It stands to reason that this branch of education has many ties with psychiatry and psychopathology.

Summing up, we can say that education as a discipline consists of the following branches: (*a*) philosophy of education; (*b*) history of education; (*c*) comparative education (which comprise educational theory); and of: (*d*) educational sociology; (*e*) educational psychology cum didactics; (*f*) remedial education (which comprise empirical education).

Education as a discipline is clearly very heterogeneous, not so much in its problems as in its theories and methods. One and the same problem may be treated from many different angles. The question of grouping in school provides an example: should pupils be grouped according to their varying scholastic ability? If so, when and how? This problem has strong political and social value implications. But we cannot understand the substance and the intensity of the commitments involved in the issue of school structure and grouping practices unless we study the historical and social background of the problem. The relationship between the general elementary school for the common people and the "learned" or Latin schools for the social élite has assumed different forms from one country to another, depending upon the degree of social heterogeneity and economic development. The International Project for the Evaluation of Educational Achievement (IEA) (Husén *et al.*, 1967) might be cited as one example of an empirically oriented study whereby advantage is taken of cross-national differences in both independent and dependent variables. Important aspects of school structure can thus be put in a deeper perspective than is possible in a study within the national confines.

Since the practical problems radiate into all branches of education as a discipline, methods can vary sharply between these branches. The study of the history of education requires a quite different research training than when statistical methods and educational tests are used to investigate, for example, the structure of ability, the accretions of knowledge and teacher-pupil interaction. In the last case one must be conversant with scientific method in the so-called behavioral sciences, such as psychology and sociology.

2. *Education as a research discipline.* Science had a long history before the assumptions and methods of education were subjected to systematic study. The first university chairs were not established until the end of the eighteenth century. The first professor of education (which also included philosophy) was appointed at Halle in Germany. This link between education and philosophy set the pattern for future university chairs in several European countries. This meant that the inquiry concentrated mainly on the "humanistic" aspects, or *objectives*, of education.

Not until the arrival of experimental psychology was the basis laid for educational psychology. The United States took the lead during the 1880s and 1890s. American psychologists who had received their experimental schooling in Germany, began to make systematic observations, conduct experiments in perception, and carry out studies in developmental psychology in order to illuminate educational problems. Mention can be made of Stanley Hall, who did pioneering work in child and adolescent psychology, and who introduced Freudian psychoanalysis into the U.S. at the beginning of this century: and of J. McKeen Cattell, who in 1890 made the first attempt to construct a so-called intelligence test (q.v.), whose primary applications were intended for the schools. In 1905 Alfred Binet, commissioned by the French Ministry of Education, constructed the first practicable intelligence test.

William James, the father of pragmatic philosophy, also made a name for himself as a psychologist. During the 1890s he held a series of lectures (published in 1899 under the title, *Talks to Teachers of Psychology*).

The same decade also witnessed the pioneering attempt at "evaluation", carried out by the American physician, Joseph M. Rice, in order to measure the results of school instruction. He travelled to schools in different parts of the country, and devised the first purely educational test, concerned with spelling.

A dissertation on the learning behavior of animals was presented at the end of the 1890s by Edward Lee Thorndike, who was to become a leading figure in American educational psychology virtually throughout the ensuing half-century. In his dissertation he expounded his law of effect. The first edition of his famous *Educational Psychology* appeared in 1903; over a long period of successive revisions its contents have greatly influenced the training of teachers.

In Germany, Ernst Meumann published in 1907 the first of his three massive volumes of *Vorlesungen zur Einführung in die experimentelle Pädagogik*, whose wide-ranging scope included developmental psychology, individual differences, scholastic ability, the psychology and hygiene of school work, and the problems encountered in teaching different subjects.

In Britain, the problem of individual differences was first studied by anthropologists and statisticians, most notably by Sir Francis Galton and Karl Pearson (the originator of the correlation method). In 1900 the German psychologist and educator, William Stern, published his *Differentielle Psychologie*, which was followed two years later by Thorndike's *Introduction to the Theory of Mental Measurements.* Thorndike introduced statistical methods into educational psychology, and also played a major role in shaping measurement theory in education, especially as applied to the construction of achievement tests. Between 1900 and 1930, education advanced as a component of almost all lived experiences. The characteristics of a central or all-embracing phenomenon are ascribed to the ego. W. Wundt uses the term to denote "the feeling of cohesion of all mental experiences". In the psychic strata theory, it appears as the final, highest layer or as the apex of a pyramid, and is therefore the essential characteristic of the structure of the personality (q.v.). W. James made an important distinction in the sphere of ego experience, when he showed the diversity of experiences comprised in the notion. According to him, there are two aspects of the ego: the knowing ego, i.e. the experience linked with the wide-ranging activities in which the individual sees himself as the subject; and the "self", or empirical ego: the latter covers all the content which the subject experiences in a special manner as belonging to himself.

2. The term acquired a completely new meaning in Freud's theory. In his opinion it is not anchored in self-perception, but in the dynamic mental process, and especially in disturbed mental conditions and conflicts. For Freud, the ego is an area or part of the psychic structure which contrasts with the id (q.v.). To begin with, he considered it to be practically equivalent to the consciousness, until he recognized that functions of the ego may also be unconscious. Originally Freud believed that the ego originated from the id but today psychoanalysis (q.v.) also refers to innate ego-mechanisms, and greater independence is ascribed to the latter (see, e.g., H. Hartmann and E. Kris). The ego permits of adaptation to reality and supports the reality principle (q.v.). Freud has compared it with the rider who "must curb the superior strength of his horse and must borrow the means to do so". Anna Freud has developed the theory of the defense mechanisms of the ego (see *Defense mechanisms*); she states that the ego appears as the decisive component of the psyche to an even greater extent than is postulated in the later writings of Freud himself. But, from the functional as well as from the experiential aspect, the ego appears to be a very complex phenomenon, and Freud found it necessary to make a distinction between the ego itself and the *super-ego*—as a special structure which is superior to the ego and represents ideals and morality, therefore corresponding broadly to what earlier psychologists had referred to as the *conscience* (q.v.).

3. To the extent that problems of the personality and motivation have been incorporated into empirical psychology primarily in connection with clinical and social psychology, the concept of the ego has again become of interest. However, in order to avoid the arguments which dominated philosophical studies and the psychology of consciousness, the term *ego* has been replaced by the word *self*. One of the classical representatives of learning psychology in the U.S.A., E. R. Hilgard, considers that the mechanisms of adaptation cannot be understood without introducing the concept of the self. Like G. Allport, who suggested the term *proprium* instead of self, Hilgard believes that this concept can establish the link between different phenomena. In this sense, however, the self does not merely denote the unity of the personality. It can best be understood as an individually characteristic centering of the personality. This definition provides the best means of understanding the different ego experiences.

In empirical research the self is now primarily understood as the perception which the subject has of himself. It is apprehended by questionnaire methods which analyze the qualities a person attributes to himself. In a summary of an extensive range of studies, R. Wylie draws attention to the wide margin of uncertainty which still remains.

4. Since the ego can only be studied as a structure, or feature on which the personality centers, research into its development is very difficult, and the results remain hypothetical. No systematic studies seem to have been made of the development of the self-image. This development does not

take place in isolation but as an aspect of the development of the personality structure as a whole. It is not possible to indicate a specific point in time at which the ego is formed. The perception of the subject's own body, which is observed through certain reactions at the end of the first year of life, recognition of his own mirror image, and use of the pronoun "I", defiant attitudes and certain roles played by small children, are initial manifestations which cannot be explained without the "ego" concept (see *Ego discover; Development*). Erikson understands the final stage of ego development as the discovery of one's own identity, and Jung's concept of individuation (q.v.) can be seen as the highest form of ego development: "becoming oneself".

Bibliography: Allport, G. W.: Pattern and growth in personality. New York, 1961. **Erikson, E. H.:** Identity: Youth and crisis. New York & London, 1968. **Freud, S.:** The ego and the id. London, [2]1962. **Hartmann, H.:** Ego psychology and the problem of adaptation. New York, 1958. **Hilgard, E. R.:** Human motives and the concept of the self, Amer. Psychol. 1949, *4*, 374–82. **Rogers, C. R.:** Client-centered therapy. Boston, 1950. **Wylie, R. C.:** The self concept. Nebraska, 1961.

R. Meili

Ego. III. According to Freud, the psychic part system which organizes the primitive and unorganized drives (urges, desires), which are included in the psychic part system known as the id (q.v.), and the drives of the super-ego (q.v.), and then contrives their satisfaction in reality. In doing this it can avail itself of the function of libidinal object cathexis (q.v.) or of object countercathexis; or, in other words, of learning about opportunities for the gratification of a motive and of unlearning about those opportunities which have either proved no longer to lead to the gratification of drives or to be linked to the deprivation of drives. In addition to learning ability, the following must be included (according to Hartmann and Rapaport) among the primary autonomous, i.e. constitutional or innate, characteristics of the ego: ability to react, perception, intelligence and motor skill, but also frustration tolerance. Different people are distinguished from one another by the degree to which they possess these characteristics. The ego is a construct, but is not identical with the experience and the perception of the self (q.v.).

Bibliography: Freud, S.: The ego and the id. London, [2]1962. **Hartmann, H., Kris, E. & Löwenstein, R. M.:** Comments on the formation of psychic structure. Psychoanalyt. Study of the Child, 1964, *2*, 11–38. **Rapaport, D.:** The structure of psychoanalytic theory: a systematizing attempt. In: **Koch, S.:** Psychology: a study of a science, Vol. 3. New York, 1959, 55–183.

W. Toman

Ego anachoresis. The withdrawal of the ego (e.g.) from non-assimilable contents of the consciousness. This is a defense (q.v.) mechanism in the psychoanalytical sense, which, according to W. T. Winkler, is primarily characteristic of psychotic experience. Ideas lose their "ego-quality" and appear as alien or remotely-controlled. The individual no longer feels responsible for the intolerable content of his consciousness and believes that it is forced upon him by the outside world (connection with projection, q.v.). A whole range of schizophrenic symptoms can be interpreted as ego anachoresis.

W. Sc.

Ego consciousness. I perceive all that I experience and sense, as well as my memories, etc., as something experienced and sensed *by me*. Knowledge of the self as the subject of experience is ego consciousness. See *Ego*. *V.M.*

Ego discovery. The process by which ego consciousness (q.v.) is acquired, generally during (pre-) puberty. A. Adler (q.v.) has used the term in a narrower sense to denote the awareness of individual existence acquired in the second year of life. *W.Sc.*

Ego function. The activity of the ego (q.v.); intelligence, perception, etc. In psychoanalysis, H. Hartmann makes a distinction between *primary autonomous* ego functions (perception, thought, reality testing, ability to judge) and *secondary autonomous* functions. See *Defense*. *W.Sch.*

Ego ideal. The person, or idea of such a person (or persons), that, on the basis of an individual's subjective experience or knowledge, superlatively embodies the tendencies and motives of his own super-ego (q.v.); the super-ego being the system of desires and motives of persons with whom the individual has identified.

Bibliography: Freud, S.: Introductory lectures on psycho-analysis. London, [3]1929. *W.T.*

Ego-ideal discrepancy. According to Rogers, a discrepancy between the (desired) self-image and actual experiences of oneself. This is a situation of tension (e.g. neurotic), because behavior is determined differently by the desire (*a*) of the whole organism, and (*b*) of the self, for fulfillment.

Bibliography: Rogers, C. R.: A theory of therapy, personality and interpersonal relationships, as developed in the client-centered framework. In: **Koch, S.** (Ed.): Psychology, a study of a science, Vol. 3. New York, 1959. *H.W.*

Ego involvement. A designation introduced by Sherif & Cantril for all those attitudes which determine the status (q.v.) of a person or assign him a role (q.v.) in relation to other individuals, groups or institutions. Behavior can be designated as ego-involved when, in the course of development, acquired attitudes related to one's own ego (q.v.) are brought into play in a certain situation by relevant objects, people or groups, so that either a high degree of participation is produced or attitudes relative to one's own ego, the image of one's ego, etc., are called upon. *W.D.F.*

Bibliography: Sherif, M. & Cantril, H.: The psychology of ego involvements. New York, 1947.

Ego strength. See *Ego*.

Ego(t)ism. Selfish, ego-centered, unsocial behavior. Various psychological theories (see *Psychoanalysis; Reinforcement*) imply that in the last analysis all behavior, even when seemingly altruistic, is actually egoistic. See *Altruism*. *D.B.*

Ehrenfels, Christian von. B. 20/6/1859 in Rodaun (Lower Austria); d. 8/9/1932 in Lichtenau (Lower Austria). Professor of Philosophy at Prague in 1900; discovered the gestalt characteristics of transposability, supersummativity, paradigms: melody), which makes him one of the pioneers of gestalt psychology. See *Ganzheit*.

Works: Uber Gestaltqualitäten, 1890 (Eng. trans.: *Soc. Res.*, 1944, *11*, 78–99). System der Werttheorie, 1898. Grundzüge der Ethik, 1907. Die Religion der Zukunft, 1929.

Bibliography: Petermann, B.: The gestalt theory. London, 1932. **Weinhandl, F.** (Ed.): Gestalthaftes Sehen. Ergebnisse und Aufgaben der Morphologie. Darmstadt, 1960. *K.E.P.*

Ehrenstein's illusion. An optical illusion in which a given square containing straight radiating lines seems to be distorted into a trapezium. See *Geometrical-optical illusions*.

Bibliography: Ehrenstein, W.: Probleme der ganzheitpsychol. Wahrnehmungslehre. Leipzig, 1947. *P.S.*

Eidesis. According to Hellpach, characteristic of a certain stage in the juvenile's development when imagination predominates.

Eidetic imagery. Vivid visual images of specific objects that are not present in actuality are "seen" by the subject (usually a child), who is generally conscious that these are not directly sensed images of the external world.

Eigenraum. In the psychology of W. Stern, *Eigenraum* is the space required for the dynamic manifestation of the individual body, which through its personal three-dimensionality determines certain qualities (up, down, in front, etc.) of that space, which is thereby differentiated from non-qualitative Euclidean space. *J.M.*

Eigenzeit. In W. Stern's "personalistic psychology" (q.v.), *Eigenzeit* is the multidimensional or polyrhythmic individual time featuring several modes within mathematical time. The personal past and the future as modes of the present, co-determine, together with the actual present, an individual life as an indivisible whole. *J.M.*

Einfühlung. See *Empathy.*

Ejaculation. The discharge of sperm during the male orgasm. Today it is no longer assumed that there is any equivalent of ejaculation in the sexual reaction cycle of women. Ejaculation is primarily a reflex process, accompanied by cortical activity. The concept of male potency includes the ability to postpone any ejaculation (see *Circumcision*). As a rule, an ejaculation is followed by a refractory period which varies in length according to the individual and terminates the erection (q.v.) relatively quickly. The object of postponing ejaculation is to avoid too early a conclusion of coitus (q.v.). Such control of ejaculation can be acquired by practice or allegedly be replaced by aphrodisiacs (q.v.). It is usually a consequence of the role (q.v.) which the male partner assumes, and its frequency increases with higher standards of education. An ejaculation which in the opinion of the couple has occurred too quickly is known as *ejaculatio praecox.* To define this concept precisely does not seem possible; in principle an ejaculation could only be diagnosed as premature if it occurred before, during or immediately after the insertion of the penis. *G.L.*

Elaborated code. See *Restricted code.*

Electra complex. The heroine of the Greek tragedy has given her name to the feminine variant of the Oedipus complex (q.v.). Just as a boy, according to Freud, in the early genital (q.v.) or Oedipal phase begins to love his mother and to compete with his father, so a girl turns from the primary object of her love, the mother, to the secondary object, the father, and competes with the mother for his favor. The Electra complex is overcome in a way similar to that of the Oedipus complex by repressing (q.v.) a part of the love-desires directed at the father and by identification with the mother. If the complex is not completely overcome, there is fixation (q.v.) which under stress (q.v.) at some later date can cause regression (q.v.) to this phase, and neurotic disorders, especially anxiety hysteria and conversion hysteria.

Bibliography: Freud, S.: Introductory lectures on psycho-analysis. London, ^{2}1929. *W.T.*

Electrocardiogram (abb. EKG). Recording the electric action potential of the heart by the use of electrocardiographs which consist of electrical activators and a writing system working on the galvanometer principle. Depending on the position of the electrode leads, the following are distinguished: W. Eindhoven's lead from the extremities, a Wilsonian lead, or a parietal lead from the chest. An electrocardiogram supplies information about the electrical phenomena in the heart which are associated with some excitation, but only qualified information about the remaining function of the heart. It is used for the diagnosis of disturbances in rhythm and the conduction of excitation, of phenomena due to oxygen deficiency, of cardiac infarcts and of changes in the tissue content. *E.D.*

Electrodiagnostics. A field of medical diagnostics. Methodologically the following fields can be distinguished: (*a*) locating and recording currents and voltages in the living organism (e.g. encephalography, q.v.); (*b*) using electric currents and voltages to test excitability; (*c*) measuring electrical properties of cells or groups of cells (see *Galvanic skin response*). See also *Electrophysiology*.

K.E.P.

Electroencephalogram. See *Encephalography*.

Electrolytic stimulus. An inadequate stimulus producing a sensory effect by electro-chemical processes.

F.-C.S.

Electrophysiology. The field of physiology which deals with the electrical phenomena in organisms and in studying the latter uses chiefly electrical techniques and methods of measurement. Applied and specialized electrophysiology has as its objects of research: (*a*) the recording of bioelectrical reactions to the general and reliable demonstration of excitations; (*b*) the relating of central or peripheral patterns of excitation derived electrically to certain functional states in the living organism. General electrophysiology works in particular on the following: (*a*) research into the conditions of artificial (especially electrical) stimulation which leads to arousal (q.v.); (*b*) study of the elementary processes which underlie resting potential as well as the actual process of arousal.

K.E.P.

Electroretinography (abb. ERG). The measurement of the electrical processes in the eye. The retina when not exposed to light has a direct voltage potential, as can be shown to be the case with the intact eyeball (cornea positive with respect to the posterior pole of the eye). This direct voltage potential is changed by the influence of light. A distinction is drawn between an a-, b-, c- and d-spike. *Electroretinogram* (ERG): the record obtained.

Bibliography: Müller-Limmroth, W.: Elektrophysiologie des Gesichtssinns. Berlin-Göttingen-Heidelberg, 1959.

R.R.

Electroshock. Generalized convulsions and unconsciousness produced by an electrical current passing through two electrodes attached to the scalp. If the indications are correctly assessed and possible contra-indications considered, complications tend to be more infrequent and harmless than with most other major medical operations. Even today, in many cases—acute catatonia and serious depression—electroshock is still the most reliable and simple treatment and the one least likely to have serious complications.

A.Hi.

Electrotonus. A term in electrophysiology for the change in state of excitable structures (e.g. nerves) when direct current with below threshold voltage is passed through. After local excitation, i.e. after the current has spread out into the region of the locally affected points ("physical electrotonus"), there occurs, simultaneously with the crossing of the threshold (the least possible conditions for intensity, duration and rapidity must be observed), an extension of the change in excitability associated with the passage of current and hence in capacity to transmit ("physiological electronus"). The nerve through which current has passed shows at the anode diminished (anelectrotonus), and at the cathode increased (catelectrotonus), excitability.

F.-C.S.

Elementarism. This term denotes in general the endeavor to describe complex phenomena or totalities as the sums of more simple elements (of which they are thought to be composed). In this sense elementarism is related to reductionism, atomism or molecularism and is used in various academic fields. Historically it denotes in particular the system of W. Wundt (q.v.), where the contents of consciousness are split up into two kinds of elements, those of sensation and those of feeling. The expression is used pejoratively by Wundt's critics. *P.M.*

Elements, psychology of. Those trends in psychology which believed that psychic events could be reduced to small units (elements) such as sensations (q.v.) and associations (q.v.) (see *Psychophysics*, and also *Wundt*). This concept of the psychology of elements is disputed, especially by gestalt psychology. See *Ganzheit*.

Bibliography: Boring, E. G.: A history of experimental psychology. New York, [2]1950. **Fechner, G. T.:** Elemente der Psychophysik. Leipzig, 1860. **Wundt, W.:** Grundzüge der physiologischen Psychol. Leipzig, [5]1902. *P.S.*

Élite. A term taken from eighteenth-century French, and meaning "the pick". It is a term used in sociology and social psychology when evaluating or analyzing small groups in some existing society who hold an important position with respect to certain activities or offices of power, or from whose ranks future holders of such positions and offices will repeatedly be drawn. Lasswell and others take the view that in the analytical sense there as many élites as there are values in any society.

Starting from Machiavelli, V. Pareto in particular put forward the anti-parliamentarian view of the cycle of élites. Expressed in very simplified terms, Pareto argues that every society has by nature an oligarchical structure. Within a (ruling) élite there are however always two tendencies the strength of which varies: the will to power by force (the "lions") and the desire to use intellectualizing tactics (the "foxes"). After some social change (e.g. a revolution), the group of the "lions" initially takes over the government; gradually, however, tactics and strategies have to be developed in order to be able to hold on to the privileges resting on power. Thus the "foxes" come into their own, and they may also be drawn from the non-élite. The assumption of power by the "foxes" mobilizes in turn the "lions" in the non-élite (the masses) among whom there are likewise "foxes" who are also joined by the foxes of the élite. These provide the masses with possible tactics and strategy so that a revolution can be initiated, to be followed by a new cycle.

Bibliography: Lasswell, H. D., Lerner, D. & Rothwell, C. E.: The comparative study of élites. Stanford (Calif.), 1952. **Pareto, V.:** Trattato di sociologia generale, 1918. *W.D.F.*

Emancipation. See *Social psychology*.

Emancipation, sexual. In contrast to sex education (q.v.), sexual emancipation can be understood to mean the endeavor to have sexuality (q.v.) regarded as a matter for purely individual concern, free from any interference by the State or any institution. This includes a critical analysis of the ways in which a society is organized socio-economically and politically and also of its sexual morality (e.g. abstinence, q.v., homosexuality, q.v., form of marriage). Sexual emancipation is usually regarded as a necessary constituent of any political revolution. In the twentieth century a further decisive impetus in this direction was given by Freud, W. Reich, H. Horkheimer and H. Marcuse.

In a narrower sense, sexual emancipation aims at helping those sections of society whose sexual behavior at any given moment is under social pressure (e.g. children, juveniles, women). Thus the sexual emancipation of woman denotes liberation from social constraints (e.g. double standards of morality) as part of a campaign for legal, social and economic equality.

Bibliography: Beauvoir, S. de: The second sex. New York & London, 1952. **Horkheimer, M.** *et al.*: Studien über Autorität und Familie. Paris, 1936. **Kursbuch No. 17:** Frau, Familie, Gesellschaft. Frankfurt, 1969. **Marcuse, H.:** Eros and civilization. Boston, 1955. **Reich, R.:** The sexual revolution: toward a self-governing character structure. New York, 1945. *J.F.*

Embedded figures. An experimental arrangement devised by Gottschaldt (1926) for the perception of figures. Simple geometrical figures have to be found in more complex ones. It is of the utmost importance that parts of the complex settings should not correspond to the embedded figures. Exercises set in this way prove very difficult to solve. Gottschaldt's figures were used by R. Meili (1943) and L. L. Thurstone (1944) in factor analyses (plasticity and flexibility of closure) and by H. A. Witkin (1954) for "field independence".

Bibliography: **Gottschaldt, K.:** Über den Einfluss der Erfahrung auf die Wahrnehmung von Figuren. Psychol. Forsch., 1926, *8*, 261–317.

P.S. & R.M.

Emergency function. Defined by Cannon as a heightened mental-physical activity which is controlled by the sympathetic division of the autonomic nervous system. It includes, e.g., the secretion of adrenaline, liberation of glycogen from the liver, an increase in the blood sugar level and an acceleration of the blood flow to the brain, heart and skeletal muscles. According to Cannon's theory (which has not been empirically confirmed in every detail), the emergency functions are accompanied by emotional reactions and prepare for flight and combat. See *Emotion.*

Bibliography: **Cannon, W. B.:** The wisdom of the body. New York, 1932.

W.Sc.

Emergency theory of the emotions. See *Emergency function.*

Emmert's law or phenomenon. A law named after F. C. Emmert: the apparent size of the afterimage changes proportionally to the change in distance of the projection screen from the observer. Formula: $l' = \frac{la'}{a}$ (l' = size of afterimage; l = size of stimulus object, a' = distance of eye from afterimage; a = distance of eye from stimulus object).

K.E.P.

Emmetropia. Normal sight in contrast to hyperopia (q.v.) and myopia (q.v.).

Emotion. The term emotion can have many meanings and has been defined in many ways. It is applied to a distinctive category of experience for which a variety of verbal labels is used: fear, anger, love, and so on. Most writers agree that it is a complex state involving heightened perception of an object or situation, widespread bodily changes, an appraisal of felt attraction or repulsion, and behavior organized toward approach or withdrawal. The urge toward action is one of the strongest subjective experiences of emotion, contained in the etymological source (Latin *e* [out] and *movere* [to move]).

Theories of emotion have been offered by existentialists, philosophers, psychiatrists, ethologists and neurophysiologists, and by many psychologists. Methods of study range from pure intuitive understanding (empathy), through the systematic study of subjective experience, to precise quantitative recordings of behavior and physiological change.

Phenomenologists have argued that we must go directly to subjective experience to understand the quality and significance of human emotion. Jaspers (1912) has outlined the method in relation to psychiatry, and there are various modern versions. These attempt to characterize the nature of man's experience of his world and himself, especially in relation to other people. The phenomenological approach has generally been regarded as antithetical to the experimental method: "Essences and facts are incommensurables" (Sartre, 1948).

Behaviorists, on the other hand, have traditionally rejected the subjective ("mentalistic") approach and have argued that the meaning of the term emotion must be limited to outwardly observable events (see Brown & Farber, 1951). Contemporary psychologists, however, are on the whole willing to encompass testimony from many sources, provided an attempt is made to scale or quantify.

1. *Assessment of emotion.* Three main categories of data are recognized: verbal, physiological and overt behavior. Most experimental work has probably been carried out on physiological changes. The role of the autonomic nervous system (q.v.) is seen as of special significance. Cannon (1929) assigned to its parasympathetic division the role of conserver of bodily energies, and to its sympathetic division an "emergency" function. This view has dominated the field. During sympathetic excitation, widespread changes occur which can be readily measured: sweating is increased, the heart beats faster, and blood is redistributed to the muscles. Further adrenergic changes include liberation of sugar into the bloodstream, improved contraction of fatigued muscle, more rapid coagulation of the blood, and so on; in this way the organism is mobilized for prompt and efficient action. Measurement of these changes has given rise to a vast literature on the assessment of emotions.

Such assessment is incomplete without examining overt emotional *behavior* and, in the case of human subjects, emotional *experience*. This latter can be inferred from verbal reports, and increasing use is being made of questionnaires, scales, feeling "thermometers", repertory grids and personal check lists. Studies of overt emotional behavior include facial and vocal expression, gesture and posture.

Approach/avoidance behavior, once linked with a simple instinct mechanism, is being analyzed in terms of subject/object relations, as well as the affective processes ("hedonic tone") which accompany it. Schneirla (1959) has postulated that stimulus intensity basically determines the direction of reaction, low intensity stimulation tending to evoke approach reactions. The attachment behavior of young mammals can be examined in this context (Bowlby, 1969).

The relationship among different measures of emotion has proved to be highly complicated. Even within autonomic changes, individual patterns of reaction occur. Lang (1967) has reported that different measures of fear taken concurrently from phobic subjects do not necessarily yield responses of the same relative strength. A subject might report extremely intense fear yet not necessarily show marked physiological changes, or behavioral avoidance of the feared object. High relationships among measures cannot be assumed. They must be examined empirically. The development of response configurations in individuals is seen to reflect the fact that different components (verbal, physiological, behavioral) are "shaped" (i.e. learned) in accordance with past reinforcement schedules. See *Anxiety*.

2. *Genesis of emotion.* Many authors have postulated the presence at birth of some diffuse excitement, which becomes differentiated and associated with certain situations and motor responses to form the separate emotions. Others have attempted to identify a single specific source of emotion in pleasure/unpleasure, anxiety, love, or a basic pair of opposites such as love and aggression. A single fund of energy capable of endless transformations has been posited repeatedly.

The opposing view is that emotions are inherited and distinct entities, and various numbers of basic passions have been proposed. Earlier instinct theories, as well as modern ethology, tend to subscribe to this view. For them, emotions provide the appropriate driving force for specific instinctual behavior. Through a process of integration and differentiation of primary feelings, an array of derived emotions can be developed.

Numerous developmental mechanisms have been proposed. Various diffuse forms of early experience are known to be relevant. Harlow (1958) has emphasized the role of sensory contact in the infant's early life; Bowlby (1969) has stressed maternal separation. In addition, a number of studies have dealt with the effect of stimulation during infancy on subsequent emotionality. Learning processes, in particular classical conditioning, have been examined by the behaviorists. The role of individual differences in basic neural functioning and ability to learn have been repeatedly stressed (Eysenck, 1967).

No very clear evidence exists for different patterns of physiological reaction in different emotional states (but see studies reviewed by Arnold, 1960, on fear and anger). It seems that human subjects tend to give an emotional label to bodily changes on the basis of prevailing situational factors. It has been suggested that it will only be possible to distinguish one emotional state from another by taking account of specific physiological, specific cognitive and specific behavioral patterns—and then only in conjunction with given eliciting conditions (Lazarus, 1968).

A large number of studies (reviewed by Goldstein, 1968) have sought the neurological structures and circuits involved in emotional behavior. Papez (1937) first proposed a theory of emotion involving the limbic system and this view has persisted. This system may serve as a "visceral brain" which processes internal information rather than external symbols. In man, neocortical-hypothalamic interrelations probably play a role in the fusion of emotional processes with those of perception, memory and learning. The role of the ascending reticular activating system has also been considered in relation to the concepts of arousal (q.v.) and emotion. It has been suggested that emotion falls on the extreme of a single arousal continuum (Duffy, 1962). However, recent authors have differentiated the arousal role of the reticular activating system from that of the limbic system (Eysenck, 1967; Gellhorn & Loufbourrow, 1963; Routtenberg, 1968). They make the point that the two systems, while interrelating physiologically, can be separated conceptually.

3. *The current position.* The shift in emphasis is toward psychological models involving cognition and information processing: the way our vocabulary of feeling is learned and used (Davitz, 1969); the narrowing of cue utilization that occurs in emotion (Easterbrook, 1959), the comparison of a perceived stimulus with the memory store (Sokolov, 1960), often leading to expectancies and uncertainties (Pribram, 1967), and to assessment and appraisal (Arnold, 1960; Lazarus, 1968).

The theme of emotion as energy, which must be discharged or released if a proper organismic balance is to be maintained, continues to be explored. Current models tend to implicate feedback and cybernetic principles in the regulation of homeostasis. Ways of releasing energy include not only catharsis and abreaction, but perhaps the recently described implosion theory (Stampfl, 1966); Pribram (1967) also suggests that the individual can exert self-control, that is, make internal adjustments that will lead to re-equilibration without recourse to action.

In spite of so much effort, the function of the emotions still remains uncertain. Recently some have asked whether all emotions fit the basic model of the "emergency" reactions, that is, follow a sequence of build-up and discharge of energy. Many have come to feel that too much attention has been concentrated on the energy-mobilizing half of the emotional spectrum, and too little on positive emotional experiences leading to growth, expansion and self-development (Arnold, 1960; Hillman, 1960; Koestler, 1964). In order to reach a more comprehensive account of human emotion, investigators in the next decade will probably give more attention to these positive, often relational properties of emotion, as well as to the more subtle categories of subjective experience.

Bibliography: Arnold, Magda, B.: Emotion and personality. 2 vols. New York, 1960. **Bowlby, J.:** Psychopathology of anxiety: the role of affectional bonds. Ch. 12. In: **Lader, M. H.** (Ed.): Studies of anxiety, Brit. J. Psychiat. Special Publication No. 3, 1969. **Brown, J. S. & Farber, I. E.:** Emotions conceptualized as intervening variables: with suggestions toward a theory of frustration. Psychol. Bull. 1951, *48*, 465–95. **Cannon, W. B.:** Bodily changes in pain, hunger, fear and rage. New York, [2]1929. **Davitz, J. R.:** The language of emotion. New York, 1969. **Duffy, Elizabeth:** Activation and behavior.

New York, 1962. **Easterbrook, J. A.:** The effect of emotion on cue utilization and the organization of behavior. Psychol. Rev. 1959, *66*, 183–201. **Eysenck, H. J.:** The biological basis of personality. London & Springfield, 1967. **Gellhorn, E. & Loofbourrow, G. N.:** Emotions and emotional disorders. New York, 1963. **Goldstein, M. L.:** Physiological theories of emotion: a critical historical review from the standpoint of behavior theory. Psychol. Bull. 1968, *69*, 23–40. **Harlow, H. F.:** The nature of love. Amer. Psychol. 1958, *12*, 673–85. **Hillman, J.:** Emotion: a comprehensive phenomenology of theories and their meanings for therapy. London, 1960. **Jaspers, K.:** The phenomenological approach in psychopathology. (Trans. of original article in the Zeitschrift fur die gesamte Neurologie und Psychiatrie, 1912, Vol. 9, 391–408). Brit. J. Psychiat. 1968, *114*, 1313–23. **Koestler, A.:** The act of creation. London, 1964. **Lang, P.:** Fear reduction and fear behaviour: problems in treating a construct. In: **Shlien, J. M.** (Ed.): Research in psychotherapy, Vol. 3, 1967. **Lazarus, R.:** Emotions and adaptation. In: **Arnold, W. J.** (Ed.): Nebraska Symposium on Motivation. Nebraska, 1968. **Papez, J. W.:** A proposed mechanism of emotion. Arch. Neurol. Psychiat. 1937, *38*, 725–43. **Pribram, K. H.:** The new neurology and the biology of emotion. Amer. Psychol. 1967, *22*, 830–38. **Routtenberg, A.:** The two arousal hypotheses: reticular formation and limbic system. Psychol. Rev. 1968, *75*, 51–80. **Sartre, J. P.:** Emotions: outline of a theory. New York, 1948. **Schneirla, T. C.:** An evolutionary and developmental theory of biphasic process underlying approach and withdrawal. In: **Jones, M. R.** (Ed.): Nebraska Symposium on Motivation. Nebraska, 1959. **Sokolov, E. N.:** Neuronal models and the orienting reflex. In: **Brazier, M. A. B.** (Ed.): The central nervous system and behavior. New York, 1960, 187–276. **Stampfl, T. G.:** Implosive therapy: the theory, the subhuman analogue, the strategy, and the technique. In: **Armitage, S. G.** (Ed.): Behavior Modification Techniques in the Treatment of Emotional Disorders. Battle Creek, Michigan: VA Publication, 1966, 12–21.

I. Martin

Emotionality. A collective concept for the individual nature of the emotional life and of the control and processing of affects. In factor-analytical personality research emotionality denotes a factor of the second order in behavioral judgments and personality questionnaires; in the relevant primary factors there are significant differences between neurotics and normal people. See *Neuroticism*. *K.P.*

Emotion, transference of. During psychotherapy (q.v.), the patient frequently transfers emotional reactions (which are often unconscious) to the psychiatrist (see *Transference*). He experiences his own feelings as though they originated in the psychiatrist (see *Projection*). While Freud considered that transference involved only wrongly-directed, infantile and repressed emotions, other psychoanalytical authors use the term "transference" to denote any emotional contact between analyst and patient. In the broader sense, the transference of emotions may denote all transference by "infection" (see *Empathy; Ideomotor law*). *W.Sc.*

Emotivity. Excessive emotional excitability. Emotivity appears as a symptom of illness in various psychopathological conditions. See *Psychopathology; Psychoses.* *P.S.*

Empathy. A term used for the endeavor to add to extraneous behavior with the object of understanding the other person. The way to experience is primarily through linguistic communication, but it can also come through a spontaneous expression of feeling. In psychological practice (*inter alia*, conversation therapy, educational guidance, q.v.), considerable importance is attached to empathy, although it has never received recognition as a scientific method, not being open to objectivization. *P.S.*

Empiricism. A philosophical doctrine according to which sensory experience, instead of reason with its organizational principles, is the source of cognition (the memory records repetition by learning, association and induction); the knowledge of things and their structure comes from without to the inquirer (Francis Bacon; Hume; J. S. Mill). In scientific methodology, empiricism no longer denotes the manner of cognition, but the experimental basis of modern science:

a free interchange between the observation of facts and the construction of hypothetico-deductive *models* (q.v.) which proves the explanatory predictive accuracy of the model. For "logical empiricism" see *Positivism*.

M.-J.B.

Encephalitis. Cerebral inflammation. An infectious (viral, bacterial, parasitical) inflammation of the cerebral tissue and frequently also of the meninges (meningoencephalitis) or of the spinal cord (encephalomyelitis), with psychological symtoms (e.g. fatigue, delirium). There is usually permanent organic and mental damage. Numerous clinical sub-forms exist.

Encephalitis, traumatic. An incorrect designation for traumatic *encephalopathy* (q.v.).

Encephalization. Increase in weight of the brain and in anatomical-physiological cerebral differentiation, especially of the cerebrum and its functions in the course of phylogenesis (q.v.) and ontogenesis (q.v.). Encephalization is linked with differentiation and the distinct emergence of the cortical function as against the brain stem (see *Brain*), and during this time there is increasing dependence of sensory and motor functions on the intactness of the cortex (progressive encephalization) and a correspondingly greater predominance of the activity of consciousness in comparison with the deep layers.

The concept of encephalization makes it possible to compare types. E. Dubois describes (1930) encephalization level as the ratio between brain weight and body weight. According to Hofstätter (1957) it is directly proportional to the attainable level of maturation and inversely proportional to the speed of maturation.

Bibliography: Dubois, E.: Die phylogenetische Grosshirnzunahme, Biologia Generalis, 1930, *6*. **Hofstätter, P. R.:** Psychologie. Frankfurt, 1957.

F.-C.S.

Encephalography. Taking a record of the living brain (q.v.). There are different techniques for recording the function and structure of the brain. In the electroencephalogram (EEG) the electrical voltage fluctuations are registered by electrodes from the undamaged human skull and, when suitably amplified, recorded. This enables the doctor to diagnose how alert the brain is and how it is functioning, whether there are any disturbances and tumors or epileptic foci (Kugler, 1966). With suitable electronic aids, responses to sensory stimuli can be recognized from the encephalogram (Keidel, 1965). Most recently, even the electrical activity of deep brain structures has been recorded by means of suitable needle electrodes (Bechterewa, 1969). With the aid of *pneumoencephalography* the cerebral ventricles can be shown with X-rays if they have previously been filled with air for this purpose (see *Ventricles*). Finally, mechanical changes in the brain such as displacement resulting from hemorrhage and tumors or from liquid in the case of hydrocephalus can be measured supersonically by means of echo-encephalography (Schiefer & Kazner, 1967). *E.D.*

Bibliography: Bechterewa, N. P. *et al.*: Physiologie und Pathophysiologie der tiefen Hirnstrukturen des Menschen. Berlin, 1969. **Keidel, W. D.:** Neuere Ergebnisse der Physiologie des Hörens. Arch. Ohren-, Nasen- und Kehlkopfheilkunde, 1965, *185*, No. 2. **Kugler, J.:** Elektroencephalographie in Klinik und Praxis. Stuttgart, 1966. **Schiefer, W. & E. Kazner:** Klinische Echo-Encephalographie. Berlin & New York, 1967.

Encephalon (see *Brain*). It consists of the parts of the central nervous system (q.v.) contained in the skull: cerebrum, diencephalon, etc. Histologically, it is composed of grey (nerve cell bodies) and white (nerve paths) matter. See *Cerebrum*. *E.D.*

Encephalopathy. A nosological term for a general cerebral illness or for a condition resulting from some brain damage, the organic basis but not the precise cause of which is obvious enough. While the medical term was already being used in the second half of the nineteenth century by various European specialists, neurologists and psychiatrists, it was not until 1904 that Brissaud and Souques used the concept "*encéphalopathie infantile*" for chronic changes in the infantile brain where the causes could not be understood more precisely.

The cause is damage of the most varied kind to the cells of the ovum and the sperm (gametopathies), to the morula and the blastula (blastopathies), to the embryo (embryopathy), to the fetus (fetopathy), all known collectively as prenatal encephalopathy, and to the brain during birth (perinatal encephalopathy), or until physiological maturity at the age of seven.

The somatic symptoms which may appear are: General retardation of physical development (somatic retardation), deformities (dysplasia), hormonal dysfunctions, autonomic dysregulations, awkward motor activity, motor weakness (nervousness) or restricted movement, slight disorders of coordination, deficient muscular tonus, irregular neural functioning, facial rigidity (hypomimia), bayonet fingers, indistinct speech, etc., together with an irregular encephalogram, albumen irregularity in the cerebral fluid and symmetrical or asymmetrical deformations of the cerebral ventricles.

The following mental and psychic symptoms appear: disturbance of the sense of reality and time; pleasure taken in disturbing, destroying, tormenting and disparaging in the sense of a basic apocritical attitude; excess or deficiency of drive with slowness of response and action; poor social behavior with marked disturbances in conforming to the social situation; incontinence of affect, sudden fluctuations of mood, performance and social behavior with a dysphoric basic mood or vague euphoria; greater irritability with a tendency to violent fits of rage, etc. A distinct disturbance of the ability to learn (as represented in the form of a minimum peak in the development profile according to C. Bühler and H. Hetzer) can appear as a major symptom. See *Brain pathology*.

Bibliography: Engels, H. J.: Über die Störung der Lernfähigkeit bei frühkindlicher Hirnschädigung. Acta Paedopsychiatrica, 1966, *33*, 67–77.

H. J. Engels

Encephalopathy, traumatic. A condition resulting from traumatic brain damage (e.g. boxer syndrome). There are three stages: slight psychic disturbances (e.g. affective disorders: irritability, lack of self-control or disturbances of the ability to learn); distinct psychopathic phenomena; serious motor and character disturbances. There are almost always autonomic symptoms as well.

F.-C.S.

Encopresis. Involuntary defecation in children even after the age when habits of cleanliness should have been learnt (approximately at the age of three) in contrast to *incontinentia alvi* (weakness of the anal sphincter muscle) due to some organic cause; analogously to enuresis (q.v.), a primary encopresis where habits of cleanliness have not yet been completely acquired is distinguished from a secondary encopresis, renewed incontinence after such habits have been learnt for a year; there are also: *diurnal encopresis* (incontinence during the day) and *nocturnal encopresis* (incontinence during the night); active, voluntary is distinct from passive, involuntary encopresis. There is affinity to psychosomatic symptoms: obstipation, colitis, diarrhea. Treatment: analysis of the supposed underlying conflict (q.v.), play and behavior therapy (q.v.).

Bibliography: Anthony, E. J.: An experimental approach to the psychopathology of childhood: Encopresis. Brit. J. med. Psychol., 1957, *30*, 146–75. **Bellmann, M.:** Studies on encopresis. Acta Paediatrica Scandinaviae. Stockholm, 1966, Suppl. 170. **Biermann, G.:** Einkotende Kinder. Psyche, 1951/52, *5*, 618–27.

W.J.S.

Enculturation. An aspect of socialization (q.v.) which can also be described as cultural education. Enculturation denotes the conscious or unconscious acquisition or acceptance of cultural standards and symbols. It differs from acculturation (q.v.) in referring to individuals, not to groups. *W.D.F.*

End action. The final phase of an instinctive action which is satisfying some urge and proceeding according to some pattern shaped by heredity, e.g. the devouring of prey. See *Instinct.* *U.H.S.*

Endocrine glands. Thyroid and parathyroid glands, thymus, adrenal glands, pancreas, ovaries, testicles and hypophysis, i.e. glands secreting internally. They represent well-defined cell complexes and are mostly independent organs. Inside their cells they form substances (see *Hormones*) which pass into the blood stream, are distributed by circulation throughout the body, and play an active part in metabolic processes. They chiefly represent part of a humoral feedback system (q.v.) and their function is controlled by the hypophysis (q.v.). *E.D.*

Endocrine psychosyndrome. This syndrome is in general characterized by anomalies of drive and mood which are not due to diffuse brain damage or some general metabolic disorder. The following symptoms are found: affective dullness and a general slowness of reaction in a case of myedema; indifference and lack of drive in a case of Simmond's cachexia or the Sheehan syndrome (insufficiency of the anterior lobe of the hypophysis, often associated with *anorexia nervosa*; there is no agreement about a possibly identical etiology); a slight tetany (electrolytic imbalance) often shows dysphoric ill humor and a tendency to fatigue; the mood fluctuates from apathy to excitement in the Cushing syndrome (over-production of glucocorticoid); fluctuations of drive and mood in Klinefelter's syndrome (outward form masculine but chromosomal sex feminine); a patient suffering from Basedow's disease is over-excitable, generally restless and experiences fluctuations of mood (over-activity of the thyroid). *U.H.S.*

Endocrinology. The study of the endocrine (q.v.) glands and the effects of hormones (q.v.).

Endoderm. See *Entoderm.*

Endogamy. A social rule prescribing that the partner in marriage should be sought inside one's own group. An individual may therefore not go too far from his family, either in a horizontal (geographical) or a vertical (in regard to social strata) direction. The rule prescribing endogamy serves, as does the rule prescribing exogamy (q.v.), to perpetuate both the particular family and the wider social structure. With mates from culturally similar groups there are fewer difficulties in mutual adaptation and the chances of a stable family are consequently greater. In addition, the continuity of group culture is maintained because the children receive a social upbringing specific to the particular group.

Bibliography: Goode, W. J.: The sociology of the family. In: **Merton, R. K., Broom, L. & Cottrell, L. S. (Eds):** Sociology today. New York, 1959. *S.K.*

Endogenous. Originating from within. The result of natural endowment and not conditioned by environmental influences. Ant. *Exogenous* (q.v.).

Endogenous psychoses. Strictly speaking, this term refers to psychoses which appear to have no precipitating environmental cause but are due to some functional change within the individual. Used chiefly to distinguish between the so-called endogenous depressions which develop "out of the blue" and reactive depressions which have a demonstrable environmental cause. This distinction has been criticized by many authorities who claim that the distinction is one of severity rather than etiology. *R.H.*

Endomorph(ic type). Growth dimension (somatotype). Main characteristics: "round, soft, fat", compact body structure with strongly pronounced digestive and respiratory organs, bones relatively fragile. The psychic correlate is viscerotonia (q.v.). The normal complete endomorphic type resembles the pyknic (q.v.).

Bibliography: Sheldon, W. H.: Varieties of human physique. New York, 1940. *W.K.*

Endopsychic. Psychoanalytical term meaning "within the mind". *Endopsychic structure* refers to the structure of the mind: id, ego, super-ego, conscious, preconscious, unconscious, and so on. *Endopsychic processes* include *endopsychic censorship* (the mechanism by which unacceptable material is prevented from reaching consciousness), and *endopsychic suicide* (mental suicide). See *Intrapsychic.* *G.D.W.*

Endothymic basis. A term from Lersch's personality theory. "Three kinds of experience" are found "in this psychic area", "the stationary states of the vital feelings" (cheerfulness, taciturnity, melancholy, anxiety) "and of self-esteem" (the feeling of one's own value and efficiency), "and the enclosed processes of aspiration" (goal-directive forces) "and emotivity". "Common to all these experiences is that they influence and overcome man." However, they can be governed by the will and mind—by the "personal superstructure" (q.v.) which represents a higher level of the "psychic life".

Bibliography: Lersch, P.: Aufbau der Person. Munich, [10]1966. *W.K.*

End pleasure. Freud's term for the feeling of pleasure accompanying the orgasm, which is followed by a reduction of libido and tension, whereas fore-pleasure creates the desire for constant increase of the intensity of pleasure. *U.H.S.*

Energetics. See *Stimulants.*

Energy, psychic or psychical. Called *libido* (q.v.) by Freud, and conceived as sexual or pleasure seeking energy. With the death instinct (q.v.), the libido (for Freud) is the source of all instinctual desires and motives. According to Freud's earlier views and according to Toman, aggressive motives can be regarded as primitive libidinal motives, and aggression as at least relatively pleasurable. Psychic energy as the source or precondition of all urges and drives, which are only manifested in behavior (q.v.) where they can be observed, would be trivial were it not supposed that a certain amount remains constant over fairly long periods of time, and differs only from one individual to another. For Freud, the amount of psychic energy is synonymous with the strength of the id or with psychic vitality. Toman expresses motive intensities as a proportion of the time since the last gratification t to the median interval of time between successive gratifications $\bar{t}$. The intensity of the motive i, $k_i = \frac{t}{\bar{t}}$. The sum of all motivational intensities k_i at any given moment, according to Toman, is $K = \frac{1}{N}\sum_{i=1}^{N} k_i$.

K corresponds to the total motivation D or the sum of all reaction potentials $\Sigma_s E_R$ (according to Hull). Increments of motivational intensity are represented by Toman as $\varepsilon_i = \frac{1}{\bar{t}_i}$ (first differential coefficient from dy to dt) and the average rate of motive differentiation as $C = f(\sum_{i=1}^{N} \varepsilon_i)$. When

C is constant, and N, the number of motives in any person which can be distinguished from one another grows with its development, the motive intensity increments ε_i are on the average smaller. This was demonstrated experimentally and empirically from samples of N (as independent of one another as possible). C can be considered as a possible operational version of the concept of psychic energy or libido. Since C is an interindividual variable, the following holds good: the greater C is, the less strain given gratification rhythms represent for the person concerned under otherwise comparable conditions (especially in the same objective state of development).

Freud's implicit assumption that libidinal object cathexes occur during motive gratifications corresponds to Hull's theory that motive reduction represents a learning step (i.e. at least a stimulus-reaction association is reinforced).

Toman postulates that there is an inverse proportion between the momentary K of any person and his simultaneous reception of knowledge or data storage. The current data stored are added to the knowledge (concerning opportunities of motive gratification) previously collected and stored, and are also classified. An individual concept of reality is constructed. The individual state of a person's information under average and comparable conditions can be conceived as a function of C and the time he has lived T: $I = f(C, T)$. Knowledge of the world thus reflects past motive gratifications and facilitates progressively the current data storage. The "effort" K_i, i.e., the amount of K which a motive in process of formation demands during its gratification, is a negative growth function with a decreasing increment: $K_i = f(K_{max}e^{-x})$. Here K_{max} is the greatest value of K so far determined for the particular individual in the gratifications of the motive i; e is the euler numeral; and x the number of gratifications so far achieved.

Jung speaks of the desexualization of libido, Freud (with the same object in mind) speaks at first of ego-drives, later of the neutralization of libidinal energy. The meaning of this is that, in the course of development, motives are increasingly "gratified" because of their instrumental gain, no matter what their intensity may be at the time. "Pleasure-seeking energy" becomes "action energy".

Bibliography: Freud, S.: Introductory lectures on psycho-analysis. London, [2]1929. **Hull, C. L.:** Principles of behavior. New York, 1943. **Jung, C. G.:** The structure and dynamics of the psyche. London, 1960. **Toman, W.:** Motivation, Persönlichkeit, Umwelt. Göttingen, 1968.

W. Toman

Engram. An enduring structural change in the nervous system resulting from temporary excitation, hypothesized as the physiological basis of memory (and inheritance, according to some writers). Also called *memory trace* and *neurogram*.

G.D.W.

Entelechy. This Aristotelian term denotes either the completed action or the cause determining the actualization of a possibility (*potentia*) (*De Anima* 11. 2, 414 a). Leibniz uses the term to denote all "simple substances or created monads" (*Monadology*, 18); in doing so, he stresses the degree of completeness and self-sufficiency of entelechy which makes it the "source of its internal actions". It is in this sense that H. Driesch (*Philosophie des Organischen*, Leipzig, 1909–28) understands the concept of entelechy as a teleological life factor subordinating physiological processes (which of course are of a physicochemical nature and therefore can be comprehended by means of the experimental sciences) in the organism to its intentions.

P.M.

Enteroceptive. Receiving information about the internal condition of the body. This is usually done through well-defined sensory organs (enteroreceptors) with a specific function, e.g. the *carotis sinus* and aortic depressor for intra-arterial blood pressure, the *glomus caroticum* for the ph-value, osmotic pressure, CO_2- and O_2- content of the blood in the carotid artery, muscle radii for the tension in the sinews. They are contrasted with the exteroreceptors, the sensory organs specifically for stimuli from the outside world. *E.D.*

Entoderm. The inner cell layer produced during gastrulation (see *Gastrula*) and all the tissues and organs which are formed later by the differentiation of this cell layer (e.g. the intestinal system). *H.Sc.*

Entonic proportion. This characterizes most clearly the barykinetic and epileptoid constitution. *Barykinetic:* abrupt (sudden, intensive), constant. *Epileptoid:* explosive (inadequately stimulable), viscous (tenacious, clinging). *W.K.*

Entoptic symptoms. Perception of processes and objects in one's own eye which occur during observation and which normally remain unconscious: e.g. dimness of the refractive media, retinal vessels, movement of the blood corpuscles in the retinal vessels. *R.R.*

Entotic symptoms. Auditory perceptions which can be produced, not by the external effect of sound but by physiological stimulation of the inner ear (e.g. circulation of the blood, muscular tension of the middle ear, etc.). Entotic phenomena are experienced as buzzing or ringing in the ears. This can also occur without any physiological stimulus when, for example, the hair cells of the inner ear are in a permanent state of excitation as a result of pathological changes. Such phenomena need to be distinguished from the buzzing which can be noticed as the aftereffect of protracted aural exposure to sound. *D.V.*

Entropy. 1. In physics, the loss of energy when this is transformed into work. **2.** As used by C. G. Jung, the tendency of psychic energy to pass from a stronger to a weaker value, until a state of equilibrium has been reached. **3.** In information theory *H* (= entropy) is the degree of chance (and hence, too, the extent of order) which exists in a certain system. *K.E.P.*

Enuresis. Urinating, bed-wetting, involuntary emptying of the bladder after the third year of age, usually bed-wetting at night (nocturnal enuresis), although voluntary control of the bladder function appears at the time to be in order. (Diurnal enuresis = inability to hold one's urine during the day.) Some think the disorder has a psychic cause (defiance, opposition, protest against a withdrawal of affection), i.e. that it results from a neurotic defect or psychopathic tendency, and is rarely the expression of a somatic anomaly. Enuresis can also occur as a symptom when there is a generalized convulsive attack. *H.N.G.*

The relatively low cure rates obtained by psychotherapeutic methods contrast strikingly with the high success rates consistently reported after the use of methods (essentially the urine-pad, electric-circuit and bell, causing the child to wake and complete urination) based on conditioning theory: i.e. enuresis is caused by a failure to learn—to acquire a conditioned response. Mowrer & Mowrer (1938) reported 100% success in their sample. But see *Behavior therapy*.

Bibliography: Lovibond, S.: The mechanism of conditioning treatment of enuresis. Behav. Res. and Ther., 1967, *5*, 11–25. **Mowrer, O. H. & Mowrer, W.:** Enuresis: a method for its study and treatment. Amer. J. Orthopsychiat., 1938, *8*, 436–59. **Turner, R. K. & Young, G. C.:** C.N.S. stimulant drugs and conditioning treatment of nocturnal enuresis: a long-term follow-up study. Behav. Res. and Ther., 1966, *4*, 225–8.

Environment. The individual's "life-space"; from the psychological viewpoint, the totality of stimuli affecting an individual from the point of fusion of sperm and ovum to the point of death.

Bibliography: **Anastasi, A.:** Differential psychology. New York, 1965, 63–7. *M.A.*

Environment, circumscribed. See *Field theory.*

Envy. The desire to possess specific attributes (or possessions) of another individual. An example is *penis envy* (q.v.), which psychoanalysis (q.v.) considers an element of the personality structure of even adult women. In his socio-psychological theory, Freud takes envy to be the origin of a sense of community, or of the desire for social equality: a person abandons something so that others will not desire the same. *U.H.S.*

Enzygotic twins. See *Monozygotic twins.*

Eonism. See *Transvestism.*

Ephebophilia. Love of youths (see *Homosexuality*).

EPI. See *Eysenck Personality Inventory.*

Epicanthus. A mongolian fold in the skin at the inner edge of the upper eyelid. It is a symptom of mongolism (q.v.), a congenital type of imbecility. *E.D.*

Epidemic, psychic. A phenomenon of mass psychology: mass hysteria of epidemic proportions which is induced psychologically by a crowd, especially when there is some specially favorable precondition (e.g. in time of crisis). Noteworthy are the heightened emotional states seen and the primitive character of the phenomenon. Such epidemics occur at all times; they are encouraged by the mass communication media, and are often incited by group interests. Examples are ecstatic rites in primitive tribes; in the Middle Ages, flagellation (q.v.), *danses macabres*, children's crusades, persecution of witches, etc.; today there are the effects of mass suggestion, such as propaganda, advertising, show business; the concept also applies to certain series of crimes. See *Crowd behavior.* *F.-C.S.*

Epilepsy. See *Abence; Grand mal; Petit mal.*

Epileptoid type. A disputed term for a psychopathic extreme state of entonic proportion (q.v.) (not necessarily connected with epilepsy). *W.K.*

Epinephrine. See *Adrenalin(e).*

Epiphysis (*Corpus pineale*). The pineal gland. An endocrine gland (q.v.) situated at the base of the brain; its function has not yet been explained. It seems to have some influence on puberty (q.v.). As it usually calcifies in adulthood, it is used by radiologists as an indicator when taking X-ray photographs of the skull. *E.D.*

Episcotister. An apparatus consisting of a rotating disc with open and closed sectors of adjustable angular width, which may be used to reduce the brightness of a visual field. Placed between the observer and a beam of light, it may also be used in the study of flicker phenomena, and as a device for measuring *critical flicker frequency* (CFF). *G.D.W.*

Epistemology. A term for a part of cognition theory (q.v.). Epistemology endeavors to

investigate cognition in the most varied fields of knowledge by throwing a critical light on the objects of investigation, the principles, methods and results, in order to determine the logical structure and objective value of each science. Epistemology itself can be a science when (in J. Piaget's sense) it is concerned with research into mechanisms of scientific knowledge (such as the "growth of knowledge" or the "historical and epigenetic genesis" of knowledge). In a wider sense the term is often used instead of *cognition theory*, or *theory of knowledge*.
M.-J.B.

Epsilon movement. An expression used to denote an apparent movement (see *Motion, apparent*): it appears when a white line on a black background turns into a black line on a white background (positive-negative movement). *K.E.P.*

Equal appearing intervals method. See *Halving methods.*

Equation, personal. Introduced by the astronomer F. W. Bessel (1784–1846) to denote the different way in which two equally competent observers observe and record the same astronomical event. On the basis of a comparison of the time estimates of a number of observers, Bessel worked out the *error of observation* (personal equation), which remains constant for a considerable length of time. Today the term is used only rarely for the constant individual error of observation recorded during an experiment (in the investigator and in the subject).

Bibliography: Boring, E. G.: A history of experimental psychology. New York, [2]1950. *A.Th.*

Equilibrium. The organ of equilibrium is made up of two functionally distinguishable systems: the statoliths (q.v.) respond to translatory acceleration, the semi-circular canals to angular acceleration (e.g. rapid turning). The sense of equilibrium functions under physiological conditions and is unaffected by consciousness. *M.S.*

Equivalence of stimuli. The equivalent stimuli method was developed by Kluever: experimental animals which have learned to respond to a specific stimulus are presented with other stimuli. Whether or not the learned response occurs, it is then possible to confirm which characteristics are decisive for the equivalence of stimuli, and to what extent they are decisive.

Bibliography: Kluever, H.: The equivalence of stimuli in the behavior of monkeys. J. genet. Psychol., 1931, *39.* *V.M.*

Equivalence, principle of. The visual perception system receives (*inter alia*) signals on the retina regarding the movement of an object, and signals regarding the position of the eye. The system uses the second type in order to eliminate the detrimental effect of one's own eye movement on proficient evaluation. This example serves to illustrate the following definition of the equivalence principle: in general, the fact that the perceptual schema utilizes an equivalent signal in order to eliminate an intrusive signal. *V.M.*

Equivalence theory. The theory that in the appreciation of art, the work of art is not taken as real, but is experienced as a substitute for reality. *V.M.*

Erection. An increase in length and volume of the penis caused by obstruction of the flow of blood in the *corpora cavernis penis.* Some have suggested the use of the term also for the increase in volume of the male and female breasts or of the *glans clitoridis* under sexual stimulation, but its use for the latter is rejected for systematic reasons. Erection is generally a prerequisite for cohabitation but not necessarily for ejaculation (q.v.). Complete erection usually occurs only just before orgasm (see *Sexual reaction cycle*). When younger men are sexually stimulated, erection is usually quick; with older men the process takes longer but there is generally a sufficient erection (contrary to the stereotyped view of the aging man). In the refractory period after orgasm, the erection disappears in two phases: before the final relaxation there is a stage (varying in duration) of diminished erection when coitus can often still take place. In the case of an older man this period may tend to occur more and more infrequently. There is supposed to be a reflex center for erection in the lumbar region of the spinal cord; case studies suggest the existence of a center inhibiting erection in the temporal regions of the cortex. For erection disturbances, see *Potency*. *G.L.*

Erethism. Morbid, excessive irritability and restlessness. *K.E.P.*

ERG. Abb. for *Electroretinography* (q.v.).

Erg. A concept in R. B. Cattell's personality theory (especially in factor-analytical research into motivation), roughly synonymous with instinct (q.v.). It denotes a motivation factor, all the features of which are directed toward a certain behavioral goal (object of drive)—independently of the stimuli released by this purposeful behavior and of the means set in train to achieve the goal. It is interpreted by Cattell as innate response readiness independent of cultural influences and directed toward some demanding terminal action (as distinguished from *metanerg*, the concrete expression of an erg under given cultural conditions). Examples of ergs are: need for sexual gratification, need for security, curiosity, self-assertion. See *Dynamic personality factors; Sentiment; Source traits.*

Bibliography: Cattell, R. B.: Personality and motivation structure and measurement. New York, 1957.

K.P.

Ergometry. Measurement of muscular performance with the aid of appliances. The *ergograph*, *ergometer* and *ergostat* are used for preference to measure how large sets of muscles move when given work to do. For example, the bicycle ergometer records the behavior of the muscles as they overcome measured resistance from the brakes. The ergograph (Mosso) supplies a work curve by constant recordings of the heights to which a weight has been raised after being pulled by the fingers. Since this curve affords an insight into the behavior of the muscles when working during a given period, the ergograph is also used to study fatigue and performance motivation. *P.S. & R.S.*

Ergonomics. The science of the relations between man and the world in which he works. An interdisciplinary science still in the process of development and based on the anatomy, physiology and psychology of work. It is subdivided into the ergonomics of the place of work and the whole area consisting of the man–machine and man–machine system (q.v.). Its field of application is the fitting of work to men, the man to the job. Industrial medicine and hygiene, and research and planning agencies play important parts here. Ergonomics is concerned to devise systems which will take account of the human factors in the work situation.

A.W.-F.

Erklärende Psychologie. In 1894, W. Dilthey contrasted "explanatory psychology" with "descriptive and analytical psychology". By *Erklärende Psychologie*, he understood psychology which worked by the natural–scientific causalistic method, as demonstrated, e.g., by G. T. Fechner in psychophysics. Bühler criticized this dualistic interpretation of psychology as an illusory problem. *P.S. & R.S.*

Erogenous. Sexually stimulating. Erogenous zones are regions of the body which can be manipulated with erogenous results. In a favorable situation, the main requirement for which is the necessary degree of harmony, any point of the body surface is suitable for sexual stimulation. Different types of stimulation are subject to taboos. See *Sexual deviations.* *U.H.S.*

Eros. The Greek god of love, defined by Hesiod in his *Theogony* as the creative force from which the world was born and to which the Orphics attributed the origin of the mystic egg laid by Night. Subsequently reduced to a mere winged angel, Eros appears again in psychoanalysis (q.v.) as the primeval, cosmic force contrasted with the death instinct (*Thanatos*). *P.M.*

Erotomania. 1. Excessive interest and desire for love and sexual intercourse. **2.** A delusional state in which the patient is convinced that some person is in love with him. This frequently leads to the person concerned receiving unwelcome attentions and communications from the patient. *P.Le.*

Error. In general the difference between an observed and a "true" or "expected" value. The deviation may be a chance effect (random error) or systematic (bias). One speaks of a *statistical* error if the statistic calculated from a random sample (q.v.) does not tally with the population (see *Expectation*; *Parameter*) where the conditions of observation for sample (q.v.) and population (q.v.) are identical. The size of the error can be standardized in accordance with the error distribution (standard error). In this context the term "error" is not used for denoting a false observation (error of observation), a false equation (error in equation) or a false conclusion in checking statistical hypotheses. *W.H.B.*

Error, margin of; probability of. See *Probable error.*

Error of estimate. 1. An error in subjective judgment. **2.** A statistical error in the rating (q.v.) of parameters. Whereas subjective errors can be checked only with difficulty, precision is possible in regard to statistical errors. The standard error (q.v.) and probable error (q.v.) are frequently used to measure statistical errors. *A.R.*

Error of the first kind. In checking statistical hypotheses, an error of the first kind is determined by means of the choice of the limit of significance α (q.v.). For example, if a choice is made of $\alpha = 0{\cdot}01$, the null hypothesis (q.v.) is rejected in 1% of all cases where it is true. This false statistical decision is known as an error of the first kind. Unlike the error of the second kind (q.v.), it increases with a rise in α. *W.H.B.*

Error of the second kind. If, following a test of significance, a statistical hypothesis (H_0) is accepted when it is false, i.e. when it should have been rejected, an error of the second kind is committed. This is also known as a *conservative* error or β-error in classical works on the statistical testing of hypotheses. The probability of an error of the second kind (β-risk) depends upon the choice of the level of significance (q.v.). An error of the second kind is quantifiable when a special alternative hypothesis H_1

exists, and when the characteristics of the distributions (see *Frequency distribution*) expected to result from H_0 and H_1, and the size of the sample are known. *W.H.B.*

Error of expectation. The individual tends to approach the future with established attitudes and behavior patterns. This anticipation is necessarily hypothetical and must be checked against reality. If the expectation fails to coincide with reality, an error of expectation has occurred. *P.S. & R.S.*

Error variance. The variance (q.v.) of an error component. This variance of the test error (departure of observed values from the "true" value established after repeated tests on the same object) is to be distinguished from the variance of *sampling error* (q.v.). A sampling error denotes that part of the difference between statistic and parameter (q.v.) due to the non-representative character of the chosen sample (q.v.). *W.H.B.*

Erythrochloropia. Blue–yellow blindness (= tritanopia or tritanomaly, q.v.; see *Color blindness*); the third receptor pigment for blue is absent or present in a reduced quantity in the retinal cones (q.v.). Occurs very rarely. *K.H.P.*

Erythropsin. The visual purple pigment which occurs in the retinal rods (q.v.). *K.H.P.*

Escapism. A major kind of *defense mechanism*, characterized by the tendency to withdraw physically and mentally from the unpleasant aspects of reality. Many neurotic symptoms (e.g. amnesia, hysterical paralysis) are interpreted by psychoanalysts as escape devices. *G.D.W.*

ESP. See *Extrasensory perception.*

ESP cards. A special pack of cards similar to playing cards used for guessing experiments. The pack consists of twenty-five cards, each card bearing one of the five symbols: circle, cross, square, star and wavy-lines; each symbol is represented five times. Hence the probability of a hit (q.v.) on any given trial with a properly shuffled pack is 1/5. Formerly known as Zener cards. *J.B.*

Many different types of cards have been used for quantitative ESP research. Such experiments can be carried out and evaluated in a relatively simple manner. The special ESP cards have led to good results in many cases. But it is unlikely that the five symbols mentioned above played a major role here. In most cases other variables, e.g. human relationships, were probably of more importance. In recent years playing or office cards as well as, e.g., postcards suitable for a particular group of subjects (e.g. children) have been used. There are also some attempts under way to select symbols and configurations for particular subjects. Further possibilities result from an exploration of the emotional values of symbols and configurations such that the selections become more accurate and meaningful with respect to particular subjects. *H.H.J.K.*

Esthesiometer. An instrument for investigating cutaneous (skin) sensation, especially sensitivity as indexed by the *two-point threshold.* One common form of esthesiometer is like a fine pair of compasses and is used to measure the minimum distance between the two points which is necessary for them to be perceived tactually as two rather than one. See also *Hair esthesiometer.* *G.D.W.*

Esthetic type. One of E. Spranger's six life-style or world-view types: an individual inclined to style and self-realization without reference to any considerations of utility. Intellectually more theoretical and concerned with personal style. Distance and self-emphasis are features of interpersonal contact. The artist approximates to the esthetic type. *W.K.*

Esthetics. See *Experimental esthetics.*

Esthetics, psychological. The branch of psychological research founded by G. T. Fechner which studies the general conditions of taste, especially of proportions (e.g. the golden section), of forms, spatial relations, colors and color combinations. See *Experimental esthetics.*

Bibliography: Fechner, G. T.: Vorschule der Ästhetik. Leipzig, 1876. *H.-J.A.*

Estrogens. Female sex hormones (q.v.). The most important estrogens formed in the ovaries are estriadol, estrone and estriol.

Bibliography: Disfalusy, E. & Lauritzen, C.: Oestrogene beim Menschen. Berlin, 1961. **Zuckerman, S.:** The ovary, Vols 1 & 2. New York, 1962. For further bibliography see *Sex hormones.* *W.J.*

Estrus; estromania. (Eng. spelling: *Oestrus*). *Heat; Rut; Estrum.* The phase in the sexual cycle of female animals which is characterized by sexual receptiveness. Usually this is accompanied by physiological changes in the reproductive organs, e.g. swelling, coloration, etc. The term is usually applied to nonhuman species since there is no clear analogy in the human female.

Estrogen: Any hormone that stimulates the female animal to estrus.

Estromania: Nymphomania. Abnormally strong heterosexual desire in the female. *G.D.W.*

Eta coefficient (syn. *Correlation ratio*). A measure of correlation for curvilinear regression. In the case of a non-linear regression of this kind, the mean values of the *Y* measurements do not rise uniformly within the *X* categories. Just as in the case of a $r<1$ correlation there are two regression lines, so there are also two expressions for η. The eta coefficient can also be used to test the linearity of a regression. *W.H.B.*

Ether. A narcotic (q.v.) in use since 1846. It has an extended introductory phase, a marked excitation stage (see *Narcosis*), and an extended recovery stage; it stimulates mucous membranes, salivary secretion, bronchial secretion, and laryngospasm. Vomiting is frequently observed. *E.L.*

Ethics. The study of the distinction between good and evil. A branch of philosophy concerned with morals; it systematically examines the characteristics of value judgments such as "good", "bad", "right", "wrong", etc., and the general principles which justify their application to a subject. Ethics as a system of relations and values is the basis of non-religious structures. *M.R.*

Ethnocentrism. An attitude and/or ideology concerning the relationship between an individual's own group and other groups (*egocentrism* concerns the interaction between an individual and other persons).

Positive characteristics of the subject's (sociological or informal) group are strongly emphasized while features and members of other groups are judged in terms of standards applicable to the subject's group, and denigrated. An easy rejection of unfamiliar things is characteristic of ethnocentrism, which therefore becomes a component of general *prejudice* (q.v.).

The *ethnocentrism scale* developed by T. W. Adorno, E. Frankel-Brunswik and co-workers shows high positive correlations with "authoritarianism", "anti-semitism" and "politico-economic conservatism" and is therefore a central variable in the authoritarian, anti-democratic syndrome. See *Authoritarian personality.*

Bibliography: Adorno, T. W., Frenkel-Brunswik, E., Levinson, D. J. & Stanford, R. N.: The authoritarian personality. New York, 1950. *H.D.S.*

Ethnography. The description of a natural society on the basis of field research (the distinction between ethnography and ethnology is rather artificial but is maintained by some authors). The discipline began with reports by travelers in modern times, but these generally only have a limited source value. Relatively objective research results have been available since about 1900. This period of monographs on tribes marks the real beginning of ethnographic or ethnological research (see *Ethnology*). *S.Kr.*

Ethnology. The descriptive and comparative science of human cultures (generally concerned with "primitive" cultures); largely identical with anthropology (q.v.) until the nineteenth century, it became a genuine science with the development of the field method and the objective compilation of tribal studies (*ethnography*). Four areas of study have developed: (*a*) technology and material culture, (*b*) social organization, (*c*) religion and magic, (*d*) games and art. In the initial period of ethnographic collections and museums (starting in about 1850), interest centered on material culture. The representatives of functionalism (q.v.) reacted against this biassed emphasis on formal aspects of culture by drawing attention to the meaningful content of material and conceptual cultural products. Early attempts to compare different cultures generally aimed at a definition of standard laws of development (evolutionary school). G. P. Murdock was the first to compare cultures on a statistical basis. More recently, research has increasingly been carried out into non-primitive cultures. The cultural transformation of the developing countries provided an opportunity to use ethnology as an applied science (ethnologists engaged on development-aid programs).

Bibliography: Benedict, R.: Patterns of culture. New York, 1934. **Boas, F.** The mind of primitive man, New York, 1938. **Id.:** Race, language and culture. New York, 1940. **Lévi-Strauss, C.:** The savage mind. London, 1966. **Id.:** Le cru et le cuit. Paris, 1964. **Lowie, R.:** History of ethnological theory. New York, 1937. **Malinowski, B.:** Culture. In: Encyclopedia of the social sciences. New York, 1951. **Mead, M.:** From the South Seas. New York, 1939. **Murdock, G. P.:** Social structure. New York, 1949. **White, A.:** The evolution of culture. New York, 1959. **Wissler, C.:** Man and culture. New York, 1923.
S.Kr.

Ethnopsychology. The psychological aspect of ethnological research, and as such a branch of social psychology (q.v.). The 2,000 or so different cultures can be considered as natural experiments in terms of the changing nature of human adaptations. M. Mead demonstrated this point with reference to sexual behavior. See *Tribal psychology*.

Bibliography: Mead, M.: Cooperation and competition among primitive peoples. New York, 1937. **Id.:** Male and female: a study of the sexes in a changing world. New York, 1949. *W.Sc.*

Ethology. Behavior research; study of the laws and causal relationships in the behavior patterns of organisms. Simple behavior patterns are direct reactions to stimuli applied to the organism by the environment. In the case of higher animals, very complex behavior patterns occur which may be inherited or acquired and are often only indirectly (if at all) released by environmental stimuli. See *Comparative psychology*.
H.S.

Euclidean space; Euclidian space. See *Linear space*.

Eugenics. The theory of the improvement of the hereditary characteristics of descendants by promoting the establishment of socially useful families enjoying good physical and mental health, and by eliminating negative hereditary characteristics through appropriate measures (danger: e.g. developments under the Third Reich, such as the murder in concentration camps of individuals deemed socially useless, and so on). See *Euthanasia*. *K.E.P.*

Eunochoidism. A form of infantilism (q.v.) in adults caused by hypofunction of the male reproductive glands, characterized by incomplete formation of the genitalia, absence of external sexual features and underdeveloped libido. Caused by congenital subdevelopment or illness, accident, castration or acquired malfunctioning of the testicles, eunochoidism is a hormone deficiency condition which can be improved by repeated replacement of the missing male reproductive gland hormones. It can also occur as a secondary condition through a gonadotropic hormone deficiency in the case of disease affecting the anterior part of the hypophysis. See *Gonads*. *E.D.*

Euphoria. An elevated mood state of extreme elation associated with feelings of well-being which may not be in accord with environmental circumstances. It is characteristically seen in mania and may occur occasionally in schizophrenia. It is often seen in coarse brain disease, especially when the frontal lobes are involved, for example in Pick's disease, presenile dementia, disseminated sclerosis, and may be a feature of intoxications such as morphine. *D.E.*

Eurhythmia. Greek concept meaning "good rhythm". Harmony of bodily movement, especially as developed with the aid of music. See *Music therapy*. *G.D.W.*

Eustachian tubes. The connection between the tympanum (tympanic cavity) and the naso-pharyngeal space is established by the eustachian tubes. The channel, with a length of about 3·5 cm, is lined with a mucous film carrying the ciliated epithelium. The tubal lumen, which is normally closed, is opened to balance pressure when the subject swallows or yawns. *M.S.*

Euthanasia. The shortening of life by suicide (q.v.) or with the assistance of a third party was permitted in antiquity and is not unusual today in non-Christian cultures. Euthanasia was forbidden by the Church but became a subject of discussion again after the publication of More's *Utopia* (1516). The general tendency for man's life span to be increased has brought interest to bear on the subject again. There is a trend to permit euthanasia for patients suffering from incurable, painful illnesses. The only legal code to allow euthanasia is the Swiss criminal code (art. 115) which states that assistance in suicide is only a punishable offence if the motives of the person giving such assistance are selfish. In England and the U.S.A. associations exist to promote the legal recognition of euthanasia.

Bibliography: Williams, G.: The sanctity of life and the criminal law. London, 1958. *P.M.*

Evaluation. The evaluation of raw experimental data is their statistical description and comparison, and can refer to qualitative or quantitative variations. The term is, however, often used generally to describe any form of expert interpretation of samples, scores, observations, results, and even case histories, etc., in order to determine their relative value. *W.H.B.*

Event. Events are results in a random experiment, i.e. they cannot be infallibly predicted in all particulars (apart from the special case of $P = 1$ or $P = 0$). The prediction of the truth of an event can therefore only take the form of a statement of probability. In contrast to a *simple* event—the occurrence of a previously defined event A in a random experiment—a *complementary* event is each result which is not classed as an event A ("not A", $\bar{A}$). A and $\bar{A}$ are complementary, i.e. the probability (q.v.) of $P(A) + P(\bar{A}) = 1$. A *certain* event is when $P(A) = 1$. In this case the complement $P(\bar{A})$ is an *impossible* event. A conditional event presupposes the occurrence of another event B where A and B may not be mutually exclusive. A *rare* event has a very slight probability of occurrence. *W.H.B.*

Evolution. A developmental mechanism by means of which (with the aid of *selection*, q.v., of those suitable for a specific environment, and *mutation*, or spontaneous genetic change) highly-complex forms of life emerge from simple organisms in the course of many generations. *H.S.*

Ewald's laws. Two laws discovered by the physiologist J. R. Ewald (1892) to define the relationship between the endolymphic flow and nystagmus (q.v.): (*a*) the eye movement (the slow component of nystagmus) takes place in the direction of the endolymphic flow which triggered the nystagmus; (*b*) the motor effect of the endolymphic flow is *not* ideal in both directions of flow. When the semicircular canal is in the horizontal position, the ampullopetal flow is stronger; in the vertical position, the ampullofugal flow dominates. *P.S.*

Ewald types. See *Biotonus*.

Examination anxiety, neurotic. The level and specificity of the individual proneness to anxiety distinguish neurotic from normal examination anxiety. As a symptom of various neurotic syndromes, neurotic examination anxiety is a specific-situational anxiety of all situations which are experienced as tests or examinations. The accompanying physical and mental symptoms and disorders of the intellectual function which is to be tested make the test or examination of questionable value. Neurotic examination anxiety is individually and psycho-socially determined in a variety of ways by the complex interaction of the triad of examinee, examiner and form of examination. The individual proneness to anxiety (of the examinee and the examiner) depends on the unconscious equation of the examination with danger situations in the individual's development (particularly in childhood) (separation; temptation from, punishment of instinctive desires; vexation). Psycho-socially, neurotic examination anxiety arises from the neurotic interaction of the examinees, or examinee and examiner (e.g. inducing anxiety in the other in order to obviate one's own anxiety), and from irrational features of the examination (institutionalized neurotic conditions). See *Anxiety*.

Bibliography: **Moeller, M. L.** Die Prüfung als Kernmodell psychosozialer Konflikte. Z. Soziol, Sozialpsychol., 1969, *21*, 355–61. **World University Service:** Student mental health. London, 1961. *M.L.M.*

Excess. A characteristic of distributions defined in terms of *kurtosis* (q.v.). *W.H.B.*

Excitability. 1. The ability of living beings to be aroused by a change in the level of stimuli. **2.** Susceptibility to irritative stimuli of an affective nature. *K.E.P.*

Excitable functional units such as nervous and muscular tissues are subject to excitation (stable potential) through the ion concentration difference (caused by metabolic processes) between the internal and external environment of the cell, which is enclosed in a functional membrane (alternating, selective permeability to potassium and sodium ions). Excitability consists in a depolarization of this membrane, which is first dependent on local stimulus intensity in the case of weak stimuli, with a measurable reduction in the stable potential. However, once a given stimulus threshold is exceeded, the cell responds with a rapidly progressing, complete depolarization; the much higher action potential (q.v.) follows the local response, and the excitation processes continue independently of the form, duration and intensity of the stimulus (see *All-or-nothing law*). Excitability is not confined to the locus of the stimulus but generally extends in both directions along a fiber axis (see *Axon*) with a specifically determined velocity. *M.S.*

Excitation. 1. Hypothetical state of stimulation of the organism or nervous system. **2.** Rapid growth of psychic stress in pleasure, enthusiasm, etc. **3.** Process by which physical energy brings about changes in a sense organ. **4.** Process causing stimulation of a nerve or muscle by nervous irritation. *K.E.P.*

Excitement phase. The first phase in the sexual reaction cycle and, achieved by effective sexual stimulation. According to Masters & Johnson, the pulse rate and blood pressure rise in man and woman as a function of the degree of sexual excitement, while voluntary and involuntary muscular tension increase and the "sex flush" occurs. The woman also has the following physiological reactions: vaginal lubrication; swelling of the nipples, clitoris, labia minora and possibly also labia majora; widening and extension of the vagina; erection of the nipples; enlargement of the breasts. In the male, the corresponding phenomena are erection (q.v.) of the penis, partial elevation of the testicles, and sometimes erection of the nipples.

Bibliography: Masters, W. H. & Johnson, V. E.: Human sexual response. Boston, 1966. **Sigusch, V.:** Exzitation und Orgasmus bei der Frau. Stuttgart, 1970. *V.S.*

Excitement type. Easily excitable; conditioned reflexes are easily provoked but difficult to countermand; reflex changes are slow. Ant. *Inhibited type.*

Bibliography: Pavlov, I. P.: Lectures on conditioned reflexes, 2 vols. New York, 1928/41. *W.K.*

Exhaustion. 1. Condition in which an organism is not able to function normally (see *Fatigue*). **2.** Appearance of a raised stimulus threshold, reduction of the frequency and intensity of reaction to stimuli. *K.E.P.*

Exhaustion threshold. The limiting condition postulated in extreme fatigue: the point at which threshold is heightened for the stimulus, but after which the response of the active system decreases in frequency and extent, or ceases.

Exhibitionism. A sexual deviation which consists in deriving pleasure from exhibiting the genital organs to other persons. In puberty and epileptic conditions, it is not considered to be a perversion (q.v.). The exhibitionist frequently achieves an orgasm through the conjunction of situational factors during exposure. Defense reactions by the involuntary spectators—generally women—are particularly effective; generally the exhibitionist himself has a defensive reaction to sexual appetence—even during an exhibition—although he usually anticipates sexual stimulation in the spectators. Psychoanalysis explains exhibitionism as a fixation in the phallic phase of libido development (see *Libido*); behavioral psychologists stress the importance of social anxieties. Exhibitionism is almost exclusively reported among men. *G.L.*

Existence analysis. Existence analysis as a science of man and as a therapy considers itself to be a further development of the psychoanalysis (q.v.) of Freud (q.v.). It is based principally on the phenomena of human behavior which were first discovered by Freud. However, it no longer explains these "metapsychologically"—pseudo-scientifically—in the manner of orthodox psychoanalytical theory, but endeavors to explain them phenomenologically. It is found that completely different meanings attach to all the phenomena which had been "prejudiced" by previous "metapsychological" concepts such as "transference" (q.v.), the "unconscious" (q.v.), "repression" (q.v.), "psychic projection", "latent and manifest dream images", etc. The new understanding thus obtained compels existence analysis when applied to therapy to deviate from the old psychoanalytical techniques wherever the "metapsychological theoretical superstructure" of Freud has an impact on practice such that the latter ceases to obey Freud's own basic therapeutic rule.

Phenomenological and existence-analytical psychology and therapy take their bearings from the philosophical *phenomenology* (q.v.) of Heidegger, whereas the philosophy of Descartes was authoritative for orthodox psychoanalytical theory. The view of existence analysis explodes above all the previous supposition of a "psyche" conceived primarily as a kind of capsule into which the objects of the outside world are thought to be reflected in the shape of imaginary images. This also puts an end to all the metapsychological concepts relating to libido processes (see *Libido*) which occur within the psyche and are just as hypothetical. Existence analysis understands what is specific about man as he exists as an "*ek-stare*" in the most literal sense, i.e., as standing outside and spanning an area of the world open to the perceptions and capable of responding to the presence of the person confronting it. To be a human being means therefore "always to be outside in the world and confronting it" and primarily to be absorbed together with one's fellow men in perceptional and responsive relationships to them. As a method of investigation, existence analysis does not suppose that there is anything behind phenomena. But it does endeavor to make manifest and increasingly differentiated those meaningful contents and referential relationships which the confronting person has acquired, until he can also move on to the next hidden essential in what has been perceived. The knowledge of the self and the world that can thus be acquired by psychoneurotic patients is the therapeutically beneficial aspect of existence analysis; it is identical with finding a worthwhile meaning in life.

Bibliography: Boss, M.: Psychoanalyse und Daseinsanalyse. Berne, 1957. **Condrau, G.:** Daseinsanalytische Psychotherapie. Berne, 1963. **Heidegger, M.:** Being and time. London, 1962.

M. Boss & Hicklin, A.

Existential analysis. A term introduced by Frankl to designate his anthropological, psychotherapeutic method of treatment and research developed from depth psychology and based on M. Heidegger's theories. Also known as *logotherapy* (q.v.), it is the third Viennese School. In analyzing biographical details, existential analysis attempts to understand individual human existence from the standpoint of its meaning and possible values. Frankl contrasts Freud's "will to pleasure" and Adler's "will to power" with the "will to meaning" which, if it is not fully achieved, is referred to as "existential frustration" and used as the starting-point for therapy. *Meaning* covers not only the positive aspects of life but also suffering and death. Frankl does not radically reject Freud's psychoanalysis, but tries to complete it. The purpose of existential analysis is less to abolish repressed urges than to arouse the "unconscious spirit" (conscience, existence, self), which may lead to neurotic disorders if it is repressed. The term is often used as a synonym for (L. Binswanger's) *Existence analysis* (q.v.).

Bibliography: Frankl, V. E.: Theorie u. Therapie der Neurosen. Vienna, 1956.

F.-C.S.

Existentialist psychology. A school of philosophical psychology which holds that the subject-matter of psychology is limited to the contents of experience (thoughts, feelings, sensations, etc.) which can be observed introspectively. Closely related to *structural psychology* in its emphasis on the analysis and classification of mental events without interpretation. *G.D.W*

Existential psychoanalysis. A therapeutic method developed from Sartre's theories which uses existential philosophy for psychotherapy; it differs from Freudian psychoanalysis. On the principle that each individual chooses what he wishes to be and expresses his choice in every aspect of his behavior, behavioral analysis serves to detect the system of values chosen originally and make it accessible to the patient, who can decide to recognize his original choice.

Bibliography: **Sartre, J. P.:** Being and nothingness. New York, 1956. **Misiak, H. & Sexton, V. S.:** History of psychology. New York & London, 1966. *F.-C.S.*

Existential psychology. Because M. Heidegger considers existence as a privileged form of access to being, the study of subjectivity is more important than in the psychology of W. Wundt, which is defined as a science of *direct* experience. Reflection on the self and phenomenological observation (see *Phenomenology*) therefore reveal realities in the psyche of the individual which are disregarded or overlooked by scientific psychology: various types of love (M. Scheler), modesty (Scheler), mood (O. F. Bollnow). This movement has led to existential analysis (q.v.) in psychotherapy. *P.M.*

Exner's spiral. An illusion of movement named after S. Exner (1846–1926): a spiral figure drawn on a rotating disk induces the impression of contraction or enlargement according to the direction of rotation. When the disk is stopped, the movement appears to be reversed. *K.E.P.*

Exocrine glands. These are all the structures which produce secreta that do not pass into the blood stream (see *Endocrine glands*), e.g. skin glands (*glandulae cutis*); sweat glands (*glandulae sudoriferae*); sebaceous glands (*glandulae sebaceae*); female mammary gland tissue (*glandula mammaria*); digestive tract glands: stomach glands (*glandulae gastricae propriae*); intestinal glands (*glandulae intestinales*). *G.A.*

Exogamy. Social rule that a marital partner must be found outside the other partner's group. This rule is the positive version of the incest (q.v.) taboo (q.v.). It applies in almost all societies to the members of the nuclear family, and is generally considered to be "natural". It is extended all the more widely to more distant relations as the latter have a functional significance for the society concerned. The rule serves to ensure unambiguous social roles in the family, and therefore the stability and continuity of society. In addition, it prevents sexual competition in the nuclear family which would bring about the latter's disorganization. When the rule applies to a larger group, it helps to extend discoveries and knowledge beyond the small group and maintains a greater social cohesion. See *Endogamy*. *S.Kr.*

Exophthalmic goiter. Protrusion of the eyeball with restriction of movement; may occur on one or both sides. Causes: mechanical forward pressure caused by retrobulbar (i.e. behind the eyeball) processes which require space, e.g. inflammation and swelling, arterial (pulsating) or venous vascular enlargement, benign or malignant tumors, parasites; the condition may also be traumatic (caused by accidents) due to lesions of the vessels or tissue, and finally hormonal (in particular, in hyperthyroidism). Hormonal goiter is not caused by the thyroidal hormones, but by an "exophthalmus producing factor" (EPF) which can be isolated from the anterior part of the hypophysis and is physically, chemically and physiologically distinct from thyrotropin(e) (thyrotropic hormone, TSH). EPF can be demonstrated in the blood in hyper- and hypothyroidism, i.e. whenever the thyroid gland regulation is disturbed. After successful treatment of the

thyroid gland disorder, the quantity of EPF may remain high and lead occasionally to "malignant exophthalmus" which may even result in the loss of the eye through paralysis of the eye muscle and disturbance of tear secretion, together with corneal ulceration.
K.H.P.

Exopsychic. Descriptive of physical or social effects in the individual's environment which can be traced back to his mental activity.
K.E.P.

Expansive type. Character type which attempts to solve difficulties "outwards" by turning toward the source of the problem. "Definite sthenic character with strong retention capacity", "egotistic", and possibly "unbridled". Primitive, "superficial/egotism" or "a more nuanced ethical sense of right". *W.K.*

Expectancy. The expectancy of the occurrence of an event is dependent on attitudes and expectations. It is therefore a subjective notion of probability. Theoretically, expectancy can be defined as the amount which a percipient is prepared to wager on the occurrence of an event. Expectancy is also the *attitude*, or *set*, of one who expects or is attentive. *K.W.*

Expectation. "The anticipation and actualization in the imagination of coming events in their relation to the objectives of our aspirations" (Lersch). This "anticipatory target reaction" (D. C. McClelland) is derived from earlier experience. The hypothetical and provisional nature of expectation is expressed in subjective experience as expectation tension. It is a function of attainability or mental distance from the goal and its influence as a motivating factor varies greatly. The expectation tension is closely related to the expectation gradient, i.e. to the difference between the present and future "real situations" and determines the expectation level. *P.S. & R.S.*

Expectation, mathematical. For any discrete random variable X and a function $g(X)$ defined for all possible values of X, the expression $E[g(X)]$ is known as the mathematical expectation value of the function $g(X)$, or the expectation of $g(X)$. In the case of a continuous distribution with density $f(X)$, the expectation of a function $g(x)$ solved for all values of X is given by:

$$E[g(x)] = \int_{\infty}^{\infty} g(x) f(x) d(x).$$

W.H.B.

Expectation value. See *Expectation, mathematical.*

Experience. Believed by many to be the best term to describe the subject-matter of psychology. May be used as a noun: the subjective (conscious) appreciation of stimulus events, or the knowledge resulting from this; or as a verb: to live through, meet with, find, feel, undergo, or be aware of any stimulus object, sensation, or internal event. Hence the term is used in psychology in the same way as in everyday language. *G.D.W.*

Experience, loss of. The process by which direct (or primary) experience is replaced by indirect (or secondary) experience not open to verification by the experiencing subjects in a technological society.

Experience types. Two response types which occur with the Rorschach test (and other shape interpretation methods). Intraverts tend to interpret movement. Their relationship to the world around them is dependent primarily on intra-mental activity. Extratensive types interpret primarily from the standpoint of color. They are very sensitive to environmental stimuli, and dependent on the latter. Rorschach defines both types solely on the basis of the type of interpretation made by them in the experiment and not on the basis of their behavior in real life, which Jung used to determine his function(al) types. *W.K.*

Experiential experiment. Unlike the normal psychological experiment, this is primarily concerned not with a manifest reaction of the individual but with subjective experiences provoked in the testee by the experimental situation. These subjective experiences must be described by the subject and therefore objectivized. The validity of the experimental data depends on the extent to which the subject is able to make objective self-observations. Quantitative determination of results is possible only to a limited extent. *P.S.*

Experiment. An experiment is the planned manipulation of variables for observation purposes; at least one of the variables, i.e. the independent or experimental variable, is altered under predetermined conditions during the experiment; the variable whose alteration is observed as a function of this change is known as the dependent variable. If an effect on the dependent variable appears possible, the other variables needed in the experiment are either held constant for the duration of observation (controlled variables, experimental parameters) or disregarded as irrelevant variables. Every controlled variable is therefore a possible independent variable for further experiments. The observation must allow a clear identification of the changes in the dependent variables within the limits of accuracy needed for a particular experiment; the observation therefore requires a measurement at least on a nominal scale level.

Experimental methods contrast with empirical methods (differential methods) in which a special set of variables is sought for observational (measurement) purposes. Since none of the variables can be manipulated in a predetermined manner during the observation, the distinction between dependent and independent variables ceases to apply; no direct conclusions can therefore be drawn from the results on the direction of the dependence. The definition of the experiment includes consideration of its purpose. An arrangement used experimentally to determine the direction and nature of relations between variables can also be used for measurement—e.g. for other experiments—as soon as these relationships are known. Experimental methods are therefore frequently also used as empirical methods (tests). See *Test theory*.

The questions asked in an experiment depend on the knowledge already available. If the latter is pre-scientific or consists merely of assumptions, we speak of a *pilot study*; in this case an attempt is often made to determine a relatively large number of variables, if it is impossible to specify adequately which effects are to be expected from the independent variables. In control experiments the results of studies conducted by the same or other workers are already known and an attempt is made to reproduce them for greater security. In generalizing experiments, the range of variation of the independent variables is increased in order to enlarge the validity of a relationship already determined. Test experiments are arranged to relate the results to previous theoretical assumptions in order to determine the range of validity of a theory.

If clear, but conflicting assumptions can be made from different theories regarding the results of an experiment so that it is possible to use it to refute one of the contradictory theories, we speak of a crucial experiment (*experimentum crucis*).

1. *Types of experiment*. In the simplest case, one independent variable is altered and the effect measured on one or more dependent variables; these univariate experiments contrast with planned or multivariate experiments, in which several independent

variables are altered in combination, in such a way that the effects of each variable can be determined separately and their interaction can be examined. Techniques are described in the literature on experimental design and evaluation (generally by analysis of variance). Further classifications of experiments can be derived from the degree of graduation of the independent variables. In bivalent experiments, the independent variable assumes only two values (e.g. dependence of calculability on the appearance or non-appearance of an interfering noise). Although such experiments have only limited value, they are still frequent and sometimes inevitable. They may show whether an effect of the experimental variables can be proved. This demonstration will not be reliable if there is a non-linear or non-monotonous relationship between the independent and dependent variable: an average noise intensity may facilitate performance while performance remains unchanged at higher and lower intensities. Multivalent experiments provide the answer in this case. In the most favorable assumption, non-monotonous relationships with the dependent variables can already be determined with three independent variables. If even more independent variables are taken in the functional experiment, it is possible to show the functional relationship with the dependent variable. The corresponding enlargement can also be made in the multivariate experiment: if the functional dependence of a variable on several independent variables is determined in this way, we speak of a parametric experiment.

In many psychological experiments, we are not so much concerned with the state assumed by the dependent variables after manipulation of the independent variables, as with the time function according to which the dependent variable reacts to changes in the independent variables (response function). Most learning experiments are examples of this. We may speak here of dynamic experiments by contrast with static forms. Generally the dependent variable changes over from one stable state to another. In the case of this type of experiment, it is necessary to record both dependent and independent variables continuously. For evaluation purposes, we associate time functions for the variables. In systems theory, we find certain well-defined formal expressions for complete analysis of the time characteristic of systems by specific stimulation functions of the independent variables (sine, rise, interval, surge); these can be directly used in some areas of psychology.

2. *History of experimental psychology*. The history of psychology (q.v.) as an independent science begins with the introduction of the experiment in about 1860 (H. L. F. von Helmholtz, W. Wundt, G. T. Fechner). However, the experimental method was never considered to be the sole method of psychology. Empirical observation and descriptive analysis of individual cases (case studies) were also used by some schools of psychology as well as the phenomenological method (philosophical psychology). It is possible to define experimental psychology as a separate discipline. Experimental psychology was first concerned mainly with problems of perception and reaction time. However, its use was rapidly extended: as long ago as 1925, I. P. Pavlov was able to show that general behavioral defects similar to human neuroses can be induced in dogs if the animals are exposed to severe, traumatic experiences (Petersburg flood, 1924) or insoluble problems. Doubts are occasionally cast on this equation of behavioral disturbances (experimental neuroses) with human neuroses. Today the experimental method is used almost universally, when there are no moral objections (damage to subject), practical difficulties (many areas of social psychology) or economic problems (cost).

Experiments were originally conducted on a small group or even on individuals, or sometimes on the research worker himself (H. Ebbinghaus, W. James). As statistical knowledge grew (e.g. "Student's test") the number of Ss needed could be rationally estimated. The development of analysis of variance (q.v.) by Fisher (1925) enabled planned experiments to be carried out; the introduction of non-parametric statistical methods (especially after 1950) simplified analysis of many experimental results, especially when the data clearly departed from the normal distribution. It is often difficult to distinguish between irrelevant and relevant variables. In addition, measurement of the dependent variable generally involves an intervention which may have an effect of its own. The addition of control groups to the experimental group was therefore an important step forward: the subject in the control group undergoes the same measurements as that in the experimental group, but without manipulation of the independent variable. Control groups were first used in 1908, and from the early 1950s about half the reported experiments have included control groups.

Our experiments have been influenced by technical as well as psychological developments. The precise mechanical apparatus initially needed for many experiments was expensive to acquire and maintain (e.g. the Hipp's chronoscope for time measurement). Since about 1950, this equipment has been rapidly replaced by electronic devices which allow precise control of the experiment and simple measurement together with reliable recording of the results. The present state of development is characterized by an emphasis on systems theory, which influences both the theory and the test set-up and analysis of results; rapid progress has also been made in electronics, and we have seen the introduction of experiments in which the dependent variable, the behavior of the subject, the further course of the experiment, i.e. the state of the independent variables, can be directly influenced.

3. *Problems of the psychological experiment.* Although the theoretical problems of psychological experimentation have been solved in principle, there remain practical problems which restrict the use of the experimental method and clear interpretation of the results; the main problems concern operational definition of the variables used, the possibility of generalizing experimental results, and limitations of a moral and legal nature.

In experiments involving human beings, the definition of the variables used is partly dependent on the interpretation of the situation by the testee; in spite of careful instruction, this interpretation is often difficult to control adequately. Personal characteristics of the experimenter, and possibly also his expectation of the subject's performance (experimenter effect) influence this interpretation so that corresponding control experiments become necessary by means of blind and double-blind tests (Rosenthal effect). In experiments in animals, attempts are made by manipulating the stimuli (frequently hunger) to determine which variables in the situation will act on the animal subject.

The possibility of generalizing experimental results depends on whether the conditions can be considered representative. There are no serious difficulties here as regards the subjects involved, although many results are based solely on experiments conducted on psychologists and students of psychology. On the other hand, the remaining conditions of psychological experiments are often representative neither of practical (biotic) experiments nor theoretical problems. So far relatively few results have been published which answer both theoretical and practical questions.

Finally, the restrictions caused by moral or legal considerations are very noticeable in the experimental techniques used. Even in relatively simple learning tests it may be necessary to delude the test subject intentionally by the instruction; experiments in schools are hampered by the failure of parents to give their agreement; and simple sociopsychological surveys are impossible to carry out because of the possible undesirable secondary effects on the group studied. Many socially important questions will only be studied experimentally and solved when a substantial section of the population becomes convinced of the value of psychological experiments.

Bibliography: Boring, E. G.: A history of experimental psychology. New York, 1929. **Cattell, R. B.** (Ed.): Handbook of multivariate experimental psychology. Chicago, 1966. **Plutchik, R.:** Foundations of experimental research. New York & London, 1968. **Sidowski, J. B.** (Ed.): Experimental methods and instrumentation in psychology. New York & London, 1966. *F. Merz*

Experimental design. The experimental testing of hypotheses in regard to the dependence and interdependence of variables. In a "design" of this kind, it is possible to plot the effects of one or more independent variables on one or more dependent variables. In general, experimental design refers to measures adopted to ensure that the planning and procedure of an experiment use all available appropriate information and as far as possible take into account all the factors implicated. In this sense, experimental design includes selection of the behaviors to be observed, precise formulation of the hypotheses to be tested (choice of the appropriate statistical procedure *before* carrying out the experiment), and selection of the sample size and of control variables in regard to the precision of the statistical tests chosen. *D.W.E. & W.H.*

Experimental drive diagnosis. L. Szondi's method (1947) of diagnosing dominant drive vectors (sexual, paroxysmal, ego and contact drives) associated in each case with two contrary drive requirements. The two most appealing and least appealing portraits must be selected from six series of eight portraits each, representing eight requirements. Differentiated conclusions are drawn by a complex process of evaluation. *R.M.*

Experimental esthetics. G. T. Fechner, generally regarded as the father of experimental psychology, was the founder of experimental esthetics. This is the application of the methods of experimental psychology to problems concerning the arts and, more generally, to the study of motivational effects of perceptual forms and qualities. Fechner advocated an esthetics "from below", in contrast to the esthetics "from above" favored by philosophical estheticians. Apart from a number of largely speculative laws, his main contributions consist of his contention that the experimenter should begin with simple stimuli, representative of the most elementary components of works of art, and his advocacy of three methods of investigation, akin to the psychophysical methods that he introduced for the measurement of sensory processes. They comprise: the *method of choice* (in which subjects are presented with several stimuli and indicate their preferences); the *method of production* (in which they perform manipulations giving rise to stimuli illustrative of their preferences); and the *method of application* (the study of artefacts as indicators of the preferences current in a particular society).

Most of the work in experimental esthetics during the century that has since elapsed has used variants of the method of choice. Recent advances in scaling theory have made available a large range of sophisticated methods of measuring preference through ratings, ranking, and so on, and of constructing mathematical models to summarize the data so obtained. Many experiments, beginning with Fechner's own, elicited judgments of visual shapes and of colors. Relatively consistent findings have been a tendency for preferences with regard to rectangles, and divisions of a line segment, to cluster—despite wide variability—around the golden section (the ratio such that $A/B = B/A + B = 0{\cdot}62$), and a tendency for red and blue to be liked more than other colors. More complex artistic material (reproducions of paintings, pictures of vases, musicalt passages, verse extracts, and so on) has been used for the investigation of individual differences in taste and of correlations of these with personality traits. Factor analysis has regularly revealed a general factor reflecting overall capacity for esthetic appreciation and a bipolar factor, which has been characterized differently by different writers (e.g. inclination toward simplicity or complexity, sensitivity to color or to form).

The impact of contemporary theoretical developments began to be felt in the 1920s and 1930s and modified the essentially empirical approach that had hitherto prevailed. Psychoanalysts interpreted artistic products, like so many other psychological phenomena, as disguised expressions of unconscious wishes and conflicts. The structural qualities to which the gestalt school attached importance in its research into perception, and especially those qualities that distinguish "good" configurations, have been seen as prime determinants of esthetic enjoyment, particularly by Arnheim. Birkhoff offered an influential mathematical treatment, ascribing esthetic value to the interaction of complexity (C) and order (O) factors.

Recent developments. Advances in psychology and neurophysiology have encouraged a distinct revival of interest in experimental esthetics in the 1960s. Studies of exploratory behavior, psychophysiological changes, and other phenomena, have drawn attention to the motivational importance of stimulus properties such as novelty, surprisingness, complexity, and ambiguity, which could be recognized as the constituents of artistic "form" or "structure. The mathematical concepts introduced by information theory have been used by Attneave, Hochberg & McAlister, and later Garner, for the quantitative treatment of "goodness" of configuration or amount of structure, and by Moles, Frank & Gunzenhäuser for a quantitative theory of esthetic value. Much has been learned about the brain processes that underlie fluctuations in emotion or "arousal", as well as about those that have to do with hedonic processes (reward and punishment, pleasurable and aversive properties of stimulus patterns). Possibilities of synthesis appeared as it became increasingly apparent that these brain processes are affected by structural or "collative" properties of stimulus patterns (novelty, complexity, and so on) and that these properties are closely related to information-theoretic concepts such as information content and uncertainty. A growing body of experiments indicates that moderate degrees of novelty and complexity tend to be favorably valued and sought out, whereas higher degrees are judged unpleasant and shunned.

In short, experimental esthetics seems to be entering a period of increasing integration with other areas of psychology, particularly motivation theory. It is also coming to rely less exclusively on verbal expressions of preference, seeking correlations between these and non-verbal measures such as spontaneous self-exposure and physiological indices of changes in arousal.

Bibliography: Berlyne, D. E.: Psychobiology and esthetics. New York, 1970. **Child, I. L.:** Esthetics. In: **Lindzey, G. & Aronson, E.** (Eds): Handbook of social psychology, Vol. 3. Reading, Mass., [2]1969, **Fechner, G. T.:** Vorschule der Ästhetik. Leipzig. 1876. **Frances, R.:** Psychologie de l'esthétique. Paris, 1968. **Frank, H.:** Informationsästhetik. Quickborn, 1959. **Moles, A.:** Information theory and esthetic perception. Urbana, Illinois, 1966. **Valentine, C. W.:** The experimental psychology of beauty. London, 1962. **Woodworth, R. S.:** Experimental esthetics. In: Experimental psychology. New York, 1938.

D. E. Berlyne

Experimental group. A sample of individuals who, under experimental conditions, in contrast to a parallel, matched control group (q.v.), feature a dependent variable which forms the object of the experiment.

D.W.E.

Experiment, planning of. See *Experimental design.*

Experimenter. One who conducts an experiment.

Explanatory psychology. See *Erklärende Psychologie.*

Exploration. A distinction can be made between three phases of explorative behavior in psychology: (*a*) a state of excitement brought about by an unsatisfied desire, internal unrest or the search for the unknown, confusion, fear, etc.; (*b*) explorative behavior (as a more or less systematic, oriented, controlled, intellectual process) aiming to discover the object or mental state which could reduce this excitement; (*c*) reduction of the state of excitement if no obstacles are encountered (material impossibility or impossibility of solving the conflict). I. P. Pavlov observed this behavior in its simplest form (orienting reflex). Animals examine their natural surroundings to satisfy their wants as does a child to discover sources of stimulation which may contribute to its development; the same goes for scholars, philosophers and mystics. A person who is unable to solve his professional, marital, educational and other problems with his own resources (exploration) can consult a psychologist who will proceed as follows:

The psychologist first analyzes the circumstances and obvious motives which have led to this request as well as the social, family and inter-human relationships. This phase (on which a written report is rarely prepared) provides guidelines for the search for determining factors and the methods of examination used. It provides the reference framework into which the results of the exploration must be translated for the benefit of the subject so that he can understand the importance of the advice given and act accordingly. The psychologist then explores the personality and its conflicts with the means at his disposal: interview, tests of individual functions (intelligence, motility, etc.), personality tests (questionnaire method, projective method: Rorschach, TAT, etc.). Some psychologists use laboratory situations (H. J. Eysenck) or interaction situations (stress interview, group situation). Others simply concentrate on psychological discussion (psychological exploration in the narrower sense) during which a subject's experiences are brought to light; this facilitates the creation of awareness and may even lead to an alteration of the personality (C. R. Rogers). Psychoanalysis and hypnosis are special processes of exploration used by depth psychologists.

The notion of exploration coincides to a varying degree with the concepts of study, evaluation, advice and diagnosis.

If we separate the two aspects of diagnosis and treatment, following the example of classical medicine, the therapy and the individual under examination become *objects* of a different kind for which the psychologist uses different methods whose validity is known. He then prepares a prognosis on the basis of an empirical correlation or establishes a clinical model to understand the individual case. However, if we adopt the notion that all exploration includes a degree of treatment then all test results are dependent on the interrelation between the patient and psychologist. By his own attitude and personality, the psychologist becomes the most important instrument of exploration, which then appears as a process of development in the existing relationship with the patient.

The activity of clinical psychologists has often been criticized. Their clinical conclusions are often unreliable and their verbal attitudes, methods and stereotypes lead to distortions which are impossible to eliminate. On the other hand the psychologist's exploratory methods are enriched by critical evaluation of clinical procedures and the use of methods enabling symptoms to be controlled by varying the environmental conditions (behavior control). Exploration is being increasingly analyzed on the pattern of sequential decision strategies. Diagnosis and treatment can therefore be combined in a comprehensive procedure.

Bibliography: Cronbach, L. J. & Gleser, G. C.: Psychological tests and personal decisions. Illinois,

1965. **Fiske, D. W. & Maddi, S. R.:** Functions of varied experience. Homewood, Ill., 1961. **Gathercole, C. E.:** Assessment in clinical psychology. Harmondsworth, 1968. **Kruboltz, J. D. & Thoresen, C. E.:** Behavioral counseling. New York, 1969. **Lesser, D.** (Ed.): Explorations in exploration: stimulation seeking. New York, 1969. **McReynolds, P.** (Ed.): Advances in psychological assessment, Vol. 1, Palo Alto, 1968. **Nahoum, C.:** L'entretien psychologique. Paris, 1952. **Rey, A.:** L'examen clinique en psychologie. Paris, 1958. **Rogers, C. R.:** Client-centered therapy. Boston, 1951. **Sundberg, N. D. & Tyler, C.:** Clinical psychology. London, 1963. **Vernon, P. E.:** Personality assessment. A critical survey. London, 1963.

G. Nahoum

Exploratory experiment. Scientific psychology arrives at its research results with the help of experimental methods based on statistics. Clear hypotheses (null and alternative hypotheses) are formulated which can be checked statistically. However the development of hypotheses already calls for a certain minimum knowledge of the object under investigation; this knowledge is obtained by preliminary exploratory experiments. *P.S.*

Explore, urge to. Interpreted as a primary, unlearned need which is found particularly in the higher mammals and in man with increasing differentiation of the cerebral cortex. This spontaneous readiness is provoked by specific groups of stimuli expressed in notions such as novelty, surprise, uncertainty, etc. Physiologically, the urge to explore can be described as a typical arousal syndrome (high-frequency EEG waves, heightened vegetative and reticular activity).

P.S. & R.S.

Exponential curve. The graphic representation of the exponential function:

$$Y = A^x = e^{bx}, A > 0$$
$$b = \ln A$$

The function can only have positive values. For $A > 1$ (i.e. $b > 0$) it rises constantly from 0 to ∞ and for $A < 1$ $(b > 0)$ it falls constantly from ∞ to 0. The curve passes through the point (0, 1) and approaches the X axis asymptotically. *W.H.B.*

Expression (Ger. *Ausdruck*). The object of the psychology of expression (psychology of modes of expression; Ger. *Ausdruckspsychologie*).

1. *Expression in psychology.* Modern expression research has inherited a number of attempts to define the concept, all of which are demonstrably inadequate in one respect or another (see Kirchhoff 1962b, 1963, 1965b) and are now obsolescent if not obsolete. Examples are tautologies sueh as "Expression is expression of the psychic", or tautological and pointlessly restrictive postulates such as "Expression is the expression of emotion".

"Expression" always implies that a "who or what" (a subject of expression; also: an essential content of expression, or, more exactly: the subject or essential content of an expressive phenomenon) is made apparent, i.e. becomes accessible to someone (the recipient of the expression). If we apply these considerations to the field of psychological expression, it is clear that a full and proficient definition can be obtained only by thematic analysis of the subject (or essential content) of psychologically relevant expressive phenomena, and of these phenomena themselves (= media of the subject of expression). If one's approach is based on a conception of psychology as the "theory of the being and being-thus of individual existents, in so far as they are scientifically and methodologically accessible in terms of their lived experience and their behavior", psychological expression may be defined primarily as the "apparent individual mode of being of men and animals": i.e. apparent or evident in the sense of being accessible in terms of specific, individual expressions and expressive of media or symptoms. Since there are no good reasons for a conceptual and/or material restriction of the individual subject of expression (e.g. merely to emotions, feelings, affects, etc.; see Kirchhoff, 1965b), in principle all actual states of mind and modes of being in the world, and all relatively enduring personality traits, in so far as they are *expressed*, are "essential contents" of psychologically expressive phenomena; the same is true of psychologically expressive media.

On systematic and practical scientific grounds (above all, conflict with psychodiagnostics, q.v.), a restriction to the actual, or "how", aspects of physically evident expressions is necessary (see Kirchhoff, 1962b). Consequently, we may define psychologically relevant expression as "the (apparent, or evident) individual mode of being of an expressive individual (man or animal), is so far as it is accessible in the actual aspects of individual phenomena" (pathognomically: *how* someone behaves, e.g. laughs, cries, stands, walks, moves expressively, speaks, and so on). This limitation marks out a further field of research which requires more precise differentiation in itself, and allows certain irrelevant phenomena (such as handwriting—a linguistic-graphic-significative artifact) to be excluded (the error of inclusion may be attributed primarily to L. Klages).

2. *The structure of psychological expression.* With this definition, the two main areas of expression, *pathognomy* and *physiognomy*, may also be precisely delineated. In classical antiquity and the Middle Ages, the two areas were confused and treated uncritically, but from the time of J. C. Lavater and G. C. Lichtenberg came increasingly to be distinguished one from the other, both conceptually and objectively; *both* are now considered to be legitimate component objects of the psychology of expression. In this process, pathognomy has come to include not only the traditional phenomena classed under *mimicry* (the play of the features) and *pantomimicry* (movement of the entire body: expressive movements), but vocal expression (phonognomy), vegetative expressions, the pathognomic elements of pragmatic, symbolic, linguistic behaviors (sound and gesture), microvibrations (q.v.), etc.

3. *The inner structure of psychological expression* comprises the relation of "expression transmitter" and "expression receiver", together with their contexts, and the individual transmitting and receiving systems. Expression exists only in terms of the transmitter-receiver relation; there is no "intrinsic expression", for it is always "by someone for someone" (more precisely: the manifestation of an expressive content peculiar to one individual for the sake of another). For the most part, the connection between transmitter and receiver is not unilinear and unipolar, but consists of interaction and social feedback between transmitter and receiver. A cybernetic model for expressive relations will probably become increasingly important. Socially relevant prototypes in this regard are, e.g., modes of visual contact (the social determination of visual expression). See *Communication.*

The following are the major problems in regard to the *transmitting* system: (*a*) How do specific physiognomic and pathognomic expressions occur under certain (actual-, onto-, and phylogenetic) conditions in the case of certain expressive systems? (*b*) How is the relation of the individual and the expressive medium to be determined? What, in particular, are the proper functional and semiotic terms to describe the relation of expressive signs and their signifieds? (*c*) What are the systematic conditions for the process of expression? What is the nature of the relation between "within" and "without", the individual expressing and the medium of his expression, the "psychic" and the "physical"? (See *Emotion.*)

The restricted nature of the earlier psychology of expression led to repeated, profitless theoretical attempts to find the origin of expressions, and in particular certain expressive movements, in non-expressive phenomena ("mere" purposive movements), and in this way (genetically) to explain the existence of "pure" expressions. Right up to the present there has been much discussion of Darwin's (1872) attempted explanations, and particularly of his first hypothesis (the "principle of serviceable associated habits" which become "mere" expressions: i.e. expressive characteristics may be derived from previous practical functions), as well as of Wundt's quasi-parallel though ultimately non-explanatory theory (see *Wundt*), and of the action theory of expression (deriving from J. J. Engel) which does contain a core of truth. Since the idea of the existence of "pure", "special" expressive phenomena (and movements), which was effective up to F. J. J. Buytendijk (1956), largely gave way to more recent data, the basic problem of a theory of expression as "transmission" has again been generally posed as the question of the (actual-, onto-, and phylogenetic) conditions of an individual system that, by means of expression, makes "subjective" essential contents accessible to a specific receiving system with its own similarly classifiable conditions.

This does not imply a more or less mysterious "transubstantiation" of non-expressive (e.g. "mere", "expressionless") into expressive actions. What is in question is rather the "emergence" of the individual essential contents of a transmission system *for* specific receiving systems, with a degree of awareness that depends on their perceptive, cognitive, and other conditions. Here, too, the constitutive basis shows that there is no such thing as "expression in itself" or "*intrinsic* expression", but only "expression *for*" specific receiving systems with their special conditions. (See Allport & Vernon, 1933.)

In the *receiving* system, the problems are in principle to be systematically arranged, formulated and answered in the same way: (*a*) phenography, (*b*) functional analysis and functional interpretation, (*c*) conditional analysis and conditional interpretation of the reception of expression and of the receiving system, together with actual-, onto-, and phylogenetic delineation of the specific individual problems.

4. *Terminology*. Until quite recently a multiplicity of terms has been in use in the psychology of expression; for the most part they were conceptually inadequate and imprecise. See Kirchhoff 1957, 1962b and 1965b for a discussion of the terminological problem.

5. *Historical outline*. In his *Ausdruckstheorie* K. Bühler (q.v.) provided an admirable survey of the basic positions and main trends of the history of expression theory from Aristotle to P. Lersch. Nevertheless, his hope that it would be possible to show a systematic development was, from the nature of the case, unrealizable. However, an historical synopsis—without reference to the actual informative content of the historical sources as such—can offer pointers for the future.

In terms of the maximal, minimal and median determination of subject and medium of expression, all concepts of expression from antiquity through the Enlightenment and Romantic periods, and the natural-scientific period of expression research in the nineteenth century, up to the present, can be ordered as peaks where expression was broadly conceived, and depressions where it was viewed in a restricted fashion.

A first "high range" of broad concepts runs from the pseudo-Aristotelian *Physiognomika* up to C. G. Carus; another from L. Klages' second, broad notion of expression up to F. J. J. Buytendijk; a third from the concepts of K. Lewin (q.v.) and G. Kafka to the present. Between these three high marks there is an initial trough extending from the beginnings of a "natural-scientific" treatment of expression by C. Bell, by way of W. Wundt, to L. Klages' first, narrow concept. A second trough is indicated by the work of researchers such as C. Landis, A. Flach, and M. Turhan, who were concerned to demonstrate that there was no such thing as an unequivocal correspondence of a specific expression to a specific essential content.

A heuristically valuable axiomatics probably lies *between* the two extremes (see Kirchhoff 1957, 1962, 1965.)

6. *Present position, results and critique.* "The work of the last few centuries contains some progressive and some static trends"—N. H. Frijda's judgment (1965) applies to expression research as a whole. Decisive progress has been evident in recent years in the conceptual, methodological, terminological and descriptive bases of psychological expression. There has also been progress in phenographic and functional (but not so much in ontogenetic) study of the reception of expressive information; and some achievements in, e.g., factor-analytical treatment of data (dimensional analysis of mimic expression; see N. H. Frijda, 1965).

The as yet incomplete separation of (though not definitive dichotomy between) fundamental scientific research and applied psychological evaluation of expression data has been less satisfactory. The theory that a premature diagnostics of expression (as well as a one-sided consideration of expression from the angle of validity) would be more harmful than helpful has not been universally influential. A pathognomic diagnostics of expression (pathognostics) established on the principles of a "universal psychological diagnostics" will be possible only on the basis of broad and solid fundamental research. The *how* and the *what* of behavior (and its effects) are only two aspects of one and the same thing; therefore neither is diagnostics itself impossible, nor is a diagnostics of expression pure and simple possible.

More than in regard to other disciplines, the existing research toward proficient principles must as yet be judged inadequate. What is lacking is not so much the fundaments themselves, and adequate methods and techniques and large-scale research programs, as the concrete possibilities for their realization. Research is carried out and results are obtained; but as a whole it is too unsystematic, scattered, and more "associative" than "coordinated and integrative". All in all, empirical expression research (and, it must be said, psychological research as a whole in Europe outside Britain) is for the most part still out-of-touch, anachronistic, and redolent of nineteenth-century paternalism. To put it positively, what we need are research centers and institutes (something like the Max Planck Institutes) which, within foreseeable periods of time, and on the basis of circumspect total strategies, would be in a position to advance and produce really significant and coherent work. We can only hope that the growing realization of the importance of science (not only technically utilizable, but individually and socially relevant science) will bring about a change in the attitude to expression research within the foreseeable future. See also *Habit; Personality; Traits.*

Bibliography: Allport, G. W. & Vernon, P. E.: Studies in expressive movements. New York, 1933. **Allport, G. W.:** Personality and social encounter. Boston, 1960. **Andrew, R.:** The origin and evolution of the calls and facial expressions of primates. Behavior, 1963, *20*, 1–109. **Bell, C.:** Anatomy and philosophy of expression. London, 1806. **Bühler, K.:** Ausdruckstheorie. Jena, 1933, [2]1968. **Buytendijk, F. J. J.:** Allgemeine Theorie der menschlichen Haltung und Bewegung. Utrecht, 1956. **Darwin, C.:** The expression of the emotions in man and animals. London, 1872. **Davitz, J. R.** (Ed.): The communication of emotional meaning. New York, 1964. **Frijda, N. H.:** De betekenis van de gelaatsexpressie. Amsterdam, [2]1958. **Id.:** Mimik und Pantomimik. In: Handbuch der Psychologie, Vol. 5. Göttingen, 1965. **Görlitz, D.:** Ergebnisse und Probleme der ausdruckpsychol. Sprechstimmforschung. Diss. Tech. Univ. Berlin, 1970. **Kafka, G.:** Grundsätzliches zur Ausdruckspsychologie. Acta Psychol., 1937, *3*, 273–314. **Kirchhoff, R.:** Allgemeine Ausdruckslehre. Göttingen, 1957. **Id.:** Vom Ausdruck des Menschenblicks. Stud. Gen, 1960, *13*. **Id.:** Die Umfelder des pathognomischen Ausdrucks. Jb. Psychol. Psychother. med. Anthropol., 1962, *9* (a). **Id.:** Methodologische und theoretische Grundprobleme der Ausdrucksforschung. Stud. Gen., 1962, *15* (b). **Id.:** Ausdruck: Begriff, Regionen. Binnenstruktur. Jb. Psychol., Psychother. med. Anthropol, 1963, *10*. **Id.:** Zur Geschichte des Ausdrucksbegriffs. In: Handbuch d. Psychol., Vol. 5. Göttingen, 1965a. **Id.:** Grundfragen der Ausdruckspsychologie. In: Handbuch d. Psychol., Vol. 5, 1965b. **Klages, L.:** Grundlegung der Wissenschaft vom Ausdruck. Bonn, [7]1950. **Lersch, P.:** Gesicht und Seele. Munich, [4]1955. **Lorenz, K.:** Studies in animal and human behaviour, Vol. 1. London, 1970. **Rudert, J.:** Vom Ausdruck der Sprechstimme. In: Handbuch d. Psychol. Vol. 5. Göttingen, 1965.

R. Kirchhoff

Expression in animals. Expression research comprises the analysis of motivation and of the transmission of information. Hence the definition: Expression is the state of a living creature in its behavior and bodily form as apparent to another creature. Animal ethology does not as yet make any distinction between a "what" and a "how" aspect. The statement "A is eating" is thought of as predicating something expressive of A, just as much as the statement "A is a hasty eater", in so far as only B apprehends the eating or mode of eating. A distinction may be made between (*a*) peripheral expressive structures (optically effective body-build characteristics, olfactory organs, skin characteristics affecting cutaneous sensibility); (*b*) non-directive expressive processes (hair and feather erection and plumage ruffling, color changes, pupillary reactions, variations in cutaneous gland secretion, changes in respiratory rhythm, sounds [in part], trembling, twitching, fidgeting); and (*c*) directive expressive actions (threat postures, aggressive displays, invitations to play, contact movements, courtship behavior, etc.).

Typical animal expressions are expressive movements, the evolution of which was favored by the requirement for unequivocal, precise, genotypically codifiable, species-specific communication units.

After 1951, the study of the motivational aspect of animal expression received an impetus from the development of the theory of conflicting impulses. Most studies emphasize expressive movements and the functional aspect of the intraspecific, species-typical expressive mode. Here there is a reflection of the considerable part played by animal expressions in the control of social behavior and the preservation of the species-typical associative and population structure. Nevertheless, future research will have to take more account of undifferentiated expression, relations between arbitrarily selected partners, and individual differences. Only in this way will it be possible to achieve a comprehensive description and causal analysis of animal expression. These viewpoints are also becoming increasingly important in applied ethology. See *Animal psychology; Comparative psychology; Instinct.*

Bibliography: Armstrong, E. A.: A study of bird song. London, 1963. **Bastock, M.:** Courtship: a zoological study. London, 1967. **Eibl, I.:** Ausdrucksformen der Säugetiere. In: **Kükenthal, W.:** Handbuch der Zoologie, Vol. 8. Berlin, 1957, *10* (6), 1–26. **Lorenz, K.:** Methods of approach to the problems of behavior (The Harvey Lectures, Series 54). New York, 1959. **Id.:** The function of color in coral reef fishes. Proc. Roy. Inst. of G.B., 1962, *39*, 282–96. **Schenkel, R.:** Ausdrucksstudien an Wölfen. Behaviour, 1947, *1*, 81–129. **Stamm, R. A.:** Perspektiven zu einer vergleichenden Ausdrucksforschung. In: Handbuch der Psychologie, Vol. 5. Göttingen, 1965, 255–88. **Tinbergen, N.:** The study of instinct. London, 1951. **Id.:** Social behavior in animals. London, 1953. **Id.:** Comparative studies of the behaviour of gulls. Behaviour, 1959, *15*, 1–70.

R. A. Stamm

Expressiveness; expressivity. 1. Richness of expression, expressive content: the degree to which an object of perception has expressive value, i.e. spontaneously releases emotional attitudes in the perceiver (see *Expression*).

2. Ability to express: the ability and willingness, which differ from individual to individual, to communicate thoughts and ideas in language. This ability is dependent on aptitude factors (divergent thinking: verbal, associative and expressive fluency, imagination) and on temperamental features which are covered by the personality factor *extraversion* (Pawlik, 1968).

3. Genetic expressiveness: the degree to which an inherited feature is phenotypically expressed in an individual (see *Heredity*).

Bibliography: Pawlik, K.: Dimensionen des Verhaltens. Berne & Stuttgart, 1968.

K.P.

Extinction. 1. In biology, the disappearance of a species or life form. **2.** In behavioristic psychology, the elimination or progressive reduction in magnitude or frequency of a *conditioned response* upon the withdrawal of *reinforcement*. The term is used in both *classical conditioning* (q.v.) (in which reinforcement is the unconditioned stimulus) and *operant conditioning* (in which reinforcement is reward or punishment contingent upon the response).

Differential extinction: a process by which one conditioned response is extinguished while one or more others are maintained.

G.D.W.

3. The disappearance of memory content (see *Memory*). An acquired ability is progressively lost through lack of reinforcement (q.v.); if the result of a specific, acquired form of behavior is not achieved, this behavior is gradually lost. *Experimental* extinction: a conditioned reflex is broken down by repeated presentation of the conditioned stimulus without reinforcement.

K.E.P.

Extinction-stimulus method. A method developed by H. von Helmholtz (q.v.) for the extinction of a sense-impression by means of a subsequent, stronger stimulus of the same stimulus class. The procedure is used, especially in tachistoscopic experiments, in order to prevent formation of an afterimage (q.v.). *F.M.*

Extirpation. Surgical removal of an organ or part of the tissue of an organ; the injury is allowed to heal spontaneously. Applied, e.g., in animal experiments: extirpation of parts or all of the brain. See *Ablation*. *F.C.S.*

Extrapyramidal motor areas. The part of the motor system of the spinal and brain situated outside the pyramidal path and not directly subject to volition. Its task is to regulate the general tone of the muscles, to coordinate movement by interaction between agonists and antagonists and simultaneous limb movement and to monitor body posture. It includes parts of the spinal cord and basal ganglia in the diencephalon and mesencephalon, e.g. striate body, *globus pallidum*, *claustrum*, *nucleus amygdalae*, *nucleus ruber* and *substantia nigra*. *E.D.*

Extrasensory perception (ESP). Paranormal cognition. The acquisition of information from the external environment otherwise than through any of the known sensory channels. In experimental parapsychology the term ESP was introduced by J. B. Rhine to embrace such phenomena as telepathy (q.v.), clairvoyance (q.v.) and precognition (q.v.). See also *Paragnosia*. *J.B.*

The term ESP, which probably goes back to Pagenstecher (*Aussersinnliche Wahrnehmung*, Halle, 1924), is freely used by writers in various fields as well as by the mass media. From a scientific point of view the choice of this term is perhaps less fortunate. Psychologists may point out with some justification that sensory perception is not fully understood and that consequently the meaning of ESP is rather obscure. However, Schmeidler (*Extrasensory Perception*, New York, 1969) pointed out that similar exclusion conditions (i.e. for ESP "no means of sensing or remembering or inferring") are used in more orthodox fields of psychology. It can also be argued that an operational definition of ESP can be formulated by providing detailed descriptions of the operations which measure ESP and which exclude "sensing, remembering and inferring". Nevertheless, the term ESP has perhaps overemphasized a difference between parapsychological phenomena and related events in orthodox areas of psychology. There is also an obvious scarcity of positive criteria for the description of ESP phenomena, and it may be reasonable to attribute some of this lack to the negative essence of the term. In some countries new expressions have been introduced (bioinformation, q.v., Russia; psychotronics, Czechoslovakia). These new terms suggest a closer association with the orthodox sciences and with monism. Dualism was more often the basic outlook in connection with ESP research. But in recent years this tendency has become less pronounced. *H.H.J.K.*

Extratensive type. An experiential type showing "an urge to live outward, excitable motility and weak affectivity" in the Rorschach test (q.v.). Coincides in large measure with C. G. Jung's extraverted type. *W.K.*

Extravert (syn. *Extrovert*). An attitude type characterized by "positive movement of subjective interest in the object" or a direct attitude to the objective world in evaluation and intention. Direction of psychic energy outward. Tends toward superficial contact. Shows "an obliging, apparently open and willing nature which easily fits in with any situation, quickly establishes relationships and ventures confidently and unhesitatingly into unknown situations without regard to possible problems". Good "adaptation" (C. G. Jung). H. J. Eysenck considers extraversion to be a statistically-proven personality dimension. The questionnaires used in his factor analysis accord with Jung's description. Close relationship with the cyclothymic (q.v.) type. See *Traits; Type.*

Bibliography: Eysenck, H. J.: The structure of human personality. London, [2]1960. **Jung, C. G.:** Psychological type. London, 1970. *W.K.*

Eye. The organ of sight. The light-refractive section is distinguished from the light-receptive section. The former includes: the cornea; the anterior and posterior chambers, which are divided by the iris and are filled with an aqueous humor; the lens; the vitreous humor. The latter includes the retina and its receptor cells, the rods and cones which transform light energy into nervous impulses, which in their turn are conveyed by the "optic nerves" (*fasciculus opticus*) to the central nervous system (CNS). The optical axis of the eye is distinguished from the visual axis. On the optical axis (*axis oculi geometrica*) are the cardinal points of the optical system (points of union, nodal points, and focal points). It connects the anterior pole of the lens with a point between the blind spot and the *fovea centralis* and corresponds approximately to the symmetrical axis of the eyeball, which is not quite symmetrical in rotation. The visual axis passes

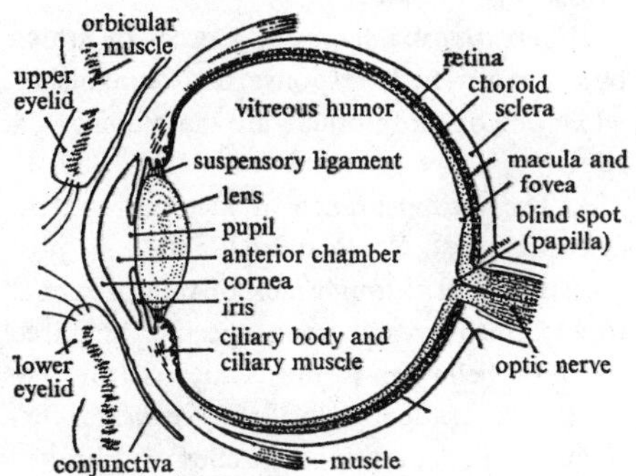

Fig. 1. Section through the eyeball.

through the middle of the fovea and bisects the optical axis in the posterior third part of the lens. See *Sense organs; Visual perception.*

Bibliography: Davson, H. (Ed.): The eye. London & New York, 1962. **Graham, C. H.:** Vision and visual perception. London, 1964. **Weale, R. A.:** From sight to light. London, 1968. *R.R.*

Eyeball. The *bulbus oculi*, situated in the orbital cavity (*orbita*). Its outer wall is formed by the cornea and the sclera, under which are the choroid membrane and the retina. It is surrounded by fatty tissue. Because of the six eye muscles attached to it, it can move on all axes (see *Fusion*). This makes the fixation of any object possible (see *Identical* [*Retinal*] *Points*). *R.R.*

Eye-blink reflex. A natural response to a blast of air that can be obtained as a conditioned response and accurately measured. Used in conditioning experiments, especially to measure traits.

Bibliography: Franks, C. M. & Trouton, D.: Effects of amobarbital sodium and dexamphetamine on the conditioning of the eyeblink response. J. Compar. Physiol. Psychol., 1958, *51*, 220–22. *J.M.*

Eyeless sight. The alleged capacity to see when the eyes are covered. Regarded by the

Mesmerists as one of the paranormal concomitants of the deep hypnotic trance (q.v.) and akin to clairvoyance (q.v.). Jules Romains coined the expression "extra-retinal" or "paroptic" vision, and attempted to give it a physiological interpretation. See *Skin vision.* *J.B.*

Eysenck Personality Inventory (abb. EPI). A revision of the Maudsley Personality Inventory (q.v.) scoring neuroticism and extraversion and including a lie scale.

Bibliography: Eysenck, H. J. & Eysenck, S. B. G.: Manual of the Eysenck Personality Inventory, London & San Diego, 1964. *J.M.*

F

Factor. In general terms, the word factor denotes a component part or a part cause. Since the introduction of factor analysis by C. Spearman, the factor is considered to be a psychological variable which has been defined with the aid of this mathematical method. A factor determines part of the overall variance of a measured characteristic. A characteristic may be determined by one or more factors. The factors are therefore psychological conditions which cause variance and establish individual differentiation. Both characteristics and individuals may be defined by factors. Depending on the method, factors are assumed to be independent of each other (orthogonal), or partially dependent, in which case they can be further analyzed. Factors are interpreted either as psychological conditions (capable of no further analysis) or causes of performance or behavior patterns (L. L. Thurstone *et al.*), or simply as principles of classification (C. Burt). Meili distinguishes between basic, or primary factors, and secondary factors originating from learning processes. The number of defined factors is impossible to evaluate and it would take more than the criteria of factor analysis to determine their general relevance. The factors are usually designated by letters or combinations of letters. See *Intelligence* for L. L. Thurstone's and R. Meili's factors, and *Intelligence, structure of* for J. P. Guilford's factors. *R.M.*

Factor analysis. I. 1. *Origins of factor analysis.* Factor analysis has two independent origins, one in psychology, and one in pure mathematics. Although the two distinct streams, represented by Spearman and Hotelling, have now united, an appreciable number of the difficulties psychologists experience with factor analysis arise from differences of assumption and emphasis between the scientific and mathematical models.

In psychology, factor analysis began as an attempt to get more out of the Galton-Pearson correlational approach than had previously been possible. Spearman developed it initially as the only instrument capable of answering the crucial question of whether there is a single, "monarchic" structure of intelligence (q.v.) or a host of "intelligences". From this concern with examining a correlation matrix for a single factor, it was further developed by Thurstone (and more briefly by Maxwell Garnett) into multiple factor analysis. After Spearman, Burt, Thomson and Thurstone used factor analysis to examine ability problems; since 1930 Cattell, Eysenck, Guilford, Horn, Hundleby, Nesselroade, Pawlik and others have used it for problems of determining structure in personality, motivation and psychological states.

2. *Nature and formulation.* The aim of factor analysis is to explain the correlations obtained among a large number, n, of variables, by variation on a smaller number, k, of underlying abstract or inferred factors. This aim is cognate with that of science generally: to go beyond appearances to a more economical set of basic concepts. In the physical sciences good guesses can be made about these underlying concepts, but in the social and biological sciences, where far

more factors are at work, factor analysis is indispensable as a preliminary concept-generating simplification. As a method, its role is both to generate hypotheses and to test them. Mathematically, the basic equations can best be expressed in matrix algebra (see *Statistics*). One begins with the experimentally given $n \times y$ correlation matrix among the variables. The mathematical process of extracting latent roots and vectors permits us to computerize this experimentally obtained $n \times n$ correlation matrix R_v ("reduced" by having communality estimates instead of unities in the diagonal) and to obtain an $n \times k$ *factor pattern matrix*, V_{fp}, which gives the loadings of each of the factors on the n variables, thus:

$$R_v = V_{fp}R_fV'_{fp} \qquad (1)$$

The R_f is in the middle in the $k \times k$ matrix of correlations among the factors, and in the special case where the factors are orthogonal it will be unity, and vanish from (1). The meaning of the loadings (or correlations in the orthogonal case) in V_{fp} is that they indicate how much the normal variance on each of the k common factors is responsible for the observed variation in each of the variables. As equation (4) below (which is a row from the V_{fp} matrix) shows, the variance of any behavioral variable must be the weighted sum of the variance on these common, broad factors (which operate on many other variables) plus that of a specific factor (F_j in equation (4)) which operates only on that specific variable. However, this "specific factor" may be a fiction stating that we do not know what other common factors to bring in.

3. *Unique resolution in the scientific model.* A major problem has been to determine the unique solution for (1), since, mathematically, there is an infinite series of equivalent solutions, which correspond, in a geometrical plot of the test variables on the coordinate axes given by the factors, to spinning the factor axis to an infinite number of positions. Consequently the problem is commonly referred to as unique rotational resolution.

Deciding on the number of factors (and communalities) and extracting them by the computer nowadays takes very little time. But the rotation, in spite of automatic programs like Oblimax, Promax, Rotoplot and Maxplane, can be long; but it is crucial for subsequent psychological meaning. The essence of rotation is the finding of the transformation matrix, L, that will convert the unrotated orthogonal matrix, V_0, which comes from the computer, into the (typical) oblique reference vector structure, V_{rs}, which has the required simple structure or other properties (see below) of the scientific model. Thus:

$$V_{rs} = V_0L \qquad (2)$$

In mathematical factor analysis, the correlations discovered between factors and variables are simply measures of "association", and all in the infinite set of equivalents are equally correct; but in the scientific use the unique values indicate that the unique position of the factor corresponds to some influence at work in nature. The hypothesis is no longer that the factor corresponds to "a mere mathematical abstraction", as some clinical critics, unfamiliar with factor analysis, have asserted, but that it is a causal influence or structure, resting on the same basis of observation as an electron or a valency in the physical sciences.

4. *Psychological meaning in the behavioral equation.* From equation (1) it is possible to pass to equations for estimating any individual's score on a given factor (or "source trait") from his performances on the variables, thus:

$$z_f = Z_vV_{fe} \qquad (3)$$

where Z_v is an N (people) $\times n$ score matrix of variables, V_{fe} is an $n \times k$ factor estimation matrix and z_f is the $N \times k$ set of factor scores (not in standard scores until a slight transformation is made). If we know both the factor pattern matrix from (1) (but including now a row for some new variable, *a*) and the individual's standard scores on the factors, from (2) we proceed to use the *specification* or *behavioral* equation, in which the individual's performance is estimated on the new variable from his factor scores, thus:

$$a_j = b_{j1}F_1 + b_{j2}F_2 + \ldots + b_{jk}F_k + b_jF_j \quad (4)$$

Here the b's are factor loadings from a row of the factor pattern matrix, and may in the psychological sense be called *behavioral indices*, for each expresses how much the given factor (or source trait) enters into the determination of the extent of the particular behavior. When the factors are motivation factors and a_j is a symptom, we have what may be called a "quantitative psycho-analysis". In any case the factor analytic model is a mathematical expression of a conceptual background in psychology that is prepared to recognize (*a*) that behavior is typically multiply determined; (*b*) that both the organism (represented by the F's in (4) above) and the stimulus situation (represented by the b's) must be invoked to determine behavior; and (*c*) that any personality concept can be operationally defined and measured only by a whole *pattern* of variables, not (typically) by any single variable. (See *Source traits.*)

In accordance with the use of factor analysis as a scientific, not only a statistical model, the factor resolution should be free to locate oblique and not merely orthogonal factors. In an interacting universe it would be strange to have factors uncorrelated. Work with plasmodes, i.e. numerical examples of a general model, where the structure is actually known (as in Thurstone's box and Cattell's ball problem), shows that simple structure yields factors corresponding to the scientific concepts in the field—length, breadth, weight, elasticity, temperature—and that an orthogonal rotation is meaningless.

5. *Oblique factors, rotational principles, higher order emergents.* Correlated factor concepts enable higher-order factors to be obtained. These are found by factoring the correlation matrix among primary (first-order factors); they have proved to have good psychological meaning. For example, Horn's factoring of Thurstone's primary abilities and others reveals the existence of two higher-order general ability factors—fluid and crystallized intelligence. The pursuit of higher-order factors has put more demands on the rotation of primaries to truly exact obliqueness. Two principles have directed such rotation: (*a*) simple structure, proposed by Thurstone, and accepting maximum simplicity, in the spirit of Newton's *natura est simplex*; and (*b*) confactor rotation, proposed by Cattell, which requires two co-ordinated factor-analytic experiments and the seeking of "proportional profiles" in the loading patterns of corresponding factors at the critical position. The latter—confactor resolution—achieves directly what simple structure aims at as secondary, namely "factor invariance", i.e. a convergence on the *same* concepts, as matchable factor patterns, from different experiments, as discussed by Meredith, Tucker and others. Lately it has become usual to separate the scientific from the mathematical model more explicitly, by calling only the former *factor analysis*, and referring to the latter as *component analysis*. Component analysis, with orthogonal principal axes, will not give the same factors from one experiment to another, since the axis of the first factor extracted will alter with biases in the choice of variables.

6. *New variants.* In the last twenty years, there have been many variants and special developments of factor analysis, such as factoring covariances and cross products (Nesselroade, 1970) instead of correlations: Guttman's non-parametric factoring; Kaiser's alpha factoring; McDonald's non-linear factor analysis; Tucker's three-way factoring; and the special scientific models called the permissive, expending and modulator models.

The three last are intended to fit the model better to certain psychological conditions. Thus the permissive model says that factor A cannot come into action at all until factor B has reached a certain level. (It brings interaction terms into equation 4 above.) The expending model, designed for motivation research, says that much discharge of a factor in one performance must reduce its availability for another. The modulator model splits the factor trait into an excitability, which alone is truly fixed for the individual and allows the stimulus situation to "modulate" the factor level itself before it operates. This offers one of the chief links between the individual difference use of factor analysis and its use in the areas of "process psychologists" in perception and learning.

7. *Impact on individual difference concepts.* The greatest impact and best understood operation of factor analysis were at first in the area of individual differences and specifically of human abilities, and soon after in the personality field. In the former it has enormously clarified the structure of primary abilities, as begun by Thurstone, and pursued by Meili, Guilford, Arnold, Horn, French and others. It has also given substantial support to certain higher-order concepts, notably those of fluid and crystallized intelligence as approached independently by Hebb in physiology and Cattell in behavior. In the personality field, operating on questionnaires and rating studies by many psychologists, and on objective, miniature situation measures, specifically in the studies of Cattell and Eysenck, it has led to a rich array of twenty or more concepts, which have proved far more stable and replicable than the numerous dimensions suggested on *a priori* or clinical grounds. They include such new concepts as surgency, independence, presmia, the self-sentiment, regression, general inhibition, parmia, affectothymia, ego strength and super ego strength. Some of these (such as the three last) are old clinical concepts, new only in the sense of being given the new outlines of experimental psychology and a basis for estimation of validity of measurement (see *Construct validity*).

8. *Diverse Referee (R, P, S, T, etc.) Techniques.* A less widely understood impact of factor analysis comes from the use of the Diverse Referee Techniques—such as *P*-, *S*-, *T*-, and *dR*-techniques. These vary the referees of measurement in the Basic Data Relation Matrix. The BDRM is a ten-dimensional "data box" having as its edges people, tests, occasions in time, etc., and illustrated as to the first three in the familiar "covariation chart" of Figure 1. The basic *R*-technique correlates tests (as relatives) over people

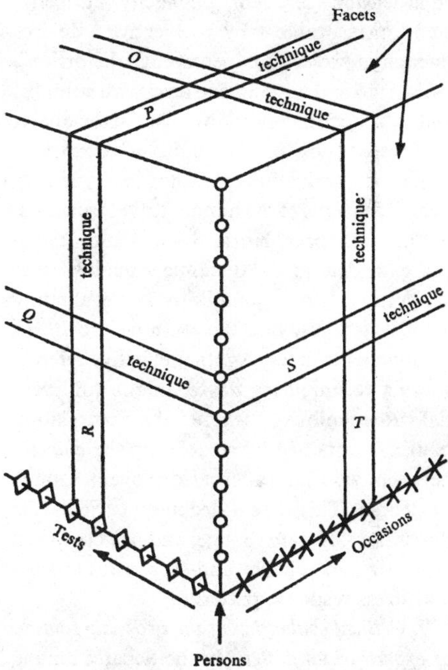

Figure 1. Possible techniques of relational analysis shown in the simpler context of the three-axis covariation chart

(as referees), while its transpose, *Q*-technique, correlates people (as relatives) over tests (as referees). For mathematical reasons, such transposes lead to essentially the same factors, but there is no reason other than some psychological lawfulness, why, say, *R*- and *P*-techniques should yield the same patterns.

In *P*-technique, as indicated in Figure 1, one factors the single person (hence *P*), by correlating behaviors ("tests") over a long enough time series of repeated measurements. Obviously the unitary dimensions so obtained should be those which describe the states of man (as Wundt attempted by *a priori* analysis), and *P*-technique has been the main means by which psychometrically useful concepts have been obtained for such states as anxiety, the depressions, stress, fatigue, etc. It has been effective in clarifying the number and nature of human drives (see *Drive*) by revealing some nine distinct dimensions of ergic tension (sex, fear, pugnacity, curiosity, etc.) measurable by objective devices (memory, projection [perceptual distortion], GSR, etc.) and varying one level with stimulus and satisfaction conditions. The factor-analytic investigation of the multivariate phenomena of motivation has not only led to clearer concepts of the human drive structures, but also (Delhees, Horn, Sweney and others) has extended to a "dynamic calculus" (see *Motivation*) for quantitatively evaluating conflict and studying the learning growth of emotional attitudes. Another effective referee-varying technique is *dR*-technique (differential *R*-technique), where the correlation matrix is obtained by correlating the *changes* between two stimulus occasions over a sample of people. This, like *P*-technique, yields the dimensions of state change, and has been used especially to define and separate anxiety and stress response patterns.

9. *Critical evaluation of the two main sources of experimental design.* In the debates among psychologists on the properties and research roles of various methods, despite half a century of use, an appropriate understanding of the role of factor analysis is only now emerging. Essentially, correlational analysis and analysis of variance divide the field, and factor analysis is the necessary culmination of any more than elementary use of correlational methods. Both factor analysis and anova are used to evaluate the significance and ultimately the magnitude of relations between variables. But anova does this two at a time (dependent and independent) whereas factor analysis handles a large number at a time. It puts the many relations in perspectives of underlying influences, whereas anova leaves it to the experimenter's unaided memory to piece together the conclusions for hypotheses and theories for many bivariate relations. Both methods create and test hypotheses, but factor analysis (where enough measures can be gathered) is much more positive and penetrating in suggesting, and more exacting in testing a hypothesis, since it tests for the reality of a whole pattern, not a divergence on a single variable.

It has been objected that factor analysis is restricted to linear relations; that it does not employ the manipulative control of the classical bivariate experiment; that it lacks various necessary checks and tests of significance; and that as a result of this last there is much disagreement among factors analysts in their substantive conceptual conclusions—examined extensively by Cattell (1966). Except for McDonald's non-linear factor analysis, which is quite complete, factor analysis is restricted to linear relations. But anova knows no more when it makes a 2-point curve; and, by a succession of tangents (loadings), a series of factor analyses over successive ranges of variables can approach a description of curvilinear relations. As to manipulation, the criticism rebounds; for there is no intrinsic reason why dependent and independent variables should not be factored together, and only the lack of enterprise of those primarily using manipulative designs is responsible for so few instances in the literature of what Cattell & Scheier (1961) have illustrated as the condition-response factor design.

On the other hand, it is true that until recently there were no effective expressions for such hypothesis-testing decisions as the significance of a primary factor loading, of a factor, of a correlation among factors, of a second-order factor, of a communality, and of a match between factors from two experiments. For the significance of a loading, Harris has suggested:

$$|a_{jf}| > t_z \sqrt{\frac{(1 - h^2{}_j)d_{ff}}{N - k - 1}} \qquad (5)$$

where d_{ff} is the element in *f*th row and column of $R^{-1}{}_f$, h^2 is the communality, *N* the number of subjects and k the number of factors. Expressions for other required significances have been developed, notably in the Lawley-Rao tests for significance of a factor. Three approaches to determining the goodness of match of purportedly the same factor in two experiments are available in Burt's congruence coefficient, Cattell's salient variable similarity index, and the configurative matching index.

10. *Factor-analytic education*. Those outside and those in the field see the differences of conclusion among factor analysts very differently. Such a difference as that between Thurstone and Guilford on primary ability structure is due to the latter retaining orthogonal factors. He asks a different question and gets a different answer. That between Cattell and Eysenck on the number and naming of personality factors is due to the latter operating at the second order, relative to the first order, which Cattell considers equally important. But if the concepts and structures which Cattell obtains at the second stage are aligned with what Eysenck obtains in a first operation, the agreement of patterns and scales is far better than between, say, the scales that two clinicians might make up for certain psychoanalytic concepts. Indeed, it must be said that the chief problem in the effective use of concepts from factor analysis in general psychological practice and research is not any inherent lack of precision or potency in the concepts themselves, but the fact that only about one-tenth of doctoral-level psychologists, even today, are trained to competence in factor analysis, conceptually or mathematically. The remaining nine-tenths develop imaginary criticisms as a defense against the unknown.

Nevertheless, the future of factor-analytic methodology in psychology is expanding rapidly. Technical procedures have been remarkably refined and enriched in the last decade, while the areas of application have spread from individual differences to social psychology (group dynamics and the dimensions of cultures; Bereiter, Gorsuch), perception (Hake, Schneewind), human and animal motivation (Delhees, Horn, Royce), physiological psychology (Fahrenberg, Mefferd), genetics (Broadhurst, Thompson), language behavior (Osgood, Miron, Papal), clinical dynamics (Cohen), learning theory (Cattell, Eysenck, Fleishman, Tucker, White) and the longitudinal study of states and processes (Baltes, Nesselroade, Scheier).

Bibliography: Burt, C. L.: Factors of the mind. London, 1940. **Cattell, R. B.:** The basis of recognition and interpretation of factors. Educ. Psychol. Measmt., 1962, *22*, 667–97. **Id.:** The configurative method for surer identification of personality dimensions, notably in child study. Psychol. Rept., 1965, *16*, 269–90. **Id.:** Handbook of multivariate and experimental psychology. Chicago, 1966. **Id.:** Confactor rotation: the central problem in structural psychology. Laboratory of Personality and Group Analysis Advance Publication, No. 1, Nov., 1966. **Id. & Dickman, K.:** A dynamic model of physical influences demonstrating the necessity of oblique simple structure. Psychol. Bull., 1962, *59*, 389–400. **Cattell, R. B. & Sullivan, W.:** The scientific nature of factors: a demonstration by cups of coffee. Behav. Sci., 1962, *7*, 184–93. **Cattell, R. B. & Scheier, I.:** The meaning and measurement of neuroticism and anxiety. New York, 1961. **Delhees, K.:** The abnormal personality: factor analysis of neurotic and delinquent behavior. In: **Cattell, R. B.** (Ed.): Handbook of modern personality theory. Chicago, 1970, 560–610. **Eysenck, H. J.:** The structure of human personality. London, [2]1960. **Guilford, J. P.:** Psychometric methods. New York, 1954. **Guttman, L.:** Some necessary conditions for common factor analysis. Psychometrika, 1954, *19*, 149–61. **Horn, J. L.:** Motivation and dynamic calculus concepts from multivariate experiment. In: **Cattell, R. B.:** Handbook of multivariate experimental psychology. Chicago, 1966, 611–41. **Hotelling, H.:** Analysis of a complex of statistical variables into principal components. J. Educ. Psychol., 1933, *24*, 417–41, 498–520. **Hundleby, J., Pawlik, K. & Cattell, R. B.:** Personality factors in objective test devices. San Diego, Calif., 1965. **Nesselroade, J. R.:** The theory of psychological states and mood action. In: **Cattell, R. B.** (Ed.): Handbook of modern personality theory. Chicago, 1970, 200–40. **Pawlik, K.:** Dimensionen des verhaltens. Berne, 1968. **Spearman, C.:** The abilities of man. London, 1932. **Thomson, G. H.:** The factorial analysis of human ability. Boston, 1939. **Thurstone, L. L.:** Multiple factor analysis. Chicago, 1947. **Überla, K.:** Faktorenanalyse. Berlin, 1968.

R. B. Cattell

II. *A critical view*. In factor analysis, correlations between series of scores (e.g.

results of different intelligence tests) are traced back to unobserved variables or factors. The level of correlation between pairs of observed variables is determined by the proportion of common factors. To determine rules of calculation for a concrete analysis, an assumption must be made concerning the type of association between the variables; traditionally it is assumed that the observed scores should be considered as the weighted total of the factor loadings. Factor analysis therefore becomes a very restrictive *model.*

1. *Critical study of the model.* The model of the linear combination of factors is convincingly simple, but this prevents its application to living systems by way of factual arguments, e.g. reference to known relationships. The introduction of more complex assumptions on the type of interaction is theoretically feasible but once again the assumption would be arbitrary. Since the number of factors is determined from the corresponding data and is unlimited, it is possible to reproduce accurately any set of data by factor analysis. The basically restrictive model therefore seems so imprecise that the results cannot be tested and are not binding.

2. *Critical study of the technique.* The model could be accepted as a "first provisional" approximation if clear results capable of interpretation could be achieved within its preconditions. This is not the case in theoretical or practical terms. This does not mean that any factor analysis leads to an infinite number of solutions which can be transferred by rotations (linear transformations). The mathematical analysis of observed scores is dependent both on the choice of variables (e.g. tests) and on the selection of the subjects. The choice of variables can be considered as an operational definition of the area under examination, and thus justified; the influence of the selection of the subjects has been wrongly contested (Meredith, 1964). It has been shown that selections which are wholly probable in empirical terms may lead to factor solutions which are not in a linear relationship with the factor structure prior to selection; in addition we find mathematically insoluble variance-covariance matrices (matrices which have not undergone "positive-semi-definite" reduction) (Kalveram, 1970). Empirically, this is only covered by statistical dispersion and the rating of communalities.

Selections of this kind may also be made for representative samples. Such samples are representative of a population but not of a hypothetical factor structure. It might therefore be argued that factor analysis was not an appropriate research method. However, if an adequate solution is found with a few factors and a large number of variables, it is useful for representing relationships in tables or graphs.

Bibliography: Meredith, W.: Notes on factorial invariance. Psychometrika, 1964, *29,* 177–85. **Kalveram, K. T.:** Über Faktorenanalyse, Arch. ges. Psychol., 1970, *122.* **Id.:** Probleme der Selektion in der Faktorenanalyse, Arch. ges. Psychol., 1970, *122.*

F.Merz.

Factorial design. An experimental arrangement for simultaneous testing of the influence of a number of independent variables on a dependent variable; applicable to all possible combinations of variable categories. This eliminates the need for a separate check on the independent variables in individual experiments and also enables possibly significant interactions to be identified. See also *Variance, analysis of.* *W.H.B.*

Fading. A term used with the same meaning as *vanishing* and *weaning* to denote a contraction technique used in the design of teaching programs; the aids (cues, prompts) contained initially in a sequence of learning units are gradually reduced and finally eliminated altogether. *L.J.I.*

Failure. In the memory research of the Lewin school, the success/failure dimension was held to be a decisive variable for memory processes. The learning psychology of the nineteen forties described failure as an intervening variable (q.v.) (E.C. Tolman; C. L. Hull). See *Aspiration level.*

False reaction. Responding in an experiment to a stimulus other than that prescribed by the experimenter, or a similar kind of response in a non-experimental situation, e.g. "jumping the gun". *G.D.W.*

Fall chronometer. An arrangement in which a falling weight is stopped by a testee and his reaction time measured. *K.E.P.*

Family. The psychological significance of the family and its members for a given person was first recognized by S. Freud and then by A. Adler and C. G. Jung. On the basis of the free thought association of his patients undergoing psychoanalytical treatment, Freud described the roles of the mother and father in relation to the child, and also of the child in relation to the parents during the early stages of its development. In the context of similar observations, Adler discussed the typical behavioral tendencies of a number of brothers and sisters, and objected that Freud's characterization of the family situation in early childhood was valid merely for only children. Jung developed his concept of archetypes (q.v.), including innate images of the father and mother which need not always coincide with the characteristics of the real mother or father.

For these reasons, W. Toman used simple combination rules to develop a model of the effects of family structures; his model had the advantage of being tested against the hard reality of social behavior in daily life; statistical tests were also carried out. In his model, psychological and behavioral effects of family members are dependent on each other and also on the persons making up the families. General characteristics of the persons in family groups are provided by the number of persons in the household and their age and sex; the duration of life in the household and the termination of this form of group life by the loss of family members are further characteristics.

The term "general effects" covers influences on the social life in the family group founded by the subject himself as well as other long-term relationships such as contacts with friends and acquaintances. Empirical evidence has been provided for a wide range of such effects which make up an important part of the family activity and form a part of the set of influences exerted by the psychological and sociological environment of an individual on his behavior. These effects of the family group on the social behavior of an individual can be roughly generalized in the "duplication theorem". This suggests that, all other conditions being equal, new long-term social relationships have more chance of success if they resemble the earlier and earliest social relationships, particularly between members of the family.

It follows that complementarity of the brother and sister roles of partners in marriage may contribute to the success of that marriage, whereas a lack of complementarity or conflict between the roles may lead to failure. Since partners in marriage are generally of similar age and the relationship between brothers and sisters provides the earliest paradigm for life with persons of similar age, the older brother of a sister *b*(*s*) and the younger sister of a brother (*b*)*s* could be defined as complementary partners in marriage. Both are accustomed (from their original family) to life with a person of the opposite sex but of much the same age. Both complement each other in age ranking. He is used to leading and taking responsibility while she is used to being led, and leaving responsibility to the partner. The same holds good with reversed leading roles for the marriage of the younger brother of a sister with the older sister of a brother (symbolically: (*s*)*b*/*s*(*b*)).

Extreme examples of non-complementarity or conflict (q.v.) between the brother and sister roles would be the marriage of the older brother of a brother with the older sister of a sister, i.e. *b(b)/s(s)*, or the marriage of the younger brother of a brother with the younger sister of a sister, i.e. *(b)b/(s)s*. In both these marriages the partners are not accustomed (from their original families) to living with persons of the opposite sex but of similar age. In addition the partners have similar age rankings. In the first marriage both will want to lead and take responsibility while in the second case each of the partners will expect the other to lead and be responsible.

Partial complementarity between the brother and sister roles occurs if the marital partners had at least one among several brothers and sisters coinciding with the family position of the marital partner (e.g. *b(bs)/(b)s(b)*, i.e. the eldest brother of a brother and sister married with the middle sister of two brothers). Conflict of ranking without sex conflict would occur, e.g. in a marriage of the elder brother of sisters with the elder sister of brothers, e.g. *b(ss)/s(bb)*, and sex conflict without rank conflict in the case of a marriage between the elder brother of one or more brothers and the youngest sister of several sisters, i.e. b(bb. .)/(ss. .)s.

Evidence exists that non-complementarity between the brother and sister roles of marital partners increases the probability of divorce, a smaller number of children, and marital or educational problems in the family. Friendships between persons of the same or of the opposite sex last longer if the partners had complementary brother and sister roles. The relationship of an individual to his parents and the relationship between the parents and their children are also determined to some extent by the brother and sister positions of the parents. Other conditions being equal, a parent will identify most easily with those of his children (of the same sex) who have an identical or similar brother and sister position to that parent (the same applies to the relationship between the child and parent). In addition, a parent will be able to establish the best direct contact with a child of the opposite sex (and vice versa) whose brother and sister position corresponds to that of a brother or sister of the parent (of the opposite sex). Other factors, such as the extent of the age differences between brothers and sisters, between the parents and between parents and children, differences in the intensity of family life, and the success or otherwise of families founded by the brothers and sisters of the parents, influence the effect of family groups on the social behavior of the persons involved. The same holds good for differences in intelligence, vitality and external appearance, as well as for socio-economic, ethnic or religious factors. All these factors complicate the relationships referred to; they may disturb, but they may also strengthen them.

The loss of persons in the original family results in greater readiness to anticipate further losses. This is expressed in a poorer selection of persons for long-term relationships (the likelihood of the latter breaking up is greater than that of other permanent relationships), but also in the tendency to choose as partners persons who have themselves suffered losses or persons whom the individual can himself leave again or by whom he or she is more likely to be left. The loss of family members is all the more serious psychologically the more recent its occurrence, the earlier it occurs in the life of a person, the older the lost person is, the greater the duration of the previous shared life with the lost person and the greater the disturbance of the balance between the sexes in the family, the smaller the number of direct family members, the greater the number of personal losses already suffered and the longer it takes to find a complete substitute for the person lost. Temporary losses are non-permanent absences of persons from the family group. The extent of their disturbing influence is governed by the same rules but depends on the duration of the absence. Partial losses are losses of certain aspects of a person in a family group (e.g. by the discovery that the father drank heavily or had served a prison sentence). The effects of permanent losses on the social development of the persons affected have been demonstrated statistically (Bowlby; Glueck & Glueck; Toman). Early losses are more likely to lead to educational problems, delinquency and criminality, neurotic disorders, unfavorable choices of marital partners, more frequent divorces and illegitimate births, and also to relatively late motherhood or parenthood.

Bibliography: Adler, A.: The practice and theory of individual psychology. London, [2]1929. **Bowlby, J.:** Maternal care and mental health. London, 1951. **Freud, S.:** Introductory lectures on psychoanalysis. London, [2]1929. **Glueck, S. & Glueck, E.:** Predicting delinquency and crime. Cambridge, Mass., 1959. **Jung, C. G.:** The structure and dynamics of the psyche. London, 1960. **Nye, F. I.:** Family relationships and delinquent behavior. New York, 1958. **O'Connor, N. & Franks, C. M.:** Childhood upbringing and other environmental factors. In: **Eysenck, H. J.** (Ed.): Handbook of abnormal psychology. London, 1960. **Parsons, T. & Bales, R. F.:** Family, socialisation and interaction process. Glencoe, Ill., 1955. **Toman, W.:** Family constellations. New York, [2]1969. **Wurzbacher, G.** (Ed.): Die Familie als Sozialisationsfaktor. Stuttgart, 1968.

W. Toman

Family group. The communal family is a form of family commonly found in feudal societies and nomadic tribes in which three generations live with their wives and children in a common household. The system is generally that of a strict patriarchate (q.v.). In Europe family groups of this kind existed only among certain Balkan peoples. As industrialization progresses, the communal family group tends to break up because of its rigid authoritarian structure and the central family (parents with dependent children) tends to dominate. One might also use the term "family group" in connection with the "communes", or communities of unrelated young people or intellectuals which have been established recently (experimentally) in certain big cities.

Bibliography: Goode, W. J.: World revolution and family patterns. New York, 1964. **Id.:** The family. New York, 1964. **McKinley, D. J.:** Social class and family life. New York, 1964. **Rosser, C. & Harris, C.:** The family and social change. London, 1965. **Shanas, E. & Streib, G. F.** (Eds): Social structure and the family: generational relations. Englewood Cliffs, 1965. **Willmott, P. & Young, M.:** Family and class in a London suburb. London, 1960. **Young, M. & Willmott, P.:** Family and kinship in East London, 1957.

N.S.-R.

Family planning. Behavior typical of developed societies, and related to their population level. By practising birth control, parents themselves determine the size of their family, bringing it into line with their social and economic standards and with their aspirations. For society as a whole, birth control is made necessary by low mortality rates (threat of population explosion, especially in developing countries). Birth control also reduces the number of abortions. See also *Contraception.*

N.S.-R.

Fanaticism. A narrow-minded, passionate and combative attitude on the part of some who are, e.g., victims of effective propaganda (q.v.), and who emphatically propagate exaggerated ideas that brook no compromise. Some adherents of religious and political sects and cure-all utopian ideologies, those who indulge in endless legal squabbles, and some health cranks and heralds of a perfect world, who zealously propound their often demented ideas and refuse to enter into any form of discussion, can be classed as fanatics.

K.T.

Fantasy. 1. *History.* The term derives from the Greek *phantasia* (making visible, capacity for imaging). Trevisa (1398) records that more fantasies are seen by night than by day. Newton mentions the power of fantasy to see colors in dreams. The term refers to subjective imagining, including waking and sleeping imagery, and hallucination. This may be visual, auditory, tactile, or a composite of these and other sense modes. Hume (1748) distinguishes images from sensations in terms of their lack of force and vivacity, but admits that in sleep, fever, and madness images may approach sensations. Galton's (1883) classic study was the first major research into imagery, and was particularly concerned with memory images, and individual differences. Freud's (1900) study of dreams was partly anticipated by Maury (1861), who also provided the name "hypnagogic" for imagery of the half-asleep state. Silberer (1909) contributed an important investigation of hypnagogic imagery.

Freud deals with fantasy under the heading of primary process, contrasted with the secondary process of goal-directed thinking. The primary process discharges itself in dreams and daydreams through wish fulfillment. An alternative terminology derives from Bleuler's concept of autism. Autistic (as opposed to realistic) thinking "may be a fleeting episode of a few seconds duration, or may fill a life and entirely replace reality" (for instance, in schizophrenia). Autism "does not insist upon testing its conclusions by realistic and logical criticism . . . it is not after truths but after the fulfillment of wishes" (Bleuler, 1922; see Rapaport, 1951). Bleuler adds that ordinary thinking is "a mixture of realistic and autistic thinking". For brevity we may speak of *A*-thinking, and *R*-thinking (McKellar, 1957). *A*-thinking may overwhelm the personality as in psychosis, or may exert temporary dominance in dreaming, the hypnagogic state, under hallucinogenic drug influence, and in sensory deprivation experiments. It also appears in daydreams, mythology, and superstition. Some projective techniques, like Murray's TAT (Thematic Apperception Test) involve standard pictures to stimulate fantasies which are then analyzed as a source of information about the personality. (See *Autism; Dream.*)

In his early studies of imagery, Galton (1883) found a "sufficient variety of cases to prove the continuity between all the forms of visualization, beginning with an almost total absence of it, and ending with complete hallucination". He observed that cultural pressures may discourage visionary activity, or may stimulate it when "faintly perceived fantasies of ordinary men become invested with the authority of reverend men with a claim to serious regard . . . they increase in definition through being habitually dwelt upon". Some spontaneous, and drug-induced or starvation-provoked, fantasies have been interpreted supernaturally. Moreover, the (British) Society for Psychical Research found that just under 10 per cent of a sample of 15,000 people reported experiences strictly classifiable as hallucinations, at least once in their lives (Sidgwick, 1894).

2. *Recent work.* A major break-through with one kind of *A*-thinking has followed the discovery that recordable effects, including rapid movement of the eyes (REMs), tend to accompany dreaming (Aserinsky & Kleitman, 1958). With REM studies we can now time dreams, and count the number of dreams in a night's sleep. Dreaming appears to be a near-universal phenomenon, and Kleitman (1963) distinguishes between recallers and non-recallers rather than dreamers and non-dreamers. Singer (1966) has extended the use of REMs to the study of waking fantasy and imagery more generally. Singer & Craven (1961) find a peak for daydreaming in the 18–29 age group, and report daydreaming—images of people and events—daily in 96 per cent of their subjects. (See *Sleep.*)

Commenting on a period of undeserved scientific neglect, Holt (1964) welcomed "the return of the ostracized". In so doing he stressed the relevance of imagery research to certain very practical problems of modern transport and engineering psychology. Rosemary Gordon's (1949) test of flexibility of visual imagery, and the Betts' (1909) test of vividness are coming into use (see Richardson, 1969). Synesthesia has been given intensive study by the Soviet psychologist Luria (1969) in his book about one individual subject to this kind of imagery.

Many substances of botanical origin that stimulate *A*-thinking processes are now known. Some are associated with Aztec and contemporary South- and Central-American religion and mythology. Research in ethnobotany (Schultes, 1963) suggests numerous largely uninvestigated sources of hallucinogens. This represents a promising area for continued study of chemically stimulated fantasy (Efron, Holmstead & Kline, 1967). In this field, as in sensory deprivation research, the word "hallucination" has been carelessly extended. "Imagery" is a general and more appropriate term for many of the phenomena reported.

Bibliography: **Efron, D. H., Holmstedt, B. & Kline, N. S.** (Eds): Ethnopharmacologic search for psychoactive drugs. Washington, 1967. **Galton, F.:** Inquiries into human faculty. London, 1883. **Holt, R. R.:** Imagery: the return of the ostracized. American Psychologist. 1964, *19*, 4. **Kleitman, N.:** Sleep and wakefulness. Chicago, 1963. **Luria, A. R.:** The mind of a mnemonist. London, 1969. **McKellar, P.:** Imagination and thinking. London & New York, 1957. **Rapaport, D.:** Organization and pathology of thought. New York, 1951. **Richardson, A.:** Mental imagery. London, 1969. **Schultes, R. E.:** The widening panorama in medical botany. Rhodora, 1963, *65*, 762. **Singer, J. L.:** Daydreaming: an introduction to the experimental study of inner experience. New York, 1966.

P. McKellar

Farsightedness. See *Hemeralopia*.

Fascination method. Used to induce hypnosis (q.v.) by staring, or getting a patient to stare, at a glittering object such as a metal or glass ball. First used in 1843 for therapeutic self-hypnosis by J. Braid, an English surgeon to whom we also owe the term "hypnosis". Today the term is usually applied to a technique for inducing hypnosis in which the patient stares fixedly into the eyes of the hypnotherapist. *H.N.G.*

Fascism. Belief in the authority principle in social relations; in the (spurious) Right-Left continuum, it equals accentuated bourgeois conservatism. The "*F*" scale for assessing the authoritarian personality (q.v.) (developed by T. W. Adorno and others) is well known. Fascism or authoritarianism involves a number of independent dimensions which are not determinable in terms of political doctrine and correlate negatively with educational level. See *Attitude*.

Bibliography: **Eysenck, H. J.:** Psychology of politics. London, 1954.

B.H.

Father fixation. An unusual, quite unconscious influence exerted by the father image (see *Imago*) throughout puberty, and beyond it, on a daughter or son. Affective or sexual fixations are often important (see *Oedipus complex*) unconscious components of this father–child relationship.

Father protest may be described as the contrary state to father fixation, being a largely unconscious attitude or "guideline" (A. Adler), perpetuated in negative attitudes toward the father, and transferred to all situations which are in any way similar to the father–child relationship (e.g. bourgeois society, a hierarchical Church). This principle of transference (q.v.) applies to father fixation as well. *W.Sch.*

Fatigue. A condition resulting from previous stress which leads to reversible impairment of performance and function, affects the organic interplay of the functions and finally may lead to disturbance of the functional structure of the personality; it is generally accompanied by a reduction in readiness to work and a heightened sensation of strain. A distinction is made between many forms of fatigue, which can be traced back to two principal areas of fatigue: physical fatigue, in particular muscular fatigue, and mental fatigue (also known as central or nervous fatigue, on account of the fact that the primarily physiological substrate of this form of fatigue is the central nervous system). Monotony and mental saturation are conditions similar to fatigue, but which have specific laws of their own. It is impossible to make a sharp distinction between physical and mental fatigue. Recent research has emphasized the complexity of this whole problem, and the interaction between different forms and causes of fatigue, to the extent that fatigue is generally understood as an alteration of the mental and physical structure of the individual under stress. Fatigue is dependent on the degree of stress or effort and on the characteristics and duration of the latter. Stress (q.v.) must be understood in the broad sense of the word. For example, an individual may be subject to greater stress resulting from tension with his environment during the performance of his work than from the activity in itself. See *Anxiety*.

1. *History of fatigue research*. Systematic research into fatigue, which began early this century, is marked by a profusion of confusing definitions, theories and research results. This is due above all to the following facts: (*a*) Some authors understand fatigue to denote the process, i.e. stress caused by an activity; and others, the state which results from stress. This second interpretation has come to be increasingly widely accepted. (*b*) Many different symptoms are reduced to a common denominator, namely the concept of fatigue, so that the concept itself covers a wide variety of notions. (*c*) The phenomenon of fatigue (interpreted in different ways) has been studied by several branches of science with widely varying theoretical assumptions and methods, and largely in isolation.

Bartley & Chute (1947) clarified the confusion by making the following distinctions: (*a*) experience of fatigue which can only be directly determined by psychological methods; (*b*) impairment of the organic structures which can only be directly determined by physiological or biochemical methods; (*c*) impaired performance. Bartenwerfer (1961) stresses that mental, physiological and performance characteristics, which may alter in the course of activity, are poorly correlated. Experiences of fatigue, changes in physiological state and variations in performance may express a mental activity but they may also express other circumstances. Reduced performance may be the sign of impending illness, and fatigue may be the consequence of a generally depressed mood. In addition, mental, physiological and performance symptoms show only slight correlation with previous activity, having regard to the difficulty and duration of that activity. There are cases in which, e.g., fatigue only sets in when the limit of exhaustion is reached, whereas in other cases it is already present at the start of an activity.

2. *Symptoms of fatigue* (according to Schmidtke, 1965). Physical fatigue: (*a*) changes in the muscle system; changes in muscular force, colloidal condition of the muscles, and disturbed peripheral coordination; (*b*) effects of muscle fatigue on the whole organism; changes in breathing, in the blood and in heart and circulatory activity. In mental fatigue: receptivity, perception and coordination disturbances, disturbed attention (q.v.) and concentration, as well as thinking, personal drive and control functions, and social relations.

3. *Causes of fatigue*. In the case of muscle fatigue, due to the impaired contractile capacity of the muscles, the cause is seen in metabolic disorders, primarily due to a lack of oxygen in the muscles. In mental fatigue, too, oxygen deficiency and resulting temporary physical and chemical changes in the cells of the CNS are considered a possible cause. In addition, research is currently being conducted to determine the extent to which functional disorders may result from specific functional stress on the brain. The question of the causes of mental fatigue is largely unresolved.

4. *Measurement of fatigue*. Muscle fatigue is measured by an ergograph, static exertion and pulse frequency. Mental fatigue is measured by methods with a physiological basis: flicker fusion frequency, optical reaction times, determination of upper auditory threshold, electroencephalogram (EEG), pulse frequency, galvanic skin response (GSR), rhythm of breathing, measurement of chronaxia, determination of muscle condition, microvibration, energy consumption. Mental fatigue

can also be measured by psychological methods: psychomotor coordination tests, motor tests, capacity tests (Pauli test), projective methods (q.v.) (Rorschach test), self-observation questionnaires, global self-analysis on the basis of comparable activities.

Bibliography: Bartenwerfer, H. G.: Beiträge zum Problem der psychischen Beanspruchung. Cologne & Opladen, 1960–63. **Id.:** Psychische Beanspruchung. In: Hdb. d. Psychol., Vol. 9. Göttingen, 1961. **Bartley, S. H. & Chute, E.:** Fatigue and impairment in man. New York, 1947. **Bornemann, E.** (Ed.): Ermüdung, Ihre Erscheinungsformen und Verhütung. Vienna, 1952. **Bracken, H. v:** Untersuchung zur Diagnose psychischer Ermüdung. Berlin, 1955. **Düker, H.:** Untersuchungen über die sogenannte Aufmerksamkeit. Berlin, 1955. **Floyd, W. F. & Welford, A. T.** (Eds): Symposium on fatigue. London, 1953. **Graf, O.:** Erforschung der geistigen E. und nervösen Belastung, Cologne & Opladen, 1955. **Lehmann, G.:** Energetik des arbeitenden Menschen. In: **Baader, E. W.** (Ed.): Hdb. d. ges. Arbeitsmedizin, Vol. 1. Berlin, 1961. **Mierke, K.:** Wille und Leistung. Göttingen, 1955. **Müller, E. A.:** Die physische Ermüdung. In: **Baader, E. W.** (Ed.): Hdb. d. ges. Arbeitsmedizin, Vol. 1, 1961. **Schafer, H.:** Physiologie der E. und Erschöpfung, Med. Klin., 1959, *54*, 159; *54*, 1109–19. **Schmidtke, H.:** Die Ermüdung. Berne, 1965.

A. Gubser

Fatigue, measurement of. An attempt quantitatively to determine the reduction in mental and physical powers resulting from continuous stress, by means of standardized test methods. The commonest methods are continuous calculation (Pauli test, q.v.; concentration capacity test) in which fatigue results in more frequent faults and a lower calculating capacity per unit of time; flicker tests in which the reduction in fusion frequency indicates the degree of fatigue, and measurements with a dynamometer (q.v.) or ergograph, in which reduced muscular energy indicates fatigue.

P.S.

Fatigue tests. Fatigue denotes a subjective condition or a reduction in capacity due to prior effort. The causes may be biochemical or psychological. There is therefore no single phenomenon of fatigue and no general fatigue test. There is little correlation between different methods of measuring fatigue. Flicker fusion and sensory threshold determination are often used. *R.M.*

Fausse reconnaissance. An illusive recognition; a new experience that seems to reproduce a previous experience. Virtually synonymous with *déja vu* (q.v.).

F distribution (R. A. Fisher). This servesas the basis of one of the major statistical test distribu tions (*F test*, q.v.). Samples of sizes N_1 and N_2 are taken repeatedly from a normally distributed population. In the process, the sum of the N_1 test values X_i—normally distributed and independent of each other—follows the χ^2 distribution (see *Chi-square distribution*). The same applies to the sum of X_i from the sample N_2. The probability $dI(F)$ of

$$F < \frac{\frac{\chi_1^2}{N_1}}{\frac{\chi_2^2}{N_2}} < (F + dF)$$

can then be determined from the area lying between F and dF of the F distribution $\varphi(F)$. $\varphi(F)$ is a single-peaked distribution skewed to the left; its skewness increases with N_2. Unlike the χ^2 distribution, it does not change into the normal distribution (q.v.). *W.H.B.*

Fear. A primitive and often intense emotion characterized by a systematic pattern of bodily changes (those resulting from arousal of the sympathetic nervous system) and by certain types of behavior, particularly flight or concealment. (See *Arousal; Anxiety*).

Fear is normally experienced in the face of threat, i.e. when danger is perceived or pain anticipated. Even normal fear is often unadaptive in humans, but fears which are persistently out of proportion to the real danger involved are called *phobias*. In psychoanalysis, a distinction is made between *real fear* and *neurotic fear;* the latter arises when instinctual urges are felt which are unacceptable to the conscious mind. *G.D.W.*

Fechner, Gustav Theodor. B. 19/4/1801 in Niederlausitz, d. 18/11/1887 in Leipzig. 1834–40 occupied the chair of physics; from 1840 philosopher, anthropologist and main founder of psychophysics (q.v.). In his philosophical works he combined scientific interests with speculative and literary efforts (pantheism, panpsychism) and rudimentary depth psychology. Fechner made pioneer contributions to psychophysics, especially in his investigations of threshold and differential values of stimuli and sensations. He followed up the findings of E. H. Weber (q.v.) concerning just-noticeable differences in stimulation, and put them into mathematical form. *F.C.S.*

Works: Zend-Avesta, 1851. Über die physikalische und philosophische Atomlehre, 1855. Elemente der Psychophysik, 1860 (Eng. trans., ed. Howes, D. H. & Boring, E. G.: Elements of psychophysics. Vol. 1 Chicago, 1966). Über die Seelenfrage, 1861. In Sachen der Psychophysik, 1877. Revision der Hauptpunkte der Psychophysik, 1882. Über die psychischen Massprinzipien und das Webersche Gesetz, 1887.

Bibliography: Boring, E. G.: A History of experimental psychology. New York & London, [2]1957. **Hall, S.:** Founders of modern psychology. New York, 1912. **Misiak, H. & Sexton, V. S.:** History of psychology. New York & London, 1966. *F.C.S.*

Fechner's law. The generalization, based on psychophysical experimentation, that the intensity of a subjective sensation (e.g. loudness) is proportional to the logarithm of the physical stimulus (sound intensity). Expressed mathematically, $S = k \log R$ where S is the sensation, k a constant, and R the stimulus (Ger., *Reiz*). This law is closely related to Weber's law, and is sometimes called the *Weber-Fechner law*.

Fechner regarded this principle as the first law of the mind since he believed that it described the exact relationship between physical and mental events. Its discovery is sometimes regarded as marking the birth of psychology as a science separate from philosophy. More recent experimentation by S. S. Stevens and others, however, has suggested that the relationship between subjective and physical intensities is better described as a *power* function, and there is some evidence that if Fechner's law holds at all, it more accurately describes the relationship between the physical stimulus and the physiological receptor response (e.g. rate of nerve firing). *G.D.W.*

Feeblemindedness. See *Mental defect; Oligophrenia.*

Feedback. 1. In computer technology, a process which, for example, enables an electronic system to maintain a constant comparison between a pre-set level (set point) and input data (actual values) (*Homeostasis*, q.v.): e.g. temperature control in a refrigerator (thermostat). **2.** In functional biology (e.g. blood pressure, body temperature): a process which serves similarly to preserve an internal balance: feedback from proprioceptive receptors. See *Reafference principle.* **3.** In the personal sphere (Martin Buber's primitive dialogue situation) the feedback principle is equally effective.

Bibliography: Wiener, N.: Cybernetics, or control and communication in the animal and machine. New York, 1948. *K.E.P.*

Feedback system (syn. *Control circuit; Control system, automatic*). A basic concept of cybernetics (q.v.). A process of automatic control (not requiring human intervention) by which the value of a quantity is continuously obtained by measurement of the actual state of the process and used to modify input and activate the control system. A well-known example is the thermostat, which keeps a temperature constant. If the temperature of a refrigerator or an electric iron is too high, the electrical current input is interrupted by means of a metal strip or a mercury column so that the temperature drops; then the mercury column also drops, and at a certain point switches the current on again, so that the temperature rises and, because of the alternate switching on and off, remains constant within a certain margin. Even without numerical values for the measurements, self-observation provides examples of series of experiences which can be interpreted as automatic (feedback) systems which keep mental states constant. One such process consists of the mental effects of frustration (q.v.), as automatic measures for maintenance of self-esteem: every diminution of self-esteem by one's own failure leads "automatically" to compensatory experiences such as rationalization (q.v.) ("I was very tired"), aggression (q.v.), substitute gratification (q.v.), and so on. Since these individual states are undoubtedly intended to restore self-confidence, it is possible to speak of a psychic feedback system (Rohracher, 1963). There is no doubt about the "automatic" nature of this control system, since the results of frustration can occur without conscious cooperation (see *Consciousness*)—even when they are apprehended as apparent "causes". The problem of "mental feedback systems" is essentially one of the immateriality of conscious lived experience, which is wholly ignored by some cyberneticians. Genuine feedback systems are to be found only in technology and in organic processes such as blood pressure, where there are material "sensing organs" and regulation devices; the mental processes, however, are not material (they do not consist of atoms or elementary particles, or of oscillations resulting from the movements of atoms or molecules; consequently, mental processes cannot be controlled by technical methods. Hence there is a further objection against the cybernetic nature of these processes: they are—in principle—non-simulable. Present knowledge does not allow us to predict that it will ever be possible to simulate conscious experiences in a machine. But cybernetic processes must, at least in principle, be technically simulable. Admittedly there are biological regulating circuits in cerebral activation (e.g. for maintenance of body temperature or for regulation of pupillary width in specific light conditions). Since all conscious experiences derive from activation processes in the ganglionic cells of the cerebral cortex (see *Cortex*), it may be assumed that it also contains material bases for the automatic regulations whose non-physical effects we experience, e.g., as the results of frustration. Because of the non-physical nature of mental behavior, it is preferable to speak of "so-called" psychic feedback systems, or of "quasi-cybernetic mental processes". See *Communication; Information theory.*

Bibliography: Aizerman, M. A.: Theory of automatic control. Oxford, 1963. **Block, H.:** The perceptron. Rev. mod. Phys., 1962, *34*. **Erismann, T. H.:** Zwischen Technik und Psychologie. Berlin & New York, 1968 **Feigenbaum, E. A. & Feldman, J.** (Eds): Computers and thought. New York, 1963. **Günther, G.:** Das Bewusstsein der Maschinen; Eine Metaphysik der Kybernetik. Krefeld, 1957. **Neumann, J. von:** The computer and the brain. New Haven, Conn., 1958. **Pask, G.:** An approach to cybernetics. London, 1961. **Rohracher, H.:** Regelprozesse im psychischen Geschehen. Forsch. Fortschr., 1963, *37*. **Id.:** Die Arbeitsweise des Gehirns und die psychischen Vorgänge. Munich, [4]1967. **Uttley, A. M.:** A theory of the mechanism of learning based on the computation of conditional probabilities. Proc. 1st Int. Cong. on Cybernetics. Namur, 1956. **Wiener, N.:** God and golem. New York & London, 1964.

H. Rohracher

Feeling. See *Emotion.*

Feeling function. According to C. G. Jung one of the four basic functions of the psyche. Together with the thinking function (q.v.), it belongs to the rational functions. It furnishes the individual value of the data registered by the sensation function (q.v.) as well as feelings like pain, anxiety, joy and love.

W.L.

Feeling type. A functional type (q.v.) in which the feeling function based on emotion is the dominant factor. Most marked in women.

Feeling is either adapted to external norms (extraverted) and therefore "rational", or subjective (introverted) and concealed so as to achieve adaptation "not extensively but intensively".

Bibliography: **Jung, C. G.:** Psychological types. In: Contributions to analytical psychology. London, 1928. *W.K.*

Fellatio. Oral contact with male genitals. Used as a method of mutual masturbation (q.v.) in homosexual relations (see also *Cunnilingus*). Fellatio is indulged in by many primates as a form of masturbation. For anatomical reasons it is in this form rare among men, although the desire is fairly often reported. A study of history shows that oral-genital contacts were not frowned upon in ancient civilizations as they are in today's Judeo-Christian culture. The spread of oral-genital contacts, especially as a prelude to coitus, increases with the level of education. They are demanded by the male more frequently than his female partner, owing to the taboo, can tolerate or carry out.

Bibliography: **Kinsey, A. C.** *et al.*: Sexual behavior in the human male. Philadelphia & London, 1948. *G.L.*

Femininity. Use is made of questionnaires (e.g. Minnesota Multiphasic Personality Inventory, q.v.) in assessing femininity. These are employed to determine the extent to which the subject's attitudes and interests depart from the norm for his or her own sex. These variables are difficult to interpret because subjects' scores depend on their social environment and occupation. The existence of a bipolar factor (q.v.)—"masculinity-femininity"—has been established by R. B. Cattell and others. *G.K.*

Feral child. The feral child legend goes back to antiquity (e.g. Romulus and Remus). Reports of "wolf", "bear", "leopard" children, and so on, are of doubtful provenanсe and trustworthiness. An essential feature is that the child grows up apart from the members of his own species during the decisive years of life (see *Imprinting*). T. A. L. Singh reported the discovery of two girls of about eighteen months and eight years of age in a termite mound inhabited by wolves in the Midnapur district of India. They lapped water like wolves, ate raw meat and carrion, bared their teeth, crawled on all fours, could neither stand nor walk, would not tolerate clothes, did not cry, and were dumb apart from basic sounds indicating excitement or agitation. The report is full of inaccuracies and contradictions.

Bibliography: **Brown, R. W.:** Words and things, Glencoe, Ill., 1957. **Köhler, O.**; "Wolfskinder," Affen im Haus und vergleichende Verhaltensforschung. Folia Phoniatrica, 1952, *4*, 29–53. **Singh, T. A. L. & Zingg, R. M.:** Wolf-children and feral man. New York, 1942. *K.F.*

Féré phenomenon. A decrease in electrical resistance (or increase in conductance) of the surface of the skin resulting in emotional arousal or heightened psychological activity of any kind. A similar effect can be obtained simply by placing two electrodes on the skin and recording changes in the potential difference across them. This is called the *Tarchanoff effect*, and is to be distinguished from the *Féré phenomenon* which involves introducing an external source of current to the skin surface. Both effects are, of course, named after the men credited with their discovery.

The Féré phenomenon is also called the *psycho-galvanic reflex* (PGR) and the *galvanic skin response* (GSR), and together the two effects are called the *electrodermal response* (EDR). The mechanism is not yet well understood, but it appears that emotional arousal stimulates sweat-gland activity, producing an increase in cell membrane permeability, which results in a polarization change and thus a change in electrical resistance. The effect is best observed using those areas of the body which are characterized by arousal or anxiety sweating rather than thermoregulation (i.e. the palms of the hands, soles of the feet, and forehead). The response is often used in psychophysiological experiments as an indicator of arousal, and is one of the components of the so-called *lie detector* (q.v.). *G.D.W.*

Fetish. A symbol for something regarded with peculiar veneration and awe which the fetish serves to embody. In sexual psychology, fetishism denotes a sexual deviation (q.v.) in which the presence of a special object and/or its handling is a condition of sexual satisfaction. Inanimate objects or parts of the body of the sexual partner can serve as fetishes. In psychoanalysis a fetish is regarded as a substitute and often treated as a cover memory. *U.H.S.*

Fetishism. 1. *Ethnological:* ritual use of specific objects (*fetishes*) to which, because of their nature or origin (e.g. the hair of an enemy), magical powers are ascribed. 2. *Clinicopsychological:* a perversion (q.v.): excitement and satisfaction are associated with parts of the body outside the genital area (breast, hair) or objects, esp. articles of clothing. See *Cultural psychology; Sexuality.* *I.L.*

Fiducial interval. See *Limits, fiducial.*

Field. An area, space, or region (physical or metaphorical) having boundaries defined in terms of relevance to a particular problem or orientation. Thus *visual field* refers to the totality of objects which are visible in a particular situation, and the *phenomenal field* refers to everything that is being experienced by an organism at a particular moment in time.

Field theory (usually associated with K. Lewin) is a general approach to psychological data which employs the notion of *fields of force* by analogy from physics. The central proposition is that the properties, objects and events are not static but are derived from or dependent upon the total field of which they are a part (see *Granzheit*).

A *field investigation* refers to the collection of data not in the laboratory or clinic, but in the natural environment of the organisms being studied. *G.D.W.*

Field dependence. A term coined by H. A. Witkin for the degree to which perception of the vertical is influenced by simultaneous perception of the ambient field. In field dependence tests (rod and frame, tilting room, tilting chair, rotating room) the subject is required to judge the vertical chiefly in the light of kinesthetic and tactile stimuli, shutting out as far as possible any irrelevant data derived from the visual sense. A number of relations with other perceptual factors are considered to have been established. Relations with personality traits, however, have not yet been satisfactorily explained.

Bibliography: Witkin, H. A. *et al.*: Personality through perception. New York, 1954. *M.A.*

Field of experience. A concept developed on the basis of Lewin's field theory (q.v.) which denotes the totality of experiential contents which appear in the context of processes and with differing degree of clarity in the consciousness. The field of experience varies from individual to individual in scope and structure and also with regard to its dynamism within the given framework.

Bibliography: Lewin, K.: A dynamic theory of personality. New York & London, 1935. *P.S.*

Field theory. A concept of Gestalt theory (esp. as developed by K. Koffka and W. Köhler) taken over and modified by K. Lewin. Individual behavior is assumed to result in every case from the grouping of psychologically relevant forces which can be localized in a mathematically reconstructible environment. Accordingly, all behavior is field behavior. Every analysis of behavior in terms of field theory starts off with the investigation of the circumstances in which that behavior occurs. These circumstances are regarded not in physical terms but exactly as they are experienced by the person concerned. *W.D.F.*

Fighting, ritualized. Combat which avoids serious injury, especially between aggressive members of the same species. It varies according to species, but frequently many elements are so similar that partial ritual combat is possible between closely related types. Frequently recurring patterns are advancing the forepart (e.g. bill sparring in birds) or the flank, circling, taking hold of the mouth, butting in the case of reptiles, mammals and fish. The fights end with the exhaustion or surrender of the weaker, who submits to the victor (see *Appeasement gestures*). There is both intraterritorial and boundary combat, the most frequent reason being the determination of territory.

Bibliography: Tinbergen, N.: Social behavior in animals. London, [2]1965. *K.F.*

Figural aftereffect. A modification in the perceived spatial characteristics of one figure (the *test figure*) following exposure to another (the *inspection figure*). E.g., continued inspection of a bowed line leads to a decrease in its apparent curvature, so that when a straight line is presented subsequently, it is perceived to be curved in the opposite direction.

Figural aftereffects are not retinal fatigue phenomena, like visual afterimages, but have been shown to be a property of the central nervous system. Thus they are more closely related to illusions, but based upon relations between *successive* stimuli rather than *simultaneous* stimulus relationships. *G.D.W.*

Figure-ground. A kind of perceptual organization in which some part of the field stands out as a unified object while the rest is relegated to the background. This relationship is not necessarily static; the figure is generally the part or parts of the field which are being attended to, and a shift in attention may result in a change of figure-ground organization (e.g. embedded and reversible figures).

Figure 1.

From: & Pauli Arnold, *Psychologisches Praktikum* (Stuttgart, [6]1957).

The phenomenon is most clearly manifested in the visual sense modality, but is known to be a general characteristic of perception. Other things being equal, those parts of the field which are regular, familiar, or need-relevant, are more likely to be perceived as figure. *G.D.W.*

Film. An audio-visual mass medium whose importance and effectiveness have undergone extensive empirical investigation since the nineteen-twenties. The effect of films appears to be to impart information rather than to alter opinions, attitudes or behavior. The aggressive behavior portrayed in films is imitated only in the presence of other conditions that are also typical of other forms of learning. Information furnished by films (just as by *Television*, q.v.) can often, under the same conditions, be better absorbed and retained than that provided by radio and printed matter. See *Aggression; Communication.*

Bibliography: Hoban, C. F. & van Ormer, E. B.: Instructional film research (Rapid mass learning) 1918–1950. Washington, D.C., 1951. **Heinrich, K.:** Filmerleben, Filmwirkung, Filmerziehung. Berlin, 1960. **Weiss, W.:** Effects of the mass media of communication. In: **Lindzey, G. & Aronson, E.** (Eds): Handbook of social psychology. Vol. 5. Reading, Mass, 1970.

H.D.S.

Film color. Unlike surface color (q.v.), film color is less consistent and compact, can be seen through up to a certain depth, and is absolutely uniform. Typical film colors are the subjective grey of the eye, fog, the hue of a clear sky, and the color of surfaces seen through a reduction screen—hence also *reduced color* (q.v.) or *aperture color* (q.v.). *G.K.*

Finger painting. A psychotherapeutic technique in which children paint directly with their finger in special colors. Since this presents no technical difficulties, the children can easily express themselves *uninhibitedly*. *R.M.*

Finger spelling (*Dactylology*). A mode of communication among deaf-mutes (see *Deaf-mutism*) of which several systems are in existence. With the *manual alphabet* spoken language is represented letter by letter by successive finger positions. This was how deaf-mutes were at one time familiarized with speech (today by optical means). For blind deaf-mutes (see *Blind deaf-mutism*) use is made of the *tactile alphabet* (H. Lorm) in which letters are symbolized by touching or brushing against certain parts of the palm. The *spell system* widely used in the U.S.A. is a kind of manual alphabet (one-hand manual alphabet) employed as an auxiliary in the training of deaf-mutes, the spelling hand being kept in the region of the mouth. Deaf-mutes also use a specially-developed gesture language to communicate with each other.

Bibliography: Moser, H. M., O'Neill, J. J., Oyer, H. J., Wolfe, S. M., Abernathy, E. A. & Showe, B. M.: Hand signals. Finger-spelling. USAF Operat. Applications Lab. tech. Rep., 1958, 58–66.

F.Ki.

Finger sucking. A habit that usually takes the form of thumb sucking and is generally regarded as harmless in infants and young children. It is particularly common in children of seven months to two years, and often associated with hunger and fatigue. Finger sucking has a soothing function.

An abnormal habit in children of five years and upward and in juveniles, it is often accompanied by nail biting and hair pulling. It is then a neurotic addiction, often the outcome of an unsatisfied craving for affection. In depth psychology, finger sucking is regarded as a return to the gratification urge of the oral phase (see *Regression*). *P.J.*

First impression. Particularly important on first meetings. This importance is due to the effect of novelty and above all the exploratory conduct triggered by the unknown person if he has valence for the observer. In general, the first impression is determined on the one hand by striking features in the expression of the unknown person and on the other by cultural standards and values of the observer. Descriptions of the first impression contain above all psychological judgments (friendly, timid, etc.) and then statements on external appearance. According to P. R. Hofstätter, the validity of the first impression is dependent on three variables: the ability of the observer, the nature of the characteristics observed, and the character of the observed person. Similar characters and members of the same sex are able to gain an impression of one another more easily. *F.Ki.*

Fisher-Yates test. The use of χ^2 as a test of independence in a double dichotomy has limitations if the cell frequencies are small. A. Yates (1934) proposed a correction for continuity (q.v.) in these circumstances and, following a suggestion by R. A. Fisher, also gave a method for computing the exact probability (q.v.) of any observed set of cell frequencies in a two-by-two table. In testing significance, it is essential to compute the probability of the frequencies observed and the probabilities of all possible extreme frequencies, and to cumulate the results. The test is also known as the *Exact* χ^2 test.

W.H.B.

Fixation. Used in two different senses: **1.** The strengthening of a tendency or response leading to the establishment of a memory or motor habit; **2.** The process of becoming, or the condition of being, set, rigid, inflexible or compulsive in some particular way of thinking, attitude, feeling, or behavior.

In psychoanalysis, used to refer to an attachment to an early stage of development, or some object at that stage, which persists in immature and neurotic form, interfering with other normal attachments (e.g. mother fixation; smoking interpreted as an oral fixation). *G.D.W.*

A tendency to regress to stages of development and spheres of motivation in which, according to Freud and Fenichel, there was too little satisfaction of certain motives, or too much or too little satisfaction following earlier excessive satisfaction of such motives. Toman considers "too much satisfaction" self-contradictory and only meaningful if neglect of other motives and other spheres of motivation is implied. Fixations are therefore always caused by frustrations, traumas and deprivation of the chance of satisfying motives, i.e. too little satisfaction. Regression (q.v.) occurs in those spheres of motivation—within such a disturbed stage of development—which were not affected by frustration (q.v.), or in the phase immediately preceding the frustrated stage. According to Freud, fixations in the early and late oral or anal phases, and in the early genital phase, can lead to neuroses (q.v.), psychoses (q.v.), perversions (q.v.) and criminality (q.v.), but not as a rule frustrations, traumas and losses experienced during later stages of development. (See also *Psychopathology*.)

Bibliography: Freud, S.: The ego and the id. London, [2]1962. **Id.:** Introductory lectures on psycho-analysis. London, [2]1929. **Toman, W.:** Introduction to psychoanalytic theory of motivation. London & New York, 1960. **Id.:** Motivation, Persönlichkeit, Umwelt. Göttingen, 1968.

W.T.

Fixation, visual. The directing or focussing of the eye toward a particular target or object of regard (the *fixation point*) so that the image falls on the retina. In *binocular fixation* both eyes are directed at the same point, but this is apparently fairly unusual. The fixation point is normally also the center of attention in the visual field, although it is also possible to attend to the periphery of vision. *G.D.W.*

Fixed attention. O. Vollmer, in particular, distinguishes between a person whose attention (q.v.) is *fixed* and one in whom it fluctuates. The first explores the field of attention systematically, step by step, taking particular note of details. The second skims over the salient features of the perceptual field and gets only a blurred impression of details. See also *Attention types*. *W.K.*

Fixed idea. See *Idée fixe*.

Flagellation. An early form of religious penance performed by scourging oneself or others. As such it is now encountered only now and then in small sects. Flagellation has a certain following as a sado-masochist sexual *deviation* (q.v.). In order to arouse or heighten sexual excitement, one partner beats the other with one of an often wide armory of appliances. Cases of reciprocal flagellation are rarer. *U.H.S.*

Flanagan Aptitude Classification Tests (FACT), developed for the USAF during the Second World War. An analysis of skills yielded 21 "critical work elements", of which 19 were embodied in the tests. Various empirically established combinations of the individual results of the tests are used to determine aptitudes for 38 professions.

Bibliography: Flanagan, J. C.: Flanagan Aptitude Classification Tests. Chicago, 1953–59. *R.M.*

Flexibilitas cerea (*Catalepsy*). Waxen flexibility, in which the patient's limbs can be made to move passively and to retain for some time the attitude forced upon them by the investigator. Patients' behavior is similar to that of wax dolls. Can be observed in organic psychoses (q.v.), hysterias (q.v.) and above all in schizophrenias (q.v.). *A.Hi.*

Flexibility. Pliancy, adaptability; ant. *rigidity* (q.v.). This factor has been studied by means of factorial analysis.

Bibliography: Guilford, J. P.: Personality. London, 1959. *W.K.*

Flicker photometry. A psychophysical method for comparing or equating different fields with respect to brightness using as an index the rate of *flicker* necessary to give *fusion* (q.v.) (the *critical flicker frequency;* CFF). This rate is known to increase as a function of both absolute brightness, and the difference in brightness between the two phases of the flicker sequence. One apparatus commonly used in flicker photometry is the *episcotister*, consisting simply of a disc with adjustable sectors which is driven by an electric motor and rotated at variable speed. *G.D.W.*

Flight into sickness. An escape, to a greater or less extent subconscious, from a reality that can be neither mastered nor endured, into a state of sickness that frees the sufferer from all responsibility. An incapacity mechanism then comes into operation, and the subject shuts himself off from the world and experiences feelings of resignation and inferiority and other neurotic complications. Neurotic symptoms are described as a flight into sickness by A. Adler and others. *H.N.G.*

Fluctuation of attention. O. Vollmer distinguishes between a person whose attention fluctuates and one in whom it is fixed. (See *Fixed attention; Attention, types of.*) *W.K.*

Fluency. A rapid flow of ideas and tendency to change direction and modify information. Characteristic for tests in which a number of answers that satisfy the same condition must be given. First defined by L. L. Thurstone as a factor of word fluency (*W*). Whether one general factor or several factors of fluency should be postulated is a point of dispute. According to Guilford, fluency belongs to "divergent thinking" (q.v.), for which he defines 24 factors. In the U.S.A., creativity (q.v.) is connected mainly with fluency.

Bibliography: Guilford, J. P.: The nature of human intelligence. New York, 1967. *R.M.*

Fluidity. Profile of the dynamic course of affect and movement with respect to intensification, transition and rhythm. In the cyclothymic type (q.v.) the process alternates smoothly, in the barykinetic type (q.v.) it is abrupt, irregular and cumulative. *W.K.*

Folk psychology (syn. *National psychology*). W. Wundt (q.v.) conceived of folk psychology as the counterpart of experimental psychology. Whereas the experimental method was to be used for the analysis of "simple psychic processes", Wundt considered that the study of "universally valid cultural products" such as language (q.v.), myth (q.v.), and morals would allow access to "higher mental processes and developments" (1913). This division was the result of Wundt's belief that experimentation was inappropriate to the investigation of "higher" mental processes such as thinking or affectivity. In this field, only "mass psychic phenomena", in contradistinction to individual products (e.g. autobiographies) were suitable objects of research directed toward "objective" findings. Because of the obvious objections against Wundt's restrictive view of experimental method, the folk psychology he proposed as an alternative was neglected. The belief that language, myth and morals were keys to the objective nature of higher intellectual processes laid the method wide open to speculative abuse. Whereas Wundt wholly neglected the social-psychological viewpoint, social psychology (q.v.) played a dominant role from the start in American folk psychology, or *ethnopsychology* (q.v.). The problem of the specific norms and value systems of a culture was preeminent. Whereas Wundt still put forward the theory of a linear evolution in folk psychology by means of which "primitive" thinking and emotions were held to display primeval stages of the same processes in civilized man (see *Cultural anthropology; Magical thought*), this was deemed highly questionable by ethnopsychologists.

A further turning-point came in folk psychology when the post-Hegelian notion of the "folk mind" or "national spirit" ("objectified spirit" for N. Hartmann) gave way to a more realistic study of the individual personality which is influenced by and incorporates the attitudes (see *Attitude*), values and knowledge of a particular culture. The quest for the "character" of a tribe or nation was replaced by that for the *basic personality structure* (A. Kardiner; R. Linton) most frequent in a specific culture (*modal personality*). Many popular hypotheses of folk psychology (e.g. "typical German industry") have become objects of social psychology (see *Prejudice; Stereotype*). At present, comparative ethnography ("ethnographic atlases") makes possible statements backed by evidence of intercultural similarities and differences (e.g. Murdock, 1967).

Bibliography: Cattell, R. B.: The dimensions of cultural patterns. J. abn. soc. Psychol., 1949, *44* **Inkeles, A. & Levinson, D. J.:** National character. In: **Lindzey, G.** (Ed.): Handbook of social psychology. New York, 1954. **Kluckhohn, C.:** Culture and behavior. In: **Lindzey, G.,** *op. cit.* **Murdock, G. P.:** The ethnographic atlas: a summary. Ethnology 1967, *6*.

W.Sc.

Forebrain. The nervous system (q.v.) develops from the ectoderm (ectoblast), passing through the neural plate, groove, and tube stages. While the neural plate is forming, the prosencephalon (forebrain) and rhombencephalon appear initially at its anterior end. The telencephalon (q.v.) and diencephalon (q.v.) develop from the forebrain. *G.A.*

Forensic psychiatry. The application of psychiatric knowledge and medical, psychiatric and psychological research techniques to the appraisal of persons whose behavior departs from social and legal canons and/or who should be confined against their will in a closed psychiatric institution on grounds of self-preservation or for the protection of the community. The subject-matter of forensic psychiatry is highly diversified and includes the assessment of soundness of mind (e.g. the administration of intelligence tests when court cases are referred for assessment of intellectual level), prognoses from the social, psychological and criminological points of view in the case of offenders and therapeutic measures for their rehabilitation, and problems of civil law such as the capacity of persons to transact business or make a will, the case for putting them under guardianship, divorce, etc.

In the legal sphere forensic psychiatry is mainly concerned with pathological disturbances of mental activity, i.e. all derangements of the mind and personality of organic origin, (*a*) based on injuries, diseases and abnormalities of the brain or of the central nervous system (e.g. cranial and brain traumas, symptomatic epilepsies, intoxications, infections, arteriosclerotic atrophy of the brain); or (*b*) known to be endogenous psychoses of the schizophrenic and manic-depressive group.

Bibliography: Glueck, S.: Law and psychiatry. Cambridge, Mass. & London, 1963. **Mayer-Gross, W.** *et al.*: Clinical psychiatry. London, 1969. **Watson, A. S.:** Psychiatry for lawyers. New York, 1968.

H.M.

Forensic psychology (*Legal psychology*) is a branch of applied psychology (q.v.). It seeks to throw light on all psychological problems arising in connection with those involved in court cases. The formulation of questions and subject-matter are governed by the law in force in a particular country or state. The requirements of the administration of justice are therefore the decisive factor. The services of psychiatrists and psychologists are today enlisted in criminal cases (expert opinions on witnesses and offender), civil cases (e.g. family law), industrial cases (e.g. labor disputes), administrative matters (e.g. assessment of aptitude of drivers), and in the execution of sentences (see *Punishment*).

In fact psychology now permeates the entire administration of justice. Almost every sphere of psychology must be taken into account by forensic psychology. The emphasis lies on developmental psychology (q.v.), social psychology (q.v.), the psychology of personality (q.v.), diagnosis, clinical psychology (q.v.), sexual psychology (q.v.), and the depth-psychology aspect.

1. *History.* In its early stages (at the turn of the century) only scant empirical material was available to researchers (e.g. W. Stern, O. Lipmann, K. Marbe). Psychological experts were seldom called upon in court and therefore had little chance of assembling cases on a large scale. If they were called at all it was usually by the defense, so that they were presented with a one-sided selection. Their activity was therefore confined to laboratory investigations of a general psychological nature. In the process the faulty nature of statements made in court became apparent. As W. Stern said in 1902: "Faulty memory is the exception, not the rule." Scarcely any attempt was made at any stage to establish the credibility of testimonies on scientific lines. In recent years experts have begun to assemble in actual practice a wide range of empirical material. To start with, their work lay mainly in delivering opinions on juvenile witnesses, chiefly in cases of sexual offenses (q.v.). The other fields earlier referred to were gradually added once it was established that psychologists could help a great deal in clearing up the facts of a case. Today both expert opinions on personality and the analysis of verbal statements can play a central role in the work of forensic psychologists.

2. *Methods.* These largely coincide with those of personality diagnosis (see *Psychodiagnostics*). An anamnesis is always carefully compiled and an analysis made of the current situation in terms of social psychology, as well as an investigation using the most effective techniques and a special exploration (q.v.) bearing on the psychology of testimony (since the forensic questions referred to a psychologist are largely bound up with the subjective data of the person on trial). In the process any admission (in the course of any statement, even a confession) must be carefully checked. Both the aspect of performance and that of motivation must invariably be taken into account.

3. *Appraisal of witnesses.* Here the emphasis has shifted from credibility (q.v.) in general terms to credibility in the case being heard. U. Undeutsch in particular described general credibility as an outdated idea of a static human character. Modern personality theories (see *Personality*) embrace all dynamic concepts. In this respect the outstanding authors are in agreement. Nonetheless, an analysis of personality that takes account of behavioral constants is indispensable. The accent lies, however, on testimony, and the psychosocial conditions that govern it.

4. *Criminal responsibility.* All legal systems make provision for diminished responsibility (see *Responsibility*) for a punishable offense. Nowadays, juvenile offenses are not tried

under retaliatory law, which aims at preventing crime in general, but are dealt with by special preventive measures, i.e. the offender is judged in the light of his individual stage of development. In Western Germany, for example, persons aged from 18 to 21 *can*, depending on their degree of maturity, be grouped among punishable juveniles (aged 14 to 18 years), and this is what in most cases happens in court. Practice varies from country to country. The best system would seem to be that the forensic psychologist is required not so much to appraise the maturity of offenders (often enough a questionable business because such assessments have to fit into an artificial idea of a "juvenile") as to put forward individual observations from case to case. At the same time he should be required to take a more active part in suggesting measures likely to lead to social rehabilitation of the individual. Achievements in the field of developmental psychology retain their importance, although the highly flexible social and cultural conditions of maturity (q.v.) should gain still more importance instead of a static and ideologically colored notion of adolescence or puberty (q.v.). This calls for close integration of psychological and criminological research, of which there is little sign today. For this purpose, statistical methods for predicting criminality (q.v.) will have to be improved. There is also a lack of educative techniques for the treatment of criminals. All scientists who have studied the problems of responsibility (q.v.) agree that the essential need is to elucidate what was going on in the wrongdoer's mind at the time of the act, and (H. Thomae) to compare his behavior and experience at that time with the model of normal behavior so often portrayed in works on psychology. In this connection, affective psychogenic disorders of consciousness (q.v.) occupy a central place in psychological assessment, which must take all available information into account. Here, too, the analysis of testimony plays an important role, since one is often thrown back on subjective data furnished exclusively by the offender. Any law which divides capacity for guilt (q.v.) into (*a*) ability to understand and (*b*) self-restraint and will-power, will tend to support differences found in the way of thinking of lawyers, psychiatrists and psychologists.

5. *Infliction of punishment*. Here the efforts of forensic psychology must obviously be directed toward social rehabilitation and special preventive measures. This calls for rational classification of groups of offenders, those needing psychotherapeutic or other treatment receiving it in special institutions. Further tasks are the diagnostic classification of prisoners, their psychological treatment, training of prison staff, occupational and educational measures, forecasts of date of release, and the provision of advice to groups and individuals.

6. *Civil law*. Here the full potential of individual diagnosis should be exhausted. Moreover, the results of research in sociology and social and developmental psychology ought to be applied and be made to embrace also the phases of the middle and later years. See *Criminality; Punishment*.

Bibliography: Blau, G. & Müller-Luckmann, E. (Eds): Gerichtliche Psychologie. Neuwied-Berlin, 1962. **Britt, S. H.:** The rules of evidence: an empirical study in psychology and law. Cornell Law Quart., 1940, *25*, 556–80. **Eysenck, H. J.:** Crime and personality. London, 1964. **Glueck, S. & Glueck, E. T.:** Unraveling juvenile delinquency. Cambridge, Mass., 1950. **Id.:** Law and psychiatry. Cambridge, Mass. & London, 1963. **Müller-Luckmann, E.:** Über die Glaubwürdigkeit kindlicher und jugendlicher Zeuginnen bei Sexualdelikten. Stuttgart, [2]1963. **Id.:** Aussagepsychologie. In: **Ponsold, A.** (Ed.): Lehrbuch der gerichtlichen Medizin. Stuttgart, [3]1967. **Münsterberg, H.:** On the witness stand. New York, 1908. **Nau, E.:** Die Persönlichkeit des jugendlichen Zeugen. Beitr. z. Sexualforschung. 1965, *33*, 27–37. **Reid, J. E. & Inbau, F. E.:** Truth and deception. Baltimore, 1966. **Trankell, A.:** Vittnespsykologins arbetsmetoder. Stockholm, 1963. **Undeutsch, U.:** Forenische Psychologie. In: Handwörterbuch der Kriminologie. Berlin, 1966. **Id.:** (Ed.): Forensische Psychologie. Hdb. d. Psychol. Vol. II. Göttingen, 1967 (Deals exhaustively with all the subjects referred to in this article and has an extensive bibliography).

E. Müller-Luckmann

Foreplay. See *Coital foreplay.*

Forepleasure. See *Anticipation; End pleasure.*

Forgetting. In psychoanalysis (q.v.), forgetting is explained by reference to the significance of affective and motivational factors for retention. Particular forms of forgetting (for Freud's disciples, tendencies to generalize originally specific data) are derived from the effect of defense (q.v.) mechanisms (see *Repression*), which inhibit memory contents that appear dangerous to the conscious ego (q.v.). See *Amnesia; Reminiscence.*

Bibliography: Rapaport, D.: Emotions and memory. New York, 1961. *H.H.*

Formal didactic(s). An algorithm for the algorithmic application of algorithmic teaching procedures, or for the production of instructional algorithms on the basis of the results of previous non-algorithmic processing of the independent didactic variables (semi-logarithmic teaching procedure). When formal didactics are programmed in a computer, they are said to be *objectivized.* The first formal didactics (Cogendi, Alzudi 1 and 2, Alskindi) were devised in 1965 at the Berlin Institut für Kybernetik and programmed for Siemens computers 303 and 3003.

Bibliography: Frank, H.: Kybernetische Grundlagen der Pädagogik, Vol. 2. Berlin, [2]1969. *H.F.*

Formal discipline. A term that corresponds to the notion of formal education broadened to embrace the process of transfer (q.v.). The practice (q.v.) of activities and the development of abilities (q.v.) are advocated not for their own sake but in order to succeed in the practice of other (similar) activities and "acquire" other abilities. The results of empirical investigations are in part contradictory. In the main they do not confirm expectations, which have been set too high. *H.Schr.*

Formatio reticularis (*Reticular formation*). A reticular structure of nerve cells and short nerve fibers in the region of the brain-stem and midbrain, reaching to the hypothalamus and forming the prolongation in the spinal cord (q.v.) of the short intermediate neurons to the extrapyramidal system. The *formatio reticularis* is provided with collateral fibers and thus with information from all centrifugal and centripetal conduction paths. By inhibiting and stimulating the thalamus and cortex (q.v.) it controls the individual's state of wakefulness and attention. Destruction of these substances in experiments on animals produces loss of consciousness which can be restored by means of LSD (lysergic acid diethylamide brings about reversible mental changes accompanied by hallucinatory symptoms). *E.D.*

Formboards. First used on the feebleminded by E. Seguin (1846), then developed as a test by Goddard (1915). A variety of wooden shapes (circles, squares, crosses, etc.) have of be fitted into matching depressions in a board. In the *casuist formboard* designed by R. Pinter & D. G. Paterson the subject is required to fill the depression by inserting into it a number of different shapes. In G. A. Lienert's *formlaying test,* four flat pieces must be put together to form specified figures. In the *Minnesota Paper Form Board* the subject must pick out the figure that can be assembled. *R.M.*

Form constancy. See *Shape constancy.*

Foster children. Children who are brought up by foster or adoptive parents. A number of studies of adopted children, their natural and their foster-parents have been made to help elucidate the development of intelligence (q.v.) and personality (q.v.) as conditioned by heredity and environment. The data suggest that environment and the methods used by the foster-parents to rear the children do influence their development, but that characteristics found in their own parents are also of some importance. A quite positive interpretation of the results is not possible because it is difficult to avoid methodological defects.

Bibliography: Anastasia, A.: Differential psychology. New York, [3]1958. *D.B.*

Foucault's law. The velocity of light through water is less than that through air. Jean Léon Foucault (1819–68) carried out the crucial experiments to determine that light passes more rapidly through rarer than denser media, thus finally refuting the emission theory (corpuscular theory), which maintained the opposite, and further confirming wave theory.

Fourier analysis. Based on a mathematical model (q.v.) (see *Fourier's law*) in which complex functions of a variable (e.g. time) are represented as the sum of an (in general) infinite series of sine and cosine terms. The resolution of the function into its components according to this model is known as Fourier analysis. See *Mathematical psychology; Statistics.*

Bibliography: Edwards, R. E.: Fourier series—a modern introduction. Oxford, 1967. *W.H.B.*

Fourier's law. A mathematical model (q.v.) of the composition of a complex periodic function (oscillation) from an (in general) infinite series of sine and cosine functions. Such an oscillation is resolved into a series of harmonic functions (see *Fourier analysis*) by means of the polynomial $Y = a_0 + a_1 \cos t + b_1 \sin t + a_2 \cos 2t + b_2 \sin 2t + \ldots$ *W.H.B.*

Four Picture Test (syn. *Lennep Test*). A projective technique (Lennep, 1930) assumed to reveal an individual's social relations as they affect his personality. It consists of four ambiguous water-color style pictures, each representing an important social situation; S. has to arrange these in a sequence so that they tell a sequacious story. Interpretation is usually qualitative and based on depth-psychological criteria; empirically obtained norms are not available.

Bibliography: Lennep, D. J.: Manual of the four picture test. Utrecht, [2]1958. *P.G.*

Fovea. A shallow pit (0·5 mm diameter) at the center of the 5 mm-diameter *macula lutea* (see *Yellow spot*). The depression is due to the absence at this point of the retinal ganglionic cell layers (ganglionic *retinae* and ganglionic *fasciculi optici*) below the sensory cells, as a result of which the neuroepithelium, here consisting entirely of cones (q.v.) and permeated with yellow pigment that is soluble in alcohol, lies exposed against the vitreous humor. The macula as a whole contains about 100,000 cones which, without converging, are each connected to a bipolar ganglionic cell and further to an optic ganglionic cell, whose prolongations reach to the *papilla fasciculi optici* (see *Blind spot*). (This contrasts with the outer edges of the retina where many cones or rods (q.v.) converge to an optic fiber, so that resolution is impaired.) Because of this, and the fact that it is unencumbered by cell layers (also refracting), the fovea is the area of the most distinct vision. *K.H.P.*

Fractionation. A method of introspection, associated with the Würzburg School, which involves the concentration of attention, according to the instructions of the experimenter, onto different parts or phases (fractions) of the total process or phenomenon which is being observed. Also, in statistics, the division of data into different groups for separate analysis. *G.D.W.*

Frame. Equivalent to *item, step;* the smallest component in a learning program (q.v.)—originally part of a program strip appearing in the window or frame of a teaching machine. A frame contains as a rule a piece of information (q.v.), a call for a response, a report (q.v.) back to the learner as to the correctness of his response, and—where the program is not computer-controlled—instructions regarding further stages of the program. The size of a frame can range from a single statement to be completed by the learner (*Skinner program*) to several paragraphs (*Crowder program*). *L.J.I.*

Frame of reference. A basis for comparison when perceiving and judging the facts of a case. (*a*) *A lasting frame of reference:* during the course of his development a person forms on the basis of his experience norms to which he unconsciously refers when judging anything. These criteria agree in large measure as between individuals as well as inside any culture, and this is one of the most important prerequisites for communication and mutual understanding. The center (also zero) of the single criteria is often termed the adaptation level (q.v.), according to Helson (1947). (*b*) *A temporary frame of reference.* This is especially constructed in perception by adaptation (q.v.) to the prevailing stimulus situation. If the stimulus factor changes, the new situation will be subject to renewed adaptation. See *Optical illusions; Weber's law.* Reference must be made to more recent investigations by Witte.

Bibliography: Helson, H.: Adaptation-level theory. In: **Koch, S.** (Ed.): Psychology, a study of a science, Vol. 1. New York, 1959, 565–621. **Witte, W.:** Zur Struktur von Bezugssystemen. Göttingen, 1956.

H.-J.A.

Frankfurt tests. Prepared and standardized for use in schools by the Hochschule für internationale pädagogische Forschung under E. Hylla, comprising verbal selection tests, tasks for reflection, analogy test (q.v.), arithmetical test, number sequences, and spelling. *R.M.*

Free association. See *Association, free.*

Free choice method (ant. *Selection method,* (q.v.). A form of programmed instruction (q.v.) in which the response of the addressee is made up of a sequence of individual responses from a pre-existing repertoire (e.g. a sequence of typewriter strokes). In the *simple* (or *word*) free choice method, an endless number of such sequences is provided for the branches (q.v.) of the learning algorithm (q.v.). In the *real* (or *event*) free choice method, classes of equivalent sequences are defined (and not merely by enumerating their elements in full). *H.F.*

Freedom. Decision and freedom of choice play a central role in the psychology of personality. All modern theories of personality (q.v.) agree as to the existence of relative, but not absolute, free will. Man is independent, and responsible for his acts, within the bounds of his personal constitution (q.v.). Freedom is a factor of special importance at law in establishing guilt and meting out punishment; i.e. in forensic psychology (q.v.).

The individual's margin of freedom is determined first by his psychophysical constitution (see *Traits; Abilities*) and then by sociocultural influences, e.g. his environment (q.v.) and the age he lives in. All physical and mental processes take place within a general ordered system that obeys the rules of cybernetics—the matching of actual and desired values (see *Homeostasis*). The biological and psychological feedback systems (q.v.), like mechanical controls, can be regulated only because they function systematically and are therefore determinable within limits and to some extent predictable (probability principle). Decisions of conscience (see *Conscience*) are also taken within an ordered system. Actual values—deeds, attitudes—have to be brought into line with desired values (commandments, virtues, norms). Degrees of freedom (q.v.) within the framework of the individual constitution vary from person to person, and the capacity for freedom of each is an individual one, i.e. indivisible. Owing to the existence of individual degrees of freedom, a man's character and personality traits are more than a system of purely reactive behavior. He is endowed with a will and the ability to take decisions. To this extent he can also act spontaneously and, within the limits of his capacity for freedom, is responsible for his acts and omissions. See *Type; Will.*

Bibliography: Arnold, W.: Freiheit und Verantwortung in psychol. Sicht. Schweiz. Z. Psychol. Anwend. No. 1/2, 1970. **Id.:** Über die sozialpsychol. Notwendigkeit der Unterscheidung von selbsttätigen, organischen und mechanischen Regelprozessen. In: Rep. of 12th Ger. Psychol. Cong. in Würzburg. Göttingen, 1963. **Eysenck, H. J.:** Crime and personality. London, 1964. **Kay, W.:** Moral development. London, 1968.

W.A.

Freedom, degrees of. See *Degrees of freedom.*

Freedom, reflex of. The reflex by which animals deprived of their usual freedom try to release themselves. Described by Pavlov as a "common trait, a general reaction of animals, and one of the most important of inborn reflexes", and exemplified for him by its unusual persistence in one dog obstinately resistant to any limitation of his freedom of movement.

Frequency. Frequency denotes the number of times that an event of a specific type or size occurs (the number of elements of a population—random sample—belonging to a specific category). Frequency $f(X)$ is brought into relation with the total number of N observations by means of the relative frequency $(pX) = f(X)/N$. See *Frequency distributions.*

W.H.B.

Frequency distributions are systematic (numerical or graphic) compilations of the observed frequencies (f_i) of all categories (X_i) of a (simple or composite) characteristic or score. In the socio-biological sciences they generally represent the first step in processing raw data. Normally, the number (N) of individual observations (on individuals, in situations, etc.) considerably exceeds the number (i) of stages or classes of the observation material. For example, the observational variable "sex" can only be recorded in two stages while "number of syllables noted" can only vary, depending on the extent of the series, in the classes "0·1 . . ." correct reproductions; on the other hand, dozens or even hundreds of cases are observed. Frequency distributions are divided according to the number of variables observed simultaneously into univariate, bivariate and multivariate types; a distinction is also made according to the type of variable (nominal, ordinal, intervening and relation variables, scaling, psychological methods). In the case of nominal variables the sequence of individual classes is immaterial or corresponds to an external convention. The commonest example in psychology is the frequency distribution of an intervening variable, e.g. distribution of points (number of correct solutions) scored by each person in a series of problems.

In the case of intervening variables, and ordinal or relational variables, the classes X_i are ranked by magnitude. If the number of cases is not much larger than the number of classes, a frequency distribution can only be obtained by assembling classes. For example, in the case of age distributions in small samples of adults, the classes (age indication in years) are grouped together in larger ten-year groups, such as 20 to 29, 30 to 39, 40 to 49, etc. If several frequency distributions have to be compared, it is useful to indicate the relative frequencies (probabilities) $p = \frac{f_i}{N}$ for the individual classes instead of the absolute frequency values.

Frequency distributions can also be represented in graphic form; the classes of the characteristic are entered on the abscissa and the frequencies on the ordinate.

Each class is defined either by its limits or by the figure X, which represents the class. In empirical distributions, X_i as abscissa values, and f_i as ordinate values, are *discrete* (discontinuous) magnitudes, i.e. they can only assume specific (e.g. whole number) values. Certain theoretical distributions are also discrete functions, e.g. the binomial distribution and Poisson's distribution. On the other hand, many distributions used in mathematical statistics (e.g. the standard distribution, the F distribution, t distribution, etc.) involve a transition from a finite number of cases N to an infinite number, and from a finite number of classes X to an infinite number; these are presented in the general form of a function $y = f(x)$ (x = abscissa value for the dimension scale, y = ordinate value for the "distribution density"). Both parameters therefore become continuously variable.

The cumulative distribution is a special form (assuming at least an ordinal scale). In this case, we do not determine the frequencies of the individual classes but the overall frequency f_i up to a specific class i (or a specific point on the scale such as the central point of each class). The cumulative distribution can also be represented as a probability distribution of the values.

The determination of an empirical frequency distribution has a practical and theoretical significance. Its practical significance is (*a*) to facilitate a general survey of all available data. Instead of individual figures, we have a frequency table with two columns containing relatively few numerical values which give a provisional impression of the position (central tendency, mean value), dispersion (variability, scatter), and course of the distribution (distribution form). (*b*) With a frequency distribution it is possible without mechanical aid to calculate much more quickly than from the individual data the different characteristics (such as mean value, scatter, skew, kurtosis). From the theoretical angle, frequency distributions are important because they enable hypotheses to be established on the occurrence of a specific, formally definable (generally by means of very few parameters) distribution type (e.g. standard distribution, logarithmic standard distribution, exponential function, power function, etc.) and further assumptions to be made on the effective mechanism which determines the processes underlying the characteristic variation.

For example, the occurrence of observed data following a precise standard distribution would show that the observed characteristic (measured in an adequate interval scale) varies as a result of random variation of a large number of independent, individual factors which make up the characteristic additively.

Theoretically recognized frequency distributions occur above all in consideration of the distributions of statistics (sampling scores). The fact that many distributions of sampling scores are theoretically known, allows a quantitative determination of the uncertainty of sample results in research (sampling error, limits of reliability, significance of differences between two or more sample values).

Bivariate frequency distributions occur if associated pairs of observations of two variables can be formed. They are found most commonly in correlational and regression statistics. The formation of observational pairs is frequently based in psychology (*a*) on the use of two types of measurement on the same individual (e.g. manual skill and performance), (*b*) on the repetition of measurements on the same individual (e.g. passing of the same intelligence test at three-year intervals).

The shape of the bivariate distribution, or better still the pattern of mean values of the regression lines (curves), gives an initial idea of the nature and degree of statistical association between two features (correlation).

For example, the linear correlation is more accurate the greater the number of values grouped around one of the two diagonals of the distribution. See *Correlational techniques; Factor analysis.* *E. Mittenecker*

Frequency histogram. This is a form of graphic representation of frequency distributions (q.v.). A rectangle is drawn over each class of score for a variable in such a way that the length of the vertical lines corresponds to the frequencies in the classes. The histogram is mainly used to represent the frequency distributions of qualitative criteria. *W.H.B.*

Frequency polygon. A diagram showing the form of a frequency distribution (q.v.) of a quantitatively recorded characteristic in a two-dimensional system of coordinates. A frequency polygon differs from a frequency histogram (q.v.) in that the frequencies plotted over the class marks are joined together by a line. The area below the frequency polygon corresponds to that shown by a histogram of the same distribution. *W.H.B.*

Freud, Sigmund. B. 6/5/1856, Freiberg, Moravia; d. 23/9/1939, London; psychiatrist. Commenced academic career in 1885; professor in Vienna from 1902. Creator (with J. Breuer) of psychoanalysis. His researches began with an attempt to treat functional psychological disorders (see *Hysteria; Neuroses*) by suggestion (q.v.) and hypnosis (q.v.). In this he was influenced by the works of J. M. Charcot, H. M. Liebault and A. A. Bernheim. Freud's "psychocathartic" treatment is based on bringing back to consciousness repressed emotions, and releasing them by abreaction. The working up of these techniques into the psychoanalytic method led to the replacement of hypnosis by dream (q.v.) interpretation, free association (q.v.) and the analysis of lapses in behavior (see *Freudian slips*). Freud's insights into the structure of drives and the significance of the unconscious for psychic activity elicited an eager response from his supporters and pupils. Even though his views were later disputed in certain points (see *Adler; Jung*), Freud became the decisive force in depth psychology (q.v.). Nor should one underestimate the influence his life and work had on the development of scientific psychology in the twentieth century. Freud's co-workers and pupils include S. Ferenczi, A. Adler, W. Stekel, P. Federn, O. Pfister, O. Rank, and his daughter Anna Freud. See *Psychoanalysis.*

Works: The Standard Edition of the Complete Psychological Works of Sigmund Freud, 24 vols, Ed. J. Strachey & A. Freud. London, 1953–70. Gesammelte Werke, London, 1948–.

Some major separate works are: An autobiographical study. London, 1935. Beyond the pleasure principle. London, ^{2}1959. Civilization and its discontents. London, ^{2}1963. The ego and the id. London, ^{2}1962. The interpretation of dreams, London, 1955. Introductory lectures on psycho-analysis. London, ^{2}1959. Jokes and their relation to the unconscious. London, 1960. New introductory lectures on psycho-analysis. London, 1933. The origins of psycho-analysis. London, 1954. An outline of psychoanalysis. London, ^{2}1959. Three essays on the theory of sexuality, London, ^{2}1962. Totem and taboo. London, 1950. Studies on hysteria (with J. Breuer). London, 1956. Dreams in folklore (with D. E. Oppenheim). New York, 1958.

Bibliography: Arlow, J. A.: The legacy of Sigmund Freud. New York, 1956. **Binswanger, L.:** Erinnerungen an Sigmund Freud. Stuttgart, 1956. **Bernfield, S.:** Freud's earliest theories and the school of Helmholtz. Psychoan. Q., 1944, *13*, 341–62. **Brinkmann, D.:** Probleme des Unbewussten. Berne, 1943. **Fromm, E.:** Sigmund Freud's mission. London, 1959. **Jones, E.:** Sigmund Freud: life and work, 3 vols. London, 1953–7. **Lee, S. G. & Herbert, M.:** Freud and psychology. Harmondsworth, 1970. **Schraml, D.:** Einführung in die Tiefenpsychologie. Stuttgart, 1968. **Shakow, D. & Rapaport, D.:** The influence of Freud on American psychology. New York, 1964. **Wollheim, R.:** Freud. London, 1971. *K.E.P.*

Freudian slips. Acts that are out of place, serve ends other than those intended, or are mistakenly left undone, including such inadvertent errors as slips of the tongue (*lapsus linguae*) and slips of the pen (*lapsus calami*). Freud described such cases of mislaying, forgetting, lapses in speech, and so on, and tried to show that they were motivated by an unconscious desire. Examples: "I welcome those present and declare the sitting closed" (for "open, but I wish it were closed"); hostess to guest glancing at his watch: "Don't stay. Can't you go?" Most everyday blunders are commonplace and lack significant motivation for those concerned, e.g. errors in typing, in totting up figures. The possible personal significance of a mistake is first brought out by the improbability of its occurrence and its relatively protracted effects, and only then justifies the time and expense involved in analysis and interpretation.

Bibliography: Freud, S.: Psychopathology of everyday life. New York, 1914. **Id.:** Introductory lectures on psycho-analysis. London, [2]1929. *W.T.*

Freudian theory embraces the dynamic model of psychic structures (id, ego, super-ego, q.v.), the schema of psychic (libidinal) development of persons (oral, anal and genital stages, q.v.), and the psychoanalytical schema of psychopathology (q.v.). These were the fruit of observation of thoughts and emotions freely expressed during the psychoanalytic treatment of mentally disturbed patients. This treatment includes the temporary transference (q.v.) of the patient's feelings toward persons of his childhood to the psychotherapist, and the overcoming of resistance to the perception and experience of his own unconscious, and often infantile, wishes and motives. See *Freud, S.*

Bibliography: Toman, W.: Dynamik der Motive. Vienna, 1954. See also *Freud, S.* *W.T.*

Friedman test. A distribution-free analysis of variance (q.v.) for the simultaneous testing of the significance (q.v.) of the results of correlating samples (q.v.) in the presence of two independent variables (q.v.). Used mainly in evaluating "Kendall designs", repeated measurements carried out on the same sample under varying conditions. *W.H.B.*

Frigidity. A woman's inability to obtain satisfaction in the performance of the sexual act. Often due merely to a lack of harmony between the partners in regard to sexual wishes and behavior, which prevents adequate stimulation. In all this, cultural rejection of various practices can also play a part. Psychoanalysis attributes frigidity to ill-managed parental love, faultily developed penis envy, and imperfect transfer of capacity for stimulation from the clitoris to the *introitus vaginae.* According to psychoanalytic theory, one can result from the other, and components of aggressive inhibition often also appear. The existence of two types of orgasm, associated respectively with the vagina and clitoris, is rejected as unproven by modern sexual psychology. *U.H.S.*

Frontal lobes (Lat. sing.: *lobus frontalis*) are among the most complicated parts of the brain (q.v.) to have evolved at a very late stage. In the lower mammals they are still rudimentary, and only in man, in whom they account for 25 per cent of the brain's bulk, are they fully developed.

The cortex of the frontal lobes covers both the premotor area, which is concerned with the functions of movement (Broadmann's areas 6 and 8) and the prefrontal (granular) cortex (Broadmann's areas 9, 10, 11, 46) which carries out the more complex functions and ensures the overall organization, within specific programs, of man's voluntary activities.

Views about the functions of the frontal lobes have changed since the early days of brain physiology and neurology (see *Neurophysiology*) and have to some extent become contradictory; the original belief was that they had no special function, the current belief is that they are the supreme organ of the brain.

Such contradictions are due to the fact that the frontal lobes—and especially their prefrontal sections—do not directly carry out rudimentary functions of feeling and movement, so that damage to them leads neither to disturbance of sensibility nor to impairment of speech or movement. Their function cannot, therefore, be described in terms of elementary neurology.

The frontal lobes, however, are crucial for the course of complicated psychological processes.

As they are closely connected with the *formatio reticularis* (q.v.), they play a vital role in the regulation of the state of activity ("wakefulness") of the cerebral cortex by maintaining the requisite tonus in expectation of information or preparation for activity. Massive damage to the frontal lobes thus leads to reduced activity and the impossibility of carrying difficult intentions into effect. In addition, after such damage the necessary program of activity ceases to play a dominant role, and casual impressions and impulses are no longer inhibited.

Patients suffering from extensive lesions of the frontal lobes are unable to carry out difficult behavioral programs, to switch from one activity to another, or to impart to their behavior a complex purposive character. Their speech is dominated by echolalias (q.v.) or perseverations (q.v.). Difficult forms of intellectual activity become disorganized and give way to uncontrolled associations or inert stereotypes. Damage of this kind also renders the sufferer unable to compare his acts with his original intentions, or to judge the effects of these acts and control their course while correcting any errors that creep in.

All this shows that the frontal lobes play a central role in self-regulation of the complicated forms of conscious psychic activity, and that they are an important component of that cerebral apparatus called the "acceptor of behavior" (P. K. Anochin) or TOTE (test/operate, text/exit—K. Pribram, J. Miller, E. Galanter). Precisely because of this, extensive damage to the frontal lobes leads to the clinically familiar symptoms of aspontaneity and "disorders of critical faculty". Limited damage to the frontal lobes, on the other hand (because of the high replacement capacity of their nerve tissue), need not cause any marked symptoms.

The latest research points to differentiation of the functions of the various areas of the frontal lobes, the outer areas being closely associated with control of movement, the mediobasal areas with the control of affective processes.

Bibliography: Luria, A. R.: Higher cortical functions in man. New York, 1962. **Id. & Pribram, K.** (Eds): The behavioral physiology of the frontal lobes. New York, 1970. **Warren, J. M. & Akezt, K.** (Eds): The frontal granular cortex and behavior. New York, 1964. **Id.:** Frontal lobe syndromes. In: **Vinken, P. J. & Bruyn, G. W.:** Handbook of clinical neurology, Vol. 2. Amsterdam, 1969. **Id. & Hornskaya, E. D.** (Eds): Frontal ideas and regulation of the psychological processes. Moscow, 1966 (in Russian).

A. R. Luria

Frustration. 1. *Terminology.* Three different meanings of the term "frustration" must be distinguished:

(*a*) *Frustrating situation.* Strict definitions have been used by Maier (1949), for whom the essential characteristics are an insoluble problem situation, impossibility of moving out of the situation, and high motivation to respond; and by Amsel (1958, 1962), for whom a frustrating situation is one in which non-rewarded trials are interspersed with, or follow, rewarded trials. Broader definitions have been summarized by Lawson & Marx (1958) and Brown & Farber (1951) who include as frustrating situations the introduction of partial or complete physical barriers, the omission or reduction of reward, delay between initiation and completion of a response sequence, failure with possibility of success implied, and infliction of punishment.

(*b*) *Frustration state.* The frustrating situation will induce a state of frustration in the organism, the degree of frustration varying between individuals. Measures of the strength of frustration should not be the same as those used to assess the reaction to the frustration state, otherwise circularity of argument is involved. This requirement has often been neglected. The frustration state may be measured directly (e.g. by GSR activity or pulse rate) or it may be treated as an intervening variable, not directly measurable. The term "frustration tolerance" (Rosenzweig, 1944) refers to individual differences (innate or acquired) in the capacity to tolerate frustrating situations.

(*c*) *Reaction to frustration.* The principal reactions to the frustration state which have been studied in detail are aggression (q.v.), regression, fixation, and increased or decreased strength of response.

2. *Frustration-aggression hypothesis.* This hypothesis, advanced by Dollard *et al.* (1939) stated that "aggression is always a consequence of frustration" and "the occurrence of aggressive behavior always presupposes the existence of frustration" (p. 1). Aggression was defined as "an act whose goal-response is injury to an organism (or organism-surrogate" (Dollard *et al.*, 1939, p. 8). The theory is circular since frustration is defined in terms of aggression, and vice versa. The strength of instigation to aggression is a function of the strength of instigation to the frustrated response, the degree of interference with the frustrated response, the number of frustrated response sequences, and the number of non-aggressive responses extinguished through non-reinforcement as frustration persists. The instigation to aggression will be inhibited as a function of the amount of punishment anticipated as a consequence of performing the aggressive act. Aggressive behavior will generalize to other objects along a generalization continuum, but may be displaced onto other objects if the behavior toward the primary object of aggression is inhibited. The occurrence of an aggressive act will reduce the instigation to aggression (catharsis). The theory has been applied more generally, particularly to the explanation of prejudice. Criticisms of the theory (Yates, 1962) have centered upon problems relating to the measurement of aggressive behavior, the generality of aggressiveness, the relationship between overt and fantasy aggressiveness, and the probability that much aggressive behavior results from learning rather than frustration.

3. *Frustration-regression hypothesis.* Barker *et al.* (1941) stated that frustration leads to regression which is defined as "a primitivation of behavior, a 'going back' to a less mature state which the individual has already outgrown" (p. 1). Regression may occur with respect to the original goal of the person, or other forms of activity. Barker *et al.* studied the constructiveness of play of children who, following a period of free play with toys of differing degrees of attractiveness, were deprived of the more attractive toys which were still visible, however, through a wire-mesh barrier. Regressive behavior was indexed by a decline in constructiveness of play with the less attractive toys, and the appearance of other forms of behavior, such as approach to the barrier. An alternative explanation in terms of competing response tendencies was put forward by Child & Waterhouse (1952). Experimental support for their position may be derived from studies of instrumental act regression (e.g. Whiting & Mowrer, 1943).

4. *Frustration-fixation hypothesis.* Using the Lashley jumping-stand technique, Maier (1949) showed that rats presented with an insoluble problem situation would develop stereotyped forms of behavior indistinguishable from the behavior of rats in a soluble problem situation. However, when the insoluble problem situation was made soluble, the rats were unable to modify their stereotyped behavior, which Maier termed "fixated". Maier considered that such fixated behavior manifested characteristics which could not be accounted for in terms of conventional

learning theory (e.g. the behavior was not modifiable by punishment; was permanent; and highly specific). Fixated behavior could be modified only by a technique known as *guidance*. Alternative explanations of Maier's results were advanced by Farber (1948) (fixations as anxiety-reducing responses); Wilcoxon (1952) (fixations as the result of partial reinforcement schedules of training); and Wolpe (fixations as learned responses reducing primary drive). Maier (1956) has rejected these alternative explanations while significantly modifying his earlier position.

5. *Frustration and learning theory.* Brown & Farber (1951) suggested that frustration

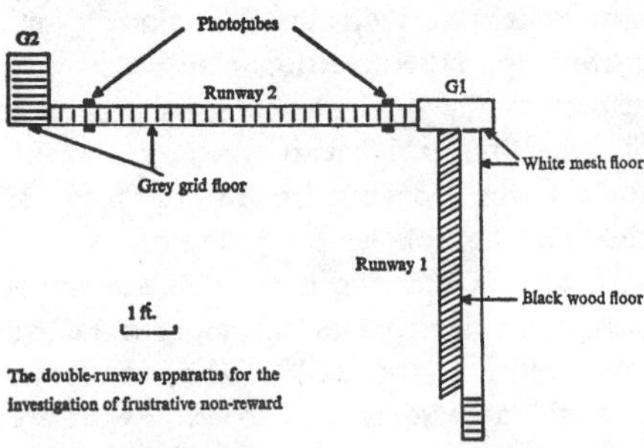

Figure 1. The double runway apparatus for the investigation of frustrative non-reward.

may produce two general effects: an increase in the general level of motivation (drive); and the production of internal drive-stimuli which serve as conditioned cues mediating escape or avoidance responses. Empirical evidence supporting both these propositions stems mainly from the work of Amsel (1958, 1962). That frustration produced drive-increment was demonstrated in the double-runway apparatus (Figure 1). After training in running through G_1 to G_2 (food being available in both goal-boxes) food was omitted in G_1 (frustrating situation defined by non-reward following reward) and an increment in running speed in runway 2 was found. The cue properties of frustration stimulation were demonstrated in a study by Adelman & Maatsch (1955) who argued that frustration as a drive-stimulus (S_f) will elicit several responses, the one which is strengthened being that which removes the organism from the frustrating situation. This approach has mediated a substantial body of experimentation and theoretical controversy (Longstreth, 1966; Hill, 1968) and has been used to explain children's reactions to non-reward in a variety of experimental situations (Ryan & Watson, 1968).

6. *Reviews of the literature.* Critical analyses of the literature on frustration may be found in Yates (1962), Lawson & Marx (1958) and Lawson (1965), while Amsel (1958, 1962) has critically analyzed the experimental work on frustrative non-reward situations.

7. *Conclusion.* Two distinct approaches to the study of frustration are discernible. First, there is the series of studies of a broad kind relating frustration to aggression, regression and fixation; second, a later series of laboratory-based investigations on the effects of frustrative non-reward producing drive and cue effects. It might have been expected that cross-fertilization would have resulted in a revival of interest in the frustration-aggression/regression/fixation hypotheses. This cross-fertilization has unfortunately not yet occurred. As Lawson (1965) has pointed out, this may be because of a belief that aggression, regression and fixation may be reducible to more fundamental operations.

Bibliography: Adelman, H. M. & Maatsch, J. L.: Resistance to extinction as a function of the type of response elicited by frustration. J.exp.Psychol., 1955, *50*, 61–5. **Amsel, A.:** The role of frustrative nonreward in noncontinuous reward situations. Psychol. Bull., 1958, *55*, 102–19. **Id.:** Frustrative nonreward in partial reinforcement and discrimination learning: some recent history and a theoretical extension. Psychol. Rev., 1962, *69*, 306–28. **Barker, R. C., Dembo, T. & Lewin, K.:** Frustration and regression: an experiment with young children. Univer. Iowa Studies in Child Welfare, 1941, *18*, No. 1. **Brown, J. S. & Farber, I. E.:** Emotions conceptualized as intervening variables—with suggestions toward a theory of frustration. Psychol. Bull., 1951, *48*, 465–95. **Child, I. L. & Waterhouse, I. K.:** Frustration and the quality of performance: I. A critique of the Barker, Dembo and Lewin experiment. Psychol. Rev., 1952, *59*, 351–62. **Dollard, J., Miller, N. E., Doob, L. W., Mowrer, O. H. & Sears, R. R.:** Frustration and aggression. New Haven, 1939. **Farber, I. E.:** Response fixation under anxiety and nonanxiety conditions. J. exp. Psychol., 1948, *38*, 111–31. **Hill, W. F.:** An attempted clarification of frustration theory. Psychol. Rev., 1968, *75*, 173–6. **Lawson, R.:** Frustration: the development of a scientific concept. New York, 1965. **Id. & Marx, M. H.:** Frustration: theory and experiment. Genet. Psychol. Monogr., 1958, *57*, 393–464. **Longstreth, L. E.:** Frustration and secondary reinforcement concepts as applied to human conditioning and extinction. Psychol. Monogr., 1966, *80*, No. 11 (whole No. 619) (pp. 29). **Maier, N. R. F.:** Frustration: the study of behavior without a goal. New York, 1949. **Id.:** Frustration theory: restatement and extension. Psychol. Rev., 1956, *63*, 370–88. **Ryan, T. J. & Watson, P.:** Frustrative nonreward theory applied to children's behavior. Psychol. Bull., 1968, *69*, 111–25. **Rosenzweig, S.:** An outline of frustration theory. In: **Hunt, J. McV.** (Ed.): Personality and the behavior disorders. New York, 1944. **Whiting, J. W. M. & Mowrer, O. H.:** Habit progression and regression—a laboratory study of some factors relevant to human socialization. J. comp. Psychol., 1943, *36*, 229–53. **Wilcoxon, H. C.:** "Abnormal fixation" and learning. J. exp. Psychol., 1952, *44*, 324–33. **Yates, A. J.:** Frustration and conflict. New York, 1962.

A. J. Yates

Frustration-aggression hypothesis. The theory that frustration always leads to aggression (although sometimes concealed or indirectly manifested, as in scapegoating), and that aggression is always a result of frustration. See *Frustration*. *G.D.W.*

Frustration-fixation hypothesis. Refers to the experimental finding that animals often persist in performing inadequate and non-adaptive responses when continually frustrated or placed in a situation of strong avoidance-avoidance conflict (the choice of two unpleasant outcomes). In a well-known experiment using the jumping-stand apparatus, rats were forced by electric shock to jump toward one of two doors. The door marked with one pattern always opened on impact, giving the rat access to a food reward, whereas the door marked with another pattern resulted only in a severe bump on the nose. When this visual discrimination problem was made particularly difficult, some rats *fixated* on a non-adaptive response such as jumping always to one side, or between the two doors. See *Frustration*. *G.D.W.*

Frustration-regression hypothesis. The hypothesis that frustration often gives rise to a reversion to primitive or early-learned responses which are usually less adaptive than other possible alternative modes of behavior (e.g. crying, throwing things around). The hypothesis also implies that regression to relatively immature behavior is normally a result of frustration. *G.D.W.*

Frustration tests. See *Picture frustration test*.

Frustration tolerance. Capacity for putting up with passing or lasting deprivation (q.v.) (see also *Frustration*) of satisfaction of motives, i.e. the postponement or forgoing of satisfaction. Dependent on constitutional characteristics such as reaction, perception and learning capacity, as well as inborn components of affective development. Under normal conditions, frustration tolerance is also largely dependent on the individual's experience, the way in which his motives have been satisfied or frustrated in the past. Frustration tolerance ranks as one of the most direct indicators of *ego strength* (q.v.). In psychopathological personality disorders, frustration tolerance declines with the severity of the disorder. According to Toman, it is finally defined in terms of (*a*) the different average rates of learning as between individuals (in Estes' sense), which indicate changes in the probability of the reactions in recurrent situations; (*b*) the individual's average rate of motive differentiation (see *Energy, psychic*); and (*c*) the individual's state of knowledge or the extent to which he has been forced by his environment to forgo satisfaction and knowledge. Frustration tolerance can be regarded as an individual's tolerance to variations in K (K = sum of all present motive intensities

K_i). When at any moment a great many motives remain unsatisfied, K is high; when many motives have just been satisfied, K is low. The mean of K,

$$K = \frac{1}{{}^nK^i} = \sum_1^{{}^nK} K_i,$$

obtained from K values of the numbeɪ ${}^nK$ measured at intervals of time, tends toward unity. When a series of further measurements of K lies clearly above unity, a stress condition exists. When the measurements lie clearly below unity, a state ranging from relaxation to boredom is present. Popular synonyms for frustration tolerance are *strength of will* and *self-discipline*.

Bibliography: **Estes, W. K.:** Toward a statistical theory of learning. Psychol. Rev. 1950, *57*, 94–106. **Freud, S.:** The ego and the id. London, [2]1962. **Toman, W.:** Motivation, Persönlichkeit, Umwelt. Göttingen, 1968. *W.T.*

FSH (*Follicle stimulating hormone*) stimulates the growth of Graafian follicle; secretion is inhibited by LH (luteinizing hormone), also known as ICSH (interstitial cell stimulating hormone)—induced estrogen formation. FSH is secreted in the anterior lobe of the pituitary, secretion being controlled by an FSH-RF (FSH releasing factor), a neurosecretion from the sexual center of the hypothalamus. FSH is a glycoprotein, FSH-RF a polypeptide. *U.H.S.*

F test. A statistical test for ensuring, with the aid of the variance ratio

$$F = \frac{S^21}{S^22}$$

that the difference between the variances (q.v.) of two (sample) distributions are not affected by a random event ($df_1 = N_1 - 1$; $df_2 = N_2 - 1$). This variance ratio is known as the F value. Its distribution (see *F distribution*) obeys R. A. Fisher's F-function and depends on the size of samples N_1 and N_2. Critical F values, which correspond to current significance limits, are given in most textbooks for df_1 and df_2. The F test is used mainly for testing the significance of mean value variations by analysis of variance. *W.H.B.*

Function. **1.** In biology, psychology, and sociology, the purpose, role, or reason for the survival of a structure (organic, mental, social, etc.). E.g., the *function* of sex drive is reproduction of the species. Thus a *functional disorder* may refer either to a disorder of some function, or to a disorder which is itself functional (i.e. provides a *secondary gain*).

2. In mathematics, a function is a relationship between two or more variables such that the value of one is dependent upon the value of others. E.g. work performance is a *function* of ability and motivation. *G.D.W.*

Functional ambivalence. G. E. Müller's term for indefinite phases of conceptual thought which attain to clarity when determinate content becomes available.

Functional area. In Uexküll's sense, the functional area (*Funktionskreis*) is an ethological concept; it comprises the inner and outer, subjective and objective world. The interaction of characteristics and effective characteristics within the functional area conditions the differentiation of the system.

Bibliography: **Uexküll, I. J.:** Umwelt and Innenwelt der Tiere. Berlin, [2]1921. *K.E.P.*

Functional autonomy. The notion of G. W. Allport that some motives originally acquired in relation to physiological needs tend to function quite independently at a later stage. This concept is used by Allport and others to explain the persistence of certain habits long after the motives which led to their acquisition have ceased to be operative (e.g. continuing to amass money after one has already made a fortune). *G.D.W.*

Functional defects. Defects of the closely interwoven psychophysical organism as a whole. These are often due to faulty control in the autonomic nervous system (q.v.). The organic system is, however, left intact (in contrast to organic defects, in which a causative organic substrate is always detected). Such defects are mostly neurotic in origin. J. H. Schultz describes neurosis as an "impairment of function of the whole living organism". *H.N.G.*

Functional drives. A term used by H. Rohracher to characterize certain "drives" featuring the need or compulsion to act in a specific way.

Functionalism. The philosophical doctrine of W. James (q.v.) which considers mental phenomena in their dynamic unity as a system of functions (geared to adapting the organism to its environment) for the satisfaction of needs that are biological in origin. Derived from this is an educational theory that sees in the exercise of these functions the primary condition for their development (J. Dewey; E. Claparède). The term is also applied to a trend, started by B. Malinowski, in Anglo-American ethnology (q.v.): if James's approach is applied to social life, this appears as an organism comprehended through the relationship existing between organs and their functions. A. R. Radcliffe-Brown (1930) lays stress on the unitary character of the social organism (leaving aside biological reduction), in which the parts function for the sake of the whole. This theory leads to structuralism, since Radcliffe-Brown's use of the function approaches that of mathematics. *M.-J.B.*

Functional pleasure. It is not the goal or the outcome of activity that produces pleasure, but the exercise of the activity itself. This view of Bühler's is an important contribution to game theory (q.v.).

Bibliography: Bühler, K.: Die Krisis der Psychologie. Jena, [2]1929. Id.: The mental development of the child. New York & London, 1930. *K.E.P.*

Functional sexual disorders occur in the course of the sexual reaction cycles, e.g. premature ejaculation (q.v.), difficult ejaculation and erection in man, and vaginism, faulty vaginal lubrication and anorgasmy (q.v.) in woman. *U.H.S.*

Functions, main. Jung defines as a function of the psyche "an activity which remains identical under different circumstances and is completely independent of given contents". He refers to four main functions: thinking, intuition, feeling, and sensation. Thinking and feeling are said to be rational functions because they both work with "value judgments". Thought proceeds by applying the criterion "true or false", whereas feeling proceeds by means of the emotional criterion of "pleasure—unpleasure". The two other functions (intuition and sensation) are termed "irrational" by Jung because they avoid reason by working with mere perceptions without value judgments or any interpretation of significance. The functional type (e.g. thinking type) of an individual is determined by the functions which predominate in any given case. Assimilation with Jung's two basic personality types, i.e. the introverted type and extraverted type, gives further psychological distinctions such as the introverted thinking type, extraverted thinking type, and so on. *W.Se.*

Functions, principal. Mental processes as distinct from the contents of experience. Pfahler describes the principal functions as consisting of the following: attention, activity, involvement of feeling, and perseveration. Jungians use the term for the rational functions of thinking and feeling, and irrational intuition and sensation.

Bibliography: Jung, C. G.: Psychological types. London & New York, 1923. **Pfahler, G.:** System der Typenlehren. Leipzig, 1943. *B.H.*

Functions, psychic. See *Psychic functions.*

Function types. Named after the four basic mental functions of thinking (q.v.), sensation (q.v.), feeling (q.v.) and intuition (q.v.). The form they assume is determined by attitude types (q.v.). *W.K.*

Fundamental colors are the phenomenologically pure or simple colors; other colors are intermediate. H. von Helmholtz defines red, green and blue as the fundamental (or primary) colors, while E. Hering refers to the four phenomenologically simple colors, red, green, yellow, blue. These are found at the four corners of the color square (q.v.). *G.Ka.*

Furor. Uncontrolled outbreaks of rage or aggression which occur in epileptics as a result of abnormal cerebral excitation. *Furor epilepticus* can occur in the prodromal stages before an epileptic attack or can replace the attack. The latter is known as an "epileptic equivalent" and may be associated with a drop in the level of consciousness. *D.E.*

Fusion. Generally, the combination or blending of two or more elements into one whole. For instance, in perception, *binocular fusion* refers to the combination of the images falling on each retina to give a single perceptual experience. In psychoanalysis, fusion refers to the balanced union of life and death instincts which is supposed to characterize the normal adult, whereas psychiatric conditions are usually supposed to involve some degree of *defusion* of the instincts. *G.D.W.*

Because the two eyes are set at a certain distance apart, only some of the points of an object in the visual field are registered at identical retinal points (q.v.). Most of them are registered at disparate retinal points, so that the image in one eye differs somewhat from that on the other. They are not perceived as double images, however, but are fused into a stereoscopic spatial impression.

Binocular fusion: based on the association of eye movements (q.v.), i.e. as a result of the mixed origin of the oculomotor fibers in the primary cores, which are connected in pairs and to the cores of the fourth (*trochlearis*) and sixth (*abducens*) cranial nerves, the eyes cannot be moved separately.

Tonal fusion: blending of two or more tones so that they appear to fuse when uniformly soft and pleasant to the ear. The result of tonal fusion can be explained largely in terms of accord and harmony. *K.H.P.*

Fusion of stimuli. Stimuli disparate in either space or time may be fused if the differences are not too great. The fusion of stimuli slightly disparate in space is the basis of depth perception and stereoscopy (see *Horizontal disparity*). The fusion of stimuli disparate in time is the basis of the *critical flicker fusion* test and the two-flash threshold, the latter being the longest interval between two flashes at which they still appear as one. The apparent movement produced by a succession of discrete stimuli, as in the cinema, is also an example of the fusion of stimuli. *C.D.F.*

G

GABA. See *Gamma-amino-butyric acid.*

Gait. Modes of walking in human and animal locomotion considered from the anatomical and physiological viewpoints. Klemm's work ([2]1954) on the rhythm and gestalt characteristics of gait is particularly well-known to psychologists. Kietz's studies ([2]1966) are especially important for the expressive psychological aspects of gait (see *Expression*). Smieskol (1968) summarizes more than 700 publications on the subject.

Bibliography: Kietz, G.: Gang und Seele. Munich, [2]1966. **Klemm, O.:** Leistung. In: Ganzheit und Struktur. Festschrift for F. Krueger. Stuttgart, [2]1954. **Smieskol, H.:** Methoden und Ergebnisse der allg. G. forschung und die Psychol. des menschlichen Ganges (Thesis, Berlin Technical Univ.). Berlin, 1968.

J.M.

Gallup, George Horace. B. 18/11/1901 in Jefferson (Iowa). Founder of the modern opinion poll. Lecturer at the University of Iowa from 1923 to 1929. Appointed professor of journalism at Drake University in 1929 and at the Northwestern University in 1931. He was Director of research in the Young and Rubicam Advertising Agency between 1932 and 1947, and Professor at the Pulitzer School of Journalism at Columbia University from 1935–37. In 1935, Gallup founded the American Institute of Public Opinion in Princeton—the first institute ever to conduct public opinion polls. He gained immediate fame in 1936 by forecasting Roosevelt's victory in the American presidential elections with an error of only 6 per cent. In the same year he also founded the British Institute of Public Opinion. He has been Editor of *The Public Opinion Quarterly* since 1936. *W.W.*

Gallup poll. A social survey or method of measuring public opinion developed by G. H. Gallup in the United States. Data are gathered by systematic sampling; an attempt is made to obtain representative results by means of personal interviews. The general validity of the method has remained unquestioned since 1936.

Bibliography: Berelson, B. & Janowitz, M.: Reader in public opinion and communication. New York, [2]1966. **Gallup, G.:** Public opinion in a democracy. Princeton, 1939. **Id. & Rae, S. F.:** The pulse of democracy. New York, 1940. **Id.:** A guide to public opinion polls. Princeton, 1944.

W.N.

Galton, Sir Francis. *Life and work* (other than psychological): B. 16/2/1822 in Birmingham (England); d. 17/1/1911 in London. Galton was a half-cousin of Darwin and is considered by many authors to have been a genius. His IQ has been estimated at 200. His psychological studies were not systematic but extremely varied and significant. After medical training at the Birmingham General Hospital and medical studies at King's College, London, he turned to mathematics, graduating from Trinity College, Cambridge. He spent most of the next ten years up to 1855 on research in South-West and North Africa, publishing a number of reports (*Art of*

Travel, 1855, etc.) for which he was awarded the Medal of the Royal Geographic Society. He then worked on meteorology, and published the first weather maps; he discovered the anticyclone, etc.

Psychological work: Impressed by Darwin's *Origin of Species*, Galton devoted increasing attention from 1860 onwards to anthropological and psychological problems. His studies were far-ranging, including research into various areas of sense phenomena, mental imagery, the origin and measurement of thought associations, free will, studies of the phenomenon of ability and its inheritance (with particular reference to genius). Galton's major contribution to psychology was in the area of methodology. He is generally considered to have founded the psychometric school of psychology. He invented the first psychological test methods for the measurement of intelligence and ability. These were primarily based on sensory discrimination and were prepared by comparing extreme groups, i.e. highly-gifted and mentally-defective individuals. He founded the first test laboratory in London (in 1882) at which visitors could take a battery of psychological tests on a fee-paying basis.

In his studies of visual imagery, Galton was one of the first authors to use questionnaires in order to study psychological characteristics. He also invented the word association test, which was later taken over by W. Wundt; and he is taken to be the founder of twin studies.

Galton originally believed that psychological traits could be inherited like physiological characteristics. He conducted a number of tests (mainly on public figures) to confirm his assumption; he tried in particular to determine the frequency of outstanding individuals among the ancestors, descendants and relatives of his subjects. Galton made a significant contribution to the development of differential psychology by suggesting—and thus opposing contemporary theories—that human characteristics are extremely varied, so that it is of value to psychologists to study the extent and causes of individual differences.

In statistics, Galton made an important contribution by developing and applying the correlation method. At his suggestion, his pupil, Pearson, later continued his work in this area and developed the product-moment correlation (q.v.) method. Galton founded the first journal of scientific statistics (*Biometrika*). His application of the normal distribution curve (q.v.) to psychological data was a major contribution to the development of psychological methodology. On the basis of his practical studies he concluded that psychological and physiological characteristics follow a standard distribution pattern throughout the population.

Major works: The telotype: a printing electric telegraph, 1850. The art of travel, or shifts and contrivances available in wild countries, [4]1872. Meteorographica, or methods of mapping the weather, 1863. Hereditary genius: an enquiry into its laws and consequences, 1869. English men of science: their nature and nurture, 1874. Address to the anthropological department of the British Association, 1878. Generic images: with autotype illustrations, 1879. Psychometric experiments, *Brain*, 1879, *2*, 149–62. Inquiries into human faculty and its development, 1883. Record of family faculties, 1884. Measurement of character, *Fortnightly Review*, 1884, *36*, 179–85. Co-relations and their measurement, chiefly from anthropometric data. *Proc. Roy. Soc.*, 1888, *15*, 135–45. Natural inheritance, 1889. Finger-prints, 1892. Finger-print directories, 1895. Index to achievements of near kinsmen of some of the fellows of the Royal Society, 1904. Eugenics: its definition, scope and aims, 1905.

Bibliography: Burt, C.: Francis Galton and his contributions to psychology. Brit. J. Stat. Psychol., 1962, *15*. **Galton, F.:** Memories of my life. London, 1908. **Pearson, K.:** The life, letters and labours of Francis Galton, Vols 1–4. London, 1914–30. *W.W.*

Galvanic skin response (abb. GSR; syn. *Electrodermal response; Psychogalvanic* *reflex*). The skin activity triggered by a sensory stimulus or motor reaction (coughing, sneezing) can be measured (*a*) as a short (0·5 to 3·5 seconds) amplification of a direct current passed through the skin (exosomatic galvanic skin reflex) due to a reduction in the basal polarization resistance; or (*b*) as a temporary, primarily negative fluctuation in the potential which can be directly derived from the skin (endosomatic galvanic skin reaction).

These electrical processes on the skin start essentially (negative deflection) as changes brought about by differing adsorption of opposingly charged ions on the surface of membranes, or by varying permeation through the membrane into the epidermal layer (in particular the *stratum lucidum*). After a certain latency, a further potential change (positive deflection) is superimposed because of depolarization of the sweat gland membrane, further amplified by incipient secretion and short-term contraction of the sweat gland passages. The epidermal cells and sweat glands may be innervated by separate sympathetic fibers; this would suggest that the galvanic skin response is a phenomenon accompanying first of all a change in the efficiency of somatosensitive receptors, and secondly an increase in the motor grasping and holding activities. In psychophysics (q.v.) the galvanic skin response based on stimuli actuated primarily in subcortical, vegetative centers is a useful measurement method, e.g. for habituation processes, conditioning, vegetative excitability, etc. Good correlation with intensity parameters for sensory stimuli is also reported.

Bibliography: Edelberg, R.: Electric properties of the skin. In: **Brown, C. C.** (Ed.): Methods in psycho-physiology. Baltimore, 1967. **Keller, P.:** Elektrophysiologie der Haut. In: **Marchioni, A.** (Ed.): Handbuch der Dermatologie. Berlin, Göttingen & Heidelberg, 1963. **Montagu, J. D. & Coles, R.:** Mechanism and measurement of the galvanic skin response. Psychol. Bull., 1966, *65*, 261–79. **Venables, P. H. & Martin, I.:** Skin resistance and skin potential. In: **Venables, P. H. & Martin, I.** (Eds): A manual of psychophysiological methods. Amsterdam, 1967. **Venables, P. H. & Sayers, E.:** On the measurement of the level of the skin potential. Brit. J. Psychol., 1963, *54*, 251–60. **Wilcott, R. C.:** The partial independence of skin potential and skin resistance from sweating. Psychophysiology, 1964, *1*, 55. *M.S.*

Gametes. Haploid sex cells which combine to form a diploid zygote representing a new individual (unicellular), or from which a new individual may develop (multicellular), which then shows a new combination of characteristics inherited from the parents (gamonts). If the two combining gametes are externally identical the process is *isogamy;* if they differ in size, *anisogamy;* and if the female gamete (then known as the ovum) is not capable of autonomous movement and is much larger than the mobile male gamete, *oogamy.* *H.S.*

Game theory. A mathematical theory which serves as a model for decision-making behavior, in so far as the result of the behavior is always determined by several decision units (individuals, groups, societies, and so on).

A "game" occurs if the decisions (or results of decisions) of at least two organisms result in a consequence for each participant, which for at least one of those concerned is not independent of the behavior of at least one of the others. The numerical values of the consequences are known as "payoffs". Since those games in particular are taken into consideration in which an increased payoff for one participant is linked to a decreased payoff for an opponent, the theory can also serve as a model for certain social conflicts (see *Conflict*).

Bibliography: Shubik, M.: (Ed.): Game theory and related approaches to social behavior. New York London, 1964. *W.H.T.*

Gamma-amino-butyric acid (*γ-aminobutyric acid;* abb. GABA). A biogenic amine (q.v.) first detected in the brain in 1950; it is produced from glutamic acid (q.v.) by biosynthesis. The biological role of GABA has not yet been determined; neurophysiological experiments on animals do, however, show that it is a significant factor in inhibiting cortical transmission.

Bibliography: Curtis, D. R. & Watkins, J. C.: The pharmacology of amino acids related to gamma-amino-butyric acids. Pharmacol. Rev., 1965, *17*, 347–91. *W.J.*

Gamma movement. An apparent movement (q.v.) of expansion and contraction which occurs if the intensity of illumination of a single figure in a dark surrounding area is suddenly increased or reduced. See *Irradiation.* *W.P.*

Ganglion. Ganglia form a collection of nerve cells (see *Ganglionic cells*) in the form of a circular, oval or irregular structure with a length of one or more millimeters. With the exception of the basal ganglia (q.v.), the ganglia are located outside the central nervous system. The spinal ganglia in the intervertebral foramina consist mainly of pseudo-unipolar ganglionic cells, and constitute the cell body of the primary, efferent neurons. The ganglia of the autonomic nervous system (q.v.) are located in the head, sympathetic nerves, and abdominal and pelvic region. In surgery the term "ganglion" is used to describe a cystic tumor of the joint membranes or tendon sheaths. *G.A.*

Ganglionic blocking agents. Substances which block the transmission of impulses in the synapses of the autonomic ganglia primarily by reaction with acetylcholine receptors. This results in a reduction of blood pressure and diminished tonicity of the smooth musculature. Ganglionic blocking agents are antagonists of nicotine (q.v.), which is a ganglionic stimulant.

Bibliography: Volle, R. L. & Koelle, G. B.: Ganglionic stimulating and blocking agents. In: **Goodman, L. S. & Gilman, A.:** The pharmacological basis of therapeutics. New York, 1965. *G.D.*

Ganglionic cells. Cells (nerve cells, neurocytes, gangliocytes, neurones) which consist of the cell body (perikaryon), the cell nucleus, and one or more extensions in the form of dendrites—which consist, like the cell body, of cytoplasm and have a receptive function, together with neurites (q.v.) which act as effectors and transmitters. A distinction is made between unipolar, pseudo-unipolar, bipolar and multipolar ganglionic cells on the basis of the configuration of the extensions. There are between 14 and 16 thousand million ganglionic cells in the human nervous system. The ganglionic cells are connected together by synapses (q.v.).

Bibliography: Porter, K. R. & Bonneville, M. A.: An introduction to the fine structure of cells and tissues. Philadelphia, 1964. *G.A.*

Ganser syndrome. Otherwise known as the "syndrome of approximate answers", this was originally described by S. J. M. Ganser. It occurs characteristically in prisoners who give silly approximate answers to questions in order to feign mental illness. An inconsistent lay impression of mental illness is presented. May be viewed as malingering or hysteria. A similar picture sometimes occurs in schizophrenia or after head injury. *D.E.*

Ganzheit; gestalt; structure. Some confusion surrounds the use of these three terms. Many authors use them as synonyms. Definitions and explanatory comments in dictionaries are also broadly similar. We shall try to distinguish between the notions on the basis of fundamental texts and suggest how they should be used in future. A more rigid distinction will be made between their substantive and attributive use than has been the case in the past.

1. *Ganzheit* (whole, wholeness, completeness, entity) is derived from the notion of "*das Ganze*" (or "the whole"), and was introduced into psychology by F. Krueger. A totality as a function of space, time or both space and time (a complex) is referred to

as "*ein Ganzes*" or "a whole" if the type, location and arrangement of the "components" are not accidental or random (as they are in an aggregate), i.e. if the totality *has a structure*, and provided that there is a real relationship between the component factors. This totality is the combination of all its parts and only exists as a "whole" (i.e. is "*ganzheitlich*") if none of these parts is lacking and if the relationship between them (as well as the distinction between this interaction and the environment) is not interrupted anywhere; this last point is generally overlooked in the literature.

A whole is only "holistic", or possesses "wholeness", if it satisfies an additional condition, which is best formulated in the following proposition of Wertheimer's (1925): "There are relationships in which all that occurs in the whole is not dependent on the nature and combination of the individual parts, but on the contrary . . . where that which occurs in a part of the whole is determined by inner structural laws of this whole". Objects which have this holistic, total character tend also to possess features which cannot be detected in any of their isolated parts (holistic or total characteristics, or complex qualities, e.g. the expression of a face). To this extent, wholes are also "super-summative".

Such phenomena can only be understood by holistic (*molar*) observation, as opposed to the atomistic (*molecular*) approach proper to non-holistic phenomena. What is the difference between these two modes of observation? In examining an object which is not holistic in the sense defined above, the "analysis" may be based on a factual ("objective") separation of individual parts from the whole, since it is justifiable to assume that these parts will behave in the same way in isolation as they do in their appropriate location in the total unit. In the holistic approach, analysis consists of an investigation of the individual parts and component processes as they are located in the whole, and with regard to their function in the whole. Behavior in isolation cannot be expected to coincide with the behavior in the whole; in addition, it is probable that local phenomena or processes will be affected both by local factors and by extralocal or translocal factors. Finally, if parts or loci are isolated or separated out, it is probable that information which is essential to the whole will be overlooked or disappear. Comparison of reactions under different conditions may of course afford valuable information; an investigation based on atomistic procedures may therefore also be of heuristic value for the study of a "whole", provided that it is carried out alongside the strictly holistic analysis.

In addition to living and animate beings whose holistic nature is immediately apparent, at least the field phenomena of the inanimate environment also require a holistic approach (Köhler, 1918). A philosophical attitude or world view in which the central notion is the fact of "wholeness" is known as "holism" (Smuts, 1926). Those personality theories which, by contrast with the idea of a multiplicity of more or less independent "factors", stress the unity of the personality and in which groups or communities are considered as supra-individual and real unities or real wholes, and individuals as "we-factors", are also known as holistic. This applies, e.g., to the "individual psychology" founded by Adler (1907).

The holistic psychological theories, in particular those of the Leipzig School (q.v.) and that of Werner (1953), assume a genetic primacy of the non- or insignificantly structured (complex, diffuse, continuous) whole over its structured (differentiated) realizations; this applies both to behavior and individual experience. The unorganized primary forms are defined as "whole" in a narrower, "more specific" sense. Their (affective) holistic characteristics are distinguished, as "complex qualities", from the "gestalt qualities" of sharply defined and (generally) organized, or structured, wholes. It is difficult to make a distinction between the two, and it does not seem fundamentally important to do so.

2. *Structure* (*Struktur*). This term originally denoted a *characteristic* of a whole, i.e. its composition, the arrangement of its parts or elements including the orderly totality of the relations between them. The word is also used with this meaning in other sciences: in chemistry, mineralogy or anatomy one may speak of the structure of a molecule, crystal or bone. W. Dilthey, who introduced the notion of structure into psychology, clearly uses it in this attributive sense when he says it is the "arrangement by which psychological facts of differing composition are connected together in the developed mental life by an internal relationship which can be experienced". In the earlier quotation, Wertheimer used the concept to describe the construction of unities of experience and action. Spranger uses it to denote the complex of interests of an individual, while L. Klages, P. Lersch and Wellek speak of the "structure of the person". See *Strata theory*.

Two special meanings have developed in pyschology, of which the second at least is objective: (*a*) in the American expression "structuralism" signifying, e.g. for E. B. Titchener, the totality of the (statically apprehended) contents of consciousness as opposed to the conditional behavioral relationships considered by the *functionalists;* (*b*) in the terminology of the Leipzig School holistic theory. A distinction is made here between two sub-concepts of the general notion of wholeness: "experiential wholes" and "structures". According to Krueger, these are the relatively permanent *premisses for the possibility of developing experiential wholes.* They form the basis of psychic functions, and are essentially "beyond consciousness", or transphenomenal, i.e. intervening variables or constructs in E. C. Tolman's terminology, but also in certain "profound individual experiences" (feelings and value judgments) only rarely accessible to direct experience. Strictly speaking, they do not exist "in themselves" or "as such" but only to the extent that they are effectively expressed in psychic phenomena (individual experiences) (Wellek, 1941). This suggests that what occurs is a hypostatization in the sense of the Platonic "idea" and the neovitalist "entelechy".

3. *Gestalt* (form, configuration). The gestalt concept is a further refinement of the notion of wholeness, which proved useful initially in perception theory, and was then more generally applied, and has tended to come increasingly to the fore in connection with the problem of the order obtaining within the whole.

(*a*) *First stage.* It has been known since classical antiquity that the specific character of the whole can be changed decisively by slight local interventions (removal, addition, alteration, displacement). In 1890, von Ehrenfels added the new notion that when changes occur which affect all the parts of a whole (exchange of material, movement to other sensory or existential areas), the specific character of this whole is maintained if its structure (i.e. the dimensional and positional relationships between the parts; and, in particular, their functions, in the case of behavioral wholes) is retained. Von Ehrenfels referred to wholes which possessed this characteristic as "gestalts" (*Gestalten*), to their supersummative property as "gestalt quality", and to the change which takes place without affecting that quality as "transposability".

(*b*) *Second stage* (Wertheimer, 1912). The whole is not, as von Ehrenfels supposed, the sum of the parts plus the holistic characteristic: $W = \Sigma p + h$, but $W = f(\Sigma p, c, l, m, n \ldots)$, in which the letters following p stand for, e.g., constitution or disposition, level of development, previous history, expectation, mode of apprehension. In other words, the whole is something other than the sum of its parts. (Example: stimulus a + stimulus b at adjacent points but at a short interval of time do not result in "sensation" A + "sensation" B + movement, but in *a* "sensation" which moves from position A to position B). In the marginal case, e.g. in visual perception, the dynamic interaction between part-stimuli determines whether and where a whole ends and whether it possesses parts, and what parts these are.

(*c*) *Third stage.* In addition to the specific characteristics of wholes, there are also specific characteristics of parts. These are characteristics which distinguish a phenomenon as the "part" of a whole from its given mode of existence as an "individual content": the function or "role" of the part in the whole (Köhler, 1918; Wertheimer, 1933).

(*d*) *Fourth stage.* Because of the dynamic interaction between the part processes, the assumption of a one to one correspondence between the locus of the stimulus and type of stimulus on the one hand, and the locus and type of phenomenon on the other has to be abandoned (the assumption of "constancy") (Köhler, 1913).

(*e*) *Fifth stage.* The structures which are most likely to develop because of this dynamic procedure are characterized by orderliness (regularity and simplicity), i.e. there is a tendency to pregnance (*Prägnanz*), i.e. to form a "good gestalt". This is not only decisive in spontaneous field formation and three-dimensional distribution in the visual modality (Kopfermann, 1930; Metzger, 1935), but also leads under certain specific conditions to disparities between perceptive and objective form and quality (illusions).

(*f*) *Sixth stage.* Order can in principle be produced and maintained in two different ways. In addition to mechanical maintenance (the sole form recognized previously) of the order of states and processes through the strengthening of a material or wall ("canalization"), it is also possible to establish order by the interaction of certain part processes, i.e. there is an order which has a "dynamic" foundation. This dynamic order brought about by the interaction of inner forces, differs from mechanical order in various respects: the same forces (i) bring the order into being, (ii) maintain it, (iii) re-establish it (within certain limits) when a disturbing factor is encountered, and (iv) restructure it under certain conditions (as a correction), e.g. in productive processes. The states of equilibrium which are finally reached also have a distinctly formal nature. The assumption of supporting factors (analogously to the postulate of entelechy) therefore becomes superfluous.

Mechanical and dynamic forms of order are not mutually exclusive; between the two extreme cases of purely dynamic and purely mechanical order, there is a continuous series of possibilities for different involvement of the two principles. The mechanical factor, e.g. in visual perception, consists (i), generally, of the anatomical structure of the receptors and conduction system, and (ii), specifically, of the instantaneous spatio-temporal configuration of stimuli. The extreme case of minimum dynamic maintenance of order, in which the event retroacts upon itself at *one* point at least, is cybernetic automation.

(*g*) *Seventh stage.* A high degree of automatic dynamic control can be assumed for all the part areas of the psyche. This holds good also for living beings as "open systems" (L. von. Bertalanffy), and for the different kinds of force fields in physics (Köhler, 1924). It is therefore possible to assume an "isomorphy" of mental and the associated physiological (psychophysical) processes. A "gestalt theory" is a psychological method which makes this possibility a psychophysical working hypothesis (Köhler, 1925).

Bibliography: Adler, A.: Organ inferiority. New York, 1907. **Ehrenfels, C. v.:** On gestalt qualities. Psychol. Rev., 1937, *44*, 521–4. **Klix, F. & Krause, B.:** Zur Definition des Begriffs Struktur, seiner Eigenschaften und Darstellungsmöglichkeiten in der Experimentalpsychologie. Z. Psychol., 1969, *176*. **Koffka, K.:** Principles of gestalt psychology, New York, 1935. **Köhler, W.:** Über umbemerkte Empfindungen und Urteilstauschungen, Z. Psychol, 1913, *66*. **Id.:** Nachweis einfacher Strukturfunktionen beim Schimpansen und beim Haushuhn. Abhandl. Preuss. Akad. Wiss. Berlin, 1918. **Id.:** Gestaltprobleme und Anfänge einer Gestalttheorie. Jber. ges. Physiol. exp. Pharmakol. für 1922, 3/1, 1925. **Id.:** Die physischen Gestalten in Ruhe und im stationärem Zustand. Erlangen, 1924. **Id.:** The mentality of apes. London, 1925. **Id.:** Gestalt psychology. New York, 1929. **Id.:** Dynamics in psychology. New York, 1940. **Kopfermann, H.:** Psychol. Untersuchungen über die Wirkung zweidimensionaler Darstellung körperlicher Gebilde. Psychol. Forsch. 1930, 13. **Krueger, F.**: Der Strukturbegriff in der Psychologie. Ber. VIII Kong. exp. Psychol. Leipzig & Jena, 1924. **Id.**: Zur Philosophie und Psychol. der Ganzheit. Berlin, 1953. **Metzger, W.**: Tiefenerscheinungen in optischen Bewegungsfeldern, Psychol. Forsch. 1935, *2*. **Petermann, B.**: The gestalt theory. London & New York, 1932. **Popper, K. R.**: The poverty of historicism. London, 1960, 76–93. **Rausch, E.**: Über Summativität und Nichtsummativität, Psychol. Forsch., 1937, *21*. **Sander, F. & Volkelt, H.**: Ganzheitspsychologie. Munich, 1962. **Smuts, J. C.**: Holism and evolution. London, 1926. **Wellek, A.**: Das Problem des seelischen Seins. Leipzig, 1941. **Werner, H.**: Einführung in die Entwicklungspsychologie. Munich, 1953. **Wertheimer, M.**: Experimentelle Studien über das Sehen von Bewegung. Z. Psychol. 1912, *61*, 161–265. **Id.**: Über Schlussprozesse im produktiven Denken. Berlin, 1920 (Productive thinking. New York, 1959). **Id.**: Untersuchungen zur Lehre der Gestalt, I. Psychol. Forsch., 1922, *1*; II. Psychol. Forsch. 1923, *4*. (Part trans.: **Beardsall, D. C. & Wertheimer, M.** (Eds): Readings in perception. Princeton, 1958, 115–35.) **Id.**: Drei Abhandlungen zur Gestalttheorie. Erlangen, 1925. **Id.**: Zum Problem der Unterscheidung von Einzelinhalt und Teil. Z. Psychol., 1933, *129*. **Id.**: On gestalt theory. Soc. Res., 1944, *11*, 78–99. **Witte, W.**: Zur Geschichte des psychol. Ganzheits- und Gestaltbegriffes. Stud. Gen., 1952.

W. Metzger

Gargoylism. A genetic disturbance of the metabolism. Metabolic products (mucopolysaccharide) are deposited in the brain and many other organs, whose development is thus impaired. Disproportionate stunted growth with contorted facial features (hence "gargoyle") and organic disorders. Generally accompanied by mental deficiency. *C.S.*

GAS (*General anxiety scale*). See *Manifest anxiety scale* (MAS).

Gastrula. In multicellular animals the blastula—a hollow sphere with a wall formed by a single cell layer—generally develops first from the fertilized ovum by cell division. The double-layered gastrula is then formed from this hollow sphere by invagination. The point of invagination remains as an opening.

H.Sch.

Gaussian curve (syn. *Gauss's curve; Normal [probability] curve*). A graphic representation of a symmetrical, bell-shaped, continuous distribution (see *Normal distribution*) with a single peak. Its probability density is determined by the following function:

$$f(x) = \frac{1}{\sigma\sqrt{2\pi}} e^{-\frac{1}{2}\left(\frac{x-\mu}{\sigma}\right)^2}$$

The distribution is therefore clearly determined by μ and N. Since many biological characteristics accord with the normal distribution, this form is often used. *W.H.B.*

Gefüge. See *Structure.*

Gegenstandstheorie. See *Object; Objective theory.*

Geisteswissenschaftliche Psychologie (Eng. *Cultural science psychology; Social science psychology*). French and English positivism (A. Comte, J. S. Mill) led to a general revision of the notion of science which had become widely accepted in Germany too. Either the natural sciences (*Naturwissenschaften*) were accepted as the only true science (Comte) or it was suggested that the social sciences (*Geisteswissenschaften*) were to be based on natural science (Mill), psychology being considered as a branch of biology.

At the end of the nineteenth and in the early twentieth century there was a very active movement in Germany which tried to establish a more balanced attitude by creating an objective, logical foundation for the cultural sciences (which, according to Dilthey, are, e.g., "history, national economy, the sciences of law and of the state, the science of religion, the study of literature and poetry, of art and music, of philosophical worldviews and systems, and finally psychology"), based on cognition theory. Because all "cultural phenomena are associated with mental phenomena" it was thought necessary to consider psychological thought processes and make a newly conceived psychology the theoretical framework and basic discipline for all the human sciences.

Since Dilthey (1883, [2]1957) the term "*Geisteswissenschaft*" had been in general use; accordingly, the term "*Geisteswissenschaftliche Psychologie*" gained currency as a collective designation for the psychological trends which—unlike the empirical research of the natural sciences—concentrated their research on the investigation of meaningful individual experiences, value factors, and purpose. All three aspects are conceivable only in the "mental" or "spiritual" sphere (*das Geistige*). However, nothing could be "explained" *causally* in this sphere (as in the natural sciences), and only the principle of "understanding" (*Verstehen*) was considered valid, the individual experience of the "soul" or "psyche" (*Seele*) being approached indirectly through "*objective mind*" or "intellectual products" (art, culture), which form the external objective expressions of the human spirit in its lived experience. Since the meaning (value) with which cultural science psychology is concerned never appears as an isolated phenomenon but only in a certain *context*, it can only be experienced by means of a "complex psychic structure" (Dilthey, 1894, [2]1957). For cultural science psychology, the principle of structure or development and the concept of *Ganzheit* (wholeness) or *gestalt* (configuration) were essential, because the structural tension and interaction of "experienced relationships" could only be described in this way. Dilthey and his followers (especially Spranger) used these notions to understand and describe feelings, aspirations, motives, character, and so on.

Methods. Understanding, re-experiencing (empathy, mimpathy), description, and interpretation are some of the methods used. Just as the natural sciences use the principle of "explanation", or "explication", cultural science psychology uses the principle of "understanding" psychologically to "penetrate" *objective* (meaningfully structured) and *personal* life (the ego), and to re-experience the confrontation of the ego with the environment. Instead of explaining mental processes by cause and effect, E. Spranger (1918) defined "understanding" (*verstehen*) as the "basic function of the percipient consciousness", and as "penetration of the value system of a psychic context". According to Scheler (1937), it is an essential aspect of understanding "that we experience the actions (speech and activities) of others from a perceptive mental idea of them as intentionally directed toward a specific end so far as we and the environment are concerned, and ourselves complete these actions . . . although this form of completion does not entail co-judgment, approval, or other sentiments". Efforts to establish an objective, theoretical foundation for these methods has led to the division of understanding into two main areas: the understanding *of persons* (contact-understanding, intuitive- or perceptive-categorial and conceptual understanding), and the understanding *of objects.*

The further development of psychological research showed that the division between natural and social scientific aspects of psychology was restrictive; nowadays it is rejected by most psychologists.

Geisteswissenschafliche Psychologie has value mainly in educational and cultural psychology. See *Verstehende Psychologie; General psychology; History of psychology.*

Bibliography: Dilthey, W.: Einleitung in die Geisteswissenschaften. Gesammelte Schriften, Vol. 4. Stuttgart, [2]1957. **Id.:** Ideen über eine beschreibende und zergliedernde Psychologie. Gesammelte Schriften, Vol. 5. Stuttgart, [2]1957. **Id.:** Pattern and meaning in history: thoughts on history and society (Ed. **Rickman, H. P.**). London, 1961; New York, 1962. **Oelrich, W.:** Geisteswissenschaftliche Psychol. und Bildung des Menschen. Stuttgart, 1950. **Scheler, M.:** Der Formalismus in der Ethik und die materiale Wertethik. Frankfurt, [3]1937. **Spranger, E.:** Types of men: the psychology and ethics of personality. Halle, 1928. **Id.:** Zur Theorie des Verstehens und zur g.P. In: Festschrift für J. Volkelt. Munich, 1918. *F. Novak*

Gemüt (Eng. *Total disposition*). The psychic and spiritual aspect of a person; the totality of emotions, basic dispositions, moods and motivations. Whereas cognitive activity is characterized by knowledge, thought and judgment, *Gemüt* is expressed in feeling and personal lived experience. Education of *Gemüt* as opposed to training of understanding has played an important role in educational theory (especially in the nineteenth century, e.g. in a particularly intense form in F. Fröbel's work). The notion of *Gemüt* acquired major philosophical significance for the German Romantics and in the sect known as "Christian Science". Recently attempts have been made, primarily by Strasser (1956), to develop the fundamentals of a phenomenological philosophy from the concept.

Bibliography: Strasser, S.: Das Gemüt. Freiburg, 1956. *E.U.*

Gene. The hypothetical component of the hereditary substance (see *De(s)oxyribonucleic acid* = DNA) which, in a simple instance, controls the formation of an individual characteristic (e.g. curly hair in a guinea-pig). In molecular terms, a gene consists of several thousand DNA components (nucleotides), and the development of a characteristic always begins with the formation of a specific simple protein which then acts as a kind of catalyst for the reaction which leads to formation of the specific characteristic. If several genes are responsible for the development of a characteristic, it is known as a "polygenic" characteristic. *H.S.*

General ability. See *Abilities; Intelligence.*

General Aptitude Test Battery (GATB). A series of twelve tests developed by Beatrice J. Dvorak in the U.S.A. (U.S. Employment Service) to determine vocational aptitude. The eight pencil-and-paper tests and four apparatus tests cover a total of nine factors, the scores for which are presented in a profile. Standard profiles for twenty-two vocational groups are available for comparison. The test battery was determined on the basis of a representative sample of about four thousand testees. According to Cronbach (p. 274), the reliability coefficients for the nine scales vary between 0·65 and 0·68.

Bibliography: Cronbach, L. J.: Essentials of psychological testing. New York, [2]1960. **Dvorak, B. J.:** The General Aptitude Test Battery. Personnel Guid. J., 1956, *35*, 145–54. *P.S.*

General factor (abb. G). If a factor which occurs in all observed variables can be extracted by means of factor analysis (q.v.), it is known as a general factor. In Spearman's factor model, there is a G (general ability) for as many specific factors (*s*) as there are variables. This assumption later proved untenable. *W.H.B.*

Generalization is a fundamental concept in learning theory. It denotes the fact that forms of behavior which were coupled with a specific stimulus situation in a learning process can be induced not only by this particular situation but also by other similar stimulus situations. The phenomenon is explained by I. P. Pavlov on the assumption of an irradiation of impulses by the cerebral cortex; C. L. Hull, on the other hand, postulates intermediate stimulus-reaction chains within the organism, while E. R. Guthrie traces the phenomenon back to common elements in stimulus situations. Generalization is used to explain phenomena such as transfer of practice (see *Transfer*), etc. The *generalization gradient* is the ranking of different stimuli according to the degree to which they evoke a response previously coupled with a specific stimulus. The generalization depends on the intensity of this association and has as many dimensions as the stimulus has variables.

Bibliography: Osgood, C. E.: Method and theory in experimental psychology. New York, 1953. *H.Ro.*

Generalized other. G. H. Mead's term for an organized group or community which (beyond relational individuals, or "significant others") endows the individual with a unified ego (q.v.) through group identity. It is assumed that the attitudes of the whole group coincide in the generalized other (e.g. the team in sport) and therefore form part of the experience of the individual group member. The actions of the individual are "controlled" by the fact that he remains himself while at the same time conforming to the attitudes of the others, i.e. is at the same time the "generalized other". A number of such groups are referred to as "generalized others"; those especially valued are "reference groups".

Bibliography: **Mead, G. H.:** Mind, self and society: from the standpoint of a social behaviorist (Ed. **Morris, C. W.**). Chicago & London, [18]1965. **Rose, A. M.** (Ed.): Human behavior and social processes. London, 1962.

W.D.F.

General psychology. I. The implied emphasis is on general principles as opposed to individual variations (*differential psychology*), species differences (*comparative psychology*), and socio-cultural factors (*social psychology*). The word "general" has been used to refer to principles underlying such processes as learning, remembering, and thinking, and such activities as attention, motivation, and emotion. Some methodologists, e.g. John Stuart Mill (1843), have argued that psychology needs to be complemented by another discipline concerned with the study of individuality. Stern (1921) underlined the same point when he wrote: "the problems set by general psychology and by the psychology of the individual are quite different". G. W. Allport (1938), in arguing for the development of a psychology of personality, adopted a highly critical assessment of the value of general psychology in arguing "to abstract a generalized human mind from a population of active prepossessing well-knit persons is a feat of questionable value. The generalized human mind is entirely mythical; it lacks the most essential characteristics of mind—locus, organic quality, reciprocal action of parts, and self-consciousness". This interest in individuality as opposed to general principles is traditional: it has a long history going back to Empedocles and Plato.

The term *general psychology* is ambiguous. A second usage is given by Chaplin (1968) as referring to "the broad synthesis of all findings and theories in the field as typified by an introductory textbook or course". (Compare the next article by Prof. P. Muller, which refers to this usage.) In this other sense, the term general psychology appears in the syllabus of many university courses, and in textbooks published at different periods of time: e.g. Murphy's *General Psychology* (1933), Valentine's *Experimental Foundations of General Psychology* (1941), Thouless's *General and Social Psychology* (1937), Kimble's *Principles of General Psychology* (1956), Das's *General Psychology* (1964). These and other such textbooks differ in content and do not necessarily exclude differential, social, and comparative psychology.

A distinction between *general* and *differential* psychology is supported by standard dictionary usage. Warren (1958 edition) defines general psychology as "the branch of psychology which seeks to discover what is true of individuals in general rather than of one individual or class of individuals as distinct from others". Warren's criterion is in terms of the goals or purposes of the investigator or writer concerned. English & English (1958 edition) similarly mention goals and purposes in distinguishing *general* from *differential* psychology. They also mention the dichotomy of *nomothetic* (concern to discover general laws) as opposed to *idiographic* (concern to understand particular events or individuals). Drever (1952) similarly defines general psychology as concerned with general principles of mental life "as distinct from peculiarities characteristic of the individual". And Chaplin (1968) similarly distinguishes general from differential psychology.

Illustrations will be taken from the main areas of the science to indicate the orientation of general psychology, and to distinguish it from other possible orientations. A number of opposing theories of learning, associated with such names as Guthrie, Hull and Skinner flourished in the 1930s and 1940s (Hilgard, 1948). These, together with the titles of leading books such as Hull's *Principles of Behavior* (1943), Skinner's *The Behavior of Organisms* (1938), and Hebb's *Organization of Behavior* (1949), exemplify the standpoint of general psychology, by contrast with, for example, Eysenck's application of Hullian theory to the elucidation of individual differences in learning, and perceiving. Within perception, the gestalt psychologists have frequently been criticized for their seemingly exclusive concern with general principles, as opposed to individual variations and personality differences. The title of one such critical paper "Where is the perceiver in perception theory?" illustrates this line of criticism (Klein & Schlesinger, 1949). In relation to memory, the early experiments of Ebbinghaus (1885) represent a significant contribution to general psychology from the standpoint of a single subject; Koffka (1935) attempted to apply general gestaltist principles to the memory field. The tradition of associationism (e.g. Bain, 1863) represents a general psychological approach to thinking as contrasted to the use of association techniques to study individual differences (e.g. Galton, 1883). Within the contributions of Soviet science may be noted the reflexology of Pavlov in its concern with general principles which have made an important impact upon the psychology of learning; this may be contrasted with Pavlov's own interest in typology, and the elaboration of this aspect of differential psychology by B. M. Teplov and his associates.

Historically, general psychology has been closely associated with the method of experiment, in the strict sense of systematic manipulation of experimental variables. By contrast, differential psychology has been historically associated with psychometric methods, and social psychology with observation of a more controlled, or less controlled kind. These connections have been historical, rather than logically necessary ones, and are much less apparent in the contemporary scene. In the early scientific period Wundt, Titchener and others made substantial use of introspective report in developing their general psychology. The classic researches of Sherif on the autokinetic effect have pioneered the by now vigorous use of experiment in social psychology (Sherif, 1936). Experimental methods received early application to personality and clinical research, in for example the study of "how a fear may be removed under laboratory conditions" by Mary Carver Jones (1924). More recent work in this tradition involving "the application of experimental method to the single case" is to be found in, for example, the study by Shapiro & Nelson (1955). Because of these developments, many of which have a long history, any equation of "scientific" psychology with either "experimental" psychology, or "general" psychology, is questionable and misleading.

The distinction between nomothetic (concern with the discovery of general laws), and idiographic (concern with a single event or specific individual), may be noted in connection with general psychology. Of interest is the fact that the size of the population studied is not necessarily a criterion to be used in differentiating the nomothetic from the idiographic. This is particularly apparent if we deal with a population of $N = 1$. Hence Ebbinghaus sought to formulate and test hypotheses, using a single subject, with a view to discovering general principles relevant to understanding, remembering and forgetting. Freud similarly sought to discover the general principles underlying dreaming, using data primarily on himself. With such work may be contrasted studies that have been made of individual cases, with a primarily idiographic orientation. In the early period, Morton Prince (1909) studied the dissociative behavior of Christine Beauchamp in this way; more recently Luria (1968) has studied, over a period of thirty years, a single case involving unusual capacity for remembering, synesthesia of a variety of kinds, and highly limited capacity for forgetting. Individuals who exhibit pain blindness merit idiographic study of a similar kind, but these also may yield information of interest to general psychology, as showing how absence of the sense of pain can affect learning as such (Mowrer, 1950). Similarly Luria's study, though primarily idiographic, may have important implications for the understanding of the general psychology of retention and forgetting.

The notion of general principles or laws of psychology, which are completely or approximately universal, is less widely adhered to than formerly. Individual variations, developmental stages, greater or lesser deviations from the normal, and both species and social differences, are all today fields of intensive, and legitimate, research. Wundtian over-preoccupation with the normal, adult, human, introspective observer, has been modified by the impact of several movements, including Watsonian behaviorism: this staked out a claim for both developmental and comparative psychology. Allport's influential book (1938) firmly established the field of personality-orientated psychology. If McDougall (1908) was concerned with instincts or propensities as generally present motivational variables, H. A. Murray and others have since developed a personality-centered approach to this same field of motivation. The functional perception movement of Bruner and others has sought to correct what the leaders of this group viewed as a narrowly general psychological approach, and to develop the differential psychology lacking in this area. Leading theorists in the field of learning, such as Mowrer (1950) and Skinner (1968), have devoted their recent attention to the study of personality differences in learning on the one hand, and the problems of the individual learner in the classroom, on the other. The concept of general psychology, though perhaps of questionable value today, provides a reference point in terms of which we can view some of these historical, and modern, developments.

Bibliography: Allport, G. W.: Personality: a psychological interpretation. London, 1938. **Chaplin, J. P.:** Dictionary of psychology. New York, 1968. **English, H. B. & English, A. C.:** A comprehensive dictionary of psychological and psychoanalytical terms. London, 1958. **Klein, G. S. & Schlesinger, H.:** Where is the perceiver in perception theory. Journal of Personality. 1949. **Koffka, K.:** Principles of gestalt psychology. London, 1935. **Luria, A. R.:** The mind of a mnemonist. (Trans. from the Russian by **Solatarff, L.**). London, 1969. **McDougall, W.:** An introduction to social psychology. London, 1908. **Mowrer, O. H.:** Learning theory and personality dynamics. New York, 1950. **Shapiro, M. B. & Nelson, E. H.:** An investigation of an abnormality of cognitive function in a co-operative young psychotic: an example of the application of the experimental method to the single case. Journal of Clinical Psychology, 1955, *11*. **Sherif, M.:** The psychology of social norms. New York, 1936. **Skinner, B. F.:** The technique of teaching. New York, 1968. **Warren, H. C.:** Dictionary of psychology (1958 edition). New York, 1934.

T. P. H. McKellar

General psychology. II. *The interdisciplinary view.* There are two accepted meanings of the term "general psychology": the first refers to the contents of an introductory course in the subject, the basic knowledge every psychologist should have before specializing in one or other of the different branches of modern psychology; "general psychologies" in this sense are to be found in various manuals (e.g. R. Kimble's *Principles of General Psychology*, New York, 1956; or the large *Handbuch der Psychologie*, I: *Allgemeine Psychologie*, edited by W. Metzger). The second meaning, the one with which this article deals, refers to problems of *method*, to the *interpretation* of psychological data, and to the *cultural* or *philosophical implications* of psychology. To be even more precise, this article is mainly concerned with the relationship between psychology and philosophy (another article discusses methodological problems, see *Philosophy and psychology*).

Psychology is a science which has existed for a long time yet possesses only a brief recorded history (Ebbinghaus, 1885); it has had some difficulty in emerging from the philosophical mold common to all traditional branches of knowledge in the West. It is now becoming apparent that psychological problems are already present in myths (in so far as these are always about man's place in the world); that they are reflected in the earliest philosophical theories; and that they then become increasingly precise in the great traditional systems of thought. Thus the "Psychology" section in Janet & Seailles' *L'Histoire de la philosophie* (1st edition, 1886) includes chapters on the following: animal life, the senses and external perception, consciousness, theories of reason, memory, association of ideas, language, sensitivity, problems of freedom, habit. Each of these chapters traces through the ages the discussion of the problems which experimental psychology, with its laboratory techniques and concern for strict verification, had taken up from 1860 onward.

A similar situation can certainly be found in the other sciences. But whereas the advent of the experimental method in physics, with deductions based on the testing of hypotheses, severed the links between physics and philosophy (at least in principle, if not in the mind of each individual physicist), nothing of the sort has happened in psychology, in spite of the constant efforts of a great number of scholars. In opposition to the earliest scientific psychology of the pioneers (1860–1912) came protests by Bergson, Dilthey, Brentano, Husserl and, finally, Natorp. In the confused era between 1912 and 1930 several psychologists expressly laid claim to philosophical methods (e.g. the "phenomenological psychology" of M. Scheler and of A. Pfänder, continued later in France by J.-P. Sartre and Merleau-Ponty). Finally, even when, from 1930 onward, there was greater unanimity concerning psychology as the "science of behavior", those who thought in depth about psychology continued animatedly to discuss the very possibility of an "objective" science of human behavior.

Philosophy aspires to conscious coherence in the concepts it uses to describe and to understand itself, and thus necessarily *reflects upon itself*. To this extent, somewhere along the line philosophy encounters objective psychology as a rival approach. The reason for this is that objective psychology includes a theory of cognition, and therefore considers the conditions governing knowledge while simultaneously itself claiming to be this knowledge. Is it possible to use concepts of objectivity borrowed from science to construct a subject capable of developing precisely the objective knowledge in question? Can "instrumental" reason of the type used in technology (Pradines) explain itself? Can it do without *dialectical reason?*

Apart from renewing this investigation into the preconditions for psychology (the *critical* question *par excellence*), general psychology should be concerned to describe the factors which make up the three things with which it is primarily concerned: behavior, experience, and other people in so far as they are personal agents. Experimental psychology always assumes that these basic problems have been resolved, whereas it is at this level that the distinction between natural ("physicalist") science and the various human sciences is worked out.

At a less fundamental level, general psychology describes the social conditions necessary for the birth of psychology, the epistemological limits implied by the three types of psychology (experimental psychology in the third person, clinical psychology in the second person, and phenomenological psychology in the first person), and the existential conditions inherent in any attempt by existence to come to terms with itself. From this point of view, scientific psychology will only become appropriately coherent by raising itself to the level of a "meta-psychology". See *Phenomenology*.

Bibliography: Binswanger, L.: Einführung in die Probleme der allgemeinen Psychologie. Berlin, 1922.

Id.: Grundformen und Erkenntnis menschlichen Daseins. Zürich, [2]1953. **Id.**: Being-in-the-world. New York, 1963. **Guillaumin, J.**: La dynamique de l'entretien psychologique. Paris, 1965. **Merleau-Ponty, M.**: The phenomenology of perception. London & New York, 1964. **Id.**: The structure of behavior. Boston, 1963. **Id.**: Les sciences de l'homme et la phénoménologie. Bull. de Psychologie, 1964, *18*, 141–70. **Muller, P.**: De la psychologie à l'anthropologie. Neuchâtel, 1946. **Id.**: La psychologie dans le monde moderne. Brussels, 1966. **Piaget, J.** (Ed.): Logique et connaissance scientifique. Paris, 1968. **Id.**: Psychology and philosophy. In: **Wolman, B. B. & Nagel, E.** (Eds): Scientific psychology: principles and approaches. New York, 1965, 28–43. **Pongratz, L. J.**: Problemgeschichte der Psychologie. Berne & Munich, 1967. **Pradines, M.**: Traité de psychologie générale, 3 vols. Paris, 1943. **Sartre, J.-P.**: Imagination: a psychological critique. Ann Arbor, Mich., 1962. **Strasser, S.**: Phénoménologie et sciences de l'homme. Louvain & Paris, 1967. *P. Muller*

Generation (*Alternation of generations; Metagenesis*). In the biological sense, a generation is the complete life cycle of an organism from the fertilized ovum (zygote) to the sexually mature individual, who himself in turn develops sex cells and produces offspring.

The *alternation of generations* is alternation between generations produced in a different manner. The term *heterogony* means that offspring are produced in different ways from the sex cells, e.g. one generation from normally fertilized ova and the next from unfertilized ova (see *Parthenogenesis*) as is the case, e.g., in water fleas and *Phylloxera vastatrix*. On the other hand, an alternation of one generation produced by a sexual and the other by an asexual process is known as *metagenesis*. E.g.: the *coelenterata*. The jelly-fish produces, by normal sexual processes, zygotes from which polyps develop. The polyp in turn produces the jelly-fish generation by asexual means, through blastogenesis. *H.S.*

Generation gap. Commonly observed problems and conflicts in the different forms of interaction between young people and members of the older generation (youthful protests against rules made by parents and teachers, sometimes also demonstrations against political decisions—which are generally made by members of the older generation). Possible explanations for these phenomena: (*a*) incompatible attitudes in the two age groups: a conservative attitude aiming to maintain the benefits of past achievements on the part of the older generation, and a tendency for the younger generation to be progressive, force changes, and improve traditional patterns by innovation; (*b*) a stereotyped approach on both sides to members of the other group; young people consider their elders to be obstinate, obstructive and outmoded, while they themselves are accused by their elders of showing an inadequate sense of responsibility, lack of experience and idleness, i.e. they are not recognized as adults. See *Authoritarian personality; Prejudice; Stereotype.*

Bibliography: Maccoby, E. E., Newcomb, T. M. & Hartley, E. L. (Eds): Readings in social psychology. New York, [3]1958. **Shanas, E. & Streib, G. F.** (Eds): Social structure and the family: generational relations. Englewood Cliffs, 1965. **Wilkins, L. T.**: Delinquent generations. London, 1960. *A.S.-M.*

Generative glands. See *Gonads.*

Genetic psychology. See *Development; Traits.*

Genetics. The theory of heredity. The physical and mental characteristics formed during the process of individualization of a living being are primarily conditioned by inherited factors (see *Gene*) in the sex cells. A secondary modification of these characteristics through environmental influences can only take place within the framework of modification determined by these inherited factors. Genetics studies both the extent to which characteristics are genetically conditioned, i.e. the extent of the modification range determined by heredity, and the way in which heredity conditions the development of characteristics by chemical and physical means (*molecular genetics*).

Bibliography: Haggis, G. M. (Ed.): Introduction to molecular biology. London, 1964. **Srb, A. M., Owen, R. D. & Edgar, R. S.:** General genetics. San Francisco & London, [2]1965. **Wagner, R. P. & Mitchell, H. K.:** Genetics and metabolism. New York & London, [2]1963. **Watson, J. D.:** The molecular biology of the gene. New York & Amsterdam, 1965. *H. S.*

Geneva scheme. Compilation of main features for work evaluation systems, developed by the ILO (International Labor Organization) in Geneva in 1950. *G.R.W.M.*

Geneva school. A designation for the branch of developmental psychology founded by J. Piaget and his co-workers (especially B. Inhelder and A. Szeminska). With its studies of the development of intelligence and perception (since 1921) and of genetic epistemology (since 1950), the Geneva school has made one of the most valuable and extensive contributions in this field. J. Piaget's theories can be understood most readily in the light of functionalism (J. Dewey, J. Mc. K. Cattell, E. Claparède).

Bibliography: Flavell, J. A.: The developmental psychology of Jean Piaget. New York, 1963. *H.Z.*

Geniology. See *Giftedness; Genius.*

Genital stage (syn. *Genital phase; Genital period*). Divided by Freud into an early and late genital phase. In the early phase, also known as the Oedipal (Oedipus) phase (app. four and five years of age), a child becomes interested (among other things) in his sexual organs. He becomes aware of the anatomical difference between the two sexes, and begins to accept the existence of two sexes and his own sex as a reality. According to Freud, this interest is connected with self-manipulation (of the sexual organs) and, in addition to previous forms of contact, with a desire for specific sexual contact with the parent of the other sex. The boy no longer looks upon his mother merely as a person who cares for him and makes demands on him, but also as a woman. He exhibits his newly discovered "manliness" (see *Phallic stage*); lays claim to his mother's sole attention; and thus comes into conflict with his father. The girl continues to look upon her mother as a person who makes demands and fulfills needs, but turns toward her father with the onset of heterosexual interest—i.e. to a person who is psychologically more novel for her—and therefore comes into conflict with the mother. The conflicts are resolved with increasing adequacy during the early genital phase, usually by partial repression of sexual interest in the parent of the opposite sex, and by identification with the parent of the same sex. These interests are generally repressed less strongly by a girl than by a boy; she remains attached to the father as an object of heterosexual love rather more strongly than a boy remains attached to the mother. The total bond between a son and his mother is, however, often somewhat stronger than a girl's attachment to her mother (or father), because he does not have to give up his primary object of love in the early genital phase as a girl must. Fixation and subsequent regression to the early genital phase may lead to hysteria (q.v.) (anxiety hysteria and phobia on the one hand, conversion hysteria on the other) and to homosexual perversion (see *Homosexuality*); and, in cases of less traumatic attachment in the early genital phase, to impotence or potency problems in the man, and to frigidity and vaginism in the woman. Instead of specific neurotic symptoms, a character change may also occur, i.e. a hysterical personality may develop. This personality type tends to a greater extent than other individuals to look upon social situations as sexual trial situations, and to satisfy his interests in a confused and apparently dishonest manner, or to react with excessive anxiety and defense. In the late genital phase, which begins after the latency phase in puberty, the young person develops an increasingly realistic interest in individuals of the opposite sex, who are generally of much the same age. The late genital phase extends throughout adult life.

Bibliography: **Fenichel, O.:** The psychoanalytic theory of neurosis. New York, 1945. **Freud, S.:** Three essays on the theory of sexuality. London, [2]1962. **Id.:** Introductory lectures on psycho-analysis. London, [2]1929. **Toman, W.:** An introduction to psychoanalytic theory of motivation. London & New York, 1960.

W. Toman

Genius. A high level of intellectual ability. Research on the subject generally takes an IQ of 135 or 140 as the lower "limit of genius". This definition would include between 0·5 and 1 per cent of the population, i.e. the most gifted. See *Giftedness; Abilities.* *K.P.*

Genome; Genome mutation. "Genome" denotes the totality of genetic material (hereditary substance) present in a cell. Since this material is localized on the chromosomes, in general all the chromosomes present in a cell are defined as the genome.

Genome mutation is the chromosomal alteration which occurs under physical or chemical environmental influences. For example, the whole set of chromosomes, or individual chromosomes, may be doubled.

H.S.

Genotype. The totality of hereditary dispositions of an individual (see *Phenotype*). Individuals with the same genotype may show varying features, because of differing environmental influences during their development, but only within the genetically fixed range of variation. *H.S.*

Geometric mean. The geometric mean (G) of a quantity of N positive values—a measurement of the central tendency of the distribution—is the Nth root of the product of these values (means):

$$G = \left(\overset{N}{\underset{i=1}{\pi}} X_i\right)^{1/N}$$

If a geometric mean exists, it is situated between the harmonic (q.v.) and the arithmetic mean (q.v.). *W.H.B.*

Geometrical-optical illusions. Geometrical-optical illusions in the wide sense represent one form of perceptual illusion. They may occur in three-, two- and one-dimensional patterns in the field of vision, in regard to size, shape and position, distance and direction of observation, and may also affect the (metric) relationship between these factors. Illusions of this kind in the narrow sense occur if, in the case of a figure presented on a frontal-parallel plane, the phenomenal distance, angular, directional or curvature characteristics deviate from their original correlates. Illusions in this narrower sense are dealt with in the remainder of this article.

Studies of these phenomena began in the mid-nineteenth century. Initially the various illusions—named after their discoverers (J. J. Oppel, F. Zollner, J. C. Poggendorff, etc.)—were only demonstrated, by means of a drawn figure. Quantitative analyses were added at the turn of the century. A figure which is still generally known as the Müller-Lyer illusion (q.v.), but was in fact developed much earlier by Oppel, was frequently adduced as an example. In figures of this kind, phenomenal equivalence is assumed between the section i which "undergoes the illusion" and a variable, isolated comparison value; the difference between i and the isolated value which appears equal to i ("equivalent" value) is the measure of (absolute) illusion. Hofmann summarized the literature on this subject in 1920. Later on, other figures were added, e.g. a parallelogram-diagonal illusion generally named after F. Sander, but already described previously by M. Luckiesh, which has been studied in particular detail.

Of the many incorrect attempts to explain such illusions, some (a) referred to the peripheral sense organ (the structure of the retina, its curvature, functional irregularity, spatial values, eye movements, etc.; and others (*b*) to previous experience relating in particular to perspective, to confusions, errors of judgment, etc. The hypotheses referred to in (*a*) above, as well as the perspective theory, are refuted by the fact that they do not also explain the analogous haptic illusions (q.v.). Although contradictory evidence does not prevent the outmoded explanations from being quoted occasionally today, it has become increasingly clear that these illusions are not determined by peripheral conditions or superimposed information from the memory or reasoning, but that their origin lies in central processes of configuration (gestalt formation). This is confirmed by the fact that there are many functional relationships between these illusions and such phenomena as apparent movement which are known to be centrally conditioned.

There has been much research into geometrical-optical illusions in recent decades, and work is still continuing. Research has concentrated on three partially overlapping areas: (*a*) *Principles* and *methods* of measurement have been developed by introducing the phenogram, i.e. the total-figural equivalent, instead of partial value equivalents; (*b*) *Functional analysis* has led to the following discoveries: the phenomenal metrics varies with the phenomenal structure; pregnance tendencies and other intra-figural forces may cause illusions; fixation and attention characteristics, contrast and adaptation, are again taken into account for explanatory purposes from new points of view; there are points of relation between geometrical-optical illusions and figural after-effects; excessively long consideration of a single figure leads to a reduction in the degree of illusion; (*c*) These illusions have been applied primarily in developmental psychology and personality theory, where it has been found that there is no general "illusion characteristic" (whose extent, varying from individual to individual, could be used to indicate a state of development or type). The principles of cognition theory which hold good for perceptual illusions are particularly applicable to geometrical-optical illusions (see *Perception, illusions of; Visual perception*).

Bibliography: Gregory, A. H.: Visual perception. London, 1970. **Hofmann, F. B.:** Die Lehre vom Raumsinn des Auges, Part 1. Berlin, 1920. **Oyama, T.:** Japanese studies on the so-called geometrical-optical illusions. Psychologia, Int. J. Psychol. Orient., 1960, *3*. **Piaget, J.:** The mechanisms of perception. London, 1969. **Rausch, E.:** Struktur und Metrik figural-optischer Wahrnehmung, Frankfurt a. M., 1952. **Id.:** Probleme der Metrik. In: **Metzger, W.** (Ed.): Hb. der Psychol., Vol. 1. Göttingen, 1966, 776–865. **Vernon, M. D.** (Ed.): Experiments in visual perception. Harmondsworth, 1966.

E. Rausch

Geopsychology. A scientific discipline and research area, in which the natural environment is studied in its relationship to behavior and mental states. A distinction is made between four principal factors (Hellpach): the influences of weather, climate, soil and landscape. After preparatory work and studies by Montesquieu and C. Lombroso, this subject is becoming increasingly important today in the context of the study of problems of human life under abnormal or atypical conditions: in the polar areas, tropics, bases on the sea-bed, interplanetary space. Some of the work of geopsychology has now been taken over by rhythm research; in biological anthropology, geopsychological problems are considered from the ecological standpoint.

Bibliography: Hellpach, W.: Die geopsychischen Erscheinungen. Leipzig, 1923. **Id.:** Geopsyche. Die Menschenseele unter dem Einfluss von Wetter und Klima, Boden und Landschaft. Stuttgart, [6]1950. **Sells, S. B. & Berry, C. A.** (Eds): Human factors in jet and space travel: a medical-psychological analysis. New York, 1961.

P.M.

Geotaxis. Alignment and movement of lower organisms as a function of gravity as the releasing stimulus. A distinction is made between movement in the direction of the force of gravity (positive geotaxis), and movement in the opposite direction (negative geotaxis). See *Taxis*. *F.C.S.*

Geriatrics. Medical research into the phenomena of old age (pathological conditions of old age) is a branch of gerontology (q.v.) and was first elevated into a scientific discipline by the work of M. Burger and E. Abderhalden in the 1930s. It provides valuable information for "social" gerontology, a field of study founded at international level in 1950, in order to help in remedying the increasing social problems encountered by the aged. See *Aging*. *F.N.*

Gerontology is the science of aging. The term derives from the Greek *geron*—old man, and came into use in the early part of the twentieth century with the increased scientific interest in the processes of aging. The appearance in 1939 of *Problems of Ageing*, edited by E. V. Cowdry, reflected the growing interest in research into aging. Technologically advanced countries now provide conditions in which large numbers of persons survive to old age; hence studies of aging are undertaken from the viewpoint of social science as well as of biology.

Gerontology can be regarded as having three major divisions: biomedical, behavioral, and social. Biomedical problems of aging clearly show the interaction of the biological aging of the organism and its susceptibility to disease. Research on the biology of aging includes the study not only of man but of lower organisms, cells and subcellular components (Comfort, 1964). The behavioral aspects of gerontology include the consideration of man psychologically (as he ages individually), and sociologically (as a member of a group) (Birren, 1959). Social gerontology is concerned particularly with the implications of man's aging in society. The presence of large numbers of retired and older persons in a society has implications for economics, social welfare, and the distribution of health and other services (Tibbitts, 1960).

Most scientists would agree at present that there is no single mechanism of aging—for example, a single *lethal gene* that governs the length of life. It is probable that the biological processes of aging are controlled by the action of many genes; but the conditions under which the animal is conceived, matures and ages are also important in accelerating or retarding the processes of aging. Important issues in gerontology include: the problem of the identification of the origins of molecular errors or faults that occur in aging cells; discovering the basis of changes in memory with age; identifying the conditions predisposing to alienation and poor life-satisfaction for older persons; and determining the extent to which continuous physical and mental activity retards regressive changes of aging. Many biomedical problems also exist in our limited understanding of the etiology of diseases associated with advancing age. Research and scholarly activity devoted to gerontology will very likely develop as industrial prosperity increases, and as the growing number of older persons in society gives cause for concern about the optimum conditions for human life in the second half of the life span (see *Aging*).

Bibliography: Birren, J. E. (Ed.): Handbook of aging and the individual. Chicago, 1959. **Comfort, A.:** Aging, the biology of senescence. New York, 1964. **Cowdry, E. V.** (Ed.): Problems of ageing. Baltimore, 1939. **Tibbitts, C.** (Ed.): Handbook of social gerontology. Chicago, 1960. *J. E. Birren*

Gerontophilia. A sexual deviation in which the age of the partner plays a decisive part: sexual attraction by and preference for much older persons. Gerontophilia is the extreme opposite of pedophilia (q.v.), in which the sexual attraction diminishes, and finally ceases altogether, as the partner grows older. Gerontophilia may also occur as a secondary phenomenon in the context of a different sexual deviation, e.g. homosexuality, or may be linked with fetishism (Kronfeld, 1923). Hirschfeld interpreted gerontophilia as an "infantile fixation on older persons". Whether it is pathological, i.e. a sexually "perverse" attitude in the clinical sense, must be determined in each individual case.

Bibliography: Kronfeld, A.: Sexualpathologie. Leipzig & Vienna, 1923. **Hirschfeld, M.:** Sexual anomalies and perversions. London, [2]1952. **Giese, H.:** Psychopathologie der Sexualität. Stuttgart, 1962. *H.M.*

Gesell, Arnold. *Life and works:* B. 21/6/1880, Alma, Wisc.; d. 29/5/1961, New Haven, Conn. He studied psychology at Clark University where he took his Ph.D. in 1906; intermittent teaching work thereafter; in 1911 he founded the Clinic of Child Development at Yale University, New Haven, which he continued to direct until his retirement in 1948. He trained in medicine while assistant professor in Yale and passed his M.D. in 1915; he edited the Journal of Genetic Psychology from 1926.

Gesell is widely considered to be the "father of child psychology". He wrote more than fifteen books on child psychology and helped this branch of psychology to gain wide popularity even among laymen. His research method consisted in simple, accurate observation of children's behavior, generally with the aid of film cameras and one-way mirrors; he also made observations under controlled test conditions. The results of his studies take the form of minute descriptions of widely varying aspects of the behavior of children and young people at different ages. The chronological development summaries prepared in this way imply standards governing the development of children in the areas of behavior under consideration and are intended to help in predicting subsequent mental development. In reality, these aims were not satisfactorily met, particularly because the observational material on which the studies were based was much too narrow (sometimes only eleven cases) for individual age groups, and unrepresentative. Gesell's approach was purely descriptive. It consisted in the description and classification of individual findings without any attempt to lay down a theory of mental development or analyze the factors which influence it. The process of development appears as something mechanical and immutable in his work. He overemphasizes the constitutional aspect and cyclical nature of development, while underestimating the significance of individual variations, and of cultural and social influences on development.

Major works: The mental growth of the pre-school child. New York, 1925. Infancy and human growth. New York, 1928. An atlas of human behavior: a systematic delineation of the forms and early growth of human behavior patterns, Vols. 1 & 2, New Haven, 1934. The feeding behavior of infants: a pediatric approach to the mental hygiene of early life. Philadelphia, 1937 (with F. L. Ilg). Reciprocal neuromotor interweaving: a principle of development evidenced in the patterning of infant behavior. *J. Comp. Neurol.*, 1939, *70*, 161–80. The first five years of life: a guide to the study of the pre-school child. New York, 1940 (with others). Twins T and C from infancy to adolescence: a biogenetic study of individual differences by the method of co-twin control. *Genet. Psychol. Monogr.*, 1941, *24*, 3–122 (with H. Thompson). Infant and child in the culture of today: the guidance of development in home and nursery school. New York, 1942 (with F. L. Ilg and others). The child from five to ten. New York, 1946 (with F. L. Ilg). Vision, its development in infant and child. New York, 1949 (with others). Child development: an introduction to the study of human growth. New York, 1949 (with F. L. Ilg). Arnold Gesell. In: Boring, E. G., *et al.* (Eds): A history of psychology in autobiography Vol. 4. Worcester, Mass., 1952, 123–42. *W.W.*

Gesell Development Schedules (GSCH), also Gesell Development Scales, Gesell Norms of Development, Gesell Tests, Pre-school Child Test, Yale Test of Child Development. The schedules were published by A. Gesell in 1925 as a "general development test" and afterwards substantially modified (Gesell & Amatruda, 1947); they led to the preparation of other development tests (H. Hetzer, C. Bühler, etc.).

Structure: selected items for key age (infants, or pre-school children), maturity and four behavior categories corresponding to the developmental concept: "the young child is as old as his behavior".

Application: GSCH were used for development diagnosis (to estimate the development quotient) of normal and impaired children between the ages of 0 and 6; they were used primarily to determine suitability for adoption and for prediction of atypical and abnormal development processes such as amentia, brain damage, blindness, etc. The *reliability coefficients* are between $r = 0{\cdot}79$ and $r = 0{\cdot}88$. *Validity* (correlation with other development tests) is quoted as $r = 0{\cdot}37$ to $r = 0{\cdot}74$.

Bibliography: **Gesell, A. & Amatruda, C. S.:** Developmental diagnosis. Normal and abnormal child development. New York, [2]1947. *F.N.*

Gestalt. See *Ganzheit; Structure.*

Gestalt form, quality. See *Ganzheit.*

Gestogens (syn. *Progestins; Progestogens*). Progestational hormones which prepare the lining of the womb to ensure that the fertilized ovum is implanted (see *Uterus*) and that pregnancy proceeds smoothly (hence known also as "pregnancy hormones"). They provide the developing ovum with optimal protection in the uterus. The most important of these natural (physiological) gestogens is *progesterone* (Micryston progesterone). Gestogens in a wider sense are synthetic hormones. They are administered as oral contraceptives (see *Contraception*) and are also used in the treatment of other disorders, such as acne and excessive menstrual bleeding. *H.M.*

g factor. A term used in the literature of factor analysis for general factor (q.v.). *W.H.B.*

G factor. A personality factor ("superego strength") derived by R. B. Cattell by factor analysis and included in Factor VI of the second order (volitional control and persistence). *W.H.B.*

Gibson effect. A group of negative aftereffects that set in after prolonged observation of special patterns (field of uniformly curved lines, pattern of oblique lines, etc.) as a result of adaptation (q.v.). The term is used in the literature to distinguish this phenomenon from figural aftereffects (q.v.) and negative aftereffects in Stratton's experiment (q.v.).

Bibliography: **Gibson, J. J.:** Adaptation, after-effect and contrast in the perception of curved lines. J. exp. Pscyhol. 1933, *16*, 1–31. *A.H.*

Giftedness, research into. The study of the causes and factors of high intellectual ability (see *Genius*) and its distribution and forms. Studies by L. M. Terman of the development of highly-gifted individuals have shown that these persons are also, e.g., emotionally more stable (less neurotic). The theory subscribed to by, e.g., Lange–Eichbaum (1928) that genius is accompanied by deficient emotional and social adaptability must therefore be rejected. Family studies have shown that giftedness occurs frequently in several members of a family; genetic factors and (above all) factors connected with the family environment are probably responsible for this. Qualitative research into giftedness (e.g. examination of the factors in thought processes and problem-solving strategy which make possible the creative achievements of genius) is still in the early stages. See *Abilities; Creativity; Intelligence.*

Bibliography: **Anastasi, A.:** Differential psychology. New York, [3]1966. **Guilford, J. P.:** The nature of human intelligence. New York, 1967. **Lange-Eichbaum, W.:** Genie, Irrsinn und Ruhm. Munich, 1928. **Terman, L. M.** *et al.*: Genetic studies of genius,

Vols 1–5. Stanford, 1926–59. **Vernon, P. E.** (Ed.): Creativity. Harmondsworth, 1970. *K.P.*

Gilbreth chronoscope. An instrument fitted with a large dial and used for measuring minute units of time. It finds application in the study of slight movements recorded cinematographically. The time units and the movements are recorded simultaneously on the film, so that the sequence of movements can be plotted against time. *A.Th.*

Glandotropic hormones. Hormones (q.v.) of the anterior lobe of the pituitary that stimulate hormone production in the endocrine glands. The most important are: *adrenocorticotropic hormone* (ACTH, q.v.), which stimulates production of adrenal hormones (corticosteroids, q.v.); *thyrotropic hormone* (thyrotropine), which stimulates production of thyroid hormones; gonadotropins (q.v.), which stimulate production of sex hormones (follicle stimulating hormone, luteinizing hormone, luteotropic hormone). The production of glandotropic hormones is governed by many factors, especially by the hormones present in the blood and produced in the peripheral glands (negative feedback) and by the releasing factors of the hypothalamus.

Bibliography: Harris, G. W.: Neural control of the pituitary gland. London, 1955. **Harris, G. W. & Donovan, D. T.:** The pituitary gland, Vols 1–3. London, 1966. **Szentagthal, J., Flerko, B., Mess, B. & Halasz, B.:** Hypothalamic control of anterior pituitary. Budapest, 1962. *W.J.*

Glands. Organs of the body which produce special secretions. *Endocrine* glands such as the thyroid gland (q.v.), the adrenal glands (q.v.), the islet cells of the pancreas, the ovaries and the testes discharge hormones into the blood stream, whereas *exocrine* glands such as the sweat, sebaceous, lacrimal, salivary, and digestive glands release their contents to outside the body, or the gastrointestinal tract. According to their histological structure, glands are divided into the acinous and the tubular, and the latter may themselves be divided into straight, coiled or branched. The masses of lymphatic tissue wrongly called "lymph glands" are more correctly described as *lymph nodes.* *E.D.*

Glandula pituitaria. See *Hypophysis.*

Glare (*Dazzle*). A diminution of visual performance (visual acuity, differential, form and color sensitivity, depth vision, etc.) as a result of inadequate lighting, or of a visual environment unfavorable to visual characteristics. In the narrower sense, glare defined by visual performance is called disability glare, or physiological glare, in contrast to discomfort glare, or psychological glare, which is defined by a diminution of the comfort, well-being, etc., of an individual or group of individuals.

Kinds of physiological glare: (*a*) absolute glare: too high light intensities, adaptation to which is impossible; (*b*) adaptation glare: sudden change of the light-intensity level; (*c*) relative glare: too great contrasts relative to the light-intensity level; (*d*) direct glare: glare coming from the light source itself; (*e*) indirect glare: reflection images, e.g., from light sources; (*f*) in-field and (*g*) peripheral field glare: cause of glare central or peripheral; (*h*) simultaneous and (*i*) successive glare: whether the cause of glare operates during or after its presence, and (*j*) fog or haze glare: the result of extensive and illuminated expanding media such as fog, smoke, curtain material, etc. For quantitative relationships see H. Schober (1964).

Bibliography: Schober, H.: Das Sehen. Leipzig, 1964. *A.H.*

Glia cells. The brain contains about ten times as many glia cells as nerve cells. Glia cells form the non-neural part of the brain tissue.

It is estimated that the human brain contains 100–130 thousand million glia cells, classified by shape into astrocytes, oligodendrocytes and microgliocytes (frequency ratio 60:30:10). Their frequency distribution varies from one region of the brain to another. They are regarded as transmitters in the process of biochemical interchange. It has not yet been determined with absolute certainty to what extent glia cells participate in neural processes. Importance attaches to the glia index N_gL/N_{neur}, where N_{gl} is the number of glia cells and N_{neur} the number of neurons. This index is useful for a comparison of the various layers and regions of the brain. Moreover, it provides an indicator for specific physical as well as mental disorders, and changes characteristically in the course of ontogenesis and phylogenesis. *M.A.*

Global learning consists in mastering the material to be studied, e.g. a poem or piece of music, by tackling it and committing it to memory as a whole. The effectiveness of this method increases with the student's familiarity with it, his intelligence, and the meaningful content of the material and the systematic way in which it is put together. It declines if the material is too lengthy, contains difficult passages, and follows a natural pattern. *G.H.*

Glucagon. A polypeptide hormone secreted in the islands of Langerhans (q.v.) in the pancreas. By breaking down glycogen in the liver it increases blood sugar concentration. Glucagon stimulates the production of insulin (q.v.). It probably exerts only a slight influence on the onset of diabetes. Glucagon is used in the treatment of severe hypoglycemic disorders.

Bibliography: **Foa, P. P.:** Glukagon. In: Ergebnisse der Physiologie, biologischen Chemie und exp. Pharmakologie, Vol. 60. Berlin, 1968. *W.J.*

Glutamic acid. A mono-amino-dicarboxylic acid manufactured as needed in the body and supplied to the organism, together with other amino acids, either in dietary albumin or in pure (or synthetic) form. It is of primary importance in the intermediate metabolism, and serves in the organism as a precursor of GABA (gamma-amino-butyric acid, q.v.). Glutamic acid has aroused special interest among psychologists because it is understood to raise mental performance among persons of low intelligence when administered over a protracted period. There have been numerous investigations, but owing to the inadequacy of the methods used, no clear interpretation is possible. No psychological effects are found after a single administration of glutamic acid.

Bibliography: **Astin, A. W. & Ross, S.:** Glutamic acid and human intelligence. Psychol. Bull., 1960, *57*, 429–34. **Lingmüller, V.:** Biochemie, Physiologie und Linik der Glutaminsäure. Aulendorf, 1955. **Vogel, W., Broverman, D. M., Dragus, J. G. & Klaiber, E. L.:** The role of glutamic acid in cognitive behaviors. Psychol. Bull., 1966, *65*, 367–82. *W.J.*

Goal gradient. C. L. Hull's term for a regular increase in efficiency while approaching a goal.

Goal orientation. The tendency to orientation toward the goal. *K.F.*

Goal orientation device. See *Maze learning.*

Golden mean (syn. *Golden section*). An esthetic ratio of division in which the *whole* bears the same proportion to the *larger* part as the latter to the *smaller*. *W.H.B.*

Gonadodysgenesia. Failure of the sex glands to develop in accordance with genetic constitution, resulting in anomalies such as an individual with XY chromosome structure manifesting female form. *G.D.W.*

Gonadotrop(h)ic hormones. Active hormonal

substances (albumin compounds) that act directly on male or female gonads (testes, ovaries), stimulating and controlling their growth as well as their endocrine function (production of male or female sex-hormones) and their exocrine function (production of semen, spermatozoa in man; ova and ovaries in woman). They are not sex-specific.

Two groups of gonadotropic hormones are distinguished:

1. *Pituitary gonadotropins*, secreted in the anterior pituitary under the influence of releasing factors of the hypothalamus: (*a*) FSH (*follicle stimulating hormone*) which stimulates the growth of ovarian follicles and, with gonadotropin, brings on the onset of LH maturity and estrogen production of the follicle; and in man the growth of mature sperms in the seminiferous tubules; (*b*) ICSH (*interstitial cell stimulating hormone;* in woman also LH, luteinizing hormone), which controls in particular the secretion of sex hormones in male and female gonads; (*c*) LTH (*luteotropic hormone*), which stimulates the growth and onset of maturity of the female breast (lactogenic hormone).

2. *Placental gonadotropins*, secreted only during pregnancy: (*a*) HCG (*human chorionic gonadotropin*), is produced in bulk in the placenta; (*b*) HPL (*human placental lactogen*), produced in the placenta, supports the action of HCG; (*c*) PMSG (*pregnant mare serum gonadotropin*), which is present in large quantities in the serum of pregnant mares (characterized biologically by a powerful follicle-stimulating effect).

Hormonal regulation mechanisms between primary stimulating centers (anterior pituitary, hypothalamus) and periphery (sex glands) are basically the same in the two sexes. The interaction of gonadotropic and sex hormones proceeds on the lines of a feedback system (e.g. FSH brings on, jointly with LH, the onset of follicular maturity and estrogen production; increasing estrogen production, in turn, slows down FSH secretion in the anterior pituitary). This feedback effect is the basis of hormonal contraception: gonadotropic production is blocked by a constant inflow of estrogens and gestogens, so that the rhythm of the female cycle is interrupted, inhibiting ovulation and, therefore, fertilization.

Bibliography: Suhl, A. M.: Gonadal hormones and social behavior in infrahuman vertebrates. In: **Young, W. C.** (Ed.): Sex and internal secretions. Baltimore, 1961. **Voigt, K. D. & Schmidt, H.:** Sexualhormone. Hamburg, 1968.

H.M.

Gonadotropins. Glandotropic hormones (q.v.) of the anterior pituitary that stimulate production of sex hormones (q.v.). The 3 main gonadotropins are the *follicle stimulating hormone* (FSH, Prolan A), the *luteinizing hormone* (LH), the *interstitial cell stimulating hormone* (ICSH, Prolan B) and the *luteotropic hormone* (LTH, prolactin). The secretory mechanism of gonadotropins is largely unaccounted for. The often alleged reduction of gonadotropins under stress has not been confirmed by recent investigations.

Bibliography: Albert, A. (Ed.): Human pituitary gonadotropins. Springfield, Ill., 1961. **Apostolakis, M. & Voigt, K. D.:** Gonadotropine. Stuttgart, 1964. **Giuliani, G.:** Studies on gonadotropin release during stressful situations and the role of the central nervous system. In: **Bajusz, E.** (Ed.): Physiology and pathology of adaptation mechanisms. Oxford, 1969.

W.J.

Gonads. *Sex glands:* in man the testis, which produces the male sex hormone (androgen); in woman the ovary, which produces the female sex hormone (estrogen and *corpus luteum* hormone). The testis also produces spermatozoa (sperm), while in the female ovary an ovum ripens every four weeks. The gonadal hormones exert considerable influence on the formation of secondary sex organs, the physique structure of both sexes, and the individual's behavior as a male or female.

E.D.

Goodenough Test (*Draw-a-Man test*, DAM). A non-verbal intelligence test for children

of 3–13 years. The child is required to draw a man. The simple evaluation technique, intelligence-age norms, and a satisfactory degree of reliability, assure the test widespread use. The existence of significant relationships with general intelligence and social adaptation factors has been established.
E.F.-K.

Gosset chart. The tabling of "Student's" t distribution of critical probability α and sample size N. With its aid the t test (q.v.) for the statistical testing of significance can be speeded up. *W.H.B.*

Gottschaldt's figures (*Embedded, hidden figures*). Complex sets of figures in which part-figures of the simplest kind can be isolated, recognized or perceived only with difficulty because of their structural embedding in the overall figure, in whose structure they lie concealed. Test figures of this kind characterize the factor "flexibility of closure".
H.H.

Gradient, approach-avoidance. According to N. E. Miller's goal gradient theory, approach and avoidance gradients are *curvilinear* functions of the *proximity of the goal* and *drive strength*. Approach and avoidance tendencies, which arise in typical conflict situations and under ambiguous stimuli, and are measured, for example, by answers in the Thematic Apperception Test (TAT), and by skin resistance, can be represented graphically as gradients. The point at which the gradients intersect is that of the maximum degree of conflict and, depending on the type of conflict, is known as *labile* or *stable* equilibrium. See *Conflict*. *F.N.*

Grammar can be understood as the *linguistic competence* of the speaker of a natural language (q.v.), and in particular as a regulative system by which relations are established between particular sound systems (see *Phonemics*), sound sequences (see *Morphemics*), rules of syntax (rules for forming sentences), and the associated meanings of sound sequences (see *Semantics*).

Every theory of grammar must try to account for the fact that a competent language user can understand, or produce in a way intelligible to others, an unlimited number of sentences never before heard. The principles that enable sentences of unlimited number or length to be assembled from a finite repertoire of elements and rules are known as *recursive rules*.

Structural description provides data on the constituents of sentences, their interrelation and sequence (*phrase-structure rules*), and on the grammatical information needed for interpreting sentences. Various grammatical models exist for structural description, e.g. *generative* (*transformational*) *grammar* (Chomsky, 1957, 1965, 1968), whose analysis in accordance with "immediate constituents" (first level: e.g. subject-predicate), or analysis by means of "transformational rules" (or rules for re-ordering and recombining sentence constituents), is concerned with the generative properties of the *basic* or *deep structure* which corresponds to the "meaning", or fundamental semantic relations, of the sentence. Actual utterances can assume other, at times more complicated, structures (*surface structure*, or structural relations between elements of a sentence) which can be formed in linguistic analysis from the basic structure by using transformational rules to re-order the fundamental constituents. In speech (q.v.) surface structures undergo phonological interpretation and are expressed phonetically (see *Phonemics*). (For the analysis of deep structure, see Chomsky, 1965.)

Language acquisition (grammar acquisition) is explained variously. The empiricist view (e.g. Skinner, 1957) is that language is mastered exclusively by *learning*. Rationalist-nativist theories (e.g. Chomsky, 1968; Chomsky & Halle, 1968) assume that language acquisition also depends on specific *predispositions.* The speed with which basic rules are derived and applied in ontogeny from pre-existing language, suggests the existence of preformed (possibly universal) formal principles of grammatical structuralization. Analyses of spoken language appear to show that linguistic competence, e.g. between the ages of 24 and 29 months (age of two- and three-word utterances), draws on only a few grammatical classes which are embodied in simple hierarchic rules:

$$S_1 \rightarrow N + N$$
$$S_2 \rightarrow P + N$$
$$S_3 \rightarrow P + NP$$
$$NP \rightarrow \{P_N\} + N$$

N = noun
P = pivot word class (containing adjectives and modifiers)
NP = noun complex
$\begin{Bmatrix} X \\ Y \end{Bmatrix}$ = either X or Y

These rules correspond to the *basic,* or *deep, structures* of adult competence. Derived, transposed structures do not yet make their appearance. Children thus seem to begin their *grammatical development* with the syntactical forms immediately associated with semantic interpretation. From the behaviorist point of view it might be expected instead that the child would first learn from the surface structures used by adults (see Braine, 1963; Brown & Bellugi, 1964; Brown & Hanlon, 1970; Miller & McNeill, 1969).

This use of Chomsky's notion of competence is criticized on the ground that it takes account only of what is systematic in speech, of *grammaticality* (q.v.), and not of the context in which utterances are made. For the competence value that verbal utterances acquire through their position in the verbal and situational context, Campbell & Wales (1970) would like to substitute "communicative competence". Consequently, the observational basis of the speech acquisition theory of McNeill (1968) also appears to be inadequate, as it includes no situational parameter. Other reasons could be adduced for the fact that children do not at first make use of any "derived" sentence structures. Brown & Hanlon (1970) try to incorporate the communicative milieu in the observation of speech development, in order to find out whether speech acquisition is partly determined by specific selections of the child from the supply of information available to it (see also Bernstein, 1961, 1965; Brown, 1965; Irwin, 1960). See *Language; Psycholinguistics; Speech; Verbal behavior; Concept.*

Bibliography: Bernstein, B.: Social class and linguistic development: a theory of social learning. In: **Halsey, A. H.** *et al.* (Eds): Education, economy and society. New York, 1961. **Id.:** A socio-linguistic approach to social learning. In: **Gould, J.** (Ed.): Penguin survey of the social sciences. Harmondsworth, 1965. **Braine, M. D. S.:** The ontogeny of English phrase structure: the first phrase. Language, 1963, *39*, 1–13. **Brown, R.:** Social psychology. New York, 1965. **Brown, R. & Bellugi, U.:** Three processes in the child's acquisition of syntax. Harv. educ. Rev., 1964, *34*, 133–51. **Brown, R. & Hanlon, C.:** Derivational complexity and order of acquisition in child speech. In: **Hays, J. R.** (Ed.): Cognition and the development of language. New York, 1970. **Campbell, R. & Wales, R.:** The study of language acquisition. In: **Lyons, J.** (Ed.): New horizons in linguistics. Harmondsworth, 1970. **Chomsky, N.:** Syntactic structures. The Hague, 1957. **Id.:** A review of B. F. Skinner's verbal behavior. Language, 1959, *35*, 26–58. **Id.:** Aspects of the theory of syntax. Cambridge, Mass., 1965. **Id.:** Language and mind. New York, 1968. **Chomsky, N. & Miller, G. A.:** Introduction to the formal analysis of natural languages. In: **Luce, R. D., Bush, R. R. & Galanter, E.** (Eds): Handbook of mathematical psychology, Vol. 2. New York, 1963. **Chomsky, N. & Halle, M.:** The sound pattern of English. New York, 1968. **Irwin, O. C.:** Language and communication. In: **Mussen, P. H.** (Ed.): Handbook of research methods in child development. New York, 1960. **McNeill, D.:** Developmental psycholinguistics. In: **Smith, F. & Miller, G. A.** (Eds): The genesis of language. Cambridge, Mass., 1968. **Miller, G. A. & McNeill, D.:** Psycholinguistics. In: **Lindzey, G. & Aronson, E.** (Eds): Handbook of social psychology, Vol. III. Reading, Mass., 1969. **Skinner, B. F.:** Verbal behavior. New York, 1957.

W. Abraham

Grammaticality. A language structure is grammatically correct when grammar (q.v.)

allows it a structural description. This presupposes that this structure can also be interpreted semantically, and if so, that the possibility of so interpreting an utterance (i.e. pragmatically) need not of itself imply proficient grammatical form. The boundary line between "correct" grammar (grammaticality) and deviant grammar (caused by sociological and redundancy factors—obvious errors where the context is situatively adequate) is a fluid one. A further distinction must be made between grammaticality and *acceptability*.

Bibliography: Halliday, M. A. K.: Categories of the theory of grammar. Word, 1961, *17*, 241–92. **Jespersen, O.:** Philosophy of grammar. London, 1924. **Leech, G. N.:** English in advertising. London, 1966. **Palmer, F.:** Grammar. Harmondsworth, 1971. **Sebeok, T. A. (Ed.):** Style in language. Cambridge, Mass., 1960. **Warburg, J. F.:** The best-chosen English. London, 1961. **Id.:** Verbal values. London, 1966. *W.A.*

Grandeur, delusion of. A false belief which qualifies as a delusion, that the person has a social position or ancestors of importance and renown, or great wealth, possessions, abilities or powers. *B.B.*

Grand mal. *Major* epileptic attack. Clinically subdivided into pre-convulsive, convulsive and post-convulsive phases. The first is characterized by prodromes (premonitory symptoms) which may take the form of irritability, moodiness, tension, or minor attacks. Alongside these general symptoms are frequently found peculiar sensations which immediately precede the onset of the fit, and to which the term *aura* is applied. This is the patient's last experience, generally accompanied by acute anxiety, before unconsciousness sets in. The seizure itself consists first of a tonic contraction, then of a clonic (tumultuous) spasm which, though usually symmetrical, can take a variety of forms. In the post-convulsive phase the patient remains for some minutes in a profound coma (q.v.). This is followed by a deep sleep lasting a few hours, in some cases by a state of semi-consciousness. The attack is followed by amnesia in regard to the entire event. The spasms can be recorded objectively by EEG (electroencephalogram, q.v.) observation of correlative electrical currents developed by the cerebral cortex. Even between attacks there are often typical indications. So far there has been no satisfactory explanation for the onset of an epileptic fit. It may be assumed that in a general way all CNS substance is spasm-prone, and that in epilepsy the normal properties of the CNS are present on an exaggerated scale. Treatment consists largely in the administration of CNS-depressant drugs. To a limited extent, recourse may be had to stereotactic (q.v.) methods, which also often have a favorable effect on the attendant psychic behavior, e.g. aggressiveness, moodiness, and so on.

Bibliography: Janz, D.: Die Epilepsien. Spezielle Pathologie und Therapie. Stuttgart, 1969. **Penfield, W. & Jasper, H.:** Epilepsy and the functional anatomy of the human brain. Boston, 1954. *M.Ad.*

Graph. A series of points joined by a line, which is the edge of the graph. Graphs are used to represent the structure of a system. A graph is finite if it has a finite number of edges and points. A graph usually shows a variable as it varies in comparison with one or more other variables. *P.-B.H.*

Graphic representation. The pictorial delineation of a numerical result. *W.H.B.*

Graphology. I. 1. *Terminology; concept.* "Graphology" is a technical term from the Greek *graphein* = to write, and *logos* = account. The word was first used by Abbé Jean-Hippolyte Michon, and is to be found in his *Système de graphologie* (1875). More recently, the expression "psychology of handwriting" has been used with the same meaning. In the U.S.A., usage varies between "grapho-analysis" and "handwriting analysis". Graphology claims to be a scientific diagnostic method for learning about the writer's personality from his handwriting. In contrast to most "psycho-technical" tests, graphology attempts to apprehend the whole personality and not merely individual characteristics. It is not itself a science, but a scientific aid in psychological diagnosis. The graphologist must be trained in psychological characterology and have some knowledge of psychiatry and neurology.

Graphology uses handwriting as its objective starting-point. No two people write in exactly the same way.

Writing represents motor activity. As such, it resembles mimicry in being a movement of the body, an individual expression (q.v.) of the personality (q.v.) in movement which writing fixes. Writing is learnt in school according to "national" models. And yet, even in the lowest class, exercise books reveal great individual differences in writing, although the collective "national" pattern may remain recognizable. It is the task of graphology to discover what each person's handwriting expresses. Some claim that inherited characteristics and those acquired later on can be recognized, and usually differentiated. Everyone's handwriting changes as he grows older and his personality develops. This is due in part to the constitution of his body and brain. A graphologist requires little equipment: an ordinary magnifying-glass and a rule are sufficient. A framed fluorescent screen can also be useful, and the work may be facilitated if a good projector is available.

In addition to establishing the details of the handwriting by analysis, a graphological diagnosis of character structure requires the use of an irrational factor—intuition (q.v.) or empathy. It is indispensable, as in all productive scientific work which is more than a mere collection of facts; however, it cannot alone justify any claim to be a science or support the reliability (q.v.) of graphology, which has been suggested in many experimental studies. Anyone who sets out to interpret handwriting by using only intuition or particularly keen "extrasensory perception" may have some success (R. Schermann), but his work can hardly be called graphology. An analytical approach must be combined with a synthetic picture of the whole, if the task is to be solved and sources of error are to be avoided.

2. *Historical survey.* By nature all people share, and indeed cannot do without, a direct understanding of what is expressed in all living movement. For that reason there was, even in antiquity, a non-scientific (or *prescientific*) interpretation of handwriting (e.g. Suetonius in the second century A.D.; in China since A.D. 1000). The first systematic approach dates from the Italian doctor C. Baldi (1622). But not until 150 years later did the Swiss pastor J. C. Lavater (1741–1801) in his *Physiognomische Fragmente zur Beförderung der Menschenkenntnis und Menschenliebe* (1775–81), make the decisive advance which was to lead to a more thorough systematic treatment of the subject. His own interpretations, however, owed too much to surmise, intuition and impression, and were often wide of the mark. But his work was widely read and proved a source of inspiration to others, especially in France (Abbé Flandrin). About a hundred years later Abbé Michon (1806–8) laid the foundations of modern graphology. He had no psychology to work on. His interpretative method was exclusively the study of individual characteristics (*signes*) of handwriting specimens. Precisely this apparent simplicity of approach awakened an almost passionate but superficial interest in large numbers of people in the nineteenth century. More responsible scientists soon attacked this frivolity. In France, for instance, J. Crépieux-Jamin (1858–1940) taught that many character traits cannot be directly established from simple graphological signs, but must be seen as combining several characteristics ("resultant theory"). Similar work was carried out in Germany by the doctors W. Preyer,

G. Meyer, etc., and above all the chemist L. Klages (1872–1956). Through his own discoveries and ideas, and those of his predecessors, he succeeded in raising graphology to a higher level. He recognized that *all handwriting characteristics had many meanings.* He sought a justifiable standpoint from which they could be judged and thought it could be found in studying the impression produced by the whole complex expression of handwriting, which he called "form level". The difficulty and relative unreliability of a study based solely on intuition caused others to split up, refine and simplify his basic concept of "form level". R. Wieser introduced the very important concept of "basic rhythm" into graphology. The Swiss M. Pulver (1889–1962), like E. Flatow-Worms and A. Mendelsohn-Teillard, introduced fundamentally psychoanalytic elements into the interpretation of handwriting. In place of "form level", as used by Klages, he endeavors to reach an integrative standpoint by the use of intuitive understanding (*Wesensschau*). Important and promising progress was made in the work of R. Pophal, Professor of Graphology at the university of Hamburg. He relates handwriting to physiological cerebral types. In so doing he creates the possibility of justifying and enriching by psychosomatic study graphological findings about personality.

3. *The present state of graphology.* At present, graphological work in the main follows the lines taken by Klages (1956), Wieser (1969) and Pophal (1965, etc.). Both mental and physiological factors are considered. Most recently, influenced by the quantifying approach of Anglo-American psychology, there has been a counter-current known as graphometry (T. Wallner, G. Gruenewald). In its practical training of graphologists, the Zürich Graphological Institute recognizes the particular significance of a psychological foundation. Graphology is also taught at some German and Dutch universities as a branch of academic psychology. A number of associations in Germany, Switzerland, Holland and Italy, some of them representing rival views, seek to further the progress of graphology by their teaching and by publishing journals.

Bibliography: Becker, M.: G. der Kinderschrift. Hamburg, 1949. **Grünewald, G.:** Graphologische Studien. Zürich, 1954. **Heiss, R.:** Die Deutung der Handschrift. Hamburg, [3]1966. **Klages, L.:** Handschrift und Charakter. Bonn, [24]1956. **Müller, W. & Enskat, A.:** Graphologie. Berlin, 1961. **Pfanne, H.:** Lehrbuch der Graphologie. Berlin, 1961. **Pokorny, K.:** Psychologie der Handschrift. Munich, 1968. **Pophal, R.:** G. in Vorlesungen, 3 Vols. Stuttgart, 1965, 1966, 1968. **Pulver, M.:** Symbolik der Handschrift. Zürich, [4]1945. **Teillard, A.:** Handschriftendeutung. Berne, [2]1963. **Wieser, R.:** Grundriss der G. Munich, 1969. **Wittich, B.:** Angewandte Graphologie. Berlin, 1951.

R. R. Pokorny

II. *Recent developments.* The more recent trend in graphological research is seen in the endeavor to do away with the confusion of pathognomy and graphology for which L. Klages and others were responsible, and to assign graphology as a diagnostic discipline to *psychodiagnostics* and not to the psychology of expression. The endeavor to objectify graphology and give it a statistical justification may be approved, if one considers the limitations of graphological diagnosis (J. P. Guilford called graphology a "useless method"; see also Müller & Enskat (1965, 562). Writing can lose its authenticity because of external factors. Other errors can be caused by inaccurate appraisal, ambiguity of characteristics, personal prejudice and systems of reference of the particular graphologist. See Allport & Vernon, 1933; Wells, 1946.

The critical justification and analysis of the basis of graphology are concerned with two sets of problems:

1. Checking the basic hypotheses (axioms) of graphological diagnostics, e.g. that the individuality of the handwriting is in essence psychologically conditioned, and that it is possible to draw conclusions from handwriting about the psyche of the writer. See *Graphology I.*

2. Studying the basic problems of the interpretation of handwriting: objectivity (q.v.), reliability (q.v.) and validity (q.v.). Graphometry, which Groffmann (1960) called the basic discipline of graphology, deals with this problem; up to now it has succeeded in objectifying the recording of graphic characteristics (more than 80 variables), grouping these with the aid of factor analysis (q.v.), and using correlational statistics to check them for stability, reliability and validity. Work in this field has so far been published by Timm (1967), Fahrenberg & Conrad (1965), Fischer (1964), Wallner (1963, 1965) and others.

The abovementioned authors all agree in the preliminary finding that, while there are quite *significant* correlations between certain characteristics found in handwriting and certain mental traits, these are nevertheless so slight that a more *critical* use of graphology is called for and that it can scarcely be recommended as the *sole test* method. This finding is largely confirmed by Eysenck's experimental work (1945, 1948). Eysenck confirmed the supposition that a personality diagnosis (e.g. of neuroticism, q.v.) is possible on the basis of a handwriting analysis (correlations with objective tests were low but significant, $v = 21$; with the psychiatric assessment, $r = 02$), but is nevertheless too time-consuming in view of the low level of accuracy. A diagnosis of intelligence with the aid of graphology hardly seems useful (Michel, 1969). A judgment on personality based on handwriting alone can rarely be justified since such fundamental dimensions as extraversion-introversion cannot be accurately diagnosed; control, irritability, etc., being the only components which can be elicited with relative certainty (Timm, 1967).

Bibliography: Allport, G. W. & Vernon, P. E.: Studies in expressive movements. New York, 1933. **Eysenck, H. J.:** Graphological analysis and psychiatry: an experimental study. Brit. J. Psychol., 1945, *35*, 70–81. **Id.:** Neuroticism and handwriting. J. Abnorm. Psychol., 1948, *43*, 94–6. **Fahrenberg, J. & Conrad, W.:** Eine explorative Faktorenanalyse graphometrischer und psychometrischer Daten. Z. exp. angew. Psychol., 1965, *12*, 223–38. **Fischer, G.:** Zur faktoriellen Struktur der Handschrift. Z. exp. angew. Psychol., 1964, *11*, 254–80. **Groffmann, K. J.:** Aus der Geschichte der Graphologie. Ciba-Zeitschrift, 1960, *98*, 3244–58. **Michel, L.:** Empirische Untersuchungen zur Frage der Übereinstimmung und Gültigkeit von Beurteilungen des intellektuellen Niveaus aus der Handschrift. Arch. ges. Psychol., 1969, *121*, 31–54. **Müller, W. H. & Enskat, A.:** Grundzüge der Graphologie. In: **Kirchhoff, R.** (Ed.): Hdb. d. Psychol., Vol. 5. Göttingen, 1965. **Timm, U.:** Graphometrie als psychol. Test. Psychol. Forschung, 1967, *30*, 307–56. **Wallner, T.:** Über die Validität graphologischer Aussagen. Diagnostica, 1963, *9*, 26–35. **Id.:** Graphologie als Objekt statistischer Untersuchungen. Psychol. Rdsch., 1965, *16*, 282–98. **Wells, F. L.:** Personal history, handwriting, and specific behaviour. J. Personality, 1946, *14*, 295–314.

F. Novak

Grasp; grasping. 1. To stretch out one's hand; a series of (purposive) simple movements of the hand and arm to grasp an object (see *Time and motion study*). **2.** Way in which an object is grasped, e.g. with the finger tips or the whole hand (see *Handedness; Manual dexterity; Work-factor system*). **3.** To understand something.

Bibliography: Mausolff, A.: Der Weg zum richtigen Griff. Berlin-Cologne-Frankfurt, 1969.

G.M.

Grasping reflex (syn. *Palmar response; Tonic grasping reflex*). A baby grasps objects which touch the hollow of its hand. The energy expended is such that the baby can be lifted up. This involuntary reflex can normally be easily demonstrated in the first two months of life, after which it then gradually begins to disappear with the increasing myelinization of the voluntary motor pathways. If the intensity of the grasp increases after the third month, or if the reflex persists longer than the fourth, it is regarded as pathological.

Bibliography: Halverson, H. M.: Studies of the grasping responses of early infancy. J. Genet. Psychol., 1937, *51*, 371–449.

K.H.P.

Grasping stage (syn. *Near space stage*). A baby begins to grasp objects at about the age of five to six months and this activity is the first indication that it is becoming aware of space. The child is now learning to control by motor maneuvers the small area within its grasp. Hence this phase of its development has been called the grasping stage or "near space stage" (Bühler). During this period visual and tactile space are combined; afterwards the visual component gradually predominates.

Bibliography: Bühler, K.: The mental development of the child. New York & London, 1930. *M.Sa.*

Gratification. See *Depth psychology.*

Graves' disease. See *Basedow's disease.*

Gravimeter. Appliance for testing sensitiveness to weights. The testee has to lift and give an estimate of various weights which look alike but are not all equally heavy. *A.Th.*

Gravity chronometer. A device used in the last century for measuring reaction time by the distance travelled by a falling weight between the time of the stimulus and the time of the response. Superseded today by precise electronic timers. *G.D.W.*

Graz school. See *Austrian school.*

Gregariousness. See *Sociability.*

Grey scale. The series of achromatic neutral colors lying between white and black. The different gradations of the scale are represented by elements between which there is a *constant* difference of brightness. *G.Ka.*

Ground; Figure-ground problem. This concerns the laws of perception which E. Rubin (1921) was the first to study systematically in the field of optics. The question why a part of the entire field takes over the role of ground, and another part that of figure, and when and why figure-ground distributions constantly vary, were investigated by W. Ehrenstein, K. Koffka, M. Metzger (in particular). See *Figure-ground.*

Bibliography: Hebb, D. O.: The organization of behavior. New York, 1949. *I.M.D.*

Group. Groups are not distinguished by fundamentally changing laws. There is no empirical justification for such a supposition, nor would it fit in with a general group theory.

A *typological* approach classifies groups according to their changing combinations of *characteristics* which can be identified operationally, such as, for example, size, density of interpersonal activity (cohesiveness), degree of formalization of roles (institutionalization); they can also be classified according to their goals: e.g. socio-emotional (R. Bales, 1953) (leisure), achievement or performance (work groups), religious, social, or racial groups, or special forms such as therapeutic groups. This mode of classification is also found in group concepts, represented by *polarities* such as big-small, institutional-autonomous, casual-lasting, etc. In spite of such differences, however, they are subject to comparable laws.

Some group concepts have proved especially useful. A genetic criterion is employed to distinguish the *primary* group (C. Cooley, 1909) from the *secondary*. The *primary group*, usually the family, is necessarily, and by the mere fact of its existence, a face-to-face group, i.e. it acts through the direct physical contact of the members. It provides the first personality-formative social experiences, impressions (see *Imprinting*), and learning processes (see *Socialization*). The *secondary group* can also result from direct contact, and is usually only one among several to which an individual belongs (school, club, work team). *Formal groups* are regulated by laws and institutions. *Informal groups* owe their continued existence to voluntary, personal and emotional relations. They are not mutually exclusive, but complementary (E. Mayo, 1933; F. Roethlisberger; W. Dickson, 1939). The concept of the *reference group* (H. Hyman, 1942) implies the identification of the individual with the standards and objects of some group. It is not necessarily identical with *membership group;* if there is agreement, the reference group is also the "ingroup"; otherwise, as an "outgroup", it is often the occasion of conflicts.

Bibliography: Cartwright, D. & Zander, A.: Group dynamics. New York, [2]1960. **Secord, P. & Backman, C.:** Social psychology. New York, 1964. *P.B.*

Group dynamics. An important object of psychological theory and practice in social, industrial, and occupational psychology (q.v.), psychotherapy (q.v.), and educational psychology (q.v.). Lewin (1936) used the term "group dynamics" to denote this field. The theory deals with groups of two or three (marriage), with educational, work or leisure groups, and with larger units such as schools, factories or military structures. It is also applied in sociology, educational and political theory, etc.

Group dynamics is *basically related to the socio-cultural context of a society* (q.v.), which helps the individual and a possible group to come together by providing given patterns of feeling, evaluating, thinking and acting. Such correspondences between the demands of the individual and the dynamic activity of the group are among the group-forming factors. They are primary determinants of reciprocal dynamic interaction between individuals who create and regulate social structures. Necessary though insufficient conditions of this kind are "*spatial proximity*" (L. Festinger, S. Schachter & K. Back, 1950) and a certain "*minimum of contacts*" (Homans, 1950; M. Sherif, 1951, 1953). In addition to external opportunities, there must be an *internal agreement* among the individuals forming the group, which transcends the above mentioned socio-cultural norms. C. B. Broderick (1956) formulated the following variables: (*a*) the nature of the area of agreement, (*b*) the degree of agreement, (*c*) the importance of the area of agreement, (*d*) the extent and number of the areas of agreement. Similarities in values and norms ("similarity of orientations") (Newcomb, 1943, 1956, 1961), and affinities of attitudes and personality traits ("similarity of attitudes") (H. M. Richardson, 1939; Winch, 1958) are reasons why certain persons are preferred to others as partners. In addition, special abilities related to the group's goals as well as intelligence increase eligibility (M. E. Bonney, 1944; B. Grossmann, J. Wrighter, 1948). Opposites, too, according to the theory of "complementary needs" (Winch & Ktsanes, 1955), favor relationships between individuals when, for example, needs felt by both are reciprocally gratified in the interaction. Secord & Backmann (1964) have combined the aspects of agreement and contrast to formulate the theory that the person is selected who will help to maintain a congruence (continuity, confirmation) of existing attitudes. The "exchange theory" (J. W. Thibaut & H. Kelley, 1959; Homans, 1961) emphasizes the outcome of cost and reward in relationships between individuals.

Groups persist when the primary conditions responsible for the grouping become a *more stable, positive interpersonal attraction.* The attraction is the measure of *group cohesiveness,* which finds expression in the frequency of contacts and the emotional and rational closeness of interpersonal relationships. *Equilibrium theories,* for example, are concerned with such processes. That of F. Helder (1946, 1958) states that in a triangular constellation of two persons who are concerned with some common object there will be a balance when (*a*) all three relationship values are positive, or (*b*) two of them are negative. But groups are determined not only by relationships between individuals but by those between dynamic processes. According to a thesis put forward by Bales (1953), group cohesion disintegrates when there are *activities in the field of performance*, whereas it increases when there is *co-operation in the socio-emotional field.*

Group cohesiveness and the structure of interpersonal relationships can be represented quantitatively as well as by graphs; this is done by using the methods of sociometry (q.v.) (J. Moreno, 1953). The so-called Q technique makes it possible to calculate a cohesiveness quotient (Hofstätter, 1965), and the measurement of "social distance" (E. S. Bogardus, 1928) throws light on efforts to establish a similar scale.

In addition to the relatively stable structure of social bonds, group dynamics determines fundamentally the actions of group members. Festinger's (1951) theory of "cognitive dissonance" (q.v.) states that activities begin when, in the cognitive field (perception, imagination, memory, thought), a decision has to be taken in regard to two simultaneous, incompatible elements (e.g. discordant items of information, irreconcilable standards). The cooperative interactions thus provoked, such as orienting behavior (gathering information, discussion), judgments and decisions, planning, differentiation of roles, checking, and actions to restructure the situation within and without, are included in the concept of "*problem-solving*" (*q.v.*) *behavior*, which culminates in the goal of the *self-preservation* of the group. There are two main phases in this process: (*a*) *the analysis of the situation* (consideration of group relationships, with feedback control of goal-attainment, etc.); and (*b*) *organizing and concluding a appropriate performance.* Observation (in the laboratory or the social field) is an example of the analytical processes. Bales (1950) suggests a list of observational categories for analyzing group processes: (*a*) the socio-emotional field: (i) positive: e.g. release of tension, (ii) negative: e.g. shows antagonism; (*b*) task area: (i) questions: e.g. asks for suggestions, (ii) answers: e.g. gives information.

The analysis of group dynamic processes is of central importance in group therapy (q.v.). Interpersonal relationships are discussed or represented in dramatic form, and it is hoped that as a result social behavior will be clarified and adjusted (J. Moreno, 1953). This method has also been successful in improving the emotional elements of interaction in group learning (Brocher, 1967).

Group leadership uses methods which vary from the autocratic model to the integrative sessions directed by the group itself, in which appropriate problems are put forward for discussion. Studies designed to elucidate the connection between leadership variables (conceived as direction or education), and modifications of behavior in the group, were reported by Lewin, Lippitt & White in 1939, and recently by Tausch & Tausch (1970). Changes in group dynamics brought about by these different kinds of *leadership* (q.v.) apply to the fields of *achievement, performance, social behavior* and *personality traits.* In spite of initial difficulties of method (determining operationally valid rating categories, practicability, and authenticity of various styles of leadership, etc.), a satisfactory uniformity was achieved in the results. The autocratic (authoritarian) style of leadership is distinguished from the socially integrative (democratic) kind by the degree of *direction and emotional aloofness* involved. The *laissez-faire* style was also examined later. As contrasted with the autocratic (authoritarian) style, the socially-integrative style brings about the following changes: (*a*) *achievement:* the amount remains the same or decreases slightly; the quality improves distinctly, becomes more creative, there is greater variety, greater keenness and independence in tackling the work; (*b*) *social behavior:* the atmosphere among group members becomes more friendly, there is less tension and aggression, more mutual appreciation, a more natural relationship with the leader is established; after six months the group members show more adaptability.

Research into leadership characteristics

has dealt with the connection between *personality and leader behavior*. In a survey of the literature (1948), Stogdill found a consensus regarding: intelligence, scholarship, reliability, sense of responsibility, activity and social sympathy (see *Leader*). Hofstätter (1957), referring also to Carter & Nixon (1949), reports three factors: competence, individual distinction, and group sociability. The leader's involvement in the group is shown in the concept of the "leadership function", which expresses group effectiveness in terms of the set goal. Krech *et al.* (1962) mention the following as functions of leadership: executive, planning, expertise, external group representation, control, reward and punishment, arbitration, example (image), ideology, etc. The specialist's role suggests that a leader's functions can also be exercised by nonleaders. In this case, leadership function and group function coincide. This type stresses the integrative running of the group by the group itself according to the criterion of self-preservation (e.g. the cybernetic growth model: Deutsch, 1949; Mills, 1969). A prominent group function is the improvement in quality of the interaction taking place in the group as, for example, success with contacts. A. Bavelas (1951) and D. D. Barrett (1951) took groups of five for examination as networks of contacts, and examined them from the point of view of possible contacts, and the importance of a central position for mediation between partners; they considered these groups as (*a*) a circle, (*b*) a chain, (*c*) a star. In the "circle", speed and accuracy of work are on a low level, but on a high level in the "chain" and the "star". In the "circle", the organization of contacts is unstable; it is more stable in the "chain", and unmistakable in the "star". Partner satisfaction is greatest in the "circle", less in the "chain", and least in the "star". The results depend on the nature of the activity. The degree of freedom of action which the group possesses, and which is related to organization, is a variable of the power relationships.

Power is manifested in very varying degrees of intensity, which may be visible or subliminal. M. Sherif (1935), using the term "autokinetic phenomenon" (q.v.), showed that individual judgment tends clearly to converge with group judgments when the individual judging is aware in advance of the others' assessments. S. E. Asch (1956) specified the following conditions for conformity of judgment: (*a*) the nature of the stimulus situation, e.g. its structural clarity; (*b*) the nature of the group forces, e.g., unanimity; (*c*) characteristics of the individual, e.g. social behavior. A more rational factor of conformity is the degree of knowledge possessed about the object of judgment. Hence those who wield power commonly resort to censorship, or the "slanting" or suppression of information. Moral defamation can also be a means of exercising power, as can sanctions and corporal punishment. Direct manifestations of power can easily lead to a state of affairs where a split or dissociation is apparent, as, e.g. on the one hand a popular leader, and on the other a leader in the field of action and authority (Hofstätter, 1965). This probably also applies to the hierarchy of motives. The exploitation of constraint to ensure group conformity, and the use of moral stereotypes and mass media, frequently combined with irrelevant appeals to the emotions, constitute some of the more subtle techniques for exerting influence, as do certain forms of propaganda and publicity. But group behavior is not always the outcome of a multiplicity and hierarchy of different goals open to the group. Situational stress (q.v.) is tolerated in order to allow achievement of more important and distant goals, which may be impracticable goals which have only been promised; if the stressful situation lasts too long, the price is not infrequently mental disorder.

The exercise of power shows that the relations between the claims of the individual and the group or society have become *one-sided*, and have resulted in displacement toward a single individual, or toward society. This unilaterality leads to conflicts and confrontations (not always immediately but, in time, inevitably), which can only be avoided by exchanging members. It disturbs the autonomous development of the natural forces at work in social structures. According to internal and external conditions, the group is either an *instrument for misuse* to gratify individual or social demands, or else an admirable means to develop and maintain mature individuals in beneficial interaction with society. Such is the danger and such the opportunity offered by group dynamics. In a positive sense it favors an (active) agreement between: (*a*) individual desires which cannot, or can only less easily, be gratified without the group; (*b*) demands and restrictions imposed by society on the individual, which are necessary in practice to achieve an equal distribution of the greatest benefits derivable from interaction.

Group dynamics is the essence of all problem-solving interaction processes which are developed by individuals conscious of relatively stable structures (e.g. norms, roles, attitudes, habits), and relatively changing forces (e.g. identified goals, cooperative actions, realization of drives, and motives) which may be subjective or standardized by society; the goal is to achieve continuous integrative development and the differentiation of social relationships. Group dynamics is not restricted to the internal working of a group; and it is not necessarily bound up with the concrete presence of a group; but the group is its primary location. See *Group formation; Attitude; Prejudice.*

Bibliography: Bales, R. F.: The equilibrium problem in small groups. In: **Parsons, T., Bales, R. F. & Schils, E. A.** (Eds): Working papers in the theory of action. New York, 1953, 111–61. **Bales, R. F. & Strodtbeck, F. L.:** Phases in group problem solving. J. abnorm. soc. Psychol., 1951, *46*, 485–95. **Brocher, T.:** Gruppendynamik und Erwachsenenbildung. Brunswick, 1967. **Carter, L. & Nixon, M.:** An investigation of the relation between four criteria of leadership ability for three different tasks. J. Psychol., 1949, *27*, 245–61. **Cartwright, D. & Zander, A.:** Group dynamics. New York, [2]1960. **Festinger, L. A.:** A theory of social comparison processes. Hum. Relat., 1954, *7*, 117–40. **Id.:** A theory of cognitive dissonance. New York, 1957. **Id., Schachter, S. & Back, K.:** Social pressures in informal groups. New York, 1950. **Hofstätter, P.:** Gruppendynamik. Munich, 1965. **Homans, G. C.:** The human group. New York, 1950. **Id.:** Social behaviour: its elementary forms. New York, 1961. **Krech, D., Crutchfield, R. S. & Ballachey, E. L.:** Individual in society. New York, 1962. **Lewin, K.:** A dynamic theory of personality. New York, 1935. **Id.:** Principles of topological psychology. New York, 1936. **Lewin, K., Lippitt, R. & White, R. K.:** Patterns of aggressive behavior in experimentally created social climates. J. soc. Psychol., 1939, *10*, 271–99. **McGrath, J. E. & Altmann, I.:** Small group research. New York, 1966. **Moreno, J. L.:** Who shall survive? New York, 1953. **Newcomb, T. M.:** The predication of interpersonal attraction. Amer. Psychologist, 1956, *11*, 575–86. **Id.:** The acquaintance process. New York, 1961. **Secord, P. F. & Backmann, C. W.:** Social psychology. New York, 1964. **Stogdill, R.:** Leadership, membership and organisation. Psychol. Bull., 1950, *47*, 1–14. **Id.:** Personal factors associated with leadership. A survey of the literature. J. of Psychol., 1948, *25*, 25–71. **Tausch, R. & A.:** Erziehungspsychologie. Göttingen, [3]1970. **Winch, R. F., Ktsanes, T. & Ktsanes, V.:** Empirical elaboration of the theory of complementary needs in mate selection. J. abnorm. soc. Psychol., 1955, *51*, 508–14. (See also *Social psychology.*)

P. Braun

Group factor. The group factor model is a predecessor of the model of several common factors (see *Factor analysis*): apart from the general factor (q.v.), and the specific factors, there are also intermediate general factors—these are group factors. The best-known method of group factor analysis is Holzinger's "bifactor method". *W.H.B.*

Group formation. A process in the course of which a group is formed from a plurality or a mere collection of individuals. Prerequisites for the formation of groups are: (*a*) individual motivation for joining a group (it may be positive, facilitating the gratification of personal needs, or negative, providing a defense against some threat to the individual concerned); (*b*) communication or contact between individuals (facilitated by spatial proximity or insignificant social distance); (*c*) mutual recognition of individuals.

As a group comes into being, the following processes can be observed: common goals appear, roles are differentiated, and taken over by individual members; common rules of behavior and norms develop, with which the behavior of the individual members begins increasingly to conform; a certain group atmosphere or special climate is engendered; auto- and hetero-stereotypes develop, i.e. a positive estimation of one's own or "our" group with reference to its capabilities, the attractiveness of its members, etc., and a rejection or disparagement of the other or "those" groups. See *Group dynamics*.

Bibliography: Hare, A. P.: Handbook of small group research. New York, 1962. **Sherif, M., Harvey, O. J., White, B. J., Hood, W. R. & Sherif, C.:** Intergroup conflict and cooperation: The robber's cave experiment. New York, 1961. *A. Schmidt-Mummendey*

Group instruction. Group instruction is education in, through, and for the group. It is the primary method used in the democratic style of education. Pupils are activated not by tasks and suggestions coming from the teacher, but by impulses originating in the members of the group. Individual behavior is determined by what the group expects from the activity and how it evaluates it. The group-dynamic forces at work are dealt with in social psychology (q.v.).

Bibliography: Fiedler, F. E.: Leader attitudes and group effectiveness. Urbana, 1958. *H.Schr.*

Group measurements. The term denotes either (*a*) the observation of a characteristic in some group (sample) with that characteristic, (*b*) the simultaneous measurement (testing) of a group of subjects (group experiment), or (*c*) the observation (quantification) of modes of behavior (performances, decisions, etc.) of a group in a socio-psychological experiment, in contrast to the modes of behavior of individuals in conditions which are otherwise similar. See *Correlational techniques*.

Group sexuality. This exists when there is equally privileged interaction of more than two persons with the goal of sexual pleasure. The activity of several directed at a single individual who responds preferentially could only be included under this head as an extreme case of sado-masochism. Promiscuity (q.v.) and the exchange of partners ("group sex") are distinct from group sexuality.

U.H.S.

Group tests. Tests which are constructed so that a fairly large number of testees can take them at the same time. The most varied tests, e.g. certain intelligence tests, tests of skills and abilities, and personality tests, have been developed as group tests. They are more economical to conduct and evaluate, and frequently more global in their results than individual tests. *E.F.-K.*

Group therapy. Psychotherapeutic methods in which several patients (usually six to twelve, half of them where possible being male, the other half female) are treated in the presence of one (or possibly several) therapists using group dynamics (q.v.). The analytical group provides opportunities, both therapeutic and diagnostic, not available in the traditional analytical situation (patient alone with psychotherapist). "Closed" groups are usually maintained for a fairly long period, but sometimes "open" groups are formed (the members of which change more or less frequently). In addition to this analytical method, other group therapies are used by psychotherapists either selectively or exclusively; for example, directive-suggestive treatment could consist of autogenic training (q.v.), psychodrama (q.v.), music therapy (q.v.) and similar methods.

Physiotherapeutic methods used in a group often achieve particularly good results because the participants spur one another on.

Bibliography: Battegay, D.: Der Mensch in der Gruppe, Vols 1–3. Berne & Stuttgart, 1968–9. **Foulkes, S. H.:** Therapeutic group analysis. London, 1964. **Id. & Anthony, E. J.:** Group psychotherapy:

the psycho-analytic approach. Harmondsworth, 1957. **Jones, M.:** Social psychiatry. London, 1952. **Id.:** Social psychiatry in practice. Harmondsworth, 1968.

H.N.G.

Group work. 1. *In industrial theory:* the direct co-operation of several workers whose efforts are interdependent in the joint execution of some task. **2.** *In education:* a method in which a given subject is not dealt with directly by the teacher standing in front of the class but by the pupils in small groups (a transition from authoritative to co-operative leadership) (see *Leadership*). Especially a form of university teaching in small tutorial or seminar groups. It has been opined that methods used in universities for lectures and discussions will be used later in public life for negotiations, speeches and conferences. *G.Ma.*

GSR. Abb. for *Galvanic skin response* (q.v.).

Guilford factors. In regard to temperament, these are fifteen primary characteristics isolated by factorial analysis from data taken from inventories; they are not wholly independent; systematized by Guilford using three areas of behavior (general, emotional, social), and five basic polar dimensions (positive-negative, controlled-uncontrolled, active-passive, etc.). For example: immaturity-maturity, confidence-inferiority, social introversion-extraversion, etc. See *Traits*.

Bibliography: Guilford, J. P.: Personality. New York, 1959.

H.H.

Guilford-Zimmermann Aptitude Survey. A test battery for intellectual aptitudes, with separate tests for verbal comprehension, general reasoning, numerical operations, perceptual speed, spatial orientation, spatial visualization and mechanical knowledge. Devised 1947–56; standardized for testees from the age of sixteen.

Bibliography: Guilford, J. P.: The nature of intelligence. New York, 1967.

R.M.

Guilford-Zimmermann Temperament Survey. On the basis of extensive factor analyses Guilford & Zimmermann produced a questionnaire for personality assessment in which the following independent characteristics are measured with thirty items each: general activity, restraint, ascendance, emotional stability, sociability, objectivity, friendliness, thoughtfulness, personal relations, masculinity. Prepared and standardized for college students and adults. *R.M.*

Bibliography: Guilford, J. P. & Zimmermann, W. S.: Fourteen dimensional temperament. Psychol. Monogr., 1956, *70*, 1–26.

Guilt. One can speak of guilt as *culpability* only on the assumption that such a thing is ascertainable in human beings within certain fixed limits. The concept and nature of guilt, when not restricted to the empirical psychological or psychopathological phenomenon of a consciousness, feeling, or sense of guilt (a subjective awareness of having offended against personal, familial, religious, or societal norms, which offense may be actual or imaginary), are defined according to philosophical anthropology, ethics and the law.

"Man is the being that is capable of guilt, and capable of perceiving his guilt" (M. Buber). The capability of guilt, or moral responsibility, implies that an individual is capable of free self-determination, responsible behavior, and the assumption of responsibility. The notion of a criminal law basing its conception of criminal responsibility on the criterion of voluntary action implies the freedom of will of the "normal" citizen as a principle. "Freedom" in this sense (as a prerequisite for all legal codes) is not the freedom that philosophers of the most varied schools have been unable to agree upon throughout the centuries. The fact that, e.g., a "normal" citizen "can" stop when the traffic light shows red, that it is impossible for him to "have to" ignore the stop signal, is assumed to be an adequate ground for postulating the "freedom" of a citizen as an inevitable and scientifically unassailable prerequisite for every legal code. Admittedly, the citizen's behavior, considered as acceptable or unacceptable in regard to the flow of traffic, is causally and finally motivated—but in the same sense as any human behavior, decision or volition. As far as the confirmation of legal responsibility is concerned, it is immaterial whether one views freedom of will as a metaphysical premiss or as an ontological prerequisite. What is in question is always no more than the empirically detectable conditions for the possibility of unfreedom. The legal code lays down the conditions beforehand in its requirement of *understanding* of the nature of an action, or of the difference between right and wrong. A psychiatrist to whom a case is referred for assessment of understanding of right or wrong, or of normality, may try to assess the determinants of the subject's behavior by physical and psychological examination and tests, even with particular reference to the action in question, but inevitably in regard to the social and criminal prognosis. Ultimately, the procedure he adopts must always be empirical. Existing ethical and legal norms permit social evaluation of a specific behavior, and to that extent form the yardstick for guilt. Ethical and legal norms enable one to confirm that a behavior does not accord with the norm. The question of *why?*, of the conditions for the abnormal behavior, is on another plane, and has to be answered by means of empirical, biological and psychological criteria. Hence, in most English-speaking countries, clinical psychologists and/or psychiatrists are hampered by the obtaining socio-legal norm. For example, the so-called McNaughten rules (which date back to a successful plea of insanity in Britain in 1843) directly involve the notions of free will, intent and moral responsibility, and, basically, hold an individual to be responsible for his socially criminal action (e.g. murder), unless he suffered from defective reason or mental disease such as to impair his understanding of the nature, quality or wrongness of the act he committed. Essentially, the law does not provide for refinements of psychological theory or evidence essentially contrary to the basic notion of free will. See also *Abnormal psychology; Alcoholism; Conscience; Criminality; Forensic psychology; Mental defect; Punishment.*

Bibliography: Burton, R. V.: The generality of honesty reconsidered. Psychol. Rev., 1963, *70*, 481–99. **Ehrhardt, H.:** Psychiatrie. In: **Sieverts, R.** (Ed.): Handwörterbuch der Kriminologie, Vol. 2. Berlin, [2]1971. **Id. & Villinger, W.:** Forensische und administrative Psychiatrie. In: **Gruhle** *et al.* (Eds): Psychiatrie der Gegenwart, Vol. 3. Berlin, 1961. **Eysenck, H. J.** (Ed.): Handbook of abnormal psychology. London, 1960; New York, 1961. **Id.:** Crime and personality. London, [2]1970. **Frey, E. R.** (Ed.): Schuld, Verantwortung, Strafe. Zürich, 1964. **Glueck, S.:** Law and psychiatry. Baltimore, 1962. **Id. & Glueck, G.:** Unravelling juvenile delinquency. New York, 1950. **Gough, H. C.:** A sociological theory of psychopathy. Amer. J. sociol., 1948, *53*, 359–66. **Guttmacher, M. S.:** The role of psychiatry in law. Springfield, Mass., 1968. **Kaufmann, A.:** Schuld und Strafe. Cologne, 1968. **Ricoeur, P.:** Philosophie de la volonté, Vol. 1, Paris, 1949. **Willett, T.:** Criminal on the road. London, 1964.

H. Ehrhardt

Guthrie's contiguous conditioning. See *Postremity theory.*

Gynagogy. Schaetzing uses the term for psychagogy as specially designed for the gynecologist during consulting hours.

Bibliography: Schaetzing, E.: Die verstandene Frau. Munich, [3]1963.

W.Sch.

Gynandromorph. An abnormal individual with some tissues genetically and structurally male, and others genetically and structurally female, as can occur through disturbance of the sex determination mechanism during embryonic development. See *Intersexuality; Hermaphroditism.* *G.D.W.*

Gynandromorphism. A type of sexual aberration in which both male and female characters are present in the same organism. The cause in man is either genetic, because of an excess of X chromosomes, or secondary, because of some psychic disorder (see *Transvestism*); in the latter case those affected try to acquire a female shape by taking female sex hormones (*apparent hermaphroditism*). Occasionally, but not necessarily, found together with homosexuality (q.v.). *W.Sc.*

Gynandry. The tendency in a female to possess male characteristics. (*Viraginity:* the tendency for a female to exhibit masculine mental characteristics.) The parallel condition in males, i.e. possessing female characteristics, is called *androgyny.* *G.D.W.*

Gynecocracy. See *Matriarchy.*

Gynecomastia. The formation of one or two breasts in a man (a *gynecomast*); in special circumstances there may be secretion of milk. It is not a disease but a symptom which has widely differing causes. The following need to be distinguished: (*a*) Puberal gynecomastia is a normal, non-morbid variant of maturation between the ages of twelve and fourteen; there is swelling of one or both mammary glands, and while this is usually transient, it can be irreversible and require an operation; occasionally puberal gynecomastia is accompanied by negative psychic effects. (*b*) Gynecomastia resulting from hormone therapy (e.g. testosterone therapy in cancer of the prostate gland). (*c*) Gynecomastia as a symptom of disease of the endocrine glandular system (e.g. estrogen-producing tumors of the adrenal glands or testicles). (*d*) Gynecomastia as a symptom of congenital intersexual conditions (real and apparent hermaphroditism). (*e*) Gynecomastia as a concomitant symptom in non-endocrine diseases (e.g. cirrhosis of the liver).

Bibliography: Jores, A. & Nowakowski, H.: Praktische Endokrinologie. Stuttgart, 1964. Monje, J.: Körperlichsexuelle Fehlentwicklungen. Hamburg, 1969. *H.M.*

Gyrus. The *gyri cerebri* (cerebral convolutions) are irregularly shaped folds 1 cm. in width and several cm. in length, separated by the cerebral fissures or *sulci cerebri.* Special terms denote position: e.g. *gyrus temporalis medius.* Some gyri have an important functional significance, as for example the *gyrus frontalis inferior*, area 44, which coordinates the muscles used in speech and is therefore known as the motor speech center (*Broca's area*, q.v.). *G.A.*

H

Haab's pupillary reflex. An ideomotor or cortical pupillary reflex (q.v.): the contraction of the pupils of both eyes when looking at a bright object in a darkened room. *K.H.P.*

Habit. The term "habit" derives from the Latin noun *habitus*, from the verb *habere*, to have. Modern dictionaries describe at least four usages, all referring to the characteristic external appearance, manner or bearing by which we may recognize an individual or class of individual: human, animal or plant. Thus one special usage refers to dress or attire, especially in relation to religious orders and other functional groups. More relevant to the present context is the usage referring to the customs or practices characteristic of a social group. Closest, however, to the technical usage within psychology is the use of the word to refer to an individual's tendency to act in customary or automatic ways, especially when these are acquired by practice or experience.

Even in this last sense, the term is used in popular language in a variety of ways. It covers many different forms of behavior, including the following:

(*a*) Mechanical, semi-automatic series of movements involved in routine actions such as dressing oneself.

(*b*) Actions related to recurrent acquired physiological cravings, e.g. the "habit" of smoking.

(*c*) Mannerisms such as "tics" and other "nervous habits".

(*d*) Characteristic modes and manners of speech.

(*e*) Characteristic ways of thinking as reflected in predictable points of view and attitudes expressed about issues and events.

(*f*) Actions evaluated on ethical grounds by others, or by society in general; that is, "good" or "bad" habits such as acts of courtesy, stealing or swearing, distinctive of an individual.

The term is also used loosely and in many different ways by psychologists. It may refer to molecular aspects of behavior such as a specific measurable component of a simple conditioned reflex or an acquired association between a pair of words, or to very broad molar patterns of behavior extended over considerable periods of time. In either case, the reactions are predictable or customary. Emphasis may be placed on the actual behavior evoked by a certain set of conditions, or on the underlying "set", disposition or readiness to respond in this way to those conditions. Habits may be seen as possessing autonomous motivating properties or as requiring appropriate motivational states for their activation. Invariably, however, habit is contrasted with pre-programmed innate reflexes or instinctual reactions in that one essential characteristic of a habit is that it is acquired, an end-product of a process of learning. Hence, an acceptable general definition of habit might be: *A customary pattern of behavioral, cognitive or emotional response, predictable according to the conditions operating at the time of response, and acquired by a process of learning* or *the underlying acquired "set" or tendency toward that pattern of response.*

1. *History.* Historically, the modern concept of habit stems from Descartes's (1596–1650) dualistic view of body and mind and his insistence on the mechanical nature of bodily events. Habit, for him, was a consequence of the easing, through usage, of the passage of "animal spirits" through the pores of the hydraulic system he proposed as a model of physiological functioning. Next, in the doctrine of association (q.v.), the English empiricist philosophers provided a central principle for a psychology of learning and placed fruitful emphasis on the importance of sensory processes. Hobbes (1588–1679) claimed that all our ideas stem from sensory experience and that association depends upon the coherence of these ideas. John Locke (1632–1704) took Hobbes's arguments further with his famous and bold assertion that the mind at birth is a "*tabula rasa*". He explained the apparent given quality of many of our ideas by the early inculcation of habits through the teaching of nurses, parents and other mentors. Hume's (1711–1776) entire philosophical system was based on the association of ideas. For him, all perceptions and experiences, even belief in relationships of cause and effect, were explained by habits established by consistencies between experiences. Habit was his universal law of mind.

The biological observations and writings of Charles Darwin (1809–1882) and, in particular, his emphasis on the adaptive nature of behavior, represent the next major relevant influence. In his *Origin of Species* (1859) Darwin discusses the effects of domestication upon animals, especially the resultant suppression of "natural instincts". While recognizing that deliberate selective breeding plays a part, he also argues that imposed habits become fixed reflexes which are then transmitted by genetic mechanisms. Later (1872) Darwin employs similar arguments to account for the acquisition of expressive characteristics from originally voluntary movements subserving practical functions. (See *Expression; Instinct.*)

These trends of thought culminated in William James's (1842–1910) brilliant exposition of psychology as an empirical science in his *Principles of Psychology* (1890). His thinking was dominated by concepts of biological utility, and he saw the function of consciousness (q.v.) as steering a highly evolved and therefore complex but plastic nervous system. James (q.v.) devotes a celebrated chapter to habit. Increased neural plasticity, it is argued, facilitates the establishment of habits whose major function is to allow the performance of routine actions with little or no attention, thus freeing the higher mental processes for more important and difficult tasks. Habit, according to James, is "the enormous fly-wheel of society, its most precious conservative agent". At the same time, James did not deny the importance and biological utility of instinctive, unlearned behavior patterns, but saw them merely as providing the opportunity for progressive, adaptive modification in the light of experience. Thus instincts become overlaid by habits which ultimately replace them. Modern views do not deviate greatly from this doctrine but phenomena such as *imprinting* (q.v.), much studied in animal species by contemporary ethologists, suggest that the relationship between instinctual and learned behavior may sometimes be of a different and equal nature. By imprinting is meant the firm linkage of an innate tendency to a specific environmental object at a critical period in the early life history of the organism, and the generalization of this linkage to other objects of the same class.

Neuro-anatomical and physiological knowledge was sufficiently advanced when James was writing for him to postulate that the neural basis of habit-formation might be the establishment of "connections" to form fixed neural "pathways" in the central nervous system (q.v.). This was an early stage in the still-continuing search for a "memory-trace". James envisaged complex pathways of this nature such that, in the execution of a complex habitual act, each new muscular contraction is instigated by the sensation evoked by the preceding contraction. Such a system would now be described as a "chain-reflex". Unfortunately, this attractively simple account of habit-formation has not survived experimental tests. Even the simplest of motor-habits do not preserve an identical form: the same strategic end may be achieved by a variety of tactical means. Similarly, ablation (q.v.) experiments demonstrate quite clearly that the preservation of a habit does not depend upon the integrity of any particular region of the brain.

Dewey and other members of the American "functionalist" school, following similar Darwinist arguments, acquired views on habit-formation very close to those of James. At about the same time, Thorndike (q.v.) (1898) was carrying out his classic experiments upon trial and error learning in which hungry cats, over a series of trials, gradually acquired the ability rapidly to unlatch the door of their specially designed "puzzle-box" cages in order to secure food placed outside. Thorndike made the point that repetition alone was insufficient to account for his findings. There is also a process of selection among the acts performed so as to increase the likelihood of those acts which yielded access to the food and resulted (so Thorndike postulated) in a state of satisfaction, and decrease the likelihood of those acts which resulted in dissatisfaction. This principle is now known as the *Law of Effect* and the rewards and punishments affecting the process of learning are now generally referred to as *reinforcements*. The Law of Effect has been subjected to much criticism but it remains clear, as argued forcibly by Skinner (1938) and his followers, who describe this type of learning as *operant conditioning* (q.v.), that behavior is modified according to its consequences, and that appropriate reinforcement is an important factor in habit formation. The recent discovery by Olds & Milner (1954) of reinforcing effects produced by electrical stimulation of the septal area of the brain suggests a neuro-physiological basis for this process.

Of equal importance to the work of Thorndike were Pavlov's (1927) investigations into the nature of *conditioned reflexes*. He showed that if a neutral stimulus, such as the sound of a bell, is presented at a very brief interval before a natural or *unconditioned stimulus* (e.g. food), evoking a natural or *unconditioned reflex* (salivation), and this pairing is repeated a number of times, presentation of the sound alone (now a *conditioned stimulus*) will evoke salivation. The latter *conditioned reflex* is qualitatively and quantitatively different from the original unconditioned response and therefore no simple stimulus-substitution theory is tenable. All the evidence points to the anticipatory nature of the conditioned reflex, and therefore suggests that what is learned is an expectancy with clear biological adaptive value. Pavlov was a physiologist, and interested in the light his experiment threw on brain functioning. He was opposed to attempts made by contemporary psychologists to build an entire systematic theory of learning upon his work. Nevertheless, J. B. Watson (q.v.) (1919), the founder of *behaviorism* (q.v.), established an entire system of psychology on this basis. For him, habits were integrated systems of conditioned reflexes built around available innate patterns of movement. Language habits were special cases in that, to some extent, speech could become "implicit", implicit speech being the behaviorist equivalent of thought. Personality, even, was considered to be merely the end-product of hierarchical habit-systems. Man was set apart from other animals only by his greater capacity for developing three of these habit-systems: laryngeal or verbal habits; manual habits; visceral or emotional habits. (See *Conditioning, classical and operant.*)

2. *Recent views.* Despite the cult-like excesses of some of Watson's arguments, a modified behaviorism has remained prominent throughout the recent history of

psychology and has yielded valuable research findings. Particularly important among the contributions of the neo-behaviorists in relation to the concept of habit are the work and theory of C. L. Hull (q.v.) (1943). He laid stress on the distinction between the actual performance of a learned act and the internalized tendency to perform the act when appropriately stimulated. He reserved the term "habit" for the latter. Those consistencies in behavior which indicate learning are only observable in appropriate stimulus conditions which may recur at long intervals. Hull inferred that some theoretically observable modification of the central nervous system, some form of "memory-trace", remains potentially active during the interval. Thus Hull's habit concept has the status of a *hypothetical construct*. It is also an *intervening variable* in his formal theory in which *habit strength* ($_{S}H_{R}$) represents the compounded effects of various antecedent variables such as the number of reinforced trials, and interacts with other intervening variables such as *drive* (D) to determine a *reaction potential* ($_{S}E_{R}$). Hence, in his quasi-mathematical presentation of the theory, Hull's fundamental equation is:

$$_{S}E_{R}=f(_{S}H_{R})\times(D)$$

This equation was further elaborated to include intervening variables representing inhibitory and other factors, but represents, as it stands, the important distinction drawn by Hull between learned habit and performance, and his view that the habit must be energized by a drive state in the presence of appropriate stimulation if an actual response is to occur.

Skinner and his co-workers are atheoretical in their approach to learning, restricting themselves entirely to observable relationships between observable events. This is entirely adequate for their aim of developing a behavioral technology, but Hull's argument concerning a modified state of the organism which persists between learning trials remains valid. Other learning theorists have elaborated aspects of Hullian theory, e.g. Spence (1956), while others, notably Tolman (1938) with his "purposive behaviorism", have presented alternative systems, stressing cognitive factors. Yet others, such as Osgood (1953), attempt to reconcile these two points of view by postulating cognitive mediating processes within a Hullian framework. All these refer to habit formation of one type or another, based on acquired associative relationships between one stimulus and another, or between stimuli and responses, brought about by appropriate conditions of contiguity and/or reinforcement. The same principles can be extended to account for higher forms of learning, such as concept learning, but the application of the term "habit" to these realms is a matter of choice. Motives can also be acquired in these ways, and there is evidence to suggest that any well-established habit can become functionally autonomous and acquire motivational properties such that the opportunity for its exercise can be used to reinforce new learning. (See *Motivation*.)

Current research and theory take many directions. One of great interest and importance is the search for a physical basis for the "memory-trace". Interesting and influential, if speculative, suggestions concerning the development of complex functional interconnections between cerebral neurons were advanced by Hebb (1949). Recently, however, considerable interest has been aroused and research stimulated by Hyden's (1959) suggestion that ribonucleic acid (RNA) might be a complex chemical mediator for memory functions. The exciting possibilities raised by the location of a "pleasure center" in the brain have already been mentioned. This is likely to give strength to already emerging hedonistic theories. The strategic context within which habits operate has also been mentioned. Miller, Galanter & Pribram's (1960) theoretical account of "plans and the structure of behavior" promises new advances in this area. (See *Memory*.)

Finally, the topic of habits should not be

left without mention of the application of planned re-educational habit-formation and habit-breaking by means of counter-conditioning carried out by the behavior therapists, and by behavior modifiers working in the field of clinical psychology (Eysenck, 1960; Ullmann and Krasner, 1965). (See *Aversion therapy; Behavior therapy*.)

Bibliography: Darwin, C.: The origin of species. London, 1859. **Id.:** Expression of the emotions in man and animals. London, 1872. **Descartes, R.:** Principles of philosophy (in Latin). Amsterdam, 1644. **Eysenck, H. J.** (Ed.): Behaviour therapy and the neuroses. London, 1960. **Hebb, D. O.:** The organization of behavior. New York, 1949. **Hobbes, T.:** Leviathan. London, 1651. **Hull, C. L.:** Principles of behavior. New York, 1943. **Hume, D.:** Enquiry concerning human understanding. London, 1751. **Hyden, H.:** Biochemical changes in glial cells and nerve cells at varying activity. Proc. of the Fourth int. Congr. of Biochemistry, Vol. III. London, 1959. **James, W.:** Principles of psychology. New York, 1890. **Locke, J.:** Essay concerning human understanding. London, 1690. **Miller, G. A., Galanter, E. & Pribram, K. H.:** Plans and the structures of behavior. New York, 1960. **Olds, J. & Milner, P. M.:** Positive reinforcement produced by electrical stimulation of septal area and other regions of rat brain. J. comp. physiol. Psychol, 1954, *47*, 419–27. **Osgood. C. E.:** Method and theory in experimental psychology. New York, 1953. **Pavlov, I. P.:** Conditioned reflexes. New York, 1927. **Skinner, B. F.:** The behavior of organisms. New York, 1938. **Spence, K. W.:** Behavior theory and conditioning. New Haven, 1956. **Thorndike, E. L.:** Animal intelligence: an experimental study of the associative processes in animals. Psychol. Rev. Monogr. Suppl., 1898, *2*, No. 4. **Tolman, E. C.:** The determiners of behaviour at a choice-point. Psychol. Rev., 1938, *45*, 1–41. **Ullmann, L. P. & Krasner, L.** (Eds.): Case studies in behavior modification. New York, 1965. **Watson, J. B.:** Psychology from the standpoint of a behaviorist. Philadelphia, 1919.

G. Jones

Habitat. An ecological term: the entire geographical environment of an organism (species; plant or animal), possibly at a certain stage in its development. The habitat consists of inanimate (biotope) and animate environmental factors. See *Biocenosis*. *H.S.*

Habitual. 1. Pertaining to, or of the nature of a *habit* (q.v.). **2.** Established by habit. **3.** Customary, regular, lasting. Pertaining to that which remains relatively the same over fairly long periods of time (e.g. *traits*, q.v.) in contrast to, e.g., states. *D.B.*

Hair esthesiometer. A hair (from human or horse) used as a fine tactile stimulus in the study of cutaneous sensation. One classical experiment is supposed to demonstrate that different points on the surface of the skin are sensitive to heat, cold, pain and pressure respectively, so that stimulation with a fine point will result in one or other of these four experiences depending upon the exact locus at which the stimulus is applied. *G.D.W.*

Half-length illusion. The phenomenon that the subjective and objective mid-points of a line do not coincide. This illusion occurs in both vision and touch. See *Kundt's bisection test*. *C.D.F.*

Hall, Granville Stanley. B. 1844 in Ashfield (Mass.); d. 1924, Worcester (Mass.). After graduating from Williams College, he studied theology at Union Theological Seminary in New York, and went on to read physiology, physics, theology and philosophy in Bonn and Berlin; he was the first person to obtain a degree in psychology proper in the USA with his doctoral thesis on "The Muscular Perception of Space" (1878). He then again studied physiology in Berlin and was Wundt's first American student in Leipzig. He also worked with Helmholtz in Berlin. He became a lecturer in 1881, and in 1884 was appointed Professor of psychology and pedagogics at Johns Hopkins University. In 1888 he became the first President of the newly-founded Clark University in Worcester, and held this post until 1920, when he resigned.

Hall was the first great organizer of

American psychology and made a substantial contribution to the expansion of psychology in the USA. In 1884 he founded what was probably the first American psychological laboratory—at Johns Hopkins University. In 1887 he established the first American journal of psychology (*American Journal of Psychology*), followed by the *Pedagogical Seminary* (later the *Journal of Genetic Psychology*) in 1891, the *Journal of Religious Psychology* in 1904, and the *Journal of Applied Psychology* in 1917. In July 1892 he was instrumental in founding the American Psychological Association (APA) of which he was the first President. In 1893, he established the National Association for the Study of the Child to foster research into child psychology.

Hall also made a major contribution to the advancement of psychoanalysis (q.v.) in America. In 1909 he invited Freud and Jung to the USA and arranged a symposium at Clark University during which he introduced leading American psychologists to the European giants.

The theory of evolution is fundamental to Hall's work. His interest in evolution was great enough to earn him the title of "Darwin of the mind". He applied, for example, the "recapitulation theory" to child development, i.e. he assumed that the individual in his ontogenetic development passes through the same stages of development as the race as a whole in its phylogenetic development ("ontogeny recapitulates phylogeny"). Hall's interest in evolution led him to consider in great detail problems of child and developmental psychology. His studies, in which he made use of Galton's questionnaire method, aroused considerable public interest and led to the "child study" movement. In addition, they played a decisive role in the development of educational psychology (q.v.), which investigates the psychological bases of child education. (See *Child psychology; History of psychology.*)

Main works: Content of children's minds. *Princeton Review*, 1883, *11*, 272–94. Adolescence: its psychology and its relations to physiology, anthropology, sociology, sex, crime, religion and education. New York, 1904. Founders of modern psychology. New York, 1912. Jesus, the Christ, in the light of psychology (2 vols.). New York, 1917. Senescence: the last half of life. New York, 1922. Life and confessions of a psychologist. New York, 1923.

Bibliography: **Burnham, J. C.:** Sigmund Freud and G. Stanley Hall: exchange of letters. Psychoanal. Quart., 1960, *29*, 307–16. **Cattell, J. M.:** The founding of the association and of the Hopkins and Clark laboratories, Psychol. Rev., 1943, *50*, 61–4. **Dennis, W. & Boring, E. G.:** The founding of APA. Amer. Psychologist, 1952, *7*, 95–7. **Starbuck, E. D.:** G. Stanley Hall as a psychologist. Psychol. Rev., 1925, *32*, 103–20.

W.W.

Hallucinations. Perceptions without corresponding external stimuli, or the absence of perception when external stimuli are presented (*negative* halucinations). Depending on the type of sensory illusion, there are: *olfactory*, *visual* or *acoustic* hallucinations. As regards etiology, the spectrum ranges from organic psychoses (frequently with elementary hallucinations), by way of exceptional psychogenic conditions, to schizophrenia (q.v.). See *Mental imagery; Psychoses, functional.*

A.Hi.

Hallucinogens. See *Psychotomimetic Drugs.*

Halo effect. A source of error in personality assessment first described by F. L. Wells (1907) and given its name by Thorndike (1920). The observer (e.g. a teacher) tends to be guided by an overall impression or an outstanding trait in rating an individual.

Bibliography: **Thorndike, E. L.:** A constant error of psychological ratings. J. appl. Psychol., 1920, *4*, 25–9.

H.Ma.

Haloperidol (*Haldol; Serenase*). The most important minor tranquilizer of the butyrophenone type (neuroleptic group). Haloperidol has a strong neuroleptic action and often has dyskinetic extrapyramidal effects in high doses. In psychological studies of healthy individuals performance and general sensation of well-being were improved rather than impaired with doses of up to 2 mg, but alcohol reinforced negative effects. See *Differential psychopharmacology.*

Bibliography: Janke, W. & Debus, G.: Experimental studies on antianxiety agents with normal subjects; methodological considerations and review of the main effects. In: **Efron, D.** (Ed.): Psychopharmacology, 1957–1967. Washington, 1968. For other literature see *Butyrophenones.* *G.D.*

Halving method. In psychophysics, a method for constructing a ratio scale of subjective magnitude. The subject is required to judge when a stimulus is perceptually half the value of a previously presented standard on the dimension being scaled, without knowledge of the relevant physical values: e.g. for scaling perceived brightness, S. is required to indicate when he thinks a variable light is half as bright as the standard (or to adjust it to this position himself). This procedure is repeated for many points along the physical scale until a stable ratio scale of subjective magnitude is achieved. *G.D.W.*

Hand. The "universal tool", an important human organ of sensation (tactile, pressure, temperature, vibratory and pain sensations), expression, communication (sign and finger language, writing), and contact (touching, stroking, gripping). Man's development into his present advanced form would have been impossible without the hand; this is reflected in the expression "*homo faber*". Industrial psychology and occupational psychology study the use of the hand in work (manual skills, motor skills, etc.)

Bibliography: Alpenfels, E. J.: The anthropology and social significance of the human hand. Artificial Limbs, 1955, *2*, 4–21. **Kiener, F.:** Hand, Gebärde und Charakter. Munich, 1962. **Rensch, B.** (Ed.): Handgebrauch und Verständigung bei Affen und Frühmenschen. Stuttgart, 1968.

Handedness. A spontaneous or acquired preference for using the right or left hand, associated with corresponding differences in dexterity. The dominance of the right hand corresponds—due to the intersection of the (motor) pyramidal pathways in the medulla or in the particular spinal-cord segments—to a dominance of the left half of the brain, and vice versa. Handedness, which Greene's studies (1943) show to be a special factor in the psychomotor system, can be determined in the simplest instance by questions, or tests such as throwing a ball, pointing, etc. See *Laterality; Motor skills.*

Bibliography: Grant, D. A. & Kaestner, N. F.: Constant velocity tracking as a function of S's handedness and the rate and direction of the target course. J. exp. Psychol., 1955, *49*, 203–8. **Greene, E. B.:** An analysis of random and systematic changes with practice. Psychometrika, 1943, *8*, 37–52. **Simon, J. R.,** *et al.*: Effects of handedness on tracking accuracy, Percept. mot. Skills Res. Exch., 1952, *4*, 53–7.

M.A.

Handicapped children. The psychological and educational problems of handicapped children include on the one hand the child's difficulty in reconciling himself with his obtrusiveness in his habitual surroundings, and his impaired physical movement, and on the other hand attempts to induce in the child, despite his handicap, a positive development of personality. Care for handicapped children concentrates on strengthening self-reliance, avoiding a succession of failures, and bringing about a positive mental attitude to the handicap. See *Child psychology; Mental defect.* *H.Schr.*

Handicapped person. An individual with innate or acquired impairment of physical function. But the term is sometimes used for the mentally, rather than the physically handicapped. See *Mental defect; Rehabilitation.* *G.R.W.M.*

Handlines. These lines appear on the palm of the hand and generally form an M-shaped pattern; they are studied in chirology (q.v.). A distinction must be made between the handlines and the papillary lines; fingerprints are taken from the papillary lines on the finger tips (dactyloscopy). The handline patterns of the palm and the lines on the sole of the foot are attracting growing attention in medicine, anthropology and genetics, and also to some extent in psychology (constitutional psychology). Chromosomal anomalies affect both the handline patterns and the psyche.

Bibliography: Penrose, L. S.: Dermatoglyphics. Scientific American, 1969, *22* (6), 72–84. *F.Ki*

Handwriting. See *Graphology*.

Haploid. By contrast with diploid (q.v.) and polyploid cells, haploid cells contain only one simple chromosome set. *Polyploid* = containing more than two chromosome sets (e.g. many cultivated plants). All the sex cells are haploid, as are many *protozoa*, lower plants and mosses. *H.S.*

Haploscope. Apparatus constructed by H. Hering for his experiments in binocular vision. The haploscope consists of two cylindrical tubes, the axes of which coincide with the line of vision of both eyes. In contrast to experiments with the *stereoscope* (q.v.), those using the haploscope are aimed not at creating effects in depth but at determining retinal orientation ratios. See *Identical retinal points*. *F.Ma.*

Haptics; haptic illusions. Haptics is the science relating to cutaneous sensation: that is, the modality of touch. There are many different types of sense organ in the skin, including receptors for pressure, temperature and pain. An example of a haptic illusion is Aristotle's illusion, in which two fingers are crossed and a small object is placed between them. Two objects are perceived since the skin on the outside of the two fingers is stimulated: normally this would result from two objects. Many of the visual illusions, e.g. *Müller-Lyer* and *tau effect*, also occur in the touch modality. *C.D.F.*

Harmonic. 1. An *overtone*, or upper partial, with a wave vibration frequency which is an integral multiple of that of the fundamental. **2.** Capable of expression in sine or cosine functions. **3.** (syn. *harmonical; harmonious*) Congruous, agreeable, pleasing.

Harmonic mean (*H*). An expression for the central tendency of a distribution: the reciprocal of the arithmetic mean of the reciprocals of a sample (series of values).

$$H = \frac{1}{\frac{1}{N}\Sigma\frac{1}{X_i}} = \frac{N}{\Sigma\frac{1}{X_i}}$$

for discrete variables, and:

$$H = \frac{1}{\int_{\infty}^{\infty}\frac{f(x)}{x}\,d_x}$$

for continuous variables. In the case of positive x values, *H* is smaller than the geometric mean or arithmetic mean. *W.H.B.*

Hashish. Cannabis (q.v.) resin: the strongest of the hemp products used as euphoriants. Hashish is normally smoked but may also be eaten. The use of hashish and other cannabis derivatives such as marihuana (q.v.) has risen constantly in recent years, especially among young people. According to Bewley (1968) consumption in England rose more than 700% in the years 1960 to 1965. The widely held opinion that persons who are labile or show other psychological anomalies are the main users of hashish could not be confirmed by Lennertz (1970) in a questionnaire study of young hashish smokers. The latter differed from a control group in their high level of tolerance, which Lennertz believes to be connected with the entire social and moral outlook of this group.

Few controlled studies have been made of the psychological effects of hashish. Evaluation of the effects is complicated by the fact that the pharmacological effectiveness of hashish varies widely while the effects are also dependent on individual experience with the substance and on the technique of smoking. In normal doses inexperienced testees generally note no subjective changes when hashish is taken, while the experienced persons report slightly euphoriant and stimulating effects. The performance of naïve testees tended to be impaired, whereas experienced marihuana smokers reported improved performance in some cases.

Hallucinogenic effects (primarily visual hallucinations linked with real perceptual objects) only occur with high doses or chronic use. See *Drug dependence; Psychotomimetic drugs.*

Bibliography: Bewley, T. H.: Recent changes in the pattern of drug abuse in London and in the United Kingdom. In: **C. W. A. Wilson** (Ed.): Adolescent drug dependence. Proceedings of the Society for the Study of Addiction. Oxford, 1968, 197–220. **Jones, R. T. & Stone, G. C.:** Psychological studies of marijuana and alcohol in man. Psychopharmacologia, 1970, *18*, 108–17. **Lennertz, E.:** Zur Frage der antisozialen Persönlichkeit jugendlicher Hashischraucher. Z. für Sozialpsychol., 1970, *1*, 48–56. **Weil, A. T., Zinberg, N. E. & Nelson, J. M.:** Clinical and psychological effects of marihuana in man. Science, 1968, *162*, 1234–42.

G.E.

Haunt. House or other locale that has become the scene of apparitions (q.v.) or similar manifestations associated with former inhabitants since deceased. *J.B.*

Hawthorne experiments. Generic name for a series of experiments to analyze the conditions of industrial output, starting with purely physiological and going on to psychological and sociological questions. The experiments were organized in 1927–32 under E. Mayo and his colleagues T. N. Whitehead, F. J. Roethlisberger, W. J. Dickson, *et al.*, in the Hawthorne Works of the Western Electric Company.

The first series of experiments (first and second Relay Assembly Test Room, Mica Splitting Test Room) showed no clear correlation between productivity and the controlled variables, i.e. wage system and general working conditions. The results of the Mass Interviewing Program (starting in 1928) led to experimental studies of human relations in the Bank Wiring Observation Room (1931–32) and to the discovery of the "informal group" (q.v.) and its significance in determining individual productivity.

Bibliography: Argyle, M.: The relay assembly test room in retrospect. Occ. Psychol., 1963, *27*, 98–103. **Roethlisberger, F. J. & Dickson, W. J.:** Management and the worker, Cambridge, Mass., 1939.

W.F.N.

Hearing. See *Auditory perception; Sense organs.*

Hearing, localized. The localization of sound depends on the difference in time taken by the sound to reach the two ears (see *Differential running time*). Because of this, localization of sound sources lying in a vertical plane at right angles to, and in the middle of, a line joining the two ears is very poor, since from all points in this plane the sound will reach both ears at the same time. *C.D.F.*

Heart beat (syn. *Heart rate*). The number of heart beats per minute. The normal value is 60 per minute. Various regulating mechanisms allow the rate to rise during physical activity (greater volume of blood supplied to the heart) up to a possible maximum of 220 beats per minute. The heart rate is determined by measuring the pulse or ECG impulses per minute (cardiochronograph, cardiograph, electrocardiograph, etc.). Recording of heart rhythms is an important part of any examination of circulatory function, and enables conclusions to be drawn on the functional condition of the heart. The rate is faster in abnormal metabolic conditions (Basedow's disease, q.v.), and slower in the case of trained athletes.

E.D.

Hebb's theory of perceptual learning. Hebb's theory (see *Attention*) that (mature) learning is dependent on interacting central neural organizations, or "cell assemblies", which form the neural basis of complex, enduring patterns required for, e.g., concept formation. The structure by which individual assemblies are related to one another is called a "phase sequence". Practice builds up these highly coordinated groups of cells in the cerebral cortex.

Bibliography: Hebb, D. O.: The organization of behavior: a neuropsychological theory. New York, 1949. **Id.:** A neuropsychological theory. In: **Koch, S.** (Ed.): Psychology: a study of a science. New York, 1959, 622–43.

Hebephilia. An abnormally passionate interest in adolescents.

Hebephrenia. One of the schizophrenic syndromes. Originally described by Hecker in 1871 as an illness of puberty which led to a silly deterioration of intellect. Hence it was similar to *dementia praecox* (q.v.) and was grouped with it by Kraepelin in 1893. The syndrome is characterized by youthful onset, affective symptoms of blunting with lability, silliness, inappropriateness, irritability, thought disorder and disturbances of volition. Poorly organized delusions and hallucinations are usually present, but motor symptoms are not. The onset is insidious and the prognosis poor. *B.B.*

Hedonism. The theory that sensual pleasure is the sole objective of all behavior. Today hedonism is mainly considered in psychoanalysis (q.v.) (the *pleasure principle*). In ethics, hedonism is contrasted or combined with *eudaemonism*, according to which the desire for happiness is the end of all (right) action.

Bibliography: James, W.: The principles of psychology, Vol. 2. New York, 1890. *M.R.*

Height disparity. See *Horizontal disparity*.

Helmholtz, Hermann von. *Life and works.* B. 31/8/1821 in Potsdam; d. 8/9/1894 in Charlottenburg, Berlin. Graduated in 1842 with a study of the origin of nerve fibers in the ganglionic cells. He then worked as an army surgeon in Potsdam. In 1847 he read his famous paper to the Physical Society of Berlin on the principle of the conservation of energy. In 1849, Helmholtz became Professor of physiology in Königsberg, where he remained until 1855. Between 1855 and 1858 he was Professor of anatomy and physiology in Bonn, and then Professor of physiology in Heidelberg until 1871. In 1871 he was appointed Professor of physics at Berlin University, and in 1887 he was appointed first Director of the newly established Imperial Institute of Physics and Technology in Charlottenburg (Berlin).

Helmholtz published more than two hundred articles and monographs in which he made a fundamental contribution to anatomy, medicine, physiology, physics and psychology. In the psychological sphere, his work on the physiology and psychology of sensation is of most interest. By far his most important works are the three volumes of his *Treatise on Physiological Optics* (1856–1867) and his study of the *Theory of Sensations of Tone as the Physiological Basis of the Theory of Music* (1862). In the first work he presents his own findings and offers a survey of the German literature on the anatomical, physiological and physical bases of visual perception; the second study contains his contribution to physiological acoustics, and in particular to the study of problems of the auditory discrimination of timbre and pitch.

Physiological psychology. Helmholtz's first important work in this sphere was the determination of the transmission velocity of nervous excitation in the sensory and motor nerve fibers (i.e. the speed of the neural impulse) by examining the "nerve-muscle preparation" of frogs and carrying out reaction-time experiments on humans. He refuted the previously held opinion that the speed of conduction in the nerve is many time greater than the speed of light. In the sphere of optics and sensory physiology Helmholtz invented the ophthalmoscope, and the ophthalmometer—a device to determine the corneal curvature of the eye. Working independently of the Dutch physiologist Cramer, Helmholtz reached the same conclusions in his description and explanation of the process of accommodation (q.v.) in the eye. In his theory of color perception he developed the view of the British physiologist T. Young. Starting from the law of specific energy of nerves (Müller), Helmholtz assumed the existence of three color-sensitive nerve substances whose excitation leads in each case to a specific color sensation (red, green, blue), while all the other color sensations are obtained by mixing these three primary colors.

Helmholtz's assumptions on space perception (q.v.) and object perception are based on Lotze's local sign theory, which he tried to harmonize with Müller's principle of specific energies. He believed that perception is a two-stage process. The basis of perception is represented by the sensations, whose quality and intensity are inborn, and which are conditioned by specific characteristics of the sense organs. Sensations themselves, however, have no significance for space and object perception but are merely "signs", which only acquire significance in the course of development by association through experience. The acquisition of meaning consists, in Helmholtz's opinion, of judgment processes which may be conscious to begin with but become automatic after repeated association—as "unconscious inferences" which, because of their compulsive character, appear as evident perceptions. Helmholtz adopted a distinctly empirical standpoint in the empiricism vs. nativism debate in perception theory (see *Perception*).

As regards audition (see *Auditory perception*), Helmholtz acquired importance primarily through his resonance theory (q.v.), in which he explained, e.g., the discrimination of pitch by assuming that the variously long fibers in the basilar membrane of the inner ear are made to vibrate by wavelengths corresponding to their natural frequency: i.e. the different hair cells vibrate in tune with the sound wave frequencies.

Main works: Treatise on physiological optics, 3 vols. Ed. J. P. C. Southall. Rochester, N.Y., 1924–5. On the rate of transmission of the nerve impulse. In: Dennis, W. (Ed.): Readings in the history of psychology. New York, 1948, 197–8. On the sensations of tone. New York, 1954.

Bibliography: Boring, E. G.: A history of experimental psychology. New York, 1950. **Gruber, H. & V.:** Hermann von Helmholtz: nineteenth century polymorph. Sci. Mon, 1956, *83*, 92–9. **Lenzen, V. F.:** Helmholtz's theory of knowledge. In: **Montague, M. F. A.** (Ed.): Studies and essays in the history of science and learning. New York, 1946, 299–320. **McKendrick, J. G.:** Hermann von Helmholtz. London, 1899. **Müller, J.:** Elements of physiology. London, 1837–42. **Warren, R. M. & R. P.:** Helmholtz on perception: its physiology and development. New York, 1968. **Young, T.:** Miscellaneous works. London, 1855.

W.W.

Helmholtz squares. This illusion principally demonstrates the effect whereby filled spaces

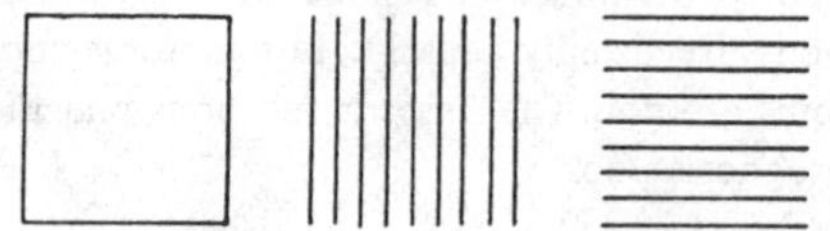

look larger than empty spaces, for the two squares composed of many parallel lines appear to have a larger surface area than the one consisting of a simple outline. However, the ends of the parallel lines give the illusion of straight edges not actually drawn so that the figure also provides an example of *closure*. *C.D.F.*

Helson-Judd effect. See *Adaptation level.*

Hemeralop[s]ia (syn. *Night-blindness*). A defect of vision at night or in twilight caused by partial or complete absence of scotopic rod vision. It may be an innate and recessive (in some case also a dominant) inherited characteristic (Trendelenburg, 1961), but is generally acquired through an alimentary deficiency of vitamin A, which is necessary for synthesis of the retinal rod pigment rhodopsin (q.v.).

Bibliography: Trendelenburg, W.: Der Gesichtssinn. Berlin, [2]1961. *K.H.P.*

Hemianopsia (syn. *Hemiopia*). Failure of the visual field on one side, which may occur in lesions of the central optical pathways between the intersection of the optic nerves (*chiasma opticum*) and the occipital lobe. Depending on the location of the lesion, hemianopsia may be homonymous (on the same side), or heteronymous (e.g. bitemporal), complete or incomplete. *C.S.*

Hemiparesis. Unilateral (motor or sensory), incomplete paralysis due to failure of the central nervous centers or pathways. Since these paths intersect, the lesion is situated on the side opposite the diseased side. *C.S.*

Hemiplegia. Paralysis of one side of the body generally caused by a stroke (see *Hemiparesis*).

Hemispheres. The two halves of the cerebrum (right and left cerebral hemispheres), which are joined together by the *corpus callosum*. *C.S.*

Hereditary characterology. A trend in psychology which developed in the nineteen twenties with the object of determining the degree to which character (q.v.) was inherited rather than dependent on environment (q.v.). The most reliable results came from twin studies (q.v.). See *Traits.* *W.K.*

Heredity, theory of. A hypothesis based on C. Darwin's *Origin of Species* (see *Darwinism*), according to which all animal and plant species have developed by evolution (q.v.) from simpler organisms. This hypothesis also implies that today's wealth of species has developed by division of species from a few organisms and ultimately, perhaps, from a single species. The essentials of heredity theory are generally recognized nowadays by serious scientists, since all the evidence is in its favor, and no refutation is available. *H.S.*

Hering, Ewald. *Life and works.* B. 5/8/1834 in Altgersdorf (Saxony); d. 27/1/1918 in Leipzig. Studied medicine in Leipzig where he was influenced by G. T. Weber and G. T. Fechner. After publishing his five-part work on space perception (q.v.), he was appointed Professor of physiology at Vienna University, where he took over C. Ludwig's post. Five years later he went to Prague as Z. Purkinje's successor, and after twenty-five years there he once again replaced C. Ludwig, this time as Professor of physiology in Leipzig.

Hering was a physiologist specializing in sensation who played a very important part as one of the pioneers of experimental physiological psychology. He was a contemporary of H. Helmholtz's (q.v.); the two shared similar interests but differed in their theoretical approaches, which led to constant controversy between them. Helmholtz was an empiricist and Hering a nativist. In his theory of space perception (published in his *Contributions to Physiology*, 1861–64), by stating that the capacity for space perception is innate and does not need to be learnt, Hering stood out against the opinion expressed by Helmholtz one year later in the third volume of *Treatise on Physiological Optics.*

Hering also differed from Helmholtz in the basis of his phenomenological studies. The observation and description of subjective, sensory experience were among his primary objectives. His nativist orientation and methodical, phenomenological approach had a strong influence on C. Stumpf, and above all on later gestalt psychology.

Hering also became important by reason of his famous theory of color vision, which was opposed to Helmholtz's three-color theory, Hering asserted that there were three color-sensitive substances in the retina (q.v.) (red/green—yellow/blue—black/white) which are in a constant state of dissimilation and assimilation, and that one of the two color sensations corresponds to each of these two processes in a substance. All possible color impressions were said to result from the combination of these fundamental colors.

Main works: Beiträge zur Physiologie, 5 vols., 1861–5, Die Lehre vom binokularen Sehen, 1868. Über das Gedächtnis als eine allgemeine Funktion der organisierten Materie, 1870. Grundzüge der Lehre vom Lichtsinn, 1920.

Bibliography: Boring, E. G.: Sensation and perception in the history of experimental psychology. New York, 1942. **Hillebrand, F.:** Ewald Hering. Leipzig, 1918.

W.W.

Hering fall test. A method for studying monocular and binocular vision in depth. In the simplest case, S. looks through a tube at a point of fixation on which the eye is focussed (see *Accommodation*). The experimenter drops small balls in front of and behind the point of fixation. S. is required to estimate the distance of the balls. *F.M.*

Hering's illusion. One of the geometric

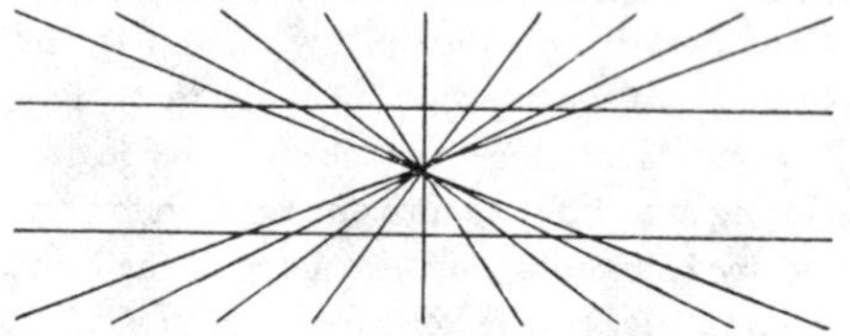

illusions. The two parallel horizontal lines are perceived as bending outwards.

C.D.F.

Hermaphrodite. An individual who has the physical characteristics (particularly sex organs) of both male and female. *Hermaphroditism* is extremely rare in humans, and only one set of sex organs is fully functional, but apparently a shift in dominance through either natural or artificial means is possible.

Hermaphroditism (syn. *Intersexuality*). Disturbed, incomplete physical sex differentiation, characterized by ambiguity or lack of agreement between external and/or internal sex characteristics (male/female). The causes of this abnormal development or malformation vary. Today a distinction is made between three principal forms of hermaphroditism: *pseudohermaphroditismus femininus* (female pseudohermaphroditism), *pseudohermaphroditismus masculinus* (male pseudohermaphroditism), and *hermaphroditismus verus* (genuine hermaphroditism). Whereas in the pseudohermaphroditisms, the genetic sex (chromosomal sex) coincides with the gonadic sex (i.e. either purely male or purely female), the external and internal sex organs are either hybrid (bisexual) or seem to belong to the other sex, in genuine hermaphroditism both sex-gland sexes are present (testicular and ovarian tissue), and the external and internal sex organs represent a mixture of male and female forms or, in external appearance, all stages from the male to the female type. The diagnosis "hermaphroditism" does not, therefore, necessarily involve specific external sex organs; the ambiguity may also be internal. The main problem of hermaphroditism lies in the psychological and psychopathological effects of the physical sexual development, above all from the angle of sex role identification and sex education.

1. *Pseudohermaphroditismus femininus:* genetically female individuals with internal

female sex organs (ovaries, fallopian tubes, uterus, vagina) and intersexual external genital organs, generally in the form of a greatly enlarged clitoris (clitoral hypertrophy), which may resemble a penis in appearance and size and is already visible at birth; the differentiation between the vagina and urethral opening is inadequate. Causes: usually a genetically conditioned overproduction of (masculinizing) androgens (q.v.); also known as the *andreno-genital syndrome* (AGS). Treatment consists in administering the hormone cortisol, which is not formed in the diseased adrenal gland. Money (1968) states early diagnosis is vital, ideally at birth. A girl can then grow up without ever knowing that she has had a special problem. The need for special sexual education is then correspondingly reduced.

2. *Pseudohermaphroditismus masculinus:* persons who are clearly male genetically and in gonadic sex; a distinction is made between two main groups, depending on the external appearance of the sex organs and the phenotype, i.e. (*a*) testicular feminization, as a relatively rare form in which the external genitalia and appearance are feminine—apart from the absence of pubic hair (hairless woman). Female development of the internal sex organs (uterus, ovaries, fallopian tubes) is not present, however. The genetic sex, sex glands and sex hormone production are male. Testicular feminization is not usually diagnosed until adolescence, when a doctor is consulted in the absence of menstrual bleeding. Cause: disturbance of all the androgen-dependent organs and tissues; clearly a hereditary defect by which the male hormones cannot influence the development of the sex organs either in the embryonic stage or in later life. Treatment: surgical extension of the vagina in or after puberty, and adequate psychological explanation of the cause of the condition and of infertility (Money, 1968). The main group of masculine pseudohermaphroditisms consists of (*b*) externally hybrid cases which come somewhere between the male and female phenotype, and which are difficult to distinguish externally from apparent female hermaphrodites. The true causes of these malformations cannot generally be explained in the individual case. Psychological and psychopathological problems are frequently encountered because (i) the external genitalia are ambiguous, and in extreme cases the patient himself has doubts about his sex role; (ii) in cases which are diagnosed at a late stage, sex characteristics may develop at puberty (e.g. breast development, absence of the secondary male sex characteristics) which do not correspond to the sex role to which the subject has become accustomed (e.g. male); (iii) certain genital malformations may prevent normal sexual behavior (failure of the erection mechanism), or make it more difficult, or alternatively—e.g. in *hypospadia scrotalis*—prevent sexually specific urination. For these and other reasons, an individual, medico-psychological treatment program must be prepared in each case of masculine hermaphroditism, as in the case of genuine hermaphroditism. There are certain basic criteria and rules for treatment (Wilkins, 1965; Money, 1968; Wallis, 1967).

3. *Genuine hermaphrodites:* the testicles and ovaries may be combined in a single organ (= ovotestes) or present separately (= lateral hermaphrodites) and both may reach fully functional maturity (sperm formation or ovulation and menstruation). The external and internal genitalia may present many different characteristics: all kinds of transitional forms from male to female types are possible (usually mixed forms). Genuine hermaphrodites may be genetically male-female or male or female (sex chromosomes XX or XY or XY/XO). Cause: probably due to disturbed nucleus division during early embryonic development. Occurrence: relatively rare. In all cases of hermaphroditism, early diagnosis is vital because medical treatment and adequate sexual education are dependent on it. The decisive factor in sexing a newly born hermaphrodite should be the anatomical appearance of the external

genitalia, even if the sex-gland sex and genetical sex do not coincide with it. Sex changes should be made at the earliest possible time (before the age of two years), and only if there is no clear phenotype. If hermaphroditism is diagnosed later on, i.e. after the fourth year of age, special medical and psychological treatment as defined by Wilkins (1965) and Money (1968) is indicated.

Bibliography: Money, J.: Cytogenetic and psychosexual incongruities with a note on spaceform blindness. Am. J. Psychiat., 1963, *119*, 820–7. **Id.** (Ed.): Sex research: new developments. Chicago, 1968. **Wilkins, L.:** The diagnosis and treatment of endocrine disorders in childhood and adolescence. Springfield, Ill., 1965. **Jores, A. & Nowakowski, H.:** Praktische Endokrinologie. Stuttgart, 1964. **Voigt, K. D. & Schmidt, H.:** Sexualhormone, Hamburg, 1968. **Wallis, H.:** Katamnestische Erhebungen bei Hermaphroditen. Jahrb. f. Psychiat., 1967, *5*, 104–111.

H. Maisch

Heroin. A semi-synthetic morphine derivative (diacetylmorphine) with highly analgesic and euphoriant action (see *Analgesics*). With chronic use there is a risk of habituation in the sense of psychological and physiological dependence. See *Drug dependence*. *G.E.*

Hertz. A unit of wave frequency equivalent to one cycle per second, especially in electricity.

Heterogamete; homogamete. The male and female differ chromosomally. They are either homogametic or heterogametic from the standpoint of the sex chromosomes. Frequently, e.g. in man and in the fruit fly *drosophila*, the female sex is of the XX and the male of the XY type (heterogamete). Some butterflies, fishes and birds have heterogametic females and homogametic males; there is also the XO type, e.g. in bed bugs. Sex, however, is not determined solely by the ratio of X:Y chromosomes but by the ratio of the number of autosome sets to the number of X chromosomes. *K.Fi.*

Heterogeneous variance. The dissimilarity of two or more sample distributions is so marked that they probably do not originate from the same basic group. See *Variance, analysis of*. *W.H.B.*

Heterohypnosis. Generally referred to simply as *hypnosis* (q.v.): a hypnotic state brought about in a subject by the suggestive influence of another person (the hypnotist) (ant. *autohypnosis*, q.v. = self-hypnosis, i.e. a state of hypnosis brought about by autosuggestion, q.v.). *H.-N.G.*

Heterosensorial (syn. *Heterosensory*). From a different sense area. Ant. *homosensorial* = from the same sense area. E.g. heterosensorial association or reproduction. See *Homosensorial reproduction.*

Heterosexual. 1. Pertaining to sexual relationships with members of the opposite sex. **2.** One who is sexually attracted to members of the opposite sex. In both cases, overt sexual behavior may or may not be involved, and the opposite is *homosexual*. *G.D.W.*

Heterosexuality, compulsive. Abnormally strong desire for heterosexual contact. Called *nymphomania* or *estromania* in females; *satyriasis*, *satyromania*, or *priapism* in males. Needless to say, the criteria for employing these diagnostic labels are ill-defined and arbitrary. *G.D.W.*

Heterostereotype. By analogy with the term as used in printing, the word *stereotype* (q.v.) denotes a relatively rigid concept of persons or groups which is resistant to change and usually simplified. *Heterostereotypes* are similar concepts of other persons or groups; *autostereotypes* are the ideas a person has of himself or of a reference, and/or membership, group. Examples: heterostereotype: "miserly Scots"; autostereotype: "self-sacrificing scientist." *H.D.S.*

Heterozygote. In a diploid (q.v.) cell, the two genes (see *Allele*) for a given feature may be identical, i.e. condition the same degree of emphasis of the feature, or different, in which case the emphasis of the feature will also differ. In the first instance, the cell or organism is said to be *homozygotic* in regard to the feature concerned, and in the second case *heterozygotic*. In heterozygotic organisms, the degree of emphasis of the feature is dependent on whether the latter is inherited by dominant-recessive or intermediary means. *H.S.*

Hexis. A term used by Guilford (in his hierarchical model of personality) for the lowest plane of habit (q.v.). Hexis designates a constant disposition, which means that an individual behaves in a similar manner in a given range of situations. *G.K.*

Hierarchy (syn. *Hierarchical structure*). **1.** A ranking of elements (e.g. persons, things, concepts, constructs) so that each rank is subordinate to the next higher rank. The subordination may be based on widely varying factors (e.g. degree of generality, level of abstraction, dominance), but must remain the same within a hierarchical system. In personality (q.v.) psychology a number of attempts have been made to describe personality as a hierarchical system of, e.g., motives or traits (q.v.). In personality research based on factor analysis the distinction between first, second and higher order factors represents a hierarchical personality model. See *Motive*. *D.B.*

2. Hierarchy of centers; hierarchy of moods. Behavioral structures are based on central coordination mechanisms with differing degrees of integration; the highest levels have been defined by Tinbergen as *instincts*. Each instinct influences the motor units and competes with other instincts for control over the latter. Tinbergen assumes a linear arrangement of centers of different orders in the hierarchy of centers, ranging from the superimposed main instinct to the end action. With the exception of the highest center, the centers are generally blocked; the lower centers are charged by higher ones and must be disinhibited by key stimuli. In Baerends' hierarchy of moods, moods of differing order influence the duration of specific behavioral spectra. A specific stimulus situation does not always release the same behavior; the mood prevailing at a given time tends to be the decisive factor. Leyhausen's relative hierarchy of moods does not include a linear arrangement of moods in order of precedence. He assumes the appetence of the final action to be the dominant factor and not the last link in the chain. Cats, for example, do not have a uniform prey-catching impulse, but specific stimuli for lying in wait, creeping, pouncing, killing, etc. Each part action may become the desired final action, and suppress the others. See *Instinct*.

Bibliography: Baerends, G. P.: Fortpflanzungsverhalten und Orientierung der Grabwespe Ammophilia campestris. Jur. Tijdschr. Entom., 1941, *84*, 71–275. **Leyhausen, P.:** Über die Funktion der relativen Stimmungshierarchie. Z. Tierpsychol., 1965, *22*, 412–94. **Tinbergen, N.:** The study of instinct. Oxford, 2969. *K.Fi.*

Hierarchy, industrial. An historically conditioned form of authority with power distributed on several different levels and a strictly defined, permanent system of command and subordination. It is undecided to what extent there are tendencies toward elimination of the hierarchical structure as a result of technical progress (automation), and to what degree an approximation to "circular" (democratic) authority structures is possible. See *Industrial psychology*.

Bibliography: Blau, P. M. & Scott, W. R.: Formal organizations: a comparative approach. San Francisco, 1962. **Simpson, R. L.:** Vertical and horizontal communication in formal organizations. Admin. Sci. Quart., 1959, *4*, 188–9. *C.B.*

Hillebrand's alley. An experimental technique for studying one aspect of the perception of three-dimensional space. Parallel lines, e.g. railway lines, appear to come together in the distance. Hillebrand constructed an alley of hanging threads and people were asked to adjust these until the two rows appeared parallel as they went into the distance. He could then measure the resulting discrepancies from true parallelism, thus discovering some of the properties of subjective space as opposed to objective space. *C.D.F.*

Hippocampus. A part of the temporal lobe which belongs to the hindbrain (see *Cerebrum*) and forms the medial wall of the inferior horn of the lateral ventricle. It consists of white and grey matter. Its functional significance has not been fully clarified; it is sometimes assumed to play a part in the ability to detect odors (olfactory processes), and sometimes to influence the function of the *formatio reticularis* (q.v.) and the development of conditioned responses. See *Neuroanatomy*. *E.D.*

Hippocratic types. The four *temperaments* (q.v.) wrongly attributed to the followers of Hippocrates and in fact described first in the Middle Ages. See *Type*. *W.K.*

Hirsutism. Abnormal growth of body hair in women (hair on the limbs, stomach, breasts; growth of a beard). Various causes: (*a*) heightened production (pathologically conditioned) of male sex hormones by the adrenal cortex (e.g. adrenogenital syndrome of female hermaphroditism, or Cushing's syndrome), or defective ovaries (e.g. Stein-Leventhal syndrome); (*b*) non-pathological excess production of male sex hormones (androgens) in the adrenal glands or ovaries; also known as idiopathic or "common" hirsutism. Psychological disturbances (e.g. uncertainty about sexual role) almost always occur, generally after and rarely before the development of the abnormal hair. Incidence: 3 to 4%.

Bibliography: Zerssen, D. von, Meyer, A. E. & Ahrens, D.: Klinische, biochemische und psychologische Untersuchungen an Patienten mit gewöhnlichem Hirsutismus. Dt. Arch. klin. Med., 1960, *206*, 234. *H.M.*

Histamine. Neurohormone or tissue hormone; a biogenic amine (q.v.) obtained by biosynthesis from histidine (decarboxylation). Histamine occurs naturally in many organs (intestine, lungs, liver, skin, central nervous system, etc.). The main physiological effects are: dilatation of the capillary blood vessels with a substantial drop in blood pressure, contraction of the smooth musculature (uterus, intestines, bronchial muscles), and strong stimulation of the secretion of gastric acid. Histamine is assumed to be important in the pathogenesis of allergies, and in the origin and conduction of pain. In antigen-antibody reactions, and in particular in anaphylactic shock, large quantities of histamine are released. Smaller amounts are released in sensory pain. The role of histamine in the central nervous system has not yet been definitively explained. Its concentration distribution is similar to that of the catecholamines. A fairly large number of centrally effective drugs block the effect of histamine (see, e.g., *Antihistamines; Neuroleptics*). See *Psychosomatics*.

Bibliography: Green, J. P.: Histamine and the nervous system. Feder. Proceed., 1964, *23*, 1095–102. **Handbuch der experimentellen Pharmakologie:** Vol. 18, Pt. 1. Histamine. Its chemistry, metabolism and physiological actions. Berlin, 1966. **Kahlson, G. & Rosengren, E.:** Histamine. Ann. Rev. Pharmacol., 1965, *5*, 305. *W.J.*

Histogram. A histogram is a graphic representation of the frequency distribution (q.v.) for a discrete variable. The frequency for each class is shown as a vertical bar. *W.H.B.*

Historical psychology. For this school (founded by J. H. van den Berg), the objects of psychological research can be determined only from their history, since they develop in the course of time. This applies in particular to the higher mental processes (needs, will, operations of the intellect, personality). This approach has led to the study of "mentalities" (L. Febvre) and recently to research into the archeology of knowledge (M. Foucauld). *P.M.*

History of psychology. I. The roots of psychology go back thousands of years and reach into many areas of knowledge. Folkways, magic, religion, philosophy and science have all contributed to the origin of psychology. It is likely that every culture had its own psychology in order to postulate causes for certain human thoughts, actions and events. But the early history of psychology, like the early history of Western thought in general, is primarily known to us through the writings of the Greek philosophers.

1. *Early Greek naturalists.* While speculating on the nature of the universe, the Greek philosophers of the sixth century B.C. were already discussing certain psychological problems. As pointed out by Esper (1964), they considered all nature as animate. Matter, animals and men were thought to be alive because they moved. Thales (c. 625 B.C.), for instance, allowed a magnet a soul because it moved iron. Anaximander (c. 610–c. 547 B.C.) proposed an evolutionary theory, suggesting that life arose from sun-heated mud. He also thought that water was basic to all substance, because it was universal, appeared in many forms, and produced movement when changing its aggregate state. Heraclitus (c. 535–c. 475 B.C.) considered fire as the primary force and "soul-substance", because it moved and transformed matter. All matter was thought to be in a constant state of flux, and only the orderliness in which change occurred presented constancy, rationality or "logos". Heraclitus also believed that all knowledge must come through the senses, a notion that formed the basis for the psychological thinking of the British empiricist philosophers of the eighteenth century, and in turn the basis for present-day methods of conditioning, reconditioning, and behavior modification.

Democritus (c. 460–c. 370 B.C.) presented the first atomic view of the universe, when he said that matter, like humans, was composed of small, mobile atoms which entered the body to give it life or soul. Different parts of the body were thought to be formed by different types of atoms responsible for a variety of functions. Democritus described the brain as the organ of thought, the heart as that of anger, and the liver as that of disease. He did not distinguish sensing from thinking, since both were based on atomic motion (Diels, 1934).

2. *Early Greek anti-naturalists.* Not all pre-Socratic philosophers believed that mind and matter, or body and soul, had equal properties and were subject to one and the same natural law. Nor did they all agree on the reliability of the senses as indicators of reality. Pythagoras (c. 582–c. 500 B.C.) and his followers were fascinated by numbers, and explained many abstract concepts by them. The Pythagoreans did not consider the soul and the body as one entity, but postulated that the soul leaves the body after death to undergo a possible succession of reincarnations. This division of body and soul was much elaborated by the Christian philosophers, who thus prepared psychology for the dualistic approach of mentalism and mechanism.

Protagoras (c. 480–c. 410 B.C.), an older contemporary of Plato, recognized the subjective value of the human senses and doubted their objectivity. He pointed out that sensations and perceptions differ between and within individuals, being subject to a constant flux of biological and social influences. Hence his famous saying, "Man is the measure of all things" (Diels, 1934).

Anti-naturalism reached its peak with Plato. He thought the senses were unreliable, because one could perceive, for instance, triangles of all shapes and sizes and still maintain an idea of triangularity. It is therefore the idea, the form, or the abstract thought which yields true knowledge. Sense perception, Plato believed, yields only probabilities and approximations. He had so much faith in reason that he preferred it to observation, a viewpoint that has often hindered the future accumulation of psychological knowledge.

The Greek philosophers established two more or less discrete philosophical approaches to psychology. One approach emphasized reason, logic, thought, theory, innate knowledge, and a mind distinct from the body. The other approach emphasized observation, experimentation, environmental learning, and unity of body and soul. Much of all future psychology has fallen into one of these two camps.

3. *Aristotle*. The views of Aristotle (384–322 B.C.) cannot be assigned to either camp. Aristotle was a theorist as well as an observer. Watson (1968) considers him to have been the first psychologist because he tried to present a systematic and integrated view of the function of the human mind. The many topics he wrote about are very similar to the titles of chapter headings in modern general psychology texts.

Unlike Plato, Aristotle thought that form cannot be separated from matter—that a bronze statue, for instance, must have matter in order to have form, and vice versa. This unifying concept is also present in Aristotle's view of the "psyche", often interpreted as "soul" or "mind". Aristotle's soul includes matter as well as the functioning of the mind. Its development is based on evolutionary principles—on a vegetative soul attributed to plants, a sensory soul attributed to animals, and a rational soul belonging to man. Aristotle's "psyche" did not have any religious or supernatural properties. Religious and supernatural properties were added over a thousand years later by the scholastic philosopher St Thomas Aquinas.

Aristotle wrote about the five senses and postulated a sixth one necessary to combine the functions of any two or more senses. He thought that we must rely on the senses to make factual observations, but warned that empirical data, no matter how correct, are useless if interpreted with false logic or wrong premisses. He also warned that correct logic is misleading if based on faulty observations. He thought knowledge was a combination of sense experience and thinking.

Many of Aristotle's hypotheses on the nature of remembering and forgetting have given rise to much experimentation in the area of learning. His doctrine of association (q.v.) stated that memory is facilitated by either similarity or dissimilarity of a present and past event, or by their close relationship in time and space. Later these hypotheses became known as the laws of similarity, contrast, and contiguity.

Aristotle formed theories about desires, appetites, pain and pleasure, reactions, and emotions. His doctrine of catharsis suggested, for instance, that fears can be transferred to the hero in a tragedy—an idea which much later formed one of the tenets of psychoanalysis and play therapy.

4. *Early Christian period and the Middle Ages*. There was little inquiry into psychology during the early Christian period and during the Middle Ages. St Augustine's (354–430) teachings were accepted for hundreds of years. He emphasized the introspective method, believing that "self-knowledge," subjective reflecting upon one's own mind, is more exact than knowledge gained through sense perception. The main force of the mind or the "self" was the power of the "will," which in turn, was responsible for habits, actions, and faith. Involuntary bodily functions, however, were not considered part of

the "self" and were to be neglected and ignored—an attitude which has remained in Western culture where autonomic functions such as sex, and gastro-intestinal activities are still preferably conducted in privacy.

St Thomas Aquinas (1225–74) accepted Augustine's concept of "faith" and "will" as well as Aristotle's "reason." In this amalgamation Augustine's "will" became subordinated to Aristotle's "reason," and Aristotle's "rational soul" became immortal and resurrectable. Aquinas also modified Aristotle's hierarchical concept of "souls" or "psyche." He postulated that there was only one soul, but that this soul was composed of a rational faculty which was non-physical and deathless, and of sensory and vegetative faculties which were physically dependent and perished with the body.

5. *Beginnings of modern psychology.* Aquinas' definitions of reason, mind, soul and body were not challenged until Descartes (1596–1650) introduced his dualistic concept of man. He held that the mind or soul is located in the brain, though it has no substance. The body, on the other hand, was thought to have substance, or "extended" qualities which, like machines, followed mechanical laws. Descartes further believed that the mind can influence the body and the body the mind, and he attempted to describe the physiological mechanisms of this interaction. Descartes is often called the first modern psychologist, because psychology would have remained speculative without the introduction and the recognition of physiological factors.

After Descartes's introduction of the concept of interaction, philosophers began to debate about the qualities and the quantities of the body's influence on the mind. They were primarily interested to know whether such mental qualities as knowing, thinking, and ideation arise within the mind, or come to the mind via the body's senses. John Locke (1632–1704) took a radical environmental view. He maintained that the mind is a "blank tablet" (*tabula rasa*), that all knowledge must enter the mind through the senses, and that ideas are, in turn, combinations and reflections of sensory impressions. Locke and other British philosophers such as Hume, Hartley, the Mills, and Bain, who held similar views, became known as the "British empiricists." They are also called "associationists," because they believed that Aristotle's principles of association play a major role in the selection, storage, and composition of all mental content such as knowledge, thought, images, and ideas.

Not all philosophers agreed with the empiricists. Berkeley (1685–1753) pointed out that the mind, as in the case of depth perception, for instance, needs to process information from retinal size differences, clearness of the image, tension from certain eye muscles, and so on—information or stimuli not directly related to depth perception. Berkeley argued that the ultimate reality lies in the mind and not in the matter found in the environment.

Psychology's major problem had been that of "body and soul." The nineteenth century superimposed on it that of "nativism vs. empiricism," or that of heredity vs. environment—a problem which still causes much discussion in the measurement and definitions of such psychological factors as temperament and intelligence.

6. *Physiology and the mind.* The physiologists of the nineteenth century gave much to the philosophers who theorized about the content and functions of the mind. Pierre Flourens (1794–1867) demonstrated that certain parts of the brain are directly responsible for certain behavioral functions. When he extirpated the cortex of a bird, for instance, he found that it could no longer fly "voluntarily," but only if thrown into the air. Paul Broca (1824–1880) attempted to locate the brain area responsible for speech, and in 1870 Fritsch and Hitzig discovered the area of the cerebral cortex related to motor functions (Boring, 1950, pp. 61–79).

The studies of sensory receptors, nerves, and muscles also contributed much to the understanding of human feelings, thoughts, and activities. Du Bois-Raymond demonstrated in 1849 that neural activity is measurable, and that it is accompanied by an electrical impulse; and Helmholtz (q.v.) showed in 1850 that neural conduction requires a specified time. Sechenov (1863) examined reflexes and found that some animals can perform "purposive" acts by means of spinal reflex actions which do not require the activity of the brain.

Physiological discoveries such as the above were important psychological "breakthroughs" because the nativists—the dominant majority—insisted that the functions of the mind had no physical correlates in space or time. Sechenov, for instance, was not allowed to publish his findings about the nature of reflexes under the title: "An attempt to establish physiological bases of psychic processes." The censorship committee of St Petersburg thought that the juxtaposition of "physiological" and "psychic" would corrupt the mores of society.

7. *Experimental psychology.* Psychology has been defined as the "product of the union of philosophy and physiology" (Keller, 1936, p. 21). Physiology brought not only physiological data but the scientific method in general to psychology, and scientists from non-physiological disciplines began to make important contributions. The physicist Gustav Fechner (q.v.) (1801–87), who was also a medical doctor and a philosopher, spent much of his lifetime investigating the relationship between the objective, physical world and the subjective, personal one. He measured the physical energy needed to produce various intensities of sensation. He found, for instance, that ten times as much energy is required to produce a tone which is heard twice as loud as before, a hundred times as much energy to hear the tone three times as loud, etc. Fechner's method became known as "psychophysics" (q.v.), and has found much use in apparatus design and human engineering.

The Dutch physician F. C. Donders (1862) attempted to measure mental activities through reaction-time experiments. To obtain a time measure for thought he deducted the reaction time required for simple from that required for more complicated tasks.

Another scientific, but non-physiological method of exploring the mind was pioneered by Hermann Ebbinghaus (q.v.) (1850–1909). He investigated rates of learning and of forgetting, such as, for instance, the relationship between number of repetitions and length of memory. Ebbinghaus created and used the "nonsense syllable". He theorized correctly that the use of meaningful words would interfere with objectivity in learning experiments.

8. *Academic psychology.* In 1879 the first psychological laboratory was founded by Wilhelm Wundt (q.v.) (1832–1920) at the University of Leipzig. Wundt was trained in medicine, physiology and philosophy. He was a prolific writer "producing a total of 491 publications ranging from one-page articles to books 2,353 pages long" (Boring, 1950, p. 345). Wundt tried to investigate the mind by studying its conscious content, and more specifically the elements of sensation, such as intensity, duration, and locality. Wundt's preferred method was that of "introspection" (q.v.), in which an individual describes his sensations and feelings in discrete, technical terms. Wundt's laboratory became the center of psychological activities. Students came to him from all over the world to investigate problems related to visual perception, hearing, touch and taste, reaction time, word associations, and so on. The variety and the volume of Wundt's contributions to psychology are unique. Boring & Boring (1948) surveyed the background of American psychologists and found that a large majority were trained by teachers who in turn were pupils of Wundt. However, Wundt's influence in his own country was less pronounced (Wesley, 1965).

9. *Diversification of psychology.* Unity in psychology was short-lived and existed

perhaps only *in statu nascendi* in the early days at Wundt's laboratory. Other psychological schools were soon to follow which emphasized different methods for studying the mind. Oswald Külpe (q.v.) (1862–1915) founded a psychological laboratory in Würzburg in 1896. He and his students examined such complex tasks as thinking, remembering, and judging. They used a more molar type of introspection, believing that the Wundtian approach was too atomistic.

The principle of "wholeness" was later stressed again by the founders of "gestalt" psychology. In 1912 Max Wertheimer (q.v.) demonstrated that two stationary lights, lit in a certain succession, will give an observer the sensation of movement. Hence, Wertheimer and the gestalt psychologists maintain that the product, the experience, is not equal to the sum of the stimuli. The gestalt school has continued to oppose atomism and elementarism in psychological research, especially in the areas of sensation and learning. (See *Ganzheit*.)

In Russia, Pavlov (q.v.) (1849–1936) followed Sechenov's work in "reflexology." His work on the conditioned reflex has given many basic rules about the nature of learning, especially those which pertain to time relationships, generalization, discrimination, extinction, reward and punishment, etc., during the process of association between stimuli and responses.

Certain psychological schools and systems which evolved around the turn of the century differed not only in methodology, but about the purpose of psychology itself. Influenced by the writings of William James (q.v.) (1842–1910), psychology in America became "functionalistic." Its research method as well as its purpose became broader. Data from animals, children, and mental patients were admitted for research, and psychologists began to make practical recommendations for child care, education, industry, and living systems in general.

John B. Watson (q.v.) (1878–1958), the behaviorist, used the Pavlovian method of conditioning to show that certain fears and desires of human infants can be conditioned by direct or indirect associations with physical pain or pleasures. Watson published experimental findings as well as much practical advice on child care (Watson, 1919, 1928). (See *Behaviorism*.)

There were other applied systems of psychology which contributed to its great diversification. The historical roots of Freud's psychoanalysis (q.v.) can be found in Greek literature, and in hypnosis and psychopathology (q.v.). Freud's practical task, the cure of neurotic and psychotic patients, produced his theories about the content and the functions of the "unconscious" (q.v.) mind.

Mental testing (q.v.), a psychological area of the most widespread and practical influence, began with the work of Francis Galton (q.v.) (1869), who tabulated the accomplishments of famous men and their offspring. The useful IQ test was developed by Binet (q.v.) & Simon (1905) to provide the Paris Schools Commission with an instrument which could predict whether or not a pupil would benefit from public instruction. In spite of revisions and modifications, the IQ tests, as used today, are essentially like the original ones designed by Binet & Simon.

Applied areas such as conditioning, psychoanalysis, and mental testing have provided, perhaps as by-products, many psychological theories. In some areas, the theories may have overshadowed experimental verification. Some psychologists feel that their science has been "oversold to an overwilling public" (Miller, 1962, p. 4).

10. *Approaches*. Three major historical works, by E. G. Boring, Gardner Murphy, and W. B. Pillsbury respectively, were published in 1929. Boring's book has been the most systematic and influential. Several historical writers (Watson, 1968; Miller, 1962) have dedicated subsequent books to Boring. Boring's approach to history was the description of an individual's accomplishment in relation to the "*Zeitgeist*." Other

texts by R. S. Woodworth (1931), Edna Heidbreder (1933) and J. C. Flugel (1933) followed soon. They described the history of psychology chronologically through the development of psychological schools and systems. More recent chronological approaches are those of Mueller (1960) and Kantor (1963).

There are also biographical, autobiographical or "great men" approaches, such as the works of Pillsbury (1929), Murchison (1930), Garrett (1951) and Watson (1968). A different approach is the doxographic or problem approach, where the histories of a number of basic and recurring problems such as body—soul, consciousness, association, intelligence, and soon, are separately discussed. Works representing this type of approach have been written by Spearman (1937), v. Schiller (1948), Pongratz (1967), and others.

Esper (1964) presents a history guided by a biophysiological theme. Histories from geographical and/or ideological viewpoints have also been written. Hearnshaw (1964) described the history of British psychology, and Roback (1964) the history of American psychology. Brožek (1969) reviewed the work of Petrovskii (1967) which centers upon the theme of the fundamental reconstruction of Russian psychology on a Marxist-Leninist basis; and that of Yaroshevskii (1966), which discusses the birth of psychological thought in Egypt, China, and India, and—in the Marxist spirit—views psychology as having developed from the practical needs of society. A useful bibliography for all major works on the history of psychology published after 1900 is given by Misiak & Sexton (1966, pp. 469–70).

11. *Past, present and future.* More than half a century ago, in his first sentence of his *Abriss der Psychologie*, Ebbinghaus (1908) said that psychology had a long past but only a short history. By "long past" he meant philosophy, by "short history," the experimental method. Much of psychology's history has been written in retrospect. In many instances the writers of psychological ideas did not show historical continuity. Esper (1964, p. 176) points out that associationism, for instance, was first discussed by Plato, later by Aristotle, millennia later by Hobbes in 1650, and again in 1695 by Locke, who thought that the principles of association had not been "hitherto considered." Esper also compares passages from the writings of William James (1890) and Hull (1930) with passages from Aristotle's *On Memory and Reminiscence* and finds many new terms, but few new ideas. He believes that psychology has led other sciences in its neglect of history.

At present the history of psychology seems no longer neglected. In the sixties there has been much renewed interest in its teaching and research. In France a history course has been included in the basic psychology curriculum. Miller (1962) has written a text to teach introductory psychology through a historical theme, and Lyman (1970) has reported on the success of such an approach. The following events have strengthened the history of psychology on the American scene:

The *Archives of the History of American Psychology* were established at the University of Akron(Ohio)in 1961 under the directorship of J. A. Poppletsone. The first volume of the *Journal of the History of the behavioral Sciences* appeared in Jan. 1965 under the editorship of R. I. Watson. The Division of the History of Psychology was established as the 26th division of the American Psychological Association in 1966. The first Summer Institute in the Teaching of the History of Psychology was held at the University of New Hampshire under the directorship of Josef Brožek in 1968. The first meeting of the International Society for the History of the Behavioral and Social Sciences (ISHOBSS) founded by Julian Jaynes was held at Princeton University in May 1969.

Research continues and certain parts of the history of psychology are still being written. For instance, Mountjoy *et al.* (1969) have recently described the falcon training techniques used by Frederick II (1194–1250). They found some striking similarities between medieval falconry and contemporary operant animal psychology.

Psychology has broadened in scope and method. Future accounts will probably include more of the histories of other disciplines, such as anthropology, chemistry, mathematics, medicine, and sociology. This diversification will make the future history of psychology more difficult, but also more obviously necessary, since the history may become the only meaningful link between the various divisions, and the basis for evaluating the many specialties which will arise.

Bibliography: Binet, A. & Simon, T.: Méthodes nouvelles pour le diagnostic du niveau intellectuel des anormaux. Année Psychologique, 1905, *11*, 191–244. **Boring, E. G.:** A history of experimental psychology. New York, [2]1950. **Boring, Mollie D. & Boring, E. G.:** Masters and pupils among the American psychologists. American Journal of Psychology, 1948, *61*, 527–34. **Brozek, J.:** Soviet contributions to history. Contemporary Psychology, 1969, *XIV* (8), 432–4. **Diels, H.:** Fragmente der Vorsokratiker (W. Krantz, Ed.). Berlin, [5]1934–1938. **Donders, F. C.:** Die Schnelligkeit psychischer Processe. Archiv. Anatomie & Physiologie, 1862, 657–81. **Ebbinghaus, H.:** Abriss der Psychologie. Leipzig, 1908. **Esper, E. A.:** A history of psychology. Philadelphia, 1964. **Flugel, J. C.:** A hundred years of psychology. London, 1933. **Garrett, H. E.:** Great experiments in psychology. New York, [3]1951. **Hearnshaw, L. S.:** A short history of British psychology, 1840–1940. New York, 1964. **Heidbreder, Edna:** Seven psychologies. New York, 1933. **Kantor, J. R.:** The scientific evolution of psychology. Vol. 1. Chicago & Ohio, 1963. **Keller, F. S.:** The definition of psychology. New York, 1937. **Lyman, B.:** Performance of introductory psychology students in an historical foundations course. J. Hist. Behav. Sci., 1970, *6*, (4), 354–7. **Miller, G. A.:** Psychology: the science of mental life. New York, 1962. **Misiak, H. & Sexton, V.:** History of psychology: an overview. New York, 1966. **Mountjoy, P. T., Bos, J. H., Duncan, M. O. & Verplank, R. B.:** Falconry: neglected aspect of the history of psychology. J. Hist. Behav. Sci., 1969, *5* (1), 59–67. **Mueller, F. L.:** Histoire de la psychologie de l'antiquité à nos jours. Paris, 1960. **Murchison, C. (Ed.):** A history of psychology in autobiography. 3 vols. Worcester, Mass., 1930–1936. **Murphy, G.:** An historical introduction to modern psychology. New York, 1929. **Petrovskii, A.:** Istoriya sovetskoi psikhologii. Moscow, 1967. **Pillsbury, W. B.:** The history of psychology. New York, 1929. **Pongratz, L. J.:** Problemgeschichte der Psychologie. Berne, 1967. **Roback, A. A.:** A history of American psychology (Rev. ed.). New York, 1964. **Schiller, P. v.:** Aufgabe der Psychologie. Eine Geschichte ihrer Probleme. Vienna, 1948. **Sechenov, I. M.:** Reflexes of the brain. Meditsinski Vestnik (Nos. 47 & 48) 1863. (English ed.: Cambridge, Mass., 1965.) **Spearman, C.:** Psychology down the ages, 2 vols. London, 1937. **Watson, J. B.:** Psychology from the standpoint of a behaviorist. Philadelphia, 1919. **Id.:** Psychological care of infant and child. New York, 1928. **Watson, R. I.:** The great psychologists from Aristotle to Freud. Philadelphia, [2]1968. **Wesley, F.:** Master and pupils among the German psychologists. J. Hist. Behav. Sci., 1965, *1* (3), 252–8. **Woodworth, R. S.:** Contemporary schools of psychology. New York, 1931. **Yaroshevskii, M. G.:** Istoriya psikhologii. Moscow, 1966.

F. Wesley

II. *Contemporary psychology.* A study of the history of contemporary psychology shows one significant feature, namely the gradual break-up of the major systems and schools such as gestalt psychology (see *Ganzheit*), behaviorism (q.v.), and, to a much lesser extent, psychoanalysis (q.v.). S. Koch, the editor of *Psychology: A Study of a Science*, noted (1959): ". . . a far more open and liberated conception of the task of psychology, the role of its investigators and systematists, than we have enjoyed in recent history." (See also the general survey of contemporary psychology in *Handbuch der Psychologie*, 1959–70.)

If we inquire more specifically into the nature of this "open and liberated conception", we see with reference to the basic assumptions and positions of psychology, as Marx observed (1963), a greatly increased interest in positivist and empirical science. As regards methods, we find that they are used eclectically and pragmatically, substantial progress having been achieved by more advanced methods of data acquisition and processing (e.g. electronic test apparatus, use of computers). The conventional areas of research in psychology are becoming more and more narrowly circumscribed, e.g. the role of motivation psychology in perception and learning. At the same time, links with neighboring disciplines such as physiology and sociology are becoming increasingly complex. New applications of psychology result from technological projects (e.g. space travel) and the more complex demands of modern social life.

While noting the growing objective and methodological diversity of psychology, the question of its theoretical unity must not be overlooked; indeed it must be stressed, as Foppa has recently suggested (1970), if psychology is to be brought closer to the aim of becoming a science of experience.

The above observations are concerned primarily with psychological research; however, it is also desirable to consider psychology as a theory and profession. As regards psychology as a theory, it has come to acquire a dual role through progressive developments in the universities: on the one hand its form and content are being questioned like other university disciplines while on the other it is called upon to remedy this unsatisfactory state of affairs. In this practical context, psychology seems not so much to lack the necessary means, when we consider the achievements of ability diagnosis, intelligence and creativity research, learning psychology (e.g. programmed learning), socio-dynamics, counseling and psychotherapy, as the ability to use the available means in an organized manner in a given practical problem situation. As regards psychology as a profession, it has taken over a wide range of social functions in the USA and become firmly established in these areas (the American Psychological Association has more than 26,000 members in some thirty sections). Professional representation in other countries is far less developed; Britain, Germany and Japan are among the few countries which approach the American example.

Bibliography: Foppa, K.: Über die Angemessenheit psychologische Beobachtungsweisen. Schweiz. Z. Psychol., 1970, *29*, 34–40. **Gottschaldt, K., Lersch, Ph., Sander, F. & Thomae, H.** (Eds.): Handbuch der Psychologie, 12 vols. Göttingen, 1959–70. **Koch, S.** (Ed.): Psychology: a study of a science, 6 vols. (Vol. 7 in preparation). New York, 1959. **Marx, M. H.** (Ed.): Theories in contemporary psychology. New York, 1963. *E. G. Wehner*

Hit. In parapsychology: a trial in which the call (q.v.) matches the target (q.v.). Every trial is either a "hit" or a "miss". Displaced hit = trial on which the call matches the target intended for a different trial either earlier than the given trial (= backward or negative displacement) or later (= forward or positive displacement). Cf. retrocognition (q.v.) and precognition. (q.v.) *J.B.*

Höfler's illusion. This illusion demonstrates the distortion induced in the perception of

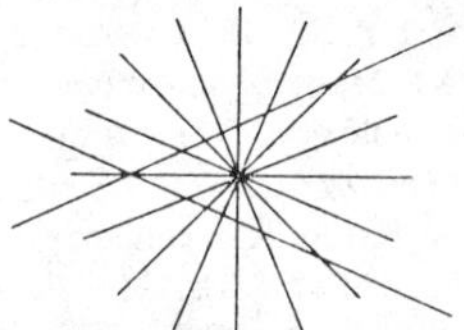

straight lines if they cross a field of radiating lines, and is thus in principle identical to *Hering's illusion.* (q.v.) *C.D.F.*

Holism. J. C. Smuts' theory that whole entities (and, above all, living beings) have specific characteristics which differ from those of their individual parts (entelechy). Holism is an integral part of biological research associated with mutationism (H. de Vries) which considers evolution as a consequence of intermittent variation that can be traced back to sudden restructuring. Against this background, the cause of evolution is to be found in internal characteristics of the organism interpreted as a structure, and in an organizational principle inherent in living matter (by comparison with chemical and physical properties). A correlation can be established between these theoretical notions and the concepts of gestalt psychology. See *Ganzheit.*

Bibliography: **Smuts, J. C.:** Holism and evolution. London, 1926. *M.J.B.*

Holmgren test. A method of determining anomalies in color vision by classifying threads of colored wool. *G.Ka.*

Homeostasis. The term homeostasis was used by the American physiologist Cannon (1932) to characterize the totality of effects responsible for maintaining a certain (relative) physiological constancy (e.g. body temperature, blood sugar). Cannon made a distinction between different hierarchical, homeostatic levels: reflex and instinctive behavior, acquired habits and adaptations, and willed actions, which serve the self-regulating system intent upon maintaining a "fluid" equilibrium (Bertalanffy, 1968). This extension of the concept made it possible to move forward from a study of organic need (deviation of an actual physiological value from the reference, or desired, value) to experimental analysis of psychological requirements within the framework of a motivational and behavioral psychology.

In cybernetics, a distinction is made between two forms of homeostasis (Ashby, 1952). In the simpler case the organic system has control or regulation circuits. But there are also complex organic systems whose mechanisms allow a transition to be made from states within which the desired value can no longer be reached, to other states, until the stability of the corresponding physiological parameters can be assured again ("ultrastability"). A technical model of this form of homeostasis is provided by the *homeostat*, whose feedback systems can compensate any slight deviation of the actual from the desired values. See *Cybernetics; Feedback system; Machine learning.*

Bibliography: **Apter, M. J.:** Cybernetics and development. Oxford, 1966. **Ashby, W. R.:** Design for a brain. London, 1952. **Bertalanffy, L. von:** General system theory. New York, 1968. **Cannon, W. B.:** The wisdom of the body. New York, 1932, [2]1939. *D.Vo.*

Homoeroticism. Erotic interest in members of one's own sex. Usually taken as being more general than *homosexuality.* *G.D.W.*

Homogeneity; homogeneity index. Similarity. The term is used in psychology primarily to characterize samples of group members, and test methods. A test manifests homogeneity if it covers only a single, narrowly defined dimension of personality. The index of homogeneity (e.g. Loevinger's homogeneity index, 1947) determines this factor quantitatively on the lines of a correlation coefficient (q.v.).

Bibliography: **Loevinger, J.:** A systematic approach to the construction and evaluation of tests of ability. Psychol. Monogr., 1947, *64,* 285. *P.S.*

Homogeneous. The term has the same meaning in statistics as in general usage. If two sample distributions have roughly similar statistics (originating from the same population) they are considered to be "homogeneous" (e.g. with reference to the mean values of their variance).

In test theory (q.v.), test problems in a sub-test are described as homogeneous if they have (*a*) a high degree of correlation (intercorrelation) in relation to items of other sub-tests and/or (*b*) retain their relative position with reference to the other items in terms of probable resolution on confrontation with varying degrees of intensity of a given feature.(gradual differences). *W.H.B.*

Homogeneous grouping. See *Ability grouping.*

Homogeneous variance. The term is used when samples originate from the same basic group. In other cases heterogeneous variance is said to occur. Homogeneous variance is assumed in using certain parametric test methods (e.g. analysis of variance). *W.H.B.*

Homology. Behavior patterns can be homologized in the same way as organs, i.e. they may be derived from common basic forms (K. Lorenz). A. Remane has compiled the homology criteria for morphological structures. According to G. P. Baerends, such behavioral elements are homologous if they have the *same neuromuscular pattern*, even if the motivation superimposed on them has changed. Behavior patterns are dependent on time, and as such are certainly the more homologous (identical) the more special features they have in common (criterion of special quality), and the more they accord in their sequence of action (criterion of position in the structural system). A distinction must be made between hereditary homology and traditional homology (Wickler, 1967).

Bibliography: Lorenz, K.: Studies in animal and human behaviour, vol. 2. London, 1971. **Wickler, W.:** Vergleichende Verhaltensforschung und Phylogenetik. In: **Heberer, G.** (Ed.): Die Evolution der Organismen, 1967, *1*, 420–508. *K.Fi.*

Homophony, mnemic. "Consonance." A term introduced by Semon (1908): *mnemic* excitation (memory) and *actual* excitation (sensation) coincide. Recognition and discrimination occur as a parallel response.

Bibliography: Semon, R.: Die Mneme als erhaltendes Prinzip im Wechsel des organischen Geschehens. Leipzig, [2]1908. *H.W.*

Homoscedasticity. The equality of sample variability. Equal variability is a prerequisite of *t* tests (q.v.) for homogeneous variance, and of analyses of variance (see *Variance, analysis of*). *D.W.E.*

Homosensorial reproduction. A term proposed by Ziehen to describe reproduction from the same sensory area as that which originally received the material, as opposed to heterosensorial (q.v.), reproduction. *C.D.F.*

Homosexuality. Sexual attraction by and sexual contact with persons of the same sex; in the narrower sense: continuous, preferred sexual attraction by such persons ("genuine homosexuality").

Attitude to homosexuality. It is socially rejected in Western societies, but for the most part accepted in tribal cultures with no written codes of conduct (64% according to Ford & Beach, 1952); homosexuality among adult males is punishable today only in a minority of countries, primarily for ideological reasons. In international, scientific discussions, proponents of the acceptance of adult homosexuality have long been in a clear majority.

Incidence. In the USA, about 4% of adult white males have *only* homosexual contacts; after puberty about 37% had at least one homosexual experience leading to orgasm. The incidence was much rarer among women (Kinsey, 1948). Temporary homosexual contacts are widespread among young males (developmental or occasional homosexuality). As yet there is no empirical evidence of an increase in homosexuality in recent decades (cf. Kinsey).

Educational and social background. Studies conducted up to now in the USA, Czechoslovakia and West Germany show a concentration of male homosexuality in the middle to upper middle social and educational stratum; in regard to socio-economic level, the lower social stratum dominates in the USA, and the middle social stratum in Europe (Giese, 1967).

Psychological–psychopathological aspects. While some studies of homosexual males revealed no neurotic symptoms (Hooker, 1957; Dean & Richardson, 1964), others have recorded slight or considerable neurotic reactions in the form of schizoid and psychasthenic character traits, mistrustful attitudes, hypochondriac, depressive and hysterical reactions, as well as approximations to neurotic test profiles in the sense of extremely labile, sensitive, dependent and anxious and uncertain (Doidge & Holtzmann, 1960; R. B. Cattell, 1962; Morony, 1962). In many homosexual groups, in particular of intelligent and "bisexual" subjects, there is no striking frequency of neurotic maladjustment (summary: Schmidt, 1968).

Social and psychological aspects. Only a minority (less than 5%) of homosexuals identify themselves with the disagreeable impression held by the general public of the male homosexual (soft, impulsive, weak, emotional, modern, light, unbalanced, unsympathetic, sick, confused, disgusting). The majority have a positive view of their own character which differs from the heterosexual male's idea of himself (Schmidt, 1967; Sigusch, 1967); although these findings are not based on a representative study of male homosexuals, they suggest that the identity and self-acceptance of many male homosexuals are less disturbed than might be expected in view of the strong prejudices held by the public at large.

Research into causes. The causes of homosexuality are still open to question. At present there are three theories concerning the origins of homosexuality. (*a*) Biologically oriented theory: homosexuality is dependent on biological factors which are not influenced by experience. (*b*) Psycho–socially oriented theory: homosexuality is conditioned by the environment, i.e. dependent on experience, and acquired (psychoanalytical theory and learning theory); (*c*) Convergence theory: homosexuality stems from a biological (learning) disposition; its occurrence in an individual is, however, dependent on environmental influences (summary: Freund, 1960).

Therapy. Many modern theorists believe that homosexuality is a variant of normal sexuality which can be treated by helping the homosexual to accept his own condition and not by attempting to convert him to heterosexual forms of conduct. On the other hand, when a homosexual wishes to change the direction of his attachment, those who consider it to be a parasympathetic response which is the chance product of conditioning, would recommend conditioning techniques that teach the homosexual to associate members of his own sex with unpleasant rather than pleasant erotic sensations. See *Aversion therapy; Behavior therapy; Sexuality.*

Bibliography: Feldman, M. P. & McCulloch, M. J.: The application of anticipatory avoidance learning to the treatment of homosexuality. Behav. Res. and Ther., 1965, *2*, 165–83. **Ford, C. S. & Beach, F. A.:** Patterns of sexual behaviour. London, 1952. **Freund, K.:** Some problems in the treatment of homosexuality. In: **Eysenck, H. J.** (Ed.): Behaviour therapy and the neuroses. Oxford, 1960. **Giese, G.** (Ed.): Homosexualität. Hamburg, 1967. **Kinsey, A. C.** *et al.*: Sexual behavior in the human male. Philadelphia & London, 1948. **Max, L.:** Breaking a homosexual fixation by the conditioned reflex technique. Psychol. Bull., 1935, *32*, 734. **McCulloch, M. J., Feldman, M. P. & Pinshoff, J. M.:** The application of anticipatory avoidance learning to the treatment of homosexuality, Behav. Res. and Ther., 1965, *3*, 21–43. **McGuire, R. J., Carlisle, J. M. & Young, B. G.:** Sexual deviations as conditioned behaviour: a hypothesis. Behav. Res. and Ther., 1965, *2*, 185–90. **Schmidt, G.:** Empirisch-psychologische Ergebnisse zur Sexualforschung. In: **Giese, H.** (Ed.): Die Sexualität des Menschen. Stuttgart, 1968. **West, D. J.:** Homosexuality. Harmondsworth, 1968.

H.M.

Honesty. The degree to which truth and respect (for others) determine behavior. Of particular practical importance in interpreting data furnished by questionnaires. In spite of largely positive correlations between various honesty tests, only Brogden has succeeded in isolating a honesty factor (q.v.) (characterized by behavior in which higher marks can be scored only by cheating, lying and exaggerating, as detected by the experimenter). See *Conscience; Child psychology; Traits.*

Bibliography: Brogden, H. E.: A factor analysis of forty character tests. Psychol. Mon., 1940, *234*, 35–55. **Hartshorne, H. & May, M. A.:** Studies in deceit. New York, 1928. **Kay, W.:** Moral development. London, 1968. **Maller, J.:** General and specific factors in character. J. soc. Psychol., 1934, *5*, 97–102. **Piaget, J.:** The moral judgement of the child. New York & London, 1960.

M.A.

Honi phenomenon. When a person is very well-known to S., he or she may fail to appear distorted in size or shape in the (Ames) distorted room (q.v.).

Horde. The primitive form of human association consisting, according to Charles Darwin and Freud, of an extended family dominated by a strong "father." Modern ethnographic field research makes it impossible to accept this reconstruction of a primitive society. Erect primates such as chimpanzees and gorillas live in loose groups (J. Goodall, G. Schaller, I. De Vore). This also applies to the remaining tribes of hunters and food gatherers, whose groups are never based on a strictly patriarchal structure and have a very flexible membership. The short life expectancy of paleolithic hunters (twenty to twenty-six years) in itself makes it difficult to believe that the younger generation was ever repressed by the "fathers." Recent field research into the various societies of Australian aborigines, which were considered for a long time to be examples of the "horde", has revealed a far more complex pattern.

Bibliography: De Vore, I. (Ed.): Primate behavior. New York, 1965. **Lévi-Strauss, C.:** The elementary structures of kinship. New York, 1967. **Lee, R. B. & De Vore, I.** (Eds.): Man the hunter. Chicago, 1968.

W.Sc.

Horizontal disparity. Because our eyes are about two inches apart, there are slight discrepancies in the two pictures of the world that they receive. These discrepancies can be used to calculate the distances of the various objects seen by the observer. The discrepancies can occur in any of the three spatial dimensions. There may be *height disparity*, *longitudinal disparity*, and *horizontal disparity*. Experiments have shown that horizontal disparities give rise to depth perception, and this, of course, is the normal disparity produced by the horizontal separation of our eyes. *C.D.F.*

Hormic psychology. In order to break with the exaggerated concern with cognitive phenomena, perceptions, ideas, cognitive development and thinking processes, many psychologists have concerned themselves since the turn of the century with research into the motivations and aims of the organism. W. McDougall (1871–1938), for example, stressed the dynamic aspects of behavior and studied the fundamental needs of the organism. This school of thought has aligned itself with psychoanalysis (q.v.) in its emphasis on the teleological aspects of all behavior(s).

Bibliography: McDougall, W.: The hormic psychology. In: **Murchison, C.** (Ed.): Psychologies of 1930. Worcester, Mass., 1930, 3–36. **Id.:** The energies of men. London, 1932.

P.M.

Hormones. 1. *Definition, formation and general effects.* Hormones are substances formed in the body in the internally secreting glands (*glandular hormones*) or in specific cell systems (*tissue* or *cell hormones*). The glandular hormones are discharged directly into the bloodstream by the corresponding gland systems, and take effect in certain organ systems or stimulate the secretion of other hormones in specific glands (see *Glandotropic hormones*). Tissue and cell hormones are generally active only at their points of formation; cell hormones are usually active only in the cell in which they are formed. Tissue or cell hormones, which are formed in the central nervous system or autonomic nervous system and act as transmitter substances (q.v.) to the synapses (q.v.) or effectors, are referred to as *neurohormones* (in particular, acetylcholine and noradrenalin, q.v.). This category is also often taken to include substances which play a decisive part in the metabolism of the nervous system (see *Biogenic amines*). The main hormone-producing glands are the anterior pituitary (adenohypophysis), posterior pituitary (neurohypophysis), pineal gland (epiphysis), thyroid gland, parathyroid gland, thymus, pancreas (Langerhans' islets), adrenal gland and adrenal cortex, ovaries and testes. The hypothalamus (q.v.) is another production center; it generates the releasing factors. These are substances whose nature has not been entirely explained; they are conveyed to the endocrine glands (q.v.) through the nerves. Several hormones are formed not only in special glands but in other systems, e.g. the catecholamines (q.v.). All known hormones are steroids, proteins or amino-acid derivatives. All the major hormones can be synthesized and introduced into the circulatory system or brain from outside (locally if necessary). Many hormones do not pass the blood–brain barrier (q.v.), or liver barrier. Hormones regulate the equilibrium of many different organ systems and perform the following main functions: (*a*) regulation of the metabolism (e.g. carbohydrate metabolism regulated by insulin); (*b*) morphogenesis, i.e. growth and maturation; (*c*) stimulation and depression of the CNS and ANS; (*d*) regulation of the inner environment for adaptation to external conditions.

2. *Effective mechanisms of hormones and interaction between different hormone systems.* Hormones have a profound influence on physiological and psychological processes. The biochemical mechanisms of these effects have been elucidated only in part. It is generally believed that hormones act locally and in the cells by altering cell permeability or by influencing the synthesis or breakdown of enzymes. Analysis of the biochemical mechanisms is made difficult by many methodological problems. Many theories are based solely on animal experiments (sometimes *in vitro*), and often merely on indirect manipulations in human beings (e.g. with pharmaceutical compounds), or on pathological symptoms occurring with under- or overproduction of specific hormones. The study of hormone effects is complicated by interaction between different hormone systems. The various hormones are sometimes *antagonistic* (e.g. adrenalin—insulin), *synergistic* (glucagon—adrenalin), or form simple or complex regulating circuits. The relationship between the glandotropic hormones and the peripherally secreted hormones can be explained on the negative feedback principle. The secretion of glandotropic hormones leads to secretion of peripheral gland hormones, which in turn block the further formation of glandotropic hormones. Several hormone systems function (in part, at least) synergistically (e.g. adrenal gland—thyroid gland).

3. *Hormones and the nervous system.* Close, though as yet incompletely explained, relationships exist between the CNS, ANS and hormone systems, and form the object of neuroendocrinological research. So far only the relationship between the hypothalamus and pituitary has been explained in any detail: vasopressin (an antidiuretic) and oxytocin are formed in certain neuron(e)s of the hypothalamus, and conveyed by the nervous system to the neurohypophysis and thence into the bloodstream. Secretion of glandotropic hormones also probably occurs with the participation of the hypothalamus (releasing factors). Electrical stimulus tests in animals have shown that localized hypothalamic stimulation leads to the secretion of specific glandotropic hormones. In addition, stimulation and elimination tests show that the peripheral secretion of catecholamines is associated with nervous excitation in the reticulo-thalamic and limbic system (e.g. *nucleus amygdalae*). The previously held assumption that the hypothalamus and pituitary are the sole links between hormones and the nervous system is therefore false. The influence of cerebral electrical activity by the peripheral and centrally localized supply of hormones, or by hormonal disturbances, may be considered certain; the mechanism on which these changes are based is, however, still unexplained. The relationship between the nervous system and hormones is particularly clear in the effective action of the neurohormones, noradrenalin(e), dopamine, acetylcholine, etc. Neurohormones are liberated when the central neuron(e)s on the synapses are stimulated (see

The most important hormones, their functions, associated disorders, and some psychologically significant findings derived from healthy individuals.

Produced by		**Hormone**	**Most important functions**	Some pathological changes with		(a) **Psychol. & physiol. effects of low doses** administered *exogenously* to healthy Ss. (b) **Change in hormone activity** in healthy Ss under stimulus variation
				Hypofunction (deficiency)	Hyperfunction (excess)	
Anterior pituitary		Growth hormone (somatotropic hormone = STH = somatotropine)	Promotion of growth, protein synthesis and fat oxidation (together with testosterone, thyroid gland hormones, insulin), RNA synthesis	*Before* completion of growth: pituitary dwarfism	*Before* completion of growth: gigantism. After completion: acromegaly	(a) increased activity (?) (b) increased production in hypoglycemia, muscular effort
	Glandotropic hormones	Thyrotropic hormone (= TSH = thyrotropin(e))	Growth of thyroid gland, promotion of biosynthesis and stimulation of thyroid gland hormone secretion	As for thyroid gland hormones	As for thyroid gland hormones	
		Adrenocorticotropic hormone (= ACTH = corticotropin(e))	Stimulation of production of cortical hormones in the adrenal cortex (exception, e.g., aldosterone)	As for adrenal cortical hormones	As for adrenal cortical hormones	(a) euphoric reactions (?) (b) increased release under all forms of trauma (stress) ("adaptation homone")
		Gonadotropic hormones (= gonadotropins: (a) follicle stimulating hormone (= FSH)	Growth and maturation of the follicle, estrogen formation; in the male: promotion of spermatogenesis	Amenorrhea, obstruction of spermatogenesis		
		(b) luteinizing hormone (= LH = interstitial cell stimulating hormone = ICSH)	Ovulation. Induction of follicular development and corpus luteum formation, stimulation of estrogen formation. In male: formation of testosterone, potentiation of effect of FSH	Amenorrhea		
		Luteotropic hormone (= LTH = prolactin)	Increases progesterone formation in corpus luteum; effect on lactation; shares in initiation of breeding behavior			
Posterior pituitary		Oxytocin	Contractions of uterus (induction of labor), lactation (release of milk in response to sucking)	Disorders of labor process		(a) decreased blood pressure, contraction of uterus
		Antidiuretic hormone = ADH = vasopressin	Antidiuresis, neurohormone, assists release of ACTH	Diabetes insipidus (polyuria)	Antidiabetes insipidus	(a) increased blood pressure, decreased diuresis (b) increased production under stress

Intermediate (?) pituitary lobe		Melanotropin (melanocyte-stimulating hormone = MSH)	Skin pigmentation, assists regulation of dark adaptation of eye	Disorder of pigment formation		(a) Increased skin pigmentation
Thyroid gland	Thyroid gland hormones	Thyroid gland hormones: triiodothyronine, tetraiodothyronine (= thyroxin)	Promotion of oxydative processes; assistance in regulation of protein synthesis, and in thermoregulation	Myxedema; with congenital or early acquired hypofunction, cretinism; adiposity; general deactivation		(a) subjective and objective activation, excitation (b) increased secretion under stress, cold stimuli
		Thyrocalcitonin (calcitonin)	Lowers blood calcium (antagonizes parathormone = parathyroid hormone)			
Parathyroid gland		Parathormone (PTH) (= parathyroid hormone)	Raises blood calcium (antagonizes thyrocalcitonin)	Hypoparathyroidism (e.g. nervous excitation, tetanic attacks)	Hyperparathyroidism (e.g. changes in bone system, renal calculi)	
Pancreas (islands of Langerhans)		Insulin	Lowers blood sugar (antagonizes adrenalin) by conversion into glycogen, influences protein, fat and carbohydrate metabolism, and hence growth	Diabetes mellitus	Hyperinsulism	(a) tiredness, dizziness, hunger, affects performance
		Glucagon	Raises blood sugar		Plays part in origin of diabetes (?)	(a) reduces hunger
Sex glands: testes	Sex gland hormones	Sex gland hormones: androgens, e.g. testosterone	Promote maturation and growth of primary and secondary sexual characteristics; promotion of general growth synergistically with growth hormone, insulin and thyroid gland hormones	Hypogonadism (e.g. delayed puberty, under-development of primary and secondary sexual characteristics)	Hypergonadism (hardly significant) (e.g. pubertas praecox)	(a) no specific psychol. effects in healthy Ss. Increased performance in exhausted Ss. (b) Reduced excretion in urine under stress
Ovaries		(a) Estrogens, e.g. estradiol, estrone, estriol	Promote maturation and growth of primary and secondary sexual characteristics in puberty; induction of menopause, regulation of cycle. Promotion of general growth	Menstrual cycle disorders Hypogonadism	Hypergonadism	(a) no specific psychol. effects in healthy women, increased performance in exhausted women
		(b) Gestogens, e.g. progesterone (progestins)	Preparation for and maintenance of pregnancy; together with estrogenic regulation of cycle			(a) impaired performance, subjective de-activation; reduced noradrenalin in CNS
Placenta		Choriongonadotropin (human chorionic gonadotropin = HCG)	Gonadotropic hormone, formed only during pregnancy. Assists effect of LH			

Produced by		Hormone	Most important functions	Some pathological changes with: Hypofunction (deficiency)	Some pathological changes with: Hyperfunction (excess)	(a) **Psychol. & physiol. effects of low doses** administered *exogenously* to healthy Ss. (b) **Change in hormone activity** in healthy Ss under stimulus variation
Adrenal medulla	Catecholamines	Adrenalin (epinephrin)	As antagonist of insulin, releases glycogen (blood sugar). "Ergotropic" regulation of organism		Increased blood pressure with tumors	(a) with small amounts: non-specific excitation (b) increased excretion under psychol. stress (anxiety)
	Catecholamines	Noradrenalin (norepinephrin)	Ergotropic regulation of organism			(a) administration of small amounts has slight or no psychol. effects (b) increased excretion under physical stress
Adrenal cortex *Zona fasciculata*	Corticoids (corticosteroids)	(a) Glucocorticoids, e.g. cortisol (hydrocortisone), cortisone, corticosterone	Regulation of carbohydrate content	Addison's disease	Cushing's disease	(a) improvement of mood (?) (b) increased excretion under physical and psychol. stress
Zona glomerulosa	Corticoids (corticosteroids)	(b) Mineralcorticoids, e.g. aldosterone, 11-desoxycorticosterone	Regulation of sodium-potassium content		Hyperaldosteronism (symptoms: e.g. hypertonia, decreased potassium rate)	(a) increased blood pressure, excitation (b) increased excretion under stress
Zona reticularis	Corticoids (corticosteroids)	(c) Androgenic cortical hormones, e.g. androsterone, androstenedione	Synergistic effect with male sex gland hormones		Adrenogenital syndrome (virilism, gynecomastia); in childhood: pubertas praecox	As for androgens
Central nervous system and vegetative nervous system (ANS)	Neurohormones or tissue hormones	(a) Acetylcholine	Transmitter substance in ANS (preganglionic fibers of the sympathetic, pre- and post-ganglionic fibers of the parasympathetic) and CNS			
	Neurohormones or tissue hormones	(b) Serotonin	Transmitter substance in CNS (transmitter of central parasympathetic system (?)). Regulation of mood; assists sleep–waking rhythm	Depression (?) Schizophrenia (?)		(a) small quantities (precursor of S.): can be stimulating. Antagonizes LSD (b) reduction of S. concentration in brain during sleep
	Neurohormones or tissue hormones	(c) Tryptamine	Biogenic amine	Depression (?)		(a) Sympathicomimetic effects, subjectively stimulating (b) Reduced excretion in urine in moody periods

Nervous system). They transmit this stimulation to other neuron(e)s or effectors, and therefore act as transmitter substances. With the liberation of the neurohormones, characteristic changes occur in the electrical activity of the nerve cell. Therefore the nervous system can also be considered as a hormone system.

4. *Hormones and psychological disorders.* Over- or under-functioning of the peripheral hormone glands are linked almost without exception not only with physiological but with psychological disorders. On the other hand, it has not been possible to show clear endocrine variations for the majority of mental disorders on the basis of hormones excreted in the urine or blood. In general, endocrine disorders do not lead to specific psychological changes. Yet relatively clear psychological changes occur in the dimension of activation (see *Arousal*) in some endocrine disorders. Promising hypotheses and theories have been put forward in the past twenty years by neuroendocrinologists and psychopharmacologists. Even if the details remain largely obscure, it may be assumed that psychiatric disorders such as schizophrenia (q.v.) and depression (q.v.) are linked with disorders of the metabolism of biogenic amines (q.v.) or neurohormones. These metabolic disorders possibly result from incorrect "programming" in the genetic code. Recent research into depression, in particular, has shown that endogenous depressions result from disorders in the metabolism of endogenous catecholamines or indolamines (see *Serotonin*).

5. *Hormones and behavior.* It is not possible to conclude from the sometimes drastic behavioral changes which occur with hormonal disorders that there is a clear relationship between hormones and normal behavior. Two methods may be followed by the endocrinological psychologist: the study of behavioral changes after the administration of hormones, or the analysis of the occurrence of specific hormones in the urine or blood as a function of systematically varied stimuli. Both methods are problematical for theoretical reasons. Hormones administered orally or intravenously do induce replicable behavior changes, but it is doubtful whether this can offer anything more than hypotheses on the relationship between natural hormones and behavior. The effective mechanisms and concentration conditions are probably not comparable for externally administered hormones and internal hormone formation. It must be remembered that most hormones introduced into the bloodstream do not pass the blood-brain barrier. Many of the observed behavioral changes probably result in part from peripheral changes. Studies using hormone secretion as a dependent variable have been conducted, in particular for the catecholamines and corticosteroids. Both hormone groups can be determined relatively easily in the urine or blood plasma with good reliability. Stress stimuli increase the excretion of catecholamines and corticosteroids. All other hormones have not yet been studied sufficiently for their significance as indicators of psychological states. Even where a correlation has been shown between hormones and behavior, generalization is difficult because only small proportions of the biologically active hormones can be detected with conventional methods, i.e. the quantity detected does not allow conclusions on the level active in the organism. In addition, the origin of the hormones detected cannot be explained with any certainty.

Bibliography: 1. *General introductions, articles and surveys:* **Bajusz, E.:** An introduction to clinical neuroendocrinology. Basle, 1967. **Bleuler, M.:** Endokrinologische Psychiatrie. Stuttgart, 1963. **Coppen, A.:** The biochemistry of affective disorders. Brit. J. Psychiatr., 1967, *113*, 1237–64. **Danowski, T. S.:** Clinical endrocrinology, Vols. 1–4. Baltimore, 1962. **Dorfman, R. I.:** Methods in hormone research, Vol. 2. New York, 1969. **Gabe, M.:** Neurosecretion. Oxford, 1969. **Hoagland, H.:** Hormones, brain function and behavior. New York, 1957, **Jores, A. & Nowakowski, N.:** Praktische Endokrinologie u. H. therapie nichtendokriner Erkrankungen. Stuttgart, 1968. **Martini, L. & Ganong, W. F. (Eds.):** Neuroendocrinology, Vols. 1 und 2. New York, 1966–67. **Pincus, G., Thiman, K. V. & Astwood, E. B. (Eds.):**

	Neurohormones or tissue hormones	(d) γ-amino-butyric (= GABA)	Biogenic amine, derived from glutamic acid, inhibition of nervous excitation (?)			
		(e) Histamine	Transmitter substance in CNS, assists in genesis of pain		Allergies Pain (?)	(a) drop in blood pressure, nausea, tiredness (b) liberation under anaphylactic shock and sensory pain
		(f) Tyramine	Biogenic amine			(a) sympathicomimetic effects, e.g. increased blood pressure, subjectively stimulating
		(g) Noradrenalin	Transmitter substance in CNS and ANS	Depression (?)		(b) increased secretion under stress
		(h) Dopamine	Transmitter substance in CNS, synergistic to noradrenalin, intermediate substance in biosynthesis of noradrenalin	Parkinson's disease (?) Depression (?)		(b) increased excretion in urine with increased activation
		(i) Angiotensin 11	Assists in blood pressure regulation; increases release of aldosterone		Essential hypertonia	(a) rise in blood pressure—increased excretion of catecholamines in urine
		(j) Substance P	Transmitter substance in CNS (?), plays part in the conduction of sensory stimuli			
		(k) Melatonin	Antagonizes melanotropin (inhibition of pigmentation), assists in regulation of light-dependent day–night rhythm			(b) reduced production under permanent lighting (animal tests)
Hypothalamus		"Releasing factors" (e.g. TRF = thyreotropic hormone releasing factor; LRF = luteotropic hormone releasing factor; CRF = corticotrophic hormone releasing factor)	Stimulate release of anterior pituitary hormones			

The hormones: physiology, chemistry, and applications. New York, 1964. **Reiss, M.:** Neuroendocrinology and psychiatry. Int. J. Neuropsychiatr., 1967, *3*, 441–63. **Scharrer, E. & Scharrer, B. V.:** Neuroendocrinology. Columbia, 1963. **Tausk, M.:** Pharmakologie der Hormone, Stuttgart, 1970. **Waelsch, H. & Weil-Malherbe, H.:** Neurochemistry and Psychiatry. In: **Gruhle, H. W.** *et al.* (Eds.): Psychiatrie der Gegenwart. Berlin, 1967. **Wigglesworth, V. B.:** Insect hormones. Edinburgh & London, 1971. **Williams, R. H.:** Textbook of endocrinology. Philadelphia, 1968. **Williams, R. J.:** Biochemical individuality. New York, 1956.

2. *Hormones and psychology:* **Bajusz, E.** (Ed.): Physiology and pathology of adaptation mechanisms. Oxford, 1969. **Bleuler, M.:** Psychische Funktionen u· vegetatives Nervensystem: Endokrine Wirkungen auf die Psyche. In: **Monnier** (Ed.): Physiologie und Pathologie des vegetativen Nervensystems, Vol. 2. Stuttgart, 1963. **Dewhurst, W. G.:** J. Psychosomatic Research, 1965, *9*, 115–27. **Eiduson, S.,** *et al.*: Biochemistry and behavior. Princeton, 1964. **Harlow, H. F. & Woolsey, C. N.:** Biological and biochemical bases of behavior. Madison, 1965. **Mandell, A. J. & Mandell, M. P.:** Psychochemical research in man. New York, 1969. **Meng, H.:** Psyche und Hormon. Berne, 1960.

W. Janke

Hormone types. Individuals featuring temperamental dispositions which occur as a function of the heightened or diminished effects of a hormone. Classification according to specific endocrine glands is possible only to a limited extent, e.g. in the case of the thyroid gland: hyperthyroidism = overexcitability; hypothyroidism = underexcitability. Otherwise the general term "endocrine psychosyndrome" is sometimes used.

Bibliography: Kretschmer, E. & Kretschmer, W.: Medizinische Psychologie. Stuttgart, [13]1970.

W.K.

Hormopathy. According to R. Brun, a primary motivational or emotive disturbance ("anergia" or "anhormia"), which may have essentially organic (endocrine or cerebral) origins or psychofunctional causes (actual neuroses [see *Actual anxiety*] and psychoneuroses, q.v.).

W.Sc.

Horner's law. J. F. Horner, a Zürich ophthalmologist (1831–86), first suggested that (most) color vision defects, like the blood disease "hemophilia", are transmitted by inheritance through apparently unaffected female "carriers", i.e. from the affected man through his apparently healthy daughter to her male descendants.

K.H.P.

Horopter. The geometrical locus of those points in the field of vision which are reproduced on corresponding (identical) retinal points. A distinction is made between *geometrical* (derived) and *empirical* (calculated) horopters. If the correspondence is complete (both longitudinally and horizontally), there is a total, point, or full horopter. With a disparation in one of the main axes, there is a partial horopter: a longitudinal or vertical horopter; or, alternatively, a transverse or horizontal horopter.

The total geometrical horopter is the Vieth–Müller circle, which passes through the fixation point and the two optical points of rotation. The empirical total horopter differs substantially from the geometrical equivalent, and already becomes a straight line in the finite range; as the fixation distance increases, it becomes a line which is convex in relation to the observer.

A.H.

Horoscope. An astrological concept; in the static sense, a summary of the personality, based on specific constellations of the sun, moon and planets at the moment of birth; in the dynamic sense, the influence of changing constellations at specific moments in time ("astral influence"). The horoscope is based on the assumption that man and the earth have a central position in the universe. In spite of complete rejection by scientists, astrology still has many proponents, who believe in aspects or trends of destiny determined by cosmic factors. The fact that many horoscopes are accurate is due not to astrology but to the diagnostic intuition of some perceptive astrologers. J. P. Guilford found that there are about 10/13 personality factors which to some extent correspond to the signs of the zodiac. A horoscope may be interpreted as an attempt to apply long-confirmed experience to the problem of reducing the wide range of individual characteristics to a relatively small system of basic qualities (P. R. Hofstätter). A distinction is to be made between the astrology of horoscope-makers and the complex cosmosophies of such figures as Paracelsus.

Bibliography: Bender, H.: Astrologie und Aberglaube. Neue Wissenschaft, 1964, *12*. **Gauquelin, M.:** Der Einfluss der Gestirne und die Statistik. Z. fur Parapsychol. u. Grenzgebiete der Psychol., 1957/58, *1–3*. **Jacobi, J.** (Ed.): Paracelsus: selected writings. New York & London, 1951. *E.U.*

Hospitalism. Generic term for all the psychological and physical disorders caused by a long stay in a hospital, clinic, or institution.

1. Hospitalism in the psychological sense is a syndrome of negative mental secondary effects which is particularly marked in small infants and other children who undergo institutional treatment for a long time or grow up in special homes. This is a progressive psychophysical process, intimately connected with development, which is explained by the failure to obtain satisfaction of the need for emotive exchange and human relations with a mother, the lack of emotional warmth and affective-emotional concern, and the absence of a family environment ("nest warmth"). Symptoms observed uniformly in the infant: tendency to cry, apathetic-depressive states, motor inhibitions or unrest, substitute satisfactions (spasmodic hand and head movements, thumb sucking, nail biting), retarded physical (standing, running) and mental development (speech, thought), and a poor state of health (susceptibility to infection, nutritional disorders) which may even lead to death. According to R. Spitz, hospitalized children in homes have a mortality rate of up to 40%. Irreversible damage occurs if the child is isolated from its mother for more than 5 months. R. Mathis has found that 75% of 1400 hospitalized children showed psychological or intellectual disturbance. The predominant characteristics are low frustration tolerance, poor ability to establish contacts and low social adaptativeness, sometimes with aggressive reactions. In puberty, hospitalism may lead to regressive and criminal behavior. The first systematic descriptions of hospitalism were given by Pfaundler (1925) (cachectic treatment damage). Spitz's and Wolf's studies ("anaclitic depression") (1945–6) have become much better known; their observations were confirmed and expanded by Bowlby (1951) and Dührssen (1958). These studies show that for a normal psychophysical development, a good mother–child relationship is more important than good hygienic conditions (cf. Harlow's experiments with monkeys). Attempts are now made to counteract hospitalism by creating closer and more stable relationships between nurses and children (small groups), and by establishing children's villages in which the children live in house communities in small groups of different age and sex, and are cared for by permanent house mothers. Arrangements are now often made to allow the mother of a hospitalized baby or small child to stay with it in the hospital. The psychological neglect of children in the family (e.g. because both parents are working), or attendance at day nurseries has been seen to lead to a "family hospitalism". Even in adult patients, hospitalism may develop after long hospitalization: i.e. in the form of increased dependence and an unwillingness to make a quick recovery. See *Child psychology.*

2. In the narrower, medical sense, "hospitalism" is a term sometimes used to denote all the damage resulting from the frequent occurrence of infection during a stay in hospital: infection either by contagion (staff, inadequate hygiene) or by resistant bacteria and viruses.

Bibliography: Bowlby, J.: Maternal care and mental health. Bull. WHO, 1951, *3*, 355–533. **Id.:** Child care and the growth of love. Harmondsworth, 1965. **Dührssen, A.:** Heimkinder und Pflegekinder in ihrer Entwicklung. Göttingen, 1958. **Harlow, H. F.:** On the meaning of love. Amer. Psychologist, 1958, *13*, 673–85. **Id. & Zimmermann, R. R.:** Affectional responses in the infant monkey. Science, 1959, *130*, 421–32. **Pfaundler, M. v.:** Klinik und Fürsorge. Gesundheitsfürsorge für das Kinderalter, 1925, *1*, 3. **Robertson, J.:** Young children in hospital. London, 1965. **Spitz, R.:** Hospitalism. Psychoanal. Stud. Child, 1945, *1*, 53. **Id. & Wolf, K. M.:** Anaclitic depression. Psychoanal. Stud. Child, 1946, *2*, 113–17.

F.-C. S.

House-Tree-Person Test (Nbb. HTP). A thematic projective test in which S. is asked to draw a house, a tree and a human being. Reliability values are satisfactory. The test is intended to supply information on intelligence, affectivity and degree of maturity, especially in children.

Bibliography: Hammer, E. F. (Ed.): The clinical application of projective drawings. Springfield, Ill., 1958.

E.F-K.

HPL. See *Human placental lactogen.*

H test. The H test is a distribution-free test method (significance test) for the simultaneous comparison of several groups of a classification variable with reference to the central tendency: i.e. differences between data are tested for statistical significance when the observations are ranked. A useful test when the conditions for a simple analysis of variance are not present. See *Variance, analysis of.* *W.H.B.*

Hue. A basic property on the basis of which a color is given a specific name. Yellow, for example, is distinguished from orange, red and blue, and in general from any other shade or tint. The phenomenon is associated with narrow wavelength bands but can also be produced by fusing two or more variations of different wavelengths. The normal human eye can distinguish 200–250 hues. *G.Ka.*

Hull, Clark Leonard. B. 25/5/1884 in Akron (N.Y.); d. 10/5/1952 in New Haven (Conn.). Hull graduated from the University of Wisconsin in 1918. He was appointed Professor of psychology at Yale University in 1929. He concentrated initially on research into abilities (q.v.) and the development of statistical methods and psychological test methods; he then devoted ten years to the study of hypnosis (q.v.) and suggestibility, on which he published thirty-two articles and a book. Through his extensive studies of learning and motivation, and because of his systematic behavioral theory, which was unique in its stringent approach to the development of psychological theories, he became the most prominent representative of neo-behaviorism (see *Behaviorism*).

Systematic theory of behavior. Hull's theory of behavior can be considered as an S–O–R theory. In addition to the objectively measurable input (stimulus) and output (response) variable, he postulates a series of hypothetical parameters in the organism, known as intervening variables (q.v.), which establish the relationship between the stimulus and response values, and whose functional interrelationship and relationship with the observed parameters Hull explained in verbal terms, and generally also in equation form, through seventeen postulates and seventeen assumptions (corollaries) derived from the postulates (hypothetico–deductive framework).

Hull's central postulate of primary reinforcement (q.v.), which is closely related to E. L. Thorndike's law of effect, states that: "Whenever an effector activity (R) is closely associated with a stimulus afferent impulse or trace (S) and the conjunction is closely associated with the rapid diminution in the motivational stimulus (S_D or S_G), there will result an increment (Δ) to a tendency for that stimulus to evoke that response." Primary reinforcement is important in the learning process; it consists of a reduction of the motivational stimulus generated by a drive (q.v.).

Hull also refers to a secondary reinforcement which occurs when a previously neutral stimulus trace is frequently and regularly associated with the rapid diminution in the motivational stimulus (S_D) and in this way takes over the function of the reinforcing agent. But a stimulus-response association through contiguity under the influence of reinforcement always forms the qualitative prerequisite for the production and reinforcement of habits (see *Habit*).

Habit strength (${}_sH_R$) (tendency of a stimulus trace to evoke an associated response) is dependent on the number of reinforcements, and increases as a rising, negatively accelerated function of this reinforced stimulus-response association. The probability of the occurrence of a response, however, depends not only on habit strength, but on additional, non-associative factors included, in addition to the habit potential (${}_sH_R$), in the reaction potential (${}_sE_R$). Whereas habit potential is an expression of associative intensity, the intensity of the reaction potential indicates the actual tendency of a stimulus to elicit a specific reaction. Reaction potential can be determined from the speed, intensity and resistance to extinction of the reaction, but cannot be identified with the reaction, since it may either be located below a threshold value (and therefore not lead to the reaction), or may interact with competing tendencies (inhibitory potential; see *Inhibition*) (and therefore lead only to an incomplete reaction).

Assuming that the conditions remain constant during the learning process and reaction formation, reaction potential is determined (*a*) by habit strength ${}_sH_R$; (*b*) by the drive D obtaining during the learning process; (*c*) by the magnitude of intensity, i.e. the stimulus value V; and (*d*) by the incentive motivation K of the reinforcement. The interaction of these factors is multiplicative: ${}_sE_R = {}_sH_R \times D \times V \times K$.

Reaction potential, on the other hand, is counteracted by the inhibitory potential (${}_sI_R$), which is made up of the reactive (I_R) and conditioned inhibition (${}_sI_R$) and, as a function of the resulting effective reaction potential (${}_s\bar{E}_R = {}_sE_R - {}_sI_R$), may weaken or neutralize the tendency to carry out specific action.

Main works: Aptitude testing. New York, 1928. Knowledge and purpose as habit mechanisms. Psychol. Rev., 1930, *37*, 511–25. Goal attraction and directing ideas conceived as habit phenomena. Psychol. Rev., 1931, *38*, 487–506. Hypnosis and suggestibility. New York, 1933. Mind, mechanism, and adaptive behavior. Psychol. Rev., *44*, 1–32. Mathematico-deductive theory of rote learning: a study in scientific methodology (with others). New Haven, 1940. Principles of behavior: an introduction to behavior theory. New York, 1943. Essentials of behavior. New Haven, 1951. Autobiography. In: Boring E. G., *et al.* (Eds.): A history of psychology in autobiography, Vol. 4. Worcester, Mass., 1952, 142–63. A behavior system: an introduction to behavior theory concerning the individual organism. New Haven, 1952.

Bibliography: Koch, S.: Clark L. Hull. In: **Estes, W. K.,** *et al.* (Eds.): Modern learning theory: a critical analysis of five examples. New York, 1954, 1–176. **Spence, K. W.:** Clark Leonard Hull: 1884–1952. Amer. J. Psychol., 1952, *65*, 639–46.

W.W.

Hull's law. The central proposition in Clark L. Hull's theory of learning, that habit strength accumulates as a direct function of the number of reinforced stimulus-response occurrences. *G.D.W.*

Human engineering. A branch of engineering science and applied psychology. Special emphasis is placed on ergonomics (q.v.) and industrial science, and above all on occupational psychology (q.v.) and industrial psychology (q.v.). Such problems as optimal working conditions, organization of men and machines, operator skills, and so on, are to the fore. See *Practice; Motor skills; Instructional technology.* *G.R.W.M.*

Human ethology is the study of the phylogenetic (innate) and ontogenetic (acquired) components of human behavior. Particularly valuable information can be obtained from the observation (e.g. by filming) of behavioral development in infants and children born deaf and blind, etc. See *Ethology; Comparative psychology*.

Bibliography: Lorenz, K.: Die angeborenen Formen möglicher Erfahrung. Z. Tierpsychol., 1943, 235–409. **Prechtl, H. F. R.:** Die Entwicklung der frühkindlichen Motorik, Inst. wiss. Film, Göttingen: Films Nos. C 651, C 652, C 653 (1955). *K.Fi.*

Humanistic psychology. I. Humanistic psychology does not set itself up as a new school, still less as "a school to end schools". It does not deny the validity of any psychological work with sound credentials, in theory and method. It insists, however (and this is its distinctive feature), that a comprehensive psychology of man cannot be delimited by particular methods (experimental or statistical), any more than a cartographer can omit oceans or mountain ranges merely because he cannot traverse the former or scale the latter.

While recognizing, on the basis of evolution, man's kinship with animals, humanistic psychology acknowledges man's essential properties: his subjectivity and selfhood; his sense of past and future which makes him at once a creature of history and a dreamer; and his universal tendency to categorize in the form of moral and other value judgments. If all this evades the method of the laboratory it nevertheless claims the utmost precision of analysis, which does justice to the *phenomena* as such. The humanistic psychologist feels that neo-positivist insistence on methodological rigor is open to suspicion, and that all too often it is indistinguishable from *rigor mortis*.

Finally, humanistic psychology asks for a reappraisal of the division of labor, as between the sciences and humanities. Such a reappraisal should serve to show that psychology can profit equally from its affiliation with history, literature, comparative religion and the arts, and from its links with neurophysiology and computer science.

Bibliography: Cohen, J.: Humanistic psychology. London, 1958.

J. Cohen

II. Humanistic psychology is the name of a new school of psychology whose main founder was A. Maslow. In 1962 the American Association for Humanistic Psychology started with a nucleus of sponsors. A year before a *Journal of Humanistic Psychology* was edited by A. Sutich.

The main reasons for the initiating of what in a few years developed into a big movement, were originally purely scientific and theoretical. Those who joined in the foundation of what Maslow called the "third force" besides the then prevailing psychoanalysis and behaviorism, felt that none of these other schools did justice to the understanding of a healthily and creatively functioning person. They felt that such a person pursued goals and values not because of a need for "homeostasis", as the more recent psychoanalysis taught, but for the purpose of what Fromm and Horney called *self-realization*, or what K. Goldstein and A. Maslow called *self-actualization*, or C. Bühler called *self-fulfillment*, which she demonstrated in studies of courses of human life.

The school, which began with a small group of sponsors, developed and spread in a very short time to become a great movement. One reason was that Carl Rogers, one of the early sponsors, demonstrated the application of humanistic psychological ideas to *psychotherapy*. He showed a completely new type of relationship between therapist and patient, in which both related as persons, instead of one being an authority and the other a sick individual who had necessarily to transfer his early emotional conflicts with his parents, as psychoanalysis had taught. Of course, this problem is still partly in discussion, and there are different concepts and many experiments in which the handling of this relationship is developed. Rogers has also the historical merit of having insisted on making tape records of psychotherapy sessions which could be made available to other therapists for inspection, comparison with their own work, and other studies. Up to then, the psychoanalysts had handled the process of therapy like an occult science which only the initiated were allowed to know about.

The opening-up of the therapy procedure to those who wanted to study it undoubtedly had many undesirable side-effects in that unqualified or semi-qualified people tried to conduct the process, and some extremists went very far in what they allowed to happen. These procedures occurred mostly in *group therapies*, which, since their early beginnings with Slavson and Moreno, had developed into the biggest movement of our time. The author considers group therapy and the related "*sensitivity training*", a group process in which people of all walks of life are assembled in groups learning to speak frankly with each other and trying to understand each other, one of the most hopeful cultural processes to take place in the present cultural crisis. Leading figures in the sensitivity training area are L. P. Bradford, J. Gibb, F. Massarik, and others who developed the procedure with industrialists, business men, administrators, educators and others.

This, as all that C. Rogers initiated, goes to show that psychotherapy is no longer considered exclusively or even primarily as a psychiatric procedure with the purpose of curing the mentally ill. Although a humanistic psychologist must be trained (and should be licensed by a supervising board) to treat neurotics, his main—and more frequent—task today is *educational* rather than curative. Together, the patient and therapist work on an understanding of themselves as *persons* and of *human life as a whole*.

Much work is just now being done in this area of educational psychotherapy. Important, however, is that humanistic psychology has gained a scientific foundation which *validates* its approach to the person as a whole, with more scientific reliability than previous psychologies were able to. A recent first international congress, in Amsterdam, was devoted to this double issue of humanistic psychology's offering a new scientific approach to the study of the person as a whole (Maslow, Rogers, C. Bühler), and help in the renewal of our Western civilization so that it offers a better self-understanding and mutual understanding of people.

Bibliography: Bühler, Charlotte & Massarik, F. (Eds.): The course of human life. A study of goals in the humanistic perspective. New York, 1968. **Maslow, A. H.:** Motivation and personality. New York, 1954. **Id.:** The psychology of science. A reconnaissance. Chicago, 1966. **Rogers, C. R.:** Client-centered therapy. Its current practice, implications and theory. Boston, 1951.

C. Bühler

Humanity. Traditionally, this term denotes a concept which covers both the totality of all characteristics innate in man and those which distinguish him from other living beings. It is used in particular to denote a moral-ethical attitude which is made up of altruism, love for one's fellow men and human understanding; it is the opposite of coercion and brute force. Since the eighteenth century, it has come to designate the revolutionary ideal of a reconciled mankind—a standard for the development of moral and political life (Declaration of Human Rights). *A.T.*

Human management. See *Management; Manipulation*.

Human nature, understanding of. A prescientific form of psychodiagnosis (q.v.), i.e. one lacking in objectivity, reliability, validity, and proficient standards. In popular language, a person who "understands human nature" is considered able to sum up an individual's personality, with particular reference to specific features—often on the basis of a first impression (q.v.). Experience is thought to be important in this "intuitive" process.

W.L.

Human placental lactogen (abb. HPL). A recently discovered extrahypophyseal gonadotropic hormone which is formed—like choriongonadotrophin(e) (q.v.)—in the placenta during pregnancy, and is similar in its effects to the hypophyseal gonadotropin: luteotropic hormone (LTH). In conjunction with other gonadotropins, HPL promotes the formation of hormones (estrogens and progesterone) in the *corpus luteum* of the ovaries and—like other placental gonadotropins—is most active in early pregnancy (second and third months). *H.M.*

Human relations. A term for interpersonal relations in work or industrial organizations. Human relations research was founded in the nineteen thirties by E. Mayo, who conducted experiments in the Hawthorne Works (USA) in the course of which informal (unplanned) structures were "discovered" in industrial concerns, and the significance of psychological and social factors (satisfaction, group standards) for productivity was shown for the first time. The human relations movement attempts to increase productivity by improving the working atmosphere; it exaggerates, however, the importance of informal structures and disregards the conflict of interests between employers and employees. See *Hawthorne experiments; Occupational psychology; Industrial psychology.* *C.B.*

Human rights. The inalienable fundamental rights of every human being: e.g. the rights to life, freedom and equality. *H.J.A.*

Humor. 1. It would not be too extreme to claim that before Freud a real interest in the phenomenon of humor and the use of the term "wit" were not met with in psychology. Before the publication of Freud's *Der Witz und seine Beziehung zum Unbewussten* (Vienna, 1905; Eng. trans., 1960), despite a few attempts to define the term (in particular, those of T. Lipps and K. Fischer), it had no precise psychological connotation.

For Freud, everything that saves psychic or muscular effort is a source of pleasure. Pleasure *sui generis*, conditioned by a joke or witticism, corresponds to an economizing on mental effort. This saving is realized on two distinct levels: that of "matter" or background, and that of "form". In terms of "matter", the pleasure afforded by the joke corresponds to a saving of psychic effort resulting either from a moderation of the censorship exercised by reason on cognitive activity (when the adult becomes a "real child" once more, he plays quite freely with words and ideas without any concern for logical constraint), or from a moderation of moral censorship over our instincts (humor allows the satisfaction of a prohibited impulse). Another source of pleasure connected with the sense of humor and the exercise of wit is to be found at the formal level. Although accessory, this is by no means a negligible source, consisting as it does in (the study of) techniques for eliciting laughter or appreciation of humor. On the basis of a large number of famous jokes and witticisms, Freud provided a detailed list of various techniques: condensation (with or without substitute-formation), repeated use of the same verbal material, punning, logical inconsistency, representation by means of the contrary, unification, allusion, omission, etc. The only factor common to all these procedures is, according to Freud, a tendency to an economy of expenditure of semantic material.

Although interested mainly in *wit*, Freud in fact represents his theory in the form of the threefold complex of *wit* (jokes), the *comic*, and *humor*. This division relies on the different underlying genetic processes: "The pleasure of wit seems to me" to arise from "an economy of expenditure of inhibition; that of the comic from an economy of expenditure of representational thought; and that of humor from an economy of expenditure of feeling."

However, as far as the last two terms are concerned, no consensus of opinion is as yet available among psychologists on their precise denotations. For Freud, humor corresponds to the economy of expenditure of a painful emotion, and therefore constitutes a means of defense against pain. For Bergson, humor is defined in contradistinction to *irony*: I am humorous when I pretend to believe that things are not as they really are, but instead as they ought really to be. "Humor" is, of course, generally used in a less precise way, and as a global term, in English: i.e. something humorous is something in any way laughable or amusing.

Bergson defines the basis of the comic as arising from the contrast between the mechanical and the organic ("*le vivant*"); he believed that comedy "is not disinterested as genuine art is. By organizing laughter, comedy accepts social life as a natural environment, it even obeys an impulse of social life. And in this respect it turns back upon art, which is a breaking away from society and a return to pure nature." Despite Bergson's insistence that all comic incongruities are examples of mechanization, the word "comic" is still without any precise psychological connotation, and has a different signification for each author. Victoroff (1953) suggests that the comic should be defined in contradistinction to the *ridiculous*, or laughable: one may elicit laughter quite intentionally, or, on the contrary, involuntarily—even bringing it upon oneself. In the first case, the comic is in question, and in the second case the ridiculous (ridicule).

Bibliography: Bergler, E.: Laughter and the sense of humor. New York, 1956. **Bergson, H.:** Laughter: an essay on the meaning of the comic. London & New York, 1911. **Eastman, M.:** The sense of humor. New York & London, 1921. **Id.:** Enjoyment of laughter. New York, 1936. **Freud, S.:** Jokes and their relation to the unconscious. London, 1960. **Victoroff, D.:** Le rire et le risible: introduction à la psychosociologie du rire. Paris, 1953.

D. Victoroff

2. The concept of humor is derived from C. Galenus' theory of temperaments (temperament as a mixture of "humors") and is used today: (*a*) in the sense of a cheerful and comprehensive attitude to life or a basic mood and (*b*) as a generic term for verbal, graphic or pantomimic expressions designed to provoke mirth and laughter (sense of humor). Factor analyses of opinions regarding humorous material showed that the sense of humor consists of at least six factors which are partly correlated with personality traits. Associations of this kind form the basis of the IPAT Humor Test of Personality (R. B. Cattell). *D.B.*

3. A distinction is sometimes made between *personal* or *orectic* (affective, conative: e.g. sex) and *impersonal* or *cognitive* (formal) aspects of humor (e.g. Kambouropoulou, 1926, 1930). Williams (1945) and Eysenck (1947) found evidence of a correlation between extraversion and preferences for orectic humor, and between introversion and preferences for cognitive humor.

Bibliography: Eysenck, H. J.: Dimensions of personality. London, 1947. **Guilford, J. P.:** Personality. New York, 1959. **Kambouropoulou, P.:** Individual differences in the sense of humor. Amer. J. Psychol., 1926, *37*, 288–97. **Id.:** Individual differences in the sense of humor and their relation to temperamental differences. Arch. Psychol., 1930, *121*, 79. **Williams, J. M.:** An experimental and theoretical study of humour in children, unpubl. Ph.D. thesis. London, 1945.

Humphrey's paradox (syn. *Arpeggio paradox*). The tendency of organisms to react to specific categories of stimuli in an identical manner, even though the objective characteristics of the stimuli vary; or the tendency of individuals, who would otherwise react differently to a specific tone, to respond identically when that tone is produced not simultaneously but in sequence, e.g. in an arpeggio. See *Generalization; Stereotype.* *H. Ro.*

Hunger. Normally refers to the desire to eat (which may or may not be associated with food deprivation), but is also used in a metaphorical sense to refer to a craving for anything, e.g. sex or affection.

Hunger drive: a hypothetical state operationally defined in terms of food deprivation, which is found to give rise to increased general activity as well as specific food-seeking behavior. (See *Instinct.*)

Hunger pangs: unpleasant sensations in the stomach associated with the need for food, and believed to be associated with contractions of the stomach wall.

Hunger-strike: refusal to eat as a means of bringing political pressure to bear upon an authority, e.g. prisoners attempting to gain improved conditions. *G.D.W.*

Husserl. See *Phenomenology.*

Hybridization. Crossing or interbreeding. In diploid (q.v.) organisms, a distinction can be made between the phenotype (q.v.) and genotype (q.v.). Individuals with pure heredity (homozygotes) have one identical allele on each (the maternal and paternal) side. Mixed hybrids (heterozygotes) differ in one gene (monohybrid), or in two (dihybrid), or three genes (trihybrid), etc. Depending on the phenotype, hybrids may be intermediate or dominant/recessive. *K. Fi.*

Hydrazines. Amine oxidase inhibitors which over a period of a week or more have a stimulant effect on mood, which would seem to correspond to the MAO inhibiting effects of the substances. Some toxic side-effects reported, e.g. with iproniazid. Hydrazines have been tried in depression (q.v.), but have now for the most part given way to dibenzazepines. See *Psychotomimetic drugs.*

Bibliography: Garattini, S. & Dukes, M.: Antidepressant drugs. Amsterdam, 1967.

Hydrocephalus. An increase of cerebrospinal fluid (csf) within the skull, usually associated with an increase in pressure. It may result from an obstruction to the flow of csf within the ventricular system, or a decreased absorption of the fluid. When it occurs in children an increase in the size of the head may follow, but in the adult this cannot occur, so that neurological and mental symptoms develop as a result of intracranial pressure. In the past, mental deficiency was a common complication in untreated cases in children, although nowadays drainage operations are possible. *D.E.*

Hydrocortisone (*Cortisol; 17-hydroxycorticosterone*, abb. *71-OHCS; Cortef; Cortril; Efcortesol;* etc.). The most important hormone (q.v.) in the adrenal cortex; belongs to the group of glucocorticoids. Hydrocortisone is very important in psychophysiological emotion research because it can be detected relatively easily and accurately (e.g. by chromatography) in the blood plasma and urine. Many studies in animals and in diseased and healthy testees have shown that all kinds of stress stimuli are associated with increased hormone secretion. Because of the high inter- and intra-individual variance, fairly large samples are often necessary to inform on significant effects. Adequate reliability can only be achieved if many factors are observed (e.g. time of day, age, sex, weight, nourishment, etc.). If these factors are taken into consideration, hydrocortisone is a sensitive indicator even for light and short-term stressors. The administration of hydrocortisone in physiological doses has only a slight effect, but experimentally induced emotions are heightened. The basal values of hydrocortisone secretion are relatively constant in a given individual. Correlation studies with personality traits show that male and anxious testees have higher values than female and non-anxious subjects. In depressive patients, hydrocortisone secretion increases with the severity of the disorder, but negative results have also been observed. See *Corticosteroids.* *W.J.*

5-hydroxytryptamine. An abbreviation for the chemical composition of serotonin (q.v.).

5-hydroxytryptophan(e). The chemical precursor of serotonin (q.v.). The conversion of 5-hydroxytryptophane into serotonin in the organism takes place under the influence of the enzyme 5-hydroxytryptophane-decarboxylase. This conversion can be blocked by specific substances, such as P-chlorophenylalanine. 5-hydroxytryptophane, unlike serotonin, passes the blood-brain barrier (q.v.). It is therefore of considerable importance for experimental or therapeutic manipulation of the serotonin concentration in the brain. See *Biogenic amines.* *W.J.*

Hygiene, mental. See *Mental hygiene.*

Hypalgesia. Hypalgesia denotes a raising of the pain threshold. This phenomenon may be explained, e.g., by the degeneration of certain nerve fibers in the affected skin area. Once the raised threshold is exceeded, the pain experienced is often even greater than normal (hyperpathy). See *Pain.* *M.S.*

Hyperacusis. Abnormally raised sensitivity to loud sounds: may be due to paralysis of the stapes muscle, which should normally raise the base of the stapes slightly above the oval window of the cochlea on exposure to extreme sound energy (protective function). Hair cell damage at high intensities is sometimes accompanied by hyperacusis. *M.S.*

Hyperal(ges)ia. If the pain threshold is lowered, even light contact may be experienced as painful. In general, the damage is confined to a limited area and the pain is described as "burning". *M.S.*

Hyperbolic type. Ant. hypobolic type or litotes type (see *Speech types*). The hyberbolic type uses drastic and exaggerated language, while the litotes type tends to underemphasize. *W.K.*

Hyperemia. Excess of blood in some part of the body, due to reactive capillary dilatation under mechanical, thermal or chemical excitation, as part of an inflammation, or in a case of venous obstruction, etc. *E.D.*

Hyperesthesia. Increased cutaneous sensitivity due to peripheral or central changes. See *Hyperalgesia.* *M.S.*

Hyperesthetic type. An extreme variant of the schizothymic character: "fickle sensitivity . . . fanatic enthusiasm for nature and art (or) persons . . . easily influenced and hurt . . . reacts oversensitively to ideas with a strong emotional coloring, tends to stick to them vehemently and for a long time." Ant. *Anesthetic type.*

Bibliography: Kretschmer, E. & Kretschmer, W.: Medizinische Psychologie. Stuttgart, [13]1970. *W.K.*

Hyperfunction(ing). The overfunctioning of organs. Often pathological and referred to by specific medical terms. The commonest condition of this kind is a hyperfunctioning of the endocrine glands. The thyroid gland is responsible for Basedow's disease (q.v.) with accelerated metabolic processes, exophthalmus and nervousness, while the adrenal gland may cause the Cushing syndrome with the following symptoms: "moon face", facial reddening, striae (pregnancy marks) and blood pressure crises. The pituitary may cause acromegaly or gigantism. Treatment is generally only possible by partial destruction of the glandular tissue. *E.D.*

Hypergeometric distribution. A hypergeometric distribution of sample values for a discrete variable is obtained by extracting X_1 elements from a finite population *without* replacement. The probability (anticipated relative frequency) of a result of exactly X occurrences of a given alternative ("successes") in a population of N elements—including M "successes"—with a sample size of n, is obtained from:

$$p(x) = \frac{\binom{M}{x}\binom{N-M}{n-x}}{\binom{N}{n}}; \quad \text{for } x = 0, 1, \ldots N.$$

The hypergeometric distribution plays the same part in samples without replacement as the binomial distribution (q.v.) for samples with replacement. It has the mean value:

$$\mu = n \cdot \frac{M}{N},$$

and the standard deviation:

$$\sigma = \frac{n \cdot M(N-M)(N-n)}{N^2(N-1)}.$$

W.H.B.

Hypergonadism; hypogonadism. In general: over- (hyper-) or under- (hypo-) functioning of the male or female sex glands with various causes. Hypogonadism is far more frequent than hypergonadism (ratio 8:1). Hypergonadism occurs very rarely when the gonadotropins (extremely uncommon) or sex gland hormones are produced in excessive quantities because of a tumor, so that there is a strong development of the secondary sexual characteristics (this does not, however, include premature puberty = see *Pubertas praecox*).

Hypogonadism plays a much more important part in clinical practice, clinical psychology, and psychopathology. A distinction is made between two main groups according to the dominant effect:

1. *Primary, hypergonadotropic hypogonadism.* Primary failure of the terminal organ (testicles, ovaries) while the regulating organs (hypophysis, hypothalamus) remain intact; also excessive production of gonadotropic hormones because of impaired functioning of the sex glands. Causes: in both sexes, chromosomal anomalies are the principal cause. Main forms: (*a*) in the male: Klinefelter syndrome; other hereditary testicular malformation syndromes, e.g. Reifenstein and male Turner syndrome are relatively uncommon; (*b*) in the female the prototype is the Turner syndrome; (*c*) special case of failure to mature in persons with external female characteristics, but primarily male sex, and failure of testicles to descend: testicular feminization syndrome.

2. *Secondary, hypogonadotropic hypogonadism.* Diminished formation of gonadotropin caused by factors in the hypophysis (q.v.) or hypothalamus (q.v.) which results in failure of the sex gland functions or even to failure of these functions to develop. Much rarer than forms of primary gonadic hypofunction. Main forms: (*a*) idiopathic eunuchoidism = failure of FSH and ICSH formation, with the result that puberty does not occur even though the testicles are essentially intact; (*b*) fertile eunuchoidism (Pasqualini syndrome); probably isolated disturbance of ICSH production with intact FSH production; so that a eunuchoidal physique with infantile genitalia develops, while the testicles reach almost normal size with well-developed spermiogenesis; hypogenitalism without marked hypogonadism (a very rare condition); (*c*) pituitary dwarfism. In all these forms puberty fails to occur and—unless treated—the patient remains sexually infantile. In addition, there is a secondary form of hypogonadism which is not innate but is acquired during the course of life (=postpuberal hypogonadism) as a partial symptom of complete failure of pituitary functions, generally caused by tumors of the hypophysis.

Chronic failure to reach puberty is more common in men than women. The psychological problem consists essentially in the need as far as possible to avoid any discrepancy between chronological age and social maturity, in spite of biological and physical retardation (childishness and immature appearance). Clinical-psychological and sexual guidance—especially in cases of infertility—are urgent necessities in such cases.

Bibliography: **Wilkins, L.:** The diagnosis and treatment of endocrine disorders in childhood and adolescence. Springfield, Mass., 1965. *H.M.*

Hyperkinesis. Abnormally excessive motility of limbs and parts of the body, caused by continuous (tonic) or intermittent (clonic) muscular contractions, which are sometimes painful; the contractions often take the form of cramp. They are due to pathological changes in the brain areas controlling movement: e.g. *nucleus niger*, *ruber* or the cerebellum (q.v.). *E.D.*

Hypermetropia. Long sight. Incident light rays are reflected only behind the retina. (*a*) *Axial hypermetropia:* the bulbus is too short. (*b*) *Refractive hypermetropia:* refraction of the light rays is insufficient. The condition can be corrected by means of convex lenses. *R.R.*

Hypermnesia. An unusually good memory (q.v.), often due to abnormal mental states of excessively acute awareness. In hypnosis (q.v.) the subject may often recall events which occurred in the distant past, but only to the extent of a heightening of the possibilities which are already present in the normal state. *Hypomnesia* = poor memory, impaired ability to recall events. *H.-N.G.*

Hypermotility. Compulsive movement, motor unrest, or exaggerated mobility of the limbs and joints, e.g. in many forms of mental deficiency. *E.D.*

Hyperopia. See *Hypermetropia.*

Hyperosmia. An extremely acute sense of smell, especially as a pathological heightening of sensitivity, e.g. in pregnancy, neurasthenia (q.v.), epilepsy (q.v.); generally due to a central cause; the mechanism is not, however, clear. *K.H.P.*

Hyperplasia. An abnormal increase in the number of cells in organs or parts of the body, sometimes associated with hyperfunctioning (q.v.). Hyperplasia is sometimes pre-cancerous and is generally caused by excessive stress or strong stimuli. *E.D.*

Hypertension. Abnormally high tension, generally used to denote high blood pressure. See *Hypertonicity.* *E.D.*

Hyperthymia. A personality trait or type characterized by cheerfulness, high activity and industry. Distinguished from *hypomania* (q.v.) by a lack of social complications and of any necessity for medical or legal restraint. The opposite pole from *dysthymia* (q.v.); together they constitute the cyclothymic personality type, which changes from one state to the other. Manic depressive patients as a group have an excess of hyperthymic or cyclothymic personalities when assessed retrospectively. Prospective studies of hyperthymic personalities who develop the psychosis are not available, and there is no evidence of any alarming relationship. *B.B.*

Hyperthyroidism. See *Basedow's disease.*

Hypertonicity (or *Hypertension*, q.v.). High blood pressure due to a variety of causes. A distinction is made between several forms of hypertonicity. Genuine red high pressure (red facial coloring) is based on constitutional factors with neural components. Pale renal high pressure (white facial coloring) is due to vascular contraction with hormonal causes, deriving mainly from kidney damage. Thyrotoxicosis, Cushing syndrome (hyperfunction of the adrenal cortex), or adrenogenic symptoms (overfunctioning of the adrenal medulla) are other possible causes. All forms of hypertonicity eventually lead to hypertrophy (q.v.) and damage to the cardiac muscle, as well as vascular sclerosis. *E.D.*

Hypertrophy. Excessive development of overloaded organs, e.g. the muscular system in athletes, the heart in cases of high blood pressure, or the uterus in pregnancy, without an increase in the cell count. These are all conditions of physiological or activity hypertrophy. On the other hand, the various pathological forms of hypertrophy, e.g. hypertrophy of the prostate gland or tonsils, are disease conditions. See *Hyperplasia*. *E.D.*

Hypnagogic hallucination. See *Sleep*.

Hypnoic mechanisms. Involuntary "functional forms" of the imagination which do not have a logical or objective basis but an emotional or subjective foundation and are reflected in (internal) "images" and in acts of expression (spheric dependence, blurring of the ego boundary, change in time and space relationships, heightened density, displacement, stylization, "picture strip" imagination, etc.). *W.K.*

Hypnolepsy. A state of abnormal sleepiness. The term is usually employed as a synonym for narcolepsy (q.v.). *J.P.*

Hypnopedia. In hypnopedia (from the Greek = education in sleep) the pupil is taught and given behavioral instructions in a hypnotic state in order to avoid difficulties in absorbing information and controlling behavior while he is awake. Experimental results confirm the possibility of teaching and learning in sleep, but precise data on increased effectiveness obtainable through hypnopedia are not available as yet. *H. Schr.*

Hypnophobia. An undue fear of sleep.

Hypnosis. "A temporary condition of altered attention in the S. which may be induced by another person and in which a variety of phenomena may appear spontaneously or in response to verbal or other stimuli. These phenomena include alterations in conscious ness and memory, increased susceptibility to suggestion and the production in the S. of responses and ideas unfamiliar to him in his usual state of mind. Further, phenomena such as anaesthesia, paralysis, and rigidity of muscles, and vasomotor changes can be produced and removed. . . ." (B.M.A., 1955, p. 191).

Hypnosis, *hypnotic state*, *hypnotic trance*, and *hypnotism* are often used interchangeably, but hypnotism may also refer specifically to *hypnotic induction* by a *hypnotist* or *operator*. *Susceptibility* is the degree to which a S. is affected by induction, and determines the *depth* of hypnosis achieved. *Hypnoidal* refers to states having at least some of the characteristics of light hypnosis.

Posthypnotic suggestions (and instructions) are made during hypnosis in order to influence the S. after hypnosis, whereas *posthypnotic phenomena* are consequences of hypnosis arising after its termination, including those resulting from posthypnotic suggestions. There may be spontaneous or induced failure of the S. to remember some or all of the events which took place during hypnosis (*posthypnotic amnesia*), and even having been hypnotized. In so far as a S. can hypnotize himself, we have *auto-hypnosis*.

Hypnosis derives from "neuro-hypnotism", a term introduced by Braid (1843) to denote a trance-like state he observed to result from prolonged visual fixation or from prolonged concentrated attention of other kinds (*monoideism*), and resembling the *sleeping-trance* described by de Puységur (1785) as resulting from the prolonged use of mesmeric passes. The fully-developed trance resembled very deep sleep, with the S. stuporous and unresponsive to stimuli. Somewhat similar states have been reported from ancient times as arising in man, often following prolonged exposure to repetitive stimuli such as rhythmical drumming and chanting. Possibly analogous states are observed in many higher animals after exposure to repetitive stimuli such as stroking and flashing lights, and to sudden inversion, forcible restraint, and pressure on body parts; hence the terms *hypnosis* and *hypnotic trance* are sometimes applied to all such trance-like states in animals and men. However, the important characteristics of sleeping trance and neurohypnosis were that if the operator started speaking to the S. while the trance was still very light, and continued to talk at frequent intervals as it deepened, a selective *rapport* developed, the S. remaining responsive to the operator's verbal suggestions yet becoming progressively less responsive to all other stimuli. The term hypnotic trance is best reserved to denote sleeping trance and similar states as modified by the effects of verbal suggestion, in which sense the hypnotic trance can be induced only in humans with at least a rudimentary command of language.

In his later work, Braid increasingly stressed the power of monoideism (resulting from concentrated attention to the operator's suggestions) to induce hypnotic trance without the help of such techniques as visual fixation. He showed that the operator's suggestions and the S.'s expectations both exerted a profound effect on the phenomena elicited during hypnosis. Liébeault and Bernheim stressed the role of such purely psychological determinants of hypnosis to the virtual exclusion of all others: "If you use suggestibility to suggest suggestibility, the result is hypnotism." But some modern work supports Braid's original view that visual fixation can lead to increased suggestibility even in the absence of suggestion or expectation.

The development of hypnosis as a field of study in the context of medicine and psychology dates from Mesmer's claims of therapeutic effects resulting from a form of convulsive seizure (*crisis*) apparently induced by magnets or (later) by mesmeric passes, and from the observations and experiments of those who sought to prove or disprove these claims. The deliberate use of direct verbal suggestion played no part in the early practice of Mesmerism, or in Mesmer's own theories.

1. *Induction and termination.* Detailed descriptions of a wide variety of induction procedures are readily available (e.g., Weitzenhoffer, 1953). The essential characteristic of most is continuous repetitive verbal suggestions, directed by the operator to the S., and normally at first designed to produce relaxation, attention to the operator's voice, drowsiness and eye closure. Subsequently, some degree of response having been observed, the operator may invite the S. to try moving his limbs gently, while at the same time confidently asserting that he will experience great disinclination and difficulty in doing so. Suggestions that the limbs, fingers, and so on, will move in specified ways without the volition of the S., and that sensations such as warmth or numbness will be experienced, may follow. Most operators believe that a crucial stage in increasing depth of hypnosis is reached when *challenge suggestions* are made, e.g. by telling S. that he will be unable to open his eyes no matter how hard he tries, and that the more he tries to open them, the more tightly they will close. Beyond this stage, the hypnosis may be said to be firmly established, and responses to further suggestions may be almost immediate, without the need for repetition; but there is no clearly marked stage at which induction can be said to terminate and the elicitation of the phenomena of hypnosis to

begin. Induction is normally a process of eliciting a continuing series of responses which themselves also constitute the phenomena, to a succession of suggestions of steadily increasing "difficulty". In a proportion of Ss., suggestions that the lethargy of the early stages is to give place to an active state with eyes open, in which strong rapport and hypersuggestibility are nevertheless retained, may be successful (*somnambulism*, q.v.). Most operators combine visual and/or auditory fixation with verbal suggestions in the initial phases of induction, but this is not essential and it is not known how much it influences rate or depth of hypnosis. Termination usually occurs when the operator commands S. to return to his normal state, specifically countermands suggestions judged to merit this, and suggests that feelings of alertness and well-being will follow the "awakening". Some Ss. may complain of disorientation and feelings of unreality, and perhaps drowsiness, for a period in which it will be exceptionally easy to re-hypnotize them. Suggestions made during hypnosis, that it will be easy to induce hypnosis again, are normally so effective, that subsequent inductions may be made almost instantaneously on an agreed signal from the operator.

2. *Susceptibility*. Suggestions can be arranged approximately along a scale of "difficulty" in the sense that if a person responds to a suggestion with any particular difficulty he is likely to respond also to all easier suggestions, whereas if he fails to respond it is unlikely that he will respond to any that are more difficult. Lists of suggestions in order of difficulty are available for measuring the depth of hypnosis achieved with any particular S. Depth tends to increase throughout the duration of any single hypnosis, and with each subsequent hypnosis, up to a maximum which differs markedly from one S. to another. Most research suggests that this maximum is not usually greatly influenced by the personality or technique of a particular operator, or by a variety of environmental factors, but there is also clear evidence that it sometimes may be. Many investigators report that about ten per cent of European adults are insusceptible, and that somnambulism can be achieved with between twenty and thirty per cent. Above-average susceptibility is more frequently found in women, and is positively correlated with high intelligence, some kinds of waking suggestibility (e.g. Eysenck's primary and tertiary suggestibilities) but not others, a tendency to vivid day-dreams and states of self–absorption, a capacity for vivid imagery, a positive attitude to the idea of being hypnotized, and addiction to narcotic drugs. A variety of relationships between susceptibility and a number of personality characteristics (particularly extraversion) have been reported, but the results of one investigation have seldom been confirmed by another: therefore it has been suggested that relationships are different for high-drive and low-drive (or high anxious and low anxious) subjects, and for men and for women. In children, susceptibility increases with the mastery of language and at about eight to ten years reaches a maximum before declining somewhat to a stable value maintained throughout maturity. Some forms of psychoneurosis may be associated with above average susceptibility, and most psychotic illness with low susceptibility, but the naturally occurring differences between normal Ss. are much larger than those between averages for groups of neurotics and normals.

3. *Phenomena*. A distinction can in principle be made between phenomena resulting from induction of itself, and those depending on specific suggestions to the hypnotized S. There is, however, ample evidence that the expectations of the S. and unintended indirect suggestions from the operator profoundly influence response to induction, so that the intrinsic characteristics of the state are difficult to elucidate. Orne has referred to the *demand characteristics* of the hypnotic situation, being the totality of the intended and unintended cues which influence the S.'s responses. He believes that the essential

characteristics of hypnosis reside in the experience of the S., rather than in his directly observable responses, and that they relate to the distortions of normal logic and normal perceptual organization which have to take place before the operator's suggestions can be accepted.

Success in demonstrating phenomena resulting from specific suggestions varies markedly from one S. to another. Among the well attested phenomena which have survived careful experimental investigation are: *responses of voluntary musculature*, inception and inhibition of contraction; paralysis resulting from simultaneous activation of opposing muscle pairs; increased tolerance of fatigue and discomfort arising from muscular activity, and thus sometimes apparently increased strength (e.g. grip) and/or work capacity; improved muscular control in relatively simple motor skills, but probably not in more complex ones; *physiological phenomena*, increased metabolic rate in relaxed S. during suggestions that muscular work was being undertaken; inhibition of hunger contractions and increased gastric acidity following suggestions that food was being eaten; changes in pepsin, trypsin, lipase and maltose production appropriate to suggested ingestion of protein, fat and carbohydrate respectively; *hallucination of sense*, absence of startle reflex and psychogalvanic reflex (PGR) on exposure to sudden loud noises or flashes following suggested deafness or blindness; appropriate changes in response to Ishihara test cards following suggestions of color-blindness; abolition of normal reactions (including PGR) to painful stimuli (including surgical operations) following suggested anesthesia or analgesia, and interruption of withdrawal reflex at level of first spinal synapse on application of noxious stimulus to hypnotically anesthetized skin; appearance of nystagmus following suggested hallucinations of rotation in a centrifuge.

4. *Memory*. Appropriate specific suggestions can often produce a post-hypnotic amnesia for material learned, or events experienced at any time before or during the hypnosis; and some degree of amnesia for the events of the hypnosis may also arise spontaneously. In so far as conditioned reflexes constitute a form of memory, it should be noted that they seem not to be abolished by direct suggestions, although the conditioned response may fail to appear after suggestions that the conditioned stimulus cannot be perceived. Hypnotic hypermnesia may involve (*a*) enhanced capacity to recall previous experiences (particularly those with strong emotional content) extending to complete recovery of repressed traumatic memories, or (*b*) improved recall of learned material, but probably only if it is meaningful, e.g. a poem or logical argument rather than an arbitrary list of words.

5. *Revivification* seems to involve the partial re-establishing of the complete psycho-physiological state existing at some time in the Subject's past. Thus in *age regression* the S. may be told that he is again an infant and may then spontaneously exhibit neo-natal reflexes such as reversed Babinski, defecation when startled, together with appropriate alterations in peripheral chronaxie; however, many responses to suggested hypermnesia and revivification are no more than plausible dramatizations of fantasy; *personality alterations*, simple changes in mood and emotions are readily induced but are often difficult to sustain post-hypnotically. Habit changes (e.g. smoking) are often short-lived but may be extended by frequent hypnosis (e.g. daily) over prolonged periods. There are reliable reports of successful experiments in the development of multiple personalities. *Organic changes* are particularly difficult to explain, but there is fair evidence for the occasional production by specific hypnotic suggestion of a variety of allergic and psychosomatic skin changes, and of skin blisters in Ss. of hysteric personality. There are also reports of such phenomena during or following abreaction, under both hypnosis and drugs. Some investigators believe that stigmata may also be produced.

6. *Hypnotherapy* is a term used rather loosely to denote several different therapeutic applications, e.g. (*a*) prolonged hypnotic "sleep" used sometimes for gastric and duodenal ulcers, hypertension, cardiac disease, and other conditions where prolonged periods free from stress might be beneficial; (*b*) *hypnoanalysis*, where classical psychoanalytic techniques are modified and shortened by using hypnosis to facilitate the emergence of memories and associations which are being repressed; (*c*) the production of cathartic abreactions, usually during revivification, as part of the treatment of post-traumatic neuroses in an attempt to relieve conversion and other symptoms such as paralysis; (*d*) direct suggestions oriented toward the relief of specified physical or mental symptoms without attempting to influence any possible underlying causes. Among the most frequently used applications, this is also the most controversial, as many psychiatrists claim that symptoms which can be removed by suggestion serve unconscious needs and help preserve the patients' psychological equilibrium. If removed without regard to etiology, substitute symptoms may soon be generated or, if not, the stability of the personality may be threatened. An influential body of psychiatric opinion, however, regards symptom removal as beneficial. Among conditions treated with apparent success have been addictions, asthma, excessive appetite, eczema, irritable bladder, stress incontinence, homosexuality, impotence, menstrual disturbances, vaginismus, headaches, stammering, warts, phobias, and conversion neuroses. There has been little success with psychosis. In Mason's celebrated case of congenital ichtysosiform erythrodermia of Broq, the photographic and clinical evidence showed that skin characteristics improved only in the limb to which the hypnotic suggestions were specifically directed.

7. *Other medical and dental applications.* The most common is probably the production of analgesia and relaxation during childbirth; the duration of labor may be reduced when this is done. Some practitioners, particularly in dentistry, use hypnosis for the alleviation of anxiety before and during treatment, and for the production of analgesia or anesthesia where using chemical agents would be difficult, inconvenient or dangerous. With some patients suffering intractable pain (e.g. in terminal cancer) hypnosis affords substantial alleviation without the side effects of chemical agents.

8. *Theories.* It is tempting to impose a classification of theories of hypnosis into two types—(*a*) those which explain the phenomena as a consequence of a special state of the central nervous system (or more generally, of the subject's condition of neuropsychological organization) usually generated by the induction, and (*b*) those which explain them as examples of the organism's normal functioning under unusual conditions of motivation, attention, expectation, and attitude, these last being influenced by the induction but by no means essentially dependent on it.

Theories of the first kind include the long established explanations of hypnosis as a form of sleep. However, in respect of a variety of measures of physiological indices such as reflexes, blood-pressure, electrical activity of the brain, oxygen consumption, etc., hypnosis has been shown to resemble wakefulness far more than sleep. There is however some evidence, particularly from electro-encephalographic studies, that it may be a specialized form of very light sleep, clearly distinguishable from both wakefulness and deep sleep. From his work on conditioned reflexes, Pavlov explained hypnosis as a state of generalized cortical inhibition within which the existence of islands of continuing excitation makes it possible to evoke responses whose bizarre characteristics result from the absence of control and modification by the cortex as a whole. Rather more vague theories speak of an inhibition of activity in the white matter of the cerebrum (Bennett), an inhibition of ganglionic cells, and a state of anemia of the frontal lobes (Völgyesi).

Janet viewed hypnosis as a state of simple or multiple dissociation in which the stream of consciousness splits into components functioning relatively independently of one another. It is tempting to see this as the psychological analogue of Pavlov's physiological explanations.

Theories of the second kind include the formulations of Bernheim and Liébeault, who saw the phenomena as special examples of waking suggestibility, produced by suggestion. Such formulations indicate the need for a theory of suggestion rather than, or as well as, of hypnosis. It is known that if the normal waking S. just thinks about certain forms of muscular activity, including speech, then very attenuated nervous impulses, appropriate to the production of that activity, are automatically generated. Such *ideomotor action* is held by some to be a sufficient basis for a theory of motor suggestibility, but it is obviously insufficient to explain the whole range of hypnotic phenomena. Conditioned reflex theories assert that the links between words and the subject's responses in hypnosis are of the same kind, and obey the same law, as those between the conditioned stimulus and the conditioned response in Pavlovian reflexology. Other theories stress the relational aspects of hypnosis. Ferenczi viewed the phenomena as resulting from a psychological regression to the infantile state of dependence on and conflict with the parents, while Freud emphasized the importance of submission, and spoke of the hypnotic relationship as the devotion of someone in love to an unlimited degree, but with sexual satisfaction excluded. More recently, Sarbin has suggested that hypnosis is a highly motivated form of role-playing. The steadily increasing evidence that most if not all kinds of hypnotic phenomena can also be demonstrated with Ss. who have not undergone induction, emphasizes the importance of theories of this kind, though not necessarily of these particular theories.

While all the formulations direct attention to interesting analogies which might help in the generation of hypotheses, none really merits the status of a theory or seems substantially explanatory or predictive. The hypnotized S. functions in modes at least as complex as does the waking S., and it is doubtful if an all-embracing "theory of hypnosis" is possible. When more is known about the determinants of normal waking activity, it should be possible to establish how these are modified in hypnosis, and in particular whether there is a specific "hypnotic state".

Bibliography: Bernheim, H.: Hypnosis and suggestion in psychotherapy. New York, 1964. **Braid, J.:** Neurypnology or the rationale of nervous sleep considered in relation with animal magnetism. London, 1843. **Chertok, M. D.:** Hypnosis. London & Edinburgh, 1966. **Ferenczi, S.:** Introjection and transference. First contributions to psychoanalysis, 1952, 39–93. **Freud, S.:** Introductory lectures on psycho-analysis. London, 1922. **Furneaux, W. D.:** The prediction of susceptibility to hypnosis. J. Pers., 1946, *14*, 281–94. **Liébeault, A.:** Du sommeil et des états analogues, etc. Paris, 1866. **Puységur, A. M. de:** Mémoires pour servir à l'histoire et à l'établissement du magnétisme animal. London, 1785. **Sarbin, T. R.:** Mental age changes in experimental regression. J. Pers., 1950, *19*, 221. **Völgyesi, F. A.:** Hypnotherapie und psychosomatische Probleme. Stuttgart, 1950. **Id.:** Schutz-, Hypnose-, Schlaf-Hemmungen und die zunehmenden Perspektiven der aktiven Psychotherapie. In: **E. Speer** (Ed.): Die Vorträge der 2. Lindauer Psychotherapiewoche 1951. Stuttgart, 1952, 210–6. **Weitzenhoffer, A.:** Hypnotism, an objective study in suggestibility. New York, 1953. For further literature, see **Stokvis, B.:** Hypnose. In: **V. E. Frankl** *et al.* (Eds.): Handbuch der Neurosenlehre und Psychotherapie. Munich & Berlin, 1959, 71–122.

W. D. Furneaux

Hypnosis research, experimental. The experimental study of hypnosis promises not only to explain a phenomenon which is interesting in itself, but also to give new insight into hitherto unsolved general psychological problems, since hypnosis allows experimental access to human experience and behavior at different levels of consciousness (see Ullmann *et al.*, 1968; Ullmann, 1971). The progress obtainable through research into hypnosis extends to such general psychological themes as cognition, perception, emotion, motivation, interpersonal relations (Barber, 1969; Orne, 1970, etc.), personality and social adaptability (McGuire, 1968), pain (Hilgard, 1967) and placebo effect (McGlashan *et al.*, 1967), and leads into central problems of psycholinguistics (q.v.) (Sarbin & Coe, 1971).

Experiments conducted by Orne (1959, 1962) have not only given useful information on problems of hypnosis as such, but have demonstrated the general influence of the experimental situation on the testee; a distinction must be made between general behavior and the specific behavior studied in a given experiment. The methodological developments of modern hypnosis research therefore go beyond the narrower subject of study (Gordon, 1967). This also applies to study of the problem of hypnotic trance. The conflicting interpretations of altered states of awareness as legitimate or impermissible constructs express the basic scientific positions of contemporary psychology (Barber, 1969, 1970; Hilgard, 1969, 1970; Sarbin, 1968; Spanos & Chaves, 1970; H. Thomae, 1962; Ullmann & Ullmann, 1966) and form the bases of paradigms of hypnosis experiments.

Sarbin and co-workers have tried to explain the phenomenon of hypnosis exclusively with the aid of social and psychological theorems; hypnotic behavior is considered in the context of a psychology of communicative influences (Sarbin & Coe, 1971), and examined empirically. In Sarbin's opinion, the experience of a trance state is not necessarily based on an objective equivalent as the cause of hypnotic phenomena. Barber adopts a similar approach; in his opinion there is no special hypnotic state of consciousness; that would be a superfluous construct which would not help one to arrive at a more comprehensive appraisal of the problem. Efforts to analyze hypnotic behavior (dependent variables), and the objective parameters which condition such behavior (independent variables), as well as the laws governing relationships between these two sets of variables in quantitative terms, are characteristic of the procedure adopted. The forms of hypnotic behavior which are to be explained, such as (*a*) behavior in response to direct suggestions, e.g. hallucinations, analgesia, amnesia, etc., (*b*) the verbal statements of the testee, and (*c*) symptoms resembling a state of trance (lack of spontaneity, retarded motor behavior), are analyzed quantitatively with the help of a standardized scale (BSS: Barber, 1965). As regards the antecedents which play a significant part in the occurrence of hypnotic behavior, Barber and co-workers have identified a number of variables which are classified as (*a*) instruction-suggestion variable, (*b*) subject variable, (*c*) hypnotizer variable, and (*d*) relationship variable (Barber, 1969). It has frequently been found that individual phenomena which occur in hypnosis can be brought about even without hypnotic induction. Barber views this result as supporting his rejection of a special hypnotic state of trance.

According to Hilgard (1965, 1969, 1970), hypnotic phenomena can in part be considered in a different light. From his standpoint of modern functionalism, subjective conditions are a legitimate object of scientific study. Referring to sleep research (see *Sleep*), Hilgard considers it desirable to distinguish between different states of consciousness. He considers that objective indicators should exist for the state of hypnosis as they do for the sleeping state. Apart from trance problems, Hilgard and co-workers have not only studied the use of hypnosis to lessen pain (Hilgard, 1967), but have developed their own scales to examine hypnotic suggestibility as an individual trait, especially from the genetic angle. In Hilgard's opinion, this characteristic can be modified by a series of variables, e.g. by expectancy attitudes of the test subject, or by adjusting the test suggestion (Barber, 1969), but results obtained so far show that this feature is relatively stable in a substantial number of cases. Like Hilgard, P. London (1970) considers the persistent proportion of individual differences in hypnotic performance to be important and attempts—as a basis for a theory of hypnosis—to find appropriate correlates. London considers that there is an empirical basis for the relationship with motivation and EEG (q.v.) patterns. Hilgard believes that the justification for abandoning the normal paradigm and examining a parameter considered in it as a dependent variable, i.e. hypnotic suggestibility, as an independent variable, lies in the additional information likely to be obtained, which can help to define important parameters in more detail.

To sum up, it can be stated that modern experimental hypnosis research is characterized by a high level of experimental plans and techniques. Some representatives of different theoretical schools have tried to determine the validity of their methods in a logical manner; it seems that the validity of the different individual positions will be clarified in the next phase of experimental activity. After the identification of several significant variables and analyzing the relationship between a number of such variables, hypnosis appears as an extremely interesting phenomenon in the broader context of general psychological studies.

Bibliography: Barber, T. X.: Hypnosis: a scientific approach. New York, 1969. **Id.:** LSD, marihuana, yoga and hypnosis. Chicago, 1970. **Gordon, J. E.** (Ed.): Handbook of clinical and experimental hypnosis. New York, 1967. **Hilgard, E. R.:** Hypnotic susceptibility. New York, 1965. **Id.:** Altered states of awareness. J. nerv. ment. Dis., 1969, *149*, 68–79. **Orne, M. T.:** On the social psychology of the psychological experiment: with particular reference to demand characteristics and their implications. Amer. Psychol., 1962, *17*, 776–83. **Sarbin, T. R. & Coe, W. C.:** Hypnotism: a social-psychological analysis. New York, 1971. **Spanos, N. S. & Chaves, J. F.:** Hypnosis research: a methodological critique of experiments generated by two alternative paradigms. Amer. J. Clin. Hypn., 1970, *13*, 108–27. **Thomae, H.:** Das Bewusstseinsproblem in der modernen Psychologie. Der Nervenarzt, 1962, *33*, 447–83. **Ullmann, J. F., Ullmann, I. M. & Klapp, W. H.:** Perspektiven psychologisch-experimenteller Hypnoseforschung bis zum Einsetzen grundsätzlicher methodischer Kritik. Arch. Ges. Psychol., 1968, *120*, 247–300. **Ullmann, J. F.** (Ed.) (with **Ullmann, I. M. & Klapp, W. H.:** Hypnose und Suggestibilität, Vol. 1: Empirische Grundlagen. Berne & Stuttgart, 1971/72; Vol. 2: Theoretische Modelle und Konzepte (in preparation).

J. F. Ullmann, I. M. Ullmann & W. H. Klapp

Hypnotics. Natural or synthetic substances which lead directly to a condition similar to sleep or facilitate its occurrence. Desirable properties: generation of a state which resembles natural sleep as closely as possible without secondary and aftereffects (hangover); no cumulative effect, habituation, or development of dependence; large therapeutic range to prevent serious risk in the event of an overdose. The hypnotics include various groups of chemical substances (some of which are no longer in use today) such as the alcohols and aldehydes (ethyl alcohol, chloralhydrate, paraldehyde), sulfones (sulfonal, methylsulfonal), urethanes (ethylurethane, ethinamate), monoureides (Bromisoval, Carbamal), cycloureides (barbiturates) and piperidine derivatives (gluthethimide, thalidomide). It is difficult to draw a clear distinction between the hypnotics and the tranquilizers (q.v.) and narcotics (q.v.). The opinion that there are only quantitative differences (Irwin, 1968) contrasts with the assertion of qualitative differences of effect (Berger). Munoz distinguishes among psychopharmaceutical drugs promoting sleep, one group with euhypnic (hypnogenic) effects, and another with hypnotic (compulsive) action. He assumes that the transition from the euhypnics to the tranquilizers, and that from the hypnotics to narcotics, are fluid. While the euhypnics facilitate sleep by anxiolytic means, the hypnotics progressively—depending on the dose—influence consciousness by general, central inhibition (primarily of the *formatio reticularis*) with a relatively fixed latency period; they lead to sedation with impaired performance, confusion, sleep, narcosis. They have a clear influence on the vegetative functions (pulse, blood pressure, temperature, respiration) and frequently lead to tolerance (also cross-tolerance), and dependence with withdrawal symptoms. The extent of a "hangover" caused by a substance (heaviness in the limbs, reduced performance) is largely dependent on the duration of action and the concentration of the substance which conditions the hypnogenic and hypnotic effect. The absence of a feeling of relaxation is accompanied by reduced body movements in sleep. In doses insufficient to induce sleep, the hypnotics are thought to bring about reversible personality changes in the sense of increasing extraversion (H. J. Eysenck). They reduce performance in many tests (Kornetsky *et al.*, 1957). However these effects on performance are difficult to demonstrate because of compensatory counter-regulation. Among the other secondary effects, the alcohol-potentiating effect and influence on driving capacity have been studied in detail.

Bibliography: Holm, E.: Der pharmakologisch induzierte Schlaf. In: **Baust, W.** (Ed.): Ermüdung, Schlaf und Traum. Stuttgart, 1970. **Irwin, S.:** Antineurotics: practical pharmacology of the sedative-hypnotics and minor tranquilizers. In: **Efron, D. H.** (Ed.): Psychopharmacology 1957–1967. Washington, 1968. **Kornetsky, C., Humphries, O. & Evarts, E. V.:** Comparison of psychological effects of certain centrally acting drugs in man. A. M. A. Arch. Neurol. Psychiat., 1957, *77*, 318–24. **Maynert, E. W.:** Sedatives and hypnotics. In: **Di Palma, J. R.:** Drill's pharmacology in medicine. New York, 1965, 169–209. **Othmer, E.:** Persönlichkeit und Schlafverhalten. Meisenheim, 1965. *E.L.*

Hypnotism. See *Hypnosis.*

Hypobulic mechanisms. Automatic, i.e. unintentional, reflex and standardized forms of movement. They occur when the higher mental (volitional) functions are disturbed, and earlier, lower psychomotor functions come to the surface and take control (rhythmic movements, violent uncontrolled movements, hysterical stupor and attacks, catalepsy, motor negativism). *W.K.*

Hypochondria. It has sometimes been suggested that hypochondria in men corresponds to hysteria (q.v.) in women. Nowadays the term is used simply to denote a syndrome encountered primarily in states of anxiety (q.v.) and depression (q.v.). The subject feels pains not only in his stomach, as the etymology of the word suggests, but in his whole body. In fact the "corporality", the "animate" body, is affected in its entirety, and perception continuously manifests unpleasant sensations, so that the patient suffers greatly. The fear and depression at the root of every hypochondriac condition have endogenous rather than reactive origins. *J.L.I.*

Hypoesthesia. Diminished cutaneous sensitivity due to peripheral or central changes. See *Hypalgesia.* *M.S.*

Hypofunction(ing). The underfunctioning of organs or parts of the body. The term is generally used in connection with the endocrine glands. Depending on the organ affected, a distinction is made between pituitary dwarfism with normal intelligence, cretinism (q.v.) caused by a thyroid condition, dwarfism accompanied by feeblemindedness, Addison's disease in the event of an adrenalin deficiency indicating underfunctioning of the adrenal medulla, and diabetes mellitus in the event of an insulin deficiency indicating underfunctioning of the pancreas, or eunuchoidism (q.v.). *E.D.*

Hypokinesis. Impaired movement of the skeletal muscular system, which occurs locally in paralysis but generally as a systemic disorder, e.g. in *paralytis agitans*, accompanied by a "mask face", and involuntary movements. *E.D.*

Hypomania. A lesser degree of *mania* (q.v.) as part of a manic depressive psychosis. It may precede or follow mania or it may constitute an episode of the illness. Hypomanic patients may be able to function for some time in some or all of their usual social activities and in fact may be very productive. Eventually, grandiose or excessive actions or decisions lead to social complications. Like mania, it has a descriptive use and overlaps with *hyperthymia* (q.v.). *B.B.*

Hypomanic type. See *Diathetic proportion.*

Hypomnesia. Weak memory: a typical symptom of organic psychoses (q.v.) and senile degeneration of the intelligence. Initially, it affects events from the recent past rather than, e.g., memories of youth ("the new dies before the old"). *W.Sc.*

Hypophysis (syn. *Glandula pituitaria; Pituitary gland*). A structure with a diameter of about 1.5 cm located in the *sella turcica* at the base of the brain. As one of the most important endocrine glands it consists of the anterior lobe (adenohypophysis), central lobe (*pars intermedia*), posterior lobe (neurohypophysis) and the *infundibulum* as a connection with the brain. The adenohypophysis originates in the ectodermal vault of the pharynx; histologically it consists of typical glandular tissue and forms several hormones (q.v.) which regulate the function of the other glands. These hormones include: growth hormone (see *Acromegaly*); gonadotropic hormones (q.v.), which influence the male and female genital glands; thyrotropic and parathyrotropic hormones, which act on the thyroid and accessory thyroid glands; corticotropic hormone, which promotes the secretion of cortisone in the adrenal medulla; the lactation hormone prolactin, and the pancreotropic hormone which influences Langerhan's cells in the pancreas. The central lobe originates in the base of the third ventricle, and consists of brain tissue (neuroglia); it forms oxytocin, which causes the uterus to contract, as well as vasopressin, which is mainly responsible for regulating the reabsorption of water in the kidney (in *tubulus contortus* II). The absence of vasopressin is responsible for diabetes insipidus; in this condition the subject may produce up to twenty liters of urine a day. *E.D.*

Hypoplasia. In general, innate or hereditary underdevelopment of an organ. It almost always leads to a reduction in, or failure of, the function of the part of the body affected. *E.D.*

Hypostasis. A process of the intellect by which an abstraction is endowed with an independent and quasi-material existence. The concept of hypostasis was developed in detail in the philosophy of Plotinus, who described the three absolute values: goodness (the infinite), intelligence, and the soul. In psychology, it is often difficult not to ascribe a material reality to the objects, terms and functions referred to (e.g. the will, ego, or superego). *M.R.*

Hypotaxia. Defective coordination of voluntary movements (see *Ataxia*). In hypnosis (q.v.), a medium state in which cataleptic rigidity and automatism are present without subsequent amnesia (q.v.). *W.Sc.*

Hypothalamus. The section of the brain belonging to the diencephalon, and situated below the thalamus, whose function consists primarily in the coordination of vegetative body functions, such as hormone functions, respiration, circulation, heat and water regulation. Close links therefore exist between the hypothalamus and the hypophysis (q.v.) and deeper parts of the brain. *E.D.*

Hypothesis. In general, a hypothesis is a statement which is assumed to be correct and is used as the basis for a discursive structure.

The word is used with the following three specific meanings: (*a*) a hypothesis is a means for logical classification of a situation: specific statements are used as the initial principles for a deductive theory (hypothetico-deductive theories); (*b*) a hypothesis is a plausible explanation preceding stringent (experimental) verification of an assumption; (*c*) a hypothesis is a heuristic means of discovering the truth. In formal systems, the terms hypothesis, axiom (q.v.) and postulate (q.v.) are equivalent. *M.J.B.*

Hypothesis testing. Statistical hypotheses refer to parameters of population distributions. By referring back to specific assumptions (degree of chance in selecting samples, distribution of random error), the chance distribution of sample values is determined numerically. See *Construct validity; Test theory.* *W.H.B.*

Hypothetical construct. A term for an assumption, i.e. of a phenomenon or process as existent even when not observable, or not observable as assumed. Hypothetical constructs have a heuristic value, i.e. they allow investigations to be made which would otherwise be virtually impossible. See *Construct validity; Test theory.* *R.Hä.*

Hypotonia. Excessively low blood pressure as a sign of defective regulation in the vegetatively labile, or in conditions of cardiac weakness. Hypotonia is reflected in weakness, fatigue and fainting. Ant. *Hypertonia.* *E.D.*

Hypotrophy. Contraction of organs as a result of inactivity. Occurs in the skeletal muscle, capsular ligaments and bones, when the limbs concerned are prevented from moving; also observed in the hearts of those who do not take enough exercise. Hypotrophy mainly affects all organs which are kept motionless, but is fully reversible, unlike hypoplasia (q.v.). *E.D.*

Hysteria. A psychogenic disorder with mental and/or physical symptoms: a reaction to experiences with a strong emotional content which are not processed normally because of an innate or acquired disposition. The following—not necessarily in conjunction—are symptoms of hysteria: semi-consciousness, hallucinations, amnesia, emotional outbursts of weeping or shouting (always in the presence of other persons), pseudo-dementia, disturbances of the senses (e.g. blindness or deafness, anesthesia), paralysis, tremor, tics and motor coordination defects (inability to stand or walk, etc.). The boundary between hysteria and simulated hysteria is often fluid. Treatment is possible by environmental therapy or psychotherapy. See *Defense; Psychopathology; Neurosis; Psychoses, functional.*

Bibliography: Kretschmer, E.: Hysteria, reflex and instinct. London, 1961. *M.A.*

Hysterical type. A term often used to denote the opposite of the dysthymic type (q.v.): extraverted; stresses are processed rapidly, although with exaggerated emphasis, as a violent reaction. This type is described by Kretschmer: impressionable with low active retentive capacity for emotions, exaggerated reaction to stress, rapid elimination of stimuli, demonstrative façade.

Bibliography: Kretschmer, E.: Hysteria, reflex and instinct. London, 1961. *W.K.*

Hysteromania. 1. State of excessive activity in patients suffering from hysteria (q.v.). **2.** An archaic synonym for *nymphomania,* which is an excessive desire in women for sexual intercourse. *P.Le.*

I

IA. Abb. for *Intelligence age* (q.v.).

Ich (Ger.). See *Ego*.

ICSH (*Interstitial cell stimulating hormone*). A gonadotropic hormone (q.v.) formed in the anterior pituitary (syn. LH, q.v., in women), which induces or maintains the formation of hormones in the male/female sex glands. In man: in the testicles: (*a*) maintenance of interstitial cells and their production of androgens (q.v.); (*b*) interaction with gonadotropic hormone FSH in spermatogenesis. In woman: (*a*) together with gonadotropic hormone FSH, induces formation of estrogens (q.v.) in the ovum, which in their turn stimulate LH secretion; (*b*) induces ovulation and the onset of the second phase in the female cycle; (*c*) conversion of the former ovum into *corpus luteum*, which produces estrogens and progesterone (q.v.) under the influence of LH and LTH (q.v.).

Bibliography: Fridhandler, L. & Pincus, G.: Pharmacology of reproduction and fertility. Ann. Rev. Pharmacol., 1964, *4*, 177. **Friesen, H. & Astwood, E.:** Hormones of the anterior pituitary body. New Eng. J. Med., 1965, *272*, 1216. **Voigt, K.-D. & Schmidt, H.:** Sexualhormone. Hamburg, *1968*. *H.M.*

Id (Ger. *Es*). A number of psychological theories assume that the whole personality contains a separate, relatively independent area in addition to the conscious "personality". This area is thought to comprise the unconscious "drives" ("impulses", "instincts") and emotions. In the strata theory (q.v.) of personality, the conscious area rests on this unconscious layer. It is sometimes suggested that ontogenetically and phylogenetically ordered structures are involved. By a vague analogy with the findings of brain physiology, we find references to "upper" and "lower" areas, the midbrain representing the second part of the personality and the cerebrum the first. F. Kraus spoke in this context of a "depth person", and based his conclusion on medico-physiological considerations. Nietzsche referred to this dark, mysterious area of the personality as the "id" (though, of course, he used the term "*Es*", properly translated as "it"; "id", however, has come to be the accepted English term). Using the layer theory of the personality, Rothacker took over Nietzsche's term and spoke of the "id" as the unconscious depth, or fundamental ground, of the person. Similarly, P. Lersch makes a distinction between an endothymic infrastructure and a noetic superstructure.

The concept of the "id" acquired its greatest importance in the context of Freud's depth-psychological interpretation of the personality (see *Depth psychology*). Freud referred to G. Groddeck's theories in using the notion of the "id". Freud developed his concept of the tripartite division of the personality into the *id*, *ego* (q.v.) and *superego* (q.v.) in *The Ego and the Id*, and later in *New Introductory Lectures on Psycho-Analysis*. The structural-topological aspect was added to the dynamic concepts of the "conscious" and "unconscious". According to Rapaport, the id, ego and superego trichotomy is the most adequate structural theory of the personality in depth psychology, and therefore of importance for psychoanalytic theory. Rapaport does not, however, view it as an independent model; for him it is merely an alternative formulation of earlier theoretical concepts of Freud regarding the nature of the conscious and the unconscious.

All processes in the id are said to be unconscious. On the other hand, the ego is not claimed to be the locus of consciousness. According to the principles of psychoanalysis, the ego also contains unconscious elements. The id is the center of the passions, extends far into the somatic, and may threaten the ego in the same way as the outside world. The ego normally controls access to motility, but frequently has to implement impulses from the id. Freud describes the relationship between the ego and the id by speaking of the ego as a rider and the id as a horse: "Just as a rider, if he does not wish to leave his mount, often has no option but to give it free rein, so the ego converts the will of the id into action as though it were itself responsible for that action." (*Werke*, Vol. 13, p. 253.) Ontogenetically, the id is the older structure; the ego arises directly from the id. The superego as the "heir of the Oedipus complex" (q.v.) also derives from the id. The id contains repressed ideas (images) and inherited "drives". Freud stresses that his concept of the id has nothing in common with C. G. Jung's "collective unconscious" (q.v.). For Freud, the ego is above all the locus of the eros and the death instinct (q.v.). The boundaries between the id and ego are fluid, and the aim of psychoanalysis is to strengthen the ego and thus to make it able to resist the dangers of the surrounding world, the punitive striving of the superego, and the temptations of the id. Psychoanalytical therapy is said to remove some of the energy (libido) from the id, by means of interpretation, "working through" and resistance analysis. Freud compares this work with the reclamation of the Zuidersee: "The ego must replace the id". (*Werke*, Vol. 15, p. 86.)

The id is one of the most often cited hypothetical constructs of psychoanalysis. It lacks precise definition, is not related to any specific behavior, and is said to be recognized only in the therapeutic process. It is, therefore, a hypothesis largely alien to the methods of modern non-psychoanalytical psychology; its theoretical value for any scientific approach is, to say the least, questionable. The use made of the "id" as a psychoanalytic concept may best be illustrated by citing Freud: "The id . . . has no means of demonstrating love or hatred to the ego. It cannot say what it wants; it has not created a uniform will. Eros and the death instinct are at odds in it; we know the means used by one instinct to combat others. We might say that it is as if the id were ruled by the silent but powerful death instincts, which are at rest and try to still the troublemaker, eros, when it seeks to obey the pleasure principle; but even then we tend to underestimate the role of eros." (*Werke*, Vol. 15, p. 289.)

Bibliography: **Freud, S.:** Werke, Vols. 13, 15. London, 1940. **Id.:** New introductory lectures on psychoanalysis. London, 1933. **Id.:** The ego and the id. London, [2]1962. **Rapaport, D.:** The structure of psychoanalytic theory: a systematizing attempt. In: **Koch, S.** (Ed.): Psychology: a study of a science, Vol. 3. New York, Toronto & London, 1959.

G. Lischke

Idea. 1. Even in modern times there is an immense number of diverse uses of the term (see **2**, below). From the Cartesian viewpoint, an idea is an individual human mental concept; for Locke, an object of conscious thinking; for Berkeley, a sensory percept; and for Hume, an image of a sense impression. For Kant (very roughly summarized), however, an idea of reason is a concept which transcends all experience and cannot be represented sensuously. In general usage, an "idea" is usually that which is perceived mentally or intellectually, and not "by the senses". In any approximation to scientific psychology the term requires precise contextual definition. See *Logical reasoning; Mental imagery; Thinking.* *J.C.*

2. "Ideas" can be concepts, attitudes, intentions, notions, images or basic models. The idea is always a product of thinking (q.v.). In philosophical usage, a distinction may be made between three principal categories: (*a*) As a model or regulating principle, the idea denotes the universal or all-embracing: a degree of perfection in which things participate and which is a measure of their reality or cohesion; (*b*) as a concept or general idea, an idea denotes an abstract class determined by its elements and also by limiting conditions; this class can only be understood in terms of its logical significance; (*c*) as a phenomenon of intellectual activity, an idea is a product or content of an intellectual process, and may be an innate form devoid of content, or an impression received from the environment. *M.J.B.*

Ideal colors. An ideal color is one obtained through a reflecting surface with a remission curve or through a color filter with a transmission curve (see *Absorption*) having values of only 1 and 0 and at most two points of discontinuity (illumination: sunlight or standard light). Example of an ideal color: a color which has the full intensity of the spectrum by mixing all wavelengths between 490 nm and 520 nm. *A.H.*

Idealized image (syn. *Guiding fiction*). See *As if; Adler, A.*

Ideal type. A complex of characteristics posited as normative and intended to be generally binding, by which individual phenomena are classified, or from which they are derived: e.g. E. Spranger's "forms of life". In a wider sense, every natural complex arrived at through correlational statistics is an "ideal type" in that, as a conceptual construct, it serves as a yardstick for classifying individual phenomena. *W.K.*

Ideation. Idea formation; cognition; thinking. See *Concept; Inner speech; Mental imagery; Psycholinguistics; Thinking.*

Idée fixe (syn. *Fixed idea*). An idea, or a series of related ideas, which dominates the mental life of a person. Occurs in certain states such as obsessional neurosis. When it occurs in a more developed form in psychotic states it is known as *monomania* (q.v.) or paranoia. See *Schizophrenia.* *R.H.*

Identical direction, law of. The law of identical direction in binocular vision was formulated by E. Hering. When an object is fixated in the field of vision, the visual axes of the two eyes are aligned so that they intersect at the fixation point; they do not terminate there, but continue after intersection. If the fixation point is defined in an appropriate experimental arrangement—a red bar for the visual axis of the right eye and a blue bar for the axis of the left eye—the bars do not appear next to each other but are fused into a single image on an imaginary median line between the two eyes. The two bars are situated "in identical visual directions", and their images are therefore received at identical (retinal) points (q.v.). *R.R.*

Identical elements, theory of. A theory of the transfer of training which supposes that the learning of one task transfers to a second task to the extent that the new task contains elements identical with those of the original task. *C.D.F.*

Identical (retinal) points (syn. *Corresponding retinal points*). If the two foveae and equivalent quadrants of the retinas of both eyes are made to coincide, an inserted needle would pass through identical retinal points; non-identical retinal points of both eyes are known as *disparate* (retinal) points. An object point whose reflected rays fall on disparate retinal points produces a double image. If the retinal points involved in the disparate image are not too far apart, the two images are fused by central coordination into a single spatial impression (see *Fusion*). This results in a three-dimensional impression (see *Depth perception*). Good spatial vision is possible in the fovea (q.v.) with a disparation of 20′ (it increases from the fovea toward the periphery), but the impression of depth disappears with a 25′ disparation: double images are then seen as such. Under normal circumstances this is not realized, because the eye constantly adjusts its accommodation (q.v.) and convergence (q.v.). Only objects fixated by the eye are seen clearly and consciously. In addition, not all the points of the object can be reflected at identical points, since the visual axes of the two eyes are in an angular relation to one another; no double images are formed: instead a spatial impression of the object appears.

Depth perception is only possible with disparation in the horizontal axis of the eye. Disparation in the vertical axis of the eye leads to double images rather than perception in depth.

The points whose reflective rays contact identical points on the two retinas are situated on the horopter (q.v.). All points which do not lie on the horopter result in a disparate image. If the disparate images are displaced in the temporal direction (i.e. outward) on the retina (bitemporal horizontal disparation), the impression appears "closer" than the horopter; but if the displacement is in the nasal direction (i.e. inward; binasal horizontal disparation) the impression appears "more distant". The horopter is always the point of reference.

The spatial impression is dependent on the distance of the objects, i.e. on the angle between the visual axes of the two eyes (convergence). Depth perception therefore diminishes as range increases.

In many oblique positions, simple vision may exist—contrary to what might be expected. New identity relations may develop, so that the fovea of one eye is not identical with that of the other, but corresponds with a point situated in the vicinity of the fovea. However, simple vision is frequently simulated in a squint because the image of one eye is suppressed in perception. See *Amblyopia*.

R.R.

Identical twins (syn. *Monozygotic*, or *monovular*, or *monochorionic twins*). Twins that develop in one chorionic sac from one split fertilized ovum (zygote). See *Twin studies*.

Identification. 1. A postulated (internal) defense (q.v.) mechanism by which a motive deprivation or motive frustration not previously experienced in its present intensity is diminished by adopting (see *Introjection*) one or more motives of other persons. The assumed motives may be substantially similar to the previous motives. Often the process centers on the person in whom the motive deprivation or frustration originated (identification with the aggressor). The direct *subjective benefit* of identification is the feeling of being at least in part the obstructive or exemplary person. The purpose of identification is to reduce the state of anxiety (q.v.) and temporary regression caused by the motive deprivation or frustration, and ultimately to forgo the opportunity for instinctual satisfaction which has been withdrawn or is threatened with punishment. The complexity of identification varies widely as a function of the frustrated motives. It ranges from thumb-sucking as a substitute for the mother's breast (identification with the mother's wish to still the child), to identification of the young girl with her mother (e.g. by playing at cooking as a substitute for direct contact with the mother), identification of the boy with his polite and reserved father (as an answer to the failure of many of his attempts to establish contact with his mother), identification of a pupil with his schoolmaster or mistress, and identification of a great pianist's pupil, a professor's assistant, or a head of government who had an outstanding or popular predecessor with the individual model. Diagnosis of the defense mechanism of identification is therefore generally meaningless without additional information on the motives which are withdrawn or assumed. Short-term identification is also possible, e.g. with an athlete, a team, or a film star; this process may be controlled by earlier identifications but its long-term effects are frequently insignificant. In social psychology (see *Socialization*), *social learning* (as identification) is a research subject in its own right (A. Bandura, 1963). The transition from imitation to identification is not clear. Continuing imitation, in particular of forms of behavior based on longer established and more complex motives, becomes identification (Miller & Dollard, 1941). Earlier forms of identification determine later identification. The totality of identifications constitutes the superego (q.v.), which includes the more primitive environmental motives which arose as reward or punishment motives in answer to individual obedience or disobedience, and were taken over by the individual as his own motives. See *Conscience*.

Bibliography: Bandura, A. & Walters, R. A.: Social learning and personality development. New York, 1963. **Freud, A.:** The ego and the mechanisms of defence. London, 1937. **Freud, S.:** Introductory lectures on psychoanalysis. London, [2]1929. **Miller, N. E. & Dollard, J.:** Social learning and imitation. New Haven, 1941. **Toman, W.:** Motivation, Persönlichkeit, Umwelt. Göttingen, 1968. *W.T.*

2. Ach used the term "identification" for the process in which both retinal images are combined and the new phenomenon of depth perception is produced. In auditory perception the analogous result is directional discrimination. Ach also suggested that (in general) the fusion of two different psychic contents leads to a new content (production principle of identification).

Identification, social. A broad approximation of the action and thought of an individual to those of a model (e.g. father—son), frequently discussed in the context of imitation (q.v.); explained in terms of the greater attention given by the model individual. Bandura refers to a generalization of the cognitive aspects of imitation. See *Identification; Socialization.* *W.D.F.*

Ideology. 1. Any set of (e.g. political, religious or philosophical) beliefs. **2.** An ineffectual, moribund set of beliefs or program. **3.** A set of beliefs acquired (e.g. by indoctrination, q.v.) and held uncritically, to the exclusion of new (or contradictory) ideas.

Ideomotor idea (syn. *Ideomotor image*). An idea or image controlled emotionally or affectively which leads involuntarily to certain motor reactions. See *Ideomotor law.* *A.Th.*

Ideomotor law (syn. *Carpenter effect; Ideoreal law*). A phenomenon described by the English physiologist W. B. Carpenter in 1879: perceptual and imaginative contents, in particular those relating to perceived and/or imagined movements, may be accompanied by partial or complete involuntary drive impulses which correspond to the motor embodiment of those contents; i.e. ideas produce motor responses by innervation of muscle groups corresponding to those ideas. *H.H. & H.Ro.*

Ideomotor reflex. Haab's reflex (q.v.): the two pupils contract when a bright object is fixated in a dark room. The term *ideomotor* (= idea of movement) denotes all movements which are elicited involuntarily by emotionally colored ideas, especially in absentminded persons, who may, e.g., involuntarily imitate others. The physiological mechanism has not been explained. *K.H.P.*

Ideo-real law. See *Ideomotor law.*

Idiocy. In non-English-speaking Europe the term is still used for a serious form of mental deficiency which is either innate or acquired through brain damage in very early childhood (e.g. birth trauma, encephalitis), characterized by an almost complete condition of ineducability (no development of speech or techniques of defense against physical danger). According to the British Mental Deficiency Act (1927) idiots were defined as representing one grade of mental deficiency (see *Deficiency, mental*), i.e. those unable to guard themselves against common physical dangers. The term has not been used other than clinically since the British Mental Health Act (1959), when "idiocy" was subsumed under "severe subnormality". See *Imbecility; Mental defect.* *M.A.*

Idiographic. According to W. Windelband, the idiographic sciences are those which, unlike the nomothetic (q.v.) natural sciences, deal with unique events and conditions (historical sciences). The aim of idiographic personality (q.v.) research is to understand and describe as fully as possible the unique nature of an individual in the totality of his forms of expression and at the same time in the unity of his determining forces. *D.B.*

Idiosyncrasy. 1. Psychological: a reaction which deviates from the norm in the form of an intense dislike for or oversensitivity to specific persons, animals, things, dishes, odors, etc. **2.** Medical: an innate or sometimes acquired hypersensitivity to certain substances (e.g. proteins, etc.) (see *Allergy; Psychosomatics*). *F.C.S.*

IEM. See *Intromission-copulation-ejaculation mechanism.*

Illusion. An alteration of actuality in subjective perception: a mistaken perception of a given object. A distinction is made between illusions and hallucinations (q.v.), in which non-existent things are perceived. Illusions induced by social perception may facilitate orientation to specific requirements. Illusions occur frequently in general and specific social spheres. Psychotherapy (q.v.) may center on different combinations of illusions. See *Fantasy; Mental imagery; Schizophrenia.* *U.H.S.*

Illusions, acoustic, optical. In the case of sense perception, an illusion is a subjective distortion of the objective content of the sense data. The many optical and acoustic illusions are experienced by most people and are not a special feature of abnormal states. Piaget has divided illusions into two classes: those in which the subjective distortion increases with age and those in which it decreases. Examples of illusions: *Müller-Lyer illusion, Hering's illusion* (q.v.). See *Geometrical-optical illusions.* *C.D.F.*

Image. 1. A mental representation: i.e. one of the senses of "idea" (q.v.). **2.** Any representation, copy, likeness, imitation or similitude. **3.** A mental copy of a sensory quality or experience in the absence of any sensory stimulus. **4.** An attitude (q.v.) toward, e.g., a national type. See *Stereotype; Mental imagery.*

Image types (syn. *Ideational types; Idea types*). In Charcot's typology these are individuals whose mental imagery (q.v.) (or ideation) is oriented to a specific sensory modality. See *Fantasy*.

Bibliography: Kiefer, T.: Der visuelle Mensch. Munich & Basle, 1956. *W.K.*

Imagination is the ability to call to mind, or "picture forth", situations, processes, objects and individuals which are not present. It includes, according to Jung, images of elementary situations, processes, objects or persons which appear as "collective human experience", supposedly without specific human experience. "Creative imagination" is the artistic or scientific combination of such elements into novel unities: e.g. as works of art, philosophic systems, or scientific hypotheses and planned experimentation. See *Fantasy; Archetypes; Imago; Literature, psychology of.* *W.T.*

Imago ("image"). A wax portrait mask placed on a corpse displayed in the forum in ancient Rome. Freud used the term "imago" to denote the idealizing or de-idealizing distortion of personality which may occur in the course of transference (q.v.): the analyst, for example, may become a father-image. Jung used the term to denote the subsequently effective "image" of a reference person. A psychoanalytical journal took the name *Imago* (later *American Imago*) from C. Spitteler's novel of that title; it deals with literary, mythological and historical subjects from a psychoanalytical standpoint. *W.Sc.*

Imbecility. The British Mental Deficiency Act (1927) defined imbeciles as "persons in whose case there exists mental defectiveness which, although not amounting to idiocy, is yet so pronounced that they are incapable of managing themselves or their affairs or, in the case of children, of being taught to do so". The term is no longer in use and since the introduction of the British Mental Health Act (1959) has been replaced by the terms "subnormality" and "severe subnormality". *V.K.J.*

Imipramine (*Tofranil; G*22355). A dibenzazepine derivative: one of the group of tricyclic antidepressants. Imipramine was used as the first tricyclic antidepressant and is generally used as a comparison substance for the effectiveness of other antidepressants. In healthy persons there are subjective symptoms of sedation with therapeutic and relatively small individual doses of imipramine. Performance changes in the form of reduced visual motor ability appear when higher therapeutic doses are administered. According to Di Mascio *et al.* (1964; 1968) the mood of healthy, depressed persons is improved, but a contrary effect is evident in some depressed patients.

Bibliography: Bättig, K. & Fischer, H.: Die Wirkung von Pharmaka auf psychische Leistungsfähigkeit und Persönlichkeitsfaktoren. Schweiz. Z. für Psychol. u. ihre Anwendung, 1964, *23*, 26–38. **Di Mascio, A., Heninger, G. & Klerman, G.:** Psychopharmacology of imipramine and desipramine. A comparative study of their effects in normal males. Psychopharmacologia, 1964, *5*, 361–71. **Di Mascio, A., Meyer, R. E. & Stifer, L.:** Effects of imipramine on individuals varying in levels of depression. Amer. J. Psychiat., 1968, *124*, 55–8. **Ideström, C.-M. & Cadenius, B.:** Imipramine–Desmethylimipramine. A pharmacological study of human beings. Psychopharmacologia, 1964, *5*, 431–39. *P.D.*

Imitation. 1. Experiments in animals, children and adults have shown that the observed behavior of a model may provoke more or less similar behavior in the observing subject (O), even when the latter did not show similar behavior patterns before (learning by imitation). The extent and nature of the imitation are dependent on features of the model, the traits and experience of the observer, and the observed reward or punishment for the model behavior ("representative reinforcement"). The acquisition of, e.g., aggressive behavior as well as standards and value scales is substantially influenced by imitation. See *Socialization; Aggression; Identification.*

2. Behavior is said to be imitative if (*a*) there is a similarity between the behavior of the model and of the imitator; and (*b*) the behavior of the model and not other stimuli is the determining factor in the behavior of the imitator. The instinct (q.v.) theory of imitation has been replaced since about 1920 by various conclusions of learning theory. Allport (1924), Piaget (1951), O. H. Mowrer (1960) emphasized the importance of associative and classical conditioning mechanisms, while N. E. Miller & J. Dollard (1941) as well as B. F. Skinner (1953) stressed instrumental mechanisms. For imitative learning, the contiguity of sensory events is essential (according to Bandura, 1968), and for imitative behavior the nature of the reinforcement. See *Conditioning, classical and operant; Imprinting; Learning.*

Bibliography: Bandura, A.: Social learning theory of identificatory processes. In: **Goslin, D. A.** (Ed.): Handbook of socialization theory and research. Chicago, 1968. **Ervin, S. M.:** Imitation and structural change in children's language. In: **Lenneberg, E. H.:** New directions in the study of language. Cambridge, Mass., 1966, 163–89. **Id. & Walters, R. H.:** Social learning and personality development. New York, 1968. **Flanders, J. P.:** A review of research on imitative behavior, Psychol. Bull, 1968, *69*, 316–37. **Foss, B. M.:** Imitation. In: **Foss, B. M.** (Ed.): Determinants of infant behavior, Vol. 3. London & New York, 1965.

D.B. & C.M.

Immediate memory (syn. *Short-term memory*). Momentary storage (duration not exceeding 30 sec. approximately) of information items and their reproduction, as compared with long-term storage (retentive or real memory). This is a genuine function of memory (q.v.). Immediate memory is very liable to disturbance; the matter is very frequently forgotten; the amount depends on the material and the particular sensory modality, and can be extended by verbal coding (Dornič, 1970). In consequence of the unusual conditions operating when the information items were acquired (e.g. a single presentation), immediate memory is treated in some research projects as a unique phenomenon, but is thought to be governed by the same processes as long-term memory (Postman, 1964). Clinical (retrograde amnesia, q.v.), neurophysiological (electric shock), cybernetic, and factor-analytical observations nevertheless suggest that an independent process (and system) is at work. Broadbent (1958) is of the opinion that the immediate memory acts as a selective filter and distributes information.

Bibliography: Broadbent, D. E.: Perception and communication. Oxford & New York, 1958. **Dornič, K.** (Ed.): Visuelles Wahrnehmen. Bratislava, 1970, 81–94. **Postman, L.:** Short-term memory and incidental learning. In: **Melton, A. W.** (Ed.): Categories of human learning. New York, 1964.

Immorality. 1. Dishonesty. **2.** Contrariety to that which a particular moral, religious, legal, political, or social system conceives as virtuous or binding behavior.

Imperceptible given. All those things which at the moment cannot be perceived by some persons and yet are experienced as being really present. For example, all the parts of a perceived object and not merely its visible aspect are experienced as being directly present. Completion phenomena, which have been closely studied by gestalt psychologists, represent an important aspect of the imperceptible given, which must be distinguished from what is only represented in the mind.

F.Ma.

Implosive therapy. A form of "learning therapy" developed by Stampfl (1968). Taking as his starting-points the two-factor theory (q.v.) of learning (q.v.) and the concept of secondary motivation (q.v.), Stampfl assumes that neurotic symptoms represent avoidance responses which are produced and maintained by a complex pattern of conditioned aversive stimuli. (See *Neurosis.*)

In contrast to other forms of therapy based

on learning theory (see *Behavior therapy*), implosive therapy makes use of suggestions from depth psychology (q.v.). Implosive theory does not set out to inhibit neurotic symptoms directly but endeavors to remove the symptoms by extinguishing the conditioned aversive stimuli which motivate the neurotic behavior. In order to do this, the maximum number of stimuli of the original conditioning, with the exception of the unconditioned aversive stimulus, are reproduced verbally or in some other form. On the principle of extinction generalization (see *Extinction; Generalization*), this diminishes the "aversiveness" if the conditioned stimuli are removed from those avoidance responses which constitute the neurotic behavior. Special attention is given to "concealed" stimuli, i.e. stimuli of which the patient cannot give an account (see *Unconscious*). Hence implosive therapy takes into account determinants of neurotic behavior neglected by other learning therapies. See *Aversion therapy*.

Bibliography: Stampfl, T. G. & Lewis, D. J.: Implosive therapy—a behavioral therapy? Behav. Res. Therapy, 1968, *6*, 31–6.

F.Ma.

Impotence. 1. Inability of the male to achieve or maintain sufficient penile erection to complete sexual intercourse. Often regarded as resulting from psychological factors, e.g. sex guilt, unfortunate early experiences, feelings of inadequacy, and so on. **2.** Inability of the male to produce offspring (*sterility*). **3.** A feeling of helplessness (inability to control events). *G.D.W.*

Impression. An overall picture of some object, say a landscape or a person, as the product of a relatively complete process of cognition or perception. In the psychology of expression (q.v.), an impression is constitutive in so far as there is no expression as such, but only an expression for someone who apprehends it as a (valid) impression. There are three main approaches:

1. *Phenography*. Study of the sensory channels by which the impression of someone's personal "thusness" is transmitted. The emphasis is on visual (see *Physiognomy; Pathognomy*) and auditory (phonognomy) access; less regard is paid to the tactile (manual pressure) or olfactory aspects of impression.

2. *Analysis of function and interpretation.* This approach deals with the question of how expressive phenomena are apperceived and interpreted. Social perception (q.v.) research is important in this regard (Graumann, 1955/56; Tajfel, 1969; Tagiuri, 1969). There are four main (in part socially conditioned) perceptive factors which go to form an impression: (*a*) *selectivity*, which, in addition to attitude (q.v.) and attention (q.v.), includes the concepts of sensitivization and perceptual defense (q.v.); (*b*) the *organizing act of perception*, underlying which are the gestalt tendencies of perceptual cognition; (*c*) *accentuation*, which modifies the impression by emphasizing a certain point of view; and (*d*) *fixation*, concentrating on points in the stimulus field selected by reason of attitude, prejudice, anxiety, etc. Research into these perceptive factors coincides in large measure with the actual-genetic aspect. From the ontogenetic angle, maturation and learning processes form part of the socio-cultural background (attitudes, stereotypes).

3. *Conditional analysis and interpretation.* This approach examines impressionability and the means by which human or animal expressions become impressions for the recipient. (*a*) The theory of association (q.v.) assumes that, when certain expressions are presented to the recipient, similar ideas (images) and emotions are (associatively) set in train; (*b*) the analogy (q.v.) theory maintains that the observer of an extraneous expression draws conclusions about it on the basis of his own behavior; (*c*) the theory of empathy (q.v.) (T. Lipps) assumes that an impression of another psyche comes about by means of "mimpathic" and "copathic" experience of others' expressions; (*d*) the

theory of rudiments—a version of "empathy"—is based on the assumption that sympathetic micro-movements (ideomotor law, q.v.) during the perception of an extraneous expression produce the elements of a corresponding inner state. Each of these theories is seriously inadequate. The problem of "impressionability" (understanding expression) is still unresolved. Interesting approaches to the phylogenetic aspect are to be found in ethology, which connects the "innate releasing mechanism" (q.v.) with the phylogenetic development of impressionability (Leyhausen, 1967). See *Emotion; Instinct*.

Bibliography: Ewert, O. M.: Zur Ontogenese des Ausdrucksverstehens. Handbuch d. Psychologie, Vol. 5. Göttingen, 1965, 289–308. **Graumann, C.-F.:** Social Perception. Z. exp. angew. Psychol., 1955/56, *3*, 605–61. **Leyhausen, P.:** Biologie von Ausdruck und Eindruck. Psychol. Forsch., 1967, *31*, 113–227. **Tagiuri, R.:** Person perception. Handbook Soc. Psychol., Vol. 3, 1969. **Tajfel, H.:** Social and cultural factors in perception. Handbook Soc. Psychol., Vol. 3, 1969.

F. Kiener

Imprinting. Many animals attach themselves only to members of their own species. But some prefer creatures of a different species which they encountered first; they follow them about, pair with them when fully grown, and try to copulate with them: "imprinting" has taken place.

1. *Definition.* (*a*) According to Lorenz (1935), imprinting is learning (q.v.) restricted to certain periods in life (sensitive or critical phases); (*b*) only the releaser, or key stimulus (q.v.), of a certain reaction (i.e. characteristics of an object in a specific functional area) is imprinted by differentiation of releasing mechanisms with—initially—low selectivity; (*c*) imprinting is *irreversible*; (*d*) not individual but species characteristics are learned; (*e*) imprinting can take place even before readiness for the corresponding responses has matured; (*f*) *readiness to learn is extinguished* when something definite has been learned, or because of internal processes of change at the termination of the critical period—even when there has been no learning.

Hess (1959) agrees with Lorenz in emphasizing that imprinting differs from associative learning: in imprinting, the animal achieves more success if practice is restricted to a short period of time; in addition, in choice situations what was learned *first* prevails over what was learned *later*. With learning by association exactly the opposite holds good. Moreover, in the latter case aversive stimuli bring about a rejection of the associated stimulus, whereas they reinforce imprinting. A further difference is the effect of the tranquilizer meprobamate on learning achievement: in hens the solution of color-discrimination tasks is not impaired, whereas imprintability drops almost to zero.

Since the concept of imprinting is based on an "injunctive definition" in Hassenstein's (1954) sense (i.e. ". . . to define the concept of life it is necessary to enumerate a number of constituent characteristics, none of which, taken by itself, constitutes life, but which taken all together, in their summation and interaction, do indeed represent the essence of life". Lorenz, 1966), continuous transitions to related and similar phenomena may be expected. Hence Eibl-Eibesfeld (1967) points to the fact that the criteria (*a*) and (*d*) are also valid for other learning processes Since the requisite basis has still not been found for statement (*e*), what remains as the distinguishing feature of imprinting is only "primacy of experience" (*c*) = irreversibility (Hess, 1959; Lannoy, 1967). However, according to Smith (1969), it cannot be generalized: the presence of an imprintable phase must be considered the crucial difference from associative learning. That such a phase does in fact exist is denied by Hinde (1955, 1962), Thorpe (1963) and Bateson (1963). Lannoy (1967) suggests a new approach: he would prefer a distinction to be made between imprinting and learning on the basis of the "facility in learning certain interactions dependent on the transmutation time", in which operation a "certain transmutation time-limit prevents animals from reaching all response levels".

2. *Incidence.* The dominance of early experience with members of a different species over later experience with members of the same species has so far been established in fish, birds and mammals (in particular). Among fish, certain mouth-breeders (*hemichromis bimaculatus*) prefer alien young to their own if, when they breed for the first time, eggs of an alien species are given them as substitutes (Myrberg, 1964). The fact that mammals reared by humans become attached to them instead of to members of their own species has been observed, e.g., by Grzimek (1949), F. Darling (1938), Hediger (1955), P. Leyhausen (1967) and L. Wilson (1966). According to Gray (1958), Thorpe (1961) and Hampson (1961) man, too, is probably imprintable. There is as yet no experimental proof; the psychoanalytical theory of childhood dreams and various ethnological observations (M. Mead) support this view, but both have only limited validity.

3. *Experimental investigations.* There are numerous accounts of experiments carried out into object imprinting (following responses and behavior toward sexual partners) and motor imprinting (learning the song of parents of an alien species) in birds.

(*a*) *Part areas and methodology.* The following were studied: beginning and end of learning ability, learning time required, influence of learning conditions on learning performance, nature of the learned phenomenon, effect of the learning processes and the matter learnt on the form of actions and their relation to objects, and the degree to which the success of later learning processes depends on earlier learning. The findings are based on comparisons of the responses of test animals when either members of the same or different species or certain objects are presented to them at time intervals or simultaneously.

(*b*) *Results.* In following experiments with a one-hour learning period, ducks are most susceptible to imprinting thirteen to sixteen hours after birth (critical period). Until they are five hours old, chicks react unspecifically; after twenty-four hours they react less and less well, until finally flight occurs (end of the sensitive period) (Fabricius, 1964; Hess, 1959). Changes in the duration of contact can have an effect on the extent to which following and sexual behavior can be released: after remaining for at least forty-eight hours with the imprinting object, two-day-old chickens prefer this in copulation experiments; shorter contact periods produce only following responses (Andrew, 1966). Apart from the *duration of contact*, successful imprinting depends, too, on the *frequency of contact:* a contact of twenty minutes repeated on five successive days produces better following imprinting with a turkey than if five contacts are arranged in the course of a single day (Hale, 1969).

Apart from time factors, successful imprinting depends on properties of the object characteristics; it can be enhanced by movement and the combination of qualitatively different stimuli and the simultaneous presentation of the imprinting characteristic and the gratification of a need. (Immelmann, 1967; Klopfer, 1968; Smith & Nott, 1970; Gottlieb, 1965; Boyd & Fabricius, 1965).

Responses to combinations of characteristics in choice experiments show that imprinting is possible on certain colors, patterns, body shapes and movements, sounds, kinds of odor and combinations of all these (Smith & Bird, 1963; Goodwin & Hess, 1969; and others). But, according to Klopfer (1968), the results of experiments can turn out differently when the same pairs of characteristics are presented; this may depend on the nature of the reward, the arrangement selected for the experiment, and the animal's innate preference for certain stimulus qualities as its internal condition varies. The strengthening or weakening of imprinting by subsequent experiences can also influence results (Schutz, 1965; Sluckin, 1964).

Imprinting always affects only the *orientation*

and never the form of the action: imprinted animals mate with members of different species but use movements peculiar to their own species (Schutz, 1965; Lannoy, 1967; von Frisch, 1957).

Subsequent learning processes can follow independently of any previous ones and produce imprinting on different objects in different functional areas (Lorenz, 1935; Schutz, 1965).

Similar conditions apply to song imprinting as to object imprinting (Thorpe, 1958; Nicolai, 1959; Immelmann, 1965).

No characteristics which might exclusively distinguish imprinting have so far been obtained from investigations based on behavioral comparisons, but there are two which stand out: the imprinting phase and the preference of what was learned first to what was learned subsequently (Lannoy, 1967; Eibl-Eibesfeld, 1967). The exact nature of the processes leading to these features is still an open question; if they were known it could perhaps be shown whether imprinting differs fundamentally from other forms of learning (Smith, 1969). See *Instinct; Animal psychology; Comparative psychology; Conditioning, classical and operant.*

Bibliography: Andrew, R. J.: Precocious adult behaviour in the young chick. Anim. Behav., 1966, *14*, 485–500. **Bateson, P. P. G.:** Filial and avoidance behaviour in chicks. Unpublished Ph.D. thesis. Cambridge, 1963. **Boyd, H. & Fabricius, E.:** Observations on the incidence of following of visual and auditory stimuli in naïve mallard ducklings (Anas platyrhynchos). Behaviour, 1965, *25*, 1–15. **Eibl-Eibesfeld, I.:** Grundriss der vergleichenden Verhaltensforschung. Munich, 1967. **Fabricius, E.:** Zur Ethologie junger Anatiden. Acta Zool. Fenn., 1951, *68*, 1–178. **Id.:** Crucial periods in the development of the following response in ducklings. Z. Tierpsychol., 1964, *21*, 326–37. **Frisch, O. von:** Mit einem Purpurreiher verheiratet. Z. Tierpsychol., 1957, *14*, 233–37. **Goodwin, E. B. & Hess, E. H.:** Stimulus generalization and responses to "supernormal" stimuli in the unrewarded pecking behaviour of young chicks. Behaviour, 1969, *34*, 223–37. **Gottlieb, G.:** Imprinting in relation to parental and species identification by avian neonates. J. comp. physiol. Psychol., 1965, *59*, 345–56. **Gray, P. H.:** Theory and evidence of imprinting in human infants. J. Psychol., 1958, *46* 155–60. **Grzimek, B.:** Ein Fohlen, das kein Pferd kannte. Z. Tierpsychol., 1949, *6*, 391–405. **Hale, E. B.:** Stages in the process of visual imprinting. Eleventh International Ethological Conference, 1969. **Hampson, J. L. & Hampson, J. G.:** The ontogenesis of sexual behaviour in man. In: **Young, W. C.** (Ed.): Sex and internal secretion. London, 1961. **Hassenstein, B.:** Abbildende Begriffe. Verh. d. Deutsch. Zool. Ges., 1954, 197–202. **Hediger, H.:** Studies of the psychology and behaviour of captive animals in zoos and circuses. London, 1955. **Hess, E. H.:** Imprinting. Science, 1959, *130*, 133–41. **Hinde, R. A.:** The following response of moorhens and coots. Brit. J. Anim. Behav., 1955, *3*, 121–22. **Id.:** Some aspects of the imprinting problem. Sym. Zool. Soc. London, 1962, *8*, 129–38. **Immelmann, K.:** Prägungserscheinungen in der Gesangsentwicklung junger Zebrafinken. Die Naturwiss., 1965, *52*, 169–70. **Id.:** Zur ontogenetischen Gesangsentwicklung bei Prachtfinken. Zool. Anz. Suppl., 1967, *30*, 320–32. **Klinghammer, E.:** Factors influencing choice of mate in altrical birds. In: **Stevenson, H. W.** (Ed.): Early behavior. New York, 1967, 5–42. **Klopfer, P. H.:** Stimulus references and discrimination in neonatal Ducklings. Behaviour, 1968, *32*, 309–14. **Lannoy, J. de:** Zur Prägung von Instinkthandlungen. Z. Tierpsychol., 1967, *24*, 162–200. **Lorenz, K.:** Der Kumpan in der Umwelt des Vogels. J. f. Ornith, 1935, *83*, 137–213. **Id.:** On aggression. London, 1966. **Myrberg, A. A.:** An analysis of preferential care of eggs and young by adult cichlid fishes. Z. Tierpsychol., 1964, *21*, 53–98. **Nicolai, J.:** Familientradition in der Gesangstradition des Gimpels (Pyrrhula pyrrhula, L.) J. f. Ornithol., 1959, *100*, 39–46. **Schutz, F.:** Sexuelle Prägung bei Anatiden. Z. Tierpsychol., 1965, *22*, 50–103. **Sluckin, W.:** Imprinting and early learning. London, 1964. **Smith, F. V. & Bird, M. W.:** The relative attraction for the domestic chick of combinations of stimuli in different sensory modalities. Anim. Behav., 1963, *11*, 300–5. **Smith, F. V.:** Attachment of the young, imprinting and other developments. Edinburgh, 1969. **Smith, F. V. & Nott, K. H.:** The "critical period" in relation to the strength of the stimulus. Z. Tierpsychol., 1970, *27*, 108–15. **Thorpe, W. H.:** Further studies on the process of song learning in the chaffinch (Fringilla coelebs). Nature, 1958, *182*, 554–57. **Id.:** Sensitive periods in learning of animals and men: a study of imprinting with special reference to the introduction of cyclic behaviour. In: **Thorpe, W. H. & Zangwill, O. L.** (Eds.): Current problems in animal behaviour. Cambridge, 1961. **Id.:** Learning and instinct in animals. London, [2]1963.

B. Tschanz

Imprinting and lactation. The concept of "imprinting" (q.v.) was first used in animal psychology. As applied to human beings it was used to express the long-lasting, "imprinted" effect of impressions received in the early months of life. In this connection the following was observed: if a baby is given a wet-nurse for the first weeks and months after birth, when the infant is weaned subsequently, it remains for a time more attached to the nurse than to its mother. It can be seen from this that the breast-feeding period has an emphatic "imprinting" effect from foster-mother to child. *M.S.*

Impulse. See *Impulsiveness; Drive; Instinct; Motivation.*

Impulsiveness (syn. *Impulsivity*). A temperamental factor classifiable as extraversion. Impulsiveness is characterized by spontaneous direct action with little regard for the consequences. There is a slight correlation between impulsivity and the intelligence factors of fluency of thought and expression. *G.K.*

Impulsive neuroses are mental disorders in which the person affected follows irresistible impulses, e.g. to start fires, wander, steal or commit certain crimes. The impulsive neurotic is often similar to the "psychopathic personality" in his behavior. See *Psychopathology.* *W.T.*

Inadequate stimuli are significant changes in the environment which do not occur under normal conditions; these changes affect excitable biological substrates and evoke reactions in them (excitation). Electrical or mechanical stimuli are inadequate for the eye whereas thermic stimuli are inadequate for the vestibular apparatus (ear); nevertheless they react with a corresponding sense impression or response if the inadequate stimulus is sufficiently strong. The threshold (minimum successful stimulus strength) is substantially higher with inadequate than with adequate stimuli. *E.D.*

Inanition. This term denotes the psychological aftereffects of the withdrawal of affective attention in early childhood. After a stay in hospital or in a children's home where the child has to do without affectionate interest, there may be a significant retardation of psychomotor development, or some regression to earlier behavior patterns, accompanied by a physical susceptibility to illness. See *Hospitalism.*

Bibliography: **Yarrow, L. J.:** Maternal deprivation: toward an empirical and conceptual revaluation. Psychol. Bull., 1961, *58*, 459–90. *M.Sa.*

Inbreeding. The mating of closely related animals, usually resulting in the magnification of certain traits. These traits may be regarded as favorable (e.g. intelligence) or unfavorable (e.g. deafness), but deleterious effects are apparently more likely because of the increased manifestation of recessive and mutated traits. Also, for some unknown reason, inbreeding tends to reduce the fertility of the offspring. The *coefficient of inbreeding* for an individual is calculated as the likelihood that he will possess identical genes at any pair of loci as a result of inheritance from both mother and father.

In sociology, *inbreeding* refers to the process by which a group or institution may tend toward stagnation or even extinction through failure to enlist new elements. *G.D.W.*

Incentive. 1. Something which incites to action (particularly higher productivity). **2.** An incidental reward. **3.** A motive (q.v.).

Incest. Sexual relations (coitus) between related individuals. Infringement of one of the oldest sexual taboos, which stems from magical and religious sources; considered as a serious sexual offence in most societies. The extent of the prohibition and the penalty threatened vary widely. There is no legal penalty in some countries (e.g. Luxembourg, Belgium,

Portugal, Turkey). The commonest forms are father-daughter and stepfather-stepdaughter incest. The proportion of concealed cases is thought to be high. Cases disclosed: primarily from the lower social strata (80%–90%); in the middle and higher social groups the "zone of secrecy" is greater. Recidivism: less than 5%. Male offenders are on average forty to forty-one years old on committing their first offense; they are primarily of average or above average intelligence (60%–85%); half of them are socially and psychopathologically unobtrusive; they are rarely psychotic (3%–6%), and in very few cases "hypersexual". The main features of offenders with striking social and psychopathological characteristics are lack of control over aggressive, oral (alcohol), and/or sexual impulses (in all about 40%), and/or maladjusted careers or lives (approximately 35%). The female "victims" are generally at the age of puberty when the offenses begin (around thirteen years old); they are of average or above-average intelligence (approximately 80%), and frequently show disturbed personality symptoms (about 70%) —but these characteristics are no more frequent after incest than before. Incestuous relationships are conditioned by many different factors. The main predisposing factor is a disturbed psychosocial relationship in the family. Incest is not a cause but a consequence of disorganized family life (approx. 80–90%).

The origin of the taboo has as yet resisted all historico-anthropological and psychological attempts at elucidation (degeneration theory, theory of instinctive incest-defense, theory of acquired disinclination, politico-economic cooperation theory, the phylogenetic theory of the incest taboo. See Maisch, 1968, for survey and summary). One sociological theory holds that in modern industrial society the incest taboo has lost any vital social significance, but nevertheless views it as an integrative element of the bourgeois family structure which may well fulfill important psychological and social functions in the development of the individual personality (Parsons' structural-functional theory).

Bibliography: Freud, S.: Totem and taboo. New York, 1918. **Maisch, H.:** Inzest, Hamburg, 1968. **Parsons, T. & Bales, R. F.:** Family, socialization and interaction process. New York, [4]1954. *H.M.*

Inclination. 1. A leaning or sloping. An angle measured from the vertical. **2.** A motivational tendency (non-technical usage). *G.D.W.*

Incontinence. Inability to retain stool or urine. Can be caused by, e.g., paraplegia (lesion of the spinal cord) after an accident; damage to the lumbar region of the spinal cord, caused by a slipped disc or carcinomal metastasis. Apart from such physiologically explicable cases, modern approaches to most forms of enuresis (q.v.) or encopresis (q.v.) treat them as faulty conditioning, variously amenable to behavior therapy (q.v.). *E.D.*

Incubation. In the study of anxiety (q.v.) and fear (q.v.), the term "incubation" has been used to describe two related phenomena. The first usage refers to "a growth of fear over a time interval which follows some aversive stimulus. The increase in fear is assumed to be spontaneous in the sense that the time interval is free of further exposure to the aversive stimulus" (McAllister & McAllister, 1967, p. 180). In a review of studies dealing with this concept of incubation of anxiety, McAllister & McAllister (1967, p. 189) conclude that "the phenomenon has yet to be convincingly demonstrated". Eysenck (1968) suggests that incubation in this sense does not deserve a special title, and can be explained in terms of a reminiscence-type theory based on consolidation of memory traces.

More recently, the term incubation has been used to refer to an increment in conditioned response (CR) over a number of trials when the conditioned stimulus (CS) is applied but without reinforcement (UCS). This second concept Eysenck (1968) prefers to call the "Napalkov phenomenon" in honor of the Russian investigator who first drew attention to it. Evidence for the Napalkov phenomenon from both animals and human Ss. is reviewed by Eysenck (1968). In these studies the CRs increase in strength over trials where the original aversive UCS was withheld. The effects are clearly in evidence and are difficult to fit into any existing learning paradigm. In the usual conditioning paradigm the CR gradually extinguishes when the CS is presented in the absence of the UCS. In the studies under discussion, the CR increased. Thus, in the first series of experiments, the CR increased over *time* without further conditioning trials; in the second series the CR increased over *unreinforced trials.*

Eysenck (1968) proposes a theory to explain the second phenomenon, laying stress on the CR being, in itself, an aversive stimulus in a feedback cycle which interferes with the usual extinction processes. He argues that an unreinforced CS will always provoke a decrement in the CR, but will also provoke an increment. The observed CR will be the resultant of these two opposing tendencies. Extinction will occur when the decrement exceeds the increment, incubation when the opposite occurs. The increment in strength of the CR is explained in the following way: in aversive conditioning, a CS is followed by a UCS which produces a variety of unconditioned responses (UCRs). After a number of pairings of CS and UCS, the CS either alone or accompanied by the UCS will produce a variety of CRs, and some of these CRs will be physiological in nature (arousal, q.v., which is termed anxiety or fear). The CS has thus acquired the function of signaling danger and impending pain. The emotional responses of fear or anxiety thus elicited are themselves aversive stimuli which, by classical conditioning, come to be associated not only with the reinforced CS but also with the unreinforced CS. By a feedback system, even unreinforced CSs are actually reinforced and tend to evoke more fear on the subsequent trials. The stimulus value of the emotional responses is in most cases small, and the resultant of the increments and decrements of unreinforced CSs will usually produce extinction. But under certain conditions, possibly when the UCS is exceptionally strong, the resultant effect will be incubation of the conditioned emotional response. A number of parametric studies are required to ascertain the conditions under which incubation instead of extinction occurs, and some hypotheses are proposed by Eysenck (1968) and Ramsay (1969).

Incubation of anxiety as seen in the laboratory has important implications for the study of neurotic behavior. The view of the development of neurosis in learning terms has long been considered inadequate to cover what the clinician observes in his patients. In humans, the processes of verbal conditioning, covert sensitization, imaginal behavior rehearsal, and cognitive factors probably play an important role in the incubation of anxiety, and the behaviorally-oriented theoretician and clinician have yet to integrate these concepts in their approaches. It is possible that a fuller investigation of the processes involved in incubation will bring theory and clinical practice more into line in the understanding and treatment of neurosis (q.v.).

Bibliography: Eysenck, H. J.: A theory of the incubation of anxiety/fear responses. Behav. Res. & Therapy, 1968, *6*, 309–21. **McAllister, D. E. & McAllister, W. R.:** Incubation of fear: an examination of the concept. J. exp. res. Person., 1967, *2*, 180–90. **Ramsay, R. W.:** Incubation of emotional responses. Unpubl. MS., Univ. of Amsterdam, 1969.

R. W. Ramsay

Incubation processes. 1. Processes during a phase of apparent rest in which a covert development takes place after which there is a distinct alteration in the general condition. **2.** Medical: processes during the time between infection and the outbreak of an illness. **3.** Psychology of thought: several "phasic" models of productive thinking use the categories (*a*) preparation, (*b*) incubation, (*c*) illumination, and (*d*) verification. *H.W.*

Incubus. A nightmare. In medieval demonology, an evil spirit which was supposed to lie upon and oppress sleeping persons, especially a male spirit which copulated with sleeping women. Cf. *Succubus*: a female spirit which seduced men during sleep, thus causing nocturnal emissions. *G.D.W.*

Independent variable. See *Variable.*

Index. Indices are ratios characteristic of a body-build and summarized in a mathematical formula; they facilitate the determination of a type (e.g. body-build indices according to H. J. Eysenck, E. Kretschmer, G. Kühnel, W. Plattner, I. Pignet, E. Strömgren, K. Westphal). See *Body-build index.* *W.K.*

Indicators, motivational. A term used to denote variables of stimuli which arouse motivation (q.v.) to a specific behavior, and those which follow some motivation, i.e. variables of motivated responses, motivated behavior. *R.Hä.*

Indifference point; indifference zone. The point of transition between opposites in experience, the neutral point in any series having positive and negative values. This point has been called the *Adaptation level* (q.v.) (Helson), since it varies with its context. A slightly more specific definition applies in the context of psychophysics (q.v.) experiments, in which the indifference point is that stimulus in a graded series which is reproduced or recognized correctly, whereas smaller ones are overestimated and larger ones underestimated. *C.D.F.*

Individual. 1. A single unit, theme, case, etc. **2.** A single, distinct organism. **3.** A person (q.v.), especially as conceived by psychoanalysis (q.v.) or individual psychology (q.v.). Adler drew specific attention to the difficulty of harmoniously integrating the individual into society (socialization, q.v.). He suggested that the child had to overcome a natural feeling of inferiority, and the way in which he managed this was dependent on the environment (parents). He considered this to be the starting point for education. See *Adler, Alfred.* *M.S.*

Individualism is the tendency to attribute independent reality to a single individual (implying nominalism) and to conceive of him as the sole basis of all values and the sole source of social achievements. The individual is both the highest value and the ultimate objective: groups, institutions and the state are simply means to allow the individual to develop. The attitude of the individualist leads to a pattern of behavior which is independent of collective standards. *M.R.*

Individuality. The unique nature of the personality (q.v.). Representatives of idiographic (q.v.) personality research (such as G. W. Allport) understand individuality as the unique *qualitative* characteristic of the individual, whereas representatives of the nomothetic variety (such as J. P. Guilford) consider it as the unique *quantitative* characteristic (in the sense of a uniqueness of the individual configuration of factor values in the relevant ability and personality factors). Apart from twin studies, no reliable empirical research data is available on the subject of individuality. But see *Abilities; Traits; Type.* *K.P.*

Individual psychology. 1. See *Differential psychology.*

2. The psychological theory of Alfred Adler

(q.v.): "The fundamental fact in human development is the dynamic and purposive striving of the psyche. . . . The unity of personality is implicit in each human being's existence. Every individual represents both a unity of personality and the individual fashioning of that unity." An approach based on the existence of an inferiority complex (q.v.), especially in neurotic individuals, and on a reaction to this complex in the form of compensation. In addition to its influence on the methods of certain psychotherapists who follow Adler's theory, "individual psychology" has had a considerable influence in some educational circles.

Bibliography: **Adler, A.:** The education of children. New York & London, 1930. *J.L.I.*

Individuation. Jung uses the term "individuation" to characterize the process of reaching maturity and developing the individual personality. The collective unconscious (q.v.) which is composed of archetypes (q.v.), is said gradually to change through individuation into the self (see *Ego*). In immature personalities the process of individuation is delayed. Some Jungian psychotherapeutic methods attempt to foster individuation by analyzing the symbols which appear in dreams and visions. *J.L.I.*

Indoctrination. Instruction in ideas or beliefs which requires their complete acceptance.

Induction. An intellectual procedure which consists of working through a finite number of given propositions in order to arrive at one proposition (the conclusion) which implies them all. In most cases the given assertions are inferred from observed facts. The induction then leads to a law which summarizes them. If the law is able to account for more than the observed facts, we speak of *ampliative induction* (or inference), and in other cases of *perfect induction*; in this case we have a deduction based on the laws of logic: what is true for each individual entity of a class is true for all other instances. On the problematical nature of the assumption of a measure of uniformity in nature (an assumption made in all inductive reasoning), see Ayer, 1956.

Bibliography: **Ayer, A. J.:** The problem of knowledge. Harmondsworth, 1956, 71–5. *J.B.G.*

Induction coil. An apparatus based on the principle of electro-magnetic induction which can be used to provide a variable but controlled amount of electric current as an aversive stimulus, usually for experiments on learning or conditioning. *G.D.W.*

Inductor. See *Token object*.

Industrial engineer. An engineer who has to solve industrial problems (systems, working times, personnel management, etc.) by analytical methods. See *Time and motion study*. *G.R.W.M.*

Industrial engineering. The work of industrial engineers in planning, implementing and supervising measures to increase productivity. This work is based not only on technical and business experience but primarily on ergonomic principles. *G.R.W.M.*

Industrial psychology. That branch of applied psychology (q.v.) which is concerned with work and economics. Its aim has often been stated as maximizing *efficiency* in the production and distribution of goods and services through the study and manipulation of "*human factors*"—the approach of *ergonomics* (q.v.)—but there is an increasing tendency for the satisfaction of workers and consumers to be regarded as an end in itself (Smith & Cranny, 1968). Though the industrial psychologist may orientate his work from the viewpoint of the individual worker, management, the organization, or the consumer, it is widely recognized that efficiency is usually best served if the interests of all parties are taken into account. There follows a brief outline of some of the problems and areas with which industrial psychologists may be concerned.

1. *Vocational guidance*. Since the choice of an occupation is one of the most critical decisions any person has to face in the course of a lifetime, he may seek the advice of a psychologist. The aims of vocational guidance are to bring the individual to a realistic awareness of his own potential, and to point out those of the various possibilities open to him which are compatible with both his talents and interests. To supplement his skill as an interviewer, the vocational counselor will probably use *objective tests* (q.v.) of general *intelligence* (e.g. Wechsler Adult Intelligence Scale, Raven Matrices), specific *aptitudes* (e.g. Differential Aptitude Test, q.v., Battery, General Aptitude Test Battery, q.v.), and *occupational interests* (e.g. Strong Vocational Interest Blank, q.v., Kuder Preference Record, q.v.). For a detailed description of these tests, see Cronbach (1960). The final decision is, of course, left with the client, and he may be so keenly motivated to attempt a particular career that he will accept as little as an estimated 10% chance of success.

2. *Employee selection and placement*. If there is a surplus of applicants for a particular job, the industrial or *personnel psychologist* may be called upon to develop a *selection program*, so that the best possible use can be made of the available talent. In this case he must take the view of the management or organization rather than that of the individual applicant. Since it is essential for the psychologist to know exactly what is entailed in the job concerned, and the skills and attributes which are relevant to effective performance, it may be necessary to start with a detailed *job analysis*. Then, in addition to the well-known tests of general intelligence and aptitudes referred to above, new tests specific to the particular situation may have to be developed and standardized for purposes of selection.

Once an applicant has been accepted by an organization, it may still have to be decided exactly what job he will do, in which department, and so on. This task of *placement* within an organization has elements of both vocational guidance and selection, remembering that work satisfaction is directly related to *productivity* and inversely related to staff *turnover*.

3. *Training*. Psychologists may also assist with the training of new employees, the retraining of old employees for new jobs, or the training of instructors in methods of instruction. Here, all the general *laws of learning* are applicable, e.g. the importance of motivation, knowledge of results, distribution of practice, etc. With *automation* has come a particular need to study methods of retraining and the variables which affect acceptance of, and resistance to change.

An effective training program presupposes a knowledge of the best and most efficient methods of work. *Time and motion study* (q.v.), associated with the names of F. W. Taylor and F. Gilbreth who introduced it into the USA in 1911, involves observing the worker at his job and carefully analyzing all his movements and the time taken to execute them with a view to reducing them and thus increasing efficiency. Although this means that with payment on the basis of productivity the worker can increase his earnings, naïve attempts to apply the method in the past have resulted in a great deal of resentment from workers who fear invasion of privacy, exploitation by management, redundancies, and loss of the freedom to do things their own way. This provides a good example of the complex psycho-social problems involving workers' attitudes, which are encountered by the industrial psychologist in his attempts to increase efficiency.

4. *Motivation, morale, and conditions of work*. Motivation is, of course, most directly manipulated by wage incentives such as piece rates and productivity bonuses, but

there is an increasing tendency for psychologists to regard the maintenance of morale (i.e. favorable attitudes) in the work situation as equally important. Morale may be facilitated in a variety of ways, e.g. by providing an avenue of communication between workers and management so that complaints can be registered, ensuring that work groups are compatible and that adequate social and recreational facilities are available. Improving the environmental conditions, e.g. by increasing illumination, reducing ambient noise, installing air conditioning, careful planning of color and decorations, provision of music, and so on, may increase productivity, depending on the personality and other characteristics of the workers concerned and the kind of work that they are doing. While this may sometimes result from direct improvement in physiological functioning, the effect more often results from the positive attitude engendered by pleasant surroundings (Maier, 1955). In the famous "Hawthorne studies" with female relay assembly workers at the Western Electric Company in the USA, it was found that the mere fact of studying workers' conditions was sufficient to exert a beneficial effect upon morale, and thus output, irrespective of the particular changes in physical conditions that were made (Roethlisberger & Dixon, 1940). (See *Hawthorne experiments.*)

5. *Fatigue.* One of the most important factors which interferes with work efficiency is *fatigue* (q.v.), which may be defined as that decrement in work performance occurring as a function of effort and time spent on the job which is recoverable through rest. The effects of fatigue upon psychomotor performance were studied in a well-known experiment conducted at Cambridge University using a simulated aeroplane cockpit. Subjects were required to sit in the "Cambridge Cockpit" for many hours at a time, making prescribed responses to signals which were complicated in their sequence, color, location, etc. The manifestations of fatigue were various, beginning with a widening indifference to signals which required action, slow reactions, and lapses in judgment, and culminating in complaints of tiredness, bodily discomfort, and emotional outbursts. Among the factors which have been found to forestall or alleviate fatigue are motivation, knowledge of results, rest pauses, and certain drugs such as caffeine (q.v.) and benzedrine (Munn, 1958).

6. *Equipment design.* However high the individual's level of aptitude, training, motivation, morale, and so on may be, his efficiency is also a function of the machines with which he works. Whereas training is concerned with adapting the man to suit the machine, the industrial psychologist may also help in designing the machine to suit the operator. This is one of the central concerns of the field sometimes called *engineering psychology*. For example, finding the best possible spatial arrangement for the controls and instruments in a motor car, aeroplane cockpit, or space craft, designing legible and unambiguous traffic signs, and so on, requires a knowledge of the perceptual and motor capabilities of human beings. Left to their own devices, engineers too often design equipment for appearance or mechanical convenience, without regard to the limitations of the persons who have to work with it.

7. *Organizational processes.* Another area which may be considered part of industrial psychology, although it overlaps the domain of *industrial sociology*, is the study of efficiency in industrial organizations (e.g. Katz & Kahn, 1966). It is now well established that large organizations have functional requirements for growth and survival which create problems of efficiency of their own, independently of the individuals and equipment which comprise the organization, e.g. problems of communication, leadership and authority. Different kinds of organizational structure have been identified (e.g. "tall" versus "flat", "rational" versus "irrational") and these have been related to the characteristic attitudes and behavior to be found within them (Smith & Cranny, 1968).

8. *Consumer research and advertising.* Finally, there is the branch of industrial psychology in which interest is focussed on the product or service itself, and its acceptability to the consumer (sometimes called "business psychology"). Consumer research is concerned with discovering the needs and motives of the public with a view to providing products and services which are appropriate to them, whereas marketing and advertising are concerned with the distribution of established commodities, e.g. by promoting public awareness of them and persuading potential consumers of their desirability. As with many other areas of applied psychology (and applied science generally) this field presents some ethical problems concerning which little agreement has been reached, e.g. the use of deliberate deception in research and advertising.

Some of the tasks frequently undertaken by consumer psychologists include: assessing the acceptability of a proposed new product, its brand name, package design, etc.; discovering the primary factors which determine brand preferences and purchasing decisions within a particular product field; assessing the public image of an established company, politician, entertainer, etc.; investigating the most effective media of communication for promoting a particular commodity; and the testing of advertising copy. Characteristic methods include: rating scales,questionnaires, extended ("depth") interviews, group discussions, panel tests, "in-home" product tests, controlled observation and actuarial studies of consumer behavior. For a review of recent trends in consumer psychology, see Perloff (1968). See *Marketing*; *Occupational psychology.*

Bibliography: Cronbach, L. J.: Essentials of psychological testing. New York, [2]1960. **Katz, D. & Kahn, R. L.:** The social psychology of organizations. New York, 1966. **Maier, N. R. F.:** Psychology in industry. Boston, 1955. **Munn, N. L.:** Psychology: The fundamentals of human adjustment. London, [3]1958. **Perloff, R.:** Consumer analysis. Ann. Rev. Psychol., 1968, *19*, 437–66. **Roethlisberger, F. J. & Dixon, W. J.:** Management and the worker. Cambridge, Mass., 1940. **Smith, P. C. & Cranny, C. J.:** Psychology of men at work. Ann. Rev. Psychol., 1968, *19*, 467–96.

G. D. Wilson

Industrial relations. 1. Human relations between all the members of staff of an industrial concern as well as their relations with the management and their own work; sometimes defined in legal and tariff provisions (labor regulations); **2.** Less commonly used to denote the relations between an industrial concern and the public (See *Public relations*). Not to be confused with *labor relations*, i.e. the relations between an industrial concern and the trade union organizations.

Bibliography: Kerr, C., Dunlop, J. T., Harbison, F. H. & Myers, C. A.: Industrialism and industrial man. New York, 1964.

G.R.W.M.

Infancy. 1. *General.* Usually the period during which the child cannot yet speak, from birth till twelve or thirteen months. Characteristic signs of this period are: development of the body and posture, development of the sensorimotor apparatus; the initial learning of emotional attitudes (attraction to the mother, anxiety); an inability to move from place to place of one's own accord, voluntarily to control behavior, to speak, or to achieve an autonomous adaptation (q.v.). This period lasts longer in human beings than in other creatures.

The *maturation* of the nervous system, as a continuation of the biological development of the embryo, determines the course of the following advances: (*a*) the reduction of sleep periods (from six to seven periods in twenty-four hours to one to three periods at the age of one year); (*b*) bent and floppy limbs become straight and firm; (*c*) disappearance of the "archaic reflexes" through the development of the cerebral cortex; (*d*) sitting with support at about four months, without support at about seven months; standing with help in the eighth month, without help in the thirteenth month; walking holding on at about eleven months, walking alone at about fifteen months.

At first the infant holds a thing just in the palm of his hand, then the thumb is bent sideways over it in about the fourth month. Binocular vision is fully attained in about the sixth month, when turning the head toward a sound source also develops. In the second month the infant can fixate moving objects, the first conditioned responses appear in connection with suckling, and he smiles at faces; in the third month he recognizes people. From three to six months he learns to watch his hands moving, to grasp things which he sees and which arouse his curiosity. At about four months he makes noises directed at other people (social noises), and, at about five months, he begins to "complain". From the sixth to the eleventh month he begins to explore objects: at first impulsively, and then to relate their different sensuous and spatial qualities (surface, relative position); shyness at strangers and the joyful recognition of members of the family, as well as involuntary imitations, begin at about seven months. From ten to thirteen months, after the infant has developed a concept of objects and discovered their "permanence" (he will look for them when they have disappeared behind a curtain), he arranges objects in relation to one another, and organizes his movements in accordance with the findings he remembers. "Instrumental (practical) intelligence" develops; he voluntarily imitates sounds and movements, and at about thirteen months can play "let's pretend"—the first sign that he is approaching the stage of symbolic imitations.

2. *Developmental mechanisms.* The important aspects here are the combined operation and significance of the *instincts, bodily maturation, learning* and interpersonal relationships. Sucking, walking, grasping and posture all have an instinctive component, but require practice in adaptation and social encouragement, and can therefore take very different forms (e.g. in "feral" children, q.v.). It used to be held that smiling at someone and certain echopraxias in the first month indicated a *social instinct*. But it is difficult to distinguish between the influences of the instincts, of maturation and of conditioning (q.v.). Conditioning can begin in the second month: situations which are associated with pleasant feelings (contentment) are reinforced; those which have aroused unpleasant feelings are feared.

Recognition of objects and persons, exploration, the realization of wishes, and the earliest form of understanding are founded upon this mechanism. However, one must also take into account the role of *circular reactions* (J. M. Baldwin, 1906): The infant is excited when he observes that his movements have caused something to happen and therefore repeats the movements. At the age of six months, even complex reactions obey this law of circularity (J. Piaget). Initiatory behavior develops in accordance with the same principle, and by playing noise and movement games with the parents. Circular reactions constitute an important source of differentiations and of discovery in the infant's exploration of his environment.

Affectivity plays a dynamogenic (i.e. initiating or changing motor responses through sensory activity) and regulating role. It develops in interpersonal reactions, principally between the infant and his mother. (See *Hospitalism*; A. Freud, R. A. Spitz, J. Bowlby). The mother appeases or gratifies urgent needs, stimulates activity by showing him things and playing with him, arouses expectations, impatience and laughter (at six months); she requires "goal-directed" behavior by teaching and showing him how (at about nine months). But she also frustrates, forbids and provokes. From the sixth month onward, strangers cause shyness, then anxiety. Psychoanalysts (N. Hartman, E. Kris) hold that object cathexis takes over from the narcissism (q.v.) of the first three months in two major phases: interest in persons (and in situations which announce these "objects"), followed by attraction to and communication with others. These object cathexes are essential to the formation of a balanced ego (q.v.) distinct from the world. The reactions of the first ten months are basic to the formation of permanent behavior patterns: e.g. (*a*) the desire to "make things happen" is strengthened by its connection with the suckling relationship, and later with motor skills; (*b*) the infant's increasing interest in sensorimotor experience leads him after ten months to regard his own image in the glass without clearly understanding the significance of what he sees; (*c*) his dependence upon his mother can turn through frustration (q.v.) to aggression (q.v.); (*d*) the affirmation of the self (q.v.) in opposition to another in the form of protests (and—after ten months—intentional provocations) is the precursor of speech.

The formation of and part played by these modes of behavior vary from infant to infant (Meili 1957; Escalona, 1968). Differences in activation (q.v.) level determine a bold or fearful approach to the environment, and therefore elicit different responses to the familiar environment: in this way definite character traits are formed. See *Arousal.*

The behavior of the person responsible for bringing the child up, and the methods used, depend upon culture and tradition. A. Kardiner, M. Mead, J. W. M. Whiting and E. H. Erikson indicate the personality (q.v.) differences caused by strict or relaxed methods of early care. The factors which determine the infant's behavior are numerous; they may be complementary or conflicting. On the one hand there is bodily (neurological) maturation (Gesell, 1934), and on the other the influence of emotional relationships. But conditioning (q.v.) (see *Learning theory*) and the active initiatives of the child, either in motor behavior (Piaget, 1952) or in emotive expressions (Wallon, 1934), must be taken into account. The interaction of these factors has still to be clarified. See *Child psychology; Development; Instinct; Traits.*

Bibliography: Baldwin, J. M.: Mental development in the child and the race: methods and processes. New York, [3]1906. **Escalona, S. K.:** The roots of individuality. Chicago, 1968. **Fantz, R. L.,** *et al.*: Maturation of pattern vision in infants during the first six months. J. comp. physiol. Psychol., 1967, *55*, 907–17. **Foss, B. M.** (Ed.): Determinants of infant behavior, 4 vols. London & New York, 1961, 1963, 1965, 1968. **Gesell, A. & Thompson, H.:** Infant behavior. New York, 1934. **Gouin Decarie, T.:** Intelligence et affectivité. Neuchâtel, 1962. **Gregoire, A.:** L'apprentissage du langage. Paris, 1937. **Lewin, K.:** A dynamic theory of personality, New York, 1935. **Lipsitt, L. P. & Spiker, C. C.** (Eds.): Advances in child development and behavior, 2 vols. New York, 1963–5. **Meili, R.:** Anfänge der Charakterentwicklung. Berne, 1957. **Piaget, J.:** The origins of intelligence in children. London, 1952. **Pratt, K. C.:** The neonate. In: **Carmichael, L.** (Ed.): Manual of child psychology. New York, [2]1954, 215–91. **Spitz, R.:** The first year of life. New York, 1965. **Wallon, H.:** Les origines du caractère. Paris, 1934. **Weir, R. H.:** Language in the crib. The Hague, 1962. **Whiting, J. W. & Child, I. L.:** Child training and personality. New Haven, Ill., 1953.

P. Malrieu

Infantile sexuality. Freudian psychoanalysis (q.v.) divides sexual expression in both sexes in early childhood into various phases: the oral phase (first year of life), the anal-urethral stage (second to fourth year—bowel training, q.v.; see *Anal stage*) and the phallic stage (q.v., fourth to seventh year) characterized by the development and overcoming of the Oedipus complex (q.v.). This early expression of infantile sexuality is said to become latent again with the maturation of the superego, until puberty—when the adolescent usually seeks heterosexual partners outside his own family.

Developmental biology might be thought to confirm certain aspects of psychoanalytical theories: in the "larval stage" of infancy there is already a hormonal difference between boys and girls. Sucking, and erection in the boy, arouse pleasure. Early childhood curiosity includes sexual questions, and children (especially in the third and fourth years) examine their genitals as part of the general process of self-exploration and understanding. Attempts at coitus are not uncommon in play. Subsequent psychosexual health depends in large measure on the examples given to children and on the security of a harmonious marriage and family environment. See *Child psychology; Sexuality.* *K.T.*

Infantile type. An individual in whom physical development has been arrested altogether (or more frequently, in part) at a childish stage of development (see *Retardation*). The term is also used in characterology since mental immaturity often goes hand in hand with physical retardation. See *Infantilism.* *W.K.*

Infantilism (syn. *Juvenilism*). **1.** If an individual fails to attain that degree of somatic growth and sexual development appropriate to his age, infantilism is said to be present. This condition is not to be confused with *dwarfism*, in which a failure of somatic growth may be accompanied by normal sexual development. Due to endocrine hypofunction (particularly of the pituitary or its connections), chronic infection, coeliac disease, renal disease, cyanotic heart disease, or is idiopathic. Intellect is not impaired, although emotional development and behavior patterns commonly retain childish characteristics.

2. The term also has psychoanalytical connotations, meaning the state of infancy. *J.P.*

Infantilism, psychosexual. A distinction is sometimes made between general *infantilism* (q.v.), which affects the whole organism, and partial or *psychosexual* infantilism: non-development of the secondary sexual characteristics, or immaturity of the sexual organs compared with the development of the rest of the body. *J.L.I.*

Infant tests. Methods which attempt to describe behavioral development as a whole or specific areas of behavior from the first month of life onward, e.g. Bühler-Hetzer tests (q.v.) for children of 0 to 6 years. See *Development tests*; *Gesell Development Schedules.* *E.F.-K.*

Infection, psychic. A sociopsychological phenomenon: stimuli are transmitted directly from individual to individual; in the simplest case this involves ideomotor reflexes, but opinions and attitudes may also be concerned. On a larger scale "psychic epidemics" may occur, e.g. rapidly propagated excitement as a reaction to music with a strong beat. See *Ideomotor law; Crowd behavior; Attitude; Stereotype.* *H.W.*

Inference. 1. A conclusion drawn from antecedent arguments or propositions accepted as true, which may be deductive or inductive. See *Deduction; Induction.* **2.** The process of drawing such a conclusion.

Inferential statistics. The theory and methods of statistics (q.v.) as applied to the "inferring" of population parameters from sample values and distributions. *W.H.B.*

Inferiority complex; inferiority, feeling of. Adler (q.v.) bases his psychotherapy on the concept of the inferiority complex. The self-realization of any human being is already colored in childhood by universal feelings of inferiority which favor or motivate a compensatory trend toward superiority. The expression "inferiority complex" denotes the weaknesses which occur in every individual and may be real or imaginary, physical, psychological or social; the term also indicates the strong tendency which exists to seek completion and totality. *J.L.I.*

Infertility. 1. The temporary or permanent inability of an organism to produce offspring

(*sterility*). **2.** The tendency for an individual or group to produce very *few* offspring.
G.D.W.

Infibulation. The stitching together of the external female genitalia (vulva or prepuce), usually in order to prevent copulation.

Inflation. The personality is "flooded" with unconscious factors or identifies with them (C. G. Jung). The clinical consequence is generally an acute psychosis. See *Psychoses, functional.*
W.Sc.

Influence. 1. That which produces an effect. **2.** Directive or modifying power (e.g. in interpersonal relations). **3.** To exert influence.

Informal group. See *Group.*

Information. The general term "information" (a synonym for news, communication) has been developed through the analysis of technical data transmission systems and communications networks into one of the basic concepts of information theory (q.v.) and cybernetics.

Starting from the principle of information transferal through technical devices with an information source (transmitter or sender), transmission channel, and receiver, problems of maximum utilization and development of foolproof codes have been examined. Information measurement according to C. E. Shannon and N. Wiener (after preliminary studies by Nyquist, Gabor and Küpfmüller) measures the invariant aspect of telecommunications in codings and signal transmissions (e.g. conversion of acoustic into electrical signals). The information of a communication, sign or event defines its news or novelty content, or more precisely its *improbability*. A sign with the probability p has the information:

$$i(p) = \mathrm{ld}\frac{1}{p}.$$

The mean information is the mean of a repertoire of r signs weighted with the individual probabilities:

$$H = \sum_{i=1}^{r} p(i)\,\mathrm{ld}\frac{1}{p(i)}.$$

In stochastic dependence, calculations are made with the limited probabilities.

Information can be interpreted as the length of the communication with optimal coding in a binary code. The information contained in one bit (q.v.) corresponds to a binary code sign or a selection process from two (equally probable) alternatives.

Because of the formal similarity with the expression for thermodynamic entropy, the mean information is frequently referred to as *entropy* (q.v.), or *negentropy*. Thermodynamic entropy is a measure of the state of order of, or degree of randomness in, a physical system, and indicates the proportion of thermal energy which cannot be converted into mechanical work at a given temperature difference in a thermal or caloric engine.

The concept of information is used not only in communications and regulation technology, but whenever the function of complex systems or the interaction between several systems implies informational processes. See *Cybernetics and psychology; Information, psychology of; Cybernetic education.*

Statistical information, objective information, syntactic(al) information and *selective information* are synonymous terms. Statistical information emphasizes the derivation from statistical characteristics; objective information the possibility of determination by external observers; syntactic(al) information the exclusion of the semantic aspect; and selective information the function of the source in generating sign sequences by selection from an ensemble of signs.

Structural information, metric information: depending on the structure of the signals (q.v.), different aspects of information dominate. Data can be conveyed in an equivalent manner by continuous signals, e.g. current fluctuations in the telephone, or by discrete signals, e.g. current impulses in a telex. In discrete signal sequences the information consists of the number of signals and their mean information. Similarly, in continuous signal sequences, the information consists of the number of distinguishable temporally sequacious signal values, and the stages distinguishable at a given degree of measurement accuracy (i.e., to a certain extent, the repertoire) of disjunctive signal values. According to D. M. McKay, the number of distinguishable signals in a signal sequence is referred to as *structural information,* whereas the information of the individual signal value is known as *metric information.*

Topological information: the information of three- or two-dimensional arrangements which can be converted into temporal signal sequences by scanning during information transferal. In topological information, a distinction is again made between structural information as the number of distinguishable grid cells and metric information derived from the intensity values of the individual cells.

Subjective information: the information content of a message for the receiver can be determined only in relation to the internal state of the receiver. In principle, this rule applies to technical receivers. In psychology, the transition to the concept of subjective information is important (K. Steinbuch, H. Frank, A. Charkewitsch, K. Weltner). It implies a change in the theoretical premisses, to the extent that information is now derived from the expectancy probabilities of the receiver which are determined in turn with the help of rate tests (Shannon, Attneave, Weltner). They enable the subjective information of given complex linguistic and other data to be studied as a function of their context, situation, attitude of the receiver, linguistic and factual understanding, and other psychological parameters.

The transition to the concept of subjective information enables not only the statistical but the *semantic* (the "information of meanings") and the *pragmatic* aspects (the information of behavioral changes elicited by data) to be analyzed. Differentiation therefore enables the semantic component of linguistic data to be isolated from the total information content by measuring the subjective information for two states of the percipient class: (*a*) significance of the unknown information; (*b*) significance of the known information.

Didactic information: in cybernetic education the amount of semantic information in the matter to be learnt; the matter must be available in verbalized form as a basal text. The information remaining when the meaning of the basal text is known is referred to as "esthetic information", which is therefore defined negatively as "non-didactic information", and constitutes a measure of the uniqueness of a particular presentation.

Theoretically precise analysis of *semantic information* is possible only on the basis of unambiguously defined language systems. Appropriate methods are to be found in the theory of logical-semantic information developed by R. Carnap and Y. Bar Hillel. See *Communication; Information theory; Instructional technology; Semantics.*

Bibliography: Attneave, F.: Applications of information theory to psychology. New York, 1959. **Bar-Hillel, Y.:** Language and information. New York, 1964. **Carnap, R.:** What is probability? Scient. Amer., 1953, *189*, 128.

K. Weltner

Information analysis, multidimensional (syn. *Multivariate information transmission*). A method described by McGill for analyzing the relationship between multidimensional (multivariate) stimulus-response sequences with the aid of information theory (q.v.), and dividing the information content of the responses into transinformation of stimuli and random components. Multidimensional information analysis may be interpreted as non-parametric analysis of variance.

Bibliography: McGill, W. J.: Multivariate information transmission. Psychometrika, 1954, *19*, 97–116.

K.W.

Information capacity of the sense organs. The upper limit of the information flow between the receptors and the projection center of the cerebrum is determined by the specific information capacity of the sense organ concerned. The following values (in bits/sec.) have been determined: optical channel: 3.10^6; acoustic channel: 2.10^4 to 5.10^4; tactile channel (with reference to the whole body surface): 2.10^5; olfactory channel: 10–100; gustatory channel: 10.

Bibliography: Gibson, J. J.: The senses considered as perceptual systems. New York, 1966. **Rosenblatt, F.:** The perceptron: a probabilistic model for information storage and organization in the brain. Psychol. Rev., 1958, *65*, 386–408. **Uttley, A. M.:** The classification of signals in the nervous system. EEG clin. Neurophysiol., 1954, *6*, 479–94. *H.R.*

Information, density of. If data are not transmitted as a sequence of signals in time, the quantity of transmitted data is indicated not as an information "flow" (q.v.), but as an information "density" which shows the number of code elements required for coding on a line, a surface, or in a given space. The density of information is measured in signals/cm (cm^2 or cm^3). The density must be determined, e.g., when adapting pictorial material to the capacity of the eye. *H.R.*

Information, esthetics of. The esthetics of information is a branch of esthetics which makes use of the concepts of information theory (q.v.) and information psychology (q.v.). The informational aspect of esthetic processes is subjective and may be described as a process of gradual acquisition; the object of esthetic perception must contain elements of surprise (information) and initially unknown as well as known organizational structures. For a summary of the field, see Bense (1969); for the basic semiological inspiration, Barthes (1967); for the psycholinguistic basis, Chomsky (1957).

Bibliography: Alsleben, K.: Ästhetische Redundanz. Quickborn, 1962. **Barthes, R.:** Elements of semiology. London, 1967. **Bense, M.:** Einführung in die informationstheoretische Ästhetik. Hamburg, 1969. **Chomsky, N.:** Syntactic structures. The Hague, 1957. **Garnier, P.:** Spatialisme et poésie concrète. Paris, 1968. **Uhr, L.** (Ed.): Pattern recognition. New York, 1966. **Wathen-Dunn, W.** (Ed.): Models for the perception of speech and visual form. Cambridge, Mass., 1967. *K.W.*

Information flow. Information flow is determined as the quantity of information transmitted through an information channel per unit of time. It is measured in "bits/sec." The upper limit is determined by the channel capacity. The concept of information flow has been adopted by information psychology (q.v.) and applied to communication (q.v.), learning, and perception. *H.R.*

Information processing (syn. *Data processing*). Any process by which received data are modified or associated with other data on the basis of specific laws so that new data are available as a result. In control, regulating or adaptation processes, this may lead to changes in the receiver's behavior. Information processing also includes the reception and transmission of data. The term "data processing" is often used only to refer to methods involving the use of a computer. When *all* the procedures in a system are bound up with a computer, the term "integrated data processing" (IDP) is applicable.

Bibliography: Feigenbaum, E.: An information processing theory of verbal behavior. Santa Monica, Calif., 1959. **Id. & Feldman, J.** (Eds.): Computers and thought. New York, 1962. *P.B.H.*

Information processing systems. A general term for all systems in which data are processed. A system of this kind can associate several different items of data on the basis of rational laws and obtain new information as the result. In general, organisms which absorb information from the environment (stimuli) and derive behavioral changes from that information can be considered as information processing systems.

P.B.H.

Bibliography: Hunt, E. B.: Concept learning: an information processing problem. New York, 1962. **Norman, D.A.:** Memory and attention: an introduction to human information processing. New York, 1969.

Information psychology. Information psychology represents an attempt to use cybernetic approaches, methods, measurements (in particular that of information) and models in psychology with a view to developing a complete theory.

Information psychology—originally conceived as a psychological basis for the esthetics of information—uses introspection as an indicator of phenomena which are arranged in an (initially qualitative) scheme (an "organogram") appropriate to the psychologically relevant aspect of the human information process. Cybernetic concepts and models (see *Cybernetics and psychology*) are also employed for descriptive ends, and the parameters used are determined quantitatively in experiments. Beyond this *descriptive* stage, the models also allow of quantitative or qualitative, empirically testable conclusions: the explanatory stage. The ultimate stage of the program of information psychology is an abstraction of all "inessential" details, and therefore the restriction of all assertions to a general cybernetic "psychostructural" model. The criterion for the "essential" is appropriateness to the proposed application (which occurs, in particular, within the framework of cybernetic education, q.v.). A series of increasingly complex psychostructural models is used in (largely programmatical) exact information psychology to obtain an approximation to man as a psychologically apprehensible existent.

Various experiments have shown (at least on average) an approximately linear relationship between reaction or perception times and the information content of stimuli. This allows the inference of a maximum reception speed ("apperception speed") of approximately 16 bits/sec. (achieved only at app. twenty years of age) for new consciously apprehended data. At the same age, the information absorption speed of the memory reaches a maximum of about 0.7 bits/sec. Several experiments have also shown that after habituation to a given probability distribution of a repertoire of signs, the subjective receptivity to a symbol reaches a peak at an occurrence probability of $p = 1/e$ (app. 37%). This "maximum effect" is explained by information psychology with the maximum of the function $p \cdot i = p \cdot \mathrm{ld}\frac{1}{p}$, i.e. with a value proportional to the apperception time. The resulting measurement for incidence has proved accurate both in the quantitative interpretation of the results of frequency ratings and in predictions of the statistical influence of examples on apparently free behavior patterns. So far, however, the approaches of information psychology have proved unsatisfactory for determining the repertoire of signs and probabilities (accommodation of information), and for constructing memory models in regard to the learning of semantic information. Above all, the suggested methods for incorporation of motivation in the model have proved inadequate.

Information psychology is, of course, essentially concerned with *models* of psychological events that are of more or less practical value. See *Instructional technology; Machine learning; Simulation.*

Bibliography: Frank, H.: Kybernetische Grundlagen der Pädagogik. Baden-Baden, ^{2}1959. (See also *Information theory.*)

H. Frank

Information reduction. The reduction of subjective information into processing data on the basis of informational accommodation and superordination by forming classes or complexes. Information reduction can help to reduce reaction times.

H.R.

Information system. All the connected means of communication employed within an organism, group or organization.

Information test. A test to estimate an individual's general or specific knowledge.

Information theory. 1. *Development.* Information theory came into being because of problems arising in connection with the transmission of information by technical systems (telegraphy, telephone, wireless). As early as 1924, H. Nyquist (1932) and K. Küpfmüller showed that for electrical transmission systems there was a quantitative connection between the band width of the transmission channel and the maximum speed of the signal. Further developments by C. E. Shannon (1948) led to information theory in its present form, which, as a part area of cybernetics as established by N. Wiener (1948) (see *Cybernetics and psychology*), is also formally connected with the inferential statistics (q.v.) of R. A. Fisher (1925). The fundamental problems are the transmission of signals, news and measurement values and the control of interference.

Shannon & Weaver (1962) deal with the problem of the optimal exploitation of communication chains and networks featuring interference, and base their theory on the objectively observable properties of signal (q.v.) or sign (q.v.) sequences. Relevant areas are the development of interference-free codes, the theory of signal transformation, and the accurate estimation of reductions in channel capacity for idealized degrees of interference.

Information theory is equivalent in many of its aspects to R. A. Fisher's inferential statistics, in so far as Fisher deals with the exclusion of interference (causal disturbances, or "noise") from measurements. Starting from the calculation of probable error (normal probability curve), inferential statistics made it possible to exclude interference from measurement data (division of disturbances into—arbitrary—classes of random and systematic errors which then become observational variables), and extended the field of relevant empirical research in education, psychology and sociology.

N. Wiener (1948) took as his starting-point the interaction, adaptation and stability of systems coupled to an unstable environment (see *Cybernetics and psychology*; *Feedback system*; *Homeostasis*). The exclusion of interference from measurements and information processing were seen as prerequisites. The result was cybernetics, which has information theory as one of its components.

2. *Theory.* The basic idea is information (q.v.) as a quantitative measure for signs (q.v.) or signals (q.v.) which are exchanged between a sender (source, transmitter, emitter) and a receiver (recipient). Sign sequences are selected by various processes from a repertoire (ensemble) available to the sender. The sign sequence can be transmitted by different physical signals (q.v.). From the repertoire of signs used, their frequency, and the selection-restrictive, statistically expressible links between the signs (*stochastic processes*, q.v.; *Markoff processes*, q.v.; grammatical rules: see *Grammar*) a measurement value is obtained for the information; it remains valid for any number of recodings (see *Code*) and signal transformations (q.v.).

In the restricted sense in which it is used in information theory, information—as a *logarithmic measure of infrequency*, or negative value of the (conditioned) probability of occurrence—is a measure for the novelty or "news" value of the sign. It is arbitrary but useful to take the two as a basis of the logarithm. Then the unit—one bit—is the amount of information of a choice of two equally probable outcomes (tossing a coin). Accordingly one bit in data processing denotes a point of a binary data medium which gives the maximum storage capacity (q.v.) of a store.

The structural content of continuous signals can also be measured. A prerequisite of mathematical information theory is the *ergodicity* of the source, i.e. its statistical properties must remain constant and independent of the point at which a sample is taken.

It is of particular interest that *unequivocal and reversible codings without loss of information* are possible not only from discrete into discrete signs (words into letters, letters into teleprinter code), from continuous into continuous signs (sound vibrations into electrical vibrations, brightness values into current values), but from discrete into continuous and from continuous into discrete sign sequences. The continuous course of a temporal (electrical oscillation) or spatial function can be replaced by a sequence of discrete numerical values if these reproduce the functional values at equidistant intervals. The distance of the intervals must be reduced in proportion to the speed at which the value of the function changes (quantal theory). Conversely, the continuous curve can be recovered from the sequence of numerical values.

Important as it is for its technical uses, this system of transfer opens up new prospects for the marginal conditions of stimulus perception and processing in biological and physiological systems (psychophysics, q.v.). In these, too, continuous physical stimuli are coded into impulse and discharge sequences of neuron(e) networks (see *Decision processes*).

When there is no interference with information transmission, an unequivocal relationship is established between the signal as it is sent and as it is received. When there is interference in the channel, the signal as it is received does not always correspond to the signal as it was sent. The information correctly received—transinformation (T)—is smaller than that which was sent. The difference—the information lost—is "*equivocation*". The information produced by interference is "*irrelevance*". Channel capacity (C) (q.v.) is determined by band width (B) (difference between the highest and lowest transmissible frequency). With a disturbed channel (almost always present), the channel capacity diminishes with an intensity proportional to that of the noise compared with the intensity of the signal.

An unexpected result of information theory is that, even in a disturbed channel, any required degree of transfer reliability can be obtained by suitable coding; then transmission speed can reach almost full channel capacity. This is surprising, since the known technical methods of interference exclusion relied on the use of control signs and, in the most trivial case, on the repetition of the data, thus producing redundancy (q.v.) artificially, and reducing transfer speed.

3. *Tasks and applications*. The measurement units and methods of information theory form the bases of data technology, data processing, theoretical optics and picture transmission (Gabor, 1950, 1963), cybernetics (Frank, 1970; Steinbuch, 1965; Wiener, 1948), and technical automation.

In addition, information theory opens up new prospects in fields in which coupling and interaction between complex systems can be regarded as a whole or in part as informational coupling. When stimuli are perceived, conducted and processed, signals are coded and decoded. Sign recognition of signs and gestalt perception may be treated as interference- and irrelevance-exclusion. Learning may be regarded as the construction of internal models by way of informational links (see *Cybernetic education*). Social processes are apprehended by measuring the entropy (information) of groups (Cube & Gunzenhäuser, 1962).

In its purely mathematical form, information theory excludes the semantic and pragmatic aspects of communication, which have to be considered when analyzing interference which has disturbed vocal or optical human intercommunication chains or networks. Such analysis requires a transition from the concept of statistical analysis to that of subjective information, which is concerned with the internal state of the receiver. In this transition, information measurement now refers not to an objective statistics (q.v.) of sign sequences which can be determined by an external observer, but to the empirically determinable probabilities expected by the percipient (Weltner, 1970). This opens up new areas of application for information theory in the analysis of the linguistic aspects and content of perception processes, and in the analysis of cognitive and learning processes, using a combination of empirical methods and the theoretically grounded measurement and relational system of information theory. In this process certain problems arise which cannot yet be treated in isolation: e.g. relevance, or the repertoire of possible references available to the perceiving recipient. See *Communication; Instructional technology*.

Bibliography: Attneave, F.: Applications of information theory to psychology. New York, 1959. **Beer, S.:** Decision and control. London, 1966. **Bellman, R. & Kalaba, R.:** Mathematical trends in control theory. New York, 1964. **Borko, H.** (Ed.): Computer applications in the behavioral sciences. Englewood Cliffs, N.J., 1962. **Brillouin, L.:** Science and information theory. New York, 1956. **Clapp, L. C. & Yilmas, H.:** Optical information processing. In: **Colborn, R.** (Ed.): Modern science and technology. New York, 1965. **Cube, F. v. & Gunzenhäuser, R.:** Die Entropie von Gruppen. Quickborn, 1962. **Frank, H.:** Kybernetik–Brücke zwischen den Wissenschaften. Frankfurt, 1970. **Gabor, D.:** Communication theory and physics. Phil. Mag., 1950, *41*, 1161. **Id:** Inventing the future. London, 1963. **Gibson, E. J.:** Principles of perceptional learning and development. New York, 1969. **Langer, D.:** Informationstheorie und Psychologie. Göttingen, 1962. **Loehlin, J. C.:** Computer models of personality. New York, 1968. **Mackay, D. M.:** Quantal aspects of scientific information. Phil. Mag., 1950, *41*, 289. **Meyer-Eppler, W.:** Grundlagen und Anwendungen der Informationstheorie. Berlin & New York, [2]1969. **Minsky, M.** (Ed.): Semantic information processing. Cambridge, Mass. & London, 1968. **Nyquist, H.:** Regeneration theory. Bell Syst. tech. J., 1932, *11*, 126. **Peters, J.:** Einführung in die allg. Informationstheorie. Berlin—Heidelberg—New York, 1967. **Pierce, J. R.:** Symbols, signals and noise. London, 1962. **Quastler, H.** (Ed.): Information theory in psychology; problems and methods. Glencoe, Ill., 1955. **Rose, J.:** Survey of cybernetics. London, 1970. **Rosenblatt, F.:** Principles of neurodynamics. New York, 1961. **Shannon, C. & Weaver, W.:** The mathematical theory of communication. Urbana, [9]1962. **Stachowiak, H.:** Denken und Erkennen im kybernetischen Modell. Berlin & New York, 1965. **Steinbuch, K.:** Automat und Mensch. Berlin & Heidelberg, [3]1965. **Tomkins, S. S. & Messik, S.:** Computer simulation of personality. New York, 1963. **Weltner, K.:** Informationstheorie und Erziehungswissenschaft. Quickborn, 1970. **Wiener, N.:** Cybernetics. New York, 1948.

K. Weltner

Information transmission (syn. *Information transfer*; *Information transferal*). The transfer of information with the help of an information medium (see *Signal*) from a transmitter to a receiver. Information (or data) transmission follows the pattern below (communication chain):

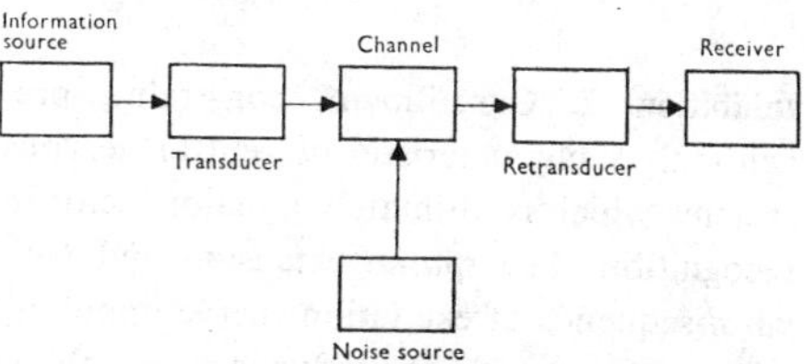

An information source generates data consisting of a sequence of signs (symbols). The latter are converted into transferable signals in a transducer. The signals pass through a data channel or transmission medium to a retransducer which reconverts the received signals and conveys them to the receiver. The noise source comprises all the interference to which the signal is subject on transmission.

Bibliography: Fano, R. M.: The transmission of information. M.I.T. Tech. Rep. 65. Cambridge, Mass., 1949. **Hartley, R. V. L.:** Transmission of information. Bell Syst. tech. J., 1928, *7*, 535.

P.B.H.

Information transmission, multivariate. See *Information analysis, multidimensional.*

Infrared. Electro-magnetic radiations of a frequency just below that of red (103–106 mμ) and therefore outside the visible spectrum. Radiant heat is transmitted in this frequency range.

C.D.F.

Infrasonic. Sounds below the frequency range detected by the ear (1/1000—16 Hz). These sounds can sometimes be detected by other senses as tremors or rhythmic beats. They may be produced by winds, earthquakes, and so on. *C.D.F.*

Inheritance. The combination of genes resulting from the fusion of the parents' cells during fertilization; in a wider sense the totality of the genetic factors which determine the structure and development (q.v.) of the individual in conjunction with environmental (q.v.) influences. See *Abilities; Differential psychology; Traits; Type.* *M.A.*

Inhibition. I. Curtailment, constraint, prevention. A characteristic of central nervous systems which is ultimately a major factor in recognition. The *spatial* extension and *temporal* sequence of excitation (nerve impulses) released by stimuli are influenced by inhibition as well as facilitation and summation processes.

1. *Local* (*lateral*) *inhibition.* The specific path originating at the receptors and running to the projection cortex is interconnected collaterally to adjacent synergistic synapses (see *Synapse*) so that an impulse tends to heighten a strong adjacent impulse, whereas a strong impulse inhibits the weak adjacent impulse. This locally effective contrast system steepens the local excitation gradient by comparison with the stimulus intensity gradient. In general, the organism is governed by the principle that a nucleus of excitation in the information transmission system of the sense organs is always accompanied by an environment with lateral inhibition. Lateral inhibition is primarily important for contrast in the eye (spatial system), and is used only in the higher central nervous layers in the ear (temporal system); in the case of the eye, lateral inhibition of neuronal "on" elements and lateral activation of neuronal "off" elements are essential for contrast recognition.

2. *Temporal inhibition.* Two parallel information channels within the specific pathway from the receptor to the cortex are so interconnected that the channel with the stronger excitation, or—after coding—with the faster action-potential sequence and shorter latency, blocks both channels through an inhibition control neuron, allowing only the first signal of the faster action potential sequence to pass; the remaining signals and above all those in the information channel which is not so strongly energized are completely suppressed.

In the acoustic sense-organ system, temporal inhibition is used, e.g., to suppress a succession of two sound stimuli in a time range in which the time difference is used for a spatial stimulus characteristic, namely the direction of the sound source.

Similarly, temporal inhibition is observed in the acoustic sense-organ system in the sense that specific action-potential intervals in a more or less completely irregular sequence can be suppressed. *M. Spreng*

II. In *neurophysiology*, inhibition is the prevention of specific nervous processes; inhibition may also denote the processes which give rise to such suppression, and which are frequently considered to be among the basic activities of the central nervous system and are interpreted as the opposite factors to excitation. In *psychology* the term is used to denote certain phenomena or the processes on which they are (hypothetically) based, above all in the psychology of memory, in the psychology of learning (see, e.g., Pavlov, 1928; Hull, 1943; Harlow, 1959; Eysenck, 1970), and in clinical psychology (q.v.) with a depth-psychological (see, e.g., Freud, 1936; Schultz-Hencke, 1951) or behavior-therapeutic orientation (see e.g. Salter, 1949; Wolpe, 1958; see *Behavior Therapy*). Although the shades of meaning sometimes vary considerably, inhibition is always the prevention or curtailment of a behavioral process by an activity of a different kind; it is generally assumed that the inhibited function may continue when the inhibiting factor has been removed.

The significance given to inhibition processes in the social or performance (achievement) context differs widely from author to author, and sometimes even within a given system. Harlow and, in certain cases (primarily differential inhibition), Pavlov attach considerable importance to the notion of inhibition, e.g. as the basis of all higher mental processes.

Reciprocal inhibition, according to Wolpe, is an essentially neutral mechanism, while internal inhibition, according to Pavlov, and reactive inhibition, according to Hull, are close to the concept of fatigue and also emphasize a possible protective function. Inhibitions of memory are generally considered to be performance-reductive influences on learning processes. In clinical psychology the need to acquire specific inhibitions in the socialization (q.v.) process is stressed, while at the same time (and more frequently) attention is drawn to the high probability of negative personality development through excessive inhibition of spontaneous impulses (Schultz-Hencke, 1951; Salter, 1949).

Studies of the associations between neurophysiological and behavioral "inhibitions" are still in their infancy. See *Arousal*; *Behaviorism*; *Conditioning, classical and operant.*

Bibliography: Eysenck, H. J.: The biological basis of personality. Springfield, Ill., [2]1970. **Freud, S.:** Inhibitions, symptoms and anxiety. London, [2]1936. **Harlow, H. F.:** Learning set and error factor theory. In: **Koch, S.** (Ed.): Psychology: A study of a science, Vol. 2. New York, 1959. **Hull, C. L.:** Principles of behavior. New York, 1943. **Pavlov, I. P.:** Lectures on conditioned reflexes, Vol. 1. New York, 1928. **Salter, A.:** Conditioned reflex therapy. New York, 1949. **Schultz-Hencke, H.:** Lehrbuch der analytischen Psychotherapie. Stuttgart, 1951. **Wolpe, J.:** Psychotherapy by reciprocal inhibition. Stanford, 1958.

L. Blöschl

Inhibition, internal (syn. *Inner inhibition*). In I.P. Pavlov's behavioral theory "internal inhibition" is a term for a group of inhibition phenomena characterized in that they are caused by changes in the conditioned association itself and, unlike the various forms of unconditioned inhibition, are acquired in learning processes. "Internal inhibition develops when the conditioned stimulus is not attended by the unconditioned, whether this be once or always, but in the latter event, only under certain circumstances. Thus come about extinction, retardation, conditioned inhibition, and differential inhibition. We see then that the same conditions are necessary for the development of sleep as for the development of internal inhibition." (Pavlov, 1928.) The following are the most important forms of internal inhibition:

1. *Extinction:* if a conditioned stimulus is not applied repeatedly, the conditioned response gradually ceases to occur. That this is inhibition and not elimination proper is shown by the results of many experiments (spontaneous restoration of the extinguished conditioned reflex after a long delay, etc.).

2. *Differential inhibition:* if one of two similar stimuli, but not the other, is applied repeatedly, the second stimulus is (differentially) inhibited as a special case of extinctive inhibition. See *Conditioning, classical and operant; Inhibition; Orienting reflex.*

Bibliography: Pavlov, I. P.: Lectures on conditioned reflexes, Vol. 1. New York, 1928. *L.B.*

Inhibition potential. See *Conditioned inhibition.*

Inhibition, social. A term for the absence (or presence in a modified form) of certain—usually aggressive—modes of behavior toward members of the same species. E.g. rats when *feigning* combat do not bite or display the threat gestures which precede serious fighting. See *Appeasement gestures*; *Aggression.* *V.P.*

Inhibition type (syn. *Inhibitory type*). More difficult to excite and less capable of achieving high performance than the excitatory, or excitement type (q.v.); conditioned reflexes are weak and unstable; changeable. "There stand out three well-defined types of nervous systems; the central or equilibrated, and the two extreme types, the excitatory and inhibitory. . . . The melancholic is evidently an inhibitory type of nervous system" (Pavlov, 1928). See *Type*.

Bibliography: Parlov, I. P.: Lectures on conditioned reflexes, Vol. 1. New York, 1928. *W.K.*

Inhibitory potential (cumulative). See *Conditioned inhibition.*

Initiation. A term taken from the Latin *initiatio*: a beginning, and used in ethnology (q.v.) to denote *rites* performed when a juvenile is received into the adult community. "Puberty rites" is another term with the same meaning. In many tribal cultures where there is no knowledge of writing, initiation rites are of greater significance than marriage. In our culture "confirmation", parties after a school-leaving examination, etc., are feeble reflections of initiation ceremonies (Hofstätter, 1963). In contrast to the vestiges of initiation rites we possess, which all relate to some achievement, the authentic rites in their highly-developed forms also perform such functions as heterosexual "education" and confirmation of sex roles by means of, e.g., circumcision (q.v.) ceremonies (e.g. the removal of the girl's clitoris or the boy's foreskin). Initiation and initiation rites emphasize the break between childhood and adulthood, and at the same time link the two chief periods in life (Chapple & Coon, 1942).

Instruction in tribal knowledge and certain skills (tribal history, mythology, mysteries, dances, pipe playing, etc.), tests of courage and self-control (piercing the nostrils, frightening experiences, etc.) serve to show whether the young member of the tribe is suitable for adult status, and at the same time to prepare him for the concomitant rights and duties. Symbolic representations and magico-religious actions play a significant part (death and rebirth) in initiation. In general, initiation does not necessarily coincide with biological sexual maturity, and can extend over several weeks or months.

Bibliography: Chapple, E. D. & Coon, C. S.: Principles of anthropology. New York, 1942. **Hofstätter, P.:** Einführung in die Sozialpsychologie. Stuttgart, 1963. **Mead, M.:** Coming of age in Samoa. New York, 1928. **Id.:** Growing up in New Guinea. New York, 1930. *H.M.*

Innate (syn. *Inborn*). **1.** That which is present at birth. **2.** Some difference between individuals which is not attributed to environmental influence. See *Differential psychology; Drive; Instinct; Traits.*

Innate releasing mechanism (abb. IRM). The instinctive, selective readiness of an animal to respond to a "releaser", or specific sign- or key-stimulus (q.v.), with a specific reaction. This hypothetical physiological (neurosensory) mechanism works as a "stimulus filter" by checking the reaction in inadequate situations. See *Imprinting; Instinct.*

Bibliography: Tinbergen, N.: An objectivistic study of the innate behaviour of animals. Biblioth. biotheor., 1942, *1*, 39–98. **Id.:** The study of instinct. Oxford, [2]1969. *I.L.*

Inner speech (syn. *Internal speech; Inner language*). Inner speech is unvoiced speech, a function in itself, and the basic form of thinking in words. The philosophers of antiquity had already noted that "thinking is speaking to oneself in silence". Plato was the first of many philosophers, linguisticians and psychologists who have tried to develop this judgment, some even going so far as to assert (unjustifiably) that thought and spoken language are one, or (in one version of behaviorism) that thinking may be defined as "subvocal" processes in the larynx (Watson, 1920; [3]1929).

Early studies of the phenomenon of inner speech were grounded on introspection (q.v.) and clinical observations of speech disorders (i.e. different forms of aphasia, q.v.). On the basis of these observations, inner speech was conceived as "verbal images" of various modalities (acoustic, motor and visual), a deficit in which could be explained in terms of aphasic dysfunctions of thought processes (disturbances of speech comprehension in sensory aphasia and of verbal memory in motor aphasia). Several theories were put forward: a motor basis for inner speech (G. Stricker, 1880); an acoustic basis (Egger, 1881); or a mixed basis (G. Ballet, 1886). In addition, visual forms were characterized as optical images of letters and schematic visual images of objects (A. Lemaitre, 1905). The Würzburg psychologists (K. Bühler, 1907–8), however, argued that perceptual mental images and verbal images did not play any essential role in thinking, and were mere sporadic phenomena.

Experimental research into inner speech is obviously very difficult because of the covert nature of all its processes. The most advantageous course would seem to be an investigation of the motor (kinesthetic) components. At first (1900–25), inadequately sensitive pneumatic and mechanical devices were used in attempts to record the micro-movements of vocal organs (Curtis, Wyczoikowska, Thorson, *et al.*). In addition, some researchers used various methods of suppressing or inhibiting external and internal articulation (A. Binet, E. Meumann, Pintner). The results of these experiments allowed of more than one interpretation; hence covert articulation was viewed not only as a general but as an individual factor in thought. The use of more sensitive recording devices (at first the string galvanometer, and later the electromyograph) made possible more exact results which indicated an increase in the tonus of the vocal musculature during all verbal functions involving difficult thinking. It was also shown that the EMG (electromyograph) potentials recorded under such conditions are local speech potentials and not merely the result of diffuse irradiation of muscular tonus. These investigations were pioneered by E. Jacobson (1929–32). The EMG method was used afterwards to study the thinking of the deaf (Max, 1937), thinking in acoustic schizophrenic hallucinations (Gould, 1948–9), in attentive hearing (Smith, Malmo & Shagass, 1954; Wallerstein, 1954), in silent reading (Faaborg-Andersen & Edfeldt, 1957–9; Hardyck *et al.*, 1966), and in verbal and perceptual problem-solving (Sokolov, 1957–68).

The results of these more recent investigations show a considerable variation in linguistic EMG reactions, which is independent of the difficulty and novelty of the conceptual problems to be solved, the degree of automatization of the thought operations to be carried out, the introduction of images (percepts and mental imagery) into mentation, and the individual inclination to a specific memory type. Vocal motor impulses are detectable not only in verbal-abstract but in "visual" thinking, even though they are weaker, or even inhibited or reduced during phases of intensive visual object-analysis. Subsequently, however, there is the phase of covert vocal motor reactions, which neither conclude nor correct the thought process. On the basis of electromyographic data it may be assumed that the main function of vocal motor (proprioceptive and tactile) afference in thinking is probably motor reinforcement or "activation" of the speech mechanisms of the brain in accordance with the "feedback" (q.v.) principle. This accords with Pavlov's (1941) conception of kinesthetic stimulations of the speech organs as the bases or fundamental components of speech, which is a second system of signalization in humans, signaling the first unified signaling system of the animal, and primarily the human, organism.

In Soviet psychology (q.v.), the problem of inner speech has been exhaustively examined in connection with a critique of the Würzburg and the behaviorist conceptions of thought. A general survey of this problem and of relevant experimental findings is available in Sokolov (1968, 1969). See also *Language; Mental imagery; Psycholinguistics; Vygotsky*.

Bibliography: Ballet, G.: Le langage intérieur. Paris, 1886. **Edfeldt, A.:** Silent speech and silent reading. Stockholm, 1959. **Jacobson, E.:** Progressive relaxation. Chicago, [2]1956. **Luria, A. R.:** The role of speech in the regulation of normal and abnormal behavior. New York, 1961. **Pavlov, I. P.:** Lectures on conditioned reflexes, Vol. 2. New York, 1941. **Sokolov, A. N.:** Internal speech and thought. Moscow, 1968. **Id.:** Studies of speech mechanisms of thinking. In: A handbook of contemporary Soviet psychology. New York & London, 1969. **Vygotsky, L. S.:** Thought and language. Cambridge, Mass., 1962. **Watson, J. B.:** Is thinking merely the action of language mechanisms? Brit. J. Psychol., 1920, *11*, 87–104. **Id.:** Psychology from the standpoint of a behaviorist. Philadelphia, [3]1929.

A. N. Sokolov

Innervation. 1. Anatomical: the development of nerve fibers in the organism. **2.** Physiological: the provision of nervous stimuli, in particular the conduction of central impulses to the effectors through (innervating) nerve fibers. In general, a distinction can be made between innervation by afferent (centripetal), efferent (centrifugal) and vegetative (sympathetic and parasympathetic) nerves. Exteroceptors and interoceptors are involved in innervation, which is regulated by the central nervous system (q.v.) *F.-C.S.*

Input. 1. The energy flowing into a system. **2.** The actual stimulus or signal received. In information theory (q.v.), a living being can be considered as an information channel (communication channel) or as a complex information system. Stimuli comprise the input and responses the output. Information theory models are frequently used to represent and interpret cognitive behavioral patterns (e.g. thought, speech). One such model is the TOTE unit (Miller, Galanter & Pribram, 1960), which includes the feedback concept. Plans (e.g. expectations) are constantly compared with environmental data. If the "plans" are considered as system states and environmental data as (information) input, the environmental influence is compared with the system state. If the two coincide a response is made (output). "Stimulus and response must be seen as phases of the organized, coordinated act . . . Stimulus and response must be considered as aspects of a feedback loop." The stimulus is seen not as preceding but as guiding the response.

Bibliography: Miller, G. A., Galanter, E. & Pribram, K. H.: Plans and the structure of behavior. New York, 1960. **Rosenblith, W. A.** (Ed.): Sensory communication. New York, 1961.

H.W.

Insanity. This term is *not* now used as a synonym for psychosis but is reserved for a medico-legal condition, namely a mental disorder which results in the patient not being responsible for his actions, or in his being unaware of the consequences of his actions. See *Mental defect; Psychoses, functional; Schizophrenia.* *R.H.*

Insects, state-forming (syn. *Social insects*). With the aid of very complex instinct (q.v.) patterns, a highly sophisticated form of social behavior has developed in certain groups of insects (hymenoptera, termites); a convergence of behavior is observed between certain species. The selective advantage for these social species consists, as in a human culture, in the possibility of answering the demands of life more rationally through the division of labor, which is determined by external influences: according to the mode of nurture, insects develop as sexually mature or retarded workers and soldiers. State-forming bees possess an unusual learning capacity and highly complex modes of exchanging information. See *Dancing language*.

Bibliography: Chauvin, R.: Animal societies from bee to gorilla. London, 1968. **Id.:** The world of ants. London, 1971. **Frisch, K. von:** Bees: their vision, chemical senses and language. London, 1968.

H.Sch.

Insight. **1.** An individual's conscious knowledge or understanding of himself or others. See *Empathy; Introspection.* **2.** An immediate understanding of a real or logico-mathematical relationship. Gestalt psychology conceives the process of insight as an organization of events such that structural relationships in the phenomenal *field* (q.v.) change in accordance with the particular phenomenon. The result of such a process is often the familiar "inspiration" or "sudden idea". (See *Aha experience.*)

Bibliography: Köhler, W.: The mentality of apes. New York, 1925.

P.T.

Insomnia (syn. *Agrypnia*). Chronic sleeplessness. First investigated by K. von Economo (1917) after an outbreak of epidemic encephalitis in Europe during World War I, which led to a reversal of the normal sleep-waking rhythm. Those suffering from the affliction are awake at night but sleep during the day. Insomnia is to be distinguished from difficulty in getting to sleep and disturbances of sleep. It is neurophysiologically conditioned by hyper-activation of neuron(e) complexes located in the reticular formation. Insomnia frequently occurs in healthy individuals as a disorder of diverse causation (over-arousal, hyper-stimulation from optical and acoustic sources, effects of caffeine ingestion). It often accompanies depressive and schizophrenic states, but can also occur in internal disorders, e.g. cardiac insufficiency, angina pectoris, high blood pressure, hyperthyroidism, etc. In old age, the sleep-waking rhythm becomes irregular; after approximately age fifty, arteriosclerotic changes can induce insomnia in about fifty per cent of individuals. See *Sleep.* *D.V.*

Inspiration. Originally a theological term: a divine influence, or a condition in which God manifests himself to man in a supernatural manner. Some psychologists have described inspiration as the manifestation of a "secondary personality" concealed in the unconscious. This personality is said to have great creative potential and to allow certain sensitive, intraverted individuals to proceed to unique achievements. Sometimes used as a synonym for genius (q.v.). See *Abilities; Creativity; Meditation.* *E.U.*

Instinct. Instinct as a word derives from the Latin *instinctus*, from *instinguere*—to incite. In some uses, the word has referred to particular behavior patterns and coordination but it is in the sense of a basic biological urge that the concept has had greatest influence. All animals maintain themselves by ingestion, digestion and elimination, and all species survive by means of reproduction. Fundamentally, the concept of instinct merely states this. Attempts to elaborate the concept, in particular the incorporation of ideas concerning innateness and subjective, purposive phenomena, have been considered controversial. Indeed the concepts of innateness and purpose are themselves as complex and confused as that of instinct.

1. *History.* The concept of biological urge or inner drive, for which the word instinct is generally used, has a history in classical antiquity. In post-Wundtian psychology the most influential instinct theorists were James (q.v.), Morgan and McDougall (q.v.), who wrote in the early part of this century, but their general influence did not extend beyond its first two decades. Freud (q.v.), the founder of psychoanalysis, is an exception, but his influence as an instinct theorist has continued only outside the mainstream of psychology.

A swing away from instinct and a preoccupation with behaviorism (q.v.) and the problem of drive (q.v.) occurred in psychology during the 1930s and 1940s. Apart from Tolman (q.v.), no influential theorist wrote on instinct, and even Tolman's following was achieved in the context of drive rather than instinct theory.

During its period of decline in psychology, work on instinctive behavior in animals was still being undertaken, mostly on the continent of Europe. The term ethology (q.v.) is now used to describe this work, carried out independently of psychology in a tradition of biology and natural history. Through the influence of this ethological work, a revival of interest in the concept of instinct occurred in comparative psychology during the 1950s. Ethologists and psychologists took renewed interest in each other's work, and the cross-fertilization of ideas has generated new research in comparative psychology (q.v.), but without, however, any widespread revival of interest in the concept in general psychology. (See *Animal psychology.*)

2. *Scientific use of the instinct concept.* Since the theory of evolution is common to all biologically oriented sciences, it is convenient to consider the scientific use of the concept as starting with Darwin. He, and others after him, have used the concept of instinct to account for behavior which is usually complex, adaptive, and often finely attuned to particular environmental conditions. Such behavior is often performed with an appearance of intelligence and aimed, with what appears to be purposiveness, toward particular goals, even though the capacities of the organism concerned make it impossible to attribute such intelligence.

No fully adequate explanation can yet be offered, in terms of physico-chemical events or known biological mechanisms, for much of this kind of behavior, particularly as it occurs in insects, fish and birds. Until research has filled obvious gaps in our knowledge, the concept of instinct will continue to be used to meet these deficiencies.

Three major scientific trends in the literature on instinct are the psychoanalytic, psychological and ethological. All have proposed models in attempts to account for instinctive behavior. Ethological models are most specific and closely linked to empirical phenomena, whereas the psychoanalytic model is more general and difficult to test empirically.

3. *Psychoanalytic views of instinct.* According to Freud, an instinct has a particular force or impetus to action. The aim of the action is to abolish the source stimuli creating the impulse, and this can be achieved in or through some object, which can vary according to its satisfying properties. Central to much of Freud's theorizing were the concepts of conflict (q.v.) and equilibrium, representing dynamic forces whereby aims and objects of instinctive behavior could be altered by repression, or sublimation. Although this represents a model of behavior, its link with reality lies in observations of clinical patients. It has proved difficult, though not impossible, to test these ideas empirically. Also, such motivational ideas as are present in Freud's scheme, in so far as they have been incorporated into general psychology, have been considered as drives rather than instincts. (See *Drive.*)

4. *Psychological views of instinct.* Psychological theorists have proposed that instinct involves some internal state disposing an organism to respond selectively to certain kinds of environmental objects or events. This basic impulse is alleged to be innate and to involve subjective, purposive excitement directed toward the ends or goal of the behavior. According to this view, an instinct is an inborn, conative-affective system.

Because of the general acceptance of the concept of evolutionary continuity existing between animals and man, it has been held that the instincts, which form an obvious part of the behavior of animals such as insects, must exist also in man. In man, however, expression of the instinct is considered to be infinitely variable.

McDougall (q.v.) was undoubtedly the most influential psychologist to write on instinct, and his books, written early in this century, were widely used in its early decades and continued in print as late as the 1950s. His system of instincts and their associated sentiments had greatest appeal to social psychologists, among whom, until relatively recently, ideas concerning social interaction seemed less amenable to empirical tests, probably because his ideas seemed simple and direct. McDougall was, however, and not without justification, criticized as confusing description with explanation.

With the hardening of behaviorist attitudes in psychology (see *Behaviorism*), the use of the concept of innateness was avoided as an inferior substitute for detailed behavioral analysis and subjective phenomena ruled out of scientific analysis. Most phenomena previously considered instinctual were redefined as drive (q.v.). The term drive was relatively free from the related concepts of innateness and purpose, yet covered many of the essential features of instinct. Apart from some areas of comparative and developmental psychology, where psychoanalytic and ethological ideas are influential, the concept of instinct is now largely ignored in psychology.

5. *Ethological views of instinct.* Ethological views of instinct, whilst owing much to the theory of evolution and to early American and European naturalists and zoologists, derive principally from the integrative work of Lorenz and Tinbergen.

Two important organizing influences stem from this work. The first is that rigid, stereotyped behavior patterns, characteristic of much instinctive behavior in animals, are potentially of equal value in taxonomy, as are structural and other factors. The second is that behavior is caused by energy specific to particular instinctive acts of fixed action patterns. When an organism, through the agency of search-like appetitive behavior, meets appropriate environmental stimuli for which the animal has special receptor and perceptual releasing mechanisms, the act is released and specific energy is dissipated. A special appeal of the energy model was that by distinguishing between appetitive behavior and the instinctive act, it could account for achievement of a set goal by variable means without incorporating the idea of purpose, because performance of the act itself was considered to be the goal.

If an animal does not meet with appropriate environmental stimuli, the energy builds up until it results in spontaneous performance of the act despite the absence of appropriate stimuli. This has been called vacuum activity and, in the examples of this kind of behavior which ethologists have described, it has the appearance of behavior performed inappropriately. Another form of inappropriate behavior has been called displacement activity. In an animal prevented from performing some instinctive act in a normal way, energy appropriate to that act is displaced, resulting in behavior inappropriate to the animal's current needs. This ethological model and attendant concepts have generated a large body of research in the field of animal behavior. The model has been severely criticized, in particular the vacuum and displacement activities, important empirical evidence for the energy model being increasingly accounted for in other terms. Concepts associated with the energy model, however, such as sensory and perceptual releasers, displacement activities and fixed action patterns, in revised form, are likely to continue to be used in behavioral analysis.

6. *Current status of the instinct concept.* A dispassionate appraisal of the current status of the concept of instinct is difficult. Considerable research activity is taking place on problems which could be described as proper to instinct, though use of the concept as such is not much in evidence. In particular, recent ideas on and research into critical periods in early behavior, whether imprinting (q.v.), primary socialization or early experience, have direct antecedents in psychoanalytic, psychological and ethological views of instinct.

Bibliography: Birney, R. C. & Teevan, R. C.: Instinct, New York, 1961. **Drever, J.:** Instinct in man. Cambridge, 1917, **Fletcher, R.:** Instinct in man. London, 1968. **McDougall, W.:** An introduction to social psychology. London, 1908. **Schiller, C. H.:** Instinctive behaviour. London, 1957. **Thorpe, W. H.:** Learning and instinct in animals. London, [2]1963. **Tinbergen, N.:** The study of instinct. Oxford, [2]1969. **Wilm, E. C.:** The theories of instinct. New Haven, 1925.

P. L. Broadhurst & J. Wilcock

Instinctive action; instinctive behavior. See *Instinct; Innate releasing mechanism.*

Instinct-taxis association (syn. *Instinctive motor co-ordination*). According to Lorenz, an instinctive action consists of innate co-ordination (a relatively rigid pattern of muscular contractions) and the taxis (q.v.) components which direct the action.

Bibliography: Lorenz, K.: Über den Begriff der Instinkthandlung. Folia biotheor., 1937, *2*, 17–50. **Id.:** Studies in animal and human behaviour, Vols. 1, 2. London, 1970–1. *K.Fi.*

Institutes of psychology. When psychology asserted its independence as an empirical and predominantly experimental discipline in its own right, a great number of university institutes and departments of psychology were established as research and teaching centers: e.g. 1879 (a milestone in the history of psychology) Leipzig, by W. Wundt (q.v.); 1881, Göttingen, by G. E. Müller (q.v.); 1883, Johns Hopkins, by G. S. Hall (q.v.); 1888, Pennsylvania, by J. McK. Cattell (q.v.); 1889, the Sorbonne, by H. Beaunis and A. Binet (q.v.); 1886, Kazan, by V. M. Bekhterev (q.v.). Important schools of psychology developed at several of these institutes (e.g. the Berlin, Leipzig and Würzburg Schools). At present, individual university institutes of psychology tend to feature a wide variety of psychological specialisms. Other institutes without any direct university connections are making an increasingly large contribution to research (e.g. the Max Planck Institutes in Germany).

Bibliography: Misiak, H. & Sexton, V. S.: History of psychology. New York, 1966. *E.G.W.*

Institution; institutionalization. A sociological concept used by H. Spencer to denote, e.g., ideas and establishments which take into account the interests or value judgments of a large cultural group through special forms of social interaction, e.g. education, marriage, property, etc. A distinction may be made between, e.g., domestic, sacred, political, professional, economic and other institutions which cover the means and activities considered necessary by a larger group to achieve specific ends. Parsons works on the basis of the internalization of values and standards with which several groups conform. If this conformity leads to satisfaction and causes others to accept these standards, this value or system of standards can be defined as "institutionalized". According to Parsons, an institution is therefore a complex of institutionalized role characteristics or status relationships which is structurally significant for the given social system and its maintenance. See *Group; System, social.*

Bibliography: Caplow, T.: Principles of organization. New York, 1964. **Feibleman, J. K.:** The institutions of society. London, 1956. **Parsons, T.:** The social system. New York, [4]1963. **Spencer, H.:** The study of sociology. London, [21]1894. *W.D.F.*

Institutionalized children. Institutionalization (in the sense of the substitution of a state or voluntary home for the natural or foster parents) can have a particularly harmful effect on young children (see *Hospitalism; Inanition*). Some studies have shown clear differences between children raised in institutions and those brought up in a family environment; these differences apply at the level of intellectual development, or that of the degree of voluntary cooperation and school progress; children brought up in institutions experience considerable difficulty in establishing and maintaining social contacts. *M.Sa.*

Instruction. 1. Directions given to the testee regarding his behavior in the experimental or test situation; he should also be motivated to conform to these indications. Even minor changes in initial instruction can lead to statistically certain differences in the test results. The tone of voice and gestures of the psychologist or experimenter during instruction can also affect results to some extent.

2. Authoritative teaching; indoctrination (q.v.). **3.** Systematic teaching. See *Instructional technology*.

Instructional technology. The study of learning should provide knowledge that can be used in designing an instructional environment and in the educational process. However, scientific findings and theories are rarely available immediately for practical use; translation and development are required for their possible application. As the study of learning becomes increasingly relevant to educational problems, an understanding is required of the relations between basic and applied science, and development, that lead to the methods and technology which can be used by the practicing educator to design conditions for learning.

The recent history of the experimental psychology of learning displays a cyclical progress toward contact between scientific endeavors and technological development. In the nineteen twenties and thirties, the work of L. Thorndike (q.v.) showed an exemplary concern with the implications of psychology for educational science (q.v.). In addition to his basic studies on the law of effect and on verbal learning. Thorndike wrote extensively on educational psychology (q.v.) and the psychology of school subjects. Following Thorndike and his associates, the psychology of learning entered a period (1940–45) of decreasing emphasis on school learning, and increasing attention to laboratory experiments and theoretical elaborations based upon them (Melton, 1941; Estes, 1960). But, beginning in the late 'fifties, experimental psychologists have been turning their thinking and their enterprises to the analysis and investigation of the educational, instructional process (Skinner, 1958; Bruner, 1960; Lumsdaine & Glaser, 1960; Bugelski, 1964; Hilgard, 1964; Suppes, 1964; Gagné, 1965; Gibson, 1965; Gilbert, 1965; Glaser, 1965; Groen & Atkinson, 1966; Moore & Anderson, 1968).

At the present time, an instructional technology based upon an underlying science of learning is emerging. Technology in this sense does not necessarily mean hardware and instrumentation, but rather an applied discipline like engineering or medicine. The techniques and procedures used by the practitioners of these technological disciplines grow out of the findings in their underlying sciences, and also develop by informing science of their needs. The major impetus for the emergence of this field of instructional technology was provided by B. F. Skinner (1954, 1958), who recognized the work of Sidney L. Pressey in the 'twenties (Pressey, 1926). While both Pressey and Skinner thought and conceptualized in terms of the broad application of behavioral science to education, their initial developments centered upon self-instructional devices as a way of making concrete certain principles of learning, and as a way of providing tools and instrumentation around which instructional innovation could take place. It is often mistakenly believed that the devices themselves, and the specifics of the early crude apparatuses, formed the major contribution. In his 1958 article, Skinner emphasized the importance of the principles of programming and the possibility of a scientific technology for instruction. Whereas an important contribution of the field of programmed instruction and instructional technology is the development of materials and instrumentation to extend the capabilities of a teacher as an instructor and the student as a learner, the field is not restricted to these products. Work in instructional technology is extended to the general design of educational environments, including teacher practices, classroom organization, and so forth (Skinner, 1968; Bruner, 1960; Hilgard, 1964).

1. *Psychological bases for instructional design.* At the present time, research and development in the field of instructional technology can be characterized in terms of

the following areas: analysis of the behavior to be learned; diagnosis of the characteristics of the learner; specification of the conditions for learning; and the assessment and optimization of the outcomes of learning.

2. *Analysis of the behavior to be learned.* A body of knowledge consists of information and of processes: information includes data, facts, concepts, and rules; processes refer to the cognitive abilities and intellectual skills by which this information is manipulated and transformed for the purposes of acquiring new knowledge and carrying out intellectual performances. From the viewpoint of instructional theory and practice, the presence of competence is inferred by reference to the behavior of an individual. For example, we infer that a student knows certain principles of physics because he can describe them, identify their application, and recall and use them where appropriate. The informational content of a body of knowledge, the ways in which this information is interrelated and structured, and the ways in which it can be processed must be analyzed and understood before the conditions involved in the acquisition of this knowledge can be meaningfully studied and implemented. As a consequence, an increasingly prominent feature of the psychology of learning is the analysis and classification of the behavior to be learned.

A particularly prominent technique for the analysis of structures of knowledge has been presented by Gagné (1962). This analysis begins with a desired instructional objective, stated in terms of student behavior, and asks in effect, "to perform this behavior, what prerequisite or component behavior(s) must the learner be able to perform?" For each behavior identified, the same question is asked, thus generating a hierarchy of behaviors based on identifiable and measurable prerequisites. Analysis of this kind attempts to provide an ordered set of tasks for inclusion in an instructional sequence. Such analyses observe the basic constraint that no objective is taught to the learner until he has met the prerequisites which facilitate learning and transfer to the next objective. These prerequisite learnings can be achieved in a variety of ways; some individuals can learn them one at a time, and others learn a number of them in larger steps. The instructional process is optimized by continuous identification of the furthest skill along the hierarchy that a student can perform at any moment; or, if a student is unsuccessful in performing a particular task objective, by determining the most immediate sub-objective at which he is successful. These hierarchies indicate transfer relationships between the elements of increasing knowledge or task competence, and make explicit what behaviors are to be observed and tested for.

The relationships between units of learning establish the subject-matter structures that are learned, e.g. concepts, rules, principles, and strategies. With increasing knowledge and with the increasing maturity of the learner, these units of behavior become progressively larger. At certain phases in the acquisition of knowledge, a structure can become a unit of a higher structure. For example, consider the progression of phases in a child learning to read. Assuming that the child has learned to speak, the first phase in the process is the discrimination of graphic symbols (printed letters). In the second phase, these discriminated objects are encoded, or mapped onto language, so that spelling-to-sound (grapheme-phoneme) correspondences are acquired. At this point, relationships are established between the discriminated symbols and speech units. In later phases, the student learns to read not letter-by-letter, but by words and paragraphs, and the previously learned units become part of higher-order structures. Such structures determine the content of a subject-matter learning that is manifested in competent subject-matter behavior; and psychological research in instruction has as a basic requirement the identification of the units and structures involved in subject-matter performance (Gagné & Gephart, 1968; Gibson, 1965, 1969). In addition to analyzing the structures of advanced knowledge, one must also determine those units and structures which serve optimally to facilitate learning for the novice (Bruner, 1964). This means that a technology of instruction must specify the ways in which a body of knowledge can be organized so that it can be most readily grasped by the learner as he progresses to more advanced competence.

3. *Diagnosis of the characteristics of a learner*. Detailed diagnosis of the initial state with which a learner comes into a particular instructional situation is necessary to further his education. In the early stages of instruction, teaching procedures adapt to the findings of this initial assessment. In this concern with initial measurement and diagnosis, an important distinction must be noted: traditional measurement practices have assumed, essentially, a "selection model" of instruction in which the aptitudes of a student are measured and used to predict his success in a relatively uniform instructional environment. In contrast, the present concern in educational technology and programmed instruction is to establish different conditions and procedures for learning, depending upon the initial state of the learner. The direction necessary to take for this purpose has been pointed to by Cronbach (1957) and by Cronbach & Gleser (1965), i.e. to move toward decision-making procedures based upon relationships between the entering behavior of a learner and the variables manipulated in instruction. Measures are taken on the basis of which a decision can be made as to what instructional environment an individual should select in order to optimize his attainment of learning outcomes.

For the most part, measures of general aptitude and general intelligence measures do not seem likely to be the most useful bases for differentiating and adapting instruction because they correlate with success in most instructional methods. As a result, psychologists are now very actively investigating the interaction between entering behavior (aptitude) measures and learning variables. Fleishman (1965, 1967) carefully studied the learning of psychomotor skills. Fleishman compared the contribution of the various abilities tested at the beginning of learning to performance scores on successive learning trials during practice and showed that the particular combinations of abilities change as practice continues, and that the different abilities existing before entering a learning task influence learning at different learning stages. The implication is that individuals with different patterns of abilities require different learning experiences at different stages of learning. In the area of verbal learning, Jensen (1966, 1967, 1968) suggested certain variables of human performance that appear to interact with the learning of verbal tasks. General reviews and analyses of the field of aptitude-method interactions have been reported by Bracht & Glass (1968), and Cronbach & Snow (1969). (See *Abilities*.)

4. *Specification of the conditions for learning*. In attaining subject-matter knowledge and intellectual skill, the learner proceeds through a novitiate and then on to relative expertise; he learns to be a good reader, a competent mathematician, a deep thinker, a quick learner, a creative person, an inquiring individual, and so on. These activities are learned according to criteria of expertise established by the school and intellectual community; more specifically by subject-matter requirements, peer group expectations, and the general social and professional criteria for what determines low, average, and high levels of competence. The educational and social community adjusts its expectations to the competence level of the learner, so that initially very awkward and incorrect performances are acceptable whereas later they are not; a young child or a novice is frequently rewarded for rather uninteresting behavior but as competence grows, his performance is attended to only in the presence of an appropriate audience or in an appropriate situational context. The process of going from ignorance to competence, from novice to expert, establishes a useful way of looking

at the processes and characteristics of instruction.

Four general properties of behavior appear to distinguish the performance of the beginner from that of the expert: (*a*) The responses of the learner move from variable, awkward, and crude to consistent, relatively fast, and precise. Responses develop from simple unitary acts into large response integrations and overall strategies. (*b*) Subject-matter stimuli change from specific instances to members of response classes, and the invariance of these classes becomes the major stimulus event. Stimulus contexts change from simple ones to complex patterns in which relevant must be distinguished from irrelevant aspects, and information must be abstracted from a context of events which are not all appropriate. (*c*) Behavior becomes increasingly symbolic and covert in the form of mediational responses and information-manipulating processes. The learner responds increasingly to internal representations of an event, to internalized standards and to internalized strategies for thinking and problem solving, all of which are manifested in terms of his behavior as an expert. (*d*) This behavior of the expert becomes increasingly self-sustaining, increasingly masterful in terms of his skillful use of the rules when they are applicable, and subtle bending of them in appropriate situations. Increasing reliance is placed on one's own ability to generate the events by which one learns and the criteria by which performance is judged and valued.

The process of instruction is concerned with implementing this growth from ignorance to competence, and the characteristics of the course of this growth determine the design of the instructional environment. As the learner interacts with the environment, certain lawful psychological processes influence the way in which this interchange (e.g. Hilgard & Bower, 1966; Skinner, 1968; Hilgard, 1964; Glaser, 1970). The conditions provided for instruction are determined by the properties of the behavior to be learned, the characteristics of the learner, and the nature of subject-matter competence. The task of an instructional technology is to design conditions for learning based upon knowledge of the learning process and upon techniques of instruction. As appropriate behavior is learned, new conditions are set up to maintain it, and use it to develop more competent and subtle behavior. A complex repertoire is taught through a series of environmental changes, during each stage of which the learner responds to extend his present competence and to prepare himself to respond at a later, more complex stage. The particular properties of the competent behavior acquired depend upon the details of the instructional environment provided in an educational setting, such as teacher practices, textbook design, teaching machines and instructional materials, peer-student interactions, and the learning skills of the student himself.

5. *Assessment and optimization of learning outcomes*. With knowledge of learner characteristics and with alternate instructional procedures available, adaptation is made to the student's performance, i.e. his mastery of prerequisites, rate of learning, requirements for amount of practice, degree of structure and prompting, scheduling of reinforcement, and so on. Different individuals are assigned to (or the student may assign to himself) different instructional conditions. These initial placement decisions reflect only initial assignment, and are corrected by further assignments as learning proceeds, so that allocation to instructional procedures becomes a multi-stage decision process defining an individual instructional path. As a student proceeds to learn, his performance is assessed at appropriate intervals, and measures of this performance are summarized and indexed. The kinds of measures of learning progress one usually obtains, and on which instructional decisions are made, consist of test-score information which measures the frequency of correct responses, errors in relation to some performance standard, and the speed of

performance. The use of measures of transfer and generalization are particularly to be encouraged. Of special interest are measures which can be obtained in the course of learning and may be predictive of future learning requirements. Work along these lines has been reported by Jensen (1966, 1967, 1968), Zeaman & House (1963), Rohwer & Levin (mimeo), and Judd & Glaser (1969).

An adaptive instructional process employs a reiterative pattern of assessment and instructional prescription where decisions are made sequentially, and decisions made early in the process affect decisions made subsequently. The task of instruction is to prescribe the most effective sequence of learner-environment interactions. Problems of this kind in other fields of endeavor have been tackled by optimization procedures (e.g. Wilde & Beightler, 1967). The optimization problem of major concern is finding a decision procedure (to be implemented by the student, teacher, and/or a teaching device, see: Atkinson & Wilson, 1969; Holtzman, 1970) for deciding which instructional alternatives to present at each stage of instruction: given the instructional alternatives available, the set of possible student responses to the previous lesson unit, and specification of the criteria to be optimized for the judgment of competence. For this, two research and development tasks are essential: First, obtain rigorous knowledge of how the system variables interact; second, obtain agreed measures of system effectiveness. The first task is to determine the kinds of experimental studies and learning theory that are most useful for discovering the relationships between individual differences and learning variables. The second task refers to the fact that criterion measures of what is to be optimized become critical. In this regard, extensive work is in progress in measurement theory and technique as related to the instructional process and learned achievement (Glaser & Nitko, 1971; Cronbach, 1963; Bormuth, 1969). This work involves techniques for the development of criterion-referenced measures of achievement in contrast to the more commonly used norm-referenced measures (Glaser, 1963; Ebel, 1962; Flanagan, 1951; Popham & Husek, 1969). Criterion-referenced measures are tests constructed to yield measurements that can be directly interpreted in terms of specified performance standards, rather than relative standards such as percentile scores or normal-curve standard scores. Serious attempts are also being made to measure what has been heretofore so difficult—those aspects of learning and knowledge that are basic to an individual's capability for continuous growth and development, including transfer of knowledge to new situations, problem solving, and self-direction.

Bibliography: Atkinson, R. C. & Wilson, H. A.: Computer-assisted instruction: A book of readings. New York, 1969. **Bormuth, J. R.:** On achievement test item theory. Chicago, 1969. **Bracht, G. H. & Glass, G. V.:** The external validity of experiments. Amer. Ed. Res. J., 1968, *5*, 437–74. **Bruner, J. S.:** The process of education. Harvard, 1960. **Id.:** Some theorems on instruction illustrated with reference to mathematics. In: Theories of learning and instruction, 63rd Yearbook, Part I, NSSE, U. of Chic., 1964, 306–35. **Bugelski, B. R.:** The psychology of learning applied to teaching. Indianapolis, 1964. **Cronbach, L. J.:** The two disciplines of scientific psychology. Amer. Psychologist, 1957, *12*, 671–84. **Id.:** Course improvement through evaluation. Teach. Col. Rec., 1963, *64*, 672–83. **Id. & Gleser, G. C.:** Psychological tests and personnel decisions. Urbana, Ill., [2]1965. **Cronbach, L. J. & Snow, R. W.:** Individual differences in learning ability as a function of instructional variables (Final Report Stanford U., School of Education), Maine, 1969. **Ebel, R. L.:** Content-standard test scores. Educ. psychol. Measmt., 1962, *22*, 15–25. **Estes, W. K.:** Learning. In: **Harris, C. W.** (Ed.): Encyclopedia of Educational Res. New York, [3]1960, 752–70. **Flanagan, J. C.:** Units, scores, and norms. In: **Lindquist, E. F.** (Ed.): Educational measurement. Washington, D.C., 1951, 695–763. **Fleishman, E. A.:** The description and prediction of perceptual-motor skill learning. In: **Glaser, R.** (Ed.): Training research and education. New York, 1965, 137–76. **Id.:** Individual differences in motor learning. In: **Gagné, R.** (Ed.): Learning and individual differences. Columbus, O., 1967, 165–91. **Gagné, R. M.:** The acquisition of knowledge. Psychol. Rev., 1962, *69*, 355–65. **Id.:** The analysis of instructional objectives for the design of instruction. In: **Glaser, R.** (Ed.):

Teaching machines and programmed learning, II: Data and directions. Washington, D.C., 1965, 21–65. **Id. & Gephart, W. J.** (Eds.): Learning research and school subjects. Itasca, Ill., 1968. **Gibson, E. J.:** Learning to read. Science, 1965, *148*, 1066–72. **Id.:** Principles of perceptual learning and development. New York, 1969. **Gilbert, T. F.:** A structure for a coordinated research and development laboratory. In: **Glaser, R.** (Ed.): Training research and education. New York, 1965, 559–78. **Glaser, R.:** Instructional technology and the measurement of learning outcomes. Amer. Psychologist, 1963, *18*, 519–21. **Id.** (Ed.): Teaching machines and programmed learning, II: Data and directions. Washington, D.C., 1965. **Id.** (Ed.): The nature of reinforcement. Columbus, O., 1970. **Id. & Nitko, A. J.:** Measurement in learning and instruction. In: **Thorndike, R. L.** (Ed.): Educational measurement. New York, 1971. **Groen, G. J. & Atkinson, R. C.:** Models for optimizing and learning process. Psychol. Bulletin, 1966, *66*, 309–20. **Hilgard, E. R.** (Ed.): Theories of learning and instruction. 63rd Yearbook, Part I, NSSE. Chicago, 1964. **Holtzman, W.** (Ed.): Computer-assisted instruction, testing, and guidance. New York, 1970. **Jensen, A. R.:** Individual differences in concept learning. In: **Klausmeier, H. J. & Harris, C. W.** (Eds.): Analyses of concept learning. New York, 1966, 139–54. **Id.:** Varieties of individual differences in learning. In: **Gagné, R. M.** (Ed.): Learning and individual differences. Columbus, O., 1967, 117–40. **Id.:** Social class and verbal learning. In: **Deutsch, M.** *et al.* (Eds.): Social class, race, and psychological development. New York, 1968, 115–74. **Judd, W. A. & Glaser, R.:** Response latency as a function of training method, information level, acquisition, and overlearning. J. educ. Psychol. Monogr., 1969, *60*, Part 2. **Lumsdaine, A. A. & Glaser, R.** (Eds.): Teaching machines and programmed learning: a source book. Washington, D.C., 1960. **Melton, A. W.:** Learning. In: **Monroe, W. S.** (Ed.): Encyclopedia of educational research. New York, 1941, 667–86. **Moore, O. K. & Anderson, A. R.:** The responsive environments project. In: **Hess, R. D. & Bear, R. M.** (Eds.): Early education: Current theory, research, and action. Chicago, 1968, 171–89. **Popham, W. J. & Husek, T. R.:** Implications of criterion-referenced measurement. J. educ. Measmt. 1969, *6*, 1–9. **Pressey, S. L.:** A simple apparatus which gives tests and scores—and teaches. School and Society, 1926, *23*, 373–6. **Rohwer, W. D. & Levin, J. R.:** Elaboration preferences and differences in learning proficiency. Institute of Human Learning, U. of California, Berkeley. (Mimeo). **Skinner, B. F.:** The science of learning and the art of teaching. Harvard Educ. Rev., 1954, *24*, 86–97. **Id.:** Teaching machines. Science, 1958, *128*, 969–77. **Id.:** The technology of teaching. New York, 1968. **Suppes, P.:** Modern learning theory and the elementary school curriculum. Amer. Educ. Res. J., 1964, *1*, 79–93. **Wilde, D. J. & Beightler, C. S.:** Foundations of optimization. Englewood Cliffs, N.J., 1967. **Zeaman, D. & House, B. J.:** The role of attention in retardate discrimination learning. In: **Ellis, N.** (Ed.): Handbook of mental deficiencies. New York, 1963, 159–223.

R. Glaser

Instrumental conditioning. See *Conditioning, classical and operant.*

Insufficiency. 1. Inadequateness to some end or purpose. **2.** A want of some ability, value, substance, etc. **3.** An individually felt inadequacy or feeling of *inferiority* (q.v.) is described by Adler (q.v.) in the context of individual psychology (q.v.) as an important factor in the origin of neuroses. Such convictions of personal inferiority are said to occur in the neurotic personality, even in the absence of organic or mental insufficiency, and to lead to "inferiority complexes". See *Neurosis.*

K.Pa.

Insula (syn. *Island of Reil*). The insula forms part of the cerebral cortex. Originally it was situated on the free surface. In the course of development it has moved downward and is covered by parts of the anterior, superior and temporal lobes. It has been suggested that the insula is an association center for acoustic thinking. *G.A.*

Insulin. A hormone (polypeptide) formed in the Langerhans islet cells (beta cells) of the pancreas with the main effect of blood sugar maintenance and control. Whereas adrenalin (epinephrine) mobilizes the stored sugar and introduces it into the blood as glucose, insulin—as an antagonist of adrenalin—promotes the development and storage of blood sugar as glycogen. Insulin deficiency leads to hyperglycemia (diabetes mellitus), and an increase in insulin secretion to hypoglycemia. Since 1963, insulin has been synthesized and can be administered intravenously. Few experimental psychologicophysiological studies have been carried out. Low doses of insulin lead to increased heart rate, higher systolic blood pressure and higher respiration frequency, and also reduce diastolic blood pressure. Subjective effects: fatigue, dizziness, hunger. Performance (calculations) is generally impaired. In higher doses, insulin causes hypoglycemic shock, and was used as a means of therapy, e.g. in schizophrenia (q.v.).

Bibliography: Davidoff, F.: Oral hypoglycemic agents and the mechanism of diabetes mellitus. New Eng. J. Med., 1968, *278*, 148. **Ferner, H.:** Das Inselsystem des Pankreas, Stuttgart, 1952. **Geller, M. R.:** The treatment of psychiatric disorders with insulin, 1936–60: a selected, annotated bibliography. Washington, 1962. **Silverman, A. J., McGough, W. E. & Bogdonoff, M. O.:** Perceptual correlates of the physiological response to insulin. Psychosom. Med., 1967, *29*, 252–64. **Sussman, K. E., Cront, J. R. & Marble, A.:** Failure of warning in insulin-induced hypoglycemic reactions. Diabetes, 1963, *12*, 38–45. *W.J.*

Insulin shock (syn. *Insulin coma; Insulin therapy*). A state of hypoglycemic shock or coma (in which the patient is unconscious) induced by administering insulin parenterally until the blood sugar is reduced to a certain level (hypoglycemia). The method has been replaced by drug therapy, primarily because the same therapeutic objective can be achieved by neuroleptics with less risk of complications.

Bibliography: Ackner, B. & Oldham, A. J.: Insulin treatment of schizophrenia. A three year follow-up of a controlled study. Lancet, 1962, i, 504–6. **Bourne, H.:** The insulin myth. Lancet, 1953, ii, 964–8. **Kalinowsky, L. B. & Hoch, P. H.:** Somatic treatments in psychiatry. New York, 1961. *A.Hi.*

Integrated type. According to E. R. Jaensch, this type is characterized by a holistic attitude and wide-ranging attention; he thinks holistically and organically and is capable of change. Ant.: *disintegrated type*. The integrated type had three further sub-groups, depending on whether the orientation is directed more strongly inward or outward. *W.K.*

Integration. In the *central nervous system* (q.v.) stimuli are processed by various means: enormous numbers of neuron(e)s of a few morphological types form synaptic networks. No less than 300,000 synapses converge at a Purkinje('s) cell in the cerebrum. Information is conveyed to chemical synapses (q.v.) through transmitter substances (noradrenalin [norepinephrine], acetylcholine, serotonin, GABA); electrical synapses function directly. Nerve cell bodies (soma) and dendrites integrate on the analogue principle through algebraic, electronic summation while nerve fibers integrate digitally on the all-or-nothing principle with pulse frequency coding. Chemical and electrical fields influence the statistical characteristics of large cell groups. A flow of stimuli with enormously high redundancy (in the order of a million bits/sec) is filtered and grouped (convergence and divergence networks); the frequencies are raised or lowered while feedback loops have a throttling effect. Plasticity is dependent on the reserve of neurons which can be physiologically activated. Hormones influence the stimulus thresholds of neurons. Neuronal excitation circuits store data for a short time while the long-term memory functions with chemical engrams (proteins, nucleotides, amino-acid sequences).

Bibliography: Gerard, R. W.: Neurophysiology: an integration (molecules, neurons, and behavior). Handbook Physiol. Neurophysiol. Vol. 3 (1919–65). Washington, 1960. **Horridge, G. A.:** Interneurons. London & San Francisco, 1968. **Quarton, G. C., Melnechuk, T. & Schmitt, F. O.** (Eds.): The neurosciences. A study program. New York, 1967. *K.Fi.*

Integration of the personality. 1. The consistency, or degree of coincidence, with which diverse individual processes or actions, and in particular the decisions of a human being, prove effective in functional dependence on each other; or the coordination of characteristics in a given situation or in contact with the environment. If we adopt A. H. Witkin's theory that the personality is an open system, i.e. closely related to the environment, integration denotes the functional relations between the system components. This integration is attributed to a complex system and therefore presupposes differentiation of the system. **2.** The making whole of the personality, either through one's own efforts (i.e. in individual development or in self-therapy, or under psychotherapy (q.v.). See *Person; Personality; Type.* *W.D.F.*

Integration, social. A general term for part processes which are necessary to complete or establish a consistent social structure. These processes include (especially in Talcott Parsons' theory): *cultural integration* as the essential consistency of normative factors; *normative integration* as the essential correlation between standards and requirements; *communicative integration* as the essential smooth transmission of standards from one individual to another; and *functional integration* as the essential harmony of requirements, expectations and actual behaviors. *W.D.F.*

Intellect. 1. The perceiving, cognizing, understanding mind. **2.** The power of understanding. **3.** Comprehension. **4.** Whatever that mental ability may be which enables man to think. **5.** High-level abstract or conceptual thought. See *Intelligence.*

Intellection: The act of understanding; using (the) intellect. *H.W.*

Intellect, structure of. The structure of intellect (i.e. intelligence) can be determined from a number of different standpoints (see *Intelligence*). In the factor-analytical sphere, the concept of the structure of intellect has acquired a special meaning as a system of factors which determine intellectual performance. A particularly well-known model for the structure of intellect or intelligence has been suggested by Guilford (1959, 1967). He distinguishes between three aspects of every act of the intelligence: operation, product and content, and also describes various modes of variation, or categories, of each dimension. In addition to the categories "figural", "symbolic", "semantic", Guilford posits a fourth category (purely theoretical) along the dimension of content, designated as "behavioral" and representing the general area of "social intelligence. Guilford's theoretical model represents (i.e. predicts) 120 distinct abilities in a cube, each cell containing a kind of problem and the corresponding factor. "If education has the general objective of developing the intellects of students, it can be suggested that each intellectual factor provides a particular goal at which to aim." (1959.)

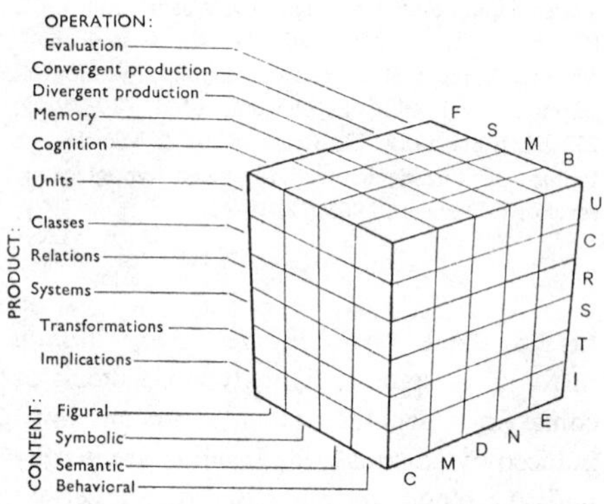

Bibliography: Guilford, J. P.: Three faces of intellect. Amer. Psychologist, 1959, *14*, 469–79. **Id.:** The nature of human intelligence. New York, 1967. *R.M.*

Intelligence. However clearly we may seem to understand what is meant by intelligence, e.g. in connection with an intelligence test, there is as yet no generally recognized definition of the term. Admittedly intelligence denotes an "ability", i.e. a condition or a complex of conditions for specific performances or achievements. But the specific types of performance which require intelligence have not yet been unambiguously defined, except to the extent that the term covers cognitive problems. Ideas on the essential, "inner" nature of this ability are even more divided. The definition of intelligence as the ability to overcome difficulties in new situations (proposed almost simultaneously by E. Claparède and W. Stern) is most widely accepted today. Since animals too can adapt to new situations for which they have no instinctive solution (W. Köhler's "intelligence tests on anthropoid apes"), thought cannot be considered to be an essential criterion for the exercise of intelligence.

1. *Research into intelligence.* There are close links between research into intelligence and the psychology of thought (processes) inasmuch as intelligence is considered as a prerequisite for individual variations in thinking; nevertheless, the two branches of research have developed separately. The aim of intelligence research is to use statistical comparisons to determine the conditions underlying various types of performance. The degree of similarity between the conditions for two types of performance is determined by correlative techniques. After 1900, Spearman (1927) was the first to develop on this basis a method of analyzing the relations between performances; his method of factor analysis (q.v.) has since been used in almost all intelligence research. These studies need not be confined to typical intellectual performance. It is largely a matter of linguistic convention which of the factors is defined as intellectual. The main problem in this research was to determine the number and nature of the factors involved. Spearman developed the two-factor theory, according to which all intellectual (in the broad sense) operations involve a single, common factor (general factor, or *g*) and a specific factor for each performance. This general factor can therefore be defined as "general intelligence", although Spearman interpreted it hypothetically as general mental energy. Since research eventually showed, however, that there are certain common features between certain types of performance which are not dependent on "g", the "hierarchical theory" of intelligence was adopted by Spearman's school. This theory assumes that there are also factors of ever-decreasing effect in the hierarchical order down to Spearman's specific factors (Vernon, 1961).

Thurstone (1938) offered a new factor model in the nineteen thirties: this provides, in addition to the specific factors, for *group factors* (but no general factor) each of which is responsible for one class of performance. Thurstone defined seven primary factors (verbal comprehension, numerical, spatial, reasoning, perceptual speed, verbal fluency, memory). With the widespread development of factor analysis, a very large number of factors have been defined (more than two hundred), which are not always wholly distinct. Guilford, who has carried out the largest number of very extensive factor analyses, suggested a three-dimensional system of one hundred and twenty factors, some eighty-two of which he considered he had defined appropriately before 1967.

Since 1946 Meili has maintained that there are only a few fundamental intellectual factors, and has so far defined four of them (complexity, plasticity, globalization and fluency), which he has verified in many experiments on subjects from the age of seven onward. These factors have been defined similarly by others; according to Meili, at least the first three of these factors play a part in all "acts of the intelligence", even though they do not always significantly determine variance in performance. Meili does not deny the possibility of defining other factors (verbal, numerical, etc.), but believes with Spearman that these are less fundamental, and arise in measure large from practice in dealing with specific types of problem. A decision for one or other of these different models cannot be made by the factor-analytical method, because every correlation matrix can be interpreted in different ways and from different approaches to the psychology of thought.

2. *Intelligence and personality.* In general, intelligence is considered today to be a characteristic, aspect or area of (the)

personality (q.v.). In the first instance, this simply implies that the personality is not completely characterized if intelligence is overlooked. But this is merely an aid toward a definition; it is more important to decide whether there are relations between cognitive and non-cognitive phenomena, the latter including primarily motivational and affective phenomena. The problem must be viewed on different levels: (*a*) Significant correlations are seldom found between performance in intelligence tests and other personality characteristics determined by means of tests or questionnaires. On the other hand, it is known that test performance may be influenced by motivation, anxiety and certain other personality characteristics. However, since these influences do not apply to all individuals to the same extent and are dependent on the test situation (i.e. are not constant) there is generally no correlation. (*b*) There seem to be correlations between personality types and forms of intelligence. Kretschmer, for example, has shown affinities between his temperament types and forms of scientific thought and literary production. On the basis of other observations, American psychologists have come to speak of "cognitive styles" (Gardner *et al.*, 1959; Gardner, 1959). They are not concerned with the level of performance but with qualitative characteristics of that performance. As yet it is impossible to decide empirically whether these characteristics can be explained by specific factor constellations, or whether they are based on the influence of non-cognitive conditions. It seems fairly certain that certain factor constellations are associated with interests (Wälti, 1970), and it can be assumed that fluency in solving certain types of problem, or ease of performance in some intellectual activities, may stimulate interest in them. In general, an interaction between the cognitive and non-cognitive spheres must be assumed. (*c*) On the factor level, therefore, factors obtained by the analysis of operations of intelligence cannot be definitely viewed as wholly intellectual: the possibility that they are interactive products (Hürsch, 1971) must be considered.

3. *Development of intelligence*. Here a distinction may be made between two lines of research: the quantitative and the qualitative. For a long time there was little doubt that the intelligence or ability required for cognitive performance was innate, and varied from individual to individual. Even if the observable ability for achievement in a given age group was thought of as acquired through learning processes, a varying ability to learn was (with a few exceptions) assumed, and defined as intelligence. This assumption of an initially given disposition or *anlage* (q.v.) then led to the question of the constancy of intelligence during development, and many studies have been made of this problem. In longitudinal studies, the intelligence of the same children was measured at various intervals after the first year of life and it was found that the IQ values (considered measures of intelligence) began to show a certain constancy only from the age of three to four. The results of different studies vary fairly widely, but it can be stated that it is only from the age of eight or nine that the intelligence level achieved at sixteen or seventeen can be anticipated with some accuracy (correlations of more than 0.80). However, since the problems used for measurement in the different age groups sometimes vary widely, this lack of consistency can be explained at least in part by the variations in the test method. Another reason for the poor correlation between IQs at different ages is the irregularity often noted in individual development. It has been found that the development (q.v.) of intellectual performance as reflected in test results, may be modified by environmental influences as by affective and physical factors. The development of intelligence must therefore be considered to be only in small measure a simple process of "growth". It tends rather to be a highly complex process of alteration of the bases of performance.

4. *Nature and nurture*. The old problem of the respective influences of innate traits and

environmental influences has still not been finally solved. The clearest answer (which still leaves certain problems) is provided by twin studies (q.v.). The correlation for intelligence between identical twins is rather more than 0.90. But if the two subjects grow up in a different environment it falls to about 0.75. The correlation for non-identical twins, or brothers and sisters, is still lower (0.54 to 0.62); and if the children grow up in different environments the correlation falls to 0.40 (Butcher, 1968). These figures suggest that the level of intelligence measured in adults is due to environment to an extent of one half or two thirds.

In conjunction with the differentiation of different factors, the question of the constancy of the factorial structure has been raised. H. E. Garrett (1946) formulated a differentiation hypothesis which was converted by G. Lienert (1961) into a divergence hypothesis. According to these hypotheses, an originally unified factor (generally identified with Spearman's "g") becomes differentiated in the course of development, and an increasing number of other factors is formed. In only about one half of some thirty studies of this problem was it possible to confirm this hypothesis. It does seem clear that certain factors associated with the school, such as "v" and "n" occur only later, but a distinction between several factors must already be made at a very early stage. This leads to a distinction between basic or primary and acquired or secondary factors. The structure of the former appears to be relatively constant (Meili, 1970).

5. *Qualitative studies.* The dominant orientation here comes from Piaget. On the basis of research over several decades, Piaget distinguishes between four main stages: (*a*) the stage of sensorimotor intelligence, up to the age of eighteen months; (*b*) the stage of preoperational thought, up to the age of about seven years; (*c*) the stage of concrete operational thought, up to eleven years; and (*d*) the stage of formal logical operations (or formal operational thought). By "intelligence", Piaget (1950, 1952) understands a mental structure which, in the course of development, achieves an increasingly comprehensive and perfect state of *equilibrium.* The different stages correspond to structures which Piaget has tried to define accurately (in the case of the two final stages, in the terminology of logistics and group theory). See *Abilities; Differential psychology; Traits; Type.*

Bibliography: Burt, C.: The factors of the mind. London, 1940. **Butcher, H. J.:** Human intelligence: its nature and assessment. London, 1968. **Gardner, R. W.:** Cognitive control principles and perceptual behavior. Bull. Meuninger Clin., 1959, *23*, 241–8. **Id.** *et al.*: Cognitive controls: a study of individual consistencies in cognitive behavior. Psychol. Issues, 1959, *1* (4), 1–186. **Garrett, H. E.:** A developmental theory of intelligence. Amer. Psychol. 1946, *1*, 372–8. **Guilford, J. P.:** The nature of human intelligence. New York, 1967. **Hürsch, L.:** Der Einfluss von Versuchsbedingungen auf die Faktorenstruktur von Intelligenzleistungen. Berne, 1971. **Köhler, W.:** The mentality of apes. New York, 1925. **Lienert, G. A.:** Überprufung und genetische Interpretation der Divergenzhypothese von Wewetzer. Vita Humana, 1961, *4*, 112–24. **Meili, R.:** L'analyse de l'intelligence. Arch. de Psychol., 1946, *31*, 1–64. **Id.:** Faktorenstruktur und Intelligenzentwicklung. Schweiz. Z. f. Psychol., 1970, *29*, 404–16. **Oléron, P.:** Les composants de l'intelligence, Paris, 1957. **Piaget, J.:** The psychology of intelligence. New York & London, 1950. **Id.:** The origins of intelligence in children. New York & London, 1952. **Spearman, C.:** The abilities of man. London, 1927. **Thurstone, L. L.:** Primary mental abilities. Chicago, 1938. **Vandenberg, S. G.:** Contribution of twin research to psychology. Psychol. Bull., 1966, *66*, 327–52. **Vernon, P. E.:** The structure of human abilities. London, 1961. **Wälti, U.:** Persönlichkeitszüge im Spiegel der Intellizgenstruktur. Berne, 1970.

R. Meili.

Intelligence age (Ger. *Intelligenzalter;* abb. *IA*). The difference between the IA and chronological age (CA) of a subject is the criterion for his advance on, or lag behind, the average intellectual development of other individuals of his age. The "intelligence age" is therefore what is usually known as *mental age* (abb. MA). *A.L.*

Intelligence quotient (abb. *IQ*). Suggested by W. Stern in 1912: $IQ = \frac{MA}{CA} \times 100$ (MA = mental age; CA = chronological age). The IQ is a measurement of the intellectual development of a testee in relation to the average value for persons of the same age group. See *Abilities; Intelligence; Intelligence tests.* *A.L.*

Intelligence, structure of. See *Intellect, structure of.*

Intelligence-structure test (abb. IST). A method of determining the general intellectual achievement level applicable to the 13–60 age group. Amthauer, the author of the test, understands intelligence as "a configuration of mental and psychological abilities"; he believes that his method helps to explain this phenomenon. The decisive feature is the test profile determined from the results of nine subtests each of which in the author's opinion represents a center of gravity in the structured totality of intelligence. The reliability (according to the halving method) of the test is r = 0.969, in the author's opinion, i.e. significantly high. In determining the validity of the method, correlations were found with teachers' opinions and school marks of r = 0.623 or r = 0.455.

Bibliography: Amthauer, R.: Intelligenz-Struktur-Test. Göttingen, [2]1955. *P.S.*

Intelligence tests. The term "intelligence tests" covers psychological test methods designed to determine interindividual differences in the sphere of human intelligence (q.v.). The testee is required to solve a series of different problems of varying complexity; the number of correct solutions gives a quantitative idea of his intellectual (performance) level by comparison with other persons of the same age. Intelligence is generally measured by the intelligence quotient (IQ) which indicates—in its commonest form—the position of S. in relation to the population as a whole on a normally divided scale (mean value 1001; dispersion 15). Normally, the designation "intelligence test" implies that the method concerned is assumed to measure "general intelligence" and not partial aspects of the latter. Psychologists are not, however, of one mind as to the performance areas covered by "g", or its structure; accordingly, the different intelligence tests are sometimes based on highly divergent models of intelligence.

The earliest attempts at a psychological diagnosis of intelligence were made in the nineteenth century. Galton (q.v.) was the first to organize relatively large-scale systematic experiments to detect interindividual differences in the sphere of intelligence. He postulated the standard distribution of intelligence generally accepted today. Pioneering work was done by Binet (q.v.) who published (with T. Simon) in 1905 the first procedures to justify the use of the term "intelligence test" in its present sense. While Binet's method was designed for educational purposes as an intelligence test for children, the first intelligence tests for adults were developed by military psychologists in America during World War I (see *Army Alpha Test; Army Beta Test*). These methods were suitable for use as group tests and were designed as test batteries; they therefore already possessed two major characteristics typical of most modern intelligence tests. The diagnostic possibilities of test batteries were subsequently extended by adding the psychological profile (test profile) formulated by the Russian psychiatrist G. J. Rossolimo. Going beyond the quantitative determination of a complex of characteristics and the various component parts of the complex (as in the case of a test battery), the psychological profile evaluated the interrelationship between individual subtests on a differential diagnostic basis.

The intelligence diagnosis method owes most of the qualitative improvements it has undergone to the use of statistical methods. These enabled the tests to be designed scientifically and standardized as measuring instruments. With the help of a statistical method, i.e. factor analysis (q.v.), it proved possible to obtain direct empirical access to the problem of intelligence, and to base intelligence tests on experimental findings.

Despite the progress made primarily through statistics, the intelligence tests in general use today are not so perfected as one would expect of precise measuring instruments. The main reason is that the extent and structure of intelligence are not as yet sufficiently well defined, while the conditions of the test situation (above all S.'s motivation) remain rather imprecise in intelligence testing as in other psychodiagnostic methods. Nevertheless, modern intelligence tests are among the most sophisticated methods available for psychological diagnosis. See *Abilities; Objective tests; Test theory; Child psychology.*

Bibliography: Anastasi, A.: Psychological testing. New York, [2]1961. **Id.:** Testing problems in perspective. New York, 1966. **Buros, O. S.:** Tests in print. New York, 1961. **Cronbach, L. J.:** Essentials of psychological testing. New York, [2]1964. **Daniels, J. C. & Diack, H.:** The standard reading tests. London, 1960. **Doll, E. A.:** The Vineland social maturity scale. Princeton, N.J., 1947. **Field, J.:** Two types of tables for use with Wechsler's intelligence. J. Clin. Psychol., 1960, *16*, 3–7. **Frostig, M.:** Testing as a basis for educational therapy. Oxford, 1967. **Littell, W. M.:** The Wechsler intelligence scale for children: a review of a decade of research. In: **Savage, R. D.:** Readings in clinical psychology. Oxford, 1966. **Maxwell, A. E.:** A factor analysis of the Wechsler intelligence scale for children. B. J. Educ. Psychol., 1959, *32*, 119–32. **Savage, R. D.:** Psychometric assessment of the individual child. Harmondsworth, 1968. **Schonell, F. S. & E.:** Scholastic diagnostic and attainment testing. London, 1960. **Terman, L. & Merrill, M. H.:** A Stanford-Binet intelligence scale: manual for form L-M. Boston, [3]1960. **Vernon, P. E.:** Intelligence and attainment tests. London, 1960. **Wechsler, D.:** Manual for the Wechsler intelligence scale for children. New York, 1949. **Id.:** The measurement and appraisal of adult intelligence. New York, [4]1965. **Id.:** The Wechsler preschool and primary intelligence scale. New York, 1966.

P. Steck

Intensification. 1. The phenomenon that certain impressions when remembered seem greatly distorted: e.g. terrible, horrific, dangerous, amazing. Artistic representation often lays considerable stress on such distortion. **2.** Reinforcement (q.v.). *H.W.*

Intensity. 1. Great attention (q.v.) **2.** The state of being forced, strained or increased. **3.** The strength of, or increase of degree of, e.g. an emotion, stimulus or response.

Intention. 1. The orientation of the mind or self toward something. **2.** Goal, purpose, objective. **3.** Close attention.

Intentional psychoses. A psychiatric term which has now gone out of general use. Inhibitions or anxieties prevent the completion of certain intended actions. The cause may be psychotic (e.g. ambivalence, negativism) or neurotic (e.g. compulsion, phobia). See *Neurosis; Psychoses, functional.* *C.Sch.*

Intention movements (syn. *Intentional responses*). Movements which are incomplete in form, intensity or frequency and show the partner or informed observer what the animal intends to do, i.e. indicate the growing motivation of an instinct. Frequently noted in conflict (q.v.) situations. *K.Fi.*

Bibliography: Heinroth, O.: Beiträge zur Biologie, namentlich Ethologie und Psychologie der Anatiden. Verh. V. Kongr. Int. Orn. Berlin, 1911. **Tinbergen, N.:** The study of instinct. Oxford, [2]1969.

Interaction. 1. A reciprocal or mutual influence between two characteristics, persons, systems, etc. **2.** In statistics (q.v.) the term *interaction* is primarily used in connection with test designs for analysis of variance. In these designs the effect of several multiple, multiclass, independent variables can be observed simultaneously. Interaction is then a measurement of the extent to which the effect of one (or more) independent variable(s) is (are) dependent on one (or more) other independent variable(s). Interactions are sometimes more interesting than the "main effects". See *Variance, analysis of.* *W.H.B.*

Interaction, psychophysical. The observable reciprocal influence of physical and mental or psychological processes, e.g. the influence of emotions (q.v.) on such functions as heart and pulse rate, respiration, and so on, or the fluctuation of performance caused by fatigue (q.v.). The theory of psychophysical interaction (E. von Hartmann, W. James, H. Lotze, E. Becher), according to which body and mind can have a causative effect upon one another, seeks to explain such phenomena in postulating that the mind can precipitate physical, and the body mental, processes. As a theory it can be traced back to Descartes's separation of mind (*res cogitans*) and body (*res extensa*), and ultimately forms part of the subject-matter of philosophy (see *Mind-body problem*). As a dualistic, causal construct it does not accord with the empirically grounded conception of relations between psychological and physiological processes. See *Physiological psychology; Psychosomatics.* *F.-C. S.*

Interaction, social (syn. *Social intercourse*). The reciprocal influence of individuals or groups through the medium of communication (q.v.). The more specific term "symbolic interaction" is used when the communicative process is specially emphasized in the context of social interaction. "Social interaction" can also denote specific phenomena in social contacts, e.g. gestures, mimicry, reading another person's letter, etc. *W.D.F.*

Interbrain. The *diencephalon* (q.v.).

Interest. 1. Concern, advantage, good, profit. **2.** A tendency to behaviors oriented toward certain objects, activities or experience, which tendency varies in intensity (and generality) from individual to individual. Factor-analytical studies of the structure of interests have shown about fifteen independent dimensions (directions of interest), e.g. for music, politics and economics, technology and natural science, art, etc. The association between interests and personality or performance tests (with the exception of tests centering purely on knowledge) is generally slight. See *Attitude; Creativity.*

Bibliography: Todt, E.: Differentieller Interessen-Test (DIT). Berne & Stuttgart, 1967. *M.A.*

Interest test (syn. *Interest inventory; Interest blank*). A test which measures interests or a questionnaire which elicits a range of interests. See *Kuder Preference Record; Strong Vocational Interest Blank.*

Interference tube. A complex sound conducting tube designed in such a way that certain components of a sound can be eliminated by a wave cancellation process, i.e. the trough of one wave being opposed to the crest of another. In this way it is possible to obtain a sound wave of increased purity. *G.D.W.*

Interindividual. Between different individuals. *Interindividual variability:* the variability of measured values observed in measurements on different individuals. *B.H.*

Intermenstrual pain. Pain occurring between successive periods of menstruation.

Intermodal qualities. Qualities of perception or imagination which are not confined to a single sensory modality. E.g. the quality "warm" is an attribute not only of sensed temperature but of visual and auditory perception; we speak of a "warm" color and of a "warm" voice. *P.T.*

Internalization. The adoption of attitudes, norms, prejudices, etc., by an individual.

Internal secretion. The release of glandular products directly into the bloodstream from glands without an outlet channel. The products are hormones (q.v.), which influence growth, development and metabolic (hormonal control) as well as psychological processes. *F.-C.S.*

Interoceptor. See *Enteroceptor.*

Interpretation. An activity as a result of which a physical or psychological datum is related to a conceptual model which assigns place and significance to the datum. *F.B.*

Interquartile range. The interquartile range takes as its "positional parameters" the measured values in a distribution between which the middle 50% of all observed cases are located. The interquartile range is therefore the interval between the first (25%) and third (75%) quartile. *W.H.B.*

Interrogation of suspects. In its psychological aspects, the examination of suspects forms part of forensic psychology (q.v.). The methods of psychology are used in an attempt to determine the subjective accuracy of verbal evidence. The methods used may be divided into two classes: (*a*) Association tests (q.v.) and other verbal reaction methods. In most cases the reaction time and word are evaluated diagnostically. These techniques were used even in the early stages of work in this area, by C. G. Jung (q.v.) and M. Wertheimer (q.v.). (*b*) Methods for recording physical side-effects during interrogation. Such techniques usually consist of questioning the suspect with a mixture of directly relevant and irrelevant questions, and of registering simultaneous physical symptoms. This latter aspect can, of course, be restricted to a mere intuitive interpretation of expressions (see *Expression*), but objective techniques for measuring physical symptoms (e.g. measurement of pulse, respiration, skin resistance, muscular activity; see *Polygraph; Lie detector*) are more sensitive. The relation between the measured physiological processes and simultaneous psychological processes allows the tester to assume a correlation between measurements and the accuracy or inaccuracy of a statement. The legal acceptability of such findings varies from country to country. See *Credibility; Criminality; Objective tests.*

Bibliography: Davis, R. C.: Physiological responses as a means of evaluating information. In: **Biderman, A. D. & Zimmer, H.** (Eds.): The manipulation of human behavior. New York, 1961. **Inbau, F. E. & Reid, J. E.:** Lie detection and criminal interrogation. Baltimore, [3]1953. **Jung, C. G.:** Zur psychol. Tatbestandsdiagnostik. Arch. Krim., 1939, *100*, 123–30. **Tent, L.:** Psychologische Tatbestandsdiagnostik. In: **Undeutsch, U.** (Ed.): Handbuch der Psychol., Vol. 11. Göttingen, 1967. **Wertheimer, M.:** Tatbestandsdiagnostik. In: **Abderhalden, E.** (Ed.): Handbuch der Biologischen Arbeitsmethoden, Section VI. Berlin, 1933. *F.M.*

Interrupted action. See *Zeigarnik effect.*

Intersexuality. The condition of being intermediate between the two sexes, especially with respect to the secondary sex characteristics (see *Hermaphroditism*).

Intersex: Abnormal individual intermediate between male and female, that has identical genetic form throughout all its cells (see *Gynandromorph*). *G.D.W.*

Interstitial cell stimulating hormone. See *ICSH.*

Intersubjectivity. 1. In E. Husserl's phenomenology (q.v.): the association of subjectivities which is necessary for an objective world to exist. **2.** Subjective experience (e.g. perception) becomes intersubjectivity when several individuals experience the same thing, e.g. report the same experience, or experimental results. *B.H.*

Interval. 1. The range of time between two events, etc. **2.** The distance between two assignable points or values. **3.** The difference in pitch between any two tones (notes). **4.** Remission of a disorder (e.g. delirium).

Interval estimate (syn. *Interval rating*). In an interval estimate two values are indicated on the basis of samples; a given parameter is situated with a known probability between these two values. An interval estimate indicates the fiducial interval (see *Limits, fiducial*) to be taken into account when a statistical index is substituted for an (unknown) parameter. It is therefore a measure of the accuracy of a sample. See *Statistics*. *W.H.B.*

Interval of uncertainty (abb. *IU*). The range of stimuli between thresholds obtained using different methods, especially ascending and descending series in the *limits method* (q.v.). *G.D.W.*

Interval scale. A unit of measurement whose multiple represents the interval magnitude is necessary to quantify an interval (defined as the distance between two values). Unlike ordinal scales, interval scales have identical distances between the scale units, but no genuine (i.e. absolute) zero point. *W.H.B.*

Intervariation characterizes the extent of differences in measured values between individuals. The opposite is the case with *intravariation*, i.e. the variability of measured values in a given individual during repeated observations. With the increasing application of statistical methods in psychology, these terms have tended to disappear from the literature. The modern equivalents represent standards of statistical variability. For the diagnosis of individual cases, *ipsative* (deviation from average value for a single person) or *normative* (deviation of one person from the average for a sample) values take over this function. *W.H.B.*

Intervening variable. A hypothetical variable and not a statistical concept, the intervening variable cannot be observed directly even though an operational definition can be given of its effect; it has an "intervening" function in the stimulus-response process, and may be considered as the *expression of a relationship* between stimulating conditions and responses (the dependent variable). *W.H.B.*

Interview. The most important of the various techniques of data collection is questioning or interviewing; a prominent factor is the use of language as a means of communication (which, of course, creates certain problems). In general, the interview is a means of obtaining verbal (and written) information. Despite the use of early, crude techniques of questioning (e.g. by ethnologists, cultural anthropologists, sociologists and psychologists), the systematic development of the interview into a research instrument and a methodically controlled observation technique occurred only in the early years of the present century. The appearance of market and public opinion research (q.v.) in the USA was followed by the gradual development of sociological research (see *Attitude; Social psychology*) dependent on planned questioning—especially for checking hypotheses. Psychology and psychoanalysis (q.v.) also use interviews in conjunction with observation, tests, experiments, etc., to obtain statements from subjects which will enable conclusions to be drawn about attitudes, actions, circumstances, conflicts, self-interpretations of a person's position in life, etc. In this sense, the interview is a planned procedure with a scientific objective, in which verbal information is elicited from testees by means of a series of deliberate questions or communicated stimuli; it can be a means (in diverse practical fields) of elucidating the situation of entire populations, or groups within a population, or merely the condition (in a wide sense) of an individual patient.

The standardized interview is the technique most often used when dealing with single persons. It allows the greatest degree of comparison. The wording, sequence of questions, possible answers, and *interviewer's behavior* are fixed in advance. Only the standardized questionnaire supplies *fully comparable data.* However, comprehensive knowledge about the subject under review is assumed. More important than the identical wording of the questions is that they should mean the same thing to all the testees. This can be achieved by standardizing the meaning in the partly standardized interview, or by "filter" questions which eliminate Ss. who do not seem to be suitable for a certain range of questions.

In the semi-standardized interview a series of questions is used which enables the interviewer to react at certain points, and to conduct a comparatively free exploration by changing the wording and explaining the questions, omitting or adding others and continuing the questioning. Such interviews (structured or semi-structured interviews, and formal questionnaires or inventories) have a detailed plan; in contrast, the *depth interview* (unstructured, open, exploratory, intensive or qualitative) leaves the shaping and development of the questioning in large measure to the discretion of the interviewer, who works to a general plan consisting especially of interview objectives, some groups of subjects, and possibly *ad hoc* questions. This type of interview is more like a free but guided conversation, with or without written note-taking or tape recording. It is suitable in various psychological disciplines, especially for obtaining a more complete account of individual cases (flexibility and more comprehensive information—more difficult quantitative evaluation).

Sets of data obtained by unstructured and intensive questioning are not comparable since standardization of significance during the course of the interview is impossible. In contrast to the form of the personal interview, the written interview consists usually of standardized questionnaires which are sent out to the testees (these may be useful in collecting more objective data, but there is not sufficient checking and possibly few replies may be received). *Group interviews* are also carried out in a written or personal form, in natural or experimental groups.

Questions vary very widely in form. The closed question allows the interviewee to give only set answers: in the alternative question these are Yes or No, in the choice question there are several possibilities to be selected from a list which is either printed or read out. The open question, on the other hand, allows free answers; other "half-open", questions allow for answers which are not prescribed but nevertheless admissible. The direct question makes the meaning and purpose of the question clear from the start; the indirect question, sometimes in conjunction with projective techniques (q.v.), conceals the orientation in order to exclude wrong and/or socially standardized answers. Batteries of questions, i.e. a number of individual questions, are useful in an optimally comprehensive investigation of a thematic complex separated from other themes by introductory and bridging questions. Follow-up questions complete the picture; filter questions are used to find out which main questions do not apply to a particular testee; control questions enable answers to be checked.

The interviewer's behavior can have considerable influence on the interview and its results. In the neutral interview the interviewer must adhere strictly to his instructions, and refrain from giving any help or making any comment. On the other hand, the interviewer has to play an active part in the "hard" interview (a "cross-examination"), or the "soft" interview (in which an atmosphere of confidence is created). In both cases the object is to get the testee to give the right answers, to prevent evasion, to detect contradictions, etc. Even an adequate training in interviewing will certainly not prevent any negative influence due to prejudice, to influencing the test subject by showing agreement, to the way in which answers are received, the interviewee classified and his responses written down. The following are some of the points which need watching in the interviewee: readiness, fluctuations of mood, alertness, education and training, expressiveness, knowledge, retention, social class, taboo subjects, evaluation of self and intimate environment, and attitude to the role of the interviewer as a stranger. How much anyone will be prepared to disclose varies considerably according to culture, class, club and other social groups. Special problems arise in depth interviews (e.g. in clinical interviewing). In research, such methods are used mainly for pilot studies (q.v.).

Reliability is the degree of consistency with which a result is obtained when the same technique is repeated. With regard to the reliability of interview data, results are available which show a value of 90% for personal interviews in the form of repeated questionings of the same persons—the panel method. The degree of reliability depends on the time lapse between the two interrogations, the groups interrogated and the subjects inquired into. There is more stability when the questions deal with more subjective matters, whereas opinions and attitudes (q.v.) are subject to varying degrees of fluctuation. Validity depends on whether the results obtained by the use of a certain technique really represent what is supposed in the interpretation. As regards the validity of interview data, only isolated material has so far been published and no comprehensive study of the subject is available. Validity may be verified by, say, comparison of the results of a questionnaire with official figures (e.g. in regard to elections and statistics of electoral behavior). The validity of interview data is no higher than their reliability; on the other hand, a high degree of reliability does not necessarily indicate an equivalent degree of validity. See *Questionnaires; Intelligence tests; Objective tests.*

Bibliography: Anastasi, A.: Psychological testing. New York, 1961. **Argyle, M.:** The scientific study of social behaviour. London, 1957. **Blum, R.. H.:** Management of the doctor-patient relationship. New York, 1960. **Cronbach, L. J. & Gleser, C. C.:** Psychological tests and personnel decisions. Chicago, 1957. **Maier, N. R. F.:** The appraisal interview. New York, 1958. **Merton, R. K.** *et al.*: The focused interview. Glencoe, Ill., 1956. **Sidney, E. & Brown, M.:** The skills of interviewing. London, 1961.

A. Bellebaum

Interviewer bias. An intruding variable to be taken into account when evaluating an interview: the effects of the interviewer's attitudes and prejudices.

Interviews, drugs in. Certain psychotropic substances with a beneficial influence on verbal behavior are used in interrogations or interviews. Hypnotic drugs, tranquilizers, antidepressants, stimulants, and hallucinogens or psychotomimetic drugs are used both for diagnostic-therapeutic purposes and also to obtain important information from potential sources. These substances may make an interrogation more productive by inducing (in various ways) some weakening of the resistance of a potential informant. Nevertheless, the validity and accuracy of the knowledge obtained are doubtful and can be confirmed only by extrinsic criteria. Not to give information does not signify that the person interrogated is not in possession of it. Facts disclosed under the influence of such drugs are usually not admissible as evidence in a court of law.

Bibliography: Gottschalk, L. A.: The use of drugs in information-seeking interviews. In: **Uhr, L. & Miller,**

J. G. (Eds.): Drugs and behavior. London, 1960; New York, 1964. *E.L.*

Intimacy. **1.** Coitus (q.v.). **2.** In gestalt psychology (usually "intimacy principle"): the interdependence of the "parts" of a gestalt, none of which may be removed or added to without changing the whole, and therefore all other parts. See *Ganzheit.*

Intimate sphere. A pre-scientific term for areas of private behavior supposedly withdrawn from social influence. *J.F.*

Intolerance. See *Tolerance; Authoritarian personality; Prejudice.*

Intonation. Speech melody: aspects of pitch (q.v.) in speech.

Intoxication. **1.** Poisoning. **2.** A temporary psychological condition resulting from poison or drugs (especially ethyl alcohol) and manifested in a variety of behaviors and symptoms ranging from exhilaration and loss of personal and social responsibility to depression, stupor or coma. See *Alcoholism; Drug dependence* (as chronic states). **3.** Usage is sometimes extended metaphorically to include similar behavioral effects of purely psychological origin, e.g. "intoxicated with joy".

Intoxicant: An agent producing the state of intoxication. *G.D.W.*

Intraindividual. Within an individual. *Intraindividual fluctuations:* fluctuations of values (e.g. body temperature) observed during repeated measurements of a particular characteristic in a given individual. *B.H.*

Intramural nervous system. A term sometimes used to describe the majority of the nerve fibers and ganglionic cells in the various layers of the intestinal wall. The most important are the *plexus myentericus* (L. Auerbach), between the intestinal musculature, and the *plexus submucosus* (G. Meissner) below the mucous membrane layer. The intramural nervous system forms part of the autonomic nervous system (q.v.) and regulates intestinal movement and secretion. The blood vessel walls also contain elements of the autonomic nervous system which affect the smooth musculature of the vessels, and thus regulate the hemodynamically effective cross-section as well as tonus.

Bibliography: **Leonhardt, H.:** Histologie und Zytologie des Menschen. Stuttgart, 1969. *G.A.*

Intrapsychic. Within the mind (endopsychic, q.v.), or the self as a whole.

Intrinsic. That which is inward, fixed in the nature of the person or thing, and therefore not dependent on external influences or accident. Ant. *extrinsic:* that which is outward and does not belong to the essential nature of the person or thing.

Intrinsic-extrinsic. A distinction of H. Heckhausen's in regard to two components of *learning motivation. Intrinsic motivation* consists of achievement motivation (q.v.); stimuli from a specialism; task stimuli (related to the degree of difficulty of the task); attainability (calculation of the probable success in performing a task); and the degree of novelty possessed by a thing or task, or attributable to it. All other motivations are extrinsic, i.e. come from without, and are posited, not with the thing or task, but by the teacher, his personality, his style of teaching, and his sanctions. Extrinsic stimuli, rewards and punishments are thought to be less effective in the long run than those deemed intrinsic. *M.H.*

Introception. The inclusion of social standards (e.g. customs, conventions, ideals) in the individual's own system of motivation; introception is not identical with socialization, where conformity (especially in behavior) is not necessarily emphasized in the dynamic structure. *B.H.*

Introjection. 1. The term is generally used with the same meaning as identification (q.v.): an individual's incorporation into his ego of an object-image representing the object as he thinks it is. The most primitive form of introjection is "oral incorporation" which is alleged to consist of fantasized incorporation of the primary love-object (the mother) by the child when in a state of oral frustration; according to Freud, Abraham and Fenichel, this is a significant factor in psychotic depression.

2. The epistemological theory that the conscious mind apprehends the external world (only) by means of (the) images (the mind generates).

Bibliography: Abraham, K.: Selected papers on psychoanalysis. London, 1927. **Fenichel, O.:** The psychoanalytic theory of neurosis. New York, 1945. **Freud, S.:** Collected papers, Vol. 4. London, 1924–5.
W.T.

Intromission-copulation-ejaculation mechanism. A concept which occurs in comparative psychology (q.v.) and sex research. The two- or three-mechanism theory attempts to explain sexual behavior patterns in the male animal, and draws on the results of experiments in mammals (mice, rats, hamsters, guinea pigs). It is suggested that at least two or three mechanisms are involved in male sexual behavior: (*a*) an *arousal mechanism* (AM), which leads to sexual excitement, followed by erection and copulation; (*b*) a *copulatory mechanism* (CM), which is activated by the first intromission (introduction) of the penis, and leads to repeated intromission which maintains the full excitement of the CM until the critical threshold of ejaculation is reached (Beach *et al.*, 1956, 1959); (*c*) the *ejaculatory mechanism*, which is triggered by ejaculation (neurologically: the "ejaculation reflex") and prevents sexual excitement (by inhibiting the AM) until a certain recovery of "drive" has taken place (McGill, 1965). AM, CM and EM, defined by certain behavioral characteristics and duration times, vary not only from one species of animal to another but (as a function of the genotype) within a given species. For a critical summary, see Bolles (1967).

Bibliography: Beach, F. A.: Characteristics of masculine sex drives. In: **Jones, M. R.** (Ed.): Nebraska symposium on motivation. Lincoln, 1956, 1–32. **Beach, F. A. & Whalen, R. E.:** Effects of ejaculation on sexual behavior in the male rat. J. comp. physiol. Psychol., 1959, *52*, 249–54. **Bolles, R. C.:** Theory of motivation. New York & London, 1967, 167–72. **McGill, T. E.:** Studies of sexual behavior of male laboratory mice: effects of genotype, recovery of sex drive, and theory. In: **Beach, F. A.** (Ed.): Sex and behavior. New York & London, 1965, 76–88. *H.M.*

Introspection. Self-observation. The contemplation of one's own experiences; sometimes, though not necessarily, implying a morbid preoccupation with one's inner thoughts and feelings. In *structural psychology*, the reporting of thought processes and sensations (either during—*simultaneous introspection*—or immediately after—*retrospective introspection*—the process) as a technique for generating psychological data. *Beschreibung* (*Ger.*): such reporting of the direct experience of the individual. *G.D.W.*

Introspective psychology. A branch of psychology which uses introspection (q.v.) as a preferred method for obtaining data. The basic assumption is that subjective elements are objectified (see *Phenomenology*). In its theoretical and experimental aspects, the school has developed several different models, e.g. for processes of the will (see *Külpe*).

B.H.

Introversion. Jung (1971) maintained that mental or psychic energy (libido) may be directed outward (extraversion) or inward (introversion). Hence there are two opposed reaction types determining the nature of behavior, subjective experience, and even compensation by the unconscious. Introversion (like extraversion) is rooted (according to Jung) in the biological constitution of the individual and is therefore difficult to alter. The definition of an individual as introverted or extraverted may be considered as remaining constant throughout his life. See *Traits; Type.*

Bibliography: Jung, C. G.: Psychological types (Collected Works, Vol. 6). London & New York, 1971.

W.S.

Introversive type. An individual who in the Rorschach test shows a "predominance of introverted behavior, intensive relationships, stabilized affectivity and motility, inadequate adaptability to reality, and inadequate extensive relationships." Partly identical with the introvert. *W.K.*

Introvert (syn. *Introverted type*). A character type defined by Jung, and having a deficient or negative relationship between the ego and object as its main feature. Tendency to distance and depth. An individual in whom "a subjective attitude is inserted between perception of the object and his own behavior which prevents behavior from assuming a character corresponding to the given objective structure." Introverts "if normal, are characterized by a hesitant, reflective, withdrawn nature; they are reserved, frightened by objects, always on the defensive and likely to hide behind mistrustful observation"; they are therefore not very adaptable. Eysenck also defines the introvert as the opposite of the extravert, but as a statistically determined personality factor (see *Type*).

Bibliography: Jung, C. G.: Psychological types. London & New York, 1971. **Eysenck, H. J.:** The structure of human personality. London, [3]1970.

W.K.

Intuition. A mode of operation of intelligence (q.v.) and its product. As a mode of operation, intuition denotes a form of direct cognition characterized by its direct and sudden nature. It is based on spontaneous internal organization, on a perception, or on an idea or image. Intuition as "sympathy" with the object (H. Bergson) may amount to nonconceptual cognition, but may also be a rapid analytical understanding of a reference system whose actual analysis would require long discursive development (E. Brunswik). Intuition is concerned with an externally (empirical) or internally (metaphysical) perceptible phenomenon. In every case the existential nature of the object is apprehended by the mind. *M.J.B.*

Intuitive type. A functional type in whom the "basic function" of intuition dominates, and judgment is only secondary. As an extravert, the intuitive type constantly seeks new possibilities and is guided by confidence in his perception. As an introvert, however, the intuitive type appears as an "imaginative, artistic person" or as a "dreamer and visionary", internal perception being directed to the esthetic or moral sphere. *W.K.*

Intuitive understanding, psychology of. See *Verstehende Psychologie.*

Invariance. A parameter or trait is said to be invariant in relation to a transformation if it remains unchanged on application of the latter. E.g. the length of a rod is an invariant factor when it is rotated in space. *K.-D.G.*

Invariance, problem of. Any problem associated with the constancy, i.e. independence, of stimuli in regard to changes in external conditions. Invariance is dealt with under terms such as "generalization of learning", "concept formation", "constancy of perception". E.g. constancy of perception is the easiest type of invariance to examine. The resulting perceptual content is independent of all changes brought about by interference. A distinction is made between: color constancy, brightness constancy, gestalt constancy, size constancy, and direction and movement constancy. *H.W.*

Inventories. See *Questionnaires.*

Inversion. A reversal of poles, e.g. top to bottom, right to left, e.g. inversion of the retinal image. In mathematics, a transform which achieves reversal of a variable or matrix. *G.D.W.*

Inversion, sexual. Assumption of the characteristics and role of the opposite sex, e.g. *transves(ti)tism* (q.v.). Has also been loosely used as a synonym for *homosexuality* (q.v.) (especially in psychoanalysis), and even *hermaphroditism* (q.v.). *Invert:* An individual with homosexual inclinations. *G.D.W.*

Inverted figures. See *Reversibility.*

Involution. On reaching maturity, the psychological development of man continues at a slower rate, and finally enters a phase of involution. At the climacteric (about the age of forty-eight), biological involution sets in as a transition to a way of life in which mental activity is more highly emphasized. Old age is a further period of involution. See *Aging; Gerontology.* *M.Sa.*

IPAT Anxiety Scale. The Ipat (Institute for Personality and Ability Testing) Anxiety Scale was developed by Cattell and Scheier on the basis of factor-analytical principles (1957). The subjective questionnaire comprises forty items which represent the secondary factor "anxiety"; anxiety, in turn, consists of five primary factors. The test—retest reliability is between r = 0.87 and 0.93 (1–2 weeks) and the split-half reliability between r = 0.84 and 0.91. The construct validity (q.v.) of the items is r = 0.92, and that of the primary factors r = 0.85. The criterion validity (correlations with other anxiety tests) is between r = 0.72/0.85.

Bibliography: Cattell, R. B. & Scheier, I. H.: Handbook for the IPAT Anxiety Scale. Champaign, Ill., 1957; [2]1963. *P.G.*

IPAT (O-A) Anxiety Battery. The Objective-Analytic (O-A) Anxiety Battery was designed by Cattell and Scheier (1960) on the basis of factor-analytical principles. The objective questionnaire with its two hundred and sixty-two items represents the primary factor "anxiety", and measures mainly the trait anxiety. The split-half reliability of the verbal subtests is between r = 0.56 and 0.90 (average: r = 0.75). The construct validity (q.v.) of the overall battery is indicated by Cattell as r = 0.94. The criterion validity (other anxiety tests) is greater than 0.80.

Bibliography: Cattell, R. B. & Scheier, I. H.: Handbook for the A-O Anxiety Battery. Champaign, Ill., 1960. *P.G.*

IPAT Objective-Analytic (O-A) Personality Test Batteries. The representative test battery in factor-analytical personality research, with objective tests by Cattell. The version for adults measures fourteen objective personality factors, with fifty-six objective tests (q.v.) (for children: eight [six to ten years], or eleven [eleven to twelve years] personality factors). Reliability coefficients are not given in the manual. The factor loadings are described by Hundleby, Pawlik & Cattell (1965). In the present state of development, the test is primarily a research instrument.

Bibliography: Cattell, R. B. *et al.*: Handbook for the O-A. Personality Test Batteries, Champaign, Ill.,

1955. **Hundleby, J. D., Pawlik, K. & Cattell, R. B.:** Personality factors in objective test devices. Champaign, Ill., 1965, 339–406. *P.G.*

Ipsation (syn. *Ipsism*). Masturbation (q.v.) or autoeroticism with reference to some particular part of the body, e.g. anal ipsation, mammary ipsation, and so on. *G.D.W.*

IQ. Abb. for *Intelligence quotient* (q.v.).

Iris. An opaque regulable diaphragm in the form of an 0.5 mm thick disk of connective tissue with a variable internal diameter, separating the anterior from the posterior chamber of the eye (see *Eye; Sense organs*). The iris is continuous peripherally with the ciliary body; its aperture is the contractile pupil, whose width can be varied between about 8 and 2 mm by the smooth *sphincter pupillae* (sphincter) and *dilatator pupillae* (dilator) muscles located in the iris. The pigmentation of its posterior pigmented surface is wholly absent in the condition of albinism. The anterior colored surface represents the "color of a person's eyes". *K.H.P.*

IRM. Abb for *Innate releasing mechanism* (q.v.).

Irradiation. 1. The influence exerted by one field on another. **2.** Physiologically: the extension of stimuli in certain regions of the brain to neighboring areas of the CNS. **3.** Psychologically, and in the sense of an optical illusion: bright objects on a dark background appear larger than dark objects of the same size on a bright background. According to T. Ziehen, irradiation occurs when neutral conscious material is influenced by emotional experiences which are present at the same time or have some associative connection with it. *K.E.P.*

Irrational. Any assertion based not on the laws of reason but on intuition is irrational, as are theories regarding an object (life, existence, will, etc.) outside reality. This is particularly true of Freud (in his late phase). *M.R.*

Irrelevant actions (syn. *Comfort movements*). Inappropriate behaviors such as stretching, yawning, scratching one's head, preening (see *Allopreening*). Although these "occur easily" (e.g. insects cleaning their antennae), by no means all such movements are autochthonous; in conflicts they often tend to be displacement activities (q.v.). As derived and ritualized movements they play a great part in the evolution of displays.

Bibliography: Bilz, R: Zur Psychophysik des Verlegenheitskratzens. Zentralbl. Psychother. u. Grenzgeb., 1941, *13*, 36–50. **Tembrock, G.:** Verhaltensforschung. Jena, 1964. *K.Fi.*

Irresponsibility. See *Guilt*.

Irritability. 1. Stimulability; excitability; the characteristic property of living matter to respond to stimuli by movement, etc. **2.** Contractability of a muscle. **3.** Affective response; emotional changeability; oversensitivity to stimulation: a strongly emotional response is given to normally acceptable stimuli. See *Arousal; Emotion*. *H.W.*

Irritation. 1. The effect of stimuli. **2.** Inflammation.

Ishihara test (syn. *Ishihara chart; Ishihara color plate*). A test for color blindness: figures are printed in varying hues against backgrounds of varying saturations and brightness. The color-blind or color-defective individual does not see the figure, or sees it imperfectly.

Island of Reil. See *Insula*.

Isolation. A hypothetical internal defense (q.v.) mechanism in which a motive which can no longer be satisfied or is forbidden can only be "abandoned" by partially satisfying it in thought or symbolically, and is therefore experienced as alien to the individual. The unsuccessful attempt at repression is reinforced by repression (q.v.) of the connection between the questionable motive and the individual. Isolation is said to occur frequently in compulsion neuroses. *W.T.*

Isolation of variables. In experiments: the intentional alteration of a condition (independent variation) in order to observe a dependent variable, while all other conditions are kept "constant", or are not altered systematically. The effect of individual conditions which are otherwise closely bound up with the phenomenon or process can then be observed in isolation. *W.H.B.*

Isolation, social. Minimal social contact or maximum social distance between individuals and/or groups. The aftereffects of social isolation in the early years of life have been described in particular by Harlow (1958) and Spitz (1958) as hospitalism (q.v.). Voluntary or planned isolation of one group in relation to alien groups is frequently used as a means of heightening the internal cohesion of the isolated group. See *Group dynamics.*

Bibliography: Harlow, H. F.: The nature of love, Amer. Psychol., 1958, *13*, 573–685. **Spitz, R. A.:** Hospitalism: an enquiry into the genesis of psychiatric conditions in early childhood. New York, 1958.

A.S.M.

Isomorphism. The theory of *isomorphy*, or correspondence of gestalts: i.e. between what is experienced perceptually and the central-physiological correlate. It is assumed that the physiological processes correspond, not in their geometrical forms, but in their dynamic structures, with the contents of experience. See *Ganzheit; Psychophysics.* *P.T.*

Item. A single exercise in a test. See *Objective tests; Test theory.*

Item analysis. The various processes used to select items for tests. See *Test theory.*

Iteration tests. Statistical test methods for checking the randomness of a sample selection.

Ixothymia. A viscous temperament (q.v.).

J

Jackson's law. After John Hughlings Jackson, English neurologist (1834–1911). The generalization that when intellectual functions are lost through disease of the nervous system, those which appeared latest in evolution are the first to disappear, that is deterioration retraces evolution in reverse. The phylogenetically developing, "stratified" structure of the CNS corresponds to a distribution of functions in the sense that the higher systems always exercise an inhibiting influence on the lower ones. The function of the higher, phylogenetically younger centers is more labile than that of the deeper, older centers. In brain damage the mental and intellectual functions (orientation, perceptual ability, memory and thought) are the most sensitive and most easily injured, and are the first to be impaired or lost. *G.D.W. & C.S.*

James-Lange theory of emotion. A theory concerned with the relationship between the physiological changes that occur with emotional arousal (q.v.) and the accompanying experience of the emotion (q.v.). The Danish philosopher C. G. Lange had argued that emotion is identical with changes in the circulatory system. The American psychologist William James (q.v.) elaborated this theory, arguing that the emotional experience results from the perception of the various bodily changes that occur in response to emotive stimuli. Thus he held that the bodily changes are neither the outcome nor the concomitants of the emotional experience, but its *cause*. It would therefore be more true to say that we are afraid because we run away, than that we run because we are afraid.

Bibliography: Lange, C. G. & James, W.: The emotions (Ed. **Dunlap, K.**). Baltimore, 1922. *G.D.W.*

James, William. B. 1/11/1842 in New York City; d. 16/8/1910 at Mount Chocorua, New Hampshire. In 1861 James enrolled at Harvard University in the Lawrence Scientific School. He first studied chemistry, then comparative anatomy, biology and physiology, and entered the Harvard Medical School in 1864. His interest in psychology was heightened by a visit to Germany in 1867–8. In Berlin he attended lectures by Du Bois-Reymond, the famous physiologist, and in Heidelberg courses given by Helmholtz and Wundt. His academic career continued at Harvard: M.D. in 1869, Instructor, 1872, and Assistant Professor of physiology in 1876, Assistant Professor of philosophy in 1880, and then Professor of philosophy in 1885; in 1889, Professor of psychology, and Professor of philosophy again from 1897 to 1907. He set up one of the first psychological laboratories in the world, in 1875. His main psychological study, *Principles of Psychology* (1890), is one of the basic works of modern psychology. James was a pioneer of American psychology and is sometimes compared with Wundt. He was a co-founder of the functionalist movement and a supporter of evolutionism; he was a friend of C. Stumpf and worked with H. Münsterberg. He was an independent thinker and not a proponent of systems or a laboratory psychologist but a man of many ideas and an intelligent critic who remained close to reality; his style was highly original. In his psychology of emotion (q.v.) and expression he represented an extreme type of physiologism but was nevertheless on the way to "a phenomenological psychology" (J. Linschoten); he advocated an experimental psychology which he did not himself practice; he stood for "radical empiricism" and also developed a pragmatic religious philosophy and psychology. Among his contributions to psychology, his theory of consciousness (q.v.) and the self (see *Ego*) deserve especial mention. James saw consciousness as a result of adaptation helping man toward species- and self-preservation. As regards the self, he made a distinction (still discussed) between the "discriminated aspects and not separate things" of "I" (the self as knower) and the social "Me" (the self as known: material, social and spiritual). He represented consciousness ("stream of consciousness") as processual rather than static (structured), and emphasized the dynamic nature of human psychology. "Consciousness, as a process in time, offers the paradoxes which have been found in all continuous change. There are no 'states' in such a thing, any more than there are facets in a circle. . . . Yet how can we do without 'states', in describing what the vehicles of our knowledge seem to be?"

Main works: Principles of psychology. New York, 1890; London, 1891. Text-book of psychology. New York & London, 1892. The will to believe. London, 1897. Human immortality. Boston & London, 1898; [2]1917. Talks to teachers on psychology, and to students on some of life's ideals. New York & London, 1899. The varieties of religious experience: a study in human nature. London, 1902. Pragmatism, London, 1897. The meaning of truth. London, 1909. A pluralistic universe. London, 1909. Some problems of philosophy. London, 1911. Essays in radical empiricism. London, 1912.

Bibliography: Allport, G. W.: The productive paradoxes of William James. Psychol. Rev., 1943, *50*, 95–120. **Id.:** William James and the behavioral sciences. J. Hist. beh. Sci., 1966, *2*, 145–7. **Boring, E. G.:** Human nature vs. sensation: William James and the psychology of the present. Amer. J. Psychol., 1942, *55*, 310–27. **Harper, R. S.:** The laboratory of William James. Harvard Alum. Bull., 1949, *52*, 169–73. **Knight, M.:** William James. London, [2]1954. **Linschoten, J.:** Auf dem Wege zu einer phänomenologischen Psychologie: die Psychologie von W. James. Berlin, 1961. **Perry, R. B.:** The thought and character of William James, 2 vols. Boston & London, 1935.

L.J.P.

Janet, Pierre. B. 29/5/1859, in Paris; d. 24/2/1947, in Paris. Studied philosophy and medicine at the University of Paris; in 1889 he gained his doctorate for philosophy with a thesis on the psychology of automatic activities; in 1890 Charcot appointed him Director of the psychological laboratory at the Salpêtrière hospital. In 1892 he received his doctorate in medicine with a thesis on the mental state of hysterics, in which he attempted a systematic classification of the different forms of hysteria, and tried to establish a concordance between hysterical symptoms and psychological theories; he taught at the Sorbonne from 1895 to 1902 and then replaced Ribot in the chair of psychology at the Collège de France, where he remained until his retirement in 1936. In 1904 Janet and G. Dumas founded the *Journal de psychologie normale et pathologique*, which Janet edited until 1937.

Janet's "psychologie de la conduite". In his behavioral theory, Janet works from the assumption that a scientific study of psychology can be meaningful only if all mental processes are interpreted as behaviors. He was one of the first to place special emphasis on the dynamic characteristics and unity of psychological phenomena. Although he had much in common with Freud (q.v.), their relationship was strained, partly because Janet claimed that Freud's psychoanalysis (q.v.) was based on his own work and that of Charcot. Janet conceived personality as a totality of tendencies which he arranged in a hierarchy on the basis of their phylogenetic and ontogenetic origins (strata theory), from the lower (reflex actions, etc.) to the higher tendencies (rational, etc.). By "tendency", Janet understood a disposition of the organism to complete a specific action; he included both external and internal or secondary actions (e.g. emotions) under the notion of action. A human being generally has access to tendencies which correspond to all the diverse stages and are normally present in a latent form. All these tendencies have specific energy loadings, which Janet derived from hereditary, physiological and psychological processes, and whose activation is manifested in behavior (actions). The lower tendencies generally have higher energy charges than the higher tendencies; they are also easy to arouse, and discharge more completely than the higher tendencies, which are only discharged successively (in this context Janet, like Freud, allows for the possibility of the inhibition and transference of instinctive [drive] energies). In general, the overall behavior of a given individual corresponds to a certain hierarchical level ("psychological or mental tension") determined both by the rank order of behaviors in the hierarchy of tendencies and by the degree of activation of those behaviors. An individual's mental tension is high if he can easily perform, frequently and accurately, actions with a high ranking in the hierarchy. The tension level is not constant but subject to continuous fluctuation. Janet emphasizes the degree of reduction of mental tension as the criterion for a classification of personality disorders. Reductions in tension which relate only to the stage of the highest tendencies are still normal; if mental tension drops below the stage of considered behavior (medium tendencies), Janet speaks of *neuroses*. If the tension falls to the level of elementary intellectual behavior, he speaks of *psychoses*; and if it drops to the level of perception and reflex actions, organic disorders of the CNS are in question.

Main works: L'automatisme. Paris, 1889. L'état mental des hysteriques. Paris, 1892 (Eng. trans. The major symptoms of hysteria. New York, [2]1920; facsimile ed., N.Y., 1965). Les obsessions et la psychasthénie. Paris, 1903. Névroses et idées fixes. Paris, [2]1904. Les névroses. Paris, 1909. De l'angoisse à l'extase. Paris, 1926. Psychological healing: a historical and clinical study, 2 vols. London, 1925. Psychological analysis. In: Murchison, C. (Ed.): Psychologies of 1930. Worcester, 1930, 369–73. Pierre Janet. In: Murchison, C. (Ed.): History of psychology in autobiography, Vol. 1. Worcester, 1930, 123–33.

Bibliography: Mayo, E.: Some notes on the psychology of Pierre Janet. Cambridge, Mass., 1948. **Zilboorg, G. & Henry, G. W.:** A history of medical psychology. New York, 1941.

W.W.

J curve. A hypothesis put forward by F. H. Allport (1934) according to which the frequency of the behavioral characteristics of a group exposed to pressure to conform—unlike groups without such pressure—follows a J distribution rather than a standard distribution (e.g. punctuality of workers in a company with fixed working hours as opposed to punctuality in a company in which the starting time may vary; or varied behavior at traffic lights). The curve of varying degrees of conformity often approximates an inverted capital J.

Bibliography: Allport, F. H.: The J-curve hypothesis of conforming behavior. J. soc. Psychol., 1934, *5*.

A.S.-M.

Jargon. 1. Incomprehensible speech. **2.** Language, vocabulary or style specific to a particular profession, political party, branch of learning, etc.

Jastrow's illusion. One of the geometric illusions. Although they are identical in size

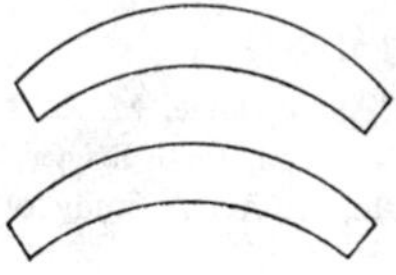

the lower of the two curved figures appears larger. *C.D.F.*

Job. 1. A task. **2.** An occupational activity performed in return for (a monetary) reward.

Job analysis. A detailed study of all the requirements and conditions of a particular occupation. Often used in management training and the preparation of interview programs. See *Industrial psychology.*

Job enlargement. Adding to an occupational activity by the inclusion of new operations (previously performed by others) in order to make the work more interesting, rational and/or responsible. *G.R.W.M.*

Job rotation. A planned change in activities and/or functions for training and vocational advancement of executives. *G.R.W.M.*

Jost's law(s). 1. The older of two associations of identical intensity diminishes less with the the passage of time. **2.** Practice is of greater benefit to the older of two associations of identical intensity. See *Association.*

Bibliography: Jost, A.: Die Assoziationsfestigkeit in ihrer Abhängigkeit von der Verteilung der Wiederholungen. Z. Psychol., 1897, *14*, 436–72. *H.H.*

Judgment. 1. The power or process of discerning the relations between one object, or concept, or term, or proposition, and another; or a propositional statement of those relations. See *Logical reasoning; Perception; Thinking.* **2.** A critical evaluation. **3.** The discernment of stimuli and their intensities (see *Psychophysics*).

Bibliography: Abercrombie, M. L. J.: The anatomy of judgment. London, 1960. **Bruner, J. S., Goodnow, J. J. & Austin, G. A.:** A study of thinking. New York, 1962.

Judgment, change of. A process of social suggestion or influence in which relatively simple verbal of symbolic "more or less" decisions on specific objects (e.g. perceptual objects) are altered: for instance, such basic judgments as "long" or "short", "positive" or "negative", "sympathetic" or "unsympathetic". A term sometimes used to characterize changes of opinion or attitude where there is no conceptual qualification beyond the basic term. See *Psychophysics.* *H.D.S*

Judicious learning. See *Learning, mechanical.*

Jung, Carl Gustav. B. 26/7/1875 in Kesswil (Switzerland); d. 6/6/1961 in Küssnacht. After obtaining his medical degree from the University of Basle in 1900, Jung was appointed assistant, and later lecturer, under Eugen Bleuler at Zürich. He gave up his university post in 1913 in order to devote himself to private practice and to research. From 1906 he corresponded regularly with Freud, whom he met for the first time in 1907, in Vienna. This was the beginning of a short-lived friendship, during which Freud for a time saw Jung as his successor. In 1909 they traveled together to Worcester, USA. In 1907 Jung founded the Freud-Gesellschaft in Zürich. In 1908 he organized the first International Psychoanalytic Congress in Salzburg. In 1911, with Freud's support, Jung was elected first president of the International Psychoanalytic Society; soon afterwards, the difficulties in his relations with Freud (primarily arising from Jung's rejection of the libido theory) increased. Their correspondence ceased in 1913; and in 1914 Jung resigned his presidency (and later his membership) of the International Psychoanalytic Society. Between 1921 and 1926 he made field expeditions to study primitive cultures in Arizona, Mexico, North Africa, and Kenya, and pursued his interest in mythology, alchemy, religion, occult practices, and so on. From 1933 to 1942 he was Professor at the Zürich

Polytechnic; and in 1944 he was appointed Professor of medical psychology at the University of Basle.

In contradistinction to Freud's more natural-scientific, mechanistic theory of personality, Jung's analytical conception of personality represents an attempt to interpret human behavior from a philosophic, religious and mystical viewpoint. Jung's theory is also distinguished from psychoanalysis (q.v.) by its stronger emphasis on teleology (q.v.) (not only causality, q.v.) as a determinant of behavior, a stress on racial and phylogenetic bases of personality, and much less emphasis on sexuality as a significant factor in the development of personality.

In explaining the dynamics of personality, Jung—like Freud—uses the concept of libido (q.v.) but—unlike Freud—does not see it as a collective concept for human sexual tendencies, but as an *undifferentiated* energy at the basis of the most varied mental processes (thinking, feeling, sensing, drive). The regulation of psychic activity is not determined by the pleasure-pain principle, but occurs autonomously by way of libido, and is determined primarily by the principles of the conservation of energy and of entropy (q.v.).

The whole personality (psyche) consists of three interacting systems: the conscious, the personal unconscious, and the collective unconscious. The midpoint of the *conscious* is constituted by the ego (q.v.), which comprises the conscious perceptions, memory contents, thoughts and feelings, and permits the individual to adapt to the environment. The *personal unconscious* consists of the personal experiences, wishes and impulses which were once conscious but were then repressed or forgotten, but are essentially capable of being once again brought to consciousness. The *collective unconscious*, the most influential psychic system, operates wholly without the conscious awareness of the individual. It is the inherited racial foundation of the structure of personality and manifests the influence of the cumulative experiences of all previous generations, and even the animal past of the human species. The structural components of the collective unconscious are the *archetypes* (q.v.), which are universal, inherited dispositions of the human imaginative faculty, which dispose the individual to experience and behave in eternally recurrent situations (birth, death, danger, fatherhood) as his ancestors experienced and behaved in them. Some archetypes are so developed that they constitute autonomous personality systems: the persona, anima, animus, and shadow.

The *self*, an archetype which is responsible for the integration and stability of the personality, occupies a central position in the Jungian theory of personality. It is expressed in the inborn striving of the human individual toward psychic wholeness, a central process which Jung calls *individuation* (q.v.), or striving toward self-realization. Since neurosis (q.v.) is said to represent a disturbance of the process of individuation, Jung's analytical therapy aims at a restoration of this natural process of development.

Jung's typology (see *Type*) is based on a distinction between function and reaction types. Whereas function types are divided into the four basic functions of thinking, intuition, feeling and sensation, the reaction type characterizes the direction of libidinous energy. According to whether libido is oriented more inwardly or outwardly, Jung distinguishes between *introversion* and *extraversion*.

Works: The Collected Works of C. G. Jung, 17 vols. Ed. Read, H., Fordham, M. & Adler, G. London & New York, 1953–.

Some major individual works are: Studies in word association. London, 1918; New York, 1919. Contributions to analytical psychology. London, 1928. Modern man in search of a soul. London & New York, 1933. Psychiatric studies (Works, Vol. 1, pt. 1), London & New York, 1957. Psychological types (vol. 6). London & New York, 1971. The structure and dynamics of the psyche (Vol. 8). London & New York, 1960. The archetypes and the collective unconscious

(Vol. 9, pt. 1). London & New York, 1959. Psychology and alchemy (Vol. 12). London & New York, [2]1969. The development of personality (Vol. 17). London & New York, 1954. The interpretation of nature and the psyche (with W. Pauli). London, 1955.

Bibliography: Clark, R. A.: Jung and Freud: a chapter in psychoanalytic history. Amer. J. Psychother., 1955, *9*, 605–11. **Fordham, F.:** An introduction to Jung's psychology. Harmondsworth, [3]1966. **Fordham, M.** (Ed.): Contact with Jung. Essays on the influence of his work and personality. London, 1963. **Gray, H. & Wheelwright, J. B.:** Jung's psychological types, including the four functions. J. Gen. Psychol., 1945, *33*, 265–84. **Hochheimer, W.:** Psychotherapy of C. J. Jung. New York, 1969. **Jacobi, J.:** Complex, archetype, symbol in the psychology of C. G. Jung. New Haven & London, 1959. **Id.:** The psychology of C. G. Jung. An introduction. New Haven & London, [7]1969. **Munroe, R. L.:** Schools of psychoanalytic thought. New York, 1955. **Progoff, I.:** Jung's psychology and its social meaning. New York, [2]1969. **Schaer, H.:** Religion and the cure of souls in Jung's psychology. London, 1951. **Serrano, M.:** C. G. Jung and Herman Hesse. A record of two friendships. London, 1966. **Wehr, G.:** Portrait of Jung. New York, 1971.

W.W.

Just-noticeable difference (abb. j.n.d.). A minute difference between stimuli which is just barely above threshold: i.e. an only just perceptible physical change in stimuli. See *Psychophysics.*

Just-not-noticeable difference (abb. j.n.n.d.). The largest difference between two stimuli which is only just imperceptible.

Juvenile delinquency. The most common offenses committed by juveniles are theft and embezzlement. In the twentieth century, and especially after World War II, juvenile crime increased far more quickly than adult crime and became an ever greater social problem. Juvenile psychology (q.v.) and criminal psychology (q.v.) investigate the causes of this development. In the practical field, child psychology (q.v.), educational counseling (q.v.), forensic psychology (q.v.), and clinical psychology (q.v.) deal with the problem of juvenile delinquency. See *Aggression; Criminality; Drug dependence.*

Bibliography: Conger, J. J. & Miller, W. C.: Personality, social class and delinquency. New York, London & Sydney, 1966. **Glueck, S. & Glueck, E. T.:** Unraveling juvenile delinquency. Cambridge, Mass., 1950. **Gottlieb, D. & Reeves, J.:** Adolescent behavior in urban areas. New York, 1963. **Mays, J. B.:** Growing up in a city. Liverpool, 1956. **Sheldon, W. H., Hartl, E. & McDermott, E.:** Varieties of delinquent youth. New York, 1949.

F.Ma.

Juvenile psychology. A part field of developmental psychology (see *Development*). Juvenile psychology studies the psychological situation and developmental processes of juveniles in pre-puberty (q.v.), puberty (q.v.), and adolescence (q.v.). The principal areas of research are psychobiological (bodily changes, personality development) and psychosocial problems (socialization, q.v.) of youth (q.v.). Special attention is given to adaptive disorders (see *Adjustment, social*) and juvenile delinquency (q.v.). See *Child psychology; Differential psychology; Educational psychology; Infancy sexuality.*

Bibliography: Gesell, A., Ilg, F. & Ames, L. B.: Youth. New York, 1956.

F.Ma.

Juvenilism. See *Infantilism.*

K

Kallikak. A pseudonym for a much-studied family with two lines of descendants: one socially respectable, the other variously defective.

Bibliography: Goddard, H. H.: The Kallikak family: a study in the heredity of feeble-mindedness. New York, 1912. **Id.:** In defense of the Kallikak study. Science, 1942, *95*, 574.

Kappa effect. If two stimuli are presented separated by a fixed temporal interval, the experienced temporal interval depends on the spatial separation of the stimuli, larger separation giving the appearance of a longer interval. This effect, which is small, occurs in both vision and touch. *C.D.F.*

Kaspar-Hauser. See *Caspar Hauser*.

Kendall's rank correlation method (syn. *Kendall tau coefficient*). A non-parametric correlation method whose use presupposes ordinal variables. The calculation is made according to

$$\tau = \frac{2S}{n(n-1)},$$

where S is the number of rank pairs of the second variables which are in the correct sequence when the first rank series is placed in its natural order. τ is not algebraically comparable with the Spearman's correlation coefficient. See *Correlational techniques*.

Bibliography: Kendall, M. G.: A new measure of rank correlation. Biometrika, 1938, *30*, 1–15. **Id.:** Rank correlation methods. London, [3]1962. *G.Mi.*

Kendall's W (syn. *Coefficient of concordance*). A non-parametric method to determine the degree of concordance of more than two rankings. The calculation is made according to:

$$W = \frac{11\,\Sigma\, D_1^2}{k^2(N^3 - N)},$$

in which k is the number of rank series and D_1 the deviations of the summed rankings of the individual components from the mean of the group rankings.

Bibliography: Kendall, M. G.: Rank correlation methods. London, [3]1962. *G.Mi.*

Kent-Rosanoff Test. A free word-association test on Jungian principles developed by G. H. Kent and A. J. Rosanoff in 1910 for psychiatric clinics. The frequencies of reaction words for the one hundred stimulus words of the test were determined in one thousand testees, and the interpretation objectivized. Other authors standardized the answers for specialized groups.

Bibliography: Buros, O. K.: The sixth mental measurement yearbook. New Jersey, 1965. *R.M.*

Keratoscope. Also known as a Placido disk after A. Placido (1882), a keratoscope is used for qualitative determination of irregular corneal curvature (see *Astigmatism*). It is a circular disk with concentric white and black rings, and a central aperture. If the cornea of a patient is viewed through the aperture, in astigmatism the reflected circles are distorted. *K.H.P.*

Keynote (syn. *Tonic*). **1.** The main, lowest note of the scale from which the passage is constructed: i.e. the first degree of the (major or minor) key, which gives the key its name. **2.** In acoustics, the lowest, overtone-free partial of a clang (q.v.) *B.S.*

Key stimulus. (syn. *Releasing stimulus; Releaser*). A trigger for an instinctive action operating through an IRM. The relevant characteristics of the stimulus object are determined in dummy sign stimuli (q.v.) experiments. E.g.: In spring the stickleback attacks rivals only when they are brilliantly colored (red belly). Although realistic stickleback dummies with no red coloration do not elicit an attack, the response occurs if a model only remotely resembling a fish but with a red base is sighted. See *Innate releasing mechanism; Instinct.* *I.L.*

Kinesiotherapy. Various kinds of movement therapy: relaxation exercises, breathing practice, rhythmic movement, gymnastics; also individual and group sports for relaxation, development of social ease, and the acquisition of new, or the recovery of previously repressed, somatic aspects of the individual personality. See *Autogenic training.* *W.T.*

Kinesthesia (syn. *Kinesthesis*). The perception of movements of parts of the body mediated by receptors in the joints, muscles and tendons. A *kinesthetic hallucination* would thus be the experience of a bodily movement which did not actually occur. Such a hallucination is sometimes experienced after traveling a long time on a boat. *C.D.F.*

Kinesthesiometer. An instrument for checking the accuracy of sensations of movement. Without visual checks, either passive movements are repeated actively or active movements of a specific type are directed to previously agreed points in space. The accuracy with which the movements are repeated or the points reached is measured. *A.T.*

Kinesthetic type (syn. *Motor type*). An ideational or one of the imagination types in whom tactile and movement images predominate. Described by Stern in 1911. *W.K.*

Kinsey report. The studies known as the Kinsey Report (Kinsey *et al.*, 1948; 1953) were conducted at the Institute for Sex Research in Bloomington (Indiana, USA) founded by A. Kinsey, and were the first comprehensive, empirical scientific studies of sexual behavior. Kinsey and his colleagues conducted surveys among 5300 white males and 5490 white females over a period of fifteen years; their subjects were of widely varying age and educational groups, social strata and religious affiliations; they were questioned about their sexual behavior: e.g. masturbation (q.v.), marital and extramarital intercourse (see *Coitus*), petting (q.v.), homosexuality (q.v.). Criticism (excluding moral rejection of the findings) has primarily been directed at the allegedly unrepresentative nature of the sample (Cochran *et al.*, 1953) and (e.g. Trilling, 1952) at the "worship of the factuality of the fact . . . the effect of suggesting a most ineffectual standard of social behavior—that is, social behavior as it exists." Beyond the results and their exemplary multivariate evaluation, the importance of the Kinsey report lies in the fact that it opened a new phase in empirical studies of sexual behavior—some of which have come from the Institute, which was continued by Gebhard after Kinsey's death. See *Sexuality.*

Bibliography: Cochran, W. G. *et al.*: Statistical problems of the Kinsey Report. J. Am. Statist. Ass., 1953, *48*, 673–716. **Gebhard, P. H., Gagnon, J. H., Pomeroy, W. B. & Christenson, C. V.:** Pregnancy, birth and abortion. New York, 1958. **Id.:** Sex offenders. New York, 1965. **Himmelhoch, J. & Fava, S. F.** (Eds.): Sexual behavior in American society. New

York, 1955. **Kinsey, A. C., Pomeroy, W. B. & Martin, C. E.:** Sexual behavior in the human male. Philadelphia, 1948. **Id. & Gebhard, P. H.:** Sexual behavior in the human female, Philadelphia, 1953. **Trilling, L.:** The Kinsey Report. Perspectives USA, 1952, *1*, 193–206. *J.F.*

Kirschmann's law of contrast. In simultaneous color contrast, if there are no differences in brightness the induced color saturation is proportional to the logarithm of the saturation of the color inducing the contrast. *W.P.*

Kjersted-Robinson law. The proportion of material learned during equal fractions of learning time is relatively constant for different lengths of material.

Klages' types. Three basic attitudes: (*a*) ego emphasis: close relationship between the ego and id; (*b*) elimination of the feeling of self: the ego and id are split apart (dissolution); (*c*) cult of images and ecstasy.

Bibliography: Klages, L.: Grundlagen der Charakterkunde. Bonn, [13]1966. *W.K.*

Klang (Ger.). See *Clang*.

Kleptomania. Compulsive pathological stealing. The objects stolen often appear to be of little value to the thief and therefore are often viewed as being of symbolic value. To a Freudian the objects would have sexually satisfying qualities. To others the thefts are seen as acts of aggression against society, to assert authority, or as a revenge against material and emotional deprivation in childhood. *D.E.*

Klinefelter's syndrome. A syndrome described by the American physician H. F. Klinefelter in 1942. Symptoms: hypogonadism with testicular atrophy, underdevelopment of the secondary sex characteristics, gynecomastia (q.v.), absence of spermiogenesis, and (frequently) eunuchoidal physique. The cause is a chromosomal anomaly with trisomia of the sex chromosomes—generally XXY. *E.D.*

Knee-jerk reflex. See *Patellar reflex.*

Knowledge. 1. *Simple knowledge:* apprehension (q.v.); perception (q.v.). **2.** *Complex knowledge*: understanding (q.v.). **3.** Certain (i.e. indubitable) apprehension or understanding. "I conclude . . . that the necessary and sufficient conditions for knowing that something is the case are first what one is said to know be true, secondly that one be sure of it, and thirdly that one should have the right to be sure. This right may be earned in various ways . . ." (Ayer, 1956). **4.** Accurate information. **5.** The relation between object and subject (see *Epistemology; Cognition*).

Knowledge, theory of: see *Cognition theory.*

Bibliography: Ayer, A. J.: The problem of knowledge. London, 1956. **Wittgenstein, L.:** Philosophical investigations. London, [2]1958.

Knowledge of results. In psychotherapy, education (especially programmed instruction), etc.: confirmation of the accuracy or inaccuracy of a response.

Koffka, Kurt. B. 18/3/1886 in Berlin; d. 22/11/1941 in Northampton, Mass. Received his doctorate in 1908 under C. Stumpf in Berlin, with a thesis on experimental studies of rhythm theory; was an assistant of J. von Fries in Freiburg (Breisgau) in 1908/09, and of O. Külpe and K. Marbe in Würzburg, in 1909/10. As research assistant to F. Schumann in Frankfurt in 1910, he met Wertheimer and Köhler, and with them founded the Berlin school of gestalt psychology. In 1919 Koffka became a private lecturer and in 1918 Extraordinary Professor in Giessen, where he remained until 1924. He left Germany in 1924 and taught at Cornell University in 1924/25, Clark University in 1925, the University of Wisconsin in 1926/27, and at Smith College from 1927 until his death.

Works: Koffka, Wertheimer and Köhler are considered to be the founders of gestalt psychology. Apart from his experimental work, Koffka's main contribution was his systematic presentation and application of gestalt principles to a wide range of phenomena from perception, learning, memory and development to social psychology.

Unlike Wertheimer and Köhler, Koffka formulated his gestaltist viewpoint at a relatively early stage, i.e. when, in 1923, he published the first of a series of twenty-five "Contributions to gestalt psychology". In 1915 he answered the critics of gestalt theory in his *Fundamentals of the Psychology of Perception: a Debate with V. Benussi*, and in 1919 with an article on the influence of experience on perception. In his *Principles of Psychological Development: An Introduction to Child Psychology* (1921), for the first time Koffka applied gestalt principles to child psychology. He believed that the development process is essentially the result of the interaction of internal and external conditions convergence hypothesis), and consists of an increasing differentiation of originally diffuse, qualitatively holistic experience.

Koffka's most important work, his *Principles of Gestalt Psychology* (1935), was the most comprehensive attempt yet to represent and integrate the results of gestalt psychological research in various fields (including the work of Lewin). His treatment of learning and memory may be considered the most systematic presentation of gestaltist ideas on the subject. (See *Ganzheit.*)

Koffka's learning theory is based on the assumption that learning, like other areas of behavior, can be explained by the gestalt principles of organization. New learning consists in the formation of "memory traces": i.e. of specific excitatory gestalts in the brain which result from previous processes (physiological correlates of direct percepts) and therefore represent past experience in the present. The memory process consists of the activation of memory traces by present processes on the basis of mutual similarity. The trace system is organized in accordance with the conventional gestalt laws and is subject to pregnance. Its time-conditioned changes do not therefore consist of a weakening of memory traces (forgetting) but in a qualitative change toward a "good gestalt" with increasing regularity and sharper accentuation of special features. The typical form of learning is learning by insight, even though this may be preceded by a testing stage. Practice brings about a consolidation and strengthening of the trace system. The "law of effect" is basically acknowledged, but reinterpreted: attainment to the goal influences learning (on the basis of the gestalt law of closure) through the completion of the action gestalt. The transfer of successful solutions to new situations (transposition) is possible if the principle of solution (i.e. the dynamic structural relation) is similar.

Main works: Perception: an introduction to the *Gestalttheorie*. Psychol. Bull., 1922, *19*, 631–85. The growth of the mind: an introduction to child psychology. London & New York, [2]1928. Principles of gestalt psychology. New York, 1935. *W.W.*

Köhler, Wolfgang. B. 21/1/1887 in Reval, Estonia; d. 11/6/1967, Lebanon, New Hampshire. Köhler received his doctorate in 1909 under C. Stumpf in Berlin; he then went to Frankfurt as an assistant to F. Schumann and became a private lecturer in 1911; he met Wertheimer and Koffka in Frankfurt and with them carried out the historic experiments that established gestalt psychology; he later became a co-founder of the Berlin school; from 1913 to 1920 he worked as director of the anthropoid station of the Prussian Academy of Sciences at Teneriffe, where he conducted his famous investigations into the "intelligence" of apes. In 1921 he took over from Stumpf as director of the Berlin psychological laboratory, and was appointed Professor of psychology and philosophy in 1922. In 1935 he left Germany because of the Nazi dictatorship and emigrated to the United States; he became Professor at Swarthmore College, where he remained until his retirement in 1955. He was President of the A.P.A., a member of the National Academy of Sciences, and in 1956 received the A.P.A.'s Distinguished Scientific Contribution Award.

Works. Together with Wertheimer and Koffka, Köhler founded gestalt psychology. His major contributions on the psychology of perception include treatises on the assumption of constancy in earlier psychology, and studies of figural aftereffects. He believed that he could use the existence of figural aftereffects indirectly to prove the existence of the cortical tension fields assumed in his neurophysiological theory of dynamic "self-distribution". In his studies of constancy, Köhler was able to show that (contrary to previous ideas) there is no constant correspondence between local sensory stimuli and experimental impressions, and that a perception is influenced not only by the local stimulus but, primarily, by the organization of the visual reference system and by the stimulus constellation of the other sense organs.

In the sphere of the psychology of learning and memory, Köhler criticized the learning theories of association psychology, and in particular the principle of association (q.v.) by contiguity; his own opinion was that associations occur under the influence of gestalt organizational tendencies: the associated contents become parts of a gestalt. Spatial and temporal contiguity was important in associations only in favoring the organization of a gestalt by sheer proximity.

Köhler's most famous works are his studies of the intelligent behavior of chimpanzees. Departing from the theory of E. L. Thorndike (who reduced animal behavior to trial-and-error learning), Köhler showed that animals are already able to act with insight, and even to use or manufacture tools to achieve their objectives.

In his gestalt theory of brain physiology, Köhler started from the assumption of a dynamic self-distribution in the physical sphere (physical gestalts) and arrived at the notion that physiological activation processes in the brain are also subject to dynamic self-distribution, and that there is a formal, topological correspondence between perceived space and the underlying physiological brain processes. See *Isomorphism; Ganzheit*.

Main works: Intelligence in apes. In: Murchison, C. (Ed.): Psychologies of 1925. Worcester, [2]1927, 145–61. The mentality of apes. New York, [2]1927. Gestalt psychology. New York, 1929. The place of value in a world of facts. New York, 1938. Dynamics in psychology. New York, 1940. On the nature of associations. Proc. Amer. phil. Soc., 1941, *84*, 489–502. Gestalt psychology: an introduction to new concepts in modern psychology. New York, [3]1957. Relational determination in perception. In: Jeffress, L. A. (Ed.): Cerebral mechanisms in behavior. New York & London, 1951, 200–43. The present situation in brain physiology. Amer. Psychologist, 1958, *13*, 150–4. Perceptual organization and learning. Amer. J. Psychol., 1958, *71*, 311–5 Gestalt psychology today. Amer. Psychologist, 1959, *14*, 727–34.

Bibliography: **Murchison, C.** (Ed.): The psychological register, Vol. 2. Worcester, 1929.

W.W.

Kolmogoroff-Smirnoff test. A non-parametric method for testing the extent to which two independent distributions match. These may be one empirical and one theoretical distribution, or, alternatively, two empirical distributions. The greatest observable difference the two summed distributions is determined as the index for matching.

Bibliography: **Kolmogoroff, A. N.:** Sulla determinazione empirica di une legge di distribuzione. Giornale Istituto Italiano Attuari, 1933, *4*, 83–91.

Smirnoff, N. W.: On the estimation of the discrepancy between empirical curves of distribution for two independent samples. Bull. Univ. Moscow. Ser. Internat., Sect. A2 (2), 1939, 3–8. *G.M.*

Korsakov's syndrome (syn. *Korsakov's psychosis*). An amnesic psychosyndrome described for the first time by K. S. Korsakov in alcohol-deranged individuals. The term was subsequently extended and is often now applied to all organic psychoses in which memory disorders are a dominant factor. The characteristic feature is a marked disturbance of perception and immediate memory, whereas long-term memory often remains adequate; there is a tendency to perseverations and confabulation. See *Alcoholism; Psychoses, functional.* *A.Hi.*

Korte's laws. Korte's laws concern apparent motion, i.e. stroboscopic motion produced by the intermittent presentation of stationary objects in different positions. If two objects are presented in this way, but appear successive, then apparent motion can be induced either by increasing the distance between the objects (Korte's first law) or by decreasing the time between presentations (Korte's second law). The third law states that an increase in separation of time can be compensated for by an increase in time or separation without regard to the quantitative relationship. *C.D.F.*

Koster's phenomenon. In artificially induced myopia (dispersion lines in front of the eyes) the colors of all (reduced) objects perceived appear fuller and more distinct. *F.C.S.*

Kraepelin, Emil. B. 15/2/1856 in Neustrelitz; d. 7/10/1926 in Munich. Kraepelin qualified as a doctor in Würzburg in 1878, then worked in the municipal mental hospital in Munich. He moved to Leipzig in 1882 in order to work with Wundt, whose friend he became while still a student, but Wundt advised him against devoting himself entirely to psychology. After a short period as a private lecturer at the university clinic in Leipzig, he was appointed Professor in Dorpat in 1885, and in Heidelberg in 1891. In 1894 he edited the periodical *Psychologische Arbeiten.* From 1903 until his death in 1926 he was Professor of psychiatry and Director of the psychiatric clinic in Munich.

Works: Kraepelin became famous mainly for his contribution to psychiatric nosology, and in particular for his classification of mental disorders. He subdivided psychoses into two main groups: dementia praecox (q.v.) and manic-depressive psychosis (q.v.); his classification is fundamentally maintained by modern authors.

Despite his friendship with Wundt, Kraepelin's standpoint on the etiology of mental disorders was primarily somatic in orientation (i.e. psychological factors play no part). He considered them to result from organic brain damage, metabolic disorders, endocrinal disturbances, or hereditary factors.

Kraepelin was also important in being the first to use the methods of psychological investigation and experimentation in psychiatry. He was the first to use objective tests (q.v.) and measurements to elucidate mental disorders. He was interested in psychological time measurements, choice reactions, associations and ergography. His studies on the work process and its forms anticipated some significant features of modern learning psychology (reactive inhibition, q.v., etc.) whose discovery (according to H. J. Eysenck) was wrongly attributed to later psychologists. Eysenck believes that Kraepelin ought to be recognized as the "father of clinical psychology".

Kraepelin's third major contribution consisted in his pioneering work in psychopharmacology (q.v.), which he virtually founded. He was the first to use experimental methods to study the effects of drugs, alcohol, nictotine, etc., on human behavior.

Main works: Compendium der Psychiatrie,

4 vols. Jena, 1883. Einführung in die psychiatrische Klinik, 3 vols. Jena, 1901. Über die Beeinflussung einfacher psychischer Vorgänge durch einige Arzneimittel. Jena, 1892. Die Arbeitskurve. Leipzig, 1902. Über geistige Arbeit. Leipzig, 1903. Lectures on clinical psychiatry. New York, 1904 (facsimile ed., N.Y., 1967).

Bibliography: Braceland, F. J.: Kraepelin: his system and its influence. Amer. J. Psychol., 1957. *W.W.*

Krause end bulb (syn. *Krause ending; Krause's corpuscle*). A rounded neuronal receptor occurring in, e.g. the conjunctiva and genitals, and thought to be a sensory end organ for cold stimuli. See *Sense organs.*

Kretschmer, Ernst. B. 8/10/18 in Wüstenrot; d. 8/2/1964, in Tübingen. Kretschmer studied medicine in Munich (where he came under the influence of Kraepelin) and at the Eppendorf Hospital in Hamburg. He received his doctorate in 1914 with a dissertation on mania and manic-depressive symptoms; he then enlisted, and was responsible for establishing a neurological department at the Bad Mergentheim military hospital. In 1918 he left Bad Mergentheim and became a private lecturer in Tübingen; in 1926 he was appointed Professor of psychiatry and neurology at Marburg University, and between 1946 and 1959 he was Director of the neurological clinic at Tübingen University.

Although Kretschmer was a highly prolific author, his name is primarily linked to his *Physique and Character* (*Körperbau und Charakter*, 1921), in which he presented his constitutional typology. After 1946 he carried out detailed studies of constitutional and developmental physiology, and of child and adolescent psychopathology, as well as research into constitutional biology. He also tried to develop new psychotherapeutic methods and hypnotic techniques. He carried out basic research in the field of criminal behavior and made recommendations for modifications of the penal law that would allow for adequate treatment.

Constitutional typology. Kretschmer's type theory has a morphological bias and is based on human physique. He makes a distinction between the leptosomic-asthenic type and the pyknic type. His major contribution in this field, beyond the distinction between physical types, was a classification of the relationship between these types and the three main forms of endogenous psychosis. On the basis of studies of two hundred and sixty mentally ill subjects, which have now been validated by examination of more than nine thousand cases, he was able to show that schizophrenic individuals are primarily leptosomic, manic-depressives are pyknic, and epileptics athletic.

Starting from the assumption that there is only a gradual, non-qualitative distinction between mental disorders and normality, Kretschmer established the existence of three character types (temperaments) with the same essential features (though in a much reduced form) as the corresponding psychoses from which they were derived. The schizothymic (split character, introversion, etc.) temperament (type) corresponds to the leptosomic physique (type); the cyclothymic (sudden changes of moods, affective responses, etc.) to the pyknic; and the viscous (cautious, slow) temperament (type) to the athletic type.

While the correlations between physique and psychosis postulated by Kretschmer appear relatively certain, there has not yet been any decisive confirmation of his assumptions concerning physique and character in normal psychology. See *Traits; Type.*

Main works: Der sensitive Beziehungswahn: ein Beitrag zur Paranoiafrage und zur psychiatrischen Charakterlehre. Berlin, [3]1950. Körperbau und Charakter, Berlin, [24]1961 (Eng. trans.: Physique and character, New York & London, 1925). Medizinische Psychologie. Stuttgart, [11]1956. Geniale Menschen. Berlin, [4]1948 (Eng. trans.: The psychology of men of genius. London, 1925). Hysterie, Reflex und Instinkt. Stuttgart, [5]1948 (Eng.

trans.: Hysteria, reflex and instinct. London, 1961). Über gestufte aktive Hypnoseübung und den Umbau der Hypnosetechnik. D. med. Wochenschrift, 1946, *71*, 29–31.

Bibliography: **Eysenck, H. J.:** Cyclothymia and schizothymia as a dimension of personality, I: historical review. J. Personal., 1950, *19*, 123–52. **Id.:** The structure of human personality. London, [2]1960.

W.W.

Kruskal–Wallis test. A non-parametric method for comparing several independent samples in regard to their central trend. The observations are ranked, and the rankings of all k samples arranged in one rank order; the rank sums (Rj) of the individual samples are compared. The critical value H is determined according to

$$H = \frac{12}{N(N+1)} \left(\sum \frac{R_j^2}{n_j} \right) - 3(N+1).$$

It is distributed at $n > 5\chi^2$ with $k-1$ degrees of freedom.

Bibliography: **Kruskal, W. H. & Wallis, W. A.:** Use of ranks in one-criterion variance analysis, J. Amer. Stat. Ass., 1952, *47*, 583–621.

G.Mi.

Kuder Preference Record. A questionnaire designed to show the relative interest for individual, comprehensive areas of vocational interest S. has to state most pleasant and most disagreeable of three activities. The test consists of ten scales presented in an interests profile, and one scale to detect dishonest answers. Standardized versions exist for children and adults. *F.G.*

Kuder-Richardson Formula 20. A formula developed by Kuder & Richardson (1937) for estimating the coefficient of consistency (see Reliability) on the basis of item difficulty (p) and test value dispersion (s_x):

$$r_{tt} = \frac{n}{n-1} \left(\frac{s_x^2 - \Sigma pq}{s_x^2} \right).$$

It presupposes that the item-intercorrelations are approximately identical. See *Test theory.*

Bibliography: **Kuder, G. F. & Richardson, M. W.:** The theory of the estimation of test reliability. Psychometrika, 1937, *2*, 151–60.

G.Mi.

Külpe, Oswald. B. 3/8/1862 in Candau (Courland); d. 30/12/1915 in Munich. Külpe began by studying history; he went on to psychology under Wundt in Leipzig, and Müller in Göttingen. He received his doctorate in 1887 (under Wundt) with a dissertation on the theory of sensory feeling. He then remained eight years in Leipzig, where he prepared a study of the "theory of will in modern psychology", and worked as a lecturer and as Wundt's assistant. In 1893 he published his *Outlines of Psychology*, a systematic presentation of psychology on Wundtian principles. He was appointed Professor at Würzburg University in 1894. In 1896 he established a psychological laboratory which, as the center of the Würzburg school (q.v.), became the most celebrated after that at Leipzig. In 1909 he was appointed Professor at Bonn. In 1913, he went to Munich.

The Würzburg school. Külpe founded the Würzburg school, which grounded the experimental psychology of thought processes. Apart from a short article "On the modern psychology of thought", Külpe wrote nothing else on this subject, but concerned himself primarily with philosophical questions in his publications: *Contemporary Philosophy in Germany* (1902), *Natural Science and the theory of Knowledge* (1910), *Realization; A Contribution to the Theory of the Realistic Sciences* (1912–1923). Külpe did, however, inspire the experimental studies of thought processes on which fifty of his Würzburg pupils published monographs. Other members of the Würzburg school (chronologically) were: A. Mayer, J. Orth, K. Marbe, H. J. Watt, N. Ach, A. Messer and K. Bühler.

The Würzburg school owed its foundation to Külpe's belief (in contrast to Wundt's) that the higher thought processes also can be studied experimentally. Külpe's approach was "systematic experimental introspection", a fractionated, retrospective account of the mental processes occurring in the course of a complex task. The main result of the Würzburg school's research work was a refutation of the previously dominant idea that thinking was a combination of quasi-perceptual images.

Külpe was able to demonstrate that thought is for the most part "imageless" and "sensation-free", and takes place with only a minimum degree of conscious awareness—so that the individual stages of the thought process are hardly "experienced". On the other hand, he showed that thought is, in general, non-associative and non-mechanical, yet directed and meaningful. The "determining tendencies" (N. Ach, 1905) which allow thought a specific orientation are either conscious *tasks* and experientially perceived *objectives*, or "conscious sets" ("*Bewusstseinslagen*": A. Messer, 1906)—attitudes, habits, long-term decisions, etc.—which may be non-perceptual or unconscious. See *Thinking*.

Main works: Grundriss der Psychologie. Leipzig, 1893 (Eng. trans.: Outlines of psychology: based upon the results of experimental investigation. New York, 1895). Vorlesungen über Psychologie. Leipzig, 1922. Die Realisierung, 3 vols. Leipzig, 1912–23.

Bibliography: Boring, E. G.: History of experimental psychology. New York, [2]1950. **Humphrey, G.:** Thinking: an introduction to its experimental psychology. London & New York,. 1951. **Ogden, R. M.:** Oswald Külpe and the Würzburg school. Amer. J. Psychol., 1951, *64*, 4–19. **Titchener, E. B.:** Experimental psychology, 2 vols. New York, 1901–5.

W.W.

Kundt's bisection test. When bisecting a horizontal line monocularly, there is a tendency to place the middle toward the nasal side. This phenomenon is also known as *Kundt's rule*. *C.D.F.*

Kundt's illusion. The illusion whereby divided distances appear greater than objectively equal undivided distances. This phenomenon is sometimes known as *Kundt's rule*. *C.D.F.*

Kundt's rule. See *Kundt's bisection test; Kundt's illusion*.

Kurtosis (Ku). The degree of flatness or peakedness (excess) about the mode of a frequency distribution (curve). If a curve has a sharper peak than the normal frequency distribution, the divergence is said to be positive (*leptokurtosis*); in the opposite case it is negative (*platykurtosis*). (An average divergence is *mesokurtosis*.) *A.R.*

Kymograph. A device consisting of a blackened drum or a moving strip of (smoked) paper used to record variations in the intensity of relatively protracted reaction processes (movements; muscular, pressure and temperature processes; electrophysiological processes: e.g. EEG, EKG, EMG). Since the drum or the paper strip moves at a constant speed, the graphic record obtained (kymogram) will indicate fluctuations. *A.Th.*

L

Lability. Flexibility; plasticity.

Labyrinth. 1. An intricate maze. 2. The complex cavity of the inner ear consisting of petrous temporal bone (the *bony labyrinth*) and a mass of sacs and tubes (the *membranous labyrinth*). Contains sense organs associated with hearing and the *static sense* (balance). *G.D.W.*

Labyrinth test. See *Maze.*

Ladd-Franklin theory of color vision. A compromise between the *Young-Helmholtz* and the *Hering* theories of color vision. A four-receptor theory is proposed with separate cone mechanisms for red, green, yellow and blue. The theory accounts for color blindness and perimetry data better than the unmodified Young-Helmholtz hypothesis. The Ladd–Franklin theory holds that the various color receptors evolved from primal achromatic receptors. See *Color vision.* *C.D.F.*

Laissez-faire (syn. *Laisser faire*). **1.** A form of leadership, particularly in education and politics, in which the main emphasis is on democracy (q.v.) and control is minimal. **2.** Neglectful or excessively permissive leadership.

Lancement experiment. One in the series of experiments by Michotte studying mechanical causality. Two objects are seen in a slit moving in the same direction, with the leading object moving more slowly. When the two objects meet, the leading one continues to move at the same speed and the following one stops. Observers spontaneously report that the following object has pushed away the leading object, thus showing the subjective perception of causality. *C.D.F.*

Landolt circles (syn. *Landolt rings*). Developed by E. Landolt, an ophthalmologist in Zürich and Paris (1876–1926) to test visual acuity: black circles of various sizes on a white ground. *K.H.P.*

Land's effect. E. H. Land succeeded in obtaining all colors of the spectrum by using only a red and a white light. He photographed the same scene once with a red filter and once with a green filter; then he projected the first through a red filter and the second with white light, thus reproducing the original scene in *all* its colors. The surprising results of this experiment seem to accord neither with the Young–Helmholtz nor the Hering theory. See *Color theories.* *G.Ka.*

Langedon-Down syndrome. See *Down syndrome.*

Lange, Friedrich Albert. B. 28/9/1828 in Wald near Solingen; d. 21/11/1875 in Marburg.

Lange obtained his doctorate at Bonn University. He taught school in Cologne and Duisburg. On account of his Socialist views he was forced to leave teaching. He moved to Winterthur in 1866. In 1869 he was made Professor of inductive philosophy in Zürich; in 1873 he went to Marburg.

Lange's position as a co-founder of modern psychology has not been sufficiently appreciated. His main work, *Geschichte des Materialismus* (History of Materialism), 2 vols., 1866–75, seemed to mark him out (and down) as a materialist, although it was a work designed, in fact, to counteract theoretical materialism. Lange developed an outline program of objective psychology about forty years before Pavlov (q.v.) and Watson (q.v.). As a neo-Kantian he fought for a non-metaphysical, physiologically based psychology, and recommended the "somatic method" and a "methodical materialism" as "preliminary" research principles. According to Lange, the *object* of psychology ought to be only that which is sensuously perceptible, together with objectively recordable responses and measurable psychological processes. His work on the principles of mathematical psychology (*Die Grundlagen der mathematischen Psychologie. Ein Versuch zur Nachweisung des grundlegenden Fehlers bei Herbart und Drobisch*, 1865) made him one of the pioneers in this field, too.

Bibliography: Pongratz, L. J.: Friedrich Albert Lange—seine psychologische Grundkonzeption. Jb. Psychol., Psychoth. u. med. Psychol., 1966, *14*, 100–11.

L.J.P.

Langerhans islet cells. Described for the first time in 1869 by the pathologist P. Langerhans, these are large, epitheloid, richly vascularized islet cells, which represent the endocrine part of the pancreas (q.v.) and produce the hormones *insulin* (q.v.) and *glucagon* (q.v.) and release them into the bloodstream. These cells play an important part in the mechanism of blood sugar regulation. Four types of cell are distinguished histologically and functionally: A, B, C and D cells. *E.D.*

Language. "Language" does not designate a clearly demarcated field of phenomena. The linguist Saussure made a distinction between *langue* (language as a system) and *parole* (language as an actual process, i.e. the act of speaking), the two composing *langage* (the general human faculty of speech). There are several differing approaches to the concept of language, which make intersubjective treatment difficult by reason of the various problems considered.

1. *Language as a system.* Linguistics is based on objectifications of specific natural languages (Bierwisch, 1966; Hörmann, 1970; Miller & McNeill, 1969), and attempts on the one hand systematically to describe the multi-level canon of rules (see *Grammar*) which linguistic products must obey (*synchronic aspect*); and on the other hand to investigate sequential regularities (*syntagmatic relations*) and relations or correspondences (*paradigmatic relations*) for linguistic units on various levels: phomenics, graphemes, significant elemental units (morphemes, words), phase structures, sentences, etc. Corresponding distinctions are made between phonetic/phonematic, semantic (see *Semantics*), and syntactic problems. Linguistic analysis may be concerned with the detection and elucidation of universal characteristics common to all natural languages (Greenberg, 1966), but also with the differentiation of specific linguistic codes within individual language systems (see *Sociolinguistics;* Ervin–Tripp, 1969; Herrmann & Stäcker, 1969). The theory of generative transformational grammar (Chomsky, 1968) has enlivened efforts to combine linguistics and psychology (see *Psycholinguistics*), so that even the basis of a universal behavioral theory has been seen as attainable in this area (Bierwisch, 1966; Dixon & Horton, 1968; Miller & McNeill, 1969). The idea that a child learning its mother-tongue is in principle faced with the same task as the linguist (he has to elaborate the rules of an existing language, according to which linguistic assertions can be made which satisfy the appropriate norms)

has greatly influenced the analysis of ontogenetic language development (Bellugi & Brown, 1964; Menyuk, 1969; Miller & McNeill, 1969; Smith & Miller, 1966).

In regard to *logic*, natural languages appear defective (Stegmüller, 1968). On the other hand, language systems which satisfy the requirements of logical analysis appear artificial to the linguist, and theoretically utilizable only to a limited degree (Bierwisch, 1966).

Mathematics provides algebraic formal structures for the description of the grammar (q.v.) of natural language systems (Miller & McNeill, 1969; Schnelle, 1968). The most general rules for programming languages (machine or computer languages) have been developed from the application of mathematics to logical automata.

Cultural anthropology (see *Ethnology; Sociology*) views a language as a system closely interwoven with the socio-cultural expressions of a particular culture or community, such as usage, social stratification, eligious views, etc. (Ervin–Tripp, 1969; Hymes, 1964; see *Whorf's hypothesis*).

2. *Semiotics and semantics*. Linguistic constructs of the most varied kind and comprehensiveness may be conceived as signs or symbols (see *Sign and symbol*), i.e. as representations of other things. Apart from this semantic area (see *Semantics*), semiotics (q.v.) deals in a very general way with the (*syntactical*) interrelations of signs and the (*pragmatic*) relations between signs and sign-users. In addition, a semantics of a more philosophico-epistemological type refers to the truth problem (Stegmüller, 1968). "General semantics" (Hayakawa, 1949) draws attention to the arbitrary arrangement of linguistic signs and objects, and rejects "word magic".

3. *Language and communication*. The basic pattern in this regard is the reciprocal exchange of information between senders and receivers. In information theory and communications research using the transmission channel model, language is a code by means of which matter worthy of transmission is encoded and the corresponding information is decoded. Attempts are made to apprehend linguistic activity on various levels by means of Markoff processes and to analyze its stochastic characteristics by means of computational or statistical linguistics (Herdan, 1960; Hörmann, 1970; Schnelle, 1968).

Understood in a somewhat vaguer sense, communication (q.v.) nevertheless takes place *non-verbally* in other channels: by means of looks, gestures, body postures (*kinesics;* Argyle, 1969; Hall, 1959; Sebeok *et al.*, 1964), and even linguistic communication is accompanied by meaningful pauses, accentuations, etc. (*paralinguistic communication:* Miller & McNeill, 1969; Moscovici, 1967; Wiener & Mehrabian, 1968).

The use of the term "language" in the case of animal communication has been much contested (e.g. Sebeok, 1968).

Communications research in an even wider sense is concerned with linguistic communication in interviews, in therapeu tic or educational counseling, within small groups (e.g. as persuasion), and the dissemination of linguistic information by mass media (e.g. in the sense of "rhetoric"), etc. (Dieckmann, 1969; Ellingworth & Clevenger, 1967; Ervin–Tripp, 1969; Herrmann & Stäcker, 1969; Jaffe & Feldstein, 1970; Moscovici, 1967; Thayer, 1967).

4. *Language and behavior*. Psychology (see *Psycholinguistics*) apprehends linguistic events primarily in the aspect of individual experience and behavior and their conditioning factors in the individual (Dixon & Horton, 1968; Hörmann, 1970; Kainz, 1941–69; Miller & McNeill, 1969). The reception, mental application and production of language (see *Speech*) are conceived as specific modes of perception, of cognitive operation and of productive activity, which are made possible by specific (to a large extent acquired) characteristics. These bases or principles and their modifications in learning processes (see *Verbal behavior, establishment and modification of*) have to be examined by experimental (Jakubowicz, 1970; Miller &

McNeill, 1969) and free observation (Ervin-Tripp, 1969) of actual behavior, or by content-analytic methods (Herrmann & Stäcker, 1969). This can occur in terms of general-psychological as well as differential-psychological and individual-diagnostic viewpoints and problems (Gottschalk & Gleser, 1969; Guilford, 1967). In this case, the relations between linguistic and other behaviors (perception, problem solving, logical thinking, motor behavior, etc.; Kleinmuntz, 1966; McGuigan, 1966; Wathen-Dunn, 1967; Vygotsky, 1962) (see *Inner speech; Whorf's hypothesis*), and competence in several linguistic systems (bilingualism, q.v.; multilingualism), as well as their functional interaction in the language user (Hörmann, 1970) are objects for investigation.

5. *Language and the biological substrate.* Human linguistic behavior is extremely complex and presupposes the existence and functional excellence of a number of organic systems (Lenneberg, 1967), whose phylogenetic development corresponds to various linguistic activities (Révész, 1946), and which can be described in terms of morphological and physiological aspects (e.g. as a second signal system). Significant information toward research in this regard is available in pathological conditions of a morphological and functional nature (see *Aphasia;* Furth, 1966; de Reuck & O'Connor, 1964; Travis, 1963).

Bibliography: Argyle, M.: Social interaction. London, 1969. **Bellugi, U. & Brown, R.** (Eds.): The acquisition of language. Monogr. Soc. Res. Child Devel., 1964, *29*, Ser. No. 92. **Bierwisch, M.:** Strukturalismus. Kursbuch, 1966, *5*, 77–152. **Chomsky, N.:** Language and mind. New York, 1968. **Crystal, D.:** Linguistics. Harmondsworth, 1971. **Dieckmann, W.:** Sprache in der Politik. Heidelberg, 1969. **Dixon, Th. R. & Horton, D. L.** (Eds.): Verbal behavior and general behavior theory. Englewood Cliffs, N.J., 1968. **Ellingworth, H. W. & Clevenger, T.:** Speech and social action. Englewood Cliffs, N.J., 1967. **Ervin–Tripp, S. M.:** Sociolinguistics. In: **Berkowitz, L.** (Ed.): Advances in experimental social psychology 4. New York, 1969, 91–165. **Furth, H. G.:** Thinking without language. New York, 1966. **Greenberg, J. H.** (Ed.): Universals of language. Cambridge, Mass., 1966. **Gottschalk, L. A. & Gleser, G. C.:** The measurement of psychological states through the content analysis of verbal behavior. Berkeley, 1969. **Guilford, J. P.:** The nature of intelligence. New York, 1967. **Hall, E. T.:** The silent language. New York, 1959. **Hayakawa, S. J.:** Language in thought and action. New York, 1949; London, 1952. **Herdan, S.:** Type-token mathematics. s'-Gravenhage, 1960. **Herriott, P.:** An introduction to the psychology of language. London, 1970. **Herrmann, T. & Stäcker, K. H.:** Sprachpsychologische Beiträge zur Sozialpsychologie. In: **Graumann, C. F.** (Ed.): Handbuch d. Psychol., Vol. 7. Göttingen, 1969, 398–474. **Hörmann, H.:** Psychologie der Sprache. Berlin, [2]1970. **Hymes, D.** (Ed.): Language in culture and society. New York, 1964. **Jaffe, J. & Feldstein, S.:** Rhythms of dialogue. New York, 1970. **Jakubowitz, C.:** Recherches récentes en psycholinguistique. L'année psychol., 1970, 247–93. **Kainz, F.:** Psychologie der Sprache. 5 vols., Stuttgart, 1941–69. **Kleinmuntz, B.** (Ed.): Problem solving: research, method and theory. New York, 1966. **Lenneberg, E. H.:** Biological foundations of language. New York, 1967. **McGuigan, F. J.:** Thinking: studies of covert language processes. New York, 1966. **Menyuk, P.:** Sentences children use. Cambridge, Mass., 1969. **Miller, G. A. & McNeill, D.:** Psycholinguistics. In: **Lindzey, G. & Aronson, E.** (Eds.): Handbook of social psychology, Vol. 3. Reading, Mass., 1969, 666–794. **Moscovici, S.:** Communication processes and the properties of language. In: **Berkowitz, L.** (Ed.): Advances in experimental social psychology, Vol. 3. New York, 1967, 225–70. **Oldfield, R. C. & Marshall, J. C.:** Language. Harmondsworth, 1968. **Reuck, A. V. S. de & O'Connor, M.** (Eds.): Disorders of language. London, 1964. **Révész, G.:** Ursprung und Vorgeschichte der Sprache. Berne, 1946. **Saussure, F. de:** Cours de linguistique générale. Paris, [5]1955. **Schnelle, H.:** Methoden mathematischer Linguistik. In: Enzyklopädie der geisteswissenschaftlichen Arbeitsmethoden: Methoden der Sprachwissenschaft. Munich, 1968, 135–60. **Sebeok, T. A.** (Ed.): Animal communication. Bloomington, 1968. **Sebeok, T. A., Hayes, A. S. & Bateson, M. C.:** Approaches to semiotics. The Hague, 1964. **Smith, F. & Miller G. A.** (Eds.): The genesis of language. Cambridge, Mass., 1966. **Stegmüller, W.:** Das Wahrheitsproblem und die Idee der Semantik. New York, 1968. **Thayer, L.** (Ed.): Communication: theory and research. Springfield, Ill., 1967. **Travis, L. E.** (Ed.): Handbook of speech pathology. London, 1963. **Vygotsky, L. S.:** Thought and language. Cambridge, Mass., 1962. **Wathen-Dunn, W.** (Ed.): Models for the perception of speech and visual form. Cambridge, Mass., 1967. **Wiener, M. & Mehrabian, A.:** Language within language. New York, 1968.

G. Kaminski

Language barrier. A language may be viewed as a system, in which case it consists of (*a*) a number of signs (e.g. phonemes, morphemes, words); (*b*) a number of rules (see *Grammar; Syntax*) which define permissible combinations. Linguistic comprehension presupposes a common repertoire of signs and rules. A *language barrier* may exist if there is no common repertoire of signs or common set of rules. In this sense there are already language barriers between different ethnic groups. In educational psychology (q.v.), the concept relates to the typical finding that working-class children tend to show considerable discrepancies between verbal IQs (Mill-Hill Vocabulary Scale) and non-verbal, language-free IQs (Raven's Progressive Matrices) (Bernstein, 1961). It is appropriate in this case to speak of "linguistic retardation" (Oevermann, 1970) (see *Restricted code*). The term "language barrier" ought to be reserved for the relation between language characteristics and school performance. The role of school achievement as a status criterion in modern industrial societies tends to make language a variable which can block social mobility. The connection between low school achievement and language characteristics results from the frequent use of linguistic features as means of social evaluation, the lack of concordance between working-class children's rule-and-sign systems and those of teachers, and the possible blocking of the speaker's problem-solving behavior by the poor flexibility of combination rules and the semantic rigidity of much working-class language. See *Sociolinguistics*.

Bibliography: Bernstein, B.: Social class and linguistic development: a theory of social learning. In: **Halsey, A. H.,** *et al.*: (Eds.): Education, economy and society. New York, 1961, 288–314. **Bernstein, B. & Brandis, W.:** Social class differences in communication and control. In: **Brandis, W. & Henderson, D.:** Primary socialisation, language and education, Vol. 1. London, 1969. **Bernstein, B. & Henderson, D.:** Social class differences in the relevance of language to socialisation. Sociology, 1969, *3*. **Oevermann, U.:** Schichtenspezifische Formen des Sprachverhaltens und ihr Einfluss auf die kognitiven Prozesse. In: **Roth, H.** (Ed.): Begabung und Lernen deutscher Bildungsrat Gutachten und Studien der Bildungskommission, Vol. 4. Stuttgart, 1970.

M.Ba.

Language development. See *Concept; Grammar; Verbal behavior; Psycholinguistics.*

Language-free tests. A group of intelligence tests which exclude verbal items and thus make no demands on oral or written language comprehension. They are appropriate for foreigners, the deaf, and the analphabetic. See *Culture-free Intelligence Tests; Progressive Matrices.* *E.F-K.*

Language laboratory. An important aid in second language instruction. Its main aim is practice to competence in the spoken language. The system uses tape recordings and multiple headphone listening systems, separate booths for each student, and a control console for the teacher, arranged so that he can monitor any student and enter into two-way communication with him. There are three main types: (*a*) group-work system, (*b*) individual system, and (*c*) mixed systems. In (*a*) the students have only a microphone and headphones, and work on a common program; only the teacher can record individual students on tape. In system (*b*) each student can work on an individual program in his own booth. In system (*c*) either course is possible. Some mini-laboratories dispense with the instructor.

Bibliography: Adam, J. B. & Shawcross, A. J.: The language laboratory. London, 1963. **Hutchinson, J. C.:** The language laboratory. Washington, 1963. **Keating, R. F.:** A study of the effectiveness of language laboratories. New York, 1963. **Moore, S. & Antrobus, A. L.:** An introduction to the language laboratory. London, 1965. **Stack, E. M.:** The language laboratory and modern language teaching. New York & London, 1966. **Turner, J. D.:** Introduction to the language laboratory. London, 1965.

H.I.

Language, psychology of. See *Language; Psycholinguistics; Grammar; Verbal behavior.*

Laryngograph. An apparatus for recording movements of the larynx, especially as produced in speech.

Lashley, Karl Spencer. B. 7/6/1890 in Davis, West Virginia; d. 7/8/1958 in Poitiers, France. Lashley obtained his doctorate in zoology from Johns Hopkins in 1914. In 1920 he was appointed Assistant Professor, and in 1924 a full Professor at the University of Minnesota. He went to Chicago in 1926, where at first he was research psychologist with the Behavior Research Fund of the Institute for Juvenile Research. In 1929 he became Professor at the University of Chicago. In 1935 he transferred to Harvard, and from 1937 held the chair of neuropsychology there. From 1942 on, Lashley succeeded R. M. Yerkes as Director of the Yale Laboratories of Primate Biology in Orange Park, Florida.

Lashley became noted above all for his neuropsychological research into the cortical bases of learning processes. He used psychological methods of animal learning research in order to study the function of cortical processes in learning and memory processes (see *Memory*). In particular, the results of his investigations of maze learning in rats had far-ranging effects on physiological psychology. He investigated mainly the relations between the complexity of the learning task and cerebral lesions, as well as the effects of different degrees and localizations of lesions on learning behavior. The basic technique of these studies was the designing of a maze or discrimination task for an animal, before and after which a lesion was introduced. Lashley also studied the effects of the lesion on retention and learning ability as a function of its extent and localization. His original intention (stimulated by Watson's behaviorism, q.v.—he had worked with Watson for some years) was to find the neural bases (i.e. localizations) of the acquired connections; he did not succeed in this, apart from a few visual discrimination operations. Instead he discovered that the learning deficits occurred independently of the location of the lesions, and depended only on the size of the damaged brain area (see *Brain pathology*). Lashley then rejected (though—as he was subsequently shown—without sufficient foundation in his own results) the assumption of the existence of specific localized connections in the brain, and tried to establish a field theory of cerebral processes, According to this theory, learning (q.v.) is not an isolated phenomenon resulting from individual, anatomically (precisely) localized neurons, but a function of the entire cortex ("mass action"), and individual parts of the brain are able to assume the functions of other, damaged brain areas ("equipotentiality"). See *Localization of psychological functions.*

Main works: The behavioristic interpretation of consciousness. Psychol. rev., 1923, *30*, 237–72, 329–53. Brain mechanisms and intelligence. Chicago, 1929. Basic neural mechanisms in behavior. Psychol. Rev., 1930, *37*, 1–24. Cerebral control versus reflexology. J. genl. Psychol. 1931, *5*, 3–20. Nervous mechanisms in learning. In: Murchison, C. (Ed.): A handbook of general experimental psychology. Worcester, Mass., 456–96. Studies of cerebral function in learning, 11: The behavior of the rat in latch box situations. Comp. psychol. Monogr., 1935, *11*, 1–42. Structural variation in the nervous system in relation to behavior. Psychol. Rev., 1947, *54*, 325–34. In search of the engram. Symp. Soc. f. Exp. Biol., IV, 1950, 454–82. The problem of serial order in behavior. In: Jeffress, L. A. (Ed.): Cerebral mechanisms in behavior: the Hixon Symposium. New York & London, 1951, 112–46.

Bibliography: Boring, E. G.: A history of experimental psychology. New York, [2]1950. **Hebb, D. O.:** Karl Spencer Lashley: 1890–1958. Amer. J. Psychol., 1959, *72*, 142–50.

W.W.

Late developer. A term for a child or adolescent whose development is seen to be rather slow, but who nevertheless finally achieves an average level of competence.

The term "late developer" is a not very accurate description for widely varying cases with many determining factors.

Bibliography: Benton, A. L.: The concept of pseudo-feeble-mindedness. In: **Trapp, E. P. & Himelstein, P.:** Readings on the exceptional child. New York, 1962, 82–95. *H.M.*

Latency period (syn. *Latency stage*). In Freud's schema of libidinal human development, the period from about the sixth to the twelfth year of life: the time between the end of the early and the beginning of the late genital stage, i.e. puberty. In this period the child's sexual interest in members of his direct family, especially the parent of the opposite sex, and conflicts with the parent of the same sex, are said to become latent. This does not mean that the child's sexual interests disappear. In the extra-family context, sublimated and occasionally direct sexual interests are pursued, and are often more clearly remembered in retrospect than the sexual interests of the early genital stage. See *Genital stage*.

Bibliography: Fenichel, O.: The psychoanalytic theory of neurosis. New York, 1945. **Toman, W.:** An introduction to psychoanalytic theory of motivation. London & New York, 1960. *W.T.*

Latent dream contents. Unconscious dream motives and wishes which are said to be expressed in the manifest dream content. In psychotherapeutic and psychoanalytic dream analysis (q.v.) they are deduced from the material of the manifest dream content and from the dreamer's memories of the manifest dream content. Errors are possible. Rejection by the dreamer is said possibly to result from his psychological resistance to conscious awareness of the latent content. See *Dream*. *W.T.*

Latent period. 1. The interval between stimulus and response. **2.** See *Latency period.*

Laterality (syn. *Cerebral dominance; Lateral dominance*). The structure or function of paired organs, or of two similarly arranged areas of a non-paired organ, distributed on the right and left sides of the body. Whereas *ambilaterality* refers to a morphological and/or functional equivalence of both sides, *lateral dominance* refers to a qualitative or quantitative primacy or preference for one side. Research into laterality is mainly concerned with functional asymmetries, and above all those that are motor or sensory, and those pertaining to the central nervous system (q.v.). *Manual dominance* is considered in terms of preferential use of one hand (see *Handedness*) and relative dexterity on a basis of, e.g., the differential excitability of paired muscles. There is a 1 to 30% range of difference in various authors' assessments of the distribution of left-handedness. An investigation by Annett (1967), which is also of theoretical interest, is based on manual practice and gives the following distribution of degrees of preference: 70% of Ss. from various populations were stable right-handers whereas 4% were stable left-handers; 26% of cases were in the unstable handedness group. Analysis of existing studies supports the suggestion that the problem of handedness also requires systematic investigation in the area of psychomotor research.

Concepts of *ocular dominance* are based on preferential eye use, directive dominance, the phi phenomenon (q.v.), relative visual acuity, and retinal rivalry phenomena. Investigations into *auditory dominance* on the basis of dichotic hearing are—like those into visual dominance—connected with problems of cerebral asymmetries of a functional nature. Existing psychological research findings and those of the appropriate neighboring disciplines together show that the cerebral functions fundamental to motor activity, sensory activity and speech feature a differentially asymmetrical distribution over the cerebral hemispheres. *Cerebral dominance* does not indicate any uniform predominance of one half of the endbrain for all cerebral functions, but a preference for one cerebral hemisphere in specific activities (Mountcastle, 1962; Zangwill, 1960, 1964; Hécaen, 1968). Investigations into the *relations* between different manifestations of lateral dominance do not as yet offer any uniform picture (Subirana, 1969). Results of clinical studies by Milner, Branch & Rasmussen (1964) regarding the relation between handedness and speech lateralization would seem to approximate conditions in the normal population: 90% of the right-handers showed a speech lateralization of the left cerebral hemisphere, and 10% one of the right hemisphere; left-handed and ambidextrous persons without any sign of an early left-side brain lesion were divided into 64% with a speech dominance of the left side, 20% with one of the right side, and 16% with a bilateral speech dominance. Left-handers and ambidextrals with an early left-side brain lesion showed a division of 22% with a left-side and 67% with a right-side speech dominance; 11% gave evidence of bilateral speech representation. Connections between laterality variables, on the one hand, and functional disorders (legasthenia, q.v.; speech disorders, etc.), accidents, personality traits, hypnotic suggestibility, etc., on the other hand, require further clarification. Experimental findings and socio-cultural manifestations appear to show that human-specific laterality is not confined to individual motor and perceptual activities, but is in many respects transferred to, and co-determines, the whole range of experience and behavior.

As a set variable, lateral dominance is a determinant of human experience and behavior (J. F. Ullmann, 1971), without which the higher forms of human performance would be impossible. Laterality research with an interdisciplinary emphasis opens up significant perspectives for human psychology (I. M. Ullmann, 1971). Recent conceptions of the functional differentiation of the endbrain hemispheres together with divergent results of reaction experiments, investigations of lateral asymmetries, visual half-fields and dichotic hearing tests suggest that differential functionality is the appropriate basis for a concept of lateral dominance offering considerable scope for further research. See *Aphasia; Brain pathology; Neuropsychology.*

Bibliography: Annett, M.: The binomial distribution of right, mixed, and left handedness. Quart. J. exp. Psychol., 1967, *19*, 327–33. **Hécaen, H.:** La dominance cérébrale. In: **Kourilsky, R. & Grapin, P.** (Eds.): Main droite et main gauche. Paris, 1968. **Kováč, D. & Horcovič, G.:** On the problem of lateral dominance. Studia Psychologica, 1966, *1*, 28–45. **Milner, B., Branch, C. & Rasmussen, T.:** Observations on cerebral dominance. In: **Dekeuck, A. V. S. & O'Connor, M. O.** (Eds.): Disorders of language: a CIBA foundation symposium. London, 1964, 200–14. **Mountcastle, V. B.** (Ed.): Interhemispheric relations and cerebral dominance. Baltimore, 1962. **Sovák, M.:** Pädagogische Probleme der Lateralität. Berlin, 1968. **Subirana, A.:** Handedness and cerebral dominance. In: **Vinken & Boyn** (Eds.): Handbook of clinical neurology, Vol. 4: Disorders of speech, perception and symbolic behavior. Amsterdam, 1969. **Ullmann, J. F.:** Psychologie lateraler Dominanz. Humanspezifische Seitigkeitsausprägung und ihre determinierende Funktion. Berne & Stuttgart, 1971. **Ullmann, I. M.:** Genese sprachlicher Bedeutungsrelation. Beitrag zur Grundlegung einer zentrierten Psycholinguistik. Würzburg, 1971. **Zangwill, O. L.:** Cerebral dominance and its relations to psychological function. London, 1960. **Id:** The current status of cerebral dominance. In: **Rioch, D. Mck. & Weinstein, E. A.** (Eds.): Disorders of communication. Baltimore, 1964. *J. F. Ullmann*

Latin square. A factorial experimental design used when individual factor combinations, as in a complete experimental plan, are not possible. In the first square, the k conditions are arranged in a $k \times k$ matrix so that they occur only once in every line and column. An example for $k = 4$ is:

A B C D
B A D C
C D A B
D C B A

G.Mi.

Latitude of acceptance. In the rating of attitudes or opinions: that range of values on the opinion or attitude scale representing values which S. still accepts or does not yet reject. A range of tolerance on either side of the individual's standpoint. Similarly, *latitude of rejection* is the range of objects of opinion which S. finds unacceptable. See *Attitude*. *H.D.S.*

Laughter. Recent findings would seem to show that laughter is genetically inborn and not specifically human, although experience and maturation make their contributions to the developed expression. See *Humor*.

Bibliography: Piddington, R.: The psychology of laughter. New York, 1963. *D.G.*

Law of averages. According to Bernoulli's theorem, when there is an infinite approximation to 1, and if the number of trials is large enough, in the long run the relative frequency f(X)/N (i.e. of occurrence of event X) will differ very little from the basic probability (of this event). *W.H.B.*

Law of comparative judgments. See *Scaling.*

Law of effect. See *Effect, law of.*

Laws in psychology. As an empirical science, psychology is based on a complex interaction of theory and empirical experience. One major aspect of this process is the formulation of hypotheses applicable to general conditions, which—after verification—are known as laws. The individual is defined approximately in a network of general laws, which is as dense as possible. Opinions differ as to the type of laws which it is possible to formulate in psychology. The prevailing concept (e.g. Brunswik, 1943; Sarris, 1967) is that because of the complexity and variability (interindividual and intraindividual variation) of the phenomena of life, laws of probability are requisite; on the other hand, authors such as Hull (1943) maintain the opposite view: i.e. that exact, natural-scientific laws are needed in psychology. Madsen (1968) integrates both positions and suggests that the exact, natural-scientific law must be considered as a positive boundary case of laws of probability.

Bibliography: Brunswik, E.: Organismic achievement and environmental probability. Psychol. Rev, 1943, *50*, 255–72. **Hull, C. L.:** The problem of intervening variables in molar behavior theory, Psychol. Rev., 1943, *50*, 273–91. **Madsen, K. B.:** Theories of motivation. Kent, 1968. **Sarris, V.:** Zum Problem der Kausalität in der Psychologie: Ein Diskussionsbeitrag. Psychol. Beitr., 1967, *10*, 173–86. **Seiffert, H.:** Einführung in die Wissenschaftstheorie, Vol. 1. Munich, 1969. *E.G.W.*

Leader. One who plays a role that varies with the course of *group formation* (q.v.) and is bound up with expectations as to the direction, control and modification of the activities of the other group members with a view to achieving group aims.

Attempts to find an enduring syndrome of personality traits describing the leader otherwise than in terms of the characteristics of his followers have failed. Researchers, therefore, focus attention on the concrete behavior of leaders of various groups in different situations (Gibb, 1954). See *Group dynamics*.

The attributes of group leaders include those that enable someone in a particular situation to contribute in a large measure to the satisfaction of group members and to the achievement of the common goal, or those that lead the other members to believe that such is the case. Where a particular group is interested mainly in performing a specific task, its leader will display in a high degree the abilities required for achieving it to the greatest advantage (task ability and task specialist, according to Bales, 1950). On the other hand, where the needs of group members tend to be of a socio-emotional kind that has to be satisfied in group activities, their leader can do even more to help gratify such needs: Bales, 1950; Thibaut & Kelley, 1959). In general, the standing of an individual within a group rises with the extent to which he identifies himself with the norms and aims of that group (Homans, 1950).

Bibliography: Bales, R. F.: Interaction process analysis, Cambridge, 1950. **Gibb, C. A.:** Leadership. In: **Lindzey, G.** (Ed.): Handbook of social psychology, Vol. 2. Reading, Mass., 1954. **Gibb, C. A.:** Leadership. Harmondsworth, 1969. **Homans, G. C.:** The human group. New York, 1950. **Thibaut, J. W. & Kelley, H. H.:** The social psychology of groups. New York, 1959. *A.S.-M.*

Learning. Even though learning has received more attention in terms of experiments than any other object of psychology, there is no one accepted definition of the term. Nevertheless, the various attempts to define it may (without too great a degree of misrepresentation) be formulated as follows: Learning consists of relatively persistent changes in possible behavior insofar as they derive from experience. This restriction of the term excludes short-term changes (adaptation, fatigue, etc.) and those which derive from certain structural alterations of the central nervous system (maturation, aging, injuries). *Possible* behaviors are in question since actual, concrete behavior is always dependent on further conditions, above all on changes in motivation; therefore a distinction is made between learning and *performance*, which raises methodological problems in regard to the assessment of *learning curves* (q.v.). Many authors replace the reference to experience with terms such as "repetition", "practice", "training", etc., in order to avoid terminology reminiscent of the psychology of *consciousness* (q.v.); nevertheless, the information theory (q.v.) model would seem to make it possible to interpret experience (without recourse to the psychology of consciousness) as the *reception and processing of information* (q.v.). The limitation of the term "learning" to *adaptive* changes of behavior is usually rejected, since the derivation of (at least objectively) unadapted behavior patterns (e.g. neuroses) from learning processes should not be excluded. The restriction of the definition to *behavior* is primarily one of method; a disadvantage is that the definition is then too far removed from everyday usage, which employs "learning" primarily in the sense of the acquisition and alteration of cognitive structures (learning in school, etc.).

Western tradition attributes learning to the establishment of associations between elements. Of the three laws of association cited by Aristotle (similarity, contrast, temporal and spatial contiguity) only the last-mentioned is still generally applied (temporal contiguity). With the rise of experimental psychology, association (q.v.) between the contents of consciousness (mental elements such as ideas and images) was replaced by association between signals (stimuli) and responses. Instead of the word "association", *conditioning* is now used, in the sense of conditioned responses and signals. The resulting connection is interpreted physiologically—though diversely (see *Association; Conditioning, classical and operant; Engram; Memory*).

Methodological and theoretical work in the field of learning is essentially indebted to the major experimental paradigms of Pavlov (q.v.) (*classical conditioning*) and Thorndike (*instrumental conditioning*). Pavlov's model posited temporal contiguity as the basic explanatory principle for the changes of behavior in question, whereas in instrumental conditioning the effect of the response (see *Effect, law of; Feedback*) is also important.

For *behaviorism* (q.v.), prediction of behavior on the basis of general laws of learning and a knowledge of the individual history of learning became the central task of psychology. A general learning theory (see *Learning theory*) was postulated for all modes of learning and behavior, in humans and in all other biological species. Experimental investigations were carried out primarily on easily manipulable laboratory animals, for the most part white rats. By far the most proficiently developed theory of learning was that of Hull (q.v.) (1943).

The original behaviorist expectation that it would be possible to elaborate *one* universal learning theory proved as generally unacceptable as the methodological and theoretical restrictions of behaviorism. Since about 1950 that initial confidence has been somewhat muted. Instead there is a concern to develop *special* theories (learning models) for individual mechanisms (e.g. the effect of *reinforcement*, q.v.), or areas of learning research (e.g. verbal or motor learning). Differences between biological species are taken into consideration, and attempts are made to classify them systematically. Experiments are carried out to determine whether special learning processes (e.g. imprinting, q.v., incidental learning, learning in sleep, q.v.) follow particular laws. Terms from the psychology of mentalism or consciousness are again employed as intervening variables (e.g. attention, q.v., expectation, fear). Instead of the search for fundamental mechanisms, learning processes which are especially important in the human socialization process (learning by instruction, imitation, etc.) or in psychological treatment (e.g. desensitization: see *Behavior therapy; Aversion therapy*) are examined directly in terms of complex variables, and classified according to the particular characteristics of the learning task. See *Educational psychology; Educational science; Instinct*.

Bibliography: Borger, R. & Seaborne, A. E. M.: The psychology of learning. Harmondsworth, 1966. **Bruner, J. S.** (Ed.): Learning about learning. Washington, 1966. **De Cecco, J. P.** (Ed.): Human learning in the school. New York, 1963. **Gagné, R. M.:** Learning and individual differences. Columbus, 1967. **Hull, C. L.:** Principles of behavior. New York, 1943. **Kimble, G. A.:** Hilgard and Marquis' conditioning and learning. New York, 1961. **Thorpe, W. H.:** Learning and instinct in animals. London, 1963.

F. Merz

Learning ability (syn. *Learning readiness*). A supposed personality trait to which individual differences in learning outcome (speed, amount, etc.) in different assignments may be attributed. Empirical investigations would seem to refute the existence of a *single* "learning" ability (cf. Pawlik, 1968, ch. 13). (See *Abilities; Begabung; Differential psychology*).

Bibliography: Pawlik, K.: Dimensionen des Verhaltens. Berne, 1968.

K.P.

Learning, associative. See *Learning, rote; Memory*.

Learning by imitation. See *Imitation; Imprinting*.

Learning by insight. As a concept, insight is central to the approach adopted by gestalt theory to the psychology of learning and thinking. Although W. Köhler sought to show as early as 1917 that insight can be defined exclusively by using behavioral data (smooth development of the solution, very sudden behavioral reorganization), this concept remained a principal point of attack for neobehaviorists. (See *Neobehaviorism.*) Osgood's approach in his mediation theory is characteristic of neobehavioral attempts to replace insight by other constructs. This argument about insight as a construct would presumably have been superfluous had the representatives of the two lines of thought clearly declared different plans of research. Gestalt theory worked chiefly in the field of the psychology of thought and studied how patterns of behavior which have already been firmly acquired are reorganized into relevant behavior for supplying a solution. The construct of *insight* was intended to explain this reorganization. As regards the choice of the word, it was certainly no coincidence that gestalt theorists approached problems in the psychology of thought from the angle of that of perception (cf. in this respect, M. Wertheimer's "rho-relation"). In the behaviorist psychology of learning, a construct such as insight was superfluous so long as S-R associations formed the exclusive subject of interest. One object of this study was the systematic exclusion of already acquired behavior patterns; "unnatural" responses were usually demanded from the animals used in the experiments (pressing bars, opening puzzle boxes, running through mazes: cf. in this connection, the criticism of Köhler and the ethologists, e.g. K. Lorenz). The organization of previously acquired behavior patterns raises problems for the behaviorist only when he examines questions posed by the psychology of thought (cf. Osgood's mediation theory and Maltzmann's habit-family-hierarchy hypothesis). It is possible that a more satisfactory explanation of the problems connected with the concept of insight will be found along the lines of subjective behaviorism as suggested by Miller. According to this, insight could be the creation of a (probably linguistic) metaprogram or solution plan which controls the application of subordinate programs (patterns of behavior) already established and available.

Bibliography: Köhler, W.: The mentality of apes. New York, [2]1927. **Maltzmann, L.:** Thinking: from a behaviorist point of view. Psychol. Rev., 1955, *62*, 275–86. **Miller, G. A., Galanter, E. & Pribram, K. H.:** Plans and the structure of behavior. New York, 1967. **Osgood, C. E.:** Method and theory in experimental psychology. New York, 1954. *M.Ba.*

Learning curves are constructed in order to represent learning progress in successive presentations of the learning material or in successive trials. Prerequisites for the construction of a learning curve are *constant* learning conditions in the individual trials (e.g. the same motivational situation) and a measure for effective learning that can be used throughout all trials. Two variables which are decisive for the type of curve selected are complexity of assignment material and stage of learning. Positively accelerated curves tend to be obtained at an earlier stage of practice and negatively accelerated curves at a later stage. There may be more or less extensive intermediate stretches without any noticeable learning increment. Interpretations of learning curves are problematical since it is not clear to what extent each learning curve is an artifact of a specific evaluation method.

Bibliography: Osgood, E.: Method and theory in experimental psychology. New York, 1953. *M.Ba.*

Learning, discriminative. Discriminative learning tries to select the characteristics of a stimulus situation which serve as guidelines for purposive behavior. In all experimental arrangements, Ss. have to learn to respond discriminatively to different stimuli. Appropriate experiments test not so much perceptual acuity for similar stimuli as attention to individual dimensions, or regularities in complex stimulus patterns.

Bibliography: Reese, H. W. & Lipsitt, I. P.: Experimental child psychology. New York & London, 1970. *H.G.*

Learning disorders (syn. *Learning disabilities*). General or partial underachievement (q.v.) or inadequate performances below the individual ability and developmental level, which are disorders in the motor (e.g. sensorimotor skills), cognitive (e.g. concentration, attentiveness), motivational (e.g. anxiety, q.v., laziness, resignation), and somatic (e.g. exhaustion, vegetative dystonia, q.v.) areas.

Theoretical explanatory models and derived therapies are offered by educational psychology (q.v.), learning psychology (see *Aversion therapy; Behavior therapy*), depth psychology (q.v.) and psychopathology (q.v.). There is an increasing tendency to view learning disorders sociologically: the excessive demands of an achievement society (q.v.) are seen as responsible for many of these educational problems. See *Child psychology; Educational guidance; Mental defect; Autism.*

Bibliography: Robinson, F. P.: Effective study. New York, 1961. **Tarnopol, L.** (Ed.): Learning disabilities. Springfield, Mass., 1969. *H.Ma.*

Learning, distributed (syn. *Distributed practice*). The total number of learning trials is distributed over a longer period by inserting intervals. In *massed learning*, on the other hand, the trials follow one another directly. See *Practice.* *F.M.*

Learning, fractionated (syn. *Part learning; Learning by parts*). If a more extensive piece of matter, e.g. a word list or a motor task (such as a piece of piano music) has to be learnt, most individuals "fractionate" the process: they divide the material into parts, each of which is to be learnt "independently". In part learning pure and simple, S. first learns all the parts separately, then in combination; in the progressive and repetitive part-learning methods (McGeoch & Irion, 1952), S. adds newly-learned parts to the recalled whole. *Global learning* (whole learning, learning by wholes) is contrasted with fractionated learning. The results of studies to find the better method are not wholly in agreement: motivation, learning level already attained and individual differences play their parts, whereas the type of assignment shows no general influence. Partial successes with fractionated learning can be encouraging; in later stages of learning the global method is more successful, and its superiority increases with developmental age and intelligence. Altogether, the findings seem to show that global learning is superior; in motor tasks the combination of the individually learned parts (e.g. for each of the two hands) can take as much time as immediate global learning.

Bibliography: Hovland, C. L.: Human learning and retention. In: **Stevens, S. S.** (Ed.): Handbook of experimental psychology. New York & London, 1951, 640–2. **McGeoch, I. A. & Irion, A. I.:** The psychology of human learning. New York, [2]1952, 499. *F.M.*

Learning, global (syn. *Whole learning; Learning by wholes*). The assignment is repeated as a whole (globally) until the learning criterion is reached. *F.M.*

Learning, incidental. In contrast to goal-directed (i.e. *intentional*) learning, incidental learning features no intention to learn on the part of the subject. The following is the operational definition used in research: Learning is incidental when no instruction is given to learn the material tested later. Experiments in incidental learning hitherto have been mounted as memory experiments: an orientation task (e.g. sorting) is used to introduce testees to the material to be tested later; in some experiments the orientation task consists of learning, but other aspects or parts of the material (e.g. colors instead of shapes) than those Ss. were instructed to learn are tested later.

Incidental learning plays a major role in everyday life. Therefore it is of interest to know whether regularities or laws found in intentional learning also occur in incidental learning. It was shown that in incidental (as compared with intentional) learning, the number of presentations plays a less important part, performance tends rather to drop with increasing motivation, and no Restorff effect (q.v.) is found in salient items; individual differences in performance seem to be greater. Proactive and retroactive inhibition (q.v.) occur comparably.

Bibliography: McLaughlin, B.: "Intentional" and "incidental" learning in human subjects. The role of instruction in learning and motivation. Psychol. Bull., 1965, *63*, 359–76. *F.M.*

Learning, insightful (syn. *Learning by insight; Judicious learning*). **1.** Insightful learning is said to occur if the change in behavior comes to pass through (spontaneous) recognition of the task structure; the contrary procedure is "blind" trial-and-error behavior. A somewhat less restrictive definition would include detour behavior not built up by trial and error. E.g.: in a maze, an animal not only acquires specific response sequences but behaves as if it knew their spatial structure: if the direct route to the goal is blocked, the longer way will be taken without any significant delay (the construction of "cognitive maps"). Accordingly, insightful learning occurs whenever, after the learning of more simple rules, behavior follows new and more general rules. If the principle of solution can be transferred, problem-solving is the typical form of insightful learning. See *Insight; Detour action*. **2**. See *Learning by insight*.

Learning, instrumental. In instrumental learning, the learner's reaction conditions subsequent signals: certain responses lead to reward or punishment, or to success (see *Conditioning*). The reinforcement by need-gratification, etc., of the responses given is cited to explain a learning increment in instrumental conditioning—in contrast to classical conditioning, where only the temporal contiguity of signals leads to learning. *Behavior shaping* is a special form of instrumental learning: in this case each approximation to the desired behavior is rewarded, so that the behavior to be acquired is formed gradually. *F.M.*

Learning, intentional (syn. *Goal-directed learning*). Learning *with intention*, as contrasted with *incidental* learning. *F.M.*

Learning, latent. Changes in behavioral possibilities which are not directly expressed in alterations of performance and therefore remain latent. Relevant experiments in latent learning (animal behavior, e.g. reinforced only in the second trial) led to a lively discussion in behaviorist circles in regard to the value of the reinforcement and contiguity principles in explaining learning (see *Reinforcement*). Latent learning would seem to show that reinforcement is *not* a necessary condition for learning. Hence even the existence of latent learning was contested, e.g. by the introduction of additional theoretical variables (e.g. curiosity or adaptation to the situation improve later learning).

In memory (q.v.) research, latent learning is admitted as existing in the form of incidental learning. Similar phenomena are *immanent* and *latent* practice (see *Practice*). Immanent practice denotes behavioral changes by repetition which lead not to improved performance but to diminished difficulty.

As in the case of latent learning, latent practice indicates an especially quick increment obtained if the preceding practice occurred under conditions adversely affecting performance (e.g. drugs capable of impairing performance), so that no improvement in performance occurred initially.

Bibliography: Düker, H.: Über latente Übung. Archiv. ges. Psychol., 1965, *117*, 54–66. *F.M.*

Learning machine. A system used to objectify learning processes. In most cases learning machines (or *automata*) simulate the formation of conditioned reflexes (see *Conditioning*) or trial-and-error learning. See *Automata theory; Machine learning; Instructional technology; Cybernetics and psychology; Learning, trial-and-error*. *H.F.*

Learning, massed (syn. *Massed practice*). Learning or practice trials may follow one another directly (*massed learning*) or (as in distributed learning, or *practice*) may be separated by intervals. This distinction is not to be confused with the similar one between *fractionated* (part) and *global* (whole) learning.

The results of investigations generally show distributed learning to be superior. Exceptions may be attributed to the following factors: the advantages of distributed learning may be concealed by warming-up effects; too long intervals may lead to complete forgetting; massed practice can prove superior if very variable behavior leads to the same success. The kind of matter assigned would seem to have no influence; nevertheless, distributed learning is relatively superior in the case of more extensive assignments. The superiority of distributed learning may be attributed to a number of factors: during intervals the tasks may be recalled quietly; intervals reduce the fatigue that has occurred; unbroken practice can reduce motivation, etc. A general theoretical concept to explain the superiority of distributed practice is *reactive inhibition* (q.v.). According to H. J. Eysenck, extraverts profit relatively more from distributed practice since they develop reactive inhibitions more quickly than introverts—a prediction confirmed by tests.

Bibliography: See *Learning; Practice.* *F.M.*

Learning, meaningful (syn. *Significant learning*). **1.** The cognitive acquisition of rules leads to the acquisition (or easier acquisition) of the learning assignment. **2.** The more general meaning of an assignment is learned without S. necessarily possessing any ability to reproduce details in full. In both cases, meaningful learning presumes that the assignment can be processed cognitively, i.e. that *rules* are derivable (see *Learning, insightful*), and therefore refers to meaningful material which may, however, also be appropriate for mechanical learning. The superiority of meaningful to mechanical learning may be seen in the fact that in meaningful learning it is necessary to store a *smaller* quantity of information (during testing it is *reconstructed*, not reproduced or retrieved from storage).

Bibliography: **Ausubel, D. P.:** Educational psychology. A cognitive view. New York & London, 1968. **Bruner, J. S.:** The process of education. New York, 1960. **Id.:** Towards a theory of instruction. New York, 1966. **Katona, G.:** Organizing and memorizing. New York & London, 1967. *F.M.*

Learning, mental (syn. *Mental training; Mental practice*). Changes in behavioral possibilities which arise without open behavior and only through *cognitive* processing of the assignment. The demarcation in regard to problem-solving and insightful learning is not unequivocal. Mental learning is most clearly evident in motor tasks. Operational definitions also differ markedly. E.g., it is defined as learning by observation of the performance of others (see *Imitation*); as "imaging" of the requisite movements; or as verbal description of the experimenter. Even though our educational and training systems depend to a large extent on such (and similar) techniques, there are only a few relevant investigations and no systematic presentations of their relative value. Clearly the type of learning task is important for the effectiveness of mental learning. Problem solutions or detour behaviors can be directly passed on by mental training. Investigations are therefore concerned mainly with motor learning. Even in such assignments, various kinds of mental training can produce quite positive results. Various factors are adduced to explain the positive effects of mental learning: implicit motor responses, verbalization, etc. See *Practice; Motor skills.*

Bibliography: **Ulich, E.:** Das Lernen sensumotorischer Fertigkeiten. In: **Bergius, R.** (Ed.): Handbuch der Psychologie, Vol. 1, ii. Göttingen, 1964, 337–9. *F.M.*

Learning method. Used in early memory research (H. Ebbinghaus) for quantitative determination of memory capacity. Memory capacity is determined by the number of presentations of the assignment needed for accurate reproduction by the testee. The learning method therefore studies the learning conditions which must be fulfilled for a clearly defined subject to be completely retained in the memory. See *Memory.* *P.S.*

Learning methods. When making learning assignments, different methods may be used, according to the (learning) type (q.v.), in order objectively or subjectively to increase effective attentiveness and retention: e.g. association of the matter with known significant phenomena, whole or partial appropriateness of content, temporal distribution of learning, and systematic alternation between the stages of acquisition and exposition.

Bibliography: **Katona, G.:** Organizing and memorizing. New York, [2]1949. *H.Schr.*

Learning motivation (syn. *Motivation to learn*). An improvement in performance without optimal motivation (q.v.) is impossible in the long run. The most primitive form of learning motivation consists in the construction of compulsive situations, in which "pressure-barrier situations" and "goal-attraction situation" interact (W. Metzger). H. Roth and W. Correll have produced further theoretical approaches (see *Intrinsic*) with the analysis of primary and secondary motives (oriented to things and persons). The notion of an intrinsic purpose-dynamics as a motivational factor in the student is, according to Rosenfeld (1966), widespread in Western educational theory and practice, whereas in the East biologistic and dialectical conceptions are the rule.

Bibliography: Rosenfeld, G.: Theorie und Praxis der Lernmotivation. Berlin, 1966. *E.U.*

Learning, motor. The acquisition of behavioral possibilities defined in terms of motor performance (e.g. piano playing, cycling, etc.). The distinction between this and other forms of learning is not always clear, since, for the most part, motor functions are also implicated (e.g. detour learning). However, other kinds or types of learning (verbal learning, the acquisition of cognitive structures) are obviously excluded. The results of motor learning are motor skills (q.v.). Motor learning is described as the formation of chains between individual movement units; however, the individual movements for highly-practiced skills occur more quickly than would be possible in a sequence of individual signal-response units. Therefore it must be supposed that the individual motor patterns are comprised in superimposed units whereby sensory control over the effect of the individual movement is partly surrendered. In simple hand movements, e.g. one assumes that movement is controlled by at least two sensory systems in the manner of control circuits: in the course of the learning process, visual control (*exteroceptive feedback*) is suppressed in favor of an inner control circuit (*proprioceptive feedback*). All motor learning processes may be conceived as the formation of increasingly complex coordinations, which relate both to the coordination between different movements and to that between muscular movement and sensory processes. Sensorimotor learning is especially important in the first twelve months of life, as Piaget (1947) emphasizes. In the course of development (q.v.), however, new sensorimotor processes occur. The relevant investigations are mostly concerned with practical and relevant questions in such fields as sport or control tasks. See *Motor skills.*

Bibliography: Fitts, P. M.: Perceptual-motor skill learning. In: **Melton, A. W.** (Ed.): Categories of human learning. New York, 1964. **Piaget, J.:** The psychology of intelligence. London, 1947. *F.M.*

Learning, operant. See *Conditioning, classical and operant.*

Learning, perceptual (syn. *Perceptive learning*). The alteration of behavioral possibilities resulting from changes in perception. The question of the existence of perceptual learning played an important part in the empiricism vs. nativism discussion within the psychology of perception. It is useful to distinguish *mental learning* (q.v.) from the perceptual variety. Spectacle experiments (see *Stratton's experiment*) are typical modes of investigation into perceptual learning. Prisms or mirrors are used systematically to disturb perception: e.g. one's image of the environment is turned upside-down; through perceptual learning the disturbance is wholly or partly compensated after some time, i.e. the testee sees the world upright again. In the meantime, however, it has been adequately proved that this reorganization of disturbed perception depends on the extent of the testee's motor activity. With reduced motor activity (S. sitting quietly, head still) there are special motor adaptation processes (e.g. the hand shows at a point corresponding to the changed perceptual conditions), without any change occurring in perception. The question whether motor or perceptual learning has occurred is decided by testing the kind of co-practice (see *Practice*). In perceptual learning, the learning sequence generalizes by way of different motor effectors, e.g. from one hand to the other. A more specialized application of the term is its use for the increasing specificity of perception with a constant physical stimulus constellation.

Bibliography: Epstein, W.: Varieties of perceptual learning. New York, 1967. **Wohlwill, J. F.:** The definition and analysis of perceptual learning. Psychol. Rev., 1958, *65*, 283–95. *F.M.*

Learning, productive. Learning with maximum transfer (Bergius, 1964). The possibility of transferring behaviors to other situations depends (among other factors, e.g. distribution of repetitions) on cognitive processing of the situation. If problem-solving is defined as a variety of learning, then productive learning may be said to occur when the solution principle that is found can be transferred to other situations.

Bibliography: Bergius, R.: Übungsübertragung und Problemlösen. In: **Bergius, R.** (Ed.): Handbuch der Psychologie, Vol. 1, ii. Göttingen, 1964, 321. *F.M.*

Learning, receptive. The insertion of meaningful material in existing knowledge. Largely synonymous with *apperception* (q.v.) or *apprehension* in Scholastic usage. *F.M.*

Learning, relational. Relational learning occurs when behavior depends not on specific individual signals but on the *relation* between two or more signals. In a typical experiment the choice of the larger (or brighter, etc.) of two objects is rewarded, and all other signal parameters (say distance or position) are varied in such a way that no direct signal-response connection can be formed. Other experiments require the selection of the deviant object from a series of similar objects (*oddity problem*) or the choice of the one of two objects that is just like a third (*matching behavior*). In somewhat more complex investigations the way in which the acquired relation is transmitted is the object of the tests. When S. has learnt to choose a square of average size, in a new series the largest one is omitted and a new, smallest square is added. If the median square is again selected, then one speaks of *transposition behavior*. Even more complex still are investigations in which signals are used which vary simultaneously in two dimensions, say color and form. In these cases the object of the test is whether relearning occurs more quickly if the change in meaning occurs within the relevant signal dimension (*reversal shift*), or if the second signal dimension is decisive for the reward (*non-reversal shift*).

The theoretical interpretation of such tests is largely concerned with the question whether learning under these particular conditions is to be assessed as the acquisition of signal-response connections or on the assumption of mediating processes. Unequivocal interpretations are difficult, since diverse assumptions on the generalization (q.v.) of learned responses (*generalization gradient*) are possible, and because the first learning attempt in each case may lead to the acquisition of learning sets which exert a specific influence on later learning.

Bibliography: Herbert, J. A. & Krantz, D. L.: Transposition. A reevaluation. Psychol. Bull., 1965, *63*, 244–57. *F.M.*

Learning, rote (syn. *Mechanical learning; Associative learning*). The impression and retention of learning matter independently of the active processing by S. of the information to be stored. Since neither motor behavior nor the cognitive processing of the situation is taken into consideration, the

memory (q.v.) processes proper. It is impossible to say as yet to what extent the development of learning theory will be determined by progress in applied learning research (in connection with behavior therapy, q.v., instructional technology, q.v., etc.). A solution of the basic problems of learning theory (Foppa, 1965) seems as little to be hoped for from this source as from a greater formalization of propositions (Foppa, 1967). It is still an open question whether approaches to date adequately represent and explain human adaptation processes. See *Learning; Behaviorism; Conditioning; Reinforcement; Soviet psychology.*

Bibliography: Anokhin, P. K.: Cybernetics and the integrative activity of the brain. In: **Cole, M. & Maltzman, I.** (Eds.): A handbook of contemporary Soviet psychology. New York, 1969, 830–56. **Atkinson, R. C. & Estes, W. K.:** Stimulus sampling theory. In: **Luce, D. R.** (Ed.): Handbook of mathematical psychology, Vol. 2. New York, 1963, 121–268. **Bandura, A. & Walters, H. W.:** Social learning and personality development. New York, 1967. **Bower, G. H.:** A model for response and training variables in paired-associate learning. Psychol. Rev., 1962, *69*, 34–53. **Bruner, J. S., Goodnow, J. J. & Austin, G. A.:** A study of thinking. New York, 1962. **Ebbinghaus, H.:** Memory: a contribution to experimental psychology. New York, [2]1964. **Feigenbaum, E. A.:** The simulation of verbal learning behavior. In: **Feigenbaum, E. A. & Feldman, J.** (Eds.): Computers and thought. New York, 1963, 297–309. **Foppa, K.:** Lernen, Gedächtnis, Verhalten. Cologne, 1965. **Id.:** Das Dilemma der Lerntheorien. 25th Congress of German Psychological Association, Berlin, 1967, 178–93. **Guthrie, E. R.:** The psychology of learning. New York, [2]1952. **Hilgard, E. R.** (Ed.): Theories of learning and instruction. Chicago, 1964. **Hull, C. L.:** Principles of behavior. New York, 1943. **Id.:** A behavior system. New Haven, 1952. **Leontiev, A. N.:** Learning as a problem in psychology. In: **O'Connor N.** (Ed.): Recent Soviet psychology. Oxford, 1961. **Osgood, C. E. & Jenkins, J. J.:** A psycholinguistic analysis of decoding and encoding. In: **Osgood, C. E. & Sebeok, T. A.** (Eds.): Psycholinguistics. J. of abnormal and social psychology, 1954, *49*, 126–35. **Pavlov, I. P.:** Lectures on conditioned reflexes, Vols. 1, 2. New York, 1928, 1941. **Postman, L.:** The history and present status of the law of effect. Psychol. Bull., 1947, *44*, 489–563. **Skinner, B. F.:** The behavior of organisms. New York, 1938. **Sluckin, W.:** Imprinting and early learning. London, 1964. **Thorndike, E. L.:** Animal intelligence. New York, 1911. **Id.:** The psychology of learning. Educational psychology, Vol. 2. 1913. **Id.:** The fundamentals of learning. New York, 1932. **Watson, J. B.:** Behavior. An introduction to comparative psychology. New York, 1914. **Young, J. Z.:** The memory system of the brain. London, 1966.

K. Foppa

Learning, trial-and-error. In situations for which no (instinctive or acquired) behaviors are at hand, activated (aroused) individuals exhibit an extremely variable, apparently undirected and random behavior. If a behavior or a sequence ultimately results in success, in successive trials this behavior gradually occurs more quickly until finally it appears immediately in the appropriate situation. Such a behavior is said to have been learnt through trial and error.

Experiments in this regard have been conducted since about 1900 using puzzle boxes and (later) mazes. The observed behavior patterns were interpreted as meaning that neither insight nor goal-directed behavior was necessary in problem situations. Learning could be explained (so it was said) by the gradual extinction of ineffective, and reinforcement by effective, behaviors (see *Effect, law of*). See *Behaviorism; Conditioning, classical and operant.* *F.M.*

Learning types. The categories used to classify learners according to readiness or a specific learning method. Everyday usage divides people into "good" and "poor" (or "bad") learners, in the sense of a relatively constant relationship between application (practice, q.v.) and successful learning. *H.S.*

Learning, verbal. The learning of verbal material by (usually) voluntary practice and memorizing. In retention testing, S. should respond to the verbal stimulus with the appropriate verbal behavior. The basis of verbal learning is that displayed in Ebbinghaus' (q.v.) classical experiment. It extends from the associative learning of two nonsense syllables to the learning by insight of the solutions to (verbally posed) complex problems. *F.-C.S.*

Learning while asleep. It was reported after a series of investigations that the presentation of (for the most part) verbal material during sleep led to successful learning. There are difficulties of method in that sleep is not defined uniformly, and that its depth is not easily measured. (See *Memory; Sleep.*)

Bibliography: Lewis, S. A.: Learning while asleep. Bull. Brit. Psychol. Soc., 1968, *21*, 23–6. *F.M.*

Least perceptible difference (syn. *Threshold difference*). That difference in the intensity of two stimuli necessary in order to produce the least possible change in sensation. *P.S.*

Le Bon,. Gustave. B. 7/5/1841 in Nogent-le-Rotrou, France; d. 15/12/1931, in Paris. Le Bon was a boy during the French Revolution of 1848 and when Napoleon III came to power. As a man in his early prime, he encountered the Paris Commune of 1871. He was forty-five when Boulanger almost took over the government of France. During the war of 1914–1918 he was an aged but still prolific writer. Between these latter crises, in 1895, he produced *The Crowd*, his *chef d'oeuvre*, which deals with broader issues of conformity, alienation, leadership, as well as with crowds in the strict sense. This work typifies Le Bon's position: he was powerfully influential, on sociologists, and psychologists from Freud downward, but remains something of a tragedy in the history of thought. He is remembered for his later social-psychological works. In these, especially those on World War I and the subsequent turmoil, his fertility and ingenuity of thought, ability to apply wide generalizations to particular problems, sensitivity in problem-finding (though his solutions were sometimes crass) are vitiated by intellectual *voltes-faces*, prejudiced conceptualization, and disjointedness of style. *The Crowd* embodies Le Bon's basic social doctrine: that in crowds the individual may rise to heights or (more usually) fall to depths of action impossible for him in isolation. The crowd is impulsive, mobile, irritable, suggestible, credulous, possessed of exaggerated and ingenuous sentiments, intolerant and dictatorial. Underlying these characteristics are the general doctrines that human action is dominated by unconscious impulses, which are irrational; and that ideas shape institutions, not the reverse. This socio-psychological contribution emerges from a previous multiphased career, in which Le Bon traveled widely, contributed to anthropology (including archeology), researched on matter and energy, developed recording instruments, and produced a substantial experimental work on equitation. Perhaps his work on variations in cranial capacity by races is the key to his development. As he aged, Le Bon became addicted to the ordering of humanity by hierarchies of races, sexes, intelligence levels, and political standpoints. Broadly speaking, as hierarchy takes over, precision and balance weaken, and the notion of race, "historically" and imprecisely conceived, appears to permeate his thought. On the "Anglo-Saxon" race Le Bon committed one of his major *voltes-faces*; but this and other aberrations should not obscure his real inventiveness and intellectual power. See *Crowd behavior*.

Main works: La psychologie des foules. Paris, 1895. La révolution française et la psychologie des révolutions. Paris, 1912. (Eng. trans.: The psychology of revolutions. London, 1913). Aphorismes du temps présent. Paris, 1913.

Bibliography: Merton, R. H.: The ambivalences of Le Bon's The Crowd. In: **Le Bon, G.** (Trans.) The crowd: a study of the popular mind. New York, 1960, v–xxxix. **Stoetzel, J.:** Le Bon, Gustave. Int. Encyc. Soc. Sci. New York, 1968, Vol. 9, 82–4. *J.A.C.*

Lee effect. Impaired vocalization resulting from delayed acoustic feedback.

Bibliography: Lee, B. S.: Effects of delayed feedback. J. Acoust. Soc. America, 1950, *22.* *K.E.P.*

Left-handedness. The preferential use of the left hand (dominance of the right half of the brain). A number of eminent men (e.g. Leonardo da Vinci) have been left-handed. A distinction is made between inherited and acquired left-handedness (e.g. encephalitis, q.v.). The degree of left-handedness is important for educational measures. If it is highly pronounced, attempts to induce the individual to "become right-handed" can result in, above all, disturbed speech and dyslexic manifestations which can in many cases be attributed to mixed dominance (the eye and hand are dominated by different halves of the brain). See *Laterality.* *H.Ma.*

Legal judgment, psychology of. One branch of forensic psychology (q.v.) concerned with external influences on, and inner phenomena and impulses operative in all human action, thinking and emotion, which may affect legal judgment. Investigations into behavior relating to legal decisions have to take into account the psychodynamics of the legal process, the personality traits and attitudes of the judge or jury, and the nature of judgments. (See *Decision processes; Attitude; Prejudice.*) Every legal judgment brings into play the social, political, cultural and vocational suasions that can affect human thought and sensitivity. Factors of place and time play a significant part. Personal experiences and impressions and their psychological correlates can affect the process. The particular mood or emotional state of a judge can modulate a decision. One vital part-concern of psychology should be to make judges, magistrates, etc., aware of the manifold extra-legal factors that can influence their decisions, and to help them to bring them under rational control. One important aim would be to exclude (by psychodiagnostic techniques) judges whose personality traits made them unsuitable, and to provide a psychological training program that would enable those exercising judgment to serve the community more effectively.

Bibliography: Schneider, H. J.: Zur Psychologie des Strafrichters. In: Grundlagen der Kriminalistik, Vol. 4. Hamburg, 1968, 133–51. See also under *Criminality; Forensic psychology; Traits; Type.* *H.J.S.*

Leipzig school. A group of psychologists including Krueger, Sander, Klemm, Volkelt and Wellek. They are sometimes referred to as "*Ganzheit*" (q.v.) psychologists to distinguish them from the "gestalt" psychologists of Berlin. *C.D.F.*

Leiter International Performance Scale. A series of "culture-free" intelligence tests (q.v.) in which local or national instruction plays as small a part as possible. The series includes picture completion, matching, analogies, discrimination tests, etc., and are available in grades from two to eighteen years. Performance is expressed in terms of mental age and IQ.

Bibliography: Leiter, R. G.: The Leiter International Performance Scale. Santa Barbara, Calif., 1940. *F.G.*

Leniency effect. A systematic error of judgment resulting from social tendencies to leniency and broadmindedness. Especially in personality assessment and rating, those exhibiting the effect tend to assess known or sympathetic individuals more favorably than less well-known or unsympathetic individuals. In the self-critical, the opposite tendency is usually to the fore. There is in most cases an additional tendency to judge favorably ("generosity error"; Cronbach, 1960).

Bibliography: Cronbach, L. J.: Essentials of psychological testing. New York, [2]1960. **Guilford, J. P.:** Psychometric methods. New York, 1954. *K.E.P.*

Lens. The lens of the eye is a biconvex, circular, transparent structure of (in the adult) approximately 1 cm diameter and 4 mm central thickness. The equator, or edge, of the lens is encircled by a number of sacculated zonular spaces, or lymph spaces, lying behind the suspensory ligaments (the zonule). The lens is situated between the iris (q.v.) and the pupil, in the hyaloid fossa on the anterior surface of the vitreous body. The curvature of the lens is varied by the ciliary muscles. The radius reduction (on contraction of the smooth muscle fibers of the ciliary muscle) of the anterior surface of the lens (in the young from about 10 to 6 mm) can be measured with an optometer. It increases refractive power and objects near to the eye are sharply imaged on the retina (q.v.) (see *Accommodation*). When constriction of the ciliary muscle is relaxed, the lens is restored to an unaccommodated condition: i.e. refractive power is diminished, producing sharp focusing of more distant objects. The refractive difference of the lens between maximal accommodation and a fully unaccommodated eye is for young persons 12 to 14 diopters; in the aged, reduced elasticity of the lens brings the accommodative mechanism to a standstill. This physiological process due to senile change produces presbyopia (q.v.) and a near point receding to infinity. *Cataract*, or opacity of the lens due in most cases to senile degeneration, can be improved by surgery and special spectacles (+12 diopters) which compensate the lost refractive power. Recently some success has been reported in the implantation of false lenses made from a material similar to plexiglass. Glass, plexiglass lenses, etc., can also be used, e.g. as spectacles in order to improve ametropic conditions (see *Ametropia*). See *Eye; Sense organs:* the eye; *Visual perception*. *K.H.P.*

Leptomorph(ic). See *Body-build*.

Leptosome (syn. *Leptosomic, leptosomatic type*). The leptosome is one of the body-build types or physiques described by E. Kretschmer (q.v.), and is characterized by slenderness, small shoulders, thin arms, fine hands and a long, small, flat chest. The type is frequently met with among the schizophrenic psychoses; among normal individuals the leptosomic physique tends to accompany a schizoid (q.v.) temperament. See *Psychoses, functional; Type*. *W.Se.*

Lesbianism. Homosexuality (q.v.) among women. Females with homosexual experiences tend on the whole to change partners less than homosexual men do. Lesbianism is tolerated in almost all societies; even in those with anti-homosexual legislation, female homosexuality is rarely punished.

Lesbianism would seem to be more widespread among students than among other females, and is more frequently met with in artistic pursuits and in those requiring dominant behavior (Gebhard, 1968). The sexual and psychosexual behavior of lesbians approximates that of heterosexual women: only a few constantly exhibit pseudomasculine behavior patterns and clothing. Most lesbians behave in a pseudomasculine manner only for a short time and experimentally, and tend to conceive their experiences according to heterosexual models (the "butch", or dominant partner; the "fem", or passive partner; although there is frequently an exchange of roles). There is often (in certain societies and circles) permanent anxiety about discovery of and social discrimination against the deviation.

The causes of lesbianism are as yet inadequately researched, but it may be asserted that only in very few cases have specific sexual experiences led to the deviation. Some hypothesize unfavorable environment and disturbed family life as influencing the tendency (Simon & Gagnon, 1970). Biological hypotheses cite physical, genetic and hormonal "errors" as determinative, although research findings to date do not support the assumption that homosexual women can be distinguished from the heterosexual by such criteria.

Bibliography: Woolf, C.: Love among women. London, 1971. **Simon, W. & Gagnon, J. H.:** Sexuelle Aussenseiter. Hamburg, 1970. See also: *Homosexuality.*

H.M.

Le Senne('s) types. A characterology based on the fundamental traits of emotionality, activity and reaction time, and extending the system developed by G. Heymans and E. Wiersma: nervous, sentimental, choleric, passionate, sanguine, phlegmatic, amorphous, apathetic.

Bibliography: Le Senne, R.: Traité de caractérologie. Paris, [4]1952.

W.K.

Lesion. A disturbance of the function of any part of the body; organic brain damage; an injury. *F.-C.S.*

Lethality; lethal factors. *Lethality*: a genetic abnormality causing the death of an organism, occurring in a homozygotism of most dominant mutations. *Lethal factors* (or lethal genes): alleles (q.v.) causing death in homozygous conditions, whereas in heterozygotes development can be impaired. *Lethal mutations* allow insight into the operation of genes (q.v.). In sickle-cell anemia in humans most of the red blood cells are sickle-shaped: homozygous children die early, heterozygous children are healthy and also resistant to malaria. Many lethal factors of drosophilia are caused by chromosomal mutations, such as deletion, inversion and translocations.

Bibliography: Hadorn, E.: Letalfaktoren. Stuttgart, 1955.

K.Fi.

Leucotomy. See *Lobotomy.*

Leveling law. Formulated and experimentally established by W. Moede, the law states that where workers perform the same task on a collective basis there is a tendency (based on "solidarity") for output to level out. Extremes tend to be eliminated while the overall group level shows a slight rise. The law does not operate in certain sociopsychological situations (e.g. in the presence of envy or rivalry within the group [see *Group dynamics*] or unusual conditions on the labor market, such as widespread unemployment). *G.R.W.M.*

Level, psychophysical. According to Köhler (1920) that area of the CNS (still to be exactly mapped out) in which the physiological processes forming the immediate correlate of the contents of consciousness occur. For example, in the course of a perceptual process, events in the terminal section of the cortex are accompanied by consciousness, but not those occurring in the sense organ and the conducting paths, which lie outside the psychophysical level.

Bibliography: Köhler, W.: Die physischen Gestalten in Ruhe und im stationären Zustand. Brunswick, 1920.

P.T.

Level-related terminology. The performance of isolated acts or a complex sequence of acts corresponding to the different levels of the instinct (q.v.) hierarchy can be brought about by electrical brain stimulation. The effects triggered off depend on stimulus parameters, the point at which the stimulus is applied, and the basic mood of the test animal, as well as on external factors. In designating the stimulus-induced behavioral elements, exact knowledge of the behavioral inventory is necessary for ethologically accurate interpretation.

Bibliography: Holst, E. v.: Zur Verhaltensphysiologie bei Tieren und Menschen. Ges. Abh. I, 1969.

K.Fi.

Levitation. Paranormal raising of an object or person; usually associated with physical mediumship. See *Medium.* *J.B.*

Lewin, Kurt. B. 9/9/1890 in Mogilno (Posen); d. 12/2/1947 in Newtonville, Mass. Lewin is remembered conceptually for his contrast of Galilean and Aristotelian psychology, field theory, topology-plus-hodology, and life-space; practically as an elucidator of culture-change, conflict (small- and large-scale), morale and minority-problems; generally as an integrator of theory and practice, and an inspiration on an unusually large scale to students who developed and applied his programs. Practically, Lewin's career was disjointed by the Nazi take-over; intellectually it was a coherent development in phases, which were expressions of the progress of his thought on basic problems. Academically, Lewin "habilitated" himself at the University of Berlin (Ph.D. 1914), following on work at Freiburg and Munich. In Berlin he taught 1921–1933. In the USA, from 1933, he held various visiting appointments, with two major permanent positions: Professor of Child Psychology at the State University of Iowa Child Welfare Research Station (1935–1945), and founder of the Research Center for Group Dynamics at the Massachusetts Institute of Technology. He became interested in motivation about 1914, working from associative bonds to intention, expectation, substitution (of tasks), and satiation. Gestalt theory he found inadequate, and developed *field theory*, the view (broadly) that events are determined by forces acting in the immediate field. Goal-seeking behavior is seen as locomotion symbolic or behavioral in a psychological life-space, (all the events that determine an individual's behavior at a time), more or less structured, the effects of motivation being represented by vectors and forces, while the data as a whole are ordered by *topology* (non-metrical geometry, with concepts inside, outside and boundary), while the direction of behavior in particular is handled through *hodology*, the science of paths. The application of these basic concepts, e.g. to conflict in marriage (1948, 84–102), and to post-war reconstruction (1948, 43–55) is the skeleton of Lewin's development from (broadly) motivation to group-behavior to social control. His major theoretical achievements were his stress on the Galilean as opposed to the Aristotelian approach (concern with function, not structure or content) in psychology, on the "two-facedness" of conceptualization (rigorous description but broad theoretical constructs), the transcending of the boundaries of the social sciences, and the use of mathematical tools in building systematic psychology. His importance is attested by the number of workers still active in developing his thought.

Main works: A dynamic theory of personality. New York, 1935. Principles of topological psychology. New York, 1936. Resolving social conflicts. New York, 1948. (G. W. Lewin, Ed., Papers dated 1935–1946.) Field theory in social science. New York, 1951. (Cartwright, D., Ed., Papers dated 1939–1947.)

Bibliography: Deutsch, M.: Field theory in social psychology. In: **Lindzey, G.** (Ed.): Handbook of social psychology, Vol. 1. Cambridge, Mass., 1954, 181–222. **Escalona, S.:** The influence of topological and vector psychology upon current research in child development: an addendum. In: **Carmichael, L.** (Ed.): Manual of child psychology. New York & London, [2]1954.

J.A.C.

Libido. According to Freud (q.v.), the sexual energy by means of which erogenous body areas arouse an individual to search for pleasure. In psychiatry, libido is often conceived more specifically as the totality and the degree of an individual's genital or love interests. Freud (1929) includes among these the pregenital interests, i.e. oral needs and the anal interests of manipulation. Libido development occurs (according to Freud) in distinct stages (see *Oral*, *Anal* and *Genital stage*). Psychic illnesses are seen as disturbances of libido development and as regressions to earlier, disturbed phases (see *Regression; Energy, mental*). According to Jung (q.v.) (1966), libido may be conceived according to the Freudian pattern but can also be desexualized. Freud, too, but above all some of his disciples (e.g. Hartmann, 1959), speak of the "neutralization" of libidinal (libidinous)—and aggressive—psychic energy. According to Toman (1960) in question here are forms of gratification of motives which are no longer sought as a function of the specific intensities of such motives (i.e. no longer for their specific value as gratification), but on account of their value for the more direct satisfaction of other motives.

Bibliography: Abraham, K.: Selected papers on psychoanalysis. London, 1927. **Freud, S.:** Introductory lectures on psycho-analysis. London, [2]1929. **Hartmann, H.:** Ego psychology and the problem of adaptation. London, 1959. **Jung, C. G.:** Symbols of transformation (Collected works, Vol. 5). Princeton & London, [2]1966. **Toman, W.:** An introduction to psychoanalytic theory of motivation. London & New York, 1960.

W.T.

Lie detectors. Polygraphs (q.v.) used in an attempt to record physiological reactions to critical questions. Findings thus obtained possess only a limited validity and objectivity, which depend to a large extent on the interrogator and the interrogation (q.v.) technique used. *P.Z.*

Lie scales. Many inventories contain built-in lie tests, designed to detect testees' tendency to falsify. Appropriate items usually contain questions or statements on socially unacceptable behaviors, which are formed so as to assume that such activities are universal. The validity (q.v.) of lie tests is difficult to check. *G.L.*

Life, course of. See *Life history; Case history method.*

Life, forms of (Ger. *Lebensformen*). **1.** Typical individual modes of life within a specific area or framework, which are correlated with the structure of the environment. **2.** According to Spranger (1966), human *ideal types* more or less intensely displaying existing cultural values. Depending upon the predominant values, Spranger distinguishes theoretical, economic, esthetic, social, religious and power forms of life, or types of men.

Bibliography: Spranger, E.: Lebensformen. Tübingen, [9]1966 (Eng. trans. of fifth Ger. ed.: Types of men: the psychology and ethics of personality. Halle, 1928).

W.K.

Life history (syn. *Study of course of life; Life cycle analysis*). A life history is a study of the life cycle, or a psychological account of the course of human life. The first attempt at such a study was made by C. Bühler in 1933. Distinctions were made between behavior and events, inner experiences and products of the course of human life. These were examined on the one hand in their interrelations, and on the other in relation to the process of physical maturation and development. Bühler distinguished *five stages* of the physical as well as the psychological process and examined various life cycle structures. Some basic theoretical assumptions were arrived at: that human life is lived with an *intentionality* that gives it direction; that men define themselves; that they are conscious not only of needs but of "tasks"; and that they wish to realize certain objectives. At approximately the same time psychoanalysts began to carry out investigations into courses of human life (see *Psychoanalysis*). Even in 1910, Freud (q.v.) published a study of Leonardo da Vinci in which he asserted the basic goal of the psychoanalytic biographical method of that time as the elucidation of the relationship between external experiences and individual reactions. In a critical report published in 1970, R. Ekstein pointed out that the biographies in the psychoanalytical literature of that time were viewed from the restricted angle of clinical theory. In modern "ego psychology" the course of life is seen as the realization of certain elective tasks, which Erikson presents in eight stages as crises of identity of human self-development (e.g. 1959).

A third kind of life study is sociologically oriented; the main representative of this school is Havighurst (1963). He sees development in the realization of developmental tasks, which result in part from the personal values and strivings of the individual, and in part from the cultural influence of society.

A fourth kind is the behavioristic and statistical method of describing a course of life, whose main representatives were at first S. C. Pressey and R. G. Kuhlen (1957). It has been more systematically and profoundly applied by Thomae (1968) in a volume containing additional studies by U. Lehr. Thomae describes the individual in an "undistorted" and "theoretically undiminished or predetermined form" (p. 103).

The fifth kind of life cycle study is the humanistic-psychological approach, as presented by Bühler (1968) in a new version of her original approach (see *Humanistic psychology*, II; *Case history method*).

Bibliography: Bühler, C. & Massarik, F. (Eds.): The course of human life. A study of goals in the humanistic perspective. New York, 1968. **Erikson, E. H.:** Identity and the life cycle. New York, 1959. **Havighurst, R. J.:** Dominant concerns in the life cycle. In.: **Schenk-Danzinger, L. & Thomae, H.** (Eds.): Gegenwartsprobleme der Entwicklungpsychologie. Göttingen, 1963. **Thomae, H.:** Das Individuum und seine Welt. Göttingen, 1968.

C. Bühler

Life instinct. Largely synonymous with psychic or mental energy and libido (q.v.). Freud conceives the life instinct as the drive toward gratification of wishes and motives, as the striving for pleasure, and as the energy behind all human (and animal) behavior. At first Freud made a distinction between the life instinct and the instinct of self-preservation, and later between the life and the death instinct. Apart from its significance in differential psychology, the term is psychologically redundant. In a sense of differential psychology, various degrees of life instinct seem more than anything to accord with diverse degrees of vitality or drive (q.v.) in a particular individual. See *Energy, psychic*.

Bibliography: Freud, S.: Beyond the pleasure principle. London, [2]1959.

W.T.

Life plan. In the individual psychology (q.v.) of Adler (q.v.), this is the structure of wholly or to some extent unconscious guiding lines which determine the individual's behavior.

W.Sch.

Life space (syn. *Living space;* Ger. *Lebensraum*). Numerous creatures defend a restricted living space, or territory, by which they subsist. However, the findings of ethnographic field research do not support the assertion of a human "territorial imperative" (R. Ardrey), i.e. the instinct (q.v.) to conquer a territory. In Lewin's topological psychology (q.v.), life space is the "field" within which individual behavior occurs and by whose positive or negative valence (q.v.) it is influenced.

W.Sch.

Light. The specific stimulus for the sense of sight (see *Sense organs:* the eye). Conceived more restrictively, light is electromagnetic radiation in the range of approximately 380–760 nm (nm = nanometer, 10^{-9} m), as evaluated by the photoreceptors (see *Cones; Rods*). Photometry is the study of light and light measurement. See *Brightness; Glare; Visual perception.*

A.Ha.

Light adaptation. Reduction in the sensitivity of the visual system to light intensity when the environment (visual field) alters spontaneously or through artificial intervention from a low to a higher level of light intensity. While the sensitivity to light intensity falls off, sensitivity to contrast, acuity, color differences, etc., rises: i.e. when the sensitivity to light intensity falls off, the capacity of the visual system improves. Opposite process: *Dark adaptation.*

A.Ha.

Lighting. Lighting is an applied discipline concerned with modes of illumination and the uses of lights, lamps, lighting systems, etc., indoors and outdoors. The method used is lighting calculation (lighting instructions derived from photometric measurements and basic knowledge of the physiology of the senses, psychophysics and psychology). Distinctions are drawn between *outdoor* or *exterior* lighting (street lighting, flood lighting, installations at sports grounds, urban lighting, and the illumination of objects, e.g. monuments, etc.), *indoor* or *interior* lighting (dwellings, places of employment, factory shops, retail stores, stages, etc.), and lighting for advertising, or with some special effect or purpose in view, etc. See *Glare; Sense organs:* the eye; *Visual perception.* *A.H.*

Likert scale. A scale giving values for individual reactive attitudes. The testee is required to choose from (at the most five) possible answers per item and thus to show his degree of agreement or disagreement with the attitudes represented. See *Attitude.*

Bibliography: Likert, R.: A technique for the measurement of attitudes. Arch. Psychol., 1932, *140,* 1–55.
W.H.B.

Limitation of consciousness. Limitation of the number of conscious contents which can be experienced clearly and simultaneously (approximately 6+2 elements in the case of simple contents of perception). See *Consciousness; Arousal.* *K.E.P.*

Limits, fiducial. The limit points on either side of a representative statistic (q.v.) giving the width of variation of the statistic on either side of the mean for given probabilities. The distance between these points is known as the *fiducial,* or *confidence, interval.* The given probability is usually $p = 0.05$ or 0.01.
D.W.E.

Limits method. A psychophysical method (see *Psychophysics*) for determining absolute thresholds and differential thresholds. Students of G. T. Fechner (q.v.) also use the term *just-noticeable-difference method.* In the limits method, the experimenter proposes to change the stimulus. In doing so he starts from a different stimulus magnitude than the one he wants. In determining absolute thresholds, the testee either says when he perceives the stimulus, or when he no longer perceives it. To determine differential thresholds, the testee says when he can find no difference between the changing stimulus and a comparative stimulus. *F.M.*

Limit value. If, for a *given* series $a_1, a_2 \ldots a_n \ldots$, there is a number A to which the terms a_n approximate as n increases, this *number A* is called the *limit value of the series*

$$A = \lim_{n \to \infty} a_n.$$

W.H.B.

Lincoln-Oseretzky Development Scale. See *Oseretzky test.*

Linear correlation. Relations between two or more variables are linear if they correspond to the linear equation $Y = a + bX$. Linear relations form a prerequisite for the use of some bivariate parametric methods. See *Product-moment correlation; Analysis of variance.* *G.Mi.*

Linear space (syn. *Euclidean space*). In contrast to *Riemannian space,* which is "curved", and a four-dimensional space-time continuum, linear space is that to which Euclidean straight-line geometry applies: this simple, "flat" space occurs in Einstein's special theory of relativity, whereas the general theory depends on "curved" space, and a "closed" rather than an "open" universe.

Linguistics. See *Psycholinguistics; Language; Grammar; Verbal behavior.*

Link Trainer (syn. *Link Instrument Trainer*). A practice chamber used mainly for pilot training, in which various flying conditions and disturbances can be simulated which the trainees have to compensate by appropriate actions. *K.D.N.*

Lip key. A device hardly used today and intended to measure reaction times in lip movements during speech. The opening or closure of the lips closes or breaks a circuit (with the aid of two contact strips) and controls a time meter. A sound hammer and similar devices are generally employed for such purposes. *A.Th.*

Lipp's illusion. One of the geometric illusions. The parallelism of main diagonals is difficult to perceive through the effect of the varying directions of lines at their ends. *C.D.F.*

Lipps, Theodor. B. 28/7/1851 at Wallhalben, Germany; d. 17/10/1914 in Munich. Philosopher and psychologist. Lipps was Professor at the Universities of Bonn (1877), Breslau (now Wroclaw, Poland) (1890) and Munich (1894). He tried to ground the basic disciplines of logic, esthetics and ethics and all psychological knowledge on the "principle of inner experience". He thought it was imperative to conceive psychology as a science of mental life and turned decisively against the application of natural-scientific methods in psychology. In order to explain the understanding of other individuals and objects as well as the comprehension of art, Lipps applied the principle of empathy (q.v.) (Ger. *Einfühlung*), which he took from the esthetician Vischer and conceived as the process of self-projection into an object of perception—for the most part by means of expressive phenomena (see *Expression*). See *Perception; Visual perception.*

Main works: Grundtatsachen des Seelenlebens. Leipzig, 1883. Raumästhetik und geometrisch-optische Täuschungen. Leipzig, 1897. Leitfaden der Psychologie. Leipzig, 1903. Psychologische Untersuchungen, 2 vols. Leipzig, 1907–12. Ästhetik, 2 vols. Leipzig, [3]1923. *W.W.*

Liquor. Medical term for a fluid, especially a fluid drug. Some body fluids are also described thus. *Liquor amnii*: the amniotic fluid which collects in the fetal amnion-sac. The *liquor cerebrospinalis* is a lymph-like fluid filling the brain cavities, the subarachnoid space (space between the brain and the *dura mater*) and the spinal cord. The cerebrospinal fluid removes waste products from nerve cells and acts as a mobile buffer. *E.D.*

Lisping. Speech impairment in which sibilants are inaccurately uttered or replaced by other sounds. Lisping results from the movement of the tongue against the upper row of teeth. Frequent causes are anomalously positioned teeth, which require appropriate orthopedic treatment of the jaw. See *Sigmatism.* *M.Sa.*

Lissajou's figures. Figures resulting from the combination of two perpendicular oscillations on an oscilloscope. Lissajou figures afford information on the frequency relation and phase sequence of two individual oscillations.

Listing's law. One of the eye-movement laws. When the eye moves from the primary position, its rotatory movements occur about an axis which is perpendicular to the initial and final lines of regard of the eyeball. This means that tertiary positions are brought about not by a *sequence* of side and upward movements, but only by both types of movement occurring simultaneously. *K.H.P.*

Literacy. The ability to read and/or write.

Literature and psychology. 1. *Psychology in literature.* Acknowledgements of psychology are so conventional in modern literature that Joyce's "They were yung and easily freudened" is almost straightforward, and Auden's "One rational voice is dumb; over a grave/The household of Impulse mourns one dearly loved" (*In Memory of Sigmund Freud*) more appropriate from a writer than Nabokov's "huge custard-colored balloon . . . inflated by Sigismond Lejoyeux, a local aeronaut" (*Speak Memory*).

The Zeno of Italo Svevo's *The Confessions of Zeno* (1923) writes an autobiographical exercise—but to show his psychiatrist is a charlatan in attributing his hypochondria to the Oedipus complex; he abandons the analysis when a physician tells him his real sickness is diabetes. Humbert Humbert begins *Lolita* (1955) in the "psychopathic ward for observation", yet Nabokov rejects "completely the vulgar, shabby, fundamentally medieval world of Freud". These two novels are correctives of a tendency to psychologism in twentieth-century literature, not because they disavow psychoanalytic methods but because they show clearly that "analysis" is only one of the interests that they arouse to produce the tension of ambiguities and possibilities peculiar to literary art, or (like sixteenth-century drama with its typology of humors) use as a *unifying principle*. There are, of course, many works of modern literature in which psychoanalysis (or the new interest in the permutations of supposedly innate myths) is put to literary ends: James Joyce's *Ulysses* (1922) and Hermann Hesse's *Steppenwolf* (1927) are examples of major fictions combining aspects of new, fashionable allegories and theories of consciousness with older introspective and associative techniques; yet the results are unique forms which cannot be reduced to a "nothing but . . .". Literary works in which the author relies wholly or largely on an untransmuted analytics appear increasingly banal as the theory becomes part of a chapter in the history of ideas.

When the insecure son in Arthur Miller's *Death of a Salesman* (1949) steals a fountain-pen, the "phallic symbolism" has a basic interpretative function in the drama that, say, Shakespeare's borrowings in *Macbeth* (1605) from the iatrochymist Paracelsus (e.g. Duncan's "golden blood") do not have to sustain. Of course psychological theories must appear in time-conditioned works whose authors rely on a common world of intellectual discourse to communicate with their audience, and the first stirrings of scientific psychology can be traced in imaginative literature: e.g. in the fourth voyage of *Gulliver's Travels* (1726), Swift makes use of contemporary perception theory (Berkeley *et al.*) when Gulliver sees an island and the sorrel nag a blue cloud—yet the reference serves the larger end of the book's literary presentation of the relations between the "passions" and reason. A simplistic theory of heredity and environmental psychology gave Zola a framework for his Rougon-Macquart novels (1871–93), the ultimate literary effects of which make a virtue of the errors of his version of the *race*, *moment* and *milieu* formula. In Zola's case, too, despite the understandable stress on alcoholism and absence of any mention of, say, phenylketonuria, the popularity of his novels helped the climate in which the importance of the scientific investigation of heredity would be more widely appreciated. In some recent semi-popular fiction the methods of behavior analysis have received attention. In, e.g., Anthony Burgess's *A Clockwork Orange* (1962), Dr Brodsky and Dr Branom induce an aversion to violence (and Beethoven) in a young delinquent and thus make him the devitalized man-machine of the title. Although this book raises the issues of moral choice and of the desirability of effective correction of socially criminal or deviant behavior, the lack of *literary* resolution and the confused portrayal of the aims and methods satirized make it a less competent essay on the subject than novels of a traditional cast which do not even refer to the techniques (e.g. Solzhenitsyn's *Cancer Ward*, 1968; Orwell's *Nineteen Eighty-Four*, 1949). The most effective use of narrative fiction to *propagandize* a psychology (behaviorism, q.v.) is to be found in B. F. Skinner's *Walden Two* (1948).

Interest in human motivation and acquaintance with, and understanding of, varieties of human behavior (if only linguistic) are necessary attainments of a literary artist; in this general sense works are often assessed for "psychological" proficiency. One might describe Benjamin Constant's *Adolphe* (1816), Swinburne's *Lesbia Brandon* (1860), Dostoevsky's *Crime and Punishment* (1866), Fedor Sologub's *The Little Demon* (1907), Proust's *A la Recherche du Temps Perdu* (1913–27), Hermann Broch's *The Bewitchment* (1935), Malcolm Lowry's *Under the Volcano* (1947) and Pinter's *The Caretaker* (1960)—all characterized repeatedly as "psychological"—as "about", respectively, emotional masochism, active and passive algolagnia, psychic conflict, persecution mania, homosexuality and the "death wish", mass hysteria, alcoholism, and electro-convulsive therapy; yet this is not all they are about. However detailed an author's observation of a disorder (Dostoevsky, e.g. has been shown to possess considerable knowledge of contemporary clinical psychology), it is conditioned by the *socio-historical symbolic* importance of an actual *or imaginary* disorder, and—above all—by the author's attempt to convey a certain ethos or to reach an artistic balance. An appropriate demonstration of how changes in science, etc., can affect the literary usage of a key psychological concept is Webster's history (1955) of the abstract noun *psyche* from Homer to the fifth century B.C.

As experimental psychology discovers more about the determinations of human personality and behavior, we may expect its insights to be *variously* imaged in literature, for literary art is essentially productive of improbability, of presemblance as well as semblance, and, by remaking it, constantly disputes the indisputable. It is not known whether greater enlightenment will produce greater literature.

2. *Psychology of literature*. The psychological investigation of literature has as its objects: (*a*) the writer's motivation; (*b*) the process of composition; (*c*) the thematic, stylistic or (psycho)linguistic analysis of works in relation to the modes of their individual or social reception and their presumed or recorded effects; (*d*) the relation of literary taste to personality; and (*e*) the investigation of the educational and therapeutic uses of literature.

(*a*) An extreme view of any *writer's psychology* is Freud's qualification (1925) of artistic activity as *fantastic compensation* rather than as a valid "real-life" pursuit—a view which, as presented, would qualify a theorist in any discipline as abnormal (see also Stekel, 1923). Kretschmer (1931) categorizes creators of prose fictions as pyknics, and manic-depressive in tendency, and creators of poetic fictions as leptosomes, and schizophrenic in tendency. Jung (1928) does not put writers into one sole category of his typology, and allows of their products being expressive sometimes of their type, sometimes of their antitype. Still met with are variations on Ribot's postulate (1906): a polarity of writers as "plastic", externally perceptive types and "diffluent", auditory, self-expressive types. None of these categorizations is conclusive. (*b*) Among investigations of *literary composition*, that of Patrick (1935) into poetry-writing, using a group of poets and another of non-poets, subjected to the same pictorial stimulus, is interesting in its characterization of the process as a form of problem-solving (q.v.) activity. It cannot, of course, be claimed that the conditions of this study allow any valid generalization. In the USSR, Jagunkova (1964) made an extensive, highly differentiated, experimental study of students' "literary abilities"; she obtained *six factors* applicable to adults and adolescents: poetic perception of actuality, emotionality, above-average intelligence, observation, imagistic thought, large vocabulary (verbal fluency). The "divergent thinking" (q.v.) of Guilford's exploration of creativity (q.v.) is not stressed.

The theory deriving from Freud, while usefully stressing the importance of verbal symbolic forms among the media by which the organism adapts to its environment, has provoked the "psychobiographical" method, which explains formal effects in works of art as expressive of known (or even unknown) proclivities or childhood experiences of the author, or turns a character in a work into a complex case-history (e.g. Jones, 1954). Hence certain scenes and word-play in *Alice in Wonderland* have been judged demonstrative of Lewis Carroll's obsessive sexual interest in pre-adolescent girls, even though his own works in symbolic logic allow of alternative decyphering. Burke (1941) summarizes critically helpful aspects of Freudian theory. Derrida (1967) and Starobinski (1971) separate the metaphysical assumptions of psychoanalytic criticism from suggestions deserving of experimental investigation.

Approaches based on the theory of Jung (1928, 1933) deliver works from overly biographical analysis to make them guardians of eternally recurrent archetypes (e.g. Bodkin, 1934). Jung also distinguishes the "psychological" or conscious from the "visionary" or primordially powered modes of artistic creation, and cites the first and second parts of *Faust* as distinctive of the two modes. But explication by reference to the collective unconscious can pointlessly replace recourse to analogous works known to an author.

In the more general area of philosophical esthetics, the problems of *creative motivation* and *audience response* are conflated in speculation on (literary) *form* as expressive of the human need to order things not only by reflection (*mimesis*) but by inventing (and reading) fictions: Vaihinger (1924) and Wittgenstein (e.g. 1966) have offered some of the most influential hypotheses in this regard, which stress the functions rather than the "meanings" of linguistic fictions.

Although the deviant cognition and expression of creative writers, especially poets, have been assessed almost as equivalent to the idiosyncrasies of some schizophrenic thinking and language (a notion not modern but classical in the characterization of the poet as divinely "possessed"—Mednick, 1962, offers an up-to-date "associative" version), precisely these creative departures from the linguistic norms and jargons of a society are the object of stylistic studies which use (statistical) surveys of spoken and written language (see *Computational linguistics*) to estimate the *degree* of originality. Intermediate to this classification of surface phenomena and ambitious descriptions of supposed underlying psychic mechanisms is the investigation (e.g. Shlovski, 1929; 1971) of literary art as the "singularization" or conscious liberation by the writer of the reader's "unconscious", automatic perception of things and actions (see also Bühler, 1921). More incisive are Horkheimer's and Adorno's (1972) post-Freudian analyses of influential "mythic" works (e.g. the Odyssey and de Sade's *Juliette*) as keys to the fatally self-destructive tendency of (scientific) enlightenment.

(*c*) The earliest, still influential, classification of literary kinds and inductive formulation of the common principle of audience reaction is Aristotle's *Poetics* (?335+ B.C.). Among other things, Aristotle discusses the psychological origin of poetry, the analysis of structure, and the emotional effects of tragedy. Plato's earlier ethical attack on the presumed ill-effects of excessive stimulus from poetry, and Aristotle's remarks on the cathartic effects of tragedy as stimulating the emotions (q.v.) in a "right" way, i.e. that which helps produce individual and social equilibrium, have grounded much later argument on the ways in which literature "rouses" the "emotions". Simplistically reduced, the two standpoints are paradigmatic for modern discussions of the effects of literary works, deemed capable of "corrupting" or "depraving", because they are "too" erotic or politically deviant.

While elaborating a theory of good literature as a "harmonious equilibrium of impulses" (and allowing it a truth of coherence, whereas science enjoys a truth of reference, e.g. 1936), Richards made a quasi-scientific attempt to detach literary criticism from biographical and historical evidence, and records (1929) the failures and extraneous suasions of undergraduates required to read unidentified texts. The validity of his findings has been criticized on the grounds that such "laboratory" conditions tend to remove the knowledge of context necessary to a full response, and therefore the duplication of typical poetry-reading conditions.

(*d*) More related to Fechner's controlled experiments in shape preference are the conclusions suggested by Burt (e.g. 1933), corroborated by Bulley (1933), and reported by Dewar (1938), Williams *et al.* (1938), and others. Burt attempted a factor analysis of esthetic cognition, using among others tests of poetical appreciation, and established a "general factor for artistic ability" operative in all expressions of esthetic taste even when differences in experiencing subjects' intelligence had been excluded (the exclusion of knowledge, convention, etc., as determinative of preference, was not shown). In more intensive research (e.g. Dewar, 1938; Eysenck, 1940*a*, *b*, 1941; Williams *et al.*, 1938), specialized factors were revealed for the esthetic appreciation of literary content, and two bipolar factors demonstrating preference for classical as against romantic, and realistic as against impressionistic style: a bipolarity interpreted as roughly identical with extraversion-introversion and radicalism-conservatism. (See *Type; Attitude.*) Eysenck postulated a *general factor of esthetic ability* ("T" factor) on the basis of these more rigorous tests, which excluded the factor of knowledge as far as possible. (See *Experimental esthetics.*)

(*e*) More educators are coming to think that the use of "good" literature in education (e.g. the teaching of language skills through reading literature and through "creative writing", the widespread conviction that "great" works—or even "socially-relevant" mediocre works—help to form a good man cf. Sartre, 1950) demands more psychologically respectable evidence as well as culturally acceptable assertion. Authors and researchers from Vygotsky (q.v.) to Bernstein (see *Language; Grammar; Psycholinguistics*) are called on variously to justify the value of literature in extending language use at crucial stages and among the disadvantaged, and the effectiveness of, e.g., verse writing as a (necessary) form of self-discovery and creation. As yet none of these large claims is any more proven than Caudwell's (1937) attempt to Marxize Freud and assert the individual and social value—even necessity—of lyric poetry by analogy with work rituals and songs. The whole area of literature in education offers much scope for psychological research.

Despite the absence of scientific evidence, it would be ludicrous to assert, however, that the modes of knowing, presenting and interpreting the ways of man that we inherit as the literary constructs of, say, Sophocles, Shakespeare and Joyce, are less privileged than certain mid-twentieth-century psychometric designs; as ludicrous as it would be to assert that psychology could not help develop strategies to tackle major, recurrent problems that literature is powerless to resolve. "O the mind, mind has mountains; cliffs of fall/Frightful, sheer, no-man-fathomed. Hold them cheap/May who ne'er hung there" (G. M. Hopkins). Typologies may be used to classify such a mind; drugs to numb its physiological substrate; a Turing machine to simulate its "faultless" operation; but without precise *literary* analyses (that those few lines may stand for) of what mind means to man, psychology fails to apprehend the nature of mind and man. (See *Humanistic psychology.*)

Bibliography: Bodkin, M.: Archetypal patterns in poetry: psychological studies of imagination. London, 1934. **Bühler, C.:** Erfindung und Entdeckung: Zwei Grundbegriffe der Literaturpsychologie. Z.f. Ästhetik, 1921, *15*, 43–87. **Bulley, M.:** Have you good taste? London, 1933. **Burke, K.:** Freud and the analysis of poetry. In: Philosophy of literary form. Baton Rouge, 1941, 258–92. **Burt, C.:** The psychology of art. In: How the mind works. London, 1933. **Caudwell, C.:** Illusion and reality. London, 1937. **Derrida, J.:** Freud et la scène de l'écriture. In: L'écriture et la différence. Paris, 1967, 293–340. **Dewar, H.:** A comparison of tests of artistic appreciation. Brit. J. educ. Psychol., 1938, *8*, 29–49. **Eiduson, B. T.:** Artist and non-artist:

a comparative study. J. Person., 1958, *26*, 13–28. **Eysenck, H. J.:** Some factors in the appreciation of poetry and their relation to temperamental qualities. Charact. and Pers., 1940*a*, *9*, 160–7. **Id.:** The general factor in aesthetic judgments. Brit. J. Psychol., 1940*b*, *31*, 94–102. **Id.:** "Type"-factors in aesthetic judgments. Brit. J. Psychol., 1941, *31*, 262–70. **Freud, S.:** The relation of the poet to day-dreaming. In: Collected papers, Vol. 4. London, 1925, 173–83. **Gunn, D. G.:** Factors in the appreciation of poetry. Brit. J. educ. Psychol., 1951, *21*, 96–104. **Horkheimer, M. & Adorno, T. W.:** Dialectic of enlightenment. New York, 1972. **Jagunkova, V. P.:** Individualno psichologitscheskoje osobienosti skolnikov, sposobnich k literaturnomu tvor cestvu. In: **Krutezki, V. A.** (Ed.): Voprosi psichologii sposobnostei skolnikov. Moscow, 1964. **Jones, E.:** Hamlet and Oedipus. Garden City, N.Y., 1954. **Jung, C. J.:** On the relation of analytical psychology to poetic art. In: Contributions to analytical psychology. London, 1928. **Id.:** Psychology and literature. In: Modern man in search of his soul. London & New York, 1933, 175–99. **Kretschmer, E.:** The psychology of men of genius. London, 1931. **Mednick, S. A.:** The associative basis of the creative process. Psychol. Rev., 1962, *69*, 220–32. **Patrick, C.:** Creative thought in poets. Arch. Psychol., 1935, *26*, 1–74. **Ribot, T.:** Creative imagination. London, 1906. **Richards, I. A.:** Practical criticism. London, 1929. **Id.:** The philosophy of rhetoric. London & New York, 1936. **Sartre, J.-P.:** What is literature? London, 1950. **Shklovski, V.:** O teorii prozy. Moscow, 1929 (Fre. trans.: **Chlovski, V.:** L'art comme procédé. In: **Todorov, T.** [Ed.]: Théorie de la littérature: textes des formalistes russes. Paris, 1966, 76–97). **Id.:** Tetiva: o neskhodstve skhodnogo. Moscow, 1971. **Starobinski, J.:** La relation critique. Paris, 1971. **Stekel, W.:** Poetry and neurosis. Psychoan. Rev., 1923, *10*, 73–96, 190–208, 316–28, 457–66. **Vaihinger, H.:** The philosophy of as if. London, 1924. **Webster, T. B. L.:** Communication of thought in ancient Greece. In: Studies in communication. London, 1955, 125–46. **Williams, E. D., Winter, L. & Woods, J. M.:** Tests of literary appreciation. Brit. J. educ. Psychol., 1938, *8*, 265–84. **Wittgenstein, L.:** Lectures on aesthetics. In: Lectures and conversations on aesthetics, psychology and religious belief. Oxford, 1966, 1–40. *J. Cumming*

Litotes type. Opposite of hyperbolic type (q.v.).

Little's disease (syn. *Spastic diplegia*). After the London surgeon W. J. Little (1846): collective term for certain forms of cerebral paralysis of childhood. Bilateral, spastic paralysis with disturbed gait, subnormality, epileptic attacks, etc. Produced by antenatal defects due to, e.g. encephalitis, congenital syphilis, or birth injuries. *E.D.*

Loading. The degree of correlation of a test with a factor. See *Factor analysis*.

Lobotomy (syn. *Lobectomy; Leucotomy*). Operations on the human frontal lobes (q.v.) by which fibers connecting them to the thalamus and hypothalamus are variously severed. The Portuguese neuropsychiatrist Egaz Moniz (together with his colleague, the neuro-surgeon, Almeida Lima) introduced the era of psychosurgery in 1935, with frontal lobotomy as the main technique. Recourse to the method in psychiatric cases reached its peak in the late nineteen forties and early fifties, since when it has increasingly declined with the use of drugs in the treatment of psychoses (q.v.). The operation is intended to remove the emotional components of disturbing conditions, such as psychotic experiences, illusions, compulsions, etc. From the start, this form of brain surgery has encountered moral and ethical objections because the irreversible defect produced can affect the most personal of the patient's mental and intellectual traits and abilities. This defect corresponds to the syndrome of a more or less considerable brain lesion with disturbed reasoning, and personality deterioration in the sense of a cerebro-organic passivity, impaired differentiation, and affective blunting. Only when all other attempts at therapy have failed, is the method indicated for critical and severe forms of paranoic and catatonic schizophrenia (q.v.), chronic depression (q.v.), and erethic forms of oligophrenia. See *Stereotactic methods*.

Bibliography: Freeman, W. & Watts, J. W.: Psychosurgery. Intelligence, emotion and social behavior following prefrontal lobotomy. Springfield, Mass., 1942. **Heimann, H. K.:** Psychochirurgie. In: Psychiatric der Gegenwart., 2 vols. Göttingen, 1963.

Häfner, H.: Psychopathologie des Stirnhirns, 1939–1955. Fortschr. Neurol., Psychiatr., 1957, *25*, 205–51. **Knight, G. C.:** Stereotactic surgery for the relief of suicidal and severe depression and intractable psychoneurosis. Postgrad. med., 1969, *3*, 45. **Levinson, F. & Meyer, V.:** Personality changes in relation to psychiatric status following orbital cortex undercutting. Brit. J. Psychiat., 1965, *111*, 42. **Mettler, F. A.:** Psychosurgical problems. London, 1952. **Sargant, W. & Slater, E.:** Physical methods of treatment in psychiatry. **Schaltenbrand, G. & Bailey, P.:** Einführung in die stereotaktischen Operationen mit einem Atlas des menschlichen Gehirns. Stuttgart, 1958. *H.Sa.*

Local excitatory potential (syn. Local excitatory state, abb. LES). The local, initial reaction of increased, superficial negative potential on a membrane on application of a stimulus.

Localization of psychological functions. The localization of psychological functions in the cerebral cortex is a major problem of neuropsychology (q.v.): it is the question of the *functional organization* of the cerebral cortex, which is the most important apparatus of psychological activity.

Over the years, conceptions of localization have changed considerably in accordance with notions of the structure of psychological processes.

When psychology was dominated by the idea that psychological functions were inborn "abilities", it was believed that not only elementary functions such as the main forms of sensation (skin, visual and auditory senses), but complicated psychological functions (speech, writing, ideation, concepts, complex needs) were located in limited areas of the brain and were a function of *isolated* groups of nerve cells. F. J. Gall (see *Phrenology*) and the "restricted localizationists" (K. Kleist in Germany and J. Nielsen in the USA) advocated these ideas. The corresponding sections of the article on *Brain pathology* discuss this "traditional aspect" of the subject. Clinical experience refuted such conceptions; it was shown that limited lesions of the cerebral cortex never lead to the "elimination" of isolated functions, but always disorganize an entire complex of complicated psychological activities, and that one and the same "function" can be disturbed through variously localized injuries of the cerebral cortex.

At present the dominant conception is that complex psychological processes are not carried out by individual nerve cells and cannot be "localized" in limited sections of the brain; they always depend on an entire complex of cortical zones operating in concert, and on the subcortical apparatus, in such a way that each of the components of this complex makes its specific contribution to the operation of the whole functional system.

Hence visual perception (q.v.) requires the participation of the occipital (visual) sections of the cortex, which cooperate with the "eye-movement fields" of the parietal-occipital and premotor area; but the lower parietal sections of the cortex also participate, producing the synthesis of the consecutive impressions to a simultaneous, organized whole, as do the speech zones of the cerebral cortex, which maintain attentiveness and inhibit secondary stimuli.

Just as complex is, e.g. the cerebral organization of movements (see *Brain pathology; Aphasia*) or even more complex forms of psychological activity (verbal behavior, intellectual processes, etc.).

In all these cases, the organization of psychological processes is contributed to, not only by the cerebral cortex, but by formations in the brainstem (especially the reticular formation), which serve to ensure constant cortical tonus and participate in the process of "imprinting" engrams (see *Memory*).

The above-mentioned views ("systematic" or dynamic localization of functions) made it possible to reformulate the problem of the organization of psychological processes in the brain; above all they provided a scientific basis for the evaluation of the disturbances of psychological processes occurring with local brain damage.

Modern ideas of the systematic localization of psychological functions make the neuropsychological analysis of local brain lesions one of the most important methods of investigation of the structure of psychological processes. See *Localization theory; Neuroanatomy.*

Bibliography: Luria, A. R.: Higher cortical functions in man. New York, 1966. *A. R. Luria*

Localization theory. The theory that specific mental functions correspond to areas of the cerebral cortex. The contrasting theory is the flexibility (or plasticity) theory, according to which each individual activity requires the cooperation of several cortical areas or the participation of the entire cerebral cortex, individual functions are *not* localizable, and each area can take over all possible functions. An elucidation of this major set of problems is still awaited from ongoing research.

Bibliography: House, E. L. & Pansky, B.: A functional approach to neuroanatomy. New York, 1967. *G.A.*

Local sign. R. Lotze (1912) defined "local signs" as local values which (in addition to qualitative contents) are present in all sense experiences and which enable consciousness to reassemble from the totality of impressions an image of their spatiality, thus allowing one sense experience to be marked off from other sensations. In his theory of complex local signs, Wundt (q.v.) (1910) described "inner tactile sensation" (sensed eye-muscle tension) and qualitative difference in retinal excitation according to the location of the receptor as essential components of visual perception (q.v.), and derived from them a theory of monocular and binocular vision. The local-sign theory has been criticized. See *Empiricism; Nativism.*

Bibliography: Lotze, H.: Grundzüge der Psychologie. Leipzig, 1912. **Wundt, W.:** Principles of physiological psychology, Vol. 2. New York, 1904. *W.P.*

Locomotion. 1. In comparative psychology: the movement from place to place of free-moving organisms under their own power (see *Taxis*); dependent on species-specific, inborn coordinations of movement (E. von Holst). **2.** In Lewin's topological psychology: the realization of behavioral possibilities by actively changing the relations or position of an individual to or in his life space (psychological locomotion), in the sense of spatial progression (physiological locomotion), of social "progress" (social locomotion, or self-development), or of cultural progress (intellectual, spiritual or cultural locomotion).

F.-C.S.

Locomotor ataxia. See *Ataxia; Romberg's sign.*

Logarithmic curve. A graphic representation of a function, generally yielded by the equation $Y = a \log X + b$. One coordinate is the natural value of a variable, and the other the logarithmic value of a variable. *G.Mi.*

Logarithmic paper. Graph paper whose measured distances on one or both axes are logarithmic, i.e. proportional to the log of the corresponding values. In the case of the logarithmic dependence of two variables ($Y = a \log X + b$ or $\log Y = a \log X + b$) the graph of the observed values of X and Y is a straight line. Logarithmic paper can therefore be used as a quick method of testing whether the dependence of two variables can be represented by a logarithmic function.

G.Mi.

Logic. See *Logical reasoning; Decision processes.*

Logical positivism (syn. *Logical empiricism*). A collective term for those views emanating from the Vienna Circle, and now associated mainly with Rudolf Carnap, that stress the unity of science; intersubjective scientific language; verifiable, factual, experiential knowledge; and the logical analysis of (especially scientific) language and knowledge as the task of philosophy.

Bibliography: Ayer, A. J.: Language, truth and logic. London, [2]1946. **Carnap, R.:** The unity of science. London, 1934. **Popper, K. R.:** The logic of scientific discovery. London, 1959.

Logical reasoning. Reasoning occurs whenever a conclusion is derived from premisses (deductive reasoning), or a generalization is established from instances (inductive reasoning). The criterion for adequate deductive reasoning is logical validity, but no such criterion exists for inductive reasoning.

1. *History.* The concept formation task, in which instances are presented by the experimenter one at a time, has traditionally been used to simulate inductive reasoning. In 1956, J. S. Bruner and his associates revolutionized this model by freeing the subjects to determine which instances they wished to test. This allowed a comparison with certain "ideal strategies". Around 1960, a further liberalization was achieved by P. C. Wason and G. A. Miller, whose tasks had a potentially infinite number of instances, and thus matched more closely the conditions of inductive reasoning in real life. Both results showed that subjects were frequently satisfied with partial solutions which they failed to test.

Gestalt psychologists, such as M. Wertheimer and K. Duncker, were eclectic in their choice of task. They stressed particularly the importance of reorganizing the perceptual field in accordance with its own internal "requirements".

2. *Present research.* Three themes characterize current research.

(*a*) *Linguistic variables.* Previous research on deductive reasoning had stressed the effect of the "atmosphere" conveyed by the linguistic form of the premisses upon the inferences made (R. S. Woodworth). The intensive development of linguistics in recent years has made psychologists much more sensitive to the role of language in reasoning. H. H. Clark's theory rests mainly on results obtained with three-term series problems (for instance, "x is worse than y"; "x is better than z"; "who is worst?"). The theory is based on the underlying linguistic properties of the premisses, specifying that certain relations will be more salient and readily processed than others.

In the same tradition, P. N. Johnson-Laird has carried out the most thorough investigation of the meaning of ambiguous quantified terms (for instance, "some", "every", and so on) and then shown that their order within a sentence predicts their interpretation in a reasoning task. Research of this kind goes well beyond global concepts such as "atmosphere effect."

(*b*) *Representational variables.* A different approach assumes that the individual constructs an abstract representation of a problem from which the solution may be read off. The pioneer work was done by C. De Soto and by J. Huttenlocher in the mid 1960s. Some doubts, however, have very recently been cast on De Soto's arguments by S. Jones, who used a task which imposed fewer constraints. The full implications of the linguistic and representational approaches are still unclear so that it is hard to formulate the evidence which would count against each.

(*c*) *Formal variables.* During the same period Wason developed a task in which the subject has to test whether a rule is true or false by selecting information from which a valid inference could be made. The task proved extremely difficult, even for the most intelligent individuals, and is still under investigation. However, in collaboration with Johnson-Laird, an information-processing model has been devised which postulates that insight is correlated with the increasing awareness that falsification is more crucial than verification.

3. *Conclusions.* The psychology of logical reasoning has recently enjoyed a modest

revival, and it will remain of absorbing interest because of its concern with the scope and limitations of man's inferential powers.

Bibliography: Clark, H. H.: Linguistic processes in deductive reasoning. Psychol. Rev., 1969, *76*, 387–404. **Huttenlocher, J.:** Constructing spatial images: a strategy in reasoning. Psychol. Rev., 1968, *75*, 550–60. **Johnson-Laird, P. N.:** On understanding logically complex sentences. Quart. J. exp. Psychol., 1969, *21*, 1–13. **Wason, P. C.:** Reasoning about a rule. Quart. J. exp. Psychol., 1968, *20*, 273–81. **Wason, P. C. & Johnson-Laird, P. N.** (Eds.): Thinking and reasoning. Harmondsworth, Mddx., 1968. *P. C. Wason*

Logopedics. The systematic treatment of inborn or acquired speech defects (e.g. stuttering, certain aphasias).

Logotherapy. A psychotherapeutic method introduced by V. Frankl of Vienna, and directed not so much to the study of conflicting drives as to the activating (motivating) mental level in the individual, in order to enable the patient to discover the meaning of his life. The noetic levels of the personality (see *Strata theory*) are multi-stimulated by means of a "paradoxical" reaction, i.e. the patient is put into extreme situations to which he is compelled to react. The method is currently achieving some success in the United States, where the first research institute devoted to logotherapy has been established.

Logotherapy mobilizes the antagonistic psychonoetic forces against neurotic symptoms; i.e. it tries to promote the specific human ability to throw off neurotic symptoms, to fill the existential vacuum of the neurotic, and to make him conscious of the full range of his actual possibilities, thus confronting the patient with the "logos" of his existence. *J.L.I.*

Long-distance hearing. This enables a person to estimate the distance of a source of sound from his ears. Essential factors are the experience of the acoustic stimulus, the intensity of the sound (the louder, the nearer) and the frequency spectrum (the deeper, the nearer; the higher, the farther away). See *Auditory perception.* *P.S. & R.S.*

Long-distance vision. This enables distances to be estimated with the aid of the optical apparatus. Essential factors are properties of the eye such as convergence (q.v.), and properties of the optical field such as apparent size of object, perspective foreshortening, shadow formation, overlapping and light absorption. Binocular estimation of distance is more accurate than monocular, as the latter can only make use of the optical field factors. See *Visual perception.* *P.S. & R.S.*

Longitudinal disparity. See *Horizontal disparity.*

Longitudinal studies. The aim of longitudinal studies is to investigate psychological and physical phenomena and behaviors in the course of development. They are contrasted with *cross-sectional studies*, in which other groups of testees are examined at each age level, in this way providing only average development curves. Investigations of physical or intellectual achievement/performance usually show that they have a rapid beginning and then rise ever more slowly, approaching their upper limit asymptotically. These development curves correspond precisely to the average learning curves. In the individual case, however, there are considerable deviations from this average pattern: the starting-point of the rise can be earlier or later, and the maximum can be reached at different points of time. In addition, the rise is seldom wholly regular, since there is a fluctuation between periods of slow and fast improvement. Only longitudinal studies can enable these changes to be viewed proficiently.

To a certain extent, biographies and diaries

kept by parents in regard to their children are longitudinal studies, but these offer no possibilities of comparison, since there is no way of determining the influences of environment and genetics. Such observations reveal the problems which have to be examined in systematic investigations. Anamnestic and catemnestic investigations can be thought of as rudimentary forms of longitudinal study. The duration and starting-point of a longitudinal study depend on the basic problem under investigation.

1. *The object of longitudinal studies.* Most such studies are basically concerned with the way in which a child with specific traits or abilities will develop. This question may be more precisely formulated according to two main emphases: (*a*) How constant is the trait? (*b*) What are the effects of the environment? Very often the two questions are treated in the same longitudinal study.

(*a*) In the background there is, of course, the question of the genetical conditioning factors, for only such a basis can allow constancy: e.g. various investigations of IQ constancy, and Gottschaldt's twin studies, which also included temperamental traits. The first major longitudinal study on this basis was carried out by M. Shirley at the end of the nineteen twenties in regard to motor, cognitive and general behaviors, using twenty-five children; the investigation lasted two years, and was undertaken from birth. Only the degree of proneness to disturbance showed any major consistency, and this was confirmed with a follow-up study after seventeen years. In general, it was shown that the correlations were less the longer the time between the compared measurements, and the earlier the date of the first one. The clearest investigations in this respect are those into intelligence (q.v.), since they can avail themselves of the best test instruments. In regard to personality variables, it has been shown that the level of correlations does not decrease gradually, but in some cases can rise again after a transient diminution. In addition, it was found that the degree of concordance for boys and girls in regard to behavior at different ages can often be quite different. All these results indicate a considerable environmental effect. The most extended longitudinal study, which has provided a large number of findings, was carried out by L. M. Terman (1925) with over one thousand gifted children (IQ over 140) in their eleventh year of age. The last results were made available after an interval of forty years. In Terman's investigation, it was a question of testing whether intelligence remained constantly at so a high a level, in order to examine the effect of environmental influence, what would become of these children, and to what factors later vocational achievements could be attributed.

(*b*) A straightforward example of this type is provided by the major investigation into German children just after World War II, carried out by C. Coerper, W. Hagen and H. Thomae. It confirmed the general influence of unfavorable developmental conditions on physical and psychological development. In most longitudinal studies concerned with environmental influences, such socio-economic modes are not to the fore, but the more specific family relations and parental attitudes (particularly those of the mother) to upbringing. Bayley's & Schaefer's (1964) and Kagan's & Moss's (1962) studies are good examples of this kind. Important, and unforeseen, results were obtained: e.g. dependence of IQ at thirteen years on maternal behavior in the first three years.

2. *Methodological problems.* The transition to longitudinal studies brought about a radical extension of the methods of developmental psychology. No longer the isolated transitory event was in the foreground, but man in the entirety of his development was a problem for empirical research. This gave rise to many new methodological questions.

(*a*) There is a purely external difficulty in the amount of labor involved, and the large number of staff required. Such studies can be carried out successfully only by specialist institutes. The first longitudinal studies were too broadly designed, since knowledge was then insufficient to show which observations or measurements would prove fruitful later on. The data from the first major longitudinal studies revealed the special problems which can be fruitfully examined in isolation. It is now possible to mount effective short-term longitudinal studies—at precisely the times when considerable changes are to be expected.

(*b*) In the field of physical, motor and intellectual behavior there are certain techniques whose relevance in infancy has not been adequately investigated. In regard to personality variables, the first years of these studies showed a concentration on observation and interviews of mothers. Very little is known about the reliability of these data, which leads one to suspect that correlational findings in part result from untrustworthy methods of data collection.

(*c*) The major difficulty is the measurability of psychological variations. They can certainly be described, and, if a parameter can be isolated (e.g. for body size or weight), measured as well. In the mental sphere this is usually not possible, for the alterations consist of the responses and the situations which release a behavior under investigation. At every age level, new intelligence tests must be given and new situations devised, in order to release aggression, frustration, joy, etc. When, in general, there are very low correlations with the data from the first months of life, this may be attributed to the poor reliability of the data, but also to the fact that the thing measured was irrelevant in comparison with the later findings. Therefore Meili (1957) has attempted another strategy for longitudinal studies of personality development. Through observation, he seeks out situations in which there are (to some extent) actually detectable individual differences in the infant, and tries to find with what later behaviors correlations exist. It is then evident that common conditions must exist in the earlier and later behaviors, however different the situations and responses may be. This technique has been shown to yield clear correlations up to seventeen years of age. Quite unexpectedly, the highest previous correlations with intelligence performance were confirmed—in fact, with responses in perception situations in the fourth month. This technique seems to avoid most of the methodological difficulties encountered with longitudinal studies.

Longitudinal studies are certainly among the most complex though sensitive methods of investigation, since they combine the developmental-psychological and the differential viewpoints, and therefore come closest to the actuality of the psychological process. See *Child psychology; Differential psychology.*

Bibliography: Bayley, N. & Schaefer, E. S.: Correlations of maternal and child behaviors with the development of mental abilities: data from the Berkeley growth study. Monogr. Soc. Res. Child Developm., 1964, *29*, No. 97. **Coerper, C., Hagen, W. & Thomae, H.:** Deutsche Nachkriegskinder. Stuttgart, 1954. **Gottschaldt, K.:** Theorie der Persönlichkeit und ihrer Entwicklung. Z. f. Psychol., 1954, *157*, 2–22. **Kagan, J. & Moss, H. A.:** Birth to maturity. A study in human development. New York, 1962. **Meili, R.:** Anfänge der Charakterentwicklung. Berne, 1957. **Oden, M. H.:** The fulfillment of promise; 40-year follow up of the Terman Gifted Group. Genetic Psychol. Monogr., 1968, *77*, 3–93. **Shirley, M.:** The first two years. A study of 25 babies, 3 Vols. Institute Child Welfare Monogr., 1931–33, *6, 7, 8*. **Stone, A. A. & Cochran, G.:** Longitudinal studies of child personality. Abstracts with index. Cambridge, Mass., 1959. **Symposium on personality consistency and change:** Perspectives from longitudinal research. Vita Humana, 1964, *7*, 65–142. **Terman, L. M.:** Genetic studies of genius, I: Mental traits of a thousand gifted children. Stanford, Cal., 1925. **Verschuer, O.:** Wirksame Faktoren im Leben des Menschen.Beobachtung an 1- und 2eiigen Zwillingen durch 25 Jahre.Wiesbaden, 1954.

R. Meili.

Lordosis. A curvature of the spine such that the back is concave. The condition is usually pathological, but it also occurs naturally as a sexual response (receptivity) in many female animals. *G.D.W.*

Lord tests. A group of statistical test methods in which range (R) is used to measure dispersion.

Bibliography: Lord, E.: The use of range in place of standard deviation in the t-test. Biometrika, 1947, *34*, 41–67.

Loudness. A term for the intensity of a sound process as judged by an individual. Sound pressure level as expressed in decibels (dB) is (approximately) numerically equal to loudness level expressed in phons for a sound of frequency 1000 Hertz (Hz) or cycles per second. The loudness of other sound processes is determined by comparison of subjectively judged sound with the reference sound of frequency 1000 Hz or with the aid of an electrical sound level meter. See *Noise exposure to.* *W.P.*

LSD. See *Lysergic acid diethylamide.*

LTH. See *Luteotropic hormone.*

Lubrication, vaginal. Usually occurs a few seconds after effective sexual stimulation, leads to moistening of the vagina and the external genital area, and probably results from seepage from congested vaginal blood vessels. The moisture (whose chemical composition is still unknown) appears initially as a "sweating" of the vaginal walls and is not, therefore (as was long supposed), produced by Bartholin's glands or, through the cervix, from the uterus. Vaginal lubrication makes the vagina receptive to intromission of the penis. See *Preejaculatory secretion; Orgasm.* *V.S.*

Luminosity. The relative brightness (q.v.) of a light source.

Luria technique. See *Conflict.*

Luteinizing hormone (abb. LH). A hormone which stimulates the formation of luteal tissue after ovulation.

Luteotropic hormone (abb. LTH; syn. *Prolactin*). A gonadotropic hormone produced by "releasing factors" in the anterior pituitary. Together with gonadotropin LH, it is said to stimulate the development of, and progesterone formation in, the *corpus luteum* (whether it does this in men as opposed to mice and rats is still contested), and, together with estrogens and progesterone (q.v.) stimulates the growth of the female breasts. At the beginning of lactation, it initiates milk formation and secretion, and is therefore sometimes known as the "lactation hormone".

Bibliography: See *Gonadotropic hormones.* *H.M.*

Lymphatic constitution. A physical constitution characterized by an especial emphasis from the lymphatic organs. A pale skin and a tendency to cutaneous inflammations are symptomatic. The lymphatic constitution is often met with in conjunction with the "hypoplastic" physique. *W.Se.*

Lysergic acid diethylamide (abb. LSD; syn. *Lysergide*). One of the psychotomimetic group: lysergic acid derivatives. There have been many psychological investigations with LSD, on account of the unusual "psychedelic" effects (especially at high doses), which are wholly novel for most Ss. The interpretation of such tests (which are often unsatisfactorily controlled) is frequently open. E.g. the confirmed diminution of intellectual performance may result from disturbances in the intellectual area, or from reduced motivation. The same is true of psychomotor impairments of performance. Effects on perception are manifold and of especial interest for study of perceptual variations resulting from psychomimetic substances (hallucinations, illusions, etc.). The following are some of the results observed: a rise in absolute visual threshold (more intense for photopic vision), an intensification of subjective color experiences with non-colored stimuli, diminution of color discrimination, changes in size, direction and distance perception and time sense (over- or under-estimation of pre-existing periods of time. LSD increases primary suggestibility (q.v.). The mechanism of the pharmacodynamic effects of LSD is as yet unexplained. One much-discussed hypothesis is that LSD enhances serotonin (q.v.) in the brain. LSD has been used in psychotherapy in the psychoanalytic treatment of neuroses, and even alcoholism (q.v.). Its effectiveness as a therapeutic aid is questioned.

Bibliography: Abrahamson, H. A. (Ed.): The use of LSD in Psychotherapy and Alcoholism. New York, 1967. **Hartmann, A. M. & Hollister, L. E.**: Effect of mescaline, lysergic acid diethylamide and psilocybin on color perception. Psychopharmacologia, 1963, *4*, 441–5. **Lienert, G. A.**: Belastung und Regression. Meisenheim, 1964. **Pollard, J. C.** *et al.*: Drugs and fantasy: The effects of LSD, psilocybin, and sernyi on college students. Boston, 1965. **Sjoberg, B. M. & Hollister, L. E.**: The effects of psychotomimetic drugs on primary suggestibility. Psychopharmacologia. 1965, *8*, 251–62. **Young, W. & Hixson, T.**: LSD on campus. New York, 1966.

G.E.

Lytic type. A subtype of Jaensch's S type, which includes chronically sick individuals, sufferers from, e.g. tuberculosis, schizophreniform thinking, or hysteriform ego-conversion.

W.K.

M

MA. Abb for *Mental age* (q.v.).

Mach, Ernst. B. 18/2/1838 in Turas (Moravia); d. 19/2/1916 in Haar (near Munich). Professor of Physics at the University of Graz from 1864 to 1867, and at the University of Prague from 1867 to 1895; Professor of Inductive Philosophy at Vienna University until 1901.

Mach represented a non-metaphysical positivistic functionalism. He believed that no finding in the natural sciences is permissible unless it has been empirically verified. His criteria for verifiability were extremely strict. He considered scientific laws to be purely descriptive, and that a choice between two alternative hypotheses about the same phenomenon should be made on the basis of economy. He thought that all mental life could be reduced to the basic components of sensations and their associations. The combination of these elements in the sense of a reinforced ideational economy occurred in the abstraction processes of thought (q.v.). Mach's experiments in the area of optical, acoustic and motor sensations were also important for psychology. The *Mach tambour*, or drum, was a rotating cylinder used to evoke illusions of movement in the enclosed subject; *Mach's ring* was a rotating disk for the detection of contrast phenomena. Lenin mounted a furious attack on Mach and Machians in his "philosophical" treatise.

Main works: Die Lehre von den Bewegungsempfindungen, 1875. Beiträge zur Analyse der Empfindungen, 1886 (Eng. trans.: The analysis of sensations, La Salle, Ill., 1914). Erkenntnis und Irrtum, [2]1906. Die Prinzipien der physikalischen Optik, 1921.

Bibliography: **Henning, H.:** Ernst Mach als Physiker, Philosoph und Psycholog. Leipzig, 1915. **Lenin, V. I.:** Materialism and empirio-criticism. Moscow, 1962. **Pearson, K.:** The grammar of science. London, [2]1900.

W.W.

Machine code. See *Machine language.*

Machine language. A program language suitable for a particular type of computer. Each computer has a fixed repertoire of operations which it can handle with given data. The operations are triggered by machine instructions written in a machine code (generally a binary code). A machine language consists of mnemotechnical abbreviations associated with the machine commands, e.g. "add price". *K.D.G.*

Machine learning. The ancient idea of learning machines has won new impetus as a result of electronic data processing and cybernetics, not only because of the newly-acquired speed and storage capacity, but because of the flexibility now attainable. Learning machines are desirable both in order to simulate organic structures (e.g. conditioned reflex behavior) and, in programming, to allow the machine itself to assemble and apply its own experiences.

Whereas the application of the concept of *thinking* to machines seems inappropriate (from a purely natural-scientific standpoint, too), there is no objection against learning in this regard, since even human learning depends on the acquisition of automatisms. To be sure, there is a profound difference between biology and technology, even though the literature in the field of engineering tends to far too easy equations of the two. The most important "technical" opposition is that between the *analog* organization of the nervous network and the *digital* machine system. In the body, magnitudes are represented by the number of nervous impulses per second, whereas digital signals represent chains of logical decisions.

Biologically and psychologically, the concept of "learning" (q.v.) is (for good reasons) somewhat imprecise, whereas the machine requires rigorous elucidation in order to carry out its formally perfect operations. Therefore it is possible to divide learning into a preliminary stage and seven varieties. The preliminary stage of *classification* is closely connected with sign recognition—which first makes learning proper possible; on the other hand, recognition is usually "linked" learning. Input signals are available to the machine, just as in the organism they are received by the sense organs (signal converters) and have to be reduced to sign classes. Learning by *storage* (1) is, e.g. learning by heart: but forgetting is the contrary. Tapes and films are rigid storage media: they neither forget nor learn. Only the computer store and logical processing permit of more than replays. Learning by *conditioned coordination* (2) is the basis of all higher combination and precise conclusions. Associative mechanisms and calculation of probabilities also come in here. *Trial-and-error* learning (3) is requisite if the stored experience is inadequate. The less there is of it, the smaller the number of presuppositions, and the greater the number of learning steps that have to be taken. Learning with *optimization* (4) mathematizes this principle with the aid of a (sought for) maximum of successful learning. But the machine has difficulty in recognizing whether it has reached a near-maximum. Learning by *imitation* (5) or *instruction* (6) presupposes very complex machines; therefore only simple marginal cases have been investigated. Learning by *comprehension* (7) is something beyond the limits of the machine.

Examples of early (i.e. *circa* 1950) learning machines are the *machina speculatrix* or *electric tortoise* of W. G. Walter—Pavlovian conditioned reflex behavior, type (2)—and C. E. Shannon's *maze-solving machine*—automatic orientation, type (3). W. R. Ashby's homoeostat—a model of ultrastability, type (3)—falls outside the present discussion, since it is an analogue device without a store. These models seemed to prove that electronics could dynamically simulate organic structures. More important than the actual automata, however, was the insight gained in developing the fundamental logical structure. Description is restricted to the essential parameters (a few values) and relations. Hence learning machines actually comprise an intermediate step toward the formal description of physical and psychological phenomena and behaviors.

Attention has also been given to the details of nervous networks and their learning characteristics; but since atomic details are important in the neurone, a precise model would require a whole computer to itself. K. Steinbuch's *learning matrix* and F. Rosenblatt's *perceptron* were conceived for technical application; to date there has been no actual industrial use, but the perceptron has become a basic mathematical model for decision theory (see *Decision processes*). The attempt to replace logical programming with statistical sequences and a definite goal failed in view of the number of steps required—despite the electronic speed possible.

Generalizations of learning machines are self-organizing automata which attempt adaptation to the environment and the development of new (learning) structures for better adaptation by means of a super-program. Whereas the improvement of model parameters can be successfully automatized on the basis of experience through actual application, difficulties multiply with the generalization of the problems. Problem-solving, game-playing and composing machines encounter such difficulties, especially when conceived as learning machines. A. L. Samuel's program, for instance, was a step forward, since it learned by the book. Further improvements have to reckon with the (hopefully not insurmountable) limits of learning machines.

Steinbuch has justly remarked that the success of learning machines depends on the quality of the image which the internal program is able to make of the external world. However, the way from this theoretical finding to its practical realization is clearly not easy. The expectations of the nineteen fifties were certainly answered with some results, but sober piecemeal research has replaced excessive hopes. See *Communication; Cybernetics and psychology; Information theory; Instructional technology; Simulation.*

Bibliography: Apter, M. J.: The computer simulation of behaviour. London, 1970. **Ashby, W. R.:** Design for a brain. New York, 1952. **Evans, G. W.,** *et al.*: Simulation using digital computers. Englewood Cliffs, N.J., 1967. **Fink, D. G.:** Computers and the human mind. London, 1968. **Friedberg, R. M.:** A learning machine. IBM J. of Research and Develpm., 1958, *2*, 2–13; 1959, *3*, 282–7. **George, F. H.:** Models of thinking. London, 1970. **Grey, W. G.:** The living brain. London, 1953. **Rosenblatt, F.:** The perceptron. Psychol. Rev., 1958, *65*, 386–408. **Samuel, A. L.:** Some studies in machine learning using the game of checkers. IBM J. of Research and Develpm., 1959, *3*, 210–29. **Id.:** Some studies in machine learning using the game of checkers. II. Recent progress. IBM J. of Research and Develpm., 1967, *11*, 601–17. **Shannon, C. W.:** Presentation of a maze-solving machine. In: **Foerster, H. von** (Ed.): Trans. Eighth Conf. on Cybernetics. New York, 1951, 173–83. **Steinbuch, K.:** Die Lernmatrix. Kybernetik, 1961, *1*, 36–45. **Tomkins, S. S. & Messick, S.** (Eds.): Computer simulation of personality. New York, 1963. **Zemanek, H.:** Lernende Automaten. In: **Steinbuch, K.** (Ed.): Taschenbuch der Nachrichtenverarbeitung. Berlin & New York, 1967. *H. Zemanek*

Machover test. See *Draw-a-person Test.*

Macula lutea. The yellow spot, with a diameter of 5 mm, surrounding the 0.5 mm *fovea centralis* at the point of intersection of the optical axis of the eye and the retina. *K.H.P.*

Magical thinking. 1. Frazer (1913) derived magic from two erroneous applications of image association: he attributed "homeopathic" magic to a misunderstanding of the law of similarity, and "contagious" magic to a misunderstanding of the law of contiguity (see *Association, laws of*). Although magical thought is by no means absent from many individuals in a developed civilization, attempts have been made to present it as a peculiarly primitive form of thinking, necessarily resulting from the fact that a "primitive" man thinks not logically but according to the principle of "mystical participation" (L. Lévy-Bruhl). Modern ethnologists (Lévi-Strauss, 1963, 1967; Malinowski) reject the view of magic as "primitive" thought. "Primitives" certainly think logically and sequaciously in other areas, and magic has many important "psychotherapeutic" functions.

Bibliography: Douglas, M.: Natural symbols. London, 1970. **Frazer, J.:** The golden bough. London, 1913. **Lévi-Strauss, C.:** Structural anthropology. New York, 1963. **Id.:** The scope of anthropology. London, 1967. **Otto, R.:** The idea of the holy. London, 1957. **Schmidbauer, W.:** Schmanismus und Psychotherapie, Psychol. Rdsch., 1969, *20*, 29–47. *W.Sch.*

2. The magical thinking and behavior of childhood are characterized not by a search for factually consistent relations, but by allowing for any possible relation between things. The child also tries to influence events by "egotistic" sets, imagining that his wishes can influence things. Magical thinking begins at some time between four and seven years of age and later becomes more differentiated. *M.Sa.*

Magnetism. See *Mesmer, Franz Anton.*

Maintenance. **1.** Maximum growth. **2.** Continuance in a state of equilibrium. **3.** Measures to ensure smooth running of, e.g. a plant, and optimal man-machine functioning.

Major principal axis. See *Principal components method.*

Make-a-picture-story test (MAPS). A thematic method described by Shneidman in 1952. Subjects are asked to build pictures from twenty-two background representations and sixty-seven individual figures, and tell accompanying stories. The advantage of individual arrangement of the stimulus field by comparison with a given field is seen by the author to lie in heightened activity of the subject, and greater personality relevance of the self-composed scene and accompanying story. See *Thematic Apperception Test.*

Bibliography: Shneidman, E. S.: Manual for the Make-a-picture-story method. Projective Techniques Monographs, 1952, *2.* *D.P.*

Maladaption. An organism's failure to develop in the way requisite for survival.

Maladjustment. An inability to adjust to one's own, social, vocational, or environmental demands.

Male protest. A tendency (which occurs in men and women in the context of compensation of feelings of inferiority) to reject apparently feminine stimuli and play a dominant, active role. The male protest occurs only in patriarchal social structures; according to Adler (q.v.) it is characterized by defiance, a desire to dominate, oversensitivity and ambition. *W.Sch.*

Mana. A Polynesian term, signifying in psychological anthropology (q.v.) a numinous, magical power which resides in certain individuals (chief, king or magician), things (word, weapon or image), or animals (lion, eagle, wolf or snake), and under certain circumstances is imparted to the faithful: positively (e.g. healing) or negatively (e.g. a curse). Figures filled with mana emanate "fascination"; they both attract and fill with awe. They are taboo (q.v.). This numinous fascination is most obvious in the cult of the "Great Mother" (icons, etc.). In popular superstition, mana also appears as a structural element of authority, especially in kings and nobles and ecclesiastical dignitaries (ordination and consecration as mana). *E.U.*

Mandala. In certain Eastern religions (Lamaism, tantric yoga) a mandala is a symbolic drawing for contemplation; it usually combines a circle and a square as the basis of various refined ornamental designs. In Jung's complex psychology the mandala is a symbol of the self-development aimed at in the individuation process. *W.Sch.*

Management. A general term for measures taken by superiors which influence cooperation, coordination and communication between all members of an organization.

Management style: general way in which an organization is managed (e.g. authoritarian, patriarchal, dictatorial-authoritarian, cooperative).

Types of modern management: participative management, internal management of the German army.

Management behavior: the management methods used by individual hierarchical superiors in everyday work.

Management method: the method of using instructional and controlling powers which is best suited to the given situation or person (e.g. command, instruction, training, discussion, personnel evaluation).

Management training: training executives in methods of leading and evaluating their colleagues. Purpose: to create a management style which is valid and binding on the whole organization.

Management problems: clarification of the principles of rule, power, misuse of power and manipulation; authority and prestige; rights and duties of the individual, the (working) group and organization as a whole; role and role expectations of the superior. See *Group dynamics; Industrial psychology; Occupational psychology.* *G.R.W.M.*

Bibliography: Dubin, R. (Ed.): Human relations in administration. New York, 1962. **Humble, J.:** Management by objectives. London, 1969. **Lupton, T.:** Management and the social sciences. Harmondsworth, [2]1971. **Tillett, A., Kempner, T. & Wills, G.** (Eds.): Management thinkers. Harmondsworth, 1970.

Mand function. Skinner's term for an imperative verbal operant. See *Conditioning, classical and operant.*

Mania. Used either as a descriptive or diagnostic label. A syndrome characterized by an elevation of mood, i.e. from optimism, hilarity and euphoria to elation and ecstasy. It is almost always accompanied by some disturbance of thought, i.e. grandiose ideas, flight of ideas, over-production of ideas and speech, and by an excess of movement. Mania is one pole of the bipolar illness *manic-depressive psychosis* (q.v.). In practice the cardinal affective symptom of elevated mood may be replaced by an irritable and suspicious mood, i.e. *irritable mania.* Its differentiation from schizophrenic excitement may be difficult, hence the need for an awareness of whether a descriptive or diagnostic label is implied. *B.B.*

Manic-depressive psychosis. Disturbed affect characterized by periods of mania, of severe depression (melancholia) and of normality. There is complete recovery between episodes, which may be manic or depressive or both in succession. The term "psychosis" suggests that the condition is both severe and endogenous, although the latter may not always be the case. Recurrent depression (episodes of depression alone) are thought to be related because of the similarity of symptoms, because patients may have several depressive episodes before developing mania, and because families are found with both manic and recurrent depressive members. The term *endogenous affective psychosis* covers both conditions, but severe reactive depression is a separate entity in most classificatory schemes, although in practice it may be indistinguishable from depressive psychosis. See *Circular psychosis.* *B.B.*

Manifest Anxiety Scale. See *Anxiety scales.*

Manifestation. 1. The appearance, disclosure or definite experience of hitherto latent affects or qualities, depending on genetic or situative factors, or—in neurotic manifestations—on, e.g. deprivation. **2.** A paranormal phenomenon. *W.Sch.*

Manifest dream. See *Dream.*

Manipulation. I. Manipulation may be defined as the management and direction of human beings by a clever use of their *desires* and *qualities* in order to control them for scientific, social or political ends not of their own choosing. This negative definition corresponds to common usage. However, a negative element is absent from the formal, abstract concept of manipulation. "A man is responsible to himself in his freedom. In this sense he should and must manipulate himself" (K. Rahner). This self-manipulation, however, needs ethical evaluation in the concrete case. It must not offend against the foundations of human dignity and freedom.

Methods of manipulation in the first sense are based on: (*a*) using the traits determined by heredity, and (*b*) changing these hereditary dispositions.

Reactions can be manipulated by intensive repeated information (propaganda, advertisements) and/or result from stress situations. Extreme over-stimulation or complete absence of stimulation (*sensory deprivation*) causes physiological and mental stress (q.v.). It results in modes of behavior which are foreign to the reflective, free consciousness. Through darkness and isolation, men can be made so eager for rewarded action, that they do or say whatever is required of them (see *Prison psychosis*). The results of such manipulation by sensory deprivation can be of long duration.

The use of sensitivity phases during development makes manipulation easier. Later behavior will be "imprinted" by the environment during these phases, which are often quite short (K. Lorenz, 1935). These "imprints" or impressions, insofar as they have been analyzed in animals, are irreversible. Periods of sensitivity of this nature are, e.g. the second half of the first year of life. During this period, through contact with the mother (or nurse), the foundations are laid for the development of "basic trust" (E. H. Erikson). The child learns that he can trust another person. Deficient contact during this period of sensibility leads to severe and irreparable physiological and psychological disturbances. (See *Hospitalization*.)

Manipulation of heredity (genetic manipulation) can take place through (*a*) selection of desired (*positive selection*), and rejection of undesired (*negative selection*) hereditary combinations; (*b*) through planned changes in the biochemical constitution of heredity (see *Genes*); (*c*) through the cultivation of selected egg cells or embryos within or outside the mother's womb. Of these possibilities only (*a*) can be realized in the current stage of genetics, e.g. through sterilization or artificial insemination with the sperm of a selected donor (in certain countries: e.g. USA, France). Methods (*b*) and (*c*) are conceivable and perhaps will become possible through progress in biology.

Ethical, legal, social and natural laws are not opposed to genetic manipulation as long as (*a*) the values and norms according to which the genes are altered or selected in a population are clearly defined and recognized by the members of a legal community; (*b*) the freedom and dignity of human beings are preserved; (*c*) the connection with the parents is maintained; and (*d*) from the point of view of natural science, the process is guarded against an unforeseeable risk of failure (production of mental or bodily abnormality).

II. *Social psychological aspects and limits of the term "manipulation"*. In its value-free usage, the term "manipulation" means *management* or *direction*. It acquires a moral overtone when the phrase "for ends not his own" is added. This moral use of the term is particularly frequent in Marxist analysis when it is applied in the theory of class struggle, to denote the direction of world views, modes of thought, etc., of the masses by the bourgeoisie.

"Manipulation" is not, however, a scientific term. It is more exact to say: where people interact they influence one another. In politics, for example, this is the explicit aim, and even scientific disciplines are sometimes expressly pursued with this end in view (education, psychiatry, clinical psychology, q.v.).

Besides brainwashing, this form of manipulation also includes the use of drugs (q.v.), planned employment of mass media (q.v.), and the possibility of surgical operations for the purpose of changing psychological structures. What is common to all these procedures is that "natural" life is brought under conscious and planned control. Still valid fictional expositions of the implications of such methods are to be found in, e.g. Zamiatin, Orwell and Huxley.

However, as a comprehensive term, "manipulation" is clearly limited. Because people always influence one another, manipulation cannot be regarded merely as a special phenomenon in contrast to other forms of influence. Methodologically, the attempts at brainwashing in Stalin's time should be regarded not as representative but as extreme cases of planned human attempts to influence one another. It is natural to human beings to form their world view with the help of others. Psychology shows that an individual is always the result of an environment, must be defined in terms of this environment, and can never be abstracted from it—as the term "human nature" implies.

Therefore, although manipulation is not a scientific term (because it is strongly moralistic), it nevertheless shows that attempts by human beings to influence one another need *legitimation*, particularly when these attempts are made in the name of a comprehensive science. The classification of modes of behavior as neurotic, psychopathic, schizophrenic or criminal is not a sufficient form of legitimation, because these terms and their opposites are not exactly enough defined. In particular, the concept of a "normal" or "healthy" human being is highly disputable. Therapeutic behavior is strictly dependent on ideology, and this ideology is often not consciously worked out in all its consequences. This becomes plain even in a so-called objective description of phenomena (see *Prejudice*).

Whereas manipulation has been a popular subject for social critics, e.g. of advertising (Packard, 1957), in scientific studies the term is hardly apparent. This shows how scientists themselves were bound up with the processes of their society, processes which sought not merely to approve certain goals of action but to present "reality" in accordance with these goals. However, the goals that men should pursue cannot be rationally established. Each individual will define manipulation in accordance with his world view, and decide which forms of influence and which tendentious presentations of reality he wishes to call by this name. (See *Aversion therapy; Behavior therapy; Humanistic psychology.*) *H. Autrum*

III. *Manipulation through drugs. Definition.* In the natural sciences, the word "manipulation" first appeared in 1716 in regard to drugs derived from plants. With the appearance of healing by "magnetism", it received the status of an art—the art of determining behavior and actions by a particular method.

1. *The problem.* Every therapeutic measure which corrects defects of body or mind with drugs or surgery contains an element of manipulation, because all interference with the nature of another person—even with the best intentions—is an act of power. However, the use of natural science to repair and heal a man has limits, because it is dealing not with a mechanistic structure but with a complicated organism and a human personality.

Modern medicine has helped to preserve life, and has therefore increased the likelihood of the inheritance of "sick" traits. A life-saving remedy can in some situations involve the danger of an undesirable and unintentional manipulation of mankind by the production of hereditary disease in coming generations. This development cannot be avoided without disregarding ethical and moral imperatives and disregarding the doctor's duty to heal.

2. *Present possibilities.* Drugs with different stimulant and depressive properties can change the content of experience. This form of manipulation has been practiced from earliest times by the use of drugs derived from plants (magic drugs, poisons) to achieve ecstasy, impassivity to pain, and heightened performance. These same drugs are used by many people today in the form of pure substances in acts of self-manipulation to avoid suffering and distress, or to improve bodily or mental performance. In the same way, a group of synthetic psycho-pharmaceutical (q.v.) drugs are used, at times unwillingly or even under duress, for legal or political ends. (See *Brainwashing.*) Such practices, because of their results, are morally and legally impermissible. Likewise, tranquilizers cannot improve the content of information in the brain, nor can they make a person permanently capable of high performance, or take away his pain and trouble for ever. With chronic misuse they may create dependence, or cause physical damage. See *Psychopharmacology; Drug dependence.* *H. Haas*

Bibliography: Brown, J. A. C.: Techniques of persuasion. Harmondsworth, 1963. **Clinard, M. B.:** Sociology of deviant behavior. New York, [3]1968. **Farber, I. E. & Harlow, H. F.:** Brainwashing, conditioning, and DDD (debility, dependency, and dread). Sociometry, 1957, *20*, **Huxley, J :** Brave new world. London, 1932. **Lorenz, K :** Der Kumpan in der Umwelt des Vogels. J. Ornithol., 1935, *83*, 137–213, 289–413. **Id.:** Evolution and modification of behavior. Chicago & London, 1965. **Marcuse, H.:** One dimensional man. Boston & London, 1964. **Miller, J. G.:** Brainwashing: present and future. J. social issues, 1957, *13*. **Orwell, G.:** Nineteen eighty-four. London, 1949. **Packard, V.:** The hidden persuaders. New York & London, 1957. **Wolstenholme, G.** (Ed.): Man and his future. London, 1963. **Zamiatin, E.:** We (trans. G. Zilboorg). New York,[2]1959.

Manipulation test. A psychological test to assess manual dexterity. It usually covers two components of movement: *precision* and *speed.* An example is the Minnesota Rate of Manipulation Test (q.v.) devised by G. L. Betts. *P.S.*

Man-machine system. A system in which typical performance by man and machine to achieve a specific goal is an important factor. Systems in which data-processing machines are involved are used to solve problems through an exchange of information between man and machine in a formal language. The machine undertakes tasks which can be described by algorithms (q.v.), while the human operator is responsible for non-objectifiable tasks of perception, thought and action (e.g. heuristic thought, selection of relevant data, decision in unforeseen cases). An example is the translation of a foreign language in a "dialogue" with an electronic dictionary. *K.D.G.*

Mann-Whitney U-Test. A non-parametric test method to compare the central tendency of two independent distributions. It presupposes ordinal variables. The scores of both distributions are ranked and the value U determined for a series; this value indicates the frequency with which a value from this distribution precedes values of the other distribution. The distribution of U is known for given sample sizes and tables are available.

Bibliography: Mann, H. B. & Whitney, D. R.: On a test of whether one of two random variables is stochastically larger than the other. Ann. Math. Statist., 1947, *18*, 50–60. *G.Mi.*

Manual dexterity tests. Tests for special motor skills (q.v.) based on manual operations. A distinction can be made between (*a*) test methods for simple movements whose accuracy or speed is measured (e.g. tremometer); (*b*) handling of objects (e.g. pearl-stringing test); (*c*) simple operations (e.g. guiding a pin along a prescribed track). The reliability of test methods in groups (*a*) and (*b*) is generally very high, while that of group (*c*) is usually lower because of the smaller series. There is generally only a slight correlation between manual dexterity tests; high specificity and low criterion validity are frequent characteristics. *K.D.N.*

Manual-genital contacts. Individual or mutual touching or sexual stimulation of the sexual organs of the partner or partners by hand (e.g. stimulation of the penis or clitoris). Active and passive manual-genital contacts are constantly increasing among young people of both sexes between the ages of two and eighteen (Schofield, 1968). Manual-genital stimulation must be considered as (*a*) one of many possible kinds of coital foreplay; (*b*) a possibility of practicing and learning heterosexual behavior; (*c*) a form of substitute heterosexual satisfaction among persons who are inexperienced in intercourse, or as an occasional possibility if coitus is impossible or undesirable for external reasons. According to Kinsey (1953) women are more reticent than men as far as manual-genital contacts are concerned. This does not apply to young people in Sweden, where there is no significant difference between the sexes from the twenty-second year on (Israel, 1970). Educational levels are clearly a significant factor; the tendency for manual-genital contacts to occur is higher among the more educated than among the less highly educated (Kinsey).

Bibliography: see *Oral-genital contacts.* **Israel, J. & Israel, M.:** Modelfall Skandinavien? Hamburg, 1970. **Schofield, M.:** The sexual behaviour of young people. Harmondsworth, 1968. *H.M.*

MAO inhibitors. See *Monoamine oxidase inhibitors.*

Marbe effect (Marbe-Thumb law, 1901). The more often an act of free association occurs in a group, the more rapid its evocation in an individual. *H.W.*

Marey tambour. An historical apparatus for recording physiological responses. It consists of a receiving drum connected by a tube to a rubber membrane which communicates movement through a stylus to be inscribed on a smoked drum or other moving surface. *G.D.W.*

Marginal contrast. A simultaneous, psychophysical (physiological) contrast phenomenon which occurs at lines of demarcation (contours) and also with planes of varying light intensity where transitions from brightness to darkness are less sharp. Both marginal contrast and inner contrast belong to the group of visual phenomena discussed under *spatial relationships* and have recently attracted much active research.

The *theory of lateral inhibition* has been suggested as an explanation for marginal contrast and a number of related phenomena.

Marginal contrast is not confined solely to the sense of sight, it occurs also with cutaneous sensitivity; and especially with respect to temperature. Tschermak-Seysenegg uses marginal contrast as an aid in correcting optical errors in image formation and constructs a physiological model for this function of contrast. According to this, marginal contrast acts counter to irradiation (q.v.). *A.Ha.*

Marginal personality (syn. *Marginal man*). A term used by the American sociologist R. E. Park to denote those individuals who are simultaneously—by personal choice or social circumstances—members of two or more groups which differ substantially in their composition and standards so that the person concerned is always in a multiple marginal position, e.g. on the boundary between two contradictory cultures. *W.D.F.*

Marijuana (syn. *Marihuana*). A South American narcotic which is prepared from the flowers, leaves and stems of the female hemp plant (see *Cannabis*). Marijuana is smoked. Its effect is qualitatively similar to that of hashish, but less strong.

Bibliography: Norton, W. A.: The marihuana habit: some observations of a small group of users. Can. Psychiat. Ass. J. 1968, 13, 163–73. See also *Cannabis; Hashish; Narcotics.* *G.E.*

Mariotte's spot. The blind spot of the eye (discovered by E. Mariotte in 1668) at which the optical nerve fibers leave the eye (*papilla fasciculi optici*), so that no photoreceptors are present at this point. It is located 12–18° nasally from the *fovea centralis.* Also known as the *optic disk.* *K.H.P.*

Marketing psychology. A branch of applied psychology dealing with the psychological laws of supply and demand and with their relations to one another.

Of its individual subdivisions, which are in part still comparatively independent (advertising, sales, product, consumer psychology, etc.), *advertising psychology* is still the largest. The reasons for this can be found in the connotations of the term, in history and in economics. If the psychological processes underlying market events can be described almost entirely as those of *information* (q.v.) and *motivation* (q.v.), then advertising (which is designed only to inform and motivate) and advertising psychology must be important.

1. *History*. The history of the subject is involved and only an outline can be given here. The psychology of marketing has not developed independently as a result of academic interest, but under the pressure of the tasks with which the economic system faced psychology. Accordingly, the questions raised dealt not so much with fundamentals and relationships, but first and foremost with immediate application and applicability. The advertising world had already seen the psychological implications at the end of the last century, at least tentatively, and a psychology of advertising began to take shape. At first the questions raised were directed primarily to "precepts for action", but they also accorded with the psychology of the period. Until the present there has been a considerable time lag between the stage of psychological research and its transfer to the practical concerns of advertising. The individual advertising medium received the whole emphasis, and, in the light of the psychotechnics of that day, interest was shown in individual aspects such as the effects of "eye-catching quality", "emotional appeal", "impression on the memory", etc. It was only much later that these questions gradually became more wide-ranging: to "get across" to the public was the interesting point, and that raised the question whether the advertising medium correctly expressed motivation—whether it was suitable for the *article* and the *public*. But a reliable answer could only be given to these questions when the *advertising medium* ceased to be the sole center of attention, and the whole background of all public pronouncements made by the enterprise came under review. In this way, whole series of advertisements, entire campaigns, and the firm's whole style came under investigation, and the transition to examination of the "public image" and motivation was made. At the same time the product itself received close attention; consumer appeal and how to "get it across" became increasingly important.

These questions were accommodated with difficulty under the concept of a psychology of advertising, and they are to some extent the reasons why some other part fields have come into being in this untidy area (product psychology and consumer psychology). It was soon realized that "advertising psychology" was not only a collective concept, but a general concept with its own theoretical foundation. Long before it had taken shape as a part discipline, advertising psychology had given rise to marketing psychology, on which it is now so dependent that it could not be meaningfully represented in isolation.

2. *Marketing and psychology*. The theory of economics is inconceivable without many psychological assumptions. As an aspect of human behavior, economic behavior, even with its supposedly rational basis, is just as much an object of psychology. True, it may be that psychology has little of *practical* import to contribute to a purely rational decision such as classical political economy postulates. But to take a decision or to act is always a matter for psychology.

In the past, in an economy of scarcity, there was no great need for a psychology of marketing, either in practice or in theory: very little supply, essentially restricted to basic commodities; a very great shortage of money on the part of the consumers, with an emphasis on supplying all one's own wants and on payment in kind; a minimal traffic in goods, with markets for a single product therefore very restricted in space and usually clearly demarcated from one another; little possibility of choice between competing goods; almost non-existent possibilities of switching to supplies of a different kind; etc. In such a situation the "rational principle" is almost completely valid. When there are *competing goods*, there are competitive prices, and these, as development proceeds and supply gradually increases, are equally gradually overlaid—if not replaced—by competition in quality. At this juncture (at the latest), subjective criteria come into play.

The late capitalist phase, on the other hand, *is distinguished on the side of the suppliers* by high production amounting to surplus capacity, as a result of which the efforts of the supplier shift increasingly from production to selling; on the side of the consumers there is high income, which is designated as freely disposable; the "affluent society", the "society of plenty", is born. The goods provided for this freely disposable income are above all commodities *which are not vitally necessary;* services with a highly elastic demand are made available. The pressure of *consumer need is comparatively slight*, and the decision whether to buy or not to buy, whether to buy this or that, is seen to be a very "arbitrary" act. "Wandering purchasing power" can end up in certain sectors, but it can also shift quickly (*market fluctuation*). The supplier endeavors to put this fickleness of consumer behavior to good account, and to influence it by adding to *competition in quality and price* a superimposed *competition in image*.

The task of the psychology of marketing is to throw light on these "irrational" processes, and, as an applied discipline, to show how some influence can be exerted on certain movements—in the economy as a whole or in specific enterprises.

If, in the economy of scarcity, the naked and overwhelming pressure of need was the crucial dimension, this has now been replaced by a differentiated network of factors which determine the particular attraction of some offer on which the profitability of a business depends. The pressure of need in the economy of scarcity depends almost exclusively on the situation of the person concerned, but the attraction experienced by the consumer in the affluent society depends on *numerous factors* extrinsic to the individual, which are not even of an economico-rational nature (e.g. the character of the product, not only its objective character, but its *image*, the name and reputation of the manufacturer and the tradesman; it depends on fashion, on the status of certain public figures who recommend the product). If the pressure of need could be neglected or taken as a universal basis, the attraction of the product no longer permits of such a wholesale theoretical approach. Marketing psychology has to replace "economic man" as a universal theoretical basis, with considered attention to the market as a social field.

Bibliography: Adams, H.: Advertising and its mental laws. New York, 1916. **Borden, N.:** The economic effects of advertising. Chicago, 1942. **Crane, E.:** Marketing communications. New York, 1965. **Galbraith, J. K.:** The affluent society. New York & London, [2]1969. **Hotchkiss, G.:** An outline of advertising. New York, 1933. **Katona, G.:** Psychological analysis of economic behavior. New York & London, 1951. **Kleppner, O.:** Advertising procedure. New York, 1925. **Schwartz, G.** (Ed.): Science in marketing. New York, 1965. **Scott, W.:** Psychology of advertising. Boston, 1908.

B. Spiegel

Market research. In principle—although at first it was not conducted in a scientific manner—market research became necessary from the moment when the practice of making single articles to order was superseded by the production of goods to be retained in stock.

In the present density and structure of often overlapping markets, and also because of the immense distribution machinery (commission agencies) which has now eliminated direct communication between buyer and manufacturer, market research represents an important instrument in the conduct of business, making it possible in places for the seller to pierce the increasing obscurity surrounding the market. According to Schäfer, its task is to carry out research into needs, the competitive situation and ways of effecting sales. One of its principal methods is *inquiry* (see *Interview*), but such a survey of psychic matters (need structures, motives, q.v.) requires to be completed by psychological methods ("interview in depth", non-directive exploration, q.v., projective tests, q.v., experiment, q.v.).

The sharp contrast which at first existed

between the "quantitative approach" of market research based on figures and the "qualitative" methods of psychology gave way to a realization that the particular nature of the subject required proficient complementary studies from both angles. Hence the "quantitative" approach increasingly developed techniques to accommodate psychological data, just as the "qualitative" approach took more account of the quantitative point of view.

Bibliography: Crisp, B.: Marketing research. New York, 1957. **Henry, H.:** Motivation research. New York, 1957. **Newman, J. W.:** Motivation research and marketing management. Boston, 1957. *B.Sp.*

Markoff chains. See *Stochastic processes.*

Markoff processes. Stochastic processes (q.v.) where the probability of an element (state) n is determined by the probability of the previous element (state) n–1. Markoff processes are therefore defined by the initial probabilities $p(X_1)$ and the transition probabilities $p_{x-1}(X_1)$ of all the elements. The transition probability is the conditioned probability of occurrence of the element X_1 under the condition $X_{(1-1)}$. *G.Mi.*

Marriage guidance. Introduced to prepare couples for married life. Its object is not merely to supply information about sex but also to show the importance of psychic, biological, legal, social and, last but not least, psychohygienic matters in married life and to explain possibilities, rights and duties.

In the last few decades, marriage guidance centers have been set up throughout the world which give information and advice about the possibilities of planned parenthood.

Matters requiring special attention in marriage guidance are the assessment of physical, psychological, mental and social health and maturity; the existence and cure of psychological problems, personal and material difficulties; the evaluation of the role played by psychological disorders and their transmissibility, the assessment of any capacity to judge, and evidence of will power. Especial care is required before pronouncing on the possible desirability of marriage where there is already an extra-marital pregnancy. In such cases the officer responsible must be especially careful to refrain from any display of sentimentality.

In many places marriage guidance also includes preparation for marriage. This is a particularly delicate problem.

In every case the marriage guidance officer must put completely out of his mind any personal inclinations. It must be remembered that obvious anatomical, biological, physiological and psychological obstacles to marriage should certainly make marriage out of the question. However, no infallible method has as yet been devised to guarantee a successful marriage with complete certainty. This banal fact needs to be considered in all marriage guidance, which can therefore not disregard the personal decision of the two partners if they have come of age and are able to look after their own affairs, provided there is no conflict with the law. *A.F.*

Bibliography: Dominian, J.: Marital breakdown. Harmondsworth, 1968.

Masculine protest. Adler's term for a will-to-power, particularly domination of another, in either a man or a woman, although the term is sometimes used for a woman's strong desire to be a man.

Masculinism; masculinization. The display of the secondary sex characteristics of the male (*masculinity*) by a female. These masculine characteristics may be physiological or psychological, or both.

Masculinization: The process of becoming masculine, i.e. the adoption of male characteristics by the female. *G.D.W.*

Masculinity. The extent to which an individual manifests the behavior patterns, interests, attitudes, and personality traits considered typical of the male sex in a given culture. *G.K.*

Masking effect, acoustic. The information contained in an acoustic message (e.g. speech) can be drowned or "masked" by the simultaneous presentation of a second sound of suitable type and intensity. Most frequently the masking sound used in experiments is *white noise* (q.v.) *C.D.F.*

Masking effect, visual. If a second visual stimulus of appropriate content is presented shortly after a previous stimulus, then the first stimulus will not be perceived. Many experimenters have investigated this phenomenon paying particular attention to the interval between the stimuli and their content. *C.D.F.*

Masochism is a sexual anomaly consisting of excitement and orgasmic response to being in pain. More loosely, the term is applied to pleasure—not specifically sexual pleasure—derived from being offended, dominated, enslaved or otherwise maltreated.

According to convoluted Freudian reasoning, masochism is a primary function proving the existence of a self-destructive tendency. Primary masochism turned outward leads to sadism (q.v.), the destructive tendency which is normally present at the anal stage of sexual development but which itself may be again directed inward. This inward direction of sadistic impulses is thought to be characteristically feminine. Aggression (sadism) is permitted for men in our society but women are encouraged to repress this tendency: that is, to become masochistic, self-effacing, and slavish. Where masochism appeared in a man, Freud considered him to be essentially feminine. One consequence of a masochistic need for punishment, according to psychoanalysts, is a strong resistance to therapy or a need for the suffering entailed in being ill. *A. Broadhurst*

Mass action principle. The principle that learning involves holistic functioning of all areas of the cortex. See *Aphasia; Brain pathology; Localization of psychological functions.*

Mass correlation. See *Product moment correlation.*

Mass media. Mass means of communication. A general term for modes of communication (channels or media, in communication theory) which can transmit the same information (messages) to a large number of individuals (receivers) relatively simultaneously.

The importance, distribution and effects of printed texts (newspapers, journals, books, comics, leaflets), radio, and audio-visual media (film and television) have been studied. The effects of records, sound and television cassettes, and wall newspapers and posters have not been studied in any detail.

Popular fears of manipulation (q.v.) by the media, and general opinions, attitudes and behavior patterns relating to mass media, contrast with empirical research results obtained by psychologists, sociologists and advertising experts. The findings show that mass communications rarely have a direct effect but frequently act through intermediary factors (e.g. persons, personal influence). They generally tend to reinforce rather than alter existing behavioral trends. Their effect is largely dependent on the characteristics of the factors involved in the communication process (source, message, receiver, intention). The importance of the mass media for giving new information and developing new forms of behavior, as well as for leisure organization, has been stressed. See *Communication; Media research; Attitude.*

Bibliography: Eysenck, H. J.: Television and the problem of violence. In: Report of the Committee of Broadcasting, Vol. 2. London, 1962, 1116–20. **Hovland, C. L.:** The effects of mass media of communication. In: **Lindsey, G.** (Ed.): Handbook of social psychology, Vol. 2. Cambridge, Mass., 1954. **Klapper, J. T.:** The effects of mass communication. Glencoe, Ill., 1960. **Weiss, W.:** The effects of mass media of communication. In: **Lindsey, G. & Aronson, E.** (Eds.): Handbook of social psychology, Vol. 5. Reading, Mass., 1970.

H.D.S.

Mass observation. A large-scale opinion poll. See *Opinion polls; Area sampling.*

Mass psychology. See *Crowd behavior.*

Mass reaction. The infant responds to stimuli with specific reactions, i.e. diffuse movements of his whole body. This form of reaction is caused by the early stage of development of the nervous system. Stimuli do not follow fixed paths but spread throughout the nervous system by a "mass reaction". This term was introduced into the American literature by G. E. Coghill. *M.Sa.*

Masson disk. A white disk with a radial series of black rectangles or squares which appear as concentric grey rings getting dimmer toward the outside when the disk is rotated. Originally designed for the study of brightness difference thresholds; now more often used to investigate attention phenomena. Certain levels of grey when fixated tend to disappear and reappear alternately. *G.D.W.*

Masturbation. Manipulation of penis or clitoris, usually to orgasm. The term is often used for other auto-erotic techniques, such as fondling of the breasts or rhythmic body movements, etc. Orgasmic masturbation starts in approximately ninety-seven per cent of males at the second puberal stage, and continues up to, and possibly beyond, the acquisition of a sexual partner. Nearly forty per cent of boys (fewer girls) indulge occasionally in mutual masturbation which is not of an essentially homosexual or morbid nature. At least fifty per cent of young girls, and many mature women, seek relief in the practice.

A taboo-ridden upbringing (especially that associated with ecclesiogenic neuroses, q.v.), while purporting to promote purity, often arouses intolerable feelings of guilt. Some would say that masturbation is a transitional "babbling" stage of love (I. H. Schultz). The frequency of masturbation depends on the strength of the drive, stimulus, inhibitions, etc., and is scarcely affected by a low-protein diet, sport or physical effort. Practiced with the partner, some think it indicates inadequate marriage relations. Scruples about masturbating involve some oversensitive, pious young people in the danger of suicide. It is anxiety felt about it, not the practice itself, that is harmful. Constructive advice on the subject should aim not at stopping the habit—always a futile endeavor—but at removing the attendant anxiety (if need be through expert hypnosis), explaining its normality, and diverting anxiety to constructive activities.

Bibliography: See *Coitus; Orgasm.* *K.T.*

Matched group (syn. *Equivalent group*). One of two experimental groups showing the same distribution on a specific variable but exposed to varying experimental conditions.

Materialization. Supposed manifestation in quasi-material form of a deceased person at a *séance* (q.v.). See *Ectoplasm.* *J.B.*

Mathematical psychology. 1. *Definition.* Mathematical psychology may be defined as psychological knowledge expressed in the language of mathematics; Fechner's law is a classical example of this knowledge. However, the range of this discipline can be extended by exchanging the functions of the two concepts "psychology" and "mathematics" and describing the mathematical language which is able to express psychological knowledge (psychological mathematics).

This extension is, however, limited if we exclude the general mathematical procedures which do not have the special characteristics of application to a psychological problem, even if they are used in psychology. This is the case with statistical methods (statistical tests, variance analysis, multivariate analysis, etc.). The boundary becomes clear by stating that the theory of Markoff chains is not a part of mathematical psychology, whereas stochastic learning models are. By reason of convention, authors leave out certain aspects, generally because these have been given more specific attention elsewhere, and are effectively independent; this is true, e.g., of test theory (q.v.) and factor analysis (q.v.). Sometimes they go beyond the definition and introduce subjects which are clearly extraneous, e.g. in the *Handbook of Mathematical Psychology* by Luce, Bush & Galanter there are three chapters dealing with mathematical linguistics (e.g. the presentation of N. Chomsky's generative grammar).

2. *Development*. The origins of mathematical psychology can be traced back to 1860, when Fechner published his *Elements of Psychophysics*. For a long time afterwards there were few developments, apart from test theory and factor analysis. However, Thurstone's contribution (1927) on the law of comparative judgment should be mentioned; he tried to define the subjective interval between two stimuli by the number of judgments in which one stimulus was given a higher ranking. The true development began after the Second World War; it was inspired by information theory (q.v.) (Shannon & Weaver's book appeared in 1949), cybernetic considerations and the theories of decision and utility, etc. Since 1950 the content of mathematical psychology has grown steadily, above all as a result of work done in the USA, where there is now a journal of mathematical psychology.

Having regard to other entries in the Encyclopedia (see *Methods of psychology*, *Information theory*, *Scaling*), mathematical psychology may be restricted to the following main headings:

(*a*) *Measurement theory*. Given a quantity of objects R and relations (or operations) r_1, r_2 . . ., we refer to the process of measurement as a transformation of R to the quantity N of real numbers, so that relations n_1, n_2 . . . corresponding to r_1, r_2 . . . coincide with the characteristics of the real numbers. After demonstrating the existence of a measurement method (representation theorem) we attempt to describe the quantity of transforms from R to N which enable the transition to be made from one numerical presentation to another: the quantity of permissible transformations. A few examples are given below:

(i) If R is associated only with equivalence relation E, the transform of R to N is possible precisely when the power of the quantity R/E of the equivalence classes is smaller than or equal to that of the continuum: any transformation of N to N is then acceptable. The process consists simply of numerical location through a nominal scale.

(ii) If R is associated with equivalence relation E and strict order relation P between the equivalence classes in infinite number, the transformation is possible precisely when the quantity R/E contains a partial quantity S which is dense in its order and also infinite. The number of legitimate transformations is that of the continuously rising transformations; the scale is therefore ordinal.

(iii) In the previous instance the order P was strict. Luce believes it would be interesting to introduce a partial order for subjective comparisons: e.g., given a quantity R of weights, let a subject be given two weights and asked which is heavier; if he replies *a is heavier than b*, we shall write $a \gg b$; the relation $\gg$ is a partial order relation; if two very similar weights are given, the subject will be unable to reply because he cannot detect the difference. This relation is not trivial, because all intervals which contain an interval of perceptible difference are themselves intervals of perceptible difference. Let us now consider three objects x, y and z and assume that $x \gg y$ and $z \ll x$; if a fourth object w is heavier than x (objectively but not necessarily subjectively), then $w \gg y$; if w is lighter than x, we have $z \ll w$. It follows that if $x \gg y$ and $z \ll x$, then $w \gg y$ or $z \ll w$. It is also apparent that if $x \gg y$ and $z \ll w$, then $x \gg w$ or $z \ll y$. A semi-order is said to exist in the quantity R if there is a strictly partial order relation which has the two properties mentioned. It can be shown that there is then a strict order relation P to be defined as follows: we obtain xPy if $z \gg x$ also gives $z \ll y$ and if $y \gg z$ also gives $x \ll z$ (irrespective of the size of z). In general, there are no representation and uniqueness theorems for the semi-arrangements.

(iv) Even if it is already provided with the binary relations E and I, the quantity R can also be associated with the quaternary relation; this will be the case if the experiments provide answers to the following questions. Is the distance between a and b greater than the distance between c and d, or is c equidistant from a and b (central)? If we assume suitable properties for these relations (e.g. transitivity of the interval sizes or archimedean axioms in order to comply with the properties of the figures) we can prove the existence of a numerical representation and see that the linearly rising transformations form the quantity of acceptable transformations (see *Intervalscale*). J. von Neumann has established axioms in a similar way which lead to cardinal numbers and introduce elements consisting of pairs (a and b) with a weighting or probability p and q ($p+q = 1$).

(v) If we define an operation which transforms $R \times R$ to R (we define the sum of the two components of R as an element of R) and establish certain characteristics (axioms), we obtain an extensive value. We can show the existence of numerical presentations which are defined up to a rising, linear, and homogeneous conversion (see *Ratio scale*).

(vi) Luce and Tukey have investigated *conjoint measurement*. If a quantity of pairs $R \times \rho$ with an order relation P is given, we try to obtain a numerical presentation $F(a, \alpha)$ in the form $f(a) + g(\alpha)$; the order relation for $R \times \rho$ would already allow conjoint measurement of R and ρ. The authors show that the assumption of 4 axioms is sufficient; the most important is the *cancellation axiom*. If a, b and c are three components of R, and α, β, γ three components of ρ, and if $(a\beta)P(c\alpha)$ and $(c\gamma)P(b\beta)$, then $(a\gamma)P(b\alpha)$.

(*b*) *Choice and decision*. Special attention has been given to the behavior patterns of choice. If a set R of objects x, y, z . . . is given, the behavior of a subject consists in selecting an object x from a finite sub-set T of R. Starting from experiments, we define the probability of choice: p_{xy} is the probability of selecting the object x in the pair (x,y); p_T is the probability that x will be selected in T; $p_T^{(S)}$ is the probability that the component selected in T will also be present in S, a sub-set of T. We now set about arranging the objects by means of a specific numerical function N(x), starting from the probabilities of choice. We decide to use one of the two following definition formulae for N(x): (1)$N(y) - N(x) = \text{probit}/p_{xy}^x$ (in which the right-hand component is the standard value corresponding to the probability p_{xy}); (2)

$$\frac{N(y)}{N(x)} = \frac{p_{xy}}{p_{xy}^x},$$

suggested by Luce (we assume that p_{xy} never reaches 0 and 1). Use of these functions requires a condition to be met relating to the probability of the choice; in Luce's function this is the condition for multiplication:

$$\frac{p_{xy}^x}{p_{xy}^y} = \frac{p_{xz}^x}{p_{xz}^z} = \frac{p_{zy}^z}{p_{zy}^y}$$

Luce has shown that this condition is met when his axiom of choice is used: let S and T be finite quantities with the property

SCTCR; we then obtain for all elements x from S:

$$p_T^{(S)} \cdot p_S^{(x)} - p_T^{(x)} \cdot$$

An example is given by selection in uncertainty, e.g. in a lottery; in this case a decision to prefer one number to another is based on comparison of the mathematical chances of winning. If we turn to psychological experiments, this rule becomes a rule of maximum anticipated benefit, if the sums of money are replaced by the utility values and the objective probabilities by subjective probabilities; these concepts of utility and subjective probability have been widely studied. One example of application is the *signal detection* model of J. A. Swets, W. P. Tanner & T. G. Birdsall.

The experimental situation is as follows: in each trial the subject is asked whether or not he has noticed the signal; in some trials the signal is really given (before white noise)—this is case SB; if no signal is given we have case B (white noise only); we assume that during a trial the testee associates subjective probabilities with SB and B and attributes utility coefficients for all experiments in which the instructions are the same, to the four pairs B yes, B no, SB yes, SB no ("yes" and "no" are the possible answers); the model of the anticipated benefit shows that the testee's reply is dependent on comparison of the relation of subjective probability with a certain expression of utility. If two appropriate standard distributions are imagined (with standard deviation = 1) which represent the frequencies of the cases XB and B as a function of the testee's expectation (dependent on the ratio of subjective probabilities) we refer to the frequency of the reply "yes" in case B (false alarm) as p_1 and the frequency of the reply "yes" in case SB (correct answer "yes") as p_2; it is apparent that probit (p_2–p_1) is a value which can be estimated and is not dependent on the degrees of utility, i.e. on the instructions; the value of the model can therefore be verified by changing the instructions.

Other models have been suggested, e.g. with choice reaction situations in which different decision criteria and latency times are taken into account.

(*c*) *Learning psychology*. Let us consider the following simple situation: the subject participates in a series of experiments; in each experiment he gives one of the two replies a_1 or a_2 (e.g. the blue or red light will flash on), after which the experimenter provides the solution e_1 or e_2 (he allows the red or blue light to flash). If this solution appears with a probability which is not dependent on the subject's replies we have what is known as an "independent" case, which we shall assume here. The models show the evolution of the subject's reply frequencies, and primarily of the frequencies after stabilization; they give reply probabilities for the nth trial, and above all asymptotic probabilities (e.g. p (a_1/e_2) is the probability of a reply a_1 after a solution e_2 in the preceding trial). A non-observable intermediate variable z is frequently used, known as the state of the subject. Frequently it is assumed that the number of possible states is finite; it may be said, e.g. that the test subject may be in the state z_0, in which there is a probability 1 that he will give a_1, in the state of complete uncertainty z_1, in which there is a probability $\frac{1}{2}$ that he will give the answer a_1, or in the state z_2 in which the probability of obtaining the reply a_1 is 0. We prepare a table of the transitional probabilities from one trial to the next (e.g. from z_i, e_j in trial n to z_h in trial n + 1); at least in the independent cases we therefore have a Markoff process between the states, and we can calculate the different reply probabilities, which are then compared with the experimental frequencies. Another possibility consists in assuming that the number of states is not finite, and each state is characterized by the probability z_1^n of the reply a_1 in the nth trial; we assume that a linear operator enables z_1^n to be calculated if z_1^{n-1} is known. These models were developed by R. R. Bush & F. Mosteller. W. K. Estes & P. Suppes consider a special model, defined as follows:

We obtain $z_1^n = (1 - V)z_1^{n-1} + V$, if the solution to the experiment n–1 was equal to e_1 and $z_1^n = (1 - V)z_1^{n-1}$, if it was e_2. A large number of stochastic teaching models of varying complexity have been developed to match different situations. It appears that Estes was the first author who managed to cover this subject in detail.

(*d*) *Social interaction.* In this case the formalization is based on various mathematical assumptions. In the first place graph theory is used to represent communications and connections between groups; an example of the notion which is useful in problems of communication analysis is given below: let R be the relation which defines the graph G; aRb signifies that a is in a direct relationship to b; if we now add the transitive relation R′ to R so that when aRb we have aR′b, and when aRb and bRc we obtain aR′c; the graph M(G), defined with R′, associates the transitive completion of G. aR′b signifies that a is directly or indirectly related to b; conversely, connections can be removed from G without altering M(G), so that we obtain a minimal graph which has the same transitive completeness as G. Matrix representations associated with graphs are often used. In addition, systems of differential equations are used for formalization.

Let us consider a quite typical example, proposed by H. A. Simon to express G. C. Homans' hypotheses on group dynamics (q.v.). If I, F, A and E represent the intensity of the interaction, the degree of friendship, the level of activity and the activity required by the environment, we have:

$$I = a_1F = a_2A, \frac{dF}{dt} = b(I - \beta t),$$

$$\frac{dA}{dt} = c_1(F - \gamma A) + c_2(E - A).$$

In this case, functions of the variables are inserted on the right-hand side; they are not precise but include partial derivations of a given sign.

Discussion of the different types of mathematical formalization is concerned primarily with their significance in psychology. Do they represent isomorphic mechanisms of the different kinds of mental activity, or are they methods of approximation and prediction for observed results? Representatives of the second position quote examples of models which fit the same conditions and are at the same time based on totally different mathematical principles. See *Decision processes; Factor analysis.*

Bibliography: Faverge, J. M.: Méthodes statistiques en psychol. appliquée, Vol. 3. Paris, 1965. **Luce, R. D., Bush, R. R. & Galanter, E.:** Handbook of mathematical psychology, 3 vols. New York, 1963–5. **Id.:** Readings in mathematical psychology, 2 vols. New York, 1965. **Restle, F. & Greeno, J. G.:** Introduction to mathematical psychology. London, 1970.

J. M. Faverge

Mating center (syn. *Sex behavior center*). The central-nervous, neuroanatomical, functional center of gravity in the autonomic hypothalamus (primarily the *nucleus ventromedialis*). The mating center plays a decisive part in the development and control of sexual behavior, in conjunction with the hormonal-sex center (McCleary & Moore, 1965) which represents the main production center of the hormonal factors RF (releasing factors) and IF (inhibiting factors), which release, synthesize and inhibit the HVL hormones (location: hypothalamus, primarily in the *nucleus infundibulus*). The mating center becomes specifically male or female through sexual hormones during the embryonal stage (in man) or shortly after birth (in various mammals) = differentiation of the hypothalamus. Recent experiments in animals have shown that predominantly male or female sexual behavior in male and female animals is later triggered exclusively by a female or male hypothalamus, and not by a sex-specific sexual hormone (Dörner, 1968). Disorders in the period of this differentiation of hypothalamic centers have a strong influence on subsequent sexual behavior (in all previously examined species of mammal, differentiation or development of these hypothalamic centers occurs after completion of the physical sexual differentiation, which occurs in man between the eighth and twelfth weeks of embryonal development). Recent research findings in this sphere have reopened the discussion as to the causes of sexually deviant behavior in man, e.g. homosexuality, transsexuality, etc.: disorders of hypothalamus differentiation dependent on the sexual hormones as a possible cause versus the theory of experience in early childhood as the cause of sexually deviant behavior (Neumann, 1970).

Bibliography: McCleary, R. A. & Moore, R. Y.: Subcortical mechanisms of behavior. New York, 1965. **Neumann, F.:** Tierexperimentelle Untersuchungen zur Transsexualitat. In: **Schmidt, G., Sigusch, V. & Schorsch, E.** (Eds.): Tendenzen der Sexualforschung. Stuttgart, 1970. **Voigt, K.-D. & Schmidt, H.:** Sexual-hormone. Hamburg, 1968. *H.M.*

Matriarchy; matriarchate. Theory developed by J. J. Bachofen (but no longer completely accepted) according to which a period of promiscuous sexual relationships as the first and original social form was followed by a matriarchate in which relationships were defined on a matrilinear basis. Hunters and collectors in ancient times did not in fact live promiscuously but primarily in stable monogamous marriages. Ethnological results cast doubt on the theory of Jung's school, according to which the matriarchate embodied an unconscious stage in the psychological development of man (and did not correspond to the supposedly "male" spirit) (E. Neumann). Recent archeological finds have shown that Bachofen was not wrong in his supposition that matriarchal social forms played an important part in the Mediterranean area in former times (Çatal Hüyük in Anatolia).

Bibliography: Mellaart, J.: Çatal Hüyük, London, 1967. **Schmidbauer, W.:** Mythos und Psychologie. Munich, 1970. *W.Sch.*

Matrices test. Non-verbal intelligence test which in the opinion of its proponents covers a general intelligence factor (see *Culture-free intelligence test; Progressive Matrices Test*). In these tests the subject is called upon to complete partial, rectangular figures, known as matrices. Several choices are offered and the correct one must be selected. Matrices tests are primarily used for intelligence testing of subjects suffering from speech defects. *P.S.*

Matrix. 1. Any two-dimensional composition of associated values. **2.** Mathematical: a form of representation for n parameters with m linear relationships; it is possible, e.g., to show linear equation systems in a matrix. The numerical solution to these equation systems presented in matrix form can be determined through the determinant. Specific rules of calculation apply in this case. The transposed matrix M. A′ is a matrix which contains the same components as the matrix A, but is reflected around the main diagonal. An inverse matrix is one which plays a similar role in the matrix calculation to the reciprocal of a number in real number algebra. It is only possible in non-singular matrices, i.e. in matrices whose determinant is not equal to zero.

Bibliography: Horst, P.: Matrix algebra for social scientists. New York, 1963. *G.Mi.*

Matrix algebra. A branch of algebra concerned with the formal treatment of matrices. Matrix calculation is dependent on specific rules, e.g. the multiplication of matrices is not commutative, i.e. in general $A \cdot B \neq B \cdot A$ holds good. *G.Mi.*

Maturation. An autonomous process of somatic, psychological and mental differentiation and integration spread over developmental stages and phases which condition and build on one another in the course of time; as a result of this process the individual's growth (see *Maturity*) is completed and consolidated somatically, mentally and spiritually as well as socially, and he can thus adapt to life; in each stage of development four phenomena can be found: latent disposition (*anlage*, q.v.), "budding", real growth, inclusion in an organization which is effective as a whole. As organ and function systems, skills and abilities develop, the organism remains active in all its parts and the person continues as a whole.

The following stages are distinguished: *new-born baby* or *neonate* (the first ten days), *suckling* or *baby* (till the end of the first year), *infant* or *pre-school child* (until 5 to 6 years), *junior* or *child* (till 12 years), *juvenile* or *adolescent* (female till 17, and male till 18 years), the *growing person* or *young adult*, the *adult* or *mature adult* and the *old man* or *woman*. There is no general agreement about terminology and precise demarcation.

Somatic, psychic and social developments take place side by side or correspond to one another, but traditional notions of psychosomatic disintegration and senile decay have been corrected in the light of the findings of the most recent research into the psychology of aging (q.v.) and geriatrics (q.v.) (see *Gerontology*). Differences specific to human ontogenesis need to be noted. The absence of any development in the testicles or the ovaries from the third to the tenth or twelfth year while psychic differentiation is continuing enables man to experience childhood; the time lag between bodily growth and full sexual development during youth and the growing period, which is due to certain hormones, allows man time for learning and for social adaptation as preconditions for the evolution of civilization. The periods of *dependence* and *dysharmony* in all areas are favorable to psychophysical humanization, language acquisition and the establishment of relationships with other people; they are important factors in the development of the individual and the anthropological structure.

In man's development, autonomous maturation and exogenous education or learning processes must blend harmoniously. For instance, a young child can learn to walk only when certain organs have matured, and thinking (q.v.) is possible only after the completion of the necessary growth in symbolic, perceptual, concrete and formal thought operations (see *Development*).

Maturation which is too rapid (somatic or psychic *acceleration*, q.v.) or too slow (*retardation*, q.v., deceleration) can often be the cause of discrepancy and dysharmony in bodily and mental and spiritual development, and it is also possible for individual phases of maturation to be too strongly emphasized endogenously, thereby causing marked disturbances in social adaptation. See *Adolescence; Child psychology; Educational psychology; Infancy; Youth; Adult psychology.*

H. J. Engels

Maturity. The state existing when somatic, psychic and mental differentiation and integration (see *Maturation*) are complete and consolidated, and when there is readiness to fulfill tasks facing the individual at any given time and to cope with the demands made by life.

While in Central Europe girls have reached sexual maturity at 15½ years of age and boys at 16 years, complete *somatic* maturity cannot be said to exist before the age of 17, and possibly not until 21.

Psychic maturity is shown in adolescent females at the age of 17 years, and in adolescent males at the age of 18, by the fact that their aspirations and will have reached lasting stability, and the search for a theme in life is over.

Social maturity in the case of growing females is reached at the age of 22 and in the case of males at the age of 24. It is marked by the appearance of a positive creative urge and the recognition of the supra-individual aspects of the socio-political life, to which may be added their final harnessing to some goal and fusion of sex and eros. The process of detachment from the parents and the still persisting state of exclusion from the civilizing but complicated adult world, as well as the divisions into groups of tyrannical and leveling sub-cultures are overcome. The individual, differentiated in body, mind and spirit and integrated in a personal whole, is ready for the community and the civilization in which he finds himself. From ancient times, people in Europe were said to have come of age on completing their twenty-fifth year; for example, that was the *legitima aetas* for the priesthood of the Roman Catholic Church, the right of the master-tradesman to train apprentices, and for full membership of gilds, companies and brotherhoods.

In all known civilizations some special ceremony has served to mark the attainment of certain degrees of maturity (confirmation, the knightly accolade, etc.).

Experience has led social bodies, collectivities and organizations to link certain degrees of maturity with definite ages, yet there have also been cases where arbitrary dates have been fixed, such as, for example, the lowering of the voting age, etc.

H. J. Engels

Maturitas praecox. Premature maturation, in particular of the sex organs (see *Pubertas praecox*). Children appear adult in their whole form of action. Their movements are often deliberately slow and their language is characterized by carefully chosen formulations which are not those of normal children. They are often concerned with religious or philosophical problems which are usually the preserve of adults. *M.Sa.*

Maudsley Personality Inventory. Developed by H. J. Eysenck in 1956. 24 items characteristic of neuroticism (N) and extraversion (E) have been selected on the basis of correlation-statistical criteria from the MMQ and tests of J. P. Guilford. (A short scale for market research purposes consists of 6 items for N and 6 for E.) The total values of the N and E scales are interpreted. The halving reliability is $r = 0.88$ for the N scale and $r = 0.83$ for the E scale. The coefficients for the short scale are $r = 0.79$ (N) and $r = 0.71$ (E). The validity of this inventory has been confirmed on the one hand by significant discriminations between normally healthy subjects and clinical groups, and on the other by major correlations between the MPI scales and other tests of the same personality dimensions (for $Er = 0.35–0.80$; for $Nr = 0.34–0.77$). See *Eysenck Personality Inventory*. *P.G.*

Maximum effect. The phenomenon (which can be explained psychologically and by information theory) according to which a sign in a given field necessarily assumes a maximum obtrusiveness when it occurs with the relative frequency $p = 0.37$. The maximum effect was first described by H. Frank and used to explain esthetic processes. *H.R.*

Maximum likelihood method. A method of statistical estimation introduced by R. A. Fisher. In this method a value is chosen as the estimation of the parameter of a data quantity at which the probability of the observed data quantity reaches a maximum. In many cases the maximum likelihood method gives estimates of maximum accuracy, i.e. with lowest standard error.

Bibliography: Fisher, R. A.: Theory of statistical estimation. Proc. Cambr. Phil. Soc., 1925, *22*, 700–25.

G.Mi.

Maxwell disks. The colored disks, split along the radius so that they can be overlapped in varying proportions, which are rotated on a *color wheel* in experiments on *color mixture*. *G.D.W.*

Mayer's waves. More or less periodic fluctuations in blood pressure which are due to vegetative sources and generally reflect physiological retardations in the blood pressure regulating mechanisms. With a cycle duration of ten or more seconds they can be distinguished—as blood pressure fluctuations of the third order—from respiratory fluctuations of the second order and heart frequency dependent fluctuations of the first order; they are linked with fluctuations in heart frequency and influence cerebral activity and awareness. *E.D.*

Maze. An experimental system used in human and animal learning and in instrumental conditioning of animals. After finding the correct pathway among the blind alleys, the animal is rewarded at the goal. Learning increments are shown by the increased speed of a run on repeated tests, and by avoidance of blind paths. One variety used with humans requires the blindfold subject to trace the maze with his finger. *P.S.*

Maze test (syn. *Labyrinth test; McCollough effect*). A specific color aftereffect described by C. McCollough (1965) and named after her.

After repeated, alternating presentations of two colored strip patterns, e.g. with vertical red and horizontal green stripes, the bright stripes in a vertical black and white striped pattern appear greenish; in a horizontal stripe pattern they are pink to red. The maze test is one of the more recent aspects of research which require cooperation between neurophysiologists and perception researchers. The effect is explained by the shape and color-specific organized, receptive fields in certain cortex neurons of the visual cortex (areas 18 and 19).

Bibliography: McCollough, C.: Color adaptation of edge-detectors in the human visual system. Science, 1965, *149*, 1115–16. **Hajos, A.:** Verlauf formspezifischer Farbadaptationen im visuellen System des Menschen. Psychol. Beitr. 1969, *11*, 95–114. *A.Ha.*

McDougall, William. B. 22/6/1871 in Lancashire; d. 28/11/1938 in Durham, frequently called himself arrogant. Some such quality of unsparingness with himself and others seems to be the key to a life of productivity and conflict. Of mixed English and Scottish (Highland) descent, educated at a German Gymnasium and at the Universities of Manchester, Cambridge (Scholar and Fellow of St John's College) and Göttingen, and at St Thomas's Hospital, London, he was a scientist and physician with an exceptionally wide background, aiming for the highest and getting nearly all he aimed for. Yet involvement in a tragedy set him to traveling (the Torres Straits Anthropological Expedition, issuing in productive field-work). As Wilde Reader in Mental Philosophy at Oxford he encountered opposition to his subject and to himself. His work in military psychiatry (World War I) he found rewarding but conflict-ridden. His move to the USA (1920) led quickly to confrontation through his incautiousness in lectures on public affairs. His involvement in parapsychology and his experiment on the inheritance of acquired characteristics were not accepted by others as by himself. McDougall began as a physiological researcher, and produced a text of merit (1905). But his speculative and scientific bents conflicted with each other, issuing in the pioneering *Social Psychology* (1908), and later in the unfortunately titled *Group Mind* (1920). Yet he also systematized with some success (*Outline of Psychology*, 1923), and produced an *Abnormal Psychology* (1926), still useful. His *Body and Mind* (1911) (argument for animism) shows his methodical advocacy of unpopular causes, and makes it difficult to believe those who claimed him as a behaviorist on the strength of *Psychology: The Study of Behavior* (1912). (His logomachy with J. B. Watson settled any such question.) Later works were mostly (e.g. *Character and the Conduct of Life*, 1927) application and popularization. McDougall is remembered intellectually for his advocacy of: hormic psychology (behavior involves purposive goal-striving, is not completely explicable in mechanistic terms); instinct (a theory of innate propensities, linked to emotions); sentiments (ordered systems of emotions, especially the self-regarding sentiment); and the "group mind" (an organized system of interacting energies, operating through the whole group). McDougall thought and lived his psychology more than most—"As a departmental chief he was beyond compare" (Adams, 1939). His work was for long influential, and in part may well be due for refinement and revaluation.

Main works: An introduction to social psychology, London, 1908 ([30]1950). The group mind. Cambridge, 1920. Autobiography, in: Murchison, C. (Ed.), A history of psychology in autobiography, Vol. 1. Worcester, Mass., 1930, 191–223.

Bibliography: Adams, D. K.: William McDougall. Psychol. Rev., 1939, *46*, 1–8. *J.A.C.*

McNemar test. A non-parametric method of testing the difference between two correlated distributions of alternative characteristics. For statistical testing purposes we determine:

$$\chi^2 = \frac{(b - c)^2}{b + c} \text{ (df = 1)}$$

in which b and c are the frequencies in the diagonal cells of the correlation schema. The χ^2 applies to the difference between the peripheral summed distributions in this schema.

Bibliography: McNemar, Q.: Note on sampling error of the differences between correlated proportions or percentages. Psychometrika, 1967, *12*, 153–4.

G.Mi.

Mean. 1. The *arithmetic mean* (q.v.). **2.** A measure of central tendency.

Meaning. A much discussed philosophical concept, which is highly ambiguous in psychology too. In particular, meaning denotes the connection between sign and signified; and, in more general usage, the signified. Analysis of context is obviously important if the meaning of meaning is to be elicited proficiently.

Meaningfulness: (according to R. Bergius) the "co-references of the concept to other data of the same or other classes". Meaningfulness is crucial in determining to what extent certain matter can be learnt.

Measurement of meaning, in the sense of connotative meaning, is chiefly carried out by two methods: (1) determining the association value (Noble, 1952): the number of associated words in a short (2″–3″) and longer (7″) period is determined; (2) by C. E. Osgood's semantic differential (q.v.) (P. R. Hofstätter: polarity profile, q.v.).

Bibliography: Bergius, R.: Einfache Lernvorgänge. Handbuch der Psychologie, Vols 1 & 2. Göttingen, 1964, 153 ff. **Noble, C. E.:** An analysis of meaning. Psychol. Rev., 1952, *59*, 421–30. **Ogden, C. K. & Richards, I. A.:** The meaning of meaning. London, 1923, [8]1946. *H.-J.A.*

Mean quartile (syn. *Quartile deviation*). A statistical characteristic for the dispersion of distributions. The mean quartile is represented symbolically by Q and is used as a dispersion measurement for ordinal variables; it represents half the distance between the third (upper) and first (lower) quartile. *G.Mi.*

Means-end relationship. A concept associated with the American learning theorist E. C. Tolman and his school of "purposive behaviorism". An object, distance, direction, etc., intervening between a means and an end (goal) which is known to the animal as a result of previous experience in the field, and is therefore a partial determinant of its behavior. *G.D.W.*

Mean square. The average of the squared values in a distribution. The mean square is an intermediate value which can be employed usefully for different calculations, e.g. in determining variances or in variance analysis. *G.Mi.*

Mean square deviation. See *Standard deviation.*

Mean values. Statistical characteristics for the central tendency of a distribution. The best known are the arithmetic mean, the median or central value, the mode, the harmonic mean and the geometric mean. Selection of the most suitable mean value to characterize a distribution is dependent on the nature of the investigated variables and on the form of the distribution. *G.Mi.*

Mean values, comparison of. The test of the difference between the characteristic values of the central trend of two or more distributions to determine statistical significance is defined as the comparison of mean values. In the case of variables with a normal distribution it is carried out in a dual sample test with a t test, or, if there are more than two samples, by variance analysis using the arithmetic mean values. In variables without normal distribution, other characteristics are compared with the central trend (e.g. median test). *G.Mi.*

Mean values, distribution of. If a number of independent samples are taken from a population, the mean values of these samples (M1, M2) are distributed with a standard deviation more or less normally around the population mean value, even if the values of the populations are not normally distributed. *G.Mi.*

Mean variation. A measurement which is used occasionally to describe the dispersion of distributions. It is the average value of the absolute deviations of the measured values from their mean. See *Standard deviation.* *G.Mi.*

Measured values. Quantitative values determined by measurement which show the degree of emphasis of a specific characteristic. Measured values may be on the quantification level of ordinal, interval or ratio scales (see *Scaling*). Derived measured values are obtained by mathematical operations to characterize the intensity of the feature concerned (e.g. percentages). *G.Mi.*

Measurement is the attribution of numerical values to objects so that specific relationships between the values correspond to similar relationships between the values correspond to similar relationships between the objects. Measurement in the narrower sense of the word presupposes a continuously variable characteristic of the object. *G.Mi.*

Measurement in psychology. In contrast to the classical natural sciences, psychology does not have at its disposal a uniform system of measurement. At the present day, the various aspects of behavior which are of psychological interest appear to be so incommensurable that very few, if any, attempts are now made to apply a uniform method of measurement to the individual psychological disciplines. That is why, in the course of the history of psychology (q.v.), different methods of measurement have been evolved for different areas or fields of psychology. Thus, in psychophysics (q.v.), for example, scaling methods (q.v.) are chiefly used, neuropsychology measures with the methods of physiology (chemistry and physics, etc.), and finally, experimental psychology (q.v.) and psychodiagnostics (q.v.) use very diverse methods of measurement which are described under the appropriate terms. See *Test theory; Psychometrics.* *R.Hä.*

Measurement theory. The theoretical basis of measurement, i.e. the representation of a quantity of given objects and the empirically observable relationship between them as a quantity of numerical values and relations between the latter. Measurement theory indicates the conditions (assumptions, peripheral conditions) under which an empirical relative value can be converted into a significant numerical relative value with the help of specific models (measurement models). Psychologists have always devoted considerable interest to measurement theory because of the problems which arise in recording psychological variables.

Bibliography: Suppes, P. & Zinnes, J. L.: Basic measurement theory. In: **Luce, R. D.,** *et al.* (Eds.): Handbook of mathematical psychology, Vol. 1. New York, 1963. **Lord, M. R. & Novick, F. M.:** Statistical theories of mental test scores. Reading, 1968.

W.-H.B.

Mechanical learning. See *Learning, rote; Memory.*

Mechanism. 1. See *Determinism* (4 & 5). **2.** A stimulus-response system. **3.** A machine or system with the predictability and limitations of a machine (see *Machine learning*). **4.** A habit (q.v.). **5.** A drive (q.v.), instinct (q.v.) or motive (q.v.).

Mecholyl test. A functional test proposed by D. H. Funkenstein (Funkenstein test) to determine the reactivity of the autonomic nervous system. The cholinergic substance methacholine chloride (Mecholyl) is adminstered intravenously to the subject. The extent and duration of the blood pressure reduction is taken as the determining factor. The test does, however, offer only limited reliability. The blood pressure reaction alone cannot be considered as a measurement of autonomic reactivity. The relationship between reaction and therapeutic success determined by Funkenstein has not been definitely confirmed. [N.B.: *Mecholyl* (methacholine chloride) is not now manufactured.]

Bibliography: Funkenstein, D. H., Greenblatt, M. & Solomon, H. C.: An autonomic nervous system test of prognostic significance in relation to electroshock treatment. Psychosom. Med., 1952, *14*, 347–62. **Rose, J. I.:** The Funkenstein Test—a review of literature. Acta. Psychiatr., 1962, *38*, 124. **Stenback, A. & Rilva, P.:** The use of histamine and methacholine in testing autonomic response. J. Psychosom. Res., 1964, 111–18.

W.J.

Median (syn. *Central value; 50th centile*). A statistical characteristic for the central trend of a distribution. The value which divides the distribution into two identical halves so that 50% of cases are situated on either side is said to be *median.* In the case of non-symmetrical distributions, the median characterizes the central trend more adequately than the arithmetic mean since it is not influenced by extreme values. *G.Mi.*

Media research. A branch of mass communications research which is concerned with those aspects of the mass media (radio, television, newspapers, etc.) which are of significance in advertising. The areas of study are (*a*) the range and socio-demographic and psychological structure of those reached by the media; (*b*) the consumption and media utilization habits of those persons; (*c*) the features of the media which are relevant to publicity (media image); (*d*) the interaction between the advertising message and medium and the effects of variations of placing and density of inclusion of advertising in the media. See *Mass media.* *H.H.*

Mediator. 1. An intervening system receiving and transmitting information (q.v.). **2.** One who assists two or more alienated individuals or groups to come to terms.

Meditation. I. The word "meditation" is derived from the Latin *meditari,* meaning both to "practice" and to "reflect". Meditation may therefore be defined as the practice of reflection. More precisely, it is the internalization process by which a man becomes aware of his deepest self and the ground of this self. It is a universal human experience. Both *cognitive* and *affective* faculties are involved, as is the body, whose posture is most important for successful meditation. The goal of this total involvement is to experience its object and not merely to contemplate it. Meditation is not the thoughts about actuality that a man might have, but a union with, and being grasped and even overwhelmed by, that reality. Rational thought can evaluate or prepare for this experience, but can never substitute for it. Yet the experience is not "thoughtless" or irrational. It involves a mode of thought which is not analytic but comprehensive and contemplative, and may therefore be called *pre-rational* or *supra-rational.* In meditation one becomes aware of one's deepest *self* (q.v.), which enables one to come to oneself, to find oneself, and be at one with self. This process of internalization is a universal human phenomenon occurring both in the pre-Christian East and in the Christian West; it has developed in different ways and stages.

1. *Meditation and related concepts.*

(*a*) *Observation or simple contemplation*, in contrast to meditation, is principally concerned with rational knowing about, or thinking about; it analyzes its objects discursively. Yet the more mature it becomes, the more it approaches meditation. Eventually it passes into, or (better) is *transformed into*, meditation.

(*b*) *Therapeutic or religious meditation.* In *therapeutic* meditation, the divided man seeks to regain possession of his self (q.v.) or unity with himself—which does not exclude union with the "ground of being". In *religious* meditation, a man seeks union with the ground of being; this presupposes union with himself, and culminates in the surrender of this found self to the ground of being. In the one case, it is a question of the *healing* of a sick man; in the other, of the *sanctification* or salvation of a sinful man. Sin is here understood as being cut off or absent from the ground of being.

(*c*) There is a distinction between the *monist* and *non-monist* views of meditation. The monist view explains the experience of union as signifying that all men and things are expressions of the one ground of being, to which they return and into which they dissolve like the waves in the sea. The non-monist form experiences in this union the particularity of things and especially of human beings; the more personalized the self of a man, the more closely he is at one with the ground of being. This is the basis of the distinction between the non-personal (monist) interpretation (held particularly in the East) and the *personal* (approaching the Christian) view of meditation.

2. *History of meditation in the West.* One might begin with the Platonic "union with God" (*Symposium*, 210e/211b), and Plotinus (*Enneads*, VI 9.11). The influence of neo-Platonism (as brought to fruition by Plotinus) was far-reaching in Christianity; it extended from Augustine (d. 430) to (especially) Meister Eckhart (d. 1327). Meditation is usually connected with supernatural mysticism (q.v.); particularly with St John of the Cross (d. 1591). The Reformation, rationalism and the Enlightenment were not favorable to the broad stream of meditation running through the Middle Ages up to the beginning of the modern age. However, it has gained new life in recent decades, both in the Catholic (Dessauer, 1961; Lotz, 1961) and in the Protestant traditions (Happich, 1948; Melzer, 1957), and has been enriched by the heritage of the East (Déchanet, 1968; Dürckheim, 1971). Methods of meditation were developed both in the East (Zen Buddhism and Yoga) and in the West (the Spiritual Exercises of Ignatius of Loyola). Although meditation corresponds to the deepest needs of human nature, and often arises spontaneously, the externally oriented Western man sometimes needs appropriate training (see *Meditation* II). If we inquire into the psychological basis of meditation, we find that the rational and conceptual idea of understanding is primarily important in the modern sciences, but not in the meditative or "contemplative" life, which arises from the pre-conceptual imagination, in which myth

(q.v.) and art are rooted. Its basis is supra-conceptual comprehension by the mind directed toward the transcendental (mystery) whence we derive philosophy and religion. See *Religion, psychology of.*

Bibliography: Bitter, W. (Ed.): Meditation in Religion und Psychotherapie. Stuttgart, 1958. **Déchanet, J. M.:** Christian Yoga. London, 1968. **Dessauer, P.:** Die naturale Meditation. Munich, 1961. **Dürckheim, K.:** Im Zeichen der grossen Erfahrung. Munich, 1951. **Id.:** Durchbruch zum Wesen. Zürich, 1964. **Id.:** The way of transformation. London, 1971. **Happich, C.:** Anleitung zur Meditation. Darmstadt, [3]1948. **James, H.:** The varieties of religious experience. Cambridge, Mass. & London, 1902. **Knowles, D.:** The English mystical tradition. London, 1964. **Lotz, J. B.:** Meditation im Alltag. Frankfurt, [3]1961. **Id.:** Der Mensch im Sein. Freiburg, 1967. **Id.:** Einübung ins Meditieren am NT. Frankfurt, [2]1968. **Melzer, F.:** Meditation in Ost und West. Stuttgart, 1957.

J. B. Lotz

II. *Eastern meditation.* Meditation is important in the East as a typical religious exercise. It has existed in India and China, the cradles of Asian culture, from the earliest times. The general name for meditation and meditative techniques in India is *Yoga* ("to bind together", "to yoke together"). A distinction is made between the yoga of knowledge (*jnana yoga*), of loving surrender (*bhakti yoga*), and of dutiful behavior (*karma yoga*). The relatively late *yoga sutra* (fifth century A.D.) names the eight steps of the way of Yoga, which are the requisite somatic and psychic behaviors. *Buddhism* has been linked with Yoga from its beginnings. In Theravada Buddhism (in Ceylon and South East Asia) meditation is joined with Yoga. The meditation texts of the Pali canon enjoin training in attention and concentration (*satipatthana*). In China, partly under the influence of Chinese meditation (particularly the Taoist form) various modes of Buddhist meditation developed: e.g. *mandala* meditation (visual concentration upon a symbol with a transcendental meaning); *amitabha* meditation (concentration upon the image or upon the names of the Amitabha Buddha, repeated in many invocations); and (most important in Mahayana Buddhism) Zen meditation, which began in China (sixth century A.D.) and reached maturity in Japan (from the thirteenth century). The Japanese word *zen* means literally "sinking" or "submersion". The two characteristic practices of Zen, *zazen* and *koan*, are intended to induce concentration. *Zazen* (= sitting in meditation) in its bodily prescriptions (a specific position with legs folded, rhythmic breathing and exclusion of sensory images, emotions and processes) is very similar to the first steps of classical Yoga, but its purpose goes beyond quietness to enlightenment. The practice of *koan*, which is often a paradoxical and intellectually insoluble task, creates a high level of concentration to prepare for the breakthrough to experience. In Zen enlightenment it is the self which is experienced, the self grounded in the ground of being and bound up in the All. The experience gives a spiritual contact with absolute reality; it has different levels of intensity, and is accompanied by strong emotions; it is experienced as a psychic liberation. Among the many other forms of meditation found in the East are *Vendanta* in Hinduism, and the Confucian and Taoistic modes in China.

The basic characteristic of Eastern meditation is the close connection of somatic and psychic elements in the process. Body posture and rhythmic breathing are held to be necessary conditions for inner realization. The anthropological concept of the unity of body and spirit in man is present, though not necessarily reflected upon, in all Eastern meditation (see *Mind-body problem*). The integration of the unified human nature reveals the way to realize the self. Moreover, Eastern meditation postulates an experience: the total (objective and subjective) experience of reality. In some (though not all) forms of Eastern meditation, intuitive knowledge is primary; in all forms a man's physical and psychic faculties are wholly applied. Sensory means are used to attain outer and inner concentration (besides body posture and rhythmic breathing, e.g. visual fixation on a point or symbol, observation of bodily processes, etc.). However, in transcendental meditation a man goes beyond the conscious ego and the objective environment to reach a state of immersion. This is a state of having broken through the world of the senses and the changing consciousness toward transcendence. In all Asian countries, meditation is regarded as a religious practice not only because of its goal but because of the ascetic struggle which accompanies it, and its place in the cult. The experience of meditation seeks liberation from ties to the phenomenal world, the fulfillment of human existence, and contact with absolute reality. The experience itself is always inexpressible; it is interpreted according to the religious and metaphysical situation of the meditating person. In Asia the interpretation is usually humanistico-ethical and cosmico-monist, although (particularly in India) theistic interpretations are also offered. In recent decades, Eastern meditation has won popularity in the West. This explains the efforts which have been made recently to introduce the techniques and methods of Eastern meditation (especially Yoga and Zen) into Christian spirituality.

Bibliography: **Benoit, H.:** The supreme doctrine. New York & London, 1955. **Boss, M.:** A psychiatrist discovers India. London, 1966. **Conze, E.:** Buddhism: its essence and development. Oxford, 1953. **Dumoulin, H.:** Östliche Meditation und christliche Mystik. Freiburg, 1966. **Id. & Sasaki, R. F.:** The development of Chinese Zen after the sixth patriarch. New York, 1953. **Eliade, M.:** Le yoga: immortalité et liberté. Paris, 1954. **Enomiya, H. M.:** Zen-Buddhismus. Cologne, 1966. **Govinda, L. A.:** Grundlagen tibetischer Mystik. Zürich, 1957. **Humphreys, C.:** Zen buddhism. London, 1949. **Id.:** Concentration and meditation. London, [3]1968. **Sato, K.:** Psychology of personality. Tokyo, [2]1953. **Suzuki, D. T.:** Essays in Zen buddhism. 3 Vols. London, 1927, 1933, 1934. **Id.:** Introduction to Zen buddhism. New York, [2]1949. **Id.:** The Zen doctrine of no-mind. London, 1949. **Id.:** Manual of Zen buddhism. London, [2]1950. **Id.:** What is Zen. London, 1971. **Watts, A.:** The spirit of Zen. London, [2]1955. **Id.:** The way of Zen. New York & London, 1957. **Wentz, W. Y. E.:** Tibetan Yoga and secret doctrines. Oxford, 1935. **Zimmer, H.:** Philosophie und Religion Indiens. Zürich, 1961.

H. Dumoulin

Medium. In spiritualism: person through whom communications purporting to come from deceased persons are obtained. Such communications are usually oral but may also be written. See *Automatist*. *Trance medium:* a medium who functions in a state of trance (q.v.). *Physical medium:* a medium who produces paranormal physical effects. *Materializing medium:* a medium who produces materializations (q.v.). *J.B.*

Medulla oblongata. The extended medulla which—as the myelencephalon—forms the section of the brain which joins the remainder of the brain to the spinal medulla, and is situated in the area of the nape of the neck. In addition to important motor (efferent) and sensory (afferent) nerve paths, the *medulla oblongata* contains many vital central areas (synaptic commutations) such as the respiratory, circulatory and other regulating centers. All life processes cease immediately if it is destroyed. *E.D.*

Megalomania. The state of having delusions of *grandeur* (q.v.). It does not imply the presence of mania used either as a disease label or as a descriptive term. *B.B.*

Meier Art Judgment Test. A test for assessment of an aspect of artistic ability—artistic judgment. The subject is presented with one hundred pairs of pictures for comparison (a reproduction of an acknowledged masterpiece and a slightly altered, inadequate copy), and has to select the esthetically better one. S. is rated according to the number of appropriate choices. *H.J.A.*

Meinong, Alexius. B. 17/7/1853 in Lemberg; d. 27/11/1920 in Graz. An Austrian philosopher and psychologist and pupil of F. Brentano (q.v.). From 1882 until his death,

Meinong was Professor of philosophy at the University of Graz; in 1894 he founded the first Austrian psychological laboratory and was the main representative of the Graz school (q.v.), which included C. von Ehrenfels (q.v.), V. Benussi and S. Witasek.

Meinong's philosophical views grew out of Brentano's philosophical psychology. His most important contribution to philosophy was his "theory of objects". According to the experiential condition, i.e. imagination, thinking, feeling and desire, Meinong distinguished four classes of object: the object proper, the objective, the dignitative and the desiderative. An object (that which is "intended" by thought) may "exist" or "subsist". Meinong's contributions to psychology often approximate to gestaltist ideas. In his work on the psychology of complexions and relations (1891) he treated the same theme examined shortly before by Ehrenfels in his work on gestalt qualities. In philosophy, Meinong's emphasis on concepts not as abstractions but as "objective realities", and his analysis of assumptions (*Annahmen*), had considerable influence on Bertrand Russell.

Main works: Über Annahmen, 1907. Über die Stellung der Gegenstandstheorie im Systeme der Wissenschaften, 1907. Über Möglichkeit und Wahrscheinlichkeit, 1915. Gesammelte Abhandlungen, Vols. 1–3, 1914.

Bibliography: Martinak, E.: Meinong als Mensch und Lehrer. Leipzig, 1925. **Russell, B.:** Introduction to mathematical philosophy. London, 1919. **Id.:** The analysis of mind. London, 1921. *W.W.*

Meissner's corpuscles. Receptors for pressure detection. Located in the papilla of the dermis and particularly numerous in the fingertips. Length about 1/10 mm, width about 1/20 mm. See *Sense organs:* skin sense. *H.L.*

Mel. A unit of a ratio scale for subjective judgment of pitch (q.v.).

Melancholic type. A slow temperament with a tendency to depression or fanatic idealism. A medieval term. See *Type.*

Bibliography: Müri, W.: Melancholie und schwarze Galle, Mus. Helv., 1953, *10;* 1953, *21.* *W.K.*

Melatonin. A hormone present in high concentrations, primarily in the pineal gland. It is, however, probably formed at several different points and not in the epiphysis itself. Melatonin can be considered as the cell and tissue hormone and is chemically related to serotonin. It is antagonistic to the melanocyte stimulating hormones (MSH) which foster the formation of skin pigments. It is very probable that melatonin plays a part in regulation of the circadian rhythm. There are close relations with the sex gland hormones; this is shown, e.g. by pineal extirpation and tumors.

Bibliography: Reiss, M.: Neuroendocrinology and psychiatry, a critical assessment of the present status. Int. J. Neuropsychiat., 1967, *3,* 441–63. *W.J.*

Mellinhoff's illusion. In this illusion the dotted line is in fact a continuation of the lower of the two parallel lines, but appears to be at a higher level between the parallel lines. *C.D.F.*

Melody. A rhythmic succession of musical notes perceived as a meaningful unit. The smallest components of the melody are known as motifs. The esthetic effect of the melody and its significance in the context of larger forms as a theme are based essentially on the unitary character maintained in certain transformations (e.g. by transposition, rhythmic enlargement and reduction, reversals). The melody as an independent quality which extends its component parts (von Ehrenfels) was a primary example in the development of the gestalt concept. See *Ganzheit.* *B.Sch.*

Membership group. See *Group.*

Membrana tympani. The tympanic membrane, which is stretched at an angle across the end of the outer auditory passage. It transmits the sound oscillations through the auditory ossicles to the inner ear. The membrane is a roughly circular disk with a diameter of about 1 cm and a thickness of about 1/10 mm. A distinction is made between a small, loose area (*the pars flaccida*) and a large taut section (the *pars tensa*). The following tissue layers of the membrane are encountered from the outside inward: the *stratum cutaneum*, the *stratum radiatum*, the *stratum circulare*, while the inner termination is formed by the *stratum mucosum*, which consists of a mucous membrane. See *Sense organs:* the ear.

Bibliography: **Couplan, R. E.:** Gray's Anatomy, London, 1967. *G.A.*

Memories, first. The earliest childhood memories (of an adult). Memory capacity is already observable on the first day of a child's life, but memory matures slowly and events can be remembered over an extended period of time only after the third year of life. The earliest (material) memories extend back to the end of the second year of life (see *Repression; Freud*). *K.E.P.*

Memory (*Retention*). **I.** A memory is an organism's unwritten record of some past event. The experimental study of memory deals with the composition of memories, their interaction, and the processes which occur over a period of time and produce forgetting as measured on retention tests. The German psychologist Ebbinghaus (q.v.) first developed laboratory methods for studying memory in 1885, and provided the first quantitative law for the rate at which memories fade with time.

1. *Methods.* Superficially, the experimental study of memory appears simple. First, to gain initial control of a memory, it is established in the laboratory by giving learning trials on a task, say, a list of words. After a period of time, the memory is measured by asking S. to recall (reproduce) the words. The number recalled is usually less than could be recalled immediately after learning. If the retention interval is further lengthened, still greater *forgetting* will be observed. But, that forgetting occurs over time needs no demonstration; this observation merely defines the problems. What causes the decline in performance? Do all memories fade at the same rate? As will be seen, attempts to answer such questions frequently require somewhat more complicated experimental procedures.

A basic fact is that the better a task is learned—the more firmly a memory is established—the slower the rate of forgetting. Most people know from experience that this is true. However, consider the question about the rate of forgetting for different kinds of tasks. A list of words is said to be highly meaningful as compared with a list of nonsense syllables (e.g. QUF, RUW, BOC). Which will be forgotten most rapidly? Initially, learning trials are given on each type of list. If the same number of trials is given on both lists, the strength of the memories will differ because learning occurs far more rapidly for a list of words than for a list of nonsense syllables. Given this, it would be expected that retention would be better for words than for syllables. Such a procedure doesn't tell us whether this difference in retention is due to the difference in level or strength of the established memories, or whether the syllables are forgotten more rapidly, or both. Obviously, if we are to discover which is forgotten more rapidly, the memories for the two types of lists must be equal in strength prior to the retention interval. When such equality is established, it is found that there is little if any difference in the rate of forgetting of different materials. A list of common words, very quickly learned, will be forgotten as rapidly as a list of nonsense syllables which are learned very slowly. But, both are forgotten. Why?

2. *Interference.* One of the factors long believed to be critically involved in the loss of memory with the passage of time is interference from other memories. This belief rests on hundreds of experiments in which interference between and among memories has been studied. The techniques of study are so fundamental that some detail is justified. Paired-associate lists may be used to illustrate a way of introducing interference. With these lists S. learns a series of response terms to a series of stimulus terms. For example, he must learn to respond with LAW when COW is presented, to respond with PEN when RUG is presented, and so on. The words COW and RUG are stimulus terms; LAW and PEN response terms. Ten to twelve such pairs may be used in a list and on successive learning trials the pairs are presented in different orders. Now, assume S. has learned such a list and then a second list is given in which the stimulus terms are the same as in the first list but the response terms are different. For example, in the second list he must learn to say LAP when COW is presented and CUP when RUG is presented. The associations between the two lists are in conflict, but the interest here is in the memories for the two lists following, say, a twenty-four hours retention interval. As a control, another group of Ss. will learn a single list with retention measured after twenty-four hours also. If the recall of the first list is compared with that of the control list, a large difference will be observed: the recall of the control list will be far superior. This difference defines a phenomenon called *retroactive inhibition.* If the recall of the second list is compared with that of the control list, the control recall will again be found to be superior and this difference is called *proactive inhibition.*

The implication of these experimental findings is that the memory for a given event may be depressed by other memories established after the acquisition of the target memory, and by memories established before the acquisition of the target memory. The illustration given above in which S. learned two successive lists with the same stimulus terms is a rather severe case of associative interference. But ideas about sources of interference should not be limited to such cases. Whenever there is conflicting information of any kind in two or more memories, the potential for interference is present. Given this conflicting information, maximum memory loss from interference will occur when there is complete overlap of other information. This overlap prevents such information from serving as a means of distinguishing among the memories. For example, temporal information has been found to act as a powerful discriminative factor even when the potential for interference is present. When the learning of two conflicting lists of associations (as illustrated earlier) is separated by several days, proactive inhibition is much less than that observed when both lists are learned on the same day. The temporal information differed sufficiently for the two lists to act as a discriminative cue. The Ss. appeared to have one set of responses appropriate to the stimulus terms for one day, and a different set for a later day. In a manner of speaking, the temporal distinctiveness made the identical stimuli different.

In the procedures used to measure retroactive and proactive inhibition, the control list—the single list—was also forgotten, but the magnitude was less than for the two conditions where two lists had been learned. This returns the discussion to the earlier question: What is responsible for the forgetting of this control list? One theory holds that it is also produced by retroactive and proactive interference from memories established prior to S.'s arrival at the laboratory and from memories established during the retention interval. This extrapolation seems reasonable, but it has been difficult to obtain evidence to account for all of the forgetting. The approach has been to use tasks which are assumed to differ in the degree to which they conflict with information contained in previously established memories. The greater the conflict, it is assumed, the greater the loss to be expected from proactive interference. No large differences in retention have been produced by such procedures. This could be interpreted to mean that the interference theory is not capable of accounting for *all* forgetting. However, it is possible that when the degree of conflict between associations is increased, other information becoming a part of the memories also changes, and in some way this information may compensate for the increased forgetting expected from the increased interference. Nevertheless, the possibility remains that there are factors other than interference, such as organic decay, which account for some forgetting.

3. *Measures of memory*. Most studies of retroactive and proactive inhibition have used recall measures of memory: S. must produce responses to stimulus terms. In severe cases of interference, it is sometimes found that S. cannot recall a single correct response. Yet if, following recall, re-learning trials are given, it is found that S. can re-learn in far fewer trials than required to master the task originally. Hence, the re-learning measure detected the fact that some components of the memory remained, whereas the recall measure did not.

Another measure of memory is recognition, a measure resulting when S. is asked to identify the correct word or correct pair from among several words or pairs. Retroactive and proactive inhibition is usually found to be much less when recognition tests (as opposed to recall tests) are employed. This indicates that the central effect of interference is an inability to produce appropriate responses. The difference in recognition and recall measures has greater theoretical importance than that implied above. A growing body of evidence suggests that decisions by S. on a recognition test may be based upon information that only partially overlaps that determining recall. This again stresses the conception that a memory may contain a variety of types of information.

In a typical recognition task, S. is presented with a long list of words, one at a time, for brief study. Then, these words are mixed with new words and S. is asked to check only the old ones (the ones shown for study). Under such procedures, S. will check 80–90% of the old ones, and very few of the new ones. How are these discriminations made? One hypothesis with considerable support holds that the discriminations are based primarily upon a frequency difference. The old items have a frequency of one in this particular situation, the new items a frequency of zero. If S. can discriminate this frequency difference, he will be correct if he chooses the words with greatest frequency. If the situation is changed slightly it can be shown that S. can discriminate this frequency difference with considerable accuracy. After presenting the long list of words for study, each is paired with a new word and S. is asked to choose the word in each pair having the highest frequency. He will be correct on about 80% of the pairs. Frequency information appears to be a part of all memories; its presence is implied whenever statements are made about differences in familiarity. It can be seen, however, that frequency information can only serve to discriminate among memories; it could not be used to produce responses as required in the recall of a paired-associate list. Other information, usually associative information, must mediate recall.

4. *Short-term memory*. In recent years, many investigators have employed short-term memory tasks as vehicles for understanding memory. In the simplest case, S. is shown a *single* item (a nonsense syllable, perhaps) for brief study. Then, an unrelated task is given to prevent rehearsal of the syllable. Finally, after perhaps thirty seconds, S. is asked to recall the syllable. If several successive syllables are given by such procedures, it is found that rather severe forgetting of the most recently presented syllable will occur over the thirty seconds. The forgetting

is most readily interpreted as a case of proactive inhibition. The previously presented syllables interfere with recall of the syllable of the moment. A number of memory phenomena can be studied by this and similar techniques; in a sense, this short-term memory situation is a microcosm of the list-type situation on which most of the foregoing discussion has been based.

One of the most ingenious uses of the short-term technique is to study the types of information which form a memory. It is assumed that the increasing proactive inhibition which occurs as successive items are presented is due to conflicting or non-discriminative information contained in the successive memories. If, then, at some point in the series, an item is given which does not contain conflicting information, proactive inhibition should sharply decrease. From such procedures it has been discovered that the memory for a common word may be based on associative information, conceptual information, affective information, and so on. These studies affirm previous conclusions; a memory is a complex set of information.

5. *Models of memory.* Much of the above discussion has been concerned with interference among memories. In recent years theorists have been producing models of memory which are at a level of theorizing quite different to that implied by interference theory. These models all have two features in common; that is, they postulate two different memory systems. One of these is a short-term system in which incoming information may be held for a very short period of time (fifteen to thirty seconds). If further processing of the information does not occur (as by rehearsal), it will be lost. Roughly, the short-term system may be said to be operating when we look up a telephone number, get a busy signal, and then, a few seconds later when we wish to dial again, find that we have forgotten the number. The second system is the long-term system, or the relatively permanent memory. Details of these theories provide mechanisms for interchange between the two systems, for search mechanisms, for the selection of incoming information, and for systematic storage in the long-term system of related memories. Also, of course, they must provide mechanisms to handle the interference among memories. Because these models represent a relatively new way of conceptualizing memory, their long-term impact on research has yet to be realized.

Bibliography: Adams, J. A.: Human memory. New York, 1967. **Atkinson, R. C. & Shiffrin, R. M.:** Human memory: A proposed system and its control processes. In: **Spence, K. W. & Spence, J. T.** (Eds.): The psychology of learning and motivation, Vol. 2. Englewood Cliffs, 1968. **Keppel, G.:** Retroactive and proactive inhibition. In: **Dixon, T. R. & Horton, D. L.** (Eds.): Verbal behavior and general behavior theory. Englewood Cliffs, 1968. **Metlon, A. W.:** Implications of short-term memory for a general theory of memory. J. of verbal Learn., verbal Behav., 1963, *2*, 1–21. **Postman, L.:** Short-term memory and incidental learning. In: **Melton, A. W.** (Ed.): Categories of human learning. New York, 1964. **Underwood, B. J.:** Attributes of memory. Psychol. Rev., 1969. **Underwood, B. J. & Postman, L.:** Extra-experimental sources of interference in forgetting. Psychol. Rev., 1960, *67*, 73–95. **Wickens, D. D. & Clark, S.:** Osgood dimensions as an encoding class in short-term memory. J. exp. Psychol., 1968, *78*, 580–4.

B. J. Underwood

II. Memory is the ability of an organism to store information from earlier learning processes (experience; retention) and reproduce that information in answer to specific stimuli. The information is reproduced in the form of conscious representation, verbal statements or motor activity.

Afterimages (eidetic imagery), illusions, hallucinations, fatigue phenomena and experiences of boredom and saturation are not generally classed as memory phenomena. A distinction must also be made between memory and fantasy (q.v.), perseveration (q.v.), and thought (q.v.). While classical memory psychology considers memory as a conscious phenomenon (H. Ebbinghaus, G. E. Müller, A. Pilzecker, E. Neumann) and ultimately as radical associations, this theory is refuted by the biological approach (E.

Hering, R. Semon, E. Mach) which attributes memory capacity solely to "organized matter" (E. Hering); the behaviorists (R. S. Woodworth) largely disregard the criterion of consciousness.

Ebbinghaus (1885), G. E. Müller and their co-workers and pupils must be considered as the founders of experimental memory psychology. Their work was continued and revised by Bartlett (1932), who also put forward new theories.

The classical distinction between perceptual ability (direct, short-term perception) and memory in the true sense of the word (long-term retention) has now given way to the distinction (which has been confirmed by a wide range of experiments) between *short-term* and *long-term* memory. Memory psychology is concerned with research into the different phases of memory: impression, retention/forgetting, reproduction (see *Memory* I), the phenomena of short- and long-term memory and, more recently, research into the neurophysiological processes within these phases.

1. *Retention.* The phase of retention, in which the actual memory function takes place, is considered formally from the complementary aspects of retention and forgetting but is viewed psychologically as a single unit. Memory in the sense of a storage unit has only a limited capacity: not all the information received previously is available in complete and unmodified form at any given time. Individual information is selected (memory as a selector) or changed (memory as a modifying agent). The retention capacity is dependent on the following factors: (*a*) on conditions of acquisition of memory content, such as the scope of the learning material (Ebbinghaus law), learning time or number of repetitions, distribution of learning (massed or distributed learning), age of the memory content (Jost's theorems), unforeseen interruption of the learning process (Zeigarnik effect), etc.; (*b*) on the nature of the learning material: formal aspects such as position in the learning series, gestalt character, etc.; content aspects such as meaning retention and differentiation, feeling tone, cognitive categorization (clustering), etc.; (*c*) on physical and motivational factors of the subject: degree of fatigue and general physical condition, attitude (set) to the learning content (warming up), attentiveness, concentration, interest, performance motivation, degree of anxiety, overall mood, responsiveness, etc.; (*d*) on reminiscence: a distinction must be made between the Ward–Hovland phenomenon and the Ballard–Williams phenomenon.

2. *Forgetting.* Forgetting must be considered as the non-availability or modification of memory content (stored information). It is a function not only of time but of the mental processes occurring over a given time. A general distinction must be made between "mechanical" processes in which the memory trace is considered hypothetically as a "passive" physiological correlate of the mental activity (Gomulicki, 1953) and "dynamic" processes in which the memory trace is considered as an "active" process which alters during the retention interval (qualitative change). The following four individual aspects must be considered: (*a*) absence of processes (repetitions) which maintain or facilitate retention (D. E. Broadbent) (forgetting curve); (*b*) extinction: by contrast with (*a*) a habit is "forgotten" in the time during which it is performed (without reinforcing stimulus); (*c*) interference (see *Memory* I); memory inhibitions: superimposed information is mutually inhibiting. Forgetting appears here as a process of re-learning and is directly dependent on the extent of a previous or subsequent information acquisition; (*d*) modification: emotional and motivational attitude factors determine to some extent what is retained and for how long. During the retention phase, memory content undergoes some deformation (modification). The gestalt psychologists consider that this is due to an "autonomous process" based on gestalt laws (*leveling* and *precision* = *pregnance*). Bartlett believes that the modification is due to creative reconstruction on the

principles of rationalization and conventionalization (avoidance of contradictions, attribution of subsequent meaning) and is clearly influenced by emotional factors, e.g. wishes and fears (rumor). Katona (1940) attempted to reconcile the two theories. According to Sintschenko (1969) forgetting is determined not only by the special nature of the material involved but, especially, by the way in which that material is considered. From the angle of depth psychology (q.v.), forgetting serves to maintain a constant psycho-dynamic equilibrium by displacing unpleasant, "tabooed" memory contents with a strong affective significance.

3. *Short-term, long-term memory.* The latest studies based on factor analysis, cybernetics, learning psychology and neuropsychology show that there is no uniform memory capacity (general memory) but a number of different memory dimensions, e.g. for specific types of material, sense modalities and storage intervals (Guilford, 1959; Katzenberger, 1967). The short-term memory—lasting at most some thirty seconds—is interpreted as a bioelectric process in the form of a closed neuronal circuit and is strongly susceptible to forgetting (filter effect; Broadbent, 1958) and interfering influences (labile phase). The long-term memory is more resistant to forgetting and faults (stable phase) and is used for the long-term storage of information in the form of biochemical patterns. These observations suggest an intermediate phase of consolidation and reinforcement at the end of the labile phase for information which is still present. Information losses occur on transfer through the different storage centers.

4. *Neurophysiological aspects.* Physiologically, the memory is primarily associated with the ganglionic cells of the grey cerebral cortex (neo-cortex) and the white fibers of the cerebrum located below it. Molecular biological and biochemical research has shown that protein synthesis, peptides, lipides and changes in ribonucleic acids (RNA) with specific base sequences play a significant role in long-term storage. Clearly, memory contents are stored in the form of a (chemical) consolidation process by alternating association of protein molecules to form different molecular chain lengths. No clear explanation is available but the old theory of "engrams" seems to be confirmed in the form of biochemical patterns with a relatively resistant structure. Forgetting, on the other hand, seems to be due to biochemical neutralization of RNS by RN-ases. The biochemical process of calling on available information (decoding) is completely unexplained as yet. Further results suggest that different learning types can be assigned different storage loci in the brain (subcortical and cortical) (Richter, 1966; John, 1967).

5. *Memory theories.* In the present state of research, memory theories are bound to remain purely speculative. A number of psychological, physiological, biochemical, cybernetic and physical models have been proposed to explain the phenomenon of "memory" but they remain unsatisfactory so long as they fail to take into account any motivational aspects of memory in the living organism (memory as a connection between sensory and motivational information circuits; Richter, 1966). The classical explanation of memory phenomena assumes as a working hypothesis that learning processes leave traces (engrams) which are renewed by repetition and form the physiological correlate for reproduction of information. The traces are considered either as changes in the ganglionic cells of the cerebrum or as being "purely psychological". The reproduction of memory contents is explained primarily by the hypothetical construct of associations; other decisive factors are logical relations and meaning associations within the memory contents and the motivational and emotional state of the organism (associative, mechanical and logical "meaning" memory). Hebb (1949) proposed a self-contained model based on forms of short- and long-term storage in neurophysiological terms. Proposed models for learning and retention in the sense

of a coding process (Müller, 1956; Ausubel, 1963) and notions of reproduction as decoding, in particular in conjunction with modern knowledge of the structure and function of the nervous system (Oldfield, 1954; Broadbent, 1958; Brown, 1958, 1964), are also important.

Bibliography: Ausubel, D. P.: Psychology of meaningful verbal reasoning. New York, 1963. **Bartlett, F. C.:** Remembering. Cambridge, 1932. **Broadbent, D. E.:** Perception and communication. London & New York, 1958. **Brown, J.:** Some tests of the decay theory of immediate memory. Quart. J. exp. Psychol., 1958, *10*, 12–21. **Id.:** Short-term memory. Brit. med. Bull., 1964, *20*, 8–11. **Ebbinghaus, H.:** Über das Gedächtnis. Leipzig, 1885 (Eng. trans.: Memory. New York, [2]1964). **Gomulicki, B. R.:** The development and present status of the trace theory of memory. Brit. J. Psychol., Monogr. Suppl. 1953, *29*. **Guilford, J. P.:** Personality. New York, 1959. **Hebb, D. O.:** The organization of behavior. New York, 1949. **Hörmann, H.:** Bedingungen für das Vergessen, Behalten und Erinnern. In: **Bergius, R.** (Ed.): Handbuch der Psychologie, Vol. 2. Göttingen, 1964, 225–83. **John, E. R.:** Mechanisms of memory. New York, 1967. **Katzenberger, G.:** Gedächtnis oder Gedächtnisse. Munich, 1967. **Neisser, U.:** Cognitive psychology. New York, 1967. **Norman, D. A.:** Memory and attention: an introduction to human information processing. New York, 1969. **Postman, L. & Keppel, G.:** (Eds.): Verbal learning and memory. Harmondsworth, 1969. **Pribram, K. H.** (Ed.): Brain and behaviour, Vol. 3: Memory mechanisms. Harmondsworth, 1969. **Richter, D.:** Aspects of learning and memory. New York, 1966. **Sintschenko, P. L.:** Probleme der Gedächtnispsychologie. In: **Hiebsch, H.** (Ed.): Ergebnisse der sowjetischen Psychologie. Stuttgart, 1969.

F.-C. Schubert

Memory afterimage. See *Afterimage; Memory.*

Memory disorders are due primarily to central (sometimes reversible) ganglionic failures caused by injury, bleeding, intoxication, pathological processes or decomposition phenomena (cerebral arteriosclerosis). Depending on the anatomico-pathological location of the disorder (and hence of the neurophysiological correlates responsible for specific memory dimensions or involved in the processes of storage or reproduction), different disorders or combinations of disorders occur. In general, a distinction must be made between qualitative (biographical; Korsakov syndrome) and quantitative (amnesia) impairment, as well as between (relatively minor) disturbance of the short-term memory, and disturbance of the long-term memory (caused by more massive processes).

Bibliography: Talland, G. A.: Disorders of memory and learning. Harmondsworth, 1968.

F.-C.S.

Memory image. See *Mental imagery; Fechner.*

Memory, immediate. See *Memory.*

Memory, inhibitions of. The classical work of the German association psychologists showed that the difficulty of retaining or remembering taught matter may be related to events which took place before or after the learning process. Reference is made in particular (although not exclusively) to interference phenomena between two successive learning processes.

Rohracher (1963) distinguishes between the following possible forms of interference: (*a*) retroactive or reactive inhibition: if further learning processes follow the learning of a series of contents the retention of the first series is thereby impaired. (*b*) Proactive inhibition: a directly preceding learning process impairs retention of subsequent contents. (*c*) Similarity, or Ranschburg's inhibition: the interference between two learning processes is particularly strong if there is a similarity of the matter taught. (*d*) Associative or reproductive inhibition: contents which were already associated in previous learning are more difficult to link with new contents than those in which this is not the case. (*e*) Ecphoric inhibition: if new material is taught shortly before the reproduction of material learnt earlier, there is a negative influence on the reproduction of material learnt earlier. (*f*) Affective inhibition: the occurrence of strong affective stimuli between the exposure to and reproduction of a content impairs reproduction of that content.

Recent work by American memory psychologists has concentrated on studies of retroactive and proactive inhibition in close relationship with problems of transfer.

L. Blöschl

Memory span. Generally defined as the period of time within which perceptions that are not connected with any learning intention can still be correctly reproduced (current memory). The reproduction time still comes within the range of "psychological presence" (W. Stern) and the typical reproduction consciousness is often lacking. In particular the memory serves to measure short-term perceptual ability (short-term memory) defined as a "memory-span method." The memory-span performance is the number of correctly reproduced elements directly after successive presentation on one single occasion of the unconnected learning elements. In adults the performance is six to ten (generally about seven) elements and is dependent on the nature of the elements (degree of acquaintance, complexity) and the overall duration of presentation. Performance in the "static" memory span (known length of learning series) was found by Pollack *et al.* (1959) to be better than in the case of a "running" memory span (unknown series length).

Bibliography: Pollack, J., Johnson, L. B. & Knaff, P. R.: Running memory span, J. exp. Psychol., 1959, *57*, 137–46.

F.-C.S.

Memory trace field. All the traces which have a dynamic connection (see *Engram*). Gestalt psychology considers that every trace can influence the others and is in turn dependent on them. In addition, a dynamic interrelation is postulated between the memory trace field and the phenomenal field.

Bibliography: Koffka, K.: Principles of gestalt psychology. New York, 1935.

P.T.

Menace. Inhibited aggression (q.v.) accompanying an activated desire for flight or sex. Usually found with enlargement of the body surface, erection of hair, feathers and fins, baring of teeth and claws. Often certain body postures have a menacing effect as, e.g. the lowering of the head with gulls and fish. Menacing sounds occur with vertebrates and insects. Syn. *Threat posture.*

Bibliography: Mertens, R.: Die Warn- und Drohreaktionen der Reptilien. Abh. Senckenberg. naturf. Ges., 1946, *471*, 1–108. **Schenkel, R.:** Ausdrucksstudien an Wölfen. Behav., 1947, *1*, 81–130.

K.Fi.

Menarche. A girl's first menstruation. Occurrence is dependent on race, constitution, climate and pattern of life; in Western civilizations the menarche occurs on average in the thirteenth year. A century ago, the average occurrence in Western countries was at the age of sixteen to seventeen. Bleeding is still irregular to begin with, and ovulation rarely takes place.

H.M.

Mendacity. A tendency consciously to conceal or falsify facts with the intention of gaining an advantage for oneself or others, or in order to avoid unpleasant consequences, or to bring these about for others. It is not a general characteristic. Its detection is a central problem in forensic psychology (q.v.) (see *Credibility; Children as witnesses*), and attempts to confirm it must depend on the particular situation and individual motivation.

M.A.

Mendelism. Mendelian laws (G. Mendel) determine the inheritance of individual characteristics in successive generations: (*a*) principle of uniformity or reciprocity: if two different pure races are crossed (Pl) the result is uniform. Male and female sex cells are equally important in inheritance. The development of features may be intermediate or dominant-recessive; (*b*) law of division: a cross between individuals of the first hybrid generation (F1) results in different individuals (F2). The hereditary features are divided in a specific ratio: 1:2:1 in the case of intermediate feature development and 3:1 in the case of dominant feature development in the F1 generation; (*c*) principle of independence (principle of recombination of the genes of different gene pairs): when races which differ in more than one feature are crossed, th alleles (q.v.) of different characteristic pairs are inherited and combined independently. *I.D.*

Meningitis. Inflammation of the meninges. May occur as *m. cerebralis* (brain), *m. spinalis* (spine) and *m. cerebro-spinalis.* Its symptoms are high temperature, headaches, disturbed consciousness, stiff neck, contraction and tightening of the stomach muscles, hyperesthesia of the skin, visual disorders, and fluid changes. It may be caused by various excitatory agents such as meningococci, tuberculous bacteria, pyogenic bacteria from the sinus or ear, syphilitic agents, viruses (e.g. Coxsackie virus) or carcinomal growths. A complete cure is possible under proper treatment, but the central nervous system is often permanently impaired. *E.D.*

Menopause. The cessation of menstruation due to the end of ovulation; the menopause marks the end of the sexually mature phase in the woman but not the end of sexual activity. It generally occurs between ages forty-five and fifty, beginning with irregular menstrual bleeding (= climacteric). The period before and after the menopause is marked by psychosomatic strains due to physiological, organic changes, also dependent in large measure on psychological factors. Symptoms of the menopause syndrome: sudden hot flushes, irregular and rapid heart beat, disturbed sleep, anxiety, depression, irritability and nervousness. See *Aged, sexuality in the.*

Bibliography: Rubin, I.: Sexual life after sixty. In: Beigel, H. G.: Advances in sex research. New York & London, 1963. *H.M.*

Menorrh(o)ea. **1.** Normal menstruation. **2.** *Menorrhagia:* Abnormally profuse or prolonged menstruation.

Amenorrh(o)ea (q.v.): Abnormal absence or cessation of menstruation, either as a result of organic disease or emotional disturbance. *Primary amenorrhea* is the failure for menstruation to appear at all; in *secondary amenorrhea,* menstruation appears at puberty but subsequently ceases. *Hypermenorrhea: Menorrhagia:* Excessive menstruation. *Hypomenorrhea:* Abnormally slight or abbreviated menstruation. *Oligomenorrhea:* Abnormal prolongation of the menstrual cycle. *G.D.W.*

Menstruation (Syn. *Period; Catamenial discharge*). The cyclic discharge of blood and sloughed-off uterine membrane that occurs at approximately four-week intervals in the sexually mature (post-puberal), non-pregnant female.

Menses is often used to refer to menstruation or the *menstrual cycle* in general, but, strictly, refers to the discharged material itself. See *Menorrh(o)ea; Premenstrual syndrome.*

G.D.W.

Mental abilities. See *Abilities.*

Mental age (abb. MA; syn. *Intelligence age*). The level of mental development expressed in terms of the chronological (life) age considered normal (i.e. that of the average child or adult for that level in a specific intelligence test). See *Abilities; Intelligence quotient.*

Mental defect. I. Mental defect (retardation or subnormality) is defined as "incomplete or insufficient general development of the mental capacities". It refers to an (arbitrary) bottom two per cent of the population: with IQ 70 and below on a test with a mean of 100 and SD (= standard deviation) 15. This IQ range is divided into profound: 0–19; severe:

20–34; moderate: 35–49; mild: 50–70, with borderline defect above 70. Three-quarters of the group lie above IQ 50, and one quarter below.

Nineteenth-century pioneers, such as Itard, Séguin and Montessori, elaborated training methods in mental deficiency, and in 1905 the study of individual differences was stimulated by Binet's development of intelligence tests (q.v.), originally designed to distinguish between educational backwardness and intellectual impairment. From Burt's appointment in 1913 as the first educational psychologist in the world, a stream of important surveys began to emerge. The multi-disciplinary study of mental deficiency has accelerated since World War II. One or more of the following general causes, separately or in interaction, are responsible for the individual case: (1) *genetic* (either normal variation in the IQ range 50–70 or resulting from an abnormal genetic factor, usually but not invariably in the IQ range 0–50); (2) *social* (subcultural) interacting with normal variation; (3) *disease or injury*, pre-, peri, or post-natal.

Research relates to description, prevention and amelioration. Recent studies of prevalence suggest a decrease in incidence of moderate, severe and profound cases largely masked by increased survival rates, particularly of mongols. It is more difficult to estimate numbers of mild cases, since these merge into normality, with the majority receiving minimal help after school age. Reducing incidence for the whole group depends on multiple factors: decline in childhood diseases, use of immunization techniques; improved social conditions, earlier completion of families, genetic counseling, decline of malnutrition, early diagnosis and treatment of rare metabolic disease, as well as specifically designed programs of education and training. Psychological contributions lie in the fields of (*a*) fact-finding surveys, (e.g. on community services and family problems); (*b*) assessment of individual abilities and disabilities; leading to (*c*) specific remediation (as well as general training) techniques; (*d*) early stimulation programs, seeking to prevent the development of backwardness or mild defect; (*e*) experimental studies of psychological processes. A majority of these use normal MA- or CA- matched controls and attempt to cast light on the question of whether defectives are qualitatively as well as quantitatively different from normals.

It seems clear that two different populations (in terms of etiology, status and prognosis) above and below about IQ 50, respectively, are to be found within the whole group; findings in the higher group may not apply to the lower. Even among the severely defective, there is a degree of responsiveness to training, and with cases of profound handicap operant conditioning has been used successfully. Many moderately retarded adults respond well to industrial and social training. Mild deficiency can often be ameliorated by special educational techniques, and among those where social factors are aetiologically relevant, there may be a reversion towards normality, either through the effects of prolonged learning or delayed maturation. The USA. is currently basing its pre-school "Headstart Programmes" for deprived and potentially backward or mildly defective children on psychological research, but such attempts appear to be of too short duration, may use inappropriate methods, and lack subsequent reinforcement (see *Abilities*).

Experiment studies show: that EEG tracings correlate with intelligence, as does reaction time; that discrimination learning is mediated in a two-stage process by attention; and that, in short-term memory, defectives are always inferior to CA-matched normals and may also be to MA-matched controls. Hence acquisition is impaired, whereas retention of well learned material (long-term recall) is often good. Defectives show greater inter- and intra-individual variability than normals, and personality factors are also important. Although defectives are particularly handicapped in verbal and conceptual abilities, even among the lower grades, passive conceptual processes can be demonstrated although there is a deficiency in verbal formulation. See *Abnormal psychology*.

Bibliography: Clarke, A. M. & Clarke, A. D. B.: Mental subnormality. In: **Eysenck, H. J.** (Ed.): Handbook of abnormal psychology. New York & London, 1970. **Stevens, H. A. & Heber, R.:** Mental retardation. Chicago & London, 1964. **Ellis, N. R.** (Ed.): International review of research in mental retardation. Vols. I, II, III. New York, 1966, 1966, 1968.

A. D.B. Clarke

II. In continental European educational theory, all children who do not have the necessary mental equipment to acquire an independent education and who cannot be helped in schools for handicapped children are described as "mentally defective". Unlike mental *retardation*, which only affects individual intellectual functions, mentally defective persons suffer from serious damage to all their abilities.

1. *Causes*. A distinction is made between a number of different causes of mental defects: there are exogenous causes due to brain disorders of all kinds (e.g. infections, birth or early-childhood trauma) and endogenous or genetic causes, the commonest being chromosomal anomaly: mongoloid idiocy is the commonest form, followed by the Klinefelter syndrome. Less frequently we encounter forms of mental defect in which the cause is a specific genetic block due to a major enzyme defect. In the forms of mental deficiency referred to so far, the brain is either unable for primary reasons to function normally or else is damaged secondarily by an external influence (trauma, infection) or organic cause (phenylalanine in phenylketonuria, q.v.).

In the case of many mentally defective individuals, no cause of this kind can be determined; there are no typical symptoms of a metabolic defect or chromosomal anomaly, nor any indication of exogenous damage. The following subdivisions are possible: (*a*) crude interventions may drastically reduce the ability of the brain to function, and therefore seriously impair the mental capacity of the individuals concerned. (*b*) These interventions may be exogenous (infection, trauma, etc.) but are often endogenous or genetic in origin. There is a further distinction between chromosomal anomalies and inborn metabolic errors. (*c*) In the majority of mentally deficient persons these crude interventions are not present. However, studies of family members and twins show the role of hereditary factors, and there are often degenerative symptoms.

2. *Behavior and social problems*. There is usually a general impairment of the mental functions in mental defectives: retardation of mental activity with infantile characteristics, apathy or erethism. Attentiveness may be limited by a tendency (of widely varying importance) to distraction, and in some cases all that remains is mere reflex attention. Frequently, perception in mental defectives is disturbed, without observable defects of the sense organs, e.g. because color impressions dominate the ability to preceive forms. Very often, there is retarded speech and speech deficiency until well beyond the normal school age, or even throughout life, e.g. stammering and paragrammatism.

Many social problems arise from the behavior characteristics and other features associated with mental deficiency. Within the family the mother is overstrained and fatigued by having to keep a constant watch on her child and there may also be financial problems. Stress situations with members of the family and the environment may arise because of destructive or aggressive behavior by the mentally deficient child, disputes between parents (accusations of guilt), or brothers and sisters (rejection, jealousy), or because of exclusion from schooling. Problems also arise for the parents in ensuring the welfare of the defective child, because they fear or see that he is mocked and harmed by others and are concerned for his future.

3. *Therapeutic possibilities*. Possibilities of medical therapy depend on the cause of the mental deficiency (e.g. dietary measures in

cases of phenylketonuria), or on its symptoms (sedatives in cases of erethism); this treatment never attacks the defect itself, but may have a favorable influence on it. Remedial education for children is vitally important. The major condition for successful education is good emotional care, which may even be successful to some extent in the case of children suffering from idiocy. Help from parents should concentrate on reducing the child's need for special care and making him more independent (keeping himself clean, eating on his own, etc.); the ultimate aim is to make the child capable of living in a community.

Motor functions and mental abilities may be trained by play (e.g. constructive games), drawing, painting and practice of all kinds. In the event of special retardation in speech, games to assist language development, and logopedic practice will be necessary.

As soon as the child reaches a level of mental development which enables it to receive outside education, or be separated for an extended period from its mother, it should be enrolled in a special school, or special nursery school, in order to enable it to join in a larger community and develop its mental capabilities. The progress made by the child, as well as the extent and quality of its ability to learn, will determine the possibility and time of its entry into a special school. If there is at least some ability to learn practical skills, simple craft activities can be acquired, enabling the child to pursue a meaningful occupation in the mental home, or even earn its own living (protective workshops). See also *Deficiency, mental* (= "mild" mental defect, but see *Mental defect*, I).

Bibliography: Tredgold, R. F. & Soddy, K.: Mental retardation. London, 1969. **Zublin, W.:** Das schwierige Kind. Stuttgart, 1967.

M. Sachs

Mental hygiene (syn. *Psychohygiene*). According to Meng's (1939) definition, mental hygiene is the *care of mental health.* Appropriate knowledge and the ability not only to preserve but to improve psychological health are requisite. This includes helping the patient to overcome psychic disorders, and to achieve the best possible adaptation to his environment and harmonious relationships within his group.

The mental hygiene now practiced began with the attempt, as far as possible, to reintegrate cured or improved mentally sick people into normal life. In particular it originated at the start of this century in C. W. Beers's *A Mind that Found Itself*, which was a self-description. His book had a profound effect, particularly upon William James (q.v.) (1842–1910), who himself underwent a development crisis after studying science (physiology and medicine). As Professor of psychology and philosophy at Harvard from 1876 till 1907, his pragmatism had a decisive influence on the psychologists of his time. Beers also affected Meyer, the leading psychiatrist of the age. James and Meyer founded mental hygiene in the USA. Its purpose was to care for the mentally and emotionally sick, to improve the treatment and care of emotionally sick epileptics, and the feebleminded, and to clarify the part played by psychological and mental disturbance in child-rearing, work, business and criminology.

H. Meng brought to his ideas on the care of mental health through human relationships the important findings of Freud's psychoanalysis (q.v.), and his own experience of somatopsychic symptoms. He succeeded in describing a pattern of symptoms which can cause serious disturbances of organic function (digestion, circulation, sexual organs), for which doctors trained in organic medicine alone could find no cause. Meng combined the study of these disorders and their cure under the term "organic psychoses" (q.v.). Research into mental hygiene has taught us the peculiarities of this "organic language" in its different forms and thus given us a better understanding of its psychic significance (see *Psychosomatics*).

Mental hygiene gained ground in the international sphere through the work of

J. R. Rees. The third International Congress on Mental Hygiene in 1948 was attended by four thousand participants from twenty-seven countries. The World Federation for Mental Health was founded, which comprised at the time eleven international organizations and one hundred and forty-six societies in fifty-three different countries.

Mental hygiene has now evolved into a "multi-disciplinary" science. In addition to psychiatry proper, the special branch of *social psychiatry* has grown under the influence of mental hygiene. Building on the foundations of Freud and Meng, the child specialist E. Schomburg defines psychological health as a relative freedom from fear, threat and feelings of hatred, so that a positive attitude to one's personality (q.v.) and ego (q.v.) and to other people and the human condition can be achieved.

The aims of mental hygiene may be delineated thus:

(1) The development of the power of self-discovery, in experience of the self and self-knowledge;

(2) the development of the struggle for a true self-affirmation;

(3) the capacity to give other people the same value as one claims for oneself;

(4) the unhampered development of a power to love, which wishes not only to possess the loved one, but to mean something to, and to enrich him or her;

(5) unhampered performance of normal functions;

(6) the development of the power to make appropriate, unprejudiced judgments.

All these aims of mental hygiene can be realized only through the cooperation of several, varied disciplines. In medicine, mental hygiene grew out of psychiatry. It not only includes the different disciplines of hygiene, as well as social hygiene and social medicine, but specialist fields of internal medicine, gynecology, pediatrics (q.v.), and even dentistry. This is particularly the case in the development of *psychosomatic medicine*. Strictly speaking, this is not a specific branch of medicine, but a particular way of looking at bodily and mental interaction in the most varied illnesses. It was practiced at first in America by Alexander (1950), and then principally by Weizsäcker (1947) in Germany. It confirmed the theses of H. Meng on organic psychoses and stressed the importance of problems and crises in the patient's life for the development of organic disorders (see *Psychosomatics*). Mental hygiene was then strongly influenced by the study of child development and law, and in turn influenced them. This was particularly true in the case of juvenile courts (q.v.), and of the borstals of Austria (Aichhorn, 1957), and the USSR (Makarenko). There has also been a fruitful cooperation between mental hygiene and psychology. Mental hygiene has come a long way from the original psychiatric after-care, and the concern with eugenics. It is associated more and more closely with psychology in social work. This is shown best by the development of a particular branch of mental hygiene in group work and group therapy (q.v.), which are themselves closely related to sociology. Group therapy was developed in Vienna in about 1912 from the mutual aid groups of prostitutes, by Moreno (1946; 1956). The first results of this psychological and educational orientation became apparent in the USA with the arrival of emigrants from European countries threatened by Hitler. At the beginning of World War II Moreno could demonstrate the significance of friendly relations within groups or between partners by the selection of aeroplane crews (see *Psychodrama*). He achieved a notable decrease in accidents compared with crews who had nothing but their technical training. In the last twenty years, group work and group therapy have made an enormous difference to the atmosphere of the most varied societies, and have adopted the aims of mental hygiene. This is true in the first place of numerous mental hospitals, where patients increasingly live as therapeutic communities. But it is also apparent in the treatment of many other social situations, from the intimate to the criminal. Mental hygiene still has much work to do. (See *Psychopathology; Gerontology.*) Many disciplines, not least psychology and social psychology, combine to bring us nearer to fulfillment of mental hygiene's demands.

Bibliography: Aichhorn, A.: Verwahrloste Jugend. Stuttgart, 1957. **Battegay, R.:** Der Mensch in der Gruppe. Berne, 1967. **Brezina, E. & Stransky, E.:** Psychische Hygiene. Berlin & Vienna, 1931. **Caplan, G.:** Preventive psychiatry. London, 1964. **David, H. P.:** Population and mental health. Berne & Stuttgart, 1964. **Id.:** Migration, mental health and community services. Berne & Stuttgart, 1966. **Federn, P. & Meng, H.:** Die Psychohygiene. Grundlagen und Ziele. Berne, 1949. **Id.:** Psychoanalyse und Alltag. Berne & Stuttgart, 1964. **Greenblatt, M.,** *et al.*: The prevention of hospitalisation. New York, 1963. **Heyer, G. R.:** Praktische Seelenheilkunde. Munich, 1950. **Jones, M.:** Social psychiatry. London, 1952. **Id.:** Social psychiatry in practice. Harmondsworth, 1968. **Meng, H.:** Die Prophylaxe des Verbrechens. Basle, 1948. **Id.:** Praxis der seelischen Hygiene. Basle, 1943. **Id.:** Psychoanalyse und Kultur. Munich, 1965. **Id.:** Psychoanalyse und Medizin. Munich, 1965. **Id.:** Psychohygienische Vorlesungen. Basle, 1939. **Moreno, J. L.:** Psychodrama. New York, 1946. **Id.:** Psychodrama, Vol. 2. New York, 1956. **Paul, B. D.** (Ed.): Health, culture and community. New York, 1955. **Rees, J. R.:** Reflections. New York, 1966. **Soddy, K. & Ahrenfeldt, R. H.:** Mental health in a changing world. London, 1965. **Id.:** Mental health and contemporary thought. London, 1967. **Id.:** Mental health in the service of the community. London, 1967. **Tramer, M.:** Allgemeine Psychohygiene. Basle, 1960. **Weizsäcker, V. von:** Fälle und Probleme. Stuttgart, 1947. **Id.:** Der kranke Mensch. Stuttgart, 1951.

A. Friedemann

Mental imagery. In one sense of "imagination", an idea may be viewed as a "mental image" or "memory copy" which, in the absence of the corresponding sensory stimuli, represents to the conscious mind previously perceived objects or processes. A *mental image* may be defined as the subjective combination of fragments of earlier perceptions. A genuinely imaginative idea would require an awareness that that which is ideated or imagined is non-existent in the external world of reality. In contradistinction to impressions derived directly from sense perceptions, the contents of mental images are usually imprecise, less detailed, and without clear localization in space. They do not possess the persistence and continuity of experiential perceptions. According to the sense modality, there are visual (optical), acoustic (auditory), kinesthetic (motor), tactile, olfactory and gustatory ideas or images (*concrete images*). When several sensory modalities combine to produce the image, it is known as a *composite image* (or *idea*). (See *Fantasy.*)

Mental imagery in the above sense must not be confused with the pseudo-perceptual, realistic character of compulsive hallucinations (see *Hallucination*). It is questionable whether, as some argue, "eidetic" phenomena are qualitatively different from intensive visual images.

Theories regarding ideas and mental imagery have played a considerable part in the history of psychology and philosophy (e.g. Locke, Hume, Leibniz, Herbart). In some older systems, any more or less "perceptible" mental content was characterized as an idea or image. Later on, there were frequent attempts to ground all intellectual life in mental imagery, and to view the laws of association and the regularities of mental images as the essential categorical principles of the intellect. Galton (q.v.) was the first to carry out anything approaching an empirical investigation of the modes and functions of mental imagery. (See *Idea.*)

In regard to the inter-individual differences in mental imagery, J. M. Charcot inspired a number of attempts to describe so-called "ideational" or "imaginative" types (the visual type or visualizer, the acoustic or auditory type, and the motor type, etc.). In order more exactly to determine the individual dominant type of ideation, several quite objective methods were developed (association analysis, appropriate distractors in selective answer tests, questionnaires, picture description, stylistic analysis, etc.; cf. Woodworth & Schlosberg, 1965). Nevertheless, the validity of these methods has often been questioned. According to Betts (1909), distinctions between ideational or imaginative types are not justified, since there would seem to be high correlations between imaginative capacities in different areas.

For a long time, preferred research topics were the laws of ideation (of image reproduction) and the significance of mental images in thought (problem-solving) processes and concept (q.v.) formation (see *Language; Thinking*). In order to explain mental imagery, association psychologists (e.g. G. E. Müller) referred mainly to the so-called laws of coexistence, succession and similarity, and perseveration (see *Association*). In order to explain arbitrary ideation and the solving of specific tasks on this basis, recourse was had, e.g. to the notion of the initial, goal or objective idea or image in connection with the theory of image complexes. On the other hand, the Würzburg school (q.v.) allowed mental imagery only a subordinate (if any) significance in thought processes proper ("imageless" or "abstract" thinking). For the Würzburg school, mental images were merely "illustrations" of the thought process. Their particular clarity or concreteness decided how far they helped or inhibited thinking. The formation or understanding of a concept can be accompanied by "mental images"; however, the concept is not identical with any specific image. Supporters of the so-called motor theory of thinking and consciousness point out that mental images (e.g. motor and visual images) are accompanied by changes in the corresponding muscular area, e.g. the arm and eye region (Jacobson, 1932; Max, 1935). With full relaxation of the specific muscles, the image should disappear, or the intellectual activity accompanying it should become impossible. Nevertheless, this cannot be safely postulated as the basis for a causal connection between muscular and ideational activity.

In the psychoanalytic view (see *Psychoanalysis*), certain images act as representations of, and safety valves for, pent-up instinctive energies, when—on account of the non-availability of the object of the drive in question, the direct release of energy by way of the instinctive action is impossible. The motivational significance of imaginative ideas results in part from their possible precursory nature. The contents of mental images, even without consciously willed intention, can arouse the impulse to carry out what is proposed in ideal or imaginary form.

Under the influence of certain toxic agents, such as mescaline (q.v.), an unusual intensification of mental imagery is noticeable. But unusual visual, acoustic and kinesthetic images can also be evoked under extreme perceptual conditions, i.e. by the drastic reduction, homogenization, monotonization and diminution of the significance of percepts (sensory deprivation; cf. Solomon *et al.*, 1961). The characterization of these phenomena as "hallucinations" may be countered by the fact that most testees do not ascribe reality to mental images, despite their emphatic character, and therefore do not derive them from specific environmental stimuli.

Bibliography: Allport, G. W.: Eidetic imagery. Brit. J. Psychol., 1924, *15*, 99–120. **Betts, G. H.:** The distribution and functions of mental imagery. New York, 1909. **Corso, J. F.:** The experimental psychology of sensory behavior. New York, 1967. **Humphrey, G.:** Thinking. London, 1951. **Jacobson, E.:** Progressive relaxation. Chicago, 1929. **Id.:** The electrophysiology of mental activities. Amer. J. Psychol., 1932, *44*, 677–94. **Max, L. W.:** An experimental study of the motor theory of consciousness III, IV. J. comp. Psychol., 1935, *19*, 469–86; 1937, *24*, 301–44. **Müller, G. E.:** Zur Analyse der Gedächtnistätigkeit und des Vorstellung verlaufes. Z. Psychol., Erg.-Bd. *5*, *8*, *9*, 1911, 1913, 1917. **Id.:** Abriss der Psychologie. Göttingen, 1924. **Solomon, P.,** *et al.* (Eds.): Sensory deprivation. Cambridge, Mass., 1961. **Traxel, W.:** Kritische Untersuchungen zur Eidetik. Arch. ges. Psychol., 1962. *114*, 260–336. **Woodworth, R. S. & Schlosberg, H.:** Experimental psychology, London, 1965.

F. Süllwold

Mental imagery therapy. Since Freud (q.v.) made the interpretation of dreams the royal road of his psychoanalytical healing method, numerous other methods of therapy with mental imagery (q.v.) have been developed.

The "*rêve éveillé dirigé*" (R. Desoille) and the "catathymic image life" (H. Leuner) are independent of dreams and introduce an informative vertical direction into mental imagery therapy. In cases of severe neurosis hallucinogenic drugs are helpful in this "psycholytic therapy" (H. Leuner, B. Berta, etc.). "Hypnotic imagogy" intensifies healing experiences with images; as "autogenic imagogy" (K. Thomas) it can be taught in groups and also practiced at home. In 1968, representatives of about four hundred methods came together in Geneva to found the "International Society for the Psychotherapeutic Application of Image Experience". See *Archetype; Hypnosis.* *K.T.*

Mental maze. The term denotes the following arrangement: pairs of one word and one syllable are given. A testee then has to find a way through these pairs of words and syllables by deciding in each case which of the two alternatives to choose (word or syllable). One of the alternatives is considered to be correct. The exercise has been done correctly if all the decisions are "correct". Mental mazes are used in research into learning (q.v.).

Bibliography: Peterson, J.: The backward elimination of errors in mental maze learning. J. exp. Psychol., 1920, *3*, 257–80. *R.Hä.*

Mental sickness. A mentally sick individual is characterized by abnormal patterns of experience and behavior. Whereas the personality is basically intact in a neurotic person, it has broken up in the mentally sick individual (psychotic). The patient can no longer distinguish between external and internal experience, imagination and perception, and the relationship between the ego and social environment is disturbed. The main forms of mental sickness are schizophrenia, manic depression, paranoid conditions (endogenous psychoses), conditions brought about by brain injury, alcohol, drugs, syphilis, aging and other external influences (exogenous psychoses), and mental sickness of a purely organic nature. Until recently persons suffering from such disorders were thought to be "possessed." The Spaniard, Father G. Jofre, was one of the first to call for them to be treated as sick persons. In 1409 he founded a "hospital dels folls" in Valencia, the first mental home in Spain and no doubt one of the first psychiatric establishments in Europe. See *Abnormal psychology; Psychopathy; Psychoses, functional.* *E.U.*

Mental training. Practice in thinking. A problem of transfer research: can sensorimotor skills be acquired by mental training alone? Early studies by R. S. Sackett (1934, 1935), H. M. Perry (1939), K. E. Baker and R. C. Wylie make a distinction between three different factors of mental training: verbalization, optical imagination, implicit motor reactions; main result: only intensive mental training has a transfer effect. *H.W.*

Menticide. See *Brainwashing; Manipulation.*

Meprobamate (*Equanil; Miltown*). The first of a new (the propanediol-carbamate) group of tranquilizers (q.v.) put into widespread use in 1954, meprobamate remained the only tranquilizer of clinical importance until the development of the benzodiazepines. Meprobamate is characterized by emotional and motor relaxing, anxiolytic action, without resulting fatigue, over a wide dosage range. Meprobamate has muscle-relaxing and anticonvulsive properties. There are no effects on the autonomic nervous system. The central effects concern primarily the thalamus and limbic structures; in relatively small doses, stimulation of the reticular formation has been observed, but when the dose is increased the opposite effect is obtained. The drug was studied in more than fifty experiments in healthy persons. Tranquilizing effects occur in doses of 200 to 800 mg, particularly in emotionally labile persons and under stress;

there is sometimes increased subjective activity and a tendency for performance to be heightened rather than impaired, in particular as regards motor and learning performance. Differences in intraindividual and interindividual effects seem less marked than in the case of the benzodiazepines and neuroleptics. Fatigue and reduced performance may occur if doses exceed 1200 mg. In combination with alcohol the effects seem merely to be additive (the opposite is the case with sedatives).

Bibliography: Berger, F. M. & Potterfield, J.: The effect of antianxiety tranquilizers on the behavior of normal persons. In: **Evans, W. O. & Kline, N. S.** (Eds.): The psychopharmacology of the normal human. Springfield, 1969. **Janke, W. & Debus, W.:** Experimental studies on antianxiety agents with normal subjects. Methodological considerations and review of the main effects. In **Efron, D.** (Ed.): Psychopharmacology, 1957–1967. Washington, 1968.

G.D.

Merkel's law. The proposition of Merkel that equal differences in sensations above threshold correspond to equal stimulus differences. This is in conflict with the more widely accepted *Weber–Fechner law* (q.v.).

G.D.W.

Merkwelt. (Ger.; syn. *Eigenwelt;* Eng. *Perceptual world*). In Uexküll's environmental theory, the environment as perceived subjectively, specifically and effectively by a particular species or animal in terms of its own sensory capacities, and reacted to in terms of a specific "*Wirkwelt*", or behavioral repertoire. See *Animal psychology; Comparative psychology.*

K.Fi.

Mescalin(e). An alkaloid of the Mexican cactus "peyote", and a derivative of phenylethylamine, mescalin has been used for centuries as a narcotic and was an essential feature of the pre-Columbian religious practices of the Aztecs and other Mexican Indians. The earliest scientific reports on mescalin were descriptions of experiments conducted by individual doctors and psychologists (e.g. Prentiss & Morgan, 1895; Beringer, 1927). In the nineteen-fifties mescalin was used to generate "model psychoses"; it was hoped to imitate a psychosis reversibly in the model, and neurochemical hypotheses concerning schizophrenia (q.v.) were prepared in this way. Mescalin has effects similar to those of other psychotomimetics but it has a comparatively prolonged effect (8 to 15 hours).

Bibliography: Beringer, K.: Der Meskalinrausch. Berlin, 1927. **Leuner, H.:** Die expt. Psychose, Berlin, 1962. **Prentiss, D. W. & Morgan, F. P.:** Anhalonium Lewinii (mescal buttons). A study of the drug with especial reference to its physiological action upon man, with report of experiments. Therap. Gaz., 1895, *19*, 577–85.

H.K.

Mesencephalon. The midbrain, a part of the brainstem situated between the diencephalon and the pons. It consists of the *tectum mesencephali*, the *tegmentum* and the *crura cerebri.* Many nerve paths and nuclei are situated in extremely close proximity in a small area.

G.A.

Mesmer, Franz Anton. B. 23/5/1734 in Iznang (Lake Constance); d. 5/3/1815 in Meersburg. Founder of Mesmerism, the theory of *animal magnetism.* He studied theology and medicine and made a name for himself as a doctor by his *theory of the curative power of magnetic iron.* From 1776, Mesmer believed he had discovered that the magnetic therapy he had so far advocated did not depend on the effect of the magnet but on some mysterious power, some fluid, by which men possessed of a special gift (magnetizers) could effect cures. This is a case of a prescientific view of the power of suggestion (q.v.). Mesmerism had a far-reaching influence on Romantic medicine and philosophy, as well as on the early forms of hypnotic treatment, the nature of which was to be investigated first by the Scottish surgeon J. Braid; he then gave this method of treatment its definitive name—hypnosis (q.v.).

Bibliography: Mesmer, F. A.: Mémoire sur la découverte du magnétisme animal. Geneva, 1779 (Eng. trans.: Mesmerism. London, 1948). *H.-N.G.*

Mesoderm. In addition to the ectoderm and entoderm, a third stage of embryonal development, i.e. the mesoderm, can be distinguished in the articulated animals and vertebrates. It is generally a derivative of the primary entoderm. It produces primarily the connective tissues and the tissues or organs derived from the latter (e.g. muscles, vertebrate skeleton). *H.Sch.*

Mesomorphy; mesomorphic type. One of the typical physical forms described by W. H. Sheldon in his typology. He believes that the different physical types result from the dominance of different primitive layers (entoderm, mesoderm, ectoderm) in the physical development of an individual. Mesomorphy is then explained by dominance of the mesoderm and is reflected in strong bone and muscle development. The phenomenon of mesomorphy corresponds largely to the athletic constitution type described by E. Kretschmer. *W.Se.*

Metalanguage. In formalization procedures, the language or languages which may be used to speak about a formal system or an objective language. It includes the names of terms and formulas of the system, and those of its classes; it is used to formulate their rules of construction and all the properties characteristic of the system. It is also possible to formalize a metalanguage by means of a meta-metalanguage; and so on. The metalanguages used in formal logic are finitistic arithmetic, set theory, and natural language. By derivation, any assertion which contains a judgment not on an object but a proposition is "metalinguistic". *M.J.B.*

Metamorphopsia. 1. A distorted view of objects, e.g. in the case of retinal detachment. See *Astigmatism*. **2.** Deviation of visual perception from reality owing to sensory illusion. *R.R.*

Metamphetamine. A central stimulant belonging to the amphetamine (q.v.) group.

Metapsychology. A branch of parapsychology which seeks transcendental causes for psychological behavior (S. Freud). *R.D.*

Metatropism. The "inversion" of emotions and feelings in sexual matters. The assumption of the specific sexual behavioral characteristics of the opposite sex causes a man to adopt a more passive role (see *Effemination*), while a woman on the other hand displays active tendencies and patterns of behavior (see *Virilism*). *K.E.P.*

Methadone. A psychotropic substance which belongs among the analgesics (q.v.). Methadone is pharmacologically similar to morphine but acts more slowly. Since 1965, methadone has been used to treat heroin addicts. It blocks the euphoria induced by heroin, and in small doses prevents withdrawal symptoms.

Bibliography: Eddy, N. B.: Methadone maintenance for the management of persons with drug dependence of the morphine type. Drug dependence, 1970, No. 3, 17–26. **Gordon, N. B.:** Reaction times of methadone treated ex-heroin addicts, Psychopharmacologia, 1970, *16*, 337–44. *W.J.*

Method of constants. A psychophysical method for determining thresholds. An object or stimulus invariable in some respect (the constant stimulus) is presented for comparison with a series of similar stimuli in random order. The percentage of correct judgments determines the threshold. This psychophysical method gives sufficient information for analysis in terms of models more complex than the simple threshold model, such as those derived from *signal detection theory*.

C.D.F.

Method of least squares (syn. *Least-square method*). A method of curve fitting in which the curve parameters are determined in such a way that the sum of the squared deviations of the curve from observed values is a minimum. The method is used for optimal adaptation of theoretical distributions to empirical distributions, e.g. regression line.

Bibliography: Guest, P. G.: Numerical methods of curve fitting. London, 1961.

G.Mi.

Methods of psychology. The methods of psychology are used in a specific problem to make observations, compare them with one another and draw conclusions in order to answer the given problem. They are instruments of psychological research and diagnosis. They have been specially developed and harmonized to deal with specific problems.

1. *General.* Since psychology deals with a totality of processes, it is based on observations. Observation is the study of a process in which at least two points of the process are studied. The aim is to determine the specific consequences which occur under specific conditions. A single observation, however precise, would never be sufficient for this purpose. It can only become significant if it is comparable with at least one other observation made of a further, comparable process. The following diagram illustrates this point:

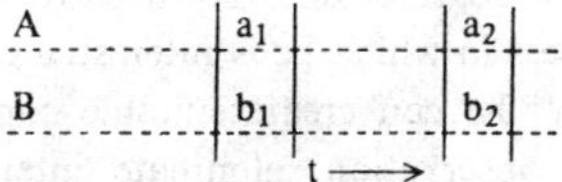

Let A and B be two processes which occur in the time t, while a_1 and a_2 are observed parts of process A, and b_1 and b_2 observed parts of process B.

The following examples from perception theory will help to illustrate this: Example for A. An individual observing a pattern as in the figure below (a_1), asserts that the two horizontal lines are *parallel* (a_2).

Example for B. The same person observes another pattern, as in the following figure (b_1). On this occasion he asserts that the two lines are *divergent*.

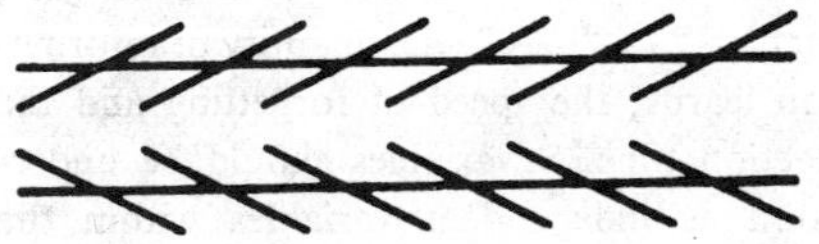

The observer now compares A with B. On the basis of their direct relationship, a_1 and a_2 on the one hand, and b_1 and b_2 on the other, are now correlated: a_2 is dependent on a_1 and b_2 on b_1. Or: a_1 leads to a_2 and b_1 to b_2.

$$a_1 \rightarrow a_2$$
$$b_1 \rightarrow b_2$$

It is clear that the difference between a_2 and b_2 is dependent on the difference between a_1 and b_1.

One of the two processes (e.g. A) requires no special study if the relevant relationship (here $a_1 \rightarrow a_2$) is already known: one knows that, "normally", parallel lines on a sheet of paper also look as if they were so. But, even then, a comparison is made—between a present observation and one in the past.

If an observed difference between a_2 and b_2 is in fact explained by the difference between a_1 and b_1, a_1 and b_1 must only differ in *a single*, precisely defined feature, i.e. in the feature which is the subject of the study. In all other features, a_1 and b_1 must be identical. Only variable conditions can be studied. A constant factor which always plays a part could not be detected. A feature therefore has at least two and generally more "degrees of intensity", "classes" or "values".

These can sometimes be determined quantitatively, i.e. by dimensional units, and sometimes only qualitatively, i.e. by terms regarding their characteristics. The variable features are known as *variables*. A distinction is made between stimulus or situation (S) variables and reaction (R) variables. S variables are, e.g. the qualitative classes of optical patterns, the length of a subject item to be learnt, or the dose of a stimulant. Examples for R variables are judgments such as "Yes" or "No", "parallel" or "divergent", "larger", "identical" or "smaller", "beautiful", "neutral" or "ugly"; the quantity of information learnt; the speed of forgetting and the reaction time. S variables should be understood as independent variables within the study concerned; R variables, on the other hand, are dependent variables. Remembering our diagram, it is possible to write:

$$S_a \rightarrow R_a$$

$$S_b \rightarrow R_b$$

S_a and S_b are defined categories for a single stimulus variable. This is only one part of a more complex stimulus situation which contains other variable components (e.g. illumination in a room, presence of other persons, etc.). The observed R variable only defines part of the total reaction which consists of more than, e.g. simply a judgment or reaction time.

Part of the process which is studied is situated between the stimulus and reaction, i.e. the inner, subjective process. It is known to the individual concerned but cannot be observed from outside. The judgment or other behavioral datum of a person (e.g. the reproduction of learnt information or a physical reaction) is simply a sign of a process which takes place within him. Nevertheless psychology is concerned with this inner process: our aim is to determine how a pattern is perceived, a subject learnt, a problem of thought solved or an action motivated. From observation of behavior and knowledge of the stimulus situation we are able to reach conclusions regarding the method of mental processing and the laws which govern it.

The reaction of an individual is not dependent solely on the given external stimuli but also on inner factors (e.g. performance of sense organs, understanding of the problem, experience, ability to concentrate, etc.). We are concerned here with another type of variable, which is defined as the O (organism) or P (person) variable. Every reaction can therefore be understood as a function of stimulus variables (S) and personality variables (P):

$$R = f(S, P).$$

Studies with S variables as independent variables form part of general psychology (q.v.); studies of P variables as an independent factor are the subject of differential psychology (q.v.).

The diagram we showed initially, which describes the procedures of psychology in a very general way, also enables the P variables to be included: if a_1 and b_1 are identical, while a_2 and b_2 differ, it is possible to conclude that there is a P variable effect which leads to differentiation. In addition, it should be stressed that this diagram not only holds good for research work but for practical operations.

2. *The experiment.* If an independent variable is intentionally varied under controlled conditions and its effect on a dependent variable observed, we have the basis for an experiment. The essential features of the experiment, i.e. its regulability, repeatability and variability, offer several methodological advantages: the observer does not need to wait for the process in which he is interested to occur naturally: he can create suitable conditions for the observation, eliminate interference and prepare aids (e.g. measuring and recording instruments); above all he can keep the experimental conditions largely under control. By repeating an experiment, earlier results can be checked and random errors will be compensated in a mean value from several observations; a high degree of objectivity can be achieved. Individual conditions

can be changed in further experiments, one variable being altered on each occasion in accordance with the rule mentioned above. It is then possible to explain gradually the significance of the individual conditions in the process as a whole and express it in the form of laws.

Special importance attaches to experiments through their interaction with the definition of theories: a theory provides a hypothesis to answer which the experiment is set up. The results of the latter may consolidate the theory or lead to its correction.

The experimenter (E) creates a given stimulus situation in a psychological experiment and studies individual variables from this complex. He observes the reactions of an experimental subject (S.) or animal. Depending on the subject's reactions, we make a distinction with W. Wundt between introspective and psychophysical experiments (or with H. Rohracher between experiential and performance experiments). In the first case the experimenter and subject are both observers and have to describe their impressions. In the second instance the reaction which is to be observed consists solely of a physical change, an expressive phenomenon. The reaction types are the same in experimental observation as in ordinary observation, but through the design of the experiment their determination is generally more precise and a better association with the releasing conditions can be ensured.

In introspective experiments, the subject may either be told to use only specific categories of judgment (fixed observation) or to make the communications which he feels important on a free basis (free observation).

To take the distinction between types of experiment further, there are also analytic and decision experiments. These are concerned primarily with the accuracy of the hypothesis, and are therefore gradual.

By a suitable arrangement of the variations in a test series, it is possible to study several independent variables very economically in a single process, but the effects of each individual variable are still distinguishable. The effects of the combination of these variables (interactions) can then also be determined (see *Variance, analysis of*).

Experiments are used effectively in almost all branches of modern psychology. They cannot, of course, be conducted if the stimulus situation cannot be established (e.g. accidental influences), and their significance may be impaired if the subject's knowledge of the strictly experimental nature of the process influences his reactions (e.g. in motivation research) or if the factors involved are difficult to control (e.g. in social psychology). The fact that many experiments cannot be repeated usefully with a single subject is of little importance in general psychology because other subjects can always be called in.

3. *The test.* Diagnostic tests are used to determine the level of individual P variables. For the results to be comparable, the test must be conducted in an identical manner for all test subjects; the derivation from S variables is not acceptable. Of course no attempts are made to change the P variables which have to be diagnosed. Provided it has purely diagnostic purposes a test can therefore be considered as a kind of measuring instrument.

The question as to whether a test can be considered as an experiment is given different answers depending on whether the condition variation is considered essential for an experiment or not. If we understand the experiment in the wider sense as every voluntary organization of a process for observational purposes and make a distinction, as Pauli does (1927), between complete experiments (with condition variation) and incomplete experiments (without such variation), the test is then seen as an incomplete experiment.

Tests are important research instruments in differential psychology. If, e.g. we wish to examine different social groups to determine differences in their intelligence structure, we shall use suitable tests for this purpose (see *Intelligence tests*; *Psychodiagnostics*).

4. *Errors.* Any alteration in a dependent variable which is not conditioned by an

alteration in the independent variable under study, is an error. The origin of errors may be traced back to every stage of the study (e.g. in planning, practical observation or in the accompanying conditions). A distinction is made between systematic (constant) and random (variable) errors. Systematic errors influence all the individual results in the same manner and therefore shift the overall result in a given direction. Random errors, on the other hand, occur in all probability just often as positive or negative deviations from a true value, and leave the mean value of several identical observations unchanged. Errors may occur—depending on the underlying causes—in different ways, e.g. as space and time errors in determining stimuli or as errors of expectation in the subject or experimenter.

Psychological methods center in large measure on the avoidance or reduction of errors. Systematic errors are countered in particular by control methods and random errors by statistical methods.

5. *Control methods.* Systematic error factors must be removed before the study begins. Control measures are therefore a part of the experimental set-up. If an interfering condition is already known (e.g. noise), it may be eliminated directly. Other interfering variables may be known but impossible to eliminate (e.g. time of day at which experiments are conducted).

They must therefore be distributed over the conditions to be studied in such a way that they have an identical influence on the results to be compared (balancing). This is possible also in the case of interfering conditions which are neither known nor possible to eliminate (e.g. aptitude and personality characteristics of test subjects), by distributing them in a random manner between the categories of variables which are studied (e.g. allocation of a subject to an experimental or control group by drawing lots). A refinement of this method, which is known as "randomizing", consists in "parallelizing" after the results of a preliminary experiment.

6. *Statistical methods.* Even if all systematic errors are eliminated by extremely careful control, the variables which are irrelevant to the purpose of the experiment remain. Except in cases where such factors are directly eliminated, their effects are simply distributed in such a way that the overall result is one of neutralization. They continue to exist but only lead to random dispersion of the results obtained under identical known conditions.

For this reason, the laws followed in psychology are statistical. Accordingly psychology must use statistical methods in processing its results.

Having regard to the relatively large random error, almost all practical findings must be taken repeatedly. A sampling of identical observations must therefore be taken. It will then be possible to determine a characteristic value which will approximate more closely than each individual result to the true value uninfluenced by errors. This characteristic value is very often the arithmetic mean or a percentage figure. (Information on this aspect of methods of psychology will be found in various articles in the Encyclopedia: e.g. *Test theory; Statistics; Correlational techniques; Significance; Hypothesis testing;* etc.).

Bibliography: Edwards, A. L.: Experimental design in psychological research. New York, 1968. **Ferguson, G. A.:** Statistical analysis in psychology and education. New York, London & Toronto, 1959. **Fraisse, P.:** Praktikum der expt. Psychol. (Ed. W. Traxel). Berne & Stuttgart, 1966. **Hays, W. L.:** Statistics for psychologists. New York, 1964. **McNemar, Q.:** Psychological statistics. New York, 1969. **Meili, R.:** Lehrbuch der psychol. Diagnostik. Berne & Stuttgart, 1965. **Plutchik, R.:** Foundations of experimental research. New York & London, 1968. **Sixtl, F.:** Messmethoden der Psychologie, Weinheim, 1967. **Traxel, W.:** Einführung in die Methodik der Psychologie. Berne & Stuttgart, 1964. **Id.:** Über Gegenstand und Methode der Psychologie. Berne & Stuttgart, 1968. **Winer, B. J.:** Statistical principles in experimental design. New York, 1962. **Zimny, G. H.:** Method in experimental psychology. New York, 1962. *W. Traxel*

Methohexital (*Methohexital sodium; Methohexitone; Brevital*). A psychotropic barbiturate.

Methohexital is very briefly acting and has been administered intravenously to support relaxation in behavior therapy (desensitization). Several studies show that methohexital may enable the duration of behavior therapy to be shortened. However, it remains to be shown whether there is then a greater probability of regression.

Bibliography: Brady, J. P.: Drugs in behavior therapy. In: **Efron, D. H.** (Ed.): Psychopharmacology, 1957–1967. Washington, 1968. *W.J.*

3-Methoxy-4-hydroxymandelic acid. The most important decomposition product of endogenous noradrenaline (q.v.), detectable in urine.

Bibliography: Crout, J. & Abraham, D.: Determination of 3-methoxy-4-hydroxymandelic acid. Clin. chem. Acta, 1962, *7*, 285. **Steinberg, H.,** *et al.*: Catecholamines and their metabolites in various states of arousal. J. Psychosom. Res., 1969, *13*, 103–8.

W.J.

Methylphenidate (*Methylphenidate hydrochloride; Ritalin*). A stimulant which has a damping effect on the limbic system but, unlike the amphetamines, does not lead to an increase in adrenalin secretion. Effects on the autonomic nervous system are less pronounced than is the case with the amphetamines and caffeine. Psychopharmacological studies have shown the following results in doses of 10–30 mg: primarily an improvement in attentiveness (especially in neurotics), mood and performance in clerical tests and in various motor tasks. Paradoxical effects occur under certain conditions. There is a complex interaction between dosage, personality features, situative factors and the effect of the substance.

Bibliography: Janke, W.: Experimentelle Untersuchungen zur Abhängigkeit der Wirkung psychotroper Substanzen von Persönlichkeitsmerkmalen. Frankfurt, 1964. *W.D.S.*

Metromania. A pathological condition characterized by the incessant writing of verse.

Metromorphy (*Metromorph*). According to Conrad's typology (1963), a physical form which represents a harmonious balance between the two typical forms of leptomorphy and pyknomorphy.

Bibliography: Conrad, K.: Der Konstitutionstypus. Berlin, 1963. *W.Se.*

Metronome. A device for marking off short periods of time, usually by means of a pendulum which produces an auditory click at the end of its arc. Most commonly used for setting the tempo in musical rehearsal, but has psychological applications, e.g. pacing of speech in the treatment of stammering.

G.D.W.

M-F index. According to L. M. Terman and C. C. Miles, as well as S. R. Hathaway and J. C. McKinley, a scale for measuring the inner masculinity or femininity of a person. It covers the relative frequency of male and female personality traits, attitudes and behavior.

Bibliography: Hathaway, S. R. & McKinley, J. C.: Minnesota Multiphasic Personality Inventory (Manual). New York, 1951. **Terman, L. M. & Miles, C. C.:** Sex and personality: studies in masculinity and femininity. New York, 1936. *W.T.*

Michotte, Albert, Baron van den Berck. B. 13/10/1881, in Brussels; d. 1965. Began his teaching career in 1905 after graduating in philosophy at Louvain University, where he was first appointed assistant, then a lecturer, and put in charge of the psychological laboratory in 1908 as Professor. He held this position for twenty-five years; in 1906 he worked in the Leipzig psychological laboratory and went to Würzburg under O. Külpe in 1907/08; in 1923 he founded the Ecole de Pédagogie et de Psychologie appliquée à l'Education at Louvain University: it was renamed the Institut de Psychologie appliquée et de Pédagogie in 1944. In 1957 he founded the Société Belge de Psychologie and in that year was appointed Chairman of the 15th International Psychological Congress. He was Chairman of the International Union for Scientific Psychology until 1960.

Works: Michotte's research activity can be divided into three periods. In the first, lasting from 1905 to 1920, he showed close affinities with the Würzburg School in research methods and content. Concentrating on the systematic introspection method, he studied higher psychological processes such as thinking and volition, determining trends, logical memory, origin of meanings, etc.

In the second period he was influenced by behaviorism and criticism of the method of systematic introspection and began to study problems such as visual and tactile-kinesthetic perception, stroboscopic perception (see *Stroboscope*), rhythm, motor learning, etc.

By far the most original and important research for which he was responsible was done between 1940 and 1965 when he studied problems of causality perception, phenomenal permanence and amodal additions to perception structures.

In his experiments in apparent causation he tried to show that the determination of causal relationships between objects, i.e. the evaluation of the influence of one object on another, is a genuine direct, perceptual phenomenon which occurs in a given stimulus configuration with the same perceptual evidence as any other perception quality. He thus opposed the previously held view that causal relationships are not perceived directly but only inferred indirectly from previous experience and the sense relationship which is apparent in a situation. His studies of amodal additions to perceptual structures were also of far-reaching importance. Michotte established a distinction from modal completions (*Hemianopsia; Blind spot*) and speaks of amodal completions when the added components have no sensory qualities in the true sense of the word (brightness and color), while the unity of the overall gestalt and the complete nature of its outline have the force of perceptual evidence. Michotte tried to refute, on the basis of his experiments, the previously held opinion that these completion phenomena do not have the qualities of perception but are conditioned solely by experience, knowledge and reasoning processes; he tried to show that they are genuine perceptual phenomena which are influenced only by the normal laws of organization of the field of perception.

Publications: La perception de la causalité. Louvain, 1946 (Eng. trans.: The perception of causality. New York, [2]1963). Autobiography. In: Boring, E. G., *et al.* (Eds.): A history of psychology in autobiography, Vol. 4. Worcester, Mass., 1952, 213–36. Causalité, permanence et réalité phénoménales. Etudes de psychologie expérimentale. Louvain, 1962 (Michotte and colleagues). Les compléments amodaux des structures perceptives. Louvain, 1964 (with G. Thines and G. Crabbé).

W.W.

Microcephaly. Abnormal reduction in the size of the head and brain with skull deformations, mental deficiency and impaired functioning of the central nervous system. Sometimes linked with hydrocephaly (an excess of cerebrospinal fluid). Microcephaly may be innate or caused by various prenatal disorders (rubella or toxoplasmosis). It is incurable. *E.D.*

Micropercepts. The perception of very small differences in any modality, e.g. pitch discrimination and *differential running time* (q.v.) in the location of sound. *C.D.F.*

Microvibration. An uninterrupted vibration of the body surface with amplitudes of 1–20 microns and frequency components of 2–60 Hz (dominant frequencies 8–20 Hz). The amplitude and frequency of the microvibration vary with the point of measurement on the body and the activity of individuals: they increase with the occurrence of affects, under mental and physical stress and after administering stimulating drugs, and fall off in relaxing situations and after administering sedatives. Microvibration probably plays a part in regulating temperature and was described for the first time by Rohracher in 1946.

Bibliography: Rohracher, H. & Inanaga, K.: Die Mikrovibration. Berne, 1969. *W.Sch.*

Middle ear. See *Auditory ossicles.*

Migration. Animal migrations are still mysterious phenomena. The parr (young salmon) recognizes the effluvial spectrum of its home river four to five years later when, having traversed thousands of miles of ocean, it returns to breed. At spawning time, toads find their original pool. The Pacific golden plover migrates from Alaska to Hawaii, and crosses 3200 km of ocean. Readiness to migrate in fish, amphibia and birds is influenced by length of day, temperature and hormonal balance. Not only landmarks but the sun, polarized light, and possibly the stars, as well as magnetic fields, play a part in distance orientation—there is also genuine navigation. Even some insects may be said to "migrate". Some 500,000 locusts per hectare fly 15 km ahead of the wind that brings them into areas where rain will fall and eggs can be laid.

Bibliography: Eastwood, E.: Radar ornithology. London, 1967. **Harden Jones, F. R.:** Fish migration. London, 1968. **Hediger, H.** (Ed.): Die Strassen der Tiere. Brunswick, 1967. **Nielsen, E. T.:** Insekten auf Reisen. Heidelberg & New York, 1967. **Salomonsen, F.:** Vogelzug. Munich, 1969. *K.Fi.*

Migration instinct. An "instinct" (q.v.) evoking and maintaining migratory behavior (in birds, fish, insects). Hormones (thyrotropine, thyroxine, prolactin) play an important part in the motivation of animal migrations, as do temperature variations and changes in the length of the day, lack of food and overpopulation (e.g. lemmings). See *Migration.*

Milieu. An imprecise designation for that aspect of an individual's environment which primarily comprises economic, cultural and inter-human factors. *M.A.*

Military psychology. The development of military psychology dates from World War I, and runs largely parallel to the differentiation of applied psychology into its various specialist branches; its tasks and the areas into which it was chiefly brought into use depended upon the needs of the changing situation in the armed forces and upon the contribution which psychological knowledge could make to those military spheres which are particularly affected by marked psychological variations in the fighting man. Starting from 1915, American psychologists (R. H. Yerkes, H. H. Goddard, L. M. Terman) succeeded in selecting some 1.75 million men for military service using the Army Alpha Test (later Army General Classification test, q.v.) to assess their intellectual and behavioral levels. The use made of research statistics in test construction (q.v.) and validation (q.v.) made this remarkable achievement possible for the first time. German war psychology enjoyed a pre-eminent position in the field of military psychology by reason of its holistic tests in real-life situations and development of personality assessment along individual diagnostic lines (Lersch, Eckstein, Rudert, Simoneit). (See *Personality.*)

During and between the two last wars the methods used in the selection of pilots, lorry drivers and specialists became more sophisticated (e.g. in the psychological laboratory before and after 1935: perception experiments based on the physiology of the senses, the development of reaction-timing devices, and also tests for assessing technical competence and determining suitability for training as wireless operators, monitors, etc.). Because of the rapid development of modern systems of weapons and leadership, with the increased demands they made on military science, logistics and infrastructure, and with the adaptation of the military forces to social systems with an emphasis on performance, military organization was confronted with completely new tasks. Which particular kind of psychology receives most attention in a given country, whether it is social, clinical, technical, or the psychology of training or aptitude, varies according to tradition (for instance, in the Latin countries medicine takes pride of place, in the Eastern it is neuropsychology, and in the Anglo-American and Scandinavian countries there is close co-operation with civilian research work. Between the military psychologists of the NATO powers (but also with countries outside this organization) there are part-agreements on the exchange of information which largely relate to the following main areas of military psychology:

1. *Man-power resources:* psychology of military reserves; selection and drafting of conscripts and volunteers by means of paper/pencil and functional tests.

2. *Personnel selection and classification:* psychological examinations and investigations of military personnel required for special duties and activities. The selection methods for pilots (begun in World War I) call for special attention: as ever more demanding aeroplane types were developed, methods with wide ramifications were worked out, including the use of flight simulators (assessment of the potential skill of the subject in visual flight and also when flying blind). (See *Aviation psychology*.) (cf. O.S.S., 1948.)

3. *Human factors engineering* (ergonomics, anthropotechnology, or the psychology of military technology): investigations by experimental psychologists to determine the optimal adaptation of a man to weapons and appliances and, on the other hand, the optimization of control devices for assessing a man's capabilities. Analyses of stress, work study and ergonomics evaluation of war material enable the degree of efficiency to be increased where man-machine systems are involved (instrument design for tanks, submarines and high performance aeroplanes).

4. *Training and military education:* development and overhaul of training methods (rational instruction planning, programmed learning, including proficiency measurement methods for calculation of levels reached by military units at different stages of their training).

5. *Human relations and morale:* socio-psychological investigations to determine human relationships in a unit (group dynamics), style of leadership (see *Leader*), motivation (q.v.), behavior in critical situations (collapse of discipline, desertion, etc.). These subjects have for decades been the subject of intensive research, the results of which have been made available only in part. In the USA almost every third publication deals with some aspect of military psychology. At NATO work conferences and international symposia the results of projects are released and discussed. See *Traits; Type.*

Bibliography: Ansbacher, H. L.: Bleibendes und Vergängliches aus der Deutschen Wehrmachtspsychologie. Mitteilungen des Berufsverbandes Deutscher Psychologen, 1949, *11*, 3–9. **Ellis, A. & Conrad, H.S.:** The validity of personality inventories in military practice. Psychol. Bull., 1948, *45*, 385–426. **O.S.S. Assessment Staff.:** Assessment of men. New York, 1948. **Simoneit, M.:** Wehrpsychologie. Berlin, 1933. **Stouffer, S. A., *et al.*:** The American soldier. Princeton, 1949. **Vernon, P. E. & Parry, J. B.:** Personnel selection in the British forces. London, 1949.

G. Mitze

Mimicry. An imitation (which occurs as a result of natural selection) of a feature which is dangerous or disagreeable to a potential enemy. For example, the markings on the back of the body of certain hovering flies are similar to those of wasps, so that these flies are not touched by certain predators which avoid wasps because of their sting.

H.Sch.

Mind. Until a psychology with a scientific orientation was created, psychological inquiry and thinking were concerned with the mind, its substantiality, spirituality and mortality. The mere fact of talking about a mind serves to distinguish it from the body to which it is bound. Thus the theory of mind raises the mind-body problem (q.v.). Investigation of the mind and its relation to the body was the special task of rational or metaphysical psychology, which was and is a branch of philosophy. When, about the middle of the nineteenth century, psychology was detached from philosophy and turned to science and its methods, it considered its subject to be those psychic processes whose totality W. Wundt sought to embrace in his *actualistic concept of mind.* The term coined by F. A. Lange, "psychology without a soul", is on the whole correct for modern scientific psychology. Nevertheless, the question concerning the real essence of the problem of mind persists. The term *mind* had *the function of a concept distinguishing it from body*, the function of a lasting substratum of psychic processes, and the mind had the *function of a standardized basis of psychic life* in the sense of continuing process, identity of subject and constancy of object recognition. These basic functions have today been transferred to the concepts "person" (q.v.) and "personality" (q.v.). As compared with the concept of mind they have the advantage that they include the relation of the psychic life to the body and the world. On the whole psychology, in so far as it considers itself a "pure", empirical science, cannot decide the problem of mind, but its voice must certainly be heard in any decision. *L.J.P.*

Mind-body problem. I. The mind-body problem is rarely defined in detail in contemporary psychology. Nevertheless it is a genuine problem and its existence can be demonstrated. Certain modern research concepts make allowance for it without acknowledging the fact. It can be considered on the basis of the principle of conflict or identity or alternatively by a combination of these two principles. This is confirmed by the history of psychology and is required by logic. From the standpoint of modern psychology the emphasis must be placed on the functional rather than the substantial aspect of the problem.

If it is approached from the principle of conflict (i.e. dualistically), the theory of interaction can be used to explain the functional relationship between mental and somatic processes: physiological processes "cause" mental correlates, and vice versa. Psychosomatics (q.v.) and psychopharmacology (q.v.) are based on this principle; traumatic experiences lead to somatic disorders of a functional and organic nature. Drugs have a specific influence on the mental state. Here we encounter an "empirical" (Jaspers, 1960) dualism of functions between which there is no bridge, because neither the Cartesian "*spiritus animales*" nor the Leibnizian "*deus ex machina*" are scientifically tenable constructs. Recently Wellek (1958) has defined an empirical dualism: "Monism is theory, dualism experience." The existence of conflicts in the personality tends to support this theory (e.g. the conflict between hunger and a desire to fast); it is also supported by the terminology concerning the mind-body problem: psychophysics, psychophysically neutral, psychosomatic, mind-body unit, etc.

From the standpoint of the identity principle in contemporary psychology only the physiological-materialistic concepts remain relevant: mental phenomena are derivatives of processes in the muscles, nerves and brain. For the development of psychology these assumptions have the advantage that they clearly emphasize the importance of the body as distinct from the metaphysical approach. The solutions to the mind-body problem indicated by most authors under the heading of "identity" are located, in accordance with the distinction made here, "substantially and functionally" between the two extreme solutions described above and therefore combine the two principles. This applies to Spinoza, who is considered as the prototypical philosopher of "identity", but only in respect of his single substance theory. To the extent that he defines the mind and body as two attributes, he obviously introduces dualism in the sense of a bilateral theory. Leibniz's concept of parallelism must be considered in the same light: he refers to unity in the substance and duality in the function (two clocks keeping time with one another). All the modern parallelists, such as G. T. Fechner, W. Wundt, G. E. Müller (with his five psychophysical axioms) as well as W. Stern (and his personalism) come under the same heading: personal processes are "psychophysically neutral", i.e. they cannot be clearly attributed to one side or the other. Empirical evidence is provided by the phenomena of expression and the motor system. Köhler's theory of isomorphy (1920—modified by Metzger, 1954) belongs to the same group: he does not refer explicitly to a substantial carrier but his theory has a dual functional basis: the cerebral and perceptual gestalts are of analogous structure. Finally the principle of complementarity taken over from physics by N. Bohr and applied to the mind-body problem deserves mention here: physical and mental processes must be described and explained individually but are complementary to the extent that they relate to the same phenomenon, as is the case with the corpuscular and wave theories of light. *Methodical dualism* would probably be acceptable as a description of the attitude to the mind-body problem in contemporary psychology: every psychologically relevant process or state must be described, analyzed and interpreted through its physical (neuro-physiological) and psychological (experiential) coordinates.

Bibliography: Blum, G.: A model of the mind. New York, 1961. **Dunbar, F.:** Mind and body. London, 1947. **Jaspers, K.:** Allgemeine Psychopathologie, Berlin–Heidelberg, 1960. **Köhler, W.:** Die physischen Gestalten in Ruhe und im stationären Zustand. Brunswick, 1920. **Id.:** Ein altes Scheinproblem in Naturwissenschaften, 1929. **Kuhlenbeck, H.:** Mind and matter. Basle & New York, 1961. **Metzger, W.:** Psychologie. Darmstadt, [2]1954. **Wellek, A.:** Das L. und die Ganzheit der Person. In: **Daumling, A.** (Ed.): Seelenleben und Menschenbild. Munich, 1958.

L. J. Pongratz

II. *The problem from the standpoint of natural science.* All our conscious processes and states are dependent on the brain, as is demonstrated by the following facts: (*a*) if the brain becomes unable to function as a result of chemical or mechanical influences (narcosis, injury), all psychological activity ceases; (*b*) changes in our brain activity due to the administration of certain substances (alcohol, opium, morphine, LSD, etc.) lead to changes in our conscious experience; (*c*) failure of specific areas of the brain (see *Brain pathology*) results in the breakdown of certain psychological functions (aphasia, agnosis, alexia, etc.); (*d*) there is a phylogenetic and ontogenetic parallel between the development of the brain and mental development. It follows that all forms of conscious experience are based on specific brain processes; brain processes form the indispensable prerequisite for psychological activity—but we do not know whether they are also a sufficient basis for it (other conditions may also have to be met before conscious experience becomes possible). The mind-body problem can therefore be reduced to two questions: "What happens in the brain when we experience something?" and "What is the causal relationship between psychological and cerebral processes?" The first question can in principle be answered reliably: during all conscious experience an enormous number of electrical and chemical processes take place in the ganglionic cells and fibers of the cerebral cortex (nervous system). The resulting "excitation constellations" must be "specific", i.e. a separate excitation constellation corresponds to each individual content of our conscious experience; there must therefore be at least as many excitation constellations as there are contents of experience.

The answer to the second question ("What is the causal relationship between psychological and cerebral processes?") is dependent in large measure on the importance attached to the "difference in nature" between the two processes; it consists in the fact that the psychological processes are non-physical (they are not made up of atoms and molecules and are largely independent of space and time), while the cerebral processes belong to the organic-material sphere. The old mind-body theories overlooked this distinction and held that there could be an interaction (interaction theory) between physical and mental processes or that they could be two aspects of the same process ("una eademque res, sed duobis modis expressa"—Spinoza's two-aspect theory). Because of the absolute dependence of the psychological processes on the brain, both theories were faced with logical difficulties: an influence of conscious experience on the brain processes in the sense defined by the interaction theory would only be possible if this experience were at least intermittently independent of the brain; the two-aspect theory does not answer the question of causal relationships. New theories have tried to explain the dependence of psychological processes on cerebral activity and the difference in nature between them by the assumption that conscious experience is an effect of the brain processes but cannot itself act on the latter ("theory of the ultimate effect," Rohracher, 1967), or that the brain processes are an indispensable (but not sufficient cause of conscious experience) which cannot develop without a further, unknown natural force which uses the brain as a tool or instrument for the production of the mental processes ("instrumental hypothesis"). The natural-scientific approach to the mind–body problem is best reflected in the "theory of the ultimate effect", which fully recognizes the special character of psychological processes—immateriality, considerable independence of space and time—as well as the absolute dependence of the psychological processes on the brain. For natural-scientific psychology, the conscious experiences are biological phenomena; they help to maintain life and individuality (e.g. the vital and social drives) as well as cultural progress (interests or cultural drives). The mental processes can be considered as the highest expression of natural development and as the ultimate effect of the organic process as a transcendental expression of the material process in immaterial subjective experience. This theory, too, leaves many questions open (above all the way in which conscious experience has developed from electro-chemical processes in the cerebral cortex); its advantage lies in the fact that it avoids the logical difficulties inherent in the assumption of a "feedback" effect of psychological processes on physical activity.

Bibliography: George, F. H.: Models of thinking. London, 1970. **Hook, S.** (Ed.): Dimensions of mind. New York, 1961. **Köhler, W.:** Psychologische Probleme. Berlin, 1933. **Lindsley, D. B.:** Attention, consciousness, sleep and wakefulness. In: Handbook of Physiol. Sect. I, Neurophysiol., Vol III. Washington, 1960. **Reeves, J. W.:** Body and mind in western thought. Harmondsworth, 1958. **Rohracher, H.:** Die Arbeitsweise des Gehirns und die psychischen Vorgänge. Munich, [4]1967. **Ryle, G.:** The concept of mind. London, 1949. **Scher, J.** (Ed.): Theories of the mind. New York, 1962. **Sluckin, W.:** Minds and machines. London, 1954. **Spatz, H.:** Gedanken über die Zukunft des Menschenhirns. In: **Benz, E.** (Ed.): Der Übermensch. Zürich–Stuttgart, 1961. **Walch, R.:** Orbitalhirn und Charakter. In: **Rehwald, E.** (Ed.): Das Hirntrauma. Stuttgart, 1956. **Wenzl, A.:** Leib-Seele-Problem. Berlin, 1933.

H. Rohracher

Minimal changes method. A standard psychophysical procedure for estimating an absolute or differential sensory threshold. The variable stimulus is progressively changed (e.g. increased in intensity) until it is either *just noticeable* or *just noticeably different* from a constant comparison stimulus. A number of such trials are run and a statistical average calculated. Syn.: *Method of limits; method of least differences; method of just noticeable differences.* *G.D.W.*

Minimum audible. The threshold of audibility; the minimum sound intensity of certain parts of the sound spectrum which is just audible. *A.Hä.*

Minimum separable. The simple separation capacity of the normal eye (see *Sense organs:* the eye). The minimum separable denotes the minimum angles between two points which are perceived as separate points: or, the least separation at which two parallel lines are perceived to be separate. It is measured in terms of vision and is dependent on many variables, such as the luminous density of the field of vision, contrast, surrounding and environmental factors, adaptation, etc.

A.Hä.

Minimum visible. Threshold of visibility: the minimum amount of light with specific duration and specific spatial extent which is just visible (see *Threshold*). The minimum visible is dependent, e.g. on the luminous density of the light, the duration of the light effect and the extent of the light stimulus.

A.Hä.

Minnesota Multiphasic Personality Inventory (abb. *MMPI*). The MMPI was developed by S. R. Hathaway and J. C. McKinley (1940, 1951). It consists of a subjective personality inventory designed according to psychiatric criteria, and has 566 questions which are summarized in the following ten clinical scales: (1) hypochondria (Hd); (2) depression (D); (3) hysteria (Hy); (4) psychopathy (Pd); (5) masculinity-femininity (Mf); (6) paranoia (Pa); (7) psychasthenia (Pt); (8) schizophrenia (Sc); (9) hypomania (Ma); (10) social introversion-extraversion (Si), and four "validity scales": (1) "?" value = questions which are not answered; (2) L (lie) value = tendency for the subject to place himself in a favorable light; (3) F value = unusual answer to questions to which almost all subjects give an identical answer; (4) K value = tendency to make a normal impression (used as a correction for other scale values). Various authors have suggested other scales (more than 200). The test profile of the personality scales is usually interpreted. The retest-reliability coefficients of the fourteen standard scales are between $r = 0.46$–9 (average value $r = 0.75$). In spite of many studies, the validity of the individual scales has not been conclusively demonstrated. See *Personality; Questionnaires; Traits; Type.* *P.G.*

Minnesota Rate of Manipulation (W. A. Ziegler). A revision of the Minnesota Manual Dexterity Test which determines the speed at which manual work is done. Pegs have to be inserted as quickly as possible into a board with sixty holes. There are five different exercises to be attempted. The test is suitable for selecting adults for jobs requiring simple manipulations. No verified standard values or authenticated pronouncements on validity (q.v.) are available. The value for repetition reliability is roughly $r = 0.8$. *F.Ma.*

Minority. A numerically small group in a society or nation which differs from the majority of the population in respect of special features, e.g. level of income, extent of political influence, skin color, religious or political beliefs are minorities; the social range in such a group is small but relatively large in relation to the rest of the population.

A minority may become a minority group if it develops into a stable sub-group within the society, representing interests which are apparently or actually different from those of the majority (hostile attitudes of the majority toward minorities). The extent of the rejection of members of a minority group is dependent among other factors on the development of certain social attitudes in the majority, e.g. ethnocentrism, authoritarianism or nationalism. See *Attitude.*

Bibliography: Horowitz, E.: Development of attitude towards negroes. In: **Newcomb, T. M. & Hartley, E. L.** (Eds.): Readings in social psychology. New York, 1947. *A.-S.M.*

Mirror writing. An experimental arrangement in transfer research. Numerous experiments in the transfer (q.v.) of sensorimotor skills have shown that children who have been trained to write with the right hand do well when they mirror-write with the left hand.

H.W.

Mirror-writing device. Used to test the coordination of hand and eye under difficult optical conditions. The test subject has to do a tracing of a more or less complicated, prepared drawing (usually a geometrical pattern made from two parallel lines) which he cannot see directly but only in a mirror, turned laterally the wrong way. For measuring the performance, the time taken to run completely through the figure and the number of occasions when the prepared tracing is touched or crossed are usually taken into consideration.

A.T.

Miosis (syn. *Myosis*). Contraction of the pupil by stimulation of the parasympathetic system or paralysis of the sympathetic system. Occurs, e.g. in neck tumors or injuries through lesions of the sympathetic nerves (Horner's syndrome), and in morphine poisoning, etc. Ant. *Mydriasis.*

R.R.

Mira myokinetic test. See *Myokinetic test.*

MMQ. Abb. for Maudsley Medical Questionnaire (Eysenck, 1947). See *Maudsley Personality Inventory; Questionnaires.*

Mneme. Memory (retention of past events). Anamnesis; recalling and reproducing stored information. According to Semon (1908) a general function of "organic matter", the totality of engrams.

Bibliography: Semon, R.: Die Mneme als erhaltendes Prinzip im Wechsel des organischen Geschehens. Leipzig, 1908.

H.W.

Mnemonics; Mnemotechnics. Improvement of memory performance, e.g. by systematic practice in particular by using special aids to learning (e.g. diagrams, rhymes, graphic presentations). Mnemometer: a memory device used by Rauschburg, N. Ach and O. Lipmann to check the time for which syllables to be learnt by a subject are presented to him and the method by which they are presented.

H.W.

Mnestic disorders. Memory disorders, in particular difficulty in retaining past occurrences.

H.W.

Mob. An uncontrolled and/or violent crowd. See *Aggression; Crowd behavior.*

Modal personality. A term offered by Linton (1945) for the personality type which is most frequently encountered in a given society or culture and by which the cultural background is formed in any given instance.

Bibliography: Linton, R.: The cultural background of personality. New York, 1945.

H.J.A.

Modal value. A statistical characteristic for the central trend. The modal value is the value in a frequency distribution which shows the highest frequency, i.e. the base of the "peak" ordinate of a distribution. Determination of the modal value is only meaningful in the case of large samples and single-peak distributions. The modal value is used as the characteristic for the central trend of a distribution of discontinuous variables.

G.Mi.

Model; model thought. A system M is known as the "model" of a prototype P if M and P are analogous but do not directly interact and if M is used to obtain information on P on the basis of the analogous relationship. The additional requirement that M should help to provide perceptual information is no longer applied as a result of the development of formal (e.g. mathematical) models. The prototype of a model in psychology is always part of its objective range. *W.H.T.*

Model psychosis. The psychopathological change induced in a normal individual by the administration of a psychotomimetic drug such as mescalin(e), LSD or psilocybin. *J.P.*

Models. 1. *Definition.* Models, or model concepts, exist in psychology wherever known, real or constructed systems are used as analogies for areas of behavior and/or experience. Model concepts associate individual behavior patterns, experiences and/or situations (stimuli) with parts of another system which generally does not originate in psychology, in such a way that specific relationships between the patterns of behavior, experiences and/or situations are illustrated by relationships in the model system. Although the model does not claim to cover completely all relationships in the given area of research, the model system nevertheless also contains "model-specific" relationships in respect of which it is not known whether they correspond to relationships in the objective range. These relationships may be used in part as the basis for deriving new research hypotheses.

2. *Development of the model concept.* According to Frey (in Kazemier & Vuysje, 1961, 89) the old High German "model" in medieval architecture represented one half the diameter of a column. The present word "model" first appeared (in Germany) in the sixteenth century as a derivative of the Italian "*modello*" and defined a pattern on the basis of which something else was manufactured. Today the term "model" denotes not only such patterns but objects which represent given patterns.

In mathematics and formal logic, a model is the interpretation of a "calculus". Object classes are associated with specific calculus signs in such a way that relationships between the object classes are represented by operators or relationship characteristics.

In the empirical sciences, a model is initially also the interpretation of a theory. To the extent that the latter contains concepts which have no observable corresponding features in the objective range, a different interpretation of the same theory may associate these concepts with better known factors which can sometimes be presented in a representational form. In Bohr's atom model, for example, electrons are represented as objects located at specific points in space and circling round an atom nucleus. Psychoanalytical theory employs the physical analogy for energy as the model of the theoretical concept of libido (q.v.).

While some authors (e.g. Dessauer, 1958, 225 ff) consider representation to be the essential feature of a model, there has been a growing tendency to define analogous systems which merely represent formalisms, as models. The multi-dimensional scaling which is widely used in psychology is based on a model in which stimuli are represented by points in a metric space in such a way that greater subjective similarity between two stimuli corresponds to a lesser distance between the associated spatial points. It is questionable whether we should speak here of "model" concepts. The representability of the spatial model is, to say the least, doubtful as soon as the space consists of more than three dimensions or has a non-Euclidean basis. In this case the model concept cannot imply that a specific model system can be represented perceptually but only that we imagine that the characteristics of the given research area behave in a manner similar to the parts of the model that is used.

3. *Black-box method.* The construction of model concepts can often be interpreted as the use of the black-box method. The black box is a box which responds through specific reactions (pointer deflections, illumination

of lights, etc.) to possible manipulations (pressure on a button, lever operation, etc.) whose content is, however, unknown. After adequate observation of its behavior a second box, i.e. the white box, with a known content and an analogous behavior, can be built. Groups of manipulations (or manipulation sequences) and groups of reactions (or reaction sequences) can then be grouped together in categories. Each category A,B . . . in the black box must correspond to a category A′, B′ . . . in the white box in such a way that the black box reacts to A with B precisely when the white box responds to A′ with B′. If common designations for the corresponding categories are introduced we can establish a sequence of manipulations in this language and complete the operations of both systems simultaneously; it must then be possible to prepare reaction reports in this language which are not distinguishable from each other (Turing criterion).

The black box and white box are parts of a model concept of model concepts. The black box should correspond to the given research subject, i.e. the living organism with its unknown inner psychological life, and the white box to the associated model. Modifications are possible if we are content—as is generally the case in practice—to consider only a few relationships ("very large box", Ashby, 1961, 109 ff), or if the relevant relationships can be observed only in part ("incompletely observable box", Ashby, 1961, 113 ff). There is then a risk that relevant aspects of the prototype will not be represented in the model, or that model-specific characteristics will be interpreted wrongly as representations of prototype aspects ("first and second order errors," according to Simon & Newell, 1963, 91 f).

4. *Types of model.* A distinction is made between physical models (material models, replica models) in which the analogous system is a perceptible object, and perceptive models or conceptual (linguistic) models. Formal models are a major special group; in this case the model system is a calculus. If the latter is obtained from an area of mathematics, we speak of a "mathematical" model.

In the last twenty years the scope and importance of mathematical models in psychology have grown considerably and led to the clear development of a "mathematical psychology" (q.v.) (Luce, Bush & Galanter, 1963/65). To characterize the part area of mathematics from which the model calculus is taken, we define a model, e.g. as algebraic, probabilistic or stochastic, etc. While some systems are used in diverse research areas (for instance, the factor analytical model), others are tailor-made for specific areas (e.g. learning models, decision models) but can still be transferred to others. In social psychology, for instance, we find forms of calculus which were first developed in general psychology (Tack, 1969, 488 ff).

We speak of a *simulation model* if fixed values are inserted in a formal model with variables in order to determine the values which are then assumed by other variables. Computers are often used for this purpose, the model being programmed on the machine. Cybernetics offers a whole range of concepts from which models can be constructed in many branches of science; these models are then referred to as "cybernetic" models. See *Cybernetics and psychology*.

5. *Function of models.* Model concepts transfer new knowledge to areas which are more familiar; therefore they represent a bridge to easier understanding. They are used for integration by representing diverse findings in a common system from which hypotheses can be derived in regard to still unknown facts. Formal models make less claim to completeness than traditional theories. On the other hand they offer more precise rules for classifying statements.

Models do not claim to represent a research subject in isomorphic form. In psychology they are limited to aspects of man or other organisms which can be represented by analogy. This form of representation of human behavior must not be misunderstood as an equation of man with a given model system. See *Decision processes; Factor analysis; Machine learning.*

Bibliography: Ashby, W. R.: An introduction to cybernetics. London, 1961. **Dessauer, F.:** Naturwissenschaftliches Erkennen. Frankfurt a.M., 1958. **Kazemier, B.H. & Vuysje, D.:** The concept and the role of the model in mathematics and natural and social sciences. Dordrecht, 1961. **Luce, R. D., Bush, R. R. & Galanter, E.** (Eds.): Handbook of mathematical psychology, Vols. 1, 2 and 3. New York & London, 1963–65. **Simon, H. A. & Newell, A.:** The use and limitations of models. In: **Marx, M. H.** (Ed.): Theories in contemporary psychology. New York & London, 1963, 89. **Smith, K. U. & Smith, M. F.:** Cybernetics: principles of learning and educational design. New York, 1966. **Stewart, D. J.** (Ed.): Automaton theory and learning systems. London, 1967. **Tack, W. H.:** Mathematische Modelle in der Sozialpsychologie. In: **Graumann, C. F.** (Ed.): Hdb. der Psychol., Vol. 7. Göttingen, 1969, 232. **Turing, A. M.:** On computable numbers, with an application to the Entscheidungs-problem. Proc. Lond. Math. Soc., 1936, *42*, 230–65. **Id.:** Computing machinery and intelligence. Mind, 1950, *59*, 433–60. *W. H. Tack*

Modesty. 1. Not presumptuousness. **2.** Self-depreciation. **3.** Conformity with the prevailing social, legal or religious norm of sexual display.

Modification. In individuals with identical hereditary characteristics, modifications may be caused by environmental influences, i.e. features may be formed differently but only within the limits of the modification range which is determined by heredity; e.g. certain plants growing in mountainous regions are smaller and have large amounts of hair while similar plants in lowland terrain are large and have no hair. *H.Sch.*

Molar. A term which psychology has borrowed from chemistry and which is used to denote larger units of behavior (events); its opposite is the term *molecular*, the name used for the smallest units of behavior (S-R relations). A stimulus-response pair can therefore be called a molecular, the running of a rat through a maze, for example, a molar unit.

Bibliography: Tolman, E. C.: Purposive behavior in animals and men. New York & London, 1932. *R.Hä.*

Molar analysis. The term denotes that form of psychological observation which carries out its investigations at a higher level than the smallest behavioral units (see *Molar*). The study of single events, of whole "episodes", right up to socio-psychological phenomena may be referred to as molar analysis.

Bibliography: Miller, D. R.: Study of social relationships. In: **Koch, S.** (Ed.): Psychology: A study of a science, Bd. 3. New York, 1963. *R.Hä.*

Molecularism. See *Atomism.*

Mongolism (syn. *Down's syndrome*). So called because the facial appearance is said to resemble that of members of the Mongolian race. It is the commonest cause of mental subnormality, accounting for about 15% of patients in subnormality hospitals. Intelligence is usually at the imbecile grade, although idiocy and feeblemindedness both occur with mongolism. The condition is caused by an extra chromosome and produces characteristic physical features such as short nose, large tongue which is fissured and often protrudes, hypotonic muscles and flabby skin. *V.K.J.*

Monoamine oxidase. A group of enzymes which act as catalysts in the oxidative decomposition of the biogenic amines (monoamines), tyramine, tryptamine, serotonin, noradrenalin, dopamine, etc. The breakdown of these substances can be inhibited by monoamine oxidase inhibitors. *W.J.*

Monoamine oxidase inhibitors. Psychopharmaceutical substances which are generally referred to in abbreviation as MAO inhibitors, MAOI, or MAO-I inhibitors, and prevent the breakdown of biogenic amines by inhibition of monoamine oxidase so that its concentration in the brain is increased. Chemically, the MAOI can be divided into the hydrazines (e.g. iproniazide, nialamide) and the non-hydrazines. MAOI cause central excitation in animals. Preliminary application of MAOI cancels damping by reserpine. The introduction of iproniazide as an anti-depressant is explained by its activating effect in human testees. The indication area of pharmacotherapy with MAOI appears to be more strictly limited than in the case of other anti-depressants. In the case of unselected depressive patients, success therefore appears more limited (Davis *et al.*, 1968), although clear effects can be observed in atypical, non-endogenous depression (Cole *et al.*, 1961); the therapeutic effect is covariant with changes in concentration of the biogenic amines.

Bibliography: Cole, J. O. *et al.*: Drug therapy. In: Progress in neurology and psychiatry, Vol. 16. New York, 1961. **Davis, J. M.** *et al.*: Drugs used in the treatment of depression. In: **Efron, D. H.** (Ed.): Psychopharmacology, 1957–1967. Washington, 1968. **Pletscher, A.**: Monoamine oxidase inhibitors; effects related to psychostimulation. In: **Efron, D. H.** (Ed.): Psychopharmacology, 1957–67. Washington, 1968.

P.D.

Monochromatic. Radiation which consists of a single wavelength or more specifically of a single wavelength range.

A color is said to be monochromatic if its stimulus basis is monochromatic radiation; antonym: polychromatic color (= mixed color). See *Chromatic*. *A.H.*

Monochromatism. An abnormality in eyesight; only differences in brightness are perceived instead of colors. In "typical" monochromatism, the retinal system of the cones does not function properly, while in "atypical" monochromatism the defect is localized in the upper nerve centers. Monochromatism is also referred to as *monochromasy*. An individual with the defect is a *monochromat*. *G.K.*

Monocular. Involving or affecting a single eye; as opposed to binocular = involving both eyes. *A.H.*

Monomania. A mental disorder in which dominating and fixed ideas are prominent. The patient is usually well integrated in other ways, and responds fairly normally to situations which do not impinge on his delusional system. *Paranoia* is a possible synonym. *R.H.*

Monotony. A state of reduced psychological activity which results in heightened fatigue and reduced ability to react, and reduced and fluctuating performance as phenomena accompanying monotonous work. On the basis of his experiments with unvarying industrial work, Wyatt (1924) showed that monotony (boredom) is a more important factor than fatigue in determining performance. Monotony is characterized by a wave-like pattern due to the intermittent falling and rising of mental activity. The reduction of activity in a state of monotony is traced back to such factors as psychological stress and degree of interest (Bartenwerfer, 1970). Lack of variety and stimuli and constant repetition of the same process can be summarized as a reduction in the range of interest. As a result of the limitation of this interest, psychological attentiveness diminishes and this leads to a reduction in mental activity. To counteract monotony, attempts are made to increase interest in boring activities, e.g. by entertainment, music, movement and changes of activity. An effort of will to avoid a state of monotony in fact has the opposite result: because of the effort to concentrate on the boring activity, the subject is all the more likely to lapse into a state of monotony (and *fatigue*, q.v.).

Bibliography: Bartenwerfer, H. G.: Psychische Beanspruchung. In: **Mayer, A. & Herwig, B.** (Eds.):

Hdb. der Psychol., Vol. 9. Göttingen, 1970. **Wyatt, S.:** Monotony. London, 1924. **Id. & Langdon, J. H.:** Fatigue and boredom in repetitive work. (Industrial Health Res. Board No. 77). London, 1937. *A.K.*

Monozygotic twins. Twins that develop from a single egg. See *Twin studies.*

Montessori method. This theory of education, named after Maria Montessori (1870–1952) elevates spontaneous action by the child into an educational principle. The aim is to educate the child freely in the manner best suited to him, using his own mental powers and manual skills without special supervision. The critical objections to Montessori education challenge its overemphasis of free development, exaggeration of the value of natural behavior of children and general idolizing of the child. *H.Sch.*

Mood. A state of feeling of some duration in which the quality of the feeling (merry, sad, optimistic mood) and natural inclination to stability or fluctuation of this quality are distinguished. Factor analysis revealed a mood stability factor which belongs among factors of temperament. See *Traits.* *G.K.*

Mood transmission. The behavior of a group of animals is influenced by mood transmission. Often expressive movements promoting this function are the only ones to have been developed. When greylag geese are in the mood to migrate, they begin to wander about, shaking their heads with necks outstretched and calling until the whole flock are seized by the mood and fly into the air together. Yawning also has an infectious, sleep-inducing effect. (See *Ideo-real law.*) *W.P.*

Morale. A term which is generally an abstraction from individual adaptive behavior and denotes a positive attitude to a group, its aims and leadership. In industrial psychology, a synonym for satisfaction in the working group with the result of a high readiness to work. *W.D.F.*

Morality. Since J. G. Fichte, two planes have been distinguished within the moral aspect of actions, one of a more subjective kind which concerns the inward observation of the rules of behavior (morality in the literal sense), and another of a more objective nature which —referring to society—embraces the totality of all kinds of behavior accepted by any cultural group. Thus morality is closely connected with that which forms the superego (q.v.) in the unconscious, or represents the basis for the ego ideal (q.v.) in consciousness. (See *Conscience*). *P.M.*

Morality principle. By analogy with the pleasure and reality principles, the controlling principle in psychological processes which seeks to establish concordance with (direct or introjected) motives of other persons, with rules and customs of groups of persons and with the norms of society. *W.T.*

Morgan's canon. The American geneticist T. H. Morgan demonstrated in studies of the fruit fly *drosophila,* how genes are inherited in groups. The number of coupled groups corresponds to the number of chromosomes in the simple set. By crossing-over, an exchange of genes may occur between corresponding coupled groups; the frequency of exchange is specific to individual species and genes. The genes are arranged on the chromosome in a linear pattern. The Morgan unit is the exchange frequency of 1%, which does not, however, correspond to the real spatial distance between the gene-loci. *K.Fi.*

Morphine. A psychotropic substance contained in opium and first isolated by Sertürner in 1804. Hypnotic in therapeutic doses (up to 15 mg); acts as a narcotic analgesic in higher doses. Morphine is a strong narcotic and leads to dependence. Physiological effects (partially antagonistic to atropine): contraction of pupils, reduction in heart frequency, inhibition of respiration, increased tonus of smooth musculature (obstipation). Psychological effects: there is some doubt whether the pain threshold is raised; pain anticipation is reduced. Euphoria occurs, especially in addicts; otherwise the main features are nausea, lethargy and dysphoria. Objectively there are improvements in performance (reaction time) in subjects habituated to morphine, especially under stress.

Bibliography: Becher, H. K.: Measurement of subjective responses. New York, 1959. **Lasagna, L.:** The clinical evaluation of morphine and its substitutes as analgesics. Pharm. rev., 1964, *16*, 47–83. **Reynolds, A. K. & Randall, L. O.:** Morphine and allied drugs. Toronto, 1957. *W.B.*

Morphology. Theory of the structure of organisms. Attempts have been made to establish correlations between physical structure and personality, frequently through a typology, e.g. Kretschmer and Sheldon. Factor-analytical studies of body structure have highlighted a number of factors: general head size, general body length, a trunk factor and a factor for muscular bulk. See *Body build index; Type.* *G.K.*

Mosaic test. A test in which square patterns must be produced from four to sixteen cubes with surfaces of different colors, which are sometimes divided diagonally. First developed by S. C. Kohs in 1923 under the title "Block Design Test", the mosaic test has been included as a non-linguistic intelligence item in various test batteries (e.g. Arthur Point Scale of Performance Tests). There is a high correlation with intelligence, but there is a greater complexity and plasticity loading depending on age and pattern. *R.M.*

Mother complex. All modes of human interest in one's mother, including those which can be satisfied, and those which are forbidden and therefore generally repressed or inhibited by other defense (q.v.) mechanisms. The term is often used only for extreme and pathological degrees of interest. It then implies disturbed relationships with other females and a reduced ability to make contact with them. *W.T.*

Mother fixation. A human being's love for his or her mother. It represents all his expectations of motive satisfaction. The term is sometimes confined to extreme forms of fixation which prevent the individual from establishing relations with others and breaking the tie with his (her) mother. According to Freud, mother fixation includes—in every person—*oral* (mothering, contact), *anal* (demanding services from the mother but giving something in return), and *early genital* (sexual interest in the mother) components, which are inhibited or repressed to a varying degree. People differ considerably in the qualitative composition and also in the intensity of their mother fixation. *W.T.*

Mother image. According to C. G. Jung, the mother image may be innate or originate from the collective unconscious, and differ from the real mother. *W.T.*

Mother substitute. Generally a female who takes over the function of a mother for a child or other person after a temporary or permanent loss of the real mother. *W.T.*

Motility. 1. A basic characteristic of all living organisms. **2.** A term used to denote the degree of facility with which an organism moves. Also used in psychodiagnostics to describe the general impression of a person. *H.Ro.*

Motion, apparent. A perception of movement with no adequate stimulus basis. In a typical arrangement designed to produce apparent motion an object is presented in the positions A and B successively. If the length of the interval of time is correctly chosen (0.04–0.08 sec.), the impression is created that the object has moved from A to B; this is a beta-movement (q.v.). In addition alpha- (q.v.), gamma- (q.v.), delta- (q.v.) and upsilon-(q.v.) movements are distinguished. In connection with apparent motion M. Wertheimer spoke of the *phi-phenomenon* (q.v.), i.e. of an elementary (irreducible) quality of movement perception. A number of theories concerning apparent motion have come from K. Marbe, M. Wertheimer, K. Koffka, P. F. Linke, T. Erismann, *et al.*

Bibliography: Graham, C. H.: Visual perception. In: **Stevens, S. S.** (Ed.): Handbook of experimental psychology. New York & London, 1963. **Id.:** Perception of movement. In: **Graham, C. H.** (Ed.): Vision and visual perception. New York & London, 1966.

W.P.

Motion, perception of. The central nervous system receives signals concerning position, weight and tensions from ends of nerves attached to muscles, sinews and joints. This information is processed, and we experience it as perception of movement. It plays a large part when we have to find our way without visual perception (e.g. in a dark room). See *Kinesthesia.*

Induced motion: the apparent movement of the moon behind the clouds, which are really moving. The clouds "induce" their movement on to the moon. Our system of perception considers the large objects to be at rest, and ascribes the movement to the smaller objects moving in any related system. *V.M.*

Motion study. See *Time-and-motion study.*

Motivation. One of the hypothetical processes (see *Intervening variable*) involved in the determination of behavior in addition to the effect of a stimulus or perceived situation, the processes of learning and certain other factors, such as abilities (q.v.). Whereas abilities primarily influence the yield or level of adaptation of a specific pattern of behavior, motivation determines its level of activation, intensity and consistency as well as general direction. Learning or acquired associations determine (for non-instinctive behavior) the concrete direction toward a given object. It is, however, clear that the effect of stimuli is not always distinctly separate from the effect of motivation. Some categories of excitation, above all those for which internal stimuli are responsible (as well as those caused by external stimuli which lead to a disagreeable condition), are often interpreted as corresponding to primary needs (homeostatic disequilibrium), while other stimuli (e.g. objects) have valences and act as motives or releasers. The state of motivation is then understood as a factor which lowers the stimulus threshold for these stimuli.

The objective phenomena which in my opinion justify consideration of the hypothetical processes of motivation, are based on the fact that behavior shows (positive or negative) preferences for the objects or situations in the environment (control), and that these objects are desired or avoided with varying degrees of intensity and perseverance.

1. *The functions of motivation.* Motivation as an energizer should explain behavior. A distinction can be made between the factors which determine the general degree of activation of the organism and its state of excitation and alertness and the question as to why an individual performs specific actions. While the first problem may be considered from the standpoint of energy sources which form the basis of vital activity in general, or from the angle of activity of the nervous system (e.g. the reticular formation), the explanation of the fact that an individual is more interested in one class of objects than another is a matter for *motivation* studies as such.

This in turn raises the problem of regulative behavior. Some authors do not wish to attribute a controlling function to motivation; in their opinion the control of behavior is a function of the learning process. Others consider that the fundamental aspect of motivation lies in the regulative influence. This problem can be solved if two different levels of control are assumed. On the one hand, control may signify the actual path followed by behavior to reach the given target which it had already achieved before, on an earlier occasion. This concrete form of control is based on learning, except in the case of innate or instinctive behavior. However the fact that an individual who is in a state of motivation or need, sets out in search of something new and turns away from certain objects in order to dwell on others, shows that motivated behavior has a general orientation or control. In this search for a relatively large category of objects or situations we can distinguish the general control of behavior which E. C. Tolman defined as its "purposiveness", and which represents nothing other than its orientation toward a specific aim. The fact that some objects or situations, unlike others, evoke a state of reduced need, satisfaction and adaptation is explained by this fundamental and implied orientation. See *Instinct; Learning*.

A third function of motivation in relation to behavior (in addition to the roles of arousal and control) resides in the fact that it endows a range of behavior with unity and comprehensive importance. In fact it is motivation which through its orientation toward a target object means that a series of movements which vary widely from the physical angle, represent behavior in the true sense of the word, i.e. an appropriate reaction to a situation.

2. *The two poles of the process and the terminology*. The terms which relate to motivation may be divided into two groups depending on whether they relate to the internal (drive and efforts of the individual) or external (valence of the object) poles of the motivational process. The first group includes concepts such as need, tension, drive, instinct, inclination, wishes, will, intention, plan, etc. The second group consists, e.g. of valence (challenge), value, affective value, incentive, cathexis, interest, etc.

Need (q.v.) is generally the fundamental concept of motivation, while a *motive* or *motivation* (in its subjective meaning) denotes the process which leads an individual toward a concrete objective. *Need* denotes in the first instance (objective meaning) the lack of specific elements in the environment; this objective lack becomes a physiological need in that it creates a deficiency in the organism, and a psychological demand because the state of the organism is perceived by the individual as a stress which influences behavior. In the psychological sense, however, this need does not necessarily refer to an organic state or physical deficiency; there may simply be a lack of specific forms of behavioral contact with the environment (Nuttin: "*théorie relationnelle des besoins*"), and this deficiency may originate from a readiness to communicate up to the point of self-sacrifice, or from sudden growth as well as from a deficit (A. H. Maslow, C. R. Rogers).

Viewed in terms of its purely dynamic significance, i.e. overlooking the aspect of "innate behavior" which has frequently been added since W. McDougall, the notion of instinct (q.v.) approximates closely to that of need.

3. *Theoretical concepts*. The actual nature of the basic needs and their effects on behavior has been considered in terms of various theoretical concepts. Often the change in the state of the organism is interpreted as a disturbance of energy or homeostatic equilibrium. This physiological state or stimulation is the origin of the drive (or tension) which triggers behavior (drive stimulus model) until an appropriate object (incentive) has been found; through the consumer reaction to this object, the homeostatic equilibrium of the organism is reestablished or the unpleasant, internal stimulus eliminated (e.g. hunger). The needs which are defined in the concepts of physiological

states (tissue needs) are termed *primary needs*. All the psycho-social needs and all specifically human needs are frequently termed *secondary needs*, as are those which result (through the influence of learning processes, socialization, sublimation, etc.) from primary needs.

The "psycho-hydraulic" need model (used by comparative psychologists such as Lorenz) assumes that a specific energy is formed for each kind of instinctive reaction and collected in the organism; the discharge of this energy then represents behavior reactions. This discharge normally occurs in the presence of the adequate object (releaser). If such a releaser is absent for an extended period, the discharge may occur in relation to inadequate stimuli and result in vacuum responses.

The neo-hedonic need theory considers the desire for pleasure (or, more accurately, to avoid disagreeable sensations) as the decisive dynamic basis of behavior. This theory (in which Freud's model can be recognized) approximates to the model of energy equilibrium and drive stimulus, since the restoration of equilibrium (or the elimination of the excessive offer of stimuli) objectively represents pleasure. According to this theory, motivation is based on affectivity (the experience of pleasure and its opposite or anxiety), since motivated behavior consists in the urge to achieve the object which previously gave pleasure (cf. also the principle of need reduction defined by C. L. Hull).

For other authors, the ultimate foundation of needs or motivation in general resides in the fact that every function of the organism is accompanied by a drive force which works toward the exercise of that function (functional pleasure according to K. Bühler). In this sense, A. Adler (1928) spoke of an auditory drive, a visual drive, etc. More recently, some authors (e.g. H. W. Nissen, 1950) have assumed that each organ has an autonomic motivation which causes it to perform those functions for which it is equipped, and that this is a characteristic of organic tissue. In this way, Nissen tries to explain the cognitive requirements as a "need" of brain cell tissue. See *Drive*.

H. F. Harlow (1953), on the other hand, suggests a distinction between two types of motivation: those which have their origin in the organism (homeostatic needs) and those whose origin lies in external objects (cognitive need, or need to explore the environment). This theory overlooks the standpoint referred to above that every motivational process can be viewed either from the angle of the subject that is motivated by a drive, or from the position of the object which triggers a motivation or exercises an attraction. However, there is certainly a distinction between the reaction effort for a homeostatic need by comparison with a cognitive need.

Several authors (H. A. Murray, G. W. Allport, etc.) make a distinction under several headings between viscerogenic and psychological needs, without, however, considering the question of the innate or derived character of the latter, while E. C. Tolman explicitly adopts the view of innate social needs. Since behavior involves a relationship to environmental objects, motivation and needs, which for the psychologist are nothing other than the dynamic aspect of behavior itself, may be viewed as types of relationship with the environment to the extent that they are necessary for the perfect (psychological and physiological) functioning of the individual. On account of the complexity of the environment it can be assumed that man has fundamental needs (i.e. types of necessary relationships) at the behavioral level relating to the psycho-social world and universe, and in regard to the biosphere. According to this concept of needs (Nuttin, 1968), based on the relationship with the environment, the fundamental needs in psychology can be seen as the dynamic aspect (active intervention of the individual in the psychological and physical environment) of those types of behavioral relationships which the individual seeks to achieve or maintain, and without which his functioning is disturbed to a greater or lesser extent, or disagreeable sensations are experienced. The dynamic nature of the relations, or the possibility and necessity of active intervention in the environment (structural and functional intervention), entail the wish or demand to achieve specific forms of relationship.

4. *Need categories and research.* As regards the question of the major categories of motivation and basic needs, several systems have been suggested which depend on the number of classification criteria adopted. The list of drives and corresponding emotions indicated in the different editions of W. McDougall's study (last edition published in 1932), shows only twenty *propensities*. Historically this list has had an important influence. At present the classifications established by H. A. Murray (1938) and E. L. Tolman (1951) have an influence on research. Murray (q.v.) distinguishes between just over ten viscerogenic and some forty psychological needs. The need to complete tasks, the need for achievement and the need for sociability in Murray's list are among those categories of needs which have provided the bases for an impressive range of studies (D. McClelland, J. Atkinson, S. Shachter, etc.). On the basis of factor analyses, R. Cattell (1950) has drawn up a list of some fifteen motivational categories (*ergs*); C. Bühler distinguishes between four groups of basic tendencies; Nuttin has prepared a classification in which the need for self-realization occurs together with the needs for contact or interaction, each of which is subdivided into three different forms of need depending on the environment in which they are manifested (the physical environment, psycho-social environment, and universe). In each of these types of environment man tries to assert himself or develop and adapt by means of a network of contacts or interactions depending on the possibilities at his disposal (cognitive, affective relationships, etc.). Among the needs on which research is concentrating at present, it is worth mentioning the need for stimulation, i.e. the harmful effect of isolation or sensory (D. O. Hebb) and affective deprivation (R. A. Spitz), as well as certain motivational states in connection with the unknown nature of objects, curiosity (D. E. Berlyne), and the needs for information, perception (H. F. Harlow), manipulation and exploration of the environment in man and animals. Work on cognitive dissonance (q.v.) (Festinger) and balance theory (F. Heider and T. Newcomb) largely belong to the sphere of social motivation. The motivational nature of aggressivity (innate or acquired) is also a problem of immediate interest (the Lorenzian view contrasting with that of K. Lewin's school and the Yale University school); experimental studies of competition and cooperation are currently important. See *Aggression.*

In "*motivation research*", the concept of motivation has a very narrow meaning. It is used in advertising psychology (see *Marketing*) to study motivations which are generally unconscious or hidden, and which must be appealed to by advertising. We cannot examine in any detail here the many individual results achieved by research into the physiological aspect of motivation and needs. See *Drive; Need.*

5. *The development of motivation.* Starting from the fundamental needs, many concrete motivations are developed as functions of widely varying cultural and individual circumstances and under the influence of many different processes. In addition to the learning processes and conditioning, channelling and socialization which are primarily active in this development, many other processes must be mentioned, such as the conscious or unconscious mechanisms supposedly discovered by psychoanalysis (q.v.) and other theories of depth psychology (q.v.). Identification, displacement, reaction formation, sublimation, and many other factors, may help a need to be satisfied in a concrete attempt to reach a specific category of objects or situations. Repression (q.v.) may cause motivational indifference toward an object which exercises an attraction on most other

people. This link between an aspiration toward a specific object and a given need may remain dark (unconscious attraction of an object) in which case we speak of an *unconscious motivation*.

On the other hand, the cognitive processes change most human needs into concrete tasks and projects. Recognition of the possibilities of achieving an aim is the concrete form in which needs control human behavior. What is commonly referred to as the will is simply the cognitively processed motivation which the individual ego prefers to other motivations, so that "my will" is the motivation favored by the conscious ego, freely or otherwise. The driving forces of the will are identical with those of other concrete motivations.

The motives and projects which exist on the bases of the developmental processes of motives in adult humans must not be considered merely as developments of forms of infantile needs. Both infantile and adult forms of motivation are embodiments of basic needs which are dependent in their concrete form on the level of development of the psychological functions in general. It is evident that each higher stage of development is influenced by the earlier stages.

G. W. Allport's theory (1937) of the development of motivation also makes a distinction between current motives and primary motives as well as those of childhood. It stresses the functional autonomy of all drives in the sense that behavior patterns which were originally motivated by specific needs (e.g. the need to earn a living) gradually find a spontaneous drive, i.e. become functionally autonomous. This opinion is reflected in Woodworth's theory that "mechanisms become drives". It remains to be determined whether the autonomous forms of behavior can be motivated by other needs which gradually find their channel, i.e. their form of embodiment, in them.

6. *Summary* (present state of knowledge). Ideas on motivation were for a long time influenced by the fact that for several decades the main research in this sphere was conducted either into animal behavior or the pathological behavior of man. Specifically human needs remained in the background for a long time, and more constructive aspects of human motivation were neglected for pathogenic processes. In addition, behavioral research veiled the role of motivation in the context of the behavioristic S-R model. While today, in clinical and applied psychology, the significance of the motivation process is scarcely disputed, some trends in experimental psychology (with a psychophysiological or behaviorist bias) generally doubt the relevance of these intervening variables. Frequently the behavioral functions which are probably attributable to motivation are ascribed to other factors (such as stimulation and physiological states, alertness and learning).

Recently, other schools of experimental and social psychology have made a thorough study of a wider range of motivations and moved beyond the opinion that human motivation is simply an extension of homeostatic needs. See *Drive; Humanistic psychology*.

Bibliography: Adler, A.: Understanding human nature. London & New York, 1928. **Allport, G. W.:** Functional autonomy of motives. Amer. J. Psychol., 1937, *50*, 141–56. **Ancona, L., Buytendijk, F. J., *et al.*:** La motivation. Paris, 1959. **Atkinson, J. W.:** An introduction to motivation. Princeton, 1964. **Berlyne, D. E.:** Conflict, arousal and curiosity. New York, 1960. **Bolles, R. C.:** Theory of motivation. New York & London, 1967. **Bühler, C. & Massarik, F.** (Eds.): The course of human life. A study of goals in the humanistic perspective. New York, 1968. **Cattell, R. B.:** Personality and motivation structure and measurement. London, 1957. **Cofer, C. N. & Appley, M. H.:** Motivation, theory and research. New York & London, 1964. **Harlow, H. F.:** Motivation as a factor in the acquisition of new responses. In: Current theory and research in motivation: a symposium. Lincoln, Neb., 1953. **Hebb, D. O.:** The organization of behavior. New York, 1949. **Hull, C. L.:** A behavior system. New Haven, 1952. **Jones, M. R. & Arnold, W. J.** (Eds.): Nebraska symposium on motivation, Vols. 1–17. Lincoln, Neb., 1953–69. **Lewin, K.:** The conceptual representation and the measurement of psychological forces. Durham, N. C., 1938. **Lorenz, K.:** The comparative method in studying innate behavior patterns. Symp. Soc. exp. Biol., 1950, *4*, 221–68. **Maslow, A. H.:** Motivation and personality. New York, 1954. **McDougall, W.:** The energies of men. London, 1932. **Murray, H. A.:** Explorations in personality. New York, 1938. **Nissen, H. W.:** Description of learned responses in discrimination behavior. Psychol. Rev., 1950, *57*, 121–31. **Nuttin, J.:** Psychoanalysis and personality: a dynamic theory of normal personality. New York, [3]1962. **Id.:** La motivation. In: **Fraisse, P. & Piaget, J.** (Eds.): Traité de psychologie expérimentale, Vol. 5. Paris, 1968, 1–83. **Spitz, R. A.:** Childhood development phenomena: the influences of the mother-child relationship and its disturbances. In: **Soddy, K.** (Ed.): Mental health and infant development. New York, 1955. **Thomae, H.:** Motivation. In: Handbuch der Psychologie, Vol. 2. Göttingen, 1965. **Tolman, E. C.:** Purposive behavior in animals and men. New York, 1932.

J. Nuttin

Motivational perception. The alteration or distortion undergone by perception because of the fact that the perceiving individual is in a state of need or emotional excitement, or the perceived object has a specific (positive or negative) value or valence for his personality. We therefore recognize that perception is a result not only of the stimulus structure and sense organs but also of the personality structure and its motivational state. Murphy formulated the theory of motivational perception in the concept of autism by which he indicated that the true image given to us by the cognitive functions of reality is distorted towards the needs and wishes of the perceiving individual (cf. M. Bleuler's "autistic thought"). Several hypothetical processes whose sequence has scarcely been studied as yet are assumed in the context of motivational perception, such as perceptual defense and projection. The new research line in this sphere has been defined as the "new look" (it began between 1945 and 1950). See *Social perception.*

Bibliography: Allport, F. H.: Theories of perception and the concept of structure. New York & London, 1955, 709. **Blake, R. R. & Ramsey, G. V.:** Perception —an approach to personality. New York, 1951, 442. **Bruner, J. S. & Krech, D.:** Perception and personality. Durham, 1950. **Grauman, C. F.:** Sich-sinnliche Bedingungen der Wahrnehmens. In: **Metzger, P. T. W.** (Ed.): Handbuch der Psychol., Vol. 1. Göttingen, 1966.

J.N.

Motivation theories. Term for theories which set out to explain or describe how a motivated (causative) stimulus, leads on to a motivated (caused) response. Motivation theories therefore must be able to explain what a motivating stimulus or a motivated response is, and also what happens between stimulus and response. See *Motivation.*

R.Hä.

Motivator. The functional block in Stachowiak's "Kybiak" psychostructural model (q.v.), which associates a form of motivation with the characteristic features of a stimulus in a given situtation; the motivation in turn triggers a program of action, or at least creates the peripheral conditions for a program of action which is to be developed by problem solving. *H.F.*

Motive. A motive is a factor which enters into arousal (activation, q.v.) and the orientation of behavior. It may designate either the object in the external world which evokes a certain tendency in the subject (an incentive), or that tendency itself. Ambition or hunger just as much as, say, nourishment, may be characterized as the motive specific to a behavior and may therefore *motivate* an action. One may speak of a "hunger motive", a "stimulus motive", or an "achievement motive" (q.v.).

Less technically, a "motive" is either the goal-object or the tendency, insofar as they are consciously, intentionally or cognitively present. In this sense, any known datum may enter into the determination or volition of an action, and hence may be designated as the motive or the "reason" for a behavior. For unconscious motives, see *Motivation.*

The influence of the motive on behavior is conceived either in terms of physical causality, or in the form of a psychological or final causation according to which the behavior itself is viewed as a physiological reaction or a meaningful response. In the latter case, certain physical or physiological factors are not excluded as causally codetermining the behavior—but such a group of factors is not characterized as a collection of *motives*. The causal action of most physical or physiological factors is apparent as conscious or unconscious tendencies, so that it seems improper to separate the two forms of behavioral determination.

Men and animals may be confronted simultaneously with several incompatible motives (goal-objects or tendencies). In this case, a *conflict* (q.v.) arises, and the strongest tendency (or, in behaviorist terms, the S-R unit possessing at this moment the most intense excitatory potential) may be thought of as inhibiting the other possible responses. Lewin (q.v.) distinguished three forms of conflict, to which much research has been devoted: approach-approach, approach-avoidance, and avoidance-avoidance (see *Conflict; Frustration*).

When the motive of an action consists not only of attaining to an object but of realizing a certain *level* of performance, the term *aspiration level* (q.v.), or *expectation*, is used; again, much research has been carried out in this area. This complex of problems is connected to that of the *achievement motive* or *motivation*: some subjects are mainly motivated by the desire for success, others by the fear of failure.

Bibliography: see *Motivation*. *J. Nuttin*

Motor aphasia. See *Aphasia*.

Motor paths. The motor paths conduct impulses to striped or smooth muscles and lead to body movements, intestinal peristaltic processes and bronchial and vascular contractions. They are among the efferent nerves. Examples: the *nervus glossapharyngeus* (glossopharyngeal nerve, 9th cranial nerve) leads to the pharyngeal muscles. A complicated pattern of impulses passes through the sciatic and femoral nerve during walking. The pyramidal paths conduct impulses of the voluntary motor system and the extrapyramidal motor system is responsible for movements which are largely automatic.

G.A.

Motor skills. Three characteristics describe motor skills: (1) The term refers to limb or body movement adjusted to spatial and temporal demands. (2) Skilled motion is controlled, and *perceptual-* or *sensorimotor* skilled motion acknowledges both sensory control and the role of movement-produced cues. Vision and proprioception are most important, and a shift from external, visual control to kinesthetic control characterizes much of skills learning. (A novice's close watch on his gear-stick placements becomes the glance—if that—an expert driver gives his rapid move.) (3) Differences from other behavior are not significant in theory.

1. *Points of view*. There are basic and applied concerns (medical, sport, musical, industrial, military) outside psychology, and there is overlapping within. Developmental study finds implications in the kind and regular sequence of skills that mature with early growth, and in the causes of loss (often sensory or cognitive) in old age. Human engineering features machine-skill problems involving time, man, and equipment. Time-and-motion is a familiar though unrepresentative field example; the problems now are to fit machine-design to human beings, and to improve selection and training techniques.

Basic work is part of experimental psychology, where classes of human behavior are less important than common concepts; therefore definition is not restrictive and may emphasize *motor* or *skill*. Behavior is not exclusively verbal, perceptual, or motor. Response takes movement, and most behavior has verbal or cognitive parts. *Motor* is substantial motion. It includes balance and steadiness, as in rail-walking and aiming;

single, repeated, serial, and successively cued all-or-none acts, as in tapping one key or several keys in a pattern; positioning, as setting a volume dial; continuous action, as in driving, writing, and running. *Skilled* action is patterned, graded in extent and ordered in time, and new sequences are accurately followed. Motor (Andreas, 1960; Bilodeau & Bilodeau, 1961) or temporal-spatial (Smith, 1962; Fitts, 1964; Bahrick & Noble, 1966), however, comes second to reliance on sensorimotor interaction and pre-set response. Information-processing models and feedback study are prominent.

2. *History and methodology.* Experimental membership has meant alternate skills stress and neglect, eclectic theory, and concentration on artificial laboratory apparatus, flexible to deliberate variation, non-existent work, play, and art skills.

Functionalism's (1890–1910) generous definition of psychology allowed the first major effort, with Woodworth, Cattell, and Stetson among the contributors. The next revival was a recent product of coincident events. Selection and training in World War II needed new apparatuses, and learning theory gave them use later on. Mathematical and computer advances permitted the scientific statement of how measured response depends on known stimulus value. Machine skills turned attention and support to tool and machine use as significant human activity. Fitts (1964), a recognized leader, credits Craik as a modern pioneer in analysis.

Research into human behavior presents a task to different groups of subjects under different conditions. An item, the experimental variable, differs for the groups, and a response index is related to the item's value. Target-size might be X, 2X, 4X for groups and accuracy at centering a stylus taken—other target (course, speed) and stylus (size, weight) aspects the same for all. As skill implies proficiency and practice, its study emphasizes learning.

3. *Research.* Tracking, the usual representative of continued adjusting, involves motion extent, pattern, choice, and speed. Discrete-trial positioning simplifies the study of adjustive motion by taking moves singly; selective learning frees pattern and choice from adjustment; work tasks, e.g. cranking, use well-learned action to measure uncomplicated effects of temporary factors such as inhibition and motivation.

(*a*) *Tracking.* Control and display are critical features of the operator tracking station in equipment-skills. Hand or foot controls steer stimuli on a display. *Pursuit* is holding a marker on a moving target—keeping a stylus on a dot as a disk rotates. *Compensatory* tracking is less accurate, as displays do not separate target input and feedback; an operator nulls pre-set stimulus-drift from a fixed point—a joystick returns a meter needle to zero or a dot to oscilloscope crosshairs. Responding is scored by pattern, direction, and amount of motion, time on target, time sharing, and information transmitted.

Control variables are number and kind (knob, stylus); plane, extent, direction of motion; elasticity, friction, and mass. Accurate moves need feel, but friction lowers precision and speed. *Display* programs set tracking courses by varying physical-stimulus input values: extent, direction, periodicity, frequency, rate of target motion; number of stimuli; noise. A single-dimensional, slow, regular course is most easily tracked. Displays give *information feedback* (IF), some representation of error between output (control × control system) and target input. Feedback stimulates corrective action and determines behavior, and the consequences of the many possible ways of transforming output-input error to display IF have wide extra-laboratory implication. *Control system* (order, lag) or *control-display* (magnification, nonlinear distortion) variables can be considered in IF transformation.

(i) *Analysis.* "Coordination", the lay term for skill, fails to show up in experiment. Part-skills combine by the law of independence. Man is exact at doing things together with chance frequency; i.e. if the azimuth tracking part has 90, elevation 80 per cent time on target, the whole-task scores 72, not 80. Transfer of training and interpart and ability-test correlation are alternative approaches to analysis.

(ii) *Other areas*. Major concerns are to determine: limits to reaction latency, rate, and extent; short- and long-term effects of practice schedules—frequent rest helps tracking, but massed practice does no permanent harm; amount and direction of transfer of training—almost invariably positive—from old to new learning for practice, display, and control factors. Tracking memory is excellent.

(*b*) *Positioning*. Drawing a line or setting a clock exemplifies a graded control move by discrete trial presentation: setting, score (IF), break, next setting.... The control, often borrowed from tracking, determines reaction characteristics (rate, latency, continuity) useful to tracking theory, but IF is the main object and the usual response scores are the extent of motion and size and sign of error in control placement.

(i) *Feedback*. The effects of IF (score) displacement in time and space get slowed-down study relative to tracking. IF comes between separate tries at a stationary target, and if control and target are out of sight, score at the end of a trial is the only IF—and is easily withheld or presented as any function of the physical size of control movement. The value of a next move, change or repetition of the last move, depends on the last IF; though learning occurs only when IF is given for responding, an established response drops out if a new IF code signals error. Extreme IF distortion can slow learning or lower accuracy, but human beings take many distortions in their stride—nonlinear relation to response extent, inexact IF. Time delay is ruinous to tracking but not to discrete-trial adjustment.

(ii) *Memory*. Unlike tracking, positioning is subject to forgetting; even the spacing of practice trials has an adverse effect on accuracy. Earlier (proactive) or later (retroactive) learning aids or interferes with memory, since earlier learning has positive or negative transfer to new learning. The combination of component-analysis with memory design in discrete-trial response yields forgetting functions for motor tasks, and shows the interdependence of components of memory. Parts are IF, correct control move, and alternative moves; what is remembered of one affects memory of the others.

4. *Comment*. Motor learning (Bilodeau & Bilodeau, 1961; Adams, 1964; Noble, 1968), engineering psychology (Melton & Briggs, 1960; Fitts, 1963; Poulton, 1966), method (Bahrick & Noble, 1966) have had recent and thorough critical evaluation; Fitts (1964) covered skills as human learning—features, history, taxonomy and theory; Bilodeau edited books on skills learning for college level (1969), and above (1966). Hence there are recent surveys of status, and reference sources to methods, facts, and theory for the full range of motor tasks and for ability, feedback, memory, information handling, instruction, and developmental variables. Recent past experience indicates the need to follow up findings and new approaches to theory under an exacting standard of stimulus and response description. The majority view plays down any uniqueness of *motor* or *skill*, and favors an analytic approach and simple situations; its rightness depends on empirical testing.

Bibliography: Adams, J. A.: Motor skills. Palo Alto: Annual Review of Psychology, 1964, *15*, 181–202. **Andreas, B. G.:** Experimental psychology. New York, 1960. **Bahrick, H. P. & Noble, M. E.:** Motor behavior. In: **Sidowski, J. B.** (Ed.): Experimental methods and instrumentation in psychology. New York, 1966, 645–75. **Bilodeau, E. A.** (Ed.): Acquisition of skill. New York, 1966. **Id.:** (Ed.): Principles of skill acquisition. New York, 1969. **Id. & Bilodeau, I. McD.:** Motor skills learning. Palo Alto: Annual Review of Psychology, 1961, *12*, 243–80. **Deese, J. & Hulse, S. H., Jr.:** The psychology of learning. New York, 1967. **Fitts, P. M.:** Engineering psychology. In: **Koch, S.** (Ed.): Psychology: A study of science. New York, 1963, 908–33. **Fitts, P. M.:** Perceptual-motor skill learning. In: **Melton, A. W.** (Ed.): Categories of human learning. New York, 1964, 244–85. **Hall, J.:** The psychology of learning. Philadelphia, 1966.

Marx, M. H.: Learning processes. London, 1969. **Melton, A. W. & Briggs, G. E.:** Engineering psychology. Palo Alto: Annual Review of Psychology, 1960, *11*, 71–98. **Noble, C. E.:** The learning of psychomotor skills. Palo Alto: Annual Review of Psychology, 1968, *19*, 203–50. **Poulton, E. C.:** Engineering psychology. Palo Alto: Annual Review of Psychology, 1966, *17*, 177–200. **Smith, K. U.:** Delayed sensory feedback and behavior. Philadelphia, 1962. **Welford, A. T.:** Ageing and human skills. London, 1958.

I. Bilodeau

Motor speech area (syn. *Broca's area*). Broca's area is synonymous with the motor speech area. It is the posterior part of the third or inferior frontal gyrus just in front of the lower part of the precentral gyrus. The name is usually applied only to this area of the dominant lobe. It is involved in the motor aspects of speech and lesions of it are associated with expressive aphasia. However, function cannot be too rigidly localized as lesions elsewhere can produce expressive aphasia (e.g. in the dominant parieto-temporal regions). See *Localization*. *B.B.*

Motor theory of consciousness. The theory supposes that the particular quality of consciousness is due to the motor response, or perhaps that the whole neural circuit from stimulus to response determines consciousness. Thus it follows that how an object is perceived will depend on how one reacts to it muscularly. *C.D.F.*

Motor type. A variant of the imagination types described by J. M. Charcot. This type designates a person whose imaginative life is clearly marked by motor (movement) images and additionally by particularly strong tactile imagery.

Mourning (syn. *Grief*). According to Freud, a reaction to the loss of an object or person. As an affect, mourning approximates a depressive mood; as a process, it is said to include the repression of all individual aspects of the lost object, and of expectation of the object's presence in all situations in which it can no longer appear. Mourning diminishes to the extent that such repressions are successful. The loss has been overcome when the object is no longer involuntarily expected, and when the image (or idea and memory) of the object no longer provokes a mourning effect, or any tears.

Bibliography: Freud, S.: Mourning and melancholy. In: Collected papers, Vol. 4. London, 1924–5. *W.T.*

Mouth rearing in fish. This characteristic has developed independently in different species of fish, e.g. lin labyrinth fish (*anabantidae*), cardinal fishes (*apogonidae*), *tachysuridae* and *osteoglossidae* and *cichlidae*. The mouth-rearing fish are an advanced stage of the "open-rearing" fish. In the course of phylogenesis their eggs have become larger and more obtrusive and the adhesive mechanism has regressed. In some types of fish the eggs are taken into the mouth so soon after spawning that special measures are necessary for successful fertilization, e.g. egg traps and genital brushes. Mouth rearing is not specific to one sex; the passive partner also participates and has to fast while the rearing process is under way. The free-swimming young fish are generally guided by the parent fish.

Bibliography: Heinrich, W.: Untersuchungen zum Sexualverhalten in der Gattung Tilapia (Cichlidae, Teleostei) und bei Artbastarden. Z. tierpsychol, 1967, *24*, 684–754. **Wickler, W.:** Ei-Attrappen und Maulbruten bei afrikanischen Cichliden. Z. Tierpsychol, 1962, *19*, 129–64. *K.Fi.*

Mouth space. Presumably the first, primitive phase of spatial awareness determined by the movements of the infant to find its mother's breast. This oral or original space is forced through into the child's awareness by feeling and movement impressions; there is as yet no connection with vision. This is a stage preceding grasping space. *M.Sa.*

Movement afterimage. Aristotle describes the following example of the afterimage: if one looks at a waterfall for some length of time and then at a motionless shore, one has the impression that the shore is moving in a direction opposite to the waterfall. This phenomenon was observed repeatedly in various forms. The system of perception has accommodated itself during the observation to the system of relations. *V.M.*

Movement formula. A plan of the sequence of movements necessary for a given action. *R.Hä.*

Movement illusion. 1. See *Motion, apparent*. **2.** The illusion that one's body is moving.

Movement, stereotyped. The uniform repetition of the same movement pattern. Even people in good health frequently show a tendency to such stereotypes, e.g. with gestures of embarrassment such as "turning buttons". It occurs in various psychic illnesses, especially obsessional neuroses (q.v.) and schizophrenia (q.v.). *A.Hi.*

MPI. See *Maudsley Personality Inventory*.

Müller, Georg Elias. B. 20/7/1850 in Grimma; d. 23/12/1934 in Göttingen. Studied history and philosophy in Leipzig and Göttingen; obtained his doctorate in 1873 under Lotze in Göttingen with a thesis on "Sensory attention"; he then became a tutor in Rötha and a private lecturer in Göttingen. In 1880 he accepted a chair of philosophy in Czernowitz but returned to Göttingen as early as 1881 as H. Lotze's successor and remained there until his retirement in 1921. His pupils in Göttingen included Külpe (q.v.), Katz, Jaensch, and Rubin.

Müller was one of the founders of experimental psychology. His major contributions were in the spheres of psychophysics, memory and visual perception.

In his monograph "On the fundamentals of psychophysics" published in 1878 and his work on "Standpoints and facts of psychophysical method" which appeared in 1903 he criticized Weber's law in detail, as well as the work of G. T. Fechner, and set out what he considered to be the fundamental psychophysical axioms of the relationship between perception and neural stimulation, which later became the bases of the gestalt-psychological principle of isomorphy. In the sphere of visual perception, Müller was particularly important for his essays on the psychophysics of visual sensations (1896–97), which contain a revision of E. Hering's theory of color perception. In 1930 he published two further monographs on the psychophysics of color sensations, which did not, however, equal the importance of his earlier works.

Müller's work on memory research met with the greatest interest. Together with F. Schumann (1894), A. Pilzecker (1900) and others, he continued Ebbinghaus's studies of memory and arrived at important results. He invented the *right associates procedure*, discovered associative and retroactive inhibitions and developed more effective learning methods, etc. Particular importance attaches to his three-volume monograph "On the analysis of memory activity and the process of imagination" (1911–17), in which he described his famous studies of the phenomenon of memory. Müller's studies of memory differ from those of Ebbinghaus, in particular through the addition of introspective reports by the subject to complete the objective data. He was able to show that even when nonsense syllables are learnt the process of learning is not mechanical and automatic; there is always a conscious and active organization of the learning assignment by the subject. With his opinion that association by contiguity not only makes learning possible but is complemented by conscious learning "sets", Müller was in close agreement with the research results achieved at much the same time in the psychology of thinking by O. Külpe and the Würzburg school. See *Memory*.

Main Works: Zur Grundlegung der Psychophysik. Berlin, 1878. Die Gesichtspunkte und die Tatsachen der psycho-physischen Methodik. Strasbourg, 1903. Experimentelle Beiträge zur Lehre vom Gedächtnis. Leipzig, 1900.

Bibliography: Boring, E. G.: Georg Elias Müller, 1850–1934. Amer. J. Psychol., 1935, *47*, 344–8. **Katz, D.:** Georg Elias Müller. Acta psychologica, 1935, *1*, 234–40. *W.W.*

Müller–Lyer illusion. The most widely studied of the geometric illusions. Although the two horizontal lines are equal in length, the arrow heads at their ends make this difficult to perceive. There are many theories accounting for this illusion, including those based on misplaced *constancy* resulting from seeing the illusion in *perspective.* However the illusion is also effective in the touch modality.

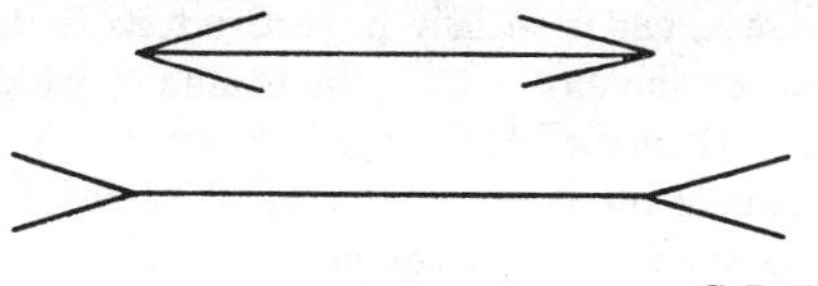

C.D.F.

Multi-dimensional diagnosis. The application of diagnostic methods which cover several personality dimensions in a single test, e.g. MPI, MMPI, 16 PF (see *Picture frustration test*), etc. *F.G.*

Multiple choice technique. A technique in programmed instruction (q.v.). The subject selects his answer from a repertoire made explicit in the step. Ant. *Free-choice method* (q.v.). Most "programmed" textbooks and programmes for teaching machines now use the MCT. *H.F.*

Multiple climax. A series of sexual climaxes which is known to occur during intercourse with some women, as opposed to the single, highly localized climax which occurs in males. See *Orgasm, multiple.* *G.D.W.*

Multiple correlation. Parametric method to determine the correlation between a (criterion) variable and a combination of other variables. The level of the multiple correlation is dependent on the level of the intercorrelation of the other variables and the correlations between those variables and the criterion variable. *G.Mi.*

Multiple sclerosis. A disorder of the spinal cord and brain in which there is a patchy loss of myelin and replacement by scar tissue. The cause is unknown, although slow viruses have been implicated. Multiple focal neurological lesions occur, the illness following a course of relapses and remissions, usually over many years. Mental symptoms are frequent. Intellectual deterioration is common together with mood changes. Euphoria was thought to be the typical mood change but depression is in fact more common. *D.E.*

Münsterberg, Hugo. B. 1/6/1863 in Danzig (now Gdansk, Poland); d. 16/12/1916 in Cambridge, Mass. Münsterberg studied medicine, philosophy and psychology in Geneva, Leipzig and Heidelberg. In 1885 he received his philosophy doctorate under Wundt (q.v.) in Leipzig; in 1887 he obtained his medical doctorate in Freiburg. In 1892, at William James's (q.v.) instigation, he was invited to Harvard, and was made director of the psychological laboratory there in 1897, in which year he was also appointed Professor of experimental psychology. He stayed at Harvard (except for one year, 1910/11, when he was exchange Professor in Berlin) until his death while lecturing.

Münsterberg's interests showed the influence of his philosophical training as well as his natural-scientific inclination. His philosophical system ("voluntary idealism") aimed at a theory of value inquiring not into cause and effect but goal and norm.

At the beginning of his scientific career Münsterberg dedicated himself mainly to experimental psychology. After 1900, he turned more and more to applied psychology (q.v.) and made pioneer contributions in this field. He preferred the description "psychotechnics" (q.v.) for this area, and defined it as the science of the practical application of psychology in the service of cultural tasks. In his last major work (1914), Münsterberg saw the tasks of psychotechnics as lying mainly in the fields of business, education, law, art, health and social order. His own research interests were correspondingly wide-ranging. He was especially interested in the applications of psychology in industry and business. He developed the first vocational selection test (1910), carried out selection investigations for various professions, tried to validate vocational aptitude tests by success criteria, and wrote the first significant book in the area of industrial and occupational psychology. He was also interested in educational and clinical psychology, and was among the first to use suggestion (q.v.) and hypnosis (q.v.) in psychotherapy. In forensic psychology (q.v.), he again performed pioneer work with his articles on credibility (q.v.) and, e.g. his investigation of the connection between blood pressure changes and the truthfulness of testimony.

Main works: Psychology and life. Boston, 1899. On the witness stand. New York, 1908. Psychology and the teacher. New York, 1909. Psychotherapy, New York, 1909. Psychology and industrial efficiency. Cambridge, Mass., 1913. Psychology; general and applied. New York, 1914. *W.W.*

Murray, Henry Alexander. B. 13/5/1893 in New York. Murray studied biology and medicine, and worked as an instructor in physiology at Harvard and as a surgeon at the Presbyterian Hospital in New York. He was an assistant for two years at the Rockefeller Institute for Medicine in New York, doing research into embryology. He obtained degrees at Harvard and Columbia, and, in 1927, a doctorate in biochemistry at Cambridge, where he first became interested in (Jungian) psychology. In the same year he became an instructor in psychology at Harvard, even though he had no academic training in the subject. In 1928 he was appointed assistant Professor and director of the Harvard Psychological Clinic; in 1937 he was made associate Professor; in 1937 he completed his psychological formation under F. Alexander and H. Sachs. He left Harvard in 1943 to serve with the U.S. Army Medical Corps and was put in charge of an Office of Strategic Services assessment service. In 1947 he returned to Harvard and was appointed Professor of clinical psychology.

Murray's importance in psychology lies mainly in his contributions to personality diagnosis and personality (q.v.) theory. He has developed a number of different techniques, and especially projective tests (q.v.), for personality investigation, among which the Thematic Apperception Test (q.v.) is pre-eminent. Murray's theory of personality is among the most complex and detailed of the existing systems. Emphasis is placed on the individual in his whole complexity, as is evident from the Murrayian term "personology". Freudian psychoanalysis (q.v.) has had a profound influence on his work, which adopts the concepts of id (q.v.), ego (q.v.) and superego (q.v.) with only slight modifications. Murray also recognized the importance of early childhood experiences for the later development of personality, which led him to accept the psychoanalytic notions of fixations (q.v.) and complexes (q.v.) (anal, oral and castration). There is also a similarity in the importance accorded to unconscious motivation (q.v.). Murray stresses more heavily than did Freud the role of sociocultural environmental influences and physiological processes in the development of personality. He also decries the overemphasis on individual drives or motives, such as

Freud's on sex, or the Adlerian will-to-power, and stresses the necessity of assuming the existence of a large number of needs in order to explain the dynamics of behavior. He has established (on the basis of projective data, interviews, etc.) a list of twenty-eight needs, which he believes occur in almost every individual, and whose relative degree of expression conditions the individual nature of each personality. Murray's needs are interrelated with "presses", or objects and events that are significant for the individual. See *Need.*

Main works: A method for investigating fantasies (with C. D. Morgan). Arch. neurol. psychiat., 1935, *34*, 289–306. Explorations in personality. New York, 1938 (with others). Assessment of men. New York, 1948 (with others). Outline of a conception of personality (with C. Kluckhohn). In: Kluckhohn, C., Murray, H. A. & Schneider, D. (Eds.): Personality in nature, society, and culture. New York, [2]1953. Preparations for the scaffold of a comprehensive system. In: Koch, S. (Ed.): Psychology: a study of a science, Vol. 3. New York, 1959, 7–54. Studies of stressful interpersonal disputations. Amer. Psychologist, 1963, *18*, 28–36. *W.W.*

Muscarine. A substance with a strong, direct energizing effect on the (cholinergic) post-ganglionic, parasympathetic synapses; chemically related to acetylcholine and with comparable effects to pilocarpine and arecoline. Muscarine is an alkaloid from the fly agaric mushroom (*Amanita muscaria*). It has a sustained effect (unlike acetylcholine). Main physiological effects: increased secretion, strong reduction of blood pressure and heart frequency even in small doses. Poisoning in high doses. Smaller doses stimulate the reticular formation and produce rapid EEG waves. This activity syndrome is much stronger than with arecoline and pilocarpine. Behavioral effects in small doses vary between excitation and sedation. Higher doses have a hallucinogenic and highly stimulating effect.

Bibliography: Riehl, J. L. & Unna, K. R.: Effects of muscarine on the nervous system. In: **Wortis,** (Ed.): Recent advances in biological psychiatry. 1960, 345–62. **Waser, P. G.:** Chemistry and pharmacology of muscarine, muscarone and some related compounds. Pharmacol. Rev., 1961, *13*, 465–515. *V.J.*

Muscle relaxants. Substances which bring about a reduction in motor activity in the skeletal muscles either centrally by inhibiting the polysynaptic reflexes or peripherally by a competitive or depolarizing effect on the stimulus transmission system (acetylcholine). Central muscle relaxants include mephenesin (Tolserol) and related substances used as tranquilizers with a psychologically sedating effect. The best known peripheral muscle relaxant is curare.

Bibliography: Donahoe, H. B. & Kimura, K. K.: Synthetic centrally acting skeletal muscle relaxants in **Burger, A.** (Ed.): Drugs affecting the central nervous system. New York, 1968. **Grob, D.:** Neuromuscular blocking drugs. In: **Root, W. S. & Hofmann, F. G.** (Eds.): Physiological pharmacology. New York, 1967. *G.D.*

Muscle senses. See *Kinesthesia.*

Muscle tonus. State of tension of a muscle. The muscle tension is regulated by means of the Aγ fibers, which originate from the reticular formation in the brain stem. Changes in tension result from alterations in the body position but may also be caused by psychological stimulation. *P.S.*

Muscular type. Designation for a physical type that is primarily characterized by muscular growth. See *Athletic type; Mesomorphy.* *W.Se.*

Musical alexia. See *Tone deafness.*

Musical aptitude test. See *Music, psychology of.*

Music, psychology of. Today psychology is generally defined as the study of the responses organisms make to stimuli. If we apply this definition of psychology to the field of music, we may say that, on the response side, we perceive music particularly through our auditory sense, we perform it and we react emotionally to it (just to give a few examples). Musical stimuli may include a sheet of music, an orchestra playing, a musical instrument, or a single note or melody.

This current conception of what constitutes the psychology of music is in contradistinction to the older notions proposed by many earlier psychologists such as Seashore (1938), who thought in terms of a "musical mind" and its contents. Such a dualistic position permeated the psychology of music from about 1915 to 1940.

1. *The dimensions of tone.* One of the simplest ways to study the responses to music is to take a single sound and consider its dimensions. To avoid a dualistic position of separating mental from physical events, we may consider sound as a stimulus to have two basic dimensions: the *vibrational* and the *tonal.* Among the vibrational dimensions we consider the sound wave, its frequency, intensity and characteristic wave form. On the tonal side, we may judge its pitch (high or low), loudness or timbre, along with some other possible dimensions, such as volume and density.

Of these, pitch has been the subject of most research. Pitch is directly related to the frequency of the sound wave. Low pitches tend to relate to slow frequencies and high pitches to rapid frequencies.

Numerous studies have been done on pitch discrimination: that is, how fine a discrimination can be made when two different pitches are sounded alternately. Seashore claimed that capacity for pitch discrimination, along with loudness, time, timbre, rhythm, discrimination and tonal memory, were set by heredity. However, Wyatt (1945), among others, demonstrated that students with poor pitch discriminations could be trained to make a great improvement, if knowledge of results was imparted in the training process.

In pitch discrimination, two tones are presented and the subject is asked to tell which is higher or lower. Another related problem is the judgment of *absolute or perfect pitch.* This demands a pitch-naming response without regard to any reference tone. If an F♯ is played the subject must identify it as such. If one has perfect pitch he should be able to name tones presented at random with little error. Again, Seashore and many psychologists and musicians have maintained that the capacity is inherited. However, Lundin & Allen (1962) have demonstrated that when subjects are given visual knowledge of results they can be trained to name correctly any random note played within a two octave range.

The tonal dimension of loudness corresponds roughly to the vibrational dimension of intensity. However, there are certain ranges of frequency between about 2000 to 4000 cycles per second where the human ear is more sensitive; therefore loudness is also related to frequency.

Timbre is a third tonal dimension and is related to the characteristic form of the sound wave. Vibrating objects, whether strings, or columns of air, emit not only a fundamental tone but other frequencies above it called partials or overtones. Hence one can tell the difference between a violin and a trumpet (even though pitch and loudness are the same) because the trumpet emits louder overtones, and this gives it its brassy quality.

2. *Tonal combinations.* When tones are combined in various ways, we find in music what we call melody and harmony; but no random combination of tones constitutes a melody. Like single tones, melodies have certain dimensions. A first attribute is *propinquity:* that is, the succession of the notes shows a close relationship. A second dimension is *repetition:* the same note or notes are frequently repeated in the melody. A third characteristic is *finality* or cadence: the

feeling of ending expressed by a falling movement of tones or a counter sequence of tones may give the feeling of conclusion. Another aspect of finality is called *tonality*. Typically, in Western music, we resolve on the tonic or beginning note of the key in which the melody is written.

In the past, psychologists have been seriously concerned with the problems of *consonance* and *dissonance* in music. One group of theories may be called "natural law" theories. Helmholtz (1912) considered tones as consonant when they possessed the same overtones. Tones sounded together which gave a rough sensation quality because of beating or beating in the overtones were judged to be dissonant.

Stumpf (1883–90) offered an alternate theory of fusion. Two tones were judged consonant to the degree that they could fuse into single tones.

An alternate type of theory of consonance has been proposed by Lundin (1947). It could be called a cultural theory and presumes that what one judges as consonant or dissonant is a matter of cultural conditioning. Individual musicians differ sharply as to what constitutes consonant and dissonant intervals. Some people confuse consonance with affective values, or what they like or dislike. Consonance is further related to the musical context in which it occurs. Finally, intervals which were judged dissonant several hundreds of years ago, and therefore before the evolution of harmonic writing, are judged consonant today.

3. *Rhythm.* Rhythm, along with melody and harmony, is considered an essential component of music. It can act both as a stimulus and a response. As a stimulus it consists of variations in time between tones (or beats) as well as accents (greater loudness) placed on some of the tones. In responding to rhythm, we perceive it and make movements to it. To be considered rhythm, the various beats must have a degree of regularity and organization. Rhythm differs from tempo in that the former defines the patterning of the tones whereas the latter is expressed in the rate at which the tones occur.

4. *Musical memory.* The ability to remember a series of tones or a melody seems to be one of the major components of musicianship. Research with several of our current musical aptitude tests indicates that a good musical memory and fine pitch and rhythm discrimination seem to be the best predictors of possible success in musical performance (Lundin, 1967).

5. *Affective responses to music.* There is a vast literature demonstrating that we react affectively when music is played. Both physiological measures and verbal reports attest to this fact. Depending on the kind of music played, changes in breathing, blood pressure and heart rate occur. Music that is strongly vigorous and rhythmic has a greater tendency to increase these physiological processes.

As to the verbal report about how one feels when certain kinds of music are played, Hevner (1936) has demonstrated a number of relationships. Music played in the major mode is more likely to be judged as happy, that in the minor mode as sad. High pitches are judged as sprightly while low ones seem to have sad qualities. Fast tempos tend to make happy music whereas slow ones have the opposite effect.

Farnsworth (1950) has studied extensively the matter of musical taste, what kinds of music we like or dislike. There tends to be a considerable stability in our tastes; and we tend to agree as to what we like or dislike, particularly as far as serious music is concerned. Over a period of twenty-five years, Farnsworth has surveyed expert musicologists and found they agree that Bach and Beethoven are the two most eminent composers of all time. Although there have been a few shifts in the ratings of the top ten composers over this period, the list remains virtually the same. There is also a reverence for the past, in that the majority of composers rated as great lived in the eighteenth and nineteenth centuries.

6. *Musical ability.* One of the major issues in the psychology of music has been what constitutes musical ability or talent. Seashore considered a *theory of specifics* in which he stated that musical ability consists of many different talents; he based his test of musical talents on that assumption. The person who ranks high in most all of these often unrelated talents is most likely to be the best musician.

An alternative theory, often called an *omnibus* theory, has been proposed by Mursell, who takes a more gestalt-psychological position. He claims that musical talent involves a more general ability. Although some other kinds of talents are involved, they also are interrelated and cannot be separated out.

The heredity-environment controversy (about which is the greater determiner of talent) persists. Lundin (1967) cites evidence on both sides but concludes that musical responses, like most other human responses, are learned, and that the environmental factors seem to be the more important.

Psychologists such as Drake (1957), Wing (1961) and Seashore (1939) have developed tests of musical talent with some degree of success; but their success in prediction has not approached that in other fields of aptitude measurement, such as intelligence.

Bibliography: Drake, R. M.: Drake musical aptitude tests. Chicago, 1957. **Farnsworth, P. R.:** Musical taste. Stanford, Calif., 1950. **Helmholtz, H. L. F. von:** On the sensations of tone (trans. Ellis). London, [4]1912. **Hevner, K.:** Experimental studies of the elements of expression in music. Amer. J. Psychol., 1936, *48*, 246–68. **Lundin, R. W. & Allen, J. D.:** A technique for training perfect pitch. Psychol. rec., 1962, *12*, 139–46. **Lundin, R. W.:** Toward a cultural theory of consonance. J. Psychol., 1947, *28*, 45–9. **Id.:** An objective psychology of music (rev. ed.). New York, 1967. **Seashore, C. E.:** Psychology of music. New York, 1938. **Id.:** Seashore measures of musical talents. New York, 1939. **Stumpf, C.:** Tonpsychologie, 2 vols. Leipzig, 1883–90. **Wing, H. D.:** A revision of the Wing musical aptitude test. J. res. Music educ., 1961, *19*, 39–47. **Wyatt, R. F.:** The improvability of pitch discrimination. Psychol. Monogr., 1945, *58*, 1–58.

R. W. Lundin

Music therapy. This is a special method of psychotherapy (q.v.), which attempts to obtain a therapeutic effect in a patient through various kinds of music, both heard and practiced. The effect is upon the mood of the patient and also upon his physiological functions.

In the earlier stages of human development music was tried as a therapy. The elementary significance of music was employed as a magical tool to control the forces of nature, propitiate gods and demons, and conquer sickness and death. One of the oldest examples of healing by music was David playing to Saul (I. Samuel, Ch. 16, v. 23). Pythagoras, Plato and Aristotle expressly mention the prophylactic and cathartic power of music. In the Middle Ages the knowledge of the ancients about the healing power of music was not given much attention. Only with the beginning of modern times did numerous authors (Kircher, in the seventeenth century, among others) speak of new theories and methods of music therapy. Sicknesses with psychic features were cited as particularly suited for cure by music. Modern psychotherapy seeks to grasp the specific significance of music as a therapeutic agent. After the Second World War two "schools" developed independently of each other. The "American school" (Illing & Benedict, 1958) may be described as a form of "musical pharmocology" in the sense of a psychotherapeutic method. The "Swedish school" (Pontivk, 1948, 1954, 1962), whose psychotherapy is strongly depth-psychological, gives music therapy an important place, by seeking to reach deeper layers of the personality (q.v.) through the specific properties of music than is possible through the spoken word. Music therapy today can be divided into individual and group therapy.

1. *Individual music therapy* is the treatment for a shorter or longer period of an individual patient by music therapy. The treatment situation is both the therapeutic partnership of doctor and patient and the planned use of

specific musical possibilities. Methods are thus evolved which:

(*a*) either set in motion an analytical process (see *Psychoanalysis*), or

(*b*) attempt to activate the individual's creative powers, or

(*c*) attempt to regulate psycho-physical tension. This is done either by asking the patient simply to listen to music or actively to practice it. There are both psychological and sociological differences between the passive listening to and active practicing of music. Listening to music need not involve the manual and technical aspects of musical activity. Playing music demands the commitment of the whole personality both to get into the music and to master the necessary manual and technical skills. The music to be played and the instruments chosen for this active music therapy are simple (pentatonics, simple rhythms and tunes, rhythm instruments, xylophone, bells, etc.). Listening and playing complement each other and together form a single therapeutic system within the psychotherapeutic treatment.

2. *Group music therapy* is a form of group therapy (q.v.). Listening and playing can both contribute. They can be used to create a therapeutically effective sociodynamics within the context of certain norms of group therapy. Examples of this form of group therapy are playing together on simple instruments, combination of music and dancing, improvised dancing to classical music.

One might note in criticism that the possible results of music therapy are for the most part not specifically ascertainable. They are more likely to be attained in conjunction with other means of concentration, release and tranquilizing (hypnosis, q.v., autogenic training, q.v., looking at pictures). But this is not to dispute the practical value of a planned music therapy.

Bibliography: Illing, H. S. & Benedict, I.: Entwicklung und Stand der amerikanischen Musiktherapie. In: **Teirich, H. R.** (Ed.): Musik in der Medizin. Stuttgart, 1958, 26–33. **Pontvik, A.:** Grundgedanken zur psychischen Heilwirkung der Musik unter besonderer Berücksichtigung der Musik von J. S. Bach. Zürich, 1948. **Id.:** Heilen durch Musik. Zürich, 1955. **Id.:** Der tönende Mensch. Psychorhythmie als gehörseelische Erziehung. Zürich & Stuttgart, 1962. **Schwabe, C.:** Musiktherapie bie Neurosen und funktionellen Störungen. Jena, 1969. *H.-N. Genius*

Mutation, genetic. A lasting change in hereditary characteristics which occurs without apparent cause. Genetic mutation is the change in a hereditary unit; the old allele is either transformed or stimulated to produce a new variant of daughter allele. A distinction is made between dominant and recessive autosomal and sex-related mutations. Somatic mutation is the change in hereditary factors affecting many or all cells. *I.M.D.*

Mutation, psychological. Sudden change in the structure of the consciousness (J. Gebser). Speculative concept which must not be confused with genetic mutation. *W.Sch.*

Mutism. Dumbness even though the speech mechanism is intact. Depending on the cause, a distinction is made between congenital and hysterical or reactive mutism. Mutism is generally encountered in children (usually caused by timidity or anxiety) and often only in relation to specific persons; in schizophrenia, mutism is primarily a symptom of catatonia, and occurs not infrequently as a secondary consequence of hospitalism. *W.Sch.*

Mydriasis. Dilatation of the pupil. The width of the pupils is determined by the interaction of the *dilatator pupillae* (innervated by the sympathetic nervous system) and *sphincter pupillae* (innervated by the parasympathetic system) muscles which are situated in the iris and are among the internal eye muscles. Mydriasis therefore occurs, e.g. on stimulation of the sympathetic system by sympathicomimetics, or on paralysis of the parasympathetic system by parasympathicolytics. *R.K.*

Myelencephalon. See *Medulla oblongata.*

Myograph. A device for measuring muscular reaction.

Myokinetic test (*Mira myokinetic test*). An objective personality test based on the theoretical assumption (held, e.g. by N. J. Oseretzky and E. Kretschmer) that motor and mental processes are closely related in man. The test problems, which have to be solved blindfolded and using the right and left hands, consist in tracing and continuing preprinted lines and shapes on the horizontal and vertical planes. There are separate standards for young people and adults, and for the two sexes. The test is used, e.g. to diagnose drives, affectivity and adaptation; it has been found that different normal and clinical groups give varying results in this test as a result of characteristic syndromes. *K.D.N.*

Myopia. Short-sightedness. With hyperopia and astigmatism, myopia is one of the main eye defects. Axially parallel light rays are united in front of the retina. Refractive myopia: the incident light rays are refracted by an excessive amount. Axial myopia: the *bulbus* is too long, generally for innate reasons. A distinction is made between: (1) *benign myopia*: this form becomes stationary with puberty; (2) *progressive malignant myopia*, which leads to changes in the area of the *fundus* (see *Retina*). It is probably caused by a pathological increase in the extensibility of the *bulbus*. *R.R.*

Mysticism. An attitude by which the mind (spirit) enters into direct, immediate and inward communion with a sacred principle inaccessible to the senses and to reason. In religions, mysticism is displayed in the orientation of one's whole being (emotions, will and intelligence) toward transcendence of the narrow confines of profane existence, which striving culminates in the illumination of ecstasy; various practices (prayer, purification and asceticism, q.v.) are used to induce this state. See *Meditation.* *A.T.*

Myth (syn. *Mythos*). A story or implied account of the characteristics of nature, or of beings with suprahuman powers and qualities, the commerce of gods with men, and the fate of gods. In contradistinction to a fairy tale, a myth is taken as true by its narrators and hearers, and formulates the world view or conception of history of a community or society, even though—in rational and causally explicative terms—it seems improbable and nonsensical.

The basic heuristic problem of research into myths is that the "experienced" and "living" myth requires and allows of no interpretation. According to W. F. Otto, the "genuine" myth cannot be interpreted in terms of, and by, a form of existence that, by recourse to a scientific approach, has lost the faculty of the mythic. Nevertheless, it is a task of science to attempt to apprehend those aspects of myth which are still "operative".

Cognitive aspect. Myth provides a closed picture of the world which, in contrast to the scientific world view, recognizes no open questions, and therefore embodies one stage in the historical development of thought. It might be said that whenever a scientific theory is put to social, political or therapeutic ends, it necessarily includes mythic elements; in the field of psychology, this is certainly true of psychoanalysis (q.v.). Here the cognitive coincides with the *functional* aspect: it offers a specific group of men supposedly universally valid and exemplary models of behavior (both that which is to be done, and that which is not to be done—by portraying the punishment attendant upon a particular misdeed or crime). Mythic behavioral models have also retained their value for "depth-psychological" theories (see *Depth psychology*); this is true especially of the unusually rich mythology of the

Greeks (see *Oedipus complex; Electra complex*). Because it has neglected the results of historical and ethnographic myth research, psychological myth interpretation is still inadequate—the major methodological error is the uncritical assumption of an analogy between myth and dream (q.v.). Similarly, there is no justification for attempts to equate mythic structures with corresponding features of the "collective unconscious" (q.v.), since they neglect the socio-cultural functions of myth.

Bibliography: Douglas, M.: Natural symbols: explorations in cosmology. London, 1970. **Firth, R.:** Tikopia ritual and belief. London, 1967. **Leach, E.** (Ed.): The structural study of myth and totemism. London, 1967. **Lévi-Strauss, C.:** The savage mind. London & New York, 1966. **Id.:** Mythologiques, I, II, III. Paris, 1964, 1966, 1968. **Id.:** Structural anthropology. London & New York, 1963; London, 1968. **Murray, A. H.** (Ed.): Myth and mythmaking. New York, 1960. **Schmidbauer, W.:** Mythos und Psychologie. Munich, 1970.

W.Sch.

Myxedema. See *Cretinism*.

N

n-achievement (syn. *Achievement need*). One of H. A. Murray's list of psychological needs. Refers to the need to be successful in competitive and creative enterprises. The concept of *achievement motivation* (q.v.) came into widespread popularity with the work of McClelland *et al.* (1953), who employed a projective measure of this need based on the Thematic Apperception Test (q.v.). See *Need.*

Bibliography: McCelland, D. C., Atkinson, J. W., Clark, R. A. & Lowell, E. L.: The achievement motive. New York, 1953. **Murray, H. A.:** Explorations in personality. Oxford, 1938. *G.D.W.*

n-affiliation (syn. *Affiliative need; Affiliation need; Need for affiliation*). The need for friendly interaction with other people, companionship, love, joining groups, etc. Included in H. A. Murray's list of psychological needs. See *Need.* *G.D.W.*

Nagel's tests. A method of testing for defective color vision, in particular dichromatopsia (q.v.). The subject is required to select those of sixteen charts which contain red, green and grey dots. Not to be confused with *Nagel's anomaloscope*: an instrument which uses spectral color lights to test color vision. *W.P.*

Nail-biting. See *Onychophagy.*

Nancy school. One of the "schools" of hypnosis research in France at the end of the nineteenth century. The leading representatives were A. A. Liébeault (1823–1904) and H. Bernheim (1837–1919) worked. The "psychic" one-sidedness of the Nancy school proved as inadequate as the "physiological" pseudo-precision of the Paris school (q.v.) under J. M. Charcot. *H.-N.G.*

Nanism (syn. *Dwarfism*). See *Pituitary dwarfism.*

Napkin ring figure. Essentially a *reversible figure* used by Wundt which can be seen with either of the circular ends facing the observer. However Wittmann claimed that there are sixty different possible interpretations of the figure. *C.D.F.*

Narcissism (syn. *Narcism*) is the characteristic of a person who places unduly high value on his own deeds and physical attributes. It is not a sexual perversion (see *Perversion*), since it is not associated with sexual gratification, and hence is to be distinguished from masturbation (q.v.) or other forms of autoeroticism. The term derives from the Greek legend of Narcissus who, spurning Echo, fell in love with his own reflection and became a waterside flower perpetually admiring himself.

Freud hypothesized that the ego takes another individual as love object but may, even in normal development, take itself as love object for a time. Full-blown narcissism is only an exaggeration of the normal course of events, and some degree of narcissism or self-love is properly maintained throughout life. Marked narcissism is, however, said to be greater in women and is also characteristic of schizophrenia (q.v.). *A. Broadhurst*

Narcoanalysis. An inquiry into a patient's experiences under the psychological effects of hypnotics (q.v.) (reduced attention, reduced anxiety, increased contact and communication, diminution of psychotic manifestations). The truthfulness and the amount of information acquired under narcoanalysis depend on many factors which are difficult to control. See *Truth drug*.

Bibliography: Kranz, H.: Die Narkoanalyse. Tübingen, 1950. *E.L.*

Narcolepsy. Characterized by periodic attacks, usually lasting minutes rather than hours, of a state resembling sleep, from which the patient may be aroused with or without difficulty. Some narcoleptics are fully conscious although unable to move a muscle. Catalepsy may occur also but is not essential to the diagnosis. Head injury and encephalitis are recognized antecedents; coexisting epilepsy is uncommon. *J.P.*

Narcosis. A pharmacologically produced, reversible loss of consciousness, in which pain and defensive reactions are absent; generally used for surgery. The effective mechanism seems to be associated with cells, but the brain cells are apparently more sensitive than others. Narcosis runs through various stages such as analgesia (absence of pain), excitation (disinhibition of the lower motor centers), tolerance (deep narcosis), and asphyxia, and can be induced by different methods. Narcosis has been used for research into consolidation in studies of animal memory (nitrous oxide narcosis directly after learning leads to a loss of retention, whereas later narcosis improves retention). In humans, narcosis has been used, e.g. to study variations in daily physiological rhythm. *E.D. & E.L.*

Narcotics. Substances of various chemical and physical composition which produce a state similar to sleep with central pain elimination. Desirable characteristics: broad therapeutic spectrum, rapid action, intensity, long-lasting effect, no respiratory depression, no influence on the cardiovascular system, no other secondary effects or aftereffects (e.g. sickness, vomiting), good toleration. None of the narcotics known today combines all these characteristics. *Inhalation narcotics* (ether, chloroform, nitrous oxide, cyclopropane), *intravenous* or *rectal narcotics* (see *Barbiturates*) are used. The distinction between narcotics and hypnotics (q.v.) is quantitative: hypnotics with a directly soporific action do produce narcosis if they are administered in suitably high doses—unlike tranquilizers (q.v.) and neuroleptics (q.v.), which do not act as narcotics but merely intensify narcosis. Narcotics have attracted psychological interest because of the post-narcotic impairment of performance (e.g. ability to drive), which may last for up to twenty-four hours.

Bibliography: Boulton, T. B., *et al.*: Progress in anaesthesiology. Amsterdam, 1970. **Dobkin, A. & Su, G.:** Newer anesthetics and their uses. Clin. Pharmacol. Ther., 1966, 7, 648. **Fraser, H. & Harris, L.:** Narcotic and narcotic antagonist analgesics. Ann. Rev. Pharmacol., 1967, 7, 277. *E.L.*

Nationalism. In social psychology (q.v.), nationalism is an attitude (q.v.) characterized by an extremely positive valuation of one's own nation. "Patriotism", "national spirit", etc., are points on an attitude continuum on which nationalism occupies an extreme position. The acquisition of a national or nationalistic attitude can occur relatively early on in the socialization process, and is similar in form to that of a prejudice (q.v.) (e.g. the development of positive reactions to symbols representative of one's own group, and the rejection of alien groups). Some research into prejudice (e.g. that of G. W. Allport) has suggested that nationalism forms the basis of further prejudices, such as anti-Semitism (q.v.) and racism. See *Authoritarian personality; Stereotype.* *H.D.S.*

Nativism. The belief that human behavior and particularly human perceptual mechanisms are inborn and determined by genetics, as opposed to the belief that they are the result of learning and experience. *C.D.F.*

Natural reflex. If a skeletal muscle is slightly stretched, e.g. by a tap on its tendon, a reflex mechanism is set in motion which causes the particular muscle to twitch. In contrast to an extraneous reflex, which is also an anatomical reaction of the organism to environmental changes, in the case of the "natural" reflex, the beginning and the end of the reflex arc (which in general includes the sensor, afferent pathway, reflex center, efferent pathway and effector) are located anatomically in the same place. The reflex arc is composed of contractile expansion receptors, sensitive nerve fibers, anterior horn cells in the spinal cord, motor nerve fibers, and diagonal skeletal muscle fibers. Its biological function is to adapt muscular contraction anatomically to the load. In medicine, it is used to study the function of the spinal cord. Most frequently the reflexes of the patellar tendons, the Achilles tendons, and the tendons of the biceps are investigated. *E.D.*

Natural retinal light. Receptors respond to perceptible stimuli by excitation. To a very small degree, such excitations in the receptors also occur constantly as physiological "spontaneous discharges", without any stimulus. Hence there is an impression of light—the "natural" light of the retina (q.v.), which becomes visible, especially in absolute darkness. *R.R.*

Natural-science psychology (syn. *Natural-scientific psychology*). Any psychology which is aware of its empirical foundation, and is thus distinguished from armchair psychology (q.v.). In a narrower sense, natural-science psychology is roughly equivalent to experimental psychology. See *Behaviorism; General psychology; History of psychology.* *R.Hä.*

Near point. The point in front of the eye which can still be clearly reproduced on the retina with maximum accommodation. At the age of ten, this point is situated about 8 cm in front of the corneal apex (50 cm at fifty, and 100 cm at seventy): i.e. it constantly retreats. This movement of the near point is caused by decreasing elasticity of the lens, reduces the range of accommodation and is known as *presbyopia* (q.v.). *K.H.P.*

Near space (Ger. *Nahraum*). Oral, visual and grasping space are at first independent but are fused by coordination of visual and oral schemata into "near space"; with the onset of locomotion, near space develops into "distance space" (eighth to twelfth months). *M.Sa.*

Necker cube. A reversible figure. The two-dimensional representation of a cube is ambiguous, and can be seen with corner A either at the front or at the back of the cube. These two percepts spontaneously alternate as the figure is fixated. *C.D.F.*

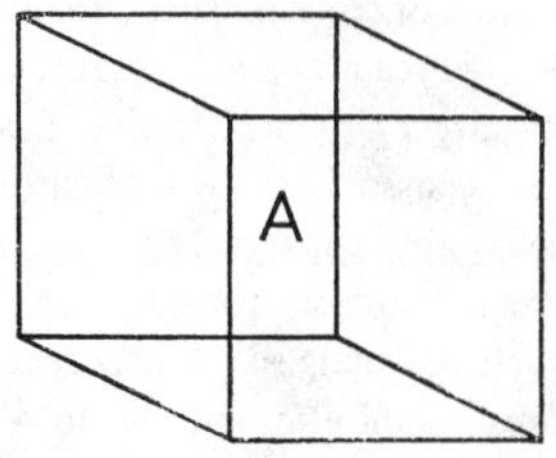

Necking, like dating (q.v.) and petting, (q.v.) forms part of heterosexual relationships. Necking generally denotes kissing, embracing and physical contact with the neck and head.

J.F.

Necrophilia (syn. *Necrophilism*). Sexual acts on or with the dead body of a person or parts of it: a very rare sexually deviant and pathological (in the clinical sense) behavior. Occurs in women as well as men. Among the genuine perversions, necrophilia is most closely related to fetishism (q.v.), both externally and in the "inner attitude" of the necrophile. An appreciable number of necrophiles are mentally subnormal or of low IQ. Forty-seven cases had been described in the literature by 1962.

Bibliography: Spoerri, T.: Nekrophilie. Basle, 1959. **Giese, H.:** Psychopathologie der Sexualität. Stuttgart, 1962.

H.M.

Need. "Need" is one of several English words (drive, motive, want, urge, wish, desire, and so on)—each in some respects unsuitable—used by psychologists today to designate an internally or externally aroused, brain-located force (often coupled with an accelerating emotion), subjectively experienced as an impulsion or felt necessity (a mild or intense urge) to act (immediately or later) so as to produce a certain specifiable terminal effect which is ordinarily expected to prove beneficial to the actor, and/or positively hedonic (less painful, more pleasurable) relative to the arousing situation. Herein implicitly ascribed to this variously named force (*need* in this article) are two indispensable, motivational properties, or powers: (*a*) the power to mobilize and select cognitive representors (image sequences) of an inviting, want-satisfying aim for action (including wish-fulfilling fantasies and long-range plans); and then (*b*), if strong enough relative to competing needs, the power to energize (initiate and sustain) the imaginally directed actional processes until if possible, by some motor, verbal, or mental skill or tactic, the aim has been sufficiently achieved. The successful exercise of the second of these two powers (resulting in an actualized need) depends on numerous facilitating states and processes (for instance, enough health, knowledge, competence, confidence, volition, and so on).

This definition must be expanded and amended to some extent to take account of such special conditions as: (*a*) need for sleep; (*b*) riddance and avoidance needs (e.g. keeping out of danger); (*c*) intellectual needs with their invisible maneuvers (e.g. composing an essay); (*d*) needs to learn or to perfect a skill; (*e*) needs to please or benefit another person; and much else besides.

Sponsored chiefly by Lewin, the word "need" was introduced into academic psychology in the early nineteen-thirties to stand for a central motivating variable: a specific desire, say, which releases energy, imparts value to certain objects, and generates a force that has both direction and magnitude. Lewin's "need" bears some resemblance to the drive (q.v.) construct as launched a little earlier by American animal psychologists, but it is very different from the referent of this term, as set forth by Hull, for instance. According to this theorist, the ultimate basis of animal motivation consists of a number of needs, or need states, each of which is a (potentially harmful) condition (for instance, pain, full bladder, deficiency of food, and so on) requiring some action to be taken (this being one dictionary definition of "need"). In Hull's language, the required action is energized by a need-produced *drive*, rather than by a *need* as we have been saying (another dictionary definition being an impulsion to act as required by some condition). In ordering varieties of human behavior, the concept of need eventually proved a quite acceptable replacement for McDougall's once-reigning but by then banished notion of instinct (q.v.). Unlike instinct, an innate need was not said to have a repertoire of inherited, unlearned action patterns, and though it was undeniably goal-oriented, this kind of teleology became scientifically respectable in the nineteen-fifties with the discovery of feedback systems (q.v.).

It is mainly in terms of the cognitive component, the aim, that four or five dozen species of needs can be most distinctly identified and systematically classified. It should be kept in mind, however, that it is the affective component (the desire for the actualization of the given aim) that moves the person. The potency of an aroused need can be roughly estimated in terms of the number and variety, intensity and duration of its observed and reported manifestations and effects. Of the many, standardized, semi-dependable, paper-and-pencil measures of need strength, none is more significant than McClelland's method of scoring the effects of the achievement need on the style and content of a subject's story compositions.

Madsen has provided an ample survey of the uses of need and drive. (See *Drive*.)

Bibliography: Hull, C. G.: Principles of behavior. New York, 1943. **Lewin, K.:** A dynamic theory of personality. New York, 1935. **Madsen, K. B.:** Theories of motivation. Copenhagen–Kent, Ohio, 1968. **McClelland, D. C.,** *et al.*: The achievement motive. New York, 1953. **McDougall, W.:** The energies of men. London, 1932. **Murray, H. A.:** Explorations in personality. New York, 1938. *H. A. Murray*

Need-drive-incentive pattern. The concept derives from W. Stern. If a specific need (q.v.) encounters an obstacle to its gratification, it is not extinguished by this deprivation, but its inherent dynamic drive must seek for some outlet or detour to accord with the basic impulse. Usually the closest approximation to the previous specific, now thwarted, form is chosen. This target is an *incentive*.

Bibliography: Stern, W.: Allgemeine Psychologie auf personalistischer Grundlage. The Hague, 1935; [2]1950. (Character and personality. London, 1938.) *R.Hä.*

Need gratification. An action which resolves or reduces the tension caused by a need (q.v.).

Neencephalon. The "new brain" or "harmonious prolongation" lying above the "old brain" or paleencephalon (q.v.). A fairly pure neencephalic area of the brain is the six-layer cerebral cortex (isocortex) in mammals. In the newly-born the medullated nerve fibers between cortex and brainstem are still immature, so that the child is visually and acoustically inactive. Voluntary motor behavior becomes possible as soon as the pyramidal tracts mature. The rate of medullary maturation increases with the phylogenic age of a system. Under narcosis or the influence of alcohol the neencephalic systems are the first to cease to operate and the paleencephalic systems are inhibited. *K.Fi.*

Negative induction (syn. *External inhibition*). In Pavlovian theory: the suppression of a conditioned response by the simultaneous effect of an unconditioned stimulus, which evokes another response. Considered to be a form of unconditioned inhibition. *L.B.*

Negative practice. Emphasizing the practice of errors in order to acquire accurate performance.

Negativism. *Active.* Performance of the opposite motor behavior to that expected from the situation or stimulus. Found in catatonia, dementia and subnormality, and called active or command negativism. It presumes that the patient understands at some level the stimulus situation.

Passive. Non-performance of any behavior that would be expected in the stimulus situation. It does not presume understanding on the part of the patient. It includes active muscular opposition to attempts to induce movement, e.g. of a limb. Bleuler used the term *inner negativism* for the behavior of patients who did not obey physiological urges such as elimination and eating. *B.B.*

Neobehaviorism. A type of behaviorism (q.v.) which (in contrast to Watsonian theory) is not restricted to objective (observable) variables and their direct relationships. Neobehaviorism uses such terms as "drive", "intelligence", "expectation", "failure", etc., which are taken from the psychology of consciousness (q.v.), and allows of the introduction of hypothetical constructs (intervening variables) to explain a relationship when there are no observable links between variables. *R.Hä.*

Neologism. A new word created by an individual who attaches a meaning to it. Normal people, writers and children create new words. Neologisms are produced by schizophrenic and brain-damaged people to label known, private and bygone concepts and experiences. New sound combinations without apparent meaning produced by brain-damaged people are not neologisms but are examples of *jargon aphasia.* Known words, or phrases of known words, to which people attach new meanings have been called neologisms, but these are better denoted by the term *paraphrasia* (q.v.). *B.B.*

Neophasia. A special form of schizophrenic language. See *Neologism; Schizophrenia.*

Neopositivism. The Vienna Circle, which formed around M. Schlick, included the psychologist O. Neurath. This school held that only those statements which were verifiable or falsifiable under stringent experimental conditions were scientific. In psychology this signifies the reduction of all mental activity to those factors which can be observed externally as action or change of place, and the elimination of all "mentalism". Neopositivism was from the outset allied to P. W. Bridgman's operationalism (q.v.), and became influential mainly in the USA, where behaviorism (q.v.) flourished around 1930. The most extreme representatives of this school can still be found in the USA (J. R. Kantor). See *Logical positivism.* *P.M.*

Neopsychoanalysis. A term first introduced in German to designate Schultz-Hencke's school of depth psychology (1951). This representative of psychoanalysis (q.v.) tried to synthesize the different branches of analysis by seeking to explain neuroses by the dynamic interaction of drives and inhibitions. The term has also been used to indicate various schools which, starting from psychoanalysis, arrived at deviant or additional concepts: e.g. the direction taken by the psychoanalysts who emigrated to the United States and took account of cultural and social phenomena in regard to the etiology and symptomatology of neuroses, and emphasized intersubjective relations (H. S. Sullivan, K. Horney, S. Rado, and F. Alexander). Some of the neopsychoanalytic schools attempt to establish a relationship between the structure of neuroses and the social structure (e.g. A. Mitscherlich, E. Fromm and H. Marcuse). See *Neurosis; Depth psychology.*

Bibliography: Mitscherlich, A.: Society without the father. London, 1969. **Schultz-Hencke, H.:** Lehrbuch der analytischen Psychotherapie. Stuttgart, 1951.

J.L.I.

Neostigmine (syn. *Prostigmine* = neostigmine methylsulfate). A parasympathetic stimulant which acts by inhibiting cholinesterase (it blocks AChE) and by directly potentiating the action of acetylcholine. Neostigmine is more effective than physostigmine (q.v.).

Bibliography: See *Cholinesterase inhibitors.* *W.J.*

Nernst-Lillie theory of excitation. Since L. Hermann (1899), J. Bernstein (1902) and E. Overton (1902), ion-concentration differences between the excitable substrate (nerve) and the immediate environment (intercellular fluid) had been considered important in the process of excitation. In 1908, W. Nernst developed a theory of excitation from the earlier studies; he described the propagation of excitation mathematically in terms of a telegraphic model. Between 1917 and 1936, R. S. Lillie conducted experiments with a nerve model of iron wire in highly concentrated nitric acid (specific gravity, 1.24) having many analogies with the nerve. Today this theory is only of historical interest since the process of nervous excitation is best explained by the "ion theory" developed by A. L. Hodgkin and A. F. Huxley, who were awarded the Nobel prize for their work in 1963. See *Axon; Nervous system.* *K.-H.P.*

Nerve. The (peripheral) nerves consist of nerve fibers (neurons) outside the central nervous system which are characteristically arranged in bundles. Nerves contain neurites (q.v.). Each neurite conducts impulses in one direction. *G.A.*

Nervousness. 1. A popular designation for over-excitability (of the autonomic nervous system, q.v.). **2.** Factor used by Guilford & Zimmerman in personality inventories, and opposed to calmness and composure. *K.P.*

Nervous system (syn. *Nerve system*). The origin, conduction and transmission of excitation. 1. *Components.* The nerve cells (neuron(e)s, q.v.) are functional units serving the process of excitation in living beings which have reached a relatively high level of development. In contrast to previous theories that protoplasmic connections combine all nerve cells in a unit without cell boundaries (syncytium) (plasmatic continuity), or that all neurons are combined by fibrillar continuity, the nerve cell is now considered as a component which is independent both in its substance and function. It is responsible for (*a*) the origin of excitation: the conversion of stimuli into nervous excitation processes by sense cells (= receptor cells) which may be thought of as specialized nerve cells; (*b*) conducting excitation on the basis of a special fault-proof principle by which impulses can be transmitted without change, even over considerable distances; (*c*) the transmission of impulses to other nerve or effector cells by means of special mechanisms. All these excitation processes do, however, follow a universally valid principle.

The basic function of the neuron consists of the reception, processing and transmission of information. A functional division of the nerve cells characterized by complex branching into an input region (dendritic zone), pericaryon (nutritive zone) and output region (neurite and axon: telodendria) is to be preferred to other classificatory theories (e.g. a division into unipolar, bipolar and multipolar nerve cells on the basis of the number of cell continuations).

The search for specific fine differentiations between nerve cells which might be responsible for the excitation process proved unsuccessful—the neuron contains the same subcellular structures as cells with other functions. Even the tigroid substance (Nissl substance) is not a special feature of the nerve cell but a multi-ribosomic endoplasmatic reticulum ("granular form") which is found in all cells with an active protein metabolism. Special differences are provided solely by the neurofibrils, small thread-like structures, which are situated in the entire cytoplasm and whose existence has repeatedly been called in question since they were first described. They are, however, immaterial as far as the mechanisms of excitation are concerned, since the latter are dependent solely on functional units of the cell membrane.

Like all cell membranes, the membrane of nerve cells consists of two lipoid layers embedded between an outer and inner protein layer ("unit membrane"). Certain substances are diffused in it with varying degrees of rapidity. The ability of the membrane to ensure active conduction is particularly important for nervous excitation: certain substances are transported against an existing concentration gradient, i.e. sodium ions are displaced from the cell to the exterior, where they are already present in a neutral state in a concentration which is ten times higher; and potassium ions are displaced toward the interior of the cell, where the concentration is some two hundred times higher than outside (the sodium–potassium ion "pump").

2. *Nervous excitation.* The fact that the nerve cell has a negative internal electrical charge in the resting state (resting potential approximately -60 mV in relation to the exterior) was tentatively explained in 1902 by J. Bernstein, who assumed the existence of a membrane with selective permeability to K^+ and Cl^- in the resting state (polarization) which changed its permeability characteristics on excitation. This ion theory of excitation, as extended by Hodgkin and Huxley, is still valid today: the resting potential (= membrane potential) can be estimated from the diffusion movements of K and Cl caused by concentration differences. In the state of excitation, on the other hand, there is increased permeability to Na^+, which (as a result of the concentration difference and potential difference) flows into the interior of the cell and brings about a reduction in resting potential (= depolarization). The resulting concentration displacements are compensated once more by the sodium–potassium "pump". This is the process of "excitation" or stimulation, as a set of electro-chemical events.

(*a*) *Origins of excitation.* Various influences (mechanical, electrical, chemical, etc.) may act as stimuli on the cell membrane. The greater their energy, the greater the change in Na permeability. If the Na input remains below a critical threshold value, there is a continuously variable depolarization of the cell membrane as a function of the stimulus intensity. This is the case if excitation is generated at the receptor, when depolarization (= generator potential) increases as the stimulus intensity rises. In the case of the receptors studied in detail to date, the generator potential is an (approximately) logarithmic function of stimulus intensity.

(*b*) *Excitation conduction.* Above a critical depolarization value, there is a sudden increase in Na permeability of the membrane to about five hundred times its original value, when the interior of the cell is for a short time positively charged (approximately $+30$ mV), only to return with equal speed to the initial state as a result of the subsequent K outflow. This voltage peak (action potential) lasts only for about 1/2 msec; its amplitude is always identical for a given nerve fiber (all-or-none law, q.v.). This stimulation is not confined to the point of origin but is propagated, thus activating the neighboring membrane regions.

The conduction of excitation on the output side of the cell follows the same principle: because of the rather lower threshold at the beginning of the output region (initial segment), action potentials are produced in an increasingly dense sequence, the higher the overall level of excitation of the relevant nerve cell (= depolarization level). The action potentials pass through fibers with a very thin covering at a uniform velocity of about 30–200 cm/sec (continuous conduction of excitation). "Myelinated" fibers, on the other hand, are enclosed in thicker covering cells which are interrupted so as to leave a narrow axon region bare at regular intervals (nodes of Ranvier). In these fibers action potentials jump from one node to the next (saltatory excitation) and a considerable increase in the speed of conduction up to 120 m/sec results.

(*c*) *Transmission of excitation.* Excitation is transmitted by the synapses: the end of the axon (q.v.) terminates in enlarged end branches (neuropodia) which are separated by an intervening space (synaptic cleft) from the sub- and post-synaptic membrane of the next cell. Chemical substances (transmitter molecules) are ready in small bubbles (synaptic vesicles) in the presynaptic membrane and are liberated by an incoming action potential; they then pass through the synaptic cleft to the sub-synaptic membrane where they lead to permeability changes. After this change (which is dependent on the transmitter) a distinction can be made between two types: (i) excitatory synapses: the transmitter substance leads to depolarization of the membrane; a positive potential is generated, i.e. the excitatory post-synaptic potential (EPSP) which increases the level of excitation of the nerve cells; (ii) inhibitory synapses: in the case of the latter, the transmitter brings about a hyperpolarization of the membrane—the inhibitory post-synaptic potential (IPSP): the negativity of the cell membrane increases and the overall level of cell excitation is reduced.

The magnitude and duration of post-synaptic potentials may cause major differences. If the post-synaptic depolarization does not reach the critical threshold value for generation of an action potential (which is generally the case in the dendritic zone), the charge is propagated electrotonically. Through simultaneous excitation of several synapses, spatial summation may occur, and through a rapid succession of activations of a single synapse summation as a function of time, the individual EPSP or IPSP being superimposed.

The interaction of all the excitatory and inhibitory stimuli may be considered as the integrative function of the individual nerve cell: the given net product of the overall excitation produces an action potential sequence in the output region (initial segments) and the excitation level of the cell is coded in the interval between the individual action potentials. The latter liberate the transmitter substance again at their destination, and thus cause the excitation to be transmitted to subsequent nerve cells (or effector cells) at which the excitation information is passed on, on approximately the same principle.

Recording of the electrical phenomena accompanying nervous excitation is of primary psychological importance. Suitable methods have been developed recently to determine correlates of specific psychological processes (e.g. perceptions) (see *Neuropsychology*). One of the major problems in psychology at present is to determine the mechanisms of information stores, i.e. the conservation of the excitation phenomenon in a permanent form which forms the basis of an actual experience or behavior (see *Engram; Memory trace*). This process of consolidation seems to be completed by means of molecular biological processes which are also responsible—and by no means accidentally—for genetic control.

Bibliography: Crosby, E. C., Humphrey, T. & Lauer, E. W.: Correlative anatomy of the nervous system. New York, 1962. **Field, J., Magoun, H. W. & Hall, V. E.** (Ed.): Handbook of physiology (Neurophysiology), Vols. 1–3. Baltimore, 1960. **Pribram, K. H.:** Brain and behaviour, Vols. 1–4. Harmondsworth, 1969. **Shadé, J. P. & Ford, D. H.:** Basic neurology. Amsterdam, London & New York, 1965. **Progress in brain research,** Vols. 1–30. Amsterdam, London & New York.

G. Guttmann

Nervous system, autonomic, parasympathetic, sympathetic, vegetative. See *Autonomic nervous system; Psychopharmacology and the ANS.*

Nervus acusticus. A frequently used, though (according to the Paris Nomenclature) anatomically incorrect, term for the eighth cranial nerve (see *Nervus statoacusticus*), and its acoustic component the *nervus cochlearis*, or *cochlear nerve.* *E.D.*

Nervus opticus. Part of the visual pathway. Since the retina and its connection to the cortex must be considered in evolutionary terms as part of the brain, the *nervus opticus* is also referred to as the *fasciculus opticus*, i.e. the connection between the retina and the *chiasma opticum* (optic chiasm). *R.R.*

Nervus statoacusticus. The statoacoustic nerve consists of the vestibular nerve and the cochlear nerve. The former brings information from the semicircular canals and the statoliths, and the latter from the cochlea of the inner ear for further processing in the brain. See *Sense organs* (*the Ear*). *E.D.*

Nest building. Nests are built to protect eggs or young, or to provide warmth, e.g. the nests in which rodents and primates sleep. Nest-building behavior is largely instinctive, and in regard to the breeding cycle its stimulation in vertebrates is largely dependent on increasing levels of sex hormones (testosterone, estrogen). *K.Fi.*

Neural. Pertaining to a nerve (q.v.).

Neuralgia. Nerve pains: paroxysmal attacks of pain in the distribution area of a sensory or mixed nerve without observable anatomical changes (unlike neuritis, q.v.); often linked with preceding unpleasant sensations (of heat or tension, itching, etc.). The commonest form is radiating facial pain (trigeminal neuralgia, tic douloureux). Possible causes: latent infections, colds, metabolic changes, poisoning, mechanical damage, etc. *F.-C.S.*

Neurasthenia. A syndrome which generally has neurotic origins, characterized by heavy fatigue, low motivation level. vegetative lability, poor concentration and general sluggishness. *G.K.*

Neurilemma. Nerve sheath. The peripheral axons are enclosed in lemnocytes (Schwann's cells). These may be richly or poorly myelinated, or non-myelinated. The lemnocytes contain cell nuclei and form a fine skin around the sheath, known as the neurilemma. This, together with an external reticular fibrous tissue, forms the endoneural sheath. *G.A.*

Neuritis. A partly inflammatory, partly degenerative condition of the peripheral nerves, accompanied by disorders of motor or sensory conduction. In contrast to neuralgia (q.v.), anatomico-pathological changes are suspected or detected. Not only subjective pain but disturbances and deficits of sensitivity and motor functions are observed. Possible causes are infections, colds, nervous lesions under pressure or strain, excessive effort, toxic action of alcohol, lead, carbon dioxide, etc. According to the number of nerves involved, a distinction is made between *mononeuritis*, *mononeuritis multiplex*, and *polyneuritis*. *F.-C.S.*

Neuroanatomy, or the anatomy of the nervous system, is a morphological science which investigates the structure and form of the nervous system and advances our understanding of the somato-cerebral bases of psychological phenomena.

The *nervous system* (NS) consists of a central organ and peripheral organs—the nerves which connect the central organ with the organism. The central organ consists of the spinal cord, the brainstem, the cerebellum, and the cerebrum (the most important part). Each hemisphere of the cerebrum is surmounted by a layer of grey matter, the cerebral cortex, which is subdivided by invaginations (fissures) into lobes and gyri. Below the cerebral cortex is the white matter, and at the center of the subcortical region are the caudate nucleus and the lenticular nucleus. Both hemispheres are connected by the corpus callosum; below it is a cavity containing the cerebrospinal fluid (*liquor cerebrospinalis*): this is the third ventricle, which is enclosed on both sides by the optic thalami (*thalami optici*), and below by the hypothalamus. The NS is made up of nerve tissue, which in its turn consists of neuron(e)s and glia cells. The points of contact between two neurons or one neuron and the stimulus emitters or (stimulus) receptors of the organism are known as synapses. The synapses

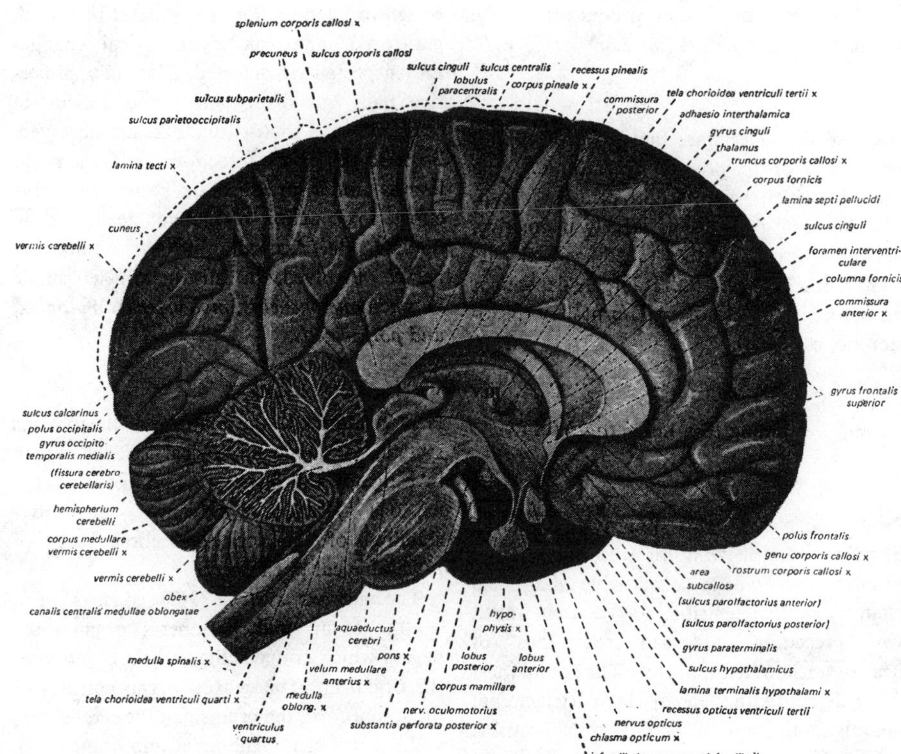

Median section through the human brain

From left to right:

1 vermis cerebelli, **2** corpus medullare vermis cerebelli, **3** hemispherium cerebelli, **4** gyrus occipitotemporalis medialis, **5** polus occipitalis, **6** sulcus calcarinus, **7** vermis cerebelli, **8** cuneus, **9** lamina tecti, **10** sulcus parietooccipitalis, **11** sulcus subparietalis, **12** precuneus, **13** splenium corporis callosi, **14** sulcus corporis callosi, **15** sulcus cinguli, **16** lobulus paracentralis, **17** sulcus centralis, **18** corpus pineale, **19** recessus pinealis, **20** commissura posterior, **21** tela chorioidea ventriculi tertii, **22** adhaesio interthalamica, **23** gyrus cinguli, **24** thalamus, **25** truncus corporis callosi, **26** corpus fornicis, **27** lamina septi pellucidi, **28** sulcus cinguli, **29** foramen interventriculare, **30** columna fornicis, **31** commissura anterior, **32** gyrus frontalis superior, **33** polus frontalis, **34** genu corporis callosi, **35** rostrum corporis callosi, **36** area subcallosa, **37** sulcus parolfactorius anterior, **38** sulcus parolfactorius posterior, **39** gyrus paraterminalis, **40** sulcus hypothalamicus, **41** lamina terminalis hypothalami, **42** recessus opticus ventriculi tertii, **43** nervus opticus, **44** chiasma opticum, **45** infundibulum recessus infundibuli, **46** lobus anterior, **47** hypophysis, **48** lobus posterior, **49** corpus mamillare, **50** nervus oculomotorius, **51** substantia perforata posterior, **52** pons, **53** aquaeductus cerebri, **54** velum medullare anterius, **55** medulla oblongata, **56** ventriculus quartus, **57** tela chorioidea ventriculi quarti, **58** medulla spinalis, **59** canalis centralis medullae oblongatae, **60** obex.

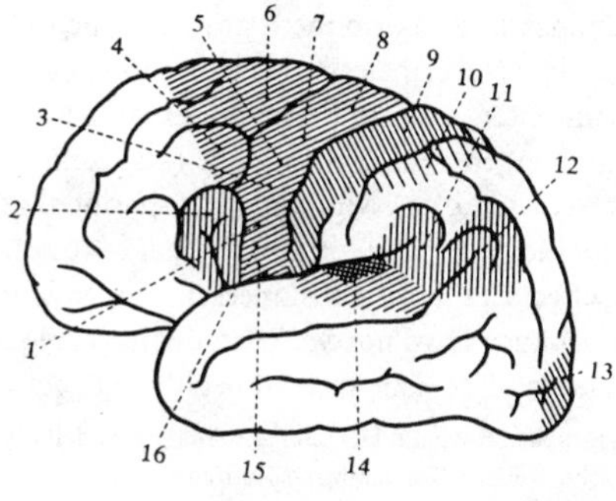

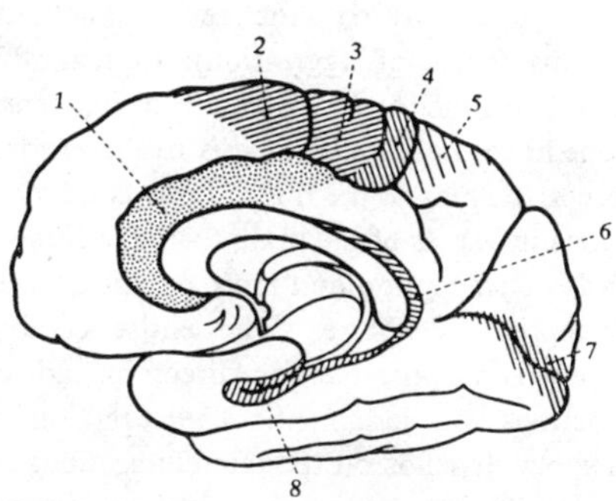

Localization of motor, sensory and autonomic centers on the cerebral cortex

Left:
1 Motor center for tongue, **2** Motor speech center, **3** Motor center for facial muscles, **4** Motor center for head and eye movements, **5** Motor center for arm, hand, finger, **6** Motor center for trunk, **7** Motor center for shoulder, **8** Motor center for leg, **9** Somesthetic region, main field, **10** Somesthetic region, secondary field, **11** Sensory speech center, **12** Visual (optic) speech center, **13** Visual center (optical memory center), **14** Auditory center, **15** Motor center for pharynx, **16** Motor center for larynx.

Right:
1 Autonomic region (vasomotor and secretory impulses), **2** Motor center (trunk), **3** Motor center (leg), **4** Somesthetic region, main field, **5** Somesthetic region, secondary field, **6** Olfactory center, **7** Visual center (perception center), **8** Gustatory center.

enable the neurons to join together to form conduction pathways; these are the substrate of the NS, which may be thought of as a totality of more or less complex and hierarchically ordered conduction channels: the more complex pathways dominate the less complex, thus affording the unity of action characteristic of the NS. The nervous impulses received at the periphery are transmitted by afferent nerves to the center of the particular conduction system; these impulses are processed in the centers, and then retransmitted by way of the efferent nerves to the periphery. This part of the system culminates in the effectors, which carry out the orders of the NS. The afferent and efferent sections consist of neurons connected more or less in series. The centers are neuronal complexes, which very frequently form circular connections. According to their particular degree of complexity, the conducting paths are subdivided into segmental, suprasegmental, and totalizing complexes. The totalizing center consists of two very important parts: the cerebrum (the center of which is the cerebral cortex, whose afferent and efferent branches, the sensory and motor pathways, are extremely complex) and the cerebellum. The segmental and suprasegmental pathways form the somatic basis of reflex actions; the cerebral system is the somatic basis of reflexive and emotional behavior: the cerebellum is a control organ for global regulation of the activity of the NS. Finally, in the brainstem there is a group of neurons, known as the reticular formation (*formatio reticularis*) which controls waking and sleeping and the "diathetic rhythm", i.e. the periodic fluctuation between states such as depression and mania. A large number of animal experiments and the investigation of inappropriate reactions in brain-damaged individuals have shown that, in regard to the biological significance of the individual parts of the totalizing cerebral system, the neurobiological processes occurring in the limbic system (which is comprised in the hypothalamic system) are the somatic correlates of the relatively elementary and primitive impulses and affects of the endothymic base, i.e. of those drives common to men and animals (e.g. hunger, thirst, the sex instinct, the various forms of aggression). In regard to cognitive functions, it is assumed that sensations have their somatic basis in the primary receptive areas of the brain; the secondary or "gnostic" areas of the brain form the cerebral basis of perception and more or less abstract perceptual complexes. The entire cerebral cortex is responsible for direct or indirect functions of judgment. The function of memory depends on the interconnections between different groups of cortical neurons and on the production of specific proteins in such fields. Finally, the "prospective" functions (formation of a plan of action and a behavioral strategy, forethought for the future, etc.) are "located" in the foremost zone of the frontal lobes (q.v.). See *Arousal; Localization of psychological functions; Neuropsychology.*

Bibliography: Gómez Bosque, P.: Organización del sistema nervioso. Estructuración General y Funciones. El Problema de la Relación Alma-Cuerpo. Madrid, 1965. **Id.** *et al.*: El sistema nervioso central, Vols. 1, 2. Valladolid, 1967–9. **Grossman, S. P.:** Textbook of physiological psychology. New York & London, 1967. **Pribram, K. H.** (Ed.): Brain and behaviour, 4 vols. Harmondsworth, 1969. **Sternbach, R. A.:** Principles of psychophysiology. New York, 1966. **Teitelbaum, P.:** Physiological psychology. New York, 1967.

P. Gómez Bosque

Neurodynamic substances. Chemical substances which "improve" the brain metabolism and probably lead to improved psychophysical performance. The concept of neurodynamic agents is essentially grounded in practical therapy and includes all substances which can bring about improvements in long-term impairment of physical and psychological performance. The neurophysiological effective mechanisms may be stimulation of the synthesis of biogenic amines in the central nervous system and/or increased cerebral blood circulation. The qualification "neurodynamic" is used only in connection with substances with a prolonged effect (days or weeks), unlike stimulants, which are active only for a few hours. Vitamins and hormones are no neurodynamic. Nevertheless there is no clearly differentiated criterion. Examples of neurodynamic agents are pyrithioxine (a substance which resembles vitamin B_6—pyridoxine hydrochloride) and glutamic acid (q.v.). The effects of both substances in improving performance have not yet been demonstrated in acute and chronic tests in healthy subjects.

Bibliography: Bochnik, H.-J., *et al.*: Analysemodell für klinische Verbundforschung: Multifaktorielle Untersuchung der Pyrithioxinwirkung nach Schlafentzug bei gesunden Studenten. Fortschr. der Neurologie und Psychiatrie, 1964, *32*, 399–425. See also *Glutamic acid.*

K.D.S.

Neuroendocrinology. A branch of endocrinology that studies the interaction of the endocrine glands and the nervous system. The main areas of study are (*a*) the influence of hormones on the nervous system; (*b*) the effect of nervous excitation on hormone secretion; and (*c*) the production and importance of hormones in the central and autonomic nervous systems. See *Hormones.*

Bibliography: Bajusz, E. (Ed.): An introduction to clinical neuroendocrinology. Basle, 1967.

W.J.

Neuroethology. Research into the neural basis of behavior with a view to establishing a synthesis of neurology and ethology. Methods used include electrical brain stimulation, derivation of action potentials from freely moving animals, elimination of areas of the brain by extirpation and coagulation, and measurement of post-operative behavioral changes. *K.Fi.*

Neurogram. See *Engram.*

Neurohormones. Chemical substances which promote or inhibit the transmission and action of impulses in the central and autonomic nervous systems. The term "neurohormones" is sometimes used as a synonym for transmitter substances (q.v.), or—more comprehensively—for all substances which play a part in the functions of nervous substrates. See *Biogenic amines.*

Bibliography: See *Hormones; Neuroendocrinology; Biogenic amines; Transmitter substances.* *W.J.*

Neurolepsy. A state characterized by hypnosis and the blocking of vegetative reflexes. This term is now seldom used. *J.P.*

Neuroleptics. Psychopharmaceutical substances which form the major group of preparations for the treatment of agitated and productive psychoses, and which are also used in severe, non-psychotic anxiety and excitation states. The term "neuroplegic" is obsolete, and it is now usual to speak of "tranquilizers", but a subdivision into major and minor tranquilizers is necessary to establish a distinction from tranquilizers (q.v.) in the narrower sense. Chemically, the neuroleptics can be divided into rauwolfia alkaloids (q.v.), butyrophenones (q.v.), phenothiazines (q.v.), and thiaxanthene derivatives (thiothixene = Navane). As regards effect, a distinction can be made between neuroleptics and hypnotics or tranquilizers by (*a*) anti-psychotic effect (reduction of high-grade excitation states of a hyper- or alkinetic type, reduction of psychotic experience phenomena such as delusions and hallucinations); (*b*) extrapyramidal symptoms (e.g. tremor, rigor, dystonic reactions—which can be prevented by anti-Parkinsonian agents); (*c*) frequent strong autonomic reactions (adrenolytic, sometimes anticholinergic); (*d*) lowering of the cramp threshold; (*e*) suppression of active, non-passive avoidance behavior (q.v.) in animal experiments. When administered concurrently with tranquilizers in therapeutic doses they do not induce sleep (unlike the hypnotics), and in higher doses do not lead to narcosis (q.v.). In low doses, the neuroleptics have tranquilizing effects. Many psychological studies have been carried out in healthy persons for chlorpromazine (q.v.), but fewer for other phenothiazines, while very few investigations have been made into reserpine (q.v.), haloperidol (q.v.), and related substances. After acute application in healthy subjects, even in low doses, neuroleptics only seldom induce motor relaxation and emotional stabilization. Impairment of performance and reduction in experienced activity are frequent. As in the case of tranquilizers, improvements are more likely to occur in cases of affective and motor stress (habitual or situative) and low psychological strain (see *Differential psychopharmacology*). The postulation of a lower degree of impairment of cognitive functions by neuroleptics than by hypnotics and tranquilizers has not been confirmed.

Bibliography: Brill, H. (Ed.): Neuro-Psychopharmacology Symposia II. Washington, 1967, 87–156. **Efron, D. H.** (Ed.): Psychopharmacology 1957–1967. Washington, 1968, 1044–181. See also *Butyrophenones; Phenothiazine; Rauwolfia alkaloids.* *G.D.*

Neurology. That branch of medicine which deals with the clinical and pathological aspects of the structure and function of the central and peripheral nervous system. *D.E.*

Neuron(e). The smallest functional unit of the nervous system (q.v.). Also known as a ganglionic cell in the brain. The neuron consists of the nerve cell body with the cell nucleus, the short dendrites (q.v.), and a generally very long axon(e). *E.D.*

Neuropathy. A term used variously: sometimes as a general term for nervous disorders, and sometimes (in a narrower sense) for an innate inclination to pathological over-excitability of the nervous system, manifested most frequently in vegetative and endocrinal disorders. The term is practically synonymous with vegetative dystonia and often indistinguishable from psychopathy (q.v.). *K.H.P.*

Neuropharmacology. A branch of pharmacology which studies changes in nervous mechanisms under the influence of drugs, in particular psychopharmaceutical substances. See *Psychopharmacology.* *W.J.*

Neuroplegics. Syn. *Neuroleptics* (q.v.).

Neuropsychiatry. The field of diagnostic and methodological problems of psychiatry in the area of the neurophysiology of brain functions. There are also close relations with neurosurgery (q.v.), experimental comparative psychology, and neurophysiology.

Bibliography: Luria, A. R.: Human brain and psychological process. New York & London, 1966. *M.Ad.*

Neuropsychology. The investigation of the correlation between experience (or behavior) and the basic biological processes. The term "neuropsychology" stresses the dominant role of the nervous system, although other systems also must sometimes be taken into account (e.g. hormones). The study of direct psychophysiological relationships (e.g. change in circulation variables under arousal, q.v., or fatigue, q.v.) is not part of the research field of neuropsychology, but belongs to the wider concept of "physiological psychology".

The abundant data on neuropsychology may be classified as follows:

1. *Elimination.* The attempt to determine biological bases of experience by eliminating the biological substrate and consequent changes in experience is the oldest method. In addition to the study of congenital malformations of the nervous system, acquired lesions (due to trauma or pathological processes), and voluntary elimination (see *Lobotomy*) by controlled destruction of cortical or subcortical neuron assemblies, or by isolating conductor paths in animal experiments, particular importance has been attached more recently to reversible function blocking, e.g. the temporary suppression of cerebral cortical activity by appropriate chemical or mechanical stimulation (see *Brain pathology*).

2. *Stimulation.* The stimulation of functions is a method which allows more accurate localization. Controlled stimulation in the human brain has allowed detailed plotting of the sensory and motor systems (since the first experiments of the last century) by systematic stimulation of the cerebral cortex during brain operations, and by controlled stimulation in the depths of the brain (see *Stereotactic methods*). Information has also been obtained on the neuronal bases of emotional and motivational processes, and on the control of learning processes (reinforcement centers) and consciousness; this has had a lasting influence on psychological theory. See *Mind-body problem.*

3. *Activity correlate.* The most useful method is, however, the observation of activity correlates. In addition to the not directly accessible biochemical correlates of neuronal activity (e.g. the concentration of substances involved in the synaptic process of stimulation transmission), the observation of electrical phenomena accompanying nervous activity is most significant. It has been shown that the spontaneous electrical activity of the brain has no certain direct link with specific psychological processes, and that only activation level is reflected in the frequency and amplitude characteristics of brain potentials. However, sophisticated techniques have recently enabled the specific stimulation components covered by the EEG (e.g. for a simple act of perception) to be isolated from spontaneous activity, which is generally some twenty times stronger; this makes it possible to analyze the specific components. In perception processes this can be done by recording the activity consequent on a sensory stimulus, and adding the values cumulatively for a series of identical, successive stimuli. In this way, the non-specific spontaneous activity is increasingly differentiated from the repeated stimuli, while the specific excitation components—however weak they may be—appear with increasing clarity. The sensory

evoked potentials obtained in this way have a typical time sequence and spatial distribution for each sense area, and also vary characteristically with stimulus quality.

It is, of course, more difficult to observe specific stimuli which do not correspond to an externally elicited process, e.g. imagery or spontaneous actions. Nevertheless, special techniques have revealed the basic specific stimuli for some of these processes (e.g. readiness potentials before a spontaneous behavior).

One of the most important current problems concerns the neuropsychological principles of learning (q.v.): the transformation of the immediate excitation process into a resistant and permanent form (consolidation process). This transformation probably takes place in several stages, which are also biologically distinct. The information set down in an action-potential sequence is maintained as nervous excitation only for a short time—possibly circulating in closed neuronal circuits. The next step seems to consist in the activation of genetically determined synthesis chains: specific qualitative changes in substances which play an important part in such biosynthesis (ribonucleic acids) have been demonstrated in the course of active learning processes. The results relating to the biochemical transfer of learning point in the same direction: if ribonucleic acid is extracted from the brain of animals which have learnt a specific behavior pattern, and is then administered to untrained animals, the latter then learn the same behavior pattern more easily. It is still not clear whether the final phase of the consolidation process consists of a growth of the cell continuations, of a facilitation of synaptic transmission, or of other changes. It has not proved possible to elucidate the number of stages in a learning process, their duration and influenceability in neuropsychological terms. Relevant studies have, however, provided the strongest evidence to date to suggest that psychological models should be based on biological principles.

Bibliography: Grossman, S. P.: Textbook of physiological psychology. New York, 1967. **Guttmann, G.:** Einführung in die Neuropsychologie. Berne, 1971. **Isaacson, R. L.** (Ed.): Basic readings in neuropsychology. New York, 1964. **Pribram, K. H.:** Brain and behavior, Vols. 1–4. Harmondsworth, 1969. **Thompson, R. F.:** Foundations of physiological psychology. New York, 1967. *G. Guttmann*

Neuropsychopharmacology. A generic term for all scientific disciplines concerned with the neurophysiological, neurochemical and psychological effects of drugs (in particular psychopharmaceutical substances) and of natural body substances (see *Hormones*). Sometimes used as a synonym for psychopharmacology (q.v.). *W.J.*

Neuroses. See *Neurosis.*

Neurosis. 1. *History.* Although the word "neurosis" only came into use about 1780, when it was introduced by William Cullen, what we now understand by the term has figured among conceptions of mental illnesses since the time of the ancient Greeks. Through the ages, explanations of the causes of mental illnesses ranged from the somewhat scientific approach of the Greeks to the supernatural explanations of medieval psychiatry; only in the eighteenth century did a fresh perspective arise, when a new philosophical system which freed thought from preoccupation with the immortal soul and the mischief of evil spirits allowed mental disorder to be seen as stemming from the mortal brain. Scientific investigation in the fields of philosophy, chemistry, medicine, and especially psychiatry itself, was responsible for this changed viewpoint.

The theories of the chemist G. E. Stahl (1660–1734) on mental illness as either caused by diseases of the organs (which he termed "sympathetic" causation), or consisting of functional disease with no organic basis ("pathetic" causation), were the core of the development of modern psychiatry. Stahl's doctrine of "animism" (q.v.) caused a rash of physiological studies designed to determine the psychogenic origins of mental disease. William Cullen (1769), spokesman for the school of "neuropathology" in Edinburgh—who had adopted the theories of "vitalism", a line of development from Stahl—tried to explain nervous disorders in terms of motion of the nerves. From that viewpoint, *neurosis* was a very appropriate name. Included under the term were a variety of otherwise inexplicable diseases such as apoplexy, palsy, dyspepsia, hypochondriasis, tetanus, epilepsy, chorea, palpitation, dyspnoea, asthma, whooping-cough, colic, cholera, diarrhea, diabetes, hysteria, and hydrophobia. Having originated in neurology, the term gained widespread psychiatric usage, but its connotation was vague and over-inclusive.

In 1778 Mesmer arrived in Paris and psychotherapy by hypnosis (q.v.) came into vogue. Using the hypnotic method, Jean Martin Charcot (1825–93) began his studies of hysteria (q.v.), the first systematic investigation of the neuroses (see Guillain, 1955). The interest generated by Charcot was maintained by Pierre Janet (q.v.) (1859–1947). In the process of hypnotizing his subjects, Janet discovered that the origin of some neuroses could be traced to forgotten traumatic events whose recall under hypnosis sometimes led to cure (see Galdston, 1967). In ascribing a psychic origin to the neuroses he separated them from other mental aberrations.

Throughout the eighteenth and early nineteenth centuries scores of classification systems for mental illness were put forth that often included subdivisions within the category of neurosis. Carl Westphal (1883–90) distinguished the obsessions, homosexuality and agoraphobia; Maudsley in 1879 spoke of *neurosis spasmodica* as a condition characterized by the disposition to sudden, singular and impulsive caprices of thought, feeling, and conduct; and Adolf Meyer referred to the "part reaction" in which only a portion of the personality is altered while the patient remains reality-oriented.

2. *Freud's psychoanalysis and its derivatives.* Undoubtedly, the most popular and influential concept of the neuroses is due to Janet's contemporary, Sigmund Freud (q.v.) (1856–1939). Freud, too, had turned to hypnotism at an early stage of his career. He and Josef Breuer (1842–1925) aroused much psychiatric interest by their *Studien über Hysterie* (*Studies in Hysteria*, 1895), which described the "cathartic method" (q.v.) whereby a neurotic patient was enabled to release emotions under hypnosis (Zilboorg & Henry, 1941). Freud later noted that his patients were preoccupied with sexual material, and went on to conclude that sexual difficulties were the cause of all neurotic disorders. He soon abandoned hypnosis and replaced it with "free association" as a means of uncovering forgotten memories thought to be "repressed" in the "unconscious". In place of the earlier simple sexual theory of neurosis, he developed a much more elaborate one that postulated a succession of stages in a child's development, during each of which traumatic events could inhibit progression to the next stage. Depending on the stage of development, the type of inhibiting trauma, and the details of the situation, the child would develop a characteristic mechanism of defense (q.v.) that would decide the type of neurosis he would eventually manifest. The childhood trauma was assumed to be retained (repressed) in the adult "unconscious" as a complex to which were attached emotional forces: these found devious outlets in neurotic responses whose form was determined by the particular defense mechanism. It followed that recovery would require the repressed complex to be released into consciousness. Free association and dream analysis were the main procedures by which this was to be brought about.

Freud's pupils, Carl Jung (q.v.) (1875–1961) and Alfred Adler (q.v.) (1870–1937), formed two dissident groups within the framework of psychoanalysis (see Bromberg,

1959). Jung theorized that instinct (q.v.), or Freud's "libido" (q.v.), was developed from primeval instinctive tendencies deposited in a "racial" or "collective unconscious" that he claimed to be represented in all men's unconscious mental functioning. Individuals could be categorized by their "racial" archetypes. For Jung, a neurosis resulted when attitudes and life goals fell outside the scope of the individual's "racial" type. Adler's Individual Psychology essentially rejected Freud's libido theory. Adler attributed neurosis to conflicting feelings of inferiority and superiority which interfered with the "life plan" or goals of the individual. Believing that man strives for superiority, he regarded neurosis as a defective means of implementing the drive toward power.

Whereas such men as Ferenczi, Jones and Fenichel remained loyal to Freud's concepts, other students of psychoanalysis proposed variations, emphasizing one or another aspect of the Freudian view of the etiology of neuroses (see Munroe; Zilboorg & Henry). Otto Rank (1929), impressed with the trauma of birth, elevated it to a position of major importance in regard to neurotic anxiety, and constructed his "will therapy" on its theme. Wilhelm Stekel sought to shorten dream analysis, and encouraged patients to control their anxiety (q.v.) and do what they were afraid to do. Wilhelm Reich proposed that anxiety was a symptom of "dammed-up libido". He claimed to have discovered the "orgone", an energy unit which he regarded as essential to orgasmic potency, and asserted that orgone deficiency, caused by a sexually suppressed environment, culminated in neurotic anxiety. Karen Horney viewed neurosis as a protective device toward feelings of helplessness in a hostile world, stressed early life social conflicts rather than infantile fears, and sought to bring the neurotic toward "self-realization". To Harry Stack Sullivan, failures of communication in important relationships are the basis of neurosis. A deep patient–therapist involvement is conceived as the vehicle for change. In fact, none of the psychoanalytic therapies has been impressively successful.

3. *Conditioning theory and behavior therapy.* In contrast to these socio-idiopathic methods of interpreting neurosis, another perspective has been evolving from the experimental laboratory in recent years.

(*a*) *Experimental neurosis.* About 1900 the states of emotional disturbance called emotional neuroses were first produced in Pavlov's laboratories (Pavlov, 1927). The basic method was to expose a spatially confined animal to a stimulus situation in which strong but incompatible action tendencies were simultaneously elicited: for instance, simultaneous tendencies to eat and not to eat. The animal would become intensely disturbed and would afterwards manifest the same disturbance whenever he was brought back into the experimental chamber, even though the conflict-producing stimuli were no longer present. Similar neuroses were later reported by many other experimenters, in some of which the initial disturbance was induced, not by conflict, but by painful electrical stimulation of the animal's legs (Wolpe, 1952; Smart, 1965).

Although the experimental neuroses were long thought to depend on some kind of stress-produced damage to the central nervous system, it is now quite evident that they are really learned emotional habits (Wolpe, 1952). The following are some of the reasons for this view: (i) The neurotic behavior consists of just such responses as have been evoked by the electrical stimulation (or conflict): pupillary dilation, pilo-erection, and other autonomic reactions, diffuse muscle tension, and motor responses such as vocalizing and crouching. By definition, these are conditioned anxiety responses (see *Anxiety*). (ii) The neurotic reactions are specifically evocable by stimuli that were present in the causal situation. They are at their strongest in the experimental cage, and can be intensified by a buzzer or other signal that regularly preceded the causative electrical stimulation. (iii) The neurotic responses show primary stimulus generalization—a characteristic of learned behavior. For example, if the animals are placed in other rooms that resemble the experimental room, neurotic reactions are aroused according to the degree of resemblance.

A striking feature of the experimental neuroses is their resistance to extinction. Though the animal is never again subjected to the neurotigenic stress, the neurotic anxiety does not diminish when the animal is put back into the experimental cage on any number of later occasions and for any length of time. Also striking is the refusal of the animal to eat in the experimental cage even after a day or two of starvation. However, if in a place where the anxiety is relatively weak—for example, a room that only slightly resembles the experimental room—he will eat, and after doing so for a while become free of all manifestations of anxiety. He will then eat in a room somewhat more like the experimental room. Advancing in stages, it eventually becomes possible for the animal to eat in the experimental room and cage and thus overcome all its anxiety conditioning there. Apparently, anxiety and eating are reciprocally inhibitory: and when feeding inhibits the anxiety, there is a diminution of the anxiety habit. Conditioned inhibition is apparently formed on the basis of reciprocal inhibition (Wolpe, 1952).

(*b*) *Human neuroses as learned emotional habits.* In all respects in which comparisons have been made, human neuroses have shown the same attributes as those experimentally induced (Wolpe, 1967). Stimuli present at the time of onset become triggers to the neurotic anxiety responses, as happens in the experimental neuroses. For example, a lawyer's fear of public speaking was traced to an occasion in law school when a lecturer humiliated him when he was speaking before a class; and a woman's phobia for sharp objects began when, after an unwanted childbirth, she became terrified at the thought that she might harm her baby with a sharp knife with which she was cutting fruit. Generalization is a feature of human neurotic reactions also. They are evocable by stimuli that resemble the primary conditioned stimuli. Other similarities to the animal neuroses include resistance to extinction and the occurrence of second-order conditioning.

Anxiety is usually overt in clinical neuroses. But there are many cases in which its presence is obscured because the patient complains of symptoms or disabilities that are more prominent or painful to him. Yet even these are really secondary results of the anxiety responses. The complaint may be of difficulty in work situations, lack of social success, attacks of asthma, impotence, frigidity, homosexuality, compulsive behavior, and stuttering, among others. The primary therapeutic target is still the deconditioning of anxiety. The only true exception appears to be classical hysteria with *la belle indifférence.*

(*c*) *Clinical derivatives of experimental methods.* The clinical methods based on experimental paradigms are called *behavior therapy* (q.v.). Counter-conditioning methods derived from the experimental therapeutic model described above have in recent years been increasingly widely adopted in the treatment of neuroses (Wolpe, 1958; 1969). Operant conditioning methods (Ayllon & Azrin, 1968; Schaefer & Martin, 1969) have also been used, but so far much less in this connection than for modifying schizophrenic behavior. The clinical counter-conditioning methods do not, as a rule, employ eating, but other responses incompatible with anxiety responses, such as anger, sexual responses, and deep muscle relaxation.

A common technique, employing muscle relaxation, is *systematic desensitization.* It consists of training the patient to relax and then having him imagine, while relaxed, the feeblest situation of a phobic theme. For example, a person with a fear of heights might at first imagine looking down from a height of ten feet. The image is given repeatedly until no more anxiety is evoked. Successively greater heights are then similarly treated, so that eventually the highest evokes no anxiety. Scenes that no longer evoke anxiety when imagined during relaxation, also no longer do so when encountered in reality. In the minority of patients whom imagined scenes do not disturb in the first place, real stimuli must be used in the therapy.

Almost 90% of neurotic patients recover or are much improved by behavior therapy in about thirty sessions (Wolpe, 1969). The relevance of the specific procedures has been impressively supported by controlled studies (e.g. Paul, 1966). The relapses and symptom substitutions predicted by psychoanalysts have not occurred.

Bibliography: Ackernecht, E. H.: A short history of psychiatry. New York, 1959. **Ayllon, T. & Azrin, N.:** The token economy. New York, 1968. **Bromberg, W.:** The mind of man: A history of psychotherapy and psychoanalysis. New York, 1959. **Culpin, M.:** The conception of nervous disorder. Brit. J. Med. Psychol., 1962, *35*, 76–7. **Galdston, I.:** Historic derivations of modern psychiatry. New York, 1967. **Garrison, F. H.:** An introduction to the history of medicine. Philadelphia, [4]1929. **Guillain, G.:** J. M. Charcot, 1825–1893, Sa vie—son oeuvre. Paris, 1955. **Hinsie, L. E. & Campbell, R. J.:** Psychiatric dictionary. New York, 1960. **Munroe, R. L.:** Schools of psychoanalytic thought. New York, 1955. **Paul, G. L. & Shannon, D. T.:** Treatment of anxiety through systematic desensitization and therapy groups. J. abnorm. Psychology, 1966, *71*, 124–33. **Pavlov, I.:** Conditioned reflex. London, 1927. **Schaefer, H. H. & Martin, P. L.:** Behavioral therapy. New York, 1969. **Smart, R. G.:** Conflict and conditioned aversive stimuli in the development of experimental responses. Canad. J. Psychol., 1965, *19*, 208–14. **Wolpe, J.:** Experimental neuroses as learned behaviour. Brit. J. Psychol., 1952, *43*, 243–68. **Id.:** Psychotherapy by reciprocal inhibition. Stanford, 1958. **Id.:** Parallels between animal and human neuroses. In: **Zubin, J. & Hunt, H. F.:** Comparative psychopathology. New York, 1967, 305–13. **Id.:** The practice of behavior therapy. New York, 1969. **Zilboorg, G. & Henry, G. W.:** A history of medical psychology. New York, 1941.

J. Wolpe

Neurosis, compensation. 1. (syn. *Indemnity neurosis.*) A term for traumatic reactions to accidents, injuries, etc. A desire for indemnification in which a lack of compensation is regarded as an insult or a deprivation of rights. **2.** See *Compensation; Neurosis; Paranoia; Schizophrenia.* *J.L.I.*

Neurosurgery. A collective term for all operative (i.e. surgical) interventions in the brain and spinal cord and, to a small extent, the peripheral nerves. Open (after removal of the vault of the cranium) or closed methods are possible, as, e.g. in stereotactic techniques (q.v.) using only burr holes. Neurosurgery uses clinico-neurological methods for localization diagnosis, as well as radioactive isotopes, EEG, myography, X-rays, and so on. Apart from stereotactic interventions, the most important indications are injuries, brain tumors and malformations (including those of cerebral vessels). Psychology and psychiatry owe many important findings to advances in neurosurgery, e.g. recognition of the fruitlessness of a point-by-point cerebral localization of psychological functions, and the high degree of potential restoration of disturbed functions after a relatively extensive loss of brain substance. See *Frontal lobes; Lobotomy; Localization of psychological functions.*

Bibliography: Merrem, G.: Lehrbuch der Neurochirurgie. Berlin, [3]1968. **Sargant, W. & Slater, E.:** Physical methods of treatment in psychiatry. Edinburgh & London, 1963. *M.A.*

Neuroticism (syn. *Neurotic tendency; Emotionality; Emotional lability*). A genotypical proneness to neurosis. The second factor after extraversion in Eysenck's personality model. This general factor corresponds largely to R. B. Cattell's second-order inventory factor ("anxiety"), and relates to intensity and control of emotional responses. According to Eysenck, neuroticism is closely bound up with ANS function, especially with the duration of adrenergic (sympathetic) excitation, and is partly inherited. See *Traits.*

Bibliography: Eysenck, H. J. & Eysenck, S.: Personality structure and measurement. London, 1969.

D.B.

Neutralization. Under the influence of Jung and Freud, the neutralizing of psychic energy has come to be regarded as a tendency to satisfy motives regardless of the present satisfaction afforded by them (Toman, 1960).

With progressive neutralization, motivated actions are used increasingly as a means of satisfying other motives. Neutralization of psychic energy is related to sublimation (q.v.) and motive differentiation. (See *Energy, psychic.*)

Bibliography: Toman, W.: Introduction to psychoanalytic theory of motivation. London & New York, 1960. *W.T.*

New York Longitudinal Study. See *Child psychology.*

Nicotine. The most important alkaloid occurring in tobacco leaves (*Nicotiana tobacum*) is related to a large number of natural and synthetic substances. In spite of the importance of nicotine as a result of the popularity of smoking, few controlled investigations have been carried out into psychological or CNS effects in *humans*. In small doses, it is said to raise briefly the level of subjective and objective activation (e.g. an increased flicker-fusion frequency). Its effects in *animals* have been widely studied, especially with a view to regulating conditioned reflexes. Small doses usually step up activity and improve the learning of avoidance reactions. Arousal is recorded in the EEG (q.v.). Larger doses impair learning ability. In both cases, however, there are contradictory findings. The difficulty of determining the effects of nicotine on behavior is possibly due to the highly complex actions in the CNS and ANS. Animal tests show that nicotine in small doses excites the cholinergic synapses in the ANS while blocking them in higher doses (depolarization). In addition, nicotine excites adrenergic systems (q.v.), releasing catecholamines (q.v.). The stimulating action of nicotine is not blocked by atropine (q.v.) but is inhibited by a series of ganglionic blocking agents. Its neurophysiological effects make it an important experimental substance in neuropsychopharmacology. Comparable cholinergic substances are described as *nicotinic* (as opposed to *muscarinic*).

Bibliography: Euler, U. S. von: Tobacco alkaloids and related compounds. Oxford, 1965. **Frankenhaeuser, M., *et al.*:** Dosage and time effects of cigarette smoking. Psychopharmacologia, 1968, *13*, 311–19. **Silvette, H., *et al.*:** The actions of nicotine on central nervous system functions. Pharm. Rev., 1962, *14*, 137–73. *W.J.*

Night blindness. See *Hemeralopia.*

Nissl bodies. Discrete granular substances occurring in the cell body of a neuron. Their high RNA content disappears with toxic or other damage, or with fatigue. Nissl bodies penetrate into the dendrites but neurite ends are free of them. They are believed to play an important part in excitation and to contribute to cellular metabolism. They can be rendered visible by staining with toluidine blue/gallocyanine. *E.D.*

Nitrous oxide (N_2O). Also called *laughing gas* by Davy (1800) because of its euphoric effect when used as an anesthetic (see *Narcosis*), nitrous oxide is the oldest narcotic given by inhalation, and has a relatively weak action. Used today in combination with O_2 and/or other narcotics (q.v.) (barbiturates, q.v.). Nitrous oxide has very short-lasting post-narcotic effects.

Bibliography: Hamilton, W.: The limited clinical pharmacology of nitrous oxide. Clin. Pharmacol. Ther., 1963, *4*, 663. *E.L.*

Nociceptor (syn. *Nocireceptor*). A *pain* receptor. The exact nature of these receptors, and whether there are receptors specifically for pain and no other sense, is as yet unknown. See *Pain.* *C.D.F.*

Noctambulism. Night- or sleep-walking in a partially conscious state with subsequent amnesia. *W.Sch.*

Nodal points of the eye. The two nodal points with the two focal points and two main points constitute the six "cardinal points" of the eye, which are important for image ray formation. A "simple optical system" has an inner focal point F_2 and an external focal point F_1 whose focal length f_1 (i.e. the distance from the corneal apex H, which is also defined as a main point) is in the same relation to the "inner focal length" f_2 as the refractive indices of the corresponding optical media. The simple nodal point N in a simple optical system is located halfway between M and F_2 on the optical axis (Fig. A).

By introducing additional refractive surfaces, in particular on the anterior and posterior surfaces of the lens (q.v.), the intact eye becomes a composite (complex) optical system with two main and two nodal points, located at a distance of 0.3 mm on the optical axis (Fig. C). For image ray formation, the eye as represented in Figure C becomes the "reduced eye" (Fig. B), in which the nodal-point ray is displaced in parallel at the nodal points N and N′.

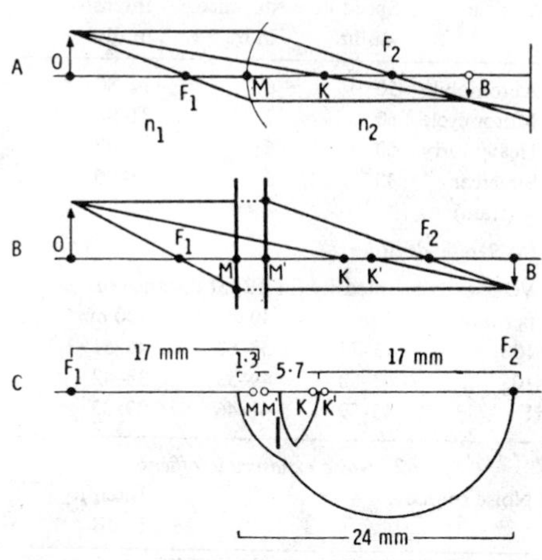

Simple (A) and reduced complex (B) optical system. Position of the reduced system in diagrammatic representation of the eye (C). M = main points; N = nodal points; F = focal points; O = object; I = image. (Dodt, 1970.)

The angle between two nodal-point rays, which originate from two object points, is the visual angle at which these object points appear; this angle must not be less than 60±10 seconds of arc (limit angle of visual acuity), so that in emmetropia (q.v.) the image points are still represented on separate cones, on account of the size of the cone pattern on the retina. *K.H.P.*

Noetic superstructure. A term applied by strata theorists, under the influence of Lersch, to individual thought processes (power of abstraction, judgment, logical reasoning, etc.) that take place, together with voluntary activities, above the endothymic basis (q.v.) (with affects, moods, drives, etc.). Lersch combines voluntary and thinking activities in the "personal superstructure" (q.v.). See *Strata theory.*

Bibliography: Lersch, P.: The levels of the mind. In: **David, H. P. & Bracken, H. von** (Eds.): Perspectives in personality theory. New York, 1957, 212–17.

B.H.

Noise. Generally "noise" refers to irrelevant or unpleasant acoustic stimulation. At high levels of intensity such noise interferes with the performance of most tasks and can even cause physical damage. At lower levels, however, noise may be beneficial for some people performing certain tasks.

Noise is used as a technical term by communications engineers to refer to background interference irrelevant to the *signal* being transmitted. If this interference is random and contains many frequency components, it is called *white noise.* This use of the term "noise" can be applied to the visual and indeed any other modality or communication system. Hence the concept of noise in this sense has been used in the interpretation of psychophysics experiments, where it may appear as internal or "neural" noise. *C.D.F.*

Noise damage. Functional or organically detectable injury caused by persistent noise (above 85 dB at more than 1000 Hz; above

95 dB at less than 1000 Hz): especially occupational or industrial deafness (a recognized form of occupational disease) and noise-conditioned functional disorders of the CNS. Early recognition by means of regular audiometric hearing tests for personnel exposed to prolonged high-intensity noise is essential. Noise damage can be prevented to some extent by noise-control measures, such as sound absorption and insulation in building premises, and careful layout of offices and workshops, damping of resonant machine-parts, redesigning or changing the weight of components, using buffered mountings, selecting new materials, or enclosing the noise source. In default of such measures, individuals can be helped by ear defenders (plugs, etc.) and planned pauses and changes of work location.

Bibliography: King, A. J.: The measurement and suppression of noise. London, 1965. **Koch, H.:** Betriebslärm, seine Folgen und seine Bekämpfung. Publication of the Bundesinstitut für Arbeitsschutz. Koblenz, n.d. **Newby, H. A.:** Audiology: principles and practice. London, 1959. **Richardson, E. G.** (Ed.): Technical aspects of sound. Amsterdam, 1953. **Sataloff, J.:** Industrial deafness. New York, 1957. **Wilson, Sir Alan:** Final report of the Committee on the Problem of Noise. London, 1963. **Wright, M. I.:** The pathology of deafness. Manchester, 1971.

G.R.W.M.

Noise, exposure to. The frequency, intensity and duration of perceived sound in a place of work can reach a level experienced as disturbing or unpleasant and thus interfere with output or even injure hearing (occupational deafness) and lead to changes in physiological balance (Broadbent, 1961) and psychological effects ranging from a diminution of attention in tasks requiring concentration, to fatigue, lethargy and abrupt changes of mood (see Bell, 1966; Glorig, 1958; Jansen, 1963; Lieber, 1964; Rodda, 1967). Whether a sound is experienced as noise in the sense of being annoying, unwanted or unbearable depends on an individual's physical and psychological type and constitution, subjective attitude to the sound source, the sound-pressure level measured in decibels (dB) duration of effect, consonance and dissonance defined in terms of individual and social habituation to qualities of timbre and tone combinations as agreeable or disagreeable, and temporal sequence (regular, irregular, rhythmic, and so on). The following table gives the general subjective judgments (perceived noise levels) of the *loudness* of sounds of certain *intensities* (measured in dB by *sound analyzers*—combined sound-level meters and frequency analyzers):

below 30 dB	= very quiet
30–40 dB	= quiet
40–50 dB	= fairly quiet
50–60 dB	= borderline between quiet and noisy
60–70 dB	= fairly noisy
over 70 dB	= very noisy

The following tables (Grandjean, 1967) give sample noise intensities in traffic, offices and various workplaces:

1. *Noise exposure from traffic*

(a) Vehicles

Vehicle	Speed in km/hr	distance in m.	Intensity in dB
Automobile	50	6	74–80
Motor cycle	60	7	81–98
Heavy lorry	50	6	85–97
Streetcar (tram)	30	5	83–90

(b) Traffic densities

Vehicles per min.	Intensity (in dB) at distance of 6 m.	30 m.	120 m.
100	73–77	58–63	46–51
10	63–68	49–53	38–42
1	55–59	41–46	29–33

2. *Noise exposure in offices*

Noise source	Intensity in dB
Back street (window closed)	45–65
Highway (main road) (window closed)	60–80
3 people	55
10 people	60
50 people	65
Telephone ringing (2 m.)	75
Normal typewriter (2 m.)	70
Noise-reduced typewriter (2 m.)	60

3. *Noise exposure in workplaces*

Noise source	Intensity in dB
Boiler shop (e.g. in navy yard/ shipyard)	90–120
Motor (engine) test stand	90–100
Automobile sheet (chassis) steel mill	90–100
Machine tools	75–90
Heavy punches	95–110
Foundry	95–115
Furniture factory	90–105
Circular saw	75–105
Hydraulic metal-planer	85–105
Textile mill (weaving shed)	95–105
Bottle-filling plant	85–95
Chocolate factory	101–106

Bibliography: Bell, A.: Noise: an occupational hazard and a public nuisance (WHO publication). Geneva, 1966. **Broadbent, D. E.:** Effects of noise on behavior. In: **Harris, C. M.** (Ed.): Handbook of noise control. New York, 1957. **Id.:** Effects of noises of high and low frequency on behaviour. Ergonomics, 1957. *1*, 21–9. **Id.:** Non-auditory effects of noise. Advmt. Sci., *1*, 1961, 406–9. **Glorig, A.:** Noise and your ear. New York, 1958. **Grandjean, E.:** Physiologische Arbeitsgestaltung. Munich, [2]1967. **Jansen, G.:** Lärm im Betrieb. Berlin, 1963. **Lieber, E.:** Occupational health. London, 1964. **Rodda, M.:** Noise and society. London, 1967. *G.R.W.M.*

Noises, animal (syn. *Animal cries*). Sounds which operate primarily as means of communication within and between species. E.g. bird sounds can act as signals of mood or status within the group, and as warning or threat cries. Bird sounds have a wide range from simple contact notes through flight calls to nesting calls and courtship songs. In addition to voiced calls, there are mechanical sounds such as the tapping of the woodpecker.

Bibliography: Armstrong, E. A.: A study of bird song. London, 1963. *V.P.*

Nominalism. The theory that abstractions or universal concepts do not represent objective real particulars but are mere names, and that only objective physical particulars ("concrete things") are (logically) real. The insistence of logical empiricism (i.e. logical positivism) on direct or indirect verification and on linguistic analysis involves a mode of nominalism. The term has also been used (pejoratively) to refer to the practice of individuals who accept the objectivity of what they have named—thus reversing its meaning. *J.C.*

Nominal scale. Used as the basis for the classification of qualitative data. The only condition that a nominal scale must satisfy is that there should be a clear correlation between event and class. The classes of a nominal scale differ qualitatively, but all instances within classes are equal. Other relations (e.g. of magnitude) do not exist between classes. The sequence of classes is without significance and merely reflects external conventions. E.g.: eye color (blue—green—brown—various); family status (single—married—widowed—divorced). See *Scale; Methods of psychology.* *G.Mi.*

Nominal value. An attributed, assumed, general, or desired, as opposed to an actual, value.

Nomothetic. That which is directed to the establishing of universal laws. The antithesis between nomothetic and idiographic (q.v.) research has been the subject of dispute among psychologists in personality research. The aims of nomothetic personality research are: (*a*) to describe individual behavior in terms of general personality dimensions present in all individuals in the same way, though in different degrees; (*b*) to explain individual behavior with the aid of general laws. Researchers make use of the quantitative, mostly multivariate and experimental, methods of psychology. See *General psychology; Nomothetic sciences.* *D.B.*

Nomothetic sciences. In a celebrated paper of 1894, W. Windelband compares the *nomothetic sciences* (aimed at establishing universal laws) with the *idiographic sciences* (q.v.) (which describe individuals or events). The two terms were adopted by G. W. Allport in his work on personality (q.v.), and owe their current importance to him.

P.M.

Non-directive therapy. 1. See *Client-centered therapy*. **2.** *Therapeutic variables:* three psychotherapeutic variables postulated by C. R. Rogers have proved effective for successful therapy: (*a*) *positive valuation* and *emotional warmth* (non-possessive warmth); (*b*) *empathic understanding* of the client's reference point, and a concern to communicate to him what is understood (accurate empathy); (*c*) *congruence* (genuineness and integration). Investigations have shown that these variables apply in other forms of therapy (Bergin & Salomon). See *Psychotherapy*. *L.J.*

Non-parametric methods. Methods of statistical inference (especially significance tests) which do not require the existence of interval or ratio scale data. They can, however, also be applied to data of this higher scale level, and independently of the type of distribution, and are also known as "distribution-free" methods. See *Non-parametric tests*. *G.Mi.*

Non-parametric tests. The term covers all statistical test methods which are not based on the concept of the normal distribution and/or on the postulate of cardinal scale measurement. In the social sciences in general, and in psychology in particular, these tests are usually concerned with variables whose distribution is either unknown or differs from the normal pattern, and/or with variables whose scale characteristics have either not been clearly defined or do not reach the necessary level (see *Scaling*). Tests based on the postulate of ordinal scale measurement which only require the observations to be independent and random and are not dependent on distributions (i.e. non-parametric), are generally more suitable for this purpose, because they are statistically more effective than the classical, parametric tests. These test methods are therefore of great methodological importance in psychology, even though they still lack a common theoretical foundation and are less effective than parametric tests in the case of variables which follow a standard distribution.

1. *Types of test.* Statisticians make a distinction between (*a*) tests to check the hypothesis of symmetry, represented primarily by the sign and sign rank tests (Wilcoxon test) (symmetry in relation to zero); (*b*) tests to check the hypothesis of randomness, consisting primarily of the U test and H test to check the randomness or significance of differences between two or more samples; and (*c*) tests to check the hypothesis of independence with Kendall's correlation and concordance tests (1962). Users of these tests distinguish between (*a*) tests to check differences in the central trend; (*b*) tests to check differences in dispersion; and (*c*) tests of relations (correlation, contingency, concordance).

2. *Principles.* The most important of these test methods are based on the ranks of the observed values, i.e. the measured values are converted into rank values. The information is supplied from the interval between observations arranged in order of magnitude; the observed values are therefore not dependent on the distribution, i.e. are distribution-free.

A good example is provided by the Wilcoxon–Mann–Whitney rank summation test (or U test). For the two samples 1 and 2 under examination, the measured values $x_1x_1x_2x_1x_2x_2$ (arranged in order of magnitude) are replaced by the rank values 1 2 *3* 4 *5 6*, and the rank totals $T_1 = 1 + 2 + 4 = 7$ (sample 1) and $T_2 = 3 + 5 + 6 = 14$ (sample 2) are calculated. For the null hypothesis H_0 (identical position) we would expect (approximately) identical rank totals, i.e. $T_1 = T_2$. For the (unilateral) alternative hypothesis (different position), we would expect different rank totals, i.e. $T_1 \neq T_2$. If the observed difference $D = T_2 - T_1$, as the test value, reaches a total which, assuming H_0 to apply, only occurs in α % (e.g. 5%) of all cases, we reject H_0 in favour of H_1. The probability of error P(D) in rejecting H_0, even though it holds good (error of the first order), is obtained by randomizing the $2 \times 3 = 6$ rank values. In the assumption H_0, every possible halving of the 6 rank values is equally probable; there are $\binom{6}{3} = 6 \times 5 \times 4/3 \times 2 \times 1 = 20$ halving possibilities, each of which gives a D value. All the D values taken together represent the test distribution for D and the highest α % D values are the rejection limits for H_0. In our example we obtain $\binom{6}{3} = 20$ combinations of 6 observations in the third class, i.e. 123456, 123456, 123456, 123456, 123456, 123456, 123456, 123456, 123456, 123456, 123456, 123456, 123456, 123456, 123456, 123456, 123456, 123456, 123456, 123456 and the D values 9 7 5 3 5 3 1 1 1 3—3—1—1—3 —5—3—5—7—9. The 5% rejection range consists of the 5% (algebraically) highest values, i.e. 5% × (20) = 1 D value, so that the unilateral 5% significance barrier $D_{0.05} = 9$. In our example this D value is not reached with D = 7, so that H_0 must be retained; the D value has an error probability of P = 2/ 20 = 0.10, since 2 D values of the null distribution for D (i.e. 7 and 9) reach or exceed the observed value of D = 7.

Non-parametric tests are based on these and similar principles. They can be understood without any knowledge of infinitesimal calculus, since they conform quite simply to the rules of combinations. Instruction in their use therefore presents no problems.

A distinction is made between exact tests (as in the test method described above) for small samples and approximation tests (asymptotic tests) for large samples (for which exact tests would be too complex). For larger N_1 and N_2 values with a mean value of zero and a variance of $N_1 N_2(N1 + N2 + 1)/3$, D follows an approximately normal distribution, so that z = D/(standard deviation of D) can be treated as a standard variable parameter. Applied to the above example, we obtain the variance var (D) = 3 × 3 (3 + 3 + 1)/3 = 21 and the standard deviation SD (D) = 21 ≈ 4.6 so that z = 7/4.6 = 1.52. This z value is smaller than z 0.05 (unilateral) = 1.65 so that, for our example, H_0 would be retained even after the asymptotic test. In general, the asymptotic test is less effective (all other considerations being equal) than the exact test.

The main tests described in handbooks on non-parametric test methods (e.g. Siegel, 1956; Walsh, 1965; Bradley, 1968; Lienert, [2]1971) are listed below.

3. *The main tests.* (*a*) The most effective test for comparing the position or location of two independent samples is the rank summation test, or its derivative—Mann–Whitney's U test; in addition to randomness and independence of the sample, the only requirement is homomerity, i.e. an identical pattern of distribution, of the associated populations. If this requirement is not met, the (weaker) median test is used to test for position differences (homologously with the t test). The most effective position test for dependent samples is Wilcoxon's matched pairs sign rank test. This is based on symmetrically distributed differences between the observational pairs and their homogeneity. If the postulate of symmetry or homogeneity is not, or not fully, met (e.g. if there are unilateral extremes in the sample of differences, or if the pairs come from different populations), the weaker sign test will be used instead of the sign rank test (by analogy with the test for differences).

(*b*) The Siegel–Tukey test is the most effective for dispersion comparison of two independent samples. This test presupposes an identical situation of the two populations and is similar to an omnibus test (responding to differences both in dispersion and in position) if the positions differ. At present there is no dispersion test which is not sensitive to position (like the homologous F test); no dispersion test has been developed for dependent samples (see Walker & Lev, 1963, 1960).

(*c*) The H test (as a global test) and Nemenyi's multiple tests for the comparison of (in each case) two samples are used to compare the positions of several independent samples (in the same manner as one-way analysis of variance). Friedman's global test and Dunn's multiple tests are used to compare several dependent samples (in the same manner as two-way analysis of variance) (see Wilcoxon & Wilcox, 1964).

(*d*) The generalized Siegel–Tukey test (Meyer-Bahlburg test) is used to compare the dispersion of several independent samples (by analogy with Bartlett's test).

(*e*) The Kolmogoroff–Smirnov test and Cramer–von Mises test are used for omnibus comparison of two independent samples (with reference to dispersion, etc.).

(*f*) The Kolmogoroff–Smirnov adaptation test is used to compare a sample distribution with a population distribution.

(*g*) Kendall's tau test or Tukey's test (instead of the r coefficient test) are used to check the relationship between two continuously distributed characteristics in a bivariate sample. Both these test methods assume a monotonous pattern for the relationship or regression lines. Non-monotonous relationships are tested by means of information statistics (Attneave, 1959).

(*h*) The relationship between two alternative or dichotomously distributed characteristics is tested by Fisher's exact fourfold test (for small samples), or asymptotically with the fourfold χ^2 test (for large samples).

(*i*) The relationship between two multi-class characteristics and k and m classes is tested exactly by means of Freeman and Halton's test (see Maxwell, 1961).

(*j*) The relationship between several multi-class characteristics or several rank evaluations for a single multi-class characteristic is determined by means of Kendall's concordance test.

4. *Conclusions.* In psychological research, non-parametric tests are preferable to conventional tests for the following reasons: (*a*) the population distributions of psychological variables are often either unknown or abnormal; (*b*) the variables rarely meet the stringent requirements of interval scale dignity for the conventional tests; (*c*) the samples are generally small and often include extreme values so that the central limit value theory (for conventional tests) no longer holds good; (*d*) the regressions between two psychological variables are rarely linear but generally monotonous. Under these four conditions, non-parametric tests are generally more efficient and valid than the conventional test methods. For descriptive purposes, the median value will be given preference over the mean value, and the interquartile or decile range (90th percentile minus 10th percentile) used instead of the standard deviation, while the rank correlation coefficient (tau or rho) will be chosen in place of the product moment coefficient.

Rating values for the population median, the median displacement from one population to another (on the basis of a given treatment effect), and for the rank correlation, can be determined on the basis of simple logical principles. Non-parametric test planning with several influencing values and interaction tests are still not fully developed. This also applies to non-parametric time series analysis and multivariate tests, and in particular to multivariate analysis of variance. It should always be remembered that non-parametric (and indeed conventional) test methods assume that samples are taken at random from their populations, but (unlike conventional tests) they make no assumptions on the pattern of distribution of the populations. See *Statistics; Statistical tests.*

Bibliography: Attneave, F.: Applications of information theory to psychology. New York, 1959. **Bradley, J. V.:** Distribution-free statistical tests. Englewood Cliffs, N.J., 1968. **Kendall, M. G.:** Rank correlation methods. London, [3]1962. **Lienert, G. A.:** Verteilungsfreie Methoden in der Statistik. Meisenheim a. G., [2]1971. **Maxwell, A. E.:** Analysing qualitative data.

London, 1961. **Siegel, S.:** Nonparametric methods for the behavioral sciences. New York, 1956. **Walker, H. M. & Lev, J.:** Statistical inference. New York, 1963. **Walsh, J. E.:** Handbook of nonparametric statistics, Vol. 2. Princeton, N.J., 1965. **Wilcoxon, F. & Wilcox, R. A.:** Some rapid approximate statistical procedures. Pearl River, N.Y., 1964.

G. A. Lienert & V. Sarris

Nonsense syllables. *Artificial syllables* first devised by Ebbinghaus (1885) and used in investigations into verbal learning; they consist of a vowel between two consonants ("CVC"), e.g. gim, joz, lur, wam, vob. In learning experiments, lists or pairs of nonsense syllables are memorized and later reproduced. Their meaninglessness is intended to guarantee that the learning and memory processes under investigation can be studied as far as possible in a "pure" state, i.e. independently of different individual responses to familiar material. (See *Memory*.)

Nonsense syllables are only *more or less devoid of meaning*. The *sense content* is frequently determined by the "association value", and this can be defined by the number of associations to a syllable which occur to a testee within a certain period of time. Other variables of nonsense syllables have also been investigated: e.g. ease of pronunciation. In general it is found that syllables can be learnt more easily as values for these variables rise.

In addition to nonsense syllables, *digrams* (two-letter combinations), *trigrams* (three-letter combinations) and *double syllables* are frequently used in investigations of verbal learning.

Bibliography: Albert, D. & Murch, G. M.: Eichung von sinnlosen Silben. Zeitschrift angewandter Psychologie, 1968, *15*, 381–403. **Ebbinghaus, H.:** Über das Gedächtnis. Leipzig, 1885 (Eng. trans.: Memory. New York, 1913). **Underwood, B. J. & Schulz, R. W.:** Meaningfulness and verbal learning. Chicago & Philadelphia, New York, 1960.

M. Hofer

Noradrenalin(e) (syn. *Norepinephrine; Arterenol*; *Levarterenol bitartrate; Levoarterenol; Levophed*). A hormone (q.v.) of the adrenal medulla and one of the catecholamines (q.v.), noradrenaline is a biogenic amine that acts as a transmitter substance in the ANS and CNS.

Bibliography: See *Catecholamines*. *W.J.*

Norepinephrin(e). See *Noradrenalin(e)*.

Norm. A representative, average value, or set of values, for a particular group. See *Norm, social; Intelligence quotient; Abilities.*

Normal distribution. A normal distribution arises when the factors that go to make up a characteristic are numerous, independent of each other and additive in combination. The mathematical equation of the normal distribution was first described by De Moivre in 1733. A normal distribution is bell-shaped, inasmuch as the highest frequency of scores is in the middle, and the frequency tapers off symmetrically on either side of the mean.

G.Mi.

Normality. 1. The state of not deviating from the norm, or the average. **2.** Approximating to a normal probability distribution; *abnormality*, therefore, is the deviation of a frequency distribution from the normal. The degree of deviation of an empirically determined distribution from the (theoretically assumed) normal distribution can be checked for statistical significance by means of the χ^2 test (q.v.). (See also *Mental defect.*) *G.Mi.*

Normalization. The transformation of an abnormal into a normal distribution (q.v.).

Normalized distribution. An originally abnormal distribution transformed into a normal distribution.

Normal probability curve. See *Gaussian curve.*

Normative efforts. According to Lersch: "strivings of obligation-carrying participation" (e.g. veracity, justice, duty) within the endothymic basis, and the attendant drive experiences; within the latter, strivings to rise beyond the self (with creative urges, interests, love of something). They serve suprapersonal needs and can compete, for example, with the instinct of self-preservation. See *Strata theory.* *B.H.*

Norm, ethico-esthetic (syn. *Cultural norm*). An ideal type or rule for arriving at value judgments. Nowadays, it denotes a behavior pattern demanded by social institutions (a result of *socialization*, q.v.). *M.R.*

Norm, social. A standard of *behavior* developed by members of a group (q.v.) to which they conform or are encouraged to comply with by penalties. Social norms, according to M. Sherif, develop gradually. If a group is faced with ambiguous information, the judgments of individual members at first vary widely. However, they gradually converge through communication (q.v.) within the group, so that the result is comparable to the *statistical norm.* In a more abstract sense norms are what group members believe ought to be done or left undone in a given situation (see *Group dynamics*). Their general binding force or soundness exerts a powerful influence on *group cohesion.* *W.D.F.*

Nosophilia; nosomania. *Nosophilia:* disease-proneness; also morbid desire to be sick.

Nosomania: an insane belief that one is diseased despite the absence of detectable symptoms. Occurs in hypochondriac psychopathy. See *Hypochondria; Depression; Anancasm; Schizophrenia.* *H.W.*

Nostalgia, or homesickness, played a major role in Romantic psychology. Until the turn of the century it was considered to be the cause of severe *depression* (q.v.). Today the term is nearly always replaced by others, such as *regression* (q.v.). *W.Sch.*

Note blindness. The inability to interpret musical symbols in a person whose general faculties of vision and apprehension remain intact. *G.M.*

Noxious stimulus. See *Anxiety.*

Nuclear and peripheral performance. Riedel's terms for work analysis: *nuclear performance* is mental performance associated directly (*dominant*) or indirectly (*non-dominant*) with the preparation of working plans and the initiative for action. *Peripheral performance* comprises all other forms of performance which support, complete and/or facilitate nuclear performance.

Bibliography: Riedel, J.: Arbeits- und Berufsanalyse, Brunswick, 1957. *G.R.W.M.*

Nuclear neurosis (I. H. Schultz, 1918). A character-dependent, "centrifugal" neurosis which impairs (almost) all areas of life (e.g. love, sleep, work, faith), and often leads to suicide. According to Schultz, the nuclear neurosis is a synonym for *psychopathy* (q.v.) but has differential-diagnostic, hereditary-constitutional degenerative stigmata related to a psychological trauma of early childhood. *Nuclear complex* is a synonym for the *Oedipus complex* (q.v.). *K.T.*

Nucleus. 1. The core of a cell. The nucleus of the ganglionic cells is large, vesicular and has a low chromatin content and a very large nucleolus. No mitoses (cell divisions) of ganglionic cells have been observed in man after birth. **2.** A cluster of nerve-cell bodies having the same or a similar function in the CNS, e.g. the *nucleus ruber* in the midbrain. *G.A.*

Null hypothesis. The statistical hypothesis (H_0) which assumes that statistics (q.v.) obtained from samples do not differ, or differ only by chance, from each other or from corresponding parameters of the population. If the null hypothesis is rejected in the light of a statistical test, the alternative hypothesis (H_1) must be accepted. The null hypothesis can be refuted but not proven. *G.Mi.*

Nutritive energy. According to Jung (q.v.), that part of the libido which activates behavior in regard to, e.g. eating and oral stimulation. Sucking, chewing, etc., are manifestations of nutritive energy. See *Oral stage.* *W.T.*

Nutritive stage. The *nutritive* or *oral* stage in the first year is characterized by the act of sucking (oral pleasure), the mouth serving as the first means of communication between mother and child. See *Oral stage.* *M.Sa.*

Nyctalopia. *Day blindness,* in which vision is more distinct at night than by day. *Congenital:* (*a*) *Albinism:* the absence of pigment to screen the light leads to dazzling by day; (*b*) total color blindness (q.v.) (disordered function of the cones, q.v.). *Acquired:* With central opacity of the cornea or lens, rays close to the axis cannot penetrate. The eye dilates the pupil excessively (see *Mydriasis*) to obtain an image with the rays at the outer edges. This leads to the admission of too much light and thus to daytime *glare* (q.v.). Not to be confused with *hemeralopia* (q.v.). The term is, however, also used in the etymologically correct sense of *night blindness.* When used in the literature, therefore, "nyctalopia" and "hemeralopia"—if they must be preferred to their English equivalents—should always be defined. *R.R.*

Nymphomania. Excessive (hetero-)sexual desire in women.

Nystagmus. Involuntary and uncontrollable eye movement made up of two components—one *slow*, the other *rapid* and acting in the opposite direction. The direction of the nystagmus is denoted by that of the rapid component. The nystagmus, which acts in the horizontal or vertical direction, serves to compensate eye positions for changes in bodily posture in space. A nystagmoid form of eye movement can also be set off involuntarily. Depending on the mechanism that triggers off the complaint, a distinction is made between: (*a*) *vestibular nystagmus*, caused by rotating the subject (rotatory nystagmus), or by irrigating the external auditory meatus with cold or warm water (calorific nystagmus); in each case the direction of the nystagmus depends on which semicircular canal of the vestibular system of the inner ear is the more intensely stimulated; (*b*) *optokinetic* (or "railroad") *nystagmus*, caused by movement of the subject or surroundings; (*c*) *cerebellar* nystagmus, the result of damage to, or disorder of, the function of the cerebellum. *R.R.*

O

Object; object theory. Egon Brunswik conceived of psychology as a science of objective relations, and stressed the fact that, in psychology, behavior can be described in strictly objective and quantitative terms. He showed how behavior can establish links between the tool objects of widely varying kinds present in the environment and biologically significant target effects.

Bibliography: Brunswik, E.: The conceptual framework of psychology. In: **Neurath, O.** *et al.* (Eds.): International Encyclopedia of Unified Science, Vol. 1. Chicago, 1952, 655–760. **Id.:** Perception and the representative design of psychological experiments. Berkeley & Los Angeles, 1956.

P.M.

Object cathexis. According to Freud, the investing of libidinal energy in an object of experience, especially a "person-object" (e.g. mother attachment). Equivalent to learning the satisfaction values of situations, things, persons, and their recollection or the idea formed of them (Rapaport, 1959; Toman, 1960). Invariances in the objective circumstances of contact with such objects lead to the object invariances and object-immanent relations of aspects of the object in the individual's world of experience and imagination (Kelly, 1955). Object cathexes are cumulative in effect, and the satisfaction of motives adds further knowledge about objects, and aspects thereof, to already developed cathexes. These play a part in determining the perception of present opportunities for satisfying motives. The totality of an individual's object cathexes is his *concept of reality*.

Object anti-cathexis is equivalent to repression (q.v.) or other forms of (inner) defense (q.v.) against objects or aspects thereof. It rules out any further attempt to seek to derive satisfaction from or experience of them, or any further cathexes, i.e. any fresh expectations of satisfaction from the object or range of objects in question. The result is that even already formed object cathexes atrophy.

Bibliography: Kelly, G. A.: The psychology of personal constructs. 2 vols. New York, 1955. **Rapaport, D.:** The structure of psychoanalytic theory: a systematizing attempt. In: **Koch, S.:** Psychology: a study of a science, Vol. 3. New York, 1959, 55–183. **Toman, W.:** Psychoanalytic theory of motivation. London & New York, 1960.

W.T.

Object choice. The choice of friends and love partners, partly determined, according to Freud, by earlier object ties. Parents and brothers and sisters represent a person's original objects; relations, acquaintances, playmates, schoolfellows and friends the extrafamilial choices, and enduring friendships and love and marriage partners the (usually) most significant examples. (See *Family; Family constellation*).

Object finding is an object choice made after a search or waiting period. It is experienced in a particularly marked manner during puberty, when a young person hankers after repressed intrafamilial personal relations but still has difficulty in perceiving opportunities for them. *W.T.*

Object constancy. An object is always recognized as the same even when the stimulus context or the spatial interval changes. Often an object can still be identified even when it is only visible in part. This constancy of an object depends on the constancy with which definite qualities are perceived, e.g. shape, size or color. To explain this constancy one may refer to the gestalt principle according to which perceived objects stand out from their surroundings as complete shapes. When such a shape has once entered the memory, it is recognized again whatever the background. *P.S.*

Object finding. See *Object choice.*

Objective anxiety. See *Real anxiety.*

Objective consciousness. The cognitive function of consciousness (knowledge "of" or "about"); i.e. the subject-object relationship, which can be equated with the distinction between two poles ("ego" and "non-ego"), is the basis of the concept of objective consciousness. The notion is implicit in most reflection theories of the consciousness and corresponds approximately to the notion that "man is conscious of all those things of which he has knowledge". Expressed differently, objective consciousness is the individual's knowledge of the object of individual experience. *F.N.*

Objective psychology. A collective term for a psychological approach that explains psychological occurrences solely on the basis of objectively determined phenomena. It largely dispenses with constructs and rejects introspection (q.v.) as a tool of research. Theories which have been formulated on these lines in the sphere of animal psychology (q.v.) and still exert influence include J. von Uexküll's environmental theory; the researches of the animal psychologists C. T. Morgan, R. M. Yerkes (q.v.) and E. L. Thorndike (q.v.); behaviorism (q.v.), founded by J. B. Watson (q.v.) in the USA; the theory of higher nervous activity developed by I. P. Pavlov (q.v.) in the USSR; and objective psychology as founded by V. M. Bekhterev (q.v.) *H.Ro.*

Objective spirit (syn. *Objective mind*). For Hegel, objective spirit is the absolute idea which only exists in itself, i.e. which is represented to the conscious mind as an array of prescriptions (right, law), of institutions (morality, ethics), or of maxims for specific actions (morals). In his general psychology (q.v.), Pradines uses the term for "works of the human spirit": technology, religion, language, art and society. *P.M.*

Objective tests. 1. *Definition.* In psychometrics, the term *objective test* is used explicitly or implicitly in at least three different ways:

(*a*) Some writers use the term to refer to tests which provide a set selection of response alternatives (e.g. yes/no, true/false, etc.) that are scored according to an agreed key or program, or tests which allow open-ended responses provided that scoring instructions are sufficiently precise for agreement between different scorers to be reached. This view of objectivity in psychometric testing centers on the question of *interscorer reliability.* A test is *objectively scored* when any competent observer can be expected to arrive at approximately the same numerical result.

(*b*) Another concept of test objectivity focuses on the *kind of behavior which is observed* rather than on the agreement between observers. In this view, a test is objective if it does not allow faking or distortion of the kind that may occur if the subject is required to give a self-report or make introspective judgments of any sort, whether objectively scored or not. Included in this category are various *behavior* or *performance* tests, some of which are used as *indirect* or *disguised* measures of apparently unrelated characteristics.

It should be noted that these two different views of what is objective in psychometric testing are often directly opposed. For example, in the measurement of humor (q.v.) preferences, the two methods which have been most frequently employed are: (i) presenting a series of jokes and having the subject rate them according to a scale of "funniness", or (ii) observing overt behavior, sometimes with the aid of videotape, and categorizing it as "disgust", "indifference", "smiling", "outright laughter", and so on. In the first case we have subjective behavior objectively scored, while the second method amounts to subjective scoring of objective behavior. Neither method is universally preferable; each has its advantages and disadvantages.

(*c*) The third view of what comprises an objective test is much broader than either of the other two, and is to some extent inclusive of them. In this more general view, a test is said to be objective if it yields measurements which are: (i) *comparable* with a body of results accumulated through a large amount of previous testing; (ii) *repeatable* in the sense that the same results would be obtained under the same conditions on another occasion of testing; and (iii) allow *prediction* of some behavior relevant to the attributes the test is designed to measure. That is to say, an objective test is one which is acceptable in terms of the criteria of *standardization, reliability*, and *validity*. The remainder of this article is devoted to an evaluation of these three concepts.

2. *Standardization*. There are two separate aspects of standardization, and a test may be "standardized" in either sense: (*a*) The detailing of precise instructions as to how the test should be administered, with what materials, under what conditions, and how the raw scores should be calculated. This *standardization of procedure* is to ensure that precisely the same test is given by different testers, at different times and in different places. (*b*) The second kind of standardization often demanded of an objective test is the provision of *normative data* so that an individual's score can be evaluated in relation to the performance of samples comparable in age, sex, occupation, or whatever variables are considered most relevant in the situation. When an individual's score is expressed in relation to the mean and variance of a larger sample, it is called a *standardized score* (e.g. modern "IQ" scores).

While both kinds of standardization are essential if a test is to be used for individual assessment, they are sometimes held to be necessary in experimental situations too. In fact, this is not so, for the experimental psychologist is often only concerned with covariation within his sample, and has no need of information concerning the performance of other groups on his tests. Also, while it may be easier to report having used a standardized procedure, the experimentalist is in no way obliged to do so, provided that his exact procedure is fully specified. Hence, while standardization of procedure and scoring is almost always useful, and sometimes essential, it should not be regarded as a prerequisite of scientific testing in psychology.

3. *Reliability*. Reliability is also an ambiguous concept in psychometric test theory, and would be better replaced by two separate concepts: (*a*) *Stability* refers to the extent to which an individual may be expected to gain the same score on different testing occasions (assuming that the attribute being measured is itself stable), and is estimated by the correlation between the scores obtained on two testing sessions with the same group of subjects. Such a correlation is called a *test-retest reliability coefficient;* (*b*) *Internal consistency* refers to the homogeneity of the test items, and is estimated by the so-called *split-half reliability coefficient*, which is the

correlation between two randomly selected halves of the test, with a correction for the fact that the number of items upon which the correlation is based has been reduced by half. A third kind of reliability coefficient, based on the correlation between *equivalent* or *parallel forms*, incorporates elements of both stability and consistency, their proportion depending upon just how equivalent the two forms of the test are.

Concerning the importance of these two types of reliability, it is essential that any test exhibit an acceptable degree of stability; otherwise, the results can have no kind of validity, and will be quite meaningless. On the other hand, internal consistency is neither an essential characteristic of a valid scientific test, nor even necessarily a good thing. Information concerning the homogeneity of a test may be important, especially when a test is hypothetically unidimensional in content; but such information is better obtained by the methods of *factor analysis* (q.v.) or *principal components* (q.v.), which provide a much more complete picture of the dimensional structure of a test.

4. *Validity*. Validity may be loosely described as the extent to which a test measures what it is supposed to measure. Traditionally, four types of validity have been identified: (*a*) *Content validity* is the extent to which the items in the test appear to be good predictors, and to represent a fair sample of the behavior domain in question. While usually regarded as adequate for the construction of achievement tests, this is not validation at all in a technical sense. (*b*) *Concurrent validity* is the extent to which scores on the test correlate with other variables which can be regarded as suitable criteria, e.g. teacher ratings, correlations with other tests. (*c*) *Predictive validity* refers to the power of test scores to predict some future outcome, e.g. examination performance, suicidal attempts, and so on. (*d*) *Construct validity* (q.v.) refers to the gradual accumulation of evidence relating to the nature of the trait or traits being measured, particularly by the experimental testing of hypotheses based on the theory underlying the test. J. Loevinger (1967) has argued that content, concurrent, and predictive validities are all essentially *ad hoc*, providing no adequate basis for test construction, and that construct validity is the whole of validity from the scientific point of view.

A correlation between scores on a test and some recognized criterion measure is often called a *validity coefficient*. It needs to be stressed, however, that there is no one such coefficient for any test, since validity is always relative to the purpose for which the test is being used. In addition, in the interpretation of both validity and reliability coefficients, it is often forgotten that the size of a correlation depends upon many factors, such as the amount of variance (heterogeneity) of the sample. See *Test theory; Validity*.

Bibliography: Anastasi, A.: Psychological testing. New York, [2]1961. **Id.:** Testing problems in perspective. New York, 1966. **Buros, O. K.** (Ed.): Tests in print. New York, 1971. **Cattell, R. B. & Warburton, F. W.:** Objective personality and motivation tests. Urbana, Ill., 1967. **Eysenck, H. J.:** Classification and the problem of diagnosis. In: **Id.** (Ed.): Handbook of abnormal psychology. London, 1960. **Nunnally, J. C.:** Tests and measurements. New York, 1959. **Id.:** Psychometric methods. New York, 1967. **White, R. W.:** What is tested by psychological tests? In: **Hoch, P. H. & Zubin, J.** (Eds.): Relation of psychological tests to psychiatry. New York, 1952.

G. D. Wilson

Objective type. Among notional or conceptual types, a type that relates to objective notions and another relating to verbal notions are distinguished, corresponding to a rather concrete (objective) type or to an abstract-theoretical way of thinking. *W.K.*

Objectivity. 1. In psychological tests: the extent to which findings are independent of the investigator as regards the ways they are obtained, evaluated and interpreted. Objectivity is usually measured by statistical correlation methods in terms of agreement between the results obtained by a number of investigators in tests on identical subjects. **2.** As against this, personality and motivation tests, whose purpose (unlike that of a questionnaire) is not disclosed to S., are called "objective tests" (q.v.). **3.** In the course of personality research, various factor analyses of questionnaire items and behavioral assessments brought to light a factor which, according to Guilford, closely resembles the hypothetical personality trait "objectivity vs. subjectivity". See *Personality*. *D.B.*

Object libido. According to Freud the totality of love interests directed toward other persons (see *Libido*). Contrasts with narcissistic libido (see *Narcissism*). *W.T.*

Object psychology. 1. The application of psychological knowledge and experience to the design of objects, e.g. operating elements (See *Coding*), control desks, drivers' cabins, indicators (see *Industrial design*). **2.** Objective psychology (q.v.). *G.M.*

Object Relations Technique (abb. ORT). A projective technique (q.v.) developed by Phillipson (1955) on lines suggested by the British psychoanalytical school (M. Klein, W. R. D. Fairbairn). The subject is required to explain, by means of stories told about thirteen pictures (see *Thematic Apperception Test*), "unconscious object-relations" (interpreted by the author) which, according to Klein and Fairbairn, were imprinted on him by early experiences with reference persons, and which have a crucial bearing on man's relations to his environment. The author provides suggestions for evaluation and provisional standards for English subjects. The problems of determining reliability and validity have not yet been satisfactorily solved.

Bibliography: Phillipson, H.: The Object Relations Technique. London, 1955. *F.J.B.*

Object transference (syn. *Sensorial transference;* Ger. *Objektion*). According to Ach (1932) the transference of individual experiential qualities, e.g. sympathy, to an object, something imagined or a set of circumstances (e.g. "the door opened invitingly"). A distinction is made between sensory, emotional and voluntary object transference. Ach sees the cause of the phenomenon in the psychic striving to relieve the ego aspect of consciousness and thus release it for other tasks. See *Empathy*.

Bibliography: Ach, N.: Finale Qualität und Objektion Archiv f.d. ges. Psychol. Supplementary vol. 1932. *H.W.*

Oblimax method. An analytical oblique method of rotating the factor matrix. It is a generalized form of the quartimax criterion (see *Factor analysis; Quartimax criterion: Rotation*). The criterion equation

$$O = \frac{\Sigma\Sigma S_{ip}^4}{(\Sigma\Sigma S_{ip}^2)^2} = \max$$

requires the steepness of the distribution of the elements of the factor structure matrix (S_{ip}, reference vector correlations) to attain a maximum. *G.Mi.*

Oblimin methods. A collective term for analytical oblique methods of rotation generalized from the quartimin method. The covariances of the squared elements of the factor structure matrix are reduced to a minimum. See *Factor analysis; Rotation*. *G.Mi.*

Observation. 1. Planned contemplation directed to changing the object of observation with the purpose of acquiring new knowledge. **2.** Knowledge of something resulting therefrom or occurring fortuitously.

Observational errors. Mistakes entering into some observation due to the inadequacy of the human sensory apparatus. Essential factors: attitude (q.v.), fluctuating attention, etc.

Self-observation. Observation directed to

the flow of one's own consciousness. Unsatisfactory as a scientific method since no precise knowledge exists of how far introspection (q.v.) influences and disturbs the normal flow of a psychological event. A second source of error is the necessarily inadequate description of what has been experienced. *H.J.A.*

Observation of behavior. The methodically controlled, non-random, purposive examination of the actions of one or several individuals in order to discover something characteristic of (their) personality. Time-sampling methods are often used in order to obviate the difficulties of continuous observation. Bales (1956) offers a proficient observational schema in his "interaction process analysis". Observation of behavior is the most important process in the validation of test criteria.

Bibliography: Bales, R. F.: Interaction process analysis. New York, 1956. *G.L.*

Observation type. See *Attention types.*

Obsession. A persistent, uncontrollable and unwelcome idea, which is associated with an unpleasant emotion, usually anxiety or fear, and which may lead to some form of thinking ritual or overt action in an attempt to reduce the anxiety level. Although the person resists the idea he cannot get rid of it. He does, however, recognize it as part of his *own* thinking. It is traditionally regarded as a neurotic rather than a psychotic symptom. See *Neurosis.* *R.H.*

Obsessional neurosis. A psychologically disturbed condition in which the individual obsessively entertains or compulsively repeats specific ideas or trains of thought which shade off into compulsions when he is unable to get rid of them. Freud considered such states to represent unconscious desires of the patient (which had not been adequately repressed but which could be gratified only in isolation, i.e. in such a way that the patient experienced them as detached from himself) as well as defense (q.v.) mechanisms acting against such desires. Some obsessional or compulsive behaviors are counting specific objects, closing doors, or continually checking to see if others have done so, while superstitious practices such as touching wood, or avoiding the number thirteen might be thought of as mild and relatively widespread obsessional symptoms. An example of an obsessional or compulsive idea is harping on the possible death of a loved one.

Bibliography: Fenichel, O.: The psychoanalytic theory of neurosis. New York, 1945. **Toman, W.:** Introduction to psychoanalytic theory of motivation. London & New York, 1960. *W.T.*

As a rule a distinction is made between *obsession* and *phobia* (q.v.), although they sometimes occur together in the same patient. A phobia is accompanied by *acute* anxiety states. This hardly ever happens with an obsession, which exhibits greater neutrality of emotional state and sometimes a reactive fear. Phobias lie very close to the ego, whereas obsessions tend to be experienced as something more external, the patient feeling rather that he is "under siege". *J.L.I.*

Obstacle sense. The capacity of certain persons, especially the blind, to perceive "noiseless", stationary objects in the environment purely by the sense of hearing, on the principle of echo location. This gift is possessed to an outstanding degree by some animal species (bat, dolphin). (See *Ultrasonics.*)

Bibliography: Griffin, D. R.: Listening in the dark. New Haven, Conn., 1958. **Kohler, L.:** Der Fernsinn der Blinden. Die Umschau, 1952, *52*, 449–51. **Supa, M., Cotzin, M. & Dallenbach, K. M.:** Facial vision. The perception of obstacles by the blind. Amer. J. Psychol., 1944, *57*, 133–83. *M.B.*

Obstruction box; obstruction method. An apparatus for measuring the strength of an animal's motivation by observing the extent to which it will voluntarily endure an unpleasant stimulus in order to reach a goal: e.g. if the animal is separated, by an electrically charged grid, from food, drink, a novel environment, or a mate, the strength of the motivation to approach these goals can be measured by the frequency of crossings or the magnitude of current that is just tolerated. Note that the situation is one of *approach-avoidance conflict* (q.v.). *G.D.W.*

Obstruction experiments. A type of experiment first used by Stratton in which perception is made abnormal, for example by wearing reversing spectacles. This was supposed to simulate early human development of vision and thus to allow controlled study of the development of normal perception. These experiments show that vision is disrupted only temporarily if the transforming spectacles are worn continuously. *C.D.F.*

Occipital. Pertaining to the occipital bone or lobe. Occasionally applied to the head in the sense of *rear*, *to the rear*. The main anatomical terms it occurs in are: *os occipitale* (occipital bone); *lobus occipitalis* (occipital lobe); *nervus occipitalis major* (greater occipital nerve); *arteria occipitalis* (occipital artery); *foramen* (*occipitale*) *magnum* (major orifice in occipital bone through which the brain and spinal cord are connected). *G.A.*

Occipital lobe. The posterior area of the cerebrum where the visual centers are located.

Occupational psychology (syn. *Psychology of work*). If work is conceived as a class of behavior patterns, then occupational psychology, or the psychology of work, is that branch of psychology concerned with the investigation of such modes of behavior, using the traditional methods of experimental, clinical and comparative psychology, and statistics. The approaches vary, but may be roughly divided into those proper to general, differential and social psychology. The object, work itself, is therefore the essential factor which sets occupational psychology apart as a unified field.

Findings about occupational behavior lead to criteria for its improvement (reduction of fatigue, q.v., raising of safety levels, increase of job satisfaction). To attain such goals, occupational psychology cooperates with other disciplines, such as physiology, sociology, engineering science, etc.

Occupational psychology is therefore both a pure and an applied science. The two aspects must be distinguished, but are interactive.

1. *Main applications.* A summary analysis of the concept of "work" will perhaps allow some idea of the implications for psychology. Work is a mode of behavior acquired through learning. This is especially true in modern society, where occupational learning is a continuous process. Work is subjected to specific demands: *technical* (e.g. precision norms, reliability), *economic* (output, yield, speed), and *social* (occupational hierarchy, working time, etc.). Work arranges men in social groups and organizations, both within and outside a business concern or factory. Hence work cannot simply be separated from its socio-technical context. The concept of work implies the interaction of men and their environment in the wider sense of objects, tools, machines and the occupational milieu. Therefore work can be considered in terms of several reference systems, two of which may be thought of as essential.

(*a*) In the first of these, the worker is conceived as a component in a *technical system*, which may be simple (a place of work) or complex (man–machine system, q.v.). Within this system the worker must perform specific tasks (his occupation); the psychologist attempts to analyze the functions of the worker: the identification and interpretation of information, decisions, and sensorimotor activities. The results of such analyses help toward the proficient design and redesigning of machines and installations, and in the various areas covered by ergonomics (design of optimal control desks and arrays, quality control, etc.). See *Motor skills; Practice.*

(*b*) The second reference-system is concerned more with the worker as an individual, and concentrates primarily on personnel and occupation in the larger sense. For a long time occupational psychology was concerned exclusively with the problems arising in this sphere of human interaction. The most characteristic example here is the investigation of individual differences among workers: the results of such analyses have been used to improve methods of personnel selection and vocational counseling. This branch of occupational psychology also extends into the area of managerial studies, which includes problems of vocational training, occupational advancement, evaluation of performance, etc. Further areas of concern are the qualitative aspects of work and change of occupation. The worker can also be considered as a (dependent) member of an organization represented by the business or factory and its various component groups, but also as a member of a social group to which he belongs by virtue of his occupation (trade union, professional organization, etc.). A further area of occupational (psychological) research is the significance of the various characteristics of a specific organization for the individual worker, and the resulting possibilities for improvement.

2. *Development of occupational psychology.* One of the initial tasks of occupational psychology would seem to have been the investigation of fatigue in order to find ways of measuring and preventing its occurrence. Experimental methods were to the fore (Kraepelin, 1905; Lahy, 1910). It soon became evident that the observational areas and tasks of this new discipline were very much more varied. (See *Fatigue.*)

Münsterberg (q.v.) (1863–1916), who is said to have been the founder of occupational psychology, defined the main lines of this new science (which he called "psychotechnics") as lying between experimental psychology and questions of political economy. Subsequently (and for a long time), psychotechnics was concerned with questions of differential psychology (q.v.). Investigations were directed mainly to personnel selection and vocational guidance (q.v.). The improvement of test methods would seem to have been the principal concern of the psychologists of that epoch—if we are to believe the evidence of the textbooks of the period 1920–50. At first, tests were concerned exclusively with work analysis, but gradually came to have only an empirical orientation in common with it—at least for some authors. Finally, test methods were to some extent abandoned in favor of the more general objectives of occupational psychology. The limits of applicability of test procedures and the urgency of other problems in the industrial area and (especially) the military field forced occupational psychologists to turn to new questions: training, performance evaluation, machine design, organizational planning, etc. Consequently occupational psychology has come to be increasingly identified with *industrial psychology* (q.v.), which is properly restricted to a much narrower field.

Since the nineteen-fifties, some branches of occupational psychology have developed almost in their own right, but have kept their place in the general science by their attempts to structure it anew. Hence ergonomic psychology (see *Ergonomics*), which is primarily concerned with the psychological aspects of systems, has much to do not only with machine design but with questions of task-directed, proficient selection and evaluation. Similarly, the psychology of organizational systems, which has evolved rapidly since the start of the nineteen-sixties, and which essentially attempts to investigate the interaction of men and organizations, has in fact examined traditional questions of occupational psychology from a new angle.

The essential problems of the discipline are no longer treated in narrowly circumscribed areas, but in a context of constant cross-reference; for instance, one is concerned less to examine the appropriateness of an individual test than to develop methods of work placement; less to improve training for a specific machine shop than to develop training methods for specific vocational areas.

This trend helps to negate the disadvantages of over-specialization. A heavy emphasis is placed on work studies and on the preliminary diagnosis of problems in order to establish valid criteria. The multifarious factors conditioning the nature of human work demand an interdisciplinary treatment of its apparent problems. The occupational psychologist working for an organization is increasingly dependent on the cooperation of other specialists. See *Social psychology.*

Bibliography: Argyle, M., Gardner, G. & Cioffi, E.: Supervisory methods related to productivity, absenteeism and labour turnover. Hum. Relat., 1958, *11*, 23–45. **Argyris, C.:** Personality and organization. New York, 1957. **Berkun, M. M.:** Performance decrement under psychological stress. Hum. Fact., 1964, *6*, 429–37. **Cyert, R. M. & March, J. G.:** A behavioral theory of the firm. Englewood Cliffs, N.J., 1963. **Davison, J. P.,** *et al.*: Productivity and economic incentives. London, 1958. **Dubin, R.** (Ed.): Human relations in administration. Englewood Cliffs, N.J., 1962. **Friedmann, G.:** The anatomy of work. Glencoe, Ill., 1961. **Goldthorpe, H. J.,** *et al.*: The affluent worker: industrial attitudes and behaviour. Cambridge, 1968. **Hertzberg, F., Mausner, B. & Synderman, B. B.:** The motivation to work. New York, 1959. **Holding, D. H.:** Principles of training. Headington, Oxford, 1965. **Katz, D. & Kahn, R. L.:** The social psychology of organizations. New York, 1966. **Katzell, R. A.:** Psychologists in industry. In: **Webb, W. B.** (Ed.): The profession of psychology. New York, 1962, 180–211. **Leontiev, A. N.:** Some prospective problems of Soviet psychology. Soviet Psychology, 1968, *6*, 112–25. **Leplat, J.:** La psychologie du travail dans le monde. In: **Reuchlin, M.** (Ed.): Traité de psychologie appliquée, Vol. 1. Paris, 1971. **Likert, R.:** The human organization. New York, 1967. **Lockman, R. F.:** An empirical description of the subfields of psychology. Amer. Psychologist, 1964, *19*, 645–53. **Mann, F. C. & Hoffman, L. R.:** Automation and the worker. New York, 1960. **McCormick, J.:** Human factors engineering. New York, 1964. **Münsterberg, H.:** Psychology and industrial efficiency. Cambridge, 1913. **Murrell, K. F. H.:** Ergonomics. London, 1965. **Nosow, J. & Form, W. H.** (Eds.): Man, work and society, New York, 1962. **Piéron, H.:** Traité de psychologie appliquée. Paris, 1959. **Pugh, D. S.,** *et al.*: A conceptual scheme for organizational analysis. Admin, Sci. Q., 1963, *8*, 288–315. **Rodgers, A.:** Occupational psychology. Harmondsworth, 1968. **Roethlisberger, F. J. & Dixon, W. J.:** Management and the worker. Cambridge, Mass., 1939. **Rüssel, A.:** Arbeitspsychologie. Berne, 1961. **Sayles, L. R.:** Behavior in industrial work groups. New York, 1958. **Tryon, R. C.:** Psychology in flux: the academic-professional bipolarity. Amer. Psychologist, 1963, *18*, 134–44. **Walker, C. R. & Guest, R. H.:** The man on the assembly line. Cambridge, Mass., 1952. **Wallon, H.:** Principes de psychologie appliqueé. Paris, 1946, 224 ff. **Zaleznik, A., Christensen, C. R. & Roethlisberger, F. J.:** The motivation, productivity and satisfaction of workers: a predictive study. Cambridge, Mass., 1958.

J. Leplat

Occupational therapy. A method introduced by H. Simon (among others) some forty years ago for use in psychiatric clinics, and based on the finding that inactivity or confinement to bed usually led to unfavorable results in the psychologically disturbed. Some form of occupational therapy is used in almost all psychiatric clinics and programs nowadays. Forms range from simple manual tasks to laundry work, agriculture or simple industrial manufacture (i.e. of consumer articles), and art therapy (drawing, painting, sculpture) and semi-artistic activities or crafts (model-making, basket-work, etc.). It is also claimed by some that occupational therapy within a group can assist insight into one's condition and improve sociability, etc., and that individual "creative" occupations assist verbal insight and self-confidence. See also *Art, psychology of; Literature, psychology of; Music therapy; Group therapy.* *A.Hi.*

Odor prism (syn. *Olfactory prism; Smell prism*). H. Henning postulated six basic (subjective) olfactory qualities (odors) which could be represented diagrammatically as a prism whose surfaces stand for the "mixed" odors. *F.N.*

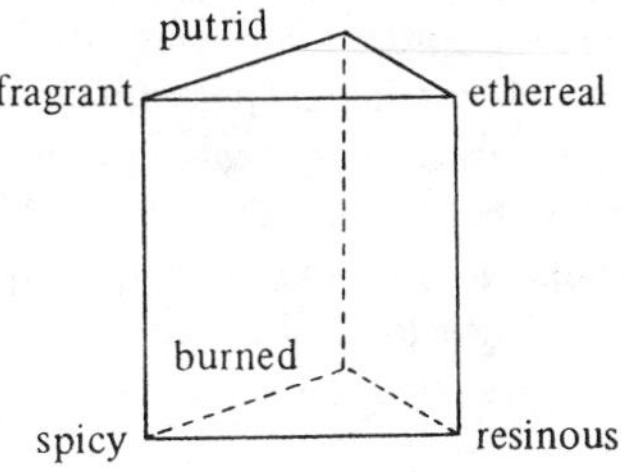

Oedipal stage. See *Oedipus complex.*

Oedipus complex. According to Freud, the special pattern of the child's relations to his parents after reaching the early genital stage (q.v.). The boy yearns to discover the anatomical sex difference of his mother, and vies with his father for her favor. He builds up a wish to dispose of his father, by whom he imagines he is threatened with castration. Renouncing some of his sexual desires, he identifies himself with the father. In this stage the girl similarly desires her father and treats her mother as a rival, later identifying herself with her and forgoing some of the sexual wishes she entertains toward her father. An incomplete breaking-down of the Oedipus complex is said to lead to psychological disorders in schoolchildren (e.g. school phobias), neuroses (q.v.) and perversions (q.v.) (genital stage). According to Adler, the brothers or sisters can complicate the Oedipus complex. Variants established by objective data on the family situation have been shown to have different long-term effects on a person's social behavior outside the family (Toman, 1969). See *Family.*

Bibliography: Adler, A.: The practice and theory of individual psychology. London, ²1929. **Freud, S.:** Introductory lectures on psycho-analysis. London, ²1929. **Toman, W.:** Family constellations. New York, ²1969. *W. Toman*

Oestrogen. See *Estrogen.*

Oestrus. See *Estrus.*

Olfactometer. An apparatus for controlling the presentation of smell stimuli to a subject, as used in psychophysical studies of smell thresholds and smell mixtures. A variety of models have been developed: some small devices, others occupying an entire room. *G.D.W.*

Olfactory bulb (syn. *Olfactory lobe*). Either one of two bulbs, which are extensions of the cerebrum toward the eyes and act as smell centers.

Olfactory cells. In the olfactory epithelium of the *regio olfactoris* (q.v.) two types of cell can be differentiated, the supporting cells and the real olfactory cells. The latter are equipped with olfactory hairs on their free surface and represent simultaneously receptor (q.v.) and nerve cell. The neurites of the olfactory cells pass as fascicles through the cribriform plate and enter the olfactory bulb. No adequate explanation has yet been advanced for the way in which the stimulus in the olfactory cells is transformed into an excitation to be transmitted. When there is only a minute concentration of a volatile material, the "perception threshold" is reached first of all, i.e. "something" is smelled, but only when the concentration increases can the nature of the material be determined (specific threshold). *R.R.*

Olfactory prism. See *Odor prism.*

Oligophrenia. Synonymous with the term *amentia* (q.v.): mental deficiency, mental defect (q.v.) and mental subnormality. *V.K.J.*

Ololuiqui (*Morning glory*). Seeds of the Mexican bindweed of the family Convolvulacea (*Rivea corymbosa* and *Pomea* *violacea*), or domestic morning glory. With "peyote" (see *Mescaline*) and "Teonanacat" (see *Psylocybin*), one of the major magical drugs of pre-Spanish Mexico. Tests with the seed or synthetically produced ololuiqui have so far failed to produce noticeable hallucinogenic effects. The main effects of ololuiqui are disagreeable vegetative sensations. Increasing the dose leads to progressive clouding of consciousness.

Bibliography: Heim, E., *et al.*: Die psychische Wirkung der mexikanischen Droge "Ololuiqui" am Menschen. Psychopharmacologia, 1968, *13*, 35–48. *G.E.*

Onanism. See *Masturbation; Coitus interruptus.*

Oneirology. See *Dream analysis.*

One-sided test of significance. Unilateral significance test. See *Significance.*

One-trial learning. The proficient acquisition of a skill, etc., on one trial. See *Practice.*

One-word sentence. A phenomenon which appears as a child develops its linguistic powers and which denotes the condensation of the meaning of a whole sentence into a single word (e.g. "balla" = I want that ball). These monoverbal sentences are normally used by the child between the ages of twelve to eighteen months, but they can occur even later. Even the adult in a state of great emotional excitement (e.g. anxiety, fury) will occasionally use the one-word sentence to communicate his needs and sensations to others. *K.E.P.*

Only child. See *Child, only.*

Ontogenesis. The individual's development from zygote to the sexually mature state. See *Biogenetic law.* *H.Sch.*

Ontology. The theory (or philosophy) of being as being, i.e. of basic principles of being.

Onychophagy. *Nail chewing* or *biting;* a behavioral disorder occurring mainly in children and occasionally persisting into adult life (especially under acute psychological stress). Can be interpreted psychoanalytically as fixation (q.v.) at the oral stage (q.v.) of libido (q.v.) development. *W.Sch.*

Operant conditioning. See *Conditioning, classical and operant.*

Operational definition (syn. *Operation(al)ism*). In grappling with the problem of simultaneity within the context of Einstein's Special Theory of Relativity, the American physicist P. W. Bridgman demanded in 1927 in *The Logic of Modern Physics* that the concepts used in science should be defined through a sufficiently accurate description of the procedures used by the investigator in establishing and testing them. The concepts "simultaneity" and "length", for example, would thus be "operational", and therefore satisfactorily defined, if the procedures adopted in establishing "simultaneity" or measuring "length" were fully described. Where general validity is assigned to this rule, the corresponding critical and methodological approach tends to be termed "operationism" or "operationalism" (synonymous terms which Bridgman repeatedly rejected on the ground that they claimed too much for the method). Bridgman hoped that by applying scientific concepts to concrete procedures he could divest scientific terminology of inconsistent and contradictory meanings, since neither of these faults exist in the actual physical situations. The interest aroused by Bridgman's theories, first among psychologists in the USA, and later in other countries, was surely due to the prospect of banishing ambiguity and obscurity from the language of science, and hence to the hopes it raised of avoiding many futile controversies. Moreover, other influential trends in American philosophy and psychology grew up around Bridgman's methodological criteria. These included American pragmatism (q.v.) or instrumentalism (C. S. Peirce, W. James, J. Dewey) and logical positivism (q.v.) or empiricism, popularized mainly by members of the Vienna School who emigrated to the USA (R. Carnap, H. Feigl, H. Reichenbach, *et al.*), who underlined the need to restrict scientific language to verifiable intersubjective propositions and create a unitary science or unitary scientific language—thus, at first, behaviorism (q.v.), which sought to limit psychology to statements about observable intersubjective behavior. (In Europe, H. Dingler propagated views closely related to Bridgman's theory.) The best-known representatives of the operationist standpoint include S. S. Stevens, E. G. Boring, E. C. Tolman and B. F. Skinner. In the psychological sphere, too, only such concepts and propositions as can be asserted and verified intersubjectively by independent observers through repeatable procedures are permissible. Thus, intelligence (q.v.) and anxiety (q.v.) would be defined by an adequate description of the procedures necessary to bring them into play and grasp them. As time went on, criticism of the theory led to its being far more loosely formulated, both by Bridgman (1959) and by other adherents of the operationist school. A central role was played by the problem of the relationship between interoperationally defined and theoretical concepts, between observational and theoretical language (Carnap, 1956). The discussion is still going on, and views on the subject among exponents of scientific psychology are far from uniform.

Bibliography: Boring, E. G., *et al.*: Symposium on operationism. Psychol. Rev., 1945, *52*, 241–94. **Bridgman, P. W.:** The logic of modern physics. New York, 1928. **Id.:** The nature of physical theory. Princeton, 1936. **Id.:** Operational analysis. Phil. Sci., 1938, *5*, 114–31. **Id.:** The way things are. Cambridge, Mass., 1959. **Carnap, R.:** The methodological character of theoretical concepts. In: **Feigl, H. & Scriven, M.:** Minnesota Studies in the Philosophy of Science, Vol. 1. Minneapolis, 1956, 38–76. **Hempel, C. G.:** A logical appraisal of operationism. Scientific Monthly, 1954, *79*, 215–20. **Pratt, C. C.:** The logic of modern psychology. New York, 1939. **Stevens, S. S.:** The operational basis of psychology. Americ. J. Psychol., 1935, *47*, 323–30. **Id.:** The operational definition of psychological concepts. Psychol. Rev., 1935, *42*, 517–27. **Id.:** Psychology and the science of science. Psychol. Bull., 1939, *36*, 221–63. **Tolman, E. C.:** Operational behaviorism and current trends in psychology. Proc. 25th Anniv. Celebr. Univ. S. Calif., 1936, 89–103.

F. Buggle

Operation(al)ism. See *Operational definition.*

Operational method. A method used in forming theories where an operational definition (q.v.) applies. The approach deliberately dispenses with any explanation of an internal relationship which direct observation cannot detect and which can therefore only be grasped intuitively. *R.Hä.*

Operator. A symbol applied to a mathematical quantity (e.g. vector, q.v.) which it transforms. An operator can be used only in connection with other quantities. *G.Mi.*

Ophthalmology. The branch of diagnostic and therapeutic medicine concerned with eye disorders and diseases.

Ophthalmometer. See *Astigmometer.*

Opiates. These are usually psychotropic substances pharmacologically related to morphine (q.v.). The term is less commonly applied to alkaloids of opium (q.v.) not resembling morphine. *W.B.*

Opinion change. A process in which an opinion is altered or replaced by another.

There would seem to be no distinction between this and what is known as "attitude change" (q.v.), except that the variables altered in that process are usually opinions, i.e. observable verbal statements about relatively complex phenomena (assertions which nevertheless derive from basic, detectable attitudes proper). *H.-D.S.*

Opinion polls (*Opinion research; Polling; Public opinion research*). In fact, this discipline is only minimally concerned with research into opinions. These misleading but widely used terms are hardly scientific. Even if the nature of the phenomenon of "public opinion" (q.v.) (still unexplained) is disregarded, the word "opinion" takes one along the wrong track: research into attitudes (q.v.), moods, "climate of opinion", must take into account not only opinions, beliefs and convictions in the widest sense, but many other things as indicators: e.g. facts, modes of behavior, or knowledge. "Opinion research" and its analogues are also applied for scientific and practical purposes which have ceased to have anything to do with public opinion. In fact, "opinion research" does not denote any definite subject of research but the employment of a certain method, the representative and statistical inquiry involving an interview (q.v.), standardized by a questionnaire, and usually a verbal interrogation. A loose division into two parts has now become common: when this method is used to study the market, the term employed is *market research* (q.v.), everything else comes under "public opinion". Different and more appropriate terms have been used: *demoscopy* (q.v.), *surveys*, and (as a general term for the scientific field of which opinion research is a partial area) *empirical social research*.

1. *History*. The method of inquiry by "opinion polls" was developed in Europe for investigations of social conditions. A questionnaire was first used by D. Davies in 1787 and was entitled "Inquiry into the Household Budget of the Working Classes in England"; in 1848, A. von Lengerke conducted the first inquiry in Germany into the conditions of farm laborers; and in the USA there were election forecasts (1824 saw the first straw poll—a sample vote to predict the result of an election). What would seem to have been the first opinion poll in the true sense of the word was conducted in 1907 by the *Chicago Journal* and concerned an order dealing with public conveyances.

In 1906 the English statistician A. L. Bowley published an account of the representative sampling method for population statistics, and he himself was the first to use it in 1912 for such an inquiry. The idea of interrogating a relatively small but statistically representative number of selected individuals, instead of conducting *mammoth* interrogations, spread throughout the world after the *Literary Digest*, an American review, used ten million voting papers to make an incorrect forecast of the presidential election in which Roosevelt and Landon were candidates, whereas G. Gallup (q.v.) (as well as E. Roper and A. Crossley) made a correct forecast after a few thousand interviews. After that, it became more and more a matter of course to collect information about the views and behavioral habits of large groups of the population with the aid of representative inquiries, which had become relatively easy to conduct. It is difficult to assess the social and political effects of the availability of this new dimension of information acquisition; according to W. Hennis (1957), it is tantamount to conducting a plebiscite by the back door.

Even today election forecasts still play an important part in opinion research, more especially as a control of the validity (q.v.) of particular methodological concepts of sampling, the preparation of questionnaires, and the organization of field work. The fact that within a few days a representative poll is followed by a general election provides, even if there is no possibility of the appearance of new influences after the conclusion of the inquiry (before the election—at any rate) a trial situation which it would be impossible to reproduce effectively. With regard to the tolerances of sample inquiries, validity control is concerned *not with a correct forecasting* of the successful candidate, but with the *size of the average deviation* and the *maximal deviation* between the forecast and the official result of the election.

2. *Methodological principles.* The methodological principles of opinion research are characterized in that the investigation is never directed at individuals, and never at a personality (q.v.) as a whole—at a character—but at collectives defined by common characteristics. It is not the *person* but the *characteristic* which is the object of the investigation. The person appears only as the bearer of characteristics, of variables (see *Methods of psychology*), and it is their frequency distribution (q.v.) and relation to other variables which must be determined.

As is appropriate to the field of investigation (majorities, characteristics), the technique of opinion research—apart from preliminary studies—is *exclusively* statistical, i.e. enumerative. The uniformity, or comparability, to which the characteristics are subordinated by this enumeration has to be accurately supported by preserving a rigorous hierarchy in the treatment of all methodological questions here first place has to be given to the requirement of invariance (q.v.) when collecting the data. This means: well-structured questionnaires to be read aloud verbatim to the interviewee; standardization of the interrogation situation; uniform central control of the interviewers; simplicity of all instructions for selecting the sample and for the interrogation. The greatest uniformity of all necessary steps when collecting data is a requisite for reliability (q.v.), repeatability and verifiability.

3. *Sampling.* When the subject of the inquiry has been determined, two questions remain to be answered: on what group of individuals, or on what social grouping (e.g. school classes, industrial concerns), is the report to be made? and secondly: is the survey to be a full one or is only a sample required?

In taking a representative sample the following principle must be observed: every unit of the whole population must have the same or a calculable chance of being included in the sample. If this principle has been followed, the probability calculation (law of large numbers) can be applied to estimate within what tolerances the result obtained can be generalized, in order to apply to the whole population. Two methods are available for representative samples.

In the *random method*, the sample is chosen from the population according to the lottery principle. For this choice to be possible, the population must be easily accessible, in a physical or symbolic form (e.g. card-indexes or lists). Disadvantages: people who are especially mobile and active, and especially young men and women, are not sufficiently contacted because they are not so frequently at home; anonymity is destroyed by the selection of addresses, and coverage, i.e. the actual interrogation of those people included in the sample, is expensive and time-consuming.

The second method for preparing a representative sample, the *quota method*, assumes that some important proportions of the population are known, e.g. the distribution according to age groups, labor groups or size of locality. Based on these data, quotas (magnitudes in a genuine random selection) are calculated and distributed to the interviewers who then select a list of people for questioning according to the quotas given to them. Disadvantages of the quota method: since the selection of people for questioning is left at the final stage to the interviewers, the method may encounter difficulties. The efficacy of the quota method has been demonstrated by a number of election forecasts. No sufficiently comprehensive scientific study of the conditions and accuracy of the different selection methods is as yet available.

4. *Types of investigation.* The most usual types of investigation used in opinion polls are:

(*a*) The *single representative inquiry* with the interview lasting from five to forty-five minutes, the average duration being thirty minutes. Usual basis: two thousand interviews for obtaining results for sub-groups as well (sex, age, employment, political sympathies, size of locality, province); if only a general picture is required, the number of interviews is limited to a few hundred. (*b*) *Trend analysis:* the questions are repeated, retaining the same words and, as far as possible, the same implications of the questions, at fixed intervals, e.g. monthly, in order to measure a government's popularity. The "decay of the instrument", in other words, a change in linguistic usage or other circumstances may be a weakness; e.g. the question used since 1952 to measure the trend in the fear of price increases can no longer be used, as more than 80% of the answers regularly state that prices will rise.

Other types of investigation: (*c*) The *multi-stage inquiry* made in areas which are fairly inaccessible or not well known, especially where motivational research is in question: a pilot study with non- or partly structured intensive interviews (q.v.) or group discussions, and subsequent, more structured and numerically more broadly based inquiries, incorporating at every stage the knowledge gained from the previous one. (*d*) The *panel investigation*, a repeated interrogation of the same group of people, which is especially suitable for research into effects, e.g. the effects of election campaigns (Lazarsfeld, Berelson & Gaudet, 1944; [3]1968), and, more generally, to study objects for investigation containing time components or processes; example: an investigation of a change in voting intentions depending on personality characteristics. The expectation that the minimally self-confident would be most likely to waver during an election campaign proved to be correct (see *Attitude; Attitude change*), but—surprisingly—even very self-assured individuals changed their intentions more often than the average.

(*e*) Investigations designed as controlled experiments are combined with all the above-mentioned methods to attempt causal explanations. In the "field experiment" of survey research—as distinguished from a laboratory experiment—interviewees remain in their accustomed surroundings; as a rule, neither they nor the interviewers know that an experiment is taking place. Lottery principles are used to make from a sample two or more test groups which do not differ from one another statistically (equalization of initial conditions); this is known as a "split ballot". The test group and control group are given the same questions and the same treatment; the experimental factor is all that is varied: e.g. the question which can be given once with, and once without, a precisely worded alternative.

If only the form of question is varied, the field experiment serves a methodological purpose, namely the investigation of the effects of types of question (the method goes back to Rugg & Cantril, 1944), and confirms the rule that alternatives must be precisely worded. Similarly, the effect of an interviewer's briefing or a method of selecting a sample is tested. Field experiments determined by content test, e.g. the influence of certain arguments, or fragments of information, on the expression of opinion.

5. *Questionnaires.* Many experiments have shown that the way questions are formulated has considerable influence on the results of opinion research, and that definition of the subject of the question and clarity and neutrality of its phrasing are very important. An additional influence is any impression carried over from previous questions, or deriving from some implication. This second point explains a principle used in constructing a demoscopic questionnaire: "An individual interview is a whole complete in itself which must be evaluated on its merits with its inner relationships (according to the interview); the individual demoscopic interview on the contrary is only a part of another 'whole', which is the survey. Every single question of the interview must be like an

identical experimental framework to which the interviewers react with their answers. The interview must, as far as possible, be not a complete whole, but ideally the *sum* of a number of questions. This explains the distinctive nature of the demoscopic interview . . . in which thematically related questions are intentionally placed at a great distance from one another, or 'obliterating' or 'buffer' questions interrupt the train of thought in order to prevent subjects just dealt with from affecting subsequent questions" (W. Schwarzenauer, in: Noelle, 1963, [5]1971, p. 49).

This is also a reason for the importance of the multiple-theme survey in opinion research —a type of survey in which quite different problems for investigation are combined without interference in one interview.

Occasionally the subject of the investigation cannot even be mentioned directly, but can only be grasped from indicators; hence the problem of validity of opinion research. New tests have constantly to be developed. Difficulties arise not so much from inhibitions preventing interviewees from speaking, but from their inability to say anything at all; the degree to which thinking and feeling are socially conditioned is also an unknown factor.

In addition to many forms of question developed by opinion research, techniques developed by psychological diagnostics are also employed in the standardized demoscopic interview: simple observation of expressions, the Thematic Apperception Test (q.v.), Rorschach charts, sign tests (E. Ring, 1965; 1967; 1970). Essential criteria of utility are the acceptability of techniques for interviewees, that interviewers should be able to use them satisfactorily, and that they should make relevant distinctions between groups of people in connection with the object of the investigation.

6. *Interviewer*. The most important qualities for an interviewer have been defined as scrupulousness and the ability to establish contact. The problem of the interviewer's influence on survey results has often been studied; it is largely a problem of the questionnaire. With "open" questions (where there are no prescribed answers), the influence is considerable, but when there is structuring, and especially when the answer is taken from lists or packs of cards, the interviewer's influence is practically excluded (see *Interview*). There is also an advantage in distributing the interview over a large number of interviewers; that is why part-time interviewers are preferred in opinion polls. Special training is not requisite if the questionnaires have been well designed (D. Rugg, in Cantril, 1947; see Moser, 1958), and indeed it is not desirable: not the interviewer but the questionnaire has to be astute.

The roles of researcher and interviewer must be strictly demarcated; one reason is exclusion of any influence of the scientist's expectations on his results.

7. *Analysis*. The data gathered by opinion research are very suitable for scale analysis, multivariable analysis (analysis of variance), or—in general—correlational analysis, factor analysis (q.v.), and segmentation; new techniques are constantly under development. There are dangers in monotonous questionnaires, which are particularly appropriate to statistical analysis. In opinion research, the interviewer and interviewee are the weakest links in the chain: therefore their mentality and motivation (q.v.) must always be taken into consideration.

Bibliography: Benny, M., Gray, A. P. & Pear, R. H.: How people vote. London, 1956. **Berelson, B. & Janowitz, M.:** Reader in public opinion and communication. New York, [2]1966. **Cantril, H.:** Gauging public opinion. Princeton, N.J. & London, [4]1947. **Cicourcel, A. V.:** Method and measurement in sociology. New York, 1964. **Hyman, H. H.,** *et al.*: Interviewing in social research. Chicago, London & Toronto, 1954. **Lazarfeld, P., Berelson, B. & Gaudet, H.:** The people's choice. New York, [3]1968. **Lippmann, W.:** Public opinion. New York, 1922. **Moser, C. A.:** Survey methods in social investigation. New York, 1958. **Noelle, E.:** Umfragen in der Massengesellschaft. Einführung in die Methoden der Demoskopie. Reinbek bei Hamburg, [5]1971. **Noelle-Neumann, E.:** Wanted: rules for wording structured questionnaires. The Public Opinion Quarterly, 1970, *34*, 191–201.

E. Noelle-Neumann

Opium. A mixture of the phenanthrene derivatives morphine (q.v., app. 10 per cent) and codeine (q.v.), both analgesics (q.v.), the benzylisochinoline derivatives narcotine and papaverine and other alkaloids, obtained from the dried juice of unripe poppy capsules (*Papaver somniferum*). Mainly smoked and eaten as a narcotic, especially in East Asia. Opium has marked hallucinatory, euphoric and analgesic effects. Chronic use leads to addiction. See *Drug dependence*.

Bibliography: See *Morphine*. *W.B.*

Oppel's illusion. A variation of the *Müller–Lyer illusion.* The two parallel lines are divided into three equal parts, but this does not appear to be so. *C.D.F.*

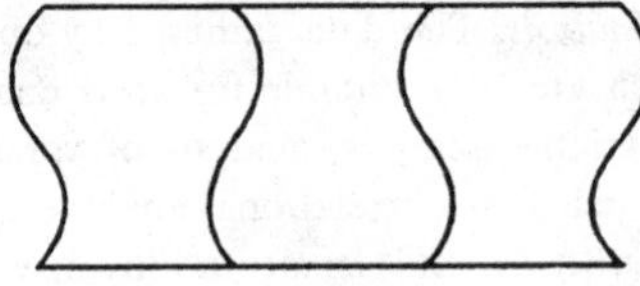

Optical axis. See *Eye.*

Optic chiasm. See *Chiasm, optic.*

Optic thalamus. See *Thalamus.*

Optic tract. The link between the retina (q.v.) and the visual centers. The first three neurons of the optic tract are in the retina (historically, a part of the brain). The fibers of the third neuron unite and emerge at the blind spot (q.v.) as the *fasciculus opticus* from the *bulbus.* As a part of the brain, the *fasciculus opticus* is surrounded by meninges (*pia mater* and *dura mater*). At the *sella turcica*, the two fasciculi cross in the *optic chiasm*, and continue as the *tractus optici.* The fibers coming from the nasal retinal halves of both eyes cross over here, the fibers of the *temporal retinal halves* continue without crossing, while the fibers of the *foveae centrales* cross in part. The two bundles of fibers which form from them leave the optic chiasm on both sides in the optic tract. The optic tract eventually divides into the *radiatio tractus optici*, which sends fibers to the lateral geniculate body and to the anterior *corpora quadrigemina.* The optic tract continues to the visual center in the *area striata* in the cortex. The ganglionic cells of the lateral geniculate body and their neurites form the fourth neuron of the optic tract. *R.R.*

Optimal performance. 1. In the occupational sphere: the working efficiency which can be achieved *temporarily* by devoting all one's energy to a specific task; fatigue sets in rapidly if effort is extended. **2.** In business and economics: production or service which can be completed in a given length of time by an organizational unit which has the best possible equipment and in which all factors liable to lead to a loss of time are eliminated. *G.R.W.M.*

Optokinetics. The study of eye movements induced by stimuli, e.g. a horizontally moving field of vertical lines. *C.D.F.*

Optometer. A device for measuring range of vision. Scheiner described the following simple test arrangement for determining variations. Two pins fitted one behind the other on an optical bench are viewed with one eye through a screen. Two holes are bored side by side in the screen at a distance from each other smaller than the pupil diameter. When the eye accommodates (see *Accommodation*) to the front pin, this is seen as single, the rear pin double. When the eye fixates the rear pin, the situation is reversed. See *Chromatoptometer.* *R.R.*

Oral character. See *Oral stage.*

Oral contraceptives. See *Ovulation inhibitors.*

Oral eroticism. See *Cunnilingus; Fellatio; Oral–genital contacts.*

Oral–genital contacts. Contact of one partner's mouth with, or oral stimulation of, the genitals of the other partner. Practiced on male genitals, *fellatio* (q.v.); on female genitals, *cunnilingus* (q.v.). One-sided or reciprocal oral–genital contacts serve for the sexual stimulation of the partner as a prelude to coitus or for full non-coital sexual satisfaction culminating in some cases in orgasm (q.v.) To the prejudiced, these forms of sexual contact rank as "unnatural" and even "perverted". Such attitudes conflict with the findings of modern sex research, which leave no doubt as to the (statistical) "normality" of these practices, although in Western countries they occur less frequently, and are as a rule learned later, than manual–genital contacts (q.v.) and coitus (q.v.). In some cultures these forms of contact were usual, or even features of religious practices. The first scientific investigations into sex habits (Kinsey, 1948/53) suggests that oral–genital contacts are practiced by about one in two married persons in the USA.

Bibliography: Beach, B. A.: Sex and behavior. New York, 1965. **Kinsey, A. C.,** *et al.*: Sexual behavior in the human male. Philadelphia & London, 1948. **Id.,** *et al.*: Sexual behavior in the human female. Philadelphia & London, 1953. *H.M.*

Oral stage (syn. *Oral phase*). According to Freud, the stage of development where the infant's interest centers on oral manipulation and stimulation, tactile stimuli and sensory reception. During the early oral stage (first four to six months) the infant has not yet built up an "object person". A change of mother under these circumstances occurs without traumatic effects. Only partial aspects of the object are already familiar to the child. During the late oral stage (lasting to the end of the first year) the child elects as "mother" the person who regularly cares for it. It gets from the mother gratuitous and unreserved attention and contact—stimulation of all sense modalities. The child learns how to move in its immediate environment, but also relies in its movements on its mother, who lifts, holds and carries it about. According to Freud, Abraham and Fenichel, fixation and subsequent regression to the *early* oral stage can lead to psychoses (q.v.). Fixation and subsequent regression to the *late* oral stage can sow the seeds of mania (q.v.), depression (q.v.) and circular psychoses, addictions, organic neuroses (q.v.), i.e. psychosomatic disorders, impulsive neuroses (psychopathic personality traits) and hypochondria (q.v.). A change of personality—the "*oral character*"—may take the place of specific neurotic symptoms. The associated characteristics include passive dependence, a craving for attention and contacts at any price, and for unconditional love, as well as egocentric sensitivity (oral eroticism). Scolding and begging for attention are further features of oral eroticism. See *Child psychology.*

Bibliography: Fenichel, O.: The psychoanalytic theory of neurosis. New York, 1945. **Freud, S.:** Three essays on the theory of sexuality. London, [2]1962. **Toman, W.:** An introduction to psychoanalytic theory of motivation. London & New York, 1960. *W.T.*

Oral zone. The mouth and the immediately adjacent area. According to Freud it is extended to the whole body during the oral stage through the contact with the mouth made by hands and feet. Seeing and hearing assume purposeful functions as "radar detectors" (W. Toman) of immediate sensory experience and physical contacts. *W.T.*

Ordering test. Any test in which the subject is required to classify a number of objects in the light of various criteria (color, shape, function, weight, size, material, surface texture, value, etc.). *H.-J.A.*

Ordinal numbers. Numbers assigned to a ranked sequence which give the quantitative or time relations existing between the elements of the rank order (q.v.), e.g. the 1st, 2nd, . . .). Ordinal numbers do not permit any statement to be made as to the size of the intervals between elements. *G.Mi.*

Ordinal scale. A scale which permits statements of the form "greater or less than" to be made about the relations of magnitude of observed units, but not about differences in size since the units of size are neither uniform nor known. E.g.: scale for school marks. *G.Mi.*

Ordinal variable. A quantitative variable to which a position has been assigned in an ordinal scale. *G.Mi.*

Orestes complex. A psychoanalytic term for the alleged development of an Oedipus complex (q.v.) into a son's (repressed) desire to kill his mother.

Organ. Any specialized bodily instrument or structural part.

Organic. 1. Pertaining to an organ. **2.** Characteristic of that which is bodily or vital, not merely, or not, mental, mechanical or functional.

Organic brain damage. All those influences which lead to organic injury to the brain (q.v.) and to a resulting reversible or irreversible reduction in mental capacity and performance controlled by the central nervous system. Damage may be a consequence, e.g. of traumatic brain damage caused by a blunt (concussion, skull fracture) or sharp blow (thrust, piercing), brain tumors, inflammation of the brain, degenerative processes of old age, hereditary or other illness, a stroke, prenatal and perinatal damage, or diseases which have a secondary effect on the brain (infections, intoxications, metabolic disorders affecting the ganglionic cells in general metabolic conditions, syphilis, etc.). Impairment of mental faculties is generally accompanied by difficulty in concentrating and remembering, impaired thinking powers, rapid fatigue and psychological lability; the symptoms are heightened by heat, alcohol, nicotine and other stresses and noxious influences. See *Aphasia; Brain pathology; Mental defect.* *F.C.S.*

Organic neurosis. According to S. Freud and O. Fenichel a psychic disorder that derives from traumatic environmental conditions or such constitutional weaknesses as occur in the late *oral stage* (q.v.). Organic neuroses are said to include those diseases of adults known as psychosomatic, e.g. asthma, gastric and intestinal disorders and ulcers, faulty blood pressure, skin ailments and disorders of the joints. All have one feature in common, i.e. that chronic psychic stress conditions, which such patients feel more acutely partly because of their early traumatic experience, are alleged to bring about physical change as a direct ("natural") reaction. As against this, hysterical conversion symptoms (see *Conversion*) fulfill for the patient a particular idiosyncratic, though unconscious, need. The relations that have been established statistically are by no means clear-cut but suggest the presence in psychosomatic diseases of intermediate links in the causative chain which include special patterns of consumption and behavior. But see *Psychosomatics.* *W.T.*

Organic psychoses. These are caused by pathological changes in the brain, as opposed to functional psychoses, where no such changes are apparent. The distinction is not clear since it is now evident that metabolic changes occur in schizophrenia (q.v.) and manic-depressive psychosis, both of which are classed as functional. Organic psychoses may be acute, usually reversible, or chronic and irreversible. See *Psychoses, functional.* *D.E.*

Organic sensations; articular sensations. Organic or visceral sensations arise in the internal organs and result in the experience of hunger, thirst, pain, etc. They are generally poorly located spatially, but can be used as cues in just the same way as any external stimulus. *Articular sensations* come from receptors in the joints and are crucial to knowledge of the position of our limbs in relation to each other and to the space around us. *C.D.F.*

Organ inferiority. In the early stages of formulating his theories (Vienna, 1907), Adler (q.v.) assumed the existence of *real* organ inferiority. Aside from its purely physiological implications, this triggers off a process of self-assertion which becomes permanent in the course of subsequent psychological development. Organ inferiority determines continuous observation and training of the organ in question whose function is regarded as inadequate. Later, Adler added the supposition that inferiority feelings (q.v.) can also be determined by social factors.

Bibliography: Adler, A.: Study of organ inferiority and its psychical implications. Washington, 1917.

J.L.I.

Organism. 1. A living animal or plant. **2.** A social group (acting in concert).

Organismic psychology. A term for any psychological approach which rejects a mind–body dualism (see *Mind–body problem*) and conceives psychology behavioristically (see *Behaviorism*) or holistically (see *Ganzheit*) as the study of a/the (biological) organism. See *General psychology.*

Organization. 1. *Sociology:* order, structure, internal cohesion, interdependence of groups. **2.** *Industrial psychology* (q.v.): the establishment of conditions, tasks, powers to issue instructions and order responsibilities in individual work sectors. See *Leadership.* **3.** *Occupational psychology:* job supervision and staff allocation, hierarchic order, and instruction, report and information channels in business enterprises. **4.** *Politics:* groupings formed at national level (e.g. trade unions, employers' associations); international or supranational level (e.g. Commission of the European Communities, ILO, UN, UNESCO), to pursue the objects laid down in their articles (programs). **5.** A business concern, or other large enterprise. **6.** Any structured whole or dynamically (inter)active system. See *Group; Role; Industrial psychology; Occupational psychology.*

Bibliography: Caplow, T.: Principles of organizations. New York, 1964. **Etzioni, A.:** Complex organizations. New York, 1961. **Blau, P. M. & Scott, W. R.:** Formal organizations. London, 1963. **Whyte, W. H.:** The organization man. New York, 1956. *G.R.W.M.*

Organizational pathology. The tendency for an organization to run down, or become essentially ineffective and non-dynamic, especially by over-formalization and impersonalization.

Organized sample. A sample (q.v.) selected so as to exhibit a specific composition in regard to one or more control characteristics, e.g. proportionality to the distribution of such characteristics in the population. Control characteristics frequently used in the organization of samples are *social status, profession* and *age.* Within the individual groups of characteristics the elements of the sample are chosen at random. See *Sampling methods.*

G.Mi.

Organ of Corti. The basilar membrane (q.v.) of the inner ear carries the organ of Corti, which consists of special supporting cells, and in which the auditory receptor cells are embedded. Because of the movements of the basilar membrane, which are dependent on sound frequency and intensity, there is a mechanical stimulation of the hairs of the sensory cells, and simultaneously a mechanico-electrical transformation and excitation of the attached fibers of the cochlear nerve. *M.S.*

Organogram. A cybernetic model of information processing in the organism. See *Cybernetics and psychology*. *G.Mi.*

Organs of sense. See *Sense organs.*

Orgasm. See *Orgasm, physiology of.*

Orgasmic phase. The third phase of the sexual response cycle (q.v.) corresponding to orgasm in man and woman. *V.S.*

Orgasmic platform. The physiological response of woman under intense sexual excitement first recorded by Masters & Johnson (1966) by physiological methods. Massive vasocongestion halves the diameter of the outer third of the vaginal barrel and environing engorged tissues through regular (three to fifteen) muscular contractions. The number, duration and strength of these are physiological measures of the subjective intensity of the orgasm. The contractions, preceded by a few seconds by an initial spasm and simultaneous consciousness of the impending orgasm, are perceived and verbalized by the woman as "pulsations" in the genital region.

Bibliography: See *Orgasm, physiology of.* *V.S.*

Orgasm, multiple. Multiple orgasm arises where several (two to thirty, or more) orgasms are achieved in a single sexual act or within a brief period (a few seconds to an hour or more). Women generally find this easier than men, who, moreover, owing to the sexual *refractory period* (q.v.), usually cannot, like women, experience orgasms in direct succession. According to Kinsey *et al.*, however, multiple orgasm is most widespread in male children and can often (15–20 per cent) occur in males aged 16 to 20, becoming progressively rarer with age. This age-dependence has not been established in women. *V.S.*

Orgasm, physiology of. Orgasm is the climax of sexual excitement and reaction which can be induced by any effective form of somatosexual or psychosexual stimulation. It represents an abrupt, involuntary discharge of psychophysical and neuromuscular tensions, and is probably accompanied by reactions in all organs and organ systems of the body. Findings to date suggest that in any *physiological definition* of the orgasm in man or woman the following reactions need to be stressed: (*a*) peak intensity of sexual pleasure; (*b*) involuntary muscular contractions in the genital and anal areas, and many extragenital muscle groups; (*c*) concentration of blood both in the genital areas (e.g. vagina or penis) and outside them (see *Sex flush*); (*d*) culmination of the reactions of heart, circulation and respiration; (*e*) partial or total loss of sensory capacities, and at times loss of consciousness for a matter of seconds or minutes. Characteristic of orgasm are the contractions of the orgasmic platform (q.v.) in woman, and of ejaculation (q.v.) in man. In physical responses (apart from ejaculation), orgasm in woman resembles that in man. The following sex-specific differences have, however, been described. A woman's subjective feelings during orgasm are more variable than a man's. The orgasm usually lasts longer in woman who, unlike man, can achieve additional orgasms immediately after the first. Moreover, more women than men need to experience a number of orgasms before achieving satisfaction. In general, women appear to possess greater *capacity*, both quantitative and qualitative, for orgastic response (see *Orgasm, multiple; Status orgasticus*), although on average more men experience orgasm more regularly.

Bibliography: Kinsey, A. C., *et al.*: Sexual behavior in the human male. Philadelphia & London, 1948. **Id.,** *et al.*: Sexual behavior in the human female. Philadelphia & London, 1953. **Masters, W. H. & Johnson, V. E.:** Human sexual response. Boston, 1966. **Sigusch, V.:** Exzitation und Orgasmus bei der Frau. Stuttgart, 1970.

V.S.

Orgies. Social occasions involving an extreme degree of indulgence in pleasurable and lustful activities, particularly drinking, feasting, dancing, and indiscriminate sexual activity. Reputed to be common in the days of the Roman Empire. *G.D.W.*

Orientation; orientation capacity; orientation loss. Orientation can have a rather limited implication as in the *orientation reflex* which refers to responses to and movements in the direction of a novel stimulus. More generally, orientation refers to the position of the body in space and in relation to its surroundings. Thus orientation loss involves the inability to tell left from right and to find one's way around. This kind of disability is particularly associated with lesions in the parietal lobe. *C.D.F.*

Orientation reflex. See *Orienting reflex.*

Orienting reflex. A novel stimulus arising in the environment evokes a number of responses in the organism. One group of these responses remains stable; the other group, which adjusts the receptor surface and brain structures for the effective perception of this stimulus, decreases and habituates gradually if the stimulus is repeatedly presented. The set of reactions increasing the perceptual capacity and referred to the novelty of the signal was called by Pavlov an *orienting reflex*, or "what is it"-reflex. The orienting reflex is an integrating part of a more complex exploratory behavior released by the uncertainty of the situation, and directed toward unfamiliar objects. The orienting reflex is a unitary functional system and has several components: somatic (movements of eyes, ears, of the head and the body, smelling movements), vegetative (cardiovascular modifications, skin, galvanic response, pupillary and respiratory effects), electroencephalographic (change of brain waves, shift of the steady potential, modifications of the evoked potentials and driving responses), sensory (increase of sensitivity and of the fusion frequency of the sensory systems). The orienting reflex is characterized by non-specificity with respect to stimulus modality, a predominance of low and medium range stimulus intensity, selective extinction with respect to the features of the repeatedly presented stimulus, spontaneous recovery from the extinction with time, and temporary disinhibition after the presentation of a novel stimulus. The orienting reflex increases the effect of the stimulus on the organism, and differs from the defensive and adaptive reflexes, which tend to diminish or to eliminate the action of the stimulus. The difference between the orienting, defensive and adaptive reflexes can be demonstrated with a parallel plethysmographic recording from the finger and from the head during extinction procedure. The first presentation of sound, electric shock, cold and warmth, as novel stimuli, evokes similar orienting reflexes: constriction of the peripheral blood vessels and dilatation of the blood vessels of the brain. After a dozen presentations, the sound evokes no response because the orienting reflex has been extinguished; electric shock produces vasoconstriction in both areas because of the preservation of the defensive reflex; cold evokes stable parallel adaptive vasoconstriction, and warmth results in stable parallel vasodilatation. A change in sound frequency, or in the location of the shock, cold, or warmth, restores the orienting reflex, which is characterized by vasodilatation at the head and vasoconstriction at the finger (Vinogradova & Sokolov, 1957).

The orienting reflex was studied initially in Pavlov's laboratory as early as 1910. These studies were carried out on animals and were devoted mainly to external inhibition of conditioned reflexes resulting from the orienting reflex. The positive effect of the orienting reflex was recorded as its motor components. Bekhterev (1932) and Ivanov-Smolensky (1933) studied the motor and vegetative components of the orienting reflex in adults and children. Using polygraphic recording, Gantt emphasized the multicomponent structure of the orienting reflex. Anokhin showed the integration of such components into a functional system. Moruzzi & Magoun's (1949) studies of arousal (q.v.) reaction stimulated electrophysiological investigation of the orienting reflex. The polygraphic recording of EEG skin galvanic response, eye movements, and so on, resulted in the differentiation of phasic and tonic, local and generalized forms of the orienting reflex (Sharpless & Jasper, 1956). The extinction of the orienting reflex is selective in respect to all properties of the repeated stimulus: its intensity, quality, duration, order of presentation, and so on. The orienting reflex is evoked by matching the stimulus against the internal trace induced during repeated presentation of the stimulus. By gradually modifying each feature of the test-stimulus, it is possible to evaluate the configuration of the internal trace and demonstrate its resemblance to an applied stimulus. This means that the brain structures build up "the neuronal model of the stimulus" (Voronin & Sokolov, 1960). The individual units participating in the orienting reflex have different dynamics of habituation. The stable "feature detectors" were found in the principal sensory pathways. The "novelty detectors" were located in the non-specific thalamus, reticular formation and hippocampus. Hence, the "novelty detectors" of the hippocampus, which respond to a variety of stimuli, are characterized by rapid selective habituation, and demonstrate on the single unit level the properties of the orienting reflex (Vinogradova, 1965). The selective habituation of the novelty detectors seems to depend on the synaptic efficiency of the terminals of the "feature detectors" in converging on the "novelty detectors" (Horn, 1967; Sokolov, 1960). The matrix of the modified synapses represents the neuronal model of stimulus. The greater the difference between the matrix of synapses used and the applied test-stimulus, the greater the response of the novelty detectors, and the greater the orienting reflex.

Pavlov wrote, emphasizing the role of the orienting reflex in man: "It expresses itself finally in the cognitive drive, which creates science, and gives and promises unlimited orientation in the surrounding world". The question of cognitive motivation as an emotional aspect of the orienting reflex opens up a new perspective and a new branch of psychology.

Bibliography: Anokhin, P. K.: Problems of higher nervous activity. Moscow, 1949 (in Russian). **Id.:** A new conception of the physiological architecture of conditioned reflex. In: **Delafresnaye, J. F.** (Ed.): Brain mechanisms and learning. Oxford, 1961, 188–229. **Bekhterev, V. M.:** General principles of human reflexology. New York, 1932. **Gantt, W. H.:** Experimental basis for neurotic behaviour. New York, 1944. **Gershuni, G. V.:** Reflexes evoked by the action of external stimuli on the sense organs as related to sensation. Physiological Journal (USSR), 1949, *35* (Russ.). **Horn, G.:** Neuronal mechanisms of habituation. Nature, 1967, *215*, 707–11. **Ivanov-Smolensky, A. G.:** The methodology of the study of the conditioned reflexes in man. Moscow, 1933 (Russ.). **Moruzzi, G. & Magoun, H. W.:** Brainstem reticular formation and activation of the EEG. Clin. Neurophys., 1949, *1*, 455–73. **Pavlov, I. P.:** Lectures on conditioned reflexes, Vols. 1, 2. New York, 1928, 1941. **Sharpless, S. & Jasper, H.:** Habituation of the arousal reaction. Brain, 1956, *79*, 655–80. **Sokolov, E. N.:** Neuronal models and the orienting reflex. In: **Brazier, M. A. B.** (Ed.): The central nervous system and behavior. New York, 1960, 187–212. **Id.:** Perception and the conditioned reflex. Oxford,

1963. **Id.:** Mechanisms of memory. Moscow, 1969. **Vinogradova, O. S.:** Dynamic classification of the single unit responses in the hippocampus in sensory stimuli. J. of higher nervous activity (USSR), 1965, *15*, 500–12 (Russ.). **Id. & Sokolov, E. N.:** The relation of the vascular responses in the hand and in the head in some unconditioned reflexes in man. Sechenov Physiol. J. (USSR), 1957, *42* (Russ.). **Voronin, L. G. & Sokolov, E. N.:** Cortical mechanisms of the orienting reflex and their relation to the conditional reflex. Proc. Int. Conf. on EEG and higher nervous activity. EEG clin. Neurophysiol., 1960, Suppl. *13*, 335–44. **Voronin, L. G. (Ed.):** Orienting reflex and exploratory behavior. Washington, 1965. *E. N. Sokolov*

Originality. A factor of *divergent* thinking (q.v.) listed by J. P. Guilford. Tests for originality require of the subject unusual ideas and suggestions for unusual applications of particular objects. *G.K.*

ORT. See *Object Relations Technique.*

Orthogenesis. A term first applied by W. Haacke (1893) to the theory that evolution is directed along definite lines. According to Schindewolf (1942) it explains the persistence and regular progress of evolutionary trends which cannot be accounted for by natural selection. Rensch (1947) attributes all orthogenic trends to undirected mutation (q.v.), selection and allele (q.v.) loss through fluctuations in population size. There is no reason to assume the existence of autonomous evolutionary forces on a physiologically unknown basis.

Bibliography: Rensch, B.: Neuere Probleme der Abstammungslehre. Stuttgart, 1947. *K.Fi.*

Orthoscopic drawing. The drawings of small children often display general regularities of imaginative experience which might be described as *orthoscopic shapes* (Bühler, 1930). Faces are mostly drawn from in front, and hands so as to display the palms. In this way the child externalizes the nature of the things it grasps actively and affectively.

Bibliography: Bühler, K.: The mental development of the child. New York & London, 1930. *M.S.*

Oscillation. 1. A periodical fluctuation showing reversal of direction. **2.** In factor analysis (q.v.): the degree of non-trend variability in responses to the same item.

Oscillograph. An instrument for producing a visual record of electrical wave-forms.

Oseretzsky test. Used to determine the motor level of development in age groups from four to sixteen years. Since its publication in 1923 it has undergone many changes and amplifications. In 1931, Oseretzsky published a group test version. The most important revision is W. Sloan's "Lincoln-Oseretzsky Motor Development Scale" for the 6–13 age groups. For this test reliability scores of $r = 0.73$ to 0.94 have been recorded.

Bibliography: Oseretzsky, N.: Eine metrische Stufenleiter zur Untersuchung der mot. Begabung bei Indern. Z. f. Kinderforschung, 1925, *30*, 300–14. **Sloan, W.:** The Lincoln-Oseretzsky motor development scale. Genet. psychol. Monogr., 1955, *51*, 183–252. *P.S.*

Osmology. See *Osphresiology.*

Osphresiology. The science of odors and the sense of smell. Syn. *Osmology.*

Ossicular chain. See *Auditory ossicles.*

Ossification. Formation of or conversion into bone. Bone is formed not directly but through conversion of cartilaginous or connective tissue. Calcium and magnesium salts are deposited in the intercellular substance. As these inorganic salts absorb more Roentgen rays than does unossified tissue, the process can be observed *in vivo* by the radiographer. The point at which bone nuclei or ossification of individual symphyses occur have been exhaustively investigated. A child's "skeletal age" can be determined with the aid of a few X-rays. Comparison with actual age—as with IQ (q.v.)—indicates whether bodily development is premature or retarded.

Bibliography: Tanner, J. M.: Education and physical growth. London, 1961. *H.L.*

Ostwald color circle. A system of color gradations comprising twenty-four colors arranged along the periphery of a circle at regular intervals. Opposite each hue along the diameter lies its complementary. Any color of the scale can be obtained by mixing equal parts of the spectral radiation of two adjacent colors.

Bibliography: Ostwald, W.: Colour science. London, 1931. *G.Ka.*

Other-directedness (syn. *Other-directed behavior*). A term used by D. Riesman for the opposite of inner-directed, as produced by a strict upbringing. Other-directedness results from a permissive upbringing in which the peer group is important. See *Child psychology; Conformity.*

Bibliography: Riesman, D., *et al.*: The lonely crowd. New Haven, Conn., 1950. *W.D.F.*

Otis Self-Administering Test of Mental Ability. An early form of brief intelligence test (q.v.) used in selecting applicants for various practical occupations at three different levels. The test largely satisfies industrial criteria but predicts ease of learning requisite skills more accurately than the likelihood of success in an occupation. It differentiates ability mainly in the medium intelligence range. *F.G.*

Otolithic apparatus. See *Sense organs:* the ear.

Outgroup. A term originated by W. G. Sumner (1906). **1.** A group other than that to which the subject belongs, this being the "ingroup". **2.** Of two or more groups, that which (from the viewpoint of an investigation) is more or most rejected, or alien.

Out-of-the-body experience (abb. OBE). Hallucination in which the subject appears to see the world including his own body (= autoscopy) from a position in space other than the position of his eyes. Of special interest to parapsychologists on account of its alleged connection with *clairvoyance* (q.v.). Celia Green distinguishes two types of "ecsomatic" or out-of-the-body experiences: the "parasomatic", where the person appears to himself to be possessed of a second duplicate body; and the "asomatic", where he feels himself to be disembodied. Also known as "astral projection" (Oliver Fox) and "traveling clairvoyance" (nineteenth-century mesmerism). *J.B.*

Output. 1. A basic term in information theory (q.v.): the signal emitted by a source. **2.** *General:* energy released by a system in a given period. **3.** *Psychological:* the response that actually occurs. See *Input.* *H.W.*

Oval window (syn. *Fenestra ovalis; Fenestra vestibuli*). An oval aperture between the middle and inner ear, which transmits vibrations to the inner ear. See *Auditory perception; Sense organs.*

Overachievement. Where the intellectual level attained by a pupil is regarded as a yardstick for predicting scholastic success, departures from the performance expected are known as *overachievement* or *underachievement.* Those who do better than their intelligence would suggest are known as overachievers, those who fall short of expectations are underachievers. Both terms denote only the ratio of expected to actual performance and give no indication of scholastic success. Cases in which this is incommensurate with intellectual capacity show that success at school depends on non-intellectual personality traits such as study behavior, learning motivation, adaptability, anxiety, neuroses, or on social factors such as approachability, attitudes and group standards. *G.B.*

Overcompensation. Originally an Adlerian term for above-average performance of an initially inferior organ (e.g. Demosthenes mastered his stutter and became the greatest orator of his time). After use in conjunction with the notion of compensation (q.v.), the term has come to indicate any positive performance which goes beyond simple compensation, without necessary reference to "organ inferiority" or any feeling of inferiority. *W.Sc.*

Overdetermination. The overdetermination of, e.g. dreams and slips is their determination by (i.e. attribution to) *several* distinct (though unconscious) wishes and motives. *W.T.*

Overlearning. The continuation of practice beyond the point of the first accurate reproduction of all the material presented for learning. Overlearning improves short-term and long-term retention (q.v.). *G.H.*

Overtones. Tonal elements whose frequencies are whole multiples of the frequency of the fundamental. The interference between a fundamental and a finite number of overtones produces a clang (q.v.). See *Auditory perception; Music, psychology of.* *W.P.*

Overt response. An overt response, unlike a covert response (q.v.), is any that is observable by another person (e.g. a verbal statement). Experiments have shown that teaching programs calling for overt responses from subjects are often more successful than those restricted to covert responses. See *Instructional technology.*

Bibliography: Glaser, R.: Teaching machines and programmed learning, II. Washington, 1965. *H.I.*

Ovulation inhibitors (syn. *Fertility inhibitors*). Hormones which are used mainly as contraceptive agents and, in their current form, are taken orally for twenty to twenty-one days from the fifth day of the cycle. They contain substances related to progesterone (q.v.) known as progestins. Estrogens (ethinyl estradiol, mestranol) are added simultaneously, or later, to support the action and improve tolerance. The most important mechanisms of the action of ovulation inhibitors are: (*a*) reduced production of luteinizing hormone from the anterior pituitary (see *Glandotropic hormone*), inhibiting ovulation; (*b*) blockage of implantation of the fertilized egg in the endometrium (mucous coat of the uterus). A large number of psychological and autonomic side-effects appear during the first few months in individuals taking ovulation inhibitors. The most frequent psychic effects are dysphoria and reduced drive, especially where the preparation has a high progestogen content. Statistical investigations show that in spite of these side-effects the influence on relations with the partner is positive.

Bibliography: Drill, C. A.: Oral contraceptives. New York, 1966. **Gäck, I. D.:** Mood and behavioral changes associated with the use of the oral contraceptive agents. A review of the literature. Psychopharmacologia, 1967, *10*, 363–74. **Pincus, G.:** The control of fertility. New York, 1965. **Segal, S.:** Research in fertility inhibition. New Eng. J. Med., 1968, *279*, 364. **Tietze, C.:** Bibliography of fertility control, 1950–1965. New York, 1966. *W.J.*

Oxazepam (*Serax*). One of the benzodiazepine derivatives, related to chlordiazepoxide (q.v.) and investigated for use as a sedative in anxiety and tension states.

Oxytocin. A hormone produced by the posterior pituitary gland which stimulates uterine contraction and the release of milk by the mammaries, and is therefore implicated in childbirth.

Bibliography: Rudinger, J. (Ed.): Oxytocin, vasopressin and their structural analogues. New York, 1964. *G.D.W.*

P

Pain. Apart from the subjective feeling of hurt, objectively pain is the total set of responses an individual makes to a harmful stimulus. These responses may be described in neurological, physiological, behavioral, or psychiatric terms.

Neurologically, the adequate stimulus for pain is a change in physical energy great enough to produce actual or impending tissue damage. Responses occur in free nerve endings and are transmitted over A-delta and C fibers to the dorsal cord, where they typically synapse, cross, and project via the lateral spinothalamic tract to the parafascicular and intralaminar thalamic nuclei, but with such overlapping of innervation and branching of transmitting fibers that no constant relationship exists between stimuli and responses. Melzack & Wall (1965) propose a gating mechanism by the cells of the *substantia gelatinosa*, modulating the membrane potentials of the terminals of afferent fibers before these affect the first central transmission cells in the dorsal horn of the cord.

The pattern of physiological responses facilitates escape or avoidance behavior. Gastro-intestinal motility is inhibited, and there is increased pulmonary alveolar ventilation and oxygen consumption. The striated muscles display greater activity, with increased muscle tension and blood flow to the area of stimulation. Cardiovascular responses are complex and variable, with elevation of both systolic and diastolic pressures, pulse rate, stroke volume, and increased peripheral vasoconstriction.

Behaviorally, those with the greatest tolerance for pain are those whose perceptual judgments of other stimuli also err on the small side, whose body images have definite boundaries, who are extraverted, not neurotic, and have relatively low anxiety. Pain tolerance decreases with lowered sensory input and exposure to frequent pain experiences. Pain tolerance increases with motivation, voluntary submission to pain, attention to another task, and anxiety reduction.

Complaints of pain as a symptom are associated on the average with older, neurotic, and intropunitive patients who come from larger laboring class families and who have a history of painful experiences. Some ethnic groups encourage complaining of pain while others discourage it. "Exaggerated" expression of pain, associated with extraversion as well as ethnic membership, is unrelated to pain tolerance.

Pain responses not only protect the body but express affect and influence interpersonal relationships. Early pain experiences associated with punishment (q.v.) and loss of parental affection shape later pain responses expressing anxiety and guilt, mimicking the behavior of a child receiving punishment. Conversely, concern about loss or guilt can elicit pain sensations. Merskey & Spear (1967) describe such psychiatric models.

Sternbach (1968) analyzes the neurological,

physiological, behavioral and psychiatric descriptions of pain responses as well as a number of pain paradoxes, and presents an integration in terms of conditioning, sensory modulation and perceptual-coping styles, with implications for both research and clinical treatment.

Bibliography: **Melzack, R. & Wall P. D.:** Pain mechanisms: a new theory. Science, 1965, *150*, 971–79. **Merskey, H. & Spear, F. G.:** Pain: Psychological and psychiatric aspects. London, 1967. **Sternbach, R. A.:** Pain: a psychophysiological analysis. New York & London, 1968. *R. A. Sternbach*

Paired comparisons. A method for determining the rank ordering of a series of stimuli on some dimension, involving the presentation of all possible pairs of the stimulus items and having the subject compare them on the variable in question. Frequently used in studies of evaluative continua, e.g. esthetic preferences. See *Scaling*.

Bibliography: **Guilford, J. P.:** Psychometric methods. New York, [2]1954. *G.D.W.*

Pair formation (syn. *Pair bonding*). A pair may form for one mating season or for life. Pairing usually begins with sexual maturation, but a bond may be terminated during the juvenile phase. Even in the first year of their lives, grey geese form pairs which remain attached although they mature sexually only in the second year. Storks exhibit a kind of "impersonal pair formation": they become attached to the nesting site but not the partner. *V.P.*

Paleencephalon (syn. *Paleoencephalon*). The terms "palencephalon" and "neencephalon" (introduced by L. Edinger) do not represent clear distinctions. The first name is used for those parts of the brain which are older phylogenetically (i.e. all sections of the brain apart from the cerebral cortex and closely associated structures); nevertheless, since the old and new elements in the brain stem (*diencephalon*, *mesencephalon* and *rhombencephalon*) are all closely connected, the above-mentioned division of the vertebrate brain is not usual, in *comparative* anatomy at least. See *Neuroanatomy*.

Bibliography: **Giersberg, H. & Rietschel, P.:** Vergleichende Anatomie der Wirbeltiere. Jena, 1967.

K.Fi.

Paleopsychology. The application of psychological hypotheses to prehistory; according to S. E. Jelliffe, a subfield of paleobiology (the study of fossils as organisms). The reconstruction of the psychological characteristics of prehistoric man relies not only on archeological finds (e.g. shackling the dead: possibly an expression of a fear that the spirits of the dead would return), but very much on the results of cultural anthropology (q.v.), where the difficulties are those peculiar to any comparative reconstruction. *W.Sch.*

Palimnesis. Recollection, bringing back into one's memory (q.v.) what had escaped it. See *Reminiscence*. *H.W.*

Pallium. That area of the cerebral cortex (cerebral hemispheres) which partly covers the brain stem is the pallium, or *pars palliaris*. By definition, the stem ganglia and the brain stem do not form part of the pallium. *G.A.*

Palmograph. Apparatus to record fatigue produced by manual movements in a straight line. *F.-C.S.*

Pancreas. A gland situated in the back of the abdomen and having both endocrine and exocrine functions. As an exocrine gland, over twenty-four hours it forms and secretes 1–1.5 liters of digestive juices which pass through the pancreatic duct into the small intestine; it is controlled by the autonomic nervous system and humorally, e.g., by secretin. The digestive juices contain proteases such as trypsin, chymotrypsin, and peptidases for digesting protein, esterases such as lipase, lecithinase, phosphatase and cholinesterase for digesting fats and lipoids, as well as carbohydrases such as amylase and maltase to digest carbohydrates. For the endocrine function, which controls carbohydrate metabolism, see *Langerhans islet cells* and *Insulin*. *E.D.*

Panel interview. See *Interview*.

Panic. A sudden state of anxiety (q.v.) ("losing one's head"), which can lead to considerable reduction of cortical control of behavior in individuals, whether alone or in a crowd. The rapid spread of such states in a crowd is explained, *inter alia*, by the effects of ideomotor mechanisms (the "Carpenter effect"; see *Ideo-real law*). *H.D.S.*

Pansexualism. The doctrine that all human behavior can be explained in terms of sexual motivation, a point of view ascribed to Freudians by their critics. See *Depth psychology; Psychoanalysis; Sexuality*. *G.D.W.*

Paper-and-pencil tests. Those tests which require only question papers, answer paper and a pencil, since the testee himself does the writing. Such tests are usually appropriate for group testing. *P.Z.*

Papillary lines. Prominent lines on the surface of the hands and feet, especially at the ends of the fingers and toes, which differ in each individual and are used in dactyloscopy as a means of identification; they have little diagnostic value. See *Handlines*. *H.W.*

Paradoxical cold; paradoxical warmth. Sensations of cold and warmth can result from stimuli not objectively considered so. Paradoxical cold can result when a stimulus of about 42°C activates a cold receptor, and paradoxical warmth when a stimulus of about 30°C activates a hot receptor. *C.D.F.*

Paradoxical intention. In logotherapy (q.v.), this method consists of compelling the patient to do what he is afraid to do. A technique used especially in treating phobias (q.v.). Paradoxical intention has been used with less success in more serious cases of obsessional and compulsive *neurosis* (q.v.) such as anancasm (q.v.).

Bibliography: **Birnbaum, F.:** Frankl's existential psychology from the viewpoint of individual psychology. J. Indiv. Psychol., 1961, *17*, 162–6. **Frankl, V. E.:** Die Psychotherapie in der Praxis. Vienna, 1961.
J.L.I.

Paragnosia. Extrasensory perception (q.v.). The term is popular with Dutch parapsychologists but is seldom encountered in the English literature. *J.B.*

Paragnost. Person who shows special ability for paragnosia (q.v.) = *sensitive* (q.v.). *J.B.*

Paragraphia. Disturbed writing due to the selection of wrong words or letters. It must be distinguished from *paragrammatism* (abnormal use of grammar), and from *apraxic agraphia* (distorted lettering or format). It is parallel to the spoken disturbance of *paraphasia* (q.v.). The degree of paragraphic disturbance may vary with the mode of writing, i.e. spontaneous, copying, or to dictation. *B.B.*

Parakinesia. The state of having bizarre and clumsily executed movements which are varied, and not repetitive as are mannerisms and stereotypies. Found in catatonic schizophrenia and organic brain disease. *Parakinetic* *catatonia* was described by Leonhard as a sub-variety of catatonia with grimacing, constant movement of limbs and trunk, handling and touching. In organic brain disorders such movements may have a conspicuous quality, and various types are recognized, e.g. chorea and athetosis. Usually parakinetic catatonia has less pronounced movements and much less disturbance of purposeful actions. *B.B.*

Paralalia. Any speaking defect, especially the habitual substitution of one sound for another. This is not an aphasia (q.v.) but a disorder of the motor mechanisms of speech (q.v.). It may be due to an imbalance of the muscle co-ordinating system of the brain stem, cerebellum or cortex. *B.B.*

Paralexia. Form of sensory *aphasia* (q.v.), in which the ability to read is affected. *F.Ma.*

Paralgesia. Any disorder or abnormality of the sensation of pain; the term is most commonly used to denote a painful paresthesia (q.v.). *J.P.*

Parallax; parallax, binocular. If an observer moves, then objects at different distances from him will appear to move relative to each other, so that the more distant the object the smaller the movement. Hence in a train those objects near the track rush past us while those in the distance move hardly at all. This parallax effect is a major cue for depth perception and shows how crucial movement of the observer is in perception. *Binocular parallax* is an identical, but much smaller, effect due to the slight difference in position of our two eyes. *C.D.F.*

Parallelism, psychophysical. A philosophical doctrine originated by Leibniz: body and soul (mind) do not influence one another reciprocally, although every state of the one corresponds to a state of the other in accordance with the state of "pre-established harmony," i.e. they run parallel courses. This doctrine reappears as a heuristic attitude with Wundt (q.v.), Claparède (q.v.) and Flournoy, who admit that every psychic (mental) phenomenon has a physiological "concomitant", but do not allow that this implies *any causal relationship* between the two series of phenomena: mental processes and nervous processes represent two "sides" (aspects) of the same event. For gestalt psychologists, the bond of concomitance is, more exactly, that of isomorphism (q.v.) (Köhler). Piaget (q.v.) adopts the same viewpoint when it is necessary to establish the mental implication of physical causality. See *Mind-body problem.* *M.-J.B.*

Parallelogram illusion. See *Sanders' parallelogram illusion.*

Paralysis. 1. An inability to move any part of the body. If a limb is affected it hangs uselessly. Causes may be physical or psychological. Hypnotic paralysis of a limb is easily produced in certain subjects. **2.** An impairment or loss of sensory function of all or part of the body. However, *anesthesia* (q.v.) would seem to be a more appropriate term. *R.H.*

Paralysis agitans (syn. *Parkinson's syndrome*). The motor weakness found in patients suffering from *Parkinson's disease* (q.v.). *C.S.*

Parameters. Statistical values of theoretical distributions or of complete populations of data. They are usually symbolized in statistical literature by Greek letters (e.g. μ, σ). *G.Mi.*

Parametric tests. Statistical methods of testing samples of interval (q.v.) or ratio variables.

Only the statistics (q.v.) of such variables represent parameter estimations (of population distribution). They are distinguished in this respect from non-parametric methods (q.v.) and, when all the prerequisites are satisfied, they are more efficient. See *Statistical tests.* *G.Mi.*

Paramnesia. An inability to remember past events correctly. The memory is distorted by the inclusion of false details or by a wrong temporal reference. *R.H.*

Paranoia. *Paranoia* and *paranoid* no longer have the simple relationship of noun and adjective. Paranoid now means *deluded:* in popular usage in English-speaking countries it is a synonym for "persecutory". A paranoid idea is a delusion, and the qualifying adjectives "persecutory", "grandiose", "religious", and so on, can all be used to precede it. Its use is not restricted to schizophrenic illnesses.

Paranoid schizophrenia is a schizophrenic syndrome in which the predominant symptoms are delusions and usually hallucinations. Thought, volitional and affective disorders may be present, but not motor symptoms. The onset varies but is usually after youth. The prognosis is variable.

Paranoia is characterized by the sole presence of delusions, i.e. paranoid ideas. At one time it was thought to be distinct from the group of schizophrenias because it did not lead to deterioration. This is not now thought to be the case. See *Schizophrenia.* *B.B.*

Paranormal healing. Healing that is assumed to be mediated by some agency unknown to science. Includes such diverse practices as "laying-on-of-hands", prayer, immersion at a religious shrine, and so on. Must not be confused with mere unorthodox medicine. *J.B.*

Paranormal phenomenon. Any phenomenon that defies explanation in terms of acknowledged scientific principles. The two main classes of paranormal phenomena are the mental (see *Extrasensory perception*), and the physical (see *Psychokinesis*). *J.B.*

Paraphrasia. Disturbed speech due to the selection of wrong words. It is parallel to the written disturbance of *paragraphia* (q.v.). *B.B.*

Paraphysics. Branch of parapsychology (q.v.) dealing with the physical aspects of paranormal phenomena (q.v.) *J.B.*

Parapraxis. The faulty performance of a purposive act, another movement being substituted for that intended. Freud applied the term to such acts as slips of the tongue and the mislaying of objects. See *Freudian slips.* *J.P.*

Parapsychology. The objective study of paranormal phenomena (q.v.). Also known as *psychical research.*

1. *Status.* The status of parapsychology remains controversial. The question of the existence of any genuinely paranormal phenomena and, if so, what implications this has for psychology, still deeply divides the scientific community. There are those who refuse to concede to parapsychology any function other than that of exposing fraudulent pretensions, but there are also those who believe that it holds clues vital to the understanding of man and nature. Three reasons may be adduced for the present isolation of parapsychology from the main body of science and of psychology: (*a*) its failure to produce any repeatable experiment of an unequivocal kind; (*b*) the outrageous character of its claims; (*c*) the lack of any coherent theory of *psi* (q.v.). As a result, findings are rarely accepted for publication in the official organs of science and there are few full-time

workers in the field. Nevertheless, parapsychology has always been able to count upon the support of scholars and scientists, sometimes of great eminence, from a wide variety of backgrounds.

2. *History*. The traditional province of the paranormal is to be found in religious miracles, in witchcraft, in magic and in occult lore of all ages and places. To these were added in the course of the nineteenth century: (*a*) the clairvoyant (q.v.) manifestations associated with Mesmerism; and (*b*) mediumistic phenomena associated with the widespread cult of *spiritualism*. The first serious attempt to subject the supernatural in all its guises to the cold scrutiny of science can be identified with the founding of the Society for Psychical Research in London in 1882 under the leadership of Sidgwick, Myers and Gurney, who were inspired by the hope that something might yet be salvaged of the belief in the immortality of the soul which had been so rudely shaken by the confrontation of science and religion in Victorian England. The early period, which we may take as extending from c. 1880 to c. 1930, was thus largely dominated by the survival (q.v.) problem. This was the period of such internationally famous physical mediums as D. D. Home and Eusapia Palladino and such brilliant mental mediums as Mrs Piper and Mrs Leonard. During this period the first systematic attempts were also made to carry out tests of extrasensory perception on selected *sensitives* (q.v.). Among the most important were the series which the American novelist Upton Sinclair carried out with his wife as subject. It was after testing Mrs Sinclair that the English psychologist, McDougall (q.v.), the Professor of Psychology at Duke University, decided that the time was ripe to set up a parapsychology laboratory there, and appointed a junior colleague, J. B. Rhine (q.v.), to be its first director in 1927. This event inaugurated the modern era in parapsychology. Mention may also be made of another outstanding sensitive, Stefan Ossowiecki, a Polish engineer who flourished in Warsaw during the 1920s and 1930s. He is best remembered for his success in reproducing drawings and inscriptions presented in opaque sealed envelopes.

The second period, which extends from c. 1930 to the present day, has been dominated by the United States, thanks largely to Rhine and to such followers as J. G. Pratt. They started from the assumption that ESP was a universal property of mind and should therefore be demonstrable with unselected populations using standardized guessing procedures and appropriate statistical analyses (see *ESP cards*). Rhine's first book *Extra-Sensory Perception* (1934) made a greater impact on scientific opinion than perhaps any parapsychological publication before or since. This was due partly to the promise it held out of achieving repeatability, and partly to the fact that, in the early days, Rhine had the good fortune of finding several "high-scorers", among whom Pearce was the most notable. Ten years later "PK" (see *Psychokinesis*) was introduced to the world when Rhine claimed that his subjects could influence the fall of dice by their volitions alone. In Britain the ESP work was taken up by S. G. Soal, a mathematician. For some years he had no success whatever, but eventually he discovered two star subjects: Shackleton and Gloria Stewart. The series of tests which he ran on these subjects during the war years is rightly regarded as among the most important in the whole history of experimental parapsychology.

Another landmark was the announcement by Gertrude Schmeidler in 1945 of a differential scoring effect such that believers in ESP (*sheep*) tended to score above chance while sceptics (*goats*) tended to score below chance. This led to the discovery of *psi-missing* (q.v.) as a distinct phenomenon, and to a spate of studies dealing with the relationship between ESP scores and personality patterns.

On the Continent of Europe, the older tradition of qualitative tests on selected sensitives persisted; its two most active exponents were W. Tenhaeff of the University of

Utrecht and H. Bender of the University of Freiburg (Breisgau).

The high hopes felt at the start of the new era have not been fulfilled. Successive claims to have discovered consistent psi-effects have often failed to be corroborated while, for whatever reason, good subjects have become ever scarcer. Recent years have witnessed a revival of interest in some of the traditional areas of parapsychology. Hypnosis, survival, reincarnation, poltergeists, haunts, out-of-the-body experiences, psychometry and psychic photography, are all traditional topics that have been tackled afresh with new techniques and more sophisticated approaches. Furthermore, M. Ullman, a psychiatrist, has staked a claim for parapsychology in the growing field of sleep-research by setting up a "Dream Laboratory" at the Maimonides Hospital, New York, where some success has been attained in attempting to influence dream imagery telepathically.

At the present moment, parapsychology confronts us with the following unresolved paradox: on the one hand, the continuing accumulation of evidence and the fact that spontaneous phenomena are as frequent and insistent as they ever were makes this field impossible to ignore; on the other hand, the prospect of any degree of experimental control or any real theoretical understanding seems as remote as ever.

For recent surveys, see the special number of the *International Journal of Neuropsychiatry* (1966) and *Rao* (1966).

Bibliography: *Main journals:* J. Proc. Amer. Soc. Psychic. Res. (New York); J. Proc. Soc. Psychic. Res. (London); J. Parapsych. (Durham [N. C.]); Tijdschrift Parapsych. (Utrecht); Z. für Parapsychol. und Grenzgebiete der Psychol. (H. Bender) Berne & Munich, 1957–1968; Freiburg & Olten, 1970ff; Int. J. Neuropsychiatry. ESP Status in 1966. Special Issue No. 5, Vol. 12. Chicago, 1966.

Books: **Bender, H.:** Parapsychologie. Entwicklung, Ergebnisse, Probleme. Darmstadt, 1966. **Id.:** Unser sechster Sinn. Stuttgart, 1971. **Broad, C.D.:** Lectures on psychical research. London, 1962. **Dingwall, E. J.:** Abnormal hypnotic phenomena, Vols. 1–4. London, 1967–68. **Gauld, A.:** The founders of psychical research. London, 1968. **Rao, K. R.:** Experimental parapsychology. Springfield, 1966. **Rhine, J. B.:** Extra-sensory perception. Boston, 1934. **Id.** *et al.*: Extrasensory perception after 60 years. Boston, 1940, [2]1960. **Schmeidler, G. R. & McConnell, R. A.:** ESP and personality patterns. New Haven, 1958. **Sinclair, U.:** Mental radio. Springfield, Ill., [2]1962. **Soal, S. G. & Bateman, F.:** Modern experiments in telepathy. London, 1954. **Tenhaeff, W. H.:** De Voorschouw (fore-knowledge). The Hague, 1962. **Tischner, R.:** Über Hellsehen und Telepathie. Munich, 1921. **Vasiliev, L. L.:** (Eng. trans.) Experiments in mental suggestion. Church Crookham, Hants., 1963. **Warcollier, R.:** La télépathie. Paris, 1921 (Eng. trans., rev. ed.: Experimental telepathy. Boston, 1938).

J. Beloff

Parasympathetic. The parasympathetic division of the autonomic nervous system (q.v.) is concerned with energy conservation effects and conditions the *tropotropic* phase of an organism—characterized by rest, recuperation, nourishment and elimination. It has opposite effects to the sympathetic (q.v.) system, which is responsible for energy expenditure effects—the *ergotrophic* phase of ANS activity. Originating and control centers of the system are the diencephalon (q.v.), medulla, and sacral marrow. A distinction is made between a *cranial* part, embracing the vagus nerve and innervating the head, neck and thorax as well as parts of the abdomen, and a *sacral* part supplying chiefly the rectum and the urogenital system. Pharmacologically, the parasympathetic is stimulated by pilocarpine, muscarine (q.v.), acetylcholine (q.v.) and physostigmine (q.v.), and inhibited by atropine (q.v.) and nicotine (q.v.). See *Arousal; Emotion; Nervous system.* *E.D.*

Parasympathicolytic. Pertaining to the action of drugs which block or inhibit parasympathetic (q.v.) activity. *Parasympathycolytics:* such drugs. See *Anticholinergic*; *Psychopharmacology and ANS.* *W.J.*

Parasympathicomimetic. Pertaining to the action of substances (*parasympathicomimetics*) affecting the parasympathetic (q.v.) in a way comparable to its natural stimulation. Some important effects are: contraction of the pupils, lowering of heart rate, dilatation of blood vessels, increase in the motility of the gastro-intestinal tract, increase in the secretion of saliva and stomach juices; as a rule these substances do not show all these symptoms. Since complex interrelationships exist between the individual systems mentioned, there are usually quite definite patterns of effect. Most parasympathicomimetics also have central effects which interact with visceral (vegetative) ones. *Cholinergic* (q.v.) is roughly synonymous with parasympathicomimetic. See *Autonomic nervous system; Psychopharmacology and ANS.* *W.J.*

Parataxic mode. H. S. Sullivan's collective term for expectancies of purely personal implication in interpersonal relations. *Parataxic distortions* are said to occur when in social contacts earlier (especially infantile) imprinting (q.v.) is activated and projected onto the partner, who is thus made to appear other than he really is. The *prototaxic mode* is characteristic of the most primitive, infantile phase of human life; the *syntaxic mode* is a "consensually validated", mature mode of communication.

Bibliography: Sullivan, H. S.: The interpersonal theory of psychiatry. New York, 1953. *W.Sch.*

Parathyroid glands. The parathyroid consists of four lentil-sized glands and is located against the back of the thyroid. It produces the vital parathyroid hormone, which plays an important part in calcium metabolism. Over-secretion (*hyperparathyroidism*) can result in *osteitis fibrosa cystica generalisata* (von Recklinghausen's bone disease), with decalcification, reduced mechanical bone strength, and increased secretion of calcium by the kidney (kidney stones, etc.). Undersecretion (*hypoparathyroidism*) leads to tetany and muscular overstimulation with a tendency to tonic cramps—once frequently incident to thyroidectomy. *E.D.*

Pareidolia. See *Schizophrenia.*

Parental attitudes. Parental attitudes to the upbringing of their children may be conceived as a system of educational measures between which there is a kind of typological relationship. A distinction is generally made between sharply contrasting attitudes: authoritarian vs. free; rejection vs. indulgence; etc. A triple division is also possible: authoritarian—democratic—laissez faire. Parental attitude determines the child's degree of freedom to make his or her own decisions and adopt personal attitudes. The difference between concepts of child rearing depends on the varying educational targets: unconditional dependence (authoritarian education), unbridled self-development (laissez faire education), or responsible integration (democratic education). See *Attitude; Educator, personality of.* *H.Schr.*

Results of experimental studies. Several attempts at classification have been based on the observation of actual parent behavior. The dimensions given in the Fels Parent Behavior Rating Scales (Baldwin *et al.*, 1945, 1949; Champney, 1941; Roff, 1949) are best known, i.e. the child's dependence on the parents, or democratic attitude to upbringing control over children's behavior. Sears, Maccoby & Levin (1957) based their appraisal of parental attitudes on interviews with parents as well as on observations. Because of the vast expenditure involved in conducting observations and interviews, it is now becoming standard practice to print questionnaires (which are submitted to the parents themselves) in order to assess parental attitudes. Bronfenbrenner (1960) uses a questionnaire for children which allows them to comment on their parents. The individual parental attitudes are then evaluated by factor analysis (q.v.) of the intercorrelations between the "education" questions. According to K. Eyferth (in Herrmann, 1966, p. 24) the different factor analyses relating to parental attitudes should coincide with W. C. Becker's system, i.e. with the following three independent dimensions: "restrictiveness-permissiveness", "warmth-hostility", "calm-anxious emotional involvement".

Recently, educational psychology has devoted considerable attention to the study of parental attitudes. In addition to defining individual dimensions and devising methods to evaluate them, the relationship between parental attitudes and the personality of the child has been studied in detail. Attitude to upbringing may be considered both as a reaction to traits in the child and as the cause of specific features (see Seitz, Wehner & Henke, 1970).

Bibliography: Baldwin, A. L., Kalhorn, J. & Breese F. H.: Patterns of parent behavior. Psychol. Monogr. 1945, *58*, 1–75. **Id.:** The appraisal of parent behavior. Psychol. Monogr., 1949, *63*, 1–85. **Bandura, A. & Walters, R. H.:** Social learning and personality development. New York, 1963. **Bronfenbrenner, U.:** Freudian theories of identification and their derivatives. **Champney, H.:** The variables of parent behavior. J. Abnorm. Soc. Psychol., 1941, *36*, 525–42. **Herrmann, T. (Ed.):** Psychologie der Erziehungsstile. Göttingen, 1966. **Mitscherlich, A.:** Society without the father. London, 1969. **Roff, M.:** A factorial study of the Fels Parent Behavior Scales. Child Develpm., 1949, *20*, 29–45. **Schaeffer, W. S. & Bayley, N.:** Maternal behavior, child behavior and their intercorrelations from infancy through adolescence. Monogr. Soc. Res. Child Develpm., 1963, *28*, 1–127. **Sears, R. R., Maccoby, E. E. & Levin, H.:** Patterns of child rearing. New York, 1957. **Seitz, W., Wehner, E. G. & Henke, M.:** Zusammenhänge zwischen elterlichem Erziehungsstil und Persönlichkeitszügen 7- bis 8 jähriger Jungen. Z. Entwicklungspsychol. päd. Psychol., 1970, 3.
W.Se.

Parent-child relationship. Life together in the family (q.v.) situation has very marked psychological consequences for children and parents. Attachment, formation of a love concept, authority (q.v.), example, the development of conscience (q.v.), implantation of attitudes (q.v.), are some of the important aspects in this field. See *Child psychology; Conscience, Criminality.*

Bibliography: Bowlby, J.: Attachment and loss, Vol. 1: Attachment. London, 1969.
K.E.P.

Paresthesia. An abnormal cutaneous sensation.

Parietal lobe (*Lobus parietalis*). One of the lobes of the cerebrum, lying wholly beneath the parietal bone. In front of it is the frontal lobe, below it the temporal lobe, and behind it the occipital. It is marked off anteriorly by the central sulcus (*sulcus centralis*), posteriorly by the parieto-occipital sulcus (*sulcus parieto-occipitalis*), and inferiorly by the posterior ramus of the lateral sulcus (*sulcus lateralis*). Its most important area is the post-central gyrus (*gyrus postcentralis*) which is the common sensation area (sensory area) for the body: its cortex contains the ends of the afferent pathways bringing information about pressure, contact, pain and temperature. *G.A.*

Paris School. A school of hypnosis research (see *Hypnosis*) formed under the direction of J.-M. Charcot (1825–93) in Paris toward the end of the nineteenth century (as distinct from the Nancy School, q.v.). It had great influence on the development of psychotherapy (q.v.) and the theory of neurosis. Freud (q.v.) studied under Charcot.

Bibliography: Owen, A. R. G.: Hysteria, hypnosis and healing: the work of J.-M. Charcot. London, 1972.
H.-N.G.

Parkinsonism. A disorder reminiscent of the symptoms of Parkinson's disease (q.v.). It occurs in arteriosclerosis of the cerebral blood vessels (arteriosclerotic Parkinsonism), after epidemic encephalitis (postencephalitic parkinsonism) and after hypoxic damage (e.g. sustained in attempts to hang oneself). In certain doses, neuroleptics (q.v.) may cause (reversible) parkinsonism as a side-effect. *Toxic parkinsonism* may occur after (carbon monoxide) poisoning. *C.Sch.*

Parkinson's disease (syn. *Parkinson's syndrome; Idiopathic parkinsonism; paralysis agitans*). A (hereditary) degenerative disease in the basal ganglia of the brain, the characteristic symptoms of which usually appear after the age of forty: slow, ineffective movement, weakness and heightened tonus (muscular rigidity, "cogwheel rigidity"), the body bent stiffly forward, a shuffling walk ("festination"), fixed expression, trembling (see *Tremor*) of the extremities and sometimes of the head. Medication often alleviates the suffering involved. Neurosurgery (see *Stereotactic methods*) may often have a favorable effect on rigor and tremor. *C.Sch.*

Parkinson's law. A part-satirical, part-sociological attempt to express in terms of rules certain phenomena in the social areas of administration and industry; e.g.: every official or employee wants to increase the number of his subordinates but not his rivals; officials or employees make work for one another; administrators expand their domains without regard to the amount of work that has to be done. This last suggestion, in particular, has not been shown to be universally true of large organizations (see Blau & Scott, 1962, for a comparative study).

Bibliography: Blau, P. M. & Scott, W. R.: Formal organizations. San Francisco, 1962. **Parkinson, C. N.:** Parkinson's law and other studies in administration. Boston & London, 1957. *G.R.W.M.*

Parthenogenesis. The reproduction of progeny from unfertilized eggs. The number of chromosomes (q.v.) is maintained either because it is not reduced by division when the egg is formed, so that the eggs are diploid (q.v.), or because haploid (q.v.) eggs are produced by haploid individuals (e.g. drones), in which, when sex cells are subsequently formed, no division by reduction takes place. *H.Sch.*

Partial correlation. A parametric method of determining the correlation between two variables when the influence of other variables on the observed correlation has been excluded. If the influence of a variable (3) on the correlation between the variables (1) and (2) is to be eliminated, the partial correlation is determined according to the following formula:

$$r_{12.3} = \frac{r_{12} - r_{13}r_{23}}{\sqrt{(1 - r_{13}^2)(1 - r_{23}^2)}}.$$

In psychology, excluded variables frequently deal with age. See *Correlational techniques.* *G.Mi.*

Partial instincts (syn. *Part-instincts; Component instincts*). Described by Freud as component instincts and instinct gratifications. According to Freud, exhibitionism, voyeurism, sadism and masochism are partial instincts of the sexual instinct and of striving for sexual gratification. More far-reaching are Freud's ideas about the differentiation and channelling of instincts and libido into an increasing number of partial instincts or instinctual derivatives. According to Toman, this kind of differentiation of motives forms part of the psychic development of the individual. See *Drive; Instinct.* *W.T*

Part-instincts. A psychoanalytic concept: specific manifestations of the libido (q.v.) in conscious experience, e.g. particular urges, desires, wishes. See *Partial instincts.* *G.D.W.*

Participation. 1. Taking part or involvement in an activity. **2.** The greater (though still limited) involvement of personnel in company policy decisions (which affect them directly). See *Industrial psychology; Occupational psychology.* *G.R.W.M.*

Partners, animal. Some vertebrates "become engaged" and "get married". Even fish, e.g. perch, form strong bonds which last a considerable time. Grey geese provide a good example of a lasting "marriage" (K. Lorenz).

It is a postulate that the individual partners should know one another. Some birds which return to the same breeding site for many years, e.g. storks, are "married" to the locality. *K.Fi.*

Part-whole relation. This became significant for psychology when the gestalt school showed that there are wholes (e.g. a melodious succession of notes) which cannot be equated with the "sum" of isolated parts. The non-summativity of a whole consists in the fact that a change in or removal of one part affects all other parts.

Bibliography: **Rausch, E.:** Über Summativität und Nichtsummativität. Psychologische Forschung, 1937, *21*, 209–89. *P.T.*

Passion. Extreme emotion of any kind, but particularly sexual love. Strong enthusiasm for a person, thing or activity. *G.D.W.*

Past, experience of the. That form of personal experience oriented to individually experienced, temporally distant events. Past experiences are usually embedded in a more or less richly structured reference system whose reference points represent striking external events and intimately self-proximate experiences. See *Memory; Reminiscence.* *P.T.*

Patellar reflex (syn. *Knee-jerk reflex*). The involuntary reaction of the thigh extensor muscle, *quadriceps femoris*. It is elicited by a sharp blow on the patellar tendon, causing the muscle and its muscle radii (acting as extension receptors) to stretch slightly. The patellar reflex is used by neurologists and psychiatrists to study the function of the spinal cord and general nervous excitability. The latter is increased when central inhibitory mechanisms are eliminated, and decreased when there is damage to the afferent neurons. *E.D.*

Pathognomy. 1. (syn. *Pathognomics*). The study of, e.g., emotion (q.v.) in terms of externally apparent *expression* (q.v.). **2.** The recognition of disease (in terms of its essential signs).

Pathology. The general theory of disease, embracing the theory of cause (etiology), origin and development (pathogenesis), outward forms and signs (symptomatology), nosology (pathological anatomy). *H.W.*

Patriarchy (syn. *Patriarchate*). A social system or type of society in which the family group is dominated by an elderly male, or more generally, a society in which males are dominant over females (ant.: *matriarchy*). *G.D.W.*

Pattern. 1. Any specimen, sample, instance or example. **2.** An archetype (q.v.). **3.** Form, in the sense of (*gestalt*) *structure* (see *Ganzheit*). **4.** More often met with in modern psychology in the sense of *model* (q.v.), *prototype*, or *frame of reference*.

Pattern analysis: the identification of test items which are in some (specific) way concordant.

Pattern discrimination: response by S. to the whole structure rather than one or more of its parts. *J.M.*

Pattern Perception Test. E.g.: L. S. Penrose's paper-and-pencil intelligence test with sixty-seven items. Every problem (item) consists of five diagrams. S. has to find those four of the five diagrams which make up a complete pattern. The test has eight grades of difficulty. It can be used with all testees from the age of six, irrespective of intelligence (q.v.). Verified data on reliability and validity are not available. See *Progressive Matrices.* *F.Ma.*

Pauli Test. ("Work curve" according to E. Kraepelin.) Standardized by R. Pauli (1938, 1943) and W. Arnold (1951–61). The test provides information about psychological capability (concentration, quality of performance, etc.) and dynamics of performance (time taken, amount done, fatigue, etc.). The testee has to add numerals from one to ten as rapidly and accurately as possible, and at three-minute intervals make a mark to show how much he has done. Retest reliability (one month) = 0.96, and for error count = 0.68.

Bibliography: Arnold, W.: Der Pauli-Test. Munich, [4]1969. *P.G.*

Pause. In industrial psychology: an interval; an important factor (especially in studying fatigue, q.v., monotony, q.v., and saturation, q.v.) when used in the sense of an intentional or unintentional interruption of some activity in order to improve or restore mental or physical capability. The effect of a pause, whether an interruption or a change of work, depends especially on the nature of the activity, number and length of pauses, time when pause is taken (preferably before great fatigue), and the worker's personality type (see *Traits; Type*). *W.L.*

Pavlov, Ivan Petrovich. B. 14/9/1849 in Rjasan (Russia); d. 27/2/1936 in Leningrad. Pavlov studied first animal physiology and then medicine at the University of St. Petersburg. His doctoral dissertation (1883) was on the function of the heart muscles. He then studied for two years under C. Ludwig in Leipzig and P. Haidenhain in Breslau. In 1890 he was appointed Professor of pharmacology at the Military Medical Academy of St. Petersburg, and Director of the department of physiology at the newly founded St. Petersburg Institute of Experimental Medicine. From 1895 to 1924 was Professor of physiology at the Academy, and from 1924 until his death in 1936 director of the Physiological Institute set up by the Russian Academy near Leningrad. He was awarded the Nobel Prize in 1904 for his research into digestion.

Pavlov was much influenced by I. M. Sechenov's belief in the reflexological nature of all psychic activity. Together with Sechenov, he regarded his field as essentially physiology and not psychology. He thought that psychology would never become an independent science. He also tried to remove all psychological terms from his own and his collaborators' vocabulary. He believed that the physiology of higher nervous activity could be investigated only if the usual psychological concepts and introspective data were replaced by a completely objective method.

Pavlov's historical importance lies in his discovery and exploration of the conditioned reflex. With this, Pavlov laid the foundations of behaviorism (q.v.) and the development of modern research into learning and learning theory (q.v.) in psychology; in fact, we are indebted to Pavlov for the fundamental notions and methodology of this area. As, e.g., an APA survey has shown, Pavlov is thought of as the scientist, after Freud who most strongly influenced modern psychology. The discovery of the conditioned reflex resulted from Pavlov's experimental research into the activity of the digestive glands, which he carried out on dogs. He found that the secretion of saliva and stomach juices occurred not only when eating began, but started before then, at the sight of the food, or even when the keeper's footsteps were heard. From these observations Pavlov concluded that a stimulus (sight of food) that was originally inadequate for eliciting a reflex can, when repeatedly associated in time with a stimulus (taste of food), be sufficient to elicit the reflex (salivation). The natural, adequate stimulus he referred to as the *unconditioned stimulus*, and the reflex occurring as a natural response to it he called the *unconditioned reflex*. The originally neutral, inadequate stimulus he called the *conditioned stimulus*, and the reflex appearing as a response, the *conditioned reflex* (see *Conditioning, classical and operant*).

Pavlov followed up this discovery by

systematic studies of the most diverse conditioning phenomena which have become the foundation for almost all learning theories: *extinction*, *reinforcement*, *generalization*, *discrimination*, etc. As a result of these investigations, Pavlov concluded that—in contrast to the genuine reflexes, which are mediated *subcortically*—the conditioned reflexes are mediated at a cortical level. He also based a theory of cortical excitation and inhibition on his results; he used this theory to explain and integrate his findings in neurophysiological terms—in this he differed from American learning theorists. Pavlov also extended his experiments into the field of psychopathy (q.v.). By conflict (q.v.) situations produced experimentally in which animals were confronted with tasks they could hardly perform but could not evade (e.g. discrimination between very similar sounds, one of which signified "food", the other "no food"), he created phenomena resembling neuroses which (in 1923) he called "experimental neuroses". (See *Neurosis.*) See *Orienting reflex; Soviet psychology.*

Main works: Collected works (in Russian). Moscow & Leningrad, 1951 (German translation: Gesammelte Werke. Berlin, 1953–55). The work of the digestive glands. New York, 1902. Conditioned reflexes: an investigation of the physiological activity of the cerebral cortex. Oxford & New York, 1927. Lectures on conditioned reflexes, Vols. 1 & 2. New York & London, 1928/41. The reply of a physiologist to psychologists. Psychol. Rev., 1932, *39*, 91–127. Selected works (in English). Moscow, 1955. Autobiography. In: Selected works (*op. cit.*), 41–4. Experimental psychology and other essays. New York, 1957.

Bibliography: Bekhterev, V. M.: General principles of human reflexology. New York, 1932. **Frolov, I. P.:** Pavlov and his school. London, 1937. **Gantt, W. H.:** Ivan P. Pavlov. In: **Pavlov, I. P.:** Lectures on conditioned reflexes, Vol. 1. New York & London, 1928, 11–31. **Wells, H. K.:** Ivan P. Pavlov. New York, 1956.

W.W.

Pavor. 1. Terror or fright. **2.** *Pavor nocturnus:* Intense fear felt during the night, especially by children. It is sometimes so strong that a child is completely terrified and upset, and can scarcely be reassured. The suggestion of latent epilepsy has very rarely been borne out. Children and adults with *pavor nocturnus* are generally "neurotic", and to some extent anxiety-prone. But this does not mean that a child who has suffered from *pavor nocturnus* for some years will necessarily become an anxiety neurotic. See *Anxiety; Neurosis.* **3.** *Pavor diurnus:* the occurrence of the same or a similar reaction during the day. *J.L.I.*

Pearson's correlation coefficient. See *Product-moment Correlation.*

Pearson, Karl. B. 1857, in London; d. 1936 in Coldharbour, Surrey, England. He read mathematics at Cambridge; appointed in 1884 to the Chair of Applied Mathematics at University College, London, where he remained until his retirement in 1933. In 1906, he took charge of the Eugenics Record Office founded by Galton at U.C.L. and combined in 1911 with the Biometric Laboratory to form the Department of Applied Statistics; he was its first director, and the first occupant of the Chair of Eugenics. Together with Galton and the zoologist Weldon, Pearson founded in 1901 the first biometric journal (*Biometrika*) and, in 1925, *The Annals of Eugenics.*

Pearson made a large number of valuable contributions to biological and psychological statistics. He introduced the term "standard deviation" (q.v.) and the symbol σ into statistics (q.v.), and developed the χ^2 test for goodness of fit. Continuing the work of Galton, who had a far-reaching influence on him, he devised a formula for calculating (Pearson's) *product-moment correlation* (q.v.), worked out the method of multiple correlation, the formula for finding the probable error of correlation coefficients (q.v.), methods to calculate the correlation in the absence of normal distributions (q.v.), the contingency coefficient (q.v.), the biserial correlation coefficient (q.v.), and published tables to facilitate statistical calculations. Pearson's aim was not merely to develop sophisticated statistical theories, but to produce methods that would make it possible to investigate biological and psychological data and relationships. He applied his methods to contemporary social questions, such as the causes of tuberculosis, alcoholism, mental retardation, etc. The results contradicted current opinion, and Pearson often had to endure attacks and hostility from medical and public authorities. Despite his considerable contribution to statistical techniques, the fact that his work awakened widespread interest in the use of statistical methods in diverse fields of science is probably more significant. See *Correlational techniques*.

Major works: The grammar of science. London, 1892; [3]1911. Mathematical contributions to the theory of evolution. London, 1894–98. Tables for statisticians and biometricians. London, 1914.

Bibliography: **Morant, G.** (Ed.): A bibliography of the statistical and other writings of Karl Pearson. Cambridge 1939. **Pearson, E. S:** Karl Pearson: an appreciation of some aspects of his life and work Cambridge, 1938.

W.W.

Pedagogy. 1. Educational science (q.v.). **2.** The study of educational methods. **3.** Classroom technique and didactic methodology. The term is usually reserved for this narrower area of education, although its use is tending to disappear altogether in the English-speaking world, where the distinction between, say, *educational psychology* (q.v.) and *pedagogical psychology* is preserved in the more precise demarcation of *instructional technology* (q.v.) from the educational sciences proper.

Bibliography: **Aebli, H.:** Didactique psychologique, application à la didactique de la psychologie de J. Piaget. Paris, 1951. **Andrey, B. & Le Men, J.:** La psychologie à l'école. Paris, 1968. **Ausubel, D. P. & Robinson, F. G.:** School learning. New York, 1970. **Claparède, E.:** L'éducation fonctionnelle. Neuchâtel, 1931. **Clark, D.:** The psychology of education. Ontario, 1967. **Dewey, J.:** Democracy and education. New York, 1916. **International Study of achievement in mathematics.** A comparison of twelve countries. Stockholm & New York, 1967. **Jadoulle, A.:** La psychologie scolaire. Paris, 1965. **Leontiev, A.:** Éducation et développement psychique. Recherches internationales à la lumière du marxisme, 1961, *28*, 3–33. **Les conditions de vie et de travail de l'ecolier.** Enseignements élémentaire, secondaire, technique. Enfance, from 1965, *1*, *2*, *3*. **Mialaret, G.:** La recherche en psycho-pédagogie. Revue de l'Enseignement Supérieur No spécial consacré à la psychologie, 1966, *2–3*. **Id.:** La formation psychologique des éducateurs. Bull. de Psychologie, 257, XX, 10–15, No Spécial de 1967, 631–635. **Piaget, J.:** Psychologie et pédagogie. (La réponse du grand psychologue aux problèmes de l'enseignement.) Paris, 1969. **Simon, B.:** Intelligence, psychology and education: a Marxist critique. London, 1971. **Skinner, B. F.:** The technology of teaching. New York, 1968. **Snyder, H.:** Contemporary educational psychology. New York, 1968. **Thorndike, E. L.:** Educational psychology. New York, 1903. **Wall, W. D.:** Psychological services for schools. Hamburg, 1956. **Wittrock, M. & Wiley, D. E.:** The evaluation of instruction. New York, 1971.

G.M.

Pedantry. 1. Excessive love of order and formalism. **2.** Fussiness and excessive attention to trifles, and inattention to essentials. **3.** Excessive attention to private interests and inattention to general matters. **4.** The ostentatious (needless) display of (needless) learning. An imprecise term in personality assessment.

Bibliography: **Sacherl, K.:** Die Pedanterie. Göttingen, 1957.

K.Pa.

Pederasty. Anal intercourse with a young male. **2.** Generally (and imprecisely): male *homosexuality* (q.v.).

Pediatrics. Branch of medicine dealing with all the diseases of children (usually up to the age of fourteen to sixteen years). *E.D.*

Pedology. The scientific study of biological, psychological, sociological and philosophico-anthropological aspects of the life and development of children. Recently the emphasis has been on the healthy child's *physiological* (morphological, functional, mental and psychological) development from birth to the end of puberty. See *Child psychology; Development; Differential psychology; Educational psychology.* *M.Sa.*

Pedophilia. 1. Sexual deviation from a socially prescribed, instinctual or sexual object (an unrelated and socially mature partner of the opposite sex). **2.** Sexual attraction for, and a preference for sexual intercourse with, children of one's own and/or of the opposite sex. Pedophilia centers upon the immaturity of the child, and is less a matter of the child's sex. The degree of immaturity is more important in homosexual than in heterosexual pedophilia. Pedophilia is a social problem since sexual use of, or intercourse with, children is a punishable offense in most countries. *H.M.*

Pemolin(e). A psychotropic (q.v.) substance, belonging to the CNS-stimulant group. In small doses, pemoline enhances performance for several hours without any manifest increase in subjective activation and motor excitation (in contrast to most other stimulants). Pemoline was investigated pharmacologically and psychologically as early as 1956, and in 1966 began to interest psychopharmacological learning research after the suggestion (Glasky & Simon) that it promoted RNA formation. There is, however, no proof of specific improvements in learning and recall, beyond a general increase in activation. Positive and negative findings are approximately equal, both in humans and in lower animals. No definite influence has been shown in cerebral disorders with reduced recall.

Bibliography: Lienert, G. A. & Janke, W.: Pharmakopsychologische Untersuchungen über 5-phenyl-2-imino-4-oxo-oxazolidin. Arzneimittel-Forsch., 1957, *7*, 436–9. **Weiss, B. & Laties, V. G.:** Behavioral pharmacology and toxicology. Ann. Rev. Pharmacol., 1969, *9*, 297–326. *W.J.*

Penis envy. 1. According to Freud, a girl's transient reaction (commencing in the early genital stage, q.v.) to the discovery of the anatomical difference between sexes. Both girl and boy are said to tend to regard the female organ as "incomplete". It is claimed that if the child has a traumatic experience at this early stage, a more realistic conception of anatomical sex difference and of the sexual role may be delayed, envy of and rivalry with men may be prolonged, and impaired female sexual response (especially frigidity, q.v., and vaginism, q.v.) may result. The notion is contested. **2.** A woman's desire to possess a penis, or to be a man. *W.T.*

Pentylenetetrazol (*Metrazol; Cardiazol; Pentetrazol*). A psychotropic substance, and one of the analeptics (q.v.); used in low dosage for, e.g., circulatory weakness or to stimulate breathing. Higher doses produce convulsions; formerly used for depression therapy. Relatively small doses, even in some normal subjects, produce an EEG spikes pattern. More recently, pentylenetetrazol has been used in psychopharmacological research into animal memory. When an injection is given up to thirty minutes after learning, there is a favorable effect on consolidation.

Bibliography: McGaugh, J.: Drug facilitation of memory and learning. In: **Efron, D. H.** (Ed.): Psychopharmacology 1957–1967. Washington, 1968. *W.J.*

Percentile. (Syn. *Centile*). **1.** A point in a distribution of scores "up to which" a certain percentage of cases can be counted. For example, fifty per cent of the scores, cases, individuals, etc., of a distribution lie in the first half up to the fiftieth percentile (the median). The twenty-fifth and seventy-fifth percentiles are also known as the first (lower) and third (upper) quartiles. Each of the divisions of a ranked distribution would contain one hundredth of the scores, and a percentile would be any point dividing the distribution into such divisions from 1 to 100. **2.** One of the actual divisions. See *Centile.* *G.Mi.*

Percentile score. The percentile score of a value, often used in standardizing test methods, denotes that percentage of those cases of a distribution below a specific raw score. *G.Mi.*

Perception. 1. *Definition.* Perception is a psychological function which (by means of the *sense organs,* q.v.) enables the organism to receive and process information on the state of, and alterations in, the environment.

2. Perception plays a very important role in *cognition theory* (q.v.), i.e. the theory of knowledge; the performance of the perceptual apparatus to a large extent determines both the information an organism has regarding its environment and the limits of direct cognition (knowledge). Theoretical studies have been made of the relationship between perception and "objective" reality; between perception and other psychological functions (understanding, q.v., motivation, q.v., etc.); and between experience and *a priori* cognitive categories. The main areas of experimental research are: the relationship between (absolute and differential) stimulus thresholds and one's picture of the environment ("*mundus sensibilis*"), the limitation of possible experience by sensory defects, illusions, etc.

3. *Historical development of perception research.* The nineteenth-century psychology of elements conceived perception as a process responsible for coordinating elementary sensations in terms of images and ideas which were then incorporated (generally as "apperceptions") into higher conceptual systems. However, under the influence of gestalt psychology (see *Ganzheit*), it was soon found that the perception of a total situation could not be interpreted as the simple summation of individual elements, but that the perception of totalities (gestalts or *Gestalten*) followed special gestalt laws. This distinction between element and gestalt psychology has been superseded now that the principles of systems analysis and cybernetics enable a "whole" or "totality" to be considered as a "system of reciprocally organized parts." Recent research has been characterized by a "perspectivist" approach, in which the basic conditions, specific properties, performance and mechanisms of perception as well as the development and learning capacity of the individual are postulated as interacting, but are usually examined separately and considered in relation to other functions of the organism. (See *History of psychology.*)

4. *Theories of perception.* The methodological differences (associated with *empiricism,* q.v.) between elemental and holistic psychology were accompanied by theoretical disagreements (associated with *nativism,* q.v.). Efforts to overcome these antitheses led, in the main, to the following theoretical assumptions: (*a*) in transactionalism (A. Ames, W. H. Ittelson), gradient theory (J. J. Gibson) and ecological probabilism (E. Brunswik), perception is considered to be largely dependent on external circumstances, i.e. an object is always viewed in relation to a physically determinate total situation; (*b*) in the theories of functional dependence (expectation theory: D. O. Hebb; motivation theory: G. Murphy, J. S. Bruner, L. Postman; hypotheses theory: Bruner, Postman, Bresson; adaptation theory: H. Helson; saturation theory: W. Köhler, H. Wallach, etc.), perception is viewed as a resultant of inner (physiological and psychological) states and therefore as dependent in many respects on the individual's "set"; (*c*) in the genetic and constructivist (learning and development) theories (actual, local and micro-genesis: F. Sanders, H. Werner; ontogenesis, constructivism, learning psychology: H. Werner, J. Piaget, E. J. Gibson, etc.), perception is interpreted as a dynamic process in which the physical characteristics of a stimulus configuration and the performance of an (active) individual together determine what is perceived and how it is perceived.

5. *Prospects.* Although they overlap at many points, the abovementioned theories are purely "local" in nature. At best, collections of scientifically confirmed data and a few partial explanations are available; this information is seldom contradictory but generally incomplete. It gives some impression of the possibilities and development of perception in

the individual but cannot provide a full picture or model of the percipient, functioning organism. See *Attention; Auditory perception; Neuroanatomy; Visual perception.*

Bibliography: Allport, F. H.: Theories of perception and the concept of structure. New York, 1955. **Boring, E. G.:** Sensation and perception in the history of psychology. New York, 1942. **Bruner, J. S., Goodnow, J. S. & Austin, G. A.:** A study of thinking. New York & London, 1956. **Brunswik, E.:** Perception and the representative design of psychological experiments. Berkeley & Los Angeles, 1956. **Dember-William, N.:** The psychology of perception. New York & London, 1965. **Dixon, N. F.:** Subliminal perception. New York, 1971. **Epstein, W.:** Varieties of perceptual learning. New York & London, 1967. **Forgus, R. H.:** Perception. New York & London, 1966. **Foss, B. M.:** Brain and behaviour: Perception and action. Baltimore, Maryland, 1969. **Fraisse, P.:** The psychology of time. New York & London, 1963. **Gibson, E. J.:** Principles of perceptual learning and development. New York, 1969. **Gibson, J. J.:** The senses considered as perceptual systems. New York, 1966. **Id.:** The perception of the visual world. Boston, 1950. **Gross, C. G. & Zeigler, H. P.:** Readings in physiological psychology. New York & London, 1969. **Hock, P. H. & Zubin, J.:** Psychopathology of perception. New York & London, 1965. **Klix, F.:** Elementaranalysen zur Psychophysik der Raumwahrnehmung. Berlin, 1962. **Koch, S.** (Ed.): Psychology: a study of a science, Vol. 1: Sensory, perceptual and physiological formulations. New York, 1959. **Laing, R. D., Phillipson, H. & Lee, A. R.:** Interpersonal perception. London & New York, 1966. **Linschoten, J.:** Strukturanalyse der binokularen Wahrnehmung. Göttingen, 1956. **Metzger, W.** (Ed.): Handbuch der Psychologie: Wahrnehmung und Bewusstsein, Vol. 1, 1. Göttingen, 1966. **Id.:** Gesetze des Sehens. Frankfurt, [2]1953. **Piaget, J.:** The mechanisms of perception. London, 1969. **Rock, I.:** The nature of perceptual adaptation. New York & London, 1966. **Sanford, F. H. & Capaldi, E. J.:** Wahrnehmung, Lernen und Konflikt. In: Moderne Psychologische Forschung, Vol. 2. Berlin & Basle, 1971. **Sheppard, J. J.:** Human color perception. New York, 1968. **Sinclair, D.:** Cutaneous sensation. London & New York, 1967. **Vernon, M. D.:** The psychology of perception. Baltimore, Maryland, 1962. **Id.:** Perception through experience. London, 1970. **Wathen-Dunn, W.:** Models for the perception of speech and visual form. London & Cambridge, Mass., 1964. **Welford, A. T. & Houssiadas, L.:** Contemporary problems in perception. London, 1970. **Zusne, L.:** Visual perception of form. New York, 1971.

R. Droz.

Perception, motivational. See *Motivational perception.*

Perception, social. See *Social perception.*

Perceptron. A learning system which processes *information* (q.v.) and may be regarded as a technical model of organic nervous networks. It can be used to simulate component processes of human cognition. Basically, simulation of cognition is achieved by arranging features into meanings: input sets are so classified as to produce the same output: i.e. from the multiplicity of signal patterns recorded and selected, a network of sensory elements forms invariant arrangements of signs to which, after the evaluating apparatus has passed through the learning phase, that meaning is assigned which possesses maximal similarity (see *Isomorphism*). Earlier assignments ensure a constant improvement in criteria. The perceptron can be used as a "diagnostic" machine for "feature detection" (i.e. for pattern recognition) in esthetics, and so on. (See *Cybernetics and psychology; Machine learning; Simulation.*)

Bibliography: Farley, B. G. & Clark, W. A.: Simulation of self-organizing systems by digital computer. Trans. IRE Professional Group on Information Theory, 1954, September, 76–84. **Rosenblatt, F.:** The perceptron: a probabilistic model for information storage and organization in man. Psychol. Rev., 1958, *65*, 386–408. **Id.:** Principles of neurodynamics. Washington, D.C., 1962. **Uhr, L.:** Pattern recognition. New York, 1966.

M.Ba.

Perceptual defense. If the subject is presented with different stimulus words on the tachistoscope, despite the similar structure of certain words he is not always able to say with the same speed what he has seen. Longer reaction times are observable particularly with "taboo" words, even when they contain the same number of letters as corresponding neutral words. This phenomenon is known as "perceptual defense"; no satisfactory explanation has yet been offered. See *Attitude; Avoidance behavior.* *R.Hä.*

Perceptual field. The part of the area in front of the testee which he can see at any given time without moving his eye (with uniform fixation: looking straight ahead); the area may be that which can be seen by one or both eyes (monocular or binocular perceptual field). The limit of the perceptual field differs for movements and colors, and depends on the state of adaptation; in general the following figures are quoted: upwards, max. 60°, downwards, max. 70°, nasal, max. 60°, temporal, max. 90°. By contrast, the field of vision (visual field) is the area which can be perceived by a moving eye (without moving the head). See *Visual perception*. *F.C.S.*

Perceptual speed. J. F. Brown's studies show that in the image-retina system the perceived speed is dependent on a number of circumstances: (*a*) the size of the object; with an identical objective speed and identical section of the field of vision, a smaller object apparently moves faster; (*b*) the size of the section of the field of vision concerned: assuming the presence of two objects of identical size, that located in the smaller field of vision appears to move faster; (*c*) distance between the eye and object: the more remote object apparently moves faster by comparison with the nearer object and the distance traveled on the retina.

Bibliography: Brown, J. F.: Über gesehene Geschwindigkeiten. Psych. Forschung, 1928, *10*, 84–101.

E.U.

Perceptual world. See *Merkwelt*.

Percipient. 1. Any individual with the power of *perception* (q.v.). **2.** The subject or receiver in a telepathy (q.v.) experiment.

Performance. 1. Behavior (q.v.). **2.** The completion of an intended or promised action. **3.** The observable exercise of a skill (see *Motor skills; Practice*). See *Abilities; Learning theory*.

Performance tests. Tests in which the subject must perform some nonverbal manual task requiring intellectual ability. Since Seguin's 1846 formboard, various test-batteries have been constructed. (See *Arthur Scale; Formboards; Pintner-Patterson Scale of Performance Tests*). Performance tests are especially useful for subjects with some speech disability. Performance in these tests decreases with age more than in verbal tests. *R.M.*

Perimeter. An apparatus for mapping the sensitivity of different parts of the retina to various visual stimuli. Stimuli are moved from the periphery inward along a semicircular arm which rotates about its center, the eye being fixated on its radial center. *Color zones* on the retina derived in this way suggest that while black and white (brightness vision) extend well toward the periphery, blue and yellow occupy smaller, more central parts of the visual field, and red and green are more foveal still. Mapping the retina in this way is called *perimetry*. *G.D.W.*

Periodic fluctuations. Changes (depending on the time of day) in physiological functions, especially body temperature, blood pressure, breathing and skin resistance, linked with the increase and decrease of physiological and psychological power in respect to performance. Investigations show in general, that, within a twenty-four hour cycle there will at any time be a performance minimum at about 3 and 15 hours, and a performance maximum at about 9 and 18 hours. Changes in physiological functions at certain times during the day are conditioned by, e.g., certain meteorological influences (day-night), but also sociological and ecological influences, and awareness of time. See *Time, psychology of*. *W.L.*

Periodic insanity. An obsolete term. See *Circular psychosis*.

Periodicity. Return of events at regular intervals. There are psychological phenomena which appear episodically or periodically (e.g. manic-depressive psychosis, q.v., circular psychosis, q.v., periodic drinking), but popular belief in the periodical recurrence of certain events (sleep-walking, centennial calendar) is thought by some to be so suggestive as to cause the event to take place. *H.J.A.*

Peripheral nervous system. All those nervous elements outside the brain and spinal cord: chiefly the afferent (sensory) and efferent (motor) nerves (nerve fibers). *E.D.*

Peripheral neurosis. Schultz (1958) classified the neuroses as *peripheral* or *nuclear*. The first category embraces all kinds of fairly superficial disturbances which are environmentally caused or provoked. The nuclear neuroses are more deeply anchored in the personality. The classification indicates a more favorable prognosis for the peripheral neuroses, for which Schultz recommended suggestive therapy, including autogenic training (q.v). See *Neurosis*.

Bibliography: **Schultz, I. H.:** Die seelische Krankenbehandlung. Stuttgart, 1958. *J.L.I.*

Peripheral vision. Outside the field of central vision, i.e. beyond an area subtending about two degrees of visual angle, the retina is filled with *rod* receptors which become more widely spaced as they approach the periphery. Hence peripheral vision has lower acuity than central vision, and is monochromatic. However there is a greater sensitivity to movement in the periphery. In the dusk, when only the rods are active, peripheral vision may be superior to central vision. *C.D.F.*

Permanent memory. Many theorists distinguish short-term and long-term memory, and separate physiological mechanisms are hypothesized to account for them. One widely held theory is that short-term memory corresponds to some kind of neural *activity*, whereas long-term memory is a function of *structural* changes in the brain (anatomical or biochemical). Although the distinction is probably arbitrary, memories do vary in permanency; the more salient psychological events, or those experiences which are likely to be relevant to future adaptation are committed to permanent memory. Such a classification of experiences and their differential assignment to memory storage has been suggested as an important function of dreaming. See *Dream; Memory; Reminiscence*. *G.D.W.*

Permissive. **1.** Granting freedom. **2.** Not hindering.

Permissive society: a (usually pejorative) term for various trends toward greater sufferance (though not necessarily approval) of freedom of choice in, e.g., dress, sexual mores, educational method, reading, entertainment.

Permutation. Any one of the possible arrangements or sequences of a number of items.

Persecution mania (syn. *Persecution, delirium of*). A lay term for people dominated by persecutory delusions A misuse of the term "mania" (q.v.). See *Paranoia; Schizophrenia*. *B.B.*

Perseverance. There is no clear distinction between persistence (q.v.) and "perseverance", which formerly indicated "perseveration" (q.v.), but is now clearly differentiated from it, since the latter means involuntary persistence, whereas perseverance implies conscious control of the attention (q.v.) (Maller, 1944, 182).

Bibliography: **Maller, J. B.:** Personality tests. In: **Hunt, J. McV.** (Ed.): Personality and the behavior disorders, Vol. 1. New York, 1944. *E.Mi.*

Perseveration; perseveration tendency. A term used by the psychiatrist Neisser (F. Soelder) to cover the various pathological forms of "clinging to earlier functions" (especially for too long a period) and for the frequent recurrence of some (sensory, motor or linguistic) mode of activity. H. Ziehen (1898) and G. E. Müller and A. Pilsecker (1900) carried out the first experimental investigations of perseveration (as "reproduction without association") in children and normal adults (see *Memory*). Gross (1901) first tried to give perseveration a theoretical foundation as a "cerebral secondary function", i.e. an unconscious after-excitation of brain cells which differs in degree with each individual and is important for the associative processing of experience. In the Netherlands, Wiersma (1906) and Heymans & Brugmans (1913) worked out methods for determining individual differences in the "sensory" secondary function (e.g. flicker-fusion frequency) and in "motor" perseveration tendency (writing letters in alternating sequence); these methods are still used, though with certain modifications. Differences in perseveration tendency (or "general mental inertia") were also looked upon as an important personality factor in German typology (O. Külpe, E. Kretschmer, G. Pfahler) and in British research into intelligence and personality (Spearman, 1927). In later investigations of the relationships between different measurements of perseveration (Eysenck, 1947; Cattel & Tiner, 1949), no general perseveration factor was found, but a number of factors were—the most important of which is often thought to be identical with "rigidity" (q.v.).

Experimental investigations of perseveration in language (Mittenecker, 1953) and the information-theoretical evaluation of perseveration-like response sequences (Mittenecker, 1960) are now being interpreted along learning-theoretical lines (disequilibrium of the intensities of response tendencies).

In clinical psychology, the significance of perseveration in brain damage (Breidt, 1969) and among epileptics (Remschmidt, 1968) is under empirical and theoretical investigation. See *Attitude; Trait; Type.*

Bibliography: Breidt, R.: Perseveration und Hirnverletzung. Phil. Diss. Tübingen, 1969. **Cattell, R. B. & Tiner, L. G.:** The varieties of structural rigidity. J. Pers., 1949, *17*, 321–42. **Eysenck, H. J.:** Dimensions of personality. London, 1947. **Gross, O.:** Die cerebrale Sekundärfunktion. Leipzig, 1902. **Heymans, G. & Brugmans, H.:** Intelligenzprüfungen mit Studierenden. Z. angew. Psychol., 1913, *7*, 232–326. **Mittenecker, E.:** Perseveration und Persönlichkeit. Z. exp. angew. Psychol., 1953, *1*, 5–31, 265–84. **Id.:** Die informationstheoretische Auswertung des Zeigeversuchs bei Psychotikern und Neurotikern. Z. exp. angew. Psychol., 1960, *7*, 392–400. **Remschmidt, H.:** Das Anpassungsverhalten der Epileptiker. Phil. Diss. Tübingen, 1968. **Soelder, F.:** Über Perseveration. Neurol. Centralbl. 1895, 14, 958. **Spearman, C.:** The abilities of man. London, 1929. **Wiersma, E.:** Die Sekundärfunktion bei Psychosen. J.f. Psychol. Neurol., 1906, *8*, 1–24.

E. Mittenecker

Persistence. Continuation in voluntarily undertaken and directed activities; a special aspect of achievement motivation (q.v.) including readiness to bear discomfort or pain (q.v.) in the pursuit of one's own or one's adopted goals.

Bibliography: French, J. W.: The validity of a persistence test. Psychometrica, 1948, *13*, 271–7.

M.A.

Person. The concept of a person might be said to be the starting point of humanistic psychology (q.v.). Etymologists trace "person" back to the Etruscan word *phersu*, meaning a being existing between the world and the underworld. The connection of *persona* (q.v.) with *mask* (Rheinfelder, 1928) also implies humanity, particularly in the sense of body and form; the intellect (or spirit) is also referred to sometimes. In the legal terminology of antiquity, "person" denoted anyone, of any rank, whether freeman or slave.

From ancient times the essential nature of a person was recognized as the unique substance of a nature endowed with reason. In the person-nature relationship there are possibilities of reference to the material and social world and to the realm of the spiritually transcendent. Heidegger asserts that man is fundamentally an active being-in-itself before which there was possible being-in-the-world. The "person" is conceived as a center of activity in the sense of man as the basic possibility of *personal encounter* (primary dialogue). Man as person is oriented to the community, in which his dignity unfolds to the full.

Drives and associated experiences are the foundation of all human experiences, and include (according to a classification principle derived from the notion of *personal* encounter) those rooted in the *self* (see *Drive*), those rooted in the *ego* (q.v.), and environmentally grounded drives, affects and moods. The concept of a "person" can be only partly or occasionally (as, e.g., in the Jungian sense) identified with the concept of a "self" (q.v.).

Whereas awareness of the *I* (*ego consciousness*, q.v.) is reflective, and represents a higher stage of development, awareness of the self is an existential fact. Not every person is *de facto* "ego-conscious", for man as an embryo or when mentally deranged is also a person. The "person" is the foundation of the process of development and unfolding which is revealed in character (q.v.) and personality (q.v.). Empirical factors and observations (e.g. the need to compensate for feelings of inferiority; conscience, q.v.) demonstrate the existence of a psychic control system within which the personal self has a psychological location. The person-mind relationship is characterized in that the mind enables the person to transcend self, and the person provides the basic moral principle of experience.

Being a person signifies an indivisible, unique and therefore non-replicable unity in human existence. It implies a living entity which embodies a complete whole and does not normally disintegrate during life; and it signifies the individual, living, entire bodily and psychic foundation of man as being (see *Mind-body problem*). Being a person concerns the "vital-biological" level, the "id" level (or *endothymic basis*, q.v.), and is related to the mental or spiritual superstructure, in that (at least) this "intellectual" structure can influence the person inwardly. (See *Strata theory*.) Recently the personal constitution of human existence has been systematically postulated by that branch of the humanistic psychology movement represented by C. Bühler. "Man as a machine or man as a person?" (A. L. Kovacs) might be thought of as the essential question of the moment.

Bibliography: Arnold, M. B. & Gasson, J. A.: The human person. New York, 1954. **Arnold, W.:** Person, Charakter, Persönlichkeit. Göttingen, [3]1970. **Bühler, C. & Massarik, F.** (Eds.): The course of human life. New York, 1968. **Chiang, H. M. & Maslow, A. H.** (Eds.): The healthy personality: readings. New York, 1970. **Eysenck, H. J.:** Psychology is about people. Harmondsworth & New York, 1972. **Langon, R. I. & Goodstein, L. D.:** Personality assessment. New York, 1971. **Lersch, P.:** The levels of the mind. In: **David, H. P. & Bracken, H. von** (Eds.): Perspectives in personality theory. New York, 1957, 212–7. **Rheinfelder, H.:** Das Wort "Persona". Beih. Zschr. f. roman. Philol., 1928.

W. Arnold

Persona. From Latin *persona* = an actor's mask. A term used by C. G. Jung (q.v.) for the "external" character which enables an individual to interrelate with the world around him so that he arrives at a kind of compromise between his individual psychological constitution (individual character) and the collective situation. This presupposes an ability to adapt to society.

Bibliography: Guilford, J. P.: Personality. New York, 1959.

J.L.I.

Personal data sheet. A list of questions about S. to be answered in writing by S. In particular, the questionnaire developed by R. S. Woodworth during World War I in order to isolate soldiers with psychological peculiarities, and considered to be the prototype of the present personality inventories. See *Questionnaires*.

H.H.

Personalism. 1. Any idealistic or "existentialist" philosophy or psychology which emphasizes the importance and uniqueness of the human individual. See *Existence analysis; Humanistic psychology; James, William; Person; Personality*.

2. A philosophico-political movement of thought developed and advanced in France by Emmanuel Mounier and put forward by the journal *Esprit*. Personalism offers a realistic psychology of the whole man apprehended in vital situations, while stressing the dynamic interaction of the individual as person (the personal aspect) with the community (the social aspect). "A person is a spiritual being constituted as such by his adhesion to a hierarchy of values, freely adopted, assimilated and lived, by a responsible self-commitment and by a constant conversion; he thus unifies all his activity in liberty and develops, moreover, by means of creative acts, his own unique vocation" (Mounier).

Bibliography: Marcel, G.: Metaphysical journal. London, 1952. **Mounier, E.:** Traité du caractère. Paris, 1947. **Id.:** Personalism. London, 1952. *P.M.*

Personality. Man is intensely interested in his own and other people's personalities. The portrayal of personalities and their interactions is the main theme of the literary, dramatic and visual arts. But despite the discussions of human nature by philosophers throughout history, the study of personality was until recently ignored by most psychologists. Partly this was due to its complexity, partly because psychology was more concerned with processes common to all organisms, such as perception and learning, which could be investigated in the laboratory, than with the whole man and his motivation. Therefore the first systematic work was carried out by psychiatrists such as Kraepelin, Janet, Freud and his followers, using clinical and intuitive rather than scientific methods.

Currently we find a welter of different theories of personality, based on different methods and constructs. There is little agreement on the data to be studied, still less on a definition. Allport listed fifty definitions in 1937, and surveys such as Hall and Lindzey's or Wepman and Heine's describe at least fifteen approaches. However, many theorists might accept (though others would reject) the following: personality is the relatively stable organization of a person's motivational dispositions, arising from the interaction between biological drives and the social and physical environment. The term implies both cognitive and physical attributes, but usually refers chiefly to the affective-conative traits, sentiments, attitudes, complexes and unconscious mechanisms, interests and ideals, which determine man's characteristic or distinctive behavior and thought. Some of the major divergent views are as follows:

1. *Social stimulus value*. Since classical times, personality has often been applied to the impression made on others rather than to the inner self. In lay usage a business director has a forceful, an actress a glamorous, personality. Clearly everyone plays varied roles, and tries to display a personality acceptable to those he meets; even his self-concept may be self-deceptive (Goffman, 1956; Vernon, 1964).

2. *Nomothetic*. Psychometrically inclined authors such as Cattell, Eysenck and Guilford accept the reality of stable personality traits of varying degrees of generality, but point out that they cannot be directly observed; they must be inferred from consistencies in speech and behavior. Their aim, then, is to isolate the main dimensions of personality through factor analysis (q.v.) of correlations between tests. Hence personality is conceived as a person's scores on all the measurable factors or common traits. (In addition Cattell proposes that unique traits and their organization can be quantified by Q or P techniques, that is, factorizing persons or occasions.) Emotional instability or anxiety and extraversion-introversion are widely accepted, but otherwise there is little agreement as to what are the major factors, or how they can be reliably measured.

3. *Idiographic*. German writers such as Dilthey and Spranger, together with most clinical psychologists, stress the need for intuitive understanding of the unique organization of each individual personality, as against measurement of his attributes. This approach is inevitably subjective, and Freudian constructs of unconscious motives are particularly

open to criticism as mythical entities, even if useful in theory-building and in psychotherapy (q.v.) (Meehl, 1954).

4. *Behaviorism* (q.v.). May and Hartshorne's studies of character and other attempts to measure general traits yielded such low correlations between tests of the same trait as to suggest that personality differences consist of specific habits of response to specific situations. This accorded with contemporary S-R learning theories. Followers of Skinner went further by dispensing wholly with inner dispositions or drives, claiming that we should study only what is directly observable and operationally definable (Lundin, 1961). Such views are important as a backing for behavior therapy (q.v.), which treats neurotic symptoms by conditioning procedures, without regard to hypothetical mental causes. Modern cybernetic behaviorism (q.v.), however, is more flexible in allowing for mediating processes or "plans": even the self might be conceived as a super-plan which guides its own reactions by estimating their likely reinforcing consequences (cf. Mischel's account of social learning theory).

5. *Anti-reductionism.* Both Freudians and learning theorists like Dollard and Miller trace back motivation to tension reduction of the biological drives and the effects of early learnings in infancy. Constitutional temperamental differences are also commonly recognized, for instance, by typologists such as Sheldon. Adler (q.v.) was the first to stress positive striving toward the future rather than determination by the past; and Allport (q.v.) argued that new interests and motives can be acquired at any time of life, becoming "functionally autonomous". The notion of the individual as creating his own personality fits in with current emphasis on curiosity and competence as basic motives, with Horney's and Fromm's accent on social influences, and with Rogers' and Maslow's theories of self-actualization as the fundamental principle in personality growth and development.

6. *Organismic and field theories,* such as Lewin's, Goldstein's and Angyal's, attribute the organism's behavior to its interaction (q.v.) with the surrounding field, rather than to its fixed dispositions. Lewin's pictorial representation of tension systems, valences and barriers in the total "life space" (q.v.) has been influential mainly in social psychology (q.v.). But Murray's theory of "press" has proved useful in conceptualizing environmental factors in personality. (See *Need.*)

7. *Phenomenology* (q.v.) considers personality wholly in terms of the person's perceptions of himself, of other people and his environment. Motivation, learning and adjustment are ascribed to man's need to resolve incongruities in his phenomenal field, and refashion his maladative interpretations. This approach, originating with Husserl, was developed by Snygg and Combs, and is implicit both in Rogers' self-theory and Kelly's psychology of personal constructs. Likewise, existentialism (though more a literary and philosophic movement than a personality theory) holds that man is free to strive for meaning and self-realization in a hostile and purposeless universe.

8. *Culture pattern theories.* Anthropologists and sociologists tend to think of personality as the product of the social groups (q.v.) in which people are reared. Thus Malinowski's and Mead's observations of the non-universality of the Oedipus complex (q.v.) and adolescent instability show that different cultures meet man's needs in different ways and lead to different modal organizations. While accepting that personality always develops in a particular social milieu (q.v.), psychologists are still more concerned with variations from the cultural norm.

9. *Current research into personality.* The search for more reliable means of personality assessment in clinical diagnosis and counseling, and in the selection of college students or employees, continues unabated, though with little signs of success. Rather such work reveals the weaknesses and biases of our instruments, whether objective tests or questionnaires, projective devices or interview techniques. Observational studies of children's

behavior and measurements of self-concepts and attitudes are making fruitful contributions to developmental psychology, though these tend to show a disappointing lack of simple causal associations between child-rearing practices or parental attitudes and such personality variables as aggression (q.v.), anxiety or authoritarianism. (See *Child psychology*.)

More carefully controlled work on therapeutic procedures and their effectiveness should help to throw light on the conflicting theories outlined above. Another noticeable trend is the growth of interdisciplinary research, since neurologists, geneticists, multivariate statisticians, and social anthropologists have much to contribute both to clinical and psychometric personality research (cf. Norbeck, *et al.*, 1968). Work on perceptual defenses and cognitive styles, and on the effects of anxiety (q.v.) and other personality variables on learning (q.v.), suggests that the gap between experimental and personality psychologists is at last being bridged.

Bibliography: Allport, G. W.: Pattern and growth in personality. New York, 1961. **Cattell, R. B.:** The scientific analysis of personality. Harmondsworth, 1965. **Dollard, J. & Miller, N. E.:** Personality and psychotherapy. New York, 1950. **Eysenck, H. J.:** The scientific study of personality. London, 1952. **Goffman, E.:** The presentation of self in everyday life. Soc. Sci. Res. Centre Monogr., 1956, *2*. **Guilford, J. P.:** Personality. New York, 1959. **Hall, C. S. & Lindzey, G.:** Theories of personality. New York, [2]1970. **Hartshorne, H. & May, M. A.:** Studies in the nature of character, Vol. I: Studies in deceit. New York, 1928. **Kelly, G. A.:** The psychology of personal constructs. New York, 1955. **Lundin, R. W.:** Personality: an experimental approach. New York, 1961. **Meehl, P. E.:** Clinical versus statistical prediction. Minneapolis, 1954. **Mischel, W.:** Personality and assessment. New York, 1968. **Murray, H. A.:** Explorations in personality: an interdisciplinary appraisal. New York, 1968. **Norbeck, E., Price-Williams, D. & McCord, W.:** The study of personality: an interdisciplinary appraisal. New York, 1968. **Rogers, C. R.:** Client-centered therapy. Boston, 1951. **Sheldon, W. H. & Stevens, S. S.:** The varieties of temperament. New York, 1942. **Snygg, D. & Combs, A. W.:** Individual behavior. New York, 1949. **Vernon, P. E.:** Personality assessment: a critical survey. London, 1964. **Wepman, J. M. & Heine, R. W.:** Concepts of personality. New York, 1963.

P. E. Vernon

II. The origins of the concept "personality" are not wholly clear, and definitions vary in emphasis. G. W. Allport conceives personality as the dynamic arrangement in the individual of those psychophysical systems which determine his unique adaptations to his environment. H. Thomae sees personality as the inclusive concept of all events which comprise an individual life history. J. P. Guilford regards an individual's personality as a unique structure of traits. R. Linton views it as the organized structure of psychological processes and states which concern the individual. For H. A. Murray, it is the controlling organ of the body, effecting change from birth to death.

The concept of *character* (q.v.) is, in the widest sense, that of the unique nature or *uniqueness* of a being. Character in the psychological sense is sometimes equated with *personality*. Both are expressions used by (almost) every psychologist today; yet no psychologist can say precisely what they really mean. Nevertheless, the concept of character has emphasized the static element more than that of personality, which has stressed the functional, dynamic, self-evolving and processual aspects. H. Rohracher characterizes the totality of the developed basic psychological disposition (*anlage*, q.v.) as the human *personality*, and the totality of all psychological *anlagen*—developed and undeveloped—as the *character*. According to Rohracher, a man's personality is that which has emerged from his character to date under the influence of his environment. His character comprises everything that (in the psychological sense) he *can* become.

Whereas science has tried to arrange human characters in typologies (see *Type*), research oriented more to the study of personality has emphasized the nature-nurture, innate traits vs. environment polarity. In his twin studies (q.v.), K. G. Gottschaldt would seem to have shown that endothymic personality traits such as affectivity, fundamental mood and vital drive, are more strongly determined by inheritance than is the intellectual superstructure.

On the basis of his twin studies, H. J.

Eysenck would allow considerable significance to heredity in the determination of personality type. The extent and direction of the environmental influence exerted on an individual depends on his genetic inheritance.

Considerable difficulties are encountered in the empirical investigation of the effects of environment on the development of the whole personality, when attempts are made to determine whether a man's personality has changed under the influence of specific environmental events. In the USA, the predominant view is that the human personality is almost wholly changeable and is formed by life history and social influences. In Europe there is more conviction that the fundamental structure of personality is relatively constant.

It can also be said, by and large, that American theoreticians view personality in terms of external behavior, superficial traits, motor components, interhuman relations and modifiability, and investigate mainly the interaction between the individual and the social environment (culture). European psychologists, on the other hand, tend to favor concepts such as profound disposition (see *Depth psychology; Person*), determination by constitution (see *Traits, Type*), fixed structure, relative independence from society, and relative unchangeability.

Bibliography: Bales, R. F.: Personality and interpersonal behavior. New York, 1970. **Eysenck, H. J.:** The structure of human personality. London, 1970. **Id. & Eysenck, S. B. G.:** Personality structure and measurement. London, 1969. **Geiwitz, P. J.:** Non-Freudian personality theories. New York, 1970. **Lynn, R.:** An introduction to the study of personality. London, 1971. **Maher, B. A.** (Ed.): Progress in experimental personality research, Vol. 5. New York, 1970. *T. Takuma*

Personality inventory; personality questionnaire. See *Questionnaires; Traits; Type.*

Personality research. A branch of psychology dealing with research into personality (q.v.) apart from abilities (q.v.). Sometimes known as "characterology" or "characterological research" in the German literature. See *Character; Differential psychology; Traits; Type.*

B.H.

Personality tests. A number of methods which do not test potential intelligence and performance, but affectivity, social attitudes, interests, proneness to neuroticism, etc. The first such tests were the questionnaires used with U.S. soldiers in World War I. Buros (1971) distinguishes projective and non-projective methods, and Anastasi projective (q.v.) methods, from questionnaires dealing with interests, attitudes and personality, the last mentioned concept here referring particularly to such dimensions of personality as extraversion-introversion and neuroticism. There are also "objective personality tests". See *Objective tests; Psychodiagnostics; Questionnaires.*

Bibliography: Anastasi, A.: Psychological Testing. New York, 1961; **Buros, O. K.:** (Ed.): Tests in print. New York, [2]1971. **Langon, R. I. & Goodstein, L. D.:** Personality assessment. New York, 1971. *G.N.*

Personality theory. A system of suppositions which represents the frame of reference in explaining or describing the human behavior and experience relevant to some particular definition of personality. Most such personality theories (in contrast to other psychological theories) refer to the whole person.

Bibliography: Hall, C. S. & Lindzey, G.: Theories of personality. New York, [2]1970. **Ruitenbeek, H. M.** (Ed.): Varieties of personality theory. New York, [2]1971. *D.Ba.*

Personality traits, constancy of. The degree to which personality traits remain unchanged in individual expression over a period of time. The same subjects take a number of tests demanding the same criteria, and their behavior throughout the tests is analyzed. See *Factor analysis; Traits; Type.* *K.P.*

Personalization. 1. Experience of one's own psychological activity, as contrasted with depersonalization. **2.** Caruso used the word more dynamically to denote the ultimate aim of psychotherapy (q.v.) or even of human life in itself. See *Conscience; Personalism; Religion, psychology of.* *J.L.I.*

Personal tempo. The preferred speed of an individual in performing motor actions with no set time limit. An important criterion in experimental typology; it was investigated particularly frequently in connection with E. Kretschmer's typology. E.g.: in a test involving free tapping on a board, leptosomes (q.v.) on average showed a higher personal tempo than athletic types and pyknics (q.v.). On the other hand, when greater accuracy was required, athletic types were the slowest. See *Kretschmer, Ernst.* *M.A.*

Personal unconscious. See *Jung; Unconscious.*

Personification. 1. The attribution of personal or human qualities to. e.g., an abstraction, a natural force (the sun as Helios on the sun chariot), or a concept (wisdom as a woman with a snake and a mirror). **2.** An individual as an especial embodiment or expression of, e.g., a quality. *W.Sch.*

Personnel management. A general term for the department in an organization responsible for, and the activity of, personnel counseling, motivation, and so on. Such a department is often put in the care of a director of the firm. See *Industrial psychology; Occupational psychology; Vocational guidance.*

Bibliography: Korman, A.: Industrial and organizational psychology. New York, 1971. **Miner, J. B.:** Personnel psychology. New York, 1969. **Sokolik, S. L.:** The personnel process: line and staff dimensions in managing people at work. New York, 1970.

G.R.W.M.

Personnel rating. Determining workers' aptitude, performance and patterns of behavior, including motives, needs, availability for certain jobs and possibilities of promotion. If a personnel rating indicates the level of competence, it can then be decided whether further training, retraining or transfer is appropriate. See *Industrial psychology; Vocational guidance.* *G.R.W.M.*

Personnel selection. The systematic selection of individuals according to certain criteria, especially with regard to their fitness for certain vocations, positions or activities (see *Vocational guidance*). Such criteria deal almost always with physical or psychological abilities, and usually with scholastic or vocational knowledge and experience, and sometimes personality variables. See *Abilities; Industrial psychology; Occupational psychology; Traits; Type; Motor skills; Practice.* *G.R.W.M.*

Personnel training. All measures which form part of *vocational training, further training,* and *retraining.* It is the function of *vocational training* to give a broadly conceived basic training, and to impart the skills and knowledge necessary in order to engage in a qualified vocational activity; to this must be added the vocational experience required by labor legislation. *G.R.W.M.*

Perspective. In perception (q.v.) theory "perspective" is one of those factors by which an impression of depth is produced in vision, and more specifically in monocular vision. The effect of differences in size of the retinal images of several positions of one and the same object is related to the depth at which the objects are seen especially when they, or their distances and positions, are arranged with a certain regularity, i.e., in changing size or density. Hence the retina registers as more distant those objects which appear smaller and areas which appear denser, an important factor in this connection being aerial perspective (blurring due to haze). In special cases one can recognize receding lines converging in depth. See *Identical (retinal) points.*

Bibliography: Gibson, J. J.: The perception of the visual world. Cambridge, Mass., 1950. *E.R.*

Persuasion; persuasion therapy. A method in psychotherapy (q.v.) put forward by P. Dubois as an alternative to suggestion (q.v.): an attempt is made to influence the patient by rational means, i.e. through the use of argument. The object is to secure a "reasonable judgment" of the illness; judgment (q.v.), as Dubois asserts, is influenced by concomitant emotional influences, which he allows only a secondary importance. Related to persuasion therapy is logotherapy (q.v.), although the latter uses psychoanalytical techniques. See *Depth psychology; Emotion.* *W.Sch.*

Perversion. Behavior, especially compulsive sexual behavior, which is subject to social condemnation. Behaviors frequently included are: bestiality (q.v.), exhibitionism (q.v.), fetishism (q.v.), homosexuality (q.v.), sadism (q.v.), masochism (q.v.), sodomy (q.v.), and even masturbation (q.v.). Rape, incest (q.v.) and promiscuity may be excluded. Hence the term perversion carries implications of abnormal sexual behavior in the sense accepted in Western culture, and has corresponding emotional overtones. With increasing awareness of the variety of human sexual behavior, the term is likely to diminish in significance, except, possibly, as an unfortunate term of abuse.

In psychoanalytic theory it is postulated that the child shows perversions or is a "polymorphous pervert". That is to say, since the child's sexual instincts have no normal outlet, they lead to various behaviors which would be called perversions in the adult. However, this only develops to actual perversion in adulthood by fixation of personality and sexual development at an early developmental stage. Fixation is said to produce perversions and neuroses. Perversions can remain in the background of normal sexual development but then will be continually detrimental to normal sexual energy or libido. *A. Broadhurst*

Petit mal. A very varied group of cerebral attacks occurring during pre-school and school age (four to fourteen years). The most frequent forms are: (*a*) *Propulsive petit mal* occurring in the first three years of life. During the seizure (which lasts a few seconds) there is a jerking forward movement of the head, sometimes accompanied by bending of the trunk and crossing of the arms; at the same time there is restriction of consciousness. This usually occurs in series, so that it is often confused with grand mal seizures. EEG records a diffuse mixed convulsion potential. Etiology: brain damage in early childhood. (*b*) *Myoclonic-astatic seizures*, occurring at the age of four years. Due to sudden loss of muscle tone children collapse as if struck by lightning. The seizure is often accompanied by twitching of the arms and the facial muscles. The EEG resembles that for propulsive petit mal. (*c*) *Pyknolepsy:* repeated "blank spells", often several hundred in one day. (*d*) *Petit-mal status:* Attacks of mental dulness which can last without interruption for hours or days. (*e*) *Impulsive petit mal* (myoclonic petit mal): patients aged between fourteen and seventeen; lightning-like jerking of the trunk and arms which lasts two to three seconds. The children are dazed for one to two seconds only with the more violent jerks. See *Absence; Grand mal.*

Bibliography: **Sargant, W. & Slater, E.:** Physical methods of treatment in psychiatry. London, 1963. **Scott, D. F.:** About epilepsy. London, 1969. *C.Sch.*

Petting. Like dating (q.v.) and necking (q.v.) a part or phase of heterosexual relations. Petting includes kissing and caressing the breasts, manual-genital contact, oral-genital (q.v.) contact apposition of sex organs without penetration and coitus (q.v.), and mutual masturbation, usually to orgasm. Petting in extra-marital sexual relations is an accepted substitute for intercourse (especially in the USA).

Bibliography: **Ehrmann, W.:** Premarital dating behavior. New York, 1959. *J.Fr.*

Pfahler types. A typology whose elements were described by Pfahler (1932) as "inherited basic functions", including *crystallized* or *fluid apperception*, or *attention* (q.v.) (restricted-broad, fixed-wandering), *tenacity of experience* (strong-weak), *emotionality* (sad-cheerful), and *vital energy* (strong-weak). Main types (out of twelve obtained by combining the above dimensions): (*a*) type with a *stable inner constitution:* receptive to a narrowly limited range of environmental influences, which are then stubbornly retained; loyalty and steadfastness of emotivity and purpose, thoroughness (perseveration). Corresponds to Kretschmer's introverted, schizothymic type. (*b*) Type with a *mobile inner constitution:* wide-ranging attention, old quickly obliterated by new impressions, emotions unstable, insufficient perseverance in purpose and little thoroughness of action. Corresponds to Kretschmer's extraverted, cyclothymic type. These main types can be subdivided according to gradations of emotion and vital energy. See *Traits; Type.*

Bibliography: Pfahler, G.: Vererbung als Schicksal. Leipzig, 1932. **Id.:** System des Typenlehren. Leipzig, 1936. *W.K.*

PGR. Abb. for *psychogalvanic reflex*. See *Skin resistance.*

Phallic cult. The cult (q.v.) of the penis continues in India and some other countries; it was very prevalent in antiquity and among primitive peoples (Egypt, Asia Minor, Greece and Italy). The phallus (q.v.) is venerated as a symbol of procreative power; opposition to such cults formed part of Jewish and Christian sexual morality. *W.Sch.*

Phallic stage (syn. *Phallic phase*). According to Freud, the beginning of the early genital or Oedipal stage (q.v.). Exhibition of the masculinity just discovered by the boy (and to a lesser extent of her femininity by the girl), boasting and a desire to impress are more noticeable than interest in the parent of the opposite sex or other such persons in the family. See *Genital stage.* *W.T.*

Phallography. A method for measuring the erection of the penis; used especially in behavior therapy (q.v.) of certain sexual deviations as a measure of success and to objectify a decision to use reinforcement. Phallography is effected telemetrically by means of a sleeve which registers the changes in penis volume. *U.H.S.*

Phallus. Originally a representation or sculptured image of the penis (or penis and testes), particularly as used as a decoration, object of veneration, or symbol of fertility and creativity in certain ancient Greek (e.g. Dionysian) and Asian cults. In psychoanalysis (q.v.), the penis itself is called a phallus, particularly during the stage of infantile sexuality when it is associated with "narcissistic love". There is an increasing tendency, both in psychoanalysis and elsewhere, to use the term as synonymous with "penis", perhaps partly as a result of euphemistic processes. *G.D.W.*

Phantom limb; phantom pain. When a limb has been amputated, the nerves that originally emanated from it will remain from the stump to the CNS. Any activity occurring in these nerves will be experienced as arising in a phantom limb from where the receptors originally associated with the nerves were. Thus various sensations of movement and pressure apparently localized in the non-existent limb may be felt and in particular pain, which, since it is localized in the non-existent limb, is called *phantom pain.* *C.D.F.*

Pharmacology. A part-discipline of medicine which deals with the effects of synthetic and natural chemical substances on animal and human organisms. The part-area of pharmacology concerned with the effects of psychopharmaceutical agents is important for psychology. See *Psychopharmacology.*

Bibliography: Goodman, L. S. & Gilman, A.: The pharmacological basis of therapeutics. New York, 1965. **Kuschinsky, G. & Lullmann, H.:** Kurzes Lehrbild der Pharmakologie. Stuttgart, 1970. **Moller, K. O.:** Pharmakologie. Basle, 1966. *W.J.*

Pharmacopsychiatry. A part-area of psychiatry which deals particularly with the study of the effects of psychotropic substances, especially psychopharmaceutical agents, on morbid conditions and behavior, as well as with the morbid (abnormal) changes in condition and behavior caused by drugs. There are no fixed boundaries with psychopharmacology (q.v.). *W.J.*

Pharmacopsychology. See *Psychopharmacology*.

Pharmacopsychopathology. A part-area of psychiatry (q.v.) which deals with abnormal or morbid changes brought about by drugs.

Bibliography: De Boor, W.: Pharmacopsychologie und Psychopathologie. Berlin, 1956. *W.J.*

Pharmacotherapy (a more accurate term is *psychiatric pharmacotherapy*) is the treatment of psychic (i.e. psychological, or mental) diseases belonging mainly to the group of endogenous *psychoses* (q.v.) and *neuroses* (q.v.), with the aid of psychopharmaceutical agents. Pharmacotherapy is usually regarded as an alternative to electroconvulsive therapy (ECT) or to psychotherapy (q.v.) and behavior therapy (q.v.), although the different methods are not mutually exclusive (Gottschalk, 1968; May, 1968). Pharmacotherapy came into use on a large scale in about 1952, and it is now widespread for the treatment of endogenous psychoses. It could be shown in a large number of cases that pharmacotherapy either gave better therapeutic results or, with the same results, left more room for maneuver in designing a therapy for a psychosis (e.g. ambulant treatment) than did the formerly prevalent ECT, or similar methods (Davis *et al.*, 1968; Hippius, 1961). If one starts from biochemical conditions of endogenous psychoses, pathogenetic part mechanisms (Hippius, 1968) are influenced by pharmacotherapy; this accords with drug therapy in other fields of medicine. Of course, pharmacotherapy does not, as a rule, produce a final cure (Kamano, 1966) but gives periods free from symptoms or shortens the phases of illness.

Pharmacotherapy in neuroses, especially with tranquilizers (q.v.), has as yet only a supportive function in regard to other techniques, particularly in reducing anxiety or tension (Rickels, 1968). Of course, the enduring effect of psychopharmaceuticals in the treatment of psychoses must be seen not only in a biochemical change in the organism but as derivable in part from learning processes induced by the drugs (Honigfeld, 1964). A crucial problem in optimizing pharmacotherapy is to obtain exact indications and details of the effects; the target symptoms are of primary importance here (Freyhan, 1959): nevertheless, it is not possible to dispense with crude nosological classifications and differentiations according to personality traits, biographical or demographic characteristics within groups with comparable target symptoms (Wittenborn & May, 1966). Determining the results of pharmacotherapy presupposes that target symptoms are definable, operationalizable and can be weighed one against the other. Clinical tests of psychopharmaceuticals are limited by the obligation of optimal treatment (e.g. a placebo test replaced in large measure by examination against a standard preparation) and by shortcomings in the secret experimental control test: a barrier to carrying out a double blind experiment because of the variation of drugs by reason of side effects (Heimann, 1969).

Bibliography: Articles by: **Davis, J. M.** et al., **Gottschalk, L. A., May, P. R. A., Rickels, K.** In: **Efron, D. H.** (Ed.): Psychopharmacology. A review of progress. Washington, 1968. **Freyhan, F. A.:** Psychopharmacology. A review. In: **Masserman, J. H.** (Ed.): Biological psychiatry. New York, 1959. **Heimann, H.:** Allgemeine meth. Probleme der klinischen Prüfung von Antidepressiva. Arzneim.-Forsch., 1969, *19*, 878–80. **Hippius, H.:** Klinische Indikation der modernen psychiatrischen Pharmakotherapie. Dtsch. med. J., 1961, *12*, 524–29. **Honigfeld, G.:** Non-specific factors in treatment. II: Review of social-psychological factors. Dis. nerv. syst., 1964, *25*, 225–39. **Kamano, D. K.:** Selective review of effects of discontinuation of drug treatment: some implications and problems. Psychol. Rep., 1966, *19*, 743–49. **Wittenborn, J. R. & May, P. R. A.:** Prediction of response to pharmacotherapy. Springfield, 1966.

R. Dietsch

Phasopathy. A reversible endogenous-episodic overemphasis of a psychic-mental developmental phase which can last for weeks or years but then disappear again; resulting difficulties in upbringing, at school and work or disturbances of social adaptation can have a pathological effect as an abnormal partial condition during the course of some psychic process. Phasopathy must be distinguished diagnostically from an inherited mental handicap, character impairments acquired from harmful environmental influences, and irreversible personal divergences toward abnormality of unmistakably somatic origin, or resulting from a post-sickness condition.

Bibliography: **Engels, H. J.:** La psychologie, science auxiliaire. Revue de Neuropsychiatrie infantile et d'Hygiène mentale de l'enfance, 1964, *12*, 747–54.

H.J.E.

Phenomenal field. The whole area of that which is experienced simultaneously; it may be divided into the phenomenal ego and the environing phenomenal field or location. The concept of field (q.v.), which gestalt theory borrowed from physics, indicates that states and processes at different positions in this area are dynamically connected and mutually determined. *P.Th.*

Phenomenal motion. An obsolescent term for any perception of movement that cannot be explained by mechanico-biological data alone (e.g.: we perceive the movement of a stone when it is thrown, although the image on the retina remains constant). *V.M.*

Phenomenology (Ger. *Phänomenologie*). The theory of *phenomena*, or *appearances*. The phenomenological approach is to examine an object from the standpoint of its appearance. This may be appearance in the external world of the senses, apprehensibility in the experiential sphere, or even the symbolic visual representation of mental structures or processes. The word "phenomenology" is used in a narrow and in a wide sense. In the narrow sense, the word stands for a philosophico-psychological method initiated by Edmund Husserl (1859–1938) that has spread significantly in philosophy and science.

1. *The "pure phenomenology" of Husserl.* For Husserl (1913) this means obtaining an immediate "*Anschauung*" (direct intuition or perception) of the bases of cognition. His appeal "back to things" meant: we must banish all preconceived theory of knowledge (q.v.) and of cognition, and obtain a *pure view of the reality of subjective experience.* From experience of direct "seeing", the phenomenologist obtains an essential, general content ("categorial perception"). The merely empirical givenness of the individual instance is stripped down to an "ideating abstraction".

Cognition, like other sense experiences, cannot be explained by means of psychologico-anatomistic analysis: like the others, it is a sensory whole. Husserl called the attempt to derive mental phenomena psychologically "psychologism" (q.v.), and showed that it was mistaken. He was convinced that only the phenomenological method could disclose the requisite basic concepts of psychology as a science. Fundamental notions cannot be proved, but only indicated. Husserl's phenomenology is grounded upon the psychology of his teacher Brentano (q.v.), according to whom the essential characteristic of consciousness is *intentionality* ("consciousness is always *consciousness of . . .*"). See *Act psychology.*

2. *Anthropological phenomenology.* Max Scheler (1874–1928), who was not a pupil of Husserl's but had similar ideas, developed a phenomenology of the "value-qualities of being", and of the vital principles of the human personality. Scheler's work was fundamental for the psychology of the "feelings", or emotion (q.v.). "Intentionality" was the central concept of his theory of the person: the person forms the center of acts and by his very nature cannot become an object. According to

Scheler's famous formulation (1916), man and animal have a fundamentally different relationship to the world: the animal has environment (*Umwelt*), man has world (*Welt*).

Martin Heidegger (1889–) found Husserl's ideas most fruitful. French existentialism also developed from Husserl and Heidegger; Merleau-Ponty (1966) developed a phenomenological anthropology.

3. *Psychological phenomenology*. A. Pfänder's (1870–1941) *Phänomenologie des Wollens* (1960), a study of the "phenomenology of volition", may be described as the classical work of psychological phenomenology, which uses an emphatic form of categorial intuition and a rigorous descriptive style.

4. *The phenomenological approach in psychological methodology*. "Categorial intuition", according to Husserl, is the means of obtaining basic psychological concepts for psychology. Such concepts as perception, volition or emotion are so postulated as to allow that which is essentially perceptual or volitional, etc., to emerge from the particular event or process as an ideating abstraction. Classification into concepts of this kind does not take place, as with categorical or area concepts, on the basis of an *either-or*, but (as with type concepts) by means of a *more-or-less*. Round about the pure case which has been seen to be the center, are grouped those processes which have been encountered as more or less according with that pure case. The individual occurrence is measured against the abstracted pure case. Binswanger (1922) has shown how important phenomenology can be for psychological methodology. Phenomenological conceptual perception is directed to meaningful wholes. A connection with the individual findings obtained by means of natural-scientific analysis is possible only if a primacy of meaningful wholes is recognized. Buytendijk's work (1953) attempts this kind of synthesis. Straus (1956) also deserves mention in this connection. See *Ganzheit; Existence analysis*.

Bibliography: Binswanger, L.: Einführung in die Probleme der allgemeinen Psychologie. Berlin, 1922. **Id.:** The case of Ellen West. In: **May, R.** *et al.* (Eds.): Existence: a new dimension in psychiatry and psychology. New York, 1958, 237–64. **Buytendijk, F. J. J.:** Die Frau, Natur, Erscheinung, Dasein. Cologne, 1953. **Id.:** Pain: its modes and functions. Chicago, 1962. **Farber, M.:** The foundation of phenomenology: Edmund Husserl and the quest for a rigorous science of philosophy. Cambridge, Mass., 1940. **Graumann, C. F.:** Grundlagen einer Phänomenologie und Psychologie der Perspektivität. Berlin, 1960. **Husserl, E.:** Logische Untersuchungen. Halle, 1900–01 (Eng. trans.: Logical investigations. London, 1970). **Id.:** Ideen zu einer reinen Phänomenologie und phänomenologischen Philosophie. Halle, 1913. **Kaam, A. van:** Existential foundations of psychology. Pittsburgh, 1966. **Lersch, P.:** The levels of the mind. In: **David, H. P. & Bracken, H. von:** (Eds.): Perspectives in personality theory. New York, 1957, 218–41. **Id.:** Aufbau der Person. Munich, [10]1966. **May, R.** (Ed.): Existential psychology. New York, 1961. **Merleau-Ponty, M.:** Phenomenology of perception. London, 1962. **Id.:** The structure of behavior. Boston, 1963. **Id.:** Les sciences de l'homme et la phénoménologie, Bull. de Psychol., 1964, *18*, 141–70. **Pfänder, A.:** Der Formalismus in der Ethik und die materiale Wertethik. Halle, 1916. **Raneurello, A. C.:** A study of Franz Brentano: his psychological standpoint and his significance in the history of psychology. New York, 1968. **Sartre, J.-P.:** Existentialism. New York, 1947. **Id.:** The psychology of imagination. New York, 1948. **Id.:** The emotions: outline of a theory. New York, 1948. **Id.:** Being and nothingness. New York, 1956. **Scheler, M.:** Der Formalismus in der Ethik und die materiale Wertethik. Halle, 1916. **Id.:** The nature of sympathy. London, 1970. **Spiegelberg, H.:** The phenomenological movement. A historical introduction. The Hague, 1960. **Straus, E.:** Vom Sinne der Sinne. Berlin, 1956.

J. Rudert

Phenothiazines. A chemical subgroup of the neuroleptics (q.v.). They are divided, according to chemical criteria, into promethazine and propylamine derivatives (promazine, chlorpromazine, trifluopromazine), propylpiperazine derivatives (perazine, prochlorperazine, fluphenazine, perphenazine, homofenazine) and alkylpiperidyl derivatives (mepazine, thioridazine). Phenothiazines have a broad spectrum of effect due to multiple impact points in the central (among others, the reticular formation (q.v.), hypothalamic regulating centers) and peripheral nervous system (adrenolytic, antichlolinergic, antihistaminic), with a varying combination and degree of intensity of effects for the individual derivatives. The clinically significant neuroleptic effect is quite varied in strength and duration (e.g. weak with promazine, strong with fluphenazine). Phenothiazines have an anti-emetic effect, increase appetite and lower the temperature (chiefly in the sense of deficient compensation; in large doses they produce extrapyramidal symptoms (also after chronic applications), and predispose to narcosis (q.v.). The effect of small doses in healthy persons is unstable, depending on the situation and person (see *Differential psychopharmacology*); in comparison with tranquilizers (q.v.), sedative effects appear quite early. Tranquilizing effects also appear after first application, but, clinically, therapeutic effects appear fully only after several applications.

Bibliography: Gordon, M.: Phenothiazines. In: **Gordon, M.** (Ed.): Psychopharmacological agents, Vol. 2. New York, 1967. **Herminger, G., DiMascio, A. & Klerman, G. L.:** Personality factors in variability of response to phenothiazines. Amer. J. Psychiat. 1965, *121*, 1011–94. *G.D.*

Phenotype. The visible type of an individual: i.e. the sum of all actually developed characteristics (see *Genotype*). Individuals with the same phenotype are not (necessarily) the same genetically: e.g. a black guinea-pig may be homozygotically or heterozygotically black with the allele (q.v.) for black dominating that for white (dominant-recessive inheritance). *H.Sch.*

Phenylalanine. An essential amino-acid, which decomposes into tyrosine (q.v.) in the organism. In certain individuals this process is disturbed because an enzyme is absent; the result is phenylketonuria (q.v.), which produces serious intelligence and personality defects if not treated during the first months of life.

Bibliography: Grüter, W.: Angeborene Stoffwechselstörungen und Schwachsinn am Beispiel der Phenylketonurie. Stuttgart, 1963. **Lyman, F. L.:** Phenylketonuria. Springfield, 1963. *W.J.*

Phenylketonuria. A recessive (q.v.) hereditary metabolic anomaly in which the conversion of phenylalanine into tyrosine (i.e. the oxidization of phenylalamines) is disturbed owing to an enzymatic deficiency. The disorder presents as a phenylpyruvic oligophrenia, or various degrees of mental defect (q.v.) and a tendency to convulsions early in life. A cure is possible only with a very early diagnosis and a phenylalanine-reduced diet beginning before three years of age. *E.D.*

Pheromones. Chemical substances which promote communication within a species. In special scent glands the female silk-moth produces a substance to which the males are extraordinarily sensitive. The exaltolides (musk-like substances) are claimed to produce similar sex-specific reactions in man. *V.Pr.*

Phi coefficient. A parametric technique for calculating the degree of interaction between two alternative variables, according to the formula

$$r_\Phi = \frac{ad - bc}{\sqrt{(a+b)(c+d)(a+c)(b+d)}},$$

in which ad and bc indicate the products of the two diagonal values in a fourfold table. *G.Mi.*

Philosophy and psychology. At the beginning of this century psychology prided itself on its newfound self-realization as a *natural science*. Today the literature would seem to be aware of the philosophical tradition of psychology as no more than an historical phenomenon.

The major question in the general discussion

of the future orientation of psychology at the time of its separation from philosophy was the problem of the "subjectivism" of self-observation (introspection or self-knowledge). Research was concerned with the processes of *consciousness* (q.v.), the *directly* experienced quality of which was available only to individual self-observation. Analysis was carried out by means of *description* and *comparison*. An attempt was made, but with the aid of *abstraction*, to formulate general laws. The result of this procedure was a *phenomenal* determination of the general nature of psychological processes (e.g. the four axioms formulated by K. Bühler for the psychology of *association* (q.v.), and *constructs* concerning the relationship of processes (e.g. the laws of association).

The *phenomenalistic* approach—a product of the prevailing "psychologism" (q.v.) (J. Locke, J. S. Mill, G. T. Fechner, W. Dilthey, *et al.*) could not, using the modes proper to philosophy, *objectify* the principle of the "subjectivism" of individual experience, as attempted in cognition theory, e.g. in Husserl's "transcendental reduction" or Hegel's "self-reflection of the thinking subject" (idealism). No philosophically satisfying future could be forecast for psychology, whereas the introduction of the category of quantity enabled scientific justice to be done to psychological phenomena.

Admittedly, the *source* of psychic events remained the *experiencing subject*. But measurement and calculation made individuals comparable according to definite criteria. In this way, a basis was created for intersubjectivity, which made it possible to think in terms of experimental-psychological arrangements. Of course these experiments were largely determined by criteria of formal logic, the various interpretations of which led to violent controversy (e.g. between W. Wundt and K. Bühler).

In psychophysics (q.v.) (E. H. Weber, G. T. Fechner) previous assertions about the nature of psychic phenomena became practically meaningless, and were supplanted by *inductively* obtained statements about general *formal* relationships of quantifiable, observed data (e.g. the intensity of physical stimuli, or experienced sensations). This was another step on the way from the psychology of consciousness to scientific psychology. If the quality of experiences was now only a fictitiously determined criterion of order, the immediacy of the experience could be dispensed with too. At this stage, European psychology began to accord with "reflexology" (I. P. Pavlov) and "behaviorism" (J. B. Watson), which replaced *self-observation* by the *observation of others*, and widened the methodological principle of intersubjectivity by the *externalization* (instrumentalization) of observational data. The determination of the general nature of psychological phenomena by analysis and abstraction was replaced by *operational definition* (q.v.) (see Nagel *et al.*, 1971; Bradley, 1971).

Psychology as a natural science now obeys the rule "*savoir pour prévoir*", and seeks to predict, plan, control; in short, to *manipulate* the processes of nature. The subjectivism of the experiencing individual would now seem (at least as a methodological problem) to have been banished from psychology.

However, the individual as the "container" or "bearer" of facts, i.e. as the *object* of psychological research, cannot be ignored, even by an extremely mechanistic psychology (Eysenck, 1972). But, together with the method, the object of psychology has undergone a conceptual transformation.

The subjective processes of the individual, his contents (i.e. his qualities) have been *reified* as *facts* related to one another by causal function. The distinctive nature of the individual at any given time can no longer be thought of on the basis of *a priori* determinations of "substance" (q.v.), of "entelechial personal development" and of "totality", but is divided into individual "parts" with random frequency and random degrees of intensity.

At this point the scientific and theoretical problem of subjectivism becomes *the* question of the theory of knowledge, which asks: Can the object "individual" still be sufficiently grasped in its reality by the rational and purposive conceptual models of a scientific psychology, or does an understanding of this object necessarily lead back to the individual as *subject* of cognition? For it *is* the individual who carries out this research into himself, and in this act devises the process of research and the categories of his own knowledge of himself. This problem of psychology is not yet wholly elucidated.

True, in modern psychology the "former" individual, with his *a priori* assumptions, is either implicitly or explicitly the subject of examination—rather as if determining fundamental nature and a purposive and rational supposition could be taken as one and the same thing. But the "totality" of psychic phenomena or their "entelechial inner laws" cannot be empirically verified; they can only be grounded on the philosophical explanation of the essence of a thing.

For example, many authors' developmental psychology presupposes a meaningful totality of the individual and a development following its inner laws, for without these postulates psychology can have no laws governing the association of facts in time: i.e. no process of development subject to any laws at all (Piaget, 1953, 1965). True, the causal relationship of component processes can be explained by means of functional models in regard to conditions defined at any particular time, but there is no causal explanation for, e.g., the sequence of definite qualities of thought (q.v.) in the development of an individual. The process of thought as development can be indicated only on the plane of *mind* conforming to law and therefore necessary. The "if" of time is not a condition for this process, is not a fact, and cannot be postulated.

A similar problem arises when examining *attitudes* (q.v.) which are objectified, i.e. typologized, by a concept of items derived from their process of development. Conditions for degrees of intensity, and positive or negative valences of attitudes, can be asserted, but the "semantic" space (see *Semantics*) of attitudes and attitude change is determined not only by conditions but by *meaning*. When an attitude originates as a meaningful relation, this cannot be explained from conditions, i.e. from facts, because it is not the facts themselves but individuals who make the connection. Freud's attempt to interpret psychological events as meaningful contexts (relationships) in depth psychology (q.v.) still deserves full consideration as a conceptual model. In this connection, the "critical theory" (q.v.) of the Frankfurt School (Horkheimer, Adorno, Marcuse, Habermas) conceives Freud's *psychoanalysis* (q.v.) as a form of "systematically generalized self-reflection" (Habermas, 1972), only to show that "this dimension (of self-reflection) is again shattered on the plane of positivism". A "legitimate path" would lead us back from "conventional theory"; such a path would be the approach of Pierce and Dilthey: i.e. "a methodology that depends upon the attitude proper to the theory of knowledge". Freud's concept of psychoanalysis as a (natural) science is seen as a "pseudo-scientific self-delusion", thus enabling the still unexplained position of psychoanalytic interpretation between hermeneutics and causal-functional thought to be explicated as "the logic of general interpretation". There is still no answer to the question of how this generalization can be legitimized, for the treatment of psychoanalysis as a form of self-reflection is a matter not only of abstractive generalization, but of grounding. This does not occur in the natural-scientific approach, nor—as self-reflection—with "critical theory" (cf. Horkheimer & Adorno, 1972).

Psychology is most akin still to philosophy when investigating psychological acts that are not of a purposive-rational nature, such as those manifestations of subjective experience which, as human *culture*, we call games and dances, and such creative phenomena as art, language and cognitive thinking. The fact that these phenomena cannot be adequately explained by modern psychology shows most clearly that the fiction of the object of psychology as a functional model has become the "as if" of the reality of an individual whose creative acts are neither predictable nor manipulable (cf. Berlinger, 1969; 1970).

When reduced to a fact, the subject of psychology is in the paradoxical situation of having deprived himself of his power of self-reflection in favor of an objectivistic methodology. Facts can say nothing about themselves or about their relationships with other facts; facts are not a subject but an object. Here psychologism becomes redundant, and here the exploration of the creative acts of the individual can go no further.

This state of affairs is not altered by an *instrumentalist formulation* of research processes and concepts. The instruments of research do become increasingly differentiated and measure more and more accurately; but instruments do not *know* what they are measuring. The object is defined by the instrument, but the instrument is designed by the still subjective individual, who, for example, selects items according to his prescientific understanding of the object. Recourse to representative sampling allows representation only in regard to the distribution of facts in the population, but not in regard to the basic factual question about the "what" of the object (e.g., in the case of intelligence tests, about the "what" of intelligence). What is *intelligence* as man understands himself in any particular epoch? A selection instrument of a certain social class, or a construct defined by its purpose and by conditions proper to specific times, and hence limited operationally? The same problems arise for concepts such as "adapted-unadapted", "neurotic-healthy", and so on. If they are taken as unproblematic facts, they become subject to arbitrary evaluation and can serve the ends of manipulation (q.v.). The situation is different if they are limited by condition and purpose.

The individual runs the risk of falling into the hands of purposive-rational manipulation, if he succumbs to a functional explanation of psychic processes (Chomsky, 1971; Horkheimer & Adorno, 1972).

But of course he remains a *subject:* the subject is not determined by facts, by a superficial concept of empiricism; instead the subject draws up the categories which determine facts. Through *consciousness* he is always involved in a relationship to himself and to the object; he not only reacts out of his involvement, but possesses the power of *conceiving* himself in this relatedness. Only on the basis of this concept of self is it possible to discern the nature not only of the conditions but of the meaning for man of purposive-rational determinations.

Bibliography: Anscombe, G. E. M.: An introduction to Wittgenstein's Tractatus. London, ³1967. **Ayer, A. J.:** The problem of knowledge. London, 1956. **Berlinger, R.:** Demiurgie als Ermächtigung zum Werk. Philosophische Perspektiven, 1969, *1*, 52–65. **Id.:** Der musikalische Weltentwurf. Philosophische Perspektiven, 1970, 2, 305–16. **Bradley, J.:** Mach's philosophy of science. London, 1971. **Chomsky, N.:** Problems of knowledge and freedom. New York, 1971; London 1972. **Eysenck, H. J.:** Psychology is about people. Harmondsworth & New York, 1972. **Habermas, J.:** Knowledge and interest. London & New York, 1972. **Horkheimer, M. & Adorno, T.:** Dialectic of enlightenment. New York, 1972. **Jaspers, K.:** The perennial scope of philosophy. New York, 1949. **Nagel, E., Bromberger, S. & Grunbaum, A.:** Observation and theory in science. Baltimore, Ud. & London, 1971. **Piaget, J.:** Logic and psychology. Manchester & New York, 1953. **Id.:** Psychology and philosophy. In: **Wolman, B. B. & Nagel, E.** (Eds.): Scientific psychology: principles and approaches. New York, 1965, 28–43. **Sartre, J.-P.:** Transcendence of the ego. New York, 1960. **Watson, J. B.:** Behaviorism. New York, 1925. **Wellek, A.:** Mathematics and intuition: the relationship between psychology and philosophy reconsidered. Acta psychologica, 1964, *22*, 413–29. **Winch, P.:** The idea of a social science and its relation to philosophy. London, ³1963.

P. Braun

Phimosis. Narrowing of the opening of the penile prepuce (foreskin) preventing it being drawn back over the glans. *Phimosis vaginalis:* narrowness of the vagina. *G.D.W.*

Phi-phenomenon. A phenomenon *sui generis* (M. Wertheimer). Denotes the optical impression of motion (apparent motion) generated when objectively stationary, relatively similar objects are presented one after the other at a certain distance in time.

Bibliography: Wertheimer, M.: Expt. Studien über das Sehen von Bewegung. Z. f. Psychol., 1912, 61.

I.M.D.

Phlegmatic. The phlegmatic person is one of the four types of temperament according to Hippocrates; that variant of personality in which water predominates. The phlegmatic character is said to be calm, constant, sluggish, not easily upset and fixed in his habits. *W.Se.*

Phobia. An abnormal fear which is either: (*a*) a fear of an object or situation which is not generally considered to be frightening, e.g. lifts, domestic animals, and so on; or (*b*) an abnormally intense fear of an object or situation which normally arouses some degree of fear in most people, e.g. surgery, dentistry, etc.

Such phobias used to be classified by adding the appropriate Greek prefix, e.g. agoraphobia, claustrophobia, zoophobia, etc. Modern classifications divide phobias into those arising from specific objects, e.g. dog phobia, cat phobia, etc., or situations, e.g. school phobia, party phobia, etc., or reactions to them such as blushing phobia, fainting phobia or vomiting phobia. Phobias can be associated with almost any psychiatric condition but are most often associated with anxiety states. Phobias associated with obsessional states can show bizarre features leading to queer compulsive behavior rituals to overcome them. See *Anxiety; Paranoia; Schizophrenia.* *P.Le.*

Phoneme. 1. An hallucinatory voice. This symptom is commonest in schizophrenia. The patient hears voices usually talking to him often abusing him, giving him instructions or commenting on his actions. **2.** Closely related vocal sounds using the same or a similar symbol. *R.H.*

Phonemics (syn. *Phonology; Phonematics*). The study of the smallest categories of sound symbols—phonemes—which can be distinguished in any particular (spoken) language. In contrast, (articulatory) phonetics deals with the so to speak still more elementary structures which can be analyzed independently of speech: sounds which can be distinguished according to the places and the special manner in which they are produced: in the larynx, the mouth or the nose. Acoustic phonetics describes, partly with the aid of depictive, technical methods (visible speech, sonagrams) the physical characteristics of sounds and sound sequences. (Linguistic) questions concerning phonemics touch partly on psychological problems (see *Language*; *Psycholinguistics; Speech*). In determining phonological *units* (phonemes), invariant, distinguishing characteristics have to be found which belong to whole classes of sound pictures, notwithstanding the variability caused by individual and regional peculiarities or by emotional color. The Prague School (Trubetzkoy, 1935) developed operational methods for this purpose. Differences between phonemes are described in terms of distinctive features (Jakobson & Halle, 1956), so that a phoneme always appears as a group of such features. Distinguishing phonemes and neglecting some differences of sound pictures in perception involves psychological problems (Hörmann, 1970).

Two stages are distinguished in the *acquisition of sounds and phonemes.* When he can only babble, the individual is able to produce all the sounds which can conceivably be articulated, but even then accent and intonation patterns exclusive to a specific language are making their appearance (Weir, 1966). After that the child gradually acquires in communication the stock of phonemes used in his native language. In the word "papa", for example, the universal basic pattern of syllable construction (consonant/vowel, closed/open) operates. The basic stock of consonants is then further differentiated in regard to the features oral/nasal, labial/dental. The stock of vowels is similarly built up. A morbid deterioration in the ability to use language (aphasia, q.v.) takes place in the reverse order.

Under what conditions and by what means individual sound structures come to have a semantic function (see *Semantics*), a connotative or denotative meaning, is open to argument. Onomatopoeic interjections (e.g. *brr, hui, pst*) are suggestive of sound symbolism. Experimental psychophonetics deals with these questions with the aid of an "impression differential": more or less elementary sound structures are rated by testees on standard scales according to "general qualities" and then related to one another and to other semantic units by the use of the Osgood three-dimensional system of general semantic "basic" components: evaluation, activity, potency (see *Semantic differential*). Diverse attempts have been made to explain the immediate semantic efficiency of more or less elementary sound structures. One starts from the (universal) covariations existing between the sound behavior of perceptible objects and certain other features (in general, large objects have a deep sound, small objects a high one), and supposes that appropriately generalizable associative connections are learnt between the feature of size and certain dimensions of sound (Brown, 1958). Another is based on covariations between sound structures and meanings as they have been formed specifically and more by chance as the individual language developed (Taylor & Taylor, 1965). In contrast to these theories based on association, the "general qualities" of sound structures (Ertel, 1969) described in the semantic differential system are traced back to the unconditioned, innate response tendencies of the autonomic nervous system, a method which recalls the interpretations of gestalt psychology (see *Ganzheit*).

Bibliography: Brown, R. W.: Words and things. Glencoe, Ill., 1958. **Ertel, S.:** Psychophonetik. Göttingen, 1969. **Hörmann, H.:** Psychologie der Sprache. Berlin, ²1970. **Jacobson, R. & Halle, M.:** Fundamentals of language. The Hague, 1956. **Taylor, K. & Taylor, M.:** Another look at phonetic symbolism. Psychol. Bull., 1965, *64*, 413–27. **Trubetzkoy, N. S.:** Anleitung zur phonologischen Beschreibung. Prague, 1935. **Weir, R. H.:** Some questions on the child's learning of phonology. In: **Smith, F. & Miller, G. A.** (Eds.): The genesis of language. Cambridge, Mass., 1966, 153–72.

B. Insam

Phonism. A phonism is an auditory sensation produced by something other than sound, e.g. an internally produced buzzing or ringing in the ears. *C.D.F.*

Phonognomics. A term which has won a certain currency since the beginning of the nineteenth century as a designation for a subdivision of the psychology of *expression* (q.v.): i.e. the part played by expression in spoken pronouncements in general, and—in a narrower sense—the part played by speech in expression ("speech analysis", etc.).

Bibliography: Davitz, J. R. (Ed.): The communication of emotional meaning. New York, 1964. *D.G.*

Photometer. An optical instrument for measuring the intensity of light (luminance or candlepower).

Photometry. A way of determining color by measurement, limited to measuring the light intensity emitted, reflected and transmitted by some object. *G.Ka.*

Photoreceptors. *Light receptors* of the eye; *cones* (q.v.) are elements of the retina (q.v.) which are sensitive to light and can perceive color; *rods* (q.v.) are insensitive to color and can only register degrees of brightness (appraise grey). The human eye possesses on average 6×10^6 cones (situated foveally and perifoveally) and 120×10^6 rods (none in the fovea, increasing towards the periphery). See *Retina.* *K.H.P.*

Phrenology. F. J. Gall and G. Spurzheim assumed that mental and emotional characteristics could be found in specific areas of the brain; that they could be detected from the external shape of the skull; and that the development of brain areas indicated the development of corresponding psychological features. See *Localization.* *H.H.*

Phylogenesis. *History of the evolution of species.* The present forms of organisms on the earth have arisen as a result of a continuous change of hereditary characteristics (see *Mutation*) and division of species from organisms which usually had a simpler structure: e.g. man's ancestors about 400 million years ago were fish-like creatures living in water and breathing through gills. *H.Sch.*

Physicalism. A term advanced by R. Carnap in 1931 and adopted by the Vienna Circle (Carnap, Neurath, Hempel, etc.: see *Logical positivism; Positivism*). It designates a thesis according to which all the sciences, and especially the human sciences, can and should be expressed in the language of the physical sciences, in order to *unify the sciences* (O. Neurath) by means of a language which is universal, homogeneous and free from any metaphysical implication, and includes only empirically manipulable propositions, i.e. those which designate observable properties of things (see *Protocol sentences*). After having explained the rules of formation and transformation so that any proposition in various sciences can be expressed in them, it is possible (by transforming the qualitative into the quantitative) to *reduce* the total number of disciplines to a small number of deductive systems, and ultimately to one such system. "The application of physicalism to psychology is the logical basis for the method of behaviorism" (Carnap).

Bibliography: Jorgensen, J.: The development of logical empiricism. In: Encyclopedia of unified science, Vol. 2 (9). Chicago, 1951, 77. **Morris, C. W.:** Logical positivism, pragmatism, and scientific empiricism. Paris, 1937. *M.-J.B.*

Physiognomic test. A general term for a test which draws conclusions about the underlying personality (q.v.) of some individual with the aid of his physiognomy (q.v.). Such tests are based on the theory that everything in the "psyche" leaves its mark on the *physiognomy.* See *Expression; Graphology; Traits.* *H.J.A.*

Physiognomy. The human face as a vehicle of expression when at rest (free from mimicry). The nature of the expression is determined by the body's structure and the imprint left by traces of habitual mimic innervation. (See *Habit.*) Physiognomic research (physiognomics as the theory of facial expression) makes use of photographs, sketches (Brunswik), average likenesses, and learning experiments. Results so far have shown that the validity of judgments based on the impression (q.v.) given by the physiognomy is slight (coefficient between 0.00 and 0.50); nevertheless, certain systematic tendencies dependent on various factors appear in judgments. *F.Ki.*

Physiological psychology. In its most general form, the theory of the relations between physical and mental (psychic) processes, including all attempts to reveal such relationships. It has as its object the scientific investigation of the mechanisms by which the 12^9 nerve cells of the human brain with their almost incalculably numerous links between one another can produce and control the behavioral variety of a living creature, which is also "infinitely" great. Physiological psychology derives from psychology; the questions it deals with rely chiefly on physiological methods for their answers. The basic problem is to elucidate behavior by the analysis of causes, behavior in this case meaning every kind of activity directed to the environment or communication with it for the purpose of exchanging information. Physiological psychology thus requires contributions from almost all subdivisions of physiology (q.v.) and a sophisticated knowledge of it requires thorough familiarity with methods and problems. *Physiopsychology* is a synonym, while *neuropsychology* (q.v.), or *neurophysiology* and *psychophysiology* (q.v.), are concerned with somewhat more narrowly defined fields, although the boundaries are often not absolute. In the English literature there has been a tendency to group "experimental psychology" and physiological psychology together; this approximation should be avoided. Physiological psychology uses methods taken from both "chemical" and "physical" physiology: the action of hormones and behavior changes resulting from them are examples related to chemistry, while the development of microelectrode techniques has made electrophysiology the most successful branch of the subject in recent years. Hence, although not a separate science, physiological psychology acts as a bridge between psychology and physiology, and is one of the most active and fruitful branches of the two parent disciplines. See *Hormones; Neuroanatomy; Neuropsychology; Psychopharmacology.*

Bibliography: Fearing, F.: Reflex action. A study in the history of physiological psychology. Cambridge, Mass., ^{2}1969. **Glickman, S. E. & Milner, P. M.** (Eds.): The neurological basis of motivation. New York, 1969. **Gross, C. G. & Zeigler, H. P.**: Readings in physiological psychology. New York & London, 1968–9. **Isaacson, R. L.** (Ed.): A primer of physiological psychology. New York, 1971. **Milner, P. M.**: Physiological psychology. New York, 1971. **Stellar, E. & Sprague, J. M.** (Eds): Progress in physiological psychology. New York, 1967 (Vol. 1); 1968 (Vol. 2); 1970 (Vol. 3). **Thompson, R. F.**: Foundations of physiological psychology. New York & London, 1967.

K. H. Plattig

Physiological clock. A mechanism which is still largely unexplained, but is presumably controlled from the brainstem, and is responsible for the primitive estimation of time demonstrated by organisms. It is presumably based on the rhythmic or periodical operations of the organic functions or of metabolism. External environmental influences such as the alternation of light and dark, temperature, dampness, etc., can affect the physiological clock just as much as interventions which accelerate or retard the metabolism. *H.Ro.*

Physiologism. A term for the tendency of certain research workers to claim that all psychic processes can be explained *physiologically*. See *Psychologism.* *H.J.A.*

Physiology includes the scientific description of the life processes in cells and organisms, and causal analysis. In research methodology, chemical physiology (biochemistry) is usually separate. *General physiology* deals with the general bases of vital processes; *special physiology* takes a special field such as animal, plant or cell physiology. In general, and for practical (medical and psychological) reasons "physiology" simply means *human physiology*, which is sub-divided into normal and pathological physiology.

Historically, physiology has developed from anatomy, from which the corresponding academic institutions split off. In teaching, largely for anatomical and functional considerations, *vegetative* is distinguished from *animal* physiology. The former deals with the life processes which take place in a comparable manner both in the stationary plant world and the animal world, and embraces "metabolism" and "reproduction", including all auxiliary nutritional and supply mechanisms (blood, heart and circulation, breathing, metabolism and energy supply, nutrition, digestion and elimination—externally by way of the intestines and kidneys/water supply, and the theory of hormones dealing with internal secretion, to which may be added reproduction, and developmental physiology). *Animal physiology*, on the other hand, embraces all the processes by which the animal is distinguished from the stationary plant, that is to say, everything which has to do, directly or indirectly, with locomotion. This comprises all such systems as the muscles, peripheral nerves, sense organs, and includes the physiology of information and regulation, and the central nervous system with the central and peripheral autonomic nervous systems, as well as the "physiology of behavior". Together with psychology and anatomy, physiology makes possible a convergent view of the human organism, which ultimately supplies a total picture within the framework of *biology;* the physiology of behavior is a link between physiology and psychology. See *Behaviorism.*

Bibliography: American Physiological Society (J. Field, Ed.): Handbook of Physiology. Washington, since 1954.

K. H. Plattig

Physiology of behavior. The "physiology of behavior" (*Verhaltensphysiologie*) is a form of comparative physiology closely associated with Erich von Holst. It combines a number of biological disciplines (e.g. sensory, movement, nervous and hormonal physiology) with ethology (q.v.) to allow analysis of animal and human behavior in accordance with natural-scientific principles. The essential concern is: "What physiological processes within an organism are responsible for a given behavior pattern and are directly expressed in it?" (Hassenstein, 1966). Typical procedure consists, first, of the quantitative measurement of certain behavior patterns under systematically "varied test conditions" and, second, of the "logical and mathematical interpretation of measurements obtained", frequently by using models (Holst, 1969). Investigations are so conducted as to leave the organism (or at least the behavior-directive system under examination) as intact as possible. Important basic data are, e.g.: the existence of innate movement sequences (inherited coordinations); the spontaneity of numerous behavior patterns not caused by external stimuli; innate stimulus selection (see *Innate releasing mechanism* = IRM; Lorenz, Tinbergen); and the inherited disposition to diverse forms of evaluation of learnable associations between forms of behavioral readiness and external stimuli (e.g. "following" imprinting, sexual imprinting, learning by experience to complete instinctive behavior sequences; see *Imprinting*). Among the main tasks of the Max Planck Institute in this field (at Seewiesen, Starnberg, Germany) are system analyses in humans and animals: e.g. the reafference principle (q.v.), constancy phenomena in optical perception, relative coordination, analyses of instinct and motivation in uninfluenced experimental animals (or in those undergoing hormone administration or cerebro-physiological stimulation), and analyses of social behavior in animals. The synthesis of behavior-determinative physiological processes in living systems according to the known laws of their association is predominantly of value to the psychology of learning and perception. See *Comparative psychology; Instinct; Animal psychology.*

Bibliography: **Eibl-Eibesfeldt, I.:** Grundriss der vergleichenden Verhaltensforschung. Munich, [2]1969. **Id.:** Love and hate. London, 1972. **Hassenstein, B.:** Kybernetik und biologische Forschung. Frankfurt, 1966. **Hinde, R. A.:** Animal behavior. New York & London, [2]1969. **Holst, E. von:** Zur Verhaltensphysiologie bei Tieren und Menschen. Gesammelte Abhandlungen, Vols. 1, 2. Munich, 1969–70. **Id. & Saint Paul, U. von:** On the functional organization of drives. Anim. Behav., 1963, *11*, 1–20. **Lorenz, K.:** Evolution and modification of behavior. Chicago & London, 1965. **Id.:** Studies in animal and human behaviour, Vols 1, 2. London, 1970–1. **Tinbergen, N.:** Animal behavior. New York, 1965. **Id.:** The study of instinct. London, ²1969. *K.E.G.*

Physostigmine (syn. *Physostigmine salicylate; Eserine*). An alkaloid which excites the parasympathetic system by inhibiting cholinesterase (see *Cholinesterase inhibitors*). Obtained from the Calabar bean. Effects last for many hours. Little used in medicine because of its undesirable effects. Most important physiological effects: miosis, promotes peristaltic action, bradycardia, increased blood pressure and perspiration. The psychic effects of physostigmine are obscure. In animal experiments small doses are credited with improved learning. With small doses there is a corresponding desynchronization of electrical activity in the EEG. See *Psychopharmacology of the ANS.*

Bibliography: see *Cholinesterase Inhibitors.* *W.J.*

Piaget, Jean. B. 9/8/1896 at Neuchâtel, Switzerland. Piaget was awarded his doctorate at the University of Neuchâtel in 1918, for a dissertation on a zoological subject. He then worked with H. Lipps and E. Bleuler, at the Sorbonne, and with A. Binet. From 1921, at the prompting of E. Claparède, he began to teach and research at the Institut J. J. Rousseau in Geneva. In 1925 he was offered a chair of philosophy in Neuchâtel, and in 1929 a professorship of scientific thought at Geneva. In addition, in 1929 Piaget became director of the Bureau International Office de l'Education, and deputy director of the Institut J. J. Rousseau, becoming its co-director (together with T. Bovet and E. Claparède) in 1932. From 1936 he was also lecturing at the university of Lausanne; in 1940 he became director of the psychological laboratory at the University of Geneva, and editor (with A. Rey and M. Lambercier) of the *Archives de psychologie.* Piaget was then elected the first president of the recently founded Swiss Society for Psychology, and edited (together with Morgenthaler) its journal *Revue Suisse de Psychologie.* In 1955 he founded the "Centre International d'Epistémologie Génétique" in Geneva, with a grant from the Rockefeller Foundation.

Piaget ranks as one of the most important developmental psychologists. His contribution to the subject is unique, both in the originality of theory and method and the variety and scope of his investigations. He is chiefly interested in the theoretical and experimental investigation of the qualitative changes in the cognitive structure occurring in the course of development, and in their description in mathematico-logical terms. As well as studying the development of intelligence, Piaget has worked (genetically) on the following subjects: perception, causality, language, moral judgment, object, space, number, time, quantity, motion, speed, geometry, logic, genetic epistemology, etc. In Piaget's theory of *intelligence* (q.v.), a distinction may be made between a general theory of cognitive function independent of any stages, and a theory of the development of intelligence linked to special stages. In his non-phasic theory of intelligence Piaget tries to derive the genesis of intelligence organically from lower forms of behavior. He starts from the assumption that all behavior, no matter whether it is an external action or an internal one in the form of a thought, represents an adaptation. *Adaptation* he considers to be a *fluid state of balance* between the *assimilation* of the environment to the individual and the *accommodation* of the individual to the environment. Whereas during biological adaptation the transfers are of a material kind, psychic life begins with the appearance of functional interaction. Piaget understands *cognitive development* to be a process of increasing equilibrium between assimilatory and the accommodatory transfers, and an accompanying generalization, differentiation and coordination of the cognitive schemata created by them. These develop from a state which was originally global and which is characterized by an imbalance between the reciprocal transfers (rhythms, e.g. in reflexes and instincts), passing through a limited state of balance ("adjustments", e.g. in perception and sensorimotor intelligence) to a form of organization possessing a mobile balance and characterized by mobility, permanence and stability of cognitive structures ("operational groupings" in logical thought). See *Development.*

In his theory of *the development of intelligence in stages*, Piaget distinguishes four different periods of development relative to the form of organization of cognitive structures, and passing organically into one another: the periods of (*a*) *sensorimotor intelligence*, (*b*) preoperational representation, (*c*) concrete operations and (*d*) formal operations. The period of sensorimotor intelligence embraces the time when development is taking place from the first reflex-like forms of behavior shortly after birth, passing through the first motor habits, the connecting of means and ends, and active experimentation, and finally reaching the stage of spontaneous invention and the internalization of what until then were sensorimotor schemata, at the age of 1½ to 2 years. The most important addition in the following period of *preoperational representation* (2 to 7 years) consists of the acquisition of the symbolic function as the product of an inward imitation of the outward world, and as a requirement for the mastery of speech. Characteristics of preoperational thinking are egocentricity, centralization, immobility, realism, irreversibility, and transductive formation of conclusions and "preconcepts". At about the age of 7, thinking loses its egocentric and unilaterally centered character and, at the stage of "concrete operations" (7–11 years), reaches a mobile state of balance marked by a system of now reversible coordinated transformations. But, whereas operations at this stage are still bound up with concrete activity, at the last stage of the development of intelligence, the period of *formal operations* (11 to 15 years), they become independent of the concrete object, and the individual acquires the capacity to draw purely formal conclusions from hypothetical assumptions.

Main works: The language and thought of the child. New York & London, 1926 Judgment and reasoning in the child. New York & London, 1928. The child's conception of the world. New York & London, 1929. The child's conception of physical causality. New York & London, 1930. The moral judgment of the child. New York & London, 1932. The psychology of intelligence. New York & London, 1950. Play, dreams and imitation in childhood. New York & London, 1951. The origins of intelligence in children. New York & London, 1952. Jean Piaget. In: Boring, E. G., *et al.* (Eds.): A history of psychology in autobiography, Vol. 4. Worcester, Mass., 1952, 237–56. The child's conception of number. New York & London, 1952. Logic and psychology. Manchester & New York, 1953. The construction of reality in the child. New York & London, 1954. Le développement de la perception de l'enfant à l'adulte, Bull. Psychol., 1954–5, *8*. The child's conception of space. New York & London, 1956 (with B. Inhelder). Les "préinférences" perceptives et leurs relations avec les schèmes sensori-moteurs et opératories. In: Etudes d'épistemologie génétique. Paris, 1958, *6* (with A. Morf). The growth of logical thinking. London & New York, 1958 (with B. Inhelder). The child's conception of geometry. London & New York, 1960 (with A. Szemiska). The early growth of logic in the child. London & New York, 1964 (with B. Inhelder). The mechanisms of perception. London & New York, 1969. Structuralism. New York & London, 1971.

Bibliography: Ausubel, D. P.: A critique of Piaget's theory of the ontogenesis of motor behavior,

J. Genet. Psychol., 1966, *109*, 119–22. **Baldwin, A. L.:** Theories of child development. London, 1967. **Brearley, M. & Hitchfield, E.:** A teacher's guide to reading Piaget. London, 1966. **Flavell, J. H.:** The developmental psychology of Jean Piaget. New York & London, 1963. *W.W.*

Pia mater. A term for the soft membrane covering the brain.

Pick's disease; Pick's syndrome. See *Dementia, presenile.*

Picrotoxin. A psychopharmaceutical agent with a highly stimulating effect on the central nervous system. Even in very small doses it causes convulsions and poisoning. The mechanism of picrotoxin is probably a blocking of inhibiting substances. It has an opposite effect to GABA, which raises the convulsion threshold. Picrotoxin is a strong circulatory analeptic. In animal experiments, subconvulsive doses of picrotoxin increased retention performance in maze problems.

Bibliography: McGaugh, J.: Drug facilitation of memory and learning. In: **Efron, D. H.** (Ed.): Psychopharmacology 1957–1967. Washington, 1968. *W.J.*

Picture arrangement test. Any test in which S. has to put pictures in an order, usually according to "content". *H.J.A.*

Picture completion test. Any test in which incomplete pictures have to be completed by S. The missing elements can either be inserted or identified. *H.J.A.*

Picture Frustration Test (*PF Test*). The PF test was developed by L. Rosenzweig as a projective (q.v.) technique (on the basis of frustration-aggression theories) for individual differences in reacting to frustration (q.v.) situations. S's reaction to problem situations drawn in cartoon form is intended to show whether he tends to reply *extrapunitively*, *impunitively* or *intropunitively* to frustrations. The *validity* of the adults' version is unsatisfactory, whereas that for children is better.

Bibliography: Rosenzweig, S.: An outline of frustration theory. In: **Hunt, J. McV.** (Ed.): Personality and the behavior disorders. New York, 1944. *G.L.*

Picture Story Test. A thematic apperception method published by Symonds (1948), which in its basic theoretical assumptions and material equipment may be compared to the Thematic Apperception Test (q.v.). The test is designed for young people between the ages of twelve and eighteen. There are twenty pictures (of a rather gloomy nature) of juveniles in situations typical of their age. For evaluation the author has proposed counting the frequency of the themes as well as making the quality of the contents a criterion. He gives frequencies resembling norms for the themes. Few estimates of validity and reliability are available.

Bibliography: Symonds, P. M.: Symonds' Picture Story Test. New York, 1948. *D.P.*

Piéron, Henri. B. 18/7/1881 in Paris; d. 6/11/1964 in Paris. Piéron was a French experimental psychologist who began as Janet's assistant in La Salpêtrière. In 1912 he succeeded Binet as Director of the Laboratory for Physiological Psychology at the Sorbonne. From 1923 he held simultaneously a professorial chair for the sensory physiology of the senses at the Collège de France which had been specially created for him. He was one of the founders of the Institut Français d'Anthropologie and of the Institut d'Etude de Travail et d'Orientation Professionnelle. In 1940 he became president of the Association Française pour L'Avancement des Sciences. He received international recognition as president of the International Congress for Psychology held in Paris in 1937, and as president of the International Union for Scientific Psychology. From 1913 until his death he was editor of the journal *L'Année Psychologique*.

Piéron's wide interests and range of research activity were remarkable, included about five hundred publications, and covered four main fields: general experimental psychology, animal psychology, psychophysiology and psychopathology. The physiology of the senses was one of his main interests for more than fifty years. He was also one of the most important representatives of applied psychology (q.v.) in France and a champion of French "psychotechnology", evidence of which is given by the foundation of the Institut d'Etude du Travail and the publication in seven volumes of the *Traité de Psychologie Appliquée* (1949) and *Examens et Docimologie* (1963). Piéron is generally considered to be the initiator of the French "psychologie du comportement", which was akin to American behaviorism in declaring the study of behavior (in contrast to that of the "contents of consciousness") to be the goal of psychology, and seeking to explain matters psychological from physiological foundations without recourse to any process of consciousness.

Main works: Le cerveau et la pensée. Paris, 1923. Psychologie expérimentale. Paris, 1927. Henri Piéron. In: Boring, E. G. *et al.* (Eds.): A history of psychology in autobiography, Vol. 4. Worcester, Mass., 1952, 257–78. Aux sources de la connaissance: la sensation, guide de vie. Paris, [3]1955 (Eng. trans. of 1st ed. of 1945: The sensations, their functions, processes and mechanisms. New Haven, Conn., 1952). Les échelles subjectives. Peuvent-elles fournir la base d'une nouvelle loi psychophysique? L'Année Psychologique, 1959, *59*, 1–34. Vocabulaire de la psychologie. Paris, 1957. De l'actinie à l'homme, Vols. 1, 2. Paris, 1958. *W.W.*

Pigment color mixture. A summative color mixture is obtained with the color op; the subtractive color mixture is produced by mixing colored powders or liquids by double absorption. The color resulting when a yellow pigment is mixed with a blue pigment is green, and not grey as would be expected according to the laws of summative color mixing. The pigments act in this case as a filter: the yellow pigment blocks blue and purple and lets red, green and yellow through; the second pigment only lets blue, purple (which however are kept back by the first pigment) and green through. In consequence the only radiations to pass the two filters are those corresponding to the color green. *G.Ka.*

Pilocarpine. A cholinergic substance which greatly increases secretion (saliva, tears, sweat, water from the anterior chamber of the eye). Other physiological effects: increased blood pressure, tachycardia. Small doses lead to excitation of the reticular formation, which is blocked by atropine. Arecoline (q.v.) and muscarine (q.v.) are related to pilocarpine. *W.J.*

Pilot study. A preliminary study carried out before a full or main study (of which it is a simplified form) in order to collect information which will help in, or even provide a decisive basis for, the main study. See *Pretest*. *H.-J.S.*

Pintner-Patterson Scale of Performance Tests. This test, devised in nineteen-seventeen, was one of the first great attempts to develop standardized series of action tests with general norms. The complete series consisted of fifteen tests of which ten were made into a shortened form. Compared with former tests it is outstanding, especially for the wide range of tasks, the standardization of the procedure and the size of the sample. *F.G.*

Piston effect. The piston effect is similar to the *tunnel effect* (q.v.) and is an example of a *kinetic screen* effect. Rectangular objects move back and forth in a slit at one end of which is a screen. With appropriate timing, one object going behind the screen followed by a second object coming from behind the screen will appear as a single object moving like a piston. *C.D.F.*

Pituitary dwarfism (syn. *Hypophyseal dwarfism; Nanosomia; Microsomia*). Underdevelopment consisting of a failure of normal growth in stature as a result of an insufficiency or an absence (very seldom isolated) of pituitary growth hormone (see *Somatotropic hormone*) conditioning delayed growth after the second to the third year of life (in untreated cases stature is 100 to 140 cm). Pituitary dwarfism usually occurs together with an inborn disturbance of pituitary gonadotrophin production, which (in addition to inadequate growth or dwarfism) evokes a sexual infantilism (secondary hypogonadism; hyper-, hypogonadism), although there are also pituitary dwarfs whose sexual development is normal. Another combination is pituitary dwarfism with hypothyroidism (secondary hypothyreosis) as a result of simultaneous insufficiency of thyreotropic pituitary hormone.

A distinction is generally made between two main forms of pituitary dwarfism: 1. The tumor form, in which tumors have destroyed the adenohypophysis (or anterior lobe of the hypophysis, q.v.) or may be localized in the hypothalamus (q.v.) = hypothalamo-hypophyseal dwarfism), and is clinically often associated with headaches, disturbed vision, vomiting, disturbances of optical field, etc. 2. The idiopathic form, the causes of which are still largely unknown but are thought to be malformations in the hypothalamo-hypophyseal area; among a small group of individuals it is a family malady. For the most part, boys are affected.

Clinically and psychopathologically, an important feature is the differential diagnostic determination of pituitary dwarfism-with-hypothyroidism as distinct from other forms, and particularly that without hypothyroidism.

Psychologically and psychopathologically, intellectual performance in non-hypothyreotic pituitary dwarfism is normal to above-average; compensatory mechanisms often help adjustment to inadequate stature and associated psycho-social stresses. It is especially burdensome if insufficient gonadotrophin production leads to delayed sexual maturation. Inadequate motivation is a marked feature of hypothyreotic dwarfism.

Prognosis and therapy: Apart from the tumor forms, the outlook is physically good, but somewhat problematic psychically. Combined medical and psychological treatment (hormone therapy, psychotherapy, q.v., and sex counseling) is advisable.

Bibliography: Gardner, L. J. (Ed.): Endocrine and genetic diseases of childhood. Philadelphia, 1967. **Jores, A. & Nowakowski, H.:** Praktische Endokrinologie. Stuttgart, 1964. **Martin, M. M. & Wilkins, L.:** Pituitary dwarfism: Diagnosis and treatment. J. clin. Endocr., 1958, *18*, 679. **Money, J.** (Ed.): Sex research: new developments. Chicago, 1968. **Wilkins, L.:** The diagnosis and treatment of endocrine disorders in childhood and adolescence. Springfield, Ill., 1965. *H. Maisch*

Placebo. Strictly speaking, a substance administered in drug tests as a biologically inactive control which resembles in perceptible qualities (form, taste, smell) the preparation under examination. In a broader sense, biologically *active* substances also are referred to as "placebos" when they have certain side-effects in common with the particular substance, but not with the principal effects under investigation (*active placebo*). Neither the subject nor the experimenter should know that a placebo is being administered (double blind test): this is an essential control in psychopharmacological and pharmacopsychiatric investigations, because the mere fact of administering a preparation usually produces unmistakable suggestive changes in almost all the dependent variables. The degree and mode of placebo action depend on many variables. Where the effects are considerable, it is more difficult to determine the significant action of the preparation.

Bibliography: Haas, H., Fink, H. & Härtfelder, G.: Das Placebo-problem. In: **Jucker, E.** (Ed.): Fortschritte der Arzneimittelforsch., 1959, *1*, 279–454. **Kissel, P. & Barrucand, D.:** Placebos et effet placebo en médecine. Paris, 1964. **Lienert, G. A.:** Die Bedeutung der Suggestion in pharmakopsychologischen Untersuchungen. Zschr. exp. angew. Psychol., 1955, *3*, 418–38. **Ross, S.,** *et al.*: Drugs and placebos: a model design. Psychol. Rep., 1962, *10*, 383–92. **Schindel, L.:** Placebo und Placebo-Effekte in Klinik und Forschung. Arzneimittel-Forsch., 1967, *17*, 892–918. *W.J.*

Placebo reactors. Individuals who react to the administration of placebos as to a biologically active substance. According to the test situation and the nature of the dependent variables, twenty to forty percent of subjects in unselected samples react to placebos. It is often supposed that such reactors are characterized by specific personality traits. Correlation studies have shown that, in comparison with non-reactors, placebo reactors register a higher score with respect to the following variables: neuroticism (q.v.), primary suggestibility (q.v.), telling lies, submission, acquiescence. Despite these correlations, there is no proof that there are placebo reactors who will habitually and generally react to a placebo. Different studies suggest that certain individuals react strongly or not at all, according to the situation, and that correlations with personality variables are specific to the situation. See *Traits; Type.*

Bibliography: Fischer, S.: The placebo reactor. Dis. nerv. syst., 1967, *28*, 510–515. **Honigfeld, G.:** Non-specific factors in treatment: 1. Review of placebo-reactors and placebo reactions. 1964, *25*, 145–56. **Steinbook, R. M. & Jones, M. B.:** Suggestibility and the placebo response. J. nerv. ment. Dis., 1965, *140*, 87–91. *W.J.*

Planned experiments. Experiments constructed according to a factorial experimental plan and evaluated by variance analysis. According to the number of independent variables considered, a distinction is drawn between simple planned experiments (two independent variables) and those which are complex (three or more independent variables). *G.Mi.*

Plasticity. 1. The *ability* of organisms during development and in concrete situations to *respond adaptively and adequately* to new environmental conditions (in the sense of relative freedom from genetic determination, educability, flexibility, and changeability). **2.** The *capacity of the organism to assume a new form* genetically. **3.** A *thought or intelligence factor* in the sense of the ability to undergo restructuring; embraces agility in thinking, readapting, discovering and deducing the essentials from stable structures. **4.** *Ability of other parts of the organism to act as substitutes* and take over functions where there has been partial failure. **5.** *Influence* which eidetic (q.v.) images may be subject to from antecedent conditions. *H.H.*

Plateau; plateau formation. See *Learning curves.*

Plateau phase. According to Masters & Johnson (1966) the second of four phases in the sexual reaction cycle, occurring after the excitement phase (q.v.) and before the orgasmic and the resolution phase. Characteristic of both sexes in the plateau phase are muscular tension, increased heart rate and blood pressure; the woman also experiences, e.g., swelling of the breasts, sex flush in the face and the upper part of the body, opening of the labia majora, and swelling and coloring of the labia minora, swelling of the outer third of the vagina, secretion of lubricating fluid; in the man there is a contraction of the anal muscle, a complete erection and an increase in testicular volume, a small increase in the diameter of the penis, and a slight secretion from Cowper's glands.

Bibliography: Masters, W. H. & Johnson, V. E.: Human sexual response. Boston & London, 1966.

J.Fr.

Play. During the child's earliest years most of his time is occupied by play, which may be defined as a joyful bodily or mental activity, which is sufficient to itself and does not seek any ulterior goal (Rüssel, 1959). The child has an urge to express himself and to play: this might be called a "play drive". Among various "theories of play", most support has been given to the ideas of K. Groos (1898), who held that play was a way of practicing important activities and acquiring skills. C. Bühler (1967) distinguishes (by content) between functional, fictional, receptive and constructive play. Developmental psychology puts functional play in the first place. It begins in the first year, and its purpose is the formation and practice of a function or skill (e.g. moving the limbs, arranging and disarranging playthings); it is characterized by a desire to acquire a function or skill.

In the middle of the second year come fictional, "pretend" or acting games. Here the child gives himself or the thing he is playing with a rôle (q.v.), and the basis of the game is a fantasy (feeding the doll and putting it to bed). Imitation (q.v.) of things seen and of one's own experiences is basic to this play form. At about the same time come the *receptive* games (looking at pictures, listening to fairy stories, etc.). The constructive games (building with bricks, drawing, playing with sand or clay) also occur in the second year. At nursery-school age, a child is ready for *games with rules*. Their distinguishing characteristic is that they are bound by strict rules ("it", "hide and seek", and ball games). Play reaches a high point in about the seventh year, when various sorts of games go through phases of popularity at different times.

Bibliography: Beach, F. A.: Current concepts of play in animals. Am. Nat., 1945, *79*, 523–41. **Berlyne, D. E.:** Conflict, arousal and curiosity. New York, 1960. **Bühler, C.:** From birth to maturity. London, 1935. **Id.:** Kindheit und Jugend. Göttingen, 1967. **Devore, I.** (Ed.): Primate behavior. New York, 1965. **Lehmann, H. C. & Witty, P. A.:** The psychology of play activities. Cranbury, N. J., 1927. **Millar, S.:** The psychology of play. Harmondsworth & New York, 1968. **O'Connor, N. & Franks, C. M.:** Childhood upbringing and other environmental factors. In: **Eysenck, H. J.** (Ed.): Handbook of abnormal psychology. London, [2]1971. **Piaget, J.:** Play, dreams and imitation in childhood. New York & London, 1951. **Rüssel, A.:** Spiel und Arbeit in der menschlichen Entwicklung. In: **Thomae, H.** (Ed.): Handbuch der Psychologie, Vol. 3. Göttingen, [2]1959, 502 ff. **Schlosberg, H.:** The concept of play. Psychol. Rev., 1947, *54*, 229–31.

M.Sa.

Playing dead. An innate behavior pattern which serves to mislead a predator. Young animals—predominantly birds leaving the nest and mammals—cease movement when danger threatens or their parents give a warning call, and use their coloring to "merge" optically with the background so that the predator can fixate them only with difficulty. Beetles draw their legs in when disturbed, and fall to the ground, where they can scarcely be detected.

V.P.

Pleasure. Enjoyment; gratification. The positive affect associated with fulfilment of needs and desires, and the attainment of goals.

G.D.W.

Pleasure principle. According to Freud, the "pleasure principle" is opposed to the "reality principle" (q.v.); it controls the "primary psychic processes", which include primitive need states and associated images said to dominate in dream, in fantasy, in psychotic conditions, in a more adequately controlled form in art, in the empathic understanding of others, and even in religious experience or mass behavior. If the reality principle predominates, e.g. in a state of self-absorption, "secondary psychic processes", the ego (q.v.) and the actual environment of the individual are more to the fore.

Bibliography: **Freud, S.:** Beyond the pleasure principle. London, [2]1959.

W.T.

Plethoric type. A term used by the Italian de Giovanni in 1877 for a person with a broad, plump physique. *W.Se.*

Plethysmograph. An instrument for recording changes in volume of some part of the body (usually due to variations in blood supply); e.g. *penile plethysmograph:* for measuring penis volume, which is sometimes used as an indicator of sexual arousal. *G.D.W.*

Plexus. A term in neuroanatomy (q.v.) for macroscopic or microscopic networks of nerve pathways or fibers. The brachial plexus is formed from the nerves C5–T1 of the spinal cord. From this emerge the nerves for the arm and the shoulder. The lumbosacral plexus contains the nerve fibers for the pelvis and the lower limbs. There are many other networks in the autonomic nervous system. The arteries are surrounded by delicate networks of the sympathetic system (q.v.). In the wall of the gastro-intestinal canal there are the intramural plexuses of the autonomic nervous system. *G.A.*

Pneumatic chamber. Used in experiments requiring different atmospheric pressures (high-, low-pressure chamber); particularly important for research in occupational psychology and medicine, but used also for special studies of aptitude and in training courses (e.g. astronauts, pilots, divers, submarine crews). *G.R.W.M.*

Pneumograph. An instrument for recording respiration.

Poetzl's phenomenon. Poetzl observed that briefly presented perceptual material which does not appear in the conscious memory may nevertheless later become part of dream content. *C.D.F.*

Poggendorff illusion. One of the geometric illusions. The diagonal line is continuous, but appears bent as it passes behind the uprights.

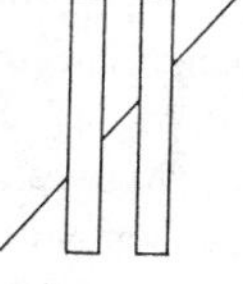

C.D.F.

Point-biserial correlation. A parametric procedure to determine the extent of the correlation between a quantitive, normally distributed (i.e. continuous) variable and a dichotomous or alternative feature. (See *Correlational techniques.*) *G.Mi.*

Point Scale of Performance Tests. A non-verbal series (consisting of eight different tests) by Arthur (1930). Used for assessing practical and concrete intelligence (q.v.) between the ages of five and sixteen years.

Bibliography: **Arthur, G.:** Point Scale of Performance Tests. New York, 1930.

H.J.A.

Poisson distribution. A highly asymmetrical distribution: the random distribution of very rare events. The Poisson distribution is a marginal case of the binomial distribution (q.v.): it occurs when N is high and when the elementary probability approximates to zero. *G.Mi.*

Polarity. A relationship between features or traits which are antithetical pairs. *K.P.*

Polarity profile. See *Semantic differential.*

Police psychology. The purpose of police psychology in the broad sense is to advise the police in their practical work. This counseling (e.g. in regard to riot control) draws upon most branches of psychology, but particularly criminal and social psychology. In the narrower sense, police psychology is concerned with the assessment of policemen, their character, attitudes (q.v.) and relationships, and with selection techniques. At present a great deal of research into police psychology is being done in West Germany. The following are only three of a number of completed Anglo-American studies: Marshall (1966) established that, by comparison with law and social welfare students, police recruits had a statistically significant more unyielding, i.e. harsher, attitude to punishment (q.v.), i.e. they more often advocated harsher punishment for criminals. It was not established whether this fiercer attitude was the result of a process of self-selection in those choosing a police career, selection by the authorities, or adaptation to a role (q.v.). Police recruits showed *greater rigidity*, one of the principal characteristics of the authoritarian personality (q.v.). Of the 282 policemen studied by Skolnick (1967), approximately 70% were concerned about their social standing, 66% considered themselves middle class, and 51% regarded it as "most important" to own a house. 250 out of 700 policemen (35%) gave other policemen as their friends. Several American criminologists already describe this remarkable social phenomenon as a "sub-culture". Most policemen believe they are able to distinguish between guilt and innocence, and do not attach much weight to the findings of the court. Cicourel (1968) showed that lay theories of the causes of delinquency form the basis of judgments made by the police. The police "know what they know", and the problem of legal proof does not arise for them in their daily routine. The North American police favor upper-class delinquent youths from "important families". Middle-class delinquent youths were not seen as actually dangerous to authority; they merely had "psychological problems". The lower-class youth, on the other hand, comes up against the full force of "law and order", particularly if he denies his delinquent behavior and belongs to a racial minority. Nevertheless, one may doubt whether so small a survey is representative of the whole US police force. The results of pertinent West German researches are still awaited. See *Abnormal psychology; Criminality; Forensic psychology; Guilt; Mental defect; Psychopathy; Social psychology.*

Bibliography: Cicourel, A. V.: The social organization of juvenile justice. New York & London, 1968. **Marshall, J.:** Law and psychology in conflict. Indianapolis & New York, 1966. **Skolnick, J. H.:** Justice without trial. Law enforcement in democratic society. New York & London, 1967. **The President's Commission on Law Enforcement and Administration of Justice:** Task force report: the police. Washington, D.C., 1967.

H. J. Schneider

Poliomyelitis (*Infantile paralysis*). An inflammatory disease of the grey substance of the spinal cord (anterior horns), its extension, and possibly also of the brain; it is caused by a virus which occurs in three forms. As a result the Nissl bodies in the plasma of the nerve cells are destroyed. The pathological symptoms, chiefly muscular paralysis, are only partly reversible, so that frequently there is permanent paralysis of single muscles or groups of muscles, and atrophy from non-use. This disease appears sporadically, but it can assume epidemic proportions—usually in the summer months; it is carried in contaminated water and enters the blood stream through the intestines. There is also an abortive form, i.e. one in which there are no paralytic symptoms. Since oral vaccination with non-virulent live viruses was introduced, the disease has practically disappeared.

E.D.

Political psychology. The study of the *personal aspect of political processes.* Various methods are used. The subject comprises: 1. Research into *techniques:* emotional means of exerting influence, forms of indoctrination, and rules for civic cognitive learning processes and socialization methods as well as processes for reaching political decisions. These techniques are governed by success criteria and their results have only a limited predictability. 2. Understanding given *uniformities* of political behavior which occur in spite of, or because of, motivational homogeneity and heterogeneity: e.g. investigations of election and electoral behavior. 3. Interpretations, especially neopsychoanalytical, monobiographical or typological aspects of political élites, basic personalities or exponents of political systems. For the most part these take as their starting point research into antidemocratic syndromes (see *Authoritarian personality*). 4. Enlightenment: i.e. making known the aspects mentioned under 1 to 4 to participants in political processes. 5. Finally, as an applied science, political psychology considers aids to orientation in the instrumental political use of knowledge. All this can be handled as by an objectively unprejudiced or a politically committed researcher.

Political psychology in its present form derives from cultural-anthropological origins. In early "culture-and-personality research", interpretations of self-perpetuating and stabilizing aspects of a culture predominated. The effect of primary institutions (children's education) is considered in neo-psychoanalysis as an irreversible form of imprinting. The corresponding social structure satisfies social expectations and fears contained in this education (see *Socialization*); it corresponds to the sociocultural needs and social perspectives of the typical personality belonging to these institutions. Between the social institutions and members—with regard to their *basic personality structure* but not to their *biographical development*—there exists a kind of "prestabilized harmony". This *stabilization hypothesis*—which is not accepted by all researchers into culture and personality—served as a starting-point for further empirical lines of research.

The object of investigation was the personality type which supports or produces fascist systems—the "authoritarian personality". This led on to research into terrorism, which may be extended to include certain aspects of group dynamics, and studies the findings of the psychology of mass observation and certain manipulative forms of language and communication (Baeyer-Katte, 1971).

Research into the political personality must begin with the *power-hungry figure* seen as a type exhibiting the exaggerated dynamic urge that so interested Alfred Adler (q.v.). But Lasswell (1950) has already begun to see interpersonal patterns of behavior (forms of influence) in which power is wielded and accepted, as typical examples of situations where power has been seized against a background of certain general sociocultural conditions.

The interpretation put forward by totalitarian systems, according to which a united political will and a consenting public opinion act in compliance with the behavioral pattern of the whole population, at first gave rise to the impression that the monolithic state had come into being voluntarily. But the real motive seemed to be less the prevailing ideology—whether with a scientific gloss or an emotional appeal—than a need for obedience and conformity (q.v.). The supposition that the family system (Horkheimer, 1936) supplied the culture-specific conditions was examined empirically in the investigations of authoritarianism (q.v.), rigidity and fascism by the Californian School and the political psychology of Eysenck (1954). The methods used were taken from the general development of empirical psychology. The pioneering work of T. W. Adorno, E. Frenkel-Brunswik, J. D. Levinson and R. N. Sandford (*The Authoritarian Personality*. New York, 1950) was based on the results of research into prejudice (Murphy & Likert, 1938) on the one hand and Fromm's hypotheses (1941) on the other. Apart from many studies in the same mold, critics have examined the method of scaling (q.v.), the special questionnaire technique and a lack of tolerance concerning the ambiguities and contradictions (a scale criterion of the F scale) to be found in the last analysis in the investigators themselves (Christie & Jahoda, 1954; Bass, 1955; K. Eyferth, 1963). The last major survey of the follow-up research pertaining to the Adorno *et al.* model was undertaken by Kirscht & Dillehay (1967). The authoritarian syndrome required a scientific basis for a typology valid for the Nazi era; it partly maintained its position after some corrections had been made (Chapman & Campbell, 1957). Roghmann (1966) provides a comprehensive critical study of these investigations.

Investigations which take the subject further follow on the one hand the Dogmatism Scale (Rokeach, 1948; 1960), on the other, the criteria, elaborated by H. J. Eysenck, of toughmindedness and tendermindedness as well as radicalism versus conservatism. Eysenck points especially to the fact that Fascists and Communists show the same authoritarian values. It is precisely this result which indicates the problems inherent in such definitions of political matters obtained from behavioral patterns. It is surely evident that, under a Fascist regime, supporters of the governing party and the Communist party will not behave alike but (politically) quite differently. The political essence of political behavior has therefore to be established functionally—in agreement or disagreement with the given social order.

If one looks back and uses the concepts of systematic theories which have in the meantime become widespread in political psychology, it may be said that three basic forms of political behavior have been dealt with: behavioral patterns which are stabilizing, conducive to change, and directed against the system (dysfunctional). Of course, like all such simplifications, this division does some violence to the whole picture. But it does show a course of development which can be recognized and substantiated in broad outline (Easton, 1965).

Change conforming to the system—the possibility of internal reform and historical development—is the way in which complicated social systems work. In the nineteen sixties Parsons (1964) and his collaborators developed the concepts which enable political psychology to group its partial findings as a plan of research into political behavior. The key concept of Parsons in this respect is the definition of the evolutionary universals in a society. It states that social systems have to be regarded as living systems: they are always developing new structures and complexes of structures by means of which they can better "adapt" to the challenge of their political environment—that is to say, deal more actively with them and assert themselves by appropriate systematic processes. *Democracy* (q.v.) is such an "invention" of political culture. Since Parsons' concept is linked to the idea of historical development, he considers democracy (representative democracy based on the right to vote) as a social universal. In different ways, but with the same function (the optimization of the political process), this discovery is made in its own time in every social order or taken over by cultural diffusion. Among other things, this means that the personal system of the democrat must correspond to the structural system of democracy. The transformation is effected by participation. The agencies of socialization possessed by democracy as a system of opinions and values are not just parents, but the whole of society without any time limit. The "political structure" of a society thus establishes the political behavior appropriate to it, and this behavior for its part supports the culture. It is a case of self-regulating processes whose political aspect is represented by institutionalized "political behavior", and not a case of an intervening control procedure outside the regular processes. Political behavior may thus be quantified, e.g. in the use of the vote, party membership, the assumption of political elective offices and the measurable state of information; in numerous studies it has been taken as evidence for the state of democratization (Kaase, 1971). Lazarsfeld, Berelson & Gaudet (1948) and Berelson, Lazarsfeld & McPhee (1954), in their studies of elections, indicate methods which can be useful, on the one hand, in election psychology and, on the other, in the connection there between elections and electoral behavior (Schenck & Wildenmann, 1963). Simultaneously, with the breakthrough in small-group research initiated by Homans (1950), the significance of the pioneer study by Levin & Lippitt (1938) increases inasmuch as it sees leadership styles as political control processes for solving problems in small groups. This approach, which is taken further by Verba (1961), lays proper emphasis on the aspect of a political control system—in addition to the studies of self-regulation which were chiefly prevalent in the school of civic cultural research. Of course, control procedures are also found in relation to political processes, but by no means only, in group leadership behavior. They always happen when there is input into the political process (Deutsch, 1969). The theoretical foundation for civic culture research in which political behavior thus receives the value of a resolution to participate after a prepolitical stage of socialization, is given by Almond in his article "Comparative political systems" (1956). *Political behavior* is not exclusively the *behavior of politicians* but includes the behavioral patterns of all men as protagonists inside the working rules of democracy. By comparing systems it is hoped to understand the requirements for participation—or, on the other hand, the conditions for apathy and loss of interest in politics. The theory that political rôles should be learnt through practice is prominent (Allport, 1945). But this is soon joined by extensive concepts based on learning theory (q.v.) and by the concept of internalization, which goes back to neo-psychoanalysis and is under modification by T. Parsons. Almond & Verba (1963) have found in empirical studies, and by comparison of cultures, a positive correlation between the standard of scholastic education, political knowledge and political participation. The conclusion was therefore quickly drawn that further scholastic education also advances democratization, especially in underdeveloped countries (see Pye, 1963). The move "into politics", that is, the crossing of a threshold by which social behavior becomes political, appears at the outset as a form of awareness of subjective competence with its roots in family participation patterns: in the assumption of responsibility in non-political social affairs. Nevertheless, a large number of studies yielded widely varying results regarding the efficiency of the individual factors in *education for citizenship*. Dennis compiled a comprehensive bibliography for the Council of Civic Education (1968). Variables such as great political interest shown by parents (Converse, 1954), the dominance of the mother or the father (who may also belong to two different parties), did reveal significant relationships, but a detailed interpretation reveals complex, multi-causal possibilities. The position is the same concerning the influence of the type of school. There is disagreement not only on the age at which instruction in politics is given (Adelson & O'Neil, 1966). The comprehensive investigations of Langton & Jennings (1968), taking eight variables into account, show only very slight relations between civics taught in school, political orientation and commitment. As long as political socialization is measured by external participation criteria, the results will always remain bogged down in formal correlation analysis. These lines are followed, too, by the two major German studies

(Masermas *et al.*, 1967; Jaide, 1970). The institutionalized agencies of socialization are not even a guarantee of loyalty to democracy (Langton, 1969). Criticism of the hypothesis of automatic processes of political socialization changes the problem of stability more and more into one of equilibrium, or into the observation of processes seeking some balance within social adaptation and integration. As early as 1969, Hyman (who offers a summary of the empirical results of political socialization as they were in 1959) criticized the relative lack of results in all quantitative assessments. This points to a difference between the unreflecting behavior of political participation, and critically reflective control behavior in the presence of this system. Political behavior of this second, higher order would consist in counter-control endeavors (as Ebert, 1970, for example, shows), or in counter-control against counter-control, i.e. in those political forms of behavior which try to make dysfunctional movements functional. Only investigations of the strategies necessary for this and the requisite degree of cognitive separation of rôles within the performance of political rôles would allow political psychology to come into its own (Johnson, 1971). Here it has much in common with the questions currently posed in conflict and peace research: namely, the effects of behavior patterns which conform or are hostile to the system, and accord systems based on threats (Boulding, 1967) or on confidence (Lukmann, 1968), and the effects of non-systematic rôle innovations.

A collection of important contributions to the sociological aspects of political behavior is offered by Allardt & Rokkan (1970). Three series appearing periodically deal with special questions in the field: the *Yearbook of Political Behavior Research* edited by H. Eulau (from 1961), *Politische Psychologie* (from 1963, containing a comprehensive subject catalog, by W. Jacobsen). The most recent effort is *Studies in Behavioral Political Science*, edited by Presthus (from 1969).

Bibliography: Adelson, J. & O'Neil, R.: The growth of political ideas in adolescence: The sense of community. J. of Pers. and Soc. Psychol., 1966, *4*, 295–306. **Adorno, T. W.,** et al.: The authoritarian personality. New York, 1950. **Allardt, E. & Rokkan, S.:** Mass politics. Studies in political sociology. New York, 1970. **Allport, G. W.:** The psychology of participation. Psychol. Rev., 1945, *53*, 117–32. **Almond, G. A.:** Comparative political systems. J. of Politics, 1956, *18*, 391–409. **Id. & S. Verba:** The civic culture. Political attitudes and democracy in five nations. Princeton, 1963. **Auwin, K., Baeyer-Katte, W. v., Jacobsen, W., Jaide, W. & Wiesbrock, H.** (Eds.): Politische Psychologie. Eine Schriftenreihe, Vols. 1–8. Frankfurt, 1963–69. **Baeyer-Katte, W. v.:** Terror. In: Soviet system and democratic society. New York & London, 1972 (in press). **Berelson, B. R., Lazarsfeld, P. F. & McPhee, W. N.:** Voting. Chicago, 1954. **Boulding, K.:** Die Parameter der Politik. Atomzeitalter, 1967, *7/8*, 362–74. **Chapman, L. J. & Campbell, D. T.:** Response set in the F-scale. J. abn. soc. Psychol., 1957, *55*. **Christie, R. & Jahoda, M.** (Eds.): Studies in the scope and method of "The Authoritarian Personality". Glencoe, Ill., 1954. **Coleman, J. S.** (Ed.): Education and political development. Princeton, 1965. **Converse, E. T.:** The nature of belief systems in mass publics. In: **Apter, D.** (Ed.): Ideology and discontent. New York, 1964. **Dennis, J.:** Major problems of political socialisation. Midwest J. of Political Science 1968, *12*, 85–114. **Deutsch, K. W.:** Politische Kybernetik. Modelle und Perspektiven. Freiburg i.Br., 1969. **Easton, D.:** A systems analysis of political life. New York, 1965. **Ebert, T.:** Gewaltfreier Aufstand – Alternative zum Bürgerkrieg. Frankfurt, 1970. **Eyferth, K.:** Typologische Aspekte des Problems der autoritären Persönlichkeit. In: Autoritarismus – Nationalismus – ein deutsches Problem? Pol. Psychol., Frankfurt, 1963, 67–74. **Eysenck, H. J.:** The psychology of politics. London, 1954. **Fromm, E.:** Escape from freedom. New York, 1941. **Habermas, J.,** *et al.*: Student und Politik. Eine soziologische Untersuchung zum politischen Bewusstsein Frankfurter Studenten. Neuwied, [2]1967. **Homans, G.:** The human group. New York, 1950. **Horkheimer, M.** (Ed.): Studien über Autorität und Familie. Paris, 1936. **Hyman, H. H.:** Political socialization. A study in the psychol. of political behavior. New York, 1969. **Jaide, W.:** Jugend und Demokratie. Politische Einstellung der westdeutschen Jugend. Munich, 1970. **Kaase, M.:.** Demokratische Einstellung in der BRD. Sozialwiss. Jahrbuch für Politik, 1971, *II*, 119–316. **Kirscht, J. P. & Dillehay, R. C.:** Dimensions of authoritarianism: a view of research and theory. Lexington, 1967. **Langton, K. P. & Jennings, M. K.:** Formal environment: The school. In: **Langton, K. P.** (Ed.): Political socialization. New York, 1969. **Lasswell, H. D. & Kaplan, A.:** Power and society. A framework of political inquiry. New Haven, 1950. **Lasswell, H. D.:** Power and personality, New York, 1946. **Lazarsfeld, P. F., Berelson, B. R. & Gandet, H.:** The people's choice. New York, 1948. **Lewin, K. & Lippitt, R.:** An experimental approach to the study of democracy and aristocracy: A preliminary note. Sociometry, 1938, *1*, 292–300. **Lipset, S. M.:** Political men. New York, 1960. **Luhmann, N.:** Vertrauen: ein Mechanismus der Reduktion sozialer Komplexität. Stuttgart, 1968. **Milbrath, L. W.:** Political participation. Chicago, 1965. **Murphy, G. & Likert, R.:** Public opinions and the individual. New York, 1938. **Parsons, T.:** Evolutionary universals in society. American sociological Rev., 1964, *29*, 339–57. **Id.:** The political aspect of social structure and process. In: **Easton, D.** (Ed.): Varieties of political theory. Englewood Cliffs, 1966. **Pye, L. W.** (Ed.): Communications and political development. Princeton, 1963. **Roghmann, K.:** Dogmatismus und Autoritarismus. Kritik der theoretischen Ansätze und Ergebnisse dreier westdeutscher Untersuchungen. Kölner Beiträge, Vol. 1, 1966; **Rokeach, M.:** Generalized mental rigidity as a factor in ethnocentrism. J. of Abn. and Soc. Psychol., 1948, *43*, 299–78. **Id.:** The open and closed mind. New York, 1960. **Scheuch, E. K. & Wildenmann, R.:** Zur Soziologie der Wahl. Cologne, 1963. **Verba, S.:** Small groups and political behavior: A study of leadership. Princeton, 1961.

W. von Baeyer-Katte

Pollution. Defilement. Non-scientifically used to refer to the discharge of semen other than during sexual intercourse. See *Masturbation*.

G.D.W.

Poltergeist. (From German, meaning "noisy spirit"). Disturbance characterized by bizarre physical effects of assumed paranormal origin suggesting mischievous or destructive intent. As opposed to a haunt (q.v.), the poltergeist phenomenon seems to depend upon the presence of a particular individual = the "poltergeist focus", usually, but not always, a child or adolescent. W. G. Roll has introduced the more neutral expression RSPK (= recurrent spontaneous psychokinesis). See *Psychokinesis*.

J.B.

Polyandry. Union of one woman with several men. It was found particularly in Ceylon and among Indian mountain tribes, but also among American Indians, where the husbands held in common had as a rule to be brothers.

W.Sch.

Polygamy. Union in marriage of more than two partners (see *Monogamy*); in the past it was much more widespread as polygyny (q.v.) than as polyandry (q.v.).

W.Sch.

Polygraph. A multipoint recorder. Used in psychology, psychophysiology (q.v.) and medicine for the simultaneous recording of several signals. According to the requirements of the task, the polygraph provides a record of: (*a*) *biosignals*, i.e. EEG (q.v.), ECG (q.v.), cardiac activity, arterial blood pressure, breathing, and gas metabolism, skin temperature and skin resistance (q.v.), body movements, electromyograms, etc.; (*b*) *stimulus values*, i.e. frequency and intensity of motor and logomotor behavioral patterns, test performances, etc.; (*c*) *general experimental conditions*, i.e. time intervals, air conditioning, acoustic level, etc. Polygraphs are widely used in medicine as electrocardiographs and electroencephalographs, in criminology as lie detectors (q.v.), and in psychophysiology for recording the physiological components of changes in *arousal* (q.v.), occurring, e.g. during periods of emotion, stress (q.v.), sleep (q.v.) and dream (q.v.).

By contrast with the old smoked and paper kymographs, or simple "event" recorders, polygraphs today are complicated electronic devices with possibly as many as thirty pre-amplifiers and monitoring systems. Each of the machines of up to sixteen final amplifiers drives a writing system whose pointer visualizes the signal pattern on a recording tape by the usual carbon paper method, or by a thermal or ink recording method. Usually there are several feed rates ranging from about 0.01 to 250 mm per second. Signals with a maximum frequency of about 200 c/s can be recorded with sufficient accuracy in this way. A polygraph is equipped with electrodes, probes and transducers for recording primary signals. The technical characteristics of these recorders and the amplifiers and writing systems have a specific influence on the quality of the signal recording.

Since the evaluation of recordings is usually very tedious, automatic data processing of bio-signals has been introduced in recent years. See *Psychophysics*.

Bibliography: Brown, C. C. (Ed.): Methods in psychophysiology. Baltimore, 1967. **Mackenzie, J.:** The ink polygraph. British Med. J., 1908, *1*, 1411. **Schönpflug, W.** (Ed.): Methoden der Aktivierungsforschung. Berne, 1969. **Venables, P. H. & Martin, I.** (Eds): A manual of psychophysiological methods. Amsterdam, 1967. *J.F.*

Polygyny. Union, resembling marriage, of one man with several women; widespread in Africa, Asia and Australia among primitive peoples and in highly civilized societies. But there is no justification for concluding purely on the basis of this ethnological material that some genetically determined "polygamous factor" exists in man (the predominance of monogamy has been established). *W.Sch.*

Polyopia. Multiple vision, monocular diplopia. Several images of an object are seen with one eye, e.g. where there is astigmatism (q.v.). *R.R.*

Polymorphous perversity. A psychoanalytic concept referring to the wide range of stimuli and activities which have erotic value to the infant, and serve as sexual outlets, but which would be considered perversions in adulthood. See *Perversion*. *G.D.W.*

Pons. A part of the occipital brain containing in part or completely the nuclei (q.v.) of the fifth, sixth, seventh, and eighth cerebral nerves. The fibers of the important pyramidal tract, into which the action potentials for voluntary movement are led, run through the pons.

Bibliography: Sidmann, R. L., Sidmann, M. & Arnold, G.: Neuroanatomy. Ein Lehrbuch in programmierter Form, Vol. 1. Berlin & New York, 1971. *G.A.*

Ponzo's illusion. One of the geometric illusions. The upper horizontal line appears longer than the lower although they are objectively equal. A common explanation of this illusion is that the two diagonals are seen as receding parallel lines and hence size *constancy* (q.v.) is misapplied to the two horizontal lines, the upper being seen as further away.

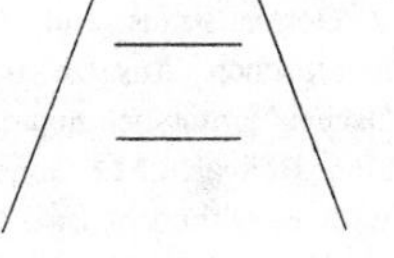

C.D.F.

Pooling. Term for combining values into classes when establishing frequency distributions (q.v.). Chance fluctuations are usually evened out by pooling. In variance analysis (q.v.) pooling is the combination of variance components the equality of which has been statistically verified. *G.Mi.*

Population. 1. The totality or number of all the possible realizations of a random variable. Characteristic statistical values of the population are known as parameters (q.v.); they are quite exact. According to the number of possible realizations, populations can be finite or infinite in extent. *G.Mi.*

2. In statistics "population" denotes a finite or infinite number of individuals (events). The area to which population applies can be laid down at will by defining its elements. For example, all the people, all the motorists, all the houses (in a town for example) constitute the population of the people, the motorists or the houses of a town.

A typical problem of inferential statistics is to give an optimal estimation of the values of a population distribution (parameter) from the values of a sample (q.v.) of that population. See *Statistics*. *W.H.B.*

Poriomania. A desire to wander which occurs without any motivation and ranges from aimlessly running away and ranging about to traveling about in a manner outwardly inconspicuous and wholly adapted to a given situation. The crucial factor is the stressful cause responsible for setting off. *A.Hi.*

Pornography. Originally the depiction of harlotry; now generalized to the expression of lewdness and obscenity of any kind, particularly through books, post-cards, films, etc. Both "obscenity" and "pornography" are to a large extent socially (and usually also legally) defined, for what violates the accepted conventions of one time and place is often regarded as completely innocuous in another.

Bibliography: Abelson, H. *et al.*: Public attitudes toward and experience with erotic materials. Technical reports of the Commission on Obscenity and Pornography (C.O.P.), Vol. 6. Washington, 1970. **Amoroso, D. M.** *et al.*: An investigation of behavioral, psychological and physiological reactions to pornographic stimuli. C.O.P., Vol. 6, Washington, 1970. **Bender, P.**: The definition of "obscene" under existing law. C.O.P., Vol. 2. Washington, 1970. **Ben-Veniste, R.**: Pornography and sex crime: the Danish experience. C.O.P., Vol. 7. Washington, 1970. **Berger, A. S.** *et al.*: Pornography: high school and college years. C.O.P., Vol. 9. Washington, 1970. **Burgess, A.**: What is pornography? in: **Hughes, D. A.** (Ed.): Perspectives on pornography. New York, 1970. **Byrne, D. & Lamberth, J.**: The effect of erotic stimuli on sex arousal evaluative responses, and subsequent behavior. C.O.P., Vol. 8. Washington, 1970. **Cairns, R. B.**: Psychological assumptions in sex censorship. C.O.P., Vol. 1. Washington, 1970. **Clor, H.**: Obscenity and public morality. Chicago, 1969. **Eliasberg, W. G. & Stuart, I. R.**: Authoritarian personality and the obscenity threshold. J. soc. psychol., 1961, *55*, 143–51. **Goldstein, M. J.** *et al.*: Exposure to pornography and sexual behavior in deviant and normal groups. C.O.P., Vol. 7. Washington, 1970. **Howard, J. L.** *et al.*: Effects of exposure to pornography. C.O.P., Vol. 8. Washington, 1970. **Money, J.**: The positive and constructive approach to pornography in general sex education, in the home and in sexological counseling. C.O.P., Vol. 10. Washington, 1970. *G.D.W.*

Porteus Labyrinth Test (syn. *Porteus Maze*). The testee has to find his way out of different labyrinths graded in order of difficulty. Used as a battery test with children to test intelligence and development, and also in diagnostics when there is no recourse to speech.

Bibliography: Porteus, S.: The Porteus Maze Test and intelligence. Palo Alto, 1950. *V.H.S.*

Positionality. The central concept of the recent theory of expression (see *Expression*) for which Frijda (1953) and Kirchhoff (1957) are chiefly responsible. Frijda defines positionality as "that structure of relations which a particular person establishes or seeks to establish at any given time with his environment. The activity structure in which and with which these relations are achieved is indivisibly linked with positionality" (1965). Kirchhoff defines the positionality of a living thing as "the (psycho-physically neutral) manner in which that being exists at any moment; this manner is defined with varying degrees of completeness and differentiation for fellow beings through the phenomenality of the subject and for the latter through his own experience" (1957). According to Kirchhoff, *pathognomic* expression is "positionality in its phenomenality". Proceeding from Kirchhoff's concept of positionality, Holzkamp proposes that Frijda's concept should be used to denote the *nature of an individual's relations* (1965).

Bibliography: Frijda, N. H.: The understanding of facial expression of emotion. Acta Psychol., *9*, 1953. **Id.:** Mimik und Pantomimik. In: **Kirchhoff, R.** (Ed.): Handbuch der Psychol., Vol. 5. Göttingen, 1965. **Holzkamp, K.:** Zur Geschichte und Systematik der Ausdruckstheorie. In: **Kirchhoff, R.** (Ed.): Handbuch der Psychol., Vol. 5. Göttingen, 1965. **Kirchhoff, R.:** Allgemeine Ausdruckslehre. Göttingen, 1957.

J.Mi.

Positivism. In the narrower sense, positivism is the doctrine associated with A. Comte (1798–1857), according to which one knows only facts, the validity of this knowledge being assured by experimental science. This notion characterizes the most advanced "state" in the history of human societies (the "positive state"). In the wider sense, positivism is any theory of knowledge (epistemology; cognition theory, q.v.) which takes into account only given data determined by a particular science, and excludes the possibility of any metaphysical apprehension of the profound nature of things (J. S. Mill, H. Spencer). *Logical positivism* (q.v.) (neo-positivism, logical empiricism) sees knowledge as consisting of "protocol sentences" (q.v.) derived from the observation of facts, and of a proficiently shaped formal and tautological language which coordinates these facts. See *Physicalism; Behaviorism.* *M.-J.B.*

Posodynics. A central concept in the characterology of Bahnsen (1867). A man's capacity for enduring pain (q.v.). Two types are distinguished: the *eucolic* with a great capacity for suffering, and the *dyscolic* who can scarcely endure any pain. *P.S.*

Postdormitium. The period of time before waking up, which may be characterized by vivid imagery. *W.Sch.*

Posthypnotic. After hypnosis (q.v.); pertaining to phenomena which last after the subject has awakened from hypnosis or which only begin to take effect then: for example, the carrying out of "posthypnotic instructions". *H.-N.G.*

Posthypnotic amnesia. See *Hypnosis.*

Posthypnotic state. Some suggestion given during hypnosis (q.v.) is carried out after the hypnotic state, i.e. in the posthypnotic state. The time elapsing between the end of the hypnosis and the performance of the suggested action can also be fixed during hypnosis by suggestion. During this time no specific physiological and emotional changes can be observed in subjects. Shortly before the suggestion is put into effect, individuals have a vague notion that they must do something important. The desired action takes place automatically. The reality of the suggestion is correspondingly reshaped hallucinatively. When the suggested action concluding the posthypnotic state has been performed, there usually occur subsequent rationalizations of the preceding action. It is extremely improbable that any criminal behavior will occur during the posthypnotic state.

Bibliography: Gill, M. M. & Brenman, M.: Hypnosis and related states. New York, 1959. **Kleitman, N.:** Sleep and awakefulness. Chicago & London, 1963.

D.Va.

Posthypnotic time suggestion. A suggestion to be carried out at a fixed time after the hypnosis (q.v.) (e.g. a suggested waking time for treatment of a nocturnal enuresis, q.v.). The date suggested can, under certain circumstances, be even a year later—sometimes a significant therapeutic advantage. *H.-N.G.*

Postremity theory (E. R. Guthrie). A theory of learning (q.v.) based on the postulate that a stimulus situation which has occurred with two or more irreconcilable responses, or has preceded these, becomes a conditioned situation only for the last response to be given.

Bibliography: Guthrie, E. R.: The psychology of learning. New York, 1952. *H.Ha.*

Postulate. An assumed, indemonstrable proposition fundamental to a deductive system. Euclid uses it on the one hand as a *request* (to the reader) to accept the existence of an object and of a specific, simple and easily grasped property pertaining to it, and on the other hand for the possibility of certain construction processes necessary to the development of the system, even though the content of that which is requested may not enjoy the same degree of evident universality as the axiom (q.v.). The content of a postulate is always specific to a given science. In the experimental sciences "postulate" is synonymous with "heuristic hypothesis". In systems theory (since the criteria of evidence and universality no longer apply), the notion of the postulate is replaced by that of the axiom. Finally, by extension, "postulate" designates any proposition admitted, whether implicitly or no, as essential for a coherent presentation. For Kant, the postulates of practical reason are metaphysical theses, which are theoretically indemonstrable though necessary to lend meaning to moral life. *M.-J.B.*

Potency. 1. Power, particularly high power; latent or potential power.

2. Ability to complete coitus (q.v.). In the case of a man this can be disturbed in particular by the diminution or the loss of erection (see *Impotence*) or by the premature ejaculation of semen when the penis is inserted into the vagina (*ejaculatio praecox*), and in the case of a woman when there are organic malformations or vaginal contraction (see *Vaginism*). This type of potency is related to the "normal working of an organic function" or to the presence or absence of frigidity (Giese, 1968, 136).

3. In general the ability to procreate or to produce a child. In the case of the man the power to produce fully developed sperm cells (begins with puberty and remains until advanced old age), in the case of the woman the ability to form fully developed ova and to carry a child for the full term (fertility); this capacity declines as the ovarian function is slowly lost (between the ages of forty-five and fifty-five). A disturbance of this type of potency (infertility) is not related to the intactness of the first type (q.v.), nor is it a generally valid norm for forming a union.

4. The ability or power to experience coitus or other sexual activities as sexually pleasurable or satisfying. This type of potency, especially in the case of women, depends in large measure on psychological and biographical factors; it is related primarily to individual behavior and psychosexual experience during coitus, and not to functional intactness (see 1 above), e.g. in men. There are men as well as women who remain sexually unsatisfied in spite of an orgasm (q.v.) or an ejaculation, and this type of potency can fail to occur especially where there are sexual perversions. See *Sexuality*. *H.M.*

Power drive (syn. *Will to power*). According to Adler (q.v.) this drive occurs as a reaction to the experience of powerlessness and inferiority of the child in its original family. To compensate this condition the individual attempts as a child (and still more as an adult) to secure his position and gain power and control over others. If the child's experience of his own powerlessness and inferiority is lessened or avoided altogether through his environment, the power drive becomes a social and community interest. If the experience of powerlessness and inferiority is particularly strong, the drive may be overcompensated and become pathological. *W.T.*

Power test. A performance test which differentiates those taking it by the varying order of difficulty of its items. The increase in difficulty from item to item should be as uniform as possible and not be too great. The principle of the power test cannot be applied to personality (q.v.) tests. Here, instead of the difficulty gradient, use is made of the graded degree to which the personality dimensions being assessed are found to be present. *P.S.*

Practical psychology. See *Applied psychology.*

Practice usually refers to repeating the same or similar overt responses, but includes single occurrences and the covert (silent rehearsal), and is nearly equivalent in scientific psychology to *experience* as a cause of behavior modification. It means much the same as in common usage: *acting, doing,* but without the connotation of preliminary try-out.

1. *Significance.* Practice is used to study molar behavior and physiological and sensory processes, and test theory. It is not a separate topic and is indexed under many labels: *theory, conditioning, learning, memory, transfer of training, rest, work, inhibition, adaptation,* and *extinction.* Repetitions change response value (error, size, rate, persistence), and all prediction takes into account existing practice-rest conditions, and amount and recency of past experience. The "nature-nurture" issue shows essentially all behavior considered in terms of dependence on practice.

Practice has high priority in theory and the psychology of learning: learning is defined by lasting behavior changes related to practice; and behaviorism bases critical distinctions between theories on the conception of practice's role in learning (Tolman, Guthrie, Hull, Estes). Components and loci of temporary effects of repetition—on drive, fatigue, adaptation—are also important, but psychology gives little attention to muscle-strengthening.

Rest is an inevitable complication, variable, and test of activity. Rest and repetition can have opposite effects on a given behavior, but theory relates them by the same constructs: accrual vs. decay of reactive inhibition; *other* learning as interference, to explain forgetting.

2. *History and methodology.* Practice has been prominent for eighty to ninety years. Its importance grew as psychology shifted from human mind to human and animal behavior; from introspection to methods that brought in practice by requiring overt action; and as learning became theory's chief issue. Repeated response has the same history as behavioral psychology: Ebbinghaus (1885), Cattell, and Functionalism, en route from Wundt to Watson (1912) and behaviorism, this century's dominant psychology; ideas, methods, tasks (Pavlov, Yerkes, Thorndike, Skinner), and inputs from mathematics, encouraged objectivity and exact statement. Task and theoretical diversity put methodological care on within-trial events; Hull made isolating and describing practice's learning and performance effects a primary research goal, and gave formal status to negative factors in repetition.

Laboratory psychology meters practice out in structured environments for a given number of units, or to a criterion response level on standard tasks that present stimuli, provide for response and scoring, and minimize unwanted stimuli and responses. Practice alternates with rest in *trial* units, defined as stimulation with opportunity to respond, constant in duration or in number of stimulations. Measured strength of the behavior studied (frequency, speed, size, e.g. to discrete, rate to continued stimuli) is related to graded values of an *experimental variable* (amount of practice or different values for groups of human or animal subjects in, e.g. stimuli, inter-trial rest, subjects' physical state); and neurophysiological variables and changes are also under study.

Behavior is related to practice variables: directly and immediately, while a difference in practice conditions obtains; directly, but later, in memory tests for change in practice residuals over time; or indirectly, in transfer of practice residuals to new tasks or practice conditions.

3. *Research.* Relating amount, duration, and direction of behavior change to what response is repeated (simple-complex, new-old), to what cues, how (ignored, rewarded, punished), and how often, is a major task. Practice has diverse effects, dependent on both positive and negative factors (adaptation, failure to reward, work inhibition, lowered drive), and much of psychology is directed to practice: repeated responding makes and breaks habits; changes vary from fleeting to permanent; temporary loss can mask lasting gain; rest causes forgetting or recovery from decrement; practicing one task helps or harms remembering, learning, or performing others.

Repetition changes reflex and already acquired behavior, but most research uses new, learning, tasks: conditioning methods analyze basic strengthening and weakening processes with simple stimulus-response tendencies; discrimination and choice add intra-task transfer of learning and inhibition; skill and serial tasks bring in timing and chaining. Task category is important, since an observed behavior, by speed or other index, depends both on the tendency to make the response on cue and on competing tendencies that can block it.

(*a*) *Assuring practice.* A trial provides opportunity; practice requires responding. The organism must be capable of the action (cats tug strings, but do not bark) and it must occur: (i) spontaneously—as operant methods take advantage of an act likely to occur (people talk, pigeons peck), or similar ones for gradual shaping to standard, and vary factors that change its probability; or (ii) by stimulation—e.g. the US in classical conditioning (food, shock). Incentive, instruction, pre-training, drive, physical restriction, and other techniques to assure stimulation, limit interference, or arouse activity, shape and steer the subject to the behavior to be practiced.

(*b*) *Learning.* Subjects practicing new tasks under certain conditions typically show gradual improvement. Error declines, amplitude and speed increase, usually as a simple exponential function of trials (for habit competition and probability indices, an ogive). The conditions vary somewhat with task category. *Conditioning* requires (i) drive, e.g. hunger, (ii) a cue-response sequence, e.g. bell-salivation, followed by (iii) a reinforcing stimulus, e.g. food, contingent on behavior (instrumental) or a US independent of response (classical). *Complex human learning* relies on social motives not always specified, and feedback follows cue-response sequences. If the conditions are not met, performance stays the same or worsens—or the response fails to occur. Extinction, memory, and transfer tests verify that the behavior trends reflect learning, and relate degree of learning to number of trials. Other variables (intra-trial stimulus and response events and temporal relations; meaningfulness in rote verbal learning; intermittent reinforcement, e.g.), influencing acquisition, retention, resistance to extinction, are a main part of the study of learning.

(*c*) *Habit breaking.* The basic procedure to weaken conditioned response by practice is *extinction:* cue, response opportunity, no reinforcement. Extinction is gradual for animal subjects, abrupt for human. But behavior recovers over rest, and can be persistent —e.g. if based on anxiety, after partial reinforcement, if instructions imply a response is expected. *Punishment* weakens if it exceeds reward, or if it—or added cues—evokes strong competing behavior e.g., but augments behavior based on aversion. *Counter-training*, combining extinction with reinforcing new responses, is an effective method, especially when it follows gradual stages in altered environments to make new behavior more, and old less, likely on return to the original situation.

(*d*) *Distribution of practice.* Continued perceptual-motor tasks (e.g. tracking) are stressed as trial/rest spacing has little effect with low work loading (e.g. verbal learning, conditioning). Output falls off with all-out work at a well-learned task and recovers with rest. Habit increments usually exceed inhibitory in new tasks and practice yields net trial-to-trial gain, but the limit of present performance grows with trial/rest spacing (in longer rest between trials or shorter trial duration). Transfer tests for lasting decrement from massed practice find behavior shift with shift to new spacing: massed practice conceals, not retards, learning. Single-rest designs vary length of rest or pre-rest practice and infer the course of accrual and dissipation of inhibition from improvement from pre- to post-rest score. Forgetting can override rest benefits or appear in warm-up decrement, despite improved performance after a rest.

4. *Comment*. Practice is evaluated with all experimental psychology in its analytic approach and use of theory to integrate varied phenomena under general principles; it is as general a term as *response*, and includes its problems of definition, elicitation, measurement, and interpretation. College texts in basic psychology (Hilgard & Atkinson, 1967; Kendler, 1968) introduce both scientific method and practice. Science's case (Nagel, 1961; in psychology, Hyman, 1964; Marx, 1963), design and experimental methods (Sidowsky; Underwood, 1966), and practice methodology and data (Deese & Hulse, 1967; Hall, 1966; Kimble, 1961; Marx, 1969; Melton, 1964) are further elaborated in other readings.

Bibliography: Corso, J. F.: The experimental psychology of sensory behavior. New York, 1967. **Deese, J. & Hulse, S. H.:** The psychology of learning. New York, [3]1967. **Floyd, W. F. & Welford, A. T.** (Eds.): Symposium on fatigue. London, 1953. **Hall, J. F.:** The psychology of learning. Philadelphia, 1966. **Hilgard, E. R. & Atkinson, R. C.:** Introduction to psychology. New York, [4]1967. **Holding, D. H.:** Principles of training. London, 1965. **Hyman, R.:** The nature of scientific inquiry. Englewood Cliffs, N.J., 1964. **Kendler, H. H.:** Basic psychology. New York, [2]1968. **Kimble, G. A.:** Hilgard and Marquis' conditioning and learning. New York, [2]1961. **Marx, M. H.** (Ed.): Theories in contemporary psychology. London, 1963. **Id.:** Learning processes. London, 1969. **Melton, A. W.** (Ed.): Categories of human learning. New York, 1964. **Nagel, E.:** The structure of science. New York, 1961. **Sidowski, J. B.** (Ed.): Experimental methods and instrumentation in psychology. New York, 1966. **Underwood, B. J.:** Experimental psychology. New York, [2]1966.

Ina McD. Bilodeau

Practice, immanent. See *Learning, latent*.

Practice period. The term *practice* refers to the repeated performance of some activity with a view to its improvement. Practice may be *massed* into one long, continuous period, or it may be *distributed* into a series of shorter periods (trials) which are interspersed with periods of rest. The latter condition is usually found to be more favorable to learning. A period of practice is used in some learning experiments in order to equate subjects for previous experience on the task, or at least to reduce this differential. *G.D.W.*

Practice therapy. An (organismic) psychotherapeutic procedure involving the use of autosuggestion (q.v.) and suggestion (q.v.), including techniques to induce increased performance, or training of the will (see *Autogenic training*), and even art therapy and psychodrama (q.v.). *F.Ma.*

Pragmatism. 1. An epistemological movement which would have the truth of any assertion reside in the consequences which it may have in our lives. There are two main varieties: (*a*) that in which the notion of truth is wholly coincident with that of individual interest (Callicles: cf. Plato's *Gorgias*); (*b*) that in which truth corresponds to the exaltation of a group (class, religious, or national truth).

2. The doctrine associated mainly with C. S. Peirce, W. James (q.v.), and J. Dewey (q.v.): "In order to ascertain the meaning of an intellectual conception one should consider what practical consequences might conceivably result by necessity from the truth of that conception; and the sum of these consequences will constitute the entire meaning of the conception." (Peirce.) "Truth lives . . . for the most part on a credit system. Our thoughts and beliefs 'pass', so long as nothing challenges them, just as bank-notes pass so long as nobody refuses them. But this all points to direct face-to-face verifications somewhere, without which the fabric of truth collapses like a financial system with no cash-basis whatever." (James.)

Bibliography: Dewey, J.: How we think. New York, 1910. **James, W.:** Pragmatism. London, 1907. **Peirce, C. S.:** Collected papers (Ed. C. Hartshorne & P. Weiss). New York, 1931–5. *F.B.*

Praise and blame. Expressions of approval and disapproval respectively, of a person or his behavior. Considered jointly in psychology as methods of manipulating human behavior (see *Reinforcement*), especially with children. *G.D.W.*

Precocity. Abnormally early development of physical and mental capacities. The term is often applied to the existence of sexual experience appropriate to a later stage of development. *K.E.P.*

Precognition. A form of ESP (q.v.) in which the target (q.v.) is some future event. Precognitive hit (q.v.) = hit with forward temporal displacement. Foreknowledge that does not depend on inference. *J.B.*

Preconscious. The system comprising all those psychic processes which can be activated at any time and without the inner resistance of the individual. See *Subconscious; Unconscious; Psi-system.* *W.T.*

Preconscious memory. A term introduced by Frank (1969) into information psychology (q.v.) and cybernetic education (q.v.) to characterize the second "temporal channel" of a *psycho-structural model* (q.v.). In this model, short-term storage (i.e. memory), as the first "temporal channel", precedes preconscious memory. In short-term storage, information becomes conscious. The information proceeds from short-term storage to preconscious memory, the latter being conceived as consisting of short- and long-term memory. Information can be recalled from the preconscious memory into the short-term store, i.e. data can become conscious memories. The term does not indicate any connection with Freud's notional pre- and un-conscious.

Bibliography: Frank, K.: Kybernetische Grundlagen der Pädagogik. Baden-Baden, [2]1969. *D.Vo.*

Prediction (syn. *Prognosis*). 1. *Definition and Methods.* Psychological prediction, strictly speaking, means forecasting the probability of future courses of action on the basis of present and past behavior. This behavior is influenced by environmental, innate and personality factors and can be consciously or unconsciously motivated. In a broader sense, *individual prediction* has its place in all fields of psychology and involves not only the personality at the time of the test but the shape it will take in the future. A distinction is drawn between *clinical, typological and statistical* predictions according to the method adopted. Statistical individual prediction makes use of prediction tables which have been compiled on the basis of a fairly wide range of experience. These tables are simply aids in the hands of an experienced psychologist when he is objectifying prediction decisions. They must not be applied mechanically or automatically. Clinical individual prediction does *not consciously* use any statistical prediction tables. However, as a preparation for deciding on some prediction, it carefully studies the life history and the family circumstances of the individual, makes a purposeful exploration (q.v.) and applies psychodiagnostic test methods. Improper forms of clinical prediction are based upon the intuition, speculation, subjectivism (prejudice) of the researcher; they cannot provide a sufficient foundation for psychological decision. Either the statistical or clinical method may be the type used for the individual prediction (this may consist of a typological application of factorial groups taken from statistics), or may be made on the basis of clinical experience.

2. *Criminal Prediction.* The most important field in which individual prediction is applied is in criminal psychology. The prognostic judgment relating to the lawbreaker is divided into two parts—its purpose and its aim. This division is partly linked to an examination at different points of the causes leading to the crime and the remedial measures to be taken. In broad outline prediction can be said to fall into the stages of *predelinquency*, *possibility of recidivism* and *prediction of treatment*. The last two stages refer only to those who are *already guilty of some criminal offense.* Criminal prediction dealing with predelinquency tries to detect children and juveniles who as yet have committed no criminal offense but who possess personality *traits* (q.v.) which make it highly likely that they will tend to become persistent criminals, as they are particularly susceptible to criminal influences.

3. *Historical survey.* Criminological prediction research began in the USA in 1923. Since then it has dealt chiefly with the problem of forecasting success (non-relapse) and the failure (relapse) during the period of parole in the case of adult convicts and occasionally also in that of juvenile convicts, but in individual cases it has also studied how to forecast success or failure when the probation system is used. Research into ways of forecasting criminal behavior at the stage of predelinquency only began relatively late, in 1940. The first useful *prediction table* was compiled by E. W. Burgess. He analyzed the files of three thousand convicts who had been placed on probation and obtained twenty-one factors on the basis of the correlation of his factors obtained from the files with the criteria of success (no relapse) and failure (relapse). S. & E. Glueck, a married couple who work together, began their prediction research in 1925, almost contemporaneously with E. W. Burgess. After carrying out comprehensive empirical investigations by the longitudinal method (q.v.) for many years, and others by the cross-sectional method since 1940, the Gluecks compiled about fifty different personality tables of all kinds. Their Social Prediction Table is the most popular table dealing with criminal prediction. Like most of their prediction tables, it consists of *five important factors:* upbringing of the boy by the father, maternal control of the boy, paternal affection for the boy, maternal affection for the boy, and closeness of the family unit. Studies of the reliability and retrospective and prospective validity of the Social Prediction Table have so far proved negative. As a result of this, a table for criminal prediction was drawn up with the following three social factors: mother's control of the boy, boy's upbringing by the mother, and closeness as a unit of the family. The first German criminal prediction table was developed by R. Schiedt. An inquiry showed that statistical methods of criminal prediction are used in only a few states in the USA (e.g. in Illinois, Ohio, California, Colorado). In Japan the tables compiled by the Gluecks have met with much approval. In the Federal German Republic and the other West European states, statistical methods of criminal prediction are only occasionally made use of. In Eastern Europe and other parts of the world research into criminal prediction is as good as unknown.

4. *Present state of research and most important results.* In essence only three methods for making criminal prediction tables were known until a short time ago: (*a*) the compilation of special stimuli configurations—mostly by using test methods devised already for other

purposes—with the aim of making a criminal prediction (such methods employ parts of tests, test profiles and batteries); (*b*) the summation of factors likely to lead to a relapse, all of which are given the same weighting (Burgess method); (*c*) the combination of a few selected personality characteristics with different ratings in a table (Glueck method).

The *main weakness* of these methods of criminal prediction, astonishingly enough, remained hidden until a few years ago; it is that they completely neglect the *interdependence and interdependence correlations of their individual factors with one another and with their criteria of success or failure.* This weakness is overcome by *structural prediction tables* which have very recently been developed afresh everywhere in North America. The classification method developed by W. T. Williams and J. M. Lambert from plant ecology was adopted and developed further by L. T. Wilkins and MacNaughton-Smith into a new and promising method for constructing criminal prediction tables. This procedure is based on the following *methodological principles:* it starts from the assumption that there is a high degree of reciprocal action which as yet has not been discovered and cannot even be studied yet with the present research methods used by criminal psychology between prediction factors and a considerable variation spread of individual dissimilarity among the criminal population. In consequence it attempts to classify the empirical data according to the presence or absence of certain characteristics and to subdivide hierarchically the heterogeneous criminal population into relatively homogeneous risk groups differing structurally from one another according to the presence or absence of characteristics which are related in different degrees to the criteria of success or failure. The personality characteristics, chiefly objective external factors, are combined for each risk group, so that something like a typology of risk groups is created. Well-known structural tables for criminal prediction have been devised quite recently by D. Glaser, K. B. Ballard and D. M. Gottfredson and T. Grygier. The first investigations of their validity have produced favorable results.

5. *Criminal prediction studied scientifically.* The method used at present is first to look especially for external factors which differentiate sharply, are accurate and can be ascertained objectively and concerning which items of information can be obtained relatively easily and then to combine them factorially in the sense of structural prediction tables. The criticism of principle made by dogmatic penologists and theoretical sociologists against the application of criminal prediction tables can be traced back to misconceptions and insufficient knowledge of the ways in which they can be applied. Important are doubts about the harmful retroactive effects of criminal prediction decisions in socio-psychological matters. For there is a serious danger that children exposed to criminal dangers will be "stigmatized", that they will commit criminal actions in a spirit of defiance, and that they will be actually forced into a delinquent rôle by unreasonable parents, siblings, teachers and school friends. The concept of "social progression" is used in this connection to denote a dynamic force which exerts on the members of some socially deviant, non-adapted group a pressure which drives them continuously to more serious social deviation (the pressure of social nonconformity). Such a negative progressive effect can be found in children and juveniles who have been the subject of an unfavorable criminal prediction, especially because as yet no new and effective methods of treatment have been devised which are suitable for preventing early criminality; the same may be said with some modifications for the prediction of recidivism. A recidivist who is unfavorably criticized runs the risk of finally giving up. Because he is being regularly sent to prison or is obliged to remain there to serve the whole of his outstanding sentence,

the team responsible for treating him can as a result of the unfavorable decision be all too easily inclined in such cases entirely to lose its educational enthusiasm. See *Conscience; Criminality; Personality; Traits; Type.*

Bibliography: Höbbel, D.: Bewährung des statistischen Prognoseverfahrens im Jugendstrafrecht. Göttingen, 1968. **Mehl, P. E.:** Clinical vs. statistical prediction. Minneapolis, 1954. **Mey, H. G.:** Prognostische Beurteilung des Rechtsbrechers. Die deutsche Forschung. In: **Undeutsch, U.** (Ed.): Handbuch der Psychologie, Vol. 11. Göttingen, 1967, 511–64. **Ohlin, L. E.:** Selection for parole. A manual of parole prediction. New York, 1951. **Schneider, H. J.:** Prognostische Beurteilung des Rechtsbrechers: Die ausländische Forschung. In: **Undeutsch, U.** (Ed.): Handbuch der Psychologie, Vol. 11. Göttingen, 1967, 397–510.

H. J. Schneider

Predictive validity, coefficient of. A special kind of validation (q.v.) of a test. If a test, e.g., is to make it possible to predict later performances, validation must be carried out in such a way that the agreement between the predicted and the observed value can be quantified. See *Test theory.* *W.H.B.*

Predormitium. Period of time before deep sleep. The concepts of pre- and post-dormitium (q.v.), which were defined phenomenologically, are now being added to by the more precise formulations of neurophysiological research into sleep (q.v.). *W.Sch.*

Pre-ejaculatory secretion. Under sexual stimulation some drops of a transparent secretion may be emitted from the orifice of the male urethra. The slightly alkaline secretion comes from the Cowper glands and neutralizes acidic traces of urine before ejaculation (q.v.). It may contain actively mobile spermatozoa. As pre-ejaculatory secretion can make the glans penis move more easily, it is also thought of as a lubricant (q.v.). *V.S.*

Pre-encephalon. See *Cerebrum.*

Preformation theory. A theory about the development of the organism prevalent until the middle of the eighteenth century. It was supposed that the embryo was not formed afresh from the protoplasm (epigenesis) but was contained in it and was already formed in all its parts. The logical consequence is the theory which states that every species was created as a pair already containing all its progeny "fitted one into the other". Growth was interpreted by preformation theory as being simply increase in size, and its origin was considered to be either in the ovum (ovulist) or the spermatozoon (animalculist). Darwinism (q.v.) demolished preformation theory; modern genetics (q.v.) has shown that, whereas the "ground plan" of the organism is already present in the hereditary factor, its development can in no way be equated with increase in size. *W.Sch.*

Pregenital stage. This phase comprises the period until the successful conclusion of the Oedipal problem (see *Oedipus complex*) at about the age of four to six years; the subsequent primacy of the genitals signifies not only a purely physical development, but psychosocially the possibility of turning toward the object, another person and experiencing feelings of pleasure. The three or four parts of the pregenital stage, according to Freud, are the oral (q.v.), the anal-sadistic (q.v.) and the phallic (q.v.). Freud discovered these phases or expressions of sexual partial instincts (q.v.) retrospectively, while analyzing his patients and by analogy from the sexual perversions (q.v.). Analytical therapeutical experience shows that neuroses (q.v.) and other psychic disturbances whose origin can be traced to a pregenital phase (autochtonous or regressive) are much more serious and more difficult to treat than disturbances which occur later. Erikson's modification of the theory of a pregenital stage emphasizes the psychosocial aspect more; he distinguishes the *zonal* (body zones), *modal* (typical forms of behavior, e.g.

embodying, retaining-eliminating, and penetrating) and the aspect of modality, "the readiness to experience exclusively the zonal and modal aspect" (to receive, take, retain, make, i.e. to show initiative). *W.Sch.*

Pregnance; pregnance, tendency to. *Pregnance* denotes clarity, an optimal state of structuring, a stage of consciousness which emphasizes the essential. A tendency to pregnance (W. Wertheimer, W. Köhler) is a tendency toward a "good gestalt" (configuration), a force resulting in the dynamic arrangement of a field or system which will produce the completeness, regularity, etc., of something perceived or will lead to the solution of a problem by "centering" or changing the functions of the parts in the whole. See *Ganzheit*; *Lewin*. *J.M.D.*

Prejudice. 1. *Definition.* The term has a similar derivation in several European languages (*préjugé, Vorurteil, prejudizio, perjudicado*). It refers to "preconceived opinion, bias (*against, in favour of*, person or thing)" (The Concise Oxford Dictionary). However, in social psychology it applies mainly to hostile attitudes towards one or more social groups (for example, racial, national, ethnic, religious). Allport (1954), for instance, defined prejudice as "an antipathy based upon a faulty and inflexible generalization. It may be felt or expressed. It may be directed toward a group as a whole, or towards an individual because he is a member of that group" (p. 9).

Prejudice is an attitude. It must be distinguished from *discrimination*, which in this context can be defined as inequitable treatment of individuals because of their membership of a particular group. Prejudice may or may not express itself in discrimination. Discrimination may or may not be caused by prejudice.

2. *The social and the individual approaches.* The distinction between prejudice and discrimination corresponds roughly to different emphases given to their study by social scientists interested mainly in social processes and those interested mainly in psychological processes. The former seek to relate the social characteristics of an intergroup situation (such as competition for resources, power and status differentials, and so on) to the social effects (such as discrimination) that these conditions may have. The latter are more interested in the genesis of prejudice in an individual, in the analysis of its various aspects, and in the relations that obtain between prejudice and the individual's overt social behavior. There is considerable overlap between these two types of interest. The traditional psychological viewpoint is exemplified by Berkowitz (1962) who stresses "the importance of individualistic considerations in the field of group relations. Dealings between groups ultimately become problems for the psychology of the individual" (p. 167). The interaction of social and cultural factors (such as social norms) with the psychological determinants of prejudice has, however, also been stressed by many social psychologists (e.g., Pettigrew, 1958).

3. *Psychological theories of prejudice.* Prejudice can be considered in terms of its motivational, cognitive and behavioral components. These approaches are complementary rather than mutually exclusive. The motivational roots of prejudice have been sought in the human response to frustration with its important derivative of displaced hostility. A synthesis of Freudian ideas and of concepts from learning theory was attempted by Dollard *et al.* (1939). The theory assumes that interference with goal-directed behavior which constitutes a frustration creates hostile impulses which, if they cannot be directed at the frustrating agent, will be displaced towards other objects. Therefore hostility and aggression following upon frustration encountered in the social environment will tend to focus on selected outgroups which provide relatively easy targets. This hostility will be accompanied

by projections and rationalizations whose function it is to "justify" to the individual his choice of substitute targets.

The frustration-aggression hypothesis was also combined with assumptions about generalization of aggression based on concepts deriving from Hullian learning theory. A recent critical analysis based on experimental research can be found in Berkowitz (1962).

An important advance in the understanding of prejudice from the point of view of its role in personality organization has been made by Adorno *et al.* (1950). They considered prejudice as a symptom which should be viewed against the background of emotional needs characteristic of individuals who display the syndrome of "authoritarian personality". Prejudice is not an isolated attitude; it is inherent "in the type of approach and outlook a subject is likely to have in a great variety of areas ranging from the most intimate features of family and sex adjustment through relationships to other people in general, to religion and to social and political philosophy" (p. 971). The background of this syndrome is to be found in the emotional problems arising in the course of early socialization.

Methodological and theoretical criticisms followed the statement of the theory and of its related assumptions about an "ethnocentric personality" characterized by a generalized hostile attitude towards outgroups. These criticisms were mainly concerned with the validity of the measures employed (e.g. Christie and Jahoda, 1954), the possibility of wider theoretical formulations (e.g. Rokeach, 1960), and the role of situational variables in the genesis of prejudice (e.g. Pettigrew, 1958; Banton, 1967).

The interest in the cognitive aspects of prejudice was first represented by studies of stereotypes: that is, the attribution of common characteristics to a group with a corresponding neglect of individual differences. Through the influence of Allport (1954) and others, this interest widened to an analysis of stereotypes as a part of the general tendency to categorize the social environment in order to be able to cope cognitively with its complexities. Hostile stereotypes have been found to be resistant to change in direct relation to the intensity of prejudice which they reflect. Social consensus in the use of stereotypes was extensively studied by Manz (1968). The system of beliefs which underlies the formation of stereotypes was considered by Tajfel (1969) in relation to an individual's attempts to understand the processes of social change by which he is affected, and to the consequences that this may have for his social behavior.

Various aspects of prejudice have been studied with a diversity of methods ranging from experiments testing some of the specific hypotheses, through attitude scales, questionnaires and surveys, to clinical depth interviews, field studies and developmental studies.

4. *Prejudice and behavior.* The relations between prejudice and behavior are complex and no simple generalizations are possible. Outstanding for their combination of attitudinal, behavioral and situational variables have been the studies of Sherif (1966) in which he related intergroup conflict and competition to the formation of intergroup attitudes and to consequent behavior. In this, perhaps Sherif's work represents an indication of future developments. The study of prejudice in its relation to social behavior, and of the conditions leading to its increase or reduction, will have to include an analysis of psychological processes carefully set against the social and cultural background of intergroup relations.

Bibliography: Adorno, T. W., *et al.*: The authoritarian personality. New York, 1950. **Allport, G. W.:** The nature of prejudice. Cambridge, Mass., 1954. **Banton, M.:** Race relations. London, 1967. **Berkowitz, L.:** Aggression: a social psychological analysis. New York, 1962. **Christie, R. & Jahoda, M.** (Eds.): Studies in the scope and method of the "authoritarian personality". Glencoe, Ill., 1954. **Dollard, G.,** *et al.*: Frustration and aggression. New Haven, 1939. **Manz, W.:** Das Stereotyp. Zur Operationalisierung eines sozialwissenschaftlichen Begriffs. Meisenheim a. G., 1968. **Pettigrew, T. F.:** Personality and sociocultural factors in intergroup attitudes: a cross, national comparison. J. Confl. Resol., 1958, *2*, 29–42. **Rokeach, M.:** The open and closed mind. New York, 1960. **Sherif, M.:** In common predicament: social psychology of intergroup conflict and cooperation. Boston, 1966. **Tajfel, H.:** Cognitive aspects of prejudice. J. Biosocial. Sci., 1969, *1*, Suppl. No. 1: Biosocial aspects of race, 173–191.

H. Tajfel

Premenstrual syndrome. A set of physiological and psychological symptoms occurring in the three or four days previous to menstruation, differing from woman to woman but characteristically involving depression and/or irritability. Also called *premenstrual tension*, and *premenstrual molimina*. *G.D.W.*

Prepuberty. (syn. *Pre-adolescence*). A stage of development lasting approximately a year and immediately preceding the beginning of puberty (q.v.). It features a non-specific emotional and behavioral lability, increased interest in intellectual matters and a sudden intensification of vertical growth (the prepuberal spurt). To this extent, prepuberty may be considered a special developmental "phase". Many specific aspects of prepuberty are conditioned not, as was once supposed, by maturation but by culture, i.e. experience. See *Adolescence; Child psychology; Development; Youth*. *H.-J.K.*

Presbyacusis. After the age of forty to fifty years, hearing can be expected to become less acute, the symptom being an increasing lowering of the upper acoustic level. At c^6 as a very crude approximation, an average deterioration in the faculty of hearing can be found amounting to about 10 to 15 db for every decade of life. Deviations admittedly lie between 4 and 25 db, so that it is scarcely possible to give exact norms for this decline due to age (presbyacoustic law). *M.Sp.*

Presbyophrenia. The loss of mental powers (in particular the ability to perceive and to remember) occurring in old age due to senile atrophy of the brain. See *Aging; Gerontology*. *C.Sch.*

Presbyopia. Owing to physical processes taking place in the lens (q.v.) as age increases, the eye loses its power of *accommodation*. Till the age of forty-five approximately, these processes often remain unnoticed, then it is suddenly realized that it has become impossible to read at the normal reading distance. Near vision, in particular, is affected. In this respect presbyopia resembles hyperopia (q.v.) but it is not a pathological process. It can be corrected by the use of convex lenses of up to 3+ diopters. *R.R.*

Pre-school age. The kindergarten or nursery-school age; the years immediately preceding entry to the infant (i.e. primary) school. The term is used largely in connection with pre-school education, but is not tied to a precise age group, since the age of entry to schooling varies from country to country, and some have more or less extensive nursery school provisions. See *Education, pre-school*. *R.O.*

Presentation, method of. A formal aspect of the psychological experiment which determines the manner in which an individual will be confronted with a stimulus or a constellation of stimuli. The main variables of the stimulus are: modality, quality, intensity, duration, etc. There are also variables such as mode of instruction, society, objects, etc.

P.S. & R.S.

Presenting (sexual). Showing the genital zone can have a soothing effect, be a greeting ceremony or indicate a rank inside a hierarchy. Sexual presenting need not necessarily be intended for someone of the opposite sex.

Male baboons of an inferior rank adopt female presenting behavior in front of a superior male. Strong males of the same species present their genitals when watching over the troop. Very probably this is the origin of the phallic cult (q.v.) of many primitive tribes.

V.P.

Pressure balance. An appliance invented by W. Wundt for measuring sensitivity to pressure.

Pressure points. Parts of the body surface which are sensitive to pressure. The receptors for pressure (Merkel's disks, Meissner's corpuscles, free nerve endings) are shaped like points and are of varying density; they are distributed over the whole surface of the body. There are about 720,000 of them, and some 80,000 are distinguished from the rest by special sensitivity (the greatest density is at the tip of the tongue, the least is at the back).

P.S.

Pressure, sense of. The sense of pressure or touch belongs, together with the sensations of pain or temperature, among the skin senses (see *Haptics*). The sensation of pressure arises from a mechanical deformation of the skin. The receptor organs for the sense of pressure are: nerve endings on the hair follicles, Meissner's corpuscles, Merkel's disks, Pacini's corpuscles (in deeper layers) and free nerve endings. *P.S.*

Pressure, sensitivity to. Excitability of the sense of pressure (q.v.), which can be determined quantitatively. It depends on the nature and the density of the pressure receptors. *P.S.*

Prestige. Social esteem in which a person is held due to the application of certain criteria (which actually or only supposedly exist). The criteria applied (e.g. income, influence, social origin, behavior), the extent to which there is general agreement with the manner of application (value consensus), and the form in which prestige is built up, may differ with individual groups, classes or societies, and influence group dynamics (q.v.) in different ways. *C.B.*

Prestige, susceptibility to (*Prestige suggestibility*). An individual tendency to change one's judgments, opinions or attitudes (q.v.), even though conditions are otherwise the same, when the *source* of the particular communication (originator or communicator) is given a positive value (esteem, influence, prestige, q.v.; indicated by professional respect, expertise, title, public service or general sympathy). The stability and situational dependence of a personality trait of susceptibility to prestige or social influence are not authenticated; in this it contrasts with an ideomotor quasi-hypnotic, susceptibility to influence (which H. J. Eysenck calls *primary suggestibility*); prestige suggestibility tends to be classified as *secondary suggestibility*. *H.D.S.*

Pretest. 1. Syn. for pilot study (q.v.). **2.** A practice run-through of a test: used to familiarize Ss. and personnel with test procedure. **3.** A preliminary test carried out in order to determine, e.g., the anticipated direction of a trend, or how great the sample range of the main test should be, or some standard for the main test.

Priapism. 1. Lewdness, licentiousness. **2.** Persistent, abnormal erection of the penis, particularly when resulting from organic disease rather than sexual desire. **3.** Sometimes used as a synonym for *satyriasis*. *G.D.W.*

Primacy-recency effect. Diametrically opposed phenomenal forms in acts involving learning or judging; it takes the form of emphasizing the stored *initial* (primacy) or *final* (recency) information in a learning or information series presented successively. *Primacy effect* (*primary law*): the first informative items in a series are learnt or retained better than those which follow (see *First impression*). *Recency effect* (*recency law*): items of information are learnt more proficiently the later they are acquired in a series. The primary effect needs to be observed when at the end of the series a judgment of the whole or a reproduction (q.v.) has to be attempted, the recency effect when each item of information in succession is used in making some judgment (e.g. judgment of personality). See *Rating*. *F.-C.S.*

Primary colors. The three colors sufficient to produce every other color when the necessary changes in intensity (mixture) have taken place. Numerous combinations are possible. Optimal results are obtained with three frequency bands of approximately 650, 530 and 460 m., corresponding to red-orange, yellow-green and purple-blue. *G.Ka.*

Primary drives. Term for a class of dynamic factors which are considered to have a physiological foundation and to be conditioned by heredity. The concept is based on a hypothetical distinction between motives which are *inherited* and others which are the *result of learning processes*. More recent research has, however, shown that it is doubtful whether there are any needs whatsoever which are related to some object or directed to some end, yet are not grounded in experience. Affects activated by certain stimuli are thought to be more probable than components of drive systems conditioned by heredity. See *Drive; Instinct; Need; Motivation*. *H.-J.K.*

Primary factors. Factors of the first order, i.e., factors which are obtained from factor analysis (q.v.) of the intercorrelations of tests. Ant.: factors of the second (third) order, which are extracted from factor analysis of the intercorrelations of factors (rotated at an oblique angle) of the first (second) order. *K.Pa.*

Primary Mental Ability Tests (PMA). Batteries of tests to assess intelligence (q.v.) in the age groups 5–7, 7–11 and 11–17 years. PMAs were constructed by Thurstone (1948, 1949, 1953) on the basis of his *multiple factor theory* of intelligence. According to his theory each of the three batteries of tests embraces five group factors of intelligence—of course, the same factors will not be found in all of the three batteries. Reliability figures for the different sub-tests of the PMA fluctuate between $r = 0.63$ and $r = 0.98$.

Bibliography: Thurstone, L. L. & Thelma, G.: SRA Primary Mental Abilities—Elementary—Ages 7 to 11: Examiner Manual. Chicago, 1948; **Id.:** SRA Primary Mental Abilities—Primary—Ages 5 to 7: Examiner Manual. Chicago, 1953. *P.S.*

Primary processes. According to Freud (q.v.) the *primary process* belongs to the unconscious (q.v.) whereas the *secondary process* characterizes the relation between the preconscious and the conscious (q.v.). In the primary process, psychic energy flows freely from one notion to another in conformity with the well-known mechanisms of condensation (q.v.), repression (q.v.), etc., with a tendency to return. In psychic processes, libido (q.v.) endeavors to gratify every desire. In contrast to this, in the secondary processes the ego endeavors to steer its libidinal energy into a somewhat more objective and moderated path. The division between primary and secondary processes is taken to be two different forms of circulation of psychic energy, one of which is *free*, the other tied (or, also, compelled). It is also possible to speak of an opposition between the pleasure principle (q.v.) and the reality principle (q.v.). See *Depth psychology*. *J.L.I.*

Primitive reaction type. Characteristic: "The experience enters the mind and immediately makes its exit in the form of a response". "A person to whom impression and expression come easily but whose memory is not good". In psychopathic states the primitive reaction type is among the "explosives" and the "unstable". *W.K.*

Principal colors. See *Fundamental colors.*

Principal-component method, a factor-analysis method introduced by H. Hotelling, widely used by psychologists. Although the calculations involved take longer, it is regarded as more accurate than the somewhat cruder centroid method. The term "principal component" (or "principal axis") was chosen so as to avoid confusion with "factor" (e.g. of a product) already current in mathematics. See *Factor analysis.* *W.H.B.*

Prismatic spectacles. Spectacles which distort the visual world (e.g. by inverting the retinal image), as used in studies of perceptual-motor adaptation. See *Stratton's experiment.* *G.D.W.*

Prism effect. See *Stratton's experiment.*

Prison psychosis. The term covers a wide variety of psychopathological symptoms and syndromes closely bound up psychologically with imprisonment, i.e. psychogenic reactions (responses to abnormal experience). The clinical picture varies with the personality of the prisoner and includes depression (q.v.), anxiety (q.v.), psychogenic semiconsciousness, agitated states. Simulation psychoses are simulated mental disorders (Ganser's syndrome, q.v., pseudodementia, clowning and attitudinizing, childish behavior, etc.). Especially characteristic are psychogenic delusions such as that of innocence or of the imminence of reprieve. After prolonged imprisonment, persecution mania and similar disorders may occur, accompanied sometimes by hallucinations, and sometimes by quarrelsomeness. See *Psychoses, functional.* *C.Sch.*

Prison psychology. The branch of psychology concerned chiefly with the psychological effects of the loss of liberty. In addition it seeks to develop methods of treatment to overcome the negative psychic effects and to prevent recidivism after discharge from prison. Such psychology differentiates corrective systems according to the different methods of therapy used. One or several classification institutions have the task of seeing that each convicted person is assigned to that corrective institution or that block inside the institution which is most likely to meet the requirements for his treatment. For this purpose classification institutions use diagnostic and prognostic methods which have been worked out by criminal psychologists. Psychologists specializing in this field are employed as therapeutic experts in prisons. Recently, methods of diagnosis and treatment have begun to be devised for sentences served outside prison. The "Community Treatment Project" in Sacramento and Stockton (California) may be quoted as an example. See *Criminality.* *H.J.S.*

Probabilism. Primarily those moral doctrines which assert that it is sufficient to act in conformity with *probable rules* (plausible rules) as (they would be) approved by respectable individuals (authority) or convention. A second use of the term is for those doctrines which affirm that it is impossible to know, not any truth, but absolute truths, and which acknowledge only *probable judgments*, mainly at the level of empirical knowledge. A "probable judgment" would then refer to the *degree* *of credibility* to be given the future occurrence of a fact; or to that which may be given hypotheses regarding past events from which facts known in reality have ensued; or, finally, to the laws which govern such known facts (induction, q.v.), or allow others to be inferred from them (prediction, q.v.) (A. Cournot, 1801–1877). *M.-J.B.*

Probabilistic psychology. In a famous article, E. Brunswik (1943) showed that in regard to the conditions that release a behavior, *and* in regard to its effects, *probabilisms* must replace the unequivocal physical schemata of the determinists.

Bibliography: Brunswik, E.: Organismic achievement and environmental probability. Psychol. Rev., 1943, *50,* 255–72. *P.M.*

Probability theory. Questions of probability were first studied seriously in the seventeenth and eighteenth centuries; they arose primarily in relation to games of chance. Many of the great European mathematicians, notably Pascal, Fermat, Laplace, de Moivre, Bernouilli and Bayes, were concerned with probability. Textbooks on the subject have been written in many languages.

There is considerable difference of opinion, even amongst experts, about the nature of probability theory. This is due in part to the different types of situation in which the word "probability" has traditionally been used. Let us take just three examples:

1. On the day of the Grand National, a man may consider the chances—or probability—of a particular horse winning, and may express his "degree of belief" by giving the horse odds of say 9 to 1: that is, a probability of 0.9 of winning.

2. A coin is tossed 100 times and gives heads 55 times. Here we may consider the likelihood of some hypothesis, for instance that the coin is unbiased, and express this in terms of a probability statement. This procedure is common in simple tests of significance.

3. We may wish to determine the relative frequencies with which the six faces of a dice occur when it is rolled a large number of times. The relative frequencies are then referred to as probabilities.

One school of thought (of which Savage, 1962, following de Finetti, is a leading proponent) believes that a theory of probability can most satisfactorily be founded on the idea of "degrees of belief", or subjective probabilities (see example 1). Another school of thought, following Fisher, maintains that statements of probability truly refer to statements about the likelihood of hypotheses: that is, of propositions about which there is uncertainty (see example 2). Although these two points of view should be kept in mind, it is the case that the term "probability theory" is most widely taken to mean the application of mathematics to the description of random events (see example 3) for which, in a long series of observations, the relative frequencies of the possible outcomes tend to stable limits.

Bibliography: Arthurs, A. M.: Probability theory. London, 1965. **Gnedenko, B. V. & Khintchine, A. Y.:** An elementary introduction to the theory of probability. London, 1961. **Lindley, D. V.:** Introduction to probability and statistics. Cambridge, 1965. **Parzen, E.:** Modern probability theory and its applications. New York, 1962. **Savage, L. J.:** The foundations of statistical inference. London & New York, 1962.

A. E. Maxwell

Probable error (abb. PE; syn. *Probable deviation; Probable discrepancy*). An index of the variability of a measure, and an index of dispersion with a limited range of applicability. Defined as equal to 0.6745 of the standard error, and used for certain purposes (e.g. test construction) because of its distinctness. In the normal distribution about half of the values (deviations from the mean) are within the range of that mean $\pm$PE.

H.J.S.

Proband. See *Testee.*

Problem box. A cage which presents a problem to the animal, which must be solved in order to gain some reward, particularly escape: e.g. Thorndike puzzle-box; Skinner box (q.v.).
G.D.W.

Problem children. A collective term with no standardized meaning for a number of behavioral disturbances found in children and juveniles and calling for special therapy. The use of the term "problem children" lays emphasis on the fact that the child is the cause of difficulties and not that it has difficulties itself. Reasons why there are problem children are, for example, education, conflict (q.v.), handicaps of various kinds (criminality, q.v.), neurosis (q.v.), neglect, psychopathy (q.v.). See *Child psychology; Criminality.*
H.M.

Problem solving. The process requisite to reach a desired goal starting from a set of initial (cognitive) conditions. By introspection (q.v.), or by the observation of behavior in solving problems, the psychology of thinking attempts to obtain information about the structure, phenomenology and course of thinking processes. Certain classes of problems (e.g. the Tower of Hanoi) can be more or less easily split up into their individual components, which on the one hand facilitates a phasic study of the underlying processes and on the other hand makes it possible to simulate the processes (within certain limits).

Bibliography: Maier, N. R. S.: Problem solving and creativity in individuals. Belmont, 1970.
R.Hä.

Process form (Ger. *Verlaufsgestalt*). A gestalt-psychological term (see *Ganzheit*), allowing for consideration of the time factor: i.e. structural alterations in time are viewed as "form" (e.g. melody). In a wider sense, the term has a "dynamic" implication, as when (especially in modern German psychology as represented by Heiss and Thomae) emphasis is laid on the "processual" aspect of the individual, when "process form" would be the kind and mode of development (q.v.) and the permanently changing existential reference of personality (q.v.).

Bibliography: Koffka, K.: Principles of gestalt psychology. New York, 1935. **Thomae, H.:** Persönlichkeit. Bonn, 1955.
K.E.P.

Production principle of identification (syn. *Compensation principle of identification*). (N. Ach). This may be observed in the phenomenon that man assigns meaning to words: a verbal symbol does not simply represent the object but represents it in apprehension and itself becomes part of the object seen as idea. Ach chanced upon this fusion of *thing* and *name* when investigating concept formation and the attribution of meaning. See *Concept; Ach-Vygotsky method.*
H.W.

Production procedure. A psychophysical method for determining subjective equality or some other perceived relationship. The subject is given control of the variable stimulus, which he adjusts until he judges it to be in a given relationship (e.g. equal) to the standard stimulus. Syn. *Adjustment procedure; Method of reproduction.*
G.D.W.

Productive thinking. Term for creative thinking which leads to something new for humanity or for the individual, even if in certain cases it was new only at the time when the thinking occurred. There are different definitions of "thinking", e.g. as a dynamic process caused by forces which effect some arrangement or restructuring inside the system, possibly of the inquiry being undertaken, of items of information, notions, etc., and which render it possible to "solve problems". See *Creativity; Thinking.*
I.M.D.

Productivity. 1. *In psychology:* a wealth of ideas, creative thinking or acting, often synonymous with *creativity* (q.v.). **2.** *In industrial theory:* the relation between expenditure and returns. An *increase in productivity* is made possible by various measures (e.g. technology, work study, marketing); it is not always the same as maximization of profit (see *Industrial psychology*). *G.R.W.M.*

Product-moment correlation. A parametric method for determining the extent of the reciprocal relationship between two quantitative variables. It is calculated as the mean standardized deviation product (standardized covariance). See *Correlational techniques*. *G.Mi.*

Product sum. The sum of the products of the homologous measurements of a bivariate (q.v.) distribution. The product sum forms a link in the calculation formulae of various statistical kinds of measurement, as, for example, in the raw value formula for determining the product-moment correlation (q.v.). *G.Mi.*

Profile. A graphic representation of the results of a test battery in order to show clearly and simultaneously the relative height of the various results of an individual. The arrangements of the test may be linear or circular. In the latter case the setting of the tests may to some extent correspond to their degree of similarity, which is not the case with linear profiles. Profiles were first used by G. J. Rossolimo (1911) for an intelligence test and later by R. Meili and D. Wechsler, etc., for interests and emotional tendencies. *R.M.*

Progesterone. Gonadotrophic hormone (q.v.). Progesterone is secreted, particularly in the second half of the cycle, from the corpus luteum; and there are large amounts during pregnancy. A single exogenous administration of progesterone has only very temporary effects (lasting a few hours). Performance is reduced and there are other deleterious subjective results. Experiments with animals tend to show that progesterone reduces the quantity of catecholamines (q.v.) in the central nervous system, and this has led to speculations about the etiology of depression (q.v.) during pregnancy. In male subjects the administration of progesterone decreases the intensity of the action of LSD. There are many natural and synthetic substances related to progesterone. See *Ovulation inhibitors*.

Bibliography: Zuckermann, S.: The ovary. Vols 1, 2. New York, 1962. *W.J.*

Program. 1. In general: plan, purpose, timetable (e.g. of research, study). **2.** In electronic data processing (EDP): instructions for a computer (q.v.), indicating the sequence in which certain operations are to be carried out; for this, special programming languages (q.v.) (e.g. Fortran, Algol, Cobol) are used by programmers. *G.R.W.M.*

Program language. Programs (q.v.) formulated with the elements of a program language can be automatically processed by a computer. A distinction is made between a *machine code* or *machine language* and a *problem-oriented program* language; the latter enables instructions to the computer (q.v.) to be formulated in the notation used in that problem area. For example, Algol uses algebraic "language" in combination with logical conditions. Computers translate automatically into the machine code. In addition to Algol, there is Fortran, which is used mainly where mathematics is required. Cobol in economics, PL 1 and Algol 68 are recent developments. *K.-D.G.*

Programmed instruction. Programmed instruction is a learning process objectified and split up into *steps* (q.v.); the individual is expected to become personally active by making an outward response. This determines, at least in part, the time when the next teaching step will begin. The steps *either* are very short, containing little information, and the response expected at any particular place is easy, *or* the individual receives some comment on his response after a very brief space of time (at least while actually working); this comment determines, at least in part, what the selection and sequence of further steps will be. See *Instructional technology*. *H.F.*

Bibliography: Coulson, J. E. (Ed.): Programmed learning and computer-based instruction. New York, 1962. **Green, E. J.:** The learning process and programmed instruction. New York, 1962. **Lange, P. C.** (Ed.): Programmed instruction. 66th Yearbook, Part II, NSSE. Chicago, 1967. **Lysaught, J. P. & Williams, C. M.:** A guide to programmed instruction. New York, 1963. **Mager, R. F.:** Preparing instructional objectives. Palo Alto, Cal., 1962. **Markle, S. M.:** Good frames and bad: a grammar of frame writing. New York, 1964. **Ofeish, G. D.:** Programmed instruction: a guide for management. New York, 1965. **Entelek-Northwester U.** Programmed instruction guide. Boston, 1967. **Joint Committee on Programmed Instruction and Teaching Machines:** Recommendations for reporting the effectiveness of programmed instruction materials. Washington, D.C., 1966. **Smallwood, R. D.:** A decision structure for teaching machines. Cambridge, Mass., 1962. **Stolurow, L. M.:** Teaching by machine. Washington, D.C., 1961. **Taber, J. I., Glaser, R., & Schaefer, H. H.:** Learning and programmed instruction. Reading, Mass., 1965. **Thomas, C. A.** *et al.*: Programmed learning in perspective: a guide to programme writing. Barking, 1963. *R.G.*

Programming. The setting up of a program (q.v.), i.e., fixing the order of the stages, actions and processes leading to certain goals. In education, programming denotes the development of teaching programs (q.v.). In electronic data processing, programming denotes the translation of a computer schedule of algorithms (q.v.) into a program language (q.v.). *K.W.*

Progressive Matrices Test. A matrices test (q.v.) (standardized by Raven, 1960, for English conditions) to determine intellectual ability. According to Raven, the method allows assessment of clear thinking and perceptual reasoning. The text exists in two versions: the standard form with matrices printed in black and white, and a colored form designed for children under eleven and for persons over sixty-five. The standard form is normalized for the age group 6–65; for the colored matrices there are norms from 5½ to 11 and from 65 to 85. Calculations of retest reliability gave values for both forms ranging between $r = 0.63$ and $r = 0.98$.

Bibliography: Raven, J. C.: Guide to the Standard Progressive Matrices. London, 1960. **Id.:** Guide to using the Coloured Progressive Matrices. London, 1965. *P.S.*

Progressive paralysis. A syphilitic inflammation of the brain tissue, which may supervene eight to ten years after infection and which occurs chiefly in the area of the frontal lobes. Chronic syphilitic encephalitis causes atrophy of the nerve cells, and as a result progressive dementia, and sometimes psychotic images, e.g. euphoria (q.v.), paranoia (q.v.), depression (q.v.), delusions (q.v.), hallucinations and impairment of reasoning. A neurological examination reveals pupillary disturbances and occasionally other morbid symptoms. The diagnosis is confirmed by blood tests. Therapy (penicillin) at an approximate stage can usually arrest the process, but cannot restore deficits. *C.Sch.*

Projection. An (inner) defense (q.v.) mechanism in which a personal motive that is forbidden or can no longer be gratified is perceived by the person concerned as a motive of one or several *other* persons. This (erroneous) perception usually contributes to diminishing anxiety about increased possibilities of gratification of the motive which can no longer be gratified or is forbidden, or to making a more effective renunciation of the gratification of this personal motive than would be possible without projection. It is not always possible to make a clear distinction between projection on the one hand and the perception or interpretation of the motives of other people on the other hand. The more outside observers agree with the affected individual about his perception of motives in another person, the more improbable it is that the case is one of projection. Working partly along the same lines as Freud, Dollard & Miller (1950), two experts on learning theory, point to the complexity of this learning mechanism. Even a child discovers that members of a community behave alike, that certain forms of behavior (e.g. friendly approach or aggression) can easily lead to similar behavior in others and that the punishment is less severe if someone else was the leading spirit, i.e. if the motive responsible for the punishment was someone else's. Prejudices, certain untried opinions and superstitions are frequently based on projections. Serious projections, i.e. such as completely ignore reality, occur in psychoses (q.v.), especially in paranoia (q.v.), depression (q.v.) and schizophrenia (q.v.). Freud's concept of projection as a defense mechanism came in for several modifications, especially during the development of projective (q.v.) methods, where its function as anxiety preventing mechanism, for example, was often disputed (H. A. Murray).

Bibliography: Miller, N. E. & Dollard, J.: Personality and psychotherapy. New York, 1950. **Toman, W.:** Psychoanalytic theory of motivation. London & New York, 1960.

W. Toman

Projection, eccentric. The introspective observation that sensory experiences are usually localized outside the body at the same position as the stimulus object, particularly as regards the visual and auditory sense modalities. Thus the blue is seen as on the sky rather than in the retina, and the sound of a radio receiver is perceived as being at its source rather than in the ears. (A rather pointless piece of philosophy associated with Helmholtz.) *G.D.W.*

Projection fibers. The projection tracts are composed of projection fibers. They join parts of the brain together and to the spinal cord. Such fibers conduct the flow of action only in one direction, either from the center in the direction of the periphery or vice versa. Projection fields are areas of the cortex at which projection fibers begin or end. Examples: anterior and posterior central convolution (q.v.), motor pathways (q.v.), gyrus (q.v.).

Bibliography: Gardner, E.: Fundamentals of neurology. Philadelphia & London, 1968.

G.A.

Projective interest test. Any interest test in which the interests of the individual are ascertained by a projective technique. *H.J.A.*

Projective techniques. Projective techniques are a group of psychological techniques and procedures that claim to disclose the basic (underlying, hidden) personality structure and motivations of a subject by having him organize, respond to, or deal with materials or stimuli in a free, unlimited way without reference to a preconceived system of correct or incorrect answers.

Projective is derived from *projection*; these terms frequently refer to techniques developed for representing three-dimensional surfaces on two-dimensional planes, as in the practical fields of cartography and map-making (for instance, Mercator projections). By the end of the sixteenth century, projection not only denoted the *action* of projection, that is, in throwing or casting forth or forward, but the less tangible mental process, as in the construction of mental projects, scheming, and planning. Actual references to projective techniques were not found until some time in the twentieth century; but around 1900, *projection* was already being used to mean "the tendency to ascribe to another person feelings, thoughts, or attitudes present in oneself, or to regard external reality as embodying such feelings, etc., in some way" (see: Random House Dictionary of the English Language, 1966).

Projection as a defense mechanism differs somewhat from projection as used in projective techniques. The former concept is generally attributed to Freud, who used it as early as 1896 (see: Freud, 1950). In this sense, projection is a defensive system or process in which impulses, wishes, and ideas are externalized because their conscious recognition would be too painful to the ego. But, as Murray (1951) and others have indicated, projections as elicited by a projective technique can actually be unrepressed, conscious, acceptable, or even admirable, and need not include defensive or anxiety-avoidant components.

For a detailed and specific account of the use of inkblots and various other projective stimuli in human affairs (inkblots, for example, were used by Leonardo da Vinci in the fifteenth century to stimulate the imagination [da Vinci, 1882]) the reader is referred to Zubin, Eron & Schumer (1965). From the beginning of recorded history, the evidence suggests that amorphous and ambiguous stimuli, for example, clouds, entrails of animals, and so on, were used for divination, reaching decisions, omens, predictions of things to come, and various sacrificial purposes. Bypassing such early use of ambiguous stimuli, we note that the majority of techniques and stimuli currently described in the literature on projective techniques have had a long history of use and study in the laboratory. Inkblots were used before Hermann Rorschach's time in experiments on imagination and in the investigation of intelligence. In the early decades of this century, Stern (see: Stern, 1938) and others employed pictures of a somewhat ambiguous nature in the investigation of testimony (*Aussage*) and Binet and Simon (1905) used them for measuring intelligence; Ebbinghaus (1897) and Ziehen (1923) employed incomplete sentences to measure intelligence, and picture completion methods were also used in this connection. Laboratory explorations of will and imagination often employed word association methods.

Historically, projective techniques arose as a protest by "dynamically" oriented clinical psychologists against what they regarded as the inability of objective methods to meet the demands of personality diagnosis. The development of these procedures, with its accompanying revolt against the rigorous framework demanded by workers in the field of intelligence and achievement testing, seemed to be based on new principles. For example, the scoring of responses as "correct" or "incorrect" was abandoned; freedom and choice in performance were introduced into the instructions; scoring procedures became more complex, as did interpretation of the responses of S; and the style and manner of S's performance began to assume importance. Some critics point out that, as a result of these more "liberal" attitudes, many scientific and psychometric standards were sacrificed.

Details of the development of projective instruments will not be presented here. Three major influences on the nature of projective techniques should be noted, however: although Hermann Rorschach's classic monograph was not published until shortly before his death in 1922 (see: third ed., 1942), he conducted his "experiments" with inkblots before World War I; Morgan & Murray published a note on the Thematic Apperception Test (TAT) about two decades later (1935); a few years later, Frank (1939) proposed his projective hypothesis and was generally credited with the labeling of projective methods as such.

In describing projective methods, Frank (1939) offered a celebrated classificatory scheme: constitutive, constructive, interpretative, cathartic, and refractive methods. Actually, many classificatory schemes have been described, so that even these can be classified into, say, those that stress the nature of the materials, the manner of interpretation, or the type of behavior or response that is required of S.

In any event, the wide variety, scope, and range of projective procedures and methods can only be indicated, not specified, because of space limitations. (For detailed references, summaries, and descriptions of a large number of projective methods, see: Rabin [1968], Schneidman [1965], Zubin, Eron, & Schumer [1965], and especially Buros [1965].) Besides the Rorschach and Thematic Apperception Technique (TAT)—the two most frequently used instruments—there are various derivatives and modifications of pictorial methods, such as the Blacky Pictures and Children's Apperception Test, many adaptations of drawing procedures, such as the House-Tree-Person technique, a wide variety of sentence completion and story-telling methods, various play kits and materials, filmed puppet materials (e.g., Rock-A-Bye, Baby), etc. Additional techniques include: the Howard Inkblot Test, Kahn Test of Symbol Arrangement, Levy Movement Blots, Lowenfeld Mosaic Test, Schneidman Make A Picture Story (MAPS) Test, Rosenweig Picture-Frustration Study, the Holtzman Inkblot Technique, and many others.

It is virtually impossible to describe the heterogeneity, methodologically speaking, of the extant techniques. They differ in terms of normative samples, amount of reliability and validity data, objectivity of scoring, scope and content of personality variables the technique is purportedly reflecting, and theoretical bias of the constructs on which the procedure seems to be based. The diversity and range of quality and quantity in this field are impressive. Even the *raison d'être* for different techniques varies: some techniques were developed because of dissatisfaction with available instruments, and were offered as "better" and more effective substitutes; other techniques were "custom-made" for specific experimental investigations (see: Lesser [1961] for a discussion of such instruments); others were introduced because they seemed to possess clinical "richness" and utility. Critical appraisal of the different methods also covers a wide range. Several reviewers are quite impressed with the clinical depth and effectiveness of some techniques (for example, the Blacky Pictures); other reviewers are more skeptical, wondering why some techniques were even put before the professional public when knowledge about them was so meager.

In general, the promise of projective techniques, according to many reviewers and critics, has not been fulfilled. Even their extensive use in cross-cultural research (Henry, 1955; Lindzey, 1961; and Zubin, Eron & Schumer, 1965) has been severely criticized. Yet some of the clinicians who question the scientific status of many of these instruments use them clinically, claiming that their use yields abundant rewards, especially in experienced hands. Nevertheless, the researcher is hard put to demonstrate this clinical effectiveness, no matter how ingenious and inventive he is in simulating the clinical situation. Moreover, the years of training required to become expert in the use of many projective methods, and the time involved in their administration, scoring, and interpretation, raise issues in regard to their efficiency and economy, especially since some psychologists feel that such techniques are often used to elicit information more readily available through other methods, such as standardized interviews or observations.

The methodological problems inherent in many of these techniques are not easily solved. Some of them have to do with the current status of personality theory, diagnosis, and the thorny issues relating to the criteria to which one presumably looks to validate projective instruments. Psychiatric diagnosis, definitions of mental health and illness, and questions concerning prediction and outcome are criterion problems filled with considerations concerning their own reliability and validity, independent of equally complex considerations concerning the instruments themselves (Zubin & Endicott [1969] summarize some of these issues).

Although projective methods are characterized by some of the most difficult problems in the psychometric field, needless to say, not all methods are thus plagued to an equal degree. Yet, ironically, the most frequently used techniques, such as the Rorschach and TAT, seem to be beset with more complex problems than many of the other instruments (Zubin, Eron, & Schumer [1965] present an exposition of some of these problems, especially with regard to considerations of reliability and validity). These include, in addition to questions of reliability, problems in connection with sampling considerations, base rates, item validity, overall validity of interpretations, cross-validation of findings, and so on. Further, to understand the projective response, the variables which have been shown to influence it must be carefully examined. For many instruments, these include not only the entire reinforcement history of S but also the parameters of the stimulus situation itself. Thus, among the variables related to the S's response are: S's verbal-expressive skills; his productivity (frequently a reflection of intellectual and socio-cultural variables); the interaction between E and S and various other examiner effects; the nature of the test situation; the manner in which S assigns cognitive and verbal meaning to perceptual events (as in the Rorschach); the set and attitude toward testing that S brings to the situation; and the nature of the stimulus materials presented to S. Needless to say, not all of the foregoing have been sufficiently studied or understood. The picture is not entirely bleak, however, and there are new developments. Some researchers, for example, are trying to solve some of the foregoing problems by constructing newer, more refined techniques (for example, the Holtzman Inkblot Technique [1961, 1968]).

Perhaps the severest criticism that can be made of the current projective techniques is the lack of a specified scientific model for their structure which can give rise to testable hypotheses for probing the tenability of both hypotheses and model. Consequently, most research is of the ad hoc variety. When such models become available it will become possible to integrate the results of projective technique investigations with the rest of the science of psychology. That these techniques have persisted despite scientific evidence of their validity is proof of the need to answer the questions they are tackling. Whether they are suitable for the task remains to be seen.

Bibliography: Binet, A. & Simon, T.: Application des méthodes nouvelles au diagnostic du niveau primaire. Année psych., 1905, *11*, 245–336. **Buros, O. K.:** The sixth mental measurements yearbook. Highland Park, N.J., 1965, 409–540. **Ebbinghaus, H.:** Über eine neue Methode zur Prüfung geistiger Fähigkeiten und ihre Anwendung bei Schulkindern. Z. Psychol., Physiol., 1897, *13*, 401–59. **Frank, L. K.:** Projective methods for the study of personality. J. Psychol., 1939, *8*, 389–413. **Henry, J.:** Symposium: projective testing in ethnography. Amer. Anthrop., 1955, *57*, 245–70. **Holtzman, W. H.:** Holtzman inkblot technique. In: **Rabin, A.** (Ed.): Projective techniques in personality assessment. New York, 1968, 136–70. **Holtzman, W. H.,** *et al.*: Inkblot perception and personality—Holtzman inkblot technique. Austin, 1961. **Lesser, G. S.:** Custom-making projective tests for research. J. proj. Tech., 1961, *25*, 21–35. **Morgan, C. D. & Murray, H. A.:** A method for investigating fantasies: the thematic apperception test. Arch. Neurol. Psychiat., 1935, *34*, 289–306. **Murray, H. A.:** Foreword. In: **Anderson, H. M. & Anderson, G. L.** (Eds.): An introduction to projective techniques. Englewood Cliffs, N.J., 1951, 11–14. **Rabin, A. I.** (Ed.): Projective techniques in personality assessment. New York, 1968. **Random House** dictionary of the English language. The unabridged edition. New York, 1966. **Rorschach, H.:** Psychodiagnostics. Berne, 1942. **Schneidman, E. S.:** Projective techniques. In: **Wolman, B. B.** (Ed.): Handbook of clinical psychology. New York, 1965,

408–521. **Stern, W.:** General psychology from the personalistic point of view. New York, 1938. **Ziehen, T.:** Die Prinzipien und Methoden der Begabungs-, insbesondere der Intelligenzprüfung bei Gesunden und Kranken. Berlin, 1923. **Zubin, J. & Endicott, J.:** From milestone to millstone to tombstone (Review of: Rapaport, D., Gill, M. M. & R. Schafer: Diagnostic psychological testing). Contem. Psychol., 1969, *14*, 280–83; **Zubin, J., Eron, L. D. & Schumer, F.:** An experimental approach to projective techniques. New York, 1965.

F. Schumer & J. Zubin

Prolepsy. A normal speech variant found in very young children which is due to the psychic conditions of a lively attentiveness outrunning the ability to speak. Word images occur more quickly than sound formations with the result that a sound belonging to a subsequent syllable breaks through before the act of speech has reached it. This phenomenon is described as *proleptic* or *anticipatory* assimilation. Example: *gugar* for *sugar*. *M.Sa.*

Promiscuity. A prescientific concept which is vague, ambiguous and often used to express a moral judgment; it refers to hetero- or homosexual intercourse with "a variety of partners". Sexual freedom, the frequent change of partners and premarital sexuality do not constitute promiscuity; they are rather attitudes and forms of behavior in the context of psychosexual learning processes necessary to obtain personal and sexual experience of hetero- or homosexual partnership. Promiscuity might possibly be defined (following Giese's argument) as apersonal (non-binding) sexual activity involving or directed at anonymous partners which does not go beyond the "purely sexual" and is largely ephemeral in character. In this sense, promiscuity is an aspect or principal feature of genuine perversions. See *Perversion; Sexuality*. *H.M.*

Prompting. (Prompts = learning aids.) Prompting denotes the *offering of learning aids* during a learning process. The method is used especially for learning paired associates (q.v.). The prompts are offered in the form of a complete or partial presentation of the response (q.v.) which has to be learnt immediately *before* the opportunity for an overt response arrives (proffered stimulus). In programmed instruction (q.v.) very frequent use is made of prompting: the context of the learning step, the sentence structure, correlative words, opposites or examples (connotative prompting) point to the correct response; or the response appears directly and is highlighted by the type of print; or it appears in fragmentary form (denotative prompting). Investigations indicate that prompting can be more important than reinforcement (q.v.) by confirmation of the answer. But at the same time there is also the danger of overprompting: the irrelevant syntax is learned instead of the substance. See *Instructional technology*.

Bibliography: Glaser, R.: Teaching machines and programmed learning. Washington, 1965. *H.I.*

Propaganda. The concept came into general use in 1622 with the institution of the Vatican *Congregatio de Propaganda Fide* (Congregation for the Propagation of the Faith); today it is frequently thought of as a variety of publicity. Propaganda is the systematic attempt to influence the attitudes of individuals or groups by spreading deliberately chosen items of information, irrespective of whether these items are true, true in part, or untrue. As distinct from education, propaganda—strictly speaking—is defined as an intentional attempt to change usual standards. In general, propaganda makes use of available patterns of thinking, feeling and acting and these are mobilized as a frame of reference, the object of propaganda being represented as if it were perceived as part of this system; other systems of reference contradicting this tendency *are not mentioned* and are avoided. The process consists of deliberately intensifying the relation between the individual and the extraneous group and thus creating prejudices and a system of stereotypes with persuasive and formalized phrases and slogans (appraisal and decision patterns). If propaganda is to be effective, the following are the most important considerations: (*a*) trustworthiness of the communicator; (*b*) absence of interfering attitudes; (*c*) coincidence with individual experience; and (*d*) absence of counter-propaganda (e.g. where there is a monopoly in totalitarian states). See *Attitude; Prejudice; Manipulation; Stereotype.*

Bibliography: Albig, W.: Modern public opinion. New York, 1956. **Katz, D.** *et al.* (Eds.): Public opinion and propaganda. New York, 1956. *W.N.*

Proportion. The numerical relation of two mathematical quantities to one another. The relative (q.v.) frequency of classes (q.v.) of values is sometimes referred to as proportional frequency. *G.Mi.*

Proprioreceptive; proprioreceptive reflex. Reflexes are divided topographically (according to where the receptor is located in the organism) into *extero-*, *intero-* and *proprioreceptive* reflexes. Proprioreceptive reflexes (known also as personal reflexes) may be regarded as special forms of interoreceptive reflexes involved in the position of the body in general, or of individual limbs. The pressure and stretching receptors in the muscles, tendons and ligaments as well as the receptors of the labyrinth (q.v.) mediate such proprioreceptive reflexes. These are important for coordinating and controlling movement. See *Motor skills.* *H.R.*

Proprium. A term used by Allport to denote the personal central area; it replaces such expressions as *ego* (q.v.), *self* (q.v.), etc., which, according to Allport, were given too specific a meaning. Even the aspect of the individual and his knowledge of himself was referred to as "self", hence Allport proposes that the "term 'proprium' should be used to denote the self as 'object' of 'knowing and feeling' ". Proprium embraces seven aspects: 1. sense of the corporal self; 2. sense of continuing self-identity; 3. self-respect, pride; 4. extension of the self; 5. self-image; 6. self as someone capable of rational action; 7. propriate striving. *H.J.A.*

Prosencephalon. See *Forebrain.*

Prostitution. The relatively indiscriminate granting of sexual favors for payment or material reward. Prostitution is not confined to one sex; in almost every society there is hetero- (female) and homo- (male) prostitution. Official and unofficial attitudes towards prostitution vary from its rejection as a "manifestation of social disease" (Società Italiana di Medicina, Rome, 1950), its banning by law (e.g. in parts of the USA), to prostitution as a legally authorized form of economic activity (e.g. in Japan). There are just as many variations in the forms taken by heterosexual prostitution: religious prostitution, temple prostitution which does not have the character of prostitution as understood in Europe, and the ancient Greek system of *hetaerae*, Roman *bonae* (low-class prostitutes), Japanese geisha girls, brothel prostitution (the "stews") from the Middle Ages to the twentieth century, street prostitution, occasional prostitution, public and clandestine prostitution, etc. There are also numerous theories about the origin of prostitution: the main lines are those of the biologico-psychological, economic and environmental theories (Bernsdorf, 1968).

1. *Heterosexual prostitution:* its structure and extent in every society are chiefly

determined by two factors: (*a*) tolerance of premarital sexuality results in young men having less intercourse with prostitutes; (*b*) the less unmarried men there are of any age, the less frequent are contacts with prostitutes. Hence, in the nineteenth and even in the twentieth century, heterosexual prostitution was a safety valve for tabooed premarital sexuality, a mechanism which bourgeois society saw as an evil necessary to preserve the "ideal of virtuous feminine purity".

2. *Homosexual prostitution* differs in certain fundamental respects from female prostitution: (*a*) homosexual prostitution is chiefly occasional; (*b*) female prostitution offers the heterosexual world a deviant sexual alternative, homosexual male prostitution provides a deviant sub-culture with a deviant form of sexual contact; (*c*) a female prostitute receives payment because her client has an orgasm (q.v.), the male prostitute is almost always paid for his own orgasm; for this reason alone, male prostitution is more infrequent than female. Furthermore, contrary to general belief, male prostitutes are mostly heterosexual and usually remain so. See *Homosexuality.*

Bibliography: Bernsdorf, W.: Soziologie der Prostitution. In: **Giese, H.** (Ed.): Die Sexualität des Menschen. Stuttgart, 1968. **Esselstyn, T. C.:** Prostitution in the United States. Annals of the American Academy of Political and Social Science, 1968, *375*, 133. *H.M.*

Protanopia. Form of color blindness (q.v.) in which the first receptor pigment of the cones which is sensitive to red is completely absent, whereas in protanomaly it has a diminished effect. See *Color vision.* *K.H.P.*

Protean behavior. Used to distract the attention of the enemy from its prey. If a lizard is seized, it frequently sheds its tail, which then writhes violently, thereby attracting attention and enabling the threatened animal to make good its escape. Many birds—chiefly those which nest on the ground—pretend that a wing has been injured when a predator comes near the nest and so entice it away. Among higher mammals a certain number of artifices reminiscent of "human" behavior and designed to deceive an enemy are known.

V.P.

Protective inhibition. In Pavlov's behaviorism protective inhibition is the diminished effectiveness of a stimulus when its intensity has exceeded a certain level. Pavlov derives the phenomenon from an inhibition process said to prevent excessive functional deterioration of cortical cells. More recent findings in brain physiology, however, tend not to support this interpretation of the phenomenon; corresponding modifications have been made in Pavlovian theory (cf. Pickenhain, 1959). Protective inhibition is conceived as a form of *unconditioned inhibition* (q.v.).

Bibliography: Pavlov, I. P.: Lectures on conditioned reflexes. Vols. 1 & 2. New York & London, 1928/41.

Protocol sentences (syn. *Basic sentences*). Carnap (1932/33) uses the term for sentences which the original protocol contains and which form the basis of an empirical system of scientific concepts ("system language"). Such sentences transcribe a *direct and actual event*, a factual being (factual stage), the elementary experience of a single individual in his unity and complex and concrete totality (sophism), "thus", "here", "now". Although they may belong to the protocol language, whose atomistic sentences they are, they are nevertheless intelligible in their *intersubjectivity*. They need no further verification and are used to check the sentences of the *system language*, or as a basis for all remaining basic sentences of a science.

Bibliography: Carnap, R.: Über Protokollsätze. Erkenntnis, 1932/33, *3*, 215–28. **Neurath, O.:** Protokollsätze. Erkenntnis, 1932/33, *3*, 204–14.

M.J.B.

Protopathic sensibility. A collective concept for sensations of pain and temperature as well as for crude sensations of pressure and contact. It is conducted along anterior nerve pathways (q.v.) in the spinal cord. By contrast, epicritic (q.v.) (gnostic) sensitivity is conducted in the phylogenically recent posterior pathways. *G.A.*

Pseudodebility. Slight feeble-mindedness affecting only a few functions and remediable given special etiological conditions (such as illness, sensory or speech defects, environmental but not hereditary factors) and the right methods of treatment and education. See *Mental defect.* *M.A.*

Pseudo-hallucination. A hallucination which lacks the quality of objectivity. Hence one may see things which have no basis in reality, but one is nevertheless aware of their unreality. Pseudo-hallucinations are particularly a feature of states produced by drugs. *C.D.F.*

Pseudo-isochromatic charts. Charts designed for the diagnosis of anomalous color vision, such as those in the *Ishihara tests* (q.v.). They are composed of various colored dots arranged so that a normal person perceives a meaningful pattern (e.g. a number or letter) whereas color-blind individuals perceive either a different pattern or none at all. The principle upon which they are based is that certain pairs of hues (especially red and green) are not distinguishable to the color-blind person, who is then forced to make his response in terms of other cues such as relative brightness, or else can make no response at all. *G.D.W.*

Pseudolism (Latin: *pseudolus* = habitual liar). A certain psychological or psychopathological phenomenon; orgiastic experience of imagined or fanciful sexual acts, usually in full knowledge of their pseudo-nature, the fictitiousness of the act—even where it is built into a real sexual incident (Giese, 1965, 12). The pseudolist uses language in a most abnormal way in the form of writing (e.g. obscene letters), speaking, reading (sexual gossip), listening (to himself or other persons) in which the fictitious sexual actions or roles are lived through in a kind of sexual waking dream in an attempt to get rid of the reality and its demands. Giese has shown the psychopathological relations between pseudolism and perversion (q.v.) on the one hand and between pseudolism and "obscene" literature on the other. See *Pornography.*

Bibliography: Giese, H.: Psychopathologie der Sexualität. Stuttgart, 1962. **Id.:** Das obszöne Buch. Beitr. z. Sexualforsch., 1965, *35.* *H.M.*

Pseudoneurosis. Frankl used the term to denote those diseases which occur with neurotic symptoms but are of somatic origin. Thus agoraphobia (fear of open spaces), for example, may be the manifestation of a disguised hyperthyreosis, the objective symptom of which is too great activity. There is much dispute about this concept of pseudoneurosis. In normal medical terminology it is used to denote cases in which a neurosis has been wrongly diagnosed but where in reality there is some somatic disease. A patient whose blood pressure is too high may have, for example, a bad headache, palpitations of the heart, and little power of concentration, but all this may be due to hypertonia (q.v.). In many cases there is a common term to describe disorders which have organic or neurotic causes; thus tachycardia can be the expression used for both heart damage and a heart neurosis. *J.L.I.*

Pseudo-pregnancy. Physical symptoms of pregnancy (missing the period, swelling of the body) without the actual state occurring.

A classic example of a psychosomatic connection (see *Psychosomatics*) which has already been described in animals (e.g. dogs).

W.Sch.

Pseudoscope. A device which reverses the normal optical relationships so that the image which normally falls on the left retina is presented to the right eye, and vice versa. Used in the investigation of retinal disparity as an important basis of the perception of visual depth; distance relations tend to be reversed so that convex surfaces appear concave, and so on. *G.D.W.*

Psi. Abbreviation of "parapsychical" (= paranormal) usually used in hyphenated expressions: for example, "psi-ability", "psi-process", etc. Introduced by J. B. Rhine as a non-committal term for the critical component in parapsychological phenomena. *J.B.*

Psi Gamma ($\psi\gamma$). Paranormal cognition. A term introduced by R. H. Thouless as more non-committal than extrasensory perception (q.v.). *J.B.*

Psi Kappa ($\psi\kappa$). Paranormal action (= psychokinesis, q.v.). A term introduced by R. H. Thouless to correspond to his psi gamma (q.v.). *J.B.*

Psilocybin. An alkaloid of the Mexican narcotic mushroom "teonanacatl". Its narcotic effects are qualitatively similar to those of LSD and mescalin; disturbances of perception, thinking and affect are experienced (see *Psychotomimetics*). It differs from the other substances mentioned in the time it takes to act (psilocybin begins to act most quickly—after about thirty minutes, and its effects wear off quite rapidly—after two to four hours).

Bibliography: Hollister, L. E. & Hartmann, A. M.: Mescalin, lysergic acid diethylamide and psilocybin: comparison of clinical syndromes, effects on color perception and biochemical measures. Comp. Psychiat., 1962, *3*, 235–41. **Wolbach, A. B.** *et al.*: Comparison of psilocin with psilocybin, mescalin and LSD-25. Psychopharmacologia, 1962, *3*, 219–23. *G.E.*

Psi missing. Score in a parapsychological experiment which is significantly below chance-expectation, suggesting a paranormal avoidance of the target (q.v.). *J.B.*

Psi-systems. According to Freud's first version of the topological structure of the psyche these are the *preconscious* system and the *unconscious* system. Both are censored by the conscious system; as a result thoughts and desires can pass from the preconscious without any internal resistance, whereas those from the unconscious cannot immediately become conscious, or can only do so in the face of internal resistance. See *Freud*. *W.T.*

Psychagogy. A term for "minor" or "clinically active" psychotherapy (Schultz, 1963), designed to develop in neurotics and persons with crisis-like disorders self-confidence and an understanding of their own worth; this it does by showing the patient some goal fitted to his personality and by supervising his progress. Hence it may be extremely useful when behaviorally disturbed children or seriously ego-disturbed patients (e.g. psychotics) are in need of treatment. Its object is to use prophylaxis to eliminate incipient wrong attitudes, to control unstable behavior by clear information and, when the principal psychotherapeutic work has been concluded, to guide the patient to the *discovery of his own personality* along the lines of "Achieve what is in you". Thus the psychagogue is in part doctor, teacher and priest—according to H. Schultz-Hencke he is a teacher trained in depth psychology. Schultz situates psychagogy between psychotherapy of the mind and the organism, whereas other writers (Kurth, 1960) lay greater emphasis on the pedagogic aspect (therapeutic education). The principal method of psychagogy is counseling in its various forms. Important supportive methods in current use are *logotherapy* (q.v.), *autogenic training* (q.v.), with graded exercises in active hypnosis (E. Kretschmer), and *rational psychotherapeutic* breathing (L. Heyer). "Bibliotherapy" is widely used in Anglo-Saxon countries; the aim here is for the patient to understand himself by special reading assignments. More ambitious is music therapy (q.v.) (Pontvik), which uses mainly Bach's organ music (possibly interspersed with jazz) to arouse the patient and induce a *cathartic* action. Therapeutic education, in which psychagogy has only an advisory function is, together with the educative special treatment of a defect, "exemplary counselling and guidance in the Socratic sense" (Kurth, 1960).

Bibliography: Kurth, W.: Psychotherapie. Munich, 1960. **Schultz, J. H.:** Die seelische Krankenbehandlung. Stuttgart, [8]1963. **Zulliger, H.:** Gespräche über Erziehung. Berne, 1960.

E.U.

Psychalgia. Every pain is accompanied by some emotional change. Pain could thus be considered as a sensation of feeling. When pain actually occurs without any physical connection, it is described as "psychalgia" ("psychic pain"). In most cases it is interpreted as a symptom of some transformation and its psychogenesis is looked for. But in reality psychalgia should be regarded as a depressive or thymopathic equivalent; examples are headaches or pain in the arm and also precordial pain. They appear as symptoms of what is actually nothing but a disguised depression. See *Psychosomatics*. *J.L.I.*

Psychasthenia. The term was introduced by Janet and denotes a general lowering of the psychic level. Psychasthenics have great difficulty in adapting to their environment and accepting reality: anxiety states, obsessions (q.v.), etc., also occur. Nowadays the word "psychasthenia" is rarely used. Janet's patients suffered chiefly from *anxiety* states, *phobias* (q.v.), and occasionally feelings of depersonalization; hence Janet wished to contrast neurasthenia (q.v.) and hysteria (q.v.). Modern psychology sometimes speaks of *asthenic psychopaths*; characteristic symptoms are a very pronounced tendency to become fatigued and hypochondriac personality traits.

J.L.I.

Psyche. For the Greeks, the personification of the vital principle: *life, soul*. A designation for the soul in the most general sense, in contrast to the material body, or *soma*. In the narrowest sense, the term represents the totality of mental acts, or psychic functions and determinants of behavior (Wundt). In psychoanalysis (q.v.) it is the totality of conscious and unconscious: *subjectivity* as opposed to that which is wholly organic. In depth psychology (q.v.) the term is used to avoid the religious and spiritualistic implications of the words "soul" and "spirit". The notion of "psyche" suggests (but does not necessarily imply) a dualism. *M.R.*

Psychesthetic proportion. Scales of temperament found in the schizothymic (q.v.) and schizoid (q.v.) constitution when the criterion of sensitivity is applied. Degrees of stimulability can occur in one individual or, one degree can decide permanently the individual style of response (E. Kretschmer). Psychesthetic proportions of the schizothymic constitution are: (*a*) sensitive (nervous), (*b*) dry, (*c*) hypesthetic (severe, cool); of the schizoid constitution: (*a*) hyperesthetic (oversensitive), (*b*) anesthetic (cold, apathetic). See *Traits*.

W.K.

Psychiatric Screening Test. Known also as the Saslow Screening Test. An inventory used to elucidate the question of how far a patient has the tendency to transform affective experiences into somatic reactions. There are two forms depending on the intellectual level of the individual. See *Psychosomatics*.

Bibliography: Saslow, G., Counts, R. & Dubois, P. H.: Evaluation of a new Psychiatric Screening Test. Psychosomatic Medicine, 1951, *13*, 242–53. *H.J.A.*

Psychiatry. That branch of medicine which is concerned with mental disorder and mental illness. *R.H.*

Psychical research. The original term for parapsychology (q.v.), still widely current in England. Ex.: "Society for Psychical Research". *J.B.*

Psychic energy. A metaphor for the dynamic aspect of behavior. Inasmuch as it refers to diverse significations of "energy" in physical theory, the term implies a particular answer to the mind-body problem (q.v.). It also stands for a Freudian model of the various forms of libido (q.v.). See *Energy, psychic or psychical* for an account of Freud's notion. *P.M.*

Psychic epidemic. An expression formerly used to characterize behavioral phenomena which spread rapidly in some population, e.g. suicide "epidemics", a general fear of certain diseases. The inclination to imitate certain critical ways of behaving seems to be greater in periods of crisis, possibly because the ground has already been prepared by more general forms of uncertainty. *H.D.S.*

Psychic functions. When a symptom, either physical or psychological, is found to offer some secondary benefit or provide emotional comfort of some kind to the patient, then it is said to have a psychic function. (Used in this sense the term *psychic* is synonymous with *psychological*, and is usually avoided in scientific psychology because of its connection with spiritualism.) Symptoms with psychic functions, e.g. *psychic blindness* and *psychic pain*, may or may not have a simple physiological basis, so long as they serve a psychological function, and are thus distinguished from *psychogenic* symptoms, which are presumed to have no physical origin. *G.D.W.*

Psychic photography. The paranormal production of images on a light-sensitive film. Also known as "thoughtography". *J.B.*

Psychic saturation. See *Saturation*.

Psychic tempo. See *Tempo, personal*.

Psychic treatment. Out-of-date term for psychotherapy (q.v.).

Psychoacoustics. The physics of sound as relating to audition and to the physiology and psychology of sound reception.

Psychoanalysis. Its founder, Freud, defined this as a scientific discipline consisting (*a*) of a method of research the object of which is to bring to light the unconscious meaning of words, actions and mental images; (*b*) of a psychotherapeutic method based on this research and employing specific means of intervention such as the interpretation of secret wishes and the resistance which seeks to prevent their free expression; and (*c*) of a system of psychological and psychopathological theories constructed on the data supplied by the method of interpretation or emerging during the treatment of patients. It may be said with good reason that psychoanalysis is the work of a single researcher, its founder.

As the starting-point for his psychodynamic theories Freud (q.v.) used the work of the French school. In 1885 he learned from J. M. Charcot, the great clinician at the Salpêtrière, that certain symptoms of illness which have apparently been caused by nerve damage are in reality related to psychic factors that may influence them; cases of hysterical paralysis which can be successfully treated by hypnosis (q.v.) are an example. A short time afterwards (1889) Freud went to Nancy where H. Bernheim was carrying out experiments with so-called post-hypnotic suggestion (see *Hypnosis*). As he reflected on the automatic mechanism at work in the actions performed as a result of instructions received during hypnosis coupled with the order completely to forget these instructions, Freud became convinced that there are psychic factors capable of determining a series of behavioral acts while remaining hidden from the person concerned. From there it was possible to go on to investigate what further actions of everyday occurrence and what further symptoms might be determined by such mysterious psychic factors with an *unconscious* and yet *very strong dynamic* action. It began to occur to Freud that many cases of so-called parapraxis (q.v.) are in reality not casual actions, the result of fatigue or absentmindedness. In fact these actions prove to be due to those very same *unconscious* factors which operate in the carrying out of post-hypnotic instructions; moreover these actions always have some meaning which the person performing them is least able to recognize. Not only is this so, but this person often shows that he has no wish to recognize this fact whereas everybody else who saw what he did knows the significance of his action, and he angrily rejects their interpretation (1901).

Having reached this point, Freud was able to establish that the unconscious facts which had been observed belong to a world shut in by a barrier making it impossible for them to get out freely. They are shut up in this world by reason of a process which Freud called "repression", and are firmly held back there by a psychic censorship; this exclusion from the consciousness is responsible for a particular form of illness. Words, actions and mental images cannot in fact be kept out of the consciousness without resulting in an impoverishment of the personality. The great discovery made by Freud concerning these facts was that everything related to the unconscious has a pulsating dynamic character and is always trying to come into the light (consciousness); and since the barrier formed by censorship does not allow it to do this, it resorts to circumventive measures.

Inside the psyche a play of forces and counter-forces thus becomes stabilized and there is a latent and lasting conflict (q.v.): when the energy on either side is quantitatively feeble, as is the case in normal psychic life, the conflict is not disturbing and a breaking of the unconscious through the censorship is accepted casually and with profound inward relief, as happens in "humor" (q.v.) and in emotional participation in works of art (see *Literature, psychology of; Sublimation*). But if, instead, the conflict becomes really intense as a result of the excessive amount of energy, a compromise is arrived at between the unconscious drive and the defense opposing it, and symptoms of illness, psychoneurotic symptoms, appear.

The concept of the dynamic unconscious therefore leads on to the notion of repression, censorship, impoverishment of the personality and its being weighed down by dynamic compromises. It is also linked to the concept of desire for the repressed elements: to the extent that they manage to break through to the surface, they determine the behavior, appetites and needs of the subject, and, correlatively, the fear and destruction of such desires result in the total extinction of all vital desire.

To uncover the unconscious motivation of normal and psychopathological behavior, to mitigate the intensity of any conflict and to enrich the personality by the recovery of those energies hitherto denied it, is a program which corresponds to the first of the three aspects with which psychoanalysis has to deal, as Freud realized.

1. *Therapeutic technique.* Considered from a therapeutic angle, psychoanalysis is derived as a new method from the abovementioned postulates; when psychic life in its neurotic forms is more or less seriously disturbed by conflicts between drives and defense, and when in its psychotic forms it may be shattered because a drive has become too strong (or a defense too weak), so that there is now a direct link between the unconscious and reality, the impulse behind the drive loses, when there is accurate interpretation, the violent and pragmatic character which it possesses from its origin in a primitive psychic world. *Interpretation* is above all a question of *understanding*, and in order to make the unconscious intelligible, Freud accomplished a major task in his major work *The Interpretation of Dreams* (1900). Dreams (q.v.) appeared immediately to Freud as a royal road to the unconscious, and it is quite clear why: the physiological relaxation of the censorship occurring during sleep allows impulses to come to the surface which either remain shut up in the unconscious or else become only indirectly visible through compromises, i.e. in parapraxis or psychoneurotic symptoms. Through long reflection on his own dreams and those of his patients Freud managed to decipher the language of dreams, to define the laws governing the dynamic activity of the unconscious world and to make available a masterly storehouse of information—which has never been bettered—for further interpretation.

Interpretation is not concerned exclusively or even to any great extent with the account the patient gives of his dreams and the circumstances of his life, but it also looks closely into all that he conceals, forgets or repeats; in addition it concentrates on his behavior, especially with regard to the psychoanalyst from whom he is receiving treatment, and on his contradictions, repetitions or anything which is strange. To help in such an analysis the patient must to the best of his ability conform to the fundamental rule of psychoanalysis, which requires him to express in words everything that occurs to him and not to be deterred by useless, improper or absurd thoughts. In this way the conversation based on "free association" that is characteristic of psychoanalysis develops and enables the analyst to interpret two basic aspects of the unconscious: what is repressed, by directly deciphering the contents expressed in words, and the repressive forces; while he is doing this, he must watch with the utmost care how the patient defends himself and endeavors to evade the obligation imposed upon him by the fundamental rule. Interpretation, it must be remembered, is a method that must be applied in stages: not when the psychoanalyst has understood, but when the patient is able to respond, and shows by his dreams, his remarks and his behavior that he is already on the point of understanding what the interpretation is bringing to the light of consciousness.

To judge the suitable moment for the interpretation, the psychoanalyst needs to have clinical sensitivity and experience and a good training; if he does not possess this, it is quite possible that the repressive forces of the material interpreted at an inappropriate moment will be intensified. The result is that *resistance* builds up and makes therapeutic work more difficult. There may in any event be strong resistance due to traits of character from the beginning of the analytical work, so that the analysis of what is repressed has to be neglected in order to enable these traits to be dealt with by character-analysis according to the teaching of W. Reich (1950). Apart from its function and its usefulness as a source of information, interpretation gives rise to a process the knowledge of which is due entirely to psychoanalysis: transference (q.v.). By that is meant the strong emotional relationship of devoted submission or bitter hostility which develops between the analyst and the subject being analyzed and which, as Freud showed, is a recrudescence of the affective links between the patient and the persons who were most important to him in the world of his earliest childhood: mother, father or substitutes for them.

Transference has to be interpreted and the patient to be shown which person is really the object of his affect; it is only by such an analysis that the patient can overcome the affect and make the transference into an instrument for achieving considerable progress toward an adult way of life. But if the patient does not analyze the affect, because he refuses to accept the interpretation that his love or his hate are directed not toward the analyst but toward other persons, then the transfer produces such violent resistance to treatment that the analysis cannot be completed (1937) and has therefore to be interrupted. The manipulation of transference is one of the difficulties of analytical technique; the analyst can fail in his task if he succumbs to the belief that the feelings which the patient expresses about him do really refer to him. This attitude, known as "counter-transference", can ruin psychoanalysis; and so that it may be avoided, it is essential that everybody intending to become a psychoanalyst should submit to a long "didactic psychoanalysis".

2. *Psychological and psychopathological theory*. The theoretical concept is based on clinical practice and experience gained from innumerable patients, on knowledge of the normal working of the psyche which was acquired in didactic psychoanalysis, on the observation of young children and for some time now on psychological experiments as well. To Freud more than to anyone else belongs the credit for having recognized that the prime cause of repression is to be found in wrongly handling (denying) the drive-impulses, the libidinous desires in early childhood. It is impossible for repressed drives to grow, that is to say, they remain primitive, and as they have a dynamic character they nevertheless have a permanent influence on the behavior of the subject who, although biologically an adult, remains infantile with respect to those drives which were repressed in childhood.

Freud described the different stages from the first to the sixth year of life through which the libido (q.v.) passes in its development (1905), and found in neurotic adults—almost in a crystallized form—the immature forms of libido development (1908, 1931). He then showed that immaturity of the libido is always bound up with a condition of "narcissism" (q.v.), i.e. with self-love which acts as a barrier to the free display of the subject's feelings towards others; only when the libido has detached itself from excessive interest in its own body and can concentrate on interpersonal relationships, does it reach maturity; this takes place as the result of a long process lasting from the sixth year of life until adolescence and terminates with it. At the end of this stage, manhood or womanhood as the case may be is reached completely, there are no neurotic or psychotic symptoms, and narcissism has been outgrown. Freud had assimilated the libido (q.v.) to eros (q.v.), the life-drive, and later (1926) he set beside the libido a further fundamental energy, aggression (q.v.), assimilating it to the death instinct (q.v.).

This last-named step did not meet with the approval of all psychoanalysts, especially from the point of view that "life serves death", however, the principle has found increasing recognition that from the earliest months of life aggression (q.v.) is an active basic energy of psychic life. The English school of psychoanalysis founded by Melanie Klein has studied these ideas in detail (1955).

Hence *libido* and *aggression* form the two poles between which the dialectic of the emotional life is conducted, and they are the material of that unconscious psychic and instinctive process, strained to the point of discharge, which Freud called the "id" (q.v.), thereby substituting this concept for the "unconscious" which preceded it. Against the "id" Freud set the "ego" as a force derived from the "id" with the object of assessing reality and calculating the suitable moment for giving effect to its impulses. And finally Freud recognized a third psychic force, the "super-ego", which in the subject represents society with its taboos, and its conventional standard of conformist perfection (1923).

Quite recently, and especially in the USA., many psychoanalysts have postulated the existence of an "ego" which is not derived from the "id" but has always been autonomous, is not bound up with conflict, and interacts with the three forces enumerated by Freud. This "ego" is credited with operating the intellectual mechanisms (H. Hartmann, 1939) which enable optimal adaptation and the synthesis of reality to take place, in other words, creativity (q.v.) and the higher operations of thought (E. Kris, 1950), which in Freud's original scheme were performed instead by sublimation (q.v.) of the instincts (Freud, 1917). But modern psychoanalysis agrees with Freud in ascribing to the "ego" the formation of those systems of alarm and protection known as defense (q.v.) mechanisms (Anna Freud, 1937). In this connection the "ego" has a double function: as a force assessing internal and external reality the "ego" notices any possible threat and mobilizes anxiety; as a force releasing responses the 'ego" determines what is the best possible defense mechanism to deal with any situation, and primarily that known as repression (1926). In English psychoanalysis, major significance is attached not to repression but to projection (q.v.) and introjection (q.v.), a mechanism which (because it appears in early childhood, pervades the whole of behavior, and has important consequences) has proved to be the factor determining the normal or pathological nature of mental functioning (M. Klein, 1955).

So, on the anthropological and psychological levels, psychoanalysis is a method by means of which it is thought by some to be possible to approach the unresolved problems of man's innermost life; the taming of primitive energies which it involves leads in fact to the removal of defenses which no longer have any reason to exist, and the subject experiences a sense of renewal and enrichment which he has never known before. His illness is said to be cured, his unconscious is gradually made conscious and his emotive personality, formerly infantile, becomes adult; the neurotic symptoms disappear, and the general orientation of the personality shifts from egocentricity to authentic, life-giving altruism. While the psychoanalysis which studies the "id" highlights above all the infrastructure of the psyche and suggests a new approach to the whole subject of human life, psychoanalysis which is directly concerned with the dynamic of the "ego" approximates increasingly to the dynamics of social life, as may be seen in E. Erikson's thought (1950–1964); it also leads to the conceptual model of ego-development in classical psychology and offers the possibility of direct experimental control. Nevertheless, the claims of psychoanalysis are contested by nearly all schools of modern scientific psychology as unproven. See *Behavior therapy; Behaviorism; Conditioning; Drive; Instinct; Need; Child psychology.*

Bibliography: Abraham, K.: Clinical papers and essays on psychoanalysis. London, 1955. **Ancona, L.:** La psicoanalisi. Brescia, 1963. **Bowlby, J.:** Attachment and loss, Vols 1, 2. London, 1969–71. **Erikson, E.:** Childhood and society. New York, 1950. **Id.:** Insight and responsibility. New York, 1964. **Eysenck, H. J.:** What is wrong with psychoanalysis? In: Uses and abuses of psychology. Harmondsworth, 1953, 221–41. **Fliess, R.** (Ed.): The psycho-analytic reader: an anthology of essential papers with critical introductions. London, 1950. **Freud, A.:** The ego and mechanisms of defence. London, 1937. **Freud, S.:** Standard edition of the complete works of Sigmund Freud, London & New York, 1953–: especially: The interpretation of dreams (Vols. 4–5); Psychopathology of everyday life (Vol. 6); Three essays on the theory of sexuality (Vol. 7); Character and anal eroticism (Vol. 9); A general introduction to psychoanalysis (Vol. 16); Beyond the pleasure principle (Vol. 18); Psychoanalysis and libido theory (Vol. 19); The ego and the id (Vol. 19); Inhibition, symptoms and anxiety (Vol. 20); Humour (Vol. 21); Libidinal types (Vol. 21); Analysis terminable and interminable (Vol. 23). **Hartmann, H.:** Ego psychology and the problem of adaptation. New York & London, 1959. **Klein, M.:** New directions in psychoanalysis. London, 1955. **Reich, W.:** Character analysis. New York & London, 1950. **Rycroft, C.:** Reich. London, 1971.

L. Ancona

Psychocatharsis. See *Cathartic method.*

Psychodiagnostics. The identification of the psychological characteristics of an individual with the aid of special methods. In the past the concept was more widely understood in the sense of *human knowledge*, that is the understanding of a person's psychological features, and the notion of "characterology" coined by J. Bahnsen in 1867 could be equated with it. Psychodiagnostics in the simply defined, narrow sense is theoretically based on Galton's (q.v.) work (1883) and its practical origin was in the diagnosis of intelligence defects by C. Rieger, a Würzburg psychiatrist (1885). This was followed by the work of E. H. Münsterberg (1891) and A. Kraepelin (1895). In the sphere of education a beginning was made by J. McK. Cattell in the USA (1888) and by A. Binet and V. Henri (1895) in France. These names are given as the initiators of the tests as well as of differential psychology, and psychodiagnostics consists in the combination of these two efforts.

1. *Fields of application.* The comprehension of a total personality in all its aspects, as befits its origin in characterology, has up to the present been widely understood by the word "psychodiagnostics" (see *Personality*). It was applied to a wide range of methods, e.g. graphology, or the form-interpretation of H. Rorschach (see *Rorschach test*), which was published under the title "Psychodiagnostics". But psychodiagnostics has quite specific functions from its origin in psychiatry and in methods of testing. The application of psychological methods in psychiatric diagnosis is of foremost importance. It is used most frequently in connection with brain damage of an endogenous or traumatic form and it has further related functions in the determination of the success of therapy in psychosomatic illnesses and in criminology (see *Prediction*). In the above function the psychologist's diagnosis complements the diagnosis of the doctor. Psychodiagnostics is also applied in educational and vocational guidance and in the determination of particular aptitudes, as for instance of pilots or in the diagnosis of exposure to the danger of accidents (see *Accident research*). This list indicates a certain difference between psychodiagnostics and medical diagnostics. In the case of the latter it is predominantly a question of the determination of a temporary condition, while psychodiagnostics on the whole ascertain lasting characteristics. Psychodiagnostics is not, therefore, for the most part diagnosis but prognosis (q.v.). Naturally the boundaries are fluid since the psychologist can also, for example, ascertain the seriousness of amnesia caused by accidents or the temporary effect of psychopharmacology. Many methodological and theoretical difficulties stem from the predominantly predictive orientation of psychodiagnostics. Psychodiagnostics relies on tests in all their forms more and more exclusively, but with a varying selection according to the questions posed at present. For problems of aptitude in school, work, the army and sport, ability tests (q.v.) (intelligence tests, concentration tests, educational-maturity tests, etc.) play a substantial part. But they are generally supplemented by personality tests (see *Projective techniques; Traits; Questionnaires*), which differ greatly according to whether the

field is criminological, clinical or vocational guidance. The following are the three main classification groups by which the tests are distinguished: (*a*) the so-called *projective techniques* (q.v.) which give information regarding above all the affective and motivational aspects; (*b*) the questionnaire (q.v.), with evaluation and observation procedures by which information is given to an appropriate third party on habits, behavioral tendencies and inclinations but also simply on personality traits. Inclination and interest tests are generally employed for the purpose of vocational guidance, the Minnesota Multiphasic Personality Inventory (q.v.) for clinical diagnostics and the Multiphasic Personality Inventory (q.v.) and the Minnesota Multiphasic Questionnaire (q.v.) for determining neurotic tendencies and the extraversion-introversion dimension (q.v.). (*c*) *Objective personality tests* are still used relatively seldom but are likely to predominate in the future. In these tests, behavior, reactions and abilities that can be objectively recorded and estimated in strictly controlled situations offer the bases for a diagnosis. E. Kraepelin's experiment in measurement, which was developed in respect of psychodiagnostics by R. Pauli (1938–1951), may be regarded as a forerunner of such tests (see *Pauli test*). Methods like graphology (q.v.) and physiognomics (q.v.) cannot easily be included in these three groups, nor can behavior observation, the interview (see *Exploration*) and anamnesis. The last three are gradually becoming more reliable in terms of evaluative procedures and are being made more accessible to scientific revision. If such conditions are fulfilled, these methods will form a very valuable part of the psychodiagnostic repertoire.

2. *Method.* The problems of psychodiagnostics stem from the fact that on the basis of scanty objective data and few test results—that is, relatively small samples of behavior—which have been obtained in a very short time and under very special conditions, assertions have to be made about behavior in quite different situations, in which a person is occupied in an entirely different way and has perhaps later experienced certain changes in development. From this it will be clear that the value of psychodiagnostics and its application depends upon data obtained by different means and also upon the means employed, in fact on the *reliability* (q.v.) and *validity* (q.v.) of the tests. There are two types of procedure in psychodiagnostics. One may be described as statistical or psychometric, the other clinical or intuitive. Also the twin concepts of nomothetic (q.v.) and idiographic (q.v.), which were employed by W. Windelband in the identification of two scientific types, describe the same difference. Using statistical methods and the most abundant data, that group of persons is defined to which the individual under examination most probably belongs. Test-norms, clinical syndromes or other data obtained from thousands of cases are used as criteria. This procedure is most clearly represented by the Minnesota Multiphasic Personality Inventory (q.v.) in regard to clinical diagnosis, and by the Strong Vocational Interest Test. A somewhat modified form of this method consists in the discovery of *syndromes* that are characteristic of certain forms of illness, personality, type, etc. These are carried out on the basis of the results of H. Rorschach's method of shape interpretation, for example, or of Wechsler's intelligence test (q.v.). Examination results must necessarily be available for the statistical method. These results define the degree of relationship between each score and a diagnosed trait. In borderline cases the diagnosis can be undertaken with the aid of the computer (q.v.), which is of course needed for aspects of medical diagnostics. Among the complexities of psychological studies the greatest deficiency is the lack of an adequate amount of reliable information and a personality theory on which psychodiagnostics might build. In the clinical or intuitive method the psychologist combines the results that have been obtained,

his observations, and his information based on psychological insight and knowledge and on his personal experience; whereas in the statistical method correct interpretation depends on the reliability and integrity of the definitions of dependence, and stands or falls, as in the clinical method, on the psychological insight and the experience of the psychologist. Objectivity and reliability of diagnosis in clinical procedure are negatively influenced principally by so-called "systematic tendencies" in personality judgments (Cohen, 1969), such as the primacy-recency effect (q.v.), leniency effect (q.v.), social desirability. A comparison would therefore necessarily favor the statistical method if the empirical basis were always reliable, and if it included all the very numerous and sometimes also fortuitous individual variations. On the basis of a great number of experiments, Meehl (1954) established that both methods lead to approximately the same number of correct results. In practice a combined method is very often applied and with advantage. In fact the clinical method in no way excludes the application of objective tests (q.v.), questionnaires, etc., nor a consultation of the research results in conjunction with the applied tests. It is desirable that psychodiagnostics should find ever wider empirically verified principles, and that the psychologist should control the diagnosis based on them and eventually correct and amplify them with individual variations which are not yet statistically classified and sometimes only occur in very rare cases. It might be said that the psychologist must work idiographically on the basis of the most nomothetic knowledge available.

3. *Results.* Nothing is more difficult than to judge whether the psychodiagnostic conclusions made about a person are correct. Here it is a question of the so-called *validity problem* (control of the verification of a diagnosis). The accuracy of the psychodiagnostic conclusions depends, on the one hand, upon the validity of the methods used (see *Test theory; Construct validity*), and, on the other hand, upon the control of verification in the various fields of psychodiagnostic practice. In the case of aptitude tests, the results of such experiments are often satisfactory, while in regard to the value of psychodiagnostics in the field of total personality the results of controlled research are quite contradictory. It may be said with certainty that the value of a conclusion which relies only on a test is generally low, but that a judgment in regard on some psychological aspects of a person, when based on scientifically sure methods, (the use of several tests) is more certain than without the application of such methods. The effectiveness of these techniques has long been overestimated, but today their field of application is better known, and certainty in the interpretation of results and an ability to differentiate are growing with the increasing extent of scientific research.

Bibliography: Anastasi, A.: Psychological testing. New York, 1954. **Brengelmann, J. C.:** Psychologische Methodik und Psychiatrie. In: **H. W. Gruble** *et al.* (Ed.): Psychiatrie der Gegenwart, Vol. 1. Berlin, 1963, 134–77. **Cattell, J. McK.:** Mental tests and measurements. Mind, 1890, *15*, 373–80. **Cattell, R. B.:** Objective personality motivation tests. Chicago, 1967. **Cohen, R.:** Systematische Tendenzen bei Persönlichkeitsbeurteilungen. Berne, 1969. **Cronbach, L. J.:** Essentials of psychological testing. New York, [2]1954. **Drenth, P. J. D.:** Der psychologische Test. Munich, 1969. **Freedman, F. S.:** Theory and practice of psychological testing. New York, 1951. **Galton, F.:** Inquiries into human faculty and its development. London, 1883. **Heiss, R.** (Ed.): Handbuch der Psychologie, Vol. 6. Göttingen, 1963. **Jenkins, J. J. & Paterson, D. G.** (Eds.): Studies in individual differences. London, 1961. **Meehl, P. E.:** Clinical vs. statistical prediction. Minneapolis, 1954. **Meili, R.:** Lehrbuch der psychol. Diagnostik. Berne, 1961. **Rapaport, D., Gill, M. M. & Schafer, R.:** Diagnostic psychological testing. New York, 1968. **Stern, E.:** Die Tests in der klinischen Psychologie. Zürich, Vol. 1, 1954; Vol. 2, 1955. **Thorndike, L. & Hagen, E.:** Measurement and evaluation in psychology and education. New York, 1961.

R. Meili

Psychodrama. The dramatic presentation of personal or general conflict (q.v.) or crisis situations for diagnostic and therapeutic purposes, together with the practice of unaccustomed modes of behavior. The distinguishing factor in the psychodramatic event is temporary adoption of a certain role (q.v.), within which more or less determined situation the players have a great deal of freedom of action. Psychodrama is used particularly as a contribution to group therapy (q.v.), but also as a method of dealing with other social psychological problems (e.g. research into opinions, training of personnel). J. R. Moreno (1914; 1959) invented psychodrama as a specific practice in group therapy. However, the therapeutic effect of acting out conflicts in the sense of an "action catharsis" has always been known. This shows that man's need to act out a rôle relieving him of his emotional tensions ("abreaction") is rooted in his nature (e.g. children's games, carnival, early theatrical forms; see *Play*). Moreno's conception of psychodrama differed sharply from Freud's psychoanalysis (q.v.), which was more concerned with words and the individual. Moreno began with the idea that spontaneity and creativity were distinguishing marks of the self realized personality. Independently of this ideology, psychodrama began to be used as a method in the most varied forms of psychotherapy. In order to illustrate and demonstrate the various theories of the time, e.g. the psychoanalytic school, the cathartic method, theories of learning, (q.v.), behavior therapy (q.v.), psychogogic (q.v.) and pedagogics, many different techniques of psychodrama were developed. In most groups, for example, they were distinguished in form and content by the type of play (patient- or theme-centered; in group problems one speaks of *sociodrama*), and by the way it was acted (monologue, exchange of parts, mirroring methods, the activating technique of Ploeger, 1968, 69), in the modes of expression (verbal, mime, use of puppets or masks), the form of intervention of the director (advising or not), etc. Psychodramatic therapy is best practiced in conjunction with other forms of individual or group therapy. (See *Group dynamics*.)

Bibliography: Blatner, H.: Psychodrama, rôle playing and action methods. Thetford, 1970. **Corsini, R. Shaw, M. E. & Blake, R. R.:** Rôle playing in business and industry, New York, 1961. **Le psychodrame:** Bulletin psychologique, *285*. Paris, 1970. **Moreno, J. L.:** Who shall survive? New York, 1963. **Ploeger, A.:** Die Stellung des Psychodrama in der Psychotherapie. Möglichkeit und Grenzen der Therapie mit dem Psychodrama, in **Batagey, R.** (Ed.): Gruppenpsychotherapie und Gruppendynamik, Vols. 2 & 3. Göttingen, 1968. See also the journal Folia Psychodramatica (Louvain, Belgium).

B. Schmidt

Psychogalvanic reflex (Abb. PGR). See *Skin resistance*.

Psychogenic disorders. Usually applied to both behavioral and physical disorders which are thought to have a psychological rather than a physiological origin. *R.H.*

Psychogenic vomiting. Vomiting of psychological origin. Also called *nervous vomiting*, and *hysterical vomiting*. This symptom is apparently most common in young women, and is supposed by psychoanalysts to be a symbolic expression of the desire to reject a hated idea or person. *G.D.W.*

Psychogram. A description of the psyche (q.v.); a full comprehensive record of all psychological data (anamnesis, remarks on behavior, tests) on a person, together with an interpretation thereof. Rules for making out a psychogram are given in the Rorschach manual. *D.Ba.*

Psychoid. 1. As a noun: a reality analogous to "being with a soul." For Driesch, it is synonymous with "entelechy" (q.v.). Bleuler used the word (in 1925) to characterize the organizing principle of lower organisms all the way down to the Protozoa. **2.** As an adjective: quasi-psychic, quasi-mental; like the psychic or mental. *P.M.*

Psychokinesis (abb. PK). Paranormal action. Physical process assumed to be of paranormal causation. In experimental parapsychology the term PK was introduced by J. B. Rhine to refer to the influence of the subject's volitions on a falling dice or similar random process. Power of mind over matter. Also called "telekinesis" (obsolete). *J.B.*

Psycholinguistics. The term is now used almost universally as a synonym for "psychology of language" (see *Language*). It first came into general use in about 1950 (Osgood & Sebeok, 1965). It comprises some very heterogeneous, interdisciplinary interests in language problems (e.g. in linguistics, communications research, information theory, psychology, and cultural anthropology), with an emphasis on the methods of experimental psychology. Traditional linguistic psychology was more descriptive and comparative, speculative and theoretical. Despite the wide variety of questions proper to psycholinguistics, it is being developed more against the background of consistent, empirically referent theories, giving rise to two partly complementary and partly opposed basic approaches (Dixon & Horton, 1968). The behaviorist S-R theory begins mainly with learning processes and results (see *Learning theory*), as detectable in significant elementary units; the cognitive approach, on the other hand, owes its stimulus more to modern linguistics, and starts from the processes of the comprehension and generation of sentences (see *Grammar; Speech*). Some psycholinguistic *research* areas, which are less well integrated theoretically, are concerned with the linguistic aspects of peripheral processes of reception and production, and the interactions between linguistic processes and diverse conditions (i.e. emotion; Davitz, 1964), thought processes (see *Inner speech*), social context (see *Language barrier; Sociolinguistics;* Ervin-Tripp, 1969; Herrmann & Stäcker, 1969; Miller & McNeill, 1969; Moscovici, 1967; Wiener & Mehrabian, 1968), and personality (q.v.) variables. Important problems and contributions arise also in various applied fields: diverse speech defects and appropriate therapies afford useful knowledge (Rieber & Brubacker, 1966), e.g. the treatment of impaired articulation, of mutism (e.g. by verbal conditioning: see *Verbal behavior, establishment and modification of;* Salzinger, 1969), etc. (see *Aphasia*). The acquisition of reading and writing, of vocabulary (in the mother tongue as well as in other languages (see *Bilingualism*), and of grammar, offer a number of problems (Crothers & Suppes, 1967; Osgood & Sebeok, 1965; Rosenberg & Koplin, 1968; Scherer & Wertheimer, 1964). Much preliminary theoretical work has been done in the field of computerized language translation.

The behavioristic variety of psycholinguistics favors simple, easily manipulable S-R systems, such as (natural or constructed) words and syllables, and to this extent recalls the older memory research. Language is conceived as "verbal behavior", which consists essentially of (open or hidden) "verbal responses" (Dixon & Horton, 1968; Mowrer, 1960; Salzinger & Salzinger, 1967; Skinner, 1957; Staats, 1968). The associative actualization of verbal responses from any stimuli and the acquisition or modification (paired or serial) of associations (verbal learning) are the fundamental processes for method and theory (Deese, 1965). More or less directly (e.g. by generalization, q.v., and transfer, q.v.) detectable associations of linguistic stimuli and responses (with one another, or with other forms of stimulus and response) are interpreted as denotative or connotative meaning (Creelman, 1966; Rommetveit, 1968) (see *Semantics*), in part by recourse to "mediating" elements (mediation theory: Dixon & Horton, 1968). Linguistic activity is apprehended as a Markoff process (q.v.), which leads to difficulties in the case of rules of syntax (Chomsky, 1968; Hörmann, 1970).

The more mentalist and cognitive form of psycholinguistics follows Chomsky in opining that the behaviorist and associationist approach must have untenable consequences (Miller & McNeill, 1969). The observable extent of interpretative and productive language competence would be explicable only in terms of the effects of grammatical rule systems (see *Grammar*), which are ontogenetically constructed as competence in a many-layered canon of comprehension and production strategies. The methodological foundation of such constructs corresponds in part to the linguistic analysis and evaluation of free utterances. An increasing number of experimental investigations (Hörmann, 1970; Jakubowicz, 1970; Miller & McNeill, 1969) are being carried out into assumptions about units of linguistic competence and their reciprocal relations. Experimental problems include, e.g., sentence structure, the psychological relevance of linguistically defined transformations, the increasing complexity of sentences, and the implications of the use of negatives. See *Communication.*

Bibliography: Brown, R. (Ed.): Psycholinguistics. Selected papers. New York, 1970. **Chomsky, K.:** Cartesian linguistics. New York, 1966. **Id.:** Language and mind. New York, 1968. **Creelman, M. B.:** The experimental investigation of meaning. New York, 1966. **Crothers, E. & Suppes, P.:** Experiments in second-language learning. New York, 1967. **Davitz, J. R.:** The communication of emotional meaning. New York, 1964. **Deese, J.:** The structure of associations in language and thought. Baltimore, 1965. **Dixon, T. R. & Horton, D. L.** (Eds.): Verbal behavior and general behavior theory. Englewood Cliffs, 1968. **Ervin-Tripp, S.:** Sociolinguistics. In: **Berkowitz, L,** (Ed.): Advances in experimental social psychology. Vol. 4. New York, 1969, 91–165. **Herrmann, T. & Stäcker, K. H.:** Sprachpsychologische Beiträge zur Sozialpsychologie. In: **Graumann, C. F.** (Ed.): Handbuch der Psychologie, Vol. 7. Göttingen, 1969, 398–474. **Hörmann, H.:** Psychologie der Sprache. Berlin, 1967. **Jakubowicz, C.:** Recherches récentes en psycholinguistique. L'année psychol., 1970, *70,* 247–93. **Miller, G. A. & McNeill, D.:** Psycholinguistics. In: **Lindzey, G. & Aronson, E.** (Eds.): Handbook of social psychology, Vol. 3. Reading, Mass., 1969, 666–794. **Lyons, J.:** An introduction to theoretical linguistics. Cambridge, 1968. **Moscovici, S.:** Communication processes and the properties of language. In: **Berkowitz, L.** (Ed.): Advances in experimental social psychology, Vol. 3. New York, 1967, 225–70. **Mowrer, O. H.:** Learning theory and the symbolic processes. New York, 1960. **Osgood, C. E. & Sebeok, T. A.** (Eds.): Psycholinguistics. Bloomington, 1965. **Rieber, R. W. & Brubaker, R. S.** (Eds.): Speech pathology. Amsterdam, 1966. **Robins, R. H.:** General linguistics: an introductory survey. London, [2]1970. **Rochford, G. & Williams, M.:** The measurement of language disorders. Speech Path. Ther., 1964, *7,* 3. **Rommetveit, R.:** Words, meanings, and messages. New York, 1968; **Rosenberg, S. & Koplin, J. H.:** Developments in applied psycholinguistic research. New York, 1968. **Salzinger, K.:** The place of operant conditioning of verbal behavior in psychotherapy. In: **Franks, C.** (Ed.): Behavior therapy: appraisal and status. New York, 1969, 375–95. **Salzinger, K. & Salzinger, S.** (Eds.): Research in verbal behavior and some neurophysiological implications. New York, 1967. **Saporta, S.** (Ed.): Psycholinguistics. New York, 1961. **Scherer, G. A. C. & Wertheimer, M.:** A psycholinguistic experiment in foreign-language teaching. New York, 1964. **Skinner, B. F.:** Verbal behavior. New York, 1957. **Slobin, D. I.:** Psycholinguistics: basic psychological concepts. New York, 1971. **Staats, A. W.:** Learning, language, and cognition. New York, 1968. **Wiener, M. & Mehrabian, A.:** Language within language. New York, 1968.

G. Kaminski

Psychological moment. A term stemming from the hypothesis that incoming information is perceived in discrete units approximately 1/6 seconds long. Within such a psychological moment all the information taken in is lumped together, so that any temporal sequence in it cannot be perceived. The length of these moments is thought to be affected by drugs and other abnormal states, and hence is related to *time sense.* *C.D.F.*

Psychologism. An attitude that wants the "psychological point of view" to dominate the specific viewpoints of other human sciences (e.g. logic, philosophy, sociology, etc.). Psychologism is therefore a variant of empiricism (Locke, Hume, J. S. Mill. Its representatives in Germany in the nineteenth century were Fries, Beneke and Sigwart). But, whether the suggested method is introspection (considered as the unique instrument of logical or philosophical knowledge), or modern experimental method, the term is mainly used *polemically* (and pejoratively) by the opponents (e.g. the Neo-Kantians, Husserl, R. Carnap, Piaget) of the view it characterizes, who assert that it is necessary to make a distinction between *normative* and *factual* problems (to assert the independence of values from psychological experience), or between the objective validity of knowledge and the actual behavior of an individual. *M.-J.B.*

Psychologists. People who, in the exercise of their profession, deal with psychic experience and behavior and with the multifarious ways in which it is expressed as well as with the causes and conditions of what is psychic. The *work of the practicing psychologist* in the most diverse fields of applied psychology can be classified into three kinds of activity, i.e. *psychodiagnostics* (q.v.) (recognition of individual peculiarities including the conditions responsible for the actualization of such characteristics; psychological reports); *counseling* (vocational guidance, q.v., educational guidance, q.v., etc.); and *psychotherapy* (treatment, changing individuals either by means of psychological influence on them or on the environmental influences to which they are subjected). *W.Se.*

Psychology as a science. There was a very strong movement in Germany at the beginning of this century which set up psychology in its own right as opposed to natural sciences such as physics or biology, without, however, denying it the rigor and objective control constitutive of any science. Erismann asserted that the natural sciences were concerned with *explanation* (*Erklären*), whereas psychology, when attempting to grasp central phenomena of the mental life, had recourse to comprehension, or *understanding* (*Verstehen*). *P.M.*

Psychology, empirical. Known also as *scientific psychology* as distinguished from speculative, academic (armchair) psychology (q.v.). It deals with actual experience and sets out to study this experimentally with exact methods. *H.J.A.*

Psychology, functional. A trend in psychology which regards psychic processes and forms of behavior more as active processes than as structures or items of consciousness. As a rule it lays special emphasis on the usefulness of such activities for the individual's survival and adaptation and in so doing is akin to biology (q.v.). In cultural anthropology (q.v.), too, there is a functional school which is concerned chiefly with the adaptive character of the cultures under investigation. The American social sciences in particular have been very strongly influenced by functionalism, the chief proponents in the history of psychology being J. R. Angell, J. M. Baldwin, J. Mc. K. Cattell, S. T. Hall and W. James.

Bibliography: Boring, E. G. *et al.*: Foundations of psychology. New York & London, 1948. *W.Sch.*

Psychology without a soul. This paradoxical term ("psychology" means "science of the soul") was used by F. A. Lange (q.v.) in his *History of Materialism* (1866) to describe scientific psychology in its first stirrings. As a science it ignored the soul as an explanatory principle, and attempted to describe "mental facts" on the basis of their elements (see *Elementarism*). The term has now lost its polemical bite and is only of historical interest. *P.M.*

Psychometrics. The application of measurement and mathematics to psychology in general and particularly mental testing and the analysis of experimental results. *G.D.W.*

Psychometry. In parapsychology: a form of ESP (q.v.) involving the use of a token-object (q.v.). Also known as "token-object reading". *J.B.*

Psychomotor reactions. See *Motor skills.*

Psychomotor tempo. See *Tempo, personal.*

Psychoneuroendocrinology. This new discipline is concerned with the neuroendocrine control of behavior, in which hormone-physiological and neurophysiological methods are employed in combination, such as the implantation of hormones (q.v.) in certain areas of the brain, and the division of action potentials under the influence of hormones, etc. *K.Fi.*

Psychoneurosis. In his earliest works Freud spoke of "actual neuroses" and "psychoneuroses" or "transfer neuroses". Among the actual neuroses he placed neurasthenia and the anxiety neuroses, tracing their origin to the damming-up of sexual secretions as a result of sexual abstinence or certain anomalies in sexual behavior. The psychoneuroses or transfer neuroses he divided into three groups: hysteria (q.v.), the phobias (q.v.), and the obsessional neuroses (q.v.). Later he added other types such as the narcissistic and character neuroses, in which the dynamic force was basically psychological and not somatic. Psychiatry, too, has distinguished the psychoneuroses from the *organic neuroses*. The latter belong to the group which today are brought together under the concept of "psychosomatic disorders". The former, on the contrary, embrace neuroses which have psychic and not internal-organic symptoms. (See *Neuroses; Psychoses, functional.*) *J.L.I.*

Psychopathia sexualis. Sexual psychopathology. Emotional illness characterized by sexual perversions. Term introduced as the title of a book by the German sexologist R. von Krafft-Ebing (1840–1903); rare in Anglo-American psychiatry. *G.D.W.*

Psychopathology. The systematic study of the etiology, symptomatology and process of mental disorders. It is that part of abnormal psychology which is concerned with illness, disease or maladjustment. *R.H.*

Psychopathology, psychoanalytic schema of. The schema, according to S. Freud (q.v.), K. Abraham and O. Fenichel, in cases of psychic illness whose cause is not organic, bacterial or some injury, results from a regression (q.v.) to those psychic phases of development in which fixation took place. The model arranges psychic illnesses of varying degrees of gravity according to (*a*) the fixation phase, (*b*) the elementary direction of the interests involved, (*c*) the elementary aspects of the personal relationships, and (*d*) the dominant anxieties of the patient, but also of the child as he passes normally through a particular phase at a particular time (see table).

The schema is in part the subject of controversy, but in principle it can be tested empirically, and has been tested in part. Among such tests are investigations of the relative frequency with which psychic illnesses of the same group occur together in the course of a single life, and also among members of the same family, in addition the relative frequency with which any mental disorders occur in the family; then investigations of the coincidences in time of traumatic environmental conditions (e.g. parental role conflicts whether emergent

Fixation stage	Elementary interests	Relations to individuals	Most primitive anxieties	Psychological disorder
Early oral stage	Oral and tactile stimulation; also stimulation of other sensory areas	No object person	Total panic; end of existence	Schizophrenia
Late oral stage	Oral, oral-aggressive, tactile and kinesthetic manipulation and stimulation	Unconditionally caring, "almighty' mother	To be lost; to "disintegrate"	Mania, depression, impulsive neuroses, organ neuroses, hypochondria
Early anal stage	Body manipulation and primitive manipulation of material including (involuntary) destruction of material; primitive manipulation of excretory function	Powerful, supportive parents; oscillation between own omnipotence and impotence	Destruction or serious mutilation	Paranoia, tics, stuttering, masochism
Late anal stage	Refined body and material manipulation; shaping of material; control of excretion	More or less just, "giving and taking", parents; realization of finer nuances of one's own power	Destruction, less serious mutilation	Compulsive neuroses, tics, stuttering, sadism
Early genital stage	Genital manipulation and stimulation; interest in all aspects of relations between men and women	Sex-specific parents; acceptance of own sex	Genital mutilation	Hysteria (anxiety or conversion hysteria); homosexuality; other deviations

or becoming manifest, the early loss of some person(s): see *Family; Family constellation*) among mental disorders of the same type, but also among all mental disorders in comparison with the average population; and finally, investigations of correlations between deteriorations of the actual life situation of the patients and actual forms of sickness, as well as transitions to other forms of illness which would have to be cured. The greater the actual deterioration of a life situation, the lower in its group and the more pronounced a particular manifestation of a mental disorder is. Improvements in the actual life situation would result in transitions in the reverse direction (toward higher, i.e. milder psychic illnesses). *W. Toman*

Psychopathy. Although the term psychopathy has been used in a variety of contexts (see: Craft, 1965), there is a growing tendency among behavioral scientists to restrict its use to a relatively specific clinical and behavioral disorder (Albert, Brigante & Chase, 1959). The disorder has been extensively described by Cleckley (1964) and Karpman (1961), and, in a broad sense, is covered by the American Psychiatric Association (1952) category: sociopathic personality disturbance—antisocial reaction.

Briefly, the psychopath (or sociopath) is an impulsive, irresponsible, hedonistic, "two-dimensional" person who lacks the ability to experience the normal emotional components of interpersonal behavior, including guilt, remorse, empathy, affection, and genuine concern for the welfare of others. Although he is often able to mimic normal emotions and to simulate affectional attachments, his social and sexual relations with others remain superficial and demanding. His judgment is poor, and he seems unable to delay the gratification of his momentary needs no matter what the consequences to himself and to others. As a result, he is frequently in trouble; in attempting to extricate himself from difficulty he often produces an intricate and contradictory web of lies and rationalizations, coupled with theatrical and sometimes convincing explanations, expressions of remorse, and promises to change. Many psychopaths are very callously predatory and aggressive; others are more typically parasitic or passively manipulative, relying upon a glib sophistication, superficial charm, and the appearance of being helpless to obtain what they want.

Although many psychopathic individuals are constantly in trouble with the law, many others manage to avoid imprisonment for long periods of time, even though their behavior may be grossly antisocial (see: Robins, 1966). They may be protected by family and friends, or operate in a sector of society that condones or tolerates their behavior. In some cases they may be charming and intelligent enough to carry out unethical and unscrupulous practices in a legal or quasi-legal manner, or to talk their way out of prosecution and conviction.

Psychopathy can be distinguished from other forms of antisocial and aggressive behavior that are more symptomatic of some basic emotional disturbance (neurotic delinquency or "psychopathy"), or that reflect socialization in a deviant subculture (subcultural delinquency or dysocial "psychopathy"). Unlike psychopaths, neurotic and subcultural delinquents are quite able to experience guilt and remorse for their behavior and to form warm affectional relationships with others. The clinical distinction between psychopathic, neurotic, and subcultural forms of antisocial behavior is supported by statistical studies of case history data, behavior ratings, and responses to questionnaires (e.g. Jenkins, 1966; Quay, 1964).

Although the general literature on psychopathy is very extensive (see bibliography by Hare & Hare, 1967), it is just beginning to receive the attention it deserves from the behavioral and biological sciences. The relevant research and theory are summarized below, with more extensive discussions being available elsewhere (Craft, 1965; Hare, 1970; McCord & McCord, 1964).

1. *Physiological studies*. A considerable number of studies has made use of electroencephalographic (EEG) recordings to determine whether psychopathy is associated with abnormalities of the brain. Although many of these studies can be criticized on methodological and conceptual grounds, their results are relatively consistent. It appears that the incidence of EEG or brain-wave abnormalities among psychopathic individuals is unusually high, the most common abnormality being the presence of an excessive amount of slow-wave (4–7 cps) activity, either widespread or, in the case of severely impulsive and aggressive psychopaths, localized in the temporal areas of the brain (e.g. Hill, 1952). Some investigators, noting that the slow-wave activity of psychopaths bears some resemblance to the EEG patterns usually found in children, have suggested that psychopathy is associated with structural or functional immaturity of the brain. A second hypothesis, based upon the presence of localized EEG abnormalities, is that psychopathy is related to some defect or malfunction of brain mechanisms concerned with emotional activity and the regulation of behavior.

The functioning of the psychopath's autonomic nervous system has attracted the interest of several investigators. The results of this line of research (reviewed by Hare, 1968a, 1970) have been somewhat equivocal. In general, however, they tend to support the hypothesis that psychopaths fall at the lower end of a dimension of autonomic arousal and lability. They are also consistent with clinical statements about the psychopath's lack of anxiety and guilt, and about his failure to respond appropriately in situations usually considered to have emotional significance for normal individuals.

2. *Psychopathy and arousal* (q.v.). In any given situation there appears to be a level of cortical arousal that is optimal for peak behavioral efficiency, hedonic tone, and awareness of the environment. However, the conditions that permit normal persons to enjoy an optimal level of arousal tend to produce a state of arousal in psychopaths that is below what for them would be an optimal level (Eysenck, 1967; Hare, 1968a; Quay, 1965). Since one of the most important determinants of arousal is stimulation, psychopaths tend to become quickly bored and restless in situations that are dull and tedious or otherwise lacking in stimulation. At the same time they appear to have an inordinate need for stimulation, particularly stimulation that is novel, varied and unpredictable (e.g. Skrzypek, 1969), or that is associated with activities that others would consider dangerous, foolhardy or frightening, but which psychopaths find exciting (e.g. Lykken, 1957). There is also some evidence that psychopaths are less attentive to weak stimulation (Hare, 1968a, 1968b) and more tolerant of strong stimulation (Thorvaldson, 1969) than are normal individuals.

3. *Learning*. There have been several attempts to account for psychopathic behavior in terms of an inability to learn the modes of behavior necessary for adequate social functioning. Eysenck (1967), for example, considers the psychopath to be an extravert, and therefore generally inferior in the acquisition of responses associated with the process of socialization. Other investigators (e.g. Lykken, 1957) have suggested that the psychopath's learning-deficit may be more specific than this, being largely confined to fear-conditioning and avoidance learning. Concerning the former, the evidence clearly indicates that psychopaths develop classically conditioned fear responses less readily than do normal persons (Lykken, 1957; Quinn, 1969). Moreover, psychopaths appear to exhibit an unusually steep "temporal gradient" of fear arousal (Hare, 1965a, 1965b; Schalling & Levander, 1967). That is, compared with normal persons, they show little fear arousal

in the interval prior to impending pain or punishment. In effect, aversive events expected in the future have no immediate emotional impact on the psychopath, a finding that has important implications for his apparent inability to stay out of trouble. Learning to inhibit behavior likely to have unpleasant consequences, for example, may be viewed as a two-stage process (Mowrer, 1947) involving the conditioning of fear to cues associated with punishment, and the subsequent reinforcement (by fear-reduction) of behavior that removes the individual from the fear-producing cues. The psychopath's apparent disregard for the future consequences of his behavior may therefore be seen as a failure of cues (verbal, symbolic, kinesthetic, visual, and so on) associated with punishment to elicit sufficient anticipatory fear for the instigation and subsequent reinforcement of avoidance responses. There is some empirical support for this position. Lykken (1957), using an ingenious "mental maze," found that psychopaths learned a sequence of rewarded responses but failed to learn to avoid responses punished with electric shock. Similar findings have been obtained by several other investigators, including Schachter & Latané (1964). An additional finding by these latter investigators was that an injection of adrenalin greatly enhanced the ability of the psychopathic subjects to avoid shocked responses. Presumably adrenalin, which increases the activity of the sympathetic nervous system, augmented the psychopaths' capacity for experiencing anticipatory fear.

Apart from fear conditioning and avoidance learning, there is little evidence that the learning ability of psychopaths differs from that of normal persons, particularly where appropriate attempts are made to motivate them to perform well (see review by Hare, 1970).

4. *Socialization.* Broken homes and disturbed family relationships, especially parental loss and rejection, have been used to account for almost every form of abnormal and antisocial behavior, including psychopathy (McCord & McCord, 1964; Wiggens, 1968). It is difficult, therefore, to determine in what ways the background of psychopaths might differ from that of other disorders. One reason for this unhappy situation is that the majority of studies made use of a retroactive approach to the problem: that is, they relied upon interviews with adult subjects to determine what took place many years before.

An extensive study by Robins (1966) largely overcame this limitation by studying the adult social and psychiatric status of persons who had been referred to a guidance clinic some thirty years earlier, and for whom a great deal of information on family background, social behavior, and so on was available. Briefly, Robins found that the childhood predictors of adult psychopathy included truancy, theft, lying, lack of guilt, refusal to obey parents, and sexual misbehavior. Although most psychopaths came from broken homes, this fact was less important than having a father who was himself psychopathic or alcoholic, a finding that is consistent with other evidence that maternal rejection and behavior have less to do with the development of antisocial behavior than do the personality and behavior of the father (e.g. Andry, 1960).

On a more theoretical level, Gough (1948) has suggested that the psychopath is pathologically unable to role-play. As a result, he is unable to see himself as a social object and to foresee the consequences of his own behavior. And because he cannot judge his own behavior from another's point of view, he is unable to experience embarrassment, loyalty, contrition, or group identification. Nor can he understand the reasons for societies' objections to his behavior.

The psychopath's low resistance to temptation and his lack of guilt have been interpreted as the result of the delayed and inconsistent administration of punishment for transgressions (Hare, 1970). Similarly, his impulsivity and inability to delay gratification have been related to a family background in which impulse-control training was generally poor, and in which parental models displayed little control over their own behavior (Arieti, 1967).

Buss (1966) has suggested that psychopathy reflects the modeling of parental behavior characterized by coldness, remoteness and the inconsistent administration of affection, rewards, and punishments.

As a final point, it is worth noting that most socialization theories, including those concerned with psychopathy, tend to view the child as a more or less passive member of the socialization process. It may be more appropriate to view the parent-child relationship as an interactive one in which the behavior and socialization techniques of the parents are partly determined by the characteristics of the child. It is possible that some of these characteristics (e.g. assertiveness, social responsiveness) are influenced by genetic and constitutional factors (Bell, 1968; Eysenck, 1967).

5. *Modification of psychopathic behavior.* The traditional psychological and biological therapeutic techniques have proved to be almost totally ineffective in the modification of psychopathic behavior. There are several reasons for this situation, including the well-known limitations of the techniques themselves. For one thing, the psychopath neither suffers from personal distress nor sees anything wrong with his behavior, and he is therefore not motivated to change. For another, his way of life can be very rewarding, at least in the short run; being periodically punished, usually well after the act, does little to offset the immediate gratification obtained. As a result, his behavior is well established, and from his own egocentric point of view, quite sensible.

It is likely that any significant modification of the psychopath's behavior would require a major restructuring of his social and psychological environment. It may be necessary, for example, to set up an intensive, long-term program, patterned after the therapeutic community concept for improving interpersonal relations (e.g. Craft, 1965; McCord & McCord, 1964; Stürup, 1964), but including attempts to increase the motivating influence of fear and anxiety and to make social reinforcements more effective.

Bibliography: Albert, R., Brigante, T. & Chase, M.: The psychopathic personality: A content analysis of the concept. J. Gen. Psychol., 1959, *60*, 17–28. **American Psychiatric Association:** Diagnostic and statistical manual: Mental disorders. Washington, 1952. **Andry, R.:** Delinquency and parental pathology. London, 1960. **Arieti, S.:** The intrapsychic self. New York, 1967. **Bell, R.:** A reinterpretation of the direction of effects in studies of socialization. Psychol. Rev., 1968, *75*, 81–95. **Buss, A.:** Psychopathology. New York, 1966. **Cleckley, H.:** The mask of sanity. St. Louis, Mo., [4]1964. **Craft, M.:** Ten studies in psychopathic personality, Bristol, 1965. **Eysenck, H. J.:** The biological basis of personality. Springfield, Ill., 1967. **Gough, H.:** A sociological theory of psychopathy. Amer. J. Sociol., 1948, *53*, 359–66. **Hare, R.:** A conflict and learning theory analysis of psychopathic behavior. J. res. Crime Delinq., 1965 (a), *2*, 12–19; **Id.:** Temporal gradient of fear arousal in psychopaths. J. abnorm. Psychol., 1965 (b), *70*, 442–45. **Id.:** Psychopathy, autonomic functioning, and the orienting response. J. abnorm. Psychol., 1968 (a), *73*, Monogr. Supp.; **Id.:** Detection threshold for electric shock in psychopaths. J. abnorm. Psychol., 1968 (b), *73*, 268–72. **Id.:** Psychopathy: theory and research. New York, 1970. **Id. & Hare, A.:** Psychopathic behavior: a bibliography. Excerpta Criminologica, 1967, *7*, 365–86. **Hill, D.:** EEG in episodic psychotic and psychopathic behavior: A classification of data. EEG clin. Neurophysiol., 1952, *4*, 419–42. **Jenkins, R.:** Psychiatric syndromes in children and their relation to family background. Amer. J. Orthopsychiat., 1966, *36*, 450–57. **Karpman, B.:** The structure of neurosis: With special differentials between neurosis, psychosis, homosexuality, alcoholism, psychopathy, and criminality. Arch. Crim. Psychodyn., 1961, *4*, 599–646. **Lykken, D.:** A study of anxiety in the sociopathic personality. J. abnorm. soc. Psychol., 1957, *55*, 6–10. **McCord, W. & McCord, J.:** The psychopath: An essay on the criminal mind. Princeton (N.J.), 1964. **Mowrer, O.:** On the dual nature of learning – a reinterpretation of "conditioning" and "problem-solving". Harvard educ. Rev., 1947, *17*, 102–48. **Quay, H.:** Personality dimensions in delinquent males as inferred from the factor analysis of behavior ratings. J. res. Crime Delinq., 1964, *1*, 33–37 **Id.:** Psychopathic personality as pathological stimulation seeking. Amer. J. Psychiatr., 1965, *122*, 180–83

Quinn, M.: Psychopathy and the conditioning of autonomic responses. Unpublished diss., University of British Columbia, 1969. **Robins, L.:** Deviant children grown up. Baltimore, 1966. **Schachter, S. & Latane, B.:** Crime, cognition, and the autonomic nervous system. **M. Jones** (Ed.): Nebraska symposium on motivation. Lincoln, 1964, 221–75. **Schalling, D. & Levander, S.:** Ratings of anxiety proneness and responses to electrical stimulation. Scand. J. Psychol., 1964, *5*, 1–9. **Skrzypek, G.:** The effects of perceptual isolation and arousal on anxiety, complexity preference, and novelty preference in psychopathic and neurotic criminals. J. abnorm. Psychol., 1969, *74*, 321–29. **Stürup, G.:** The treatment of chronic criminals. Bull. Menninger Clin., 1964, *28*, 229–43. **Throvaldson, S.:** Detection threshold and tolerance level for electric shock in psychopaths. Unpublished M.A. thesis, University of British Columbia, 1969. **Wiggens, J.:** Inconsistent socialization. Psychol. Reports, 1968, *23*, 303–36.

R. D. Hare

Psychopharmacology. 1. *Definition, demarcation and development of psychopharmacology.* This, strictly speaking, is a sub-field of psychology, which investigates psychic and correlative physiological effects of natural and synthetic chemical substances (chiefly psychopharmaceuticals) after these have been introduced into the organism—whether a "healthy" human individual, or an animal. To classify psychopharmacology among the usual fields of psychology does not seem possible. In so far as it is regarded as complementary to pharmacotherapy (q.v.), it is thought of as applied or clinical psychology (q.v.). If it is considered as a discipline dealing with the physiological bases of behavior, it is general or physiological psychology. No sharp demarcation of psychopharmacology from other disciplines (such as pharmacology, pharmacopsychiatry or pharmacotherapy) dealing with psychotropic (q.v.) substances is possible.

Although psychopharmaceuticals have been known for centuries, psychopharmacology as a science is less than a century old. The psychiatrist E. Kraepelin (1856–1926) is considered to be its founder and it was under him that, from the end of the nineteenth century, numerous investigations were conducted into the effect of stimulants (q.v.) and sedatives (q.v.), etc., on a series of arithmetical performances, memory and learning processes and processes requiring attention. In spite of isolated studies on a larger scale which dealt in particular with the effect of narcotics (q.v.), stimulants (q.v.), opiates (q.v.) and gonadotropic hormones (q.v.), the researches on which Kraepelin had embarked did not subsequently lead to the foundation of any systematic partial discipline of psychology. But when completely new types of preparation were developed which proved effective (see *Pharmacotherapy*) in cases of psychosis (see *Neuroleptics*) and neurosis (see *Tranquilizers*), interest in psychopharmacological research grew extremely rapidly. Whereas in pharmacopsychiatry interest is concentrated on the therapeutic efficacy of the new substances, especially in cases of schizophrenia (q.v.), as well as on hypotheses concerning the biochemistry of mental disorders (Wooley & Shaw, 1955), psychopharmacology attempts to explain inter- and intraindividual variation in reaction when tranquilizers are used. The considerable variability of effect found with these preparations in comparison with those known hitherto led to numerous studies of the relationship between reaction to pharmaceuticals and personality factors (Eysenck, Kornetsky, Dimascio, Janke—cf. bibliography) as well as situational factors (see *Differential psychology*).

Practical work to be done in assessing the action of psychotropic substances in healthy individuals may be grouped under the following headings: 1. Classification of new substances, of tranquilizers (q.v.), stimulants (q.v.), antidepressives (q.v.), sedatives (q.v.) and soporifics on the basis of their relative action. 2. Development of hypotheses concerning possible therapeutical indications. 3. Analysis of psychic side-effects of pharmaceuticals used in the treatment of somatic diseases. Analgesics (q.v.), antihistamines (q.v.), antihypertonics (q.v.), remedies for colds and many other medicines do not merely remove the target symptoms but also frequently induce fairly pronounced psychic changes the exact understanding of which is very important, e.g. in deciding whether a person is fit to drive. 4. Relatively healthy individuals constitute a considerable proportion of consumers of tranquilizers, stimulants and other medicines. Pharmacopsychological studies make it possible by suitably planned multifactorial experiments to give considered recommendations for certain situations and persons when disturbances are to be expected in particular circumstances. It is very important to analyze the effects of soporifics (q.v.) (aftereffects), tranquilizers (q.v.) and alcohol on fitness to drive.

2. *Psychopharmacology and psychological research.* For all partial disciplines of non-applied psychology, psychopharmacology is a basic discipline pursued under special aspects and to be considered in conjunction with physiological psychology (q.v.). In principle every pharmacopsychological study makes a contribution to the question of the inter- and intraindividual variability of psychic processes. Pharmaceuticals (biochemical variations derived from them) are regarded as a special class of stimuli (independent variables) which may be fundamentally compared to all other stimuli in psychology. A systematic understanding of the relations between drug-induced "biochemical lesions" (Russell, 1966) and behavior is, however, at the present moment in its earliest stages because the influence of psychopharmaceuticals on biochemical processes is largely unknown in detail. *Human* psychopharmacology in particular is chiefly dependent on speculation and analogies with animal psychopharmacology. Nevertheless, above all other fields of psychology, it provides the opportunity to use in its interpretations the biochemical processes that take place between the stimulus (drug) and the response (behavior). The importance of psychopharmacology as a basic psychological discipline will increase in proportion as biochemical correlates of behavior are found in animal experiments, because as a rule in human beings biochemical processes can be varied only indirectly and as a result of administering pharmaceuticals. The following lines of research in modern psychopharmacology are examples of the use of psychotropic substances as "tools" of psychological basic research:

(*a*) Psychopharmaceutical agents, biochemical "lesions" and behavior: present research is concentrated mainly on the relations between variations of the substances found in the body such as acetylcholine (q.v.), serotonin (including those which are similar, e.g. tryptophan, q.v., tryptamine) and noradrenalin (q.v.) (including those which are similar, e.g. dopa, q.v., dopamine, q.v.) and variations of behavior. Substances most commonly used in experiments are cholinesterase (q.v.) inhibitors and cholinergic (q.v.) substances for the manipulation of acetylcholine in the central and autonomic nervous systems. Monoaminooxydase (q.v.) inhibitors for varying noradrenalin and serotonin concentrations and reserpine (q.v.) and LSD for manipulating serotonin. Learning and memory (acetylcholin, serotonin) moods and affects (noradrenalin, serotonin) and experimentally induced "psychotic" behavior (serotonin) are used as major psychological variables.

(*b*) Psychopharmaceuticals and covariations of physical and psychic processes: numerous psychophysiological models (e.g. activation theory), as well as the consequent diagnostic applications, are based on the correlations between physiological and psychological variables which have been obtained under normal conditions. Investigations with psychopharmaceuticals can make a contribution to the adequacy of such models. Several investigations show that under the influence of certain preparations correlations are found quite different to those under normal conditions. With a large number of preparations (e.g. anticholinergics, q.v., barbiturates, q.v.), there occur dissociations between behavior and physiological processes (see EEG; *Skin resistance*; *Pulse rate*; etc.) as well as dissociations inside different physiological systems.

(*c*) Psychopharmaceuticals and learning. Main points of research in this field are; (i) Relations between learning and memory and ribonucleic acid (RNA), substances inhibiting and promoting the synthesis of RNA (see *Antibiotics*); (ii) Pharmaceuticals and consolidation: whereas certain substances (e.g. strychnine, picrotoxin, pentetrazol) which stimulate the central nervous system seem to improve retention when administered immediately after some learning process, hypnotics and narcotics (e.g. ether) given in large doses cause retention to deteriorate. The analysis of the relation "learning and time when preparation was administered" can provide fresh knowledge about the consolidation or perseveration theory of memory. Because of their selective action, psychopharmaceuticals are undoubtedly superior to other stimuli (e.g. electric shocks, hypothermia, anoxia).

(*c*) State-dependent learning: behavior learnt under the influence of pharmaceuticals is reproduced less well in conditions where pharmaceuticals are not used than when the experimental conditions are kept constant. It is evident that an organismic condition induced by pharmaceuticals has to be regarded as a conditioned stimulus. So far, however, no results of experiments with human beings are available.

(*d*) Psychopharmaceutical agents and personality: psychological personality models should make it possible to predict individual differences in reaction to psychopharmaceuticals. The best-known personality model which has made use of such differences is that of H. J. Eysenck.

(*e*) Psychopharmaceuticals and emotion: the most important fields of research deal with the question of how far psychotropic substances can induce emotional variations of specific emotional qualities going beyond a general heightening or lowering of arousal. The possibility of specific changes results from the fact that many preparations have a relatively specific action on hypothalamic, thalamic or limbic structures. Special importance is attached to studies in which pharmaceuticals acting on the autonomic nervous system are used to change autonomic reaction patterns whereas cognitive-situational factors are kept constant or varied (Schachter, 1966). As different pharmaceuticals have different periphero-physiological action patterns, physiological (James-Lange theory) and physiologico-cognitive (Schachter, 1966) emotion theories can be tested by psychopharmacological studies (see *Emotions*). Other investigations are concerned with the question whether depressions are to be studied in connection with the central serotonin and catecholamine metabolism.

(*f*) Psychopharmaceuticals and motivation: the central topic of psychopharmacological research into motivation is how the action of the pharmaceutical agent administered is processed by the individual in accordance with the habitual or temporary motivational situation. Pharmaceuticals may be considered as stimuli which disturb the normal adaptation level, i.e. the optimal activation (q.v.) level. As differential psychopharmacology (q.v.) has shown, many individuals under certain situational conditions respond to such disturbances with paradoxical reactions (e.g. excitation in the case of tranquilizers, q.v., or heightened performance in the case of sedatives, q.v., and narcotics, q.v.). Paradoxical reactions are the result of complex interactions between situational conditions, personality characteristics and the nature and dose of the preparation. In this research pharmaceuticals are seen as tools for studying motivational processes. A further range of problems dealt with by psychopharmacological research into motivation is how pharmaceuticals influence central "reward" and "punishment" systems. The autostimulation rate, following a technique devised by L. Olds, can be modified by numerous drugs.

3. *Planning and execution of psychopharmacological investigations* of the only slight constancy of intra- and interindividual action of psychotropic substances, psychopharmacological investigations yield results that can be interpreted and reproduced only when numerous factors have been eliminated or checked. The following table shows the most important of these factors as well as some methods for eliminating and checking them:

Factors	*Control or elimination method*
1. Spontaneous changes and changes conditioned by learning and practice	Comparison with placebo substance: if possible, comparison with standard preparations (especially in clinical tests)
2. Suggestion	
(a) Knowledge that some substance has been administered	Comparison with placebo; comparison with the action of preparation when administered without subject's knowledge
(b) Uncertainty whether a placebo or an active substance has been administered	Standardization, by disclosure ("instruction"), of the subjective probability that a placebo or an active substance will be received
(c) General awareness of the mode of action of psychoactive substances	Interindividual standardization by disclosure of the degree of information
(d) Awareness of the way in which the substance is expected to act	(a) Disclosure, but not of the specific action (e.g. "mode of operation so far unknown") (b) Specific instruction (e.g. "the preparation has a sedative effect")
(e) Expectation of psychic action on account of fairly strong somatic side-effects	Comparison with "active" placebo, i.e. a substance with the somatic side-effects but not the main psychic effects
3. Subjects' characteristics	
(a) Age, sex, weight, habitual personality traits, etc.	Homogenization of the sample by selection (e.g. only "neuroticism"); parallelization with independent groups, factorial experimental designs
(b) Health characteristics	Elimination of testees with certain diseases (e.g. liver or gastro-intestinal diseases)
(c) Voluntary cooperation of testees	Check on personality traits of volunteer testees
(d) Initial individual disposition	Elimination of diverse initial dispositions by adaptation (test cycle before administration of the preparation), habituation (practice tests) or standardization (e.g. standard meals). Subsequent correction by regression methods (e.g. covariance analysis) in order to take initial disposition into account
(e) Experiences with psychopharmaceuticals and psychopharmacological investigations, attitudes, expectations	Standardization by instruction. Elimination of testees with "considerable experience"
(f) Antecedent activities	Standardization. Inquiry into particularities. Possible elimination of testees
4. Situational conditions	
(a) Experimenter's knowledge (as under 2)	As for 2
(b) Sex and behavior of experimenter	Homogenization (elimination) or control by factorial experimental designs
(c) Social conditions	Standardization: group or individual experiments
(d) Spatial conditions	Standardization: same space for testees, freedom from interruption
(e) Time conditions (day, week, year)	Restriction to short periods, compensation, factorial test designs
5. Dosage: characteristic effects	Use of minimum of three doses
6. Time: characteristic effects	Several measurements during an investigation
7. Characteristic effects in comparison with other substances	Use of standard preparations
8. Test instruments	
(a) Selective effects of psychopharmaceuticals	Abstention from "global measurements, multivariant test batteries in the areas of experience, behavior and physiological processes
(b) Ambiguity of effects	Use of tests that are factorially as simple as possible. Control of complex tests by factorially simple tests
(c) Varying sensitivity of tests with different types of preparation, e.g. insensitivity of speed tests with sedatives	Use of different batteries according to mode of effect; in speed tests, control of motivational factors by scaling techniques
(d) "Unreliability" of certain tests against a placebo	(a) Control of ceiling effects by "no preparation" conditions (b) No use of tests with high incidence of placebo effect
(e) Reinforcement effects by using several tests	Use of batteries with least possible correlation

Bibliography: (1) *Journals and lit.:* Psychopharmacologia. Berlin, from 1960. International Pharmacopsychiatry. Basle, from 1968; Pharmakopsychiatrie—Neuropsychopharmakologie. Stuttgart, from 1968. Psychopharmacological Abstracts. Bethesda, from 1961. Neuro-Psycho-Pharmacology. Amsterdam, from 1958. **Caldwell, A. E.:** Psychopharmaca. A bibliography of psychopharmacology. Washington, 1958. **Kobo-yashi, T.:** International bibliography on psychopharmacology, Vol. 1. Tokio, 1968. **Wortis, J.** (Ed.): Recent advances in biological psychiatry. New York, from 1960. (2) *General introductions:* **Black, P.:** Drugs and the brain. Baltimore, 1969. **Clark, W. G. & del Guidice, J.** (Eds.): Principles of psychopharmacology. New York, 1970. **Dews, P. B.:** Psychopharmacology. In: **Bachrach, A. J.** (Ed.): Experimental foundations of clinical psychology. New York, 1962. **Efron, D. H.** (Ed.): Psychopharmacology. A review of progress 1957–67. Washington, 1968. **Elkes, J.:** Behavioral pharmacology in relation to psychiatry. In: **Gruhle, H. W.** *et al.* (Eds.): Psychiatrie der Gegenwart in Forschung und Praxis, Vol. I/1. Berlin, 1967. **Eysenck, H. J.** (Ed.): Experiments with drugs. Oxford, 1963. **Goodman, L. S. & Gilman, A.** (Eds.): The pharmacological basis of therapeutics. New York, 1965. **Joyce, C. R. B.** (Ed.): Psychopharmacology—Dimensions and perspectives. London, 1968. **Lippert, H.:** Einführung in die Pharmakopsychologie. Bern, 1959. **Nordine, J. H. & Siegler, P. E.:** Animal and clinical pharmacological techniques in drug evaluation, Vol. 1. Chicago, 1964. **Ross, S. & Cole, J. O.:** Psychopharmacology. Ann. Rev. Psychol., 1960, *11*, 415–38. **Russell, R. W.:** Psychopharmacology. Ann. Rev. Psychol., 1964, *15*, 87–114. **Siegler, P. E. & Moyer, J. H.:** Animal and clinical pharmacologic techniques in drug evaluations, Vol. 2. Chicago, 1967. **Solomon, P.:** Psychiatric drugs. New York, 1966. **Steinberg, H.** (Ed.): Animal behavior and drug action. London, 1964. **Thompson, T. & Schuster, C. R.:** Behavioral pharmacology. New York, 1968; **Uhr, L. & Miller, J. G.:** Drugs and behavior. New York, 1960. (3) *Drugs, biochemistry and behavior:* **Deutsch, S. A.:** The physiological basis of memory. Ann. Rev. Psychol., 1969, *20*, 85–104. **Domagk, G. F. & Zippel, H. P.:** Biochemie der Gedächtnisspeicherung. Naturwissensch., 1970, 57, 152–62. **Eiduson, S.** *et al.*: Biochemistry and behavior. Princeton, 1964. **Freedman, D. X.:** Aspects of the biochemical pharmacology of psychotropic drugs. In: **Solomon, P.** (Ed.): Psychiatric drugs. New York, 1966. **Mandell, A. S. & Mandell, M. P.** (Eds.): Psychochemical research in man. New York, 1969. **Young, R. D.:** Developmental psychopharmacology: a beginning. Psychol. Bull., 1967, *67*, 73–86. **Russell, R. W.:** Effects of "biochemical lesions" on behavior. Acta Psychol., 1958, *14*, 281–94. **Russell, R. W.:** Biochemical substrats of behavior. In: **Russell, R. W.** (Ed.): Frontiers in physiological psychology. New York, 1966. **Weiss, B. & Laties, V. G.:** Behavioral pharmacology and toxicology. Ann. Rev. Pharmacol., 1969, *9*, 297–326. (4) *Special topics:* **Baker, R. R.:** The effects of psychotropic drugs on psychological testing. Psychol. Bull., 1968, *69*, 377–89. **Corning, W. C. & Ratner, S. C.:** Chemistry of learning. New York, 1967; **Düker, H.:** Über reaktive Anspannungssteigerung. Zschr. exp. angew. Psychol., 1963, *10*, 46–72. **Gaito, J.:** Molecular psychobiology. Springfield, 1966. **Kimble, D. P.** (Ed.): The anatomy of memory. Palo Alto, 1965. **Janke, W.:** Experimentelle Untersuchungen zur Abhängigkeit der Wirkung psychotroper Substanzen von Persönlichkeitsmerkmalen. Frankfurt, 1964. **Janke, W. & Debus, G.:** Experimental studies on anti-anxiety drugs with normal subjects: methodological considerations and review of the main effects. In: **Efron, D. H.** (Ed.): Psychopharmacology 1957–67. Washington, 1968. **Janke, W.:** Methoden der Induktion von Aktiviertheit. In: **Schönpflug, W.** (Ed.): Methoden der Aktivierungsforschung. Berne, 1969. **Lennard, H. L.:** A proposed program of research in sociopharmacology. In: **Leiderman, P. H. & Shapiro, D.** (Eds.): Psychobiological aspects to social behavior. London, 1965. **McGaugh & Petrinovich, L. F.:** Effects of drugs on learning and memory. Int. Rev. Neurobiol., 1965, *8*, 139–96. **Mikhel'son, M. Y. & Longo, V. G.:** Pharmacology of conditioning, learning and retention. Oxford, 1965. **Miller, N. E. & Barry, H.:** Motivational effects of drugs. Psychopharmacologia, 1960, *1*, 169–99. **Overton, D.:** Dissociated learning in drug states (state-dependent learning). In: **Efron, D. H.** (Ed.): Psychopharmacology 1957–67. Washington, 1968. **Schachter, S.:** The interaction of cognitive and physiological determinants of emotional state. In: **Spielberger C.** (Ed.): Anxiety and behavior. New York, 1966. **Stein, L.:** Chemistry of reward and punishment. In: **Efron, D. H.** (Ed.): Psychopharmacology 1957–67. Washington, 1968. **Trouton, D. T. & Eysenck, H. J.:** The effects of drugs on behavior. In **Eysenck, H. J.** (Ed.): Handbook of abnormal psychology. London & New York, [2]1971.

W. Janke

Psychopharmacology of the ANS. ANS drugs, i.e. pharmaceuticals, are substances which lead to alterations of the activity of the *autonomic nervous system* (q.v.). Most ANS drugs also affect the CNS, and many influence the endocrine system. A distinction is made between

ANS drugs which take effect primarily in the central autonomic regulation centers (hypothalamus, q.v.; limbic system), and those which take effect primarily in the peripheral autonomic neuron(e)s. This division is, however, only conditionally useful, since many ANS drugs take effect both centrally and peripherally, and of course a wholly straightforward separation of the peripheral and central ANS is not possible. Other possibilities of division of ANS drugs correspond to the separation of the ANS into the *sympathetic* and *parasympathetic* divisions. Sympathetic-stimulant substances are known as *sympathicomimetic* (q.v.), sympathetic-inhibiting substances as *sympathicolytic* (q.v.). By analogy, within the parasympathetic system, *parasympathicomimetic* are differentiated from *parasympathicolytic* substances. The tables below list a selection of ANS substances.

The effective mechanism of ANS drugs may be described (in somewhat simplified terms) as the influencing of the natural body transmitter substances acetylcholine (parasympathetic ganglia, preganglionic fibers of the sympathetic division, neuromuscular connections) and noradrenalin(e) (postganglionic fibers of the sympathetic division). The effect on the natural-body acetylcholine and noradrenalin(e) action may be *direct* or *indirect*.

Examples of drugs with pronounced effects on the sympathetic system

(sympathicomimetic)

Direct effect:

Many substances (app. 500), e.g.:
adrenalin(e) (epinephrine)
noradrenalin(e) (norepinephrine)
isopropylnoradrenalin(e) (isoprenalin(e))
phenylephrin(e)
synephrin(e)
angiotensin
vasopressin
LSD
psilocybin

Alpha receptor blockers:
dibenamine
ergot alkaloids (e.g. ergotamine)
phentolamine
tolazolanine
yohimbine

(sympathicolytic)

phenoxybenzamine

Beta receptor blockers:
dichlorisopropylnoradrenalin(e) (dichlorisoprenaline)
propanolol
pronethanol

Cholinergics:
acetylcholine (ACh)
methacholine (mecholyl)
carbachol
bethanechol
muscarine
pilocarpine
arecoline
tremorine

Anticholinergics:
atropine, scopalamine, homatropine, and numerous related substances

Inhibit acetylcholine at muscle end plates:
curare
D-tubocurarine
gallamine
toxiferine

Indirect effect:

phenylethylamine
tyramine
tryptamine
amphetamine, methamphetamine
metaraminol, mephentermine
cocaine

Inhibit enzymatic breakdown:
monoaminooxidase inhibitors
e.g. isoproniazid (antidepressive)
e.g. tranylcypromine
ephedrine
o-methyl-transferase-inhibitors
(e.g. pyrrogallol)

Inhibit enzymatic build-up:
alpha-methyldopa
alpha-methyltyrosine

Inhibit storage:
reserpine
guanethidine
bretylium

False transmitter formation:
alpha-methyldopa

Anticholinesterase, cholinesterase inhibitors:
neostigmine (Prostigmine)
edrophonium (Tensilon)
physostigmine (Eserine)
pyridostigmine
diisopropylfluorophosphate (DFP)
various nerve poisons (e.g. tabune)
parathione (E 605) and many pesticides

Promote enzymatic build-up:
dimethylaminoethanol
deanol

Promote enzymatic breakdown:
cholinesterase-related substances

The most important mechanisms are: (*a*) drugs work in principle in a manner similar to that of transmitter substances; (*b*) drugs intensify the effect of transmitter substances by inhibition of their enzymatic breakdown; (*c*) drugs weaken the action of transmitter substances (i) by blocking them in the post-ganglionic fibers or at the receptors, (ii) by inhibition of their enzymatic build-up, or (iii) by promoting their breakdown; (*d*) drugs intensify or weaken the action of transmitter substances by influencing their suitability for storage; (*e*) drugs replace the natural transmitters by 'false" transmitters; (*f*) blockade of acetylcholine action at the muscle end plates. The effects of ANS drugs differ considerably according to their effective mechanisms and modes of action (central or peripheral). They are used therapeutically, e.g., as: antidepressives (q.v.), antihypertonics (q.v.), hypertonics (q.v.), antihistamines (q.v.), circulation regulators, spasmolytics (q.v.), muscle relaxants (q.v.), stimulants (q.v.), or neuroleptics (q.v.). It is psychologically significant that the diverse ANS substances induce different autonomic patterns and combinations of autonomic and central-psychic variations, making it possible to use them as "tools" in emotion research (see *Psychopharmacology*), e.g. to block autonomic feedback in stress experiments. See *Emotions; Stress.*

Bibliography: Fawaz, G.: Cardiovascular pharmacology. Ann. Rev. Pharmacol., 1963, *3*, 57–90. **Koelle, G. B.:** Cholinesterases and anticholinesterase agents. Handbuch expt. Pharmakol., 15, Berlin, 1963. **Langemann, H.:** Pharmakologie des VNS. In: Akt. Fragen Psychiatr., 1966, *3*, 74–105. **Marley, E.:** The adrenergic system and sympathicomimetic amines. Advanc. Pharmacol., 1964, *3*, 167–266. **Volle, R. L.:** Pharmacology of the autonomic nervous system. Ann. Rev. Pharmacol., 1963, *3*, 129–52. **Zaimis, E.:** Pharmacology of the autonomic system. Ann. Rev. Pharmacol., 1964, *4*, 365–400. **Nickerson, M.:** The pharmacology of adrenergic blockade. Pharmacol. Rev., 1949, *1*, 27–101.

W. Janke

Psychophysical law. See *Weber-Fechner law.*

Psychophysics. Psychophysics concerns the manner in which living organisms respond to the energetic configurations of the environment. Stimulus energy in many forms affects the organisms through one or another of its specialized sensory receptors. Therefore many of the problems of psychophysics relate to the operation and behavior of sensory systems. A central problem is to determine the quantitative relation between stimulus input and response output—the so-called operating characteristic of the sensory system. Efforts to determine the functional relation between perceptual experience and the physical stimulus that produces it have given rise to a variety of psychophysical methods, many of which have found uses in other fields, ranging from the scaling of preferences to the measurement of the public consensus concerning the seriousness of various crimes.

1. *History.* In an early attempt at psychophysical scaling (about 150 B.C.), Hipparchus proposed that a useful measurement of stellar magnitude could be based on the apparent brightness of the stars. The brightest star was assigned to the first magnitude and the dimmest to the sixth. The distance between those limits was then partitioned in such a way that the apparent distances from one star magnitude to the next appeared equal. This scale of equal appearing intervals, based on six categories of apparent brightness, served astronomy for many centuries. When the development of photometry finally produced physical measurements of the light intensity, each of the steps on the visual scale of stellar magnitude turned out to be approximately four decibels, a value that represents a constant distance on a logarithmic scale. The logarithmic scale of stellar magnitude was hailed by Fechner as an important confirmation of the psychophysical law that bears his name. Only in recent decades has it become clear that the scale obtained by partitioning stellar magnitudes into categories is not an adequate test of Fechner's law.

In 1860 G. T. Fechner published his monumental *Elements of Psychophysics*. Although he argued that a direct measurement of sensation remains impossible, Fechner saw the possibility of an indirect approach. Instead of measuring sensation, he proposed to measure just noticeable differences, JND, which increase, as E. H. Weber had shown, in proportion to stimulus intensity. Fechner assumed that there is a fixed increment in sensation, corresponding to each JND in the stimulus. Hence, when the stimulus ϕ increased by constant ratios, the sensation ψ would increase by constant differences, and the result would be a logarithmic relation

$$\psi = k \log \phi$$

In the absence of any serious alternative, Fechner's logarithmic relation became the accepted psychophysical law. Alternatives had been suggested, however, for the relation between percept and stimulus has long engaged man's attention. In 1728, for example, the mathematician Gabriel Cramer conjectured that the perceived value of money, often called "utility", may grow as the square root of the number of, say, dollars. This early suggestion of a power function was followed in the 1850s by a similar conjecture when J. A. F. Plateau proposed that the apparent lightness of a surface grows as a power function of the reflectance. Plateau reasoned that, since the apparent relation among different shades of gray remains essentially the same when the level of the illumination changes, the *ratios*, not the *differences* (as Fechner argued), among the sensations produced by the shades of gray must remain constant. If the ratios remain fixed, then sensation must follow a power law. But Plateau eventually abandoned his conjecture when further experiments seemed not to bear him out.

A major procedural advance was made by J. Merkel when he undertook in 1888 to determine the stimulus that would appear to be double a given standard stimulus. That method was the forerunner of what is now called ratio production, and it was a method that could have settled the matter of the psychophysical law if it had been fully exploited. But Merkel's work had little effect on the course of psychophysics.

It was not until the 1930s that Merkel's procedures were re-invented and used with other procedures to determine a loudness scale. Many workers in acoustics had become aware that Fechner's logarithmic law was defective, because Fechner's law would predict that the decibel scale could serve as a loudness scale. In particular, Fechner's law predicts that 100 decibels should sound twice as loud as 50 decibels. Actually, 100 decibels sounds about twice as loud as 90 decibels.

2. *The power law*. Definitive evidence for the power law emerged in 1953 when S. S. Stevens employed the methods of equisection, ratio production, and magnitude estimation to demonstrate that the sensations of both loudness and brightness obey a power law. Following that demonstration, Stevens undertook to explore the other sense modalities and to devise additional experimental procedures with which to validate the power law. As a result of that undertaking, together with the work of many other laboratories, the psychophysical power law now stands as the most pervasive and perhaps the best-supported quantitative generalization in psychology. There appears to be no exception to the rule that on all prothetic continua the subjective magnitude ψ grows as the stimulus magnitude ϕ raised to a power. Hence the formula may be written

$$\psi = k\phi^{\alpha}$$

where α is the exponent. Conveniently, in double logarithmic coordinates, this equation becomes a line whose slope corresponds to the exponent.

Each sense modality tends to have its characteristic exponent, ranging from 0·33 for apparent brightness to 3·5 for the sensation produced by electric current through the fingers. The exact value of the exponent may depend on various parameters, such as the duration of the stimulus, the state of sensory adaptation, the presence of inhibiting stimuli (contrast), and so on. The exponent is also affected by the method of measurement, and an unbiased measure of the exponent can be approximated only with the aid of multiple experiments in counterbalanced designs. The apparent inclination. Prothetic continua include, but are not limited to, those continua on which discrimination is mediated by an additive process at the physiological level. Increasing loudness, for example, involves the addition of excitation to excitation. Increasing pitch, however, involves a metathetic process in which new excitation is substituted for old, thereby changing the locus of the excitation.

Measured exponents and their possible fractional values for power functions relating subjective magnitude to stimulus magnitude

Continuum	Measured Exponent	Possible Fraction	Stimulus Condition
Loudness	0·67	2/3	3000 Hertz tone
Brightness	0·33	1/3	5° target in dark
Brightness	0·5	1/2	very brief flash
Smell	0·6	2/3	heptane
Taste	1·3	3/2	sucrose
Taste	1·4	3/2	salt
Temperature	1·0	1	cold on arm
Temperature	1·5	3/2	warmth on arm
Vibration	0·95	1	60 Hertz on finger
Vibration	0·6	2/3	250 Hertz on finger
Duration	1·1	1	white noise stimuli
Finger span	1·3	3/2	thickness of blocks
Pressure on palm	1·1	1	static force on skin
Heaviness	1·45	3/2	lifted weights
Force of handgrip	1·7	5/3	hand dynamometer
Vocal effort	1·1	1	vocal sound pressure
Electric shock	3·5	3	current through fingers
Tactual roughness	1·5	3/2	feeling emery cloths
Tactual hardness	0·8	4/5	squeezing rubber
Visual length	1·0	1	projected line
Visual area	0·7	2/3	projected square

Table above gives representative values of the exponents thus far obtained for a variety of perceptual continua.

In addition to the measured values of the exponents, an attempt has been made in the Table to suggest the rational fraction that would correspond to the exponent under ideal conditions. Many of the measured values have been obtained by the method of magnitude estimation, which, because of a regression effect, tends to underestimate the exponent.

3. *Two kinds of continua.* Most continua, including those in the Table, belong to the class called prothetic. They concern the question *how much* (quantity) as opposed to *what kind* or *where* (quality). Only a few continua belong to the class called metathetic. Examples are pitch, apparent azimuth, and

The main difference between the two kinds of continua resides in the functional relations observed among the three principal kinds of scaling measures. On metathetic continua a linear relation may be obtained among all the measures. On prothetic continua the three types of measures are non-linearly related.

4. *Three kinds of measure.* Most of the measures that have been used for scaling perceptual continua fall into one or another of three classes.

(*a*) *Magnitude scales.* Ratio scales of apparent magnitude have been erected by several methods. The most direct method is the matching of values on a perceptual continuum to values on some standard or reference continuum, such as length or number. For example, ten observers adjusted the length of a line of light projected on a wall in order to make its length appear proportional to five different loudnesses presented in random order. The geometric means of the lengths produced were found to be related to the sound pressures of the stimuli by a power function with an exponent of 0·69, a value very close to the exponent for loudness listed in the table.

A more convenient procedure is to ask the observer to match numbers to a series of stimuli. He then assigns numbers proportional to the apparent magnitude of the stimuli presented by the experimenter. This matching procedure is called *magnitude estimation.* In a reverse procedure, called *magnitude production*, the experimenter assigns a set of numbers in irregular order and the observer adjusts the stimuli to produce what he judges to be a sensation proportional to each number. Because all matching procedures are characterized by a regression effect, or centering tendency, the exponent obtained by magnitude estimation is smaller than that obtained by magnitude production.

Magnitude scales may also be constructed by Merkel's method of ratio production, which he called the method of doubled stimulus. In fact, there are many variations on the procedures that can be used to determine apparent or subjective ratios. Fractionation is a name applied to some of them.

Cross-modality matching may be used to validate the scaling of various continua. Thus, if numbers have been matched to two continua, say, loudness and brightness, the two resulting power functions can be used to predict what observers will do when they match loudness to brightness directly. The exponent of the predicted matching function is given by the ratio of the two exponents obtained with number matching. The results of many such cross-modality comparisons show that the power functions meet the test of transitivity: the exponents of two such functions can be used to predict a third.

Cross-modality matching uses the procedures that have long been used within a single modality, for instance, for determining equal loudness contours, photometric matches, and heterochromatic equations.

(*b*) *Partition scales.* As noted above, stellar magnitudes and the lightness of grays were scaled by dividing a continuum into finite segments. On metathetic continua, observers can make such partitions without a systematic bias, but on prothetic continua the partition scale gives a smaller exponent than the magnitude scale; that is, relative to the magnitude scale, the partition scale is curved. The degree of non-linearity in the partition scale depends very much on the methods used. Under favorable conditions, the observer may bisect the distance between two fixed values with only a small net bias. But even there, the results depend on the order of presentation, with the result that a strong hysteresis effect is observed: the bisection point is set higher in ascending than in descending order.

In the most common form of the partition scale, the category rating scale, the observer assigns one of a finite set of numbers or adjectives to each stimulus, for example, the numbers 1 to 7, or the adjectives, small, medium, and large. The resulting category scale is usually highly curved relative to the magnitude scale, except, of course, on metathetic continua. Limiting the observer's response to a finite set of numbers forces him to partition the continuum. He is thereby prevented from making a proportional number assignment in a way that would preserve ratios. On prothetic continua, the restriction to a finite set of numbers or categories produces a dramatic curvature in the scale.

(*c*) *Confusion scales.* This class includes such scales as JND, discrimination, paired comparisons, and successive intervals. The common feature of these scales is that some measure of variability or confusion is taken as the unit. Fechner's JND, which became the unit of his scale, is essentially a measure of variability or "noise". If there were no noise or confusion in human judgments, the JND would become infinitely small. Similar to the JND scales are the scales that L. L. Thurstone built on the method of paired comparisons, which make use of the dispersions among the observer's judgments in order to derive a unit for the scale.

On metathetic continua, the confusion scale may be linearly related to the magnitude scale. For example, the JND for pitch is a constant size when measured in mels, the subjective unit of pitch. On prothetic continua, however, the confusion scale approximates a logarithmic function of the magnitude scale. In numerous experiments by G. Ekman, this logarithmic relation has been shown to hold not only for sensory scales, but for scales involving attitudes, preferences, esthetic judgments, and so on.

5. *Other problems.* Although scaling has always been the central problem of psychophysics, other topics have commanded interest. Among the important topics are the measurement of thresholds and the so-called neural quantum, the application of information theory to the channel capacity of sensory systems, the application of decision theory to the study of signal detectability, and the use of proximity analysis in the development of multidimensional scaling. These and other branches of psychophysics have become major subjects in their own right, and the methods of psychophysics have found important uses in many applied areas.

Bibliography: d'Amato, M. R.: Experimental psychology: methodology, psychophysics, and learning. New York, 1970. **Ekman, G. & Sjöberg, G.:** Scaling. Annual Rev. Psychol., 1965, *16*, 451–74. **Fechner, G. T.:** Elemente der Psychophysik, 1860 (Eng. trans. Elements of psychophysics. New York, 1966). **Stevens, S. S.:** On the brightness of lights and the loudness of sounds. Science, 1953, *118*, 576. **Stevens, S. S.:** On the psychophysical law. Psychol. Rev., 1957, *64*, 153–81. **Stevens, S. S.:** Psychophysics of sensory function. In: **Rosenblith, W. A.** (Ed.): Sensory communication. Cambridge, Mass., 1961, 1–33. **Stevens, S. S.:** Ratio scales of opinion. In: **Whitla, D. K.** (Ed.): Handbook of measurement and assessment in behavioral sciences. Reading, Mass., 1968, 171–99. **Stevens, S. S.:** Le quantitatif et la perception. Bull. de Psychol., 1968–69, *22*, 696–715.

S. S. Stevens

Psychophysiological methods. A combination of psychological and physiological methods the purpose of which is to be able to give a valid description of psychophysiological phenomena. Under conditions which can be described psychologically, e.g. anxiety, physiological processes (e.g. secretion of catecholamine) are measured, or under conditions which can be described physiologically, e.g. muscular work on the ergometer, psychological data (e.g. calculation of internal tension) are collected. Only by looking at it from these dual aspects is a complete picture of the states and responses of organisms and their constitutional relationships obtained (see *Psychophysiology*).

Whereas practically all psychological methods, including observations of behavior, tests and introspection, can be used for certain psychophysiological inquiries, there are in the case of physiological methods several limitations that apply especially to some of the methods which are reliable technically as measurements. Since psychophysiological investigations are usually carried out on people free as far as possible from disabilities and in as natural a situation as possible, painful or complicated methods, e.g. direct measurement of arterial blood flow and determination of blood volume per heart beat, measurement of blood-flow through the muscles, catheters and probes, are generally all unsuitable because they may give rise to considerable psychophysiological sideeffects.

Most biosignals can be recorded with a well-equipped polygraph (q.v.), others require additional devices.

A second category of variables consists of clinical and chemical laboratory methods: differential blood picture and drop in blood pressure, electrolyte and pH value of the body

Psychophysiological Methods

Biosignal	Abbreviation	Recording device	Most important parameters
Cortical potentials, spontaneous or evoked (electroencephalogram)	EEG, EVP	Electrodes	Frequency band (α, β, δ, ϑ), DC components, change of frequency, e.g. alpha-block, SW complex, other patterns
Cardiac potentials (electrocardiogram, cardiotachogram)	EKG (ECG)	Electrodes	Pulse rate, irregularity of pulse, and other parameters
Blood pressure, arterial		Indirect: microphone Direct: sphygmomanometer (pressure cuff)	Systolic and diastolic blood pressure; blood pressure amplitude
Pulse waves (pulse pressure), e.g. radial and femoral pulse (sphygmogram, oscillogram)		Sphygmograph, or photoelectric device	Pulse frequency, systolic and diastolic phases, pulse wave speed
Pulse volume (rating of blood flow) (finger plethysmogram, as volume-, rheo-, or photo-plethysmogram)		Sphygmograph, impedance meter or photoelectric device	Pulse volume change
Respiration, respiration-conditioned thoracic movements (pneumogram)		Thermistor, pneumograph, thoracic recorder	Respiratory frequency, duration of inspiration and expiration
Respiration speed (pneumotachogram)		Breathing (oxygen) mask and differential pressure variator	Respiration speed
Respiratory volume, metabolism (spirogram)	RQ	Breathing mask, spirometer and gas analysis apparatus	Breathing volume, minute volume of air, respiratory quotient (CO_2/O_2)
Blood gases	pO_2 pCO_2 pH	Special-purpose electrodes	gas partial-pressures, pH value (hydrogen-ion concentration)
Body temperature, Skin and body cavities		Resistance thermometer, thermoelement, thermistor	Absolute value and local temperature differences
Skin resistance, skin conductance, psychogalvanic reactions (galvanic skin response) (electrodermatogram)	SR, SC, GSR (PGR)	Electrodes	Skin conductance, GSR latency, amplitude and frequency
Skin potential, skin potential reactions	SP, SPR	Electrodes	Latency, amplitude and frequency of SPR
Body movements, tremor (actiogram, mechanogram, tremogram)		Movement and acceleration recording devices, tremograph	Frequency and amplitude
Muscle action potentials Electromyogram	EMG	Skin or needle electrodes Electromyograph	Frequency and amplitude, Amplitude frequency product, electromyointegral
Eyelid reflex		Electrodes or photoelectric recorder	Frequency
Eye movements (electrooculogram, electronystagmogram)	EOG, ENG	Electrodes	Amplitude, direction Frequency
Pupillary reflex (pupillogram)		Photographic techniques or photoelectric recording	Size of pupil
Gastro-intestinal motility (electrogastrogram)	EGG	Magnetic detectors, electrodes or radio probes	
Gastro-intestinal-pH-value		Radio probes	pH value (hydrogen-ion concentration as expression of acidity or alkalinity)

fluids: blood serum, urine, saliva; biochemical parameters such as creatinin, uric acid, albumen, lipids, blood sugar, cholinesterase and other enzymes. Particular attention must be given to work in determining enzymes and hormones which will become more important as further progress is made in chemical laboratory methods. Finally those methods of vegetative-endocrinal and neuromuscular diagnostics are still available which, in order to test some dynamic function, apply a stress to the body by sensory stimuli, change of position, muscular effort or some drug, and then attempt to determine individual control quality (vegetative (q.v.) lability or stability) from counter-regulation.

The physiological methods mentioned above differ very considerably from one another with respect to reliability and definition. There is still no methodical line of discussion in this field comparable to test theory (q.v.) and test construction in psychology. Of course, checking methods is made more difficult by several problems:

1. Marked functional fluctuation depending on the time of day, season, weather, nutrition, nicotine, so that the classical reliability concept of parallel or repeated measurements can scarcely be employed.

2. Major difficulties of standardization, since the investigations should be conducted in rooms shielded from electro-magnetic forces (so-called Faraday cage), and which are sound and fire-proof and air-conditioned; a watch must be kept for effects due to habituation and situation.

3. Relatively large errors of measurement due to methods concerning biochemical quantities, e.g. in determining hormones.

4. Absence of absolute comparability—at most it is intraindividual—of precisely those methods which are frequently used because they are sensitive to psychologically induced changes in condition: the recording of skin resistance and the finger plethysmogram.

5. Phasic time-lags due to varying latencies of the effector organs or to the time needed to collect urine.

6. Quite excessive number of polygraph recordings required to cover fully the wealth of information.

7. Possibility of response patterns specific to the individual and the stimulus.

8. Dependence of an interpretation on the initial values of the function in question and on the other system parameters, as a change in value represents the displacement of a multiple dynamic balance.

9. Necessity for a multivariate strategy and non-linear models if counter-regulating, compensatory processes are to be described at all appropriately.

In many psychophysiological investigations there is a somewhat superficial and uncritical analysis of biosignals, whose conditions, measurement and implications have to be regarded as most doubtful from a physiological standpoint. In addition there exists a manifest uncertainty whether certain characteristics are sufficient (just what can a change of skin resistance, q.v., tell us?) or whether individual physiological values can rank as more or less valid indicators of dimensions of latent states (arousal, activation, q.v., stress, q.v., etc.), or of lasting dimensions of characteristics (vegetative lability, q.v.; sympathicotony, q.v., etc.). The theoretical interpretations and the practical consequences (e.g. a validity check on such "indicators") have not yet become sufficiently clear. To suppose that there is one uniform activating dimension seems in any case out-of-date idea. The dimensional approach is also open to question, for physiological values represent functional patterns (synergisms) adapted to changing demands which arise because of more or less complex integration achievements on higher or lower planes of the central nervous system. The study of these integrative achievements, their coordination or dissociation, promises to give better results than the superficial inspection of pulse, and GSR.

A standard combination of physiological techniques is impossible. In each inquiry criteria such as repeatability, reasonableness, economy and physiological meaningfulness will call for a different selection: during inner tension and emotional excitation as well as during a multiplicity of tasks many writers are agreed that—largely independently of the quality of the emotions—a relatively distinct covariation of the following physiological values may be observed: pulse rate, breathing, systolic blood pressure (automatic recording difficult), skin resistance and peripheral blood flow (standardization problems), body movements (recording problems), frequency change in brain potential fluctuations (accurate EEG analysis difficult), corticosteroid and catecholamine secretion (rather less reliability, and in the case of urine values only as the mean value of the collecting period).

How many-sided psychophysiological methods are can only be sketched here: in addition to the above methods there are also those dependent on the type of constitution, inventories to list physical infirmities or the momentary state of physical activation, methods for conditioning (q.v.) autonomic and motor responses (e.g. eyelid movement) methods for determining sensory thresholds or orientation response (see *Orientation reflex*) and habituation, as well as many special procedures which have proved their worth in this field bordering on various disciplines. Psychophysiological methods also depend on technological progress: the construction of new measuring instruments, the development of biotelemetric systems for recording biosignals in everyday situations, the use of laboratory computers for the more rapid and exhaustive processing of biosignals and the automatic control of experiments.

The special problems of psychophysiological methods must not be underestimated, but a steadily increasing application of these combined methods can be expected; they

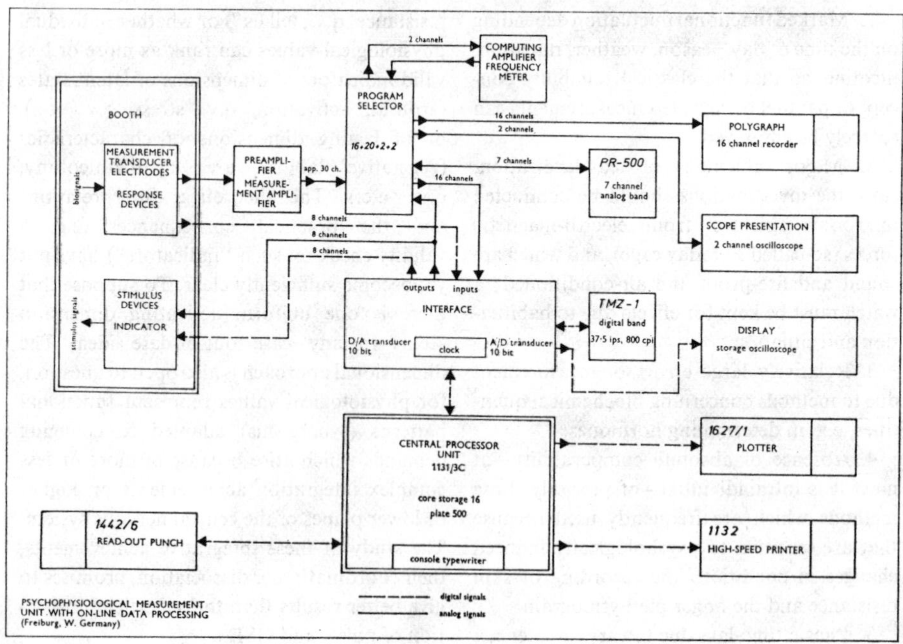

PSYCHOPHYSIOLOGICAL MEASUREMENT UNIT WITH ON-LINE DATA PROCESSING (Freiburg, W. Germany)

have great theoretical merit and can be used in many practical ways.

Bibliography: Brown, C. C. (Ed.): Methods in psychophysiology. Baltimore, 1967. **Fahrenberg, J.**: Psychophysiologische Persönlichkeitsforschung. Göttingen, 1967. **Mackay, R. S.**: Biomedical telemetry. New York, ²1970. **Tompson, P. N. & Yarbrongh, R. B.**: The shielding of electroencephalographic laboratories. Psychophysiology, 1967, *4*, 244–8. **Venables, P. H. & Martin, I.** (Eds.): Manual of psychophysiological methods. Amsterdam, 1967. *Journals:* Computer Programs in Biomedicine, Amsterdam. Das Ärztliche Laboratorium, Berlin. GIT Fachschrift für das Laboratorium, Darmstadt. EDV in Medizin und Biologie, Stuttgart. Elektromedizin, Berlin (from 1971: Biomedical Engineering). Psychophysiology, Baltimore.

J. Fahrenberg

Psychophysiology is concerned with psychophysical processes, i.e. those life processes which are susceptible to psychological, physiological and biological methods. In this field which borders on various traditional disciplines, theories are still at variance. Other areas have partly impinged upon the territory of the old concept of physiological psychology and relieved it of certain fields of research: the physiology of the brain and psychophysics, psychosomatics, the physiology of behavior, psycho-endocrinology, psychomorphology, the study of constitutional types, neuropsychology and psychophysiology in the narrower sense. Common to these already partly independent disciplines is the question of the physiological and biological bases of experience (state of health and consciousness) and of behavior. Differences exist in regard to the quantity and kind of permissible variables (central nervous, peripheral, vegetative-endocrine and motor functions, observation of behavior, psychological tests), in regard to selection and general applicability of experimental situations (from the anesthetized uterus in labor to telemetrical studies on a person in an everyday situation), and consideration of individual differences, and in regard to the question of whether types of behavior and experience can be explained physiologically. Extreme "physiologism": that is, the reduction of psychologically definable models to neurophysiological terms, is certainly seldom encountered today.

The distinguishing mark of psychophysiology is psychological-physiological double interpretation. This dualism in the method of definition emerges from the peculiar position (peculiar historically and in relation to the theory of perception) of the methods of both techniques, especially if the methods of experiential psychology and the style of interpretation proper to a commentator on the arts are accepted as psychological methods. However, the use of such means of definition which differ in their terms of reference conveys nothing in respect of the duality or identity of the observed life processes (bodily functions, behavior, q.v., experienced subjectivity). The different systems of classification are looked upon as complementary forms which are equally necessary to the description of the higher life processes.

A theory of the organism relating to the psychophysical individuality of a person is only possible by the mutual supplementation of psychological and physiological methods and if it is based on a synopsis of different areas of data.

Themes of *general psychophysiology* are—apart from the mind-body problem and the theory of the organism—general methodology and the bases of a psychophysiological double interpretation and systems analysis.

The chief functions of *specialized* psychophysiology are the definition and classification of psychophysical phenomena such as orientation reaction (q.v.), perception of pain, anxiety (q.v.), hunger, trauma (q.v.), exhaustion, nervousness. Many authors have sought to classify the extraordinary diversity of psychophysical phenomena within certain concepts: activation (q.v.), arousal, stress (q.v.), ergotropy-trophotropy, psychovegetative lability, and other concepts of dimension.

These notions are useful indeed, yet on the one hand they are still held in too general a sense to be employed without qualification, and on the other hand, from the psychological or physiological point of view, they are too one-sided in meaning. Multivariate analyses have hitherto hardly been tried; because of the special problems of psychological method they are additionally complicated. Therefore the formulated questions of psychophysiology are still often determined from single phenomena and from certain functions which seem specially interesting, for example, secretion of catecholamine, EEG (encephalography, q.v.), or even only from very special classification techniques, e.g. skin resistance to electrical impulses (PGR) (q.v.) and evoked potentials. On the other hand, a number of significant studies have been published which demonstrate the theoretical value and the practical possibilities of application. The present position of research is represented by many catch-words: emotion impact (q.v.), activation (q.v.), fatigue (q.v.), hormone research (q.v.), noise research (q.v.), psychosomatic medicine (q.v.), sleep and dream research (q.v.), stress research (q.v.). Specific physiological patterns of certain emotions could hitherto—contrary to the interpretation of many representatives of psychosomatic medicine—not be established with certainty, also the concept of a dimension of psycho-vegetative lability (nervousness, neuroticism, q.v.), as well as the question of a co-variation of central nervous (EEG) arousal and peripheral ergotropic inversion of function, are still debated. Clearly more progress must first be made in the simple definition of psychophysical correlates before, as the second step, more differentiated theoretical concepts can be developed: e.g. a clearer analysis of dimension, and before taxonomy can be undertaken.

Practical applications will follow chiefly in clinical psychophysiology in relation to psychosomatic medicine, then first on the basis of broadly-planned and fundamental longitudinal (q.v.) (time series) studies of psychophysical correlates the success of a certain therapy might be judged: psychoanalysis of psychosomatic disorders, classical and operant conditioning (q.v.) of vegetative and motor forms of behavior, influence through autogenic training (q.v.), hypnosis (q.v.), psychopharmacology, methods of physical medicine, investigation into subjective observation of disturbances in bodily function, and also studies in response correlation or self-control of biorhythm.

All in all, psychophysiology can be regarded as a basic discipline of psychosomatic medicine and of all biologically orientated personality research.

Bibliography: Ax, A. F.: Goals and methods of psychophysiology. Psychophysiology, 1964, *1*, 8–25. **Black, P.:** (Ed.): Physiological correlates of emotion. New York, 1970. **Cattell, R. B.:** A brief survey of present knowledge and hypotheses on psychophysiological state dimensions. In: **Cattell, R. B.** (Ed.): Handbook of multivariate experimental psychology. Chicago, 1966. **Delius, L. & Fahrenberg, J.:** Psychovegetative Syndrome. Stuttgart, 1966. **Eysenck, H. J.:** The biological basis of personality. Springfield, Ill., 1967. **Fahrenberg, J.:** Psychophysiologische Persönlichkeitsforschung. Göttingen, 1967. **Hess, W. R.:** Psychologie in biologischen Sicht. Stuttgart, [2]1968. **Jung, R.:** Neurophysiologie und Psychiatrie. In: **H. W. Gruhle** *et al.* (Eds.): Psychiatrie der Gegenwart, Vol. 1, Pt. 1 A. Berlin, 1967. **Levi, L.** (Ed.): Emotional stress. Basle, 1967. **Martin, I.:** Somatic reactivity. In: **Eysenck, A. J.** (Ed.): Handbook of abnormal psychology. London, [2]1971; **Rothschuh, K. E.:** Theorie des Organismus. München, [2]1963. **Royce, J. R.:** Concepts generated in comparative and physiological observations. In: **Cattell, R. B.** (Ed.): Handbook of multivariate experimental psychology. Chicago, 1966. **Schönpflug, W.** (Ed.): Methoden der Aktivierungsforschung. Berne, 1969. **Sternbach, R. A.:** Principles of psychophysiology. New York, 1966.

J. Fahrenberg

Psychoprophylaxis. Prevention of mental disturbances (psychohygiene, q.v.) by appropriate measures; it always corresponds to a particular theory of *neurosis* (q.v.) and is an important aim of educational counselling (q.v.). *W.Sch.*

Psychoreflexology. Also known as *objective psychology*. Developed by W. Bekhterev and J. P. Pavlov. According to this theory, all mental disorders are to be explained as neuropsychological; they all originate in physical causes and are to be classified as such. Fundamental concept of the method: the object of scientific psychology can be observed, classified and measured only in its physical aspects. *H.W.*

Psychoses, functional. *Psychopathology* may be described as the branch of psychological science concerned with the systematic investigation of deviant behavior. It involves the application of the principles of learning, perception, motivation and physiological psychology in order to understand the abnormal. Some of the usual criteria of deviancy are personal distress, disabling behavioral tendencies and disturbances of motor behavior, mood and thinking. The disturbances that reflect greater deviancy, severity and disorganization of the personality are called *psychoses*. When the individual fails to take care of himself or seems likely to injure himself or others, society puts him in hospital or locks him up. Hence the fact of institutionalization also constitutes a definition of the psychotic condition.

Classification of the psychotic disorders is based primarily on the symptom syndromes exhibited, and secondarily on life history data such as type of onset, duration, age, sex and number of recurrences. Attempts at classification based on the concept of physical disease have so far proved unsatisfactory because no organism has been implicated, no lesions have been demonstrated, and no consistent central nervous system changes have been identified. Although there are several biochemical theories regarding causal agents, and there is some evidence of genetic determinants, on the whole there is no systematic basis for regarding the psychoses as physical diseases. The 18th International Classification of Diseases (ICD-8) recognizes the present status of the psychoses as disorders without any known organic etiology.

1. *The elementary syndromes.* The standard psychiatric nomenclature is widely regarded as comparatively unsatisfactory for decision making or as a schema for research. One important defect is poor agreement among classifiers through non-objective criteria for category membership. A related defect is the absence of decision rules for combining multiple indicators in a diagnostic decision. In addition, there are questions whether some of the categories overlap too much, some are too broad, and others are invalid. Finally there is the complaint that most of the diagnostic classes are of little or no value for prognosis or for treatment selection.

The defects in nomenclature have produced a wide variety of strategies for solving them. Investigators have sought to objectify the vague terms by use of rating scales, and to make the diagnostic procedure uniform by structured interviews. Another approach has been to establish existing categories more firmly by providing more objective definitions of terms and by establishing consensual validation for the accepted psychiatric classes. Finally, some investigators have sought to establish a descriptive system on the basis of currently discernible symptoms, by using modern multivariate statistical procedure; this consists of interviewing patients before treatment and rating them immediately afterwards on observable behaviors defined in a standardized rating schedule. The relations among the behaviors and symptoms are rated and then analyzed to isolate all independent syndromes (symptom clusters) to be found.

Twelve psychotic syndromes have been identified in numerous independent studies of hospitalized U.S. patients (Lorr, Klett & McNair, 1963). The equivalence of the syndromes observed in U.S. samples to those found in patients observed in six countries

(England, France, Germany, Italy, Japan and Sweden) have recently been established (Lorr & Klett, 1969). The same symptom groupings may be found in women as well as in men.

Brief descriptions of each of the twelve psychotic syndromes or dimensions are given below. Each variable is regarded as present in all patients to some degree. A low score on a syndrome implies a mild, and a high score a severe, disturbance. For additional details and for description of the scales the reader is referred to Lorr & Klett (1966).

(*a*) *Excitement*. Speech is hurried, loud and difficult to stop. The level of mood and self-esteem is elevated. Emotional expression tends to be unrestrained and histrionic. (*b*) *Hostile belligerence*. Expressions of complaints, hostility and resentment concerning others are common. Difficulties and failures are blamed on others. (*c*) *Paranoid projection*. There is evidence of unwarranted fixed beliefs that attribute a hostile, persecutory or controlling intent to persons around the patient. (*d*) *Grandiosity*. An attitude of superiority is associated with unwarranted beliefs of possessing unusual powers. Divine missions may also be reported. (*e*) *Perceptual distortions*. There are reports of false perceptions in the form of voices that threaten, accuse or demand. (*f*) *Obsessional-phobic*. Uncontrollable acts and rituals, recurrent unwanted thoughts, specific fears, and ideas of personal change and unreality are reported. (*g*) *Anxious-depression*. Vague anxiety as well as specific concerns are reported. The mood is dysphoric and the attitudes towards the self are derogatory. In addition, feelings of guilt and remorse for real and imagined faults are evident. (*h*) *Functional impairment*. There are complaints of inability to concentrate, work or to make decisions. Interest in people, sex and social activity is much reduced or lacking. (*i*) *Retardation*. Speech, ideation and motor activity are slowed or blocked. There are also apathy and disinterest in the future. (*j*) *Disorientation*. There is a functional disorientation with respect to time, place and season. There may be failure to recognize persons the patient should know well. (*k*) *Motor disturbances*. Bizarre postures are assumed and maintained. Peculiar and manneristic facial and body movements are manifested repeatedly. (*l*) *Conceptual disorganization*. Speech is rambling, incoherent, or unrelated to the question asked. The same words or phrases are repeated in a stereotyped fashion. New words (neologisms) may be invented and incorporated in speech.

An important characteristic of this descriptive system is that all patients are uniformly assessed for all behaviors and symptoms. Conventional procedures are unsystematic in that each case is examined with respect to a slightly different set of symptoms. Furthermore, since life-history events are excluded from definition of the syndromes there is no confounding of data sources as in conventional diagnoses. This means that it is possible to evaluate the independent contribution of each towards the prediction of some specified outcome. The procedure also provides the psychiatrist with a distinctive profile or configuration of scores on the twelve syndromes.

2. *The major syndromes*. The elementary syndromes are by no means completely independent of one another. They combine in meaningful ways into more inclusive dimensions. For example, anxious depression is often associated with functional impairment and retardation. Recent efforts (Lorr *et al.*, 1967; Overall *et al.*, 1967) to define the major psychotic disorders or syndromes in terms of disturbances of thinking mood and behavior have converged. When the correlations among the scores defining the elementary syndromes are analyzed by multivariate statistical procedures, five more inclusive behavioral dimensions emerge. The same patterns have been isolated in U.S. data, and in ratings obtained in cross-national studies. Sex differences are negligible with respect to the nature of these

disorders, although men and women may differ in severity (Lorr & Klett, 1968).

Each of the major syndromes will be characterized in terms of the elementary symptom clusters. Of course, in practice, the elementary syndrome scores defining each disorder are weighted and then summed to yield a measure of severity.

(*a*) *Schizophrenic disorganization*. This disorder is characterized by psychomotor retardation and apathy, functional disorientation and motor disturbances. Conceptual disorganization is also present but to a lesser degree. (*b*) *Paranoid process*. Characterized by the joint presence of paranoid projection, perceptual distortion (hallucinations), grandiosity and obsessive thinking. (*c*) *Hostile paranoia*. Somewhat narrower than the previous two described. It is defined by hostile belligerence and paranoid projection. (*d*) *Psychotic depression*. Characterized by anxious depression, functional impairment and by obsessional and phobic symptoms. (*e*) *Disorganized hyperactivity*. Primarily characterized by excitement, conceptual disorganization and motor disturbances. Grandiosity may also be evident but not uniformly.

3. *Conventional diagnostic classes*. The major psychoses not attributed to physical conditions, as listed in ICD-8, include Schizophrenia, the Affective disorders, the Paranoid states and a miscellaneous category. These groupings are typically defined by a combination of current symptoms and life-history events. Included are such differentia as type of onset, premorbid personality, duration of the disturbance, age, and number of episodes. Each major disorder and the subtypes subsumed under it will be described briefly and then compared with the syndromes delineated earlier.

Schizophrenia is characterized as a thought disorder. Disturbances in thinking are reflected in delusions and hallucinations. The mood is ambivalent, constricted or marked by apathy. Behavior is withdrawn and sometimes bizarre. Typically, there is a loss of empathy with others. The withdrawn subtypes are called simple, hebephrenic, catatonic (withdrawn) and schizo-affective (depressed). The excited subtypes are called acute, catatonic (excited) and schizo-affective (excited). The paranoid subtype is recognized as being differentiable into the hostile, the grandiose and the hallucinatory.

The simple subtype is recognizable symptomatically only by the lack of interests or attachments, and by apathy and indifference. The hebephrenic is characterized by disorganized thinking, inappropriate affect and manneristic movements. The catatonic exhibits stupor, mutism, negativism, and occasionally a resistance to movement called "waxy flexibility". The symptoms of these withdrawn and apathetic subtypes appear to correspond to what was identified earlier as schizophrenic disorganization.

The paranoid subtypes are characterized primarily by delusions of persecution and grandiosity associated with hallucinations, and occasionally by excessive religiosity. The syndrome previously described as Paranoid Process appears to include the symptom pattern included here under the paranoid subtype. The paranoid schizophrenics are commonly differentiated from the non-paranoid because this separation is useful for prognosis, for treatment, and for sound theoretical reasons. The paranoid subtypes and the withdrawn subtypes correspond well to this separation. However, the allocation of the excited subtypes is presently in doubt although it is possible to regard these as transient states.

The *Affective psychoses* represent the second major grouping of disorders. This group is characterized by deviation in mood, in the form of elation or depression, unrelated apparently to any precipitating life event. Included here are involutional melancholia and manic-depressive illness, depressed type. Both are described as exhibiting depressed mood with retardation or agitation, and thus may be differentiated only on the basis of age or the presence or absence of previous episodes. The manic subtype is characterized by excessive motor activity. There is also a circular or bipolar subtype which involves both a depressive episode and a manic episode. The major syndrome (identified statistically) corresponding to the excited subtype is disorganized hyperactivity. This syndrome, however, is also defined by motor disturbances and thus represents both the excited catatonic and the so-called manic-depressive, manic subtype. On the depressive side the subtype symptomatology is seen in psychotic depression.

The third major grouping of psychotic disorders is called *paranoid states*; these include paranoia and Involutional paranoid state. These are disorders in which a persecutory or grandiose delusion is primary. Disturbances in mood, behavior, perception and thinking are said to derive from these delusions. The diagnostic manual acknowledges that many authorities question whether the paranoid states are truly distinct or merely variants of schizophrenia or paranoid personality. It does seem that the evidence for this set of disorders is quite shaky.

In summary, it can be said that there is a rough correspondence between the major syndromes of psychotic behavior (statistically determined) and the major psychotic disorders (clinically established). Yet it is important that the elementary and major syndromes constitute a dimensional rather than a typological conception of the psychotic disorders. The psychiatric subtypes are presumably homogeneous subgroups of individuals, characterized by a common set of symptoms and behaviors. Classification of a fresh case in a diagnostic subtype is done on an all-or-none basis; that is, the individual either belongs or does not belong to the category. The process is similar to diagnosing a disease such as pneumonia; either one has or does not have pneumonia. In contradistinction, the dimensional approach is quantitative in character. Every person receives a score on each syndrome, and thus has a "profile" or set of scores.

4. *Emerging models.* The modern model of the behavior disorders is both dimensional and typological. Most of the symptoms and behaviors defining the psychoses are not qualitative and discrete but quantitative and continuous in character. Therefore a behavior disorder and those changes resulting in it from natural causes or treatment should be assessed by quantitative and continuous variables. The dimensional approach offers an objectively defined minimal set of non-overlapping descriptors (syndromes) to represent the domain of deviant behavior. It also provides a more useful and objective basis for evaluating changes in a disorder.

In the typological approach individuals are described on all the syndromes of behavior deviation. They are then grouped together into mutually exclusive subgroups on the basis of similarity of syndrome score profile. Each subgroup is thus objectively defined in terms of possession of a common score profile. There have been investigations concerned with the development of such psychotic typologies, but none has as yet been tested sufficiently to warrant description here. It should be noted that members of two diagnostic classes may differ in their life history antecedents and yet be quite similar symptomatically. For example, involutional melancholia and the depressive subtype of manic-depressive psychosis appear to have similar syndrome score patterns even though they differ with respect to age and number of previous episodes of disturbance.

Bibliography: Lorr, M. & Klett, C. J.: Cross-cultural comparison of psychotic syndromes. J. Abnorm. Psychol., 1969, *74*, 531–43. **Id.:** Major psychotic disorders. Arch. Gen. Psychiat., 1968, *19*, 652–8. **Id.:** Inpatient multidimensional psychiatric scale. Manual. Palo Alto, Calif., 1966. **Id.:** Higher level psychotic syndromes. J. Abnorm. Psychol., 1967, *72*, 74–7. **Lorr, M., Klett, C. J. & McNair, D. M.:** Syndromes of psychosis. Oxford, 1963. **Overall, J. E., Hollister, L. E. & Pichot, P.:** Major psychiatric disorders. Arch. Gen. Psychiat., 1967, *16*, 146–51. *M. Lorr*

Psychosis of association. If a person who has hitherto been of sound mind becomes deranged under the influence of a deranged person with whom he is closely associated (*paranoid schizophrenia*), and if he himself experiences the same hallucinations and changes in mood as the first subject, the latter (inducent) is said to have "induced" the second subject (induced person). A study of psychoses has shown that only psychoses of delusion are transmitted in this way (Scharfetter, 1970). Because of their hereditary disposition, the induced persons are liable to the psychoreactive development of schizophrenic psychoses under differing psychodynamic conditions. See *Paranoia; Schizophrenia.* *C.S.*

Psychosomatics. 1. *Definition.* The term psychosomatics is used with different meanings. The commonest and narrowest use is to signify a limited number of diseases which have certain characteristics. Less commonly it means a holistic philosophy of medicine, which regards disease as a relation between the individual and his environment, both considered as integrations of the psychological and material aspects. Its practical application is seen in the approach of the physician to the treatment and management of the patient, whatever the disorder. An outcome of this, and perhaps a third meaning, underlines the recent researches which regard disease as an ecological problem. Different schools of psychology agree with the general definition, i.e. the range of the subject, although they concentrate on different aspects, e.g. psychoanalysis is concerned with unconscious dynamics, and learning theory studies the conditioning of the autonomic nervous system.

2. *Psychosomatic disorders.* The characteristics of these disorders are:

(*a*) They show disturbances of function together with damage in the organs of the body. In this they differ from mental disorders. (*b*) Emotional disturbances play an essential part in them, in precipitating the onset, recurrence or exacerbation of symptoms. This distinguishes them from purely "organic" disorders. (*c*) They are chronic disorders with a phasic course. (*d*) They tend to be associated with other psychosomatic disorders. This may occur in the family or at different periods of life in one patient. (*e*) They show a great difference in the incidence between the sexes. Thus, asthma is twice as common in boys as in girls, before puberty; after, it is less common in men than in women. Duodenal ulcer is much more common in men and thyrotoxicosis is commoner in women.

There is no universal agreement as to which conditions should be included as being psychosomatic, but the following brief list (in systems) is generally accepted.

Respiratory: asthma, vasomotor rhinitis. *Gastro-intestinal:* peptic ulcer, colonic disorders. *Cardio-vascular:* hypertension, coronary disease, migraine. *Skin:* urticaria, rosacea, neurodermatitis (atopic eczema). *Endocrine:* thyrotoxicosis, diabetes mellitus, menstrual disturbances. *Other:* rheumatoid arthritis. There is much debate whether pulmonary tuberculosis and ulcerative colitis should be included. There is some evidence that emotional factors play a part in the onset and course of the former (Kissen, 1958), but it is doubtful if this is true of the latter.

3. *Physiology of the emotions.* It is an empirical fact that emotional disturbances are associated with the onset of psychosomatic disorders and exacerbations of their symptoms; there is also good evidence that such disturbances play a part in the etiology. The philosophical problem of how mental changes can produce damage to bodily organs can be evaded by taking into account the fact that emotional changes are always accompanied by bodily changes. The emotional reactions

and bodily changes can be therefore regarded as different aspects of the reaction of the individual to stresses; it remains only to consider how the bodily changes can give rise to lesions in the organs.

The function of the internal organs is controlled by the autonomic nervous system (ANS). Most of the organs have a double supply, consisting of adrenergic and cholinergic fibers with opposing actions. Under normal conditions the two act together; thus, when the heart accelerates it can be shown that there is an increased activity in its sympathetic (adrenergic) supply and a decreased activity of its parasympathetic (cholinergic) supply.

Some of the simpler reflexes which affect the activity of the internal organs are mediated by those parts of the ANS which lie outside the central nervous system (CNS), e.g. peristalsis of the intestine. Most of the others involve the spinal cord. The low level reflexes are integrated in hierarchical systems at higher levels of the CNS, in order to maintain internal conditions at an optimum level. With exposure to stress, e.g. extremes of temperature, asphyxia, pain, or situations of danger, a wide discharge of impulses occurs through the whole of the ANS, and the changes produced can be seen to be those associated with fear or rage. The Cannon-Bard theory of the emotions regards such changes as an adjustment of the individual to an emergency. The center which organizes this discharge is the hypothalamus, and it is linked through the amygdaloid nucleus, hippocampus and anterior nucleus of the thalamus to the cingulate gyrus of the cerebral cortex. These higher nuclei form the "limbic system" which links the organization of emotional responses to the activities of the rest of the CNS.

The discharge through the ANS is accompanied by activity in a parallel system: the endocrine glands. Stimulation of the autonomic supply to the medulla of the adrenal gland produces a release of adrenalin and noradrenalin into the circulation and these hormones produce in each organ the same effect as direct stimulation of the autonomic nervous supply. In addition, the hypothalamus controls the activity of the pituitary gland, which releases hormones which stimulate other endocrine glands, especially, from the present viewpoint, the adrenal cortex and the thyroid. The former plays an essential part in the reaction of tissues to damage and the latter increases metabolism and potentiates the effect of adrenalin.

The response to stress can be divided into three stages:

(*a*) An immediate response (taking about a second) via the ANS, (*b*) A delayed response (of the order of a minute) via the secretions of the adrenal medulla. (*c*) A long-term reaction to chronic stress via the adrenal cortex and thyroid.

These emergency reactions can be directly related to the manifestations of the psychosomatic disorders. Stimulation of the parasympathetic supply to the bronchioles causes contraction of the muscle fibers and narrowing of the lumen of the bronchioles, and this is the first stage of an attack of asthma. Stimulation of the autonomic supply to the stomach leads to engorgement of the gastric mucous membrane, which becomes friable and easily injured. Such injuries do not heal unless the membrane returns to normal. Wolff & Wolf (1947) demonstrated in the human subject that these phenomena occurred in states of anxiety and anger. One of the hormones of the adrenal cortex, cortisone, is now used therapeutically, and two well-known complications of its use are the development of peptic ulcer and the flare-up of pulmonary tuberculosis.

4. *Specificity*. Not all individuals develop psychosomatic disturbances in response to (psychological) stress and, furthermore, they suffer from different disorders. Much research and theorizing has been devoted to the problems of "specificity" and, considering only the psychological aspects, this may be viewed in

terms of the predisposing personality, the nature of precipitating stress and specific aspects of the intermediate mechanisms.

Many of the earlier researches were based on the theory that certain types of personality were particularly liable to develop specific psychosomatic disorders. Various "personality profiles" were described, but it became clear in time that the resemblances between the profiles were much greater than the differences. Most of these types of personality were variations of the "obsessional" or "anancastic" personality. Since most of the original work lacked adequate controls, or even any at all, and since the obsessional personality is a common normal type, it is not surprising that subsequent work largely discounted the earlier findings. In some cases it would appear that the personality of the patient is better regarded as the result of the illness rather than the cause, for example, in ulcerative colitis. Despite much criticism, some of the research findings have been confirmed, but they are not specific, for example, sufferers from duodenal ulcer tend to be of an anxious disposition. Much the same may be said of the studies on the nature of the psychological stresses which precipitate illness.

Much research has been devoted to the mechanism by which emotional disturbances can effect the activity of an organ. In summary, there are very few functions which are not under the control of the CNS, either through the ANS or the hypothalamus-pituitary endocrine system. Earlier researches demonstrated easily that the response to stress showed a different pattern between individuals. It was also shown that different stresses, evoking fear or resentment, had different patterns of response. Attempts were made to show that the pattern was fixed for each individual, but even if this is true, it is not important. The autonomic response is not only related to ongoing activity but also to the (voluntary) patterns of behavior evoked. The ANS is easily conditioned, and therefore its response will depend also on the history of the individual. Not only is this true of classical conditioning (q.v.), but also of operant conditioning and the latter implies that modification of the ANS plays a part, not only in the development of psychosomatic disorders, but in their recurrence and recovery.

Psychological mechanisms have been studied from the psychoanalytical point of view. The unconscious mechanisms described do not differ essentially from those which underlie the neuroses and personality disorders; this is to be expected, since the response of an individual to stress is based on the totality of his life-experiences. Psychotherapy must be based on his individuality. As controlled trials of psychotherapy are extremely difficult to carry out, the evidence that such treatment plays a significant role in the recovery of the patient is still tenuous.

5. *Recent developments*. The most important aspect of new work is the increasing rigor of research techniques: for instance, comparison with appropriate control groups and the use of psychometric methods for assessment of personality. Scales have even been devised to measure life-stresses. New techniques for continuous recording of physiological changes, including multiple recording and telemetering, have given much more detailed information about the response to stress. Intensive research on operant conditioning of autonomic function has not only illuminated problems of mechanism, but has opened up important possibilities for treatment (Miller, 1969).

Epidemiological studies have investigated the role of genetic and environmental factors and have attempted to identify vulnerable groups. Whole populations have been studied intensively (Essen-Moller, 1956) and followed up for a considerable period (Hagnell, 1966). A special development is based on an ecological approach. An early paper is that of Hinckle & Wolff (1958). They demonstrated the existence of a group of disease-susceptible individuals. With an increasing number of illnesses, type, variety (including mental illnesses), and severity increase. Although each individual has a fairly steady rate of illness, there are episodes of increased rate which occur when the individual feels he is threatened, when life is unsatisfying and full of conflict, and no satisfactory solution is possible. This work has been extended by Holmes Rahe (1967), who quantified life change by means of a schedule of recent experiences. They were able to show that a significant increase of life changes preceded a clustering of severe illnesses. It also succeeded a cluster (Rahe & Arthur, 1965). This work has given specific content to the holistic notion that disease is a reaction to environmental changes, and that the difference between somatic and mental disease is less than current tradition maintains. The study of psychosomatic disorders is entering a new and interesting period.

Bibliography: Essen-Moller, E.: Individual traits and morbidity in Swedish rural population. Acta Psychiat. et neurol. Scand., 1956, Suppl., 100. **Hagnell, O.:** A prospective study of the incidence of mental disorders. Stockholm, 1966. **Hamilton, M.:** Psychosomatics. London, 1955. **Hinckle, L. E. & Wolff, H. G.:** Ecologic investigations of the relationship between illness, life experiences and the social environment. Ann. intern. Med., 1958, *49*, 1373–88. **Holmes, T. H. & Rahe, R. H.:** The social readjustment rating scale. J. psychosom. Res., 1967, *11*, 213–8. **Kissen, D. M.:** Emotional factors in pulmonary tuberculosis. London, 1958. **Leigh, D. & Marley, E. M.:** Bronchial asthma Oxford, 1967. **Miller, N. E.:** Learning of visceral and glandular responses. Science, 1969, *163*, 434–45. **Rahe, R. H. & Arthur, R. J.:** Life-change patterns surrounding illness experience. J. psychosom. Res., 1968, *11*, 341–5. **Wolff, H. G. & Wolf, S.:** An experimental study of changes in gastric function in response to varying life experiences. Rev. Gastroenteral., 1947, *14*, 419–34. **Wretmark, G.:** Peptic ulcer individual: study in heredity, physique, and personality. Acta psychiat. et neurol. Scand., 1953, Suppl., 84.

M. Hamilton

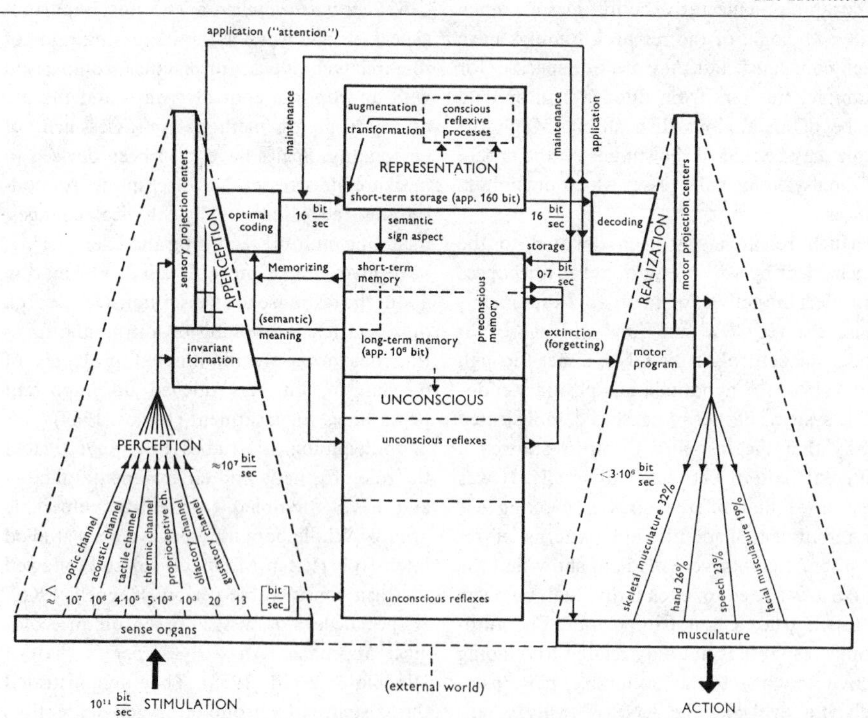

An organogram for human information processing

Psychosomimetics. See *Psychotomimetic drugs.*

Psychostructural model. Every physical model of a mental phenomenon realized through a means of communication, and every model that can be programmed mathematically for a computer is a "psychostructural" model. The starting-point of the psychostructural model within cybernetic education is the "organogram" of information psychology (q.v.). From this, in itself very rough, concept of a model, different more or less far-reaching simplifications were simulated on a computer and applied as the basis for the production of instructional algorithms (Frank, 1966). The most complex psychostructural model at present in existence underlies the formal didactics of Cogendi (q.v.). Here optimal coding was simulated through a deterministic automaton representing informational accommodation; short-term storage was simulated through a probabilistic coordinator, and short-term memory through a probabilistic automaton. (See diagram on previous page.)

Bibliography: **Frank, H.:** Ansätze zum algorithmischen Lehralgorithmieren. Lehrmaschinen, 1966, *4*, 70–112. **Riedel, H.:** Psychostruktur. Quickborn, 1967. *H.F.*

Psychosyndrome, endocrine (M. Bleuler). Mental disturbances occurring in different endocrine (internal secretion) malfunctioning show the same range of symptoms (and are similar to the so-called local psychosyndrome of the brain). They are recognized by disturbances in the *control of impulses* (excitatory-inhibitory), of *affect* (anxious, manic, depressive, irritable, liable to outbursts of temper), of *individual urges* (increase or inhibition of the need to move, of hunger, thirst and sexuality). Intellectual functions, however, are not impaired. *C.S.*

Psychosyndrome, organic (E. Bleuler). *Amnesic syndrome* (q.v.); *Korsakov's syndrome* (q.v.).

Psychosynthesis. Form of psychotherapy (q.v.) regarded as the complement of a psychoanalysis (q.v.). It aims above all at the reconstruction of the personality after defense mechanisms and resistances have been corrected by analytical methods. Regarded as superfluous by S. Freud, who asserted that psychosynthesis took place automatically as soon as neurotic conflicts were resolved, but emphasized by C. G. Jung and authors of similar views (A. Maeder, P. Tournier, H. Trueb). The causes of psychiatric illness are not greatly clarified when seen from the aspect of development possibilities and the self-discovery of the patient. Appellative methods supplement the therapy. (See *Psychagogy.*) *W.Sch.*

Psychotechnics. A theory introduced to psychology in 1903 by Stern for the classification of the terms of reference of applied psychology (q.v.) necessary to psychological judgment (psychognostics), i.e. for the provision of aids in psychological treatment (psychotechnics). For Münsterberg (1912), who attempted to define the field of psychotechnics, it is "the science of the practical application of psychology in the service of cultural problems. It should be a kind of psychological technique which helps people to achieve all the cultural aims they aspire to (for example in the industrial, social, educational, scientific, medical and legal fields) by the control of the mental mechanism." As in the course of time the application of the psychotechnics theory and related psychology gained acceptance, O. Lipmann condemned them (without lasting success) using the concept of *technopsychology* (also known as *psychotechnology*). The latter was intended to make the pure application of psychological perceptions more intelligible in practice. Giese in 1925 distinguished between *subject psychotechnics*, i.e. "adaptation of environment to the character of the human mental life" (e.g. arrangement of place of work, shape of tools, organization of work, etc.). The theory of psychotechnics has today lost its significance and therefore also its problems. It is now often equated with applied psychology or used as a special expression for practical industrial and vocational psychology (q.v.). *A. Thomas*

Psychotherapy, literally "treatment of the mind", refers to any of a variety of psychological means used to modify mental, emotional, and behavior disorders. This may occur in individual interviews where therapist and patient verbally explore the patient's conflicts, feelings, memories and fantasies in order to attain insight into the causes of the presenting problems, or it may be conducted in small groups of six to twelve patients, or, in the case of children, may take the form of play between child and therapist during which the child expresses feelings and learns new behavior patterns through his relationship with the therapist.

Psychotherapy is distinguished from medical techniques such as chemotherapy (q.v.) or electroconvulsive therapy (q.v.), which are often employed in treating mental disorders, particularly in the more severe forms found among patients in mental hospitals.

1. *History*. Psychological methods of influence have been employed in primitive forms for thousands of years to remedy psychological disorders. These methods include witchcraft, religious healing, and diverse forms of punishment. In the late nineteenth century scientific systems of intervention were devised, based in part upon the pioneering efforts of psychiatrists such as Philippe Pinel in France, who argued that insanity resulted from social and psychological stresses. Early systems focused upon the importance of a therapeutic social influence created by the physician, and upon various forms of persuasion and suggestion, including hypnosis, which was applied as a therapeutic technique by eminent physicians such as Jean Charcot in France and Josef Breuer in Austria.

This nineteenth-century work culminated in the development between 1895 and 1939 of *psychoanalysis* (q.v.) by Sigmund Freud, who had worked with both Charcot and Breuer. Freud, however, gave up hypnosis and turned to the key techniques of *free association* (q.v.) by the patient, *interpretation* by the therapist, and formation of a *transference relationship* between patient and therapist. Psychoanalysis may be considered to be the first and most elaborate *system* of psychotherapy. Freud's method gradually gave way to numerous variants of his technique espoused by his pupils, such as Carl Jung, Otto Rank, and Alfred Adler. Other approaches, such as those devised by Karen Horney, Harry Stack Sullivan, Franz Alexander, and so on, were greatly influenced by his writings. Even those who depart considerably from Freud's assumptions regarding the *unconscious* (q.v.), *psychic structure*, free association, and so on, such as Carl Rogers, Albert Ellis, and Viktor Frankl, still employ as their chief mode of intervention the verbal self-exploration interview format which Freud invented.

2. *Current therapies*. Several dozen systems of therapy are now in vogue in addition to those which derive more directly from the Freudian traditions. These range widely from *existential therapy* (q.v.), which focuses upon philosophical and religious issues such as values, meaning, and purpose in life, to *behavior therapies* which utilize conditioning techniques, and are far more specific and mechanistic in style (see *Behaviorism*). In addition, a wide variety of group methods has emerged which range from the verbal self-exploratory psychoanalytic type to more active *encounter groups* in which confrontation, touching and other actions are common, and in which the goals include intensive experiencing of strong feelings as opposed to insights *per se*.

Therapists affiliated with differing positions divide on a number of important issues. Some are interested in making unconscious experience conscious, and in probing the early history of the patient's life, whereas others are more concerned with modifying conscious attitudes or overt behaviors in the present. Some, such as *client-centered therapists* (q.v.), believe that if the therapist provides a warm and understanding relationship for the patient this will suffice to stimulate positive personality change. Many others agree that such a relationship is necessary but that it is not sufficient for change; technical interventions such as interpretation and advice are necessary. Behavior therapists believe that such techniques as reinforcement, desensitization or aversive conditioning are most important, and that the "ideal" therapeutic relationship is neither necessary nor sufficient. Others argue that the results of all (including behavioral) therapies are due to non-specific influences such as the aura which surrounds the treatment techniques and settings of prestigious practitioners publicly identified as "healers". Advocates of this "placebo" effect oppose those who believe in specific effects of specific techniques. (See *Behaviour therapy*.)

Another controversy is whether overt symptomatic behavior such as that involved in phobias and sexual disorders can be changed directly by re-conditioning without full self-exploration and insight, and without thereby harming the patient. A related point of debate focuses upon divergent models of pathology, with psychoanalysts arguing that an underlying, unconscious conflict produces symptoms, and behaviorists positing that symptoms are learned behaviors which follow ordinary laws of reinforcement and conditioning. This contention often centers on the issue of whether intrapsychic private events or external behavioral ones predominate in the control of behavior. Theorists and practitioners also divide in their emphasis upon the biological determinants of disturbed behavior, with environmentalists advocating the primacy of social and psychological factors in the patient's history, and the more genetically and biochemically oriented arguing for the predominance of biological predispositions, defects, and temporary chemical imbalances. The latter more frequently use some combination of psychotherapy and chemotherapy.

Classifying the divergent range of techniques and systems is difficult, but they may be arranged crudely in terms of the extent to which they focus respectively upon: (*a*) conceptual restructuring (attitude change or insight), (*b*) changing emotional states or emotional responsiveness and sensitivity, or (*c*) modifying behavior. Although all therapies touch upon each of these domains, different ones are known for their emphasis on a particular area. For example, psychoanalysis is noted for its emphasis upon insight, client-centered therapy for its focus upon feeling states, and behavior therapy for its attention to behavior modification.

Historically, the divergent approaches have competed and contended for primacy and influence, each one claiming to be helpful for a wide range of disorders; but in recent years there has been a more concentrated effort to isolate from these broad-gauged techniques or systems the specific ingredients, agents or influences which are most efficacious in relation to specific patient syndromes. Therefore, instead of asking which system is best, inquiry increasingly focuses upon which specific influences have what effects upon which symptoms under what conditions. This development is similar to the advances made in medical therapy when it became possible to make precise chemical analyses of various potions and remedies in common use. Results of that line of investigation revealed that nineteenth-century medical compounds were composed of largely inert, useless or harmful agents and a small number of truly therapeutic chemicals.

Although psychological therapies are inherently more complex than drug treatment, similar investigations in psychotherapy have begun to yield an analogous picture, and modern therapies are beginning to emerge which have specific potency in relation to given pathologies. For example, *systematic desensitization* has become a popular method for treating phobias; although it was devised by behavior therapists, it is being increasingly endorsed by adherents of opposing schools such as psychoanalysis and client-centered therapy. Such actions, unthinkable in the past, mark the growing maturity and scientific commitment of the field. School affiliations and clinical "wisdom" are gradually being retired as arbiters of therapist behavior in favor of a more empirical basis for devising and selecting techniques.

3. *Psychotherapy research.* In 1952, psychotherapists were stunned by H. J. Eysenck's analysis of statistical studies of therapy, in which he concluded that there was no evidence that psychotherapy had any unique effect upon patients beyond that attributable to non-specific everyday-life influences. At about the same time, Carl Rogers and his students had been conducting pioneering research studies on the therapeutic process and were calling for a more rigorous empirical approach to treatment. These and similar influences stimulated an outpouring of research studies which attempted to bring psychological treatment more fully within the framework of science by demonstrating therapy's specific effects and objectifying the processes leading to its outcomes.

Outcome research has revealed that the average cross-section of therapy as normally practiced has only modest effects when compared to the spontaneous changes occurring among untreated control group cases; however, this conclusion is based upon data averaged across heterogeneous samples of patients and therapists. When these samples are subdivided according to various criteria, interesting results emerge. For example, patients seen by more warm and empathic therapists show a higher than average improvement rate, whereas those seen by less warm and empathic therapists show lower than average improvement. Similar differences in outcomes appear between cases whose therapists differ in degree of personal adjustment and in amount of professional experience. It has also been found that outcomes vary considerably across patient types and across techniques. For example, more severely disturbed patients respond less well than the moderately disturbed, and behavioral desensitization techniques appear to be more effective with specific phobias than relationship and insight oriented techniques. It is currently more evident than before that outcome is a complex function of patient characteristics, therapist characteristics, and technique. The measurement of therapeutic effects in research studies is therefore entering a stage of specificity in which more homogeneous samples of therapists are treating more homogeneous sets of patients with more precisely defined procedures and, in each case, with respect to a previously selected specific criterion.

Process research examines the "live" or recorded interaction of therapist and patient in order to discover the precise types of interactions, influences, and responses which produce change. To illustrate, it has been found that therapists who have personal conflicts in areas such as dependency or hostility tend to avoid discussion of these topics and thus impede exploration of them by their patients. On the other hand, less anxious therapists are better at encouraging self-exploration, which leads to personality change. It has also been found that when therapists probe too deeply in sensitive areas patients defend themselves by silence or by changing to a different topic.

Therapist research evaluates therapist characteristics which are related to both process and outcome, for example, the role of therapist adjustment levels or conflict areas as noted above. The evaluation of therapist traits includes studies revealing that those treating schizophrenics have varying success rates which are discriminable by their scores on the *Strong Vocational Interest Blank*, and studies showing that therapist values tend to shape the direction of value changes in patients over the course of therapy.

Patient research has established that responsiveness to therapeutic interventions is a function of longstanding traits and presenting symptoms. These include: motivation for change; severity of disturbance, symptom complexity and duration; degree of psychological and environmental resources; cultural, educational, economic status; openness to emotional experience; and so on.

Analogue research explores therapy phenomena by recreating elements of clinical situations under experimental control, so that causes and consequences can be more firmly established. Frequently, this involves isolating a procedure from its context to determine whether it has certain predicted consequences. Behavior therapy researchers have used this method particularly well, for example, by testing which ingredients of desensitization do the work of producing change such as relaxation induction, hierarchy item presentation, and personal contact with the therapist. They have also pioneered in setting-up analogues of treatment based directly upon bodies of pure experimental work which then lead toward the invention of entirely new techniques. Some scholars argue that this will be the primary mode of therapy research in the future. New methods will come from laboratories in learning, personality, social psychology, and so on, rather than from the clinic itself.

4. *Psychotherapy, psychology, and society.* Psychotherapy is an applied area of psychology and as such influenced by the methods and principles of the field in general. It in turn has had a fertilizing effect upon thought and inquiry in nearly every basic field of psychology. The problem of measuring personality change has stretched the boundaries of the measurement field; analyses of psychodynamics have stimulated interest in the effect of motives on perceptions; case history material has posed hypotheses for developmental psychology; and the concept of therapeutic change as re-education has in part prompted developments in learning, such as renewed interests in social learning and mediational processes, and so on.

On the other hand, psychotherapy is criticized by modernists as being far too limited in scope to resolve the increasingly frequent pathologies rooted in social decay, changing mores, international conflicts, inflexible institutions, and harmful community structures. Those moving toward *community psychology*, in which intervention occurs in the community and often at the level of social structure, consider psychotherapy to be a miniscule influence in the backwash of a time of turbulent upheaval and social crises. Theirs is an ecological model rather than one focusing upon individual change.

However history may deal with the social significance of psychotherapy, it is unlikely that its contribution to an understanding of the mechanisms of personality change will be erased. The fact that social and political influences preoccupy many minds today does not obscure the fact that powerful psychological processes transpire between pairs of individuals, in families, and in small groups.

Bibliography: Bandura, A.: Principles of behavior modification. New York & London, 1969. **Bergin, A. E. & Garfield, S. L.:** Handbook of psychotherapy and behavior change. New York & London, 1970. **Eysenck, H. J.:** The effects of psychotherapy. New York, 1966. **Ford, D. H. & Urban, H. B.:** Systems of psychotherapy. New York & London, 1963. **London, P.:** The modes and morals of psychotherapy. New York & London, 1964. **Rogers, C. R.:** Client-centered therapy. Boston, 1964. **Strupp, H. H.:** Psychotherapy and the modification of abnormal behavior: an introduction to theory and research. New York & London, 1970. **Strupp, H. H. & Bergin, A. E.:** Some empirical and conceptual bases for coordinated research in psychotherapy. International Journal of Psychiatry, 1969, 7, no. 2, 18–90; no. 3, 116–68. **Strupp, H. H. & Bergin, A. E.:** Research in individual psychotherapy: a bibliography. (National Clearing

House for Mental Health Information, National Institute of Mental Health.) Washington, D.C., 1969. **Truax, C. B. & Carkhuff, R. R.:** Toward effective counseling and psychotherapy. Chicago, 1967. **Wolberg, L. R.:** The techniques of psychotherapy, 2 Vols. New York, 1967.

A. E. Bergin

Psychoticism. A factor evolved by Eysenck (1971) through an analysis of criteria, which distinguishes three groups of normal, schizophrenic and manic-depressives Ss. from each other (with scores increasing in that order). Psychoticism tests are, for instance, judgment of spatial distance, reading speed, level of proficiency in mirror drawing, and adding rows of numbers. See *Traits; Type.*

Bibliography: Eysenck, H. J.: Classification and the problem of diagnosis. In: **Eysenck, H. J.** (Ed.): Handbook of abnormal psychology. London, [2]1971.

M.A.

Psychotomimetic drugs. Psychotropic drugs (q.v.) which can produce temporary conditions similar to psychosis. They are also known as *psychosomimetic drugs*, *hallucinogenic*, *fantastic*, *eidetic*, *psychotogenic*, *psychodysleptic* and *psychedelic* drugs. *Chemically* they are classified under *indolalkaloids* (derivates of lysergine, dimethyltryptamine, bufotenin, psilocybin, ibogaine, harmine), derivates of *phenylethylamine* (mescalin), derivates of *piperidine* (belladonna-alkaloids, q.v., and other anticholinergic substances, phencyclidine) and *tetracannabinols* (which produce the effect of cannabis, q.v.). In connection with *psychotomimetic effects*, LSD (q.v.), mescalin (q.v.) and psilocybin have hitherto been studied at greatest depth. The patterns of effect of these are similar. Differences occur mainly in the duration of the effect, (psilocybin—peak effect after about 30 minutes, duration of effect 2–4 hours; LSD—peak effect after 1–1½ hours, duration of effect 5–6 hours; mescalin—peak effect 2–2½ hours, duration of effect 8 hours and longer). With chronic use, tolerance and cross-tolerance can be developed to these substances. The psychological changes affect perception, and cognitive and affective functions. Possible disturbances of perception are hallucination, illusion (mainly in the visual field), intensification of the perception of colour, synesthesia, changes in form and space perception, disturbances of physical patterns, etc. In the cognitive field, depersonalization phenomena, loss of control over thoughts, etc., can occur. The affective changes can, according to the subject's original state of health, consist of euphoria (q.v.), dysphoria or extreme variations of mood. Before mental changes begin, dizziness, feelings of weakness, nausea, tremor, sleepiness or other somatic symptoms can occur. Observable autonomic effects are, on the whole, however, relatively few (dilation of pupils, increased muscular tension, and so on). EEG research indicates a slight increase of alpha-rhythm or the desynchronization pattern. The similarity of mental changes provoked by these substances with schizophrenic psychosis inspired the hope that some light might be thrown on the origins of schizophrenia (q.v.) by the pattern of effect of these drugs (see *Psychopharmacology*). This hope has not been fulfilled up to the present. The view commonly held today is that the conditions induced by these drugs differ from schizophrenia even in their symptoms.

Bibliography: Downing, D. F.: Psychotomimetic compounds. In: **Gordon, M.** (Ed.): Psychopharmacological agents, Vol. 1. New York & London, 1964. **Efron, D. H.** (Ed.): Psychopharmacology: a review of progress 1957–67. Washington, 1968. **Hollister, L. E.:** Chemical psychoses. Springfield, 1968. **Leuner, H.:** Die experimentelle Psychose. Berlin & Göttingen, 1962. **Levine, J.:** LSD – a clinical overview. In: **Black, P.** (Ed.): Drugs and the brain. Baltimore, 1969.

G.E.

Psychotomimetic effect. The result of psychotropic drugs (q.v.) which consists in the creation of a psychosis-type (see *Psychoses*) condition. Substances whose main effect is psychotomimetic are known as psychotomimetic drugs (q.v.). As a consequence of overdosage when taken chronically, psychotomimetic effects can persist in the case of many psychotropic drugs. *G.E.*

Psychotonic drugs. Synonym for *stimulants* (q.v.).

Psychotonolytic drugs. Synonym for *tranquilizers* (q.v.).

Psychotropic drugs. Chemically differing, natural and synthetic substances, whose principal effects are psychotropic, i.e., they induce in the nervous system behavioral and experiential changes which are at present mainly reversible. Their effect is for the most part neurophysiologically selective in various regions of the central nervous system (for example the limbic system, reticular system, thalamus, cortex) and they interact with different neurohumeral substances (see *Transmitter substances* and *Biogenic amines*). Psychologically, the motivational and emotional learning, retention and integration aspects of behavior are affected most of all. They are usually classified under hypnotics (q.v.), stimulants (q.v.), neuroleptics (q.v.), antidepressives (q.v.), tranquilizers (q.v.) and psychotomimetic drugs (q.v.) (cf. table). *Substances* with psychotropic sideeffects which are not included under psychotropic drugs are: analgesics (q.v.), antiallergics, antibiotics (q.v.), antiemetics (q.v.), antiepileptics, antihistamine (q.v.), antihypertensives (q.v.), anticonvulsives (q.v.), anti-Parkinson drugs, antipyretics, antitussives, aphrodisiacs (q.v.), hormones (q.v.), muscle-relaxants (q.v.), narcotics (q.v.), spasmolytics (q.v.), autonomic drugs, vitamins (q.v.). In the absence of a strict division, centrally induced effects are often hardly distinguishable from indirect effects of the afferent input of peripherally induced changes, e.g. in the autonomic nervous system. The general, rough classification of psychotropic drugs takes into account dosage, situation, actual and habitual personality traits (see Differential psychopharmacology), and such major clinical-therapeutic characteristics as symptoms treated, therapeutic dose, side-effects, and addiction. The classification which is generally used in the application of drug therapy with reference to its effect on animals gives species-specific differences. Forecasts of the effects in patients are more successful in tests on more highly developed organisms, and of behavior under model experimental conditions (for example, aggressive behavior, active and passive evasive reaction, resistance to stress). Classification according to chemical similarity admits rough partial subdivisions into families of substances, but allows no specific forecast of effects. New psychotropic drugs are discovered partly by chance observation but developed mainly with regard to optimal therapy of specific target symptoms through systematic variation of the chemical composition of known drugs. Possibilities of applying and studying psychotropic drugs exist in various practical and scientific disciplines. (See *Pharmacopsychiatry*; *Pharmacotherapy; Psychopharmacology; Pharmacopsychology; Neuropharmacology*). The identification of psychotropic drugs usually follows the international chemical abbreviation (as in this encyclopedia) or one or more trade-names, according to whether the substance is commercially obtainable.

Bibliography: Black, P.: Drugs and the brain. Baltimore, 1969. **Burger, A.** (Ed.): Drugs affecting the central nervous system. Medical Research, Vol. 2. New York, 1968. **Clark, W. G. & del Giudice, J.** (Eds.): Principles of psychopharmacology. Ch. 4: Structure and metabolism of psychotropic drugs. New York, 1970. **Dietsch, P.:** Versuchssituation und Tranquilizerwirkung. Arzneimittel-Forsch., 1969, *19*, 472–4. **Elkes, J.:** Behavioral pharmacology in relation to psychiatry. In: **Gruhle, H. W.** *et al.* (Eds.): Psychiatrie der Gegenwart I/1A. Berlin, 1967. **Ippen, H.:**

A selection of psychotropic drugs, mainly from those which are of significance in pharmacotherapy (q.v.). The shortened, non-proprietary names are listed, together with a sample "trade" name, and letters indicating class and (if the drug appears in a separate encyclopedia entry) the family of substances. Abbreviations: H = hypnotics; N = neuroleptics; T = tranquilizers; S = stimulants; A = antidepressives; P = psychotomimetic drugs; Mo = monoaminooxidase inhibitors; Ba = barbiturates; Ph = phenothiazines; Ra = rauwolfia alkaloids; Bu = butyrophenones; Am = amphetamines.

Shortened, non-proprietary name	Trade name	Class
Allobarbital	Dial	H-Ba
Amitriptyline	Elavil	A
Amobarbital	Amytal	H-Ba
Amphetamine	Benzedrine	S-Am
Azacyclonol	Frenquel	T
Barbital	Veronal	H-Ba
Benactyzine	Suavitil	T
Benperidol		N-Bu
Bromisovalum	Bromural	H
Butabarbital	Butisol	H
Caffeine		S
Captodiamine	Suvren	T
Carbromal	Adalin	H
Carisoprodol	Soma	T
Chloral hydrate		H
Chlordiazepoxide	Librium	T
Chlorpromazine	Thorazine	N-Ph
Chlorprothixine	Taractan	N
Cocaine		P
Cyclobarbital	Phanodorn	H-Ba
Deserpine	Harmonyl	N-Ra
Desipramine	Pertofrane	A
Dextroamphetamine	Dexedrine	S-Am
Diacetylmorphine	(Heroin)	P
Diazepam	Valium	T
Dibenzepin		A
Droperidol	Inapsine	N-Bu
Emylcamate	Striatron	T
Ethinamate	Valmid	H
Ethyl-iso-butrazine	Ditran	N-Ph
Fluphenazine	Prolixin	N-Ph
Glutethimide	Doriden	H
Haloperidol	Haldol	N-Bu
Heptabarbital	Medomin	H-Ba
Hexobarbital	Sombucaps	H-Ba
Hydroxyzine	Atarax	T
Imipramine	Tofranil	A
Iproniazid	Marsilid	A-A-Mo
Isocarboxazid	Marplan	A-Mo
Lysergide (LSD -αS)	Pacatal	P
Mepazine	Pacatal	N-Ph
Meperone		N-Bu
Mephenesin	Tolserol	T
Meprobamat	Miltown	T
Mescaline		P
Methamphetamine	Desoxyn	S-Am
Methohexital	Brevital	H-Ba
Methotrimeprazine	Levoprome	N-Ph
Methylphenidate	Ritalin	S
Methyprylon	Noludar	H
Nialamide	Niamid	A-Mo
Nitrazepam	Mogadon	T/H
Nortriptyline	Aventyl	A
Opipramol	Ensidon	A
Oxazepam	Serax	T
Paraldehyde		H
Pentobarbital	Nembutal	H-Ba
Perphenazine	Trilafon	N-Ph
Phenaglycodol	Ultran	T
Phencyclidin	Sernyl	P
Phenmetrazin	Preludin	S
Phenobarbital	Luminal	H-Ba
Pipradol	Meratran	S
Prochlorperazine	Compazine	N-Ph
Promazine	Sparine	N-Ph
Promethazine	Phenergan	N-Ph
Psilocin		P
Psilocybin		P
Rescinnamine	Moderil	N-Ra
Reserpine	Reserpoid	N-Ra
Secobarbital	Seconal	H-Ba
Tetrahydrocannabinol		P
Thalidomide	Distaval	H
Thioridazine	Mellaril	N-Ph
Thiothixene	Navane	N
Triflupromazine	Vesprin	N-Ph
Trifluoperazine	Stelazine	N-Ph
Trifluperidol	Triperidol	N-Ph
Trimipramine	Surmontil	A
Tybamat	Solacen	T

Index Psychopharmacorum. Stuttgart, 1968. **Janke, W.:** Verwendungsmöglichkeiten einiger multivariater statistischer Verfahren für die Klassifikation von Psychopharmaka. Arzneimittel-Forsch., 1964, *14*, 582–4. **Pöldinger, W. & Schmidlin, P.:** Index psychopharmacorum 1966. Berne, 1966. **Wandrey, D. & Leutner, V.:** Neuro-Psychopharmaca in Klinik und Praxis. Stuttgart, 1965.

G. Debus

P technique. When measurements are made concerning a single individual at *S* different points in time (or under *S* different conditions) in respect of *m* variables where *S* is greater than *m*, and the variables in the situation correlate and factorize, this technique is known as a *P* technique. The factors evolved in a *P* technique are state factors. In the same factor, weighted variables show similar profiles. (See *Factor analysis*.)

G. M.

Pubertas praecox. Precocious puberty.—Abnormally rapid maturation in children, manifested in the premature development of the secondary sex characteristics and onset of functioning of the primary sex organs, usually with accompanying sex interest. May occur as a result of *pituitary gland* malfunction.

G.D.W.

Puberty. A second independent stage, which at first takes a negative form, introduces the age of puberty. It is an age of uncertainty of direction together with introversion in defence against outside influences. Eventually new values begin to be stabilized. The latter stage is announced by more extraverted tendencies, such as joining youth groups and forming friendships with the opposite sex. The goal of puberty is independence and adaptation to adult life. These changes cause "inner turmoils" (S. Freud), that is to say strong conflicts of the child with himself. The working out of these conflicts often causes difficulties, which lead to aggression (q.v.) directed against the self, as in disturbances of bodily and sexual development. One symptom of such conflicts is the puberty slimming craze. It is most common in girls and its symptoms are: psychologically determined refusal of food, loss of weight usually accompanied by constipation and amenorrhea. See *Child psychology; Youth.* *M. Sa.*

Publicity. In its psychological aspect, publicity ("advertising" in the larger sense) is concerned to *inform* and to "*motivate*". It offers information about the existence of a commodity, and sometimes about its purpose, but in competitive situations about the "unique" or special nature of the "product", in which case non-thematic information is very important. In consumer motivation there are at least three conceptually and formally distinct possibilities: (*a*) motivation by increasing the "appeal" of the product (e.g. by emphasizing the degree of its "reality"); (*b*) by adapting the "image" to the consumer; (*c*) by adapting the consumer to the "image"—largely by manipulation of his attitudes (the "standardization of needs" effect); (*b*) and (*c*) represent a diminution of "semantic distance" (see *Semantics*) between image and consumers. Each of the three measures leads to a steeper gradient of appeal.

The psychology of publicity (a division of marketing or consumer psychology) is concerned with the psychological "laws" of publicity. In principle it may be considered as a branch of applied social psychology. It developed from a not wholly psychotechnically oriented and autonomous aspect of advertising (consumer) psychology into a part aspect of marketing psychology (q.v.). It became more exact as the findings of general psychology found increasing acceptance. Psychologists in the service of (or concerned scientifically to examine) publicity, study its media in terms of the findings of communications (information) and motivation research into the psychological structure of (the) consumers (in question).

Bibliography: Britt, S. H. (Ed.): Psychological experiments in consumer behavior. New York, 1971. **Brückner, P.:** Die informierende Funktion der Wirtschaftswerbung. Berlin, 1967. **Dichter, E.:** Motivating human behavior. New York & London, 1971. **Ehrenberg, A. S. C. & Pugh, F. C.:** Consumer behavior. Harmondsworth, 1971. **Horkheimer, M. & Adorno, T.:** Dialectic of enlightenment. New York, 1972. **Perloff, R.:** Consumer analysis. Ann. Rev. Psychol., 1968, *19*, 437–66. See also *Marketing*.

B.Sp.

Public opinion. "Opinion publique" (J. J. Rousseau, 1750), closely related to the English "climate of opinion" (Glanville, 1661), "law of opinion" (J. Locke, 1671). All three concepts were formulated in (pre)revolutionary periods, i.e. in times when the government and the popular will were at odds. Its limitation to political matters (Lippmann, 1922; Hennis, 1956; Habermas, 1962) is more recent; in the eighteenth and nineteenth centuries public opinion was recognized as a social force (exerting an influence both on an individual member of society and on the rulers in order to compel action in conformity with prevailing views (F. v. Holtzendorff, 1879). The reciprocal integrating effect was forgotten when E. A. Ross (1896) introduced the concept of *social control* for the pressure which public opinion brings to bear on the individual (Noelle, 1966).

At the moment there is no generally accepted definition of public opinion (Schmidtchen, 1959, 236; W. P. Davison: International Encyclopaedia of the Social Sciences, vol. 13, 1969, 188), but it is hardly likely that the proposal to do away with the concept (H. Schelsky, 1967, and others) will be achieved now that demoscopy (q.v.) has come into being. Results of opinion polls (q.v.) are not yet a reflection of public opinion. The existence or development of a prevailing opinion, the conviction that this opinion is shared by a majority (cf. also Hofstätter, 1949, 53 ff.), the conviction that the prevailing demands may be achieved, and expectations that developments are moving in the direction of these demands—the conjunction of these factors which may be measured by opinion polls leads to a sociopsychological dynamism, the perception of which probably led in the beginning to the formation of the concept.

Bibliography: Habermas, J.: Strukturwandel der Öffentlichkeit. Neuwied, 1962, [5]1969. **Hennis, W.:** Meinungsforschung und repräsentative Demokratie. Tübingen, 1957. **Hofstätter, P. R.:** Die Psychologie der öffentlichen Meinung. New York, 1922; Munich, 1964. **Noelle, E.:** Offentliche Meinung und Soziale Kontrolle. Tübingen, 1966. *E.N.-N.*

Public relations. (Abb. PR). **1.** Leading public relations experts define public relations as "the conscious, planned and permanent striving to build and maintain mutual understanding and trust in public activities". Public relations work is the dialogue which each group (q.v.) in society or each individual must hold in social intercourse. Public relations work is the effort of social groups with different opinions to reach some form of agreement. It cannot solve conflicts, but can free them from misunderstandings so that their factual solution becomes possible. Daily discussion shows how many emotional obstacles there are to understanding and how important public relations are to the solution of problems by a proper formulation of them. The task and aim of public relations is thus the reassurance of social groups through recognition and trust.

In contrast to advertising, whose purpose is to maximize sales, the work of public relations is to win social acceptance for the group or firm. Hence information which is an aid to understanding in socio-political life is part of public relations, whereas information which helps to sell the goods is proper to publicity (q.v.). In its preliminary analysis of the situation and subsequent attempts to deal with it, public relations uses the methods of empirical social research, from the depth psychology interview (q.v.) to broad field studies.

2. The exchange of communication between organizations, such as firms, businesses, groups and so forth, and the public, and in particular the attitudes (q.v.) and opinions of the public concerning these organizations. Public relations in the active sense aims to maintain and create favorable relations with the public. It seeks through publicity, activities, services, etc. to win interest, sympathy, regard and trust for the organization. *B.Sp.*

Puerilism. 1. A state of childishness: that stage which follows infancy and precedes puberty. **2.** An abnormal state in an adult when the mind appears to revert to its childhood state. *J.P.*

Puerperal psychosis. A term used loosely to refer to psychic disturbance in a woman after childbirth. It does not characterize any specific condition.

Pulfrich effect (*C. Pulfrich*, 1858–1927). An object oscillating in the frontal plane viewed binocularly seems to describe a horizontal ellipse if one eye is partially covered by a grey or colored filter. The stereoscopic effect is explained as follows. Different time intervals occur between stimulus and perception (perception times) for the right and left eye according to the varying light intensities. The resulting disparity of diagonals leads to a perception of depth. *W.P.*

Pulse. The number of arterial fluctuations of blood-pressure produced by the heart per minute. It is normally 70 a minute, but in extreme cases of trained athletes at rest it can fall to 50 a minute and with extreme excitement and certain circulatory diseases it can rise to 200 a minute. The pulse can be felt in the superficial arteries synchronously with the frequency of the heart-beat. In the past it was much more important evidence than today in the diagnosis of circulation. The characteristic deviations from the norm were therefore given special names like *pulsus frequens* or *rarus* (frequency), *regularis* or *irregularis*, *celer* or *tardus* (rising fast or slowly), *altus* or *parvus* (large or small pressure fluctuations), *durus* or *mollis* (high or low blood pressure). *E.D.*

Punishment. Punishment is the presentation of an aversive event contingent upon a response. In practice, most studies of punishment employ events that are unquestionably aversive. Electric shock has been used in a large majority of studies of punishment of animal subjects, since its physical characteristics are easily measured and controlled. The withdrawal of a positive reinforcement contingent upon a response has also been used as an aversive event.

Punishment may also be defined as the presentation of an event contingent upon a response that reduces the probability of that response. This, of course, parallels the familiar functional definition of a positive reinforcement.

Although several theories of punishment emphasize a symmetrical opposition between punishment and positive reinforcement, the term "negative reinforcement" is no longer used as a synonym for punishment. This term is now used to describe the withdrawal of an aversive stimulus contingent upon a response (that is, the escape operation).

The technical uses of the word "punishment" in psychology are closely related to the general use of the word, but several differences should be noted. The aversive event need not be administered by an animate agent, and there is no implication of retribution.

Although the relationship between a response and an aversive event is central to all contemporary definitions of punishment, some definitions emphasize the contiguity between a response and an aversive event rather than the contingency between the response and the aversive event.

1. *History.* Punishment has been used for two major purposes: to facilitate the acquisition of new responses, and to suppress the performance of established responses. The early research on discrimination learning of rats demonstrated that punishment of erroneous responses facilitates learning. In addition, punishment can also suppress ongoing responses. Such suppression is particularly rapid when an alternative response is rewarded. Some concern has been expressed about undesirable sideeffects of punishment, particularly in child rearing.

2. *Severity.* The severity of a punishment may be specified in terms of its intensity, duration, and frequency. If the punishment is extremely mild (for example, an external inhibitor) response suppression may be temporary and complete recovery may follow, but if the punishment is severe, the effects of punishment are permanent.

3. *Relationship between response and aversive event.* An aversive event that is contingent upon a response (punishment) has a greater effect on that response than an aversive event that is independent of a response. In

addition, contiguity is important. The shorter the temporal interval between the response and the aversive event the greater the effect of the punishment upon the response (the delay-of-punishment gradient). In contrast, there is some evidence that various measures of emotional upset (ulcers, interference with learned discriminations, and so on) may be greater when the aversive event is unpredictable and uncontrollable.

4. *Paradoxical effects of punishment.* Under some conditions punishment may paradoxically increase the response it was designed to suppress. For example, mild punishment of the correct (rewarded) response in a relatively difficult two-choice discrimination can facilitate the learning of the discrimination. Punishment of an escape or avoidance response can also result in facilitation of the response, and if positive reinforcement is associated with punishment an animal may appear to be masochistic. To resolve such paradoxes it is necessary to recognize that a punishing event has varied effects (it serves as a discriminative stimulus, a fear-arousing stimulus, it elicits competing motor responses, and so on).

5. *Applications in behavior therapy.* Basic research on the principles of punishment and the conditioned emotional response has had important applications in the development of effective behavior therapy (q.v.). Prominent among behavior therapies are punishment procedures designed to suppress maladaptive instrumental acts. Numerous case studies have been reported in which punishment has led to a marked alleviation of such problems as stuttering, writer's cramp, head-banging, and sexual fetishes. See *Aversion therapy.*

Bibliography: Azrin, N. H. & Holz, W. C.: Punishment. In: **Honig, W. K.** (Ed.): operant behavior: Areas of research and application. New York, 1966, 380–447. **Bandura, A.:** Principles of behavior modification. New York, 1969. **Boe, E. E. & Church, R. M.:** Punishment: issues and experiments. New York, 1969. **Brush, F. R.:** Aversive conditioning and learning. New York, 1970. **Campbell, B. A. & Church, R. M.:** Punishment and aversive behavior. New York, 1969. **Church, R. M.:** The varied effects of punishment on behavior. Psychol. Rev., 1963, 70, 369–402.

R. M. Church

Pupillary reflex. The width of the pupils (central aperture in the iris, q.v.) is regulated by the fluctuation of the muscles *dilator* (enlargement, innervated by the sympathetic nerve) and *sphincter* (contraction, innervated by the parasympathetic nerve) *pupillae.* When a strong light strikes only one eye the width of of the pupil is immediately reduced (see *Miosis*), and not only of the eye on which the light falls (direct reaction to light) but also of the eye that has not been exposed to the light (consensual reaction to light). This purely reflexive, unconscious, unexposed reaction is a pupillary reflex. This is to be distinguished from *pupil reaction* in convergence (q.v.) In accommodation (q.v.), which leads to a convergent movement of both eyes, it comes about by the linked innervation of the parasympathetic component of the *nervus oculomotorius* at the same time as a contraction of the pupils of both eyes. In this way the amount of light entering the eye is reduced (near objects are brighter) and depth of focus increased (by the dimming of marginal rays, spherical aberration). *R.R.*

Purkinje figure; Purkinje (-Sanson) image; Purkinje phenomenon (effect). Three materially different things which are named after J. E. Purkinje (1787–1869). **1.** *Figure:* by entoptic observation an observer can make the blood vessels of his retina visible. Entoptic observation can be undertaken with the help of a diaphanoscope (sclera illuminator) or a small lamp moved near the sclera or with a perforated screen moved backwards and forwards near to the eyeball in front of the aperture of the pupil. A movement of the light or of the perforated screen is needed to counteract the adaptation of the receptors (see *Stabilized retinal image*). The entoptic image perceived by the observer of the blood vessels of his retina is the Purkinje figure.

2. *Image:* also known as Purkinje–Sanson image. Reflexions of a light are made by the cornea and lens which are observable when a suitable light shines on someone else's eye. (Painters often depict this image as the characteristic light of the eye.) Generally only three images are observable: one reflected by the anterior surface of the cornea and two by the lens surface. The image reflected by the posterior surface of the cornea is very weak and only visible in optimal conditions. Of the four images three are upright, the image from the posterior surface of the lens being upside-down. This image is used to determine the curvature of the lens in accommodation (q.v.).

3. *Phenomenon:* the function of spectral sensitivity to light is dependent upon the eye's adaptability. Accordingly the sensitivity maximum fluctuates with adaptation to the dark from the wavelength range 555 NM to 505 NM. To demonstrate Purkinje's phenomenon two colors are chosen, one orange-red, the second blue-green (or simply red and blue), so that in bright illumination the orange-red is brighter than the blue-green, and when the light is gradually dimmed the blue-green seems brighter to the observer. (See *Duplicity theory*). *A.H.*

Puromycin. An antibiotic (q.v.).

Purposivism. An active animal's purposive behaviour is decisive; it learns to anticipate the result of its actions.

Bibliography: Tolman, E. C.: Purposive behaviour in animals and man. New York & London, 1932.

K.Fi.

Pursuit-rotor. A more or less large spot moving in a circle must be followed by a pointer so that the pointer does not leave the spot. The method was developed in the U.S.A. during research into motor learning.

Bibliography: Cronbach, L. J.: Essentials of psychological testing. New York, [2]1960. *K.M.*

Puzzle box. A box used by Thorndike (q.v.) to investigate the behavior (learning) of animals. The box is fitted with a mechanism which opens a door when actuated. Animals, e.g. cats, are put in the box so that their attempts to leave it can be observed. At first the exit mechanism is set off by chance, but its operation is then learnt (over several trials), and finally occurs systematically. The puzzle box was a forerunner of the Skinner box (q.v.).

Bibliography: Thorndike, E. L.: Animal intelligence. Psychol. Rev. Monogr. Suppl., 1898, No. 8 (reprinted in *Animal intelligence*, New York, 1911). *R.Hä.*

Pyknic (type). One of the classifications of human *body build* (q.v.) described by E. Kretschmer. It is characterized by a medium-sized, squat figure, a soft, broad face on a short, massive neck. The deep, barrel chest expands below into a portly paunch. The face is soft and broad, presenting from the front a flat pentagon. The nose is broad with a fleshy to thick snub end. The pyknic type is especially often observed among patients with manic-depressive psychosis. Among normal people the pyknic body structure is often correlated with a cyclothymic (q.v.) temperament. See *Traits; Type.* *W.Se.*

Pyknolepsy. Petit-mal epilepsy (q.v.).

Pyknomorphy. One of the typical forms of body structure described by K. Conrad, which is to be traced back to a primary growth tendency toward thickness to the detriment of length. Primary growth tendency to length at the expense of thickness causes its opposite, leptomorphy. K. Conrad explains the primary variants of the leptomorphic and pyknomorphic bodybuilds by the development of temperament, dependent on genes, by a propulsive or conservative growth tendency. According to this, pyknomorphy occurs as a result of a conservative development which comes to a halt on the threshold of harmonization after the first but before the second change of shape. The appearance of pyknomorphy conforms to a large extent with the pyknic body structure described by E. Kretschmer. See *Traits; Type.* *W.Se.*

Pyramidal tract. Formerly (Holms & May, 1909) the suggestion that fiber paths exclusively from the large pyramid-shaped Betz cells of area IV of the brain were responsible for the voluntary motor system was connected with the "pyramidal tract" concept. After overlapping on the opposite side of the body in the "pyramids" (so called after their outward shape) above the *medulla oblongata,* the paths extend to the motor cells of the anterior horn. These pathways of voluntary movement were contrasted with the so-called *extra-pyramidal system* (see *Parkinsonism*). Today we know that only 30 per cent of the fibers of the pyramidal tract originate in the large Betz cells. A great proportion of the fibers do not cross to the opposite side; even ascending fibers are found in this tract. The opposition of involuntary movements (see *Extrapyramidal system*) and voluntary motor (pyramidal) movement is pointless. Voluntary movement sequences are explained today neurophysiologically by control systems which go beyond the bounds of the earlier theory. *M.A.*

Q

Q correlation. A correlation in which n individuals are correlated in regard to m characteristics where m is greater than n. This kind of correlational technique, which statistically is no different from the usual R correlation (q.v.), derives from W. Stephenson. It is used especially in clinical psychology (q.v.). *G.Mi.*

Q sorting. A rating technique (q.v.) in which a large number of statements are sorted into a series of categories so that the resulting frequency distribution (q.v.) corresponds to a defined distribution. The advantage of Q sorting is that it guards against faulty use of the rating scale. Originally (in investigations by W. Stephenson) a testee sorted some 100 statements written on cards (e.g. dealing with traits) according to their accuracy or their correctness with reference to different concepts (e.g. self-concept); he then went on to calculate the results with the Q technique (q.v.). (See *Scaling*.)

Bibliography: Stephenson, W.: The study of behavior. Chicago, 1953. *G.Mi.*

Q technique. Synonymous with Q analysis. A factor analysis (q.v.) which starts from Q correlations (q.v.). Individuals are factorized and the extracted factors can be interpreted as types. The factor matrix of a Q technique thus contains the factor loadings of the individual persons in the type factors. There is reciprocity between R and Q techniques in so far as the factor matrix of R technique (q.v.) is equivalent to the factor-value matrix of Q technique, and *vice versa.* *G.Mi.*

Qualitative characteristics. Those characteristics which can be exclusively grouped into categories differing in content and between which there are numerical relations. Qualitative characteristics can only be classified by means of nominal scales (q.v.). According to the number of possible classes a distinction is made between alternative (q.v.) (e.g. sex) and multiple-class characteristics (eye color, employment). Qualitative characteristics are discrete (q.v.) or discontinuous variables. *G.Mi.*

Quality. 1. In general: kind, nature, goodness; as opposed to quantity (q.v.), it cannot be measured and can be quantified only to a limited degree.

2. In the psychology of perception a characteristic of sensory perception together with intensity and duration. Whereas the last two largely depend directly on the stimulus, quality depends on the sensation felt by the receptor, the sensory cell which has been excited.

3. In psychodiagnostics (q.v.) the quality and quantity of a performance in conjunction with time are the predominant criteria for evaluation. The quality of a performance includes

both the latter's merit and its degree of difficulty (complexity), whereas quantity includes speed of performance, or the number of answers (solutions) in a certain time.
H.J.A.

Quality of gestalt (Ger. *Gestaltqualität*). The essential character or form of a whole when apprehended as a configuration of parts. See *Ganzheit*.

Quantification. A term used for the grouping of numbers into characteristics. If the characteristics are qualitative (q.v.), quantification is possible only by enumeration, i.e. by determining the class frequencies. Where the characteristics are quantitative (q.v.), quantification is synonymous with measurement (q.v.). *G.Mi.*

Quantitative characteristics. The characteristics which vary in their degree of distinctness and are therefore (fundamentally) capable of being measured. It is assumed that they are continuous, even when the methods of measurement employed enable only discrete values to be obtained (e.g. memory: the number of elements noticed). According to the nature of the possible quantification, a distinction is made between ordinal (q.v.), interval (q.v.), and proportional (q.v.) variables. (See *Scaling; Methods of psychology.*) *G.Mi.*

Quantity. In general: amount, size, number. As opposed to quality (q.v.), the characteristic of a phenomenon which permits it to be measured or counted. In psychodiagnostics (q.v.), a quantity in performance is a score, i.e. the speed of the performance (time as measure), or the number of tasks solved (answers) in a given period of time. *H.J.A.*

Quantization. The splitting up of a complex or a quantity into elements which in the given connection may be considered the maximum possible. Signal transformation (q.v.) of *continuous signals* into *discrete* signals and in the coding (q.v.) of a news item with a multidimensional signal function so that it can be transmitted over a one-dimensional channel. Example: two-dimensional copies of pictures are reduced at the transmitting end to lines and then to image-dots (information quanta) and subsequently reconverted at the receiving end into a two-dimensional complex. *H.R.*

Quartile. The three points by which a frequency distribution (q.v.) can be divided into equal quarters are known as quartiles. The first quartile of a distribution therefore contains 25% of all the cases, the second, the median, contains 50%, and the third, 75%. The first and third quartiles are known as the lower and upper quartiles. *G.Mi.*

Quartimax methods. Analytical, *orthogonal* rotation methods of rotating the factor matrix. See *Factor analysis.* *G.Mi.*

Quasi-experiment. An experiment, the results of which are invalid on account of a defective experimental design. A quasi-experiment allows no conclusions to be drawn regarding the connection between dependent and independent variables, since the independent variables were inadequately conceived and controlled.

Bibliography: **Campbell, D. T. & Stanley, J. C.:** Experimental and quasi-experimental designs for research in teaching. In: **Gage, N. L.** (Ed.): Handbook of research on teaching. Chicago, 1963. *F.Ma.*

Quasi-need. A distinction was made by Lewin (1926) between quasi-needs and "real" needs. The former are "intended acts" or "purposive thoughts", and depend on "real" needs. The latter can be traced back to instincts (q.v.) or "central desires". Zeigarnik is of the opinion that quasi-needs are aftereffects of unaccomplished acts. *H.M.*

Questioning. The first phase of questioning occurs around the second year when a child wants to know the names of things, the questions being related to the designating function of language (K. Bühler). The second phase (questioning proper, i.e. questions prefaced by "why") starts during the third year and represents the child's attempt to classify the world around him.

Bibliography: Bühler, K.: Die geistige Entwicklung des Kindes. Jena, [3]1922. **Stern, C. & Stern, W.:** Kindersprache. Leipzig, [2]1920. *S.Kr.*

Questionnaires. "Questionnaire" describes a variety of instruments and techniques. Often it consists of a printed form containing a structured set of questions, all of which the subject is required to answer—usually in writing, but sometimes orally, as in public opinion surveys and market research. Form, method of administration and subject matter may all vary widely. The content areas in psychology found most suitable to questionnaire methods have been: biographical data, opinions, attitudes, values, and personality traits. Some cognitive tests might be classed as questionnaires, but the term is rarely applied to them.

An important distinction is between open-ended and objectively scored items. To the first type the subject phrases his response with little constraint from the experimenter, and analysis of the results will be to some extent subjective. In the second type the questionnaire constructor will pre-determine a few response categories and require the respondent to endorse one or other. This restricts variety of response, but facilitates objective coding and analysis.

1. *Item construction.* Constructing good items is not simple and is more art than science, objective principles being few and dependence upon experience considerable. Evaluation and scaling of items can, however, more readily be reduced to a set of rules. Common faults found in questionnaire items are bias, ambiguity, over-elaboration and lack of discriminative power. Crude bias may be obvious; for example, questions like the Latin words *nonne* and *num*, may pre-dispose the subject in the direction of "Yes" or "No". This may occur also in subtle forms, so that whether a question is slanted is not easily detectable.

Ambiguity is also a matter of degree. It is worth noting that the following words often require careful placement to make quite clear what they qualify: "always", "only", "often", "sometimes", "usually", "many", "most", and so on. Moser (1958) quotes another instance of faulty question construction. In one survey women were asked, "Is your work made more difficult because you are expecting a baby?", irrespective of whether they *were* expecting a baby. The answer "No" would then be ambiguous because it might mean either "not expecting a baby" or "work not made more difficult". Over-elaborate syntax and phrasing should be avoided; items should be as plain and spare as is consistent with lucidity. An especially undesirable form of elaboration results in double-barrelled statements: for example, "Are you satisfied with the service and prices in this restaurant?" Many people may be satisfied with service but not with prices, or *vice versa*. These and other dangers apply to all questionnaire construction; when the questionnaire is to be administered to a cross-section of a national population or to any unselected sample of subjects, special care should be taken to make the questions clear, simple and unambiguous.

Many writers (for instance, Jahoda, Cook & Deutsch, 1951) have made useful distinctions between different kinds of information to be elicited. According to type of information, modifications in questionnaire design may well be necessary, as between those designed to tap facts and those concerned with, e.g. beliefs, feelings, standards of action, reasons for beliefs.

2. *Opinion questionnaires.* Innumerable opinion and attitude questionnaires have been constructed, particularly in the USA. "Opinion" and "attitude" have become almost synonymous in this context. Three main attitude-scaling techniques are available, devised by Thurstone, Likert and Guttman respectively. Each of these has its merits, and the first two methods have been very widely used. The technique of equal-appearing intervals (Thurstone & Chave, 1929) extends methods already used in psychophysical studies of perception and sensation. It enables the questionnaire constructor to assign a "scale value" to each item and to place each respondent on the required attitude continuum according to the median scale value of the items he endorses. The Likert technique is similar to those used in constructing ability tests, but a distinctive feature is that the respondent is presented with five alternative degrees of endorsement of each item. The Guttman scaling technique (Stouffer, 1950) produces short, highly homogeneous scales.

3. *Personality questionnaires.* These have been developed on different lines from those concerned with attitudes and are of considerable theoretical importance. They vary even more widely in type, being essentially means of classifying people according to the personality theory of the constructor, which may be based on clinical syndromes, on ideal types, or on traits and dimensions. The best known instrument of the first type is the Minnesota Multiphasic Personality Inventory, a huge amalgam from which less general instruments have been developed; for example, the Taylor Manifest Anxiety Test.

Classification of personality by discrete types is open to criticism; consequently, few questionnaires are based on this approach. An interesting exception is the Myers-Briggs inventory, based on the two-by-four Jungian typology of "introvert" and "extravert", and the cross-classification into "sensation", "perception", "intuition" and "feeling" types.

Many personality questionnaires are based on the dimensional approach, and attempt to assess the most important general traits, in the sense of accounting for maximum variance in an unselected sample of people. Identifying such traits has depended largely upon the technique of factor analysis (q.v.). The most important measures of this kind are those of Cattell, Eysenck and Guilford, particularly the two former. All these are derived from factor-analytical studies, but with different presuppositions. Cattell's questionnaire for adults assesses sixteen dimensions, Eysenck's only two. Each approach has some advantages: Cattell provides a more detailed profile, but Eysenck gives factors that are probably more reliable and pervasive (Eysenck & Eysenck, 1969).

4. *Criteria of good questionnaires.* The requirements for good single items have been discussed in an earlier section; in addition, questionnaires employed as psychological tests should satisfy the usual criteria of reliability and validity. If they are carefully constructed and item-analyzed, adequate reliability should be assured. Validity, however, whether of attitude or of personality questionnaires, is difficult to evaluate, since there will typically be no simple real-life criterion with which to compare the test score. The evaluator is therefore more dependent on construct validity and on a network of indirect inferences. As stated, many questionnaires in this area are valuable exploratory instruments, but their validity should never be taken for granted, least of all by non-psychologists. (See *Objective tests.*)

Bibliography: Eysenck, H. J. & Eysenck, S. B. G.: Personality structure and measurement. London, 1969. **Jahoda, M., Cook, S. W. & Deutsch, M.:** Research methods in social relations. New York, 1951. **Moser, C. A.:** Survey methods in social investigation. London, 1958. **Stouffer, S. A.:** Measurement and prediction. Princeton, 1950. **Thurstone, L. L. & Chave, E. J.:** The measurement of attitude. Chicago, 1929.

H. J. Butcher

Quotidian cycle. In order to give a clear picture of how individual behavioral items are distributed and change during the first year of life, Bühler (1967) introduced the "quotidian cycle". In a cycle corresponding to the twenty-four-hour day, individual forms of behavior, such as sleep, feeding, state of semi-consciousness and wakefulness, are divided into sectors according to the percentage of time they occupy. Such cycles show that sleep, which at birth takes up more than three-quarters of the total cycle, has by the end of the first year fallen to barely one half, reflecting the increasing alertness of the young infant.

Bibliography: Bühler, C.: Kindheit und Jugend. Göttingen, 1967.

M.Sa.

R

Race. A group of individuals of a species who, while they are distinguished from one another by individual hereditary characteristics (e.g. skin color), can nevertheless produce fertile young. For a long time the significance of race for human psychology has been exaggerated, partly for ideological reasons (anti-Semitism, q.v., in Europe, prejudice, q.v., against negroes in the USA). In the opinion of many modern anthropologists, typical racial characteristics can be shown to exist only in the field of physical anthropology, while in psychological matters the genetically determined "racial traits" can scarcely be distinguished from cultural influences. This seems to confirm the complete assimilation of a new culture in a few generations (for instance by American immigrants). See *Abilities; Differential psychology.* *W.Sch.*

Radiatio optica. L.-P. Gratiolet (1958) described this part of the optic tract (q.v.) of which it constitutes the fourth neurone, passing from the *corpus geniculatum laterale* to the *area striata* of the occipital lobe, which represents primary cortical field V1. *K.H.P.*

Radio. One of the mass media of communication (q.v.), important for the direct transmission of the latest information. Although it is now much less used owing to the competition of audio-visual media (especially where light entertainment is concerned), radio retains its pre-eminence for "live" broadcasts, news, and "background" music. Given equal conditions, information communicated by radio makes less impact and is remembered less well than where communication is personal and audio-visual, but it is more effective than purely visual communication (e.g. by the printed word). *A.D.S.*

Ragoni-Scina contrast. Two black squares, each on white backgrounds, are viewed simultaneously one through a sheet of colored glass and the other by reflection from the surface of the same sheet. This is by having the squares in planes at right-angles to each other and the glass in between them at 45 degrees to each. The square viewed by reflection appears the same colour as the glass sheet while the square viewed through the sheet appears in its complementary color. *C.D.F.*

Randomizer. A device used in electronic data processing to produce random numbers and simulate stochastic processes. *F.M.*

Random sample. A random sample occurs when every element of the population has an equal chance of being included in the sample. *H.-J.S.*

Range. The interval between the highest and the lowest observed value in a sample. As the size of the sample increases, it supplies less and less information about the details of the range. Lord tests (q.v.) use range instead of standard deviation. *A.R.*

Rank order. A quantitative classification of a continuous variable the interval magnitudes of which are unlike or unknown. Rank orders are used with variables which vary with respect to their degree of distinctness but for the measurement of which there are no exact methods, so that only "greater or smaller" judgments are possible. *G.Mi.*

Rank-order correlation. A non-parametric correlational technique the use of which postulates ordinal variables (q.v.). Rank-order correlations were developed by Spearman and Kendall. (See *Correlational techniques.*) *G.Mi.*

Rapport. A (verbal) relationship existing in the state of restricted consciousness between the hypnotist and the hypnotized individual; it represents a particular kind of inward dependence and a willingness to carry out any suggestions (q.v.) which may have been made. See *Hypnosis.* *H.N.G.*

Rate tests. Techniques for determining empirically the subjective information (q.v.) of news by finding the expectancy probability of the signs (news elements). In a Shannon rate test, a test is predicted sign by sign and replaced by the sequence of the rate tests necessary for each sign, and from it an upper and lower limit for the subjective information can be derived. By using branching models to fix the prediction strategy, Weltner (1970) has extended and defined arbitrary sign repertoires and also indicated important simplified methods for practical use. F. Attneave has applied rate tests to pictures and graphic representations.

Bibliography: Weltner, K.: Informationstheorie und Erziehungswissenschaft. Schnelle, Quickborn, 1970.

H.F.

Rating. 1. A term for a subjective assessment made on an established scale. It enables rough information to be obtained about the degree to which continuous characteristics exist for the comprehension of which no exact methods are available. Ratings are the bases of direct scaling methods. Data obtained by ratings have the character of ordinal scales (q.v.) but can be converted by suitable scaling techniques into scales with higher values. See *Scaling.* *G.Mi.*

2. The result of a statistical rating technique. *A.R.*

Rating scale. A multi-stage scale on which degrees of a characteristic are arranged subjectively by a rater. Such scales usually have five, six or seven stages which can be formulated verbally or shown by numbers; they are used, for example, in Q sorting (q.v.) and polarity profiles (q.v.). They have the standard of ordinal scales (q.v.) and form the starting point for direct scaling techniques (see *Successive intervals*) by means of which they can be converted into scales with higher values. See *Scaling.* *A.R.*

Rating techniques. Methods for rating parameters on the basis of statistics calculated from samples (q.v.). The best known rating techniques of mathematical statistics are the maximum likelihood and the minimum chi-square methods. The former, using normally distributed scores, leads on to the method of smallest squares. *A.R.*

Rationalism. In general this term designates those systems which, being grounded in reason, hold to its primacy over faith, feeling (sentiment) or experience, and conceive understanding as the establishment of coherent and necessary connections. More specifically, in regard to the value of knowledge, rationalism postulates the intelligibility of everything (everything has its "*raison d'être*" or "reason for being"), or the capacity of human intelligence to know the truth because the laws of being are not distinct from the laws of thought. In regard to the origin of knowledge, the term denotes the existence of systematic and normative (forms of) knowledge *within* the (absolute or human) mind (spirit). In the theory of voluntary behavior, rationalism is opposed to any irrational impulsion of the will. *M.-J.B.*

Rationalization. 1. The process of interpreting the reasons why certain events took place. In psychoanalysis (q.v.): a defense (q.v.) mechanism in which apparent reasons tolerated by the superego take the place of real reasons which are not admitted.

2. The process of systematic improvement of business structures. In economics and in industrial psychology (q.v.): the optimization of the relation between performance and necessary expenditure. Essential measures in rationalization are *specialization* (reducing the range of work by the division of labor), standardization (establishing norms for work processes), and mechanization or automation (the transfer of human functions to substitute technical devices). Special problems of industrial psychology arise from changes in work requirements due to rationalization (more attention must be given to construction, servicing, controlling and supervising), and in consequence a special study must be made of educational programs and stress factors (increase of psychic as compared with physical stress). *J.N.*

Ratio scale. A ratio scale represents the most complete form of metric classification. As in the interval scale (q.v.), its units of measurement are constant; it has an absolute zero point, at which the measured variable is in fact zero. Therefore statements such as "A is twice as big as B" are also possible. A weighing scale is a ratio scale. *G.Mi.*

Rauwolfia alkaloids. Alkaloids (numbering about a hundred) deriving from the plant *Rauwolfia Serpentina*, indigenous to India and used for centuries as a folk medicine (see *Reserpine*). Since the isolation in 1952 of reserpine as a psychotropic drug with emotional and motor inhibitory effects, hydrogen-oxygen compounds from these alkaloids have formed a chemical subdivision of neuroleptics (q.v.). Neurochemically, the reserpine-type alkaloids increase central storage capacity (mainly indicated in the area of the hypothalamus, q.v.) for noradrenaline (q.v.) (also for noradrenaline in the peripheral sympathetic nerves) and serotonin. In higher doses, rauwolfia alkaloids induce extrapyramidal arousal (pseudo-Parkinson effect: see *Parkinson's disease*), and a considerable drop in blood pressure (hence they are used as antihypertonics), but not narcosis. Action commences slowly and is long-lasting (up to twenty hours).

Bibliography: Schlittler, E. & Plummer, A. J.: Tranquilizing drugs from rauwolfia. In **Gordon, M.** (Ed.): Psychopharmacological agents. Vol. 1. New York, 1964. *G.D.*

Raw scores. Quantitative values which originally obtained in a measurement and not converted algebraically. The magnitude of the statistical values of raw scores is determined by these alone and is not subject to any external convention, as is the case, e.g., with standard scores. *G.Mi.*

R correlation. In the R technique of factor analysis (q.v.) an intercorrelation matrix is factorized whose coefficients have been calculated by correlation of m characteristics to n individuals where n is greater than m. It represents the most general kind of correlation or factor-analytic technique, and is reciprocal to Q technique in so far as its factor matrix corresponds to the factorial value matrix of the Q technique. The factors extracted by the use of an R correlation are interpreted as *characteristic factors.* *G.Mi.*

Reaction formation. An internal defense mechanism in which a no longer gratifiable motive (or one gratifiable only under threat of punishment) is replaced by a motive at the other end of the existing continuum. Primitive manipulation wishes (e.g. daubing) no longer satisfiable as formerly are released through violent desire for contact (which occurs much more often because of its minimal satisfaction value), prodigality through thrift, obscenity through extreme politeness, disappointed love through malevolent pursuit of the beloved. Characteristics of reaction formation are the lack of ordinary, average forms of motive satisfaction and the inability to take advantage of the many possibilities of satisfaction as circumstances change, except by rigid adherence to extreme forms of gratification. *W.T.*

Reaction time. The amount of time taken by a subject in responding to a stimulus. In the classical experiment, the subject makes a predetermined response (usually lifting his finger off a telegraph key) as quickly as possible upon receiving a pre-arranged signal (e.g. the onset of a light). The interval between stimulus and response is measured by some kind of chronometer, today usually an electronic timer.

Simple reaction time involves only one stimulus and one prescribed response. Of the various forms of *complex reaction time*, *discrimination R.T.* involves alternative stimuli, response being made to some of them but not others, and *choice R.T.* refers to a situation of alternative responses as well as stimuli. Subjects may be classified in terms of *reaction types* depending upon the characteristic direction of their attention; the *motor type* concentrates on the response that is to be made, giving faster R.T.s, but a greater number of false reactions, whereas the *sensory type* is set to appraise the stimulus. An important variable in determining the speed of R.T. is the *preparatory interval,* i.e. the amount of time elapsing between warning the subject to be ready and the actual occurrence of the stimulus.

An early application of the reaction time experiment was in the rough calculation of the speed of nerve transmission by estimating the total distance that the message and command would have to travel between receptors and muscles. The early hypothesis that R.T. might constitute a very fundamental measure of intelligence has not been supported, and it is even doubtful that laboratory-measured R.T. has any validity in predicting adaptive responses in real-life situations, e.g. stopping an automobile in an emergency. *G.D.W.*

Reaction timers. Instruments for testing the behavioral reactions of the subject to a given stimulus. There are very many reaction timers with the help of which the time between stimulus and response in the case of simple reactions, and choice and simple reaction can be measured. The reaction timer developed by Mierke (also known as the "*Kieler determination instrument*") and, similar to this, the "*Vienna determination instrument*" are used to ascertain time-related reaction capacities. The task of the subject consists in responding with a specific reaction inside a fixed length of time to a variable number of optimal stimuli (for example different colored stimuli, or stimuli consisting of different geometric patterns) and acoustic stimuli (higher and deeper sound). The number of signals given and the speed of the signal sequence can be varied in this way. The number of correct responses within a test series serves as a criterion of capacity. In traffic psychology (q.v.), industrial psychology (q.v.) and psychopharmacology (q.v.), reaction timers or determination instruments are used to establish certainty and exactitude in the performance of multiple reaction, in the level and load capacity of individual efficiency, in individual behavior under risk and stress circumstances, and all the psychological factors of work behavior, e.g., fatigue, distraction, attention, etc.

Bibliography: Mierke, K.: Wille und Leistung. Göttingen, 1955. **Müller, A. & Uslar, D. von:** Ergebnisse mit dem Determinationsgerät nach Mierke bei Fahrtauglichkeitsuntersuchungen. Diagnostica, 1963, **9**, 156–70.

A. Thomas

Reaction types. Traits relating to speed, strength, fluidity, economy, harmony, etc. of reaction (e.g. Ewald types: see *Biotonns*). The concept of reaction types is also related to mental processes: hysterical (q.v.), primitive (q.v.), sensitive (q.v.), anancastic (q.v.), etc.

W.K.

Reactive inhibition. The tendency (postulated by Hull in 1943 in his hypothetico-deductive theory of learning, q.v.) of every reaction to engender in the organism a (fatigue-like) state opposed to the recurrence of that reaction. Reactive inhibition is defined as a negative impulse; i.e. its reduction (through the conclusion of existing activity) has an intensifying effect and can become part of the foundation of the learning process (see *Conditioned inhibition*).

Bibliography: Hull, C. L.: Principles of behavior. New York, 1943.

L.B.

Readiness. A physiological condition, also variously defined as "tendency", "urge", "impulse", as a result of which certain actions are carried out in preference to all others. The causes, as yet scarcely analyzed, lie in the activity of certain brain structures, in concentrations of hormones and transmitter substances, etc. (See *Action-specific energy.*) Readiness is subject to hypertrophy and atrophy. It is rare for an instinctive action to be motivated by only one manifestation of readiness; the motivation is for the most part multiple. See *Arousal; Drive; Instinct; Vigilance.*

Bibliography: Hinde, R. A.: Animal behavior. A synthesis of ethology and comparative psychology. New York & London, [2]1970.

K.Fi.

Reading is the optical (in the case of Braille, tactile) perception of written symbols and their arrangement as specific meaningful content. Reading disorders consist of an inability to apprehend signs as configurations and/or inadequate association of signs and meaningful contents. Methods of learning how to read are usually either *synthetic* (based on the letters) or *analytic* (based on whole words, sentences, or meaningful wholes). Tinker (1965) summarizes research into the psychological factors fundamental to proficient reading, including the *appearance* of the reading material (type, light, color, etc.).

Bibliography: Carter, H. L. J. & McGinnis, D. J.: Diagnosis and treatment of the disabled reader. New York & London, 1970. **Deboer, J. J. & Dallman, M.:** The teaching of reading. New York & London, [3]1970. **Dechant, E.:** Diagnosis and remediation of reading disability. New York & London, 1969. **Roswell, F. G. & Natchez, G.:** Reading disability: diagnosis and treatment. New York & London, [2]1971. **Smith, F.:** Understanding reading. A psycholinguistic analysis of reading and learning to read. New York & London, 1971. **Tinker, M. A.:** Bases for effective reading. Minneapolis, 1965.

H.Sch.

Reafference principle. Overall connection system of the organism which at every level of efferent synaptic information processing collates the issue of instructions and their execution, and in the case of a discrepancy makes possible a retransmission for correction at the higher centers. As orders (the results of action potential) go out from a superordinate central nervous center (for example the pyramidal pathways) by way of synapses to an effector (e.g. a muscle), a temporarily delayed stimulus (efference engram) is detached from the efferent signal sequence at the connection point and collated with the retransmission concerning the execution of orders by the effector (*reafference*). When the efference engram and reafference disagree, a message (*exafference*) is sent back to the superordinate centers and corrects the original efference. At the most the retransmissions can ascend partly as far as the central nervous system and there cause a *conscious correction-decision.* A clear example of the reafference principle is eye movement and the coordination of the eye-hand system.

Bibliography: Holst, E.v. & Mittelstaedt, H.: Das Reafferenzprinzip. Naturwiss., 1950, 37, 256–72.

M.S.

Real anxiety (syn. *Actual anxiety*). Freud (q.v.) distinguishes real from neurotic *anxiety* (q.v.). The neurotic variety derives from inner releasers, whereas the "real" kind is the product of external phenomena. According to Freud, civilized man has to be educated to a condition of real anxiety. No child exhibits it initially. He sees children's real anxiety in the face of parental punishment as a predecessor of the later anxiety of *conscience* (q.v.). Real anxiety as an isolated phenomenon is problematical in view of the differential probability and intensity of avoidance reactions to similar objects or situations offered on diverse occasions by different individuals. *U.H.S.*

Reality, denial of. Ignoring the relevance of essential part-aspects of one's own physical, psychic and/or social environment; effectively similar to repression and isolation. Examples: a soldier under fire who suddenly behaves as if he were on a dance floor, or a political detainee who makes light of his captor's threats. Denial of reality often occurs in psychoses, especially in mania (q.v.), depression (q.v.), and schizophrenia (q.v.). *W.T.*

Realization (Ger. *Realisierung*). A scientific method founded by O. Külpe. The real is recognized as, or postulated as, true. Perception (q.v.) is enunciated as a basic principle of experience. Thought mediates the structures and laws of that which is perceived. See *Würzburg school.* *H.W.*

Reality. The world independent of consciousness. In the broader sense the term also embraces the *experienced world;* as subjective reality it is contrasted with objective reality. The term often serves to distinguish certain parts of the experienced world from others: e.g. the indirectly encountered from the merely visualized. *P.T.*

Reality principle. According to Freud (q.v.), opposed to the pleasure principle (q.v.). It controls the secondary psychological processes. Under its influence (and through experience and learning; according to Freud, through object cathexis and object anticathexis), the primary processes are modified and made adaptable. While the primary psychological processes are attributed to the *id* (q.v.), the secondary processes belong, according to Freud, to the *ego* (q.v.). In waking life these latter rule over dream and sleep conditions, in adult life over childhood, in a refreshed condition over fatigue, in a state of health over conditions of mental illness. The development of the individual may be defined as a continuous transition to an ever higher share of the secondary processes in the whole life of the mind and to a growing dominance of the reality principle over the pleasure principle. *W.T.*

Reason (Lat. *ratio;* Fre. *raison;* Ger. *Vernunft*). **1.** A philosophical term, synonymous with understanding (q.v.), or insight. It denotes intellectual ability as a whole in contrast to sensory capacity. In psychology, "reason" is often opposed to intuition (q.v.), instinct (q.v.) or emotion (q.v.). **2.** The power to proceed from premisses to consequences. **3.** Clarity of mind, of thinking. **4.** A cause, ground or principle; an efficient cause; a final cause. **5.** (Kant) That mental faculty which transcends conditions of possible experience, and not including understanding (*Verstand*) or sensibility (sense experience).

H.J.A. & J.M.

Receptors. In earlier literature on the subject the term "receptors" often has the same meaning as organs of the brain or parts of the brain's organs. Receptors were postulated in regard to different parts of the brain (i.e. organs for the perception of stimuli which could be invested with certain subjective qualities). In the physiology of the brain, especially "objective" physiology, the concept of "receptor" is understood broadly as to extent and narrowly in respect of capacity. A sensory organ, i.e. an organ perceptive of signals or stimuli, is also called a receptor when no phenomenal (perceptive) experiences result from its activity (see Hensel, 1966). Pavlov described receptors as the analyzers of *primary* signal systems, and defined these as points of contact between the environment and mental activity. In the general use of the term, the influence of cybernetic and communications models is increasingly influential. In this view, the receptor is less an organ, or part of an organ, and more a biological, cybernetic (or biocybernetic) function.

As a rule, however, such receptor functions clearly also correspond to specialized organs (see *Psychophysics*). The receptor is an information transformer: a function of transformation, which transforms a signal, a stimulus or physically measurable event into a specific stimulus for the nervous system, or is in a position to transform the former into the latter.

The receptors may be classified as follows: (*a*) *exteroceptors:* information transformers for exterior stimuli. (*b*) *interoceptors:* information transformers for interior stimuli as, for example, *proprioceptors* for stress conditions, changes of muscle tension, sinew tension, changes of position and arrangement of joints; *visceroceptors* which transfer signals through inner organs, such as blood vessels, the heart, etc. Much more difficult and at the same time more problematic is the coordination of specific receptors with qualities of experience (e.g., in the case of skin receptors).

Bibliography: Hensel, H.: Allgemeine Sinnesphysiologie: Hautsinne. Geschmack, Geruch. Berlin & New York, 1966. **Field, J., Magoun, H. W. & Hall, V. E.** (Eds.): Handbook of Physiology. Vol. 1: Neurophysiology. Baltimore, 1959. *A.Ha.*

Recessive. Those features are recessive which cannot be distinctly marked as heterozygous since they are suppressed by dominant genes (q.v.). Many hereditary diseases are recessive: e.g. albinism, diseases of the blood, and sickle-cell anemia. They first become manifest when they appear as homozygous. *K.Fi.*

Recidivism. The repetition of an offense by someone already punished for it. Criminal psychology (q.v.) investigates the conditions for recidivism. See *Criminality; Punishment.*

Bibliography: Glueck, S. & E. T.: Ventures in criminology. London, 1964.

Reciprocal innervation (Sherrington). Involuntary stimulation of the motor neurons of a spinal segment activates the muscular agents and inhibits their antagonists in the innervated extremity: contraction of the flexor muscles with simultaneous repose of the extensor, and *vice versa*. *K.-H.P.*

Reciprocal inhibition. Wolpe (1958) developed the theory and psychotherapeutic method of reciprocal inhibition (which accords with Sherrington's neurophysiological concept of mutual inhibition, q.v., of reflexes, 1906) as a possibility of forgetting inadequate modes of behavior. At the moment of appearance of a desired reaction, another reaction is caused which is basically incompatible with the desired mode of behavior (e.g. relaxation with reaction to anxiety), and therefore checks it. With frequent association, the reaction to be eliminated will be increasingly weakened and finally disappear. The method has been mainly applied during recent years in the psychotherapy (q.v.) of phobias (q.v.), but also in the treatment of many other behavioral disturbances. (See *Aversion therapy; Behavior therapy.*)

Bibliography: Sherrington, C. S.: Integrative action of the nervous system. New Haven, 1906. **Wolpe, J.:** Psychotherapy by reciprocal inhibition. Stanford, 1958. *L.B.*

Recognition. The ability to judge a datum according to whether it is identical with one perceived on an earlier occasion. It might be said to require less effort than remembering proper. See *Memory; Reminiscence.*

Recollection, part(ial). A memory image which offers only part of the event remembered, and whose full significance cannot be immediately recognized. Recollections from early childhood are mostly partial in character. They are isolated, but when the event is reconstructed (possibly by "psychoanalyzing" what a person knows or thinks), the connection with that person's relevant interests can often be recognized. In a certain sense, contemporary (and perhaps all) recollections are really partial. The significant aspect can usually be made more easily conscious than is the case when the recollection is very early or, if later, very isolated. In general, reminiscences represent the beginning, the end, or the resumption of an interrupted series of events. See *Memory; Reminiscence.*

Bibliography: Adler, A.: Erste Kindheitserinnerungen. Internat. Z.f. Individual-Psychol., 1933, **11. Freud, S.:** Introductory lectures on psycho-analysis. London, [2]1929. **Toman, W.:** Das Erinnerungsbild und seine motivationstheoretische Bedeutung. Z.f.exp. und angew. Psychol., 1963, **10,** 125–39. *W.T.*

Reconstruction method. A memory research technique to test how well structures are remembered. Items previously learned in a certain sequence are given to the testee as a disordered series; he is required to restore them to the original sequence. The number of correct ascriptions is a measure of the memory performance. *E.H.*

Recreation. Leisure activity engaged in for its own sake. Refreshment, relaxation, pastime, sport, holiday, amusement. To indulge in these activities is said to *recreate* one (as in popular usage. (See *Vacation.*)

Recreational therapy (J. E. Davis): Recreation "prescribed by a medical authority as an adjuvant in treatment" (includes drama, music, dancing, painting, excursions, discussion groups, athletic games, and so on). *G.D.W.*

Rectangular distribution. A distribution in which (*a*) the density for a defined sphere of a continuous characteristic is uniform, and (*b*) the values of the function (e.g. frequencies) are uniform for a defined number of classes of a discrete variable. E.g. every distribution transformed according to a percentile rank scale is a rectangular distribution. *W.H.B.*

Rectangular frequency polygon. A graphic representation of rectangular frequencies. Rectangular frequencies are incorporated in intervals since it is assumed that observations are distributed equally over an interval. *A.R.*

Red-green blindness. Color blindness in which red and green are confused; usually associated with protanopia (q.v.) but less frequently with deuteranopia (q.v.). *K.H.P.*

Redirection activity. An ethological concept referring to behavior elicited by two different stimulus situations but directed toward only one. For instance, some male birds will defend their territory against intruders only after they have acquired a mate. Hence two conditions are necessary to evoke this aggressive behavior: the intrusion of a rival, and the presence of a mate, although the behavior is directed only toward the rival. *G.D.W.*

Reductionism. The term denotes a viewpoint which, in the sciences or in philosophy, accounts for the superior by means of the inferior, or postulates a causal link between levels of reality which, in their very specificity, ought to depend only on the mode of explanation proper to them. That type of materialism which reduces mind to matter is a form of reductionism, as are the empiricism and psychologism which would reduce problems of validity to questions of fact. The same is true of those theories which try to account for mental phenomena in terms of biological control systems, or physico-chemical mechanisms (reflexes); or of those which see human societies as extensions of the "natural state" of animal societies, or which explain the diversity of the same as derived from conditions of the physical environment. *M.-J.B.*

Redundancy. A term from information theory which describes quantitively the possible abbreviation of a sequence of symbols when using an optimal coding, and of the same repertoire of symbols. The redundancy of a code allows transmission of information to take place without disturbance. Without redundancy, an error in the transmission of code elements always leads to the coding of another symbol and consequently cannot be discovered. Redundancy can be used to discover, locate and even correct errors. The redundancy of human speech, which is relatively secure against disturbance, stands at 0.7–0.8. The disadvantage of redundancy in the discovery and correction of errors is that the length of the code words increases with the degree of redundancy and safety from disturbance. *P.-B.H.*

Reference, association of. See *Association, laws of.*

Reference group. See *Group.*

Referral and reports. Only those expressions of opinion which satisfy the following conditions usually come under the heading of psychological reports: (*a*) the judgments are made after intensive preliminary studies; (*b*) the preliminary studies make use of the most recent findings of psychological research in the field of the report, and of empirical studies specially made to support the judgments; (*c*) the judgments should furnish an answer to an actual question.

The questions asked in a psychological report can relate to individuals and to their environment; hence a distinction is made between individual diagnostic reports and those dealing with the environment.

1. *Individual diagnostic reports.* In almost all fields of applied psychology (q.v.), psychologists are concerned with the diagnostic

judgment of people, either in vocational selection, school counseling, educational guidance (q.v.), clinical psychology (q.v.), military psychology (q.v.), forensic psychology (q.v.) (e.g. law relating to guardians and children, determining legal maturity and responsibility, judging the credibility, q.v., of witnesses), and traffic psychology (q.v.).

According to the specific purpose the psychologist has in mind, Heiss (1964) distinguishes three forms of report: (*a*) a report as a *representation* and picture of a personality; (*b*) a report as expressing an attitude and a judgment; (*c*) a report giving advice. A description of the personality as an aim in itself is, in practice, rare. The report expressing attitude and judgment demands from the psychologist that he should compare the findings on some individual with a more or less *clearly defined standard value*, e.g. in the case of a report on juvenile responsibility with a developmental norm; hence it comes about that many reports expressing some attitude make an interindividual comparison.

The counseling report (e.g. dealing with school, education, life, marriage) has a strong individual reference. It is not oriented toward an objective norm independent of the individual concerned, but deals with the individual himself, with *intraindividual* matters. It must take into account all those factors in the environment and personal relationships which can be seen to have caused a behavior, to be influencing the course it is taking, and whose influence is expected to continue. Such reports give some individual advice which ought to include predictions (q.v.) about constancy and change of behavior as time and situation vary.

Of the three purpose-based forms of applied diagnostics according to Cronbach (1964) "selection" is a case of the report expressing an attitude and a judgment, "deciding on suitable therapy" a case of advice giving; the third form, according to Cronbach (namely, diagnostics as "classification"), can precede both the expression of an attitude and a decision about treatment.

In practice, the different purpose-based forms do not occur independently but together. However, according to the case, one or the other purpose will be more prominent. There are also always special problems which basic psychological research has not yet been able to solve satisfactorily, and which go beyond purely diagnostic psychology. The necessity for empirically devised personality criteria for selection and classification, for statements of job requirements, for vocational profiles and for factors concerning ability and credibility of witnesses is an urgent matter, because they would lead to more efficient diagnostic reporting. (See *Personality; Traits; Type.*)

The problem of the counseling report is the decision as to how the present diagnostic state of the person in question can be transformed into a future desirable state (the object of treatment). An explicit and detailed behavioral theory seems necessary from which a suitable form of treatment could be logically derived. The hypothetical constructions used by the diagnostician must allow description of changes in a person: e.g. attitude change (q.v.), clarified habits, ideas, roles, skills, etc. Hence the diagnostician needs a consistent, proficiently researched, experience-based theory dealing with all such processes of change in an individual.

Unfortunately, there is scarcely any guidance for practical psychological diagnosis. Two groups stand out among the diverse practical methods of procedure: *one is more inductive and the other more deductive*. Someone drawing up a report inductively bases all the detailed pronouncements on the traits and behavior of an individual exclusively (or at any rate largely) on individual diagnostic data which have been collected empirically. Where the method is more deductive, some findings are based on diagnostic observation (the starting point is thus inductive), but after that, further characteristics of the individual not noticed during the investigation are derived from relevant personality theories.

The method used in preparing the report depends very much on the writer's attitude to personality theory. There are various possible ways of observing behavior, but (according to Heiss, 1964) the report should deal with (*a*) the interpretation as a characteristic of the behavioral form observed during diagnosis, (*b*) the question of what conditioned the behavior, (*c*) a causal analysis of the behavior, (*d*) a genetic interpretation of the behavior, (*e*) summary consideration of the behavior. Another important standpoint is a record of the specific form of behavior that it is thought will appear under certain conditions. Seitz (1971) has attempted to produce as comprehensive a classification as possible based on personality theory.

A special problem of individual diagnostic reporting is the fact that so far diagnostic investigation methods are still hardly suitable for checking by a systematic comparison the manifestation of a characteristic where environmental conditions vary, or the same characteristic exists on different behavioral planes (see *Psychodiagnostics*). Hence diagnostic psychology needs to refine its existing psychological methods or construct new and more differentiated ones based on a comprehensive though precise personality theory. Of course, reports on an individual diagnosis can *never express more than probability*. The degree of probability the report possesses is determined by the reliability (q.v.) and the specific validity (q.v.) of the investigation techniques employed. The report should mention the degree of probability; no certainty should be falsely claimed for it.

2. *Reports on the individual's environment.* Environment here always refers to its *effect on* the individual. What is important is not the objective description and recording of the environment but its psychological relevance. If so far a comprehensive behavioral theory has been demanded as the basis for making an effective report, what is now required from this behavioral theory is that it should also embrace the complex interaction of the individual with his varied environment. The possible subjects of a psychological report on the environment could be arranged according to a classification of all the possible environmental factors, but this can only be one of emphasis. Sells (1963) mentions the following main aspects of the total stimulus situation, which are involved in behavioral variance, and whose action in forming behavior can therefore also be considered: (*a*) natural aspects of the environment (e.g. reports on the effect of weather, geographical, nutritional conditions on the behavior of individuals); (*b*) aspects of the environment due to man (e.g. reports on the influence of group membership, the influence of education, politics, art and literature on the formation of personality); (*c*) problems, situations and circumstances in which they occur (e.g. reports on accidents and their causes); (*d*) external reference characteristics of the individual (e.g. reports on the dependence of behavior on biologically defined factors such as age, sex; on socially defined factors such as family's importance, social status, etc.); (*e*) behavior of the individual in relation to others (e.g. reports on the effect of varying techniques of group leadership on the well-being of the individual in the group).

Such reports may be provided by private and public authorities (e.g. employers, school authorities, transport ministry). They serve partly to criticize conditions already in existence, especially where unsatisfactory (e.g. analysis of why accidents happen), but also afford a basis for a purposeful planning and shaping of the environment (e.g. design of traffic signs, development of new housing patterns).

The basic difficulties in this area of report compilation are the same as those found with individual diagnostic reports, especially the attempts to note and record general psychological facts and considerations without checking them sufficiently with regard to their applicability to any object of the report that is limited to certain conditions. Without this specific synchronization, a report loses its effectiveness. This depends also on the degree to which theoretical or empirical preliminary studies enable the writer to make judgments representing a decision rather than a measurement. Of course, certain decisions will never be possible in psychology, but there will be those with a higher or lower degree of probability and where the degree of probability can also be calculated; the difficulty will be greater where complex psychological considerations determine the attitude to be taken in the report. Since, in practice, recording and processing of data will usually be restricted for economic reasons, a complex process of judgment will remain a judgment of measurement to a certain degree (in relation to the clarity and validity of existing norms, theories, knowledge, etc., and to the methods used in drawing up the report).

Bibliography: Anastasi, A.: Psychological testing. New York, 1961. **Cronbach, L. J.:** Essentials of psychological testing. New York & London, [3]1971. **Hörmann, H.,** *et al.*: Symposion 111: Die Beziehungen zwischen psychologischer Diagnostik und Grundlagenforschung. In: **Merz, F.** (Ed.): Bericht uber den 25. Kongress der Deutschen Gesellschaft für Psychologie in Münster, 1966. Göttingen, 1967. **Heiss, R.:** Über den Begriff des Verhaltens und das Modell der Persönlichkeit in der diagnostischen Psychologie. In: **Heiss, R.** (Ed.): Handbuch der Psychologie, Vol. 6, Psychologische Diagnostik. Göttingen, 1964. **Johnson, D. E. & Vestermark, M. J.:** Barriers and hazards in counseling. New York & London, 1971. **Rapaport, D.** *et al.*: Diagnostic psychological testing. New York & London, [2]1971. **Sells, S. B.:** Dimensions of stimulus situations which account for behavior variance. In: **Sells, S. B.** (Ed.): Stimulus determinants of behavior. New York, 1963. **Tredgold, R. F. & Wolff H. H.:** U. C. H. notes on psychiatry. London, 1970.

W. Seitz

Reflective psychology. For Karl Bühler the various aspects of psychology were: psychology of experience, psychology of conduct, and psychology of works. The method of the first of these must be one of the modes of reflection, which gives access to that which is lived and elucidates the conditions of possibility. This approach is related to *Geisteswissenschaftliche Psychologie* (q.v.), phenomenology (q.v.) and existentialist psychology (q.v.). *P.M.*

Reflex. An involuntary automatic response to an environmental change acting as a stimulus to the organism. This response is mainly of a motor type, and manifests itself in a *reflex movement* of a muscle or limb. The nervous excitation runs along a well-defined track down the *reflex* arc whose entry is represented by the sensory receptor transmitting the stimulus from the environment into nervous arousal. By way of afferent centripetal nerves, the stimulus reaches the reflex center which, according to the kind of reflex, consists of a simple synapse or a complicated system of nerve cells containing many synapses and connective neurons. By way of efferent centrifugal fibers, the stimulus arrives at the organ. See *Conditioning, classical and operant*. *E.D.*

Reflex inhibition occurs with the activation of neurones which inhibit other nerve cells or gradually compensate their activity. See *Arousal; Inhibition.* *U.H.S.*

Refraction. The normal-sighted (emmetropic) individual possesses a refraction strength of 58 diopters, which result from the surface shape and refraction indices of the refractory media (see *Cornea; Aqueous humour; Lens; Vitreous humour*). With these 58 diopters and with a normal eyeball length of 24 millimeters, the eye is capable of forming on the retina (q.v.) a clear image of an object at more than 4 meters from the eye; rays of light from the object strike the eye (to all intents and purposes) parallel with the axis. Through accommodation (q.v.) by means of the lens, an eye can increase its refractive strength by 14 to 72 diopters. *R.R.*

Refractory phase. The *non-arousable period* of the activity phase of an excitable cell. It serves the replenishment of exhausted energy reserves and varies widely in duration according to the speed of the metabolism. While nerve and skeletal muscles are refractory for only a few milliseconds after stimulation commences, the heart muscle is refractory for the whole period of its action, and even *absolutely refractory* during its *contraction*, and *relatively* during repose. In this relative reflex the heart is excitable only by supranormally large stimuli, a circumstance which leads to extrasystoles. *E.D.*

Refractory period. According to Masters & Johnson (1966), an observable part of the resolution phase of the male sexual excitement cycle. The refractory period begins after ejaculation and ends with the decline of sexual excitement. It is characterized by the relaxation of the penis and diminished psychophysiological sexual arousability. In women, however, a new plateau phase is linked to the orgasmic phase throughout which, given adequate sexual stimulation, they are capable of further orgasms.

Bibliography: Masters, W. H. & Johnson, V. E.: Human sexual response. Boston, 1966. *J.F.*

Regio olactoria. An area in the region of the upper part of the nasal cavity in which the olfactory epithelium and olfactory cells are situated. The olfactory epithelium is surrounded by a static layer of air. Odors normally reach the regio olfactoria by diffusion of normal breath into this layer of air. If olfactory sensitivity is intensified, the air is moved about ("sniffing"). *R.R.*

Regression. 1. An inner defense (q.v.) mechanism which usually appears when others do not suffice to achieve and sustain renunciation of satisfaction necessitated by the real or psychologically induced environment. It consists in the return of the person to earlier phases of motive development. According to Freud (q.v.) and his disciples, mental disorders such as regression derive from earlier phases of mental or motive development, and sometimes those phases succeeded by traumatizations, though remedies could be found (substitution satisfaction), or those phases which directly preceded the traumatic phases. All states of extreme deprivation or frustration (q.v.) in which defense mechanisms are (even though not completely) established, represent states of temporary regression (Toman, 1954, 1968). Anxiety (q.v.) and aggression (q.v.) are to be interpreted for the course of their duration as states of regression. Also states of fatigue, of physical weakness caused by illness bring about regression states of motive satisfaction; after a long day's work, for example, one can sustain only the lighter type of conversation. Regression has been described by Freud and Kris (1952) as a part of the creative process. Scientists and artists have often adopted primitive attitudes towards new advances within their own professional fields. They temporarily abandon conventional and established ways of thinking to pursue unexpected ideas and summarily reject current notions. But after this regression (or incubation, q.v.) phase, those concerned rediscover the path to the full and complex reality of their sphere of activity. Regression as part of the creative process may be described as "regression in the service of the ego" (Kris, 1952). Regression also serves the ego (q.v.) as part of a psychopathological process. Indeed its consequences cannot easily be erased, and it affects the ego itself for a long period.

Bibliography: Freud, S.: The ego and the id. London, [2]1962. **Id.:** Introductory lectures on psychoanalysis. London, [2]1929. **Kris, E.:** Psychoanalytic explorations in art. New York, 1952. **Toman, W.:** Dynamik der Motive. Vienna & Frankfurt, 1954. **Id.:** Introduction to psychoanalytic theory of motivation. London & New York, 1960. *W. Toman*

2. *In statistics* regression represents the fact that the estimated or predicted standard values of a dependent variable are nearer the sample mean than the corresponding standard values of the independent variable. The term "regression" was introduced by Galton (q.v.) ("*law of filial regression*"). *G. Mikula*

Regression analysis. Statistical analysis of the functional dependence of an incidental variable on one or several independent variables. Regression analysis permits the prediction of the unknown values of dependent variables on the basis of knowledge of the corresponding values of independent variables. Both dependent and independent variables must be measured on an interval scale (q.v.). Simple and multiple regression are distinguished according to the number of independent variables, and linear and curvilinear (non-linear) regression according to the equation of the line of regression (q.v.). *G.Mi.*

Regression, atavistic. See *Atavistic regression.*

Regression coefficients are the two coefficients a and b of the regression line (q.v.), although the term is usually applied only to b. In the case of linear regression (q.v.), a represents the distance of the point of intersection of the straight line of regression with the ordinate from the origin of the coordinates, and b represents the rise of the straight line of regression. *G.Mi.*

Regression equation. The regression equation of the line of regression permits the prediction of the value of the dependent variables on the basis of an arbitrary (also unobserved intermediate) value of the independent variables. *G.Mi.*

Regression lines. In the case of simple *regression* (q.v.), those lines are regression lines which, according to the *method of least squares* (q.v.) are so disposed that the sum of deviations of the empirical values from it is minimal. In linear regression it is a straight line. The angle formed by both regression lines of a bivariate distribution designates the level of correlation existing between both variables. In a correlation $r = \pm 1$, both regression lines occur together. *G.Mi.*

Regulation. Setting, maintaining or changing the conditions of a system by external determination of the input values without feedback. Examples are the regulation of a computer (q.v.) by a program (q.v.), and regulation of learning by a film or broadcast lecture. See *Feedback system.* *K.-D.G.*

Rehabilitation. The prevention, removal or reduction of a physical, mental or social disability, development of remaining potentialities, and attempt to put a person into a position where he can dispose fully of his physical and mental faculties to achieve his own aims and contribute to the needs of society or (if this is not possible, or only with extreme discomfort) to live with whatever help is necessary. The following are associated with rehabilitation: recovery or substitution of the physical and mental faculties necessary to everyday life; balanced training for the particular handicap, (pre-) school and vocational education; acquisition and retention of a proper place of work, living quarters, car, etc.; foundation and continuation of satisfactory social contact; where necessary financial assistance and care. Rehabilitation is proposed when a person is disabled, i.e. in the case of an illness or injury which means a break in social life and necessitates the building of a new career or, in the case of congenital damage, a special way of life. Rehabilitation is the care of disabled in all respects and is therefore planned and carried out with the cooperation of all the appropriate specialists, certainly with a medical specialist, a psychologist and if possible a sociologist, along with others according to the circumstances of the case: a specialist in the training of handicapped people, a special schoolteacher, careers adviser, a social worker, an accountant, a technical teacher, an occupational therapist, a physiotherapist and a physical educationist. The practical tasks of the psychologist in rehabilitation are educational, vocational and marriage guidance, the removal of psychosocial factors that tend to hinder rehabilitation and that promote activation in the disabled, investigation of his social environment, individual and group discussion with the disabled and his dependents, other psychagogic procedures (see *Psychagogy*), behavior therapy (q.v.), and psychotherapy (q.v.), communication and companionship. The scientific psychology of rehabilitation inquires into the mental determinants of the success of rehabilitation and their interaction with physical and social factors. It is concerned with the creation of procedures for the diagnosis of these determinants, and for the prognosis and improvement of successful rehabilitation. Outstanding work is being done especially in the USA, yet there is a lack of integrated and comprehensive research.

H.D.L.

Reid's movement illusion. A kinesthetic illusion corresponding to the *horizontal-vertical illusion.* A person is asked to move a stick from left to right a certain distance and then through the same distance at right-angles. The former distance is underestimated in comparison to the latter. *C.D.F.*

Reincarnation. A form of survival (q.v.) in which the individual is supposed to recommence a new life cycle after death by being reborn. A rebirth. *J.B.*

Reinforcement may be viewed either as a procedure or as a process. As a procedure, reinforcement is an event which either naturally in the environment or artificially by experimental arrangement is contingent upon the occurrence of some specified response, and which then maintains the performance of that response. In this arrangement there is a two-way interaction between the individual and its environment. The response operates upon the environment, and the environment in turn supplies the reinforcement event which maintains the behavior. The resulting behavior is said to be operant, because it operates upon the environment, or instrumental, because it alone produces the reinforcing event. What kind of event will be reinforcing in a given instance may have to be determined. Here it may be easy to maintain some behavior in a dog or a small boy with a pat on the head, but difficult to get the same reinforcing effect in a rat or a grown man.

Procedurally, we may distinguish two kinds of reinforcers: positive reinforcers, e.g. food, are those whose presentation maintains behavior, whereas negative reinforcers, e.g. painful stimulation, are those whose removal has the same effect. The two kinds of reinforcers have other effects upon behavior, of course, which are quite different. Negative reinforcement should be, but often is not, carefully distinguished from punishment. The latter is, procedurally, making the onset of an aversive stimulus contingent upon some response, and, in terms of process, what weakens the response with this procedure.

Conceptually, at least, we may distinguish between primary and secondary (acquired, or conditioned) reinforcers, according to whether the reinforcing effect of an event requires no prior experience with it, or whether some prior learning is necessary. Food is said to be a primary reinforcer for the hungry rat, but some kind of experience in the situation, with deprivation, or with the particular food, may be necessary in this instance. Smiling is said to be an acquired reinforcer for humans, the acquisition supposedly being based upon the prior association of smiling with primary reinforcement, but it seems more likely that the reinforcing effect of a smile can be demonstrated in infants prior to any appropriate learning. The distinction between primary and secondary reinforcement may only have merit when a previously neutral stimulus is established as a reinforcer within the context of a particular experiment. Even in this case it is possible that the critical stimulus may have associative or informational effects in addition to, or instead of, a reinforcement effect. Experimental studies have left considerable uncertainty both as to how the secondary reinforcers are established, and as to how they function.

Some psychologists, most notably the followers of B. F. Skinner, argue that the well-known reinforcement principles used in maintaining behavior are now sufficiently well understood and sufficiently effective that little else need be considered in predicting and regulating behavior. The two main principles involved in reinforcement are (*a*) differential reinforcement, i.e. a routine for ensuring that reinforcement is given only when the desired response occurs in the presence of a particular stimulus configuration, and (*b*) a schedule of reinforcement, i.e. a routine for reinforcing the desired response only on certain occasions, such as every tenth time it occurs. Armed with these principles, a number of psychologists of Skinnerian persuasion have recently made dramatic inroads into the behavior problems presented by autism and retardation, speech defects, neurosis, and psychosis (Ullman & Krasner, 1965). Although reinforcement can be used to explain the acquisition of new responses, often the response in question is already in the individual's repertoire, but occurs inappropriately. Hence the emphasis in practice upon differential reinforcement, and upon maintaining an appropriate rate of response.

Other psychologists, while not denying the practical effectiveness of reinforcement in regulating behavior, consider its effect to be cognitive rather than directly on performance. The individual is said to know that his behavior produces reinforcement; and if the reinforcement is needed or desired, then the individual will perform the response to obtain it. Thus reinforcement can be viewed as a utilitarian reward for appropriate behavior.

Most psychologists assume that reinforcement is more than a procedure. They regard it as a process, something which happens in the individual's nervous system to make learning occur when a response is followed by reinforcement. It is said to be a mechanism which, somehow, connects a particular response to particular stimuli. Current accounts of reinforcement derive from Thorndike's (1911) law of effect, which states that a response will or will not be learned depending upon the pleasant or unpleasant effect of the response. There have been specific theories of the reinforcement process. The most famous theory is Hull's (1943) hypothesis that reinforcement is necessary and sufficient for the acquisition of instrumental behavior. Hull proposed, in addition, that reinforcement invariably involved drive reduction. Reinforcing events were those, like food, which reduced the individual's hunger drive, or termination of shock, which reduced the pain and fear drives. Hull's theory fails to explain many experimental findings, such as learning based upon saccharin (which is non-nutritive, and cannot reduce hunger), sexual excitation, exploration, or brain stimulation. Such evidence has led Miller (1963) and others to suggest that reinforcement may consist of a sudden increase in excitation (q.v.). Hope of finding the physiological basis of reinforcement followed Olds' (1961) work on the apparent reinforcing effect of electrical stimulation in certain parts of the septal area of the brain. This hope may ultimately be realized.

It may be noted that even the most thoroughgoing reinforcement theorists, for example, Hull and Skinner, admit that there are other mechanisms of learning which do not require reinforcement; classical or Pavlovian conditioning is one instance.

Bibliography: Hull, C. L.: Principles of behavior. New York, 1943. **Miller, N. E.:** Some reflections on the law of effect produce a new alternative to drive reduction. In: **Jones, M. R.** (Ed.): Nebraska symposium on motivation. Lincoln, 1963. **Olds, J.:** Hypothalamic substrates of reward. Physiol. Rev., 1962, *42*, 554–604. **Thorndike, E. L.:** Animal intelligence. New York, 1911. **Ullman, L. P. & Krasner, L.:** Case studies in behavior modification. New York, 1965.

R. C. Bolles

Rejection. (Social) rejection is a somewhat ambiguous term used sometimes in social psychology and personality study to characterize the negative pole of a continuum between rejection and acceptance (when the word "rejectance" is occasionally used for emphasis). M. Rokeach's studies of dogmatism see readiness to reject experiences, objects, individuals or groups (e.g. ethnic minorities) as a sign of a consciousness operating as a closed system (closed mind; closedness) as opposed to an open system (open mind; openness), the latter then being identical with acceptance. The term is also used to describe social relations within a family (E. H. Erikson), and a person's attitude to himself (self-rejection, A. H. Maslow). Repression (q.v.) is often invoked by analytic theorists to explain the phenomenon.

W.D.F.

Relation theory. The perception of a gestalt depends on the apprehension of relations rather than the component parts between which the relations occur. Thus a tune is recognized as the same in many different keys. See *Ganzheit; Structure.* *C.D.F.*

Relative frequencies. The class frequencies of a frequency distribution (q.v.) related to the full extent of the sample. Column (q.v.) or sector diagrams are used to show relative frequencies. *G.Mi.*

Relative frequency, cumulative. The summated relative frequencies of a distribution which are calculated by the successive addition of class frequencies of an entire random sample; these classes are the successive classes of a distribution. Cumulative relative frequency is used for determining the percentile rank of a value. *G.Mi.*

Relativity, principle of; relativism. The principle that any aspect of behavior or experience can only be understood within its context (background stimuli, antecedent conditions, etc.). *Gestalt theory* and *adaptation level theory* (H. Helson) in the areas of perception and psychophysics are examples of approaches which acknowledge the importance of relativity. The *Weber-Fechner law* has sometimes been referred to as the *principle of relativity*, although it is a very special case. *Cultural relativism:* the view that human behavior generally, and concepts such as *morality* and *deviance* in particular, are very much dependent upon the nature of the society in question. *G.D.W.*

Relaxants. Non-specific and inexact term for tension-reductive pharmaceuticals. See *Tranquilizers.*

Relaxation. In cybernetic terms, the return of a system to the normal state due to trophotropic adjustment after ergotropic actuation. The effect of relaxation pauses diminishes with the pause length with negative acceleration. To counter fatigue, especially in intensely fatiguing activities, several short pauses (to eliminate fatigue peaks, favourable motivation effect) are preferable to a greater number of long pauses (see *Fatigue*). *J.N.*

Relaxation therapy. 1. Psychotherapeutic methods the object of which is to reduce intrapsychic tensions and physical cramps. In addition to hypnosis (q.v.), treatment consists of the relaxation exercises of *autogenic training* (q.v.) as well as other (auto-) suggestive techniques. **2.** Physiotherapeutic methods are predominantly those designed to relax the muscles: e.g. active exercises or passive gymnastics for the sick.

Bibliography: Stokvis, B. & Wiesenhütter, E.: Der Mensch in der Entspannung. Lehrbuch autosuggestiver und übender Verfahren in der Psychotherapie und Psychosomatik. Stuttgart, [2]1963. *H.N.G.*

Releaser. J. von Uexküll (1909) was of the opinion that an animal's whole environment is stored in its brain as nerve models in the shape of simplified images. K. Lorenz (1935) regarded as an "innate releaser" the "receptor correlate", i.e. the ability to respond to a certain code combination. N. Tinbergen (1942) translated "innate releaser" as "innate releasing mechanism". By "releasing mechanism" (R.M.), Schleidt (1962) understands an agency which directly triggers off a certain response and can accomplish the following performances: selectivity for certain stimuli, integration of various stimuli, linkage of stimulus and response, dependence of moods, coupling of learning mechanisms. The innate releasing mechanism (IRM) has been selected by phylogenetic adaptation and is thus present at birth. An acquired releasing mechanism (ARM) is developed ontogenetically by the individual. An IRM modified by experience (IRME) is an IRM completed by habit and learning. If an experienced animal reacts to simple traps (q.v.), that is a case of IRM, if it reacts selectively, IRME suggests itself, and this probably is usually the case with vertebrates. A releasing mechanism as a neurosensory device has yet to be localized.

Bibliography: Schleidt, W.: Die historische Entwicklung der Begriffe "Angeborenes auslösendes Schema" und "Angeborener Auslösemechanismus". Zeitschrift für Tierpsychologie. 1962, *19*, 697–722. **Tembrock, G.:** Grundriss der Verhaltenswissenschaften. Grundbegriffe der modernen Biologie, Vol. 3. Stuttgart, 1968. **Tinbergen, N.:** The study of instinct. Oxford, [2]1971. *K. Fi.*

Releasing factors. Neurohormones (see *Hormones*) detected in the hypothalamus (q.v.); chemical polypeptides which contribute to the excretion of glandotropic hormones (q.v.). The chemical structures and function of RFs are not as yet wholly clear. They probably provoke the synthesis of glandotropic hormones.

Bibliography: Bajusz, E. & Jasmin, E. (Eds.): Major problems in neuroendocrinology. Basle, 1964. *W.J.*

Reliability. 1. In the measurement of variables, that part of the result derivable from systematic and non-erroneous effects. Total variance therefore consists of permissible (true) variance and erroneous variance. The term is used mainly in factor analysis (q.v.) and test construction. See *Test theory*. *H.-J.S.*

2. The accuracy with which a measurement technique measures a characteristic. Reliability is expressed by the relation between error variance (q.v.) and total variance of the measurement scores. Different aspects of reliability can be distinguished, and these are also shown in the methods used for determining reliability: (*a*) *the stability of a measurement technique;* this is determined by the test or test-repetition method; (*b*) *the parallel test reliability* which is determined on the basis of the correlation of the measurement results with two equivalent methods of measuring; (*c*) the *internal consistency* (q.v.) which is determined by the split-half method (q.v.) and consistency analysis (see *Kuder-Richardson* formula 20). (See *Test theory.*)

Bibliography: Guilford, J. P.: Psychometric methods. New York, 1954. *G.Mi.*

Religion, psychology of. I. 1. *Concept.* The psychology of religion investigates the psychological laws governing religious attitudes; its object is not the truth about the divine (theology), but the human reality in which belief in a divine revelation comes into being. According to its particular function, the psychology of religion may form part of the comparative study of religions, of the phenomenology of religion, of theology (theological anthropology, pastoral psychology), or generally of psychology in the context of the human sciences.

As *pastoral psychology*, the psychology of religion may be of service—though from a critical standpoint—to the church and religion in its pastoral ministry to society and individuals. The founders of modern pastoral psychology include A. T. Boisen, S. Hiltner, C. A. Wise, P. E. Johnson, O. Pfister and W. Gruehn.

2. *History.* Interest in psychology, and with it in the psychology of religion, originated in observation of and reflection on the self, which was the result of a growth in awareness of the complexity of consciousness (q.v.) and the consequent development of perception of the psychic as a separate element in human existence. Hence the psychology of religion is as old as the idea of the "soul" (q.v.).

An interest in the psychology of religion may be found in early Christian writing, in, e.g., Paul (Epistles, c. 49–56), Tertullian (*De anima*, c. 210–211), Gregory of Nyssa (*Dialogue with Macrina on the Soul and Resurrection*, c. 380) and Augustine (*Confessions*, c. 400). In particular, the mystics of various periods may be regarded as predecessors of the psychology of religion in the modern sense, although there was at first no sense of the psychology of religion as a study distinct from theology, and empirical and metaphysical statements are found side by side. This can be seen particularly in Luther, whose observations on the psychology of religion always have for him also a theological and anthropological significance: "*Sicut de Deo cogitas, sic ipse.*" A direct line leads from Luther to Kierkegaard (*Either–or*, 1843; *the Concept of Dread*, 1844) and *also* to, among others, Feuerbach (*the Essence of Christianity*, 1841; *The Essence of Religion*, 1851). Luther's fellow reformer, Melanchthon, also wrote "on the soul" (*De anima*, 1540). Relevant also are Pascal's *Pensées* (1670) and Schleiermacher's *Reden über die Religion* (1799). Nietzsche must also be included among the predecessors of the modern psychology of religion.

The psychology of religion as a separate discipline in the modern sense begins with the "race" psychology of W. Wundt (q.v.) (1832–1920). Wundt put forward the hypothesis of four stages in the development of religion (from the primitive stage, through totemism, to the cult of heroes and gods, and that of humanity). Related to the ethnologico-genetic approach are the theories on the history of religion of N. Söderblom (*Das Werden des Gottesglaubens*, 1915), F. Heiler (*Das Gebet*, 1918), R. Otto (*The Idea of the Holy*, 1917), T. Andrae (*Die letzten Dinge*, 1940), and others.

The USA produced an empirical and experimental psychology of religion, whose main representatives are G. S. Hall (1881), Starbuck (1903), G. A. Coe (*The Spiritual Life*, 1900; *The Psychology of Religion*, 1916), James (1902), E. S. Ames (*The Psychology of Religious Experience*, 1910) and J. H. Leuba (*A Psychological Study of Religion*, 1912). J. B. Pratt's *The Religious Consciousness*, like James's *Varieties*, is one of the classics of modern psychology of religion. In Europe, the experimental psychology of religion became known through the work of the Würzburg school (q.v.): O. Külpe, K. Bühler, K. Marbe, W. Stählin, K. Girgensohn, W. Gruehn. This school made especial use of questionnaires (q.v.) and interviews (q.v.), diaries and other autobiographical material; the objects of investigation were at first striking religious phenomena, such as conversion and mysticism, but later included more ordinary phenomena. Independent of the Würzburg school was the work of Durkheim (1912), Beth (1926ff), Dehn (1923), W. Frühauf and E. Eichele. Many investigations in the USA and in Europe have studied religion among children and young people. In this field a close connection can be seen between the psychology of religion and the psychology of *development* (q.v.): see the works of, among others, Piaget (q.v.) and Goldman (1964).

The contribution of depth psychology (q.v.) to the psychology of religion has generally received too little recognition. The work of Sigmund Freud (q.v.) and his school (Pfister, 1944, etc.), and the later works of Fromm (1965) and E. H. Erikson, are of great importance for the psychology of religion, as are the investigations of C. G. Jung (q.v.) and authors influenced by him (e.g. Schär, 1950; Rudin, 1960). The individual psychology (q.v.) developed by A. Adler (q.v.) has also influenced contemporary thinking in the psychology of religion (especially through the work of Künkel, 1957).

3. *Methods.* On the basic assumption that the phenomenon of religion in all its forms, collective, ethnological and individual, is something that can be empirically described and analyzed, any particular branch of research can call on all the modern methods of the human sciences. Due correlation and interdependence in this field of medical, sociological, ethnological, historical-genetic and psychological approaches are important. Only through cooperation between the whole range of anthropological methods is an adequate psychology of religion possible, just as the psychology of religion itself can only be properly understood as an aspect of or factor in the wider field of anthropology. Whether there are any methods specific to the psychology of religion may be doubted, although a psychology which takes account of the hermeneutical circle (W. Dilthey, E. Spranger) will be more suitable for the investigation of religion than an experimental psychology which isolates individual facts and phenomena; nevertheless, the value of the latter as an auxiliary discipline should not be underestimated. No less important than the concepts of depth psychology are the findings of social psychology (q.v.), especially group dynamics (q.v.), and of medicine. Efforts are being made to find out how the empirically accessible aspect of religion may be determined and changed by a person's social relationships, and to understand its psychosomatic role as both cause and effect of chemo-physiological and other processes (cf. the current problem of hallucinogenic drugs).

In the past, interest was concentrated on genetic problems. Investigations have been made into the origin of religion in human history (W. Wundt, q.v., S. Freud, q.v., historians of religion), and in the life of the individual, and especially of the child ("genetic" psychology of religion: H. Clavier, 1913; Goldman, 1964; Piaget, 1945); while it is true that all stages have to be taken into account, religious awareness in man nevertheless clearly shows age-specific characteristics in every stage of life. Investigations related to particular occupations (Dehn, 1923; Demal, 1953; Piechowski, 1927; Rudin, 1966; Rey, 1969, etc.), to particular denominations (the affinity of Catholicism with oral sexuality and of Protestantism with anal sexuality would be an interesting study), or to sex (Hainz, 1932, etc.) should all provide valuable information.

In this field, the psychology of religion must work closely with sociology (sociology of religion). Since the individual's religious attitude cannot be considered in isolation from his environment, representative results are more likely to be produced by social psychology and depth psychology than by the experimental (associative) methods of the Würzburg school. In this connection it should be remembered that in a pluralistic society very different stages of religious development may exist side by side, from primitive animism through the institutional forms of the so-called higher religions to an assertion of individual autonomy which regards itself as "beyond all religion"; from observance of taboos and magical attitudes, through a religious morality, to liberal outlooks among groups of some intellectual distinction. This means that at the same time and in the same society, or even within the same denomination, one may find every stage and form known to the history of religions. The same is true of "styles" in religion, the sensuousness of a thoroughly magical worship of images, and the bleak austerity of iconoclastic asceticism, pietism, liberalism, orthodoxy, etc. These are expressions of religious group norms (see also *Meditation*) which recur in all religions, and obviously correspond to some basic structures or human needs.

4. *Research.* One of the most important tasks of the psychology of religion is the criticism of religion. This may be regarded as a special case of the criticism of ideology, which in its turn may be regarded as a secularized criticism of religion. Today the psychology of religion must concern itself with the secular forms of human religious awareness, such as mass hysteria in politics, the manipulation of opinion and uncritical adulation of idols, unthinking acceptance of authority, all the forms of unconscious dependence, etc. Critical attention should also be devoted to the political use of religion, e.g. by means of the concept of "psychological defense" or by the exploitation of primitive stages of religious feeling, e.g. in courts (crucifix, oath), or in other circumstances in which obligations or restrictions are to be imposed. The psychology of religion might be said to have political responsibilities. The results of the historical psychology of religion are relevant here; this is concerned with investigating the psychological background of crusades, wars of religion, the persecution of witches, forced conversions, etc., but reveals structures which are still effective.

Among these structures are the role of religion as projection and wish-fulfilment and the rationalizing function of the—usually unconscious—interests of the corresponding theologies at various periods, in which individual and collective needs motivate the community. Other structures in this category are taboo (q.v.), prejudice (q.v.) and dogma, and all defense mechanisms, which are found in many forms in religions as means of overcoming anxiety (q.v.). This makes the basic phenomenon of fear an important object of research in the psychology of religion. In this connection one should also mention anthropological phenomena which occur in the context of religion, such as fanaticism, tolerance and intolerance, missionary activity, asceticism, monasticism, hedonism, forms of sublimation (Jesus the beloved, Marian mysticism, devotion to the saints), conversion (which as an object of research marked the beginning of the modern psychology of religion), voices and visions, castration (q.v.) and prostitution (q.v.) performed for religious motives, martyrdom and sadomasochism (q.v.), inspired dreams in sanctuaries, ecstasy, religious devotion to the sexual organs, ancestor-worship, etc. Tendencies to monistic or dualistic ways of thought may also be investigated by psychological techniques.

In connection with the phenomena of dogmatism and ideologically oriented security tendencies, the categories of law and gospel

(Paul, Luther) are of interest, as are individual dogmatic propositions and their background and content in relation to collective mythology (e.g. virgin birth, the Resurrection, the dogma of the Trinity). So also are changes in the meaning of dogmas and their function in the psychological system of individual believers, e.g. "great" theologians, whose lives cannot be viewed in isolation from their theology (and *vice versa*). Examples are the doctrine of justification in the context of Luther's life and its different function in the case of Melanchthon or Osiander, or in the case of the "orthodox" Lutherans of Karl Barth. Other topics are the categories of obedience and maturity, the role of women in Christian tradition (including the question of their eligibility for the ministry), the therapeutic function of confession and absolution for individuals and groups, the investigation by psychology of religion and comparative religious studies of the relation of the individual to the collective (and *vice versa*) in the categories of guilt, sin (separation), conscience, morality, and so on.

Finally apocalyptics—the relationship of which to the ideas of schizophrenics (see *Schizophrenia*) was pointed out in particular by Boisen (1936), is an important area of investigation for the psychology of religion, as is Christian and non-Christian eschatology, including the secularized forms of Marxism, and the meaning of goal projections and "real utopias" (E. Bloch, 1970) for individual life styles. The psychology of religion also investigates the way in which religious experiences are objectified—e.g. mythological and poetical statements, religious art, dogmas, messiahs, sacred texts, persons and objects, metaphysics or attempts to avoid it, and of course all ritual or cultic expressions of "religious" experience, sacred meals, washings, ceremonies, etc. Office-holders in religions also have to be studied, and the expectations associated with them by believers (father-figures: "Father" as a title for priests, obligatory wearing of beards, celibacy; archetypes (q.v.) and "representatives" of deities; religious communities of men and women ("brothers" and "sisters"); father- and mother-goddesses, religious groups as "families", etc.).

The psychology of religion also studies the function of animals and animal symbols. Lastly, it must also investigate the basic experience of the human search for meaning, which, like fear, is—in psychological terms—at the root of religious feeling. Nor can psychology of religion ignore the fact that all men have some sort of idea of transcendence, some sort of "faith", and that their health depends on the form of their religion, which is a particular way of coping with conflict (q.v.), and it must be aware of the influence which religions exercise on the relations between human groups, including whole nations (wars of religion, alliances, etc.). It is possible that certain dogmas which impose restrictions on aggression (q.v.), in fact have exactly the opposite effect to their apparent intention of establishing peace, but no conclusive evidence is yet available. This is another example of the political responsibilities of the psychology of religion.

5. *Future possibilities*. The psychology of religion is in its early stages as an independent scientific discipline and there is immense scope for development. Teaching posts in the subject are rare. In the form of analytical pastoral psychology with a critical attitude to the churches, the psychology of religion can make an important contribution to overcoming the churches' identity crises, and even those of religions, by revealing the unconscious roots of the crises and finding new methods of communication. The psychology of religion can help to stimulate freedom and creativity where authoritarianism and legalism, conservatism and dogmatism have restricted thought and feeling.

The psychology of religion may be able to offer the ecumenical movement a way of breaking down denominational barriers by increasing each denomination's awareness of its historical identity. A similar approach may also have an effect on the barriers between the higher religions, and even between religions at different stages of historical development. In this way, the psychology of religion will be at the service, not of a destructive positivistic critique of religion, but of a testing of spirits whose aim is human emancipation.

Bibliography: Archiv für Religions-psychologie founded by **W. Stählin,** 1914 ff. **Berggrav, E.:** Religionens terskel. 1924 (Ger. trans.: Der Durchbruch der Religion im menschlichen Seelenleben. 1929). **Berguer, G.:** Traité de la Psychologie de la Religion. Geneva, 1946. **Bernet, W.:** Inhalt und Grenzen der religiösen Erfahrung, 1955. **Beth, K.** (Ed.): Zeitschrift f. R., 1926 ff. **Birk, K.:** Sigmund Freud und die Religion. Münsterschwarzach, 1970. **Bloch, E.:** Philosophy of the future. New York, 1970. **Boisen, A. T.:** The exploration of the inner world. Chicago, 1936. **Id.:** Religion in crisis and custom. New York, 1955. **Id.:** Out of the depths. New York, 1960. **Canziani, W.:** Religion als empirische Wissenschaft. In: Der Psychologe, Vol. 2. (1959), 409–80. **Clark, W. H.:** The psychology of religion. New York, 1958. **Deconchy, J. P.:** Structure génétique de l'idée de Dieu chez des catholiques francais. Garçons et filles de 8 à 16 ans. Brussels, 1967. **Dehn, G.:** Die religiöse Gedankenwelt der Proletarierjugend. Leipzig, 1923. **Demal, W.:** Praktische Pastoralpsychologie. Vienna, [2]1953. **Durkheim, E.:** The elementary forms of the religious life. London, 1915. **Freud, S.:** Totem and taboo. London & New York, 1950. **Id.:** Moses and monotheism. London, 1939. **Fromm, E.:** Das Christus-Dogma und andere Essays. Munich, 1965. **Id.:** Psychoanalysis and religion. New York & London, 1950. **Girgensohn, K.:** Der seelische Aufbau des religiösen Erlebens. Gütersloh, 1921. **Glasenapp, H. von,** Die fünf grossen Religionen, 2 vols. Düsseldorf, [2]1954. **Goldman, R.:** Religious thinking from childhood to adolescence. London, 1964. **Grensted, L. W.:** The psychology of religion. 1952. **Griesl, G.:** Pastoralpsychologische Studien. Innsbruck, 1966. **Gronbaek, V.:** Religionspsykologi. Copenhagen, 1958. **Id.:** Seelsorge an alten Menschen. Göttingen, 1969. **Id.: Gruehn, W.:** Werterlebnis. Gütersloh, 1924. **Id.:** Religionspsychologie. Breslau, 1926. **Id.:** Die Frömmigkeit der Gegenwart. Münster, 1956. **Hainz, J.:** Das religiöse Erleben der weiblichen Jugend. Düsseldorf, 1932. **Harsch, H.:** Das Schuldproblem in Theologie und Tiefenpsychologie. Heidelberg, 1965. **Hellpach, W.:** Grundriss der Religionspsychologie. 1951. **Hermann, W.:** Zur Frage des religionspsychol. Experiments. In: Beiträge zur Förderung Christlicher Theologie, 1922, *26*, 5. **Hiltner, S.:** Religion and health. New York, 1943. **Hollweg, A.:** Theologie und Empirie. Stuttgart, 1971. **Hostie, R.:** C. G. Jung und die Religion. Freiburg, 1957. **Johnson, P. E.:** Psychology of religion. New York, 1945. **Jung, C. G.:** Psychology and religion: west and east. London & New York, 1951. **Keilbach, W.:** Die Problematik der Religionen. Paderborn, 1936. **Kietzig, O.:** Religiös, kirchlich, gläubig. Göttingen, 1934. **Kretschmer, W.:** Psychologische Weisheit der Bibel. München, 1955. **Künkel, F.:** Die Schöpfung geht weiter. Eine psychologische Auslegung des Matthäus-Evangelium. Evangeliums. 1957. **Langeveld, M. J.:** Das Kind und der Glaube. Braunschweig, 1959. **van der Leeuw, G.:** Phänomenologie der Religion. Tübingen, 1933. **Leitner, H.:** Psychologie jugendlicher Religiosität innerhalb des deutschen Methodismus. Munich, 1930. **McKenzie, J. G.:** Souls in the making. New York, 1929. **Meng, H. & Frued, E. L.** (Eds.): Psychoanalysis and faith: The letters of Sigmund Freud and Oskar Pfister. London, 1963. **Mensching, G.:** Die Religion. Stuttgart, 1959. **Müller-Freienfels, R.:** Psychologie der Religion, 2 Vols. 1920. **Oates, W. E.:** The religious dimensions of personality. New York, 1957. **Pfister, O.:** Das Christentum und die Angst. Zürich, 1944. **Piaget, J.:** La formation du symbole chez l'enfant. Neuchâtel & Paris, 1945. **Id.:** Le jugement et le raisonnement chez l'enfant. Neuchâtel & Paris, 1947. **Piechowski, P.:** Protestantischer Glaube. Berlin, 1927. **Pöll, W.:** Religionspsychologie. Münich, 1965. **Potempa, R.:** Persönlichkeit und Religiosität. 1958. **Pratt, J. B.:** The religious consciousness. New York, 1920. **Preuss, H. G.:** Illusion und Wirklichkeit. Stuttgart, 1971. **Pruyser, P. W.:** A dynamic psychology of religion. New York, 1968. **Rey, K. G.:** Das Mutterbild des Priesters. Zürich, 1969. **Richter, L.:** Zum Situationsbewusstsein der gegenwärtigen Religionspsychologie. In: ThLZ, 1960, *85*, 333–42. **Rudin, J.:** Psychotherapie und Religion. Olten, 1960. **Id.:** Fanatismus. Olten, 1961. **Schär, H.:** Erlösungsvorstellungen und ihre psychol. Aspekte. Zürich, 1950. **Id.:** Religion und Seele in der Psychol. C. G. Jungs. Zürich, 1956. **Id.:** Was ist Wahrheit? Zürich, 1970. **Scharfenberg, J.:** Sigmund Freud und seine Religionskritik als Herausforderung für den christlichen Glauben. Göttingen, 1968. **Schmid, L.:** Religiöses Erleben unserer Jugend. Zollikon, 1960. **Spinks, G. S.:** Psychology and religion. London, 1963. **Spranger, E.:** Die Magie der Seele. Gotha, 1947. **Starbuck, E. D.:** The psychology of religion. New York, [2]1903. **Stewart, C. W.:** Adolescent religion.

New York, 1966. **Stollberg, D.:** Therapeutische Seelsorge. München, 1969. **Id.:** "Religionspsychologie pädagogisch". In: Pädagogisches Lexikon. Stuttgart, [6]1971. **Sundén, H.:** Die Religion und die Rollen. Berlin, 1966. **Thouless, R. H.:** An introduction to the psychology of religion. Cambridge, 1923. **Thun, T.:** Die Religion des Kindes. Stuttgart, 1959. **Id.:** Die religiöse Entscheidung der Jugend. Stuttgart, 1963. **Id.:** Das religiöse Schicksal des alten Menschen. Stuttgart, 1969. **Trillhaas, W.:** Die innere Welt. Munich, 1946. **Vergote, A.:** Psychologie religieuse. Brussels, 1966. **Wiemann, H. N. & R. W.:** Normative psychology of religion. New York, 1935. **Wise, C. A.:** Religion in illness and health. New York, 1942. **Wobbermin, G.:** Systematische Theologie nach religionspsychol. Methode, 2 Vols. Leipzig, 1921/22. **Wunderle, G.:** Das religiöse Erleben. 1922.

D. Stollberg

II. *Origins of religious experience.* Religion is a universal phenomenon prompted by motivations as common to men at all cultural levels as is sex. Religion existed for hundreds of thousands of years before any of the great religions came into existence, hence religion is motivated by the same psychological functions as mankind. There is no instinct or emotion exclusively peculiar to the religious nature. Psychologists, to explain the nature of religion, must be acquainted with comparative religion. The great religions of the world—Hinduism, Buddhism, Confucianism, Christianity, Islam—have their roots in the religions of prehistory. In spite of esthetic differences, all religions subscribe to certain basic beliefs such as a Supernatural Being(s), immortal souls, moral codes, and after death, an assessment of the individual's life. Religion, therefore, has everywhere a common psychological nature. Some of the most stimulating studies in the psychology of religion derive from Sigmund Freud and C. G. Jung, though their views of religion are diametrically opposed. Various authors: William James (*Varieties of Religious Experience*, 1902) was an important American psychologist writing on religion before Freud and Jung. J. H. Leuba (*A Psychological Study of Religion*, 1912) collected forty-eight different definitions of religion. J. Bissett Pratt (*The Religious Consciousness*, 1930) argued that religion is not one department of psychic life but involves the whole man. L. W. Grensted (*The Psychology of Religion*, 1952) said that "The material for the psychologist lies not in the existence of God. . . . Our beliefs and worship lie open to the inspection of the psychologist, but God does not" (p. 16). According to Freud (*Totem and Taboo*, 1913), the Oedipus complex is closely associated with the origins of religion, but Ian Suttie (*Origins of Love and Hate*, 1939) suggested that the Oedipus complex is not, as Freud said, universal. The matriarchal preceded the patriarchal forms of religion. Bronislaw Malinowski (*Sex and Repression in Savage Society*, 1937) asserted that in matrilineal societies the Oedipus complex is not present in the same forms as in patrilineal societies. All religions have their female and male psychological aspects.

Worship is objective when performed only in order to gratify (the) God(s). On the other hand, subjective worship exists for the benefit of the worshipper rather than for the gratification of deities. Prayer, psychologically, promotes human personality; it is beyond autosuggestion. If it passes over into worship, and from worship into communion, the Divine is viewed psychologically as the satisfaction of a being whose profoundest need is completeness. See: F. Heiler, *Prayer, a Study in the History and Psychology of Religion*, 1932.

The technique most productive of religious experience is contemplation. A crucifix for Christian contemplatives, the use of the *mandala* for Buddhist contemplatives and of the *yantra* for Hindu and oriental yogi, are means by which the mind of the experient is detached from the phenomenal world and brought to spiritual focus. Psychologically, contemplation is the means by which the phenomena of daily life arouse a sense of the mystery of being. See: R. C. Zaehner, *Mysticism—Sacred and Profane*, 1957 (see *Meditation*).

The concept of archetypes (q.v.) is one of Jung's most important contributions to the psychology of religion. According to Jung, the archetypes, which are primitive, non-personal and common to mankind and time, are the means by which the significant contents of dogmas and doctrines are most satisfactorily expressed. The instinct-emotion associations most active in religion, produce sentiments which are more unconsciously instinctual than consciously intellectual, and help us to understand psychologically that religion is in many ways a matter of feeling rather than of reason, though reason is not incompatible with it. See *Emotion; Instinct.*

Bibliography: Eliade, M.: Patterns in comparative religion. London, 1958. **Freud, S.:** Totem and taboo. London, 1938. **Id.:** Moses and monotheism. London, 1939. **Fromm, E.:** Psycho-analysis and religion. London, 1950. **James, W.:** The varieties of religious experience. London & New York, 1902. **Jung, C. G.:** Modern man in search of a soul. London, 1936. **Id.:** Psychology and religion: west and east. London, 1958. **Id.:** Memories, dreams, reflections. London, 1963. **Pratt, J. B.:** The religious consciousness. London, 1930. **Spinks, G. S.:** Psychology and religion. London, 1963; Boston, 1965; Utrecht, 1966; Tokyo, 1969.

G. S. Spinks

III. As a form of methodical scientific enquiry into religious experience the psychology of religion began towards the end of the nineteenth century. It was the result of the growth of the science of comparative religion and of the ever deeper probings of the psychology of experience. In order to clarify the psychic significance of the religious experience, the psychology of religion makes use of the methods of empirical psychology.

The following stages may be distinguished in the development of *method.* W. Wundt (1832–1920), in accordance with current evolutionary theories, employed the "anthropological" method. It did not attempt to describe the course of religious experience in the present but was chiefly concerned with the historical origins of religious images and the accompanying forms of religious rites. Wundt's law of four stages (religion of primitive man, totemism, gods and heroes, the development of humanism) is not the result of his research but a preliminary schema for it. In America, E. D. Starbuck (1866–1947) and W. James (1842–1910) won popularity for the psychology of religion, firstly by their method of questioning its basis and their research into the phenomenon of conversion, secondly by their description of so-called ideal cases and biographical details of conversions. The interpretation of religious material was still under the tutelage of philosophy; immanentist, biologistic and pragmatist tendencies were not admissible. In French Switzerland, T. Flournoy (1854–1920) attempted a purely observational approach, but observed chiefly sick and eccentric people. His positivistic and pathologistic approach led him to regard mysticism as a cousin of epilepsy (q.v.) and hysteria (q.v.). He was more interested in parapsychical phenomena than in natural and spontaneous religious experiences. Evangelical theology tried to describe systematic theology in terms of the psychology of religion, and even to justify it, e.g. G. Wobbermin (1869–1943). The expression "transcendental religion" shows that this method owes more to philosophy than to empirical research. In accordance with the findings of O. Külpe (q.v.) on the specific nature of religious experience, K. Girgensohn (1875–1925) and W. Gruehn (1887–1961) studied its empirical foundations. They agree that there is no such thing as an elementary religous feeling, that to be precise, religious experience is a complex structure, a process in which an *intellectual moment* is of paramount importance and involves a relationship to totality (ego-function). The validity of this theory has been questioned on numerous counts and the emotional side of religious experience accorded more significance than the intellectual. It must be assumed that religious feeling is not to be equated with any one basic emotion.

Others who have contributed to the study of piety as a psychic phenomenon are S. Freud (q.v.) through psychoanalysis (q.v.), A. Adler (q.v.) through his individual psychology (q.v.), and C. G. Jung (q.v.) through his analytic or complex psychology (q.v.). Their researches ran into difficulties because they did not clearly distinguish the empirical and therapeutic aspects from the a-priori and metaphysical aspects of religion. Freud saw religion as a temporary "human compulsive neurosis". Adler tried to explain God as exclusively immanent in human instinct. Jung described religion and God as purely functional archetypes, or constructs of the psyche. V. E. Frankl's logotherapy (q.v.) or existential analysis (q.v.) sees its therapeutic task as a theoretical confrontation with the spiritual problems of the patient, seeking to arouse his willingness to take responsibility without making the decision for him.

Recent work in the psychology of religion seeks to establish it upon a broad methodological basis and to experiment with new methods of research, which have been tried in other branches of experimental psychology. Work is being done at present particularly in social psychology (q.v.) and personality research (q.v.). (See also *Attitude; Role; Group dynamics; Prejudice; Authoritarian personality.*)

Research is particularly interested in the genuineness of religious experience, with special reference to the current popularity of hallucinogenic drugs, and also in the problem of the manipulation (q.v.) of people through religion.

Bibliography: Berguer, G.: Traité de la Psychologie de la Religion. Geneva, 1946. **Clark, W. H.:** The psychology of religion. New York, [5]1963. **Frankl, V. E.:** Ärztliche Seelsorge. Vienna, [6]1952. **Girgensohn, K.:** Der seelische Aufbau des religiösen Erlebens. Gütersloh, [2]1930. **Griesl, G.:** Pastoralpsychologische Studien. Innsbruck, 1966. **Gruehn, W.:** Die Frömmigkeit der Gegenwart. Constance, [2]1960. **Hostie, R.:** C. G. Jung und die Religion. Freiburg, 1957. **James, W.:** The varieties of religious experience. London & New York, 1902. **Johnson, P. E.:** Psychology of religion. New York, 1959. **Keilbach, W.:** Die Problematik der Religionen. Paderborn, 1936. **Leuner, H.:** Die toxische Ekstase. Bibl. psychiat. neurol. 1968, *134*, 73–114. **Pöll, W.:** Religionspsychologie. Munich, 1965. **Pruyser, P. W.:** A dynamic psychology of religion. New York, 1968. **Rudin, J.:** Psychotherapie und Religion. Olten-Freiburg, 1960. **Starbuck, E. D.:** The psychology of religion. London, 1899; New York, [2]1903. **Sunden, H.:** Die Religion und die Rollen. Berlin, 1966. **Thun, T.:** Die Religion des Kindes. Stuttgart, 1959. **Id.:** Die religiöse Entscheidung der Jugend. Stuttgart, 1963. **Id.:** Das religiöse Schicksal des alten Menschen. Stuttgart, 1969. **Trillhaas, W.:** Die innere Welt. München, [2]1953. **Vergote, A.:** Psychologie religieuse. Bruxelles, 1966. Journal: Psychologie religieuse. Brussels, from 1957.

W. Keilbach

IV. *The genetic psychology of religion.* The first specific researches into the psychology of religion in children (H. Clavier, 1913) were concerned with the genesis of the idea of God: material anthropomorphism (6–7 years), mixed anthropomorphism (8–11 years), and spiritualization (from 12 years) were later established as the distinguishing factors in the child's idea of God (influence of Piaget, q.v.).

According to R. Goldman, the development of the idea of God passes from the *intuitive* (up to 7–8 years), via the *concrete* (from 7–8 till 13–14 years) to the *formal* (after 13–14 years). J. P. Deconchy, as a result of his free-association researches, differentiates between phases of *attribution* (9–10 years), *personalization* (12–13 years), and *internalization* (15–16 years).

The Louvain center for the psychology of religion conducted researches into the connection between the child's image of God and that of his parents, and has established: the specificity of the symbolic father-and-mother image, the comprehensive nature of the God image, a difference between various groups. Research based on Piaget's work has been carried out into the connection between the growth of moral consciousness (see *Conscience*) and belief in God (Caruso,

Havighurst, Jahoda, A. Godin). Research has been carried out in Louvain into the perception of the symbolic communication of religious attitudes in religious rites between the ages of six and twelve (J. M. Dumoulin, J. M. Jaspard).

Four fields of current psychological research into the genetic psychology of religion may be distinguished: (*a*) Research into different situations, perceptions and experiences which can be seen and expressed in terms of specific elements of religious language (e.g. God who reveals himself as witness, judge, merciful, protective . . .). For each of these experiences and categories the implicit psychological processes must be analyzed (see *Motivation; Symbolization; Identification*, etc.). (*b*) The connection of religious behavior with a specific image of God and the recognized attributes of the parental image, throws light on the structure of religious behavior and the recurrence of the Oedipus complex. (*c*) By means of semantic scales (see *Semantic differential*) the connotations of religious language are compared with those of profane language. This can reveal the agreements and conflicts between human and religious realities, and provide useful data for clinical psychology (q.v.) (see *Depth psychology; Psychoanalysis*). (*d*) The connection between types of religious behavior and personality structures (q.v.), has been the subject of various works of research, particularly in clinical and social psychology, e.g. the contrast between a "authoritarian" or "dogmatic" religion and "liberal" or "humanistic" forms (Allport, Rokeach, Siegman). Only a few works have appeared to date on the varieties of religious and atheistic behavior in relation to different personality traits.

Bibliography: Deconchy, J. P.: Structure génétique de l'idée de Dieu chez des catholiques français. Garçons et filles de 8 à 16 ans. Brussels, 1967. **Goldman, R.:** Religious thinking from childhood to adolescence. London, 1964. **Vergote, A.:** Psychologie religieuse, Brussels, 1966.

A. Vergote & J. M. Jaspard

Religious type. One of the ideal types, which E. Spranger describes in his "forms of life" (q.v.). It is characterized by striving for the highest spiritual values. People of the religious type are chiefly intent upon ethical aims and seek for knowledge. They regard economic affairs as of secondary importance and tend to shun the use of force. *W.K.*

Reminiscence. Reminiscence may be defined as an improvement, attributable to rest, in the performance of a partially learned act. The basic experimental design for studying reminiscence is:

Experimental Group	Practice	Rest	Recall
Control Group	Practice	No Rest	Recall

If the experimental group performs better than the control group in recall, reminiscence has occurred.

It will be recognized that reminiscence is a special and limiting case of a phenomenon that has long been known. Very often, performance is better under conditions of distributed than under conditions of massed practice. The benefits of distributed practice result from the interpolation of a *series* of rests, while reminiscence is defined in terms of the effects of a *single* rest. Because it is the simple, limiting case of a range of phenomena, considerable theoretical importance has attached to the explanation of reminiscence.

Reminiscence, as distinct from the phenomena of distributed practice, was not identified until Ballard's (1913) study of the memorization of poetry by children. Careful studies of reminiscence in the verbal learning situation, such as those by Ward (1937) and Hovland (1938), reveal small reminiscence gains over rest periods that may not be longer than a few minutes. Although the reminiscence effect tends to be small and transitory in verbal learning situations, large reminiscence benefits are found in motor learning situations (Bell, 1942) and these gains have been shown to occur over rest periods of up to two years in length (Koonce, Chambliss, & Irion, 1964).

Reminiscence is a function of a number of variables and conditions:

1. Length of rest interval: Amount of reminiscence increases to a maximum and then decreases as length of rest increases (Ward, 1937; Ammons, 1947). Optimum length of rest is much longer in motor learning than in verbal learning situations.

2. Amount of pre-rest practice: As amount of pre-rest practice increases, amount of reminiscence at first increases and then decreases (Ammons, 1947; Irion, 1949). The decrease with large amounts of pre-rest practice may reflect the fact that a performance asymptote is being approached.

3. Previous distribution of practice: Much more reminiscence is obtained following massed pre-rest practice than following distributed pre-rest practice (Hovland, 1938). If pre-rest practice were to be very widely distributed, it is probable that the introduction of a single additional rest would have no effect at all.

4. Chronological and mental age: Reminiscence appears to increase and then to decrease as a function of increasing chronological age. For the chronological ages that yield most reminiscence (early adulthood), amount of reminiscence appears to be an increasing function of mental age (Thumin, 1962).

Early explanations of distribution and reminiscence gains centered upon various forms of two theories, the fatigue theory and the perseveration theory. In simplest form, the fatigue theory holds that the learner becomes tired during practice. Rest allows him to recover from fatigue, then his performance improves. The perseveration theory was first advanced by Müller and Pilzecker (1900). It holds that, after the termination of formal practice, some kind of learning process continues to operate which, in effect, gives additional, unintended practice to the learner. Rehearsal might be one example of such a perseverative process, but it is not necessary to the theory that the perseveration be intentional or that the learner be able to report that it is occurring. To these two general theoretical approaches can be added the differential forgetting theory in which it is held that, during practice, the learner acquires two sets of habits: correct ones and a set of competing and incorrect ones. It is further held that, during a rest, all habits lose strength through forgetting, but that weak habits are forgotten at a *faster rate* than strong habits. Since training situations are usually arranged so that correct habits will be stronger than incorrect ones, a rest period should weaken the interfering habits more than the correct ones, and this differential forgetting should result in less interference and better performance following a rest. (See *Habit.*)

In more recent times, Hull's theory has had a strong influence on interpretations of reminiscence. Hull (1943) introduced two inhibitory constructs: *reactive inhibition* and *conditioned inhibition.* Reactive inhibition has the property of increasing as a function of the amount of work performed during practice and of dissipating spontaneously during rest periods. Therefore, although reactive inhibition is defined more precisely than fatigue, it possesses properties similar to those that are intuitively ascribed to fatigue. Performance is degraded in proportion to the amount of reactive inhibition that has accumulated. Conditioned inhibition also acts to degrade performance, but conditioned inhibition is held to be more permanent than reactive inhibition. Since conditioned inhibition does not dissipate spontaneously in time, an accumulation of it should be associated with a failure of reminiscence to occur.

A number of studies pertinent to Hull's

theory have appeared. Kimble and Horenstein (1948) measured the growth of reminiscence in time and fitted these data to Hull's theoretical formula for the decay of reactive inhibition. Moreover, an experiment by Adams and Reynolds (1954) demonstrated that very nearly *all* of the reminiscence gains in a motor learning situation could be accounted for in terms of the decay of a *single* inhibitory factor (such as reactive inhibition). This finding has been confirmed by several investigators.

However, some of the other theoretical explanations of reminiscence retain their attractiveness—partly because of their reasonableness, partly because of supporting data obtained in special situations, and partly because the theoretical ideas seem to have validity in other contexts (as witness the usefuless of the idea of perseveration or consolidation in contemporary treatments of short-term memory). Eysenck (1965) has advanced a three-factor theory of reminiscence that employs the concepts of perseveration, reactive inhibition, and conditioned inhibition. Very possibly, some such complex explanation of the phenomena of reminiscence will be required when all the learning situations in which reminiscence has been studied are taken into account. Perhaps, for example, reactive inhibition will account for most of reminiscence gains in motor learning situations while perseveration might play a more prominent role in the explanation of reminiscence in verbal memorization situations.

Further material and extensive lists of references may be found in Bilodeau & Bilodeau (1961), Irion (1966), and McGeoch & Irion (1952). See *Memory*.

Bibliography: Adams, J. A. & Reynolds, B.: Effect of shift in distribution of practice conditions following interpolated rest. J. Exp. Psychol., 1954, *47*, 32–6. **Ammons, R. B.:** Acquisition of motor skill: II. Rotary pursuit performance with continuous practice before and after a single rest. J. exp. Psychol., 1947, *37*, 393–411. **Ballard, P. B.:** Obliviscence and reminiscence. Brit. J. Psychol., Monogr. Suppl, 1913, *1*, No. 2. **Bell, H. M.:** Rest pauses in motor learning as related to Snoddy's hypothesis of mental growth. Psychol. Monogr., 1942, *54*, No. 1, No. 243. **Bilodeau, E. A. & I. McD.:** Motor-skills learning. Ann. Rev. Psychol., 1961, *12*, 243–80. **Eysenck, H. J.:** A three-factor theory of reminiscence. Brit. J. Psychol., 1965, *56*, 163–81. **Hovland, C. I.:** Experimental studies in rote-learning theory. I. Reminiscence following learning by massed and distributed practice. J. exp. Psychol., 1938, *22*, 201–24. **Hull, C. L.:** Principles of behavior. New York, 1943. **Irion, A. L.:** Reminiscence in pursuit-rotor learning as a function of length of rest and of amount of pre-rest practice. J. exp. Psychol., 1949, *39*, 492–9. **Irion, A. L.:** A brief history of research on the acquisition of skill. In: **Bilodeau, E. A.** (Ed.): Acquisition of skill. New York, 1966. **Kimble, G. A. & Horenstein, B. R.:** Reminiscence in motor learning as a function of length of interpolated rest. J. Exp. Psychol., 1948, *38*, 239–44. **Koonce, J. M., Chambliss, D. J. & Irion, A. L.:** Long-term reminiscence in the pursuit-rotor habit. J. exp. Psychol., 1964, *67*, 498–500. **McGeoch, J. A. & Irion, A. L.:** The psychology of human learning. New York, [2]1952. **Müller, G. E. & Pilzecker, A.:** Experimentelle Beiträge zur Lehre vom Gedächtnis. Z. Psychol., 1900, *1*, 1–300. **Thumin, F. J.:** Reminiscence as a function of chronological and mental age. J. Geront., 1962, *17*, 392–6. **Ward, L. B.:** Reminiscence and rote learning. Psychol. Monogr., 1937, *49*, whole No. 220.

A. L. Irion

REM phase. See *Dream; Sleep*.

Repellants. Chemical substances emitted as a warning to members of the same or other species of an enemy, or in order to make the latter's prey uninviting for the future. Minnows when injured secrete a repellant to warn other fish. Many species of beetle squirt foul-smelling liquid from their extremities or spit out a corrosive gastric fluid which makes them inedible as prey. *V.P.*

Repercussion. The effect of emotional occurrences on vegetative activities (e.g. profuse sweating, dilatation of the blood vessels). (See *Emotion; Stress*.) *H.W.*

Repertoire (syn *Repertory*). In information theory (q.v.) the quantity of well-defined, reliable signals within a code (q.v.), or a number of events which, broadly speaking, are incompatible as pairs.

If a repertoire has only a finite number of elements, it is *finite*. A repertoire *in some order* is an alphabet.

Before a code (q.v.) is drawn up or the information (q.v.) calculated, the repertoire must be determined, e.g. the repertoire of letters, words, sounds or perceptual elements. *P.-B.H.*

Repetition compulsion (syn. *Compulsive repetition*). According to Freud, the more or less irresistible tendency of an individual to repeat unpleasurable, even partly painful and traumatic experiences. Repetition compulsion is said to control the death instinct (q.v.). Freud "explained" the phenomena of recurrent nightmares or anxiety dreams, neurotic symptoms and transference as the effects of compulsive repetition. It has been claimed that it is possible to show that anxiety dreams derive from "libidinous" pleasurable motives (see *Libido*) that could not be fully gratified in reality. The nightmare itself is the answer to, and defense of, this libidinous motive produced by the dreamer from the introjected punishment (q.v.) tendencies of the environment. It seems possible to demonstrate the gratification value of symptomatic behaviors even in neurotic symptoms. The symptomatic actions partly gratify, in a minimal form, even the forbidden or no longer gratifiable motive. Toman has indicated repetitions of all primary drive and motive gratifications, and has explained phenomena characterized as "repetition compulsions"as emphatic repetitions of more primitive and aggressive motive gratifications. See *Obsession*.

Bibliography: Toman, W.: Repetition and repetition compulsion. Internat. Journ. Psychoanalysis, 1956, *37*, 347–50. **Id.:** Introduction to psychoanalytic theory of motivation. London & New York, 1960.

W.T.

Representation, principle of. Klages' term for a thesis conceived within graphology (q.v.), and at first related only to handwriting but later generalized only in regard to human expression: man's urge toward representation, which is rooted in his experience of the world he perceives, follows a personal (unconscious) guiding image: "Man's every voluntary movement is partly determined by his personal guiding image" (Klages). *B.K.*

Representative. Samples (q.v.) are representative if their composition corresponds to the population from which they were taken. To obtain representative samples, random techniques (random samples, q.v., random numbers) or controlled techniques (see *Organized sample*) may be used. Conclusions about the population can only be drawn on the basis of the results of samples when the latter are representative of the population. (See *Sampling techniques; Opinion polls.*) *G.Mi.*

Representative conclusion. A conclusion which concerns the basic population and which is drawn on the basis of a representative sample (q.v.). Thus, for example, on the basis of a statistic, a conclusion is drawn about the size of the corresponding parameter (q.v.) of the population. *G.Mi.*

Representative poll/sampling. The use of a partial sample which in its essential structural characteristics corresponds to the population from which it was drawn. The results of the sampling as embodied in the *representational poll* are held to be valid for the population. The elements (people interrogated) of the sample (q.v.) are either selected by *random control* (e.g. by lot) or by random control (e.g. *quota technique*) from the population. See *Opinion polls.* *A.H.*

Repression. In psychoanalytic theory: an inner defense (q.v.) mechanism by means of which a motive that is no longer gratifiable (or gratifiable only in the case of subsequent punishment) is replaced by similar gratifiable motives. The removal of a motive from the continuum of related motives accelerates the gratification sequences of still gratifiable motives. This state is experienced psychically as an *anxiety-aggression state*; it can become aggression if there is still a prospect of gratifying the blocked motive, and anxiety if environmental conditions seem insurmountable. This anxiety-aggression state may be equated with a transient *regression* (q.v.), which, like the anxiety-aggression state itself, comes to an end when a new pattern of gratifications of the persistent motives becomes fixed. Renunciation of the non-gratifiable motive would then be assessed as provisionally successful. A successful renunciation enables the individual in question automatically to resist opportunities of weaker and average intensity for gratification of the original motive. Finally he no longer perceives them as such opportunities. Only opportunities of above-average intensity for gratification of the repressed motive (those stronger than all opportunities since to gratify the repressed motive since repression) are experienced as recent temptation situations. In this case, subsequent repressions, additional repression work, and additional substitute gratifications are needed to maintain renunciation, and to avoid future temptation by even these more intense opportunities for gratification of the repressed motive. Should such a motive be gratified, the individal experiences guilt feelings, and introjected punishment motives occur. Examples of repression are weaning a baby, bereavement, or giving up cigarettes. Repression is successful and the state of unrest (provided by the accelerated gratification sequences of related motives) ceases, when the child no longer experiences the need to suck even when the breast is directly presented; when the thought or memory of the lost person no longer evokes any feeling of mourning or regret; when the former smoker can smoke a cigarette (maximal temptation situation) and it no longer appeals to him. Cases of repression in everyday life, e.g. "Freudian slips" (q.v.), are relatively transient and can be relatively slight phenomena. They are secondary repressions, which are codetermined by older, primary repressions. See *Depth psychology; Psychoanalysis.*

Bibliography: Freud, A.: The ego and the mechanisms of defence. London, 1937. **Freud, S.:** Inhibitions, symptoms and anxiety. London, [2]1936. **Toman, W.:** Introduction to psychoanalytic theory of motivation. London & New York, 1960. *W. Toman*

Reproduction. Voluntary reminiscence (q.v.). A term for the recall of items of information which have been noted at some earlier time and stored in the memory (material of experience and learning). Reproduction must be distinguished from recognition (q.v.). (See *Memory.*) *F.-C.S.*

Reproduction methods. A broad term for a series of methods in the psychology of memory in which, as opposed to recognition methods, a free reactivation of retention is required. The retention performance is determined according to the amount of freely reproduced material previously learned. *E.H.*

Reserpine. The best-known member of the rauwolfia alkaloids (q.v.), a chemical subgroup of the neuroleptics (see *Psychopharmaceuticals*). Its importance as a therapeutic agent has decreased today because of possible massive side-effects (extra-pyramidal excitation, depression, q.v., circulatory strain). Because of its action on the central storage of catecholamines (q.v.) and serotonin, as well as its antagonism to LSD, reserpine has been used experimentally in numerous investigations. In healthy persons reserpine (1–2 mg) remained active for a long time (up to 12 hours) and caused no impairment of function but enhanced sensitivity to afterimages (q.v.); after about three hours the period of sleep was prolonged (paradoxical sleep). When the dose was increased to 5 mg there was a deterioration of performance and subjective sedation.

Bibliography: **Brown, J. W., DiMascio, A. & Klerman, G. L.:** Exploratory study on the effects of phrenotropic drugs on competitive paired-associate learning. Psychol. Rep., 1958, *4*, 583–9. **Hartmann, E.:** Reserpine: its effect on the sleep-dream cycle in man. Psychopharmacologia, 1966, *9*, 242–7. **Lehmann, H. E. & Csank, J.:** Differential screening of phenotropic agents in man: psychophysiological test data. J. clin. exp. Psychopath., 1957, *18*, 225–35. *G. D.*

Residuum. 1. An *engram* or *trace* which—according to the psychology of association and the classical psychology of memory—every experience leaves and which forms the substratum for the reproduction (q.v.) of this experience. (See *Engram; Reminiscence; Memory*.)

2. *Factor analysis:* the correlation left over when factors have been extracted. *F.-C.S.*

Resistance in the psychological sense is an individual's refusal to acknowledge as such unconscious motives which tend to affect his behavior and (in hidden form) his subjective experience. All defense (q.v.) mechanisms specific to a person can be diminished or removed only in the face of his own involuntary psychic resistance. In psychotherapy the patient is helped by a slow process intended to remove his defense mechanisms. Whereas Freud (q.v.) and his disciples were inclined (in the first years of psychoanalysis, q.v.) to confront patients initially and directly with the "contents" of their most repressed motives, afterwards care was taken to ensure a *gradual* cancellation of the client's inner defenses. Too intense confrontations with unconscious motives can so increase a patient's resistance, and frighten or tax him, that he insists on abandoning the therapy.

Bibliography: **Toman, W.:** Introduction to psychoanalytic theory of motivation. London & New York, 1960. *W.T.*

Resolution. The final part of an act of will which is followed directly by a readiness to act. It presupposes deliberation and consideration of the aspects relevant to the decision and implies knowledge of the personal responsibility for this decision. To that extent resolution needs to be distinguished from a *spontaneous* decision resulting from an emotional situation. *P.S.*

Resolution phase. The term given by Masters and Johnson (1966) to the fourth and last phase in the sexual reaction cycle, coming after the excitation phase (q.v.), the plateau phase (q.v.), and the orgasmic phase (q.v.). Characteristics of this phase common to both sexes are a return to a normal blood pressure and a normal heart rate. In addition there are in the woman, the following: disappearance of the sex flush, shrinking of the nipple area; diminution of the labia minora, return to original position of the labia majora, the clitoris and the uterus, shrinking of the orgasmic platform in the vagina; in the man there are: shrinking of the penis in two stages, reduction of testicles and return to normal position (see *Refractory period*).

Bibliography: **Masters, W. H. & Johnson, V. E.:** Human sexual response. Boston, 1966. *J.F.*

Resonance technique. A global method of perceiving expressive phenomena. The technique is characterized by a somewhat "intuitive" procedure based on impressions. *D.G.*

Resonance, theory of. The supposition, first expressed by H. von Helmholtz, that in the hearing process a tone is split up into its components because the fibers of the basilar membrane together with the liquid surrounding them behave like a set of resonators. According to this theory the resonance frequency of the fibers decreases from the base to the top of the basilar membrane as the length of the fibers and the strain from the column of liquid becomes greater towards the top and the tension of the fibers decreases. This theory of resonance was criticized by G. von Békésy and O. F. Ranke and replaced by the so-called *dispersion* or *hydrodynamic theory*. (See *Sense organs: the ear*.) *W.P.*

Resonator. A hollow object (e.g. cylinder or box), open at one end, which is used to magnify the loudness of a tone in accordance with its natural frequency. *G.D.W.*

Respiration. Synonymous with breathing, this represents the process whereby O_2 is inhaled and CO_2 exhaled by the respiratory system. By means of the different muscles of respiration (see *Respiratory organs*) pressure is alternately decreased (*inspiration, drawing in of breath*) and increased (*expiration, expelling of air*), and as a result fresh air is taken in and spent air is breathed out. The volume of air breathed is controlled by means of the CO_2 regulating cycle through the respiratory center in the wall of the fourth ventricle in the medulla oblongata. Sensory vagus fibers of the lung make it possible to control the kind and depth of breathing and offer the possibility of influencing subjectively (voluntarily) the autonomic nervous system. *E.D.*

Respiratory system. All those organs which together are responsible for external respiration. They consist of a series of air passages including nasal chambers, mouth, throat, pharynx, larynx with epiglottis, trachea, bronchi and bronchioles and the pulmonary vesicles which constitute the major part of the lung. This system is contained in the thoracic cavity which by expanding and contracting produces the increase and decrease in pressure necessary for the movement of air which is breathed (see *Respiration*). The muscles which accomplish this are transverse and can be innervated at will. In the main they are the intercostal muscles and the diaphragm, which in warm-blooded animals also serves to separate the abdomen from the thoracic cavity. *E.D.*

Response set. Any of those influences which, as specific answer tendencies of the testee, falsify the intended dimensions of a test. Two basic forms are distinguished: *formal* response sets include all those conditioned by the particular form of the question (see *Acquiescence tendency*); *content* response sets are those which evoke a false answer by reason of the specific content of an item or test. The most important sets of this kind are: simulation and dissimulation, defensive attitudes, lying.

The influence of response sets can constitute a considerable part of the variance of a test procedure and therefore has to be taken into account in test construction. A variety of scales have been developed to guard against the content form: e.g. in the MMPI, or A. L. Edwards' "Social Desirability Scale".

Bibliography: Adams, G. S.: Techniques de minimisation ou d'exploitation des tendences de réponse dans les inventaires structurés d'auto-évaluation. Res. de Psychol. appl., 1961, *11*, 233–62; 303–41. *P.Z.*

Responsibility. The ability to commit a (punishable) offense, insofar as that action is dependent on the mental state of the individual in question. Responsibility (see *Guilt*) in this sense is a legal construction but unknown in psychopathology; its varieties can be defined only in relation to an actual legal code.

Legal norms usually rely on the assumption of the existence of *freedom* of human decision, and of responsibility for such decision. According to Knobloch (1965), the most frequent causes of lack of responsibility are: (*a*) mental sickness in the sense of a mental disturbance of fairly long duration, characterized by more or less typical onset, course and possible cessation; (*b*) chronic mental sickness without a specific beginning, course and progression (this category includes developmental disorders and retardations, psychopathies, oligophrenias, and some cases of deaf-muteness); (*c*) short-term mental disturbances (these are most often pathic affects or intoxications, severe cases of disturbed consciousness, episodic disturbances in the course of chronic nervous illnesses, mental disturbances after brain concussion, etc. See *Alcoholism; Childpsychology; Criminality; Deficiency, mental; Mental defect; Psychopathy; Schizophrenia; Traits; Type.*

Bibliography: Blau, G. & Müller-Luckman, E.: Gerichtliche Psychologie. Neuwied, 1962. **Ehrhardt, H. & Villinger, W.:** Forensische und administrative Psychiatrie. In: Psychiatrie der Gegenwart, Vol. 2. Berne, 1961. **Knobloch, F. & J.:** Soudní psychiatrie pro právníky a lékare. Prague, 1965. **Thomae, H. & Schmidt, E.:** Psychologische Aspekte der Schuldfähigkeit. In: **Undeutsch, U.** (Ed.): Handbuch der Psychologie, Vol. 11. Göttingen, 1967. *O.T.*

Restitution of psychological functions (*higher cortical*). The restitution of functions after brain damage (see *Brain pathology*) is one of the major problems of *neuropsychology* (q.v.). Traditional conceptions, according to which mental processes are functions of isolated sectors of the brain, led to the conclusion that since damaged nerve-cells of the cortex do not regenerate themselves, functions disturbed because of multiple brain damage are lost for ever and cannot be recovered (see *Localization*).

Clinical practice has shown, however, that functions disturbed because of brain damage can be restored or can redevelop. This phenomenon required an explanation, which was given by a series of papers in neurology and neuropathology during the last century. Multiple brain damage can lead to two main types of functional disturbance: the pathological center can put the cellular tissue in a temporary state of inactivity or disturb it irrevocably.

In the first case, the pathological condition leads to disturbance of the synaptic conductability of a stimulus; this disturbance is induced by biochemical changes, above all by a reduced secretion of acetylcholine (q.v.), which ensures the transmission of the stimulus to the synapse (see *Nervous system*); possibly a mechanism of the reflector inhibition (or inhibition caused by irradiation, q.v.) of functions in the damaged nervous tissue is also involved. Such a temporary inhibition can occur both in the cortical sectors which border directly on the center of the damage, and in the cortical areas situated well away from but connected to the center by the nervous system (for example the areas which are situated symmetrically with the center), or in the deeper subcortical formations. This temporary type of inhibition has been described as "diaschisis" by K. Monakov. To restore the temporarily inhibited function the synaptic connectability of the cells which exist in the condition of diaschisis must be restored. To this end substances can be used which overcome acetylcholine antagonists (cholinesterase, q.v.) and restore the active effect of acetylcholine. Such substances are eserine, prostigmine and galantamine, etc. Wartime experience has shown that the introduction of these substances into the bloodstream leads to the disinhibition of temporarily inhibited functions (e.g. of movement), while it has no influence on the functions disturbed by damage to the nerve cells. In the event of a unilateral hemiplegia, for example, produced because of an injury to the cortical motor area of the arm, the introduction of these substances restores the temporarily impaired motor functions of the leg but not of the arm. An essential role in the removal of inhibitory states is also played by the *exercise* of corresponding functions. This contributes to the reactivation of the uninjured but temporarily inhibited cells. In all these cases the disturbed function is restored to its earlier form.

The second kind of functional disturbance takes place because of destruction of the corresponding nervous apparatus (or area of the cerebral cortex). In these cases also, however, the disturbed functions can be restored. This is explained by the fact that the highest cortical functions (perception, behavior, speech, writing, calculation, etc.), are never a function of one isolated, limited sector of the brain (see *Localization*). Accordingly, diffuse brain damage disturbs only one of the conditions necessary for the normal working of the whole functional system (e.g. the synthesis of stimuli in one whole simultaneous or successive structure, spatial and temporary analysis and synthesis, the entire tone of the cortex, etc.) and yet leads secondarily to the failure of the whole system. Such an explanation of a disturbance to the highest cortical functions in the event of local damage of the brain shows why the disturbed functions can be restored and allows a means of restoration. In this sense a restoration of the disturbed functions can be achieved only through the functional reconstruction of the system, in other words the disturbed member of the functional system must be replaced by one of the uninjured members. Training for the restoration of psychological functions of patients with diffuse brain injuries is based on this principle.

The restoration of speech or writing ability to a patient with damage to the cortical area (see *Broca's area*) serves as an example of such training. Here the disturbed speech—(phonematic) hearing is replaced by *visual* or *kinesthetic analysis* of perceived speech. A further example would be the restoration of spatial orientation, disturbed because of injury to the parietal-occipital sector of the cortex, by successive verbal-logical analysis of spatial relations.

The training, whose object is to restore functions lost because of injuries to different parts of the brain, must be differentiated and backed up by a special program, which begins with a neuropsychological analysis of the disturbance.

Bibliography: Bethe, A.: Plastizität und Zentrumlehre. In: **Bethe, A.** (Ed.): Handbuch der normalen und pathologischen Physiologie. Vol. 15. Berlin, 1931. **Monakow, C. von:** Lokalization im Grosshirn und der Abbau der Funktionen durch lokale Herde. Wiesbaden, 1914. **Goldstein, K.:** Aftereffects of brain injuries in war. New York, 1942. **Luria, A. R.:** Restoration of functions after brain trauma. Oxford, 1963. **Id.** *et al.* Restoration of higher cortical functions following brain damage. In: **Vinken, P. J. & Bruyn, G. W.** (Eds.): Handbook of clinical neurology. Amsterdam, Vol. 3. 368–433.

A. R. Luria

Restorff effect. If the data of a learning series differ materially, those items which contrast categorically with the majority of others, are retained better than those which resemble categorically most of the others.

Bibliography: Restorff, H. Von: Analyse von Vorgängen im Spurenfeld: 1. Uber die Wirkung von Bereichsbildung im Spurenfeld. Psychol. Forsch., 1933, *18*, 299–342.

E.H.

Resultant. The sum of adjusted quantities or vectors (q.v.).

Resumption of interrupted actions. A phenomenon studied by M. Ovsiankina (1928), a pupil of Lewin's, and traced to a "quasi-need", characterizable in dynamic terms as a *tension system* (q.v.). The intensity of the need to resume depends, *inter alia*, on the structure of the behavior, on the stage in which it is broken off, and on the attitudes of the subject.

See *Lewin; Need; Attitude; Achievement level.* *J.M.D.*

Retardation. Delayed development. "Retardation" is mainly applied to measuring the differences between intellectual ability and the statistical age-norm (see *Intelligence*). Some authors also assess temporary "developmental inhibitions" and disharmonious lapses in the physical sphere as "retardation". The concept implies nothing concerning the origins of retardation: for example emotional disturbances, conditions of upbringing, cultural deprivation, sensory and motor handicaps, illnesses, inherited factors, damage to parts of the brain. See *Autism; Deficiency, Mental; Mental defect.*

Bibliography: Heber, R.: Manual of terminology and classification in mental retardation. Amer. J. ment. Defic. Monograph. Suppl., 1959, *64*, No. 2. **Zigler, E.:** Mental retardation: Current issues and approaches. In: **Hoffman, M. L. & L. W.:** Child development research, Vol. 2. New York, 1966, 107–68. *H.M.*

Retention. In contrast to forgetting, "what remains in the memory". Retention, according to R. S. Woodworth and H. Schlosberg, is one form of the four processes of memory: memorizing, retention, recall, and recognition. A distinction is also made between immediate retention (for seconds or at most minutes) and memory (q.v.) (for hours and years). (See *Memory; Reminiscence*). *H.-J.A.*

Retention curve. A graphic representation of retention (see *Learning; Memory; Reminiscence*): e.g. the relative frequency of correct reproductions of learned items after variously long intervals from the point of attainment of the learning criterion. Retention R at any point in time T is usually expressed by an exponential function ($R = a \cdot e^{-bt}$ for $t > 0$). The intensity of the falling off b is dependent on the learning process investigated (verbal, motor), on the kind of retention measurement (e.g. reproduction, recognition), and the kind of learning assignment (meaningful, nonsense) and the learning conditions (Bahrick, 1964). In conditioned learning, the drop in the intensity of learned response with time is characterized not as forgetting but as extinction. The speed of extinction depends on the number of unconditioned (or unrewarded) rehearsals after the attainment of the learning criterion or on the length of the interval of time in which there was no further response (latent extinction). A learned behavior can often be elicited after its extinction. (See *Conditioning, classical and operant*). Forgetting is mainly explained in that old and new associations suppress the learned associations (interference theory; see *Memory; Inhibition*).

Bibliography: Bahrick, H. P.: Retention curves: facts or artifacts? Psychol. Bull., 1964, *61*, 188–94. **Kintsch, W.:** Learning, memory, and conceptual processes. New York, 1970. *M. Hofer*

Reticular activating system (abb. RAS). A term introduced in 1958 by W. H. Magoun (USA) and G. Maruzzi (Italy) for the *formatio reticularis* or reticular formation (q.v.). Magoun and Maruzzi discovered its arousal function: sensory nerve bundles from parts of the body supply the cortex (q.v.) directly, but also send branches to the formation which, when there is excitation, selectively dispatch signals to the cortex. The signals reaching the cortex from the formation have an "arousal function"; they produce the activation of the brain which does not take place by direct excitation of the cortex. The formation continues to maintain the aroused state (attention) of the cortex. Different results show that it is probable that the RAS plays some part in mental disturbances. The RAS inhibits and promotes not only sensory but motor impulses, it modifies voluntary and reflex movements which—when regulated by the cortex alone—are jerky and convulsive. See *Arousal*. *H.W.*

Retina. The inner layer of the eye's wall. The non-percipient portion (*pars caeca retinae*) in the area of the ciliary body (see *Lens*); it is clearly divided from the remaining, far bigger percipient area (*pars optica retinae*) by a jagged line (*ora serrata*). The retina is normally located apart from the pigment epithelium and is close to the vitreous humour. The retina is fixed only at the blind spot (q.v.) (the optic nerve papilla) and at the *ora serrata*. The pale reddish colour of the retina is caused by visual purple (rhodopsin). Near the posterior ocular pole lie the blind spot (q.v.) and the *macula lutea* (or yellow spot) whose centers are about 4 mm. from each other.

Anatomically, the retina has ten layers. But it is more practical to give the distribution according to function: (*a*) pigment epithelium; (*b*) rods and cones; (first neuron); (*c*) bipolar ganglionic cells (second neuron), or *ganglion retinae*; (*d*) large ganglionic cells (third neuron) or *ganglion fasciculi optici* (working from the outer to the inner layers). Between these extends the glia membrane (supporting membrane). The light must first penetrate a part of the retinal layers until it reaches the light-sensitive rods and cones. The retina originates developmentally from a protrusion of the brain.

In the retina, stimuli (light is a physiological stimulus) are changed by chemical reaction into nervous impulses, which are then conducted in the *fasciculus opticus* to the optic centers. The retina exhibits an electronic potential, which in the healthy eye can be detected as an electroretinogram.

With the aid of an ophthalmoscope (H. von Helmholtz) the vessels of the retina (arteries and veins) may be clearly distinguished from the *macula lutea* (q.v.), the blind spot and the rest of the retina, and pathological variations from the physiological image. The size of the retinal image depends on the type of ophthalmoscope. An upright and inverted representation can be obtained. *R.R.*

Retroactive inhibition. See *Memory*.

Retrocognition. A form of ESP (q.v.) in which the target (q.v.) is some past event. Retrocognitive hit (q.v.) = hit with backward temporal displacement. Knowledge about the past that does not depend on either memory or inference. *J.B.*

Retrograde amnesia. Amnesia for memories of events which occurred before the cause of that amnesia. For example retrograde amnesia can occur for events which led up to an accident involving head injury, one of the results of which is the amnesia. *R.H.*

Reversibility; reversible figures. A class of figures for which there is more than one perceptual interpretation. In these circumstances, rather than all interpretations being seen simultaneously, a single interpretation is seen which abruptly gives way to some other. These changes in interpretation are called reversals. One class of reversible figures includes the *Necker cube* (q.v.) and the *Schröder staircase* (q.v.) for which there are two three-dimensional interpretations of two-dimensional representations. Another class of reversible figure includes *Rubin's figure* (q.v.) in which reversal involves an alteration in which part is seen as *figure* and part is seen as *ground*. *C.D.F.*

Reversible lenses. See *Stratton's experiment*.

Reversion. An inner defense (q.v.) mechanism in which, apparently because of the impossibility, or fear of a specific form, of motive satisfaction, its opposite is sought. Insofar as reversion is not reaction formation, it is considered as more vaguely defined and less worthy of interpretation than other defense mechanisms. *W.T.*

Reward. In behaviorism, reward and reinforcement (q.v.) are frequently used as synonyms. A *reward* has a motivating function. In human individuals it increases in addition the feeling of self-esteem and social status. Its efficacy depends on its size, its frequency, the time lapse between it and previous behavior as well as on various personality variables. See *Punishment.*

Bibliography: Skinner, B. F.: Science and human behavior. New York, 1958. *B.L.*

Rhathymia. A dimension of temperament developed by Guilford (1959) based on factor analysis and represented by the Rhathymia scale of the Guilford-Zimmerman temperament survey (1947). Rhathymia manifests itself in an unconcerned, carefree merry attitude; antipole: prudent seriousness and conscientiousness. Rhathymia correlates closely with Eysenck's extraversion/introversion dimension. See *Traits; Type.*

Bibliography: Guilford, J. P.: Personality. New York, 1959. *H.H.*

Rheobase and chronaxie. Units of measurement in testing peripheral nerve functions. Electrode stimuli are applied over the nervous regions or put right into the nerve and the latter is stimulated by electrical rectangular impulses of varying duration (0·01–8 msec.) and intensity. For the stimulus threshold (the smallest stimulus that produces any excitement, e.g. a movement of the appropriate muscle) the Nernst rule applies: $I\,.\,t$ = constant. This relation is called the stimulus time span curve and is different for every individual nerve. To describe this function the smallest impulse current strength to have an effect over the desired rectangular impulse duration is referred to as *rheobase* and the smallest rectangular stimulus duration to effect a stimulus at double rheobase is referred to as "chronaxie". *E.D.*

Rhine, Joseph Banks. B. 29/9/1895 in Tuniata, Pennsylvania. Director of the "Foundation for Research on the Nature of Man" (Durham, N.C.). 1928: instructor in philosophy and psychology; 1930: assistant Professor; 1934: associate Professor; 1937 to 1950: full Professor and director of the parapsychology laboratory at Duke University. In 1937 founded (with W. McDougall's support) the *Journal of Parapsychology.*

Rhine has carried out research into the most varied areas of parapsychology. In 1928 he began, under McDougall's direction, to investigate the hypothesis of life after death, and until 1940 was principally concerned with the investigation of clairvoyance (q.v.). Subsequently he intensified his interest in questions of precognition (foreknowledge) and psychokinesis (q.v.) and (from 1945) problems of telepathy (q.v.). In order to explain paranormal phenomena, Rhine postulates a psychic(al) function (psi-function, q.v.), which is supposed to operate outside physical laws proper, and whose mode of operation he has tried to investigate, with—since 1950—animal experiments.

Main works: Extra-sensory perception. Boston, 1934. Extra-sensory perception after 60 years. Boston, 1940; New York, ²1960 (with others). The reach of the mind. New York, 1947. Parapsychology: from Duke to FRNM. New York, 1965. Parapsychology today. New York, 1968 (with others). *W.W.*

Rhodopsin. Also known as erythropsin or visual purple. Red-violet coloring material of the rods (q.v.) which above all determines the red colour of the back of the eye. This substance is a chromoproteid, i.e., the combination of the protein (albumin) "opsin" with the (added non-protein) group "neoretinal b". Neoretinal b is chemically "11 cis retinal" which derives stereoisomerically from "all-trans-retinal", the vitamin A aldehyde. Opsin only induces retinal in cis-form to combine and to form rhodopsin with it. When this combination is exposed to the light then c-trans-configuration of the retina takes place; the resulting trans-retinal is released from the opsin; stereo-configuration, dependent on the quantities of light, and the separation have the following effect: (*a*) membrane depolarization together with stimulus of the rods, (*b*) the visual purple pales to visual white. Lack of vitamin A prejudices regeneration in rhodopsin and consequently leads to hemeralopia (q.v.). *K.H.P.*

Rhombencephalon. A general term which embraces the *metencephalon* and *myelencephalon*. The metencephalon consists of the pons (q.v.) and cerebellum (q.v.). Higher up, the rhombencephalon adjoins the mesencephalon and lower down, the spinal cord. The term indicates an evolutionary process. Initially, at the cerebral end of the neural duct, there are two main sections, the prosencephalon and the rhombencephalon, which then become more differentiated.

Bibliography: Clara, M.: Entwicklungsgeschichte des Menschen. Leipzig, 1966. *G.A.*

Rhythm. 1. In general the time structure of a series where there is change. **2.** In biological systems especially the natural (autonomous) time structure of some functional operation (e.g. bioelectrical processes in the conduction of excitation, pulse frequency, rate of breathing, body movements, menstruation cycle, fluctuations of attention). Biological rhythms can be partly explained by the adaptation which is necessary for life of the biological functional operations to rhythmic processes in the physical environment (inter alia fluctuations of ultra-violet irradiation during the year, change of light intensities during the day and—especially for man—also in the social environment (certain time conventions); in part they represent the homeostatically regulated utilization of organ capacities within their natural limits, i.e. in general the constant alternation of work and rest, of *ergotropic* and *trophotropic* functional proclivities. Rhythmic processes form the basis of performances with a time orientation (sense of time, "biological clock"; time indicator, time consciousness; (see *Time*). For arranging work it is especially advisable to take into account the fluctuations in daily rhythm of the "physiological readiness for work" (O. Graf, circadian rhythms). Rhythm disturbances and desynchronization of different internal and external rhythms represent an important area in diagnostic activity. *J.N.*

Ribonucleic acid(s). I. (RNA) Found in nucleic protein substances as an important component of chromosomes (q.v.) and acts as a carrier of inherited characteristics to the amino acid sequences of specific proteins. Like desoxyribonucleic acid (DNA) it consists of a nucleic acid, a sugar (ribosis), phosphoric acid and one of the four nucleic bases: *adenin*, *guanin*, *cytosin* or *uracil*. (See *Desoxyribonucleic acid.*) *E.D.*

II. High molecular substances (nucleic acids) present in all cells (mainly cytoplasm), also in viruses and bacteria. Ribonucleic acid is of fundamental importance for protein synthesis. At least three kinds are to be distinguished: *ribosomal* RNA (rRNA) which represents about 80–90% of cell RNA, *messenger* RNA (mRNA) and *transfer* RNA (tRNA). The three RNAs form differen substances in protein synthesis. mRNA forms the first substance in which it supplies to rRNA the information deposited in desoxyribonucleic acid (DNA) for proteinsynthesis. tRNA places the specific amino acid requested at disposal for the formation of protein. Since McConnell's experiments with planaria, RNA has occupied a central position in biochemical research. RNA extracted from the brains of conditioned animals and injected into the brain of an unsophisticated animal leads to behavior which corresponds to that of the trained animal, (see *Psychopharmacology*). Transfers of brain extracts have been carried out on many other animals besides planaria (goldfish, rats, mice, etc.). Many of these experiments have proved negative, but those which took place under carefully controlled conditions were largely positive. Experiments with the supply of yeast RNA produced varying results. RNA was used by Hyden as a dependent variable, especially through the working group. From these experiments it emerged that learning (q.v.) leads to increased RNA synthesis (see *Memory*). Disturbance of RNA synthesis by antibiotics (q.v.) prevents the retention of learning material. It has not hitherto been made clear which of the following hypotheses regarding the meaning of RNA is to be accepted: (*a*) RNA has a special significance beyond the normal protein synthesis in respect of learning and its retention; (*b*) RNA has a special significance in respect of learning and its retention only as a link; (*c*) RNA has a special role only in learning and not in retention; (*d*) RNA has no special role in learning or its retention.

Bibliography: Cantoni, G. L. & Davies, D. R.: Procedures in nucleic acid research. New York, 1966. **Corning, W. C. & Ratner, S. C.:** Chemistry of learning. New York, 1967. **Domagk, G. F. & Zippel, H. P.:** Biochemie der Gedächtnisspeicherung. Naturwiss., 1970, *57*, 152–62. **Gaito, J.:** Molecular psychobiology. Springfield, 1966. **Gaito, J. M.:** Macromolecules and learning. In: **Bourne, J. H.** (Ed.): The structure and function of nervous tissues. New York, 1969. **Glassman, E.:** The biochemistry of learning: an evaluation of the role of RNA and protein. Ann. Rev. Biochem., 1969, *38*, 605–46. **Id.:** The biochemistry of learning: an evaluation of the role of RNA and protein. Ann. Rev. Biochem., 1969, *38*, 605–46. **Walas, O.** (Ed.): Molecular basis of some aspects of mental academy. London, 1966. *W.J.*

Ribot's law. Formulated by the French psychologist Ribot (1839–1916) (q.v.): the loss of memorized material which occurs in old age, or when there are organic or traumatic disturbances of memory (q.v.), takes place in an order inverse to that in which it was accumulated: material memorized at a later date, such as experiences, kinds of behavior, learning material, is the first to be lost, and the last is material acquired at an (ontogenetically) early date (e.g. childhood memories) and primitive emotions.

Bibliography: Ribot, T.: Les maladies de la mémoire. Paris, 1881. *F.C.S.*

Ribot, Théodule. B. 18/12/1839 in Guingamp; d. 9/12/1916 in Paris. From 1889, professor of experimental psychology at the Collège de France in Paris. Ribot is considered to be the founder of French psychology. He was the first scholar in France who endeavored to detach psychology from philosophy and to introduce the principles of experimental psychology. In his two early monographs *La psychologie anglaise contemporaine* (1870) and *La psychologie allemande contemporaine* (1879) (Eng. trans.: English psychology. London, 1873. German psychology of today. New York & London, 1886), he brought to the notice of his fellow countrymen English associationism and German experimental psychology as it was at the time of Wundt (q.v.). Among those who studied under him were Pierre Janet (q.v.), his successor at the Collége de France, and Georges Dumas.

Although Ribot introduced experimental psychology into France, he was not an experimental psychologist in the same sense as Wundt. He was fundamentally a pure theorist who neither had a psychological laboratory nor supported his theories with experimental investigations. Even his publications in his main field of work, psychopathology, were scarcely based on clinical experience, so that he had to admit to Janet that he had taught psychopathology without having seen the patient (Misiak & Sexton, 1966).

His works dealt on the one hand with pathological disorders of memory (q.v.) (*Les maladies de la mémoire*, 1881), of volition (*Les maladies de la volonté*, 1883), and of personality (q.v.) (*Les maladies de la personnalité*, 1885). Ribot sought to show that these abnormalities were due to disturbances of cerebral function. In his later publications he was more concerned with the psychology of affective and emotional states (*Psychologie des sentiments*, 1896. *La logique des sentiments*, 1905. *Essai sur les passions*, 1907. *Problèmes de psychologie affective*, 1910).

Bibliography: Misiak, H. & Sexton, U. S.: History of psychology: an overview. New York, 1966. *W.W.*

Riemann(ian) space. After the mathematician B. Riemann (1826–66): the curved space of Riemannian geometry (see *Linear space*). The concept of n-dimensional, Riemannian space occupies a central position in the binocular vision theory of R. K. Luneburg (1903–49). Luneberg's theory concerns the prerequisites for scaling of subjectively perceived spatial relations (see *Space perception*). For this purpose, he distinguishes between a physical space (with a Euclidian geometrical structure) and a visual space (with a Riemannian geometrical structure). On the basis of this theory a better explanation is possible of some phenomena in the perception of spatial relations (e.g. Hillebrand's alley, q.v.).

Bibliography: Luneburg, R. K.: Mathematical analysis of binocular vision. Princeton, 1947. **Raschewski, P. K.:** Riemannsche Geometrie und Tensoranalysis.

F.Ma.

Right associates procedure (syn. *Paired associates; Retained members method*). A method for testing the retention of material presented in pairs during the learning phase. One item (e.g. a word) acts as stimulus, the other as response. S. has to give the right response on re-presentation of the stimulus item. See *Memory; Reminiscence.* *E.H.*

Rigidity. Inappropriate adherence to a habit, set, or action when objective conditions demand change. The word is ambiguous, and research has revealed different types of rigidity. For example, Cattell and Tiner (1949), with seventeen tests from past studies, found two factors: dispositional rigidity (persistence of a response through inability to shift to another), and ideational inertia (inability to give up perceptual or thought habits). Dispositional rigidity is identified with perseveration (mental inertia), a term introduced by Neisser (1894) and also called "secondary factor" (Wiersma, 1906). Guilford (1957) distinguishes adaptive flexibility (ability to alter a set with changing problems) from spontaneous flexibility (diversity of ideas in unstructured situations). In brain injury, Goldstein (1943) differentiates primary rigidity (inability to change set) from secondary rigidity (in a too difficult task S. sticks to a previous task). Rokeach (1960) distinguishes dogmatic thinking (resistance to changing single beliefs) from rigid thinking (resistance to change of a system of beliefs or set).

Tests of rigidity include Einstellung water jar problems (Zener & Duncker, 1920; Luchins, 1942); fluctuations of Necker cube (McDougall, 1929); Gottschaldt's embedded figures; card sorting; and pencil and paper tests (e.g. Gough-Sanford scale, 1952). Performances on such tests and tasks may provide operational definitions of rigidity. The Californian authoritarianism scale (F-scale) has been used as a measure of personality rigidity. Both semantic and empirical problems in this field are numerous.

Bibliography: **Cattell, R. B. & Tiner, L. G.:** The varieties of structural rigidity. J. Personal. 1949, *17*, 321–41. **Chown, S. M.:** Rigidity—a flexible concept. Psychol. Bull. 1959, *56:3*, 195–223. **Rokeach, M.:** The open and closed mind. New York, 1960.

P. McKellar

Rigor. Increase of muscular tonus; "wax-like" stiffness. It persists from the beginning to the end of the examination when movement is passive. It is a symptom of diseases of the extrapyramidal system, especially in Parkinsonism (q.v.) and Parkinson's disease (q.v.). *H.W.*

Ring sector illusion. An illusion produced by color contrast. A ring of uniform grey lies on a field which is half red and half green. If the boundary between red and green is covered by a thin strip then the two halves of the ring appear to be different shades because of contrast with the surrounding colours.

C.D.F.

Risk taking. Despite the extensive research on risk-taking behavior carried out over approximately the past fifteen years, the construct itself is quite elusive and, in fact, defies explicit definition. Indeed, Kogan and Wallach (1967) describe risk-taking behavior on the basis of the kinds of situations in which it is likely to be elicited. For those authors, behavior reflective of risk-taking dispositions occurs in "situations where there is a desirable goal and a lack of certainty that it can be attained. The situation may take the form of requiring a choice between more and less desirable goals, with the former having a lower probability of attainment than the latter. A further possible, but not necessary, characteristic of such situations is the threat of negative consequences for failure so that the individual at the postdecisional stage might find himself worse off than he was before he made the decision" (p. 115). The following sections consider the various kinds of influences impinging upon the risk-taking domain. These include task and situational factors, personal characteristics, and influences deriving from group interaction.

1. *Task and Situational Influences.* Decision-making situations vary in the degree to which their outcomes involve aspects of chance and skill.

Where tasks of a chance nature are concerned—gambling decisions in this case—the most sophisticated work has been carried out by Slovic and his associates. On the basis of several empirical studies, Slovic & Lichtenstein (1968) reinterpret the findings on gambling choices in terms of two fundamental processes: (*a*) the relative importance that subjects assign to the various probability and pay-off components of a bet, and (*b*) limitations on information-processing capacities which lead the decision-maker to focus on particular components of a bet to the exclusion of other components.

Comparisons of decision making in chance and skill contexts has been a major concern of the British psychologist John Cohen (e.g. 1960). In decision-making situations offering equiprobable chance vs. skill alternatives, subjects tend to prefer the latter. Presumably, equal objective probabilities are not subjectively equal, subjects apparently biasing probabilities upward when they believe they have control over outcomes.

Unlike bets in which all the necessary information is available to the subject, much decision making involves the accumulation of additional information. The amount of information sought will be a function of the gravity of the decision (i.e. the nature of the positive or negative outcomes contingent upon it), the cost of obtaining the information, and the consistency of the information being gathered (Irwin & Smith, 1957). Studies of this kind are highly relevant to risk taking, for individuals must decide when a decision is most optimal in the face of progressively increasing costs and decreasing value of the incentive. Wide individual variation reflective of differences in risk-taking dispositions seems to be a common feature of information-seeking activity (e.g. Lanzetta & Kanareff, 1962).

A central issue in the study of risk taking concerns the relative predominance of gain maximization and loss minimization in arriving at decisions. Rettig & Rawson (1963), working with hypothetical ethical dilemmas, have shown that severity of censure—if apprehended in an unethical act—has greater influence than potential gain in the prediction and actual occurrence of unethical ("risky") behavior. Comparable findings in other decision contexts, some involving monetary gain and loss (e.g., Atthowe, 1960), reinforce the conclusion that university students tend toward conservatism in decision making.

In regard to the issue of prior gains and losses on subsequent decisions, contrary to Edwards' (1962) claim that previous outcomes have negligible impact, investigators working in both naturalistic and laboratory contexts have obtained sequential effects. McGlothlin (1956) in a study of race-track betting found that prior losses facilitated risk taking, whereas prior winnings enhanced conservatism. Kogan and Wallach (1964) obtained similar results in the laboratory.

Comparisons of risk taking in naturalistic and laboratory contexts point to higher risk levels in the former. Differences can be traced to competitive elements in the naturalistic situation, for the introduction of competition in the laboratory (Preston & Baratta, 1948) yields risk levels highly similar to those obtained in field settings.

2. *Effect of Personal Characteristics.* Sex, age and social-class differences in risk taking have been reported. Sex differences indicative of greater risk taking in males have been found for children (e.g. Kass, 1964), but such differences appear to be attenuated in adulthood (Kogan & Wallach, 1964). Less is known about age differences, for psychologists have not studied risk taking across the entire life span. Wallach & Kogan (1961) obtained higher risk levels in university students relative to a gerontological sample of comparable education. Comparisons of subjects differing in social class—university students vs. enlisted military personnel—have indicated stronger risk-taking dispositions in the latter group (Scodel, Ratoosh & Minas, 1959).

The bulk of research on personality and motivational correlates of risk taking has been focused on the achievement motive (e.g. Atkinson, 1957). It must be noted that this work concerns the development of a theory of achievement motivation (q.v.), not a theory of risk taking as such, and accordingly will not be treated here.

Central to the psychology of risk taking is the issue of its generality vs. specificity. An initial empirical attack on this "convergent validation" issue by Slovic (1962) revealed little generality across risk-taking measures. A subsequent large-scale study devoted to the same issue by Kogan & Wallach (1964) also failed to show much generality. The latter authors, however, by resorting to a moderator variable analysis, were able to demonstrate generality for some individuals and specificity for others. Generality was most typical of those "motivationally disturbed" subjects who were highly test anxious and defensive. In contrast, subjects low in test anxiety and defensiveness manifested a high degree of specificity, in the sense that risk-taking levels were not constant across different decision situations. The Kogan-Wallach research also offers evidence for maladaptive irrationality in the subgroup strongest in "motivational disturbance"—for example, adhering to a risky strategy despite a high rate of failure.

3. *Risk Taking and Interaction in Groups.* A stable and oft-cited social-psychological phenomenon—the "risky-shift effect"—has generated a great deal of research and theoretical controversy over the past decade. The effect states that group interaction has a

risk-enhancing influence on prior individual decisions. This shift toward risk in groups has now been demonstrated in a variety of decision contexts and in numerous countries, though it should be noted that cautious shifts sometimes occur.

Various interpretations of the "risky-shift effect" have been advanced: (*a*) diffusion of responsibility: group influenced decisions are more risky because the blame for failure of a risky choice will not fall upon a single person but rather will be diffused across the members of a group (e.g. Wallach & Kogan, 1965); (*b*) the risk-taker as group leader—groups become more risky because leaders are more inclined to take risks and they persuade the other group members to follow that course (e.g. Hoyt & Stoner, 1968); (*c*) the familiarization explanation—thorough individual study of the decision situations produces shifts toward risk, and hence the risky-shift effect is not truly a group phenomenon (e.g. Bateson, 1966); (*d*) risk as a cultural value—individuals in Western society value risk more highly than caution and believe that they are no less risky than their peers, but discover in the group context that some of their peers are more risky, thereby offering a rationale for shifts toward greater risk.

The final interpretation listed above, first advanced by Brown (1965), has gained the greatest acceptance in part because it has been able to account for both risky and cautious shifts in groups (e.g., Stoner, 1968). A review of the "risky-shift" literature is contained in Kogan & Wallach (1967), and a more up-to-date review in Dion, Baron, & Miller (1971).

Bibliography: Atkinson, J. W.: Motivational determinants of risk-taking behavior. Psychol. Rev., 1957, *64*, 359–72. **Atthowe, J. M.:** Types of conflict and their resolution: A reinterpretation. J. exp. Psychol., 1960, *59*, 1–9. **Bateson, N.:** Familiarization, group discussion, and risk taking. J. exp. soc. Psychol., 1966, *2*, 119–29. **Brown, R.:** Social psychology. New York, 1965. **Cohen, J.:** Chance, skill, and luck. Baltimore, 1960. **Dion, K. L., Baron, R. S. & Miller, N.:** Why do groups make riskier decisions than individuals? In: **Berkowitz, L.** (Ed.): Advances in experimental social psychology, Vol. 5. New York & London, 1971. **Edwards, W.:** Subjective probabilities inferred from decisions. Psychol. Rev., 1962, *69*, 109–35. **Hoyt, G. C. & Stoner, J. A. F.:** Leadership and group decisions involving risk. J. exp. soc. Psychol., 1968, *4*, 275–84. **Irwin, F. W. & Smith, W. A. S.:** Value, cost, and information as determiners of decision. J. exp. Psychol., 1957, *54*, 229–32. **Kass, N.:** Risk in decision-making as a function of age, sex, and probability preference. Child Develpm., 1964, *35*, 577–82. **Kogan, N. & Wallach, M. A.:** Risk taking: A study in cognition and personality. New York, 1964. **Id.:** Risk taking as a function of the situation, the person, and the group. In: New directions in psychology, III. New York 1967, 111–278. **Lanzetta, J. T. & Kanareff, V. T.:** Information cost, amount of payoff, and level of aspiration as determinants of information seeking in decision making. Behav. Sci., 1962, *7*, 459–73. **McGlothlin, W. H.:** Stability of choices among uncertain alternatives. Amer. J. Psychol., 1956, *69*, 604–15. **Preston, M. G. & Baratta, P.:** An experimental study of the auction-value of an uncertain outcome. Amer. J. Psychol., 1948, *61*, 183–93. **Rettig, S. & Rawson, H. E.:** The risk hypothesis in predictive judgments of unethical behavior. J. abnorm. soc. Psychol., 1963, *66*, 243–8. **Scodel, A., Ratoosh, P. & Minas, J. S.:** Some personality correlates of decision making under conditions of risk. Behav. Sci., 1959, *4*, 19–28. **Slovic, P.:** Convergent validation of risk taking measures. J. abnorm. soc. Psychol., 1962, *65*, 68–71. **Slovic, P. & Lichtenstein, S.:** Relative importance of probabilities and payoffs in risk taking. J. exp. Psychol. Monogr., 1968, *78*, (No. 3, Part 2). **Stoner, J. A. F.:** Risky and cautious shifts in group decisions:The influence of widely held values. J. exp. soc. Psychol., 1968, *4*, 442–59. **Wallach, M. A. & Kogan, N.:** Aspects of judgment and decision-making: Interrelationships and changes with age. Behav. Sci., 1961, *6*, 23–36. **Id.:** The roles of information, discussion, and consensus in group risk taking. J. exp. soc. Psychol., 1965, *1*, 1–19.

N. Kogan

Ritualization (The formalization of instinctual acts.) The term was first used by Huxley to designate every change in a kind of behavior intended to improve signalling function. There are many possible causes: change of external stimuli, of motivation, of orientation components, of movement sequence, of co-ordination, intensity and rapidity of movements; striking characteristics of shape and color, etc. are formed. Wickler (1967) suggests the term "*semanticization*". Semanticization *on the part of the sender* is the clarification of a signal, *on the part of the receiver* it is the improvement of sense-organs, releasing devices and learning mechanisms. When semanticization is positive, there is an improvement, when it is negative, there is a deterioration of communication until desemanticization takes place. There is both ontogenetic and phylogenetic semanticization. Ritualization in the old sense is phylogenetic semanticization on the part of the sender.

Bibliography: Tinbergen, N.: "Derived" activities, their causation, biological significance, origin and emancipation during evolution. Quart. Rev. Biol., 1952, *27*, 1–32. **Wickler, W.:** Vergleichende Verhaltensforschung und Phylogenetik. In: **Heberer, G.** (Ed.): Die Evolution der Organismen. Stuttgart, [3]1967, 420–508.

K.Fi.

Roborants. A rarely used synonym for *stimulants* (q.v.) or neurodynamic substances (q.v.).

Rods. Elongated elements in the retina (q.v.), sensitive to light but not to color (see *Photoreceptors*), about 60μ long, with a diameter of about $1–2\mu$. They consist of an outer and an inner member, and can scarcely change their shape or their position (in the primates almost not at all). The rod fiber, with its nuclear swelling, is attached to the rod on the inside of the eyeball; together they form the rod cell, of which there are estimated to be approximately 120 million arranged round, not in, the *fovea centralis* (q.v.) in each eye; they increase in relative density toward the periphery of the retina. That their spatial breakdown power does not increase concurrently is connected with the fact that a larger number of rods are attached to a single nerve fiber at the periphery of the retina. Rods contain the light-sensitive pigmented material *rhodopsin* (q.v.) which helps to transform grey values (intensity degrees of brightness) into membrane depolarizations of the rod cell analogous to stimulus intensity. In this process, approximately 10^3 stimulus intensity units (e.g. apostilb or lux) can be transmitted out of the total number of rods. The sensitivity of the rods is greater and their threshold is lower than those of the color-sensitive *cones*. When they are not functioning properly, e.g. because of a vitamin A deficiency, night blindness (see *Hemeralopia*) develops; physiologically, this is "central scotoma" (failure of the central field of vision), which always occurs when the light densities in the surrounding field necessary for stimulation of the rods are not reached, since the *fovea centralis* (q.v.) contains only cones (q.v.) but no rods. (See *Sense organs: the eye*.)

K.H.P.

Role. A term used mainly in social psychology, where it occurs in its principal sense of "social role". It has to do with the very essence of this area of psychology, which is in fact the meeting place of sociology and psychology, since it implies both socially determined individual behaviors and social models defined and practiced by actual individuals. Its acceptations are linked with the origin of the term and its historical development.

1. *Origin of the term.* Etymologically, the term "role", derived from the medieval Latin word "*rotulus*" (Latin "*rota*" = wheel), signifies on the one hand a rolled-up script, and on the other hand the lines an actor recites in a theater. From the eleventh century, the term "*rôle*" has been used in French in the sense of "social function", or "profession".

Here we already have the model (and interpretation of a model) of individual behavior and social function, but current usage adds other derived meanings: role as a —usually inauthentic—individual attitude ("mere role-playing!"), and rôle as the major aspect of an individual in a social context ("he plays a political rôle"). These different meanings of the term (dramatic, personal, social) reappear in small in its acceptations in social psychology; hence their diversity and complexity.

2. *History.* Before appearing under the actual term "role", the concept itself occurred intermittently in the human sciences, under various titles, in the USA and in France and Germany. In psychology, the notion was emphasized when man was considered as an individual in relation to another or the group. Often the "dramatic" aspect of the human individual, the distance between "being" and "appearance", or the importance of the other in the determination of self is underlined. Sociologists arrive at the concept from the basis of the function and task of the individual in the social group.

After this first stage, the term "role" was used systematically by G. H. Mead, who studied the processes of communication and founded them on "role-taking", i.e. on mental substitution for one's partner, and adoption of his attitude. Role-taking allows a forecast of another's actions so that one's attitude can adapt to them, but it can also reveal self as self appears to the other. The personality (q.v.) is formed in the course of a whole series of "role-takings", which allow a gradual integration of the roles presented by those surrounding the child. All those mental activities which depend on an inward flexion (such as reflection, introspection, and so on) are founded on such "role-taking". Role, as defined thus by G. H. Mead, is close to attitude (q.v.), and is located in an essentially horizontal and interpersonal dimension.

Linton studied roles in relation not only to other individuals but to the group. For Linton, the concept of role is connected with that of *status*, of social position within a particular system. Role is the actualization or dynamic aspect of status, or the conduct prescribed for individuals on the basis of their status.

Whereas Linton associates role with sociological concepts such as status, T. M. Newcomb locates it more exactly in the sociological sphere. For him the term ought strictly to denote the theoretical model which actual individuals translate more or less faithfully into their role behavior. If these models, associated with social positions, represent constraint for the individual, that is due to the agreement, or consensus, of individuals in the group who expect a specific behavior from all those with a given status.

J. L. Moreno considers role not only as a constraining model, but as deriving from the very spontaneity of the individual who creates and grounds it: in Moreno's work it appears with all its personal, dramatic and social implications, and in the perpetual melée of action.

Among the foremost theoreticians of role one might cite Parsons, who analyzes the notion in the social system (relations between individuals are structured by roles), and in the personality system (which can interiorize various roles).

3. *Definition.* The notion of role has been taken up by many authors, but their definitions are not unambiguous; they diverge significantly in regard to the following: (*a*) the aspect of psychosocial reality to which they apply, which is either the individual or the group, or the interaction itself; (*b*) their range: sometimes they comprise a very limited area (in one of his definitions, Linton suggests the practice of the rights and duties associated with status), and sometimes they designate all socially determined behaviors; (*c*) their level of abstraction: for some, role is a theoretical model directing from without the actual behaviors of an individual; for others, it is the observable actions themselves.

An additional difficulty is met in regard to the dramatic (or, more exactly, the psychological) connotations of the word. Among the diverse definitions available, certain general examples use "role" as an organized model of behaviors, relative to a certain position of the individual in an interactional whole. Several specific cases may be envisaged on this basis.

Social role: position becomes status; the model of behavior is defined by the consensus of group members and has a functional value for the group. *Dramatic role:* the position is provided by the play's theme: the model defining the actor's performance was created by the dramatist. *Personal role:* the individual determines his own position in relation to others, and acts in accordance with his own model of behavior—which he uses as a standard for intersubjective relations.

4. *Position of the concept.* The marginal position of this concept, located as it is between psychology and sociology, raises a number of problems. Is role a social function or the character assumed by the individual? What is the relation between social and personal role? between prescribed and actual role? between role and status? . . .

It seems useful to distinguish several perspectives in the study of the notion: the *sociological* standpoint of the model and of theoretical role; that of *interaction,* where social and personal determining factors influence role behavior; and the *psychological* perspectives of the personality which perceives and interprets roles, and can even interiorize them.

At present "role theory" comes increasingly under discussion; the term stands for more than one concept, and in fact a number of interconnected notions (such as *norm, model, status, consensus*) are grouped round about the concept of role. There have been some interesting attempts to apply a mathematical model to the theory. The notion of role offers the main link between anthropologists' and sociologists' analyses of group behavior and psychologists' and psychiatrists' analyses of individual motivation (Kluckhohn & Murray): this makes it a conceptual tool of value throughout the human sciences (anthropology, sociology and psychology).

Bibliography: Banton, M.: Roles: an introduction to the study of social relations. London, 1965. **Biddle, B. J.:** Role theory: concepts and research. New York, 1966. **Dahrendorf, R.:** Homo sociologicus: Ein Versuch zur Geschichte, Bedeutung und Kritik der Kategorie der sozialen Rolle. Kölner Z. Soziol. Soz.-psychol., 1958, *2,* 178–208; *3,* 345–78. **Gross, N., Mason, W. S. & McEachern, A. W.:** Explorations in role analysis. New York, 1958. **Linton, R.:** The cultural background of personality. New York, 1945. **Mead, G. H.:** Mind, self and society. Chicago, 1934. **Moreno, J. L.:** Who shall survive? A new approach to the problem of human interrelations. Washington, 1934. **Newcomb, T. M.:** Social psychology. New York, 1950. **Parsons, T.:** Essays in sociological theory, pure and applied. Glencoe, Ill., 1954. **Rocheblave-Spenlé, A. M.:** La notion de rôle en psychologie sociale. Paris, 1962. **Sader, M.:** Rollentheorie. In: **Graumann, C. F.** (Ed.): Handbuch der Psychol., Vol. 7, Göttingen, 1969, 204–31. **Sarbin, T. R.:** Role theory. In: **Lindzey, G.** (Ed.): Handbook of social psychology. New York, 1954, 223–66.

A. M. R-S

Role conflict. Occurs when a person is faced, occasionally or constantly, with mutually contradictory and competing role expectations (q.v.) which result from his membership of several different groups, and make it difficult for him to behave in conformity with individual role expectations. *A.S.-M.*

Role expectations. Certain notions concerning the behavior of an individual occupying a *formally* or *informally* defined position in a group. A distinction is made between expectations involving (*a*) *prescribed* and (*b*) *predicted* role behavior. Hence role expectations reflect (*a*) norms and aims of the group (q.v.) and describe how the occupant of a role (q.v.) has to behave in certain situations; and (*b*) refer to the probability that a role bearer will actually behave in a certain way in certain situations. Both kinds of role expectations refer both to expectations in respect to the behavior of other individuals in the group, and also to those in respect to the individual's own behavior in the group.

Bibliography: Thibaut, J. W. & Kelley, H. H.: The social psychology of groups. New York, 1959.

A.S.-M.

Role playing. 1. Adoption by an individual of any social *role* (q.v.). **2.** A form of children's play in which different social roles (q.v.) are imitated by the child, either in groups (e.g. cops and robbers) or individually. It is an important element in the socialization process of a society with a differentiated structure. Moreno uses role playing (1959) in psychodrama (q.v.) for psychotherapeutic purposes; by changing roles, the patient learns to recognize the motivation of the other actors, and abreacts his emotions cathartically. *W.Sch.*

Role theory. Sarbin (1954) considers role theory to be an interdisciplinary theory involving cultural anthropology, sociology and psychology. Its aim is to examine human behavior or social interactions on a relatively complex level, and it consists of pronouncements about the combination of the concepts of "role" (q.v.) "position" as a system of role expectations with and "self". A survey of the work so far done in the field of social interaction which uses role concepts shows, however, that there is no system of postulates, which might satisfy the conditions for a theory (Sader, 1969).

Bibliography: Sarbin, T. R.: Role theory. In: **Lindzey, G.** (Ed.): Handbook of social psychology. Vol. 1. Cambridge, Mass., 1954, 223–58. *A.S.-M.*

Romberg's sign. If an individual can stand still with his feet close together and his eyes open, but starts to sway when he closes his eyes, then he is said to exhibit Romberg's sign. It is a sign of *tabes dorsalis*, but may be seen also in other disorders of the posterior columns and in hysteria. *J.P.*

Rorschach test. A technique developed by H. Rorschach (1922) which consists of ten plates or cards containing ink-blots, five of which are in black and white and the other five in colors; the subject has to interpret them freely. The interpretations are encoded with the aid of a system of signs according to localization, determination by form, color, movement, etc., frequency and content; they are then evaluated with a projection hypothesis to obtain a personality assessment (see *Projective techniques*). There are a number of parallel forms (q.v.) and modifications by S. Behn, C. Drey-Fuchs, H. Zulliger, M. R. Harrower & M. E. Steiner, W. H. Holtzman, etc.

Bibliography: Klopfer, B. *et al.*: Developments in the Rorschach technique, Vols. 1 & 2. Yonkers on Hudson, 1954/1956. **Rorschach, H.:** Psychodiagnostics. Berne, 1942. **Spitznagel, A. & Vogel, H.:** Formdeuteverfahren. In: **Heiss, R.** (Ed.): Handbuch der Psychologie, Vol. 6. Göttingen, [3]1966, 556–634.

H.H.

Rotation. A term for the analytical or graphic transformation of a factor matrix with the object of interpreting the content of the extracted factors. The rotation criterion most commonly used is that of L. L. Thurstone's simple structure. It requires the factors to be rotated so that on or near them are the greatest possible number of end-points of characteristic vectors. In graphic (visual) rotation this is done by subjective evaluation of the factor structure, in analytical rotation by the mathematical definition of maximum or minimum optimal values. Rotation methods can be subdivided, according to the angle made by the factors with one another, into orthogonal and oblique. See *Factor analysis*. *G.Mi.*

Rotation tachistoscope. A device for momentary presentation of visual stimuli. In contrast to the tachistoscope (q.v.) proper, a perforated rotating disc is used in this version in order to elicit multiple visual impressions at predetermined intervals. *F.Ma.*

R-p diagram. Traxel's graphic presentation of the findings of threshold tests in psychophysics (q.v.). The diagram represents the distribution of categories of judgment (e.g. perceived/not perceived). The stimuli values (Ger. *Reiz* = stimulus = R) appear on the abscissa, and the frequencies of judgments (p values) on the ordinate. The diagram allows the compensation of random deviations and enables one to estimate the relative frequency of judgments for all other stimulus intensities between the presented stages.

F.Ma.

R-R relation. An association between two response (reaction) events such that the first response represents one of the conditions for the second response.

Rubin's figure. Rubin constructed many figures which showed ambiguity as to which part of the diagram was figure and which part ground. He used these figures to investigate the factors which allow us to differentiate figure from ground in the things we normally perceive.

For diagram see *Figure-ground* in Vol. 1.

C.D.F.

Ruleg ("Rule" + "e.g."). A term used for the rule-example technique, a didactic programing strategy evolved by Evans, Glaser & Homme, which divides subject matter into rules and examples for instructional purposes. Incomplete examples and rules which have to be completed by the pupil himself, and others which are expressed negatively, are formulated. Each learning step contains either one element (a rule or example), or a combination of two or three elements. See *Instructional technology.*

Bibliography: Evans, J. L., Glaser, R. & Homme, L.: The RULEG system for the construction of programmed verbal learning sequences. J. Educ. Res., 1962, *55*, 515–20. **Glaser, R.:** Teaching machines and programmed learning, Vol. II. Washington, 1965.

H.I.

Rutz typology. A typology of expression, based on body build, carriage and muscle tension, alleged to be applicable to artistic modes of representation, including speech: (*a*) the *spherical type:* a Caesarean type, sturdy frame, "easily excitable, hot-blooded, inconstant", compliant, mutable, dependent on outside influences; (*b*) the *parabolic type:* small, slim, "persevering and single-minded", not easily influenced, rational and orderly; (*c*) the *pyramidal type:* hard, "jerky, inflexible", cool, forcible; markedly narrow loins and angular waist.

Bibliography: Rutz, O.: Neue Wege zur Menschenkenntnis. Kampen, 1935.

W.K.

Rybakoff's figures. Irregular geometrical figures that have to be divided in two so that the two segments can be formed into a square. Originally suggested by the Russian psychiatrist T. Rybakoff (1911) and developed further by various authors.

Bibliography: Meili, R.: Lehrbuch der psychologischen Diagnostik. Berne, [5]1965. **Id.:** Figuren von Rybakoff. Berne, 1956.

R.M.

S

S. Abbreviation for *subject*.

Sadism. A sexual anomaly in which sexual satisfaction is achieved by inflicting pain. The intensity of the anomaly varies from those who are sexually aroused by pained facial expressions to those who achieve organismic relief only from blood, pain, torture and even death. Loosely, the term sadism is used also for pleasure in cruelty without obvious sexual arousal or satisfaction. The word originated from the eighteenth-century French Marquis de Sade who in his debauched life and writings presented examples of sadism as well as many other perversions (q.v.).

Followers of Freud find sadism to be normally associated with the second, or anal, (hence anal-sadistic) stage of infantile sexual development, when the cutting of teeth and strengthening of muscles allows the child to feel power and the ability to hurt others. This sadism can be destructive or possessive. It is said to be normally a "polymorphous perverse" phase that is superseded by the genital phase of sexual development.

Anne Broadhurst

Sadomasochism. A term used in sexual science, introduced by von Krafft-Ebing in 1907 and derived from the work of the Marquis de Sade (1740–1814) and the Austrian short-story writer Ritter von Sacher-Masoch (1836–95). Sadomasochism denotes in the first instance sexually deviant forms of behavior which occur relatively infrequently (e.g. by comparison with homosexuality, q.v.), incur relatively weak social sanctions and do not lead to the formation of sexual subcultures (Simon & Gagnon, 1970). Sadomasochism is reflected in pornography (films, photographs, sadomasochistic appliances and devices), and to some extent in art. The general meaning of the term can be defined through its two components: (*a*) sadism: sexual excitement and satisfaction obtained by a person who inflicts pain, maltreatment and humiliation on a partner. In a wider sense: obtaining pleasure by tormenting and humiliating others. Etiology: defense against (unconscious) fears of castration (q.v.); (*b*) masochism (q.v.): sexual excitement and satisfaction by experiencing and tolerating pain, torment and humiliation. In the wider sense: all pleasure obtained through pain, setbacks, disappointment or humiliation.

The characteristic component of these sexually deviant behavior patterns is the general process of sadistic, masochistic and usually sadomasochistic interaction; Freud (1924) and more recently Schorsch (1971) have drawn attention to the "play" aspect of this behavior. Phenomenologically the psychopathology of the sadomasochistic arrangement is characterized by the following typical features of the partners' roles: behavior resembles a game with specific rules and parts (e.g. master and slave) which are completely artificial (the roles can be adopted or abandoned at any time; there is no personal commitment and the "punishment" is administered without emotional involvement); the artificial aspect of the "role playing" always remains conscious. "The decisive factor is the fiction of complete submission or domination; the administration or suffering of physical pain is not an essential feature" (Schorsch, 1971). The decisive importance of fantasy (q.v.) in sadomasochism, sadism and masochism was recognized at an early date but different explanations have been given: psychiatrists and sexual scientists have sought an explanation in the "artificial character of these games" (Schorsch, 1971), while psychoanalysts have referred to the psychogenesis and psychodynamics of the personality. The importance of masochistic masturbation fantasies has also been highlighted, above all as a defense against the feelings of guilt and anxiety which block the "ultimate pleasure" (Fenichel, 1960, 358–65).

From the criminological angle, sadomasochism is a very rare phenomenon. The extensive surveys of sexual delinquents conducted by the Kinsey Institute have not shown a single "modern Sade" (Gebhard *et al.*, 1965, 134). Sadomasochism in the narrower sense, as the interdependence and interaction of sadists and masochists in an artificial game situation, is a sexual deviation which cannot generally be equated with sexual aggression, brutality in crimes of indecent assault or sadistic killing. Murder as an integrative component of sexual satisfaction (e.g. murder of a child) is estimated to be very rare (one in one million) by sexual scientists (Gebhard, 1965, 134). Sadistic or masochistic masturbation fantasies are most common—by comparison with other groups of sexual delinquents—in delinquents who commit their offenses with menace or violence (9–17%) (Gebhard *et al.*, 1965, 504).

Etiology: Freud considered sadism and masochism to be sexual perversions resulting from a fixation—conditioned by guilt feelings or fear of castration—on an originally normal, active or passive attitude to sexual experience and the sexual object, which is then exaggerated and becomes the sole center of interest. He assumed to begin with that masochism developed out of sadomasochism—through regression from the object to one's own ego and to pregenital stages of sexual development in early childhood—and not simply "an extension of sadism turned against the individual's own person, which takes the place of the sexual object". Freud subsequently revised his theory and differentiated between three main forms of masochism with complex hypotheses: (*a*) erogenous masochism = pleasure experienced through pain = a component of the residual "death wish" in the organism which has libidinal connotations and persists through all phases of libido development; erogenous masochism is the basis of the two other forms; (*b*) feminine masochism = expression of a "situation which is characteristic of femininity" and of the feminine "nature" (= "being castrated, used as the object of copulation or bearing children"); (*c*) moral masochism (the most important form) = satisfaction of an unconscious guilt feeling or need for punishment of the ego; moral masochism is generally subconscious and the relationship with sexuality (q.v.) is blurred; pain, humiliation, debasement or self-punishment become the important factor, regardless of whether they are inflicted by a loved person, by an individual toward whom the "victim" is indifferent, or by anonymous powers (affinity with asceticism). In severe cases of moral masochism in which no connection with sexuality is demonstrable and the person concerned torments himself unconsciously, there can be no question of sexual perversion (Fenichel, 1960).

The etiological concept of sadism, masochism and sadomasochism is closely related to the psychoanalytical theory of infantile sexuality, and the psychoanalytical concept of neurosis (summarized by Fenichel, 1960). In spite of the psychoanalytical theories, knowledge of the origins of sadism, masochism and sadomasochism is still very scanty.

Bibliography: Fenichel, O.: The psychoanalytical theory of neuroses. London, 1960. **Gebhard, P. G.,** *et al.*: Sex offenders. London, 1965. **Giese, H.:** Psychopathologie der Sexualität. Stuttgart, 1962. **Schorsch, E.:** Sexualstraftäter. Stuttgart, 1971.

H. Maisch

Salivary reflex. A congenital physiological mechanism necessary for the digestion of food. Stimulation of the mucous membrane of the mouth or the nose leads to the direct (unconditioned) secretion of saliva. Indirect (conditioned) triggering of the salivary reflex can come about by the perception (real or imagined) of food, its signs or symbols. The salivary reflex became famous in the psychology of learning because it was the means whereby the Russian physiologist Pavlov (q.v.) discovered and studied the process of classical conditioning. *H.Ro.*

Salpêtrière School. Its founder, J. M. Charcot the neurologist, was particularly interested for administrative reasons in bringing all patients suffering from convulsions together to be cared for in a special department. Most patients were epileptics (see *Epilepsy*) and hysterics. The study of hysteric syndromes had engaged the attention of French medicine for many years. Charcot described four phases in an attack of hysteria and thus established a certain analogy with an attack of epilepsy. But he also insisted that hysteria (q.v.) is not just a woman's illness but can occur equally in men. The therapy he used was hypnosis (q.v.) and other suggestive methods. The Salpêtrière was a large hospital which, in addition to medical patients, had formerly admitted prostitutes, criminals and other kinds of asocial cases. Later, when Pinel was the principal, it was converted into a psychiatric clinic. *J.L.I.*

Sample. If G is a number of articles of the same kind, the population (q.v.), a sample is a part of this number selected from the population according to certain criteria. The number of elements in this selected part are called N (the sample size). In statistics (q.v.) one looks at random samples because it is only in these that the sampling error can be found. When planning experiments, a distinction is made between independent and dependent (q.v.) samples. In the case of dependent (correlating) samples, these or approximately identical objects according to some control characteristic are examined in order to decrease the sampling error. Sampling methods (q.v.) are used in order to obtain samples (see *Opinion polls*). *A.R.*

Sampling. The selection for study of a small group of people, animals, or items from a larger group (the *population*) in such a way that it is *representative* of that larger group, i.e. that conclusions based on the sample can be generalized to the population from which the sample was drawn. *Sampling theory*, which is a part of *statistics* (q.v.) and the mathematics of *probability* (q.v.), is concerned with ensuring that the sample is selected in such a way that valid *inferences* can be made about the nature of the population from an examination of the sample. In *random sampling* every item in the population has an equal chance of being drawn. *Quota sampling* implies randomness within the restriction that certain sub-groups of the population (e.g. male and female; social class categories) are proportionately represented. *G.D.W.*

Sampling error (syn. *Sample bias*). The extent to which the sample bias of a parameter constructed on the basis of a sample deviates from the true value. The sampling error can be systematic or random. The random sampling error decreases as the size of the sample increases. It can be estimated by the standard error (q.v.). In variance analysis (q.v.) the variance between the groups is the sampling error. *A.R.*

Sampling techniques. The sampling technique determines the extent to which measurements made of the sample hold good for the population as a whole. Greater accuracy can always be achieved by increasing the size of the random sample. However, to obtain twice the degree of accuracy it is necessary to quadruple the size of the sample; choice of the sampling technique is therefore determined to some extent by cost. A distinction can be made between sampling techniques based on the principle of random sampling (probability sampling) and those based on non-random (non-probability) sampling. Non-random samples are generally chosen by experts using their own judgment while in the case of random samples there is a known probability of each element of the population being included in the sample. Although it is conceivable that more accurate results may be obtained by non-random sampling, this is not generally confirmed by practical experience; the decisive factor, however, is that an indication on the accuracy of results can only be given in the case of random selection.

The random methods can be divided into simple, limited and multi-stage categories. In the simple method, every element of the population has the same likelihood of being included in the sample. The choice can be made by drawing lots or by simulation with random numbers. Simple random samples are also sometimes taken to include systematic selection in which individuals are selected at given intervals from a list of all the population elements. The most important techniques using limited random selection are the stratified sample and cluster sample.

In the stratified sample, the basic population is divided into strata which must be as homogeneous as possible; selection is then effected on a strictly random basis within the individual strata. The number of individuals selected from each stratum must not correspond to the share accounted for by this stratum in the basic population; if it does correspond to that share we speak of a proportional sample. In a cluster sample we refer to groupings already present in the population (e.g. school classes, houses, towns) which must be as non-homogeneous as possible. Random clusters are then chosen and used as the sample. By comparison with pure random samples, stratified samples result in an increase in accuracy which is all the more substantial the more homogeneous the strata are and the more clearly they are separated from each other. On the other hand the cluster method is less accurate than the purely random procedure. The reduction in accuracy is smaller the greater the lack of homogeneity in the composition of the clusters and the smaller the differences between individual clusters. The cluster method is characterized by low sampling costs. Multi-stage sampling generally takes the form of a sequence of cluster selections, e.g. villages may be selected first and individual houses then chosen at random in the villages. The stratified and cluster methods may also be combined. In non-random sampling the quota method plays an important part, since it is successfully used by opinion research institutes. Each interviewer is required to question a number (quota) of individuals having characteristics selected with a given code, e.g. a specific number of persons of a particular sex with a specific income level and political attitudes, etc. The quotas are determined proportionately to the structure of the population as a whole, to the extent that this is known. The quota method therefore has some similaritiy to the stratified sampling technique, with the important difference that within the quotas selection is left to the skill of the interviewer. Common errors are: e.g. that more intelligent persons tend to be consulted because they can be expected to answer the questions more quickly, and that telephone subscribers tend to be chosen because it is easier to contact them in advance and so avoid any loss of time, etc. Because of these distortions, quota sampling cannot be classified as a random method. A further type of non-random sampling is frequently used for preliminary studies where a sample may be taken simply because it is easily accessible, e.g. students at an institute of psychology may be used as subjects. This method is known as opportunity sampling. It is not really possible to generalize from the results achieved.

A special sampling technique is the sequential method, which is particularly advantageous if the study of an individual entails very high costs or is only rarely possible (e.g. in medicine).

Bibliography: Cochran, W. G.: Sampling techniques. New York, 1953.

A. Rausche

Sander's parallelogram illusion. One of the geometric illusions. The diagonal AB appears shorter than BC although they are objectively equal.

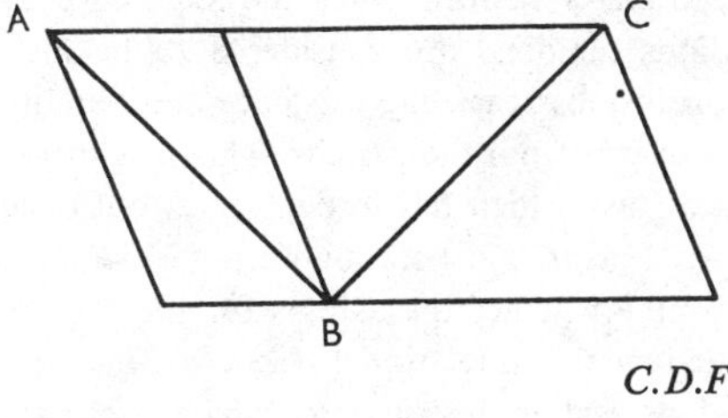

C.D.F.

Sanguine temperament. A concept of temperament which goes back to Galen but was presumably defined as a psychological term only in modern times: hasty temperament (q.v.), impressionable, unstable. The word "sanguine" has been in common use since the sixteenth century. See *Type*. *W.K.*

Sapphism. Lesbianism (q.v.). Female homosexuality. (After the Ancient Greek poetess Sappho, queen of the island of Lesbos).

G.D.W.

Satiation. Psychic satiation denotes a state of affect-colored aversion from an action which is performed repeatedly or a monotonous situation which has been lasting a long time. It must be distinguished from fatigue (q.v.), which does not primarily cause psychic satiation although it may appear as an accompanying phenomenon during the process of satiation (Lewis, 1928; Karsten, 1928). Even a behavior which initially has an element of pleasure does not by any means always produce a greater fixation of pleasure when it is repeated several times, but causes unpleasure. Instead of satisfaction and an inclination to repeat the act, psychic satiation makes its appearance, the positive challenging character disappears and is replaced by a negative challenging character. In experiments with simple repetition exercises the following observations were made as satiation began to develop (Karsten, 1928): variation in execution, execution as a subsidiary act, arrangement of the exercise into subdivisions, digression, physical fatigue, worsening of performance, structural disintegration, sense of futility, the feeling of marking time, emotional outbursts and finally discontinuance. The increasing emotional tension spreads to acts belonging to adjacent areas (associated satiation); the aversion turns not only against drawing lines but against drawing in general.

To the extent to which the challenging character of the task becomes negative, other, extremely "contrary tasks" take on a positive challenging character. Or the psychic satiation is removed when the task is embedded in a new meaningful context and is given a new target (earning money, competitive struggle), in which case the work which had previously caused satiation is taken up with renewed zest.

Bibliography: Karsten, A.: Psychische Sättigung. Psychol. Forsch., 1928, *10*, 142–254. **Lewin, K.:** Bedeutung der psychischen Sättigung für einige Probleme der Psychotechnik. Psychotechn. Z., 1928, *3*, 182–8. **Kounin, J. S.:** Experimental studies of rigidity. Character and Pers., 1941, *9*, 251–82. **Rivera, J. de** (Ed.): Gestalt. Contributions to the dynamics of behavior. New York, 1970.

A. Karsten

Saturation. In colors: the state of fulness of hue or color. It can range from a very slight degree of intensity where a certain color can only just be recognized as such and is not easily distinguishable from grey up to a maximum where this color has its full strength and life. In this sense the *degree of saturation* of a color can also be defined as its "distance" from grey, i.e. from the absence of color in a restricted sense. Saturation is in proportion to the composition of the spectrum of the stimulus: the greater the purity of the radiation, the more intense is the phenomenal saturation.

G.Ka.

Satyriasis; satyromania. Abnormally strong heterosexual desire in a male. Cf. *nymphomania* (female equivalent). Personal noun: *satyromaniac*. *G.D.W.*

Scales, major and minor. In the Western tradition, the usual systems of succession of notes in an octave. These scales can begin at any pitch and are characterized by definite changes of interval which, however, are distributed differently. *B.S.*

Scaling. In psychology, the term "scaling" denotes the theory and practice of associating numbers with objects. Since the characteristics of psychological objects (e.g. relative willingness to cooperate) are in the great majority of cases not fixed with reference to time and place, scaling is the basis of any comparative psychological statement. A strict definition of scaling must be based on measurement theory.

Measurement of a characteristic implies mapping a set of objects onto a subset of real numbers; the relationship between the associated numbers must correspond to the relationship between the characteristics of the objects which are being studied. Let M be a set of objects and R a relationship with M; (M, R) is then known as an empirical, relational system (Tarski, 1954). Example: let M be a class of pupils and R designate the characteristic "more cooperative than". If M is a subset of real numbers we speak of a numerically relational system.

Measurement consists in transforming an empirical system onto a numerically relational system. A one-to-one mapping f of a relational system (M, R) onto another (N, S) is known as an isomorphism if aRb applies only when $f(a)Sf(b)$ is also realized, i.e. if both systems have identical structures. If x = (M, R) is an empirical relational system y = (N, S) a numerically relational system while f is an isomorphism of on, then (, f) is a scale. Scaling consists in preparing a scale.

In preparing a scale, the existence and validity of the transform f must be demonstrated. For this purpose we set out from a relational system in which the required conditions (axioms) are considered to be met. Conclusions regarding existence and validity are drawn from the axioms. This is a theoretical task which has to be carried out once only. For practical scaling purposes we must examine whether the axioms for the investigated empirical relational system are met and follow scaling instructions which associate scale values with the objects.

Example: Thurstone (1927) postulated that on repeated presentation each stimulus from a set of stimuli to be scaled assumed a position which oscillated on the continuum of sensations. The probability density of the position corresponded to a standard distribution. The dispersions for the stimuli under examination were identical. It follows that the frequency with which stimulus *a* is given a higher ranking than stimulus *b* in relation to a particular characteristic, corresponds to the subjective distance between *a* and *b* (law of comparative judgment). If the standard distribution and a number of additional axioms are assumed to be accurate for the stimulus scaling, by comparing the order of magnitude of pairs, we obtain with the Thurstone scale, a scale of relative subjective distances between the evaluated objects.

From the scale level it is possible to conclude which statements concerning scale values are meaningful. A statement is said to be meaningful if its validity remains constant with the permissible transformations; otherwise it is said to be meaningless. In certain circumstances, rank relationships are sufficient for measurement at interval scale level. Suppes & Winet (1955) showed that an interval scale may be based on rank orders of differences (higher ordered metric scales).

The BTL system (Bradley-Terry-Luce) of scaling, based on Luce's selection axiom (1963) is particularly important. The BTL scaling leads on to the theory of signal detection and to developments in the sphere of probabilistic learning models.

Further variants of scaling methods may be classified as follows: stimulus-centered scaling only considers the differences between objects to be evaluated, whereas reaction-centered scaling covers both judging individuals and their judgments. The first group (e.g. application of Thurstone's law of comparative judgment, 1927) originates primarily from psychophysics, while the latter (e.g. Guttman scales) has been primarily determined by social psychology. Direct scaling differs from the indirect version in that it requires the judgment to be given directly in numerical terms. No satisfactory measurement models are available for these methods (e.g. categorial and magnitude scales) while the indirect methods, which are generally based on judgment frequencies, sometimes have an axiomatic basis. Deterministic scaling attempts to convert the empirical system directly into its numerical equivalent, while probabilistic scaling introduces probability functions as an intermediate stage. The distinction between one-dimensional and multidimensional methods of scaling is significant; in the former instance a single, subjective judgment continuum is postulated to distinguish between objects while in the latter several independent distinguishing features are assumed. The problem of defining axioms for multidimensional scaling has not yet been completely solved. Torgerson (1958) suggested a generalization of Thurstone's model for multidimensional scaling, which does, however, contain certain inherent contradictions. Shepard (1966) developed the principles of a multi-dimensional scaling based solely on rank judgments, but nevertheless arrived at a presentation at interval level. Further development then led to conjoint measurement (Luce and Tukey) which has tried more recently to determine simultaneously the effect of several parameters involved. See *Test theory*.

Bibliography: Coombs, C. H.: A theory of data. New York, 1964. **Luce, R. D.** *et al.* (Eds.): Handbook of mathematical psychology, Vol. 1. New York, 1963. **Pfanzagl, J.:** Theory of measurement. Würzburg & Vienna, 1968. **Shepard, R. N.:** Metric structures in ordinal data. Journal of Mathematical Psychol., 1966, *3*, 280–315. **Sixtl, F.:** Messmethoden der Psychologie. Weinheim, 1967. **Suppes, P. & Winet, M.:** An axiomalization of utility based on the notion of utility differences. Management Science, 1955, *1*, 259–70. **Tarski, A.:** Contributions to the theory of models. Indagationes Mathematicae, 1954, *16*, 572–81. **Torgerson, W. S.:** Theory and methods of scaling. New York, 1958. **Thurstone, L. L.:** A law of comparative judgment. Psychol. Review, 1927, *34*, 273–86.

K. Eyfuth

Scalogram analysis. A method for constructing an attitude scale from items in accumulated form (according to L. A. Guttman) with the object of the *unidimensionality of the scale*. This object is obtained when to each individual item (q.v.) from a person with a more extreme attitude (q.v.) a response is given which is more extreme (or at least equally decided) than that of a person with a less extreme attitude. Thus the degree of the attitude to be measured is expressed in the response to each individual item; ideally, too, the constellation of the responses is reproducible from each attitude scale score (total score). The Guttman scale appears all the more problematic, the more complex in regard to material the attitudes to be measured appear. *H.D.S.*

Scanning. A method of research and exploration used in electronics, data processing and video-technique by which measurements and calculations are processed to obtain information (q.v.) from definite information carriers.

Picture material, for example, chiefly in screen plates which include different grey values, is analyzed by mechanical symbol recognition in a way similar to the working method of the retina. If there are complex structures they are explored by a point of light produced by a cathode ray tube according to an exploration program and arranged as both black and white values. *B.R.*

Scatter. The appearance of different test results, observations, abilities, qualities, etc., generally understood as the deviation from the mean value. Also a synonym for standard deviation (q.v.). *A.R.*

Sceno test. Developed by the child psychotherapist G. von Staab in 1939. According to the depth-psychology conception of the test, the construction of figures by means of the child's projections and identifications (q.v.) evokes a representation of his (unconscious) conflicts. The child builds something with plasticene figures (potential representations of real persons) and with animals, plants, bricks, etc. The course of the building and the final result, which the child comments on, are recorded. Non-standardized evaluation and interpretation follow with reference to matter and quality.

Bibliography: Staab, G. von: Sceno-test. Berne, 1964. *P.G.*

Schafer-Murphy effect. The effect whereby reward can determine the perception of an ambiguous figure. Whereas normally the two aspects of an ambiguous figure may be seen equally often, if one of them is associated with a reward then that aspect of the figure will later be seen more often. *C.D.F.*

Schicksal analysis (*Analysis of destiny; Analysis of the past*). Szondi (1948) introduced this term for a method which tries to find the secrets of destiny in the personality, and to locate, in addition to the personal unconscious, the "family unconscious" and the circumstances connected with it (choice of career, choice of friends, etc.) which influence every person's life. The main method used, in addition to family research, is the Szondi test (q.v.). Schicksal analysis in general and the Szondi test are based on the thesis that two persons whose hereditary endowment includes concealed analogous, recurrent inherited factors will attract one another.

Bibliography: Szondi, L.: Experimentelle Triebdiagnostik. Berne, 1947. Id.: Schicksalsanalyse. Basle, [2]1948. Id.: Schicksalsanalytische Theorie. Berne, 1963. *J.L.I.*

Schizoid. According to Bleuler (1922), the schizoid "retains his independence of his social surroundings . . . and endeavors to withdraw from the effective influences of the living and dead environment and to pursue his own goals". "Because he does not respect reality and the existing order, he is led on the one hand to endeavor to change it and on the other to turn it upon himself". According to Kretschmer (1970), the term indicates an extreme type of temperament located in psychesthetic proportion (q.v.) which frequently correlates with the leptosomic (q.v.) and asthenic body build.

Bibliography: Bleuler, E.: Die Probleme der Schizoidie und der Syntonie. Zeitschrift neurologischer Psychiatrie, 1922, *78*, 375. **Kretschmer, E. & Kretschmer, W.:** Medizinische Psychologie. Stuttgart, [13]1970. *W.K.*

Schizophrenia. This term covers a group of severe, common and often incapacitating mental illnesses, which although manifest in a wide variety of psychological symptoms and abnormal behavior, are thought to have enough in common to justify their being grouped together. More patients are in hospital with schizophrenia than with any other medical or surgical condition, and since its maximum incidence is around 30 years of age it must be regarded as one of the major incapacitating illnesses of mankind; the world total of schizophrenics is probably about 9,000,000.

1. *History.* The term schizophrenia was introduced by E. Bleuler in 1911, but under "*dementia praecox*" Kraepelin had previously brought together Morel's "*démence précoce*", Kahlbaum's "catatonia" and Hecker's "hebephrenia" (Kraepelin, 1899). Kraepelin showed that this group of conditions could be differentiated from manic-depressive insanity by its special symptoms and its worse prognosis. In general, the majority of manic-depressives recover completely from or between their illnesses, in contrast to most schizophrenics, who show residual symptoms such as emotional blunting and loss of drive and initiative. This differentiation is still the basis of the present international classification of psychoses and other mental disorders (WHO., 1965).

2. *Clinical features.* (The descriptions given here are based upon the British glossary to the 8th Revision of the I.C.D. (WHO., 1965) and are probably close to current German and Scandinavian usage.) The disturbance that is thought to underlie the various types of schizophrenia shows itself as an utterly unfamiliar experience, in clear consciousness, whereby the person's innermost thoughts, feelings or acts seem to be known to, shared with or caused by others. This experience is often accompanied or followed by delusions that individuals, organizations, or natural or unnatural forces (e.g. television, hypnosis, witchcraft) are responsible. Hallucinations are common, particularly auditory, as voices in the third person or commenting upon the patient's thoughts and actions. Thought processes may be disturbed, so that thinking becomes vague, with unusual logic and idiosyncratic use of words or association of ideas. There may be sudden breaks in the flow of thought or speech, which may become incomprehensible. Perception may be disturbed so that normally irrelevant features of a percept become important, and may lead to delusions of reference in which the patient believes that everyday objects and situations (e.g. statements on television or in the press) possess a special, usually sinister, meaning intended specially for him. The emotional state may become capricious and inappropriate, and there may be extreme abnormalities of motor behavior, such as stupor or over-activity. A wide variety of other symptoms of less diagnostic importance may occur, and may be all that can be detected at any one time (e.g. delusions of persecution, grandiose and religious delusions; hallucinations of smell, taste and touch; sensations of bodily change, sexual change or interference; depersonalization; changed perception of the surroundings).

3. *Classification.* The symptoms may change during one illness, or from one illness to another, but many clinicians still traditionally follow Kraepelin and divide schizophrenia

descriptively into several sub-types, the commonest being *paranoid*, in which delusions (frequently of persecution) and hallucinations dominate the clinical picture. In the *hebephrenic* form, thought disorder and capricious affect, such as silly giggling, predominate. The *catatonic* type is characterized mainly by psychomotor manifestations such as hyperkinesis, stupor, repetitive movements, or automatic obedience. Other varieties such as *simple*, *latent* and *residual* have been described, but their usefulness has been questioned. The term "schizo-affective" is used to describe a small minority of patients showing typical symptoms of both schizophrenia and manic-depressive psychosis. *Paraphrenia* is a term introduced by Kraepelin (1899) to designate patients intermediate between his categories of dementia praecox and paranoia; the predominantly delusional illness develops later and produces less social deterioration than in *dementia praecox*, but the presence of auditory hallucinations eliminates the use of the term paranoia. More recently, the term has been used loosely to be almost synonymous with paranoid schizophrenia, particularly in elderly patients. Kraepelin considered dementia praecox, paraphrenia and paranoia to be separate disease entities, but this was not supported by later work on their outcome and hereditary basis. The historical development of the concept of schizophrenia has always been closely linked with that of paranoia (Lewis, 1970).

Kleist & Leonhart (1961) have developed complicated classifications of schizophrenia into subgroups according to detailed symptoms. The disorder is believed to be basically physical, affecting different parts of the nervous system, singly or in various combinations. This work has not found supporters outside Germany, with the exception of Fish (1962). Langfeld (1956) has proposed a much simpler and more widely accepted division into a "nuclear" group having typical symptoms and a poor prognosis, contrasted with a "schizophreniform" group with less typical symptoms and a much better prognosis.

4. *Diagnosis*. Kurt Schneider has been particularly influential in Europe with his view that diagnosis should rest upon simple description of the above symptoms (Schneider, 1958), in contrast to Bleuler who proposed that diagnosis should depend upon the presence of four inferred primary processes underlying the observed symptoms. These are: (i) loosening of thought associations; (ii) disturbances of affect; (iii) autistic thinking; (iv) ambivalence (Bleuler, 1950). These concepts have never been clearly defined, and followers of Bleuler tend to develop a wide concept of schizophrenia, particularly when also influenced by prominent American teachers such as A. Meyer and H. S. Sullivan, who regarded schizophrenia as the end result of a gradually developing reaction to life experiences and interpersonal relationships.

The diagnosis of schizophrenia still relies entirely upon descriptions of the patient's history, mental state and behavior, since the neurophysiological or biochemical mechanisms responsible for schizophrenia remain uncertain and no structural abnormality of the brain has ever been reliably demonstrated. This lack of reliable, quantifiable data has allowed different concepts of the nature of schizophrenia to arise, so that diagnosis between psychiatrists can be unreliable unless precautions are taken to ensure uniformity of interviewing and consistent use of descriptive terms. Most European psychiatrists use diagnostic criteria similar to those described here, but in North America the use of much broader concepts often results in the diagnosis of schizophrenia being given to patients who have any type of delusion or hallucination, or marked difficulties with interpersonal relationships and self-expression. In Europe, such patients would probably receive a diagnosis of atypical affective illness or personality disorder (Kendell *et al.*, 1971). Any figures quoted in the following sections must be viewed in the light of the underlying diagnostic uncertainties.

5. *Epidemiology.* By European statistics, the annual incidence of new cases is about 150 per 100,000 population, and just under one per cent of the population will receive this diagnosis at some time in their lives. The peak incidence is between 25 and 35 years. Schizophrenia is common in all races and cultures (Mischler & Scott, 1963), and is commonest in the lower socio-economic groups in dilapidated areas of large cities. A downward social drift due to incapacitating residual symptoms is the probable explanation of this (Goldberg & Morrison, 1963).

6. *Etiology and mechanisms.* No single general cause of schizophrenia is known. Both environmental stress and genetic predisposition seem to play a part in many patients, but in others neither of these influences is evident: *Genetic predisposition:* The near relatives of schizophrenics have a much greater incidence (about 12% in siblings) than the general population, and monozygotic twins have a greater concordance rate (about 60%) for the illness than dizygotic twins. Selection bias makes the interpretation of surveys of twins difficult (Rosenthal, 1962) but an important genetic component in schizophrenia is generally accepted, probably with a polygenic mode of inheritance (Shields, 1967). A monogenic theory involving partial penetrance has also been proposed (Slater, 1958). Since schizophrenia results in the genetic loss of so many fertile individuals, carriers of the predisposition who do not manifest the illness should have some compensatory advantage, but this has not yet been identified.

Family and environment: Much recent work from the USA is based upon the assumption that schizophrenia is caused by parents who submit the child to conflicting emotional relationships and illogical confusing habits of verbal and non-verbal communication. This work remains theoretical, since the suggested abnormal styles of communication have not been shown to be specific to schizophrenia (Mischler & Waxler, 1965). In adults, objective evidence has at last been obtained to confirm the simple but important observation that schizophrenic illnesses may be precipitated by stressful events (Brown & Birley, 1968).

Biochemical: Some hereditary conditions are known to be associated with metabolic abnormalities arising from the lack of dysfunction of specific enzymes, but widespread and enthusiastic biochemical investigations of schizophrenic patients have up to now produced only theories. Much attention has been given to the metabolic pathways of noradrenaline, an important substance found in all parts of the nervous system, since it bears a tantalizing resemblance to mescaline and other compounds which can cause hallucinations and delusions. The skin pigment melanin, the amino-acid methionine, and transmethylation reactions, have all been of recent interest. Unfortunately, the negative conclusions expressed in Kety's review of 1959 still hold.

Psycho-physiological: Slowness is characteristic of many chronic schizophrenics, and this has led to the investigation of their reaction time and state of arousal by means of skin potential levels, and fusion thresholds of auditory and visual stimuli. Strong evidence has emerged that, contrary to expectation, social withdrawal is associated with excessive cortical arousal (Kornetsky & Mursky, 1966; Venables, 1968). This could mean that chronic schizophrenics are either quick to develop or slow to dissipate reactive inhibition, but this and other interpretation of these findings can only be tentative since the concepts of arousal and inhibition are complex and debatable, and chronic schizophrenics are unlikely to be a homogeneous group. This line of inquiry seems likely to be rewarding.

Cognitive disorder: Early descriptive studies of schizophrenic thought disorder suggested an inability to form abstract concepts ("concrete thinking"), plus an inability to preserve conceptual boundaries ("over-inclusive thinking"; Cameron, 1954). Subsequently Payne developed a theory of schizophrenic thought disorder involving over-inclusiveness and slowness (Payne, 1960), but the discrimination of schizophrenics from other psychiatric patients by Payne's battery of tests has not been confirmed by others. A more recent but more complex approach has been Bannister's utilization of Kelly's Repertory Grid, a sorting test in which the relationships between conceptual categories are measured statistically (Bannister, 1965). Cognitive disorders on all these measures are associated with the hebephrenic type of schizophrenia, and are usually absent in patients with systematized delusions. As in the psychophysiological studies, concepts of arousal, attention and distractability are brought into discussions of the test results. These tests have not yet proved to be of much value in clinical diagnosis, but they are important in the investigation and understanding of some of the symptoms of schizophrenia viewed as disorders of short-term handling and retrieval of information.

7. *Other theories of schizophrenia.* Psychoanalytic concepts have not proved helpful in either the understanding or treatment of schizophrenia. In psychoanalytic terms schizophrenia is regarded as a disturbance of ego organization and object relations, arising from abnormal early interaction between mother and child. There is regression back to the very early narcissistic level at which the self is not differentiated from the environment. Paranoid delusions are regarded as a repressed form of homosexual wishes. Federn (1952) and Klein (1952) have produced modern variations of psychoanalytic theories, but even convinced psychoanalysts usually accept that interpretative psychotherapy is of no use with schizophrenic patients, a view confirmed by a large-scale clinical investigation (May, 1968). Jung's use of his "word-association test" in schizophrenia is historically important as an early example of clinical experimental psychology, and he did a great deal of descriptive work on the relationship between the symbolism of schizophrenic symptoms and mythology. His belief that schizophrenia is due to emergence of the unconscious due to weakening of the will had no special impact. Kretschmer (1925) proposed a constitutional theory of mental illness, in which schizophrenia is one extreme of a continuum, the other end being normality; schizoid personality disorder occupies an intermediate position between. Body type is said to vary in the same way, the tall thin (asthenic) type being associated with schizophrenia. Kretschmer's theories have influenced the thinking of many clinicians, but reliable evidence for the importance of these fairly weak correlations has not been produced. Existential theories and therapy have recently arisen in Germany but are not widely accepted or used (Binswanger, 1958).

8. *Treatment of schizophrenia.* The modern treatment of schizophrenia that has evolved over the last fifteen years is empirical, and consists of phenothiazine drugs for the acute phases (commonly chlorpromazine or trifluorperazine), followed by a planned program of social stimulation and work training or re-training, often aimed at achieving a less ambitious level than before the acute illness. Ideally, a system of in-patient units, day hospitals, assessment and training workshops, supervised hostels and sheltered employment facilities should be available, which together with long-term psychiatric follow-up form a comprehensive system aimed at keeping the patient as much in contact with normal community life as possible. Positive contact with the patient needs to be maintained, to avoid a drift into an isolated, vagrant or institutionalized existence. This concept of community care has greatly improved the prognosis of all forms of schizophrenia, and even with the limited facilities usually available, only a small proportion of patients now remain in hospital for more than two years, the majority being

discharged within six months; this often remains so even when re-admissions are necessary. It is easy to overestimate the role of phenothiazines in this improved prognosis, and there are good grounds for believing that improvement in daily social care and living conditions in mental hospitals has been just as important (Hoenig, 1967; Wing & Birley, 1970).

Electroconvulsive therapy is effective in the acute catatonic forms of schizophrenia, but its use in other forms is debatable. Insulin coma and leucotomy are no longer widely used. The rise and fall in popularity of insulin coma treatment, which was the treatment of choice all over the world for about twenty years between 1935 and 1955, is one of the most striking recent examples of how a non-specific treatment effect can be universally accepted by clinicians in spite of the lack of objective and controlled evidence of its efficacy (Ackner, 1952).

The recent development of therapy based upon modern learning theories has resulted in the successful application of operant conditioning techniques and token economies to both verbal and social behavior of chronic schizophrenics (e.g. Allyon, T. & Azrin, N., 1968). Surprisingly encouraging results have often been obtained but adequate control of the ward environment is often difficult to achieve, and the major problem is how to obtain generalization of the response to other environments. This appears to be a promising area for further research.

9. *Future developments.* It is likely that new drugs and more refined techniques of physiological and biochemical investigation will allow the identification of subgroups of patients with different underlying etiology or mechanisms of symptom production. These sub-divisions will presumably reflect disturbances in the biochemical reactions and inter-neuronal connections which determine how the brain stores, retrieves and integrates information.

Bibliography: Ackner, B. & Oldham, A. J.: Insulin treatment of schizophrenia, Lancet (i), 1962, 504–506. **Allyon, T. & Azrin, N.:** The token economy: a motivational system for therapy and rehabilitation. New York, 1968. **Bannister, D.:** The genesis of schizophrenic thought disorder, Brit. J. Psychiat., 1965, *111*, 377. **Binswanger, L.:** Schizophrenie. Pfüllingen, 1958. **Bleuler, E. P.:** Dementia praecox and the group of schizophrenias. New York, 1950. **Brown, G. W. & Birley, J. L. T.:** Crises and life changes and the onset of schizophrenia. J. of Health & Social Behavior, 1968, *9*, 203. **Cameron, N.:** Experimental analysis of schizophrenic thinking. In: **Kasanin** (Ed.): Language and thought in schizophrenia. California, 1944. **Federn, P.:** Ego psychology and the psychoses. London, 1952. **Fish, F.:** Schizophrenia. Bristol, 1962. **Goldberg, E. M. & Morrison, S. L.:** Schizophrenia & social class. Brit. J. Psychiat, 1963, *109*, 785–802. **Hoenig, J.:** The prognosis of schizophrenia. In: Recent developments in schizophrenia. Brit. J. Psychiat. Special Publ. No. 1, 1967. **Kendell, R. E., Cooper, J. E., Gourlay, A. J., Copeland, J. R. M., Sharpe, L. & Gurland, B. J.:** The diagnostic criteria of American and British psychiatrists. Archiv. Gen. Psychiat, 1971 **Kety, S. S.:** Biochemical theories of schizophrenia. Science, 1959, *129*, 1528–96. **Klein, M., Heimann, P., Isaacs, S. & Riviere, J.:** Developments in psychoanalysis. London, 1952. **Kleist, K.:** Schizophrenic symptoms and cerebral pathology. J. Ment. Sci., 1960, *106*, 246. **Kornetsky, C. & Mursky, A. F.:** On certain psychopharmacological and physiological differences between schizophrenic and normal persons. Psychopharmacologia (Berl.), 1966, *8*, 309–18. **Kraepelin, E.:** Lehrbuch der Psychiatrie. Leipzig, [8]1899. **Kretschmer, E.:** Physique and character, trans. **Sprott, W. J. H.,** London, 1925. **Langfelt, G.:** The prognosis in schizophrenia. Acta Psychiat. Scand. Suppl., 1956, *110*. **Leonhard, K.** Cycloid psychoses—endogenous psychoses which are neither schizophrenic or manic depressive. J. Ment. Sci., 1961, *107*, 633. **Lewis, A. J.:** Paranoia and paranoid—a historical perspective. Psychological Medicine, 1970, *1*, 2–12. **May, P. R. A.:** Treatment of schizophrenia—a comparative study of five treatment methods. New York, 1968. **McGhie, A.:** Studies of cognitive disorder in schizophrenia. In: Recent developments in schizophrenia. Brit. J. Psychiat. Special Publ. No. 1, 1967. **Mischler, E. G. & Scotch, N. A.:** Sociocultural factors in the epidemiology of schizophrenia. Psychiatry, 1953, *26*, 315. **Mischler, E. G. & Waxler, N. E.:** Family interaction process and schizophrenia—a review of current theories. Merrill-Palmer Quart., 1965, *II*, 269. **Payne, R. W.:** Cognitive abnormalities.

In: **Eysenck, H. J.** (Ed.): Handbook of abnormal psychology. London, 1960, 193–261. **Rosenthal, D.:** Problems of sampling and diagnosis in the major twin studies of schizophrenia. Psychiat. Res., 1962, *1*, 116–134. **Roth, M.:** The natural history of mental disorder in old age. J. Ment. Sci., 1955, *101*, 281–301. **Schneider K.:** Clinical psychopathology (trans. **Hamilton, M.**). New York, 1958. **Shields, J.:** The genetics of schizophrenia in historical context. In: Recent developments in schizophrenia. Brit. J. Psychiat. Special Publ. No. 1, 1967. **Slater, E. T. O.:** The monogenic theory of schizophrenia. Acta genet. (Basle), 1958, *8*, 50–56. **Smythies, J. R.:** Recent advances in the biochemistry of schizophrenia. In: Recent developments in schizophrenia. Brit. J. Psychiat. Special Publ. No. 1, 1967. **Venables, P. H.:** Experimental psychological studies of chronic schizophrenia. In: **Shepherd & Davies** (Eds.): Studies in psychiatry. London, 1968. **W.H.O.:** International statistical classification of diseases (section V), 8th Revision, W.H.O., Geneva, 1965. **Wing, J. K. & Brown, G. W.:** Institutionalism and schizophrenia. Cambridge, 1970. **Yates, A. J :** Behavior therapy. New York, 1970. Ch. 14.

J. E. Cooper

Schizothyme. A constitutional temperament having some affinity with the leptosomic (q.v.), asthenic type and in which introversion (q.v.) and psychesthetic proportion (q.v.) are strongly marked. The schizothyme is characterized by a "very sharply defined individual zone", "a conscious contrast between the ego and the outside world", "a touchy or indifferent withdrawal from the mass of his fellow men", the predominance of "dreams, ideas or principles". *W.K.*

School counselor. A person who gives advice to all those concerned with the education of young people at school and to the pupils themselves. He assists the parents and teachers when important decisions concerning school admission and school course have to be taken; he helps also to remove difficulties at school and to solve educational problems. The student is given advice commensurate with his specific abilities in the choice of subjects, in deciding on a career and in coping with difficulties which appear as work progresses and his personality develops. The duties which a school counselor is required to perform are so extensive that anybody taking up this work should have had some training in psychology, educational theory and practical teaching. See *Vocational guidance*.

H.S.

School neurosis. The term indicates a neurotic weakness of behavior which shows up in the area covered by school or is triggered by it. Occasionally the forms this behavioral disorder takes can only be seen when the individual is at school (school mutism, cramp, phobia, aphasia), but usually they appear both in and out of school (separation anxiety, performance anxiety, difficulties with learning, weakness of concentration, social difficulty). To cure the behavior due to school neurosis is one of the tasks of the school psychologist (q.v.) and the school counselor (q.v.). See *Neurosis; Educational psychology.* *H.S.*

School psychologist. As a rule this officer is assigned to an educational authority or to a large school; his duties are to decide the suitability of a child for school (see *School readiness*), to determine the reason for failure at school and to show what are the specific areas in which the pupils are gifted (q.v.) or possess ability (q.v.). In addition to these tasks, which are primarily diagnostic, the school psychologist has also chiefly to look ahead (advice on school career) and to counsel. See *Vocational guidance.* *H.S.*

School readiness. The term should not—as the concept of readiness might suggest—be understood as being relatively independent of the environment in the sense of biologistico-automatic growth models. School readiness is rather *that state of development necessary for a certain rudimentary instruction* which is more the result of learning than of maturation processes.

School readiness has to be considered as a relational concept which is determined partly by the demands of society (teaching aims and methods, school organization), which the latter makes on the school beginner, and partly by the particular state of the child's development. Three more or less prognostic groups of school readiness criteria are specified for the school system at present in existence:

1. *Somatic criteria:* the general state of health (nutritional standard, functional efficiency of the organs and senses), change of structure (Zeller criteria), growth of second teeth.

2. *Psychic criteria:* ability to arrange, to think, language capacity, learning motivation. It is believed that these criteria can be determined with the tests of school readiness in use nowadays.

3. *Sociological criteria:* family situation, school education and occupation of the parents, number of children, attendance at nursery school, social behavior.

There are no established criteria for predicting success in the first school year. School readiness tests in general only possess validity coefficients of up to $v = 0.60$. No decision about keeping any individual child down can be taken with such tests. But in proficiently organized primary schools there is no definite need for selection procedures but only for recommending certain treatment. See *Educational psychology.* *H.Ma.*

Schroeder's staircase. A *reversible figure* which appears alternately as the top of a staircase seen from above or the underneath of a staircase seen from below. *C.D.F.*

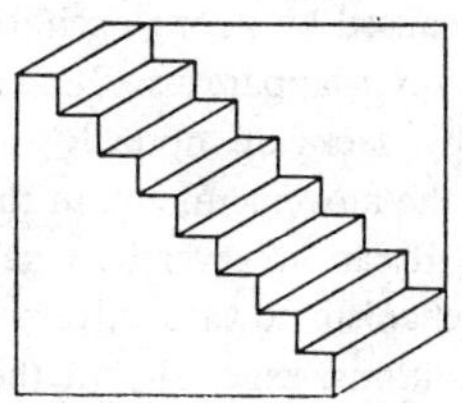

Scientific management. A system of the American engineer F. W. Taylor (1856–1915) according to a scientifically based method of industrial management for the purpose of rationalization and increasing productivity. Taylor believed that maximization of gain and harmonious cooperation could be achieved for both social partners, if each worker had a definite task ("pensum") which had to be fulfilled in a standard time ("normal time") and in a standard way ("the one best way"), (substituted for individually obtained "rules of thumb"). His study of the loading of unwrought iron (1899) is famous. *Criticism:* treatment of men as extension of the machine with disregard of physiological (see *Fatigue*, etc.), psychological (individual differences) and social factors (see *Hawthorne experiment*). See *Industrial psychology.* *W.F.N.*

Sclera. The outer layer of the eye (q.v.). Its thickness varies locally and ranges between 0.3 mm and 1.5 mm. About 15 circular degrees nasally from the posterior pole of the eye it is traversed by the optic nerve and joins on to the cornea with a circular boundary line (limbus corneae). Adhesive fibers in the sclerotic wall form a dense fibrous network comparable to the fibrous network of a balloon. That is why the sclera possesses such an extraordinarily tough elasticity; together with the intraocular pressure it fixes the shape of the eyeball. *R.R.*

Scopolamine (synonym for hyoscine). An anticholinergic substance with strong central and psychological effects, occurring in solanacene and one of the belladonna alkaloids (q.v.). Scopolamine is comparable to *atropine* (q.v.) in many of its effects (e.g. dilatation of the pupils, storage reduction, reduction of the EEG—arousal under stimulation, slow EEG waves). Psychological effects are, however, to some extent different: its effects in humans, in contrast to those of atropine, are to induce fatigue and inhibit the faculties (especially extended concentration, reduction of vigilance). Altogether, the peripheral physiological effects of the two substances are comparable, but psychologically the effect of scopolamine is stronger. The effects persist for several hours (more than five). With higher doses, scopolamine has psychosomatic effects. The amnesic effects often attributed to it are not sufficiently attested. In animal research, surprisingly, no sedative effects have been discovered. Many experiments (in rats) show an increase in activity. Faculties are usually impeded. Scopolamine in animal experiments leads to delay in habituation to new stimuli; it is often applied for therapeutic purposes, e.g. in conditions of excitation (usually in combination with other sedatives).

Bibliography: Colquhoun, W. P.: Effects of hyoscine and meclozine on vigilance and short term memory. Brit. J. Industr. Med., 1962, *19*, 287–96. **Helmann, H.:** Die Scopolaminwirkung. Basle, 1952. **Longo, V. G.:** Behavioral and electroencephalographic effects of related compounds. Pharmacol. Rev. 1966, *18*, 965–96. **Ostfeld, A. M. & Aruguete, A.:** Central nervous system effects of hyoscine in man. J. Pharmacol. exp. Therapeut., 1969, *137*, 133–9. **Parkes, M. W.:** An examination of central actions characteristic of scopolamine: comparison of central and peripheral activity in scopolamine, atropine and some synthetic basic esters. Psychopharmaciologia, 1965, 1–19.

W.J.

Score. Number (generally a total of points) assigned to an individual on the basis of an objective measurement (e.g. a test) or a subjective judgment (see *Rating; Scaling*). *A.R.*

Scotoma. An area in the visual field which is blind or partially blind. All people have one blind spot, since the region where the optic nerve leaves the retina has no receptors. Scotomata can result from damage to the retina or to the brain. *C.D.F.*

Scotopia (*Twilight vision*). Twilight vision has different properties from day vision since it is mediated by the *rods* rather than the *cones*. The existence of these two systems is indicated by the discontinuity in the dark adaptation curve. With twilight vision a person is insensitive to color and his periperhal vision is better for fine detail than his central vision, since there are no rods in the fovea. *C.D.F.*

Screen effect. 1. *Static screen effect.* An effect whereby we strongly perceive the continuation of objects behind screens although there is no immediate or objective evidence for the particular continuation we perceive.

2. *Kinetic screen effect.* This is the same effect concerning the way we perceive the continuation of moving objects behind a screen. The *piston effect* (q.v.) and the *tunnel effect* (q.v.) are examples of kinetic screen effects. *C.D.F.*

Scribbling stage. The first stage in the development of drawing in a child. Normally it occurs at the age of 2 or 3, but there can be considerable variations in time, since an essential role is played by perception, sensory motor activity, imagination, memory, motivation and intelligence in acquiring the ability to draw.

Séance. Meeting at which a medium (q.v.) officiates. Also called "sitting" or "session". *J.B.*

Sea sickness. A kinetosis released by the movement of the ship (movement sickness), which manifests itself in giddiness, nausea (indisposition), vomiting and other vegetative disturbances like perspiration, weakness and palor. It is caused by strong excitation of the vestibular (q.v.) apparatus. Its effects are increased by lack of optical information concerning the movement, e.g. in the interior of the ship. It can however be regarded as a defense mechanism toward adverse environmental conditions, especially in the case of discrepancy of mental impressions comparable to the automatic reflexes of dead insects.

E.D.

Seashore test. See *Music, psychology of.*

Secondary drives. Motive forces in human behavior which are not innate (*primary drives*) but learnt. The psychology of learning explains their origin as follows: situations which often occur together with a condition of reduction of primary drives can eventually occur on their own and are then striven for by the organism on their own account. There is also the explanation of "vicarious reinforcement" in the process of the creation of secondary drives, or *introjection.* This helps the transmission of ethical and esthetic values in the process of nurture. (See *Drive.*) *A.Ro.*

Secondary, primary function. In behavior accompanying attention we note two opposite processes. Fluctuation or distraction (oscillation) is a "primary function" and perseverance (q.v.) is a "secondary function". (K. Gross, G. Heymans.) *H.W.*

Secondary processes. According to S. Freud these are set against the *primary processes* (q.v.), motives (q.v.), opinions of a man which accord with his reality and can be striven for or satisfied in real situations. They are controlled by the "reality principle" (q.v.).

W.T.

Second sight (syn. *Deuteroscopy*). Form of precognition (q.v.) in which the sensitive (q.v.) sees a person's double situated alongside that person. This is taken to portend his imminent demise. Associated with Scottish folklore. *J.B.*

Secrecy, obligation of. For the psychologist this is largely covered by a professional code of ethics. In some countries, a breach of the vow of secrecy on the part of a psychologist can result in proceedings in a court of civil or criminal law. *H.J.S.*

Secretion. Discharge or emission of products of the glands. A distinction is made between *external secretions* of the exocrine glands such as the salivary, digestive, tear and sweat glands and the *internal secretions* of the endocrine (q.v.) or hormone glands. *E.D.*

Security. A general human need for stability in existence; it is a matter of contention whether it is a vital need (such as hunger or thirst motivation), or socio-cultural in nature (see *Drive; Need; Motivation*). Cantril's (1965) list of human hopes and fears based on questionnaires (twenty thousand individuals from thirteen countries) begins with (*a*) gratification of those needs oriented toward survival; (*b*) securing of what has been achieved hitherto; and (*c*) aspiration to order and certainty in one's own life, and to the calculability of existence. Concern for the satisfaction of survival needs is an experience which draws on all the energies and thoughts of those under such pressure. The need for security in all areas of life leads men to devise various methods to anticipate regulation of danger and disorder: in industrial societies we have, e.g., "social security" and "insurance" and "assurance" (economic security), and "industrial security" or "industrial safety". See *Anxiety; Accident proneness; Accident research.*

Bibliography: **Cantril, H.:** The pattern of human concerns. New Brunswick, N.Y., 1965. **Thomae, H.:** Das Individuum und seine Welt. Göttingen, 1968.

G.R.W.M.

Sedation threshold. A pharmacopsychological test introduced by Shagass (1957) for diagnosis and prognosis. The barbiturate (q.v.) amobarbital natricum (sodium amytal r) is administered intravenously with a speed of 0.5 mg/kg body weight per 40 sec. During the injection an EEG is taken frontally. The sedation threshold is defined as the amobarbital quantity (in mg/kg bodyweight) experienced during the fast wave in the region of 17–25 Hz, a strong increase of amplitudes. The occurrence of slurred speech correlates roughly with it. Repetition reliability and objectivity of the procedure is high. The sedation threshold correlates *inter alia* with manifest anxiety (q.v.), it is higher in reactive than endogenous depressions (q.v.) and lower in hysterical (see *Hysteria*) than in dysthymic (see *Dysthymia*) subjects (in H. J. Eysenck's interpretation).

Bibliography: Shagass, C.: A neurophysiological test for psychiatric diagnosis: results in 750 patients. Amer. J. Psychiatr., 1957, *114*, 1002–10. **Id.:** Sedation threshold: technique and concept. In: **Brill, H.** (Ed.): Proceed. 5. Intern. Congr. Neuro-Psycho-Pharmacology. Amsterdam, 1967. *W.J.*

Sedatives. Substances which are applied therapeutically in higher doses as hypnotics (q.v.), in lower doses for the purpose of affective and motor inhibition. They have been used much less since the development of tranquilizers (q.v.), because of their frequent tendency to induce fatigue and hinder faculties. However they have more in common pharmacologically with tranquilizers than with neuroleptics. *E.L.*

Segmental innervation. The whole surface of the human body can be divided into skin areas (dermatome, Read's zones) each of which is sensorily innervated by one and the same *segment of the spinal cord.* The internal organs also can be associated with segments of the spinal cord so that when painful diseases of an organ occur, it happens not infrequently that corresponding dermatomes are also irritated and cause pain. *E.D.*

Segment illusion. Of two identical segments of circles placed one above the other, the upper will appear larger. In addition, if monocularly fixated, the lower one will appear nearer. The trapezium illusion is identical except that the segments are replaced by trapezia. *C.D.F.*

Selection (syn. *Natural selection*). A term used in genetics. Selection, together with mutation, plays a decisive part in the evolution of species. Selection takes place because creatures that are more fitted to survive in their environment have more offspring than those not so well fitted to survive. Selection is used to refer not only to the choice of genetic types in breeding but to the singling out of specific *personality traits* in the development of the individual. See *Traits.* *W.L.*

Selective perception. Because of the volume and complexity of stimulation with which a person is continually bombarded, all perception is selective, but in some circumstances it can become abnormally so. A person will selectively perceive those aspects of his experience that he has found most important in the past. Hence the attaching of extreme importance to various aspects of the world through stress, psychiatric disturbance, poverty or even a strong expectation induced by experimental manipulation can result in selective perception of an extreme kind. People see only what they want to see or what they expect. *C.D.F.*

Selectivity. The ability of a test item to differentiate between testees in whom a given feature is emphasized to a greater or lesser extent. Selectivity is often defined as the correlation between a test item and the total point value. There is a clear relationship between difficulty and selectivity. See *Test theory.* *A.R.*

Self. The individual, as subject to his own contemplation or action. According to Hegel: "Consciousness first finds itself in self-consciousness—the notion of mind—its turning-point, where it leaves the particolored show of the sensuous immediate, passes from the dark void of the transcendent and remote super-sensuous, and steps into the spiritual daylight of the present." (*Phenomenology of Spirit.*) Williams James makes a distinction between the self as known, or the *me*, the empirical ego, and the self as knower, or the *I*, the pure ego: "Whatever I may be thinking of, I am always at the same time more or less aware of myself, of my personal existence. At the same time it is I who am aware; so that the total self of me, being as it were duplex, partly known and partly knower, partly object and partly subject, must have two aspects discriminated in it, of which for shortness we may call one the *Me* and the other the *I*". (*Textbook of Psychology.*) But Wittgenstein observes: ". . . James' introspection showed, not the meaning of the word 'self' (so far as it means something like 'person', 'human being', 'he himself', 'I myself'), nor any analysis of such a thing, but the state of a philospher's attention when he says the word 'self' to himself and tries to analyze its meaning. (And a good deal could be learned from this.)" (*Philosophical Investigations.*) *J.M.*

Self concept. The totality of attitudes (q.v.), judgments, and values of an individual relating to his behavior, abilities (q.v.) and qualities. "Self concept" embraces the awareness of these variables and their evaluation. Self concept has been investigated by the use of the Q sorting method (q.v.), which distinguishes between first *the real self-description* and second the discrepancy between this and an *ideal self-description.*

Among theories of the self and the self concept we may mention that of C. Rogers, whose client-centered psychotherapy (non-prescriptive psychotherapy) is founded upon his theories of the self. These theories elicited numerous empirical studies on the self concept which show, for example, that parental behavior during upbringing has a strong influence on the appearance of the self concept and that the measure of ego-ideal discrepancy is closely connected with the measure of failure in adjustment. (See *Ego.*)

Bibliography: Byrne, D.: An introduction to personality. A research approach. Englewood Cliffs, N.J., 1966. *D.B.*

Self-knowledge. I. Kant considered self-knowledge to be the beginning of all human wisdom, yet the academic psychology of the nineteen-seventies does not include the term among its basic concepts and it does not appear in contemporary dictionaries of psychology. The main concern of psychology is the attempt to apprehend others psychologically. Only the various branches of depth psychology (q.v.) still insist that anyone who seeks to analyze others must first undergo a training analysis. It would seem reasonable that the assessment of others should be preceded by self-assessment.

According to Hector (1971), self-knowledge is one of the two pillars of psychology. Self-knowledge begins with a survey of one's own life, taking into account outward stages and inner conditions, and enabling one to reach an understanding of one's personal development and a critical judgment of one's spiritual and intellectual existence. Any theoretical scientific question about the truth and error of self-knowledge can produce only flexible answers. Of course it is possible to arrive at an essentially erroneous self-image (self-deception). However, the probability of such deception drops when the process is psychologically controlled. *H. Hector*

II. "Self-knowledge" is found as an entry in dictionaries of philosophy, where it is defined as the knowledge of the ego (q.v.), of the self, of the dispositions (see *Anlagen*), abilities, errors and weaknesses, suasions and response patterns of one's own person (q.v.). Hector (1971) believes that any judgment of an other ought to be preceded by self-knowledge in the form of one's own case history (q.v.). Such a life history (q.v.) can certainly help one toward self-knowledge, but hardly resolves the complex problem of self-knowledge posed by the requirement "Know thyself!" (inscription above the temple of Apollo at Delphi) and the "*individuum ineffabile*" thesis. For the psychology of the twentieth century—when it became clear that there could be no self-knowledge without self-deception—"self-knowledge" became (if reflected upon at all) a pre-scientific (lay) term for more precisely conceived (and operationally definable) psychological concepts such as: self-judgment, self-assessment, self-image, and self-concept. Self-concept research has shown that what each individual knows about himself and how he sees himself, derives from the way in which he has been and is considered by others (role, q.v., role expectations, mirror-image). If one's own self is falsely assessed, this leads to difficulties and conflicts with one's fellows and the environment (see *Conflict*). The therapeutic effect of the psychological (analytic, exploratory) interview, of psychoanalysis (q.v.) and, above all, of non-directive therapy (q.v.) resides ultimately in the fact that clients correct their erroneous self-image in the course of psychotherapy, and thus attain once more to personal and social harmony. See *Abilities; Differential psychology; Personality; Philosophy and psychology; Traits; Type; Meditation.*

Bibliography: Hector, H.: Selbsterkenntnis als fehlender Psychologie-Begriff. Praktische Psychol., 1971, *25*, 97–8. **Kierkegaard, S.:** Either/or. Princeton, N.J., 1944.

F. Novak

Semantic differential. A method developed by C. E. Osgood (1952, 1957) and P. R. Hofstätter (1957) to allow rating of an idea, concept or object on a series of scales. A series of dimensions (e.g. soft-hard, strong-weak) is divided into stages (usually seven). A subject's ratings of a concept may be represented as a "polarity profile". The average values of a concept assigned a position by a number of subjects reflect a group idea or opinion (see *Stereotype*). Well-known "stereotypes" of this kind are e.g., sex roles and national characters. The degree of similarity of two concepts may be determined by correlational techniques (e.g. "love" and "red," $r = +0.89$). According to Hofstätter, the matrices of similarity correlations of a number of assigned concepts from the sphere of personality yield factors, which he interprets thus: F_1 = *positive* outward orientation; F_2 = *negative* outward orientation; F_3 = *inward* orientation. Osgood's three basic dimensions, or factors, reduced from a large number of scales, are: *potency*, (strong-weak, etc.), *activity* (fast-slow, etc.), *evaluation* (good-bad, etc.). See *Attitude; Psycholinguistics.*

Bibliography: Hofstätter, P. R.: Psychologie. Frankfurt, 1957. **Osgood, C. E.:** The nature and measurement of meaning. Psychol. Bull., 1952, *49*, 197–237. **Id., Suci, G. J. & Tannenbaum, P. H.:** The measurement of meaning. Urbana, Ill., 1957.

P.G.

Semantization (syn. *Ritualization*). The development of a behavior pattern into a pure signal. Even human greeting ceremonies are thought to have developed from combat rituals. Raising one's hat derives from removing a helmet, and a military salute from raising one's visor. Both gestures indicate trust.

V.P.

Semantics. The noun "semantics", derived from the Greek adjective σημαντικόγ ("significant"), in the sense of science of meaning or of signification, is a modern creation. It is used by different authors within a wide range of connotations. Many use it as synonymous with "semiotic", the general study of signs, in particular of linguistic signs, others as denoting only that subfield of semiotic which deals with such relations of signs to things other than signs as denotation, connotation, reference, designation, and the like, with "pragmatics" reserved for the subfield that deals with the relations of signs to their users, while "syntax" deals with the relations of signs among themselves. Synonyms for "semantics" in its narrow linguistic use are "semology", "semasiology", and "semantology", but these terms are rarely used.

In logical semantics, one often distinguishes, with Mill, between denotation and connotation, or with Frege and Quine, between denotation and sense, or with Carnap, between extension and intension. Carnap also distinguishes between descriptive semantics, the empirical study of meaning in natural languages, and pure semantics, the analytical study of meaning in constructed language-systems. Whereas descriptive semantics is the result of an abstraction from descriptive pragmatics, the psychological, sociological, and ethnological study of actual speech behavior, pure semantics is independent of pragmatics, though the choice of rules for the semantic systems to be investigated may be guided by pragmatic facts, and is so in general for those systems that are meant to stand in "close correspondence" with natural languages.

In linguistics, the development of theoretical semantics is only in its beginnings. It was long hampered by certain philosophical and, in particular, ontological preconceptions, from which many linguists thought to escape by retreating into the study of meaning change and etymology, subjects still often identified with semantics in general. But there still exists little unanimity on even the most basic issues in theoretical semantics such as whether words (or morphemes) are to be regarded as the fundamental carriers of meaning so that the meaning of larger units (up to sentences) is to be treated as resulting from the meanings of their component words by some combinatory rules (sometimes called rules of projection), or whether sentences should be regarded as the fundamental meaning carriers, with the meanings of their component words considered to be some function of the meanings of the sentences in which they may occur.

Componential meaning analysis works reasonably well in some simple cases, and there seems little wrong in looking at the meanings of "father", "mother", "son", and "daughter" as simple conjuncts of the meanings of "parent" and "male", "parent" and "female", "child" and "male", and "child" and "female", respectively. How far this kind of analysis can be usefully driven and how universal it is, are questions under active discussion. It seems that the treatment of semantic fields, in the sense of Trier-Weisgerber, requires not only componential rules, but also rules of quite different kinds, of various degrees of universality, such as the rules that "parent-of" and "child-of" denote converse relations, as do "greater-than" and "smaller-than", "sells-to" and "buys-from", or the rules that "male" and "female" are antonyms, that "father-of" and "parent-of" are hyponyms, and of many other much more complex kinds.

The meaning of metaphorical and idiomatic expressions are clear instances of cases which cannot be handled by simple combinatorial-componential techniques exclusively. Other phenomena, that sometimes create difficulties in communication, are semantic ambiguity, whether of the accidental type—homonymy—or of the more essential one—polysemy—, and vagueness. How these difficulties are overcome, through utilization of linguistic context or of extra-linguistic, situational context, is still little understood.

Insufficiently understood is also so far the functioning of indexical (cotext- and context-dependent) expressions, whether of the deictic type ("I", "you", "now", "here", etc.), of the anaphoric type (pro-elements of various kinds, pro-nouns, pro-verbs, pro-adjectives, pro-sentences, etc.), or of still other types. Their treatment transcends semantics and belongs rather to pragmatics, since for understanding their role in communication the cotexts and contexts of their utterances have to be taken into account.

In standard modern generative-transformational linguistic theory (originating with Chomsky), the semantic component of the total grammar of a language is considered to operate on certain structures generated by the syntactic component, sometimes called deep structures, interpretatively, providing them with one or more semantic representations (or readings), while the phonological component provides other structures generated by the syntactic component, sometimes called surface structures, with their phonological representations.

In another version of this theory, the semantic component itself is supposed to directly generate semantic representations. It should be noted that in this version these representations are often modelled along norms provided by logical systems developed independently by modern symbolic logicians for mathematical and philosophical, but not necessarily for linguistic, reasons. These developments throw new light on the problem of the precise relationship between semantics and logic and may support attempts made (e.g., by Bar-Hillel) to identify logic with universal (or transcendental) semantics.

Since all these theories are still in active development, the last word on the relations between deep structure, semantic representation, and cognitive content has not yet been said.

A recent subfield of applied semantics is computational semantics, in which the use of computers for the determination of the semantic representation(s) of sentences of natural languages, as well as of constructed languages, is investigated.

Due to the lack of adequate semantic theories, the field of psychosemantics, that brand of psycholinguistics which deals with the psychological aspects of meaning, is still in its very first beginnings. Experimental studies in this field, using quantitative techniques, have not yet gone beyond studying the strengths of meaning association of various expressions, usually of single verbs or small phrases (Osgood's "semantic differential").

Various measures of the meaning content, or of the semantic information, carried by declarative sentences of natural or constructed languages, defined on the basis of absolute and conditional logical probability measures of these sentences (not to be confused with the statistical probabilities of the utterances of these sentences) have been proposed (e.g. by Carnap and Bar-Hillel), but so far the applications have been rather restricted.

Bibliography: Bar-Hillell Y.: Language and information. Reading, Mass. & Jerusalem, 1964. **Id.:** Aspects of language. Amsterdam & Jerusalem, 1970. **Carnap, R.:** Replies and expositions, III. In: **Schilpp, P. A.** (Ed.): The philosophy of Rudolf Carnap. La Salle (Ill.), 889–944. **Chomsky, N.:** Aspects of the theory of syntax. Cambridge, Mass., 1965. **Cohen, L. J.:** The diversity of meaning. London, 1962. **Creelman, M. B.:** The experimental investigation of meaning. New York, 1966. **Katz, J. J.:** The philosophy of language. New York & London, 1966. **Lakoff, G.:** Generative semantics. New York, 1971. **Lorenz, K.:** Elemente der Sprachkritik. Frankfurt a/M, 1970. **Lyons, J.:** Introduction to theoretical linguistics. Cambridge, 1968. **Quinel, W. V. O.:** Word and object. New York & London, 1970. **Schaff, A.:** Introduction to semantics. Oxford & Warsaw, 1962. **Ullman, S.:** The principles of semantics. Glasgow, [2]1957. **Weinreichl, U.:** Explorations in semantic theory. In: **Sebeok, T. A.** *et al.* (Eds.): Current trends in linguistics, III. The Hague, 1966, 395–477. **Ziff, P.:** Semantic analysis. Ithaca, N.Y., 1960.

Y. Bar-Hillel

Semicircular canals are filled with liquid, stand vertically one on top of the other, lie at any given time in a spatial plane, and serve as part of the organ of balance for the reception of acceleration. Inside the canal on both sides are movable tufts of hair in a colloid mass (*cupulae*) which during accelerations are turned outwards by the liquid flowing into the arcades and which impart a mechanical stimulus to the sensory cells situated at their lower end. *M.S.*

Semiotic(s). The general theory of signs, which can derive from *natural* and *artificial* languages. Three aspects are usually distinguished:

Syntax is concerned with the relations between signs and other signs or series of signs. The syntactic rules of a language enable the permissible associations of basic elements to develop into more complex structures (sentences). See *Grammar.*

Semantics (q.v.) studies the connection between signs and their meanings.

Pragmatics is concerned with the relation between linguistic signs and their users, the human transmitters and receivers of information. According to K. Bühler's model of language, the signal and symptom functions are the main objects of pragmatic investigation. The factor of evaluation disclosed by the semantic differential (q.v.) technique (good-bad, beautiful-ugly, etc.) also lies in this area. *B.R.*

Senility (syn. *Decrepitude*). Terms for the physical and mental decline of performance which usually occurs in old age. This aging process of the mind and body is accompanied by an enfeeblement of vitality and activity, and the psychic tempo slows down. Attention (q.v.) and initiative are usually reduced, and the capacity for self-control is partly lost. An old person's powers of observation suffer (see *Memory*), especially with regard to new impressions, and frequently there are impaired powers of judgment and comprehension. (See *Aging; Gerontology.*) *M.Sa.*

Sensation. "Sensation is a psychic phenomenon incapable of further division and is produced by external stimuli acting on the sensory organs; in its intensity it depends on the strength of the stimuli, and in its quality on the nature of the sensory organs." That is how H. Rohracher paraphrased the concept of sensation in the classical sense, and he distinguished sensation from perception (q.v.) as follows: "Perception is a complex psychic phenomenon consisting of sensory sensations and *components of experience*, the cause or content of which is located in space and so leads to the apprehension of objects belonging to the outside world." Of course, this separation of sensation and perception is scarcely feasible in practice, and the boundary between the two concepts in the literature is becoming increasingly obscure (cf. S. H. Bartley).

After Heraclitus and Protagoras had spoken of sensation and the communication of knowledge by means of sensation as early as the fifth century B.C., the problem of sensation in the eighteenth century became urgent for classical science because of empiricism.

The physiologists Bell (1811) and F. Magendie (1822) showed that the afferent (q.v.) nerves transmitting sensation are different from the motor nerves; the former reach the spinal cord by way of the posterior roots, the latter leave it by way of the anterior roots. W. Wundt (1874) had begun to distinguish between sensations and perceptions: sensation is an element, perception is composed of complexes of these elements (see *Psychology of Elements*). He said that in sensation there is intensity and quality, but in perception space and time. Thus Wundt agrees with the psychology of association in opposition to gestalt psychology, in which sensation is understood as a part of perception or is completely absorbed by it (while in physiological psychology sensation has absorbed perception) (cf. E. G. Boring). Finally behaviorism examines the sensations of humans and animals through their "distinctive behavior", and therefore uses "discriminating reaction" as an expression of sensation. The psychology of information (q.v.) uses the possibilities created by information theory (q.v.) to interpret the information content of sensations mathematically.

The senses as conveyors of sensations. Using the word in its strict physiological meaning it may be said that sensation is the primary direct psychic correlate of an excitation of the senses by stimuli and contains information (q.v.) about the quality and quantity of these stimuli. Aristotle had been the first to state without the help of any apparatus that there were five senses, namely, sight, hearing, smell, taste and touch. Subsequent detailed study with improved apparatus subdivided the main sense of touch into the sense of pressure and contact (somesthetics), the sense of heat and the sense of pain; to these were added the sense of position and movement (kinesthetics) as a special form of somesthetics, and the sense of balance (see *Sense organs*). The senses are characterized by the following psychological and physiological criteria: (*a*) their excitation leads to a single class of experience with mostly different qualities of sensation. (*b*) Their adequate excitation is only possible if there is an amount of energy exceeding a certain minimum (threshold value). For an inadequate excitation even far greater amounts of energy are required. (*c*) The single senses or sensory channels have specific intakes (sensory cells, sensory receptor cells, neuro-epithelium). (*d*) From these specific sensory receptors a direct neuron path leads by way of synapses to certain areas of the cerebral cortex which are known as primary projection fields (q.v.) and in the direct vicinity of which there lie secondary projection fields (short and long term storage).

If the dimensions of experience and memory (q.v.) which in classical definitions of sensation are associated with perception are excluded, one must then say that sensations occur when these primary projection fields are excited, and that it does not matter whether they are excited adequately by way of the specific and relevant sensory channel or inadequately, i.e., by some direct electrical stimulus. The so-called "reflection theory" of Soviet writers could therefore be valid only if one ignored that cortical projection fields are excited inadequately, i.e., after by-passing the sensory cells (see *Hallucination*).—Cf. Lenin, quoted according to B. G. Ananiev, p. 5: "Sensation is an image of matter in motion."

The physiological mechanism of sensation. A stimulus (q.v.) (a physico-chemical state with an energy content) impinges—usually after passing through an organ that carries stimuli (eyeball, external auditory channel and middle ear, nasal passages, derma and subcutaneous fatty tissue)—on a specific sensory receptor cell which becomes excited if the energy of the stimulus is above the threshold. Sechenov was probably the first to state that sensations represent some kind of transformation of external energy in the sensory organs and finally in the brain (q.v.) itself. Continuing from there, Pavlov called the sensory organs the "transformers of external energy" and recognized correctly that each functional act of these organs, which he classified as "peripheral ends of the analysators", represents a transformation of external energy into a process of nervous "excitement". The excitement expresses itself in physico-chemical changes in the cell membrane which lead to a change of the "membrane potential" and hence to the creation of a receptor potential (= generator potential) which is necessarily dependent on stimulus intensity (intensity functions, according to E. H. Weber, q.v., G. T. Fechner, q.v., S. S. Stevens, W. D. Keidel). The generator potential releases a salvo of neuro-action potentials (NAP) on the adjoining efferent nerve fiber, the frequency being proportional to the amplitude of the generator potential (coding of the stimulus intensity "continuous-analogous" in the amplitude of the generator potential and "discrete analogous" in the frequency of the

NAP). Several further synapses are passed in which there is each time a reduction of the NAP frequency (Keidel speaks of the reductive behavior of the synapses) by way of the necessary recoding (discrete-analogous into continuous-analogous and finally at the postsynaptic axon once more discrete-analogous). The excitation of the cortical projection fields can be directly demonstrated in the electrocorticogram (electric potential lead direct from the exposed cerebral cortex) as an "evoked potential" with a latency of approximately 10 m sec after the sensory cell excitation. This can also be proved indirectly by an EEG message from the intact, unopened scalp. The amplitudes of these evoked cerebral potentials are proportional to the degree of the receptor cells, which of course are subject to influences of adaptation, contrast, etc., and can therefore not give any simple "reflection" of the environment. In addition, these amplitudes are altered by central nervous, psychic

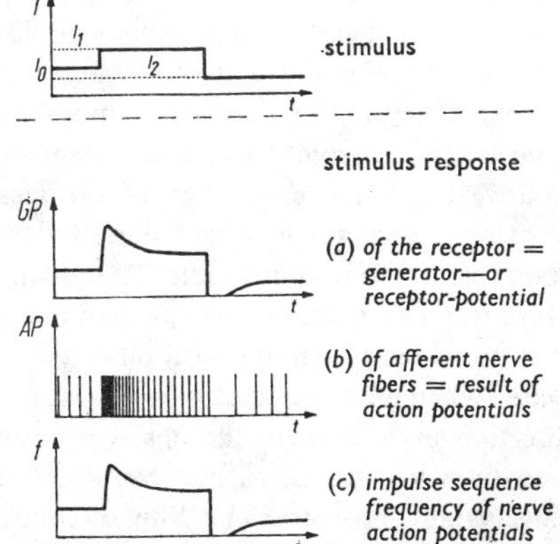

Schematic representation of connections between stimulus and physiological stimulus responses. Abscissa: time (standardized for all four axes). Ordinates: I: stimulus intensity; GP: amplitude of generator potential; AP: amplitude of action potentials measured on nerve fibers for a typical time sequence; f: frequency, number of action potentials passing over a point on the afferent nerve fibers in the set time unit. Upward movement of stimulus from I_0 to I_1, then downward from I_1 to I_2, so that I_2 (as here) is less than I_0. (Plattig, 1968.)

influences such as attention (q.v.), vigilance (q.v.), expectation, etc. Altogether, however, they represent a sufficiently accurate and objective correlate of sensation (W. D. Keitel, M. Spreng, K. H. Plattig, G. Guttmann). But how a sensation becomes conscious remains a complete mystery.

Bibliography: **Ananiev, B. G.**: Psychologie der sinnlichen Erkenntnis. Berlin, 1963. **Boring, E. G.**: Sensation and perception in the history of experimental psychology. New York, 1942. **Keidel, W. D. & Spreng, M.**: Elektronisch gemittelte langsame Rindenpotentiale des Menschen bei akustischer Reizung. Acta Oto-Laryngologica, Stockholm, 1963, *56*, 318–28. **Plattig, K. H.**: Über den elektrischen Geschmack. Reizstärkeabhängige evozierte Hirnpotential nach elektrischer Reizung der Zunge des Menschen. Z. Biol. 1969, *116*, 161–211. **Rohracher, H.**: Einführung in die Psychologie. Vienna & Innsbruck, [9]1965.

K. H. Plattig

Sensation function. According to C. G. Jung one of the four basic functions of the psyche. Together with intuition (q.v.) it is one of the irrational functions because it bypasses reason and transmits facts only without their meaning or value. *W.L.*

Sensation type. A functional type (q.v.) corresponding to the leading "irrational" psychic "basic function" of sensation ("conscious perception") which is linked "concretely" to sensory impression or "abstractly" to subjective "esthetic" evaluation. Hence it appears extraverted as naïve realism or introverted as an experience of the profoundly "portentous" and of the "significant". *W.K.*

Sense organs. The universe contains atoms and molecules which cause vibrations and radiation by means of regular movements; in so far as they affect the sense organs, they are called *stimuli*. The sense organs contain specifically reactive receptors (q.v.) (selection of stimuli) in which (adequate) stimuli evoke a potential which expands within the receptor. If it exceeds a critical value, it brings about total depolarization and action potentials in the nerve fibers. By analogy with communications technology a stimulus may be conceived as information encoded by means of a frequency code and broadcast over the nerves. The quantity of information depends on impulse frequency and the number of receptors.

1. *The eye.* The eye (q.v.) mediates most information concerning the environment. It produces an image of the environment on its light-sensitive layer, the retina (q.v.). Since the eye is a living structure, in addition to the physically conditioned faults, errors occur which distort the image. Physiological *contrast* (q.v.) (cf. Fig. 1) serves to correct the

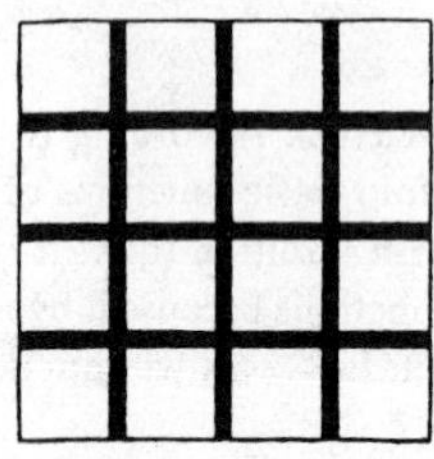

Fig. 1. Lattice contrast (L. Hermann). Bright spots appear at the points where the black lines intersect.

image: the retinal elements on which the light stimulus falls produce a contrasting effect (*inhibition*) in their environment; hence the difference between the object and its environment is enlarged; contrast largely compensates for dioptric imperfections, and thus affords the prerequisite for the proficient operation of the eye.

The eye's sense of space comes from its ability to perceive two separate points (see *Corresponding retinal points*). Its power of analysis, or *visual activity*, is greatest in the *fovea centralis* (q.v.). The limit of visual activity is reached when two cones are excited which are separated by an element excited by about twenty-five per cent less. Since recent anatomical research suggests that the diameter of a cone is smaller than had earlier been assumed, J. J. Oppel conjectures that the individual cone is not linked to the center by a separate fiber, but that several cones unite as an aggregate which is possibly sensitive to different colors. Hence visual activity is independent of the color of the test sign.

In the focused eye visual activity is measured at a distance of 5 m., since the light-sensitive layer of cones has a thickness that allows a shifting of the object within limits. Moreover, the dispersion circles at 5 m. are still too small to cause any substantial disturbance to physiological correction through contrast. The eye's power of analysis is still the same even at a shorter distance, if the experimental conditions are constantly maintained. It is optimal if illumination exceeds 1000 lx (König).

In the periphery of the retina, visual activity decreases quickly (to one-third at a distance from the center of the retina of 5°, and to one fifth at 10°). The decrease is smaller if presentation time is reduced, because a counter-effect sets in with the stimulus: this causes the threshold to give way (local adaptation). The influence of presentation time is evident also in foveal vision; the product of the angle of vision and presentation time is constant (photo-chemical principle: R. Bunsen & H. E. Roscoe). Processes take place in the eye that are similar to those on a photographic plate. When an object moves in a horizontal direction in relation to the observer, visual activity at first increases, but then decreases considerably (fast traffic). With a circular movement of the object (radar set) it decreases more slowly; there is a regular connection between it and the number of rotations.

If an object approaches the observer ($<$5 m.), its image on the retina will quickly be so indistinct that contrast no longer suffices for compensation. Alteration of the distance between lens and retina is possible only in lower animals (cuttlefish). In mammals and young humans, the lens (q.v.) is soft and elastic; under the influence of colloidal forces, it can approximate a globular shape, if a bundle of fibers attached to its equator slackens (see *Accommodation*).

The radius of curvature of the (less elastic) anterior surface of the lens decreases in the process by about one half (from 10 mm. to 5.33 mm.), and that of the posterior surface by only 0.67 mm. However, this does not mean that the posterior surface is not involved in the accommodation process. Since the volume of the lens cannot change, its anterior surface can become flatter under distance adjustment of the eye, only if the mass of the lens can give way against the (more elastic) posterior surface. Therefore the posterior surface is already dilated with distance adjustment. According to Gullstrand, the change in the shape of the lens is insufficient to explain the entire increase in refractive powers of the young eye; he attributes a third of it to a displacement of more strongly refractive masses within the lens from the periphery back to the center (intracapsular accommodation mechanism).

The suspensory ligament is slackened when ciliary muscle contracts on excitation of the oculomotor nerve (*nervous oculomotorius*), which belongs to the parasympathetic nervous system. Von Helmholtz thought it improbable that contraction of the radial fibers in the ciliary muscle restored distance adjustment of the eye. Recently, however, the presence of sympathetic nerve fibers between the small muscle cells of the ciliary muscle has been reported. The influence of the sympathetic was investigated in experiments by Meesmann, Monjé, Siebeck and others, and may now be taken as established. Therefore adjustment of the eye to ∞ should not be described as loss of accommodation, but as near and distance accommodation.

When at rest, the eye adjusts to a finite distance, as in short sight (see *Myopia*), e.g., in fog, and in darkness, when there is no cue for fixation (empty space or night myopia). Since the lens grows constantly throughout life, like the hair and nails, but cannot get rid of the old substance, the substance of the lens thickens to form the inelastic lenticular nucleus, which increases with age and makes the lens progressively less elastic. The ability to adjust the eye to near objects therefore constantly decreases, and the range of accommodation is reduced: in the young it is ten to fourteen diopters, but at sixty drops to one diopter.

Two further processes are linked to that of accommodation: the *convergence* movement of the eyes and the *contraction of the pupils*. Just to see with both eyes an object situated close at hand, it is necessary to bring it into the *foveae centrales* so that images can be formed bilaterally. The axes of vision of both eyes must be directed to the object; the eyes must carry out a convergence movement (see *Convergence*). If they do not, double images occur. Whether the convergence movement or the accommodation adjustment is the first process, is not yet clear. The extent of convergence (in contrast to accommodation width) is practically independent of age; the near point in convergence is ten cm. away from the eye. Variation of pupil width (see *Pupillary reflex*) is linked with convergence. The pupil is formed from the iris; its pigment is responsible for the particular color of the eye. It "screens off" marginal rays and reduces the effect of lens errors. It contracts when the eyes converge and are adjusted to close surroundings, and thus assists near accommodation. Depth of focus increases when the pupil is contracted; at a pupil width of two mm. at reading distance it amounts to three cm.; with near work no change of eye focus is necessary. The width of the pupil is also influenced by the incidence of light (on the second eye too) and by age. Since its width constantly fluctuates, it is natural to regard pupillary movement as the result of an automatic control circuit, and not as a reflex in response to the stimulus of light. The retina serves as an antenna, the pupillary center as a regulator. The diameter of the pupil fluctuates between eight and two mm., and the incidence of light in the ratio of 16:1. In very strong light the pupils can contract violently and cause the pain of dazzle or glare (q.v.). The maximal pupillary diameter diminishes with age. The contraction of the pupil after the incidence of light lasts 4″, widening 16″. Widening is the first stage of dark adaptation (q.v.).

The totality of objects that can be perceived simultaneously by the unmoving eye is the *field of vision*, or *visual field*. The field of vision is limited by the orbital roof, the bridge of the nose and the cheeks. The periphery is color-blind; then comes a zone in which blue and yellow are discerned; farthest towards the center are the limits for red and green. The limits of the field of vision, especially those for color, are dependent on the luminance of the test signs, their size and saturation. The point at which the nerve fibers leave the eye (*papilla nervi optici*) is blind. It is situated in the field of vision between 10° and 20° away from the middle of the retina. Even in the case of unilateral vision, the blind spot (q.v.) is not noticed, since its environment is of too little importance. Outside the limits of the field of vision, sensitivity at individual points of the retina can be measured by the method of light perception perimetry (see *Perimeter*). Refraction anomalies can be easily adjusted in this way. Deficiencies of the visual field help doctors to locate, e.g., tumors.

Twilight and night vision. Print on white paper appears black even when the letters in the midday sun throw back into our eyes three times as much light as the paper at dawn. The reason is the accommodation of the eye to the different proportions of light. The sensitivity of the eye (see *Dark adaptation*) increases with diminishing light. If the eye was previously adapted to daylight, after a longer period in complete darkness its increase can exceed 10,000 times. The curve is appropriately represented as a logarithmic scale. It is dependent on the area of the retina in question. The greatest increase in sensitivity is found in an area 10° to 20° away from the middle of the retina, and the least at the very center. The increase is further dependent on the color of the light stimulus (least in the case of red, most in the case of green), on the size of the test sign (number of elements) and on the age of the subject. Adaptation to darkness decreases with increasing age, as is the case with near accommodation, after age fifty. It is greater binocularly than monocularly, yet the adaptation of the one eye does not influence that of the other. Adaptation to darkness starts with the widening of the pupil; in the following phase of five to ten minutes the aftereffect of the previous light adaptation must first be overcome (it has nothing to do with the transition from cones-vision to rod-vision). After forty-five minutes, the eye has practically adapted to the darkness; in the case of a longer period the sensitivity increase is only smaller. The speed of the adaptation process allows no conclusions regarding the degree of sensitivity achieved after complete adaptation. It is clear that speed of adaptation and the terminal condition are two different and independent processes. The sensitivity in different adaptation conditions is studied by perimetry.

The discovery of visual purple by L. Kühne in the nineteenth century seemed to afford an explanation of dark adaptation. *Rhodopsin* (q.v.) occurs mainly in the rods of the retina; therefore the adaptation capacity of the middle of the retina is also small. It is assumed today that only a part of the adaptation process (not perhaps the largest) takes place because of visual purple.

In the human retina there are two kinds of light-sensitive receptors: *cones* (q.v.) and *rods* (q.v.). This finding grounded the theory of the double function of the retina, "duplicity theory" (q.v.), which states that the rods mediate night vision, and the cones day (and color) vision. Many observations, which were previously interpreted in the sense of the duplicity theory, can be explained in other ways. Therefore it is now thought that the duplicity theory is to be understood less crudely. Cones and rods work together so that information is conducted to the brain by a minimum of conduction pathways.

Electric potentials are discharged from every living tissue. From the potential difference between retina and cornea, a resting current is created in which, during exposure to light, an action current, the *electroretinogram* (ERG; see *Electroretinography*) is set up. The ERG has a complicated course caused by different processes. Hopes of being able to associate one of these processes with the cones and another with the rods remain unfulfilled. It has not yet proved possible even to derive the action potential from human brain cells. ERG plays a special part in medical diagnosis.

Sensitivity to light. Between the incidence of a stimulus on the eye and the occurrence of sensitivity there is a time-lapse of at least 0.035 seconds (*Sensitivity time*, Fröhlich, 1929). Its duration is dependent on the course of the light stimulus, its duration and strength, the adaptation condition of the observer and his attention, and it can increase to above two seconds. As a part of reaction time it is important for the car driver and in rapid flight. Fig. 2 shows that the abovementioned factors also influence the duration of sensitivity and its course in time. Maximum sensitivity does not occur at the beginning of sensitivity; the position of maximum sensitivity and the duration of sensitivity play a part in the fusion of two stimuli, which changes with the logarithm of the intensity of the light stimulus. In daylight the fusion frequency amounts to sixty; even in twilight, twenty stimuli fuse per second. The luminance corresponds to the sum of the luminances of the fused stimuli (Talbot-Plateau law).

For the peculiarities and theories of *sensitivity to color*, see *Color perception; Color vision; Color blindness*.

Eye movements. By virtue of its globular shape, the eye can (without any movement of the head) turn to an object incident in the periphery of the retina (peripheral vision, q.v.). The totality of objects that can be included (without any head movement) in direct vision is called the *field of vision*, or visual field. Eye movement depends on three

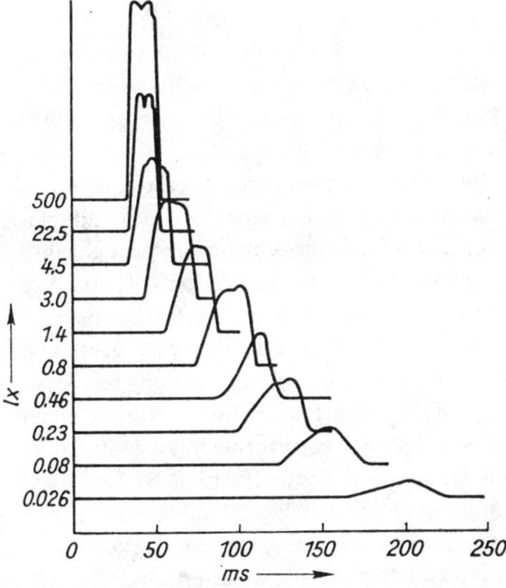

Fig. 2. Temporal sequence of visual sensation process as dependent on stimulus intensity. The abscissas give the time in msec, the ordinates show intensity of light.

pairs of muscles. The eyes can revolve about 50–60° outwards and 70–80° inward. The power of movement continuously diminishes with age; only inward and downward movement increases up to the thirtieth year of life, and remains constant from then on. Generally only 18° of possible movement are used; the field of vision is extended by the additional movement of the head. Rotation of the eye on its axis is also possible by means of the oblique eye muscles. The same position of the eye, however, always accords with a definite position of the line of vision (Donders' *law of constant orientation*). Listing's law (q.v.) gives us some information about this position. In studying eye movements, it is necessary to distinguish the voluntary from the involuntary. Those movements made during the observation of an object show no relationship with the object, except in following contours, when the movements are interrupted by occasional pauses and backward "leaps" (saccades). Similar eye movements occur in reading; a line of 12 cm. is explored in five leaps at reading distance. Only half is seen sharply (foveal vision). The letters seen indistinctly are "made up"; hence misprints are easily overlooked. Regular eye movements (possible up to 30°) are unusual under physiological conditions. During pauses, the eye adapts very quickly to the different light intensities (local adaptation). Rhythmic movements are brought into relationship with innervation of the eye muscles. Similar movements are to be observed during the mere imagination of objects and during dreams (q.v.). An (initially, at least) voluntary movement leads to fixation of an object. Fixation is performed by a central area of the fovea of about 100 mm. By backward movements, which last about 20 msec., and often occur in groups, the eye avoids having to travel through slow deviations. Fixation point and the beginning of rough correction movements depend on the appearance of the object. Fixation movements are related to rhythmic head movements. Involuntary movements occur when the eye is no longer in a position to keep in view the object under observation. It then makes a backward movement (nystagmus), and seeks a new viewing point. Nystagmus is influenced by optical and psychological factors (psycho-optic reflex). It is used in the objective study of dark adaptation and visual acuity. Similar eye movements can be caused independently of the optic stimulus of the vestibular apparatus. During sleep (q.v.) the eyes move outward and upward (Bell's phenomenon), and are thus protected from the incidence of light; the pressure of the eyelids on the eye is also reduced.

The localization of static objects is effected by means of the retinal point. As this changes, the perception of an object movement occurs. Although a similar movement of the image on the retina can be caused by eye movements, both can be easily distinguished one from the other. Errors are rare, since image fluctuation on the retina follows either an impulse current from the center (efference), which then adjusts the return message resulting from the movement (reafference), or this adjustment fails and the return message reaches the center. In the first case the eye has moved, in the second the object.

Eye movements control one's ability to estimate the height and width of an object. The precision with which one can assess the parallelism of two lines is well-known. Eye movements can, however, lead to "illusions". Undivided lines, surfaces or angles can be thought to be smaller when subdivided. According to Fröhlich (1929), even the Müller-Lyer illusion (q.v.) is due to eye movements. Other "illusions" (see *Kundt's illusion* and *Münsterberg's illusion*) can be explained by different width values of the retinal halves. Similarly with the subjective vertical (set up in the dark with the help of a line of light), which diverges outward about 1° with its upper end in the middle. All illusions of this kind can be interpreted on the basis of physiological conditions (see *Geometrical-optical illusions*).

An object is seen singly with both eyes when portrayed at "identical" points. Objects do not form at *identical points of the retina* (q.v.) if they are seen double. Objects which deviate from one another on the horizontal only up to 9 minutes of arc are an exception. Transversely disparate deviations within these limits do not as a rule lead to double images, but are given a new meaning in a spatial impression. Diversity of image in binocular vision is (according to C. Wheatstone) the origin of *depth perception* (q.v.). Since this theory cannot explain the dependence of depth of focus on time and many other observations, M. Monjé assumes that eye movements or their intention are the real reason for depth of vision, in which case transverse disparation may be the ruling factor. Looking corresponds in the optical field to "exploration" in the tactile field (dynamic theory of sight). According to this theory the eye does not have a special position; it functions according to the same principle as other sense organs (taste, touch). See *Visual perception.*

2. *The ear.* The ear communicates information in the same way as the eye. The origin of the information is in the environment. Like the eye, the ear is an exteroceptor. Its main task is the mediation of speech, which is impossible without constant supervision by the ear (see *Deaf mutism*). The adequate stimuli are longitudinal vibrations in which the air is displaced by sound sources. The human larynx is also one of these sound sources. The real organ of hearing is situated in *the labyrinth*, which is hollowed out of the hard substance of the petrosal bone and filled with fluid (perilymph). Since the perilymph's resistance to sound waves is about 3500 times greater than that of air, the air waves must be adjusted closely to the proportion of the perilymph. Via the external ear, sound reaches the external auditory canal, which is closed at the end by the tympanic membrane (characteristic sound 2000 Hz). The tympanic membrane vibrates as a rigid mass about an axis situated on its upper edge. It transfers its vibrations to an angular lever formed by the three *auditory ossicles*. The long shaft of the *hammer* is attached to the tympanic membrane. It is situated on the extension of the incus, which transfers the vibration to the foot of the stapes (stirrup) in the ratio of 1.3:1. Since the active part of the tympanic membrane is in the ratio of 17:1 to the surface of the foot of the stapes, strength is increased up to twenty-two times, and movement amplitude declines simultaneously. The characteristic frequency of the whole system is between 1200 and 1400 Hz; the system is well muffled and especially suitable for the transmission of low frequencies in the field of human speech (80–600 Hz). Since the tympanic membrane stops reacting entirely at 2000 Hz, the transmission of energy at this frequency rapidly declines; bone conduction replaces air conduction. The tension of the tympanic membrane is not changed by the muscles of the middle ear but the chain of auditory ossicles is stiffened, and its vibration muffled. That part of the labyrinth which assists hearing is called the *cochlea* because of its shape. Around the bony bar of the axis the *scala vestibuli* ascends from the oval window (the foot of the stapes) to the end of the cochlea, and changes into the *scala tympani*. Both are divided by a sac containing viscous endolymph; the foundation of this sac is formed by the basilar membrane, which bears the sense cells. The basilar membrane is 33.5 mm. long; its width is 0.5 mm. at its end, but this declines to 0.04 mm. in the area of the foot of the stapes. No principle of frequency analysis except that of resonance was known at the time of Helmholtz, he therefore believed that it also applied to the basilar membrane of the ear. Ranke and Békésy were the first to realize that the inner ear is full of fluid. Since the canal depth near the foot of the stapes is small in comparison with the sound wavelengths, these are transmitted proportionately at first; very soon the canal depth is equal to the shortest wave length. When an added force occurs perpendicularly to the direction of locomotion, vertices are formed; the smaller the frequency, the later this phenomenon—it is latest when the frequency near the end of the cochlea is deepest. Moreover the basilar membrane is narrowest (and therefore hardest) in the area of the oval window, and becomes softer as its width increases. But its flexibility increases at the same time, and the frequency of the conducted waves is again dependent on flexibility. Since energy cannot be lost, it induces a maximal bend in the basilar membrane and at the same time a maximal stimulus to the associated hair cells. The measurement at the

maximal point of maxism in the ear of a corpse shows an approximate logarithmic dependence on the amount of vibrations from the stimulus, i.e., the increase of a sound at a certain percentage rate signifies a definite distance of the new stimulus from the original one, at 2.6 mm. an octave. Since the basilar membrane is 30 mm. long, according to the hearing distance, it can take 11.5 octaves.

When the waves occur up to 800 Hz, the whole head vibrates. Compression waves are created by the rhythmic compression of the labyrinth walls. These waves (like those caused by the foot of the stapes) lead to a bulging of the basilar membrane (bone conduction). The origin of this is the difference in the volumes of both scales and their elasticity.

The adequate stimulus for the excitation of sense cells is their curvature. The inner hair cells are situated in a row on the bony ledge and have an isolated connection with the auditory center. A row of external hair cells corresponds to each cell. A nerve fiber links cells over 1–2 mm. of the basilar membrane. Neighboring areas overlap. They are more sensitive than the inner hair cells, but can communicate only a rough location; however, the continuous linkage with the center is attributed to the inner hair cells. They may be compared to the cones of the eye. The hair cells are not distributed regularly over the basilar membrane, and their number is at its greatest in the middle area, corresponding to selectivity of frequency.

The intensity threshold and the possibility of variation difference in volume must be distinguished from the possibility of variation in sounds of different frequency and selectivity. The absolute threshold for different sounds is dependent on frequency. At 18 Hz a pressure of 1 dyn/cm.^{2} is necessary to cause sound sensitivity. The pressure which is necessary to reach threshold falls with increasing frequency, at 1000 Hz to 2.10^{-4} dyn/cm.^{2}. This value corresponds to a sound intensity of 10^{-16} Watts, (see Fig. 4). Since the auditory field at 1000 Hz contains 10^{13} divisions of energy it is advantageous to choose a logarithmic system of comparison. The "bell" (after A. G. Bell) serves as a unit. By this is understood the logarithmic proportion of sound power in relation to the absolute threshold at 1000 hz (1 decibel [db] = 1/10 bel). The upper frequency limit for the young is 22,000 Hz; the upper limit declines constantly with increasing age (down to one octave), and finally (at the

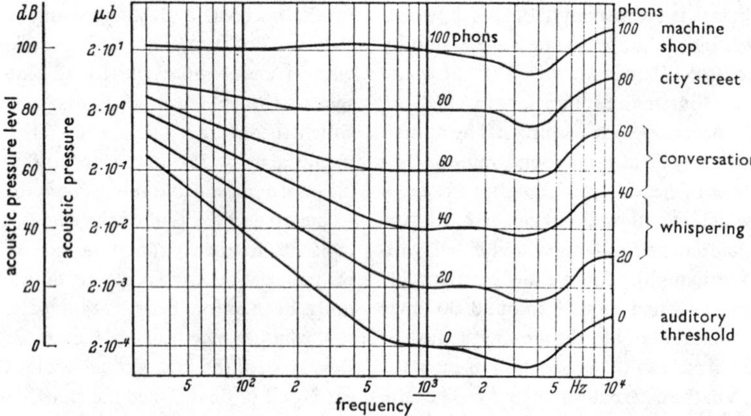

Fig. 3. Curves of equal loudness. The loudness of a sound in phons corresponds to the decibel value of a 1000 Hz sound ("normal noise") that sounds equally loud (E. Schütz).

age of 70) is 10,000–12,000 Hz. Selectivity is at its greatest in the vocal field when the duration of sound and its intervals is limited to 1″. In the area from 500–2000 Hz it is optimal (0.3%) and fluctuates up and down. As the maximum for the basilar membrane is very wide, this selectivity can be achieved only by a physiological process (contrast). 1500 individual sounds can be distinguished. The variation threshold for two sounds of equal frequency amounts to approximately 10% (= 1 db). The upper limit of the auditory field is actually not an auditory limit but one of *pain* (q.v.). The whole auditory field contains 340,000 sounds. The "loudness" (q.v.) of a sound sensation is measured in *phons*. The phon scale differs from the decibel scale, in that the latter is independent of the frequency of its zero point at a sound pressure of 2.10^{-4} dyn/cm.^{2}, whereas the phon scale is dependent on frequency; its zero position corresponds at every sound to the absolute threshold (see Fig. 4). At 1000 Hz the scales agree. The loudness of whispering amounts to 20, of conversation to 40–60 phons; a car horn at a distance of 1 m. is 90 phons. In the case of a steady load of 65 phons, the natural protective mechanisms of the ear are already overtaxed; If 95 phons is exceeded, protective measures are necessary (see *Noise level*). The ear can adapt to a sound lasting a longer time. *Adaptation* is not to be confused with fatigue (q.v.). Rather the alternation of stimulus material in *adaptation* is arranged so that the intensity threshold is at its greatest in the given conditions. The extent of adaptation in the ear is substantially less than in the eye.

The *sensation time*, the period between the incidence of a stimulus and the occurrence of sensation, is in the same dimension as in the eye; dependent on sound intensity, it is between 35 and 150 msec. Since the motor constituent of a reaction is not influenced by the sensory stimulus, the reaction time must also occur under comparable conditions within the same order of magnitude. But, whereas in the eye not only the initial but the maximum sensation time follows a logarithmic regularity (see Fig. 2), in the ear only the sensation time follows such a system, and the maximum is reached for all magnitudes of stimulus after 180 msec. (Monjé, 1926).

Using one ear, the *direction* from which the sound comes is established by gauging the sound source. In both ears, a sound not emanating from the median plane is distinguished by its *intensity and the time of incidence*. Since the sensation time does not play a part in both ears, Monjé (1935) attributes localization to the fluctuation of sensation maxima. The distance of a sound wave can be known with considerable certainty

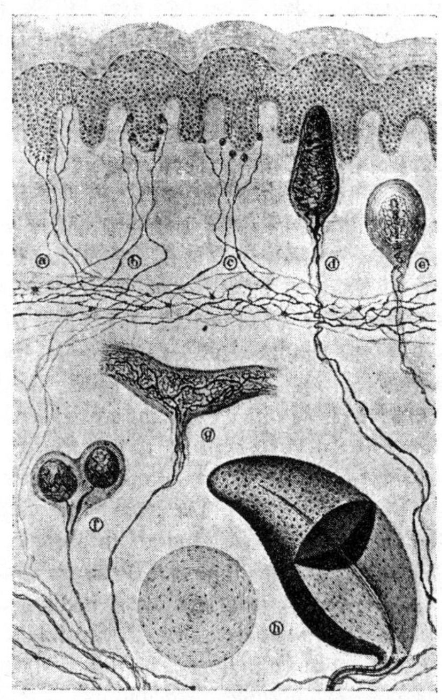

Fig. 4. The sense organs of the skin (Kahn). (*a*) free nerve endings (pain); (*b*) cells of epidermis; (*c*) cells in hypodermis; (*d*) tactile apparatus (pressure sensation); (*e*) Krause end bulbs (cold?); (*f*) Golgi-Mazzoni terminal corpuscles (itching?); (*g*) Ruffini's brushes (heat?); (*h*) lamellar corpuscle left, cross-section right.

independently of its intensity by the diversity of the frequency spectrum. The speed of the flow of air is perceptible with near sound waves but not with distant waves. The ear, therefore, reacts more to quality than to quantity. See *Auditory perception.*

3. *Skin senses* (*a*) *Touch.* The "skin senses", or "cutaneous senses", include several senses which as a rule act together, (see Fig. 4). In feeling an object, an *excitation* of the *pressure and touch receptors* of the *organs of the sense of temperature* and eventually those also of the sense of *pain* (q.v.) occurs simultaneously. The sensation of touch is communicated by a plexus of nerves in the area of the hair follicles. The Meissner corpuscles are found mainly on hairless parts of the skin in the papillae of the derma. They are particularly numerous at the extremities of the body, at the end of the tongue, the lips, the ends of the fingers, but sparse, e.g., on the skin of the back. Their number declines with age. As the spatial sense is empowered by its capacity to perceive two separate points, it must be especially equipped at the ends of the body. The sense of pressure communicates a great deal of information concerning the environment. Pressure and touch are further mediated by Merkel's and Vater's or Pacini's corpuscles, and possibly by independent nerve endings in hairless parts of the skin. The absolute threshold amounts to 0.03 erg, and the variation threshold to 3%; hence the former is very small in comparison with other sense organs, and the latter comes between those of the eye and the ear. The time necessary for the creation of sensation in respect of rapid (electric) skin stimulus is in the same proportion as with the eye and the ear; it is inversely proportional to the logarithm of stimulus intensity (Fröhlich, 1929).

Besides its contributions to spatial sensation, the sense of touch carries a large quantity of information concerning the condition of the body. In this regard, deformation of the skin provides the major stimulus. The organism can adapt itself very quickly to a continuous stimulus. The sensation of touch is especially affected by adaptation; electrophysiological tests show that the thin nerve fibers which communicate pressure sensation go on firing after initial adaptation.

Rhythmic stimuli induce a particular sensation, "prickling" (vibration sensation). A stimulus somewhat in excess of threshold travelling over the skin causes the tickling sensation (especially on the lips, the palms of the hands and the soles of the feet).

Perception of depth is communicated by the Vater–Pacini particles, the Golgi apparatus, and the receptors which branch out with their non-myelinated, tree-like ramifications in muscular sheaths, and wind around the tendons. The position of limbs is not communicated by muscle sense, but mainly by the sense organs of the skin and the Pacini corpuscles.

(*b*) *Pain* (q.v.). A shift of metabolic into pathological processes, whether caused by damage to the skin or by chemical substances, leads to the sensation of pain through depolarization in fine nerve fibers situated in the upper layers of the epithelium. Pain (q.v.) is not communicated by special sense organs; hence there is no *specific* stimulus (as with light in the case of the eye). The release of pain sensation requires much greater energy; there is also no summation and no adaptation to pain; its sensation time is long.

Two kinds of pain are distinguished: *superficial* and *deep pain.* The former is conducted by medullated nerve fibers at a mean speed of 20–30 msec., and the deep pain is conveyed by thin non-myelinated, slow-conducting fibers. Superficial pain can be more easily located than deep pain, because the density of the nerve fibers is less in deep pain than in superficial, and therefore the possibility of contrast formation is smaller. The sensations within the body are not so delicate as on the skin. They inhibit above all the voluntary motor system and therefore bring about relaxation or protection of a diseased organ. The fluctuation of vegetative tonus is substantial;

dominance of sympathetic tonus occurs (see *Autonomic nervous system*) together with rising blood pressure and heart beat, increased clarity of consciousness, and defense and flight readiness. The temporal course of the stimulus plays an important part in deep pain. The stomach, the intestine and bladder are, e.g., insensitive to a cut, but react violently to stretching, spasms and lack of oxygen.

If pain nerves are destroyed, reduced pain sensitivity is produced (hypesthesia), and is often linked with increased painfulness (*hyperpathy*); then, with regeneration, there is a stage of altered sensitivity (*paresthesia*).

No special organ has hitherto been found for the sensation of *itching*. One hypothesis is a combination of weak pain stimuli and touch stimuli. Its origin is also related to protopathic pain, or attributed to a still undiscovered "mediator substance", formed by means of an axon reflex, which only then effects a change in tissue chemistry. In spite of considerable similarity, there is a big difference between pain and itching; pain induces defense, itching causes tickling. Morphine relieves pain but promotes itching; on the other hand heat causes pain but prevents itching.

Sense of temperature. The cold (*Krause's end bulb*) and heat receptors (*Ruffini's corpuscles*) are sense organs (the former situated at a depth of 0.1 mm in the skin, the latter at 9.5 mm.) which ensure a constant body temperature. Today it is assumed that, instead of the end particles, independent nerve endings operate as receptors (H. Hensel). Cold stimuli, since they are not situated so deep down in the skin, are easier to locate. Their contribution to the representation of the environment is greater than that of the heat receptors. The heat receptors react in temperatures above the mean and the cold ones in those below it. Sudden changes lead to an excessive reaction which then declines to a constant value (adaptation). "Burning heat" and "biting cold" are not pure temperature sensations but mixed sensations on the edge of the temperature scales. The sensation of variation is dependent on surface (spatial summation) and on the speed of the change (temporal summation). Therefore wood feels warmer than metal at the same temperature, and water seems colder than air at the same temperature. (When small cutaneous areas cool down because of a draught, the counteraction of the body can fail, and encourage a cold.) Internal parts of the body seem to be insensitive to temperature.

4. *Taste*. The spectrum of taste sensation consists of four fundamental qualities: *sweet* (the end of the tongue), *salty* and *sour* (the edge of the tongue), and *bitter* (the base of the tongue). Further sensations are formed from a combination of these tastes. Smell and the co-stimuli of touch-, temperature-, and pain-receptors make a further contribution to taste. The taste buds are embedded in the papillae of the tongue. There are approximately twenty sense cells grouped in a bud and each one of these bears an easily broken peg which projects into a small hole. To be able to reach these holes, the matter to be tasted must be water-soluble and diffusible. However, it is still impossible to understand all the basic sensations from their physical and chemical properties. The sour sensation is linked with the presence of H-ions, and the salty sensation tastes of sodium chloride. Other salts, e.g., magnesium sulphate, cause a salty sensation at the end of the tongue but a bitter sensation at its base. The bitter sensation alone is induced by quinine. The sweet sensation can be caused by inorganic (diluted lead solution) and quite different organic compounds (cane sugar, saccharine). Levorotatory aminoacids taste sweet, dextrorotatory bitter, or they are tasteless. It has therefore been thought that the sweet taste occurs when neighboring hydroxide groups possess excessive cohesive forces which, because of the geometrical structure of the molecule, cannot be neutralized and react to the atom groups in the nerve ends of the taste buds (R. S. Schallenberger). The

term "contrast" is sometimes used in connection with taste, as is "aftertaste" or "change" (e.g., by means of 2% sulphuric acid) and "insensitivity". The individual parts of the tongue are supplied by different nerves; according to recent findings, excitation in respect of salty, sour and bitter is conducted via different nerves, and on a quantitatively different scale. The individual reaction is greatest for sweetness; the sensory nerves of the soft palate also participate in this reaction. It is concluded from the evidence of electrophysiological tests that receptors with a narrow field and a wide field must be distinguished. The significance of areas of taste for the composition of saliva must also be noted.

5. *Smell.* Although in the history of development the sense of smell is to be reckoned among the oldest functions of the senses, hitherto it has not been possible to explain all its physiological processes. In the *regio olfactoria*, an area of the human nasal roof measuring about 25 mm.^{2}, the extensions of the *olfactory cells* are situated between yellow-pigmented supporting cells; they bear 6–8 ciliary-type hairs and are covered with a special watery mucus which, besides its rinsing function, could perhaps affect the selection of odiferous substances. Since breath passes chiefly over the second and third nasal muscles, the movement of air at the *regio olfactoria* is slight; the latter is thus protected against too strong a concentration of odors and too low an air temperature. The movement can be increased and accelerated by sniffing. Among the elements, only halogens smell, together with about thirty inorganic compounds; organic compounds also smell. Carbon monoxide and ammonium do not smell. We distinguish about ten thousand qualities of sensation. It is clear that this large number does not correspond to a similarly large number of receptors but that it is created by combination and by stimulation patterns. On the other hand there must be a definite specificity of olfactory cells, for adaptation to individual odors is possible. H. Henning has postulated the existence of six basic smells (see *Odor prism*). The *stereochemical theory*, which proceeds from the molecular structure of smells, postulates a similar number of basic smells which do not, however, entirely coincide with Henning's. As with colors, an absolute threshold can also be distinguished from the specific threshold in the case of olfactory sensations. Olfactory sensations can combine, and smell changes with the concentration of the substance and the duration of its effect. Adaptation to a smell follows quickly at first, and then slowly. There are *hyposmias* (q.v.) and *anosmias* (q.v.).

Contact and touch sensations, pain, temperature sensation and taste have no *fields of projection* distributed according to the sense organs; instead, the primary sensory cortex is distributed according to organs so that, for example, touch and taste stimuli to a large extent overlap. Confusions are therefore not excluded.

Bibliography: Bauer, I.: Unsere gegenwärtigen Kenntnisse über den Geruchssinn und deren Prüfung. Diss. Med. Fac., Kiel, 1962. **Fröhlich, F. W.:** Die Empfindungszeit. Jena, 1929. **Gross, C. G. & Zeigler, H. P.** (Eds.): Readings in physiological psychology, Vols. 1–3. New York & London, 1969. **Gulick, W. L.:** Hearing: physiology and psychophysics. New York & London, 1970. **Haber, R. N.** (Ed.): Contemporary theory and research in visual perception. New York, 1968. **Hensel, H.:** Allgemeine Sinnesphysiologie. Hautsinne, Geschmack, Geruch. Berlin, 1969. **Keidel, W. D.:** Physiologie der Hautsinne. In: Handbuch der Haut- und Geschlechtskrankheiten. Suppl. Vol. I, Pt. 3. Berlin, 1963, 157. **Milner, P. M.:** Physiological psychology. New York & London, 1970. **Monjé, M.:** Empfindungszeit und zeitlicher Verlauf der Gehörempfindung bei Verwendung kurzdauernder Schallreize. Z. Biol., 1926, *85*, 349. **Id.:** Ein Beitrag zur Frage der Richtungslokalisation von Schallreizen. Z. Sinnesphysiol., 1935, *66*, 7. **Id.:** Physiologie des Auges. In: Handbuch der Zoologie, Vol. 8(2). Berlin, 1968. **Id.:** Lichtsinn. Physiologie des Auges. In: **Velhagen, K.** (Ed.): Der Augenarzt. Vol. 1, Leipzig, ²1969, 173. **Moray, N.:** Attention: selective processes in vision and hearing. London, 1970. **Noton, D. & Stark, L.:** Eye movements and visua perception. Scient. Amer., 1971, *6*, 35–43. **Polyak, S.:** The retina. Chicago, 1941. **Ranke, O. F. & Lullies, H.:** Gehör, Stimme, Sprache. Berlin, 1953. **Schober, H.:** Das Sehen. Leipzig, [3]1960, (Vol. 1); 1964, (Vol. 2). **Trendelenburg, W.:** Der Gesichtssinn (Monjé, Schmidt, Schütz). Berlin, 1961. **Trincker, D.:** Physiologie des Hörens und die Reiztransformation im Innenohr. J. Audiological Technique, 1967, *6*, 158.

M. Monjé

Senses. See *Sense organs.*

Sense types. These are characterized by the preference of a certain sensory area for perception (q.v.), but also for imagination (q.v.) and for remembering and thinking (q.v.) (see *Ideational types*). J. M. Charcot distinguished the optic (visual), acoustic (auditive) and motor type. *W.K.*

Sensibility. 1. *In psychology* sensibility is sensitivity, delicacy of or capacity for feeling. 2. *In physiology*, sensibility denotes the ability to feel and to process sensory stimuli. Sensibility may be either superficial (pressure, temperature, pain) or deep-seated (muscular tonus, etc.) (see *Sense organs*).

Disturbances of sensibility. Physiologically three forms may be distinguished: (*a*) *anesthesia* (q.v.): absence of sensibility; (*b*) *hypesthesia*: diminished sensibility; (*c*) *hyperesthesia* (q.v.): excessive sensibility (see also *Analgesia*). *H.-J.A.*

Sensitive. Person with special ability for ESP (q.v.). In experimental parapsychology is often referred to as a "high scorer". *J.B.*

Sensitive delusion of reference. Kretschmer used the phrase *sensitiver Beziehungswahn* to describe a delusion of reference occurring in a person who is self-conscious, easily upset and prone to feel that he is conspicuous or remarked upon. The delusion may or may not develop after some humiliating or upsetting experience, and is usually accompanied by other delusions and symptoms of anxiety. These delusional states may not be related to schizophrenia if they follow some traumatic experience and if they are not accompanied by personality disintegration. *B.B.*

Sensitiveness; sensitivity. In general: the degree to which a person is capable of receiving influences from the outside world. *In sensory perception and psychophysics:* the capability of receiving sensory stimuli. *In technology:* the relation between output and input magnitudes of a measuring instrument or plant (cybernetics: a system), etc. G. T. Fechner (q.v.) defined the sensitiveness of the sensory organs as the reciprocal value of the stimulus which was just sufficient (in 50% of cases [threshold]) to produce a sensation. The number 1 in the counter ($1/S$, S = stimulus intensity) indicates the unit in experience, that intensity of sensation which is just perceptible. This makes the Fechner definition a special case of the definition in technology.

Sensitiveness is often divided into *sensitivity* (sensitiveness to some stimulus) and *sensibility* (sensitiveness to differences in stimuli). In general linguistic usage sensitive is also used in the sense of sentimental, and sensible in the sense of having delicacy of feeling. Psychophysics (q.v.) sometimes uses for sensitivity the expression *absolute sensitiveness*, and for sensibility the expression *relative sensitiveness*. *Sensitiveness functions* (function of spectrally clear sensitiveness, linear, logarithmic, etc.; graphs of sensory systems in bio- and psychocybernetics) show the rules governing the relation between stimuli and their effects on the sensory system. On change of sensitiveness see *Adaptation*. *A.Ha.*

Sensitive reaction type. The almost schizoid personality. Manifests itself in oversensitive impressionability to the stimuli of experience and in defective, uneven power of expression and behavior, i.e. conscious complex formation. The impact of sthenic sensation, pride and ambition spurs the personality on in spite of its feeling of insufficiency (see *Experience of insufficiency*) to a struggle with agonizing experience. Self torture and moral scruple are the typical responses to "humiliating insufficiency" and "moral defeat". Development to sensitive delusion concerning relationships (q.v.) is possible.

Bibliography: Kretschmer, E. & Kretschmer, W.: Medizinische Psychologie. Stuttgart, 1970. *W.K.*

Sensitivity training. A method closely connected with group therapy which has entered into the sphere of industrial psychology and must be regarded as an important step toward widespread adult education in the pure communication of knowledge. Sensitivity training takes place today in group therapy sessions where completely free expression is encouraged of individual emotional reactions to a gathering of fellow participants. In this way those who undergo the training learn how to give themselves, and how others react to them. It is thus possible to break down fixed reactions (see *Communication*) toward other people and to achieve social sensitivity (Tannenbaum *et al.*, 1953).

Bibliography: Tannenbaum, R., Wechsler, I. R. & Massarik, F.: Leadership and organisation. New York, 1953. **Corsini, R. J.:** Methods of group psychotherapy. New York, 1957. *W.Sch.*

Sensorimotor activity or behavior. Field of research, oriented partly to behaviorism but recently more to cybernetics, concerning the connection between the sensory (q.v.) and motor systems. The chief problems of the sensorimotor are: (*a*) by which processes are sensory and motor information linked with each other (*sensorimotor coordination*, e.g., between sense of vision and ocular motor, sense of vision and hand motor, hand sense and proprioceptors of the hand, etc.)? (*b*) Which stabilizing processes guarantee that information provided by the sensorium leads to the effect of motor action (sensorimotor adaptation processes)? (*c*) What role has movement (motor action) for perception, etc?

Bibliography: Ashby, W. R.: Design for a brain London, 1960. **Taylor, J. G.:** The behavioral basis of perception. New Haven & London, 1962. *A.Ha.*

Sensory. The sensory system of organisms (*sensorium*), consisting of peripheral receptors (q.v.) sensory nerves and central nervous processing planes, performs the task of transmission of information between the physical environment and the central nervous system. By way of numerous types of information processing, special central nervous arousal patterns occur which are collated in association centers and finally become conscious as primary acts of judgment. *M.S.*

Sensory-perceptual function. In C. Jung's theory, one of the four basic "functions" of behavior (the others being the *feeling*, *thinking*, and *intuitive* functions). Overdevelopment of this function is said to produce a sensory-perceptual bias of the personality. *J.M.*

Sensory physiology. The theory of the normal functioning of the sense organs (q.v.). A distinction is made between exteroreceptors and enteroceptors. The former process information from the body's general environment and include the senses dealing with distant sources, such as sight, hearing and smell, as well as those dealing with immediate sources such as taste and feeling (reception of temperature, vibration, contact, pain, burning and itching) and the organ of balance (q.v.). In contrast to the above, the enteroceptors are located inside the body and give information concerning the condition of the internal organs. They include the sinew and muscle spindles, the mechanoreceptors of the joints, the pressure receptors in the arterial vascular system and the heart as well as the osmo- and chemoreceptors in the different regions of the body; temperature receptors located in the central nervous system can also be grouped here. (See *Receptors.*) *E.D.*

Sensualism. The doctrine according to which all our knowledge (including rational knowledge) originates in sensation. One of the possible forms of empiricism (Condillac, 1715–80; Dewey, 1859–1952). *M.J.B.*

Sensuality. 1. Devotion to the senses, i.e., predominantly to sensory pleasure. See *Sensation.* 2. Addiction to or dependence on physical, especially sexual, pleasure. See *Alcoholism; Drug dependence; Sexuality.*

Sentence completion tests. These tests, published almost exclusively in English-speaking countries, belong to the group of verbal completion methods (e.g., projective questions, continuation of stories) and are based on the concept of projection. It is assumed that the spontaneous completion of incomplete sentences will reveal the attitudes, inclinations, needs of an individual. Experimental investigations (A. C. Carr, 1956) have shown that sentence completion tests with regard to their stimulus material (projection of unconscious material) come between personality inventories and picture interpretation methods. In the majority of sentence completion tests the results are interpreted subjectively (e.g. A. E. Payne, 1928; A. D. Tendler, 1930; OSS Assessment Staff, 1948). For some of them objective standards of assessment are available (e.g., A. R. Rohde & G. H. Hildreth, 1947; J. B. Rotter *et al.*, 1949). See *Projective techniques.* *P.G.*

Sentiment (*Feeling, attitude*: W. McDougall). In R. B. Cattell's study of motivation by factor analysis, sentiment has the same significance as a motive aim through which various motives can be satisfied (e.g., the self, q.v., parents, marital partner, one's own profession, etc.). *K.P.*

Sentimentality. A special form of emotional reaction which finds expression in an *excessive* degree of emotional excitability and response to experience. *P.S. & R.S.*

Sequential analysis. A type of statistical test developed by A. Wald during two world wars. The basic principle is as follows: to establish errors of the first and second kind with a given difference of observed populations, the sample area which is necessary for the statistical recording of this difference, is confined to random variables with a definite expectation value. Thus the sample range necessary for the decision can be minimized. In sequential analysis one observation is made after another, and after each observation one of the three following decisions is reached: (*a*) accept H_0; (*b*) accept H_1; (*c*) carry out a further observation. Observations continue in this way until the decision turns out in favor of H_0 or H_1.

Bibliography: Wald, A.: Sequential analysis. New York, 1947.

A.R.

Serial photography. A phototechnical procedure to represent movements: (*a*) by arrangement in series; (*b*) by superimposing several single shots on each other; the industrial and scientific uses of serial photography are as for cyclography. Both procedures are also used to good effect today by the media of visual communication (e.g. television, advertising). Sheldon's types were ascertained by superimposition.

Bibliography: Sheldon, W. H.: The varieties of human physique. New York & London, 1940.

G.R.W.M.

Serotonin (*5-hydroxytryptamine*), 5-HT, *Enteramine* (= previous name) belonging to the *Indoleamine* class. Substances peculiar to the body (see *Biogenic amines*) which are found up to 90–95% in Darminukosa. The substance already discovered in the thirties and called enteramine has been the subject of neuropsychiatric research since the middle fifties, when it was proved to be in the brain (chiefly in the hypothalamus, q.v., the limbic system and the epiphysis, q.v.). Serotonin is formed in the body with the participation of different enzyme systems by a catalyst (5-hydroxytrytophan) from tryptophan (q.v.). Certain psychotropic drugs (e.g. reserpine, q.v., LSD, q.v.), by the emptying of the central store, cause a serotonin deficiency in the tissue, which is accompanied by behavioral changes (e.g. depression q.v. and hallucinations, q.v.). Substances such as 5-chlorophenylalanine, which by a process of selection block biosynthesis, are theoretically significant. Biological inactivation of serotonin is brought about by monoaminoxydase (q.v.). MAO-inhibitor therefore increases the effect of serotonin. Since serotonin does not pass the blood-brain barrier, the element 5-hydroxytryptophan is used to manipulate the serotonin content of the central nervous system. Many experiments indicate that depressions are linked to a diminished content of serotonin in the brain (q.v.) (hypothalamus, nucleus amygdalae, septum nucleus). At the same time there are areas which produce a high content of biogenic amines.

The hypothesis of a relationship between lack of serotonin in the brain and schizophrenia (D. W. Woolley & D. A. Shaw) advanced in the fifties because of the ill-effects of LSD is totally rejected. Serotonin has the effect of increasing blood pressure and contracting blood vessels and is spasmogenic. Small quantities have an inhibitory effect on the nervous system, large quantities a stimulating effect. It is certainly difficult to understand the effects of serotonin on the nervous system, since *inter alia* it scarcely passes the blood-brain barrier (q.v.) and many interactions with catecholamine (q.v.) occur. Animal experiments suggest that serotonin acquires significance in the consolidation of learned material. More plausibly serotonin plays an important role in the waking-sleeping rhythm and for the duration of sleep (REM-phases; see *Sleep*; Jouvet, 1969). During sleep a smaller quantity is produced in the brain than in waking hours. The role of serotonin as a transmitter substance (q.v.) is disputed. The assertion made by B. B. Brodie and P. A. Shaw (1957) that serotonin is the transmitter substance of the central parasympathetic nervous system (see *Autonomic nervous system*) is not yet sufficiently substantiated. There are many substances occurring in plants (alkaloids) which are related to and derive from serotonin; these have partly psychomimetic effects (LSD, q.v., bufotenin, ibogaine, psilocybin, harmine).

Bibliography: Erspamer, V. (Ed.): Handbuch d. expt. Pharmakologie, Vol. 19: 5-Hydroxytryptamine and related indolealkylamines. Berlin, 1966. **Garrattini, S. & Valzelli, L.:** Serotonin. Amsterdam, 1965. **Jouvet, M.:** Biogenic amines and the states of sleep. Science 1969, *163*, 32–41. **Kawka, Z. M.:** A review of the central actions of serotonin and its implications in schizophrenia. Amer. J. Pharmac., 1967, *19*, 136–54. **Koe, B. K. & Weissman, A.:** p-Chlorphenylanaline: a specific depletor of brain serotonin. J. Pharmacol. exp. Ther., 1966, *154*, 499–516. **Lewis, G. P.** (Ed.): 5-Hydroxytryptamine. Oxford, 1968. **Scheving, L. E.** *et al.*: Daily fluctuation (circadian and ultradian) in biogenic amines of the rat. Amer. J. Physiol., 1968, *214*, 166–73. **Woolley, D. W.:** The biochemical basis of psychoses. New York, 1962.

W.J.

Set. 1. A temporary orientation, expectation, or state of readiness to respond in a particular way to a particular stimulus situation: e.g. *Perceptual set:* readiness to perceive the environment in a particular way; *Motor set:* readiness to perform a particular muscular response; *Neural set:* a temporary sensitization of a particular neural circuit (usually hypothetical); *Instructional set:* a perceptual, cognitive, or motor orientation induced by instructions from the experimenter. (Cf. *Attitudes* and *habits* which are relatively enduring dispositions.)

2. A fixed or rigid mode of responding.

3. A group or aggregate. In mathematical *set theory*, the totality of objects or elements which satisfy a given condition: e.g. the set of all female depressives over the age of thirty.

G.D.W.

Sex. See *Sexuality*.

Sex chromosomes. In genetic sex determination, one pair of chromosomes differ (XY type) in one sex but are identical (XX) in the other sex. If a Y chromosome is present in the zygote chromosomes, the zygote will develop into a male (e.g. in the mammals) or female (many species of butterflies and birds). This Y chromosome is known as the sex chromosome. *H.Sch.*

Sex cycle, in women. See *Menstruation*.

Sex differences. Members of the different sexes achieve varying results in personality and ability tests, as well as interest and attitude tests. The origin of these differences (e.g. better results achieved by men in tests of the coarse motor system, spatial orientation, mechanical understanding and by women as regards perception speed, accuracy and verbal flow) is as yet unexplained; presumably an interaction between biological and cultural factors is involved.

Bibliography: Anastasi, A.: Differential psychology. New York, [3]1958. *G.K.*

Sex education. Instruction (especially in schools) in the physiology of male–female differences and reproduction, and/or the social ethics relating to sexual behavior. The aim of such instruction is usually stated as helping the individual toward a happy, healthy and socially acceptable sexual adjustment.

G.D.W.

Sex, extramarital, postmarital, premarital. Extramarital sex is regarded as objectionable by many societies which demand monogamous marriage, in spite of the fact that it often occurs. When it is allowed, the man is nearly always given more rights than the woman. According to Kinsey and his collaborators, (See *Kinsey report*), extramarital petting (q.v.) occurs quite frequently (about 50% of married men and 25% of married women up to the age of forty). In working-class men extramarital intercourse decreases with age (from 45% at age 21–22 to 27% at age 36–40). In middle- and upper-class men, on the other hand, it increases (from 20% to 30%). Education and social class do not make significant differences in the figures for women. The percentage of women with extramarital sexual contacts was twice as high in those with premarital experience than in those without. This is probably due to an (acquired) stronger appetite for sex and to more liberal attitudes.

Postmarital sex refers to the sexual behavior and attitudes of separated living spouses, the divorced and the widowed. According to Kinsey and others, postmarital sexual behavior is not very different from behavior when married, the average frequency of intercourse being somewhere between the celibate and the married (according to their age, 85–54% of women and 96–82% of men had intercourse). Frequency of *masturbation* (q.v.) was above that of the married (29–13% of women, 56–33% of men). *Homosexuality* (q.v.) occurred in 10% of women and 28% of the men. Extramarital sex relations were more dependent on age than any other.

"Premarital sex" refers to sex relations before marriage.

Bibliography: Bell, R. R.: Premarital sex in a changing society. Englewood-Cliffs, N.J., 1966. **Gebhard, P. H.** *et al.*: Pregnancy, birth, and abortion. New York, 1958. **Kinsey, A. C.** *et al.*: Sexual behavior in the human male. Philadelphia, 1948. **Id.:** Sexual behavior in the human female. Philadelphia, 1953. *J.Fr.*

Sex flush. Reddening of particular areas of the skin: e.g. stomach, breast, face, back, resulting from an increased blood supply caused by sexual stimulation. Sex flush is more common in women than in men.

Bibliography: Masters, W. H. & Johnson, V. E.: Human sexual response. Boston, 1966. *V.S.*

Sex gland hormones. Hormones (q.v.) formed in the testes of man and the ovaries of woman which are of fundamental importance to the formation and development of primary and secondary sex features as well as for general growth. A distinction is made between female and male sex hormones on the basis of their effects. Androgens are produced not only in the testes but in the adrenal cortex, and to some extent in the ovaries. The formation of sex gland hormones is stimulated by the gonadotropic hormones of the HVL. The relationship between sex gland hormones and physical as well as personality development is undisputed, at least in terms of broadly parallel characteristics. Hypofunction or hyperfunction of the gonads or hypophysis leads to retarded or accelerated development. In adults, underfunctioning (e.g. castration) leads to reduced sexual activity in the male, although this is often not the case in the female. At an advanced age, the sexual drive in women is increased by androgens and reduced in men by estrogens. Little is known about the relationship between psychological characteristics and sex gland hormones in the case of persons with a healthy hormonal balance. The correlation is, however, probably slight. It seems likely on the other hand that estrogens and androgens play a part in the general level of activity of an individual. This is confirmed by the higher noradrenalin content in the central nervous system after the administration of estrogen or androgen. Behavioral fluctuations in the menstrual cycle have also not been clearly associated with the production of sex gland hormones. There is also no certain link between androgen or estrogen administration in males and sexual behavior.

Bibliography: Broverman, D. M. *et al.*: Roles of activation and inhibition in sex differences of cognitive abilities. Psychol. Rev., 1968, *75*, 23–50. **Diamond, M.** (Ed.): Perspectives in reproduction and sexual behavior. Bloomington, 1968. **Düker, H.:** Leistungsfähigkeit und Keimdrüsenhormone. Munich, 1957. **Giese, H.** (Ed.): Die Sexualität des Menschen. Stuttgart, 1955. **Lloyd, C. W.** (Ed.): Human reproduction and sexual behavior. Philadelphia, 1964. See also *Androgens; Estrogens.* *W.J.*

Sex offenses. Blanket term for all behavior contravening the current sexual laws of a state or country, by persons of indictable age. Legally, criminologically and socially this term covers an enormous variety of behavior, from rape to the—possibly socially damaging —"dissemination of obscene literature." At the centre of the legal, psychiatric and psychological research are the (usually male) delinquent, his personality traits, life history, (social background, psychic, sexual, social development), specific sexual offenses and their relation to the age of the delinquent or victim and to other variables (e.g. circumstances of the crime, behavior which preceded and followed it, etc., prognosis for its repetition, resocialization, pre-delinquent prognosis, q.v.). Different scientific disciplines are engaged in research and practice: psychology, psychiatry, sociology, criminology. In West Germany scientific research has been lacking. In the USA, Gebhard (1965), for example, has engaged in it.

Bibliography: **Gebhard, P. H.:** Sex offenders. New York & London, 1965. **Karpman, B.:** The sexual offender and his offenses: etiology, pathology, psychodynamics and treatment. New York, 1954. *H.M.*

Sex roles. In every society, specific behavioral expectations and standards are applied to men and women; deviations are generally subject to negative sanctions. On the basis of biological and physiological differences between the sexes, psychological reactions and social behavior patterns are formed which in turn are dependent on the socio-economic organization of a society, in particular on the division of labor. As a function of this division of labor, research suggests that the sex roles can be traced back to a learning process in which an increasing range of activities are standardized as typical of a particular sex, without reference to biological differences being noticeable (D'Andrade, 1966). The sex roles almost always lead to unequal power relationships, expressed in property ownership laws, inheritance laws, residence after marriage and sexual standards.

Since the sex roles are learnt in the process of socialization and generally unconsciously internalized, they come to be taken for granted culturally. Intercultural comparisons (and comparisons between different social strata in a given society) show the extreme variability of the sex roles. The following activities are almost always pursued by men and rarely by women: hunting, metal working, weapon manufacture and boat building, mining; the opposite is true of: child rearing, housework, work in the fields, weaving and preparation of food (Murdock, 1949, 1967). Opposite examples are provided by societies in which women do all the physical work (cultures of Micronesia and Melanesia) or where the traditional, western sex roles are reversed (Tschambuli). The change in sex roles in industrial societies is reflected in the increasing economic equality of woman, sexual emancipation, a lessening of dual moral standards, i.e. in a reduction of all (male) privileges.

Bibliography: **D'Andrade, R. C.:** Sex differences and cultural institutions. In: **Maccoby, E. E.** (Ed.): The development of sex differences. Stanford, 1966. **Ford, C. S. & Beach, F. A.:** Patterns of sexual behavior. New York, 1951. **Mead, M.:** Sex and temperament in three primitive societies. New York, 1936. **Murdock, G. P.:** Social structure. New York, 1949. **Id.:** Ethnographic atlas. Pittsburg, 1967. *J.F.*

Sex, science of. The application of the scientific approach (detached, logical, empirical, and usually quantitative) to the study of the physiological and psychological aspects of sex. Also called *sexology*. *G.D.W.*

Sex skin phenomenon. Coloring of the labia minora pink or pale to dark red caused by the increased blood supply in sexual stimulation. Because of this reaction (which takes place during the plateau stage of the sexual reaction cycle, q.v., and is characteristic of the coming orgasm) the labia minora are called the *sex skin*. *V.S.*

Sexual. Pertaining to sex. Broad and variable usage encompassing the biology of male–female differences, reproduction involving male and female gametes (as opposed to *asexual reproduction*), the behavior of organisms relating to reproduction and sex drive, and the conscious experiences relating to sex, e.g. *eroticism*. *G.D.W.*

Sexual arousal mechanism (abb. SAM). A term from animal-experimental comparative psychology, and an element in a theory regarding the mechanisms of sexual behavior in male laboratory animals, "SAM" designates the hypothetical mechanism responsible for the onset or beginning of sexual behavior (AM = arousal mechanism; see *Arousal*). The measure of the AM is the time from the sight of a receptive female animal to the mounting and intromission response of the male animal (=ML = "mount latency": Beach & Whalen, 1959). By successive intromission, the AM and CM (=copulation mechanism) are sensitized and kept at full excitation level until the ejaculation threshold is reached after a critical period of time, and the male ejaculation ensues. Other researchers have postulated a further mechanism (EM = ejaculation mechanism, triggered off on ejaculation), which exerts an influence on the AM and prevents an immediate, renewed sensitization of the AM until the recovery phase of the EM (McGill, 1965). On renewed presentation of a receptive female, the sensitization of the AM (and CM) becomes manifest in reduced ML and reduced genital stimulation until a second ejaculation. Experiments shows that the AM (like the other mechanisms) is to a large extent dependent on genotype. See *Intromission–copulation–ejaculation mechanism; Drive; Instinct.* *H.M.*

Sexual characteristics. A general designation for all external and internal physical features which distinguish between the male and female sexes. In general a distinction is made between two kinds of sexual characteristics: primary characteristics, i.e. the sexual organs as such (gonads: testicles, and sperm ducts in the man; womb, ovaries and fallopian tubes in the woman); accessory sexual organs: penis, vagina, vulva, etc., and secondary characteristics, i.e. specific male and female features of bodily development (e.g. beard, body hair in men; breasts and rounded hips in women). Apart from the different sexual organs, other differences are also classified as sexual characteristics and referred to by some authors as "tertiary" characteristics (e.g. physical size, bone structure, specific blood cells, development and position of the organs, cardiac and respiratory activity).

Bibliography: Money, J.: Sex research. New York, 1965. *H.M.*

Sexual deviations. Various kinds of sexual behavior may be considered deviant in three different, though usually overlapping, senses: (*a*) abnormal in the statistical sense, i.e. relatively unusual, (*b*) abnormal in the pathological sense, i.e. as symptomatic of some physical or psychological disease, and (*c*) socially unacceptable, perhaps to the extent of being illegal. See *Perversions, sexual.* *G.D.W.*

Sexual disorders. Disorders of procreative (*impotentia generandi*) and coital (*impotentia coeundi*) capacity. Both forms of impairment frequently occur together, but only disorders of sexual efficacy (functional sexual disorders) are relevant to psychology. These may be divided into two main groups: (*a*) symptoms of physical and mental sickness; (*b*) symptoms of disturbed partner relationships. The most important functional sexual disorders are inadequate libido control, isolated libido reduction (see *Libido*), disorders of erection (q.v.), and of ejaculation (q.v.), anorgasmy (q.v.). Functional sexual disorders are often delimited by the terms *impotence* (q.v.: in men), and *frigidity* (q.v.: in women). In general, sexual disorders are separated from *unconventional* sexual behavior (see *Perversions; Sexuality*). *F.Ma.*

Sexual economy. A theory of sexuality developed by Wilhelm Reich in connection with psychoanalysis (q.v.). According to Reich, it is an independent discipline comprising psychological, physiological, biological and sociological approaches. In a narrower sense, the term refers to the regulation of the energy flow of the organism (regulation of the "life energy" or "sexual energy"). The orgasm (q.v.) is considered most important in this regard. A reduced capacity to make love ("orgasmic potency") is said to bring about a disturbance of the total energy flow resulting in neurotic disorders or a "deformed character structure". The so-called psychotherapeutic technique recommended in "sexual economy" is "character-analytic vegetotherapy". Reich's importance would seem to have been his emphasis on the socially-conditioned nature of mental disorders.

Bibliography: Reich, W.: Character analysis. New York & London, 1950. **Id.:** Selected writings. London & New York, 1960. **Id.:** The sexual revolution. London & New York, [2]1969. Rycroft, C.: Reich. London, 1971.
F.Ma.

Sexual inheritance. If sex is determined by hereditary factors (as opposed to phenotypical sex determination, i.e. development into male or female organism determined by different environmental influences), the sex is determined either by the YX type or XO type; in the latter case the decisive factor in determining sex is the presence of one or two X chromosomes in the zygote. *H.Sch.*

Sexuality. Biologically, sex is the combination of characteristics that differentiate the two forms or parts of organisms reproducing themselves by the fusion of gametes and hence of genetic material from two different sources. Female gametes are eggs and male gametes sperms. They may be produced by a single individual (hermaphrodite) or by the sexes separately.

Psychologically, sex is the behavior directly associated with the meeting of the two sexes, and in some species their copulation, to allow the fusion of the gametes (fertilization) to take place. In humans, sex may refer specifically to the act of copulation or heterosexual intercourse, but may extend to the related behaviors of two individuals of the same morphological sex (homosexuality).

Genetically, sex is determined by the presence or absence of the smaller Y chromosome in the relevant chromosomal pair. In mammals (including humans) females have the XX pair of chromosomes and males the XY form.

Sex identification by inspection ranges from impossible in some species, to unmistakable, as normally in humans. Five methods of sex identification are: (i) assay of the chromatin content of cell nuclei—the additional X chromosome in women forming an identifiable chromatin body not found in men with the Y chromosome; (ii) examination of the sex organs—external genitalia; (iii) examination of the internal accessory sex organs; (iv) examination of the gonads, the gamete-producing organs, ovaries and testes; (v) investigation of hormonal state. Since human sexual morphology is distinctly bimodal, errors of sex assignment are rare. Genetically determined anomalies do, however, occur, giving a continuum of maleness–femaleness and individuals in whom there is inconsistency of sex as determined by the above methods. These difficult cases provide investigators with evidence on the development of psychological awareness of sex.

1. *Psychosexual differentiation and gender role.* There are behavioral differences between the two sexes, apart from actual sexual activity, which give rise to the concept of sex or gender role. Clearly, men and women have different roles in society, in reproduction and the associated family structure, and in their occupational choices and ambitions, their peer groupings and social behavior. That sex roles differ markedly from one society to another even to the extent of reversal indicates the importance of culture as a determinant of sex role behavior. Nevertheless, the problem of the assimilation of sex role is raised by individuals who do not adopt the sex-appropriate behavior of their society.

Cases of intersexuality and hermaphroditism, including some brought up with incorrect gender assignment by parents puzzled by the sexual morphology, show instances of unquestioning acceptance of the sex of up bringing—even when contrary to biological sex. This led to statements of the paramount importance of environmental over biological factors of sex determination where the two were at variance. It has been proposed that human sexuality is essentially neutral at birth, and develops as male or female according to the environmental pressures which bring about learning of the gender rôle. This view has been criticized because evidence from intersex abnormalities may not apply to normal individuals. Moreover, there are intersex individuals who rebel against their assigned sex. It is now generally agreed that environmental factors in sex role determination are important, but that powerful hormonal influences operate and all factors interact with genetic sex.

2. *Development of sexual behavior.* Because sexual behavior in lower animals is seen as instinctive, and because in human society, owing to prudery and ignorance, there are few formal lessons in sexual and reproductive behavior, human sexual performance has also been thought to be instinctive. However, mammalian sexual behavior is generally found to become more efficient with experience and the effects of learning are apparent here also.

Freud (1934) employed the instinct (q.v.) concept in his theory of infantile sexual development, with implications for normal and abnormal personality formation. His major achievement was to reintroduce the notion of a continuity of sexual development throughout the life of the child, including the "latent period" in which sexual behavior had been thought to be absent. In the earliest infantile stage of sexual development the child takes pleasure in oral exploration—sucking and chewing. In the second stage the child develops his strength and power; with increasing sensitivity of the anal region sexual responsivity becomes anal and aggressive (see *Sadism*). In the final stage of sexual development, the centre of sexual awareness moves to the genital regions.

Freud adds hypotheses of personality and pathology development based upon the normal progression through the stages stated, or alternatively, a fixation at, or regression to, earlier, inappropriate stages of sexual development. This theory of pathology and the link between sexuality and pleasure derived from non-genital zones of the body have not remained unquestioned scientifically. Much remains speculative or has been discredited for lack of confirmatory evidence. For example, the lack of major sexual abnormality in neurotic patients argues against the Freudian position.

Since human experimentation is fraught with difficulties, studies using non-human subjects can advance our knowledge of the development of sexual behavior. Animals reared in social isolation from others of their own kind show later deficiencies of sexual behavior. Harlow has reared rhesus monkeys in isolation from infant peer groups, combined with isolation from the mother. This was found to be much more disruptive of adult socio-sexual behavior than was isolation from the mother only. Reared in complete isolation from infancy, neither sex showed the normal sexual approach behavior nor the mounting or presenting behavior characteristic of males and females respectively. Females mated with normal males could conceive and give birth but were inadequate and cruel in the secondary sexual behavior of infant care. Hence, at least for infrahuman primates, experience of peer contacts and early sexual play with other infants is a necessary prerequisite for normal development of sexual behavior.

3. *Evidence on human sexual behavior.* Despite the difficulties of studying the intimate and until recently largely taboo topics of human sexuality, methods have gradually progressed from insecure clinical generalizations to large-scale surveys giving factual data. Kinsey pioneered the use of trained interviewers with very large samples in the United States, and achieved a remarkable degree of

cooperation from his interviewees. The results, mainly tabulated to show sexual outlets including intercourse, masturbation, nocturnal emissions and perversions (q.v.), show a marked discrepancy between social expectations and actual behavior. These surveys provide normative data for many human sexual activities and have not been seriously disconfirmed in the numerous smaller replications carried out in other countries.

4. *Disorders of sexual behavior*. Homosexuality ranks first in popular view as a major disorder of sexual behavior and yet Kinsey (1948, 1953) showed clearly that incidents of homosexuality in the population are frequent (males, 37%) and that there is no clear distinction between the homosexual and the heterosexual. The findings suggest that there is a continuum from pure homosexuality to pure heterosexuality with the majority of men showing interest in both directions. The same is true of women homosexuals, or lesbians. Although homosexuals rarely wish to change their sexual orientation, society exerts such pressures towards heterosexuality—the social norm—that sexual reorientation may be desired to relieve the psychiatric distress and depression thus caused. While psychoanalytic or another psychotherapy (q.v.) can offer a greater acceptance of the self, behavior therapy (q.v.) is increasingly able to effect a change of sexual interests in selected patients.

As with homosexuality, other disorders of sexuality are notably more frequent in men than in women. This is more than a greater societal tolerance for female deviation and may be related to a sex difference in sexual arousal. Males are more arousable generally and by visual stimuli in particular.

5. *Research*. Research into sexuality is in its infancy. There is currently a growth of serious interest, and surveys are more ably carried out than formerly, but problems of theory and of measurement remain. Little true experimentation has been carried out but the therapeutic application of findings from comparative and general psychology gives hope of further rapid developments in the future.

Bibliography: Beach, F. A. (Ed.): Sex and behavior New York, 1968. **Broadhurst, A.**: Abnormal sexual behaviour female. In: **Eysenck, H. J.** (Ed.): Handbook of abnormal psychology. London, ²1971. **Diamond, M.**: A critical evaluation of the ontogeny of human sexual behavior. Quart. Rec. Biol., 1965, *40*, 147–74 **Ellis, H. & Abarbanel, A.** (Eds.): The encyclopedia of sexual behavior. 2 vols., New York, 1961. **Feldman, M. P.**: Abnormal sexual behaviour male. In: **Eysenck, H. J.** (Ed.): Handbook of abnormal psychology. London, ²1971. **Id. & MacCulloch, M. J.**: Homosexual behaviour: therapy and assessment. Oxford, 1970. **Freud, S.**: Collected papers. London, 1934. **Gagnon, J. H.**: Sexuality and sexual learning in the child. Psychiatry, 1965, *28*, 212–227. **Green, R. & Money, J.** (Eds.): Transsexualism and sex reassignment. Baltimore, 1969. **Harris, G. W. & Levine, S.**: Sexual differentiation and its experimental control. J. Physiol., 1965, *181*, 379–400. **Kenyon, F. E.**: Homosexuality in the female. Brit. J. Hosp. Med., 1970, *3*, 183–296. **Kinsey, A. C.** *et al.*: Sexual behavior in the human male. Philadelphia, 1948. **Id.**: Sexual behavior in the human female. Philadelphia, 1953. **Maccoby, E. E.** (Ed.): The development of sex differences. London, 1967. **Masters, W. H. & Johnson, V. E.**: Human sexual response. Boston, 1966. **Rheingold, H. L.**: Maternal behavior in mammals. New York, 1963. **Sackett, G. P.**: Abnormal behavior in laboratory-reared rhesus monkeys. In: **Fox, M. W.** (Ed.): Abnormal behavior in animals. Philadelphia, 1968, 293–331. **Winokur, G.** (Ed.): Determinants of human sexual behavior. Springfield, Ill., 1963.

A. Broadhurst

Sexual neurosis. A form of neurosis (q.v.) in which the sexual functions are disturbed and a cause of distress. The patient who becomes uncertain of his sexuality (q.v.) reacts oversensitively to a demand for sexual performance. The causative factor may be the situation, the partner or the patient himself. The most frequent symptom of a sexual neurosis is impotence (q.v.).

Bibliography: Wolman, B. B.: Handbook of clinical psychology. New York & London, 1965. *F.Ma.*

Sexual reaction cycle. According to Masters & Johnson (1966), the physiological reactions to a sexual act such as coitus (q.v.) or masturbation (q.v.) go in a cycle which can be arbitrarily divided into four phases: excitement (q.v.), plateau phase (q.v.), orgasm (q.v.), detumescence (q.v.). These phases, even the orgasm, cannot be exactly defined either in terms of objective reactions or of subjective experience.

Bibliography: Masters, W. H. & Johnson, V. E.: Human sexual response. Boston, 1966. **Sigusch, V.:** Exzitation und Orgasmus bei der Frau. Stuttgart, 1970. *V.S.*

Sexual socialization. This is the adaptation of the individual to society by internalizing its values and learning the appropriate modes of behavior. Sexual socialization is made more difficult by the gap between the age of puberty and the attainment of social adult status. This brands youthful sex relations ("premarital") as deviant. Sexual socialization is also made more difficult by the gap between the sexual norms of a bourgeois society (taboo on sex, denial of instinct, monopolizing of sex by marriage), and the need to satisfy sexual drives, which is particularly strong in youth. It is paradoxical that children brought up to respect these inhibiting standards before they marry are expected to achieve a full flowering of sex within marriage: that is to say, they are expected at a single moment to become experts in a skill which they were forbidden to learn. The tone of sexual explanations and education is correspondingly ambivalent. *N.S.-R.*

Sexual symbolism. The representation by any object or event of the sex organs or sexual behavior. Thus in psychoanalytic dream interpretation, narrow, pointed objects, such as knives, keys, chimneys and snakes, are often taken as *phallic symbols*, while soft, round and indented objects, such as hats and vases, are treated as female symbols. Intercourse is said to be represented by many activities, such as climbing stairs and riding horses. According to Freudian theory, this kind of symbolism has the function of disguising the sexual meaning from the conscious mind where it would otherwise be unacceptable. *G.D.W.*

Sexual trauma. General definition: a trauma is an experience or event which (directly or indirectly) has a damaging influence in the psychological and/or psychosexual sphere. The term "sexual trauma" is used in two branches of science with a slightly different meaning: in psychoanalysis, where it has undergone a number of changes for empirical and theoretical reasons, in the context of the theory of neuroses, and in forensic psychology and psychiatry, where it is the subject of empirical research in the special sector of victimology, concerned with children who are victims of sexual offenses.

1. *Psychoanalysis.* The notion of the sexual trauma was first introduced specifically by Freud in 1896 ("Weitere Bemerkungen über die Abwehr-Neuropsychosen"). Freud assumed at the time (on the basis of thirteen analyses of cases of hysteria) that a predisposition toward neurosis (q.v.) may occur as a result of actual sexual experiences in early childhood (between the second and tenth years of life). However, he considered that the traumatic effect did not lie in the early experiences themselves but in subsequent recollections of them after puberty; these recollections are not conscious but lead to emotional ties and repression. These sexual traumata of childhood, accompanied by "real irritation of the genitalia", consisted, in the case of hysteria, in sexual passivity of the child (which was sexually seduced: frequently sibling incest) and, in the case of a compulsion neurosis, in sexual activity of the child, i.e. in "aggression performed with pleasure and pleasurable participation in sex acts" (Freud).

The theory that sexual traumas of early

childhood were the etiological bases of defense neuroses had to be abandoned, however, as experience of analysis grew: Freud realized that these childhood recollections of his adult patients did not entirely correspond to genuine experience. The pathogenic memories which repeatedly come to light during analysis are (wish) phantasies consisting of a blend of reality and imagination. The real aspects of these phantasies are events which the child is as yet unable to understand: (*a*) "with the seduction phantasy when there has been no actual seduction, the child generally conceals the auto-erotic period of its sexual activity. It spares itself shame over masturbation by inventing the existence of a desired object in this early period." (*b*) The child deduces the threat of castration "from his knowledge that auto-erotic satisfaction is forbidden and under the impression of his discovery of the female genitalia" and builds up a corresponding phantasy. (*c*) The primal scene, i.e. observation of sexual intercourse between the parents, is considered a historical fact which is then embellished "on the strength of observations of intercourse in animals (dogs), motivated by the child's unsatisfied voyeurism in the years of puberty". The trauma is always triggered by a conflict between drive stimuli and drive-inhibiting ideas. (*d*) The attempt to master the traumatic libido energy by repetition in order to re-establish satisfaction at an earlier, pleasurable stage of libido development cannot succeed and makes a decisive contribution to neurotic development.

2. *Victimology*. Although a number of case studies have been made on the subject of the harmful effects of sexual crimes against children, there have so far been no methodical studies of sexual trauma and their consequences in the case of sexual crimes. Results obtained so far are contradictory and of differing value. *H. Maisch*

S factor. The specific ability factor in Spearman's two-factor intelligence theory, according to which there is a "g" or general factor common to all performance, and every individual performance possesses an "s" or specific factor. See *Abilities*. *H.J.A.*

Shadow. A term found in the complex psychology of C. G. Jung (q.v.) for the totality of those personal and collective-unconscious tendencies (see *Unconscious*) which are incompatible with the conscious life form and are therefore not integrated into the ego (q.v.). The shadow functions as a relatively autonomous partial personality which acts as compensation for the consciousness; however, it embodies not only negatively repressed influences but also tendencies pointing to the future. To make the shadow conscious is the first task of any Jungian analysis. *W.Sch.*

Shannon-Wiener entropy formula. See *Information; Communication.*

Shape constancy. The perceived shape of an object is relatively independent of changes in the stimuli exciting the retina (q.v.) brought about in the projected image by spatial adjustment. Usually the set of stimuli furnish information about the spatial situation, e.g. through the distribution of brightness, perspective, texture, and above all the surroundings of an object. Shape constancy is impaired when such information is withdrawn.

Bibliography: Epstein, W. & Park, J.: Shape constancy; functional relationships and theoretical formulations. Psychol. Bull. 1963, *60*, 265–88. *J.Z.*

Sheldon types. Sheldon (1942) distinguished three dimensions of physical constitution, or three main clusters of traits of temperament, each cluster consisting of twenty traits: *viscerotonia*, *somatotonia* and *cerebrotonia*. Each cluster was related to bodily functions. See *Type; Traits*.

Bibliography: Sheldon, W. H.: The varieties of temperament. New York & London, 1942. **Id.:** The varieties of delinquent youth: an introduction to constitutional psychiatry. New York & London, 1949. *M.H.*

Shock. A complex syndrome with physical and psychic components brought about by a sudden, intense influence on the organism. The main characteristic of shock is the vascular crisis (an acute circulatory insufficiency). There is frequently a disturbance of consciousness, or a loss of consciousness. Two basic forms are distinguished: organic shock (e.g. in a cardiac infarction, or *commotio cerebri*), and shock as a general reaction (e.g. anaphylactic shock brought about by inappropriate protein; insulin or hypoglycemia shock—reduction of blood sugar; psychic shock).

Since a shock can cause long-lasting alterations, especially of a psychological nature, it is used, as "shock therapy", to treat psychoses artificially. See *Psychoses, functional; Schizophrenia.* *F.Ma.*

Shock, apperceptive. In his characterology, Lersch places this among the "excitations of feeling directed toward self-preservation" (as a sub-group of the excitations of emotion of the individual as he exists for himself), a "shock condition of fright", a disturbance in grouping perceptional material into some orderly connection based on experience and accompanied by a loss of orientation and diminished capability of performing a purposive act. *A.G.*

Shock inducer. An instrument on the principle of electro-magnetic induction (induction coil) which makes it possible to produce a variable aversive stimulus whose intensity can be regulated; it is used especially in learning and conditioning experiments (q.v.). *J.M.*

Shock therapy. Treatment of severe mental illness by inducing some kind of shock to the nervous system. At one time drugs which induced an epileptic fit were used for this purpose. Since the late 1930s an electric current passed through the brain has been found to produce the same effect with less unpleasantness for the patient. Used mainly for the treatment of severe depression, and less often for schizophrenia or mania. *R.H.*

Shortsightedness. See *Myopia.*

Short-term memory. In interpreting the findings of memory psychology, the model of a short and long-term memory has been adopted. W. James already spoke of a primary memory which is used for short-term retention and a secondary memory corresponding to the psychological past. Tests of immediate retention capacity generally show little correlation with tests of the long-term memory. Time estimates of the short-term memory range from 2–3 to 10 seconds (Rohracher, 1968; Frank, 1969). Frank developed a model which showed a short-term memory with an intake speed C of 16 bits per second and a capacity of 160 bits, a short memory ($C = 0.4 - 0.8$ bits/sec) and a long-term memory ($C = 0.05$ bits/sec). See *Memory.* *R.R.*

Short-term therapy. In many neuroses, analysis or other forms of long-term psychotherapy are not necessary. For this reason, and also because of the actual therapeutic requirements, short-term therapy has been introduced for less severe neuroses in which it is generally necessary to defuse the conflict situation and disintegrate it without the need for long-term analysis of the past. *J.L.I.*

Sight. The faculty of vision; seeing; the sense mediated by the eyes. The visual modality is often considered the dominant one in humans and is characteristically and especially concerned with the perception of space and spatial relations. See *Eye; Visual perception.* *G.D.F.*

Sigmatism. Incorrect formation of the S sound. The most prevalent forms are: *sigmatismus interdentalis* (tongue between rows of teeth); *sigmatismus addentalis* (tongue on upper row of teeth); *sigmatismus lateralis* (air escaping on either side of tongue). The most difficult to treat is lateral sigmatism. *H.B.*

Sign. A sign is usually understood as a perceptual content effected by a signal (q.v.) which refers beyond itself to a referent—a cause or meaning. Signs are distinguished as indicators (signs *of*. . .) and representational signs (signs *for* . . .). When a sign indicates, the referent is the cause of the sign: hence a higher body temperature is a sign (indication) of an infection. When a sign represents, the referent is the meaning of the sign: hence a spoken word is a physical signal sequence which becomes a sign only by virtue of the associated meaning. A common repertoire of signs (letters, words, etc.) is the prerequisite for information exchange and transmission. Three sign functions are distinguished: the *syntactic, semantic* and *pragmatic*, whose study is the object of semiotics (q.v.), or semiology. See *Sign and symbol; Communication.*

P.-B.H.

Sign and symbol. Signs and symbols are information bearers which, by virtue of their meaning, stand for that which they symbolize or designate; they *represent* that which they designate. Both terms may be used synonymously or in different acceptations; there is no one mind in the diverse research traditions as to the definition or psychological function of the words.

1. *Behaviorism* (q.v.). In this area, signs and symbols are considered predominantly in regard to their function as signals. Under the influence of Pavlov's first and second signal systems, H. Mead and O. H. Mowrer described those stimuli that elicit responses as signs, and those stimuli that stand for stimuli eliciting responses as symbols. According to C. E. Osgood, a stimulus becomes the sign of a stimulus object when it exerts a mediating, fractional response exerted originally by the stimulus object. Osgood calls signs that stand for other signs, "assigns". In neo-behaviorism (q.v.) it is emphasized that the part response released by a symbol is not an instrumental action but serves merely to "stimulate" further responses (D. E. Berlyne). The production and association of such symbolic part responses are known as symbolic processes; they are adduced to explain information processing in learning and thinking.

2. *Depth psychology.* Symbols are viewed as isomorphic and usually pictorial manifestations of the unconscious, and are studied in order to analyze pathological states, dreams and myths. For Freud, a symbol is (*a*) a mental representation of physical processes, e.g. an hysterical symptom (see *Hysteria*); (*b*) a disguised expression of repressed objects and wishes, especially in infantile, primitive or regressive thinking (O. Rank, T. Reik, W. Stekel, M. Klein). For Jung, a symbol is the individual concretization of an archetype, and does not merely serve to mask something but unites the conscious and the unconscious, the productivity-favoring flow of the libido (q.v.) and the manifestation of phylogenetic experiences.

3. *Cognitive psychology.* Signs and symbols are considered to be of major importance in perception (q.v.), thinking (q.v.) and memory (q.v.), and to be means of understanding these processes as well as characteristics of diverse levels of thought and abstraction. Whereas the term "sign" is usually applied to representations with a denotative, and conventionally fixed meaning, the term "symbol" is used to characterize representation by means of

convention, isomorphisms, expressive traits, associations, and so on. Piaget (1959), for example, speaks of *social* symbols (with an acquired meaning), and of *private* symbols (which are understood since they are a part of, or like, that which is designated). Extending K. Goldstein's classification (concrete, asymbolic and abstract, symbolic thinking), J. S. Bruner distinguishes between *enactive* representation (which forms part of an action and controls further actions), *iconic* representation (which serves concrete description and apprehension), and *symbolic* representation (i.e. signs to represent abstract relations). Gestalt psychologists (W. Köhler, H. Werner) take into account especially the implications for the psychology of thinking of the fusion (in concrete representations) of the symbol and that which is symbolized, and consider even abstract symbols to be expressive agents. The level of abstraction of the designatum (Kahn's symbol test), or of its representativeness (R. Brown), are used to classify thought processes. See also *Language; Grammar; Semantics.*

4. *Synthesis.* The agreement about the term "sign" and the chaotic state of definition of the term "symbol" would seem to be conditioned, among other things, by the fact that symbols are viewed as *bearers of connotative meaning*, so that on the one hand a specific symbol symbolizes various things, and on the other hand a specific designatum can be variously symbolized. The consequent large number of forms of symbolization allowed research workers to take into account only those kinds of symbol that accorded with their intention. For the purpose of a more unified classification of different forms of symbol, and to allow the study of their interrelations, symbolization experiments were carried out, and the means of symbolization in each case was analyzed: ten symbol categories resulted (Kreitler, 1965). Most like the sign are symbolizations whose meaning is afforded by lexical explanations (category 1), e.g. Osgood's "assign", Piaget's "social symbol", Goldstein's and Bruner's "abstract symbols", etc. Predominantly isomorphic symbolizations, e.g. by representation of the referent by means of an individual case or detail, a situation, a scenic action or real consequence (categories 2, 3, 4 and 6), correspond to Bruner's "enactive" and "iconic", Piaget's "private" and von Domarus' "*pars-pro-toto*" symbols. Symbolization by means of the sensations elicited by the referent (category 7) correspond to gestalt-psychological criteria. The symptoms of hysteria conceived by Freud as symbols are symbolizations by means of physical expression (category 5), whereas his dream symbols are isomorphous allegories (category 9). Jung's archetypal symbols are in part verbal or pictorial indications (category 8) of individual or collective behavior patterns, and in part the synthesis of a contradiction and its resolution in a good gestalt (category 10) as the representation of an immanent dynamic.

Bibliography: Jacobi, J.: Complex, archetype and symbol in the psychology of C. G. Jung. Princeton & London, 1959. **Kreitler, S.:** Symbolschöpfung und Symbolerfassung. Munich & Basle, 1965. **Piaget, J.:** La formation du symbole chez l'enfant. Neuchâtel, [2]1959. **Werner, H. & Kaplan, B.:** Symbol formation. New York, 1963.

S. Kreitler & H. Kreitler

Signal. A stimulus in any modality intended to convey information; often contrasted to *noise* used in the sense of conveying no information. *C.D.F.*

Signals, animal. Communication within or between species in animals employ signals which are bodily structures, sounds, smells and specific patterns of behavior. Signals usually have a releasing function, e.g.: The red breast of the robin releases aggression in males of the same species. When signals are copied from other species this is called *mimicry*. Non-stinging hymenoptera are avoided as if they were wasps when they have a black and yellow striped body. *V.P.*

Signal transformation. By the process of signal transformation a given signal (q.v.) is transformed into another. The transformation must take place in such a way that the original signal can be reconstructed (through "reversed transformation"). Signal transformation is a physical process which makes use of a clearly understood transformable *code* (q.v.). It is used, e.g., to transform the signals of a sender to suit a given channel of communication.

P.B.H.

Significance. Statistical (q.v.) tests are also called significance tests, because they test the significance (that is to say relevance) of differences. We distinguish between *statistical* and *practical* significance. Statistical significance (provable by a test) is a necessary but not a sufficient condition of practical significance. Very large samples may reveal very small practically insignificant differences, in which case the taking of a smaller sample is quite sufficient to reveal the same practically significant differences. *A.R.*

Significance level. The probability of error which is allowed for in a statistical (q.v.) test is called the significance level. In psychology this is usually set at 5%. *A.R.*

Significance, limits of. The numbers in statistical tests which at a given significance level (q.v.) must be exceeded or fallen short of to make these tests significant (q.v.). *A.R.*

Significant. When a hypothesis is adopted from observed data, the probability of error is calculated as a number which is called the significant difference. *A.R.*

Sign language. A means of communication based on signs for use in cases where normal speech must be replaced. Sign languages developed among the North American Indians (to enable different tribes to communicate), Neapolitans (as a secret language) and Trappist monks (because of the rule of silence). These languages form the basis of the sign language used for deaf and dumb people which, however, has been enlarged by conventional signs (the French Method was founded by Abbé Charles Michel de l'Eppée in about 1770). Recently the American Sign Language has been successfully used to train chimpanzees and establish a broader means of communication between men and chimpanzees (attempts to teach spoken language proved unsuccessful).

Bibliography: **Gardner, R. A. & B. T.:** Acquisition of sign language in the chimpanzee. Progr. Report, Reno, 1967. *F.Ki.*

Simplicity structure. A concept from factor analysis. If, following extraction, all common factors (q.v.) are rotated according to the criteria of simplicity structure, the following characteristics are attributed to the factor matrix: (*a*) the factorial solutions rotated in this way (see *Rotation*) are, given certain assumptions, unspecific for random samples. (*b*) This structure makes possible a particularly simple content interpretation of the factors. According to the criterion of the simplicity structure, rotated factor matrices are usually no longer orthogonal. *W.H.B.*

Simulation. See *Lie scale*.

Simulation of psychological (mental) processes. The process by which pseudo-empirical data are produced from an abstract psychological theory. The familiar representation of psychological regularities (laws) as curves in a Cartesian coordinate system stand for statistics already calculated from observations but not the data themselves (e.g. see *Learning* *curves*). Individual observations are dispersed around these mean values in a way that is generally not closely considered. All oppositions of theory and observation consist mainly in the comparison of theoretical with empirical statistics. The simulation of psychological processes enables any desired number of learning curves to be produced. Their points are pseudoempirical since they represent a set of data which, although produced theoretically, should correspond to experimental data. It is therefore evident that the simulation of psychological processes can be applied to the validation of theories. The pseudoempirical data produced can be contrasted item for item with the experimental data. The prerequisite for the use of simulation is a noncontradictory formulation of psychological theory. This is usually impossible if one is restricted to natural languages (e.g. German, English, etc.). In order to formulate theories, special languages are used: e.g. mathematics (cf. Atkinson, Bower & Crothers, 1965), or a computer or program language (Algol, Fortran, etc.). A simulation whose set of pseudoempirical data cannot be distinguished from a set of genuine experimental data even by an expert has passed the "Turing test".

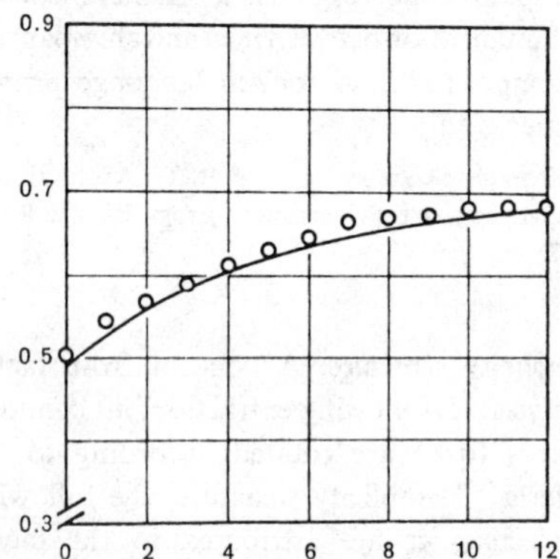

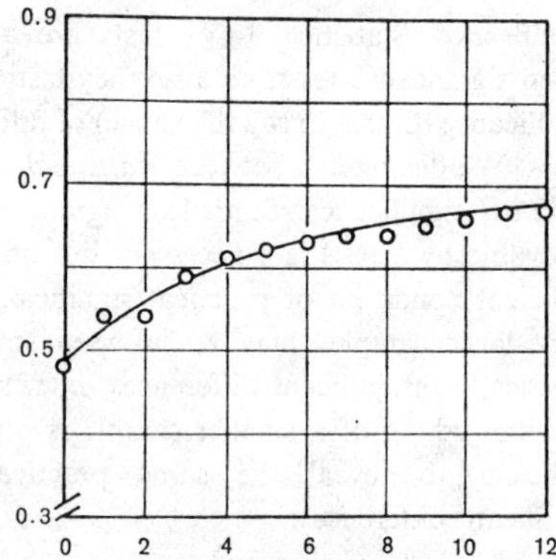

Empirical results (Fig. left) and simulation data (Fig. right) for a learning experiment. In the ordinate direction, the cumulative total of mistakes improved on spontaneously by the subject is set off against the actual errors (abscissa). The simulation data were obtained using the Bush-Mosteller model and parameters estimated from experimental data (Drösler, 1964).

By its use as an instrument for validation of a theory, or in prognosis, simulation is itself used as a *medium in the construction of theories*. Psychological regularities often do not allow of a mathematical representation in a consistent form. In the areas of cognitive psychology (see *Thinking*) and social psychology, for example, the theoretical consequences of an aggregate of individual mathematical-logical assertions are sought for by the use of simulation. Newell, Shaw & Simon (1957) compiled their deliberations in the process of solving a simple logical problem. The system shows such a high degree of complexity that its consequences can be surveyed only by means of simulation. Hence extensive theoretical constructions show the useful application of electronic data-processing installations (see *Computer*). Simulation is often used with mainly pragmatic aims: human working potentials must be mechanized for industrial purposes. Here the criterion for realization consists only of successful automation, whereas the psychologist is just as interested in the errors of the "automaton", in order to compare them qualitatively with human errors. Hence in the simulation of letter recognition not only success in the form of probable score is considered, but all the mistakes that occur. A psychological theory is needed which in practice would (through simulation) produce an error matrix which is indistinguishable from an empirical one.

The first experiments in simulation related to the behavior of parts of the organism (individual nerve cells—"neuron models"—and reflexes). Electronic control circuits were used for simulation in these instances. Later, an electromechanical simulation of conditioned responses was produced. The availability of electronic data-processing makes a wide variety of behaviors, such as perception (q.v.), learning (q.v.) and thinking (q.v.) accessible to simulation. The search for the widely ramified consequences of a developed simulation model is in itself tantamount to being an empirical pursuit. This may have contributed to the fact that in published work on simulation the experimental aspect is sometimes too restricted.

The emphasis of present-day research is on the field of perception and the psychology of thinking. Sign recognition is of major importance in perception (cf. Uhr, 1966). The incentive for such investigations is to be seen in the fact that each item of information still has to be prepared manually before it is accessible to electronic data-processing, and because an army of workmen has to be employed for this purpose in industry and administration. The gain to psychology in the use of simulation in sign recognition is still small, since the procedures applied are oriented more toward technological than psychological data. In the psychology of thinking, approaches to simulation have led to the first precise formulations of certain extensive areas, and a clear view of the connections between learning, concept formation and problem solving (Hunt, 1966). With the help of simulation, for example, an exact analysis of heuristic behavior is possible for the first time. The realization of similar programs on electronic computers leads to pseudo-data in areas which not long ago were quite impenetrable: for example, the use of arguments in elementary logic or the practice of two-dimensional geometry, problem solving, or the course of dialogues.

Developments of this kind are occasionally known as "artificial intelligence", though this term is misleading, and threatens to divert us from the scientific aim of simulation. Simulation generates fallacies as soon as aspects of pseudo-empirical sets of data are uncritically generalized. Details peculiar to the simulation may easily be mistaken for psychological regularities. Precautions are necessary so that pseudo-empirical data are compared in as many aspects as possible with experimental results. This requirement is often not observed today. It is therefore sometimes difficult to estimate the psychological-theoretical content of simulation findings as they are reported in the literature. Nevertheless, the heuristic value of the simulation of psychological processes is recognized as high (Gregg & Simon, 1967). See *Communication; Cybernetics and psychology; Machine learning; Instructional technology.*

Bibliography: Anderson, A. R. (Ed.): Minds and machines. New York, 1964. **Atkinson, R. C., Bower, G. H. & Crothers, E. J.:** An introduction to mathematical learning theory. New York, 1965. **Bernstein, J.:** The analytical engine: computers—past, present and future. **Bush, R. R. & Mosteller, F.:** Stochastic models for learning. New York & London, 1955. **Drösler, J.:** Ein besonders empfindlicher Indikator für den Lernfortschritt und der Bush-Mosteller-Operator. Z.f. exp. angew. Psychol., 1964, *11*, 238–253. **Id.:** Künstliche Intelligenz. In: **Irle, M.** (Ed.): Bericht über den 26. Kongress der DGP. Göttingen, 1969, 37–52. **Gregg, L. W. & Simon, H. A.:** Process models and stochastic theories of simple concept formation. J. of mathematical Psychol., 1967, *4*, 246–76. **Hunt, E. B., Malin, J. & Stone, P. J.:** Experiments in induction. New York & London, 1966; **Loehlin, J. C.:** Computer models of personality. New York, 1968. **Meltzer, B. & Michie, D.** (Eds.): Machine intelligence 4. Edinburgh, 1969. **Minsky, M.:** Artificial intelligence. Scientific American. 1966, *215*, 246–63. **Id.** (Ed.): Semantic information processing. Cambridge, Mass., 1968.

J. Drösler

Simultaneous contrast. See *Contrast*.

Sitter. Person at a *séance* (q.v.) who is the recipient of a communication from the medium (q.v.). *J.B.*

Situation, social. A general term for the field of reference (stimuli, objects, fellow men, groups, values, including those of the individual self) of the orientation of a person acting in society. Looked at from this standpoint, the social situation may be defined by three categories of data and the manner in which they are linked: (*a*) the actual data which influence the acting person, (*b*) the attitudes (q.v.) which are brought into play at the time of the act, and (*c*) the degree of ego involvement (q.v.) or awareness of the actual data and attitudes on the part of the acting person. T. Parsons and E. A. Shills designate all those data of the environment which have some meaning for the acting person as constituents of the social situation. *W.D.F.*

Sixteen Personality Factor Questionnaire. (*16 PF*). R. B. Cattell devised this representative test of factor analytical personality research with subjective tests. Among the 16 factors designated by the letters A–O (without D) and Q_1–Q_4 can be found: B = intelligence; C+ = emotional stability; E+ = dominance; O+ = trust; L+ = composure; N+ = naïveté. Each factor is represented by 20–26 items. The standard form for adults consists of the forms A and B (of 6 possible forms A–F) each with a different half of the items. The forms A and B can be regarded as *parallel tests* (q.v.). (Equivalence coefficients lie between r = 0.34–0.76 when N = 230). For the test ratings calculated per factor different norms are available. For interpretation of the factors the manual can be consulted, where descriptions of them will be found. By means of a special calculation, scores can also be obtained for the secondary factors: (i) anxiety; (ii) introversion/extraversion; (iii) emotionality; (iv) submission versus independence. The test-retest reliability of the factors ranges between r = 0.78–0.93 (6 days; N = 146) and r = 0.63–0.88 (2 months; N = 132), the bisection reliability between r = 0.06–0.78 (form A), r = 0.12–0.81 (B) when N = 218. The factorial validities (multiple correlation of the items [q.v.] with the factor representing them) lie between r = 0.74–0.92.

Bibliography: Cattell, R. B. & Eber, H. W.: Manual for forms A and B Sixteen Personality Factor Questionnaire (16 PF). Champaign, Ill., [5]1962. *P.G.*

Size perception. An important and much studied phenomenon in the psychology of optical perception (visual perception). Size perception in human beings cannot be described and explained by physical laws: in spite of the identical size of different *retinal* (images) the corresponding objects can be perceived as different in size. The phenomenon of size constancy (q.v.) in spatial perception (q.v.) is involved here. *R.Hä.*

Skaggs-Robinson hypothesis. Formulated by E. B. Skaggs and E. S. Robinson, this hypothesis deals with the effect which the similarity of two amounts of material to be learned (when presented successively) has on the retention performance (retroactive inhibition, q.v.). The effect of the inhibition of the retention performance is maximal when there is "average similarity" between the interpolated and the original material and it decreases towards the poles of maximal and minimal similarity, the retention performance with minimal similarity not equalling that with maximal similarity. *F.-C.S.*

Skepticism. The name of a school of Greek philosophy whose teaching was taken up again by M. de Montaigne and P. Charron ("What do I know?") and later by L. Klages, G. Jünger *et al.* *Absolute* skepticism considers man to be incapable of arriving at the truth in any area of knowledge whatsoever; those who believe this recommend the suspension of all judgment. *Relative* skepticism excludes from some areas any possibility of knowing the truth (metaphysical, religious, scientific skepticism, etc.). The word is commonly used to signify the attitude of a person who does not regard some datum as certain, and to indicate the basic attitude of a mind inclined to doubt. *M.R.*

Skewness. A measure for the deviation of a distribution from symmetry. Most commonly used in the moment coefficient $a_3 = m_3/m_2{}^{3/2}$: (m_2 and m_3 are the second and third powers of the distribution based on the arithmetic mean). The Pearson skewness coefficients are now only of historical interest, as in more recent times the percentile coefficients are more commonly used. *A.R.*

Skiascopy. A method taken from ophthalmology to determine *refraction anomalies* (see *Refraction*) and astigmatism (q.v.). It consists of moving a perforated convex mirror in front of the eye of the person being examined and observing the movement of the light ray and its shadow in the red illumination of the pupil. *E.D.*

Skin. The skin (*integumentum commune*) consists of three main layers, the *epidermis*, *corium* and *tela subcutanea.* The skin provides protection against physical, chemical and microbiological influences; it is also involved in the process of water and temperature regulation. *G.A.*

Skin diseases. The skin (as the external boundary of a human being) has always been considered as a privileged centre of expression for emotional processes (blushing, losing color, goose pimples). Many psychological factors may be involved in the various disturbances of the functional relationship between the skin gland reaction and the vascular and pilo-activity; however, the assumption of a direct psychological cause seems inexact. It is simply possible to observe multifactorial complementarity functions between personality variables and skin diseases. It is difficult to make a distinction between psychological changes which have contributed to the skin disease and those which are merely a result of the latter (e.g. feeling of inferiority).

Psychosomatic symptoms: acne occurs primarily at puberty as a result of abnormal secretion by the sebaceous glands due to a disturbance of the endocrine equilibrium. If the condition continues, adult patients frequently show a delay in reaching effective and psychosexual maturity. Traumatic conflict situations are often responsible for the sudden occurrence of acne. This also applies to skin diseases which become secondary symptoms as a result of intense itching and scratching. Diseases of this kind include *acne excoriée des jeunes filles* (L. Brocq) encountered frequently among female patients. The skin is damaged by crushing or scratching and large flat scars develop which are liable to become inflamed. These forms of self-aggression have a compulsory character and serve to break down mental stress in the case of neurotic patients. In patients suffering from neurodermatitis (= endogenous eczema) in which organic factors played an important part (constitution, nutritional and metabolic disorders, allergy factors), the following psychosyndrome has been observed: heightened irritability, unsociable behavior and depression, strong attachment to the mother and masochistic trends. These mental factors play a decisive part in the reappearance or disappearance of the neurodermatitis but they need not necessarily be psychological causes of the disorder.

In the case of urticaria (chronic nettle-rash) whose organic factors have not yet been clearly determined, psychopathological changes may be observed: repressed aggression, exhibitionist (see *Exhibitionism*) and masochistic (see *Masochism*) trends.

Because of their demonstrative social protest against the withdrawal of affection and love (skin as an organ of contact and expression), patients tend to inflict punishment on themselves. Highly unspecific psychological changes (heightened anxiety, feelings of inferiority) are found in the case of psoriasis, alopecia, etc. Some patients develop phobias, e.g. zoophobia (illusion of small animals penetrating into the skin, and particles which must constantly be scratched out), luophobia and gonococcal phobia (fear of venereal disease), or cancerophobia (fear of cancer).

Treatment: medication and changed diet, supported by psychotherapy (psychoanalytic focal therapy, client-centered discussion therapy, autogenic training). See *Psychosomatics*.

D. Vaitl

Skinner box. A wooden box for experiments with animals in *operant* conditioning (q.v.). A lever device is fitted to it and when this is depressed, a pellet of food drops into the cage or a door is opened through which the test animal can escape. The Skinner box is a variant of the experiment, vexation (q.v.) or problem cage (q.v.) developed by E. L. Thorndike, and owes its name to R. F. Skinner, the American researcher into behavior and learning. *H.Ro.*

Skin resistance. I. The resistance to a direct current flowing through the skin corresponds in very small measure only to a true ohmic resistance (13–95 kohms). It is caused primarily by a combination of several different kinds of variable polarization voltage (1.5–800 kohm polarization resistance). The reflectoral changes in the skin resistance caused by sensory stimuli or motor reactions are due solely to changes in the adsorption and permeation characteristics of membranes or to changes in polarization capacities. The capacitative proportion of the skin impedance consists of a "diffusion capacity" and a "double layer capacity" and can be determined by alternating current measurements or by recording the cut-in characteristic of a DC current. *M.S.*

II. *Skin potential:* the resistance and potential difference vary as a function of the subject's condition. At different times in the day, when solving problems and in conjunction with emotional changes, long-term alterations may be noted (basal values, basal level). In addition external or internal stimulation leads to brief reductions in the skin potential and multiphase fluctuations (skin galvanic or psychogalvanic reactions, phenomena, reflexes). In psychophysiology short-term changes are used to demonstrate orienting and defensive behavior.

Bibliography: Venables, P. H. & Martin, I.: Skin resistance and skin potential. In: **Venables, P. H. & Martin, I.** (Ed.): Manual of psycho-physiological methods. Amsterdam, 1967. *W.Sch.*

Skin vision. The alleged capacity to be able to discriminate brightness and colour by means of touch. Also known as "finger vision" and "dermo-optical perception" or DOP (G. Razran). See *Eyeless sight*. *J.B.*

Slavery, reflex of. Pavlov's term for an "inborn reflex of slavish submission" opposed to the reflex of freedom (q.v.), related to appeasement gestures (q.v.) in animals, and having a similar effect in decreasing the destructive ambition of the strong. Pavlov suggests that insight into the condition, and systematic measures, will enable the reflex to be controlled and suppressed, whereas ineffective resistance will only increase aggression (q.v.). *J.C.*

Sleep is a recurrent, healthy state of inertia and unresponsiveness. Observable responses are less easily elicited, and so also, it would appear, are the internal responses underlying perception. Sleep must be distinguished from hibernation, in which activity declines during long periods of low body temperature. Sleep should also be distinguished from the hypnotic trance, in which responsiveness to external stimuli (from the hypnotist) is not reduced, and in which the physiology is that of wakefulness.

In recent years, it has become known that there are two different kinds of sleep (Oswald, 1962) which alternate throughout mammalian sleep. The normal human passes from wakefulness into "orthodox" sleep, and later into the "paradoxical" phase of sleep. These phases will be described subsequently. There appears to be a physiological and psychological continuum embracing intense alertness, relaxed wakefulness, drowsiness and the successive stages of orthodox sleep. The transition into paradoxical sleep, however, usually appears abrupt and discontinuous.

1. *Historical perspective and methods*. Sleep can be studied by simple observation, an approach that still provides interesting comparative data (Hediger, 1960). Questionnaires too can provide subjective estimates of delay to sleep, duration of sleep, number of awakenings and so on. The method of intermittent stimuli, to which the subject must respond, has the disadvantage of potentially interfering with the sleep process. Motility during the night was for long a principal tool, but the advent of the electroencephalograph (EEG) has stimulated extensive research.

Bremer (1935) made a cut through the lower medulla oblongata of the cat, producing the *encéphale isolé*, in which EEG and ocular signs of alternating wakefulness and sleep persisted. A cut made through the upper mesencephalon resulted in the *cerveau isolé*, in which signs resembling perpetual sleep were seen. Bremer's belief that the signs of wakefulness were contingent solely on greater afferent inflow was discounted following the finding by Moruzzi & Magoun (1949) that electrical stimulation of the central core of the brainstem would cause signs of wakefulness to replace those of sleep in the *encéphale isolé*.

There came the formulation of the concept of the ascending activating reticular formation (Delafresnaye, 1964). The brainstem reticular formation, in the central core of the brain stem, from medulla to thalamus, was found to receive collateral afferent nervous inflow from all the main sensory pathways. Impulses arriving by these afferents, or descending from the cortex, would exite the reticular formation, from which activating impulses would then ascend to the cerebral cortex. These impulses did not convey specific information but increased the cortical vigilance or efficiency, making possible perception and controlled response, together with EEG signs of wakefulness. Sleep was conceptualized as a negative state resulting from a decline in the up-flow of activating impulses from the reticular formation.

The concept of the activating reticular formation can still be considered valid for orthodox sleep but not for paradoxical sleep. The controlling-mechanisms for the latter are in the pons (Jouvet, 1965). Sleep induced by drugs such as barbiturates has been explained in terms of a depressant action on the reticular formation. It is now realized that such drugs cause an enhancement of orthodox sleep but a suppression of paradoxical sleep.

There is currently no comprehensive theory of the sleep mechanism. A possible chemical hypnotoxin is still the subject of conflicting reports. Any satisfactory theory will need to embrace the rapid provocation of sleep by intense, repetitive, sensory stimuli; the provocation of sleep by electrical stimulation of some forebrain areas (Clemente & Sterman, 1967); the circadian rhythmicity of the desire for sleep; and the probability that there is a delicate balance between the two different kinds of sleep.

2. *The present state of knowledge.* Sleep is accompanied by characteristic EEG features. In man the waking alpha (Berger) rhythm, at 10 c/sec. gives way in drowsiness (stage 1 sleep) to irregular low voltage waves of 4–6 c/sec. with rolling eyeball movements, succeeded by stage 2 sleep with sleep spindles at 12–14 c/sec. and high voltage slow wave complexes, and then stages 3 and 4 with predominant high voltage 1–2 c/sec. waves (Rechtschaffen & Kales, 1968). These are all stages of orthodox sleep (or NREM, slow-wave, or synchronized sleep). Paradoxical sleep (or REM, desynchronized, or activated sleep) is accompanied by a low voltage EEG with 4–10 c/sec. waves and frequent bursts of conjugate rapid eye movements. A burst of eye movements is often preceded by a few "saw-tooth" EEG waves at 2–3 c/sec.

In orthodox sleep, the breathing, heart rate and blood pressure are regular, the brain blood flow is reduced and the brain temperature falls slightly. The skeletal muscles retain some tone, and the penis is flaccid. The thresholds for arousal (q.v.), and for respiratory response to carbon dioxide are raised, but electrically induced reflexes of the lower limbs are still present.

Paradoxical sleep in man makes up about 20–25% of total sleep and recurs about five times per night. The first period, after about one hour of orthodox sleep, is brief, but later periods are longer, lasting some 20–40 minutes. In paradoxical sleep the breathing, heart rate and blood pressure are irregular, and more brief body and facial movements are made. A major body movement often precedes by a minute or two each period of paradoxical sleep, which again often terminates with a movement. The penis is erect unless there is accompanying severe dream anxiety (Karacan *et al.*, 1966) and most skeletal muscles are flaccid. There is abolition of limb reflexes because of descending inhibitory impulses in the spinal cord. The inhibition is maximal at the moment of each rapid eye movement burst. The brain blood flow is greater than in wakefulness, and the brain temperature rises, whereas the blood flow through red muscles is greatly reduced.

The total duration of sleep is about fourteen hours per twenty-four in the newborn human. The proportion spent as paradoxical sleep is greatest just before birth, declines in the weeks after birth, declines steeply again in senility, and is low in mental defectives. Stages 3 and 4 are accompanied by increased secretion of human growth hormone, are enhanced after physical exercise, but are much reduced in middle and old age. In old age, total sleep is somewhat reduced and is frequently interrupted.

In wakefulness, sporadic galvanic skin responses will occur "spontaneously" but these are reduced during drowsiness, are occasional in stage 2 and in paradoxical sleep, but in some people become very large and almost continuous in stages 3 and 4 sleep.

Total deprivation of sleep leads to diminished ability to sustain attention (Williams *et al.*, 1959) and, after about sixty hours, to occasional visual and auditory hallucinations or paranoid ideas. Selective deprivation of paradoxical sleep causes it to be subsequently enhanced in both its duration and its intensity. Selective deprivation of stages 3 and 4 sleep is followed by similar enhancement.

3. *Psychological features of sleep.* The terms "light" and "deep" sleep are no longer valid: in paradoxical sleep especially, concordance between differing criteria is lost. Progression from wakefulness through stages 1 to 4 of orthodox sleep is associated with progressive decline in responsiveness to auditory stimuli, but in paradoxical sleep responsiveness is governed by the meaningfulness of the stimuli (Williams *et al.*, 1966). Meaningful stimuli are often woven into dream content on an assonant basis without causing awakening (Berger, 1963). Complex auditory discriminations and selective responses can be made during sleep (Oswald *et al.*, 1960).

Memory of the psychological events of sleep, or of external stimuli presented during sleep, is poor (Hoskovec & Cooper, 1967), but awakenings from any stage of sleep can usually elicit recall of some immediately preceding mental life. In drowsiness there occur *hypnagogic hallucinations*, namely brief, disconnected and often bizarre sensory experiences, coupled with internal verbal productions of schizophrenia-like nature. Awakenings from orthodox sleep usually elicit fragmentary reports, often characterized as "thinking", whereas awakenings from paradoxical sleep usually elicit lengthy, colorful and adventuresome reports often characterized as "dreaming" (Dement & Kleitman, 1957). The experienced observer can discriminate the type of sleep from which the dream was elicited (Monroe *et al.*, 1965). (See *Dream.*)

4. *Aberrations of sleep.* Insomnia is the commonest complaint about sleep. It occurs in association with older age, especially in women, with introversion, with anxiety and depression, or with states of mood elevation, whether spontaneous or caused by drugs such as amphetamine. The consumption of drugs to promote sleep is widespread and increasing. Many drugs, including alcohol, suppress paradoxical sleep, and if the individual has grown accustomed to a drug and it is then withdrawn, a "rebound" increase of paradoxical sleep occurs which takes up to two months to resolve (Oswald, 1969) and is accompanied, in the case of hypnotic drugs, by insomnia, restless sleep and vivid dreams.

Sleep-walking, sleep-talking, and enuresis are phenomena of orthodox sleep, whereas head-banging, body-rocking, and nightmares can occur in either kind of sleep. Among these only the nightmares are recallable by the subject, and he may remember the paralysis that accompanied a period of paradoxical sleep. Idiopathic narcolepsy is characterized by short periods of irresistible day-time sleep and, often, cataplectic attacks, namely sudden loss of muscular tone following an emotional stimulus specific to the individual. The cataplexy is probably a form of partial paradoxical sleep. The narcoleptic is unusual in that he will often pass immediately into paradoxical sleep instead of first into orthodox sleep.

Sleep is important in psychology because its study shows that the degree and the quality of a response are governed by a generalized state of the nervous system which can vary between extreme alertness and profound unresponsiveness. The role of sleep in the physiological economy is uncertain, but it is probable that the two kinds of sleep subserve different restorative functions, and that paradoxical sleep, with its intense brain blood flow, is especially related to synthesis for growth, plasticity and renewal in the brain (Oswald, 1969).

Bibliography: Berger, R. J.: Experimental modification of dream content by meaningful verbal stimuli. Brit. J. Psychiat., 1963, *109*, 722–40. **Bremer, F.:** Cerveau isolé et physiologie du sommeil. C. R. Soc. Biol. (Paris), 1935, *118*, 1235–41. **Clemente, C. D. & Sterman, M. B.:** Basal forebrain mechanisms for internal inhibition and sleep. Res. Publ. Ass. nerv. ment. Dis., 1967, *45*, 127–47. **Delafresnaye, J. F.** (Ed.): Brain mechanisms and consciousness. Oxford, 1954. **Dement, W.C. & Kleitman, N.:** The relation of eye movements during sleep to dream activity, an objective method for the study of dreaming. J. exp. Psychol., 1957, *53*, 339–47. **Fisher, K. C.** *et al.* (Eds.): Mammalian hibernation III. Edinburgh, 1967. **Foulkes, D.:** The psychology of sleep. New York, 1966. **Hediger, H.:** Comparative observations on sleep. Proc. roy. Soc. Med., 1969, *62*, 153–6. **Hoskovec, J. & Cooper, L. M.:** Comparison of recent experimental trends concerning sleep learning in the USA and the Soviet Union. Activ. nerv. sup. (Prague), 1967, *9*, 93–6. **Jouvet, M.:** Paradoxical sleep. In: **Akert, K.** *et al.* (Eds.): Sleep mechanisms. Amsterdam, 1965, 20–62. **Kales, A.** (Ed.): Sleep: physiology and pathology. Philadelphia, 1969. **Karacan, I.** *et al.*: Erection cycle during sleep in relation to dream anxiety. Arch. gen. Psychiatr., 1966, *15*, 183–9. **Monroe, L. J.** *et al.*: Discriminability of REM and NREM reports. J. pers. soc. Psychol., 1965, *2*, 456–60. **Moruzzi, G. & Magoun, H. W.:** Brain stem reticular formation and activation of the EEG. Electroenceph. clin. Neurophysiol., 1949, *1*, 455–73. **Oswald, I.:** Sleep mechanisms recent advances. Proc. roy. Soc. Med., 1962, *55*, 1910–1912. **Id.:** Human brain protein, drugs and dreams. Nature, 1969, *223*, 893–7. **Id.:** Sleep. Harmondsworth, 1970. **Id., Taylor, A. M. & Treisman, M.:** Discriminative responses to stimulation during human sleep. Brain, 1960, *83*, 440–53. **Rechtschaffen, A. L. & Kales, A.** (Ed.): A manual of standardized terminology, techniques and scoring system for sleep stages of human subjects. Washington, D.C., 1968. **Williams, H. L., Lubin, A. & Goodnow, J. J.:** Impaired performance with acute sleep loss. Psychol. Monogr., 1959, *73*, No. 14. **William, H. L., Morlock, H. C. & J. V.:** Discriminative responses to auditory signals during sleep. Psychophysiology, 1966, *2*, 208–15.

I. Oswald

Sleeping pills. See *Hypnotics*.

Sleep-walking (syn. *Somnabulism*). Sleep-walking may occur spontaneously; the somnambulist acts unconsciously in a kind of semi-conscious state. Sleep-walkers used to be referred to as "moonstruck" but it has been impossible to demonstrate any real influence of the moon on their behavior. Somnambulism can be generated artificially by hypnosis (q.v.). The concordance between depth hypnosis and sleep-walking was already discovered by J. M. Charcot and H. M. Bernheim. Holzschuher (1955) has a bipolar interpretation of sleep-walking as action and reaction in the purely primitive consciousness, while the ego-consciousness is eliminated in sleep. In this state, the primitive person functions quasi-independently. Sleep-walking is observed in neurotic personalities and is fairly common in children.

E.U.

Smell. See *Sense organs*.

Smelling, colored. An example of *synesthesia*. The spontaneous tendency found in some people to interpret smells consistently in terms of certain colors. *C.D.F.*

Smell, intensity of. The intensity of a smell is dependent on the concentration of the gas carrier and is particularly important from the methodological angle, since quality perception is influenced by intensity. Other qualities are modified in addition to the intensity, e.g. by adaptation. The absolute thresholds of smells —examined primarily olfactometrically (see *Olfactometer*)—are very low (= high sensitivity of the sense of smell (see *Sense organs:* sense of smell). On the other hand the ability of human beings to differentiate between pure gradations of intensity seems very poor. *F.N.*

Smile, first. An expressive movement which appears above all on perception of a human countenance between about the third and sixth months. According to A. Gesell, it occurs in ninety-eight per cent of six-month-old infants. The first smile underlies positive and negative reinforcement. C. Bühler (1921) saw it as the first social reaction. According to investigations carried out by Spitz (1946) and R. Meili, it is, less specifically, an expression of pleasurable states. These effects are clearly heredity-conditioned responses to specific stimuli, above all to the eye-nose-forehead schema, which acts as a releaser (q.v.) or key stimulus.

Bibliography: Spitz, R.: The smiling response. Genet. Psychol. Monogr., 1946, *34*. *H.J.K.*

Snellen charts. Charts with letters of a certain shape and varying in size to test visual acuity.

R.R.

Sociability. 1. Literally, the capacity of the individual to adapt himself to social conditions; more generally, the inclination or the need for social life and human contact.

2. Also "gregariousness"; the desire for friendly relations with other people or for participation with them in common activities. Sociability was described by Cattell and Guilford as a motivation factor defined in factor-analytical terms.

Bibliography: Cattell, R. B.: Personality and motivation structure and measurement. New York, 1957.

D.B.

Social anthropology. A term used in association with cultural anthropology (q.v.), ethnology (q.v.), and ethnography to signify the study of the early history of forms of human society. Under the influence of E. Durkheim it has come to mean specifically and in contrast to ethnology the science of the general laws which are to be found behind the development of cultures (syn.: *Socio-cultural anthropology*). *W.D.F.*

Social desirability. This is one of the most important response sets (q.v.). It contains the tendency to answer an item independently of the reply which would be appropriate for the individual by giving that which, in the individual's opinion, is the most desirable by the criterion of social norms. In order to check this reply tendency, suitable scales of social desirability (SD) were constructed, e.g. the SD scales of A. L. Edwards, O. P. Corwen & D. Marlowe. *P.Z.*

Social hygiene. The science dealing with health in social life. See *Mental hygiene*. *W.Sch.*

Socialization refers to the process whereby individuals develop the qualities essential to function effectively in the society in which they live. As indicated in this definition, socialization is concerned with the characteristics that individuals acquire and the psychological mechanisms through which the desired changes are brought about. These issues have been studied most extensively in the context of child socialization.

1. *Outcomes of socialization.*

(*a*) *Primary socialization.* During early childhood, efforts at socialization are principally directed at developing in children basic psychological functions that are necessary for acquisition of more elaborate patterns of behavior. Among other things, children must develop cognitive skills that will enable them to deal intelligently with complex and changing requirements of everyday life; they must gain proficiency in verbal communication by which they can influence others and be influenced by them; they must become adept in intricate social behaviors that are conducive to reciprocally satisfying relationships; and they must learn to value social approval and other symbolic rewards which make them amenable to social influence.

As children become more versatile, their wishes inevitably come into conflict with those of other group members. No longer can they express their desires when and how they please, but they must learn to regulate their actions partly on the basis of the consequences these can have for others. Whereas self-controlling behavior contributes to the well-being of other people, it generally detracts from the person's own rewarding outcomes. For example, self-control often involves relinquishing expedient means of gaining satisfactions because, for one reason or another, they are socially prohibited. At other times it requires postponing rewarding activities in the pursuit of goals requiring expenditure of considerable time and effort. On most occasions, the performance of desired activities must be channeled through irksome routines and time schedules. Because of the unfavorable immediate consequences associated with self-controlling behavior it is difficult to establish, even though in the long run it may benefit all group members in varying degrees.

(*b*) *Internalization and self-regulatory processes.* The ultimate aim of successful socialization is the substitution of internal controls for external sanctions. Once a self-regulatory system is developed, a person's self-demands and self-reactions to his own behavior serve as his main guides and deterrents. At this level of development, adherence to societal norms occurs in the absence of external pressures and social surveillance.

It is commonly assumed that self-regulatory systems are established through internalization of attitudes and values. This type of explanation, however, rarely specifies the manner in which attitudes govern action. There is, in fact, some dispute whether attitudes control behavior or whether a change in behavior produces attitudinal accommodations. Experimental evidence (Festinger, 1964; Bandura, 1969a) favors the latter causal sequence. Behavior is also sometimes spoken of as being internalized. Actually, after behavior has been acquired it cannot undergo any further interiorization. The process of internalization is, therefore, less concerned with the locus of behavior than with the manner in which it is maintained. See *Attitude*.

According to social learning theory (Bandura, 1970), internalized control is largely mediated through anticipated consequences for prospective actions. These self-produced consequences may take two major forms. As a result of experiencing differential outcomes in conjunction with different patterns of behavior, a person eventually comes to expect that a given course of action will be rewarded, ignored, or punished. Anticipated reward facilitates performance of behavior, whereas anticipated punishment usually has an inhibitory effect. Through symbolic representation, future consequences can be converted into current events that are functionally similar to actual outcomes in their capacity to influence action.

Behavior can be self-regulated not only by anticipated external consequences but by self-evaluative responses to one's own actions. People typically set themselves certain behavioral standards, and respond to their own performances in self-rewarding and self-punishing ways in accordance with their self-imposed demands. Anticipation of self-disapproval for personally devalued actions provides an additional motivating influence to keep behavior in line with adopted standards. Self-generated and externally occurring consequences often conflict, as when certain behaviors are approved and encouraged by others, but if performed would give rise to self-critical and self-devaluative reactions. Under these circumstances, the effects of self-reinforcement may prevail over external influences. Conversely, response patterns may be maintained by self-reward under conditions of minimal external support.

It is not difficult to explain why people might reward themselves for praiseworthy accomplishments. A more challenging, but inadequately explored, question is why they punish themselves for transgressive behavior or for performances they judge to be inadequate? There are several factors that may cause people to punish themselves. Reprehensible or self-disappointing performances provoke distressing thoughts that are likely to persist until amends have been made. Self-punishment can thus provide relief from self-generated distress that is enduring and often more painful than the self-administered reprimand. This phenomenon is most vividly illustrated in extreme cases where people torment themselves for years over relatively minor transgressions and do not achieve equanimity until they have made some kind of reparation. Having criticized or punished themselves for undesirable actions, individuals are likely to stop upsetting themselves by thinking about that behavior.

Although self-punishing behavior is partly maintained because it can stop self-generated distress, it often receives external support as well. Self-censure can serve as an effective means of reducing reprimands from others that might otherwise be even more unpleasant. In this case, self-punishment is the lesser of two evils. Moreover, adherence to high standards of behavior is actively supported through a vast system of societal rewards, whereas few accolades are bestowed on people for rewarding themselves on the basis of reprehensible performances. Self-regulative behavior is most effectively sustained when the standards adopted for self-reinforcement result in selective association with persons who share similar behavioral norms, thus providing social support for one's own system of self-evaluation.

(*c*) *Socialization as a reciprocal influence process*. When socialization is discussed in terms of psychological changes occurring in the learner, it provides a one-sided view of the process, which may erroneously convey the impression that individuals merely learn to conform to societal requirements. A number of writers (Cottrell, 1969; Goslin, 1969; Inkeles, 1968) have therefore stressed socialization as a two-way process. Although behavior is regulated to some extent by environmental influences, equally, individuals play an active rôle in altering their environment. In primary socialization, for example, children exercise some degree of control over parents as well as being influenced by them. Socialization therefore involves a continuous reciprocal influence between individuals' behavior and societal demands. Because of reciprocal control societal agencies often encounter formidable difficulties in inculcating in their members the characteristics they value. Not infrequently the social system fails to surmount the countercontrol exerted by its members, and is then altered in accordance with their wishes.

(*d*) *Transmission of cultural patterns by familial and other social systems*. Socialization is often depicted as a process that is largely achieved in childhood, with the family serving as the principal agency. In fact, socialization is a life-long process in which a wide variety of social agents plays an influential role. As Brim & Wheeler (1966) point out, childhood experiences do not adequately prepare one for meeting the demands of adult life. New modes of behavior have to be learned in later years as individuals assume various marital, occupational, and social roles. Even at the adult level, under conditions of rapid social and technological change, behavior patterns that had functional values may have to be replaced by new skills appropriate to the altered circumstances. Moreover, when cultural discontinuities exist, early social learning must be modified; sometimes drastically, in later years. In American society, for example, childhood sexual behavior is negatively sanctioned, but adults are expected to engage in appropriate sexual activities without anxiety or guilt. Hence, the more successfully parents inhibit their children's sexual behavior, the more likely sexual disorders are to occur in adulthood. Other cultures similarly involve training discontinuities (Hsu, 1961), notably in the areas of dependency, aggression, and affectional behavior, which necessitate re-socialization experiences.

It is evident that the diverse outcomes of socialization cannot be established solely within the family agency, no matter how versatile its members may be. Social, legal, educational, and religious organizations, mass media influences, and a host of other extra-familial agents, contribute, in varying degrees, to the types of values and response patterns instilled in group members. Socialization is further complicated by the fact that these multiple sources of influence frequently act in conflicting directions.

2. *Modes of socialization*. Socialization outcomes are achieved through a variety of means.

(*a*) *Differential reinforcement*. There is abundant documentation in psychological research (Bandura, 1969a; Staats & Staats, 1963) to show that human behavior is largely controlled by its consequences. Behaviors that produce rewarding outcomes tend to be adopted, whereas those that are punished or ignored are generally discarded. Differential reinforcement is, therefore, widely employed by socialization agents to promote desired patterns of behavior.

(*b*) *Vicarious reinforcement*. In everyday life, people repeatedly observe the actions of others and their consequences for them. As will be shown later, observed rewards and punishments can play an influential rôle in regulating behavior in much the same way as outcomes which are directly experienced (Bandura, 1970; Kanfer, 1965).

Observed consequences also provide a reference standard that determines whether a particular outcome will assume positive or negative value. The same compliment, for instance, is likely to be punishing for persons who have seen similar performances by others highly acclaimed, but rewarding when others have been less generously praised. Thus, observation of other people's outcomes can drastically alter the effectiveness of direct reinforcement.

(*c*) *Verbal guidance*. Socialization would be exceedingly laborious if individuals had to discover the appropriate cultural patterns solely through trial and error responses and their associated consequences. Other forms of influence are therefore used to accelerate the process of social learning. Verbal guidance is one such technique. After children have acquired linguistic skills, they can be taught, by verbal instructions, advantageous ways of behaving, and the societal rules and prohibitions.

Instructional control and reinforcing sanctions are most effective when combined. The power of sanctions is often enhanced if the reinforcement contingencies are verbally specified (Aronfreed, 1968); conversely, instructions have no enduring effects or go unheeded if they are not backed up with appropriate sanctions.

(*d*) *Modeling*. Socialization is to a large extent effected through modeling processes. Research conducted within the framework of social-learning theory (Bandura, 1969a, b; Flanders, 1968) demonstrates that virtually all learning phenomena resulting from direct experiences can occur on a vicarious basis through observation of other people's behavior and its consequences for them. Intricate response patterns can be acquired by observing the performances of live or symbolic models; emotional and attitudinal responses can be developed observationally by witnessing the affective reactions of others undergoing painful or pleasurable experiences; fearful and defensive behavior can be eliminated vicariously by observing others perform the threatening behavior without experiencing any adverse consequences; inhibitions can be induced by witnessing the behavior of others punished; and, finally, the incidence of group members' engagement in given activities can be socially regulated through the actions of influential models.

The provision of models not only serves to accelerate the learning process but, in cases where errors are dangerous or costly, becomes an essential means of transmitting behavioral patterns. Social behavior, of course, is most rapidly acquired and modified through the combined influence of modeling, verbal guidance, and differential reinforcement.

Bibliography: Aronfreed, J.: Conscience and conduct. New York, 1968. **Bandura, A.:** Principles of behavior modification. New York, 1969a. **Id.:** Social-learning theory of identificatory processes. In: **Goslin, D. A.** (Ed.): Handbook of socialization theory and research. Chicago, 1969b, 213–62. **Id.:** Vicarious and self-reinforcement processes. In: **Glaser, R.** (Ed.): The nature of reinforcement. Columbus, Ohio, 1970. **Brim, O. G. & Wheeler, S.:** Socialization after childhood, two essays. New York, 1966. **Cottrell, L. S.:** Interpersonal interaction and the development of self. In: **Goslin, D. A.** (Ed.): Handbook of socialization theory and research. Chicago, 1969, 543–70. **Festinger, L.:** Behavioral support for opinion change. Publ. Opin. Quart., 1964, *28*, 404–17. **Flanders, J. P.:** A review of research on imitative behavior. Psychol. Bull., 1968, *69*, 316–37. **Goslin, D. A.:** Handbook of socialization theory and research. Chicago, 1969. **Hsu, F. L. K.:** Psychological anthropology. Homewood, Ill., 1961. **Inkeles, A.:** Society, social structure, and child socialization. In: **Clausen, J.** (Ed.): Socialization and society. Boston, 1968, 74–129. **Kanfer, F. H.:** Vicarious human reinforcement: a glimpse into the black box. In: **Krasner, L. & Ullmann, L. P.** (Ed.): Research in behavior modification. New York, 1965, 244–67. **Staats, A. W. & Staats, C. K.:** Complex human behavior. New York, 1963. *A. Bandura*

Social motivation test (SMT). A method published by Müller in 1966 for diagnosing the structure of social motivations and the social awareness of values in children whose ages range from nine to fourteen years. The method which is available in two parallel forms consists of twenty-four items (q.v.) in which social problem situations differing in clearness and closeness to experience are verbalized. An objective evaluation according to six different motivational forms is guaranteed by a choice between several responses. There are differential norms in percentage ranks and test scores. The objectivity of the evaluation and interpretation is assessed as follows: parallel test reliability when $N = 309$ individuals is $r = 0.71$. With high *content validity* there are some indications of construct validity based on age and sex differences.

Bibliography: Müller, R.: Der soziale Motivationstest. Weinheim, 1966. *G.P.*

Social neurosis. Social illnesses are said to occur when the affective life of the members of a society is either excessively stimulated or repressed. Under the heading of social neuroses may be grouped, for example, compensation neuroses (q.v.) as well as the neurotic reactions which may be caused by social mobility of one kind or another that the individual finds unbearable (retraining late in life, unemployment among older workers, removal to an uncongenial district due to work requirements (see *Neurosis*). *J.L.I.*

Social norms. These *denote* (*a*) behavioral patterns which the population regards as of positive worth and which are to be striven for because they represent a *value*, an *obligation* or an *ideal*; social norms *describe* (*b*) as real norms what individuals know or imagine they know about the actual behavior of the other members of the population. *Statistical* social norms are data obtained by a selected sample of individuals which describe in figures the extent or distribution of the real behavior investigated. *I.M.D.*

Social perception. Social perception as a branch of social psychology (q.v.) may be defined in narrow or wide terms: the narrower definition takes as its theme the influence by personal and social factors while the wider definition not only considers the dependence of perception on social environment but also its relationship to that environment (in particular to man, i.e. person perception). The discrepancy between these two definitions is continued in the interpretation of the notion of perception. In the narrower definition, in spite of all methodological difficulties, emphasis is still placed to a greater extent on the direct experience of the senses whereas in the wider definition the concept of perception is used in a very loose sense to include all processes of information acquisition and processing right up to the most complex judgment processes. In the wider version, social perception therefore represents a very vague sphere of study. But even if the narrower definition is adopted, studies often go beyond the range of perception based on direct experience. Allport (1955) draws attention to the fact that social perception is frequently taken to denote the whole range of the individual's understanding of his social situation. The difficulty of setting down a precise definition was accurately described by Taijfel (1969, 316) when he pointed out that the transition from perception to such cognitive activities as drawing conclusions, establishing categories or making judgments was always difficult. There is in fact a continuum with no sharp distinctions. In the central area of perception, attempts to make a clear distinction between perception and non-perception will probably fail, all the more so as in recent years the rôle of establishing conclusions and categories has been considered centrally important to the act of perception. The result is that in many studies, the precise point of reference cannot be identified (for instance in many studies of distortions of perception the question arises as to whether it is in fact perception and not memory which has been distorted). This may be one of the reasons why many studies are not classified under the heading of social perception, but considered primarily from the angle of the social variables. Example: the problem raised by Asch (1952) of the distortion of perception under group pressure is certainly a problem of social perception but is frequently dealt with under the heading of "conformity", i.e. as a special example of influence of the group on the individual, and in this genuine example of perception, the same explanations are given as for the problem of attitude changes under group pressure (see *Group dynamics*). The lack of integration of the object sphere is apparent in a particularly important area which is generally dealt with separately, namely that of language. B. L. Whorf has developed the theory that language shapes perception of the environment (see *Whorf's hypothesis*). We therefore arrive at a new principle of relativity indicating that observers will not arrive at the same images of the universe through the same physical evidence, unless their linguistic background is similar or could be calibrated in some way (Whorf, 1940). But the majority of existing studies do not differentiate between cognition and perception.

While it is apparent that different languages cannot represent the environment in the same way (e.g. have different color differentiations), this does not mean that the perceptions themselves must therefore be different too. Whorf's theory is, however, confirmed by the classical work of Brown & Lenneberg (1958) who showed a correlation between the codability of colors (i.e. the association between individual colors and the names given to them) and the repeated recognition of these colors, i.e. a positive relationship between linguistic and non-linguistic behavior.

In the nineteen-forties and fifties, social perception was referred to by many authors as the "new look" because—by contrast with gestalt psychology—it placed great emphasis on motivational factors which had hitherto received little attention in perception psychology. A considerable step forward was taken by comparison with the theory based on inherent factors of the perception process (such as stimulus, nerve excitation, etc.) as is shown by some of the hypotheses developed in this connection:

Physical needs determine what is perceived. Studies did, however, show that while physiological needs influence perception, this influence cannot be heightened at will; on the contrary as needs increase, the influence may be reduced. Values which are characteristic for the individual influence the speed with which words associated with these values are perceived. Some authors did, however, attempt to reduce the significance of values to the variable of word frequencies. According to this assumption, the value structure of an individual leads to heightened interest in the relevant stimuli and therefore to a greater degree of familiarity with these stimuli. A more recent study (Johnson *et al.*, 1960) has, however, shown both the influence of the degree of familiarity and that of the value in lowering the recognition thresholds. At the same time this study revealed a clear relationship between the value of a word and the frequency with which this word is used in a particular country.

The influence of value attributes was also found in the sphere of distortion of perception. In a perception experiment conducted by Wittreich & Radcliffe (1956), authoritative personalities showed less distortion than non-authoritative personalities; the variable of familiarity was controlled during this experiment.

Verbal stimuli which are emotionally disturbing or threatening to the individual, require a longer perception time than neutral words and are sometimes perceived with such heavy distortion that their significance is radically changed and characteristic emotional reactions provoked before they are perceived.

This phenomenon assumed a central position in the discussion of social perception and led to the concept of perceptual defense. While the phenomenon of defense against memory contents was well-known from depth psychology (q.v.), the problem was encountered in a paradoxical formulation here in the sphere of precisely defined perception psychology: how is it possible for an individual to repress, distort or delay perceptions which he has not yet perceived? Put like this, the problem can only be solved by postulating a "homunculus theory", i.e. the existence of a kind of "censor" in the percipient individual which checks the contents of perception before allowing them to be "perceived". To avoid this dilemma, hypotheses were developed which were based essentially on the availability of response patterns and confirmed experimentally. One of the few portmanteau theories in social perception was developed by J. S. Bruner and L. Postman; it takes into account considerations of probability theory as well as motivational factors (see the summary report by Allport, 1955). The idea underlying this hypothesis testing theory is that perception consists essentially in testing specific hypotheses. Perception is based on a process of experience which leads the individual to expect certain objects and specific characteristics for these objects. According to this theory, the strength of a hypothesis is determined by: (*a*) the frequency of the confirmations obtained of it; (*b*) the number of simultaneously available hypotheses; (*c*) the motivational backing; (*d*) the cognitive backing. While these factors determine the strength of a hypothesis, the strength itself is defined by the quantity of corresponding stimulus information needed to confirm or refute the hypothesis.

Criticism of social perception concentrates on three points: (*a*) Most studies do not take into account personality differences while differential psychological (see *Differential psychology*) studies have tried to demonstrate that subjects include both sensitizers (i.e. subjects who react with heightened attention and can therefore be described as sensitized) and repressors (subjects who tend to be characterized by perceptual defense). The general and differential psychological theories have not as yet been integrated.

(*b*) Jones and Gerald (1967) have drawn attention to the fact that previous studies of perceptual defense have failed to take the experimental situation adequately into account in the interpretation. In their opinion, perceptual defense is only present beyond dispute when perception itself is the ultimate objective; if, however, perception has an instrumental function in a decision on action, the categories both for preferred and rejected values by comparison with neutral categories will be more easily available to the observer, i.e. the perception threshold will be lowered both for positive and negative values as opposed to neutral ones. This theory can be confirmed experimentally.

(*c*) The third point of criticism concerns the importance to be attributed to the theory of social perception. It must be remembered that the theory cannot explain social perception as such but can only attempt to clarify the influence of social factors on perception. In many experiments the emphasis is therefore not placed on the accuracy of perception but on the social factors which influence it. An extreme example is provided by Sherif's autokinetic effect, where testees are required to describe in the dark, without any aid to structuration, the position of a point which does not move but is experienced as moving because of the experimental set-up; in a situation of this kind, social influences can become the dominant factor. In order to ensure the action of social factors, the perception process is often made quite difficult, and, e.g., images have to be reconstructed from memory, which in many studies raises the question as to which particular psychological function has in fact been tested. In addition many studies were organized from the outset in order to demonstrate the influence of social factors and clearly reflect their origins. As a result the theory of social perception has ceased to be of immediate importance and the phenomena involved are grouped together under social factors (e.g. reference group, stereotype, q.v., prejudice, q.v., conformity, etc.).

Bibliography: Allport, F. H.: Theories of perception and the concept of structure. New York, 1955. **Asch, S. E.:** Social psychology. Englewood Cliffs, 1952. **Brown, R. W. & Lenneberg, E. H.:** Studies in linguistic relativity. In: **Maccoby, N., Newcomb, T. & Hartley, E. L.** (Eds.): Readings in social psychology. New York, [3]1958. **Carpenter, B., Wiener, M. & Carpenter, J. T.:** Predictability of perceptual defense behavior. J. Abn. Soc. Psychol., 1956, *52*, 380–3. **Eriksen, C. W.:** Defense against ego threat in memory and perception. J. Abn. Soc. Psychol., 1952, *47*, 230–5. **Graumann, C, F.:** Social perception. Exp. Angew. Psychol., 1956, *3*, 605–61. **Hörmann, H.:** Psychologie der Sprache. Berlin, 1967. **Johnson, R. C., Thomsen, C. W. & Frincke, G.:** Word values, word frequency, and visual duration thresholds. Psychol. Rev., 1960, 6, *67*. **Jones, E. E. & Gerald, H. B.:** Foundations of social psychology. New York, 1967. **McDavid, J. W. & Harari, H.:** Social psychology. New York, 1968. **Secord, P. F. & Backman, C. W.:** Social psychology. New York, 1964. **Sherif, M.:** Group influences upon the formation of norms and attitudes. In: **Maccoby. N., Newcomb, T. & Hartley, E. L.** (Eds.): **Taijfel, H.:** Social and cultural factors in perception. In: **Lindzey, G. & Aronson, E.** (Eds.): Handbook of social psychology. Reading, Mass., 1969. **Whorf, B. L.:** Science and linguistics. In: **Maccoby, N., Newcomb, T. & Hartley, E. L.** (Eds.): **Wittreich, W. J. & Radcliffe, K. B.:** Differences in the perception of an authority figure and a non-authority figure by Navy recruits. J. Abn. Soc. Psychol., 1956.

J. Schenk

Social power. The extent to which an individual has the ability or authority through his position or status in a group, to control other individuals, prescribe forms of behavior for them and demand obedience.

Social power is determined less by special personality features than by the type of social relations in the group. It is therefore considered as a decisive aspect for explanation of social interaction and the distribution of costs and rewards among members of the group (see *Group dynamics*). At present three variables are generally mentioned which determine the extent of social power: (*a*) the resources which enable an individual to influence the subjective rewards and costs of others. The value of these resources is in turn determined by (*b*) the extent of dependency of others on this individual, which in turn is a function of (*c*) the number of possible alternatives for other individuals which are reward sources.

Bibliography: Cartwright, D. (Ed.): Studies in social power. Ann. Arbor, Mich., 1959. **Emersin, R. M.:** Power-dependence relations, Amer. sociol. Rev. 1962. *27*, 31–41.

A.S.-M.

Social psychology. I. Social psychology is identified as a branch of psychology, and as a branch of sociology. Anthropologists are also concerned with this field, most commonly calling it the study of "culture and personality". It has been variously defined as a function of the prevailing conceptions concerning the nature of man and the theoretical orientation of the particular writer. Thus, when human behavior was thought of as representing an essentially physiological process, social psychology was the analysis of social factors that influenced the individual, as in the heredity-environment controversies in the study of intelligence. The more sociologically oriented conceive of social psychology as representing those aspects of behavior defined by the participation of the individual in a structured society. The more behavioristic students emphasize the study of interaction, or responses to social stimuli. In essence, the field may be defined operationally by noting that study of the following topics tends to be identified with social psychology: social influences on abilities and behavior, attitudes, social norms, group dynamics, communication, role and status, leadership, conflict and co-operation, intergroup relations, crime and delinquency, authoritarianism and machiavellianism, belief systems and value orientations, socialization, person perception, social learning, and conformity.

As with other fields of psychology, we find some authors making a molecular and others a molar approach; some emphasizing learning theories, some using a cognitive orientation, and others relying on conative processes to explain behavior. There is currently little interest in social philosophy or theoretical speculation. In order to secure reliable information, instead of opinions, about important issues, the almost universal concern is with empirical analyses of problems, preferably using experimental methods with the requirement that variables be identified and controlled, with manipulation of the independent variable by the experimenter, the assignment of subjects to treatment categories by chance, and the objective assessment of the dependent variables with proper statistical treatment of the data. There are, of course, field studies as well as laboratory studies, correlational as well as experimental analyses, studies of simulations as well as of significant social processes and matrices. As might be expected, there is considerable emphasis on the applied aspects of social psychology as well as on the development of the scientific principles. Here we can only offer a very brief introduction to a few of the special topics in social psychology, in order to illustrate what might be found if one explored more broadly and more deeply in the field.

1. *Social attitudes*. The early traditions of modern psychology included experimental analyses of reaction time. In these studies, the importance of "set" (*Einstellung*) as a determinant of performance was clearly established. Subjects who were paying attention to the motor response they were going to make (a response set), responded more rapidly than those who were focusing on the stimulus that would set off the response (stimulus set). In the research on the laws of association, the instructions given the subjects, for example "opposites" or "part-whole relations", determined what word was associated with the stimulus word. The early studies of the reliability of testimony indicated that people "saw" what they were set to see. In such a context, it was not surprising that the early decades of the nineteenth century saw the concept of "attitude" as the core concept for social psychology. Attitudes were the determiners of behavior; they were thought of as enduring sets which accounted for the consistencies in behavior. When behavior was not consistent, or when the behavior did not correspond to what was expected on the basis of verbalized attitude, it was because the attitudes could not be expressed in the particular situation. After the war of 1914–1918, psychology was marked by the development of psychometrics. During the war, a notable achievement by psychologists was the successful development of group intelligence testing. After the war, this success led to applications in personal selection in industry as well as to the extension of the concepts of measurement to a wide array of skills and personal attributes. By the nineteen thirties several different methods of measuring attitudes had been developed, demonstrated, and used in research. The increased attention paid to social psychology during the economic collapse of the time led to the widespread use of these new techniques in many different areas of study. Studies of morale, race prejudice, and liberalism-conservatism in economic and political affairs, were undertaken with objective measuring instruments. With the development of the war of 1939–1945, new researches were defined on the basis of applied problems, and new measurement techniques were devised. Public opinion study flourished, but it was almost completely descriptive and unrelated to any theory.

With the post-war trend towards an emphasis on observable behavior rather than on mentalistic events, the importance of attitude study declined. The neo-behaviorists had little use for the construct. Those having a conative orientation tended to conceive attitudes in the form of ego defense systems. The cognitively oriented often established attitudes as another way of referring to the perceptual structuring of a field. That mental images of the people of other nations, or stereotypes, existed, was unquestioned. But what the significance of such stereotypes was in psychological theory was completely uncertain. The prevailing emphasis on empirical investigation could not lend itself to encouraging preoccupation with the definition of attitudes as such. Instead, a new development emerged in the form of studies of attitude change—and the problem of what is an attitude was subordinated to the question of how attitudes are modified.

The learning theorists presented their particular emphases in their analyses of attitude change. Studies demonstrated the importance of classical conditioning and of reinforcement theory. Similarly, the field theorists demonstrated the modification of attitudes by the manipulation of the field forces impinging on the individual. The psychoanalytically oriented elaborated the rôle of tension reduction and the functions of attitudes in facilitating responses which reduce tensions and resolve conflicts among motives. However, it was largely among the cognitively oriented that the studies of attitude change developed most significance, for these studies established a motivational component within the cognitive domain. The fundamental proposition is that inconsistent cognitions lead to activities which contribute to the reduction of the inconsistency, the establishment of consistency. The consistency theories are varied and are known by various names, e.g., cognitive inbalance, congruity theory, cognitive dissonance. The research generated by the consistency theories has been very extensive and their contributions have implications for the understanding of a broad range of social behavior. With respect to attitude change, they have analyzed such problems as the effects of information at variance with one's own position on an issue (if it varies too much, it loses credibility), the effects of taking a public position at variance with private beliefs (under what conditions do one's opinions change?), the effects of failure of prophecies, and so on.

2. *Group processes*. The study of collective behavior is a specialization within sociology. The study of differentiations within a group, the behavior of individuals in a social group, the analysis of the effects of group membership on the individual, the development of group norms and group productivity all illustrate the concerns of social psychology. In the nineteen thirties, J. L. Moreno introduced sociometry with a technique for studying the patterning of interpersonal attractions and repulsions among the members of a group. This led to the study of "real" groups with analyses of their psychological structures. At about the same time, K. Lewin extended his field theoretical approach by establishing small groups in the laboratory and exposing them to various kinds of experimental manipulation. Both approaches had profound impacts on subsequent developments of social psychology. Moreno's work, however, overlapped with his contributions to group psychotherapy and seemed to find more of a place in the clinical setting, whereas the students of Lewin remained identified with social psychology and contributed to the founding of the specialization in group dynamics.

An aggregate of individuals interacting to achieve a common goal form a group. In time, the differentiations within the group become stabilized, and a pattern of relations emerges which defines the group structure. The behavior expected of an individual occupying a particular position in a group is known as a social rôle. Some rôles derive from the activities needed to achieve the group goal, and are known as task rôles. Other rôles have the function of maintaining the cohesiveness of the group and are known as group maintenance rôles. The various rôles in a group are perceived as forming a prestige hierarchy or status system; and some rôles, and some individuals, achieve relatively high status, whereas others are perceived as having lower status. Stratification in small groups is paralleled in the larger society by the ranking of occupations, people of different ethnic and religious backgrounds, degrees of affluence and education.

The difficulty in achieving a sound understanding of group processes is illustrated in the efforts to solve the applied problems of selecting leaders for business and industry, the military, educational systems, and so on. Early researches studied leaders in an effort to identify those attributes which differentiated them from others and which could account for their success. Literally hundreds and hundreds of studies were done without significant success. Not until the nineteen forties did the theoretical conception of group structure and function, combined with the failure of the earlier approaches, lead to the appreciation of the fact that one could not be a leader without followers. It became clear that the question of leadership was in part the question of what the followers were seeking. Therefore, the problem was transformed from a study of characteristics of individuals, to the analysis of processes with an emphasis on the consequences of the leadership behavior for the group.

3. *Communication.* Early studies were concerned with the development of language in the child, verbal imagery in mental content, bilingualism and intelligence, language and thought, the influence of naming on perception, the influence of propaganda on attitudes. Only quite recently, however, has communication been confronted as the field for study. As might be expected from the heterogeneity among social psychologists, a complex field like communication study has not been given simple and uniform treatment. In some discussions, for example, communication is examined with a cybernetics model emphasizing a feedback system in interpersonal relations; other approaches examine varieties of communication materials to study social influence; and others use mathematical models, and apply information theory with the reduction of uncertainty as their point of departure. And of course there are those who study language, psycholinguistics (and sociolinguistics and ethnolinguistics), and semantics. The applied problems of persuasive communication in industrial advertising, political campaigning and international maneuvering have led to considerable research. These studies have tended to focus on such variables as one-sided versus two-sided presentations, primacy and recency factors in the comparative effectiveness of arguments, "sleeper" or delayed effects of communication materials, factors associated with enhanced communicator credibility. However, this research has contributed little to the development of general theory.

Much attention has been paid in recent years to the effects of the mass media in shaping the perceptions, values and behaviors of the mass audiences, particularly children. The recent attacks of concerned community groups on the television industry are very similar to those made on the motion pictures and radio in earlier years. Content analysis of the media reveals a large component of violence in the entertainment offered. The lay concern is that such presentations brutalize the audience and encourage children in such display. Some controlled laboratory studies have demonstrated a modeling effect which might lead one to suspect that the pictured violence could increase the violence behavior of the audience. However, field studies show no such effects on the normal child, and more careful analyses of the laboratory studies show many significant differences between the naturalistic setting in which programs are commonly seen and the controlled laboratory conditions.

4. *Methodology*. The problem of extrapolation from the laboratory to the community has been considered in various contexts, but never really settled. Laboratory studies of social attitudes show that they are readily manipulated, easily influenced. The field studies, particularly in the political and economic realms, find attitudes very resistant to change. Laboratory studies of group dynamics often fail to be confirmed when findings are extended to the community. Apparently there is a social psychology of the experiment that has to be further explored in order that we may understand more fully the true meanings of our findings. There may well be a "guinea pig role" adopted by subjects in an experiment which alters the relations that may obtain when subjects are playing other roles. In addition, the ego involvement in real decision making is very poorly reflected in the laboratory decision making.

Methodological improvements have been sought along many lines. In the laboratories, advanced technology has been used for instrumentation. Great ingenuity has been used in devising "games" and social simulations in order to provide analogs for the processes deemed of significance in the larger community. The social psychological literature can hardly now be read unless one is familiar with the "prisoner's dilemma", a game which permits the study of trust-distrust and is used to analyze the bases for co-operation. In addition, there are simulations that represent international relations, inner city functions, land use, and generalized societal organization. These simulations have become useful teaching devices and are also advanced as research techniques in that they permit representation in the laboratory of important societal variables that are commonly excluded from the conventional small group research.

Research developments in the field have been proceeding along two significant lines. On the one hand, there have been ingenious experiments designed in natural settings—sometimes by intervention in the community, and sometimes by complete formal experiment building. Another development of particular interest is the use of unobtrusive measures of behavior. In these studies, the design involves focusing observations and collecting data so that the entire study is perceived as part of the natural setting, yet without the invasion of privacy of the subjects being observed. Illustrative of these studies, for example, is the one in which stamped, addressed envelopes were dropped on the street in different parts of a city. It was possible easily to observe the comparative proportions of "letters" picked up and mailed in the different sections (with their known social characteristics), and thus to study a form of helpfulness and co-operation.

Another development of promise has been in the field of cross-cultural research. Though using subjects from different cultures is old in the history of psychology, the modern approach includes increased sophistication. Though it is true that there is still interest in simple comparative studies, a number of studies are devised because of the search for social variables in a context where they may not be confounded as they are in Western society. Though it is still too early in the emergence of this field to predict with confidence, it seems likely that this specialization will have much of significance to contribute in the future.

As we head into the nineteen-seventies, peace and conflict research is becoming more accepted as a focus for research and theory. In the past, social psychology has addressed itself to the study of competition and co-operation, to the nature of industrial conflict, race relations, and in times of crisis to the problems of human nature and enduring peace. These, however, have tended to be relatively transitory and specialized concerns. In recent years, however, there has been a growing peace research movement and academicians in increasing numbers are dedicating themselves to systematic work in this field. Social psychologists are extending their professional field and addressing themselves to the systematic analysis of conflict resolution, of problems in international relations. While it would obviously be the height of academic imperialism to claim that war is a psychological problem, wars do begin in the minds of men—and, increasingly, social psychologists are implementing their social concerns by means of professional and scientific applications toward the construction of the defenses of peace.

Bibliography: Asch, S. E.: Social psychology. Englewood Cliffs, 1952. **Bales, R. F.:** Interaction process analyses. Cambridge Cliffs, 1952. **Dexter, L. A. & White, D. M.:** People, society and mass communications. London, 1964. **Deutsch, M., Katz, J. & Jensen, A. R.:** Social class, race and psychological development. New York & London, 1968. **Deutsch, M. & Krauss, R. M.:** Theories in social psychology. New York & London, 1965. **Dohrenwend, B. P. & Dohrenwend, B. S.:** Social status and psychological disorder. London & New York, 1969. **Edward, E. J. & Harold, B. G.:** Foundations of social psychology. New York & London, 1967. **Eysenck, H. J.:** The psychology of politics. London, 1963. **Feldman, S.:** Cognitive consistency. New York & London, 1966. **Festinger, L., Schachter, S. & Bach, K.:** Social pressures in informal groups. London, 1963. **Fiedler, F. E.:** A Theory of leadership effectiveness. New York & London, 1967. **Flavell, J. H.:** The development of role taking and communication skills in children. New York & London, 1968. **Freedman, J. L., Carlsmith, J. M. & Sears, D. O.:** Social psychology. London & Toronto, 1970. **Gnetzkow, H.:** Groups, leadership and man. New York, 1963. **Graumann, C. F.** (Ed.): Hdb der Psychol., 7. Göttingen, 1969. **Greenstein, F. J.:** Personality and politics. Chicago, 1969. **Grennwald, A. G., Brock, T. C. & Ostrom, T. M.:** Social status and psychological disorder: A causal inquiry. New York & London, 1969. **Grey, A. L.:** Class and personality in society. New York, 1969. **Harvey, O. J.:** Motivation and social interaction. New York, [4]1963. **Heidner, F.:** The psychology of interpersonal relations. New York & London, [5]1967. **Hofstätter, P. R.:** Einführung in die Sozialpsychologie. Stuttgart, 1963. **Kretch, D. S. & Crutchfield, R. S.:** Theory and problems of social psychology. New York & London, 1948. **Lewin, K.:** Feldtheorie in der Sozialwissenschaften. Stuttgart, 1963. **Lindgren, H. C.:** Contemporary research in social psychology. London & New York, 1969. **Lindzey, G. & Aronson, L. J.:** The handbook of social psychology, vols. 1–5. Reading, Mass. & London, [2]1969f. **Proshanky, H. & Seidenberg, B.:** Basic studies in social psychology. London & New York, 1969. **Secord, P. F. & Backman, C. W.:** Social psychology. New York, 1964. **Sherif, M. & C. W.:** An outline of social psychology. New York, 1956.

E. L. Hartley

II. The literature that goes under the title of "social psychology" is now quite vast and yields numerous definitions of a fairly diverse nature. It is not easy to offer a satisfactory inclusive definition of social psychology. Nevertheless, most specialists in the field would certainly admit that the notion of *social interaction*—a concept mediating between individual and group qualities—is central to their interests. It is justifiable to describe the essential object of social psychology as the study of interaction processes: interaction between individuals, between individuals and groups, and between groups.

The following are some of the research areas: *communications* in a group (discussion) (interactions between individuals); *attitudes and opinions* (interactions between the individual and the group); *co-operation or competition* between two or more groups (interactions between groups). In most cases the three varieties of interaction occur simultaneously.

1. *History*. The term "social psychology" dates from the beginning of the present century. A notable user of the concept was Durkheim (1858–1915): "As for the laws of collective ideation, they are still wholly . . . ignored. The 'social psychology' which should be used to ascertain what they are is only a phrase which denotes all kinds of generalities. . . ." (1901). The first books using the term as a title appeared in 1908 (E. A. Ross: *Social Psychology. An Outline and Source Book*, New York, and W. McDougall, *Introduction to Social Psychology*, London). But the real work in social psychology only came after 1925.

Admittedly, people from very different

fields (dramatists, philosophers, historians, economists, politicians, and so on) have always addressed themselves to the problems with which social psychology is now concerned. Yet those earlier "studies" lacked the objectivity and precision of scientific work. For a long time, social psychology was considered only as an appendix of psychology or of sociology. This considerably delayed the development of investigations into psycho-sociological questions.

The mutual lack of understanding between psychologists and sociologists had to cease before social psychology could become an independent discipline. The French sociologist Marcel Mauss (1872–1950) bears much of the credit for this. His paper to the French Psychological Society in 1924 ("Actual and practical connections between psychology and sociology", published in the *Journal de Psychologie* in the same year) stated that psychology and sociology enjoy major common ground, and that close collaboration between the two disciplines was not only desirable but necessary in this area of mutual interest. At about the same time, Max Weber (1864–1920) and Max Scheler (1874–1928) in Germany, and Charles H. Cooley (1867–1929) and George H. Mead (1863–1931) in the United States, bore witness to the same desire to coordinate the viewpoints of psychology and sociology. Mead's contribution was especially important: his theory proved effective in empirical research, and his posthumous work, *Mind, Self and Society* (Chicago, 1934), exerted (and continues to exert) considerable influence on American research-workers. The diffusion of his ideas probably had much to do with the advance won by American social psychologists over their European equivalents.

The experimental work which most obviously contributed to awareness of the autonomy of social psychology may be attributed to Americans, or to researchers who lived and worked in the USA. The change of consciousness would seem to have occurred in the nineteen thirties, for the first sociometric inquiry was conducted by Moreno (born 1892) in 1930, in the Hudson Institution, a delinquents' home near New York. The famous Hawthorne experiments (q.v.) were carried out by Elton Mayo (1880–1949) at the Western Electric Company at almost the same time, as was the study of aggressive behavior in four groups of five ten-year-olds, by Kurt Lewin (1890–1947) and co-workers (results published in 1939). The first opinion polls were in action around 1936. The main effort of these pioneers of social psychology related to the development of concepts, methods and techniques appropriate to the study of the specific problems facing the young science. Social psychology became an autonomous human science in its own right once it had a proper conceptual apparatus and adequate research instruments.

2. *Main research areas*. The general definition already offered reveals the gamut of ambitions of social psychology. All the levels and aspects of human activity can, in fact, provide socio-psychological research subjects. This great variety of problems has brought about a certain diversification of methods, and it is now legitimate to distinguish different areas whose limits vary according to one's viewpoint. Methodologically, these are:

Sociometry, which uses two specific approaches, the sociometric test, a quantitative technique employing statistical procedures to describe attractions and repulsions, and modes of indifference between individuals in a small group; and psychodrama (q.v.) and sociodrama, psychotherapeutic techniques in which a group of individuals directed by a play-leader (who should be an experienced clinical psychologist) becomes the essential therapeutic instrument.

Group dynamics (q.v.), which studies the play of forces and takes into account the formation and transformation of restricted groups. It draws on ideas developed by gestalt psychology, and uses mathematical models. Group practice and discussion have served to popularize this branch of social psychology. Some specialists in group dynamics are much indebted to psychoanalytic concepts.

The *study of opinions and attitudes*, which makes use of psychological and statistical surveys.

The *study of communication processes*, which is based on information theory (q.v.), is certainly the most promising of the branches of contemporary social psychology.

The following, according to the French social psychologist Jean Stoetzel (born 1910) are the main centers of interest:

Problems of relations between the individual and culture (civilization); the study of psychological behavior under social conditions; personality (q.v.) from the psycho-social viewpoint; the study of various aspects of interindividual interaction; behavior in large groups.

But the ambition of social psychology is not restricted to the acquisition of theoretical knowledge. It also seeks *practical* knowledge which might help men to resolve actual problems. In addition to general social psychology, there is an *applied* social psychology which now extends into almost all the major spheres of contemporary social life: politics, management, medicine, religion, mass media, leisure, consumption, publicity, etc.

Social psychology, of all the branches of psychology, would seem to be the most alive today and to have made the greatest progress. This is probably the result of two factors: the relatively unresearched state of this area, despite the historical stirrings already noted; and the richness of the instruments available to social psychology. In fact the late appearance of social psychology enables it to benefit, apart from its own methods, from all those developed in other areas, and in particular from those proper to psychology and sociology.

Bibliography: Klineberg, O. & Christie, R. (Eds.): Perspectives in social psychology. New York, 1965. **Lazarsfeld, P. F., Berelson, B. & Gaudet, H.:** The people's choice. New York, 1948. **Mead, G. H.:** Mind, self and society. Chicago, 1934. **Moreno, J. L.:** Who shall survive? New York, [2]1953. **Stoetzel, J.:** La psychologie sociale. Paris, 1963.

D. Victoroff

Social medicine. A term used in many senses. In his "Lectures on the tasks and aims of social medicine" L. Teleky (1909) uses the term principally for social hygiene (q.v.); social medicine was the term used in England, "preventive medicine" in the USA. The term is often used in contrast to individual medicine to mean "public health", "communal hygiene". Sociologically, social medicine covers the social security of the individual in sickness, accident and disablement. *H.W.*

Social sciences. The totality of sciences which seek to use experimental methods of studying the behavior of man in society. Historically, they were preceded by the work of the humanists and the great syntheses of the nineteenth century. They attained a scientific status only in the twentieth century, particularly through World War II (industrial development, ideological conditions, integration of minorities, decolonization, etc.). Methods were refined (quantitative methods, field studies), branches became specialized (economics, political sciences, sociology, social psychology, ethnology, anthropology as a natural science, linguistics, etc.). Nowadays these separate disciplines are coming together again, as man is seen more and more as a totality. *M.J.B.*

Social structure. All the social relations of a formal (organization) or informal (group dynamics) nature, between individuals and groups (q.v.) in businesses. See *Management*.

G.R.W.M.

Social system. The kind and form of mutual relations (interactions) of the members of a group or larger community of a certain system of action, in the context of which the individual group members orientate themselves as acting according to compulsory norms or expectations connected with them. This concept occurs especially in the work of Parsons & Shils (1951) where it includes interaction, orientation towards another person with his aims and norms and the consensus in respect of norms and norm expectations between the individual(s) and others. Norm and norm expectations define the roles (q.v.) of the individual member so that the social system can be represented as *role structure*. See *Group dynamics*.

Bibliography: Parsons, T. & Shils, E. E.: Towards a general theory of action. Cambridge, Mass. 1951.

W.D.F.

Social therapy. Therapy which seeks to make changes in the patient's environment or conditions of life (*milieu* or *situation therapy*). The term is also sometimes used in the sense of *group therapy* (q.v.) or *psychodrama* (q.v.).

W.D.F.

Social type. One of the six *life forms* described by E. Spranger. A person who loves his fellow men, who finds his chief satisfaction in being of service to others. Its opposite is the misanthrope who has been disappointed in love. *W.K.*

Sociatry. A term is used in the branch of psychiatry expecially concerned with conflicts of a socio-psychological nature. During World War II, sociatry was understood as a form of "spiritual counseling". At the moment, sociatry is being vigorously developed as psychiatry is influenced more and more by socio-psychological and sociological viewpoints: e.g. in research into psychiatric communities (clinics, institutions for treatment and care, hospitals). *J.L.I.*

Society. A term used with increasing frequency since the development of sociology as a separate branch of science in the mid-nineteenth century, but for which no general definition is available; society is held to be an entity which is "more" than a mere social aggregate. If a distinction is made between a specific society and "society" as such, most definitions are based on descriptions of the given structures of social relations or cultural peculiarities. Accordingly social sciences are those which are concerned with the organizational and relational structures as well as the cultural and institutional differences between cultures or cultural groups. *W.D.F.*

Sociogram. Illustration or diagram representing the findings of sociometric tests (Moreno, 1953): the (desired) relationships of a positive or negative nature or interaction frequencies of the members of a group (q.v.). (See *Sociometry*.)

In a sociogram, individuals are represented as circles or squares connected by lines or arrows of varying lengths. The length of the line or arrow is analogous to the social (emotional) distance between two individuals. The arrows show the direction of choice. In this way some of the distinguishing factors of the sociometric structure of a group (outsiders, central figures, clique formation, group comparisons, etc.) are illustrated. In large groups, a representation by sociogram is not easy to read, and so in these cases other methods of representation (matrix analysis, index analysis) are used.

Bibliography: Moreno, J. L.: Who shall survive? New York, 1953. **Proctor, C. H. & Loomis, C. P.:** Analysis of sociometric data. In: **Jahoda, M., Deutsch, M. & Cook, S. W.** (Ed.): Research methods in social relations, Vol. 2. New York, 1951.

A.S.-M.

Sociolinguistics is virtually identical with "sociology of language", and comprises the relations of language (q.v.) to culture; sociolinguisticians may be said to study the relations between language and social structure.

The only contemporary sociolinguistic theory founded on empirical evidence, Bernstein's "language barrier" (q.v.) theory, distinguishes between a "restricted code" possessed by all social classes but spoken mainly by the lower (or working) class, and an "elaborated code" spoken only by (a) privileged class(es). A man's code is the socio-culturally determined inventory of meanings, signs and rules that controls his language. Characteristics of the restricted code are: simple, often incomplete sentences in the active form, a rigid sentence structure, abrupt orders and questions, simple adjectives, adverbs and conjunctions ("then", "and"), conventional locutions, gestures. Characteristics of the elaborated code are: complex sentence structure, conjunctions and prepositions with logical functions, impersonal pronouns, a highly differentiated vocabulary, individual usage. According to the theory, these differences and their consequences for thought development are conditioned in childhood by class socialization processes. The resulting linguistically disadvantaged condition of the underprivileged may sometimes (it is thought by some) be improved by compensatory or even "emancipatory" English teaching. Problematic aspects of the theory are: the underlying class concept (an impermissible degree of?), generalization from imprecise samples, the use of an implicit middle-class language norm in the selection of linguistic characteristics, and an absence of socio-theoretical foundation in the definition of the goals of compensatory language work. See *Language; Psycholinguistics.*

Bibliography: Bernstein, B.: Class, codes and control, Vol. 1. London, 1972. **Crystal, D.:** Linguistics. Harmondsworth, 1971. **Douglas, M.:** Natural symbols: explorations in cosmology. London, 1970. **Lawton, D.:** Social class, language and education. London, 1968. *G.S.*

Sociology. The study of society. The term comes from A. Comte: the overlap between sociology and social psychology (q.v.) is so substantial that the two disciplines must be regarded as two aspects of the same field. Social psychology starts with the individual and tries to ascertain how he reacts upon his environment, influences other people and is in turn influenced by them, whereas sociology starts with the group (q.v.), its specific forms, structures and norms, and then tries to tackle the laws of human community directly. Sociology also has close ties with cultural anthropology (q.v.) and folk psychology. Sociology may be described as the cultural anthropology of industrial societies, whereas cultural anthropology is often understood as sociology applied to illiterate (or "primitive") societies. *W.Sch.*

Sociometry. A blanket term for techniques, particularly the "*sociometric test*" (Moreno, 1953) used to make a quantitative analysis of the emotional structure of a group (q.v.). The emotional structure is measured on the basis of mutual choices of the group members, what they feel and think about one another.

Two components are of crucial importance for the results of a sociometric test: (1) the prescribed form of choice, and (2) the criteria of choice. The resulting emotional structure is a function of the criterion employed.

At the present the term is used not only for the analysis of emotional structure but for the assessment of other aspects of the relationships between group members. See *Sociogram.*

Bibliography: Moreno, J. L.: Who shall survive? New York, [2]1953. *A.S.-M.*

Sociopath. A term often used as a synonym for *psychopath*, but suggests that anti-social behavior is caused primarily by socio-cultural factors rather than constitutional elements. Two main kinds of sociopath have been described. The first group are of extravert personality and have difficulty in forming conditioned responses. The second group condition normally but are exposed to an abnormal delinquent subculture which shapes their behavior anti-socially. *D.E.*

Sodomy. In some countries, the term signifies sexual intercourse between men and animals (see *Bestiality*). In English-speaking countries "sodomy" is mainly used for *anal coitus*. From ancient times, there have been laws (Hittite Book of Laws, Old Testament, Talmud) which expressly tabooed sodomy. *H.M.*

Solipsism. That position in the theory of knowledge according to which reality exists only in cognition by the individual. Only the individual ego (q.v.) and its psychic states really exist; neither others nor the outside world have any reality. Max Stirner is the most famous solipsist. The standpoint reappears in the neo-positivistic (see *Neopositivism*) concept of *elementary experience*. *M.R.*

Somatic. Pertaining to the body, bodily; ant.: "psychic", mental, referring to the psyche. *H.W.*

Somatization. It is supposed that the "transformation reaction", the "conversion reaction" (see *Conversion*) presupposes the transformation of an experience together with its emotional charge into a somatic change. This may consist of some change in the nervous system, when, for example, a hysterical paralysis appears, or of some psychosomatic disorder, e.g. diarrhea, dysuria, asthma, etc. The expression somatization is preferred when referring to this kind of relations between the psychic events and the accompanying somatic correlates. *J.L.I.*

Somatogenic. In *biology*: changes in individuals due to body cells (not from hereditary factors); in *medicine* and *psychology*: conditioned or produced by bodily causes. Ant.: *psychogenic*, conditioned or caused by the mind. *H.W.*

Somatology. The science of the general properties and characteristics of the body. Ant.: *psychology* *H.W.*

Somatopsychology. The branch of psychology which investigates the bodily phenomena accompanying and following psychic events. (See *Psychosomatics*.) *H.W.*

Somatotherapy. A treatment for somatic disorders which may be accompanied by pathological psychic changes as is the case, for example, with the exogenous psychoses (q.v.). It is used also in cases of endogenous psychoses when a somatic cause, although not definitely known, is suspected none the less. In cases of neurosis (q.v.), too, somatotherapeutic methods are currently being used together with psychotherapy (q.v.) as, for instance, in aversion therapy (see *Behavior therapy*), and where special psychopharmaceuticals (q.v.) such as ataraxics (see *Tranquilizers*) and thymeretics (see *Antidepressants*) are being tried.

J. H. Schultz uses the word "somatization" to signify the integration of the individual body, which can be undertaken with the help of hypnosis (q.v.), *autogenic training* (q.v.) or under other conditions. *J.L.I.*

Somatotonia. A temperament related to the mesomorphic growth tendency: extraverted, energetic, fond of exercise, straightforward and simple.

Bibliography: Sheldon, W. H.: The varieties of temperament. New York, 1942. *W.K.*

Somatotropic hormone (*Somatotropin, growth hormone*, abbreviation STH). A polypeptide formed in the adenohypophysis (see *Hypophysis*) and carried from there in the blood stream to the peripheral tissue. The secretion of somatotropic hormone is stimulated, *inter alia*, by hypoglycemia (heightened level of insulin, q.v., in the blood) and physical and mental stress. STH, like the androgens (q.v.), has an anabolic action. It stimulates, *inter alia*, the formation of ribonucleic acids (q.v.) and the synthesis of protein and mobilizes fat (in the form of free fatty acids). In adolescents it increases the activity of the epiphysis (q.v.) and thus promotes growth. STH deficiency in childhood and adolescence results in pituitary dwarfism, over-production of the growth hormone in adolescents results in gigantism. In adults overproduction is responsible for the condition known as acromegaly (q.v.). STH acts synergistically to numerous other hormones, especially gonadotropic hormones (q.v.) and catecholamines (q.v.)

Bibliography: Pecile, A. & Müller, E. E. (Eds.): Growth hormone. Amsterdam, 1967.

W.J.

Somatotropin. A term for somatotropic hormone (q.v.) (STH).

Somnabulism. Sleepwalking in a state of partial consciousness, followed by amnesia (q.v.) and often accompanied by other complex activities.

W.S.

Sophistry. 1. Sophistic argument (sophism)—literally: inference which has been falsely drawn but which is given out as correct with the intention to deceive; in a wider sense, "paralogism": inference which has been drawn falsely but unintentionally; or "paradox": an inference starting from correct premises and rightly drawn, but leading, however to an unacceptable and irrefutable conclusion.

2. Sophistic attitude (sophist)—this is the attitude of the person who (*a*) has skilfully mastered the tricks of speaking, (*b*) gives out that he is teaching the truth, and (*c*) uses sophisms: a charlatan who seeks rather to persuade than to find the truth.

3. Sophistic school—its teaching set out to impart by the use of language (q.v.) (formal science of language) a practical (political) affectiveness with a skeptical and pragmatic perspective (fifth to fourth centuries B.C.).

M.-J.B.

Sorting. In sorting, Ss. have to select from a series of comparison stimuli the one which most readily accords with a predetermined standard stimulus. Sorting techniques are used both in language-free and in verbal tests, but hardly at all in psychological scaling, where the results would be affected by the conditions of similarity varying from instance to instance within the pool of comparison stimuli.

W.H.B.

Soul (Gre. *psyche;* Ger. *Seele;* Fre. *âme*). In the widest sense, the "soul" is all states of consciousness of an individual or a group. It also designates the principle of moral or religious life. More specifically, among "primitives" and in ancient philosophy, the soul was conceived as the vital principle, or principle of life (Lat. *anima*): that which animates bodies and departs at the moment of death. This belief conditions the *animist* attitude and *vitalist* doctrines. It recurs in the concept of a "world soul" or dynamic principle of unity of the sensible world (Plato, Plotinus). But, in the same context, the soul is also conceived as the seat of feeling, of volition (will) and thought (*animus*), which is contrasted with the body and vegetative functions (the Aristotelian theory of the soul: see *Entelechy*). This conception grounds "spiritualistic" doctrines according to which the soul dominates the body and, being immortal, seeks to escape from it (Plato), and those "dualisms" which address themselves to the problem of the union of the soul and the body (Descartes). See *Mind-body problem; History of psychology; Philosophy and psychology.* *F.B.*

Sound. Mechanical vibrations in a given medium (e.g. air) conduct energy in the form of longitudinal waves.

We become sensitive to sound within a definite frequency (16–20,000) and field of amplitude (lower or higher hearing threshold). According to the number of frequencies and the regularity of the phase vibrations various kinds of sound occur. Sound localization is the localization of the distance and direction of a sound wave. Localization of the direction of a sound wave is rendered possible by: (*a*) the time difference between both ears; (*b*) the left-right intensity difference. See *Auditory perception; Noise.* *M.B.*

Bibliography: Bekesy, G. v.: Experiments in hearing. New York, 1960. **Stevens, S. S.:** Bibliography on hearing. Cambridge, Mass., 1955. *B. Schmidt*

Sound image theory. Theory of auditory perception (q.v.) formulated by G. Ewald. Ewald stretched a rubber membrane over a frame and made this vibrate by means of a tuning fork. Waves formed on the membranes, which produced an image characteristic of a particular sound, the so-called sound image. Ewald assumed that the basilar membrane operated in the same way and that appropriate receptors conducted the structure of vibrations into the brain, where the individual sound images were distinguished by central processing. *R.Hä.*

Source traits. Traits (q.v.) are the descriptive attributes of personality research. They may appear as *surface* traits or as *source* traits. Source traits constitute the elements of personality theory, forming the major constructs for models of personality. Source traits are latent variables accounting for the covariation between observed scores on personality tests, and may be regarded as "sources" or "causes" of the observed scores (Cattell, 1957). Thus an observed act of hostility would be regarded as resulting from several more fundamental sources of variance: perhaps anxiety, some learned pattern favoring aggressive responses, and extraversion, to name three possible sources.

An important issue is the extent to which the same source traits may be identified in different areas of measurement (e.g. questionnaires, morphological measures, performance tests, ratings). The evidence on this is still incomplete.

Whether some score is to be regarded as a measure of a source trait must be resolved on empirical grounds. Some criteria of source trait measures that have been suggested (Hundleby, 1970) are: (1) aspects of factor validity; (2) consistency over situations and persons; (3) circumstantial relations to other constructs; and (4) predictive validity in terms of personality-relevant criteria.

There is not, as yet, complete agreement on a set of source traits, though in some areas, notably questionnaires, much integration is taking place. Works by R. B. Cattell, H. J. Eysenck, and J. P. Guilford may be consulted to appreciate links between systems.

Bibliography: Cattell, R. B.: Personality and motivation structure and measurement. New York, 1957. **Hundleby, J. D.:** The structure of personality: surface and source traits. In: **Dreger, R.** (Ed.): Multivariate personality research. Claitor, 1970.

J. D. Hundleby

Soviet psychology. I. In the USSR, psychology is defined as the study of mental ("psychic") activity viewed as a function of the brain, determined by the conditions of life, reflecting objective reality, and regulating the interaction between man and his environment. It incorporates the dialectical materialist concept of the unity of the physical and the mental, inseparability of the mind from the physiological processes of the brain, and the vital role of the mind. Man's consciousness is regarded as the product of a prolonged historical development in which a decisive rôle was played by man's work and by verbal communication (Kostyuk, 1966).

The results of psychological research are considered to have a theoretical and a practical significance. The scientific knowledge of the mind (*psikhika*) constitutes an important component of our understanding of the nature of man. Psychology contributes to the theory of knowledge and to the formulation of a philosophical view of the world. It shares in the scientific organization of human work and is an essential ingredient of the theory and practice of education, both as regards the acquisition of information and skills (*obuchenie*), and the development of personality (*vospitanie*).

In the sense of political geography, Russian psychology became a "Soviet psychology" overnight, so to speak, as a result of the 1917 October political revolution. Russian psychology and, in its early years, the psychology of the USSR, were not essentially different from equivalents abroad. Psychology of this period, in and out of Russia, was characterized by a multiplicity of approaches and points of view.

Although it was, indeed, a branch of European psychology, Russian psychology developed in a distinct intellectual, political and socio-economic environment. Intellectually, this environment was characterized by a long-lasting struggle between "materialism" and "idealism". Historically, in Russia, "idealism" stood for metaphysical speculation, "materialism" for science. This was a local, autochthonous tradition, which can be traced back to M. V. Lomonosov (1711–1765), a many-sided scientist, scholar and man of letters, and A. N. Radischchev, a revolutionary writer. In the nineteenth century, materialism was the philosophical credo of the influential group of revolutionary democrats (A. J. Gertsen, V. G. Belinsky, N. A. Dobrolyubov, N. G. Chernyshevsky) and of such influential scientists as I. M. Sechenov (1829–1905), the "father of Russian physiology" and a proponent (*Reflexes of the Brain*, in Russian, 1863) of a physiologically oriented psychology. Materialism, historical and dialectical, is one of the bases of Marxism-Leninism, which became the sole and official philosophy of the Soviet Union. The question of what constitutes a "truly Marxist-Leninist" psychology was not answered readily in the Soviet Union. In fact, the issue represented the focus of search and debate, frequently acrimonious, for many years. There was a whole file of "candidates", including several varieties of "objective psychology": Bekhterev's reflexology, Vagner's biopsychology (human psychology as a part of comparative psychology), Blonsky's behavioral human psychology, and Kornilov's reactology.

In the nineteen-twenties and early thirties, Pavlov's (and I. M. Sechenov's) views on the reflex nature of the mind tended to be rejected by Soviet Marxist psychologists as "mechanistic". Only later, Pavlov's concept of mental activities as the processing of signals by the brain became regarded not only as compatible with Marxism–Leninism but as a premiss (*predposylka*) of the interpretation of the mind (*psikhika*) in the framework of (Soviet) dialectical materialism. But it could be argued that the R in the S-R (stimulus-response) formula is an artificial "interruption of what is uninterruptable"; consequently, the concept would be contrary to the principles of dialectical materialism. It was the physiologist, P. K. Anokhin (1935), anticipating the cyberneticists' concept of feedback, who pointed out that each R is followed, in turn, by afferent impulses ("return afferentation") which constitute information concerning the response act. At about the same time N. A. Bernstein formulated the concept of the "reflex circle", replacing the traditional "reflex arc". These were important new ideas in the physiology of behavior, but it was some time before they were incorporated, as its organic parts, into Soviet psychology.

In the nineteen-thirties *consciousness* was affirmed, *ex officio*, as the subject matter of orthodox Marxist psychology. In those years the Soviet psychologists began to consider in earnest the implications for psychology of the thought of V. I. Lenin, especially as formulated in his *Materialism and Empiriocriticism* and *Philosophical Notebooks*. It is the express acceptance of Lenin's theory of reflection as psychology's philosophical basis that contributes, in part, to the distinctiveness of Soviet psychology. The theory, not to be confused with I. P. Pavlov's theory of conditional (conditioned) reflexes, views mind, a product of highly organized matter, as an active (not passive, not mirror-like) *reflection* of external reality.

Also in the nineteen-thirties, L. S. Vygotsky stressed an historical, socio-cultural approach to the study of man's mind. The thesis of socio-historical conditionality of human consciousness became one of the basic tenets of Soviet psychology.

In 1940 S. L. Rubinstein published his *Foundations of General Psychology*, with emphasis on the dialectical *unity* of consciousness and activity (all mental processes not only manifesting themselves in activity but having their origin in activity).

Hence the reconstruction (*perestroika*) of "bourgeois" Russian psychology as truly "Soviet" psychology, based on Marxism–Leninism, proved to be a complex undertaking stretching over years and decades. In Payne's formulation (1968, p. 168) this has meant "not merely adherence to its [Marxism–Leninism's] principles but even to the very words used by the 'Classics'—Marx, Engels, Lenin—when referring to psychological subjects. This has acted as a brake on the normal development of psychological theory, has forced Soviet psychology into a theoretical straightjacket and produced a vast crop of purely exegetical problems."

The Soviet authors view the issue differently. To Petrovsky (1967), Marxism–Leninism represents the only theoretical (philosophical) platform that could provide a unifying framework and could have led Soviet psychology out of the "crisis" of the nineteen-twenties, initially shared with the West and expressed in the chaos of the warring "schools" of psychology. In view of the dissolution and virtual disappearance of the schools and global systems in the West, without the benefit of a universally shared philosophical underpinning, Petrovsky's argument is not convincing.

In any case, the general methodological (philosophical) "foundations" of Soviet psychology in Marxism–Leninism are a *sine qua non*, and will remain so in the visible future. A non-partisan, comprehensive assessment of the effects of the insistence on ideological uniformity and orthodoxy on the development of psychology in the Soviet Union has yet to be attempted.

In the mid 'thirties, psychology began to dry on the vine. One after another, the psychological journals withered away. The July 4, 1936 decree of the Central Committee of the Communist Party, directed against "pedology", originally conceived as an interdisciplinary study of child development, had disastrous effects on applied psychology in general, and suppressed psychometrics for decades. Psychologists, lacking a journal of their own for some twenty years, sought refuge in the journals of education and philosophy.

In the early 'fifties, the insistence on the "Pavlovization" of psychology created further confusion and stress. In this "general-methodological" crisis, dogmatic Pavlovism threatened to "liquidate" psychology, since, it was argued, psychology lacked a valid subject matter. For ideological reasons, the development of whole fields of psychology (e.g., social and animal) were suppressed as "reactionary" and "lacking promise". Animal psychology was charged with being out of tune with Pavlovian principles. Stalin's death in 1953 provided relief from the pressures of "the cult of personality".

The outward symbols of rapid recovery were the foundation of a scientific journal of psychology (*Voprosy psikhologii*, in 1955) and of a scientific society (*Obshchestvo psikhologov*, in 1957), the first all-Union psychological congress (in 1959), and the publication of a two-volume, historically oriented handbook reviewing the accomplishments of Soviet psychologists (Ananjev *et al.*, 1959, 1960).

Contacts with colleagues abroad were re-established, and Soviet psychologists familiarized themselves, through an impressive number of translations, with the work accomplished during their isolation from the "West". The new trends, including a rapid advance in the area of engineering psychology and a hesitant exploration of the area of social psychology, were clearly visible in the program of the second all-Union congress held in 1963 in Leningrad.

The culminating event in this process of "opening the windows to the West" (and vice versa) was the eighteenth International Congress of Psychology, held in Moscow in August 1966. The same year saw the establishment, in Moscow and in Leningrad, of the first Colleges of Psychology—first not only in the Soviet Union but in the world.

Current research activities are reflected in the program of the third all-Union congress of the Soviet Psychological Society, held in Kiev in June 1968 (Brožek, 1969). The percentages ($N = 906$) of papers presented in different areas were as follows: philosophical-theoretical topics, 1.0; history, 1.2; psychophysiology, 2.2; general experimental, 20.7; personality and differential psychology, 5.9; engineering and industrial, 12.8; medical (incl. neuropsychology, psychopathology, and abnormal child psychology), 15.2; social, 3.8; comparative, 0.7; and physical education and sports, 7.8.

A major advance in the status of psychology was represented by the establishment, in 1968, of doctoral degrees in psychology. Prior to this, psychologists could receive a doctoral degree (denoting a substantially higher level of demonstrated competence than the European or the American Ph.D. degrees) "in pedagogical sciences, with specialization in psychology". Administratively, the 1968 decree marked psychology's coming of age in the Soviet Union.

Bibliography: Ananjev, B. G. *et al.* (Eds.): Psikhologischeskaya nauka v SSSR. Moscow, Vol. 1, 1959; Vol. 2, 1960 (Eng. trans.: Psychological science in the USSR. Washington, D.C., Vol. 1, 1961; Vol. 2, 1962). **Bauer, R. A.:** The new man in Soviet psychology. Cambridge, Mass., 1952. **Id.** (Ed.): Some views on Soviet psychology. Washington, D.C., 1962. **Brožek, J.:** Spectrum of Soviet psychology: 1968. Model. Amer. Psychologist, 1969, *24*, 944–6. **Id.** (Ed.): Fifty years of Soviet psychology: An historical perspective. Soviet Psychology, 1968, *6* (3–4), 1–127 und *7* (1), 1–72. **Id.** (Ed.): Special issue on Georgian psychology. Soviet Psychology, 1968/69, *7* (2), 1–55. **Cole, M. & Maltzman, M.:** A handbook of contemporary Soviet psychology. New York, 1969. **Kostyuk, G. S.:** Psikhologija, Vol. 3. In: Pedagogicheskaja entsiklopedija. Moscow, 1966. **Molino, J. L.:** Is there a new Soviet psychology? In: **Simirenko, A.** (Ed.): Chicago, 1969, 300–27. **O'Connor, N.** (Ed.): Present-day Russian psychology. Oxford, England, 1966. **Payne, T. R.:** S. L. Rubinstejn and the philosophical foundations of Soviet psychology. New York, 1968. **Petrovskij, A. V.:** Istorija sovetskoi psikhologii. Moscow, 1967. **Razran, G.:** Russian physiologists' psychology and American experimental psychology. Psychol. Bulletin, 1965, *63*, 42–64. In: **Rubinstein, S. L.:** Psychology. In: Social Sciences in the USSR. New York, 1965, 120–6. **Slobin, D. I.** (Ed.): Handbook of Soviet psychology. Soviet Psychology and Psychiatry 1966, *4* (3–4), 1–146. **Wolman, B. B.** (Ed.): Historical roots of contemporary psychology. New York, 1968,

J. Brožek

Brožek, J.: Soviet contributions to history. Contemp. Psychol., 1969, *14*, 432–4. **Golann, S. E.:** Ethical standards for psychology, Ann. New York Acad. Sci., 1970, *169*, 398–405.

J.G.

II. The main task of psychology as it has developed in the USSR is the scientific (materialistic) investigation of the highest forms of human psychic (mental) activity, of their evolution in the process of socio-historical development, and of the fundamental laws of their operation. Consequently psychology in the USSR has always stood in a close relationship to the social sciences on the one hand, and to the physiology of higher nervous activity on the other, and has always been subject to the guidance of the philosophy of dialectical and historical materialism.

The most important task of psychology in the USSR has always been the investigation of the process of the development of the highest forms of psychic activity, in other words, their differentiation in the process of socio-historical development. A decisive part in the performance of this task was played by the work of the prominent Soviet psychologist L. S. Vygotsky (q.v.) (1896–1934), who established the scientific analysis of the development of the highest mental processes.

Vygotsky's initial thesis, which has decisively influenced the further development of psychology in the USSR, was the realization that the highest mental processes in man are to be viewed as *complex functional systems*, which are socio-historical in origin, mediated in structure (i.e. dependent on corresponding aids, e.g. language), and self-regulating as far as their mode of operation is concerned. A child always develops in the course of exchanges with adults. Even relations to things are mediated for the child by relations to adults. Through language acquisition, the child begins to organize its own behavior. The highest mental functions then arise; they are social in origin and dependent on a system of signs that comes into existence in the process of human intercourse, and—above all—on language.

In the further course of development, the child interiorizes slowly developed behaviors, i.e. they now depend not on external aids and on external, audible language but on inner language (inner speech, q.v.) and the conceptual system formed in language. A process begins: i.e. the appropriation of universal human knowledge and of modes of behavior which have developed in history and have now become the major human behavior patterns. This approach to research has been extended by a great number of investigations carried out by Soviet psychologists and pre-eminently by A. N. Leontiev, A. V. Zaporozhec, P. J. Galperin and D. B. Elkonin, who have made a major contribution to the extension of the theory of the structure of human activity with its complex motives and needs, and auxiliary operations leading to the production of complex "inner behaviors". The investigation of different stages in the gradual development of "inner behaviors" proved to be very productive not only in regard to theory, but in regard to educational practice, and became the basis of a scientifically grounded transformation of educational methods put into effect in a number of Soviet schools. The psychological theory of the gradual development of intellectual activities and concepts is also at the basis of the principles of programmed learning (see *Instructional technology*) as elaborated in Soviet psychology.

The second characteristic of psychology in the USSR is the constant search for the physiological mechanisms of complex psychic processes. This direction of research was established by I. M. Sechenov and realized in the investigations of I. P. Pavlov (q.v.), A. A. Uchtomskii and V. M. Bekhterev, who developed the theory of the reflexive basis of psychic processes. In the last few decades, a number of physiologists and psychologists have actively developed this field. P. K. Anokhin has established a theory of functional systems and of a behavior "acceptor", which play an active part in the regulation of complex behaviors. S. V. Kravkov elaborated a theory of the organization of sensory processes and their interaction; L. A. Orbeli grounded the theory of the interaction of afferent systems, which was further developed by his pupils, in particular by G. V.

Gershuni, who worked out an unusually precise theory of the construction of sensory (and above all auditory) functions, and was the first to establish the scientific basis for an objective investigation of subsensory processes. An important part in the investigation of the reflexive bases of sensory processes was played by E. N. Sokolov's studies of the orienting reflex (q.v.) and those of complex forms of orientation and information-seeking behavior by A. V. Zaporozhec and co-workers.

Also important for the development of Soviet psychophysiology was the research work of B. M. Teplov and co-workers, who developed exact methods for the investigation of the main characteristics of nervous processes, and a concept for the objective study of types of human nervous activity and interindividual differences.

A new branch of neuropsychology developed by A. R. Luria and co-workers has also won considerable importance: it is concerned with the investigation of the changes in psychic processes occurring with local lesions of the brain (see *Aphasia; Brain pathology; Restitution of psychological functions*).

Further important contributions to the development of psychology in the USSR have been made by, e.g., P. A. Blonskii, S. L. Rubinstein, A. A. Smirnov and B. G. Ananiev.

Present-day psychology in the USSR is a complex and differentiated research system extending throughout general psychology (q.v.) (A. N. Leontiev, A. A. Smirnov, B. G. Ananiev, A. N. Sokolov, etc.), genetic and child psychology (q.v.) (A. V. Zaporozhec, L. I. Bozhovich, N. A. Mechinskaia, D. B. Elkonin), psychosomatic disorders (J. M. Soloviev, M. I. Zemcova, Z. S. Sif), medical psychology (B. V. Zeigarnik), psychophysiology (E. N. Sokolov, V. D. Nebylicyn), and engineering psychology (B. D. Lomov, V. D. Zinchenko).

The most important work in psychology is carried out in the Psychological Institute of the Academy of Educational Sciences in Moscow, and in the Faculty of Psychology of the Universities of Moscow and Leningrad. Original work is also produced in Georgia—in the D. N. Uznadze Institute for Psychology of the Academy of Sciences of the Georgian SSR and by the Professors of Psychology at the University of Tiflis. Another important center is the Psychological Institute of the Ukrainian Ministry of Education in Kiev.

Bibliography: Psichologicheskaia nauka v. SSSR. Edited by the Academy of Educational Sciences. Moscow. **Leontiev, A. N., Luria, A. R. & Semivnov,** A. (Eds.): Psychological research in the USSR. Moscow, 1966. **Masucco Costa, A.**: Psicologica Sovietica. Turin, 1963.

A. R. Luria

Space perception. The study of space perception is concerned with our registration of sensory information about the spatial layout of the environment: that is, the distance and directions of objects from one another. This is ordinarily accomplished by seeing, hearing, and/or feeling. Interest in the subject can be traced to Greek philosophers who worried about how things at a distance could be sensed. However, it was not until British associationism of the seventeenth and eighteenth centuries that a systematic and, in fact, quite contemporary analysis was made. Berkeley proposed a solution to the paradox that distance or depth, i.e. the third dimension, is registered, although stimulation from the world falls on a two-dimensional surface such as the retina of the eye, or the skin. His answer was that cue sensations, such as the strain of convergence of the two eyes, are associated with the distance one must reach or walk towards an object. For example, one learns that when the eyes strain to converge on an object, it must be close, whereas if they are relaxed in converging, the object is more distant.

During the mid-nineteenth century, when psychology as a self-conscious discipline was born, problems of space perception were among the first to be tackled. The perception of visual distance and depth was studied by severely restricting all stimulation from the environment that could possibly provide information about distance. Then specific stimulation was provided to see how much perception of distance was possible. The use of eye convergence, for example, was studied by estimating the distance of a single point of light in the dark. Accurate judgments on the basis of convergence were possible only up to a few meters. In a similar manner, a number of other "cues" for depth were identified, for example: binocular disparity—the disparity between the images in the two eyes from a single object due to the slight difference between the eyes in viewpoint; and motion parallax—the different rates of apparent motion of near and far objects with head movement. Certain pictorial cues were identified also, for example, linear perspective—the convergence of pictorial representation of parallel lines as they recede from us.

In the study of the perception of the *direction* of objects in space, local sign was a central concept during the nineteenth century. Every point on a receptor surface such as the skin or retina of the eye was said to have a unique quality which innately, or through experience, specified direction in vision, or locus in touch. The concept of local sign generated much careful research into the acuity of our sense of direction.

Contemporary work on perception of distance and of direction has shifted from assessment of acuity or of capacity to analysis of process. Consider binocular disparity again: that two slightly different views of an object to the two eyes do provide depth information can be demonstrated with a Wheatstone stereoscope. With this device, a slightly different flat picture can be presented to each eye: a solid three-dimensional object is vividly perceived. The two disparate views are fused as one if the amount of disparity is small. If the amount of disparity is too large, double images are perceived. When the eyes are stimulated by radically different pictures, rivalry occurs and one sees, in alternation, first the right eye picture, then the left, or a constantly changing intermixture of the two.

Closely related to binocular disparity is the problem of visual direction. Since the two eyes are at slightly different positions in space, the direction of an object from each eye will be slightly different. How is the direction of an object from us determined? Research indicates that visual direction is judged as if from a point between the two eyes. It may be, but is not generally, exactly midway.

Our ability to register the direction of sounds has been shown to depend on the fact that there are time and intensity differences in the stimulation reaching the two ears. If a sound source is to our right, the right ear receives a slightly stronger sound signal, slightly sooner than the left. As in vision, two similar sounds to the two ears are fused in perception. There is no auditory phenomenon exactly like binocular rivalry. However, if two different messages are presented one to each ear, we cannot perceive both as well as we could one alone.

Little is known about the mechanism of distance and direction perception by feeling (haptic perception), except that it is probably mediated primarily by neural receptors in the joints rather than by muscle receptors. Haptic directional perception, as evidenced by pointing, is good, but not as precise as visual or auditory. Haptic is also less precise than visual, but probably better than auditory distance perception, and, of course, it only functions close to the body.

There has been considerable interest in the calibration between the visual, haptic, and auditory modes of distance and direction perception. It has been found, for example, that we are very precise in aligning a light with a sound, or in pointing to either. One technique for studying the mechanism underlying this calibration is to disturb it by optical distortion. Errors made initially in pointing after optical distortion may be quickly corrected as our directional systems recalibrate to such disruption. See *Visual perception*.

Bibliography: Bekesy, G. von: Sensory inhibition. Princeton, N.J., 1967. **Boring, E. G.:** Sensation and perception in the history of experimental psychology. New York, 1942. **Broadbent, D. E.:** Perception and communication. London, 1958. **Gibson, E. J.:** Principles of perceptual learning and development. New York, 1969. **Gibson, J. J.:** The perception of the visual world. New York, 1950. **Harris, C. S.:** Perceptual adaptation to inverted, reversed, and displaced vision. Psychological Review. 1965, 72: 419–444. **Hochberg, J. E.:** Perception. Englewood Cliffs, N.J., 1966. **Howard, I. P., Templeton, W. B.:** Human spatial orientation. New York, 1966. *H. L. Pick*

Spaltbarkeit; Spaltungsfähigkeit (Ger.). The analytical ability, inherent in one's constitution, to dissect impressions and acts or to analyze several separate intentions in juxtaposition; said to be most marked in schizothymes. *W.K.*

Span of consciousness. 1. The consciousness of incoming information is severely limited. Experiments in the awareness of several streams of incoming information (e.g. several speakers) suggest that people can be conscious of little more than one such source at a time, although additional information may be stored temporarily below the level of consciousness. There is a similarly limited span of consciousness with regard to time. See *Psychological moment*.

2. Studies of immediate retention show that the extent of simultaneously apprehended conscious contents is limited. Tachistoscopic experiments revealed a span of approximately five to eight units (figures, letters, geometrical shapes, etc.). The degree of redundancy of sign sequences plays an important part in the phenomenon. Sequences containing less information are identified more readily (Miller, Bruner & Postman, 1954). By appropriate coding, larger quantities of data can be consciously surveyed for a short period of time. See *Memory; Reminiscence*.

Bibliography: Miller, G. A.: The magical number seven, plus or minus two: some limits on our capacity of processing information. Psychol. Rev., 1956, *63*, 81–97. **Miller, G. A., Bruner, J. S. & Postman, L.:** Familarity of letter sequences and tachistoscopic identification. J. gen. Psychol., 1954, *50*, 129–139.

B.R.

Spasm (*cramp*). An increased, involuntary state of tension (*tonic* spasm) lasting for some time and, or, a quick succession of irregular, involuntary contractions (*clonic* spasm) of a muscle or group of muscles, especially in diseases of the brain or spinal cord (lesion of the pyramidal tract). *F.-C.S.*

Spasmolytics. Substances which produce a decrease in tonus of the smooth musculature, in particular of the gastro-intestinal tract. The chemistry and pharmacology of the different spasmolytics varies; most of them belong to the anticholinergic (q.v.) or sympathicomimetic (q.v.) substances. Depending on their points of attack, there can frequently be disagreeable side-effects (e.g. anticholinergic substances can cause dryness of the mouth).

Bibliography: Miller, S. W. & Lewis, S. E.: Drugs affecting smooth muscle. Annals of the Pharmacological Review, 1969, *9*, 147–72. *W.J.*

Spastic (*convulsive*). Contracting after the manner of a spasm (q.v.). Impairment of the normal coordination of movement.

Spastic paralysis: paralysis in which the ability of a large skeletal musculature to move at will is lost although the muscle is not slack, but tonically contracted. *F.-C.S.*

Spatial symbolism. Theory applied particularly to graphology, according to which spatial grouping of features in handwriting, drawings,

sculpture, etc., give a key to expression and coordination of individual personality traits of the author. Thus in handwriting the lower half of a letter corresponds to the area of desire and affect and the upper half to intellectual interests. Spatial symbolism also plays a part in the interpretation of dreams (q.v.) in many depth psychology schools (see *Depth psychology*) (e.g. C. G. Jung), which usually hold that the unconscious is allied with the lower, the conscious (q.v.) with the upper, the past with the left and the future with the right.
W.Sch.

Spatial threshold. The necessary minimum distance between two stimulus points, such that they are experienced as two different stimuli. The spatial threshold is measured in the optical and tactile sensory modalities. In the measurement of simultaneous spatial thresholds, the stimuli are simultaneous; in the measurement of successive spatial thresholds (successive threshold) they are successive.
F.Ma.

Spearman, C. E. B. 10/9/1863 in London; d. 17/9/1945 in London. It was only relatively late, in 1897, after leaving the English army where he had served as an officer, that Spearman turned to psychology. He subsequently spent several years in Germany, first under W. Wundt (q.v.), under whom he graduated in 1904 with an investigation of spatial perception (q.v.), and subsequently at the universities of Würzburg, Göttingen and Berlin, where he completed his studies of physiology, experimental psychology and philosophy. While in Germany he published in 1904 his famous article "General intelligence objectively determined and measured", in which for the first time he clearly expounded the fundamental ideas of factor analysis (q.v.). In 1907, Spearman was appointed to a lectureship, and in 1911 to a professorial chair, at University College, London, which he occupied until 1931.

Spearman's historical significance can be seen in two facts which are closely interrelated: on the one hand the development of the factor analytical method, the beginnings of which can admittedly be found in K. Pearson's work but which Spearman was the first to set out explicitly, and, on the other hand, the two-factor theory of intelligence (q.v.) which, together with A. Binet's work, represents the starting point for the development of the theory and measurement of intelligence in the twentieth century. The basic assumption of the two-factor theory is that every cognitive performance represents a function of two factors: (*a*) a *general intelligence factor* g which underlies every performance of the intelligence and (*b*) specific ability factors which only come into play at any time in particular kinds of tasks. In subsequent revisions of his theory Spearman recognized in addition the existence of individual group factors, without however abandoning his basic concept of g and s factors. (See *Abilities*.)

Other significant contributions by Spearman were the development of Spearman rank correlation (q.v.) and Spearman–Brown formula (q.v.). On the other hand, his attempts to state fundamental laws of psychology and the human mind on the basis of his g factor concept ("The nature of intelligence and the principles of cognition", 1923; "G and after —a school to end schools", 1930) must be regarded as somewhat exaggerated.

Other works: The abilities of man, their nature and measurement. London, 1927. Creative mind. London, 1930. Psychology down the ages. London, 1937.

Bibliography: Murchison, C. (Ed.): A history of psychology in autobiography, Vol. 1. Worcester, Mass., 1930, 299–333.
W.W.

Spearman–Brown formula. If the reliability (q.v.) r_{tt} of a test of a given extent is known, then the reliability of a test extended *n*-fold can be calculated according to this formula. It is as follows:

$$r_{nn} = \frac{n \, . \, r_{tt}}{1 + (n - 1)r_{tt}}$$

Of special importance is the case where $n = 2$, which occurs when calculating the reliability according to the *split-half* method (q.v.).

Bibliography: **Guilford, J. P.:** Psychometric methods. New York, 1954. *A.R.*

Spearman rank correlation coefficient. A method of comparison of two rank orders for agreement. In the following, r_s = correlation between ranks over things ranked:

$$r_s = 1 - \frac{6(\Sigma D_i^2)}{N(N^2 - 1)}$$

when N = number of things observed, and D_i = the difference between ranks associated with a specific observed object i. This computational method applies when no ties in rank exist. r_s is, therefore, a normal correlation coefficient calculated on ranks (see *Correlational techniques*).

Bibliography: **Kendall, M. G.:** Rank correlation methods. London, 1962. *A.K.*

Special school. An institution, either private or run by the State, which has as its object to care both for the health and the education of children and adolescents who because of some organic or mental defect can respond only inadequately or not at all to primary school instruction and yet are *capable of development*. The term special schools embraces institutions of the most diverse kinds, such as schools for the deaf and hard of hearing, schools for children with language difficulties, for the blind and partially blind, schools for those with learning disabilities and the mentally handicapped (see *Mental defect*), and in addition institutions for those with behavioral disorders, for the subnormal, adolescents serving a sentence, the physically handicapped and those suffering from some disease. The first special schools were for the deaf (Paris, 1770; Leipzig, 1778), then followed those for the blind (Paris, 1780). It was only in about 1900 that institutions for those with learning disabilities began really to appear as a result of the psychological and psychiatric discoveries of the nineteenth century. Schools for those serving a prison sentence have been in existence since 1921. Quite recently dyslexia (q.v.) has also begun to be treated in special classes. The organization of the special school system varies; for some types there are preparatory institutions, primary and intermediate schools, senior sections, vocational classes, and courses for adults. Instruction at special schools is an educational problem of the first order since it makes great demands on teachers' skill and requires outstanding human qualities (leader figures). See *Child psychology; Educational psychology*. *E.U.*

Species. 1. A natural class, a single order of beings. **2.** Any class, sort, or subdivision of a general term. **3.** In particular: a class narrower than a genus, yet wider than a variety.

Specific energy of sensations, law of. A doctrine proposed by Müller in 1826. He stated that each sensory nerve has its own characteristic type of activity, so that the optic nerve signals light and color, the auditory nerve sound and the olfactory nerve odor, and so on. In accord with this theory is the fact that most receptors respond to electrical stimulation in just this way, resulting in reports of light, sound, and smell respectively. The current view is that the specific activity depends not so much on the nerve, but on the locality in the brain at which the signal the nerve is transmitting eventually arrives. Hence electrical stimulation of the occipital lobe gives an experience of light. *C.D.F.*

Spectrum. **1.** In general: periodic but also aperiodic fluctuating partial oscillations distributed in time or space can be split up into harmonic partial oscillations, of differing frequency. If, in a system of coordinates, the amplitudes of the partial oscillations (ordinates), for example, are plotted as a function of the frequency (abscissa), a representation is obtained which is known as a spectrum. In the case just mentioned, the spectrum is called the *amplitude spectrum.* If, instead of the amplitude, the amplitude squared is plotted on the ordinate, a *performance spectrum* is obtained.

2. In a literal sense the concept of spectrum is used for the range of electromagnetic oscillations with a wavelength between 380 and 780 nm, which is also known as *visible spectrum.* In this case the radiation energy (light current, etc.) as ordinate is plotted as a function of the wavelength (lambda) on the abscissa.

The energy-like spectrum in all wavelength ranges (visible) has a constant energy. A spectrum can be made from a reflected radiation: *reflection spectrum.* Also analogous are: emission spectrum, absorption spectrum, etc. (see *Absorption*). Sound spectra are also referred to in the field of acoustics when the frequency range between 16 Hertz and 20, sometimes, as much as 40 thousand Hertz (20 k Hertz): is understood (above 20 kHz, *ultrasonic spectrum*). In this case a performance spectrum is usually meant (pressure fluctuations in microbar or dyn/cm^2 as a function of the frequency). *R.R.*

Speculative psychology. A branch of philosophical psychology which dispenses with experiments (q.v.) and systematic observations and describes the essential dimensions of mental life in connection with a comprehensive philosophical system. Thus Thomism, for example, includes a speculative psychology. See *Philosophy and psychology.* *P.M.*

Speech (syn. *Speaking; Linguistic behavior; Verbal behavior*). In everyday usage, "speech" appears to be a clearly demarcated form of behavior. In varying conceptions of language (q.v.), however, speech (whether as a whole or in part) is variously conceived theoretically: e.g. as the emission of verbal responses, as encoding, as communication, as performance (see *Psycholinguistics; Expression; Verbal behavior, establishment and modification of*).

The linguistic concept of "competence" unites the most diversely nuanced ideas of the dispositional bases of language acquisition (see *Grammar;* Miller & McNeill, 1969). The complementary concept of "performance", in the sense of language use, is any processual application of competence in language or in the reception of linguistic utterances, and requires correspondingly differentiated ideas of speech and speech perception (Bierwisch, 1966; Wales & Marshall, 1966). Accordingly, a psychological theory of linguistic performance would have consistently to interpret at least the following part functions individually and in their functional interactions (Hörmann, 1970; Osgood & Sebeck, 1965): (*a*) in speech *production*: the actualization of meanings and meaningful linguistic units (see *Semantics*); the selection, formation and arrangement of such units according to grammatical rules (see *Grammar*); and the vocal realization of available linguistic structures (see *Phonemics*) in the interaction of respiration, phonation and articulation (or graphic realization by means of writing). In speech *perception*: the perception of sound sequences (or of written sequences) and their decoding as phoneme sequences (or grapheme sequences); the constitution of meaningful units (morphemes, words), including the actualization of meanings, the decoding of their grammatical relations, the construction of integrative meaningful contexts (e.g. of sentences and more extensive linguistic structures).

Psychological theories and investigations are concerned primarily with some of the performance components (Goodman, 1968; Lashley, 1951; Morse, Ballintine & Dixon, 1968; Wathen-Dunn, 1967); and in addition with specific aspects of speech and speech perception, such as the effect of emotional conditions and/or social interactions down to the most varied formal and substantial parameters of speech, interactions between speech and non-verbal forms of communication (body postures, movements, visual contact), between speech and thought (see *Inner speech*), and the identification of affective states, social and individual-specific characteristics in the partner in communication by means of perceived utterance and/or intervals and disturbances in the same (Argyle, 1969; Davitz, 1964; Ellingworth & Clevenger, 1967; Ervin-Tripp, 1969; Goldman-Eisler, 1968; Knapp, 1963; Paivio, 1965; Wiener & Mehrabian, 1968), and effects of the limited nature of the actual storage capacity and processing speed on linguistic performance. For methodological and theoretical reasons, speech and speech perception are usually treated together, since both processes would seem to include common part processes or, to some extent, to imply one another. Under differential-psychological and individual-diagnostic-pathognostic aspects, in addition to content (Gottschalk & Gleser, 1969), the most diverse formal characteristics of speech production and its voiced or graphic realization come into play: e.g. tempo, duration, duration and type of pauses and disturbances, pitch, volume, intensity, intonation, accentuation, breathing, and so on (Ellingworth & Clevenger, 1967; Rudert, 1965). The formal variables of graphic realization are studied in the psychology of handwriting (see *Graphology*). Techniques for the detection of the interindividual variability of speech perception can also be used for the differentiation of such aspects as readability, comprehensibility, etc.

Bibliography: Argyle, M.: Social interaction. London, 1969. **Bierwisch, M.:** Strukturalismus. Kursbuch, 1966, 5, 77–152. **Davitz, J. R.:** The communication of emotional meaning. New York, 1964. **Ellingworth, H. W. & Clevenger, T.:** Speech and social action. Englewood Cliffs, N.J., 1967. **Ervin-Tripp, S. M.:** Sociolinguistics. In: **Berkowitz, L.** (Ed.): Advances in experimental social psychology, Vol. 4. New York & London, 1969, 91–165. **Goldman-Eisler, F.:** Psycholinguistics. London, 1968. **Goodman, K. S.** (Ed.): The psycholinguistic nature of the reading process. Detroit, 1968. **Gottschalk, L. A. & Glese, G. C.:** The measurement of psychological states through the content analysis of verbal behavior. Berkeley, 1969. **Hörmann, H.:** Psychologie der Sprache. Berlin, [2]1970. **Knapp, P. H.** (Ed.): Expression of the emotions in man. New York, 1963. **Lashley, K. S.:** The problem of serial order in behavior. In: **Jeffress, L. A.** (Ed.): Cerebral mechanism in behavior. New York, 1951. **Miller, G. A. & McNeill, D.:** Psycholinguistics. In: **Lindzey, G. & Aronson, E.** (Eds.): Handbook of social psychology, 3. Reading, Mass., 1969, 666–794. **Morse, W. C., Ballantine, F. A. & Dixon, W.:** Studies in the psychology of reading. New York, 1968. **Osgood, C. E. & Sebeok, T. A.** (Eds.): Psycholinguistics. Bloomington, 1965. **Paivio, A.:** Personality and audience influence. In: **Maher, B. A.** (Ed.): Progress in experimental personality research, Vol. 2. New York, 1965, 127–73. **Rudert, J.:** Vom Ausdruck der Sprechstimme. In: **Kirchhoff, R.** (Ed.): Hdb. d. Psychol., Vol. 5. Göttingen, 1965, 422–64. **Wales, R. J. & Marshall, J. C.:** The organisation of linguistic performance. In: **Lyons, J. & Wales, R. J.** (Eds.): Psycholinguistic papers. Edinburgh, 1966, 29–80. **Wathen-Dunn, W.** (Ed.): Models for the perception of speech and visual form. Cambridge, Mass.), 1967. **Wiener, M. & Mehrabian, A.:** Language within language. New York, 1968.

G. Kaminski

Speech center. A cortical field in the left cerebral hemisphere (in the right-handed) the destruction of which leads to an inability to speak (see *Aphasia*). The motor speech center was described by P. Broca (see *Broca's area*) in the *pars opercularis* of the inferior frontal gyrus. Its destruction leads to motor aphasia with an inability to translate thoughts into spoken words. The sensory speech center was discovered by K. Wernicke in the rear temporal area. Its destruction leads to sensory aphasia, an inability to understand words. But see *Brain pathology; Localization of psychological functions.*

E.D.

Speech disorders. See *Aphasia; Aphrasia.*

Speech types. A division of modes of speech according to body posture, rhythm, clang, tension, etc. Sievers (1912) and Drach (1928) offer elaborate categorizations.

Bibliography: Drach, E.: Sprechausdruck und Charakterkunde. Päd. Zbl., 1928. **Sievers, E.:** Rhythmisch-melodische Studien. Heidelberg, 1912.

W.K.

Speed test. A test of psychological performance in which the rapidity with which one or several tasks are solved is the crucial criterion. As far as possible the difficulty of the tasks should not enter into consideration and it is therefore kept uniformly low. To determine the score for the performance there are two possibilities: either the time required for a certain number of tasks or the number of tasks performed for each unit of time. The tests of this kind currently in use select chiefly the second alternative. Speed tests are usually employed in the diagnosis of attentiveness and concentration, endurance and motor skill.

P.S.

Spence, Kenneth Wartinbee (1907–1967) "demanding of others, . . . much more of himself," a personality "drawn in bold lines; strong attitudes, powerful opinions, prodigious worker" (Kendler, 1967). Born in Chicago, Illinois, Spence was raised in Canada, was educated at McGill University, Montreal (B.A., 1929; M.A., 1930) and Yale (Ph.D., 1933), worked as National Research Council Fellow at the Yale Laboratories of Primate Biology, Orange, Florida (1933–37), the University of Virginia (1937–38), and the University of Iowa (1938–64) (Professor and Head of Department in 1942). From 1964 he was Professor at the University of Texas. Both alone and in collaboration his experimental output was formidable, which for some may have obscured his vital contribution to theory: "I do not consider myself a philosopher, even an amateur one," said Spence (1960, 7). This denial suggests an awareness evident in a careful theoretical progress from the identification of events deemed unitary and elementary to theory which can be extended to more complex, "higher" behaviors. Often regarded as a reviser of Hull's learning theory, Spence appears instead a theorist of a superior class, especially in his views on contiguity and reinforcement (1960, 185–201). His most visible scholarly monuments are his Silliman Lectures (*Behavior and Conditioning*, 1956), and the later collection *Behavior Theory and Learning* (1960). The latter covers methodology (five papers), learning theory extending to, e.g., anxiety (ten papers) and discrimination learning (seven papers), including an outstanding handling of the intervening variable. In his distinction between earlier and later behaviorism (1960, 40), exposition of developing views of the subject matter of psychology (1960, 72), and discussion of the shift of interest from complex to simple learning (1959, 89), there is more historical insight than has been commonly allowed. Spence was explicitly laboratory oriented, but appears more aware of applied psychology and more balanced in approach than has been sometimes thought. Hence, on learning theory and educational technology: "We psychologists have been asked to solve practical problems before we had the laws of behavior necessary to do so . . . the applied psychologist has found it necessary to proceed in much the same fashion as the basic research psychologist instead of operating in the manner of the typical engineer" (1959, 87); on "cultural" psychology: "knowledge . . . based on introspective observation or empathic projection . . . differs from scientific knowledge." This may be developed, e.g. regarding personality, but it should not be represented as being one of the natural sciences (1960, 81). Balanced contribution deserves balanced evaluation: Spence's position with psychologists, whether scientific or humanistic, remains secure.

Works: Behavior theory and conditioning. New Haven, 1956. The relation of learning theory to the technology of education. Harvard Educ. Rev., 1959, *29*, 84–95. Behavior theory and learning. Englewood Cliffs, N.J., 1960.

Bibliography: Kendler, H. H.: Kenneth W. Spence. Psychol Rev., 1967, *74*, 335–41. *J.A.C.*

Sphere (*sphere of consciousness*). A concept of Schilder (1920) and E. Kretschmer which is related to the "marginal consciousness" (M. Prince) and "marginal zone" (M. Dessoir). E. Kretschmer describes the sphere as the "periphery of the field of consciousness" with "its beclouded orbit of associated conscious notions and feelings which has some obscure influence at the birth of every action and spoken sequence". These imprecise processes are indispensable not only for empathy and tact, but for intuitive, productive and artistic thinking. *W.K.*

Sphygmograph. An instrument for graphical recording of the strength and frequency of the pulse. *G.D.W.*

Sphygmography. A technique for recording changes in pulse beat with the aid of suitable measuring devices and the partly mechanical, partly pneumatic, partly electrical or optical transference of the fluctuations of blood pressure on to a writing system. A *sphygmogram* is the record of the fluctuations of pulsatory blood pressure. *E.D.*

Sphygmomanometer. An instrument for measuring arterial blood pressure (both *systolic* and *diastolic*). A rubber tube connected to an air bulb is wound tightly around the upper arm and air pumped into it until circulation is blocked off (heart sounds are no longer heard through a stethoscope placed on the arm just below the tube). As pressure is released, a pulse is heard first (the systolic pressure), but this disappears again as the blood begins to course more freely (the diastolic pressure). *G.D.W.*

Spinal cord. That part of the central nervous system (*medulla spinalis*) located in the spinal canal of the vertebral column. Its function is on the one hand to provide links in the shape of nerve pathways between the brain (q.v.) and the body's periphery and on the other hand to form reflex centers as well as synapses for coordinating simple series of motor movements. Accordingly it consists of white (pathways) and grey matter (collections of nerve cells) which are absolutely separate from one another. When a cross-section of the spinal cord about as large as a small coin is examined, the pathways outside the butterfly-shaped grey matter can be easily recognized and assigned to the different cords (e.g. pyramidal anterior and posterior cord, Flechsig, Gower, Burdach and Goll cords). See *Nervous system.* *E.D.*

Spinal ganglion. See *Ganglion.*

Spiritual exercises. Ignatius of Loyola (1535) developed the medieval "*Exercitia spiritualia*" as the classical "spiritual exercises" of the Catholic Church. Under the guidance of a leader, a few days (originally four weeks) are spent in examination of conscience, followed by meditation on the life of Jesus and his grace. With the general tendency to intellectualization, the ability of meditative devotional prayer to change the personality has become very rare. See *Meditation.* *K.T.*

Spiritualism. A cult centered upon belief in survival (q.v.), and upon the practice of communicating with deceased persons through a medium (q.v.). Hence "spiritualist" = devotee of spiritualism. *J.B.*

Spirometer. An instrument which measures the volume of air that can be expired at one breath (usually taken as an indication of lung capacity). *G.D.W.*

Split-half method. A method of assessing the reliability (q.v.) of a psychometric test. The items are arbitrarily split into two equal parts (e.g. by taking all the odd and all the even numbers) and a score given to each half of the test. The correlation between the two halves of the test gives a reliability assessment which is half as great as the original test. By means of the Spearman-Brown formula this reliability score can be converted to apply to the original test. This method can only be used for power tests. Reliability tested in this way is called split-half reliability. See *Test theory.*

Bibliography: **Guilford, J. P.:** Psychometric methods. New York, 1954. *A.R.*

Spontaneous psi phenomenon. A paranormal phenomenon (q.v.) that occurs spontaneously in the real-life situation as opposed to an experimental psi-phenomenon of the parapsychological laboratory. *J.B.*

Sport, psychology of. The investigation of the psychological processes and their manifestations present in people during and after sporting activity. It tries to investigate the causes and effects of these processes but not the sport itself; it investigates the player not the game. In every sporting performance the personality is involved as a whole, both with the physical and psychic factors of ability to perform, and with the affective and voluntary factors of willingness to perform (see *Motivation*). Every sporting activity is also the behavior (q.v.) of an individual in an environment (q.v.).

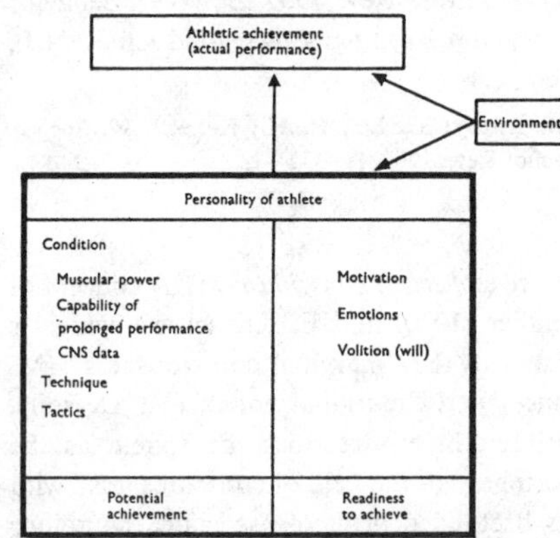

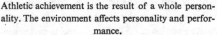

Athletic achievement is the result of a whole personality. The environment affects personality and performance.

Psychosomatic medicine and pediatric psychology are still working on the fundamental soul-body problem which concerns us in every sporting activity. New incentives came from various attempts continually to improve sporting performance and bring it to perfection. Sports medicine has contributed to this process of improvement, but the physical readiness of top athletes is approaching an optimum. The technical contribution to sport (biomechanics, equipment and apparatus) is also approaching perfection. The task of the psychology of sport is therefore to use the findings of general psychology (q.v.) and its own researches to help the performer to develop his sporting capacity and preparation to the full, so that he can be at his best at the critical moment.

The relationship between the practice and psychology of sport is mutual. The practice of sport can be perfected through the findings of psychology, and psychological knowledge can be increased by the practice of sport. Sport allows the observation of behavior which cannot easily be studied in everyday life. Questions of skill, for example, or the socio-psychological problems of group dynamics (q.v.) are of great importance in sport. The athlete, particularly in sport of a high standard, experiences psychologically extreme conditions with corresponding drives, e.g. aggression (q.v.), self-approval, fear. The athlete in training subjects himself to ordeals (see *Stress*) and makes demands upon himself which reach the limits of his personal capacities. "Neither in professional work nor in psychological studies in general can such an unreserved commitment of all a man's capacities be found, not only bodily but also psychic capacities." (Feige, 1964.) The psychology of sport investigates psychic behavior and capacity at the limits of normal performance" (Feige, 1964). This special task makes the psychology of sport a special branch of psychology.

Methods. The psychology of sport employs the usual methods of general psychology: the observation of experience (self-observation), the observation of others through questioning (see *Exploration*), and free association (see *Psychoanalysis*). Experiments (q.v.) and tests (see *Psychodiagnostics; Objective tests; Intelligence tests*) may be conducted in direct conjunction with sporting activity. Experiments and tests in the laboratory must always be ratified by field studies because the laboratory cannot reproduce the competitive situation very closely.

Aims. Basic research seeks through work which is not practice-directed to reach a deeper understanding of the psychic phenomena of sporting activity. In this sphere are the mind-body problem (q.v.), developmental psychology (see *Development; Maturation*), psycho-mechanics, high-performance psychology and depth psychology (q.v.): problems concerning biology and physiology on the one hand, and psychology on the other.

Research directed toward the practice of sport seeks to reach a deeper understanding of the participant, and proceeds as in traffic psychology (q.v.) or occupational psychology (q.v.). It is particularly concerned with problems of adaptation of the player, motivation, performance and social psychology. There is a constant interchange between the basic and applied research. The relationship between research and practice is most important. Research, particularly applied research, must be directed toward practice, yet must not only describe but explain psychic phenomena, and pass on findings to the practice of sport. In a teaching department, the psychology of sport aims to give teachers and trainers a basic psychological knowledge. They are also shown what psychic factors are involved in a sporting performance. The attempt is made to arouse their interest and sense of responsibility, and to develop their understanding of problems in the psychology of sport.

As well as this research and teaching work, the psychology of sport is also directly engaged in the practice of sport, particularly in counseling. This counseling may be individual, or (in groups and clubs) a form of group therapy (q.v.).

Bibliography: Bally, G.: Vom Ursprung und von den Grenzen der Freiheit. Eine Deutung des Spiels bei Tier und Mensch. Basle Stuttgart, [2]1966. **Feige, K.:** Aufgaben und Bedeutung der Sportpsychologie für die Theorie der Leibeserziehung. Die Leibeserziehung, 1964, *4*, 111–25. **Fischel, W.:** Psychologie. In: **Arnold, A.** (Ed.): Lehrbuch der Sportmedizin. Leipzig, 1960, 374–299. **Hegg, J. J.:** Tiefenpsychol. des Hochleistungssportes. Schweiz. Z. für Sportmedizin, 1969, *3*, 89–112. **Kleibert, G. & Elssner, G.:** Einige grundlegende Bemerkungen zur Entwicklung einer wiss. Psychol. des Sports. Theorie und Praxis der Körperkultur, 1954, *4*, 318–30. **Kohlmann, T.:** Die Psychologie der motorischen Begabung. Vienna, Stuttgart, 1958. **Kunath, P.:** Psychologie. Leipzig, 1965. **Lorenz, K. & Leyhausen, P.:** Antriebe tierischen und menschlichen Verhaltens. Munich, 1968. **Lotz, F.:** Sport–Leibeserziehung–Psychol. Die Leibeserziehung, 1965, *8*, 280–5. **Macak, J.:** The psychological aspects of the control of the prestart state and the possibilities of its valuation. Bratislava: Acta facultatis educationis fisicae, *VI*, 1967. **Neumann, O.:** Die leibseelische Entwicklung im Jugendalter. Múnich, 1964. **Ogilvie,**

B. & Tutko, T. A.: Problem athletes and how to handle them. London, 1966. **Puni, A. Z.:** Abriss der Sportpsychologie. Berlin, 1961. **Singer, R. N.:** Motor learning and human performance. New York & London, 1968. **Steinbach, M.:** Uber konkrete Möglichkeiten einer Zusammenarbeit von Ärzten und Psychologen im Sport. Schweiz. Z. für Sportmedizin, 1968, *3/4*, 145–55. **Vanek, M.:** Medelovan trénink. Psychologické priprava sportovce, Metodicky dopis CSTV, 1963. **Widmer, K.:** Das sportliche Training in psychologisch-soziologischer Sicht. Jugend und Sport, 1967, *10*, 277–83. **Winter, E. de & Dubreuil, J.:** La relaxation comme psychothérapie sportive. 1st International Congress of Sports Psychology, 1965.

G. Schilling

Square illusion. The illusion by which a square standing on one corner looks larger than an

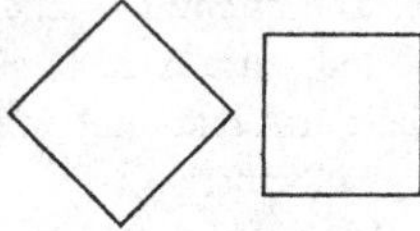

objectively equal square standing on one side.

C.D.F.

Squinting (*Strabismus*). When an object is fixated, the visual axes of both eyes are directed at it. Thus the image-forming rays fall on the identical retinal positions (q.v.). If a person is unable to direct the visual axes of both eyes simultaneously on a fixated object, he suffers from squinting. Squinting can occur when the pivots of both eyes are in their normal position and also when this position is abnormal (caused by tumors). In the following four cases of squinting the pivots of both eyes and hence both eyes themselves are in the normal position with respect to the orbits: (*a*) "eccentric fixation"; identical retinal positions: especially the foveae are located anomalously. (*b*) "Simple squinting". (*c*) "Paralytic squinting" (*strabismus paralyticus*), due to paralysis or contraction (shortening) of one or several muscles. (*d*) Anomalous attachment of the muscles at the bulbus, as a result of which the pull of the eye muscles acts at the wrong place physiologically.

The visual axes can deviate from one another both in a horizontal and in a vertical direction. When there is deviation in the horizontal plane, a distinction is made between inward squinting (*strabismus convergens*) and outward squinting (*strabismus divergens*). In the vertical plane (elevation squinting) one visual axis may deviate *upwards* (*strabismus ascendens*) or *downwards* (*strabismus descendens*). Usually the visual axis of one eye is directed correctly at the object fixated (the leading eye), whereas the visual axis of the other eye deviates. If the *leading eye alternates*, the term "*strabismus alternans*" is used. When both eyes squint, the case is one of *strabismus binocularis. Strabismus concomitans* occurs with hyperopia (q.v.) and myopia (q.v.). The eye tries to compensate for the hyperopia, for example, by near accommodation (see *Accommodation*). But, because of the nervous displacement caused in this near accommodation, the visual axes simultaneously turn inward (see *Convergence*).

Vision in the squinting eye is frequently poor (see *Amblyopia*). This amblyopia can be either the cause (absence of fusion stimulus) or the result of the squinting.

Strabismus latens indicates a tendency to squint. The squinting is irregular and varies in degree. "Heterophoria" is a term also used for such cases; it may be *esophoria* (deviating inward), *exophoria* (deviating outward), *hyperphoria* or *hypophoria* (deviating upward or downward).

R. Rix

S-R, S-R-S, S-S models. The attempt is made through the *S-R model* to explain all behavior of organisms as a response to preceding stimulation. It forms the basis of all behavioristic theories of learning (q.v.) and behavior (q.v.). The basic units of S-R theory are the innate S-R associations, which are known as *unconditioned reflexes*. If the association of S and R is produced because they repeatedly occur together or close in time to one another, then a conditioned reflex is formed by the method of classical conditioning (q.v.). The model which is adduced to explain how the association comes about in this way is known as the *S-R contiguity model.* If the association is explained as having occurred because a reward followed the appearance together of S and R, then the case is said to be one of a *S-R reinforcement model* or—particularly since the reinforcement represents the action of a stimulus—an *S-R-S model.* According to the so-called S-S theory of E. C. Tolman, it is not the associations between the S and the R which are learned, but those between the external stimuli leading to the reward (S_1) and the desired stimulus of the reward (S_2). E. R. Guthrie is famous as the proponent of the S-R contiguity theory and C. L. Hull (q.v.) as the proponent of the S-R reinforcement theory. See *Behaviorism.* *H.Ro.*

S-R psychology. An inclusive term for most psychological research activities with a scientific orientation. This term was given to them because of their common theoretical basic model, according to which all behavior is explained as a response (R) to a certain stimulus (S). *H.Ro.*

S-R relation. The connection between stimulus and response in an individual, where the stimulus represents a condition for the response. Study of the S-R relation is at the center of stimulus-response psychology, or S-R psychology, which is especially concerned with problems of learning (q.v.). See *Behaviorism; Conditioning, classical and operant; Learning theory.* *F.Ma.*

Stabilized retinal image. Using special experimental techniques (e.g. an extremely bright flash inducing long-lasting afterimages) it is possible to stabilize a visual image so that it stimulates only one fixed part of the retina. Viewed under these conditions, the visual image disappears within a few seconds. The exact nature of this disappearance depends on the structure of the stimulus, some parts of the stimulus remaining visible longer than others. These results show that normal vision depends on continual small movements of the eyes, thus revealing a particular inadequacy in the analogy between the eye and a camera. *C.D.F.*

Stammering. A speech impediment involving blockages and hesitations which interrupt the even flow of words. Is sometimes equated with *stuttering*, with which it is often associated. Normally distinguished from disorders of articulation such as *dysarthria* and *anarthria* which result from lesions in the speech areas of the brain. Believed to be influenced by psychological factors, although some emotional conditions may be secondary results of the stammering, e.g. shyness and withdrawal. *G.D.W.*

Standard. The mean measure or *norm* (q.v.).

Standard deviation (abb. SD; syn. *Variation; Mean square deviation*). A measure for the standard deviation of a distribution from the arithmetic mean:

$$SD = \sqrt{\frac{\Sigma x^2}{N}}$$

x being a score minus the mean, $N =$ the number of items, and $\Sigma =$ sum of. *A.R.*

Standard error. Measure of the sample error (q.v.). It is the standard deviation (q.v.) of a statistic (q.v.) expressed from a sample calculated to the size N. Simple relations are often valid between the standard deviation of a feature in the population, the N size of the sample and the S. *A.R.*

Standardization. Sometimes used as a synonym for *normalization*; transformation of rough data into units of measurement which fulfil certain conditions (e.g. they have a given mean value and given deviations). *A.R.*

Standard score. A numerical value derived from a raw value, which plays an important part in test construction. Standard scores have the mean value 0 and the standard deviation 1; they have no dimensions. If x is a raw value, $\bar{x}$ the arithmetic mean of distribution of x and s its standard deviation, then $z = (x - \bar{x})/s$. Standard scores allow the comparison of performances in different tests, but only in relation to a standard sample applied to the calculation of $\bar{x}$ and s; they are therefore dependent upon distribution. See *Test theory*. *A.R.*

Standards, sexual. Attitudes and values which define sexual behavior. The term and classification of sexual standards were originated by Reiss (1960) and are based on attitude data from empirical surveys in the USA. Reiss distinguishes from sexual standards: (*a*) *abstinence* (q.v.), (*b*) orthodox and traditional *dual morality* (q.v.), (*c*) *permissiveness with affection*: heterosexual relationships are permitted on the basis of love without having to be directly connected with marriage. (*d*) *Permissiveness without affection:* heterosexual relationships are accepted unconditionally. In a later publication (1967) Reiss reduced the standards to a one-dimensional scale: "restrictiveness-permissiveness".

Bibliography: Reiss, I. L.: Premarital sexual standards in America. Glencoe, Ill., 1960. **Id.:** The social context of premarital sexual permissiveness. New York, 1967.

J.F.

Stanford Intelligence Test. Stanford-Binet tests in the 1937 edition. The procedure applies the well-known Binet model of arrangement of tests according to age order. The calculation of intelligence age and intelligence quotients likewise takes place in the traditional form. The tests are used for children from 3–14, and without differentiation for adolescents and adults. *P.S.*

Stationary wheel illusion. If a moving object is illuminated intermittently at such a rate that it is always in exactly the same position during the illumination, then it will appear to be stationary. This stroboscopic technique is used in industry to obtain a stationary view of moving parts without having to stop them moving. Before the availability of stroboscopic light, this phenomenon was sometimes observed when a wheel happened to move at the right speed behind a fence, the slits in the fence providing the intermittent view. *C.D.F.*

Statistic. Statistics are units of measurement which are calculated from sample observations. The parameter which can be estimated by statistics corresponds to statistics in the population. Statistics often in use are, for example, the arithmetic mean $\bar{x}$ and the standard deviation s. *A.R.*

Statistical sign test. A non-parametric technique by means of which two independent samples may be tested for differences in regard to their central trend. It is indicated when the samples are observed under different conditions, and these observational data can be grouped in pairs.

Bibliography: Dixon, W. J. & Mood, A. M.: The statistical sign test. J. Amer. Statist. Assoc., 1946, *41*, 557–66.

H.-J.S.

Statistical certainty. The probability which an estimate or an assertion made on the basis of statistical methods has of being correct. The

opposite of statistical certainty is probability of error. They are mutually complementary to 100%.
A.R.

Statistical inference. That branch of mathematical statistics (q.v.) concerned with the inferences possible in respect of a population on the basis of sample observations. Procedures for estimating credibility intervals and hypothesis testing form part of statistical inference.
A.R.

Statistics. 1. *General.* Given a set of elements and a variable, the association of a specific number or percentage of elements from the set with each value of the variable in such a way that only one value of the variable corresponds to a particular element is a basic aspect of statistics. A distinction is made between descriptive and inductive (analytical or sample) statistics. Descriptive statistics is concerned with finite values of real quantities, e.g. the number of workers in a country classified by profession or region, whereas inductive statistics considers the actual quantities as samples taken from a basic group (in the form of random samples) to allow the methods of probability calculation to be used.

Three developments in the history of statistics deserve especial mention: the theory of measurement errors formulated in the law of P. S. Laplace and F. K. Gauss, F. Galton's application of statistical concepts to the biological sciences, and Fisher's theoretical innovations. More recently, computers have facilitated the development of complex methods.

2. *Fundamental concepts of statistics.* (*a*) Distributions of a variable. Given a set of elements E and a variable x, the distribution of x in E is represented graphically by plotting a *histogram* (q.v.). It is assumed that the values are discontinuous either because of their effective nature or by dividing them into categories. The values are entered on an axis, and each of them corresponds to a segment which forms the base of a rectangle whose height is proportional to the number of associated elements E. A number calculated from the values X in E is a statistic (this term was proposed by Fisher; it is often referred to as a *parameter*). For a cardinal variable, the commonest statistic is the mean $\bar{x}$ of the values for X from all the elements of E. With ordinal variables, we consider the *median* (*central value*), i.e. the value of X on either side of which there are identical numbers of smaller and larger values. These statistics are said to measure the *central trend* (or tendency). There are also *dispersion statistics. Variance* is the mean value of the squares of the deviations from the mean; its square root, which has the advantage that it can be expressed in the same unit as the variable, is the *standard deviation.* Other dispersion measurements must be used for non-cardinal variables, e.g. entropy in the case of a nominal variable (see *Information theory; Communication*): $H = -\Sigma f_i \log f_i$, where f_i is the frequency of the values for X; this number is alone in having the properties expected of a dispersion measurement in this case. In addition, the central moment can be defined for a cardinal variable; the central moment of the order r is the mean value of the r-th power of the deviations from the mean, i.e. μ_r; the quotient μ_3/σ^3 is often taken to measure the asymmetry of the distribution (gestalt parameter).

Let us consider E from the standpoint of inductive statistics as a random sample, extracted from a basic set U; we can then define the distribution of X in U by working from a frequency distribution in which the area located between the curve and the ordinates of two random points X_1 and X_2 on the abscissa corresponds to the proportion of elements X of U for which X is situated between X_1 and X_2 (this is the case with a cardinal and continuous variable). We then define the mean μ as the mathematical expectation of X, the variance as the mathematical expectation of $(X - \mu)^2$, and the centered moment of the order r as the expectation of $(X - \mu)^r$. These concepts can also be applied to the discontinuous case by associating the corresponding frequency with each value X. Among the frequency distributions (q.v.), standard distributions are particularly important. Their density function is dependent on the two parameters μ and σ (see *Standard deviation*); μ is also the abscissa of the axis of symmetry of the distribution and $\mu \pm \sigma$ the abscissa of the points at which its direction changes. The curve is asymptotic to the X axis. If the variables X are replaced by the variables $\frac{X - \mu}{\sigma}$, we obtain the standardized distribution (mean = 0, standard deviation $\sigma = 1$), for which tables are drawn up showing, e.g., that 95% of the elements have values between -1.96 and $+1.96$, and 99% of the elements values between -2.58 and $+2.58$. Other highly important distributions can be derived from the standard distributions: the sum of the squares of ν standardized independent standard variables is known as the χ^2 distribution with ν degrees of freedom; if χ^2_ν with ν degrees of freedom and $\chi^2_{\nu^1}$ with ν^1 degrees of freedom are distributed independently, the function

$$F(\nu,\nu^1) = \frac{\chi^2_\nu/\nu}{\chi^2_{\nu^1}/\nu^1}$$

is known as Snedecor's distribution with ν and ν^1 degrees of freedom; the distribution of the variables $t = \sqrt{F(1,\nu)}$ is a Student distribution with ν degrees of freedom.

(*b*) Special *discontinuous distributions*. If n balls with two colors and invariable composition are drawn from an urn, the probability of drawing r balls of one color with proportion p is $C^r_n p^r q^{n-r}$, in which $q = 1 - p$; the distribution of the value r is known as the *binomial distribution* (q.v.); its mean is np and its variance npq. Poisson's curve is another significant distribution. It is obtained by assuming that $p = \frac{m}{n}$ with m constant and n tending to infinity; it is then clear that

$$C^r_n p^r q^{n-r} \rightarrow \frac{m\, e^{r-m}}{r}$$

The mean and variance of a Poisson distribution are both equal to m.

In applied psychology (q.v.), special methods of standardization are frequently applied to empirical distributions (stepped scaling); the variables, e.g. test performance results, are often only ordinal. This fact is utilized to convert the distribution into a step scale by suitable methods of conversion. If the distribution has a rectangular form and ten subdivisions are sufficient, we obtain a decile scale. This is obtained by fixing the criterion X_1 in such a way that ten percent of the testees have a better performance, X_2 in such a way that twenty percent have a better performance, and so on. Greater precision can, of course, be obtained with a centile scale. If the selected form is a standard distribution, we obtain a standardized scale; for example, with the following percentages: 4.0%, 10.6%, 22.7%, 40.2%, 59.8%, 77.3%, 89.4%, 96.0%, we should obtain a standard scale with nine classes (stages). This procedure enables, e.g., the *profile* of an individual to be recorded in a set of variables. Comparison of the performances for two variables is meaningful since it expresses the classification in a given population. The stepped scale provides an interpretation of an isolated performance result with reference to the population as a whole.

(*c*) *Multivariate distributions*. Let us first consider an example with two variables X and Y. In the (X, Y) plane, each element in the set E is represented by a point M and the resultant system of points is the dispersion or correlation diagram. The distribution of Y values corresponding to a given X value is known as the *partial* distribution of Y for this particular X value; the distributions of all X or Y values are *marginal* distributions. If we have a straight line D on the surface and consider the distance Mm, i.e. from M to this line, calculated parallel to OY, the line for which the $\Sigma\, Mm^2$ values are least is known as the line of least squares; its gradient is:

$$a = \frac{\Sigma (X - \bar{X})(Y - \bar{Y})}{\Sigma (X - \bar{X})^2}$$

in which $\bar{X}$ and $\bar{Y}$ are the means of the marginal distributions. This gradient is the regression coefficient from Y to X. If the variance of the distribution of Y is given, the lines of the least squares will match all the more accurately, the closer the absolute value of

$$r = \frac{\Sigma (X - \bar{X})(Y - \bar{Y})}{\sqrt{\Sigma (X - \bar{X})^2 \Sigma (Y - \bar{Y})^2}}$$

approximates to 1. r is known as the *correlation coefficient*. Inductive statistics distinguishes between the area of the frequency distribution of (X, Y), the partial distributions and the marginal distributions. If $\bar{Y}_x$ is the mean of the partial distribution of Y for a value of X, the equation $\bar{Y}_x = f(X)$ is the *regression* equation from Y to X, and the curve representing it is the regression line from Y to X. The most important distribution of two variables is the *bivariate standard distribution.* In addition to the product-moment correlation coefficient referred to above, there are other measurements of dependence, e.g. the *biserial, tetrachoric* and *Spearman's* correlation coefficients (see *Correlational techniques*). The regression equation from Y to X also enables Y to be forecast from X. If the regression is linear, the quality of the forecast is measured by the correlation coefficient r. Generalizing, a forecast is made of a variable z—starting from n variables—when the distributions of these variables are standardized and the regression is linear. The coefficients of the regression equation are the standardized coefficients of the partial regression and the accuracy of the forecast is measured by the multiple correlation coefficient. Partial correlation coefficients measure the association between two variables when the influence of one or more variables has been eliminated. Let us assume n variables in a set of N elements (designated in this case as subjects). Using matrix terminology, let Z be the matrix (n, N) of the values of the standardized variables and R the matrix of the intercorrelations (with 1 in all the fields of the diagonals). We now obtain $R = \frac{ZZ'}{N}$ (X′ is the transposed value of X). Let R* be a symmetrical real matrix with the order (n, n) of rank r (which need not necessarily only contain 1 in the diagonals); the determination of a real matrix F so that FF' = R* is then defined as factorizing R. F necessarily has the rank r. In factor analysis we look for diagonal elements which reduce r to a minimum. Thurstone and Hotelling have proposed solutions to the above equation. We obtain the solution by linear rotation (conversion) of the axes.

(*d*) *Methods of estimation.* From now on we shall be concerned solely with the statistics of samples. Let us assume a basic set, in which a variable X is present in standard distribution, with a mean value and a standard deviation. These are parameters which we wish to estimate by starting from a sample of N elements. This sample is one of the random samples of N elements which can be taken from the basic set under consideration. Let $\bar{X}$ be the (statistical) mean value of such a sample. For the population as a whole, $\bar{X}$ is normally distributed around the mean value μ, with a standard deviation $\frac{\sigma}{\sqrt{N}}$. If N is infinitely great, $\bar{X}$ tends toward μ. In such a case, $\bar{X}$ is said to be a *consistent* estimation of μ. In addition the mean value of the distribution of $\bar{X}$ is the parameter μ. In such a case, X is said to be an estimation of μ which is true to expectation. The standard deviation $\frac{\sigma}{\sqrt{N}}$ is known as the mean error (standard error) of the mean value, and gives information on the effectiveness of the estimation. For 95% of the samples, the interval $(\bar{X} - 1.96 \frac{\sigma}{\sqrt{N}}, \bar{X} + 1.96 \frac{\sigma}{\sqrt{N}})$ contains the parameter μ. This interval is known as the confidence range, with a threshold of $P = 0.05$, and its limits are known as "confidence limits" on this threshold. In practice these limits are calculated by replacing σ by its estimated value $\hat{\sigma}$. Fisher has developed a technique known as the *maximum likelihood method* for obtaining the most effective statistic, if it exists. It can be shown, e.g. that to obtain an estimate of variance σ which is true to expectation, $\Sigma (X - \bar{X})$ must be divided by $N - 1$ rather than by N.

(*e*) *Statistical significance tests.* Let us now consider the difference d between a statistic and a norm, or between two statistics. Let us assume that $d = X - \bar{X}'$ is the difference between the means of two samples. We now make the *null hypothesis*, i.e. we assume that the basic sets of the two samples have the same mean value. If we use additional hypotheses (e.g. that the two basic sets follow a standard distribution and have the same variance) to determine the sample distribution of d, it is possible to indicate the limits of an interval in such a way that 2.5% of the subjects are situated outside it on the right and 2.5% on the left (bilateral test). If the empirical value of d is situated outside this interval, we say that the null hypothesis is rejected or that the difference on the $P = 0.5$ threshold is significant (by which we mean the risk that the null hypothesis is correct and that the empirical value is one of the 5% groups which would normally fall outside the limits). A test of significance has been made. Some significance tests require no additional hypotheses concerning the forms of distribution; they are referred to as "*non-parametric*" tests (q.v.). Conventional parametric tests use the standard distribution, the "Student's distribution" (comparison of mean values), the Snedecor distribution (see *Variance, analysis of*) and the X^2 distribution (frequency comparison).

Statistics are particularly important in psychology because of the variability of psychological measurements (especially inter-individual measurements). See *Mathematical psychology; Test theory; Factor analysis.*

Bibliography: **Cramer, H.:** Mathematical methods of statistics. Princeton, 1945. **Faverge, J. M.:** Méthodes statistiques en psychologie appliquée. Paris, 1960. **Ferguson, G. A.:** Statistical analysis in psychology and education. New York & London, [3]1971. **Fisher, R. A.:** Statistical methods for research workers. Edinburgh, 1954. **Glass, G. V. & Stanley, J. C.:** Statistical methods in education and psychology. New York & London, 1970. **Guilford, J. P.:** Fundamental statistics in psychology and education. New York, 1958. **Kendall, M. G. & Stuart, A.:** The advanced theory of statistics. London, Vol. 1 1963; Vol. 2 1961; Vol. 3 1966. **Lewis, D. G.:** The analysis of variance. Manchester, 1971. **McCall, R. B.:** Fundamental statistics for psychology. New York & London, 1970. **McNemar, Q.:** Psychological statistics. New York, 1955. **Minium, E. W.:** Statistical reasoning in psychology and education. New York & London, 1970.

J. M. Faverge

Stato-acoustic sense organ. Fluid-filled parts of the inner ear (cochlea and basilar membrane) and of the organ of balance (the semicircular canals, sacculus and utriculus). Starting at the corresponding sense cells (ear: organ of corti; organ of balance; *cristae* or *maculae*) nerve fibers (*nervus cochlearis* and *nervus vestibularis*) meet in the *nervus statoacusticus*, the VIIIth brain nerve. The central nervous processing areas are, however, separate in respect of sense of balance and hearing. *M.S.*

Statoliths. The statolithic organ consists of a sack (*sacculus*) in the petrosal bone of the skull, which is linked with the semicircular canal system and is full of *statoliths* (small grains on the sensory cilia of the statolithic organ). When the head is in a perpendicular position these press on the cilia of their base on the floor of the sack. *E.D.*

Status arises in the process of group formation, and is based upon the differentiation of roles (q.v.) and the division of social power (in animals it is called the "pecking order"). It has a decisive influence on the interaction and communication of the group.

Through his status each individual is allotted a sphere of action. According to the type of group, status may be one-dimensional, i.e. based on a single criterion of status (e.g. military ranks) or multi-dimensional, i.e. based on several criteria of status (e.g. "high" society).

In groups with multi-dimensional status criteria, a member may have a high status in one respect and a relatively low status in another. In these cases there is usually a tendency for the two positions to draw together (Benoit-Smullyan, 1944), i.e. an attempt is made to bring the lower position up to the level of the higher (e.g. a newly rich person seeks to raise his educational and cultural level to that of his purse.)

Variables which determine the social status of a person are similar to those which determine his level of *social power*.

Bibliography: Benoit-Smullyan, E.: Status types and status interrelations. American sociological Review, 1944, 9. **Whyte, W. F.:** Street corner society. Chicago, 1943. *A.S.-M.*

Status orgasmus. Sigusch gave this name to an orgasmic form of reaction, first recorded physiologically by Masters & Johnson, which objectively and subjectively accompanies the highest intensity. *Status orgasmus* was observed only in women, lasts 20 to more than 50 seconds and is to be conceived as either a series of orgasms rapidly succeeding each other or as a long-drawn-out orgasmic episode.

Bibliography: Masters, W. H. & Johnson, V. E.: Human sexual response. Boston, 1966. **Sigusch, V.:** Exzitation und Orgasmus bei der Frau. Stuttgart, 1970. *V.S.*

Stencil Design Test. A non-verbal intelligence test (individual test) developed by G. Arthur. Tests are available with various difficulty gradings and may be used on subjects above the age of six. S. must reproduce geometrical patterns (designs) by superimposing paper stencils. There are two forms of test, one with colored and one with black and white materials. Standard values are available for each age group. *F.Ma.*

Step size. A term for the size of a learning step which can be measured in (typewriter) strokes in the average time taken to work through it or by the contents seen as transinformation of the basic text.

Step size in teaching programs (q.v.) of the Skinner type (non-branching q.v.) amounts to an average of 200 typewriter impressions, or to 20–40 seconds for working through, or to 10–15 bits (q.v.) of medium semantic information. With teaching steps in branching programs the size is on average five times as large. See *Instructional technology*. *H.F.*

Stereokinesis. The perception of the three-dimensionality of an object induced by its movement. Experiments have shown that the shadow of certain three-dimensional solids will only be perceived as three-dimensional when the object is in motion. It has also been found that for the moving shadow to have this three-dimensional quality it must contain contours or lines which change length and direction simultaneously. *C.D.F.*

Stereophonia. The sensation of the direction of sounds and hence three-dimensionality in the experience of sounds depends on the subtle difference in the sounds reaching the two ears (see *Differential running time*). Hence an illusion of fully three-dimensional sound (stereophonic sound) can be produced by sounds recorded by two microphones simulating the two ears. *C.D.F.*

Stereoscope. A viewing instrument through which two different stimuli (e.g. pictures) can be presented simultaneously, one to each eye. If the two stimuli are *anaglyphs*, i.e. disparate in the same way that the two retinal images are when a three-dimensional scene is viewed, then they will fuse to give an impression of *visual depth*. The easiest way to obtain anaglyphic pictures is by use of a *stereoscopic camera*, which takes two slightly different pictures of the same scene simultaneously through lenses separated by the same distance as the two eyes are apart. *G.D.W.*

Stereotactic techniques (syn. *Stereotaxic methods*). Methods used in human medical diagnosis and therapy by which potential variations from predictable structures, located by means of a probe, can be traced back and eliminated. The method is based on a pattern used in animal experiments, developed by Horsley & Clark around 1910 and introduced to human medicine in 1947 by Spiegel & Wyels.

Atlases of the brain provide the basis of stereotactic techniques derived from opened brains. Points can be selected from a map which are related to certain basic lines. After the patient's cerebral ventricle has been filled with air, the relationship between point, basis and lines is ascertained with standard X-rays. When the patient's brain and the atlas brain have been arranged in relation to each other, real values are obtained in respect of the patient's points. Two developments of stereotactic methods are (*a*) *focussed proton-beam elimination* of a point which in its precision resembles the usual stereotactic procedure, without any further surgical technique being necessary; (*b*) "*chronically*" *implanted electrodes:* with these a large number of electrodes, up to 60 per brain, with a diameter in each case of 100μt can be left in the brain for up to two years. During this time electric brain currents can be observed in relation to behavior, and elimination can thus be controlled and followed more exactly.

Recently stimulation has been conducted telemetrically by these deep electrodes, i.e. without a wire connection, with patients living in completely natural circumstances. The indications are mainly in Parkinsonism (q.v.). Tremor and rigor experienced in this illness can be removed almost equally easily, but not drive disorders. Other disturbances of movement, e.g. *torticollus spasticus*, *hemiballism*, essential tremor, can also be treated by stereotactic methods. The procedure was used at an early stage in psychiatric disturbances and indeed in schizophrenia (q.v.), compulsive illnesses, etc. The non-specific therapeutic effect consists partly in a form of leucotomy: the original nuclei of the tracts, which are cut in leucotomy, are destroyed. Unlike the effects of leucotomy, the side-effects of stereotactic techniques are slight, with a somewhat similar therapeutic sequel. The possibilities of application in psychiatric disorders, however, relate to a specific effect in relatively easily isolated functional structures of the brain, e.g. within the so-called limbic system, when elimination takes place in the amygdalum, fornix, and other points.

Psychiatric indications will probably increase in the future. If this proves to be the case the method of chronic implantation, with its independence of the operating theater and with the possibility it allows of observing the patient under natural conditions, offers substantial prospects of psychiatric treatment. For example, methods have been devised which allow patients to stimulate themselves in different regions of the brain; these are similar to the methods used in animal experiments by Olds. With these, pleasurable and unpleasurable centers were found, as in animal experiments, but excluding the appearance of excessive additive excitation. Drugs (see *Psychopharmacology*) were injected by micro-cannulae, implanted chronically, and at the same time permanent electrodes were applied to diverse regions of the brain. The many individual results of these experiments show clearly the first elements of a coherent therapy (Heath & Mickle, 1960). Surprisingly, the side-effects of this technique are slight, and consist essentially in negligible and transient memory disturbances and in the possibility of bleeding, which according to past experiments (more than 10,000) occurs in less than 1% of cases. It has been said that side-effects in chronic implantations are less than in normal stereotactic treatment (Bechterewa *et al.*, 1969). In addition to the direct clinical effects, new approaches to an understanding of the brain (q.v.) can result from these diagnostic and therapeutic techniques. Here anatomical, neurophysiological and psychological structural areas are directly linked with each other, and structural equivalences are already apparent between neurophysiological and psychological areas, for example in the sense that relationships exist on both sides which obey probability functions rather than deterministic controls. In this way, monistic conceptions capable of precise formalization form the basis of clinical and experimental "mind-body" research.

Bibliography: Bechterewa, N. P., Bondartschuk, A. N., Smirnow, W. M. & Trochatschow, A. J.: Physiologie und Pathophysiologie der tiefen Hirnstrukturen des Menschen. Berlin, 1969. **Heath, R. G. & Mickle, W. A.:** Evaluation of seven years experience with depth electrode studies in human patients. Electr. Studies on the unaesth. brain. New York, 1960. **Mundinger, F. & Riechert, T.:** Die stereotaktischen Hirnoperationen zur Behandlung extrapyramidaler Bewegungsstörungen und ihre Resultate. Fortschr. Neurol. Psychiat., 1963, *31*, 1–120. **Spiegel, E. A. & Wycis, H. T.:** Stereoeucephalotomy. New York, 1962. **Umbach, W.:** Elektrophysiol. und negative Phänomene bei stereotaktischen Hirnoperationen. Berlin & New York, 1966.

M. Adler

Stereotype. A term whose meaning varies. It is most commonly used in the sense formulated by M. Jahoda among others, and according to which a stereotype denotes opinions about classes of individuals, groups or objects which are "preconceived", i.e. which do not derive from new judgments of each single phenomenon but are pattern-like forms of perceiving and judging. Accordingly, the Germans, for example, are hardworking and negroes are musical, etc. But beyond this common denominator, emphases differ.

Stereotypes can be examined as to origin, when expressly *defined as group judgments*, i.e. they are judgments on which a sufficiently large number of the members of a group (q.v.) or a social category are agreed; for this reason Sherif & Sherif, 1969 called them *a priori group stereotypes*, and placed them in the context of relations between groups.

Emphasis can also be placed on the element of truth in the stereotype. In this case stereotypes are often defined as over-simplified concepts which are false for the reason that they are over-generalized (Allport, 1955; Katz & Stotland, 1959; Lindgren, 1969; Hilgard & Atkinson, 1967; Morgan & King, 1966). Arguments against this are: (*a*) whether a reason is right or wrong can only be decided when there is sufficient knowledge. But this knowledge does not often exist. What, however, is certain is that all people's ideas, in so far as they have been generalized, are more or less false. One could however adhere to the evaluation of opinions from the aspect that as a rule certain knowledge of any subject is too scanty or that general experience shows that the subjects judged are as a rule too variable to justify a relatively simple and unchangeable judgment in the form of a stereotype (Katz & Stotland, 1959). Of course, the concept then becomes inflationary since it holds good for all everyday opinions.

(*b*) Investigations, however, show that stereotypes are by no means necessarily false. For instance, comparisons of studies of the intelligence of Americans seemed to show that American negroes on average have a lower IQ than whites (see *Abilities*). Admittedly, differentiated studies might show that this result is not due to race but, among other factors, to the conditions of life of the testees, for as a rule these are far more unfavorable for negroes. In this connection, Pettigrew (1964) speaks of a self-fulfilling prophecy: the opinion held about a population group influences the behavior shown to this group, and this behavior in turn provokes in the group the alleged behavior. For example, because negroes are held to be less intelligent, they do not need such good schools, and because they are not given such schools, they have less chance to develop and so stay less intelligent. It is clear that on the one hand opinions about others may be perfectly correct, but it is also clear that public opinion and the kinds of behavior resulting from it have a part in determining the behavior of the relevant group and thus bring their influence to bear on the social system.

(*c*) Whether a stereotype is appropriate is shown not only by its agreement with a fictitious "reality" but is dependent on the background to the judgment in a particular instance. For certain questions the precise knowledge of a certain subject may be necessary, for other questions it may be superfluous, indeed even confusing. It is certain that everyone must generalize, for events or persons do not return in all their detail, but as long as we cannot discern any repetitions, we cannot plan for the future and anticipate it (Brown, 1965). How sharply individual objects are to be delineated must therefore be determined by the aims of the individual concerned. In an extreme case a stereotype alone may be taken as a justification for the oppression of a certain social group; then very different evaluations are possible, depending on whether one thinks of the appropriateness to reality of the judgment or of the element of justification it possesses.

Empirical statistical studies as a rule are based predominantly on the approach of group psychology (Katz & Braly, 1933; Gilbert, 1951; Buchanan, 1953; Sodhi & Bergius, 1953), which has nevertheless been heavily criticized.

(*a*) Eysenck (1950) showed (from a study on the lines of the classical work of Katz & Braly, 1933) that many subjects admit they only repeat clichés which do not represent their own opinion. And, in fact, even when a certain group are agreed about what they say, this cannot be taken as a proof that the corresponding judgment is widely shared.

(*b*) As Asch (1968) showed, an inquiry does not lead to any unequivocal pronouncement. It may be that the pronouncement is based on all the members of the category; it may, however, for example, be based only on a higher percentage of the group in some particular respect. See *Prejudice; Attitude*.

Bibliography: Allport, G. W.: The nature of prejudice. Boston, 1955. **Asch, S. E.:** Social psychology. Englewood Cliffs, [8]1965. **Brown, R.:** Social psychology. New York, 1965. **Buchanan, W. & Cantril, H.:** How nations see each other. Urbana, 1953. **Duiker, H. & Frijda, N.:** National character and national stereotype. Amsterdam, 1960. **Eysenck, H. J. & Crown, S.:** National stereotype: an experimental and methodological study. Int. J. Opinion Attitude Res., 1948, *2*. **Eysenck, H. J.:** War and aggressiveness. In: **Pear, T. H.** (Ed.): Psychological factors of peace and war. London, 1950. **Gilbert, G. M.:** Stereotype persistence and change among college students. J. Hbn. Soc. Psychol., 1951, *46*. **Hilgard, E. R. & Atkinson, R. C.:** Introduction to psychology. New York, [4]1967. **Hofstätter, P. R.:** Einführung in die Sozialpsychologie. Stuttgart, 1966. **Jahoda, M.:** Stereotype. In: **Gould, J. & Kolb, W. L.** (Eds.): A dictionary of the social sciences. New York, [3]1965. **Katz, D. & Braly, K. W.:** Racial stereotypes of one hundred college students. J. Abn. Soc. Psychol., 1933, *28*. **Katz, D. & Stotland, E.:** A preliminary statement to a theory of attitude structure and change. In: **Koch, S.** (Ed.): Psychology: A study of a science. Vol. 3, 1959. **Lindgren, H. C.:** Psychology of personal development. New York, [2]1969. **Lippmann, W.:** Public opinion. New York, 1922. **McDavid, J. W. & Harari, H.:** Social psychology. New York, 1968. **Morgan, C. T. & King, R. A.:** Introduction to psychology. New York, [3]1966. **Rice, S. A.:** Stereotypes: a source of error in judging human characters. J. Pers. Res., *5*, 1926. **Sherif, M. & Sherif, C. W.:** Social psychology. New York & London, 1969. **Sodhi, Bergius:** Nationale Vorurteile. Berlin, 1953. **Wells, W. D., Goi, F. J. & Seader, S. A.:** A change in a product image. J. Appl. Psychol., 1958, *42*. **Shuey, A. M.**: The testing of Negro intelligence. Lynchburg, 1958. **Pettigrew, T. F.**: A profile of the Negro American. Princeton, 1964. *J. Schenk*

Sterilization. 1. Making aseptic. Freeing a part of the environment of bacteria and other living matter.

2. Rendering an organism incapable of sexual reproduction on a more or less permanent basis, usually by means of surgical intervention (cf. *contraception*). The most simple methods currently employed are *vasectomy* (cutting and tying the vas deferens in males) and *salpingectomy* (tying the fallopian tubes in females), but *castration* (removal of the gonads, particularly the testes) and *hysterectomy* (removal of the uterus) also prevent reproduction. Only the first two of these methods are ever used as *birth control* techniques with humans: neither interferes to any degree with sexual performance or enjoyment. *G.D.W.*

Stern, William Louis. B. 29/4/1871 in Berlin; d. 27/3/1938, in Durham (North Carolina). Stern studied in Berlin, became a lecturer in Breslau and was a university reader until 1916. But it was Hamburg which he made into a center for psychological research. In 1916 he succeeded Wundt's (q.v.) pupil E. Meumann at the Hamburg Lecture Institute, was one of those most active in founding Hamburg University in 1919, set up the Psychological Department and Laboratory of Hamburg University (which in 1930 became the Psychological Institute of Hamburg University) and was its director until 1933. Then he was obliged because of racial persecution to emigrate to the USA; he lectured at Harvard and Duke universities.

Works. Stern was one of the great pioneers of modern psychology. His work in three volumes *Person und Sache* (1916, 1918, 1924) was, as its enlarged title "*System der philosophischen Weltanschauung*" says, primarily philosophical in essence, but formed the basis of his psychological thought; his *Allgemeine Psychologie auf personalistischer Grundlage* (1935) is proof of this. Stern attempted a synthesis of experimental and academic psychology, and defined psychology, in contrast to behaviorism (q.v.), as "the science of the individual as he experiences and is capable of experiencing", made a vital contribution with his theory of personalism to the solution of the problem of mind and mind-body (q.v.), disposed finally of "capability theory" with his concept of tendency, decided the problem of nature and nurture with his theory of convergence (q.v.), and built a bridge between elementarism and the theory of wholes, between natural science and philosophy. No less outstanding were his pioneer achievements in other departments of psychology; he was the founder of *Differentielle Psychologie* (1900, 1911); the term "intelligence quotient" (see IQ) was invented by Stern. Together with C. Stern he initiated research into developmental psychology with his study of child language (*Die Kindersprache*) 1907, and his psychology of early childhood (*Psychologie der frühen Kindheit*), 1914. Stern is regarded as the founder of applied psychology (q.v.): his two volumes *Beiträge zur Psychologie der Aussage* (Contributions to the Psychology of Testimony) 1903, belong to the history of the foundation of forensic psychology (q.v.); he advanced the cause of educational psychology (q.v.) by collaborating in the *Zeitschrift für pädagogische Psychologie* (joint editor, 1916) and the cause of the psychology of occupational and vocational by editing in part the *Schriften zur Psychologie der Berufseignung und des Wirtschaftslebens* (documents on the psychology of vocational aptitude and careers in industry), 1918.

Bibliography: Stern, W.: Selbstdarstellung. In: **Schmidt, R.** (Ed.): Die Philosophie in Selbstdarstellungen. Vol. 6, 1927; Das Psychologische Institut der Hamburgischen Universität in seiner gegenwärtigen

Gestalt. Leipzig, 1931. William Stern: Festschrift. Leipzig, 1931. **Stern-Anders, G.:** Bild meines Vaters und. **Cassirer, E.:** William Stern. In: **Stern, W.** (Ed.): Allgemeine Psychologie. The Hague, ²1950. **Pongratz, L. J.:** Problemgeschichte der Psychologie. Berne & Munich, 1967, 43 ff., 65 ff. *L.J.P.*

STH. Abb. for *somatotropic hormone* (q.v.).

Sthenic type. "A predominant feeling of superiority, power, mastery and energy, a tendency to arrogance, activity, ruthlessness, aggressiveness." Conflicts are tackled head on. Ant.: *asthenic* (q.v.). *W.K.*

Sthenoplastic type. Thin, fragile organism (see *Leptosome*). *W.K.*

Stigma. *A general functional disorder* of the circulation or of certain organs, caused by an abnormal sensitivity and eccentricity of the autonomic nervous system (e.g. tendency to faint) and by hysterical reactions (anesthesia, paralysis, convulsions, etc.).

Stigmatization: special hysterical reactions in the shape of certain visible markings on the body (e.g. cutaneous hemorrhage), which often appear as an indication of identification—in Christian cultural circles with the crucified Christ and his stigmata—and are considered by believers to be of supernatural origin (e.g. in the case of saints).

Bibliography: Biot, R.: Das Rätsel der Stigmatisierten. Aschaffenburg, 1957. *F.-C.S.*

Stilling test; Stilling charts. Devised by J. Stilling, an ophthalmologist in Strasbourg. Stilling-Hertel or Isihara charts are used to test color sensitivity in the normal eye. *K.H.P.*

Stimulants. Psychotropic drugs with a generally *activating effect*: they are *subjectively animating, tend to postpone sleep*, and usually *improve psychophysical performance*. Unlike the gradual and long-lasting effects of neurodynamics (q.v.), the effects of stimulants are rapid in onset, and limited to so many hours. When higher doses of stimulants are taken, appetite declines, tremor increases and longer sleeplessness can be induced. Chronic ingestion can lead to dependence (see *Drug dependence*) and psychotic states. Overdoses act to some extent like convulsive poisons. Stimulants possess a chemically diverse structure and are therefore difficult to classify; amphetamines (q.v.) are the most important group: e.g. methamphetamine hydrochloride = Desoxyn, Methedrine, Pervitin, etc., amphetamine sulfate = Benzedrine. Individual substances in other groups are: pemoline, caffeine (q.v.), methylphenidate hydrochloride (Ritalin), phenmetrazine hydrochloride (Preludin). Stimulants affect the central nervous system variously. Many stimulants also have effects on the autonomic nervous system (see *Psychopharmaceuticals and the ANS*); in this case the relationship of psychological to peripheral-autonomic effects varies considerably. Preparations whose main effects are on circulation and breathing are known as "analeptics" (q.v.). Substances which have a stimulating effect on the central nervous system but a convulsive effect even in relatively small doses (e.g. strychnine), are not counted as psychostimulants. Stimulants were used therapeutically before the development of antidepressives to improve mood and increase the motivation of depressive patients suffering from depression. They are now used mainly by healthy people to improve performance acutely (e.g. as a means of "doping") and temporarily to suppress fatigue and sleep, or to curb appetite. Psychological tests using stimulants (e.g. caffeine) were often carried out in the early stages of psychopharmacology (q.v.), but less after the development of antipsychotic and antineurotic drugs; they are now becoming useful again in research into learning and memory (see *Psychopharmacology*). Results in healthy people after one dose: mainly subjective activation; improvement of mood; feeling of improved performance, even when that is not so objectively (overestimation of one's own performance); in the sensorimotor field, effects are diverse. Activation is most clearly evident in purely sensory activities (e.g. flicker fusion frequency, afterimage sensitivity. The greater the degree of requisite motor security (e.g. steadiness of the hand), and the higher the dosage, the less performance is improved and the more it declines. The effects of stimulants depend on S.'s condition before administration, and particularly on the degree of previous stress and the amount of sleep deprivation (see *Sleep*). But they seem to be less dependent on habitual personality traits than the effects of tranquilizers (q.v.) and neuroleptics (q.v.). (See *Differential psychopharmacology*.)

Bibliography: Ehlers, T.: Zur quantitativen Differenzierung pharmakonbedingter Leistungsmotiviertheit. Arztneimittelforsch., 1966, *16*, 306–8. **Wenzel, D. G. & Rutledge, C.:** Effects of centrally acting drugs on human motor and psychomotor performance. J. Pharmaceut. Sci., 1962, *51*, 631–44. *K.-D.S.*

Stimulation. The effect of an internal or external stimulus in activating the nervous system. The additional stimulation of the brain by micro-electrodes is sometimes used as an independent variable in learning experiments. *H.Ro.*

Stimulus (Ger. *Reiz*). A variation in physical energy inside or outside an organism capable of influencing the afferent nervous system through receptors (when appropriate receptors exist), or (more narrowly defined) which activates a receptor (*stimulus transformation*). If the difference between these definitions is ignored, and it is assumed that a sensation must correspond to every external stimulus, a source of error (*stimulus error*) is present in investigations. The entire process from the activation of a receptor up to sensation is *stimulus processing*. To activate a receptor the stimulus must be between *stimulus intensity thresholds* and within *stimulus quality thresholds*. *Stimulus generalization* occurs when a conditioned response does not clearly succeed a narrowly defined stimulus intensity but a specific area on the stimulus continuum; *stimulus response generalization*, on the other hand, occurs when every stimulus of a distinct area of the stimulus continuum can evoke a specific response from an area of similar responses. If an individual stimulus is insufficient to release a sensation or a reflex, stimulation repeated over a certain period of time, or a combination of individual stimuli in the sense of *stimulus summation*, finally sets off the process. However, a diminished stimulus effect can occur by reason of *stimulus habituation* arising from, e.g., repeated presentation. (See *Arousal; Nervous system; Learning; Conditioning, classical and operant*.) *H.Ro.*

Stimulus conduction. The transmission of excitation from a receptor; arousal (q.v.).

Stimulus continuum. A hierarchical series of stimuli.

Stimulus sensation. See *Selective perception*.

Stimulus summation rule. Dummy experiments show that external and internal stimuli and excitations are calculated equivalently. Hence, given a state of acute readiness, minor external stimuli, such as dummies with a reduced number of apparent features, suffice for a response to be given. Movement seldom improves ineffective dummies significantly. The precise mode of calculation is unknown, but it is not a question of simple summation.

Bibliography: Seitz, A.: Die Paarbildung bei einigen Cichliden I. Z. Tierpsychol., 1940, *4*, 40–84. **Tinbergen, N.:** The study of instinct. London, [2]1969. *K.Fi.*

Stimulus word. A word requiring a response and presented acoustically or optically to S.

Stochastic dependence. The connection between two or more random variables. An investigation of stochastic dependence will lead to regression and correlational analysis. Two random events A and B are stochastically independent if the probability of their incidence is: P(AB) = P(A)P(B). See *Correlational techniques.* *A.R.*

Stochastic process. A process is stochastic when the sequence of events or procedures is governed by laws of probability. The events may be stochastically independent (e.g. radioactive decay) or stochastically dependent (e.g. the probability of a consonant occurring after a vowel). In communications theory the production of symbol sequences is analyzed by a stochastic process. Sequences of signs in which each sign preceding *r* codetermines the probability of the following sign constitute a Markov-chain *r* order. In 1913, A. Markov made statistical studies of associations of letters in printed texts. Letter sequences, like word sequences, are brought about by syntactic or semantic associations. Stochastic processes are characteristic of stochastic automata, whose behavior is not determined solely by momentary condition and input signals, so that output signals are determined to a greater or lesser extent by random processes. If no part is played by random processes, the stochastic automaton becomes a determined automaton. The theory of stochastic processes and of stochastic automata concerns psychology inasmuch as it allows models to be constructed which approximate behavioral phenomena. See *Communication; Correlational techniques; Information theory; Machine learning.* *K.W.*

Storage capacity. The maximum input capacity of a store (q.v.) is expressed in terms of the storage (the number of words or "bits") it can accommodate. *B.R.*

Store; storage. A store retains information for recall. Its function corresponds to that of memory (q.v.).

Analogue storage is distinguished from *digital* storage. In the former, items of information are preserved as analogue measurement values, in the latter as series of digits. Punched cards and strips represent *permanent* storage. After verification their contents can no longer be changed. The contents of impermanent storage media can be changed. *B.R.*

Strain. 1. In general, a process in a biological system accompanying any changed stability in relation to the maximum stability of that system (stress). **2.** In a narrower sense, a biological process which may be experienced as psychic tension and is manifested physiologically in vegetative tonus in connection with response to particular psychic demands. Psychic strain is sometimes understood more in the sense of response to a specific demand, and sometimes as a state of fatigue (q.v.) in the sense of a debilitation of powers and functions. Investigations suggest that biological systems tend to avoid prolonged over- as well as under-strain. Apart from use to refer generally to tension in or injury to a muscle or joint, the term is, however, restricted to popular usage. See *Stress.* *J.N.*

Strata theory (syn. *Layer theory; Levels of personality theory*). The strata concept was introduced into psychology in about 1920. It follows the principle of the Platonic theory of the mind, according to which the *logos* is associated with the head, the *thymos* ("heart") with the breast, and the *epithymia* (desire) with the abdomen. As early as 1916, Scheler (1923) distinguished (in reverse order) a *vital* or *body stratum*, a *psychovital stratum of emotions* and aspirations, and a stratum of *intellectual activities*. Freud (q.v.) tended not to use this image of "strata" or "layers", yet in his demarcation of a *sub*conscious, and not simply an *unconscious*, he implicitly postulated a layer theory (see *Id; Ego*). Klages, again not explicitly a strata theorist, adopted a similar approach. Kraus of Vienna (1926) postulated the existence of two personalities in one: the "*depth personality*" (born of the genetically older, "more original" "sectors" of the central nervous system) and the "*cortical personality*" (controlled by the genetically recent central nervous area, the cortex). In his theory of the character and person (after Plato), Lersch (1966) united the approaches of Scheler, Kraus and Freud and opposed the "endothymic basis" (q.v.) to the "noetic" or (more broadly conceived) the "personal superstructure" (1942). Later (1951), like Scheler, he added another "*vital basis*" beneath the "endothymic basis". The theory of stratification (analogously with geology) was taken to an extreme by Scheler's pupil Rothacker (1938), who based his approach mainly on Kraus's "dual personality". Rothacker divided the "depth personality" into "life-in-me", "animal-in-me", "child-in-me", and an emotional layer; the "cortical person" into a person or character layer, and an ego layer, the latter being a mere organizational center, expressed as an "ego point". Rothacker stressed his belief that stratification represents a developmental process in which the personality's early stages are not dissolved or replaced by later phases, but are superimposed upon, and effectively retained. Correspondingly, the "deep personality" (the "id", the "unconscious") must be regarded "as an independent creature, which, though 'below' higher centers, is in many cases directly expressed in the behavior of the whole person". On this supposition, Rothacker's theory (as he admits) conflicts with the hypothesis of the unity or wholeness of the personality.

Strata theory in these more recent formulations is partly accepted by such American authors as G. W. Allport and A. Gilbert. A. Wellek pointed out in 1941 that the image of a stratified pattern of personality must not be related unequivocally and unilaterally to the analogy of earth stratification, but to that of an onion (onion skin model): the "deep" layers ought to be called "*primitive layers*", and—if the term "person(ality)" were to be used at all—"*primitive person(ality)*" would be more appropriate. This term has been used by L. Holzschuher as the basis of a theoretical and "practical psychology" in which both the "deep" and the "primitive" person(alities) are invoked.

Wellek emphasized a "core character" or "kernel of personality" corresponding to the onion model, and divided it into four areas: *disposition* (*Gemüt*), *conscience*, *refined intuition* (*Gespür*) and *taste*. The "existence" of such "nuclei" is, according to him, demonstrated by the fact of a "character barrier" observable in hypnosis experiments when a conflict occurs between hypnotist and hypnotized, and the latter reacts to a suggestion that his "character" finds unacceptable (particularly one that is criminal or distasteful), by breaking even the most profound rapport. The existence of "disposition" cannot be wholly comprised in the statement that man "lives from" a deep or primitive personality; it is not a matter of the "higher life of the mind" in any quasi-vertical sense. The personality condition described as "heartlessness" or coldness of disposition signifies neither a lack of cortical control nor a lack of emotionality. For example, in the case of a murderer neither the "deep" person(ality) nor the cortical person(ality) is to be held responsible: i.e. there is no lack of control (which may on the contrary be superbly exercised, as in the case of malice), or of emotionality, not to mention still "deeper", i.e. lower, "strata". Affects in particular can "simmer", so to speak, "under the surface" of an apparently "cold" individual, who may be touchy, mistrustful, envious, jealous, prestige-conscious, spiteful, irascible and even—in certain circumstances—sentimental. When viewed as "stratified" in the conventional (one-dimensional) sense, such people (especially the insignificant petty criminal—can seem quite "all right". The inadequacy—the "gap" in the structure—does not appear in the simplistic schema.

In double stratification it is a question not only of two (or more) different strata, but of two further diverse dimensions: double stratification is "two-dimensional", i.e. "vertical-horizontal". "Superstructure", "animation", "intensification" and "profundity" depend on the "disposition", or "core", of personality. This is to be understood not only on the level of individual psychology but in terms of social structures. Like most other strata theorists, Rothacker tends to identify deep (i.e. primitive) strata with the "unconscious" (q.v.). Admittedly, in Rothacker's, and certainly in Scheler's sense, the "deep layers" are less precise and less conscious; in many ways consciousness is even inimical to them, as—above all—in Freud's theory. But this does not apply to the "core": disposition (as well as conscience and taste: both are connected with temperament) is a consciously protected and respected area in a well-formed personality. Disposition and refined intuition, however, are to some extent comprised functionally in Rothacker's "deep areas", e.g. in the "need for tenderness".

On the other hand, lower strata or layers are not in a position to formulate "prospective" intentions but only to take them over and carry them out at an appointed time. The locus of intention is that of *insight:* the ego (q.v.). As an interpretative model, "strata theory" has nevertheless been useful in many ways. By this method authentic and spurious expression (q.v.) and character have been traced by Lersch to agreement or disagreement between basis and superstructure, and by Wellek to accord or lack of it between core and casing, depths and surface. In addition, the concept of *identity* in recent American theories presupposes the stratification or even reconciliation of conscious and subconscious, though not in the sense of "pure" strata theory. A. Gilbert does adopt a stratification concept in his "*stratification discrepancy*", which is alleged to correspond to neuroticism (q.v.).

The present position of strata theory in regard to personality (q.v.) may be summarized as follows:

(*a*) Strata theory is a *genetic* theory: the strata develop out of one another.

(*b*) There are two basically different concepts of "depth" in use. The only legitimate candidate is the older one, which intends a "core" or "kernel" model.

(*c*) Equal attention to both dimensions of "depth" leads to a so to speak "two-dimensional" stratum uniting the *vertical* and the *horizontal*.

(*d*) A merely one-dimensional, "vertical" arrangement does not accord with the complexity of personality and its most decisive aspects.

(*e*) The conventional theory of a "deep person(ality)" confuses aspects of vertical and horizontal stratification.

(*f*) The (supposed) depth of a deep, i.e. primitive, person(ality) is *not identical* with the *unconscious*. The primitive layers and their functions may be conscious, and the high (like the core) layers and their functions may be unconscious.

(*g*) The "cortical person" is active even in deep hypnosis (as in deep sleep).

(*h*) It would seem to be unanimously accepted among "strata theorists" that the concept of a "stratum" or "layer" is an image of restricted applicability. See *Depth psychology; Dream; Consciousness; Traits; Type.*

Bibliography: David, H. P. & Bracken, H. von (Eds.): Perspectives in personality theory. New York, 1957. **Gilbert, A. R.:** On the stratification of personality. In: **David & Bracken,** *op. cit.*, 218–41. **Kraus, F.:** Allgemeine und spezielle Pathologie der Person, II. Leipzig, 1926. **Lersch, P :** Aufbau der Person. München, [11]1966. **Id :** The levels of the mind. In: **David & Bracken,** *op. cit.*, 212–7. **Rothacker, E.:** Die Schichten der Persönlichkeit. Leipzig, [2]1941. **Scheler, M.:** Wesen und Formen der Sympathie. Bonn, 1923. **Wellek, A.:** Die Polarität im Aufbau des Charakters. Berne, [3]1966.

A. Wellek

Stratton's experiment. 1. A classical experiment on perceptual learning conducted by G. E. Stratton, using himself as subject. For many days he went about wearing a pair of spectacles which inverted the visual world. One of the most remarkable findings was that as he began to reorient himself and regain visual-motor coordination, he reached a stage when the world no longer looked upside-down. When he eventually removed the spectacles he experienced a certain degree of disorientation again. Stratton's technique has since been widely adopted as an approach to the investigation of the developmental basis of perception. *G.D.W.*

2. The spectacles experiment as a method is described by Kohler (1951, 1956) In general, it consists of the transformation of visual signals by optical means (lenses, mirrors, prisms, color filters, etc.). The optical media are maintained for relatively a long time in front of the eyes by means of spectacles. The state of perception (q.v.) and behavior while looking through the spectacles (acquisition of new constancy standards), and for a brief period while looking without spectacles (negative aftereffects, spectacle effects), are observed and measured. A distinction is made between the experiment in which spectacles are worn continuously for days and weeks, while the subject goes about his affairs, and that in which habituation varies from a few minutes to several hours in a controlled stimulus situation According to the nature of the questioning, a spectacles experiment can be a reaction experiment (the criterion of observation and measurement is the improvement in the testee's sensorimotor behavior), or a perception experiment (acquired perceptual constancy), or both. Since the nineteen fifties, spectacles methods have been applied to new problems: sensorimotor coordinations (Held, 1962), problems of form and figure perception (Kohler, 1951; Hajos, 1965), etc.; major contributions have been made to perception theory, and a bridge has been built between perception research and biological and biocybernetic models (e.g., reafference principle, q.v., homoeostasis models, etc.).

Bibliography: Hajos, A.: Nacheffekte unter kovariierenden Reizbedingungen und deren interoculare und intersensorische Auswirkungen. In: **Heckhausen, H.** (Ed.) Bericht 24. Kongress Deutscher Gestalt Psychologen. Göttingen, 1965. **Held, R.:** Adaptation to rearrangement and visual-spatial aftereffects. Psychol. Beitr. 1962, *6*, 439–50. **Helmholtz, H. von:** Handbuch der Physiologischen Optik, Vol. 3. Leipzig, 1910. **Kohler, I.:** Über Aufbau und Wandlungen der Wahrnehmungswelt. Österreichische Akademie der Wissenschaften: philosophisch-historische Klasse 227/1. Vienna, 1951, 1–118. **Id.:** Der Brillenversuch in der Wahrnehmungswelt mit Bemerkungen zur Lehre von der Adaption. Zeitschrift experimenteller und angewandter Psychologie, 1956, *3*, 381–417. **Id.:** Interne und externe Organization in der Wahrnehmung. Psychol. Beitr., 1962, *8*, 259–64. **Stratton, G. M.:** Upright vision and the retinal image. Psychol. Rev., 1897, *4*, 182–7.

A.Ha.

Stream of consciousness. Experiences, recollections, feelings, aspirations, fancies, etc., seem to the individual to be a "stream" which, in the last resort, is independent of him. James calls this the "stream of consciousness".

Bibliography: James, W.: The principles of psychology.

V.M.

Stress. The term "stress" has been widely and indiscriminately used; its most precise definition is that of Selye (1950). He restricts the concept of stress to a characteristic physiological response, differentiating this from "stressors"—the agents which produce stress.

This bodily reaction is manifested through the symptoms of a general adaptation syndrome. When the stress is prolonged, the syndrome typically includes three stages: (*a*) an alarm reaction, including an initial shock phase of lowered resistance and a countershock phase, in which defensive mechanisms begin to operate; (*b*) a stage of resistance in which adaptation is optimal; and (*c*) a stage of exhaustion, marked by the collapse of the adaptive response.

The features of this reaction are organized around the pituitary-adrenal cortical axis. Selye describes the triad of the alarm reaction as enlargement of the adrenals, shrinkage of the thymus and lymph nodes, and gastrointestinal ulceration.

This, like Cannon's earlier proposal of a sympathetic nervous system/adrenal medulla stress reaction (Cannon, 1932), was made within the concept of systemic equilibration. The general effect of the stress syndrome appears to be the modification of bodily processes so as to make available the energy resources normally kept in reserve or used for other functions such as digestion or anabolism (Cofer & Appley, 1964). Selye describes antecedents of the stress concept in the Hippocratic view of disease not only as suffering but as toil: the fight of the body to restore itself. A recurring theme is a finite amount of "adaptation energy" which gets "used up" (Selye, 1950); or physiological and psychological integrative capacities which are taxed to the limit (Basowitz *et al.*, 1955).

The nature of pituitary-adrenal involvement has been much debated, and the physiological (hormonal, metabolic, and so on) mechanisms involved in the stress reaction have been extensively investigated (Goldstein & Ramey, 1957; Oken, 1967).

Attempts to extend Selye's idea of systemic stress to include psychological aspects have met with many problems. Firstly, the nature of stressors is very different: Selye discussed such systemic stressor agents as heat, cold, infections, intoxicants, injury, shock, and surgical trauma. The range of psychological stressors is so wide as to be virtually endless. Cofer & Appley argue that these are effective only when they threaten the life or integrity of the individual exposed to them. They offer a definition of stress as "the state of an organism when he perceives that his well-being (or integrity) is endangered and that he must elevate all of his energies to its protection" (Cofer & Appley, 1964, p. 453).

Secondly, the nature of the physiological reaction is not now seen as a general, well-defined pattern. The results of decades of research suggest that individual differences, styles, patterns of response and pre-potent tendencies lead to idiosyncratic response patterns. These may relate to inherited responsivity (for example, of the sympathetic nervous system [Eysenck, 1967]) and possibly to various personality characteristics which determine stress thresholds and stress tolerance.

Central issues in psychological stress are the conditions and processes (*a*) that lead the individual to differentiate between benign and damaging conditions, and (*b*) that determine the kind of coping behavior which ensues. Recent analyses emphasize the role of cognitive appraisal (Lazarus, 1966). Once a stimulus has been appraised as threatening, various methods of coping are adopted. Pribram (1967) has suggested that cognitive re-evaluation may obviate the necessity for overt behavioral adjustment: that is, an individual's appraisal of the situation can reduce the stress reaction.

When examined in a psychological context, the stress reaction must therefore take account of complex cognitive processes as well as physiological reactions, and feedback from the effects of these reactions. In such circumstances it is difficult to retain Selye's clear though perhaps over-simplified view of stress, and of late the meaning of the term has tended to widen again. For example it is often undifferentiated from anxiety, conflict, emotion, frustration, and arousal (q.v.).

Perhaps some order could be restored if more attention were paid to the time course of the physiological reactions, and to the original implication of a balance between catabolic and anabolic processes. We should discriminate between the immediate physiological disturbance produced by a stimulus, and a chronic, long-term stress reaction where basic physiological changes are produced which result in a detrimental shift in equilibratory processes. Psychological stresses of an inescapable kind may lead to a sustained stress reaction eventuating in tissue damage, disruption of adreno-cortical functioning, and psychosomatic disorder. This type of reaction differs from a neurotic reaction in which sustained tissue damage is avoided by some behavioral solution—for example, the use of escape mechanisms.

Bibliography: Basowitz, H., Persky, H., Korchin, S. J. & Grinker, R. R.: Anxiety and stress. New York, 1955. **Cannon, W. B.:** The wisdom of the body. New York, 1932. **Cofer, C. N. & Appley, N. H.:** Frustration, conflict, and stress. In: Motivation: theory and research. New York, 1964, 412–65. **Eysenck, H. J.:** Biological basis of personality. Springfield, 1967. **Goldstein, M. S. & Ramey, E. R.:** Nonendocrine aspects of stress. Perspectives in Biol. & Med., 1957, *1*, 33–47. **Lazarus, R. S.:** Psychological stress and the coping process. New York, 1966. **Oken, D.:** The psychophysiology and psychoendocrinology of stress and emotion. In: **Appley, M. H. & Trumbull, R.** (Eds.): Psychological stress. Issues in Research. New York, 1967. **Pribram, K. H.:** The new neurology and the biology of emotion. A structural approach. Amer. Psychol., 1967, *22*, 830–8. **Selye, H.:** Stress. Montreal, 1950.

I. Martin

Stress type. This type burdens the ego (q.v.) aspect of consciousness with slow or stubborn objection, especially noticeable in schizothymes. *W.K.*

Striate body (syn. *Corpus striatum*). A term applied collectively to the *nucleus lentiformis* (lenticular nucleus) and its parts, the *putamen* and *globus pallidus*, and the *nucleus caudatus* (caudate nucleus), all of which form part of the brainstem (q.v.). *E.D.*

Strivings (syn. *Aspirations*). According to Lersch (1954), "strivings" are human drives originating in the "endothymic basis" (q.v.) and directed to the attainment of definite aims; thus they are not indefinite instinctual impulses. Lersch speaks of strivings as the highest degree of drive experience. See *Strata theory*.

Bibliography: Lersch, P.: Aufbau der Person. Munich, [2]1962. *B.H.*

Stroboscope. An instrument for producing and observing *stroboscopic effects*, i.e. illusions of movement resulting from intermittent stimulus exposure such as that produced by a light flashing on and off. The most familiar example of this effect is that seen in Western movies when the wheels of a wagon are perceived to be moving backward. This occurs because the interval between successive picture-frame exposures is of such a length that each new position of the spokes is more parsimoniously seen as just behind the previous one, rather than in front of it. The stroboscopic effect can be employed as an indicator of the speed of rotation of an object, e.g. the ring of radial stripes surrounding the labels of some gramophone records which provide a check on the turntable speed. *G.D.W.*

Strong Vocational Interest Blank. One of the most widely used American *tests of vocational interests*, the 399 items of which (careers, preferences, career-related activities, etc.) have to be answered, chiefly along the lines of like-dislike, or to be placed in order of preference, after which they are evaluated diagnostically on the basis of their correlation with the relative answer requirements of a large number of different career groups.

Bibliography: Strong, E. K. & Campbell, D. P.: Manual for Strong Vocational Interest Blanks. Stanford, 1966. *H.H.*

Stroop word-color test. See *Color-word test.*

Structuralism. 1. Any theory (e.g. *strata theory,* q.v.) which conceives mind or personality in terms of its structure (q.v.). **2.** Atomism (q.v.). **3.** Gestalt psychology. **4.** A science of signs, and of systems of signs (see *Semantics; Sign and symbol*). **5.** The study of that which has a systematic nature: of any whole, one element of which cannot be altered without bringing about an alteration in all the other elements (see *Ganzheit*).

Bibliography: Ducrot, O., Qu'est-ce que le structuralisme? Paris, 1968. **Lévi-Strauss, C.:** Structural anthropology. New York, 1963. **Piaget, J.:** Structuralism. New York & London, 1971. *J.G.*

Structure. The underlying organization of components. Structure usually refers to the relationship between the components that make up some complex stimulus. These relationships are independent of the nature of the component parts: e.g. a melody has the same structure even if played in different keys. The concept of structure is central to gestalt psychology, since it emphasizes the organization of complex wholes rather than their component parts in isolation. Structure in its more general sense is also used in other areas of psychology, e.g. personality and memory. See *Ganzheit; Strata theory.* *C.D.F.*

Strychnine. A substance which stimulates circulation and breathing; an alkaloid, obtained from the seeds of *nux vomica,* it produces convulsions when taken in large doses. Because of this danger, strychnine is of very restricted therapeutic value. It has a strongly exciting action on the central nervous system, probably because it blocks inhibition systems. Recently it has been shown that strychnine, administered in subconvulsive doses, improves the retention performance of rats, but so far the mechanism of these improvements in memory has not been explained.

Bibliography: Dusser de Barenne, J. G.: Mode and site of action of strychnine in nervous system. Physiol. Rev., 1933, *13,* 325–35. **McGaugh, J.:** Drug facilitation of memory and learning. In: **Efron, D.** (Ed.): Psychopharmacology, 1957–1967. Washington, 1968. *W. Janke*

Study of values. A method devised by G. W. Allport and P. E. Vernon in 1931 to cover the range of interests, attitudes and values to be found in an individual. The test is based on the value philosophy of E. Spranger (life forms, 1925) with its six *a priori* value areas: theoretical, social, economic, political, esthetic and religious. The test consists of two parts with thirty or fifteen alternative or multiple choice questions. The six test scores, which can be combined to form a profile are interpreted according to standardized norms. The test-retest reliability ranges from r = 0.84 to r = 0.93. *Pointers of validity* are: the clear discrimination of selected careers by the test and successful predictions of the behavior of individuals in different tests.

Bibliography: Allport, G. W., Vernon, P. E. & Lindzey, G.: Study of values. Boston, 1960. *P.G.*

Stumpf, Carl. B. 21/4/1848 in Wiesentheid; d. 25/12/1936 in Berlin. Stumpf studied philosophy under Brentano (q.v.) in Würzburg and Lotze in Göttingen; he received his doctorate in Göttingen in 1868, was a lecturer in Göttingen from 1870 to 1873, and from then on held the following posts: 1873, professor in

Würzburg; 1879, professor of philosophy in Prague; 1884, in Halle; 1889, in Munich; from 1894 to 1921, in Berlin. In Berlin he founded the Psychological Institute of Berlin University, with F. Schumann and N. Ach as his assistants. When he retired in 1921, W. Köhler succeeded him in his Chair.

Stumpf was influenced by Brentano's act psychology (q.v.); his theoretical approach was directly opposed to that of Wundt (q.v.) and, together with Brentano, he ranks as the founder of *functional psychology*. He made a distinction between the act of hearing and the heard content. The study of functions was in his opinion the sole province of psychology, whereas the study of contents belonged more to phenomenology (q.v.). Going beyond Brentano, he subjected act psychology to experimentation for the first time. His functional approach was diametrically opposed to Wundt's emphasis on contents, and Stumpf was in continual conflict with Wundt. One such controversy was in regard to differing views of the nature of the introspective method (see *Introspection*).

Stumpf's most significant contributions to knowledge were in the field of the psychology of music (q.v.) and comparative musicology, which he may be considered to have established as a sub-discipline. He won special recognition for his treatise on the songs of the Bellakula Indians (*Lieder der Bellakula Indianer*, 1886), a pioneer study in comparative musicology, for his main two-volume work on the psychology of sound (*Tonpsychologie*, Leipzig, 1883–1890), and for his later work on the beginnings of music (*Die Anfänge der Musik*, Leipzig, 1911). His other contributions to psychology, however, are less important. He wrote, *inter alia*, a treatise on the psychological origin of the idea of space (1873), and he was responsible for a theory of emotion (q.v.), in which, proceeding from the James-Lange theory, he reduced the emotions to a special form of organic sensations—the "emotional sensations".

Among Stumpf's pupils (many of whom were opposed to his basic scientific position, which they criticized very strongly) were W. Köhler (q.v.), K. Koffka (q.v.), M. Wertheimer (q.v.), C. J. von Allesch, W. Poppelreuter and H. S. Langfeld.

Other writings: Psychologie und Erkenntnistheorie. Leipzig, 1891. Erscheinungen und psychische Funktionen. Leipzig, 1907. Die Sprachlaute: experimentellphonetische Untersuchungen nebst einem Anhang über Instrumental-Klänge. Berlin, 1926. Gefühl und Gefühlsempfindung. Berlin, 1928. Erkenntnislehre, Vols. 1, 2 (Ed. F. Stumpf). Leipzig, 1939–40.

Bibliography: **Langfeld, H. S.:** Carl Stumpf: 1848–1936. Amer. J. of Psychol., 1937, *49*, 316–20. **Murchison, C.** (Ed.): A history of psychology in autobiography. Vol. 1. Worcester, Mass. 1930, 389–441.

W.W.

Stupor. An inhibited or suppressed ability to respond due to psychic causes, although consciousness remains clear (and reflexes can be demonstrated). The most diverse inner states may underlie the external symptoms: apathy, inhibitions, terror; but there may also be a high degree of ambivalence and ambitendency. An "examination stupor" (see *Examination anxiety, neurotic*) is a recognized condition. Stuporous syndromes can be caused reactively or psychogenically, but they also occur in cases of brain diseases, epilepsy (q.v.), depression (q.v.), and schizophrenia (q.v.). *A.Hi.*

Stuttering. A speech impediment, sometimes equated with *stammering*, but strictly consisting in the rapid repetition of consonants and vowels at the beginning of words. Believed to be strongly influenced by emotional factors if not entirely psychogenic in origin. The incidence of stuttering is considerably higher in males than females, and there is some evidence that it is also associated with right hemispheric cerebral dominance. *G.D.W.*

Style. Mode of presentation. The term has a specific meaning in the "individual psychology" (q.v.) of Adler (q.v.), where "life-style" stands for the way feelings of inferiority are handled. Far-reaching attempts to rationalize personal style have been made only in regard to verbal style. E. Mittenecker attempted to develop the degree of perseveration of style as an instrument in clinical diagnosis. The use of computers to quantify stylistic characteristics in written tests has become a major feature of linguistic and literary research in recent years. See *Experimental esthetics; Literature and psychology; Music, psychology of.*

Bibliography: Wisbey, R. A. (Ed.) Uses of the computer in literary research. Cambridge, 1972. *B.H.*

S type. A characterization according to the typology elaborated by Jaensch (1929). The central concept is synesthesia (q.v.). It is a question of the simultaneous response of two senses to a single stimulus. "S" indicates an ability of this type to associate color and auditory impressions, i.e. to "hear" colors. Jaensch differentiates the "S type" from the "I type", or *integrated type* (q.v.), because of the more intense inner coherence in experience of the environment. The inner world dominates absolutely and is projected onto the outer world, hence the S type is also (as a "projective type") contrasted with the "receptive type" of the integrative series. *M.H.*

Subconscious. The subconscious is sometimes assumed to be identical with the "preconscious", and is then a part-system of the psyche (in addition to the system of "conscious" and "unconscious"). It includes all psychic contents, memories, motives and readiness to act which are (momentarily) not activated, but when required can always be reactivated. Unconscious psychic contents, on the other hand, can be activated only with difficulty and against the inner resistance of the person in question (Freud). The subconscious as the "co-consciousness" (Rohracher)—as a consciousness without an attention cathexis (Freud)—comprises those psychic contents which exist among already conscious contents and in cases of necessity are made conscious more readily than other subconscious contents. See *Consciousness; Unconscious; Depth psychology.*

Bibliography: Freud, S.: Introductory lectures on psycho-analysis. London, [2]1959. *W.T.*

Subject (abb. S.). The person or animal upon whom the experiment is being conducted. The subject is not expected to benefit personally from any treatment applied in the course of the experiment; at least if he does so it is purely incidental. *G.D.W.*

Subjective colors. If the eye is stimulated by intermittent white light at a frequency of approximately five impulses per second, it begins to see colors which are not highly saturated, and which follow one another with a certain regularity. A similar phenomenon, but with brighter color tones, results when a color top with white and black sectors is rotated at a speed of about forty r.p.s., i.e. in the stage before fusion (colored flicker).

Bibliography: Cohen, J. & Gordon, D. A.: The Prevost–Fechner–Benham subjective colors. Psychol. Bull., 1949, *46*. *G.K.*

Subjective stage. In dream interpretation, according to Jung (q.v.), the elucidation of dream images and events as representations of factors and situations within the dreamer. *W.T.*

Sublimation. According to Sigmund Freud (q.v.) a psychic process; according to Anna Freud, an inner defense (q.v.) mechanism, by means of which more primitive and socially less acceptable forms of motive gratification are replaced and then further developed by socially more acceptable forms. Hence a dauber may become an artist, a dissector of toys a surgeon, or a bawler a singer. If sublimation is to mean something more than the process of uninterrupted motive differentiation and correction of this process by people in the environment, then demonstrably greater renunciations of motive gratifications must be linked with especially unusual forms or degrees of sublimation. In practice, proof of this is often not possible in cases where sublimation is said to be present. Sublimation is related to socialization (q.v.) and enculturation: "We believe that civilization has been built up, under the pressure of the struggle for existence, by sacrifices in gratification of the primitive impulses, and that it is to a greater extent for ever being re-created, as each individual, successively joining the community, repeats the sacrifice of his instinctive pleasures for the common good. The sexual are amongst the most important of the instinctive forces thus utilized . . ." (Freud, 1929).

Bibliography: **Freud, A.:** The ego and the mechanisms of defence. London, 1937. **Freud, S.:** Introductory lectures on psycho-analysis. London, [2]1929. *W.T.*

Subliminal. Appertaining (e.g. "subliminal perception") to stimuli which cannot be perceived or distinguished under the given conditions; in particular, those which, though they cannot be consciously apprehended or named (e.g. because presented for too short a time), nevertheless give rise to either conscious or unconscious stimulus-specific effects.

Bibliography: **McConnell, J. V.** *et al.:* Subliminal stimulation: an overview. American Psychologist, 1958, *13*, 239–42. *W.H.*

Substance. 1. *History of the substance problem.* From the time of the Greek philosophers of nature, various aspects of this problem have come to the forefront of discussion: the material element as a bearer of substance; motion, change and development, especially in regard to living creatures; the question of essence (*ousia*). In addition to the theory of substance, the history of philosophy also features a substrate (*substratum; hypokeimenon*) theory. Heraclitus (536–470 B.C.) wrote of a substrate-less succession of things, and thought of it as most clearly "embodied" in the consuming movement of fire. Parmenides (*c.* 6th century B.C.), on the other hand, distinguished being from consciousness and explained thinking and being as wholly identical. Descartes made a distinction between conscious and spatial substances; Locke, as an empiricist, declared substance to be unknowable; Kant used it as a category and allowed it a metaphysical character; and Fichte gave it a secondary position in his theory of ideas.

2. *Substance and substrate.* Wundt (q.v.) brought about a change in the conception of substance by subjecting it wholly to a natural-scientific treatment. In physics and chemistry the term is used for any kind of matter. Such material substances, whether atoms, molecules, or compounds, are always entities. In biochemistry, substances which are changed in cell metabolism under the influence of enzymes, are known as substrates. In psychology, the substrates of cerebral and nerve cells are the most important.

3. *Present situation.* Recently, substantial being in the inorganic, organic and mental spheres has been more closely related. Physics does not stop at the detection of elementary particles, whose real existence can be revealed by special methods, but is constantly intent on passing new limits—possible only in terms of ever smaller hypothetical particles. This is a search for "what lies behind things"—for substance.

Similarly, biochemistry looks for the elements of living substance. Modern gene research has revealed the fundamental significance of desoxyribonucleic acid (DNA) for the individual development of all forms of life, and hence as a supportive principle for biological and psychological occurrence. But, here too, it has proved necessary to look for further bases, since DNA, like any other chemical compound, comes to be only by virtue of energy. The search for a prime base constantly comes up against certain limits; hence in modern psychology the substance problem has been obscured though not resolved, for it persists existentially. Inasmuch as characteristics of the nervous substrate have been detected which go to explain certain personality traits, and these characteristics have a general character, both somatologically and psychologically, the substance problem recurs for both areas simultaneously. Recent findings of Soviet psychological research conducted by B. Teplov emphasize this: "Whereas Pavlovian psychology postulated three main characteristics of the nervous system, i.e. intensity, mobility and equilibrium, with excitation and inhibition processes", recently the dominant conception has been that of an "equilibrium of the excitation and inhibition process as a relationship of two intensity characteristics of the nervous substrate". This "nervous substrate" is seen as a psychophysiological model of personality (q.v.); the characteristics of intensity, mobility and equilibrium are ascribed to it.

Independently of this Soviet research, in 1970 W. Arnold published a formula that arrived at the same basic factors in the motivational sphere: emotional tension (E), motivational intensity (I), inhibition (R). This gives the formula $I = E/R$, which is demonstrable in various modalities. The fact that these three factors tend in the same direction (and even coincide nominally) in neuropsychological research, i.e. empirically, and in theoretical considerations based on psychophysics (q.v.), allows one to suggest that the different scientific aspects derive from one and the same substantial unity and whole, which has specific rules within one and the same ordered system, different aspects of which are apprehended from time to time by research workers in diverse fields.

4. *Self, person and substance.* Dynamic psychology has tended to disregard the substantial approach. In reality, neither a functionally nor a motivationally oriented psychology can be concerned only with experience and behavior patterns, without taking into account the foundation that supports these modes of happening. Experiences and responsibilities are inconceivable without substance and substrate. Today, too, man is a questioner and a seeker in regard to the problem of substance. That and how he questions are psychological facts; why he questions is a philosophical question. Man seeks for causes and grounds of being and occurrence: in psychological terms, for the supportive principle of experience and behavior. In this perspective, it is not enough to see only drive (q.v.)—say, sexual drive—as a "spiritual" extreme from which all experience and behavior would develop; nor would reflexes or primary motives, or behavioral dispositions, suffice to explain the case. Neither molar nor molecular behaviorism (q.v.) can offer a satisfactory answer. From all these viewpoints there has been continual reflection and "self-observation" in an attempt to discover the substantial basis of things. Humanistic psychology (q.v.) identifies the *person* (q.v.) (Stern, C. Bühler), as a constitutional basis, with the self that bears all subjective experiences.

What are we to understand by "substance" in contemporary psychology? A supportive basic principle for all individual being and happening, the unity that establishes and makes observable in spatial and temporal reality all drives and motives, all action and permission. It is consistent in the true sense of the word. Within this consistency all these events and occurrences are related or diffugient. In the phenomena observed and described by psychology one thing persists: the individual person with his or her thus-ness (basic character) and specific constitution, with his or her self-ness, with his or her individually specific communication with the world of others, the co-world, and the world of objects, the environment. The many traits that the individual personal being displays in this process are externalities, or behavior patterns, which would, however, be impossible without a basic supportive principle: "*Substantia est id quod substat accidentibus*" (substance is that which underlies the accidents). See *General psychology; History of psychology; Philosophy and psychology.*

Bibliography: Arnold, W.: Person, Charakter, Persönlichkeit. Göttingen, [3]1969. **Id.:** Ein vorläufig-theoretisches Motivationsmodell more psycho-physico. Psychol. Beitr., 1970, *12*, 2. **Jordan, P.:** Schöpfung und Geheimnis. Oldenburg, [2]1971. **Monod, J.:** Chance and necessity. London & New York, 1972. **Nebylizyn, W.:** Die Haupteigenschaften des Nervensystems. Ideen des exakten Wissens, Wissenschaft und Techniks in der Sowjetunion. Stuttgart, 1971, *8*, 545–54.

W. Arnold

Substance P. A polypeptide isolated from extracts of tissues (brain, viscera) whose biological significance has not yet been explained. Substance P possibly acts as a transmitter (q.v.) in the central nervous system. High concentrations are found in the hypothalamus (q.v.), thalamus (q.v.) and basal nuclei. Substance P is one of those substances which most dilate the blood vessels; it also influences the smooth musculature. Its central effects have not yet been established, because not many investigations have been carried out with pure substance P. It probably plays a part in the transmission of sensory information. Pointers in this direction are an increase in substance P concentration under sensory stimulation, and the high content of substance P in the dorsal roots of the spinal cord.

Bibliography: Stern, P.: Substance P as a sensory transmitter and its other central effects. Ann. N.Y. Acad. Sciences, 1962, 403–14.

W.J.

Substitute formation. The formation of a substitute motive, action or satisfaction (gratification) to replace something that is intolerable for reasons of external situation or internal defense. Tolerance of this process is limited in the neurotic (see *Neurosis*), who is also less able to accept a substitute. According to psychoanalytical theory (see *Psychoanalysis*), a repressed motive is constantly searching for substitute objectives to allow its continuation. The conversion of the original motive, etc., into the substitute is effected with the aid of the mechanisms described in connection with "dream work". The "normal" individual generally has different appropriate and possible substitutes for an "urge" which cannot be satisfied for the time being, neurotic substitutes on the other hand, usually prove inadequate. This fact, as well as the neurotic individual's helplessness in a failure situation because of his inflexibility in the matter of choice, may be used to establish a distinction between the normal and neurotic structure. The neurotic symptom is a substitute for something which has been repressed or cannot be faced in reality because of a specific neurotic structure. See *Depth psychology; Dream; Instinct.*

U.H.S.

Substitute reactions (syn. *Substitute movements*). Not only intention movements and redirection activities but substitute reactions appear frequently in conflicts. The reaction is inhibited in regard to the initiator, and is abreacted onto a substitute: e.g. the appearance of a human in a herring-gull colony triggers off unmotivated attacks on other herring gulls. See *Conflict; Aggression.*

Bibliography: Bastock, M., Morris, D. & Moynihan, M.: Some comments on conflicts and thwarting in animals. Behaviour, 1958, *12*, 234–84.

K.Fi.

Substitution therapy. Treatment by means of the substitution of substances which the body itself is failing to produce, e.g. the administration of thyroxine (q.v.) in cases of cretinism (q.v.). *E.D.*

Substrate (syn. *Substratum*). **1.** Substance (q.v.). **2.** The subject of prediction. **3.** The "matter" underlying a "form". **4.** A foundation, in the sense of one layer underlying another. (See *Strata theory.*)

Success. The positive confirmation of hypotheses. In subjective experience it appears as an activating variable and as such influences motivation (q.v.), cognition and behavior. Success can be represented as a function of actual performance capability, of the degree of difficulty of the task set and of the standard aimed at. See *Achievement motive; Achievement motivation.* *P.S. & R.S.*

Successive. E.g.: as in *successive contrast*, *successive gestalts*, = following upon one another.

Successive contrast: Contrast (q.v.): influence exerted upon a phenomenon by a perception directly preceding it in time, e.g. an *afterimage* (q.v.) appearing in the complementary color of a previously perceived object.

Successive gestalts: Successions, whose characteristics are determined from the specific temporal order of their elements, e.g. the melody obtained from a sound sequence. *E.H.*

Successive intervals (syn. *Successive categories; Methods of absolute scaling*). A procedure in scaling (q.v.), in which a subject is invited to categorize stimuli in a sequence of given categories. It is assumed that these categories are classified. The arrangement of the test corresponds to that used in the method of apparently equal intervals. But it is not supposed that the categories cover equally large areas of the subjective continuum. The procedure depends on the "law of comparative judgment"; Stevens includes it as one of the "confusion" methods. See *Mathematical psychology; Psychophysics.*

Bibliography: **Sixtl, F.:** Messmethoden der Psychologie. Weinheim, 1967. **Torgerson, W. S.:** Theory and methods of scaling. New York, 1958.

A.R.

Suggestibility. The individual degree of susceptibility to influence by suggestion (q.v.) and hypnosis (q.v.). The correlative connections between suggestibility and personality do not yet permit clear conclusions on a definite dimension of suggestibility. In 1947, H. J. Eysenck suggested three factors: *primary suggestibility*, *secondary suggestibility* and "*prestige suggestibility*". States of heightened suggestibility can be induced by means of hypnosis and drugs. If by suggestion we understand the insinuation of ideas into the unconscious, then suggestibility may be aroused and heightened by ceremonial ritual, by the Carpenter effect (mass suggestion), by persistent repetition of the same word ("Hitler", "Stalin"), or by conversation in a subdued, agreeable atmosphere (colors, music), by appealing to sexuality (sex appeal), which are methods used by political and commercial propaganda. In medicine, suggestibility is eliminated during the testing of pharmaceuticals by the placebo effect (q.v.). When both suggestibility and credulity (or superstition and magic) combine, "faith cures" can occur. Learning processes are probably linked with suggestibility.

Bibliography: **Guilford, J. P.:** Personality. New York, [4]1970. **Hull, C. L.:** Hypnosis and suggestibility. New York, 1933. **Schjelderup, H.:** Das Verborgene in uns. Stuttgart & Berne, 1964. **Schmitz, K.:** Was ist, was kann, was nützt Hypnose? Munich, 1964. *E.U.*

Suggestibility, primary and secondary. *Primary suggestibility* is susceptibility to influence by (autosuggestion and) heterosuggestion, as demonstrated in Hull's Body Sway Test of Suggestibility (q.v.), Chevreul's sway test, and the "press-and-release" test.

Secondary suggestibility signifies susceptibility to influence by heterosuggestion, as demonstrated in the ink-blot suggestion test, Lindberg's smelling test, the picture-report test, Binet's test of progressive lines and weights, and the heat illusion test.

Bibliography: Eysenck, H. J. & Furneaux, W. D.: Primary and secondary suggestibility: an experimental and statistical study. J. exp. Psychol., 1945, *35*, 485–502. **Ferguson, L. W.:** An analysis of the generality of suggestibility to group opinion. Char. and Person., 1944, *12*, 237–44. **Hull, C. L.:** Hypnosis and suggestibility. New York, 1933. **Stukat, K. G.:** Suggestibility: a factorial and experimental analysis. Stockholm, 1958.

S.M.D.

Suggestion. A process of communication during which one or more persons cause one or more individuals to change (without critical response) their judgments, opinions, attitudes, etc., or patterns of behavior. The process can take place without being noticed by the individual to be influenced; nonhypnotic differs from hypnotic suggestion by being practised in a waking state. There is no consistently close connection between individual suggestibility in the hypnotic and in the waking condition.

Occasionally "suggestion" is also used to denote the communication content of social suggestion. See *Hypnosis; Suggestibility.*

Bibliography: Stukat, K. G.: Suggestibility. Stockholm, 1958.

H.D.S.

Suggestion therapy. Interhuman influence whereby suggestions appealing to the emotions but lacking rational foundation are made to another person; preconditions are trust and "experience of community" (B. Stokvis). Many psychological and physical processes are more effectively influenced by suggestion than by conscious intention (see *Hypnosis*). *Suggestion therapy* consists in communicating to the patient positive suggestions which change according to his condition. Therapeutic suggestions must always be positively formulated. A less passive attitude in the patient than in pure (hetero-) suggestion therapy is sought for in autosuggestive techniques (see *Relaxation therapy; Autosuggestion*), which are often coupled with formal autosuggestions (e.g. *Autogenic training*, q.v.). Suggestion therapy is probably the oldest form of treatment of mental sickness; it is closely related to magic. Magic may be understood as suggestion transposed outside the individual, and suggestion as magic confined to the range of an individual nervous system. See *Psychoanalysis; Attitude; Stereotype.*

Bibliography: Schultz, J. H.: Die Seelische Krankenbehandlung. Stuttgart, 1963. **Schmidbauer, W.:** Schamanismus und Psychotherapie. Psychologischer Rundschau., 1969, *20*, 29–47.

W.Sch.

Suicide. In most countries suicide is among the ten most frequent causes of death; however, official statistics are not always accurate or clear. They show the relative frequency of suicide in big cities (especially Berlin), and in certain countries (Austria, Switzerland and Sweden).

Methods of suicide are significant (in attempted suicide, usually pills; in successful suicide, forty percent by hanging).

Certain philosophical theories attempt to explain the phenomenon of "freely-chosen death" (in reality a sick compulsion). Psychoanalytic, sociological, pathologico-anatomical and theological theories can only offer suggestions. Those who threaten suicide are not acting in accordance with a Freudian "death instinct" (q.v.), but nearly all (ninety-six percent) are making a dramatic call for help.

E. Ringel advanced the psychiatric theory of a presuicidal syndrome (withdrawal, aggression, flight into unreality), particularly in his "International Union for the Prevention of Suicide". Some universities in the USA teach a course in the theory of suicide, i.e. "suicidology".

Suicide is the only destructive action in which actor and victim are one and the same person. As actor, a suicide is mentally sick (and therefore not responsible or sinful); as victim, he requires protection from himself. Hence the most important problem in connection with suicide is its *prevention.*

Among five thousand threatened suicides, we found fifty percent depressives and thirty-three percent neurotics, and the remainder schizophrenics, manics, psychopathics, etc. Nearly all were at the time in a state of conflict: more than fifty percent through love, marriage or sexual conflict; the rest, in authority, family, money, legal or vocational conflicts. Many seek religious, philosophic or similar answers (meaning of life and death; forgiveness of guilt, and so on).

Suicide prevention means psychiatric or psychoanalytic treatment, then a psychological approach to conflict resolution, including pastoral care (care by telephone helps to establish contact but cannot act as treatment). See *Aggression; Accident research; Alcoholism; Conflict; Criminality; Neurosis.*

Bibliography: Camus, A.: The myth of Sisyphus. London & New York, 1955. **Durkheim, E.:** Suicide. London & New York, 1952. **Kessel, N. & McCulloch, W.:** Repeated acts of self-poisoning and self-injury. Proc. Roy. Soc. Med., 1966, *59*, 89. **Stengel, E.:** Suicide and attempted suicide. Harmondsworth, 1964. **Watson, A. S.:** Psychiatry for lawyers. New York & London, 1968. **Williams, G.:** The sanctity of human life and the criminal law. London, 1955.

K. Thomas

Sulcus. The *sulci cerebri* are groove-shaped hollows between the cerebral convolutions. In human beings they grow from the second half of the embryonic period. The cortex is considerably enlarged because of them. On the cerebellum (q.v.) fissure-type hollows can be observed: *fissurae cerebelli.* The *sulcus centralis* runs diagonally over the cerebral hemisphere (see *Central convolution*). The visual cortex is situated in the occipital lobe in the area of the *sulcus calcarinus.* See *Neuroanatomy.* *G.A.*

Summated rating. One of the fundamental types of test. The test value is formed as the sum of the response items, or of response importance, without the items being clearly arranged in a basic continuum. The items indicate the existence of a definite feature. See *Test theory.* *P.Z.*

Summation (syn. *Summativity*). **1.** Any aggregate or total. **2.** A term from gestalt psychology. The opposite is suprasummation (q.v.). The first definition of summation is found in the work of W. Köhler (q.v.): "A whole is a pure sum of 'parts' or 'fragments' only when it can be produced from them, one after the other, without one of the parts changing because of the combination . . ." By analogy, this applies to the separation of parts. A comprehensive description of the theory is given by Rausch (1937). See *Ganzheit.*

Bibliography: Köhler, W.: Die physischen Gestalten in Ruhe und im stationären Zustand. Brunswick, 1920. **Rausch, E.:** Über Summativität und Nichtsummativität. Psychol. Forschung, 1937, *21*, 209–89.

A.R.

Summation curves. Graphic representations of the distribution function in constant random variables. A summation curve rises steadily. With a normal distribution it is S-shaped. Mean values and deviations, as well as deviations from the norm, can be derived from a summation curve. *A.R.*

Summation tone. The combined tone resulting from the simultaneous sounding of two tones at a frequency corresponding to the sum of frequencies of primary tones. Summation tones were discovered by H. von Helmholtz in 1857. See *Difference tone.*

Bibliography: Helmholtz, H. von: Die Lehre von den Tonempfindungen. Brunswick, 1896. *R.S.*

Summativity. See *Summation.*

Superego. The superego is one of the aspects of personality which Freud (q.v.) described in his second theory of the psyche. Its role is comparable with that of a judge or censor in regard to the ego (q.v.). Among its functions, Freud includes the formation of a moral *conscience* (q.v.), and that of ideals and self-observation (see *Self-knowledge*). It is an inheritance from the Oedipus complex (q.v.), since it is constituted by the incorporation of all parental prohibitions. Klein (1948) suggests that the formation of the superego occurs in the pre-Oedipal stage.

Bibliography: Freud, S.: The ego and the id. London, [2]1962. **Klein, M.:** The importance of symbol-formation in the development of the ego. London, 1948.
J.L.I.

Superformation. The formation of *supersigns* (q.v.). Because of the reduction of information, superformation permits both a restriction of reaction times, and a scanning of relatively complex information despite a restricted span of consciousness (q.v.). *A.R.*

Superposition effect. In 1941, E. von Holst discovered that the rhythmic fin movements of a fish feature a special automatism. The individual rhythms can be linked with one another by relative coordination. Hence the rhythms of the pectoral fins are independent and influence the beat frequency of the dorsal fin by *superposition.* The independent rhythm can respond to the dependent rhythm to the extent of almost complete dominance.

Bibliography: Holst, E. von: Entwurf eines Systems der lokomotorischen Periodenbildungen bei Fischen. Ein kritischer Beitrag zum Gestaltproblem. Z. vergl. Physiol., 1941, *26*, 481–529. *K.Fi.*

Supersign. Created by the combination of several signs of a simple sign repertoire (complex formation or classification) by the receiver. For example, sounds or letters are formed by complex formation into a word as a supersign of the first order, and words into a sentence or proposition as a supersign of the second order. Details of a printed letter are not distinguished when one reads, but are formed into a class and perceived as one and the same letter. The information of the supersign is always less than the total information of the subsigns. *H.R.*

Superstition. 1. An inappropriate or unnecessary fear or scruple requiring the observance of a rite or practice that it is supposed will ward off a usually non-existent danger. **2.** Such a rite or practice. **3.** The postulation of cause-and-effect relationships without good reason. **4.** Religion without morality, or tradition, or faith, or philosophy, etc. (pejorative usage). See *Attitude; Obsession; Religion, psychology of.*

Bibliography: Jahoda, G.: The psychology of superstition. London, 1969.

Suppression. Effective repression (q.v.), sublimation (q.v.), defense (q.v.), or censorship (q.v.). See *Depth psychology; Psychoanalysis.*

Suppressor fields. Areas of the cerebral cortex (e.g. *gyrus cingularis*), whose stimulation (electrical, chemical or mechanical) leads (*a*) to an *inhibition* or suppression of a motor activity evoked *simultaneously* by stimulation, and (*b*) to a transient inhibition occurring *shortly thereafter*, or to a diminution of spontaneous, local electrical activity in the cortex.

The postulation of the existence of these areas and their effect goes back to Dusser de Barenne and his school (1941), and especially to McCulloch (1944), but the experimental evidence for the regions has been called in question (Meyers & Knott, 1953). *Neurologically*, the suppressor effect may be interpreted as regulation of cortical activity; and *psychologically*, as an attention (q.v.) mechanism (inhibition of receptiveness to other sensory impressions).

Bibliography: Dusser de Barenne, J. C. & McCulloch, W. S.: Suppression of a motor response obtained from area 4 by stimulation of area 4 S.J. Neurophysiol., 1941, *4*, 311–23. **McCulloch, W. S.:** Corticocortical connections. In: **Bucy, P. C.** (Ed.): The pre-central motor cortex. Urbana, Ill., 1944, 211 ff. **Meyers, R. & Knott, J.:** On the question as to the existence of a suppressor mechanism. 5th Intern. Neurol. Congr., Lisbon, Vol. 2, 1953.

F.-C.S.

Suppressor variable (syn. *Suppressor test*). A test in a battery which indicates high correlation with a part test and no correlation with the criterion. Hence it suppresses a part of the variance (q.v.) which is without significance in the criterion. *R.M.*

Supranormal stimuli. Stimulus situations which exceed the "natural" key or signal stimulus of an innate releasing mechanism (IRM) in effectiveness. Example: the male *Eumenis semele*, or grayling, responds more intensively to black butterfly models than to naturally colored ones. The oyster-catcher rolls into its nest giant eggs which it prefers to its own. The capacity of the central evaluation apparatus would seem to be greater than necessary. See *Dummy sign stimuli; Instinct; Releaser*.

Bibliography: Magnus, D.: Zum Problem der überoptimalen Schlüsselreize (Versuche am Kaisermantel Argynnis paphia). Zool. Anz. Suppl. 1954, *18*, 317–25. **Tinbergen, N.:** The study of instinct. London, [2]1969. *H.H. & K.Fi.*

Suprarenin(e). Epinephrine hydrochloride (adrenalin, q.v.) obtained synthetically.

Suprasummation (syn. *Suprasummativity*). The effect by which it is supposed that the perception of a gestalt cannot be predicted from the perception of its individual parts. This is because perception depends on the relationships between the components of a gestalt rather than on the components themselves. See *Ganzheit; Transposition of gestalts; Structure.* *C.D.F.*

Surface colors. Katz (1911) distinguished various modes of appearance of colors according to their location in space. In addition to *film colors* (endowed with a loose spatial structure) and *solid colors* (occupying three-dimensional space), he speaks of "surface colors" localized at the site of the object bearing them, e.g. colored paper. Surface colors have a firm surface "structure".

Bibliography: Katz, D.: Die Erscheinungsweisen der Farben und ihre Beeinflussung. Z.f. Psychol., 1911, *7*.

A.Ha.

Surface traits. When several personality measures show some degree of cohesion or correlation with each other, such a cluster is called a surface trait (Cattell, 1957). A score on such a trait may be obtained by forming a simple linear composite of the measures. An added refinement would be to extract a factor from the intercorrelations between the measures and then obtain scores on the factor by one of the several factor estimation methods.

Surface traits can be useful in the description of personality. However, they are not considered to be fundamental in the development of theoretical models of personality. It is in this sense of not being basic to theory that they are distinguished from *source traits* (q.v.). Use of a surface trait is often determined by practical and conventional considerations.

The variance of a surface trait is to be thought of as potentially reducible to a set of more basic explanatory constructs. Thus, it might be observed that several different tests of, say, "cautiousness" co-vary together. A set of trait scores, based on these tests, could be generated. This new variable could then be introduced into a factor analysis (q.v.) including measures known to be associated with source traits. It would be expected that if the test of cautiousness involves a surface trait, its variance will be distributed among several different factors. In this way, many of the variables in common usage in personality research—such as the clinical scales of the MMPI—may be expressed in terms of more fundamental influences. See *Personality; Traits; Type.*

Bibliography: Cattell, R. B.: Personality and motivation: structure and measurement. New York, 1957.

J. D. Hundleby

Surprisal value. The surprise evoked by an item of information (news) depends not only on the actual information but on the rest of the field. In information esthetics, Frank's (1964) surprisal value gives the relation of the information (q.v.) of an item to the uncertainty that this item removes. Information with the value $s > 1$ is described as "surprizing" and that with $s < 1$ as "banal".

Bibliography: Frank, H.: Kybernetische Analysen subjektiver Sachverhalte. Schnelle, 1964. *H.R.*

Survey. The determination of characteristics and their prominence in units of a whole. If not all the units of a whole but only a random sample of units selected on representative, statistical principles, are covered, we speak of a ***representative survey.*** See *Area sampling; Demoscopy; Opinion polls.* *E.N.-N.*

Survival. The doctrine that the individual person may continue to exist in some form after destruction of his body. Life after death. See *Spiritualism.* *J.B.*

Susceptibility tests. Tests to measure the susceptibility of a subject to hypnotism. Recent susceptibility tests have been published by Hilgard & Weitzenhoffer. The researcher notes on prepared report sheets S.'s reactions to various hypnotic suggestions; S.'s susceptibility is obtained from the sum of reactions to different items. On the basis of his experiments, Hilgard rejects the stages of hypnosis (q.v.) as understood by, say, A. Forel.

Bibliography: Weitzenhoffer, A. M. & Hilgard, E. A.: Revised Stanford profile scales of hypnotic susceptibility. Palo Alto, 1967. *G.L.*

Swarming. Animals in groups of at least two to three thousand individuals can display synchronous behavior, especially when in swimming or flight formations. Usually individuals in a swarm remain at a certain distance from one another, but this tends to diminish when there is any sign of danger. Shoals of fish or swarms of birds, e.g. starlings, can envelop predators and prevent them from attacking. The survival value of swarm formations lies in the increasing difficulty of mounting attacks on individuals. The swarm has no leader; instead movements are usually carried out as a result of optical mood signalling, which is reinforced by striking patterns.

Bibliography: Eibl-Eibesfeldt, I.: Grundriss der vergleichenden Verhaltensforschung: Ethologie. Munich, 1967. **Horstmann, E.:** Schwarm und Phalanx als überindividuelle Lebensformen. J. Forsch. Spiekeroog. **Id.:** Schwarmstudien unter Ausnutzung einer optomotorischen Reaktion bei Mugil cephalus (CUV.) Pubbl. Staz. Zool. Napoli, 1967, *XXXI/I, 25–35.* *K.Fi.*

Symbiosis. The "cohabitation" of two, generally quite different, forms of organism, both of which obtain advantages from this association. In the intestines of termites, for example, there are unicellular organisms which produce cellulose-splitting enzymes which enable the termites to digest wood, their main item of diet; at the same time, the termites' intestinal tract, with its ideal environmental conditions and adequate food intake, is a paradise for the unicellular organisms. *H.Sch.*

Symbol. 1. In information theory (q.v.), usually synonymous with sign (q.v.), or with a sign whose referent is a part signal. If all disjunctive part signals are codes by means of symbols proper, statistical statements about signal sequences may be replaced by statements about symbol sequences. **2.** An abstract or compendium. **3.** That which figuratively represents something else. **4.** A sign that relies upon a convention accepted by its users. See *Sign and symbol; Communication.* *K.W.*

Symmetrical distribution. A frequency or probability distribution, for which the following applies: $f(X - \bar{X}) = f(\bar{X} - X)$. In symmetrical distributions, the arithmetic mean $\bar{X}$ and the median (q.v.) coincide (see *Normal distribution*). A non-symmetrical distribution is a skew distribution. *A.R.*

Sympathicolytic (syn. *Sympatholytic*). Appertaining to the mode of effect of chemical substances which inhibit or block sympathetic activity (see *Autonomic nervous system*). The sympathicolytic effect of drugs vary according to the basic mechanisms of action and varied physiological systems. A common characteristic of sympathicolytic substances is neurophysiological and chemical inhibition of the effect of biogenic catecholamines, especially noradrenalin (norepinephrine), in the peripheral ANS. According to the active mechanisms, the sympathicolytic substances which directly affect the receptors (q.v.) can be distinguished from those which influence biosynthesis or catecholamine storage. Alpha or beta receptor inhibitors can be distinguished according to the site of action. The effects of sympathicolytic substances on behavior vary considerably. Both stimulating and sedative effects are found.

Bibliography: See *Psychopharmaceuticals and the ANS.* *W.J.*

Sympathicolytics (syn. *Sympatholytics*). Chemical substances with a predominantly sympathicolytic effect. For examples, see *Psychopharmaceuticals and the ANS.*

Sympathicomimetic. Appertaining to the mode of effect of chemical substances which arouse the sympathetic division of the ANS. Effects differ according to whether the alpha or beta receptors are aroused. Stimulation of the alpha receptors (e.g. by adrenalin) induces, *inter alia:* contraction of blood vessels (only in a few parts, e.g. the skeletal muscles, skin, kidneys), reduced salivation, inhibition of gastric juice secretion, localized (adrenergic) sweating and the mobilization of glycogen. Excitation of beta receptors (e.g. by isopropylnoradrenalin) leads, *inter alia,* to increased heart rate, enlargement of the heart beat volume, dilation of the blood vessels of the skeletal muscles, and reduced intestinal motility.

Bibliography: See *Psychopharmaceuticals and the ANS.* *W.J.*

Sympathicomimetics. Substances whose predominant effect is to stimulate the sympathetic division. The comparison of sympathicomimetics to adrenergics (q.v.), though often made, is problematic since (*a*) the sympathetic system is not aroused only by noradrenalin and adrenalin (q.v.) or related substances, and (*b*) adrenergic substances also affect the central nervous system without arousal of the peripheral sympathetic system. Many sympathicomimetics also have strong central effects, and may be classed as stimulants.

Bibliography: See *Psychopharmaceuticals and the ANS.* *W.J.*

Sympathicotony. A clinical syndrome described by Eppinger & Hess (1910). A shift (induced by unilateral heightening of sympathetic tonus) of equilibrium in the autonomic nervous system to the sympathetic side with increased sympathetic excitability, so that normally subliminal stimuli capable of sympathetic arousal cause abnormally increased reactions (increased vasomotor excitability, dilated pupils, tachycardia, q.v., and increased secretion of sweat). The reactions correlate with psychological traits: according to Birkmeyer & Winkler, increased psychological excitability and lability of affect, disturbances of concentration and sleep, inclination to anxiety states. Ant. *Vagotonia* (q.v.).

Bibliography: Eppinger, H. & Hess, L.: Die Vagotonie. Berlin, 1910. *F.-C.S.*

Symptom. In the psychological sense, an attitude, thought or subjective experience with a significance beyond or different from itself. As a rule, unconscious though not wholly suppressed wishes and motives are indicated by symptoms (Freud, 1929). Hence sudden states of anxiety are alleged possibly to show that an individual is at a crucial stage in regard to a forbidden motive, or that he was prevented from avoiding such situations in his usual way or from using the necessary inner defense mechanisms. Compulsive washing is supposed to indicate aggressive impulses, stuttering a power conflict with relatives, and a hysterical paralysis a (forbidden) wish to touch a certain person.

Symptomatic actions are actions which are said to indicate something more than, or other than, the mere conscious and intended object of behavior. Unconscious motives and impulses are supposed to have contributed to their origin. "Freudian" slips (q.v.) are also symptomatic actions in this sense. See *Syndrome.*

Bibliography: Fenichel, O.: The psychoanalytic theory of neurosis. New York, 1945. Freud, S.: Introductory lectures on psycho-analysis. London, [2]1969. *W.T.*

Synapses. Nerve fibers (axons) of other nerve cells or receptors terminate at several points (*end feet*) of the nerve cell body, or neuron(e), and at the dentrites. These fibers transmit excitation (nerve impulses) by way of *synapses*; similarly, the link between nerve and muscle is formed by a kind of synapse. A synapse is, therefore, a *transfer point*. Essentially, a neuron can be regulated by a few up to several hundred synapses. A structural distinction is made between the *presynaptic fiber* terminating in an extension on the cell body, the *subsynaptic membrane* (membrane part of the cell), and the narrow gap (*synaptic cleft*) between them (width 200–300 Å).

1. *Excitatory synapses* with chemical transmitter substances. In spite of the narrow gap, pre- and postsynaptic structures are thoroughly linked by electricity. The chemical *transmitter substance* molecules (q.v.) stored in the presynaptic part, and released in appropriate quantity by the incident electrical excitation has, after diffusion through the gap, the effect of depolarizing that part of the subsynaptic membrane near the synapse; the excitatory postsynaptic potential (EPSP), delayed by about 0.3–0.6 ms, arises intracellularly. EPSP is not identical with the action potential (q.v.), which represents the further conducted excitation of the neuron, but stands primarily for a purely local change of potential (about 10 mV). EPSP follows a characteristic course: a rapid rise (1–20 ms), an approximate exponential drop (1–20 ms). The amplitude, and not the course, is influenced by the sequential frequency of the impulse: *summation* (decoding), to be explained by repeated secretion of

transmitter substance and a corresponding rise in concentration. If the amplitude of the EPSP, or the integral above the amplitudes of all EPSPs in the neuron, reaches a critical threshold, then excitation of the whole neuron takes place and an action potential (80–140 mV) is created as an input signal to the conductor axon. Hence the excitation of the whole neuron depends on the number of excited afferent fibers and their action potential frequency.

2. *Excitatory synapse; electrical transmission.* Synapses of this relatively infrequent type have a narrower gap, and almost no latency of EPSP in relation to presynaptic action potential (< 0.1 ms). A direct transmission of the depolarizing current from the presynaptic to the subsynaptic membrane is assumed to occur here, though only in one direction.

3. *Inhibitory synapse with chemical transmitter substance.* The excitation which generally arrives by way of an intermediate neuron with a short axon creates (by means of a chemical transmitter substance, e.g. γ-aminoperbutyric acid in invertebrates) a hyperpolarization of the synaptic membrane and an inhibitory postsynaptic potential (IPSP). The latter is directed electrically against EPSP and reduces the excitability of the nerve cells.

4. *Inhibitory synapse; electrical transmission.* In a few nerve cells (Mauthner cells), the axon is surrounded by a fine nerve tissue which exerts an electrotonic influence on the excitation conducted in the axon, and in certain cases inhibits it. (See *Axon; Nervous system.*)

Bibliography: Eccles, J. C.: The mechanism of synaptic transmission. Ergebnisse der Physiologie, 1961, *51*, 300–429. **Grossman, S. P.:** Physiological psychology. New York, 1967. **Pritbam, K. H.** (Ed.): Brain and behavior. Harmondsworth, 1969.

M. Spreng

Synchronicity. Jung (q.v.) introduced the concept of synchronicity to describe the correlation between external and internal facts, which cannot be explained "causally". According to Jung, this correlation is based on archetypes (q.v.). Coincidences often occur between certain factors in an individual's life and mythological patterns, where at first sight a causality may be inferred. Yet it is a question not of strict causality but of a special synchronous variation. Jung and his disciples, above all E. Neumann, gave the theory a chronological, "evolutionary" dimension.

J.L.I.

Syndrome. A concurrence of a set of abnormal signs and/or symptoms. Syndromes are given names which are either descriptive or eponymic (that is, they bear the name of one or more individuals who described or clarified them).

J.P.

Synesthesia. In some people, sensory systems other than the one actually being stimulated can share in the perception of the stimulus. Hence musical notes may give rise to the perception of colors or odors. *C.D.F.*

Synop(s)ia. A subvariety of synesthesia (q.v.) in which the visual modality is influenced by non-visual stimuli or images See *Mental imagery.* *F.Ma.*

Synthesis, creative. According to Wundt (q.v.), a universal principle of psychic activity. It indicates that a "psychic structure" represents more than the sum of its elements ("pure feelings" or "pure sensations"). The product of several elements is something wholly new in relation to its parts. The principle of creative synthesis refers not to objective circumstances but to subjective values and goals; nevertheless it does not contradict physical laws. The creative synthesis is most evident in the "higher" psychic processes ("apperceptive synthesis"). See *Ganzheit.*

Bibliography: Wundt, W.: Grundriss der Psychologie. Leipzig, [12]1914.

F.Ma.

Syntonia. A term coined by Bleuler in 1922 to replace cyclothymia (q.v.), and meaning that "affectivity toward the outside world . . . is in harmony with that of the human environment and corresponds to the conditions of the outside world; actual emotions are harmonious within, and—like aspirations—are unified." Kretschmer's concept of a "midpoint" of the diathetic proportion (q.v.) of adequately balanced, non-extreme feeling and thought has been more influential; "healthy human understanding, traditional manner, practical instinct . . . skill . . . in friendly communication."

Bibliography: **Bleuler, E.:** Die Probleme der Schizoidie und Syntonie. Zschr. ges. Neur. Psychiatr., 1922, *78*, 373 ff. **Kretschmer, E. & W.:** Medizinische Psychologie. Stuttgart, [13]1970.

W.K.

Systematic error. See *Bias.*

Systole; diastole. *Systole:* contraction of a hollow muscular organ, in particular of the heart. Part of the cardiac cycle; contraction of the heart muscle rhythmically alternating with diastole: pumping out of the blood.

Diastole: enlargement of the heart muscle alternating with systole; phase of refilling of ventrical with blood.

H.W.

Szondi test. Devised by L. Szondi and published in 1947. The original purpose of the test was to discover the motivational nature of the "familiar unconscious", but experience shows that it throws more light on questions of individual motivation. The test consists of forty-eight pictures (six series of eight) of persons lacking in motivation; these the testee is required to arrange in two groups (four pictures per group) in terms of relative attractiveness or unattractiveness. These sympathy/antipathy choices are projections (q.v.) of inner need and motive tensions. The reliability of the test is difficult to assess. Its validity, despite much research, is doubtful.

Bibliography: **Heinelt, G.:** Bildwahlverfahren. In: **Heiss, R.** (Ed.): Handbuch der Psychologie, Vol. 6. Göttingen, 1963.

P.G.

T

Tabes dorsalis (syn. *Locomotor ataxia*). A third-stage sequel of syphilis (and rarely due to other causes): posterior spinal sclerosis. It appears five to fifteen years after the first infection with *Treponema pallidum* (*Spirochaeta pallida*) and is characterized by degeneration of sensory neurons in the spinal cord, sensory ganglia, and nerve roots. Characteristic symptoms are: alterations in pupils (see *Argyll-Robertson pupil*); disturbances of sensibility, such as lightning pains; analgesia (q.v.) and heat sensations in particular areas of the body; disturbed movement (see *Ataxia*) and especially gait, as a result of faulty information to the brain about the position of the limbs and the contact of the soles of the feet with the ground; failure of tendon (ankle and knee) reflexes; and personality changes. The disease develops slowly, and over the years leads (if the causative syphilis is untreated) to tabetic paralysis and *dementia paralytica*. *E.D.*

Table. An arithmetic representation of scores, so arranged as to reveal relations of time, frequency, etc.

Taboo (syn. *Tabu*). Originally a term for a "primitive", solemn prohibition of certain actions (e.g. looking at or touching certain objects or persons). From this arose the magical religious belief that violation of a taboo brings harm to a community. Punishment for ignoring the taboo was often violent expulsion from the (tribal) group, or death.

In social psychology, the term "taboo" is applied to certain usually unofficial but highly regarded norms in a group or society. It is applied in particular to social prohibitions of an irrational nature when punishment is threatened if they are violated. There are many similarities between "taboo" objects in modern and in primitive societies (e.g. the tabooing of aspects of certain vital functions such as some forms of eating, drinking, elimination, sexual taboos, taboos on strangers and property, etc.)

Freud held that taboos arose through an instinctual conflict, with a resulting repression of the attractive but forbidden behavioral tendencies into the "unconscious" (q.v.). The repression had features in common with neurotic compulsions not to touch certain things. Social psychology, however, sees the taboo as a special instance of group norms by which the community can control an individual's behavior—sometimes very strictly (e.g. the increased effectiveness of a religious or military group through certain sexual taboos. See *Incest*).

Bibliography: Freud, S.: Totem and taboo. New York & London, 1918. *H.D.S.*

Taboo death. The sudden or gradual death of a person who knows (or thinks he knows) he has offended against a taboo and therefore must die. Because he believes himself bewitched or guilty—excluded from the law, and therefore from life—he dies. His responsibility is wholly bound up with the observance of the prohibition.

This phenomenon is observed almost exclusively in archaic cultures, in which the psychosomatic connection is very close. The individual is subject to an almost pure affectivity, which can pass directly from excess to exhaustion. He can die through the effect of a shock of joy or fear, or of a death wish. If he is bewitched and cast out of society, he can avoid sudden death or pining away only through exorcism or the conjuration of "counter magic". For the physiological effects of these phenomena and the clinical causes of such deaths, see C. Lévi-Strauss's *Structural Anthropology* (New York, 1963). They are due to a kind of paralysis of the sympathetic nervous system. *M.R.*

Tachistoscope. An apparatus for presenting visual stimuli for very brief and accurately timed periods. Various mechanisms have been employed, but most operate either on a shutter system like that of a camera, or on a principle of selective illumination. The instrument has a wide variety of uses in the field of *perception*, but it best known in connection with studies of *pattern recognition* and the influences of motivation upon perception, e.g. *perceptual defense*. *Tachistoscopic projector:* A slide projector with the addition of a shutter mechanism for timing brief presentations of the slide on the screen, and usually also the interval between slide presentations. *G.D.W.*

Tachycardia. An increased heart beat above the rate of a hundred beats a minute is normal in bodily exertion and in childhood. Tachycardia, or an abnormally rapid heart beat, is unhealthy in the case of heart attack (*paroxysmal tachycardia*); in cases of acute or chronic occurrence through psychic excitement, heart weakness, endocarditis and myocarditis; and in hormone poisoning, and poisoning from drugs and eating and drinking, and in long-term infections. There is no fixed boundary between heart flutter and the mortal heart murmur. *E.D.*

Talbot-Plateau law. If the eye is stimulated by a light flickering at a frequency above that of flicker-fusion frequency, the brightness created by the flickering light is the same as that which would result if the total amount of light had been uniformly distributed over the whole period of the intermittence. In other words: a light of intensity a, shining for the period t, has the same effect as a light of intensity a/n shining for the period nt. If the flickering lights are colored (i.e. of different wavelengths), the resulting color tone is that to be expected from a summative color mixture (q.v.), and its brightness (q.v.) conforms to the Talbot law. See *Flicker photometry*. *G.Ka.*

Talent. Great or outstanding ability. See *Giftedness, research into; Abilities; Creativity.*

Talisman. An object which is supposed to bring its owner luck or give him protection (see *Fetishism*). *J.L.*

Tapping. An experimental or test procedure in which S. has to carry out simple tapping movements or depress keys with the fingers and hands as rapidly as possible, or at a speed convenient to him. Tapping is a psychomotor test which has been introduced in several variations: for instance, as simple tapping (knocking with the bare finger, a pencil on a paper pad, etc.), and as purposive tapping, when S. has to hit target points (circles, parts of figures, etc.) at a prescribed speed, or at any speed he chooses. Usually a tapping test serves to determine "personal tempo", that is, the speed of work preferred by the individual, and to test delicate motor precision. See *Motor skills; Practice.*

Bibliography: Whipple, G. M.: Manual of mental and physical tests. Baltimore, [2]1914. *A.T.*

Tapping test. A test to measure the abilities requisite to learn typewriting and similar activities, and to predict individual scores. *F.Gr.*

Tarchanoff phenomenon. See *Galvanic skin response.*

Target. In parapsychology (q.v.): the particular object, symbol or property that has to be identified in an ESP experiment. *J.B.*

Taste nerves. The taste receptors are longish cells with a diameter of 3 to 8 μ, combined in groups of ten to forty in taste buds. The latter are situated in elevations of the mucous membrane of the tongue, or papillae, and also in isolated groups on the hard and soft gum, the pharynx and even the larynx. It may be assumed that there are four different kinds of receptors for the four qualities of taste, i.e. *sweet, sour, salt* and *bitter*, since sweet tastes are detected primarily by the tip of the tongue, bitter tastes by the base of the tongue, and salt and sour tastes on the edges of the tongue (the former at the front and the latter further back). Thin, afferent (myelinated) nerve fibers of the Aδ group according to Erlanger & Gasser, are synaptically connected to the bases of the taste buds and lead into the central nervous system. The fibers originating in the front two-thirds of the tongue lead through the *nervus lingualis* (*n. trigeminus* 3/1) to the *chorda tympani*, and with the latter through the middle ear to the *n. facialis*; the fibers from the base of the tongue lead to the *n. glossopharyngicus* and those from all remaining areas which are sensitive to taste to the *n. vagus.* All these nerves lead in turn to the *nucl. terminalis tract. solitarii,* which is located in the bulbo-pontine cerebrum in the vicinity of the *vestibularis nuclei,* and is frequently referred to as the *nucl. gustatorius.* Above the thalamus (*nucl. ventr. posteromedialis*) Brodmann area 43 is reached at the lower end of the *gyrus postcentralis* in the immediate vicinity of the primary somesthetic projection of the tongue and mucous membrane of the mouth (Brodmann areas 1, 2 and 3); Brodmann area 43 is considered to be the primary cortical taste center. Previous assumptions that the taste center was located in the *gyrus* and *uncus hippocampi* or in the *insula Reili* or *operculum* have been superseded.

Bibliography: Plattig, K. H.: Über den elektrischen Geschmack, Z. Biol., 1969, *116*, 161–211. *K.H.P.*

Tau effect. See *Gelb phenomenon.*

Taxis. The response in space of freely moving living creatures to external stimuli. There are the following subforms:

(*a*) Grouped according to the basic tendency of the movement: (i) *positive taxis* (seeking, turning toward); (ii) *negative taxis* (avoiding, turning away from).

(*b*) Grouped according to the quality of the operative stimulus: (i) *phototaxis:* irradiation by light; (ii) *chemotaxis:* concentration of diverse substances; (iii) *thermotaxis:* temperature, drops in; (iv) *geotaxis:* gravity; (v) *rheotaxis:* direction of current; (vi) *thigmotaxis:* tactile contact with solid bodies, etc.

(*c*) Grouped according to the kind of movement evoked, or the relation to the stimulus source striven after by the organism: (i) *phobotaxis*—movement of flight on the principle of trial and error, on the basis of a time-differential intensity. Success is shown by the time spent in a zone of optimal conditions. (ii) *topotaxis:* directional movements in the stimulus field on the basis of a spatial difference of intensity. According to the final position achieved by the body with respect to the stimulus source, subgroups are distinguished among which are: (*a*) *tropotaxis:* the object is an excitation equilibrium between two receptors (q.v.), arranged symmetrically like a mirror-image (e.g. left and right eye); (*b*) *telotaxis:* heading in a straight line for a target that can be fixed; (*c*) *menotaxis:* the object is the maintenance of a certain angle between the axis of the body and the direction of stimulus action; (*d*) *mnemotaxis:* the orientation movement is directed toward a number of stimulus sources (e.g. path markers), which are headed for in succession and whose space and time relationships are stored in the memory. But it is a matter of controversy whether such complex orientation behavior should be included under taxis.

Whereas taxis was formerly regarded as a reflex-like set of movements with some direction in view, modern behavioral research separates the directive component, taxis in the more limited sense, from the automatic movement controlled by the central nervous system. Only the combination of the two (successively or joined simultaneously) will produce the space-oriented action.

Bibliography: Kühn, A.: Die Orientierung der Tiere im Raum. Jena, 1919. **Tinbergen, N:** The study of instinct. Oxford, [2]1969.

I. Lindner

Taxonomy. The *taxonomy of learning goals* dispenses with the description of teaching content in instruction. Instead it endeavors to take account of all the elementary psychological processes of the pupil and to classify the instruction according to them. See *Educational psychology; Instructional technology.*

G.B.

Taylor system. Methods and principles of organization worked out by F. W. Taylor (1903) for scientific management: the first attempt at a global concept for solving human problems in large-scale industry. The system went through the following phases: (*a*) increase of individual productivity by a differential wage-system (until 1895); (*b*) investigation of work by time-and-motion studies (part-time work was measured but the workers concerned were specially picked); (*c*) reorganization and division of work between shop-floor and office on a functional basis (until 1903); (*d*) change of the whole factory organization by substituting for overseers a system of several foremen with special functions.

Taylorism: the further development of the Taylor system, especially by F. B. Gilbreth, H. L. Gantt, J. Hopkins, C. G. Garth, H. K. Hathway, etc. See *Industrial psychology; Occupational psychology.*

Bibliography: Taylor, F. W.: Shop management. New York, 1903. **Id.:** Principles of scientific management. New York, 1911.

W.F.N.

t distribution. A distribution for average values of samples from normally distributed populations; devised by W. S. Gosset in 1908, but under the pseudonym "Student". The t distribution allows, e.g., significance testing of average value differences in the case of smaller samples.

Bibliography: Student: The probable error of a mean. Biometrika, 1908, *6*, 1–25.

D.W.E.

Tea. A beverage brewed from the dried young leaves, buds and blossom of the tea shrub contains the stimulating substance *theine*, which is identical with caffeine (q.v.). *H.-D.S.*

Teaching machines. See *Instructional technology; Programmed learning; Machine learning; Cybernetics and psychology; Cybernetic education.*

Teaching program. In the sense of programmed instruction, a number of complex steps which unequivocally determine a teaching algorithm. A *linear program* is the type of program devised by Skinner (1960), in which the learner has to work through short frames (steps) according to a pre-determined sequence. An individual frame or a group of frames cannot be repeatedly circumvented, and in any case only under special conditions. Usually only those assignments are linearly programmed that allow of one possible solution. The *branched* form of program derives from Crowder (1960). In contrast to the linear method, this method uses remedial tracks and branches allowing repetition, circumvention of frames, and other possible solutions. The remedial tracks depend on a series of alternative questions or selective answers (multiple-choice responses), which anticipate total and partial erroneous solutions. In the case of a false answer, the learner is led out of the main program, informed of his error, and referred back to the initial question. The branching technique allows for individual learning speeds, and is specially suited to assignments capable of several modes of solution. Linear and branched programs are now often found in combination. See *Instructional technology*.

Bibliography: Crowder, N. A.: Automatic tutoring by intrinsic programming. In: **Lumsdaine, A. A. & Glaser, R.** (Eds.): Teaching machines and programmed learning. Washington, 1960. **Skinner, B. F.:** The science of learning and the art of teaching. In: **Lumsdaine & Glaser,** *op. cit.* *H.F. & E.U.*

Team. A form of division of labor in which (in contrast to the traditional *hierarchical* organizational model) cooperation of formal equals takes the place of orders received from a superior. See *Democracy; Group.* *P.B.*

Teamwork. 1. A term for any work done by a group (q.v.). **2.** A special form of direct cooperation where every member of the group is a specialist but has constantly to rely on coordination and communication with the others, and where success cannot be achieved by anyone alone. *G.R.W.M.*

Tectum opticum. The terminus of the optic pathway in fish, amphibians, reptiles, and birds. It is here that optical, olfactory, static and somatic items of information are integrated and converted into behavioral patterns. In mammals the visual cortex dominates over the *tectum opticum.* *K.Fi.*

Telekinesis. In parapsychology (q.v.), the exertion of a psychological influence on external objects. Driesch (1967) places telekinesis in the group of paranormal "physical" phenomena, which he distinguishes from "intellectual" paranormal phenomena. In a series of studies, Rhine (1962) tried to demonstrate individual telekinetic activities using "psychokinetic" tests, e.g. when testees were asked to roll dice, any significant deviation from random results could be explained by a psychic influence.

Bibliography: Bender, H.: Parapsychologie: ihre Ergebnisse und Probleme. Bremen, 1970. **Driesch, H.:** Parapsychologie. Munich, 1967. **Rhine, J. B. & Pratt, J. G.:** Parapsychology. Springfield, 1962. *K.E.P.*

Telencephalon. The human brain (q.v.) is divided into the telencephalon, diencephalon (q.v.), mesencephalon (q.v.), metencephalon (consisting of the pons, q.v., and cerebellum, q.v., and myelencephalon (see *Medulla oblongata*). From the evolutionary point of view the telencephalon is the most advanced; in man it has reached the highest point of development. It can be divided into a *pars basalis* (basal brain) and a *pars palliaris* (pallium, q.v.). The telencephalon consists of the hemispheres of the cerebrum, the *corpus callosum*, the *fornix cerebri*, lateral ventricles and the *corpus striatum*. Between the two hemispheres of the cerebrum is the longitudinal fissure of the brain, the *fissura longitudinalis cerebri*. See *Neuroanatomy*. *G.A.*

Teleology. In philosophy, the science of *finality*. In a wider sense, *finality* itself, i.e. the fact of striving for some goal—whether intentional (*volition*) or unintentional (*entelechy*—a purpose which is realized by organic development, the arrangement of the parts in a whole). The term can also mean *finalism*, i.e. the doctrine according to which the world is thought of as a system of relations between means and end. In the Aristotelian theory of "four causes", teleology refers to the "*causa finalis*", or final cause. *Vitalism* is one of the forms of finalism (H. Bergson); it is opposed to any mechanistic interpretation.

Bibliography: Monod, J.: Chance and necessity. London & New York, 1972. *M.J.B.*

Telepathy. A form of ESP (q.v.) where the information acquired by the subject is assumed to derive from the mind or brain of some other person (see *Clairvoyance*). A term introduced by Frederic Myers which has superseded earlier expressions such as "thought-transference" or "teleasthesia". *J.B.*

Television. An audiovisual mass medium whose importance and effectiveness have undergone extensive empirical investigation since the beginning of the nineteen-fifties. The assumption that prolonged viewing as such is harmful (e.g. impairs concentration or encourages crime) has not been established in general either for children and juveniles or adults. The effectiveness of the medium in spreading knowledge appears to be greatest in combination with other media communication. In this respect the importance of television for education is constantly increasing. The question of the beneficial or harmful effects of television obviously depends on the view held of the esthetic value and/or educative, moral, etc. value of the ethic, information, etc., of a specific program in regard to a specific age group, personality type, environment, and so on.

Bibliography: Benton, C. W. et al.: Television in urban education: its application to major educational problems in sixteen cities. New York, 1970. **Eysenck, H. J.:** Television and the problem of violence. In: Report of the Committee on broadcasting, Vol. 2. London, 1962, 1116–20. **Hancock, A.:** Planning for educational television. London, 1971.

H.D.S. & W.A.

Temperament. A basic characteristic of the personality as a whole. The classical descriptions of temperament (melancholic, phlegmatic, choleric and sanguine) derive from ancient cosmology and pathology. According to Kretschmer ([13]1970), temperament is "the overall attitude of the affectivity characteristic of an individual . . . measured by sensitivity and impulses" or "the profile of activity and sensitivity, the dominant ranges and outlets". It is the result of the "combination of affective, vegetative, humoral and morphological factors". See *Personality; Traits; Type*. *W.K.*

Temperature. See *Body temperature*.

Temporal lobe. The *lobus temporalis* of the brain (q.v.) is situated in the center of the cranial cavity, and bordered above by the lateral cerebral fissure (*Sulcus lateralis*) and connected posteriorly and above to the parietal and occipital lobes (q.v.). The convolutions of the temporal lobe are the *Gyrus temporalis superior*, *medius et inferior* (the superior, middle and inferior temporal convolutions) and the *Gyri temporales transversi* (the transverse temporal convolutions = Heschl's gyrus), which are responsible for hearing. In the *gyrus temporalis superior* is the sensory speech center; its removal or failure produces aphasia (q.v.). In the right-handed, the sensory speech center is on the left-hand side, and in the left-handed, it is on the right of the *gyrus temporalis superior*. *G.A.*

Temptation. Guilt (q.v.) is said to arise after the commission of a previously punished act. Temptation corresponds to the anxiety (q.v.) and conflict (q.v.) experienced before the commission of forbidden acts. Guilt feelings can occur if they occur independently of the direct threat of external punishment (q.v.). If corresponding feelings are associated with an external source of punishment, one speaks of *shame*. See *Conscience; Criminality; Traits; Type.*

Bibliography: Mowrer, O. H.: Learning theory and the symbolic processes. New York, 1960. *F.Ma.*

Tenacity. Used of attention (q.v.): a difference between individuals in the length of time for which they can perform correctly tasks which require a high degree of attention. Tenacity is generally measured by crossing-out tests (q.v.). *K.P.*

Tendencies (determining, anticipatory, persevering). **1.** *Determining tendencies:* A term in the psychology of thinking and volition invented by N. Ach. Thought (q.v.) does not proceed in any direction, like association (q.v.), but is given a firm direction by attitudes to, or ideas of, a goal or task; sometimes these are part of observable experience, and sometimes unobservable and unconscious.

2. *Anticipatory tendencies:* If a learning process is divided into a sequence of individual associations, it is found that the steps in the sequence are not independent of one another. For example, if when memorizing nonsense syllables a particular response to a stimulus is learnt, subjects show a tendency to react before the stimulus if the response is demanded.

3. *Persevering tendencies:* Reproductive tendencies: the dependence of one step in a learning process on its predecessors. Appears in experiments with nonsense syllables, when a syllable recently learnt is reproduced instead of the correct one, which was learnt earlier. *H.W.*

Tendermindedness. An idealistic attitude toward social, political and philosophical problems; ant.: *toughmindedness.* Whereas the tenderminded person will make judgments and perform actions according to principles, and try to solve problems by reason or argument, the toughminded person adopts a position based on facts and tries to solve problems by manipulation or the use of force (pragmatism). H. J. Eysenck (1963) claims a correlation between tendermindedness and introversion, and between toughmindedness (q.v.) and extraversion. See *Traits; Type; Authoritarian personality.* *I.L.*

Tension. 1. *Muscular tension* (*hypertension:* increased tension; *hypotension:* reduced tension). **2.** *Condition of an organism:* restless, tense activity (see *Stress*). **3.** Emotional condition resulting from unsatisfied needs or blocked desires (see *Conflict; Frustration*). *F.-C.S.*

Tension, psychic. Psychoanalytic term referring to a state or condition marked by high arousal, anxiety, restlessness, and undirected drive. Also called *psychentonia.* Similar to popular concepts of "nervous tension" and "emotional tension". *G.D.W.*

Tension system. According to K. Lewin, mental activity can be visualized in terms of topological concepts, such as *region, path* and *boundary* (see *Field theory; Topological psychology*). The ego and life-space can be regarded as an internally differentiated field in a number of regions interconnected by paths. Under extreme stress the tension systems, or part-regions of the differentiated personality, "de-differentiate": i.e. energy levels in the various tension systems are equated because of the flow from one to the other, and there is something like (e.g. when a man loses his head in a fit of rage) a return to the poorly differentiated child personality.

Bibliography: Lewin, K.: A dynamic theory of personality. New York, 1935. **Id.:** Principles of topological psychology. New York, 1936. *P.M.*

Terman, Lewis Madison. B. 15/1/1877 in Johnson County (Ind.); d. 21/12/1956 in Stanford. Ph.D. 1905, under Stanley Hall at Clark University; 1910, assistant Professor in the Department of Education at Stanford University; 1916, full Professor; from 1922, until his death, Professor of psychology at Stanford University.

Terman was a very prolific scholar, and his bibliography lists over two hundred publications. He is mainly known, however, for his famous investigations into the measurement and development of intelligence (q.v.).

In his *The Measurement of Intelligence. An explanation of and a complete guide for the use of the Stanford revision and extension of the Binet-Simon Intelligence Scale* (1916) he took a revised form of the Binet-Simon intelligence test and adapted it to North-American conditions. This "Stanford Revision", which was later revised a number of times, acquired great importance, particularly through its use by the US Army during World War I for the selection of gifted personnel.

Besides his work on intelligence tests, Terman devoted particular attention to famous and gifted people. In the second volume of his *Genetic Studies of Genius* (1926) (together with U. Miles) he examined the lives of three hundred famous historical figures and awarded them intelligence quotients based on an examination of their letters, sayings and actions. Sample assessments are: Goethe, 210; Descartes, 180; Napoleon, 145. The remaining four volumes of *Genetic Studies of Genius* (1925–29) describe a longitudinal investigation (q.v.) of the development (q.v.) of over 1000 gifted children with an IQ of over 140 into adulthood (age 45). Among Terman's conclusions was that, contrary to previously held beliefs, gifted children were open, effective and socially active, and retained these characteristics throughout development.

Other studies of Terman's were concerned with the relation between masculinity and femininity in groups of different age, sex and occupation (*Sex and Personality*, 1936), and with the contribution of psychological factors to marital happiness (*Psychological Factors in Marital Happiness*, 1938). In the presentation of his research findings, Terman generally remained on the purely descriptive level and avoided general theoretical statements.

Bibliography: Boring, E. G.: Lewis Madison Terman: 1877–1956. In: National Academy of Sciences, Biographical Memoirs, Vol. 33. Washington, 1959, 414–61. **Hilgard, E. R.:** Lewis Madison Terman: 1877–1956. Amer. J. of Psychol., 1957, *70*, 472–9. **Lewis, W. B.:** Professor Lewis M. Terman. Brit. J. of Stat. Psychol., 1957, *10*, 65–8. *W.W.*

Terminal depression. A depression (q.v.) which appears after the discharge of some difficult task or a release from worry or deprivation. The decisive factor is that those affected were initially wholly absorbed in some task, and feel "empty" after its completion. *A.Hi.*

Termination of pregnancy. See *Abortion*.

Terminology. In the strict sense, the *study of technical terms* used by any theoretical discipline concerned to reduce a totality of contents to a logically ordered and systematic form. In general, terminology is also the *total* *range of such terms*, or the technical vocabulary of such disciplines. A "term" is an expression which defines an object of thought by describing its specific content. "Term" is sometimes also used to mean "word" in contexts where the content in question is loosely described. *M.J.B.*

Test. 1. *Definition.* The term "test" has several meanings in psychology. In addition to specific mathematical and statistical test methods (see *Statistics*), the test material used in all studies and the process of testing, considerable importance attaches to psychodiagnostic testing (see *Psychodiagnostics*). Lienert defines the latter as "a routine scientific method of studying one or more empirically defined personality traits in order to draw quantitative conclusions on the relative importance of the particular features in the individual." In this sense, psychodiagnostic testing is a specific form of psychological experimentation. (See *Traits*).

2. *History.* Diagnostic psychology employing tests was not founded by a particular individual or publication. Interest in differential psychology (q.v.) led certain research workers in the late nineteenth century to develop and use measuring instruments to determine interindividual differences; interest centered first on intellectual differentiations (see *Abilities*) and intelligence tests, for educational (McK. Cattell, 1890; H. Münsterberg, 1891; H. Ebbinghaus, 1897; A. Binet, 1905, etc.), psychopathological (C. Rieger, 1888; E. Kraepelin, 1896; T. Ziehen, 1897, etc.), or philanthropic (F. Galton, 1883, who already used fundamental statistics in his work) reasons. It is significant that many of these psychologists were influenced directly (e.g. Cattell, Kraepelin and Münsterberg), or indirectly (e.g. Binet through his colleague V. Henri), by W. Wundt and his experimental psychology. Binet's test methods (the "échelle métrique" for individual testing) were used in many countries (USA, Germany, Switzerland, Sweden, etc.) and the development after 1917 of group testing methods (see *Army Alpha Test; Army Beta Test*) in the USA (L. M. Terman, G. M. Whipple, R. M. Yerkes *et al.*), which proved extremely useful in the selection of soldiers, played an important part in earning recognition for prediction of performance by means of tests. The simultaneous development of the classical test theory (H. O. Gulliksen) made it possible to provide a full theoretical foundation for these methods.

The development of methods to determine emotional, motivational and—in the broadest sense—characterological components (see *Projective techniques*) began with psychoanalysis (q.v.). Jung's word association test (1904) may be considered the starting-point of this development, which culminated in Rorschach's shape interpretation method (1921).

Today psychodiagnostic tests form an essential part of practical and scientific psychology. They are used for individual diagnosis and in the academic sector for developing, verifying and refuting theories.

3. *Test criteria.* Literature on the subject (Anastasi, 1966; Cronbach, 1971, *et al.*) lists criteria which must be met by a test: (*a*) *standardization:* the test material, instructions and the test situation must be standardized sufficiently for each subject to be confronted with identical conditions, so that his own behavior is the only variable; in this way, interindividual comparability of the test results is guaranteed; (*b*) *norms:* to make quantitative statements on the degree of development of a given feature in an individual, comparable results from other individuals are needed in order to determine the relative position of an individual on a scale. A number of different normative scales are used in psychodiagnostics. The requirement of standardization is met only by *psychometric tests*, i.e. test methods which allow a particular feature to be measured (numerical determination); (*c*) the *objectivity* (one of the main quality criteria, in addition to *reliability* and

validity) of a test is defined in a variety of ways in the literature. Lienert understands this term to denote the degree to which different evaluators are in agreement, i.e. arrive at the same results; Watson, on the other hand, suggests (1959) that the test material should have the same stimulus value for every testee, while Cattell (1957) stipulates that subjective, distorting influences on the part of the subject must be eliminated; (*d*) *reliability:* for proper interpretation of a test value, it is necessary first of all for this value to be characteristic of an individual. Reliability determines the accuracy of the measurement, regardless of what is measured. Reliability (generally represented in numerical terms by a reliability coefficient) characterizes the proportion of interindividual dispersion for a test result which is explained by "true" interindividual differences, by comparison with the proportion of total variance which can be explained by measurement errors and intervening factors in the test record (*error variance*). Two different sources of error must be taken into consideration here: the inaccuracy of a test as a measuring instrument (lack of consistency and inadequate evaluative objectivity), and changes in test conditions (inadequate objectivity in test arrangements, motivational influences, situational interference, etc.). The effect of these sources of error varies as a function of the different operational possibilities of determining a reliability coefficient. When tests are repeated with the same or an equivalent test form, the two sources of error come into play, whereas when reliability is determined by a method of test halving, the conditions of implementation may be considered more or less constant, so that any lack of consistency and objectivity in evaluation are particularly important here. Test halving gives a more optimistic estimate of reliability than determination of repeat reliability. *It is impossible to speak of the reliability of a test in an absolute sense.* The commonest techniques to determine reliability are:

(i) *test repetition:* (with the same test form —test-retest; with equivalent test form— parallel test); (ii) halving techniques (split-half): halving as a function of the test time— in speed tests; random halving; odd-even-split-half—division into items with odd and even indexes; halving on the basis of analysis data—items of identical selectivity and difficulty in each test half (inter-item consistency).

In the English-language literature, reliability coefficients determined by halving techniques are generally referred to as *consistency coefficients*, whereas coefficients obtained by repetition with the same test form are *stability coefficients;* if there is repetition with a parallel form, we speak of *equivalence*.

Reliability coefficients enable the standard measurement error of a score to be calculated, and the confidence interval to be estimated (taking into account also the mean value and test dispersion); in this interval there is a specific probability that a "true" test value can be found.

(*e*) *Validity*. Whereas reliability concerns only the formal accuracy of measurements, validity determines the degree of accuracy with which a test measures the parameters it is designed to measure. A distinction is made between three different validation concepts: *criterion-related validity*, *content validity* and *construct validity* (q.v.); for diagnostic practice the most important of these is criterion-related validity. Here validity is defined empirically as the correlation with a criterion; many different comparisons may be used as criteria, ranging from objective notations of performance (e.g. production figures) to subjective appraisals (e.g. by a superior).

In the case of criterion-related validation, a distinction is made between *concurrent validity* and *predictive validity*. In concurrent validity, the test values are measured simultaneously with the criterion values; this allows a diagnosis to be made. A prognosis of anticipated behavior is not possible from this validation. In the case of predictive validity, psychological test results are used to predict criterion values measured after the test values. The period of prediction may vary widely, as may the validity coefficients determined for different time intervals. Under certain circumstances validation of a test may not be necessary, i.e. when the validity of a test is logically or psychologically evident (e.g. a spelling test for the criterion "spelling"), if a test is more comprehensive than a criterion (e.g. the task of continuing a series of numbers gives a better impression of the "ability to abstract" than a score in mathematics), if no practical criterion exists (e.g. in interest questionnaires), or if the criterion is much less reliable than the test (e.g. a teacher's appraisal of intelligence). In all these cases it is assumed that the test problems are themselves the best possible criteria. We then speak of *content validity*.

A third, more theoretical than pragmatic, concept of validation is that of *construct validity* (q.v.). This is concerned less with practical-diagnostic relevance than with the clarification of the actual factors measured in a test.

In addition to these main criteria of quality, a test must be comparable, economical and useful.

4. *Classification of psychodiagnostic tests.* Psychodiagnostic tests can be classified on the basis of a range of factors concerning *content* or *form*. Performance tests are sometimes contrasted with personality tests, although this dichotomy is rarely encountered in personality psychology. This division corresponds to Cronbach's (1971) distinction between maximum and typical performance tests. The classification of psychometric and projective methods does not take into account the fact that different classification standpoints are used, and that these two possibilities are certainly not mutually exclusive. Clearer classifications may be established from formal criteria: e.g. standardized—non-standardized tests; one-dimensional—multi-dimensional tests; speed tests; power tests; individual tests; group tests; etc.

5. *Test construction.* We cannot examine in detail here the many theoretical and technical problems of test construction, and confine ourselves to the individual stages of construction: (*a*) *Planning* covers the selection of the type of problem best suited to the aim of the study (correct—wrong, free answer, multiple choice, etc.), as well as the test time and test length. (*b*) *Test design:* bearing in mind the range of applicability of the test (which also determines to some extent the type of validation), the plan must be provisionally implemented. Very great importance attaches here to the content of the test problems, the structural design of the test (questionnaire, test battery, etc.), the test instruction and problems of test evaluation. (*c*) *Construction of the test problems:* problem concepts are designed having regard to the aim of the study and then broken down into concrete individual problems. These are subsequently built up into a first provisional test form. (*d*) *Problem analysis:* an analysis sample is used to check the test problems for utility (with regard to reliability and validity). The criteria for a good test problem are difficulty, selectivity, and—less frequently—the validity relationship between individual problems and the degree of characterization of a particular feature). Item analysis is used to eliminate unsuitable problems, and the problems as a whole are revised as far as necessary. The instructions are also tested under practical conditions. (*e*) *Distribution analysis* of the raw values. A standard distribution is generally the aim, but in special cases an oblique distribution may be desirable because of the better differentiation obtained in specific areas. (*f*) Preparation of the *final test form.* The nature of the material, problem arrangement, test time and instructions, instructions for arranging and evaluating the tests are now defined in detail. (*g*) Check on *quality criteria, reliability* and *validity* by various methods. (*h*) *Test calibration,* as the final stage in standardizing a test, is carried out on a calibrated sample; the results are

then to draw up test norms. See *Objective tests; Test theory.*

Bibliography: Anastasi, A.: Psychological testing. New York, [2]1966. **Bormuth, J. R.:** On the theory of achievement test items. Chicago & London, 1970. **Cattell, R. B.:** Personality and motivation: structure and measurement. New York, 1957. **Cronbach, L. J.:** Essentials of psychological testing. New York & London, [3]1971. **Lyman, H. B.:** Test scores and what they mean. New York & London, [2]1971. **Rapaport, D.** *et al.*: Diagnostic psychological testing. New York & London, [2]1971. **Thorndike, R. L.:** Personal selection test, and measurement methods. New York, 1949. **Watson, R. I.:** Historical review of objective personality testing: the search for objectivity. In: **Bass, B. M. & Berg, I. A.** (Eds.): Objective approaches to personality assessment. New York, 1959, 1–23. *D. Pfau*

Test battery. A group of different tests designed to test a broad ability (general intelligence level, aptitude for specific schools or professions, etc.). The intercorrelations between the individual tests should not be too high, but the correlation between the overall result and the criterion should be higher than that of the individual test. See *Test theory.* *R.M.*

Test economy. One of the secondary quality criteria for a test. A distinction is made between three major aspects: implementation, evaluation and interpretation economy. In general all three economy conditions are more stringent for objective than for projective methods. They constitute an important criterion in selecting tests for routine and group purposes. *P.Z.*

Testicles (*testes; testiculi*). See *Gonads; Sex gland hormones.*

Testicular feminization. See *Hermaphroditism.*

Test norms. In the methodological context, the term "norms" usually denotes *test norms* (= standardized raw score). In psychology, on the other hand, the "norms" refers to different aspects of behavioral "normality".

1. *Significance of test norms.* The score (raw score) calculated initially in a test evaluation consists of units chosen arbitrarily with a zero point selected at will. The raw score in test (A) is not directly comparable with the score obtained in test (B). The raw score usually does not enable the relative position of a testee in his group to be determined directly. To eliminate these drawbacks, test psychology has developed transformation methods by means of which the raw score can be converted into standardized values. The task of establishing norms is one of the main problems of calibration in the final test construction phase. It should be noted that test norms acquire major importance only if the reliability of the test is sufficiently high, as this is the only way of obtaining statistical references for inter-individual and intraindividual differences along a test scale. The lower the empirical reliability, the less accurate the standardization scale need be, and *vice versa.*

2. *Classification of test norms:* depending on the particular problem, test norms may be classified in a variety of ways.

(*a*) *Simple* and *multiple norms:* if separate norms are established for the overall sample (standardized sample) and/or for individual subgroups within it, we refer to simple norms. If both overall and group norms are formed, we refer to multiple norms. Representativity (because of small samples) is particularly important for group norms.

(*b*) *Equivalent* and *variability norms:* while equivalent norms refer to the mean values for different groups which can be classified according to a sociologically relevant criterion (e.g. age, school year, etc.), the most common variability norms are based on variability within a given standardized sample.

(*c*) *Non-parametric and parametric norms:* from this formal angle, a distinction may be made between test norms as a function of the transformation process on which they are based.

(i) *Non-parametric norms* are used for raw scores which do not conform to a standard statistical distribution. Percent rank norms are obtained by converting the raw score into a rank between 1 and 100. Although these norms are still used, they have the drawback that the actual individual test differences are exaggerated in the medium scale range, and underestimated in the extreme ranges. Percent rankings therefore undergo further transformation. From the statistical angle, test norms merely require an asymptotic raw score distribution.

(ii) *Parametric norms* are used for scores following a standard statistical distribution of the type normally encountered in carefully constructed psychometric procedures. These linear transform methods always refer to a basic distribution, i.e. to the standard or z transformation, based on the well-known equation $z = (x - \bar{x})/s$. To avoid negative values, preference is given to the following test norms: Z norms, obtained through $Z = 100 + 10z$; IQ (intelligence quotient) norms, obtained through $\text{IQ} = 100 + 15z$; school mark norms, obtained through $S = 3z$. See *Test theory; Objective tests.*

V. Sarris & G. A. Lienert

Testosterone. The most important male sex hormone. The administration of testosterone often leads to an improvement in persons with a disturbed endocrine metabolism. The effect in healthy persons is uncertain. Extensive studies by H. Düker show an improvement in performance in slightly exhausted individuals, whereas the improvement is only temporary in completely normal subjects. Only a small percentage (about 1%) of active testosterone is excreted unchanged in the urine. The percentage differs from individual to individual, but is relatively constant. Under stress (q.v.) conditions, the amount of testosterone excreted in urine appears to be reduced.

Bibliography: **Rose, R. M.:** Androgen excretion in stress. In: **Bourne, P. G.** (Ed.): The psychology and physiology of stress. New York, 1969. See also *Sex gland hormones.*

W.J.

Test profile. A graphic representation of test results. Test profiles are popular because of their clarity and generally make for much easier interpretation. Specific forms of intelligence, professional profiles, etc. are associated with the individual profile forms, as a function of the particular test concerned.

H.J.A.

Test projectif d'intérêts vocationnels. A test developed by F. Bemelmans to clarify vocational interests. The test is designed on the TAT principle. It consists of two series of thirty small photographs, differing according to sex; the testee is asked to answer six questions concerning the activity of the persons illustrated in each photograph.

Bibliography: **Bemelmans, F.:** Test projectif d'intérêts vocationnels. Schweiz. Z. f. Psychol., 1953, *12*, 283–94.

H.J.A.

Test theory. 1. *A basis for definition.* As it is used in psychology and related behavioral sciences, the term "test theory" has a number of quite distinct connotations. At the core of the most widely accepted meaning, however, there is reference to conditions under which numbers are assigned to objects in ways that will ensure that the numbers will reliably and validly represent amounts (i.e. magnitudes) of an attribute of the objects. In specifying these conditions, many theories are elaborated: test theory refers to a collection of theories developed under the headings of reliability, standardization, levels of measurement, validity, item characteristic curves, corrections for chance success, scaling, and norms. Entire books (see bibliography) are written to explicate these various theories. There is thus a domain of test theory. But because the elements of this domain are quite diverse, are sometimes in competition, and are not closely interlocked in a single unifying system, it can be a bit misleading to imply that there is *a* (singular) test theory. Here the term is defined by referring to some of the important kinds of theories considered under headings such as those mentioned above.

2. *Axioms and levels of measurement.* In one important set of test theories, the focus is upon specifying fundamental relationships between meta-theories of mathematics, and procedures whereby numbers may be assigned to objects to represent amounts of an attribute. In such theories the position of formal axiomatics is implicitly accepted. It is assumed that number systems and number operations defined within subsections of mathematics exist quite independently of empirical observations (including those which, historically, led to the development of the system of mathematics). The task of measurement is then viewed as one of forming a one-to-one (isomorphic) link-up between magnitudes of an attribute and the numbers of an established system of numbers.

Four characteristics of the number system of scalar algebra are singled out as having particular relevance for defining the essential nature of measurement. These are referred to as the properties of identity, order, order of difference, and true zero. By *identity* is meant simply that a number symbol, such as 5, is distinct from all other number symbols, and represents the same thing regardless of the context in which it appears. The order *property* refers to the fact that of all numbers that are not identical, one is either larger or smaller than another. It is sometimes convenient to think of an ordered number as representing magnitude of an attribute of numerosity of the number system. The order of *difference characteristic* then represents the fact that differences (and sums) of numerosity are defined explicitly as numbers which, as all other numbers, are ordered. The *zero characteristic* refers to the fact that the number system contains a unique number, zero, which represents the idea of no numerosity, or none of the attributes represented by other numbers.

Levels of measurement are defined by specifying which of these characteristics of a number system are, or (as is more common) are assumed to be, isomorphically related to magnitudes of an attribute of objects. If, when all of a set of objects have the same amount of an attribute, the same number is consistently assigned, the identity property is used. If only this property is used, a nominal level of measurement is said to obtain. To use the order property, it is necessary that the order of numbers assigned to objects be the same as (or the exact reverse of) the order of magnitudes of an attribute. This kind of an assignment of numbers is referred to as an ordinal level of measurement. The order of difference property is used when numbers are assigned to objects in such a way that the order of differences between numbers is consistently the same as the order of differences in magnitudes of an attribute of the objects. When numbers are assigned in this way, theorists speak of an interval level of measurement. If an object has none of an attribute, or such an object can be conceived of as an extrapolation from observations, and the zero number is assigned, then either ordinal level measurement with a true zero, or interval level measurement with a true zero, is said to obtain. The latter is most often referred to as the ratio level of measurement.

3. *Combinative models and item characteristic theories.* The basic element of most psychological measurements is a response to an identifiable stimulus. In itself, however, a response is usually too small a sample from the responder's repertoire of possible responses to be a reliable and valid indicator of a magnitude of an attribute: a single response is usually a rather unstable, complex, and trivial indicator of many attributes. In most behavioral measurement, therefore, it is necessary to combine several responses. There are

many ways to do this, and therefore many combinative models, but by far the most commonly used procedure is merely to count the number of responses of a particular kind (e.g. "correct responses") to a set of stimuli all of which are assumed to provoke responses that are indicative of the attribute in question. The measurement obtained by counting the number correct in an ability test is typical. This procedure is part of what is frequently referred to as the summative model.

A theory about the relationship between the probability of responding in a particular way to a stimulus and magnitude of an attribute is an item characteristic theory. Several of these are considered in books on test theory. They are usefully cross-classified as either monotonic or non-monotonic and as either probabilistic or deterministic. The theory implicit in most applications of the summative model, and therefore the one most commonly accepted, belongs to the class of monotonic probabilistic theories. According to this kind of theory, as magnitude of an attribute increases, the probability of a response counted to measure that attribute should increase: if several responses to a stimulus are recorded and assigned different numbers (such as 1, 2, 3 and 4) before being summed with numbers representing responses to other stimuli, then there should be a positive monotonic relationship between the item numbers assigned and the total sum-score.

4. *Error theory and concepts of reliability.* If the assumptions of the summative model and a monotonic item characteristic theory are warranted, then it is reasonable to suppose that, in summing responses, the indications of irrelevant attributes will function as random errors which cancel out; and that there will be an accumulation of information on the non-random influence represented by the positive relationship between stimulus response and total score. This idea of a cancelling of random influences and convergence in a non-random influence is basic to many theories of reliability. In the particular application outlined here, the concept of internal consistency reliability is indicated: a set of stimuli is said to be internally consistent if response to each stimulus reliably indicates the same attribute as does response to all other stimuli of the set. A measurement operation may be reliable in this sense without being reliable in the sense that a subject obtaining a high score on one day would obtain a correspondingly high score on another day. Consistency in measurements obtained at distinctly different times is referred to as "stability" reliability. Measurements of thirst might show high internal consistency reliability, but low stability reliability. Consistency in measurements obtained with distinctly different measurement operations—as, for example, different tests—indicates equivalency reliability. When measurements depend upon complex judgments made by raters, it is useful to assess consistency across raters. This is referred to as "inter-rater" or "conspect" reliability. Conspect reliability and equivalency reliability can be high when internal consistency and stability reliability are low. (See also *Construct validity.*)

5. *Dynamic nature of test theory.* This sampling of some of the basic concepts of test theory can only adumbrate the outlines of a broad and complex field within the behavioral sciences. There is much activity and change within this field. The assumptions outlined above are being considered evermore carefully by an increasing number of investigators; a variety of non-linear, non-Euclidean and multivariate theories for representing responses in measurements are being studied; unusual theories of error are being tried out; attempts are being made to specify more clearly the conditions required to assume ratio-level measurement; and many other basic questions are being asked. Yet in much of this activity there would appear to be a trend toward conceptual integration of poorly related areas. Test theory, a complex medley of loosely related theories, is developing into

an even more complex but perhaps symphonically arranged set of theories.

Bibliography: **Cattell, R. B.:** Validity and reliability: a proposed more basic set of concepts. J. Educ. Psychol., 1964, *55*, 1–22. **Id. & Tsujioka, B.:** The importance of factor-trueness and validity versus homogeneity and orthogonality, in test scales. Educational and Psychological Measurement, 1964, *24*, 3–30. **Ghiselli, E. E.:** Theory of psychological measurement. New York, 1964. **Gullicksen, H.:** Theory of mental tests. New York, 1950. **Horn, J. L.:** Equations representing combinations of components in scoring psychological variables. Acta Psychologica, 1963, *21*, 184–217. **Id.:** Integration of concepts of reliability and standard error of measurement. Educational and Psychological Measurement, 1971, *31*. **Horst, P.:** Psychological measurement and prediction. Belmont, Calif., 1960. **Lord, F. M.:** A theory of test scores. Psychometric Monographs, 1952, *7*. **Id.:** An approach to mental test theory. Psychometrika, 1959, *24*, 283–302. **Nunnally, J. C.:** Psychometric theory. New York, 1967.

J. L. Horn

Tetanus. **1.** The rhythmic contraction of the striated skeletal muscle which occurs under normal conditions. As a function of the frequency of contraction, a distinction is made between incomplete tetanus with visible tremor, and complete tetanus with uniform, flowing movements.

2. Lockjaw: an acute, severe infection caused by the toxic influence of the tetanus bacilli, characterized by tonic muscle cramps which begin in the face (*risus sardonicus*) and spread throughout the muscular system, so that there is a risk of asphyxia and of bone fractures. Passive and active vaccination is possible and advisable. *E.D.*

Tetrachoric correlation. An estimate of the relationship between two normally distributed, continuous variables obtained from the information contained in a two-class table. The tetrachoric correlation is a two-class correlation coefficient. See *Correlational techniques*. *D.W.E.*

Thalamus. The largest subdivision of the diencephalon, consisting chiefly of an ovoid mass of nuclei in each lateral wall of the third ventricle, and divisible into an anterior and medial group of nuclei constituting the paleothalamus; concerned with primitive correlations in connection with the *corpus striatum* but not the cerebral cortex, and a center for the crude perception of pain and affective qualities of other sensations: it is the major relay center between the cerebral cortex and various sensory and optic pathways. *E.D.*

Thanatos instinct. See *Death instinct*.

Thematic Apperception Test (*abb. TAT*). A psychodiagnostic (q.v.) procedure developed by Morgan & Murray and published in 1935. The TAT is based on the hypothesis that, in imaginary stories centering upon pictorial material open to several interpretations, an individual expresses motives (q.v.), needs (q.v.), attitudes (q.v.), and conflicts (q.v.), which throw light on his own personality. Procedures of this kind are known as "thematic apperception techniques" (Kornadt, 1964). The widely circulated test material from the TAT revision published by Murray in 1943 consists of a manual describing the test, its use and evaluation, and thirty picture cards with a simplified representation in black and white of mainly social and human situations, together with a blank card. The cards were selected according to a clinical test (which is not precisely defined), and some of them are intended for certain reference groups (male or female—under or over fourteen years of age), and bear appropriate markings. It is allegedly possible for the test to be used with subjects from the age of approximately eight years (Revers & Taeuber, 1968). In each of two sessions S. is given ten picture cards in a predetermined sequence, and is asked to tell an exciting story about each picture; at least twenty-four hours should elapse between the two sessions. Because time is limited, it often happens in practice that only a smaller number of cards is used (Bell, 1948; and others). Very different techniques have been developed to evaluate TAT stories; they can be put into three groups: (*a*) evaluation by content; (*b*) formal counting methods based on content; (*c*) purely formal counting methods. In practice, techniques belonging to the third category are chiefly used, whereas methods of the second and third kind have become particularly relevant in research.

First technique: Murray himself has proposed an evaluation technique based on content and going back to a general personality model which he devised in 1938 and which has become known as "need-press analysis": the needs (q.v.), feelings, wishes of the principal figure in each story, and the environmental influences ("press") to which he is exposed, are recorded with a numerical weighting; the sum of these loadings in the whole test then gives for each variable a numerical value which expresses its prominence. Other evaluative techniques based on content have been proposed by Tomkins (1947), Stein (1955) and Rapaport (1943). Bellak with his "inspection technique" (Bellak, 1954), and an outline evaluation schedule (Bellak, 1947), responded to the need for a less time-consuming interpretation. A proposal for a shortened evaluation has been made by Revers (Revers, 1958; Revers & Taeuber, ²1968).

Second technique: Proposals for a formal counting method based on content were made by Dana (1959). McClelland *et al.* (1953). The technique of motive measurement—especially in the area of performance motivation—as developed by McClelland and others, was taken up and elaborated in German-speaking countries by, among others, Heckhausen (1963), Sader & Keil (1968) and Vontobel (1970).

Third technique: the purely formal counting methods exclude considerations of content in evaluating the story and are based solely on structural characteristics. One of the most extreme proposals taking this line comes from Balken & Masserman (1940).

The development of *norms* for TAT was neglected for a long time (Kornadt, 1964), although as early as 1943 Murray had published norms for "need-press" analysis; other attempts to construct norms were directed to the formulation of "common stories", frequent stories concerning certain cards (Stein, 1948, etc.) and the identification of cliché stories and deviations from them (Rapaport, 1943).

The results of investigations to determine reliability and to validate TAT findings are not unanimous (Kornadt, 1964), and are so strongly influenced by the questions or picture selection forming the object of the particular study that general pronouncements are not possible. See *Protective techniques.*

Bibliography: Balken, E. R. & Masserman, J. H.: The language of phantasy. J. Psychol., 1940, *10*, 75–86. **Bell, J. E.:** Projective techniques. New York, 1948, 207–38. **Bellak, L.:** Thematic Apperception Test blank. Psychological Corporation, New York, 1947. **Id.:** The Thematic Apperception test and the children's apperception test in clinical use. New York, 1954. **Dana, R. H.:** Proposal for objective scoring of the TAT. Perceptual and Motor Skills, 1959, *9*, 27–43. **Heckhausen, H.:** Hoffnung und Furcht in der Leistungsmotivation. Meisenheim, 1963. **Kornadt, H. J.:** Thematische Apperzeptionsverfahren. In: **Heiss, R.** (Ed.): Handbuch der Psychologie, Vol. 6. Göttingen, 1964, ²1966. **McClelland,** *et al.*: The achievement motive. New York, 1953. **Morgan, C. D. & Murray, H. A.:** Method of investigating fantasies: the Thematic Apperception Test. Arch. Neurol. Psychiatr., 1935, *34*, 289–306. **Murray, H. A.:** Explorations in personality. New York, 1938. **Id.:** Thematic Apperception Test manual. Cambridge, 1943. **Rapaport, D.:** The clinical application of the Thematic Apperception Test. Bull. Menninger Clin., 1943, *7*, 106–13. **Revers, W. J. & Taeuber, K.:** Der Thematische Apperzeptionstest. Berne, ²1968. **Sader, M. & Keil, W.:** Faktorenanalytische Untersuchungen zur Projektion der Leistungsmotivation. Arch. Ges. Psychol., 1968, *120*, 25–53. **Stein, M. I.:** The Thematic Apperception Test. Cambridge, 1948. **Tomkins, S. S.:** The Thematic Apperception Test. New York, 1947. **Vontobel, J.:** Leistungsbedürfnis und soziale Umwelt. Berne, 1970.

F.J.B.

Thematic sign tests. Tests in which S. is asked to draw a specific theme (e.g. tree, man, family, house, person, etc.). The test is then used to reach conclusions concerning S's. social behavior, intelligence, etc., on the assumption of personality projection. See *Projective techniques*. *H.J.A.*

Theoretical frequency. Theoretical frequencies are frequency indices calculated on the basis of hypotheses or known basic entities. Distributions of theoretical frequencies can always be described by distribution functions. *D.W.E.*

Theoretical type. One of Spranger's six "forms of life", denoting persons who are always concerned to find the truth and arrive at general laws. They are interested in intellectual matters and not in "a bed to sleep in" (Helwig, 1957, 82). They search for truth as the sole value, and their emotions are oriented to this goal.

Bibliography: Helwig, P.: Charakterologie. Stuttgart, 1957. *W.K.*

Theory. In philosophy, a construct deduced logically by the intelligence and isolated from action; a consistent group of concepts and statements derived from principles, built up methodically and systematically and detached from their application. In science, laws expressed in a systematic form, which are based on observation and remain true until they are superseded by new data; they are therefore dependent on a specific state of knowledge. The purpose of a theory is not only to explain the known but to forecast the unknown. In the narrower sense, a theory is a system of axiomatic mathematical statements which serves as a model for a set of empirical laws (hypothetico-deductive theory). Examples: theory of reminiscence (q.v.); theory of relativity. *M.J.B.*

Thermoreceptors. There are two kinds of receptor in the skin which respond to heat; they are known as *cold spots* and *hot spots*. Respectively, these respond to temperatures above and below skin temperature. *C.D.F.*

Thinking. I. Thinking is defined operationally as the establishing of order(s) in the apprehended world. This ordering relates to objects as well as to representations of the world of objects. Thinking is also the ordering of relations between objects, and the ordering of relations between representations of objects.

The figurative or pictorial representation (imagery) of what has been perceived makes it possible to order according to *equality*, *similarity*, or *difference:* objects with the same visual, acoustic, haptic or kinesthetic qualities are treated as belonging together; inequalities lead to separation from the grouping of similar objects. The action of ordering with figurative and pictorial images is called *intuitive thinking*.

The younger subjects are, the more stubbornly they adhere to intuitive orders, and are unable to classify the material or representations of it in any new way (principle of reversibility: Piaget, 1948).

Thought is said to be "*autistic*" (but see *Autism*) if the ordering of the experienced world takes place according to states conditioned by feeling or motivation so that it *arbitrarily* links persons, things or objects coinciding fortuitously with these inner states. If *wish-fulfilment* tendencies determine the results of thinking, the thought processes are defined as *primary*; if, on the other hand, *rational* ordering techniques determine the result of thinking, the thought processes are defined as *secondary* (S. Freud).

Magical thinking orders the relations of image, sign or symbol to the object as if objects, animals or plants, as well as representations of them, were capable of acting like human beings. This way of thinking is frequently found in younger children, uninformed adults, and in exceptional existential states.

If the representations, thoughts and their relations which are being ordered can no longer be expressed in imagery or figuratively, then thinking is non-intuitive, abstract or conceptual (Selz, 1913). An experimental example is searching for words which are subordinated, co-ordinated, or superordinated to a given stimulus word. In such thinking activity the *task* determines the direction thinking will take: "determining tendency" (Ach, 1905), or "convergent and divergent thinking" (J. P. Guilford). The simulation of thinking processes by means of binary-functioning electronic models makes use of the thinking steps expressed audibly by testees.

The establishing of ordered relations between representations or thoughts is conceptual behavior. Rules, thought patterns and operators are developed, or those already known are applied in a formalized model (orientation experiment on maps, Bartlett, 1958) (actualization of knowledge). An experimental example: Kendler (1970): testees learn that the choice of two large squares, then that the choice of two small squares and finally that the choice of two black squares, is correct. The relearning required to change from the concept "big" to the concept "small" can be managed by adults; that from big to black by children up to the age of six; then the verbalization of rules of thinking enables them to proceed like adults. In the response method, different objects are given words until the testee defines the order set with a comprehensive concept. Both reinforced and non-reinforced reactions lead to the formation of concepts; concepts are verbal mediators between perceived material and attempts to arrange the material (C. E. Osgood). In the mechanized or electronic stimulus-response experiment of complex thinking behavior, the testee orders stimuli in classes, and simultaneously decides verbally or in accordance with stimulus what he supposes to be the order system stored in the sequence of stimuli. A success or a mistake is indicated or corrected as the case may be, so that with each reaction one "bit" (q.v.) of information-growth can be used. The quotient of the optimal and the observed increment of knowledge indicates the strategy of information-assembly. Multiple response-sequence analyses with fixed alternating selection possibilities reveal individual styles of deciding and thinking.

Bibliography: Ach, N.: Über die Willenstätigkeit und das Denken. Göttingen, 1905. **Bartlett, F.:** Thinking. New York, 1958. **Bruner, J. S.** *et al.*: A study of thinking. New York, 1962. **Duncan, C. P.** (Ed.): Thinking: current experimental studies. New York, 1967. **Graumann, C. F.** (Ed.): Denken. Berlin, 1965. **Hedinger, U.:** Die Faktorenstruktur komplexer Denkaufgaben. Zschr. exp. angew. Psychol., 1965, *12*, 337–403. **Kendler, H. H.** *et al.*: Stimulus control and memory loss in reversal shift behavior. J. exp. Psychol., 1970, *83*, 84–8. **Külpe, O.:** Versuche über Abstraktion. Ber. l. Kongr. exp. Psychol. Giessen, 1904. **Selz, O.:** Über die Gesetze des geordneten Denkverlaufs. Stuttgart, 1913.

E. Jorswieck

II. In the USSR, psychological research into thinking is developing on the bases of cognition theory (q.v.), dialectical materialism, logic, the physiology of higher nervous activity, information theory (q.v.), cybernetics (q.v.), and other sciences adjacent to psychology. Soviet psychology rejects all idealistic and metaphysical interpretations of thinking as "purely mental" or "spontaneous activity", and supports instead the Marxist socio-historical theory of the development of thinking in the process of practical activity and human intercourse. The production of ideas, notions and of the consciousness is primarily interwoven directly with the material activity and the material intercourse of human beings; it is the language of real life (Marx & Engels). In the further course of socio-historical development it becomes possible to abstract from real actions, to replace them with mental actions, or those described with words (other, different signs are also used for this purpose).

On this foundation the highest—abstract and generalized—form of thinking arises. Simultaneously, a separation of cognition takes place: it becomes a special theoretical activity, which nevertheless remains linked to practice as the source and criterion of accuracy, and the place where the results of thinking will be used. From the start, thinking is an active, purposeful process of cognition, a creative activity, a search for the solutions to practical and subsequently to theoretical problems.

These general principles relate not only to the socio-historical but also to the ontogenetic development of thinking, which from the time proceeds by paths of its inception goes along ways different to those of the biological evolution of thinking in the animal world. The latter is only the "prehistory of the intellect", which remains restricted by the limits of biological needs, these being satisfied by elementary forms of intuitive-practical thinking (practical analysis and practical synthesis). But social factors are of crucial importance in the ontogenetic development of thinking, a child's conversation with adults, social forms of play, participation in ongoing work, school instruction, etc.; their influence determines not only the content but the structure of thinking operations. Age "norms" for the mental development of the child are relative, and can vary within a very wide range—independently of any system of education and training. In this connection, Soviet psychologists criticize the formal evaluation of the intellect with the aid of tests which usually do not consider the possibilities of a child's mental development during training and practical activity. Hence long-term observation of children undergoing instruction at school remains the principal means of determining mental development and its prognosis. The use of short-term intelligence tests can have only a limited significance. (See *Abilities*).

From the psychological angle, thinking is characterized as a complex analytical-synthetic activity of the brain, its cortical and subcortical mechanisms, which process all the objective and linguistic information reaching the brain (the first and second systems, according to I. P. Pavlov) and correct it with the mechanisms of *feedback* (q.v.) or *retroactive afference.* In this process, according to Pavlov, different degrees of correlation between the first and second signal systems are possible; different types of thinking can then develop (intuitive or "artistic", abstract or "verbal", or mixed). This difference of types of thinking (q.v.) is, however, relative, and depends on many factors (e.g. the kind of objects being thought about, experience, diverse subjective attitudes, etc.). Such conditions apply also to the early ontogenetic stages of thinking, which are termed merely "sensorimotor" or "intuitive-practical", since in reality even in the second year of a child's life not only direct sensorimotor influences but verbal stimuli and verbal responses from the child himself which are bound up with them, become increasingly important in the development of his intellect. Soviet psychological research reveals the complicated and contradictory nature of the relations between thought and language (q.v.), and proves that language is not only a means for expressing thoughts but *a basic element or mechanism of thinking*, with the aid of which abstractions are made from immediate objective impressions and behaviors, which are replaced by thought-images and schemata in combination with outer or inner language.

The most complete presentation of these theoretical theses will be found in the works of L. S. Vygotsky (1934; Eng. trans., 1962), S. L. Rubinstein (1946, 1958) and A. N. Leontiev (1959, 1964), in which early and modern theories of the intellect, the theories about thinking of the Würzburg school (q.v.), of gestalt psychology, behaviorism (q.v.), and J. Piaget's approach are critically analyzed. Experimental research into thinking follows various paths in the Soviet Union, the most important of which are: (*a*) the *phylogenetic* investigation of the mental development of animals, including the genetics of higher nervous activity, animal psychology, ecology and ethology (I. P. Pavlov and his school, N. N. Ladyna-Kots, N. J. Voitonis, N. A. Tich, A. D. Slonim, L. V. Krusinski); (*b*) ontogenetic research into the mental development of children (P. P. Blonski, A. V. Zaporozhek, D. N. Usnadze, B. I. Chashapuridze, N. Ch. Shvashkin, M. M. Kolzova); (*c*) *structural-functional and operational* research into thinking in different kinds of teaching and practical activity (P. A. Shevarev, G. S. Kostiuk, P. J. Galperin, N. A. Menshinskaia); (*d*) research into *heuristics* and the *model construction* of thinking operations with electronic computers (V. N. Pushkin, D. A. Pospelov, O. K. Tichomirov); (*e*) *psycho-physiological and clinical research* (A. R. Luria, V. N. Miasichshcev, E. I. Bojko, B. V. Zeigarnik); (*f*) psycholinguistic investigations into the problem of the interrelations of language and thought, the psychological foundations of nomenclature and the understanding of meaning, the acquisition of foreign languages and translating (D. N. Usnadze, V. A. Artemov, N. I. Zhinkin); (*g*) *defectological* research specializing in the specific nature of thinking, and the ways in which it is compensated with different defects of mental development (L. V. Zankov, I. M. Solovev), and when there is either damage to hearing or some other defect (N. G. Morozova, Z. I. Shif). The results of this research work are published in psychological and other reviews, monographs and volumes with different contributions on special topics; they are also announced at scientific symposia, conferences and meetings.

Bibliography: Bartlett, F.: Thinking. London, 1958. **Blonski, P. P.:** Memory and thinking (Russian). Moscow, 1935. **Duncan, C. P.:** Thinking: current experimental studies. New York, 1967. **Graumann, C. F.:** Denken. Cologne–Berlin, 1965. **Humphrey, G.:** Thinking. London, 1951. **Ladygina-Kots, N. N.:** Research into the cognitive abilities of the chimpanzee (Russian). Moscow, 1923. **Id.:** Prerequisites for human thinking (Russian). Moscow, 1965. **Leontiev, A. N.:** Problems of psychic development (Russian). Moscow, 1959. **Luria, A. R.:** The human brain and psychological processes (Russian). Moscow, 1963. **Pushkin, V. N., Pospelov, D. A. & Sadovski, V. N.** (Eds.): Problems of heuristics (Russian). Moscow, 1969. **Rohr, A.:** Komplexes Denken. Weinheim & Basle, 1968. **Rubinstein, S. L.:** Thinking and research (Russian). Moscow, 1958. **Sokolov, A N :** Inner language and thinking (Russian). Moscow, 1968. **Usnadze, D. N.:** Psychological research (Russian). Moscow, 1966. **Voitonis, N. J.:** Prehistory of the intellect (Russian). Moscow, 1934. **Vygotsky, L. C.:** Thought and language. Cambridge, Mass., 1962. **Watson, P. C. & Johnson-Laird, P. N.** (Eds.): Thinking and reasoning. Harmondsworth, 1968. **Werner, H. & Kaplan, B :** Symbol formation. New York & London, 1963.

A. N. Sokolov

Thinking, abstract. From the viewpoint of association (q.v.) psychology, any thought process makes use of "images" or raw ideational material presented pictorially in the conscious mind. Since the Würzburg school's research into thought processes, non-pictorial or abstract thinking has been supposed to be characteristic and constitutive of thought processes. Images are often only the stimulus and starting-point of a thought process; they are accompanied by specific abstract contents (or elements of consciousness) and determinative tendencies which exert a decisive effect on the course of thinking. *H.W.*

Thinking function. According to C. G. Jung (q.v.) one of the four basic functions of the psyche. Like the feeling function, it helps us to understand our own significance and that of the world. *W.L.*

Thinking, psychology of. A collective term for several lines of research into cognitive functions, especially in solving human and animal problems. The Würzburg School (q.v.) showed (in experiments with introspection, and departing from the Aristotelian view that thinking is only a linking of images) that thinking is possible non-intuitively and without images, being controlled by "determining

background. Some are made to approach or removed to a greater distance from the eye, until all appear equidistant from it. *J.G.*

Three-sided intercourse (syn. *Triangular sex*). Heterosexual or homosexual contacts between three individuals. One of the three partners may act as a voyeur. A variation consists in one partner being heterosexually selected but homosexual, and engaging in homosexual relations with a third partner of the same sex while the first watches the activity. The association of three-sided intercourse and voyeurism is quite often a feature of genuine perversions (see *Perversion*); however, three-sided intercourse is not intrinsically perverted, but a variant sexual activity subject to strong societal taboos, and therefore less well-known. *H.M.*

Threshold. The value of a quantitative variable (e.g. sound intensity) at which a stimulus is just detectable (*absolute threshold*) or the minimum difference between two stimuli on either a quantitative or qualitative variable (e.g. hue) that is detectable (*difference or differential threshold*). In both cases it is usually necessary to express the threshold as a statistical average even for an individual subject. Also called *limen*; hence abbreviations AL and DL for absolute and difference thresholds respectively, and *subliminal perception:* referring to stimuli below the threshold of conscious perception which are nevertheless supposed to influence behavior. The *psychophysical methods* were developed originally as means for determining thresholds. See also: *Signal-detection theory*, which is a modern approach to the problem of measuring sensory thresholds. *G.D.W.*

Thurstone, Louis Leon. B. 29/5/1887 in Chicago; d. 29/9/1955 in Chapel Hill, USA. Thurstone studied electrical engineering at Cornell University and worked as an assistant of Edison's at the East Orange (N.J.) laboratory. In 1914 he began to study psychology at Chicago and at the Carnegie Institute of Technology. His initial interest was research into learning. In 1923 he worked for a year at the Institute of Government Research in Washington, and returned in 1924 to Chicago as Associate Professor of psychology; three years later he was appointed a full professor; he established a psychometric laboratory. Thorndike was among the founders of the "Psychometric Society" and its journal *Psychometrika*; in 1932 he became president of the APA, and in 1936 first president of the Psychometric Society.

Thurstone was essentially a psychometrician, and in this capacity made important contributions to many areas of psychology. In intelligent research he became well-known for his factor-analytic approach: he came out against Spearman's "g" and tried instead to derive cognitive performance from several group factors (see *Abilities; Intelligence*). After a considerable amount of factor-analytic work, he postulated his seven "primary mental abilities": verbal comprehension, numerical ability, spatial visualization, perceptual ability, memory, reasoning and word fluency. He was able to extract similar factors in corresponding investigations in other areas, e.g. in perception.

Beyond the field of intelligence, Thurstone is best known for his work on "simple structure" and many other contributions to the development of multiple factor analysis, and for the construction of modern scaling techniques and their use in attitude (q.v.) measurement. See *Factor analysis.*

Main works: The measurement of attitude: a psychophysical method and some experiments with a scale for measuring attitude toward the church. Chicago, 1929. The vectors of mind: multiple-factor analysis for the isolation of primary traits. Chicago, 1935. Primary mental abilities. Chicago, 1938. A factorial study of perception. Chicago, 1944.

Multiple-factor analysis: a development and expansion of the vectors of mind. Chicago, 1947. L. L. Thurstone. In: Boring, E. G. *et al.* (Eds.): A history of psychology in autobiography. Vol. 4. Worcester, Mass., 1952, 295–321. An analytical method for simple structure. Chicago, 1954. A method of factoring without communalities. Chicago, 1955. The measurement of values. Chicago, 1959.

Bibliography: Atkins, D. C.: Louis Leon Thurstone: creative thinker, dedicated teacher, eminent psychologist. In: **Frederiksen, N. & Gulliksen, H.** (Eds.): Contribution to mathematical psychology. New York, 1964, 1–39. *W.W.*

Thymeretics. A subgroup of the antidepressives (q.v.).

Thymoleptics. A subgroup of the antidepressives (q.v.).

Thymopsyche. A term used in A. Gemelli's personality psychology. The thymopsyche forms the layer of the personality in which drives and inclinations are formed. It lies between the layer of organic functions (constitution) and that of higher feelings, thought and will. See *Strata theory*. *W.K.*

Thymus. An endocrine organ (see *Endocrine glands*) behind the breast-bone which grows only until the individual reaches sexual maturity and then gradually degenerates into fatty tissue. Its function affects growth, calcium balance, and the development of the gonads and the entire lymphatic system. Recent research shows that the thymus is also very important for the development of immunities. *E.D.*

Thyrocalcitonin. A thyroid gland hormone which normalizes the extracellular calcium level when it becomes too high. Thyrocalcitonin is an antagonist of parathyroid hormone. The secretion and effect mechanisms of thyrocalcitonin are as yet unexplained.

Bibliography: Russell, R. G. G. & Fleisch, H. (Eds.): Thyrocalcitonin. London, 1967. *W.J.*

Thyroid gland (*Glandula thyreoidea*). A dual inner secretory gland situated on the anterior side of the neck, to the right and left of the larynx, and producing the hormone thyroxin. Histologically, it consists of epithelial follicles. Many thyroid diseases are connected with the formation of a goiter. *E.D.*

Thyroid hormones. Hormones stored by the thyroid gland. The most prominent effect is that on *metabolism*. Hyperfunction leads to increased basal metabolism. Substantial hypofunction characterizes the myxedema syndrome. In the case of innate hyperfunction, or where it appears during early youth, cretinism occurs. Slight hyperfunction often leads to adiposity. The primary thyroid hormones are *thyroxin* (tetraiodthyroxin) and the more active *triiodthyronine*. The storage of thyrotropin(e) is inhibited by both hormones. Recently, a further thyroid hormone, *thyrocalcitinon*, which causes a drop in blood calcium, was discovered. There have been few psychological tests of thyroid hormone. Under stress (q.v.) conditions, slight variable increases in storage after initial decrease have been demonstrated.

Bibliography: Klein, E.: Die Schilddrüse. Berlin, 1969. **Mason, J. W.:** A review of psychoendocrine research on the pituitary-thyroid system. Psychosom. Med., 1968, *30*, 666–81. **Pitt-Rivers, R. & Trotter, W. R.:** The thyroid gland. Washington, 1964. *W.J.*

Thyrotoxicosis. See *Basedow's disease.*

Thyrotropic hormone (TSH). See *Thyrotropin.*

Thyrotropin (*Thyropar*). A glandotropic hormone which stimulates the secretion of thyroid hormones. Secretion is regulated under the influence of the neurohormone TRH (thyrotropin-releasing hormone) produced in the hypothalamus, and by the quantity of thyroid gland hormones present in the blood. *W.J.*

Tic. A brief jerk in the muscles usually of the upper part of the body such as the face, neck or shoulder. May be due to psychological causes but may also be associated with brain damage. *P.Le.*

Time-and-motion study. The methodical investigation, analysis and synthesis of movement (using appropriate recording devices) during some work process. See *Time study*.

Time, estimation of. All reactions to the discrimination of the duration of (or between two) events, whether through comparative or absolute judgment, production or reproduction. As a specific process, time estimation is the direct assessment of duration with the aid of a subjectively numerical scale (e.g. seconds or minutes). Sometimes the term is used for events of longer duration (more than the directly experienced present of a few seconds), and thus set over against time perception. But this phenomenal distinction is not functionally straightforward.

Bibliography: Fraisse, P : Psychologie du temps. Paris, [2]1967. *A.L.*

Time, experience of. The experience of time may be defined as the representation of time in the human consciousness (q.v.).

The perception of temporal duration requires a simultaneous apprehension of successive aspects of an occurrence without the participation of memory (q.v.). The process of learning to harmonize physiological processes without environmental changes makes possible orientation in time (the "internal clock") and the anticipation of external events. "Empty" stretches of time are perceived as shorter than "full" ones. The perception of "empty" and "full" periods of time is influenced by stimulus intensity, frequency, duration and location of stimuli. Psychic (psychological) time does not elapse continuously but discretely. The shortest perceptible form of temporal duration is the "moment".

A temporal perspective develops out of the interaction of recurrent needs with environmental influences in the sense of *conditioning* (q.v.). The expectation of a need gratification already experienced at an earlier date produces the connections between past, present and future. The separation of temporal from spatial succession is a prerequisite for the perception of time. Around the eighth year of age, the ability to reconstruct events in correct time sequence and the idea of an abstract unit of time as the basis for a perspective of time corresponding to the adult level come into being. The stability of time assessment increases with age.

Old people assess a given stretch of time as shorter than young people would. For older people, time passes — subjectively — more quickly. This tendency becomes more obvious with increasing age. Women tend to be less proficient than men in the exactitude and stability of their estimation of time, and are more inclined than men to overestimate.

Time seems to pass more quickly, the higher the activation level of the organism. Low motivation for an actual event (boredom) accompanies spontaneous overassessment of periods of time, just as high motivation for a future activity accords with momentary inactivity (waiting). Spontaneous underassessment occurs with high motivation for actual events. These conditions are reversed in reminiscence (q.v.).

The variable length of hypothetical inner units of time conditions interindividual variations in the processing of temporal information. The length of these units can be altered by external circumstances (e.g. stress, q.v.).

Hallucinogens (mescalin, psilocybin, LSD-25) and thyroxin, caffeine and methamphetamine can cause overestimation of periods of time. Phenothiazine, tranquilizers (e.g. chlorpromazine), quinine and laughing gas can produce underestimation.

Phenomena of pathological time perception are: (*a*) extreme acceleration or deceleration of time perception; (*b*) loss of temporal sense of reality: absence of any awareness of a temporal continuum; (*c*) the proportions of past, present and future are displaced: one or more of these dimensions may be missing.

The perception of temporal sequences may be traced to fluctuations of attention (q.v.), whose intermediate periods are experienced as "present", and whose rhythm may depend on motivation. The hypothesized existence of a subcortical "pacemaker" center dependent on the relation between excitation and inhibition processes explains the ability of the nervous system to reproduce a series of excitations as sequential experience. See *Arousal.*

Time perception alters with fluctuations in body temperature: the basis for this process is thought to be the speed of chemical processes. Personality-dependent differences in time perception are explicable in terms of a hypothetical, individually diverse input level of chemical processes in the organism. See *Time, psychology of; Memory; Reminiscence.*

Bibliography: Fraisse, P.: Psychology of time. New York, 1963. **Id :** Zeitwahrnehmung und Zeitschätzung. In: **Metzger, W.** (Ed.): Handbuch der Psychologie, Vol. 1/1. Göttingen, 1966, 656–90. **Orme, J. E.:** Time, experience and behaviour. London, 1969. **Ornstein, R. E.:** On the experience of time. Harmondsworth, 1969.

J. Wittkowski

Time, psychology of. As an object of psychology, time is bound up with happenings as they appear to an individual (*awareness of time*), which affect or influence him (*relation to time*), or in relation to which he orientates his action (*time perspective*). *Psychic* or *psychological time* designates the totality of before-and-after relations between the individual and such events. The events are thought of as foreseen or planned (*future*), or engaged in, or accomplished (*present*), or remembered or stored (*past*). They can arise in the organism or its environment, and may be noticed or unnoticed. In their temporal aspect, all events for an individual follow an irreversible order. A given event in this series can only occur once, lasts for a shorter or longer time (*duration*), and stands in a particular relationship of order to other events (*simultaneous* or *successive*). This series and the socio-culturally conditioned relationship of its elements to each other make possible the *temporal orientation* of the individual in the world and in society.

The psychology of time does not seek to establish the philosophical nature of time, but to determine the means by which it is possible to form a concept of, and relationship to, time. It also seeks to discover the laws underlying this means, and its diverse modes of operation. Traditionally, time is real though mysterious (Augustine), but in the calendar and the clock as well as the parameters of Newtonian physics it has been made successfully operational.

Kant defined time as a "form of perception", and thus made it a central problem of psychology. The ordinary procedure of the psychology of time is to compare and contrast "objective" clock time and "subjective time", which is understood in many different ways.

1. *Duration.* The early psychophysics (q.v.) of duration investigated the awareness of time as a "sense of time" (E. H. Weber, Czermak) which, by analogy with the other senses, apprehended duration as its object. The researches of Vierordt, E. Mach, G. J. Fechner, W. Wundt and their disciples showed that

subjective time is related in a peculiar way to clock time. Hence the *difference threshold* (between time as a sense object and clock time) is smaller the shorter the duration to be apprehended. At 0.6–1 seconds it is at a minimum of 1.5–15%, according to conditions and the methods employed; it increases irregularly as the duration increases. Under optimal conditions (training and repeated presentation of the sense object), the minimum difference threshold becomes about 1% at about 100 milli-seconds.

The relation between subjective and objective duration is also unclear because the methods most frequently used of comparing, reproducing and verbally communicating the processes of apprehension (q.v.) and attention (q.v.) are various and uncorrelated.

Pronounced individual differences make the usual averages and the subjective scales derived from them appear artificial. In most studies the shorter intervals are presented in relationship to the longer, and the longer to the shorter. (Concepts of over- and underestimation are ambivalent because the relative difference is not the same in different cases.) The rate of constant error in the assessment of a length of time so that clock time agrees with subjective time is *indifference point.* This was at one time held to be a constant in the order of 0.6–0.8 seconds, or up to 1.5 seconds. More recent research shows that it is not constant but relative to the interval in question. Therefore the time or "tempo" of the "internal clock" is *dependent on the duration* of the objective length of time to be assessed. Frequent repetition of objectively the same interval effects cumulative changes in subjective duration. Unlike the immediate experience of duration, a period which seemed to pass slowly can seem in retrospect to have been short, and *vice versa.* The apprehension of, and relationship to, time can be influenced in uncertain ways by *situational conditions,* such as instruction, a context of aspiration, the nature of the stimulus, the intensity of the stimulus, a change of stimulus, a changed interpretation of the stimulus, and *organic conditions* such as the mode of apprehension, hormonal condition, psychopharmacological factors, the time of day, body temperature (q.v.), activation level (q.v.), motivation, age, intelligence (q.v.), personality traits (q.v.), psychopathological categories, and so on. The hope of using the apprehension of time as a diagnostic element in personality psychology and psychopathology, has not been fulfilled.

In the peculiar relationship between subjective and objective time there is also a phenomenological difference between immediately experienced duration (psychic *present time,* in the range of 0.5 to a few seconds; W. Stern) and longer, apparently cognitively apprehended (or not immediately experienced), periods (Fraisse, 1967). This difference cannot be functionally ascertained. With respect to the *cognitive process* (in the apprehension of duration), it is clear that under conditions of sleep (q.v.) or hypnosis (q.v.), and in animals, the relationship to time is more exact. At any rate in rhythmic behavior and experience, a frequency of one to two heart beats (corresponding to periods of 1.5 to one second) appears in many cases to be acceptable, comfortable and natural.

Early theoretical studies stressed the eventual fading of a sense impression; the extent to which a memory had faded was regarded as a temporal sign (T. Lipps). They also described apparent continuities (with the smallest difference threshold, indifference point, personal tempo, etc.) as playing a time-structuring role. In obvious analogy to the mechanical clock, the "internal clock" was thought of as the *measure of individual duration* (H. Münsterberg, W. James).

2. *Simultaneity and succession.* Under optimal conditions a practiced listener can distinguish an acoustical stimulus as two sounds with an interruption between them of a minimum of 2 msec. With optical stimuli on the same retinal image, about 50 msec are

necessary. In order to distinguish clearly between two signals distinct in place, nature of stimulus or the sense by which it is to be apprehended, a pause of 100–60 msec is necessary. Practiced observers can reduce this to about 20 msec (F. Exner, D. J. Hirsch). Events occurring at objectively different times can (within a certain span which has not been clearly determined) be subjectively experienced as simultaneous. Numerous serial interactions, usually dependent upon *temporal integration*, can be distinguished in the reception of two or more signals at a short interval.

Although the question of an absolute threshold between simultaneity and succession cannot be given a clear and general answer, the functional apprehensibility of the time dimension is of great importance for the renewal of the unitary single-number theory of the "internal clock", which is held today either explicitly or implicitly by most authors. According to this theory, subjective time is made up of a series of elements, by the "counting" of which the duration of events can be assessed and reproduced. The units are defined as apprehended internal or external occurrences in themselves (Fraisse, 1967; M. Frankhaeuser), numerous biological oscillatory and subsidiary processes of a (quasi-) periodical (for example the Alpha-rhythm: N. Wiener) or excitatory (Creelman) nature. The most commonly advanced theory (von Baier, H. Bergson, von Uexküll, Stroud) is of a cumulative series of so-called "psychic moments", together with assumed additional mechanisms to explain the special articulation of the duration dimension and its functional dependencies. These additional mechanisms are, e.g., a variable length of psychological moments, distortion of the counting process in storage, etc. (Triesman, 1963; Michon, 1967; Cohen, 1967). The discontinuity of one's apprehension of the sense object is thus assured. However, there is no proof of the relevance of this series of moments to the problem of coping with time.

3. *Orientation in time*. Research is being carried out into the so-called *time perspective* (K. Lewin; H. Frank), particularly into time span, but also into articulation, intensity, consistency and division (particularly in the experience of the future: R. Bergius), factors which are psychically active in present experience and behavior. Such research uses questionnaires and many projective (q.v.) tests both as functions and determinants of diverse social, cultural, constitutional, personal and developmental factors. The results of research to date show the relevance of temporal orientation, particularly in motivational and social psychology. But empirically tested detailed knowledge is still lacking because of the lack of any real consistency of method.

In contrast to the functional discrepancy and irregularity of subjective time, the *subjective concept of time* takes the form of an idealized, homogeneous continuum. Subjective time narrows the distant past and future to the point of immobility; the conceptual continuum continues both ways everlastingly. Accordingly, the concept of time in classical physics takes time-and-space as an absolute presupposition of the rapidity of movement dependent on them. Researches into the ontogenesis of the concept of time (J. Piaget) and the complex relationships between time, distance and speed known as the *tau phenomenon* (q.v.) and kappa effect, are undertaken on the basis of relativist physics. According to this, psychic time is constituted by the tempo of endogenous life processes, and the processes in the environment which they use for the purpose of synchronization.

Bibliography: Bindra, D. & Waksberg, H.: Methods and terminology in studies of time estimation. Psychol. Bull., 1956, *53*, 155–9. **Cohen, J.:** Psychological time in health and disease. Springfield, Ill., 1967. **Fischer, R.** (Ed.): Interdisciplinary perspectives of time. Ann. N.Y. Acad. Sci., 1967, *138* (2), 367–915. **Fraisse, P.:** Psychologie du temps. Paris, [2]1967. **Fraser, J. T.** (Ed.): The voices of time. New York, 1966. **Michon, J. A.:** Timing in temporal tracking. Soesterberg (Holland), 1967. **Mönks, F. J.:** Zeitperspektive als psychologische

Variable. Arch. ges. Psychol., 1967, *119*, 131–61. **Treisman, M.:** Temporal discrimination and the indifference interval: implications for a model of the "internal clock". Psychol. Monogr., 1963, *77* (13). No. 576. **Wallace, M. & Rabin, A. I.:** Temporal experience. Psychol. Bull., 1960, *57*, 213–36. **White, C. T.:** Temporal numerosity and the psychological unit of duration. Psychol. Monogr., 1963, *77* (12), No. 575.

A. Lang

Time sampling. A systematic or "fractionated" short-term observation method in which a subject is observed repeatedly for only a few minutes at a time in the course of a longer investigation, and the observed behavior is simultaneously or subsequently recorded. Distribution of the observations for each subject takes into account the comparability of conditions in the observation situation. Multiple short-term observation allows of a higher reliability of observational data. See *Observation; Test theory.*

Bibliography: Cronbach, L. J.: Essentials of psychological testing. New York & London, [2]1960. *J.O.*

Time sense. The mechanism by which people can estimate the passage of time is still obscure. "Primitive" time estimation, i.e. during sleep and hypnosis, is more accurate than conscious estimation. Time sense is affected by the activity being carried out during estimation and also by drugs, fever and certain psychiatric states. These latter effects suggest that metabolism may play a role in time estimation.

C.D.F.

Time-sharing systems. A computer is a time-sharing system (abb. TSS) when it is accessible simultaneously to several users by way of their own on-line service devices ("on-line" means that the user's requirements are directly processed by the computer's central unit).

K.-D.G.

Time study. Part of a work study or analysis. Among other things, a time study ascertains the time required for human work. The time spent on the task is measured and assessed experientially. Various kinds of stop watch and recording device may be used that are actuated by the worker or observers (industrial engineers), or even automatically. Cinematic records may also be made. See *Industrial psychology; Occupational psychology.*

G.R.W.M.

Titchener, E. B. Edward Bradford Titchener (1867–1927) "donned his gown, the assistant brushed his coat for fear of ashes from the ever-present cigar, the staff went out the door for apparatus and took front seats, and Titchener then appeared on the platform from the office door" (Boring, 1927). This was Titchener at Cornell, where he *was* psychology from 1892 until his death. His psychology was intellectually pure and professionally separatist. Titchener left no school behind him, though he deeply influenced many in American psychology. The determining force in his intellectual life was his time at Leipzig with Wundt (1890–92). Though he spent more years at Oxford (1875–90), taking a double first in Greats (classics and philosophy) and reading physiology, this period furnished background rather than professional orientation. Yet his English university and public school (Malvern) background and the long-established status of his family in Chichester, Sussex, probably combined to furnish a feeling for history and a scholarly exactitude which appear in his *Experimental Psychology* (1901–05), a book which Boring was inclined to accept as "the most erudite psychological work in the English language", "astonishingly accurate". Probably Titchener's most seminal theoretical doctrine was that the point of view is basic to psychology, that in it experience is treated as "dependent upon the experiencing individual" (1950, p. 417), so that a psychologist who deserts the psychological point of view commits the stimulus-error. His contributions to feeling, attention, and thought were also notable. In Titchener's immense production (7 books, 216 articles, 176 publications from the Cornell laboratory, 54 doctorates supervised), there is only one comprehensive outline of his doctrine, the *Text-book* (1909-10). His proposed systematic work never appeared, though Weld was able to put together its *Prolegomena* (1929). Of this, the opening section, on Wundt and Brentano (also in *Amer. J. Psychol.*, 1921) is now seen to be historically important. Himself a redoubtable translator (e.g. of Külpe and Wundt) Titchener was much translated. His life and work appear as a series of dualisms: psychology and not-psychology; mental process and meaning; structure and function, graciousness versus dominance; experimental rigor versus delight in music and tennis—not to mention numismatics; American residence versus British nationality (plus German appearance); a certain exclusiveness versus controversial editorship and informal leadership of the group known as the "Experimental Psychologists": a paradoxical and great man.

Bibliography: Boring, E. G.: Edward Bradford Titchener, 1867–1927. Amer. J. Psychol., 1927, *38*, 489–506. **Id.:** A history of experimental psychology. New York, [2]1950, 410–20; 435–7. **Titchener, E. B.:** A primer of psychology (rev. ed.). New York, 1903 (1899). **Id.:** Systematic psychology: prolegomena (Ed. H. P. Weld). New York, 1927. *J.A.C.*

Titchener's illusion. A contrast illusion. Two identical circles are surrounded by large and small circles respectively. The one surrounded by large circles appears smaller. *C.D.F.*

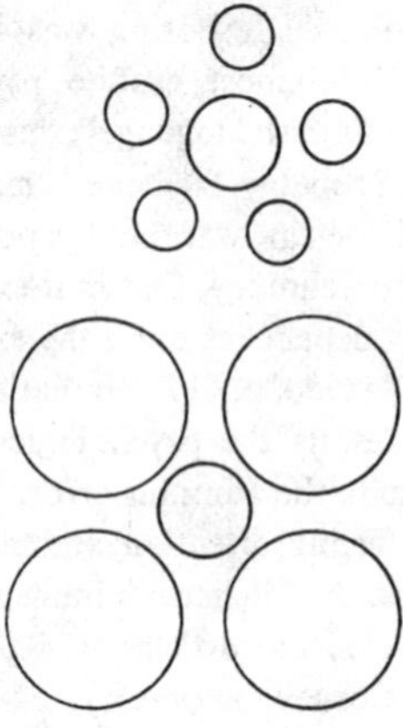

Toilet training. See *Bowel training.*

Token-object (syn. *Inductor*). Object used to elicit paranormal information concerning its owner. Sometimes used at a *séance* (q.v.) as a proxy for an absent sitter (q.v.) *J.B.*

Tolerance. A term descriptive of social attitudes and/or behaviors of an individual which —in contrast to intolerant attitudes or behaviors—show no offense at the opinions, attitudes and so on of other individuals (e.g. members of minority groups), which are divergent in substance and objective from those of the majority; "tolerance" also indicates an active seeking to prevent the rejection or repression of other or alien ways of thought and behavior.

E. Frenkel-Brunswik's (1949) term "tolerance of ambiguity" is restricted to a specific cognitive style characterized by a more or less limited ability to offer nuanced judgments and balance them in ambiguous situations. "Intolerance of ambiguity" occurs, e.g. as a tendency to prejudge an issue prematurely (see *Prejudice; Stereotype*); and to withdraw, or to resort to an authority rather than try to understand and cope with a situation.

Investigations indicate positive relations between intolerance of ambiguity and "authoritarian personality" (q.v.) traits; but these findings have not yet been confirmed.

Bibliography: Frenkel-Brunswik, E.: Intolerance of ambiguity as an emotional and perceptual personality variable. J. Pers., 1949, *18*, 108–43. **Martin, J. G.:** The tolerant personality. Detroit, 1964. *A.S.-M.*

Tolman, Edward Chace. B. 14/4/1886 in Newton, Mass.; d. 19/11/1959 in Berkeley. Tolman received his doctorate in 1915 at

Harvard. He taught until 1918 at Northwestern University, where he became interested in abstract thought, retroactive inhibition and similar phenomena of memory. From 1918 (with only short breaks, when he taught at Harvard and Chicago) he was Professor at the University of California at Berkeley. His investigations of learning and goal-directed behavior made him one of the most prominent representatives of neobehaviorism and American learning psychology. In 1937 he became president of the APA.

Cognitive learning theory. Tolman's theory of cognitive learning is distinct from the other behaviorist learning theories in a number of features: (*a*) it describes behavior not on the molecular but on the molar level; (*b*) all behavior is seen as purposive; (*c*) the individual learns not sequences of movements but *expectations*, i.e. meaningful connections between two given stimuli: the actual situation S1 (sign) and the situation arising in the course of the action (the signified, the goal); (*d*) reinforcement (q.v.) is replaced by the principle of "confirmation".

In addition to objectively measurable stimulus and response variables, Tolman postulates a series of (not directly observable) factors: "intervening variables", which as internal processes in the organism establish connections between factors: the need (q.v.) system, the "belief-value matrix", and immediate actual "behavior space".

In contrast to C. L. Hull (q.v.), who experimented mainly with problem boxes and runways, Tolman used the most diverse maze situations in his investigations. For an individual in the maze, the situation is subdivided by means of "choice points": signs which denote the way to the goal and allow orientation. On repeated trials the animal develops specific "expectations" for the different signs, i.e. differences in the probability that specific behaviors in this situation will lead to the goal. If the expectation that the way taken leads to the goal is "confirmed", the probability of its occurrence (and therefore, indirectly, the probability of the behavior in question) is increased. If the expectation is not confirmed, its probability is reduced. All that is required for confirmation is reaching the goal, and not a reduction of need tension in Hull's sense.

The signs encountered on the way to the goal are emphasized by the confirmation and become sub-goals which are themselves liable to confirm expectations. Ultimately the organism establishes a kind of "cognitive map" of all the signs in the maze situation and their meanings, and then orientates its behavior by this map.

Main works: Purposive behavior in animals and men. New York, 1932. Drives toward war. New York, 1942. Cognitive maps in rats and men. Psychol. Rev., 1948, *55*, 189–208. E. C. Tolman. In: Boring, E. G. (Ed.): A history of psychology in autobiography, Vol. 4. Worcester, Mass., 323–39. Collected papers in psychology. New York, 1951. Principles of purposive behavior. In: Koch, S. (Ed.): Psychology: a study of a science, Vol. 2. New York, 1959, 92–157.

Bibliography: Hilgard, E. R. & Bower, G. H.: Theories of learning. New York, [3]1966. *W.W.*

Tone-deafness. The inability to recognize the different pitches of musical notes. The term is often generalized to include other musical disabilities, such as the inability to recognize tunes. *C.D.F.*

Tone psychology, or the psychology of sound, is the theory of the psychophysical prerequisites for, and processes of, auditory perceptions and experiences, which originate as the result of diverse sound impressions, and in particular those with simple musical stimulus structures (e.g. clang, interval, rhythmical units). The real progenitor of tone psychology was H. von Helmholtz (1863); it was established as a discipline by Carl Stumpf (1883; 1890). The onesided nature of the study of psychoacoustics in that era was followed after the turn of the century by the development of the psychology of music, which considered music and its effective context as a complex whole and tended to question the validity of a psychology of sound oriented to physiological psychology. Later, however, tone psychology became more important, not least as the necessary basis for a psychology of music, and as a relatively independent discipline open to the varied approaches of phenomenology (q.v.), information theory (q.v.), cybernetics (see *Cybernetics and psychology*), etc. See *Experimental esthetics; Music, psychology of; Auditory perception; Sense organs: the ear; Noise.*

Bibliography: Bekesy, G. von: Experiments in hearing. New York, 1960. **Stevens, S. S.:** Bibliography on hearing. Cambridge, Mass., 1955. **Stumpf, C.:** Tonpsychologie, 2 Vols. Leipzig, 1883–90, [2]1965. *B.S.*

Tonolytics. Syn. for *Spasmolytics* (q.v.) and *Muscle relaxants* (q.v.).

Tonus (syn. *Tonicity*). A state of slight muscular tension. In striate skeletal muscles tonus is known as "contractile tonus" when produced by tetanic contraction, i.e. by rhythmic contractions of individual muscle fibers. Tonus in this case depends on the number of nervous impulses emanating from the spinal cord, is higher in a waking state, and (especially) under arousal (q.v.), and lower in sleep (q.v.). In the case of the smooth musculature (of, e.g., the blood vessels), there is a "plastic tonus", which depends on the particular regular state of arousal of the individual muscular fibers and their mutual location. *E.D.*

Topological and vector psychology. A comprehensive psychology of behavior developed by K. Lewin (q.v.).

1. *Basic principles.* Working on the basis of gestalt psychology, Lewin devised a "field theory", which he described as a "method for the analysis of causal relations and the synthesis of scientific constructs".

An essential component of this theory is Lewin's "constructive" or "genetic method" of concept (q.v.) formation. In contrast to the classificatory method, it attempts to explain phenomena by way of their conditions, and to group them according to their conditions: i.e. "genotypical identity" is posited as fundamental to concept formation. In this way one attains to functional concepts ("function" is conceived here as a relational concept—analogously to the mathematical concept of function), which comprise the dynamic aspect and can be represented mathematically. It is possible in this way to bridge the gap between the general and the particular, since the essence of the constructive method lies "in the representation of an individual case with the aid of a few constructional elements". Lewin looked for psychological concepts that would adequately comprehend not the "objective" (physical) but the *behaviorally relevant* facts.

Lewin oriented the construction of his theories toward the findings of the "philosophy of science". A system of empirical constructs is allocated to a specific formal system by means of coordinate definitions. For his formal system Lewin drew on a few fundamental terms from topology and vector mathematics, and evolved "hodology" (a "theory of the way").

(*a*) *Topology* is a science of spatial relations based on the relationship between the "part" and the "whole." It is concerned with the reciprocal locations of areas (regions). Lewin uses topology to represent the structure of a psychological field.

(*b*) In order to explain the changes in, and hence the dynamic characteristics of, a psychological field, Lewin uses mainly the concepts of vector mathematics. Associated vectors are determined by size, direction and point of access. The psychological forces from which changes in field structure derive, are ascribed to vectors.

(*c*) Hodology represents a substantial union of both formal systems. It extends topology by defining the (topologically non-apprehensible) concepts of "direction" and "distance".

2. *Topology of life space.* (*a*) *Structure.* The behavior (B) of an individual is dependent on (a function of) all the psychological facts, the psychological field, or life space (L): B = f(L).

The life space of an individual comprises all that which, at a specific point in time, has "psychological life" for this person: "that which is real is that which is effective". Life space (L) is a function of the person (P) and environment (E):

L = f(P, E); applied to behavior:
B = f(L) = f(P, E).

Life space is divided into regions (areas). The regions represent possible events (in most cases, possible behaviors). Life space may therefore be characterized as an inclusive concept of all possible occurrences, "containing the person and his psychological environment".

(*b*) *Structural change and dynamics.* If a person moves from one region to another, then psychological "*locomotion*" is said to occur. However, other forms of restructuration are possible: e.g. those in which other regions are moved. These are equivalent to locomotion. Locomotion is the most important structural alteration of life space, and depends on the individual's pattern of movement. Within the area of freedom of movement the boundaries between the individual regions are relatively easy to cross. However, the sphere of movement itself is determined by especially rigid and almost impassable boundaries, or "*barriers*". A barrier is defined by the resistance it offers to locomotion. The degree of resistance of a barrier varies according to the kind of locomotion and the point of approach to the barrier, and also depends on the direction in which the barrier is to be crossed. Barriers, and therefore freedom of movement, are conditioned primarily by two aspects: specific goals cannot be reached, (i) because they are forbidden (the intensity of prohibition determines the fixedness of the boundary, the extent of the prohibition the inaccessible area), and (ii) because of a lack of intellectual and physical ability.

The direct cause of locomotion is the "*power*" with which an individual aspires to a goal. This power is the resultant of all field forces which exert an effect on the individual at a given point in time. This force is represented mathematically by a *vector*. The access point and direction are obtained from the topological structure, and the degree of force from the "*valence*" of the goal object and its (psychological or topological) distance.

A region has valence when it attracts or repels the individual (positive or negative valence, symbolized by + or −). Valence is determined by the perceived quality of the goal region and the total state of the individual (tension conditions within the individual).

3. *Topology of the person*(*ality*). (*a*) *Structure.* Like the environment, personal structure can be represented topologically. This is necessary, since behavior is conditioned not only environmentally but, to the same extent, personally. Lewin distinguishes between the "inner personal" and "sensorimotor" areas. In the topological schema, the sensorimotor area is the transitional zone between the inner personal area and the environment. The sensorimotor area comprises, e.g.: language and expression (efferent) and the whole perceptual system (afferent). In the inner-personal area, Lewin distinguishes between central (e.g. drives, emotions) and peripheral (e.g. thoughts, attitudes) regions.

(*b*) *Structural change and dynamics.* In contrast to the environment, locomotion in the person is not a fundamental dynamic quantity (for determination of structure). In the case of the person, another dynamic relation is applied—the degree of dynamic dependence (degree of communication). Dynamic dependence is the greater the more intensely the state of the area affects the other. Lewin calls the dynamic characteristics of the individual personal areas "*tension*". Tension is the state of an area in relation to the state of another area. Tension is dependent on, e.g. *needs* and *quasi-needs* (see *Need; Tension system*).

(*c*) *Interindividual differences*. The most important topologically apprehensible interindividual differences are obtained from the degree of individual difference (a child compared with an adult has less part-areas), and the type of personal structure (arrangement of part-areas and the intensity of their association).

4. *Criticism*. (*a*) *Critique of mathematical bases*. An objection often brought against topological and vector psychology is that it uses only a few of the terms but not the propositions of topology (London, 1944). Basically, Lewin uses an incomplete formal system of his own construction (Madsen, 1958) that is not explicit (Koch, 1941). According to Lewin (1963), it is not a matter of the extent to which a formal system is invoked for interpretation, but of the utility (e.g. predictive value) of the presupposed coordinations.

(*b*) *Formal critique*. Here criticism is directed against the terminology and the whole propositional system. The key concepts of topological and vector psychology are not precise enough (Deutsch, 1954), since they are largely without empirical substantiation (Estes, 1954). Individual propositions cannot be deduced unequivocally (London, 1944; Estes, 1954).

(*c*) *Substantial critique*. The practical value of the life space concept is questioned, since it is scarcely possible to represent all behaviorally-relevant facts as components of life space (London, 1944). Brunswick (1943) criticizes the inadequate attention paid to external (physical) factors. He calls life space "post-perceptual" and "pre-behavioral", and indicates the danger of the phenomenal "encapsulation" of the field. Lewin counters this criticism in his emphasis on the necessity for a psychological *ecology*, which has the task of determining the peripheral zone of life space (or of the individual personality), i.e. the relevance of all external factors for life space.

Bibliography: Brunswick, E.: Organismic achievement and environmental probability. Psychol. Rev., 1943, *50*, 225–72. **Cartwright, D.**: Lewinian theory as a contemporary systematic framework. In: **Koch, S.** (Ed.): Psychology: a study of a science, Vol. 2. New York, 1959. **Deutsch, M.**: Field theory in social psychology. In: **Lindzey, G.** (Ed.): Handbook of social psychology. Reading, Mass., 1954. **Escalona, S.**: The influence of topological and vector psychology upon current research in child development: an addendum. In: **Carmichael, L.** (Ed.): Manual of child psychology. New York & London, 1954, 971–83. **Estes, W. K.**: Kurt Lewin. In: **Estes, W. K.** *et al.* (Eds.): Modern learning theory. New York, 1954. **Koch, S.**: The logical character of the motivation concept. Psychol. Rev., 1941, *48*, 15–38. **Lewin, K.**: Der Richtungsbegriff in der Psychologie: Der spezielle und der allg. hodologische Raum. Psychol. Forsch., 1034, *19*, 249–99. **Id.**: Dynamic theory of personality. New York & London, 1935. **Id.**: Principles of topological psychology. New York, 1936. **Id.**: The conceptual representation and the measurement of psychological forces. Contr. Psychol. Theory, Vol. I, 1938. **Id.**: Frontiers in group dynamics. Human Relations, 1947, *1*, 5–41; 143–53. **Id.**: Resolving social conflicts. New York, 1948. **London, I. D.**: Psychologists' misuse of the auxiliary concepts of physics and mathematics. Psychol. Rev., 1944, *51*, 266–91. **Madsen, K. B.**: Theories of motivation. Copenhagen, [4]1968. **Marx' M. H. & Hillix, W. A.**: Systems and theories in psychology. New York & London, 1963.

F. Mattejat & E. G. Wehner

Topological mnemonics (syn. *Topological learning*). The "art" of remembering, used as an aid in spatial and situational recall. The assignment is made more accessible by (imaged or actual) spatial arrangement, or made more imprintable by associative pictorial images (e.g. diagrams). *H.W.*

Totem. Totemism is a principle of social organization among "primitive" peoples. The cohesiveness of a group (clan) is attributed to a mythic process in animal form (sometimes also a plant or some other natural object). The members of the group are under the protection of the totem as long as they obey certain commandments (e.g. exogamy) and prohibitions (e.g. that of killing the totemic animal). See *Taboo.*

Bibliography: Freud, S.: Totem and taboo. New York & London, 1918. Lévi-Strauss, C.: Totemism. London & Boston, 1963.

I.L.

TOTE units. According to Miller *et al.*, TOTE units are elements of behavioral process. As an alternative to reflex arcs, they may be thought of as more flexible "foundation stones" in the hierarchical structure of a behavior. "TOTE" is the abbreviation for the characteristic course of events: "*Test operate test exit*". "Test" is the comparison of an actual value ("state of organism") with a desired value ("state to be tested"). Should both stages prove incongruent, a correction takes place in the shape of a reduction of difference (operate), a new test, and in the case of adequate congruence the end response ("exit"). TOTE units are used to study behavior on various levels of abstraction from the operation of simple cellular membranes all the way to cognitive processes. See *Cybernetics and psychology.*

Bibliography: Miller, G. A., Galanter, E. & Pribram, K. H.: Plans and structure of behavior. New York, 1960.

W.H.B.

Touch receptors. Receptors for the sensation of contact. See *Sense organs.*

Tough-mindedness. A pragmatic attitude (q.v.) to social, political and philosophical problems, associated with more extraverted personality traits. See *Traits; Type; Authoritarian personality; Prejudice.*

J.L.

Tourism. Tourism research came into being some forty years ago, but at first was concerned only with economic questions. With the rapid development of modern tourism since the nineteen-fifties, there has been growing interest in a psychologically and sociologically oriented form of tourism research. The object of psychological research in this area is not the "journey" or travel as such, but "psychological traveling time" as a whole (Böhm), which includes all activities and influences (before and after setting out) conditioned by traveling. Among the main topics are: analyses of the conditions for travelling (including motivational and social emphases); analyses of experience and behavior during a tour (specific vacation habits, role playing, role expectations, etc.); effects of the holiday (e.g. on educational, leisure and consumption interests; changes in attitudes to other nations; changes in experience of self). Apart from these questions of individual and social psychology, there are other aspects of tourism which come into the areas of medicine (the psychophysical value of traveling), education, and economics (advertising and publicity).

Bibliography: Hahn, H. (Ed.): Motives, Meinungen, Verhaltensweisen. Starnberg, 1969. Id. (Ed.): Jugendtourismus. Munich, 1965.

B.S.

Tracing test. A test of fine motor co-ordination involving the tracing of life drawings and measurement of the resultant deviations.

C.D.F.

Traction effect. One of Michotte's experiments on mechanical causality. An object A approaches and passes a stationary object B. Thereafter the two objects move together. Under the right conditions, object A appears to observers to be pulling object B in its wake. *C.D.F.*

Tractus opticus. The two *tractus optici*, or optic tracts, begin at the *chiasma opticum* or chiasma in the region of the *sella turcica* (behind the optic groove) and divide near the geniculate bodies into a lateral and a medial root, which then pass into the lateral and medial geniculate bodies. Fibers are carried in the *radiatio tractus optici*, or optic radiation, to the sight center in the occipital cortex. Injury to an optic tract can cause blindness of the corresponding half of each eye. *R.R.*

Tradition. The (or a) totality of opinions, attitudes, habits and customs handed down (primarily informally) by oral communication or imitation from one generation to another, in such a way that the self-obviousness and accepted value of such traditions usually increase with their age. The term "traditionalism" stands for tendencies to overvalue traditional opinions, etc., or to exclude them from (rational) evaluation. See *Attitude; Habit; Authoritarian personality; Social psychology; Prejudice; Stereotype.* *A.S.-M.*

Traffic psychology. Traffic psychology may be thought of as a subdivision of applied psychology (q.v.). It is concerned with the scientific study of psychological problems arising from conditions of motor, rail and air travel (see *Aviation psychology*). The main emphasis of research is on motor traffic. The driving of motor vehicles (driving behavior), which is the primary concern of traffic psychology (the behavior of pedestrians and others has received less attention), is considered as a comprehensive *man-machine system* (MMS) consisting of *street* (roadway), *driver* and *vehicle* and symbolically represented as in Fig. 1. In cybernetic terms, this is a dynamic system of interactive elements, and with multiple feedback (q.v.). Although it seems appropriate when describing the problems of traffic psychology to begin with the input of the system and then progressively to discuss its components, it is in fact advisable to start with an analysis and description of driving behavior, i.e. with the *output* of the driver or of the whole system, in order initially to appreciate the object of traffic psychology, i.e. *traffic behavior*.

Whereas a few investigations have tried to evaluate drivers' statements on driving behavior, most studies are based on direct

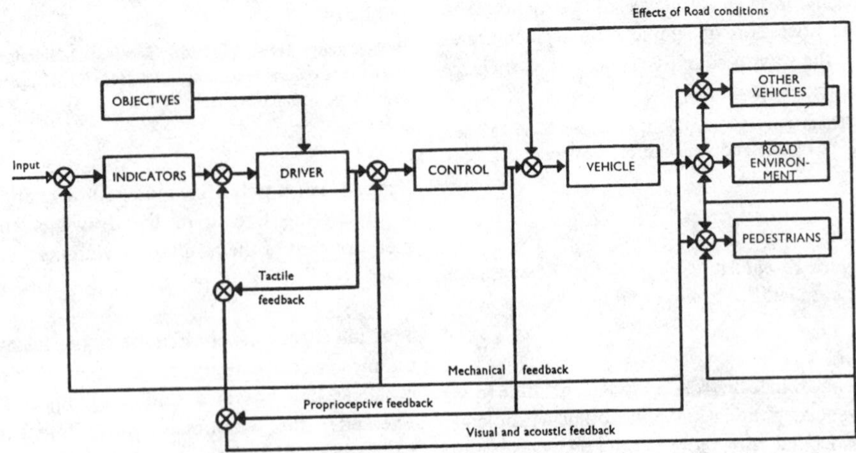

observations of the driver or the vehicle, usually by passenger observers. Scales have been devised for systematic recording of observed driving behavior. In part, control movements (e.g. braking) are recorded by instruments with simultaneous registration of the vehicle's position in relation to the roadside or other vehicles.

Observations in normal traffic are complemented by observations in simulated traffic situations. Simulated studies are especially suitable for the investigation of behavior in dangerous situations, under the effect of alcohol, etc. Some large simulators, especially in the USA, attempt optimal truth-to-life, and represent reality by means of TV pictures of a miniature landscape, or movies, the subject being able to exercise control. In many cases, only selected aspects of traffic are simulated, e.g. a roadway.

A description of driving behavior is meaningful only when it is judged in regard to the goals or aims of the MMS, among which traffic safety and traffic flow are the main criteria. Both criteria have to be brought into an optimal reciprocal relation, since, e.g. increased traffic safety correlates with impaired traffic flow, and *vice versa.* The evaluation of traffic behavior in terms of safety is very difficult since few indices for traffic safety are available, and the accessible criteria, such as accidents, near-accidents and offenses against regulations, can be recorded only imprecisely and have unfavorable psychometric characteristics. Therefore indirect criteria are also used, such as maintaining distance, sign recognition, and so on. Traffic flow, on the other hand, is more precisely recorded, since it can be estimated from the capacity of a streetcar (tram), the average speed of the stream of traffic, the throughput of a crossing, etc.

Input is the most important of the determinants of system-output. It consists of street, traffic signs, and other vehicles, pedestrians, etc., and of feedback signals from the vehicle. From the ergonomic viewpoint, the question of the configuration of traffic routes, signals, etc. on system performance is of primary interest. Little is known about the visual characteristics of traffic routes, yet basic findings of the psychology of perception may be applied to roadway design. The concept of optical direction—by special guidelines, etc.—is especially important. For future traffic design, it will be important to give warning of not directly visible sections of roadway by means of better indicators.

On the other hand, the legibility of signs and plates of all kinds has been thoroughly investigated, and the excessive demand on the driver made by the conventional forest of signs has often been pointed out. Other vehicles produce relevant visual input as a leading vehicle, as an obliquely crossing vehicle, and so on. The brake warning lights (stop lights) of preceding vehicles indicate speed changes in the leading vehicle. Response speed is improved if three pairs of rear lights are used (green: maintenance of uniform speed or acceleration; orange: moderate braking; red: sharp braking). The driver receives a great deal of information if he directly observes the roadway and uses the rear view mirror. Further information—especially regarding the condition of the vehicle—is supplied by indicators (e.g. the speedometer) which are being intensively studied at present with a view to optimal improvement (e.g. by indication of the distance from a preceding vehicle, or of stopping distance). Since the information relevant for the driver is for the most part visual (acoustic and tactile information essentially inform him only of the state of the vehicle), the functions of the optical apparatus (resolution, accommodation, sensitivity to dazzle and glare, day and twilight vision, color vision, depth vision) are of basic importance, but are not solely determinative of safe driving behavior, since inadequacies can to a large extent be compensated. A normative variable, which has been adequately assessed only recently, is the driver's active detection and scanning performance with the aid of eye movements. Significant variations in fixation were shown, e.g. between normal driving and overtaking. The change of fixation from distant to near space, and *vice versa*, is also important. Attempts have been made to assess the general channel capacity of the driver in information reception, and the not impressively high rate of 4–6 bits a second has been obtained.

The processing of received information takes place by means of the selection of relevant signals, comparison with known quantities, and reference to instructions, rules, etc. Processes of this kind were examined to some extent from the viewpoint of "mental load", distraction, and aspects of stress (q.v.). The driver's *reactions* (responses) consist partly of automatic, i.e. highly practiced and not consciously intended, behavior patterns, the nature of which is as yet inadequately explained. A large number of inputs require a decision in regard to the kinds of response. These decisions may be confined to limited aspects of driving (e.g. braking, overtaking), or may be of a basic kind (e.g. avoidance of night driving, or driving after taking alcohol) and are considered primarily in terms of the risk the driver is prepared to take (see *Risk taking; Alcoholism*). There is a broad variation in risk taking, the course of which may be interpreted according to standard decision models (see *Decision processes*), and the origin of which is examined in terms of the psychology of personality (see *Personality; Traits; Type*).

The above-mentioned processes give rise to *driving behavior*, which may be divided into several components. Among the cybernetic aspects, the transfer characteristics of the human part-system are of interest. The driver's actions are also influenced by the kind and arrangement of the control and operation devices to which he has access. The conventional motor vehicle is poorly constructed from an ergonomic viewpoint, since, for example, it requires movement in the same direction for opposed activities (acceleration and braking); the devices are often operated only with difficulty (there would seem to be no appropriate, relevant anthropometric measurements); and switches are poorly coded (functions may be confused).

The functioning of the "driver" part-system is of primary interest to the traffic psychologist, and is affected by several temporally variable and temporally constant conditions which have already evoked a considerable amount of research. One of the most consequential time-variable conditions is certainly drunken driving (see *Alcoholism*). The degree of drunkenness determines inadequacies in driving performance, but also in decision about erroneous judgment of internal and external magnitudes. In the field of decisions, it is necessary to investigate why individuals with restricted driving capacity actually take to their vehicles.

Analogous problems arise in regard to time-variable conditions, such as the influence of drugs, vigilance (q.v.), and fatigue (q.v.), and to a certain extent in regard to transient moods. Intelligence (q.v.) and mental abilities, motor abilities and personality variables of the most varied kind have been correlated with accidents and other data obtained from traffic and driving behavior; with only a few exceptions, however, only minor correlations have been revealed. Only biographical information on social characteristics has been shown to be a useful predictor of driving behavior (see *Accident research*). The relative failure of these investigations may be attributed in part to methodological difficulties. Since data from personality tests were usually compared directly with external criteria, it remains unclear where and how the functional structure can be influenced by a personality variable. On the other hand, the accident (on account of its inadequate psychometric aspects) is an uncertainty factor. Further studies will have to concentrate more on system analysis of the driver, and take new, improved criteria into account. Simulation experiments may be of use here. Some success would seem to be promised by attempts to detect the influence of sets and attitudes on driving behavior. Major attitudes deserving of research are those toward safety and authority.

The driver's age is an essential factor among influences on driving behavior. Young drivers and those of an advanced age have proved of especial interest to researchers. The adequately proven higher accident rate among members of the group up to age twenty-five is explainable largely in terms of inappropriate attitudes and sets, and a lack of experience in regard to the performance limits of the system. Older drivers frequently exhibit performance deficits which can considerably restrict driving fitness.

Bibliography: Arthur D. Little, Inc.: The state of art of traffic safety. Cambridge, Mass., 1966. **Bena, E., Hoskovec, J. & Stikar, J.:** Psychologie a fyziologie ridice. Prague, [2]1968. **Hoyos, C. (Ed.):** Psychologie des Strassenverkehrs. Berne, 1965. **Mittenecker, E.:** Methoden und Ergebnisse der psychologischen Unfallforschung. Vienna, 1962. **O'Day, J. (Ed.):** Driver behavior—cause and effect. Washington, D.C., 1968. **Selzer, M. L., Gikas, P. W. & Huelko, D. F. (Eds.):** The prevention of highway injury. Ann Arbor, Mich., 1967. **Wagner, K. & Wagner, H.-J. (Eds.):** Handbuch der Verkehrsmedizin. Berlin & Heidelberg, 1968.

C. Hoyos

Training. Systematic and extensive practice (q.v.) in order to reach a state of optimal physical, manual and/or mental and spiritual capability, or to maintain the same. "Training on the job" is short though intensive systematic introductory practice at the work place itself.

G.R.W.M.

Training, animal. The acquisition of certain behaviors (by animals) using associative methods. The training procedure endeavors by frequent repetition and reinforcement (see *Conditioning, classical and operant*) to produce specific reactions to definite stimuli. A prerequisite for any attempt at training is a certain measure of "teachability" (or contionability). See *Behaviorism.*

Bibliography: Thorndike, E. L. : Animal intelligence; an experimental study of the associative processes in animals. Psychol. Rev. Monog., 1898, Suppl. 2.

K.E.P.

Training method. A procedure for controlling behavior. Desired behavior is "reinforced" (rewarded or praised); undesired behavior is punished. With this method any "breaking out" of the situation is prevented by the erection of real or social barriers. With the aid of a well-planned method, behavior can be selected and channelled at will. The acquisition of automated knowledge is most economically promoted with this method. See *Conditioning, classical and operant; Aversion therapy; Behavior therapy; Manipulation.*

B.L.

Training within industry (abb. TWI). A systematic technique of instruction used in connection with conversion from one form of production to another, or a change of processes.

G.R.W.M.

Traits. The concept of "personality" (q.v.) is too all-embracing to be of much direct use to the empirical investigator; we require more specific concepts which will point the way towards measurable entities. These are found in the concepts of *abilities* in the cognitive field, and in those of *traits* and *types* (q.v.) in the non-cognitive field. All these concepts presuppose some form of nomothetic approach; the idiographic approach would deny that traits or abilities appearing in any two individuals were in fact only *quantitatively* different, and would argue that the actual behaviors involved were unique. An alternative criticism, often made by behaviorists, insists that all stimulus-response bonds or habits are *specific,* and that consequently general traits cannot exist. As Thorndike

(1913) has put it, "there are no broad, general traits of personality, no general and consistent forms of conduct which, if they existed, would make for consistency of behavior and stability of personality, but only independent and specific stimulus-response bonds or habits." These criticisms will be considered after we have defined the concept itself more closely.

Language and the man in the street have always incorporated traits in their characterization of people; Allport & Odbert (1936) have listed some 4,500 trait terms in the English language. Many typologists, from Galen to Jung and Kretschmer, used trait terms to characterize their ideal "types". Among modern writers, Stern (1921) was perhaps the foremost advocate of a trait psychology; he wrote: "We have the right and the obligation to develop a concept of trait as a definitive doctrine; for in all activity of the person, there is beside a variable portion, likewise a constant purposive portion, and this latter we isolate in the concept of trait." Allport (1937) introduced this doctrine into the English-speaking countries; here is his description of how traits are discovered: "Traits . . . are discovered not by deductive reasoning, not by fiat, not by naming, and are themselves never directly observed. They are discovered in the individual life—the only place where they can be discovered—only through an inference (or interpretation) made necessary by the demonstrable consistency of the separate observable acts of behavior." This insistence on *behavioral consistency* is even stronger in another quotation: "Traits are not directly observable; they are inferred (as any kind of determining tendency is inferred). Without such an inference the stability and consistency of personal behavior could not possibly be explained. Any specific action is a product of innumerable determinants, not only of traits but of momentary pressures and specialized influences. But it is the repeated occurrence of actions having the *same significance* (equivalence of response) following upon a definable range of stimuli having the same personal significance (equivalence of stimuli) that makes necessary the postulation of traits as states of being. Traits are not at all times active, but they are persistent even when latent, and are distinguished by low thresholds of arousal".

Consistency of behavior can be conceptualized best in terms of statistical *correlations;* consistency implies (1) test-retest reliability, that is, the same or at least similar behavior should appear on temporally separate occasions when the same stimuli are presented, and (2) inter-test correlations when different but functionally identical or similar stimuli are presented. Thus a person who is *persistent* in situation A should also be persistent in situation A′, that is, the same situation on another occasion; he should also be persistent in situations B, C. . . N, that is, situations which call for and enable persistence to be shown. These are testable propositions, and their investigation should enable us to decide between this hypothesis and Thorndike's notion of *response specificity* mentioned above.

The literature on these points is now very large; a historically oriented account is given by Eysenck (1970). The first large-scale experimental attack on this problem was mounted by Hartshorne & May (1928, 1929; Hartshorne & Shuttleworth, 1930) in their Character Education Enquiry; their concern was with the problem of honesty and other morally and ethically desirable qualities, and with ways and means of improving these. They administered objectively designed tests to thousands of school children; these dealt with honesty (lying and cheating), co-operation, inhibition of impulses, and persistence. In devising these tests, they followed certain rules: the test situation should be natural as well as controlled, all subjects should have equal opportunity for showing the behavior in question, children should not be subjected to undue moral strain, and the tests should have low "visibility", i.e. they should not be recognized for what they were by the children. They also inquired into knowledge of moral conduct, and collected "reputation" scores for their children; finally, they assessed the "integration" of the children, a term by which they mean "consistency of performance"—"by *integration* is often intended a certain dependability or stability of moral conduct". The statistical treatment of the data was beyond cavil, and in view of the brilliance of the design and the technical excellence of the execution, this study has rightly been regarded as crucial in respect to the theory of specificity. When therefore Hartshorne & May found very low intercorrelations between their tests (averaging 0.20–0.25), and discovered that children who were honest, or persistent, or co-operative in one test-situation were not always so in another, their conclusion that these alleged qualities were "groups of specific habits rather than general traits" was very widely accepted as finally settling the issue in favor of specificity.

Eysenck (1970) has re-examined the detailed results, and argues that the conclusion does not follow from the data. Single tests do not correlate very highly, but if they are regarded as parts of a battery it can be shown that the battery is in fact a very reliable measure. The reliability of a battery of nine tests of honesty is 0.72, that for a battery of five service tests was only slightly lower. Validities of these batteries were investigated by correlating scores with ratings; these were 0.4 for honesty, 0.6 for service, figures which are not all that much lower than correlations between intelligence test results and teachers' ratings for IQ. Finally, the batteries intercorrelated positively, correlations going up to as high as 0.5, thus giving some support for the concept of "integration"; integration itself was shown to be quite highly correlated with honesty, co-operation, and the other desirable moral qualities. Hartshorne & May may have been misled by certain assumptions which is fact do not hold. Thus they find that a given child may succeed in one test of honesty and fail on another; this, they argue, is evidence of specificity. But this is not necessarily true; a child may succeed with an easy IQ problem and fail with a difficult one, without demonstrating that intelligence does not exist! A child may cheat (in the schoolroom situation), but may not steal, in another test; this demonstrates merely that the tests differ in the amount of stress which they put on a child's moral nature. Most children find it easier to cheat than to steal; little (often no) blame attaches to the former, but a great deal to the latter. Thus the tests may be ranged in order of "difficulty", much like intelligence tests; some children "pass" many items, others few, others yet are intermediate. All this does not prove the specificity of moral behavior.

Another argument relates to the age of the children; moral behavior has to be learned, and young children are still in the early stages of learning; older children and adults may show greater consistency of conduct. McKinnon (1933) later showed that this was in fact so, and that with older subjects very high correlations were found. It would thus seem that consistency may develop through a process of learning or conditioning, and evidence should be looked for in older rather than in younger subjects. Even so, work with very young children of two years or younger has shown marked consistencies in such behavior traits as activity, or withdrawn behavior, or frequency of crying, and some of these consistencies correlate with behavior many years later; this suggests that much of behavior depends on inherited patterns of conduct, a point to be taken up presently.

The ready acceptance of Hartshorne & May's proposition regarding specificity of conduct was probably due to the wide recognition of Thorndike's associationist position; if all learning was of specific S-R bonds, then general traits should not exist. There was also Thorndike's disproof of the doctrine of "transfer of training", associated with his doctrine of identical elements; when transfer of learning took place, this was supposed to be due to the presence of identical elements in the original and the second task. Modern learning theory has effectively abolished the first of the positions; not only do we have many alternatives to a simple S-R model (which indeed is put forward by fewer and fewer people), but in addition stimulus and response generalization provide means by which simple S-R connections could be built up into general traits. The second of these positions has been heavily criticized by Allport (1937), and is now of purely historical interest. Theoretical support for the specifist position has been dwindling, at the same time as its main empirical support has been shown to be wanting; nowadays it would be difficult to find any proponents of it among experts in the personality field. This fact, however, should not cause the pendulum to swing too much in the opposite direction; conduct certainly is less general than the man in the street imagines, and there is a considerable degree of specificity about it. What was wrong in Thorndike's position was its denial of *all* generality; this whole question has been shown to be a graded, dimensional problem, not an all-or-none one. There are both generality and specificity; it becomes an empirical research problem in each case to decide for a given trait, and for a given population, at a given time, just how general and how specific conduct really is.

The same conclusion may apply to the idiographic argument; as Spinoza already pointed out, everything that exists is unique, and personality is thus not exceptional. But there are also similarities and identities between persons, and only in so far as these exist can we begin to treat personality as an experimental problem. It is unnecessary to lay down on an arbitrary and *a priori* basis just how much of personality can be suitably treated in this way; such information will emerge at the end, not at the beginning of scientific work. Even in the study of subatomic particles, the Heisenberg principle sets limitations to prediction and accuracy of measurement; it seems likely that in due course we shall understand better than we do now the limitations placed on the accurate measurement of human traits. But the idiographic position is wrong in so far as it declares impossible all nomothetic investigations; the success of many such studies adequately proves this point (Eysenck, 1970).

Research into traits has in the main used the following lines of research: (1) Personality inventories (self-ratings); (2) Ratings by peers, teachers, and other persons with knowledge of the candidate; (3) Miniature situations, i.e. laboratory replicas of life-situations calling into action the trait to be measured; (4) Laboratory situations making use of some hypothetico-deductive system to predict objective manifestations theoretically linked with a given trait. Personality inventories and ratings are perhaps most frequently used because they are particularly easy to collect; laboratory studies are more laborious but more objective, and possibly in the long run more fruitful. The differentiation between (3) and (4) is not always easy, but an example may make the matter clear. Persistence is a personality trait or quality calling for continuance of effort against fatigue, pain or boredom; it is easy to set up in the laboratory a situation requiring persistence in this sense. We may instruct the subject to pull against a dynamometer at half his full strength, or ask him to solve problems some of which are insoluble; great differences are observed between people in the length of time during which they pull against the dynamometer (although their strength differences have been averaged out), or the length of time which they spend on insoluble (but not obviously so) problems. Furthermore, such tasks correlate together to form a general factor of persistence, and do not correlate with IQ, thus ruling out the possibility that we are merely measuring intelligence. As an example of a hypothetico-deductive test, consider the work of Witkin *et al.* (1962) on the assumed trait of field dependence—field independence; they used tests such as the rod-and-frame and the embedded figures test, neither of which would have been thought of as a measure of a personality trait in the absence of Witkin's theory. Thus a theoretical framework may provide the basis for the experimental testing of laboratory tests as measures of personality traits.

It cannot of course be assumed that because a trait name exists, a corresponding trait must also exist; statistical methods are required which will translate observations into scientifically meaningful and objective concepts. The main method in use at present is factor analysis (q.v.); starting with a matrix of intercorrelations between all measures used, this method condenses the existing pattern of covariation into orthogonal factors which, after rotation, may or may not resemble the hypothetical traits postulated by the investigator. It is sometimes objected that "you only get out of a factor analysis what you put into it", but this is only partially true. If no tests of certain traits or abilities are contained in the battery, then of course these will not emerge from the analysis; just in the same way, qualitative analysis in chemistry will not disclose the presence of substances not contained in the sample. But the obverse is not true; in most cases we do not in fact know what we "put into" the analysis, and the statistical treatment often gives results not anticipated. Several outcomes are in fact possible when a series of tests supposedly measuring a given trait is intercorrelated and factor analyzed. (1) The tests form a matrix of rank one, thus confirming the hypothesis that they all measure the same trait; we also obtain information in this case about the degree to which each test measures the hypothetical trait (through its factor loadings). (2) The tests fail to intercorrelate, thus disproving the hypothesis completely. (3) The tests show patterns of intercorrelations suggesting the existence of two or more independent traits. (4) The tests intercorrelate as in (1), but with an additional breakdown into smaller factors which suggest further subdivisions of the hypothetical trait.

Examples of these various outcomes are given by Eysenck (1970); a few of these are quoted here. (1) is illustrated in the work of Gould (1939) on level of aspiration; he found that several tests of this trait intercorrelated in such a way as to give rise to one single general factor. (2) is relatively rare, as tests seldom fail to intercorrelate completely; usually something can be salvaged, unless the original choice of tests was exceptionally poor. A good example of complete failure is the work of Payne (1955) on Kretschmer's conception of the trait of "*Spaltungsfähigkeit*". (3) is illustrated by the work of Eysenck and Furneaux (1945) on suggestibility; instead of one single factor they found two independent ones, called primary or ideomotor and secondary or perceptual suggestibility, with a possible third type, tertiary or social suggestibility, less well established. (4) is illustrated by work on persistence, McArthur (1955), where a general factor is found, but also additional factor differentiating "ideational" persistence and "physical" persistence, i.e. persistence on cognitive and on physical (endurance) tests respectively. This type of solution merges into a multiple-factor one, in which a larger number of sub-factors are found; personal tempo is a good example of this. Rimoldi (1951), using 59 tests, obtained 9 factors which were, however, not independent; their intercorrelations in turn gave rise to 4 second-order factors (motor speed, speed of perception, speed of cognition, reaction time). Thus the outcome of a factor analysis is not predetermined by the hypotheses to be tested; it can and often does deviate very considerably from the preconceptions which led to the setting up of the experiment. Factor analysis is indispensable in the testing of hypotheses regarding traits, as without it there is no proper statistical check on the experimenter's preconceptions;

it also serves the additional purpose of generating new and previously unconsidered hypotheses.

Within factor analysis Cattell has drawn a distinction between surface traits and source traits. A surface trait is defined as "a set of personality characteristics which are correlated but do not form a factor, hence are believed to be determined by more than one influence or source". A source trait is defined as a "factor dimension, stressing the proposition that variations in value along it are determined by a single, unitary influence or source". Statistically, the distinction is between rotation of factors through clusters (surface traits) or through hyperplanes (source traits). This view is not widely held, and it may be regarded as doubtful if factor analysis by itself can ever decide about the presence or absence of "a single, unitary influence or source". More specialized hypotheses and experimental designs are likely to be required for this purpose.

Traits are not independent; they tend to correlate and give rise to higher-order factors (superfactors) which resemble the *types* of writers like Jung and Kretschmer (see notation on *Type*). American writers tend to concentrate on the trait level; European and British writers tend to concentrate on the type level. This sometimes gives the impression that factor analysis does not give identical results in different hands, and that it is therefore not an objective method. This is not true; Eysenck & Eysenck (1969) have analyzed correlations between tests used by Cattell, Guilford & Eysenck, and have shown that considerable similarities (almost amounting to identity) exist at the higher-order level. Analyses should always include both levels, as otherwise the study is incomplete and difficult to interpret; American studies have in the past often sinned in this respect, in spite of the categorical statements to this effect by Thurstone and other pioneers of the statistical methods employed in these studies.

Are traits determined by heredity or by environment? Such a question is meaningless; all observed behavior is of course *phenotypic*, that is, determined by genetic causes acting in interaction with environmental ones. Nevertheless it is permissible to try to assess the relative importance of these two factors in particular cases, i.e. particular traits, in a particular environment, for a particular sample, at a particular time. Extrapolation beyond these limitations is dangerous. The method used in the majority of studies is that of comparing the intraclass correlations of monozygotic and dizygotic twins, of identical sex; better methods are now available, thanks to the efforts of biometrical geneticists. Cattell & Scheier (1961) review the extensive work of the former author, and Fuller & Thompson (1960) give a good review of the general field. Unlikely as it may seem, animal work has also been prominent in this field (Eysenck & Broadhurst, 1964; Scott & Fuller, 1965); it is of course more difficult to measure and interpret "personality traits" in dogs or rats, but it is much easier to conduct breeding experiments (e.g. diallel crosses) in animals, thus enabling proper genetic analysis of such factors as dominance to be made. The outcome of such studies in humans or animals is too complex to be reviewed here; heredity certainly plays an important part in the genesis of many traits, but the respective contribution of environment and heredity differs from trait to trait, and much further work is required before any very definitive generalization becomes possible.

The whole notion of traits is sometimes attacked (e.g. Lundin, 1961) on the same grounds as that of instincts. We start with some piece of behavior which we class, say, as sociable; we then explain it by inventing an instinct, or trait, of sociability. But nothing has in fact been explained by this circular bit of argument; all the evidence we have for our "trait" is still the behavior, which thus remains unexplained. This type of criticism is not admissible; trait psychology does not in fact try to give a *causal* analysis, but rather a *descriptive* one. Before we can say what *causes* a given trait, we must analyze the myriad items of ordinary, everyday behavior into meaningful units which can be measured and handled with sufficient ease to permit further analysis. To analyze physical entitles into elements, as in Mendeleff's Table, does not tell us *why* these elements are as they are; it merely describes them in a systematic fashion. That is all that trait analysis sets out to do, and it is unreasonable to blame it for not doing more. Nor is it correct to suggest that the argument is circular; we use the term "sociability" as if it were a unitary trait, but Eysenck & Eysenck (1969) have shown that there are at least two quite separate types of sociability; introverted lack of sociability (I don't care to be with other people) and neurotic lack of sociability (I am afraid to be with other people), and there is perhaps yet a third type (psychotic lack of sociability—I hate other people). These are factual results of statistical analysis of behavior; they are not implicit in the term "sociability" or in the simple observations which formed the lay use of that term. We conclude that this type of criticism is not damaging to the concept of "trait", which remains fundamental to the analysis and discussion of personality.

Bibliography: Allport, G. W.: Personality. London, 1937. **Allport, G. W. & Odbert, H. S.:** Trait names: a psycho-lexical study. Psychol. Monogr., 1936, *47*, 171. **Cattell, R. B. & Scheier, I. H.:** The meaning and measurement of neuroticism and anxiety. New York, 1961. **Eysenck, H. J.:** The structure of human personality. London, [3]1970. **Eysenck, H. J. & Broadhurst, P. L.:** Experiments with animals. In: **Eysenck, H. J.** (Ed.): Experiments in motivation. Oxford, 1964. **Eysenck, H. J. & Eysenck, S. B. G.:** The structure and measurement of personality. London, 1969. **Eysenck, H. J. & Furneaux, W. D.:** Primary and secondary suggestibility. An experimental and statistical study. J. exper. Psychol., 1945, *35*, 485–503. **Fuller, J. R. & Thompson, W. R.:** Behavior genetics. New York, 1960. **Gould, R.:** An experimental analysis of "level of aspiration". Genet. Psychol. Monogr., 1939, *21*, 3–15. **Hartshorne, H. & May, M. A.:** Studies in deceit. New York, 1928. **Id.:** Studies in service and self-control. New York, 1929. **Hartshorne, H., May, M. A. & Shuttleworth, F. K.:** Studies in the organization of character. New York, 1930. **Lundin, R. V.:** Personality. New York, 1961. **MacArthur, R. S.:** An experimental investigation of persistence in secondary school boys. Canad. J. Psychol., 1955, *9*, 47–54. **McKinnon, D. V.:** The violation of prohibitions in the solving of problems. In: Ph.D. thesis: Harvard University Library, 1933. **Payne, R. W.:** Experimentelle Untersuchung zum Spaltungsbegriff von Kretschmer. Z. exp. angew. Psychol., 1953, *3*, 65–97. **Rimoldi, H. J. A.:** Personal tempo. J. abnorm. soc. Psychol., 1951, *44*, 283–303. **Scott, J. P. & Fuller, J. L.:** Genetics and the behavior of the dog. Chicago, 1965. **Stern, W.:** Differentielle Psychologie. Hamburg, 1921. **Thorndike, E. L.:** Educational psychology. New York, 1913. **Witkin, H. A., Dyke, R. B., Goodenough, D. R. & Harp, S. A.:** Psychological differentiation. New York, 1962.

H. J. Eysenck

Trance. 1. A state of dissociation in which the individual is oblivious of his situation and surroundings. Can be induced by hypnosis, drugs, meditation, and so on. Sometimes associated with ESP (q.v.) experiences.

2. A transition (Lat. *transitus*) into a state of psychic abstraction characterized by restricted consciousness and (often) subsequent amnesia. Studied experimentally largely in connection with hypnosis (q.v.), and induced by concentration on a fragment of experience, possibly together with monotonous, rhythmic stimulation, physical exhaustion and emotional strain or expectation, as in the "archaic ecstasy" techniques described by Mircea Eliade (dancing to a drum or to rhythmic singing). Trance has a close connection with religious ecstasy or rapture and visionary experiences (see *Meditation; Religion, psychology of*). In functional terms, it is related to the normal, reality-oriented state as a mutation is to inheritance. It enables the affected individual to obtain release from everything he has learned to date, and makes possible achievements (both mental and physical) that he would not otherwise attempt.

Bibliography: Eliade, M.: Patterns in comparative religion. London & New York, 1958. **Ludwig, A. M.:** Trance. Comprehensive psychiatry, 1967, *8*. **Schmidbauer, W.:** Zur Psychologie des Orakels. Psychol. Rdsch., 1970, *21*, 88–98. *J.B. & W.Sch.*

Tranquilizers (syn. *Anxiolytics; Ataractic drugs; Relaxants; Happy pills;* etc.). Psychopharmaceutical substances used in pharmacotherapy on account of their anxiolytic and relaxing effects. In contrast to the neuroleptics (or *major tranquilizers*), which also have a tranquilizing effect in low doses, but are primarily anti-psychotic, the tranquilizers proper (or *minor tranquilizers*) are used mainly for the treatment of neurotics, and healthy individuals under emotional stress. Tranquilizers have much in common with hyponotics in low doses, which (as "sedatives") in the past fulfilled the function of the tranquilizers and neuroleptics at present in use. An essential difference is the absence of the sleep-inducing, unpleasant effects of high doses of tranquilizers. Chemically, the tranquilizers are divided into the therapeutically important glycol derivatives (meprobamate, tybamate, phenylglycodol) and benzodiazepine (chlordiazepoxide, oxazepam, diazepam, nitrazepam), and into the less important glycerine derivatives (mephinisine), diphenolmethane derivatives (phenyltoloxamine, captodiamine, hydroxycine), and the carbonols (emylcamate). Neurophysiologically, the primary result is an attenuation in the limbic and thamamic system, and in high doses an extension to other areas, but no narcotization. Autonomic effects are hardly noticeable. Central muscle-relaxant and spasmolytic effects are frequent. A large number of psychological investigations in healthy individuals have been carried out for meprobamate and chlordiazepoxide. With low to middling doses there are no, or only slight, impairments of performance, and to some extent improvements in motor functions (tremor tests), and emotional stabilization without (or with only slight) fatigue. Differences in effect are related to neuroticism, extraversion (in the Eysenckian sense; see *Drug postulate, Eysenck's; Trait; Type*) and situative factors (stress, mental strain).

The tranquilizing effect is reinforced if the individual condition is habitually or situatively oriented to emotional lability. Sedation is emphasized in the case of mental strain (see *Differential psychopharmacology*). Factorial test plans have been used in investigations.

Bibliography: Barret, J. E. & Dimascio, A.: Comparative effects on anxiety of the "minor tranquilizers" in "high" and "low" anxious student volunteers. Dis. nerv. Syst., 1966, *27*, 483–6. **Berger, F. M.:** The relation between the pharmacological properties of meprobamate and the clinical usefulness of the drug. In: **Efron, D. H.** (Ed.): Psychopharmacology, 1957–1967. Washington, 1968. **Berger, F. M. & Potterfield, J.:** The effect of antianxiety tranquilizers on the behavior of normal persons. In: **Evans, W. O. & Kline, N. S.:** The psychopharmacology of the normal human. Springfield, 1969. **Eysenck, H. J.:** Experiments with drugs. Oxford, 1963. **Janke, W.:** Expt. Untersuchungen zur Abhängigkeit der Wirkung psychotroper Substanzen von Persönlichkeitsmerkmalen. Frankfurt, 1964. **Janke, W. & Debus, G.:** Experimental studies on antianxiety agents with normal subjects. Methodological considerations and review of the main effects. In: **Efron, D. H.** (Ed.): Psychopharmacology 1957–1967. Washington, 1968. **Rickels, K.:** Antineurotic agents: specific and non-specific effects. In: **Efron, D. H.** (Ed.): Psychopharmacology 1957–1967. Washington, 1968. **Zbinden, G. & Randall, L. O.:** Pharmacology of benzodiazepines: laboratory and clinical correlations. In: **Garattini, S. & Shore, P. A** (Eds.): Advances in pharmacology, 1967, *5*, 213–91. *G. Debus*

Transaction, social. In relation to "interaction", a social transaction is a process presupposing individual dynamic participation, which is not necessarily the case with interaction. *W.D.F.*

Transducer. An instrument which converts energy from one form into another. Hence the human ear is a transducer because it converts sound waves into nerve impulses. *G.D.W.*

Transfer occurs if the acquisition of an assignment (material B) is influenced by the previous learning of another assignment (material A). The influence of the assignment learned first on that learned second, may be an improvement (positive transfer) or an impairment (negative transfer: see *Proactive inhibition*). The positive transfer effect is the more emphatic the greater the similarity between learning assignments. A negative transfer occurs if the stimulus situation for both assignments is similar, but differing responses are required (Osgood, 1953). A negative transfer is noticeable, e.g. if a new, like task is to be solved in a way different from the first. But the "similarity" of learning assignments is quite variously defined.

In the case of conditioned learning, the notion of positive transfer is identical with that of *stimulus generalization* (q.v.). See *Conditioning, classical and operant.*

One may distinguish between the transfer of elements (e.g. in serial learning), when the elements of an assignment learned first make the learning of the second easier, and the transfer of rules (e.g. in problem-solving, when the principle for solving one task is transferred to the other ("learning set"). These specific transfer effects are to be distinguished from non-specific transfer effects, which consist merely of an increased general readiness to learn ("warming-up effect", or "learning to learn").

An unproven theory of formal education derives positive transfer from the improvement of individual functions, e.g. from the extension of memory (q.v.), will (q.v.), and logical thinking (q.v.). See *Memory; Reminiscence; Learning; Instructional technology.*

Bibliography: Kintsch, W.: Learning, memory and conceptual processes. New York, 1970. **Osgood, C.:** Method and theory in experimental psychology. New York, 1953.

H. Hofer

Transference. A general phenomenon of the perception or interpretation of current situations in the light of past experiences or similar past situations. Approximately identical with the concept of generalization (q.v.) in learning theory. In psychoanalytical terminology (see *Psychoanalysis*), the term indicates primarily the phenomenon of emotional adjustment of the patient to the psychotherapist in analogy to the emotional adjustment of the patient to his early and earliest (intrafamilial) reference persons. Feelings of love, devotion, respect (*positive transference*), but also of hate, fear, or abasement (*negative transference*) are directed to the psychotherapist without the latter having actually given any "cause" to elicit them. Hence, as a rule, specific emotions of the patient toward the psychotherapist, and his ideas of the psychotherapist's feelings, are interpreted as transferences from past relations. They are referred to as such during treatment, if the patient uses them (inwardly) to resist an acknowledgement of his or her own unconscious motives, desires and aspirations.

If the psychotherapist has given the patient some concrete occasion for such feelings, he may find himself in a state of *counter-transference:* the psychotherapist misinterprets his relation to the patient in the light of his own irrational needs and his own unresolved conflicts. If the psychotherapist succumbs to such tendencies to counter-transference, he can seriously endanger the proficiency of psychotherapy and psychoanalysis. Hence one of the most important aspects of a psychotherapist's training is control of his own tendencies to counter-transference, ensured by an appropriate training analysis.

In psychotherapy and psychoanalysis, positive transferences of the patient in regard to his past are requisite. Extremely positive and negative transferences often impair the process.

Transference neuroses (in contrast to "narcissistic neuroses"; see *Neurosis; Psychoses, functional*) are psychic illnesses, the analytical treatment of which includes transference, or development of an emotional relation to the psychotherapist. Those said to be suffering from narcissistic neuroses are hardly capable of such an emotional relationship, since they are scarcely (or not at all) capable of it "in reality". Therefore treatment by Freudian psychoanalysis (q.v.) is not possible. Transference neuroses are said to be quite accessible to therapy; their interpretation uncovers the infantile factors in a disturbed development. See *Depth psychology; Psychotherapy*.

Bibliography: Freud, S.: Introductory lectures on psychoanalysis. London, 1922. **Toman, W.:** Introduction to psychoanalytic theory of motivation. London & New York, 1960. *W. Toman*

Transfert (Fre.). According to J. M. Charcot, the treatment of hysteria (q.v.) consists in an alteration of the moral medium, and in mental hygiene, and physical therapy. It seemed clear to him that treatment with static electricity should have an assured place among such methods. His basic idea was the production of an analogy ("*transfert*") between suggestion and hypnosis (q.v.), and such treatments. The basic conception of *transfert* goes back to the notion of a psychic fluid, as postulated by Mesmer (q.v.). *J.L.I.*

Transformation. The conversion of data in accordance with a prescription (usually simple functions), so that a transformed value corresponds to every initial value. The purpose is an alteration of a measurement scale, usually in order to correct empirical data according to the demands of the selected mathematical model, and to simplify data processing, mainly in the comparison of relative with theoretical frequencies. *D.W.E.*

Transformation, area. The transformation (q.v.) of raw values on the basis of the relative portion of the area lying between a particular raw value and a reference value derived from a theoretical or observed distribution. Hence in a distribution that has undergone area transformation the new scale units correspond to units of area of the distribution that has not been transformed. An example of area transformation is percentile rank. *W.H.B.*

Transformed standard values are obtained from a z scale by means of linear transformation, in order to avoid negative values and to compare scores with differing average values and dispersions. Example: IQ scores. *D.W.E.*

Transinformation. The amount of information (q.v.) correctly received in data transmission, and thus the information common to the transmitted and received signal sequences. In the absence of interference or noise, transinformation can equal information sent; the information flow, however, is limited by channel capacity.

Semantic transinformation is the amount of meaning common to two signal sequences, or that correctly transmitted in data transmission. A special case of semantic transinformation in cybernetic education (q.v.; see *Instructional technology*) is *didactic transinformation*—the didactic information conveyed by instructional techniques and acquired by the student. Didactic transinformation is employed as a measure of learning achievement in the information-theoretical process of "transinformation analysis". See *Sign and symbol*. *K.W.*

Transmitter substances. Transmitter substances (sometimes known as *neurohormones*) are substances formed in the organism which make possible or assist a transmission, and/or further transmission, of nervous excitation in the ANS or CNS (see *Nervous system*). The transmission may be from neurone to effector or from neurone to neurone (see *Synapses*). It is generally acknowledged nowadays that the transmission of impulses occurs chemically by means of the release of transmitter substances in the synapses. Since the identification and demarcation of transmitter substances from other body substances is relatively difficult, the following criteria for the characterization of a substance as a transmitter have been formulated: (*a*) the substance must be detectable in neurones whose action is transmitted to another neurone or effector; (*b*) the neurone must contain the enzyme system requisite for synthesis; (*c*) the transmitter is stored in the neurone in a physiologically inactive form; (*d*) an impulse entering the neurone releases the transmitter substance; (*e*) the transmitter substance reacts with specific receptors of the effector organ; (*f*) the application of the transmitter substance in the immediate neighborhood of the receptor must imitate the action of neurone stimulation; (*g*) an inactivation system must be present to make possible a limitation of duration of effect.

For the peripheral ANS, the transmitter substance in the pre- and post-ganglionic fibers of the sympathetic is acetylcholin(e) (q.v.). In the postganglionic fibers of the sympathetic, the transmitter substance is noradrenalin(e) (noreprinephrine), and possibly also adrenalin(e) (with a few exceptions). For some years the major emphasis of interdisciplinary transmitter research (biochemistry, pharmacology, clinical medicine, comparative psychology) has been on the search for transmitters in the CNS. The most important (and certainly present) transmitter substances in the CNS are acetylcholin(e) and noradrenalin(e). There is as yet no adequate information on the extent to which other substances (see *Biogenic amines*) definitely act as transmitters in the CNS (see *Serotonin; Gamma-amino-butyric acid; Histamine; Substance P*). Synthesis and inactivation of transmitters usually occur in several stages by means of various metabolites, with the participation of diverse enzymatic systems. Transmitter research is of considerable practical importance in the following respects: (*a*) the attribution of transmitter systems to specific behavior patterns; (*b*) disturbance of the synthesis or decomposition of transmitters and psychoses; (*c*) the replacement of natural transmitters by substances which take over or alter their functions (false transmitters, substitute transmitters, e.g. alpha-methyldopa, q.v.); (*d*) the alteration of the function of transmitters by psychopharmaceutical means.

Bibliography: Eccles, J. C.: The physiology of synapses. New York, 1964. **Ehrenpreis, S. & Solnitzky, O. C.:** Neurosciences research, Vol. 1. New York, 1968. **Kappers, J. A.** (Ed.): Neurohormones and neurohumors. Amsterdam, 1969. **McLennan, H.:** Synaptic transmission. Philadelphia, 1963. **Phillis, J. W.:** The pharmacology of synapses. Oxford, 1970. See also: *Biogenic amines.*

W. Janke

Transparency. If the rays emanating from an object penetrate a second object lying on top of it, e.g. a sheet of glass, there is transparency in a physical sense, as contrasted with a transparency which is either psychic or experienced when objectively non-transparent things are perceived as transparent. To explain this, one has recourse to the gestalt laws of perception, and especially the law of pregnance (q.v.).

Bibliography: Kanizsa, G.: Die Erscheinungsweisen der Farben. Handbuch der Psychologie, Vol. 1/1. Göttingen, 1966, 161–91. **Michotte, A., Thinès, G. L. & Grabbe, G.:** Die amodalen Ergänzungen von Wahrnehmungsstrukturen. Handbuch der Psychologie, Vol. 1/1. Göttingen, 1966, 978–1002.

P.S. & R.S.

Transport effect. A phenomenon studied by Michotte whereby a transported object, e.g. an apple on a plate, appears stationary because it is seen only in relation to the object transporting it. It is difficult to demonstrate the effect experimentally since it is crucial that the transported and the transporting objects be seen as separate entities. Michotte achieved this by having a white screen and a black patch moving together horizontally while the black patch made irregular vertical oscillations in relation to the screen. The black patch was then seen as transported by the screen.

C.D.F.

Transposition of gestalts. Since a gestalt is a pattern of relationships between components, the components can be changed without altering the gestalt. Thus a gestalt can be transposed into a different set of components. For example, a tune can be recognized in many different keys. See *Structure; Ganzheit*. *C.D.F.*

Transsexualism. A term first used by Benjamin for physically normal people who are convinced that they belong to the opposite sex. They are driven by a compulsion to have their sexual organs, ordinary appearance and social status changed to those of the opposite sex. Several transsexuals are not homosexuals; many have little interest in sexual activity. Hormonal treatment and psychological support are usually helpful. In appropriate cases plastic genital surgery after surgical castration in the male usually gives satisfactory results. In several parts of the world, after castration and plastic surgery, such patients have obtained a change of name certificate. After a so-called change-of-sex operation a few cases are known to have married in their new sex role. See *Hermaphroditism.*

Bibliography: Green, R. & Money, J.: Transsexualism and sex reassignment. Baltimore, 1969. **Hamburger, C., Stürup, G. K. & Dahl-Iversen, E.:** Transvestism. Hormonal, psychiatric and surgical treatment. J.A.M.A., 1953, *152*, 391–6.

G.K.S.

Transvestite. The term used for those who derive pleasure from wearing the clothes of the opposite sex. In practice mostly applied to a male who uses female dress. First described by Hirschfeld (Germany, 1910); called (by Havelock Ellis) Eonism, after Chevalier d'Eon de Beaumont (famous French T., 1728–1810). The need to dress thus is not always of the same strength, and is often activated by a sexual stimulus. Both heterosexual and homosexual T.'s are met with. Transvestism should not be confused with fetishism, or with homosexuals using the dress of the opposite sex as an element in erotic situations. See also *Transsexualism; Hermaphroditism.*

Bibliography: H. M.: Die Transvestiten. Eine Untersuchung über den erotischen Verkleidungstrieb. Berlin, 1910. **Ellis, H.:** Eonism. Studies in the psychology of sex, Vol. 7. Philadelphia, 1928.

G.K.S.

Trapezium illusion. See *Segment illusion.*

Trauma, psychic. A psychic trauma may be any painful individual experience, especially if that experience is associated with permanent environmental change(s). As a rule psychic trauma involves a loss of possible motive gratification. This is "painful", i.e. it evokes an anxiety-aggression state that some claim can be cancelled only by aggressive restoration of the threatened possibilities of gratification, or by the development of inner defense (q.v.) mechanisms and an ultimate renunciation of possible gratifications (see *Object cathexis*).

W.T.

Traumatic neuroses are neuroses that derive from for the most part unexpected and short-term, frightening or painful environmental influences (e.g. accident neuroses, war neuroses, animal phobias, etc.). Despite the short-term nature of the environmental effect and the speedy restoration of the original objective state, the frightening or painful experience and the expectation of a recurrence of such occasions (e.g. that an accident will happen any moment, that a bomb will fall or a dog bite are retained). The neurotic behavior (say an hysterical paralysis, or an excessive anxiety reaction to every kind of noise or to dogs) is promoted by secondary advantages by illness (see *Defense; Object cathexis;*

Advantage by illness; Psychopathology, psychoanalytic schema of).

Freud assumed initially that all psychoneuroses were preceded by traumatic events (the trauma hypothesis). He rejected this supposition in favor of the "wish theory" of neurosis, according to which infantile wishes can introduce psychoneuroses after traumatic events. It is, however, a matter for debate how some individuals of this type develop such infantile desires when others do not.

Today it is assumed that traumatic factors may also be present at the commencement of psychoneuroses, but that the severity of the trauma depends on the extent of painful change in the affected individual's environment. See *Family; Psychoanalysis; Depth psychology.*

Bibliography: Freud, S.: Inhibitions, symptoms and anxiety. London, [2]1936. **Toman, W.:** Introduction to psychoanalytic theory of motivation. London & New York, 1960.

W.T.

Tremograph; tremometer. Devices for testing and measurement of tremor (q.v.). Tremographs are used to record the tremor as a curve on a kymograph by applying the device to the bodily organ. With a tremometer a pin has to be inserted in a small aperture, or retained there so that it does not touch the sides of the hole. The number of times it does touch the edge is a measure of the intensity of tremor of the organ in question. In his factor-analytical studies, E. A. Fleishman tried to isolate an "arm-hand steadiness" factor.

Bibliography: Fleishman, E. A.: Dimensional analysis of movement reactions. J. exp. Psychol., 1958, *55*, 438–53.

A.T.

Tremor. Shaky movements of individual parts of the body caused by varying contraction of antagonistic muscle groups. Tremors can occur in conditions of cold, intense fatigue, stimulation, in the aged as *tremor senilis*, and in various cases of poisoning (by alcohol, lead, mercury and nicotine); it may be inherited and is a symptom of various diseases, such as Parkinsonism (q.v.), *paralysis agitans*, multiple sclerosis (q.v.), and Basedow's disease (q.v.).

E.D.

Trend. A systematic variation in time in a basic variable, in terms of a rise, drop, or a constant, intermittent, monotonous or phasic change. Dispersions and other parameters can underlie a trend. *D.W.E.*

Trend analysis. An analysis made at different points in time in order to establish the significance of a trend (q.v.) *D.W.E.*

Trial and error. A term applied by L. Morgan to behaviors which occur when an organism is presented with tasks which it is unable to solve because of its lack of appropriate behavior patterns. C. L. Hull (q.v.) called such behaviors "operants". Complex behavior patterns are developed by means of directed, positive reinforcement (q.v.) of desired, and negative reinforcement of non-desired, trials (operant conditioning, or "shaping"). See *Learning, trial-and-error; Conditioning, classical and operant.* *H.Ro.*

Triangular conflict (syn. *Three-sided conflict*). In many animals courtship arises from a conflict between urges to aggression, flight and sex, but others such as the urge to build or care for the young may also be activated. Conflicting instincts led during phylogenesis to typical compromises, which are represented in typical intensities of movement patterns.

Bibliography: Morris, D. L.: The function and causation of courtship ceremonies. In: **Grassé, P. P.** (Ed.): L'Instinct dans le comportement des animaux et de l'homme. Paris, 1956, 261–87.

K.Fi.

Tribadism. Lesbianism; sapphism; female homosexuality. *Tribade:* a woman with an abnormally large clitoris who adopts the male role in homosexual behavior. *G.D.W.*

Trichromatism. Normal color vision.

Triple-X Syndrome. A sex chromosome abnormality in which an extra X chromosome is added to the usual XX structure of the female. Occurs in about 0.12% of the female population, and tends to be associated with mental retardation. Yet more Xs are possible (e.g. XXXX), and with each addition the probability of retardation is increased. Only two cases of pento-X chromosome structure have been reported. *G.D.W.*

Tritanomaly. A defect of color vision in which the third, blue-violet sensitive cone pigment is only moderately effective. *K.H.P.*

Tritanopia. Color blindness, in which the third (blue-sensitive) cone pigment is wholly absent. *K.H.P.*

Tropism. The directive response of an organism to a stimulus or a stimulus source. The absolute stimulus intensity is less decisive than the spatial or temporal intensity. *Positive tropism:* toward; *negative tropism:* away from. Other distinctions are made according to the kind of stimulus: toward light radiation: *phototropism;* the sun: *heliotropism*; a concentration of various substances: *chemotropism*; temperature: *thermotropism*; and so on. The term "tropism" is usually applied to fixed plants, immobile animals, etc. *Taxis* is the term for freely mobile organisms. Sometimes, however, both terms are used synonymously. *I.L.*

True value. A term occurring mainly in test theory, where it indicates the expectation value of an observed variable obtained by measuring an individual with a specific test. As a rule the true value is not identical with the observed value, since measurements include an error. Therefore the true value may be characterized as the difference between the observed value and the error in measurement. In principle, the concept of true value may also be applied to other parameters of a variable. *H.-J.S.*

Truth drug. A chemical substance supposed to compel an individual to disclose all information. Experimental studies on the validity of information given oppose the existence of such drugs. In 1932, House asserted of scopalamine (q.v.), a drug related to atropine (q.v.), that no one under its influence could lie, and introduced the term "truth drug". See *Narcoanalysis; Lie detector.* *E.L.*

Tryptamine. A neurohormone and biogenic amine formed from the aromatic amino-acid tryptophan(e) (q.v.) by decarboxylation. Tryptamine passes the blood-brain barrier and can therefore be administered extra-cerebrally. It has sympathicomimetic (q.v.) qualities (e.g. increased heart rate and blood pressure). Related drugs (dimethyltryptamine) have psychotomimetic (q.v.) qualities.

Bibliography: Dewhurst, W. G.: On the chemical basis of mood. J. Psychosom. Res., 1965, *9*, 115–27. See also *Biogenic amines.* *W.J.*

Tryptophan(e). An aromatic amino-acid from which serotonin (q.v. = 5-hydroxytryptamine) is formed by way of the intermediate substance 5-hydroxytryptophan(e) (see *Biogenic amines*). Tryptophan(e) is also to some extent transformed by decarboxylation into tryptamine, which counts as a neurohormone. Oral administration of tryptophan(e) to healthy subjects can induce very slight parathymia after a short time (app. one hour). *W.J.*

Tsédek test. A test by H. Baruk for moral insight. S. has to judge the behavior of persons from the moral viewpoint in a series of summarized everyday situations. The judgments offered are assessed in order to arrive at S's moral attitude. *H.J.A.*

TSH. Abb. for *Thyroid stimulating hormone.* See *Hormones.*

T-technique. A factor-analytical technique based on correlation coefficients determined by means of the correlation of the measurements of a characteristic at t different times in regard to n individuals, in which $n > t$. The factors extracted are interpreted as situational. The technique is applied in developmental psychology and learning studies. See *Factor analysis.* *G.Mi.*

Tunnel effect. An example of a *kinetic screen effect* similar to the *piston effect* (q.v.). Two lights appear successively at points some distance apart. A screen is placed between and in front of the lights. In these conditions observers see one light travelling from one side of the screen to the other as if it had gone through a tunnel. This effect continues even after the screen has been removed. However, if the observer is never aware of the existence of the screen, the effect does not occur. *C.D.F.*

Turner syndrome (syn. *Albright-Turner syndrome; Morgagni-Turner syndrome; XO syndrome*). An intersexual syndrome named after the American physician H. H. Turner (b. 1892) and featuring dysgenesia (= underdevelopment) or agenesia (= complete absence) of sex glands (see *Gonads*). The classic genetic sex-chromosome constitution is XO; there are, however, also mosaic structures (XO/XX, XO/XY). Further symptoms are: physical appearance usually female; internal and external genitals usually female, but infantile; secondary sex characteristics often underdeveloped; sex chromatin more often negative (male) than positive (female); inadequate growth or dwarfism; multiple deformations; *ptergyium colli;* primary amenorrhea (q.v.); often increased gonadotrophin and decreased estrogen excretion in urine; average intelligence.

Bibliography: Jores, A. & Nowakowski, H.: Praktische Endokrinologie. Stuttgart, 1968. Leiber, B. & Olbrich, G.: Die klinischen Syndrome. Munich, [4]1966. Overzier, C.: Intersexuality. New York, 1963. *V.S.*

t value. A normalized standard value from non-normal distributions named after L. Terman by McCall (1939). See *Test theory.*

Bibliography: McCall, W. A.: Measurement. New York, 1939. *D.W.E.*

Twilight sleep. A state of dream-like semi-consciousness which is associated with some psychopathological conditions such as hysteria and epilepsy, and may be induced by certain drugs. It is normally transitory, but is of highly variable duration. *G.D.W.*

Twin studies. When Galton (1875, 1883) introduced twins into scientific research toward the end of the nineteenth century, they already had a rich history in mythology, legends and superstition. In the age of Darwinian theorizing and research, a major question was that of the "supremacy" of heredity; recourse was had to twins in order to substantiate this supremacy.

1. *Classic method of twin research.* Classically defined, the method of twin study used in scientific research is very simple. The basis

is the existence of two kinds of twins: namely, one-egg and two-egg twins. Genuine one-egg (*monozygotic*) twins (*MZ twins*) come from a single zygote—a single egg cell (or ovum) fertilized by a single sperm cell (spermatozoon). They represent two copies of a single individual. Their inherited basis (*anlage*, q.v.) is wholly identical.

Two-egg (*dizygotic*) twins (*DZ twins*) come from two zygotes (i.e. from two egg cells (ova), fertilized by two sperm cells). Genetically, their similarity is like that between two usual (genuine) siblings. But, in both MZ and DZ twins, the members of a pair are of the same age and depend upon the same environment. The only difference is that in one kind the genetic inheritance is identical, and in the other it is not.

The classic twin study method consists of taking a given (intellectual or physical) characteristic or trait and comparing the average differences between individuals from MZ and DZ pairs. The difference noticeable in MZ twins is to be ascribed only to the very small difference in environmental influences. The difference between DZ twins is attributable to the same influences, but also (and above all) to the difference in genetic inheritance. If one then demarcates the differences between MZ twins from those between DZ twins, the role of inheritance in regard to the characteristic under examination should be clear.

Numerous research projects have been carried out in accordance with this classic method. Nevertheless, they have been unable to answer the following question: "What are the respective contributions of inheritance and environment in the formation of individual differences?" The reason is simply that the question is wrongly put. There is no real "contribution" or "share", but a complex interaction between genetic and environmental factors. This interaction varies according to the characteristics under investigation, the age of the subjects, and the methods of comparison used. On the other hand, this method has made it possible to draw the main lines of the structure of mental and physical characteristics from the viewpoint of inheritance.

Body build and intelligence (defined according to the Binet-Simon test) are the characteristics most closely associated with inheritance. The correlation in regard to intelligence is of course zero between individuals who are not related and who have no environmental influences in common. It is approximately 0.25 between non-related children who were nevertheless reared together, and 0.50 between parents and their children and between siblings. The correlation reaches a value of some 0.55 for DZ twins reared together, and a value of almost 0.90 for MZ twins who have grown up together. School success also depends on inheritance, but to a much less noticeable degree. On the other hand, the hypothesis according to which there are genetically conditioned special abilities for mathematics, science, literature, history and so on, could not be verified. The results in regard to affective or volitional characteristics are often uncertain, and are contested. This is perhaps attributable to the fact that in this area the concepts are unclear and the test methods insufficiently validated.

Newman, Freeman & Holzinger, who were the first to use the twin method to any real point, came to the following conclusion (1937): in so far as personality and temperamental traits are concerned, MZ twins are hardly any more alike than DZ twins.

By using more complex methods (mainly factor analysis, q.v.), more recent studies have nevertheless been able to demonstrate the essential role of inheritance for certain personality factors. Hence, e.g. Vandenberg (1962) found very significant differences between MZ and DZ twins for the four factors of Thurstone's temperament inventory ("active", "vigorous", "impulsive", "sociable"), and for four factors of one of Cattell's inventories ("emotional sensitivity", "nervous tension", "neuroticism", and "will control").

Eysenck's (1952) work on neuroticism is, however, by far the most convincing and fruitful in this area. Eysenck defines neuroticism (q.v.) as a normal personality (q.v.) variable, extending from extreme stability to extreme instability. There is no difference between the MZ and DZ groups in regard to neuroticism. On the other hand, the correlations between DZ pairs are 0.21, and between MZ pairs 0.85. Variance analysis shows that, for the neuroticism factor, 80% of the individual differences are to be attributed to inheritance and only 20% to environmental influences.

2. *Control method.* The "co-twin control method" is associated with the name of a major child psychologist, A. Gesell (1941). The method consists in comparing MZ twins by subjecting one (experimental) partner to intensive training, whereas the (control) partner continues in his "spontaneous" development, i.e. without any special training. It is no longer a question, as in the classic method of twin studies, of comparing the respective parts played by inheritance and environment, but of comparing the effects of maturation (q.v.) and education (upbringing) (q.v.). In other words: Can learning and training—in short, education—accelerate the child's maturation process? This method has not often been used, and only with children of pre-school age, and most often in the areas of motor and linguistic development (q.v.).

Gesell's central experiment is well known. It consists of training the experimental twin in stages over a period of several weeks. The training gives the experimental twin an incontestable advantage, yet by the end of the experiment this head start is compensated by the control twin thanks to mere maturation.

The co-twin control method has tackled the old problem of "nature" and "nurture" in terms of the more dynamic concepts of maturation and learning, and usefully questioned the American ideology of the nineteen-thirties, which ascribed predominance to education.

The essential point of Gesell's observation is to be found elsewhere, however: namely in the demonstration that the maturation process of MZ twins is never wholly identical. Hence MZ twins no longer appear as a single being divided into two exemplars, but as two individualities. The twin method allows clarification of the maturation process (as a multiplicity of factors subjected to a general regulative principle), and simultaneously poses (yet again) the question of the inheritance and genesis of the human individual.

3. *Twin pair method.* The twin pair method is concerned predominantly with the genesis of individuality. It is a matter of a new problem whose formulation, however, puts in question the other problems of inheritance and maturation. The twin pair method starts from a critique of the other research methods.

The control and the classic twin study methods treat the partners of each pair of twins as two independent individuals, and not as a pair. It is, however, obvious (or at least a hypothesis is feasible) that life in a pair-bond has certain consequences. This form of existence determines similarities which have nothing to do with genetic inheritance (mutual imitation), and differences which are not attributable to environmental differences (role difference, dominance and submission relations, etc.). Hence it would seem possible to explain why in certain personality tests genuine twins are not more, and sometimes even less, alike than usual siblings.

But here, as in the foregoing perspectives, the interest of twin studies is that (thanks to their specific characteristics) they provide a generally applicable research method. The complete identity of MZ twins grounds the investigation of inheritance in classic twin research.

Twins—as complete pairs—offer the unique opportunity not only of carrying out research into the psychology of the pair, but of investigating the fundamental processes of the development of human individuality. Child psychologists have long been aware that it is not the individual in the sense of the *I* or *ego* (q.v.) that is "original" or "fundamental", but the undifferentiated "we", the "confusion" between mother and child; and that a consciousness of the self and of others forms only gradually (though simultaneously). (See *Self-knowledge.*) Whereas, however, a fundamental difference lies at the basis of the mother-child pair (as in the case of every other freely-formed pair), in a pair of twins (above all in a MZ pair) there is, at first, practically no difference between the partners. For this reason, any ascertainable differences between partners may be ascribed to the (direct and indirect) consequences of living in the pair bond.

The twin pair method is relatively new. Its rough lines were suggested by Gedda (1948), applied by von Bracken (1934) before it had been developed in its own right, and have been defined and developed by Zazzo (1960). This method makes it possible to investigate the negative or positive (and differentiating) effects of existence in the pair bond on the development and structure of personality. The noticeable delay in language development and the frequent occurrence of secret languages—chiefly with MZ twins—clearly indicate the danger of alienation in or through the pair. Both partners are their mutual prisoners, and social needs are gratified and exhausted in the twin relationship. In spite of this "mirror effect", and in spite of identity in regard to inheritance and environment, an individualization process does take place. The fact that a pair is a structure allows it a differentiating effect. Above all, it is possible to observe how oppositions, rivalries and completions occur, and how role division and ego-consciousness are formed; in short, it is possible to observe the formation of a specific individuality in the case of each partner.

Twin studies are not restricted to one method. A distinction has been made here between three methods, which correspond to the many problems and to the historic sequence of questions raised by scientific psychology. The methods of twin research are not the only ones that allow investigation of such problems. Nevertheless, the application of a "naturally" available method in an area where experiment research proper was impossible, enabled at least an entry to be made into some of the most difficult areas of human psychology.

Bibliography: Bracken, H. von: Mutual intimacy in twins. Char. and Pers., 1934, *4*, 293–309. **Id.:** Zwilling und Psychologie des Gemeinschaftslebens. Report of 14th German Psycho. Soc. Jena, 1935. **Burlingham, D. T.:** The relationship of twins to each other. Psychoanal. Stud. Child, 1939, *3–4*. **Burt, C.:** The genetic determination of differences in intelligence: a study of monozygotic twins reared together and apart. Brit. J. Psychol., 1966, *57*, 137–53. **Cattell, R. B.:** Methodological and conceptual advances in evaluating hereditary and environmental influences and their interaction. In: **Vandenberg, S. G.** (Ed.): Methods and goals in human behavior genetics. New York, 1965. **Day, E. J.:** The development of language in twins. Child Developm., 1932, 179–99; 298–316. **Eysenck, H. J.:** The scientific study of personality. London, 1952. **Id.:** The biological basis of personality. Springfield, 1967. **Id.:** Intelligence assessment: a theoretical and experimental approach, Brit. J. Educ. Psychol., 1967, *37*, 81–98. **Galton, F.:** The history of twins as a criterion of the relative powers of nature and nurture. Fraser's Magazine, 1875, *12*, 566–76. **Id.:** Inquiries into human faculty and its development. London, 1883. **Gedda, L.:** Psicologica della società intrageminale. Riv. di Psicol., 1948, *4*, 10–44. **Id.:** Studio dei gemelli. Roma, 1951. **Id.:** Twins in history and in science. New York, 1961. **Gesell, A. & Thompson, H.:** Twins T and C from infancy to adolescence: a biogenetic study of individual differences by the method of co-twin control. Provincetown, Mass., 1941. **Gottschaldt, K.:** Das Problem der Phänogenetik der Persönlichkeit. In: **Lersch, P. & Thomas, H.** (Eds.): Handbuch der Psychologie, Vol. 4. Göttingen, 1960. **Husén, T.:** Analyse de facteurs héréditaires et de milieu determinant la réussite scolaire par l'étude de jumeaux élevés ensemble. Bull. Psychol., 1967, *20*, 772–81. **Id.:** Über die Begabung von Zwillingen. Psychol. Beitr., 1953, *1*. **Luria, A. R. & Yudovitch, F. I.:** Speech and the development of mental processes in the child. London, 1959. **Mittler, P.:** The study of twins. Harmondsworth, 1971. **Newman, H. H., Freeman, F. N. & Holzinger, R. J.:** Twins: a study of heredity and environment. Chicago, 1937. **Pire, G.:** Application des techniques sociométriques à l'étude des jumeaux. Enfance, 1966, *1*, 23–48. **Vandenberg, S. G.**: The hereditary abilities study: hereditary components in a psychological test battery. Amer. J. Hum. Genet., 1962, *14*, 220–237. **Id.** (Ed.): Methods and goals in human behavior genetics. New York, 1965. **Zazzo, R.**: Les jumeaux, le couple, et la personne. Paris, 1960. **Id.**: Sur le postulat de la comparabilité dans la méthode des jumeaux. Acta genet. med. gemellolog., 1955, *4*. *R. Zazzo*

Two-factor theory of learning. A theory of O. H. Mowrer's that he has since abandoned. It separates the areas of application of classical and instrumental learning: (*a*) *sign learning:* emotions, autonomic responses, movements of the smooth musculature are acquired in accordance with the law of contiguity (q.v.); (*b*) *solution learning:* voluntary responses, movements of the striate musculature are acquired by instrumental learning. See *Learning theory; Conditioning, classical and operant.* *H.W.*

Tympanic membrane (syn. *Tympanum; Eardrum*). The tympanic membrane lies between the external auditory canal and the middle ear. The hammer of the first auditory ossicle is joined to it. Recent objective studies of middle-ear functioning have been carried out by measuring input wave resistance on the membrane. See *Auditory perception; Sense organs: the ear.* *M.S.*

Type. In common parlance, the terms "type" and "trait" (q.v.) are used almost interchangeably. We may say that a person possesses the trait of sociability, or that he is "the sociable type", meaning in both instances that he is sociable, that is, behaves in a sociable manner. Many psychologists, particularly in the USA, make little difference in their usage of these terms, except with respect to the hypothetical distribution of the behavior in question; it is often said that the concept of *type* requires a bimodal distribution of test scores, or even a clear separation of members of the opposite sides of the typology, whereas the concept of *trait* requires a unimodal and probably even a normal Gaussian form of distribution. This point will be discussed presently; the best modern usage certainly distinguishes clearly between the two concepts, as will be pointed out later, but nevertheless much of what has been said about traits in this book also applies to types, and the two articles should be read together in order to clarify all the relevant points.

Typology may be said to have begun with Galen's theory of the four temperaments (choleric, sanguine, phlegmatic, melancholic) in the second century A.D., although the roots of this typology are said to go back to Hippocrates, and traces of it are certainly found in ancient Greece (Roback, 1931). In his *Anthropologie*, Kant adopted and adapted this doctrine, and his version became official doctrine until the end of the nineteenth century. One essential feature of this typology was its categorical character; a person belonged to one type or another, and no mixtures were allowed. It is this feature of the Galen-Kant view which gave rise to the mistaken notion that distribution of scores discriminated between types and traits; this is only true if we accept a categorical view of type concepts. As we shall see, none of the well-known exponents of modern typology (Jung, Kretschmer) has in fact adopted such a view.

The alternative to a categorical view is a dimensional one, and such a position seems to have been adumbrated by Wundt (1903), who argued that two of the four types were characterized by high emotionality (cholerics and melancholics), whereas the other two were characterized by low emotionality; he consequently suggested a dimension of "emotionality" along which people could be graded continuously. He provided a second dimension by noting that cholerics and sanguines were "changeable", melancholics and phlegmatics "unchangeable"; this dimension was independent of the first. Wundt's dimensional system thus locates the four temperaments in the four quadrants generated by these two dimensions; they have lost their categorical character, and normal or unimodal distributions along the two dimensions, while not a necessary feature of the model, would certainly not be counter to Wundt's thinking. Combining Kant's description of the personality traits characterizing the four temperaments, and the dimensional system of Wundt, gives us a picture of what might be called "classical typology" which is reproduced as Fig. 1 (Eysenck, 1967).

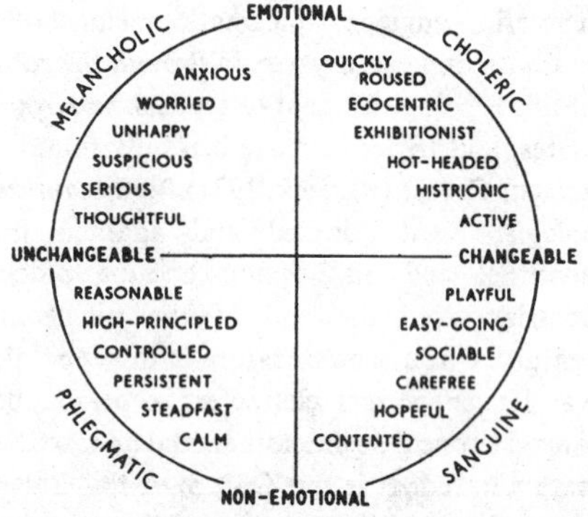

Fig. 1. Diagram showing combination of the Galen-Kant theory of the four temperaments and Wundt's dimensional hypothesis

Distribution of scores is thus not the distinguishing mark as between type and trait concepts; it would in any case be a meaningless one from a purely statistical point of view (Eysenck, 1970). Scores measure error variance as well as true variance; indeed in psychology, particularly the psychology of personality, they probably contain more error variance than true variance. But error variance is by definition normally distributed, so that even if the distribution of "true" scores happened to be bimodal, the addition of normally distributed error variance could easily make the combined distribution unimodal. Furthermore, arguments from distributions require a proper, rational metric; no such metric has ever been suggested for measures of personality. Observed scores are arbitrary, and can be transformed in any desired way through the use of logarithms or other mathematical functions; none of the resulting distributions, however different they may be, can be said to be more correct than any other. Arguments from distributions are a quagmire which more cautious writers avoid; no possible conclusions could be drawn from them, even if the argument happened to be relevant, which it is not (Eysenck, 1970).

If the distribution of scores does not mark the distinction between type and trait concepts, what does? Eysenck (1947) has suggested that traits are the subordinate concept, type the supraordinate concept; typologies are created to account for the observed intercorrelations between traits. This suggestion forms part of a general hierarchical concept of personality structure, which is shown diagrammatically in Fig. 2, using the type "extraversion-introversion" as the example. At the lowest level we have specific responses to specific stimuli, i.e. isolated bits of behavior; these are integrated into habitual responses when they can be shown to be regular, i.e. to have statistical reliability. These habitual responses are in turn integrated into traits, such as sociability, impulsiveness, activity, liveliness, or excitability; evidence for the existence of such traits is provided by observed intercorrelations among habitual responses. If these traits themselves are found to intercorrelate in representative samples of the population, in the manner predicted by the theory, then we have evidence of the supraordinate type concept; in the case shown in diagram form in Fig. 2, the concept of "extraversion" implies, and is based on, positive intercorrelations between the various traits listed.

As in the case of traits (q.v.), the statistical technique best adapted to the exploration of typological hypotheses is that of factor analysis (q.v.). Thurstone's use of oblique primary factors, the intercorrelations between which can again be factored to give rise to second-order factors, fits the situation very well; traits are primary factors, types second-order ones, and both levels of the hierarchy can be investigated simultaneously by modern computerized rotation methods. Of these, varimax is often used but is not appropriate as it imposes orthogonality on the solution; this automatically rules out type factors conceived as second-order factors. Promax or some such program which allows the angles between primary factors to align themselves according

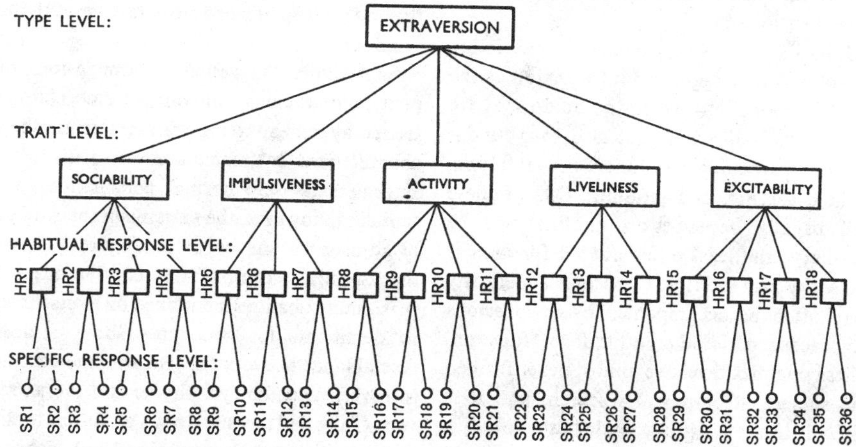

Fig. 2. Diagram showing hierarchical hypothesis of type and trait concepts

to simple structure principles without additional requirements of orthogonality is mandatory for the proper exploration of the factor space. Apparent contradictions between different writers can often be traced to the use of clearly inappropriate methods of rotation.

Historically, the first to use quasi-statistical methods for the elaboration of a descriptive system of personality were Heymans & Wiersma (1906–9); on the basis of ratings of some 2,523 individuals by their doctors on various personality traits, they arrived at a system of classification using three main dimensions: emotionality, activity, and primary as opposed to secondary function; this last dimension resembles extraversion-introversion and is based on certain pseudo-physiological speculations of the Austrian psychiatrist O. Gross (1902). Eysenck (1970), who gives a detailed account of these studies, has recalculated the original data and has shown that activity is in fact correlated quite highly with primary-secondary function, so that the only two independent dimensions which emerge are emotionality and primary-secondary function, or extraversion; this result is in good agreement with Wundt's hypothesis as shown in Fig. 1. (It is assumed here that "changeableness" can be identified with extraversion; this seems likely from the personality descriptions given, and also from experimental work done, e.g. Eysenck, 1967.)

Better known than Heymans and Wiersma's typology (which is widely used only in South Africa at the present time) is the work of Jung (1921) and Kretschmer (1948). Jung's exclusively theoretical and speculative writing was not influenced by empirical studies, and his particular hypotheses did not give rise to much experimental work; Kretschmer's first book appeared in 1921, and ran into twenty-five editions by 1968, having inspired a tremendous amount of empirical research, and being changed in many ways by the results of this research, much of which was done by Kretschmer and his students. Detailed reviews are given of these theories in Eysenck (1970) and by Hall and Lindzey (1957); the latter work gives prominence to Sheldon's (1940, 1942) version of Kretschmer's teachings, mixed as it is with Jungian notions, and hardly does justice to Kretschmer's pioneering investigations. The details of these two typologies cannot of course be discussed here, but there are certain features of them which require consideration.

Jung's system is very complex, postulating not only extraversion and introversion as the two directions into which the libido may be preferentially directed, but also four fundamental psychological functions: thinking, feeling, sensing, and intuiting. One of these will usually be superior, another will be auxiliary; the least differentiated function is called by him inferior. Conscious superiority may often be accompanied by unconscious dominance of another attitude or function. These complexities have almost never formed the subject of empirical research, and it is difficult to see how they could; attention has usually only been paid to what Jung would consider an extremely superficial caricature of his system, namely the behavioral dimension of extraversion-introversion; this closely resembles Wundt's "changeableness" and Heymans and Wiersma's primary vs. secondary function, and is by no means original in conception.

Jung suggested that the two types of neurotic illness which emerged from Janet's investigations (hysteria and psychasthenia) were characteristically found in extraverted and introverted personalities respectively; this proposition was verified by Eysenck (1947). The same investigation tested another proposition implicit in Jung's account, but never discussed by him. If two types of neurotic illness are at opposite ends of the extraversion-introversion continuum, then we must posit another dimension, orthogonal to the first one, ranging from neurotic to stable; this dimension was called "neuroticism", and is in nature very similar to Wundt's emotionality. Fittingly, psychasthenics (now more usually called "dysthymics", i.e. anxiety states, reactive depressions, obsessional and compulsive patients, and phobics) fall into the "melancholic" quadrant, hysterics and psychopaths into the "choleric" quadrant, as do criminals. Thus empirical results support the Wundtian doctrine, and accommodate Jung's hypothesis (in this rather superficial form) in one and the same scheme.

Kretschmer suggested a dimension of personality ranging from one extreme, characterized by schizophrenic disorders, to another, characterized by manic-depressive disorder. Intermediate were normal personalities, resembling, however, the extreme in their mode of adjustment and behavior. Figure 3 shows the essential nature of this continuum; the personality qualities mentioned by Kretschmer to demarcate his two types show a close resemblance between the schizothyme and the introvert, and the cyclothyme and the extravert. (Jung had already drawn attention to the affinity between introversion and schizophrenia.) Here too it is obvious that the existence of psychotic patients at both ends of the continuum requires the postulation of another dimension, orthogonal to the first, ranging from psychosis to normality; this dimension may be named "psychoticism" and there is considerable evidence for its existence (Eysenck & Eysenck, 1968).

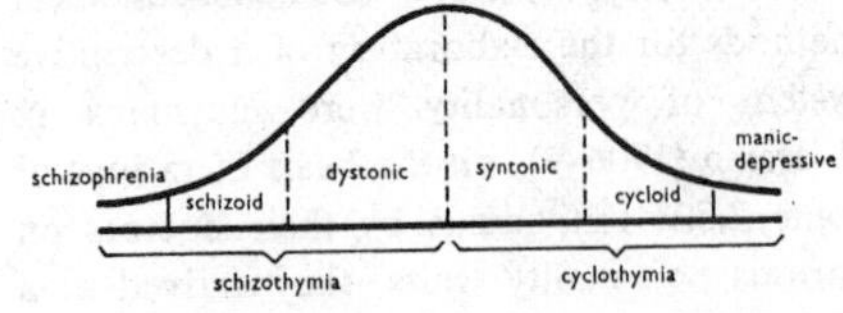

If we can identify, as is probably permissible, introversion with schizothymia and extraversion with cyclothymia, the question remains of whether we can identify, as the Freudians would do, neuroticism with psychoticism, regarding psychotic illness as a more serious form of neurotic illness. The evidence fairly conclusively suggests that this hypothesis is false, and that the two dimensions are in fact orthogonal (Eysenck, 1964; Cattell & Scheier, 1961). In general, tests which discriminate between normals and psychotics do not discriminate between normals and neurotics, and vice versa; discriminant function analyses demonstrate the existence of two significant latent roots. Hence at the type level a minimum of three independent dimensions seems to be required to represent human personality: extraversion, emotionality-neuroticism, and psychoticism. (The Heymans and Wiersma dimension of *activity* may be similar to psychoticism; the slowness and retardation of psychotics may appear as the opposite of activity.)

Kretschmer introduced the notion of body-build into his system, associating leptomorph, linear physique with schizothymia and pyknic, broad physique with cyclothymia. There is probably a low correlation of 0.3–0.4 between introversion and leptomorph physique, but the association with psychotic disorder is largely an experimental artefact, produced by the different ages at which schizophrenics and manic-depressives succumb to their respective illnesses; body build becomes more pyknic with age, and manic-depressive patients are considerably older than schizophrenic ones. Sheldon found a very high correlation between physique and temperament, but these have not been replicated by other investigators, and are almost certainly due to contamination of one measure by knowledge of the other.

Giese (1939), conscious of the multiplicity of typologies, pleaded for a single typology; his wish is gradually coming true as experimental studies and refined statistical techniques clear away many of the obstacles which have hitherto stood in the way of such a unified account of human typology. Cattell, Guilford and Eysenck all find evidence for extraversion-introversion and emotionality-stability in their studies (Eysenck & Eysenck, 1969), and there is also a good deal of agreement on psychoticism, and on the position within this dimensional framework of various psychiatric diagnostic groups. Much still remains to be done, but better methods and more objective measures are gradually narrowing the range of dispute. Models are becoming more sophisticated, largely by becoming more quantified, and questions are being asked the answers to which were being taken for granted by earlier writers. Thus for instance the distinction between normals and neurotics, or normals and psychotics, may be quantitative, i.e. along a continuum, or qualitative, i.e. categorical; one answer or the other was usually assumed by psychiatric and other intuitive writers, but no method was available to provide cogent evidence one way or the other. The method of criterion analysis (Eysenck, 1950) was designed specially with this problem in mind, and has shown that the quantitative hypothesis is in fact the correct one, both for neurosis and psychosis.

Empirical work on typologies makes use of the same methods as work on traits (q.v.); ratings, self-ratings (questionnaires), miniature situation tests and laboratory tasks based on theoretical systems and deductions therefrom are all being used, as well as physiological recordings. As in the case of traits, the question arises whether a person's position on a typological dimension is determined more by hereditary or environmental causes. A detailed survey of the evidence is given by Eysenck (1967), who concludes that in the Western type of culture, at the present time, the average contribution of heredity to individual differences in extraversion, emotionality and psychoticism is roughly between 60% and 80%, with the majority of well designed studies giving values in the neighborhood of 75%, a value very similar to that found in the case of intelligence tests. There are many different methods in use, in addition to the study of monozygotic and dizygotic twins, and results are in good agreement. The same may be said of concordance studies of neurotic, psychotic and criminal twins; concordance of identical twins is considerably greater than that of fraternal twins.

A central problem in genetic studies of this kind is connected with the question of what is inherited—clearly we cannot inherit function, only structure. This raises the fundamental problem of causality; types, like traits, are merely descriptive, yet we would like to know more precisely why a particular person is situated at the extraverted end of the continuum, or at the stable end, or the psychotic. Such questions are difficult to answer, and attempts have been made either by using psychological concepts like Hull's reactive inhibition (Eysenck, 1957) or Pavlov's "excitation-inhibition" (Gray, 1964), or physiological notions like the ascending reticular activating system and the visceral brain (Eysenck, 1967). Such theories generate testable hypotheses, particularly the physiological types of theory, and many experiments have been reported in which such deductions have been subjected to test. Such deductions may be along physiological or psychological lines. As an example of the first type, consider the hypothesis that extraverts have higher thresholds of A.R.A.S. activity, so that cortical arousal will be lower in them; this leads immediately to the deduction that EEG alpha activity will be of greater amplitude, and characteristically of lower frequency. Similarly, it can be predicted that sedation thresholds are low in extraverts, high in introverts. Both predictions have in fact received strong support. Psychological predictions derive from knowledge of behavioral consequences of high and low arousal states; conditioning is facilitated by high arousal, impaired by low arousal, and introverts do as predicted show better conditioning than do extraverts on eyeblink or GSR conditioning. Many other predictions relating to orienting responses, figural aftereffects, sensory thresholds, reminiscence, blocking, vigilance, tolerance of pain and sensory deprivation, rote learning, time errors, perceptual defense, motor movements, level of aspiration, autonomic reactions, and so on have been tested in efforts to provide evidence relating to the causal hypothesis mentioned, usually with positive results (Eysenck, 1967). It seems likely that work along these lines, i.e. using the hypothetico-deductive method, will succeed in the long run to put the whole study of typology on a higher level than the largely intuitive, subjective kind of impressionism which characterized the earlier writers. At present we have reached a half-way house, with a fair number of well established facts, but also with a number of puzzling discrepancies; with fair agreement on the outline of the general picture, but with disagreement on specific points. Resolution of these disagreements will be the next stage in the development of typological theories.

Types, like traits, may be investigated with animals as well as with humans; rats may be bred for emotionality, using the open field tests, and emotionally reactive animals compared with emotionally non-reactive ones on a variety of experimental tests, or with respect to physiological functioning and biochemical make-up. It cannot of course be assumed without proof that the meaning of emotionality is identical in humans and in animals, but the hypothesis that this is so can be experimentally tested, and predictions made on this basis have been largely validated. Experimental work along these lines promises to add considerably to our knowledge; animal analogues of human types offer advantages (breeding studies for genetic analysis; physiological analysis *in vivo*; biochemical analysis and anatomical study after dissection) which make them of considerable value to the experimenter. Possibly dogs and monkeys will in due course supplant rats, being closer to man in their make-up; to date, most work has in fact been done with rats (Eysenck & Broadhurst, 1964).

Although the various dimensions of personality which constitute the basis of modern typology are independent of each other, and of intelligence, nevertheless they may interact, and this interaction requires the use of special techniques of *zone analysis*. Consider as an example work done on expansiveness of movements; low N extraverts show much expansiveness, low N introverts little. High N extraverts show little expansiveness, high N introverts much. If the results are averaged over all high E vs. high I groups, no differences appear; similarly when all high N groups are contrasted with all low N groups. It is only when we plot all four zones (high E, high N; low E, high N; high E, low N; low E, low N) that highly significant results emerge. Taking only extremes of this kind, and using our three dimensions plus intelligence, we have sixteen sub-groups which require to be compared with each other; if we took three samples for each dimension (high, medium and low) in order to test linearity of regression (which should not simply be assumed), then we have 81 groups to compare. It will be clear that typological studies, properly carried out in line with the principles of zone analysis, require considerable thought, special design and complex statistical treatment; many failures to replicate previous studies, or to find results in line with hypothesis, may be due to insufficient care being taken with the design of the experiment. Typology is such an important part of psychology that greater care in this respect will undoubtedly repay the trouble taken.

Bibliography: Cattell, R. B. & Scheier, I. H.: The meaning and measurement of neuroticism and anxiety. New York, 1961. **Eysenck, H. J.:** Dimensions of personality. London, 1947. **Id.:** Criterion analysis—an application of the hypothetico-deductive method in factor analysis. Psychol. Rev., 1950, *57*, 38–53. **Id.:** The dynamics of anxiety and hysteria. London, 1957. **Id.:** Principles and methods of personality description, classification and diagnosis. Brit. J. Psychol., 1964, *55*, 284–94. **Id.:** The biological basis of personality. Springfield, 1967. **Id.:** The structure of human personality. London, [3]1970. **Eysenck, H. J. & Broadhurst, P. L.:** Experiments with animals. Oxford, 1964. **Eysenck, H. J. & Eysenck, S. B. G.:** Structure and measurement of personality. London, 1969. **Eysenck, S. B. G. & Eysenck, H. J.:** The measurement of psychoticism: a study of factor stability and reliability. Brit. J. soc. clin. Psychol., 1968, *7*, 286–94. **Giese, F.:** Lehrbuch der Psychologie. Tübingen, 1939. **Gray, J. A.:** Pavlov's typology. Oxford, 1964. **Gross, O.:** Die cerebrale sekundärfunktion. 1902. **Hall, C. S. & Lindsey, G.:** Theories of personality. New York, 1957. **Heymans, G. & Niersma, E.:** Beiträge zur speziellen Psychologie auf Grund einer Massenuntersuchung. Z. Psychol., 1906, *42*, 81–127; *43*, 321–73; 1907, *45*, 1–42; 1908, *47*, 321–33; *49*, 414–39; 1909, *51*, 1–72. **Jung, C. G.:** Psychologische Typen. Zürich, 1921. **Kretschmer, E.:** Körperbau und Charakter. Berlin, 1948. **Roback, A. A.:** The psychology of character. New York, 1931. **Sheldon, W. H.:** The varieties of temperament. New York, 1942. **Id.:** The varieties of human physique. New York, 1940. **Wundt, W.:** Grundzüge der physiologischen Psychologie. Vol. 3. Leipzig, 1903.

H. J. Eysenck

Typical intensity. In order to reach a formal constancy of ritualized movements, a typical intensity which excludes ambiguity was "discovered" in the course of phylogenesis (Morris, 1957). The basis is variable intensity. In typical intensity there is constancy over a wide range and variability only with very low and very high frequencies. Constant intensity is independent of frequency: e.g. the telephone.

Bibliography: Morris, D.: "Typical intensity" and its relation to the problem of ritualization. Bevaviour, 1957, *11*, 1–12.

K.Fi.

Tyramine. A neurohormone obtained from tyrosine by decarboxylization, which is counted among the biogenic amines (q.v.). It is also a substance with a sympathicomimetic effect; it is weaker though more long-lasting in effect than adrenalin, with a pronounced circulation effect, and especially increased blood pressure. Numerous similar substances are produced synthetically (phenylephrine-tyramine group) and are used as vasoconstrictors, bronchodilatators, mydriatic drugs (see *Mydriasis*), and therapeutically. Tyramine's sympathicomimetic effect probably occurs indirectly through the release of noradrenalin(e) (norepinephrine). *W.J.*

Tyrosine. An aromatic amino-acid, and an important protein component. A precursor in the formation of hormones, for instance in the catecholamines (q.v.; see also *Biogenic amines*). Tyrosine is introduced into the organism in food (protein); in the organism it is formed, e.g., from phenylalanine (q.v.).

Bibliography: Acheson, G. H. (Ed.): Second symposium on catecholamines. Pharmacol. Rev., 1966, *18*, 1–804.

U

Ultrared. Also known as "infrared": electromagnetic radiation shorter in vibration frequency than the visible red portion of the spectrum. *W.P.*

Ultrasound; ultrasonics. Mechanical vibrations and waves above the frequency range that can be perceived by the human ear, on account of its mode of operation: from 2×10^4 to 10^9 Hz; beyond that is "hypersound" up to 10^{13} Hz. Some species (e.g. bats) hear in ultrasound, and locate objects in the environment by echolocation. Psychologically relevant experiments try to imitate the bat principle by technical means and use it in the service of the blind.

Bibliography: Griffin, D. R.: Listening in the dark. New Haven, 1958. Kay, L.: Ultrasonic mobility aids for the blind. In: Clark, L. L. (Ed.): Proceedings of the Rotterdam mobility research conference. Rotterdam, 1965, 61–71. *M.B.*

Ultraviolet. The electromagnetic radiation shorter than extreme violet and beyond the violet portion of the visible spectrum. *W.P.*

Unburdening type. This type unburdens the ego aspect of consciousness by a readiness to prepare and change objects; this is especially the case with the cyclothymic temperament. *W.K.*

Unconditioned inhibition. In Pavlov's behavioral theory: a collective term for inhibition phenomena which, in contrast to forms of conditioned inhibition, need not first be acquired by learning. Among the varieties of unconditioned inhibition are external inhibition or negative induction and protective inhibition. See *Inhibition; Conditioning, classical and operant; Pavlov.* *L.B.*

Unconscious. The *personal unconscious* is all those experiences and memories of situations of motive gratification which, from specific points in time in the development of the individual in question, were no longer available (or only with subsequent punishment), and were therefore repressed. It is all the object cathexes of an individual at a given point in his development; the sum of all opportunities for motive gratification that were once available but are so no longer. This repressed totality may be assessed directly by psychotherapy or psychoanalysis, and indirectly in terms of observable gaps or deficits in the reality concept of the individual concerned. According to Toman (1960) it may be defined in relation to the given age and motive differentiation rate of an individual as the extent by which that individual's knowledge is behind the optimal state (see *Energy, mental*).

The personal environment is clinically and socio-psychologically important. Experiences with individuals are (according to Freud, by the process of object cathexis; and, in general terms, by means of data storage and learning of meaning) precipitated as knowledge. Gaps in knowledge may relate to authority figures, individuals (of approximately the same age) of the other sex, of the same sex, children, and so on. Part aspects of individuals, such as their readiness to co-operate, conscientiousness or power, may be ignored.

By means of defense (q.v.) mechanisms, *subconscious* and *preconscious* experiences become unconscious (see *Preconscious*). The now unconscious motives may (according to Freud) become evident in behavior or in the conscious mind. In dreams, in fantasy (q.v.), and in mental illnesses, the individual's reduced control allows such unconscious motives to become manifest. Their indication in psychotherapy is supposed to help the patient reporting such dreams or fantasies to make these supposedly unconscious motives conscious, and to learn to some extent to gratify them in reality, and to some extent to find substitute gratifications for them if they are no longer gratifiable, or to do without them more successfully than hitherto.

According to Jung (q.v.) the *collective unconscious* is the totality of certain innate modes of response to typical objects and occasions, such as danger, death, woods, water, etc., but also to persons, such as the old man, the child, the woman, the man, the mother or the father. Certain discrepancies may arise between concrete experiences and archetypally pre-existent expectations; these may be attenuated by psychoanalysis of preferences and wishes arising from the collective unconscious. Analogous phenomena from comparative psychology would be instinctive behaviors (see *Instinct*) that can be evoked (without experience) by certain key stimulus schemata. In psychotherapy and psychoanalysis the term is sometimes used as a *deus ex machina*, and then prevents further analysis of the experiential components of supposedly archetypal responses.

The *familiar unconscious* is all those unconscious wishes and tendencies at least in part taken over from parents and other members of the family (by identification or introjection). As a rule the familiar unconscious represents a part of the personal unconscious, and especially unconscious fragments of the superego (q.v.). See *Freud; Jung; Depth psychology; Dream.*

Bibliography: Toman, W.: Introduction to psychoanalytic theory of motivation. London & New York, 1960.

W. Toman

Unconsciousness. A condition in which the ability to perceive and to act consciously is in abeyance. The deepest state of unconsciousness is *coma*. Unconsciousness results from a threat to the whole organism (e.g. in fevers, heart attacks, cases of poisoning), or from a direct disturbance of brain functioning (*exogenous:* concussion, the paralysing effect of narcotics (q.v.), alcohol, etc.; or *endogenous:* epileptic fits). *V.M.*

Underachievement. See *Overachievement*.

Understanding. 1. The ability to think, i.e. to apprehend being and relations non-pictorially. In this acceptation often synonymous with intellect (q.v.). Frequently conceived as the capability of purposeful, insightful behavior, though not necessarily connected with highly "conceptual" thought. **2.** Apprehension of a meaning. **3.** The awareness of a logical connection; the apprehension of a meaningful connection between sign and signified; the meaningful apprehension of a sign in semantics (q.v.). **4.** Knowledge of that which is not expressed. **5.** Automatic interpretation of an expression (q.v.). **6.** Thinking (q.v.). *H.W.*

Undoing. An (inner) defense (q.v.) mechanism which allows appeasement of a guilt feeling about a forbidden motive gratification that has already occurred. It usually consists of the gratification of those introjected motives which in the past followed forbidden motive gratifications in the form of punishment by others. Examples: being particularly friendly to someone to whom one has already shown hatred; compulsive washing to compensate for supposedly unclean actions (even if only intended) or thoughts. *W.T.*

Uroboros. According to Neumann (1956), the ur-archetype, represented by a serpent biting its own tail. The symbol of the primal situation, in which the consciousness and ego of the individual have still to develop. It includes contradictory principles—positive and negative, male and female—and represents primal chaos and the totality of the psyche.

Bibliography: **Neumann, E.:** Die grosse Mutter. Zürich, 1956. *J.L.I.*

Urolagnia. A kind of sexual deviation in which urine, urination, or the sight of others urinating, are sources of erotic enjoyment. Drinking one's own urine is another behavior which usually comes under this label. *G.D.W.*

Usnadze's volume illusion. This illusion discovered by Usnadze is the prototype of a series of demonstrations of *set* which is the basis of the Georgian (USSR) school of psychology. The illusion requires the repeated presentation to each hand of two spheres of unequal volume, the subject indicating each time which is the smaller. Finally, two equal spheres are presented, and it appears to the subject that the sphere in the hand that previously held the larger sphere is smaller than the other.

C.D.F.

Utopia. Thomas More's term for an imaginary world, and the title of his prose fiction *Utopia* (Latin version, Louvain 1516). Utopia aims at an ateration of society even though it can never be achieved; it strives to approximate to the ideal by (as far as possible) human means. Utopian socialism intends a better world than capitalist society without offering a concrete programme for its attainment. In general usage, a "utopia" is any system or project which seems incapable of realization; a "utopian" is an unrealistic dreamer.

Bibliography: **Bloch, E.:** The spirit of utopia. New York, 1972. **More, T.:** Utopia (first Eng. trans.). London, 1551. *M.R.*

Utriculus. See *Statoliths.*

V

Vacation. A period of time free from work commitments and extending beyond the daily or weekly rest period; for the most part the minimum vacation is now legally determined. With the present increasing trend to solution of technico-economic problems there is a tendency toward longer vacations. The problem of the future in this regard will be the provision of appropriate activities for an "achieving society" during enforced leisure time. See *Aging; Industrial psychology.*

Bibliography: Kleemeier, R. W. (Ed.): Ageing and leisure. New York, 1957. **McLellan, D.:** Marx's Grundrisse. London, 1971. **Mott, P. E.:** Shift work: the social, psychological and physical consequences. Ann Arbor, Mich., 1965. **Murrell, K. F. H.:** Ergonomics. London, 1965. **Sergean, R.:** Managing shift-work. London 1971. *G.R.W.M.*

Vacuum neurosis. A term sometimes used for what V. E. Frankl (Vienna) has called the "existential vacuum", which causes many, and especially young, people in most contemporary cultures to suffer from a feeling of essential meaninglessness: "Today we are no longer, as at the time of Freud, living in an age of sexual frustration, but in one of existential frustration" (Frankl, 1970).

Bibliography: Frankl, V. E.: Der Mensch auf der Suche nach Sinn. Universitas, 1970, *25*, 369–76. *G.H.*

Vacuum response. In behaviorism, a response which occurs in the absence of the stimulus which usually evokes it. *G.D.W.*

Vagina, artificial. An artificial vagina is supplied mechanically or surgically in cases of congenital absence of a natural vagina or if a "sex change" is thought possible and desirable. It is requisite that an artificial organ should allow almost the same physiological reactions to sexual stimulation as a natural vagina. See *Hermaphroditism.*

Bibliography: Masters, W. H. & Johnson, V. E.: The artificial vagina. Western J. Surg., 1961, *69*, 192–212. **Id.:** Human sexual response, Boston, 1966. *V.S.*

Vaginism (syn. *Vaginismus*). A contraction or spasm (adductor spasm) of the pelvic and vaginal orifice musculature which either prevents the introduction of the penis into the vagina (and therefore coitus), or hinders withdrawal of the penis during coitus. In very rare cases, the latter condition can be arrested only by narcosis of the woman.

Bibliography: Ellison, C.: Psychosomatic factors in the unconsummated marriage. J. Psychosom. Res., 1968, *12*, 61. **Friedman, L. J.:** Virgin wives: a study of unconsummated marriages. London, 1962. *H.M.*

Vagotonia. According to Eppinger & Hess (1910), a shift (brought about by unilateral increased tonus of the parasympathetic system) of equilibrium in the autonomic nervous system to the parasympathetic side. It tends to cause increased parasympathetic excitability, so that normally subthreshold, parasympathetically exciting stimuli evoke abnormally intensified responses (low blood pressure, inclination to cold hands and feet, increased assimilation, over-acidification of the stomach), which are also evident psychically (according to Birkmeyer & Winkler, 1951).

Bibliography: Eppinger, H. & Hess, L.: Die Vagotonie. Berlin, 1910. **Birkmeyer, W. & Winkler, W.:** Klinik und Therapie der vegetativen Funktionsstörungen. Berlin, 1951. *F.-C.S.*

Vagus. The tenth cranial nerve; the motor and secretory fibers arise in the *medulla oblongata* and the sensory fibers in two ganglia on the nerve-trunk. Part of the parasympathetic nervous system. *E.D.*

Valence. Lewin's term for the psychological attraction, or drawing-power, of a thing. Valence may be positive or negative. See *Lewin, Kurt; Tension system; Topological and vector psychology*.

Validity. A vitally important concept in the theory of psychological testing. A test is valid when it actually measures the characteristic it is supposed to. Accordingly the validity of a test can vary gradually. See *Test theory; Objective tests; Traits; Type.* *W.H.B.*

Variability. See Dispersion.

Variable. In the mathematical acceptation, an alterable value, and frequently used as a short form of "random variable". A variable represents a basis for the notation of functions (in the function $x = f(y)$, x represents the independent and y the dependent variable). In general, "variable" is a term for a factor which has some effect or exerts an influence during the observation or measurement of some phenomenon. *D.W.E.*

Variables, continuous. As opposed to discrete variables, these may assume any value within a certain interval of real even numbers. In practice the distinction between continuous and discrete variables is more a question of degree than of principle, since continuous variables, too, can be measured only in stages. *A.R.*

Variance. A measure of variability or dispersion; the square of the standard deviation (s^2) used to determine the degree of difference from one another of certain values (scores) in a set. *D.W.E.*

Variance, analysis of, may be characterized as a collection of procedures by which the variation of a measure relative to its mean is resolved as the sum of two or more distinct sums of squares each corresponding to a source, real or suspect, of variation.

It may also be regarded as a family of linear regression models in which a single dependent variable is expressed as a linear combination of a number of independent variables. The independent variables represent either potential sources of variation (factors) or products of such factors (interactions).

These views lead to very piecemeal treatments of the subject in which the reader is confronted with a vast array of cookbook techniques each with its own computational formulae and set of rules of thumb for the determination of appropriate error terms.

Key papers by Eisenhart (1947), Mann (1949), and Bock (1963) as well as the book by Scheffé (1958) have led to a more unified treatment of the subject. Bock outlines in detail a general model which leads directly to powerful, flexible, yet highly efficient computer codes for the analysis of variance. Such programs perform univariate and multivariate linear estimation and tests of hypotheses for any crossed and/or nested design, with or without concomitant variables or covariates, and with equal, proportional, disproportionate, and even zero subclass frequencies. The multivariate tests for repeated measurements designs make much less unrealistic assumptions on the data than do the now standard univariate trend analyses in common use.

It should be emphasized, however, that the availability of such powerful programs is not an unmixed blessing. That very flexibility which allows the skilled and experienced worker to fit a carefully considered model to his data and to test its appropriateness also allows the naïve, inexperienced worker to fit a variety of ill-conceived and inappropriate models and to grasp at that one which just happens to yield statistical significance.

Yates (1964) has outlined the early development by R. A. Fisher of the analysis of variance in the context of agricultural field trials, and has emphasized the extent to which it developed concurrently with the study of the design of experiments. The reader is referred to the extensive bibliography in Scheffé (1958) for further reading.

Bibliography: Bock, R. D.: Programming univariate and multivariate analysis of variance. Technometrics, 1963, *5*. **Eisenhart, C.:** The assumptions underlying the analysis of variance. Biometrics, 1947, *3*. **Mann, H. B.:** Analysis and design of experiments. New York, 1949. **Scheffé, H.:** The analysis of variance. New York, 1958. **Yates, F.:** Sir Ronald Fisher and the design of experiments. Biometrics, 1964, *20*. *O. White*

Variation. 1. A term for the possibilities of combining *n* different elements as *k* elements, including the possibility of repetitions of the elements. 2. Any difference or change. *G.Mi.*

Variation coefficient (syn. *Variability coefficient*). A measure of relative variability given by the formula

$$V = \frac{100 \times S}{\bar{x}}.$$

The variation coefficient allows of comparison of dispersions of groups of differing sample size and scale units. *D.W.E.*

Varimax method. An orthogonal analytic rotation method developed by H. F. Kaiser (see *Factor analysis*).

Bibliography: Kaiser, H. F.: The varimax criterion for analytic rotation in factor analysis. Psychometrika, 1958, *23*, 187–200. *D.W.E.*

Vasoconstriction; vasodilatation. Constriction and expansion of the diameter of blood vessels. *H.W.*

Vasolability. A weakness of the vascular muscles evident, e.g., in inadequate vascular contraction when standing up after lying down. *E.D.*

Vasopressin (*Pitressin*). A posterior pituitary hormone; also known as *antidiuretic hormone*, or ADH, because it inhibits diuresis. Vasopressin tends to raise blood pressure (peripheral vasoconstriction) and is excreted more profusely under physical and psychic stress. See *Stress*.

Bibliography: Heller, H. (Ed.): The neurohypophysis. London, 1957. *W.J.*

Vater's corpuscle (syn. *Pacinian corpuscle*). One of the oval, lamellated corpuscles (discovered by A. Vater in 1741, and rediscovered by F. Pacini in 1842) in the skin of the hands and feet, acting as terminal capsules for sensory nerve fibers and sense organs for depth sensibility and pressure. See *Sense organs*. *E.D.*

Vector. A symbol representing a force or an abient or adient suasion toward an incentive. See *Topological psychology; Lewin*. *D.W.E.*

Vegetative dystonia (syn. *Vegetative dystony*). A term introduced by B. Wichmann in 1934, and largely synonymous with "neurasthenia", "vegetative lability", "vegetative stigmatatization". It is an inexact collective term for disturbances of vegetative functions of the most varied etiology, and disorders resulting from faulty regulation or lability of an antagonistic "tonic equilibrium" in the autonomic nervous system formed by the *nervus vagus* and *nervus sympathicus*. There are many contributory factors in the etiology of the condition: it is affected by constitution and to a considerable extent psychogenically conditioned, but may also arise from non-physiological sources: e.g. work and environmental conditions. Vegetative dystonia is always the symptom of an underlying sickness. *F.-C.S.*

Vegetative lability. A disorder of the autonomic nervous system (q.v.). See *Psychosomatics; Neurosis; Traits; Type.*

Ventricle. Any cavity within a body organ, but more especially one of the chambers of the heart.

Verbal behavior, establishment and modification of. This article is concerned with the establishment and expansion of verbal behavior, and the modification of inadequate verbal behavior in the impaired. Verbal behavior submits to Skinner's three-term contingency paradigm. A behavioral event, verbal or other, is seen in terms of the *stimulus setting* in which a *performance* occurs, and the following *consequential changes in the environment* of the performing organism. Unlike behaviors with which an organism operates *directly* on his physical environment (moving objects), verbal behavior effects changes through the agency of *other* organisms with a corresponding verbal repertoire. Since the probability of emission of any performance in a specific stimulus setting is a function of the consequences, study of these consequences permits prediction and control of the probability of recurrence of a performance in a given stimulus setting. The primary data are the shifts in *probability* and *topography* of the behavior as functions of the relationships between *stimulus settings*, *performance* and *consequences*. Crucial is the discrimination of two discrete repertoires; a *receptive verbal repertoire* of behaviors of *any* class occurring under the stimulus control of some organism's *verbal* behavior, and a *productive repertoire* of verbal behaviors that control the behavior of any organism displaying a corresponding receptive repertoire. This discrimination allows issues of receptive repertoires to be viewed as problems of bringing behavior under specific *verbal stimulus control* ("understanding"), and issues of productive repertoires ("speaking") as problems of *shaping* verbal behavior having operant function in a verbal community. Primary principles include: analysis of response topographies in terms of *function* rather than form; rigorous management of stimulus settings and consequences relative to a performance; fine analysis of terminal behavior in terms of *requisite antecedent behaviors;* building complex behaviors through the successive establishment of antecedent behaviors.

Bibliography: Sapon, S. M.: Operant studies in the expansion and refinement of verbal behavior. Reports from the Verbal Behavior Lab., Univ. of Rochester, Rochester, N.Y., 1969. **Skinner, B. F.:** Verbal Behavior. New York, 1957. *S. M. Sapon*

Verbal suggestion. Suggestion (q.v.) by means of spoken words. The patient's responsiveness to verbal suggestion is individually diverse. See *Hypnosis*. *H.N.G.*

Verstehende Psychologie (Ger.). The "psychology of understanding" is an inclusive term for those human-scientific modes of interpretation which try to offer insight into the mental life of a human individual or the social configuration of a group (q.v.). The procedure of "understanding" is *deductive* and *descriptive*, and aims at the apprehension and knowledge of personality structures, of dispositions to certain abilities and levels of performance, and of social formations and "forms of life". The approach arose out of philosophical phenomenology and epistemology, yet is concerned primarily with practical human knowledge and life experience. Intuitive apprehension of essences and "mimpathy" are necessarily, in every act of understanding, under the control of critical understanding itself. The method emphasizes the importance of an attentive, wholly observant procedure in which the essence of a thing is fixated by means of analysis, formally ordered by synthesis, inserted in a meaningful context, and precisely described by means of appropriate concepts or symbols and unambiguous linguistic formulations. See *Geisteswissenschaftliche Psychologie.*

The principles and procedures of *verstehende Psychologie* play a dominant role in structural psychology (Dilthey, *et al.*; see *Ganzheit*), in characterology (Lersch), in typology (Spranger, Jung, q.v., Kretschmer, q.v.; see *Type*), and in strata theory (q.v.). It also has important consequences for the psychology of expression (Klages, *et al.*) and of achievement (Mierke). "Understanding" under specific conditions is characteristic of the empirical and analytic methods of experimental (Wundt), gestalt (Krueger) and social psychology (Lewin, Gehlen). Depth psychology (q.v.) attempts to describe and *understand* drive-conditioned behavior, elementary "urges" and needs, and reaction and compensation tendencies.

The cybernetic theory of information (see *Information theory*) adds natural-scientific explanations to human-scientific analyses. It orders experiences obtained in informational processes into a systematic pattern, and tries to examine their causal or final connections. Similarly, differential psychology (q.v.) and developmental psychology (C. Bühler) unite empathic understanding and "mimpathy" with inductive causistic or statistical methods. The same is true of Russian ability and achievement research (N. S. Leites, S. A. Samarin, L. J. Vygotsky).

Behavioral research, behaviorism (q.v.; see *Watson*, *Thorndike*), and operationism (see *Tolman*) basically reject the methods of *verstehende Psychologie*, since subjective moods and feelings, intuitions and self-observations offer diverse sources of error.

Nevertheless, the psychology of understanding still has an important position among diagnostic methods (see *Psychodiagnostics*), and would seem to be essential in areas where certain practical problems of human management arise (e.g. in learning and occupational psychology, in educational and forensic psychology, and so on. In practical psychology, "understanding" is invoked in terms of the evidence offered by studies of courses of human life (case histories), and analyses of abilities, behavior and expression.

Bibliography: Dilthey, W.: Ideen über eine beschreibende und zergliedernde Psychologie. Leipzig, 1894. **Hinde, R.** (Ed.): Non-verbal communication. Cambridge, 1972. **Mierke, K.:** Psychologische Diagnostik. **In: Ach, N.** (Ed.): Lehrbuch der Psychologie. Bamberg, 1944.

K. Mierke

Vertical center line illusion. One of the geometric illusions. Although objectively equal, the vertical line looks longer than the horizontal line, especially if it starts from the center of the horizontal line. *C.D.F.*

Vertigo. 1. Subjective sensation after rapid and frequent rotation of the body round its own axis. After the end of the rotation one receives the impression that one is moving in the opposite direction or that the environment is turning in the same direction as the previous turning movement. Pronounced vertigo can indicate disturbances of balance (q.v.). Suitability as a pilot, suggestibility (q.v.), etc. can be investigated with the aid of the Barany (rotating chair) procedure.

2. A state characterized by a feeling of disturbed balance, an impression of a world oscillating and revolving, accompanied by an inclination to fall, a feeling of being ill, sweating, of nausea and other vegetative disturbances. In labyrinthine vertigo the feeling that one is turning round and round, that one is about to fall, and some characteristic symptoms such as nystagmus (q.v.) (rapid sideways movements of the eyes), and bending the head and body, are predominant. They occur as a result of the false information received from the organ of balance (q.v.) in the osseous labyrinth of the petrosal bone. Similar symptoms are caused by disorders such as inflammation and tumors in the nervous processing apparatus, e.g. in the cerebellum (q.v.) or brain stem. Attacks of vertigo with a circulatory origin should be regarded more as a decrease in functioning of cerebral activity, while in symptoms of brain pressure, feelings of vertigo are replaced by other autonomic disorders. As there may be many possible causes, treatment is correspondingly difficult.
M.B. & E.D.

Vestibule. A cavity forming part of the inner ear; the "vestibule" of the labyrinth, consisting of the saccule and utricle, two sacs whose hair cells convey sensations. *E.D.*

Vibration, sense of. See *Sense organs.*

Vicarious instigation. A term from learning theory for a response to the evocation of emotional responses. A human or animal subject observes the evocation of an unconditioned emotional response (EUR) in an "object" testee by an unconditioned stimulus (UCS). The perception of the UCS and the consequent UER leads to an emotional response (ER) in the observer. The concept of vicarious instigation enables socio-psychologically interesting phenomena, e.g. empathy, or envy, to be assessed more proficiently.

Bibliography: Berger, S. M.: Conditioning through vicarious suggestion. Psychol. Rev., 1962, *69.*
F.Ma.

Vicarious trial and error (abb. *VTE*). Symbolic trial-and-error behavior. It occurs during discrimination and maze learning when subjects have to choose between several possible behaviors (e.g. between right and left-hand turns in the *T* maze). In such situations the subject delays, looks to right and left, before selecting an alternative (Muenzinger, 1938). These "symbolic" responses are interpreted as orientation and trial movements. Nevertheless there would seem to be no unambiguous support for Muenzinger's & Tolman's assumption that VTE behavior makes learning easier (Goss & Wischner, 1956).

Bibliography: Goss, A. E. & Wischner, G. J.: Vicarious trial and error and related behavior. Psychol. Bull., 1956, *53*, 35–54. **Muenzinger, K. F.:** Vicarious trial and error at a point of choice: 1. a general survey of its relation to learning efficiency. J. genet. Psychol., 1938, *53*, 75–86.
M.H.

Victimology is concerned with the victims of criminal acts from two main viewpoints: (*a*) victims of sex crimes, traffic accidents, suicide, deception and theft. The main question is what group of individuals with what traits is potentially in danger of becoming the victims of this or that criminal tendency? (*b*) The objectification of social, psychological, psychopathological factors of groups of individuals who have already become victims. The main problems here are the pre-disposing factors (post-hoc data) and personality traits, the attitude of the victim and his behavior toward criminals, and injury to the victim by the crime (immediate and delayed psychological damage).

Bibliography: Huffman, A. V.: Violent behavior—possibilities of prediction and control. Police, 1964, *8*, 13–6. **Maisch. H.:** Inzest. Hamburg, 1968. **Schönfelder, T.:** Die Rolle des Mädchens bei Sexualdelikten. Beiträge z. Sexualforschung, 1968, No. 42.

H.M.

Vienna School. 1. *Philosophy:* the neopositivism (q.v.) and operationalism (q.v.) founded by K. P. Moritz and M. Schlick, which maintained that philosophy had no specific content, but, by means of mathematical logic, helped to clarify conceptual contradictions in the empirical and experimental sciences, and to improve their propositional systems. Some of Schlick's pupils are R. Carnap, K. Popper, P. Frank, H. Reichenbach, V. Kraft.

2. *Psychology:* that psychodynamic orientation of psychology dependent on the theories of Freud (q.v.), or that deriving from A. Adler (q.v.). See *Depth psychology; Psychoanalysis.*

W.T.

Vieth-Müller circle. When an object is viewed with both eyes a certain angle of convergence between the eyes is required for a single image of the object to be seen. Thus for any given angle of convergence there will be a surface in which objects have a single image, while objects nearer than or beyond this surface have a double image. This surface is known as the Vieth-Müller circle or horopter. Theoretically it should be a sphere which passes through the point of fixation and the centers of revolution of the two eyes. In practice, however, the situation is found to be more complicated.

C.D.F.

Vigilance (Lat. *vigilantia*). Literally: "wakefulness"; but "vigilance" is more precisely defined, and includes the maintenance of a specific activity for a fairly long period, usually accompanied by voluntary attention (q.v.).

1. *Various definitions and acceptations.* Behaviorally, vigilance is most simply defined as performance in observational and inspection tasks. Since attention processes undoubtedly play a considerable part in vigilance, the term may also be applied to the central process which determines achievement in various vigilance tasks, and which may be characterized as long-term or extended *attention* (Haider, 1962). Finally, a specific state of the organism may be described as vigilance in either a physiological or a psychological sense. Physiologically, Head (1926) defines vigilance as a state of the CNS which makes possible a speedy and purposive reaction. Psychologically, Mackworth (1957) defines vigilance as readiness to detect and respond to specific, restricted environmental changes which occur at randomly distributed intervals. This readiness may be characterized by performance criteria, such as percentages of non-observed signals, reaction latencies for observed signals, and inappropriate reactions to non-signals (neutral stimuli).

2. *Historical survey.* Systematic investigations of this special kind of signal detection over fairly extended periods of time were first carried out during World War II in connection with problems of radar observation. Vigilance research has also won practical significance in automated industrial processes and in traffic and space travel. Neurophysiological investigations into cerebral vigilance were carried out mainly in the course of developing electroencephalographic techniques.

3. *Present state of research.* In vigilance tasks, the probability of signal detection decreases over the course of time and the length of reaction latencies increases. The decrease in performance can begin after even a few minutes, and usually reaches a plateau after about 30 to 60 minutes, when stabilization occurs. Rest pauses can keep observational

performance at a higher level. Total performance and course of performance depend on many variables, which can both be environmentally determined and derive from the organism itself.

(*a*) *Environmental variables and vigilance.* Most important here are the characteristics of the task situations. Complex task situations with several indicational elements usually lead to a reduced total performance, but to less emphatic drops in performance than simple vigilance tasks. Increased intensity and length of signals bring about improvements in vigilance, but do not always prevent the drop in performance. Increased signal frequency and the introduction of "random" stimuli increase the probability of detection. If the signals occur regularly (removal of temporal uncertainty) and only in a specific location (removal of spatial uncertainty), the probability of detection is high. The relation of neutral stimuli ("non-signals") to signals is also significant.

General environmental influences are also important. Hence noise and temperature have differential effects on vigilance with an optimum in the comfort range. Isolation tends to bring about a decrease in performance, whereas, e.g., the mere presence of the experimenter can prevent drops in vigilance.

(*b*) *Organismic variables and vigilance.* Individual differences are very great. Nevertheless, despite several investigations, no reliable methods of prediction were elicited. Age and experience show little influence. Introductory signal frequency and information about one's own performance play an important part. Sleep deprivation leads to an intensified reduction of performance. The effects of drugs have been demonstrated. Evoked potentials obtainable from EEG by computer analysis may be selectively analyzed as correlates for detected and non-detected signals, but also for neutral stimuli. In vigilance situations, pulse rates tend to drop, whereas activities requiring movement (spontaneous movements) tend to increase. See *Activation; Arousal.*

4. *Theoretical considerations.* (*a*) *Attention and vigilance.* The vigilance situation may be considered as an extended controlled attention situation without warning of the occurrence of signals. This situation has to be distinguished from, e.g., attention tasks with warning of the occurrence of the signals and free attention situations. Errors in detection may perhaps be ascribed in all situations to similar mechanisms, in terms of distractions, blocks, fluctuations, and so on, using, e.g., the filter theory model (Broadbent, 1958).

(*b*) *Expectation, learning and vigilance.* Mainly in view of the temporal distribution of signals, it can be shown that observers extrapolate to the future on the basis of their individual experiences. This may be conceived as the "construction of expectation structures."

Traditional conditioning experiments were drawn on for inhibition (q.v.) (thought to play a similar role in extinction processes) as an explanation (Mackworth, 1950), and for the concept of "reactive inhibition" (Frankman & Adams, 1962). The efficacy of instrumental learning in influencing behavior was demonstrated for observational reactions (Holland, 1958).

(*c*) *Activation and vigilance.* Activation processes play a role in vigilance (as in many other aspects of performance) in the sense that optimal arousal (q.v.) is associated with good performance, and hyper-arousal and non-arousal with performance deficits. The simple assumption that vigilance is dependent on the number and variation of neutral stimuli has not been confirmed. More complex approaches are more appropriate to the empirical findings. Among such theories is the postulate that arousal variables can follow divergent courses during vigilance experiments (Groll, 1966). A hierarchical theory of arousal (Haider, 1969) offers neuropsychological approaches to attention, expectation and vigilance processes, and a common basis for physiological and psychological vigilance research. See *Attention; Arousal.*

Bibliography: Broadbent, D. E.: Perception and communication. London, 1958. **Buckner, D. N. & McGrath, J. J.:** Vigilance: A symposium. New York & London, 1963. **Frankman, J. P. & Adams, J. A.:** Theories of vigilance. Psychol. Bull. 1962, *59*, 257–72. **Groll, E.:** Zentralnervöse und periphere Aktivierungsvariable bei Vigilanzleistungen. Z. exp. angew. Psychol., 1966, *13*, 248–64. **Haider, M.:** Ermüdung, Beanspruchung und Leistung. Vienna, 1962. **Id:** Elektrophysiologische Indikatoren der Aktivierung. In: **Schönpflug, W.** (Ed.): Methoden der Aktivierungsforschung. Berne, 1969. **Haider, M., Spong, P. & Lindsley, D. B.:** Attention, vigilance and cortical evoked potentials in humans. Science, 1964, *145*, 180–82. **Head, H.:** Aphasia. Cambridge, 1926. **Holland, J. G.:** Human vigilance. Science, 1958, *128*, 61–3. **Jerison, H. J. & Pickett, R. M.:** Vigilance: A review and re-evaluation. Human Factors, 1963, *5*, 211–38. **Mackworth, N. H.:** Researches on the measurement of human performance. M. R. C. Spez. Rep. Ser. N. 268 (H. M. S. O.) London, 1950. **ders.:** Some factors affecting vigilance. The advancement of Science, 1957, *53*, 389–93. **Studies of human vigilance.** Human Factors Res. Santa Barbara, 1968. **Wyatt, S. & Langdon, J. N.:** Inspection processes in industry. Rep. Ind. Health Res. Vol. 63. London, 1932.

M. Haider

Vincent curves. Graphic representations of average learning processes, dependent on relativized individual learning scores. In learning experiments discontinued according to a specific criterion (e.g. after three faultless trials), in general individuals require a varying number of trials to reach the criterion. If the learning curves of individual testees are to be compared or summarized in a single learning curve, it was thought useful to establish a universal standard number of trials. An equal part of the total time or number of trials needed by an individual is treated as equivalent to the same part of another individual's total. The method is hardly ever used in modern research projects.

Bibliography: Hilgard, E. R.: A summary and evaluation of alternative procedures for the construction of Vincent curves. Psychol. Bull., 1938, *35*, 282–97. **Hunter, W. S. & Yarbrough, J. N.:** The interference of auditory habits in the white rat. J. anim, Beh., 1917, *7*, 49–65. **Vincent, S. B.:** The function of the vibrissae in the behaviour of the white rat. Beh. Monogr., 1912, *1*, No. 5.

M.H.

Vineland Social Maturity Scale. A scale designed to assess social maturity in terms of the ability to come to terms with one's social needs and assume responsibility. Norms are available up to age twenty-five. One scale may also be used with younger or retarded people. A "social age" (SA) and a "social quotient" may be answered from the 117 items. *F.G.*

Virginity. The condition of never having had experienced sexual intercourse, particularly (though not necessarily) with reference to the female. *G.D.W.*

Virile. Manly. Possessed of *virility*, masculine characteristics generally, and especially strength, vigor, procreative power, and (most specifically) the capacity to repeat sexual intercourse at short intervals. *G.D.W.*

Virilism. The development by a woman of masculine secondary sex characteristics.

G.D.W.

Visceral nervous system. See *Autonomic nervous system.*

Viscerotonia. A temperament associated with the endomorphic type. Tolerant, peaceful, rather slow. See *Traits; Type.*

Bibliography: Sheldon, W. H.: The varieties of temperament. New York, 1942. *W.K.*

Viscous type. One of the three types of constitution in Kretschmer's typology. The viscous type has an athletic body-build. Psychically, he is characterized by vacillation between an explosive and a phlegmatic temperament. See *Kretschmer; Traits; Type.*

M.H.

Vision, angle of. Two points of an object appear in an optical system at a certain angle (angle of vision), the size of which depends on the ratio of the size of the object to its distance. Hence the angle of vision increases with the distance of the two points from one another and diminishes with the increasing distance of the object. *R.R.*

Vision test. Determination of visual acuity. In vision tests, use is made of charts with letters (Hess, Snellen charts, q.v., Landolt circles, q.v.), animal pictures or pictures with easily recognizable subjects of different sizes. A vision test is carried out at a standard distance (3–5 meters), and in standard illumination (according to H. Schober, 1000 lux). Visual acuity is stated in a common fraction. The denominator represents the distance (in meters), at which the test ought to be seen normally; the numerator gives the distance at which the test is actually seen by the person being examined. *R.R.*

Visual center. The end of the visual pathway (q.v.) in the areas of the *fissura calcarina.* The *corpus geniculatum laterale* (thalamus) is also known as the primary visual center. It is in these centers that the items of information received from visual perception (q.v.) are processed. *R.R.*

Visual focusing. The ability to bring perceptual objects into focus which develops gradually in the new-born child. There are normally four stages in this process of development: (*a*) diffuse eye movements; (*b*) attraction by light stimuli of the line of sight; (*c*) reflex movement; (*d*) voluntary focusing.

K.E.P.

Visual illusions, unlike illusions of *memory* (q.v.), have nothing to do with the relation of an experiential content evoked by trace reactivation to a chronologically past event or phenomenon, or—like illusions of memory occurring during logical thinking—with the relation of an ongoing conceptual act to the appropriate logical content, but are concerned with the relation of (*a*) an actual perception to (*b*) a particular part-area of its actual causative complex. The following applies to both aspects of this relationship:

(*a*) The perception has two characteristics: it has a general phenomenal similarity to imagery, but is distinguished from images and ideas conditionally and genetically, in that (i) it is evoked by a sensory stimulus occurring simultaneously, and (ii) phenomenologically, in that it is oriented to something present at the same time and in the immediate spatial environment. As far as the spatial extension of the sensory stimulation occurring in visual illusions is concerned, a fundamental role is always played by the whole stimulus field, which is also in certain cases *factually* relevant: often, however, apprehension of a specific sector is enough. The analogy in the case of (ii) is experiential: as a rule the intention concerns a more or less extensive, figuratively effective part of the phenomenal field. The distinction between two modes of experience remains significant: an active-apprehensive mode and a passive-sensitive mode: in most cases of visual illusion the perception is of the first variety.

(*b*) If, in the functional analysis of a specific visual illusion, "correctness" is in question, only one area of the complex of conditions is taken into consideration. This is that providing the norm for a "correct" perception of the type in question, but absent in the case of an illusion. When such a norm and possible deviations of visual illusions from it exist, it is assumed that both aspects of functional content (the phenomenon and the part-area of conditions) are comparable and —under certain conditions—genuinely commensurable. In optical illusions, retinal data make a comparison with the phenomenon possible: for psychological purposes, however, it is usually more appropriate when seeking the norm to follow the causal chain right back to the stimulus *source* (enriched by the characteristics of the direction and distance of observation).

One may distinguish three main areas of visual illusion:

(*a*) Phenomena in the case of which there is objectively "absolutely nothing" to be seen at the intended position in the spatial environment. Such phenomena depend on central processes and include hallucinations. More frequent are the everyday experiences of (modal and amodal) completion: gaps are filled by the illusion, etc. In autokinesis (see *Autokinetic phenomenon*), the new product is formed not by figurative components but by movements. The same is true of the gamma phenomenon (see *Gamma movement*)—which has, of course, a different origin.

(*b*) Other effects may be classed as "exchange". In beta movement (q.v.) the aspect of movement instead of that of succession is actualized. In induced movement, of the two participating elements (one may be the observer's body-ego), the false one becomes the bearer of movement. Even (illusory) phenomenal causality, which is sometimes taken at first as absolute novelty, is an example of exchange, or confusion.

(*c*) In the third class, illusions of alteration, the illusion accords basically with the object, but not in specific details, which act as variables. Examples are contrast (q.v.) effects, or the geometrical-optical illusions. In such cases the phenomenon is "altered" in relation to the object.

Visual illusions should be considered not only as "erroneous" but as meaningful and purposeful; for example: the great significance of completion phenomena for the construction of the phenomenal world.

The theory of visual illusions has specific epistemological presuppositions. The dualistic approach that sets a phenomenon over against its presentation, depends on a critical form of realism. A purely phenomenalistic viewpoint does not do justice to visual illusions. This is true also when the illusions concern the observer's body, e.g. his orientation in space, the location of pressure or pain, etc. In such cases, one's own body belongs both to the phenomenal and to the presentational area. See *Geometrical-optical illusions; Perception; Visual perception.*

Bibliography: Aarons, L.: Visual apparent movement research: Review 1935–55; Bibliography 1955–63; Perc. Mot. Skills, 1964, *18*, 239–74. **Metzger, W.:** Gesetze des Sehens. Frankfurt a.M., [2]1953. **Michotte, A., Thinès, G. & Crabbé, G.:** Die amodalen Ergänzungen von Wahrnehmungsstrukturen. In: **Metzger, W.** (Ed.): Handbuch der Psychologie, Vol. 1/1. Göttingen, 1966, 978–1002. **Rausch, E.:** Probleme der Metrik. In: **Metzger, W.** (Ed.): Handbuch der Psychol, Vol. 1/1. Göttingen, 1966, 776–865. **Royce, J. R.,** *et al.*: The autokinetic phenomenon: A critical review. Psychol. Bull., 1966, *65*, 243–60.

E. Rausch

Visual nerve damage. Complete or partial paralysis of the mimic muscles controlled by the *nervus facialis*. Generally one half of the face is affected; it is very rare for both sides to be involved. A distinction is made between central (supra-nuclear) and peripheral (nuclear and infra-nuclear) visual nerve damage, or (by etiology) between traumatic, toxic, rheumatic and inborn visual nerve damage. *F.C.S.*

Visual perception. Perception through the sense of vision is one of the oldest research areas in the history of psychology. Both the phenomenological and psychophysical methods are used. Gestalt psychology had a great influence on the development of this area.

1. *Simplest visual perception.* The perception obtained through a uniform retinal stimulation may be regarded as the simplest form of visual perception. The sight of a cloudless sky covering the whole visual field, and visual experience in the midst of thick fog or in a completely dark room, are examples. We see neither a form nor a rigid surface, but a soft, filmy field of uniform color which is not localized at a definite distance.

2. *Emergence of a figure.* A heterogeneous area in the visual field produces the perception of a figure. A perceived figure in general differs from its background in that: the figure has form and the character of an object or thing, whereas the ground is formless and appears as a substance; the figure is localized at a definite distance and its surface looks hard, but the ground is soft and not definitely localized; the figure seems usually to stand out in front of the ground, which appears to extend continuously behind it; the contours are perceived as belonging to the figure, not to the ground.

3. *Interactions among figures.* When more than one figure appears in a visual field they interact in various ways. For example, if several figures or objects are presented simultaneously, they are perceived neither singly nor as a chaotic total mass, but in groups. The following factors are found important for such grouping: (*a*) objects relatively close together (proximity); (*b*) objects of the same color or shape (similarity); (*c*) objects constituting a closed area (closure); (*d*) objects constituting continuous sequence (good continuity); or (*e*) objects moving in the same direction (common fate) are readily seen as a group. In some circumstances, the shape or size of a perceived figure which is presented with other figures appears different to that of the same figure presented singly. Geometrical illusions may be regarded as such an interaction among figures or figural elements; and figural aftereffects as a kind of interaction which occurs if two figures are presented successively. See *Afterimages; Aftersensation.*

4. *Perceptual constancies.* A figure or visual object generally has shape, size, color and brightness as its perceptual properties, and appears to be positioned with a certain slant, at a certain distance, and under the illumination of a certain color and brightness. When the slant, distance and illumination vary physically, the shape and size of the retinal image and the quality and intensity of light in it vary correspondingly, but the perceived shape, size, color and brightness usually do not vary so much. There are consistent tendencies which keep these perceptual properties constant. These tendencies are called shape, size, color and brightness constancies, respectively. They all make the perceptual world stable, in spite of the continuous change of the positions of many objects relative to the observer, and of the illumination affecting them. The cues for depth perception are thought to be important factors for constancies of shape and size, interrelations in the distribution of light in the visual field, and constancies of color and brightness.

5. *Perception of movement.* A figure or object may be seen as it moves. The displacement of a retinal image is neither a necessary nor a sufficient condition for the perception of movement. If we fixate a moving object, its retinal image will be stationary, but its motion will be perceived. On the other hand, if we move our eyes, the retinal images of stationary objects will move, but we will not perceive them as in motion. Rather, the displacement of an object relative to greater objects (frame of reference) is important for the perception of movement. However, the perception of movement occurs even without any relative displacement (apparent movement, autokinetic phenomenon, aftermage of movement).

Bibliography: Boring, E. G.: Sensation and perception in the hstoiry of experimental psychology. New York,

1942. **Gibson, J. J.:** Perception of the visual world. New York, 1950. **Graham, C. H.:** Vision and visual perception. New York, 1965. **Koffka, K.:** Principles of gestalt psychology. London & New York, 1935. **Metzger, W.:** Gesetze des Sehens. Frankfurt am Main, *2*, 1953. **Vernon, M. D.:** The psychology of perception. Harmondsworth & Baltimore, 1962. *T. Oyama*

Visual registration. Procedures for registering ocular movements and hence the path of vision have been developed by restricting experimental conditions until they have come close to *biotic* procedures (see *Biotic experiment*). Visual registration was first used in ophthalmology and reading psychology (B. Erdmann & R. Dodge), and was later taken over by other disciplines with more refined methods and increasingly less harm to the testee; such disciplines are industrial psychology (q.v.) (e.g. ocular movements of the pilot during blind-flying to establish the optimal arrangement of the instruments, forensic psychology (q.v.), and consumer psychology (e.g. advertising appeal, ocular response to packaging, etc.). *B.S.*

Visual type. An imaginative type (q.v.) in whom the visual aspect is dominant. *W.K.*

Vitalism. The assumption of a special force (*vis vitalis*) at the basis of the phenomenon of life, and inexplicable (in principle) in mechanistic or physicochemical terms. *W.Sch.*

Vitality. Life-force; the energy required for the functions of life. In personality (q.v.) psychology, a popular term for a quality shown by more easily arousable individuals. See *Arousal; Traits; Type.* *W.Sch.*

Vitamins. Substances which exert catalytic functions within the framework of normal metabolism. They are essential nutrients, but are only partly manufactured by the body itself. Therefore they have to be ingested with food, and in the case of some deficiencies administered in a concentrated form. Vitamin deficiencies are largely "vitamin-specific"

Vitamins of psychological interest

Traditional term	Short chemical designation	Selected physical symptoms in deficiency conditions
A	retinol	disturbed vision, debility and drying up of sebaceous and sweat glands, hyperkeratosis
B_1	thiamin	beri-beri, polyneuritis, oedema
B_2	riboflavin	arrested growth in babies; cracked lips; diminished visual acuity
B_6	pyridoxine	alterations in skin
P	pantothenic acid	myasthenia
PP	niacinamide	pellagra, dermatitis, diarrhea
H	biotin	alterations in skin and hair
B_{12} group	cyanocobalamin, etc.	anemia
C	ascorbic acid	scurvy, reduced capacity of resistance, loss of appetite, digestive disorders, inclination to bleeding, loosening of teeth, rheumatic pains, susceptibility to infections
D	calcipherol	rickets, disorders of growth, hypertonia, disorders of fertility
E	tocopherol	muscular dystrophy

and have largely physical, though also psychic symptoms. It is, however, usually unclear how far the effects in question are primary or secondary (resulting from somatic changes). The tabular summary above shows a selection of vitamin substances of interest to psychologists; both the traditional names are given and those introduced since 1960 as a result of international-level discussions. The table also gives physical symptoms for deficiency states. Influences on behavior have been investigated and demonstrated in animal experiments, primarily for pyridoxine and for cynanocobalamin. There has been no systematic investigation of the psychological effects of vitamins in normal individuals. See *Avitaminosis*. *K.-D.S.*

Vocational guidance (Syn. *Vocational counseling; Careers advice*). One of the chief fields of applied psychology (q.v.). Advice and help are given to adolescents and those entitled to education, but also to enterprises in industry, commerce and trade, and to schools, and mainly to those seeking work or a career.

The organization of vocational guidance varies from country to country, e.g., in France it is linked with the school, in Germany with labor administration and charitable organizations, in England and the USA both with the labor authorities, and in large measure with independent bodies. But in all countries there is also vocational guidance in large industrial and administrative concerns and in banks (railways, aviation companies, insurance and the like). Qualified vocational guidance officers are mostly psychologists, but other professional experience is recognized as a prerequisite, to be accompanied by a recognized form of psychological-diagnostic training and training in vocational work.

By far the largest number of cases dealt with are adolescents about to leave school. The purpose of vocational guidance is to set them on the right vocational track, taking into consideration personality (q.v.), inclination and aptitude for a given vocation or employment (see *Abilities; Traits; Type*).

Over and above this, vocational guidance is concerned with the rehabilitated (e.g., the disabled who can be brought back into employment), with adults seeking another vocation (retraining, change of employer), with those aspiring to promotion (e.g., electricians anxious to become engineers by taking the necessary training). The function of vocational guidance is primarily to help. Unlike the school, it conducts no examinations to determine performance but uses aptitude tests (q.v.), nor does it at any stage make any selection of the best (vocational selection q.v.), but is interested in the normal distribution of ability. Vocational guidance has been established by law in most countries (freedom of vocational choice). Measures to control vocations are possible only in dictatorial state systems in which the supreme guideline is not the right of the individual but the priority of society.

In its diagnostic work, i.e. in its endeavors to establish vocational aptitude, vocational guidance uses verifiable methods and data (abilities, q.v., intelligence tests, q.v., specimens of work, interviews, exploration, q.v.). It must be able to substantiate its advice; for estimates of aptitude with a purely subjective value have no greater prognostic value than "expressions of opinion". Vocational guidance must be social and humane; but this can still be achieved only by a scientifically based psychodynamics (q.v.), aware not only of its possibilities but also of its limitations. Hence vocational guidance makes use of scientifically guaranteed investigation procedures; it is also aware of its educational and therapeutic functions (e.g. finding employment for those who haver eceived therapeutic treatment). Therefore it must always work in close conjunction with remedial medicine. Vocational guidance is closely connected with school and university counseling.

School counseling is guidance in the school career; its task consists in finding the kind of school suited for child or adolescent: whether private or state primary school, above all which specially oriented intermediate school, and secondary "technical" or "academic" course (classical, modern language, science, art). Investigations into readiness to attend school and into the aptitude and attainment needed for secondary or tertiary education are among the essential tasks of vocational guidance; since a child's real aptitudes are often revealed gradually, school counseling comes before vocational guidance both in time and content.

The object of university counseling is to help and guide during academic life. In content, university counseling is determined by vocational choice, then by the aptitude of the student (if he has already selected a profession) as well as by the educational facilities available for realizing the vocational decision taken and enabling one to enter a particular profession. Crucial prerequisites for school counseling are full expert information about the vocation in question, and plans of study approved by panels of experts, i.e. lists of studies necessary in each of the academic years (lectures, practical work, advanced tutorials).

In contrast to vocational guidance, school and university counseling have still not received full official recognition outside the USA, and their development is very restricted. But such counseling assumes special importance in view of the increasing differentiation of vocational tasks and the wider variety of schools, and because of the need to be able to change from one school system to another.

Experts constantly affirm that it is essential to develop an effective system of school and university counseling. See *Industrial psychology; Occupational psychology; Educational psychology; Traits; Type.*

Bibliography: Adams, J. F. (Ed.): Counseling and guidance. New York, 1965. **Armor, D. J.**: The American school counselor: a case study in the sociology of professions. New York, 1969. **Borrow, H.** (Ed.): Man in a world at work. New York, 1954. **Cramer, S. H.** *et al.*: Research and the school counselor. New York, 1971. **Crites, J. O.**: Vocational psychology. New York, 1969. **Holden, A.**: Teachers as counsellors. London, 1969. **Id**: Counseling in secondary schools. London, 1971. **Hopson, B. & Hayes, J.** (Eds.): The theory and practice of vocational guidance. Oxford, 1968. **Jackson, R. & Juniper, D. F.**: A manual of educational guidance. New York, 1971. **Johnson, D. E. & Vestermark, M. J.**: Barriers and hazards in counseling. New York, 1971. **Jones, A.**: School counseling in practice. London, 1970. **Jones, A. J.**: Principles of guidance. New York, 1970. **Kell, B. L. & Burrow, J. M.**: Developmental counseling and therapy. New York, 1970. **Ligon, M. G. & McDaniel, S. W.**: The teacher's role in counseling. Englewood Cliffs, 1970. **Ohlsen, M. M.**: Group counseling. Chicago, 1970. **Osipow, S. H.**: Theories of career development. New York, 1968. **Peters, R. J.**: The guidance process. A perspective. New York, 1970. **Peters, H. J. & Hanson, J. C.** (Eds.): Vocational guidance and careers development. New York, 1966. **Peters, H. J. & Shertzer, B.**: Guidance, program development and management. New York, [2]1970. **Pietrofesa, J. J. & Vriend, J.**: The school counselor as a professional. New York, 1971. **Taylor, J. H. F.**: School counseling. London, 1971.

W. Arnold

Vocational Interest Blanks. For the purpose of vocational guidance (q.v.) questionnaires have to list in as much detail as possible interests in special subjects, activities, etc., so that the most suitable vocational line can be deduced. There are numerous inventories of this kind, but in most cases the validation problem has not been solved. See *Kudor Preference Record; Strong Vocational Interest Blank.* *R.M.*

Vocational research. An area of industrial psychology (q.v.) dealing with requirements in individual occupations, vocational analysis, vocational guidance (q.v.), procedural techniques in vocational guidance, vocational training, and producing literature in which the mental and physical requirements of any particular occupation are described. See *Occupational psychology.* *W.Sp.*

Vocational selection. A procedure which aims at a choice of a certain group and type of vocation, but usually a technique which presupposes a determination of the quality of the candidates for employment or a profession, and excludes those found unsuitable (negative selection) or prefers those found to be best suited (selection of the best). These decisions are determined by subjective and objective factors. *Subjective factors* are interest, inclinations, abilities and social prestige; *objective factors* are chiefly social security and economic vocational prospects (pay, salary, possibilities of promotion). Subjective factors depend on how far one is inwardly attracted by a certain vocational activity, its purpose, significance and value, and much less by the economic, material weighting. In choosing employment, firm location and colleagues, the worker is primarily concerned with optimum pay, social advantages and how easy the job is. Vocational and labor selection are controlled by industrial, commercial and trade enterprises. Parents, teachers and vocational guidance officers have only a subsidiary influence.

Vocational guidance experts or counselors, usually subsidized by the State, assist in deciding the choice of a vocation. The special facilities which may be offered by vocational guidance to adolescents seeking advice and to their parents are investigations of psychological aptitude; the determinants of professional aptitude established by research in the vocational field afford a certain normative decision criterion for vocational advice as well as for vocational decisions by employers, schools and parents. Vocational selection and choice presuppose specialist knowledge of vocational matters which is best supplied by trained officers but can also come from vocational literature, illustrations, films, etc. See *Abilities; Intelligence; Educational psychology; Industrial psychology; Occupational psychology.* *W.A.*

Voice key. An instrument which enables a vocal sound to start or stop some other mechanism. *G.D.W.*

Volition. See *Will.*

Voluntarism. In philosophy: a metaphysical doctrine which conceives ultimate reality as "will": i.e. as an obscure, irrational, independent power, or one opposed to the idea of an intelligible ground of things (Schopenhauer). Also a moral doctrine which sees will as the source of action, and more specifically so than intellectual thought (Nietzsche); also an epistemological theory for which any judgment is true only inasmuch as it is affirmed voluntarily (Descartes). In psychology, voluntarists see cognitive and representational (linguistic) functions as subject to affectivity, feeling and voluntary commitment (psychoanalytic viewpoint). See *Will.* *F.B.*

Voyeur; voyeurism. Voyeurs obtain sexual satisfaction and stimulation from the observation (in secret) of sexual objects or situations. Pleasure in sexual observation becomes voyeurism when it is the only, or the dominant, sexual goal in an individual's sexual behavior. The voyeur is usually male (average age about twenty-four years), and tries to preserve his anonymity when watching women naked or undressing, or acts of coitus, and thus (with or without masturbation) obtains sexual gratification. Most habitual voyeurs appear to lead an inadequate heterosexual life, are seldom married, and become delinquent at a relatively early age (Gebhard *et al.*, 1965). As a sexually deviant behavior, voyeurism evokes relatively weak social responses (compared with, e.g., incest), and is relatively infrequent (compared, e.g., with male homosexuality). See *Perversion; Sexuality*.

Bibliography: Gebhard, P., *et al.*: Sex offenders. London, 1965. **Giese, H.:** Psychopathologie der Sexualität. Stuttgart, 1962. *H.M.*

Vygotsky, Lev Semenovich. B. 1896; d. 1934. A Soviet psychologist who developed one of the most highly-nuanced and influential socio-historical theories of language and concept (q.v.) development. Vygotsky studied at Moscow University and did research in educational and developmental psychology and psychopathology (q.v.). His major work, *Thought and Language*, was suppressed in 1936, inasmuch as it offended against the peculiar lines of the pseudo-psychology recommended by Stalinism (see *Soviet psychology*), but Vygotsky influenced and continues to influence some of the most fruitful Soviet psychological thinking. Vygotsky conceived of thought as deriving from overt action in an internalized form (see *Inner speech*), and particularly from the internalization of external dialogue. He based his work on K. Bühler, W. Stern and the early Piaget, and viewed inner speech as inner representation. Vygotsky's emphasis on the human ability to replace and revivify earlier conceptual structures is also an emphasis on the multiplicity of individual modes of linguistic, conceptual and personal development. See *Act psychology*.

Bibliography: Hanfmann, E. & Kasanin, J.: A method for the study of concept formation. J. Psychol., 1937, *3*, 521–40. **Vygotsky, L. S.:** Thought and language. Cambridge, Mass., 1962. *J.C.*

Vygotsky test. A variant of Ach's method of studying concept (q.v.) formation, developed by Sakharov, a co-worker of Vygotsky's, for use especially with schizophrenic subjects. Twenty-two wooden blocks (Vygotsky blocks) have to be related conceptually to the same number of nonsense syllables. *F.-C.S.*

W

Waking, artificial. Deprivation of sleep achieved by chemical effects or repeated waking in order to vary sleep requirement. An independent variable for investigation of the part played by sleep in the course of diverse mental functions. See *Dream; Sleep.* *H.Ro.*

Waking dream; waking vision. See *Daydream.*

Wald-Wolfowitz test. A non-parametric test for testing whether two independent samples differ in regard to their form of distribution (central trend, dispersion, skew, excess). The scores of both samples are ranked in a common series and characterized alternatively according to sample (e.g. A, B). The variable measured must be continuously distributed, and at least ordinally scalable.

Bibliography: Wald, A. & Wolfowitz, J.: On a test of whether two samples are from the same population. Annals of Mathematical Statistics, 1940, *11*, 147–62.

H.-J.S.

Walking. In general, the first free step is observable at the end of the first year of life, and usually occurs by chance in place of previous walking "along" the wall or other objects. On acquiring an upright carriage, a child considerably extends his life space to date ("distance space") and begins the process of release from the mother-child bond.

M.Sa.

Wallon, Henri. B. 15/6/1879 in Paris; d. Paris, 1962. French psychologist. Studied philosophy and medicine. He began his career as a psychiatrist, but later took up developmental psychology, and became its leading representative in France. He taught at the Sorbonne and at the Collège de France. In 1927 he founded the Laboratory of Child Psychobiology in Paris, and edited the journal *Enfance.* Wallon entered into many lively discussions with Piaget on development. Whereas Piaget was concerned primarily with the mental development of the child, Wallon was more interested in his emotional ("affective") development. He emphasized especially the importance of the degree of maturation of the CNS linked with social influences. Wallon believed that development was marked by "crises" involving a new organization of mental structures.

Main works: Evolution psychologique de l'enfant. Paris, 1941. De l'acte à la pensée. Paris, 1942. L'enfant turbulent. Paris, 1945. Les origines de la pensée chez l'enfant. Paris, 1947. Les origines du caractère chez l'enfant. Paris, 1949.

Bibliography: Zazzo, R.: Portrait d'Henri Wallon (1879–1962). J. psychol. norm. path., 1963, *60*, 386–400.

W.W.

Walsh test. A non-parametric technique used to test two dependent samples for differences in central trend. Used when both sample distributions are symmetric (though not necessarily identical). See *Non-parametric tests.*

Bibliography: Walsh, J. E.: Some significance tests for the medium, which are valid under very general conditions. Annals of Mathematical Statistics. 1949, *20,* 64–81.

H.-J.S.

Ward-Hovland phenomenon. A phenomenon of reminiscence (q.v.) named after Ward (1937) and Hovland (1938): an increase in retention is observable after an interval of two to ten minutes after a rote-learning trial.

Bibliography: Hovland, C. I.: Experimental studies in rote-learning theory. I, II. J. exp. Psychol., 1938, *23,* 201–24, 338–63. **Ward, L. B.:** Reminiscence and rote learning. Psychol. Monogr., 1937, *49,* 4 (whole No. 220).

F.-C.S.

Warfare, psychological. A term introduced in the USA during World War II as part of military and political strategy on the basis of learning, social, advertising and depth psychology. Features: defense and attack ritual, optically and acoustically effective intimidation, propaganda with a view to changing existing structures. Planning for psychological warfare, and military propaganda, are determined by a large number of psychologically relevant reference variables. Psychological warfare is used primarily in the preparatory stages for war (diplomacy of dramatic intimidation), or as carefully planned support for military actions. A distinction is made between open (white), camouflaged (black), strategic, tactical and defensive, divisive and counter propaganda. Technical aids are provided by the mass media and also by balloons and rockets to distribute propaganda leaflets. The aim is to win the opponent over, or to outlaw and intimidate him (war of nerves), and to paralyze the opponent's will to fight and disintegrate the cohesion of the group by fostering uncertainty.

In peacetime, psychological warfare makes a contribution to the intensive presentation of state ideologies, and helps to provide immunity against outside influences, e.g. by "mental armament," by arousing trust in the leadership and in the protagonist's own ability to fight and to consolidate morale.

G.Mi.

Warming-up period. A short period before the actual activity (e.g. verbal or motor learning) is begun, which produces an introductory set and adaptation to the task, without direct reinforcement (e.g. of the S–R connection to be learned (or practice, q.v.). Warming-up leads to an increase of the total (learning or reproduction) performance.

Warm(ing)-up decrement: cessation or diminution of warming-up during a rest or retention interval. The effect of warming-up would seem to depend on the extent of the period, the similarity between warming-up activity and learning task, and the interval between warming-up and the task or reproduction (McGeoch & Irion, 1952). See *Memory; Reminiscence; Learning.*

Bibliography: Adams, J. A.: The second facet of forgetting: a review of warm-up decrement. Psychol. Bull., 1961, *58,* 257–73. **McGeoch, J. A. & Irion, A. L.:** The psychology of human learning. New York, 1952.

F.-C.S.

Warning cries, or cries of distress, draw the attention of members of the same or different species to the presence of a predator. The response to such a cry may be acquired or inborn. Unhatched chicks cease scratching the shell at the sound of a chicken's warning cry. Young snipe, on the other hand, must first learn to associate the warning with the enemy's image. Minnows warn other fishes by emitting warning substances. *V.P.*

Watson, John Broadus. B. 9/1/1878 in Greenville; d. 25/9/1958 in New York City. Watson studied at Furman University and (philosophy) at the University of Chicago. He received his doctor's degree in 1903 under the functionalist James Angell and the neurologist H. H. Donaldson for a dissertation on "animal education". He then devoted himself largely to animal psychology (q.v.), and in 1908 became a full Professor in experimental and comparative psychology at the Johns Hopkins University (Baltimore), where he was also director of the psychological laboratory. He left the university in 1920, and pursued a career in consumer psychology until 1945, although he exerted considerable influence on modern psychology through his popular lectures and his widely-read books.

Watson is considered to be the founder of behaviorism (q.v.). His fundamental works *Psychology as the Behaviorist sees it* (1913), *Behavior: an introduction to animal psychology* (1914), *Psychology from the Standpoint of a Behaviorist* (1919), *Behaviorism* (1925), and *Psychological Care of Infant and Child* (1928) had a revolutionary effect on the traditional psychology of consciousness. Watson's provocative theses and his quasi-journalistic defense of them helped in their dissemination. In addition, his uncompromising assertion that psychology was to be conceived and practiced wholly as a natural science, and especially on the model of physics, that the introspective method (see *Introspection*) was pointless, that an objectivist terminology was to be used, and that psychology should be restricted to the examination of measurable, tangible, visible and audible behavior, accorded with the spirit of the times and the tendencies of young scholars. Even though it can be shown that Watson's decisive ideas were put forward before him (by, e.g., J. Rush, F. A. Lange, q.v., W. McDougall, q.v.), and especially by Russian reflexologists (W. Bekhterev, J. P. Pavlov, q.v.), his service to psychology is undiminished, since he was responsible for propagating this view of the science and for helping worldwide psychological research on objective lines really to get under way.

Watson's optimistic ideas about education relied on an extreme environmental theory, and amounted to a belief in human malleability. They also influenced the development of psychotherapy (q.v.). After Pavlov, Watson may also be considered as one of the founding fathers of modern behavior therapy (q.v.). See *Conditioning, classical and operant; Aversion therapy.*

Bibliography: Murchison, C.: History of psychology in autobiography. Vol. 3. London, 1936, 271–81. **Skinner, B. F.:** John Broadus Watson, behaviorist. Science, 1959, *129*, 197–8. **Woodworth, R. S.:** John Broadus Watson: 1878–1958. Amer. J. Psychol., 1959, *72*, 301–10.

L.J.P.

Weber, Ernst Heinrich. B. 24/6/1795 in Wittenberg; d. 26/1/1878 in Leipzig. Weber was Professor of anatomy (1818) and physiology (1840) in Leipzig, and is considered by many to be the co-founder of modern sensory physiology and psychophysics (q.v.).

Weber's investigations of touch and muscular sense formed the starting-point for the quantitative assessment of the relations between stimulus and response and hence for the development of psychophysics. The method of "just-noticeable differences" used in his investigations was the first psychophysical method. Weber tried to confirm the least difference that could be distinguished by a testee with two weights laid on the back of his hands. The results showed that stimuli that differ only insignificantly are experienced as equivalent, and that the ability to distinguish between two stimuli varies with their size or intensity, and is finer in the case of smaller than greater stimulus intensities. Analogous conditions were revealed in all the sensory areas that Weber examined. The quantitative formulation of this stimulus-response relation is presented in the law known (by G. T. Fechner, q.v.) as "Weber's law" (q.v.). Weber's experiments were continued and extended by Fechner (see *Fechner's law*).

In other experiments, Weber was able to show the distance between two pressure points on the skin at which the impression of two separate pressure sensations goes over into that of a single sensation. Weber was able to demonstrate therefore that tactile sensitivity is different at different points on the body surface ("two-point discrimination" or "two-point threshold"). He explained this in terms of "sensory circles", or skin areas where there is no perception of "doubleness" because of the stimulation of immediately adjacent tactile nerve fibers.

Main works: De aure et auditu hominis et animalium. Leipzig, 1820. De pulsu, resorptione, auditu et tactu. Annotationes anatomicae et physiologicae. Leipzig, 1834. Der Tastsinn und das Gemeingefühl. In: Wagner, R. (Ed.): Handwörterbuch der Physiologie, Vol. 3. Brunswick, 1846, 481–588. Über den Raumsinn und die Empfindungskreise in der Haut und im Auge. Berichte d. kön.-sächs. Ges. d. Wissenschaften z. Leipzig: Klasse 4, 1852, 87–105. *W.W.*

Weber-Fechner Law. See *Fechner's Law.*

Weber's law. An early psychophysical generalization stating that a *just-noticeable difference* (q.v.) is a constant proportion of the magnitude of the original stimulus, i.e., the more intense the stimulus the greater the increase must be to be perceptible. Also called the *Weber fraction:* $\Delta R/R$, where ΔR is the change of stimulus that is just noticeable and R is the magnitude of the stimulus. This fraction has generally been found to be fairly constant at least for stimuli of middle-range intensity. Weber's basic law was elaborated later by Fechner; see *Fechner's law.* *G.D.W.*

We-break. A term from individual psychology (q.v.) for a suddenly experienced opposition between the ego and the community. A we-break is favored by a neglectful or authoritarian education, and is alleged to be a frequent precursor of neurosis (q.v.). *W.Sch.*

Wechsler-Bellevue Test. A test battery of ten subtests for general intelligence. The selection of subtests and their grouping in a verbal scale and a performance scale extended, according to D. Wechsler, the diagnostic possibilities of the battery in comparison with earlier intelligence tests, especially in the clinical sense. The test is for use between ages ten to fifty-nine. The author suggests that the retest reliability of the whole test is 0.94. See *Abilities; Intelligence.*

Bibliography: **Wechsler, D.:** The measurement of adult intelligence. Baltimore, 1939. *P.S.*

Weighting coefficient. Coefficient attached to an observation (by multiplication or addition) in order that it shall assume a desired degree of importance in a function of all the observations of the set. A further example of the application of weighting coefficients is in predicting a criterion based on a multiple regression. In the process, the weighting coefficients of test data in the individual variables are obtained from the intercorrelations of the variables and the correlations between the criterion and the variables. See *Test theory.* *W.H.B.*

Weight, sensitivity to. Sensitivity to weight depends on both the *haptic* and the *kinesthetic* senses. A passively felt weight will depend largely on the haptic senses such as pressure, whereas an actively lifted weight will depend on the kinesthetic senses of movement and muscular tension. See *Kinesthesia.* *C.D.F.*

Weltanschauung types (syn. *World-view types*). Those manifesting a form of judgment of the environment characterized by personal emotions, aspirations, values and experiences as well as rational considerations, and described by Dilthey, Spranger, Jaspers, etc. See *Type*. *W.K.*

Wertheimer, Max. B. 15/4/1880 in Prague; d. 12/10/1943 in New York. Wertheimer obtained his doctorate under Külpe (q.v.) in Würzburg in 1904 with a thesis on the investigation of credibility (q.v.), in the sense of the detection of guilty knowledge. Subsequently he carried out independent psychological research in Prague, Berlin and Vienna without any fixed academic post. From 1910 to 1916 he was a Reader in Frankfurt University, and met W. Köhler (q.v.) and Koffka (q.v.), who were assistants at the Psychological Institute. With his investigations of the perception of stroboscopic apparent movements (see *Phi-phenomenon*), Wertheimer provided the basis for the development of gestalt psychology. From 1916 to 1929 he was *Privatdozent* at the University of Berlin. Together with Köhler and Koffka and the neurologists K. Goldstein and H. W. Gruhle (the Berlin School), he continued his gestalt research and became the first editor of the journal *Psychologische Forschung* in 1921. In 1929 he returned to Frankfurt as Professor. In 1933, with the onset of the Nazi dictatorship, he left Germany, and after a short stay in Marienbad received a teaching appointment in the graduate school of the New School of Social Research, New York; he taught there until his death in 1943.

Together with Köhler and Koffka, Wertheimer is acknowledged to be one of the founders of gestalt psychology, which may be dated from the publication of his investigation into "Experimental Studies of the Perception of Movement" as a research paper in 1912. In this paper, Wertheimer examined the phi-phenomenon (an apparent movement which arises as a result of the successive presentation of two usually equivalent optical elements in different positions), which became the starting-point of the holistic mode of examining psychological phenomena (a mode characteristic of gestalt psychology), and the associated critique of elementarist psychology. Wertheimer was able to show that the phenomenon could not be explained by the existing theories of perception: i.e. neither by reduction to local sensory sensations, nor by the assumption of summative associations of individual sensations; therefore he viewed the phenomenon as an example of the operation of a dynamic whole whose individual parts are influenced by the structural determinative constellation of the total form ("gestalt-as-a-whole"). See *Ganzheit*, *Gestalt*, *Structure*.

Associated with this experiment was Wertheimer's assumption regarding the neurophysiological activation processes basic to the phenomenon. He ascribed a unified, holistic character to these, as to the perceptions themselves. This conception of brain processes as physiological gestalts was later more precisely conceived and extended by Köhler in his theory of isomorphism (q.v.).

In an article of 1923 on "Investigations of gestalt theory", Wertheimer showed for the first time how, through a series of organizational principles (the gestalt laws of proximity, equivalence and closure), perception has a spontaneous tendency to configural structuration.

Wertheimer also detected the effects of tendencies to organization on gestalt principles in areas of behavior other than perception, as is evidenced in the posthumous publication *Productive Thinking* (1959). In particular, he attributed a significant role in the thinking process to the tendency to *pregnance* (q.v.), which he understood as essentially a transition from a bad to a good gestalt.

Main works: Experimentelle Studien über das Sehen von Bewegung. Z. Psychol. 1912,

61, 161–265. Untersuchungen zur Lehre von der Gestalt. Psychol. Forsch., 1921, *1*, 47–58; 1923, *4*, 301–50 (part-trans. in: Ellis, W. D. (Ed.): A sourcebook of gestalt psychology. New York, 1938, 12–16; and in: Beardsall, D. C. & Wertheimer, M. (Eds.): Readings in perception. Princeton, 1958, 115–35). A story of three days. In: Anshen, R. N. (Ed.): Freedom: its meaning. New York, 1940, 555–69. Some problems in the theory of ethics. Soc. Res., 1935, 2, 353–67. Productive thinking (Ed. Michael Wertheimer). New York, [2]1959.

Bibliography: Helson, H.: The fundamental propositions of gestalt psychology. Psychol. Rev., 1933, *40*, 13–32. **Newman, E. B.:** Max Wertheimer: 1880–1943. Amer. J. Psychol. 1944, *57*, 428–35. *W.W.*

White noise. Noise composed of a random mixture of sounds of many different wave lengths (term derived by imperfect analogy from white light, which occurs naturally as a mixture of spectral wave lengths). The sound of a waterfall approximates to a white noise, but in the laboratory it is electronically created by a *white noise generator*. *G.D.W.*

Whole learning. An analytical method: a progression in teaching and learning from the given total units of sense, experience and objects to their constituent elements. Many teaching goals call for subsequent synthesis. Initial tuition in reading using the whole-learning method starts with whole sentence and word units and proceeds to analyze the individual letters in order to reassemble words and sentences. *G.H.*

Whorf's hypothesis (syn. *Sapir-Whorf hypothesis*). A theory put forward by the linguisticians B. L. Whorf, E. Sapir and H. Hoijer. Whorf started from undeniable differences in the vocabularies and structures of different languages, especially those of American Indian languages (e.g. Hopi) and "standard average European" (SAE). He asserted that language (q.v.) determined thought, so that variations in languages were derivable from diverse world-views (the thesis of linguistic relativity), and therefore diverse cultures or civilizations. Whorf tried to demonstrate this in terms of the concepts of "time", "space" and "matter", and accordant behaviors. He compared (for the most part) individual word-thing relations in different languages, in a largely anecdotal and exemplary manner. The less emphatic version of the hypothesis states that language influences perception and memory by specific encoding of areas of reality. In the planning of experimental tests of the Whorf hypothesis, three criteria need to be taken into consideration (in terms of the example of color coding): (*a*) *Variation*. It is necessary first of all to confirm in the linguistic and in the non-linguistic behavioral inventory, areas of variation between which covariation is expected (e.g. color codability, i.e. codability of colors by means of color terminology, performance in recognizing colors). (*b*) *Universality*. The object under investigation must be present in each of the cultures under comparison (e.g. the universal pre-existence of the physical color spectrum). (*c*) *Simplicity*. The object of investigation ought as far as possible to be comparable in terms of some one-dimensional characteristic (e.g. the localization of colored areas on the color circle). A covariation of color codability/color recognition has been shown to be intra- as well as intercultural. A correspondingly positive association has been reported for mimic emotional expressions in perception. The testing of covariance between linguistic and behavioral criteria (e.g. between color coding and classification by means of free object sorting) provided only ambiguous or negative results.

Critics of Whorf's hypothesis emphasize the following points especially: (*a*) the association of influence between language and thought is to be seen as interactive and not unilateral. (*b*) The over-emphasis on the word-thing relation in Whorf's conception of language is accompanied by a neglect of overlapping significant linguistic contexts (e.g. no attention is paid to the semantic dependency of the sentence on the context). (*c*) The universals of languages (linguistic universals) are undervalued in favor of their differences.

Bibliography: Brown, R. W. & Lenneberg, E. H.: A study in language and cognition. J. Abn. Soc. Psychol., 1954, *49*, 454–62. **Hymes, D.** (Ed.): Language in culture and society. New York, 1964. **Lenneberg, E. H. & Roberts, J. M.:** The language of experience. Bloomington, Ind., 1956. **Miller, G. A. & McNeill, D.:** Psycholinguistics. In: **Lindzey G. & Aronson, E.** (Eds.): The handbook of social psychology, Vol. 3. Reading, Mass., [2]1969, 666–794. **Whorf, B. L.:** Language, thought and reality. Cambridge, Mass., 1956.

H. Bosbach

Wiggly-block test. A test by O'Connor for assessment of space apprehension. A rectangular block about 20 cm long is divided into nine smaller blocks each cut by irregular wavy lines. The testee has to reassemble them as quickly as possible. *H.J.A.*

Wilcoxon's test. A non-parametric technique used to test two dependent samples for differences in regard to central trend. Its use is indicated when the individuals in both samples can be grouped in homogeneous pairs or there are two observations for each individual.

Bibliography: Wilcoxon, F.: Individual comparisons by ranking methods. Biometrics, 1945, *1*, 80–3.

H.-J.S.

Wilcoxon-White test. See *Mann-Whitney U-test.*

Will. Wundt considered "will" or "volition" to be a basic function of psychic existence, which he conceived of as a dynamic structure—in contradistinction to the substantial concept of mind put forward by association (q.v.) psychologists. The theory of will ("voluntarism," F. Tönnies) he developed was experimentally founded, and has been extended by his many pupils and disciples, and especially by the Würzburg school (O. Külpe, N. Ach, J. Lindworski, K. Bühler, A. Messer, O. Selz). Voluntarism also influenced American motivational and behavioral research (C. L. Hull, q.v., J. B. Watson, q.v., E. L. Thorndike, q.v., E. C. Tolman, q.v., R. B. Cattell, G. W. Allport, q.v.), who nevertheless reject the method of self-observation as too prone to subjective error. *Verstehende Psychologie* (q.v.) either sees will as a formal principle (L. Klages, P. Lersch) or divides it according to effect: will to learn, will to life, will to achievement, will to value (E. Spranger). Empirical investigations have derived will from ideas and thought processes (T. Ziehen; E. Meumann, 1908) or elementary emotions (H. Ebbinghaus). In its structural psychological orientation (K. Lewin, q.v., H. Rohracher, G. W. Allport, q.v.), motivational theory is convinced that genuine volitional motives are conscious, or that hidden motives can be made conscious in an act of recall.

Ach (1905) showed in experiments that the concept of will indicates a special energy potential which is able to overcome strong contrary forces such as associative inhibitions, fatigue, etc. A motivational act results in a decision, which then gives rise to "determining tendencies" controlled by a goal or target idea, but remaining effective for long periods of time and despite intervals. The expenditure of volitional energy is measurable (Arnold, 1969). Weakness of volition may be innate or acquired, and may be compensated by educational or psychotherapeutic measures (see *Adler, Alfred*).

Ach (1935) discovered the law of difficulty of motivation and the effects of guiding ideas and motivational limits. The law of special determination indicates that an intention is the more easily realized the more specialized the determining target idea is.

Volitional impulses may increase achievement level for some time during continuous operations. They show that "will" is able to convert potential into kinetic energies, and that it may therefore be viewed as a genuine force (Mierke, 1955). The impelling and affective energies which arise from the "vital layers" can be sublimated by the central ego (q.v.), which represents the "spirit" and its value associations, and thus become a will to achieve. A value-oriented will is said to change the elementary "achievement eros" into an "achievement ethos". Volitional acts may be directed inwards; they are directed outwards when they mobilize abilities and achievement energies for spontaneous or persistent activity (A. Wellek). Many think that in the consciousness of "I will!", men experience the freedom of a personal decision. See *Conscience; Drive; Instinct; Emotions; Personality; Traits; Type.*

Bibliography: Ach, N.: Über den Willenakt und das Temperament. Leipzig, 1910. **Id.:** Analyse des Willens. Berlin, 1935. **Arnold, W.:** Person, Charakter, Persönlichkeit. Göttingen, [3]1969. **Cattell, R. B.:** Personality and motivation structure and measurement. New York, 1957. **Hull, C. L.:** Principles of behavior. New York, 1943. **Klages, L.:** Der Geist als Widersacher der Seele. Leipzig, 1933. **Lewin, K.:** Vorsatz, Wille und Bedürfnis. Psychol. Forsch., 1920, *7*, 330–85. **Lindworski, J.:** Der Wille. Seine Erscheinung und seine Beherrschung. Leipzig, 1923. **Meumann, E.:** Intelligenz und Wille. Leipzig, 1908. **Mierke, K.:** Wille und Leistung, Göttingen, 1955. **Wundt, W.:** An introduction to psychology. New York, 1912. *K. Mierke*

Wing Standardized Tests of Musical Intelligence. Tests of musical ability (see *Music, psychology of*).

Winzen's proposition. Put forward by Winzen in 1921: the formation of an association between two learning elements is made easier if the more impressive, better-known element appears (as a stimulus) in first place. F. D. Sheffield came to the opposite conclusion in 1947. *F.-C.S.*

Wire-bending test. A prescribed shape has to be copied with a piece of wire. The purpose is to measure the manual skill shown in adapting the material in order to reproduce the shape correctly. See *Motor skills.*

Bibliography: Lienert, G.: Drahtbiegeprobe. Die Drahtbiegeprobe als standardisierter Test. Göttingen, 1961. *R.M.*

Wish. According to Freud (q.v.), the concrete form (enriched by individual experience) of a drive (q.v.) or motive (q.v.). Wishes may be repressed and unconscious. (See *Energy, mental; Object cathexis*). According to Freud's original conception, a "wish dream" can be any dream. Later, he excepted anxiety dreams (at whose start the dreamer's positive wishes play a definite though small part). The function of such a dream is alleged to be the maintenance of sleep (q.v.) and the protection of sleep from disturbing external and internal stimuli. See *Dream; Depth psychology.*

Withdrawal symptoms. Physical or psychic symptoms which set in during or after the process of withdrawal from dependence on an addictive drug. Among the drugs which can cause effects of this kind are narcotics and certain opiates. In the case of the opiates, such symptoms can include: extreme pain, fainting, diarrhea, shivering, vomiting, sensation of coldness, violent yawning, discharge of watery mucus, sleeplessness, restlessness, fear and anxiety. The popular terms for withdrawal, "kicking the habit" and "going cold turkey", are indicative of the symptoms. See *Drug dependence.* *A.Hn.*

Witnesses. Evidence provided by a witness may be said to be not merely a recalling of an experienced action but a performance reflecting the whole personality (q.v.) of the witness. A witness is often able to remember only insignificant aspects of an event, which are unimportant for the judicial process. In some cases he is able only to recall certain fragments of a process, and cannot connect them chronologically. The ability of children and adolescents to act as witnesses is conditioned by the simplicity or complicated nature of the event and the development of the witness's intellect. For instance, a twelve-year-old boy with a passionate interest in cars (automobiles) can (under certain conditions) offer qualitatively better evidence than a much older person with a quite different orientation. The effectiveness of witnesses is much reduced by intense emotion (especially by anxiety or fear). See *Abilities; Child psychology; Forensic psychology; Credibility; Conscience; Guilt.* *O.T.*

Bibliography: Davis, R. C.: Physiological responses as a means of evaluating information. In: **Biderman A. D. & Zimmer, H.** (Eds.): The manipulation of human behavior. New York, 1961. **Inbau, F. E. & Reid, J. E.:** Lie detection and criminal interrogation, Baltimore, [3]1953. **Jung, C. G.:** Zur psychol. Tatbestandsdiagnostik. Arch. Krim., 1939, *100*, 123–30. **Tent, L.:** Psychologische Tatbestandsdiagnostik. In: **Undeutsch, u.** (Ed.): Handbuch der Psychologie, Vol. 11. Göttingen, 1967. **Wertheimer, M.:** Tatbestandsdagnostik. In: **Abderhalden, E.** (Ed.): Handbuch der Biologischen Arbeitsmethoden, Section 6. Berlin, 1933. *F.M.*

Witte-König effect. A paradoxical fusion effect. If S's eyes are variously stimulated the sensations fuse into one percept. Either one stimulus dominates, or the percept alternates from one stimulus to the other. If *S.* is presented (by means of a stereoscope) with two circles one of which is incomplete, *S.* sees the break only if it is relatively small. A larger break in the circle is not perceived.

Bibliography: Helson, H. & Wilkinson, A. E.: A study of the Witte-König paradoxical fusion effect. Amer. J. Psychol, 1958, *71*, 316–20. **König, E.:** Experimentelle Beiträge zur Theorie des binocularen Einfach- und Tiefensehens. Meisenheim, 1962. *F.Ma.*

Woodworth Personal Data Sheet. The prototype of all personality inventories or questionnaires, devised by R. Woodworth in World War I in order to single out neurotics unfit for military service. The test was not validated at the time. See *Questionnaires; Personality.*

Bibliography: Symonds, P. M.: Diagnosing personality and conduct. New York, 1931. *R.M.*

Woodworth, Robert Sessions. B. 17/10/1869 in Belchertown, Mass.; d. 4/7/1962 in New York. Woodworth obtained his M.A. at Harvard in 1897, having studied philosophy and psychology. He received his Ph.D. under J. McK. Cattell (q.v.) in 1899 with a dissertation on "The Accuracy of Voluntary Movement". He widened the scope of his knowledge with studies in anthropology and statistics under F. Boas and in physiology under H. Bowditch in New York, Sarpey-Schafer in Edinburgh (1900), and as Sherrington's assistant in Liverpool (1902). He went to Germany in 1912, where he visited Külpe in Bonn and Wundt in Leipzig. From 1903 until his retirement in 1958 at the age of eighty-nine, he worked as Cattell's successor at Columbia. In 1956 he received the first Gold Medal award of the American Psychological Foundation for his exceptional contribution as an integrator and organizer of psychological science.

Woodworth achieved a worldwide reputation, above all by his publications, which have become standard works. Especially important are the following: the revised edition of Ladd's *Physiological Psychology* (1911); *Dynamic Psychology* (1918), the first systematic presentation of his scientific position; the introductory manual *Psychology* (1921), which went into five editions before 1947, and after Boring's work of 1950 was for twenty-five years the most frequently consulted textbook of psychology; *Contemporary Schools of Psychology*, which appeared in Mary R. Sheehan's revision two years after his death (1964); *Experimental Psychology* (1938), which in Schlosberg's revision (1954) is still among the standard works on experimental psychology; and his last work, *Dynamics of Behavior* (1958), which Woodworth published at the age of eighty-nine.

Woodworth's standpoint was essentially functionalist, even though he did not belong to the functionalist school of J. R. Angell and H. A. Carr. On the one hand, Woodworth was eclectic enough to shun the narrowness of partisan attachment to a school, on the other he integrated quite considerable elements of dynamic psychology into his functionalist conceptions.

His dynamic psychology was concerned with the conditions determining human behavior. He did not think it sufficient to explain behavior solely in terms of stimuli and responses without taking the living organism into consideration. Therefore, even in behavioral analysis, he recognized introspection as a legitimate psychological method. The concepts invoked by Woodworth to explain motivated behavior were drives and mechanisms. His decisive assumption in this regard, later taken over in the principle of functional autonomy by G. W. Allport (q.v.), was that a mechanism, as soon as it was aroused, itself represented a drive (q.v.), and was also in a position to activate other associated mechanisms.

Bibliography: Poffenberger, A. T.: Robert Sessions Woodworth: 1896–1962. Amer. J. of Psychol., 1962, *75*, 677–92. **Seward, G. H.:** Woodworth, the man: a "case history". In: **Georgene, H. & Seward, J. P.** (Eds.): Current psychological issues. New York, 1958, 3–20.
W.W.

Word association. A collective term for a number of psychodiagnostic techniques used to make diagnostic conclusions on the basis of subjects' responses to specific stimulus words. Reaction time is also measured. The method goes back to suggestions from C. G. Jung (q.v.) and L. Binswanger at the turn of the century. See *Association; History of psychology.* *G.L.*

Word blindness. See *Alexia.*

Word-choice tests. Tests to assess part-aspects of verbal intelligence. Usually employed as subtests in larger general intelligence test-batteries. By definitions or synonymns, *S.* indicates his mastery of the term in question. *P.S.*

Word fluency. A factor ("W") described by E. L. Thurstone (1938) and replicated on several later occasions. It is defined operationally by means of tests in which as many words as possible must be named which satisfy specific formal and symbolic conditions (e.g. those ending with specific letters).

Bibliography: Guilford, J. P.: The nature of human intelligence. New York, 1967.
H.H.

Word-salad. A disturbance of thinking with complete loss of the connection between individual words. Because of the absence of association, words—often from different languages—are related quite haphazardly. Above all a schizophrenic symptom. See *Schizophrenia.* *A.Hi.*

Work-factor system. A time-study system from the USA, used to analyze a work process according to predetermined guidelines, to classify individual movements, and provide a tabular summary of their time or energy demands. *G.R.W.M.*

World test; world technique. A therapeutic game devised by M. Lowenfeld, and standardized by C. Bühler (1941) in regard to material, directions and evaluation. The world test is a projective technique (q.v.) which allows some insight into the (prelogical) world-picture of a child. The game contains, e.g., more than a hundred items (houses, trees, human, animals). The child is asked to build something. The process is recorded and finally photographed. *P.G.*

Writer's cramp. Formerly called *scrivener's palsy*, this is a condition in which various muscles involved in writing go into spasm whenever the patient tries to write, or after he has been writing for a short time. It is one of many occupational cramps, another being violinist's cramp. *P.Le.*

Wundt's napkin ring. See *Napkin ring figure.*

Wundt, Wilhelm. B. 18/6/1832 in Neckarau near Mannheim; d. 31/8/1920 in Grossbothen near Leipzig. After a year at Tübingen University, Wundt moved in 1852 to Heidelberg, where he obtained his medical doctorate in 1856, became *Privatdozent* in 1857, and was appointed Professor in 1864. From 1858 to 1871, H. von Helmholtz (q.v.) held the chair of physiology at Heidelberg. The two giants of scientific psychology lived at close quarters for thirteen years without any real personal or scientific contact. In 1874, Wundt was appointed to the chair of inductive philosophy at the University of Zürich, and in 1875 to the University of Leipzig, where he remained until his death forty-five years later. Wundt is considered to be the founder of modern psychology. He enabled psychology to become an independent discipline in terms of its object and methods, and developed it in accordance with the natural-scientific model. He defined it as the "science of inward and immediate experience", and grounded psychological research on experiments and "pure observation". He offered a systematic presentation of the principles and results of psychology. In 1874 he published the first version of the eventual three volumes of his main work, *Principles of Physiological Psychology.* In 1883, he founded the first psychological journal under the title *Philosophische Studien* (Philosophical Studies). His ten-volume work *Völkerpsychologie* (Folk Psychology) was intended to complement individual, experimental psychology with a psychology of communal life and research into the higher products of human consciousness. This immense work (now largely outdated) bears witness to an immensely knowledgeable mind. In 1879, Wundt founded the world's first psychological institute, which soon achieved international rank. Psychologists went there from all leading countries in order to study experimental psychology under Wundt (see *Titchener; History of psychology*).

Main works: Lectures on human and animal psychology. London, 1894. Outlines of psychology, Leipzig, 1896; New York, 1897. Principles of physiological psychology. New York, 1904. An introduction to psychology. New York, 1912. Elements of folk psychology: outlines of a psychological history of the development of mankind. New York, 1916.

Bibliography: Boring, E. G.: A history of experimental psychology. New York, ^{2}1957, 316–47. **Id.:** On the subjectivity of important historical dates: Leipzig, 1879, J. Hist. Behav. Sci., 1965, *1*, 5–9. **Feldman, S.:** Wundt's psychology. Amer. J. of Psychol., 1932, *44*, 615–29. **Fernberger, S. W.:** Wundt's doctorate students, Psychol. Bull., 1933, *30*, 80–3. **Hall, G. S.:** Founders of modern psychology. New York, 1912, 311–458. **Petersen, P.:** Wilhelm Wundt und seine Zeit. Stuttgart, 1924. **Tinker, M. A.:** Wundt's doctorate students and their theses (1875–1920). Amer. J. Psychol., 1932, *44*, 630–7. **Titchener, E. B.:** Wilhelm Wundt, Amer. J. Psychol., 1921, *32*, 161–78. **Wolman, B. B.:** Historical roots of contemporary psychology. New York, 1968, 275–97. *L.J.P.*

Würzburg School. The school of thought psychologists deriving from the ideas of O. Külpe (q.v.). Other main representatives: N. Ach, K. Bühler, K. Marbe, A. Messer, O.

Selz. The Würzburg School opposed the sensualist and mechanist axiom of association psychology, and carried out experimental investigations of many acts that had until then been subjected to no such research, such as thought processes and forms of judgment, or goal ideas. See *Act psychology; History of psychology.* *H.W.*

Xanthocyanopsia. Yellow-blue vision, color weakness or blindness, in which the second and the third cone color substance is intact, and the functioning of the first is non-existent or limited. See *Color blindness.* *K.H.P.*

Xanthopsia. Yellow vision in digitalis, phenacetin, santonin and other forms of poisoning, etc. *K.H.P.*

Xenoglossy. Speech occurring during a trance (q.v.) in a language ostensibly unknown to the speaker. "Responsive xenoglossy": ability to answer questions appropriately in the unknown language. *J.B.*

Y Z

Yates correction. A special continuity correction for fourfold χ^2 scores. An improvement on the Pearson χ^2 test only for 1 degree of freedom. Included in the equation for the McNemar test, the Yates correction is as follows.

$$\chi^2 = \frac{(|b - c| - 1)^2}{b + c},$$

so that the difference between the observed and the expected frequencies is reduced by 0.5 for every category before squaring.

H.-J.S.

Yerkes-Dodson Law. A rule deriving from a publication of Yerkes and J. D. Dodson (1908), in which they reported on experiments in mice. With increased intensity of electrical shock, the mice learned more difficult assignments less readily than easy ones. The "law" was examined anew by H. J. Eysenck in 1955, and more generally formulated by, e.g., Broadhurst in 1959: the optimal motivation for a learning assignment decreases with the increasing difficulty of the task.

Bibliography: Broadhurst, P. L.: The interaction of task difficulty and motivation. The Yerkes-Dodson law revived. Acta psychol., 1959, *16*, 321–38.

Yerkes, Robert Mearns. B. 26/5/1876 in Bucks County, Pennsylvania; d. 1956. Yerkes studied zoology and psychology. He obtained his doctorate in 1902 at Harvard. From 1902 he was an instructor and later Professor at Harvard. From 1912 to 1917 he also worked at the Boston Psychopathic Hospital, and in 1917 he took up a Professorship in psychology at the University of Minnesota but was called up for military service in the same year. In the Army Medical Department, within eighteen months and together with a number of coworkers, he developed the Army Alpha Test (q.v.). From the end of the war until 1924 Yerkes was active in the National Research Council in Washington. In 1924 he became Professor at Yale. From 1930 to 1941 he was director of the Yale laboratories of primate biology, founded at his instigation in Orange Park, Florida, which was a research center for the comparative psychobiology of infrahuman primates.

Yerkes was one of the founders of modern animal research, and of comparative primate psychobiology. His laboratories were a model for animal psychology (q.v.) laboratories throughout the world (see *Comparative psychology*). Yerkes stressed the importance of understanding the anatomical, physiological and neurological bases of animal behavior in psychological experimentation. Summaries of his ideas are to be found in his two most significant books *The Great Apes* (1929, with his wife Ada W. Yerkes) and *Chimpanzees: a Laboratory Colony* (1943). Further contributions to this area were: "The dancing mouse: a study in animal behavior" (1907); a report published together with J. Watson: "Methods of studying vision in animals" (1911); *Chimpanzee Intelligence and its Vocal Expressions* (1925, with B. Learned); and *The Mind of a Gorilla* (1927, 1928). Yerkes also wrote an *Introduction to Psychology* (1911) and together with G. V. Hamilton devised the multiple-choice method for psychological diagnostics. His Army-alpha research was written up in the two publications *Army Mental Tests* (1920, with C. Yoakum), and *Psychological Examining in the United States Army* (1921).

Bibliography: Murchison, C.: History of psychology in autobiography, Vol. 2. New York, 1932, 381–407.

W.W.

Yohimbine (syn. *Quebrachine; Corynine; Aphrodine*). An alkaloid obtained from a West African tree, *Coryanthe johimbe*. Related to the rauwolfia alkaloids, yohimbine blocks the alpha receptors in the sympathetic division, and is therefore grouped as a sympathicolytic substance. However, physiological and psychological investigations offer no unified picture. In low doses, there are sympathicomimetic as well as sympathicolytic effects; only with a higher dosage are sympathicolytic effects readily obtained. The psychic effects are unclear. Several investigations report conditions approaching anxiety (q.v.). There is no experimental foundation for the frequent recommendations of yohimbine as an aphrodisiac.

Bibliography: Holmberg, G. & Gershon, S.: Autonomic and psychic effects of yohimbine hydrochloride. Psychopharmacologia, 1961, *2*, 93–106.

W.J.

Young-Helmholtz theory. See *Color perception.*

Youth. The terms "youth" and "adolescence" (q.v.) cover a section of the human life-span which has not been precisely defined, but extends from the age of about eleven to over twenty years. The German word "*Adoleszenz*" covers the period from eighteen to the mid-twenties.

1. *Cognitive performance.* Development of the intelligence begins to slow down at the beginning of the second decade of life and reaches its climax in many types of performance in adolescence (formal logical operations in the sense defined by Piaget, thinking with semantically denotative and connotative symbols). The differences in intelligence which develop in adolescence are generally final and can be traced back partially to inherited factors and partly to social conditions (sociological stratification, sex differences).

2. *Physical development.* Important physical changes occur in adolescence. At the beginning of puberty there is a strong tendency for fat to develop and about one year after gonadotropine secretion begins, a sharp growth is generally noted. Puberty itself is triggered by the influence of the hypothalamus, which must have reached a certain level of maturity (Tanner, 1962). However, sexual maturation and sudden growth are caused by hormonal processes. The interaction between endocrinal processes is still relatively obscure (Tanner, 1962). As a result of muscular growth physical strength and speed are increased and motor coordination improves. Early sexual and physical maturation or accelerated growth (see *Acceleration*) and late maturation or retarded growth (see *Retardation*) are dependent on dispositional factors (see *Twin studies*), cultural and civilization conditions, sociological factors and nutritional influences. They may promote or retard development of personality.

3. *Social development.* Sexual behavior in youth is largely dependent on social and cultural factors. The standard of sexual continence which prevails in our cultures leads to forms of behaviour which conflict with the norm, e.g. masturbation (q.v.) (in more than

90% of male adolescents) and petting (q.v.). Sexual behavior varies with the sociological group (Kinsey, 1948). In relation to personality development and social adaptation, adolescence is frequently marked by conflicts and crises. This is in particular the case when a young person is prevented by adults from substituting the adult role for the childhood role, and when there is a discrepancy between different influences (e.g. values enforced in and out of school). In our culture, the difficulties in making the transition to adulthood are greater than in primitive societies where the transition is often made in a matter of days or weeks (see *Initiation rites*). The development of attitudes (q.v.) in adolescence is marked less by a complete break and new structures than by revision and modification of values already accepted at an earlier stage. Efforts are noted on the one hand to develop independent opinions often associated with radicalism and remoteness from reality, and on the other by attempts to take over the adult culture—with some liberal and relativistic features. In his efforts for "self-achievement" (Maslow, 1954), the adolescent frequently moves towards a *peer-group culture*, i.e. a subculture in which factors (requirements, interests, values) are represented which distinguish the youth sharply from children on the one hand and adults on the other. The importance of *models* no longer seems so important in adolescence as in earlier periods of life. Many adolescents cannot even name a "hero" (Jaide, 1963). A distinction between phases and stages does not seem justified because these may occur at very different periods for typical features (such as lability).

4. *Abnormal development in adolescence.* In addition to social maladjustment (juvenile delinquence, neglect), mental sicknesses also first appear in a pronounced form in adolescence. See *Child psychology; Development; Educational psychology; Neurosis.*

Bibliography: Jaide, W.: Aus empirischen Untersuchungen über Vorbilder heutiger Jugendlicher. In: **Schenk-Danzinger, L.,** and **Thomae, H.** (Eds.): Gegenwartsprobleme der Entwicklungspsychologie, Göttingen, 1963. **Kinsey, A.,** *et. al*: Sexual behavior in the human male, Philadelphia & London, 1948. **Kuhlen, R. G.:** The psychology of adolescent development, New York, 1952. **Maslow, A. H.:** Motivation and personality, New York, 1954. **Staton, T. F.:** Dynamics of adolescent adjustment, New York, 1963.

R. Oerter

Zeigarnik effect. A phenomenon named after Lewin's pupil Zeigarnik, who showed in 1927 that interrupted tasks are remembered more proficiently than uninterrupted tasks, depending on involvement in the dynamic field. *I.M.D.*

Zero absolute. The point on a measuring scale at which a psychological variable ceases to exist. This point is supposedly analogous to absolute zero of temperature in physics.

C.D.F.

Zipf's laws. Zipf (1932) obtained data from the application of statistical methods to linguistic material from various languages and diverse literary genres, and asserted that they showed the following tendencies (usually referred to as "Zipf's laws"): the more frequently words are used in a language, the shorter they become; the most frequent words of a language are probably also the shortest, oldest, morphologically most simple, and those with the greatest semantic extension.

Bibliography: Lepschy, G. C.: Die strukturale Sprachwissenschaft. Munich, 1969. **Mandelbrot, B.:** Information theory and psycholinguistics. In: **Wolman, B. B. & Nagel, E.** (Eds.): Scientific psychology. New York, 1965. **Meyer-Eppler, W.:** Grundlagen und Anwendungen der Informationstheorie. Berlin, [2]1969. **Miller, G. A. & Chomsky, N.:** Finitary models of language users. In: **Bush, R. R., Luce, R. D. & Galanter** (Eds.): Handbook of mathematical psychology, Vol. 2. New York, 1963. **Zipf, G. K.:** Selected studies of the principle of relative frequency in language. Cambridge, Mass., 1932. **Id.:** Psychobiology of language. An introduction to dynamic philology.

Boston, 1935. **Id.:** Human behavior and the principle of least effort. An introduction to human ecology. Cambridge, Mass., 1949. *D.Vo.*

Zöllner illusion. One of the geometric illusions. The small diagonals make it difficult to perceive that the vertical lines are parallel.

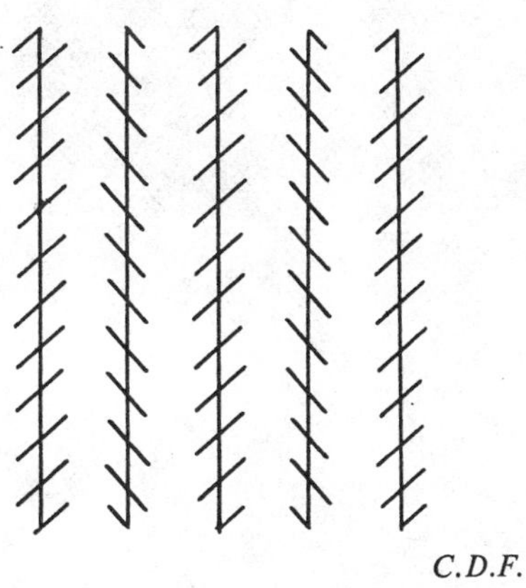

C.D.F.

Zoophilia. A term now seldom used and deriving from Krafft-Ebing: contact between humans and animals (stroking or beating) which give those concerned sexual pleasure (in contrast to direct sexual contacts with animals). *H.M.*

z scale. A linear transformation of scores according to the formula

$$z = \frac{(X - \overline{X})}{s}.$$

The scale basic to the resulting standard distribution has a medium value of 0 and a standard deviation of 1. The z transformation is most often used for normally distributed scores. *H.-J.S.*

z test. 1. A statistical test used as a test distribution for the standard normal distribution. It may be used as an approximation to various other statistical tests, since many test distributions are—with increasing degrees of freedom—transformed into a normal distribution.

2. A projective test (q.v.) procedure using screen projections and a Rorschach interpretative schema. *H.-J.S.*

Zwaardemaker, Hendrik. B. 1857; d. 1930. Dutch physiologist. Worked as an army surgeon and then succeeded Engelmann as Professor of physiology at Utrecht University. Zwaardemaker became widely known mainly for his experimental research into smell, using large samples (*Physiologie des Geruchs*, 1895), and his invention of the olfactometer (q.v.). He also carried out investigations of acoustic perception, some in conjunction with his friend, the Belgian psychologist A. Michotte (q.v.). *W.W.*

Zygote. A fertilized cell, which is always diploid, formed by the union of a male with a female gamete. A new individual develops from the zygote, which is therefore the starting-point of a new generation. *H.Sch.*